DIAMOND
FRENCH
DICTIONARY

FRENCH · ENGLISH   ENGLISH · FRENCH

Pierre-Henri Cousin

This edition published 1994 by
Diamond Books
77–85 Fulham Palace Road
Hammersmith, London W6 8JB

Reprinted 1992

Latest reprint 1994

---

contributors
Claude Nimmo, Lorna Sinclair,
Philippe Patry, Hélène Lewis, Elisabeth Campbell,
Renée Birks

editorial staff
Catherine Love, Lesley Robertson

Printed and bound in Finland

INTRODUCTION

L'usager qui désire comprendre l'anglais – qui déchiffre – trouvera dans ce dictionnaire un vocabulaire moderne et très complet, comprenant de nombreux composés et locutions appartenant à la langue contemporaine. Il trouvera aussi dans l'ordre alphabétique les principales formes irrégulières, avec un renvoi à la forme de base où figure la traduction, ainsi qu'abréviations, sigles et noms géographiques choisis parmi les plus courants.

L'usager qui veut s'exprimer – communiquer – dans la langue étrangère trouvera un traitement détaillé du vocabulaire fondamental, avec de nombreuses indications le guidant vers la traduction juste, et lui montrant comment l'utiliser correctement.

The user whose aim is to read and understand French will find in this dictionary a comprehensive and up-to-date wordlist including numerous phrases in current use. He will also find listed alphabetically the main irregular forms with a cross-reference to the basic form where a translation is given, as well as some of the most common abbreviations, acronyms and geographical names.

The user who wishes to communicate and to express himself in the foreign language will find clear and detailed treatment of all the basic words, with numerous indications pointing to the appropriate translation, and helping him to use it correctly.

CONTENTS

adjectif, locution adjective	a	adjective, adjectival phrase
abréviation	ab(b)r	abbreviation
adverbe, locution adverbiale	ad	adverb, adverbial phrase
administration	ADMIN	administration
agriculture	AGR	agriculture
anatomie	ANAT	anatomy
architecture	ARCHIT	architecture
l'automobile	AUT(O)	the motor car and motoring
aviation, voyages aériens	AVIAT	flying, air travel
biologie	BIO(L)	biology
botanique	BOT	botany
anglais de Grande-Bretagne	Brit	British English
conjonction	cj	conjunction
langue familière (! emploi vulgaire)	col (!)	colloquial usage (! particularly offensive)
commerce, finance, banque	COMM	commerce, finance, banking
construction	CONSTR	building
nom utilisé comme adjectif, ne peut s'employer ni comme attribut, ni après le nom qualifié	cpd	compound element: noun used as an adjective and which cannot follow the noun it qualifies
cuisine, art culinaire	CULIN	cookery
déterminant: article, adjectif démonstratif ou indéfini etc	dét, det	determiner: article, demonstrative etc.
économie	ECON	economics
électricité, électronique	ELEC	electricity, electronics
exclamation, interjection	excl	exclamation, interjection
féminin	f	feminine
langue familière (! emploi vulgaire)	fam (!)	colloquial usage (! particularly offensive)
emploi figuré	fig	figurative use
(verbe anglais) dont la particule est inséparable du verbe	fus	(phrasal verb) where the particle cannot be separated from main verb
dans la plupart des sens; généralement	gén, gen	in most or all senses; generally
géographie, géologie	GEO	geography, geology
géométrie	GEOM	geometry
invariable	inv	invariable
irrégulier	irg	irregular
domaine juridique	JUR	law
grammaire, linguistique	LING	grammar, linguistics
masculin	m	masculine
mathématiques, algèbre	MATH	mathematics, calculus
médecine	MED	medical term, medicine
masculin ou féminin, suivant le sexe	m/f	either masculine or feminine depending on sex
domaine militaire, armée	MIL	military matters
musique	MUS	music
nom	n	noun
navigation, nautisme	NAVIG, NAUT	sailing, navigation
adjectif ou nom numérique	num	numeral adjective or noun
	o.s.	oneself
péjoratif	péj, pej	derogatory, pejorative
photographie	PHOT(O)	photography
physiologie	PHYSIOL	physiology
pluriel	pl	plural
politique	POL	politics
participe passé	pp	past participle
préposition	prép, prep	preposition
psychologie, psychiatrie	PSYCH	psychology, psychiatry

temps du passé	**pt**	past tense
nom non comptable: ne peut s'utiliser au pluriel	**q**	collective (uncountable) noun: is not used in the plural
quelque chose	**qch**	
quelqu'un	**qn**	
religions, domaine ecclésiastique	**REL**	religions, church service
	sb	somebody
enseignement, système scolaire et universitaire	**SCOL**	schooling, schools and universities
singulier	**sg**	singular
	sth	something
subjonctif	**sub**	subjunctive
sujet (grammatical)	**su(b)j**	(grammatical) subject
techniques, technologie	**TECH**	technical term, technology
télécommunications	**TEL**	telecommunications
télévision	**TV**	television
typographie	**TYP(O)**	typography, printing
anglais des USA	**US**	American English
verbe	**vb**	verb
verbe ou groupe verbal à fonction intransitive	**vi**	verb or phrasal verb used intransitively
verbe ou groupe verbal à fonction transitive	**vt**	verb or phrasal verb used transitively
zoologie	**ZOOL**	zoology
marque déposée	**®**	registered trademark
indique une équivalence culturelle	**≈**	introduces a cultural equivalent

v

FRANÇAIS-ANGLAIS
FRENCH-ENGLISH

A

a *vb voir* avoir.

à (*à* + *le* = au, *à* + *les* = aux) [a, o] *prép* (*situation*) at, in ; (*direction, attribution*) to ; (*provenance*) from ; (*moyen*) with, by ; **payé au mois** paid by the month ; **100 km/unités à l'heure** 100 km/units per hour ; **à 3 heures/minuit** at 3 o'clock/midnight ; **au mois de juin** in the month of June ; **se chauffer au gaz** to heat one's house with gas ; **à bicyclette** by bicycle *ou* on a bicycle ; **l'homme aux yeux bleus** the man with the blue eyes ; **à la semaine prochaine!** see you next week! ; **à la russe** the Russian way, in the Russian fashion.

abaisser [abese] *vt* to lower, bring down ; (*manette*) to pull down ; (*fig*) to debase ; to humiliate ; **s'~** *vi* to go down ; (*fig*) to demean o.s. ; **s'~ à faire/à qch** to stoop *ou* descend to doing/to sth.

abandon [abādɔ̃] *nm* abandoning ; deserting ; giving up ; relinquishing ; (*SPORT*) withdrawal ; (*fig*) lack of constraint ; relaxed pose *ou* mood ; **être à l'~** to be in a state of neglect.

abandonné, e [abɑ̃dɔne] *a* (*solitaire*) deserted.

abandonner [abɑ̃dɔne] *vt* to leave, abandon, desert ; (*projet, activité*) to abandon, give up ; (*SPORT*) to retire *ou* withdraw from ; (*céder*) to surrender, relinquish ; **s'~** *vi* to let o.s. go ; **s'~ à** (*paresse, plaisirs*) to give o.s. up to.

abasourdir [abazurdir] *vt* to stun, stagger.

abat-jour [abaʒuR] *nm inv* lampshade.

abats [aba] *nmpl* (*de bœuf, porc*) offal *sg* ; (*de volaille*) giblets.

abattage [abataʒ] *nm* cutting down, felling ; (*entrain*) go, dynamism.

abattement [abatmɑ̃] *nm* enfeeblement ; dejection, despondency ; (*déduction*) reduction ; **~ fiscal** ≈ tax allowance.

abattis [abati] *nmpl* giblets.

abattoir [abatwaR] *nm* abattoir, slaughterhouse.

abattre [abatR(ə)] *vt* (*arbre*) to cut down, fell ; (*mur, maison*) to pull down ; (*avion, personne*) to shoot down ; (*animal*) to shoot, kill ; (*fig*) to wear out, tire out ; to demoralize ; **s'~** *vi* to crash down ; **s'~ sur** to beat down on ; to rain down on.

abbaye [abei] *nf* abbey.

abbé [abe] *nm* priest ; (*d'une abbaye*) abbot ; **M. l'~** Father.

abc, ABC [abese] *nm* alphabet primer ; (*fig*) rudiments *pl*.

abcès [apsɛ] *nm* abscess.

abdication [abdikasjɔ̃] *nf* abdication.

abdiquer [abdike] *vi* to abdicate // *vt* to renounce, give up.

abdomen [abdɔmɛn] *nm* abdomen ; **abdominal, e, aux** *a* abdominal // *nmpl* : **faire des abdominaux** to do exercises for the stomach muscles.

abécédaire [abesedɛR] *nm* alphabet primer.

abeille [abɛj] *nf* bee.

aberrant, e [abɛRɑ̃, -ɑ̃t] *a* absurd.

abêtir [abetir] *vt* to turn into a half-wit.

abhorrer [abɔRe] *vt* to abhor, loathe.

abîme [abim] *nm* abyss, gulf.

abîmer [abime] *vt* to spoil, damage ; **s'~** *vi* to get spoilt *ou* damaged ; (*tomber*) to sink, founder.

abject, e [abʒɛkt] *a* abject, despicable.

abjurer [abʒyRe] *vt* to abjure, renounce.

ablation [ablasjɔ̃] *nf* removal.

ablutions [ablysjɔ̃] *nfpl* : **faire ses ~** to perform one's ablutions.

abnégation [abnegasjɔ̃] *nf* (self-) abnegation.

aboiement [abwamɑ̃] *nm* bark, barking *q*.

abois [abwa] *nmpl* : **aux ~** at bay.

abolir [abɔliR] *vt* to abolish ; **abolition** *nf* abolition.

abominable [abɔminabl(ə)] *a* abominable.

abondance [abɔ̃dɑ̃s] *nf* abundance ; (*richesse*) affluence.

abondant, e [abɔ̃dɑ̃, -ɑ̃t] *a* plentiful, abundant, copious.

abonder [abɔ̃de] *vi* to abound, be plentiful ; **~ en** to be full of, abound in ; **~ dans le sens de qn** to concur with sb.

abonné, e [abɔne] *nm/f* subscriber ; season ticket holder.

abonnement [abɔnmɑ̃] *nm* subscription ; (*pour transports en commun, concerts*) season ticket.

abonner [abɔne] *vt* : **s'~ à** to subscribe to, take out a subscription to.

abord [abɔR] *nm* : **être d'un ~ facile** to be approachable ; **~s** *nmpl* surroundings ; **au premier ~** at first sight, initially ; **d'~** *ad* first.

abordable [abɔRdabl(ə)] *a* approachable ; reasonably priced.

abordage [abɔRdaʒ] *nm* boarding.

aborder [abɔRde] *vi* to land // *vt* (*sujet, difficulté*) to tackle ; (*personne*) to approach ; (*rivage etc*) to reach ; (*NAVIG: attaquer*) to board ; (: *heurter*) to collide with.

aborigène [abɔRiʒɛn] *nm* aborigine, native.

aboulique [abulik] *a* totally lacking in willpower.

aboutir [abutiR] *vi* (*négociations etc*) to succeed ; **~ à/dans/sur** to end up at/in/on ; **aboutissants** *nmpl voir* tenants.

aboyer [abwaje] *vi* to bark.

abracadabrant, e [abRakadabRɑ̃, -ɑ̃t] *a* incredible, preposterous.

abrasif, ive [abRazif, -iv] *a, nm* abrasive.

abrégé [abReʒe] *nm* summary.

abréger [abReʒe] *vt* (*texte*) to shorten, abridge ; (*mot*) to shorten, abbreviate ; (*réunion, voyage*) to cut short, shorten.

abreuver [abʀœve] *vt* to water ; *(fig)*: ~ qn de to shower *ou* swamp sb with ; s'~ *vi* to drink ; **abreuvoir** *nm* watering place.

abréviation [abʀevjɑsjɔ̃] *nf* abbreviation.

abri [abʀi] *nm* shelter ; à l'~ under cover ; à l'~ de sheltered from ; *(fig)* safe from.

abricot [abʀiko] *nm* apricot ; **abricotier** *nm* apricot tree.

abriter [abʀite] *vt* to shelter ; *(loger)* to accommodate ; s'~ to shelter, take cover.

abroger [abʀɔʒe] *vt* to repeal, abrogate.

abrupt, e [abʀypt] *a* sheer, steep ; *(ton)* abrupt.

abruti, e [abʀyti] *nm/f (fam)* idiot, moron.

abrutir [abʀytiʀ] *vt* to daze ; to exhaust ; to stupefy.

abscisse [apsis] *nf* abscissa, X axis.

absence [apsɑ̃s] *nf* absence ; *(MÉD)* blackout ; mental blank.

absent, e [apsɑ̃, -ɑ̃t] *a* absent ; *(chose)* missing, lacking ; *(distrait: air)* vacant, faraway // *nm/f* absentee ; **absentéisme** *nm* absenteeism ; **s'absenter** *vi* to take time off work ; *(sortir)* to leave, go out.

absinthe [apsɛ̃t] *nf (boisson)* absinth(e) ; *(BOT)* wormwood, absinth(e).

absolu, e [apsɔly] *a* absolute ; *(caractère)* rigid, uncompromising ; ~ment *ad* absolutely.

absolution [apsɔlysjɔ̃] *nf* absolution.

absolutisme [apsɔlytism(ə)] *nm* absolutism.

absolve *etc vb voir* **absoudre**.

absorbant, e [apsɔʀbɑ̃, -ɑ̃t] *a* absorbent.

absorbé, e [apsɔʀbe] *a* engrossed, absorbed.

absorber [apsɔʀbe] *vt* to absorb ; *(gén MÉD: manger, boire)* to take.

absoudre [apsudʀ(ə)] *vt* to absolve.

abstenir [apstəniʀ]: s'~ *vi (POL)* to abstain ; s'~ de qch/de faire to refrain from sth/from doing ; **abstention** *nf* abstention ; **abstentionnisme** *nm* abstentionism.

abstinence [apstinɑ̃s] *nf* abstinence.

abstraction [apstʀaksjɔ̃] *nf* abstraction ; faire ~ de to set *ou* leave aside.

abstraire [apstʀɛʀ] *vt* to abstract ; **abstrait, e** *a* abstract.

absurde [apsyʀd(ə)] *a* absurd // *nm* absurdity ; absurd ; par l'~ *ad* absurdio ; **absurdité** *nf* absurdity.

abus [aby] *nm (excès)* abuse, misuse ; *(injustice)* abuse ; ~ de confiance breach of trust ; embezzlement.

abuser [abyze] *vi* to go too far, overstep the mark // *vt* to deceive, mislead ; ~ de *vt (force, droit)* to misuse ; *(alcool)* to take to excess ; *(violer, duper)* to take advantage of ; s'~ *(se méprendre)* to be mistaken ; **abusif, ive** *a* exorbitant ; excessive ; improper.

acabit [akabi] *nm*: de cet ~ of that type.

académicien, ne [akademisjɛ̃, -jɛn] *nm/f* academician.

académie [akademi] *nf (société)* learned society ; *(école: d'art, de danse)* academy ; *(ART: nu)* nude ; *(SCOL: circonscription)* ≈ regional education authority ; l'A~ (française) the French Academy ; **académique** *a* academic.

acajou [akaʒu] *nm* mahogany.

acariâtre [akaʀjɑtʀ(ə)] *a* sour(-tempered).

accablement [akɑblamɔ̃] *nm* despondency, depression.

accabler [akɑble] *vt* to overwhelm, overcome ; *(suj: témoignage)* to condemn, damn ; ~ qn d'injures to heap *ou* shower abuse on sb ; ~ qn de travail to overburden sb with work ; **accablé de dettes/soucis** weighed down with debts/cares.

accalmie [akalmi] *nf* lull.

accaparer [akapaʀe] *vt* to monopolize ; *(sujet: travail etc)* to take up (all) the time *ou* attention of.

accéder [aksede]: ~ à *vt (lieu)* to reach ; *(fig: pouvoir)* to accede to ; *(: poste)* to attain ; *(accorder: requête)* to grant, accede to.

accélérateur [akseleʀatœʀ] *nm* accelerator.

accélération [akseleʀɑsjɔ̃] *nf* speeding up ; acceleration.

accélérer [akseleʀe] *vt (mouvement, travaux)* to speed up // *vi (AUTO)* to accelerate.

accent [aksɑ̃] *nm* accent ; *(inflexions expressives)* tone (of voice) ; *(PHONÉTIQUE, fig)* stress, aux ~s de *(musique)* to the strains of ; mettre l'~ sur *(fig)* to stress ; ~ aigu/grave acute/grave accent.

accentuation [aksɑ̃tɥɑsjɔ̃] *nf* accenting ; stressing.

accentuer [aksɑ̃tɥe] *vt (LING: orthographe)* to accent ; *(: phonétique)* to stress, accent ; *(fig)* to accentuate, emphasize ; to increase ; s'~ *vi* to become more marked *ou* pronounced.

acceptable [aksɛptabl(ə)] *a* satisfactory, acceptable.

acceptation [aksɛptɑsjɔ̃] *nf* acceptance.

accepter [aksɛpte] *vt* to accept ; ~ de faire to agree to do ; *(tolérer)*: ~ que qn fasse to agree to sb doing, let sb do.

acception [aksɛpsjɔ̃] *nf* meaning, sense.

accès [aksɛ] *nm (à un lieu)* access ; *(MÉD)* attack ; fit, bout ; outbreak // *nmpl (routes etc)* means of access, approaches ; d'~ facile easily accessible ; ~ de colère fit of anger ; ~ de joie burst of joy ; donner ~ à *(lieu)* to give access to ; *(carrière)* to open the door to ; avoir ~ auprès de qn to have access to sb.

accessible [aksesibl(ə)] *a* accessible ; *(livre, sujet)*: ~ à qn within the reach of sb ; *(sensible)*: ~ à la pitié/l'amour open to pity/love.

accession [aksesjɔ̃] *nf*: ~ à accession to ; attainment of.

accessit [aksesit] *nm (SCOL)* ≈ certificate of merit.

accessoire [akseswaʀ] *a* secondary, of secondary importance ; incidental // *nm* accessory ; *(THÉÂTRE)* prop ; **accessoiriste** *nm/f (TV, CINÉMA)* property man/girl.

accident [aksidɑ̃] *nm* accident ; par ~ by chance ; ~ de la route road accident ; **accidenté, e** *a* damaged *ou* injured (in an accident) ; *(relief, terrain)* uneven ; hilly ; **accidentel, le** *a* accidental.

acclamation [aklamɑsjɔ̃] *nf*: par ~

(vote) by acclamation; ~s nfpl cheers, cheering ag.
acclamer [aklame] vt to cheer, acclaim.
acclimatation [aklimatasjɔ̃] nf acclimatization.
acclimater [aklimate] vt to acclimatize; s'~ vi to become acclimatized.
accointances [akwɛ̃tɑ̃s] nfpl: avoir des ~ avec to have contacts with.
accolade [akɔlad] nf (amicale) embrace; (signe) brace; donner l'~ à qn to embrace sb.
accoler [akɔle] vt to place side by side.
accommodant, e [akɔmɔdɑ̃, -ɑ̃t] a accommodating.
accommodement [akɔmɔdmɑ̃] nm compromise.
accommoder [akɔmɔde] vt (CULIN) to prepare; (points de vue) to reconcile; s'~ de to put up with; to make do with.
accompagnateur, trice [akɔ̃paɲatœr, -tris] nm/f (MUS) accompanist; (de voyage: guide) guide; (: d'enfants) accompanying adult; (: de voyage organisé) courier.
accompagnement [akɔ̃paɲmɑ̃] nm (MUS) accompaniment.
accompagner [akɔ̃paɲe] vt to accompany, be ou go ou come with; (MUS) to accompany.
accompli, e [akɔ̃pli] a accomplished.
accomplir [akɔ̃plir] vt (tâche, projet) to carry out; (souhait) to fulfil; s'~ vi to be fulfilled; accomplissement nm carrying out; fulfilment.
accord [akɔr] nm (entente, convention, LING) agreement; (entre des styles, tons etc) harmony; (consentement) agreement, consent; (MUS) chord; se mettre d'~ to come to an agreement (with each other); être d'~ to agree; parfait (MUS) tonic chord.
accordéon [akɔrdeɔ̃] nm (MUS) accordion; accordéoniste nm/f accordionist.
accorder [akɔrde] vt (faveur, délai) to grant; (harmoniser) to match; (MUS) to tune; s'~ to get on together; to agree; (LING) to agree; accordeur nm (MUS) tuner.
accoster [akɔste] vt (NAVIG) to draw alongside; (personne) to accost // vi (NAVIG) to berth.
accotement [akɔtmɑ̃] nm (de route) verge, shoulder; ~s non stabilisés soft verges.
accoter [akɔte] vt: ~ qch contre/à to lean ou rest sth against/on; s'~ contre/à to lean against/on.
accouchement [akuʃmɑ̃] nm delivery, (child)birth; labour.
accoucher [akuʃe] vi to give birth, have a baby; (être en travail) to be in labour // vt to deliver; ~ d'un garçon to give birth to a boy; accoucheur nm: (médecin) accoucheur obstetrician; accoucheuse nf midwife.
accouder [akude]: s'~ vi: s'~ à/contre to rest one's elbows on/against; accoudoir nm armrest.
accouplement [akuplɑ̃] nm mating, coupling.
accoupler [akuple] vt to couple; (pour la reproduction) to mate; s'~ to mate.

accourir [akurir] vi to rush ou run up.
accoutrement [akutrəmɑ̃] nm (péj) getup, rig-out.
accoutumance [akutymɑ̃s] nf (gén) adaptation; (MED) addiction.
accoutumé, e [akutyme] a (habituel) customary, usual.
accoutumer [akutyme] vt: ~ qn à qch/faire to accustom sb to sth/to doing; s'~ à to get accustomed ou used to.
accréditer [akredite] vt (nouvelle) to substantiate; ~ qn (auprès de) to accredit sb (to).
accroc [akro] nm (déchirure) tear; (fig) hitch, snag.
accrochage [akrɔʃaʒ] nm hanging (up); hitching (up); (AUTO) (minor) collision, bump; (MIL) encounter, engagement; (dispute) clash, brush.
accroche-cœur [akrɔʃkœr] nm kiss-curl.
accrocher [akrɔʃe] vt (suspendre): ~ qch à to hang sth (up) on; (attacher: remorque): ~ qch à to hitch sth (up) to; (heurter) to catch; to catch on; to hit; (déchirer): ~ qch (à) to catch sth (on); (MIL) to engage; (fig) to catch, attract; s'~ (se disputer) to have a clash ou brush; s'~ à (rester pris à) to catch on; (agripper, fig) to hang on ou cling to.
accroissement [akrwasmɑ̃] nm increase.
accroître [akrwatr(ə)] vt to increase; s'~ vi to increase.
accroupi, e [akrupi] a squatting, crouching (down).
accroupir [akrupir]: s'~ vi to squat, crouch (down).
accru, e [akry] pp de **accroître**.
accu [aky] nm abr de accumulateur.
accueil [akœj] nm welcome; comité d'~ reception committee.
accueillir [akœjir] vt to welcome; (loger) to accommodate.
acculer [akyle] vt: ~ qn à ou contre to drive sb back against; ~ qn dans to corner sb in; ~ qn à (faillite) to drive sb to the brink of.
accumulateur [akymylatœr] nm accumulator.
accumulation [akymylasjɔ̃] nf accumulation; chauffage/radiateur à ~ (night-)storage heating/heater.
accumuler [akymyle] vt to accumulate, amass; s'~ vi to accumulate; to pile up.
accusateur, trice [akyzatœr, -tris] nm/f accuser // a accusing; (document, preuve) incriminating.
accusatif [akyzatif] nm (LING) accusative.
accusation [akyzasjɔ̃] nf (gén) accusation; (JUR) charge; (partie): l'~ the prosecution; mettre en ~ to indict.
accusé, e [akyze] nm/f accused; defendant; ~ de réception acknowledgement of receipt.
accuser [akyze] vt to accuse; (fig) to emphasize, bring out; to show; ~ qn de to accuse sb of; (JUR) to charge sb with; ~ qch de (rendre responsable) to blame sth for; ~ réception de to acknowledge receipt of.
acerbe [asɛrb(ə)] a caustic, acid.

acéré, e [aseʀe] a sharp.

achalandé, e [aʃalɑ̃de] ɔ: **bien ~** well-stocked; well-patronized.

acharné, e [aʃaʀne] a (lutte, adversaire) fierce, bitter; (travail) relentless, unremitting.

acharnement [aʃaʀnəmɑ̃] nm fierceness; relentlessness.

acharner [aʃaʀne]: **s'~** vi: **s'~ sur** to go at fiercely, hound; **s'~ contre** to set o.s. against; to dog, pursue; **s'~ à faire** to try doggedly to do; to persist in doing.

achat [aʃa] nm buying q; purchase; **faire l'~ de** to buy, purchase; **faire des ~s** to do some shopping, buy a few things.

acheminer [aʃmine] vt (courrier) to forward, dispatch; (troupes) to convey, transport; (train) to route; **s'~ vers** to head for.

acheter [aʃte] vt to buy, purchase; (soudoyer) to buy; **~ qch à** (marchand) to buy ou purchase sth from; (ami etc: offrir) to buy sth for; **acheteur, euse** nm/f buyer; shopper; (COMM) buyer; (JUR) vendee, purchaser.

achevé, e [aʃve] a: **d'un ridicule ~** thoroughly ou absolutely ridiculous.

achèvement [aʃɛvmɑ̃] nm completion; finishing.

achever [aʃve] vt to complete, finish; to end; (blessé) to finish off; **s'~** vi to end.

achoppement [aʃɔpmɑ̃] nm: **pierre d'~** stumbling block.

acide [asid] a acid, sharp; (CHIMIE) acid(ic) // nm (CHIMIE) acid; **acidifier** vt to acidify; **acidité** nf acidity; sharpness; **acidulé, e** a slightly acid; **bonbons acidulés** acid drops.

acier [asje] nm steel; **aciérie** nf steelworks sg.

acné [akne] nf acne.

acolyte [akɔlit] nm (péj) confederate.

acompte [akɔ̃t] nm deposit; (versement régulier) instalment; (sur somme due) payment on account; **un ~ de 100 F** 100 F on account.

acoquiner [akɔkine]: **s'~ avec** vt (péj) to team up with.

à-côté [akote] nm side-issue; (argent) extra.

à-coup [aku] nm (du moteur) (hic)cough; (fig) jolt; **sans ~s** smoothly; **par ~s** by fits and starts.

acoustique [akustik] nf (d'une salle) acoustics pl; (science) acoustics sg // a acoustic.

acquéreur [akeʀœʀ] nm buyer, purchaser.

acquérir [akeʀiʀ] vt to acquire; (par achat) to purchase, acquire; (valeur) to gain; **ce que ses efforts lui ont acquis** what his efforts have won ou gained (for) him.

acquiescer [akjese] vi (opiner) to agree; (consentir): **~ (à qch)** to acquiesce ou assent (to sth).

acquis, e [aki, -iz] pp de **acquérir** // nm (accumulated) experience; **être ~ à** (plan, idée) to fully agree with; **son aide nous est ~e** we can count on ou be sure of her help.

acquisition [akizisjɔ̃] nf acquisition; purchase; **faire l'~ de** to acquire; to purchase.

acquit [aki] vb voir **acquérir** // nm (quittance) receipt; **pour ~** received; **par ~ de conscience** to set one's mind at rest.

acquittement [akitmɑ̃] nm acquittal; payment, settlement.

acquitter [akite] vt (JUR) to acquit; (facture) to pay, settle; **s'~ de** to discharge; to fulfil, carry out.

âcre [ɑkʀ(ə)] a acrid, pungent.

acrobate [akʀɔbat] nm/f acrobat.

acrobatie [akʀɔbasi] nf (art) acrobatics sg; (exercice) acrobatic feat; **~ aérienne** aerobatics sg; **acrobatique** a acrobatic.

acte [akt(ə)] nm act, action; (THÉÂTRE) act; **~s** nmpl (compte-rendu) proceedings; **prendre ~ de** to note, take note of; **faire ~ de présence** to put in an appearance; **l'~ d'accusation** the charges; the bill of indictment; **~ de naissance** birth certificate.

acteur, trice [aktœʀ, -tʀis] nm/f actor/actress.

actif, ive [aktif, -iv] a active // nm (COMM) assets pl; (fig): **avoir à son ~** to have to one's credit; **mettre à son ~** to add to one's list of achievements.

action [aksjɔ̃] nf (gén) action; (COMM) share; **une bonne ~** a good deed; **~ en diffamation** libel action; **actionnaire** nm/f shareholder; **actionner** vt to work; to activate.

active [aktiv] a voir **actif**; **~ment** ad actively.

activer [aktive] vt to speed up; **s'~** vi to bustle about; to hurry up.

activiste [aktivist(ə)] nm/f activist.

activité [aktivite] nf activity; **volcan en ~** active volcano.

actrice [aktʀis] nf voir **acteur**.

actualiser [aktɥalize] vt to actualize; to bring up to date.

actualité [aktɥalite] nf (d'un problème) topicality; (événements): **l'~** current events; **les ~s** (CINÉMA, TV) the news.

actuel, le [aktɥɛl] a (présent) present; (d'actualité) topical; (non virtuel) actual; **~lement** ad at present; at the present time.

acuité [akɥite] nf acuteness.

acuponcteur, acupuncteur [akypɔ̃ktœʀ] nm acupuncturist.

acuponcture, acupuncture [akypɔ̃ktyʀ] nf acupuncture.

adage [adaʒ] nm adage.

adagio [adadʒjo] nm adagio.

adaptateur, trice [adaptatœʀ, -tʀis] nm/f adapter // nm (ÉLEC) adapter.

adaptation [adaptusjɔ̃] nf adaptation.

adapter [adapte] vt to adapt; **~ qch à** (approprier) to adapt sth to (fit); **~ qch sur/dans/à** (fixer) to fit sth on/into/to; **s'~ (à)** (suj: personne) to adapt (to).

additif [aditif] nm additional clause; (CHIMIE) additive.

addition [adisjɔ̃] nf addition; (au café) bill; **additionnel, le** a additional.

additionner [adisjɔne] vt to add (up); **~**

un produit d'eau to add water to a product.

adepte [adɛpt(ə)] nm/f follower.

adéquat, e [adekwa, -at] a appropriate, suitable.

adhérence [aderɑ̃s] nf adhesion.

adhérent, e [aderɑ̃, -ɑ̃t] nm/f (de club) member.

adhérer [adere] vi (coller) to adhere, stick; ~ à vt (coller) to adhere ou stick to; (se rallier à: parti, club) to join; to be a member of; (: opinion, mouvement) to support; **adhésif, ive** a adhesive, sticky // nm adhesive; **adhésion** nf joining; membership; support.

ad hoc [adɔk] a ad hoc.

adieu, x [adjø] excl goodbye // nm farewell; **dire ~ à qn** to say goodbye ou farewell to sb.

adipeux, euse [adipø, -øz] a bloated, fat; (ANAT) adipose.

adjacent, e [adʒasɑ̃, -ɑ̃t] a adjacent.

adjectif [adʒɛktif] nm adjective; ~ attribut adjectival complement; ~ épithète attributive adjective.

adjoindre [adʒwɛ̃dR(ə)] vt: ~ qch à to attach sth to; to add sth to; ~ qn à (personne) to appoint sb as an assistant to; (comité) to appoint sb to, attach sb to; s'~ (collaborateur etc) to take on, appoint; **adjoint, e** nm/f assistant; **adjoint au maire** deputy mayor; **directeur adjoint** assistant manager; **adjonction** nf attaching; addition; appointment.

adjudant [adʒydɑ̃] nm (MIL) warrant officer.

adjudicataire [adʒydikatɛR] nm/f successful bidder, purchaser; successful tenderer.

adjudication [adʒydikɑsjɔ̃] nf sale by auction; (pour travaux) invitation to tender.

adjuger [adʒyʒe] vt (prix, récompense) to award; (lors d'une vente) to auction (off); s'~ vt to take for o.s.

adjurer [adʒyRe] vt: ~ qn de faire to implore ou beg sb to do.

adjuvant [adʒyvɑ̃] nm adjuvant; additive; stimulant.

admettre [admɛtR(ə)] vt (visiteur, nouveau-venu) to admit, let in; (candidat: SCOL) to pass; (TECH: gaz, eau, air) to admit; (tolérer) to allow, accept; (reconnaître) to admit, acknowledge.

administrateur, trice [administratœR, -tRis] nm/f (COMM) director; (ADMIN) administrator.

administratif, ive [administratif, -iv] a administrative.

administration [administrɑsjɔ̃] nf administration; l'A~ ≈ the Civil Service.

administré, e [administre] nm/f: ses ~s the citizens in his care.

administrer [administre] vt (firme) to manage, run; (biens, remède, sacrement etc) to administer.

admirable [admirabl(ə)] a admirable, wonderful.

admirateur, trice [admiratœR, -tRis] nm/f admirer.

admiratif, ive [admiratif, -iv] a admiring.

admiration [admirɑsjɔ̃] nf admiration.

admirer [admire] vt to admire.

admis, e pp de **admettre**.

admissible [admisibl(ə)] a (candidat) eligible; (comportement) admissible, acceptable.

admission [admisjɔ̃] nf admission; acknowledgement; tuyau d'~ intake pipe; demande d'~ application for membership.

admonester [admɔnɛste] vt to admonish.

adolescence [adɔlesɑ̃s] nf adolescence.

adolescent, e [adɔlesɑ̃, -ɑ̃t] nm/f adolescent.

adonner [adɔne]: s'~ à vt (sport) to devote o.s. to; (boisson) to give o.s. over to.

adopter [adɔpte] vt to adopt; (projet de loi etc) to pass; **adoptif, ive** a (parents) adoptive; (fils, patrie) adopted; **adoption** nf adoption.

adoration [adɔRɑsjɔ̃] nf adoration; worship.

adorer [adɔRe] vt to adore; (REL) to worship, adore.

adosser [adose] vt: ~ qch à ou contre to stand sth against; s'~ à ou contre to lean with one's back against.

adoucir [adusiR] vt (goût, température) to make milder; (avec du sucre) to sweeten; (peau, voix) to soften; (caractère, personne) to mellow; (peine) to soothe, allay; s'~ vi to become milder; to soften; to mellow.

adresse [adRɛs] nf (voir adroit) skill, dexterity; (domicile) address; à l'~ de (pour) for the benefit of.

adresser [adRese] vt (lettre: expédier) to send; (: écrire l'adresse sur) to address; (injure, compliments) to address; ~ qn à un docteur/bureau to refer ou send sb to a doctor/an office; ~ la parole à qn to speak to ou address sb; s'~ à (parler à) to speak to, address; (s'informer auprès de) to go and see, go and speak to; (: bureau) to enquire at; (suj: livre, conseil) to be aimed at.

Adriatique [adRiatik] nf: l'~ the Adriatic.

adroit, e [adRwa, -wat] a (joueur, mécanicien) skilful, dext(e)rous; (politicien etc) shrewd, skilled; **adroitement** ad skilfully; dext(e)rously.

aduler [adyle] vt to adulate.

adulte [adylt(ə)] nm/f adult, grown-up // a (chien, arbre) fully-grown, mature; (attitude) adult. grown-up; l'âge ~ adulthood.

adultère [adyltɛR] a adulterous // nm/f adulterer/adulteress // nm (acte) adultery; **adultérin, e** a born of adultery.

advenir [advəniR] vi to happen; qu'est-il advenu de what has become of.

adverbe [advɛRb(ə)] nm adverb.

adversaire [advɛRsɛR] nm/f (SPORT, gén) opponent, adversary; (MIL) adversary, enemy; (non partisan): ~ de opponent of.

adverse [advɛRs(ə)] a opposing.

adversité [advɛRsite] nf adversity.

aérateur [aeRatœR] nm ventilator.

aération [aeRɑsjɔ̃] nf airing; ventilation;

conduit d'~ ventilation shaft ; bouche d'~ air-vent.

aéré, e [aeRe] a (pièce, local) airy, well-ventilated ; (tissu) loose-woven.

aérer [aeRe] vt to air ; (fig) to lighten ; s'~ vi to get some (fresh) air.

aérien, ne [aeRjɛ̃ -jɛn] a (AVIAT) air cpd, aerial ; (câble, métro) overhead ; (fig) light.

aéro... [aeRɔ] préfixe: ~-club nm flying club ; ~drome nm aerodrome ; ~dynamique a aerodynamic, streamlined // nf aerodynamics sg ; ~gare nf airport (buildings) ; (en ville) air terminal ; ~glisseur nm hovercraft ; ~nautique a aeronautical // nf aeronautics sg ; ~naval, e a air and sea cpd // nf the Fleet Air Arm ; ~phagie nf aerophagy ; ~port nm airport ; ~porté, e a airborne, air-lifted ; ~sol nm aerosol ; ~spatial, e, aux a aerospace ; ~train nm hovertrain.

affable [afabl(ə)] a affable.

affadir [afadiR] vt to make insipid ou tasteless.

affaiblir [afebliR] vt to weaken ; s'~ vi to weaken, grow weaker ; affaiblissement nm weakening.

affaire [afɛR] nf (problème, question) matter ; (criminelle, judiciaire) case ; (scandaleuse etc) affair ; (entreprise) business ; (marché, transaction) (business) deal ; (piece of) business q ; (occasion intéressante) good deal, bargain ; ~s nfpl affairs ; (activité commerciale) business sg ; (effets personnels) things, belongings ; ce sont mes ~s (cela me concerne) that's my business ; ceci fera l'~ this will do (nicely) ; avoir ~ à to be faced with ; to be dealing with ; les A~s étrangères (POL) Foreign Affairs ; s'affairer vi to busy o.s., bustle about ; affairisme nm (political) racketeering.

affaisser [afese]: s'~ vi (terrain, immeuble) to subside, sink ; (personne) to collapse.

affaler [afale]: s'~ vi: s'~ dans/sur to collapse ou slump into/onto.

affamer [afame] vt to starve.

affectation [afɛktɑsjɔ̃] nf allotment ; appointment ; posting ; (voir affecté) affectedness.

affecté, e [afɛkte] a affected.

affecter [afɛkte] vt (émouvoir) to affect, move ; (feindre) to affect, feign ; (telle ou telle forme etc) to take on, assume ; ~ qch à to allocate ou allot sth to ; ~ qn à to appoint sb to ; (diplomate) to post sb to ; ~ qch d'un coefficient etc to modify sth by a coefficient etc, tag a coefficient etc onto sth.

affectif, ive [afɛktif, -iv] a emotional, affective.

affection [afɛksjɔ̃] nf affection ; (mal) ailment ; affectionner vt to be fond of.

affectueux, euse [afɛktyø, -øz] a affectionate.

afférent, e [afeRɑ̃, -ɑ̃t] a: ~ à pertaining ou relating to.

affermir [afɛRmiR] vt to consolidate, strengthen.

affichage [afiʃaʒ] nm billposting ; (électronique) display ; ~ numérique ou digital digital display.

affiche [afiʃ] nf poster ; (officielle) (public) notice ; (THÉÂTRE) bill.

afficher [afiʃe] vt (affiche) to put up, post up ; (réunion) to announce by (means of) posters ou public notices ; (électroniquement) to display ; (fig) to exhibit, display ; s'~ (péj) to flaunt o.s.

affilée [afile]: d'~ ad at a stretch.

affiler [afile] vt to sharpen.

affilier [afilje] vt: s'~ à to become affiliated to.

affiner [afine] vt to refine ; s'~ vi to become (more) refined.

affinité [afinite] nf affinity.

affirmatif, ive [afiRmatif, -iv] a affirmative // nf: répondre par l'affirmative to reply yes ou in the affirmative ; dans l'affirmative if (the answer is) yes, if he does (ou you do etc).

affirmation [afiRmɑsjɔ̃] nf assertion.

affirmer [afiRme] vt (prétendre) to maintain, assert ; (autorité etc) to assert.

affleurer [aflœRe] vi to show on the surface.

affliction [afliksjɔ̃] nf affliction.

affligé, e [afliʒe] a distressed, grieved ; ~ de (maladie, ta~e) afflicted with.

affliger [afliʒe] vt (peiner) to distress, grieve.

affluence [aflyɑ̃s] nf crowds pl ; heures d'~ rush hours ; jours d'~ busiest days.

affluent [aflyɑ̃] nm tributary.

affluer [aflye] vi (secours, biens) to flood in, pour in ; (sang) to rush, flow ; afflux nm flood, influx ; rush.

affoler [afɔle] vt to throw into a panic ; s'~ vi to panic.

affranchir [afRɑ̃ʃiR] vt to put a stamp ou stamps on ; (à la machine) to frank ; (esclave) to enfranchise, emancipate ; (fig) to free, liberate ; affranchissement nm franking ; freeing ; tarifs d'affranchissement postal rates ; affranchissement insuffisant insufficient postage.

affres [afR(ə)] nfpl: dans les ~ de in the throes of.

affréter [afRete] vt to charter.

affreux, euse [afRø, -øz] a (laid) hideous, ghastly ; (épouvantable) dreadful, awful.

affriolant, e [afRijɔlɑ̃, -ɑ̃t] a tempting, arousing.

affront [afRɔ̃] nm affront.

affronter [afRɔ̃te] vt to confront, face.

affubler [afyble] vt (péj): ~ qn de to rig ou deck sb out in ; (surnom) to attach to sb.

affût [afy] nm (de canon) gun carriage ; à l'~ (de) (gibier) lying in wait (for) ; (fig) on the look-out (for).

affûter [afyte] vt to sharpen, grind.

afin [afɛ̃]: ~ que cj so that, in order that ; ~ de faire in order to do, so as to do.

a fortiori [afɔRsjɔRi] ad all the more, a fortiori.

A.F.P. sigle f = Agence France Presse.

africain, e [afRikɛ̃, -ɛn] a, nm/f African.

Afrique [afRik] nf: l'~ Africa ; l'~ du Sud South Africa.

agacer [agase] vt to pester, tease ; (involontairement) to irritate, aggravate ; (aguicher) to excite, lead on.

âge [ɑʒ] nm age; quel ~ as-tu? how old are you?; prendre de l'~ to be getting on (in years), grow older; l'~ ingrat the awkward ou difficult age; l'~ mûr maturity, middle age; âgé, e a old, elderly; âgé de 10 ans 10 years old.

agence [aʒɑ̃s] nf agency, office; (succursale) branch; ~ immobilière estate agent's (office); ~ matrimoniale marriage bureau; ~ de voyages travel agency.

agencer [aʒɑ̃se] vt to put together; to arrange, lay out.

agenda [aʒɛ̃da] nm diary.

agenouiller [aʒnuje]: s'~ vi to kneel (down).

agent [aʒɑ̃] nm (aussi: ~ de police) policeman; (ADMIN) official, officer; (fig: élément, facteur) agent; ~ d'assurances insurance broker; ~ de change stockbroker; ~ (secret) (secret) agent.

agglomération [aglɔmeʀɑsjɔ̃] nf town; built-up area; l'~ parisienne the urban area of Paris.

aggloméré [aglɔmeʀe] nm (bois) chipboard; (pierre) conglomerate.

agglomérer [aglɔmeʀe] vt to pile up; (TECH: bois, pierre) to compress.

agglutiner [aglytine] vt to stick together; s'~ vi to congregate.

aggraver [agʀave] vt to worsen, aggravate; (JUR: peine) to increase; s'~ vi to worsen.

agile [aʒil] a agile, nimble; **agilité** nf agility, nimbleness.

agir [aʒiʀ] vi (se comporter) to behave, act; (faire quelque chose) to act, take action; (avoir de l'effet) to act; il s'agit de it's a matter ou question of; it is about; (il importe que): il s'agit de faire we (ou you etc) must do; **agissements** nmpl (gén péj) schemes, intrigues.

agitateur, trice [aʒitatœʀ, -tʀis] nm/f agitator.

agitation [aʒitasjɔ̃] nf (hustle and) bustle; agitation, excitement; (politique) unrest, agitation.

agité, e [aʒite] a fidgety, restless; agitated, perturbed; (journée) hectic; une mer ~e a rough ou choppy sea; un sommeil ~ (a) disturbed ou broken sleep.

agiter [aʒite] vt (bouteille, chiffon) to shake; (bras, mains) to wave; (préoccuper, exciter) to trouble, perturb; s'~ vi to bustle about; (dormeur) to toss and turn; (enfant) to fidget; (POL) to grow restless.

agneau, x [aɲo] nm lamb.

agonie [agɔni] nf mortal agony, pangs pl of death; (fig) death throes pl.

agonir [agɔniʀ] vt: ~ qn d'injures to hurl abuse at sb.

agoniser [agɔnize] vi to be dying.

agrafe [agʀaf] nf (de vêtement) hook, fastener; (de bureau) staple; **agrafer** vt to fasten; to staple; **agrafeuse** nf stapler.

agraire [agʀɛʀ] a agrarian; (mesure, surface) land cpd.

agrandir [agʀɑ̃diʀ] vt (magasin, domaine) to extend, enlarge; (trou) to enlarge, make bigger; (PHOTO) to enlarge, blow up; s'~ vi to be extended; to be enlarged; **agrandissement** nm extension; enlarge-

ment; **agrandisseur** nm (PHOTO) enlarger.

agréable [agʀeabl(ə)] a pleasant, nice.

agréé, e [agʀee] a: concessionnaire ~ registered dealer.

agréer [agʀee] vt (requête) to accept; ~ à vt to please, suit; veuillez ~ ... (formule épistolaire) yours faithfully.

agrégation [agʀegɑsjɔ̃] nf highest teaching diploma in France (competitive examination); **agrégé, e** nm/f holder of the agrégation.

agréger [agʀeʒe]: s'~ vi to aggregate.

agrément [agʀemɑ̃] nm (accord) consent, approval; (attraits) charm, attractiveness; (plaisir) pleasure.

agrémenter [agʀemɑ̃te] vt to embellish, adorn.

agrès [agʀɛ] nmpl (gymnastics) apparatus sg.

agresser [agʀese] vt to attack.

agresseur [agʀesœʀ] nm aggressor, attacker; (POL, MIL) aggressor.

agressif, ive [agʀesif, -iv] a aggressive.

agression [agʀesjɔ̃] nf attack; (POL, MIL, PSYCH) aggression.

agressivité [agʀesivite] nf aggressiveness.

agreste [agʀɛst(ə)] a rustic.

agricole [agʀikɔl] a agricultural, farm cpd.

agriculteur [agʀikyltœʀ] nm farmer.

agriculture [agʀikyltyʀ] nf agriculture, farming.

agripper [agʀipe] vt to grab, clutch; (pour arracher) to snatch, grab; s'~ à to cling (on) to, clutch, grip.

agronome [agʀɔnɔm] nm/f agronomist.

agronomie [agʀɔnɔmi] nf agronomy, agronomics sg.

agrumes [agʀym] nmpl citrus fruit(s).

aguerrir [ageʀiʀ] vt to harden.

aguets [agɛ]: aux ~ ad: être aux ~ to be on the look-out.

aguicher [agiʃe] vt to entice.

ahurissement [ayʀismɑ̃] nm stupefaction.

ai vb voir avoir.

aide [ɛd] nm/f assistant // nf assistance, help; (secours financier) aid; à l'~ de (avec) with the help ou aid of; aller à l'~ de qn to go to sb's aid ou to help sb; venir en ~ à qn to help sb, come to sb's assistance; appeler (qn) à l'~ to call for help (from sb); ~ comptable nm accountant's assistant; ~ électricien nm electrician's mate; ~ familiale nf mother's help, home help; ~ de laboratoire nm/f laboratory assistant; ~ sociale nf (assistance) ≈ social security; ~ soignant, e nm/f auxiliary nurse; ~-mémoire nm inv memoranda pages pl (key facts) handbook.

aider [ede] vt to help; ~ à qch (faciliter) to help (towards) sth; s'~ de (se servir de) to use, make use of.

aie etc vb voir avoir.

aïe [aj] excl ouch.

aïeul, e [ajœl] nm/f grandparent, grandfather/grandmother; forbear.

aïeux [ajø] nmpl grandparents; forbears, forefathers.

aigle [ɛgl(ə)] nm eagle.

aigre [ɛgʀ(ə)] a sour, sharp; (fig) sharp, cutting; ~-doux, douce a bitter-sweet; ~-let, te a sourish, sharpish; **aigreur** nf sourness; sharpness; **aigreurs** d'estomac heartburn sg; **aigrir** vt (personne) to embitter; (caractère) to sour; s'aigrir vi to become embittered; to sour; (lait etc) to turn sour.

aigu, ë [egy] a (objet, arête) sharp, pointed; (son, voix) high-pitched, shrill; (note) high(-pitched); (douleur, intelligence) acute, sharp.

aigue-marine [ɛgmaʀin] nf aquamarine.

aiguillage [egɥijaʒ] nm (RAIL) points pl.

aiguille [egɥij] nf needle; (de montre) hand; ~ à tricoter knitting needle.

aiguiller [egɥije] vt (orienter) to direct; (RAIL) to shunt; **aiguilleur** nm (RAIL) pointsman; **aiguilleur du ciel** air traffic controller.

aiguillon [egɥijɔ̃] nm (d'abeille) sting; (fig) spur, stimulus; **aiguillonner** vt to spur ou goad on.

aiguiser [egize] vt to sharpen, grind; (fig) to stimulate; to sharpen; to excite.

ail [aj] nm garlic.

aile [ɛl] nf wing; **ailé, e** a winged; **aileron** nm (de requin) fin; (d'avion) aileron; (de voiture) aerofoil; **ailette** nf (TECH) fin; blade; wing; **ailier** nm winger.

aille etc vb voir **aller**.

ailleurs [ajœʀ] ad elsewhere, somewhere else; partout/nulle part ~ everywhere/nowhere else; d'~ ad (du reste) moreover, besides; par ~ ad (d'autre part) moreover, furthermore.

aimable [ɛmabl(ə)] a kind, nice; ~ment ad kindly.

aimant [ɛmɑ̃] nm magnet.

aimant, e [ɛmɑ̃, -ɑ̃t] a loving, affectionate.

aimanter [ɛmɑ̃te] vt to magnetize.

aimer [eme] vt to love; (d'amitié, affection, par goût) to like; (souhait): j'aimerais... I would like...; bien ~ qn/qch to quite like sb/sth; j'aime mieux ou autant vous dire que I may as well tell you that; j'aimerais autant y aller maintenant I'd sooner ou rather go now; j'aimerais mieux y aller maintenant I'd much rather go now.

aine [ɛn] nf groin.

aîné, e [ene] a elder, older; (le plus âgé) eldest, oldest // nm/f eldest child ou one, oldest boy ou son/girl ou daughter; il est mon ~ (de 2 ans) (rapports non familiaux) he's (2 years) older than me, he's 2 years my senior; ~s nmpl (fig: anciens) elders; **aînesse** nf: droit d'aînesse birthright.

ainsi [ɛ̃si] ad (de cette façon) like this, in this way, thus; (ce faisant) thus // cj thus, so; ~ que (comme) (just) as; (et aussi) as well as; pour ~ dire so to speak, as it were; et ~ de suite and so on (and so forth).

air [ɛʀ] nm air; (mélodie) tune; (expression) look, air; en l'~ (up) into the air; tirer en l'~ to fire shots in the air; prendre l'~ to get some (fresh) air; (avion) to take off; avoir l'~ (sembler) to look, appear; avoir l'~ de to look like; avoir l'~ de faire to look as though one is doing, appear to be doing.

aire [ɛʀ] nf (zone, fig, MATH) area; (nid) eyrie; ~ d'atterrissage landing strip; landing patch; ~ de jeu play area; ~ de lancement launching site; ~ de stationnement parking area; (d'autoroute) lay-by.

aisance [ɛzɑ̃s] nf ease; (richesse) affluence; être dans l'~ to be well-off, be affluent.

aise [ɛz] nf comfort // a: être bien ~ que to be delighted that; ~s nfpl: aimer ses ~s to like one's (creature) comforts; prendre ses ~s to make o.s. comfortable; frémir d'~ to shudder with pleasure; être à l'~ ou à son ~ to be comfortable; (pas embarrassé) to be at ease; (financièrement) to be comfortably off; se mettre à l'~ to make o.s. comfortable; être mal à l'~ ou à son ~ to be uncomfortable; to be ill at ease; mettre qn mal à l'~ to make sb feel ill at ease; à votre ~ please yourself, just as you like; en faire à son ~ to do as one likes; **aisé, e** a easy; (assez riche) well-to-do, well-off; **aisément** ad easily.

aisselle [ɛsɛl] nf armpit.

ait vb voir **avoir**.

ajonc [aʒɔ̃] nm gorse q.

ajouré, e [aʒuʀe] a openwork cpd.

ajournement [aʒuʀnəmɑ̃] nm adjournment; deferment; postponement.

ajourner [aʒuʀne] vt (réunion) to adjourn; (décision) to defer, postpone; (candidat) to refer; (conscrit) to defer.

ajout [aʒu] nm addition.

ajouter [aʒute] vt to add; ~ à (accroître) to add to; s'~ à to add to; ~ foi à to lend ou give credence to.

ajustage [aʒystaʒ] nm fitting.

ajusté, e [aʒyste] a: bien ~ (robe etc) close-fitting.

ajustement [aʒystəmɑ̃] nm adjustment.

ajuster [aʒyste] vt (régler) to adjust; (vêtement) to alter; (coup de fusil) to aim; (cible) to aim at; (TECH, gén: adapter): ~ qch à to fit sth to; **ajusteur** nm metal worker.

alambic [alɑ̃bik] nm still.

alanguir [alɑ̃giʀ]: s'~ vi to grow languid.

alarme [alaʀm(ə)] nf alarm; donner l'~ to give ou raise the alarm; **alarmer** vt to alarm; s'alarmer vi to become alarmed.

Albanie [albani] nf: l'~ Albania.

albâtre [albɑtʀ(ə)] nm alabaster.

albatros [albatʀos] nm albatross.

albinos [albinos] nm/f albino.

album [albɔm] nm album.

albumen [albymɛn] nm albumen.

albumine [albymin] nf albumin; avoir ou faire de l'~ to suffer from albuminuria.

alcalin, e [alkalɛ̃, -in] a alkaline.

alchimie [alʃimi] nf alchemy; **alchimiste** nm alchemist.

alcool [alkɔl] nm: l'~ alcohol; un ~ a spirit, a brandy; ~ à brûler methylated spirits; ~ à 90° surgical spirit; ~ique a, nm/f alcoholic; ~isé, e a alcoholic; ~isme nm alcoholism; **alco(o)test** ® nm breathalyser; (test) breath-test.

alcôve [alkov] nf alcove, recess.

aléas [alea] *nmpl* hazards ; **aléatoire** *a* uncertain.

alentour [alɑ̃tuʀ] *ad* around (about) ; **~s** *nmpl* surroundings ; **aux ~s de** in the vicinity *ou* neighbourhood of, around about ; *(temps)* (a)round about.

alerte [alɛʀt(ə)] *a* agile, nimble ; brisk, lively // *nf* alert ; warning ; **donner l'~** to give the alert ; **alerter** *vt* to alert.

alèse [alɛz] *nf* (*drap*) undersheet, drawsheet.

aléser [aleze] *vt* to ream.

alevin [alvɛ̃] *nm* alevin, young fish.

algarade [algaʀad] *nf* row, dispute.

algèbre [alʒɛbʀ(ə)] *nf* algebra ; **algébrique** *a* algebraic.

Alger [alʒe] *n* Algiers.

Algérie [alʒeʀi] *nf* Algeria ; **algérien, ne** *a, nm/f* Algerian.

Algérois, e [alʒeʀwa, -waz] *nm/f* inhabitant *ou* native of Algiers // *nm*: **l'~** the Algiers region.

algorithme [algɔʀitm(ə)] *nm* algorithm.

algue [alg(ə)] *nf* (*gén*) seaweed *q* ; (*BOT*) alga (*pl* algae).

alibi [alibi] *nm* alibi.

aliénation [aljenɑsjɔ̃] *nf* alienation.

aliéné, e [aljene] *nm/f* insane person, lunatic (*péj*).

aliéner [aljene] *vt* to alienate ; (*bien, liberté*) to give up ; **s'~** *vt* to alienate.

alignement [aliɲmɑ̃] *nm* alignment ; lining up ; **à l'~** in line.

aligner [aliɲe] *vt* to align, line up ; (*idées, chiffres*) to string together ; (*adapter*): **~ qch sur** to bring sth into alignment with ; **s'~** (*soldats etc*) to line up ; **s'~ sur** (*POL*) to align o.s. on.

aliment [alimɑ̃] *nm* food ; **alimentaire** *a* food *cpd* ; (*péj: besogne*) done merely to earn a living, done as a potboiler ; **produits alimentaires** foodstuffs, foods.

alimentation [alimɑ̃tɑsjɔ̃] *nf* feeding ; supplying ; (*commerce*) food trade ; (*produits*) groceries *pl* ; (*régime*) diet.

alimenter [alimɑ̃te] *vt* to feed ; (*TECH*): **(en)** to supply (with) ; to feed (with) ; (*fig*) to sustain, keep going.

alinéa [alinea] *nm* paragraph ; **'nouvel ~'** new line.

aliter [alite]: **s'~** *vi* to take to one's bed.

alizé [alize] *a, nm*: (*vent*) **~** trade wind.

allaiter [alete] *vt* to (breast-)feed, nurse ; (*suj: animal*) to suckle.

allant [alɑ̃] *nm* drive, go.

allécher [aleʃe] *vt*: **~ qn** to make sb's mouth water ; to tempt sb, entice sb.

allée [ale] *nf* (*de jardin*) path ; (*en ville*) avenue, drive. **~s et venues** *nfpl* comings and goings.

allégation [alegɑsjɔ̃] *nf* allegation.

alléger [aleʒe] *vt* (*voiture*) to make lighter ; (*chargement*) to lighten ; (*souffrance*) to alleviate, soothe.

allégorie [alegɔʀi] *nf* allegory.

allègre [alɛgʀ(ə)] *a* lively, jaunty ; gay, cheerful.

allégresse [alegʀɛs] *nf* (*joie*) elation, gaiety.

alléguer [alege] *vt* to put forward (as proof *ou* an excuse).

Allemagne [aləmaɲ] *nf*: **l'~** Germany ; **l'~ de l'Est/Ouest East/West Germany** ; **allemand, e** *a, nm/f, nm* (*langue*) German.

aller [ale] *nm* (*trajet*) outward journey ; (*billet*) single *ou* one-way ticket // *vi* (*gén*) to go ; **~ à** (*convenir*) to suit ; (*suj: forme, pointure etc*) to fit ; **~ avec** (*couleurs, style etc*) to go (well) with ; **je vais y aller/me fâcher** I'm going to go/to get angry ; **~ voir** to go and see, go to see ; **comment allez-vous** *ou* **ça va?** how are you? ; **comment ça va?** (*affaires etc*) how are things? ; **il va bien/mal** he's well/not well, he's fine/ill ; **ça va bien/mal** (*affaires etc*) it's going well/not going well ; **il y va de leur vie** their lives are at stake ; **s'en ~** *vi* (*partir*) to be off, go, leave ; (*disparaître*) to go away ; **~ et retour** *nm* (*trajet*) return trip *ou* journey ; (*billet*) return (ticket).

allergie [alɛʀʒi] *nf* allergy ; **allergique** *a* allergic ; **allergique à** allergic to.

alliage [aljaʒ] *nm* alloy.

alliance [aljɑ̃s] *nf* (*MIL, POL*) alliance ; (*mariage*) marriage ; (*bague*) wedding ring ; **neveu par ~** nephew by marriage.

allié, e [alje] *nm/f* ally ; **parents et ~s** relatives and relatives by marriage.

allier [alje] *vt* (*métaux*) to alloy ; (*POL, gén*) to ally ; (*fig*) to combine ; **s'~** to become allies ; (*éléments, caractéristiques*) to combine ; **s'~ à** to become allied to *ou* with.

allô [alo] *excl* hullo, hallo.

allocataire [alɔkatɛʀ] *nm/f* beneficiary.

allocation [alɔkɑsjɔ̃] *nf* allowance ; **~ (de) chômage** unemployment benefit ; **~ (de) logement** rent allowance *ou* subsidy ; **~s familiales** family allowance(s).

allocution [alɔkysjɔ̃] *nf* short speech.

allonger [alɔ̃ʒe] *vt* to lengthen, make longer ; (*étendre: bras, jambe*) to stretch (out) ; **s'~** *vi* to get longer ; (*se coucher*) to lie down, stretch out ; **~ le pas** to hasten one's step(s).

allouer [alwe] *vt*: **~ qch à** to allocate sth to, allot sth to.

allumage [alymaʒ] *nm* (*AUTO*) ignition.

allume... [alym] *préfixe*: **~-cigare** *nm inv* cigar lighter ; **~-gaz** *nm inv* gas lighter.

allumer [alyme] *vt* (*lampe, phare, radio*) to put *ou* switch on ; (*pièce*) to put *ou* switch the light(s) on in ; (*feu*) to light ; **s'~** *vi* (*lumière, lampe*) to come *ou* go on.

allumette [alymɛt] *nf* match.

allumeuse [alyméz] *nf* (*péj*) teaser, vamp.

allure [alyʀ] *nf* (*vitesse*) speed ; pace ; (*démarche*) walk ; (*maintien*) bearing ; (*aspect, air*) look ; **avoir de l'~** to have style *ou* a certain elegance ; **à toute ~** at top *ou* full speed.

allusion [alyzjɔ̃] *nf* allusion ; (*sous-entendu*) hint ; **faire ~ à** to allude *ou* refer to ; to hint at.

alluvions [alyvjɔ̃] *nfpl* alluvial deposits, alluvium *sg*.

almanach [almana] *nm* almanac.

aloi [alwa] *nm*: **de bon ~** of genuine worth *ou* quality.

alors [alɔʀ] *ad* then, at that time // *cj* then, so ; **~ que** *cj* (*au moment où*) when, as ; (*pendant que*) while, when ; (*tandis que*) whereas, while.

alouette [alwɛt] *nf* (sky)lark.
alourdir [aluʀdiʀ] *vt* to weigh down, make heavy.
aloyau [alwajo] *nm* sirloin.
alpage [alpaʒ] *nm* high mountain pasture.
Alpes [alp(ə)] *nfpl*: les ~ the Alps; **alpestre** *a* alpine.
alphabet [alfabɛ] *nm* alphabet; (*livre*) ABC (book), primer; **alphabétique** *a* alphabetic(al); **alphabétiser** *vt* to teach to read and write; to eliminate illiteracy in.
alpin, e [alpɛ̃, -in] *a* alpine; **alpinisme** *nm* mountaineering, climbing; **alpiniste** *nm/f* mountaineer, climber.
Alsace [alzas] *nf* Alsace; **alsacien, ne** *a*, *nm/f* Alsatian.
altérer [alteʀe] *vt* to falsify; to distort; to debase; to impair; (*donner soif à*) to make thirsty; s'~ *vi* to deteriorate; to spoil.
alternance [altɛʀnɑ̃s] *nf* alternation; en ~ alternately.
alternateur [altɛʀnatœʀ] *nm* alternator.
alternatif, ive [altɛʀnatif, -iv] *a* alternating // *nf* (*choix*) alternative; **alternativement** *ad* alternately.
alterner [altɛʀne] *vt* to alternate // *vi*: ~ (avec) to alternate (with); (**faire**) ~ qch avec qch to alternate sth with sth.
Altesse [altɛs] *nf* Highness.
altier, ière [altje, -jɛʀ] *a* haughty.
altimètre [altimɛtʀ(ə)] *nm* altimeter.
altiste [altist(ə)] *nm/f* viola player, violist.
altitude [altityd] *nf* altitude, height; à 1000 m d'~ at a height *ou* an altitude of 1000 m; en ~ at high altitudes.
alto [alto] *nm* (*instrument*) viola // *nf* (contr)alto.
altruisme [altʀɥism(ə)] *nm* altruism.
aluminium [alyminjɔm] *nm* aluminium.
alunir [alyniʀ] *vi* to land on the moon.
alvéole [alveɔl] *nf* (*de ruche*) alveolus; **alvéolé, e** *a* honeycombed.
amabilité [amabilite] *nf* kindness, amiability; il a eu l'~ de he was kind *ou* good enough to.
amadou [amadu] *nm* touchwood, amadou.
amadouer [amadwe] *vt* to coax, cajole; to mollify, soothe.
amaigrir [amegʀiʀ] *vt* to make thin *ou* thinner; **régime amaigrissant** slimming diet.
amalgamer [amalgame] *vt* to amalgamate.
amande [amɑ̃d] *nf* (*de l'amandier*) almond; (*de noyau de fruit*) kernel; **amandier** *nm* almond (tree).
amant [amɑ̃] *nm* lover.
amarre [amaʀ] *nf* (NAVIG) (mooring) rope *ou* line; ~s moorings; **amarrer** *vt* (NAVIG) to moor; (*gén*) to make fast.
amas [amɑ] *nm* heap, pile.
amasser [amase] *vt* to amass; s'~ *vi* to pile up; to accumulate; to gather.
amateur [amatœʀ] *nm* amateur; en ~ (*péj*) amateurishly; **musicien/sportif** ~ amateur musician/sportsman; ~ **de musique/sport** *etc* music/sport *etc* lover; ~**isme** *nm* amateurism; (*péj*) amateurishness.

amazone [amazon] *nf*: en ~ sidesaddle.
ambages [ɑ̃baʒ]: sans ~ *ad* without beating about the bush, plainly.
ambassade [ɑ̃basad] *nf* embassy; (*mission*): en ~ on a mission; **ambassadeur, drice** *nm/f* ambassador/ambassadress.
ambiance [ɑ̃bjɑ̃s] *nf* atmosphere.
ambiant, e [ɑ̃bjɑ̃, -ɑ̃t] *a* (*air, milieu*) surrounding; (*température*) ambient.
ambidextre [ɑ̃bidɛkstʀ(ə)] *a* ambidextrous.
ambigu, ë [ɑ̃bigy] *a* ambiguous; **ambiguïté** *nf* ambiguousness q, ambiguity.
ambitieux, euse [ɑ̃bisjø, -øz] *a* ambitious.
ambition [ɑ̃bisjɔ̃] *nf* ambition; **ambitionner** *vt* to have as one's aim *ou* ambition.
ambivalent, e [ɑ̃bivalɑ̃, -ɑ̃t] *a* ambivalent.
ambre [ɑ̃bʀ(ə)] *nm*: ~ (**jaune**) amber; ~ **gris** ambergris.
ambulance [ɑ̃bylɑ̃s] *nf* ambulance; **ambulancier, ière** *nm/f* ambulance man/woman.
ambulant, e [ɑ̃bylɑ̃, -ɑ̃t] *a* travelling, itinerant.
âme [ɑm] *nf* soul; ~ **sœur** kindred spirit.
améliorer [ameljɔʀe] *vt* to improve; s'~ *vi* to improve, get better.
aménagement [amenaʒmɑ̃] *nm* fitting out; laying out; developing; ~s *nmpl* developments; l'~ **du territoire** ≈ town and country planning; ~s **fiscaux** tax adjustments.
aménager [amenaʒe] *vt* (*agencer, transformer*) to fit out; to lay out; (: *quartier, territoire*) to develop; (*installer*) to fix up, put in; **ferme aménagée** converted farmhouse.
amende [amɑ̃d] *nf* fine; **mettre à l'~** to penalize; **faire ~ honorable** to make amends.
amender [amɑ̃de] *vt* (*loi*) to amend; (*terre*) to enrich; s'~ *vi* to mend one's ways.
amène [amɛn] *a* affable; **peu** ~ unkind.
amener [amne] *vt* to bring; (*causer*) to bring about; (*baisser: drapeau, voiles*) to strike; s'~ *vi* (*fam*) to show up, turn up.
amenuiser [amənɥize]: s'~ *vi* to grow slimmer, lessen; to dwindle.
amer, amère [amɛʀ] *a* bitter.
américain, e [ameʀikɛ̃, -ɛn] *a*, *nm/f* American.
Amérique [ameʀik] *nf* America; l'~ **centrale** Central America; l'~ **latine** Latin America; l'~ **du Nord** North America; l'~ **du Sud** South America.
amerrir [ameʀiʀ] *vi* to land (on the sea).
amertume [amɛʀtym] *nf* bitterness.
améthyste [ametist(ə)] *nf* amethyst.
ameublement [amœbləmɑ̃] *nm* furnishing; (*meubles*) furniture; **articles d'~** furnishings; **tissus d'~** soft furnishings, fabrics.
ameuter [amøte] *vt* (*badauds*) to draw a crowd of; (*peuple*) to rouse, stir up.
ami, e [ami] *nm/f* friend; (*amant/maîtresse*) boyfriend/girlfriend // *a*: **pays/groupe** ~ friendly country/group; **être (très)** ~ **avec qn** to be (very)

good friends with sb ; être ~ de l'ordre to be a lover of order ; un ~ des arts a patron of the arts ; un ~ des chiens a dog lover.

amiable [amjabl(ə)]: à l'~ ad (JUR) out of court ; (gén) amicably.

amiante [amjɑ̃t] nm asbestos.

amibe [amib] nf amoeba (pl ae).

amical, e, aux [amikal, -o] a friendly // nf (club) association.

amidon [amidɔ̃] nm starch ; **amidonner** vt to starch.

amincir [amɛ̃siR] vt (objet) to thin (down) ; ~ qn to make sb thinner ou slimmer ; s'~ vi to get thinner ; to get slimmer.

amiral, aux [amiral, -o] nm admiral ; **amirauté** nf admiralty.

amitié [amitje] nf friendship ; **prendre en ~** to take a liking to, befriend ; **faire** ou **présenter ses ~s** à qn to send sb one's best wishes ou kind regards.

ammoniac [amɔnjak] nm: (gaz) ~ ammonia.

ammoniaque [amɔnjak] nf ammonia (water).

amnésie [amnezi] nf amnesia ; **amnésique** a amnesic.

amnistie [amnisti] nf amnesty ; **amnistier** vt to amnesty.

amoindrir [amwɛ̃dRiR] vt to reduce.

amollir [amɔliR] vt to soften.

amonceler [amɔ̃sle] vt, s'~ vi to pile ou heap up ; (fig) to accumulate.

amont [amɔ̃]: en ~ ad upstream ; (sur une pente) uphill ; en ~ de prép upstream from ; uphill from, above.

amorce [amɔRs(ə)] nf (sur un hameçon) bait ; (explosif) cap ; primer ; priming ; (fig: début) beginning(s), start ; **amorcer** vt to bait ; to prime ; to begin, start.

amorphe [amɔRf(ə)] a passive, lifeless.

amortir [amɔRtiR] vt (atténuer: choc) to absorb, cushion ; (bruit, douleur) to deaden ; (COMM: dette) to pay off, amortize ; (: mise de fonds) to write off ; (: matériel) to write off, depreciate ; ~ un abonnement to make a season ticket pay (for itself).

amour [amuR] nm love ; (liaison) love affair, love ; (statuette etc) cupid ; **faire l'~** to make love ; s'~acher de (péj) to become infatuated with ; ~ette nf passing fancy, ~eux, euse a (regard, tempérament) amorous ; (vie, problèmes) love cpd ; (personne): ~eux (de qn) in love (with sb) // nm/f lover // nmpl courting couple(s) ; être ~eux de qch to be passionately fond of sth ; un ~eux de la nature a nature lover ; ~-propre nm self-esteem, pride.

amovible [amɔvibl(ə)] a removable, detachable.

ampère [ɑ̃pɛR] nm amp(ere) ; ~mètre nm ammeter.

amphibie [ɑ̃fibi] a amphibious.

amphithéâtre [ɑ̃fiteɑtR(ə)] nm amphitheatre ; (d'université) lecture hall ou theatre.

amphore [ɑ̃fɔR] nf amphora.

ample [ɑ̃pl(ə)] a (vêtement) roomy, ample ; (gestes, mouvement) broad ; (ressources) ample ; ~ment ad amply ; ~ment

suffisant ample, more than enough ; **ampleur** nf (importance) scale, size ; extent, magnitude.

amplificateur [ɑ̃plifikatœR] nm amplifier.

amplifier [ɑ̃plifje] vt (son, oscillation) to amplify ; (fig) to expand, increase.

amplitude [ɑ̃plityd] nf amplitude ; (des températures) range.

ampoule [ɑ̃pul] nf (électrique) bulb ; (de médicament) phial ; (aux mains, pieds) blister.

ampoulé, e [ɑ̃pule] a (péj) turgid, pompous.

amputation [ɑ̃pytasjɔ̃] nf amputation.

amputer [ɑ̃pyte] vt (MÉD) to amputate ; (fig) to cut ou reduce drastically ; ~ qn d'un bras/pied to amputate sb's arm/foot.

amulette [amylɛt] nf amulet.

amusant, e [amyzɑ̃, -ɑ̃t] a (divertissant, spirituel) entertaining, amusing ; (comique) funny, amusing.

amusé, e [amyze] a amused.

amuse-gueule [amyzgœl] nm inv appetizer, snack.

amusement [amyzmɑ̃] nm (voir amusé) amusement ; (voir amuser) entertaining, amusing ; (jeu etc) pastime, diversion.

amuser [amyze] vt (divertir) to entertain, amuse ; (égayer, faire rire) to amuse ; (détourner l'attention de) to distract ; s'~ vi (jouer) to amuse o.s., play ; (se divertir) to enjoy o.s., have fun ; (fig) to mess about ; s'~ de qch (trouver comique) to find sth amusing ; s'~ avec ou de qn (duper) to make a fool of sb ; **amusette** nf idle pleasure, trivial pastime ; **amuseur** nm entertainer ; (péj) clown.

amygdale [amidal] nf tonsil ; **opérer qn des ~s** to take sb's tonsils out.

an [ɑ̃] nm year.

anachronique [anakRɔnik] a anachronistic ; **anachronisme** nm anachronism.

anagramme [anagRam] nf anagram.

anal, e, aux [anal, -o] a anal.

analgésique [analʒezik] nm analgesic.

analogie [analɔʒi] nf analogy.

analogue [analɔg] a: ~ (à) analogous (to), similar (to).

analphabète [analfabɛt] nm/f illiterate.

analyse [analiz] nf (gén) analysis ; (MÉD) test ; **faire l'~ de** to analyse ; ~ **grammaticale** grammatical analysis, parsing (SCOL) ; **analyser** vt to analyse ; (MÉD) to test ; **analyste** nm/f analyst ; (psych-analyste) (psycho)analyst ; **analytique** a analytical.

ananas [anana] nm pineapple.

anarchie [anaRʃi] nf (gén, POL) anarchy ; **anarchisme** nm anarchism ; **anarchiste** a anarchistic // nm/f anarchist.

anathème [anatɛm] nm: **jeter l'~ sur**, **lancer l'~ contre** to anathematize, curse.

anatomie [anatɔmi] nf anatomy ; **anatomique** a anatomical.

ancestral, e, aux [ɑ̃sɛstRal, -o] a ancestral.

ancêtre [ɑ̃sɛtR(ə)] nm/f ancestor ; (fig): l'~ de the forerunner of ; ~s nmpl (aïeux) ancestors, forefathers.

anche [ɑ̃ʃ] nf reed.

anchois [ɑ̃ʃwa] nm anchovy.

ancien, ne [ɑ̃sjɛ̃, -jɛn] a old; (de jadis, de l'antiquité) ancient; (précédent, ex-) former, old // nm/f (dans une tribu) elder; **un ~ ministre** a former minister; **être plus ~ que qn dans une maison** to have been in a firm longer than sb; to be senior to sb (in a firm); **anciennement** ad formerly; **ancienneté** nf oldness; antiquity; (ADMIN) (length of) service; seniority.

ancrage [ɑ̃kRaʒ] nm anchoring; (NAVIG) anchorage; (CONSTR) cramp(-iron), anchor.

ancre [ɑ̃kR(ə)] nf anchor; **jeter/lever l'~** to cast/weigh anchor; **à l'~** at anchor.

ancrer [ɑ̃kRe] vt (CONSTR: câble etc) to anchor; (fig) to fix firmly; **s'~** vi (NAVIG) to (cast) anchor.

Andorre [ɑ̃dɔR] n Andorra.

andouille [ɑ̃duj] nf (CULIN) sausage made of chitterlings; (fam) clot, nit.

âne [ɑn] nm donkey, ass; (péj) dunce, fool.

anéantir [aneɑ̃tiR] vt to annihilate, wipe out; (fig) to obliterate, destroy; to overwhelm.

anecdote [anɛkdɔt] nf anecdote; **anecdotique** a anecdotal.

anémie [anemi] nf anaemia; **anémié, e** a anaemic; (fig) enfeebled; **anémique** a anaemic.

anémone [anemɔn] nf anemone; **~ de mer** sea anemone.

ânerie [ɑnRi] nf stupidity; stupid ou idiotic comment etc.

ânesse [ɑnɛs] nf she-ass.

anesthésie [anɛstezi] nf anaesthesia; **faire une ~ locale à qn** to give sb a local anaesthetic; **anesthésier** vt to anaesthetize; **anesthésique** a anaesthetic; **anesthésiste** nm/f anaesthetist.

anfractuosité [ɑ̃fRaktyozite] nf crevice.

ange [ɑ̃ʒ] nm angel; **être aux ~s** to be over the moon; **~ gardien** guardian angel; **angélique** a angelic(al).

angélus [ɑ̃ʒelys] nm angelus.

angine [ɑ̃ʒin] nf sore throat, throat infection (tonsillitis or pharyngitis); **~ de poitrine** angina (pectoris).

anglais, e [ɑ̃glɛ, -ɛz] a English // nm/f: **A~, e** Englishman/woman // nm (langue) English; **les A~** the English; **~es** nfpl (cheveux) ringlets; **filer à l'~e** to take French leave.

angle [ɑ̃gl(ə)] nm angle; (coin) corner; **~ droit/obtus/aigu** right/obtuse/acute angle.

Angleterre [ɑ̃glətɛR] nf: **l'~** England.

anglican, e [ɑ̃glikɑ̃, -an] a Anglican.

anglicisme [ɑ̃glisism(ə)] nm anglicism.

angliciste [ɑ̃glisist(ə)] nm/f English scholar; student of English.

anglo... [ɑ̃glɔ] préfixe Anglo-, anglo(-); **~phile** a anglophilic; **~phobe** a anglophobic; **~phone** a English-speaking; **~-saxon, ne** a Anglo-Saxon.

angoisse [ɑ̃gwas] nf: **l'~** anguish q; **angoisser** vt to harrow, cause anguish to.

anguille [ɑ̃gij] nf eel; **~ de mer** conger (eel).

angulaire [ɑ̃gylɛR] a angular.

anguleux, euse [ɑ̃gylø, -øz] a angular.

ancroche [ɑ̃kRɔʃ] nf hitch, snag.

animal, e, aux [animal, -o] a, nm animal; **~ier** a: **peintre ~ier** animal painter.

animateur, trice [animatœR, -tRis] nm/f (de télévision, music-hall) compère; (de maison de jeunes) leader, organizer.

animation [animɑsjɔ̃] nf (voir animé) business; liveliness; (CINÉMA: technique) animation.

animé, e [anime] a (rue, lieu) busy, lively; (conversation, réunion) lively, animated; (opposé à inanimé, aussi LING) animate.

animer [anime] vt (ville, soirée) to liven up, enliven; (mettre en mouvement) to drive; (stimuler) to drive, impel; **s'~** vi to liven up, come to life.

animosité [animozite] nf animosity.

anis [ani] nm (CULIN) aniseed; (BOT) anise.

ankyloser [ɑ̃kiloze]: **s'~** vi to get stiff, to ankylose.

annales [anal] nfpl annals.

anneau, x [ano] nm (de rideau, bague) ring; (de chaîne) link.

année [ane] nf year; **l'~ scolaire/fiscale** the school/tax year; **~-lumière** nf light year.

annexe [anɛks(ə)] a (problème) related; (document) appended; (salle) adjoining // nf (bâtiment) annex(e); (de document, ouvrage) annex, appendix; (jointe à une lettre, un dossier) enclosure.

annexer [anɛkse] vt (pays, biens) to annex; **~ qch à** (joindre) to append sth to; **annexion** nf annexation.

annihiler [aniile] vt to annihilate.

anniversaire [anivɛRsɛR] nm birthday; (d'un événement, bâtiment) anniversary // a: **jour ~** anniversary.

annonce [anɔ̃s] nf announcement; (signe, indice) sign; (aussi: **~ publicitaire**) advertisement; (CARTES) declaration; **les petites ~s** the classified advertisements, the small ads.

annoncer [anɔ̃se] vt to announce; (être le signe de) to herald; **s'~ bien/difficile** to look promising/difficult; **annonceur, euse** nm/f (TV, RADIO: speaker) announcer; (publicitaire) advertiser; **l'Annonciation** nf the Annunciation.

annotation [anɔtɑsjɔ̃] nf annotation.

annoter [anɔte] vt to annotate.

annuaire [anɥɛR] nm yearbook, annual; **~ téléphonique** (telephone) directory, phone book.

annuel, le [anɥɛl] a annual, yearly; **~lement** ad annually, yearly.

annuité [anɥite] nf annual instalment.

annulaire [anylɛR] nm ring ou third finger.

annulation [anylɑsjɔ̃] nf cancellation; annulment; quashing.

annuler [anyle] vt (rendez-vous, voyage) to cancel, call off; (mariage) to annul; (jugement) to quash; (résultats) to declare void; (MATH, PHYSIQUE) to cancel out.

anoblir [anɔbliR] vt to ennoble.

anode [anɔd] nf anode.

anodin, e [anɔdɛ̃, -in] a harmless; insignificant, trivial.

anomalie [anɔmali] nf anomaly.

ânonner [unɔne] vi, vt to read in a drone ; to read in a fumbling manner.

anonymat [anɔnima] nm anonymity.

anonyme [anɔnim] a anonymous ; (fig) impersonal.

anorak [anɔʀak] nm anorak.

anormal, e, aux [anɔʀmal, -o] a abnormal ; (insolite) unusual, abnormal.

anse [ɑ̃s] nf (de panier, tasse) handle ; (GÉO) cove.

antagoniste [ɑ̃tagɔnist(ə)] a antagonistic // nm antagonist.

antan [ɑ̃tɑ̃]: **d'~** a of yesteryear, of long ago.

antarctique [ɑ̃taʀktik] a Antarctic // nm: l'A~ the Antarctic.

antécédent [ɑ̃tesedɑ̃] nm (LING) antecedent ; **~s** nmpl (MÉD etc) past history sg.

antédiluvien, ne [ɑ̃tedilyvjɛ̃, -jɛn] a (fig) ancient, antediluvian.

antenne [ɑ̃tɛn] nf (de radio, télévision) aerial ; (d'insecte) antenna (pl ae), feeler ; (poste avancé) outpost ; (petite succursale) sub-branch ; **passer à l'~** to go on the air ; **prendre l'~** to tune in ; **2 heures d'~** 2 hours' broadcasting time.

antépénultième [ɑ̃tepenyltjɛm] a antepenultimate, last but two.

antérieur, e [ɑ̃teʀjœʀ] a (d'avant) previous, earlier ; (de devant) front ; **~ à** prior ou previous to ; **passé/futur ~** (LING) past/future anterior ; **~ement** ad earlier, previously ; **~ement à** prior ou previous to ; **antériorité** nf precedence (in time).

anthologie [ɑ̃tɔlɔʒi] nf anthology.

anthracite [ɑ̃tʀasit] nm anthracite.

anthropo... [ɑ̃tʀɔpɔ] préfixe: **~centrisme** nm anthropocentrism ; **~logie** nf anthropology ; **~logue** nm/f anthropologist ; **~métrie** nf anthropometry ; **~morphisme** nm anthropomorphism ; **~phage** a cannibalistic, anthropophagous.

anti... [ɑ̃ti] préfixe anti... ; **~aérien, ne** a anti-aircraft ; **~abri ~aérien** air-raid shelter ; **~alcoolique** a against alcohol ; **ligue ~alcoolique** temperance league ; **~atomique** a: **abri ~atomique** fallout shelter ; **~biotique** nm antibiotic ; **~brouillard** a: **phare ~brouillard** fog lamp ; **~cancéreux, euse** a cancer cpd.

antichambre [ɑ̃tiʃɑ̃bʀ(ə)] nf antechamber, anteroom ; **faire ~** to wait (for an audience).

antichar [ɑ̃tiʃaʀ] a anti-tank.

anticipation [ɑ̃tisipasjɔ̃] nf anticipation ; payment in advance ; **livre/film d'~** science fiction book/film.

anticipé, e [ɑ̃tisipe] a (règlement, paiement) early, in advance ; (joie etc) anticipated, early ; **avec mes remerciements ~s** thanking you in advance ou anticipation.

anticiper [ɑ̃tisipe] vt (événement, coup) to anticipate, foresee ; (paiement) to pay ou make in advance // vi to look ou think ahead ; to jump ahead ; to anticipate ; **~ sur** to anticipate.

anticlérical, e, aux [ɑ̃tikleʀikal, -o] a anticlerical.

anticonceptionnel, le [ɑ̃tikɔ̃sɛpsjɔnɛl] a contraceptive.

anticorps [ɑ̃tikɔʀ] nm antibody.

anticyclone [ɑ̃tisiklɔn] nm anticyclone.

antidater [ɑ̃tidate] vt to backdate, predate.

antidérapant, e [ɑ̃tideʀapɑ̃, -ɑ̃t] a non-skid.

antidote [ɑ̃tidɔt] nm antidote.

antienne [ɑ̃tjɛn] nf (fig) chant, refrain.

antigel [ɑ̃tiʒɛl] nm antifreeze.

Antilles [ɑ̃tij] nfpl: **les ~** the West Indies.

antilope [ɑ̃tilɔp] nf antelope.

antimilitariste [ɑ̃timilitaʀist(ə)] a antimilitarist.

antimite(s) [ɑ̃timit] a, nm: **(produit) ~** mothproofer ; moth repellent.

antiparasite [ɑ̃tipaʀazit] a (RADIO, TV) anti-interference ; **dispositif ~** suppressor.

antipathie [ɑ̃tipati] nf antipathy ; **antipathique** a unpleasant, disagreeable.

antiphrase [ɑ̃tifʀaz] nf: **par ~** ironically.

antipodes [ɑ̃tipɔd] nmpl (GÉO): **les ~** the antipodes ; (fig): **être aux ~ de** to be the opposite extreme of.

antiquaire [ɑ̃tikɛʀ] nm/f antique dealer.

antique [ɑ̃tik] a antique ; (très vieux) ancient, antiquated.

antiquité [ɑ̃tikite] nf (objet) antique ; **l'A~** Antiquity ; **magasin d'~s** antique shop.

antirabique [ɑ̃tiʀabik] a rabies cpd.

antiraciste [ɑ̃tiʀasist(ə)] a antiracist, antiracialist.

antirides [ɑ̃tiʀid] a (crème) anti-wrinkle.

antirouille [ɑ̃tiʀuj] a inv: **peinture ~** anti-rust paint ; **traitement ~** rustproofing.

antisémite [ɑ̃tisemit] a anti-semitic ; **antisémitisme** nm anti-semitism.

antiseptique [ɑ̃tisɛptik] a, nm antiseptic.

antitétanique [ɑ̃titetanik] a tetanus cpd.

antithèse [ɑ̃titɛz] nf antithesis.

antituberculeux, euse [ɑ̃titybɛʀkylø, -øz] a tuberculosis cpd.

antivol [ɑ̃tivɔl] a, nm: **(dispositif) ~** anti-theft device.

antre [ɑ̃tʀ(ə)] nm den, lair.

anus [anys] nm anus.

anxiété [ɑ̃ksjete] nf anxiety.

anxieux, euse [ɑ̃ksjø, -øz] a anxious, worried.

aorte [aɔʀt(ə)] nf aorta.

août [u] nm August.

apaisement [apɛzmɑ̃] nm calming ; soothing ; appeasement ; **~s** nmpl soothing reassurances ; pacifying words.

apaiser [apeze] vt (colère) to calm, quell, soothe ; (faim) to appease, assuage ; (douleur) to soothe ; (personne) to calm (down), pacify ; **s'~** vi (tempête, bruit) to die down, subside.

apanage [apanaʒ] nm: **être l'~ de** to be the privilege ou prerogative of.

aparté [apaʀte] nm (THÉÂTRE) aside ; (entretien) private conversation ; **en ~** ad in an aside ; in private.

apathie [apati] nf apathy ; **apathique** a apathetic.

apatride [apatʀid] nm/f stateless person.

apercevoir [apɛʀsəvwaʀ] vt to see ; **s'~ de** vt to notice ; **s'~ que** to notice that.

aperçu [apɛʀsy] *nm* (*vue d'ensemble*) general survey; (*intuition*) insight.

apéritif, ive [aperitif, -iv] *nm* (*boisson*) aperitif; (*réunion*) pre-lunch (*ou* -dinner) drinks *pl* // **a** which stimulates the appetite; **prendre l'~** to have drinks (before lunch *ou* dinner) *ou* an aperitif.

apesanteur [apəzɑ̃tœʀ] *nf* weightlessness.

à-peu-près [apøpʀɛ] *nm inv* (*péj*) vague approximation.

apeuré, e [apœʀe] **a** frightened, scared.

aphone [afɔn] **a** voiceless.

aphrodisiaque [afʀɔdizjak] **a,** *nm* aphrodisiac.

aphte [aft(ə)] *nm* mouth ulcer.

aphteuse [aftøz] **af: fièvre ~** foot-and-mouth disease.

apiculteur [apikyltœʀ] *nm* beekeeper.

apiculture [apikyltyʀ] *nf* beekeeping, apiculture.

apitoyer [apitwaje] *vt* to move to pity; **~ qn sur** to move sb to pity for, make sb feel sorry for; **s'~ (sur)** to feel pity *ou* compassion (for).

aplanir [aplaniʀ] *vt* to level; (*fig*) to smooth away, iron out.

aplati, e [aplati] **a** flat, flattened.

aplatir [aplatiʀ] *vt* to flatten; **s'~** *vi* to become flatter; to be flattened; (*fig*) to lie flat on the ground; (: *fam*) to fall flat on one's face; (: *péj*) to grovel.

aplomb [aplɔ̃] *nm* (*équilibre*) balance, equilibrium; (*fig*) self-assurance; nerve; **d'~** a steady; (*CONSTR*) plumb.

apocalypse [apɔkalips(ə)] *nf* apocalypse.

apogée [apɔʒe] *nm* (*fig*) peak, apogee.

apolitique [apɔlitik] **a** apolitical.

apologie [apɔlɔʒi] *nf* vindication, praise.

apoplexie [apɔplɛksi] *nf* apoplexy.

a posteriori [apɔsteʀjɔʀi] **ad** after the event, with hindsight, a posteriori.

apostolat [apɔstɔla] *nm* (*REL*) apostolate, discipleship; (*gén*) proselytism, preaching; **apostolique** a apostolic.

apostrophe [apɔstʀɔf] *nf* (*signe*) apostrophe; (*appel*) interpellation.

apostropher [apɔstʀɔfe] *vt* (*interpeller*) to shout at, address sharply.

apothéose [apɔteoz] *nf* pinnacle (of achievement); grand finale.

apôtre [apotʀ(ə)] *nm* apostle, disciple.

apparaître [apaʀɛtʀ(ə)] *vi* to appear // *vb avec attribut* to appear, seem; **il apparaît que** it appears that.

apparat [apaʀa] *nm*: **tenue/dîner d'~** ceremonial dress/dinner; **~ critique** (*d'un texte*) critical apparatus.

appareil [apaʀɛj] *nm* piece of apparatus, device; appliance; (*politique, syndical*) machinery; (*avion*) (aero)plane, aircraft *inv*; (*téléphonique*) phone; (*dentier*) brace; **~ digestif/reproducteur** digestive/reproductive system *ou* apparatus; **qui est à l'~?** who's speaking?; **dans le plus simple** ~ in one's birthday suit; **~ de photographie, ~(-photo)** *nm* camera; **~ 24 x 36 ou petit format** 35mm. camera.

appareillage [apaʀɛjaʒ] *nm* (*appareils*) equipment; (*NAVIG*) casting off, getting under way.

appareiller [apaʀeje] *vi* (*NAVIG*) to cast off, get under way // *vt* (*assortir*) to match up.

apparemment [apaʀamɑ̃] **ad** apparently.

apparence [apaʀɑ̃s] *nf* appearance; **en ~** apparently, seemingly.

apparent, e [apaʀɑ̃, -ɑ̃t] **a** visible; obvious; (*superficiel*) apparent; **coutures ~es** topstitched seams; **poutres ~es** exposed beams.

apparenté, e [apaʀɑ̃te] **a: ~ à** related to; (*fig*) similar to.

appariteur [apaʀitœʀ] *nm* attendant, porter (*in French universities*).

apparition [apaʀisjɔ̃] *nf* appearance; (*surnaturelle*) apparition.

appartement [apaʀtəmɑ̃] *nm* flat.

appartenance [apaʀtənɑ̃s] *nf*: **~ à** belonging to, membership of.

appartenir [apaʀtəniʀ]: **~ à** *vt* to belong to; (*faire partie de*) to belong to, be a member of; **il lui appartient de** it is up to him to, it is his duty to.

apparu, e *pp de* **apparaître**.

appas [apɑ] *nmpl* (*d'une femme*) charms.

appât [apɑ] *nm* (*PÊCHE*) bait; (*fig*) lure, bait; **appâter** *vt* (*hameçon*) to bait; (*poisson, fig*) to lure, entice.

appauvrir [apovʀiʀ] *vt* to impoverish; **s'~** *vi* to grow poorer, become impoverished.

appel [apɛl] *nm* call; (*nominal*) roll call; (: *SCOL*) register; (*MIL: recrutement*) call up; (*JUR*) appeal; **faire ~ à** (*invoquer*) to appeal to; (*avoir recours à*) to call on; (*nécessiter*) to call for, require; **faire ou interjeter ~** (*JUR*) to appeal, lodge an appeal; **faire l'~** to call the roll; to call the register; **sans ~** (*fig*) final, irrevocable; **~ d'air** in-draught; **~ d'offres** (*COMM*) invitation to tender; **faire un ~ de phares** to flash one's headlights; **~ (téléphonique)** (tele)phone call.

appelé [aple] *nm* (*MIL*) conscript.

appeler [aple] *vt* to call; (*faire venir: médecin etc*) to call, send for; (*fig: nécessiter*) to call for, demand; **être appelé à** (*fig*) to be destined to; **~ qn à comparaître** (*JUR*) to summon sb to appear; **en ~ à** to appeal to; **s'~: elle s'appelle Gabrielle** her name is Gabrielle, she's called Gabrielle; **comment ça s'appelle?** what is it called?

appellation [apelasjɔ̃] *nf* designation, appellation.

appendice [apɛ̃dis] *nm* appendix; **appendicite** *nf* appendicitis.

appentis [apɑ̃ti] *nm* lean-to.

appesantir [apəzɑ̃tiʀ]: **s'~** *vi* to grow heavier; **s'~ sur** (*fig*) to dwell at length on.

appétissant, e [apetisɑ̃, -ɑ̃t] **a** appetizing, mouth-watering.

appétit [apeti] *nm* appetite; **avoir un gros/petit ~** to have a big/small appetite; **bon ~!** enjoy your meal!

applaudir [aplodiʀ] *vt* to applaud // *vi* to applaud, clap; **~ à** (*décision*) to applaud, commend; **applaudissements** *nmpl* applause *sg*, clapping *sg*.

application [aplikɑsjɔ̃] *nf* application.

applique [aplik] *nf* wall lamp.

appliqué, e [aplike] *a* (*élève etc*) industrious, assiduous; (*science*) applied.

appliquer [aplike] *vt* to apply; (*loi*) to enforce; **s'~** *vi* (*élève etc*) to apply o.s.; **s'~ à faire qch** to apply o.s. to doing sth, take pains to do sth.

appoint [apwɛ̃] *nm* (extra) contribution *ou* help; **avoir/faire l'~** (*en payant*) to have/give the right change *ou* money; **chauffage d'~** extra heating.

appointements [apwɛ̃tmɑ̃] *nmpl* salary.

appontement [apɔ̃tmɑ̃] *nm* landing stage, wharf.

apport [apɔʀ] *nm* supply; contribution.

apporter [apɔʀte] *vt* to bring.

apposer [apoze] *vt* to append; to affix.

apposition [apozisjɔ̃] *nf* appending; affixing; (*LING*): **en ~** in apposition.

appréciable [apʀesjabl(ə)] *a* (*important*) appreciable, significant.

appréciation [apʀesjɑsjɔ̃] *nf* appreciation; estimation, assessment; **~s** (*avis*) assessment *sg*, appraisal *sg*.

apprécier [apʀesje] *vt* to appreciate; (*évaluer*) to estimate, assess.

appréhender [apʀeɑ̃de] *vt* (*craindre*) to dread; (*arrêter*) to apprehend; **~ que** to fear that; **~ de faire** to dread doing.

appréhension [apʀeɑ̃sjɔ̃] *nf* apprehension.

apprendre [apʀɑ̃dʀ(ə)] *vt* to learn; (*événement, résultats*) to learn of, hear of; **~ qch à qn** (*informer*) to tell sb (of) sth; (*enseigner*) to teach sb sth; **~ à faire qch** to learn to do sth; **~ à qn à faire qch** to teach sb to do sth; **apprenti, e** *nm/f* apprentice; (*fig*) novice, beginner; **apprentissage** *nm* learning; (*COMM, SCOL: période*) apprenticeship.

apprêt [apʀɛ] *nm* (*sur un cuir, une étoffe*) dressing; (*sur un mur*) size; (*sur un papier*) finish.

apprêté, e [apʀete] *a* (*fig*) affected.

apprêter [apʀete] *vt* to dress, finish.

appris, e *pp de* **apprendre**.

apprivoiser [apʀivwaze] *vt* to tame.

approbateur, trice [apʀobatœʀ, -tʀis] *a* approving.

approbation [apʀobɑsjɔ̃] *nf* approval.

approche [apʀɔʃ] *nf* approaching; approach; **à l'~ du bateau/de l'ennemi** as the ship/enemy approached *ou* drew near.

approché, e [apʀɔʃe] *a* approximate.

approcher [apʀɔʃe] *vi* to approach, come near // *vt* (*vedette, artiste*) to come close to, approach; (*rapprocher*): **~ qch (de qch)** to bring *ou* put *ou* move sth near (to sth); **~ de** *vt* to draw near to; (*quantité, moment*) to approach; **s'~ de** *vt* to approach, go *ou* come *ou* move near to.

approfondi, e [apʀɔfɔ̃di] *a* thorough, detailed.

approfondir [apʀɔfɔ̃diʀ] *vt* to deepen, make deeper; (*fig*) to go (deeper *ou* further) into.

approprié, e [apʀɔpʀije] *a*: **~ (à)** appropriate (to), suited to.

approprier [apʀɔpʀije]: **s'~** *vt* to appropriate, take over.

approuver [apʀuve] *vt* to agree with; (*autoriser: loi, projet*) to approve, pass; (*trouver louable*) to approve of.

approvisionnement [apʀɔvizjɔnmɑ̃] *nm* supplying; (*provisions*) supply, stock.

approvisionner [apʀɔvizjɔne] *vt* to supply; (*compte bancaire*) to pay funds into; **~ qn en** to supply sb with; **s'~ en** to stock up with.

approximatif, ive [apʀɔksimatif, -iv] *a* approximate, rough; vague; **approximativement** *ad* approximately, roughly; vaguely.

Appt *abr de* **appartement**.

appui [apɥi] *nm* support; **prendre ~ sur** to lean on; to rest on; **à l'~ de** (*pour prouver*) in support of; **l'~ de la fenêtre** the windowsill, the window ledge; **appui-tête** *nm*, **appuie-tête** *nm inv* headrest.

appuyer [apɥije] *vt* (*poser*): **~ qch sur/contre** to lean *ou* rest sth on/against; (*soutenir: personne, demande*) to support, back (up); **~ sur** (*bouton*) to press, push; (*frein*) to press on, push down; (*mot, détail*) to stress, emphasize; (*suj: chose: peser sur*) to rest (heavily) on, press against; **s'~ sur** *vt* to lean on; to rely on; **~ à droite** to bear (to the) right.

âpre [ɑpʀ(ə)] *a* acrid, pungent; (*fig*) harsh; bitter; **~ au gain** grasping, greedy.

après [apʀɛ] *prép* after // *ad* afterwards; **2 heures ~** 2 hours later; **~ qu'il est ou soit parti/avoir fait** after he left/having done; **d'~** *prép* (*selon*) according to; **~ coup** *ad* after the event, afterwards; **~ tout** *ad* (*au fond*) after all; **et (puis) ~?** so what?; **~-demain** *ad* the day after tomorrow; **~-guerre** *nm* postwar years *pl*; **~-midi** *nm ou nf inv* afternoon; **~-ski** *nm inv* (*chaussure*) snow boot; (*moment*) après-ski.

à-propos [apʀopo] *nm* (*d'une remarque*) aptness; **faire preuve d'~** to show presence of mind, do the right thing.

apte [apt(ə)] *a*: **~ à qch/faire qch** capable of sth/doing sth; **~ (au service)** (*MIL*) fit (for service); **aptitude** *nf* ability, aptitude.

aquarelle [akwaʀɛl] *nf* (*tableau*) watercolour; (*genre*) watercolours *pl*, aquarelle.

aquarium [akwaʀjɔm] *nm* aquarium.

aquatique [akwatik] *a* aquatic, water *cpd*.

aqueduc [akdyk] *nm* aqueduct.

aqueux, euse [akø, -øz] *a* aqueous.

arabe [aʀab] *a* Arabic; (*désert, cheval*) Arabian; (*nation, peuple*) Arab // *nm/f*: **A~** Arab // *nm* (*langue*) Arabic.

arabesque [aʀabɛsk(ə)] *nf* arabesque.

Arabie [aʀabi] *nf*: **l'~ (Séoudite)** Saudi Arabia.

arable [aʀabl(ə)] *a* arable.

arachide [aʀaʃid] *nf* (*plante*) groundnut (plant); (*graine*) peanut, groundnut.

araignée [aʀeɲe] *nf* spider; **~ de mer** spider crab.

araser [aʀɑze] *vt* to level; to plane (down).

aratoire [aʀatwaʀ] *a*: **instrument ~** ploughing implement.

arbalète [aʀbalɛt] *nf* crossbow.

arbitrage [aʀbitʀaʒ] *nm* refereeing; umpiring; arbitration.

arbitraire [aʀbitʀɛʀ] a arbitrary.

arbitre [aʀbitʀ(ə)] nm (SPORT) referee; (: TENNIS, CRICKET) umpire; (fig) arbiter, judge; (JUR) arbitrator; **arbitrer** vt to referee; to umpire; to arbitrate.

arborer [aʀbɔʀe] vt to bear, display; to sport.

arboriculture [aʀbɔʀikyltyʀ] nf arboriculture.

arbre [aʀbʀ(ə)] nm tree; (TECH) shaft; ~ **généalogique** family tree; ~ **de transmission** (AUTO) driveshaft; **arbrisseau**, x nm shrub.

arbuste [aʀbyst(ə)] nm small shrub, bush.

arc [aʀk] nm (arme) bow; (GÉOM) arc; (ARCHIT) arch; ~ **de cercle** arc of a circle; **en ~ de cercle** a semi-circular; **A~ de triomphe** Triumphal Arch.

arcade [aʀkad] nf arch(way); ~**s** arcade sg, arches; ~ **sourcilière** arch of the eyebrows.

arcanes [aʀkan] nmpl mysteries.

arc-boutant [aʀkbutɑ̃] nm flying buttress.

arc-bouter [aʀkbute]: **s'~** vi: **s'~ contre** to lean ou press against.

arceau, x [aʀso] nm (métallique etc) hoop.

arc-en-ciel [aʀkɑ̃sjɛl] nm rainbow.

archaïque [aʀkaik] a archaic; **archaïsme** nm archaism.

arche [aʀʃ(ə)] nf arch; ~ **de Noé** Noah's Ark.

archéologie [aʀkeɔlɔʒi] nf archeology; **archéologique** a archeological; **archéologue** nm/f archeologist.

archer [aʀʃe] nm archer.

archet [aʀʃɛ] nm bow.

archevêché [aʀʃəveʃe] nm arch-bishopric; archbishop's palace.

archevêque [aʀʃəvɛk] nm archbishop.

archi... [aʀʃi] préfixe (très) dead, extra; ~**simple** dead simple; ~**bondé** chock-a-block, packed solid.

archipel [aʀʃipɛl] nm archipelago.

architecte [aʀʃitɛkt(ə)] nm architect.

architecture [aʀʃitɛktyʀ] nf architecture.

archives [aʀʃiv] nfpl archives; **archiviste** rm/f archivist.

arçon [aʀsɔ̃] nm voir **cheval**.

arctique [aʀktik] a Arctic // nm: **l'A~** the Arctic; **l'océan A~** the Arctic Ocean.

ardemment [aʀdamɑ̃] ad ardently, fervently.

ardent, e [aʀdɑ̃, -ɑ̃t] a (soleil) blazing; (fièvre) raging; (amour) ardent, passionate; (prière) fervent; **ardeur** nf blazing heat; fervour, ardour.

ardoise [aʀdwaz] nf slate.

Ardt abr de **arrondissement**.

ardu, e [aʀdy] a arduous, difficult.

are [aʀ] nm are, 100 square metres.

arène [aʀɛn] nf arena; ~**s** nfpl bull-ring sg.

arête [aʀɛt] nf (de poisson) bone; (d'une montagne) ridge; (GÉOM, gén) edge (where two faces meet).

argent [aʀʒɑ̃] nm (métal) silver; (monnaie) money; ~ **liquide** ready money, (ready) cash; ~ **de poche** pocket money; **argenté, e** a silver(y); (métal) silver-plated; **argenter** vt to silver(-plate); **argenterie** nf silverware; silver plate.

argentin, e [aʀʒɑ̃tɛ̃, -in] a (son) silvery; (d'Argentine) Argentinian, Argentine // nm/f Argentinian, Argentine.

Argentine [aʀʒɑ̃tin] nf: **l'~** Argentina, the Argentine.

argile [aʀʒil] nf clay; **argileux, euse** a clayey.

argot [aʀgo] nm slang; **argotique** a slang cpd; slangy.

arguer [aʀgɥe]: ~ **de** vt to put forward as a pretext ou reason.

argument [aʀgymɑ̃] nm argument.

argumenter [aʀgymɑ̃te] vi to argue.

argus [aʀgys] nm guide to second-hand car prices.

arguties [aʀgysi] nfpl pettifoggery sg, quibbles.

aride [aʀid] a arid.

aristocrate [aʀistɔkʀat] nm/f aristocrat.

aristocratie [aʀistɔkʀasi] nf aristocracy; **aristocratique** a aristocratic.

arithmétique [aʀitmetik] a arithmetic(al) // nf arithmetic.

armateur [aʀmatœʀ] nm shipowner.

armature [aʀmatyʀ] nf framework; (de tente etc) frame; (de soutien-gorge) bone, wiring.

arme [aʀm(ə)] nf weapon; (section de l'armée) arm; ~**s** nfpl (blason) (coat of) arms; **les ~s** (profession) soldiering sg; **passer par les ~s** to execute (by firing squad); **en ~s** up in arms; **prendre/présenter les ~s** to take up/present arms; **se battre à l'~ blanche** to fight with blades; ~ **à feu** firearm.

armée [aʀme] nf army; ~ **de l'air** Air Force; **l'~ du Salut** the Salvation Army; ~ **de terre** Army.

armement [aʀməmɑ̃] nm (matériel) arms pl, weapons pl; (: d'un pays) arms pl, armament.

armer [aʀme] vt to arm; (arme à feu) to cock; (appareil-photo) to wind on; ~ **qch de** to fit sth with; to reinforce sth with; ~ **qn de** to arm ou equip sb with.

armistice [aʀmistis] nm armistice.

armoire [aʀmwaʀ] nf (tall) cupboard; (penderie) wardrobe.

armoiries [aʀmwaʀi] nfpl coat sg of arms.

armure [aʀmyʀ] nf armour q, suit of armour.

armurier [aʀmyʀje] nm gunsmith; armourer.

aromates [aʀɔmat] nmpl seasoning sg, herbs (and spices).

aromatisé, e [aʀɔmatize] a flavoured.

arôme [aʀom] nm aroma; fragrance.

arpège [aʀpɛʒ] nm arpeggio.

arpentage [aʀpɑ̃taʒ] nm (land) surveying.

arpenter [aʀpɑ̃te] vt (salle, couloir) to pace up and down.

arpenteur [aʀpɑ̃tœʀ] nm land surveyor.

arqué, e [aʀke] a bow, bandy; arched.

arrachage [aʀaʃaʒ] nm: ~ **des mauvaises herbes** weeding.

arrache-pied [aʀaʃpje]: **d'~** ad relentlessly.

arracher [aʀaʃe] vt to pull out; (page etc) to tear out, tear out; (déplanter: légume) to lift; (: herbe, souche) to pull up; (bras etc: par explosion) to blow off; (: par accident) to tear off; ~ qch à qn to snatch sth from sb; (fig) to wring sth out of sb, wrest sth from sb; ~ qn à (solitude, rêverie) to drag sb out of; (famille etc) to tear ou wrench sb away from; s'~ vt (article très recherché) to fight over.

arraisonner [aʀɛzɔne] vt (bateau) to board and search.

arrangeant, e [aʀɑ̃ʒɑ̃, -ɑ̃t] a accommodating, obliging.

arrangement [aʀɑ̃ʒmɑ̃] nm arrangement.

arranger [aʀɑ̃ʒe] vt (gén) to arrange; (réparer) to fix, put right; (régler) to settle, sort out; (convenir à) to suit, be convenient for; s'~ (se mettre d'accord) to come to an agreement ou arrangement; je vais m'~ I'll try and manage; ça va s'~ it'll sort itself out; s'~ pour faire to manage so that one can do; **arrangeur** nm (MUS) arranger.

arrestation [aʀɛstɑsjɔ̃] nf arrest.

arrêt [aʀɛ] nm stopping; (de bus etc) stop; (JUR) judgment, decision; (FOOTBALL) save; ~s nmpl (MIL) arrest sg; être à l'~ to be stopped, have come to a halt; rester ou tomber en ~ devant to stop short in front of; sans ~ without stopping, non-stop; continually; ~ de travail stoppage (of work).

arrêté [aʀete] nm order, decree.

arrêter [aʀete] vt to stop; (chauffage etc) to turn off, switch off; (fixer: date etc) to appoint, decide on; (criminel, suspect) to arrest; ~ de faire to stop doing; s'~ vi to stop.

arrhes [aʀ] nfpl deposit sg.

arrière [aʀjɛʀ] nm back; (SPORT) fullback // a inv: siège/roue ~ back ou rear seat/wheel; à l'~ ad behind, at the back; en ~ ad behind; (regarder) back, behind; (tomber, aller) backwards; en ~ de prép behind; arrière, e a (péj) backward // nm (d'argent) arrears pl; ~-boutique nf back shop; ~-garde nf rearguard; ~-goût nm aftertaste; ~-grand-mère nf great-grandmother; nm great-grandfather; ~-pays nm inv hinterland; ~-pensée nf ulterior motive; mental reservation; ~-petits-enfants nmpl great-grandchildren; ~-plan nm background; ~-saison nf late autumn; ~-train nm hindquarters pl.

arrimer [aʀime] vt to stow; to secure, fasten securely.

arrivage [aʀivaʒ] nm arrival.

arrivée [aʀive] nf arrival; (ligne d'arrivée) finish; ~ d'air/de gaz air/gas inlet; à mon ~ when I arrived.

arriver [aʀive] vi to arrive; (survenir) to happen, occur; il arrive à Paris à 8h he gets to ou arrives at Paris at 8; ~ à (atteindre) to reach; ~ à faire qch to succeed in doing sth; il arrive que it happens that; il lui arrive de faire he sometimes does; **arriviste** nm/f go-getter.

arrogance [aʀɔgɑ̃s] nf arrogance.

arrogant, e [aʀɔgɑ̃, -ɑ̃t] a arrogant.

arroger [aʀɔʒe]: s'~ vt to assume (without right).

arrondi, e [aʀɔ̃di] a round // nm roundness.

arrondir [aʀɔ̃diʀ] vt (forme, objet) to

round; (somme) to round off; s'~ vi to become round(ed).

arrondissement [aʀɔ̃dismɑ̃] nm (ADMIN) ≈ district.

arrosage [aʀozaʒ] nm watering; **tuyau d'**~ hose(pipe).

arroser [aʀoze] vt to water; (victoire) to celebrate (over a drink); (CULIN) to baste; **arroseuse** nf water cart; **arrosoir** nm watering can.

arsenal, aux [aʀsənal, -o] nm (NAVIG) naval dockyard; (MIL) arsenal; (fig) gear, paraphernalia.

arsenic [aʀsənik] nm arsenic.

art [aʀ] nm art; ~s et métiers applied arts and crafts; ~s ménagers homecraft sg, domestic science sg.

artère [aʀtɛʀ] nf (ANAT) artery; (rue) main road; **artériel, le** a arterial; **artériosclérose** nf arteriosclerosis.

arthrite [aʀtʀit] nf arthritis.

arthrose [aʀtʀoz] nf (degenerative) osteoarthritis.

artichaut [aʀtiʃo] nm artichoke.

article [aʀtikl(ə)] nm article; (COMM) item, article; à l'~ de la mort at the point of death; ~ de fond (PRESSE) feature article.

articulaire [aʀtikylɛʀ] a of the joints, articular.

articulation [aʀtikylɑsjɔ̃] nf articulation; (ANAT) joint.

articuler [aʀtikyle] vt to articulate; s'~ (sur) (ANAT, TECH) to articulate (to).

artifice [aʀtifis] nm device, trick.

artificiel, le [aʀtifisjɛl] a artificial; ~lement ad artificially.

artificier [aʀtifisje] nm pyrotechnist.

artificieux, euse [aʀtifisjø, -øz] a guileful, deceitful.

artillerie [aʀtijʀi] nf artillery, ordnance; **artilleur** nm artilleryman, gunner.

artisan [aʀtizɑ̃] nm artisan, (self-employed) craftsman; l'~ de la victoire the architect of victory; **artisanal, e, aux** a of ou made by craftsmen; (péj) cottage industry cpd, unsophisticated; **artisanat** nm arts and crafts pl.

artiste [aʀtist(ə)] nm/f artist; (de variétés) entertainer; performer; singer; actor/actress; **artistique** a artistic.

aryen, ne [aʀjɛ̃, -jɛn] a Aryan.

as vb [a] voir avoir // nm [ɑs] ace.

ascendance [asɑ̃dɑ̃s] nf (origine) ancestry.

ascendant, e [asɑ̃dɑ̃, -ɑ̃t] a upward // nm ascendancy; ~s nmpl ascendants.

ascenseur [asɑ̃sœʀ] nm lift.

ascension [asɑ̃sjɔ̃] nf ascent; climb; l'A~ (REL) the Ascension.

ascète [asɛt] nm/f ascetic; **ascétique** a ascetic.

asepsie [asɛpsi] nf asepsis; **aseptique** a aseptic; **aseptiser** vt to sterilize; to disinfect.

asiatique [azjatik] a, nm/f Asiatic, Asian.

Asie [azi] nf Asia.

asile [azil] nm (refuge) refuge, sanctuary; (POL): droit d'~ (political) asylum; (pour malades mentaux) home, asylum; (pour vieillards) home.

aspect [aspɛ] nm appearance, look; (fig) aspect, side; (LING) aspect; **à l'~ de** at the sight of.

asperge [aspɛrʒ(ə)] nf asparagus q.

asperger [aspɛrʒe] vt to spray, sprinkle.

aspérité [aspeRite] nf excrescence, protruding bit (of rock etc).

aspersion [aspɛrsjɔ̃] nf spraying, sprinkling.

asphalte [asfalt(ə)] nm asphalt; **asphalter** vt to asphalt.

asphyxie [asfiksi] nf suffocation, asphyxia, asphyxiation; **asphyxier** vt to suffocate, asphyxiate; (fig) to stifle.

aspic [aspik] nm (ZOOL) asp; (CULIN) aspic.

aspirant, e [aspiRɑ̃, -ɑ̃t] a: **pompe ~e** suction pump // nm (NAVIG) midshipman.

aspirateur [aspiRatœR] nm vacuum cleaner, hoover.

aspiration [aspiRɑsjɔ̃] nf inhalation; sucking (up); drawing up; **~s** nfpl (ambitions) aspirations.

aspirer [aspiRe] vt (air) to inhale; (liquide) to suck (up); (suj: appareil) to suck ou draw up; **~ à** vt to aspire to.

aspirine [aspiRin] nf aspirin.

assagir [asaʒiR] vt, **s'~** vi to quieten down, sober down.

assaillant, e [asajɑ̃, -ɑ̃t] nm/f assailant, attacker.

assaillir [asajiR] vt to assail, attack; **~ qn de** (questions) to assail ou bombard sb with.

assainir [aseniR] vt to clean up; to purify.

assaisonnement [asɛzɔnmɑ̃] nm seasoning.

assaisonner [asɛzɔne] vt to season.

assassin [asasɛ̃] nm murderer; assassin.

assassinat [asasina] nm murder; assassination.

assassiner [asasine] vt to murder; to assassinate.

assaut [aso] nm assault, attack; **prendre d'~** to (take by) storm, assault; **donner l'~** to attack; **faire ~ de** (rivaliser) to vie with ou rival each other in.

assécher [aseʃe] vt to drain.

assemblage [asɑ̃blaʒ] nm assembling; (MENUISERIE) joint; **un ~ de** (fig) a collection of.

assemblée [asɑ̃ble] nf (réunion) meeting; (public, assistance) gathering; assembled people; (POL) assembly; **l'A~ Nationale** the (French) National Assembly.

assembler [asɑ̃ble] vt (joindre, monter) to assemble, put together; (amasser) to gather (together), collect (together); **s'~** vi to gather, collect.

assener, asséner [asene] vt: **~ un coup à qn** to deal sb a blow.

assentiment [asɑ̃timɑ̃] nm assent, consent; approval.

asseoir [aswaR] vt (malade, bébé) to sit up; to sit down; (autorité, réputation) to establish; **~ qch sur** to build sth on; to base sth on; **s'~** vi to sit (o.s.) down.

assermenté, e [asɛRmɑ̃te] a sworn, on oath.

asservir [asɛRviR] vt to subjugate, enslave.

assesseur [asesœR] nm (JUR) assessor.

asseye etc vb voir **asseoir**.

assez [ase] ad (suffisamment) enough, sufficiently; (passablement) rather, quite, fairly; **est-il ~ fort/rapide?** is he strong/fast enough ou sufficiently strong/fast?; **il est passé ~ vite** he went past rather ou quite ou fairly fast; **~ de pain/livres** enough ou sufficient bread/books; **travailler ~** to work sufficiently (hard), work (hard) enough.

assidu, e [asidy] a assiduous, painstaking; regular; **assiduités** nfpl assiduous attentions.

assied etc vb voir **asseoir**.

assiéger [asjeʒe] vt to besiege, lay siege to; (suj: foule, touristes) to mob, besiege.

assiérai etc vb voir **asseoir**.

assiette [asjɛt] nf plate; (contenu) plate(ful); (équilibre) seat; seating; trim; **~ anglaise** assorted cold meats; **~ creuse** (soup) dish, soup plate; **~ à dessert** dessert plate; **~ de l'impôt** basis of (tax) assessment; **~ plate** (dinner) plate.

assigner [asiɲe] vt: **~ qch à** (poste, part, travail) to assign ou allot sth to; (limites) to set ou fix sth to; (cause, effet) to ascribe ou attribute sth to; **~ qn à** (affecter) to assign sb to; **~ qn à résidence** (JUR) to assign a forced residence to sb.

assimiler [asimile] vt to assimilate, absorb; (comparer): **~ qch/qn à** to liken ou compare sth/sb to; **ils sont assimilés aux infirmières** (ADMIN) they are classed as nurses; **s'~** vi (s'intégrer) to be assimilated ou absorbed.

assis, e [asi, -iz] pp de **asseoir** // a sitting (down), seated // nf (CONSTR) course; (GÉO) stratum (pl a); (fig) basis (pl bases), foundation; **~es** nfpl (JUR) assizes; (congrès) (annual) conference.

assistance [asistɑ̃s] nf (public) audience; (aide) assistance; porter **~ à qn** to give sb assistance; **l'A~ (publique)** (-1953) ≈ National Assistance; Child Care.

assistant, e [asistɑ̃, -ɑ̃t] nm/f assistant; (d'université) probationary lecturer; **les ~s** nmpl (auditeurs etc) those present; **~e sociale** social worker.

assisté, e [asiste] a (AUTO) power assisted.

assister [asiste] vt to assist; **~ à** vt (scène, événement) to witness; (conférence, séminaire) to attend, be (present) at; (spectacle, match) to be at, see.

association [asɔsjɑsjɔ̃] nf association.

associé, e [asɔsje] nm/f associate; partner.

associer [asɔsje] vt to associate; **~ qn à** (profits) to give sb a share of; (affaire) to make sb a partner in; (joie, triomphe) to include sb in; **~ qch à** (joindre, allier) to combine sth with; **s'~** (suj pl) to join together; (COMM) to form a partnership; **s'~** vt (collaborateur) to take on (as a partner); **s'~ à qn pour faire** to join (forces) ou join together with sb to do; **s'~ à** to be combined with; (opinions, joie de qn) to share in.

assoiffé, e [aswafe] a thirsty.

assolement [asɔlmɑ̃] nm (systematic) rotation of crops.

assombrir [asɔ̃bʀiʀ] vt to darken ; (fig) to fill with gloom ; s'~ vi to darken ; to cloud over ; to become gloomy.

assommer [asɔme] vt to batter to death ; (étourdir, abrutir) to knock out ; to stun ; (fam: ennuyer) to bore stiff.

Assomption [asɔ̃psjɔ̃] nf: l'~ the Assumption.

assorti, e [asɔʀti] a matched, matching ; fromages/légumes ~s assorted cheeses/vegetables ; ~ à matching.

assortiment [asɔʀtimɑ̃] nm assortment, selection.

assortir [asɔʀtiʀ] vt to match ; ~ qch à to match sth with ; ~ qch de to accompany sth with ; s'~ de to be accompanied by.

assoupi, e [asupi] a dozing, sleeping ; (fig) (be)numbed ; dulled ; stilled.

assoupir [asupiʀ]: s'~ vi to doze off.

assouplir [asupliʀ] vt to make supple ; (fig) to relax.

assourdir [asuʀdiʀ] vt (bruit) to deaden, muffle ; (suj: bruit) to deafen.

assouvir [asuviʀ] vt to satisfy, appease.

assujettir [asyʒetiʀ] vt to subject, subjugate ; ~ qn à (règle, impôt) to subject sb to.

assumer [asyme] vt (fonction, emploi) to assume, take on.

assurance [asyʀɑ̃s] nf (certitude) assurance ; (confiance en soi) (self-)confidence ; (contrat) insurance (policy) ; (secteur commercial) insurance ; ~ maladie health insurance ; ~ tous risques (AUTO) comprehensive insurance ; ~s sociales ≈ National Insurance ; ~-vie nf life assurance ou insurance.

assuré, e [asyʀe] a (victoire etc) certain, sure ; (démarche, voix) assured, (self-)confident ; (certain): ~ de confident of // nm/f insured (person) ; ~ social ≈ member of the National Insurance scheme ; ~ment ad assuredly, most certainly.

assurer [asyʀe] vt (COMM) to insure ; (stabiliser) to steady ; to stabilize ; (victoire etc) to ensure, make certain ; (frontières, pouvoir) to make secure ; (service, garde) to provide ; to operate ; (garantir): ~ qch à qn to secure ou guarantee sth for sb ; (certifier) to assure sb of sth ; ~ à qn que to assure sb that ; ~ qn de to assure sb of ; s'~ (contre) (COMM) to insure o.s. (against) ; s'~ de/que (vérifier) to make sure of/that ; s'~ (de) (aide de qn) to secure (for o.s.) ; assureur nm insurance agent ; insurers pl.

astérisque [asteʀisk(ə)] nm asterisk.

asthmatique [asmatik] a asthmatic.

asthme [asm(ə)] nm asthma.

asticot [astiko] nm maggot.

astiquer [astike] vt to polish, shine.

astre [astʀ(ə)] nm star.

astreignant, e [astʀɛɲɑ̃, -ɑ̃t] a demanding.

astreindre [astʀɛ̃dʀ(ə)] vt: ~ qn à qch to force sth upon sb ; ~ qn à faire to compel ou force sb to do.

astringent, e [astʀɛ̃ʒɑ̃, -ɑ̃t] a astringent.

astrologie [astʀɔlɔʒi] nf astrology ; astrologue nm/f astrologer.

astronaute [astʀɔnot] nm/f astronaut.

astronautique [astʀɔnotik] nf astronautics sg.

astronome [astʀɔnɔm] nm/f astronomer.

astronomie [astʀɔnɔmi] nf astronomy ; astronomique a astronomic(al).

astuce [astys] nf shrewdness, astuteness ; (truc) trick, clever way ; (plaisanterie) wisecrack ; astucieux, euse a shrewd, clever, astute.

asymétrique [asimetʀik] a asymmetric(al).

atelier [atəlje] nm workshop ; (de peintre) studio.

athée [ate] a atheistic // nm/f atheist.

Athènes [atɛn] n Athens.

athlète [atlɛt] nm/f (SPORT) athlete ; (costaud) muscleman ; athlétique a athletic ; athlétisme nm athletics sg.

atlantique [atlɑ̃tik] a Atlantic // nm: l'(océan) A~ the Atlantic (Ocean).

atlas [atlɑs] nm atlas.

atmosphère [atmɔsfɛʀ] nf atmosphere ; atmosphérique a atmospheric.

atome [atom] nm atom ; atomique a (bombe, pile) atomic, nuclear ; (usine) nuclear ; (nombre, masse) atomic.

atomiseur [atɔmizœʀ] nm atomiser.

atone [atɔn] a lifeless.

atours [atuʀ] nmpl attire sg, finery sg.

atout [atu] nm trump ; (fig) asset ; trump card ; '~ pique/trèfle' spades/clubs are trumps.

âtre [ɑtʀ(ə)] nm hearth.

atroce [atʀɔs] a atrocious ; dreadful ; atrocité nf atrocity.

atrophie [atʀɔfi] nf atrophy.

atrophier [atʀɔfje]: s'~ vi to atrophy.

attabler [atable]: s'~ vi to sit down at (the) table.

attachant, e [ataʃɑ̃, -ɑ̃t] a engaging, lovable, likeable.

attache [ataʃ] nf clip, fastener ; (fig) tie ; à l'~ (chien) tied up.

attaché, e [ataʃe] a: être ~ à (aimer) to be attached to // nm (ADMIN) attaché ; ~-case nm inv attaché case.

attachement [ataʃmɑ̃] nm attachment.

attacher [ataʃe] vt to tie up ; (étiquette) to attach, tie on ; (souliers) to do up // vi (poêle, riz) to stick ; s'~ à (par affection) to become attached to ; s'~ à faire qch to endeavour to do sth ; ~ qch à to tie ou fasten ou attach sth to.

attaquant, e [atakɑ̃] nm (MIL) attacker ; (SPORT) striker, forward.

attaque [atak] nf attack ; (cérébrale) stroke ; (d'épilepsie) fit.

attaquer [atake] vt to attack ; (en justice) to bring an action against, sue ; (travail) to tackle, set about // vi to attack ; s'~ à to attack ; (épidémie, misère) to tackle, attack.

attardé, e [ataʀde] a (passants) late ; (enfant) backward ; (conceptions) old-fashioned.

attarder [ataʀde]: s'~ vi to linger ; to stay on.

atteindre [atɛ̃dʀ(ə)] vt to reach; (blesser) to hit; (contacter) to reach, contact, get in touch with; (émouvoir) to affect.

atteint, e [atɛ̃, -ɛ̃t] a (MÉD): être ~ de to be suffering from // nf attack; hors d'~e out of reach; porter ~e à to strike a blow at; to undermine.

attelage [atlaʒ] nm (de remorque etc) coupling; (animaux) team; (harnachement) harness; yoke.

atteler [atle] vt (cheval, bœufs) to hitch up; (wagons) to couple; s'~ à (travail) to buckle down to.

attelle [atɛl] nf splint.

attenant, e [atnɑ̃, -ɑ̃t] a: ~ (à) adjoining.

attendre [atɑ̃dʀ(ə)] vt (gén) to wait for; (être destiné ou réservé à) to await, be in store for // vi to wait; s'~ à (ce que) (escompter) to expect (that); ~ un enfant to be expecting (a baby); ~ de faire/d'être to wait until one does/is; ~ que to wait until; ~ qch de to expect sth of; en attendant ad meanwhile, in the meantime; be that as it may.

attendri, e [atɑ̃dʀi] a tender.

attendrir [atɑ̃dʀiʀ] vt to move (to pity); (viande) to tenderize; s'~ (sur) to be moved ou touching (by); **attendrissant, e** a moving, touching; **attendrissement** nm emotion; pity.

attendu [atɑ̃dy] nm: ~s reasons adduced for a judgment; ~ que cj considering that, since.

attentat [atɑ̃ta] nm assassination attempt; ~ à la bombe bomb attack; ~ à la pudeur indecent exposure q; indecent assault q.

attente [atɑ̃t] nf wait; (espérance) expectation.

attenter [atɑ̃te]: ~ à vt (liberté) to violate; ~ à la vie de qn to make an attempt on sb's life.

attentif, ive [atɑ̃tif, -iv] a (auditeur) attentive; (travail) scrupulous; careful; ~ à paying attention to; mindful of; careful to.

attention [atɑ̃sjɔ̃] nf attention; (prévenance) attention, thoughtfulness q; à l'~ de for the attention of; faire ~ (à) to be careful (of); faire ~ (à ce) que ou make sure that; ~! careful!, watch ou mind (out)!; **attentionné, e** a thoughtful, considerate.

attentisme [atɑ̃tism(ə)] nm wait-and-see policy.

attentivement [atɑ̃tivmɑ̃] ad attentively.

atténuer [atenɥe] vt to alleviate, ease; to lessen; to mitigate the effects of; s'~ vi to ease; to abate.

atterrer [ateʀe] vt to dismay, appal.

atterrir [ateʀiʀ] vi to land; **atterrissage** nm landing; **atterrissage sur le ventre** belly landing.

attestation [atɛstasjɔ̃] nf certificate; ~ médicale doctor's certificate.

attester [atɛste] vt to testify to, vouch for; (démontrer) to attest, testify to; ~ que to testify that.

attiédir [atjediʀ]: s'~ vi to become lukewarm; (fig) to cool down.

attifé, e [atife] a (fam) got up, rigged out.

attique [atik] nm: appartement en ~ penthouse (flat).

attirail [atiʀaj] nm gear; (péj) paraphernalia.

attirance [atiʀɑ̃s] nf attraction; (séduction) lure.

attirant, e [atiʀɑ̃, -ɑ̃t] a attractive, appealing.

attirer [atiʀe] vt to attract; (appâter) to lure, entice; ~ qn dans un coin/vers soi to draw sb into a corner/towards one; ~ l'attention de qn (sur) to attract sb's attention (to); to draw sb's attention (to); s'~ des ennuis to bring trouble upon o.s., get into trouble.

attiser [atize] vt (feu) to poke (up), stir up; (fig) to fan the flame of, stir up.

attitré, e [atitʀe] a qualified; accredited; appointed.

attitude [atityd] nf attitude; (position du corps) bearing.

attouchements [atuʃmɑ̃] nmpl touching sg; (sexuels) fondling sg, stroking sg.

attraction [atʀaksjɔ̃] nf (gén) attraction; (de cabaret, cirque) number.

attrait [atʀɛ] nm appeal, attraction; lure; éprouver de l'~ pour to be attracted to; ~s nmpl attractions.

attrape [atʀap] nf voir farce // préfixe: ~-nigaud nm con.

attraper [atʀape] vt (gén) to catch; (habitude, amende) to get, pick up; (fam: duper) to take in.

attrayant, e [atʀɛjɑ̃, -ɑ̃t] a attractive.

attribuer [atʀibɥe] vt (prix) to award; (rôle, tâche) to allocate, assign; (imputer): ~ qch à to attribute sth to, ascribe sth to, put sth down to; s'~ vt (s'approprier) to claim for o.s.

attribut [atʀiby] nm attribute; (LING) complement.

attribution [atʀibysjɔ̃] nf awarding; allocation, assignment; attribution; ~s nfpl (compétence) attributions.

attrister [atʀiste] vt to sadden.

attroupement [atʀupmɑ̃] nm crowd, mob.

attrouper [atʀupe]: s'~ vi to gather.

au [o] prép + dét voir à.

aubade [obad] nf dawn serenade.

aubaine [obɛn] nf godsend; (financière) windfall.

aube [ob] nf dawn, daybreak; à l'~ at dawn ou daybreak; à l'~ de (fig) at the dawn of.

aubépine [obepin] nf hawthorn.

auberge [obɛʀʒ(ə)] nf inn; ~ de jeunesse youth hostel.

aubergine [obɛʀʒin] nf aubergine.

aubergiste [obɛʀʒist(ə)] nm/f inn-keeper, hotel-keeper.

aucun, e [okœ̃, -yn] dét no, tournure négative + aucun; (positif) any // pronom none, tournure négative + any; any(one); il n'y a ~ livre there isn't any book, there is no book; je n'en vois ~ qui I can't see any which, I (can) see none which; sans ~ doute without any doubt; plus qu'~ autre more than any other; ~ des deux neither of the two; ~ d'entre eux none of them; d'~s (certains) some;

aucunement ad in no way, not in the least.
audace [odas] nf daring, boldness; (péj)
audacity; **audacieux, euse** a daring, bold.
au-delà [odla] ad beyond // nm: l'~ the
beyond; ~ **de** prép beyond.
au-dessous [odsu] ad underneath;
below; ~ **de** prép under(neath), below;
(limite, somme etc) below, under; (dignité,
condition) below.
au-dessus [odsy] ad above; ~ **de** prép
above.
au-devant [odvã]: ~ **de** prép: aller ~ **de**
(personne, danger) to go (out) and meet;
(souhaits de qn) to anticipate.
audience [odjãs] nf audience; (JUR:
séance) hearing; **trouver** ~ **auprès de** to
arouse much interest among, get the (interested) attention of.
audio-visuel, le [odjovizɥɛl] a audio-
visual.
auditeur, trice [oditœR, -tRis] nm/f (à la
radio) listener; (à une conférence) member
of the audience, listener; ~ **libre** unregis-
tered student (attending lectures).
audition [odisjɔ̃] nf (ouïe, écoute) hearing;
(JUR: de témoins) examination; (MUS,
THÉÂTRE: épreuve) audition; **auditionner** vt,
vi to audition.
auditoire [oditwaR] nm audience.
auditorium [oditɔrjɔm] nm (public)
studio.
auge [oʒ] nf trough.
augmentation [ɔgmãtasjɔ̃] nf increasing; raising; increase; ~ (**de salaire**) rise
(in salary).
augmenter [ɔgmãte] vt (gén) to increase;
(salaire, prix) to increase, raise, put up;
(employé) to increase the salary of, give
a (salary) rise to // vi to increase.
augure [ɔgyR] nm soothsayer, oracle; **de
bon/mauvais** ~ of good/ill omen.
augurer [ɔgyRe] vt: ~ **qch de** to foresee
sth (coming) out of; ~ **bien de** to augur
well for.
auguste [ɔgyst(ə)] a august, noble,
majestic.
aujourd'hui [oʒuRdɥi] ad today.
aumône [omon] nf alms sg (pl inv); **faire
l'~** (à qn) to give alms (to sb); **faire l'~
de qch à qn** (fig) to favour sb with sth.
aumônerie [omonRi] nf chaplaincy.
aumônier [omonje] nm chaplain.
auparavant [oparavã] ad before(hand).
auprès [opRɛ]: ~ **de** prép next to, close
to; (recourir, s'adresser) to; (en
comparaison de) compared with, next to.
auquel [okɛl] prép + pronom voir **lequel.**
aurai etc vb voir **avoir.**
auréole [ɔReɔl] nf halo; (tache) ring.
auriculaire [ɔRikylɛR] nm little finger.
aurons etc vb voir **avoir.**
aurore [ɔRɔR] nf dawn, daybreak; ~
boréale northern lights pl.
ausculter [ɔskylte] vt to auscultate.
auspices [ɔspis] nmpl: **sous les** ~ **de**
under the patronage ou auspices of; **sous
de bons/mauvais** ~ under fa-
vourable/unfavourable auspices.
aussi [osi] ad (également) also, too; (de
comparaison) as // cj therefore, consequently; ~ **fort que** as strong as; **moi**

~ **me too**, so do I; ~ **bien que** (de même
que) as well as.
aussitôt [osito] ad straight away, immediately; ~ **que** as soon as; ~ **envoyé**
as soon as it is (ou was) sent.
austère [ɔstɛR] a austere; **austérité** nf
austerity.
austral, e [ɔstral] a southern.
Australie [ɔstrali] nf Australia;
australien, ne a, nm/f Australian.
autant [otã] ad so much; (comparatif): ~
(**que**) as much (as); (nombre) as many
(as); ~ (**de**) so much (ou many); as much
(ou many); ~ **partir** we (ou you etc) had
better leave; **y en a-t-il** ~ (**qu'avant**)?
are there as many (as before)?; **is there
as much** (as before)?; **il n'est pas
découragé pour** ~ he isn't discouraged
for all that; **pour** ~ **que** cj assuming, as
long as; **d'**~ **plus/mieux** (**que**) all the
more/the better (since).
autarcie [otarsi] nf autarchy.
autel [otɛl] nm altar.
auteur [otœR] nm author; **l'**~ **de cette
remarque** the person who said that; ~-
compositeur nm composer-songwriter.
authentifier [otãtifje] vt to authenticate.
authentique [otãtik] a authentic, genuine.
auto [oto] nf car.
auto... [oto] préfixe auto..., self-;
~**biographie** nf autobiography.
autobus [otobys] nm bus.
autocar [otokaR] nm coach.
autochtone [otoktɔn] nm/f native.
auto-collant, e [otokolã, -ãt] a self-
adhesive; (enveloppe) self-seal // nm
sticker.
auto-couchettes [otokuʃɛt] a: **train** ~
car sleeper train.
autocratique [otokRatik] a autocratic.
autocritique [otokRitik] nf self-criticism.
autodéfense [otodefãs] nf self-defence;
groupe d'~ vigilance committee.
autodidacte [otodidakt(ə)] nm/f self-
taught person.
auto-école [otoekɔl] nf driving school.
autofinancement [otofinãsmã] nm self-
financing.
autogestion [otoʒɛstjɔ̃] nf self-
management.
autographe [otoɡRaf] nm autograph.
automate [otomat] nm automaton.
automatique [otomatik] a automatic //
nm: **l'**~ ≈ subscriber trunk dialling;
~**ment** ad automatically; **automatiser** vt
to automate: **automatisme** nm
automatism.
automne [otɔn] nm autumn.
automobile [otomɔbil] a motor cpd // nf
(motor) car; ~ **motoring**; **the car
industry**; **automobiliste** nm/f motorist.
autonome [otonɔm] a autonomous;
autonomie nf autonomy; (POL) self-
government, autonomy; **autonomie de
vol** range.
autopsie [otopsi] nf post mortem
(examination), autopsy.
autorisation [otoRizasjɔ̃] nf permission,
authorization; (papiers) permit; **avoir l'**~
de faire to be allowed ou have permission
to do, be authorized to do.

autorisé, e [ɔtɔrize] *a* (*opinion, sources*) authoritative.

autoriser [ɔtɔrize] *vt* to give permission for, authorize ; (*fig*) to allow (*of*), sanction ; ~ qn à faire to give permission to sb to do, authorize sb to do.

autoritaire [ɔtɔritɛr] *a* authoritarian.

autorité [ɔtɔrite] *nf* authority ; faire ~ to be authoritative.

autoroute [ɔtɔrut] *nf* motorway.

auto-stop [ɔtɔstɔp] *nm*: l'~ hitch-hiking ; faire de l'~ to hitch-hike ; prendre qn en ~ to give sb a lift ; ~peur, euse *nm/f* hitch-hiker, hitcher.

autour [otur] *ad* around ; ~ de *prép* around ; (*environ*) around, about ; tout ~ *ad* all around.

autre [otR(ə)] *a* other ; un ~ verre (*supplémentaire*) one more glass, another glass ; (*différent*) another glass, a different glass ; un ~ another (one) ; l'~ the other (one) ; les ~s (*autrui*) others ; l'un et l'~ both (of them) ; se détester *etc* l'un l'~/les uns les ~s to hate *etc* each other/one another ; se sentir ~ to feel different ; d'une semaine à l'~ from one week to the next ; (*incessamment*) any week now ; ~ chose something else ; ~ part ad somewhere else ; d'~ part ad on the other hand ; entre ~s among others ; among other things ; nous/vous ~s us/you (lot).

autrefois [otRəfwa] *ad* in the past.

autrement [otRəmɑ̃] *ad* differently ; in another way ; (*sinon*) otherwise ; ~ dit in other words.

Autriche [otRiʃ] *nf* Austria ; **autrichien, ne** *a, nm/f* Austrian.

autruche [otRyʃ] *nf* ostrich.

autrui [otRɥi] *pronom* others.

auvent [ovɑ̃] *nm* canopy.

aux [o] *prép* + *dét voir* à.

auxiliaire [ɔksiljɛr] *a, nm, nf* auxiliary.

auxquels, auxquelles [okɛl] *prép* + *pronom voir* **lequel**.

av. *abr de* **avenue.**

avachi, e [avaʃi] *a* limp, flabby.

aval [aval] *nm* (*accord*) endorsement, backing ; (GÉO): en ~ downstream, downriver ; (*sur une pente*) downhill ; en ~ de downstream ou downriver from ; downhill from.

avalanche [avalɑ̃ʃ] *nf* avalanche ; ~ poudreuse powder snow avalanche.

avaler [avale] *vt* to swallow.

avance [avɑ̃s] *nf* (*de troupes etc*) advance ; progress ; (*d'argent*) advance ; (*opposé à retard*) lead ; being ahead of schedule ; ~s *nfpl* overtures ; (*amoureuses*) advances ; **une ~ de 300 m/4 h** (SPORT) a 300 m/4 hour lead ; (**être**) en ~ (to be) early ; (*sur un programme*) (to be) ahead of schedule ; **payer d'~** to pay in advance ; **à l'~** in advance, beforehand.

avancé, e [avɑ̃se] *a* advanced ; well on ou under way // *nf* projection ; overhang ; jutting part.

avancement [avɑ̃smɑ̃] *nm* (*professionnel*) promotion.

avancer [avɑ̃se] *vi* to move forward, advance ; (*projet, travail*) to make progress ; (*être en saillie*) to overhang ; to project ; to

jut out ; (*montre, réveil*) to be fast ; to gain // *vt* to move forward, advance ; (*argent*) to advance ; **s'~** *vi* to move forward, advance ; (*fig*) to commit o.s. ; to overhang ; to project ; to jut out ; **j'avance (d'une heure)** I'm (an hour) fast.

avanies [avani] *nfpl* snubs.

avant [avɑ̃] *prép* before // *ad*: trop/plus ~ too far/further forward // *a inv*: siège/roue ~ front seat/wheel // *nm* (*d'un véhicule, bâtiment*) front ; (SPORT: *joueur*) forward ; ~ qu'il parte/de faire before he leaves/doing ; ~ tout (*surtout*) above all ; à l'~ (*dans un véhicule*) in (the) front ; en ~ *ad* forward(s) ; en ~ de *prép* in front of.

avantage [avɑ̃taʒ] *nm* advantage ; (TENNIS): ~ service/dehors advantage ou van in/out ; ~s sociaux fringe benefits ; **avantager** *vt* (*favoriser*) to favour ; (*embellir*) to flatter ; **avantageux, euse** *a* attractive ; attractively priced.

avant-bras [avɑ̃bra] *nm inv* forearm.

avant-centre [avɑ̃sɑ̃tr(ə)] *nm* centre-forward.

avant-coureur [avɑ̃kurœr] *a*: signe ~ forerunner.

avant-dernier, ère [avɑ̃dɛrnje, -jɛr] *a, nm/f* next to last, last but one.

avant-garde [avɑ̃gard(ə)] *nf* (MIL) vanguard ; (*fig*) avant-garde.

avant-goût [avɑ̃gu] *nm* foretaste.

avant-hier [avɑ̃tjɛr] *ad* the day before yesterday.

avant-poste [avɑ̃pɔst(ə)] *nm* outpost.

avant-première [avɑ̃prəmjɛr] *nf* (*de film*) preview.

avant-projet [avɑ̃prɔʒɛ] *nm* pilot study.

avant-propos [avɑ̃prɔpo] *nm* foreword.

avant-veille [avɑ̃vɛj] *nf*: l'~ two days before.

avare [avar] *a* miserly, avaricious // *nm/f* miser ; ~ de (*compliments etc*) sparing of ; **avarice** *nf* avarice, miserliness ; **avaricieux, euse** *a* miserly, niggardly.

avarié, e [avarje] *a* rotting, going off.

avaries [avari] *nfpl* (NAVIG) damage *sg*.

avatar [avatar] *nm* misadventure ; metamorphosis (*pl* phoses).

avec [avɛk] *prép* with ; (*à l'égard de*) to(wards), with.

avenant, e [avnɑ̃, -ɑ̃t] *a* pleasant ; à l'~ *ad* in keeping.

avènement [avɛnmɑ̃] *nm* (*d'un roi*) accession, succession ; (*d'un changement*) advent, coming.

avenir [avnir] *nm* future ; à l'~ in future ; politicien d'~ politician with prospects ou a future.

Avent [avɑ̃] *nm*: l'~ Advent.

aventure [avɑ̃tyr] *nf* adventure ; (*amoureuse*) affair ; **s'aventurer** *vi* to venture ; **aventureux, euse** *a* adventurous, venturesome ; (*projet*) risky, chancy ; **aventurier, ère** *nm/f* adventurer // *nf* (*péj*) adventuress.

avenu, e [avny] *a*: nul et non ~ null and void.

avenue [avny] *nf* avenue.

avérer [avere] : **s'~** *vb avec attribut* to prove (to be).

averse [avɛʀs(ə)] *nf* shower.

aversion [avɛʀsjɔ̃] *nf* aversion, loathing.

averti, e [avɛʀti] *a* (well-)informed.

avertir [avɛʀtiʀ] *vt*: ~ qn (de qch/que) to warn sb (of sth/that); (renseigner) to inform sb (of sth/that); **avertissement** *nm* warning; **avertisseur** *nm* horn, hooter.

aveu, x [avø] *nm* confession.

aveugle [avœgl(ə)] *a* blind; ~**ment** *nm* blindness; **aveuglément** *ad* blindly; **aveugler** *vt* to blind; **à l'aveuglette** *ad* groping one's way along; (fig) in the dark, blindly.

aviateur, trice [avjatœR, -tRis] *nm/f* aviator, pilot.

aviation [avjɑsjɔ̃] *nf* aviation; (sport) flying; (MIL) air force.

avide [avid] *a* eager; (péj) greedy, grasping; **avidité** *nf* eagerness; greed.

avilir [aviliʀ] *vt* to debase.

aviné, e [avine] *a* intoxicated, drunken.

avion [avjɔ̃] *nm* aeroplane; **aller (quelque part) en ~** to go (somewhere) by plane, fly (somewhere); **par ~** by airmail; ~ **à réaction** jet (aeroplane).

aviron [aviʀɔ̃] *nm* oar; (sport): l'~ rowing.

avis [avi] *nm* opinion; (notification) notice; **être d'~ que** to be of the opinion that; **changer d'~** to change one's mind; **jusqu'à nouvel ~** until further notice.

avisé, e [avize] *a* sensible, wise; **être bien/mal ~ de faire** to be well-/ill-advised to do.

aviser [avize] *vt* (voir) to notice, catch sight of; (informer): ~ qn de/que to advise *ou* inform sb of/that // *vi* to think about things, assess the situation; s'~ **de qch/que** to become suddenly aware of sth/that; s'~ **de faire** to take it into one's head to do.

avocat, e [avɔka, -at] *nm/f* (JUR) barrister; (fig) advocate, champion // *nm* (CULIN) avocado (pear); l'~ **de la défense/partie civile** the counsel for the defence/plaintiff; ~ **d'affaires** business lawyer; ~ **général** assistant public prosecutor; ~**stagiaire** *nm* ≈ barrister doing his articles.

avoine [avwan] *nf* oats *pl*.

avoir [avwaʀ] *nm* assets *pl*, resources *pl* // *vt* (gén) to have; (fam: duper) to do // *vb auxiliaire* to have; ~ **à faire qch** to have to do sth; **il a 3 ans** he is 3 (years old); *voir* **faim, peur** *etc*; ~ **3 mètres de haut** to be 3 metres high; **il y a** there is + *sg*, there are + *pl*; (temporel): **il y a 10 ans** 10 years ago; **il y a 10 ans/longtemps que je le sais** I've known it for 10 years/a long time; **il y a 10 ans qu'il est arrivé** it's 10 years since he arrived; **il ne peut y en ~** qu'un there can only be one; **il n'y a qu'à** we (*ou* you *etc*) will just have to; **qu'est-ce qu'il y a?** what's the matter?, what is it?; **en ~ à** *ou* **contre qn** to have a down on sb.

avoisinant, e [avwazinɑ̃, -ɑ̃t] *a* neighbouring.

avoisiner [avwazine] *vt* to be near *ou* close to; (fig) to border *ou* verge on.

avortement [avɔʀtəmɑ̃] *nm* abortion.

avorter [avɔʀte] *vi* (MÉD) to have an abortion; (fig) to fail.

avorton [avɔʀtɔ̃] *nm* (péj) little runt.

avoué, e [avwe] *a* avowed // *nm* (JUR) ≈ solicitor.

avouer [avwe] *vt* (crime, défaut) to confess (to); ~ **avoir fait/que** to admit *ou* confess to having done/that.

avril [avʀil] *nm* April.

axe [aks(ə)] *nm* axis (pl axes); (de roue etc) axle; (fig) main line; ~ **routier** trunk road, main road; ~ **de symétrie** symmetry axis; **axer** *vt*: **axer qch sur** to centre sth on.

ayant droit [ɛjɑ̃dʀwa] *nm* assignee; ~ **à** (pension etc) person eligible for *ou* entitled to.

ayons *etc vb voir* **avoir**.

azalée [azale] *nf* azalea.

azimut [azimyt] *nm* azimuth; **tous ~s** *a* (fig) omnidirectional.

azote [azɔt] *nm* nitrogen; **azoté, e** *a* nitrogenous.

azur [azyʀ] *nm* (couleur) azure, sky blue; (ciel) sky, skies *pl*.

azyme [azim] *a*: **pain ~** unleavened bread.

B

B.A. *sigle f* (= bonne action) good deed (for the day).

babiller [babije] *vi* to prattle, chatter; (bébé) to babble.

babines [babin] *nfpl* chops.

babiole [babjɔl] *nf* (bibelot) trinket; (vétille) trifle.

bâbord [babɔʀ] *nm*: **à** *ou* **par ~** to port, on the port side.

babouin [babwɛ̃] *nm* baboon.

bac [bak] *nm* (SCOL) abr de baccalauréat; (bateau) ferry; (récipient) tub; tray; tank; ~ **à glace** ice-tray.

baccalauréat [bakalɔʀea] *nm* ≈ GCE A-levels.

bâche [baʃ] *nf* tarpaulin, canvas sheet.

bachelier, ère [baʃəlje, -ljɛʀ] *nm/f* holder of the baccalauréat.

bâcher [baʃe] *vt* to cover (with a canvas sheet *ou* a tarpaulin).

bachot [baʃo] *nm* abr de baccalauréat.

bacille [basil] *nm* bacillus (pl i).

bâcler [bakle] *vt* to botch (up).

bactérie [bakteʀi] *nf* bacterium (pl ia); **bactériologie** *nf* bacteriology.

badaud, e [bado, -od] *nm/f* idle onlooker, stroller.

baderne [badɛʀn(ə)] *nf* (péj): (vieille) ~ old fossil.

badigeon [badiʒɔ̃] *nm* distemper; colourwash; **badigeonner** *vt* to distemper; to colourwash; (barbouiller) to daub.

badin, e [badɛ̃, -in] *a* light-hearted, playful.

badinage [badinaʒ] *nm* banter.

badine [badin] *nf* switch (stick).

badiner [badine] *vi*: ~ **avec qch** to treat sth lightly.

badminton [badmintɔn] *nm* badminton.

baffe [baf] *nf* (fam) slap, clout.

bafouer [bafwe] *vt* to deride, ridicule.

bafouiller [bafuje] *vi, vt* to stammer.

bâfrer [bɑfʀe] vi, vt (fam) to guzzle, gobble.

bagage [bagaʒ] nm: ~s luggage sg ; ~ littéraire (stock of) literary knowledge ; ~s à main hand-luggage.

bagarre [bagaʀ] nf fight, brawl ; il aime la ~ he loves a fight, he likes fighting ; se bagarrer vi to have a fight ou scuffle, fight.

bagatelle [bagatɛl] nf trifle, trifling sum ou matter.

bagnard [baɲaʀ] nm convict.

bagne [baɲ] nm penal colony.

bagnole [baɲɔl] nf (fam) car, motor.

bagout [bagu] nm glibness ; avoir du ~ to have the gift of the gab.

bague [bag] nf ring ; ~ de fiançailles engagement ring ; ~ de serrage clip.

baguenauder [bagnode]: se ~ vi to trail around, loaf around.

baguer [bage] vt to ring.

baguette [bagɛt] nf stick ; (cuisine chinoise) chopstick ; (de chef d'orchestre) baton ; (pain) stick of (French) bread ; ~ magique magic wand ; ~ de tambour drumstick.

bahut [bay] nm chest.

baie [bɛ] nf (GÉO) bay ; (fruit) berry ; ~ (vitrée) picture window.

baignade [bɛɲad] nf bathing.

baigné, e [beɲe] a: ~ de bathed in ; soaked with ; flooded with.

baigner [beɲe] vt (bébé) to bath // vi: ~ dans son sang to lie in a pool of blood ; ~ dans la brume to be shrouded in mist ; se ~ vi to have a swim, go swimming ou bathing ; baigneur, euse nm/f bather ; baignoire nf bath(tub).

bail, baux [baj, bo] nm lease.

bâillement [bɑjmɑ̃] nm yawn.

bâiller [bɑje] vi to yawn ; (être ouvert) to gape.

bailleur [bajœʀ] nm: ~ de fonds sponsor, backer.

bâillon [bɑjɔ̃] nm gag ; bâillonner vt to gag.

bain [bɛ̃] nm bath ; prendre un ~ to have a bath ; ~ de foule walkabout ; ~ de soleil sunbathing q ; prendre un ~ de soleil to sunbathe ; ~s de mer sea bathing sg ; ~-marie nm double boiler ; faire chauffer au ~-marie (boîte etc) to immerse in boiling water.

baïonnette [bajɔnɛt] nf bayonet.

baisemain [bɛzmɛ̃] nm kissing a lady's hand.

baiser [beze] nm kiss // vt (main, front) to kiss ; (fam!) to screw (!).

baisse [bɛs] nf fall, drop ; '~ sur la viande' 'meat prices down'.

baisser [bese] vt to lower ; (radio, chauffage) to turn down ; (AUTO: phares) to dip // vi to fall, drop, go down ; se ~ vi to bend down.

bajoues [baʒu] nfpl chaps, chops.

bal [bal] nm dance ; (grande soirée) ball ; ~ costumé fancy-dress ball ; ~ musette dance (with accordion accompaniment).

balade [balad] nf walk, stroll ; (en voiture) drive.

balader [balade] vt (traîner) to trail round ; se ~ vi to go for a walk ou stroll ; to go for a drive.

baladeuse [baladøz] nf inspection lamp.

baladin [baladɛ̃] nm wandering entertainer.

balafre [balafʀ(ə)] nf gash, slash ; (cicatrice) scar ; balafrer vt to gash, slash.

balai [balɛ] nm broom, brush ; ~-brosse nm deck scrubber.

balance [balɑ̃s] nf scales pl ; (de précision) balance ; (signe): la B~ Libra, the Scales ; être de la B~ to be Libra ; ~ des comptes/forces balance of payments/power ; ~ romaine steelyard.

balancer [balɑ̃se] vt to swing ; (lancer) to fling, chuck ; (renvoyer, jeter) to chuck out // vi to swing ; se ~ vi to swing ; to rock ; to sway ; se ~ de (fam) not to care about ; balancier nm (de pendule) pendulum ; (de montre) balance wheel ; (perche) (balancing) pole ; balançoire nf swing ; (sur pivot) seesaw.

balayer [baleje] vt (feuilles etc) to sweep up, brush up ; (pièce) to sweep ; (chasser) to sweep away ; to sweep aside ; (suj: radar) to scan ; (: phares) to sweep across ; balayeur, euse nm/f roadsweeper // nf (engin) roadsweeper ; balayures nfpl sweepings.

balbutier [balbysje] vi, vt to stammer.

balcon [balkɔ̃] nm balcony ; (THÉÂTRE) dress circle.

baldaquin [baldakɛ̃] nm canopy.

baleine [balɛn] nf whale ; (de parapluie, corset) rib ; baleinière nf whaleboat.

balise [baliz] nf (NAVIG) beacon ; (marker) buoy ; (AVIAT) runway light, beacon ; (AUTO, SKI) sign, marker ; baliser vt to mark out (with beacons ou lights etc).

balistique [balistik] nf ballistics sg.

balivernes [balivɛʀn(ə)] nfpl twaddle sg, nonsense sg.

ballade [balad] nf ballad.

ballant, e [balɑ̃, -ɑ̃t] a dangling.

ballast [balast] nm ballast.

balle [bal] nf (de fusil) bullet ; (de sport) ball ; (du blé) chaff ; (paquet) bale ; ~ perdue stray bullet.

ballerine [balʀin] nf ballet dancer ; ballet shoe.

ballet [balɛ] nm ballet.

ballon [balɔ̃] nm (de sport) ball ; (jouet, AVIAT) balloon ; (de vin) glass ; ~ de football football.

ballonner [balɔne] vt: j'ai le ventre ballonné I feel bloated.

ballon-sonde [balɔ̃sɔ̃d] nm sounding balloon.

ballot [balo] nm bundle ; (péj) nitwit.

ballottage [balɔtaʒ] nm (POL) second ballot.

ballotter [balɔte] vi to roll around ; to toss // vt to shake ou throw about ; to toss.

balluchon [balyʃɔ̃] nm bundle (of clothes).

balnéaire [balneɛʀ] a seaside cpd.

balourd, e [baluʀ, -uʀd(ə)] a clumsy, doltish ; balourdise nf clumsiness, doltishness ; blunder.

balte [balt] a Baltic.

Baltique [baltik] *nf*: la (mer) ~ the Baltic (Sea).

baluchon [baly ʃɔ] *nm* = **balluchon**.

balustrade [balystʀad] *nf* railings *pl*, handrail.

bambin [bɑbɛ̃] *nm* little child.

bambou [bɑbu] *nm* bamboo.

ban [bɑ̃] *nm* round of applause, cheer; ~s *nmpl* (*de mariage*) banns; **être/mettre au ~ de** to be outlawed/to outlaw from; **le ~ et l'arrière-~ de sa famille** every last one of his relatives.

banal, e [banal] *a* banal, commonplace; (*péj*) trite; four/moulin ~ village oven/mill; ~**ité** *nf* banality; truism, trite remark.

banane [banan] *nf* banana; ~**raie** *nf* banana plantation; **bananier** *nm* banana tree; banana boat.

banc [bɑ̃] *nm* seat, bench; (*de poissons*) shoal; ~ **des accusés** dock; ~ **d'essai** (*fig*) testing ground; ~ **de sable** sandbank; ~ **des témoins** witness box.

bancaire [bɑ̃kɛʀ] *a* banking, bank *cpd*.

bancal, e [bɑ̃kal] *a* wobbly; bandy-legged.

bandage [bɑ̃daʒ] *nm* bandaging; bandage; ~ **herniaire** truss.

bande [bɑ̃d] *nf* (*de tissu etc*) strip; (*MÉD*) bandage; (*motif*) stripe; (*magnétique etc*) tape; (*groupe*) band; (*péj*): ~ **de** bunch ou crowd of; **par la** ~ in a roundabout way; **donner de la** ~ to list; **faire** ~ **à part** to keep to o.s.; ~ **dessinée** strip cartoon; ~ **perforée** punched tape; ~ **de roulement** (*de pneu*) tread; ~ **sonore** sound track.

bandeau, x [bɑ̃do] *nm* headband; (*sur les yeux*) blindfold; (*MÉD*) head bandage.

bander [bɑ̃de] *vt* (*blessure*) to bandage; (*muscle*) to tense; ~ **les yeux à qn** to blindfold sb.

banderole [bɑ̃dʀɔl] *nf* banner, streamer.

bandit [bɑ̃di] *nm* bandit; **banditisme** *nm* violent crime, armed robberies *pl*.

bandoulière [bɑ̃duljɛʀ] *nf*: **en** ~ (slung ou worn) across the shoulder.

banjo [bɑ̃(d)ʒo] *nm* banjo.

banlieue [bɑ̃ljø] *nf* suburbs *pl*; lignes/quartiers de ~ suburban lines/areas; **trains de** ~ commuter trains.

bannière [banjɛʀ] *nf* banner.

bannir [baniʀ] *vt* to banish.

banque [bɑ̃k] *nf* bank; (*activités*) banking; ~ **d'affaires** merchant bank.

banqueroute [bɑ̃kʀut] *nf* bankruptcy.

banquet [bɑ̃kɛ] *nm* dinner; (*d'apparat*) banquet.

banquette [bɑ̃kɛt] *nf* seat.

banquier [bɑ̃kje] *nm* banker.

banquise [bɑ̃kiz] *nf* ice field.

baptême [batɛm] *nm* christening; baptism; ~ **de l'air** first flight; **baptiser** *vt* to christen.

baquet [bakɛ] *nm* tub, bucket.

bar [baʀ] *nm* bar.

baragouin [baʀagwɛ̃] *nm* gibberish.

baraque [baʀak] *nf* shed; (*fam*) house; ~ **foraine** fairground stand.

baraqué, e [baʀake] *a* well-built, hefty.

baraquements [baʀakmɑ̃] *nmpl* huts (for refugees, workers etc).

baratin [baʀatɛ̃] *nm* (*fam*) smooth talk, patter; **baratiner** *vt* to chat up.

barbare [baʀbaʀ] *a* barbaric // *nm/f* barbarian.

barbe [baʀb(ə)] *nf* beard; **quelle** ~ (*fam*) what a drag ou bore; ~ **à papa** candyfloss.

barbelé [baʀbəle] *nm* barbed wire *q*.

barbiche [baʀbiʃ] *nf* goatee.

barbiturique [baʀbityʀik] *nm* barbiturate.

barboter [baʀbɔte] *vi* to paddle, dabble // *vt* (*fam*) to filch.

barboteuse [baʀbɔtøz] *nf* rompers *pl*.

barbouiller [baʀbuje] *vt* to daub; **avoir l'estomac barbouillé** to feel queasy ou sick.

barbu, e [baʀby] *a* bearded.

barda [baʀda] *nm* (*fam*) kit, gear.

barde [baʀd(ə)] *nf* (*CULIN*) sliver of fat bacon.

bardé, e [baʀde] *a*: ~ **de médailles** *etc* bedecked with medals *etc*.

barder [baʀde] *vi* (*fam*): **ça va** ~ sparks will fly, things are going to get hot.

barème [baʀɛm] *nm* scale; table; ~ **des salaires** salary scale.

barguigner [baʀgiɲe] *vi*: **sans** ~ without (any) humming and hawing ou shilly-shallying.

baril [baʀil] *nm* barrel; keg.

barillet [baʀijɛ] *nm* (*de revolver*) cylinder.

bariolé, e [baʀjɔle] *a* many-coloured, rainbow-coloured.

baromètre [baʀɔmɛtʀ(ə)] *nm* barometer.

baron [baʀɔ̃] *nm* baron; **baronne** *nf* baroness.

baroque [baʀɔk] *a* (*ART*) baroque; (*fig*) weird.

baroud [baʀud] *nm*: ~ **d'honneur** gallant last stand.

barque [baʀk(ə)] *nf* small boat.

barrage [baʀaʒ] *nm* dam; (*sur route*) roadblock, barricade.

barre [baʀ] *nf* bar; (*NAVIG*) helm; (*écrite*) line, stroke; (*JUR*): **comparaître à la** ~ to appear as a witness; ~ **fixe** (*GYM*) horizontal bar; ~ **à mine** crowbar; ~**s parallèles** (*GYM*) parallel bars.

barreau, x [baʀo] *nm* bar; (*JUR*): **le** ~ the Bar.

barrer [baʀe] *vt* (*route etc*) to block; (*mot*) to cross out; (*chèque*) to cross; (*NAVIG*) to steer; **se** ~ *vi* (*fam*) to clear off.

barrette [baʀɛt] *nf* (*pour cheveux*) (hair) slide.

barreur [baʀœʀ] *nm* helmsman; (*aviron*) coxswain.

barricade [baʀikad] *nf* barricade; **barricader** *vt* to barricade; **se barricader chez soi** (*fig*) to lock o.s. in.

barrière [baʀjɛʀ] *nf* fence; (*obstacle*) barrier.

barrique [baʀik] *nf* barrel, cask.

baryton [baʀitɔ̃] *nm* baritone.

bas, basse [bɑ, bɑs] *a* low // *nm* bottom, lower part; (*chaussette*) stocking // *nf* (*MUS*) bass // *ad* low; **plus** ~ lower down; (*dans un texte*) further on, below; (*parler*) more softly; **au** ~ **mot** at the lowest estimate; **enfant en** ~ **âge** infant, young child ; **en ~** down below ; at (ou to) the bottom ; (dans une maison) downstairs ; **en ~ de** at the bottom of ; **mettre ~** vi to give birth ; **à ~ ...!** 'down with ...!' ; **~ morceaux** nmpl (viande) cheap cuts.

basalte [bazalt(ə)] nm basalt.

basané, e [bazane] a tanned, bronzed.

bas-côté [bakote] nm (de route) verge ; (d'église) (side) aisle.

bascule [baskyl] nf: (jeu de) **~** seesaw ; (balance à) **~ scales** pl ; **fauteuil à ~** rocking chair ; **système à ~** tip-over device ; rocker device.

basculer [baskyle] vi to fall over, topple (over) ; (benne) to tip up // vt (gén: **faire ~**) to topple over ; to tip out, tip up.

base [baz] nf base ; (POL) rank and file ; (fondement, principe) basis (pl bases) ; **de ~** basic ; **à ~ de café** etc coffee etc -based ; **baser** vt to base ; **se baser sur** (données, preuves) to base one's argument on.

bas-fond [bafɔ̃] nm (NAVIG) shallow ; **~s** (fig) dregs.

basilic [bazilik] nm (CULIN) basil.

basilique [bazilik] nf basilica.

basket(-ball) [basket(bol)] nm basketball.

basque [bask(ə)] a, nm/f Basque.

bas-relief [bərəljɛf] nm bas relief.

basse [bas] a, nf voir **bas** ; **~-cour** nf farmyard.

bassin [basɛ̃] nm (cuvette) bowl ; (pièce d'eau) pond, pool ; (de fontaine, GÉO) basin ; (ANAT) pelvis ; (portuaire) dock.

bassiste [basist(ə)] nm/f (double) bass player.

bastingage [bastɛ̃gaʒ] nm (ship's) rail.

bastion [bastjɔ̃] nm bastion.

bas-ventre [buvɑ̃tR(ə)] nm (lower part of the) stomach.

bat vb voir **battre**.

bât [ba] nm packsaddle.

bataille [bataj] nf battle ; fight.

bataillon [batajɔ̃] nm battalion.

bâtard, e [butar, -ard(ə)] nm/f illegitimate child, bastard (péj).

bateau, x [bato] nm boat, ship.

batelier, -ière [batəlje, -jɛR] nm/f (de bac) ferryman.

bat-flanc [baflɑ̃] nm inv raised boards for sleeping, in cells, army huts etc.

bâti, e [buti] a: **bien ~** well-built // nm (armature) frame.

batifoler [batifɔle] vi to frolic ou lark about.

bâtiment [butimɑ̃] nm building ; (NAVIG) ship, vessel ; (industrie) building trade.

bâtir [butiR] vt to build.

bâtisse [butis] nf building.

bâton [butɔ̃] nm stick ; **à ~s rompus** informally.

bâtonnier [butɔnje] nm ≈ president of the Bar.

batraciens [batRasjɛ̃] nmpl amphibians.

bats vb voir **battre**.

battage [bataʒ] nm (publicité) (hard) plugging.

battant [batɑ̃] nm (de cloche) clapper ; (de volets) shutter, flap ; (de porte) side ; **porte à double ~** double door.

battement [batmɑ̃] nm (de cœur) beat ; (intervalle) interval (between classes, trains etc) ; **~ de paupières** blinking q (of eyelids) ; **10 minutes de ~** 10 minutes to spare.

batterie [batri] nf (MIL, ÉLEC) battery ; (MUS) drums pl, drum kit ; **~ de cuisine** pots and pans pl, kitchen utensils pl.

batteur [batœR] nm (MUS) drummer ; (appareil) whisk ; **batteuse** nf (AGR) threshing machine.

battre [batR(ə)] vt to beat ; (suj: pluie, vagues) to beat ou lash against ; (œufs etc) to beat up, whisk ; (blé) to thresh ; (passer au peigne fin) to scour // vi (cœur) to beat ; (volets etc) to bang, rattle ; **se ~** vi to fight ; **~ la mesure** to beat time ; **~ en brèche** to demolish ; **~ son plein** to be at its height, be going full swing ; **~ pavillon britannique** to fly the British flag ; **~ des mains** to clap one's hands ; **~ des ailes** to flap its wings ; **~ en retraite** to beat a retreat.

battue [baty] nf (chasse) beat ; (policière etc) search, hunt.

baume [bom] nm balm.

bauxite [boksit] nf bauxite.

bavard, e [bavar, -ard(ə)] a (very) talkative ; gossipy ; **bavardage** nm chatter q ; gossip q ; **bavarder** vi to chatter ; (indiscrètement) to gossip ; to blab.

bave [bav] nf dribble ; (de chien etc) slobber, slaver ; (d'escargot) slime ; **baver** vi to dribble ; to slobber, slaver ; **bavette** nf bib ; **baveux, euse** a dribbling ; (omelette) runny.

bavure [bavyR] nf smudge ; (fig) hitch, flaw.

bayer [baje] vi: **~ aux corneilles** to stand gaping.

bazar [bazar] nm general store ; (fam) jumble ; **bazarder** vt (fam) to chuck out.

B.C.G. sigle m (= bacille Calmette-Guérin) BCG.

bd. abr de **boulevard**.

B.D. sigle f = **bande dessinée**.

béant, e [beɑ̃, -ɑ̃t] a gaping.

béat, e [bea, -at] a showing open-eyed wonder ; blissful ; **béatitude** nf bliss.

beau(bel), belle, beaux [bo, bɛl] a beautiful, fine, lovely ; (homme) handsome // nf (SPORT) decider // ad: **il fait ~** the weather's fine ou fair ; **un ~ jour** one (fine) day ; **de plus belle** more than ever, even more ; **on a ~ essayer** however hard ou no matter how hard we try ; **faire le ~** (chien) to sit up and beg.

beaucoup [boku] ad a lot ; much (gén en tournure négative) ; **il ne boit pas ~** he doesn't drink much ou a lot ; **~ de** (nombre) many, a lot of ; (quantité) a lot of, much ; **~ plus/trop** etc far ou much more/too much ; **de ~** by far.

beau-fils [bofis] nm son-in-law ; (remariage) stepson.

beau-frère [bofRɛR] nm brother-in-law.

beau-père [bopɛR] nm father-in-law ; stepfather.

beauté [bote] nf beauty ; **de toute ~** beautiful ; **en ~** with a flourish, brilliantly.

beaux-arts [bozaR] nmpl fine arts.

beaux-parents [bopaRɑ̃] *nmpl* wife's/husband's family *sg ou pl*, in-laws.
bébé [bebe] *nm* baby.
bec [bɛk] *nm* beak, bill; (*de plume*) nib; (*de récipient*) spout; lip; (*fam*) mouth; ~ **de gaz** (street) gaslamp; ~ **verseur** pouring lip.
bécane [bekan] *nf* bike.
bécasse [bekas] *nf* (*ZOOL*) woodcock; (*fam*) silly goose.
bec-de-lièvre [bɛkdəljɛvR(ə)] *nm* harelip.
bêche [bɛʃ] *nf* spade; **bêcher** *vt* to dig.
bécoter [bekɔte]: **se** ~ *vi* to smooch.
becquée [beke] *nf*: **donner la** ~ **à** to feed.
becqueter [bɛkte] *vt* to peck (at).
bedaine [bədɛn] *nf* paunch.
bedeau, x [bəd'ɔ] *nm* beadle.
bedonnant, e [bədɔnɑ̃, -ɑ̃t] *a* paunchy, potbellied.
bée [be] *a*: **bouche** ~ gaping.
beffroi [befRwa] *nm* belfry.
bégayer [begeje], *vt*, *vi* to stammer.
bègue [bɛg] *nm/f*: **être** ~ to have a stammer.
bégueule [begœl] *a* prudish.
béguin [begɛ̃] *nm*: **avoir le** ~ **de** *ou* **pour** to have a crush on.
beige [bɛʒ] *a* beige.
beignet [bɛɲɛ] *nm* fritter.
bel [bɛl] *a voir* **beau**.
bêler [bele] *vi* to bleat.
belette [bəlɛt] *nf* weasel.
belge [bɛlʒ(ə)] *a*, *nm/f* Belgian.
Belgique [bɛlʒik] *nf* Belgium.
bélier [belje] *nm* ram; (*engin*) (battering) ram; (*signe*): **le B**~ Aries, the Ram; **être du B**~ to be Aries.
belle [bɛl] *af*, *nf voir* **beau**; ~**-fille** *nf* daughter-in-law; (*remariage*) stepdaughter; ~**-mère** *nf* mother-in-law; stepmother; ~**-sœur** *nf* sister-in-law.
belligérant, e [beliʒeRɑ̃, -ɑ̃t] *a* belligerent.
belliqueux, **euse** [belikø, -øz] *a* aggressive, warlike.
belvédère [bɛlvedɛR] *nm* panoramic viewpoint (*or small building at such a place*).
bémol [bemɔl] *nm* (*MUS*) flat.
bénédiction [benediksjɔ̃] *nf* blessing.
bénéfice [benefis] *nm* (*COMM*) profit; (*avantage*) benefit; **bénéficiaire** *nm/f* beneficiary; **bénéficier de** *vt* to enjoy; to benefit by *ou* from; to get, be given; **bénéfique** *a* beneficial.
benêt [bənɛ] *nm* simpleton.
bénévole [benevɔl] *a* voluntary, unpaid.
bénin, **igne** [benɛ̃, -iɲ] *a* minor, mild; (*tumeur*) benign.
bénir [benir] *vt* to bless; **bénit**, e *a* consecrated; **eau bénite** holy water; **bénitier** *nm* stoup, font (*for holy water*).
benjamin, e [bɛ̃ʒamɛ̃, -in] *nm/f* youngest child.
benne [bɛn] *nf* skip; (*de téléphérique*) (cable) car; ~ **basculante** tipper.
benzine [bɛ̃zin] *nf* benzine.
béotien, ne [beɔsjɛ̃, -jɛn] *nm/f* philistine.
B.E.P.C. *sigle m voir* **brevet**.
béquille [bekij] *nf* crutch; (*de bicyclette*) stand.

bercail [bɛRkaj] *nm* fold.
berceau, x [bɛRso] *nm* cradle, crib.
bercer [bɛRse] *vt* to rock, cradle; (*suj: musique etc*) to lull; ~ **qn de** (*promesses etc*) to delude sb with; **berceuse** *nf* lullaby.
béret (**basque**) [bɛRɛ(bask(ə))] *nm* beret.
berge [bɛRʒ(ə)] *nf* bank.
berger, **ère** [bɛRʒe, -ɛR] *nm/f* shepherd/shepherdess; **bergerie** *nf* sheep pen.
berline [bɛRlin] *nf* (*AUTO*) saloon (car).
berlingot [bɛRlɛ̃go] *nm* (*emballage*) carton (*pyramid shaped*).
berlue [bɛRly] *nf*: **j'ai la** ~ I must be seeing things.
berne [bɛRn(ə)] *nf*: **en** ~ at half-mast.
berner [bɛRne] *vt* to fool.
besogne [bəzɔɲ] *nf* work q, job; **besogneux**, **euse** *a* hard-working.
besoin [bəzwɛ̃] *nm* need; (*pauvreté*): **le** ~ need, want; ~**s** (**naturels**) nature's needs; **faire ses** ~**s** to relieve o.s.; **avoir** ~ **de qch/faire qch** to need sth/to do sth; **au** ~ if need be; **pour les** ~**s de la cause** for the purpose in hand.
bestial, e, **aux** [bɛstjal, -o] *a* bestial, brutish.
bestiaux [bɛstjo] *nmpl* cattle.
bestiole [bɛstjɔl] *nf* (tiny) creature.
bétail [betaj] *nm* livestock, cattle *pl*.
bête [bɛt] *nf* animal; (*bestiole*) insect, creature // *a* stupid, silly; **il cherche la petite** ~ he's being pernickety *ou* overfussy; ~ **noire** pet hate, bugbear; ~ **sauvage** wild beast; ~ **de somme** beast of burden.
bêtise [betiz] *nf* stupidity; stupid thing (to say *ou* do).
béton [betɔ̃] *nm* concrete; ~ **armé** reinforced concrete; **bétonner** *vt* to concrete (over); **bétonnière** *nf* cement mixer.
betterave [bɛtRav] *nf* (*rouge*) beetroot; ~ **fourragère** mangel-wurzel; ~ **sucrière** sugar beet.
beugler [bøgle] *vi* to low; (*radio etc*) to blare // *vt* (*chanson etc*) to bawl out.
beurre [bœR] *nm* butter; **beurrer** *vt* to butter; **beurrier** *nm* butter dish.
beuverie [bœvRi] *nf* drinking session.
bévue [bevy] *nf* blunder.
bi... [bi] *préfixe* bi... , two-.
biais [bjɛ] *nm* (*moyen*) device, expedient; (*aspect*) angle; **en** ~, **de** ~ (*obliquement*) at an angle // (*fig*) indirectly; **biaiser** *vi* (*fig*) to sidestep the issue.
bibelot [biblo] *nm* trinket, curio.
biberon [bibRɔ̃] *nm* (feeding) bottle; **nourrir au** ~ to bottle-feed.
bible [bibl(ə)] *nf* bible.
biblio... [biblijɔ] *préfixe*: ~**bus** *nm* mobile library van; ~**graphie** *nf* bibliography; ~**phile** *nm/f* booklover; ~**thécaire** *nm/f* librarian; ~**thèque** *nf* library; (*meuble*) bookcase.
biblique [biblik] *a* biblical.
bicarbonate [bikaRbɔnat] *nm*: ~ (**de soude**) bicarbonate of soda.
biceps [bisɛps] *nm* biceps.
biche [biʃ] *nf* doe.

bichonner [biʃɔne] vt to groom.
bicolore [bikɔlɔR] a two-coloured.
bicoque [bikɔk] nf (péj) shack.
bicorne [bikɔRn(ə)] nm cocked hat.
bicyclette [bisiklɛt] nf bicycle.
bide [bid] nm (fam: ventre) belly ; (THÉÀTRE) flop.
bidet [bidɛ] nm bidet.
bidon [bidɔ̃] nm can // a inv (fam) phoney.
bidonville [bidɔ̃vil] nm shanty town.
bielle [bjɛl] nf connecting rod.
bien [bjɛ̃] nm good ; (patrimoine) property q ; faire du ~ à qn to do sb good ; dire du ~ de to speak well of ; changer en ~ to turn to the good ; ~s de consommation consumer goods // ad (travailler) well ; ~ jeune rather young ; ~ assez quite enough ; ~ mieux very much better ; ~ du temps/ des gens quite a time/a number of people ; j'espère ~ y aller I do hope to go ; je veux ~ le faire (concession) I'm (quite) willing to do it ; il faut ~ le faire it has to be done ; ~ sûr certainly ; c'est ~ fait (mérité) it serves him (ou her etc) right ; croyant ~ faire thinking he was doing the right thing // a inv (à l'aise): être ~ to be fine ; ce n'est pas ~ de it's not right to ; cette maison est ~ this house is (very) good ; elle est ~ (jolie) she's good-looking ; des gens ~ (parfois péj) respectable people ; être ~ avec qn to be on good terms with sb ; ~ que cj although ; ~aimé, e a, nm/f beloved ; ~être nm well-being ; ~faisance nf charity ; ~faisant, e a (chose) beneficial ; ~fait nm act of generosity, benefaction ; (de la science etc) benefit ; ~faiteur, trice nm/f benefactor/benefactress ; ~fondé nm soundness ; ~fonds nm property ; ~heureux, euse a happy ; (REL) blessed, blest.
biennal, e, aux [bjenal, -o] a biennial.
bienséance [bjɛ̃seɑ̃s] nf propriety, decorum q.
bienséant, e [bjɛ̃seɑ̃, -ɑ̃t] a proper, seemly.
bientôt [bjɛ̃to] ad soon ; à ~ see you soon.
bienveillance [bjɛ̃vɛjɑ̃s] nf kindness.
bienveillant, e [bjɛ̃vɛjɑ̃, -ɑ̃t] a kindly.
bienvenu, e [bjɛ̃vny] a welcome // nm/f: être le ~/la ~e to be welcome // nf: souhaiter la ~e à to welcome ; ~e à welcome to.
bière [bjɛR] nf (boisson) beer ; (cercueil) bier ; ~ blonde lager ; ~ brune brown ale ; ~ (à la) pression draught beer.
biffer [bife] vt to cross out.
bifteck [biftɛk] nm steak.
bifurcation [bifyRkasjɔ̃] nf fork (in road).
bifurquer [bifyRke] vi (route) to fork ; (véhicule) to turn off.
bigame [bigam] a bigamous ; **bigamie** nf bigamy.
bigarré, e [bigaRe] a multicoloured ; (disparate) motley.
bigorneau, x [bigɔRno] nm winkle.
bigot, e [bigo, -ɔt] (péj) a churchy // nm/f church fiend.
bigoudi [bigudi] nm curler.
bijou, x [biʒu] nm jewel ; ~terie nf

jeweller's (shop) ; jewellery ; ~tier, ière nm/f jeweller.
bikini [bikini] nm bikini.
bilan [bilɑ̃] nm (COMM) balance sheet(s) ; end of year statement ; (fig) (net) outcome ; (: de victimes) toll ; faire le ~ de to assess ; to review ; déposer son ~ to file a bankruptcy statement.
bilatéral, e, aux [bilateRal, -o] a bilateral.
bile [bil] nf bile ; se faire de la ~ (fam) to worry o.s. sick.
biliaire [biljɛR] a biliary.
bilieux, euse [biljø, -jøz] a bilious ; (fig: colérique) testy.
bilingue [bilɛ̃g] a bilingual.
billard [bijaR] nm billiards sg ; billiard table.
bille [bij] nf (gén) ball ; (du jeu de billes) marble ; (de bois) log.
billet [bijɛ] nm (aussi: ~ de banque) (bank)note ; (de cinéma, de bus etc) ticket ; (courte lettre) note ; ~ circulaire round-trip ticket ; ~ de faveur complimentary ticket ; ~ de loterie lottery ticket ; ~ de quai platform ticket.
billion [biljɔ̃] nm billion.
billot [bijo] nm block.
bimensuel, le [bimɑ̃sɥɛl] a bimonthly, two-monthly.
bimoteur [bimɔtœR] a twin-engined.
binaire [binɛR] a binary.
binocle [binɔkl(ə)] nm pince-nez.
binôme [binom] nm binomial.
bio... [bjɔ] préfixe bio... ; ~dégradable a biodegradable ; ~graphe nm/f biographer ; ~graphie nf biography ; ~graphique a biographical ; ~logie nf biology ; ~logique a biological ; ~logiste nm/f biologist.
bipède [bipɛd] nm biped, two-footed creature.
biplan [biplɑ̃] nm biplane.
biréacteur [biReaktœR] nm twin- engined jet.
bis, e [bi, biz] a (couleur) greyish brown // ad [bis]: 12 ~ 12a ou A // excl, nm [bis] encore // nf (baiser) kiss ; (vent) North wind.
bisannuel, le [bizanɥɛl] a biennial.
bisbille [bisbij] nf: être en ~ avec qn to be at loggerheads with sb.
biscornu, e [biskɔRny] a crooked, weird(-looking).
biscotte [biskɔt] nf rusk.
biscuit [biskɥi] nm biscuit ; sponge cake.
bise [biz] a, nf voir bis.
biseau, x [bizo] nm bevelled edge ; en ~ bevelled ; ~ter vt to bevel.
bison [bizɔ̃] nm bison.
bisque [bisk(ə)] nf: ~ d'écrevisses shrimp bisque.
bissectrice [bisɛktRis] nf bisector.
bisser [bise] vt to encore.
bissextile [bisɛkstil] a: année ~ leap year.
bissexué, e [bisɛksɥe] a bisexual.
bistouri [bistuRi] nm lancet.
bistre [bistR(ə)] a bistre.
bistro(t) [bistRo] nm bistrot, café.

bitte [bit] *nf*: ~ **d'amarrage** bollard (*NAUT*).
bitume [bitym] *nm* asphalt.
bivouac [bivwak] *nm* bivouac; **bivouaquer** *vi* to bivouac.
bizarre [bizaʀ] *a* strange, odd.
blafard, e [blafaʀ, -aʀd(ə)] *a* wan.
blague [blag] *nf* (*propos*) joke; (*farce*) trick; **sans** ~! no kidding!; ~ **à tabac** tobacco pouch.
blaguer [blage] *vi* to joke // *vt* to tease; **blagueur, euse** *a* teasing // *nm/f* joker.
blaireau, x [blɛʀo] *nm* (*ZOOL*) badger; (*brosse*) shaving brush.
blâmable [blɑmabl(ə)] *a* blameworthy.
blâme [blɑm] *nm* blame; (*sanction*) reprimand.
blâmer [blɑme] *vt* to blame.
blanc, blanche [blɑ̃, blɑ̃ʃ] *a* white; (*non imprimé*) blank; (*innocent*) pure // *nm/f* white, white man/woman // *nm* (*couleur*) white; (*linge*): **le** ~ whites *pl*; (*espace non écrit*) blank; (*aussi*: ~ **d'œuf**) (egg-)white; (*aussi*: ~ **de poulet**) breast, white meat; (*aussi*: **vin** ~) white wine // *nf* (*MUS*) minim; **chèque en** ~ blank cheque; **à** ~ *ad* (*chauffer*) white-hot; (*tirer, charger*) with blanks; ~-**bec** *nm* greenhorn; **blancheur** *nf* whiteness.
blanchir [blɑ̃ʃiʀ] *vt* (*gén*) to whiten; (*linge*) to launder; (*CULIN*) to blanch; (*fig: disculper*) to clear // *vi* to grow white; (*cheveux*) to go white; **blanchissage** *nm* (*du linge*) laundering; **blanchisserie** *nf* laundry; **blanchisseur, euse** *nm/f* launderer.
blanc-seing [blɑ̃sɛ̃] *nm* signed blank paper.
blaser [blaze] *vt* to make blasé.
blason [blazɔ̃] *nm* coat of arms.
blasphème [blasfɛm] *nm* blasphemy; **blasphémer** *vi* to blaspheme // *vt* to blaspheme against.
blatte [blat] *nf* cockroach.
blazer [blazɛʀ] *nm* blazer.
blé [ble] *nm* wheat; ~ **en herbe** wheat on the ear.
bled [blɛd] *nm* (*péj*) hole; (*en Afrique du nord*): **le** ~ the interior.
blême [blɛm] *a* pale.
blennorragie [blenɔʀaʒi] *nf* blennorrhoea.
blessant, e [blesɑ̃, -ɑ̃t] *a* hurtful.
blessé, e [blese] *a* injured // *nm/f* injured person; casualty.
blesser [blese] *vt* to injure; (*délibérément: MIL etc*) to wound; (*suj: souliers etc, offenser*) to hurt; **se** ~ to injure o.s.; **se** ~ **au pied etc** to injure one's foot *etc*.
blessure [blesyʀ] *nf* injury; wound.
blet, te [blɛ, blɛt] *a* overripe.
bleu [blø] *a* blue; (*bifteck*) very rare // *nm* (*couleur*) blue; (*novice*) greenhorn; (*contusion*) bruise; (*vêtement: aussi*: ~**s**) overalls *pl*; **au** ~ (*CULIN*) au bleu.
bleuet [bløɛ] *nm* cornflower.
bleuir [bløiʀ] *vt, vi* to turn blue.
bleuté, e [bløte] *a* blue-shaded.
blindage [blɛ̃daʒ] *nm* armour-plating.
blinder [blɛ̃de] *vt* to armour; (*fig*) to harden.
blizzard [blizaʀ] *nm* blizzard.

bloc [blɔk] *nm* (*de pierre etc*) block; (*de papier à lettres*) pad; (*ensemble*) group, block; **serré à** ~ tightened right down; **en** ~ as a whole; wholesale; ~ **opératoire** operating theatre suite.
blocage [blɔkaʒ] *nm* blocking; jamming; freezing; (*PSYCH*) hang-up.
bloc-moteur [blɔkmɔtœʀ] *nm* engine block.
bloc-notes [blɔknɔt] *nm* note pad.
blocus [blɔkys] *nm* blockade.
blond, e [blɔ̃, -ɔ̃d] *a* fair, blond; (*sable, blés*) golden // *nm/f* fair-haired *ou* blond man/woman; ~ **cendré** ash blond; **blondeur** *nf* fairness.
bloquer [blɔke] *vt* (*passage*) to block; (*pièce mobile*) to jam; (*crédits, compte*) to freeze; (*regrouper*) to group; ~ **les freins** to jam on the brakes.
blottir [blɔtiʀ]: **se** ~ *vi* to huddle up.
blouse [bluz] *nf* overall.
blouson [bluzɔ̃] *nm* lumber jacket; ~ **noir** (*fig*) ≈ teddy boy.
blues [bluz] *nm* blues *pl*.
bluet [blyɛ] *nm* = **bleuet**.
bluff [blœf] *nm* bluff; ~**er** *vi, vt* to bluff.
boa [bɔa] *nm* boa.
bobard [bɔbaʀ] *nm* (*fam*) tall story.
bobèche [bɔbɛʃ] *nf* candle-ring.
bobine [bɔbin] *nf* reel; (*machine à coudre*) spool; (*ÉLEC*) coil.
bocage [bɔkaʒ] *nm* grove, copse.
bocal, aux [bɔkal, -o] *nm* jar.
bock [bɔk] *nm* (beer) glass; glass of beer.
bœuf [bœf, *pl* bø] *nm* ox (*pl* oxen), steer; (*CULIN*) beef.
bohème [bɔɛm] *a* happy-go-lucky, unconventional.
bohémien, ne [bɔemjɛ̃, -jɛn] *nm/f* gipsy.
boire [bwaʀ] *vt* to drink; (*s'imprégner de*) to soak up; ~ **un verre** to have a drink.
bois [bwa] *nm* wood; **de** ~, **en** ~ wooden; ~ **de lit** bedstead.
boisé, e [bwaze] *a* wooded.
boiser [bwaze] *vt* (*galerie de mine*) to timber; (*chambre*) to panel; (*terrain*) to plant with trees.
boiseries [bwazʀi] *nfpl* panelling *sg*.
boisson [bwasɔ̃] *nf* drink; **pris de** ~ drunk, intoxicated; ~**s alcoolisées** alcoholic beverages *ou* drinks; ~**s gazeuses** fizzy drinks.
boîte [bwat] *nf* box; **aliments en** ~ canned *ou* tinned foods; ~ **de sardines/petits pois** can *ou* tin of sardines/peas; ~ **d'allumettes** box of matches; (*vide*) matchbox; ~ **de conserves** can *ou* tin (of food); ~ **crânienne** cranium, brainpan; ~ **à gants** glove compartment; ~ **aux lettres** letterbox; ~ **de nuit** night club; ~ **postale (B.P.)** P.O. Box; ~ **de vitesses** gear box.
boiter [bwate] *vi* to limp; (*fig*) to wobble; to be shaky; **boiteux, euse** *a* lame; wobbly; shaky.
boîtier [bwatje] *nm* case; ~ **de montre** watch case.
boive *etc vb voir* **boire**.
bol [bɔl] *nm* bowl; **un** ~ **d'air** a dose of fresh air.

bolet [bɔlɛ] nm boletus (mushroom).

bolide [bɔlid] nm racing car; **comme un ~** at top speed, like a rocket.

bombance [bɔ̃bɑ̃s] nf: **faire ~** to have a feast, revel.

bombardement [bɔ̃baʀdəmɑ̃] nm bombing.

bombarder [bɔ̃baʀde] vt to bomb; **~ qn de** (cailloux, lettres) to bombard sb with; **~ qn directeur** to thrust sb into the director's seat; **bombardier** nm bomber.

bombe [bɔ̃b] nf bomb; (atomiseur) (aerosol) spray; **faire la ~** (fam) to go on a binge.

bombé, e [bɔ̃be] a rounded; bulging; cambered.

bomber [bɔ̃be] vi to bulge; to camber // vt: **~ le torse** to swell out one's chest.

bon, bonne [bɔ̃, bɔn] a good; (charitable): **~** (envers) good (to), kind (to); (juste): **le ~ numéro/moment** the right number/moment; (approprié): **~ à/pour** fit to/for // nm (billet) voucher; (aussi: **~ cadeau**) gift coupon ou voucher // nf (domestique) maid // ad: **il fait ~** it's ou the weather's fine; **sentir ~** to smell good; **tenir ~** to stand firm, hold out; **pour de ~** for good; **de bonne heure** early; **~ anniversaire!** happy birthday!; **~ voyage!** have a good journey!, enjoy your trip!; **bonne chance!** good luck!; **bonne année!** happy New Year!; **bonne nuit!** good night!; **~ enfant** a inv accommodating, easy-going; **~ d'essence** nm petrol coupon; **~ marché** a inv, ad cheap; **~ mot** nm witticism; **~ sens** nm common sense; **~ à tirer** nm pass for press; **~ du Trésor** nm Treasury bond; **~ vivant** nm jovial chap; **bonne d'enfant** nf nanny; **bonne femme** nf (péj) woman; female; **bonne à tout faire** nf general help; **bonnes œuvres** nfpl charitable works; charities.

bonasse [bɔnas] a soft, meek.

bonbon [bɔ̃bɔ̃] nm (boiled) sweet.

bonbonne [bɔ̃bɔn] nf demijohn; carboy.

bonbonnière [bɔ̃bɔnjɛʀ] nf sweet box, bonbonnière.

bond [bɔ̃] nm leap; **faire un ~** to leap in the air.

bonde [bɔ̃d] nf (d'évier etc) plug; (: trou) plughole; (de tonneau) bung; bunghole.

bondé, e [bɔ̃de] a packed (full).

bondir [bɔ̃diʀ] vi to leap.

bonheur [bɔnœʀ] nm happiness; porter **~** (à qn) to bring (sb) luck; **au petit ~** haphazardly; **par ~** fortunately.

bonhomie [bɔnɔmi] nf goodnaturedness.

bonhomme [bɔnɔm] nm (pl **bonshommes** [bɔ̃zɔm]) fellow // a goodnatured; **aller son ~ de chemin** to carry on in one's own sweet way; **.~ de neige** snowman.

boni [bɔni] nm profit.

bonification [bɔnifikasjɔ̃] nf bonus.

bonifier [bɔnifje] vt to improve.

boniment [bɔnimɑ̃] nm patter q.

bonjour [bɔ̃ʒuʀ] excl, nm good morning (ou afternoon); hello; **dire ~ à qn** to say hello ou good morning/afternoon to sb.

bonne [bɔn] a, nf voir bon; **~-meat** ad: tout **~-ment** quite simply.

bonnet [bɔnɛ] nm bonnet, hat; (de soutien-gorge) cup; **~ d'âne** dunce's cap; **~ de bain** bathing cap; **~ de nuit** nightcap.

bonneterie [bɔnɛtʀi] nf hosiery.

bon-papa [bɔ̃papa] nm grandpa, grandad.

bonsoir [bɔ̃swaʀ] excl good evening.

bonté [bɔ̃te] nf kindness q; **avoir la ~ de** to be kind ou good enough to.

borborygme [bɔʀbɔʀigm] nm rumbling noise.

bord [bɔʀ] nm (de table, verre, falaise) edge; (de rivière, lac) bank; (de route) side; (monter) **à ~** (to go) on board; **jeter par-dessus ~** to throw overboard; **le commandant/les hommes du ~** the ship's master/crew; **au ~ de la mer** at the seaside; **être au ~ des larmes** to be on the verge of tears.

bordage [bɔʀdaʒ] nm planking q, plating q.

bordeaux [bɔʀdo] nm Bordeaux (wine) // a inv maroon.

bordée [bɔʀde] nf broadside; **une ~ d'injures** a volley of abuse.

bordel [bɔʀdɛl] nm brothel.

border [bɔʀde] vt (être le long de) to border; to line; (garnir): **~ qch de** to line sth with; to trim sth with; (qn dans son lit) to tuck up.

bordereau, x [bɔʀdəʀo] nm docket; slip; statement, invoice.

bordure [bɔʀdyʀ] nf border; (sur un vêtement) trim(ming), border; **en ~ de** on the edge of.

borgne [bɔʀɲ(ə)] a one-eyed; **hôtel ~** shady hotel.

borne [bɔʀn(ə)] nf boundary stone; (gén: **~ kilométrique**) kilometre-marker, ≈ milestone; **~s** nfpl (fig) limits; **dépasser les ~s** to go too far; **sans ~(s)** boundless.

borné, e [bɔʀne] a narrow; narrowminded.

borner [bɔʀne] vt to limit; to confine; **se ~ à faire** to content o.s. with doing; to limit o.s. to doing.

bosquet [bɔskɛ] nm copse, grove.

bosse [bɔs] nf (de terrain etc) bump; (enflure) lump; (du bossu, du chameau) hump; **avoir la ~ des maths** etc to have a gift for maths etc; **il a roulé sa ~** he's been around.

bosseler [bɔsle] vt (ouvrer) to emboss; (abîmer) to dent.

bosser [bɔse] vi (fam) to work; to slog (hard).

bossu, e [bɔsy] nm/f hunchback.

bot [bo] am: **pied ~** club foot.

botanique [bɔtanik] nf: **la ~** botany // a botanic(al).

botaniste [bɔtanist(ə)] nm/f botanist.

botte [bɔt] nf (soulier) (high) boot; (ESCRIME) thrust; (gerbe): **~ de paille** bundle of straw; **~ de radis/d'asperges** bunch of radishes/asparagus; **~s de caoutchouc** wellington boots.

botter [bɔte] vt to put boots on; to kick; (fam): **ça me botte** I fancy that.

bottier [bɔtje] nm bootmaker.
bottin [bɔtɛ̃] nm directory.
bottine [bɔtin] nf ankle boot, bootee.
bouc [buk] nm goat; (barbe) goatee; ~ émissaire scapegoat.
boucan [bukɑ̃] nm din, racket.
bouche [buʃ] nf mouth; **faire le ~ à ~ à qn** to give sb the kiss of life, to practise mouth-to-mouth resuscitation on sb; ~ **de chaleur** hot air vent; ~ **d'égout** manhole; ~ **d'incendie** fire hydrant; ~ **de métro** métro entrance.
bouché, e [buʃe] a (temps, ciel) overcast; (péj: personne) thick; (JAZZ: trompette) muted; **avoir le nez** ~ to have a blocked (-up) nose.
bouchée [buʃe] nf mouthful; ~**s à la reine** chicken vol-au-vents.
boucher [buʃe] nm butcher // vt (pour colmater) to stop up; to fill up; (obstruer) to block (up); **se** ~ **le nez** to hold one's nose; **se** ~ (tuyau etc) to block up, get blocked up.
bouchère [buʃɛʀ] nf (woman) butcher; butcher's wife.
boucherie [buʃʀi] nf butcher's (shop); butchery; (fig) slaughter.
bouche-trou [buʃtʀu] nm (fig) stop-gap.
bouchon [buʃɔ̃] nm (en liège) cork; (autre matière) stopper; (fig: embouteillage) holdup; (PÊCHE) float; ~ **doseur** measuring cap.
bouchonner [buʃɔne] vt to rub down.
boucle [bukl(ə)] nf (forme, figure) loop; (objet) buckle; ~ (de cheveux) curl; ~ **d'oreilles** earring.
bouclé, e [bukle] a curly; (tapis) uncut.
boucler [bukle] vt (fermer: ceinture etc) to fasten up; (: magasin) to shut; (terminer) to finish off; to complete; (: budget) to balance; (enfermer) to shut away; to lock up; (: quartier) to seal off // vi to curl.
bouclier [buklije] nm shield.
bouddhiste [budist(ə)] nm/f Buddhist.
bouder [bude] vi to sulk // vt to turn one's nose up at; to refuse to have anything to do with; **bouderie** nf sulking q; **boudeur, euse** a sullen, sulky.
boudin [budɛ̃] nm (CULIN) black pudding; (TECH) roll.
boudoir [budwaʀ] nm boudoir.
boue [bu] nf mud.
bouée [bwe] nf buoy; ~ (de sauvetage) lifebuoy.
boueux, euse [bwø, -øz] a muddy // nm refuse collector.
bouffe [buf] nf (fam) grub, food.
bouffée [bufe] nf puff; ~ **de fièvre/de honte** flush of fever/shame; ~ **d'orgueil** fit of pride.
bouffer [bufe] vi (fam) to eat; (COUTURE) to puff out // vt (fam) to eat.
bouffi, e [bufi] a swollen.
bouffon, ne [bufɔ̃, -ɔn] a farcical, comical // nm jester.
bouge [buʒ] nm (low) dive; hovel.
bougeoir [buʒwaʀ] nm candlestick.
bougeotte [buʒɔt] nf: **avoir la** ~ to have the fidgets.
bouger [buʒe] vi to move; (dent etc) to

be loose; (changer) to alter; (agir) to stir // vt to move.
bougie [buʒi] nf candle; (AUTO) sparking plug.
bougon, ne [bugɔ̃, -ɔn] a grumpy.
bougonner [bugɔne] vi, vt to grumble.
bougre [bugʀ(ə)] nm chap; (fam): **ce** ~ **de** that confounded.
bouillabaisse [bujabɛs] nf bouillabaisse.
bouillant, e [bujɑ̃, -ɑ̃t] a (qui bout) boiling; (très chaud) boiling (hot); (fig: ardent) hot-headed.
bouilleur de cru [bujœʀdəkʀy] nm (home) distiller.
bouillie [buji] nf gruel; (de bébé) cereal; **en** ~ (fig) crushed.
bouillir [bujiʀ] vi, vt to boil; ~ **de colère** etc to seethe with anger etc.
bouilloire [bujwaʀ] nf kettle.
bouillon [bujɔ̃] nm (CULIN) stock q; (bulles, écume) bubble; ~ **de culture** culture medium.
bouillonner [bujɔne] vi to bubble; (fig) to bubble up; to foam.
bouillotte [bujɔt] nf hot-water bottle.
boulanger, ère [bulɑ̃ʒe, -ɛʀ] nm/f baker // nf (woman) baker; baker's wife.
boulangerie [bulɑ̃ʒʀi] nf bakery, baker's (shop); (commerce) bakery; ~ **industrielle** bakery; ~**-pâtisserie** nf baker's and confectioner's (shop).
boule [bul] nf (gén) ball; (pour jouer) bowl; ~ **de neige** snowball; **faire** ~ **de neige** to snowball.
bouleau, x [bulo] nm (silver) birch.
bouledogue [buldɔg] nm bulldog.
boulet [bulɛ] nm (aussi: ~ **de canon**) cannonball; (de bagnard) ball and chain; (charbon) (coal) nut.
boulette [bulɛt] nf ball.
boulevard [bulvaʀ] nm boulevard.
bouleversement [bulvɛʀsəmɑ̃] nm (politique, social) upheaval.
bouleverser [bulvɛʀse] vt (émouvoir) to overwhelm; (causer du chagrin) to distress; (pays, vie) to disrupt; (papiers, objets) to turn upside down, upset.
boulier [bulje] nm abacus; (de jeu) scoring board.
boulimie [bulimi] nf compulsive eating, bulimia.
boulon [bulɔ̃] nm bolt; **boulonner** vt to bolt.
boulot [bulo] nm (fam: travail) work.
boulot, te [bulo, -ɔt] a plump, tubby.
bouquet [bukɛ] nm (de fleurs) bunch (of flowers), bouquet; (de persil etc) bunch; (parfum) bouquet; (fig) crowning piece.
bouquetin [buktɛ̃] nm ibex.
bouquin [bukɛ̃] nm book; **bouquiner** vi to read; to browse around (in a bookshop); **bouquiniste** nm/f bookseller.
bourbeux, euse [buʀbø, -øz] a muddy.
bourbier [buʀbje] nm (quag)mire.
bourde [buʀd(ə)] nf (erreur) howler; (gaffe) blunder.
bourdon [buʀdɔ̃] nm bumblebee.
bourdonnement [buʀdɔnmɑ̃] nm buzzing.

bourdonner [buʀdɔne] vi to buzz.

bourg [buʀ] nm town.

bourgade [buʀgad] nf township.

bourgeois, e [buʀʒwa, -waz] a (souvent péj) ≈ (upper) middle class; bourgeois // nm/f (autrefois) burgher.

bourgeoisie [buʀʒwazi] nf ≈ upper middle classes pl; bourgeoisie; petite ~ middle classes.

bourgeon [buʀʒɔ̃] nm bud; bourgeonner vi to bud.

Bourgogne [buʀgɔɲ] nf: la ~ Burgundy // nm: b~ burgundy (wine).

bourguignon, ne [buʀgiɲɔ̃, -ɔn] a of ou from Burgundy, Burgundian; bœuf ~ bœuf bourguignon.

bourlinguer [buʀlɛ̃ge] vi to knock about a lot, get around a lot.

bourrade [buʀad] nf shove, thump.

bourrage [buʀaʒ] nm: ~ de crâne brainwashing; (SCOL) cramming.

bourrasque [buʀask(ə)] nf squall.

bourratif, ive [buʀatif, -iv] a filling, stodgy.

bourreau, x [buʀo] nm executioner; (fig) torturer; ~ de travail glutton for work.

bourreler [buʀle] vt: être bourrelé de remords to be racked by remorse.

bourrelet [buʀlɛ] nm draught excluder; (de peau) fold ou roll (of flesh).

bourrer [buʀe] vt (pipe) to fill; (poêle) to pack; (valise) to cram (full); ~ de to cram (full) with; to stuff with; ~ de coups to hammer blows on, pummel.

bourrique [buʀik] nf (âne) ass.

bourru, e [buʀy] a surly, gruff.

bourse [buʀs(ə)] nf (subvention) grant; (porte-monnaie) purse; la B~ the Stock Exchange; boursier, ière a (COMM) Stock Market cpd // nm/f (SCOL) grant-holder.

boursouflé, e [buʀsufle] a swollen, puffy; (fig) bombastic, turgid.

boursoufler [buʀsufle] vt to puff up, bloat; se ~ vi (visage) to swell ou puff up; (peinture) to blister.

bous vb voir **bouillir**.

bousculade [buskylad] nf rush; crush.

bousculer [buskyle] vt to knock over; to knock into; (fig) to push, rush.

bouse [buz] nf: ~ (de vache) (cow) dung q.

bousiller [buzije] vt (fam) to wreck.

boussole [busɔl] nf compass.

bout [bu] vb voir **bouillir** // nm bit; (extrémité..d'un bâton etc) tip; (: d'une ficelle, table, rue, période) end; au ~ de (après) at the end of, after; pousser qn à ~ to push sb to the limit (of his patience); venir à ~ de to manage to overcome ou finish (off); à ~ portant at point-blank range; ~ filtre filter tip.

boutade [butad] nf quip, sally.

boute-en-train [butɑ̃tʀɛ̃] nm inv live wire.

bouteille [butɛj] nf bottle; (de gaz butane) cylinder.

boutique [butik] nf shop; boutiquier, ière nm/f shopkeeper.

bouton [butɔ̃] nm (BOT) bud; (MÉD) spot; (électrique etc) button; (de porte) knob; ~ de manchette cuff-link; ~ d'or butter-

cup; **boutonner** vt to button up, do up; boutonneux, euse a spotty; boutonnière nf buttonhole; ~-pression nm press stud, snap fastener.

bouture [butyʀ] nf cutting.

bouvreuil [buvʀœj] nm bullfinch.

bovidé [bɔvide] nm bovine.

bovin, e [bɔvɛ̃, -in] a bovine; ~s nmpl cattle.

bowling [bɔliŋ] nm (tenpin) bowling; (salle) bowling alley.

box [bɔks] nm lock-up (garage); cubicle; (d'écurie) loose-box; le ~ des accusés the dock.

boxe [bɔks(ə)] nf boxing; boxer vi to box; boxeur nm boxer.

boyau, x [bwajo] nm (corde de raquette etc) (cat) gut; (galerie) passage(way); (narrow) gallery; (pneu de bicyclette) tubeless tyre // nmpl (viscères) entrails, guts.

boycotter [bɔjkɔte] vt to boycott.

B.P. sigle de **boîte postale**.

bracelet [bʀaslɛ] nm bracelet; ~-montre nm wristwatch.

braconner [bʀakɔne] vi to poach; braconnier nm poacher.

brader [bʀade] vt to sell off, sell cheaply.

braguette [bʀagɛt] nf fly, flies pl.

brailler [bʀaje] vi to bawl, yell // vt to bawl out, yell out.

braire [bʀɛʀ] vi to bray.

braise [bʀɛz] nf embers pl.

braiser [bʀeze] vt to braise.

bramer [bʀame] vi to bell; (fig) to wail.

brancard [bʀɑ̃kaʀ] nm (civière) stretcher; (bras, perche) shaft; brancardier nm stretcher-bearer.

branchages [bʀɑ̃faʒ] nmpl branches, boughs.

branche [bʀɑ̃f] nf branch; (de lunettes) side-piece.

brancher [bʀɑ̃fe] vt to connect (up); (en mettant la prise) to plug in.

branchies [bʀɑ̃fi] nfpl gills.

brandir [bʀɑ̃diʀ] vt to brandish, wield.

brandon [bʀɑ̃dɔ̃] nm firebrand.

branle [bʀɑ̃l] nm: donner le ~ à to set in motion.

branle-bas [bʀɑ̃lba] nm inv commotion.

branler [bʀɑ̃le] vi to be shaky, be loose // vt: ~ la tête to shake one's head.

braquage [bʀakaʒ] nm (fam) stick-up; (AUTO): rayon de ~ turning circle.

braquer [bʀake] vt (AUTO) to turn (the wheel) // vt (revolver etc): ~ qch sur to aim sth at, point sth at; (mettre en colère): ~ qn to antagonize sb, put sb's back up.

bras [bʀa] nm arm // nmpl (fig: travailleurs) labour sg, hands; saisir qn à ~-le-corps to take hold of sb (a)round the waist; à ~ raccourcis with fists flying; ~ droit (fig) right-hand man; ~ de levier lever arm; ~ de mer arm of the sea, sound.

brasero [bʀazeʀo] nm brazier.

brasier [bʀazje] nm blaze, (blazing) inferno.

brassage [bʀasaʒ] nm mixing.

brassard [bʀasaʀ] nm armband.

brasse [bʀas] nf (nage) breast-stroke;

(*mesure*) fathom ; ~ **papillon** butterfly (-stroke).

brassée [bʀase] *nf* armful.

brasser [bʀase] *vt* to mix ; ~ **l'argent/les affaires** to handle a lot of money/business.

brasserie [bʀasʀi] *nf* (*restaurant*) brasserie ; (*usine*) brewery.

brasseur [bʀasœʀ] *nm* (*de bière*) brewer ; ~ **d'affaires** big businessman.

brassière [bʀasjɛʀ] *nf* (baby's) vest.

bravache [bʀavaʃ] *nm* blusterer, braggart.

bravade [bʀavad] *nf*: **par** ~ out of bravado.

brave [bʀav] *a* (*courageux*) brave ; (*bon*, *gentil*) good, kind.

braver [bʀave] *vt* to defy.

bravo [bʀavo] *excl* bravo // *nm* cheer.

bravoure [bʀavuʀ] *nf* bravery.

break [bʀɛk] *nm* (*AUTO*) estate car.

brebis [bʀəbi] *nf* ewe ; ~ **galeuse** black sheep.

brèche [bʀɛʃ] *nf* breach, gap ; **être sur la** ~ (*fig*) to be on the go.

bredouille [bʀəduj] *a* empty-handed.

bredouiller [bʀəduje] *vi*, *vt* to mumble, stammer.

bref, brève [bʀɛf, bʀɛv] *a* short, brief // *ad* in short // *nf*: (**voyelle**) **brève** short vowel ; **d'un ton** ~ sharply, curtly ; **en** ~ in short, in brief.

brelan [bʀəlɑ̃] *nm* three of a kind ; ~ **d'as** three aces.

brème [bʀɛm] *nf* bream.

Brésil [bʀezil] *nm* Brazil ; **b**~**ien, ne** *a*, *nm/f* Brazilian.

Bretagne [bʀətaɲ] *nf* Brittany.

bretelle [bʀətɛl] *nf* (*de fusil etc*) sling ; (*de combinaison*, *soutien-gorge*) strap ; (*autoroute*) slip road ; ~**s** *nfpl* (*pour pantalon*) braces.

breton, ne [bʀətɔ̃, -ɔn] *a*, *nm/f* Breton.

breuvage [bʀœvaʒ] *nm* beverage, drink.

brève [bʀɛv] *a*, *nf voir* **bref**.

brevet [bʀave] *nm* diploma, certificate ; ~ (**d'invention**) patent ; ~ **d'apprentissage** certificate of apprenticeship ; ~ **d'études du premier cycle** (**B.E.P.C.**) ≈ O levels ; **breveté, e** *a* patented ; (*diplômé*) qualified ; **breveter** *vt* to patent.

bréviaire [bʀevjɛʀ] *nm* breviary.

bribes [bʀib] *nfpl* bits, scraps ; snatches ; **par** ~ piecemeal.

bric-à-brac [bʀikabʀak] *nm inv* bric-a-brac, jumble.

bricolage [bʀikɔlaʒ] *nm*: **le** ~ do-it-yourself (jobs).

bricole [bʀikɔl] *nf* trifle ; small job.

bricoler [bʀikɔle] *vi* to do D.I.Y. jobs ; to potter about ; to do odd jobs // *vt* to fix up ; to tinker with ; **bricoleur, euse** *nm/f* handyman, D.I.Y. enthusiast.

bride [bʀid] *nf* bridle ; (*d'un bonnet*) string, tie ; **à** ~ **abattue** flat out, hell for leather ; **tenir en** ~ to keep in check ; **lâcher la** ~ **à, laisser la** ~ **sur le cou à** to give free rein to.

bridé, e [bʀide] *a*: **yeux** ~**s** slit eyes.

brider [bʀide] *vt* (*réprimer*) to keep in check ; (*cheval*) to bridle ; (*CULIN: volaille*) to truss.

bridge [bʀidʒ(ə)] *nm* bridge.

brièvement [bʀijɛvmɑ̃] *ad* briefly.

brièveté [bʀijɛvte] *nf* brevity.

brigade [bʀigad] *nf* (*POLICE*) squad ; (*MIL*) brigade ; (*gén*) team.

brigand [bʀigɑ̃] *nm* brigand.

brigandage [bʀigɑ̃daʒ] *nm* robbery.

briguer [bʀige] *vt* to aspire to.

brillamment [bʀijamɑ̃] *ad* brilliantly.

brillant, e [bʀijɑ̃, -ɑ̃t] *a* brilliant ; bright ; (*luisant*) shiny, shining // *nm* (*diamant*) brilliant.

briller [bʀije] *vi* to shine.

brimade [bʀimad] *nf* vexation, harassment *q* ; bullying *q*.

brimbaler [bʀɛ̃bale] *vb* = **bringue-baler**.

brimer [bʀime] *vt* to harass ; to bully.

brin [bʀɛ̃] *nm* (*de laine, ficelle etc*) strand ; (*fig*): **un** ~ **de** a bit of ; ~ **d'herbe** blade of grass ; ~ **de muguet** sprig of lily of the valley ; ~ **de paille** wisp of straw.

brindille [bʀɛ̃dij] *nf* twig.

bringuebaler [bʀɛ̃gbale] *vi* to shake (about) // *vt* to cart about.

brio [bʀijo] *nm* brilliance ; (*MUS*) brio ; **avec** ~ brilliantly, with panache.

brioche [bʀijɔʃ] *nf* brioche (bun) ; (*fam*: *ventre*) paunch.

brique [bʀik] *nf* brick // *a inv* brick red.

briquer [bʀike] *vt* to polish up.

briquet [bʀikɛ] *nm* (cigarette) lighter.

brisant [bʀizɑ̃] *nm* reef ; (*vague*) breaker.

brise [bʀiz] *nf* breeze.

brise-glace [bʀizglas] *nm inv* icebreaker.

brise-jet [bʀizʒɛ] *nm inv* tap swirl.

brise-lames [bʀizlam] *nm inv* breakwater.

briser [bʀize] *vt* to break ; **se** ~ *vi* to break ; **briseur, euse de grève** *nm/f* strike-breaker.

britannique [bʀitanik] *a* British // *nm/f* British person ; **les B**~**s** the British.

broc [bʀo] *nm* pitcher.

brocanteur, euse [bʀɔkɑ̃tœʀ, -øz] *nm/f* junkshop owner ; junk dealer.

broche [bʀɔʃ] *nf* brooch ; (*CULIN*) spit ; (*fiche*) spike, peg ; **à la** ~ spit-roast, roasted on a spit.

broché, e [bʀɔʃe] *a* (*livre*) paper-backed.

brochet [bʀɔʃɛ] *nm* pike *inv*.

brochette [bʀɔʃɛt] *nf* skewer ; ~ **de décorations** row of medals.

brochure [bʀɔʃyʀ] *nf* pamphlet, brochure, booklet.

broder [bʀɔde] *vt* to embroider // *vi* to embroider the facts ; **broderie** *nf* embroidery.

bromure [bʀɔmyʀ] *nm* bromide.

broncher [bʀɔ̃ʃe] *vi*: **sans** ~ without flinching ; without turning a hair.

bronches [bʀɔ̃ʃ] *nfpl* bronchial tubes ; **bronchite** *nf* bronchitis ; **broncho-pneumonie** [bʀɔ̃kɔ-] *nf* bronco-pneumonia *q*.

bronze [bʀɔ̃z] *nm* bronze.

bronzé, e [bʀɔ̃ze] *a* tanned.

bronzer [bʀɔ̃ze] *vt* to tan // *vi* to get a tan ; **se** ~ to sunbathe.

brosse [bʀɔs] *nf* brush ; **donner un coup de** ~ **à qch** to give sth a brush ; **coiffé**

en ~ with a crewcut; ~ à cheveux hairbrush; ~ à dents toothbrush; ~ à habits clothesbrush; **brosser** vt (nettoyer) to brush; (fig: tableau etc) to paint; to draw.

brouette [bʀuɛt] nf wheelbarrow.

brouhaha [bʀuaa] nm hubbub.

brouillard [bʀujaʀ] nm fog.

brouille [bʀuj] nf quarrel.

brouiller [bʀuje] vt to mix up; to confuse; (RADIO) to cause interference to; to jam; (rendre trouble) to cloud; (désunir: amis) to set at odds; **se** ~ vi (ciel, vue) to cloud over; (détails) to become confused; **se** ~ (avec) to fall out (with).

brouillon, ne [bʀujɔ̃, -ɔn] a disorganised; unmethodical // nm draft.

broussailles [bʀusɑj] nfpl undergrowth sg: **broussailleux, euse** a bushy.

brousse [bʀus] nf: la ~ the bush.

brouter [bʀute] vt to graze on // vi to graze; (AUTO) to judder.

broutille [bʀutij] nf trifle.

broyer [bʀwaje] vt to crush; ~ du noir to be down in the dumps.

bru [bʀy] nf daughter-in-law.

brucelles [bʀysɛl] nfpl: (pinces) ~ tweezers.

bruine [bʀɥin] nf drizzle.

bruiner [bʀɥine] vb impersonnel: il bruine it's drizzling, there's a drizzle.

bruire [bʀɥiʀ] vi to murmur; to rustle.

bruit [bʀɥi] nm: un ~ a noise, a sound; (fig: rumeur) a rumour; le ~ noise; pas/trop de ~ no/too much noise; **sans** ~ without a sound, noiselessly; ~ de fond background noise.

bruitage [bʀɥitaʒ] nm sound effects pl; **bruiteur, euse** nm/f sound-effects engineer.

brûlant, e [bʀylɑ̃, -ɑ̃t] a burning (hot); (liquide) boiling (hot); (regard) fiery; (sujet) red-hot.

brûlé, e [bʀyle] a (fig: démasqué) blown // nm: odeur de ~ smell of burning.

brûle-pourpoint [bʀylpuʀpwɛ̃]: à ~ ad point-blank.

brûler [bʀyle] vt to burn; (suj: eau bouillante) to scald; (consommer: électricité, essence) to use; (feu rouge, signal) to go through (without stopping) // vi to burn; (jeu) to be warm; **se** ~ to burn o.s.; to scald o.s.; **se** ~ la cervelle to blow one's brains out; ~ (d'impatience) de faire qch to burn with impatience ou be dying to do sth.

brûleur [bʀylœʀ] nm burner.

brûlure [bʀylyʀ] nf (lésion) burn; (sensation) burning (sensation); ~s d'estomac heartburn sg.

brume [bʀym] nf mist; **brumeux, euse** a misty; (fig) hazy.

brun, e [bʀœ̃, -yn] a brown; (cheveux, personne) dark // nm (couleur) brown; **brunir** vi to get a tan // vt to tan.

brusque [bʀysk(ə)] a (soudain) abrupt, sudden; (rude) abrupt, brusque; ~ment ad (soudainement) abruptly; suddenly; **brusquer** vt to rush; **brusquerie** nf abruptness, brusqueness.

brut, e [bʀyt] a raw, crude, rough; (COMM) gross // nf brute; (champagne) ~ brut

champagne; (pétrole) ~ crude (oil).

brutal, e, aux [bʀytal, -o] a brutal; ~iser vt to handle roughly, manhandle; ~ité nf brutality q.

brute [bʀyt] a, nf voir brut.

Bruxelles [bʀysɛl] n Brussels.

bruyamment [bʀɥijamɔ̃] ad noisily.

bruyant, e [bʀɥijɑ̃, -ɑ̃t] a noisy.

bruyère [bʀɥijɛʀ] nf heather.

bu, e pp de boire.

buanderie [bɥɑ̃dʀi] nf laundry.

buccal, e, aux [bykal, -o] a: par voie ~e orally.

bûche [byʃ] nf log; prendre une ~ (fig) to come a cropper; ~ de Noël Yule log.

bûcher [byʃe] nm pyre; bonfire // vb (fam) vi to swot, slog away //. vt to swot up.

bûcheron [byʃʀɔ̃] nm woodcutter.

bucolique [bykɔlik] a bucolic, pastoral.

budget [bydʒɛ] nm budget; **budgétaire** [bydʒetɛʀ] a budgetary, budget cpd.

buée [bɥe] nf (sur une vitre) mist; (de l'haleine) steam.

buffet [byfɛ] nm (meuble) sideboard; (de réception) buffet; ~ (de gare) station buffet.

buffle [byfl(ə)] nm buffalo.

buis [bɥi] nm box tree; (bois) box(wood).

buisson [bɥisɔ̃] nm bush.

buissonnière [bɥisɔnjɛʀ] af: faire l'école ~ to play truant.

bulbe [bylb(ə)] nm (BOT, ANAT) bulb; (coupole) onion-shaped dome.

bulgare [bylgaʀ] a, nm/f Bulgarian.

Bulgarie [bylgaʀi] nf Bulgaria.

bulldozer [buldozɛʀ] nm bulldozer.

bulle [byl] nf bubble; (papale) bull; ~ de savon soap bubble.

bulletin [byltɛ̃] nm (communiqué, journal) bulletin; (papier) form; ticket; (SCOL) report; ~ d'informations news bulletin; ~ météorologique weather report; ~ de santé medical bulletin; ~ (de vote) ballot paper.

buraliste [byʀalist(ə)] nm/f tobacconist; clerk.

bure [byʀ] nf homespun; frock.

bureau, x [byʀo] nm (meuble) desk; (pièce, service) office; ~ de change (foreign) exchange office ou bureau; ~ de location box office; ~ de poste post office; ~ de tabac tobacconist's (shop); ~ de vote polling station; ~crate nm bureaucrat; ~cratie [-kʀasi] nf bureaucracy; ~cratique a bureaucratic.

burette [byʀɛt] nf (de mécanicien) oilcan; (de chimiste) burette.

burin [byʀɛ̃] nm cold chisel; (ART) burin.

buriné, e [byʀine] a (fig: visage) craggy, seamed.

burlesque [byʀlɛsk(ə)] a ridiculous; (LITTÉRATURE) burlesque.

burnous [byʀnu(s)] nm burnous.

bus vb [by] voir boire // nm [bys] bus.

buse [byz] nf buzzard.

busqué, e [byske] a: nez ~ hook(ed) nose.

buste [byst(ə)] nm (ANAT) chest; bust; (sculpture) bust.

but [by] vb voir **boire** // nm (parfois byt) (cible) target ; (fig) goal ; aim ; (FOOTBALL etc) goal ; de ~ en blanc point-blank ; avoir pour ~ de faire to aim to do ; dans le ~ de with the intention of.

butane [bytan] nm butane ; calor gas.

buté, e [byte] a stubborn, obstinate // nf (TECH) stop ; (ARCHIT) abutment.

buter [byte] vi: ~ contre/sur to bump into ; to stumble against // vt to antagonize ; se ~ vi to get obstinate ; to dig in one's heels.

buteur [bytœR] nm striker.

butin [bytɛ̃] nm booty, spoils pl ; (d'un vol) loot.

butiner [bytine] vi to gather nectar.

butor [bytɔR] nm (fig) lout.

butte [byt] nf mound, hillock ; être en ~ à to be exposed to.

buvais etc vb voir **boire**.

buvard [byvaR] nm blotter.

buvette [byvɛt] nf refreshment room ; refreshment stall.

buveur, euse [byvœR, -øz] nm/f drinker.

byzantin, e [bizɑ̃tɛ̃, -in] a Byzantine.

C

c' [s] dét voir **ce**.

ça [sa] pronom (pour désigner) this ; (: plus loin) that ; (comme sujet indéfini) it ; ~ m'étonne que it surprises me that ; ~ va? how are you? ; how are things? ; (d'accord?) OK?, all right? ; c'est ~ that's right.

çà [sa] ad: ~ et là here and there.

caban [kabɑ̃] nm reefer jacket, donkey jacket.

cabane [kaban] nf hut, cabin.

cabanon [kabanɔ̃] nm chalet ; (country) cottage.

cabaret [kabaRɛ] nm night club.

cabas [kaba] nm shopping bag.

cabestan [kabɛstɑ̃] nm capstan.

cabillaud [kabijo] nm cod inv.

cabine [kabin] nf (de bateau) cabin ; (de plage) (beach) hut ; (de piscine etc) cubicle ; (de camion, train) cab ; (d'avion) cockpit ; ~ d'ascenseur) lift cage ; ~ d'essayage fitting room ; ~ spatiale space capsule ; ~ (téléphonique) call ou (tele)phone box, (tele)phone booth.

cabinet [kabinɛ] nm (petite pièce) closet ; (de médecin) surgery ; (de notaire etc) office ; (: clientèle) practice ; (POL) Cabinet ; (d'un ministre) advisers pl ; ~s nmpl (w.-c.) toilet sg, loo sg ; ~ d'affaires business consultants' (bureau), business partnership ; ~ de toilette toilet ; ~ de travail study.

câble [kabl(ə)] nm cable.

câbler [kable] vt to cable.

cabosser [kabɔse] vt to dent.

cabotage [kabɔtaʒ] nm coastal navigation ; **caboteur** nm coaster.

cabotinage [kabɔtinaʒ] nm playacting ; third-rate acting, ham acting.

cabrer [kabRe]: se ~ vi (cheval) to rear up ; (avion) to nose up ; (fig) to revolt, rebel ; to jib.

cabri [kabRi] nm kid.

cabriole [kabRijɔl] nf caper ; somersault.

cabriolet [kabRijɔlɛ] nm convertible.

cacahuète [kakaɥɛt] nf peanut.

cacao [kakao] nm cocoa (powder) ; (boisson) cocoa.

cachalot [kaʃalo] nm sperm whale.

cache [kaʃ] nm mask, card (for masking) // nf hiding place.

cache-cache [kaʃkaʃ] nm: jouer à ~ to play hide-and-seek.

cachemire [kaʃmiR] nm cashmere // a: dessin ~ paisley pattern.

cache-nez [kaʃne] nm inv scarf, muffler.

cache-pot [kaʃpo] nm inv flower-pot holder.

cacher [kaʃe] vt to hide, conceal ; ~ qch à qn to hide ou conceal sth from sb ; se ~ to hide ; to be hidden ou concealed ; il ne s'en cache pas he makes no secret of it.

cachet [kaʃɛ] nm (comprimé) tablet ; (sceau: du roi) seal ; (: de la poste) postmark ; (rétribution) fee ; (fig) style, character ; **cacheter** vt to seal.

cachette [kaʃɛt] nf hiding place ; en ~ on the sly, secretly.

cachot [kaʃo] nm dungeon.

cachotterie [kaʃɔtRi] nf mystery ; faire des ~s to be secretive.

cactus [kaktys] nm cactus.

cadastre [kadastR(ə)] nm cadastre, land register.

cadavérique [kadaveRik] a deathly (pale), deadly pale.

cadavre [kadavR(ə)] nm corpse, (dead) body.

cadeau, x [kado] nm present, gift ; faire un ~ à qn to give sb a present ou gift ; faire ~ de qch à qn to make a present of sth to sb, give sb sth as a present.

cadenas [kadna] nm padlock ; **cadenasser** vt to padlock.

cadence [kadɑ̃s] nf (MUS) cadence ; rhythm ; (de travail etc) rate ; ~s nfpl (en usine) production rate sg ; en ~ rhythmically ; in time ; **cadencé, e** a rhythmic(al).

cadet, te [kadɛ, -ɛt] a younger ; (le plus jeune) youngest // nm/f youngest child ou one, youngest boy ou son/girl ou daughter ; il est mon ~ (de deux ans) (rapports non familiaux) he's (2 years) younger than me, he's 2 years my junior ; les ~s (SPORT) the minors (15 - 17 years).

cadran [kadRɑ̃] nm dial ; ~ solaire sundial.

cadre [kadR(ə)] nm frame ; (environnement) surroundings pl ; (limites) scope // nm/f (ADMIN) managerial employee, executive // a: loi ~ outline ou blueprint law ; ~ moyen/supérieur (ADMIN) middle/senior management employee, junior/senior executive ; rayer qn des ~s to discharge sb ; to dismiss sb ; dans le ~ de (fig) within the framework ou context of.

cadrer [kadRe] vi: ~ avec to tally ou correspond with // vt (CINÉMA) to centre.

caduc, uque [kadyk] a obsolete ; (BOT) deciduous.

cafard [kafaʀ] nm cockroach; **avoir le ~** to be down in the dumps, be feeling low.

café [kafe] nm coffee; (*bistro*) café // a inv coffee-coloured; **~ au lait** white coffee; **~ noir** black coffee; **~ tabac** tobacconist's or newsagent's also serving coffee and spirits; **~ine** nf caffeine; **cafetier, ière** nm/f café-owner // nf (*pot*) coffee-pot.

cafouiller [kafuje] vi to get in a shambles; to work in fits and starts.

cage [kaʒ] nf cage; **~ (des buts)** goal; **en ~** in a cage, caged up ou in; **~ d'ascenseur** lift shaft; **~ d'escalier** (stair)well; **~ thoracique** rib cage.

cageot [kaʒo] nm crate.

cagibi [kaʒibi] nm shed.

cagneux, euse [kaɲø, -øz] a knock-kneed.

cagnotte [kaɲɔt] nf kitty.

cagoule [kagul] nf cowl; hood; (*SKI etc*) cagoule.

cahier [kaje] nm notebook; (*TYPO*) signature; **~ de revendications/doléances** list of claims/grievances; **~ de brouillons** roughbook, jotter; **~ des charges** schedule (of conditions); **~ d'exercices** exercise book.

cahin-caha [kaẽkaa] ad: **aller ~** to jog along; (*fig*) to be so-so.

cahot [kao] nm jolt, bump; **cahoter** vi to bump along, jog along.

cahute [kayt] nf shack, hut.

caïd [kaid] nm big chief, boss.

caille [kaj] nf quail.

caillé, e [kaje] a: **lait ~** curdled milk, curds pl.

cailler [kaje] vi (*lait*) to curdle; (*sang*) to clot.

caillot [kajo] nm (blood) clot.

caillou, x [kaju] nm (little) stone; **~ter** vt (*chemin*) to metal; **~teux, euse** a stony; pebbly.

Caire [kɛʀ] nm: **le ~** Cairo.

caisse [kɛs] nf box; (*où l'on met la recette*) cashbox; till; (*où l'on paye*) cash desk; check-out; (*de banque*) cashier's desk; teller's desk; (*TECH*) case, casing; **~ enregistreuse** cash register; **~ d'épargne** savings bank; **~ de retraite** pension fund; **caissier, ière** nm/f cashier.

caisson [kɛsɔ̃] nm box, case.

cajoler [kaʒɔle] vt to wheedle, coax; to surround with love and care, make a fuss of.

cake [kɛk] nm fruit cake.

calaminé, e [kalamine] a (*AUTO*) coked up.

calamité [kalamite] nf calamity, disaster.

calandre [kalɑ̃dʀ(ə)] nf radiator grill; (*machine*) calender, mangle.

calanque [kalɑ̃k] nf rocky inlet.

calcaire [kalkɛʀ] nm limestone // a (*eau*) hard; (*GÉO*) limestone cpd.

calciné, e [kalsine] a burnt to ashes.

calcium [kalsjɔm] nm calcium.

calcul [kalkyl] nm calculation; **le ~** (*SCOL*) arithmetic; **~ différentiel/intégral** differential/integral calculus; **~ (biliaire)** (gall)stone; **~ (rénal)** (kidney) stone; **~ateur** nm, **~atrice** nf calculator.

calculer [kalkyle] vt to calculate, work out, reckon; (*combiner*) to calculate.

cale [kal] nf (*de bateau*) hold; (*en bois*) wedge, chock; **~ sèche** dry dock.

calé, e [kale] a (*fam*) clever, bright.

calebasse [kalbɑs] nf calabash, gourd.

caleçon [kalsɔ̃] nm pair of underpants, trunks pl; **~ de bain** bathing trunks pl.

calembour [kalɑ̃buʀ] nm pun.

calendes [kalɑ̃d] nfpl: **renvoyer aux ~ grecques** to postpone indefinitely.

calendrier [kalɑ̃dʀije] nm calendar; (*fig*) timetable.

cale-pied [kalpje] nm inv toe clip.

calepin [kalpɛ̃] nm notebook.

caler [kale] vt to wedge, chock up; **~ (son moteur/véhicule)** to stall (one's engine/vehicle).

calfater [kalfate] vt to caulk.

calfeutrer [kalføtʀe] vt to (make) draughtproof; **se ~** to make o.s. snug and comfortable.

calibre [kalibʀ(ə)] nm (*d'un fruit*) grade; (*d'une arme*) bore, calibre; (*fig*) calibre; **calibrer** vt to grade.

calice [kalis] nm (*REL*) chalice; (*BOT*) calyx.

califourchon [kalifuʀʃɔ̃]: **à ~** ad astride; **à ~ sur** astride, straddling.

câlin, e [kalɛ̃, -in] a cuddly, cuddlesome; tender.

câliner [kaline] vt to fondle, cuddle.

calleux, euse [kalø, -øz] a horny, callous.

calligraphie [kaligʀafi] nf calligraphy.

calmant [kalmɑ̃] nm tranquillizer, sedative; painkiller.

calme [kalm(ə)] a calm, quiet // nm calm(ness), quietness; **~ plat** (*NAVIG*) dead calm.

calmer [kalme] vt to calm (down); (*douleur, inquiétude*) to ease, soothe; **se ~** to calm down.

calomnie [kalɔmni] nf slander; (*écrite*) libel; **calomnier** vt to slander; to libel; **calomnieux, euse** a slanderous; libellous.

calorie [kalɔʀi] nf calorie.

calorifère [kalɔʀifɛʀ] nm stove.

calorifique [kalɔʀifik] a calorific.

calorifuge [kalɔʀifyʒ] a (heat-) insulating, heat-retaining.

calot [kalo] nm forage cap.

calotte [kalɔt] nf (*coiffure*) skullcap; (*gifle*) slap; **~ glaciaire** icecap.

calque [kalk(ə)] nm (*dessin*) tracing; (*fig*) carbon copy.

calquer [kalke] vt to trace; (*fig*) to copy exactly.

calvaire [kalvɛʀ] nm (*croix*) wayside cross, calvary; (*souffrances*) suffering, martyrdom.

calvitie [kalvisi] nf baldness.

camaïeu [kamajø] nm: (*motif en*) **~** monochrome motif.

camarade [kamaʀad] nm/f friend, pal; (*POL*) comrade; **~rie** nf friendship.

cambouis [kɑ̃bwi] nm engine oil.

cambrer [kɑ̃bʀe] vt to arch; **se ~** to arch one's back; **pied très cambré** foot with high arches ou insteps.

cambriolage [kɑ̃bʀijɔlaʒ] nm burglary.

cambrioler [kɑ̃bʀijɔle] vt to burgle; **cambrioleur, euse** nm/f burglar.

cambrure [kɑ̃bʀyʀ] nf (*de la route*) camber.

cambuse [kɑ̃byz] nf storeroom.

came [kam] nf: **arbre à ~s** camshaft; **arbre à ~s en tête** overhead camshaft.

camée [kame] nm cameo.

caméléon [kamele3̃] nm chameleon.

camelot [kamlo] nm street pedlar.

camelote [kamlɔt] nf rubbish, trash, junk.

caméra [kameʀa] nf camera; (*d'amateur*) cine-camera.

camion [kamj3̃] nm lorry, truck; (*plus petit, fermé*) van; **~-citerne** nm tanker; **camionnage** nm haulage; **camionnette** nf (small) van; **camionneur** nm (*entrepreneur*) haulage contractor; (*chauffeur*) lorry ou truck driver; van driver.

camisole [kamizɔl] nf: **~ (de force)** strait jacket.

camomille [kamɔmij] nf camomile; (*boisson*) camomile tea.

camouflage [kamufla3] nm camouflage.

camoufler [kamufle] vt to camouflage; (*fig*) to conceal, cover up.

camouflet [kamuflɛ] nm snub.

camp [kɑ̃] nm camp; (*fig*) side; **~ de nudistes/vacances** nudist/holiday camp; **~ de concentration** concentration camp.

campagnard, e [kɑ̃paɲaʀ, -aʀd(ə)] a country cpd // nm/f countryman/woman.

campagne [kɑ̃paɲ] nf country, countryside; (*MIL, POL, COMM*) campaign; **à la ~** in the country; **faire ~ pour** to campaign for.

campement [kɑ̃pmɑ̃] nm camp, encampment.

camper [kɑ̃pe] vi to camp // vt to pull ou put on firmly; to sketch; **se ~ devant** to plant o.s. in front of; **campeur, euse** nm/f camper.

camphre [kɑ̃fʀ(ə)] nm camphor.

camping [kɑ̃piŋ] nm camping; (*terrain de*) **~** campsite, camping site; **faire du ~** to go camping.

camus, e [kamy, -yz] a: **nez ~** pug nose.

Canada [kanada] nm: **le ~** Canada; **canadien, ne** a, nm/f Canadian // nf (*veste*) fur-lined jacket.

canaille [kanaj] nf (*péj*) scoundrel // a raffish, rakish.

canal, aux [kanal, -o] nm canal; (*naturel*) channel; (*ADMIN*): **par le ~ de** through (the medium of), via.

canalisation [kanalizasj3̃] nf (*tuyau*) pipe.

canaliser [kanalize] vt to canalize; (*fig*) to channel.

canapé [kanape] nm settee, sofa; (*CULIN*) canapé, open sandwich.

canard [kanaʀ] nm duck.

canari [kanaʀi] nm canary.

cancans [kɑ̃kɑ̃] nmpl (malicious) gossip sg.

cancer [kɑ̃sɛʀ] nm cancer; (*signe*): **le C~** Cancer, the Crab; **être du C~** to be Cancer; **cancéreux, euse** a cancerous; suffering from cancer; **cancérigène** a carcinogenic.

cancre [kɑ̃kʀ(ə)] nm dunce.

cancrelat [kɑ̃kʀəla] nm cockroach.

candélabre [kɑ̃delabʀ(ə)] nm candelabrum; street lamp, lamppost.

candeur [kɑ̃dœʀ] nf ingenuousness, guilelessness.

candi [kɑ̃di] a inv: **sucre ~** (sugar-)candy.

candidat, e [kɑ̃dida, -at] nm/f candidate; (*à un poste*) applicant, candidate; **candidature** nf candidature; application; **poser sa candidature** to submit an application, apply.

candide [kɑ̃did] a ingenuous, guileless, naïve.

cane [kan] nf (female) duck.

caneton [kant3̃] nm duckling.

canette [kanɛt] nf (*de bière*) (flip-top) bottle; (*de machine à coudre*) spool.

canevas [kanva] nm (*COUTURE*) canvas (for tapestry work); (*fig*) framework, structure.

caniche [kaniʃ] nm poodle.

canicule [kanikyl] nf scorching heat; midsummer heat, dog days pl.

canif [kanif] nm penknife, pocket knife.

canin, e [kanɛ̃, -in] a canine // nf canine (tooth), eye tooth; **exposition ~e** dog show.

caniveau, x [kanivo] nm gutter.

canne [kan] nf (walking) stick; **~ à pêche** fishing rod; **~ à sucre** sugar cane.

canné, e [kane] a (*chaise*) cane cpd.

cannelle [kanɛl] nf cinnamon.

cannelure [kanlyʀ] nf flute, fluting q.

cannibale [kanibal] nm/f cannibal.

canoë [kanɔe] nm canoe; (*sport*) canoeing.

canon [kan3̃] nm (*arme*) gun; (*d'une arme: tube*) barrel; (*fig*) model; canon // a: **droit ~** canon law; **~ rayé** rifled barrel.

cañon [kaɲ3̃] nm canyon.

canoniser [kanɔnize] vt to canonize.

canonnade [kanɔnad] nf cannonade.

canonnier [kanɔnje] nm gunner.

canonnière [kanɔnjɛʀ] nf gunboat.

canot [kano] nm boat, ding(h)y; **~ pneumatique** rubber ou inflatable ding(h)y; **~ de sauvetage** lifeboat; **canoter** vi to go rowing.

canotier [kanɔtje] nm boater.

cantate [kɑ̃tat] nf cantata.

cantatrice [kɑ̃tatʀis] nf (opera) singer.

cantine [kɑ̃tin] nf canteen.

cantique [kɑ̃tik] nm hymn.

canton [kɑ̃t3̃] nm *district regrouping several communes*; (*en Suisse*) canton.

cantonade [kɑ̃tɔnad]: **à la ~** ad to everyone in general; from the rooftops.

cantonner [kɑ̃tɔne] vt (*MIL*) to billet; to station; **se ~ dans** to confine o.s. to.

cantonnier [kɑ̃tɔnje] nm roadmender, roadman.

canular [kanylaʀ] nm hoax.

caoutchouc [kautʃu] nm rubber; **~ mousse** foam rubber; **caoutchouté, e** a rubberized; **caoutchouteux, euse** a rubbery.

cap [kap] nm (*GÉO*) cape; headland; (*fig*) hurdle; watershed; (*NAVIG*): **changer de ~** to change course; **mettre le ~ sur** to head ou steer for.

C.A.P. sigle m = Certificat d'aptitude professionnelle (obtained after trade apprenticeship).

capable [kapabl(ə)] a able, capable; ~ de qch/faire capable of sth/doing; **livre ~ d'intéresser** book liable ou likely to be of interest.

capacité [kapasite] nf (compétence) ability; (JUR, contenance) capacity; ~ (en droit) basic legal qualification.

cape [kap] nf cape, cloak; **rire sous ~** to laugh up one's sleeve.

C.A.P.E.S. [kapɛs] sigle m = Certificat d'aptitude au professorat de l'enseignement du second degré.

capharnaüm [kafaʀnaɔm] nm shambles sg.

capillaire [kapilɛʀ] a (soins, lotion) hair cpd; (vaisseau etc) capillary; **capillarité** nf capillarity.

capilotade [kapilɔtad]: **en ~** ad crushed to a pulp; smashed to pieces.

capitaine [kapitɛn] nm captain; ~ **des pompiers** fire chief, firemaster; ~**rie** nf (du port) harbour master's (office).

capital, e, aux [kapital -o] a major; of paramount importance; fundamental; (JUR) capital // nm capital; (fig) stock; asset // nf (ville) capital; (lettre) capital (letter); // nmpl (fonds) capital sg, money sg; ~ (social) authorized capital; ~**iser** vt to amass, build up; (COMM) to capitalize; ~**isme** nm capitalism; ~**iste** a, nm/f capitalist.

capiteux, euse [kapitø, -øz] a heady; sensuous, alluring.

capitonner [kapitɔne] vt to pad.

capitulation [kapitylɑsjɔ̃] nf capitulation.

capituler [kapityle] vi to capitulate.

caporal, aux [kapɔʀal, -o] nm lance corporal.

capot [kapo] nm (AUTO) bonnet.

capote [kapɔt] nf (de voiture) hood; (de soldat) greatcoat.

capoter [kapɔte] vi to overturn.

câpre [kupʀ(ə)] nf caper.

caprice [kapʀis] nm whim, caprice; passing fancy; ~**s** (de la mode etc) vagaries; **capricieux, euse** a capricious; whimsical; temperamental.

Capricorne [kapʀikɔʀn] nm: **le ~** Capricorn, the Goat; **être du ~** to be Capricorn.

capsule [kapsyl] nf (de bouteille) cap; (amorce) primer; cap; (BOT etc, spatiale) capsule.

capter [kapte] vt (ondes radio) to pick up; (eau) to harness; (fig) to win, capture.

captieux, euse [kapsjø, -øz] a specious.

captif, ive [kaptif, -iv] a captive // nm/f captive, prisoner.

captiver [kaptive] vt to captivate.

captivité [kaptivite] nf captivity; **en ~** in captivity.

capture [kaptyʀ] nf capture, catching q; catch.

capturer [kaptyʀe] vt to capture, catch.

capuche [kapyʃ] nf hood.

capuchon [kapyʃɔ̃] nm hood; (de stylo) cap, top.

capucin [kapysɛ̃] nm Capuchin monk.

capucine [kapysin] nf (BOT) nasturtium.

caquet [kakɛ] nm: **rabattre le ~ à qn** to bring sb down a peg or two.

caqueter [kakte] vi (poule) to cackle; (fig) to prattle, blether.

car [kaʀ] nm coach // cj because, for; ~ **de reportage** broadcasting ou radio van.

carabine [kaʀabin] nf carbine, rifle.

caracoler [kaʀakɔle] vi to caracole, prance.

caractère [kaʀaktɛʀ] nm (gén) character; **en ~s gras** in bold type; **en petits ~s** in small print; **avoir du ~** to have character; **avoir bon/mauvais ~** to be good-/ill-natured ou -tempered; **caractériel, le** a (of) character // nm/f emotionally disturbed child.

caractérisé, e [kaʀakterize] a: **c'est une grippe/de l'insubordination ~e** it is a clear(-cut) case of flu/insubordination.

caractériser [kaʀakterize] vt to characterize; **se ~ par** to be characterized ou distinguished by.

caractéristique [kaʀakteʀistik] a, nf characteristic.

carafe [kaʀaf] nf decanter; carafe.

carambolage [kaʀɑ̃bɔlaʒ] nm multiple crash, pileup.

caramel [kaʀamɛl] nm (bonbon) caramel, toffee; (substance) caramel; **caraméliser** vt to caramelize.

carapace [kaʀapas] nf shell.

carat [kaʀa] nm carat; **or à 18 ~s** 18-carat gold.

caravane [kaʀavan] nf caravan; **caravanier** nm caravanner; **caravaning** nm caravanning; (emplacement) caravan site.

carbone [kaʀbɔn] nm carbon; (feuille) carbon, sheet of carbon paper; (double) carbon (copy).

carbonique [kaʀbɔnik] a: **gaz ~** carbonic acid gas; **neige ~** dry ice.

carbonisé, e [kaʀbɔnize] a charred.

carboniser [kaʀbɔnize] vt to carbonize; to burn down, reduce to ashes.

carburant [kaʀbyʀɑ̃] nm (motor) fuel.

carburateur [kaʀbyʀatœʀ] nm carburettor.

carburation [kaʀbyʀɑsjɔ̃] nf carburation.

carcan [kaʀkɑ̃] nm (fig) yoke, shackles pl.

carcasse [kaʀkas] nf carcass; (de véhicule etc) shell.

carder [kaʀde] vt to card.

cardiaque [kaʀdjak] a cardiac, heart cpd // nm/f heart patient.

cardigan [kaʀdigɑ̃] nm cardigan.

cardinal, e, aux [kaʀdinal, -o] a cardinal // nm (REL) cardinal.

cardiologie [kaʀdjɔlɔʒi] nf cardiology; **cardiologue** nm/f cardiologist, heart specialist.

carême [kaʀɛm] nm: **le C~** Lent.

carence [kaʀɑ̃s] nf incompetence, inadequacy; (manque) deficiency; ~ **vitaminique** vitamin deficiency.

carène [kaʀɛn] nf hull.

caréner [kaʀene] vt (NAVIG) to careen; (carrosserie) to streamline.

caressant, e [kaʀɛsɑ̃, -ɑ̃t] *a* affectionate; caressing, tender.

caresse [kaʀɛs] *nf* caress.

caresser [kaʀese] *vt* to caress, stroke, fondle; (*fig: projet, espoir*) to toy with.

cargaison [kaʀgɛzɔ̃] *nf* cargo, freight.

cargo [kaʀgo] *nm* cargo boat, freighter.

caricatural, e, aux [kaʀikatyʀal, -o] *a* caricatural, caricature-like.

caricature [kaʀikatyʀ] *nf* caricature; (*politique etc*) (satirical) cartoon; **caricaturiste** *nm/f* caricaturist; (satirical) cartoonist.

carie [kaʀi] *nf*: **la ~ (dentaire)** tooth decay; **une ~** a hole (in a tooth); **carié, e** *a*: **dent cariée** bad *ou* decayed tooth.

carillon [kaʀijɔ̃] *nm* (*d'église*) bells *pl*; (*pendule*) chimes *pl*; (*de porte*): **~ (électrique)** (electric) door chime *ou* bell; **carillonner** *vi* to ring, chime, peal.

carlingue [kaʀlɛ̃g] *nf* cabin.

carnage [kaʀnaʒ] *nm* carnage, slaughter.

carnassier, ière [kaʀnasje, -jɛʀ] *a* carnivorous // *nm* carnivore.

carnation [kaʀnɑsjɔ̃] *nf* complexion; **~s** (*PEINTURE*) flesh tones.

carnaval [kaʀnaval] *nm* carnival.

carné, e [kaʀne] *a* meat *cpd*, meat-based.

carnet [kaʀnɛ] *nm* (*calepin*) notebook; (*de tickets, timbres etc*) book; (*d'école*) school report; (*journal intime*) diary; **~ de chèques** cheque book; **~ de commandes** order book; **~ à souches** counterfoil book.

carnier [kaʀnje] *nm* gamebag.

carnivore [kaʀnivɔʀ] *a* carnivorous // *nm* carnivore.

carotide [kaʀɔtid] *nf* carotid (artery).

carotte [kaʀɔt] *nf* carrot.

carpe [kaʀp(ə)] *nf* carp.

carpette [kaʀpɛt] *nf* rug.

carquois [kaʀkwa] *nm* quiver.

carre [kaʀ] *nf* (*de ski*) edge.

carré, e [kaʀe] *a* square; (*fig: franc*) straightforward // *nm* (*de terrain, jardin*) patch, plot; (*NAVIG: salle*) wardroom; (*MATH*) square; **élever un nombre au ~** to square a number; **mètre/kilomètre ~** square metre/kilometre; (*CARTES*): **~ d'as/de rois** four aces/kings.

carreau, x [kaʀo] *nm* (*en faïence etc*) (floor) tile; (*au mur*) (wall) tile; (*de fenêtre*) (window) pane; (*motif*) check, square; (*CARTES: couleur*) diamonds *pl*; (: *carte*) diamond; **tissu à ~x** checked fabric.

carrefour [kaʀfuʀ] *nm* crossroads *sg*.

carrelage [kaʀlaʒ] *nm* tiling.

carreler [kaʀle] *vt* to tile.

carrelet [kaʀlɛ] *nm* (*poisson*) plaice.

carreleur [kaʀlœʀ] *nm* (floor) tiler.

carrément [kaʀemɑ̃] *ad* straight out, bluntly; straight; definitely.

carrer [kaʀe]: **se ~** *vi*: **se ~ dans un fauteuil** to settle o.s. comfortably *ou* ensconce o.s. in an armchair.

carrier [kaʀje] *nm*: **(ouvrier) ~** quarryman, quarrier.

carrière [kaʀjɛʀ] *nf* (*de roches*) quarry; (*métier*) career; **militaire de ~** professional soldier; **faire ~ dans** to make one's career in.

carriole [kaʀjɔl] *nf* (*péj*) old cart.

carrossable [kaʀɔsabl(ə)] *a* suitable for (motor) vehicles.

carrosse [kaʀɔs] *nm* (horse-drawn) coach.

carrosserie [kaʀɔsʀi] *nf* body, coachwork *q*; (*activité, commerce*) coachbuilding; **atelier de ~ coachbuilder's workshop**; (*pour réparations*) body repairs shop, panel beaters' (yard); **carrossier** *nm* coachbuilder; (*dessinateur*) car designer.

carrousel [kaʀuzɛl] *nm* (*ÉQUITATION*) carousel; (*fig*) merry-go-round.

carrure [kaʀyʀ] *nf* build; (*fig*) stature, calibre.

cartable [kaʀtabl(ə)] *nm* (*d'écolier*) satchel, (school)bag.

carte [kaʀt(ə)] *nf* (*de géographie*) map; (*marine, du ciel*) chart; (*de fichier, d'abonnement etc, à jouer*) card; (*au restaurant*) menu; (*aussi:* **~ postale**) (post)card; (*aussi:* **~ de visite**) (visiting) card; **avoir/donner ~ blanche** to have/give carte blanche *ou* a free hand; **à la ~** (*au restaurant*) à la carte; **~ de crédit** credit card; **~ d'état-major** ≈ Ordnance Survey map; **la ~ grise** (*AUTO*) the (car) registration book; **~ d'identité** identity card; **~ perforée** punch(ed) card; **la ~ verte** (*AUTO*) the green card; **la ~ des vins** the wine list; **~-lettre** *nf* letter-card.

carter [kaʀtɛʀ] *nm* (*AUTO: d'huile*) sump; (: *de la boîte de vitesses*) casing; (*de bicyclette*) chain guard.

cartilage [kaʀtilaʒ] *nm* (*ANAT*) cartilage.

cartographe [kaʀtɔgʀaf] *nm/f* cartographer.

cartographie [kaʀtɔgʀafi] *nf* cartography, map-making.

cartomancien, ne [kaʀtɔmɑ̃sjɛ̃, -ɛn] *nm/f* fortune-teller (*with cards*).

carton [kaʀtɔ̃] *nm* (*matériau*) cardboard; (*boîte*) (cardboard) box; (*d'invitation*) invitation card; (*ART*) sketch; cartoon; **faire un ~** (*au tir*) to have a go at the rifle range; to score a hit; **~ (à dessin)** portfolio; **cartonnage** *nm* cardboard (packing); **cartonné, e** *a* (*livre*) hardback, cased; **~-pâte** *nm* pasteboard; **de ~-pâte** (*fig*) cardboard *cpd*.

cartouche [kaʀtuʃ] *nf* cartridge; (*de cigarettes*) carton; **cartouchière** *nf* cartridge belt.

cas [kɑ] *nm* case; **faire peu de ~/grand ~ de** to attach little/great importance to; **en aucun ~** on no account, under no circumstances (whatsoever); **au ~ où** in case; **en ~ de** in case of, in the event of; **en ~ de besoin** if need be; **en tout ~** in any case, at any rate; **~ de conscience** matter of conscience.

casanier, ière [kazanje, -jɛʀ] *a* stay-at-home.

casaque [kazak] *nf* (*de jockey*) blouse.

cascade [kaskad] *nf* waterfall, cascade; (*fig*) stream, torrent.

cascadeur, euse [kaskadœʀ, -øz] *nm/f* stuntman/girl.

case [kɑz] *nf* (*hutte*) hut; (*compartiment*) compartment; (*pour le courrier*) pigeonhole ; (*sur un formulaire, de mots croisés, d'échiquier*) square.

casemate [kazmat] *nf* blockhouse.

caser [kaze] *vt* to put ; to tuck ; to put up ; (*péj*) to find a job for ; to find a husband for.

caserne [kazɛrn(ə)] *nf* barracks *sg ou pl* ; ~-**ment** *nm* barrack buildings *pl*.

cash [kaʃ] *ad*: **payer** ~ to pay cash down.

casier [kazje] *nm* (*à journaux etc*) rack ; (*de bureau*) filing cabinet ; (: *à cases*) set of pigeonholes ; (*case*) compartment ; pigeonhole ; (: *à clef*) locker ; (*PÊCHE*) lobster pot ; ~ **à bouteilles** bottle rack ; ~ **judiciaire** police record.

casino [kazino] *nm* casino.

casque [kask(ə)] *nm* helmet ; (*chez le coiffeur*) (hair-)drier ; (*pour audition*) (head-)phones *pl*, headset.

casquette [kaskɛt] *nf* cap.

cassant, e [kasɑ̃, -ɑ̃t] *a* brittle ; (*fig*) brusque, abrupt.

cassate [kasat] *nf*: (**glace**) ~ cassata.

cassation [kasasjɔ̃] *nf*: **recours en** ~ appeal to the Supreme Court.

casse [kas] *nf* (*pour voitures*): **mettre à la** ~ to scrap, send to the breakers ; (*dégâts*): **il y a eu de la** ~ there were a lot of breakages.

casse... [kas] *préfixe*: ~-**cou** *a inv* daredevil, reckless ; **crier** ~-**cou à qn** to warn sb (*against a risky undertaking*) ; ~-**croûte** *nm inv* snack ; ~-**noisette(s)**, ~-**noix** *nm inv* nutcrackers *pl* ; ~-**pieds** *a, nm/f inv* (*fam*): **il est** ~-**pieds, c'est un** ~-**pieds** he's a pain (in the neck).

casser [kase] *vt* to break ; (*ADMIN: gradé*) to demote ; (*JUR*) to quash // *vi*, **se** ~ to break.

casserole [kasrɔl] *nf* saucepan ; **à la** ~ (*CULIN*) braised.

casse-tête [kastɛt] *nm inv* (*fig*) brain teaser ; headache (*fig*).

cassette [kasɛt] *nf* (*bande magnétique*) cassette ; (*coffret*) casket.

cassis [kasis] *nm* blackcurrant ; (*de la route*) dip, bump.

cassonade [kasɔnad] *nf* brown sugar.

cassoulet [kasulɛ] *nm* cassoulet.

cassure [kasyr] *nf* break, crack.

castagnettes [kastaɲɛt] *nfpl* castanets.

caste [kast(ə)] *nf* caste.

castor [kastɔr] *nm* beaver.

castrer [kastre] *vt* to castrate ; to geld ; to doctor.

cataclysme [kataklism(ə)] *nm* cataclysm.

catacombes [katakɔ̃b] *nfpl* catacombs.

catadioptre [katadjɔptr(ə)] *nm* = **cataphote**.

catafalque [katafalk(ə)] *nm* catafalque.

catalogue [katalɔg] *nm* catalogue.

cataloguer [katalɔge] *vt* to catalogue, to list ; (*péj*) to put a label on.

catalyse [kataliz] *nf* catalysis ; **catalyseur** *nm* catalyst.

cataphote [katafɔt] *nm* reflector.

cataplasme [kataplasm(ə)] *nm* poultice.

catapulte [katapylt(ə)] *nf* catapult ; **catapulter** *vt* to catapult.

cataracte [katarakt(ə)] *nf* cataract ;

opérer qn de la ~ to operate on sb for (a) cataract.

catarrhe [katar] *nm* catarrh.

catastrophe [katastrɔf] *nf* catastrophe, disaster ; **catastrophique** *a* catastrophic, disastrous.

catch [katʃ] *nm* (all-in) wrestling ; ~-**eur, euse** *nm/f* (all-in) wrestler.

catéchiser [kateʃize] *vt* to catechize ; to indoctrinate ; to lecture ; **catéchisme** *nm* catechism ; **catéchumène** [katekymɛn] *nm/f* catechumen (*trainee convert*).

catégorie [kategɔri] *nf* category.

catégorique [kategɔrik] *a* categorical.

cathédrale [katedral] *nf* cathedral.

cathode [katɔd] *nf* cathode.

catholicisme [katɔlisism(ə)] *nm* (Roman) Catholicism.

catholique [katɔlik] *a, nm/f* (Roman) Catholic ; **pas très** ~ a bit shady *ou* fishy.

catimini [katimini]: **en** ~ *ad* on the sly, on the quiet.

cauchemar [koʃmar] *nm* nightmare ; ~-**desque** *a* nightmarish.

caudal, e, aux [kodal, -o] *a* caudal, tail *cpd*.

causal, e [kozal] *a* causal ; ~-**ité** *nf* causality.

cause [koz] *nf* cause ; (*JUR*) lawsuit, case ; brief ; **à** ~ **de** because of, owing to ; **pour** ~ **de** on account of ; owing to ; (**et**) **pour** ~ and for (a very) good reason ; **être en** ~ to be at stake ; to be involved ; to be in question ; **mettre en** ~ to implicate ; to call into question ; **remettre en** ~ to challenge, call into question.

causer [koze] *vt* to cause // *vi* to chat, talk.

causerie [kozri] *nf* talk.

caustique [kostik] *a* caustic.

cauteleux, euse [kotlø, -øz] *a* wily.

cautériser [koterize] *vt* to cauterize.

caution [kosjɔ̃] *nf* guarantee, security ; (*JUR*) bail (bond) ; (*fig*) backing, support ; **payer la** ~ **de qn** to stand bail for sb ; **libéré sous** ~ released on bail.

cautionnement [kosjɔnmɑ̃] *nm* (*somme*) guarantee, security.

cautionner [kosjɔne] *vt* to guarantee ; (*soutenir*) to support.

cavalcade [kavalkad] *nf* (*fig*) stampede.

cavalerie [kavalri] *nf* cavalry.

cavalier, ère [kavalje, -jɛr] *a* (*désinvolte*) offhand // *nm/f* rider ; (*au bal*) partner // *nm* (*ÉCHECS*) knight ; **faire** ~ **seul** to go it alone.

cave [kav] *nf* cellar ; (*cabaret*) (cellar) nightclub // *a*: **yeux** ~**s** sunken eyes.

caveau, x [kavo] *nm* vault.

caverne [kavɛrn(ə)] *nf* cave.

caverneux, euse [kavɛrnø, -øz] *a* cavernous.

caviar [kavjar] *nm* caviar(e).

cavité [kavite] *nf* cavity.

CC *sigle voir* **corps**.

C.C.P. *sigle m voir* **compte**.

CD *sigle voir* **corps**.

ce(c'), cet, cette, ces [sə, sɛt, se] *dét* (*gén*) this ; these *pl* ; (*non-proximité*) that ; those *pl* ; **cette nuit** (*qui vient*) tonight ; (*passée*) last night // *pronom*: ~ **qui**, ~

que what; (*chose qui ...*): **il est bête, ~
qui me chagrine** he's stupid, which
saddens me; **tout ~ qui bouge**
everything that *ou* which moves; **tout ~
que je sais** all I know; **~ dont j'ai parlé**
what I talked about; **ce que c'est grand
how big it is!, what a size it is!; c'est
petit/grand** it's ou it is small/big; **~ est
un peintre, ce sont des peintres** he's *ou*
he is a painter, they are painters; **c'est
le facteur** *etc* (*à la porte*) it's the postman
etc; **c'est une voiture** it's a car; **qui est-
ce?** who is it?; (*en désignant*) who is
he/she?; **qu'est-ce?** what is it?; *voir aussi*
-ci, est-ce que, n'est-ce pas, c'est-à-dire.

ceci [səsi] *pronom* this.

cécité [sesite] *nf* blindness.

céder [sede] *vt* to give up // *vi* (*pont,
barrage*) to give way; (*personne*) to give
in; **~ à** to yield to, give in to.

cédille [sedij] *nf* cedilla.

cèdre [sɛdʀ(ə)] *nm* cedar.

C.E.E. *sigle f* (= *Communauté économique
européenne*) EEC (European Economic
Community).

ceindre [sɛ̃dʀ(ə)] *vt* (*mettre*) to put on,
don; (*entourer*): **~ qch de qch** to put sth
round sth.

ceinture [sɛ̃tyʀ] *nf* belt; (*taille*) waist;
(*fig*) ring; belt; circle; **~ de sécurité**
safety *ou* seat belt; **~ (de sécurité) à
enrouleur** inertia reel seat belt; **ceinturer**
vt (*saisir*) to grasp (round the waist);
(*entourer*) to surround; **ceinturon** *nm* belt.

cela [səla] *pronom* that; (*comme sujet
indéfini*) it; **~ m'étonne que** it surprises
me that; **quand/où ~?** when/where (was
that)?

célèbre [selɛbʀ] *a* famous.

célébrer [selebʀe] *vt* to celebrate; (*louer*)
to extol.

célébrité [selebʀite] *nf* fame; (*star*)
celebrity.

céleri [sɛlʀi] *nm*: **~(-rave)** celeriac; **~
(en branche)** celery.

célérité [seleʀite] *nf* speed, swiftness.

céleste [selɛst(ə)] *a* celestial; heavenly.

célibat [seliba] *nm* celibacy;
bachelor/spinsterhood.

célibataire [selibatɛʀ] *a* single, unmarried
// *nm/f* bachelor/unmarried *ou* single
woman.

celle, celles [sɛl] *pronom voir* **celui.**

cellier [selje] *nm* storeroom.

cellophane [selɔfan] *nf* cellophane.

cellulaire [selylɛʀ] *a* (*BIO*) cell *cpd*,
cellular; **voiture** *ou* **fourgon ~** prison *ou*
police van.

cellule [selyl] *nf* (*gén*) cell.

cellulite [selylit] *nf* excess fat, cellulitis.

cellulose [selyloz] *nf* cellulose.

celui, celle, ceux, celles [səlɥi, sɛl, sø]
pronom the one; **~ qui bouge** the one
which *ou* that moves; (*personne*) the one
who moves; **~ que je vois** the one (which
ou that) I see; the one (whom) I see; **~
dont je parle** the one I'm talking about;
~ qui veut (*valeur indéfinie*) whoever
wants, the man *ou* person who wants; **~
du salon/du dessous** the one in (*ou* from)
the lounge/below; **~ de mon frère** my

brother's; **celui-ci/-là, celle-ci/-là**
this/that one; **ceux-ci, celles-ci** these
ones; **ceux-là, celles-là** those (ones).

cénacle [senakl(ə)] *nm* (literary) coterie *ou*
set.

cendre [sɑ̃dʀ(ə)] *nf* ash; **~s** (*d'un foyer*)
ash(es), cinders; (*volcaniques*) ash *sg*;
(*d'un défunt*) ashes; **sous la ~** (*CULIN*) in
(the) embers; **cendré, e** *a* (*couleur*) ashen;
(*piste*) **cendrée** cinder track; **cendrier** *nm*
ashtray.

cène [sɛn] *nf*: **la ~** (Holy) Communion;
(*ART*) the Last Supper.

censé, e [sɑ̃se] *a*: **être ~ faire** to be
supposed to do.

censeur [sɑ̃sœʀ] *nm* (*SCOL*) vice-principal,
deputy-head; (*CINÉMA, POL*) censor.

censure [sɑ̃syʀ] *nf* censorship.

censurer [sɑ̃syʀe] *vt* (*CINÉMA, PRESSE*) to
censor; (*POL*) to censure.

cent [sɑ̃] *num* a hundred, one hundred;
centaine *nf*: **une centaine (de)** about a
hundred, a hundred or so; (*COMM*) a
hundred; **plusieurs centaines (de)**
several hundred; **des centaines (de)**
hundreds (of); **centenaire** *a* hundred-year-
old // *nm/f* centenarian // *nm*
(*anniversaire*) centenary; **centième** *num*
hundredth; **centigrade** *nm* centigrade;
centigramme *nm* centigramme;
centilitre *nm* centilitre; **centime** *nm*
centime; **centimètre** *nm* centimetre;
(*ruban*) tape measure, measuring tape.

central, e, aux [sɑ̃tʀal, -o] *a* central //
nm: **~** (*téléphonique*) (telephone)
exchange // *nf*: **~e électrique/nucléaire**
electric/nuclear power-station; **~e
syndicale** group of affiliated trade unions.

centraliser [sɑ̃tʀalize] *vt* to centralize.

centre [sɑ̃tʀ(ə)] *nm* centre; **~ de gravité**
centre of gravity; **~ de tri** (*POSTES*) sorting
office; **le ~-ville** the town centre;
centrer *vt* to centre // *vi* (*FOOTBALL*) to
centre the ball.

centrifuge [sɑ̃tʀifyʒ] *a*: **force ~**
centrifugal force; **centrifuger** *vt* to
centrifuge.

centripète [sɑ̃tʀipɛt] *a*: **force ~**
centripetal force.

centuple [sɑ̃typl(ə)] *nm*: **le ~ de qch** a
hundred times sth; **au ~** a hundredfold;
centupler *vi, vt* to increase a hundredfold.

cep [sɛp] *nm* (vine) stock; **cépage** *nm*
(type of) vine.

cèpe [sɛp] *nm* (edible) boletus.

cependant [səpɑ̃dɑ̃] *ad* however, nevertheless.

céramique [seʀamik] *nf* ceramic; (*art*)
ceramics *sg*.

cercle [sɛʀkl(ə)] *nm* circle; (*objet*) band,
hoop; **~ vicieux** vicious circle.

cercueil [sɛʀkœj] *nm* coffin.

céréale [seʀeal] *nf* cereal.

cérébral, e, aux [seʀebʀal, -o] *a* (*ANAT*)
cerebral, brain *cpd*; (*fig*) mental, cerebral.

cérémonial [seʀemɔnjal] *nm* ceremonial.

cérémonie [seʀemɔni] *nf* ceremony; **~s**
(*péj*) fuss *sg*, to-do *sg*; **cérémonieux, euse**
a ceremonious, formal.

cerf [sɛʀ] *nm* stag.

cerfeuil [sɛRfœj] *nm* chervil.

cerf-volant [sɛRvɔlɑ̃] *nm* kite.

cerise [səRiz] *nf* cherry; **cerisier** *nm* cherry (tree).

cerné, e [sɛRne] *a*: **les yeux ~s** with dark rings *ou* shadows under the eyes.

cerner [sɛRne] *vt* (*MIL etc*) to surround; (*fig*: *problème*) to delimit, define.

cernes [sɛRn(ə)] *nfpl* (dark) rings, shadows (under the eyes).

certain, e [sɛRtɛ̃, -ɛn] *a* certain; (*sûr*): **~ (de/que)** certain *ou* sure (of/ that) // *dét* certain; **d'un ~ âge** past one's prime, not so young; **un ~ temps** (quite) some time; **~s** *pronom* some; **certainement** *ad* (*probablement*) most probably *ou* likely; (*bien sûr*) certainly, of course.

certes [sɛRt(ə)] *ad* admittedly; of course; indeed (yes).

certificat [sɛRtifika] *nm* certificate; **le ~ d'études** the school leaving certificate.

certifié, e [sɛRtifje] *a*: **professeur ~** qualified teacher.

certifier [sɛRtifje] *vt* to certify, guarantee; **~ à qn que** to assure sb that, guarantee to sb that.

certitude [sɛRtityd] *nf* certainty.

cerveau, x [sɛRvo] *nm* brain.

cervelas [sɛRvəla] *nm* saveloy.

cervelle [sɛRvɛl] *nf* (*ANAT*) brain; (*CULIN*) brain(s).

cervical, e, aux [sɛRvikal, -o] *a* cervical.

ces [se] *dét voir* **ce**.

césarienne [sezaRjɛn] *nf* caesarean (section), section.

cessantes [sɛsɑ̃t] *afpl*: **toutes affaires ~** forthwith.

cessation [sɛsɑsjɔ̃] *nf*: **~ des hostilités** cessation of hostilities: **~ de paiements/commerce** suspension of payments/trading.

cesse [sɛs]: **sans ~** *ad* continually, constantly; continuously; **il n'avait de ~ que** he would not rest until.

cesser [sese] *vt* to stop // *vi* to stop, cease; **~ de faire** to stop doing.

cessez-le-feu [seselfø] *nm inv* ceasefire.

cession [sɛsjɔ̃] *nf* transfer.

c'est-à-dire [sɛtadiR] *ad* that is (to say).

cet [sɛt] *dét voir* **ce**.

cétacé [setase] *nm* cetacean.

cette [sɛt] *dét voir* **ce**.

ceux [sø] *pronom voir* **celui**.

C.F.D.T. *sigle f* = *Confédération française et démocratique du travail* (a major association of French trade unions).

C.G.C. *sigle f* = *Confédération générale des cadres* (union of managerial employees).

C.G.T. *sigle f* = *Confédération générale du travail* (a major association of French trade unions).

chacal [ʃakal] *nm* jackal.

chacun, e [ʃakœ̃, -yn] *pronom* each; (*indéfini*) everyone, everybody.

chagrin, e [ʃagRɛ̃, -gRin] *a* ill-humoured, morose // *nm* grief, sorrow; **avoir du ~** to be grieved *ou* sorrowful; **chagriner** *vt* to grieve, distress; (*contrarier*) to bother, worry.

chahut [ʃay] *nm* uproar; **chahuter** *vt* to

rag, bait // *vi* to make an uproar; **chahuteur, euse** *nm/f* rowdy.

chai [ʃɛ] *nm* wine and spirit store(house).

chaîne [ʃɛn] *nf* chain; (*RADIO, TV*: *stations*) channel; **travail à la ~** production line work; **faire la ~** to form a (human) chain; **~ (haute-fidélité ou hi-fi)** hi-fi system; **~ (de montage ou de fabrication)** production *ou* assembly line; **~ (de montagnes)** (mountain) range; **chaînette** *nf* (small) chain; **chaînon** *nm* link.

chair [ʃɛR] *nf* flesh // *a*: (*couleur*) **~** flesh-coloured; **avoir la ~ de poule** to have goosepimples *ou* gooseflesh; **bien en ~** plump, well-padded; **~ à saucisses** sausage meat.

chaire [ʃɛR] *nf* (*d'église*) pulpit; (*d'université*) chair.

chaise [ʃɛz] *nf* chair; **~ de bébé** high chair; **~ longue** deckchair.

chaland [ʃalɑ̃] *nm* (*bateau*) barge.

châle [ʃal] *nm* shawl.

chalet [ʃalɛ] *nm* chalet.

chaleur [ʃalœR] *nf* heat; (*fig*) warmth; fire, fervour; heat.

chaleureux, euse [ʃalœRø, -øz] *a* warm.

challenge [ʃalɑ̃ʒ] *nm* contest, tournament.

chaloupe [ʃalup] *nf* launch; (*de sauvetage*) lifeboat.

chalumeau, x [ʃalymo] *nm* blowlamp, blowtorch.

chalut [ʃaly] *nm* trawl (net); **chalutier** *nm* trawler; (*pêcheur*) trawlerman.

chamailler [ʃamaje]: **se ~** *vi* to squabble, bicker.

chamarré, e [ʃamaRe] *a* richly coloured *ou* brocaded.

chambarder [ʃɑ̃baRde] *vt* to turn upside down, upset.

chambranle [ʃɑ̃bRɑ̃l] *nm* (door) frame.

chambre [ʃɑ̃bR(ə)] *nf* bedroom; (*TECH*) chamber; (*POL*) chamber, house; (*JUR*) court; (*COMM*) chamber; federation; **faire ~ à part** to sleep in separate rooms; **stratège en ~** armchair strategist; **~ à un lit/deux lits** (*à l'hôtel*) single-/double- *ou* twin-bedded room; **~ d'accusation** court of criminal appeal; **~ à air** (*de pneu*) (inner) tube; **~ d'amis** spare *ou* guest room; **~ à coucher** bedroom; **la C~ des députés** the Chamber of Deputies, ≈ the House (of Commons); **~ forte** strongroom; **~ froide** *ou* **frigorifique** cold room; **~ des machines** engine-room; **~ meublée** bed-sitter, furnished room; **~ noire** (*PHOTO*) dark room.

chambrée [ʃɑ̃bRe] *nf* room.

chambrer [ʃɑ̃bRe] *vt* (*vin*) to bring to room temperature.

chameau, x [ʃamo] *nm* camel.

chamois [ʃamwa] *nm* chamois // *a*: (*couleur*) **~** fawn, buff (-coloured).

champ [ʃɑ̃] *nm* field; (*PHOTO*): **dans le ~** in the picture; **prendre du ~** to draw back; **~ de bataille** battlefield; **~ de courses** racecourse; **~ de mines** minefield.

champagne [ʃɑ̃paɲ] *nm* champagne.

champêtre [ʃɑ̃pɛtR(ə)] *a* country *cpd*, rural.

champignon [ʃɑ̃piɲɔ̃] nm mushroom; (terme générique) fungus (pl i); ~ **de couche** ou **de Paris** cultivated mushroom; ~ **vénéneux** toadstool, poisonous mushroom.

champion, ne [ʃɑ̃pjɔ̃, -jɔn] a, nm/f champion; **championnat** nm championship.

chance [ʃɑ̃s] nf: **la** ~ luck; **une** ~ a stroke ou piece of luck ou good fortune; (occasion) a lucky break; ~**s** nfpl (probabilités) chances; **avoir de la** ~ to be lucky; **il a des** ~**s de gagner** he has a chance of winning.

chanceler [ʃɑ̃sle] vi to totter.

chancelier [ʃɑ̃səlje] nm (allemand) chancellor; (d'ambassade) secretary.

chanceux, euse [ʃɑ̃sø, -øz] a lucky, fortunate.

chancre [ʃɑ̃kR(ə)] nm canker.

chandail [ʃɑ̃daj] nm (thick) jumper ou sweater.

Chandeleur [ʃɑ̃dlœR] nf: **la** ~ Candlemas.

chandelier [ʃɑ̃dəlje] nm candlestick; (à plusieurs branches) candelabra, candlestick.

chandelle [ʃɑ̃dɛl] nf (tallow) candle; **dîner aux** ~**s** candlelight dinner.

change [ʃɑ̃ʒ] nm (COMM) exchange; **opérations de** ~ (foreign) exchange transactions; **contrôle des** ~**s** exchange control.

changeant, e [ʃɑ̃ʒɑ̃, -ɑ̃t] a changeable, fickle.

changement [ʃɑ̃ʒmɑ̃] nm change; ~ **de vitesses** gears; gear change.

changer [ʃɑ̃ʒe] vt (modifier) to change, alter; (remplacer, COMM, rhabiller) to change // vi to change, alter; **se** ~ to change (o.s.); ~ **de** (remplacer: adresse, nom, voiture etc) to change one's; (échanger, alterner: côté, place, train etc) to change + npl; ~ **de couleur/direction** to change colour/direction; ~ **d'idée** to change one's mind; ~ **de place avec qn** to change places with sb; ~ **(de train** etc**)** to change (trains etc); ~ **qch en** to change sth into.

changeur [ʃɑ̃ʒœR] nm (personne) moneychanger; ~ **automatique** change machine; ~ **de disques** record changer, autochange.

chanoine [ʃanwan] nm canon.

chanson [ʃɑ̃sɔ̃] nf song.

chansonnier [ʃɑ̃sɔnje] nm cabaret artist (specializing in political satire); song book.

chant [ʃɑ̃] nm song; (art vocal) singing; (d'église) hymn; (de poème) canto; (TECH): **de** ~ on edge.

chantage [ʃɑ̃taʒ] nm blackmail; **faire du** ~ to use blackmail; **soumettre qn à un** ~ to blackmail sb.

chanter [ʃɑ̃te] vt, vi to sing; **si cela lui chante** (fam) if he feels like it ou fancies it.

chanterelle [ʃɑ̃tRɛl] nf chanterelle (edible mushroom).

chanteur, euse [ʃɑ̃tœR, -øz] nm/f singer.

chantier [ʃɑ̃tje] nm (building) site; (sur une route) roadworks pl; **mettre en** ~ to put in hand, start work on; ~ **naval** shipyard.

chantonner [ʃɑ̃tɔne] vi, vt to sing to oneself, hum.

chanvre [ʃɑ̃vR(ə)] nm hemp.

chaos [kao] nm chaos; **chaotique** a chaotic.

chaparder [ʃapaRde] vt to pinch, pilfer.

chapeau, x [ʃapo] nm hat; ~ **mou** trilby; ~**x de roues** hub caps.

chapeauter [ʃapote] vt (ADMIN) to head, oversee.

chapelet [ʃaplɛ] nm (REL) rosary; (fig): **un** ~ **de** a string of; **dire son** ~ to tell one's beads.

chapelle [ʃapɛl] nf chapel; ~ **ardente** chapel of rest.

chapelure [ʃaplyR] nf (dried) breadcrumbs pl.

chaperon [ʃapRɔ̃] nm chaperon; **chaperonner** vt to chaperon.

chapiteau, x [ʃapito] nm (ARCHIT) capital; (de cirque) marquee, big top.

chapitre [ʃapitR(ə)] nm chapter; (fig) subject, matter; **avoir voix au** ~ to have a say in the matter.

chapitrer [ʃapitRe] vt to lecture.

chaque [ʃak] dét each, every; (indéfini) every.

char [ʃaR] nm (à foin etc) cart, waggon; (de carnaval) float; ~ **d'assaut** tank.

charabia [ʃaRabja] nm (péj) gibberish, gobbledygook.

charade [ʃaRad] nf riddle; (mimée) charade.

charbon [ʃaRbɔ̃] nm coal; ~ **de bois** charcoal; **charbonnage** nm: **les charbonnages de France** the (French) Coal Board sg; **charbonnier** nm coalman.

charcuterie [ʃaRkytRi] nf (magasin) pork butcher's shop and delicatessen; (produits) cooked pork meats pl; **charcutier, ière** nm/f pork butcher.

chardon [ʃaRdɔ̃] nm thistle.

charge [ʃaRʒ(ə)] nf (fardeau) load, burden; (explosif, ÉLEC, MIL, JUR) charge; (rôle, mission) responsibility; ~**s** nfpl (du loyer) service charges; **à la** ~ **de** (dépendant de) dependent upon, supported by; (aux frais de) chargeable to, payable by; **j'accepte, à** ~ **de revanche** I accept, provided I can do the same for you (in return) one day; **prendre en** ~ to take charge of; (suj: véhicule) to take on; (dépenses) to take care of; ~ **utile** (AUTO) live load; ~**s sociales** social security contributions.

chargé [ʃaRʒe] nm: ~ **d'affaires** chargé d'affaires; ~ **de cours** ≈ senior lecturer.

chargement [ʃaRʒmɑ̃] nm (action) loading, charging; (objets) load.

charger [ʃaRʒe] vt (voiture, fusil, caméra) to load; (batterie) to charge // vi (MIL etc) to charge; **se** ~ **de** to see to, take care ou charge of; ~ **qn de qch/faire qch** to give sb the responsibility for sth/of doing sth; to put sb in charge of sth/doing sth.

chariot [ʃaRjo] nm trolley; (charrette) waggon; (de machine à écrire) carriage; ~ **élévateur** fork-lift truck.

charitable [ʃaRitabl(ə)] a charitable; kind.

charité [ʃaRite] nf charity; **faire la** ~ **to**

give to charity; to do charitable works; faire la ~ à to give (something) to.

charlatan [ʃaʀlatɑ̃] nm charlatan.

charmant, e [ʃaʀmɑ̃, -ɑ̃t] a charming.

charme [ʃaʀm(ə)] nm charm; **charmer** vt to charm; **je suis charmé de l'm delighted to**; **charmeur, euse** nm/f charmer; **charmeur de serpents** snake charmer.

charnel, le [ʃaʀnɛl] a carnal.

charnier [ʃaʀnje] nm mass grave.

charnière [ʃaʀnjɛʀ] nf hinge; (fig) turning-point.

charnu, e [ʃaʀny] a fleshy.

charogne [ʃaʀɔɲ] nf carrion q; (fam!) bastard (!).

charpente [ʃaʀpɑ̃t] nf frame(work); (fig) structure, framework; build, frame; **charpentier** nm carpenter.

charpie [ʃaʀpi] nf: en ~ (fig) in shreds ou ribbons.

charretier [ʃaʀtje] nm carter.

charrette [ʃaʀɛt] nf cart.

charrier [ʃaʀje] vt to carry (along); to cart, carry.

charrue [ʃaʀy] nf plough.

charte [ʃaʀt(ə)] nf charter.

chas [ʃa] nm eye (of needle).

chasse [ʃas] nf hunting; (au fusil) shooting; (poursuite) chase; (aussi: ~ d'eau) flush; la ~ est ouverte the hunting season is open; ~ **gardée** private hunting grounds pl; **prendre en** ~, **donner la** ~ à to give chase to; **tirer la** ~ (d'eau) to flush the toilet, pull the chain; ~ **à courre** hunting; ~ **à l'homme** manhunt; ~ **sous-marine** underwater fishing.

châsse [ʃas] nf reliquary, shrine.

chassé-croisé [ʃasekʀwaze] nm (DANSE) chassé-croisé; (fig) mix-up where people miss each other in turn.

chasse-neige [ʃasnɛʒ] nm inv snowplough.

chasser [ʃase] vt to hunt; (expulser) to chase away ou out, drive away ou out; (dissiper) to chase ou sweep away; to dispel, drive away; **chasseur, euse** nm/f hunter // nm (avion) fighter; (domestique) page (boy), messenger (boy); **chasseurs alpins** mountain infantry sg ou pl.

chassieux, ieuse [ʃasjø, -øz] a sticky, gummy.

châssis [ʃasi] nm (AUTO) chassis; (cadre) frame; (de jardin) cold frame.

chaste [ʃast(ə)] a chaste; ~**té** nf chastity.

chasuble [ʃazybl(ə)] nf chasuble.

chat [ʃa] nm cat; ~ **sauvage** wildcat.

châtaigne [ʃatɛɲ] nf chestnut; **châtaignier** nm chestnut (tree).

châtain [ʃatɛ̃] a inv chestnut (brown); chestnut-haired.

château, x [ʃato] nm castle; ~ **d'eau** water tower; ~ **fort** stronghold, fortified castle; ~ **de sable** sandcastle.

châtier [ʃatje] vt to punish, castigate; (fig: style) to polish, refine; **châtiment** nm punishment, castigation.

chatoiement [ʃatwamɑ̃] nm shimmer(ing).

chaton [ʃatɔ̃] nm (ZOOL) kitten; (BOT) catkin; (de bague) bezel; stone.

chatouiller [ʃatuje] vt to tickle; (l'odorat, le palais) to titillate; **chatouilleux, euse** a ticklish; (fig) touchy, over-sensitive.

chatoyer [ʃatwaje] vi to shimmer.

châtrer [ʃatʀe] vt to castrate; to geld; to doctor.

chatte [ʃat] nf (she-)cat.

chaud, e [ʃo, -od] a (gén) warm; (très chaud) hot; (fig) hearty; keen; heated; **il fait** ~ it's warm; it's hot; **manger** ~ to have something hot to eat; **avoir** ~ to be warm; to be hot; **ça me tient** ~ it keeps me warm; **rester au** ~ to stay in the warmth; **chaudement** ad warmly; (fig) hotly.

chaudière [ʃodjɛʀ] nf boiler.

chaudron [ʃodʀɔ̃] nm cauldron.

chaudronnerie [ʃodʀɔnʀi] nf (usine) boilerworks; (activité) boilermaking; (boutique) coppersmith's workshop.

chauffage [ʃofaʒ] nm heating; ~ **central** central heating.

chauffant, e [ʃofɑ̃, -ɑ̃t] a: **couverture** ~**e** electric blanket; **plaque** ~**e** hotplate.

chauffard [ʃofaʀ] nm (péj) reckless driver; roadhog; hit-and-run driver.

chauffe-bain [ʃofbɛ̃] nm, **chauffe-eau** [ʃofo] nm inv water-heater.

chauffer [ʃofe] vt to heat // vi to heat up, warm up; (trop chauffer: moteur) to overheat; **se** ~ (se mettre en train) to warm up; (au soleil) to warm o.s.

chaufferie [ʃofʀi] nf boiler room.

chauffeur [ʃofœʀ] nm driver; (privé) chauffeur.

chaume [ʃom] nm (du toit) thatch; (tiges) stubble.

chaumière [ʃomjɛʀ] nf (thatched) cottage.

chaussée [ʃose] nf road(way); (digue) causeway.

chausse-pied [ʃospje] nm shoe-horn.

chausser [ʃose] vt (bottes, skis) to put on; (enfant) to put shoes on; (suj: soulier) to fit; ~ **du 38/42** to take size 38/42; ~ **grand/bien** to be big-/well-fitting; **se** ~ to put one's shoes on.

chaussette [ʃosɛt] nf sock.

chausseur [ʃosœʀ] nm (marchand) footwear specialist, shoemaker.

chausson [ʃosɔ̃] nm slipper; ~ (aux pommes) (apple) turnover.

chaussure [ʃosyʀ] nf shoe; (commerce) shoe industry ou trade; ~**s montantes** ankle boots; ~**s de ski** ski boots.

chaut [ʃo] vb: peu me ~ it matters little to me.

chauve [ʃov] a bald.

chauve-souris [ʃovsuʀi] nf bat.

chauvin, e [ʃovɛ̃, -in] a chauvinistic; jingoistic; **chauvinisme** nm chauvinism; jingoism.

chaux [ʃo] nf lime; **blanchi à la** ~ whitewashed.

chavirer [ʃaviʀe] vi to capsize, overturn.

chef [ʃɛf] nm head, leader; (de cuisine) chef; **en** ~ (MIL etc) in chief; ~ **d'accusation** charge, count (of indictment); ~ **d'atelier** (shop) foreman; ~ **de bureau** head clerk; ~ **de clinique** senior hospital lecturer; ~ **d'entreprise**

company head; ~ **d'équipe** team leader; ~ **d'état** head of state; ~ **de famille** head of the family; ~ **de file** (de parti etc) leader; ~ **de gare** station master; ~ **d'orchestre** conductor; ~ **de rayon** department(al) supervisor; ~ **de service** departmental head.

chef-d'œuvre [ʃɛdœvR(ə)] nm masterpiece.

chef-lieu [ʃɛfljø] nm county town.

cheftaine [ʃɛftɛn] nf (guide) captain.

cheik [ʃɛk] nm sheik.

chemin [ʃəmɛ̃] nm path; (itinéraire, direction, trajet) way; **en** ~ on the way; ~ **de fer** railway; **par** ~ **de fer** by rail; **les** ~**s de fer** the railways.

cheminée [ʃəmine] nf chimney; (à l'intérieur) chimney piece, fireplace; (de bateau) funnel.

cheminement [ʃəminmɑ̃] nm progress; course.

cheminer [ʃəmine] vi to walk (along).

cheminot [ʃəmino] nm railwayman.

chemise [ʃəmiz] nf shirt; (dossier) folder; ~ **de nuit** nightdress; ~**rie** nf (gentlemen's) outfitters'; **chemisette** nf short-sleeved shirt.

chemisier [ʃəmizje] nm blouse.

chenal, aux [ʃənal, -o] nm channel.

chêne [ʃɛn] nm oak (tree); (bois) oak.

chenet [ʃənɛ] nm fire-dog, andiron.

chenil [ʃənil] nm kennels pl.

chenille [ʃənij] nf (zool) caterpillar; (auto) caterpillar track; **véhicule à** ~**s** tracked vehicle, caterpillar; **chenillette** nf tracked vehicle.

cheptel [ʃɛptɛl] nm livestock.

chèque [ʃɛk] nm cheque; ~ **barré/sans provision** crossed/bad cheque; ~ **au porteur** cheque to bearer; **chéquier** nm cheque book.

cher, ère [ʃɛR] a (aimé) dear; (coûteux) expensive, dear // ad: **cela coûte** ~ it's expensive, it costs a lot of money // nf: **la bonne chère** good food; **mon** ~, **ma chère** my dear.

chercher [ʃɛRʃe] vt to look for; (gloire etc) to seek; **aller** ~ to go for, go and fetch; ~ **à faire** to try to do.

chercheur, euse [ʃɛRʃœR, -øz] nm/f researcher, research worker; ~ **de** seeker of; hunter of; ~ **d'or** gold digger.

chère [ʃɛR] a,nf voir **cher**.

chéri, e [ʃeRi] a beloved, dear; (mon) ~ darling.

chérir [ʃeRiR] vt to cherish.

cherté [ʃɛRte] nf: **la** ~ **de la vie** the high cost of living.

chérubin [ʃeRybɛ̃] nm cherub.

chétif, ive [ʃetif, -iv] a puny, stunted.

cheval, aux [ʃəval, -o] nm horse; (auto): ~ **(vapeur) (C.V.)** horsepower q; **50 chevaux (au frein)** 50 brake horsepower, 50 b.h.p.; **10 chevaux (fiscaux)** 10 horsepower (for tax purposes); **faire du** ~ to ride; **à** ~ on horseback; **à** ~ **sur** astride, straddling; (fig) overlapping; ~ **d'arçons** vaulting horse.

chevaleresque [ʃəvalRɛsk(ə)] a chivalrous.

chevalerie [ʃəvalRi] nf chivalry; knighthood.

chevalet [ʃəvalɛ] nm easel.

chevalier [ʃəvalje] nm knight; ~ **servant** escort.

chevalière [ʃəvaljɛR] nf signet ring.

chevalin, e [ʃəvalɛ̃, -in] a of horses, equine; (péj) horsy; **boucherie** ~**e** horsemeat butcher's.

cheval-vapeur [ʃəvalvapœR] nm voir **cheval**.

chevauchée [ʃəvoʃe] nf ride; cavalcade.

chevaucher [ʃəvoʃe] vi (aussi: **se** ~) to overlap (each other) // vt to be astride, straddle.

chevelu, e [ʃəvly] a with a good head of hair, hairy (péj).

chevelure [ʃəvlyR] nf hair q.

chevet [ʃəvɛ] nm: **au** ~ **de qn** at sb's bedside; **lampe de** ~ bedside lamp.

cheveu, x [ʃəvø] nm hair; // nmpl (chevelure) hair sg; **avoir les** ~**x courts** to have short hair.

cheville [ʃəvij] nf (anat) ankle; (de bois) peg; (pour enfoncer un clou) plug; ~ **ouvrière** (fig) kingpin.

chèvre [ʃɛvR(ə)] nf (she-)goat.

chevreau, x [ʃəvRo] nm kid.

chèvrefeuille [ʃɛvRəfœj] nm honeysuckle.

chevreuil [ʃəvRœj] nm roe deer inv; (culin) venison.

chevron [ʃəvRɔ̃] nm (poutre) rafter; (motif) chevron, v(-shape); **à** ~**s** chevron-patterned; herringbone.

chevronné, e [ʃəvRɔne] a seasoned, experienced.

chevrotant, e [ʃəvRɔtɑ̃, -ɑ̃t] a quavering.

chevrotine [ʃəvRɔtin] nf buckshot q.

chewing-gum [ʃwiŋgɔm] nm chewing gum.

chez [ʃe] prép (à la demeure de): ~ **qn** at (ou to) sb's house ou place; (parmi) among; ~ **moi** at home; (avec direction) home; ~ **le boulanger** (à la boulangerie) at the baker's; ~ **ce musicien** (dans ses œuvres) in this musician; ~**-soi** nm inv home.

chic [ʃik] a inv chic, smart; (généreux) nice, decent // nm stylishness; **avoir le** ~ **de** to have the knack of; **de** ~ ad off the cuff; ~**!** great!, terrific!

chicane [ʃikan] nf (obstacle) zigzag; (querelle) squabble.

chiche [ʃiʃ] a niggardly, mean // excl (à un défi) you're on!

chicorée [ʃikɔRe] nf (café) chicory; (salade) endive.

chicot [ʃiko] nm stump.

chien [ʃjɛ̃] nm dog; (de pistolet) hammer; **en** ~ **de fusil** curled up; ~ **de garde** guard dog.

chiendent [ʃjɛ̃dɑ̃] nm couch grass.

chien-loup [ʃjɛ̃lu] nm wolfhound.

chienne [ʃjɛn] nf dog, bitch.

chier [ʃje] vi (fam!) to crap (!).

chiffe [ʃif] nf: **il est mou comme une** ~, **c'est une** ~ **molle** he's spineless ou wet.

chiffon [ʃifɔ̃] nm (de ménage) (piece of) rag.

chiffonner [ʃifɔne] vt to crumple, crease.
chiffonnier [ʃifɔnje] nm ragman, rag-and-bone man ; (meuble) chiffonier.
chiffre [ʃifʀ(ə)] nm (représentant un nombre) figure ; numeral ; (montant, total) total, sum ; (d'un code) code, cipher ; ~s romains/arabes roman/arabic figures ou numerals ; en ~s ronds in round figures ; écrire un nombre en ~s to write a number in figures ; ~ d'affaires turnover ; **chiffrer** vt (dépense) to put a figure to, assess ; (message) to (en)code, cipher.
chignole [ʃiɲɔl] nf drill.
chignon [ʃiɲɔ̃] nm chignon, bun.
Chili [ʃili] nm: le ~ Chile ; **chilien, ne** a, nm/f Chilean.
chimère [ʃimɛʀ] nf (wild) dream, chimera ; pipe dream, idle fancy.
chimie [ʃimi] nf: la ~ chemistry ; **chimique** a chemical ; **produits chimiques** chemicals ; **chimiste** nm/f chemist.
Chine [ʃin] nf: la ~ China.
chiné, e [ʃine] a flecked.
chinois, e [ʃinwa, -waz] a Chinese ; (fig: péj) pernickety, fussy // nm/f Chinese // nm (langue): le ~ Chinese.
chiot [ʃjo] nm pup(py).
chipoter [ʃipɔte] vi to nibble ; to quibble ; to haggle.
chips [ʃips] nfpl (aussi: pommes ~) crisps.
chique [ʃik] nf quid, chew.
chiquenaude [ʃiknod] nf flick, flip.
chiquer [ʃike] vi to chew tobacco.
chiromancien, ne [kiʀɔmɑ̃sjɛ̃, -ɛn] nm/f palmist.
chirurgical, e, aux [ʃiʀyʀʒikal, -o] a surgical.
chirurgie [ʃiʀyʀʒi] nf surgery ; ~ esthétique plastic surgery ; **chirurgien, ne** nm/f surgeon.
chiure [ʃjyʀ] nf: ~s de mouche fly specks.
chlore [klɔʀ] nm chlorine.
chloroforme [klɔʀɔfɔʀm(ə)] nm chloroform.
chlorophylle [klɔʀɔfil] nf chlorophyll.
choc [ʃɔk] nm impact ; shock ; crash ; (moral) shock ; (affrontement) clash ; ~ opératoire/nerveux post-operative/(nervous) shock.
chocolat [ʃɔkɔla] nm chocolate ; (boisson) (hot) chocolate ; ~ à croquer plain chocolate ; ~ au lait milk chocolate.
chœur [kœʀ] nm (chorale) choir ; (OPÉRA, THÉÂTRE) chorus ; (ARCHIT) choir, chancel ; en ~ in chorus.
choir [ʃwaʀ] vi to fall.
choisi, e [ʃwazi] a (de premier choix) carefully chosen ; select ; **textes** ~s selected writings.
choisir [ʃwaziʀ] vt to choose, select.
choix [ʃwa] nm choice ; selection ; **avoir le** ~ to have the choice ; **premier** ~ (COMM) class ou grade one ; **de** ~ choice, selected ; **au** ~ as you wish ou prefer.
choléra [kɔleʀa] nm cholera.
chômage [ʃomaʒ] nm unemployment ; **mettre au** ~ to make redundant, put out of work ; **être au** ~ to be unemployed ou

out of work ; ~ **partiel** short-time working ; ~ **technique** lay-offs pl ; **chômer** vi to be unemployed, be idle ; **jour chômé** public holiday ; **chômeur, euse** nm/f unemployed person, person out of work.
chope [ʃɔp] nf tankard.
choquer [ʃɔke] vt (offenser) to shock ; (commotionner) to shake (up).
choral, e [kɔʀal] a choral // nf choral society, choir.
chorégraphe [kɔʀegʀaf] nm/f choreographer.
chorégraphie [kɔʀegʀafi] nf choreography.
choriste [kɔʀist(ə)] nm/f choir member ; (OPÉRA) chorus member.
chorus [kɔʀys] nm: faire ~ (avec) to voice one's agreement (with).
chose [ʃoz] nf thing ; **c'est peu de** ~ it's nothing (really) ; it's not much.
chou, x [ʃu] nm cabbage // a inv cute ; **mon petit** ~ (my) sweetheart ; ~ **à la crème** cream bun (made of choux pastry).
choucas [ʃuka] nm jackdaw.
chouchou, te [ʃuʃu, -ut] nm/f (SCOL) teacher's pet.
choucroute [ʃukʀut] nf sauerkraut.
chouette [ʃwɛt] nf owl // a (fam) great, smashing.
chou-fleur [ʃuflœʀ] nm cauliflower.
chou-rave [ʃuʀav] nm kohlrabi.
choyer [ʃwaje] vt to cherish ; to pamper.
chrétien, ne [kʀetjɛ̃, -ɛn] a, nm/f Christian ; **chrétiennement** ad in a Christian way ou spirit ; **chrétienté** nf Christendom.
Christ [kʀist] nm: le ~ Christ ; **c~** (crucifix etc) figure of Christ ; **christianiser** vt to convert to Christianity ; **christianisme** nm Christianity.
chromatique [kʀɔmatik] a chromatic.
chrome [kʀom] nm chromium ; **chromé, e** a chromium-plated.
chromosome [kʀɔmozom] nm chromosome.
chronique [kʀɔnik] a chronic // nf (de journal) column, page ; (historique) chronicle ; (RADIO, TV): la ~ sportive/théâtrale the sports/theatre review ; **la** ~ **locale** local news and gossip ; **chroniqueur** nm columnist ; chronicler.
chronologie [kʀɔnɔlɔʒi] nf chronology ; **chronologique** a chronological.
chronomètre [kʀɔnɔmɛtʀ(ə)] nm stopwatch ; **chronométrer** vt to time.
chrysalide [kʀizalid] nf chrysalis.
chrysanthème [kʀizɑ̃tɛm] nm chrysanthemum.
chu, e [ʃy] pp de **choir**.
chuchoter [ʃyʃɔte] vt, vi to whisper.
chuinter [ʃɥɛ̃te] vi to hiss.
chut [ʃyt] excl sh!
chute [ʃyt] nf fall ; (de bois, papier: déchet) scrap ; **la** ~ **des cheveux** hair loss ; **faire une** ~ (de 10 m) to fall (10 m) ; ~s de pluie/neige rain/snowfalls ; ~ (d'eau) waterfall ; ~ **libre** free fall.

Chypre [ʃipʀ] *n* Cyprus; **chypriote** *a*, *nm/f* = **cypriote**.

-ci, ci- [si] *ad voir* par, **ci-contre**, **ci-joint** *etc* // *dét*: **ce garçon-ci/-là** this/that boy; **ces femmes-ci/-là** these/those women.

ci-après [siapʀɛ] *ad* hereafter.

cible [sibl(ə)] *nf* target.

ciboire [sibwaʀ] *nm* ciborium (*vessel*).

ciboule [sibul] *nf* (large) chive; **ciboulette** *nf* (smaller) chive.

cicatrice [sikatʀis] *nf* scar.

cicatriser [sikatʀize] *vt* to heal; **se ~** to heal (up), form a scar.

ci-contre [sikɔ̃tʀ(ə)] *ad* opposite.

ci-dessous [sidəsu] *ad* below.

ci-dessus [sidəsy] *ad* above.

ci-devant [sidəvɑ̃] *nm/f* aristocrat who lost his/her title in the French Revolution.

cidre [sidʀ(ə)] *nm* cider.

Cie *abr de* **compagnie**.

ciel [sjɛl] *nm* sky; (REL) heaven; **~s** *nmpl* (PEINTURE *etc*) skies; **cieux** *nmpl* sky *sg*, skies; (REL) heaven *sg*; **à ~** **ouvert** open-air; (*mine*) opencast; **~ de lit** canopy.

cierge [sjɛʀʒ(ə)] *nm* candle.

cigale [sigal] *nf* cicada.

cigare [sigaʀ] *nm* cigar.

cigarette [sigaʀɛt] *nf* cigarette.

ci-gît [siʒi] *ad* + *vb* here lies.

cigogne [sigɔɲ] *nf* stork.

ciguë [sigy] *nf* hemlock.

ci-inclus, e [siɛ̃kly, -yz] *a*, *ad* enclosed.

ci-joint, e [siʒwɛ̃, -ɛt] *a*, *ad* enclosed.

cil [sil] *nm* (eye)lash.

ciller [sije] *vi* to blink.

cimaise [simɛz] *nf* picture rail.

cime [sim] *nf* top; (*montagne*) peak.

ciment [simɑ̃] *nm* cement; **~ armé** reinforced concrete; **cimenter** *vt* to cement; **cimenterie** *nf* cement works *sg*.

cimetière [simtjɛʀ] *nm* cemetery; (*d'église*) churchyard; **~ de voitures** scrapyard.

cinéaste [sineast(ə)] *nm/f* film-maker.

ciné-club [sineklœb] *nm* film club; film society.

cinéma [sinema] *nm* cinema; **~scope** *nm* cinemascope; **~thèque** *nf* film archives *pl* *ou* library; **~tographique** a film *cpd*, cinema *cpd*.

cinéphile [sinefil] *nm/f* film *ou* cinema enthusiast.

cinétique [sinetik] *a* kinetic.

cinglé, e [sɛ̃gle] *a* (*fam*) barmy.

cingler [sɛ̃gle] *vt* to lash; (*fig*) to sting // *vi* (NAVIG): **~ vers** to make *ou* head for.

cinq [sɛ̃k] *num* five.

cinquantaine [sɛ̃kɑ̃tɛn] *nf*: **une ~ (de)** about fifty.

cinquante [sɛ̃kɑ̃t] *num* fifty; **~naire** *a*, *nm/f* fifty-year-old; **cinquantième** *num* fiftieth.

cinquième [sɛ̃kjɛm] *num* fifth.

cintre [sɛ̃tʀ(ə)] *nm* coat-hanger; (ARCHIT) arch; **~s** *nmpl* (THÉÂTRE) flies.

cintré, e [sɛ̃tʀe] *a* curved; (*chemise*) fitted, slim-fitting.

cirage [siʀaʒ] *nm* (shoe) polish.

circoncision [siʀkɔ̃sizjɔ̃] *nf* circumcision.

circonférence [siʀkɔ̃feʀɑ̃s] *nf* circumference.

circonflexe [siʀkɔ̃flɛks(ə)] *a*: **accent ~** circumflex accent.

circonscription [siʀkɔ̃skʀipsjɔ̃] *nf* district; **~ électorale** (*d'un député*) constituency.

circonscrire [siʀkɔ̃skʀiʀ] *vt* to define, delimit; (*incendie*) to contain.

circonspect, e [siʀkɔ̃spɛkt] *a* circumspect, cautious.

circonstance [siʀkɔ̃stɑ̃s] *nf* circumstance; (*occasion*) occasion; **~s atténuantes** attenuating circumstances.

circonstancié, e [siʀkɔ̃stɑ̃sje] *a* detailed.

circonstanciel, le [siʀkɔ̃stɑ̃sjɛl] *a*: **complément/proposition ~(le)** adverbial phrase/clause.

circonvenir [siʀkɔ̃vniʀ] *vt* to circumvent.

circonvolutions [siʀkɔ̃vɔlysjɔ̃] *nfpl* twists, convolutions.

circuit [siʀkɥi] *nm* (*trajet*) tour, (round) trip; (ÉLEC, TECH) circuit; **~ automobile** motor circuit; **~ de distribution** distribution network.

circulaire [siʀkylɛʀ] *a*, *nf* circular.

circulation [siʀkylɑsjɔ̃] *nf* circulation; (AUTO): **la ~** (the) traffic; **mettre en ~** to put into circulation.

circuler [siʀkyle] *vi* to drive (along); to walk along; (*train etc*) to run; (*sang, devises*) to circulate; **faire ~** (*nouvelle*) to spread (about), circulate; (*badauds*) to move on.

cire [siʀ] *nf* wax.

ciré [siʀe] *nm* oilskin.

cirer [siʀe] *vt* to wax, polish; **cireur** *nm* shoeshine-boy; **cireuse** *nf* floor polisher.

cirque [siʀk(ə)] *nm* circus; (*arène*) amphitheatre; (GÉO) cirque; (*fig*) chaos, bedlam; carry-on.

cirrhose [siʀoz] *nf*: **~ du foie** cirrhosis of the liver.

cisaille(s) [sizaj] *nf(pl)* (gardening) shears *pl*; **cisailler** *vt* to clip.

ciseau, x [sizo] *nm*: **~ (à bois)** chisel; // *nmpl* (pair of) scissors; **sauter en ~x** to do a scissors jump; **~ à froid** cold chisel.

ciseler [sizle] *vt* to chisel, carve.

citadelle [sitadɛl] *nf* citadel.

citadin, e [sitadɛ̃, -in] *nm/f* city dweller // *a* town *cpd*, city *cpd*, urban.

citation [sitɑsjɔ̃] *nf* (*d'auteur*) quotation; (JUR) summons *sg*; (MIL: *récompense*) mention.

cité [site] *nf* town; (*plus grande*) city; **~ ouvrière** (workers') housing estate; **~ universitaire** students' residences *pl*.

citer [site] *vt* (*un auteur*) to quote (from); (*nommer*) to name; (JUR) to summon.

citerne [sitɛʀn(ə)] *nf* tank.

cithare [sitaʀ] *nf* zither.

citoyen, ne [sitwajɛ̃, -ɛn] *nm/f* citizen; **citoyenneté** *nf* citizenship.

citron [sitʀɔ̃] *nm* lemon; **~ vert** lime; **citronnade** *nf* lemonade; **citronnier** *nm* lemon tree.

citrouille [sitʀuj] *nf* pumpkin.

civet [sivɛ] *nm* stew; **~ de lièvre** jugged hare.

civette [sivɛt] *nf* (*BOT*) chives *pl*; (*ZOOL*) civet (cat).

civière [sivjɛʀ] *nf* stretcher.

civil, e [sivil] *a* (*JUR, ADMIN, poli*) civil; (*non militaire*) civilian // *nm* civilian; **en ~ in** civilian clothes; **dans le ~ in** civilian life.

civilisation [sivilizasjɔ̃] *nf* civilization.

civiliser [sivilize] *vt* to civilize.

civique [sivik] *a* civic.

civisme [sivism(ə)] *nm* public-spiritedness.

claie [klɛ] *nf* grid, riddle.

clair, e [klɛʀ] *a* light; (*chambre*) light, bright; (*eau, son, fig*) clear // *ad*: **voir ~** to see clearly; **bleu ~** light blue; **tirer qch au ~** to clear sth up, clarify sth; **mettre au ~** (*notes etc*) to tidy up; **le plus ~ de son temps/argent** the better part of his time/money; **en ~** (*non codé*) in clear; **~ de lune** *nm* moonlight; **~ement** *ad* clearly.

claire-voie [klɛʀvwa]: **à ~** *ad* letting the light through; openwork *cpd*.

clairière [klɛʀjɛʀ] *nf* clearing.

clairon [klɛʀɔ̃] *nm* bugle; **claironner** *vt* (*fig*) to trumpet, shout from the rooftops.

clairsemé, e [klɛʀsəme] *a* sparse.

clairvoyant, e [klɛʀvwajɑ̃, -ɑ̃t] *a* perceptive, clear-sighted.

clameur [klamœʀ] *nf* clamour.

clandestin, e [klɑ̃dɛstɛ̃, -in] *a* clandestine; (*POL*) underground, clandestine.

clapier [klapje] *nm* (rabbit) hutch.

clapoter [klapɔte] *vi* to lap; **clapotis** *nm* lap(ping).

claquage [klakaʒ] *nm* pulled *ou* strained muscle.

claque [klak] *nf* (*gifle*) slap.

claquer [klake] *vi* (*drapeau*) to flap; (*porte*) to bang, slam; (*coup de feu*) to ring out // *vt* (*porte*) to slam, bang; (*doigts*) to snap; **se ~ un muscle** to pull *ou* strain a muscle.

claquettes [klakɛt] *nfpl* tap-dancing *sg*.

clarifier [klaʀifje] *vt* (*fig*) to clarify.

clarinette [klaʀinɛt] *nf* clarinet.

clarté [klaʀte] *nf* lightness; brightness; (*d'un son, de l'eau*) clearness; (*d'une explication*) clarity.

classe [klɑs] *nf* class; (*SCOL: local*) class(room); (: *leçon*) class; (: *élèves*) class, form; **~ touriste** economy class; **faire ses ~s** (*MIL*) to do one's (recruit's) training; **faire la ~** (*SCOL*) to be a *ou* the teacher; to teach; **aller en ~** to go to school.

classement [klɑsmɑ̃] *nm* classifying; filing; grading; closing; (*rang: SCOL*) place; (: *SPORT*) placing; (*liste: SCOL*) class list (in order of merit); (: *SPORT*) placings *pl*; **premier au ~ général** (*SPORT*) first overall.

classer [klɑse] *vt* (*idées, livres*) to classify; (*papiers*) to file; (*candidat, concurrent*) to grade; (*JUR: affaire*) to close; **se ~ premier/dernier** to come first/last; (*SPORT*) to finish first/last.

classeur [klɑsœʀ] *nm* (*cahier*) file; (*meuble*) filing cabinet.

classification [klasifikasjɔ̃] *nf* classification.

classifier [klasifje] *vt* to classify.

classique [klasik] *a* classical; (*sobre: coupe etc*) classic(al); (*habituel*) standard, classic // *nm* classic; classical author.

claudication [klodikasjɔ̃] *nf* limp.

clause [kloz] *nf* clause.

claustrer [klostʀe] *vt* to confine.

claustrophobie [klostʀɔfɔbi] *nf* claustrophobia.

clavecin [klavsɛ̃] *nm* harpsichord.

clavicule [klavikyl] *nf* clavicle, collarbone.

clavier [klavje] *nm* keyboard.

clé *ou* **clef** [kle] *nf* key; (*MUS*) clef; (*de mécanicien*) spanner // *a*: **problème ~** key problem; **~ de sol/de fa** treble/bass clef; **~ anglaise** (monkey) wrench; **~ de contact** ignition key; **~ à molette** adjustable spanner; **~ de voûte** keystone.

clémence [klemɑ̃s] *nf* mildness; leniency.

clément, e [klemɑ̃, -ɑ̃t] *a* (*temps*) mild; (*indulgent*) lenient.

cleptomane [klɛptɔman] *nm/f* = **kleptomane**.

clerc [klɛʀ] *nm*: **~ de notaire** solicitor's clerk.

clergé [klɛʀʒe] *nm* clergy.

clérical, e, aux [kleʀikal, -o] *a* clerical.

cliché [kliʃe] *nm* (*PHOTO*) negative; print; (*TYPO*) (printing) plate; (*LING*) cliché.

client, e [klijɑ̃, -ɑ̃t] *nm/f* (*acheteur*) customer, client; (*d'hôtel*) guest, patron; (*du docteur*) patient; (*de l'avocat*) client; **clientèle** *nf* (*du magasin*) customers *pl*, clientèle; (*du docteur, de l'avocat*) practice; **accorder sa clientèle à** to give one's custom to.

cligner [kliɲe] *vi*: **~ des yeux** to blink (one's eyes); **~ de l'œil** to wink.

clignotant [kliɲɔtɑ̃] *nm* (*AUTO*) indicator.

clignoter [kliɲɔte] *vi* (*étoiles etc*) to twinkle; (*lumière: à intervalles réguliers*) to flash; (: *vaciller*) to flicker.

climat [klima] *nm* climate; **climatique** *a* climatic.

climatisation [klimatizasjɔ̃] *nf* air conditioning; **climatisé, e** *a* air-conditioned.

clin d'œil [klɛ̃dœj] *nm* wink; **en un ~** in a flash.

clinique [klinik] *a* clinical // *nf* nursing home, (private) clinic.

clinquant, e [klɛ̃kɑ̃, -ɑ̃t] *a* flashy.

cliqueter [klikte] *vi* to clash; to jangle, jingle; to chink.

clitoris [klitɔʀis] *nm* clitoris.

clivage [klivaʒ] *nm* cleavage.

clochard, e [klɔʃaʀ, -aʀd(ə)] *nm/f* tramp.

cloche [klɔʃ] *nf* (*d'église*) bell; (*fam*) clot; **~ à fromage** cheese-cover.

cloche-pied [klɔʃpje]: **à ~** *ad* on one leg, hopping (along).

clocher [klɔʃe] *nm* church tower; (*en pointe*) steeple // *vi* (*fam*) to be *ou* go wrong; **de ~** (*péj*) parochial.

clocheton [klɔʃtɔ̃] *nm* pinnacle.

clochette [klɔʃɛt] *nf* bell.

cloison [klwazɔ̃] *nf* partition (wall); **cloisonner** *vt* to partition (off); to divide up; (*fig*) to compartmentalize.

cloître [klwatʀ(ə)] nm cloister.
cloîtrer [klwatʀe] vt: **se ~** to shut o.s. up ou away; (REL) to enter a convent ou monastery.
clopin-clopant [klɔpɛ̃klɔpɑ̃] ad hobbling along; (fig) so-so.
cloporte [klɔpɔʀt(ə)] nm woodlouse (pl lice).
cloque [klɔk] nf blister.
clore [klɔʀ] vt to close; **clos, e** a voir **maison, huis, vase //** nm (enclosed) field.
clôture [klotyʀ] nf closure, closing; (barrière) enclosure, fence; **clôturer** vt (terrain) to enclose, close off; (festival, débats) to close.
clou [klu] nm nail; (MÉD) boil; **~s** nmpl = **passage clouté; pneus à ~s** studded tyres; **le ~ du spectacle** the highlight of the show; **~ de girofle** clove; **~er** vt to nail down ou up; (fig): **~er sur/contre** to pin to/against; **~té, e** a studded.
clown [klun] nm clown; **faire le ~** (fig) to clown (about), play the fool.
club [klœb] nm club.
C.N.R.S. sigle m = Centre national de la recherche scientifique.
coaguler [kɔagyle] vi, vt, **se ~** to coagulate.
coaliser [kɔalize]: **se ~** vi to unite, join forces.
coalition [kɔalisjɔ̃] nf coalition.
coasser [kɔase] vi to croak.
cobaye [kɔbaj] nm guinea-pig.
cocagne [kɔkaɲ] nf: **pays de ~** land of plenty; **mât de ~** greasy pole (fig).
cocaïne [kɔkain] nf cocaine.
cocarde [kɔkaʀd(ə)] nf rosette.
cocardier, ère [kɔkaʀdje, -ɛʀ] a jingoistic, chauvinistic.
cocasse [kɔkas] a comical, funny.
coccinelle [kɔksinɛl] nf ladybird.
coccyx [kɔksis] nm coccyx.
cocher [kɔʃe] nm coachman // vt to tick off; (entailler) to notch.
cochère [kɔʃɛʀ] af: **porte ~** carriage entrance.
cochon, ne [kɔʃɔ̃, -ɔn] nm pig // nm/f (péj) (filthy) pig; beast; swine // a (fam) dirty, smutty; **cochonnerie** nf (fam) filth; rubbish, trash.
cochonnet [kɔʃɔnɛ] nm (BOULES) jack.
cocktail [kɔktɛl] nm cocktail; (réception) cocktail party.
coco [kɔko] nm voir **noix**; (fam) bloke, geezer.
cocon [kɔkɔ̃] nm cocoon.
cocorico [kɔkɔʀiko] excl, nm cock-a-doodle-do.
cocotier [kɔkɔtje] nm coconut palm.
cocotte [kɔkɔt] nf (en fonte) casserole; **~ (minute)** pressure cooker; **~ en papier** paper shape; **ma ~** (fam) sweetie (pie).
cocu [kɔky] nm cuckold.
code [kɔd] nm code // a: **éclairage ~, phares ~s** dipped lights; **se mettre en ~(s)** to dip one's (head)lights; **~ civil** Common Law; **~ pénal** penal code; **~ postal** (numéro) postal code; **~ de la route** highway code; **coder** vt to (en)code; **codifier** vt to codify.

coefficient [kɔefisjɑ̃] nm coefficient.
coercition [kɔɛʀsisjɔ̃] nf coercion.
cœur [kœʀ] nm heart; (CARTES: couleur) hearts pl; (: carte) heart; **avoir bon ~** to be kind-hearted; **avoir mal au ~** to feel sick; **~ de laitue/d'artichaut** lettuce/artichoke heart; **de tout son ~** with all one's heart; **en avoir le ~ net** to be clear in one's own mind (about it); **par ~** by heart; **de bon ~** willingly; **avoir à ~ de faire** to make a point of doing; **cela lui tient à ~** that's (very) close to his heart.
coffrage [kɔfʀaʒ] nm (CONSTR: action) coffering; (: dispositif) form(work).
coffre [kɔfʀ(ə)] nm (meuble) chest; (d'auto) boot; **avoir du ~** (fam) to have a lot of puff; **~(-fort)** nm safe.
coffrer [kɔfʀe] vt (fam) to put inside, lock up.
coffret [kɔfʀɛ] nm casket; **~ à bijoux** jewel box.
cogner [kɔɲe] vi to knock.
cohabiter [kɔabite] vi to live together.
cohérent, e [kɔeʀɑ̃, -ɑ̃t] a coherent, consistent.
cohésion [kɔezjɔ̃] nf cohesion.
cohorte [kɔɔʀt(ə)] nf troop.
cohue [kɔy] nf crowd.
coi, coite [kwa, kwat] a: **rester ~** to remain silent.
coiffe [kwaf] nf headdress.
coiffé, e [kwafe] a: **bien/mal ~** with tidy/untidy hair; **~ d'un béret** wearing a beret; **~ en arrière** with one's hair brushed ou combed back.
coiffer [kwafe] vt (fig) to cover, top; **~ qn** to do sb's hair; **~ qn d'un béret** to put a beret on sb; **se ~** to do one's hair; to put on a ou one's hat.
coiffeur, euse [kwafœʀ, -øz] nm/f hairdresser // nf (table) dressing table.
coiffure [kwafyʀ] nf (cheveux) hairstyle, hairdo; (chapeau) hat, headgear q; (art): **la ~** hairdressing.
coin [kwɛ̃] nm corner; (pour graver) die; (pour coincer) wedge; (poinçon) hallmark; **l'épicerie du ~** the local grocer; **dans le ~** (les alentours) in the area, around about; locally; **au ~ du feu** by the fireside; **regard en ~** side(ways) glance.
coincer [kwɛ̃se] vt to jam; (fam) to catch (out); to nab.
coïncidence [kɔɛ̃sidɑ̃s] nf coincidence.
coïncider [kɔɛ̃side] vi: **~ (avec)** to coincide (with).
coing [kwɛ̃] nm quince.
coït [kɔit] nm coitus.
coite [kwat] af voir **coi**.
coke [kɔk] nm coke.
col [kɔl] nm (de chemise) collar; (encolure, cou) neck; (de montagne) pass; **~ du fémur** neck of the thighbone; **~ roulé** polo-neck; **~ de l'utérus** cervix.
coléoptère [kɔleɔptɛʀ] nm beetle.
colère [kɔlɛʀ] nf anger; **une ~** a fit of anger; **coléreux, euse** a, **colérique** a quick-tempered, irascible.
colifichet [kɔlifiʃɛ] nm trinket.
colimaçon [kɔlimasɔ̃] nm: **escalier en ~** spiral staircase.

colin [kɔlɛ̃] *nm* hake.

colique [kɔlik] *nf* diarrhoea ; colic (pains).

colis [kɔli] *nm* parcel.

collaborateur, trice [kɔlabɔratœr, -tris] *nm/f* (*aussi POL*) collaborator ; (*d'une revue*) contributor.

collaboration [kɔlabɔrasjɔ̃] *nf* collaboration.

collaborer [kɔlabɔre] *vi* to collaborate ; ~ à to collaborate on ; (*revue*) to contribute to.

collant, e [kɔlɑ̃, -ɑ̃t] *a* sticky ; (*robe etc*) clinging, skintight ; (*péj*) clinging // *nm* (*bas*) tights *pl* ; (*de danseur*) leotard.

collation [kɔlasjɔ̃] *nf* light meal.

colle [kɔl] *nf* glue ; (*à papiers peints*) (wallpaper) paste ; (*devinette*) teaser, poser.

collecte [kɔlɛkt(ə)] *nf* collection.

collecter [kɔlɛkte] *vt* to collect ; **collecteur** *nm* (*égout*) main sewer.

collectif, ive [kɔlɛktif, -iv] *a* collective ; (*visite, billet etc*) group *cpd*.

collection [kɔlɛksjɔ̃] *nf* collection ; (*EDITION*) series ; **pièce de ~** collector's item ; **faire (la) ~ de** to collect ; **collectionner** *vt* (*tableaux, timbres*) to collect ; **collectionneur, euse** *nm/f* collector.

collectivité [kɔlɛktivite] *nf* group ; **la ~** the community, the collectivity ; **les ~s locales** local communities.

collège [kɔlɛʒ] *nm* (*école*) (secondary) school ; (*assemblée*) body ; **collégial, e, aux** *a* collegiate ; **collégien, ne** *nm/f* schoolboy/girl.

collègue [kɔlɛg] *nm/f* colleague.

coller [kɔle] *vt* (*papier, timbre*) to stick (on) ; (*affiche*) to stick up ; (*enveloppe*) to stick down ; (*morceaux*) to stick *ou* glue together ; (*fam: mettre, fourrer*) to stick, shove ; (*SCOL: fam*) to keep in, give detention to // *vi* (*être collant*) to be sticky ; (*adhérer*) to stick ; ~ **qch sur** to stick (*ou* paste *ou* glue) sth on(to) ; ~ **à** to stick to ; (*fig*) to cling to.

collerette [kɔlrɛt] *nf* ruff ; (*TECH*) flange.

collet [kɔlɛ] *nm* (*piège*) snare, noose ; (*cou*): **prendre qn au ~** to grab sb by the throat ; ~ **monté** *a inv* straight-laced.

collier [kɔlje] *nm* (*bijou*) necklace ; (*de chien, TECH*) collar ; ~ (**de barbe**), **barbe en ~** narrow beard along the line of the jaw.

colline [kɔlin] *nf* hill.

collision [kɔlizjɔ̃] *nf* collision, crash ; **entrer en ~** (**avec**) to collide (with).

colloque [kɔlɔk] *nm* colloquium, symposium.

colmater [kɔlmate] *vt* (*fuite*) to seal off ; (*brèche*) to plug, fill in.

colombe [kɔlɔ̃b] *nf* dove.

colon [kɔlɔ̃] *nm* settler ; (*enfant*) boarder (*in children's holiday camp*).

côlon [kɔlɔ̃] *nm* colon.

colonel [kɔlɔnɛl] *nm* colonel ; (*armée de l'air*) group captain.

colonial, e, aux [kɔlɔnjal, -o] *a* colonial ; ~**isme** *nm* colonialism.

colonie [kɔlɔni] *nf* colony ; ~ (**de vacances**) holiday camp (*for children*).

colonisation [kɔlɔnizasjɔ̃] *nf* colonization.

coloniser [kɔlɔnize] *vt* to colonize.

colonne [kɔlɔn] *nf* column ; **se mettre en ~ par deux/quatre** to get into twos/fours ; **en ~ par deux** in double file ; ~ **de secours** rescue party ; ~ (**vertébrale**) spine, spinal column.

colophane [kɔlɔfan] *nf* rosin.

colorant [kɔlɔrɑ̃] *nm* colouring.

coloration [kɔlɔrasjɔ̃] *nf* colour(ing).

colorer [kɔlɔre] *vt* to colour.

colorier [kɔlɔrje] *vt* to colour (in) ; **album à ~** colouring book.

coloris [kɔlɔri] *nm* colour, shade.

colossal, e, aux [kɔlɔsal, -o] *a* colossal, huge.

colporter [kɔlpɔrte] *vt* to hawk, peddle ; **colporteur, euse** *nm/f* hawker, pedlar.

colza [kɔlza] *nm* rape(seed).

coma [kɔma] *nm* coma ; **être dans le ~** to be in a coma ; ~**teux, euse** *a* comatose.

combat [kɔ̃ba] *nm* fight ; fighting *q* ; ~ **de boxe** boxing match ; ~ **de rues** street fighting *q*.

combatif, ive [kɔ̃batif, -iv] *a* of a fighting spirit.

combattant [kɔ̃batɑ̃] *nm* combatant ; (*d'une rixe*) brawler ; **ancien ~** war veteran.

combattre [kɔ̃batr(ə)] *vt* to fight ; (*épidémie, ignorance*) to combat, fight against.

combien [kɔ̃bjɛ̃] *ad* (*quantité*) how much ; (*nombre*) how many ; (*exclamatif*) how ; ~ **de** how much ; how many ; ~ **de temps** how long, how much time ; ~ **coûte/pèse ceci?** how much does this cost/weigh?

combinaison [kɔ̃binɛzɔ̃] *nf* combination ; (*astuce*) device, scheme ; (*de femme*) slip ; (*d'aviateur*) flying suit ; (*d'homme-grenouille*) wetsuit ; (*bleu de travail*) boilersuit.

combine [kɔ̃bin] *nf* trick ; (*péj*) scheme, fiddle.

combiné [kɔ̃bine] *nm* (*aussi*: ~ **téléphonique**) receiver.

combiner [kɔ̃bine] *vt* to combine ; (*plan, horaire*) to work out, devise.

comble [kɔ̃bl(ə)] *a* (*salle*) packed (full) // *nm* (*du bonheur, plaisir*) height ; ~**s** *nmpl* (*CONSTR*) attic *sg*, loft *sg* ; **c'est le ~!** that beats everything!, that takes the biscuit!

combler [kɔ̃ble] *vt* (*trou*) to fill in ; (*besoin, lacune*) to fill ; (*déficit*) to make good ; (*satisfaire*) to gratify, fulfil ; ~ **qn de joie** to fill sb with joy ; ~ **qn d'honneurs** to shower sb with honours.

combustible [kɔ̃bystibl(ə)] *a* combustible // *nm* fuel.

combustion [kɔ̃bystjɔ̃] *nf* combustion.

comédie [kɔmedi] *nf* comedy ; (*fig*) playacting *q* ; ~ **musicale** musical ; **comédien, ne** *nm/f* actor/actress ; (*comique*) comedy actor/actress, comedian/comedienne ; (*fig*) sham.

comestible [kɔmɛstibl(ə)] *a* edible.

comète [kɔmɛt] *nf* comet.

comique [kɔmik] *a* (*drôle*) comical ; (*THÉÂTRE*) comic // *nm* (*artiste*) comic, comedian; le ~ de qch the funny ou comical side of sth.

comité [kɔmite] *nm* committee; ~ d'entreprise work's council.

commandant [kɔmɑ̃dɑ̃] *nm* (*gén*) commander, commandant; (*MIL: grade*) major; (*armée de l'air*) squadron leader; (*NAVIG, AVIAT*) captain.

commande [kɔmɑ̃d] *nf* (*COMM*) order; ~s *nfpl* (*AVIAT etc*) controls; **passer une** ~ (de) to put in an order (for); **sur** ~ to order; ~ **à distance** remote control.

commandement [kɔmɑ̃dmɑ̃] *nm* command; (*ordre*) command, order; (*REL*) commandment.

commander [kɔmɑ̃de] *vt* (*COMM*) to order; (*diriger, ordonner*) to command; ~ **à** (*MIL*) to command; (*contrôler, maîtriser*) to have control over; ~ **à qn de faire** to command ou order sb to do.

commanditaire [kɔmɑ̃ditɛR] *nm* sleeping partner.

commandite [kɔmɑ̃dit] *nf*: (**société en**) ~ limited partnership.

commando [kɔmɑ̃do] *nm* commando (squad).

comme [kɔm] *prép* like; (*en tant que*) as // *cj* as; (*parce que, puisque*) as, since // *ad*: ~ **il est fort/c'est bon!** how strong he is/good it is!; **faites-le** ~ **cela** *ou* **ça** do it like this *ou* this way; ~ **ci** ~ **ça** so-so, middling; **joli** ~ **tout** ever so pretty.

commémoration [kɔmemɔRasjɔ̃] *nf* commemoration.

commémorer [kɔmemɔRe] *vt* to commemorate.

commencement [kɔmɑ̃smɑ̃] *nm* beginning; start; commencement; ~s (*débuts*) beginnings.

commencer [kɔmɑ̃se] *vt* to begin, start, commence; (*être placé au début de*) to begin // *vi* to begin, start, commence; ~ **à** *ou* **de faire** to begin *ou* start doing.

commensal, e, aux [kɔmɑ̃sal, -o] *nm/f* companion at table.

comment [kɔmɑ̃] *ad* how; ~? (*que dites-vous*) (I beg your) pardon?

commentaire [kɔmɑ̃tɛR] *nm* comment; remark; ~ (**de texte**) (*SCOL*) commentary.

commentateur, trice [kɔmɑ̃tatœR, -tRis] *nm/f* commentator.

commenter [kɔmɑ̃te] *vt* (*jugement, événement*) to comment (up)on; (*RADIO, TV: match, manifestation*) to cover, give a commentary on.

commérages [kɔmeRaʒ] *nmpl* gossip *sg*.

commerçant, e [kɔmɛRsɑ̃, -ɑ̃t] *a* commercial; shopping; trading; commercially shrewd // *nm/f* shopkeeper, trader.

commerce [kɔmɛRs(ə)] *nm* (*activité*) trade, commerce; (*boutique*) business; le **petit** ~ small shopowners *pl*, small traders *pl*; **faire** ~ **de** to trade in; (*fig: péj*) to trade on; **vendu dans le** ~ sold in the shops; **vendu hors-**~ sold directly to the public; **commercial, e, aux** *a* commercial, trading; (*péj*) commercial; **commercialiser** *vt* to market.

commère [kɔmɛR] *nf* gossip.

commettre [kɔmɛtR(ə)] *vt* to commit.

commis [kɔmi] *nm* (*de magasin*) (shop) assistant; (*de banque*) clerk; ~ **voyageur** commercial traveller.

commisération [kɔmizeRasjɔ̃] *nf* commiseration.

commissaire [kɔmisɛR] *nm* (*de police*) ≈ (police) superintendent; (*de rencontre sportive etc*) steward; ~-**priseur** *nm* auctioneer.

commissariat [kɔmisaRja] *nm* police station; (*ADMIN*) commissionership.

commission [kɔmisjɔ̃] *nf* (*comité, pourcentage*) commission; (*message*) message; (*course*) errand; ~s *nfpl* (*achats*) shopping *sg*; **commissionnaire** *nm* delivery boy (*ou* man); messenger.

commissure [kɔmisyR] *nf*: les ~s des lèvres the corners of the mouth.

commode [kɔmɔd] *a* (*pratique*) convenient, handy; (*facile*) easy; (*air, personne*) easy-going; (*personne*): **pas** ~ awkward (to deal with) // *nf* chest of drawers; **commodité** *nf* convenience.

commotion [kɔmɔsjɔ̃] *nf*: ~ (**cérébrale**) concussion; **commotionné, e** *a* shocked, shaken.

commuer [kɔmɥe] *vt* to commute.

commun, e [kɔmœ̃, -yn] *a* common; (*pièce*) communal, shared; (*réunion, effort*) joint // *nf* (*ADMIN*) commune, ≈ district; (: *urbaine*) ≈ borough; ~s *nmpl* (*bâtiments*) outbuildings; **cela sort du** ~ it's out of the ordinary; le ~ **des mortels** the common run of people; **en** ~ (*faire*) jointly; **mettre en** ~ to pool, share; **communal, e, aux** *a* (*ADMIN*) of the commune, ≈ (district ou borough) council *cpd*.

communauté [kɔmynote] *nf* community; (*JUR*): **régime de la** ~ communal estate settlement.

commune [kɔmyn] *a, nf voir* **commun**.

communiant, e [kɔmynjɑ̃, -ɑ̃t] *nm/f* communicant; **premier** ~ child taking his first communion.

communicatif, ive [kɔmynikatif, -iv] *a* (*personne*) communicative; (*rire*) infectious.

communication [kɔmynikasjɔ̃] *nf* communication; ~ (**téléphonique**) (telephone) call; **vous avez la** ~ this is your call, you're through; **donnez-moi la** ~ **avec** put me through to; ~ **interurbaine** trunk call; ~ **en PCV** reverse charge call.

communier [kɔmynje] *vi* (*REL*) to receive communion; (*fig*) to be united.

communion [kɔmynjɔ̃] *nf* communion.

communiqué [kɔmynike] *nm* communiqué.

communiquer [kɔmynike] *vt* (*nouvelle, dossier*) to pass on, convey; (*maladie*) to pass on; (*peur etc*) to communicate; (*chaleur, mouvement*) to transmit // *vi* to communicate; **se** ~ **à** (*se propager*) to spread to.

communisme [kɔmynism(ə)] *nm* communism; **communiste** *a, nm/f* communist.

commutateur [kɔmytatœR] *nm* (*ÉLEC*) (change-over) switch, commutator.

compact, e [kɔ̃pakt] a dense ; compact.
compagne [kɔ̃paɲ] nf companion.
compagnie [kɔ̃paɲi] nf (firme, MIL) company ; (groupe) gathering ; (présence): **la ~ de qn** sb's company ; **tenir ~ à qn** to keep sb company ; **fausser ~ à** to give sb the slip, slip ou sneak away from sb ; **en ~ de** in the company of ; **Dupont et ~, Dupont et Cie** Dupont and Company, Dupont and Co.
compagnon [kɔ̃paɲɔ̃] nm companion ; (autrefois: ouvrier) craftsman ; journeyman.
comparable [kɔ̃paʀabl(ə)] a: **~ (à)** comparable (to).
comparaison [kɔ̃paʀɛzɔ̃] nf comparison ; (métaphore) simile.
comparaître [kɔ̃paʀɛtʀ(ə)] vi: **~ (devant)** to appear (before).
comparatif, ive [kɔ̃paʀatif, -iv] a comparative.
comparé, e [kɔ̃paʀe] a: **littérature etc ~e** comparative literature etc.
comparer [kɔ̃paʀe] vt to compare ; **~ qch/qn à ou et** (pour choisir) to compare sth/sb with ou and ; (pour établir une similitude) to compare sth/sb to.
comparse [kɔ̃paʀs(ə)] nm/f (péj) associate, stooge.
compartiment [kɔ̃paʀtimɑ̃] nm compartment ; **compartimenté, e** a partitioned ; (fig) compartmentalized.
comparution [kɔ̃paʀysjɔ̃] nf appearance.
compas [kɔ̃pa] nm (GÉOM) (pair of) compasses pl ; (NAVIG) compass.
compassé, e [kɔ̃pase] a starchy, formal.
compassion [kɔ̃pasjɔ̃] nf compassion.
compatible [kɔ̃patibl(ə)] a compatible.
compatir [kɔ̃patiʀ] vi: **~ (à)** to sympathize (with).
compatriote [kɔ̃patʀijɔt] nm/f compatriote.
compensation [kɔ̃pɑ̃sɑsjɔ̃] nf compensation ; (BANQUE) clearing.
compenser [kɔ̃pɑ̃se] vt to compensate for, make up for.
compère [kɔ̃pɛʀ] nm accomplice.
compétence [kɔ̃petɑ̃s] nf competence.
compétent, e [kɔ̃petɑ̃, -ɑ̃t] a (apte) competent, capable ; (JUR) competent.
compétition [kɔ̃petisjɔ̃] nf (gén) competition ; (SPORT: épreuve) event ; **la ~** competitive sport ; **la ~ automobile** motor racing.
compiler [kɔ̃pile] vt to compile.
complainte [kɔ̃plɛ̃t] nf lament.
complaire [kɔ̃plɛʀ]: **se ~** vi: **se ~ dans/parmi** to take pleasure in/in being among.
complaisance [kɔ̃plɛzɑ̃s] nf kindness ; (péj) indulgence ; **attestation de ~** certificate produced to oblige a patient etc ; **pavillon de ~** flag of convenience.
complaisant, e [kɔ̃plɛzɑ̃, -ɑ̃t] a (aimable) kind ; obliging ; (péj) over-obliging, indulgent.
complément [kɔ̃plemɑ̃] nm complement ; supplement ; remainder ; (LING) complement ; **~ d'information** (ADMIN) supplementary ou further information ; **~ d'agent** agent ; **~** (d'objet) **direct/indirect** direct/indirect object ; **~**

(circonstanciel) **de lieu/temps** adverbial phrase of place/time ; **~ de nom** possessive phrase ; **complémentaire** a complementary ; (additionnel) supplementary.
complet, ète [kɔ̃plɛ, -ɛt] a complete ; (plein: hôtel etc) full // nm (aussi: **~-veston**) suit ; **compléter** vt (porter à la quantité voulue) to complete ; (augmenter) to complement, supplement ; to add to ; **se compléter** vt réciproque (personnes) to complement one another // vi (collection etc) to be building up.
complexe [kɔ̃plɛks(ə)] a complex // nm (PSYCH) complex, hang-up ; (bâtiments): **~ hospitalier** hospital complex ; **complexé, e** a mixed-up, hung-up ; **complexité** nf complexity.
complication [kɔ̃plikɑsjɔ̃] nf complexity, intricacy ; (difficulté, ennui) complication.
complice [kɔ̃plis] nm accomplice ; **complicité** nf complicity.
compliment [kɔ̃plimɑ̃] nm (louange) compliment ; **~s** nmpl (félicitations) congratulations ; **complimenter qn** (sur ou de) to congratulate ou compliment sb (on).
compliqué, e [kɔ̃plike] a complicated, complex, intricate ; (personne) complicated.
compliquer [kɔ̃plike] vt to complicate ; **se ~** vi (situation) to become complicated ; **se ~ la vie** to make life difficult ou complicated for o.s.
complot [kɔ̃plo] nm plot ; **comploter** vi, vt to plot.
comportement [kɔ̃pɔʀtəmɑ̃] nm behaviour ; (TECH: d'une pièce, d'un véhicule) behaviour, performance.
comporter [kɔ̃pɔʀte] vt to be composed of, consist of, comprise ; (être équipé de) to have ; (impliquer) to entail, involve ; **se ~** vi to behave ; (TECH) to behave, perform.
composant [kɔ̃pozɑ̃] nm component, constituent.
composante [kɔ̃pozɑ̃t] nf component.
composé, e [kɔ̃poze] a (visage, air) studied ; (BIO, CHIMIE, LING) compound // nm (CHIMIE, LING) compound.
composer [kɔ̃poze] vt (musique, texte) to compose ; (mélange, équipe) to make up ; (faire partie de) to make up, form ; (TYPO) to set // vi (SCOL) to sit ou do a test ; (transiger) to come to terms ; **se ~ de** to be composed of, be made up of ; **~ un numéro** (au téléphone) to dial a number.
composite [kɔ̃pozit] a heterogeneous.
compositeur, trice [kɔ̃pozitœʀ, -tʀis] nm/f (MUS) composer ; (TYPO) compositor, typesetter.
composition [kɔ̃pozisjɔ̃] nf composition ; (SCOL) test ; (TYPO) typesetting, composition ; **de bonne ~** (accommodant) easy to deal with ; **amener qn à ~** to get sb to come to terms.
composter [kɔ̃pɔste] vt to date stamp ; to punch ; **composteur** nm date stamp ; punch ; (TYPO) composing stick.
compote [kɔ̃pɔt] nf stewed fruit q ; **~ de pommes** stewed apples ; **compotier** nm fruit dish ou bowl.
compréhensible [kɔ̃pʀeɑ̃sibl(ə)] a comprehensible ; (attitude) understandable.

compréhensif, ive [kɔ̃pʀeɑ̃sif, -iv] *a* understanding.

compréhension [kɔ̃pʀeɑ̃sjɔ̃] *nf* understanding ; comprehension.

comprendre [kɔ̃pʀɑ̃dʀ(ə)] *vt* to understand ; (*se composer de*) to comprise, consist of.

compresse [kɔ̃pʀɛs] *nf* compress.

compresseur [kɔ̃pʀɛsœʀ] *am voir* **rouleau.**

compression [kɔ̃pʀɛsjɔ̃] *nf* compression ; reduction.

comprimé, e [kɔ̃pʀime] *a*: **air ~** compressed air // *nm* tablet.

comprimer [kɔ̃pʀime] *vt* to compress ; (*fig: crédit etc*) to reduce, cut down.

compris, e [kɔ̃pʀi, -iz] *pp de* **comprendre** // *a* (*inclus*) included ; **~ entre** (*situé*) contained between ; **la maison ~e/non ~e,** y/non **~ la maison** including/excluding the house ; **service ~** service (charge) included ; **100 F tout ~** 100 F all inclusive *ou* all-in.

compromettre [kɔ̃pʀɔmɛtʀ(ə)] *vt* to compromise.

compromis [kɔ̃pʀɔmi] *nm* compromise.

compromission [kɔ̃pʀɔmisjɔ̃] *nf* compromise, deal.

comptabilité [kɔ̃tabilite] *nf* (*activité, technique*) accounting, accountancy ; (*d'une société: comptes*) accounts *pl*, books *pl*; (: *service*) accounts office *ou* department.

comptable [kɔ̃tabl(ə)] *nm/f* accountant // *a* accounts *cpd*, accounting.

comptant [kɔ̃tɑ̃] *ad*: **payer ~** to pay cash ; **acheter ~** to buy for cash.

compte [kɔ̃t] *nm* count, counting ; (*total, montant*) count, (right) number ; (*bancaire, facture*) account ; **~s** *nmpl* accounts, books ; (*fig*) explanation *sg* ; **faire le ~ de** to count up, make a count of ; **en fin de ~** (*fig*) all things considered, weighing it all up ; **à bon ~** at a favourable price ; (*fig*) lightly ; **avoir son ~** (*fig: fam*) to have had it ; **pour le ~ de** on behalf of ; **travailler à son ~** to work for oneself ; **rendre ~ (à qn) de qch** to give (sb) an account of sth ; **~ chèques postaux (C.C.P.)** ≈ (Post Office) Giro account ; **~ courant** current account ; **~ de dépôt** deposit account ; **~ à rebours** countdown.

compte-gouttes [kɔ̃tgut] *nm inv* dropper.

compter [kɔ̃te] *vt* to count ; (*facturer*) to charge for ; (*avoir à son actif, comporter*) to have ; (*prévoir*) to allow, reckon ; (*espérer*): **~ réussir/revenir** to expect to succeed/return // *vi* to count ; (*être économe*) to economize ; (*être non négligeable*) to count, matter ; (*valoir*): **pour** to count for ; (*figurer*): **~ parmi** to be *ou* rank among ; **~ sur** *vt* to count (up)on ; **~ avec qch/qn** to reckon with *ou* take account of sth/sb ; **sans ~ que** besides which ; **à ~ du 10 janvier** (*COMM*) (as) from 10th January.

compte-rendu [kɔ̃tʀɑ̃dy] *nm* account, report ; (*de film, livre*) review.

compte-tours [kɔ̃ttuʀ] *nm inv* rev(olution) counter.

compteur [kɔ̃tœʀ] *nm* meter ; **~ de vitesse** speedometer.

comptine [kɔ̃tin] *nf* nursery rhyme.

comptoir [kɔ̃twaʀ] *nm* (*de magasin*) counter ; (*de café*) counter, bar ; (*colonial*) trading post.

compulser [kɔ̃pylse] *vt* to consult.

comte, comtesse [kɔ̃t, kɔ̃tɛs] *nm/f* count/countess.

con, ne [kɔ̃, kɔn] *a* (*fam!*) bloody stupid (!).

concave [kɔ̃kav] *a* concave.

concéder [kɔ̃sede] *vt* to grant ; (*défaite, point*) to concede ; **~ que** to concede that.

concentration [kɔ̃sɑ̃tʀasjɔ̃] *nf* concentration.

concentrationnaire [kɔ̃sɑ̃tʀasjɔnɛʀ] *a* of *ou* in concentration camps.

concentré [kɔ̃sɑ̃tʀe] *nm* concentrate.

concentrer [kɔ̃sɑ̃tʀe] *vt* to concentrate ; **se ~** to concentrate.

concentrique [kɔ̃sɑ̃tʀik] *a* concentric.

concept [kɔ̃sɛpt] *nm* concept.

conception [kɔ̃sɛpsjɔ̃] *nf* conception.

concerner [kɔ̃sɛʀne] *vt* to concern ; **en ce qui me concerne** as far as I am concerned ; **en ce qui concerne ceci** as far as this is concerned, with regard to this.

concert [kɔ̃sɛʀ] *nm* concert ; **de ~** ad in unison ; together.

concerter [kɔ̃sɛʀte] *vt* to devise ; **se ~** (*collaborateurs etc*) to put one's heads together, consult (each other).

concertiste [kɔ̃sɛʀtist(ə)] *nm/f* concert artist.

concerto [kɔ̃sɛʀto] *nm* concerto.

concession [kɔ̃sesjɔ̃] *nf* concession.

concessionnaire [kɔ̃sesjɔnɛʀ] *nm/f* agent, dealer.

concevoir [kɔ̃svwaʀ] *vt* (*idée, projet*) to conceive (of) ; (*méthode, plan d'appartement, décoration etc*) to plan, devise ; (*enfant*) to conceive ; **appartement bien/mal conçu** well-/badly-designed *ou* -planned flat.

concierge [kɔ̃sjɛʀʒ(ə)] *nm/f* caretaker.

concile [kɔ̃sil] *nm* council, synod.

conciliabules [kɔ̃siljabyl] *nmpl* (private) discussions, confabulations.

conciliation [kɔ̃siljasjɔ̃] *nf* conciliation.

concilier [kɔ̃silje] *vt* to reconcile ; **se ~ qn/l'appui de qn** to win sb over/sb's support.

concis, e [kɔ̃si, -iz] *a* concise ; **concision** *nf* concision, conciseness.

concitoyen, ne [kɔ̃sitwajɛ̃, -jɛn] *nm/f* fellow citizen.

conclave [kɔ̃klav] *nm* conclave.

concluant, e [kɔ̃klyɑ̃, -ɑ̃t] *a* conclusive.

conclure [kɔ̃klyʀ] *vt* to conclude ; **~ à l'acquittement** to decide in favour of an acquittal ; **~ au suicide** to come to the conclusion (*ou* (*JUR*) to pronounce) that it is a case of suicide.

conclusion [kɔ̃klyzjɔ̃] *nf* conclusion ; **~s** *nfpl* (*JUR*) submissions ; findings.

conçois *etc vb voir* **concevoir.**

concombre [kɔ̃kɔ̃bʀ(ə)] *nm* cucumber.

concordance [kɔ̃kɔʀdɑ̃s] *nf* concordance ; **la ~ des temps** (*LING*) the sequence of tenses.

concorde [kɔ̃kɔʀd(ə)] *nf* concord.

concorder [kɔ̃kɔʀde] *vi* to tally, agree.
concourir [kɔ̃kuʀiʀ] *vi* (*SPORT*) to compete; ~ à *vt* (*effet etc*) to work towards.
concours [kɔ̃kuʀ] *nm* competition; (*SCOL*) competitive examination; (*assistance*) aid, help; **recrutement par voie de** ~ recruitment by (competitive) examination; ~ **de circonstances** combination of circumstances; ~ **hippique** horse show.
concret, ète [kɔ̃kʀɛ, -ɛt] *a* concrete.
concrétiser [kɔ̃kʀetize] *vt* (*plan, projet*) to put in concrete form; **se** ~ *vi* to materialize.
conçu, e [kɔ̃sy] *pp de* **concevoir.**
concubinage [kɔ̃kybinaʒ] *nm* (*JUR*) cohabitation.
concupiscence [kɔ̃kypisɑ̃s] *nf* concupiscence.
concurremment [kɔ̃kyʀamɑ̃] *ad* concurrently; jointly.
concurrence [kɔ̃kyʀɑ̃s] *nf* competition; **jusqu'à** ~ **de** up to; ~ **déloyale** unfair competition.
concurrent, e [kɔ̃kyʀɑ̃, -ɑ̃t] *a* competing // *nm/f* (*SPORT, ÉCON etc*) competitor; (*SCOL*) candidate.
condamnation [kɔ̃danasjɔ̃] *nf* condemnation; sentencing; sentence; conviction; ~ **à mort** death sentence.
condamner [kɔ̃dane] *vt* (*blâmer*) to condemn; (*JUR*) to sentence; (*porte, ouverture*) to fill in, block up; (*obliger*): ~ **qn à qch/faire** to condemn sb to sth/to do; ~ **qn à 2 ans de prison** to sentence sb to 2 years' imprisonment; ~ **qn à une amende** to impose a fine on sb, request sb to pay a fine.
condensateur [kɔ̃dɑ̃satœʀ] *nm* condenser.
condensation [kɔ̃dɑ̃sasjɔ̃] *nf* condensation.
condensé [kɔ̃dɑ̃se] *nm* digest.
condenser [kɔ̃dɑ̃se] *vt*, **se** ~ *vi* to condense.
condescendre [kɔ̃desɑ̃dʀ(ə)] *vi*: ~ **à** to condescend to.
condiment [kɔ̃dimɑ̃] *nm* condiment.
condisciple [kɔ̃disipl(ə)] *nm/f* school fellow, fellow student.
condition [kɔ̃disjɔ̃] *nf* condition; ~**s** *nfpl* (*tarif, prix*) terms; (*circonstances*) conditions; **sans** ~ *a* unconditional // *ad* unconditionally; **sous** ~ **que** on condition that; **à** ~ **de/que** provided that; **conditionnel, le** *a* conditional // *nm* conditional (tense); **conditionner** *vt* (*déterminer*) to determine; (*COMM: produit*) to package; (*fig: personne*) to condition; **air conditionné** air conditioning; **réflexe conditionné** conditioned reflex.
condoléances [kɔ̃dɔleɑ̃s] *nfpl* condolences.
conducteur, trice [kɔ̃dyktœʀ, -tʀis] *a* (*ELEC*) conducting // *nm/f* driver // *nm* (*ELEC*) conductor.
conduire [kɔ̃dɥiʀ] *vt* (*véhicule, passager*) to drive; (*délégation, troupeau*) to lead; **se** ~ *vi* to behave; ~ **vers/à** to lead towards/to; ~ **qn quelque part** to take sb somewhere; to drive sb somewhere.

conduit [kɔ̃dɥi] *nm* (*TECH*) conduit, pipe; (*ANAT*) duct, canal.
conduite [kɔ̃dɥit] *nf* (*en auto*) driving; (*comportement*) behaviour; (*d'eau, de gaz*) pipe; **sous la** ~ **de** led by; ~ **forcée** pressure pipe; ~ **à gauche** left-hand drive; ~ **intérieure** saloon (car).
cône [kon] *nm* cone.
confection [kɔ̃fɛksjɔ̃] *nf* (*fabrication*) making; (*COUTURE*): **la** ~ the clothing industry, the rag trade; **vêtement de** ~ ready-to-wear *ou* off-the-peg garment.
confectionner [kɔ̃fɛksjɔne] *vt* to make.
confédération [kɔ̃fedeʀasjɔ̃] *nf* confederation.
conférence [kɔ̃feʀɑ̃s] *nf* (*exposé*) lecture; (*pourparlers*) conference; ~ **de presse** press conference; **conférencier, ère** *nm/f* lecturer.
conférer [kɔ̃feʀe] *vt*: ~ **à qn** (*titre, grade*) to confer on sb; ~ **à qch/qn** (*aspect etc*) to endow sth/sb with, give (to) sth/sb.
confesser [kɔ̃fese] *vt* to confess; **se** ~ (*REL*) to go to confession; **confesseur** *nm* confessor.
confession [kɔ̃fɛsjɔ̃] *nf* confession; (*culte: catholique etc*) denomination; **confessionnal, aux** *nm* confessional; **confessionnel, le** *a* denominational.
confetti [kɔ̃feti] *nm* confetti *q.*
confiance [kɔ̃fjɑ̃s] *nf* confidence, trust; faith; **avoir** ~ **en** to have confidence *ou* faith in, trust; **mettre qn en** ~ to win sb's trust; ~ **en soi** self-confidence.
confiant, e [kɔ̃fjɑ̃, -ɑ̃t] *a* confident; trusting.
confidence [kɔ̃fidɑ̃s] *nf* confidence.
confident, e [kɔ̃fidɑ̃, -ɑ̃t] *nm/f* confidant/confidante.
confidentiel, le [kɔ̃fidɑ̃sjɛl] *a* confidential.
confier [kɔ̃fje] *vt*: ~ **à qn** (*objet en dépôt, travail etc*) to entrust to sb; (*secret, pensée*) to confide to sb; **se** ~ **à qn** to confide in sb.
configuration [kɔ̃figyʀasjɔ̃] *nf* configuration, layout.
confiné, e [kɔ̃fine] *a* enclosed; stale.
confiner [kɔ̃fine] *vt*: **se** ~ **dans** *ou* **à** to confine o.s. to; ~ **à** *vt* to confine to.
confins [kɔ̃fɛ̃] *nmpl*: **aux** ~ **de** on the borders of.
confirmation [kɔ̃fiʀmasjɔ̃] *nf* confirmation.
confirmer [kɔ̃fiʀme] *vt* to confirm.
confiscation [kɔ̃fiskasjɔ̃] *nf* confiscation.
confiserie [kɔ̃fizʀi] *nf* (*magasin*) confectioner's *ou* sweet shop; ~**s** *nfpl* (*bonbons*) confectionery *sg*, sweets; **confiseur, euse** *nm/f* confectioner.
confisquer [kɔ̃fiske] *vt* to confiscate.
confit, e [kɔ̃fi, -it] *a*: **fruits** ~**s** crystallized fruits // *nm*: ~ **d'oie** conserve of goose.
confiture [kɔ̃fityʀ] *nf* jam; ~ **d'oranges** (orange) marmalade.
conflit [kɔ̃fli] *nm* conflict.
confluent [kɔ̃flyɑ̃] *nm* confluence.
confondre [kɔ̃fɔ̃dʀ(ə)] *vt* (*jumeaux, faits*) to confuse, mix up; (*témoin, menteur*) to confound; **se** ~ *vi* to merge; **se** ~ **en**

excuses to offer profuse apologies, apologize profusely.

confondu, e [kɔ̃fɔ̃dy] a (stupéfait) speechless, overcome.

conformation [kɔ̃fɔʀmɑsjɔ̃] nf conformation.

conforme [kɔ̃fɔʀm(ə)] a: ~ à in accordance with ; in keeping with ; true to.

conformé, e [kɔ̃fɔʀme] a: bien ~ well-formed.

conformer [kɔ̃fɔʀme] vt: ~ qch à to model sth on ; se ~ à to conform to ; conformisme nm conformity ; conformiste a, nm/f conformist.

conformité [kɔ̃fɔʀmite] nf conformity ; agreement ; en ~ avec in accordance with ; in keeping with.

confort [kɔ̃fɔʀ] nm comfort ; tout ~ (COMM) with all mod cons ; confortable a comfortable.

confrère [kɔ̃fʀɛʀ] nm colleague ; fellow member ; confrérie nf brotherhood.

confrontation [kɔ̃fʀɔ̃tɑsjɔ̃] nf confrontation.

confronté, e [kɔ̃fʀɔ̃te] a: ~ à confronted by, facing.

confronter [kɔ̃fʀɔ̃te] vt to confront ; (textes) to compare, collate.

confus, e [kɔ̃fy, -yz] a (vague) confused ; (embarrassé) embarrassed.

confusion [kɔ̃fyzjɔ̃] nf (voir confus) confusion ; embarrassment ; (voir confondre) confusion ; mixing up ; (erreur) confusion.

congé [kɔ̃ʒe] nm (vacances) holiday ; (arrêt de travail) time off q ; leave q ; (MIL) leave q ; (avis de départ) notice ; en ~ on holiday ; off (work) ; en ~ semaine/jour de ~ week/day off ; prendre ~ de qn to take one's leave of sb ; donner son ~ à to hand ou give in one's notice to ; ~ de maladie sick leave ; ~s payés paid holiday.

congédier [kɔ̃ʒedje] vt to dismiss.

congélateur [kɔ̃ʒelatœʀ] nm freezer, deep freeze.

congeler [kɔ̃ʒle] vt to freeze.

congénère [kɔ̃ʒenɛʀ] nm/f fellow (bear ou lion etc), fellow creature.

congénital, e, aux [kɔ̃ʒenital, -o] a congenital.

congère [kɔ̃ʒɛʀ] nf snowdrift.

congestion [kɔ̃ʒɛstjɔ̃] nf congestion ; ~ cérébrale stroke ; ~ pulmonaire congestion of the lungs.

congestionner [kɔ̃ʒɛstjɔne] vt to congest ; (MED) to flush.

congratuler [kɔ̃gʀatyle] vt to congratulate.

congre [kɔ̃gʀ(ə)] nm conger (eel).

congrégation [kɔ̃gʀegɑsjɔ̃] nf (REL) congregation ; (gén) assembly ; gathering.

congrès [kɔ̃gʀɛ] nm congress.

congru, e [kɔ̃gʀy] a: la portion ~e the smallest ou meanest share.

conifère [kɔnifɛʀ] nm conifer.

conique [kɔnik] a conical.

conjecture [kɔ̃ʒɛktyʀ] nf conjecture, speculation q.

conjecturer [kɔ̃ʒɛktyʀe] vt, vi to conjecture.

conjoint, e [kɔ̃ʒwɛ̃, -wɛ̃t] a joint // nm/f spouse.

conjonctif, ive [kɔ̃ʒɔ̃ktif, -iv] a: tissu ~ connective tissue.

conjonction [kɔ̃ʒɔ̃ksjɔ̃] nf (LING) conjunction.

conjonctivite [kɔ̃ʒɔ̃ktivit] nf conjunctivitis.

conjoncture [kɔ̃ʒɔ̃ktyʀ] nf circumstances pl ; la ~ (économique) the economic climate ou circumstances.

conjugaison [kɔ̃ʒygɛzɔ̃] nf (LING) conjugation.

conjugal, e, aux [kɔ̃ʒygal, -o] a conjugal ; married.

conjuguer [kɔ̃ʒyge] vt (LING) to conjugate ; (efforts etc) to combine.

conjuration [kɔ̃ʒyʀɑsjɔ̃] nf conspiracy.

conjuré, e [kɔ̃ʒyʀe] nm/f conspirator.

conjurer [kɔ̃ʒyʀe] vt (sort, maladie) to avert ; ~ qn de faire qch to beseech ou entreat sb to do sth.

connaissance [kɔnɛsɑ̃s] nf (savoir) knowledge q ; (personne connue) acquaintance ; (conscience, perception) consciousness ; être sans ~ to be unconscious ; perdre ~ to lose consciousness ; à ma/sa ~ to (the best of) my/his knowledge ; avoir ~ de to be aware of ; prendre ~ de (document etc) to peruse ; en ~ de cause with full knowledge of the facts.

connaisseur, euse [kɔnɛsœʀ, -øz] nm/f connoisseur // a expert.

connaître [kɔnɛtʀ(ə)] vt to know ; (éprouver) to experience ; (avoir) to have ; to enjoy ; ~ de nom/vue to know by name/sight ; ils se sont connus à Genève they (first) met in Geneva.

connecter [kɔnɛkte] vt to connect.

connexe [kɔnɛks(ə)] a closely related.

connexion [kɔnɛksjɔ̃] nf connection.

connu, e [kɔny] a (célèbre) well-known.

conquérant, e [kɔ̃keʀɑ̃, -ɑ̃t] nm/f conqueror.

conquérir [kɔ̃keʀiʀ] vt to conquer, win ; conquête nf conquest.

consacrer [kɔ̃sakʀe] vt (REL): ~ qch (à) to consecrate sth (to) ; (fig: usage etc) to sanction, establish ; (employer): ~ qch à to devote ou dedicate sth to ; se ~ à qch/faire to dedicate ou devote o.s. to/to doing.

consanguin, e [kɔ̃sɑ̃gɛ̃, -in] a between blood relations.

conscience [kɔ̃sjɑ̃s] nf conscience ; (perception) consciousness ; avoir/prendre ~ de to be/become aware of ; perdre ~ to lose consciousness ; avoir bonne/mauvaise ~ to have a clear/guilty conscience ; ~ professionnelle professional conscience ; consciencieux, euse a conscientious ; conscient, e a conscious ; conscient de aware ou conscious of.

conscription [kɔ̃skʀipsjɔ̃] nf conscription.

conscrit [kɔ̃skʀi] nm conscript.

consécration [kɔ̃sekʀɑsjɔ̃] nf consecration.

consécutif, ive [kɔ̃sekytif, -iv] *a* consecutive ; ~ **à** following upon.

conseil [kɔ̃sɛj] *nm* (*avis*) piece of advice, advice *q* ; (*assemblée*) council ; (*expert*): ~ **en recrutement** recruitment consultant // a: **ingénieur-**~ consulting engineer, engineering consultant ; **tenir** ~ to hold a meeting ; to deliberate ; **prendre** ~ (**auprès de qn**) to take advice (from sb) ; ~ **d'administration** board (of directors) ; ~ **de discipline** disciplinary committee ; ~ **de guerre** court-martial ; **le** ~ **des ministres** ≈ the Cabinet ; ~ **municipal** town council.

conseiller [kɔ̃seje] *vt* (*personne*) to advise ; (*méthode, action*) to recommend, advise.

conseiller, ère [kɔ̃seje, kɔ̃sɛjɛʀ] *nm/f* adviser ; ~ **matrimonial** marriage guidance counsellor ; ~ **municipal** town councillor.

consentement [kɔ̃sɑ̃tmɑ̃] *nm* consent.

consentir [kɔ̃sɑ̃tiʀ] *vt*: ~ (**à qch/faire**) to agree *ou* consent (to sth/to doing) ; ~ **qch à qn** to grant sb sth.

conséquence [kɔ̃sekɑ̃s] *nf* consequence, outcome ; ~**s** *nfpl* consequences, repercussions ; **en** ~ (*donc*) consequently ; (*de façon appropriée*) accordingly ; **ne pas tirer à** ~ to be unlikely to have any repercussions.

conséquent, e [kɔ̃sekɑ̃, -ɑ̃t] *a* logical, rational ; **par** ~ consequently.

conservateur, trice [kɔ̃sɛʀvatœʀ, -tʀis] *a* conservative // *nm/f* (*POL*) conservative ; (*de musée*) curator.

conservation [kɔ̃sɛʀvasjɔ̃] *nf* preserving ; preservation ; retention ; keeping.

conservatoire [kɔ̃sɛʀvatwaʀ] *nm* academy.

conserve [kɔ̃sɛʀv(ə)] *nf* (*gén pl*) canned *ou* tinned food ; ~**s de poisson** canned *ou* tinned fish ; **en** ~ canned, tinned ; **de** ~ (*ensemble*) in convoy ; in concert.

conserver [kɔ̃sɛʀve] *vt* (*faculté*) to retain, keep ; (*amis, livres*) to keep ; (*maintenir en bon état, aussi CULIN*) to preserve ; **conserverie** *nf* canning factory.

considérable [kɔ̃sideʀabl(ə)] *a* considerable, significant, extensive.

considération [kɔ̃sideʀasjɔ̃] *nf* consideration ; (*estime*) esteem, respect ; ~**s** *nfpl* (*remarques*) reflections ; **prendre en** ~ to take into consideration *ou* account ; **en** ~ **de** given, because of.

considéré, e [kɔ̃sideʀe] *a* respected.

considérer [kɔ̃sideʀe] *vt* to consider ; (*regarder*) to consider, study ; ~ **qch comme** to regard sth as.

consigne [kɔ̃siɲ] *nf* (*COMM*) deposit ; (*de gare*) left luggage (office) ; (*punition: SCOL*) detention ; (: *MIL*) confinement to barracks ; (*ordre, instruction*) orders *pl*.

consigner [kɔ̃siɲe] *vt* (*note, pensée*) to record ; (*punir*) to confine to barracks ; to put in detention ; (*COMM*) to put a deposit on.

consistance [kɔ̃sistɑ̃s] *nf* consistency.

consistant, e [kɔ̃sistɑ̃, -ɑ̃t] *a* thick ; solid.

consister [kɔ̃siste] *vi*: ~ **en/dans/à faire** to consist of/in/in doing.

consœur [kɔ̃sœʀ] *nf* (lady) colleague ; fellow member.

consolation [kɔ̃sɔlasjɔ̃] *nf* consolation *q*, comfort *q*.

console [kɔ̃sɔl] *nf* console.

consoler [kɔ̃sɔle] *vt* to console ; **se** ~ (**de qch**) to console o.s. (for sth).

consolider [kɔ̃sɔlide] *vt* to strengthen, reinforce ; (*fig*) to consolidate.

consommateur, trice [kɔ̃sɔmatœʀ, -tʀis] *nm/f* (*ÉCON*) consumer ; (*dans un café*) customer.

consommation [kɔ̃sɔmasjɔ̃] *nf* consumption ; (*JUR*) consummation ; (*boisson*) drink ; ~ **aux 100 km** (*AUTO*) (fuel) consumption per 100 km, ≈ miles per gallon (m.p.g.).

consommé, e [kɔ̃sɔme] *a* consummate // *nm* consommé.

consommer [kɔ̃sɔme] *vt* (*suj: personne*) to eat *ou* drink, consume ; (*suj: voiture, usine, poêle*) to use (up), consume ; (*JUR*) to consummate // *vi* (*dans un café*) to (have a) drink.

consonance [kɔ̃sɔnɑ̃s] *nf* consonance ; **nom à** ~ **étrangère** foreign-sounding name.

consonne [kɔ̃sɔn] *nf* consonant.

consorts [kɔ̃sɔʀ] *nmpl*: **et** ~ (*péj*) and company, and his bunch *ou* like.

conspirateur, trice [kɔ̃spiʀatœʀ, -tʀis] *nm/f* conspirator, plotter.

conspiration [kɔ̃spiʀasjɔ̃] *nf* conspiracy.

conspirer [kɔ̃spiʀe] *vi* to conspire, plot.

conspuer [kɔ̃spɥe] *vt* to boo, shout down.

constamment [kɔ̃stamɑ̃] *ad* constantly.

constant, e [kɔ̃stɑ̃, -ɑ̃t] *a* constant ; (*personne*) steadfast.

constat [kɔ̃sta] *nm* (*d'huissier*) certified report (*by bailiff*) ; (*de police*) report.

constatation [kɔ̃statasjɔ̃] *nf* noticing ; certifying ; (*remarque*) observation.

constater [kɔ̃state] *vt* (*remarquer*) to note, notice ; (*ADMIN, JUR: attester*) to certify ; (*dégâts*) to note ; ~ **que** (*dire*) to state that.

constellation [kɔ̃stelasjɔ̃] *nf* constellation.

constellé, e [kɔ̃stele] *a*: ~ **de** studded *ou* spangled with ; spotted with.

consternation [kɔ̃stɛʀnasjɔ̃] *nf* consternation, dismay.

constipation [kɔ̃stipasjɔ̃] *nf* constipation.

constipé, e [kɔ̃stipe] *a* constipated ; (*fig*) stiff.

constitué, e [kɔ̃stitɥe] *a*: ~ **de** made up *ou* composed of ; **bien** ~ of sound constitution ; well-formed.

constituer [kɔ̃stitɥe] *vt* (*comité, équipe*) to set up, form ; (*dossier, collection*) to put together, build up ; (*suj: éléments, parties: composer*) to ' make up, constitute ; (*représenter, être*) to constitute ; **se** ~ **prisonnier** to give o.s. up.

constitution [kɔ̃stitysjɔ̃] *nf* setting up ; building up ; (*composition*) composition, make-up ; (*santé, POL*) constitution ; **constitutionnel, le** *a* constitutional.

constructeur [kɔ̃stʀyktœʀ] *nm* manufacturer, builder.

construction [kɔ̃stʀyksjɔ̃] *nf* construction, building.

construire [kɔ̃stʀɥiʀ] *vt* to build, construct.

consul [kɔ̃syl] *nm* consul; **~aire** *a* consular; **~at** *nm* consulate.

consultation [kɔ̃syltɑsjɔ̃] *nf* consultation; **~s** *nfpl* (*POL*) talks; **aller à la ~** (*MÉD*) to go to the surgery; **heures de ~** (*MÉD*) surgery hours.

consulter [kɔ̃sylte] *vt* to consult // *vi* (*médecin*) to hold surgery.

consumer [kɔ̃syme] *vt* to consume; **se ~** *vi* to burn; **se ~ de chagrin/douleur** to be consumed with sorrow/grief.

contact [kɔ̃takt] *nm* contact; **au ~ de** (*air, peau*) on contact with; (*gens*) through contact with; **mettre/couper le ~** (*AUTO*) to switch on/off the ignition; **entrer en ~** (*fils, objets*) to come into contact, make contact; **se mettre en ~ avec** (*RADIO*) to make contact with; **prendre ~ avec** (*relation d'affaires, connaissance*) to get in touch *ou* contact with; **~er** *vt* to contact, get in touch with.

contagieux, euse [kɔ̃taʒjø, -øz] *a* contagious, infectious.

contagion [kɔ̃taʒjɔ̃] *nf* contagion.

container [kɔ̃tɛnɛʀ] *nm* container.

contaminer [kɔ̃tamine] *vt* to contaminate.

conte [kɔ̃t] *nm* tale; **~ de fées** fairy tale.

contempler [kɔ̃tɑ̃ple] *vt* to contemplate, gaze at.

contemporain, e [kɔ̃tɑ̃pɔʀɛ̃, -ɛn] *a, nm/f* contemporary.

contenance [kɔ̃tnɑ̃s] *nf* (*d'un récipient*) capacity; (*attitude*) bearing, attitude; **perdre ~** to lose one's composure; **se donner une ~** to give the impression of composure.

contenir [kɔ̃tniʀ] *vt* to contain; (*avoir une capacité de*) to hold.

content, e [kɔ̃tɑ̃, -ɑ̃t] *a* pleased, glad; **~ de** pleased with; **contentement** *nm* contentment, satisfaction; **contenter** *vt* to satisfy, please; (*envie*) to satisfy; **se contenter de** to content o.s. with.

contentieux [kɔ̃tɑ̃sjø] *nm* (*COMM*) litigation; litigation department; (*POL etc*) contentious issues *pl*.

contenu [kɔ̃tny] *nm* (*d'un bol*) contents *pl*; (*d'un texte*) content.

conter [kɔ̃te] *vt* to recount, relate.

contestable [kɔ̃tɛstablə] *a* questionable.

contestation [kɔ̃tɛstasjɔ̃] *nf* questioning, contesting; (*POL*): **la ~** anti-establishment activity, protest.

conteste [kɔ̃tɛstə]: **sans ~** *ad* unquestionably, indisputably.

contester [kɔ̃tɛste] *vt* to question, contest // *vi* (*POL, gén*) to protest, rebel (against established authority).

conteur, euse [kɔ̃tœʀ, -øz] *nm/f* storyteller.

contexte [kɔ̃tɛkstə] *nm* context.

contigu, ë [kɔ̃tigy] *a*: **~ (à)** adjacent (to).

continent [kɔ̃tinɑ̃] *nm* continent; **continental, e, aux** *a* continental.

contingences [kɔ̃tɛ̃ʒɑ̃s] *nfpl* contingencies.

contingent [kɔ̃tɛ̃ʒɑ̃] *nm* (*MIL*) contingent; (*COMM*) quota; **contingenter** *vt* (*COMM*) to fix a quota on.

continu, e [kɔ̃tiny] *a* continuous; (*courant*) **~** direct current, DC.

continuation [kɔ̃tinɥasjɔ̃] *nf* continuation.

continuel, le [kɔ̃tinɥɛl] *a* (*qui se répète*) constant, continual; (*continu*) continuous.

continuer [kɔ̃tinɥe] *vt* (*travail, voyage etc*) to continue (with), carry on (with), go on (with); (*prolonger: alignement, rue*) to continue // *vi* (*pluie, vie, bruit*) to continue, go on; (*voyageur*) to go on; **~ à ou de faire** to go on *ou* continue doing.

continuité [kɔ̃tinɥite] *nf* continuity; continuation.

contorsion [kɔ̃tɔʀsjɔ̃] *nf* contortion; **se contorsionner** *vi* to contort o.s., writhe about.

contour [kɔ̃tuʀ] *nm* outline, contour; **~s** *nmpl* (*d'une rivière etc*) windings.

contourner [kɔ̃tuʀne] *vt* to bypass, walk (*ou* drive) round.

contraceptif, ive [kɔ̃tʀasɛptif, -iv] *a, nm* contraceptive.

contraception [kɔ̃tʀasɛpsjɔ̃] *nf* contraception.

contracté, e [kɔ̃tʀakte] *a* (*muscle*) tense, contracted; (*personne: tendu*) tense, tensed up.

contracter [kɔ̃tʀakte] *vt* (*muscle etc*) to tense, contract; (*maladie, dette, obligation*) to contract; (*assurance*) to take out; **se ~** *vi* (*métal, muscles*) to contract; **contraction** *nf* contraction.

contractuel, le [kɔ̃tʀaktɥɛl] *a* contractual // *nm/f* (*agent*) traffic warden; (*employé*) contract employee.

contradiction [kɔ̃tʀadiksjɔ̃] *nf* contradiction; **contradictoire** *a* contradictory, conflicting; **débat contradictoire** (open) debate.

contraignant, e [kɔ̃tʀɛɲɑ̃, -ɑ̃t] *a* restricting.

contraindre [kɔ̃tʀɛ̃dʀ(ə)] *vt*: **~ qn à faire** to force *ou* compel sb to do.

contraint, e [kɔ̃tʀɛ̃, -ɛ̃t] *a* (*mine, air*) constrained, forced // *nf* constraint; **sans ~e** unrestrainedly, unconstrainedly.

contraire [kɔ̃tʀɛʀ] *a, nm* opposite; **~ à** contrary to; **au ~** *ad* on the contrary.

contrarier [kɔ̃tʀaʀje] *vt* (*personne*) to annoy, bother; (*fig*) to impede; to thwart, frustrate; **contrariété** *nf* annoyance.

contraste [kɔ̃tʀast(ə)] *nm* contrast; **contraster** *vi* to contrast.

contrat [kɔ̃tʀa] *nm* contract.

contravention [kɔ̃tʀavɑ̃sjɔ̃] *nf* (*infraction*): **~ à** contravention of; (*amende*) fine; (*P.V. pour stationnement interdit*) parking ticket; **dresser ~ à** (*automobiliste*) to book; to write out a parking ticket for.

contre [kɔ̃tʀ(ə)] *prép* against; (*en échange*) (in exchange) for // *préfixe*: **~-amiral, aux** *nm* rear admiral; **~-attaque** *nf* counter-attack; **~-attaquer** *vi* to counter-attack; **~-balancer** *vt* to counter-balance; (*fig*) to offset.

contrebande [kɔ̃tʀabɑ̃d] *nf* (*trafic*) contraband, smuggling; (*marchandise*) contraband, smuggled goods *pl*; **faire la ~ de** to smuggle; **contrebandier** *nm* smuggler.

contrebas [kɔ̃trəba]: **en ~** ad (down) below.

contrebasse [kɔ̃trəbas] nf (double) bass ; **contrebassiste** nm/f (double) bass player.

contrecarrer [kɔ̃trəkaʀe] vt to thwart.

contrecœur [kɔ̃trəkœʀ]: **à ~** ad (be)grudgingly, reluctantly.

contrecoup [kɔ̃trəku] nm repercussions pl.

contre-courant [kɔ̃trəkuʀɑ̃]: **à ~** ad against the current.

contredire [kɔ̃trədiʀ] vt (personne) to contradict ; (témoignage, assertion, faits) to refute.

contrée [kɔ̃tre] nf region ; land.

contre-écrou [kɔ̃trekʀu] nm lock nut.

contre-espionnage [kɔ̃trɛspjɔnaʒ] nm counter-espionage.

contre-expertise [kɔ̃trɛkspɛrtiz] nf second (expert) assessment.

contrefaçon [kɔ̃trəfasɔ̃] nf forgery.

contrefaire [kɔ̃trəfɛʀ] vt (document, signature) to forge, counterfeit ; (personne, démarche) to mimic ; (dénaturer: sa voix etc) to disguise.

contrefait, e [kɔ̃trəfɛ, -ɛt] a misshapen, deformed.

contreforts [kɔ̃trəfɔʀ] nmpl foothills.

contre-indication [kɔ̃trɛdikasjɔ̃] nf contra-indication.

contre-jour [kɔ̃trəʒuʀ]: **à ~** ad against the sunlight.

contremaître [kɔ̃trəmɛtʀ(ə)] nm foreman.

contre-manifestation [kɔ̃trəmanifɛstasjɔ̃] nf counter-demonstration.

contremarque [kɔ̃trəmaʀk(ə)] nf (ticket) pass-out ticket.

contre-offensive [kɔ̃trɔfɑ̃siv] nf counter-offensive.

contrepartie [kɔ̃trəparti] nf compensation ; **en ~** in compensation ; in return.

contre-performance [kɔ̃trəpɛrfɔrmɑ̃s] nf below-average performance.

contrepèterie [kɔ̃trəpetri] nf spoonerism.

contre-pied [kɔ̃trəpje] nm: **prendre le ~ de** to take the opposing view of ; to take the opposite course to ; **prendre qn à ~** (SPORT) to wrong-foot sb.

contre-plaqué [kɔ̃trəplake] nm plywood.

contre-plongée [kɔ̃trəplɔ̃ʒe] nf low-angle shot.

contrepoids [kɔ̃trəpwa] nm counterweight, counterbalance ; **faire ~** to act as a counterbalance.

contrepoint [kɔ̃trəpwɛ̃] nm counter point.

contrer [kɔ̃tre] vt to counter.

contresens [kɔ̃trəsɑ̃s] nm misinterpretation ; mistranslation ; nonsense q ; **à ~** ad the wrong way.

contresigner [kɔ̃trəsiɲe] vt to countersign.

contretemps [kɔ̃trətɑ̃] nm hitch, contretemps ; **à ~** ad (MUS) out of time ; (fig) at an inopportune moment.

contre-terrorisme [kɔ̃trətɛrɔrism(ə)] nm counter-terrorism.

contre-torpilleur [kɔ̃trətɔrpijœr] nm destroyer.

contrevenir [kɔ̃trəvniʀ]: **~ à** vt to contravene.

contribuable [kɔ̃tribɥabl(ə)] nm/f taxpayer.

contribuer [kɔ̃tribɥe]: **~ à** vt to contribute towards ; **contribution** nf contribution ; **les contributions** (bureaux) ≈ the Tax Office, the Inland Revenue ; **contributions directes/indirectes** (impôts) direct/indirect taxation ; **mettre à contribution** to call upon.

contrit, e [kɔ̃tri, -it] a contrite.

contrôle [kɔ̃trol] nm checking q, check ; supervision ; monitoring ; **perdre le ~ de son véhicule** to lose control of one's vehicle ; **~ d'identité** identity check ; **~ des naissances** birth control.

contrôler [kɔ̃trole] vt (vérifier) to check ; (surveiller) to supervise ; to monitor, control ; (maîriser, COMM: firme) to control ; **contrôleur, euse** nm/f (de train) (ticket) inspector ; (de bus) (bus) conductor/tress.

contrordre [kɔ̃trɔrdr(ə)] nm counter-order, countermand ; **sauf ~** unless otherwise directed.

controverse [kɔ̃trɔvɛrs(ə)] nf controversy ; **controversé, e** a much debated.

contumace [kɔ̃tymas]: **par ~** ad in absentia.

contusion [kɔ̃tyzjɔ̃] nf bruise, contusion.

convaincre [kɔ̃vɛkr(ə)] vt: **~ qn (de qch)** to convince sb (of sth) ; **~ qn (de faire)** to persuade sb (to do) ; **~ qn de** (JUR: délit) to convict sb of.

convalescence [kɔ̃valesɑ̃s] nf convalescence ; **maison de ~** convalescent home.

convalescent, e [kɔ̃valesɑ̃, -ɑ̃t] a, nm/f convalescent.

convenable [kɔ̃vnabl(ə)] a (décent) acceptable, proper ; (assez bon) decent, acceptable ; adequate, passable.

convenance [kɔ̃vnɑ̃s] nf: **à ma/votre ~** to my/your liking ; **~s** nfpl proprieties.

convenir [kɔ̃vniʀ] vi to be suitable ; **~ à** to suit ; **il convient de** it is advisable to ; (bienséant) it is right ou proper to ; **~ de** vt (bien-fondé de qch) to admit (to), acknowledge ; (date, somme etc) to agree upon ; **~ que** (admettre) to admit that, acknowledge the fact that ; **~ de faire qch** to agree to do sth ; **il a été convenu que** it has been agreed that ; **comme convenu** as agreed.

convention [kɔ̃vɑ̃sjɔ̃] nf convention ; **~s** nfpl (convenances) convention sg, social conventions ; **de ~** conventional ; **~ collective** (ÉCON) collective agreement ; **conventionné, e** a (ADMIN) ≈ National Health cpd ; **conventionnel, le** a conventional.

conventuel, le [kɔ̃vɑ̃tɥɛl] a monastic ; monastery cpd ; conventual, convent cpd.

convenu, e pp de **convenir**.

convergent, e [kɔ̃vɛrʒɑ̃, -ɑ̃t] a convergent.

converger [kɔ̃vɛrʒe] vi to converge.

conversation [kɔ̃vɛrsasjɔ̃] nf conversation ; **avoir de la ~** to be a good conversationalist.

converser [kɔ̃vɛʀse] *vi* to converse.

conversion [kɔ̃vɛʀsjɔ̃] *nf* conversion; (*SKI*) kick turn.

convertir [kɔ̃vɛʀtiʀ] *vt*: ~ qn (à) to convert sb (to); ~ qch en to convert sth into; se ~ (à) to be converted (to).

convexe [kɔ̃vɛks(ə)] *a* convex.

conviction [kɔ̃viksjɔ̃] *nf* conviction.

convienne *etc vb voir* **convenir.**

convier [kɔ̃vje] *vt*: ~ qn à (*dîner etc*) to (cordially) invite sb to; ~ qn à faire to urge sb to do.

convive [kɔ̃viv] *nm/f* guest (*at table*).

convocation [kɔ̃vɔkasjɔ̃] *nf* convening, convoking; invitation; summoning; (*document*) notification to attend; summons *sg.*

convoi [kɔ̃vwa] *nm* (*de voitures, prisonniers*) convoy; (*train*) train; ~ (*funèbre*) funeral procession.

convoiter [kɔ̃vwate] *vt* to covet; **convoitise** *nf* covetousness; (*sexuelle*) lust, desire.

convoler [kɔ̃vɔle] *vi*: ~ (en justes noces) to be wed.

convoquer [kɔ̃vɔke] *vt* (*assemblée*) to convene, convoke; (*subordonné, témoin*) to summon; ~ qn (à) (*réunion*) to invite sb (to attend).

convoyer [kɔ̃vwaje] *vt* to escort; **convoyeur** *nm* (*NAVIG*) escort ship; convoyeur de fonds security guard.

convulsions [kɔ̃vylsjɔ̃] *nfpl* convulsions.

coopératif, ive [kɔɔpeʀatif, -iv] *a, nf* cooperative.

coopération [kɔɔpeʀasjɔ̃] *nf* cooperation; (*ADMIN*): la C~ ≈ Voluntary Service Overseas (*sometimes done in place of Military Service*).

coopérer [kɔɔpeʀe] *vi*: ~ (à) to cooperate (in).

coordination [kɔɔʀdinasjɔ̃] *nf* coordination.

coordonné, e [kɔɔʀdɔne] *a* coordinated // *nf* (*LING*) coordinate clause; ~s *nmpl* (*vêtements*) coordinates; ~es *nfpl* (*MATH*) coordinates.

coordonner [kɔɔʀdɔne] *vt* to coordinate.

copain, copine [kɔpɛ̃, kɔpin] *nm/f* mate, pal // *a*: être ~ avec to be pally with.

copeau, x [kɔpo] *nm* shaving; (*de métal*) turning.

copie [kɔpi] *nf* copy; (*SCOL*) script, paper; exercise.

copier [kɔpje] *vt* to copy; **copieuse** *nf* photo-copier.

copieux, euse [kɔpjø, -øz] *a* copious, hearty.

copilote [kɔpilɔt] *nm* (*AVIAT*) co-pilot; (*AUTO*) co-driver, navigator.

copine [kɔpin] *nf voir* **copain.**

copiste [kɔpist(ə)] *nm/f* copyist, transcriber.

coproduction [kɔpʀɔdyksjɔ̃] *nf* coproduction, joint production.

copropriété [kɔpʀɔpʀijete] *nf* coownership, joint ownership; acheter en ~ to buy on a co-ownership basis.

copulation [kɔpylasjɔ̃] *nf* copulation.

coq [kɔk] *nm* cock, rooster.

coq-à-l'âne [kɔkalɑn] *nm inv* abrupt change of subject.

coque [kɔk] *nf* (*de noix, mollusque*) shell; (*de bateau*) hull; à la ~ (*CULIN*) boiled.

coquelicot [kɔkliko] *nm* poppy.

coqueluche [kɔklyʃ] *nf* whooping-cough.

coquet, te [kɔkɛ, -ɛt] *a* flirtatious; appearance-conscious; pretty.

coquetier [kɔktje] *nm* egg-cup.

coquillage [kɔkijaʒ] *nm* (*mollusque*) shellfish *inv*; (*coquille*) shell.

coquille [kɔkij] *nf* shell; (*TYPO*) misprint; ~ de beurre shell of butter; ~ de noix nutshell; ~ St Jacques scallop.

coquin, e [kɔkɛ̃, -in] *a* mischievous, roguish; (*polisson*) naughty // *nm/f* (*péj*) rascal.

cor [kɔʀ] *nm* (*MUS*) horn; (*MÉD*): ~ (au pied) corn; réclamer à ~ et à cri (*fig*) to clamour for; ~ anglais cor anglais; ~ de chasse hunting horn.

corail, aux [kɔʀaj, -o] *nm* coral *q.*

Coran [kɔʀɑ̃] *nm*: le ~ the Koran.

corbeau, x [kɔʀbo] *nm* crow.

corbeille [kɔʀbɛj] *nf* basket; (*à la Bourse*): la ~ the stockbrokers' central enclosure; ~ de mariage (*fig*) wedding presents *pl*; ~ à ouvrage work-basket; ~ à pain bread-basket; ~ à papier waste paper basket *ou* bin.

corbillard [kɔʀbijaʀ] *nm* hearse.

cordage [kɔʀdaʒ] *nm* rope; ~s *nmpl* (*de voilure*) rigging *sg.*

corde [kɔʀd(ə)] *nf* rope; (*de violon, raquette, d'arc*) string; (*trame*): la ~ the thread; (*ATHLÉTISME, AUTO*): la ~ the rails *pl*; semelles de ~ rope soles; ~ à linge washing *ou* clothes line; ~ lisse (climbing) rope; ~ à nœuds knotted climbing rope; ~ raide tight-rope; ~ à sauter skipping rope; ~s vocales vocal cords.

cordeau, x [kɔʀdo] *nm* string, line; tracé au ~ as straight as a die.

cordée [kɔʀde] *nf* (*d'alpinistes*) rope, roped party.

cordial, e, aux [kɔʀdjal, -jo] *a* warm, cordial; ~ité *nf* warmth, cordiality.

cordon [kɔʀdɔ̃] *nm* cord, string; ~ sanitaire/de police sanitary/police cordon; ~ bleu cordon bleu; ~ ombilical umbilical cord.

cordonnerie [kɔʀdɔnʀi] *nf* shoe repairer's *ou* mender's (shop).

cordonnier [kɔʀdɔnje] *nm* shoe repairer *ou* mender, cobbler.

coreligionnaire [kɔʀəliʒjɔnɛʀ] *nm/f* (*d'un musulman, juif etc*) fellow Mahometan/Jew *etc.*

coriace [kɔʀjas] *a* tough.

cormoran [kɔʀmɔʀɑ̃] *nm* cormorant.

cornac [kɔʀnak] *nm* elephant driver.

corne [kɔʀn(ə)] *nf* horn; (*de cerf*) antler; ~ d'abondance horn of plenty; ~ de brume (*NAVIG*) foghorn.

cornée [kɔʀne] *nf* cornea.

corneille [kɔʀnɛj] *nf* crow.

cornélien, ne [kɔʀneljɛ̃, -jɛn] *a* (*débat etc*) where love and duty conflict.

cornemuse [kɔʀnəmyz] *nf* bagpipes *pl.*

corner nm [kɔʀnɛʀ] (FOOTBALL) corner (kick) // vb [kɔʀne] vt (pages) to make dog-eared // vi (klaxonner) to blare out.
cornet [kɔʀnɛ] nm (paper) cone; (de glace) cornet, cone; ~ à piston cornet.
cornette [kɔʀnɛt] nf cornet (headgear).
corniaud [kɔʀnjo] nm (chien) mongrel; (péj) twit, clot.
corniche [kɔʀniʃ] nf cornice.
cornichon [kɔʀniʃɔ̃] nm gherkin.
cornue [kɔʀny] nf retort.
corollaire [kɔʀɔlɛʀ] nm corollary.
corolle [kɔʀɔl] nf corolla.
coron [kɔʀɔ̃] nm mining cottage; mining village.
coronaire [kɔʀɔnɛʀ] a coronary.
corporation [kɔʀpɔʀasjɔ̃] nf corporate body; (au moyen-âge) guild.
corporel, le [kɔʀpɔʀɛl] a bodily; (punition) corporal; soins ~s care sg of the body.
corps [kɔʀ] nm (gén) body; (cadavre) (dead) body; à son ~ défendant against one's will; à ~ perdu headlong; perdu ~ et biens lost with all hands; prendre ~ to take shape; faire ~ avec to be joined to; to form one body with; ~ d'armée army corps; ~ de ballet corps de ballet; le ~ consulaire (CC) the consular corps; ~ à ~ ad hand-to-hand // nm clinch; le ~ du délit (JUR) corpus delicti; le ~ diplomatique (CD) the diplomatic corps; le ~ électoral the electorate; le ~ enseignant the teaching profession; ~ étranger (MÉD) foreign body; ~ de garde guardroom.
corpulent, e [kɔʀpylɑ̃, -ɑ̃t] a stout, corpulent.
correct, e [kɔʀɛkt] a (exact) accurate, correct; (bienséant, honnête) correct; (passable) adequate; ~ement ad accurately; correctly.
correcteur, trice [kɔʀɛktœʀ, -tʀis] nm/f (SCOL) examiner, marker; (TYPO) proof-reader.
correction [kɔʀɛksjɔ̃] nf (voir corriger) correction; marking; (voir correct) correctness; (rature, surcharge) correction, emendation; (coups) thrashing; ~ (des épreuves) proofreading.
correctionnel, le [kɔʀɛksjɔnɛl] a (JUR): chambre ~le ≈ police magistrate's court.
corrélation [kɔʀelɑsjɔ̃] nf correlation.
correspondance [kɔʀɛspɔ̃dɑ̃s] nf correspondence; (de train, d'avion) connection; ce train assure la ~ avec l'avion de 10 heures this train connects with the 10 o'clock plane; cours par ~ correspondence course; vente par ~ mail-order business; **correspondancier, ère** nm/f correspondence clerk.
correspondant, e [kɔʀɛspɔ̃dɑ̃, -ɑ̃t] nm/f correspondent.
correspondre [kɔʀɛspɔ̃dʀ(ə)] vi (données, témoignages) to correspond, tally; (chambres) to communicate; ~ à to correspond to; ~ avec qn to correspond with sb.
corrida [kɔʀida] nf bullfight.
corridor [kɔʀidɔʀ] nm corridor, passage.

corrigé [kɔʀiʒe] nm (SCOL) correct version; fair copy.
corriger [kɔʀiʒe] vt (devoir) to correct, mark; (texte) to correct, emend; (erreur, défaut) to correct, put right; (punir) to thrash; ~ qn de (défaut) to cure sb of.
corroborer [kɔʀɔbɔʀe] vt to corroborate.
corroder [kɔʀɔde] vt to corrode.
corrompre [kɔʀɔ̃pʀ(ə)] vt (soudoyer) to bribe; (dépraver) to corrupt.
corrosion [kɔʀɔzjɔ̃] nf corrosion.
corruption [kɔʀypsjɔ̃] nf bribery; corruption.
corsage [kɔʀsaʒ] nm bodice; blouse.
corsaire [kɔʀsɛʀ] nm pirate, corsair; privateer.
corse [kɔʀs(ə)] a, nm/f Corsican // nf: la C~ Corsica.
corsé, e [kɔʀse] a vigorous; full-flavoured; (fig) spicy; tricky.
corselet [kɔʀsəlɛ] nm corselet.
corset [kɔʀsɛ] nm corset; bodice.
corso [kɔʀso] nm: ~ fleuri procession of floral floats.
cortège [kɔʀtɛʒ] nm procession.
corvée [kɔʀve] nf chore, drudgery q; (MIL) fatigue (duty).
cosmétique [kɔsmetik] nm hair-oil; beauty care product.
cosmique [kɔsmik] a cosmic.
cosmonaute [kɔsmɔnot] nm/f cosmonaut, astronaut.
cosmopolite [kɔsmɔpɔlit] a cosmopolitan.
cosmos [kɔsmɔs] nm outer space; cosmos.
cosse [kɔs] nf (BOT) pod, hull.
cossu, e [kɔsy] a opulent-looking, well-to-do.
costaud, e [kɔsto, -od] a strong, sturdy.
costume [kɔstym] nm (d'homme) suit; (de théâtre) costume; **costumé, e** a dressed up.
cote [kɔt] nf (en Bourse etc) quotation; quoted value; (d'un cheval): la ~ de the odds pl on; (d'un candidat etc) rating; (mesure: sur une carte) spot height; (: sur un croquis) dimension; (de classement) (classification) mark; reference number; insc. it à la ~ quoted on the Stock Exchange; ~ d'alerte danger ou flood level.
côte [kot] nf (rivage) coast(line); (pente) slope; (: sur une route) hill; (ANAT) rib; (d'un tricot, tissu) rib, ribbing q; ~ à ~ ad side by side; la C~ (d'Azur) the (French) Riviera.
côté [kote] nm (gén) side; (direction) way, direction; de tous les ~s from all directions; de quel ~ est-il parti? which way ou in which direction did he go?; de ce/de l'autre ~ this/the other way; du ~ de (provenance) from; (direction) towards; du ~ de Lyon (proximité) the Lyons way, near Lyons; de ~ ad side-ways; on one side; to one side; aside; laisser de ~ to leave on one side; mettre de ~ to put on one side, put aside; à ~ ad (right) nearby; beside; next door; (d'autre part) besides; à ~ de beside, next to; (fig) in comparison to; à ~ (de la cible) off target, wide (of the mark); être aux ~s de to be by the side of.

coteau, x [kɔto] *nm* hill.
côtelé, e [kotle] *a* ribbed ; **pantalon en velours** ~ corduroy trousers *pl*.
côtelette [kotlɛt] *nf* chop.
coter [kɔte] *vt* (*en Bourse*) to quote.
coterie [kɔtRi] *nf* set.
côtier, ière [kotje, -jɛR] *a* coastal.
cotisation [kɔtizasjɔ̃] *nf* subscription, dues *pl* ; (*pour une pension*) contributions *pl*.
cotiser [kɔtize] *vi*: ~ (**à**) to pay contributions (to) ; **se** ~ to club together.
coton [kɔtɔ̃] *nm* cotton ; ~ **hydrophile** (absorbent) cotton-wool.
côtoyer [kotwaje] *vt* to be close to ; to rub shoulders with ; to run alongside ; to be bordering *ou* verging on.
cotte [kɔt] *nf*: ~ **de mailles** coat of mail.
cou [ku] *nm* neck.
couard, e [kwaR, -aRd] *a* cowardly.
couchage [kuʃaʒ] *nm voir* **sac.**
couchant [kuʃɑ̃] *a*: **soleil** ~ setting sun.
couche [kuʃ] *nf* (*strate: gén, GÉO*) layer, stratum (*pl* a) ; (*de peinture, vernis*) coat ; (*de poussière, crème*) layer ; (*de bébé*) nappy, napkin ; (*MÉD*) confinement *sg* ; ~**s sociales** social levels *ou* strata ; ~**-culotte** *nf* disposable nappy and waterproof pants in one.
coucher [kuʃe] *nm* (*du soleil*) setting // *vt* (*personne*) to put to bed ; (: *loger*) to put up ; (*objet*) to lay on its side ; (*écrire*) to inscribe, couch // *vi* (*dormir*) to sleep, spend the night ; (*fam*): ~ **avec qn** to sleep with sb, go to bed with sb ; **se** ~ *vi* (*pour dormir*) to go to bed ; (*pour se reposer*) to lie down ; (*soleil*) to set, go down ; **à prendre avant le** ~ (*MÉD*) take at night *ou* before going to bed ; ~ **de soleil** sunset.
couchette [kuʃɛt] *nf* couchette ; (*de marin*) bunk.
coucou [kuku] *nm* cuckoo // *excl* peek-a-boo.
coude [kud] *nm* (*ANAT*) elbow ; (*de tuyau, de la route*) bend ; ~ **à** ~ *ad* shoulder to shoulder, side by side.
cou-de-pied [kudpje] *nm* instep.
coudre [kudR(ə)] *vt* (*bouton*) to sew on ; (*robe*) to sew (up) // *vi* to sew.
couenne [kwan] *nf* (*de lard*) rind.
couettes [kwɛt] *nfpl* bunches.
couffin [kufɛ̃] *nm* Moses basket ; (straw) basket.
couiner [kwine] *vi* to squeal.
coulant, e [kulɑ̃, -ɑ̃t] *a* (*indulgent*) easy-going ; (*fromage etc*) runny.
coulée [kule] *nf* (*de lave, métal en fusion*) flow ; ~ **de neige** snowslide.
couler [kule] *vi* to flow, run ; (*fuir: stylo, récipient*) to leak ; (*sombrer: bateau*) to sink // *vt* (*cloche, sculpture*) to cast ; (*bateau*) to sink ; (*fig*) to ruin, bring down ; **se** ~ **dans** (*interstice etc*) to slip into ; **il a coulé une bielle** his big-end went.
couleur [kulœR] *nf* colour ; (*CARTES*) suit.
couleuvre [kulœvR(ə)] *nf* grass snake.
coulisse [kulis] *nf* (*TECH*) runner ; ~**s** *nfpl* (*THÉÂTRE*) wings ; (*fig*): **dans les** ~**s** behind the scenes ; **porte à** ~ sliding door ; **coulisser** *vi* to slide, run.

couloir [kulwaR] *nm* corridor, passage ; (*de bus*) gangway ; (*SPORT: de piste*) lane ; (*GÉO*) gully ; ~ **de navigation** shipping lane.
coulpe [kulp(ə)] *nf*: **battre sa** ~ to repent openly.
coup [ku] *nm* (*heurt, choc*) knock ; (*affectif*) blow, shock ; (*agressif*) blow ; (*avec arme à feu*) shot ; (*de l'horloge*) chime ; stroke ; (*SPORT*) stroke ; shot ; blow ; (*ÉCHECS*) move ; ~ **de coude/genou** nudge (with the elbow)/with the knee ; **à** ~**s de hache/marteau** (hitting) with an axe/a hammer ; ~ **de tonnerre** clap of thunder ; ~ **de sonnette** ring of the bell ; ~ **de crayon/pinceau** stroke of the pencil/brush ; **donner un** ~ **de balai** to sweep up, give the floor a sweep ; **donner un** ~ **de chiffon** to go round with the duster ; **avoir le** ~ (*fig*) to have the knack ; **boire un** ~ to have a drink ; **d'un seul** ~ (*subitement*) suddenly ; (*à la fois*) at one go ; in one blow ; **du premier** ~ first time *ou* go, at the first attempt ; **du même** ~ at the same time ; **à** ~ **sûr** definitely, without fail ; **sur** ~ in quick succession ; **sur le** ~ outright ; **sous le** ~ **de** (*surprise etc*) under the influence of ; **tomber sous le** ~ **de la loi** to constitute a statutory offence ; ~ **de chance** stroke of luck ; ~ **de couteau** stab (of a knife) ; ~ **dur** hard blow ; ~ **d'envoi** kick-off ; ~ **d'essai** first attempt ; ~ **d'état** coup d'état ; ~ **de feu** shot ; ~ **de filet** (*POLICE*) haul ; ~ **franc** free kick ; ~ **de frein** (sharp) braking *q* ; ~ **de fusil** rifle shot ; ~ **de grâce** coup de grâce ; ~ **de main:** **donner un** ~ **de main à qn** to give sb a (helping) hand ; ~ **d'œil** glance ; ~ **de pied** kick ; ~ **de poing** punch ; ~ **de soleil** sunburn ; ~ **de téléphone** phone call ; ~ **de tête** (*fig*) (sudden) impulse ; ~ **de théâtre** (*fig*) dramatic turn of events ; ~ **de vent** gust of wind.
coupable [kupabl(ə)] *a* guilty ; (*pensée*) guilt. culpable // *nm/f* (*gén*) culprit ; (*JUR*) guilty party ; ~ **de** guilty of.
coupe [kup] *nf* (*verre*) goblet ; (*à fruits*) dish ; (*SPORT*) cup ; (*de cheveux, de vêtement*) cut ; (*graphique, plan*) (cross) section ; **être sous la** ~ **de** to be under the control of ; **faire des** ~**s sombres dans** to make drastic cuts in.
coupé [kupe] *nm* (*AUTO*) coupé.
coupe-circuit [kupsiRkɥi] *nm inv* cutout, circuit breaker.
coupée [kupe] *nf* (*NAVIG*) gangway.
coupe-papier [kuppapje] *nm inv* paper knife.
couper [kupe] *vt* to cut ; (*retrancher*) to cut (out), take out ; (*route, courant*) to cut off ; (*appétit*) to take away ; (*fièvre*) to take down, reduce ; (*vin, cidre*) to blend ; (: *à table*) to dilute (with water) // *vi* to cut ; (*prendre un raccourci*) to take a short-cut ; (*CARTES: diviser le paquet*) to cut ; (: *avec l'atout*) to trump ; **se** ~ (*se blesser*) to cut o.s. ; (*en témoignant etc*) to give o.s. away ; ~ **la parole à qn** to cut sb short.
couperet [kupRɛ] *nm* cleaver, chopper.
couperosé, e [kupRoze] *a* blotchy.
couple [kupl(ə)] *nm* couple ; ~ **de torsion** torque.

coupler [kuple] *vt* to couple (together).

couplet [kuplɛ] *nm* verse.

coupole [kupɔl] *nf* dome; cupola.

coupon [kupɔ̃] *nm* (*ticket*) coupon; (*de tissu*) remnant; roll; ~-réponse international international reply coupon.

coupure [kupyʀ] *nf* cut; (*billet de banque*) note; (*de journal*) cutting; ~ de courant power cut.

cour [kuʀ] *nf* (*de ferme, jardin*) (court)yard; (*d'immeuble*) back yard; (*JUR, royale*) court; faire la ~ à qn to court sb; ~ d'assises court of assizes, ≈ Crown Court; ~ de cassation Court of Cassation; ~ martiale court-martial.

courage [kuʀaʒ] *nm* courage, bravery; **courageux, euse** *a* brave, courageous.

couramment [kuʀamɑ̃] *ad* commonly; (*avec aisance: parler*) fluently.

courant, e [kuʀɑ̃, -ɑ̃t] *a* (*fréquent*) common; (*COMM, gén: normal*) standard; (*en cours*) current // *nm* current; (*fig*) movement; trend; être au ~ (de) (*fait, nouvelle*) to know (about); mettre qn au ~ (de) (*fait, nouvelle*) to tell sb (about); (*nouveau travail etc*) to teach sb the basics (of); se tenir au ~ (de) (*techniques etc*) to keep o.s. up-to-date (on); dans le ~ de (*pendant*) in the course of; le 10 ~ (*COMM*) the 10th inst; ~ d'air draught; ~ électrique (electric) current, power.

courbature [kuʀbatyʀ] *nf* ache; **courbaturé, e** *a* aching.

courbe [kuʀb(ə)] *a* curved // *nf* curve; ~ de niveau contour line.

courber [kuʀbe] *vt* to bend; ~ la tête to bow one's head; se ~ *vi* (*branche etc*) to bend, curve; (*personne*) to bend (down).

courbette [kuʀbɛt] *nf* low bow.

coureur, euse [kuʀœʀ, -øz] *nm/f* (*SPORT*) runner (*ou* driver); (*péj*) womaniser/ manhunter; ~ cycliste/automobile racing cyclist/driver.

courge [kuʀʒ(ə)] *nf* (*BOT*) gourd; (*CULIN*) marrow.

courgette [kuʀʒɛt] *nf* courgette, zucchini.

courir [kuʀiʀ] *vi* (*gén*) to run; (*se dépêcher*) to rush; (*fig: rumeurs*) to go round; (*COMM: intérêt*) to accrue // *vt* (*SPORT: épreuve*) to compete in; (*risque*) to run; (*danger*) to face; ~ les cafés/bals to do the rounds of the cafés/dances; le bruit court que the rumour is going round that; ~ après qn to run after sb, chase (after) sb.

couronne [kuʀɔn] *nf* crown; (*de fleurs*) wreath, circlet.

couronnement [kuʀɔnmɑ̃] *nm* coronation, crowning; (*fig*) crowning achievement.

couronner [kuʀɔne] *vt* to crown.

courons *etc vb voir* **courir**.

courre [kuʀ] *vb voir* **chasse**.

courrier [kuʀje] *nm* mail, post; (*lettres à écrire*) letters *pl*; (*rubrique*) column; long/moyen ~ *a* (*AVIAT*) long-/medium-haul; ~ du cœur problem page.

courroie [kuʀwa] *nf* strap; (*TECH*) belt; ~ de transmission/de ventilateur driving/fan belt.

courrons *etc vb voir* **courir**.

courroucé, e [kuʀuse] *a* wrathful.

cours [kuʀ] *nm* (*leçon*) lesson; class; (*série de leçons*) course; (*cheminement*) course; (*écoulement*) flow; (*avenue*) walk; (*COMM*) rate; price; donner libre ~ à to give free expression to; avoir ~ (*monnaie*) to be legal tender; (*fig*) to be current; (*SCOL*) to have a class ou lecture; en ~ (*année*) current; (*travaux*) in progress; en ~ de route on the way; au ~ de in the course of, during; le ~ du change the exchange rate; ~ d'eau water course, generic term for streams, rivers; ~ du soir night school.

course [kuʀs(ə)] *nf* running; (*SPORT: épreuve*) race; (*trajet: du soleil*) course; (: *d'un projectile*) flight; (: *d'une pièce mécanique*) travel; (*excursion*) outing; climb; (*d'un taxi, autocar*) journey, trip; (*petite mission*) errand; ~s *nfpl* (*achats*) shopping *sg*; (*HIPPISME*) races.

court, e [kuʀ, kuʀt(ə)] *a* short // *ad* short // *nm*: ~ (de tennis) (tennis) court; tourner ~ to come to a sudden end; à ~ de short of; prendre qn de ~ to catch sb unawares; tirer à la ~e paille to draw lots; ~-bouillon *nm* court-bouillon; ~-circuit *nm* short-circuit.

courtier, ère [kuʀtje, -jɛʀ] *nm/f* broker.

courtisan [kuʀtizɑ̃] *nm* courtier.

courtisane [kuʀtizan] *nf* courtesan.

courtiser [kuʀtize] *vt* to court, woo.

courtois, e [kuʀtwa, -waz] *a* courteous; **courtoisie** *nf* courtesy.

couru, e *pp de* **courir**.

cousais *etc vb voir* **coudre**.

cousin, e [kuzɛ̃, -in] *nm/f* cousin.

coussin [kusɛ̃] *nm* cushion.

cousu, e [kuzy] *pp de* **coudre** // *a*: ~ d'or rolling in riches.

coût [ku] *nm* cost; le ~ de la vie the cost of living.

coûtant [kutɑ̃] *am*: au prix ~ at cost price.

couteau, x [kuto] *nm* knife; ~ à cran d'arrêt flick-knife; ~ de poche pocket knife; ~-scie *nm* serrated-edged knife.

coutellerie [kutɛlʀi] *nf* cutlery shop; cutlery.

coûter [kute] *vt, vi* to cost; combien ça coûte? how much is it?, what does it cost?; coûte que coûte at all costs; **coûteux, euse** *a* costly, expensive.

coutume [kutym] *nf* custom; **coutumier, ère** *a* customary.

couture [kutyʀ] *nf* sewing; dress-making; (*points*) seam.

couturier [kutyʀje] *nm* fashion designer, couturier.

couturière [kutyʀjɛʀ] *nf* dressmaker.

couvée [kuve] *nf* brood, clutch.

couvent [kuvɑ̃] *nm* (*de sœurs*) convent; (*de frères*) monastery; (*établissement scolaire*) convent (school).

couver [kuve] *vt* to hatch; (*maladie*) to be sickening for // *vi* (*feu*) to smoulder; (*révolte*) to be brewing; ~ qn/qch des yeux to look lovingly at; to look longingly at.

couvercle [kuvɛʀkl(ə)] *nm* lid; (*de bombe aérosol etc, qui se visse*) cap, top.

couvert, e [kuvɛʀ, -ɛʀt(ə)] *pp de* **couvrir**
// a (*ciel*) overcast; (*coiffé d'un chapeau*)
wearing a hat // *nm* place setting; (*place
à table*) place; (*au restaurant*) cover
charge; ~s *nmpl* place settings; cutlery
sg; ~ **de** covered with *ou* in; **bien** ~
(*habillé*) well wrapped up; **mettre le** ~
to lay the table; **à** ~ under cover; **sous
le** ~ **de** under the shelter of; (*fig*) under
cover of.

couverture [kuvɛʀtyʀ] *nf* (*de lit*) blanket;
(*de bâtiment*) roofing; (*de livre, fig: d'un
espion etc*) cover.

couveuse [kuvéz] *nf* (*à poules*) sitter,
brooder; (*de maternité*) incubator.

couvre... [kuvʀ(ə)] *préfixe*: **~-chef** *nm*
hat; **~-feu** *nm* curfew; **~-lit** *nm*
bedspread.

couvreur [kuvʀœʀ] *nm* roofer.

couvrir [kuvʀiʀ] *vt* to cover; **se** ~ (*ciel*)
to cloud over; (*s'habiller*) to cover up,
wrap up; (*se coiffer*) to put on one's hat;
(*par une assurance*) to cover o.s.; **se** ~ **de**
(*fleurs, boutons*) to become covered in.

crabe [kʀab] *nm* crab.

crachat [kʀaʃa] *nm* spittle *q*, spit *q*.

cracher [kʀaʃe] *vi* to spit // *vt* to spit out;
(*fig: lave etc*) to belch (out); ~ **du sang**
to spit blood.

crachin [kʀaʃɛ̃] *nm* drizzle.

crachoir [kʀaʃwaʀ] *nm* spittoon; (*de
dentiste*) bowl.

craie [kʀɛ] *nf* chalk.

craindre [kʀɛ̃dʀ(ə)] *vt* to fear, be afraid
of; (*être sensible à: chaleur, froid*) to be
easily damaged by; ~ **de/que** to be afraid
of/that.

crainte [kʀɛ̃t] *nf* fear; **de** ~ **de/que** for
fear of/that; **craintif, ive** a timid.

cramoisi, e [kʀamwazi] a crimson.

crampe [kʀɑ̃p] *nf* cramp; ~ **d'estomac**
stomach cramp.

crampon [kʀɑ̃põ] *nm* (*de semelle*) stud;
(*ALPINISME*) crampon.

cramponner [kʀɑ̃pɔne]: **se** ~ *vi*: **se** ~
(**à**) to hang *ou* cling on (to).

cran [kʀɑ̃] *nm* (*entaille*) notch; (*de
courroie*) hole; (*courage*) guts *pl*; ~
d'arrêt safety catch; ~ **de mire** bead.

crâne [kʀɑn] *nm* skull.

crâner [kʀɑne] *vi* (*fam*) to swank, show
off.

crânien, ne [kʀɑnjɛ̃, -jɛn] a cranial, skull
cpd, brain *cpd*.

crapaud [kʀapo] *nm* toad.

crapule [kʀapyl] *nf* villain.

craquelure [kʀaklyʀ] *nf* crack, crackle *q*.

craquement [kʀakmɑ̃] *nm* crack, snap;
(*du plancher*) creak, creaking *q*.

craquer [kʀake] *vi* (*bois, plancher*) to
creak; (*fil, branche*) to snap; (*couture*) to
come apart, burst; (*fig*) to break down //
vt: ~ **une allumette** to strike a match.

crasse [kʀas] *nf* grime, filth.

crassier [kʀasje] *nm* slag heap.

cratère [kʀatɛʀ] *nm* crater.

cravache [kʀavaʃ] *nf* (*riding*) crop;
cravacher *vt* to use the crop on.

cravate [kʀavat] *nf* tie; **cravater** *vt* to put
a tie on; (*fig*) to grab round the neck.

crawl [kʀol] *nm* crawl; **dos crawlé**
backstroke.

crayeux, euse [kʀɛjé, -éz] a chalky.

crayon [kʀɛjõ] *nm* pencil; (*de rouge à
lèvres etc*) stick, pencil; **écrire au** ~ to
write in pencil; ~ **à bille** ball-point pen;
~ **de couleur** crayon, colouring pencil.

créance [kʀeɑ̃s] *nf* (*COMM*) (financial)
claim, (recoverable) debt; **créancier, ière**
nm/f creditor.

créateur, trice [kʀeatœʀ, -tʀis] a
creative // *nm/f* creator.

création [kʀeasjõ] *nf* creation.

créature [kʀeatyʀ] *nf* creature.

crécelle [kʀesɛl] *nf* rattle.

crèche [kʀɛʃ] *nf* (*de Noël*) crib; (*garderie*)
crèche, day nursery.

crédence [kʀedɑ̃s] *nf* (small) sideboard.

crédit [kʀedi] *nm* (*gén*) credit; ~s *nmpl*
funds; **payer/acheter à** ~ to pay/buy on
credit *ou* on easy terms; **faire** ~ **à qn** to
give sb credit; **créditer** *vt*: **créditer un
compte (de)** to credit an account (with);
créditeur, trice a in credit, credit *cpd* //
nm/f customer in credit.

crédule [kʀedyl] a credulous, gullible;
crédulité *nf* credulity, gullibility.

créer [kʀee] *vt* to create; (*THÉÂTRE*) to
produce (for the first time).

crémaillère [kʀemajɛʀ] *nf* (*RAIL*) rack;
(*tige crantée*) trammel; **direction à** ~
(*AUTO*) rack and pinion steering; **pendre
la** ~ to have a house-warming party.

crémation [kʀemasjõ] *nf* cremation.

crématoire [kʀematwaʀ] a: **four** ~
crematorium.

crème [kʀɛm] *nf* cream; (*entremets*)
cream dessert // a *inv* cream(-coloured);
un (café) ~ ≈ a white coffee; ~
fouettée whipped cream; ~ **à raser**
shaving cream; **crèmerie** *nf* dairy;
(*tearoom*) teashop; **crémeux, euse** a
creamy; **crémier, ière** *nm/f* dairy-
man/woman.

créneau, x [kʀeno] *nm* (*de fortification*)
crenel(le); (*fig*) gap; slot; (*AUTO*): **faire un**
~ to reverse into a parking space (*between
cars alongside the kerb*).

créole [kʀeɔl] a, *nm*, *nf* Creole.

crêpe [kʀɛp] *nf* (*galette*) pancake // *nm*
(*tissu*) crêpe; (*de deuil*) black mourning
crêpe; black armband (*ou* hatband *ou*
ribbon); **semelle (de)** ~ crêpe sole;
crêpé, e a (*cheveux*) backcombed; **~rie**
nf pancake shop *ou* restaurant.

crépi [kʀepi] *nm* roughcast; **crépir** *vt* to
roughcast.

crépiter [kʀepite] *vi* to sputter, splutter;
to crackle; to rattle out; to patter.

crépon [kʀepõ] *nm* seersucker.

crépu, e [kʀepy] a frizzy, fuzzy.

crépuscule [kʀepyskyl] *nm* twilight, dusk.

crescendo [kʀeʃɛndo] *nm*, ad (*MUS*)
crescendo; **aller** ~ (*fig*) to rise higher and
higher, grow ever greater.

cresson [kʀesõ] *nm* watercress.

crête [kʀɛt] *nf* (*de coq*) comb; (*de vague,
montagne*) crest.

crétin, e [kʀetɛ̃, -in] *nm/f* cretin.

cretonne [kʀətɔn] *nf* cretonne.

creuser [kRøze] vt (trou, tunnel) to dig; (sol) to dig a hole in; (bois) to hollow out; (fig) to go (deeply) into; **cela creuse** (l'estomac) that gives you a real appetite; **se ~ (la cervelle)** to rack one's brains.

creuset [kRøzε] nm crucible; (fig) melting pot; (severe) test.

creux, euse [kRø, -øz] a hollow // nm hollow; (fig: sur graphique etc) trough; **heures creuses** slack periods; off-peak periods; **le ~ de l'estomac** the pit of the stomach.

crevaison [kRəvεzɔ̃] nf puncture.

crevasse [kRəvas] nf (dans le sol) crack, fissure; (de glacier) crevasse; (de la peau) crack.

crevé, e [kRəve] a (fatigué) fagged out, worn out.

crève-cœur [kRεvkœr] nm inv heartbreak.

crever [kRəve] vt (papier) to tear, break; (tambour, ballon) to burst // vi (pneu) to burst; (automobiliste) to have a puncture; (abcès, outre, nuage) to burst (open); (fam) to die; **cela lui a crevé un œil** it blinded him in one eye.

crevette [kRəvεt] nf: **~ (rose)** prawn; **~ grise** shrimp.

cri [kRi] nm cry, shout; (d'animal: spécifique) cry, call; **c'est le dernier ~** (fig) it's the latest fashion.

criant, e [kRijɑ̃, -ɑ̃t] a (injustice) glaring.

criard, e [kRijaR, -aRd(ə)] a (couleur) garish, loud; yelling.

crible [kRibl(ə)] nm riddle; (mécanique) screen, riddle; **passer qch au ~** to put sth through a riddle; (fig) to go over sth with a fine-tooth comb.

criblé, e [kRible] a: **~ de** riddled with.

cric [kRik] nm (AUTO) jack.

crier [kRije] vi (pour appeler) to shout, cry (out); (de peur, de douleur etc) to scream, yell; (fig: grincer) to squeal, screech // vt (ordre, injure) to shout (out), yell (out); **crieur de journaux** nm newspaper seller.

crime [kRim] nm crime; (meurtre) murder; **criminaliste** nm/f specialist in criminal law; **criminalité** nf criminality, crime; **criminel, le** a criminal // nm/f criminal; murderer; **criminel de guerre** war criminal; **criminologiste** nm/f criminologist.

crin [kRε̃] nm hair q; (fibre) horsehair; **à tous ~s, à tout ~** diehard, out-and-out.

crinière [kRinjεR] nf mane.

crique [kRik] nf creek, inlet.

criquet [kRikε] nm locust; grasshopper.

crise [kRiz] nf crisis (pl crises); (MÉD) attack; fit; **~ cardiaque** heart attack; **~ de foi** crisis of belief; **~ de foie** bilious attack; **~ de nerfs** attack of nerves.

crispation [kRispasjɔ̃] nf twitch; contraction; tenseness.

crisper [kRispe] vt to tense; (poings) to clench; **se ~** to tense; to clench; (personne) to get tense.

crisser [kRise] vi (neige) to crunch; (tissu) to rustle; (pneu) to screech.

cristal, aux [kRistal, -o] nm crystal // nmpl (objets) crystal(ware) sg; **~ de plomb** (lead) crystal; **~ de roche** rock-crystal; **cristaux de soude** washing soda sg.

cristallin, e [kRistalε̃, -in] a crystal-clear // nm (ANAT) crystalline lens.

cristalliser [kRistalize] vi, vt, **se ~** vi to crystallize.

critère [kRitεR] nm criterion (pl ia).

critique [kRitik] a critical // nm/f (de théâtre, musique) critic // nf criticism; (THÉÂTRE etc: article) review; **la ~** (activité) criticism; (personnes) the critics pl.

critiquer [kRitike] vt (dénigrer) to criticize; (évaluer, juger) to assess, examine (critically).

croasser [kRoase] vi to caw.

croc [kRo] nm (dent) fang; (de boucher) hook.

croc-en-jambe [kRokɑ̃ʒɑ̃b] nm: **faire un ~ à qn** to trip sb up.

croche [kRoʃ] nf (MUS) quaver; **double ~** semiquaver.

crochet [kRoʃε] nm hook; (clef) picklock; (détour) detour; (BOXE): **~ du gauche** left hook; (TRICOT: aiguille) crochet-hook; (: technique) crochet; **~s** nmpl (TYPO) square brackets; **vivre aux ~s de** qn to live ou sponge off sb; **crocheter** vt (serrure) to pick.

crochu, e [kRoʃy] a hooked; claw-like.

crocodile [kRokodil] nm crocodile.

crocus [kRokys] nm crocus.

croire [kRwaR] vt to believe; **~ qn honnête** to believe sb (to be) honest; **se ~ fort** to think one is strong; **~ que** to believe ou think that; **~ à, ~ en** to believe in.

crois vb voir **croître**.

croisade [kRwazad] nf crusade.

croisé, e [kRwaze] a (veston) double-breasted // nm (guerrier) crusader // nf (fenêtre) window, casement; **~e d'ogives** intersecting ribs; **à la ~e des chemins** at the crossroads.

croisement [kRwazmɑ̃] nm (carrefour) crossroads sg; (BIO) crossing; crossbreed.

croiser [kRwaze] vt (personne, voiture) to pass; (route) to cross, cut across; (BIO) to cross // vi (NAVIG) to cruise; **~ les jambes/bras** to cross one's legs/fold one's arms; **se ~** (personnes, véhicules) to pass each other; (routes) to cross, intersect; (lettres) to cross (in the post); (regards) to meet.

croiseur [kRwazœR] nm cruiser (warship).

croisière [kRwazjεR] nf cruise; **vitesse de ~** (AUTO etc) cruising speed.

croisillon [kRwazijɔ̃] nm: **motif/fenêtre à ~s** lattice pattern/window.

croissance [kRwasɑ̃s] nf growing, growth; **maladie de ~** growth disease; **~ économique** economic growth.

croissant, e [kRwasɑ̃, -ɑ̃t] a growing; rising // nm (à manger) croissant; (motif) crescent.

croître [kRwatR(ə)] vi to grow; (lune) to wax.

croix [kRwa] nf cross; **en ~** a, ad in the form of a cross; **la C~ Rouge** the Red Cross.

croquant, e [kRokɑ̃, -ɑ̃t] a crisp, crunchy // nm/f (péj) yokel, (country) bumpkin.

croque... [kʀɔk] *préfixe:* ~-**mitaine** *nm* bog(e)y-man ; ~-**monsieur** *nm inv* toasted ham and cheese sandwich ; ~-**mort** *nm* (*péj*) pallbearer.

croquer [kʀɔke] *vt* (*manger*) to crunch ; to munch ; (*dessiner*) to sketch // *vi* to be crisp *ou* crunchy.

croquet [kʀɔkɛ] *nm* croquet.

croquette [kʀɔkɛt] *nf* croquette.

croquis [kʀɔki] *nm* sketch.

cross(-country) [kʀɔs(kuntʀi)] *nm* cross-country race *ou* run ; cross-country racing *ou* running.

crosse [kʀɔs] *nf* (*de fusil*) butt ; (*de revolver*) grip ; (*d'évêque*) crook, crosier ; (*de hockey*) hockey stick.

crotte [kʀɔt] *nf* droppings *pl*.

crotté, e [kʀɔte] *a* muddy, mucky.

crottin [kʀɔtɛ̃] *nm:* ~ (**de cheval**) (horse) dung *ou* manure.

crouler [kʀule] *vi* (*s'effondrer*) to collapse ; (*être délabré*) to be crumbling.

croupe [kʀup] *nf* croup, rump ; **en** ~ pillion.

croupier [kʀupje] *nm* croupier.

croupir [kʀupiʀ] *vi* to stagnate.

croustillant, e [kʀustijɑ̃, -ɑ̃t] *a* crisp ; (*fig*) spicy.

croustiller [kʀustije] *vi* to be crisp *ou* crusty.

croûte [kʀut] *nf* crust ; (*du fromage*) rind ; (*de vol-au-vent*) case ; (*MÉD*) scab ; **en** ~ (*CULIN*) in pastry, in a pie ; ~ **aux champignons** mushrooms on toast ; ~ **au fromage** cheese on toast *q* ; ~ **de pain** (*morceau*) crust (of bread) ; ~ **terrestre** earth's crust.

croûton [kʀutɔ̃] *nm* (*CULIN*) crouton ; (*bout du pain*) crust, heel.

croyance [kʀwajɑ̃s] *nf* belief.

croyant, e [kʀwajɑ̃, -ɑ̃t] *nm/f* believer.

C.R.S. *sigle fpl* = **Compagnies républicaines de sécurité** (a state security police force) // *sigle m* member of the C.R.S..

cru, e [kʀy] *pp de* **croire** // *a* (*non cuit*) raw ; (*lumière, couleur*) harsh ; (*paroles, description*) crude // *nm* (*vignoble*) vineyard ; (*vin*) wine // *nf* (*d'un cours d'eau*) swelling, rising ; **de son** (*propre*) ~ (*fig*) of his own devising ; **du** ~ local ; **en** ~**e** in spate.

crû *pp de* **croître**.

cruauté [kʀyote] *nf* cruelty.

cruche [kʀyʃ] *nf* pitcher, (earthenware) jug.

crucial, e, aux [kʀysjal, -o] *a* crucial.

crucifier [kʀysifje] *vt* to crucify.

crucifix [kʀysifi] *nm* crucifix.

cruciforme [kʀysifɔʀm(ə)] *a* cruciform, cross-shaped.

cruciverbiste [kʀysivɛʀbist(ə)] *nm/f* crossword puzzle enthusiast.

crudité [kʀydite] *nf* crudeness *q* ; harshness *q* ; ~**s** *nfpl* (*CULIN*) salads.

crue [kʀy] *nf voir* **cru.**

cruel, le [kʀyɛl] *a* cruel.

crus *etc*, **crûs** *etc vb voir* **croire, croître.**

crustacés [kʀystase] *nmpl* shellfish.

crypte [kʀipt(ə)] *nf* crypt.

cubage [kybaʒ] *nm* cubage, cubic content.

cube [kyb] *nm* cube ; (*jouet*) brick, building block ; **mètre** ~ cubic metre ; **2 au** ~ = **8 2 cubed is 8** ; **élever au** ~ to cube ; **cubique** *a* cubic.

cueillette [kœjɛt] *nf* picking, gathering ; harvest *ou* crop (of fruit).

cueillir [kœjiʀ] *vt* (*fruits, fleurs*) to pick, gather ; (*fig*) to catch.

cuiller *ou* **cuillère** [kɥijɛʀ] *nf* spoon ; ~ **à café** coffee spoon ; (*CULIN*) ≈ teaspoonful ; ~ **à soupe** soup-spoon ; (*CULIN*) ≈ tablespoonful ; **cuillerée** *nf* spoonful.

cuir [kɥiʀ] *nm* leather ; (*avant tannage*) hide ; ~ **chevelu** scalp.

cuirasse [kɥiʀas] *nf* breastplate ; **cuirassé** *nm* (*NAVIG*) battleship.

cuire [kɥiʀ] *vt* (*aliments*) to cook ; (*poterie*) to fire // *vi* to cook ; (*picoter*) to smart, sting, burn ; **bien cuit** (*viande*) well done ; **trop cuit** overdone.

cuisine [kɥizin] *nf* (*pièce*) kitchen ; (*art culinaire*) cookery, cooking ; (*nourriture*) cooking, food ; **faire la** ~ to cook, make a *ou* the meal ; **cuisiner** *vt* to cook ; (*fam*) to grill // *vi* to cook ; **cuisinier, ière** *nm/f* cook // *nf* (*poêle*) cooker.

cuisse [kɥis] *nf* (*ANAT*) thigh ; (*CULIN*) leg.

cuisson [kɥisɔ̃] *nf* cooking ; firing.

cuistre [kɥistʀ(ə)] *nm* prig.

cuit, e *pp de* **cuire.**

cuivre [kɥivʀ(ə)] *nm* copper ; **les** ~**s** (*MUS*) the brass ; **cuivré, e** *a* coppery ; bronzed.

cul [ky] *nm* (*fam!*) arse (!), bum ; ~ **de bouteille** bottom of a bottle.

culasse [kylas] *nf* (*AUTO*) cylinder-head ; (*de fusil*) breech.

culbute [kylbyt] *nf* somersault ; (*accidentelle*) tumble, fall ; **culbuter** *vi* to (take a) tumble, fall (head over heels) ; **culbuteur** *nm* (*AUTO*) rocker arm.

cul-de-jatte [kydʒat] *nm/f* legless cripple.

cul-de-sac [kydsak] *nm* cul-de-sac.

culinaire [kylinɛʀ] *a* culinary.

culminant, e [kylminɑ̃, -ɑ̃t] *a:* **point** ~ highest point.

culminer [kylmine] *vi* to reach its highest point ; to tower.

culot [kylo] *nm* (*d'ampoule*) cap ; (*effronterie*) cheek, nerve.

culotte [kylɔt] *nf* (*pantalon*) pants *pl*, trousers *pl* ; (*de femme*): (**petite**) ~ knickers *pl* ; ~ **de cheval** riding breeches *pl*.

culotté, e [kylɔte] *a* (*pipe*) seasoned ; (*cuir*) mellowed ; (*effronté*) cheeky.

culpabilité [kylpabilite] *nf* guilt.

culte [kylt(ə)] *nm* (*religion*) religion ; (*hommage, vénération*) worship ; (*protestant*) service.

cultivateur, trice [kyltivatœʀ, -tʀis] *nm/f* farmer.

cultivé, e [kyltive] *a* (*personne*) cultured, cultivated.

cultiver [kyltive] *vt* to cultivate ; (*légumes*) to grow, cultivate.

culture [kyltyʀ] *nf* cultivation ; growing ; (*connaissances etc*) culture ; (**champs de**) ~**s** land(s) under cultivation ; ~ **physique** physical training ; **culturel, le** *a* cultural ; **culturisme** *nm* body-building.

cumin [kymɛ̃] nm (CULIN) caraway seeds pl, cumin.

cumul [kymyl] nm (voir cumuler) holding (ou drawing) concurrently; ~ de peines sentences to run consecutively.

cumuler [kymyle] vt (emplois, honneurs) to hold concurrently; (salaires) to draw concurrently; (JUR: droits) to accumulate.

cupide [kypid] a greedy, grasping.

curatif, ive [kyratif, -iv] a curative.

cure [kyʀ] nf (MÉD) course of treatment; (REL) cure, ≈ living; presbytery, ≈ vicarage; faire une ~ de fruits to go on a fruit cure ou diet; n'avoir ~ de to pay no attention to; ~ de sommeil sleep therapy q.

curé [kyʀe] nm parish priest; M. le ~ ≈ Vicar.

cure-dent [kyʀdã] nm toothpick.

cure-pipe [kyʀpip] nm pipe cleaner.

curer [kyʀe] vt to clean out.

curieux, euse [kyʀjø, -øz] a (étrange) strange, curious; (indiscret) curious, inquisitive; (intéressé) inquiring, curious // nmpl (badauds) onlookers, bystanders; **curiosité** nf curiosity, inquisitiveness; (objet) curio(sity); (site) unusual feature ou sight.

curiste [kyʀist(ə)] nm/f person taking the waters at a spa.

curriculum vitae [kyʀikylɔmvite] nm inv (abr C.V.) curriculum vitae.

curry [kyʀi] nm curry; poulet au ~ curried chicken, chicken curry.

curseur [kyʀsœʀ] nm (de règle) slide; (de fermeture-éclair) slider.

cursif, ive [kyʀsif, -iv] a: écriture cursive cursive script.

cutané, e [kytane] a cutaneous, skin cpd.

cuti-réaction [kytiʀeaksjɔ̃] nf (MÉD) skin-test.

cuve [kyv] nf vat; (à mazout etc) tank.

cuvée [kyve] nf vintage.

cuvette [kyvɛt] nf (récipient) bowl, basin; (du lavabo) (wash)basin; (des w.-c.) pan; (GÉO) basin.

C.V. sigle m (AUTO) voir cheval; (COMM) = curriculum vitae.

cyanure [sjanyʀ] nm cyanide.

cybernétique [sibɛʀnetik] nf cybernetics sg.

cyclable [siklabl(ə)] a: piste ~ cycle track.

cyclamen [siklamɛn] nm cyclamen.

cycle [sikl(ə)] nm cycle.

cyclique [siklik] a cyclic(al).

cyclisme [siklism(ə)] nm cycling.

cycliste [siklist(ə)] nm/f cyclist // a cycle cpd.

cyclomoteur [siklɔmɔtœʀ] nm moped; **cyclomotoriste** nm/f moped-rider.

cyclone [siklon] nm hurricane.

cygne [siɲ] nm swan.

cylindre [silɛ̃dʀ(ə)] nm cylinder; moteur à 4 ~s en ligne straight-4 engine; **cylindrée** nf (AUTO) (cubic) capacity; une (voiture de) grosse cylindrée a big-engined car; **cylindrique** a cylindrical.

cymbale [sɛ̃bal] nf cymbal.

cynique [sinik] a cynical; **cynisme** nm cynicism.

cyprès [sipʀɛ] nm cypress.

cypriote [sipʀijɔt] a, nm/f Cypriot.

cyrillique [siʀilik] a Cyrillic.

cystite [sistit] nf cystitis.

cytise [sitiz] nm laburnum.

D

d' prép, dét voir de.

dactylo [daktilo] nf (aussi: ~graphe) typist; (aussi: ~graphie) typing, typewriting; ~graphier vt to type (out).

dada [dada] nm hobby-horse.

daigner [deɲe] vt to deign.

daim [dɛ̃] nm (fallow) deer inv; (peau) buckskin; (imitation) suede.

dallage [dalaʒ] nm paving.

dalle [dal] nf paving stone, flag(stone); slab.

daltonien, ne [daltɔnjɛ̃, -jɛn] a colour-blind.

dam [dam] nm: au grand ~ de much to the detriment ou annoyance of.

dame [dam] nf lady; (CARTES, ÉCHECS) queen; ~s nfpl (jeu) draughts sg.

damer [dame] vt to ram ou pack down; ~ le pion à (fig) to get the better of.

damier [damje] nm draughtboard; (dessin) check (pattern).

damner [dane] vt to damn.

dancing [dãsiŋ] nm dance hall.

dandiner [dãdine]: se ~ vi to sway about; to waddle along.

Danemark [danmaʀk] nm Denmark.

danger [dãʒe] nm danger; mettre en ~ to endanger, put in danger; **dangereux, euse** a dangerous.

danois, e [danwa, -waz] a Danish // nm/f: D~, e Dane // nm (langue) Danish.

dans [dã] prép in; (direction) into, to; (à l'intérieur de) in, inside; je l'ai pris ~ le tiroir/salon I took it out of ou from the drawer/lounge; boire ~ un verre to drink out of ou from a glass; ~ 2 mois in 2 months, in 2 months' time, 2 months from now; ~ les 20 F about 20 F.

dansant, e [dãsã, -ãt] a: soirée ~e evening of dancing; dinner dance.

danse [dãs] nf: la ~ dancing; (classique) (ballet) dancing; une ~ a dance; **danser** vi, vt to dance; **danseur, euse** nm/f ballet dancer/ballerina; (au bal etc) dancer; partner; en danseuse (à vélo) standing on the pedals.

dard [daʀ] nm sting (organ).

darder [daʀde] vt to shoot, send forth.

date [dat] nf date; faire ~ to mark a milestone; ~ de naissance date of birth; **dater** vt, vi to date; dater de to date from, go back to; à dater de (as) from.

datif [datif] nm dative.

datte [dat] nf date; **dattier** nm date palm.

dauphin [dofɛ̃] nm (ZOOL) dolphin; (du roi) dauphin; (fig) heir apparent.

daurade [dɔʀad] nf gilt-head.

davantage [davãtaʒ] ad more; (plus longtemps) longer; ~ de more.

DCA [desea] sigle f (= défense contre avions): la ~ anti-aircraft defence.

de (*de* + *le* = **du**, *de* + *les* = **des**) [də, dy, de] *prép* of; (*provenance*) from; (*moyen*) with; **la voiture d'Élisabeth/de mes parents** Elizabeth's/my parents' car; **un mur de brique/bureau d'acajou** a brick wall/mahogany desk; **augmenter** etc **de 10F** to increase by 10F; **une pièce de 2 m de large** *ou* **large de 2 m** a room 2 m wide *ou* in width, a 2 m wide room; **un bébé de 10 mois** a 10-month-old baby; **un séjour de 2 ans** a 2-year stay; **12 mois de crédit/travail** 12 months' credit/work // *dét*: **du vin, de l'eau, des pommes** (some) wine, (some) water, (some) apples; **des enfants sont venus** some children came; **a-t-il du vin?** has he got any wine?; **il ne veut pas de pommes** he doesn't want any apples; **il n'a pas d'enfants** he has no children, he hasn't got any children; **pendant des mois** for months.

dé [de] *nm* (*à jouer*) die *ou* dice (*pl* dice); (*aussi*: ~ **à coudre**) thimble; ~**s** *nmpl* (*jeu*) (game of) dice; **un coup de** ~**s** a throw of the dice.

déambuler [deɑ̃byle] *vi* to stroll about.

débâcle [debakl(ə)] *nf* rout.

déballer [debale] *vt* to unpack.

débandade [debɑ̃dad] *nf* rout; scattering.

débarbouiller [debaʀbuje] *vt* to wash; **se** ~ to wash (one's face).

débarcadère [debaʀkadɛʀ] *nm* landing stage.

débardeur [debaʀdœʀ] *nm* docker, stevedore; (*maillot*) slipover, tank top.

débarquement [debaʀkəmɑ̃] *nm* unloading; landing; disembarcation; (*MIL*) landing.

débarquer [debaʀke] *vt* to unload, land // *vi* to disembark; (*fig*) to turn up.

débarras [debaʀa] *nm* lumber room; junk cupboard; outhouse; **bon** ~**!** good riddance!

débarrasser [debaʀase] *vt* to clear; ~ **qn de** (*vêtements, paquets*) to relieve sb of; (*habitude, ennemi*) to rid sb of; ~ **qch de** (*fouillis* etc) to clear sth of; **se** ~ **de** *vt* to get rid of; to rid o.s. of.

débat [deba] *nm* discussion, debate; ~**s** (*POL*) proceedings, debates.

débattre [debatʀ(ə)] *vt* to discuss, debate; **se** ~ *vi* to struggle.

débauche [deboʃ] *nf* debauchery; **une** ~ **de** (*fig*) a profusion of; a riot of.

débaucher [deboʃe] *vt* (*licencier*) to lay off, dismiss; (*entraîner*) to lead astray, debauch.

débile [debil] *a* weak, feeble; ~ **mental, e** *nm/f* mental defective.

débit [debi] *nm* (*d'un liquide, fleuve*) (rate of) flow; (*d'un magasin*) turnover (of goods); (*élocution*) delivery; (*bancaire*) debit; **avoir un** ~ **de 10 F** to be 10 F in debit; ~ **de boissons** drinking establishment; ~ **de tabac** tobacconist's (shop); **débiter** *vt* (*compte*) to debit; (*liquide, gaz*) to yield, produce, give out; (*couper: bois, viande*) to cut up; (*vendre*) to retail; (*péj: paroles* etc) to come out with, churn out; **débiteur, trice** *nm/f* debtor // *a* in debit.

déblai [deblɛ] *nm* earth (*moved*).

déblaiement [deblɛmɑ̃] *nm* clearing; **travaux de** ~ earth moving *sg*.

déblayer [debleje] *vt* to clear.

débloquer [debloke] *vt* (*frein*) to release; (*prix, crédits*) to free.

déboires [debwaʀ] *nmpl* setbacks.

déboiser [debwaze] *vt* to clear of trees; to deforest.

déboîter [debwate] *vt* (*AUTO*) to pull out; **se** ~ **le genou** etc to dislocate one's knee etc.

débonnaire [debonɛʀ] *a* easy-going, good-natured.

débordé, e [debɔʀde] *a*: **être** ~ **de** (*travail, demandes*) to be snowed under with.

débordement [debɔʀdəmɑ̃] *nm* overflowing.

déborder [debɔʀde] *vi* to overflow; (*lait* etc) to boil over // *vt* (*MIL, SPORT*) to outflank; ~ (**de**) **qch** (*dépasser*) to extend beyond sth; ~ **de** (*joie, zèle*) to be brimming over with *ou* bursting with.

débouché [debuʃe] *nm* (*pour vendre*) outlet; (*perspective d'emploi*) opening; (*sortie*): **au** ~ **de la vallée** where the valley opens out (onto the plain); **au** ~ **de la rue Dupont** (*sur le boulevard*) where the rue Dupont meets the boulevard.

déboucher [debuʃe] *vt* (*évier, tuyau* etc) to unblock; (*bouteille*) to uncork, open // *vi*: ~ **de** to emerge from, come out of; ~ **sur** to come out onto; to open out onto; (*fig*) to arrive at, lead up to.

débourser [debuʀse] *vt* to pay out, lay out.

debout [dəbu] *ad*: **être** ~ (*personne*) to be standing, stand; (: *levé, éveillé*) to be up (and about); (*chose*) to be upright; **être encore** ~ (*fig: en état*) to be still going; to be still standing; **se mettre** ~ to get up (on one's feet); **se tenir** ~ to stand; ~**!** stand up!; (*du lit*) get up!; **cette histoire ne tient pas** ~ this story doesn't hold water.

déboutonner [debutɔne] *vt* to undo, unbutton; **se** ~ *vi* to come undone *ou* unbuttoned.

débraillé, e [debʀaje] *a* slovenly, untidy.

débrayage [debʀɛjaʒ] *nm* (*AUTO*) clutch; (: *action*) disengaging the clutch; (*grève*) stoppage; **faire un double** ~ to double-declutch.

débrayer [debʀeje] *vi* (*AUTO*) to declutch, disengage the clutch; (*cesser le travail*) to stop work.

débridé, e [debʀide] *a* unbridled, unrestrained.

débris [debʀi] *nm* (*fragment*) fragment // *nmpl* (*déchets*) pieces; rubbish *sg*; debris *sg*.

débrouillard, e [debʀujaʀ, -aʀd(ə)] *a* smart, resourceful.

débrouiller [debʀuje] *vt* to disentangle, untangle; (*fig*) to sort out, unravel; **se** ~ *vi* to manage.

débroussailler [debʀusaje] *vt* to clear (of brushwood).

débusquer [debyske] *vt* to drive out (from cover).

début [deby] *nm* beginning, start ; ~s *nmpl* beginnings ; début *sg*.

débutant, e [debytɑ̃, -ɑ̃t] *nm/f* beginner, novice.

débuter [debyte] *vi* to begin, start ; (*faire ses débuts*) to start out.

deçà [dəsa]: **en ~ de** *prép* this side of.

décacheter [dekaʃte] *vt* to unseal, open.

décade [dekad] *nf* (*10 jours*) (period of) ten days ; (*10 ans*) decade.

décadence [dekadɑ̃s] *nf* decadence ; decline.

décaféiné, e [dekafeine] *a* decaffeinated, caffeine-free.

décalage [dekalaʒ] *nm* gap ; discrepancy ; move forward *ou* back ; shift forward *ou* back ; ~ **horaire** time difference (between time zones) ; time-lag.

décalcomanie [dekalkɔmani] *nf* transfer.

décaler [dekale] *vt* (*dans le temps: avancer*) to bring forward ; (: *retarder*) to put back ; (*changer de position*) to shift forward *ou* back ; ~ **de 2 h** to bring *ou* move forward 2 hours ; to put back 2 hours.

décalquer [dekalke] *vt* to trace ; (*par pression*) to transfer.

décamper [dekɑ̃pe] *vi* to clear out *ou* off.

décanter [dekɑ̃te] *vt* to (allow to) settle (and decant) ; **se ~** to settle.

décapant [dekapɑ̃] *nm* acid solution ; scouring agent ; paint stripper.

décaper [dekape] *vt* to clean ; (*avec abrasif*) to scour ; (*avec papier de verre*) to sand.

décapiter [dekapite] *vt* to behead ; (*par accident*) to decapitate ; (*fig*) to cut the top off ; to remove the top men from.

décapotable [dekapɔtabl(ə)] *a* convertible.

décapoter [dekapɔte] *vt* to put down the top of.

décapsuler [dekapsyle] *vt* to take the cap *ou* top off ; **décapsuleur** *nm* bottle-opener.

décathlon [dekatlɔ̃] *nm* decathlon.

décédé, e [desede] *a* deceased.

décéder [desede] *vi* to die.

déceler [desle] *vt* to discover, detect ; to indicate, reveal.

décélération [deselerɑsjɔ̃] *nf* deceleration.

décembre [desɑ̃br(ə)] *nm* December.

décemment [desamɑ̃] *ad* decently.

décence [desɑ̃s] *nf* decency.

décennie [desni] *nf* decade.

décent, e [desɑ̃, -ɑ̃t] *a* decent.

décentraliser [desɑ̃tralize] *vt* to decentralize.

décentrer [desɑ̃tre] *vt* to decentre ; **se ~** to move off-centre.

déception [desɛpsjɔ̃] *nf* disappointment.

décerner [desɛrne] *vt* to award.

décès [desɛ] *nm* death, decease.

décevoir [desvwar] *vt* to disappoint.

déchaîner [deʃene] *vt* (*passions, colère*) to unleash ; (*rires etc*) to give rise to, arouse ; **se ~** *vi* to rage ; to burst out, explode ; (*se mettre en colère*) to fly into a rage, loose one's fury.

déchanter [deʃɑ̃te] *vi* to become disillusioned.

décharge [deʃarʒ(ə)] *nf* (*dépôt d'ordures*) rubbish tip *ou* dump ; (*électrique*) electrical discharge ; (*salve*) volley of shots ; **à la ~ de** in defence of.

déchargement [deʃarʒəmɑ̃] *nm* unloading.

décharger [deʃarʒe] *vt* (*marchandise, véhicule*) to unload ; (*ÉLEC*) to discharge ; (*arme: neutraliser*) to unload ; (: *faire feu*) to discharge, fire ; ~ **qn de** (*responsabilité*) to relieve sb of, release sb from.

décharné, e [deʃarne] *a* bony, emaciated, fleshless.

déchausser [deʃose] *vt* (*personne*) to take the shoes off ; (*skis*) to take off ; **se ~** to take off one's shoes ; (*dent*) to come *ou* work loose.

déchéance [deʃeɑ̃s] *nf* degeneration ; decay, decline ; fall.

déchet [deʃɛ] *nm* (*de bois, tissu etc*) scrap ; (*perte: gén COMM*) wastage, waste ; ~s *nmpl* (*ordures*) refuse *sg*, rubbish *sg*.

déchiffrer [deʃifre] *vt* to decipher.

déchiqueter [deʃikte] *vt* to tear *ou* pull to pieces.

déchirant, e [deʃirɑ̃, -ɑ̃t] *a* heart-breaking, heart-rending.

déchirement [deʃirmɑ̃] *nm* (*chagrin*) wrench, heartbreak ; (*gén pl: conflit*) rift, split.

déchirer [deʃire] *vt* to tear ; (*mettre en morceaux*) to tear up ; (*pour ouvrir*) to tear off ; (*arracher*) to tear out ; (*fig*) to rack ; to tear ; to tear apart ; **se ~** *vi* to tear, rip ; **se ~ un muscle** to tear a muscle.

déchirure [deʃiryr] *nf* (*accroc*) tear, rip ; ~ **musculaire** torn muscle.

déchoir [deʃwar] *vi* (*personne*) to lower o.s., demean o.s.

déchu, e [deʃy] *a* fallen ; deposed.

décibel [desibɛl] *nm* decibel.

décidé, e [deside] *a* (*personne, air*) determined ; **c'est ~** it's decided ; **être ~ à faire** to be determined to do.

décidément [desidemɑ̃] *ad* undoubtedly ; really.

décider [deside] *vt:* ~ **qch** to decide on sth ; ~ **de faire/que** to decide to do/that ; ~ **qn** (*à faire qch*) to persuade *ou* induce sb (to do sth) ; ~ **de qch** to decide upon sth ; (*suj: chose*) to determine sth ; **se ~** (*à faire*) to decide (to do), make up one's mind (to do) ; **se ~ pour** to decide on *ou* in favour of.

décilitre [desilitr(ə)] *nm* decilitre.

décimal, e, aux [desimal, -o] *a, nf* decimal.

décimer [desime] *vt* to decimate.

décimètre [desimɛtr(ə)] *nm* decimetre ; **double ~** (20 cm) ruler.

décisif, ive [desizif, -iv] *a* decisive ; (*qui l'emporte*): **le facteur/ l'argument ~** the deciding factor/ argument.

décision [desizjɔ̃] *nf* decision ; (*fermeté*) decisiveness, decision ; **emporter** *ou* **faire la ~** to be decisive.

déclamation [deklamasjɔ̃] *nf* declamation ; (*péj*) ranting, spouting.

déclaration [deklarɑsjɔ̃] *nf* declaration ; registration ; (*discours: POL etc*) statement ; ~ (**d'amour**) declaration ; ~ **de décès**

registration of death; ~ **de guerre** declaration of war; ~ **(d'impôts)** statement of income, tax declaration, ≈ tax return; ~ **(de sinistre)** (insurance) claim.

déclarer [deklaRe] vt to declare, announce; (revenus, marchandises) to declare; (décès, naissance) to register; **se** ~ (feu, maladie) to break out; ~ **que** to declare that.

déclassement [deklasmɑ̃] nm (RAIL etc) change of class.

déclasser [deklase] vt to relegate; to downgrade; to lower in status.

déclenchement [deklɑ̃ʃmɑ̃] nm release; setting off.

déclencher [deklɑ̃ʃe] vt (mécanisme etc) to release; (sonnerie) to set off, activate; (attaque, grève) to launch; (provoquer) to trigger off; **se** ~ vi to release itself; to go off.

déclic [deklik] nm trigger mechanism; (bruit) click.

déclin [deklɛ̃] nm decline.

déclinaison [deklinɛzɔ̃] nf declension.

décliner [dekline] vi to decline // vt (invitation) to decline, refuse; (responsabilité) to refuse to accept; (nom, adresse) to state; (LING) to decline.

déclivité [deklivite] nf slope, incline; **en** ~ sloping, on the incline.

décocher [dekɔʃe] vt to throw; to shoot.

décoder [dekɔde] vt to decipher, decode.

décoiffer [dekwafe] vt: ~ **qn** to disarrange ou mess up sb's hair; to take sb's hat off; **se** ~ to take off one's hat.

décoincer [dekwɛse] vt to unjam, loosen.

déçois etc vb voir **décevoir**.

décolérer [dekɔleRe] vi: **Il ne décolère pas** he's still angry, he hasn't calmed down.

décollage [dekɔlaʒ] nm (AVIAT) takeoff.

décoller [dekɔle] vt to unstick // vi (avion) to take off; **se** ~ to come unstuck.

décolletage [dekɔltaʒ] nm (TECH) cutting.

décolleté, e [dekɔlte] a low-necked, low-cut; wearing a low-cut dress // nm low neck(line); (bare) neck and shoulders; (plongeant) cleavage.

décolorant [dekɔlɔRɑ̃] nm decolorant, bleaching agent.

décoloration [dekɔlɔRasjɔ̃] nf: **se faire une** ~ (chez le coiffeur) to have one's hair bleached ou lightened.

décolorer [dekɔlɔRe] vt (tissu) to fade; (cheveux) to bleach, lighten; **se** ~ vi to fade.

décombres [dekɔ̃bR(ə)] nmpl rubble sg, debris sg.

décommander [dekɔmɑ̃de] vt to cancel; (invités) to put off; **se** ~ to cancel one's appointment etc, cry off.

décomposé, e [dekɔ̃poze] a (visage) haggard, distorted.

décomposer [dekɔ̃poze] vt to break up; (CHIMIE) to decompose; (MATH) to factorize; **se** ~ vi (pourrir) to decompose; **décomposition** nf breaking up; decomposition; factorization; **en décomposition** (organisme) in a state of decay, decomposing.

décompression [dekɔ̃pResjɔ̃] nf decompression.

décompte [dekɔ̃t] nm deduction; (facture) breakdown (of an account), detailed account.

déconcentration [dekɔ̃sɑ̃tRasjɔ̃] nf (des industries etc) dispersal.

déconcentré, e [dekɔ̃sɑ̃tRe] a (sportif etc) who has lost (his/her) concentration.

déconcerter [dekɔ̃sɛRte] vt to disconcert, confound.

déconfit, e [dekɔ̃fi, -it] a crestfallen, downcast.

déconfiture [dekɔ̃fityR] nf failure, defeat; collapse, ruin.

décongeler [dekɔ̃ʒle] vt to thaw (out).

décongestionner [dekɔ̃ʒɛstjɔne] vt (MÉD) to decongest; (rues) to relieve congestion in.

déconnecter [dekɔnɛkte] vt to disconnect.

déconseiller [dekɔ̃seje] vt: ~ **qch (à qn)** to advise (sb) against sth; ~ **à qn de faire** to advise sb against doing.

déconsidérer [dekɔ̃sideRe] vt to discredit.

déconsigner [dekɔ̃sine] vt (valise) to collect (from left luggage); (bouteille) to return the deposit on.

décontenancer [dekɔ̃tnɑ̃se] vt to disconcert, discountenance.

décontracter [dekɔ̃tRakte] vt, **se** ~ to relax.

déconvenue [dekɔ̃vny] nf disappointment.

décor [dekɔR] nm décor; (paysage) scenery; ~**s** nmpl (THÉÂTRE) scenery sg, décor sg; (CINÉMA) set sg.

décorateur [dekɔRatœR] nm (interior) decorator; (CINÉMA) set designer.

décoratif, ive [dekɔRatif, -iv] a decorative.

décoration [dekɔRasjɔ̃] nf decoration.

décorer [dekɔRe] vt to decorate.

décortiquer [dekɔRtike] vt to shell; (riz) to hull; (fig) to dissect.

décorum [dekɔRɔm] nm decorum, étiquette.

découcher [dekuʃe] vi to spend the night away from home.

découdre [dekudR(ə)] vt to unpick, take the stitching out of; **se** ~ to come unstitched; **en** ~ (fig) to fight, do battle.

découler [dekule] vi: ~ **de** to ensue ou follow from.

découpage [dekupaʒ] nm cutting up; carving; (image) cut-out (figure); ~ **électoral** division into constituencies.

découper [dekupe] vt (papier, tissu etc) to cut up; (volaille, viande) to carve; (détacher: manche, article) to cut out; **se** ~ **sur** (ciel, fond) to stand out against.

découplé, e [dekuple] a: **bien** ~ well-built, well-proportioned.

découpure [dekupyR] nf: ~**s** (morceaux) cut-out bits; (d'une côte, arête) indentations, jagged outline sg.

découragement [dekuRaʒmɑ̃] nm discouragement, despondency.

décourager [dekuRaʒe] vt to discourage, dishearten; (dissuader) to discourage, put off; **se** ~ to lose heart, become discouraged; ~ qn de faire/de qch to discourage sb from doing/from sth, put sb off doing/sth.

décousu, e [dekuzy] a unstitched; (fig) disjointed, disconnected.

découvert, e [dekuvɛʀ, -ɛʀt(ə)] a (tête) bare, uncovered; (lieu) open, exposed // nm (bancaire) overdraft // nf discovery; à ~ ad (MIL) exposed, without cover; (fig) openly // a (COMM) overdrawn; **aller à la** ~**e de** to go in search of.

découvrir [dekuvʀiʀ] vt to discover; (apercevoir) to see; (enlever ce qui couvre ou protège) to uncover; (montrer, dévoiler) to reveal; se ~ to take off one's hat; to take off some clothes; (au lit) to uncover o.s.; (ciel) to clear; ~ **que** to discover that, find out that.

décrasser [dekrase] vt to clean.

décrépi, e [dekrepi] a peeling; with roughcast rendering removed.

décrépit, e [dekrepi, -it] a decrepit; **décrépitude** nf decrepitude; decay.

decrescendo [dekreʃɛndo] nm (MUS) decrescendo; **aller** ~ (fig) to decline, be on the wane.

décret [dekrɛ] nm decree; **décréter** vt to decree; to order; to declare; ~**-loi** nm statutory order.

décrié, e [dekrije] a disparaged.

décrire [dekriʀ] vt to describe; (courbe, cercle) to follow, describe.

décrochement [dekrɔʃmɑ̃] nm (d'un mur etc) recess.

décrocher [dekrɔʃe] vt (dépendre) to take down; (téléphone) to take off the hook; (: pour répondre): ~ **(le téléphone)** to pick up ou lift the receiver; (fig: contrat etc) to get, land // vi to drop out; to switch off.

décroître [dekrwatr(ə)] vi to decrease, decline, diminish.

décrue [dekry] nf drop in level (of the waters).

décrypter [dekripte] vt to decipher.

déçu, e [desy] pp de **décevoir**.

déculotter [dekylɔte] vt: ~ qn to take off ou down sb's trousers.

décuple [dekypl(ə)] nm: le ~ de ten times; au ~ tenfold; **décupler** vt, vi to increase tenfold.

dédaigner [dedeɲe] vt to despise, scorn; (négliger) to disregard, spurn; ~ de faire to consider it beneath one to do; not to deign to do; **dédaigneux, euse** a scornful, disdainful.

dédain [dedɛ̃] nm scorn, disdain.

dédale [dedal] nm maze.

dedans [dədɑ̃] ad inside; (pas en plein air) indoors, inside // nm inside; au ~ on the inside; inside; en ~ (vers l'intérieur) inwards; voir aussi **là**.

dédicace [dedikas] nf dedication; (manuscrite, sur une photo etc) inscription; **dédicacer** vt: ~ (à qn) to sign (for sb), autograph (for sb), inscribe (to sb).

dédier [dedje] vt to dedicate.

dédire [dediʀ]: se ~ vi to go back on one's word; to retract, recant.

dédit [dedi] nm (COMM) forfeit, penalty.

dédommagement [dedɔmaʒmɑ̃] nm compensation.

dédommager [dedɔmaʒe] vt: ~ qn (de) to compensate sb (for); (fig) to repay sb (for).

dédouaner [dedwane] vt to clear through customs.

dédoublement [dedubləmɑ̃] nm splitting; (PSYCH): ~ **de la personnalité** split ou dual personality.

dédoubler [deduble] vt (classe, effectifs) to split (into two); (couverture etc) to unfold; (manteau) to remove the lining of; ~ **un train/les trains** to run a relief train/additional trains.

déduction [dedyksjɔ̃] nf (d'argent) deduction; (raisonnement) deduction, inference.

déduire [deduiʀ] vt: ~ **qch (de)** (ôter) to deduct sth (from); (conclure) to deduce ou infer sth (from).

déesse [deɛs] nf goddess.

défaillance [defajɑ̃s] nf (syncope) blackout; (fatigue) (sudden) weakness q; (technique) fault, failure; (morale etc) weakness; ~ **cardiaque** heart failure.

défaillant, e [defajɑ̃, -ɑ̃t] a (JUR: témoin) defaulting.

défaillir [defajiʀ] vi to faint; to feel faint; (mémoire etc) to fail.

défaire [defɛʀ] vt (installation, échafaudage) to take down, dismantle; (paquet etc, nœud, vêtement) to undo; se ~ vi to come undone; **se** ~ **de** vt (se débarrasser de) to get rid of; (se séparer de) to part with.

défait, e [defɛ, -ɛt] a (visage) haggard, ravaged // nf defeat.

défaitiste [defetist(ə)] a, nm/f defeatist.

défalquer [defalke] vt to deduct.

défaut [defo] nm (moral) fault, failing, defect; (d'étoffe, métal) fault, flaw, defect; (manque, carence): ~ **de** lack of; shortage of; en ~ at fault; in the wrong; **faire** ~ (manquer) to be lacking; à ~ **ad** failing that; à ~ **de** for lack ou want of; **par** ~ (JUR) in his (ou her etc) absence.

défaveur [defavœʀ] nf disfavour.

défavorable [defavɔʀabl(ə)] a unfavourable.

défavoriser [defavɔʀize] vt to put at a disadvantage.

défectif, ive [defɛktif, -iv] a: **verbe** ~ defective verb.

défection [defɛksjɔ̃] nf defection, failure to give support ou assistance; failure to appear; **faire** ~ (d'un parti etc) to withdraw one's support, leave.

défectueux, euse [defɛktɥø, -øz] a faulty, defective; **défectuosité** nf defectiveness q; defect, fault.

défendre [defɑ̃dʀ(ə)] vt to defend; (interdire) to forbid; ~ à qn qch/de faire to forbid sb sth/to do; se ~ to defend o.s.; **il se défend** (fig) he can hold his own; **ça se défend** (fig) it holds together; se ~ **de/contre** (se protéger) to protect o.s. from/against; se ~ **de** (se garder de) to refrain from; (nier): se ~ **de vouloir** to deny wanting.

défense [defɑ̃s] nf defence; (d'éléphant etc) tusk; '~ **de fumer/cracher**' 'no smoking/ spitting', 'smoking/spitting prohibited'; **défenseur** nm defender ; (JUR) counsel for the defence ; **défensif, ive** a, nf defensive.

déférent, e [defeʀɑ̃, -ɑ̃t] a (poli) deferential, deferent.

déférer [defeʀe] vt (JUR) to refer ; ~ à vt (requête, décision) to defer to ; ~ qn à la justice to hand sb over to justice.

déferlement [defɛʀləmɑ̃] nm breaking ; surge.

déferler [defɛʀle] vi (vagues) to break ; (fig) to surge.

défi [defi] nm (provocation) challenge ; (bravade) defiance.

défiance [defjɑ̃s] nf mistrust, distrust.

déficience [defisjɑ̃s] nf deficiency.

déficit [defisit] nm (COMM) deficit ; (PSYCH etc: manque) defect ; **être en** ~ to be in deficit, be in the red.

défier [defje] vt (provoquer) to challenge ; (fig) to defy, brave ; **se** ~ **de** (se méfier de) to distrust, mistrust ; ~ qn de faire to challenge ou defy sb to do ; ~ qn à (jeu etc) to challenge sb to.

défigurer [defigyʀe] vt to disfigure ; (suj: boutons etc) to mar ou spoil (the looks of) ; (fig: œuvre) to mutilate, deface.

défilé [defile] nm (GÉO) (narrow) gorge ou pass ; (soldats) parade ; (manifestants) procession, march ; **un** ~ **de** (voitures, visiteurs etc) a stream of.

défiler [defile] vi (troupes) to march past ; (sportifs) to parade ; (manifestants) to march ; (visiteurs) to pour, stream ; **se** ~ vi (se dérober) to slip away, sneak off.

défini, e [defini] a definite.

définir [definiʀ] vt to define.

définitif, ive [definitif, -iv] a (final) final, definitive ; (pour longtemps) permanent, definitive ; (sans appel) final, definite // nf: **en définitive** eventually ; (somme toute) when all is said and done.

définition [definisjɔ̃] nf definition ; (de mots croisés) clue ; (TV) (picture) resolution.

définitivement [definitivmɑ̃] ad definitively ; permanently ; definitely.

déflagration [deflagʀasjɔ̃] nf explosion.

déflation [deflɑsjɔ̃] nf deflation ; **déflationniste** a deflationist, deflationary.

déflecteur [deflɛktœʀ] nm (AUTO) quarter-light.

déflorer [defloʀe] vt (jeune fille) to deflower ; (fig) to spoil the charm of.

défoncer [defɔ̃se] vt (caisse) to stave in ; (porte) to smash in ou down ; (lit, fauteuil) to burst (the springs of) ; (terrain, route) to rip ou plough up.

déformant, e [defɔʀmɑ̃, -ɑ̃t] a: **glace ou miroir** ~(e) distorting mirror.

déformation [defɔʀmɑsjɔ̃] nf loss of shape ; deformation ; distortion ; ~ **professionnelle** conditioning by one's job.

déformer [defɔʀme] vt to put out of shape ; (corps) to deform ; (pensée, fait) to distort ; **se** ~ vi to lose its shape.

défouler [defule]: **se** ~ vi (PSYCH) to work off one's tensions, release one's pent-up feelings ; (gén) to unwind, let off steam.

défraîchir [defreʃiʀ]: **se** ~ vi to fade ; to become worn.

défrayer [defreje] vt: ~ **qn** to pay sb's expenses ; ~ **la chronique** to be in the news, be the main topic of conversation.

défricher [defriʃe] vt to clear (for cultivation).

défroquer [defʀɔke] vi (gén: se ~) to give up the cloth, renounce one's vows.

défunt, e [defœ̃, -œ̃t] a: **son** ~ **père** his late father // nm/f deceased.

dégagé, e [degaʒe] a clear ; (ton, air) casual, jaunty.

dégagement [degaʒmɑ̃] nm emission ; freeing ; clearing ; (espace libre) clearing ; passage ; clearance ; (FOOTBALL) clearance ; **voie de** ~ slip road ; **itinéraire de** ~ alternative route (to relieve traffic congestion).

dégager [degaʒe] vt (exhaler) to give off, emit ; (délivrer) to free, extricate ; (MIL: troupes) to relieve ; (désencombrer) to clear ; (isoler: idée, aspect) to bring out ; **qn de** (engagement, parole etc) to release ou free sb from ; **se** ~ vi (odeur) to emanate, be given off ; (passage, ciel) to clear ; **se** ~ **de** (fig: engagement etc) to get out of ; to go back on.

dégaine r [degene] vt to draw.

dégarnir [degaʀniʀ] vt (vider) to empty, clear ; **se** ~ vi to empty ; to be cleaned out ou cleared ; (tempes, crâne) to go bald.

dégâts [degu] nmpl damage sg.

dégazer [degɑze] vi (pétrolier) to clean its tanks.

dégel [deʒɛl] nm thaw.

dégeler [deʒle] vt to thaw (out) ; (fig) to unfreeze // vi to thaw (out).

dégénéré, e [deʒeneʀe] a, nm/f degenerate.

dégénérer [deʒeneʀe] vi to degenerate ; (empirer) to go from bad to worse.

dégingandé, e [deʒɛ̃gɑ̃de] a gangling, lanky.

dégivrage [deʒivʀaʒ] nm defrosting ; de-icing.

dégivrer [deʒivʀe] vt (frigo) to defrost ; (vitres) to de-ice ; **dégivreur** nm defroster de-icer.

déglutir [deglytiʀ] vi to swallow.

dégonflé, e [degɔ̃fle] a (pneu) flat.

dégonfler [degɔ̃fle] vt (pneu, ballon) to let down, deflate ; **se** ~ vi (fam) to chicken out.

dégouliner [deguline] vi to trickle, drip ; ~ **de** to be dripping with.

dégoupiller [degupije] vt (grenade) to take the pin out of.

dégourdi, e [deguʀdi] a smart, resourceful.

dégourdir [deguʀdiʀ] vt to warm (up) ; **se** ~ (les jambes) to stretch one's legs (fig).

dégoût [degu] nm disgust, distaste.

dégoûtant, e [degutɑ̃, -ɑ̃t] a disgusting.

dégoûter [degute] vt to disgust ; **cela me dégoûte** I find this disgusting ou revolting ; ~ **qn de qch** to put sb off sth.

dégoutter [degute] vi to drip ; ~ **de** to be dripping with.

dégradé, e [degʀade] a (couleur) shaded off // nm (PEINTURE) gradation.

dégrader [degʀade] vt (MIL: officier) to degrade ; (abîmer) to damage, deface ;

(*avilir*) to degrade, debase ; **se** ~ (*relations, situation*) to deteriorate.

dégrafer [degʀafe] vt to unclip, unhook, unfasten.

dégraissage [degʀɛsaʒ] nm: ~ **et nettoyage à sec** dry cleaning.

dégraisser [degʀese] vt (*soupe*) to skim ; (*vêtement*) to take the grease marks out of.

degré [dəgʀe] nm degree ; (*d'escalier*) step ; **brûlure au 1er/2ème** ~ 1st/2nd degree burn ; **équation du 1er/2ème** ~ linear/quadratic equation ; **alcool à 90** ~**s** 90% proof alcohol (*on Gay-Lussac scale*) ; **vin de 10** ~**s** 10° wine (*on Gay-Lussac scale*) ; **par** ~(**s**) ad by degrees, gradually.

dégressif, ive [degʀesif, -iv] a on a decreasing sliding scale, degressive.

dégrever [degʀave] vt to grant tax relief to ; to reduce the tax burden on.

dégringoler [degʀɛ̃gɔle] vi to tumble (down).

dégriser [degʀize] vt to sober up.

dégrossir [degʀosiʀ] vt (*bois*) to trim ; (*fig*) to work out roughly ; to knock the rough edges off.

déguenillé, e [dɛgnije] a ragged, tattered.

déguerpir [degɛʀpiʀ] vi to clear off, scarper.

déguisement [degizmɑ̃] nm disguise.

déguiser [degize] vt to disguise ; **se** ~ (*se costumer*) to dress up ; (*pour tromper*) to disguise o.s.

dégustation [degystɑsjɔ̃] nf tasting ; sampling ; savouring ; (*séance*): ~ **de vin(s)** wine-tasting session.

déguster [degyste] vt (*vins*) to taste ; (*fromages etc*) to sample ; (*savourer*) to enjoy, savour.

déhancher [deɑ̃ʃe]: **se** ~ vi to sway one's hips ; to lean (one's weight) on one hip.

dehors [dəɔʀ] ad outside ; (*en plein air*) outdoors, outside // nm outside // nmpl (*apparences*) appearances, exterior sg ; **mettre** ou **jeter** ~ (*expulser*) to throw out ; **au** ~ outside ; outwardly ; **au** ~ **de** outside ; **en** ~ (*vers l'extérieur*) outside ; outwards ; **en** ~ **de** (*hormis*) apart from.

déjà [deʒa] ad already ; (*auparavant*) before, already ; **quel nom,** ~? what was the name again?

déjanter [deʒɑ̃te]: **se** ~ vi (*pneu*) to come off the rim.

déjeté, e [dɛʒte] a lop-sided, crooked.

déjeuner [deʒœne] vi to (have) lunch ; (*le matin*) to have breakfast // nm lunch ; (*petit déjeuner*) breakfast.

déjouer [deʒwe] vt to elude ; to foil, thwart.

delà [dəla] ad: **par** ~, **en** ~ (**de**), **au** ~ (**de**) beyond.

délabrer [delabʀe]: **se** ~ vi to fall into decay, become dilapidated.

délacer [delase] vt to unlace, undo.

délai [delɛ] nm (*attente*) waiting period ; (*sursis*) extension (of time) ; (*temps accordé*) time limit ; **sans** ~ without delay ; **à bref** ~ shortly, very soon ; at short notice ; **dans les** ~**s** within the time limit ; **comptez un** ~ **de livraison de 10 jours** allow 10 days for delivery.

délaisser [delese] vt to abandon, desert.

délasser [delase] vt (*reposer*) to relax ; (*divertir*) to divert, entertain ; **se** ~ to relax.

délateur, trice [delatœʀ, -tʀis] nm/f informer.

délation [delɑsjɔ̃] nf denouncement, informing.

délavé, e [delave] a faded.

délayer [deleje] vt (*CULIN*) to mix (with water etc) ; (*peinture*) to thin down ; (*fig*) to pad out, spin out.

delco [dɛlko] nm (*AUTO*) distributor.

délecter [delɛkte]: **se** ~ vi: **se** ~ **de** to revel ou delight in.

délégation [delegɑsjɔ̃] nf delegation.

délégué, e [delege] a delegated // nm/f delegate ; representative.

déléguer [delege] vt to delegate.

délester [delɛste] vt (*navire*) to unballast.

délibération [deliberɑsjɔ̃] nf deliberation.

délibéré, e [delibeʀe] a (*conscient*) deliberate ; (*déterminé*) determined, resolute.

délibérément [deliberemɑ̃] ad deliberately.

délibérer [delibeʀe] vi to deliberate.

délicat, e [delika, -at] a delicate ; (*plein de tact*) tactful ; (*attentionné*) thoughtful ; (*exigeant*) fussy, particular ; **procédés peu** ~**s** unscrupulous methods ; **délicatement** ad delicately ; (*avec douceur*) gently ; **délicatesse** nf delicacy, delicate nature ; tactfulness ; thoughtfulness ; **délicatesses** nfpl attentions, consideration sg.

délice [delis] nm delight.

délicieux, euse [delisjø, -jøz] a (*au goût*) delicious ; (*sensation, impression*) delightful.

délictueux, euse [deliktɥø, -ɥøz] a criminal.

délié, e [delje] a nimble, agile ; slender, fine // nm: **les** ~**s** the upstrokes (*in handwriting*).

délier [delje] vt to untie ; ~ **qn de** (*serment etc*) ` free ou release sb from.

délimitation [delimitɑsjɔ̃] nf delimitation, demarcation.

délimiter [delimite] vt to delimit, demarcate ; to determine ; to define.

délinquance [delɛ̃kɑ̃s] nf criminality ; ~ **juvénile** juvenile delinquency.

délinquant, e [delɛ̃kɑ̃, -ɑ̃t] a, nm/f delinquent.

déliquescence [delikesɑ̃s] nf: **en** ~ in a state of decay.

délire [deliʀ] nm (*fièvre*) delirium ; (*fig*) frenzy ; lunacy.

délirer [deliʀe] vi to be delirious ; (*fig*) to be raving, be going wild.

délit [deli] nm (*criminal*) offence ; ~ **de droit commun** violation of common law ; ~ **politique** political offence ; ~ **de presse** violation of the press laws.

délivrance [delivʀɑ̃s] nf freeing, release ; (*sentiment*) relief.

délivrer [delivʀe] vt (*prisonnier*) to (set) free, release ; (*passeport, certificat*) to issue ; ~ **qn de** (*ennemis*) to set sb free from, deliver ou free sb from ; (*fig*) to relieve sb of ; to rid sb of.

déloger [delɔʒe] vt (*locataire*) to turn out ; (*objet coincé, ennemi*) to dislodge.

déloyal, e, aux [delwajal, -o] a disloyal; unfair.

delta [dɛlta] nm (GÉO) delta.

déluge [delyʒ] nm (biblique) Flood, Deluge; (grosse pluie) downpour, deluge; (grand nombre): ~ de flood of.

déluré, e [delyre] a smart, resourceful; (péj) forward, pert.

démagnétiser [demaɲetize] vt to demagnetize.

démagogie [demagɔʒi] nf demagogy, demagoguery; démagogique a demagogic, popularity-seeking; vote-catching; démagogue a demagogic // nm demagogue.

démaillé, e [demaje] a (bas) laddered, with a run, with runs.

demain [dəmɛ̃] ad tomorrow.

demande [dəmɑ̃d] nf (requête) request; (revendication) demand; (ADMIN, formulaire) application; (ÉCON): la ~ demand; '~s d'emploi' situations wanted; ~ en mariage (marriage) proposal; ~ de naturalisation application for naturalization; ~ de poste job application.

demandé, e [dəmɑ̃de] a (article etc): très ~ (very) much in demand.

demander [dəmɑ̃de] vt to ask for; (question: date, heure etc) to ask; (requérir, nécessiter) to require, demand; ~ qch à qn to ask sb for sth; to ask sb sth; ~ à qn de faire to ask sb to do; ~ que/pourquoi to ask that/why; se ~ si/pourquoi etc to wonder if/why etc; (sens purement réfléchi) to ask o.s. if/why etc; on vous demande au téléphone you're wanted on the phone, someone's asking for you on the phone.

demandeur, euse [dəmɑ̃dœr, -øz] nm/f: ~ d'emploi job-seeker; (job) applicant.

démangeaison [demɑ̃ʒɛzɔ̃] nf itching.

démanger [demɑ̃ʒe] vi to itch; la main me démange my hand is itching; l'envie me démange de I'm itching to.

démanteler [demɑ̃tle] vt to break up; to demolish.

démaquillant [demakijɑ̃] nm make-up remover.

démaquiller [demakije] vt: se ~ to remove one's make-up.

démarcage [demarkaʒ] nm = démarquage.

démarcation [demarkasjɔ̃] nf demarcation.

démarchage [demarʃaʒ] nm (COMM) door-to-door selling.

démarche [demarʃ(ə)] nf (allure) gait, walk; (intervention) step; approach; (fig: intellectuelle) thought processes pl; approach; faire des ~s auprès de qn to approach sb.

démarcheur, euse [demarʃœr, -øz] nm/f (COMM) door-to-door salesman/woman.

démarquage [demarkaʒ] nm mark-down.

démarqué, e [demarke] a (FOOTBALL) unmarked.

démarquer [demarke] vt (prix) to mark down; (joueur) to stop marking.

démarrage [demaraʒ] nm starting q, start; ~ en côte hill start.

démarrer [demare] vi (conducteur) to start (up); (véhicule) to move off; (travaux) to get moving; (coureur: accélérer) to pull away; démarreur nm (AUTO) starter.

démasquer [demaske] vt to unmask.

démâter [demɑte] vt to dismast // vi to be dismasted.

démêler [demele] vt to untangle, disentangle.

démêlés [demele] nmpl problems.

démembrer [demɑ̃bre] vt to slice up, tear apart.

déménagement [demenaʒmɑ̃] nm (du point de vue du locataire) move; (: du déménageur) removal; entreprise/camion de ~ removal firm/van.

déménager [demenaʒe] vt (meubles) to (re)move // vi to move (house); déménageur nm removal man; (entrepreneur) furniture remover.

démence [demɑ̃s] nf dementia; madness, insanity.

démener [demne]: se ~ vi to thrash about; (fig) to exert o.s.

démenti [demɑ̃ti] nm denial, refutation.

démentiel, le [demɑ̃sjɛl] a insane.

démentir [demɑ̃tir] vt (nouvelle) to refute; (suj: faits etc) to belie, refute; ~ que to deny that; ne pas se ~ not to fail; to keep up.

démériter [demerite] vi: ~ auprès de qn to come down in sb's esteem.

démesure [demǝzyr] nf immoderation, immoderateness; démesuré, e a immoderate, disproportionate.

démettre [demɛtr(ə)] vt: ~ qn de (fonction, poste) to dismiss sb from; se ~ (de ses fonctions) to resign (from) one's duties; se ~ l'épaule etc to dislocate one's shoulder etc.

demeurant [dəmœrɑ̃]: au ~ ad for all that.

demeure [dəmœr] nf residence; mettre qn en ~ de faire to enjoin ou order sb to do; à ~ ad permanently.

demeurer [dəmœre] vi (habiter) to live; (séjourner) to stay; (rester) to remain.

demi, e [dəmi] a: et ~: trois heures/bouteilles et ~es three and a half hours/bottles, three hours/bottles and a half; il est 2 heures/midi et ~e it's half past 2/12 // nm (bière) ≈ half-pint (.25 litre); (FOOTBALL) half-back; à ~ ad half-; ouvrir à ~ to half-open; à ~ fini half-completed; à la ~e (heure) on the half-hour.

demi... [dəmi] préfixe half-, semi..., demi-; ~-cercle nm semicircle; en ~-cercle a semicircular // ad in a half circle; ~-douzaine nf half-dozen, half a dozen; ~-finale nf semifinal; ~-fond nm (SPORT) medium-distance running; ~-frère nm half-brother; ~-gros nm wholesale trade; ~-heure nf half-hour, half an hour; ~-jour nm half-light; ~-journée nf half-day, half a day.

démilitariser [demilitarize] vt to demilitarize.

demi-litre [dəmilitr(ə)] nm half-litre, half a litre.

demi-livre [dəmilivʀ(ə)] nf half-pound, half a pound.

demi-longueur [dəmilɔ̃gœʀ] nf (SPORT) half-length, half a length.

demi-lune [dəmilyn] ad: en ~ semicircular.

demi-mesure [dəmimzyʀ] nf half-measure.

demi-mot [dəmimo]: à ~ ad without having to spell things out.

déminer [demine] vt to clear of mines; **démineur** nm bomb disposal expert.

demi-pension [dəmipɑ̃sjɔ̃] nf (à l'hôtel) half-board.

demi-pensionnaire [dəmipɑ̃sjɔnɛʀ] nm/f (au lycée) half-boarder.

demi-place [dəmiplas] nf half-fare.

démis, e [demi, -iz] a (épaule etc) dislocated.

demi-saison [dəmisɛzɔ̃] nf: vêtements de ~ spring ou autumn clothing.

demi-sel [dəmisɛl] a inv (beurre, fromage) slightly salted.

demi-sœur [dəmisœʀ] nf half-sister.

démission [demisjɔ̃] nf resignation; **donner sa** ~ to give ou hand in one's notice, hand in one's resignation; **démissionner** vi (de son poste) to resign, give ou hand in one's notice.

demi-tarif [dəmitaʀif] nm half-price; (TRANSPORTS) half-fare.

demi-tour [dəmituʀ] nm about-turn; **faire un** ~ (MIL etc) to make an about-turn; **faire** ~ to turn (and go) back; (AUTO) to do a U-turn.

démobilisation [demɔbilizusjɔ̃] nf demobilization.

démocrate [demɔkʀat] a democratic // nm/f democrat.

démocratie [demɔkʀasi] nf democracy; ~ **populaire/libérale** people's/liberal democracy.

démocratique [demɔkʀatik] a democratic.

démocratiser [demɔkʀatize] vt to democratize.

démodé, e [demɔde] a old-fashioned.

démographie [demɔgʀafi] nf demography.

démographique [demɔgʀafik] a demographic; **poussée** ~ increase in population.

demoiselle [dəmwazɛl] nf (jeune fille) young lady; (célibataire) single lady, maiden lady; ~ **d'honneur** bridesmaid.

démolir [demɔliʀ] vt to demolish.

démolisseur [demɔlisœʀ] nm demolition worker.

démolition [demɔlisjɔ̃] nf demolition.

démon [demɔ̃] nm demon, fiend; evil spirit; (enfant turbulent) devil, demon; **le D~** the Devil.

démoniaque [demɔnjak] a fiendish.

démonstrateur, trice [demɔ̃stʀatœʀ, -tʀis] nm/f demonstrator.

démonstratif, ive [demɔ̃stʀatif, -iv] a (aussi LING) demonstrative.

démonstration [demɔ̃stʀusjɔ̃] nf demonstration; (aérienne, navale) display.

démonté, e [demɔ̃te] a (fig) raging, wild.

démonter [demɔ̃te] vt (machine etc) to take down, dismantle; (fig: personne) to disconcert; **se** ~ vi (personne) to lose countenance.

démontrer [demɔ̃tʀe] vt to demonstrate, show.

démoraliser [demɔralize] vt to demoralize.

démordre [demɔʀdʀ(ə)] vi: **ne pas** ~ **de** to refuse to give up, stick to.

démouler [demule] vt (gâteau) to turn out.

démoustiquer [demustike] vt to clear of mosquitoes.

démultiplication [demyltiplikasjɔ̃] nf reduction; reduction ratio.

démuni, e [demyni] a (sans argent) impoverished; ~ **de** without, lacking in.

démunir [demyniʀ] vt: ~ **qn de** to deprive sb of; **se** ~ **de** to part with, give up.

dénatalité [denatalite] nf fall in the birth rate.

dénaturer [denatyʀe] vt (goût) to alter (completely); (pensée, fait) to distort, misrepresent.

dénégations [denegasjɔ̃] nfpl denials.

dénicher [denife] vt to unearth; to track ou hunt down.

dénier [denje] vt to deny.

dénigrer [denigʀe] vt to denigrate, run down.

dénivellation [denivɛlasjɔ̃] nf, **dénivellement** [denivɛlmɑ̃] nm ramp; dip; difference in level.

dénombrer [denɔ̃bʀe] vt (compter) to count; (énumérer) to enumerate, list.

dénominateur [denɔminatœʀ] nm denominator; ~ **commun** common denominator.

dénomination [denɔminasjɔ̃] nf designation, appellation.

dénommer [denɔme] vt to name.

dénoncer [denɔ̃se] vt to denounce; **se** ~ to give o.s. up, come forward; **dénonciation** nf denunciation.

dénoter [denɔte] vt to denote.

dénouement [denumɑ̃] nm outcome, conclusion; (THÉÂTRE) dénouement.

dénouer [denwe] vt to unknot, undo.

dénoyauter [denwajote] vt to stone; **appareil à** ~, **dénoyauteur** nm stoner.

denrée [dɑ̃ʀe] nf food(stuff); ~**s alimentaires** foodstuffs.

dense [dɑ̃s] a dense.

densité [dɑ̃site] nf denseness; density; (PHYSIQUE) density.

dent [dɑ̃] nf tooth (pl teeth); **faire ses** ~**s** to teethe, cut (one's) teeth; **en** ~**s de scie** serrated; jagged; ~ **de lait/sagesse** milk/wisdom tooth; **dentaire** a dental; **denté, e** a: **roue dentée** cog wheel.

dentelé, e [dɑ̃tle] a jagged, indented.

dentelle [dɑ̃tɛl] nf lace q.

dentier [dɑ̃tje] nm denture.

dentifrice [dɑ̃tifʀis] nm, a: (pâte) ~ toothpaste.

dentiste [dɑ̃tist(ə)] nm/f dentist.

dentition [dɑ̃tisjɔ̃] nf teeth pl; dentition.

dénudé, e [denyde] a bare.

dénuder [denyde] vt to bare.

dénué, e [denɥe] *a*: ~ **de** devoid of; lacking in.

dénuement [denymɑ̃] *nm* destitution.

déodorant [deɔdɔRɑ̃] *nm* deodorant.

dépannage [depanaʒ] *nm*: **service de ~** (AUTO) breakdown service.

dépanner [depane] *vt* (*voiture, télévision*) to fix, repair ; (*fig*) to bail out, help out ; **dépanneuse** *nf* breakdown lorry.

déparer [depaRe] *vt* to spoil, mar.

départ [depaR] *nm* leaving *q*; departure ; (SPORT) start ; (*sur un horaire*) departure ; **à son ~** when he left.

départager [depaRtaʒe] *vt* to decide between.

département [depaRtəmɑ̃] *nm* department.

départir [depaRtiR]: **se ~ de** *vt* to abandon, depart from.

dépassé, e [depɑse] *a* superseded, outmoded.

dépassement [depɑsmɑ̃] *nm* (AUTO) overtaking *q*.

dépasser [depɑse] *vt* (*véhicule, concurrent*) to overtake ; (*endroit*) to pass, go past ; (*somme, limite*) to exceed ; (fig: *en beauté etc*) to surpass, outshine ; (*être en saillie sur*) to jut out above (*ou* in front of) // *vi* (AUTO) to overtake ; (*jupon*) to show.

dépaysement [depeizmɑ̃] *nm* disorientation ; change of scenery.

dépayser [depeize] *vt* to disorientate.

dépecer [depase] *vt* to joint, cut up ; to dismember.

dépêche [depeʃ] *nf* dispatch ; ~ **(télégraphique)** wire.

dépêcher [depeʃe] *vt* to dispatch ; **se ~** *vi* to hurry.

dépeindre [depɛ̃dR(ə)] *vt* to depict.

dépendance [depɑ̃dɑ̃s] *nf* dependence, dependency.

dépendre [depɑ̃dR(ə)] *vt* (*tableau*) to take down ; ~ **de** *vt* to depend on ; (*financièrement etc*) to be dependent on.

dépens [depɑ̃] *nmpl*: **aux ~ de** at the expense of.

dépense [depɑ̃s] *nf* spending *q*, expense, expenditure *q*; (*fig*) consumption ; expenditure ; **une ~ de 100 F** an outlay *ou* expenditure of 100 F ; ~ **physique** (physical) exertion ; ~**s publiques** public expenditure.

dépenser [depɑ̃se] *vt* to spend ; (*gaz, eau*) to use ; (*fig*) to expend, use up ; **se ~** (*se fatiguer*) to exert o.s.

dépensier, ière [depɑ̃sje, -jɛR] *a*: **il est ~** he's a spendthrift.

déperdition [depɛRdisjɔ̃] *nf* loss.

dépérir [depeRiR] *vi* to waste away ; to wither.

dépêtrer [depetRe] *vt*: **se ~ de** to extricate o.s. from.

dépeupler [depœple] *vt* to depopulate ; **se ~** to be depopulated ; (*rivière, forêt*) to empty of wildlife *etc*.

déphasé, e [defaze] *a* (ELEC) out of phase ; (*fig*) out of touch.

dépilatoire [depilatwaR] *a* depilatory, hair removing.

dépistage [depistaʒ] *nm* (MÉD) detection.

dépister [depiste] *vt* to detect ; (*voleur*) to track down ; (*poursuivants*) to throw off the scent.

dépit [depi] *nm* vexation, frustration ; **en ~ de** *prép* in spite of ; **en ~ du bon sens** contrary to all good sense ; **dépité, e** *a* vexed, frustrated.

déplacé, e [deplase] *a* (*propos*) out of place, uncalled-for.

déplacement [deplasmɑ̃] *nm* moving ; shifting ; transfer ; trip, travelling *q*; ~ **d'air** displacement of air ; ~ **de vertèbre** slipped disc.

déplacer [deplase] *vt* (*table, voiture*) to move, shift ; (*employé*) to transfer, move ; **se ~** *vi* to move ; (*organe*) to be displaced ; (*voyager*) to travel // *vt* (*vertèbre etc*) to displace.

déplaire [deplɛR] *vi*: **ceci me déplaît** I don't like this, I dislike this ; **il cherche à nous ~** he's trying to displease us *ou* be disagreeable to us ; **se ~ quelque part** to dislike it somewhere ; **déplaisant, e** *a* disagreeable, unpleasant.

déplaisir [depleziR] *nm* displeasure, annoyance.

dépliant [deplijɑ̃] *nm* leaflet.

déplier [deplije] *vt* to unfold.

déplisser [deplise] *vt* to smooth out.

déploiement [deplwamɑ̃] *nm* deployment ; display.

déplorer [deplɔRe] *vt* to deplore ; to lament.

déployer [deplwaje] *vt* to open out, spread ; to deploy ; to display, exhibit.

dépoli, e [depɔli] *a*: **verre ~** frosted glass.

déportation [depɔRtasjɔ̃] *nf* deportation.

déporté, e [depɔRte] *nm/f* deportee ; (39-45) concentration camp prisoner.

déporter [depɔRte] *vt* (POL) to deport ; (*dévier*) to carry off course.

déposant, e [depozɑ̃, -ɑ̃t] *nm/f* (*épargnant*) depositor.

dépose [depoz] *nf* taking out ; taking down.

déposer [depoze] *vt* (*gén: mettre, poser*) to lay down, put down, set down ; (*à la banque, à la consigne*) to deposit ; (*passager*) to drop (off), set down ; (*démonter: serrure, moteur*) to take out ; (: *rideau*) to take down ; (*roi*) to depose ; (ADMIN: *faire enregistrer*) to file ; to lodge ; to submit ; to register // *vi* to form a sediment *ou* deposit ; (JUR): ~ **(contre)** to testify *ou* give evidence (against) ; **se ~** *vi* to settle ; **dépositaire** *nm/f* (JUR) depository ; (COMM) agent ; **déposition** *nf* (JUR) deposition.

déposséder [deposede] *vt* to dispossess.

dépôt [depo] *nm* (*à la banque, sédiment*) deposit ; (*entrepôt, réserve*) warehouse, store ; (*gare*) depot ; (*prison*) cells *pl*; ~ **légal** registration of copyright.

dépotoir [depɔtwaR] *nm* dumping ground, rubbish dump.

dépouille [depuj] *nf* (*d'animal*) skin, hide ; (*humaine*): ~ **(mortelle)** mortal remains *pl*.

dépouillé, e [depuje] *a* (*fig*) bare, bald ; ~ **de** stripped of ; lacking in.

dépouiller [depuje] *vt* (*animal*) to skin ; (*spolier*) to deprive of one's possessions ; (*documents*) to go through, peruse ; ~

qn/qch de to strip sb/sth of ; ~ **le scrutin** to count the votes.

dépourvu, e [depuʀvy] a: ~ **de** lacking in, without ; **au** ~ ad unprepared.

dépoussiérer [depusjeʀe] vt to remove dust from.

dépravation [depʀavɑsjɔ̃] nf depravity.

dépraver [depʀave] vt to deprave.

dépréciation [depʀesjɑsjɔ̃] nf depreciation.

déprécier [depʀesje] vt, **se** ~ vi to depreciate.

déprédations [depʀedɑsjɔ̃] nfpl damage sg.

dépression [depʀɛsjɔ̃] nf depression ; ~ **(nerveuse)** (nervous) breakdown.

déprimer [depʀime] vt to depress.

dépuceler [depysle] vt (fam) to take the virginity of.

depuis [dəpɥi] prép (temps: date) since ; (: période) for ; (espace) since, from ; (quantité, rang: à partir de) from // ad (ever) since ; ~ **que** (ever) since ; ~ **quand le connaissez-vous?** how long have you known him? ; **je le connais** ~ **3 ans** I've known him for 3 years ; ~ **lors** since then.

députation [depytɑsjɔ̃] nf deputation ; (fonction) position of deputy, ≈ Parliamentary seat.

député, e [depyte] nm/f (POL) deputy, ≈ Member of Parliament.

députer [depyte] vt to delegate ; ~ **qn auprès de** to send sb (as a representative) to.

déraciner [deʀasine] vt to uproot.

déraillement [deʀɑjmɑ̃] nm derailment.

dérailler [deʀɑje] vi (train) to be derailed ; **faire** ~ to derail.

dérailleur [deʀɑjœʀ] nm (de vélo) dérailleur gears pl.

déraisonnable [deʀɛzɔnabl(ə)] a unreasonable.

déraisonner [deʀɛzɔne] vi to talk nonsense, rave.

dérangement [deʀɑ̃ʒmɑ̃] nm (gêne) trouble ; (gastrique etc) disorder ; (mécanique) breakdown ; **en** ~ (téléphone) out of order.

déranger [deʀɑ̃ʒe] vt (personne) to trouble, bother ; to disturb ; (projets) to disrupt, upset ; (objets, vêtements) to disarrange ; **se** ~ to put o.s. out ; to (take the trouble to) come ou go out ; **est-ce que cela vous dérange si** do you mind if.

dérapage [deʀapɑʒ] nm skid, skidding q.

déraper [deʀape] vi (voiture) to skid ; (personne, semelles, couteau) to slip ; (fig) to go out of control.

dératiser [deʀatize] vt to rid of rats.

déréglé, e [deʀegle] a (mœurs) dissolute.

dérégler [deʀegle] vt (mécanisme) to put out of order, cause to break down ; (estomac) to upset ; **se** ~ vi to break down, go wrong.

dérider [deʀide] vt, **se** ~ vi to brighten up.

dérision [deʀizjɔ̃] nf: **tourner en** ~ to deride.

dérisoire [deʀizwaʀ] a derisory.

dérivatif [deʀivatif] nm distraction.

dérivation [deʀivɑsjɔ̃] nf derivation ; diversion.

dérive [deʀiv] nf (de dériveur) centre-board ; **aller à la** ~ (NAVIG, fig) to drift.

dérivé, e [deʀive] a derived // nm (LING) derivative ; (TECH) by-product // nf (MATH) derivative.

dériver [deʀive] vt (MATH) to derive ; (cours d'eau etc) to divert // vi (bateau) to drift ; ~ **de** to derive from ; **dériveur** nm sailing dinghy.

dermatologie [dɛʀmatɔlɔʒi] nf dermatology ; **dermatologue** nm/f dermatologist.

dernier, ière [dɛʀnje, -jɛʀ] a last ; (le plus récent) latest, last ; **lundi/le mois** ~ last Monday/month ; **du** ~ **chic** extremely smart ; **les** ~s **honneurs** the last tribute ; **en** ~ ad last ; **ce** ~ the latter ; **dernièrement** ad recently ; ~-**né, dernière-née** nm/f (enfant) last-born.

dérobade [deʀɔbad] nf side-stepping q.

dérobé, e [deʀɔbe] a (porte) secret, hidden ; **à la** ~**e** surreptitiously.

dérober [deʀɔbe] vt to steal ; ~ **qch à (la vue de)** qn to conceal ou hide sth from sb('s view) ; **se** ~ vi (s'esquiver) to slip away ; to shy away ; **se** ~ **sous** (s'effondrer) to give way beneath ; **se** ~ **à** (justice, regards) to hide from ; (obligation) to shirk.

dérogation [deʀɔgɑsjɔ̃] nf (special) dispensation.

déroger [deʀɔʒe]: ~ **à** vt to go against, depart from.

dérouiller [deʀuje] vt: **se** ~ **les jambes** to stretch one's legs (fig).

déroulement [deʀulmɑ̃] nm (d'une opération etc) progress.

dérouler [deʀule] vt (ficelle) to unwind ; (papier) to unroll ; **se** ~ vi to unwind ; to unroll, come unrolled ; (avoir lieu) to take place ; (se passer) to go on ; to go (off) ; to unfold.

déroute [deʀut] nf rout ; total collapse ; **mettre en** ~ to rout.

dérouter [deʀute] vt (avion, train) to reroute, divert ; (étonner) to disconcert, throw (out).

derrière [dɛʀjɛʀ] ad behind // prép behind // nm (d'une maison) back ; (postérieur) behind, bottom ; **les pattes de** ~ the back legs, the hind legs ; **par** ~ from behind ; (fig) in an underhand way, behind one's back.

des [de] dét, prép + dét voir **de**.

dès [dɛ] prép from ; ~ **que** cj as soon as ; ~ **son retour** as soon as he was (ou is) back ; ~ **lors** ad from then on ; ~ **lors que** cj from the moment (that).

D.E.S. sigle m = **diplôme d'études supérieures**.

désabusé, e [dezabyze] a disillusioned.

désaccord [dezakɔʀ] nm disagreement.

désaccordé, e [dezakɔʀde] a (MUS) out of tune.

désaffecté, e [dezafɛkte] a disused.

désaffection [dezafɛksjɔ̃] nf: ~ **pour** estrangement from.

désagréable [dezagʀeable(ə)] a unpleasant, disagreeable.

désagréger [dezagʀeʒe]: se ~ vi to disintegrate, break up.

désagrément [dezagʀemɑ̃] nm annoyance, trouble q.

désaltérer [dezalteʀe] vt: se ~ to quench one's thirst; **ça désaltère** it's thirst-quenching, it takes your thirst away.

désamorcer [dezamɔʀse] vt to remove the primer from; (fig) to defuse; to forestall.

désappointé, e [dezapwɛ̃te] a disappointed.

désapprobation [dezapʀɔbasjɔ̃] nf disapproval.

désapprouver [dezapʀuve] vt to disapprove of.

désarçonner [dezaʀsɔne] vt to unseat, throw; (fig) to throw, nonplus.

désarmement [dezaʀməmɑ̃] nm disarmament.

désarmer [dezaʀme] vt (MIL, aussi fig) to disarm; (NAVIG) to lay up.

désarroi [dezaʀwa] nm helplessness, disarray.

désarticulé, e [dezaʀtikyle] a (pantin, corps) dislocated.

désarticuler [dezaʀtikyle] vt: se ~ (acrobate) to contort (o.s.).

désassorti, e [dezasɔʀti] a unmatching, unmatched.

désastre [dezastʀ(ə)] nm disaster; **désastreux, euse** a disastrous.

désavantage [dezavɑ̃taʒ] nm disadvantage; (inconvénient) drawback, disadvantage; **désavantager** vt to put at a disadvantage; **désavantageux, euse** a unfavourable, disadvantageous.

désavouer [dezavwe] vt to disown, repudiate, disclaim.

désaxé, e [dezakse] a (fig) unbalanced.

désaxer [dezakse] vt (roue) to put out of true.

desceller [desele] vt (pierre) to pull free.

descendance [desɑ̃dɑ̃s] nf (famille) descendants pl, issue; (origine) descent.

descendant, e [desɑ̃dɑ̃, -ɑ̃t] nm/f descendant.

descendre [desɑ̃dʀ(ə)] vt (escalier, montagne) to go (ou come) down; (valise, paquet) to take ou get down; (étagère etc) to lower; (fam: abattre) to shoot down // vi to go (ou come) down; (chemin) to go down; (passager: s'arrêter) to get out, alight; (niveau, température) to go ou come down, fall, drop; ~ à pied/en voiture to walk/drive down, to go down on foot/by car; ~ de (famille) to be descended from; ~ du train to get out of ou off the train; ~ d'un arbre to climb down from a tree; ~ de cheval to dismount, get off one's horse.

descente [desɑ̃t] nf descent, going down; (chemin) way down; (SKI) downhill (race); **au milieu de la** ~ halfway down; **freinez dans les** ~s use the brakes going downhill; ~ **de lit** bedside rug; ~ **(de police)** (police) raid.

description [dɛskʀipsjɔ̃] nf description.

désembuer [dezɑ̃bɥe] vt to demist.

désemparé, e [dezɑ̃paʀe] a bewildered, distraught; (véhicule) crippled.

désemparer [dezɑ̃paʀe] vi: **sans** ~ without stopping.

désemplir [dezɑ̃pliʀ] vi: **ne pas** ~ to be always full.

désenchantement [dezɑ̃ʃɑ̃tmɑ̃] nm disenchantment; disillusion.

désenfler [dezɑ̃fle] vi to become less swollen.

désengagement [dezɑ̃gaʒmɑ̃] nm (POL) disengagement.

désensibiliser [desɑ̃sibilize] vt (MÉD) to desensitize.

déséquilibre [dezekilibʀ(ə)] nm (position): **être en** ~ to be unsteady; (fig: des forces, du budget) imbalance; (PSYCH) unbalance.

déséquilibré, e [dezekilibʀe] nm/f (PSYCH) unbalanced person.

déséquilibrer [dezekilibʀe] vt to throw off balance.

désert, e [dezɛʀ, -ɛʀt(ə)] a deserted // nm desert.

déserter [dezɛʀte] vi, vt to desert; **déserteur** nm deserter; **désertion** nf desertion.

désertique [dezɛʀtik] a desert cpd; barren, empty.

désescalade [dezɛskalad] nf (MIL) de-escalation.

désespéré, e [dezɛspeʀe] a desperate; ~ment ad desperately.

désespérer [dezɛspeʀe] vt to drive to despair // vi, se ~ vi to despair; ~ de to despair of.

désespoir [dezɛspwaʀ] nm despair; **faire le** ~ **de qn** to be the despair of sb; **en** ~ **de cause** in desperation.

déshabillé, e [dezabije] a undressed // nm négligée.

déshabiller [dezabije] vt to undress; **se** ~ to undress (o.s.).

déshabituer [dezabitɥe] vt: **se** ~ **de** to get out of the habit of.

désherbant [dezɛʀbɑ̃] nm weed-killer.

déshériter [dezeʀite] vt to disinherit.

déshérités [dezeʀite] nmpl: **les** ~ the underprivileged.

déshonneur [dezɔnœʀ] nm dishonour, disgrace.

déshonorer [dezɔnɔʀe] vt to dishonour, bring disgrace upon.

déshydraté, e [dezidʀate] a dehydrated.

desiderata [deziderata] nmpl requirements.

désignation [deziɲasjɔ̃] nf naming, appointment; (signe, mot) name, designat on.

désigner [deziɲe] vt (montrer) to point out, indicate; (dénommer) to denote, refer to; (nommer: candidat etc) to name, appoint.

désillusion [dezilyzjɔ̃] nf disillusion(ment).

désinence [dezinɑ̃s] nf ending, inflexion.

désinfectant, e [dezɛ̃fɛktɑ̃, -ɑ̃t] a, nm disinfectant.

désinfecter [dezɛ̃fɛkte] vt to disinfect.

désinfection [dezɛfɛksjɔ̃] nf disinfection.

désintégrer [dezɛ̃tegʀe] vt, se ~ vi to disintegrate.

désintéressé, e [dezɛ̃teʀese] a disinterested, unselfish.

désintéresser [dezɛ̃teʀese] vt: se ~ (de) to lose interest (in).

désintoxication [dezɛ̃tɔksikɑsjɔ̃] nf treatment for alcoholism.

désinvolte [dezɛ̃vɔlt(ə)] a casual, off-hand; **désinvolture** nf casualness.

désir [deziʀ] nm wish; (fort, sensuel) desire.

désirer [deziʀe] vt to want, wish for; (sexuellement) to desire; **je désire** ... (formule de politesse) I would like ...; **il désire que tu l'aides** he would like ou he wants you to help him; ~ **faire** to want ou wish to do.

désireux, euse [deziʀø, -øz] a: ~ de **faire** anxious to do.

désistement [dezistəmɑ̃] nm withdrawal.

désister [deziste]: se ~ vi to stand down, withdraw.

désobéir [dezɔbeiʀ] vi: ~ (à qn/qch) to disobey (sb/sth); **désobéissance** nf disobedience; **désobéissant**, e a disobedient.

désobligeant, e [dezɔbliʒɑ̃, -ɑ̃t] a disagreeable, unpleasant.

désodorisant [dezɔdɔʀizɑ̃] nm air freshener, deodorizer.

désœuvré, e [dezœvʀe] a idle; **désœuvrement** nm idleness.

désolation [dezɔlɑsjɔ̃] nf distress, grief; desolation, devastation.

désolé, e [dezɔle] a (paysage) desolate; **je suis** ~ I'm sorry.

désoler [dezɔle] vt to distress, grieve.

désolidariser [desɔlidaʀize] vt: se ~ de ou d'avec to dissociate o.s. from.

désopilant, e [dezɔpilɑ̃, -ɑ̃t] a screamingly funny, hilarious.

désordonné, e [dezɔʀdɔne] a untidy, disorderly.

désordre [dezɔʀdʀ(ə)] nm disorder(liness), untidiness; (anarchie) disorder; ~s nmpl (POL) disturbances, disorder sg; **en** ~ in a mess, untidy.

désorganiser [dezɔʀganize] vt to disorganize.

désorienté, e [dezɔʀjɑ̃te] a disorientated; (fig) bewildered.

désormais [dezɔʀmɛ] ad in future, from now on.

désosser [dezɔse] vt to bone.

despote [dɛspɔt] nm despot; tyrant; **despotisme** nm despotism.

desquels, desquelles [dekɛl] prép + pronom voir **lequel**.

dessaisir [deseziʀ]: se ~ de vt to give up, part with.

dessaler [desale] vt (eau de mer) to desalinate; (CULIN) to soak.

desséché, e [deseʃe] a dried up.

dessécher [deseʃe] vt to dry out, parch; se ~ vi to dry out.

dessein [desɛ̃] nm design; **dans le** ~ **de** with the intention of; **à** ~ intentionally, deliberately.

desserrer [deseʀe] vt to loosen; (frein) to release; (poing, dents) to unclench; (objets alignés) to space out.

dessert [desɛʀ] nm dessert, pudding.

desserte [desɛʀt(ə)] nf (table) sideboard table; (transport): **la** ~ **du village est assurée par autocar** there is a coach service to the village.

desservir [desɛʀviʀ] vt (ville, quartier) to serve; (nuire à) to go against, put at a disadvantage; ~ (**la table**) to clear the table.

dessin [desɛ̃] nm (œuvre, art) drawing; (motif) pattern, design; (contour) (out)line; ~ **animé** cartoon (film); ~ **humoristique** cartoon.

dessinateur, trice [desinatœʀ, -tʀis] nm/f drawer; (de bandes dessinées) cartoonist; (industriel) draughtsman.

dessiner [desine] vt to draw; (concevoir: carrosserie, maison) to design.

dessoûler [desule] vt, vi to sober up.

dessous [dəsu] ad underneath, beneath // nm underside // nmpl (sous-vêtements) underwear sg; **en** ~, **par** ~ underneath; **below**; **au**—**below**; **de** ~ **le lit** from under the bed; **au**—**de below**; (peu digne de) beneath; **avoir le** ~ to get the worst of it; ~-**de-plat** nm inv tablemat.

dessus [dəsy] ad on top; (collé, écrit) on it // nm top; **en** ~ above; **par** ~ ad over it // prép over; **au**—~ above; **au**—**de** above; **avoir le** ~ to get the upper hand; ~-**de-lit** nm inv bedspread.

destin [dɛstɛ̃] nm fate; (avenir) destiny.

destinataire [dɛstinatɛʀ] nm/f (POSTES) addressee; (d'un colis) consignee.

destination [dɛstinɑsjɔ̃] nf (lieu) destination; (usage) purpose; **à** ~ **de** bound for, travelling to.

destinée [dɛstine] nf fate; (existence, avenir) destiny.

destiner [dɛstine] vt: ~ **qn à** (poste, sort) to destine sb for, intend sb to + verbe; ~ **qn/qch à** (prédestiner) to mark sb/sth out for, destine sb/sth to + verbe; ~ **qch à** (envisager d'affecter) to intend to use sth for; ~ **qch à qn** (envisager de donner) to inte... to give sth to sb, intend sb to have sth; (adresser) to intend sth for sb; to aim sth at sb; se ~ **à l'enseignement** to intend to become a teacher; **être destiné à** (sort) to be destined to + verbe; (usage) to be intended ou meant for; (suj: sort) to be in store for.

destituer [dɛstitɥe] vt to depose.

destructeur, trice [dɛstʀyktœʀ, -tʀis] a destructive.

destruction [dɛstʀyksjɔ̃] nf destruction.

désuet, ète [desɥɛ, -ɛt] a outdated, outmoded; **désuétude** nf: **tomber en désuétude** to fall into disuse, become obsolete.

désuni, e [dezyni] a divided, disunited.

détachant [detaʃɑ̃] nm stain remover.

détachement [detaʃmɑ̃] nm detachment.

détacher [detaʃe] vt (enlever) to detach, remove; (délier) to untie; (ADMIN): ~ **qn** (auprès de/à) to send sb on secondment (to); (MIL) to detail; se ~ vi (tomber) to come off; to come out; (se défaire) to come undone; (SPORT) to pull ou break away; **se**

~ **sur** to stand out against; **se** ~ **de** (*se désintéresser*) to grow away from.

détail [detaj] *nm* detail; (*comm*): **le** ~ retail; **au** ~ **ad** (*comm*) retail; separately; **donner le** ~ **de** to give a detailed account of; (*compte*) to give a breakdown of; **en** ~ in detail.

détaillant [detajã] *nm* retailer.

détaillé, e [detaje] *a* (*récit*) detailed.

détailler [detaje] *vt* (*comm*) to sell retail; to sell separately; (*expliquer*) to explain in detail; to detail; (*examiner*) to look over, examine.

détartrant [detartrã] *nm* descaling agent.

détaxer [detakse] *vt* to reduce the tax on; to remove the tax from.

détecter [detɛkte] *vt* to detect; **détecteur** *nm* detector; **détection** *nf* detection.

détective [detɛktiv] *nm* (*Brit: policier*) detective; ~ (**privé**) private detective *ou* investigator.

déteindre [detɛ̃dʀ(ə)] *vi* (*tissu*) to lose its colour; (*fig*): ~ **sur** to rub off on.

dételer [detle] *vt* to unharness; to unhitch.

détendre [detɑ̃dʀ(ə)] *vt* (*fil*) to slacken, loosen; (*relaxer*) to relax; **se** ~ to lose its tension; to relax.

détenir [detniʀ] *vt* (*fortune, objet, secret*) to be in possession of, have (in one's possession); (*prisonnier*) to detain, hold; (*record*) to hold; ~ **le pouvoir** to be in power.

détente [detɑ̃t] *nf* relaxation; (*POL*) détente; (*d'une arme*) trigger; (*d'un athlète qui saute*) spring.

détenteur, trice [detɑ̃tœʀ, -tʀis] *nm/f* holder.

détention [detɑ̃sjɔ̃] *nf* possession; detention; holding; ~ **préventive** (pretrial) custody.

détenu, e [detny] *nm/f* prisoner.

détergent [detɛʀʒɑ̃] *nm* detergent.

détérioration [deteʀjɔʀasjɔ̃] *nf* damaging; deterioration, worsening.

détériorer [deteʀjɔʀe] *vt* to damage; **se** ~ *vi* to deteriorate.

déterminant [detɛʀminɑ̃] *nm* (*LING*) determiner.

détermination [detɛʀminasjɔ̃] *nf* determining; (*résolution*) determination.

déterminé, e [detɛʀmine] *a* (*résolu*) determined; (*précis*) specific, definite.

déterminer [detɛʀmine] *vt* (*fixer*) to determine; (*décider*): ~ **qn à faire** to decide sb to do; **se** ~ **à faire** to make up one's mind to do.

déterrer [detɛʀe] *vt* to dig up.

détersif [detɛʀsif] *nm* detergent.

détestable [detɛstabl(ə)] *a* foul, ghastly; detestable, odious.

détester [detɛste] *vt* to hate, detest.

détonant, e [detɔnɑ̃, -ɑ̃t] *a*: **mélange** ~ explosive mixture.

détonateur [detɔnatœʀ] *nm* detonator.

détonation [detɔnasjɔ̃] *nf* detonation, bang, report (of a gun).

détoner [detɔne] *vi* to detonate, explode.

détonner [detɔne] *vi* (*MUS*) to go out of tune; (*fig*) to clash.

détour [detuʀ] *nm* detour; (*tournant*) bend, curve; **sans** ~ (*fig*) without beating

about the bush, in a straightforward manner.

détourné, e [detuʀne] *a* (*moyen*) roundabout.

détournement [detuʀnəmɑ̃] *nm* diversion, rerouting; ~ **d'avion** hijacking; ~ (**de fonds**) embezzlement *ou* misappropriation (of funds); ~ **de mineur** corruption of a minor.

détourner [detuʀne] *vt* to divert; (*avion*) to divert, reroute; (: *par la force*) to hijack; (*yeux, tête*) to turn away; (*de l'argent*) to embezzle, misappropriate; **se** ~ to turn away.

détracteur, trice [detʀaktœʀ, -tʀis] *nm/f* disparager, critic.

détraquer [detʀake] *vt* to put out of order; (*estomac*) to upset; **se** ~ *vi* to go wrong.

détrempe [detʀɑ̃p] *nf* (*ART*) tempera.

détrempé, e [detʀɑ̃pe] *a* (*sol*) sodden, waterlogged.

détresse [detʀɛs] *nf* distress.

détriment [detʀimɑ̃] *nm*: **au** ~ **de** to the detriment of.

détritus [detʀitys] *nmpl* rubbish *sg*, refuse *sg*.

détroit [detʀwa] *nm* strait.

détromper [detʀɔ̃pe] *vt* to disabuse.

détrôner [detʀone] *vt* to dethrone, depose; (*fig*) to oust, dethrone.

détrousser [detʀuse] *vt* to rob.

détruire [detʀɥiʀ] *vt* to destroy.

dette [dɛt] *nf* debt.

D.E.U.G. [dœg] *sigle m* = **diplôme d'études universitaires générales**.

deuil [dœj] *nm* (*perte*) bereavement; (*période*) mourning; (*chagrin*) grief; **porter le/être en** ~ to wear/be in mourning.

deux [dø] *num* two; **les** ~ both; **ses** ~ **mains** both his hands, his two hands; **les** ~ **points** the colon *sg*; **deuxième** *num* second; ~-**pièces** *nm inv* (*tailleur*) two-piece suit; (*de bain*) two-piece (swimsuit); (*appartement*) two-roomed flat; ~-**roues** *nm inv* two-wheeled vehicle; ~-**temps** *a* two-stroke.

devais *etc vb voir* **devoir**.

dévaler [devale] *vt* to hurtle down.

dévaliser [devalize] *vt* to rob, burgle.

dévaloriser [devalɔʀize] *vt*, **se** ~ *vi* to depreciate.

dévaluation [devalɥasjɔ̃] *nf* depreciation; (*ÉCON: mesure*) devaluation.

dévaluer [devalɥe] *vt* to devalue.

devancer [dəvɑ̃se] *vt* to be ahead of; to get ahead of; to arrive before; (*prévenir*) to anticipate; ~ **l'appel** (*MIL*) to enlist before call-up; **devancier, ière** *nm/f* precursor.

devant [dəvɑ̃] *ad* in front; (*à distance: en avant*) ahead // *prép* in front of; ahead of; (*avec mouvement: passer*) past; (*fig*) before, in front of; faced with, in the face of; in view of // *nm* front; **prendre les** ~**s** to make the first move; **les pattes de** ~ the front legs, the forelegs; **par** ~ (*boutonner*) at the front; (*entrer*) the front way; **aller au-**~ **de qn** to go out to meet sb ; **aller au-~ de** (*désirs de* qn) to anticipate.

devanture [dəvɑ̃tyʀ] *nf* (*façade*) (shop) front ; (*étalage*) display ; (shop) window.

dévastation [devastɑsjɔ̃] *nf* devastation.

dévaster [devaste] *vt* to devastate.

déveine [devɛn] *nf* rotten luck q.

développement [devlɔpmɑ̃] *nm* development.

développer [devlɔpe] *vt* to develop ; **se ~** *vi* to develop.

devenir [dəvniʀ] *vb avec attribut* to become ; **~ instituteur** to become a teacher ; **que sont-ils devenus?** what has become of them?

dévergondé, e [devɛʀgɔ̃de] *a* wild, shameless.

devers [dəvɛʀ] *ad*: **par ~ soi** to oneself.

déverser [devɛʀse] *vt* (*liquide*) to pour (out) ; (*ordures*) to tip (out) ; **se ~ dans** (*fleuve, mer*) to flow into ; **déversoir** *nm* overflow.

dévêtir [devetiʀ] *vt*, **se ~** to undress.

devez *etc vb voir* **devoir**.

déviation [devjɑsjɔ̃] *nf* (*aussi* AUTO) diversion ; **~ de la colonne** (**vertébrale**) curvature of the spine.

dévider [devide] *vt* to unwind ; **dévidoir** *nm* reel.

devienne *etc vb voir* **devenir**.

dévier [devje] *vt* (*fleuve, circulation*) to divert ; (*coup*) to deflect // *vi* to veer (off course) ; (**faire**) **~** (*projectile*) to deflect ; (*véhicule*) to push off course.

devin [dəvɛ̃] *nm* soothsayer, seer.

deviner [dəvine] *vt* to guess ; (*prévoir*) to foretell ; to foresee ; (*apercevoir*) to distinguish.

devinette [dəvinɛt] *nf* riddle.

devins *etc vb voir* **devenir**.

devis [dəvi] *nm* estimate, quotation.

dévisager [devizaʒe] *vt* to stare at.

devise [dəviz] *nf* (*formule*) motto, watchword ; (ÉCON: *monnaie*) currency ; **~s** *nfpl* (*argent*) currency *sg*.

deviser [dəvize] *vi* to converse.

dévisser [devise] *vt* to unscrew, undo ; **se ~** *vi* to come unscrewed.

dévoiler [devwale] *vt* to unveil.

devoir [dəvwaʀ] *nm* duty ; (SCOL) piece of homework, homework q ; (: *en classe*) exercise // *vt* (*argent, respect*): **~ qch (à** qn) to owe (sb) sth ; (*suivi de l'infinitif: obligation*): **il doit le faire** he has to do it, he must do it ; (: *intention*): **il doit partir demain** he is (due) to leave tomorrow ; (: *probabilité*): **il doit être tard** it must be late.

dévolu, e [devɔly] *a*: **~ à** allotted to // *nm*: **jeter son ~ sur** to fix one's choice on.

dévorant, e [devɔʀɑ̃, -ɑ̃t] *a* (*faim, passion*) raging.

dévorer [devɔʀe] *vt* to devour ; (*suj: feu, soucis*) to consume.

dévot, e [devo, -ɔt] *a* devout, pious.

dévotion [devɔsjɔ̃] *nf* devoutness ; **être à la ~ de** qn to be totally devoted to sb.

dévoué, e [devwe] *a* devoted.

dévouement [devumɑ̃] *nm* devotion, dedication.

dévouer [devwe]: **se ~** *vi* (*se sacrifier*): **se ~** (*pour*) to sacrifice o.s. (for) ; (*se consacrer*): **se ~ à** to devote ou dedicate o.s. to.

dévoyé, e [devwaje] *a* delinquent.

devrai *etc vb voir* **devoir**.

dextérité [dɛksteʀite] *nf* skill, dexterity.

diabète [djabɛt] *nm* diabetes *sg* ; **diabétique** *nm/f* diabetic.

diable [djɑbl(ə)] *nm* devil ; **diabolique** *a* diabolical.

diabolo [djabɔlo] *nm* (*boisson*) lemonade and fruit (*ou* mint *etc*) cordial.

diacre [djakʀ(ə)] *nm* deacon.

diadème [djadɛm] *nm* diadem.

diagnostic [djagnɔstik] *nm* diagnosis *sg* ; **diagnostiquer** *vt* to diagnose.

diagonal, e, aux [djagɔnal, -o] *a, nf* diagonal ; **en ~e** diagonally ; **lire en ~e** to skim through.

diagramme [djagʀam] *nm* chart, graph.

dialecte [djalɛkt(ə)] *nm* dialect.

dialogue [djalɔg] *nm* dialogue ; **dialoguer** *vi* to converse ; (POL) to have a dialogue.

diamant [djamɑ̃] *nm* diamond ; **diamantaire** *nm* diamond dealer.

diamètre [djamɛtʀ(ə)] *nm* diameter.

diapason [djapazɔ̃] *nm* tuning fork.

diaphragme [djafʀagm] *nm* (ANAT, PHOTO) diaphragm ; (*contraceptif*) diaphragm, cap ; **ouverture du ~** (PHOTO) aperture.

diapositive [djapozitiv] *nf* transparency, slide.

diapré, e [djapʀe] *a* many-coloured.

diarrhée [djaʀe] *nf* diarrhoea.

diatribe [djatʀib] *nf* diatribe.

dictaphone [diktafɔn] *nm* Dictaphone.

dictateur [diktatœʀ] *nm* dictator ; **dictatorial, e, aux** *a* dictatorial ; **dictature** *nf* dictatorship.

dictée [dikte] *nf* dictation ; **prendre sous ~** to take down (*sth dictated*).

dicter [dikte] *vt* to dictate.

diction [diksjɔ̃] *nf* diction, delivery ; **cours de ~** speech production lesson.

dictionnaire [diksjɔnɛʀ] *nm* dictionary ; **~ bilingue/encyclopédique** bilingual/encyclopaedic dictionary.

dicton [diktɔ̃] *nm* saying, dictum.

didactique [didaktik] *a* technical ; didactic.

dièse [djɛz] *nm* sharp.

diesel [djezɛl] *nm, a inv* diesel.

diète [djɛt] *nf* (*jeûne*) starvation diet ; (*régime*) diet ; **être à la ~** to be on a starvation diet.

diététicien, ne [djetetisjɛ̃, -jɛn] *nm/f* dietician.

diététique [djetetik] *nf* dietetics *sg* ; **magasin ~** health food shop.

dieu, x [djø] *nm* god ; **D~** God ; **le bon D~** the good Lord.

diffamation [difamɑsjɔ̃] *nf* slander ; (*écrite*) libel ; **attaquer** qn **en ~** to sue sb for libel (*ou* slander).

diffamer [difame] *vt* to slander, defame ; to libel.

différé [difeʀe] *nm* (TV): **en ~** (pre-)recorded.

différence [diferɑ̃s] nf difference ; à la ~ de unlike.

différencier [diferɑ̃sje] vt to differentiate ; se ~ vi (organisme) to become differentiated ; se ~ de to differentiate o.s. from ; to differ from.

différend [diferɑ̃] nm difference (of opinion), disagreement.

différent, e [diferɑ̃, -ɑ̃t] a: ~ (de) different (from) ; ~s objets different ou various objects.

différentiel, le [diferɑ̃sjɛl] a, nm differential.

différer [difere] vt to postpone, put off // vi: ~ (de) to differ (from) ; ~ de faire to delay doing.

difficile [difisil] a difficult ; (exigeant) hard to please, difficult (to please) ; ~ment with difficulty ; ~ment lisible difficult ou hard to read.

difficulté [difikylte] nf difficulty ; en ~ (bateau, alpiniste) in trouble ou difficulties ; avoir de la ~ à faire to have difficulty (in) doing.

difforme [difɔrm(ə)] a deformed, misshapen ; **difformité** nf deformity.

diffracter [difrakte] vt to diffract.

diffus, e [dify, -yz] a diffuse.

diffuser [difyze] vt (chaleur, bruit) to diffuse ; (émission, musique) to broadcast ; (nouvelle, idée) to circulate ; (COMM) to distribute ; **diffuseur** nm diffuser ; distributor ; **diffusion** nf diffusion ; broadcast(ing) ; circulation ; distribution.

digérer [diʒere] vt to digest ; (fig: accepter) to stomach, put up with ; **digestible** a digestible ; **digestif, ive** a digestive // nm (after-dinner) liqueur ; **digestion** nf digestion.

digital, e, aux [diʒital, -o] a digital.

digne [diɲ] a dignified ; ~ de worthy of ; ~ de foi trustworthy.

dignitaire [diɲitɛr] nm dignitary.

dignité [diɲite] nf dignity.

digue [dig] nf dike, dyke.

dilapider [dilapide] vt to squander, waste.

dilater [dilate] vt to dilate ; (gaz, métal) to cause to expand ; (ballon) to distend ; se ~ vi to expand.

dilemme [dilɛm] nm dilemma.

diligence [diliʒɑ̃s] nf stagecoach, diligence ; (empressement) despatch.

diligent, e [diliʒɑ̃, -ɑ̃t] a prompt and efficient, diligent.

diluer [dilɥe] vt to dilute.

diluvien, ne [dilyvjɛ̃, -jɛn] a: pluie ~ne torrential rain.

dimanche [dimɑ̃ʃ] nm Sunday.

dimension [dimɑ̃sjɔ̃] nf (grandeur) size ; (cote, de l'espace) dimension.

diminuer [diminɥe] vt to reduce, decrease ; (ardeur etc) to lessen ; (personne: physiquement) to undermine ; (dénigrer) to belittle // vi to decrease, diminish, diminutif nm (LING) diminutive ; (surnom) pet name ; **diminution** nf decreasing, diminishing.

dinde [dɛ̃d] nf turkey.

dindon [dɛ̃dɔ̃] nm turkey.

dîner [dine] nm dinner // vi to have dinner.

dingue [dɛ̃g] a (fam) crazy.

diode [djɔd] nf diode.

diphtérie [difteri] nf diphtheria.

diphtongue [diftɔ̃g] nf diphthong.

diplomate [diplɔmat] a diplomatic // nm diplomat ; (fig) diplomatist.

diplomatie [diplɔmasi] nf diplomacy ; **diplomatique** a diplomatic.

diplôme [diplom] nm diploma, certificate ; (diploma) examination ; **diplômé, e** a qualified.

dire [dir] nm: au ~ de according to ; leur ~s what they say // vt to say ; (secret, mensonge) to tell ; ~ l'heure/la vérité to tell the time/the truth ; ~ qch à qn to tell sb sth ; ~ que to say that ; ~ à qn que to tell sb that ; ~ à qn qu'il fasse ou de faire to tell sb to do ; on dit que they say that ; si cela lui dit (plaire) if he fancies it ; que dites-vous de (penser) what do you think of ; on dirait que it looks (ou sounds etc) as though.

direct, e [dirɛkt] a direct // nm (TV): en ~ live ; ~ement ad directly.

directeur, trice [dirɛktœr, -tris] nm/f (d'entreprise) director ; (de service) manager/eress ; (d'école) headmaster/mistress ; ~ de thèse (SCOL) supervisor.

direction [dirɛksjɔ̃] nf management ; conducting ; supervision ; (AUTO) steering ; (sens) direction ; sous la ~ de (MUS) conducted by.

directive [dirɛktiv] nf directive, instruction.

dirent vb voir **dire**.

dirigeable [diriʒabl(ə)] a, nm: (ballon) ~ dirigible.

dirigeant, e [diriʒɑ̃, -ɑ̃t] a managerial ; ruling // nm/f (d'un parti etc) leader ; (d'entreprise) manager, member of the management.

diriger [diriʒe] vt (entreprise) to manage, run ; (véhicule) to steer ; (orchestre) to conduct ; (recherches, travaux) to supervise, be in charge of ; (braquer: regard, arme): ~ sur to point ou level ou aim at ; (fig: critiques): ~ contre to aim at ; se ~ (s'orienter) to find one's way ; se ~ vers ou sur to make ou head for.

dirigisme [diriʒism(ə)] nm (ÉCON) state intervention, interventionism.

dis etc vb voir **dire**.

discernement [disɛrnəmɑ̃] nm discernment, judgment.

discerner [disɛrne] vt to discern, make out.

disciple [disipl(ə)] nm/f disciple.

disciplinaire [disiplinɛr] a disciplinary.

discipline [disiplin] nf discipline ; **discipliné, e** a (well-)disciplined ; **discipliner** vt to discipline ; to control.

discontinu, e [diskɔ̃tiny] a intermittent.

discontinuer [diskɔ̃tinɥe] vi: sans ~ without stopping, without a break.

disconvenir [diskɔ̃vnir] vi: ne pas ~ de qch/que not to deny sth/that.

discordance [diskɔrdɑ̃s] nf discordance ; conflict.

discordant, e [diskɔrdɑ̃, -ɑ̃t] a discordant ; conflicting.

discorde [diskɔRd(ə)] *nf* discord, dissension.

discothèque [diskɔtɛk] *nf* (*disques*) record collection ; (: *dans une bibliothèque*) record library ; (*boîte de nuit*) disco(thèque).

discourir [diskuRiR] *vi* to discourse, hold forth.

discours [diskuR] *nm* speech.

discréditer [diskRedite] *vt* to discredit.

discret, ète [diskRɛ, -ɛt] *a* (*fig*) unobtrusive ; quiet ; **discrètement** *ad* discreetly.

discrétion [diskResjɔ̃] *nf* discretion ; **être à la ~ de qn** to be in sb's hands ; **à ~** unlimited ; as much as one wants.

discrimination [diskRiminasjɔ̃] *nf* discrimination ; **sans ~** indiscriminately ; **discriminatoire** *a* discriminatory.

disculper [diskylpe] *vt* to exonerate.

discussion [diskysjɔ̃] *nf* discussion.

discuté, e [diskyte] *a* controversial.

discuter [diskyte] *vt* (*contester*) to question, dispute ; (*débattre: prix*) to discuss // *vi* to talk ; (*ergoter*) to argue ; **~ de** to discuss.

dise *etc vb voir* **dire**.

disert, e [dizɛR, -ɛRt(ə)] *a* loquacious.

disette [dizɛt] *nf* food shortage.

diseuse [dizøz] *nf*: **~ de bonne aventure** fortuneteller.

disgrâce [disgRɑs] *nf* disgrace.

disgracieux, euse [disgRasjø, -jøz] *a* ungainly, awkward.

disjoindre [diswɛ̃dR(ə)] *vt* to take apart ; **se ~** *vi* to come apart.

disjoncteur [disʒɔ̃ktœR] *nm* (*ÉLEC*) circuit breaker, cutout.

dislocation [dislɔkasjɔ̃] *nf* dislocation.

disloquer [dislɔke] *vt* (*membre*) to dislocate ; (*chaise*) to dismantle ; (*troupe*) to disperse ; **se ~** *vi* (*parti, empire*) to break up ; **se ~ l'épaule** to dislocate one's shoulder.

disons *vb voir* **dire**.

disparaître [dispaRɛtR(ə)] *vi* to disappear ; (*à la vue*) to vanish, disappear ; to be hidden *ou* concealed ; (*être manquant*) to go missing, disappear ; (*se perdre: traditions etc*) to die out ; **faire ~** to remove ; to get rid of.

disparate [dispaRat] *a* disparate ; ill-assorted.

disparité [dispaRite] *nf* disparity.

disparition [dispaRisjɔ̃] *nf* disappearance.

disparu, e [dispaRy] *nm/f* missing person ; (*défunt*) departed.

dispendieux, euse [dispɑ̃djø, -jøz] *a* extravagant, expensive.

dispensaire [dispɑ̃sɛR] *nm* community clinic.

dispense [dispɑ̃s] *nf* exemption ; **~ d'âge** special exemption from age limit.

dispenser [dispɑ̃se] *vt* (*donner*) to lavish, bestow ; (*exempter*): **~ qn de** to exempt sb from ; **se ~ de** to avoid ; to get out of.

disperser [dispɛRse] *vt* to scatter ; (*fig: son attention*) to dissipate ; **se ~** *vi* to scatter ; (*fig*) to dissipate one's efforts.

disponibilité [disponibilite] *nf* availability ; (*ADMIN*): **être en ~** to be on leave of absence.

disponible [disponibl(ə)] *a* available.

dispos [dispo] *am*: (*frais et*) **~** fresh (as a daisy).

disposé, e [dispoze] *a* (*d'une certaine manière*) arranged, laid-out ; **bien/mal ~** (*humeur*) in a good/bad mood ; **~ à** (*prêt à*) willing *ou* prepared to.

disposer [dispoze] *vt* (*arranger, placer*) to arrange ; (*inciter*): **~ qn à qch/faire qch** to dispose *ou* incline sb towards sth/to do sth // *vi*: **vous pouvez ~** you may leave ; **~ de** *vt* to have (at one's disposal) ; to use ; **se ~ à faire** to prepare to do, be about to do.

dispositif [dispozitif] *nm* device ; (*fig*) system, plan of action ; set-up.

disposition [dispozisjɔ̃] *nf* (*arrangement*) arrangement, layout ; (*humeur*) mood ; (*tendance*) tendency ; **~s** *nfpl* (*mesures*) steps, measures ; (*préparatifs*) arrangements ; (*testamentaires*) provisions ; (*aptitudes*) bent *sg*, aptitude *sg* ; **à la ~ de qn** at sb's disposal.

disproportion [dispRopoRsjɔ̃] *nf* disproportion ; **disproportionné, e** *a* disproportionate, out of all proportion.

dispute [dispyt] *nf* quarrel, argument.

disputer [dispyte] *vt* (*match*) to play ; (*combat*) to fight ; (*course*) to run, fight ; **se ~** *vi* to quarrel, have a quarrel ; **~ qch à qn** to fight with sb for *ou* over sth.

disquaire [diskɛR] *nm/f* record dealer.

disqualification [diskalifikasjɔ̃] *nf* disqualification.

disqualifier [diskalifje] *vt* to disqualify.

disque [disk(ə)] *nm* (*MUS*) record ; (*forme, pièce*) disc ; (*SPORT*) discus ; **~ d'embrayage** (*AUTO*) clutch plate.

dissection [disɛksjɔ̃] *nf* dissection.

dissemblable [disɑ̃blabl(ə)] *a* dissimilar.

disséminer [disemine] *vt* to scatter.

disséquer [diseke] *vt* to dissect.

dissertation [disɛRtasjɔ̃] *nf* (*SCOL*) essay.

disserter [disɛRte] *vi*: **~ sur** to discourse upon.

dissident, e [disidɑ̃, -ɑ̃t] *a, nm/f* dissident.

dissimulation [disimylasjɔ̃] *nf* concealing ; (*duplicité*) dissimulation.

dissimuler [disimyle] *vt* to conceal ; **se ~** to conceal o.s. ; to be concealed.

dissipation [disipasjɔ̃] *nf* squandering ; unruliness ; (*débauche*) dissipation.

dissiper [disipe] *vt* to dissipate ; (*fortune*) to squander, fritter away ; **se ~** *vi* (*brouillard*) to clear, disperse ; (*doutes*) to disappear, melt away ; (*élève*) to become undisciplined *ou* unruly.

dissolu, e [disɔly] *a* dissolute.

dissolution [disɔlysjɔ̃] *nf* dissolving ; (*POL, JUR*) dissolution.

dissolvant, e [disɔlvɑ̃, -ɑ̃t] *a* (*fig*) debilitating // *nm* (*CHIMIE*) solvent ; **~ (gras)** nail varnish remover.

dissonant, e [disonɑ̃, -ɑ̃t] *a* discordant.

dissoudre [disudR(ə)] *vt* to dissolve ; **se ~** *vi* to dissolve.

dissuader [disɥade] *vt*: **~ qn de faire/de qch** to dissuade sb from doing/from sth.

dissuasion [disчuzjɔ̃] *nf* dissuasion; **force de ~** deterrent power.

dissymétrique [disimetʀik] **a** dissymmetrical.

distance [distɑ̃s] *nf* distance; *(fig: écart)* gap; **à ~** at *ou* from a distance; **à une ~ de 10 km, à 10 km de ~** 10 km away, at a distance of 10 km; **à 2 ans de ~** with a gap of 2 years; **garder ses ~s** to keep one's distance; **tenir la ~** *(SPORT)* to cover the distance, last the course; **distancer** *vt* to outdistance, leave behind.

distant, e [distɑ̃, -ɑ̃t] **a** *(réservé)* distant, aloof; *(éloigné)* distant, far away; **~ de** *(lieu)* far away *ou* a long way from; **~ de 5 km** *(d'un lieu)* 5 km away (from a place).

distendre [distɑ̃dʀ(ə)] *vt*, **se ~** *vi* to distend.

distillation [distilɑsjɔ̃] *nf* distillation, distilling.

distillé, e [distile] **a**: **eau ~e** distilled water.

distiller [distile] *vt* to distil; *(fig)* to exude; **to ·** elaborate: **distillerie** *nf* distillery.

distinct, e [distɛ̃(kt), distɛ̃kt(ə)] **a** distinct; **distinctement** *ad* distinctly; **distinctif, ive a** distinctive.

distinction [distɛ̃ksjɔ̃] *nf* distinction.

distingué, e [distɛ̃ge] **a** distinguished.

distinguer [distɛ̃ge] *vt* to distinguish.

distraction [distʀaksjɔ̃] *nf* *(manque d'attention)* absent-mindedness; *(oubli)* lapse (in concentration *ou* attention); *(détente)* diversion, recreation; *(passe-temps)* distraction, entertainment.

distraire [distʀɛʀ] *vt* *(déranger)* to distract; *(divertir)* to entertain, divert; *(détourner: somme d'argent)* to divert, misappropriate; **se ~** to amuse ou enjoy o.s.

distrait, e [distʀɛ, -ɛt] **a** absent-minded.

distribuer [distʀibчe] *vt* to distribute; to hand out; *(CARTES)* to deal (out); *(courrier)* to deliver; **distributeur** *nm* *(COMM)* distributor; *(automatique)* (vending *ou* slot) machine; **distribution** *nf* distribution; *(postale)* delivery; *(choix d'acteurs)* casting, cast; **distribution des prix** *(SCOL)* prize giving.

district [distʀik(t)] *nm* district.

dit, e [di, dit] *pp de* **dire** *// a (fixé):* **le jour ~** the arranged day; *(surnommé):* **X, ~ Pierrot** X, known as *ou* called Pierrot.

dites *vb voir* **dire**.

dithyrambique [ditiʀɑ̃bik] **a** eulogistic.

diurétique [djyʀetik] **a** diuretic.

diurne [djyʀn(ə)] **a** diurnal, daytime *cpd*.

divagations [divagɑsjɔ̃] *nfpl* wanderings, ramblings; ravings.

divaguer [divage] *vi* to ramble; to rave.

divan [divɑ̃] *nm* divan; **~-lit** *nm* divan (bed).

divergence [divɛʀʒɑ̃s] *nf* divergence.

divergent, e [divɛʀʒɑ̃, -u] **a** divergent.

diverger [divɛʀʒe] *vi* to diverge.

divers, e [divɛʀ, -ɛʀs(ə)] **a** *(varié)* diverse, varied; *(différent)* different, various, *// dét (plusieurs)* various, several; **(frais) ~** sundries, miscellaneous (expenses);

diversement *ad* in various *ou* diverse ways; **diversifier** *vt* to diversify.

diversion [divɛʀsjɔ̃] *nf* diversion; **faire ~** to create a diversion.

diversité [divɛʀsite] *nf* diversity; variety.

divertir [divɛʀtiʀ] *vt* to amuse, entertain; **se ~** to amuse *ou* enjoy o.s.; **divertissement** *nm* entertainment; *(MUS)* divertimento, divertissement.

dividende [dividɑ̃d] *nm* *(MATH, COMM)* dividend.

divin, e [divɛ̃, -in] **a** divine; **diviniser** *vt* to deify; **divinité** *nf* divinity.

diviser [divize] *vt* *(gén, MATH)* to divide; *(morceler, subdiviser)* to divide (up), split (up); **diviseur** *nm* *(MATH)* divisor; **division** *nf* *(gén)* division.

divorce [divɔʀs(ə)] *nm* divorce; **divorcé, e** *nm/f* divorcee; **divorcer** *vi* to get a divorce, get divorced; **divorcer de** *ou* **d'avec qn** to divorce sb.

divulgation [divylgɑsjɔ̃] *nf* disclosure.

divulguer [divylge] *vt* to divulge, disclose.

dix [dis] *num* ten; **dixième** *num* tenth.

dizaine [dizɛn] *nf* (10) ten; *(environ 10):* **une ~ (de)** about ten, ten or so.

do [do] *nm* *(note)* C; *(en chantant la gamme)* do(h).

docile [dɔsil] **a** docile; **docilité** *nf* docility.

dock [dɔk] *nm* dock.

docker [dɔkɛʀ] *nm* docker.

docte [dɔkt(ə)] **a** learned.

docteur [dɔktœʀ] *nm* doctor.

doctoral, e, aux [dɔktɔʀal, -o] **a** pompous, bombastic.

doctorat [dɔktɔʀa] *nm:* **~ d'Université ≈** Ph.D.; **~ d'état ≈** Higher Doctorate.

doctoresse [dɔktɔʀɛs] *nf* lady doctor.

doctrinaire [dɔktʀinɛʀ] **a** doctrinaire; pompous, sententious.

doctrine [dɔktʀin] *nf* doctrine.

document [dɔkymɑ̃] *nm* document.

documentaire [dɔkymɑ̃tɛʀ] **a**, *nm* documentary.

documentaliste [dɔkymɑ̃talist(ə)] *nm/f* archivist; researcher.

documentation [dɔkymɑ̃tɑsjɔ̃] *nf* documentation, literature; *(PRESSE, TV: service)* research.

documenté, e [dɔkymɑ̃te] **a** well-informed, well-documented; well-researched.

documenter [dɔkymɑ̃te] *vt:* **se ~ (sur)** to gather information *ou* material (on *ou* about).

dodeliner [dɔdline] *vi:* **~ de la tête** to nod one's head gently.

dodo [dɔdo] *nm:* **aller faire ~** to go to bye-byes.

dodu, e [dɔdy] **a** plump.

dogmatique [dɔgmatik] **a** dogmatic.

dogme [dɔgm(ə)] *nm* dogma.

dogue [dɔg] *nm* mastiff.

doigt [dwa] *nm* finger; **à deux ~s de** within an ace *ou* an inch of; **un ~ de lait/whisky** a drop of milk/whisky; **~ de pied** toe.

doigté [dwate] *nm* *(MUS)* fingering; fingering technique; *(fig: habileté)* diplomacy, tact.

doigtier [dwatje] *nm* fingerstall.
doit *etc vb voir* **devoir**.
doléances [dɔleɑ̃s] *nfpl* complaints;
grievances.
dolent, e [dɔlɑ̃, -ɑ̃t] *a* doleful, mournful.
dollar [dɔlaR] *nm* dollar.
D.O.M. [*parfois* dɔm] *sigle m ou mpl* =
département(s) d'outre-mer.
domaine [dɔmɛn] *nm* estate, property;
(*fig*) domain, field; **tomber dans le ~**
public (*JUR*) to be out of copyright.
domanial, e, aux [dɔmanjal, -jo] *a* (*forêt,*
biens) national, state *cpd*.
dôme [dom] *nm* dome.
domesticité [dɔmɛstisite] *nf* (domestic)
staff.
domestique [dɔmɛstik] *a* domestic //
nm/f servant, domestic.
domestiquer [dɔmɛstike] *vt* to
domesticate.
domicile [dɔmisil] *nm* home, place of
residence; **à ~** at home; **domicilié, e** *a*:
être domicilié à to have one's home in
ou at.
dominant, e [dɔminɑ̃, -ɑ̃t] *a* dominant;
predominant.
dominateur, trice [dɔminatœR, -tRis] *a*
dominating; domineering.
domination [dɔminasjɔ̃] *nf* domination.
dominer [dɔmine] *vt* to dominate;
(*passions etc*) to control, master;
(*surpasser*) to outclass, surpass;
(*surplomber*) to tower above, dominate //
vi to be in the dominant position; **se ~**
to control o.s.
dominical, e, aux [dɔminikal, -o] *a*
Sunday *cpd*, dominical.
domino [dɔmino] *nm* domino; **~s** *nmpl*
(*jeu*) dominoes *sg*.
dommage [dɔmaʒ] *nm* (*préjudice*) harm,
injury; (*dégâts, pertes*) damage *q*; **c'est ~**
de faire/que it's a shame *ou* pity to
do/that; **~s-intérêts** *nmpl* damages.
dompter [dɔ̃te] *vt* to tame; **dompteur,**
euse *nm/f* trainer; liontamer.
don [dɔ̃] *nm* (*cadeau*) gift; (*charité*)
donation; (*aptitude*) gift, talent; **avoir des**
~s pour to have a gift *ou* talent for.
donateur, trice [dɔnatœR, -tRis] *nm/f*
donor.
donation [dɔnasjɔ̃] *nf* donation.
donc [dɔ̃k] *cj* therefore, so; (*après une*
digression) so, then.
donjon [dɔ̃ʒɔ̃] *nm* keep, donjon.
donné, e [dɔne] *a* (*convenu*) given // *nf*
(*MATH, gén*) datum (*pl* data); **étant ~ ...**
given ... .
donner [dɔne] *vt* to give; (*vieux habits etc*)
to give away; (*spectacle*) to show; to put
on; **~ qch à qn** to give sb sth, give sth
to sb; **~ sur** (*suj: fenêtre, chambre*) to look
(out) onto; **~ dans** (*piège etc*) to fall into;
se ~ à fond (à son travail) to give one's
all (to one's work); **s'en ~ à cœur joie**
(*fam*) to have a great time (of it).
donneur, euse [dɔnœR, -øz] *nm/f* (*MÉD*)
donor; (*CARTES*) dealer; **~ de sang** blood
donor.
dont [dɔ̃] *pronom relatif*: **la maison ~ je**
vois le toit the house whose roof I can
see, the house I can see the roof of; **la**

maison ~ le toit est rouge the house
whose roof is red *ou* the roof of which is
red; **l'homme ~ je connais la sœur** the
man whose sister I know; **10 blessés, ~**
2 grièvement 10 injured, 2 of them
seriously; **2 livres, ~ l'un est** 2 books,
one of which is; **il y avait plusieurs**
personnes, ~ Gabrielle there were
several people, among whom was
Gabrielle; **le fils ~ il est si fier** the son
he's so proud of; **ce ~ je parle** what I'm
talking about; *voir adjectifs et verbes à*
complément prépositionnel: **responsable**
de, souffrir de *etc*.
dorade [dɔrad] *nf* = **daurade.**
doré, e [dɔRe] *a* golden; (*avec dorure*) gilt,
gilded.
dorénavant [dɔRenavɑ̃] *ad* from now on,
henceforth.
dorer [dɔRe] *vt* (*cadre*) to gild; (*faire*) **~**
(*CULIN*) to brown (in the oven).
dorloter [dɔRlɔte] *vt* to pamper, cosset.
dormant, e [dɔRmɑ̃, -ɑ̃t] *a*: **eau ~e** still
water.
dormeur, euse [dɔRmœR, -øz] *nm/f* sleeper.
dormir [dɔRmiR] *vi* to sleep; (*être endormi*)
to be asleep.
dorsal, e, aux [dɔRsal, -o] *a* dorsal.
dortoir [dɔRtwaR] *nm* dormitory.
dorure [dɔRyR] *nf* gilding.
doryphore [dɔRifɔR] *nm* Colorado beetle.
dos [do] *nm* back; (*de livre*) spine; '**voir**
au ~' 'see over'; **de ~** from the back,
from behind; **à ~ de chameau** riding on
a camel.
dosage [dozaʒ] *nm* mixture.
dos-d'âne [dodɑn] *nm* humpback.
dose [doz] *nf* dose.
doser [doze] *vt* to measure out; to mix
in the correct proportions; (*fig*) to expend
in the right amounts *ou* proportion; to
strike a balance between; **doseur** *nm*
measure.
dossard [dosaR] *nm* number (*worn by*
competitor).
dossier [dosje] *nm* (*renseignements, fichier*)
file; (*enveloppe*) folder, file; (*de chaise*)
back.
dot [dɔt] *nf* dowry.
doter [dɔte] *vt*: **~ qn/qch de** to equip
sb/sth with.
douairière [dwɛRjɛR] *nf* dowager.
douane [dwan] *nf* (*poste, bureau*) customs
pl; (*taxes*) (customs) duty; **passer la ~**
to go through customs; **douanier, ière** *a*
customs *cpd* // *nm* customs officer.
doublage [dublaʒ] *nm* (*CINÉMA*) dubbing.
double [dubl(ə)] *a, ad* double // *nm* (*2 fois*
plus): **le ~ (de)** twice as much (*ou* many)
(as), double the amount (*ou* number) (of);
(*autre exemplaire*) duplicate, copy; (*sosie*)
double; **en ~ (exemplaire)** in duplicate;
faire ~ emploi to be redundant; **~**
carburateur twin carburettor; **à ~s com-**
mandes dual-control; **~ messieurs/**
mixte men's/mixed doubles *sg*; **~ toit** (*de*
tente) fly sheet.
doublé, e [duble] *a* (*vêtement*): **~ (de)**
lined (with).
doublement [dubləmɑ̃] *nm* doubling;

twofold increase // ad doubly; in two ways, on two counts.

doubler [duble] vt (*multiplier par 2*) to double; (*vêtement*) to line; (*dépasser*) to overtake, pass; (*film*) to dub; (*acteur*) to stand in for // vi to double, increase twofold // ~ (**la classe**) (*scol*) to repeat a year.

doublure [dublyʀ] nf lining; (*cinéma*) stand-in.

douce [dus] a *voir* **doux**; ~**âtre** a sickly sweet; ~**ment** ad gently; slowly; ~**reux**, **euse** a (*péj*) sugary, suave; **douceur** nf mildness; gentleness; softness; sweetness; **douceurs** nfpl (*friandises*) sweets.

douche [duʃ] nf shower; ~**s** nfpl (*salle*) shower room sg; **se doucher** to have ou take a shower.

doué, e [dwe] a gifted, talented; ~ **de** endowed with.

douille [duj] nf (*ÉLEC*) socket; (*de projectile*) case.

douillet, te [dujɛ, -ɛt] a cosy; (*péj*) soft.

douleur [dulœʀ] nf pain; (*chagrin*) grief, distress; **il a eu la ~ de perdre son père** he suffered the grief of losing his father; **douloureux, euse** a painful.

doute [dut] nm doubt; **sans ~** ad no doubt.

douter [dute] vt to doubt; ~ **de** vt (*allié*) to doubt, have (one's) doubts about; (*résultat*) to be doubtful of; **se ~ de qch/que** to suspect sth/that; **je m'en doutais** I suspected as much.

douteux, euse [dutø, -øz] a (*incertain*) doubtful; (*discutable*) dubious, questionable; (*péj*) dubious-looking.

douve [duv] nf (*de château*) moat; (*de tonneau*) stave.

Douvres [duvʀ(ə)] n Dover.

doux, douce [du, dus] a (*lisse, moelleux, pas vif: couleur, non calcaire: eau*) soft; (*sucré, agréable*) sweet; (*peu fort: moutarde etc, clément: climat*) mild; (*pas brusque*) gentle.

douzaine [duzɛn] nf (*12*) dozen; (*environ 12*): **une ~ (de)** a dozen or so, twelve or so.

douze [duz] num twelve; **douzième** num twelfth.

doyen, ne [dwajɛ̃, -ɛn] nm/f (*en âge, ancienneté*) most senior member; (*de faculté*) dean.

draconien, ne [dʀakɔnjɛ̃, -ɛn] a draconian; stringent.

dragage [dʀagaʒ] nm dredging.

dragée [dʀaʒe] nf sugared almond; (*MÉD*) (sugar-coated) pill.

dragon [dʀagɔ̃] nm dragon.

drague [dʀag] nf (*filet*) dragnet; (*bateau*) dredger; **draguer** vt (*rivière*) to dredge; to drag // vi (*fam*) to try and pick up girls; to chat up birds; **dragueur de mines** nm minesweeper.

drainage [dʀɛnaʒ] nm drainage.

drainer [dʀene] vt to drain.

dramatique [dʀamatik] a dramatic; (*tragique*) tragic // nf (*TV*) (television) drama.

dramatiser [dʀamatize] vt to dramatize.

dramaturge [dʀamatyʀʒ(ə)] nm dramatist, playwright.

drame [dʀam] nm (*THÉÂTRE*) drama; (*catastrophe*) drama, tragedy.

drap [dʀa] nm (*de lit*) sheet; (*tissu*) woollen fabric.

drapeau, x [dʀapo] nm flag; **sous les ~x** with the colours, in the army.

draper [dʀape] vt to drape.

draperies [dʀapʀi] nfpl hangings.

drapier [dʀapje] nm (*woollen*) cloth manufacturer; (*marchand*) clothier.

dresser [dʀese] vt (*mettre vertical, monter: tente*) to put up, erect; (*fig: liste, bilan, contrat*) to draw up; (*animal*) to train; **se ~** vi (*falaise, obstacle*) to stand; to tower (up); (*personne*) to draw o.s. up; ~ **qn contre qn d'autre** to set sb against sb else.

dresseur, euse [dʀesœʀ, -øz] nm/f trainer.

dressoir [dʀeswaʀ] nm dresser.

dribbler [dʀible] vt, vi (*sport*) to dribble.

drogue [dʀɔg] nf drug; la ~ drugs pl.

drogué, e [dʀɔge] nm/f drug addict.

droguer [dʀɔge] vt (*victime*) to drug; (*malade*) to give drugs to; **se ~** (*aux stupéfiants*) to take drugs; (*péj: de médicaments*) to dose o.s. up.

droguerie [dʀɔgʀi] nf hardware shop.

droguiste [dʀɔgist(ə)] nm keeper (ou owner) of a hardware shop.

droit, e [dʀwa, dʀwat] a (*non courbe*) straight; (*vertical*) upright, straight; (*fig: loyal, franc*) upright, straight(forward); (*opposé à gauche*) right, right-hand // ad straight // nm (*prérogative*) right; (*taxe*) duty, tax; (: *d'inscription*) fee; (*lois, branche*): **le ~** law // nf (*ligne*) straight line; **avoir le ~ de** to be allowed to; **avoir ~ à** to be entitled to; **être en ~ de** to have a ou the right to; **faire ~ à** to grant, accede to; **être dans son ~** to be within one's rights; **à ~e on the right**; (*direction*) (to the) right; **de ~e** (*POL*) right-wing; ~ **d'auteur** copyright; ~**s d'auteur** royalties; **le ~ de vote** the (right to) vote.

droitier, ière [dʀwatje, -jɛʀ] nm/f right-handed person.

droiture [dʀwatyʀ] nf uprightness, straightness.

drôl! [dʀol] a (*amusant*) funny, amusing; (*bizarre*) funny, peculiar.

dromadaire [dʀɔmadɛʀ] nm dromedary.

dru, e [dʀy] a (*cheveux*) thick, bushy; (*pluie*) heavy.

drugstore [dʀœgstɔʀ] nm drugstore.

D.S.T. sigle f = **direction de la surveillance du territoire** (the French internal security service).

du [dy] prép + dét, dét *voir* **de**.

dû, due [dy] vb *voir* **devoir** // a (*somme*) owing, owed; (: *venant à échéance*) due; (*causé par*): ~ **à** due to // nm due; (*somme*) dues pl.

dubitatif, ive [dybitatif, -iv] a doubtful, dubious.

duc [dyk] nm duke; **duché** nm dukedom; **duchesse** nf duchess.

duel [dyɛl] nm duel.

dûment [dymɑ̃] ad duly.

dune [dyn] *nf* dune.
Dunkerque [dœkɛʀk] *n* Dunkirk.
duo [dɥo] *nm* (*MUS*) duet ; (*fig: couple*) duo, pair.
dupe [dyp] *nf* dupe // *a*: (**ne pas**) **être** ~ **de** (not) to be taken in by.
duper [dype] *vt* to dupe, deceive.
duperie [dypʀi] *nf* deception, dupery.
duplex [dyplɛks] *nm* (*appartement*) split-level appartment, duplex.
duplicata [dyplikata] *nm* duplicate.
duplicateur [dyplikatœʀ] *nm* duplicator.
duplicité [dyplisite] *nf* duplicity.
duquel [dykɛl] *prép* + *pronom voir* **lequel**.
dur, e [dyʀ] *a* (*pierre, siège, travail, problème*) hard ; (*lumière, voix, climat*) harsh ; (*sévère*) hard, harsh ; (*cruel*) hard(-hearted) ; (*porte, col*) stiff ; (*viande*) tough // *ad* hard ; ~ **d'oreille** hard of hearing.
durable [dyʀabl(ə)] *a* lasting.
durant [dyʀɑ̃] *prép* (*au cours de*) during ; (*pendant*) for ; ~ **des mois, des mois** ~ for months.
durcir [dyʀsiʀ] *vt, vi, se* ~ *vi* to harden.
durcissement [dyʀsismɑ̃] *nm* hardening.
durée [dyʀe] *nf* length ; (*d'une pile etc*) life ; (*déroulement: des opérations etc*) duration ; **pour une** ~ **illimitée** for an unlimited length of time.
durement [dyʀmɑ̃] *ad* harshly.
durer [dyʀe] *vi* to last.
dureté [dyʀte] *nf* hardness ; harshness ; stiffness ; toughness.
durit [dyʀit] *nf* ® (*radiator*) hose (*for car*).
dus *etc vb voir* **devoir**.
duvet [dyvɛ] *nm* down ; (**sac de couchage en**) ~ down-filled sleeping bag.
dynamique [dinamik] *a* dynamic.
dynamisme [dinamism(ə)] *nm* dynamism.
dynamite [dinamit] *nf* dynamite.
dynamiter [dinamite] *vt* to (blow up with) dynamite.
dynamo [dinamo] *nf* dynamo.
dynastie [dinasti] *nf* dynasty.
dysenterie [disɑ̃tʀi] *nf* dysentery.
dyslexie [dislɛksi] *nf* dyslexia, word-blindness.
dyspepsie [dispɛpsi] *nf* dyspepsia.

E

eau, x [o] *nf* water // *nfpl* waters ; **prendre l'**~ to leak, let in water ; **faire** ~ to leak ; **tomber à l'**~ (*fig*) to fall through ; ~ **de Cologne** Eau de Cologne ; ~ **courante** running water ; ~ **douce** fresh water ; ~ **de Javel** bleach ; ~ **minérale** mineral water ; ~ **salée** salt water ; ~ **de toilette** toilet water ; **les E**~**x et Forêts** (*ADMIN*) ≈ the National Forestry Commission ; ~**-de-vie** *nf* brandy ; ~**-forte** *nf* etching.
ébahi, e [ebai] *a* dumbfounded, flabbergasted.
ébats [eba] *nmpl* frolics, gambols.
ébattre [ebatʀ(ə)]: **s'**~ *vi* to frolic.
ébauche [eboʃ] *nf* (*rough*) outline, sketch.
ébaucher [eboʃe] *vt* to sketch out, outline ; **s'**~ *vi* to take shape.

ébène [ebɛn] *nf* ebony.
ébéniste [ebenist(ə)] *nm* cabinetmaker ; **ébénisterie** *nf* cabinetmaking ; (*bâti*) cabinetwork.
éberlué, e [ebɛʀlɥe] *a* astounded, flabbergasted.
éblouir [eblwiʀ] *vt* to dazzle.
éblouissement [ebluismɑ̃] *nm* dazzle ; (*faiblesse*) dizzy turn.
éborgner [ebɔʀɲe] *vt*: ~ **qn** to blind sb in one eye.
éboueur [ebwœʀ] *nm* dustman.
ébouillanter [ebujɑ̃te] *vt* to scald ; (*CULIN*) to blanch.
éboulement [ebulmɑ̃] *nm* falling rocks *pl*, rock fall.
ébouler [ebule]: **s'**~ *vi* to crumble, collapse.
éboulis [ebuli] *nmpl* fallen rocks.
ébouriffé, e [eburife] *a* tousled, ruffled.
ébranler [ebʀɑ̃le] *vt* to shake ; (*rendre instable: mur*) to weaken ; **s'**~ *vi* (*partir*) to move off.
ébrécher [ebʀeʃe] *vt* to chip.
ébriété [ebʀijete] *nf*: **en état d'**~ in a state of intoxication.
ébrouer [ebʀue]: **s'**~ *vi* to shake o.s. ; to snort.
ébruiter [ebʀɥite] *vt* to spread, disclose.
ébullition [ebylisjɔ̃] *nf* boiling point ; **en** ~ boiling ; (*fig*) in an uproar.
écaille [ekaj] *nf* (*de poisson*) scale ; (*de coquillage*) shell ; (*matière*) tortoiseshell ; (*de roc etc*) flake.
écailler [ekaje] *vt* (*poisson*) to scale ; (*huître*) to open ; **s'**~ *vi* to flake ou peel (off).
écarlate [ekaʀlat] *a* scarlet.
écarquiller [ekaʀkije] *vt*: ~ **les yeux** to stare wide-eyed.
écart [ekaʀ] *nm* gap ; (*embardée*) swerve, sideways leap ; (*fig*) departure, deviation ; **à l'**~ *ad* out of the way ; **à l'**~ **de** *prép* away from ; (*fig*) out of ; ~ **de conduite** misdemeanour.
écarté, e [ekaʀte] *a* (*maison, route*) out-of-the-way, remote ; (*ouvert*): **les jambes** ~**es** legs apart ; **les bras** ~**s** arms outstretched.
écarteler [ekaʀtəle] *vt* to quarter ; (*fig*) to tear.
écartement [ekaʀtəmɑ̃] *nm* space, gap ; (*RAIL*) gauge.
écarter [ekaʀte] *vt* (*séparer*) to move apart, separate ; (*éloigner*) to push back, move away ; (*ouvrir: bras, jambes*) to spread, open ; (: *rideau*) to draw (back) ; (*éliminer: candidat, possibilité*) to dismiss ; **s'**~ *vi* to part ; to move away ; **s'**~ **de** to wander from.
ecchymose [ekimoz] *nf* bruise.
ecclésiastique [eklezjastik] *a* ecclesiastical // *nm* ecclesiastic.
écervelé, e [esɛʀvəle] *a* scatterbrained, featherbrained.
échafaud [eʃafo] *nm* scaffold.
échafaudage [eʃafodaʒ] *nm* scaffolding ; (*fig*) heap, pile.
échafauder [eʃafode] *vt* (*plan*) to construct.

échalas [eʃala] *nm* stake, pole.
échalote [eʃalɔt] *nf* shallot.
échancrure [eʃɑ̃kRyR] *nf* (de robe) scoop neckline; (de côte, arête rocheuse) indentation.
échange [eʃɑ̃ʒ] *nm* exchange; **en ~ de** in exchange *ou* return for.
échanger [eʃɑ̃ʒe] *vt*: **~ qch (contre)** to exchange sth (for); **échangeur** *nm* (AUTO) interchange.
échantillon [eʃɑ̃tijɔ̃] *nm* sample; **échantillonnage** *nm* selection of samples.
échappatoire [eʃapatwaR] *nf* way out.
échappée [eʃape] *nf* (vue) vista; (CYCLISME) breakaway.
échappement [eʃapmɑ̃] *nm* (AUTO) exhaust.
échapper [eʃape]: **~ à** *vt* (gardien) to escape (from); (punition, péril) to escape; **~ à qn** (détail, sens) to escape sb; (objet qu'on tient) to slip out of sb's hands; **s'~** *vi* to escape; **l'~ belle** to have a narrow escape.
écharde [eʃaRd(ə)] *nf* splinter (of wood).
écharpe [eʃaRp(ə)] *nf* scarf (pl scarves); (de maire) sash; **avoir un bras en ~** to have one's arm in a sling; **prendre en ~** (dans une collision) to hit sideways on.
écharper [eʃaRpe] *vt* to tear to pieces.
échasse [eʃas] *nf* stilt.
échassier [eʃasje] *nm* wader.
échauffement [eʃofmɑ̃] *nm* overheating.
échauffer [eʃofe] *vt* (métal, moteur) to overheat; (fig: exciter) to fire, excite; **s'~** (SPORT) to warm up; (dans la discussion) to become heated.
échauffourée [eʃofuRe] *nf* clash, brawl.
échéance [eʃeɑ̃s] *nf* (d'un paiement: date) settlement date; (: somme due) financial commitment(s); (fig) deadline; **à brève/longue ~** *a* short-/long-term // *ad* in the short/long run.
échéant [eʃeɑ̃]: **le cas ~** *ad* if the case arises.
échec [eʃɛk] *nm* failure; (ÉCHECS): **~ et mat/au roi** checkmate/check; **~s** *nmpl* (jeu) chess *sg*; **tenir en ~** to hold in check; **faire ~ à** to foil *ou* thwart.
échelle [eʃɛl] *nf* ladder; (fig, d'une carte) scale; **à l'~ de** on the scale of; **sur une grande ~** on a large scale; **faire la courte ~ à qn** to give sb a leg up.
échelon [eʃlɔ̃] *nm* (d'échelle) rung; (ADMIN) grade.
échelonner [eʃlɔne] *vt* to space out, spread out.
écheveau, x [eʃvo] *nm* skein, hank.
échevelé, e [eʃəvle] *a* tousled, dishevelled; wild, frenzied.
échine [eʃin] *nf* backbone, spine.
échiquier [eʃikje] *nm* chessboard.
écho [eko] *nm* echo; **~s** *nmpl* (potins) gossip *sg*, rumours.
échoir [eʃwaR] *vi* (dette) to fall due; (délais) to expire; **~ à** *vt* to fall to.
échoppe [eʃɔp] *nf* stall, booth.
échouer [eʃwe] *vi* to fail // *vt* (bateau) to ground; **s'~** *vi* to run aground.
échu, e [eʃy] *pp voir* **échoir**.
éclabousser [eklabuse] *vt* to splash.

éclair [eklɛR] *nm* (d'orage) flash of lightning, lightning *q*; (fig) flash, spark; (gâteau) éclair.
éclairage [eklɛRaʒ] *nm* lighting.
éclaircie [eklɛRsi] *nf* bright *ou* sunny interval.
éclaircir [eklɛRsiR] *vt* to lighten; (fig) to clear up; to clarify; (CULIN) to thin (down); **s'~ la voix** to clear one's throat; **éclaircissement** *nm* clearing up; clarification.
éclairer [eklɛRe] *vt* (lieu) to light (up); (personne: avec une lampe de poche etc) to light the way for; (fig) to enlighten; to shed light on // *vi*: **~ mal/bien** to give a poor/good light; **s'~ à la bougie/l'électricité** to use candlelight/have electric lighting.
éclaireur, euse [eklɛRœR, -øz] *nm/f* (scout) (boy) scout/(girl) guide // *nm* (MIL) scout; **partir en ~** to go off to reconnoitre.
éclat [ekla] *nm* (de bombe, de verre) fragment; (du soleil, d'une couleur etc) brightness, brilliance; (d'une cérémonie) splendour; (scandale): **faire un ~** to cause a commotion; **des ~s de verre** broken glass; flying glass; **~ de rire** burst *ou* roar of laughter; **~ de voix** shout.
éclatant, e [eklatɑ̃, -ɑ̃t] *a* brilliant, bright.
éclater [eklate] *vi* (pneu) to burst; (bombe) to explode; (guerre, épidémie) to break out; (groupe, parti) to break up; **~ de rire** to burst out laughing.
éclipse [eklips(ə)] *nf* eclipse.
éclipser [eklipse] *vt* to eclipse; **s'~** *vi* to slip away.
éclopé, e [eklɔpe] *a* lame.
éclore [eklɔR] *vi* (œuf) to hatch; (fleur) to open (out).
écluse [eklyz] *nf* lock; **éclusier** *nm* lock keeper.
écœurer [ekœRe] *vt*: **~ qn** to make sb feel sick.
école [ekɔl] *nf* school; **aller à l'~** to go to school; **faire ~** to collect a following; **~ de dessin/danse** art/dancing school; **~ hôtelière** catering college; **~ normale** (d'instituteurs) teachers' training college; **~ de secrétariat** secretarial college; **écolier, ière** *nm/f* schoolboy/girl.
écologie [ekɔlɔʒi] *nf* ecology; environmental studies *pl*; **écologique** *a* ecological; environmental; **écologiste** *nm/f* ecologist; environmentalist.
éconduire [ekɔ̃dɥiR] *vt* to dismiss.
économat [ekɔnɔma] *nm* bursar's office.
économe [ekɔnɔm] *a* thrifty // *nm/f* (de lycée etc) bursar.
économie [ekɔnɔmi] *nf* (vertu) economy, thrift; (gain: d'argent, de temps etc) saving; (science) economics *sg*; (situation économique) economy; **~s** *nfpl* (pécule) savings; **économique** *a* (avantageux) economical; (ÉCON) economic.
économiser [ekɔnɔmize] *vt, vi* to save.
économiste [ekɔnɔmist(ə)] *nm/f* economist.
écoper [ekɔpe] *vi* to bale out; (fig) to cop it; **~ (de)** *vt* to get.
écorce [ekɔRs(ə)] *nf* bark; (de fruit) peel; **écorcer** *vt* to bark.

écorché [ekɔʀʃe] *nm* cut-away drawing.
écorcher [ekɔʀʃe] *vt* (*animal*) to skin;
(*égratigner*) to graze; **écorchure** *nf* graze.
écossais, e [ekɔsɛ, -ɛz] *a* Scottish // *nm/f*: E~, e Scot.
Écosse [ekɔs] *nf* Scotland.
écosser [ekɔse] *vt* to shell.
écot [eko] *nm*: **payer son** ~ to pay one's share.
écouler [ekule] *vt* to sell; to dispose of;
s' ~ *vi* (*eau*) to flow (out); (*jours, temps*) to pass (by).
écourter [ekuʀte] *vt* to curtail, cut short.
écoute [ekut] *nf* (*RADIO, TV*): **temps/heure**
d' ~ listening (*ou* viewing) time/hour;
prendre l' ~ to tune in; **rester à l'** ~ (**de**)
to stay listening (to) *ou* tuned in (to); ~s
téléphoniques phone tapping *sg*.
écouter [ekute] *vt* to listen to; **écouteur**
nm (*TÉL*) receiver; (*RADIO*) headphones *pl*,
headset.
écoutille [ekutij] *nf* hatch.
écran [ekʀɑ̃] *nm* screen.
écrasant, e [ekʀazɑ̃, -ɑ̃t] *a* overwhelming.
écraser [ekʀaze] *vt* to crush; (*piéton*) to
run over; **s'** ~ (**au sol**) to crash; **s'** ~
contre to crash into.
écrémer [ekʀeme] *vt* to skim.
écrevisse [ekʀavis] *nf* crayfish *inv*.
écrier [ekʀije]: **s'** ~ *vi* to exclaim.
écrin [ekʀɛ̃] *nm* case, box.
écrire [ekʀiʀ] *vt* to write; **ça s'écrit**
comment? how is it spelt?, how do you
write that?; **écrit** *nm* document; (*examen*)
written paper; **par écrit** in writing.
écriteau, x [ekʀito] *nm* notice, sign.
écritoire [ekʀitwaʀ] *nf* writing case.
écriture [ekʀityʀ] *nf* writing; (*COMM*)
entry; ~s *nfpl* (*COMM*) accounts, books;
l'É~ (sainte), les É~s the Scriptures.
écrivain [ekʀivɛ̃] *nm* writer.
écrou [ekʀu] *nm* nut.
écrouer [ekʀue] *vt* to imprison; to
remand in custody.
écrouler [ekʀule]: **s'** ~ *vi* to collapse.
écru, e [ekʀy] *a* (*toile*) raw, unbleached.
écueil [ekœj] *nm* reef; (*fig*) pitfall;
stumbling block.
écuelle [ekɥɛl] *nf* bowl.
éculé, e [ekyle] *a* (*chaussure*) down-
at-heel; (*fig: péj*) hackneyed.
écume [ekym] *nf* foam; (*CULIN*) scum;
écumer *vt* (*CULIN*) to skim; (*fig*) to plunder
// *vi* (*mer*) to foam; (*fig*) to boil with rage;
écumoire *nf* skimmer.
écureuil [ekyʀœj] *nm* squirrel.
écurie [ekyʀi] *nf* stable.
écusson [ekysɔ̃] *nm* badge.
écuyer, ère [ekɥije, -ɛʀ] *nm/f* rider.
eczéma [ɛgzema] *nm* eczema.
édenté, e [edɑ̃te] *a* toothless.
E.D.F. *sigle f* = *Électricité de France*, ≈
Electricity Board.
édifice [edifis] *nm* building, edifice.
édifier [edifje] *vt* to build, erect; (*fig*) to
edify.
édiles [edil] *nmpl* city fathers.
édit [edi] *nm* edict.
éditer [edite] *vt* (*publier*) to publish;
(: *disque*) to produce; (*préparer: texte*) to

edit; **éditeur, trice** *nm/f* editor;
publisher; **édition** *nf* editing *q*; edition;
(*industrie du livre*) publishing.
éditorial, aux [editɔʀjal, -o] *nm* editorial,
leader; ~**iste** *nm/f* editorial *ou* leader
writer.
édredon [edʀadɔ̃] *nm* eiderdown.
éducatif, ive [edykatif, -iv] *a* educational.
éducation [edykasjɔ̃] *nf* education;
(*familiale*) upbringing; (*manières*) (good)
manners *pl*; **l'É~ (Nationale)** ≈ The
Department of Education; ~ **physique**
physical education.
édulcorer [edylkɔʀe] *vt* to sweeten; (*fig*)
to tone down.
éduquer [edyke] *vt* to educate; (*élever*) to
bring up; (*faculté*) to train.
effacer [efase] *vt* to erase, rub out; **s'** ~
vi (*inscription etc*) to wear off; (*pour laisser
passer*) to step aside; ~ **le ventre** to pull
one's stomach in.
effarement [efaʀmɑ̃] *nm* alarm.
effarer [efaʀe] *vt* to alarm.
effaroucher [efaʀuʃe] *vt* to frighten *ou*
scare away; to alarm.
effectif, ive [efɛktif, -iv] *a* real; effective
// *nm* (*MIL*) strength; (*SCOL*) total number
of pupils, size; ~s *nmpl* numbers,
strength *sg*; **effectivement** *ad* effectively;
(*réellement*) actually, really; (*en effet*)
indeed.
effectuer [efɛktɥe] *vt* (*opération, mission*)
to carry out; (*déplacement, trajet*) to make,
complete; (*mouvement*) to execute, make.
efféminé, e [efemine] *a* effeminate.
effervescent, e [efɛʀvesɑ̃, -ɑ̃t] *a* (*cachet,
boisson*) effervescent; (*fig*) agitated, in a
turmoil.
effet [efɛ] *nm* (*résultat, artifice*) effect;
(*impression*) impression; ~s *nmpl*
(*vêtements etc*) things; **faire de l'** ~
(*médicament, menace*) to have an effect, be
effective; **en** ~ *ad* indeed.
effeuiller [efœje] *vt* to remove the leaves
(*ou pétals*) from.
efficace [efikas] *a* (*personne*) efficient;
(*action, médicament*) effective; **efficacité**
nf efficiency; effectiveness.
effigie [efiʒi] *nf* effigy.
effilé, e [efile] *a* slender; sharp;
streamlined.
effiler [efile] *vt* (*cheveux*) to thin (out);
(*tissu*) to fray.
effilocher [efilɔʃe]: **s'** ~ *vi* to fray.
efflanqué, e [eflɑ̃ke] *a* emaciated.
effleurer [eflœʀe] *vt* to brush (against);
(*sujet, idée*) to touch upon; (*suj: idée,
pensée*): ~ **qn** to cross sb's mind.
effluves [eflyv] *nmpl* exhalation(s).
effondrement [efɔ̃dʀamɑ̃] *nm* collapse.
effondrer [efɔ̃dʀe]: **s'** ~ *vi* to collapse.
efforcer [efɔʀse]: **s'** ~ **de** *vt*: **s'** ~ **de faire**
to try hard to do.
effort [efɔʀ] *nm* effort; **faire un** ~ to
make an effort.
effraction [efʀaksjɔ̃] *nf* breaking-in;
s'introduire par ~ **dans** to break into.
effrangé, e [efʀɑ̃ʒe] *a* fringed; (*effiloché*)
frayed.
effrayant, e [efʀɛjɑ̃, -ɑ̃t] *a* frightening,
fearsome; (*sens affaibli*) dreadful.

effrayer [efʀeje] vt to frighten, scare; (rebuter) to put off; s'~ (de) to be frightened ou scared (by).

effréné, e [efʀene] a wild.

effriter [efʀite]: s'~ vi to crumble.

effroi [efʀwa] nm terror, dread q.

effronté, e [efʀɔ̃te] a insolent, brazen.

effroyable [efʀwajabl(ə)] a horrifying, appalling.

effusion [efyzjɔ̃] nf effusion; sans ~ de sang without bloodshed.

égailler [egaje]: s'~ vi to scatter, disperse.

égal, e, aux [egal, -o] a (identique, ayant les mêmes droits) equal; (plan: surface) even, level; (constant: vitesse) steady; (équitable) even // nm/f equal; être ~ à (prix, nombre) to be equal to; ça lui est ~ it's all the same to him, it doesn't matter to him; he doesn't mind; sans ~ matchless, unequalled; à l'~ de (comme) just like; d'~ à ~ as equals; ~ement ad equally; evenly; steadily; (aussi) too, as well; ~er vt to equal; ~iser vt (sol, salaires) to level (out); (chances) to equalize // vi (SPORT) to equalize; ~itaire a egalitarian; ~ité nf equality; evenness; steadiness; (MATH) identity; être à ~ité (de points) to be level; ~ité de droits equality of rights; ~ité d'humeur evenness of temper.

égard [egaʀ] nm: ~s nmpl consideration sg; à cet ~ in this respect; eu ~ à in view of; par ~ pour out of consideration for; sans ~ pour without regard for; à l'~ de prép towards; concerning.

égarement [egaʀmɑ̃] nm distraction, aberration.

égarer [egaʀe] vt (objet) to mislay; (moralement) to lead astray; s'~ vi to get lost, lose one's way; (objet) to go astray; (fig: dans une discussion) to wander.

égayer [egeje] vt (personne) to amuse; to cheer up; (récit, endroit) to brighten up, liven up.

égide [eʒid] nf: sous l'~ de under the aegis of.

églantier [eglɑ̃tje] nm wild ou dog rose(-bush).

églantine [eglɑ̃tin] nf wild ou dog rose.

églefin [egləfɛ̃] nm haddock.

église [egliz] nf church; aller à l'~ (être pratiquant) to go to church, be a churchgoer.

égocentrique [egɔsɑ̃tʀik] a egocentric, self-centred.

égoïsme [egɔism(ə)] nm selfishness, egoism; **égoïste** a selfish, egoistic // nm/f egoist.

égorger [egɔʀʒe] vt to cut the throat of.

égosiller [egozije]: s'~ vi to shout o.s. hoarse.

égout [egu] nm sewer; **égoutier** nm sewer worker.

égoutter [egute] vt (linge) to wring out; (vaisselle) to drain // vi, s'~ vi to drip; **égouttoir** nm draining board; (mobile) draining rack.

égratigner [egʀatiɲe] vt to scratch; **égratignure** nf scratch.

égrener [egʀəne] vt: ~ une grappe, ~ des raisins to pick grapes off a bunch.

égrillard, e [egʀijaʀ, -aʀd(ə)] a ribald, bawdy.

Égypte [eʒipt(ə)] nf Egypt; **égyptien, ne** a, nm/f Egyptian; **égyptologie** nf Egyptology.

eh [e] excl hey!; ~ bien well.

éhonté, e [eɔ̃te] a shameless, brazen.

éjaculation [eʒakylɑsjɔ̃] nf ejaculation.

éjaculer [eʒakyle] vi to ejaculate.

éjectable [eʒɛktabl(ə)] a: siège ~ ejector seat.

éjecter [eʒɛkte] vt (TECH) to eject; (fam) to kick ou chuck out.

élaboration [elabɔʀɑsjɔ̃] nf elaboration.

élaborer [elabɔʀe] vt to elaborate.

élaguer [elage] vt to prune.

élan [elɑ̃] nm (ZOOL) elk, moose; (SPORT: avant le saut) run up; (de véhicule ou objet en mouvement) momentum; (fig: de tendresse etc) surge; **prendre son** ~/**de l'~** to take a run up/gather speed.

élancé, e [elɑ̃se] a slender.

élancement [elɑ̃smɑ̃] nm shooting pain.

élancer [elɑ̃se]: s'~ vi to dash, hurl o.s.; (fig: arbre, clocher) to soar (upwards).

élargir [elaʀʒiʀ] vt to widen; (vêtement) to let out; (JUR) to release; s'~ vi to widen; (vêtement) to stretch.

élasticité [elastisite] nf (aussi ÉCON) elasticity.

élastique [elastik] a elastic // nm (de bureau) rubber band; (pour la couture) elastic q.

électeur, trice [elɛktœʀ, -tʀis] nm/f elector, voter.

élection [elɛksjɔ̃] nf election; ~s nfpl (POL) election(s); ~ partielle ≈ by-election.

électoral, e, aux [elɛktɔʀal, -o] a electoral, election cpd.

électorat [elɛktɔʀa] nm electorate.

électricien, ne [elɛktʀisjɛ̃, -jɛn] nm/f electrician.

électricité [elɛktʀisite] nf electricity; **allumer/éteindre l'~** to put on/off the light; ~ **statique** static electricity.

électrifier [elɛktʀifje] vt (RAIL) to electrify.

électrique [elɛktʀik] a electric(al).

électriser [elɛktʀize] vt to electrify.

électro... [elɛktʀɔ] préfixe: ~-aimant nm electromagnet; ~cardiogramme nm electrocardiogram; ~choc nm electric shock treatment; ~cuter vt to electrocute; ~cution nf electrocution; électrode nf électrode; ~encéphalogramme nm electroencephalogram; ~gène a: groupe ~gène generating set; ~lyse nf electrolysis sg; ~magnétique a electromagnetic; ~ménager a: appareils ~ménagers domestic (electrical) appliances.

électron [elɛktʀɔ̃] nm electron.

électronicien, ne [elɛktʀɔnisjɛ̃, -jɛn] nm/f electronics engineer.

électronique [elɛktʀɔnik] a electronic // nf electronics sg.

électrophone [elɛktʀɔfɔn] nm record player.

élégance [elegɑ̃s] nf elegance.

élégant, e [elegɑ̃, -ɑ̃t] a elegant; (solution)

neat, elegant; (attitude, procédé) courteous, civilized.

élément [elemɑ̃] nm element; (pièce) component, part; ~s nmpl (aussi: rudiments) elements; **élémentaire** a elementary; (CHIMIE) elemental.

éléphant [elefɑ̃] nm elephant.

élevage [ɛlvaʒ] nm breeding; (de bovins) cattle breeding ou rearing.

élévateur [elevatœʀ] nm elevator.

élévation [elevasjɔ̃] nf (gén) elevation; (voir élever) raising; (voir s'élever) rise.

élève [elɛv] nm/f pupil; ~ **infirmière** nf student nurse.

élevé, e [ɛlve] a (prix, sommet) high; (fig: noble) elevated; **bien/mal** ~ well-/ill-mannered.

élever [ɛlve] vt (enfant) to bring up, raise; (bétail, volaille) to breed; (abeilles) to keep; (hausser: immeuble, taux, niveau) to raise; (fig: âme, esprit) to elevate; (édifier: monument) to put up, erect; **s'**~ vi (avion, alpiniste) to go up; (niveau, température, aussi: cri etc) to rise; (survenir: difficultés) to arise; **s'**~ **à** (suj: frais, dégâts) to amount to, add up to; **s'**~ **contre qch** to rise up against sth; ~ **une protestation/critique** to raise a protest/make a criticism; ~ **la voix** to raise one's voice; ~ **qn au rang de** to raise ou elevate sb to the rank of; **éleveur, euse** nm/f cattle breeder.

élidé, e [elide] a elided.

éligible [eliʒibl(ə)] a eligible.

élimé, e [elime] a worn (thin), threadbare.

élimination [eliminasjɔ̃] nf elimination.

éliminatoire [eliminatwaʀ] a eliminatory; disqualifying // nf (SPORT) heat.

éliminer [elimine] vt to eliminate.

élire [eliʀ] vt to elect; ~ **domicile à** to take up residence in ou at.

élision [elizjɔ̃] nf elision.

élite [elit] nf elite.

elle [ɛl] pronom (sujet) she; (: chose) it; (complément) her; it; ~s (sujet) they; (complément) them; ~-**même** herself; it-self; ~s-**mêmes** themselves; voir note sous **il**.

ellipse [elips(ə)] nf ellipse; (LING) ellipsis sg; **elliptique** a elliptical.

élocution [elɔkysjɔ̃] nf delivery; **défaut d'**~ speech impediment.

éloge [elɔʒ] nm praise (gén q); **faire l'**~ **de** to praise; **élogieux, euse** a laudatory, full of praise.

éloigné, e [elwaɲe] a distant, far-off.

éloignement [elwaɲmɑ̃] nm removal; putting off; estrangement; distance.

éloigner [elwaɲe] vt (objet): ~ **qch (de)** to move ou take sth away (from); (personne): ~ **qn (de)** to take sb away ou remove sb (from); (échéance) to put off, postpone; (soupçons, danger) to ward off; **s'**~ (**de**) (personne) to go away (from); (véhicule) to move away (from); (affectivement) to become estranged (from).

élongation [elɔ̃gasjɔ̃] nf strained muscle.

éloquence [elɔkɑ̃s] nf eloquence.

éloquent, e [elɔkɑ̃, -ɑ̃t] a eloquent.

élu, e [ely] pp de **élire** // nm/f (POL) elected representative.

élucider [elyside] vt to elucidate.

élucubrations [elykybʀasjɔ̃] nfpl wild imaginings.

éluder [elyde] vt to evade.

émacié, e [emasje] a emaciated.

émail, aux [emaj, -o] nm enamel.

émaillé, e [emaje] a enamelled; (fig): ~ **de** dotted with.

émanation [emanasjɔ̃] nf emanation, exhalation.

émanciper [emɑ̃sipe] vt to emancipate; **s'**~ (fig) to become emancipated ou liberated.

émaner [emane]: ~ **de** vt to come from; (ADMIN) to proceed from.

émarger [emaʀʒe] vt to sign; ~ **de 1000 F à un budget** to receive 1000 F out of a budget.

émasculer [emaskyle] vt to emasculate.

emballage [ɑ̃balaʒ] nm wrapping; packaging.

emballer [ɑ̃bale] vt to wrap (up); (dans un carton) to pack (up); (fig: fam) to thrill (to bits); **s'**~ vi (moteur) to race; (cheval) to bolt; (fig: personne) to get carried away.

embarcadère [ɑ̃baʀkadɛʀ] nm landing stage, pier.

embarcation [ɑ̃baʀkasjɔ̃] nf (small) boat, (small) craft inv.

embardée [ɑ̃baʀde] nf swerve; **faire une** ~ to swerve.

embargo [ɑ̃baʀgo] nm embargo; **mettre l'**~ **sur** to put an embargo on, embargo.

embarquement [ɑ̃baʀkəmɑ̃] nm embarkation; loading; boarding.

embarquer [ɑ̃baʀke] vt (personne) to embark; (marchandise) to load; (fam) to cart off; to nick // vi (passager) to board; (NAVIG) to ship water; **s'**~ vi to board; **s'**~ **dans** (affaire, aventure) to embark upon.

embarras [ɑ̃baʀa] nm (obstacle) hindrance; (confusion) embarrassment; (ennuis): **être dans l'**~ to be in a predicament ou an awkward position; ~ **gastrique** stomach upset.

embarrasser [ɑ̃baʀase] vt (encombrer) to clutter (up); (gêner) to hinder, hamper; (fig) to cause embarrassment to; to put in an awkward position; **s'**~ **de** to burden o.s. with.

embauche [ɑ̃boʃ] nf hiring; **bureau d'**~ labour office.

embaucher [ɑ̃boʃe] vt to take on, hire; **s'**~ to get o.s. hired.

embauchoir [ɑ̃boʃwaʀ] nm shoetree.

embaumer [ɑ̃bome] vt to embalm; to fill with its fragrance; ~ **la lavande** to be fragrant with (the scent of) lavender.

embellir [ɑ̃beliʀ] vt to make more attractive; (une histoire) to embellish // vi to grow lovelier ou more attractive.

embêtements [ɑ̃bɛtmɑ̃] nmpl trouble sg.

embêter [ɑ̃bete] vt to bother; **s'**~ vi (s'ennuyer) to be bored; **il ne s'embête pas!** (ironique) he does all right for himself!

emblée [ɑ̃ble]: **d'**~ ad straightaway.

emblème [ãblɛm] nm emblem.

emboîter [ãbwate] vt to fit together; s'~ dans to fit into; s'~ (l'un dans l'autre) to fit together; ~ le pas à qn to follow in sb's footsteps.

embolie [ãbɔli] nf embolism.

embonpoint [ãbɔ̃pwɛ̃] nm stoutness.

embouché, e [ãbuʃe] a: mal ~ foul-mouthed.

embouchure [ãbuʃyʀ] nf (GÉO) mouth; (MUS) mouthpiece.

embourber [ãbuʀbe]: s'~ vi to get stuck in the mud.

embourgeoiser [ãbuʀʒwaze]: s'~ vi to adopt a middle-class outlook.

embout [ãbu] nm (de canne) tip; (de tuyau) nozzle.

embouteillage [ãbutɛjaʒ] nm traffic jam, (traffic) holdup.

emboutir [ãbutiʀ] vt (TECH) to stamp; (heurter) to crash into, ram.

embranchement [ãbʀãʃmã] nm (routier) junction; (classification) branch.

embraser [ãbʀaze]: s'~ vi to flare up.

embrassades [ãbʀasad] nfpl hugging and kissing sg.

embrasser [ãbʀase] vt to kiss; (sujet, période) to embrace, encompass; (carrière, métier) to take up, enter upon.

embrasure [ãbʀazyʀ] nf: dans l'~ de la porte in the door(way).

embrayage [ãbʀɛjaʒ] nm (mécanisme) clutch.

embrayer [ãbʀeje] vi (AUTO) to let in the clutch.

embrigader [ãbʀigade] vt to recruit.

embrocher [ãbʀɔʃe] vt to (put on a) spit.

embrouillamini [ãbʀujamini] nm (fam) muddle.

embrouiller [ãbʀuje] vt (fils) to tangle (up); (fiches, idées, personne) to muddle up; s'~ vi (personne) to get in a muddle.

embroussaillé, e [ãbʀusaje] a overgrown, bushy.

embruns [ãbʀœ̃] nmpl sea spray sg.

embryon [ãbʀijɔ̃] nm embryo; embryonnaire a embryonic.

embûches [ãbyʃ] nfpl pitfalls, traps.

embué, e [ãbɥe] a misted up.

embuscade [ãbyskad] nf ambush; tendre une ~ à to lay an ambush for.

embusquer [ãbyske] vt to put in ambush; s'~ vi to take up position (for an ambush).

éméché, e [emeʃe] a tipsy, merry.

émeraude [ɛmʀod] nf emerald // a inv emerald-green.

émerger [emɛʀʒe] vi to emerge; (faire saillie, aussi fig) to stand out.

émeri [ɛmʀi] nm: toile ou papier ~ emery paper.

émérite [emeʀit] a highly skilled.

émerveiller [emɛʀveje] vt to fill with wonder; s'~ de to marvel at.

émetteur, trice [emɛtœʀ, -tʀis] a transmitting; (poste) ~ transmitter.

émettre [emɛtʀ(ə)] vt (son, lumière) to give out, emit; (message etc: RADIO) to transmit; (billet, timbre, emprunt) to issue; (hypothèse, avis) to voice, put forward //

vi: ~ sur ondes courtes to broadcast on short wave.

émeus etc vb voir émouvoir.

émeute [emøt] nf riot; émeutier, ère nm/f rioter.

émietter [emjete] vt to crumble; (fig) to split up, to disperse.

émigrant, e [emigʀã, -ãt] nm/f emigrant.

émigré, e [emigʀe] nm/f expatriate.

émigrer [emigʀe] vi to emigrate.

éminemment [eminamã] ad eminently.

éminence [eminãs] nf distinction; (colline) knoll, hill; Son É~ his (ou her) Eminence.

éminent, e [eminã, -ãt] a distinguished.

émir [emiʀ] nm emir; ~at nm emirate.

émissaire [emisɛʀ] nm emissary.

émission [emisjɔ̃] nf emission; transmission; issue; (RADIO, TV) programme, broadcast.

emmagasiner [ãmagazine] vt to (put into) store; (fig) to store up.

emmailloter [ãmajɔte] vt to wrap up.

emmanchure [ãmãʃyʀ] nf armhole.

emmêler [ãmele] vt to tangle (up); (fig) to muddle up; s'~ to get into a tangle.

emménager [ãmenaʒe] vi to move in; ~ dans to move into.

emmener [ãmne] vt to take (with one); (comme otage, capture) to take away; (SPORT, MIL: joueurs, soldats) to lead; ~ qn au cinéma to take sb to the cinema.

emmerder [ãmɛʀde] (fam!) vt to bug, bother; s'~ (s'ennuyer) to be bored stiff.

emmitoufler [ãmitufle] vt to wrap up (warmly).

emmurer [ãmyʀe] vt to wall up, immure.

émoi [emwa] nm (agitation, effervescence) commotion; (trouble) agitation.

émoluments [emɔlymã] nmpl remuneration sg, fee sg.

émonder [emɔ̃de] vt to prune.

émotif, ive [emɔtif, -iv] a emotional.

émoti: ɔn [emosjɔ̃] nf emotion; avoir des ~s (fig) to get a fright; émotionnel, le a emotional.

émoulu, e [emuly] a: frais ~ de fresh from, just out of.

émousser [emuse] vt to blunt; (fig) to dull.

émouvoir [emuvwaʀ] vt (troubler) to stir, affect; (toucher, attendrir) to move; (indigner) to rouse; (effrayer) to disturb, worry; s'~ vi to be affected; to be moved; to be roused; to be disturbed ou worried.

empailler [ãpaje] vt to stuff.

empaler [ãpale] vt to impale.

empaqueter [ãpakte] vt to pack up.

emparer [ãpaʀe]: s'~ de vt (objet) to seize, grab; (comme otage, MIL) to seize; (suj: peur, doute) to take hold of.

empâter [ãpate]: s'~ vi to thicken out.

empattement [ãpatmã] nm (AUTO) wheelbase; (TYPO) serif.

empêchement [ãpɛʃmã] nm (unexpected) obstacle, hitch.

empêcher [ãpɛʃe] vt to prevent; ~ qn de faire to prevent ou stop sb (from) doing; ~ que qch (n')arrive/qn (ne)

fasse to prevent sth from happening/sb from doing; **il n'empêche que** nevertheless, be that as it may; **il n'a pas pu s'~ de rire** he couldn't help laughing.

empêcheur [ɑ̃pɛʃœʀ] nm: **~ de danser en rond** spoilsport, killjoy.

empeigne [ɑ̃pɛɲ] nf upper(s).

empereur [ɑ̃pʀœʀ] nm emperor.

empesé, e [ɑ̃pəze] a (fig) stiff, starchy.

empeser [ɑ̃pəze] vt to starch.

empester [ɑ̃pɛste] vt (lieu) to stink out // vi to stink, reek; **~ le tabac/le vin** to stink ou reek of tobacco/wine.

empêtrer [ɑ̃petʀe] vt: **s'~ dans** (fils etc) to get tangled up in.

emphase [ɑ̃faz] nf pomposity, bombast.

empierrer [ɑ̃pjeʀe] vt (route) to metal.

empiéter [ɑ̃pjete]: **~ sur** vt to encroach upon.

empiffrer [ɑ̃pifʀe]: **s'~** vi (péj) to stuff o.s.

empiler [ɑ̃pile] vt to pile (up), stack (up).

empire [ɑ̃piʀ] nm empire; (fig) influence.

empirer [ɑ̃piʀe] vi to worsen, deteriorate.

empirique [ɑ̃piʀik] a empirical.

emplacement [ɑ̃plasmɑ̃] nm site.

emplâtre [ɑ̃plɑtʀ(ə)] nm plaster; (fam) twit.

emplette [ɑ̃plɛt] nf: **faire l'~ de** to purchase; **~s** nfpl shopping sg.

emplir [ɑ̃pliʀ] vt to fill; **s'~ (de)** to fill (with).

emploi [ɑ̃plwa] nm use; (COMM. ÉCON) employment; (poste) job, situation; **d'~ facile** easy to use; **~ du temps** timetable, schedule.

employé, e [ɑ̃plwaje] nm/f employee; **~ de bureau/banque** office/bank employee ou clerk.

employer [ɑ̃plwaje] vt (outil, moyen, méthode, mot) to use; (ouvrier, main-d'œuvre) to employ; **s'~ à faire** to apply ou devote o.s. to doing; **employeur, euse** nm/f employer.

empocher [ɑ̃pɔʃe] vt to pocket.

empoignade [ɑ̃pwaɲad] nf row, set-to.

empoigne [ɑ̃pwaɲ] nf: **foire d'~** free-for-all.

empoigner [ɑ̃pwaɲe] vt to grab; **s'~** (fig) to have a row ou set-to.

empoisonnement [ɑ̃pwazɔnmɑ̃] nm poisoning.

empoisonner [ɑ̃pwazɔne] vt to poison; (empester: air, pièce) to stink out; (fam): **~ qn** to drive sb mad.

emportement [ɑ̃pɔʀtəmɑ̃] nm fit of rage, anger q.

emporte-pièce [ɑ̃pɔʀtəpjɛs] nm inv (TECH) punch; à l'~ a (fig) incisive.

emporter [ɑ̃pɔʀte] vt to take (with one); (en dérobant ou enlevant, emmener: blessés, voyageurs) to take away; (entraîner) to carry away ou along; (arracher) to tear off; to carry away; (MIL: position) to take; (avantage, approbation) to win; **s'~** vi (de colère) to fly into a rage, lose one's temper; **l'~ (sur)** to get the upper hand (of); (méthode etc) to prevail (over); **boissons à (l')~** take-away drinks.

empourpré, e [ɑ̃puʀpʀe] a crimson.

empreint, e [ɑ̃pʀɛ̃, -ɛ̃t] a: **~ de** marked with; tinged with // nf (de pied, main) print; (fig) stamp, mark; **~e (digitale)** fingerprint.

empressé, e [ɑ̃pʀese] a attentive; (péj) overanxious to please, overattentive.

empressement [ɑ̃pʀɛsmɑ̃] nm (hâte) eagerness.

empresser [ɑ̃pʀese]: **s'~** vi to bustle about; **s'~ auprès de qn** to surround sb with attentions; **s'~ de faire** (se hâter) to hasten to do.

emprise [ɑ̃pʀiz] nf hold, ascendancy; **sous l'~ de** under the influence of.

emprisonnement [ɑ̃pʀizɔnmɑ̃] nm imprisonment.

emprisonner [ɑ̃pʀizɔne] vt to imprison, jail.

emprunt [ɑ̃pʀœ̃] nm borrowing q, loan (from debtor's point of view); (LING etc) borrowing; **~ public à 5%** 5% public loan.

emprunté, e [ɑ̃pʀœ̃te] a (fig) ill-at-ease, awkward.

emprunter [ɑ̃pʀœ̃te] vt to borrow; (itinéraire) to take, follow; (style, manière) to adopt, assume; **emprunteur, euse** nm/f borrower.

empuantir [ɑ̃pɥɑ̃tiʀ] vt to stink out.

ému, e [emy] pp de **émouvoir** // a excited; touched; moved.

émulation [emylasjɔ̃] nf emulation.

émule [emyl] nm/f imitator.

émulsion [emylsjɔ̃] nf emulsion.

en [ɑ̃] prép in; (avec direction) to; (moyen): **~ avion/taxi** by plane/taxi; (composition): **~ verre** made of glass, glass cpd; **se casser ~ plusieurs morceaux** to break into several pieces; **~ dormant** while sleeping, as one sleeps; **~ sortant** on going out, as he went out; **~ réparation** being repaired, under repair; **~ T/étoile** T-/star-shaped; **~ chemise/chaussettes** in one's shirt/socks; **peindre qch ~ rouge** to paint sth red; **~ soldat** as a soldier; **le même ~ plus grand** the same only ou but bigger // pronom (provenance): **j'~ viens** I've come from there; (cause): **il ~ est malade** he's ill because of it; (complément de nom): **j'~ connais les dangers** I know its dangers; (indéfini): **j'~ ai/veux** I have/want some; **~ as-tu?** have you got any?; **je n'~ veux pas** I don't want any; **j'~ ai assez** I've got enough (of it ou them); (fig) I've had enough; **j'~ ai 2** I've got 2 (of them); **combien y ~ a-t-il?** how many (of them) are there?; **j'~ suis fier/ai besoin** I am proud of it/need it: voir le verbe ou l'adjectif lorsque 'en' correspond à 'de' introduisant un complément prépositionnel.

E.N.A. [ena] sigle f = École Nationale d'Administration: one of the Grandes Écoles; **énarque** nm/f former E.N.A. student.

encablure [ɑ̃kablyʀ] nf (NAVIG) cable's length.

encadrement [ɑ̃kadʀəmɑ̃] nm framing; training; (de porte) frame.

encadrer [ɑ̃kadʀe] vt (tableau, image) to frame; (fig: entourer) to surround; to flank; (*personnel, soldats etc*) to train; **encadreur** *nm* (picture) framer.

encaisse [ɑ̃kɛs] *nf* cash in hand; ~ **or/métallique** gold/gold and silver reserves.

encaissé, e [ɑ̃kese] *a* steep-sided; with steep banks.

encaisser [ɑ̃kese] *vt* (*chèque*) to cash; (*argent*) to collect; (*fig: coup, défaite*) to take; **encaisseur** *nm* collector (*of debts etc*).

encan [ɑ̃kɑ̃]: **à l'~** *ad* by auction.

encanailler [ɑ̃kɑnɑje]: **s'~** *vi* to become vulgar *ou* common; to mix with the riff-raff.

encart [ɑ̃kaʀ] *nm* insert.

encastrer [ɑ̃kastʀe] *vt*: ~ **qch dans** (*mur*) to embed sth in(to); (*boîtier*) to fit sth into; **s'~ dans** to fit into; (*heurter*) to crash into.

encaustique [ɑ̃kostik] *nf* polish, wax; **encaustiquer** *vt* to polish, wax.

enceinte [ɑ̃sɛ̃t] *af*: ~ (**de 6 mois**) (6 months) pregnant // *nf* (*mur*) wall; (*espace*) enclosure; ~ (**acoustique**) speaker system.

encens [ɑ̃sɑ̃] *nm* incense; **encenser** *vt* to (in)cense; (*fig*) to praise to the skies; **encensoir** *nm* thurible.

encercler [ɑ̃sɛʀkle] *vt* to surround.

enchaîner [ɑ̃ʃene] *vt* to chain up; (*mouvements, séquences*) to link (together) // *vi* to carry on.

enchanté, e [ɑ̃ʃɑ̃te] *a* delighted; enchanted; ~ (**de faire votre connaissance**) pleased to meet you, how do you do?.

enchantement [ɑ̃ʃɑ̃tmɑ̃] *nm* delight; (*magie*) enchantment; **comme par ~** as if by magic.

enchanter [ɑ̃ʃɑ̃te] *vt* to delight.

enchâsser [ɑ̃ʃase] *vt*: ~ **qch (dans)** to set sth (in).

enchère [ɑ̃ʃɛʀ] *nf* bid; **faire une ~** to (make a) bid; **mettre/vendre aux ~s** to put up for (sale by)/sell by auction.

enchevêtrer [ɑ̃ʃvetʀe] *vt* to tangle (up).

enclave [ɑ̃klav] *nf* enclave; **enclaver** *vt* to enclose, hem in.

enclencher [ɑ̃klɑ̃ʃe] *vt* (*mécanisme*) to engage; **s'~** *vi* to engage.

enclin, e [ɑ̃klɛ̃, -in] *a*: ~ **à** inclined *ou* prone to.

enclore [ɑ̃klɔʀ] *vt* to enclose.

enclos [ɑ̃klo] *nm* enclosure.

enclume [ɑ̃klym] *nf* anvil.

encoche [ɑ̃kɔʃ] *nf* notch.

encoignure [ɑ̃kɔɲyʀ] *nf* corner.

encoller [ɑ̃kɔle] *vt* to paste.

encolure [ɑ̃kɔlyʀ] *nf* (*tour de cou*) collar size; (*col, cou*) neck.

encombrant, e [ɑ̃kɔ̃bʀɑ̃, -ɑ̃t] *a* cumbersome, bulky.

encombre [ɑ̃kɔ̃bʀ(ə)]: **sans ~** *ad* without mishap *ou* incident.

encombrement [ɑ̃kɔ̃bʀəmɑ̃] *nm* (*d'un lieu*) cluttering (up); (*d'un objet: dimensions*) bulk.

encombrer [ɑ̃kɔ̃bʀe] *vt* to clutter (up); (*gêner*) to hamper; **s'~ de** (*bagages etc*) to load *ou* burden o.s. with; ~ **le passage** to block *ou* obstruct the way.

encontre [ɑ̃kɔ̃tʀ(ə)]: **à l'~ de** *prép* against, counter to.

encorbellement [ɑ̃kɔʀbɛlmɑ̃] *nm* corbelled construction; **fenêtre en~** oriel window.

encore [ɑ̃kɔʀ] *ad* (*continuation*) still; (*de nouveau*) again; (*restriction*) even then *ou* so; (*intensif*): ~ **plus fort/mieux** even louder/better; **pas ~** not yet; ~ **une fois** (once) again; ~ **deux jours** still two days, two more days; **si** ~ if only.

encouragement [ɑ̃kuʀaʒmɑ̃] *nm* encouragement.

encourager [ɑ̃kuʀaʒe] *vt* to encourage.

encourir [ɑ̃kuʀiʀ] *vt* to incur.

encrasser [ɑ̃kʀase] *vt* to foul up; to soot up.

encre [ɑ̃kʀ(ə)] *nf* ink; ~ **de Chine** Indian ink; ~ **sympathique** invisible ink; **encrer** *vt* to ink; **encreur** *am*: **rouleau encreur** inking roller; **encrier** *nm* inkwell.

encroûter [ɑ̃kʀute]: **s'~** *vi* (*fig*) to get into a rut, get set in one's ways.

encyclique [ɑ̃siklik] *nf* encyclical.

encyclopédie [ɑ̃siklɔpedi] *nf* encyclopaedia; **encyclopédique** *a* encyclopaedic.

endémique [ɑ̃demik] *a* endemic.

endetter [ɑ̃dete] *vt*, **s'~** *vi* to get into debt.

endeuiller [ɑ̃dœje] *vt* to plunge into mourning; **manifestation endeuillée par** event over which a tragic shadow was cast by.

endiablé, e [ɑ̃djable] *a* furious, boisterous.

endiguer [ɑ̃dige] *vt* to dyke (up); (*fig*) to check, hold back.

endimancher [ɑ̃dimɑ̃ʃe] *vt*: **s'~** to put on one's Sunday best.

endive [ɑ̃div] *nf* chicory *q*.

endocrine [ɑ̃dɔkʀin] *af*: **glande ~** endocrine (gland).

endoctriner [ɑ̃dɔktʀine] *vt* to indoc⁺⁺inate.

endommager [ɑ̃dɔmaʒe] *vt* to damage.

endormi, e [ɑ̃dɔʀmi] *a* asleep; (*fig*) sleepy, drowsy; sluggish.

endormir [ɑ̃dɔʀmiʀ] *vt* to put to sleep; (*MÉD: dent, nerf*) to anaesthetize; (*fig: soupçons*) to allay; **s'~** *vi* to fall asleep, go to sleep.

endosser [ɑ̃dose] *vt* (*responsabilité*) to take, shoulder; (*chèque*) to endorse; (*uniforme, tenue*) to put on, don.

endroit [ɑ̃dʀwa] *nm* place; (*opposé à l'envers*) right side; **à l'~** right side out; the right way up; (*vêtement*) the right way out; **à l'~ de** *prép* regarding, with regard to.

enduire [ɑ̃dɥiʀ] *vt* to coat; ~ **qch de** to coat sth with; **enduit** *nm* coating.

endurance [ɑ̃dyʀɑ̃s] *nf* endurance.

endurant, e [ɑ̃dyʀɑ̃, -ɑ̃t] *a* tough, hardy.

endurcir [ɑ̃dyʀsiʀ] *vt* (*physiquement*) to toughen; (*moralement*) to harden; **s'~** *vi* to become tougher; to become hardened.

endurer [ɑ̃dyʀe] *vt* to endure, bear.

énergétique [enɛʀʒetik] *a* (*ressources etc*) energy *cpd*.

énergie [enɛʀʒi] *nf* (*PHYSIQUE*) energy; (*TECH*) power; (*fig: physique*) energy;

(: *morale*) vigour, spirit; **énergique** a energetic; vigorous; (*mesures*) drastic, stringent.

énergumène [enɛʀgymɛn] nm rowdy character ou customer.

énerver [enɛʀve] vt to irritate, annoy; s'~ vi to get excited, get worked up.

enfance [ɑ̃fɑ̃s] nf (*âge*) childhood; (*fig*) infancy; (*enfants*) children pl; petite ~ infancy.

enfant [ɑ̃fɑ̃] nm/f child (pl children); ~ de chœur nm (REL) altar boy; ~ prodige child prodigy; **enfanter** vi to give birth // vt to give birth to; **enfantillage** nm (*péj*) childish behaviour q; **enfantin, e** a childlike; child cpd.

enfer [ɑ̃fɛʀ] nm hell.

enfermer [ɑ̃fɛʀme] vt to shut up; (*à clef, interner*) to lock up.

enferrer [ɑ̃feʀe]: s'~ vi: s'~ dans to tangle o.s. up in.

enfiévré, e [ɑ̃fjevʀe] a (*fig*) feverish.

enfilade [ɑ̃filad] nf: une ~ de a series ou line of (interconnecting).

enfiler [ɑ̃file] vt (*vêtement*): ~ qch to slip sth on, slip into sth; (*insérer*): ~ qch dans to stick sth into; (*rue, couloir*) to take; (*perles*) to string; (*aiguille*) to thread; s'~ dans to disappear into.

enfin [ɑ̃fɛ̃] ad at last; (*en énumérant*) lastly; (*de restriction, résignation*) still; well; (*pour conclure*) in a word.

enflammer [ɑ̃flame] vt to set fire to; (MÉD) to inflame; s'~ to catch fire; to become inflamed.

enflé, e [ɑ̃fle] a swollen; (*péj: style*) bombastic, turgid.

enfler [ɑ̃fle] vi to swell (up); s'~ vi to swell; enflure nf swelling.

enfoncer [ɑ̃fɔ̃se] vt (*clou*) to drive in; (*faire pénétrer*): ~ qch dans to push ou knock ou drive sth into; (*forcer: porte*) to break open; (: *plancher*) to cause to cave in; (*fam: surpasser*) to lick // vi (*dans la vase etc*) to sink in; (*sol, surface porteuse*) to give way; s'~ vi to sink; s'~ dans to sink into; (*forêt, ville*) to disappear into.

enfouir [ɑ̃fwiʀ] vt (*dans le sol*) to bury; (*dans un tiroir etc*) to tuck away; s'~ dans/sous to bury o.s. in/under.

enfourcher [ɑ̃fuʀʃe] vt to mount.

enfourner [ɑ̃fuʀne] vt: ~ qch dans to shove ou stuff sth into.

enfreindre [ɑ̃fʀɛ̃dʀ(ə)] vt to infringe, break.

enfuir [ɑ̃fɥiʀ]: s'~ vi to run away ou off.

enfumer [ɑ̃fyme] vt to smoke out.

engagé, e [ɑ̃gaʒe] a (*littérature etc*) engagé, committed.

engageant, e [ɑ̃gaʒɑ̃, -ɑ̃t] a attractive, appealing.

engagement [ɑ̃gaʒmɑ̃] nm taking on, engaging; starting; investing; (*d'un écrivain etc, professionnel, financier*) commitment; (*promesse*) agreement, promise; (MIL: *combat*) engagement; prendre l'~ de faire to undertake to do; sans ~ (COMM) without obligation.

engager [ɑ̃gaʒe] vt (*embaucher*) to take on, engage; (*commencer*) to start; (*lier*) to bind, commit; (*impliquer, entraîner*) to

involve; (*investir*) to invest, lay out; (*faire intervenir*) to engage; (*inciter*): ~ qn à faire to urge sb to do; (*faire pénétrer*): ~ qch dans to insert sth into; s'~ (*s'embaucher*) to hire o.s., get taken on; (MIL) to enlist; (*promettre, politiquement*) to commit o.s.; (*débuter*) to start (up); s'~ à faire to undertake to do; s'~ dans (*rue, passage*) to enter, turn into; (*s'emboîter*) to engage ou fit into; (*fig: affaire, discussion*) to enter into, embark on.

engelures [ɑ̃ʒlyʀ] nfpl chilblains.

engendrer [ɑ̃ʒɑ̃dʀe] vt to father; (*fig*) to create, breed.

engin [ɑ̃ʒɛ̃] nm machine; instrument; vehicle; (AVIAT) aircraft inv; missile; ~ (*explosif*) (explosive) device.

englober [ɑ̃glɔbe] vt to include.

engloutir [ɑ̃glutiʀ] vt to swallow up; s'~ to be engulfed.

engoncé, e [ɑ̃gɔ̃se] a: ~ dans cramped in.

engorger [ɑ̃gɔʀʒe] vt to obstruct, block; s'~ vi to become blocked.

engouement [ɑ̃gumɑ̃] nm (sudden) passion.

engouffrer [ɑ̃gufʀe] vt to swallow up, devour; s'~ dans to rush into.

engourdi, e [ɑ̃guʀdi] a numb.

engourdir [ɑ̃guʀdiʀ] vt to numb; (*fig*) to dull, blunt; s'~ vi to go numb.

engrais [ɑ̃gʀɛ] nm manure; ~ (*chimique*) (chemical) fertilizer.

engraisser [ɑ̃gʀese] vt to fatten (up) // vi (*péj*) to get fat(ter).

engrenage [ɑ̃gʀənaʒ] nm gears pl, gearing; (*fig*) chain.

engueuler [ɑ̃gœle] vt (*fam*) to bawl out.

enhardir [ɑ̃aʀdiʀ]: s'~ vi to grow bolder.

énigmatique [enigmatik] a enigmatic.

énigme [enigm(ə)] nf riddle.

enivrer [ɑ̃nivʀe] vt: s'~ to get drunk; s'~ de (*fig*) to become intoxicated with.

enjambée [ɑ̃ʒɑ̃be] nf stride.

enjamber [ɑ̃ʒɑ̃be] vt to stride over; (*suj: pont etc*) to span, straddle.

enjeu, x [ɑ̃ʒø] nm stakes pl.

enjoindre [ɑ̃ʒwɛ̃dʀ(ə)] vt: ~ à qn de faire to enjoin ou order sb to do.

enjôler [ɑ̃ʒole] vt to coax, wheedle.

enjoliver [ɑ̃ʒɔlive] vt to embellish; enjoliveur nm (AUTO) hub cap.

enjoué, e [ɑ̃ʒwe] a playful.

enlacer [ɑ̃lase] vt (*étreindre*) to embrace, hug; (*suj: lianes*) to wind round, entwine.

enlaidir [ɑ̃lediʀ] vt to make ugly // vi to become ugly.

enlèvement [ɑ̃lɛvmɑ̃] nm removal; abduction, kidnapping; l'~ des ordures ménagères refuse collection.

enlever [ɑ̃lve] vt (*ôter: gén*) to remove; (: *vêtement, lunettes*) to take off; (: MÉD: *organe*) to remove, take out; (*emporter: ordures etc*) to collect, take away; (*prendre*): ~ qch à qn to take sth (away) from sb; (*kidnapper*) to abduct, kidnap; (*obtenir: prix, contrat*) to win; (MIL: *position*) to take; (*morceau de piano etc*) to execute with spirit ou brio.

enliser [ɑ̃lize]: s'~ vi to sink, get stuck.

enluminure [ɑ̃lyminyʀ] *nf* illumination.

enneigé, e [ɑ̃neʒe] *a* snowy; snowed-up.

enneigement [ɑ̃nɛʒmɑ̃] *nm* depth of snow, snowfall; **bulletin d'~** snow report.

ennemi, e [ɛnmi] *a* hostile; (MIL) enemy *cpd* // *nm, nf* enemy; **être ~ de** to be strongly averse *ou* opposed to.

ennoblir [ɑ̃nɔbliʀ] *vt* to ennoble.

ennui [ɑ̃nyi] *nm* (*lassitude*) boredom; (*difficulté*) trouble *q*; **avoir des ~s** to be in trouble; **ennuyer** *vt* to bother; (*lasser*) to bore; **s'ennuyer** to be bored; **s'ennuyer de** (*regretter*) to miss; **ennuyeux, euse** *a* boring, tedious; annoying.

énoncé [enɔ̃se] *nm* terms *pl*; wording; (LING) utterance.

énoncer [enɔ̃se] *vt* to say, express; (*conditions*) to set out, state.

enorgueillir [ɑ̃nɔʀgœjiʀ]: **s'~ de** *vt* to pride o.s. on; to boast.

énorme [enɔʀm(ə)] *a* enormous, huge; **énormément** *ad* enormously, tremendously; **énormément de neige/gens** an enormous amount of snow/number of people; **énormité** *nf* enormity, hugeness; outrageous remark.

enquérir [ɑ̃keʀiʀ]: **s'~ de** *vt* to inquire about.

enquête [ɑ̃kɛt] *nf* (*de journaliste, de police*) investigation; (*judiciaire, administrative*) inquiry; (*sondage d'opinion*) survey; **enquêter** *vi* to investigate; to hold an inquiry; to conduct a survey; **enquêteur, euse** *ou* **trice** *nm/f* officer in charge of the investigation; person conducting a survey.

enquiers *etc vb voir* **enquérir**.

enraciné, e [ɑ̃ʀasine] *a* deep-rooted.

enragé, e [ɑ̃ʀaʒe] *a* (MÉD) rabid, with rabies; (*fig*) fanatical.

enrageant, e [ɑ̃ʀaʒɑ̃, -ɑ̃t] *a* infuriating.

enrager [ɑ̃ʀaʒe] *vi* to be furious, be in a rage.

enrayer [ɑ̃ʀeje] *vt* to check, stop; **s'~** *vi* (*arme à feu*) to jam.

enregistrement [ɑ̃ʀʒistʀəmɑ̃] *nm* recording; (ADMIN) registration; **~ des bagages** (*à l'aéroport*) luggage check-in.

enregistrer [ɑ̃ʀʒistʀe] *vt* (MUS *etc*) to record; (*remarquer, noter*) to note, record; (*fig: mémoriser*) to make a mental note of; (ADMIN) to register; (*bagages: par train*) to register; (: *à l'aéroport*) to check in.

enrhumer [ɑ̃ʀyme]: **s'~** *vi* to catch a cold.

enrichir [ɑ̃ʀiʃiʀ] *vt* to make rich(er); (*fig*) to enrich; **s'~** to get rich(er).

enrober [ɑ̃ʀɔbe] *vt*: **~ qch de** to coat sth with; (*fig*) to wrap sth up in.

enrôler [ɑ̃ʀole] *vt* to enlist; **s'~** (**dans**) to enlist (in).

enrouer [ɑ̃ʀwe]: **s'~** *vi* to go hoarse.

enrouler [ɑ̃ʀule] *vt* (*fil, corde*) to wind (up); **~ qch autour de** to wind sth (a)round; **s'~** to coil up; to wind; **enrouleur** *nm voir* **ceinture**.

enrubanné, e [ɑ̃ʀybane] *a* trimmed with ribbon.

ensabler [ɑ̃sable] *vt* (*port, canal*) to silt up, sand up; (*embarcation*) to strand (on a sandbank); **s'~** *vi* to silt up; to get stranded.

ensanglanté, e [ɑ̃sɑ̃glɑ̃te] *a* covered with blood.

enseignant, e [ɑ̃sɛɲɑ̃, -ɑ̃t] *a* teaching // *nm/f* teacher.

enseigne [ɑ̃sɛɲ] *nf* sign // *nm*: **~ de vaisseau** lieutenant; **à telle ~ que** so much so that; **~ lumineuse** neon sign.

enseignement [ɑ̃sɛɲmɑ̃] *nm* teaching; (ADMIN): **~ primaire/secondaire** primary/secondary education.

enseigner [ɑ̃sɛɲe] *vt, vi* to teach; **~ qch à qn/à qn que** to teach sb sth/sb that.

ensemble [ɑ̃sɑ̃bl(ə)] *ad* together // *nm* (*assemblage*, MATH) set; (*totalité*): **l'~ du/de la** the whole *ou* entire; (*vêtement féminin*) ensemble, suit; (*unité, harmonie*) unity; (*résidentiel*) housing development; **impression/idée d'~** overall *ou* general impression/ idea; **dans l'~** (*en gros*) on the whole; **~ vocal/musical** vocal/musical ensemble.

ensemblier [ɑ̃sɑ̃blije] *nm* interior designer.

ensemencer [ɑ̃smɑ̃se] *vt* to sow.

enserrer [ɑ̃seʀe] *vt* to hug (tightly).

ensevelir [ɑ̃səvliʀ] *vt* to bury.

ensoleillé, e [ɑ̃sɔleje] *a* sunny.

ensoleillement [ɑ̃sɔlɛjmɑ̃] *nm* period *ou* hours of sunshine.

ensommeillé, e [ɑ̃sɔmeje] *a* sleepy, drowsy.

ensorceler [ɑ̃sɔʀsəle] *vt* to enchant, bewitch.

ensuite [ɑ̃sɥit] *ad* then, next; (*plus tard*) afterwards, later; **~ de quoi** after which.

ensuivre [ɑ̃sɥivʀ(ə)]: **s'~** *vi* to follow, ensue.

entaille [ɑ̃taj] *nf* (*encoche*) notch; (*blessure*) cut.

entailler [ɑ̃taje] *vt* to notch; to cut; **s'~ le doigt** to cut one's finger.

entamer [ɑ̃tame] *vt* (*pain, bouteille*) to start; (*hostilités, pourparlers*) to open; (*fig: altérer*) to make a dent in; to shake; to dam...

entartrer [ɑ̃taʀtʀe]: **s'~** *vi* to fur up; (*dents*) to scale.

entassement [ɑ̃tasmɑ̃] *nm* (*tas*) pile, heap.

entasser [ɑ̃tase] *vt* (*empiler*) to pile up, heap up; (*tenir à l'étroit*) to cram together; **s'~** *vi* to pile up; to cram.

entendement [ɑ̃tɑ̃dmɑ̃] *nm* understanding.

entendre [ɑ̃tɑ̃dʀ(ə)] *vt* to hear; (*comprendre*) to understand; (*vouloir dire*) to mean; (*vouloir*): **~ être obéi/que** to intend *ou* mean to be obeyed/that; **j'ai entendu dire que** I've heard (it said) that; **~ raison** to see sense; **s'~** *vi* (*sympathiser*) to get on; (*se mettre d'accord*) to agree; **s'~ à qch/à faire** (*être compétent*) to be good at sth/doing.

entendu, e [ɑ̃tɑ̃dy] *a* (*réglé*) agreed; (*au courant: air*) knowing; (*c'est*) **~!** all right, agreed; **c'est ~** (*concession*) all right, granted; **bien ~!** of course!

entente [ɑ̃tɑ̃t] *nf* (*entre amis, pays*) understanding, harmony; (*accord, traité*) agreement, understanding; **à double ~** (*sens*) with a double meaning.

entériner [ûteRine] vt to ratify, confirm.

entérite [ûteRit] nf enteritis q.

enterrement [ûtɛʀmô] nm burying; (cérémonie) funeral, burial.

enterrer [ûteRe] vt to bury.

entêtant, e [ûtɛtâ, -ât] a heady.

en-tête [ûtɛt] nm heading; **papier à ~** headed notepaper.

entêté, e [ûtete] a stubborn.

entêter [ûtete]: **s'~** vi: **s'~ (à faire)** to persist (in doing).

enthousiasme [ûtuzjasm(ə)] nm enthusiasm; **enthousiasmer** vt to fill with enthusiasm; **s'enthousiasmer (pour qch)** to get enthusiastic (about sth); **enthousiaste** a enthusiastic.

enticher [ûtiʃe]: **s'~ de** vt to become infatuated with.

entier, ère [ûtje, -jɛR] a (non entamé, en totalité) whole; (total, complet) complete; (fig: caractère) unbending, averse to compromise // nm (MATH) whole; **en ~** totally; in its entirety; **lait ~** full-cream milk; **pain ~** wholemeal bread; **entièrement** ad entirely, completely, wholly.

entité [ûtite] nf entity.

entonner [ûtone] vt (chanson) to strike up.

entonnoir [ûtonwaR] nm (ustensile) funnel; (trou) shell-hole, crater.

entorse [ûtɔRs(ə)] nf (MÉD) sprain; (fig): **~ à la loi/au règlement** infringement of the law/rule.

entortiller [ûtɔRtije] vt (envelopper): **~ qch dans/avec** to wrap sth in/with; (enrouler): **~ qch autour de** to twist ou wind sth (a)round; (fam): **~ qn** to get round sb; to hoodwink sb.

entourage [ûtuRaʒ] nm circle; family (circle); entourage; (ce qui enclôt) surround.

entourer [ûtuRe] vt to surround; (apporter son soutien à) to rally round; **~ de** to surround with; (trait) to encircle with.

entourloupettes [ûtuRlupɛt] nfpl mean tricks.

entracte [ûtRakt(ə)] nm interval.

entraide [ûtRɛd] nf mutual aid ou assistance; **s'entraider** to help each other.

entrailles [ûtRaj] nfpl entrails; bowels.

entrain [ûtRɛ] nm spirit; **avec/sans ~** spiritedly/half-heartedly.

entraînant, e [ûtRɛnâ, -ât] a (musique) stirring, rousing.

entraînement [ûtRɛnmâ] nm training; (TECH): **~ à chaîne/galet** chain/wheel drive.

entraîner [ûtRene] vt (tirer: wagons) to pull; (charrier) to carry ou drag along; (TECH) to drive; (emmener: personne) to take (off); (mener à l'assaut, influencer) to lead; (SPORT) to train; (impliquer) to entail; (causer) to lead to, bring about; **~ qn à faire** (inciter) to lead sb to do; **s'~** (SPORT) to train; **s'~ à qch/à faire** to train o.s. for sth/to do; **entraîneur, euse** nm/f (SPORT) coach, trainer // nm (HIPPISME) trainer // nf (de bar) hostess.

entrave [ûtRav] nf hindrance.

entraver [ûtRave] vt (circulation) to hold up; (action, progrès) to hinder, hamper.

entre [ûtR(ə)] prép between; (parmi) among(st); **l'un d'~ eux/nous** one of them/us; **ils se battent ~ eux** they are fighting among(st) themselves.

entrebâillé, e [ûtRəbaje] a half-open, ajar.

entrechoquer [ûtRəʃɔke]: **s'~** vi to knock ou bang together.

entrecôte [ûtRəkot] nf entrecôte ou rib steak.

entrecouper [ûtRəkupe] vt: **~ qch de** to intersperse sth with.

entrecroiser [ûtRəkRwaze] vt, **s'~** vi intertwine.

entrée [ûtRe] nf entrance; (accès: au cinéma etc) admission; (billet) (admission) ticket; (CULIN) first course; **d'~** ad from the outset; **'~ interdite'** 'no admittance ou entry'; **'~ libre'** 'admission free'; **~ des artistes** stage door; **~ en matière** introduction; **~ de service** service entrance.

entrefaites [ûtRəfɛt]: **sur ces ~** ad at this juncture.

entrefilet [ûtRəfilɛ] nm paragraph (short article).

entregent [ûtRəʒâ] nm: **avoir de l'~** to have an easy manner.

entrejambes [ûtRəʒâb] nm crotch.

entrelacer [ûtRəlase] vt, **s'~** vi to intertwine.

entrelarder [ûtRəlaRde] vt to lard.

entremêler [ûtRəmele] vt: **~ qch de** to (inter)mingle sth with.

entremets [ûtRəmɛ] nm cream dessert.

entremetteur, euse [ûtRəmɛtœR, -ɛz] nm/f go-between.

entremettre [ûtRəmɛtR(ə)]: **s'~** vi to intervene.

entremise [ûtRəmiz] nf intervention; **par l'~ de** through.

entrepont [ûtRəpô] nm steerage.

entreposer [ûtRəpoze] vt to store, put into storage.

entrepôt [ûtRəpo] nm warehouse.

entreprenant, e [ûtRəpRənâ, -ât] a (actif) enterprising; (trop galant) forward.

entreprendre [ûtRəpRâdR(ə)] vt (se lancer dans) to undertake; (commencer) to begin ou start (upon); (personne) to buttonhole; to tackle; **~ de faire** to undertake to do.

entrepreneur [ûtRəpRənœR] nm: **~ (en bâtiment)** (building) contractor; **~ de pompes funèbres** (funeral) undertaker.

entreprise [ûtRəpRiz] nf (société) firm, concern; (action) undertaking, venture.

entrer [ûtRe] vi to go (ou come) in, enter; (faire) **~ qch dans** to get sth into; **~ dans** (gén) to enter; (pièce) to go (ou come) into, enter; (club) to join; (heurter) to run into; (partager: vues, craintes de qn) to share; (être une composante de) to go into; to form part of; **~ à l'hôpital** to go into hospital; **laisser ~ qn/qch** to let sb/sth in; **faire ~** (visiteur) to show in.

entresol [ûtRəsɔl] nm entresol, mezzanine.

entre-temps [ûtRətâ] ad meanwhile, (in the) meantime.

entretenir [ûtRətniR] vt to maintain; (amitié) to keep alive; (famille, maîtresse) to support, keep; **~ qn (de)** to speak to sb (about); **s'~ (de)** to converse (about).

entretien [ɑ̃tʀətjɛ̃] *nm* maintenance ; *(discussion)* discussion, talk ; *(audience)* interview.

entrevoir [ɑ̃tʀəvwaʀ] *vt (à peine)* to make out ; *(brièvement)* to catch a glimpse of.

entrevue [ɑ̃tʀəvy] *nf* meeting ; *(audience)* interview.

entr'ouvert, e [ɑ̃tʀuvɛʀ, -ɛʀt(ə)] *a* half-open.

énumérer [enymeʀe] *vt* to list, enumerate.

envahir [ɑ̃vaiʀ] *vt* to invade ; *(suj: inquiétude, peur)* to come over ; **envahissant, e** *a (péj: personne)* interfering, intrusive ; **envahisseur** *nm* (MIL) invader.

enveloppe [ɑ̃vlɔp] *nf (de lettre)* envelope ; (TECH) casing ; outer layer ; **mettre sous ~** to put in an envelope.

envelopper [ɑ̃vlɔpe] *vt* to wrap ; *(fig)* to envelop, shroud.

envenimer [ɑ̃vnime] *vt* to aggravate.

envergure [ɑ̃vɛʀgyʀ] *nf (d'un oiseau, avion)* wingspan ; *(fig)* scope ; calibre.

enverrai *etc vb voir* envoyer.

envers [ɑ̃vɛʀ] *prép* towards, to // *nm* other side ; *(d'une étoffe)* wrong side ; **à l'~** upside down ; back to front ; *(vêtement)* inside out.

envie [ɑ̃vi] *nf (sentiment)* envy ; *(souhait)* desire, wish ; *(tache sur la peau)* birthmark ; *(filet de peau)* hangnail ; **avoir ~ de** to feel like ; *(désir plus fort)* to want ; **avoir ~ de faire** to feel like doing ; to want to do ; **avoir ~ que** to wish that ; **donner à qn l'~ de faire** to make sb want to do ; **ça lui fait ~** he would like that ; **envier** *vt* to envy ; **envieux, euse** *a* envious.

environ [ɑ̃viʀɔ̃] *ad*: **~ 3 h/2 km, 3 h/2 km ~** (around) about 3 o'clock/2 km, 3 o'clock/2 km or so ; **~s** *nmpl* surroundings ; **aux ~s de** around.

environnement [ɑ̃viʀɔnmɑ̃] *nm* environment.

environner [ɑ̃viʀɔne] *vt* to surround.

envisager [ɑ̃vizaʒe] *vt (examiner, considérer)* to view, contemplate ; *(avoir en vue)* to envisage ; **~ de faire** to consider *ou* contemplate doing.

envoi [ɑ̃vwa] *nm* sending ; *(paquet)* parcel, consignment.

envol [ɑ̃vɔl] *nm* takeoff.

envolée [ɑ̃vɔle] *nf (fig)* flight.

envoler [ɑ̃vɔle]: **s'~** *vi (oiseau)* to fly away *ou* off ; *(avion)* to take off ; *(papier, feuille)* to blow away ; *(fig)* to vanish (into thin air).

envoûter [ɑ̃vute] *vt* to bewitch.

envoyé, e [ɑ̃vwaje] *nm/f* (POL) envoy ; *(PRESSE)* correspondent.

envoyer [ɑ̃vwaje] *vt* to send ; *(lancer)* to hurl, throw ; **~ chercher** to send for ; **envoyeur, euse** *nm/f* sender.

éolien, ne [eɔljɛ̃, -jɛn] *a* wind *cpd*.

épagneul, e [epaɲœl] *nm/f* spaniel.

épais, se [epɛ, -ɛs] *a* thick ; **épaisseur** *nf* thickness ; **épaissir** *vt*, **s'épaissir** *vi* to thicken.

épanchement [epɑ̃ʃmɑ̃] *nm*: **un ~ de sinovie** water on the knee ; **~s** *nmpl (fig)* (sentimental) outpourings.

épancher [epɑ̃ʃe] *vt* to give vent to ; **s'~** *vi* to open one's heart ; *(liquide)* to pour out.

épandage [epɑ̃daʒ] *nm* manure spreading.

épanouir [epanwiʀ]: **s'~** *vi (fleur)* to bloom, open out ; *(visage)* to light up ; *(fig)* to blossom (out), bloom ; to open up ; **épanouissement** *nm* blossoming ; opening up.

épargnant, e [epaʀɲɑ̃, -ɑ̃t] *nm/f* saver, investor.

épargne [epaʀɲ(ə)] *nf* saving.

épargner [epaʀɲe] *vt* to save ; *(ne pas tuer ou endommager)* to spare // *vi* to save ; **~ qch à qn** to spare sb sth.

éparpiller [epaʀpije] *vt* to scatter ; *(pour répartir)* to disperse ; *(fig: efforts)* to dissipate ; **s'~** *vi* to scatter ; *(fig)* to dissipate one's efforts.

épars, e [epaʀ, -aʀs(ə)] *a* scattered.

épatant, e [epatɑ̃, -ɑ̃t] *a (fam)* super, splendid.

épaté, e [epate] *a*: **nez ~** flat nose (with wide nostrils).

épater [epate] *vt* to amaze ; to impress.

épaule [epol] *nf* shoulder.

épaulement [epolmɑ̃] *nm* escarpment ; retaining wall.

épauler [epole] *vt (aider)* to back up, support ; *(arme)* to raise (to one's shoulder) // *vi* to (take) aim.

épaulette [epolɛt] *nf* (MIL) epaulette ; *(de combinaison)* shoulder strap.

épave [epav] *nf* wreck.

épée [epe] *nf* sword.

épeler [eple] *vt* to spell.

éperdu, e [epɛʀdy] *a* distraught, overcome ; passionate ; frantic.

éperon [epʀɔ̃] *nm* spur ; **éperonner** *vt* to spur (on) ; *(navire)* to ram.

épervier [epɛʀvje] *nm* (ZOOL) sparrowhawk ; *(PÊCHE)* casting net.

éphèbe [efɛb] *nm* beautiful young man.

éphémère [efemɛʀ] *a* ephemeral, fleeting.

éphéméride [efemeʀid] *nf* block *ou* tear-off calendar.

épi [epi] *nm (de blé, d'orge)* ear ; **stationnement en ~** angled parking.

épice [epis] *nf* spice ; **épicé, e** *a* highly spiced, spicy ; *(fig)* spicy.

épicéa [episea] *nm* spruce.

épicer [epise] *vt* to spice ; *(fig)* to add spice to.

épicerie [episʀi] *nf (magasin)* grocer's shop ; *(denrées)* groceries *pl* ; **~ fine** delicatessen (shop) ; **épicier, ière** *nm/f* grocer.

épidémie [epidemi] *nf* epidemic.

épiderme [epidɛʀm(ə)] *nm* skin, epidermis ; **épidermique** *a* skin *cpd*, epidermic.

épier [epje] *vt* to spy on, watch closely ; *(occasion)* to look out for.

épieu, x [epjø] *nm* (hunting-)spear.

épilatoire [epilatwaʀ] *a* depilatory, hair-removing.

épilepsie [epilɛpsi] *nf* epilepsy ; **épileptique** *a*, *nm/f* epileptic.

épiler [epile] *vt (jambes)* to remove the hair from ; *(sourcils)* to pluck ; **se faire ~** to get unwanted hair removed.

épilogue [epilɔg] *nm* (*fig*) conclusion, dénouement.

épiloguer [epilɔge] *vi*: ~ **sur** to hold forth on.

épinard [epinaʀ] *nm* spinach q.

épine [epin] *nf* thorn, prickle ; (*d'oursin etc*) spine, prickle ; ~ **dorsale** backbone ; **épineux, euse** a thorny, prickly.

épingle [epɛ̃gl(ə)] *nf* pin ; **virage en** ~ **à cheveux** hairpin bend ; ~ **de cravate** tie pin ; ~ **de nourrice** *ou* **de sûreté** *ou* **double** safety pin.

épingler [epɛ̃gle] *vt* (*badge, décoration*): ~ **qch sur** to pin sth on(to) ; (*fam*) to catch, nick.

épinière [epinjɛʀ] *af voir* **moelle**.

Épiphanie [epifani] *nf* Epiphany.

épique [epik] *a* epic.

épiscopal, e, aux [episkɔpal, -o] *a* episcopal.

épiscopat [episkɔpa] *nm* bishopric, episcopate.

épisode [epizɔd] *nm* episode ; **film/roman à** ~**s** serialized film/novel, serial ; **épisodique** *a* occasional.

épissure [episyʀ] *nf* splice.

épistolaire [epistɔlɛʀ] *a* epistolary.

épitaphe [epitaf] *nf* epitaph.

épithète [epitɛt] *nf* (*nom, surnom*) epithet ; **adjectif** ~ attributive adjective.

épître [epitʀ(ə)] *nf* epistle.

éploré, e [eplɔʀe] *a* in tears, tearful.

épluche-légumes [eplyʃlegym] *nm inv* potato peeler.

éplucher [eplyʃe] *vt* (*fruit, légumes*) to peel ; (*comptes, dossier*) to go over with a fine-tooth comb ; **éplucheur** *nm* (automatic) peeler ; **épluchures** *nfpl* peelings.

épointer [epwɛ̃te] *vt* to blunt.

éponge [epɔ̃ʒ] *nf* sponge ; **éponger** *vt* (*liquide*) to mop *ou* sponge up ; (*surface*) to sponge ; (*fig: déficit*) to soak up, absorb ; s' **éponger le front** to mop one's brow.

épopée [epɔpe] *nf* epic.

époque [epɔk] *nf* (*de l'histoire*) age, era ; (*de l'année, la vie*) time ; **d'**~ *a* (*meuble*) period cpd.

épouiller [epuje] *vt* to pick lice off ; to delouse.

époumoner [epumɔne]: s' ~ *vi* to shout o.s. hoarse.

épouse [epuz] *nf* wife (*pl* wives).

épouser [epuze] *vt* to marry ; (*fig: idées*) to espouse ; (: *forme*) to fit.

épousseter [epuste] *vt* to dust.

époustouflant, e [epustuflɑ̃, -ɑ̃t] *a* staggering, mind-boggling.

épouvantable [epuvɑ̃tabl(ə)] *a* appalling, dreadful.

épouvantail [epuvɑ̃taj] *nm* (*à moineaux*) scarecrow ; (*fig*) bog(e)y ; bugbear.

épouvante [epuvɑ̃t] *nf* terror ; **film d'**~ horror film ; **épouvanter** *vt* to terrify.

époux [epu] *nm* husband // *nmpl* (married) couple.

éprendre [epʀɑ̃dʀ(ə)]: s' ~ **de** *vt* to fall in love with.

épreuve [epʀœv] *nf* (*d'examen*) test ; (*malheur, difficulté*) trial, ordeal ; (*PHOTO*) print ; (*d'imprimerie*) proof ; (*SPORT*) event ;

à l'~ **des balles** bulletproof ; **à toute** ~ unfailing ; **mettre à l'**~ to put to the test.

épris, e [epʀi, -iz] *vb voir* **éprendre**.

éprouver [epʀuve] *vt* (*tester*) to test ; (*mettre à l'épreuve*) to put to the test ; (*marquer, faire souffrir*) to afflict, distress ; (*ressentir*) to feel.

éprouvette [epʀuvɛt] *nf* test tube.

épuisé, e [epɥize] *a* exhausted ; (*livre*) out of print.

épuisement [epɥizmɑ̃] *nm* exhaustion ; **jusqu'à** ~ **des stocks** while stocks last.

épuiser [epɥize] *vt* (*fatiguer*) to exhaust, wear *ou* tire out ; (*stock, sujet*) to exhaust ; s' ~ *vi* to wear *ou* tire o.s. out, exhaust o.s. (*stock*) to run out.

épuisette [epɥizɛt] *nf* landing net ; shrimping net.

épurer [epyʀe] *vt* (*liquide*) to purify ; (*parti, administration*) to purge ; (*langue, texte*) to refine.

équarrir [ekaʀiʀ] *vt* (*pierre, arbre*) to square (off) ; (*animal*) to quarter.

équateur [ekwatœʀ] *nm* equator ; (**la république de**) **l'É**~ Ecuador.

équation [ekwasjɔ̃] *nf* equation ; **mettre en** ~ to equate.

équatorial, e, aux [ekwatɔʀjal, -o] *a* equatorial.

équerre [ekɛʀ] *nf* (*à dessin*) (set) square ; (*pour fixer*) brace ; **en** ~ at right angles ; **à l'**~, **d'**~ straight.

équestre [ekɛstʀ(ə)] *a* equestrian.

équidistant, e [ekɥidistɑ̃, -ɑ̃t] *a*: ~ (**de**) equidistant (from).

équilatéral, e, aux [ekɥilateʀal, -o] *a* equilateral.

équilibrage [ekilibʀaʒ] *nm* (*AUTO*): ~ **des roues** wheel balancing.

équilibre [ekilibʀ(ə)] *nm* balance ; (*d'une balance*) equilibrium ; **garder/perdre l'**~ to keep/lose one's balance ; **être en** ~ to be balanced ; **équilibré, e** *a* (*fig*) well-balanced, stable ; **équilibrer** *vt* to balance ; s'**équilibrer** (*poids*) to balance ; (*fig: défauts etc*) to balance each other out ; **équilibriste** *nm/f* tightrope walker.

équinoxe [ekinɔks] *nm* equinox.

équipage [ekipaʒ] *nm* crew.

équipe [ekip] *nf* team ; (*bande: parfois péj*) bunch.

équipée [ekipe] *nf* escapade.

équipement [ekipmɑ̃] *nm* equipment ; ~**s** *nmpl* amenities, facilities ; installations.

équiper [ekipe] *vt* to equip ; (*voiture, cuisine*) to equip, fit out ; ~ **qn/qch de** to equip sb/sth with ; s' ~ (*sportif*) to equip o.s., kit o.s. out.

équipier, ière [ekipje, -jɛʀ] *nm/f* team member.

équitable [ekitabl(ə)] *a* fair.

équitation [ekitasjɔ̃] *nf* (horse-)riding.

équité [ekite] *nf* equity.

équivalence [ekivalɑ̃s] *nf* equivalence.

équivalent, e [ekivalɑ̃, -ɑ̃t] *a, nm* equivalent.

équivaloir [ekivalwaʀ]: ~ **à** *vt* to be equivalent to ; (*représenter*) to amount to.

équivoque [ekivɔk] *a* equivocal, ambiguous ; (*louche*) dubious // *nf* ambiguity.

érable [eʀabl(ə)] nm maple.

érafler [eʀafle] vt to scratch; éraflure nf scratch.

éraillé, e [eʀaje] a (voix) rasping, hoarse.

ère [ɛʀ] nf era; en l'an 1050 de notre ~ in the year 1050 A.D.

érection [eʀɛksjɔ̃] nf erection.

éreinter [eʀɛ̃te] vt to exhaust, wear out; (fig: critiquer) to slate.

ergot [ɛʀgo] nm (de coq) spur; (TECH) lug.

ériger [eʀiʒe] vt (monument) to erect; s'~ en critique to set o.s. up as a critic.

ermitage [ɛʀmitaʒ] nm retreat.

ermite [ɛʀmit] nm hermit.

éroder [eʀɔde] vt to erode; érosion nf erosion.

érotique [eʀɔtik] a erotic; érotisme nm eroticism.

erratum, a [ɛʀatɔm, -a] nm erratum (pl a).

errer [ɛʀe] vi to wander.

erreur [ɛʀœʀ] nf mistake, error; (morale) error; être dans l'~ to be mistaken; par ~ by mistake; ~ judiciaire miscarriage of justice; ~ de jugement error of judgment.

erroné, e [ɛʀɔne] a wrong, erroneous.

éructer [eʀykte] vi belch, eructate.

érudit, e [eʀydi, -it] a erudite, learned // nm/f scholar; érudition nf erudition, scholarship.

éruptif, ive [eʀyptif, -iv] a eruptive.

éruption [eʀypsjɔ̃] nf eruption; (cutanée) outbreak.

es vb voir être.

ès [ɛs] prép: licencié ~ lettres/sciences ≈ Bachelor of Arts/Science.

escabeau, x [ɛskabo] nm (tabouret) stool; (échelle) stepladder.

escadre [ɛskadʀ(ə)] nf (NAVIG) squadron; (AVIAT) wing.

escadrille [ɛskadʀij] nf (AVIAT) flight.

escadron [ɛskadʀɔ̃] nm squadron.

escalade [ɛskalad] nf climbing q; (POL etc) escalation.

escalader [ɛskalade] vt to climb, scale.

escale [ɛskal] nf (NAVIG) call; port of call; (AVIAT) stop(over); faire ~ à to put in at, call in at; to stop over at.

escalier [ɛskalje] nm stairs pl; dans l'~ ou les ~s on the stairs; ~ roulant escalator; ~ de service backstairs.

escalope [ɛskalɔp] nf escalope.

escamotable [ɛskamɔtabl(ə)] a retractable; fold-away.

escamoter [ɛskamɔte] vt (esquiver) to get round, evade; (faire disparaître) to conjure away.

escapade [ɛskapad] nf: faire une ~ to go on a jaunt; to run away ou off.

escargot [ɛskaʀgo] nm snail.

escarmouche [ɛskaʀmuʃ] nf skirmish.

escarpé, e [ɛskaʀpe] a steep.

escarpement [ɛskaʀpəmɑ̃] nm steep slope.

escarpin [ɛskaʀpɛ̃] nm flat(-heeled) shoe.

escarre [ɛskaʀ] nf bedsore.

escient [esjɑ̃] nm: à bon ~ advisedly.

esclaffer [ɛsklafe] s'~ vi to guffaw.

esclandre [ɛsklɑ̃dʀ(ə)] nm scene, fracas.

esclavage [ɛsklavaʒ] nm slavery.

esclave [ɛsklav] nm/f slave; être ~ de (fig) to be a slave of.

escompte [ɛskɔ̃t] nm discount.

escompter [ɛskɔ̃te] vt (COMM) to discount; (espérer) to expect, reckon upon; ~ que to reckon ou expect that.

escorte [ɛskɔʀt(ə)] nf escort; escorter vt to escort; escorteur nm (NAVIG) escort (ship).

escouade [ɛskwad] nf squad.

escrime [ɛskʀim] nf fencing; escrimeur, euse nm/f fencer.

escrimer [ɛskʀime] s'~ vi: s'~ à faire to wear o.s. out doing.

escroc [ɛskʀo] nm swindler, conman.

escroquer [ɛskʀɔke] vt: ~ qn (de qch)/qch (à qn) to swindle sb (out of sth)/sth (out of sb); escroquerie nf swindle.

espace [ɛspas] nm space; ~ vital living space.

espacer [ɛspase] vt to space out; s'~ vi (visites etc) to become less frequent.

espadon [ɛspadɔ̃] nm swordfish inv.

espadrille [ɛspadʀij] nf rope-soled sandal.

Espagne [ɛspaɲ(ə)] nf: l'~ Spain; espagnol, e a Spanish // nm/f: Espagnol, e Spaniard // nm (langue) Spanish.

espagnolette [ɛspaɲɔlɛt] nf (window) catch; fermé à l'~ resting on the catch.

espèce [ɛspɛs] nf (BIO, BOT, ZOOL) species inv; (gén: sorte) sort, kind, type; (péj): ~ de maladroit/de brute! you clumsy oaf/brute!; ~s nfpl (COMM) cash sg; (REL) species; en l'~ ad in the case in point.

espérance [ɛspeʀɑ̃s] nf hope; ~ de vie (DÉMOGRAPHIE) life expectancy.

espérer [ɛspeʀe] vt to hope for; j'espère (bien) I hope so; ~ que/faire to hope that/to do; ~ en to trust in.

espiègle [ɛspjɛgl(ə)] a mischievous; ~rie nf mischievousness; piece of mischief.

espion, ne [ɛspjɔ̃, -ɔn] nm/f spy; avion ~ spy plane.

espionnage [ɛspjɔnaʒ] nm espionage, spying.

espionner [ɛspjɔne] vt to spy (up)on.

esplanade [ɛsplanad] nf esplanade.

espoir [ɛspwaʀ] nm hope.

esprit [ɛspʀi] nm (pensée, intellect) mind; (humour, ironie) wit; (mentalité, d'une loi etc, fantôme etc) spirit; l'~ d'équipe/de compétition team/competitive spirit; faire de l'~ to try to be witty; reprendre ses ~s to come to; perdre l'~ to lose one's mind; ~s chagrins faultfinders.

esquif [ɛskif] nm skiff.

esquimau, de, x [ɛskimo, -od] a, nm/f Eskimo.

esquinter [ɛskɛ̃te] vt (fam) to mess up.

esquisse [ɛskis] nf sketch; l'~ d'un sourire/changement the suggestion of a smile/of change.

esquisser [ɛskise] vt to sketch; s'~ vi (amélioration) to begin to be detectable; ~ un sourire to give a vague smile.

esquive [ɛskiv] nf (BOXE) dodging; (fig) side-stepping.

esquiver [ɛskive] *vt* to dodge ; **s'~** *vi* to slip away.

essai [esɛ] *nm* testing ; trying ; *(tentative)* attempt, try, *(RUGBY)* try ; *(LITTÉRATURE)* essay ; **~s** *(AUTO)* trials ; **~ gratuit** free trial ; **à l'~** on a trial basis.

essaim [esɛ̃] *nm* swarm ; **essaimer** *vi* to swarm ; *(fig)* to spread, expand.

essayage [esɛjaʒ] *nm (d'un vêtement)* trying on, fitting.

essayer [eseje] *vt (gén)* to try ; *(vêtement, chaussures)* to try (on) ; *(tester: ski, voiture)* to test ; *(restaurant, méthode)* to try (out) // *vi* to try ; **~ de faire** to try *ou* attempt to do ; **s'~ à faire** to try one's hand at doing.

essence [esɑ̃s] *nf (de voiture)* petrol ; *(extrait de plante, PHILOSOPHIE)* essence ; *(espèce: d'arbre)* species *inv* ; **prendre de l'~** to get petrol ; **~ de citron/rose** lemon/rose oil.

essentiel, le [esɑ̃sjɛl] *a* essential ; **emporter l'~** to take the essentials ; **c'est l'~** *(ce qui importe)* that's the main thing ; **l'~ de** *(la majeure partie)* the main part of.

esseulé, e [esœle] *a* forlorn.

essieu, x [esjø] *nm* axle.

essor [esɔʀ] *nm (de l'économie etc)* rapid expansion ; **prendre son ~** *(oiseau)* to fly off.

essorer [esɔʀe] *vt (en tordant)* to wring (out) ; *(par la force centrifuge)* to spin-dry ; **essoreuse** *nf* mangle, wringer ; spin-dryer.

essouffler [esufle] *vt* to make breathless ; **s'~** *vi* to get out of breath.

essuie-glace [esɥiglas] *nm inv* windscreen wiper.

essuie-mains [esɥimɛ̃] *nm inv* hand towel.

essuyer [esɥije] *vt* to wipe ; *(fig: subir)* to suffer ; **s'~** *(après le bain)* to dry o.s. ; **~ la vaisselle** to dry up, dry the dishes.

est [ɛst] *vb* [ɛ] *voir* **être** // *nm* : **l'~** the east // *a* east ; *(côte)* east(ern) ; **à l'~** in the east ; *(direction)* to the east, east(wards) ; **à l'~ de** (to the) east of.

estafette [ɛstafɛt] *nf (MIL)* dispatch rider.

estafilade [ɛstafilad] *nf* gash, slash.

est-allemand, e [ɛstalmɑ̃, -ɑ̃d] *a* East German.

estaminet [ɛstaminɛ] *nm* tavern.

estampe [ɛstɑ̃p] *nf* print, engraving.

estampille [ɛstɑ̃pij] *nf* stamp.

est-ce que [ɛska] *ad* : **~ c'est cher/c'était bon?** is it expensive/was it good? ; **quand est-ce qu'il part?** when does he leave?, when is he leaving? ; **qui est-ce qui le connaît/a fait ça?** who knows him/did that? ; *voir aussi* **que**.

esthète [ɛstɛt] *nm/f* aesthete.

esthéticienne [ɛstetisjɛn] *nf* beautician.

esthétique [ɛstetik] *a* attractive ; aesthetically pleasing // *nf* aesthetics *sg*.

estimation [ɛstimasjɔ̃] *nf* valuation ; assessment.

estime [ɛstim] *nf* esteem, regard.

estimer [ɛstime] *vt (respecter)* to esteem, hold in high regard ; *(expertiser)* to value ; *(évaluer)* to assess, estimate ; *(penser)* : **~ que/être** to consider that/o.s. to be ; **j'estime la distance à 10 km** I reckon the distance to be 10 km.

estival, e, aux [ɛstival, -o] *a* summer *cpd*.

estivant, e [ɛstivɑ̃, -ɑ̃t] *nm/f (summer)* holiday-maker.

estocade [ɛstɔkad] *nf* death-blow.

estomac [ɛstɔma] *nm* stomach.

estomaqué, e [ɛstɔmake] *a* flabbergasted.

estompe [ɛstɔ̃p] *nf* stump ; stump-drawing.

estomper [ɛstɔ̃pe] *vt (ART)* to shade off ; *(fig)* to blur, dim ; **s'~** *vi* to soften ; to become blurred.

estrade [ɛstʀad] *nf* platform, rostrum.

estragon [ɛstʀagɔ̃] *nm* tarragon.

estropié, e [ɛstʀɔpje] *nm/f* cripple.

estropier [ɛstʀɔpje] *vt* to cripple, maim ; *(fig)* to twist, distort.

estuaire [ɛstɥɛʀ] *nm* estuary.

estudiantin, e [ɛstydjɑ̃tɛ̃, -in] *a* student *cpd*.

esturgeon [ɛstyʀʒɔ̃] *nm* sturgeon.

et [e] *cj* and ; **~ lui?** what about him? ; **~ alors!** so what!.

étable [etabl(ə)] *nf* cowshed.

établi [etabli] *nm* (work)bench.

établir [etabliʀ] *vt (papiers d'identité, facture)* to make out ; *(liste, programme)* to draw up ; *(gouvernement, artisan etc: aider à s'installer)* to set up, establish ; *(entreprise, atelier, camp)* to set up ; *(réputation, usage, fait, culpabilité)* to establish ; **s'~** *vi (se faire: entente etc)* to be established ; **s'~** *(à son compte)* to set up one's own business ; **s'~ à/près de** to settle in/near.

établissement [etablismɑ̃] *nm* making out ; drawing up ; setting up, establishing ; *(entreprise, institution)* establishment ; **~ de crédit** credit institution ; **~ industriel** industrial plant, factory ; **~ scolaire** school, educational establishment.

étage [etaʒ] *nm (d'immeuble)* storey, floor ; *(de fusée)* stage ; *(GÉO: de culture, végétation)* level ; **au 2ème ~** on the 2nd floor ; **de bas ~** a low ; **étager** *vt (cultures)* to lay out in tiers ; **s'étager** *vi (prix)* to range ; *(zones, cultures)* to lie on different levels.

étagère [etaʒɛʀ] *nf (rayon)* shelf ; *(meuble)* shelves *pl*, set of shelves.

étai [etɛ] *nm* stay, prop.

étain [etɛ̃] *nm* tin ; *(ORFÈVRERIE)* pewter *q*.

étais *etc vb voir* **être**.

étal [etal] *nm* stall.

étalage [etalaʒ] *nm* display ; display window ; **faire ~ de** to show off, parade ; **étalagiste** *nm/f* window-dresser.

étale [etal] *a (mer)* slack.

étalement [etalmɑ̃] *nm* spreading, staggering.

étaler [etale] *vt (carte, nappe)* to spread (out) ; *(peinture, liquide)* to spread ; *(échelonner: paiements, dates, vacances)* to spread, stagger ; *(exposer: marchandises)* to display ; *(richesses, connaissances)* to parade ; **s'~** *vi (liquide)* to spread out ; *(fam)* to come a cropper ; **s'~ sur** *(suj: paiements etc)* to be spread out over.

étalon [etalɔ̃] *nm (mesure)* standard ; *(cheval)* stallion ; **étalonner** *vt* to calibrate.

étamer [etame] vt (casserole) to tin(plate) ; (glace) to silver.

étamine [etamin] nf (BOT) stamen ; (tissu) butter muslin.

étanche [etɑ̃ʃ] a (récipient) watertight ; (montre, vêtement) waterproof.

étancher [etɑ̃ʃe] vt (liquide) to stop (flowing) ; ~ sa soif to quench ou slake one's thirst.

étang [etɑ̃] nm pond.

étant [etɑ̃] vb voir être, donné.

étape [etap] nf stage ; (lieu d'arrivée) stopping place ; (: CYCLISME) staging point ; faire ~ à to stop off at.

état [eta] nm (POL, condition) state ; (d'un article d'occasion etc) condition, state ; (liste) inventory, statement ; (condition professionnelle) profession, trade ; (: sociale) status ; en mauvais ~ in poor condition ; en ~ (de marche) in (working) order ; remettre en ~ to repair ; hors d'~ out of order ; être en ~/hors d'~ de faire to be in a/in no fit state to do ; en tout ~ de cause in any event ; être dans tous ses ~s to be in a state ; faire ~ de (alléguer) to put forward ; en ~ d'arrestation under arrest ; en ~ de grâce (REL) in a state of grace ; (fig) inspired ; ~ civil civil status ; ~ des lieux inventory of fixtures ; ~ de santé state of health ; ~ de siège/d'urgence state of siege/emergency ; ~s d'âme moods ; ~s de service service record sg ; étatiser vt to bring under state control.

état-major [etamaʒɔʀ] nm (MIL) staff ; (d'un parti etc) top advisers pl ; top management.

États-Unis [etazyni] nmpl: les ~ (d'Amérique) the United States (of America).

étau, x [eto] nm vice.

étayer [eteje] vt to prop ou shore up ; (fig) to back up.

et c(a)etera [ɛtseteʀa], etc. ad et cetera, and so on, etc.

été [ete] pp de être // nm summer.

éteignoir [etɛɲwaʀ] nm (candle) extinguisher ; (péj) killjoy, wet blanket.

éteindre [etɛ̃dʀ(ə)] vt (lampe, lumière, radio) to turn ou switch off ; (cigarette, incendie, bougie) to put out, extinguish ; (JUR: dette) to extinguish ; s'~ vi to go out ; to go off ; (mourir) to pass away ; éteint, e a (fig) lacklustre, dull ; (volcan) extinct.

étendard [etɑ̃daʀ] nm standard.

étendre [etɑ̃dʀ(ə)] vt (appliquer: pâte, liquide) to spread ; (déployer: carte etc) to spread out ; (sur un fil: lessive, linge) to hang up ou out ; (bras, jambes, par terre: blessé) to stretch out ; (diluer) to dilute, thin ; (fig: agrandir) to extend ; (fam: adversaire) to floor ; s'~ vi (augmenter, se propager) to spread ; (terrain, forêt etc): s'~ jusqu'à/de ... to stretch as far as/from ... to ; s'~ (sur) (s'allonger) to stretch out (upon) ; (se reposer) to lie down (on) ; (fig: expliquer) to elaborate ou enlarge (upon).

étendu, e [etɑ̃dy] a extensive // nf (d'eau, de sable) stretch, expanse ; (importance) extent.

éternel, le [etɛʀnɛl] a eternal ; les neiges ~les perpetual snow.

éterniser [etɛʀnize]: s'~ vi to last for ages ; to stay for ages.

éternité [etɛʀnite] nf eternity ; de toute ~ from time immemorial.

éternuer [etɛʀnɥe] vi to sneeze.

êtes vb voir être.

étêter [etete] vt (arbre) to poll(ard) ; (clou, poisson) to cut the head off.

éther [etɛʀ] nm ether.

éthique [etik] a ethical // nf ethics sg.

ethnie [ɛtni] nf ethnic group.

ethnographie [ɛtnɔgʀafi] nf ethnography.

ethnologie [ɛtnɔlɔʒi] nf ethnology ; ethnologue nm/f ethnologist.

éthylisme [etilism(ə)] nm alcoholism.

étiage [etjaʒ] nm low water.

étiez vb voir être.

étinceler [etɛ̃sle] vi to sparkle.

étincelle [etɛ̃sɛl] nf spark.

étioler [etjɔle]: s'~ vi to wilt.

étique [etik] a skinny, bony.

étiqueter [etikte] vt to label.

étiquette [etikɛt] nf label ; (protocole): l'~ etiquette.

étirer [etiʀe] vt to stretch ; (ressort) to stretch out ; s'~ vi (personne) to stretch ; (convoi, route): s'~ sur to stretch out over.

étoffe [etɔf] nf material, fabric.

étoffer [etɔfe] vt, s'~ vi to fill out.

étoile [etwal] nf star ; à la belle ~ in the open ; ~ filante shooting star ; ~ de mer starfish ; étoilé, e a starry.

étole [etɔl] nf stole.

étonnant, e [etɔnɑ̃, -ɑ̃t] a amazing.

étonnement [etɔnmɑ̃] nm surprise, amazement.

étonner [etɔne] vt to surprise, amaze ; s'~ que/de to be amazed that/at ; cela m'étonnerait (que) (j'en doute) I'd be very surprised (if).

étouffant, e [etufɑ̃, -ɑ̃t] a stifling.

étouffée [etufe]: à l'~ ad (CULIN) steamed ; braised.

étouffer [etufe] vt to suffocate ; (bruit) to muffle ; (scandale) to hush up // vi to suffocate ; (avoir trop chaud) to feel stifled ; s'~ vi (en mangeant etc) to choke.

étourderie [etuʀdəʀi] nf heedlessness ; thoughtless blunder.

étourdi, e [etuʀdi] a (distrait) scatterbrained, heedless.

étourdir [etuʀdiʀ] vt (assommer) to stun, daze ; (griser) to make dizzy ou giddy ; étourdissant, e a staggering ; étourdissement nm dizzy spell.

étourneau, x [etuʀno] nm starling.

étrange [etʀɑ̃ʒ] a strange.

étranger, ère [etʀɑ̃ʒe, -ɛʀ] a foreign ; (pas de la famille, non familier) strange // nm/f foreigner ; stranger // nm: à l'~ abroad ; de l'~ from abroad ; ~ à (fig) unfamiliar to ; irrelevant to.

étranglement [etʀɑ̃glamɑ̃] nm (d'une vallée etc) constriction, narrow passage.

étrangler [etʀɑ̃gle] vt to strangle ; s'~ vi (en mangeant etc) to choke ; (se resserrer) to make a bottleneck.

étrave [etrav] *nf* stem.

être [ɛtr(ə)] *nm* being // *vb avec attribut,* *vi* to be // *vb auxiliaire* to have (*ou parfois* be) ; **il est instituteur** he is a teacher ; ~ **à qn** (*appartenir*) to be sb's, to belong to sb ; **c'est à moi/eux** it is *ou* it's mine/theirs ; **c'est à lui de le faire** it's up to him to do it ; ~ **de** (*provenance, origine*) to be from ; (*appartenance*) to belong to ; **nous sommes le 10 janvier** it's the 10th of January (today) ; **il est 10 heures, c'est 10 heures** it is *ou* it's 10 o'clock ; **c'est à réparer** it needs repairing ; **c'est à essayer** it should be tried ; ~ **humain** human being ; *voir aussi* **est-ce que, n'est-ce pas, c'est-à-dire, ce.**

étreindre [etrɛ̃dr(ə)] *vt* to clutch, grip ; (*amoureusement, amicalement*) to embrace ; **s'**~ to embrace ; **étreinte** *nf* clutch, grip ; embrace.

étrenner [etrene] *vt* to use (*ou* wear) for the first time.

étrennes [etrɛn] *nfpl* Christmas box *sg* (*fig*).

étrier [etrije] *nm* stirrup.

étriller [etrije] *vt* (*cheval*) to curry ; (*fam: battre*) to trounce.

étriper [etripe] *vt* to gut ; (*fam*): ~ **qn** to tear sb's guts out.

étriqué, e [etrike] *a* skimpy.

étroit, e [etrwa, -wat] *a* narrow ; (*vêtement*) tight ; (*fig: serré*) close, tight ; **à l'**~ *ad* cramped ; ~ **d'esprit** narrow-minded ; **étroitesse** *nf* narrowness.

étude [etyd] *nf* studying ; (*ouvrage, rapport*) study ; (*de notaire: bureau*) office ; (: *charge*) practice ; (*SCOL: salle de travail*) study room ; ~**s** *nfpl* (*SCOL*) studies ; **être à l'**~ (*projet etc*) to be under consideration ; **faires des** ~**s de droit/médecine** to study *ou* read law/medicine.

étudiant, e [etydjɑ̃, -ɑ̃t] *nm/f* student.

étudié, e [etydje] *a* (*démarche*) studied ; (*système*) carefully designed.

étudier [etydje] *vt, vi* to study.

étui [etɥi] *nm* case.

étuve [etyv] *nf* steamroom ; (*appareil*) sterilizer.

étuvée [etyve] : **à l'**~ *ad* braised.

étymologie [etimɔlɔʒi] *nf* etymology ; **étymologique** *a* etymological.

eu, eue [y] *pp voir* **avoir.**

eucalyptus [økaliptys] *nm* eucalyptus.

eugénique [øʒenik] *a* eugenic // *nf* eugenics *sg.*

euh [ø] *excl* er.

eunuque [ønyk] *nm* eunuch.

euphémisme [øfemism(ə)] *nm* euphemism.

euphonie [øfɔni] *nf* euphony.

euphorie [øfɔri] *nf* euphoria ; **euphorique** *a* euphoric.

eurasien, ne [ørazjɛ̃, -ɛn] *a, nm/f* Eurasian.

Europe [ørɔp] *nf* Europe ; **européen, ne** *a, nm/f* European.

eus *etc vb voir* **avoir.**

euthanasie [øtanazi] *nf* euthanasia.

eux [ø] *pronom* (*sujet*) they ; (*objet*) them.

évacuation [evakɥasjɔ̃] *nf* evacuation.

évacuer [evakɥe] *vt* (*salle, région*) to evacuate, clear ; (*occupants, population*) to evacuate ; (*toxine etc*) to evacuate, discharge.

évadé, e [evade] *a* escaped // *nm/f* escapee.

évader [evade] : **s'**~ *vi* to escape.

évaluation [evalɥasjɔ̃] *nf* assessment, evaluation.

évaluer [evalɥe] *vt* to assess, evaluate.

évangélique [evɑ̃ʒelik] *a* evangelical.

évangéliser [evɑ̃ʒelize] *vt* to evangelize.

évangile [evɑ̃ʒil] *nm* gospel.

évanouir [evanwir] : **s'**~ *vi* to faint, pass out ; (*disparaître*) to vanish, disappear.

évanouissement [evanwismɑ̃] *nm* (*syncope*) fainting fit ; (*dans un accident*) loss of consciousness.

évaporation [evapɔrasjɔ̃] *nf* evaporation.

évaporé, e [evapɔre] *a* giddy, scatterbrained.

évaporer [evapɔre] : **s'**~ *vi* to evaporate.

évaser [evaze] *vt* (*tuyau*) to widen, open out ; (*jupe, pantalon*) to flare ; **s'**~ *vi* to widen, open out.

évasif, ive [evazif, -iv] *a* evasive.

évasion [evazjɔ̃] *nf* escape ; **littérature d'**~ escapist literature.

évêché [eveʃe] *nm* bishopric ; bishop's palace.

éveil [evɛj] *nm* awakening ; **être en** ~ to be alert.

éveillé, e [eveje] *a* awake ; (*vif*) alert, sharp.

éveiller [eveje] *vt* to (a)waken ; **s'**~ *vi* to (a)waken ; (*fig*) to be aroused.

événement [evɛnmɑ̃] *nm* event.

éventail [evɑ̃taj] *nm* fan ; (*choix*) range ; **en** ~ fanned out ; fan-shaped.

éventaire [evɑ̃tɛr] *nm* stall, stand.

éventer [evɑ̃te] *vt* (*secret*) to discover, lay open ; (*avec un éventail*) to fan ; **s'**~ *vi* (*parfum*) to go stale.

éventrer [evɑ̃tre] *vt* to disembowel ; (*fig*) to tear *ou* rip open.

éventualité [evɑ̃tɥalite] *nf* eventuality ; possibility ; **dans l'**~ **de** in the event of.

éventuel, le [evɑ̃tɥɛl] *a* possible ; ~**lement** *ad* possibly.

évêque [evɛk] *nm* bishop.

évertuer [evɛrtɥe] : **s'**~ *vi*: **s'**~ **à faire** to try very hard to do.

éviction [eviksjɔ̃] *nf* ousting, supplanting ; (*de locataire*) eviction.

évidemment [evidamɑ̃] *ad* obviously.

évidence [evidɑ̃s] *nf* obviousness ; obvious fact ; **de toute** ~ quite obviously *ou* evidently ; **en** ~ conspicuous ; **mettre en** ~ to highlight ; to bring to the fore.

évident, e [evidɑ̃, -ɑ̃t] *a* obvious, evident.

évider [evide] *vt* to scoop out.

évier [evje] *nm* (kitchen) sink.

évincer [evɛ̃se] *vt* to oust, supplant.

évitement [evitmɑ̃] *nm*: **place d'**~ (*AUTO*) passing place.

éviter [evite] *vt* to avoid ; ~ **de faire/que qch ne se passe** to avoid doing/sth happening ; ~ **qch à qn** to spare sb sth.

évocateur, trice [evɔkatœR, -tRis] a evocative, suggestive.

évocation [evɔkasjɔ̃] nf evocation.

évolué, e [evɔlye] a advanced.

évoluer [evɔlye] vi (enfant, maladie) to develop; (situation, moralement) to evolve, develop; (aller et venir: danseur etc) to move about, circle; **évolution** nf development; evolution; **évolutions** nfpl movements.

évoquer [evɔke] vt to call to mind, evoke; (mentionner) to mention.

ex... [ɛks] préfixe ex-.

exacerber [ɛgzasɛRbe] vt to exacerbate.

exact, e [ɛgzakt] a (précis) exact, accurate, precise; (correct) correct; (ponctuel) punctual; **l'heure ~e** the right ou exact time; **~ement** ad exactly, accurately, precisely; correctly; (c'est cela même) exactly.

exactions [ɛgzaksjɔ̃] nfpl exactions.

exactitude [ɛgzaktityd] nf exactitude, accurateness, precision.

ex aequo [ɛgzeko] a equally placed; classé 1er ~ placed equal first.

exagération [ɛgzaʒeRasjɔ̃] nf exaggeration.

exagéré, e [ɛgzaʒeRe] a (prix etc) excessive.

exagérer [ɛgzaʒeRe] vt to exaggerate // vi (abuser) to go too far; overstep the mark; (déformer les faits) to exaggerate.

exaltation [ɛgzaltasjɔ̃] nf exaltation.

exalté, e [ɛgzalte] a (over)excited // nm/f (péj) fanatic.

exalter [ɛgzalte] vt (enthousiasmer) to excite, elate; (glorifier) to exalt.

examen [ɛgzamɛ̃] nm examination; (SCOL) exam, examination; **à l'~** under consideration; (COMM) on approval; **~ blanc** mock exam(ination); **~ de la vue** sight test.

examinateur, trice [ɛgzaminatœR, -tRis] nm/f examiner.

examiner [ɛgzamine] vt to examine.

exaspération [ɛgzaspeRasjɔ̃] nf exasperation.

exaspérer [ɛgzaspeRe] vt to exasperate; to exacerbate.

exaucer [ɛgzose] vt (vœu) to grant, fulfil; **~ qn** to grant sb's wishes.

excavateur [ɛkskavatœR] nm excavator, mechanical digger.

excavation [ɛkskavasjɔ̃] nf excavation.

excavatrice [ɛkskavatRis] nf = excavateur.

excédent [ɛksedɑ̃] nm surplus; **en ~** surplus; **~ de bagages** excess luggage; **excédentaire** a surplus, excess.

excéder [ɛksede] vt (dépasser) to exceed; (agacer) to exasperate.

excellence [ɛksɛlɑ̃s] nf excellence; (titre) Excellency.

excellent, e [ɛksɛlɑ̃, -ɑ̃t] a excellent.

exceller [ɛksele] vi: ~ (dans) to excel (in).

excentricité [ɛksɑ̃tRisite] nf eccentricity; **excentrique** a eccentric; (quartier) outlying.

excepté, e [ɛksɛpte] a, prép: **les élèves ~s, ~ les élèves** except for ou apart from the pupils; **~ si** except if.

excepter [ɛksɛpte] vt to except.

exception [ɛksɛpsjɔ̃] nf exception; **à l'~ de** except for, with the exception of; **d'~** (mesure, loi) special, exceptional; **exceptionnel, le** a exceptional.

excès [ɛksɛ] nm surplus // nmpl excesses; **à l'~** (méticuleux, généreux) to excess; **~ de vitesse** speeding q, exceeding the speed limit; **~ de zèle** overzealousness q; **excessif, ive** a excessive.

exciper [ɛksipe]: **~ de** vt to plead.

excitant [ɛksitɑ̃] nm stimulant.

excitation [ɛksitasjɔ̃] nf (état) excitement.

exciter [ɛksite] vt to excite; (suj: café etc) to stimulate; **s'~** vi to get excited; **~ qn à** (révolte etc) to incite sb to.

exclamation [ɛksklamasjɔ̃] nf exclamation.

exclamer [ɛksklame]: **s'~** vi to exclaim.

exclure [ɛksklyR] vt (faire sortir) to expel; (ne pas compter) to exclude, leave out; (rendre impossible) to exclude, rule out; **exclusif, ive** a exclusive; **exclusion** nf expulsion; **à l'exclusion de** with the exclusion ou exception of; **exclusivement** ad exclusively; **exclusivité** nf exclusiveness; (COMM) exclusive rights pl; **film passant en exclusivité à** film showing only at.

excommunier [ɛkskɔmynje] vt to excommunicate.

excréments [ɛkskRemɑ̃] nmpl excrement sg, faeces.

excroissance [ɛkskRwasɑ̃s] nf excrescence, outgrowth.

excursion [ɛkskyRsjɔ̃] nf (en autocar) excursion, trip; (à pied) walk, hike; **faire une ~** to go on an excursion ou a trip; to go on a walk ou hike; **excursionniste** nm/f tripper; hiker.

excuse [ɛkskyz] nf excuse; **~s** nfpl apology sg, apologies.

excuser [ɛkskyze] vt to excuse; **s'~ (de)** to apologize (for); **'excusez-moi'** 'I'm sorry'; (pour attirer l'attention) 'excuse me'.

exécrable [ɛgzekRabl(ə)] a atrocious.

exécrer [ɛgzekRe] vt to loathe, abhor.

exécutant, e [ɛgzekytɑ̃, -ɑ̃t] nm/f performer.

exécuter [ɛgzekyte] vt (prisonnier) to execute; (tâche etc) to execute, carry out; (MUS: jouer) to perform, execute; **s'~** vi to comply; **exécuteur, trice** nm/f (testamentaire) executor // nm (bourreau) executioner; **exécutif, ive** a, nm (POL) executive; **exécution** nf execution; carrying out; **mettre à exécution** to carry out.

exégèse [ɛgzeʒɛz] nf exegesis.

exemplaire [ɛgzɑ̃plɛR] a exemplary // nm copy.

exemple [ɛgzɑ̃pl(ə)] nm example; **par ~** for instance, for example; **donner l'~** to set an example; **prendre ~ sur** to take as a model; **à l'~ de** just like.

exempt, e [ɛgzɑ̃, -ɑ̃t] a: **~ de** (dispensé de) exempt from; (ne comportant pas de) free from.

exempter [ɛgzɑ̃te] vt: **~ de** to exempt from.

exercé, e [ɛgzɛʀse] a trained.

exercer [ɛgzɛʀse] vt (pratiquer) to exercise, practise; (faire usage de: prérogative) to exercise; (effectuer: influence, contrôle, pression) to exert; (former) to exercise, train // vi (médecin) to be in practice; s'~ (sportif, musicien) to practise; (se faire sentir: pression etc) to be exerted.

exercice [ɛgzɛʀsis] nm practice; exercising; (tâche, travail) exercise; (activité, sportive, physique): l'~ exercise; (MIL): l'~ drill; (COMM, ADMIN: période) accounting period; en ~ (juge) in office; (médecin) practising; dans l'~ de ses fonctions in the discharge of his duties.

exhaler [ɛgzale] vt to exhale; to utter, breathe; s'~ vi to rise (up).

exhaustif, ive [ɛgzostif, -iv] a exhaustive.

exhiber [ɛgzibe] vt (montrer: papiers, certificat) to present, produce; (péj) to display, flaunt s'~ to parade; (suj: exhibitionniste) to expose o.s.; exhibitionnisme nm exhibitionism.

exhorter [ɛgzɔʀte] vt: ~ qn à faire to urge sb to do.

exhumer [ɛgzyme] vt to exhume.

exigeant, e [ɛgziʒɑ̃, -ɑ̃t] a demanding; (péj) hard to please.

exigence [ɛgziʒɑ̃s] nf demand, requirement.

exiger [ɛgziʒe] vt to demand, require.

exigu, ë [ɛgzigy] a (lieu) cramped, tiny.

exil [ɛgzil] nm exile; en ~ in exile; ~é, e nm/f exile; ~er vt to exile; s'~er to go into exile.

existence [ɛgzistɑ̃s] nf existence.

exister [ɛgziste] vi to exist; il existe un/des there is a/are (some).

exode [ɛgzɔd] nm exodus.

exonérer [ɛgzɔneʀe] vt: ~ de to exempt from.

exorbitant, e [ɛgzɔʀbitɑ̃, -ɑ̃t] a exorbitant.

exorbité, e [ɛgzɔʀbite] a: yeux ~s bulging eyes.

exorciser [ɛgzɔʀsize] vt to exorcize.

exotique [ɛgzɔtik] a exotic; exotisme nm exoticism; exotic flavour ou atmosphere.

expansif, ive [ɛkspɑ̃sif, -iv] a expansive, communicative.

expansion [ɛkspɑ̃sjɔ̃] nf expansion.

expatrier [ɛkspatʀije] vt: s'~ to leave one's country, expatriate o.s.

expectative [ɛkspɛktativ] nf: être dans l'~ to be still waiting.

expectorer [ɛkspɛktɔʀe] vi to expectorate.

expédient [ɛkspedjɑ̃] nm (péj) expedient; vivre d'~s to live by one's wits.

expédier [ɛkspedje] vt (lettre, paquet) to send; (troupes) to dispatch; (péj: travail etc) to dispose of, dispatch; expéditeur, trice nm/f sender.

expéditif, ive [ɛkspeditif, -iv] a quick, expeditious.

expédition [ɛkspedisjɔ̃] nf sending; (scientifique, sportive, MIL) expedition.

expéditionnaire [ɛkspedisjɔnɛʀ] a: corps ~ task force.

expérience [ɛksperjɑ̃s] nf (de la vie) experience; (scientifique) experiment; avoir de l'~ to have experience, be experienced; avoir l'~ de to have experience of.

expérimental, e, aux [ɛksperimɑ̃tal, -o] a experimental.

expérimenté, e [ɛksperimɑ̃te] a experienced.

expérimenter [ɛksperimɑ̃te] vt (technique) to test out, experiment with.

expert, e [ɛkspɛʀ, -ɛʀt(ə)] a, nm expert; ~ en assurances insurance valuer; ~-comptable nm ≈ chartered accountant.

expertise [ɛkspɛʀtiz] nf valuation; assessment; valuer's (ou assessor's) report; (JUR) (forensic) examination.

expertiser [ɛkspɛʀtize] vt (objet de valeur) to value; (voiture accidentée etc) to assess damage to.

expier [ɛkspje] vt to expiate, atone for.

expiration [ɛkspiʀasjɔ̃] nf expiry; breathing out q.

expirer [ɛkspiʀe] vi (venir à échéance, mourir) to expire; (respirer) to breathe out.

explétif, ive [ɛkspletif, -iv] a expletive.

explicatif, ive [ɛksplikatif, -iv] a explanatory.

explication [ɛksplikasjɔ̃] nf explanation; (discussion) discussion; argument; ~ de texte (SCOL) critical analysis (of a text).

explicite [ɛksplisit] a explicit; expliciter vt to make explicit.

expliquer [ɛksplike] vt to explain; s'~ (discuter) to discuss things; to have it out; son erreur s'explique one can understand his mistake.

exploit [ɛksplwa] nm exploit, feat.

exploitant [ɛksplwatɑ̃] nm farmer.

exploitation [ɛksplwatasjɔ̃] nf exploitation; running; ~ agricole farming concern.

exploiter [ɛksplwate] vt (mine) to exploit, work (entreprise, ferme) to run, operate; (clients, ouvriers, erreur, don) to exploit; exploiteur, euse nm/f exploiter.

explorateur, trice [ɛksplɔʀatœʀ, -tʀis] nm/f explorer.

exploration [ɛksplɔʀasjɔ̃] nf exploration.

explorer [ɛksplɔʀe] vt to explore.

exploser [ɛksploze] vi to explode, blow up; (engin explosif) to go off; (fig: joie, colère) to burst out, explode; (personne: de colère) to explode, flare up; explosif, ive a, nm explosive; explosion nf explosion.

exportateur, trice [ɛkspɔʀtatœʀ, -tʀis] a export cpd, exporting // nm exporter.

exportation [ɛkspɔʀtasjɔ̃] nf exportation; export.

exporter [ɛkspɔʀte] vt to export.

exposant [ɛkspozɑ̃] nm exhibitor; (MATH) exponent.

exposé, e [ɛkspoze] nm talk // a: ~ au sud facing south, with a southern aspect; bien ~ well situated; très ~ very exposed.

exposer [ɛkspoze] vt (marchandise) to display; (peinture) to exhibit, show; (parler de: problème, situation) to explain, set out; (mettre en danger, orienter, PHOTO) to expose; ~ qn/qch à to expose sb/sth to ; **exposition** *nf* displaying ; exhibiting ; setting out ; (*voir exposé*) aspect, situation ; (*manifestation*) exhibition ; (*PHOTO*) exposure.

exprès [ɛkspʀɛ] *ad* (*délibérément*) on purpose ; (*spécialement*) specially ; **faire ~ de faire qch** to do sth on purpose.

exprès, esse [ɛkspʀɛs] *a* (*ordre, défense*) express, formal // *a inv, ad* (*PTT*) express.

express [ɛkspʀɛs] *a, nm*: (**café**) **~** espresso ; (**train**) **~** fast train.

expressément [ɛkspʀɛsemɑ̃] *ad* expressly ; specifically.

expressif, ive [ɛkspʀesif, -iv] *a* expressive.

expression [ɛkspʀɛsjɔ̃] *nf* expression.

exprimer [ɛkspʀime] *vt* to express ; (*jus, liquide*) to press out ; **s'~** *vi* (*personne*) to express o.s.

expropriation [ɛkspʀɔpʀijɑsjɔ̃] *nf* expropriation ; **frapper d'~** to put a compulsory purchase order on.

exproprier [ɛkspʀɔpʀije] *vt* to buy up (*ou* buy the property of) by compulsory purchase, expropriate.

expulser [ɛkspylse] *vt* to expel ; (*locataire*) to evict ; (*FOOTBALL*) to send off ; **expulsion** *nf* expulsion ; eviction ; sending off.

expurger [ɛkspyʀʒe] *vt* to expurgate, bowdlerize.

exquis, e [ɛkski, -iz] *a* exquisite ; delightful.

exsangue [ɛksɑ̃g] *a* bloodless, drained of blood.

extase [ɛkstɑz] *nf* ecstasy ; **s'extasier sur** to go into ecstasies *ou* raptures over.

extenseur [ɛkstɑ̃sœʀ] *nm* (*SPORT*) chest expander.

extensible [ɛkstɑ̃sibl(ə)] *a* extensible.

extensif, ive [ɛkstɑ̃sif, -iv] *a* extensive.

extension [ɛkstɑ̃sjɔ̃] *nf* (*d'un muscle, ressort*) stretching ; (*MÉD*) **à l'~** in traction ; (*fig*) extension ; expansion.

exténuer [ɛkstenɥe] *vt* to exhaust.

extérieur, e [ɛksteʀjœʀ] *a* (*porte, mur etc*) outer, outside ; (*au dehors: escalier, w.-c.*) outside ; (*commerce*) foreign ; (*influences*) external ; (*apparent: calme, gaieté etc*) surface *cpd* // *nm* (*d'une maison, d'un récipient etc*) outside, exterior ; (*d'une personne: apparence*) exterior ; (*d'un groupe social*): **l'~** the outside world ; **à l'~** outside ; (*à l'étranger*) abroad ; **~ement** *ad* on the outside ; (*en apparence*) on the surface ; **extérioriser** *vt* to show ; to exteriorize.

exterminer [ɛkstɛʀmine] *vt* to exterminate, wipe out.

externat [ɛkstɛʀna] *nm* day school.

externe [ɛkstɛʀn(ə)] *a* external, outer // *nm/f* (*MÉD*) non-resident medical student ; (*SCOL*) day pupil.

extincteur [ɛkstɛ̃ktœʀ] *nm* (fire) extinguisher.

extinction [ɛkstɛ̃ksjɔ̃] *nf* extinction ; (*JUR: d'une dette*) extinguishment ; **~ de voix** loss of voice.

extirper [ɛkstiʀpe] *vt* (*tumeur*) to extirpate ; (*plante*) to root out, pull up.

extorquer [ɛkstɔʀke] *vt*: **~ qch à qn** to extort sth from sb.

extra [ɛkstʀa] *a inv* first-rate ; top-quality // *nm inv* extra help.

extraction [ɛkstʀaksjɔ̃] *nf* extraction.

extrader [ɛkstʀade] *vt* to extradite ; **extradition** *nf* extradition.

extraire [ɛkstʀɛʀ] *vt* to extract ; **extrait** *nm* (*de plante*) extract ; (*de film, livre*) extract, excerpt.

extra-lucide [ɛkstʀalysid] *a*: **voyante ~** clairvoyant.

extraordinaire [ɛkstʀaɔʀdinɛʀ] *a* extraordinary ; (*POL: mesures*) special ; **ambassadeur ~** ambassador extraordinary.

extravagance [ɛkstʀavagɑ̃s] *nf* extravagance *q* ; extravagant behaviour *q*.

extravagant, e [ɛkstʀavagɑ̃, -ɑ̃t] *a* extravagant ; wild.

extraverti, e [ɛkstʀavɛʀti] *a* extrovert.

extrême [ɛkstʀɛm] *a, nm* extreme ; **~ment** *ad* extremely ; **~-onction** *nf* last rites *pl*, Extreme Unction ; **E~-Orient** *nm* Far East ; **extrémiste** *a, nm/f* extremist.

extrémité [ɛkstʀemite] *nf* end ; (*situation*) straits *pl*, plight ; (*geste désespéré*) extreme action ; **~s** *nfpl* (*pieds et mains*) extremities ; **à la dernière ~** (*à l'agonie*) on the point of death.

exubérant, e [ɛgzybeʀɑ̃, -ɑ̃t] *a* exuberant.

exulter [ɛgzylte] *vi* to exult.

exutoire [ɛgzytwaʀ] *nm* outlet, release.

ex-voto [ɛksvɔto] *nm inv* ex-voto.

F

F *abr de* franc.

fa [fa] *nm inv* (*MUS*) F ; (*en chantant la gamme*) fa.

fable [fabl(ə)] *nf* fable ; (*mensonge*) story, tale.

fabricant [fabʀikɑ̃] *nm* manufacturer, maker.

fabrication [fabʀikasjɔ̃] *nf* manufacture, making.

fabrique [fabʀik] *nf* factory.

fabriquer [fabʀike] *vt* to make ; (*industriellement*) to manufacture, make ; (*fig*): **u'est-ce qu'il fabrique?** what is he doing?

fabulation [fabylasjɔ̃] *nf* fantasizing.

fabuleux, euse [fabylø, -øz] *a* fabulous, fantastic.

façade [fasad] *nf* front, façade ; (*fig*) façade.

face [fas] *nf* face ; (*fig: aspect*) side // *a*: **le côté ~ heads** ; **perdre la ~** to lose face ; **en ~ de** *prép* opposite ; (*fig*) in front of ; **de ~** *ad* from the front ; **face on** ; **~ à** *prép* facing ; (*fig*) faced with, in the face of ; **faire ~ à** to face ; **~ à ~** *ad* facing each other // *nm inv* encounter ; **~-à-main** *nm* lorgnette.

facéties [fasesi] *nfpl* jokes, pranks.

facétieux, euse [fasesjø, -øz] *a* mischievous.

facette [fasɛt] *nf* facet.

fâché, e [fɑʃe] *a* angry ; (*désolé*) sorry.

fâcher [fɑʃe] *vt* to anger ; **se ~** *vi* to get angry ; **se ~ avec** (*se brouiller*) to fall out with.

fâcheux, euse [faʃó, -éz] a unfortunate, regrettable.

facial, e, aux [fasjal, -o] a facial.

faciès [fasjɛs] nm features pl, facies.

facile [fasil] a easy; (accommodant) easy-going; ~ment ad easily; facilité nf easiness; (disposition, don) aptitude; facilités nfpl facilities; facilités de paiement easy terms; faciliter vt to make easier.

façon [fasɔ̃] nf (manière) way; (d'une robe etc) making-up; cut; ~s nfpl (péj) fuss sg; de quelle ~? (in) what way?; de ~ à so as to; de ~ à ce que so that; de toute ~ anyway, in any case.

faconde [fakɔ̃d] nf loquaciousness, volubility.

façonner [fasɔne] vt (fabriquer) to manufacture; (travailler: matière) to shape, fashion; (fig) to mould, shape.

fac-similé [faksimile] nm facsimile.

facteur, trice [faktœʀ, -tʀis] nm/f postman/woman // nm (MATH, fig: élément) factor; ~ d'orgues organ builder; ~ de pianos piano maker.

factice [faktis] a artificial.

faction [faksjɔ̃] nf (groupe) faction; (surveillance) guard ou sentry (duty); watch; en ~ on guard; standing watch; factionnaire nm guard, sentry.

factoriel, le [faktɔʀjɛl] a factorial.

factotum [faktɔtɔm] nm odd-job man, dogsbody.

facture [faktyʀ] nf (à payer: gén) bill; (: COMM) invoice; (d'un artisan, artiste) technique, workmanship; facturer vt to invoice.

facultatif, ive [fakyltatif, -iv] a optional; (arrêt de bus) request cpd.

faculté [fakylte] nf (intellectuelle, d'université) faculty; (pouvoir, possibilité) power.

fadaises [fadɛz] nfpl twaddle sg.

fade [fad] a insipid.

fading [fadiŋ] nm (RADIO) fading.

fagot [fago] nm (de bois) bundle of sticks.

fagoté, e [fagɔte] a (fam): drôlement ~ in a peculiar getup.

faible [fɛbl(ə)] a weak; (voix, lumière, vent) faint; (rendement, intensité, revenu etc) low // nm weak point; weakness, soft spot; ~ d'esprit feeble-minded; faiblesse nf weakness; faiblir vi to weaken; (lumière) to dim; (vent) to drop.

faïence [fajɑ̃s] nf earthenware q; piece of earthenware.

faignant, e [fɛɲɑ̃, -ɑ̃t] nm/f = fainéant, e.

faille [faj] vb voir falloir // nf (GÉO) fault; (fig) flaw, weakness.

faillible [fajibl(ə)] a fallible.

faim [fɛ̃] nf hunger; avoir ~ to be hungry; rester sur sa ~ (aussi fig) to be left wanting more.

fainéant, e [fɛneɑ̃, -ɑ̃t] nm/f idler, loafer.

faire [fɛʀ] vt to make; (effectuer: travail, opération) to do; vraiment? fit-il really? he said; fait à la main/machine hand-/machine-made; ~ du bruit/des taches to make a noise/marks; ~ du rugby/piano to play rugby/play the piano; ~ le malade/l'ignorant to act the

invalid/the fool; ~ de qn un frustré/avocat to make sb a frustrated person/a lawyer; cela ne me fait rien (m'est égal) I don't care ou mind; (me laisse froid) it has no effect on me; cela ne fait rien it doesn't matter; je vous le fais 10 F (j'en demande 10 F) I'll let you have it for 10 F; que faites-vous? (quel métier etc) what do you do?; (quelle activité: au moment de la question) what are you doing?; comment a-t-il fait pour how did he manage to; qu'a-t-il fait de sa valise? what has he done with his case?; 2 et 2 font 4 2 and 2 are ou make 4 // vb avec attribut: ça fait 10 m/15 F it's 10 m/15 F // vb substitut: ne le casse pas comme je l'ai fait don't break it as I did // vb impersonnel voir jour, froid etc; ça fait 2 ans qu'il est parti it's 2 years since he left; ça fait 2 ans qu'il y est he's been there for 2 years; faites! please do!; il ne fait que critiquer (sans cesse) all he (ever) does is criticize; (seulement) he's only criticizing; ~ vieux/démodé to look old/old-fashioned // ~ faire: ~ réparer qch to get ou have sth repaired; ~ tomber/bouger qch to make sth fall/move; cela fait dormir it makes you sleep; ~ travailler les enfants to make the children work, get the children to work; ~ punir les enfants to have the children punished; ~ démarrer un moteur/chauffer de l'eau to start up an engine/heat some water; se ~ examiner la vue/opérer to have one's eyes tested/have an operation; il s'est fait aider (par qn) he got sb to help him; il va se ~ tuer/punir he's going to get himself killed/get (himself) punished; se ~ faire un vêtement to get a garment made for o.s. // se ~ vi (fromage, vin) to mature; se ~ à (s'habituer) to get used to; cela se fait beaucoup/ne se fait pas it's done a lot/not done; comment se fait-il/faisait-il que how is it/was it that; se ~ vieux to be getting old; se ~ des amis to make friends; il ne s'en fait pas he doesn't worry.

faisable [fəzabl(ə)] a feasible.

faisan [fəzɑ̃, -an] nm/f pheasant.

faisandé, e [fəzɑ̃de] a high.

faisceau, x [fɛso] nm (de lumière etc) beam; (de branches etc) bundle.

faiseur, euse [fəzœʀ, -éz] nm/f (gén: péj): ~ de maker of // nm (bespoke) tailor.

faisons vb voir faire.

fait [fɛ] nm (événement) event, occurrence; (réalité, donnée: s'oppose à hypothèse) fact; le ~ que/de manger the fact that/of eating; être le ~ de (causé par) to be the work of; être au ~ (de) to be informed (of); au ~ (à propos) by the way; en venir au ~ to get to the point; de ~ a (opposé à: de droit) de facto // ad in fact; du ~ de ceci/qu'il a menti because of ou on account of this/his having lied; de ce ~ therefore, for this reason; en ~ in fact; en ~ de repas by way of a meal; prendre ~ et cause pour qn to support sb, side with sb; prendre qn sur le ~ to catch sb in the act; ~ d'armes feat of arms; ~ divers (short) news item; les ~s et gestes de qn sb's actions ou doings.

fait, e [fɛ, fɛt] a (mûr: fromage, melon) ripe; un homme ~ a grown man; c'en est ~ de notre tranquillité that's the end of our peace.

faîte [fɛt] nm top; (fig) pinnacle, height.

faites vb voir **faire**.

faîtière [fɛtjɛʀ] nf (de tente) ridge pole.

fait-tout nm inv, **faitout** nm [fɛtu] stewpot.

fakir [fakiʀ] nm wizard.

falaise [falɛz] nf cliff.

fallacieux, euse [falasjø, -øz] a fallacious; deceptive; illusory.

falloir [falwaʀ] vb impersonnel: il va ~ 100 F we'll (ou I'll) need 100 F; il doit ~ du temps that must take time; il me faudrait 100 F I would need 100 F; il vous faut tourner à gauche après l'église you have to ou want to turn left past the church; nous avons ce qu'il (nous) faut we have what we need; il faut qu'il parte/a fallu qu'il parte (obligation) he has to ou must leave/had to leave; il a fallu le faire it had to be done // s'en ~: il s'en est fallu de 100 F/5 minutes we (ou they) were 100 F short/5 minutes late (ou early); il s'en faut de beaucoup qu'il soit he is far from being; il s'en est fallu de peu que cela n'arrive it very nearly happened.

falot, e [falo, -ɔt] a dreary, colourless // nm lantern.

falsifier [falsifje] vt to falsify; to doctor.

famé, e [fame] a: mal ~ disreputable, of ill repute.

famélique [famelik] a half-starved.

fameux, euse [famø, -øz] a (illustre) famous; (bon: repas, plat etc) first-rate, first-class.

familial, e, aux [familjal, -o] a family cpd // nf (AUTO) estate car.

familiariser [familjaʀize] vt: ~ qn avec to familiarize sb with.

familiarité [familjaʀite] nf informality; familiarity; ~ avec (sujet, science) familiarity with; ~s nfpl familiarities.

familier, ière [familje, -jɛʀ] a (connu, impertinent) familiar; (dénotant une certaine intimité) informal, friendly; (LING) informal, colloquial // nm regular (visitor).

famille [famij] nf family; il a de la ~ à Paris he has relatives in Paris.

famine [famin] nf famine.

fan [fan] nm/f fan.

fanal, aux [fanal, -o] nm beacon; lantern.

fanatique [fanatik] a fanatical // nm/f fanatic; **fanatisme** nm fanaticism.

faner [fane]: se ~ vi to fade.

faneur, euse [fanœʀ, -øz] nm/f hay-maker.

fanfare [fɑ̃faʀ] nf (orchestre) brass band; (musique) fanfare.

fanfaron, ne [fɑ̃faʀɔ̃, -ɔn] nm/f braggart.

fange [fɑ̃ʒ] nf mire.

fanion [fanjɔ̃] nm pennant.

fanon [fanɔ̃] nm (de baleine) plate of baleen; (repli de peau) dewlap, wattle.

fantaisie [fɑ̃tezi] nf (spontanéité) fancy, imagination; (caprice) whim; extravagance; (MUS) fantasia // a: bijou/pain ~ fancy jewellery/bread;

fantaisiste a (péj) unorthodox, eccentric // nm/f (de music-hall) variety artist ou entertainer.

fantasme [fɑ̃tasm(ə)] nm fantasy.

fantasque [fɑ̃task(ə)] a whimsical, capricious; fantastic.

fantassin [fɑ̃tasɛ̃] nm infantryman.

fantastique [fɑ̃tastik] a fantastic.

fantoche [fɑ̃tɔʃ] nm (péj) puppet.

fantomatique [fɑ̃tɔmatik] a ghostly.

fantôme [fɑ̃tom] nm ghost, phantom.

faon [fɑ̃] nm fawn.

farce [faʀs(ə)] nf (viande) stuffing; (blague) (practical) joke; (THÉÂTRE) farce; ~s et attrapes jokes and novelties; **farceur, euse** nm/f practical joker; **farcir** vt (viande) to stuff; (fig): **farcir qch de** to stuff sth with.

fard [faʀ] nm make-up.

fardeau, x [faʀdo] nm burden.

farder [faʀde] vt to make up.

farfelu, e [faʀfəly] a cranky, hare-brained.

farfouiller [faʀfuje] vi (péj) to rummage around.

farine [faʀin] nf flour; **farineux, euse** a (sauce, pomme) floury // nmpl (aliments) starchy foods.

farouche [faʀuʃ] a shy, timid; savage, wild; fierce.

fart [faʀ(t)] nm (ski) wax; **farter** vt to wax.

fascicule [fasikyl] nm volume.

fascination [fasinɑsjɔ̃] nf fascination.

fasciner [fasine] vt to fascinate.

fascisme [fasism(ə)] nm fascism; **fasciste** a, nm/f fascist.

fasse etc vb voir **faire**.

faste [fast(ə)] nm splendour // a: c'est un jour ~ it's his (ou our) lucky day.

fastidieux, euse [fastidjø, -øz] a tedious, tiresome.

fastueux, euse [fastɥø, -øz] a sumptuous, luxurious.

fat [fa] am conceited, smug.

fatal, e [fatal] a fatal; (inévitable) inevitable; ~isme nm fatalism; fatalistic outlook; ~ité nf fate; fateful coincidence; inevitability.

fatidique [fatidik] a fateful.

fatigant, e [fatigɑ̃, -ɑ̃t] a tiring; (agaçant) tiresome.

fatigue [fatig] nf tiredness, fatigue.

fatiguer [fatige] vt to tire, make tired; (TECH) to put a strain on, strain; (fig: importuner) to wear out // vi (moteur) to labour, strain; se ~ to get tired; to tire o.s. (out).

fatras [fatʀa] nm jumble, hotchpotch.

fatuité [fatɥite] nf conceitedness, smugness.

faubourg [fobuʀ] nm suburb.

fauché, e [foʃe] a (fam) broke.

faucher [foʃe] vt (herbe) to cut; (champs, blés) to reap; (fig) to cut down; to mow down; **faucheur, euse** nm/f, nf (machine) reaper, mower.

faucille [fosij] nf sickle.

faucon [fokɔ̃] nm falcon, hawk.

faudra vb voir **falloir**.

faufiler [fofile] vt to tack, baste; se ~ vi: se ~ dans to edge one's way into; se ~

parmi/entre to thread one's way among/between.

faune [fon] nf (zool) wildlife, fauna // nm faun.

faussaire [foseʀ] nm forger.

fausse [fos] a voir faux.

faussement [fosmɑ̃] ad (accuser) wrongly, wrongfully; (croire) falsely, erroneously.

fausser [fose] vt (objet) to bend, buckle; (fig) to distort.

fausset [fosɛ] nm: voix de ~ falsetto voice.

faussete [foste] nf wrongness; falseness.

faut vb voir falloir.

faute [fot] nf (erreur) mistake, error; (péché, manquement) misdemeanour; (FOOTBALL etc) offence; (TENNIS) fault; (responsabilité): par la ~ de through the fault of, because of; c'est de sa/ma ~ it's his/my fault; être en ~ to be in the wrong; ~ de (temps, argent) for ou through lack of; sans ~ without fail; ~ de frappe typing error; ~ d'orthographe spelling mistake; ~ professionnelle professional misconduct q.

fauteuil [fotœj] nm armchair; ~ club (big) easy chair; ~ d'orchestre seat in the front stalls; ~ roulant wheelchair.

fauteur [fotœʀ] nm: ~ de troubles trouble-maker.

fautif, ive [fotif, -iv] a (incorrect) incorrect, inaccurate; (responsable) at fault, in the wrong; guilty // nm/f culprit.

fauve [fov] nm wildcat // a (couleur) fawn.

faux [fo] nf scythe.

faux, fausse [fo, fos] a (inexact) wrong; (falsifié) fake; forged; (sournois, postiche) false // ad (MUS) out of tune // nm (copie) fake, forgery; (opposé au vrai): le ~ falsehood; le ~ numéro/la fausse clef the wrong number/key; faire ~ bond à qn to stand sb up; ~ col detachable collar; ~ frais nmpl extras, incidental expenses; ~ mouvement awkward movement; ~ nez funny nose; ~ pas tripping q; (fig) faux pas; ~ témoignage (délit) perjury; fausse alerte false alarm; fausse couche miscarriage; ~-filet nm sirloin; ~-fuyant nm equivocation; ~-monnayeur nm counterfeiter, forger.

faveur [favœʀ] nf favour; (ruban) ribbon; traitement de ~ preferential treatment; à la ~ de under cover of; thanks to; en ~ de in favour of.

favorable [favoʀabl(ə)] a favourable.

favori, te [favoʀi, -it] a, nm/f favourite; ~s nmpl (barbe) sideboards, sideburns.

favoriser [favoʀize] vt to favour.

favoritisme [favoʀitism(ə)] nm (péj) favouritism.

FB sigle = franc belge.

fébrile [febʀil] a feverish, febrile.

fécal, e, aux [fekal, -o] a voir matière.

fécond, e [fekɔ̃, -ɔ̃d] a fertile; **féconder** vt to fertilize; **fécondité** nf fertility.

fécule [fekyl] nf potato flour.

fédéral, e, aux [fedeʀal, -o] a federal; **fédéralisme** nm federalism.

fédération [fedeʀɑsjɔ̃] nf federation.

fée [fe] nf fairy; ~rie nf enchantment; ~rique a magical, fairytale cpd.

feignant, e [fɛɲɑ̃, -ɑ̃t] nm/f = fainéant, e.

feindre [fɛ̃dʀ(ə)] vt to feign // vi to dissemble; ~ de faire to pretend to do.

feinte [fɛ̃t] nf (SPORT) dummy.

fêler [fele] vt to crack.

félicitations [felisitɑsjɔ̃] nfpl congratulations.

félicité [felisite] nf bliss.

féliciter [felisite] vt: ~ qn (de) to congratulate sb (on).

félin, e [felɛ̃, -in] a feline // nm (big) cat.

félon, ne [felɔ̃, -ɔn] a perfidious, treacherous.

fêlure [felyʀ] nf crack.

femelle [fəmɛl] a (aussi ÉLEC, TECH) female // nf female; souris ~ female mouse, she-mouse.

féminin, e [feminɛ̃, -in] a feminine; (sexe) female; (équipe, vêtements etc) women's // nm feminine; **féministe** a feminist; **féminité** nf femininity.

femme [fam] nf woman; (épouse) wife (pl wives); **devenir** ~ to attain womanhood; ~ de chambre cleaning lady; ~ de ménage domestic help, cleaning lady.

fémur [femyʀ] nm femur, thighbone.

fenaison [fənɛzɔ̃] nf haymaking.

fendre [fɑ̃dʀ(ə)] vt (couper en deux) to split; (fissurer) to crack; (fig: traverser) to cut through; to cleave through; se ~ vi to crack; **fendu, e** a (sol, mur) cracked; (jupe) slit.

fenêtre [fənɛtʀ(ə)] nf window.

fenouil [fənuj] nm fennel.

fente [fɑ̃t] nf (fissure) crack; (de boîte à lettres etc) slit.

féodal, e, aux [feodal, -o] a feudal; **féodalité** nf feudality.

fer [fɛʀ] nm iron; (de cheval) shoe; au ~ rouge with a red-hot iron; ~ à cheval horseshoe; ~ forgé wrought iron; ~ de lance spearhead; ~ (à repasser) iron; ~ à souder soldering iron.

ferai etc vb voir faire.

fer-blanc [fɛʀblɑ̃] nm tin(plate); **ferblanterie** nf tinplate making; tinware; **ferblantier** nm tinsmith.

férié, e [feʀje] a: jour ~ public holiday.

ferions etc vb voir faire.

férir [feʀiʀ]: sans coup ~ ad without meeting any opposition.

ferme [fɛʀm(ə)] a firm // ad (travailler etc) hard // nf (exploitation) farm; (maison) farmhouse.

fermé, e [fɛʀme] a closed, shut; (gaz, eau etc) off; (fig: personne) uncommunicative; (: milieu) exclusive.

ferment [fɛʀmɑ̃] nm ferment.

fermentation [fɛʀmɑ̃tɑsjɔ̃] nf fermentation.

fermenter [fɛʀmɑ̃te] vi to ferment.

fermer [fɛʀme] vt to close, shut; (cesser l'exploitation de) to close down, shut down; (eau, lumière, électricité, robinet) to put off, turn off; (aéroport, route) to close // vi to close, shut; to close down, shut down; se

~ vi (yeux) to close, shut ; (fleur, blessure) to close up.

fermeté [fɛRməte] nf firmness.

fermeture [fɛRmətyR] nf closing ; shutting ; closing ou shutting down ; putting ou turning off ; (dispositif) catch ; fastening, fastener ; **heure de ~** (COMM) closing time ; **jour de ~** (COMM) day on which the shop (etc) is closed ; **~ éclair** ® ou **à glissière** zip (fastener), zipper.

fermier, ière [fɛRmje, -jɛR] nm farmer // nf woman farmer ; farmer's wife // a: **beurre/cidre ~** farm butter/cider.

fermoir [fɛRmwaR] nm clasp.

féroce [feRɔs] a ferocious, fierce.

ferons vb voir **faire.**

ferraille [fɛRaj] nf scrap iron ; **mettre à la ~** to scrap ; **ferrailleur** nm scrap merchant.

ferré, e [fɛRe] a hobnailed ; steel-tipped ; (fam): **~ en** well up on, hot at.

ferrer [fɛRe] vt (cheval) to shoe ; (chaussure) to nail ; (canne) to tip ; (poisson) to strike.

ferreux, euse [fɛRø, -øz] a ferrous.

ferronnerie [fɛRɔnRi] nf ironwork ; ~ **d'art** wrought iron work ; **ferronnier** nm craftsman in wrought iron ; ironware merchant.

ferroviaire [fɛRɔvjɛR] a rail(way) cpd.

ferrure [fɛRyR] nf (ornamental) hinge.

ferry-boat [fɛRebot] nm ferry.

fertile [fɛRtil] a fertile ; ~ **en incidents** eventful, packed with incidents ; **fertiliser** vt to fertilize ; **fertilité** nf fertility.

féru, e [feRy] a: ~ **de** with a keen interest in.

férule [feRyl] nf: **être sous la ~ de qn** to be under sb's (iron) rule.

fervent, e [fɛRvã, -ãt] a fervent.

ferveur [fɛRvœR] nf fervour.

fesse [fɛs] nf buttock ; **fessée** nf spanking.

festin [fɛstɛ̃] nm feast.

festival [fɛstival] nm festival ; **~ier** nm festival-goer.

festivités [fɛstivite] nfpl festivities, merry-making sg.

feston [fɛstɔ̃] nm (ARCHIT) festoon ; (COUTURE) scallop.

festoyer [fɛstwaje] vi to feast.

fêtard [fɛtaR] nm (péj) high liver, merry-maker.

fête [fɛt] nf (religieuse) feast ; (publique) holiday ; (en famille etc) celebration ; (kermesse) fête, fair, festival ; (du nom) feast day, name day ; **faire la ~** to live it up ; **faire ~ à qn** to give sb a warm welcome ; **les ~s (de fin d'année)** the Christmas and New Year holidays, the festive season ; **la salle/le comité des ~s** the village hall/ festival committee ; ~ **foraine** (fun) fair ; ~ **mobile** movable feast (day) ; **la F~ Nationale** the national holiday ; **la Fête-Dieu** Corpus Christi ; **fêter** vt to celebrate ; (personne) to have a celebration for.

fétiche [fetiʃ] nm fetish ; **fétichisme** nm fetishism.

fétide [fetid] a fetid.

fétu [fety] nm: ~ **de paille** wisp of straw.

feu [fø] a inv: ~ **son père** his late father.

feu, x [fø] nm (gén) fire ; (signal lumineux) light ; (de cuisinière) ring ; (sensation de brûlure) burning (sensation) // nmpl (éclat, lumière) fire sg ; (AUTO) (traffic) lights ; à ~ **doux/vif** over a slow/brisk heat ; à **petit ~** (CULIN) over a gentle heat ; **faire** ~ to fire ; **tué au** ~ killed in action ; **mettre à** ~ (fusée) to fire off ; **prendre** ~ to catch fire ; **mettre le** ~ **à** to set fire to, set on fire ; **faire du** ~ to make a fire ; **avez-vous du** ~ ? (pour cigarette) have you (got) a light? ; ~ **rouge/vert/orange** red/green/ amber light ; ~ **arrière** rear light ; ~ **d'artifice** firework ; (spectacle) fireworks pl ; ~ **de camp** campfire ; ~ **de cheminée** chimney fire ; ~ **de joie** bonfire ; ~ **de paille** (fig) flash in the pan ; ~x **de brouillard** fog-lamps ; ~x **de croisement** dipped headlights ; ~x **de position** sidelights ; ~x **de route** head-lights, headlamps.

feuillage [fœjaʒ] nm foliage, leaves pl.

feuille [fœj] nf (d'arbre) leaf (pl leaves) ; ~ **(de papier)** sheet (of paper) ; ~ **d'or/de métal** gold/metal leaf ; ~ **d'impôts** tax form ; ~ **morte** dead leaf ; ~ **de température** temperature chart ; ~ **de vigne** (BOT) vine leaf ; (sur statue) fig leaf ; ~ **volante** loose sheet.

feuillet [fœjɛ] nm leaf (pl leaves), page.

feuilleté, e [fœjte] a (CULIN) flaky.

feuilleter [fœjte] vt (livre) to leaf through.

feuilleton [fœjtɔ̃] nm serial.

feuillu, e [fœjy] a leafy ; ~s nmpl (BOT) broad-leaved trees.

feulement [følmã] nm growl.

feutre [føtR(ə)] nm felt ; (chapeau) felt hat ; **feutré, e** a feltlike ; (pas, voix) muffled ; **feutrer** vt to felt ; (fig) to muffle // vi, se **feutrer** vi to felt ; **feutrine** nf (lightweight) felt.

fève [fɛv] nf broad bean.

février [fevRije] nm February.

FF sigle = **franc français.**

F.F.I. sigle fpl = **Forces françaises de l'intérieur** (1942-45) // sigle m member of the F.F.I.

fi [fi] excl: **faire** ~ **de** to snap one's fingers at.

fiacre [fjakR(ə)] nm (hackney) cab ou carriage.

fiançailles [fjãsaj] nfpl engagement sg.

fiancé, e [fjãse] nm/f fiancé/fiancée // a: **être** ~ (à) to be engaged (to).

fiancer [fjãse]: **se** ~ vi: **se** ~(avec) to become engaged (to).

fibre [fibR(ə)] nf fibre ; ~ **de verre** fibre-glass, glass fibre ; **fibreux, euse** a fibrous ; (viande) stringy.

ficeler [fisle] vt to tie up.

ficelle [fisɛl] nf string q ; piece ou length of string.

fiche [fiʃ] nf (pour fichier) (index) card ; (formulaire) form ; (ÉLEC) plug.

ficher [fiʃe] vt (pour un fichier) to file ; (POLICE) to put on file ; (planter): ~ **qch dans** to stick ou drive sth into ; (fam) to do ; to give ; to stick ou shove ; **fiche(-moi) le camp** (fam) clear off ; **fiche-moi la paix** (fam) leave me alone ; **se** ~ **dans** (s'enfoncer) to get stuck in, embed itself in ; se ~ de (fam) to make fun of ; not to care about.

fichier [fiʃje] nm file ; card index.

fichu, e [fiʃy] pp de ficher (fam) // a (fam: fini, inutilisable) bust, done for ; (: intensif) wretched, darned // nm (foulard) (head)scarf (pl scarves) ; mal ~ (fam) feeling lousy ; useless.

fictif, ive [fiktif, -iv] a fictitious.

fiction [fiksjɔ̃] nf fiction ; (fait imaginé) invention.

fidèle [fidɛl] a : ~ (à) faithful (to) // nm/f (REL): les ~s the faithful ; (à l'église) the congregation ; **fidélité** nf faithfulness ; fidélité conjugale marital fidelity.

fief [fjɛf] nm fief ; (fig) preserve ; strong-hold.

fiel [fjɛl] nm gall.

fiente [fjɑ̃t] nf (bird) droppings pl.

fier [fje]: se ~ à vt to trust.

fier, fière [fjɛʀ] a proud ; ~ de proud of ; avoir fière allure to cut a fine figure ; ~té nf pride.

fièvre [fjɛvʀ(ə)] nf fever ; avoir de la ~/39 de ~ to have a high temperature/a temperature of 39°C ; ~ typhoïde typhoid fever ; **fiévreux, euse** a feverish.

fifre [fifʀ(ə)] nm fife ; fife-player.

figer [fiʒe] vt to congeal ; (fig: personne) to freeze, root to the spot ; se ~ vi to congeal ; to freeze ; (institutions etc) to become set, stop evolving.

figue [fig] nf fig ; **figuier** nm fig tree.

figurant, e [figyʀɑ̃, -ɑ̃t] nm/f ; (THÉÂTRE) walk-on ; (CINÉMA) extra.

figuratif, ive [figyʀatif, -iv] a a representational, figurative.

figuration [figyʀasjɔ̃] nf walk-on parts pl ; extras pl.

figure [figyʀ] nf (visage) face ; (image, tracé, forme, personnage) figure ; (illustration) picture, diagram ; faire ~ de to look like.

figuré, e [figyʀe] a (sens) figurative.

figurer [figyʀe] vi to appear // vt to represent ; se ~ que to imagine that.

figurine [figyʀin] nf figurine.

fil [fil] nm (brin, fig: d'une histoire) thread ; (du téléphone) cable, wire ; (textile de lin) linen ; (d'un couteau: tranchant) edge ; au ~ des années with the passing of the years ; au ~ de l'eau with the stream ou current ; donner/recevoir un coup de ~ to make/get a phone call ; ~ à coudre (sewing) thread ou yarn ; ~ électrique electric wire ; ~ de fer wire ; ~ de fer barbelé barbed wire ; ~ à pêche fishing line ; ~ à plomb plumbline ; ~ à souder soldering wire.

filament [filamɑ̃] nm (ÉLEC) filament ; (de liquide) trickle, thread.

filandreux, euse [filɑ̃dʀø, -øz] a stringy.

filasse [filas] a inv white blond.

filature [filatyʀ] nf (fabrique) mill ; (policière) shadowing q, tailing q.

file [fil] nf line ; ~ (d'attente) queue ; prendre la ~ to join the (end of the) queue ; prendre la ~ de droite (AUTO) to move into the right-hand lane ; se mettre en ~ to form a line ; (AUTO) to get into

lane ; en ~ indienne in single file ; à la ~ ou (d'affilée) in succession.

filer [file] vt (tissu, toile, verre) to spin ; (dérouler: câble etc) to pay ou let out ; to veer ou (prendre en filature) to shadow, tail ; (fam: donner): ~ qch à qn to slip sb sth // vi (bas, maille, liquide, pâte) to run ; (aller vite) to fly past ou by ; (fam: partir) to make off ; ~ doux to behave o.s., toe the line.

filet [file] nm net ; (CULIN) fillet ; (d'eau, de sang) trickle ; ~ (à provisions) string bag.

filetage [filtaʒ] nm threading ; thread.

fileter [filte] vt to thread.

filial, e, aux [filjal, -o] a filial // nf (COMM) subsidiary.

filiation [filjasjɔ̃] nf filiation.

filière [filjɛʀ] nf: passer par la ~ to go through the (administrative) channels ; suivre la ~ (dans sa carrière) to work one's way up (through the hierarchy).

filiforme [filifɔʀm(ə)] a spindly ; thread-like.

filigrane [filigʀan] nm (d'un billet, timbre) watermark ; en ~ (fig) showing just beneath the surface.

filin [filɛ̃] nm rope.

fille [fij] nf girl ; (opposé à fils) daughter ; ~ de joie prostitute ; ~ de salle waitress ; ~-mère (péj) unmarried mother ; **fillette** nf (little) girl.

filleul, e [fijœl] nm/f godchild, godson/daughter.

film [film] nm (pour photo) (roll of) film ; (œuvre) film, picture, movie ; (couche) film ; ~ muet/parlant silent/talking picture ou movie ; ~ d'animation animated film ; **filmer** vt to film.

filon [filɔ̃] nm vein, lode ; (fig) lucrative line, money spinner.

fils [fis] nm son ; ~ de famille moneyed young man.

filtre [filtʀ(ə)] nm filter ; '~ ou sans ~?' 'tipped or plain?' ; ~ à air (AUTO) air filter ; **filtrer** vt to filter ; (fig: candidats, visiteurs) to screen // vi to filter (through).

fin [fɛ̃] nf end ; ~s nfpl (but) ends ; à (la) ~ mai at the end of May ; en ~ de semaine at the end of the week ; prendre ~ to come to an end ; mettre ~ à to put an end to ; à la ~ ad in the end, eventually ; sans ~ a endless // ad endlessly.

fin, e [fɛ̃, fin] a (papier, couche, fil) thin ; (cheveux, poudre, pointe, visage) fine ; (taille) neat, slim ; (esprit, remarque) subtle ; shrewd // ad (moudre, couper) finely // nf (alcool) liqueur brandy ; ~ prêt/soûl quite ready/drunk ; un ~ tireur a crack shot ; avoir la vue/l'ouïe ~e to have sharp eyes/ears, have keen eyesight/hearing ; or/linge/vin ~ fine gold/linen/wine ; repas ~ gourmet meal ; une ~e mouche (fig) a sharp customer ; ~es herbes mixed herbs.

final, e [final] a, nf final ; quarts de ~e quarter finals ; 8èmes/16èmes de ~e 2nd/1st round (in 5 round knock-out competition) ; ~ement ad finally, in the end ; (après tout) after all ; ~iste nm/f finalist.

finance [finɑ̃s] *nf* finance ; **~s** *nfpl* (*situation financière*) finances ; (*activités financières*) finance *sg* ; **moyennant ~** for a fee *ou* consideration ; **financer** *vt* to finance ; **financier, ière** *a* financial // *nm* financier.

finaud, e [fino, -od] *a* wily.

finesse [finɛs] *nf* thinness ; fineness ; neatness, slimness ; subtlety ; shrewdness ; **~s** *nfpl* (*subtilités*) niceties ; finer points.

fini, e [fini] *a* finished ; (*MATH*) finite ; (*intensif*): **un égoïste ~** an egotist through and through // *nm* (*d'un objet manufacturé*) finish.

finir [finiʀ] *vt* to finish // *vi* to finish, end ; **~ quelque part** to end *ou* finish up somewhere ; **~ de faire** to finish doing ; (*cesser*) to stop doing ; **~ par faire** to end *ou* finish up doing ; **il finit par m'agacer** he's beginning to get on my nerves ; **~ en pointe/tragédie** to end in a point/in tragedy ; **en ~ avec** to be *ou* have done with ; **il va mal ~** he will come to a bad end.

finish [finiʃ] *nm* (*SPORT*) finish.

finissage [finisaʒ] *nm* finishing.

finition [finisjɔ̃] *nf* finishing ; finish.

finlandais, e [fɛ̃lɑdɛ, -ɛz] *a* Finnish // *nm/f* Finn.

Finlande [fɛ̃lɑd] *nf*: **la ~** Finland ; **finnois** *nm* Finnish.

fiole [fjɔl] *nf* phial.

fiord [fjɔʀ(d)] *nm* = **fjord**.

fioriture [fjɔʀityʀ] *nf* embellishment, flourish.

firmament [fiʀmamɑ̃] *nm* firmament, skies *pl*.

firme [fiʀm(ə)] *nf* firm.

fis *vb voir* **faire**.

fisc [fisk] *nm* tax authorities *pl*, ≈ Inland Revenue ; **~al, e, aux** *a* tax *cpd*, fiscal ; **~alité** *nf* tax system ; (*charges*) taxation.

fission [fisjɔ̃] *nf* fission.

fissure [fisyʀ] *nf* crack.

fissurer [fisyʀe] *vt*, **se ~** *vi* to crack.

fiston [fistɔ̃] *nm* (*fam*) son, lad.

fit *vb voir* **faire**.

fixateur [fiksatœʀ] *nm* (*PHOTO*) fixer ; (*pour cheveux*) hair cream.

fixatif [fiksatif] *nm* fixative.

fixation [fiksasjɔ̃] *nf* fixing ; fastening ; setting ; (*de ski*) binding ; (*PSYCH*) fixation.

fixe [fiks(ə)] *a* fixed ; (*emploi*) steady, regular // *nm* (*salaire*) basic salary ; **à heure ~** at a set time ; **menu à prix ~** set menu.

fixé, e [fikse] *a*: **être ~ (sur)** (*savoir à quoi s'en tenir*) to have made up one's mind (about) ; to know for certain (about).

fixement [fiksəmɑ̃] *ad* (*regarder*) fixedly, steadily.

fixer [fikse] *vt* (*attacher*): **~ qch (à/sur)** to fix *ou* fasten sth (to/on) ; (*déterminer*) to fix, set ; (*CHIMIE, PHOTO*) to fix ; (*poser son regard sur*) to look hard at, stare at ; **se ~** (*s'établir*) to settle down ; **se ~ sur** (*suj: attention*) to focus on.

fjord [fjɔʀ(d)] *nm* fjord, fiord.

flacon [flakɔ̃] *nm* bottle.

flageller [flaʒele] *vt* to flog, scourge.

flageoler [flaʒɔle] *vi* (*jambes*) to sag.

flageolet [flaʒɔlɛ] *nm* (*MUS*) flageolet ; (*CULIN*) dwarf kidney bean.

flagorneur, euse [flagɔʀnœʀ, -øz] *nm/f* toady, fawner.

flagrant, e [flagʀɑ̃, -ɑ̃t] *a* flagrant, blatant ; **en ~ délit** in the act, in flagrante delicto.

flair [flɛʀ] *nm* sense of smell ; (*fig*) intuition ; **flairer** *vt* (*humer*) to sniff (at) ; (*détecter*) to scent.

flamand, e [flamɑ̃, -ɑ̃d] *a, nm* (*langue*) Flemish // *nm/f* Fleming ; **les F~s** the Flemish.

flamant [flamɑ̃] *nm* flamingo.

flambant [flɑbɑ̃] *ad*: **~ neuf** brand new.

flambé, e [flɑbe] *a* (*CULIN*) flambé // *nf* blaze ; (*fig*) flaring-up, explosion.

flambeau, x [flɑbo] *nm* (flaming) torch.

flamber [flɑbe] *vi* to blaze (up) // *vt* (*poulet*) to singe ; (*aiguille*) to sterilize.

flamboyant, e [flɑbwajɑ̃, -ɑ̃t] *a* flashing, blazing ; flaming.

flamboyer [flɑbwaje] *vi* to blaze (up) ; to flame.

flamingant, e [flamɛ̃gɑ̃, -ɑ̃t] *a* Flemish-speaking.

flamme [flam] *nf* flame ; (*fig*) fire, fervour ; **en ~s** on fire, ablaze.

flammèche [flamɛʃ] *nf* (flying) spark.

flan [flɑ̃] *nm* (*CULIN*) custard tart *ou* pie.

flanc [flɑ̃] *nm* side ; (*MIL*) flank ; **à ~ de colline** on the hillside ; **prêter le ~ à** (*fig*) to lay o.s. open to.

flancher [flɑ̃ʃe] *vi* to fail, pack up.

flanelle [flanɛl] *nf* flannel.

flâner [flɑne] *vi* to stroll ; **flânerie** *nf* stroll.

flanquer [flɑ̃ke] *vt* to flank ; (*fam: mettre*): **~ qch sur/dans** to bung *ou* shove sth on/into ; (: *jeter*): **~ par terre/à la porte** to fling to the ground/chuck out.

flapi, e [flapi] *a* dog-tired.

flaque [flak] *nf* (*d'eau*) puddle ; (*d'huile, de sang etc*) pool.

flash, pl flashes [flaʃ] *nm* (*PHOTO*) flash ; **~ (d'information)** newsflash.

flasque [flask(ə)] *a* flabby.

flatter [flate] *vt* to flatter ; (*caresser*) to stroke ; **se ~ de qch** to pride o.s. on sth ; **flatterie** *nf* flattery *q* ; **flatteur, euse** *a* flattering // *nm/f* flatterer.

fléau, x [fleo] *nm* scourge, curse ; (*de balance*) beam ; (*pour le blé*) flail.

flèche [flɛʃ] *nf* arrow ; (*de clocher*) spire ; (*de grue*) jib ; **monter en ~** (*fig*) to soar, rocket ; **flécher** *vt* to arrow, mark with arrows ; **fléchette** *nf* dart ; **fléchettes** *nfpl* (*jeu*) darts *sg*.

fléchir [fleʃiʀ] *vt* (*corps, genou*) to bend ; (*fig*) to sway, weaken // *vi* (*poutre*) to sag, bend ; (*fig*) to weaken, flag ; **fléchissement** *nm* bending ; sagging ; flagging.

flegmatique [flɛgmatik] *a* phlegmatic.

flegme [flɛgm(ə)] *nm* composure.

flemmard, e [flemaʀ, -aʀd(ə)] *nm/f* lazybones *sg*, loafer.

flétrir [fletʀiʀ] *vt* to wither ; (*stigmatiser*) to condemn (in the most severe terms) ; **se ~** *vi* to wither.

fleur [flœʀ] nf flower; (d'un arbre) blossom, bloom; être en ~ (arbre) to be in blossom ou bloom; tissu à ~s flowered ou flowery fabric; à ~ de terre just above the ground; ~ de lis fleur-de-lis.

fleurer [flœʀe] vt: ~ la lavande to be fragrant with the scent of lavender.

fleuret [flœʀɛ] nm (arme) foil; (sport) fencing.

fleuri, e [flœʀi] a in flower ou bloom; surrounded by flowers; (fig) flowery; florid.

fleurir [flœʀiʀ] vi (rose) to flower; (arbre) to blossom; (fig) to flourish ; / vt (tombe) to put flowers on; (chambre) to decorate with flowers.

fleuriste [flœʀist(ə)] nm/f florist.

fleuron [flœʀɔ̃] nm jewel (fig).

fleuve [flœv] nm river.

flexible [flɛksibl(ə)] a flexible.

flexion [flɛksjɔ̃] nf flexing, bending; (LING) inflection.

flibustier [flibystje] nm buccaneer.

flic [flik] nm (fam: péj) cop.

flirter [flœʀte] vi to flirt.

F.L.N. sigle m = Front de libération nationale (during the Algerian war).

flocon [flɔkɔ̃] nm flake; (de laine etc: boulette) flock; ~s d'avoine oatflakes.

flonflons [flɔ̃flɔ̃] nmpl blare sg.

floraison [flɔʀɛzɔ̃] nf flowering; blossoming; flourishing.

floral, e, aux [flɔʀal, -o] a floral, flower cpd.

floralies [flɔʀali] nfpl flower show sg.

flore [flɔʀ] nf flora.

florissant, e [flɔʀisɑ̃, -ɑ̃t] vb voir **fleurir** // a flourishing.

flot [flo] nm flood, stream; (marée) flood tide; ~s nmpl (de la mer) waves; être à ~ (NAVIG) to be afloat; (fig) to be on an even keel; entrer à ~s to be streaming ou pouring in.

flottage [flɔtaʒ] nm (du bois) floating.

flottaison [flɔtɛzɔ̃] nf: ligne de ~ waterline.

flottant, e [flɔtɑ̃, -ɑ̃t] a (vêtement) loose (-fitting); (cours, barème) floating.

flotte [flɔt] nf (NAVIG) fleet; (fam) water; rain.

flottement [flɔtmɑ̃] nm (fig) wavering, hesitation.

flotter [flɔte] vi to float; (nuage, odeur) to drift; (drapeau) to fly; (vêtements) to hang loose; (monnaie) to float // vt to float; faire ~ to float; flotteur nm float.

flottille [flɔtij] nf flotilla.

flou, e [flu] a fuzzy, blurred; (fig) woolly, vague.

flouer [flue] vt to swindle.

fluctuation [flyktɥasjɔ̃] nf fluctuation.

fluet, te [flyɛ, -ɛt] a thin, slight.

fluide [flɥid] a fluid; (circulation etc) flowing freely // nm fluid; (force) (mysterious) power; **fluidité** nf fluidity; free flow.

fluor [flyɔʀ] nm fluorine.

fluorescent, e [flyɔʀesɑ̃, -ɑ̃t] a fluorescent.

flûte [flyt] nf flute; (verre) flute glass; (pain) long loaf (pl loaves); ~! drat it!;

petite ~ piccolo (pl s); ~ à bec recorder; ~ de Pan panpipes pl; **flûtiste** nm/f flautist, flute player.

fluvial, e, aux [flyvjal, -o] a river cpd, fluvial.

flux [fly] nm incoming tide; (écoulement) flow; le ~ et le reflux the ebb and flow.

fluxion [flyksjɔ̃] nf: ~ de poitrine pneumonia.

FM sigle voir **modulation**.

F.M.I. sigle m voir **fonds**.

foc [fɔk] nm jib.

focal, e, aux [fɔkal, -o] a focal // nf focal length.

fœtal, e, aux [fetal, -o] a foetal, fetal.

fœtus [fetys] nm foetus, fetus.

foi [fwa] nf faith; **sous la ~ du serment** under ou on oath; **ajouter ~ à** to lend credence to; **digne de ~** reliable; **sur la ~ de** on the word ou strength of; **être de bonne/mauvaise ~** to be sincere/insincere.

foie [fwa] nm liver; ~ gras foie gras.

foin [fwɛ̃] nm hay; **faire les ~s** to make hay; **faire du ~** (fig: fam) to kick up a row.

foire [fwaʀ] nf fair; (fête foraine) (fun) fair; **faire la ~** (fig: fam) to whoop it up; ~ (exposition) trade fair.

fois [fwa] nf: **une/deux ~** once/twice; **trois/vingt ~** three/twenty times; **2 ~ 2** twice 2, 2 times 2; **deux/quatre ~ plus grand (que)** twice/four times as large (as); **une ~** (dans le passé) once; (dans le futur) sometime; **une ~ pour toutes** once and for all; **une ~ que c'est fait** once it's done; **une ~ parti** once he had left; **des ~** (parfois) sometimes; **cette ~** this (ou that) time; **à la ~** (ensemble) (all) at once; **à la ~ grand et beau** both tall and handsome.

foison [fwazɔ̃] nf: **une ~ de** an abundance of; **à ~** ad in plenty.

foisonner [fwazɔne] vi to abound; ~ en ou de to abound in.

fol [fɔl] a voir **fou**.

folâtre [fɔlɑtʀ(ə)] a playful.

folâtrer [fɔlɑtʀe] vi to frolic (about).

folie [fɔli] nf (d'une décision, d'un acte) madness, folly; (état) madness, insanity; (acte) folly; **la ~ des grandeurs** delusions of grandeur; **faire des ~s** (en dépenses) to be extravagant.

folklore [fɔlklɔʀ] nm folklore; **folklorique** a folk cpd; (fam) weird.

folle [fɔl] a, nf voir **fou**; ~ment ad (très) madly, wildly.

follet [fɔlɛ] am: **feu ~** will-o'-the-wisp.

fomenter [fɔmɑ̃te] vt to stir up, foment.

foncé, e [fɔ̃se] a dark; **bleu ~** dark blue.

foncer [fɔ̃se] vt to make darker // vi to go darker; (fam: aller vite) to tear ou belt along; ~ sur to charge at.

foncier, ière [fɔ̃sje, -jɛʀ] a (honnêteté etc) basic, fundamental; (malhonnêteté) deep-rooted; (COMM) real estate cpd; **foncièrement** ad basically; thoroughly.

fonction [fɔ̃ksjɔ̃] nf (rôle, MATH, LING) function; (emploi, poste) post, position; ~s (professionnelles) duties; **entrer en ~s** to take up one's post ou duties; to take up office ; **voiture de ~** car provided with the post ; **être ~ de** (*dépendre de*) to depend on ; **en ~ de** (*par rapport à*) according to ; **faire ~ de** to serve as ; **la ~ publique** the public *ou* state service.

fonctionnaire [fɔ̃ksjɔnɛʀ] *nm/f* state employee, local authority employee ; (*dans l'administration*) ≈ civil servant.

fonctionnel, le [fɔ̃ksjɔnɛl] *a* functional.

fonctionnement [fɔ̃ksjɔnmɑ̃] *nm* functioning.

fonctionner [fɔ̃ksjɔne] *vi* to work, function ; (*entreprise*) to operate, function ; **faire ~** to work, operate.

fond [fɔ̃] *nm voir aussi* **fonds** ; (*d'un récipient, trou*) bottom ; (*d'une salle, scène*) back ; (*d'un tableau, décor*) background ; (*opposé à la forme*) content ; (*SPORT*): **le ~** long distance (running) ; **au ~ de** at the bottom of ; at the back of ; **à ~** *ad* (*connaître, soutenir*) thoroughly ; (*appuyer, visser*) right down *ou* home ; **à ~** (**de train**) *ad* (*fam*) full tilt ; **dans le ~, au ~** *ad* (*en somme*) basically, really ; **de ~ en comble** *ad* from top to bottom ; **~ sonore** background noise ; **~ de teint** make-up base.

fondamental, e, aux [fɔ̃damɑ̃tal, -o] *a* fundamental.

fondant, e [fɔ̃dɑ̃, -ɑ̃t] *a* (*neige*) melting ; (*poire*) that melts in the mouth ; (*chocolat*) fondant.

fondateur, trice [fɔ̃datœʀ, -tʀis] *nm/f* founder ; **membre ~** founder member.

fondation [fɔ̃dɑsjɔ̃] *nf* founding ; (*établissement*) foundation ; **~s** *nfpl* (*d'une maison*) foundations ; **travaux de ~** foundation works.

fondé, e [fɔ̃de] *a* (*accusation etc*) well-founded ; **mal ~** unfounded ; **être ~ à croire** to have grounds for believing *ou* good reason to believe ; **~ de pouvoir** *nm* authorized representative ; (*banking*) executive (*having the signature*).

fondement [fɔ̃dmɑ̃] *nm* (*derrière*) behind ; **~s** *nmpl* foundations ; **sans ~** *a* (*rumeur etc*) groundless, unfounded.

fonder [fɔ̃de] *vt* to found ; (*fig*): **~ qch sur** to base sth on ; **se ~ sur** (*suj: personne*) to base o.s. on.

fonderie [fɔ̃dʀi] *nf* smelting works *sg*.

fondeur [fɔ̃dœʀ] *nm*: (**ouvrier**) **~** caster.

fondre [fɔ̃dʀ(ə)] *vt* to melt ; (*dans l'eau: sucre, sel*) to dissolve ; (*fig: mélanger*) to merge, blend // *vi* to melt ; to dissolve ; (*fig*) to melt away ; (*se précipiter*): **~ sur** to swoop down on ; **faire ~** to melt ; to dissolve ; **~ en larmes** to burst into tears.

fondrière [fɔ̃dʀijɛʀ] *nf* rut.

fonds [fɔ̃] *nm* (*de bibliothèque*) collection ; (*COMM*): **~** (**de commerce**) business ; (*fig*): **~ de probité** *etc* fund of integrity *etc* // *nmpl* (*argent*) funds ; **à ~ perdus** *ad* with little or no hope of getting the money back ; **F~ Monétaire International** (**FMI**) International Monetary Fund (IMF) ; **~ de roulement** *nm* float.

fondu, e [fɔ̃dy] *a* (*beurre, neige*) melted ; (*métal*) molten // *nm* (*CINÉMA*): **~** (**enchaîné**) dissolve // *nf* (*CULIN*) fondue.

font *vb voir* **faire**.

fontaine [fɔ̃tɛn] *nf* fountain ; (*source*) spring.

fonte [fɔ̃t] *nf* melting ; (*métal*) cast iron ; **la ~ des neiges** the (spring) thaw.

fonts baptismaux [fɔ̃batismo] *nmpl* (baptismal) font *sg*.

football [futbol] *nm* football, soccer ; **~ de table** table football ; **~eur** *nm* footballer, football *ou* soccer player.

footing [futiŋ] *nm* jogging.

for [fɔʀ] *nm*: **dans son ~ intérieur** in one's heart of hearts.

forage [fɔʀaʒ] *nm* drilling, boring.

forain, e [fɔʀɛ̃, -ɛn] *a* fairground *cpd* // *nm* stallholder ; fairground entertainer.

forçat [fɔʀsa] *nm* convict.

force [fɔʀs(ə)] *nf* strength ; (*puissance: surnaturelle etc*) power ; (*PHYSIQUE, MÉCANIQUE*) force ; **~s** *nfpl* (*physiques*) strength *sg* ; (*MIL*) forces ; (*effectifs*): **d'importantes ~s de police** big contingents of police ; **à ~ d'insister** by dint of insisting ; **as he** (*ou* **I**) **kept on insisting** ; **de ~** *ad* forcibly, by force ; **par la ~** using force ; **faire ~ de rames/voiles** to ply the oars/cram on sail ; **être de ~ à faire** to be up to doing ; **de première ~** first class ; **~ d'âme** fortitude ; **~ de frappe** strike force ; **~ d'inertie** force of inertia ; **la ~ publique** the authorities responsible for public order ; **~s d'intervention** peacekeeping force *sg* ; **les ~s de l'ordre** the police.

forcé, e [fɔʀse] *a* forced ; unintended ; inevitable.

forcément [fɔʀsemɑ̃] *ad* necessarily ; inevitably ; (*bien sûr*) of course.

forcené, e [fɔʀsəne] *a* frenzied // *nm/f* maniac.

forceps [fɔʀsɛps] *nm* forceps *pl*.

forcer [fɔʀse] *vt* (*contraindre*): **~ qn à faire** to force sb to do ; (*porte, serrure, plante*) to force ; (*moteur, voix*) to strain // *vi* (*SPORT*) to overtax o.s. ; **~ la dose/l'allure** to overdo it/increase the pace ; **~ l'attention/le respect** to command attention/respect.

forcing [fɔʀsiŋ] *nm*: **faire le ~** to pile on the pressure.

forcir [fɔʀsiʀ] *vi* (*grossir*) to broaden out ; (*vent*) to freshen.

forer [fɔʀe] *vt* to drill, bore.

forestier, ière [fɔʀɛstje, -jɛʀ] *a* forest *cpd*.

foret [fɔʀɛ] *nm* drill.

forêt [fɔʀɛ] *nf* forest.

foreuse [fɔʀøz] *nf* (electric) drill.

forfait [fɔʀfɛ] *nm* (*COMM*) fixed *ou* set price ; all-in deal *ou* price ; (*crime*) infamy ; **déclarer ~** to withdraw ; **gagner par ~** to win by a walkover ; **travailler à ~** to work for a lump sum ; **forfaitaire** *a* inclusive ; set ; **~-vacances** *nm* (all-inclusive) holiday package.

forfanterie [fɔʀfɑ̃tʀi] *nf* boastfulness *q*.

forge [fɔʀʒ(ə)] *nf* forge, smithy.

forger [fɔʀʒe] *vt* to forge ; (*fig: personnalité*) to form ; (: *prétexte*) to contrive, make up ; **être forgé de toutes pièces** to be a complete fabrication.

forgeron [fɔʀʒəʀɔ̃] *nm* (black)smith.

formaliser [fɔʀmalize]: **se ~** *vi*: **se ~ (de)** to take offence (at).

formalité [fɔʀmalite] *nf* formality.

format [fɔʀma] *nm* size; **petit ~** small size; (*PHOTO*) 35 mm (film).

formation [fɔʀmasjɔ̃] *nf* forming; training; (*MUS*) group; (*MIL, AVIAT, GÉO*) formation; **la ~ professionnelle** professional training.

forme [fɔʀm(ə)] *nf* (*gén*) form; (*d'un objet*) shape, form; **~s** *nfpl* (*bonnes manières*) proprieties; (*d'une femme*) figure *sg*; **en ~ de poire** pear-shaped, in the shape of a pear; **être en ~** (*SPORT etc*) to be on form; **en bonne et due ~** in due form; **prendre ~** to take shape.

formel, le [fɔʀmɛl] *a* (*preuve, décision*) definite, positive; (*logique*) formal; **~lement** *ad* (*absolument*) positively.

former [fɔʀme] *vt* (*gén*) to form; (*éduquer: soldat, ingénieur etc*) to train; **se ~** *vi* to form.

formidable [fɔʀmidabl(ə)] *a* tremendous.

formol [fɔʀmɔl] *nm* formalin, formol.

formulaire [fɔʀmylɛʀ] *nm* form.

formule [fɔʀmyl] *nf* (*gén*) formula; (*formulaire*) form; **~ de politesse** polite phrase; letter ending.

formuler [fɔʀmyle] *vt* (*émettre: réponse, vœux*) to formulate; (*expliciter: sa pensée*) to express.

fort, e [fɔʀ, fɔʀt(ə)] *a* strong; (*intensité, rendement*) high, great; (*corpulent*) stout // *ad* (*serrer, frapper*) hard; (*sonner*) loud(ly); (*beaucoup*) greatly, very much; (*très*) most // *nm* (*édifice*) fort; (*point fort*) strong point, forte; **c'est un peu ~!** it's a bit much!; **avoir ~ à faire pour faire** to have a hard job doing; **se faire ~ de ... to** claim one can ...; **~ bien/peu** very well/few; **au plus ~ de** (*au milieu de*) in the thick of, at the height of.

forteresse [fɔʀtəʀɛs] *nf* fortress.

fortifiant [fɔʀtifjɑ̃] *nm* tonic.

fortifications [fɔʀtifikasjɔ̃] *nfpl* fortifications.

fortifier [fɔʀtifje] *vt* to strengthen, fortify; (*MIL*) to fortify.

fortin [fɔʀtɛ̃] *nm* (small) fort.

fortiori [fɔʀtjɔʀi]: **à ~** *ad* all the more so.

fortuit, e [fɔʀtɥi, -it] *a* fortuitous, chance *cpd*.

fortune [fɔʀtyn] *nf* fortune; **faire ~** to make one's fortune; **de ~** a makeshift; chance *cpd*.

fortuné, e [fɔʀtyne] *a* wealthy, well-off.

forum [fɔʀɔm] *nm* forum.

fosse [fos] *nf* (*grand trou*) pit; (*tombe*) grave; **la ~ aux lions/ours** the lions' den/bear pit; **~ commune** common *ou* communal grave; **~** (*d'orchestre*) (orchestra) pit; **~ à purin** cesspit; **~s nasales** nasal fossae *pl*.

fossé [fose] *nm* ditch; (*fig*) gulf, gap.

fossette [fosɛt] *nf* dimple.

fossile [fosil] *nm* fossil // *a* fossilized, fossil.

fossoyeur [foswajœʀ] *nm* gravedigger.

fou(fol), folle [fu, fɔl] *a* mad; (*déréglé etc*) wild, erratic; (*fam: extrême, très grand*) terrific, tremendous // *nm/f* mad-man/woman // *nm* (*du roi*) jester, fool; (*ÉCHECS*) bishop; **être ~ de** to be mad *ou* crazy about; **faire le ~** (*enfant etc*) to play *ou* act the fool; **avoir le ~ rire** to have the giggles.

foudre [fudʀ(ə)] *nf* lightning; **~s** *nfpl* (*colère*) wrath *sg*.

foudroyant, e [fudʀwajɑ̃, -ɑ̃t] *a* lightning *cpd*, stunning.

foudroyer [fudʀwaje] *vt* to strike down; **il a été foudroyé** he was struck by lightning.

fouet [fwɛ] *nm* whip; (*CULIN*) whisk; **de plein ~** *ad* (*se heurter*) head on; **~ter** *vt* to whip; to whisk.

fougère [fuʒɛʀ] *nf* fern.

fougue [fug] *nf* ardour, spirit; **fougueux, euse** *a* fiery, ardent.

fouille [fuj] *nf* search; **~s** *nfpl* (*archéologiques*) excavations; **passer à la ~** to be searched.

fouiller [fuje] *vt* to search; (*creuser*) to dig // *vi*: **~ dans/parmi** to rummage in/among.

fouillis [fuji] *nm* jumble, muddle.

fouine [fwin] *nf* stone marten.

fouiner [fwine] *vi* (*péj*): **~ dans** to nose around *ou* about in.

fouisseur, euse [fwisœʀ, -øz] *a* burrowing.

foulante [fulɑ̃t] *af*: **pompe ~** force pump.

foulard [fulaʀ] *nm* scarf (*pl* scarves).

foule [ful] *nf* crowd; **la ~** crowds *pl*; **les ~s** the masses; **une ~ de** masses of.

foulée [fule] *nf* stride.

fouler [fule] *vt* to press; (*sol*) to tread upon; **se ~** (*fam*) to overexert o.s.; **se ~ la cheville** to sprain one's ankle; **~ aux pieds** to trample underfoot.

foulure [fulyʀ] *nf* sprain.

four [fuʀ] *nm* oven; (*de potier*) kiln; (*THÉÂTRE: échec*) flop.

fourbe [fuʀb(ə)] *a* deceitful; **~rie** *nf* deceitfulness; deceit.

fourbi [fuʀbi] *nm* (*fam*) gear, clobber.

fourbir [fuʀbiʀ] *vt*: **~ ses armes** (*fig*) to get ready for the fray.

fourbu, e [fuʀby] *a* exhausted.

fourche [fuʀʃ(ə)] *nf* pitchfork; (*de bicyclette*) fork.

fourchette [fuʀʃɛt] *nf* fork; (*STATISTIQUE*) bracket, margin.

fourchu, e [fuʀʃy] *a* split; forked.

fourgon [fuʀgɔ̃] *nm* van; (*RAIL*) wag(g)on; **~ mortuaire** hearse.

fourgonnette [fuʀgɔnɛt] *nf* (delivery) van.

fourmi [fuʀmi] *nf* ant; **~s** *nfpl* (*fig*) pins and needles; **~lière** *nf* ant-hill.

fourmiller [fuʀmije] *vi* to swarm; **~ de** to be teeming with; to be swarming with.

fournaise [fuʀnɛz] *nf* blaze; (*fig*) furnace, oven.

fourneau, x [fuʀno] *nm* stove.

fournée [fuʀne] *nf* batch.

fourni, e [fuʀni] *a* (*barbe, cheveux*) thick; (*magasin*): **bien ~ (en)** well stocked (with).

fournir [fuʀniʀ] *vt* to supply; (*preuve, exemple*) to provide, supply; (*effort*) to put in; **~ qch à qn** to supply sth to sb, to supply *ou* provide sb with sth; **~ qn en**

(COMM) to supply sb with ; **fournisseur, euse** nm/f supplier.

fourniture [furnityr] nf supply(ing) ; ~s nfpl supplies ; ~s de bureau office supplies, stationery ; ~s scolaires school stationery.

fourrage [fura3] nm fodder, forage.

fourrager [fura3e] vi: ~ dans/ parmi to rummage through/among.

fourrager, ère [fura3e, -ɛʀ] a fodder cpd.

fourré, e [fure] a (bonbon, chocolat) filled ; (manteau, botte) fur-lined // nm thicket.

fourreau, x [furo] nm sheath ; (de parapluie) cover.

fourrer [fure] vt (fam): ~ qch dans to stick ou shove sth into ; se ~ dans/sous to get into/under.

fourre-tout [furtu] nm inv (sac) holdall ; (péj) junk room ou cupboard ; (fig) rag-bag.

fourreur [furœʀ] nm f. ~ier.

fourrière [furjɛʀ] nf pound.

fourrure [furyr] nf fur ; (sur l'animal) coat ; manteau/col de ~ fur coat/collar.

fourvoyer [furvwaje]: se ~ vi to go astray, stray ; se ~ dans to stray into.

foutre [futr(ə)] vt (fam!) = **ficher** (fam) ; **foutu, e** a (fam!) = **fichu, e** a.

foyer [fwaje] nm (de cheminée) hearth ; (fig) seat, centre ; family ; home ; (social) club ; hostel ; (salon) foyer ; (OPTIQUE, PHOTO) focus sg ; lunettes à double ~ bi-focal glasses.

fracas [fraka] nm din ; crash ; roar.

fracassant, e [frakasɑ̃, -ɑ̃t] a sensational, staggering.

fracasser [frakase] vt to smash.

fraction [fraksjɔ̃] nf fraction ; **fractionner** vt to divide (up), split (up).

fracture [fraktyr] nf fracture ; ~ du crâne fractured skull ; ~ de la jambe broken leg.

fracturer [fraktyre] vt (coffre, serrure) to break open ; (os, membre) to fracture.

fragile [fra3il] a fragile, delicate ; (fig) frail ; **fragilité** nf fragility.

fragment [fragmɑ̃] nm (d'un objet) fragment, piece ; (d'un texte) passage, extract ; **fragmentaire** a sketchy ; **fragmenter** vt to split up.

frai [frɛ] nm spawn ; spawning.

fraîche [frɛʃ] a voir frais ; ~ment ad coolly ; freshly, newly ; **fraîcheur** nf coolness ; freshness ; **fraîchir** vi to get cooler ; (vent) to freshen.

frais, fraîche [frɛ, frɛʃ] a (air, eau, accueil) cool ; (petit pois, œufs, souvenir, couleur, troupes) fresh // ad (récemment) newly, fresh(ly) ; il fait ~ it's cool ; servir ~ chill before serving, serve chilled // nm: mettre au ~ to put in a cool place ; prendre le ~ to take a breath of cool air // nmpl (débours) expenses ; (COMM) costs ; charges ; faire des ~ to spend ; to go to a lot of expense ; ~ de déplacement travel(ling) expenses ; ~généraux overheads ; ~ de scolarité school fees.

fraise [frɛz] nf strawberry ; (TECH) countersink (bit) ; (de dentiste) drill ; ~ des bois wild strawberry ; **fraiser** vt to countersink ; **fraisier** nm strawberry plant.

framboise [frɑ̃bwaz] nf raspberry ; **framboisier** nm raspberry bush.

franc, franche [frɑ̃, frɑ̃ʃ] a (personne) frank, straightforward ; (visage, rire) open ; (net: refus, couleur) clear ; (: coupure) clean ; (intensif) downright ; (exempt): ~ de port post free, postage paid, carriage paid // ad: parler ~ to be frank ou candid // nm franc.

français, e [frɑ̃sɛ, -ɛz] a French // nm/f: F~, e Frenchman/woman // nm (langue) French ; les F~ the French.

France [frɑ̃s] nf: la ~ France.

franche [frɑ̃ʃ] a voir franc ; ~ment ad frankly ; clearly ; (tout à fait) downright.

franchir [frɑ̃ʃir] vt (obstacle) to clear, get over ; (seuil, ligne, rivière) to cross ; (distance) to cover.

franchise [frɑ̃ʃiz] nf frankness ; (douanière, d'impôt) exemption ; (ASSURANCES) excess.

franciser [frɑ̃size] vt to gallicize, Frenchify.

franc-maçon [frɑ̃masɔ̃] nm freemason ; **franc-maçonnerie** nf freemasonry.

franco [frɑ̃ko] ad (COMM) carriage paid, postage paid.

franco... [frɑ̃ko] préfixe: ~phile a francophile ; ~phone a French-speaking // nm/f French speaker ; ~phonie nf French-speaking communities.

franc-parler [frɑ̃parle] nm inv outspokenness.

franc-tireur [frɑ̃tirœr] nm (MIL) irregular ; (fig) freelance.

frange [frɑ̃3] nf fringe.

frangipane [frɑ̃3ipan] nf almond paste.

franquette [frɑ̃kɛt]: à la bonne ~ ad without (any) fuss.

frappe [frap] nf (d'une dactylo, pianiste, machine à écrire) touch ; (BOXE) punch ; (péj) hood, thug.

frappé, e [frape] a iced.

frapper [frape] vt to hit, strike ; (étonner) to strike ; (monnaie) to strike, stamp ; se ~ (s'inquiéter) to get worked up ; ~ à la porte to knock (at) the door ; ~ dans ses mains to clap one's hands ; ~ du poing sur to bang one's fist on ; frappé de stupeur dumbfounded.

frasques [frask(ə)] nfpl escapades.

fraternel, le [fraternɛl] a brotherly, fraternal.

fraterniser [fraternize] vi to fraternize.

fraternité [fraternite] nf brotherhood.

fratricide [fratrisid] a fratricidal.

fraude [frod] nf fraud ; (SCOL) cheating ; passer qch en ~ to smuggle sth in (ou out) ; ~ fiscale tax evasion ; **frauder** vi, vt to cheat ; **fraudeur, euse** nm/f person guilty of fraud ; candidate who cheats ; tax evader ; **frauduleux, euse** a fraudulent.

frayer [freje] vt to open up, clear // vi to spawn ; (fréquenter): ~ avec to mix ou associate with ; se ~ un passage dans to clear o.s. a path through, force one's way through.

frayeur [frɛjœr] nf fright.

fredaines [frədɛn] nfpl mischief sg, escapades.

fredonner [frədɔne] vt to hum.

freezer [frizœr] nm freezing compartment.

frégate [fregat] nf frigate.

frein [frɛ̃] nm brake; **mettre un ~ à** (fig) to put a brake on, check; **~ à main** handbrake; **~ moteur** engine braking; **~s à disques** disc brakes; **~s à tambour** drum brakes.

freinage [frɛnaʒ] nm braking; **distance de ~** braking distance; **traces de ~** tyre marks.

freiner [frene] vi to brake // vt (progrès etc) to check.

frelaté, e [frəlate] a adulterated; (fig) tainted.

frêle [frɛl] a frail, fragile.

frelon [frəlɔ̃] nm hornet.

frémir [fremir] vi to tremble, shudder; to shiver; to quiver.

frêne [frɛn] nm ash.

frénésie [frenezi] nf frenzy; **frénétique** a frenzied, frenetic.

fréquemment [frekamɑ̃] ad frequently.

fréquence [frekɑ̃s] nf frequency.

fréquent, e [frekɑ̃, -ɑ̃t] a frequent.

fréquentation [frekɑ̃tasjɔ̃] nf frequenting; seeing; **~s** nfpl company sg.

fréquenté, e [frekɑ̃te] a: **très ~** (very) busy; **mal ~** patronized by disreputable elements.

fréquenter [frekɑ̃te] vt (lieu) to frequent; (personne) to see (frequently).

frère [frɛr] nm brother.

fresque [frɛsk(ə)] nf (ART) fresco.

fret [frɛ] nm freight.

fréter [frete] vt to charter.

frétiller [fretije] vi to wriggle.

fretin [frətɛ̃] nm: **le menu ~** the small fry.

friable [frijabl(ə)] a crumbly, friable.

friand, e [frijɑ̃, -ɑ̃d] a: **~ de** very fond of.

friandise [frijɑ̃diz] nf sweet.

fric [frik] nm (fam) cash.

fric-frac [frikfrak] nm break-in.

friche [friʃ]: **en ~** a, ad (lying) fallow.

friction [friksjɔ̃] nf (massage) rub, rub-down; (chez le coiffeur) scalp massage; (TECH, fig) friction; **frictionner** vt to rub (down); to massage.

frigidaire [friʒidɛr] nm ® refrigerator.

frigide [friʒid] a frigid; **frigidité** nf frigidity.

frigo [frigo] nm fridge.

frigorifier [frigɔrifje] vt to refrigerate; **frigorifique** a refrigerating.

frileux, euse [frilø, -øz] a sensitive to (the) cold.

frimas [frima] nmpl wintry weather sg.

frimousse [frimus] nf (sweet) little face.

fringale [frɛ̃gal] nf: **avoir la ~** to be ravenous.

fringant, e [frɛ̃gɑ̃, -ɑ̃t] a dashing.

fripé, e [fripe] a crumpled.

fripier, ère [fripje, -jɛr] nm/f secondhand clothes dealer.

fripon, ne [fripɔ̃, -ɔn] a roguish, mischievous // nm/f rascal, rogue.

fripouille [fripuj] nf scoundrel.

frire [frir] vt, vi, **faire ~** to fry.

frise [friz] nf frieze.

frisé, e [frize] a curly, curly-haired; (chicorée) **~e** curly endive.

friser [frize] vt, vi to curl; **se faire ~** to have one's hair curled.

frisson [frisɔ̃] nm shudder, shiver; quiver; **frissonner** vi to shudder, shiver; to quiver.

frit, e [fri, frit] pp de **frire** // a fried // nf: **(pommes) ~es** chips, French fried potatoes; **friteuse** nf chip pan; **friture** nf (huile) (deep) fat; (plat): **friture (de poissons)** fried fish; (RADIO) crackle, crackling q.

frivole [frivɔl] a frivolous.

froid, e [frwa, frwad] a, nm cold; **il fait ~** it's cold; **avoir ~** to be cold; **prendre ~** to catch a chill ou cold; **jeter un ~** (fig) to cast a chill; **être en ~ avec** to be on bad terms with; **froidement** ad (accueillir) coldly; (décider) coolly.

froisser [frwase] vt to crumple (up), crease; (fig) to hurt, offend; **se ~** vi to crumple, crease; to take offence ou umbrage; **se ~ un muscle** to strain a muscle.

frôler [frole] vt to brush against; (suj: projectile) to skim past; (fig) to come within a hair's breadth of; to come very close to.

fromage [frɔmaʒ] nm cheese; **~ blanc** soft white cheese; **~ de tête** pork brawn; **fromager, ère** nm/f cheesemonger; **fromagerie** nf cheese dairy.

froment [frɔmɑ̃] nm wheat.

froncer [frɔ̃se] vt to gather; **~ les sourcils** to frown.

frondaisons [frɔ̃dɛzɔ̃] nfpl foliage sg.

fronde [frɔ̃d] nf sling; (fig) rebellion, rebelliousness.

front [frɔ̃] nm forehead, brow; (MIL) front; **avoir le ~ de faire** to have the effrontery ou front to do; **de ~ ad** (se heurter) head-on; (rouler) together (i.e. 2 or 3 abreast); (simultanément) at once; **faire ~ à** to face up to; **~ de mer** (sea) front; **frontal, e,** aux a frontal.

frontalier, ière [frɔ̃talje, -jɛr] a border cpd, frontier cpd // nm/f: (travailleurs) **~s** workers who cross the border to go to work, commuters from across the border.

frontière [frɔ̃tjɛr] nf (GÉO, POL) frontier, border; (fig) frontier, boundary.

frontispice [frɔ̃tispis] nm frontispiece.

fronton [frɔ̃tɔ̃] nm pediment; (de pelote basque) (front) wall.

frottement [frɔtmɑ̃] nm rubbing, scraping; rubbing ou scraping noise.

frotter [frɔte] vi to rub, scrape // vt to rub; (pour nettoyer) to rub (up); to scrub; **~ une allumette** to strike a match.

frottoir [frɔtwar] nm (d'allumettes) friction strip; (pour encaustiquer) (long-handled) brush.

fructifier [fryktifje] vi to yield a profit; **faire ~** to turn to good account.

fructueux, euse [fryktyø, -øz] a fruitful; profitable.

frugal, e, aux [fʀygal, -o] a frugal.

fruit [fʀɥi] nm fruit (gén q); ~s de mer seafood(s); ~s secs dried fruit sg; **fruité, e** a fruity; **fruitier, ière** a: arbre fruitier fruit tree // nm/f fruiterer, greengrocer.

fruste [fʀyst(ə)] a unpolished, uncultivated.

frustration [fʀystʀɑsjɔ̃] nf frustration.

frustrer [fʀystʀe] vt to frustrate.

FS sigle = franc suisse.

fugace [fygas] a fleeting.

fugitif, ive [fyʒitif, -iv] a (lueur, amour) fleeting; (prisonnier etc) fugitive, runaway // nm/f fugitive.

fugue [fyg] nf (d'un enfant) running away q; (MUS) fugue; **faire une ~** to run away, abscond.

fuir [fɥiʀ] vt to flee from; (éviter) to shun // vi to run away; (gaz, robinet) to leak.

fuite [fɥit] nf flight; (écoulement) leak, leakage; (divulgation) leak; **être en ~** to be on the run; **mettre en ~** to put to flight; **prendre la ~** to take flight.

fulgurant, e [fylgyʀɑ̃, -ɑ̃t] a lightning cpd, dazzling.

fulminer [fylmine] vi: ~ (contre) to thunder forth (against).

fume-cigarette [fymsigaʀɛt] nm inv cigarette holder.

fumé, e [fyme] a (CULIN) smoked; (verres) (grey-)tinted // nf smoke.

fumer [fyme] vi to smoke; (soupe) to steam // vt to smoke; (terre, champ) to manure.

fumerie [fymʀi] nf: ~ d'opium opium den.

fumerolles [fymʀɔl] nfpl gas and smoke (from volcano).

fûmes vb voir être.

fumet [fymɛ] nm aroma.

fumeur, euse [fymœʀ, -øz] nm/f smoker.

fumeux, euse [fymø, -øz] a (péj) woolly.

fumier [fymje] nm manure.

fumigation [fymigɑsjɔ̃] nf fumigation.

fumigène [fymiʒɛn] a smoke cpd.

fumiste [fymist(ə)] nm (ramoneur) chimney sweep // nm/f (péj) shirker; phoney.

fumisterie [fymistəʀi] nf (péj) fraud, con.

fumoir [fymwaʀ] nm smoking room.

funambule [fynɑ̃byl] nm tightrope walker.

funèbre [fynɛbʀ(ə)] a funeral cpd; (fig) doleful; funereal.

funérailles [fyneʀɑj] nfpl funeral sg.

funéraire [fyneʀɛʀ] a funeral cpd, funerary.

funeste [fynɛst(ə)] a disastrous; deathly.

funiculaire [fynikylɛʀ] nm funicular (railway).

fur [fyʀ]: **au ~ et à mesure** ad as one goes along; **au ~ et à mesure que** as, as soon as; **au ~ et à mesure de leur progression** as they advance (ou advanced).

furet [fyʀɛ] nm ferret.

fureter [fyʀte] vi (péj) to nose about.

fureur [fyʀœʀ] nf fury; (passion): ~ de passion for; **faire ~** to be all the rage.

furibond, e [fyʀibɔ̃, -ɔ̃d] a furious.

furie [fyʀi] nf fury; (femme) shrew, vixen; **en ~** (mer) raging; **furieux, euse** a furious.

furoncle [fyʀɔ̃kl(ə)] nm boil, furuncle.

furtif, ive [fyʀtif, -iv] a furtive.

fus vb voir être.

fusain [fyzɛ̃] nm (BOT) spindle-tree; (ART) charcoal.

fuseau, x [fyzo] nm (pour filer) spindle; ~ horaire time zone.

fusée [fyze] nf rocket; ~ éclairante flare.

fuselage [fyzlaʒ] nm fuselage.

fuselé, e [fyzle] a slender; tapering.

fuser [fyze] vi (rires etc) to burst forth.

fusible [fyzibl(ə)] nm (ÉLEC: fil) fuse wire; (: fiche) fuse.

fusil [fyzi] nm (de guerre, à canon rayé) rifle, gun; (de chasse, à canon lisse) shotgun, gun; **fusilier** [-lje] nm rifleman; **fusillade** [-jad] nf gunfire q, shooting q; shooting battle; **fusiller** vt to shoot; ~-**mitrailleur** nm machine gun.

fusion [fyzjɔ̃] nf fusion, melting; (fig) merging; (COMM) merger; **en ~** (métal, roches) molten; **fusionner** vi to merge.

fustiger [fystiʒe] vt to denounce.

fut vb voir être.

fût [fy] nm (tonneau) barrel, cask; (de canon) stock; (d'arbre) bole, trunk; (de colonne) shaft.

futaie [fytɛ] nf forest, plantation.

futile [fytil] a futile; frivolous.

futur, e [fytyʀ] a, nm future; **au ~** (LING) in the future; ~-**iste** a futuristic.

fuyant, e [fɥijɑ̃, -ɑ̃t] vb voir fuir // a (regard etc) evasive; (lignes etc) receding; (perspective) vanishing.

fuyard, e [fɥijaʀ, -aʀd(ə)] nm/f runaway.

G

gabardine [gabaʀdin] nf gabardine.

gabarit [gabaʀi] nm (fig) size; calibre; (TECH) template.

gabegie [gabʒi] nf (péj) chaos.

gâcher [gaʃe] vt (gâter) to spoil, ruin; (gaspiller) to waste; (plâtre) to temper; (mortier) to mix.

gâchette [gaʃɛt] nf trigger.

gâchis [gaʃi] nm waste q.

gadoue [gadu] nf sludge.

gaffe [gaf] nf (instrument) boat hook; (erreur) blunder; **faire ~** (fam) to be careful; **gaffer** vi to blunder.

gag [gag] nm gag.

gage [gaʒ] nm (dans un jeu) forfeit; (fig: de fidélité) token; ~s nmpl (salaire) wages; (garantie) guarantee sg; **mettre en ~** to pawn; **laisser en ~** to leave as a security.

gager [gaʒe] vt: ~ que to bet ou wager that.

gageure [gaʒyʀ] nf: c'est une ~ it's attempting the impossible.

gagnant, e [gaɲɑ̃, -ɑ̃t] a: billet/ numéro ~ winning ticket/number // nm/f winner.

gagne-pain [gaɲpɛ̃] nm inv job.

gagner [gaɲe] vt to win; (somme d'argent, revenu) to earn; (aller vers, atteindre) to reach // vi to win; (fig) to gain; ~ du temps/de la place to gain time/save space; ~ sa vie to earn one's living; ~ du terrain to gain ground; ~ à faire (s'en trouver bien) to be better off doing.

gai, e [ge] a gay, cheerful; (un peu ivre) merry.

gaieté [gete] nf cheerfulness; ~s nfpl (souvent ironique) delights; de ~ de cœur with a light heart.

gaillard, e [gajaʀ, -aʀd(ə)] a (robuste) sprightly; (grivois) bawdy, ribald // nm/f (strapping) fellow/wench.

gain [gɛ̃] nm (revenu) earnings pl; (bénéfice: gén pl) profits pl; (au jeu: gén pl) winnings pl; (fig: de temps, place) saving; avoir ~ de cause to win the case; (fig) to be proved right.

gaine [gɛn] nf (corset) girdle; (fourreau) sheath; (de fil électrique etc) outer covering; ~-culotte nf pantie girdle; **gainer** vt to cover.

gala [gala] nm official reception; soirée de ~ gala evening.

galant, e [galɑ̃, -ɑ̃t] a (courtois) courteous, gentlemanly; (entreprenant) flirtatious, gallant; (aventure, poésie) amorous; en ~-e compagnie with a lady friend/gentleman friend.

galaxie [galaksi] nf galaxy.

galbe [galb(ə)] nm curve(s); shapeliness.

gale [gal] nf scabies sg.

galéjade [galeʒad] nf tall story.

galère [galɛʀ] nf galley.

galerie [galʀi] nf gallery; (THÉÂTRE) circle; (de voiture) roof rack; (fig: spectateurs) audience; ~ marchande shopping arcade; ~ de peinture (private) art gallery.

galérien [galeʀjɛ̃] nm galley slave.

galet [galɛ] nm pebble; (TECH) wheel; ~s nmpl pebbles, shingle sg.

galette [galɛt] nf flat cake.

galeux, euse [galø, -øz] a: un chien ~ a mangy dog.

galimatias [galimatja] nm (péj) gibberish.

Galles [gal] n: le pays de ~ Wales.

gallicisme [galisism(ə)] nm French idiom; (tournure fautive) gallicism.

gallois, e [galwa, -waz] a, nm (langue) Welsh // nm/f: G~, e Welshman/woman.

galon [galɔ̃] nm (MIL) stripe; (décoratif) piece of braid.

galop [galo] nm gallop; au ~ at a gallop.

galopade [galɔpad] nf stampede.

galoper [galɔpe] vi to gallop.

galopin [galɔpɛ̃] nm urchin, ragamuffin.

galvaniser [galvanize] vt to galvanize.

galvauder [galvode] vt to debase.

gambader [gɑ̃bade] vi (animal, enfant) to leap about.

gamelle [gamɛl] nf mess tin; billy can; (fam): ramasser une ~ to come a cropper.

gamin, e [gamɛ̃, -in] nm/f kid // a mischievous, playful.

gamme [gam] nf (MUS) scale; (fig) range.

gammé, e [game] a: croix ~e swastika.

gang [gɑ̃g] nm gang.

ganglion [gɑ̃glijɔ̃] nm ganglion.

gangrène [gɑ̃gʀɛn] nf gangrene.

gangue [gɑ̃g] nf coating.

ganse [gɑ̃s] nf braid.

gant [gɑ̃] nm glove; ~ de toilette (face) flannel; ~s de boxe boxing gloves; **ganté, e** a: ganté de blanc wearing white gloves; **ganterie** nf glove trade; glove shop.

garage [gaʀaʒ] nm garage; ~ à vélos bicycle shed; **garagiste** nm/f garage owner; garage mechanic ou man.

garant, e [gaʀɑ̃, -ɑ̃t] nm/f guarantor // nm guarantee; se porter ~ de to vouch for; to be answerable for.

garantie [gaʀɑ̃ti] nf guarantee; (gage) security, surety; (bon de) ~ guarantee ou warranty slip.

garantir [gaʀɑ̃tiʀ] vt to guarantee; (protéger): ~ de to protect from; je vous garantis que I can assure you that; garanti 2 ans/pure laine guaranteed for 2 years/pure wool.

garçon [gaʀsɔ̃] nm boy; (célibataire) bachelor; (jeune homme) boy, lad; ~ boucher/coiffeur butcher's/hairdresser's assistant; ~ de courses messenger; ~ d'écurie stable lad; **garçonnet** nm small boy; **garçonnière** nf bachelor flat.

garde [gaʀd(ə)] nm (de prisonnier) guard; (de domaine etc) warden; (soldat, sentinelle) guardsman // nf guarding; looking after; (soldats, BOXE, ESCRIME) guard; (faction) watch; (d'une arme) hilt; (TYPO): (page de) ~ endpaper; flyleaf; de ~ a, ad on duty; monter la ~ to stand guard; être sur ses ~s to be on one's guard; mettre en ~ to warn; prendre ~ (à) to be careful (of); ~ champêtre nm rural policeman; ~ du corps nm bodyguard; ~ d'enfants nf child minder; ~ des enfants nf (après divorce) custody of the children; ~ forestier nm forest warden; ~ mobile nm, nf mobile guard; ~ des Sceaux nm ≈ Lord Chancellor; ~ à vue nf (JUR) ≈ police custody; ~-à-vous nm inv: être/se mettre au ~-à-vous to be at/stand to attention.

garde... [gaʀd(ə)] préfixe: ~-barrière nm/f level-crossing keeper; ~-boue nm inv mudguard; ~-chasse nm gamekeeper; ~-fou nm railing, parapet; ~-malade nf home nurse; ~-manger nm inv meat safe; pantry, larder; ~-meuble nm furniture depository; ~-pêche nm inv water bailiff; fisheries protection ship.

garder [gaʀde] vt (conserver) to keep; (surveiller: prisonnier, enfants) to look after; (: immeuble, lieu) to guard; ~ le lit/la chambre to stay in bed/indoors; se ~ (aliment: se conserver) to keep; se ~ de faire to be careful not to do; pêche/chasse gardée private fishing/hunting (ground).

garderie [gaʀdəʀi] nf day nursery, crèche.

garde-robe [gaʀdəʀɔb] nf wardrobe.

gardeur, euse [gaʀdœʀ, -øz] nm/f (d'animaux) cowherd; goatherd.

gardien, ne [gaʀdjɛ̃, -jɛn] nm/f (garde) guard; (de prison) warder; (de domaine, réserve) warden; (de musée etc) attendant; (de phare, cimetière) keeper; (d'immeuble) caretaker; (fig) guardian; ~ de but

goalkeeper; ~ de nuit night watchman;
~ de la paix policeman.
gare [gaʀ] nf (railway) station // excl
watch out!; ~ à ne pas ... mind you don't
...; ~ maritime harbour station; ~
routière coach station.
garenne [gaʀɛn] nf voir lapin.
garer [gaʀe] vt to park; se ~ to park;
(pour laisser passer) to draw into the side.
gargariser [gaʀgaʀize]: se ~ vi to
gargle; **gargarisme** nm gargling q; gargle.
gargote [gaʀgɔt] nf cheap restaurant.
gargouille [gaʀguj] nf gargoyle.
gargouiller [gaʀguje] vi to gurgle.
garnement [gaʀnəmɑ̃] nm tearaway,
scallywag.
garni, e [gaʀni] a (plat) served with
vegetables (and chips or pasta or rice) //
nm furnished accommodation q.
garnir [gaʀniʀ] vt to decorate; to fill; to
cover; ~ qch de (orner) to decorate sth
with; to trim sth with; (approvisionner) to
fill ou stock sth with; (protéger) to fit sth
with; (CULIN) to garnish sth with.
garnison [gaʀnizɔ̃] nf garrison.
garniture [gaʀnityʀ] nf (CULIN) vegetables
pl; trimmings pl; filling; (décoration)
trimming; (protection) fittings pl; ~ de
frein brake lining; ~ intérieure (AUTO)
interior trim.
garrot [gaʀo] nm (MÉD) tourniquet;
(torture) garrotte.
garrotter [gaʀɔte] vt to tie up; (fig) to
muzzle.
gars [ga] nm lad; guy.
gas-oil [gazɔjl] nm diesel oil.
gaspillage [gaspijaʒ] nm waste.
gaspiller [gaspije] vt to waste.
gastrique [gastʀik] a gastric, stomach cpd.
gastronome [gastʀɔnɔm] nm/f gourmet.
gastronomie [gastʀɔnɔmi] nf gastronomy.
gâteau, x [gato] nm cake; ~ sec biscuit.
gâter [gate] vt to spoil; se ~ vi (dent, fruit)
to go bad; (temps, situation) to change for
the worse.
gâterie [gatʀi] nf little treat.
gâteux, euse [gatø, -øz] a senile.
gauche [goʃ] a left, left-hand; (maladroit)
awkward, clumsy // nf (POL) left (wing);
à ~ on the left; (direction) (to the) left;
à ~ de (on ou to the) left of; à la ~ de
to the left of; **gaucher, ère** a left-handed;
~rie nf awkwardness, clumsiness;
gauchir vt to warp; **gauchisant, e** a with
left-wing tendencies; **gauchiste** nm/f
leftist.
gaufre [gofʀ(ə)] nf waffle.
gaufrer [gofʀe] vt (papier) to emboss;
(tissu) to goffer.
gaufrette [gofʀɛt] nf wafer.
gaule [gol] nf (long) pole.
gaulois, e [golwa, -waz] a Gallic; (grivois)
bawdy // nm/f: G~, e Gaul.
gausser [gose]: se ~ de vt to deride.
gaver [gave] vt to force-feed; (fig): ~ de
to cram with, fill up with.
gaz [gaz] nm inv gas; mettre les ~ (AUTO)
to put one's foot down; ~ lacrymogène
tear gas; ~ de ville town gas.

gaze [gaz] nf gauze.
gazéifié, e [gazeifje] a aerated.
gazelle [gazɛl] nf gazelle.
gazer [gaze] vt to gas // vi (fam) to be
going ou working well.
gazette [gazɛt] nf news sheet.
gazeux, euse [gazø, -øz] a gaseous; eau
gazeuse soda water.
gazoduc [gazɔdyk] nm gas pipeline.
gazomètre [gazɔmɛtʀ(ə)] nm gasometer.
gazon [gazɔ̃] nm (herbe) turf; grass;
(pelouse) lawn.
gazouiller [gazuje] vi to chirp; (enfant)
to babble.
geai [ʒɛ] nm jay.
géant, e [ʒeɑ̃, -ɑ̃t] a gigantic, giant;
(COMM) giant-size // nm/f giant.
geindre [ʒɛ̃dʀ(ə)] vi to groan, moan..
gel [ʒɛl] nm frost; freezing.
gélatine [ʒelatin] nf gelatine; **gélatineux,
euse** a jelly-like, gelatinous.
gelé, e [ʒəle] a frozen.
gelée [ʒəle] nf jelly; (gel) frost; ~
blanche hoarfrost, white frost.
geler [ʒəle] vt, vi to freeze; il gèle it's
freezing; **gelures** nfpl frostbite sg.
Gémeaux [ʒemo] nmpl: les ~ Gemini,
the Twins; être des ~ to be Gemini.
gémir [ʒemiʀ] vi to groan, moan;
gémissement nm groan, moan.
gemme [ʒɛm] nf gem(stone).
gênant, e [ʒɛnɑ̃, -ɑ̃t] a annoying;
embarrassing.
gencive [ʒɑ̃siv] nf gum.
gendarme [ʒɑ̃daʀm(ə)] nm gendarme;
~rie nf military police force in countryside
and small towns; their police station or
barracks.
gendre [ʒɑ̃dʀ(ə)] nm son-in-law.
gène [ʒɛn] nf (à respirer, bouger)
discomfort, difficulty; (dérangement)
bother, trouble; (manque d'argent)
financial difficulties pl ou straits pl;
(confusion) embarrassment.
gêné, e [ʒene] a embarrassed.
généalogie [ʒenealɔʒi] nf genealogy;
généalogique a genealogical.
gêner [ʒene] vt (incommoder) to bother;
(encombrer) to hamper; to be in the way;
(déranger) to bother; (embarrasser): ~ qn
to make sb feel ill-at-ease; se ~ to put
o.s. out.
général, e, aux [ʒeneʀal, -o] a, nm
general //nf: (répétition) ~e final dress
rehearsal; en ~ usually, in general; ~
ement ad generally.
généralisation [ʒeneʀalizasjɔ̃] nf
generalization.
généralisé, e [ʒeneʀalize] a general.
généraliser [ʒeneʀalize] vt, vi to
generalize; se ~ vi to become widespread.
généraliste [ʒeneʀalist(ə)] nm/f general
practitioner, G.P.
généralités [ʒeneʀalite] nfpl generalities;
(introduction) general points.
générateur, trice [ʒeneʀatœʀ, -tʀis] a:
~ de which causes ou brings about // nf
generator.
génération [ʒeneʀasjɔ̃] nf generation.

génèreusement [ʒeneʀøzmɑ̃] ad generously.

généreux, euse [ʒeneʀø, -øz] a generous.

génèrique [ʒeneʀik] a generic // nm (CINÉMA) credits pl, credit titles pl.

générosité [ʒeneʀozite] nf generosity.

genèse [ʒanɛz] nf genesis.

genêt [ʒanɛ] nm broom q.

génétique [ʒenetik] a genetic // nf genetics sg.

Genève [ʒanɛv] n Geneva; **genevois, e** a, nm/f Genevan.

génial, e, aux [ʒenjal, -o] a of genius.

génie [ʒeni] nm genius; (MIL): **le ~** the Engineers pl; **~ civil** civil engineering.

genièvre [ʒanjɛvʀ(ə)] nm juniper (tree); (boisson) geneva; **grain de ~** juniper berry.

génisse [ʒenis] nf heifer.

génital, e, aux [ʒenital, -o] a genital.

génitif [ʒenitif] nm genitive.

genou, x [ʒnu] nm knee; **à ~x** on one's knees; **se mettre à ~x** to kneel down; **genouillère** nf (SPORT) kneepad.

genre [ʒɑ̃ʀ] nm kind, type, sort; (allure) manner; (LING) gender; (ART) genre; (ZOOL etc) genus.

gens [ʒɑ̃] nmpl (f in some phrases) people pl.

gentil, le [ʒɑ̃ti, -ij] a kind; (enfant: sage) good; (sympa: endroit etc) nice; **gentillesse** nf kindness; **gentiment** ad kindly.

génuflexion [ʒenyflɛksjɔ̃] nf genuflexion.

géographe [ʒeɔgʀaf] nm/f geographer.

géographie [ʒeɔgʀafi] nf geography; **géographique** a geographical.

geôlier [ʒolje] nm jailer.

géologie [ʒeɔlɔʒi] nf geology; **géologique** a geological; **géologue** nm/f geologist.

géomètre [ʒeɔmɛtʀ(ə)] nm/f: (arpenteur-) (land) surveyor.

géométrie [ʒeɔmetʀi] nf geometry; **à ~ variable** (AVIAT) swing-wing; **géométrique** a geometric.

gérance [ʒeʀɑ̃s] nf management; **mettre en ~** to appoint a manager for.

géranium [ʒeʀanjɔm] nm geranium.

gérant, e [ʒeʀɑ̃, -ɑ̃t] nm/f manager/manageress; **~ d'immeuble** managing agent.

gerbe [ʒɛʀb(ə)] nf (de fleurs) spray; (de blé) sheaf (pl sheaves); (fig) shower, burst.

gercé, e [ʒɛʀse] a chapped.

gerçure [ʒɛʀsyʀ] nf crack.

gérer [ʒeʀe] vt to manage.

gériatrie [ʒeʀjatʀi] nf geriatrics sg; **gériatrique** a geriatric.

germain, e [ʒɛʀmɛ̃, -ɛn] a: **cousin ~** first cousin.

germanique [ʒɛʀmanik] a Germanic.

germe [ʒɛʀm(ə)] nm germ.

germer [ʒɛʀme] vi to sprout; to germinate.

gésier [ʒezje] nm gizzard.

gésir [ʒeziʀ] vi to be lying (down); voir aussi **ci-gît**.

gestation [ʒɛstasjɔ̃] nf gestation.

geste [ʒɛst(ə)] nm gesture; move; motion.

gesticuler [ʒɛstikyle] vi to gesticulate.

gestion [ʒɛstjɔ̃] nf management.

gibecière [ʒibsjɛʀ] nf gamebag.

gibet [ʒibɛ] nm gallows pl.

gibier [ʒibje] nm (animaux) game; (fig) prey.

giboulée [ʒibule] nf sudden shower.

giboyeux, euse [ʒibwajø, -øz] a well-stocked with game.

gicler [ʒikle] vi to spurt, squirt.

gicleur [ʒiklœʀ] nm (AUTO) jet.

gifle [ʒifl(ə)] nf slap (in the face); **gifler** vt to slap (in the face).

gigantesque [ʒigɑ̃tɛsk(ə)] a gigantic.

gigogne [ʒigɔɲ] a: **lits ~s** pull-out ou stowaway beds; **tables/poupées ~s** nest of tables/dolls.

gigot [ʒigo] nm leg (of mutton ou lamb).

gigoter [ʒigɔte] vi to wriggle (about).

gilet [ʒilɛ] nm waistcoat; (pull) cardigan; (de corps) vest; **~ pare-balles** bulletproof jacket; **~ de sauvetage** life jacket.

gin [dʒin] nm gin.

gingembre [ʒɛ̃ʒɑ̃bʀ(ə)] nm ginger.

girafe [ʒiʀaf] nf giraffe.

giratoire [ʒiʀatwaʀ] a: **sens ~** roundabout.

girofle [ʒiʀɔfl(ə)] nm: **clou de ~** clove.

girouette [ʒiʀwɛt] nf weather vane ou cock.

gisait etc vb voir **gésir**.

gisement [ʒizmɑ̃] nm deposit.

gît vb voir **gésir**.

gitan, e [ʒitɑ̃, -an] nm/f gipsy.

gite [ʒit] nm home; shelter; **~ rural** farmhouse accommodation q (for tourists).

givrage [ʒivʀaʒ] nm icing.

givre [ʒivʀ(ə)] nm (hoar) frost.

glabre [glabʀ(ə)] a hairless; clean-shaven.

glace [glas] nf ice; (crème glacée) ice cream; (verre) sheet of glass; (miroir) mirror; (de voiture) window; **~s** nfpl (GÉO) ice sheets, ice sg.

glacé, e [glase] a icy; (boisson) iced.

glacer [glase] vt to freeze; (boisson) to chill, ice; (gâteau) to ice; (papier, tissu) to glaze; (fig): **~ qn** to chill sb; to make sb's blood run cold.

glaciaire [glasjɛʀ] a ice cpd; glacial.

glacial, e [glasjal] a icy.

glacier [glasje] nm (GÉO) glacier; (marchand) ice-cream maker.

glacière [glasjɛʀ] nf icebox.

glaçon [glasɔ̃] nm icicle; (pour boisson) ice cube.

glaïeul [glajœl] nm gladiola.

glaire [glɛʀ] nf (MÉD) phlegm q.

glaise [glɛz] nf clay.

gland [glɑ̃] nm acorn; (décoration) tassel; (ANAT) glans.

glande [glɑ̃d] nf gland.

glaner [glane] vt, vi to glean.

glapir [glapiʀ] vi to yelp.

glas [glɑ] nm knell, toll.

glauque [glok] a dull blue-green.

glissade [glisad] nf (par jeu) slide; (chute) slip; (dérapage) skid.

glissant, e [glisɑ̃, -ɑ̃t] a slippery.

glissement [glismɑ̃] nm sliding; (fig) shift; **~ de terrain** landslide.

glisser [glise] vi (avancer) to glide ou slide along; (coulisser, tomber) to slide; (déraper) to slip; (être glissant) to be slippery // vt: ~ qch sous/dans/à to slip sth under/into/to; ~ sur (fig: détail etc) to skate over; se ~ dans/entre to slip into/between; glissière nf slide channel; à glissière sliding; glissoire nf slide.

global, e, aux [glɔbal, -o] a overall.

globe [glɔb] nm globe; sous ~ under glass; ~ oculaire eyeball; le ~ terrestre the globe.

globule [glɔbyl] nm (du sang): ~ blanc/rouge white/red corpuscle.

globuleux, euse [glɔbylø, -øz] a: yeux ~ protruding eyes.

gloire [glwaʀ] nf glory; (mérite) distinction, credit; (personne) celebrity; glorieux, euse a glorious; glorifier vt to glorify, extol.

glossaire [glɔsɛʀ] nm glossary.

glousser [gluse] vi to cluck; (rire) to chuckle.

glouton, ne [glutɔ̃, -ɔn] a gluttonous, greedy.

glu [gly] nf birdlime.

gluant, e [glyɑ̃, -ɑ̃t] a sticky, gummy.

glycine [glisin] nf wisteria.

go [go]: tout de ~ ad straight out.

G.O. sigle = grandes ondes.

gobelet [gɔblɛ] nm tumbler; beaker; (à dés) cup.

gober [gɔbe] vt to swallow.

godet [gɔdɛ] nm pot.

godiller [gɔdije] vi to scull.

goéland [gɔelɑ̃] nm (sea)gull.

goélette [gɔelɛt] nf schooner.

goémon [gɔemɔ̃] nm wrack.

gogo [gɔgo] nm (péj) mug, sucker; à ~ ad galore.

goguenard, e [gɔgnaʀ, -aʀd(ə)] a mocking.

goguette [gɔgɛt] nf: en ~ on the binge.

goinfre [gwɛ̃fʀ(ə)] nm glutton; se goinfrer vi to make a pig of o.s.; se goinfrer de to guzzle.

goitre [gwatʀ(ə)] nm goitre.

golf [gɔlf] nm golf; golf course; ~ miniature crazy ou miniature golf.

golfe [gɔlf(ə)] nm gulf; bay.

gomme [gɔm] nf (à effacer) rubber, eraser; (résine) gum; gommer vt to erase; to gum.

gond [gɔ̃] nm hinge; sortir de ses ~s (fig) to fly off the handle.

gondole [gɔ̃dɔl] nf gondola.

gondoler [gɔ̃dɔle] vi, se ~ vi to warp; to buckle.

gondolier [gɔ̃dɔlje] nm gondolier.

gonflage [gɔ̃flaʒ] nm inflating, blowing up.

gonflé, e [gɔ̃fle] a swollen; bloated.

gonfler [gɔ̃fle] vt (pneu, ballon) to inflate, blow up; (nombre, importance) to inflate // vi to swell (up); (CULIN: pâte) to rise; gonfleur nm air pump.

gong [gɔ̃g] nm gong.

goret [gɔʀɛ] nm piglet.

gorge [gɔʀʒ(ə)] nf (ANAT) throat; (poitrine) breast; (GÉO) gorge; (rainure) groove.

gorgé, e [gɔʀʒe] a: ~ de filled with; (eau) saturated with // nf mouthful; sip; gulp.

gorille [gɔʀij] nm gorilla; (fam) bodyguard.

gosier [gozje] nm throat.

gosse [gɔs] nm/f kid.

gothique [gɔtik] a gothic.

goudron [gudʀɔ̃] nm tar; goudronner vt to tarmac.

gouffre [gufʀ(ə)] nm abyss, gulf.

goujat [guʒa] nm boor.

goujon [guʒɔ̃] nm gudgeon.

goulée [gule] nf gulp.

goulet [gulɛ] nm bottleneck.

goulot [gulo] nm neck; boire au ~ to drink from the bottle.

goulu, e [guly] a greedy.

goupillon [gupijɔ̃] nm (REL) sprinkler.

gourd, e [guʀ, guʀd(ə)] a numb (with cold).

gourde [guʀd(ə)] nf (récipient) flask.

gourdin [guʀdɛ̃] nm club, bludgeon.

gourmand, e [guʀmɑ̃, -ɑ̃d] a greedy; gourmandise nf greed; (bonbon) sweet.

gourmet [guʀmɛ] nm epicure.

gourmette [guʀmɛt] nf chain bracelet.

gousse [gus] nf: ~ d'ail clove of garlic.

gousset [gusɛ] nm (de gilet) fob.

goût [gu] nm taste; prendre ~ à to develop a taste ou a liking for.

goûter [gute] vt (essayer) to taste; (apprécier) to enjoy // vi to have (afternoon) tea // nm (afternoon) tea; ~ à to taste, sample; ~ de to have a taste of.

goutte [gut] nf drop; (MÉD) gout; (alcool) brandy; ~s nfpl (MÉD) (nose) drops.

goutte-à-goutte [gutagut] nm (MÉD) drip; alimenter au ~ to drip-feed.

gouttelette [gutlɛt] nf droplet.

gouttière [gutjɛʀ] nf gutter.

gouvernail [guvɛʀnaj] nm rudder; (barre) helm, tiller.

gouvernante [guvɛʀnɑ̃t] nf governess.

gouverne [guvɛʀn(ə)] nf: pour sa ~ for his guidance.

gouvernement [guvɛʀnəmɑ̃] nm government; membre du ~ ≈ Cabinet member; gouvernemental, e, aux a government cpd; pro-government.

gouverner [guvɛʀne] vt to govern; gouverneur nm governor; commanding officer.

grâce [gʀɑs] nf grace; favour; (JUR) pardon; ~s nfpl (REL) grace sg; dans les bonnes ~s de qn in favour with sb; faire ~ à qn de qch to spare sb sth; rendre ~(s) à to give thanks to; demander ~ to beg for mercy; droit de ~ right of reprieve; ~ à prép thanks to; gracier vt to pardon; gracieux, euse a graceful.

gracile [gʀasil] a slender.

gradation [gʀadasjɔ̃] nf gradation.

grade [gʀad] nm rank; monter en ~ to be promoted.

gradé [gʀade] nm officer.

gradin [gʀadɛ̃] nm tier; step; ~s nmpl (de stade) terracing sg.

graduation [gʀadɥasjɔ̃] nf graduation.

graduel, le [gʀadɥɛl] a gradual; progressive.

graduer [gRadɥe] vt (effort etc) to increase gradually ; (règle, verre) to graduate ; **exercices gradués** exercises graded for difficulty.

graffiti [gRafiti] nmpl graffiti.

grain [gRɛ̃] nm (gén) grain ; (NAVIG) squall ; ~ **de beauté** beauty spot ; ~ **de café** coffee bean ; ~ **de poivre** peppercorn ; ~ **de poussière** speck of dust ; ~ **de raisin** grape.

graine [gRɛn] nf seed ; ~**tier** nm seed merchant.

graissage [gRɛsaʒ] nm lubrication, greasing.

graisse [gRɛs] nf fat ; (lubrifiant) grease ; **graisser** vt to lubricate, grease ; (tacher) to make greasy ; **graisseux, euse** a greasy ; (ANAT) fatty.

grammaire [gRamɛR] nf grammar ; **grammatical, e, aux** a grammatical.

gramme [gRam] nm gramme.

grand, e [gRɑ̃, gRɑ̃d] a (haut) tall ; (gros, vaste, large) big, large ; (long) long ; (sens abstraits) great // ad: ~ **ouvert** wide open ; **son** ~ **frère** his older brother ; **il est assez** ~ **pour** he's old enough to ; **au** ~ **air** in the open (air) ; ~**s blessés/brûlés** casualties with severe injuries/burns ; ~ **angle** nm (PHOTO) wide-angle lens sg ; + **écart** splits pl ; ~ **ensemble** housing scheme ; ~ **magasin** department store ; ~**e personne** grown-up ; ~**es écoles** prestige schools of university level, with competitive entrance examination ; ~**es lignes** (RAIL) main lines ; ~**es vacances** summer holidays ; **grand-chose** nm/f inv: **pas grand-chose** not much ; **Grande-Bretagne** nf: **la Grande-Bretagne** (Great) Britain ; **grandeur** nf (dimension) size ; magnitude ; (fig) greatness ; **grandeur nature** life-size ; **grandir** vi (enfant, arbre) to grow ; (bruit, hostilité) to increase, grow // vt: **grandir qn** (suj: vêtement, chaussure) to make sb look taller ; (fig) to make sb grow in stature ; ~**mère** nf grandmother ; ~**messe** nf high mass ; ~**père** nm grandfather ; ~**route** nf main road ; ~**rue** nf high street ; ~**s-parents** nmpl grandparents.

grange [gRɑ̃ʒ] nf barn.

granit [gRanit] nm granite.

granulé [gRanyle] nm granule.

granuleux, euse [gRanylø, -øz] a granular.

graphie [gRafi] nf written form.

graphique [gRafik] a graphic // nm graph.

graphisme [gRafism(ə)] nm graphic arts pl ; graphics sg.

graphologie [gRafɔlɔʒi] nf graphology ; **graphologue** nm/f graphologist.

grappe [gRap] nf cluster ; ~ **de raisin** bunch of grapes.

grappiller [gRapije] vt to glean.

grappin [gRapɛ̃] nm grapnel ; **mettre le** ~ **sur** (fig) to get one's claws on.

gras, se [gRɑ, gRɑs] a (viande, soupe) fatty ; (personne) fat ; (surface, main) greasy ; (toux) loose, phlegmy ; (rire) throaty ; (plaisanterie) coarse ; (crayon) soft-lead ; (TYPO) bold // nm (CULIN) fat ; **faire la** ~**se matinée** to have a lie-in ;

~**sement** ad: ~**sement payé** handsomely paid ; ~**souillet, te** a podgy, plump.

gratification [gRatifikasjɔ̃] nf bonus.

gratifier [gRatifje] vt: ~ **qn de** to favour sb with, reward sb with ; (sourire etc) to favour sb with.

gratin [gRatɛ̃] nm (CULIN) cheese-topped dish ; cheese topping.

gratiné, e [gRatine] a (CULIN) au gratin ; (fam) hellish.

gratis [gRatis] ad free.

gratitude [gRatityd] nf gratitude.

gratte-ciel [gRatsjɛl] nm inv skyscraper.

grattement [gRatmɑ̃] nm (bruit) scratching (noise).

gratte-papier [gRatpapje] nm inv (péj) penpusher.

gratter [gRate] vt (frotter) to scrape ; (enlever) to scrape off ; (bras, bouton) to scratch ; **grattoir** nm scraper.

gratuit, e [gRatɥi, -ɥit] a (entrée, billet) free ; (fig) gratuitous.

gratuitement [gRatɥitmɑ̃] ad free.

gravats [gRava] nmpl rubble sg.

grave [gRav] a (maladie, accident) serious, bad ; (sujet, problème) serious, grave ; (air) grave, solemn ; (voix, son) deep, low-pitched // nm (MUS) low register ; **blessé** ~ seriously injured person ; ~**ment** ad seriously ; gravely.

graver [gRave] vt to engrave ; **graveur** nm engraver.

gravier [gRavje] nm gravel q ; **gravillons** nmpl gravel sg, loose chippings ou gravel.

gravir [gRaviR] vt to climb (up).

gravitation [gRavitasjɔ̃] nf gravitation.

gravité [gRavite] nf seriousness ; gravity ; (PHYSIQUE) gravity.

graviter [gRavite] vi: ~ **autour de** to revolve around.

gravure [gRavyR] nf engraving ; (reproduction) print ; plate.

gré [gRe] nm: **à son** ~ to his liking ; **as he** p..ases ; **au** ~ **de** according to, following ; **contre le** ~ **de qn** against sb's will ; **de son (plein)** ~ of one's own free will ; **de** ~ **ou de force** whether one likes it or not ; **de bon** ~ willingly ; **de** ~ **à** ~ (COMM) by mutual agreement ; **savoir** ~ **à qn de qch** to be grateful to sb for sth.

grec, grecque [gRɛk] a Greek ; (classique: vase etc) Grecian // nm/f Greek.

Grèce [gRɛs] nf: **la** ~ Greece.

gréement [gRemɑ̃] nm rigging.

greffe [gRɛf] nf grafting q, graft ; transplanting q, transplant // nm (JUR) office.

greffer [gRefe] vt (BOT, MÉD: tissu) to graft ; (MÉD: organe) to transplant.

greffier [gRefje] nm clerk of the court.

grégaire [gRegɛR] a gregarious.

grège [gRɛʒ] a: **soie** ~ raw silk.

grêle [gRɛl] a (very) thin // nf hail.

grêlé, e [gRele] a pockmarked.

grêler [gRele] vb impersonnel: **il grêle** it's hailing.

grêlon [gRelɔ̃] nm hailstone.

grelot [gRəlo] nm little bell.

grelotter [gRəlɔte] vi (trembler) to shiver.

grenade [grənad] nf (explosive) grenade ; (BOT) pomegranate ; ~ **lacrymogène** teargas grenade.

grenadier [grənadje] nm (MIL) grenadier ; (BOT) pomegranate tree.

grenat [grəna] a inv dark red.

grenier [grənje] nm attic ; (de ferme) loft.

grenouille [grənuj] nf frog.

grenu, e [grəny] a grainy, grained.

grès [grɛ] nm sandstone ; (poterie) stoneware.

grésiller [grezije] vi to sizzle ; (RADIO) to crackle.

grève [grɛv] nf (d'ouvriers) strike ; (plage) shore ; **se mettre en/faire** ~ to go on/be on strike ; ~ **de la faim** hunger strike ; ~ **sauvage** wildcat strike ; ~ **sur le tas** sit-down strike ; ~ **tournante** strike by rota ; ~ **du zèle** work-to-rule q.

grever [grəve] vt to put a strain on ; **grevé d'impôts** crippled by taxes.

gréviste [grevist(ə)] nm/f striker.

gribouiller [gribuje] vt to scribble, scrawl // vi to doodle.

grief [grijɛf] nm grievance ; **faire** ~ **à qn de** to reproach sb for.

grièvement [grijɛvmɑ̃] ad seriously.

griffe [grif] nf claw ; (fig) signature.

griffer [grife] vt to scratch.

griffonner [grifɔne] vt to scribble.

grignoter [griɲɔte] vt to nibble ou gnaw at.

gril [gril] nm steak ou grill pan.

grillade [grijad] nf grill.

grillage [grijaʒ] nm (treillis) wire netting ; wire fencing.

grille [grij] nf (portail) (metal) gate ; (d'égout) (metal) grate ; (fig) grid.

grille-pain [grijpɛ̃] nm inv toaster.

griller [grije] vt (aussi: **faire** ~: pain) to toast ; (: viande) to grill ; (fig: ampoule etc) to burn out, blow.

grillon [grijɔ̃] nm cricket.

grimace [grimas] nf grimace ; (pour faire rire): **faire des** ~s to pull ou make faces.

grimer [grime] vt to make up.

grimper [grɛ̃pe] vi, vt to climb.

grincement [grɛ̃smɑ̃] nm grating (noise) ; creaking (noise).

grincer [grɛ̃se] vi (porte, roue) to grate ; (plancher) to creak ; ~ **des dents** to grind one's teeth.

grincheux, euse [grɛ̃ʃø, -øz] a grumpy.

grippe [grip] nf flu, influenza ; **grippé, e** a: **être grippé** to have flu.

gripper [gripe] vt, vi to jam.

gris, e [gri, griz] a grey ; (ivre) tipsy.

grisaille [grizaj] nf greyness, dullness.

grisant, e [grizɑ̃, -ɑ̃t] a intoxicating, exhilarating.

griser [grize] vt to intoxicate.

grisonner [grizɔne] vi to be going grey.

grisou [grizu] nm firedamp.

grive [griv] nf thrush.

grivois, e [grivwa, -waz] a saucy.

grog [grɔg] nm grog.

grogner [grɔɲe] vi to growl ; (fig) to grumble.

groin [grwɛ̃] nm snout.

grommeler [grɔmle] vi to mutter to o.s.

grondement [grɔ̃dmɑ̃] nm rumble.

gronder [grɔ̃de] vi to rumble ; (fig: révolte) to be brewing // vt to scold.

gros, se [gro, gros] a big, large ; (obèse) fat ; (travaux, dégâts) extensive ; (large: trait, fil) thick, heavy // ad: **risquer/gagner** ~ to risk/win a lot // nm (COMM): **le** ~ the wholesale business ; **prix de** ~ wholesale price ; **par** ~ **temps/** ~ **se mer** in rough weather/heavy seas ; **le** ~ **de** the main body of ; the bulk of ; **en** ~ roughly ; (COMM) wholesale ; ~ **intestin** large intestine ; ~ **lot** jackpot ; ~ **mot** coarse word, vulgarity ; ~ **plan** (PHOTO) close-up ; ~ **sel** cooking salt ; ~ **se caisse** big drum.

groseille [grozɛj] nf: ~ **(rouge)/(blanche)** red/white currant ; ~ **à maquereau** gooseberry ; **groseillier** nm red ou white currant bush ; gooseberry bush.

grosse [gros] a voir gros.

grossesse [grosɛs] nf pregnancy.

grosseur [grosœr] nf size ; fatness ; (tumeur) lump.

grossier, ière [grosje, -jɛr] a coarse ; (travail) rough ; crude ; (évident: erreur) gross ; **grossièrement** ad coarsely ; roughly ; crudely ; (en gros) roughly.

grossir [grosir] vi (personne) to put on weight ; (fig) to grow, get bigger ; (rivière) to swell // vt to increase ; to exaggerate ; (au microscope) to magnify ; (suj: vêtement): ~ **qn** to make sb look fatter ; **grossissement** nm (optique) magnification.

grossiste [grosist(ə)] nm/f wholesaler.

grosso modo [grosomɔdo] ad roughly.

grotte [grɔt] nf cave.

grouiller [gruje] vi to mill about ; to swarm about ; ~ **de** to be swarming with.

groupe [grup] nm group ; ~ **sanguin** blood group.

groupement [grupmɑ̃] nm grouping ; group.

grouper [grupe] vt to group ; **se** ~ to get together.

gruau [gryo] nm: **pain de** ~ wheaten bread.

grue [gry] nf crane.

grumeaux [grymo] nmpl lumps.

grutier [grytje] nm crane driver.

Guadeloupe [gwadlup] nf: **la** ~ Guadeloupe.

gué [ge] nm ford ; **passer à** ~ to ford.

guenilles [gənij] nfpl rags.

guenon [gənɔ̃] nf female monkey.

guépard [gepar] nm cheetah.

guêpe [gɛp] nf wasp.

guêpier [gepje] nm (fig) trap.

guère [gɛr] ad (avec adjectif, adverbe): **ne** ... ~ hardly ; (avec verbe): **ne** ... ~ **tournure** négative + much ; hardly ever ; **tournure** négative + (very) long ; **il n'y a** ~ **que/de** there's hardly anybody (ou anything) but/hardly any.

guéridon [geridɔ̃] nm pedestal table.

guérilla [gerija] nf guerrilla warfare.

guérillero [gerijero] nm guerrilla.

guérir [gerir] vt (personne, maladie) to cure ; (membre, plaie) to heal // vi (*personne*) to recover, be cured; (*plaie, chagrin*) to heal; ~ **de** to be cured of, recover from; ~ **qn de** to cure sb of; **guérison** *nf* curing; healing; recovery; **guérissable** *a* curable; **guérisseur, euse** *nm/f* healer.

guérite [genit] *nf* sentry box.

guerre [gɛʀ] *nf* war; (*méthode*): ~ **atomique/de tranchées** atomic/ trench warfare q; **en** ~ **at war; faire la** ~ **à** to wage war against; **de** ~ **lasse** finally; ~ **civile/ mondiale** civil/world war; ~ **d'usure** war of attrition; **guerrier, ière** *a* warlike // *nm/f* warrior; **guerroyer** *vi* to wage war.

guet [gɛ] *nm:* **faire le** ~ to be on the watch *ou* look-out.

guet-apens [gɛtapɑ̃] *nm* ambush.

guêtre [gɛtʀ(ə)] *nf* gaiter.

guetter [gete] *vt* (*épier*) to watch (intently); (*attendre*) to watch (out) for; to be lying in wait for; **guetteur** *nm* lookout.

gueule [gœl] *nf* mouth; (*fam*) face; mouth; ~ **de bois** (*fam*) hangover.

gueuler [gœle] *vi* (*fam*) to bawl.

gueux [gø] *nm* beggar; rogue.

gui [gi] *nm* mistletoe.

guichet [giʃɛ] *nm* (*de bureau, banque*) counter, window; (*d'une porte*) wicket, hatch; **les** ~**s** (*à la gare, au théâtre*) the ticket office; **guichetier, ière** *nm/f* counter clerk.

guide [gid] *nm* guide.

guider [gide] *vt* to guide.

guidon [gidɔ̃] *nm* handlebars *pl*.

guignol [giɲɔl] *nm* ≈ Punch and Judy show; (*fig*) clown.

guillemets [gijmɛ] *nmpl:* **entre** ~ in inverted commas *ou* quotation marks; ~ **de répétition** ditto marks.

guilleret, te [gijʀɛ, -ɛt] *a* perky, bright.

guillotine [gijɔtin] *nf* guillotine; **guillotiner** *vt* to guillotine.

guindé, e [gɛ̃de] *a* stiff, starchy.

guirlande [giʀlɑ̃d] *nf* garland; (*de papier*) paper chain.

guise [giz] *nf:* **à votre** ~ as you wish *ou* please; **en** ~ **de** by way of.

guitare [gitaʀ] *nf* guitar; **guitariste** *nm/f* guitarist, guitar player.

gustatif, ive [gystatif, -iv] *a* gustatory; *voir* papille.

guttural, e, aux [gytyʀal, -o] *a* guttural.

Guyane [gɥijan] *n:* **la** ~ Guiana.

gymkhana [ʒimkana] *nm* rally.

gymnase [ʒimnɑz] *nm* gym(nasium).

gymnaste [ʒimnast(ə)] *nm/f* gymnast.

gymnastique [ʒimnastik] *nf* gymnastics *sg*; (*au réveil etc*) keep fit exercises *pl*.

gynécologie [ʒinekɔlɔʒi] *nf* gynaecology; **gynécologue** *nm/f* gynaecologist.

gypse [ʒips(ə)] *nm* gypsum.

H

h. *abr de* heure.

habile [abil] *a* skilful; (*malin*) clever; ~**té** *nf* skill, skilfulness; cleverness.

habilité, e [abilite] *a:* ~ **à faire** entitled to do, empowered to do.

habillé, e [abije] *a* dressed; (*chic*) dressy; (*TECH*): ~ **de** covered with; encased in.

habillement [abijmɑ̃] *nm* clothes *pl*; (*profession*) clothing industry.

habiller [abije] *vt* to dress; (*fournir en vêtements*) to clothe; **s'**~ to dress (o.s.); (*se déguiser, mettre des vêtements chic*) to dress up; **s'**~ **de/en** to dress in/dress up as; **s'**~ **chez/à** to buy one's clothes from/at.

habit [abi] *nm* outfit; ~**s** *nmpl* (*vêtements*) clothes; ~ (**de soirée**) tails *pl*; evening dress.

habitable [abitabl(ə)] *a* (in)habitable.

habitacle [abitakl(ə)] *nm* cockpit; (*AUTO*) passenger cell.

habitant, e [abitɑ̃, -ɑ̃t] *nm/f* inhabitant; (*d'une maison*) occupant, occupier; **loger chez l'**~ to stay with the locals.

habitat [abita] *nm* housing conditions *pl*; (*BOT, ZOOL*) habitat.

habitation [abitasjɔ̃] *nf* living; residence, home; house; ~**s à loyer modéré** (HLM) low-rent housing *sg*, ≈ council flats.

habité, e [abite] *a* inhabited; lived in.

habiter [abite] *vt* to live in; (*suj: sentiment*) to dwell in // *vi:* ~ **à/dans** to live in *ou* at/in.

habitude [abityd] *nf* habit; **avoir l'**~ **de faire** to be in the habit of doing; (*expérience*) to be used to doing; **d'**~ usually; **comme d'**~ as usual.

habitué, e [abitɥe] *a:* **être** ~ **à** to be used *ou* accustomed to // *nm/f* regular visitor; regular (customer).

habituel, le [abitɥɛl] *a* usual.

habituer [abitɥe] *vt:* ~ **qn à** to get sb used to; **s'**~ **à** to get used to.

*****hâbleur, euse** [ɑblœʀ, -øz] *a* boastful.

*****hache** [ˈaʃ] *nf* axe.

*****haché, e** [ˈaʃe] *a* minced; (*fig*) jerky.

*****hacher** [ˈaʃe] *vt* (*viande*) to mince; (*persil*) to chop.

*****hachis** [ˈaʃi] *nm* mince q.

*****hachisch** [ˈaʃiʃ] *nm* hashish.

*****hachoir** [ˈaʃwaʀ] *nm* chopper; (*meat*) mincer; chopping board.

*****hachures** [ˈaʃyʀ] *nfpl* hatching *sg*.

*****hagard, e** [ˈagaʀ, -aʀd(ə)] *a* wild, distraught.

*****haie** [ˈɛ] *nf* hedge; (*SPORT*) hurdle; (*fig: rang*) line, row; **200 m** ~**s** 200 m hurdles; ~ **d'honneur** guard of honour.

*****haillons** [ˈajɔ̃] *nmpl* rags.

*****haine** [ˈɛn] *nf* hatred; **haineux, euse** *a* full of hatred.

*****haïr** [ˈaiʀ] *vt* to detest, hate.

*****halage** [ˈalaʒ] *nm:* **chemin de** ~ towpath.

*****hâle** [ˈɑl] *nm* (sun)tan; *****hâlé, e** *a* (sun)tanned, sunburnt.

haleine [alɛn] *nf* breath; **hors d'**~ out of breath; **tenir en** ~ to hold spellbound; to keep in suspense; **de longue** ~ a long-term.

*****haleter** [ˈalte] *vi* to pant.

*****hall** [ˈol] *nm* hall.

*****hallali** [alali] *nm* kill.

*****halle** [ˈal] *nf* (covered) market; ~**s** *nfpl* central food market *sg*.

hallucinant, e [alysinɑ̃, -ɑ̃t] a staggering.
hallucination [alysinasjɔ̃] nf hallucination.
halluciné, e [alysine] nm/f person suffering from hallucinations; (raving) lunatic.
*halo ['alo] nm halo.
*halte ['alt(ə)] nf stop, break; stopping place; (RAIL) halt // excl stop!; faire ~ to stop.
haltère [altɛʀ] nm dumbbell, barbell; ~s nmpl (activité) weight lifting sg; haltérophile nm/f weight lifter.
*hamac ['amak] nm hammock.
*hameau, x ['amo] nm hamlet.
hameçon [amsɔ̃] nm (fish) hook.
*hampe ['ɑ̃p] nf shaft.
*hamster ['amstɛʀ] nm hamster.
*hanche ['ɑ̃ʃ] nf hip.
*hand-ball ['ɑ̃dbal] nm handball.
*handicap ['ɑ̃dikap] nm handicap; *~é, e a handicapped // nm/f physically (ou mentally) handicapped person; ~é moteur spastic; *~er vt to handicap.
*hangar ['ɑ̃gaʀ] nm shed.
*hanneton ['antɔ̃] nm cockchafer.
*hanter ['ɑ̃te] vt to haunt.
*hantise ['ɑ̃tiz] nf obsessive fear.
*happer ['ape] vt to snatch; (suj: train etc) to hit.
*haranguer ['aʀɑ̃ge] vt to harangue.
*haras ['aʀɑ] nm stud farm.
harassant, e ['aʀasɑ̃, -ɑ̃t] a exhausting.
*harceler ['aʀsəle] vt (MIL, CHASSE) to harass, harry; (importuner) to plague.
*hardes ['aʀd(ə)] nfpl rags.
*hardi, e ['aʀdi] a bold, daring.
*hareng ['aʀɑ̃] nm herring.
*hargne ['aʀɲ(ə)] nf aggressiveness.
*haricot ['aʀiko] nm bean; ~ vert/blanc French/haricot bean.
harmonica [aʀmɔnika] nm mouth organ.
harmonie [aʀmɔni] nf harmony; harmonieux, euse a harmonious; harmonique nm ou nf harmonic; harmoniser vt to harmonize.
*harnaché, e ['aʀnaʃe] a (fig) rigged out.
*harnacher ['aʀnaʃe] vt to harness.
*harnais ['aʀnɛ] nm harness.
*harpe ['aʀp(ə)] nf harp; *harpiste nm/f harpist.
*harpon ['aʀpɔ̃] nm harpoon; *harponner vt to harpoon; (fam) to collar.
*hasard ['azaʀ] nm: le ~ chance, fate; un ~ a coincidence; a stroke of luck; au ~ aimlessly; at random; haphazardly; par ~ by chance; à tout ~ just in case; on the off chance.
*hasarder ['azaʀde] vt (mot) to venture; (fortune) to risk; se ~ à faire to risk doing, venture to do.
*hasardeux, euse ['azaʀdø, -øz] a hazardous, risky; (hypothèse) rash.
*haschisch ['aʃiʃ] nm hashish.
*hâte ['ɑt] nf haste; à la ~ hurriedly, hastily; en ~ posthaste, with all possible speed; avoir ~ de to be eager ou anxious to; *hâter vt to hasten; se hâter to hurry; se hâter de to hurry ou hasten to.

*hâtif, ive ['ɑtif, -iv] a hurried; hasty; (légume) early.
*hausse ['os] nf rise, increase; (de fusil) backsight adjuster; en ~ rising.
*hausser ['ose] vt to raise; ~ les épaules to shrug (one's shoulders).
*haut, e ['o, 'ot] a high; (grand) tall; (son, voix) high(-pitched) // ad high // nm top (part); de 3 m de ~ 3 m high, 3 m in height; des ~s et des bas ups and downs; en ~ lieu in high places; à ~e voix aloud, out loud; du ~ de from the top of; de ~ en bas up and down; downwards; plus ~ higher up, further up; (dans un texte) above; (parler) louder; en ~ up above; at (ou tc) the top; (dans une maison) upstairs; en ~ de at the top of; la ~e couture/coiffure haute couture/coiffure; ~e fidélité hi-fi, high fidelity.
*hautain, e ['otɛ̃, -ɛn] a (personne, regard) haughty.
*hautbois ['obwa] nm oboe.
*haut-de-forme ['odfɔʀm(ə)] nm top hat.
*hautement ['otmɑ̃] ad highly.
*hauteur ['otœʀ] nf height; (GÉO) height, hill; (fig) loftiness; haughtiness; à ~ des yeux at eye level; à la ~ de (sur la même ligne) level with; by; (fig) equal to; à la ~ (fig) up to it, equal to the task.
*haut-fond ['ofɔ̃] nm shallow, shoal.
*haut-fourneau ['ofuʀno] nm blast ou smelting furnace.
*haut-le-cœur ['olkœʀ] nm inv retch, heave.
*haut-parleur ['opaʀlœʀ] nm (loud)speaker.
*hâve ['ɑv] a gaunt.
*havre ['ɑvʀ(ə)] nm haven.
*Haye ['ɛ] n: la ~ the Hague.
*hayon ['ɛjɔ̃] nm tailgate.
hebdomadaire [ɛdbɔmadɛʀ] a, nm weekly.
héberger [ebɛʀʒe] vt to accommodate, lodge; (réfugiés) to take in.
hébété, e [ebete] a dazed.
hébraïque [ebʀaik] a Hebrew, Hebraic.
hébreu, x [ebʀø] am, nm Hebrew.
H.E.C. sigle fpl = Hautes études commerciales.
hécatombe [ekatɔ̃b] nf slaughter.
hectare [ɛktaʀ] nm hectare, 10,000 square metres.
hectolitre [ɛktolitʀ] nm hectolitre.
hégémonie [eʒemɔni] nf hegemony.
*hein ['ɛ̃] excl eh?
*hélas ['elas] excl alas! // ad unfortunately.
*héler ['ele] vt to hail.
hélice [elis] nf propeller.
hélicoïdal, e, aux [elikɔidal, -o] a helical; helicoid.
hélicoptère [elikɔptɛʀ] nm helicopter.
héliogravure [eljogʀavyʀ] nf heliogravure.
héliport [elipɔʀ] nm heliport.
héliporté, e [elipɔʀte] a transported by helicopter.
hellénique [elenik] a Hellenic.
helvétique [ɛlvetik] a Swiss.

hématome [ematom] *nm* haematoma.
hémicycle [emisikl(ə)] *nm* semicircle; (*POL*): l'~ ≈ the benches (of the Commons).
hémiplégie [emipleʒi] *nf* paralysis of one side, hemiplegia.
hémisphère [emisfɛR] *nf:* ~ nord/sud northern/southern hemisphere.
hémophile [emɔfil] *a* haemophiliac.
hémorragie [emɔRaʒi] *nf* bleeding q, haemorrhage.
hémorroïdes [emɔRɔid] *nfpl* piles, haemorrhoids.
***hennir** [ʼeniR] *vi* to neigh, whinny.
hépatite [epatit] *nf* hepatitis, liver infection.
herbe [ɛRb(ə)] *nf* grass; (*CULIN, MÉD*) herb; en ~ unripe; (*fig*) budding; **herbeux, euse** *a* grassy; **herbicide** *nm* weed-killer; **herbier** *nm* herbarium; **herboriser** *vi* to collect plants, botanize; **herboriste** *nm/f* herbalist; **herboristerie** *nf* herbalist's shop; herb trade.
***hère** [ʼɛR] *nm:* pauvre ~ poor wretch.
héréditaire [eRediteR] *a* hereditary.
hérédité [eRedite] *nf* heredity.
hérésie [eRezi] *nf* heresy; **hérétique** *nm/f* heretic.
***hérissé, e** [ʼeRise] *a* bristling; ~ de spiked with; (*fig*) bristling with.
***hérisser** [ʼeRise] *vt:* ~ qn (*fig*) to ruffle sb; se ~ *vi* to bristle, bristle up.
***hérisson** [ʼeRisɔ̃] *nm* hedgehog.
héritage [eRitaʒ] *nm* inheritance; (*fig*) heritage; legacy; **faire un (petit)** ~ to come into (a little) money.
hériter [eRite] *vi:* ~ de qch (de qn) to inherit sth (from sb); ~ de qn to inherit sb's property; **héritier, ière** *nm/f* heir/heiress.
hermétique [ɛRmetik] *a* airtight; watertight; (*fig*) abstruse; impenetrable; ~ment *ad* tightly, hermetically.
hermine [ɛRmin] *nf* ermine.
hernie [ʼɛRni] *nf* hernia.
***héroïne** [eRɔin] *nf* heroine; (*drogue*) heroin.
héroïque [eRɔik] *a* heroic.
héroïsme [eRɔism(ə)] *nm* heroism.
***héron** [ʼeRɔ̃] *nm* heron.
***héros** [ʼeRo] *nm* hero.
***herse** [ʼɛRs(ə)] *nf* harrow; (*de château*) portcullis.
hésitant, e [ezitɑ̃, -ɑ̃t] *a* hesitant.
hésitation [ezitɑsjɔ̃] *nf* hesitation.
hésiter [ezite] *vi:* ~ (à faire) to hesitate (to do).
hétéroclite [eteRɔklit] *a* heterogeneous; (*objets*) sundry.
***hêtre** [ʼɛtR(ə)] *nm* beech.
heure [œR] *nf* hour; (*SCOL*) period; (*moment, moment fixé*) time; c'est l'~ it's time; quelle ~ est-il? what time is it? être à l'~ to be on time; (*montre*) to be right; mettre à l'~ to set right; à toute ~ at any time; 24 ~s sur 24 round the clock, 24 hours a day; à l'~ qu'il est at this time (of day); by now; sur l'~ at once; ~ locale/d'été local/summer time; ~s de bureau office hours; ~s supplémentaires overtime *sg*.

heureusement [œRézmɑ̃] *ad* (*par bonheur*) fortunately, luckily.
heureux, euse [œRé, -éz] *a* happy; (*chanceux*) lucky, fortunate; (*judicieux*) felicitous, fortunate.
***heurt** [ʼœR] *nm* (*choc*) collision; ~s *nmpl* (*fig*) clashes.
***heurté, e** [ʼœRte] *a* (*fig*) jerky, uneven.
***heurter** [ʼœRte] *vt* (*mur*) to strike, hit; (*personne*) to collide with; (*fig*) to go against, upset; se ~ à *vt* to collide with; (*fig*) to come up against; **heurtoir** *nm* door knocker.
hexagone [ɛgzagɔn] *nm* hexagon.
***hiatus** [ʼjatys] *nm* hiatus.
hiberner [ibɛRne] *vi* to hibernate.
***hibou, x** [ʼibu] *nm* owl.
***hideux, e**[1]**se** [ʼidé, -éz] *a* hideous.
hier [jɛR] *ad* yesterday; ~ matin/soir yesterday morning/ evening; toute la journée d'~ all day yesterday; toute la matinée d'~ all yesterday morning.
***hiérarchie** [ʼjeRaRʃi] *nf* hierarchy; ***hiérarchique** *a* hierarchic; ***hiérarchiser** *vt* to organize into a hierarchy.
hiéroglyphe [jeRɔglif] *nm* hieroglyphic.
hilare [ilaR] *a* mirthful; **hilarité** *nf* hilarity, mirth.
hindou, e [ɛ̃du] *a, nm/f* Hindu; Indian.
hippique [ipik] *a* equestrian, horse *cpd*.
hippisme [ipism(ə)] *nm* (horse) riding.
hippodrome [ipodRom] *nm* racecourse.
hippopotame [ipɔpɔtam] *nm* hippopotamus.
hirondelle [iRɔ̃dɛl] *nf* swallow.
hirsute [iRsyt] *a* hairy; shaggy; tousled.
hispanique [ispanik] *a* Hispanic.
***hisser** [ʼise] *vt* to hoist, haul up; se ~ sur to haul o.s. up onto.
histoire [istwaR] *nf* (*science, événements*) history; (*anecdote, récit, mensonge*) story; (*affaire*) business q; (*chichis: gén pl*) fuss q; ~s *nfpl* (*ennuis*) trouble *sg*; **historien, ne** *nm/f* historian; **historique** *a* historic.
hiver [ivɛR] *nm* winter; ~nal, e, aux *a* winter *cpd*; wintry; ~ner *vi* to winter.
H.L.M. *sigle m ou f voir* **habitation**.
***hocher** [ʼɔʃe] *vt:* ~ la tête to nod; (*signe négatif ou dubitatif*) to shake one's head.
***hochet** [ʼɔʃɛ] *nm* rattle.
***hockey** [ʼɔkɛ] *nm:* ~ (sur glace/gazon) (ice/field) hockey; ***hockeyeur** *nm* hockey player.
holding [ʼɔldiŋ] *nm* holding company.
hold-up [ʼɔldœp] *nm inv* hold-up.
***hollandais, e** [ʼɔldɛ, -ɛz] *a, nm* (*langue*) Dutch // *nm/f:* H~, e Dutchman/ woman; les H~ the Dutch.
***Hollande** [ʼɔlɑ̃d] *nf* Holland.
***homard** [ʼɔmaR] *nm* lobster.
homéopathie [ɔmeɔpati] *nf* homoeopathy; **homéopathique** *a* homoeopathic.
homérique [ɔmeRik] *a* Homeric.
homicide [ɔmisid] *nm* murder // *nm/f* murderer/eress; ~ **involontaire** manslaughter.
hommage [ɔmaʒ] *nm* tribute; ~s *nmpl:* présenter ses ~s to pay one's respects;

rendre ~ à to pay tribute ou homage to ; faire ~ de qch à qn to present sb with sth.

homme [ɔm] nm man ; ~ **d'affaires** businessman ; ~ **d'État** statesman ; ~ **de main** hired man ; ~ **de paille** stooge ; ~-**grenouille** nm frogman ; ~-**orchestre** nm one-man band.

homogène [ɔmɔʒɛn] a homogeneous ; **homogénéité** nf homogeneity.

homologue [ɔmɔlɔg] nm/f counterpart, opposite number.

homologué, e [ɔmɔlɔge] a (SPORT) officially recognized, ratified ; (tarif) authorized.

homonyme [ɔmɔnim] nm (LING) homonym ; (d'une personne) namesake.

homosexualité [ɔmɔsɛksɥalite] nf homosexuality.

homosexuel, le [ɔmɔsɛksɥɛl] a homosexual.

*****Hongrie** [ˈɔ̃gʀi] nf: **la** ~ Hungary ; *****hongrois, e** a, nm/f, nm (langue) Hungarian.

honnête [ɔnɛt] a (intègre) honest ; (juste, satisfaisant) fair ; ~**ment** ad honestly ; ~**té** nf honesty.

honneur [ɔnœʀ] nm honour ; (mérite): l'~ **lui revient** the credit is his ; **en l'~ de** in honour of ; (événement) on the occasion of ; **faire** ~ **à** (engagements) to honour ; (famille) to be a credit to ; (fig: repas etc) to do justice to ; **être à l'**~ to be in the place of honour ; **être en** ~ to be in favour ; **membre d'**~ honorary member ; **table d'**~ top table.

honorable [ɔnɔʀabl(ə)] a worthy, honourable ; (suffisant) decent ; ~**ment** ad honorably ; decently.

honoraire [ɔnɔʀɛʀ] a honorary ; ~**s** nmpl fees pl ; **professeur** ~ professor emeritus.

honorer [ɔnɔʀe] vt to honour ; (estimer) to hold in high regard ; (faire honneur à) to do credit to ; **s'**~ **de** to pride o.s. upon ; **honorifique** a honorary.

*****honte** [ˈɔ̃t] nf shame ; **avoir** ~ **de** to be ashamed of ; **faire** ~ **à qn** to make sb (feel) ashamed ; *****honteux, euse** a ashamed ; (conduite, acte) shameful, disgraceful.

hôpital, aux [ɔpital, -o] nm hospital.

*****hoquet** [ˈɔkɛ] nm hiccough ; **avoir le** ~ to have (the) hiccoughs ; **hoqueter** vi to hiccough.

horaire [ɔʀɛʀ] a hourly // nm timetable, schedule.

*****horions** [ˈɔʀjɔ̃] nmpl blows.

horizon [ɔʀizɔ̃] nm horizon ; (paysage) landscape, view ; **sur l'**~ on the skyline ou horizon.

horizontal, e, aux [ɔʀizɔ̃tal, -o] a horizontal ; ~**ement** ad horizontally.

horloge [ɔʀlɔʒ] nf clock ; l'~ **parlante** the speaking clock ; **horloger, ère** nm/f watchmaker ; clockmaker ; ~**rie** nf watch-making ; watchmaker's (shop) ; clockmaker's (shop) ; **pièces d'**~**rie** watch parts ou components.

*****hormis** [ˈɔʀmi] prép save.

hormonal, e, aux [ɔʀmɔnal, -o] a hormonal.

hormone [ɔʀmɔn] nf hormone.

horoscope [ɔʀɔskɔp] nm horoscope.

horreur [ɔʀœʀ] nf horror ; **avoir** ~ **de** to loathe ou detest ; **horrible** a horrible ; **horrifier** vt to horrify.

horripiler [ɔʀipile] vt to exasperate.

*****hors** [ˈɔʀ] prép except (for) ; ~ **de** out of ; ~ **pair** outstanding ; ~ **de propos** inopportune ; **être** ~ **de soi** to be beside o.s. ; ~-**bord** nm inv speedboat (with outboard motor) ; ~-**concours** a ineligible to compete ; (fig) in a class of one's own ; ~-**d'œuvre** nm inv hors d'œuvre ; ~-**jeu** nm inv offside ; ~-**la-loi** nm inv outlaw ; ~-**taxe** a duty-free ; ~-**texte** nm inv plate.

hortensia [ɔʀtɑ̃sja] nm hydrangea.

horticulteur, trice [ɔʀtikyltœʀ, -tʀis] nm/f horticulturalist.

horticulture [ɔʀtikyltyʀ] nf horticulture.

hospice [ɔspis] nm (de vieillards) home.

hospitalier, ière [ɔspitalje, -jɛʀ] a (accueillant) hospitable ; (MÉD: service, centre) hospital cpd.

hospitaliser [ɔspitalize] vt to take (ou send) to hospital, hospitalize.

hospitalité [ɔspitalite] nf hospitality.

hostie [ɔsti] nf host.

hostile [ɔstil] a hostile ; **hostilité** nf hostility ; **hostilités** nfpl hostilities.

hôte [ot] nm (maître de maison) host ; (invité) guest ; (client) patron ; (fig) inhabitant, occupant.

hôtel [otɛl] nm hotel ; **aller à l'**~ to stay in a hotel ; ~ (**particulier**) (private) mansion ; ~ **de ville** town hall ; **hôtelier, ière** a hotel cpd // nm/f hotelier, hotel-keeper ; ~**lerie** nf hotel business ; (auberge) inn.

hôtesse [otɛs] nf hostess ; ~ **de l'air** air hostess ou stewardess.

*****hotte** [ˈɔt] nf (panier) basket (carried on the back) ; (de cheminée) hood ; ~ **aspirante** cooker hood.

*****houblon** [ˈublɔ̃] nm (BOT) hop ; (pour la bière) hops pl.

*****houille** [ˈuj] nf coal ; ~ **blanche** hydroelectric power ; *****houiller, ère** a coal cpd ; coal-bearing.

*****houle** [ˈul] nf swell.

*****houlette** [ˈulɛt] nf: **sous la** ~ **de** under the guidance of.

*****houleux, euse** [ˈulø, -øz] a heavy, swelling ; (fig) stormy, turbulent.

*****houppe** [ˈup] nf, *****houppette** [ˈupɛt] nf powder puff.

*****hourra** [ˈuʀa] nm cheer // excl hurrah!

*****houspiller** [ˈuspije] vt to scold.

*****housse** [ˈus] nf cover ; dust cover ; loose ou stretch cover ; ~ (**penderie**) hanging wardrobe.

*****houx** [ˈu] nm holly.

*****hublot** [ˈyblo] nm porthole.

*****huche** [ˈyʃ] nf: ~ **à pain** bread bin.

*****huées** [ˈɥe] nfpl boos.

*****huer** [ˈɥe] vt to boo.

huile [ɥil] nf oil ; (ART) oil painting ; (fam) bigwig ; ~ **de foie de morue** cod-liver oil ; ~ **de table** salad oil ; **huiler** vt to oil ; **huileux, euse** a oily.

huis [ɥi] nm: **à** ~ **clos** in camera.

huissier [ɥisje] nm usher ; (JUR) ≈ **bailiff**.
huit ['ɥit] num eight ; **samedi en ~ a**
week on Saturday ; **dans ~ jours** in a
week('s time) ; **une huitaine de jours** a
week or so ; **huitième** num eighth.
huître [ɥitr(ə)] nf oyster.
humain, e [ymɛ̃, -ɛn] a human ;
(compatissant) humane // nm human
(being) ; **humaniser** vt to humanize ;
humanitaire a humanitarian ; **humanité**
nf humanity.
humble [œ̃bl(ə)] a humble.
humecter [ymɛkte] vt to dampen ; **s'~**
les lèvres to moisten one's lips.
humer ['yme] vt to smell ; to inhale.
humeur [ymœr] nf mood ; (tempérament)
temper ; (irritation) bad temper ; **de**
bonne/mauvaise ~ in a good/bad mood.
humide [ymid] a damp ; (main, yeux)
moist ; (climat, chaleur) humid ; (route)
wet ; **humidificateur** nm humidifier ;
humidifier vt to humidify ; **humidité** nf
humidity ; dampness ; **traces d'humidité**
traces of moisture ou damp.
humiliation [ymiljɑsjɔ̃] nf humiliation.
humilier [ymilje] vt to humiliate.
humilité [ymilite] nf humility,
humbleness.
humoriste [ymɔrist(ə)] nm/f humorist.
humoristique [ymɔristik] a humorous ;
humoristic.
humour [ymur] nm humour ; **avoir de**
l'~ to have a sense of humour ; **~ noir**
sick humour.
huppé, e ['ype] a crested ; (fam) posh.
hurlement ['yrləmɑ̃] nm howling q,
howl, yelling q, yell.
hurler ['yrle] vi to howl, yell.
hurluberlu [yrlybɛrly] nm (péj) crank.
hutte ['yt] nf hut.
hybride [ibrid] a hybrid.
hydratant, e [idratɑ̃, -ɑ̃t] a (crème)
moisturizing.
hydrate [idrat] nm: **~s de carbone** carbohydrates.
hydraulique [idrolik] a hydraulic.
hydravion [idravjɔ̃] nm seaplane,
hydroplane.
hydro... [idrɔ] préfixe: **~carbures** nmpl
hydrocarbon oils ; **~cution** nf immersion
syncope ; **~électrique** a hydroelectric ;
~gène nm hydrogen ; **~glisseur** nm
hydroplane ; **~graphie** nf (fleuves) hydro-
graphy ; **~phile** a voir **coton**.
hyène [jɛn] nf hyena.
hygiène [iʒjɛn] nf hygiene ; **~ intime**
personal hygiene ; **hygiénique** a hygienic.
hymne [imn(ə)] nm hymn ; **~ national**
national anthem.
hypermarché [ipɛrmarʃe] nm hyper-
market.
hypermétrope [ipɛrmetrɔp] a long-
sighted, hypermetropic.
hypertension [ipɛrtɑ̃sjɔ̃] nf high blood
pressure, hypertension.
hypnose [ipnoz] nf hypnosis ;
hypnotique a hypnotic ; **hypnotiser** vt to
hypnotize.
hypocrisie [ipɔkrizi] nf hypocrisy.
hypocrite [ipɔkrit] a hypocritical // nm/f
hypocrite.

hypotension [ipotɑ̃sjɔ̃] nf low blood
pressure, hypotension.
hypothécaire [ipotekɛr] a hypothecary ;
garantie/prêt ~ mortgage security/loan.
hypothèque [ipotɛk] nf mortgage ;
hypothéquer vt to mortgage.
hypothèse [ipotɛz] nf hypothesis ;
hypothétique a hypothetical.
hystérie [isteri] nf hysteria ; **hystérique**
a hysterical.

I

ibérique [iberik] a: **la péninsule ~** the
Iberian peninsula.
iceberg [isbɛrg] nm iceberg.
ici [isi] ad here ; **jusqu'~** as far as this ;
until now ; **d'~ là** by then ; **in the**
meantime ; **d'~ peu** before long.
icône [ikon] nf icon.
iconographie [ikɔnɔgrafi] nf
iconography ; (collection of) illustrations.
idéal, e, aux [ideal, -o] a ideal // nm
ideal ; ideals pl ; **~iser** vt to idealize ;
~iste a idealistic // nm/f idealist.
idée [ide] nf idea ; **avoir dans l'~** que to
have an idea that ; **~ fixe** idée fixe,
obsession ; **~s noires** black ou dark
thoughts ; **~s reçues** accepted ideas.
identification [idɑ̃tifikɑsjɔ̃] nf
identification.
identifier [idɑ̃tifje] vt to identify ; **~**
qch/qn à to identify sth/sb with ; **s'~ à**
(héros etc) to identify with.
identique [idɑ̃tik] a: **~ (à)** identical (to).
identité [idɑ̃tite] nf identity.
idéologie [ideɔlɔʒi] nf ideology.
idiomatique [idjɔmatik] a: **expression ~**
idiom, idiomatic expression.
idiot, e [idjo, idjɔt] a idiotic // nm/f idiot ;
idiotie [-si] nf idiocy ; idiotic remark etc.
idiotisme [idjɔtism(ə)] nm idiom,
idiomatic phrase.
idolâtrer [idolɑtre] vt to idolize.
idole [idɔl] nf idol.
idylle [idil] nf idyll ; **idyllique** a idyllic.
if [if] nm yew.
I.F.O.P. [ifɔp] sigle m = Institut français
d'opinion publique.
igloo [iglu] nm igloo.
ignare [iɲar] a ignorant.
ignifugé, e [iɲifyʒe] a fireproof(ed).
ignoble [iɲɔbl(ə)] a vile.
ignominie [iɲɔmini] nf ignominy ;
ignominious ou base act.
ignorance [iɲɔrɑ̃s] nf ignorance.
ignorant, e [iɲɔrɑ̃, -ɑ̃t] a ignorant.
ignorer [iɲɔre] vt (ne pas connaître) not
to know, be unaware ou ignorant of ; (être
sans expérience de: plaisir, guerre etc) not
to know about, have no experience of ;
(bouder: personne) to ignore ; **j'ignore**
comment/si I do not know how/if ; **~**
que to be unaware that, not to know that.
il [il] pronom he ; (animal, chose, en tournure
impersonnelle) it ; NB: en anglais les navires
et les pays sont en général assimilés aux
femelles, et les bébés aux choses, si le sexe
n'est pas spécifié ; **~s** they ; **il neige** it's
snowing ; voir aussi **avoir**.

ile [il] *nf* island ; les ~s anglo-normandes the Channel Islands ; les ~s Britanniques the British Isles.

illegal, e, aux [ilegal, -o] *a* illegal, unlawful ; ~ité *nf* illegality, unlawfulness ; être dans l'~ité to be outside the law.

illégitime [ileʒitim] *a* illegitimate ; (*optimisme, sévérité*) unjustified ; unwarranted ; illégitimité *nf* illegitimacy ; gouverner dans l'illégitimité to rule illegally.

illettré, e [iletre] *a, nm/f* illiterate.

illicite [ilisit] *a* illicit.

illimité, e [ilimite] *a* (*immense*) boundless, unlimited ; (*congé, durée*) indefinite, unlimited.

illisible [ilizibl(ə)] *a* illegible ; (*roman*) unreadable.

illogique [iloʒik] *a* illogical.

illumination [ilyminasjɔ̃] *nf* illumination, floodlighting ; flash of inspiration ; ~s *nfpl* illuminations, lights.

illuminer [ilymine] *vt* to light up ; (*monument, rue: pour une fête*) to illuminate, floodlight ; s'~ *vi* to light up.

illusion [ilyzjɔ̃] *nf* illusion ; se faire des ~s to delude o.s. ; faire ~ to delude ou fool people ; ~ d'optique optical illusion ; illusionniste *nm/f* conjuror ; illusoire *a* illusory, illusive.

illustrateur [ilystratœr] *nm* illustrator.

illustration [ilystrasjɔ̃] *nf* illustration ; (*d'un ouvrage: photos*) illustrations *pl*.

illustre [ilystr(ə)] *a* illustrious, renowned.

illustré, e [ilystre] *a* illustrated // *nm* illustrated magazine ; comic.

illustrer [ilystre] *vt* to illustrate ; s'~ to become famous, win fame.

îlot [ilo] *nm* small island, islet ; (*de maisons*) block.

image [imaʒ] *nf* (*gén*) picture ; (*comparaison, ressemblance, OPTIQUE*) image ; ~ de marque brand image ; (*d'un politicien*) public image ; ~ pieuse holy picture ; imagé, e *a* full of imagery.

imaginaire [imaʒinɛr] *a* imaginary.

imagination [imaʒinasjɔ̃] *nf* imagination ; (*chimère*) fancy ; avoir de l'~ to be imaginative, have a good imagination.

imaginer [imaʒine] *vt* to imagine ; (*inventer: expédient, mesure*) to devise, think up ; s'~ *vt* (*se figurer: scène etc*) to imagine, picture ; s'~ que to imagine that ; ~ de faire (*se mettre dans l'idée de*) to dream up the idea of doing.

imbattable [ɛ̃batabl(ə)] *a* unbeatable.

imbécile [ɛ̃besil] *a* idiotic // *nm/f* idiot ; (*MÉD*) imbecile ; imbécillité *nf* idiocy ; imbecility ; idiotic action (*ou remark etc*).

imberbe [ɛ̃bɛrb(ə)] *a* beardless.

imbiber [ɛ̃bibe] *vt*: ~ qch de to moisten ou wet sth with ; s'~ de to become saturated with.

imbriquer [ɛ̃brike]: s'~ *vi* to overlap (each other) ; (*fig*) to become interlinked ou interwoven.

imbu, e [ɛ̃by] *a*: ~ de full of.

imbuvable [ɛ̃byvabl(ə)] *a* undrinkable.

imitateur, trice [imitatœr, -tris] *nm/f* (*gén*) imitator ; (*MUSIC-HALL*: d'une personnalité*) impersonator.

imitation [imitasjɔ̃] *nf* imitation ; (*sketch*) imitation, impression ; impersonation ; sac ~ cuir bag in imitation ou simulated leather.

imiter [imite] *vt* to imitate ; (*contrefaire: signature, document*) to forge, copy ; (*avoir l'aspect de*) to look like ; il se leva et je l'imitai he got up and I did likewise.

immaculé, e [imakyle] *a* spotless ; immaculate.

immangeable [ɛ̃mɑ̃ʒabl(ə)] *a* inedible, uneatable.

immanquable [ɛ̃mɑ̃kabl(ə)] *a* (*cible*) impossible to miss.

immatriculation [imatrikylasjɔ̃] *nf* registration.

immatriculer [imatrikyle] *vt* to register ; faire/se faire ~ to register ; voiture immatriculée dans la Seine car with a Seine registration (number).

immédiat, e [imedja, -at] *a* immediate // *nm*: dans l'~ for the time being ; immédiatement *ad* immediately.

immense [imɑ̃s] *a* immense.

immergé, e [imɛrʒe] *a* submerged.

immerger [imɛrʒe] *vt* to immerse, submerge ; to lay under water ; s'~ *vi* (*sous-marin*) to dive, submerge.

immérité, e [imerite] *a* undeserved.

immeuble [imœbl(ə)] *nm* building // *a* (*JUR*) immovable, real ; ~ locatif block of rented flats.

immigrant, e [imigrɑ̃, -ɑ̃t] *nm/f* immigrant.

immigration [imigrasjɔ̃] *nf* immigration.

immigré, e [imigre] *nm/f* immigrant.

immigrer [imigre] *vi* to immigrate.

imminent, e [iminɑ̃, -ɑ̃t] *a* imminent, impending.

immiscer [imise]: s'~ *vi*: s'~ dans to interfere in ou with.

immobile [imɔbil] *a* still, motionless ; (*pièce de machine*) fixed ; (*fig*) unchanging.

immobilier, ière [imɔbilje, -jɛr] *a* property *cpd*, in real property // *nm*: l'~ the property ou the real estate business.

immobilisation [imɔbilizasjɔ̃] *nf* immobilization ; ~s *nfpl* (*COMM*) fixed assets.

immobiliser [imɔbilize] *vt* (*gén*) to immobilize ; (*circulation, véhicule, affaires*) to bring to a standstill ; s'~ (*personne*) to stand still ; (*machine, véhicule*) to come to a halt ou standstill.

immobilité [imɔbilite] *nf* stillness ; immobility.

immodéré, e [imɔdere] *a* immoderate, inordinate.

immoler [imɔle] *vt* to immolate, sacrifice.

immonde [imɔ̃d] *a* foul.

immondices [imɔ̃dis] *nmpl* refuse *sg* ; filth *sg*.

immoral, e, aux [imɔral, -o] *a* immoral.

immortaliser [imɔrtalize] *vt* to immortalize.

immortel, le [imɔrtɛl] *a* immortal.

immuable [imyabl(ə)] *a* immutable ; unchanging.

immunisé, e [imynize] a: ~ **contre** immune to.

immuniser [imynize] vt to immunize.

immunité [imynite] nf immunity; ~ **diplomatique** diplomatic immunity; ~ **parlementaire** parliamentary privilege.

impact [ɛpakt] nm impact.

impair, e [ɛpɛʀ] a odd // nm faux pas, blunder.

imparable [ɛpaʀabl(ə)] a unstoppable.

impardonnable [ɛpaʀdɔnabl(ə)] a unpardonable, unforgivable.

imparfait, e [ɛpaʀfɛ, -ɛt] a imperfect // nm imperfect (tense).

impartial, e, aux [ɛpaʀsjal, -o] a impartial, unbiased; ~**ité** nf impartiality.

impartir [ɛpaʀtiʀ] vt: ~ **qch à qn** to assign sth to sb; to bestow sth upon sb.

impasse [ɛpas] nf dead-end, cul-de-sac; (fig) deadlock.

impassible [ɛpasibl(ə)] a impassive.

impatience [ɛpasjɑs] nf impatience.

impatient, e [ɛpasjɑ̃, -ɑ̃t] a impatient; **impatienter** vt to irritate, annoy; **s'impatienter** to get impatient; **s'impatienter de/contre** to lose patience at/with, grow impatient at/with.

impayable [ɛpɛjabl(ə)] a (drôle) priceless.

impayé, e [ɛpeje] a unpaid.

impeccable [ɛpekabl(ə)] a faultless, impeccable; spotlessly clean; impeccably dressed; (fam) smashing.

impénétrable [ɛpenetrabl(ə)] a impenetrable.

impénitent, e [ɛpenitɑ̃, -ɑ̃t] a unrepentant.

impensable [ɛpɑ̃sabl(ə)] a unthinkable; unbelievable.

impératif, ive [ɛpeʀatif, -iv] a imperative; (JUR) mandatory // nm (LING) imperative; ~**s** nmpl requirements; demands.

impératrice [ɛpeʀatris] nf empress.

imperceptible [ɛpɛʀsɛptibl(ə)] a imperceptible.

imperfection [ɛpɛʀfɛksjɔ̃] nf imperfection.

impérial, e, aux [ɛpeʀjal, -o] a imperial // nf upper deck; **autobus à ~e** double-decker bus.

impérialiste [ɛpeʀjalist(ə)] a imperialist.

impérieux, euse [ɛpeʀjø, -øz] a (caractère, ton) imperious; (obligation, besoin) pressing, urgent.

impérissable [ɛpeʀisabl(ə)] a undying; imperishable.

imperméabiliser [ɛpɛʀmeabilize] vt to waterproof.

imperméable [ɛpɛʀmeabl(ə)] a waterproof; (GÉO) impermeable; (fig): ~ **à** impervious to // nm raincoat; ~ **à l'air** airtight.

impersonnel, le [ɛpɛʀsɔnɛl] a impersonal.

impertinence [ɛpɛʀtinɑ̃s] nf impertinence.

impertinent, e [ɛpɛʀtinɑ̃, -ɑ̃t] a impertinent.

imperturbable [ɛpɛʀtyʀbabl(ə)] a imperturbable; unruffled; unshakeable.

impétrant, e [ɛpetʀɑ̃, -ɑ̃t] nm/f (JUR) applicant.

impétueux, euse [ɛpetɥø, -øz] a fiery.

impie [ɛpi] a impious, ungodly; **impiété** nf impiety.

impitoyable [ɛpitwajabl(ə)] a pitiless, merciless.

implacable [ɛplakabl(ə)] a implacable.

implanter [ɛplɑ̃te] vt (usine, industrie, usage) to establish; (colons etc) to settle; (idée, préjugé) to implant; **s'~ dans** to be established in; to settle in; to become implanted in.

implication [ɛplikasjɔ̃] nf implication.

implicite [ɛplisit] a implicit.

impliquer [ɛplike] vt to imply; ~ **qn (dans)** to implicate sb (in).

implorer [ɛplɔʀe] vt to implore.

implosion [ɛplozjɔ̃] nf implosion.

impoli, e [ɛpɔli] a impolite, rude; ~**tesse** nf impoliteness, rudeness; impolite ou rude remark.

impondérable [ɛpɔ̃deʀabl(ə)] nm imponderable.

impopulaire [ɛpɔpylɛʀ] a unpopular.

importance [ɛpɔʀtɑ̃s] nf importance; **avoir de l'~** to be important; **sans ~** unimportant.

important, e [ɛpɔʀtɑ̃, -ɑ̃t] a important; (en quantité) considerable, sizeable; extensive; (péj: airs, ton) self-important // nm: l'~ the important thing.

importateur, trice [ɛpɔʀtatœʀ, -tʀis] a importing // nm importer; **pays ~ de blé** wheat-importing country.

importation [ɛpɔʀtasjɔ̃] nf importation; introduction; (produit) import.

importer [ɛpɔʀte] vt (COMM) to import; (maladies, plantes) to introduce // vi (être important) to matter; ~ **à qn** to matter to sb; **il importe qu'il fasse** he must do, it is important that he should do; **peu m'importe** I don't mind; I don't care; **peu importe (que)** it doesn't matter (if); voir aussi **n'importe**.

import-export [ɛpɔʀɛkspɔʀ] nm import-export business.

importun, e [ɛpɔʀtœ̃, -yn] a irksome, importunate; (arrivée, visite) inopportune, ill-timed // nm intruder; **importuner** vt to bother.

imposable [ɛpozabl(ə)] a taxable.

imposant, e [ɛpozɑ̃, -ɑ̃t] a imposing.

imposer [ɛpoze] vt (taxer) to tax; ~ **qch à qn** to impose sth on sb; **s'~** (être nécessaire) to be imperative; (montrer sa prominence) to stand out, emerge; (artiste: se faire connaître) to win recognition, come to the fore; **en ~ à** to impress.

imposition [ɛpozisjɔ̃] nf (ADMIN) taxation.

impossibilité [ɛpɔsibilite] nf impossibility; **être dans l'~ de faire** to be unable to do, find it impossible to do.

impossible [ɛpɔsibl(ə)] a impossible; **il m'est ~ de le faire** it is impossible for me to do it, I can't possibly do it; **faire l'~ (pour que)** to do one's utmost (so that).

imposteur [ɛpɔstœʀ] nm impostor.

imposture [ɛpɔstyʀ] nf imposture, deception.

impôt [ɛpo] nm tax; (taxes) taxation; taxes pl; ~s nmpl (contributions) (income) tax sg; payer 1000 F d'~s to pay 1,000 F in tax; ~ sur le chiffre d'affaires corporation tax; ~ foncier land tax; ~ sur les plus-values capital gains tax; ~ sur le revenu income tax.

impotent, e [ɛpotɑ̃, -ɑ̃t] a disabled.

impraticable [ɛpratikabl(ə)] a (projet) impracticable, unworkable; (piste) impassable.

imprécation [ɛprekasjɔ̃] nf imprecation.

imprécis, e [ɛpresi, -iz] a (contours, souvenir) imprecise, vague; (tir) inaccurate, imprecise.

imprégner [ɛprene] vt (tissu, tampon): ~ (de) to soak ou impregnate (with); (lieu, air): ~ (de) to fill (with); (suj: amertume, ironie) to pervade; s'~ de to become impregnated with; to be filled with; (fig) to absorb.

imprenable [ɛpranabl(ə)] a (forteresse) impregnable; vue ~ unimpeded outlook.

impresario [ɛpresarjo] nm manager, impresario.

impression [ɛpresjɔ̃] nf impression; (d'un ouvrage, tissu) printing; (PHOTO) exposure; faire bonne ~ to make a good impression.

impressionnant, e [ɛpresjonɑ̃, -ɑ̃t] a impressive; upsetting.

impressionner [ɛpresjone] vt (frapper) to impress; (troubler) to upset; (PHOTO) to expose.

impressionnisme [ɛpresjonism(ə)] nm impressionism.

imprévisible [ɛprevizibl(ə)] a unforeseeable.

imprévoyant, e [ɛprevwajɑ̃, -ɑ̃t] a lacking in foresight; (en matière d'argent) improvident.

imprévu, e [ɛprevy] a unforeseen, unexpected // nm unexpected incident; en cas d'~ if anything unexpected happens.

imprimé [ɛprime] nm (formulaire) printed form; (POSTES) printed matter q; (tissu) printed fabric.

imprimer [ɛprime] vt to print; (apposer: visa, cachet) to stamp; (empreinte etc) to imprint; (publier) to publish; (communiquer: mouvement, impulsion) to impart, transmit; **imprimerie** nf printing; (établissement) printing works sg; (atelier) printing house, printery; **imprimeur** nm printer; **imprimeur-éditeur/-libraire** printer and publisher/bookseller.

improbable [ɛprɔbabl(ə)] a unlikely, improbable.

improductif, ive [ɛprɔdyktif, -iv] a unproductive.

impromptu, e [ɛprɔ̃pty] a impromptu; sudden.

impropre [ɛprɔpr(ə)] a inappropriate; ~ à unsuitable for; **impropriété** nf (de langage) incorrect usage q.

improvisé, e [ɛprɔvize] a makeshift, improvised; (jeu etc) scratch, improvised.

improviser [ɛprɔvize] vt, vi.to improvise; s'~ (secours, réunion) to be improvised; s'~ cuisinier to (decide to) act as cook.

improviste [ɛprɔvist(ə)]: à l'~ ad unexpectedly, without warning.

imprudemment [ɛprydamɑ̃] ad carelessly; unwisely, imprudently.

imprudence [ɛprydɑ̃s] nf carelessness; imprudence; act of carelessness; foolish ou unwise action.

imprudent, e [ɛprydɑ̃, -ɑ̃t] a (conducteur, geste, action) careless; (remarque) unwise, imprudent; (projet) foolhardy.

impubère [ɛpybɛr] a below the age of puberty.

impudent, e [ɛpydɑ̃, -ɑ̃t] a impudent; brazen.

impudique [ɛpydik] a shameless.

impuissance [ɛpɥisɑ̃s] nf helplessness; ineffectiveness; impotence.

impuissant, e [ɛpɥisɑ̃, -ɑ̃t] a helpless; (sans effet) ineffectual; (sexuellement) impotent // nm impotent man; ~ à faire powerless to do.

impulsif, ive [ɛpylsif, -iv] a impulsive.

impulsion [ɛpylsjɔ̃] nf (ÉLEC, instinct) impulse; (élan, influence) impetus.

impunément [ɛpynemɑ̃] ad with impunity.

impur, e [ɛpyr] a impure; ~eté nf impurity.

imputation [ɛpytasjɔ̃] nf imputation, charge.

imputer [ɛpyte] vt (attribuer): ~ qch à to ascribe ou impute sth to; (COMM): ~ à ou sur to charge to.

imputrescible [ɛpytresibl(ə)] a which does not rot.

inabordable [inabɔrdabl(ə)] a (lieu) inaccessible; (cher) prohibitive.

inaccentué, e [inaksɑ̃tɥe] a (LING) unstressed.

inacceptable [inaksɛptabl(ə)] a unacceptable; inadmissible.

inaccessible [inaksesibl(ə)] a inaccessible; unattainable; (insensible): ~ à impervious to.

inaccoutumé, e [inakutyme] a unaccustomed.

inachevé, e [inaʃve] a unfinished.

inactif, ive [inaktif, -iv] a inactive, idle.

inaction [inaksjɔ̃] nf inactivity.

inactivité [inaktivite] nf (ADMIN): en ~ out of active service.

inadapté, e [inadapte] a (gén): ~ à not adapted to, unsuited to; (PSYCH) maladjusted.

inadmissible [inadmisibl(ə)] a inadmissible.

inadvertance [inadvɛrtɑ̃s]: par ~ ad inadvertently.

inaliénable [inaljenabl(ə)] a inalienable.

inaltérable [inalterabl(ə)] a (matière) stable; (fig) unchanging; ~ à unaffected by; couleur ~ (au lavage/à la lumière) fast colour/fade-resistant colour.

inamovible [inamɔvibl(ə)] a fixed; (JUR) irremovable.

inanimé, e [inanime] a (matière) inanimate; (évanoui) unconscious; (sans vie) lifeless.

inanité [inanite] nf futility.

inanition [inanisjɔ̃] nf: tomber d'~ to faint with hunger (and exhaustion).

inaperçu, e [inapɛʀsy] *a*: **passer** ~ to go unnoticed.

inappliqué, e [inaplike] *a* lacking in application.

inappréciable [inapʀesjabl(ə)] *a* (*service*) invaluable; (*différence, nuance*) inappreciable.

inapte [inapt(ə)] *a*: ~ **à** incapable of; (*MIL*) unfit for.

inattaquable [inatakabl(ə)] *a* (*MIL*) unassailable; (*texte, preuve*) irrefutable.

inattendu, e [inatɑ̃dy] *a* unexpected.

inattentif, ive [inatɑ̃tif, -iv] *a* inattentive; ~ **à** (*dangers, détails*) heedless of; **inattention** *nf* inattention; **faute d'inattention** careless mistake.

inaugural, e, aux [inɔgyʀal, -o] *a* (*cérémonie*) inaugural, opening; (*vol, voyage*) maiden.

inauguration [inɔgyʀasjɔ̃] *nf* opening; unveiling.

inaugurer [inɔgyʀe] *vt* (*monument*) to unveil; (*exposition, usine*) to open; (*fig*) to inaugurate.

inavouable [inavwabl(ə)] *a* shameful; undisclosable.

inavoué, e [inavwe] *a* unavowed.

incalculable [ɛ̃kalkylabl(ə)] *a* incalculable.

incandescence [ɛ̃kɑ̃desɑ̃s] *nf* incandescence; **porter à** ~ to heat white-hot.

incantation [ɛ̃kɑ̃tasjɔ̃] *nf* incantation.

incapable [ɛ̃kapabl(ə)] *a* incapable; ~ **de faire** incapable of doing; (*empêché*) unable to do.

incapacité [ɛ̃kapasite] *nf* incapability; (*JUR*) incapacity; **être dans l'** ~ **de faire** to be unable to do; ~ **permanente/de travail** permanent/industrial disablement; ~ **électorale** ineligibility to vote.

incarcérer [ɛ̃kaʀseʀe] *vt* to incarcerate.

incarnation [ɛ̃kaʀnasjɔ̃] *nf* incarnation.

incarné, e [ɛ̃kaʀne] *a* incarnate; (*ongle*) ingrown.

incarner [ɛ̃kaʀne] *vt* to embody, personify; (*THÉÂTRE*) to play; (*REL*) to incarnate.

incartade [ɛ̃kaʀtad] *nf* prank, escapade.

incassable [ɛ̃kɑsabl(ə)] *a* unbreakable.

incendiaire [ɛ̃sɑ̃djɛʀ] *a* incendiary; (*fig: discours*) inflammatory // *nm/f* fire-raiser, arsonist.

incendie [ɛ̃sɑ̃di] *nm* fire; ~ **criminel** arson q; ~ **de forêt** forest fire.

incendier [ɛ̃sɑ̃dje] *vt* (*mettre le feu à*) to set fire to, set alight; (*brûler complètement*) to burn down.

incertain, e [ɛ̃sɛʀtɛ̃, -ɛn] *a* uncertain; (*temps*) uncertain, unsettled; (*imprécis: contours*) indistinct, blurred; **incertitude** *nf* uncertainty.

incessamment [ɛ̃sɛsamɑ̃] *ad* very shortly.

incessant, e [ɛ̃sɛsɑ̃, -ɑ̃t] *a* incessant, unceasing.

inceste [ɛ̃sɛst(ə)] *nm* incest.

inchangé, e [ɛ̃ʃɑ̃ʒe] *a* unchanged, unaltered.

incidemment [ɛ̃sidamɑ̃] *ad* in passing.

incidence [ɛ̃sidɑ̃s] *nf* (*effet, influence*) effect; (*PHYSIQUE*) incidence.

incident [ɛ̃sidɑ̃] *nm* incident; ~ **de parcours** minor hitch ou setback; ~ **technique** technical difficulties *pl*.

incinérateur [ɛ̃sineʀatœʀ] *nm* incinerator.

incinérer [ɛ̃sineʀe] *vt* (*ordures*) to incinerate; (*mort*) to cremate.

incise [ɛ̃siz] *nf* (*LING*) interpolated clause.

incisif, ive [ɛ̃sizif, -iv] *a* incisive, cutting // *nf* incisor.

incision [ɛ̃sizjɔ̃] *nf* incision; (*d'un abcès*) lancing.

inciter [ɛ̃site] *vt*: ~ **qn à faire** to incite ou prompt sb to do.

inclinaison [ɛ̃klinɛz] *nf* (*déclivité: d'une route etc*) incline; (: *d'un toit*) slope; (*état penché: d'un mur*) lean; (: *de la tête*) tilt; (: *d'un navire*) list.

inclination [ɛ̃klinɑsjɔ̃] *nf* (*penchant*) inclination, tendency; ~ **de (la) tête** nod (of the head); ~ **(de buste)** bow.

incliner [ɛ̃kline] *vt* (*tête, bouteille*) to tilt; (*inciter*): ~ **qn à qch/à faire** to encourage sb towards sth/to do // *vi*: ~ **à qch/à faire** to incline towards sth/doing; to tend towards sth/to do; **s'** ~ (*route*) to slope; **s'** ~ (*devant*) to bow (before); (*céder*) to give in ou yield (to); ~ **la tête** ou **le front** to give a slight bow.

inclure [ɛ̃klyʀ] *vt* to include; (*joindre à un envoi*) to enclose; **jusqu'au 10 mars inclus** until 10th March inclusive.

incoercible [ɛ̃kɔɛʀsibl(ə)] *a* uncontrollable.

incognito [ɛ̃kɔɲito] *ad* incognito.

incohérence [ɛ̃kɔeʀɑ̃s] *nf* inconsistency.

incohérent, e [ɛ̃kɔeʀɑ̃, -ɑ̃t] *a* inconsistent; incoherent.

incollable [ɛ̃kɔlabl(ə)] *a*: **il est** ~ he's got all the answers.

incolore [ɛ̃kɔlɔʀ] *a* colourless.

incomber [ɛ̃kɔ̃be]: ~ **à** *vt* (*suj: devoirs, responsabilité*) to rest ou be incumbent upon; (: *frais, travail*) to be the responsibility of.

incombustible [ɛ̃kɔ̃bystibl(ə)] *a* incombustible.

incommensurable [ɛ̃kɔmɑ̃syʀabl(ə)] *a* immeasurable.

incommode [ɛ̃kɔmɔd] *a* inconvenient; (*posture, siège*) uncomfortable.

incommoder [ɛ̃kɔmɔde] *vt*: ~ **qn** to bother ou inconvenience sb; (*embarrasser*) to make sb feel uncomfortable ou ill at ease.

incomparable [ɛ̃kɔ̃paʀabl(ə)] *a* not comparable; (*inégalable*) incomparable, matchless.

incompatibilité [ɛ̃kɔ̃patibilite] *nf* incompatibility; ~ **d'humeur** (mutual) incompatibility.

incompatible [ɛ̃kɔ̃patibl(ə)] *a* incompatible.

incompétent, e [ɛ̃kɔ̃petɑ̃, -ɑ̃t] *a* (*ignorant*) inexpert; (*JUR*) incompetent, not competent.

incomplet, ète [ɛ̃kɔ̃plɛ, -ɛt] *a* incomplete.

incompréhensible [ɛ̃kɔ̃pʀeɑ̃sibl(ə)] *a* incomprehensible.

incompréhensif, ive [ɛ̃kɔ̃pʀeɑ̃sif, -iv] *a* lacking in understanding; unsympathetic.

incompris, e [ɛ̃kɔ̃pʀi, -iz] *a* misunderstood.

inconcevable [ɛ̃kɔ̃svabl(ə)] *a* inconceivable.

inconciliable [ɛ̃kɔ̃siljabl(ə)] *a* irreconcilable.

inconditionnel, le [ɛ̃kɔ̃disjɔnɛl] *a* unconditional; (*partisan*) unquestioning.

inconduite [ɛ̃kɔ̃dɥit] *nf* wild behaviour q.

inconfortable [ɛ̃kɔ̃fɔʀtabl(ə)] *a* uncomfortable.

incongru, e [ɛ̃kɔ̃gʀy] *a* unseemly.

inconnu, e [ɛ̃kɔny] *a* unknown; new, strange // *nm/f* stranger; unknown person (*ou* artist *etc*) // *nm*: l'~ the unknown // *nf* (*MATH*) unknown; (*fig*) unknown factor.

inconsciemment [ɛ̃kɔ̃sjamɑ̃] *ad* unconsciously; thoughtlessly.

inconscience [ɛ̃kɔ̃sjɑ̃s] *nf* unconsciousness; thoughtlessness, recklessness.

inconscient, e [ɛ̃kɔ̃sjɑ̃, -ɑ̃t] *a* unconscious; (*irréfléchi*) thoughtless, reckless // *nm* (*PSYCH*): l'~ the subconscious, the unconscious; ~ de unaware of.

inconsidéré, e [ɛ̃kɔ̃sideʀe] *a* illconsidered.

inconsistant, e [ɛ̃kɔ̃sistɑ̃, -ɑ̃t] *a* flimsy, weak; runny.

inconstant, e [ɛ̃kɔ̃stɑ̃, -ɑ̃t] *a* inconstant, fickle.

incontestable [ɛ̃kɔ̃tɛstabl(ə)] *a* indisputable.

incontesté, e [ɛ̃kɔ̃tɛste] *a* undisputed.

incontinence [ɛ̃kɔ̃tinɑ̃s] *nf* incontinence.

incontinent, e [ɛ̃kɔ̃tinɑ̃, -ɑ̃t] *a* incontinent // *ad* forthwith.

incontrôlable [ɛ̃kɔ̃tʀolabl(ə)] *a* unverifiable.

inconvenant, e [ɛ̃kɔ̃vnɑ̃, -ɑ̃t] *a* unseemly, improper.

inconvénient [ɛ̃kɔ̃venjɑ̃] *nm* (*d'une situation, d'un projet*) disadvantage, drawback; (*d'un remède, changement etc*) risk, inconvenience; **si vous n'y voyez pas d'~** if you have no objections.

incorporation [ɛ̃kɔʀpɔʀasjɔ̃] *nf* (*MIL*) callup.

incorporer [ɛ̃kɔʀpɔʀe] *vt* ~ (**à**) to mix in (with); (*paragraphe etc*): ~ (**dans**) to incorporate (in); (*territoire, immigrants*): ~ (**à**) to incorporate (into); (*MIL*: *appeler*) to recruit, call up; (: *affecter*): ~ **qn dans** to enlist sb into.

incorrect, e [ɛ̃kɔʀɛkt] *a* (*impropre, inconvenant*) improper; (*défectueux*) faulty; (*inexact*) incorrect; (*impoli*) impolite; (*déloyal*) underhand.

incorrigible [ɛ̃kɔʀiʒibl(ə)] *a* incorrigible.

incorruptible [ɛ̃kɔʀyptibl(ə)] *a* incorruptible.

incrédule [ɛ̃kʀedyl] *a* incredulous; (*REL*) unbelieving.

increvable [ɛ̃kʀəvabl(ə)] *a* (*pneu*) puncture-proof; (*fam*) tireless.

incriminer [ɛ̃kʀimine] *vt* (*personne*) to incriminate; (*action, conduite*) to bring

under attack; (*bonne foi, honnêteté*) to call into question.

incroyable [ɛ̃kʀwajabl(ə)] *a* incredible; unbelievable.

incroyant, e [ɛ̃kʀwajɑ̃, -ɑ̃t] *nm/f* nonbeliever.

incrustation [ɛ̃kʀystasjɔ̃] *nf* inlaying q; inlay; (*dans une chaudière etc*) fur q, scale q.

incruster [ɛ̃kʀyste] *vt* (*ART*): ~ **qch dans/qch de** to inlay sth into/sth with; (*radiateur etc*) to coat with scale *ou* fur; **s'~** *vi* (*invité*) to take root; (*radiateur etc*) to become coated with fur *ou* scale; **s'~ dans** (*suj*: *corps étranger, caillou*) to become embedded in.

incubateur [ɛ̃kybatœʀ] *nm* incubator.

incubation [ɛ̃kybasjɔ̃] *nf* incubation.

inculpation [ɛ̃kylpasjɔ̃] *nf* charging q; charge.

inculpé, e [ɛ̃kylpe] *nm/f* accused.

inculper [ɛ̃kylpe] *vt*: ~ (**de**) to charge (with).

inculquer [ɛ̃kylke] *vt*: ~ **qch à** to inculcate sth in *ou* instil sth into.

inculte [ɛ̃kylt(ə)] *a* uncultivated; (*esprit, peuple*) uncultured; (*barbe*) unkempt.

incurable [ɛ̃kyʀabl(ə)] *a* incurable.

incurie [ɛ̃kyʀi] *nf* carelessness.

incursion [ɛ̃kyʀsjɔ̃] *nf* incursion, foray.

incurvé, e [ɛ̃kyʀve] *a* curved.

Inde [ɛ̃d] *nf*: l'~ India.

indécence [ɛ̃desɑ̃s] *nf* indecency; indecent remark (*ou* act *etc*).

indécent, e [ɛ̃desɑ̃, -ɑ̃t] *a* indecent.

indéchiffrable [ɛ̃deʃifʀabl(ə)] *a* indecipherable.

indécis, e [ɛ̃desi, -iz] *a* indecisive; (*perplexe*) undecided; **indécision** *nf* indecision; indecisiveness.

indéfendable [ɛ̃defɑ̃dabl(ə)] *a* indefensible.

indéfini, e [ɛ̃defini] *a* (*imprécis, incertain*) undefined; (*illimité, LING*) indefinite; ~**ment** *ad* indefinitely; ~**ssable** *a* indefinable.

indéformable [ɛ̃defɔʀmabl(ə)] *a* that keeps its shape.

indélébile [ɛ̃delebil] *a* indelible.

indélicat, e [ɛ̃delika, -at] *a* tactless; dishonest.

indémaillable [ɛ̃demɑjabl(ə)] *a* run-resist.

indemne [ɛ̃dɛmn(ə)] *a* unharmed.

indemniser [ɛ̃dɛmnize] *vt*: ~ **qn (de)** to compensate sb (for).

indemnité [ɛ̃dɛmnite] *nf* (*dédommagement*) compensation q; (*allocation*) allowance; ~ **de licenciement** redundancy payment; ~ **de logement** housing allowance; ~ **parlementaire** ≈ M.P.'s salary.

indéniable [ɛ̃denjabl(ə)] *a* undeniable, indisputable.

indépendamment [ɛ̃depɑ̃damɑ̃] *ad* independently; ~ **de** (*abstraction faite de*) irrespective of; (*en plus de*) over and above.

indépendance [ɛ̃depɑ̃dɑ̃s] *nf* independence.

indépendant, e [ɛ̃depɑ̃dɑ̃, -ɑ̃t] *a* independent; ~ **de** independent of;

chambre ~e room with private entrance.
indescriptible [ɛ̃dɛskʀiptibl(ə)] a indescribable.
indésirable [ɛ̃deziʀabl(ə)] a undesirable.
indestructible [ɛ̃dɛstʀyktibl(ə)] a indestructible; (marque, impression) indelible.
indétermination [ɛ̃detɛʀminɑsjɔ̃] nf indecision; indecisiveness.
indéterminé, e [ɛ̃detɛʀmine] a unspecified; indeterminate; indeterminable.
index [ɛ̃dɛks] nm (doigt) index finger; (d'un livre etc) index; **mettre à l'~ to blacklist.
indexé, e [ɛ̃dɛkse] a (ÉCON): ~ (sur) index-linked (to).
indicateur [ɛ̃dikatœʀ] nm (POLICE) informer; (livre) guide; directory; (TECH) gauge; indicator; **~ des chemins de fer** railway timetable; **~ de direction** (AUTO) indicator; **~ immobilier** property gazette; **~ de rues** street directory; **~ de vitesse** speedometer.
indicatif, ive [ɛ̃dikatif, -iv] a: **à titre ~** for (your) information // nm (LING) indicative; (d'une émission) theme ou signature tune; (téléphonique) dialling code; **~ d'appel** (RADIO) call sign.
indication [ɛ̃dikasjɔ̃] nf indication; (renseignement) information q; **~s** nfpl (directives) instructions.
indice [ɛ̃dis] nm (marque, signe) indication, sign; (POLICE: lors d'une enquête) clue; (JUR: présomption) piece of evidence; (SCIENCE, TECH) index; (ADMIN) grading, rating; **~ d'octane** octane rating; **~ des prix** price index; **~ de traitement** salary grading.
indicible [ɛ̃disibl(ə)] a inexpressible.
indien, ne [ɛ̃djɛ̃, -jɛn] a Indian // nm/f: **I~, ne** (d'Amérique) Red Indian; (d'Inde) Indian.
indifféremment [ɛ̃difeʀamɑ̃] ad (sans distinction) equally (well); indiscriminately.
indifférence [ɛ̃difeʀɑ̃s] nf indifference.
indifférent, e [ɛ̃difeʀɑ̃, -ɑ̃t] a (peu intéressé) indifferent; **~ à** (insensible à) indifferent to, unconcerned about; (peu intéressant pour) indifferent to; immaterial to.
indigence [ɛ̃diʒɑ̃s] nf poverty.
indigène [ɛ̃diʒɛn] a native, indigenous; local // nm/f native.
indigent, e [ɛ̃diʒɑ̃, -ɑ̃t] a destitute, poverty-stricken; (fig) poor.
indigeste [ɛ̃diʒɛst(ə)] a indigestible.
indigestion [ɛ̃diʒɛstjɔ̃] nf indigestion q.
indignation [ɛ̃diɲasjɔ̃] nf indignation.
indigne [ɛ̃diɲ] a unworthy.
indigner [ɛ̃diɲe] vt to make indignant; **s'~** (de/contre) to be (ou become) indignant (at).
indignité [ɛ̃diɲite] nf unworthiness q; shameful act.
indiqué, e [ɛ̃dike] a (adéquat) appropriate, suitable; (conseillé) suitable, advisable.
indiquer [ɛ̃dike] vt (désigner): **~ qch/qn à qn** to point sth/sb out to sb; (suj: pendule, aiguille) to show; (suj: étiquette, plan) to show, indicate; (faire connaître:

médecin, restaurant): **~ qch/qn à qn** to tell sb of sth/sb; (renseigner sur) to point out, tell; (déterminer: date, lieu) to give, state; (dénoter) to indicate, point to; **pourriez-vous m'~ les toilettes/l'heure?** could you direct me to the toilets/tell me the time?
indirect, e [ɛ̃diʀɛkt] a indirect.
indiscipline [ɛ̃disiplin] nf lack of discipline; **indiscipliné, e** a undisciplined; (fig) unmanageable.
indiscret, ète [ɛ̃diskʀɛ, -ɛt] a indiscreet; **indiscrétion** nf indiscretion.
indiscutable [ɛ̃diskytabl(ə)] a indisputable.
indispensable [ɛ̃dispɑ̃sabl(ə)] a indispensable; essential.
indisponible [ɛ̃dispɔnibl(ə)] a unavailable.
indisposé, e [ɛ̃dispoze] a indisposed, unwell.
indisposer [ɛ̃dispoze] vt (incommoder) to upset; (déplaire à) to antagonize.
indistinct, e [ɛ̃distɛ̃, -ɛ̃kt(ə)] a indistinct; **indistinctement** ad (voir, prononcer) indistinctly; (sans distinction) without distinction, indiscriminately.
individu [ɛ̃dividy] nm individual; **~aliser** vt to individualize; (personnaliser) to tailor to individual requirements; **~aliste** nm/f individualist.
individuel, le [ɛ̃dividɥɛl] a (gén) individual; (opinion, livret, contrôle, avantages) personal; **chambre ~le** single room; **maison ~le** detached house; **propriété ~le** personal ou private property.
indocile [ɛ̃dɔsil] a unruly.
indolent, e [ɛ̃dɔlɑ̃, -ɑ̃t] a indolent.
indolore [ɛ̃dɔlɔʀ] a painless.
indomptable [ɛ̃dɔ̃tabl(ə)] a untameable; (fig) invincible, indomitable.
Indonésie [ɛ̃donezi] nf Indonesia; **indonésien, ne** a, nm/f Indonesian.
indu, e [ɛ̃dy] a: **à des heures ~es** at some ungodly hour.
indubitable [ɛ̃dybitabl(ə)] a indubitable.
induire [ɛ̃dɥiʀ] vt: **~ qch de** to induce sth from; **~ qn en erreur** to lead sb astray, mislead sb.
indulgence [ɛ̃dylʒɑ̃s] nf indulgence; leniency.
indulgent, e [ɛ̃dylʒɑ̃, -ɑ̃t] a (parent, regard) indulgent; (juge, examinateur) lenient.
indûment [ɛ̃dymɑ̃] ad wrongfully; without due cause.
industrialiser [ɛ̃dystʀijalize] vt to industrialize; **s'~** to become industrialized.
industrie [ɛ̃dystʀi] nf industry; **~ du spectacle** entertainment business; **industriel, le** a industrial // nm industrialist; manufacturer.
industrieux, euse [ɛ̃dystʀijø, -øz] a industrious.
inébranlable [inebʀɑ̃labl(ə)] a (masse, colonne) solid; (personne, certitude, foi) steadfast, unwavering.
inédit, e [inedi, -it] a (correspondance etc)

hitherto unpublished; (*spectacle, moyen*) novel, original.

ineffable [inefabl(ə)] *a* inexpressible, ineffable.

ineffaçable [inefasabl(ə)] *a* indelible.

inefficace [inefikas] *a* (*remède, moyen*) ineffective; (*machine, employé*) inefficient; **inefficacité** *nf* ineffectiveness; inefficiency.

inégal, e, aux [inegal, -o] *a* unequal; uneven.

inégalable [inegalabl(e)] *a* matchless.

inégalé, e [inegale] *a* unmatched, unequalled.

inégalité [inegalite] *nf* inequality; unevenness *q*; ~ **de 2 hauteurs** difference *ou* disparity between 2 heights.

inélégant, e [inelegɑ̃, -ɑ̃t] *a* inelegant; (*indélicat*) discourteous.

inéligible [ineliʒibl(ə)] *a* ineligible.

inéluctable [inelyktabl(ə)] *a* inescapable, ineluctable.

inemployé, e [inɑ̃plwaje] *a* unused.

inénarrable [inenaʀabl(ə)] *a* hilarious.

inepte [inɛpt(ə)] *a* inept; **ineptie** [-si] *nf* ineptitude; nonsense *q*.

inépuisable [inepɥizabl(ə)] *a* inexhaustible.

inerte [inɛʀt(ə)] *a* lifeless; (*apathique*) passive, inert; (*PHYSIQUE, CHIMIE*) inert. **inertie** [inɛʀsi] *nf* inertia.

inespéré, e [inɛspeʀe] *a* unhoped-for.

inesthétique [inɛstetik] *a* unsightly.

inestimable [inɛstimabl(e)] *a* priceless; (*fig: bienfait*) invaluable.

inévitable [inevitabl(ə)] *a* unavoidable; (*fatal, habituel*) inevitable.

inexact, e [inɛgzakt] *a* inaccurate, inexact; unpunctual; ~**itude** *nf* inaccuracy.

inexcusable [inɛkskyzabl(ə)] *a* inexcusable, unforgivable.

inexécutable [inɛgzekytabl(ə)] *a* impracticable, unworkable; (*MUS*) unplayable.

inexistant, e [inɛgzistɑ̃, -ɑ̃t] *a* nonexistent.

inexorable [inɛgzɔʀabl(ə)] *a* inexorable.

inexpérience [inɛkspeʀjɑ̃s] *nf* inexperience, lack of experience.

inexplicable [inɛksplikabl(ə)] *a* inexplicable.

inexpliqué, e [inɛksplike] *a* unexplained.

inexploité, e [inɛksplwate] *a* unexploited, untapped.

inexpressif, ive [inɛkspʀesif, -iv] *a* inexpressive; expressionless.

inexprimable [inɛkspʀimabl(ə)] *a* inexpressible.

inexprimé, e [inɛkspʀime] *a* unspoken, unexpressed.

inextensible [inɛkstɑ̃sibl(ə)] *a* (*tissu*) nonstretch.

in extenso [inɛkstɛ̃so] *ad* in full.

inextricable [inɛkstʀikabl(ə)] *a* inextricable.

in extremis [inɛkstʀemis] *ad* at the last minute // *a* last-minute; (*testament*) death bed *cpd*.

infaillibilité [ɛ̃fajibilite] *nf* infallibility.

infaillible [ɛ̃fajibl(ə)] *a* infallible; (*instinct*) infallible, unerring.

infâme [ɛ̃fɑm] *a* vile.

infanterie [ɛ̃fɑ̃tʀi] *nf* infantry.

infanticide [ɛ̃fɑ̃tisid] *nm/f* child-murderer/eress // *nm* (*meurtre*) infanticide.

infantile [ɛ̃fɑ̃til] *a* (*MÉD*) infantile, child *cpd*; (*ton, réaction, péj*) infantile, childish.

infarctus [ɛ̃faʀktys] *nm*: ~ (**du myocarde**) coronary (thrombosis).

infatigable [ɛ̃fatigabl(ə)] *a* tireless, indefatigable.

infatué, e [ɛ̃fatɥe] *a* conceited; ~ **de** full of.

infécond, e [ɛ̃fekɔ̃, -ɔ̃d] *a* infertile, barren.

infect, e [ɛ̃fɛkt] *a* vile, foul; (*repas, vin*) revolting, foul.

infecter [ɛ̃fɛkte] *vt* (*atmosphère, eau*) to contaminate; (*MÉD*) to infect; **s'**~ to become infected *ou* septic; **infectieux, euse** [-sjø, -øz] *a* infectious; **infection** [-sjɔ̃] *nf* infection.

inféoder [ɛ̃feode] *vt*: **s'**~ **à** to pledge allegiance to.

inférer [ɛ̃feʀe] *vt*: ~ **qch de** to infer sth from.

inférieur, e [ɛ̃feʀjœʀ] *a* lower; (*en qualité, intelligence*) inferior // *nm/f* inferior; ~ **à** (*somme, quantité*) less *ou* smaller than; (*moins bon que*) inferior to; (*tâche: pas à la hauteur de*) unequal to; **infériorité** *nf* inferiority.

infernal, e, aux [ɛ̃fɛʀnal, -o] *a* (*chaleur, rythme*) infernal; (*méchanceté, complot*) diabolical.

infester [ɛ̃fɛste] *vt* to infest; **infesté de moustiques** infested with mosquitoes, mosquito-ridden.

infidèle [ɛ̃fidɛl] *a* unfaithful; (*REL*) infidel; **infidélité** *nf* unfaithfulness *q*.

infiltration [ɛ̃filtʀɑsjɔ̃] *nf* infiltration.

infiltrer [ɛ̃filtʀe]: **s'**~ *vi*: **s'**~ **dans** to penetrate into; (*liquide*) to seep into; (*fig: noyauter*) to infiltrate.

infime [ɛ̃fim] *a* minute, tiny; (*inférieur*) lowly.

infini, e [ɛ̃fini] *a* infinite // *nm* infinity; **à l'**~ (*MATH*) to infinity; (*discourir*) ad infinitum, endlessly; (*agrandir, varier*) infinitely; (*à perte de vue*) endlessly (into the distance); ~**ment** *ad* infinitely; **infinité** *nf*: **une infinité de** an infinite number of.

infinitif, ive [ɛ̃finitif, -iv] *a, nm* infinitive.

infirme [ɛ̃fiʀm(ə)] *a* disabled // *nm/f* disabled person; ~ **de guerre** war cripple; ~ **du travail** industrially disabled person.

infirmer [ɛ̃fiʀme] *vt* to invalidate.

infirmerie [ɛ̃fiʀməʀi] *nf* sick bay.

infirmier, ière [ɛ̃fiʀmje, -jɛʀ] *nm/f* nurse; **infirmière chef** sister; **infirmière diplômée** registered nurse; **infirmière visiteuse** ≈ district nurse.

infirmité [ɛ̃fiʀmite] *nf* disability.

inflammable [ɛ̃flamabl(ə)] *a* (in)flammable.

inflammation [ɛ̃flamɑsjɔ̃] *nf* inflammation.

inflation [ɛflɑsjɔ̃] *nf* inflation; **inflationniste** *a* inflationist.

infléchir [ɛfleʃiʀ] *vt* (*fig: politique*) to reorientate, redirect.

inflexible [ɛflɛksibl(ə)] *a* inflexible.

inflexion [ɛflɛksjɔ̃] *nf* inflexion; ~ **de la tête** slight nod (of the head).

infliger [ɛfliʒe] *vt*: ~ **qch (à qn)** to inflict sth (on sb); (*amende, sanction*) to impose sth (on sb).

influençable [ɛflyɑ̃sabl(ə)] *a* easily influenced.

influence [ɛflyɑ̃s] *nf* influence; (*d'un médicament*) effect; **influencer** *vt* to influence; **influent, e** *a* influential.

influer [ɛflye]: ~ **sur** *vt* to have an influence upon.

influx [ɛfly] *nm*: ~ **nerveux** (nervous) impulse.

informaticien, ne [ɛfɔʀmatisjɛ̃, -jɛn] *nm/f* computer scientist.

information [ɛfɔʀmɑsjɔ̃] *nf* (*renseignement*) piece of information; (*PRESSE, TV: nouvelle*) news *sg*; (*diffusion de renseignements, INFORMATIQUE*) information; (*JUR*) inquiry, investigation; **voyage d'**~ fact-finding trip; **agence d'**~ news agency; **journal d'**~ quality newspaper.

informatique [ɛfɔʀmatik] *nf* (*techniques*) data processing; (*science*) computer science; **informatiser** *vt* to computerize.

informe [ɛfɔʀm(ə)] *a* shapeless.

informer [ɛfɔʀme] *vt*: ~ **qn (de)** to inform sb (of) // *vi* (*JUR*): ~ **contre/sur** to initiate inquiries about; **s'**~ **(sur)** to inform o.s. (about); **s'**~ **(de/si)** to inquire *ou* find out (about/whether *ou* if).

infortune [ɛfɔʀtyn] *nf* misfortune.

infraction [ɛfʀaksjɔ̃] *nf* offence; ~ **à** violation *ou* breach of; **être en** ~ to be in breach of the law.

infranchissable [ɛfʀɑ̃ʃisabl(ə)] *a* impassable; (*fig*) insuperable.

infrarouge [ɛfʀaʀuʒ] *a, nm* infrared.

infrastructure [ɛfʀastʀyktyʀ] *nf* (*d'une route etc*) substructure; (*AVIAT, MIL*) ground installations *pl*; (*ÉCON: touristique etc*) infrastructure.

infroissable [ɛfʀwasabl(ə)] *a* crease-resistant.

infructueux, euse [ɛfʀyktɥø, -øz] *a* fruitless, unfruitful.

infus, e [ɛfy, -yz] *a*: **avoir la science** ~**e** to have innate knowledge.

infuser [ɛfyze] *vt* (*thé*) to brew; (*tisane*) to infuse // *vi* to brew; to infuse; **infusion** *nf* (*tisane*) infusion, herb tea.

ingambe [ɛgɑ̃b] *a* spry, nimble.

ingénier [ɛʒenje]: **s'**~ *vi*: **s'**~ **à faire** to strive to do.

ingénieur [ɛʒenjœʀ] *nm* engineer; ~ **agronome/chimiste** agricultural/chemical engineer; ~ **du son** sound engineer.

ingénieux, euse [ɛʒenjø, -øz] *a* ingenious, clever; **ingéniosité** *nf* ingenuity.

ingénu, e [ɛʒeny] *a* ingenuous, artless // *nf* (*THÉÂTRE*) ingénue.

ingérer [ɛʒeʀe]: **s'**~ *vi*: **s'**~ **dans** to interfere in.

ingrat, e [ɛgʀa, -at] *a* (*personne*) ungrateful; (*sol*) barren, arid; (*travail, sujet*) arid, thankless; (*visage*) unprepossessing; **ingratitude** *nf* ingratitude.

ingrédient [ɛgʀedjɑ̃] *nm* ingredient.

inguérissable [ɛgeʀisabl(ə)] *a* incurable.

ingurgiter [ɛgyʀʒite] *vt* to swallow.

inhabile [inabil] *a* clumsy; (*fig*) inept.

inhabitable [inabitabl(ə)] *a* uninhabitable.

inhabité, e [inabite] *a* (*régions*) uninhabited; (*maison*) unoccupied.

inhabituel, le [inabitɥɛl] *a* unusual.

inhalateur [inalatœʀ] *nm* inhaler; ~ **d'oxygène** oxygen mask.

inhalation [inalɑsjɔ̃] *nf* (*MÉD*) inhalation; **faire des** ~**s** to use an inhalation bath.

inhérent, e [ineʀɑ̃, -ɑ̃t] *a*: ~ **à** inherent in.

inhibition [inibisjɔ̃] *nf* inhibition.

inhospitalier, ière [inɔspitalje, -jɛʀ] *a* inhospitable.

inhumain, e [inymɛ̃, -ɛn] *a* inhuman.

inhumation [inymɑsjɔ̃] *nf* interment, burial.

inhumer [inyme] *vt* to inter, bury.

inimaginable [inimaʒinabl(ə)] *a* unimaginable.

inimitable [inimitabl(ə)] *a* inimitable.

inimitié [inimitje] *nf* enmity.

ininflammable [inɛflamabl(ə)] *a* non-flammable.

inintelligent, e [inɛteliʒɑ̃, -ɑ̃t] *a* unintelligent.

inintelligible [inɛteliʒibl(ə)] *a* unintelligible.

inintéressant, e [inɛteʀɛsɑ̃, -ɑ̃t] *a* uninteresting.

ininterrompu, e [inɛtɛʀɔ̃py] *a* (*file, série*) unbroken; (*flot, vacarme*) uninterrupted, non-stop; (*effort*) unremitting, continuous.

iniquité [inikite] *nf* iniquity.

initial, e, aux [inisjal, -o] *a, nf* initial.

initiateur, trice [inisjatœʀ, -tʀis] *nm/f* initiator; (*d'une mode, technique*) innovator, pioneer.

initiative [inisjativ] *nf* initiative; **prendre l'**~ **de qch/de faire** to take the initiative for sth/of *ou* in doing; **avoir de l'**~ to have initiative, show enterprise.

initier [inisje] *vt*: ~ **qn à** to initiate sb into; (*faire découvrir: art, jeu*) to introduce sb to.

injecté, e [ɛʒɛkte] *a*: **yeux** ~**s de sang** bloodshot eyes.

injecter [ɛʒɛkte] *vt* to inject; **injection** [-sjɔ̃] *nf* injection; **à injection** *a* (*AUTO*) fuel injection *cpd*.

injonction [ɛʒɔ̃ksjɔ̃] *nf* injunction, order.

injure [ɛʒyʀ] *nf* insult, abuse *q*.

injurier [ɛʒyʀje] *vt* to insult, abuse; **injurieux, euse** *a* abusive, insulting.

injuste [ɛʒyst(ə)] *a* unjust, unfair; **injustice** *nf* injustice.

inlassable [ɛlɑsabl(ə)] *a* tireless, indefatigable.

inné, e [ine] *a* innate, inborn.

innocence [inɔsɑ̃s] *nf* innocence.

innocent, e [inɔsɑ̃, -ɑ̃t] *a* innocent // *nm/f*

innocent person ; **innocenter** vt to clear, prove innocent.

innombrable [inɔ̃bʀabl(ə)] a innumerable.

innommable [inɔmabl(ə)] a unspeakable.

innover [inɔve] vi to break new ground.

inobservation [inɔpsɛʀvasjɔ̃] nf non-observation, inobservance.

inoccupé, e [inɔkype] a unoccupied.

inoculer [inɔkyle] vt: ~ qch à qn (volontairement) to inoculate sb with sth ; (accidentellement) to infect sb with sth ; ~ qn contre to inoculate sb against.

inodore [inɔdɔʀ] a (gaz) odourless ; (fleur) scentless.

inoffensif, ive [inɔfɑ̃sif, -iv] a harmless, innocuous.

inondation [inɔ̃dasjɔ̃] nf flooding q ; flood.

inonder [inɔ̃de] vt to flood ; (fig) to inundate, overrun ; ~ de (fig) to flood ou swamp with.

inopérable [inɔpeʀabl(ə)] a inoperable.

inopérant, e [inɔpeʀɑ̃, -ɑ̃t] a inoperative, ineffective.

inopiné, e [inɔpine] a unexpected, sudden.

inopportun, e [inɔpɔʀtœ̃, -yn] a ill-timed, untimely ; (moment) inappropriate ; inopportune.

inoubliable [inublijabl(ə)] a unforgettable.

inouï, e [inwi] a unheard-of, extraordinary.

inoxydable [inɔksidabl(ə)] a stainless ; (couverts) stainless steel cpd.

inqualifiable [ɛ̃kalifjabl(ə)] a unspeakable.

inquiet, ète [ɛ̃kjɛ, -ɛt] a (par nature) anxious ; (momentanément) worried.

inquiétant, e [ɛ̃kjetɑ̃, -ɑ̃t] a worrying, disturbing.

inquiéter [ɛ̃kjete] vt to worry, disturb ; (harceler) to harass ; s'~ to worry, become anxious ; s'~ de to worry about ; (s'enquérir de) to inquire about.

inquiétude [ɛ̃kjetyd] nf anxiety ; **donner de l'~ ou des ~s à** to worry ; **avoir de l'~ ou des ~s au sujet de** to feel anxious ou worried about.

inquisition [ɛ̃kizisjɔ̃] nf inquisition.

insaisissable [ɛ̃sezisabl(ə)] a elusive.

insalubre [ɛ̃salybʀ(ə)] a insalubrious, unhealthy.

insanité [ɛ̃sanite] nf madness q, insanity q.

insatiable [ɛ̃sasjabl(ə)] a insatiable.

insatisfait, e [ɛ̃satisfɛ, -ɛt] a (non comblé) unsatisfied ; unfulfilled ; (mécontent) dissatisfied.

inscription [ɛ̃skʀipsjɔ̃] nf (sur un mur, écriteau etc) inscription ; (à une institution: voir s'inscrire) enrolment ; registration.

inscrire [ɛ̃skʀiʀ] vt (marquer: sur son calepin etc) to note ou write down ; (: sur un mur, une affiche etc) to write ; (: dans la pierre, le métal) to inscribe ; (mettre: sur une liste, un budget etc) to put down ; ~ qn à (club, école etc) to enrol sb at ; s'~ (pour une excursion etc) to put one's name down ; s'~ (à) (club, parti) to join ; (université) to register ou enrol (at) ; (examen, concours) to register ou enter (for) ; s'~ en faux contre to challenge.

insecte [ɛ̃sɛkt(ə)] nm insect ; **insecticide** nm insecticide.

insécurité [ɛ̃sekyʀite] nf insecurity, lack of security.

I.N.S.E.E. [inse] sigle m = Institut national de la statistique et des études économiques.

insémination [ɛ̃seminasjɔ̃] nf insemination.

insensé, e [ɛ̃sɑ̃se] a insane.

insensibiliser [ɛ̃sɑ̃sibilize] vt to anaesthetize.

insensible [ɛ̃sɑ̃sibl(ə)] a (nerf, membre) numb ; (dur, indifférent) insensitive ; (imperceptible) imperceptible.

inséparable [ɛ̃sepaʀabl(ə)] a inseparable.

insérer [ɛ̃seʀe] vt to insert ; s'~ dans to fit into ; to come within.

insidieux, euse [ɛ̃sidjø, -øz] a insidious.

insigne [ɛ̃siɲ] nm (d'un parti, club) badge // a distinguished ; ~s nmpl (d'une fonction) insignia pl.

insignifiant, e [ɛ̃siɲifjɑ̃, -ɑ̃t] a insignificant ; trivial.

insinuation [ɛ̃sinɥasjɔ̃] nf innuendo, insinuation.

insinuer [ɛ̃sinɥe] vt to insinuate, imply ; s'~ dans to seep into ; (fig) to worm one's way into ; to creep into.

insipide [ɛ̃sipid] a insipid.

insistance [ɛ̃sistɑ̃s] nf insistence ; **avec ~** insistently.

insister [ɛ̃siste] vi to insist ; (s'obstiner) to keep trying ; ~ sur (détail, note) to stress.

insociable [ɛ̃sɔsjabl(ə)] a unsociable.

insolation [ɛ̃sɔlasjɔ̃] nf (MÉD) sunstroke q ; (ensoleillement) period of sunshine.

insolence [ɛ̃sɔlɑ̃s] nf insolence q.

insolent, e [ɛ̃sɔlɑ̃, -ɑ̃t] a insolent.

insolite [ɛ̃sɔlit] a strange, unusual.

insoluble [ɛ̃sɔlybl(ə)] a insoluble.

insolvable [ɛ̃sɔlvabl(ə)] a insolvent.

insomnie [ɛ̃sɔmni] nf insomnia q, sleeplessness q.

insondable [ɛ̃sɔ̃dabl(ə)] a unfathomable.

insonore [ɛ̃sɔnɔʀ] a soundproof ; **insonoriser** vt to soundproof.

insouciance [ɛ̃susjɑ̃s] nf carefree attitude ; heedless attitude.

insouciant, e [ɛ̃susjɑ̃, -ɑ̃t] a carefree ; (imprévoyant) heedless.

insoumis, e [ɛ̃sumi, -iz] a (caractère, enfant) rebellious, refractory ; (contrée, tribu) unsubdued.

insoumission [ɛ̃sumisjɔ̃] nf rebelliousness ; (MIL) absence without leave.

insoupçonnable [ɛ̃supsɔnabl(ə)] a above suspicion.

insoupçonné, e [ɛ̃supsɔne] a unsuspected.

insoutenable [ɛ̃sutnabl(ə)] a (argument) untenable ; (chaleur) unbearable.

inspecter [ɛ̃spɛkte] vt to inspect.

inspecteur, trice [ɛ̃spɛktœʀ, -tʀis] nm/f inspector ; ~ d'Académie ≈ Chief Education Officer ; ~ des finances ≈ Treasury Inspector.

inspection [ɛ̃spɛksjɔ̃] nf inspection.

inspiration [ɛ̃spiʀasjɔ̃] nf inspiration ; breathing in q ; sous l'~ de prompted by.

inspirer [ɛspiʀe] vt (gén) to inspire // vi (aspirer) to breathe in; s'~ de (suj: artiste) to draw one's inspiration from; (suj: tableau) to be inspired by; ~ à qn (œuvre, action) to inspire sb with; (dégoût, crainte) to fill sb with; ça ne m'inspire pas I'm not keen on the idea.

instable [ɛstabl(ə)] a (meuble, équilibre) unsteady; (population, temps) unsettled; (paix, régime, caractère) unstable.

installation [ɛstalɑsjɔ̃] nf installation; putting in ou up; fitting out; settling in; (appareils etc) fittings pl, installations pl; ~s nfpl installations, plant sg; facilities.

installer [ɛstale] vt (loger): ~ qn to get sb settled, install sb; (placer) to put, place; (meuble) to put in; (rideau, étagère, tente) to put up; (gaz, électricité etc) to put in, install; (appartement) to fit out; s'~ (s'établir: artisan, dentiste etc) to set o.s. up; (se loger) to settle (o.s.); (emménager) to settle in; (sur un siège, à un emplacement) to settle (down); (fig: maladie, grève) to take a firm hold ou grip.

instamment [ɛstamɑ̃] ad urgently.

instance [ɛstɑ̃s] nf (JUR: procédure) (legal) proceedings pl; (ADMIN: autorité) authority; ~s nfpl (prières) entreaties; affaire en ~ matter pending; être en ~ de divorce to be awaiting a divorce; en seconde ~ on appeal.

instant [ɛstɑ̃] nm moment, instant; dans un ~ in a moment; à l'~ this instant; à tout ~ at any moment; constantly; pour l'~ for the moment, for the time being; par ~s at times; de tous les ~s perpetual.

instantané, e [ɛstɑ̃tane] a (lait, café) instant; (explosion, mort) instantaneous // nm snapshot.

instar [ɛstaʀ]: à l'~ de prép following the example of, like.

instaurer [ɛstɔʀe] vt to institute.

instigateur, trice [ɛstigatœʀ, -tʀis] nm/f instigator.

instigation [ɛstigɑsjɔ̃] nf: à l'~ de qn at sb's instigation.

instinct [ɛstɛ̃] nm instinct; ~ de conservation instinct of self-preservation; **instinctif, ive** a instinctive.

instituer [ɛstitɥe] vt to institute, set up.

institut [ɛstity] nm institute; ~ de beauté beauty salon; I~ Universitaire de Technologie (IUT) ≈ Polytechnic.

instituteur, trice [ɛstitytœʀ, -tʀis] nm/f (primary school) teacher.

institution [ɛstitysjɔ̃] nf institution; (collège) private school.

instructeur, trice [ɛstʀyktœʀ, -tʀis] a (MIL): sergent ~ drill sergeant; (JUR): juge ~ examining magistrate // nm/f instructor.

instructif, ive [ɛstʀyktif, -iv] a instructive.

instruction [ɛstʀyksjɔ̃] nf (enseignement, savoir) education; (JUR) (preliminary) investigation and hearing; (directive) instruction; ~s nfpl (mode d'emploi) directions, instructions; ~ civique civics sg; ~ religieuse religious instruction; ~ professionnelle vocational training.

instruire [ɛstʀɥiʀ] vt (élèves) to teach; (recrues) to train; (JUR: affaire) to conduct the investigation for; s'~ to educate o.s.; ~ qn de qch (informer) to inform ou advise sb of sth; instruit, e a educated.

instrument [ɛstʀymɑ̃] nm instrument; ~ à cordes/vent stringed/wind instrument; ~ de mesure measuring instrument; ~ de musique musical instrument; ~ de travail (working) tool.

insu [ɛsy] nm: à l'~ de qn without sb knowing (it).

insubmersible [ɛsybmɛʀsibl(ə)] a unsinkable.

insubordination [ɛsybɔʀdinɑsjɔ̃] nf rebelliousness; (MIL) insubordination.

insuccès [ɛsyksɛ] nm failure.

insuffisance [ɛsyfizɑ̃s] nf insufficiency; inadequacy; ~s nfpl (lacunes) inadequacies; ~ cardiaque cardiac insufficiency q.

insuffisant, e [ɛsyfizɑ̃, -ɑ̃t] a insufficient; (élève, travail) inadequate.

insuffler [ɛsyfle] vt: ~ qch dans to blow sth into; ~ qch à qn to inspire sb with sth.

insulaire [ɛsylɛʀ] a island cpd; (attitude) insular.

insulte [ɛsylt(ə)] nf insult; **insulter** vt to insult.

insupportable [ɛsypɔʀtabl(ə)] a unbearable.

insurgé, e [ɛsyʀʒe] a, nm/f insurgent, rebel.

insurger [ɛsyʀʒe]: s'~ vi: s'~ (contre) to rise up ou rebel (against).

insurmontable [ɛsyʀmɔ̃tabl(ə)] a (difficulté) insuperable; (aversion) unconquerable.

insurrection [ɛsyʀɛksjɔ̃] nf insurrection, revolt.

intact, e [ɛtakt] a intact.

intangible [ɛtɑ̃ʒibl(ə)] a intangible; (principe) inviolable.

intarissable [ɛtaʀisabl(ə)] a inexhaustible.

intégral, e, aux [ɛtegʀal, -o] a complete // nf (MATH) integral; ~ement ad in full.

intégrant, e [ɛtegʀɑ̃, -ɑ̃t] a: faire partie ~e de to be an integral part of, be part and parcel of.

intègre [ɛtɛgʀ(ə)] a upright.

intégrer [ɛtegʀe] vt: ~ qch à/dans to integrate sth into; s'~ à/dans to become integrated into.

intégrité [ɛtegʀite] nf integrity.

intellect [ɛtelɛkt] nm intellect.

intellectuel, le [ɛtelɛktɥɛl] a intellectual // nm/f intellectual; (péj) highbrow.

intelligence [ɛteliʒɑ̃s] nf intelligence; (compréhension): l'~ de the understanding of; (complicité): regard d'~ glance of complicity; (accord): vivre en bonne ~ avec qn to be on good terms with sb; ~s nfpl (MIL, fig) secret contacts.

intelligent, e [ɛteliʒɑ̃, -ɑ̃t] a intelligent.

intelligible [ɛteliʒibl(ə)] a intelligible.

intempérance [ɛtɑ̃peʀɑ̃s] nf intemperance q; overindulgence q.

intempéries [ɛtɑ̃peʀi] nfpl bad weather sg.

intempestif, ive [ɛ̃tɑ̃pɛstif, -iv] *a* untimely.

intenable [ɛ̃tnabl(ə)] *a* (*chaleur*) unbearable.

intendance [ɛ̃tɑ̃dɑ̃s] *nf* (MIL) supply corps; supplies office; (SCOL: *bureau*) bursar's office.

intendant, e [ɛ̃tɑ̃dɑ̃, -ɑ̃t] *nm/f* (MIL) quartermaster; (SCOL) bursar; (*d'une propriété*) steward.

intense [ɛ̃tɑ̃s] *a* intense; **intensif, ive** *a* intensive; **intensifier** *vt*, **s'intensifier** to intensify; **intensité** *nf* intensity.

intenter [ɛ̃tɑ̃te] *vt*: ~ **un procès contre** *ou* **à** to start proceedings against.

intention [ɛ̃tɑ̃sjɔ̃] *nf* intention; (JUR) intent; **avoir l'~ de faire** to intend to do, have the intention of doing; **à l'~ de** *prép* for; (*renseignement*) for the benefit *ou* information of; (*film, ouvrage*) aimed at; **à cette** ~ with this aim in view; **intentionné, e** *a*: **bien intentionné** well-meaning *ou* -intentioned; **mal intentionné** ill-intentioned; **intentionnel, le** *a* intentional, deliberate.

inter [ɛ̃tɛʀ] *nm* (TÉL) *abr de* **interurbain**; (SPORT): ~-**gauche**/ -**droit** inside-left/-right.

intercalaire [ɛ̃tɛʀkalɛʀ] *a*: **feuillet** ~ insert; **fiche** ~ divider.

intercaler [ɛ̃tɛʀkale] *vt* to insert; **s'~ entre** to come in between; to slip in between.

intercéder [ɛ̃tɛʀsede] *vi*: ~ (**pour qn**) to intercede (on behalf of sb).

intercepter [ɛ̃tɛʀsɛpte] *vt* to intercept; (*lumière, chaleur*) to cut off; **interception** [-sjɔ̃] *nf* interception; **avion d'interception** interceptor.

interchangeable [ɛ̃tɛʀʃɑ̃ʒabl(ə)] *a* interchangeable.

interclasse [ɛ̃tɛʀklɑs] *nm* (SCOL) break (between classes).

interdiction [ɛ̃tɛʀdiksjɔ̃] *nf* ban; ~ **de séjour** (JUR) *order banning ex-prisoner from frequenting specified places.*

interdire [ɛ̃tɛʀdiʀ] *vt* to forbid; (ADMIN: *stationnement, meeting, passage*) to ban, prohibit; (: *journal, livre*) to ban; ~ **qch à qn** to forbid sb sth; ~ **à qn de faire** to forbid sb to do, prohibit sb from doing; (*suj: empêchement*) to prevent *ou* preclude sb from doing.

interdit, e [ɛ̃tɛʀdi, -it] *a* (*stupéfait*) taken aback // *nm* interdict, prohibition.

intéressant, e [ɛ̃tɛʀɛsɑ̃, -ɑ̃t] *a* interesting.

intéressé, e [ɛ̃tɛʀese] *a* (*parties*) involved, concerned; (*amitié, motifs*) self-interested; **les** ~**s** those concerned *ou* involved.

intéressement [ɛ̃tɛʀɛsmɑ̃] *nm* (COMM) profit-sharing.

intéresser [ɛ̃tɛʀese] *vt* (*captiver*) to interest; (*toucher*) to be of interest *ou* concern to; (ADMIN: *concerner*) to affect, concern; (COMM: *travailleur*) to give a share in the profits to; (: *partenaire*) to interest (in the business); **s'~ à** to take an interest in, be interested in.

intérêt [ɛ̃tɛʀɛ] *nm* (*gén, aussi* COMM) interest; (*égoïsme*) self-interest; **avoir des** ~**s dans** (COMM) to have a financial interest *ou* a stake in; **avoir** ~ **à faire** to be well-advised to do.

interférer [ɛ̃tɛʀfeʀe] *vi*: ~ (**avec**) to interfere (with).

intérieur, e [ɛ̃teʀjœʀ] *a* (*mur, escalier, poche*) inside; (*commerce, politique*) domestic; (*cour, calme, vie*) inner; (*navigation*) inland // *nm* (*d'une maison, d'un récipient etc*) inside; (*d'un pays, aussi: décor, mobilier*) interior; (POL): **l'I**~ the Interior, ≈ the Home Office; **à l'~ (de)** inside; (*fig*) within; **en** ~ (CINÉMA) in the studio; **vêtement d'**~ indoor garment.

intérim [ɛ̃teʀim] *nm* interim period; **assurer l'~ (de)** to deputize (for); **par** ~ *a* interim // *ad* in an interim capacity; ~**aire** *a* temporary, interim.

intérioriser [ɛ̃teʀjɔʀize] *vt* to internalize.

interjection [ɛ̃tɛʀʒɛksjɔ̃] *nf* interjection.

interligne [ɛ̃tɛʀliɲ] *nm* space between the lines // *nf* lead; **simple/double** ~ single/double spacing.

interlocuteur, trice [ɛ̃tɛʀlɔkytœʀ, -tʀis] *nm/f* speaker; **son** ~ the person he was speaking to.

interlope [ɛ̃tɛʀlɔp] *a* shady.

interloquer [ɛ̃tɛʀlɔke] *vt* to take aback.

interlude [ɛ̃tɛʀlyd] *nm* interlude.

intermède [ɛ̃tɛʀmɛd] *nm* interlude.

intermédiaire [ɛ̃tɛʀmedjɛʀ] *a* intermediate; middle; half-way // *nm/f* intermediary; (COMM) middleman; **sans** ~ directly; **par l'~ de** through.

interminable [ɛ̃tɛʀminabl(ə)] *a* never-ending.

intermittence [ɛ̃tɛʀmitɑ̃s] *nf*: **par** ~ sporadically, intermittently.

intermittent, e [ɛ̃tɛʀmitɑ̃, -ɑ̃t] *a* intermittent.

internat [ɛ̃tɛʀna] *nm* (SCOL) boarding school.

international, e, aux [ɛ̃tɛʀnasjɔnal, -o] *a* international // *nm/f* (SPORT) international player.

interne [ɛ̃tɛʀn(ə)] *a* internal // *nm/f* (SCOL) boarder; (MÉD) houseman.

interner [ɛ̃tɛʀne] *vt* (POL) to intern; (MÉD) to confine to a mental institution.

interpellation [ɛ̃tɛʀpelɑsjɔ̃] *nf* interpellation; (POL) question.

interpeller [ɛ̃tɛʀpele] *vt* (*appeler*) to call out to; (*apostropher*) to shout at; (POLICE) to take in for questioning; (POL) to question.

interphone [ɛ̃tɛʀfɔn] *nm* intercom.

interposer [ɛ̃tɛʀpoze] *vt* to interpose; **s'~** *vi* to intervene; **par personnes interposées** through a third party.

interprétariat [ɛ̃tɛʀpʀetaʀja] *nm* interpreting.

interprétation [ɛ̃tɛʀpʀetɑsjɔ̃] *nf* interpretation.

interprète [ɛ̃tɛʀpʀɛt] *nm/f* interpreter; (*porte-parole*) spokesman.

interpréter [ɛ̃tɛʀpʀete] *vt* to interpret.

interrogateur, trice [ɛ̃teʀɔgatœʀ, -tʀis] *a* questioning, inquiring // *nm/f* (SCOL) (oral) examiner.

interrogatif, ive [ɛ̃teʀɔgatif, -iv] *a* (LING) interrogative.

interrogation [ɛterɔgusjɔ̃] nf question; (scol) (written ou oral) test.

interrogatoire [ɛterɔgatwaʀ] nm (police) questioning q; (jur) cross-examination.

interroger [ɛterɔʒe] vt to question; (données, ordinateur) to consult; (scol) to test.

interrompre [ɛterɔ̃pʀ(ə)] vt (gén) to interrupt; (travail, voyage) to break off, interrupt; s'~ to break off.

interrupteur [ɛteryptœʀ] nm switch.

interruption [ɛterypsjɔ̃] nf interruption; sans ~ without a break; ~ de grossesse termination of pregnancy.

intersection [ɛtɛʀsɛksjɔ̃] nf intersection.

interstice [ɛtɛʀstis] nm crack; slit.

interurbain [ɛteryʀbɛ̃] nm (tél) trunk call service.

intervalle [ɛtɛʀval] nm (espace) space; (de temps) interval; dans l'~ in the meantime.

intervenir [ɛtɛʀvəniʀ] vi (gén) to intervene; (survenir) to take place; ~ auprès de to intervene with; la police a dû ~ police had to be called in; les médecins ont dû ~ the doctors had to operate.

intervention [ɛtɛʀvɑ̃sjɔ̃] nf intervention; ~ chirurgicale (surgical) operation.

intervertir [ɛtɛʀvɛʀtiʀ] vt to invert (the order of), reverse.

interview [ɛtɛʀvju] nf interview; **interviewer** vt [-ve] to interview.

intestin, e [ɛtɛstɛ̃, -in] a internal // nm intestine; ~ grêle small intestine; **intestinal, e,** aux a intestinal.

intime [ɛtim] a intimate; (vie, journal) private; (conviction) inmost; (dîner, cérémonie) held among friends, quiet // nm/f close friend.

intimer [ɛtime] vt (jur) to notify; ~ à qn l'ordre de faire to order sb to do.

intimider [ɛtimide] vt to intimidate.

intimité [ɛtimite] nf intimacy; privacy; private life; dans l'~ in private; (sans formalités) with only a few friends, quietly.

intitulé [ɛtityle] nm title.

intituler [ɛtityle] vt: comment a-t-il intitulé son livre? what title did he give his book?; s'~ to be entitled; (personne) to call o.s.

intolérable [ɛtɔleʀabl(ə)] a intolerable.

intolérance [ɛtɔleʀɑ̃s] nf intolerance.

intolérant, e [ɛtɔleʀɑ̃, -ɑ̃t] a intolerant.

intonation [ɛtɔnusjɔ̃] nf intonation.

intouchable [ɛtuʃabl(ə)] a (fig) above the law, sacrosanct; (rel) untouchable.

intoxication [ɛtɔksikusjɔ̃] nf poisoning q; (fig) brainwashing; ~ alimentaire food poisoning.

intoxiquer [ɛtɔksike] vt to poison; (fig) to brainwash.

intraduisible [ɛtʀaduizibl(ə)] a untranslatable; (fig) impossible to render.

intraitable [ɛtʀɛtabl(ə)] a inflexible, uncompromising.

intransigeance [ɛtʀɑ̃ziʒɑ̃s] nf intransigence.

intransigeant, e [ɛtʀɑ̃ziʒɑ̃, -ɑ̃t] a intransigent; (morale, passion) uncompromising.

intransitif, ive [ɛtʀɑ̃zitif, -iv] a (ling) intransitive.

intransportable [ɛtʀɑ̃spɔʀtabl(ə)] a (blessé) unable to travel.

intraveineux, euse [ɛtʀavɛnø, -øz] a intravenous.

intrépide [ɛtʀepid] a dauntless.

intrigant, e [ɛtʀigɑ̃, -ɑ̃t] nm/f schemer.

intrigue [ɛtʀig] nf intrigue.

intriguer [ɛtʀige] vi to scheme // vt to puzzle, intrigue.

intrinsèque [ɛtʀɛ̃sɛk] a intrinsic.

introduction [ɛtʀɔdyksjɔ̃] nf introduction.

introduire [ɛtʀɔduiʀ] vt to introduce; (visiteur) to show in; (aiguille, clef): ~ qch dans to insert ou introduce sth into; s'~ (techniques, usages) to be introduced; s'~ dans to gain entry into; to get o.s. accepted into; (eau, fumée) to get into.

introniser [ɛtʀɔnize] vt to enthrone.

introspection [ɛtʀɔspɛksjɔ̃] nf introspection.

introuvable [ɛtʀuvabl(ə)] a which cannot be found; (comm) unobtainable.

introverti, e [ɛtʀɔvɛʀti] nm/f introvert.

intrus, e [ɛtʀy, -yz] nm/f intruder.

intrusion [ɛtʀyzjɔ̃] nf intrusion; interference.

intuitif, ive [ɛtyitif, -iv] a intuitive.

intuition [ɛtyisjɔ̃] nf intuition.

inusable [inyzabl(ə)] a hard-wearing.

inusité, e [inyzite] a not in common use; unaccustomed.

inutile [inytil] a useless; (superflu) unnecessary; **inutilisable** a unusable; **inutilité** nf uselessness.

invaincu, e [ɛ̃vɛ̃ky] a unbeaten; unconquered.

invalide [ɛ̃valid] a disabled; ~ de guerre disabled ex-serviceman; ~ du travail industrially disabled person.

invalider [ɛ̃valide] vt to invalidate.

invalidité [ɛ̃validite] nf disability.

invariable [ɛ̃vaʀjabl(ə)] a invariable.

invasion [ɛ̃vuzjɔ̃] nf invasion.

invectiver [ɛ̃vɛktive] vt to hurl abuse at // vi: ~ contre to rail against.

invendable [ɛ̃vɑ̃dabl(ə)] a unsaleable; unmarketable; **invendus** nmpl unsold goods.

inventaire [ɛ̃vɑ̃tɛʀ] nm inventory; (comm: liste) stocklist; (: opération) stocktaking q; (fig) survey.

inventer [ɛ̃vɑ̃te] vt to invent; (subterfuge) to devise, invent; (histoire, excuse) to make up, invent; ~ de faire to hit on the idea of doing; **inventeur** nm inventor; **inventif, ive** a inventive; **invention** [-sjɔ̃] nf invention.

inventorier [ɛ̃vɑ̃tɔʀje] vt to make an inventory of.

inverse [ɛ̃vɛʀs(ə)] a reverse; opposite; inverse // nm inverse, reverse; en proportion ~ in inverse proportion; dans l'ordre ~ in the reverse order; en sens ~ in (ou from) the opposite direction; ~ment ad conversely; **inverser** vt to invert, reverse; (élec) to reverse; **inversion** nf inversion; reversal.

inverti, e [ɛ̃vɛʀti] *nm f* homosexual.

investigation [ɛ̃vɛstigɑsjɔ̃] *nf* investigation, inquiry

investir [ɛ̃vɛstiʀ] *vt* to invest; **investissement** *nm* investment; **investiture** *nf* investiture; (à une élection) nomination.

invétéré, e [ɛ̃veteʀe] *a* (habitude) ingrained; (bavard, buveur) inveterate.

invincible [ɛ̃vɛ̃sibl(ə)] *a* invincible, unconquerable.

invisible [ɛ̃vizibl(ə)] *a* invisible.

invitation [ɛ̃vitɑsjɔ̃] *nf* invitation.

invité, e [ɛ̃vite] *nm/f* guest.

inviter [ɛ̃vite] *vt* to invite; ~ **qn à faire** to invite sb to do; (suj: chose) to induce ou tempt sb to do.

involontaire [ɛ̃vɔlɔ̃tɛʀ] *a* (mouvement) involuntary; (insulte) unintentional; (complice) unwitting.

invoquer [ɛ̃vɔke] *vt* (Dieu, muse) to call upon, invoke; (prétexte) to put forward (as an excuse); (témoignage) to call upon; (loi, texte) to refer to; ~ **la clémence de qn** to beg sb ou appeal to sb for clemency.

invraisemblable [ɛ̃vʀɛsɑ̃blabl(ə)] *a* unlikely, improbable; incredible.

invulnérable [ɛ̃vylneʀabl(ə)] *a* invulnerable.

iode [jɔd] *nm* iodine.

ion [jɔ̃] *nm* ion.

ionique [jɔnik] *a* (ARCHIT) Ionic; (SCIENCE) ionic.

irai etc *vb voir* aller.

Irak [iʀak] *nm* Iraq; **irakien, ne** *a, nm/f* Iraqi

Iran [iʀɑ̃] *nm* Iran; **iranien, ne** *nm/f* Iranian.

irascible [iʀasibl(ə)] *a* short-tempered, irascible

irions etc *vb voir* aller.

iris [iʀis] *nm* iris.

irisé, e [iʀize] *a* iridescent.

irlandais, e [iʀlɑ̃dɛ, -ɛz] *a, nm* (langue) Irish // *nm/f*: I~, e Irishman/woman; **les I~** the Irish

Irlande [iʀlɑ̃d] *nf* Ireland; ~ **du Nord** Northern Ireland

ironie [iʀɔni] *nf* irony; **ironique** *a* ironical. **ironiser** *vi* to be ironical.

irons etc *vb voir* aller.

irradier [iʀadje] *vi* to radiate // *vt* to irradiate.

irraisonné, e [iʀɛzɔne] *a* irrational, unreasoned.

irrationnel, le [iʀasjɔnɛl] *a* irrational.

irréalisable [iʀealizabl(ə)] *a* unrealizable; impracticable.

irréconciliable [iʀekɔ̃siljabl(ə)] *a* irreconcilable.

irrécupérable [iʀekypeʀabl(ə)] *a* unreclaimable, beyond repair; (personne) beyond redemption ou recall.

irrécusable [iʀekyzabl(ə)] *a* unimpeachable.

irréductible [iʀedyktibl(ə)] *a* indomitable, implacable; (MATH) irreducible.

irréel, le [iʀeɛl] *a* unreal.

irréfléchi, e [iʀeflefi] *a* thoughtless.

irréfutable [iʀefytabl(ə)] *a* irre-futable.

irrégularité [iʀegylaʀite] *nf* irregularity; unevenness q.

irrégulier, ière [iʀegylje, -jɛʀ] *a* irregular; uneven; (élève, athlète) erratic.

irrémédiable [iʀemedjabl(ə)] *a* irreparable.

irremplaçable [iʀɑ̃plasabl(ə)] *a* irreplaceable.

irréparable [iʀepaʀabl(ə)] *a* beyond repair; (fig) irreparable.

irrépressible [iʀepʀesibl(ə)] *a* irrepressible, uncontrollable.

irréprochable [iʀepʀɔfabl(ə)] *a* irreproachable, beyond reproach; (tenue, toilette) impeccable.

irrésistible [iʀezistibl(ə)] *a* irresistible; (preuve, logique) compelling.

irrésolu, e [iʀezɔly] *a* irresolute.

irrespectueux, euse [iʀɛspɛktɥø, -øz] *a* disrespectful.

irrespirable [iʀɛspiʀabl(ə)] *a* unbreathable; (fig) oppressive, stifling.

irresponsable [iʀɛspɔ̃sabl(ə)] *a* irresponsible.

irrévérencieux, euse [iʀeveʀɑ̃sjø, -øz] *a* irreverent.

irréversible [iʀevɛʀsibl(ə)] *a* irreversible.

irrévocable [iʀevɔkabl(ə)] *a* irrevocable.

irrigation [iʀigɑsjɔ̃] *nf* irrigation.

irriguer [iʀige] *vt* to irrigate.

irritable [iʀitabl(ə)] *a* irritable.

irritation [iʀitɑsjɔ̃] *nf* irritation.

irriter [iʀite] *vt* (agacer) to irritate, annoy; (MÉD: enflammer) to irritate; s'~ contre/de to get annoyed ou irritated at/with.

irruption [iʀypsjɔ̃] *nf* irruption q; **faire** ~ **dans** to burst into.

Islam [islam] *nm* Islam; **islamique** *a* Islamic.

islandais, e [islɑ̃dɛ, -ɛz] *a, nm* (langue) Icelandic // *nm/f* Icelander.

Islande [islɑ̃d] *nf* Iceland.

isocèle [izɔsɛl] *a* isoceles.

isolant, e [izɔlɑ̃, -ɑ̃t] *a* insulating; (insonorisant) soundproofing.

isolation [izɔlɑsjɔ̃] *nf* insulation.

isolé, e [izɔle] *a* isolated; insulated.

isolement [izɔlmɑ̃] *nm* isolation; solitary confinement.

isoler [izɔle] *vt* to isolate; (prisonnier) to put in solitary confinement; (ville) to cut off, isolate; (ELEC) to insulate; **isoloir** *nm* polling booth.

Israël [isʀaɛl] *nm* Israel; **israélien, ne** *a, nm/f* Israeli; **israélite** *a* Jewish // *nm/f* Jew/Jewess.

issu, e [isy] *a*: ~ **de** descended from; (fig) stemming from // *nf* (ouverture, sortie) exit; (solution) way out, solution; (dénouement) outcome; **à l'~e de** at the conclusion ou close of; **rue sans ~e** dead end, no through road.

isthme [ism(ə)] *nm* isthmus.

Italie [itali] *nf* Italy; **italien, ne** *a, nm, a* Italian.

italique [italik] *nm*: **en** ~ in italics.

itinéraire [itineʀɛʀ] *nm* itinerary, route.

itinérant, e [itinerɑ̃, -ɑ̃t] a itinerant, travelling.

I.U.T. sigle m voir **institut**.

ivoire [ivwaʀ] nm ivory.

ivre [ivʀ(ə)] a drunk; ~ **de** (colère, bonheur) wild with; **ivresse** nf drunkenness; **ivrogne** nm/f drunkard.

J

j' [ʒ] pronom voir **je**.

jabot [ʒabo] nm (ZOOL) crop; (de vêtement) jabot.

jacasser [ʒakase] vi to chatter.

jachère [ʒaʃɛʀ] nf: (être) en ~ (to lie) fallow.

jacinthe [ʒasɛ̃t] nf hyacinth.

jade [ʒad] nm jade.

jadis [ʒadis] ad in times past, formerly.

jaillir [ʒajiʀ] vi (liquide) to spurt out, gush out; (fig) to rear up; to burst out; to flood out.

jais [ʒɛ] nm jet; (d'un noir) de ~ jet-black.

jalon [ʒalɔ̃] nm range pole; (fig) milestone; **jalonner** vt to mark out; (fig) to mark, punctuate.

jalouser [ʒaluze] vt to be jealous of.

jalousie [ʒaluzi] nf jealousy; (store) (venetian) blind.

jaloux, se [ʒalu, -uz] a jealous.

jamais [ʒamɛ] ad never; (sans négation) ever; ne ... ~ never.

jambage [ʒɑ̃baʒ] nm (de lettre) downstroke; (de porte) jamb.

jambe [ʒɑ̃b] nf leg; **jambières** nfpl leggings; (SPORT) shin pads.

jambon [ʒɑ̃bɔ̃] nm ham.

jante [ʒɑ̃t] nf (wheel) rim.

janvier [ʒɑ̃vje] nm January.

Japon [ʒapɔ̃] nm Japan; **japonais, e** a, nm, nf Japanese.

japper [ʒape] vi to yap, yelp.

jaquette [ʒakɛt] nf (de cérémonie) morning coat; (de livre) dust cover, dust jacket.

jardin [ʒaʀdɛ̃] nm garden; ~ **d'acclimatation** zoological gardens pl; ~ **d'enfants** nursery school; ~ **public** (public) park, public gardens pl; **jardinage** nm gardening; **jardinier, ière** nm/f gardener // nf (de fenêtre) window box; **jardinière d'enfants** nursery school teacher.

jargon [ʒaʀgɔ̃] nm jargon.

jarre [ʒaʀ] nf (earthenware) jar.

jarret [ʒaʀɛ] nm back of knee, ham; (CULIN) knuckle, shin.

jarretelle [ʒaʀtɛl] nf suspender.

jarretière [ʒaʀtjɛʀ] nf garter.

jaser [ʒaze] vi to chatter, prattle; (indiscrètement) to gossip.

jasmin [ʒasmɛ̃] nm jasmin.

jaspe [ʒasp(ə)] nm jasper.

jatte [ʒat] nf basin, bowl.

jauge [ʒoʒ] nf (capacité) capacity, tonnage; (instrument) gauge; **jauger** vt to gauge the capacity of; (fig) to size up; **jauger 3000 tonneaux** to measure 3,000 tons.

jaune [ʒon] a, nm yellow // nm/f Asiatic // ad (fam): **rire** ~ to laugh on the other side of one's face; ~ **d'œuf** (egg) yolk; **jaunir** vi, vt to turn yellow.

jaunisse [ʒonis] nf jaundice.

javel [ʒavɛl] nf voir **eau**.

javelot [ʒavlo] nm javelin.

jazz [dʒaz] nm jazz.

J.-C. sigle voir **Jésus-Christ**.

je, j' [ʒ(ə)] pronom I.

jean [dʒin] nm jeans pl.

jérémiades [ʒeʀemjad] nfpl moaning sg.

jerrycan [ʒeʀikan] nm jerrycan.

jersey [ʒɛʀzɛ] nm jersey.

Jésus-Christ [ʒezykʀi(st)] n Jesus Christ; **600 avant/après** ~ **ou J.-C.** 600 B.C./A.D.

jet [ʒɛ] nm (lancer) throwing q, throw; (jaillissement) jet; spurt; (de tuyau) nozzle; (avion) [dʒɛt] jet; **arroser au** ~ to hose; **du premier** ~ at the first attempt or shot; ~ **d'eau** fountain; spray.

jetée [ʒəte] nf jetty; pier.

jeter [ʒəte] vt (gén) to throw; (se défaire de) to throw away ou out; (son, lueur etc) to give out; ~ **qch à qn** to throw sth to sb; (de façon agressive) to throw ou hurl sth at sb; ~ **un coup d'œil (à)** to take a look (at); ~ **l'effroi parmi** to spread fear among; ~ **un sort à qn** to cast a spell on sb; **se** ~ **dans** (fleuve) to flow into.

jeton [ʒətɔ̃] nm (au jeu) counter; (de téléphone) token; ~**s de présence** (director's) fees.

jette etc vb voir **jeter**.

jeu, x [ʒø] nm (divertissement, TECH: d'une pièce) play; (défini par des règles, TENNIS: partie, FOOTBALL etc: façon de jouer) game; (THÉÂTRE etc) acting; (au casino): **le** ~ gambling; (fonctionnement) working, interplay; (série d'objets, jouet) set; (CARTES) hand; **en** ~ at stake; at work; (FOOTBALL) in play; **remettre en** ~ to throw in; **entrer/mettre en** ~ to come/bring into play; ~ **de boules** game of bowls; (endroit) bowling pitch; (boules) set of bowls; ~ **de cartes** card game; (paquet) pack of cards; ~ **de construction** building set; ~ **d'échecs** chess set; ~ **de hasard** game of chance; ~ **de mots** pun; **le** ~ **de l'oie** snakes and ladders sg; ~ **d'orgue(s)** organ stop; ~ **de société** parlour game; **J**~**x olympiques** (J.O.) Olympic Games.

jeudi [ʒødi] nm Thursday.

jeûn [ʒœ̃]: **à** ~ ad on an empty stomach.

jeune [ʒœn] a young; **les** ~**s** young people, the young; ~ **fille** nf girl; ~ **homme** nm young man; ~ **premier** leading man; ~**s gens** nmpl young people.

jeûne [ʒøn] nm fast.

jeunesse [ʒœnɛs] nf youth; (aspect) youthfulness; youngness; (jeunes) young people pl, youth.

J. O. sigle mpl voir **jeu**.

joaillerie [ʒɔajʀi] nf jewel trade; jewellery; **joaillier, ière** nm/f jeweller.

jobard [ʒɔbaʀ] nm (péj) sucker, mug.

jockey [ʒɔkɛ] nm jockey.

joie [ʒwa] *nf* joy.

joindre [ʒwɛ̃dʀ(ə)] *vt* to join; *(à une lettre):* ~ **à** to enclose sth with; *(contacter)* to contact, get in touch with; ~ **les mains/talons** to put one's hands/heels together; **se ~ à** to join.

joint [ʒwɛ̃] *nm* joint; *(ligne)* join; *(de ciment etc)* pointing *q*; ~ **de cardan** cardan joint; ~ **de culasse** cylinder head gasket; ~ **de robinet** washer.

joli [ʒɔli] *a* pretty, attractive; **c'est du ~!** *(ironique)* that's very nice!; ~**ment** *ad* prettily, attractively; *(fam: très)* pretty.

jonc [ʒɔ̃] *nm* (bul)rush.

joncher [ʒɔ̃ʃe] *vt (suj: choses)* to be strewed on; **jonché de** strewn with.

jonction [ʒɔ̃ksjɔ̃] *nf* joining; *(point de)* ~ junction; **opérer une** ~ *(MIL etc)* to rendezvous.

jongler [ʒɔ̃gle] *vi* to juggle; **jongleur, euse** *nm/f* juggler.

jonquille [ʒɔ̃kij] *nf* daffodil.

Jordanie [ʒɔʀdani] *nf:* **la** ~ Jordan.

joue [ʒu] *nf* cheek; **mettre en** ~ to take aim at.

jouer [ʒwe] *vt (partie, carte, coup, MUS: morceau)* to play; *(somme d'argent, réputation)* to stake, wager; *(pièce, rôle)* to perform; *(film)* to show; *(simuler: sentiment)* to affect, feign // *vi* to play; *(THÉÂTRE, CINÉMA)* to act, perform; *(bois, porte: se voiler)* to warp; *(clef, pièce: avoir du jeu)* to be loose; ~ **sur** *(miser)* to gamble on; ~ **de** *(MUS)* to play; ~ **du couteau/des coudes** to use knives/one's elbows; ~ **à** *(jeu, sport, roulette)* to play; ~ **au héros** to play the hero; ~ **avec** *(risquer)* to gamble with; **se ~ de** *(difficultés)* to make light of; **se ~ de qn** to deceive *ou* dupe sb; ~ **un tour à qn** to play a trick on sb; ~ **serré** to play a close game; ~ **de malchance** to be dogged with ill-luck.

jouet [ʒwɛ] *nm* toy; **être le ~ de** *(illusion etc)* to be the victim of.

joueur, euse [ʒwœʀ, -øz] *nm/f* player; **être beau/mauvais** ~ to be a good/bad loser.

joufflu, e [ʒufly] *a* chubby-cheeked, chubby.

joug [ʒu] *nm* yoke.

jouir [ʒwiʀ] ~ **de** *vt* to enjoy; **jouissance** *nf* pleasure; *(JUR)* use; **jouisseur, euse** *nm/f* sensualist.

joujou [ʒuʒu] *nm (fam)* toy.

jour [ʒuʀ] *nm* day; *(opposé à la nuit)* day, daytime; *(clarté)* daylight; *(fig: aspect)* light; *(ouverture)* opening; openwork *q*; **au** ~ **le** ~ from day to day; **de nos** ~**s** these days, nowadays; **il fait** ~ it's daylight; **au** ~ in daylight; **au grand** ~ *(fig)* in the open; **mettre au** ~ to uncover, disclose; **mettre à** ~ to bring up to date, update; **donner le** ~ **à** to give birth to; **voir le** ~ to be born; **se faire** ~ to become clear.

journal, aux [ʒuʀnal, -o] *nm* (news)paper; *(personnel)* journal, diary; ~ **parlé/télévisé** radio/television news *sg*; ~ **de bord** log.

journalier, ière [ʒuʀnalje, -jɛʀ] *a* daily; *(banal)* everyday // *nm* day labourer.

journalisme [ʒuʀnalism(ə)] *nm* journalism; **journaliste** *nm/f* journalist.

journée [ʒuʀne] *nf* day; **la** ~ **continue** the 9 to 5 working day (with short lunch break).

journellement [ʒuʀnɛlmɑ̃] *ad* daily.

joute [ʒut] *nf* duel.

jouvence [ʒuvɑ̃s] *nf:* **bain de** ~ rejuvenating experience.

jovial [ʒɔvjal] *a* jovial, jolly.

joyau, x [ʒwajo] *nm* gem, jewel.

joyeux, euse [ʒwajø, -øz] *a* joyful, merry; ~ **Noël!** merry *ou* happy Christmas!; ~ **anniversaire!** many happy returns!

jubilé [ʒybile] *nm* jubilee.

jubiler [ʒybile] *vi* to be jubilant, exult.

jucher [ʒyʃe] *vt:* ~ **qch sur** to perch sth (up)on // *vi (oiseau):* ~ **sur** to perch (up)on; **se** ~ **sur** to perch o.s. (up)on.

judaïque [ʒydaik] *a (loi)* Judaic; *(religion)* Jewish.

judaïsme [ʒydaism(ə)] *nm* Judaism.

judas [ʒyda] *nm (trou)* spy-hole.

judiciaire [ʒydisjɛʀ] *a* judicial.

judicieux, euse [ʒydisjø, -øz] *a* judicious.

judo [ʒydo] *nm* judo; ~**ka** *nm/f* judoka.

juge [ʒyʒ] *nm* judge; ~ **d'instruction** examining magis-trate; ~ **de paix** justice of the peace; ~ **de touche** linesman.

jugé [ʒyʒe]: **au** ~ *ad* by guesswork.

jugement [ʒyʒmɑ̃] *nm* judgment; *(JUR: au criminel)* sentence; (: *au civil)* decision; ~ **de valeur** value judgment.

jugeote [ʒyʒɔt] *nf (fam)* gumption.

juger [ʒyʒe] *vt* to judge; ~ **qn/qch satisfaisant** to consider sb/sth (to be) satisfactory; ~ **que** to think *ou* consider that; ~ **bon de faire** to consider it a good idea to do, see fit to do; ~ **de** *vt* to appreciate.

jugulaire [ʒygylɛʀ] *a* jugular // *nf (MIL)* chinstrap.

juif, ive [ʒɥif, -iv] *a* Jewish // *nm/f* Jew/Jewess.

juillet [ʒɥijɛ] *nm* July.

juin [ʒɥɛ̃] *nm* June.

jumeau, elle, x [ʒymo, -ɛl] *a, nm/f* twin; **jumelles** *nfpl* binoculars.

jumeler [ʒymle] *vt* to twin; **roues jumelées** double wheels.

jumelle [ʒymɛl] *a, nf voir* **jumeau.**

jument [ʒymɑ̃] *nf* mare.

jungle [ʒɔ̃gl(ə)] *nf* jungle.

jupe [ʒyp] *nf* skirt; ~**-culotte** *nf* divided skirt, culotte(s).

jupon [ʒypɔ̃] *nm* waist slip *ou* petticoat.

juré, e [ʒyʀe] *nm/f* juror, juryman/woman // *a:* **ennemi** ~ sworn enemy.

jurer [ʒyʀe] *vt (obéissance etc)* to swear, vow // *vi (dire des jurons)* to swear, curse; *(dissoner):* ~ *(avec)* to clash (with); *(s'engager):* ~ **de faire/que** to swear *ou* vow to do/that; *(affirmer):* ~ **que** to swear *ou* vouch that; ~ **de qch** *(s'en porter garant)* to swear to sth.

juridiction [ʒyʀidiksjɔ̃] *nf* jurisdiction; court(s) of law.

juridique [ʒyʀidik] *a* legal.

juriste [ʒyʀist(ə)] nm/f jurist ; lawyer.
juron [ʒyʀɔ̃] nm curse, swearword.
jury [ʒyʀi] nm (JUR) jury ; (SCOL) board (of examiners), jury.
jus [ʒy] nm juice ; (de viande) gravy, (meat) juice ; ~ de fruits fruit juice ; ~ de raisin/tomates grape/tomato juice.
jusant [ʒyzɑ̃] nm ebb (tide).
jusque [ʒysk(ə)]: **jusqu'à** prép (endroit) as far as, (up) to ; (moment) until, till ; (limite) up to ; ~ sur/dans up to, as far as ; (y compris) even on/in ; jusqu'à présent until now, so far.
juste [ʒyst(ə)] a (équitable) just, fair ; (légitime) just, justified ; (exact, vrai) right ; (étroit, insuffisant) tight // ad right ; tight ; (chanter) in tune ; (seulement) just ; ~ assez/au-dessus just enough/above ; pouvoir tout ~ faire to be only just able to do ; au ~ exactly, actually ; le ~ milieu the happy medium ; ~ment ad rightly ; justly ; (précisément): c'est ~ment ce que that's just ou precisely what ; **justesse** nf (précision) accuracy ; (d'une remarque) aptness ; (d'une opinion) soundness ; de justesse just, by a narrow margin.
justice [ʒystis] nf (équité) fairness, justice ; (ADMIN) justice ; rendre la ~ to dispense justice ; obtenir ~ to obtain justice ; rendre ~ à qn to do sb justice ; se faire ~ to take the law into one's own hands ; (se suicider) to take one's life.
justiciable [ʒystisjabl(ə)] a: ~ de (JUR) answerable to.
justicier, ière [ʒystisje, -jɛʀ] nm/f judge, righter of wrongs.
justifiable [ʒystifjabl(ə)] a justifiable.
justification [ʒystifikɑsjɔ̃] nf justification.
justifier [ʒystifje] vt to justify ; ~ de vt to prove.
jute [ʒyt] nm jute.
juteux, euse [ʒytø, -øz] a juicy.
juvénile [ʒyvenil] a young, youthful.
juxtaposer [ʒykstapoze] vt to juxtapose.

K

kaki [kaki] a inv khaki.
kaléidoscope [kaleidɔskɔp] nm kaléidoscope.
kangourou [kɑ̃guʀu] nm kangaroo.
karaté [kaʀate] nm karate.
karting [kaʀtiŋ] nm go-carting, karting.
kayac, kayak [kajak] nm kayak.
képi [kepi] nm kepi.
kermesse [kɛʀmɛs] nf bazaar, (charity) fête ; village fair.
kérosène [keʀozɛn] nm jet fuel ; rocket fuel.
kibboutz [kibuts] nm kibbutz.
kidnapper [kidnape] vt to kidnap.
kilogramme [kilɔgʀam] nm, **kilo** nm kilogramme.
kilométrage [kilɔmetʀaʒ] nm number of kilometres travelled, ≈ mileage.
kilomètre [kilɔmɛtʀ(ə)] nm kilometre.
kilométrique [kilɔmetʀik] a (distance) in kilometres ; compteur ~ ≈ mileage indicator.

kilowatt [kilɔwat] nm kilowatt.
kinésithérapeute [kineziteʀapøt] nm/f physiotherapist.
kiosque [kjɔsk(ə)] nm kiosk, stall.
kirsch [kiʀʃ] nm kirsch.
klaxon [klaksɔn] nm horn ; **klaxonner** vi, vt to hoot.
kleptomane [klɛptɔman] nm/f kleptomaniac.
km. abr de kilomètre ; km./h (= kilomètres-heure) ≈ m.p.h. (miles per hour).
knock-out [nɔkawt] nm knock-out.
K.-O. [kao] a inv (knocked) out, out for the count.
kolkhoze [kɔlkoz] nm kolkhoz.
kyrielle [kiʀjɛl] nf: une ~ de a stream of.
kyste [kist(ə)] nm cyst.

L

l' [l] dét voir le.
la [la] nm (MUS) A ; (en chantant la gamme) la.
la [la] dét voir le.
là [la] (voir aussi -ci, celui) ad there ; (ici) here ; (dans le temps) then ; est-ce que Catherine est ~? is Catherine there ou in? ; elle n'est pas ~ she isn't in ou here ; c'est ~ que this is where ; ~ où where ; de ~ (fig) hence ; par ~ (fig) by that ; tout est~ (fig) that's what it's all about ; ~-bas ad there.
label [label] nm stamp, seal.
labeur [labœʀ] nm toil q, toiling q.
labo [labo] nm (abr de laboratoire) lab.
laborantin, e [labɔʀɑ̃tɛ̃, -in] nm/f laboratory assistant.
laboratoire [labɔʀatwaʀ] nm laboratory ; ~ de langues/ d'analyses language/(medical) analysis laboratory.
laborieux, euse [labɔʀjø, -øz] a (tâche) laborious ; (personne) hard-working, industrious.
labour [labuʀ] nm ploughing q ; ~s nmpl ploughed fields ; cheval de ~ plough- ou cart-horse ; bœuf de ~ ox (pl oxen).
labourer [labuʀe] vt to plough ; (fig) to make deep gashes ou furrows in ; **laboureur** nm ploughman.
labyrinthe [labiʀɛ̃t] nm labyrinth, maze.
lac [lak] nm lake.
lacer [lase] vt to lace ou do up.
lacérer [laseʀe] vt to tear to shreds, lacerate.
lacet [lasɛ] nm (de chaussure) lace ; (de route) sharp bend ; (piège) snare.
lâche [lɑʃ] a (poltron) cowardly ; (desserré) loose, slack // nm/f coward.
lâcher [lɑʃe] nm (de ballons, oiseaux) release // vt to let go of ; (ce qui tombe, abandonner) to drop ; (oiseau, animal: libérer) to release, set free ; (fig: mot, remarque) to let slip, come out with ; (SPORT: distancer) to leave behind // vi (fil, amarres) to break, give way ; (freins) to fail ; ~ les amarres (NAVIG) to cast off (the moorings) ; ~ les chiens to unleash the dogs ; ~ prise to let go.

lâcheté [laʃte] nf cowardice ; lowness.
lacis [lasi] nm maze.
laconique [lakɔnik] a laconic.
lacrymogène [lakrimɔʒɛn] a voir gaz, grenade.
lacté, e [lakte] a (produit, régime) milk cpd.
lacune [lakyn] nf gap.
lacustre [lakystr(ə)] a lake cpd, lakeside cpd.
lad [lad] nm stable-lad.
là-dedans [ladədɑ̃] ad inside (there), in it ; (fig) in that ; **là-dehors** ad out there ; **là-derrière** ad behind there ; (fig) behind that ; **là-dessous** ad underneath, under there ; (fig) behind that ; **là-dessus** ad on there ; (fig) at that point ; about that ; **là-devant** ad there (in front).
ladite [ladit] dét voir ledit.
ladre [ladr(ə)] a miserly.
lagon [lagɔ̃] nm lagoon.
lagune [lagyn] nf lagoon.
là-haut [la'o] ad up there.
laïc [laik] a, nm/f = **laïque**.
laïciser [laisize] vt to secularize.
laid, e [lɛ, lɛd] a ugly ; (fig: acte) mean, cheap ; **laideron** nm ugly girl ; **laideur** nf ugliness q ; meanness q.
laie [lɛ] nf wild sow.
lainage [lɛnaʒ] nm woollen garment ; woollen material.
laine [lɛn] nf wool ; ~ **de verre** glass wool ; **laineux, euse** a woolly.
laïque [laik] a lay, civil ; (SCOL) state cpd (as opposed to private and Roman Catholic) // nm/f layman/woman.
laisse [lɛs] nf (de chien) lead, leash ; **tenir en** ~ to keep on a lead.
laisser [lɛse] vt to leave // vb auxiliaire : ~ **qn faire** to let sb do ; **se** ~ **exploiter** to let o.s. be exploited ; **se** ~ **aller** to let o.s. go ; **laisse-toi faire** let me (ou him) do it ; **cela ne laisse pas de surprendre** nonetheless it is surprising ; **~-aller** nm carelessness, slovenliness ; **laissez-passer** nm inv pass.
lait [lɛ] nm milk ; **frère/sœur de** ~ foster brother/sister ; ~ **écrémé/concentré** skimmed/evaporated milk ; ~ **démaquillant/de beauté** cleansing/beauty lotion ; **laitage** nm milk food ; **laiterie** nf dairy ; **laiteux, euse** a milky ; **laitier, ière** a milk cpd // nm/f milkman/dairywoman.
laiton [lɛtɔ̃] nm brass.
laitue [lety] nf lettuce.
laïus [lajys] nm (péj) spiel.
lambeau, x [lɑ̃bo] nm scrap ; **en** ~**x** in tatters, tattered.
lambin, e [lɑ̃bɛ̃, -in] a (péj) slow.
lambris [lɑ̃bri] nm panelling q ; **lambrissé, e** a panelled.
lame [lam] nf blade ; (vague) wave ; (lamelle) strip ; ~ **de fond** ground swell q ; ~ **de rasoir** razor blade.
lamé [lame] nm lamé.
lamelle [lamɛl] nf thin strip ou blade ; (de champignon) gill.
lamentable [lamɑ̃tabl(ə)] a appalling ; pitiful.
lamentation [lamɑ̃tasjɔ̃] nf wailing q, lamentation ; moaning q.

lamenter [lamɑ̃te] : **se** ~ vi : **se** ~ **(sur)** to moan (over).
laminer [lamine] vt to laminate ; **laminoir** nm rolling mill.
lampadaire [lɑ̃padɛr] nm (de salon) standard lamp.
lampe [lɑ̃p(ə)] nf lamp ; (TECH) valve ; ~ **à pétrole** paraffin lamp ; ~ **de poche** torch ; ~ **à souder** blowlamp.
lampée [lɑ̃pe] nf gulp, swig.
lampe-tempête [lɑ̃ptɑ̃pɛt] nf storm lantern.
lampion [lɑ̃pjɔ̃] nm Chinese lantern.
lampiste [lɑ̃pist(ə)] nm light (maintenance) man ; (fig) underling.
lance [lɑ̃s] nf spear ; ~ **d'incendie** fire hose.
lancée [lɑ̃se] nf: **être/continuer sur sa** ~ to be under way/keep going.
lance-flammes [lɑ̃sflam] nm inv flamethrower.
lance-grenades [lɑ̃sgrənad] nm inv grenade launcher.
lancement [lɑ̃smɑ̃] nm launching.
lance-pierres [lɑ̃spjɛr] nm inv catapult.
lancer [lɑ̃se] nm (SPORT) throwing q, throw ; (PÊCHE) rod and reel fishing // vt to throw ; (émettre, projeter) to throw out, send out ; (produit, fusée, bateau, artiste) to launch ; (injure) to hurl, fling ; (proclamation, mandat d'arrêt) to issue ; (moteur) to send roaring away ; ~ **qch à qn** to throw sth to sb ; (de façon aggressive) to throw ou hurl sth at sb ; **se** ~ vi (prendre de l'élan) to build up speed ; (se précipiter) : **se** ~ **sur/contre** to rush at ; **se** ~ **dans** (discussion) to launch into ; (aventure) to embark on ; ~ **du poids** nm putting the shot ; **lance-roquettes** nm inv rocket launcher ; **lance-torpilles** nm inv torpedo tube.
lancinant, e [lɑ̃sinɑ̃, -ɑ̃t] a (regrets etc) haunting ; (douleur) shooting, throbbing.
landau [lɑ̃do] nm pram.
lande [lɑ̃d] nf moor.
langage [lɑ̃gaʒ] nm language.
lange [lɑ̃ʒ] nm flannel blanket ; ~**s** swaddling clothes.
langer [lɑ̃ʒe] vt to change (the nappy of) ; **table à** ~ changing table.
langoureux, euse [lɑ̃gurø, -øz] a languorous.
langouste [lɑ̃gust(ə)] nf crayfish inv ; **langoustine** nf Dublin Bay prawn.
langue [lɑ̃g] nf (ANAT, CULIN) tongue ; (LING) language ; (bande) : ~ **de terre** spit of land ; **tirer la** ~ **(à)** to stick out one's tongue (at) ; **de** ~ **française** French-speaking ; ~ **maternelle** native language ; **mother tongue** ; ~ **verte** slang ; ~ **vivante** living language ; ~**-de-chat** nf finger biscuit, sponge finger.
languette [lɑ̃gɛt] nf tongue.
langueur [lɑ̃gœr] nf languidness.
languir [lɑ̃gir] vi to languish ; (conversation) to flag ; **faire** ~ **qn** to keep sb waiting.
lanière [lanjɛr] nf (de fouet) lash ; (de valise, bretelle) strap.
lanterne [lɑ̃tɛrn(ə)] nf (portable) lantern ;

(électrique) light, lamp; (de voiture) (side)light; ~ rouge (fig) tail-ender.
lapalissade [lapalisad] nf statement of the obvious.
laper [lape] vt to lap up.
lapereau, x [lapRo] nm young rabbit.
lapidaire [lapidɛR] a (fig) terse.
lapider [lapide] vt to stone.
lapin [lapɛ̃] nm rabbit; (peau) rabbitskin; ~ de garenne wild rabbit.
laps [laps] nm: ~ de temps space of time, time q.
lapsus [lapsys] nm slip.
laquais [lakɛ] nm lackey.
laque [lak] nf lacquer; (brute) lac, shellac // nm lacquer; piece of lacquer ware; laqué, e a lacquered; with lacquer finish.
laquelle [lakɛl] pronom voir lequel.
larbin [laRbɛ̃] nm (péj) flunkey.
larcin [laRsɛ̃] nm theft.
lard [laR] nm (graisse) fat; (bacon) (streaky) bacon.
larder [laRde] vt (CULIN) to lard.
lardon [laRdɔ̃] nm (CULIN) lardon.
large [laRʒ(ə)] a wide; broad; (fig) generous // ad: calculer/voir ~ to allow extra/think big // nm (largeur): 5 m de ~ 5 m wide ou in width; (mer): le ~ the open sea; en ~ ad sideways; au ~ de off; ~ d'esprit broad-minded; ~ment ad widely; greatly; easily; amply; generously; **largesse** nf generosity; largesses liberalities; **largeur** nf (qu'on mesure) width; (impression visuelle) wideness, width; breadth; broadness.
larguer [laRge] vt to drop; ~ les amarres to cast off (the moorings).
larme [laRm(ə)] nf tear; (fig): une ~ de a drop of; en ~s in tears; **larmoyant**, e a tearful; **larmoyer** vi (yeux) to water; (se plaindre) to whimper.
larron [laRɔ̃] nm thief (pl thieves).
larve [laRv(ə)] nf (ZOOL) larva (pl ae); (fig) worm.
larvé, e [laRve] a (fig) latent.
laryngite [laRɛ̃ʒit] nf laryngitis.
laryngologiste [laRɛ̃gɔlɔʒist(ə)] nm/f throat specialist.
larynx [laRɛ̃ks] nm larynx.
las, lasse [lu, lɑs] a weary.
lascar [laskaR] nm character; rogue.
lascif, ive [lasif, -iv] a lascivious.
laser [lazɛR] a, nm: (rayon) ~ laser (beam).
lasse [lɑs] af voir las.
lasser [lɑse] vt to weary, tire; se ~ de to grow weary ou tired of.
lassitude [lɑsityd] nf lassitude, weariness.
lasso [laso] nm lasso.
latent, e [latɑ̃, -ɑ̃t] a latent.
latéral, e, aux [lateRal, -o] a side cpd, lateral.
latex [latɛks] nm latex.
latin, e [latɛ̃, -in] a, nm, nf Latin; **latiniste** nm/f Latin scholar (ou student); **latino-américain, e** a Latin-American.
latitude [latityd] nf latitude; (fig): avoir la ~ de faire to be left free ou be at liberty to do; à 48° de ~ Nord at latitude 48° North.

latrines [latRin] nfpl latrines.
latte [lat] nf lath, slat; (de plancher) board.
lattis [lati] nm lathwork.
lauréat, e [lɔRea, -at] nm/f winner.
laurier [lɔRje] nm (BOT) laurel; (CULIN) bay leaves pl; ~s nmpl (fig) laurels.
lavable [lavabl(ə)] a washable.
lavabo [lavabo] nm (de salle de bains) washbasin; ~s nmpl toilet sg.
lavage [lavaʒ] nm washing q, wash; ~ d'estomac/d'intestin stomach/intestinal wash; ~ de cerveau brainwashing q.
lavande [lavɑ̃d] nf lavender.
lavandière [lavɑ̃djɛR] nf washerwoman.
lave [lav] nf lava q.
lave-glace [lavglas] nm (AUTO) windscreen washer.
lavement [lavmɑ̃] nm (MÉD) enema.
laver [lave] vt to wash; (tache) to wash off; (fig: affront) to avenge; se ~ to have a wash, wash; se ~ les mains/dents to wash one's hands/clean one's teeth; ~ qn de (accusation) to clear sb of; **laverie** nf: laverie (automatique) launderette.
lavette [lavɛt] nf dish cloth.
laveur, euse [lavœR, -øz] nm/f cleaner.
lave-vaisselle [lavvɛsɛl] nm inv dishwasher.
lavis [lavi] nm (technique) washing; (dessin) wash drawing.
lavoir [lavwaR] nm wash house; washtub.
laxatif, ive [laksatif, -iv] a, nm laxative.
laxisme [laksism(ə)] nm laxity.
layette [lɛjɛt] nf layette.
le(l'), la, les [l(ə), la, le] dét the // pronom (personne: mâle) him; (: femelle) her; (animal, chose) it; (remplaçant une phrase) it ou non traduit; (indique la possession): se casser la jambe etc to break one's leg etc; voir note sous il; les them; je ne le savais pas I didn't know (about it); il était riche et ne l'est plus he was once rich but no longer is; levez la main put your hand up; avoir les yeux gris/le nez rouge to have grey eyes/a red nose; le jeudi etc ad (d'habitude) on Thursdays etc; (ce jeudi-là) on the Thursday etc; le matin/soir ad in the morning/evening; mornings/ evenings; 10 F le mètre/kilo 10 F a ou per metre/kilo; le tiers/quart de a third/quarter of.
lécher [leʃe] vt to lick; (laper: lait, eau) to lick ou lap up; ~ les vitrines to go window-shopping.
leçon [ləsɔ̃] nf lesson; faire la ~ to teach; faire la ~ à (fig) to give a lecture to; ~s de conduite driving lessons; ~s particulières private lessons ou tuition sg.
lecteur, trice [lɛktœR, -tRis] nm/f reader; (d'université) foreign language assistant // nm (TECH): ~ de cassettes cassette player.
lecture [lɛktyR] nf reading.
ledit [ladi], **ladite** [ladit], mpl **lesdits** [ledi], fpl **lesdites** [ledit] dét the aforesaid.
légal, e, aux [legal, -o] a legal; ~ement ad legally; ~iser vt to legalize; ~ité nf legality, lawfulness; être dans/sortir de la ~ité to be within/step outside the law.
légataire [legatɛR] nm: ~ universel sole legatee.

légation [legɑsjɔ̃] nf legation.

légendaire [leʒɑ̃dɛʀ] a legendary.

légende [leʒɑ̃d] nf (mythe) legend; (de carte, plan) key, legend; (de dessin) caption, legend.

léger, ère [leʒe, -ɛʀ] a light; (bruit, retard) slight; (superficiel) thoughtless; (volage) free and easy; flighty; blessé ~ slightly injured person; à la légère ad (parler, agir) rashly, thoughtlessly; légèrement ad lightly; thoughtlessly, rashly; légèrement plus grand slightly bigger; légèreté nf lightness; thoughtlessness.

légiférer [leʒifeʀe] vi to legislate.

légion [leʒjɔ̃] nf legion; ~ étrangère foreign legion; ~ d'honneur Legion of Honour; légionnaire nm legionnaire.

législateur [leʒislatœʀ] nm legislator, lawmaker.

législatif, ive [leʒislatif, -iv] a legislative.

législation [leʒislasjɔ̃] nf legislation.

législature [leʒislatyʀ] nf legislature; term (of office).

légiste [leʒist(ə)] a: médecin ~ forensic surgeon.

légitime [leʒitim] a (JUR) lawful, legitimate; (fig) justified, rightful, legitimate; en état de ~ défense in self-defence; ~ment ad justifiably, rightfully; légitimité nf (JUR) legitimacy.

legs [lɛg] nm legacy.

léguer [lege] vt: ~ qch à qn (JUR) to bequeath sth to sb; (fig) to hand sth down ou pass sth on to sb.

légume [legym] nm vegetable.

lendemain [lɑ̃dmɛ̃] nm: le ~ the next ou following day; le ~ matin/soir the next ou following morning/evening; le ~ de the day after; au ~ de in the days following; in the wake of; penser au ~ to think of the future; sans ~ short-lived; de beaux ~s bright prospects.

lénifiant, e [lenifjɑ̃, -ɑ̃t] a soothing.

lent, e [lɑ̃, lɑ̃t] a slow; lentement ad slowly; lenteur nf slowness q.

lentille [lɑ̃tij] nf (OPTIQUE) lens sg; (BOT) lentil.

léopard [leɔpaʀ] nm leopard.

lèpre [lɛpʀ(ə)] nf leprosy; lépreux, euse nm/f leper // a (fig) flaking, peeling.

lequel [ləkɛl], **laquelle** [lakɛl], mpl **lesquels**, fpl **lesquelles** [lekɛl] (avec à, de: **auquel**, **duquel** etc) pronom (interrogatif) which, which one; (relatif: personne: sujet) who; (: objet, après préposition) whom; (: chose) which // a: auquel cas in which case.

les [le] dét voir le.

lesbienne [lɛsbjɛn] nf lesbian.

lesdits [ledi], **lesdites** [ledit] dét voir ledit.

léser [leze] vt to wrong.

lésiner [lezine] vt: ~ (sur) to skimp (on).

lésion [lezjɔ̃] nf lesion, damage q; ~s cérébrales brain damage.

lesquels, lesquelles [lekɛl] pronom voir lequel.

lessive [lesiv] nf (poudre) washing powder; (linge) washing q, wash; (opération) washing q; faire la ~ to do the washing.

lessivé, e [lesive] a (fam) washed out; cleaned out.

lessiver [lesive] vt to wash.

lessiveuse [lesivøz] nf (récipient) (laundry) boiler.

lest [lɛst] nm ballast.

leste [lɛst(ə)] a sprightly, nimble.

lester [lɛste] vt to ballast.

léthargie [letaʀʒi] nf lethargy.

léthargique [letaʀʒik] a lethargic.

lettre [lɛtʀ(ə)] nf letter; ~s nfpl literature sg; (SCOL) arts (subjects); à la ~ literally; en toutes ~s in words, in full; ~ de change bill of exchange.

lettré, e [letʀe] a well-read, scholarly.

leu [lø] voir queue.

leucémie [løsemi] nf leukaemia.

leur [lœʀ] dét their // pronom them; le(la) ~, les ~s theirs; à ~ approche as they came near; à ~ vue at the sight of them.

leurre [lœʀ] nm (appât) lure; (fig) delusion; snare.

leurrer [lœʀe] vt to delude, deceive.

levain [ləvɛ̃] nm leaven.

levant, e [ləvɑ̃, -ɑ̃t] a: soleil ~ rising sun // nm: le L~ the Levant.

levé, e [ləve] a: être ~ to be up.

levée [ləve] nf (POSTES) collection; (CARTES) trick; ~ de boucliers general outcry; ~ du corps collection of the body from house of the deceased, before funeral; ~ d'écrou release from custody; ~ de terre levee; ~ de troupes levy.

lever [ləve] vt (vitre, bras etc) to raise; (soulever de terre, supprimer: interdiction, siège) to lift; (séance) to close; (impôts, armée) to levy; (CHASSE) to start; to flush; (fam: fille) to pick up // vi (CULIN) to rise // nm: au ~ on getting up; se ~ vi to get up; (soleil) to rise; (jour) to break; (brouillard) to lift; ça va se ~ the weather will clear; ~ du jour daybreak; ~ du rideau curtain; ~ de rideau curtain raiser; ~ de soleil sunrise.

levier [ləvje] nm lever; faire ~ sur to lever up (ou off); ~ de changement de vitesse gear lever.

lèvre [lɛvʀ(ə)] nf lip; petites/grandes ~s (ANAT) labia minora/majora.

lévrier [levʀije] nm greyhound.

levure [ləvyʀ] nf yeast.

lexicographie [lɛksikɔgʀafi] nf lexicography, dictionary writing.

lexique [lɛksik] nm vocabulary; lexicon.

lézard [lezaʀ] nm lizard.

lézarde [lezaʀd(ə)] nf crack; lézarder: se lézarder vi to crack.

liaison [ljɛzɔ̃] nf (rapport) connection, link; (RAIL, AVIAT etc) link; (amoureuse) affair; (PHONÉTIQUE) liaison; entrer/être en ~ avec to get/be in contact with; ~ radio radio contact.

liane [ljan] nf creeper.

liant, e [ljɑ̃, -ɑ̃t] a sociable.

liasse [ljas] nf wad, bundle.

Liban [libɑ̃] nm: le ~ (the) Lebanon; libanais, e a, nm/f Lebanese.

libations [libasjɔ̃] nfpl libations.

libelle [libɛl] nm lampoon.

libeller [libele] vt (chèque, mandat): ~ (au nom de) to make out (to); (lettre) to word.

libellule [libelyl] *nf* dragonfly.

libéral, e, aux [liberal, -o] *a*, *nm/f* liberal; **~iser** *vt* to liberalize; **~isme** *nm* liberalism.

libéralité [liberalite] *nf* liberality *q*, generosity *q*.

libérateur, trice [liberatœr, -tris] *a* liberating // *nm/f* liberator.

libération [liberasjɔ̃] *nf* liberation, freeing; release; discharge.

libérer [libere] *vt* (*délivrer*) to free, liberate; (: *moralement*, PSYCH) to liberate; (*relâcher*) to release; to discharge; (*dégager: gaz, cran d'arrêt*) to release; **se ~** (*de rendez-vous*) to try and be free, get out of previous engagements; **~ qn de** to free sb from; (*promesse*) to release sb from.

libertaire [libɛrtɛr] *a* libertarian.

liberté [libɛrte] *nf* freedom; (*loisir*) free time; **~s** *nfpl* (*privautés*) liberties; **mettre/être en ~** to set/be free; **en ~ provisoire/surveillée/conditionnelle** on bail/ probation/parole; **~ d'esprit** independence of mind; **~ d'opinion** freedom of thought; **~ de réunion** right to hold meetings; **~s individuelles** personal freedom *sg*.

libertin, e [libɛrtɛ̃, -in] *a* libertine, licentious; **libertinage** *nm* licentiousness.

libidineux, euse [libidinø, -øz] *a* libidinous, lustful.

libido [libido] *nf* libido.

libraire [librɛr] *nm/f* bookseller.

librairie [libreri] *nf* bookshop.

libre [libr(ə)] *a* free; (*route*) clear; (*pas pris ou occupé: place etc*) vacant; empty; not engaged; not taken; (SCOL) private and Roman Catholic (*as opposed to 'laïque'*); **~ de qch/de faire** to be free from sth/ to do; **~-échange** *nm* free trade; **~ment** *ad* freely; **~-service** *nm* self-service store.

librettiste [libretist(ə)] *nm/f* librettist.

Libye [libi] *nf*: **la ~** Libya; **libyen, ne** *a*, *nm/f* Libyan.

licence [lisɑ̃s] *nf* (*permis*) permit; (*diplôme*) (first) degree; (*liberté*) liberty; licence; licentiousness; **licencié, e** *nm/f* (SCOL): **licencié ès lettres/en droit** ≈ Bachelor of Arts/Law; (SPORT) member of a sports federation.

licenciement [lisɑ̃simɑ̃] *nm* dismissal; laying off *q*; redundancy.

licencier [lisɑ̃sje] *vt* (*renvoyer*) to dismiss; (*débaucher*) to make redundant; to lay off.

licencieux, euse [lisɑ̃sjø, -øz] *a* licentious.

lichen [likɛn] *nm* lichen.

licite [lisit] *a* lawful.

licorne [likɔrn(ə)] *nf* unicorn.

licou [liku] *nm* halter.

lie [li] *nf* dregs *pl*, sediment.

lié, e [lje] *a*: **très ~ avec** very friendly with *ou* close to; **~ par** (*serment*) bound by.

liège [ljɛʒ] *nm* cork.

lien [ljɛ̃] *nm* (*corde, fig: affectif*) bond; (*rapport*) link, connection; **~ de parenté** family tie.

lier [lje] *vt* (*attacher*) to tie up; (*joindre*) to link up; (*fig: unir, engager*) to bind; (CULIN) to thicken; **~ qch à** to tie sth to;

to link sth to; **~ conversation avec** tó strike up a conversation with; **se ~ avec** to make friends with.

lierre [ljɛr] *nm* ivy.

liesse [ljɛs] *nf*: **être en ~** to be celebrating *ou* jubilant.

lieu, x [ljø] *nm* place // *nmpl* (*habitation*) premises; (*endroit: d'un accident etc*) scene *sg*; **en ~ sûr** in a safe place; **en premier ~** in the first place; **en dernier ~** lastly; **avoir ~** to take place; **avoir ~ de faire** to have grounds *ou* good reason for doing; **tenir ~ de** to take the place of; **to serve as**; **donner ~ à** to give rise to, give cause for; **au ~ de** instead of; **au ~ qu'il y ailie** instead of him going; **~ commun** commonplace; **~ géométrique** locus.

lieu-dit *nm*, *pl* **lieux-dits** [ljødi] locality.

lieue [ljø] *nf* league.

lieutenant [ljøtnɑ̃] *nm* lieutenant.

lièvre [ljɛvr(ə)] *nm* hare.

liftier [liftje] *nm* lift boy.

ligament [ligamɑ̃] *nm* ligament.

ligature [ligatyr] *nf* ligature; **ligaturer** *vt* to ligature.

lige [liʒ] *a*: **homme ~** (*péj*) henchman.

ligne [liɲ] *nf* (*gén*) line; (TRANSPORTS: *liaison*) service; (: *trajet*) route; (*silhouette féminine*): **garder la ~** to keep one's figure; **'à la ~'** 'new paragraph'; **entrer en ~ de compte** to be taken into account; to come into it; **~ de but/médiane** goal/halfway line; **~ d'horizon** skyline.

lignée [liɲe] *nf* line; lineage; descendants *pl*.

ligneux, euse [liɲø, -øz] *a* ligneous, woody.

lignite [liɲit] *nm* lignite.

ligoter [ligɔte] *vt* to tie up.

ligue [lig] *nf* league; **se liguer** *vi* to form a league; **se liguer contre** (*fig*) to combine against.

lilas [lila] *nm* lilac.

limace [limas] *nf* slug.

limaille [limaj] *nf*: **~ de fer** iron filings *pl*.

limande [limɑ̃d] *nf* dab.

lime [lim] *nf* file; **~ à ongles** nail file; **limer** *vt* to file (down); (*ongles*) to file; (*fig: prix*) to pare down, trim.

limier [limje] *nm* bloodhound; (*détective*) sleuth.

liminaire [liminɛr] *a* (*propos*) introductory.

limitation [limitɑsjɔ̃] *nf* limitation, restriction.

limite [limit] *nf* (*de terrain*) boundary; (*partie ou point extrême*) limit; **charge/vitesse ~** maximum speed/load; **cas ~** borderline case; **date ~** deadline.

limiter [limite] *vt* (*restreindre*) to limit, restrict; (*délimiter*) to border, form the boundary of.

limitrophe [limitrɔf] *a* border *cpd*; **~ de** bordering on.

limoger [limɔʒe] *vt* to dismiss.

limon [limɔ̃] *nm* silt.

limonade [limɔnad] *nf* (fizzy) lemonade.

limpide [lɛ̃pid] *a* limpid.

lin [lɛ̃] *nm* flax.

linceul [lɛ̃sœl] *nm* shroud.

linéaire [lineɛʀ] *a* linear.

linge [lɛ̃ʒ] *nm* (*serviettes etc*) linen ; (*pièce de tissu*) cloth ; (*aussi*: ~ **de corps**) underwear ; (*aussi*: ~ **de toilette**) towel ; (*lessive*) washing ; ~ **sale** dirty linen.

lingerie [lɛ̃ʒʀi] *nf* lingerie, underwear.

lingot [lɛ̃go] *nm* ingot.

linguiste [lɛ̃gɥist(ə)] *nm/f* linguist.

linguistique [lɛ̃gɥistik] *a* linguistic // *nf* linguistics *sg*.

lino(léum) [lino(leɔm)] *nm* lino(leum).

lion, ne [ljɔ̃, ljɔn] *nm/f* lion/lioness ; (*signe*): **le L~** Leo, the Lion ; **être du L~** to be Leo ; **lionceau, x** *nm* lion cub.

lippu, e [lipy] *a* thick-lipped.

liquéfier [likefje] *vt*, **se** ~ *vi* to liquefy.

liqueur [likœʀ] *nf* liqueur.

liquidation [likidasjɔ̃] *nf* liquidation ; (*COMM*) clearance (sale).

liquide [likid] *a* liquid // *nm* liquid ; (*COMM*): **en** ~ in ready money *ou* cash.

liquider [likide] *vt* (*société, biens, témoin gênant*) to liquidate ; (*compte, problème*) to settle ; (*COMM*: articles) to clear, sell off.

liquidités [likidite] *nfpl* (*COMM*) liquid assets.

liquoreux, euse [likɔʀø, -øz] *a* syrupy.

lire [liʀ] *nf* (*monnaie*) lira // *vt, vi* to read ; ~ **qch à qn** to read sth (out) to sb.

lis *vb* [li] *voir* **lire** // *nm* [lis] = **lys**.

liseré [lizʀe] *nm* border, edging.

liseron [lizʀɔ̃] *nm* bindweed.

liseuse [lizøz] *nf* book-cover.

lisible [lizibl(ə)] *a* legible.

lisière [lizjɛʀ] *nf* (*de forêt*) edge ; (*de tissu*) selvage.

lisons *vb voir* **lire**.

lisse [lis] *a* smooth ; **lisser** *vt* to smooth.

liste [list(ə)] *nf* list ; **faire la** ~ **de** to list, make out a list of ; ~ **électorale** electoral roll.

lit [li] *nm* (*gén*) bed ; **faire son** ~ to make one's bed ; **aller/se mettre au** ~ to go to/get into bed ; **prendre le** ~ to take to one's bed ; **d'un premier** ~ (*JUR*) of a first marriage ; ~ **de camp** campbed.

litanie [litani] *nf* litany.

literie [litʀi] *nf* bedding ; bedclothes *pl*.

lithographie [litɔgʀafi] *nf* lithography ; (*épreuve*) lithograph.

litière [litjɛʀ] *nf* litter.

litige [litiʒ] *nm* dispute ; **litigieux, euse** *a* litigious, contentious.

litre [litʀ(ə)] *nm* litre ; (*récipient*) litre measure.

littéraire [liteʀɛʀ] *a* literary.

littéral, e, aux [liteʀal, -o] *a* literal.

littérature [liteʀatyʀ] *nf* literature.

littoral, e, aux [litɔʀal, -o] *a* coastal // *nm* coast.

liturgie [lityʀʒi] *nf* liturgy ; **liturgique** *a* liturgical.

livide [livid] *a* livid, pallid.

livraison [livʀɛzɔ̃] *nf* delivery.

livre [livʀ(ə)] *nm* book // *nf* (*poids, monnaie*) pound ; ~ **de bord** logbook ; ~ **d'or** visitors' book ; ~ **de poche** paperback (*cheap and pocket size*).

livré, e [livʀe] *a*: ~ **à soi-même** left to o.s. *ou* one's own devices // *nf* livery.

livrer [livʀe] *vt* (*COMM*) to deliver ; (*otage, coupable*) to hand over ; (*secret, information*) to give away ; **se** ~ **à** (*se confier*) to confide in ; (*se rendre*) to give o.s. up to ; (*s'abandonner à: débauche etc*) to give o.s. up *ou* over to ; (*faire: pratiques, actes*) to indulge in ; (: *travail*) to be engaged in, engage in ; (: *sport*) to practise ; (: *enquête*) to carry out ; ~ **bataille** to give battle.

livresque [livʀɛsk(ə)] *a* bookish.

livret [livʀɛ] *nm* booklet ; (*d'opéra*) libretto (*pl s*) ; ~ **de caisse d'épargne** (savings) bank-book ; ~ **de famille** (official) family record book ; ~ **scolaire** (school) report book.

livreur, euse [livʀœʀ, -øz] *nm/f* delivery boy *ou* man/girl *ou* woman.

lobe [lɔb] *nm*: ~ **de l'oreille** ear lobe.

lobé, e [lɔbe] *a* (*ARCHIT*) foiled.

lober [lɔbe] *vt* to lob.

local, e, aux [lɔkal, -o] *a* local // *nm* (*salle*) premises *pl* // *nmpl* premises.

localiser [lɔkalize] *vt* (*repérer*) to locate, place ; (*limiter*) to localize, confine.

localité [lɔkalite] *nf* locality.

locataire [lɔkatɛʀ] *nm/f* tenant ; (*de chambre*) lodger.

locatif, ive [lɔkatif, -iv] *a* (*charges, réparations*) incumbent upon the tenant ; (*valeur*) rental ; (*immeuble*) with rented flats, used as a letting concern.

location [lɔkasjɔ̃] *nf* (*par le locataire*) renting ; (*par l'usager: de voiture etc*) hiring ; (*par le propriétaire*) renting out, letting ; hiring out ; '~ **de voitures**' 'car hire *ou* rental' ; ~**-vente** *nf* form of hire purchase for housing.

lock-out [lɔkawt] *nm inv* lockout.

locomotion [lɔkɔmosjɔ̃] *nf* locomotion.

locomotive [lɔkɔmɔtiv] *nf* locomotive, engine ; (*fig*) pacesetter, pacemaker.

locution [lɔkysjɔ̃] *nf* phrase, locution.

logarithme [lɔgaʀitm(ə)] *nm* logarithm.

loge [lɔʒ] *nf* (*THÉÂTRE: d'artiste*) dressing room ; (: *de spectateurs*) box ; (*de concierge, franc-maçon*) lodge.

logement [lɔʒmɑ̃] *nm* accommodation *q*, flat ; housing *q* ; **chercher un** ~ to look for a flat *ou* for accommodation ; **construire des** ~**s** **bon marché** to build cheap housing *sg ou* flats ; **crise du** ~ housing shortage.

loger [lɔʒe] *vt* to accommodate // *vi* to live ; **se** ~: **trouver à se** ~ to find accommodation ; **se** ~ **dans** (*suj: balle, flèche*) to lodge itself in ; **logeur, euse** *nm/f* landlord/landlady.

loggia [lɔdʒja] *nf* loggia.

logiciel [lɔʒisjɛl] *nm* software.

logique [lɔʒik] *a* logical // *nf* logic ; ~**ment** *ad* logically.

logis [lɔʒi] *nm* home ; abode, dwelling.

logistique [lɔʒistik] *nf* logistics *sg*.

loi [lwa] *nf* law ; **faire la** ~ to lay down the law.

loin [lwɛ̃] *ad* far ; (*dans le temps*) a long way off ; a long time ago ; **plus** ~ further ; **moins** ~ (que) not as far (as) ; ~ **de far**

from; **pas ~ de 1000 F** not far off a 1000 F; **au ~ far off**; **de ~** ad from a distance; *(fig: de beaucoup)* by far; **il vient de ~** he's come a long way; he comes from a long way away.

lointain, e [lwɛ̃tɛ̃, -ɛn] a faraway, distant; *(dans le futur, passé)* distant, far-off; *(cause, parent)* remote, distant // nm: **dans le ~** in the distance.

loir [lwaʀ] nm dormouse *(pl mice).*

loisir [lwaziʀ] nm: **heures de ~** spare time; **~s** nmpl leisure sg; leisure activities; **avoir le ~ de faire** to have the time ou opportunity to do; **à ~** at leisure; at one's pleasure.

londonien, ne [lɔ̃dɔnjɛ̃, -jɛn] a London cpd, of London // nm/f: **L~, ne** Londoner.

Londres [lɔ̃dʀ(ə)] n London.

long, longue [lɔ̃, lɔ̃g] a long // ad: **en savoir ~** to know a great deal // nm: **de 3 m de ~** 3 m long, 3 m in length // nf: **à la longue** in the end; **faire ~ feu** to fizzle out; **ne pas faire ~ feu** not to last long; **du ~ cours** *(NAVIG)* ocean cpd, ocean-going; **être ~ à faire** to take a long time to do; **en ~** ad lengthwise; **(tout) le ~ de** (all) along; **tout au ~ de** *(année, vie)* throughout; **de ~ en large** *(marcher)* to and fro, up and down.

longanimité [lɔ̃ganimite] nf forbearance.

longe [lɔ̃ʒ] nf *(corde)* tether; lead; *(CULIN)* loin.

longer [lɔ̃ʒe] vt to go *(ou* walk *ou* drive) along(side); *(suj: mur, route)* to border.

longévité [lɔ̃ʒevite] nf longevity.

longiligne [lɔ̃ʒiliɲ] a long-limbed.

longitude [lɔ̃ʒityd] nf longitude; **à 45° de ~ ouest** at 45° longitude west.

longitudinal, e, aux [lɔ̃ʒitydinal, -o] a longitudinal, lengthways; running lengthways.

longtemps [lɔ̃tɑ̃] ad (for) a long time, (for) long; **avant ~** before long; **pour/pendant ~** for a long time/long; **mettre ~ à faire** to take a long time to do.

longue [lɔ̃g] af voir **long**; **~ment** ad for a long time, at length.

longueur [lɔ̃gœʀ] nf length; **~s** nfpl *(fig: d'un roman etc)* lengthy ou drawn-out parts; **sur une ~ de 10 km** for ou over 10 km; **en ~** ad lengthwise; **tirer en ~** to drag on; **à ~ de journée** all day long; **~ d'onde** wavelength.

longue-vue [lɔ̃gvy] nf telescope.

lopin [lɔpɛ̃] nm: **~ de terre** patch of land.

loquace [lɔkas] a loquacious, talkative.

loque [lɔk] nf *(personne)* wreck; **~s** nfpl *(habits)* rags.

loquet [lɔkɛ] nm latch.

lorgner [lɔʀɲe] vt to eye; to have one's eye on.

lorgnon [lɔʀɲɔ̃] nm lorgnette.

loriot [lɔʀjo] nm *(golden)* oriole.

lors [lɔʀ]: **~ de** prép at the time of; during; **~ même que** even though.

lorsque [lɔʀsk(ə)] cj when, as.

losange [lɔzɑ̃ʒ] nm diamond; *(GÉOM)* lozenge; **en ~** diamond-shaped.

lot [lo] nm *(part)* share; *(de loterie)* prize; *(fig: destin)* fate, lot.

loterie [lɔtʀi] nf lottery; raffle.

loti, e [lɔti] a: **bien/mal ~** well-/badly off *(as regards luck, circumstances).*

lotion [losjɔ̃] nf lotion.

lotir [lɔtiʀ] vt *(terrain)* to divide into plots; to sell by lots; **lotissement** nm housing development; plot, lot.

loto [lɔto] nm lotto; numerical lottery.

louable [lwabl(ə)] a praiseworthy, commendable.

louage [lwaʒ] nm: **voiture de ~** hired car; hire car.

louange [lwɑ̃ʒ] nf: **à la ~ de** in praise of; **~s** nfpl praise sg.

louche [luʃ] a shady, fishy, dubious // nf ladle.

loucher [luʃe] vi to squint; *(fig)*: **~ sur** to have one's eye on.

louer [lwe] vt *(maison: suj: propriétaire)* to let, rent (out); *(: locataire)* to rent; *(voiture etc)* to hire out, rent (out); to hire, rent; *(réserver)* to book; *(faire l'éloge de)* to praise; **'à louer'** 'to let'; **~ qn de** to praise sb for; **se ~ de** to congratulate o.s. on.

loufoque [lufɔk] a crazy, zany.

loulou [lulu] nm *(chien)* spitz.

loup [lu] nm wolf *(pl* wolves); **~ de mer** *(marin)* old seadog.

loupe [lup] nf magnifying glass; **~ de noyer** burr walnut.

louper [lupe] vt *(manquer)* to miss; *(gâcher)* to mess up, bungle.

lourd, e [luʀ, luʀd(ə)] a, ad heavy; **~ de** *(conséquences, menaces)* charged ou fraught with; **lourdaud, e** a *(péj)* clumsy; oafish; **lourdement** ad heavily; **lourdeur** nf heaviness; **lourdeur d'estomac** indigestion q.

loutre [lutʀ(ə)] nf otter.

louve [luv] nf she-wolf.

louveteau, x [luvto] nm wolf-cub; *(scout)* cub.

louvoyer [luvwaje] vi *(NAVIG)* to tack; *(fig)* to hedge, evade the issue.

lover [lɔve]: **se ~** vi to coil up.

loyal, e, aux [lwajal, -o] a *(fidèle)* loyal, faithful; *(fair-play)* fair; **loyauté** nf loyalty, faithfulness; fairness.

loyer [lwaje] nm rent.

lu, e [ly] pp de **lire**.

lubie [lybi] nf whim, craze.

lubrifiant [lybʀifjɑ̃] nm lubricant.

lubrifier [lybʀifje] vt to lubricate.

lubrique [lybʀik] a lecherous.

lucarne [lykaʀn(ə)] nf skylight.

lucide [lysid] a *(conscient)* lucid, conscious; *(perspicace)* clear-headed; lucid; **lucidité** nf lucidity.

luciole [lysjɔl] nf firefly.

lucratif, ive [lykʀatif, -iv] a lucrative; profitable; **à but non ~** non profit-making.

luette [lɥɛt] nf uvula.

lueur [lɥœʀ] nf *(chatoyante)* glimmer q; *(métallique, mouillée)* gleam q; *(rougeoyante, chaude)* glow q; *(pâle)* (faint) light; *(fig)* glimmer; gleam.

luge [lyʒ] nf sledge.

lugubre [lygybʀ(ə)] a gloomy; dismal.

lui [lчi] *pronom (chose, animal)* it; *(personne: mâle)* him; (: *en sujet)* he; (: *femelle)* her; *voir note sous* il; ~-**même** himself; itself.

luire [lчiʀ] *vi* to shine; to glow; to gleam.

lumbago [lɔbago] *nm* lumbago.

lumière [lymjɛʀ] *nf* light; ~**s** *nfpl (d'une personne)* knowledge *sg*, wisdom *sg*; à la ~ **de** by the light of; *(fig)* in the light of; **fais de la** ~ let's have some light, give us some light; **mettre en** ~ *(fig)* to bring out *ou* to light; ~ **du jour/soleil** day/sunlight.

luminaire [lyminɛʀ] *nm* lamp, light.

lumineux, euse [lyminé, -éz] *a (émettant de la lumière)* luminous; *(éclairé)* illuminated; *(ciel, journée, couleur)* bright; *(relatif à la lumière: rayon etc)* of light, light *cpd*; *(fig: regard)* radiant; **luminosité** *nf (TECH)* luminosity.

lunaire [lynɛʀ] *a* lunar, moon *cpd*.

lunatique [lynatik] *a* whimsical, temperamental.

lunch [lœntʃ] *nm (réception)* buffet lunch.

lundi [lœdi] *nm* Monday; ~ **de Pâques** Easter Monday.

lune [lyn] *nf* moon; ~ **de miel** honeymoon.

luné, e [lyne] *a*: **bien/mal** ~ in a good/bad mood.

lunette [lynɛt] *nf*: ~**s** *nfpl* glasses, spectacles; *(protectrices)* goggles; ~ **d'approche** telescope; ~ **arrière** *(AUTO)* rear window; ~**s noires** dark glasses; ~**s de soleil** sunglasses.

lurette [lyʀɛt] *nf*: **il y a belle** ~ ages ago.

luron, ne [lyʀɔ̃, -ɔn] *nm/f* lad/lass; **joyeux** *ou* **gai** ~ gay dog.

lus *etc vb voir* **lire**.

lustre [lystʀ(ə)] *nm (de plafond)* chandelier; *(fig: éclat)* lustre.

lustrer [lystʀe] *vt (faire briller)* to lustre; *(poil d'un animal)* to put a sheen on; *(user)* to make shiny.

lut *vb voir* **lire**.

luth [lyt] *nm* lute; **luthier** *nm* (stringed-)instrument maker.

lutin [lytɛ̃] *nm* imp, goblin.

lutrin [lytʀɛ̃] *nm* lectern.

lutte [lyt] *nf (conflit)* struggle; *(sport)* wrestling; **lutter** *vi* to fight, struggle; to wrestle; **lutteur** *nm* wrestler; *(fig)* battler, fighter.

luxation [lyksasjɔ̃] *nf* dislocation.

luxe [lyks(ə)] *nm* luxury; **de** ~ *a* luxury *cpd*.

Luxembourg [lyksɑ̃buʀ] *nm*: **le** ~ Luxemburg.

luxer [lykse] *vt*: **se** ~ **l'épaule** to dislocate one's shoulder.

luxueux, euse [lyksцé, -éz] *a* luxurious.

luxure [lyksyʀ] *nf* lust.

luxuriant, e [lyksyʀjɑ̃, -ɑ̃t] *a* luxuriant, lush.

luzerne [lyzɛʀn(ə)] *nf* lucerne, alfalfa.

lycée [lise] *nm* (state) secondary school; **lycéen, ne** *nm/f* secondary school pupil.

lymphatique [lɛ̃fatik] *a (fig)* lethargic, sluggish.

lymphe [lɛ̃f] *nf* lymph.

lyncher [lɛ̃ʃe] *vt* to lynch.

lynx [lɛ̃ks] *nm* lynx.

lyophilisé, e [ljɔfilize] *a* freeze-dried.

lyre [liʀ] *nf* lyre.

lyrique [liʀik] *a* lyrical; *(OPÉRA)* lyric; **comédie** ~ comic opera; **théâtre** ~ opera house *(for light opera)*; **lyrisme** *nm* lyricism.

lys [lis] *nm* lily.

M

m' [m] *pronom voir* **me**.

M. [ɛm] *abr de* **Monsieur**.

ma [ma] *dét voir* **mon**.

maboul, e [mabul] *a (fam)* loony.

macabre [makɑbʀ(ə)] *a* macabre, gruesome.

macadam [makadam] *nm* tarmac.

macaron [makaʀɔ̃] *nm (gâteau)* macaroon; *(insigne)* (round) badge.

macaronis [makaʀɔni] *nmpl* macaroni *sg*.

macédoine [masedwan] *nf*: ~ **de fruits** fruit salad.

macérer [maseʀe] *vi, vt* to macerate; *(dans du vinaigre)* to pickle.

mâchefer [maʃfɛʀ] *nm* clinker, cinders *pl*.

mâcher [maʃe] *vt* to chew; **ne pas** ~ **ses mots** not to mince one's words.

machin [maʃɛ̃] *nm (fam)* thingummy, whatsit; contraption, thing.

machinal, e, aux [maʃinal, -o] *a* mechanical, automatic.

machination [maʃinasjɔ̃] *nf* scheming, frame-up.

machine [maʃin] *nf* machine; *(locomotive)* engine; *(fig: rouages)* machinery; **faire** ~ **arrière** *(NAVIG)* to go astern; ~ **à laver/coudre/tricoter** washing/sewing/knitting machine; ~ **à écrire** typewriter; ~ **à sous** fruit machine; ~ **à vapeur** steam engine; ~-**outil** *nf* machine tool; ~**rie** *nf* machinery, plant; *(d'un navire)* engine room; **machinisme** *nm* mechanization; **machiniste** *nm (THÉÂTRE)* scene shifter; *(de bus, métro)* driver.

mâchoire [maʃwaʀ] *nf* jaw; ~ **de frein** brake shoe.

mâchonner [maʃɔne] *vt* to chew (at).

maçon [masɔ̃] *nm* bricklayer; builder.

maçonner [masɔne] *vt (revêtir)* to face, render (with cement); *(boucher)* to brick up.

maçonnerie [masɔnʀi] *nf (murs)* brickwork; masonry, stonework; *(activité)* bricklaying; building.

maçonnique [masɔnik] *a* masonic.

maculer [makyle] *vt* to stain; *(TYPO)* to mackle.

Madame [madam], *pl* **Mesdames** [medam] *nf*: ~ X Mrs ['misiz] X; **occupez-vous de** ~/**Monsieur**/ **Mademoiselle** please serve this lady/gentleman/(young) lady; **bonjour** ~/**Monsieur**/**Mademoiselle** good morning; *(ton déférent)* good morning Madam/Sir/Madam; *(le nom est connu)* good morning Mrs/Mr/Miss X; ~/**Monsieur**/ **Mademoiselle!** *(pour appeler)* Madam/Sir/Miss! ~/**Monsieur**/**Mademoiselle** *(sur lettre)* Dear Madam/Sir/Madam; **chère** ~/**cher**

Monsieur/chère **Mademoiselle** Dear Mrs/Mr/Miss X.

Mademoiselle [madmwazɛl], pl **Mesdemoiselles** [medmwazɛl] nf Miss; voir aussi Madame.

madère [madɛʀ] nm Madeira (wine).

madone [madɔn] nf madonna.

madré, e [madʀe] a crafty, wily.

madrier [madʀije] nm beam.

madrilène [madʀilɛn] a of ou from Madrid.

maestria [maɛstʀija] nf (masterly) skill.

maf(f)ia [mafja] nf Maf(f)ia.

magasin [magazɛ̃] nm (boutique) shop; (entrepôt) warehouse; (d'une arme) magazine; en ~ (COMM) in stock; **magasinier** nm warehouseman.

magazine [magazin] nm magazine.

mage [maʒ] nm: **les Rois M~s** the Magi, the (Three) Wise Men.

magicien, ne [maʒisjɛ̃, -jɛn] nm/f magician.

magie [maʒi] nf magic; **magique** a magic; (enchanteur) magical.

magistral, e, aux [maʒistʀal, -o] a (œuvre, adresse) masterly; (ton) authoritative; (gifle etc) sound, resounding; (ex cathedra): **enseignement ~** lecturing, lectures pl.

magistrat [maʒistʀa] nm magistrate.

magistrature [maʒistʀatyʀ] nf magistracy, magistrature.

magma [magma] nm (GÉO) magma; (fig) jumble.

magnanerie [maɲanʀi] nf silk farm.

magnanime [maɲanim] a magnanimous.

magnat [magna] nm tycoon, magnate.

magnésie [maɲezi] nf magnesia.

magnésium [maɲezjɔm] nm magnesium.

magnétique [maɲetik] a magnetic.

magnétiser [maɲetize] vt to magnetize; (fig) to mesmerize, hypnotize.

magnétisme [maɲetism(ə)] nm magnetism.

magnéto [maɲeto] nf (ÉLEC) magneto.

magnétophone [maɲetɔfɔn] nm tape recorder; ~ **à cassettes** cassette recorder.

magnétoscope [maɲetɔskɔp] nm video-tape recorder.

magnificence [maɲifisɑ̃s] nf (faste) magnificence, splendour.

magnifique [maɲifik] a magnificent.

magnolia [maɲɔlja] nm magnolia.

magnum [magnɔm] nm magnum.

magot [mago] nm (argent) pile (of money); nest egg.

mahométan, e [maɔmetɑ̃, -an] a Mohammedan, Mahometan.

mai [mɛ] nm May.

maigre [mɛgʀ(ə)] a (very) thin, skinny; (viande) lean; (fromage) low-fat; (végétation) thin, sparse; (fig) poor, meagre, skimpy // ad: **faire ~** not to eat meat; **jours ~s** days of abstinence, fish days; **maigreur** nf thinness; **maigrir** vi to get thinner, lose weight.

maille [maj] nf stitch; **avoir ~ à partir avec qn** to have a brush with sb.

maillet [majɛ] nm mallet.

maillon [majɔ̃] nm link.

maillot [majo] nm (aussi: ~ **de corps**) vest; (de danseur) leotard; (de sportif) jersey; ~ **de bain** bathing costume, swimsuit; (d'homme) bathing trunks pl.

main [mɛ̃] nf hand; **à la ~** in one's hand; **se donner la ~** to hold hands; **donner ou tendre la ~ à qn** to hold out one's hand to sb; **se serrer la ~** to shake hands; **serrer la ~ à qn** to shake hands with sb; **sous la ~** to ou at hand; **à ~ levée** (ART) freehand; **à ~s levées** (voter) with a show of hands; **attaque à ~ armée** armed attack; **à ~ droite/gauche** to the right/left; **à remettre en ~s propres** to be delivered personally; **de première ~** (renseignement) first-hand; (COMM: voiture etc) second-hand with only one previous owner; **faire ~ basse sur** to help o.s. to; **mettre la dernière ~ à** to put the finishing touches to; **se faire/perdre la ~** to get one's hand in/lose one's touch; ~ **courante** handrail.

mainate [mɛnat] nm myna(h) bird.

main-d'œuvre [mɛ̃dœvʀ(ə)] nf manpower, labour.

main-forte [mɛ̃fɔʀt(ə)] nf: **prêter ~ à qn** to come to sb's assistance.

mainmise [mɛ̃miz] nf seizure; (fig): ~ **sur** complete hold on.

maint, e [mɛ̃, mɛ̃t] a many a; ~**s** many; **à ~es reprises** time and (time) again.

maintenant [mɛ̃tnɑ̃] ad now; (actuellement) nowadays.

maintenir [mɛ̃tniʀ] vt (retenir, soutenir) to support; (contenir: foule etc) to keep in check, hold back; (conserver) to maintain, uphold; (affirmer) to maintain; **se** ~ vi to hold; to keep steady; to persist.

maintien [mɛ̃tjɛ̃] nm maintaining, upholding; (attitude) bearing.

maire [mɛʀ] nm mayor.

mairie [meʀi] nf (résidence) town hall; (administration) town council.

mais [mɛ] cj but; ~ **non!** of course not!; ~ **enfin** but after all; (indignation) look here!

maïs [mais] nm maize.

maison [mɛzɔ̃] nf house; (chez-soi) home; (COMM) firm // a inv (CULIN) home-made; made by the chef; (fig) in-house, own; (fam) first-rate; **à la ~** at home; (direction) home; ~ **d'arrêt** ≈ remand home; ~ **close** brothel; ~ **de correction** reformatory; ~ **des jeunes** ≈ youth club; ~ **mère** parent company; ~ **de repos** convalescent home; ~ **de retraite** old people's home; ~ **de santé** mental home; **maisonnée** nf household, family; **maisonnette** nf small house, cottage.

maitre, esse [mɛtʀ(ə), mɛtʀɛs] nm/f master/mistress; (SCOL) teacher, schoolmaster/mistress // nm (peintre etc) master; (titre): **M~ (Me) Maitre**, term of address gen for a barrister // nf (amante) mistress // a (principal, essentiel) main; **être ~ de** (soi-même, situation) to be in control of; **se rendre ~ de** (pays, ville) to gain control of; (situation, incendie) to bring under control; **une maitresse femme** a managing woman; ~ **d'armes** fencing master; ~ **chanteur** blackmailer;

~ de chapelle choirmaster; ~ de conférences ≈ senior lecturer; ~/maîtresse d'école teacher, schoolmaster/ mistress; ~ d'hôtel (domestique) butler; (d'hôtel) head waiter; ~ de maison host; ~ nageur lifeguard; ~ à penser intellectual leader; ~ queux chef; maîtresse de maison hostess; housewife (pl wives); ~-autel nm high altar.

maîtrise [metriz] nf (aussi: ~ de soi) self-control, self-possession; (habileté) skill, mastery; (suprématie) mastery, command; (diplôme) ≈ master's degree.

maîtriser [metrize] vt (cheval, incendie) to (bring under) control; (sujet) to master; (émotion) to control, master; se ~ vt réfléchi to control o.s.

majesté [maʒeste] nf majesty.

majestueux, euse [maʒestɥø, -øz] a majestic.

majeur, e [maʒœr] a (important) major; (JUR) of age; (fig) adult // nm/f person who has come of age ou attained his/her majority // nm (doigt) middle finger; en ~e partie for the most part.

major [maʒɔr] nm (SCOL): ~ de la promotion first of one's year.

majordome [maʒɔrdɔm] nm majordomo.

majorer [maʒɔre] vt to increase.

majorette [maʒɔrɛt] nf majorette.

majoritaire [maʒɔritɛr] a majority cpd: système/scrutin ~ majority system/ ballot.

majorité [maʒɔrite] nf (gén) majority; (parti) party in power; en ~ mainly.

majuscule [maʒyskyl] a, nf: (lettre) ~ capital (letter).

mal, maux [mal, mo] nm (opposé au bien) evil; (tort, dommage) harm; (douleur physique) pain, ache; (maladie) illness, sickness q // ad badly // a: c'est ~ (de faire) it's bad ou wrong (to do); être ~ to be uncomfortable; être ~ avec qn to be on bad terms with sb; il comprend ~ he has difficulty in understanding; il a ~ compris he misunderstood; dire du ~ de to speak ill of; ne voir aucun ~ à to see no harm in, see nothing wrong in; craignant ~ faire fearing he was doing the wrong thing; faire du ~ à qn to hurt sb; to harm sb; se faire ~ to hurt o.s.; se faire ~ au pied to hurt one's foot; ça fait ~ it hurts; j'ai ~ (ici) it hurts (here); j'ai ~ au dos my back aches, I've got a pain in my back; avoir ~ à la tête/aux dents/au cœur to have a headache/have toothache/feel sick; avoir le ~ de l'air to be airsick; avoir le ~ du pays to be homesick; prendre ~ to be taken ill, feel unwell; ~ de mer seasickness; ~ en point a inv in a bad state; maux de ventre stomach ache sg.

malade [malad] a ill, sick; (poitrine, jambe) bad; (plante) diseased // nm/f invalid, sick person; (à l'hôpital etc) patient; tomber ~ to fall ill; être ~ du cœur to have heart trouble ou a bad heart; ~ mental mentally sick ou ill person.

maladie [maladi] nf (spécifique) disease, illness; (mauvaise santé) illness, sickness; (fig: manie) mania; ~ de peau skin disease; maladif, ive a sickly; (curiosité, besoin) pathological.

maladresse [maladrɛs] nf clumsiness q; (gaffe) blunder.

maladroit, e [maladrwa, -wat] a clumsy.

malaise [malɛz] nm (MÉD) feeling of faintness; feeling of discomfort; (fig) uneasiness, malaise.

malaisé, e [maleze] a difficult.

malappris, e [malapri, -iz] nm/f ill-mannered ou boorish person.

malaria [malarja] nf malaria.

malavisé, e [malavize] a ill-advised, unwise.

malaxer [malakse] vt to knead; to mix.

malchance [malʃɑ̃s] nf misfortune, ill luck q; par ~ unfortunately; malchanceux, euse a unlucky.

malcommode [malkɔmɔd] a impractical, inconvenient.

maldonne [maldɔn] nf (CARTES) misdeal; il y a ~ (fig) there's been a misunderstanding.

mâle [mal] a (aussi ELEC, TECH) male; (viril: voix, traits) manly // nm male; souris ~ male mouse, he-mouse.

malédiction [malediksjɔ̃] nf curse.

maléfice [malefis] nm evil spell.

maléfique [malefik] a evil, baleful.

malencontreux, euse [malɑ̃kɔ̃trø, -øz] a unfortunate, untoward.

malentendu [malɑ̃tɑ̃dy] nm misunderstanding.

malfaçon [malfasɔ̃] nf fault.

malfaisant, e [malfəzɑ̃, -ɑ̃t] a evil, harmful.

malfaiteur [malfɛtœr] nm lawbreaker, criminal; burglar, thief (pl thieves).

malfamé, e [malfame] a disreputable, of ill repute.

malformation [malfɔrmasjɔ̃] nf malformation.

malfrat [malfra] nm villain, crook.

malgache [malgaʃ] a, nm/f Madagascan, Malagasy // nm (langue) Malagasy.

malgré [malgre] prép in spite of, despite; ~ tout ad all the same.

malhabile [malabil] a clumsy.

malheur [malœr] nm (situation) adversity, misfortune; (événement) misfortune; disaster, tragedy; malheureux, euse a (triste) unhappy, miserable; (infortuné, regrettable) unfortunate; (malchanceux) unlucky; (insignifiant) wretched // nm/f poor soul; unfortunate creature; les malheureux the destitute.

malhonnête [malɔnɛt] a dishonest; (impoli) rude; ~té nf dishonesty; rudeness q.

malice [malis] nf mischievousness; (méchanceté) par ~ out of malice ou spite; sans ~ guileless; malicieux, euse a mischievous.

malin, igne [malɛ̃, -iɲ] a (futé: f gén: maline) smart, shrewd; (MÉD) malignant; faire le ~ to show off; éprouver un ~ plaisir à to take malicious pleasure in.

malingre [malɛ̃gr(ə)] a puny.

malle [mal] nf trunk.

malléable [maleabl(ə)] a malleable.

malle-poste [malpɔst(ə)] nf mail coach.
mallette [malɛt] nf (small) suitcase ;
overnight case ; attaché case.
malmener [malməne] vt to manhandle ;
(fig) to give a rough handling to.
malodorant, e [malɔdɔrɑ̃, -ɑ̃t] a foul- ou
ill-smelling.
malotru [malɔtry] nm lout, boor.
malpoli, e [malpɔli] nm/f rude individual.
malpropre [malprɔpr(ə)] a dirty.
malsain, e [malsɛ̃, -ɛn] a unhealthy.
malséant, e [malseɑ̃, -ɑ̃t] a unseemly,
unbecoming.
malsonnant, e [malsɔnɑ̃, -ɑ̃t] a offensive.
malt [malt] nm malt.
maltais, e [maltɛ, -ɛz] a, nm/f Maltese.
Malte [malt(ə)] nf Malta.
maltraiter [maltrete] vt (brutaliser) to
manhandle, ill-treat.
malveillance [malvɛjɑ̃s] nf (animosité) ill
will ; (intention de nuire) malevolence ; (JUR)
malicious intent q.
malveillant, e [malvɛjɑ̃, -ɑ̃t] a
malevolent, malicious.
malversation [malvɛrsɑsjɔ̃] nf
embezzlement, misappropriation (of
funds).
maman [mamɑ̃] nf mum, mother.
mamelle [mamɛl] nf teat.
mamelon [mamlɔ̃] nm (ANAT) nipple ;
(colline) knoll, hillock.
mammifère [mamifɛr] nm mammal.
mammouth [mamut] nm mammoth.
manche [mɑ̃ʃ] nf (de vêtement) sleeve ;
(d'un jeu, tournoi) round ; (GÉO): la M ~
the Channel // nm (d'outil, casserole)
handle ; (de pelle, pioche etc) shaft ; (de
violon, guitare) neck ; (fam) clumsy oaf ; ~
à air nf (AVIAT) wind-sock ; ~ à balai nm
broomstick ; (AVIAT) joystick.
manchette [mɑ̃ʃɛt] nf (de chemise) cuff ;
(coup) forearm blow ; (titre) headline.
manchon [mɑ̃ʃɔ̃] nm (de fourrure) muff ;
~ à incandescence incandescent (gas)
mantle.
manchot [mɑ̃ʃo] nm one-armed man ;
armless man ; (ZOOL) penguin.
mandarine [mɑ̃darin] nf mandarin
(orange), tangerine.
mandat [mɑ̃da] nm (postal) postal ou
money order ; (d'un député etc) mandate ;
(procuration) power of attorney, proxy ;
(POLICE) warrant ; ~ d'amener summons
sg ; ~ d'arrêt warrant for arrest ; ~ de
dépôt committal order ; **mandataire** nm/f
representative ; proxy.
mander [mɑ̃de] vt to summon.
mandibule [mɑ̃dibyl] nf mandible.
mandoline [mɑ̃dɔlin] nf mandolin(e).
manège [manɛʒ] nm riding school ; (à la
foire) roundabout, merry-go-round ; (fig)
game, ploy.
manette [manɛt] nf lever, tap.
manganèse [mɑ̃ganɛz] nm manganese.
mangeable [mɑ̃ʒabl(ə)] a edible, eatable.
mangeaille [mɑ̃ʒaj] nf (péj) grub.
mangeoire [mɑ̃ʒwar] nf trough, manger.
manger [mɑ̃ʒe] vt to eat ; (ronger: suj:
rouille etc) to eat into ou away // vi to
eat ; **mangeur, euse** nm/f eater.

mangouste [mɑ̃gust(ə)] nf mongoose.
mangue [mɑ̃g] nf mango.
maniable [manjabl(ə)] a (outil) handy ;
(voiture, voilier) easy to handle.
maniaque [manjak] a finicky, fussy ;
suffering from a mania // nm/f maniac.
manie [mani] nf mania ; (tic) odd habit.
maniement [manimɑ̃] nm handling ; ~
d'armes arms drill.
manier [manje] vt to handle.
manière [manjɛr] nf (façon) way,
manner ; ~s nfpl (attitude) manners ;
(chichis) fuss sg ; de ~ à so as to ; de telle
~ que in such a way that ; de cette ~
in this way ou manner ; d'une ~ générale
generally speaking, as a general rule ; de
toute ~ in any case ; **adverbe de** ~
adverb of manner.
maniéré, e [manjere] a affected.
manif [manif] nf demo (pl s).
manifestant, e [manifɛstɑ̃, -ɑ̃t] nm/f
demonstrator.
manifestation [manifɛstɑsjɔ̃] nf (de joie,
mécontentement) expression, demonstration ; (symptôme) outward sign ; (fête etc)
event ; (POL) demonstration.
manifeste [manifɛst(ə)] a obvious,
evident // nm manifesto (pl s).
manifester [manifɛste] vt (volonté,
intentions) to show, indicate ; (joie, peur)
to express, show // vi to demonstrate ; se
~ vi (émotion) to show ou express itself ;
(difficultés) to arise ; (symptômes) to
appear ; (témoin etc) to come forward.
manigance [manigɑ̃s] nf scheme.
manigancer [manigɑ̃se] vt to plot, devise.
manioc [manjɔk] nm cassava, manioc.
manipuler [manipyle] vt to handle ; (fig)
to manipulate.
manivelle [manivɛl] nf crank.
manne [man] nf (REL) manna ; (fig)
godsend.
mannequin [mankɛ̃] nm (COUTURE)
dummy ; (MODE) model.
manœuvre [manœvr(ə)] nf (gén)
manœuvre // nm labourer.
manœuvrer [manœvre] vt to manœuvre ;
(levier, machine) to operate // vi to
manœuvre.
manoir [manwar] nm manor ou country
house.
manomètre [manɔmɛtr(ə)] nm gauge,
manometer.
manquant, e [mɑ̃kɑ̃, -ɑ̃t] a missing.
manque [mɑ̃k] nm (insuffisance): ~ de
lack of ; (vide) emptiness, gap ; (MÉD)
withdrawal ; ~s nmpl (lacunes) faults,
defects ; ~ à gagner loss of profit ou
earnings.
manqué, e [mɑ̃ke] a failed ; garçon ~
tomboy.
manquement [mɑ̃kmɑ̃] nm: ~ à
(discipline, règle) breach of.
manquer [mɑ̃ke] vi (faire défaut) to be
lacking ; (être absent) to be missing ;
(échouer) to fail // vt to miss // vb
impersonnel: il (nous) manque encore 100
F we are still 100 F short ; il manque des
pages (au livre) there are some pages
missing ou some pages are missing (from
the book) ; l'argent qui leur manque the

money they need *ou* are short of; **le pied/la voix lui manqua** he missed his footing/his voice failed him; ~ **à qn** (*absent etc*): **il/cela me manque** I miss him/this; ~ **à** vt (*règles etc*) to be in breach of, fail to observe; ~ **de** vt to lack; **ne pas ~ de faire: il n'a pas manqué de le dire** he sure enough said it, he didn't fail to say it; ~ **(de) faire: il a manqué (de) se tuer** he very nearly got killed.

mansarde [mɑ̄saʀd(ə)] nf attic; **mansardé, e** a attic cpd.

mansuétude [mɑ̄sɥetyd] nf leniency.

mante [mɑ̄t] nf: ~ **religieuse** praying mantis.

manteau, x [mɑ̄to] nm coat; ~ **de cheminée** mantelpiece.

mantille [mɑ̄tij] nf mantilla.

manucure [manykyʀ] nf manicurist.

manuel, le [manɥɛl] a manual // nm/f manually gifted pupil *etc* (*as opposed to intellectually gifted*) // nm (*ouvrage*) manual, handbook.

manufacture [manyfaktyʀ] nf factory.

manufacturé, e [manyfaktyʀe] a manufactured.

manuscrit, e [manyskʀi, -it] a handwritten // nm manuscript.

manutention [manytɑ̄sjɔ̄] nf (COMM) handling; **manutentionnaire** nm/f warehouseman/woman, packer.

mappemonde [mapmɔ̄d] nf (*plane*) map of the world; (*sphère*) globe.

maquereau, x [makʀo] nm (ZOOL) mackerel inv; (*fam*) pimp.

maquerelle [makʀɛl] nf (*fam*) madam.

maquette [makɛt] nf (*d'un décor, bâtiment, véhicule*) (scale) model; (*d'une page illustrée*) paste-up.

maquignon [makiɲɔ̄] nm horse-dealer.

maquillage [makijaʒ] nm making up; faking; (*crème etc*) make-up.

maquiller [makije] vt (*personne, visage*) to make up; (*truquer: passeport, statistique*) to fake; (: *voiture volée*) to do over (*respray etc*); **se ~** to make up (one's face).

maquis [maki] nm (GÉO) scrub; (*fig*) tangle; (MIL) maquis, underground fighting q.

marabout [maʀabu] nm (ZOOL) marabou(t).

maraîcher, ère [maʀeʃe, maʀɛʃɛʀ] a: **cultures maraîchères** market gardening sg // nm/f market gardener.

marais [maʀɛ] nm marsh, swamp; ~ **salant** salt pen, saltern.

marasme [maʀasm(ə)] nm stagnation, slump.

marathon [maʀatɔ̄] nm marathon.

marâtre [maʀɑtʀ(ə)] nf cruel mother.

maraude [maʀod] nf pilfering, thieving (*of poultry, crops*); (*dans un verger*) scrumping; (*vagabondage*) prowling; **en ~** on the prowl; (*taxi*) cruising.

marbre [maʀbʀ(ə)] nm (*pierre, statue*) marble; (*d'une table, commode*) marble top; (TYPO) stone, bed; **rester de ~** to remain stonily indifferent; **marbrer** vt to mottle, blotch; (TECH: *papier*) to marble; **~rie** nf monumental mason's yard; **marbrier** nm monumental mason.

marc [maʀ] nm (*de raisin, pommes*) marc; ~ **de café** coffee grounds pl ou dregs pl.

marcassin [maʀkasɛ̄] nm young wild boar.

marchand, e [maʀʃɑ̄, -ɑ̄d] nm/f shopkeeper, tradesman/woman; (*au marché*) stallholder; (*spécifique*): ~ **de cycles/tapis** bicycle/carpet dealer; ~ **de charbon/vins** coal/wine merchant // a: **prix/valeur ~(e)** market price/value; ~ **de biens** real estate agent; ~ **de couleurs** ironmonger; ~**/e de fruits** fruiterer, fruit merchant; ~**/e de journaux** newsagent; ~**/e de légumes** greengrocer; ~**/e de poisson** fishmonger, fish merchant; ~**e de quatre saisons** costermonger; ~ **de tableaux** art dealer.

marchander [maʀʃɑ̄de] vt (*article*) to bargain *ou* haggle over; (*éloges*) to be sparing with // vi to bargain, haggle.

marchandise [maʀʃɑ̄diz] nf goods pl, merchandise q.

marche [maʀʃ(ə)] nf (*d'escalier*) step; (*activité*) walking; (*promenade*, *trajet*, *allure*) walk; (*démarche*) walk, gait; (MIL *etc*, MUS) march; (*fonctionnement*) running; (*progression*) progress; course; **ouvrir/fermer la ~** to lead the way/bring up the rear; **dans le sens de la ~** (RAIL) facing the engine; **en ~** (*monter etc*) while the vehicle is moving *ou* in motion; **mettre en ~** to start; **remettre qch en ~** to set *ou* start sth going again; **se mettre en ~** (*personne*) to get moving; (*machine*) to start; ~ **arrière** reverse (gear); **faire ~ arrière** to reverse; (*fig*) to backtrack, back-pedal; ~ **à suivre** (correct) procedure; (*sur notice*) (step by step) instructions pl.

marché [maʀʃe] nm (*lieu*, COMM, ÉCON) market; (*ville*) trading centre; (*transaction*) bargain, deal; **M~ commun** Common Market; ~ **aux fleurs** flower market; ~ **noir** black market; **faire du ~ noir** to buy and sell on the black market; ~ **aux puces** flea market.

marchepied [maʀʃəpje] nm (RAIL) step; (AUTO) running board; (*fig*) stepping stone.

marcher [maʀʃe] vi to walk; (MIL) to march; (*aller*: *voiture*, *train*, *affaires*) to go; (*prospérer*) to go well; (*fonctionner*) to work, run; (*fam*) to go along, agree; to be taken in; ~ **sur** to walk on; (*mettre le pied sur*) to step on *ou* in; (MIL) to march upon; ~ **dans** (*herbe etc*) to walk in *ou* on; (*flaque*) to step in; **faire ~ qn** to pull sb's leg; to lead sb up the garden path; **marcheur, euse** nm/f walker.

mardi [maʀdi] nm Tuesday; **M~ gras** Shrove Tuesday.

mare [maʀ] nf pond; ~ **de sang** pool of blood.

marécage [maʀekaʒ] nm marsh, swamp; **marécageux, euse** a marshy, swampy.

maréchal, aux [maʀeʃal, -o] nm marshal; ~ **des logis** (MIL) sergeant.

maréchal-ferrant [maʀeʃalfɛʀɑ̄] nm blacksmith, farrier.

maréchaussée [maʀeʃose] nf constabulary.

marée [maʀe] nf tide; (*poissons*) fresh (sea) fish; ~ **haute/basse** high/low tide;

~ montante/ descendante rising/ebb tide.

marelle [maʀɛl] nf: (jouer à) la ~ (to play) hopscotch.

marémotrice [maʀemɔtʀis] af tidal.

mareyeur, euse [maʀɛjœʀ, -øz] nm/f wholesale (sea) fish merchant.

margarine [maʀgaʀin] nf margarine.

marge [maʀʒ(ə)] nf margin; en ~ in the margin; en ~ de (fig) on the fringe of; cut off from; connected with; ~ bénéficiaire profit margin.

margelle [maʀʒɛl] nf coping.

margeur [maʀʒœʀ] nm margin stop.

marginal, e, aux [maʀʒinal, -o] a marginal.

marguerite [maʀgəʀit] nf marguerite, (oxeye) daisy.

marguillier [maʀgije] nm churchwarden.

mari [maʀi] nm husband.

mariage [maʀjaʒ] nm (union, état, fig) marriage; (noce) wedding; civil/religieux civil ou registry office/church wedding; un ~ de raison/d'amour a marriage of convenience/love match; ~ blanc unconsummated marriage; ~ en blanc white wedding.

marié, e [maʀje] a married // nm/f (bride)groom/bride; les ~s the bride and groom; les (jeunes) ~s the newly-weds.

marier [maʀje] vt to marry; (fig) to blend; se ~ (avec) to marry, get married (to); (fig) to blend (with).

marin, e [maʀɛ̃, -in] a sea cpd, marine // nm sailor // nf navy; (ART) seascape; ~e de guerre navy; ~e marchande merchant navy; ~e à voiles sailing ships pl.

marinade [maʀinad] nf marinade.

marine [maʀin] af, nf voir marin // a inv: navy (blue) // nm (MIL) marine.

mariner [maʀine] vi, vt to marinate, marinade.

marinier [maʀinje] nm bargee.

marinière [maʀinjɛʀ] nf smock // a inv: moules ~ mussels in white wine.

marionnette [maʀjɔnɛt] nf puppet.

marital, e, aux [maʀital, -o] a marital, husband's; ~ement ad as husband and wife.

maritime [maʀitim] a sea cpd, maritime.

marjolaine [maʀʒɔlɛn] nf marjoram.

mark [maʀk] nm mark.

marmaille [maʀmaj] nf (péj) (gang of) brats pl.

marmelade [maʀməlad] nf stewed fruit, compote; en ~ (fig) crushed (to a pulp).

marmite [maʀmit] nf (cooking-)pot.

marmiton [maʀmitɔ̃] nm kitchen boy.

marmonner [maʀmɔne] vt, vi to mumble, mutter.

marmot [maʀmo] nm brat.

marmotte [maʀmɔt] nf marmot.

marmotter [maʀmɔte] vt (prière) to mumble, mutter.

marne [maʀn(ə)] nf marl.

Maroc [maʀɔk] nm: le ~ Morocco; **marocain, e** a, nm/f Moroccan.

maroquin [maʀɔkɛ̃] nm morocco (leather); (fig) (minister's) portfolio.

maroquinerie [maʀɔkinʀi] nf leather craft; fine leather goods pl.

marotte [maʀɔt] nf fad.

marquant, e [maʀkɑ̃, -ɑ̃t] a outstanding.

marque [maʀk(ə)] nf mark; (SPORT, JEU: décompte des points) score; (COMM: de produits) brand; make; (: de disques) label; à vos ~s! (SPORT) on your marks! de ~ a (COMM) brand-name cpd; proprietary; (fig) high-class; distinguished; ~ déposée registered trademark; ~ de fabrique trademark.

marqué, e [maʀke] a marked.

marquer [maʀke] vt to mark; (inscrire) to write down; (bétail) to brand; (SPORT: but etc) to score; (: joueur) to mark; (accentuer: taille etc) to emphasize; (manifester: refus, intérêt) to show // vi (événement, personnalité) to stand out, be outstanding; (SPORT) to score; ~ les points (tenir la marque) to keep the score.

marqueterie [maʀkətʀi] nf inlaid work, marquetry.

marquis, e [maʀki, -iz] nm/f marquis ou marquess/marchioness // nf (auvent) glass canopy ou awning.

marraine [maʀɛn] nf godmother.

marrant, e [maʀɑ̃, -ɑ̃t] a (fam) funny.

marre [maʀ] ad (fam): en avoir ~ de to be fed up with.

marrer [maʀe]: se ~ vi (fam) to have a (good) laugh.

marron [maʀɔ̃] nm (fruit) chestnut // a inv brown // am (péj) crooked; bogus; ~s glacés marrons glacés; **marronnier** nm chestnut (tree).

mars [maʀs] nm March.

Mars [maʀs] nf ou m Mars.

marsouin [maʀswɛ̃] nm porpoise.

marsupiaux [maʀsypjo] nmpl marsupials.

marteau, x [maʀto] nm hammer; (de porte) knocker; ~-piqueur nm pneumatic drill.

martel [maʀtɛl] nm: se mettre ~ en tête to worry o.s.

marteler [maʀtəle] vt to hammer.

martial, e, aux [maʀsjal, -o] a martial.

martien, ne [maʀsjɛ̃, -jɛn] a Martian, of ou from Mars.

martinet [maʀtinɛ] nm (fouet) small whip; (ZOOL) swift.

martingale [maʀtɛ̃gal] nf (COUTURE) half-belt; (JEU) winning formula.

Martinique [maʀtinik] nf: la ~ Martinique.

martin-pêcheur [maʀtɛ̃pɛʃœʀ] nm kingfisher.

martre [maʀtʀ(ə)] nf marten.

martyr, e [maʀtiʀ] nm/f martyr // a martyred; enfants ~s battered children.

martyre [maʀtiʀ] nm martyrdom; (fig: sens affaibli) agony, torture.

martyriser [maʀtiʀize] vt (REL) to martyr; (fig) to bully; to batter.

marxisme [maʀksism(ə)] nm Marxism.

mascarade [maskaʀad] nf masquerade.

mascotte [maskɔt] nf mascot.

masculin, e [maskylɛ̃, -in] a masculine; (sexe, population) male; (équipe, vêtements) men's; (viril) manly // nm masculine.

masochisme [mazɔʃism(ə)] *nm* masochism.

masque [mask(ə)] *nm* mask ; ~ **à gaz** gas mask.

masqué, e [maske] *a* masked.

masquer [maske] *vt* (*cacher: paysage, porte*) to hide, conceal ; (*dissimuler: vérité, projet*) to mask, obscure.

massacrant, e [masakrɑ̃, -ɑ̃t] *a*: **humeur ~e** foul temper.

massacre [masakʀ(ə)] *nm* massacre, slaughter.

massacrer [masakʀe] *vt* to massacre, slaughter ; (*fig: texte etc*) to murder.

massage [masaʒ] *nm* massage.

masse [mas] *nf* mass ; (*péj*): **la ~** the masses *pl* ; (*ÉLEC*) earth ; (*maillet*) sledgehammer ; **~s** *nfpl* masses ; **une ~ de, des ~s de** (*fam*) masses *ou* loads of ; **en ~** *ad* (*en bloc*) in bulk ; (*en foule*) en masse // *a* (*exécutions, production*) mass *cpd* ; **~ salariale** aggregate remuneration (of employees).

massepain [maspɛ̃] *nm* marzipan.

masser [mase] *vt* (*assembler*) to gather ; (*pétrir*) to massage ; **se ~** *vi* to gather ; **masseur, euse** *nm/f* masseur/masseuse.

massicot [masiko] *nm* guillotine.

massif, ive [masif, -iv] *a* (*porte*) solid, massive ; (*visage*) heavy, large ; (*bois, or*) solid ; (*dose*) massive ; (*déportations etc*) mass *cpd* // *nm* (*montagneux*) massif ; (*de fleurs*) clump, bank.

massue [masy] *nf* club, bludgeon.

mastic [mastik] *nm* (*pour vitres*) putty ; (*pour fentes*) filler.

mastiquer [mastike] *vt* (*aliment*) to chew, masticate ; (*fente*) to fill ; (*vitre*) to putty.

masturbation [mastyʀbɑsjɔ̃] *nf* masturbation.

masure [mɑzyʀ] *nf* tumbledown cottage.

mat, e [mat] *a* (*couleur, métal*) mat(t) ; (*bruit, son*) dull // *a inv* (*ÉCHECS*): **être ~** to be checkmate.

mât [mɑ] *nm* (*NAVIG*) mast ; (*poteau*) pole, post.

match [matʃ] *nm* match ; **~ nul** draw ; **faire ~ nul** to draw.

matelas [matla] *nm* mattress ; **~ pneumatique** air bed *ou* mattress ; **~ à ressorts** spring *ou* interior-sprung mattress.

matelasser [matlase] *vt* to pad ; to quilt.

matelot [matlo] *nm* sailor, seaman.

mater [mate] *vt* (*personne*) to bring to heel, subdue ; (*révolte*) to put down.

matérialiser [mateʀjalize]: **se ~** *vi* to materialize.

matérialiste [mateʀjalist(ə)] *a* materialistic.

matériau, x [mateʀjo] *nm* material // *nmpl* material(s).

matériel, le [mateʀjɛl] *a* material // *nm* equipment *q* ; (*de camping etc*) gear *q* ; **~ d'exploitation** (*COMM*) plant.

maternel, le [matɛʀnɛl] *a* (*amour, geste*) motherly, maternal ; (*grand-père, oncle*) maternal // *nf* (*aussi*: **école ~le**) (state) nursery school.

maternité [matɛʀnite] *nf* (*établissement*) maternity hospital ; (*état de mère*) motherhood, maternity ; (*grossesse*) pregnancy.

mathématicien, ne [matematisjɛ̃, -jɛn] *nm/f* mathematician.

mathématique [matematik] *a* mathematical ; **~s** *nfpl* (*science*) mathematics *sg*.

matière [matjɛʀ] *nf* (*PHYSIQUE*) matter ; (*COMM, TECH*) material, matter *q* ; (*fig: d'un livre etc*) subject matter, material ; (*SCOL*) subject ; **en ~ de** as regards ; **donner ~ à** to give cause to ; **~ plastique** plastic ; **~s fécales** faeces ; **~s grasses** fat content *sg* ; **~s premières** raw materials.

matin [matɛ̃] *nm, ad* morning ; **matinal, e, aux** *a* (*toilette, gymnastique*) morning *cpd* ; (*de bonne heure*) early ; **être matinal** (*personne*) to be up early ; to be an early riser.

matinée [matine] *nf* morning ; (*spectacle*) matinée, afternoon performance.

mâtiner [mɑtine] *vt* to cross.

matois, e [matwa, -waz] *a* wily.

matou [matu] *nm* tom(cat).

matraque [matʀak] *nf* cosh ; (*de policier*) truncheon ; **matraquer** *vt* to beat up (with a truncheon) ; to cosh ; (*fig: disque*) to plug.

matriarcal, e, aux [matʀijaʀkal, -o] *a* matriarchal.

matrice [matʀis] *nf* (*ANAT*) womb ; (*TECH*) mould ; (*MATH etc*) matrix.

matricule [matʀikyl] *nf* (*aussi*: **registre ~**) roll, register // *nm* (*aussi*: **numéro ~**) (*MIL*) regimental number ; (*ADMIN*) reference number.

matrimonial, e, aux [matʀimɔnjal, -o] *a* marital, marriage *cpd*.

mâture [mɑtyʀ] *nf* masts *pl*.

maturité [matyʀite] *nf* maturity ; (*d'un fruit*) ripeness, maturity.

maudire [modiʀ] *vt* to curse.

maudit, e [modi, -it] *a* (*fam: satané*) blasted, confounded.

maugréer [mogʀee] *vi* to grumble.

Mauresque [mɔʀɛsk] *a* Moorish.

mausolée [mozɔle] *nm* mausoleum.

maussade [mosad] *a* sullen.

mauvais, e [mɔvɛ, -ɛz] *a* bad ; (*faux*): **le ~ numéro/moment** the wrong number/moment ; (*méchant, malveillant*) malicious, spiteful // *ad*: **il fait ~** the weather is bad ; **sentir ~** to have a nasty smell, smell bad *ou* nasty ; **la mer est ~e** the sea is rough ; **~ coup** (*fig*) criminal venture ; **~ garçon** tough ; **~ plaisant** hoaxer ; **~ traitements** ill treatment *sg* ; **~e herbe** weed ; **~e langue** gossip, scandalmonger ; **~e passe** difficult situation ; bad patch ; **~e tête** rebellious *ou* headstrong customer.

mauve [mov] *a* mauve // *nf* mallow.

mauviette [movjɛt] *nf* (*péj*) weakling.

maux [mo] *nmpl voir* **mal.**

maximal, e, aux [maksimal, -o] *a* maximal.

maxime [maksim] *nf* maxim.

maximum [maksimɔm] *a, nm* maximum ; **au ~** *ad* (*le plus possible*) to the full ; as much as one can ; (*tout au plus*) at the (very) most *ou* maximum.

mayonnaise [majɔnɛz] nf mayonnaise.

mazout [mazut] nm (fuel) oil.

me, m' [m(ə)] pronom me ; (réfléchi) myself.
Me abr de **Maître.**

méandres [meɑ̃dʀ(ə)] nmpl meanderings.

mec [mɛk] nm (fam) bloke.

mécanicien, ne [mekanisjɛ̃, -jɛn] nm/f
mechanic ; (RAIL) (train ou engine) driver ;
~-dentiste nm/f dental technician.

mécanique [mekanik] a mechanical // nf
(science) mechanics sg ; (technologie)
mechanical engineering ; (AUTO): **s'y
connaître en ~** to be mechanically
minded ; (mécanisme) mechanism ;
engineering ; works pl ; **ennui ~** engine
trouble q ; **mécaniser** vt to mechanize.

mécanisme [mekanism(ə)] nm
mechanism.

mécanographie [mekanɔgʀafi] nf
(mechanical) data processing.

mécène [mesɛn] nm patron.

méchanceté [meʃɑ̃ste] nf nastiness,
maliciousness ; nasty ou spiteful ou
malicious remark (ou action).

méchant, e [meʃɑ̃, -ɑ̃t] a nasty, malicious,
spiteful ; (enfant: **pas sage**) naughty ;
(animal) vicious ; (avant le nom: **valeur
péjorative**) nasty ; miserable ; (: intensive)
terrific.

mèche [mɛʃ] nf (de lampe, bougie) wick ;
(d'un explosif) fuse ; (de vilebrequin,
perceuse) bit ; (de fouet) lash ; (de cheveux)
lock ; **vendre la ~** to give the game away ;
de ~ avec in league with.

méchoui [meʃwi] nm whole sheep barbecue.

mécompte [mekɔ̃t] nm miscalculation ;
(déception) disappointment.

méconnaissable [mekɔnɛsabl(ə)] a
unrecognizable.

méconnaissance [mekɔnɛsɑ̃s] nf
ignorance.

méconnaître [mekɔnɛtʀ(ə)] vt (ignorer)
to be unaware of ; (mésestimer) to
misjudge.

mécontent, e [mekɔ̃tɑ̃, -ɑ̃t] a: ~ (de)
discontented ou dissatisfied ou displeased
(with) ; (contrarié) annoyed (at) ;
mécontentement nm dissatisfaction,
discontent, displeasure ; annoyance ;
mécontenter vt to displease.

médaille [medaj] nf medal ; **médaillé, e**
nm/f (SPORT) medal-holder.

médaillon [medajɔ̃] nm (portrait)
medallion ; (bijou) locket ; (CULIN)
médaillon ; **en ~ a** (carte etc) inset.

médecin [medsɛ̃] nm doctor ; ~
généraliste general practitioner, G.P.

médecine [medsin] nf medicine ; ~ **légale**
forensic medicine ; ~ **du travail**
occupational ou industrial medicine.

médian, e [medjɑ̃, -an] a (MATH) median.

médiateur, trice [medjatœʀ, -tʀis] nm/f
mediator ; arbitrator.

médiation [medjusjɔ̃] nf mediation ; (dans
conflit social etc) arbitration.

médical, e, aux [medikal, -o] a medical.

médicament [medikamɑ̃] nm medicine,
drug.

médicinal, e, aux [medisinal, -o] a
medicinal.

médico-légal, e, aux [medikɔlegal, -o]
a forensic.

médiéval, e, aux [medjeval, -o] a
medieval.

médiocre [medjɔkʀ(ə)] a mediocre, poor ;
médiocrité nf mediocrity.

médire [mediʀ] vi: ~ **de** to speak ill of ;
médisance nf scandalmongering ; piece of
scandal ou of malicious gossip.

méditatif, ive [meditatif, -iv] a
thoughtful.

méditation [meditasjɔ̃] nf meditation.

méditer [medite] vt (approfondir) to
meditate on, ponder (over) ; (combiner) to
meditate // vi to meditate ; ~ **de faire** to
contemplate doing, plan to do.

Méditerranée [meditɛʀane] nf: **la** (mer)
~ the Mediterranean (Sea) ;
méditerranéen, ne a, nm/f Mediterranean.

médium [medjɔm] nm medium (person).

médius [medjys] nm middle finger.

méduse [medyz] nf jellyfish.

méduser [medyze] vt to dumbfound.

meeting [mitiŋ] nm (POL, SPORT) rally ; ~
d'aviation air show.

méfait [mefɛ] nm (faute) misdemeanour,
wrongdoing ; ~s nmpl (ravages) ravages,
damage sg.

méfiance [mefjɑ̃s] nf mistrust, distrust.

méfiant, e [mefjɑ̃, -ɑ̃t] a mistrustful,
distrustful.

méfier [mefje]: **se ~** vi to be wary ; to
be careful ; **se ~ de** vt to mistrust,
distrust, be wary of ; (faire attention) to be
careful about.

mégarde [megaʀd(ə)] nf: **par ~**
accidentally ; by mistake.

mégère [meʒɛʀ] nf shrew.

mégot [mego] nm cigarette end.

meilleur, e [mɛjœʀ] a, ad better ; (valeur
superlative) best // nm: **le ~** (celui qui ...)
the best (one) ; (ce qui ...) the best // nf:
la ~e the best (one) ; **le ~ des deux** the
better of the two ; ~ **marché** cheaper.

mélancolie [melɑ̃kɔli] nf melancholy,
gloom ; **mélancolique** a melancholic,
melancholy.

mélange [melɑ̃ʒ] nm mixture.

mélanger [melɑ̃ʒe] vt (substances) to
mix ; (vins, couleurs) to blend ; (mettre en
désordre) to mix up, muddle (up).

mélasse [melas] nf treacle, molasses sg.

mêlée [mele] nf mêlée, scramble ; (RUGBY)
scrum(mage).

mêler [mele] vt (substances, odeurs, races)
to mix ; (embrouiller) to muddle (up), mix
up ; **se ~** to mix ; to mingle ; **se ~ à** (suj:
personne) to join ; to mix with ; (: odeurs
etc) to mingle with ; **se ~ de** (suj:
personne) to meddle with, interfere in ; ~
qn à (affaire) to get sb mixed up ou
involved in.

mélodie [melɔdi] nf melody ; **mélodieux,
euse** a melodious, tuneful ; **mélodique** a
melodic.

mélodrame [melɔdʀam] nm melodrama.

mélomane [melɔman] nm/f music lover.

melon [məlɔ̃] nm (BOT) (honeydew) melon ;
(aussi: **chapeau ~**) bowler (hat) ; ~ **d'eau**
watermelon.

mélopée [melɔpe] *nf* monotonous chant.
membrane [mɑ̃bʀɑn] *nf* membrane.
membre [mɑ̃bʀ(ə)] *nm* (ANAT) limb; (*personne, pays, élément*) member // *a* member; ~ (**viril**) (male) organ.
même [mɛm] *a* same // *pronom:* **le(la)** ~ the same (one) // *ad* even; **en ~ temps** at the same time; **ce sont ses paroles/celles-là** ~s they are his very words/the very ones; **il n'a ~ pas pleuré** he didn't even cry; **ici** ~ at this very place; **à ~ la bouteille** straight from the bottle; **à ~ la peau** next to the skin; **être à ~ de faire** to be in a position *ou* be able to do; **mettre qn à ~ de faire** to enable sb to do; **faire de ~** to do likewise; **lui de ~** so does (*ou* did *ou* is) he; **de ~ que** just as; **il en va/est allé de ~** pour the same goes/happened for.
mémento [memɛto] *nm* (*agenda*) engagement diary; (*ouvrage*) summary.
mémoire [memwaʀ] *nf* memory // *nm* (ADMIN, JUR) memorandum (*pl* a); (SCOL) dissertation, paper; ~s *nmpl* memoirs; **avoir la ~ des chiffres** to have a good memory for figures; **à la ~ de** to the *ou* in memory of; **pour ~** *ad* for the record; **de ~ d'homme** in living memory; **de ~** *ad* from memory.
mémorable [memɔʀabl(ə)] *a* memorable.
mémorandum [memɔʀɑ̃dɔm] *nm* memorandum (*pl* a).
mémorial, aux [memɔʀjal, -o] *nm* memorial.
menaçant, e [mənasɑ̃, -ɑ̃t] *a* threatening, menacing.
menace [mənas] *nf* threat.
menacer [mənase] *vt* to threaten.
ménage [menaʒ] *nm* (*travail*) housekeeping, housework; (*couple*) (married) couple; (*famille*, ADMIN) household; **faire le** ~ to do the housework; **faire des** ~s to go out charring; **monter son** ~ to set up house; **se mettre en** ~ (**avec**) to set up house (with); **heureux en** ~ happily married; **faire bon** ~ **avec** to get on well with; ~ **de poupée** doll's kitchen set; **à trois** love triangle.
ménagement [menaʒmɑ̃] *nm* care and attention; ~s *nmpl* (*égards*) consideration *sg*, attention *sg*.
ménager [menaʒe] *vt* (*traiter*) to handle with tact; to treat considerately; (*utiliser*) to use sparingly; to use with care; (*prendre soin de*) to take (great) care of, look after; (*organiser*) to arrange; (*installer*) to put in; to make; ~ **qch à qn** (*réserver*) to have sth in store for sb.
ménager, ère [menaʒe, -ɛʀ] *a* household *cpd*, domestic // *nf* housewife (*pl* wives).
ménagerie [menaʒʀi] *nf* menagerie.
mendiant, e [mɑ̃djɑ̃, -ɑ̃t] *nm/f* beggar.
mendicité [mɑ̃disite] *nf* begging.
mendier [mɑ̃dje] *vi* to beg // *vt* to beg (for).
menées [məne] *nfpl* intrigues, manœuvres.
mener [məne] *vt* to lead; (*enquête*) to conduct; (*affaires*) to manage // *vi*: ~ (**à la marque**) to lead, be in the lead; ~ **à/dans** (*emmener*) to take to/into; ~ **qch à terme** *ou* **à bien** to see sth through (to

a successful conclusion), complete sth successfully.
meneur, euse [mənœʀ, -øz] *nm/f* leader; (*péj*) agitator; ~ **d'hommes** born leader; ~ **de jeu** compère; quizmaster.
méningite [menɛ̃ʒit] *nf* meningitis *q*.
ménopause [menɔpoz] *nf* menopause.
menotte [mənɔt] *nf* (*main*) mitt, tiny hand; ~s *nfpl* handcuffs; **passer les** ~s **à** to handcuff.
mensonge [mɑ̃sɔ̃ʒ] *nm* lie; lying *q*; **mensonger, ère** *a* false.
mensualité [mɑ̃syalite] *nf* monthly payment; monthly salary.
mensuel, le [mɑ̃sɥɛl] *a* monthly.
mensurations [mɑ̃syʀysjɔ̃] *nfpl* measurements.
mental, e, aux [mɑ̃tal, -o] *a* mental.
mentalité [mɑ̃talite] *nf* mentality.
menteur, euse [mɑ̃tœʀ, -øz] *nm/f* liar.
menthe [mɑ̃t] *nf* mint; ~ (**à l'eau**) peppermint cordial.
mention [mɑ̃sjɔ̃] *nf* (*note*) note, comment; (SCOL): ~ **bien** *etc* ≈ grade B *etc* (*ou* upper 2nd class *etc*) pass; **faire** ~ **de** to mention; **mentionner** *vt* to mention.
mentir [mɑ̃tiʀ] *vi* to lie; to be lying.
menton [mɑ̃tɔ̃] *nm* chin.
menu, e [məny] *a* slim, slight; tiny; (*frais, difficulté*) minor // *ad* (*couper, hacher*) very fine // *nm* menu; **par le** ~ (*raconter*) in minute detail; ~e **monnaie** small change.
menuet [mənɥɛ] *nm* minuet.
menuiserie [mənɥizʀi] *nf* (*travail*) joinery, carpentry; woodwork; (*local*) joiner's workshop; (*ouvrage*) woodwork *q*.
menuisier [mənɥizje] *nm* joiner, carpenter.
méprendre [mepʀɑ̃dʀ(ə)]: **se** ~ *vi*: **se** ~ **sur** to be mistaken (about).
mépris [mepʀi] *nm* (*dédain*) contempt, scorn; (*indifférence*): **le** ~ **de** contempt *ou* disregard for; **au** ~ **de** regardless of, in defiance of.
méprisable [mepʀizabl(ə)] *a* contemptible, despicable.
méprisant, e [mepʀizɑ̃, -ɑ̃t] *a* contemptuous, scornful.
méprise [mepʀiz] *nf* mistake, error; misunderstanding.
mépriser [mepʀize] *vt* to scorn, despise; (*gloire, danger*) to scorn, spurn.
mer [mɛʀ] *nf* sea; (*marée*) tide; **en** ~ at sea; **prendre la** ~ to put out to sea; **en haute** ~ off shore, on the open sea; **la** ~ **du Nord/Rouge** the North/Red Sea.
mercantile [mɛʀkɑ̃til] *a* (*péj*) mercenary.
mercenaire [mɛʀsənɛʀ] *nm* mercenary, hired soldier.
mercerie [mɛʀsəʀi] *nf* haberdashery; haberdasher's shop.
merci [mɛʀsi] *excl* thank you // *nf*: **à la** ~ **de qn/qch** at sb's mercy/the mercy of sth; ~ **beaucoup** thank you very much; ~ **de** thank you for; **sans** ~ merciless.
mercier, ière [mɛʀsje, -jɛʀ] *nm/f* haberdasher.
mercredi [mɛʀkʀədi] *nm* Wednesday; ~ **des Cendres** Ash Wednesday.
mercure [mɛʀkyʀ] *nm* mercury.

merde [mɛʀd(ə)] (fam!) nf shit (!) // excl bloody hell (!).

mère [mɛʀ] nf mother; ~ célibataire unmarried mother.

méridien [meʀidjɛ̃] nm meridian.

méridional, e, aux [meʀidjɔnal, -o] a southern // nm/f Southerner.

meringue [məʀɛ̃g] nf meringue.

merisier [məʀizje] nm wild cherry (tree).

méritant, e [meʀitɑ̃, -ɑ̃t] a deserving.

mérite [meʀit] nm merit; le ~ (de ceci) lui revient the credit (for this) is his.

mériter [meʀite] vt to deserve.

méritoire [meʀitwaʀ] a praiseworthy, commendable.

merlan [mɛʀlɑ̃] nm whiting.

merle [mɛʀl(ə)] nm blackbird.

merveille [mɛʀvɛj] nf marvel, wonder; faire ~ to work wonders; à ~ perfectly, wonderfully.

merveilleux, euse [mɛʀvɛjø, -øz] a marvellous, wonderful.

mes [me] dét voir **mon**.

mésalliance [mezaljɑ̃s] nf misalliance, mismatch.

mésange [mezɑ̃ʒ] nf tit(mouse) (pl mice); ~ bleue blue tit.

mésaventure [mezavɑ̃tyʀ] nf misadventure, misfortune.

Mesdames [medam] nfpl voir **Madame**.

Mesdemoiselles [medmwazɛl] nfpl voir **Mademoiselle**.

mésentente [mezɑ̃tɑ̃t] nf dissension, disagreement.

mésestimer [mezɛstime] vt to underestimate, underrate; to have low regard for.

mesquin, e [mɛskɛ̃, -in] a mean, petty; **mesquinerie** nf pettiness q, meanness q.

mess [mɛs] nm mess.

message [mesaʒ] nm message; ~ téléphoné telegram dictated by telephone; **messager, ère** nm/f messenger; **messageries** nfpl parcels service sg; distribution service sg.

messe [mɛs] nf mass; aller à la ~ to go to mass, ~ de minuit midnight mass.

messie [mesi] nm: le M— the Messiah.

Messieurs [mesjø] nmpl (abr Messrs) voir **Monsieur**

mesure [məzyʀ] nf (évaluation, dimension) measurement; (étalon, récipient, contenu) measure; (MUS: cadence) time, tempo; (: division) bar; (retenue) moderation; (disposition) measure, step; sur ~ (costume) made-to-measure; à la ~ de (fig) worthy of; on the same scale as; dans la ~ où insofar as, inasmuch as; à ~ que as; en ~ (MUS) in time ou tempo; être en ~ de to be in a position to; dépasser la ~ (fig) to overstep the mark.

mesurer [məzyʀe] vt to measure; (juger) to weigh up, assess; (limiter) to limit, ration; (modérer) to moderate; (proportionner): ~ qch à to match sth to, gear sth to; se ~ avec to have a confrontation with; to tackle; il mesure 1 m 80 he's 1 m 80 tall.

met vb voir **mettre**.

métairie [meteʀi] nf smallholding.

métal, aux [metal, -o] nm metal; ~lique a metallic; ~lisé, e a (peinture) metallic; ~lurgie nf metallurgy; ~lurgiste nm/f steel ou metal worker; metallurgist.

métamorphose [metamɔʀfoz] nf metamorphosis (pl oses).

métaphore [metafɔʀ] nf metaphor.

métaphysique [metafizik] nf metaphysics sg // a metaphysical.

métayer, ère [meteje, metɛjɛʀ] nm/f (tenant) farmer.

météo [meteo] nf weather report; ≈ Met Office.

météore [meteɔʀ] nm meteor.

météorologie [meteɔʀɔlɔʒi] nf meteorology; **météorologique** a meteorological, weather cpd.

métèque [metɛk] nm (péj) wop.

méthode [metɔd] nf method; (livre, ouvrage) manual, tutor; **méthodique** a methodical.

méticuleux, euse [metikylø, -øz] a meticulous.

métier [metje] nm (profession: gén) job; (: manuel) trade; (: artisanal) craft; (technique, expérience) (acquired) skill ou technique; (aussi: ~ à tisser) (weaving) loom; être du ~ to be in the trade ou profession.

métis, se [metis] a, nm/f half-caste, half-breed.

métisser [metise] vt to cross.

métrage [metʀaʒ] nm (de tissu) length, ≈ yardage; (CINÉMA) footage, length; long/moyen/court ~ full-length/ medium-length/short film.

mètre [mɛtʀ(ə)] nm metre; (règle) (metre) rule; (ruban) tape measure; **métrique** a metric // nf metrics sg.

métro [metʀo] nm underground, subway.

métropole [metʀɔpɔl] nf (capitale) metropolis; (pays) home country; **métropolitain, e** a a metropolitan.

mets [mɛ] nm dish.

metteur [metœʀ] nm: ~ en scène (THÉÂTRE) producer; (CINÉMA) director; ~ en ondes producer.

mettre [mɛtʀ(ə)] vt (placer) to put; (vêtement: revêtir) to put on; (: porter) to wear; (installer: gaz, l'électricité) to put in; (faire fonctionner: chauffage, électricité) to put on; (noter, écrire) to say, put down: **mettons que** let's suppose ou say that; ~ en bouteille/en sac to bottle/put in bags ou sacks; y ~ du sien to pull one's weight; ~ du temps/2 heures à faire to take time/2 hours doing; ~ à: n'avoir rien à se ~ to have nothing to wear; se ~ de l'encre sur les doigts to get ink on one's fingers; se ~ au lit to get into bed; se ~ au piano (s'asseoir) to sit down at the piano; (apprendre) to start learning the piano; se ~ à faire to begin ou start doing ou to do; se ~ au travail/à l'étude to get down to work/one's studies.

meublant, e [mœblɑ̃, -ɑ̃t] a (tissus etc) effective (in the room), decorative.

meuble [mœbl(ə)] nm piece of furniture; furniture q // a (terre) loose, friable; (JUR) biens ~s movables; **meublé** nm furnished room (ou flatlet); **meubler** vt to furnish;

(fig): **meubler qch (de)** to fill sth (with); **se meubler** to furnish one's house.

meugler [møgle] *vi* to low, moo.

meule [møl] *nf (à broyer)* millstone; *(à aiguiser)* grindstone; *(à polir)* buffwheel; *(de foin, blé)* stack; *(de fromage)* round.

meunerie [mønʀi] *nf* flour trade; milling; **meunier, ière** *nm* miller // *nf* miller's wife // *af inv (CULIN)* meunière.

meure *etc vb voir* **mourir**.

meurtre [mœʀtʀ(ə)] *nm* murder; **meurtrier, ière** *a (arme etc)* deadly; *(fureur, instincts)* murderous // *nm/f* murderer/eress // *nf (ouverture)* loophole.

meurtrir [mœʀtʀiʀ] *vt* to bruise; *(fig)* to wound; **meurtrissure** *nf* bruise; *(fig)* scar.

meus *etc vb voir* **mouvoir**.

meute [møt] *nf* pack.

mexicain, e [mɛksikɛ̃, -ɛn] *a, nm/f* Mexican.

Mexico [mɛksiko] *n* Mexico City.

Mexique [mɛksik] *nm*: **le ~** Mexico.

MF *sigle f voir* **modulation**.

Mgr *abr de* **Monseigneur**.

mi [mi] *nm (MUS)* E; *(en chantant la gamme)* mi.

mi... [mi] *préfixe* half(-); mid-; **à la ~-janvier** in mid-January; **~-bureau, ~-chambre** half office, half bedroom; **à ~-jambes/-corps** (up ou down) to the knees/waist; **à ~-hauteur/-pente** halfway up ou down/up ou down the hill.

miauler [mjole] *vi* to mew.

mica [mika] *nm* mica.

mi-carême [mikaʀɛm] *nf*: **la ~** the third Thursday in Lent.

miche [miʃ] *nf* round ou cob loaf.

mi-chemin [miʃmɛ̃]: **à ~** *ad* halfway, midway.

mi-clos, e [miklo, -kloz] *a* half-closed.

micmac [mikmak] *nm (péj)* carry-on.

micro [mikʀo] *nm* mike, microphone.

microbe [mikʀɔb] *nm* germ, microbe.

microfiche [mikʀɔfiʃ] *nf* microfiche.

microfilm [mikʀɔfilm] *nm* microfilm.

microphone [mikʀɔfɔn] *nm* microphone.

microscope [mikʀɔskɔp] *nm* microscope; **au ~** under ou through the microscope.

midi [midi] *nm* midday, noon; *(moment du déjeuner)* lunchtime; **à ~** at 12 (o'clock) ou midday ou noon; *(sud)* south; **en plein ~** (right) in the middle of the day; facing south.

mie [mi] *nf* crumb (of the loaf).

miel [mjɛl] *nm* honey.

mielleux, euse [mjɛlø, -øz] *a (péj)* sugary, honeyed.

mien, ne [mjɛ̃, mjɛn] *pronom*: **le(la) ~(ne)**, **les ~s** mine; **les ~s** my family.

miette [mjɛt] *nf (de pain, gâteau)* crumb; *(fig: de la conversation etc)* scrap; **en ~s** *(fig)* in pieces ou bits.

mieux [mjø] *ad* better // *a* better; *(plus joli)* better-looking // *nm (progrès)* improvement; **le ~** the best (thing); **le(la) ~**, **les ~** the best; **le ~ des deux** the better of the two; **les livres les ~ faits** the best made books; **de mon/ton ~** as best I/you can *(ou* could); **de ~ en ~** better and better; **pour le ~** for the best;

au ~ at best; **au ~ avec** on the best of terms with.

mièvre [mjɛvʀ(ə)] *a* mawkish, sickly sentimental.

mignon, ne [miɲɔ̃, -ɔn] *a* sweet, cute.

migraine [migʀɛn] *nf* headache; migraine.

migrateur, trice [migʀatœʀ, -tʀis] *a* migratory.

migration [migʀasjɔ̃] *nf* migration.

mijaurée [miʒɔʀe] *nf* pretentious girl.

mijoter [miʒɔte] *vt* to simmer; *(préparer avec soin)* to cook lovingly; *(affaire, projet)* to plot, cook up // *vi* to simmer.

mil [mil] *num* = **mille**.

mildiou [mildju] *nm* mildew.

milice [milis] *nf* militia; **milicien, ne** *nm/f* militia man/woman.

milieu, x [miljø] *nm (centre)* middle; *(fig)* middle course ou way; happy medium; *(BIO, GÉO)* environment; *(entourage social)* milieu; background; circle; *(pègre)*: **le ~** the underworld; **au ~ de** in the middle of.

militaire [militɛʀ] *a* military, army *cpd* // *nm* serviceman.

militant, e [militɑ̃, -ɑ̃t] *a, nm/f* militant.

militer [milite] *vi* to be a militant; **~ pour/contre** *(suj: faits, raisons etc)* to militate in favour of/against.

mille [mil] *num a ou* one thousand // *nm (mesure)*: **~ (marin)** nautical mile; **mettre dans le ~** to hit the bull's-eye; to be bang on target; **~-feuille** *nm* cream ou vanilla slice; **millénaire** *nm* millennium // *a* a thousand-year-old; *(fig)* ancient; **~-pattes** *nm inv* centipede.

millésime [milezim] *nm* year; **millésimé, e** *a* vintage *cpd*.

millet [mijɛ] *nm* millet.

milliard [miljaʀ] *nm* milliard, thousand million; **milliardaire** *nm/f* multi-millionaire.

millier [milje] *nm* thousand; **un ~ (de)** a thousand or so, about a thousand; **par ~s** in (their) thousands, by the thousand.

milligramme [miligʀam] *nm* milligramme.

millimètre [milimɛtʀ(ə)] *nm* millimetre; **millimétré, e** *a*: **papier millimétré** graph paper.

million [miljɔ̃] *nm* million; **deux ~s de** two million; **toucher cinq ~s** to get five million; **riche à ~s** worth millions; **millionnaire** *nm/f* millionaire.

mime [mim] *nm/f (acteur)* mime(r) // *nm (art)* mime, miming.

mimer [mime] *vt* to mime; *(singer)* to mimic, take off.

mimétisme [mimetism(ə)] *nm (BIO)* mimicry.

mimique [mimik] *nf (funny)* face; *(signes)* gesticulations *pl*, sign language *q*.

mimosa [mimoza] *nm* mimosa.

minable [minabl(ə)] *a* shabby (-looking); pathetic.

minauder [minode] *vi* to mince, simper.

mince [mɛ̃s] *a* thin; *(personne, taille)* slim, slender; *(fig: profit, connaissances)* slight, small // *excl* drat it!; **minceur** *nf* thinness; slimness, slenderness.

mine [min] nf (physionomie) expression, look; (extérieur) exterior, appearance; (de crayon) lead; (gisement, exploitation, explosif) mine; ~s nfpl (péj) simpering airs; **avoir bonne ~** (personne) to look well; (ironique) to look an utter idiot; **avoir mauvaise ~** to look unwell ou poorly; **faire ~ de faire** to make a pretence of doing; to make as if to do; **~ de rien** ad with a casual air; although you wouldn't think so; **~ de charbon** coalmine; **~ à ciel ouvert** opencast mine.

miner [mine] vt (saper) to undermine, erode; (MIL) to mine.

minerai [minRɛ] nm ore.

minéral, e, aux [mineral, -o] a mineral; (CHIMIE) inorganic // nm mineral.

minéralogie [mineralɔʒi] nf mineralogy.

minéralogique [mineralɔʒik] a mineralogical; **plaque ~** number plate; **numéro ~** registration number.

minet, te [minɛ, -ɛt] nm/f (chat) pussy-cat; (péj) young trendy/dollybird.

mineur, e [minœR] a minor // nm/f (JUR) minor, person under age // nm (travailleur) miner; **~ de fond** face worker.

miniature [minjatyR] a, nf miniature; **miniaturiser** vt to miniaturize.

minibus [minibys] nm minibus.

mini-cassette [minikasɛt] nf cassette (recorder).

minier, ière [minje, -jɛR] a mining.

mini-jupe [miniʒyp] nf mini-skirt.

minimal, e, aux [minimal, -o] a minimum.

minime [minim] a minor, minimal // nm/f (SPORT) junior.

minimiser [minimize] vt to minimize; (fig) to play down.

minimum [minimɔm] a, nm minimum; **au ~** (au moins) at the very least; **~ vital** living wage; subsistance level.

ministère [ministɛR] nm (aussi REL) ministry; (cabinet) government; **~ public** (JUR) Prosecution, State Prosecutor; **ministériel, le** a cabinet cpd; ministerial.

ministre [ministR(ə)] nm (aussi REL) minister; **~ d'État** senior minister (of the Interior or of Justice).

minium [minjɔm] nm red lead paint.

minois [minwa] nm little face.

minoritaire [minɔRitɛR] a minority cpd.

minorité [minɔRite] nf minority; **être en ~** to be in the ou a minority; **mettre en ~** (POL) to defeat.

minoterie [minɔtRi] nf flour-mill.

minuit [minɥi] nm midnight.

minuscule [minyskyl] a minute, tiny // nf: (lettre) **~** small letter.

minute [minyt] nf minute; (JUR: original) minute, draft; **à la ~** (just) this instant; there and then; **steak ~** minute steak; **minuter** vt to time; **minuterie** nf time switch.

minutieux, euse [minysjø, -øz] a meticulous; minutely detailed; requiring painstaking attention to detail.

mioche [mjɔʃ] nm (fam) nipper, brat.

mirabelle [miRabɛl] nf (cherry) plum; (eau-de-vie) plum brandy.

miracle [miRakl(ə)] nm miracle; **miraculé, e** a who has been miraculously cured (ou rescued); **miraculeux, euse** a miraculous.

mirador [miRadɔR] nm (MIL) watchtower.

mirage [miRaʒ] nm mirage.

mire [miR] nf: **point de ~** target; (fig) focal point; **ligne de ~** line of sight.

mirer [miRe] vt (œufs) to candle; **se ~** vi: **se ~ dans** to gaze at one's reflection in; to be mirrored in.

mirifique [miRifik] a wonderful.

mirobolant, e [miRɔbɔlɑ̃, -ɑ̃t] a fantastic.

miroir [miRwaR] nm mirror.

miroiter [miRwate] vi to sparkle, shimmer; **faire ~ qch à qn** to paint sth in glowing colours for sb, dangle sth in front of sb's eyes.

miroiterie [miRwatRi] nf mirror factory; mirror dealer's (shop).

mis, e [mi, miz] pp de **mettre** // a: **bien ~** well dressed // nf (argent: au jeu) stake; (tenue) clothing; attire; **être de ~e** to be acceptable ou in season; **~e de fonds** capital outlay; **~e à mort** kill; **~e en plis** set; **~e au point** (fig) clarification (voir aussi **point**); **~e en scène** production.

misaine [mizɛn] nf: **mât de ~** foremast.

misanthrope [mizɑ̃tRɔp] nm/f misanthropist.

mise [miz] a, nf voir **mis**.

miser [mize] vt (enjeu) to stake, bet; **~ sur** vt (cheval, numéro) to bet on; (fig) to bank ou count on.

misérable [mizeRabl(ə)] a (lamentable, malheureux) pitiful, wretched; (pauvre) poverty-stricken; (insignifiant, mesquin) miserable // nm/f wretch; (miséreux) poor wretch.

misère [mizɛR] nf (extreme) poverty, destitution; **~s** nfpl woes, miseries; little troubles; **être dans la ~** to be destitute ou poverty-stricken; **salaire de ~** starvation wage; **miséreux, euse** nm/f down-and-out.

miséricorde [mizeRikɔRd(ə)] nf mercy, forgiveness; **miséricordieux, euse** a merciful, forgiving.

misogyne [mizɔʒin] a misogynous // nm/f misogynist.

missel [misɛl] nm missal.

missile [misil] nm missile.

mission [misjɔ̃] nf mission; **partir en ~** (ADMIN, POL) to go on an assignment; **missionnaire** nm/f missionary.

missive [misiv] nf missive.

mit vb voir **mettre**.

mitaine [mitɛn] nf mitt(en).

mite [mit] nf clothes moth; **mité, e** a moth-eaten.

mi-temps [mitɑ̃] nf inv (SPORT: période) half (pl halves); (: pause) half-time; **à ~** a, ad part-time.

miteux, euse [mitø, -øz] a seedy, shabby.

mitigé, e [mitiʒe] a lukewarm; mixed.

mitonner [mitɔne] vt to cook with loving care; (fig) to cook up quietly.

mitoyen, ne [mitwajɛ̃, -ɛn] a common, party cpd; **maisons ~nes** semi-detached houses; (plus de deux) terraced houses.

mitraille [mitʀɑj] nf grapeshot ; shellfire.
mitrailler [mitʀɑje] vt to machine-gun ; (fig: photographier) to take shot after shot of ; ~ qn de to pelt sb with, bombard sb with ; **mitraillette** nf submachine gun ; **mitrailleur** nm machine gunner ; **mitrailleuse** nf machine gun.
mitre [mitʀ(ə)] nf mitre.
mitron [mitʀɔ̃] nm baker's boy.
mi-voix [mivwa]: à ~ ad in a low ou hushed voice.
mixage [miksaʒ] nm (CINÉMA) (sound) mixing.
mixer [miksœʀ] nm (food) mixer.
mixité [miksite] nf (SCOL) coeducation.
mixte [mikst(ə)] a (gén) mixed ; (SCOL) mixed, coeducational ; à usage ~ dual-purpose ; **cuisinière** ~ gas and electric cooker ; **équipe** ~ combined team.
mixture [mikstyʀ] nf mixture ; (fig) concoction.
M.L.F. sigle m = mouvement de libération de la femme, ≈ Women's Lib.
Mlle, pl **Mlles** abr de **Mademoiselle**.
MM abr de **Messieurs**.
Mme, pl **Mmes** abr de **Madame**.
mnémotechnique [mnemɔtɛknik] a mnemonic.
Mo abr de **métro**.
mobile [mɔbil] a mobile ; (pièce de machine) moving ; (élément de meuble etc) movable // nm (motif) motive ; (œuvre d'art) mobile ; (PHYSIQUE) moving object ou body.
mobilier, ière [mɔbilje, -jɛʀ] a (JUR) personal // nm furniture ; **valeurs mobilières** transferable securities ; **vente mobilière** sale of personal property ou chattels.
mobilisation [mɔbilizɑsjɔ̃] nf mobilization.
mobiliser [mɔbilize] vt (MIL, gén) to mobilize.
mobilité [mɔbilite] nf mobility.
mocassin [mɔkasɛ̃] nm moccasin.
moche [mɔʃ] a (fam) ugly ; rotten.
modalité [mɔdalite] nf form, mode ; ~s nfpl (d'un accord etc) clauses, terms.
mode [mɔd] nf fashion ; (commerce) fashion trade ou industry // nm (manière) form, mode ; (LING) mood ; (MUS) mode ; à la ~ fashionable, in fashion ; ~ d'emploi directions pl (for use) ; ~ de vie way of life.
modèle [mɔdɛl] a, nm model ; (qui pose: de peintre) sitter ; ~ déposé registered design ; ~ réduit small-scale model ; ~ de série production model.
modelé [mɔdle] nm relief ; contours pl.
modeler [mɔdle] vt (ART) to model, mould ; (suj: vêtement, érosion) to mould, shape ; ~ qch sur/d'après to model sth on.
modérateur, trice [mɔdeʀatœʀ, -tʀis] a moderating // nm/f moderator.
modération [mɔdeʀɑsjɔ̃] nf moderation.
modéré, e [mɔdeʀe] a, nm/f moderate.
modérer [mɔdeʀe] vt to moderate ; se ~ vi to restrain o.s.
moderne [mɔdɛʀn(ə)] a modern // nm modern style ; modern furniture ; **moderniser** vt to modernize.

modeste [mɔdɛst(ə)] a modest ; **modestie** nf modesty.
modicité [mɔdisite] nf: **la** ~ **des prix** etc the low prices etc.
modification [mɔdifikɑsjɔ̃] nf modification.
modifier [mɔdifje] vt to modify, alter ; (LING) to modify ; **se** ~ vi to alter.
modique [mɔdik] a modest.
modiste [mɔdist(ə)] nf milliner.
modulation [mɔdylɑsjɔ̃] nf modulation ; ~ **de fréquence (FM** ou **MF)** frequency modulation.
module [mɔdyl] nm module.
moduler [mɔdyle] vt to modulate ; (air) to warble.
moelle [mwal] nf marrow ; (fig) pith, core ; ~ **épinière** spinal chord.
moelleux, euse [mwalø, -øz] a soft ; (au goût, à l'ouïe) mellow.
moellon [mwalɔ̃] nm rubble stone.
mœurs [mœʀ] nfpl (conduite) morals ; (manières) manners ; (pratiques sociales, mode de vie) habits ; **passer dans les** ~ to become the custom ; **contraire aux bonnes** ~ contrary to proprieties.
mohair [mɔɛʀ] nm mohair.
moi [mwa] pronom me ; (emphatique): ~, je for my part, I, I myself.
moignon [mwaɲɔ̃] nm stump.
moi-même [mwamɛm] pronom myself ; (emphatique) I myself.
moindre [mwɛ̃dʀ(ə)] a lesser ; lower ; **le(la)** ~, **les** ~s the least, the slightest.
moine [mwan] nm monk, friar.
moineau, x [mwano] nm sparrow.
moins [mwɛ̃] ad less // cj: ~ **2** minus 2 ; ~ **je travaille, mieux je me porte** the less I work the better I feel ; ~ **grand que** not as tall as, less tall than ; **le(la)** ~ **doué(e)** the least gifted ; **le** ~ the least ; ~ **de** (sable, eau) less ; (livres, gens) fewer ; ~ **de 2 ans/100 F** less than 2 years/100 F ; ~ **de midi** not yet midday ; **100 F/3 jours de** ~ 100 F/3 days less ; **3 livres en** ~ 3 books fewer ; **3 books too few** ; **de l'argent en** ~ less money ; **le soleil en** ~ but for the sun, minus the sun ; **à** ~ **que** cj unless ; **à** ~ **de faire** unless we do (ou he does) ; **à** ~ **de** (imprévu, accident) barring any ; **au** ~ at least ; **de** ~ **en** ~ less and less ; **pour le** ~ at the very least ; **du** ~ at least ; **il est** ~ **cinq** it's five to ; **il fait** ~ **cinq** it's five below (freezing) ou minus five.
moiré, e [mwaʀe] a (tissu, papier) moiré, watered ; (reflets) shimmering.
mois [mwa] nm month ; ~ **double** (COMM) extra month's salary.
moïse [mɔiz] nm Moses basket.
moisi, e [mwazi] a mouldy, mildewed // nm mould, mildew ; **odeur de** ~ musty smell.
moisir [mwaziʀ] vi to go mouldy ; (fig) to rot ; to hang about.
moisissure [mwazisyʀ] nf mould q.
moisson [mwasɔ̃] nf harvest ; (fig): **faire une** ~ **de** to gather a wealth of ; **moissonner** vt to harvest, reap ; (fig) to collect ; **moissonneur, euse** nm/f harvester, reaper // nf (machine)

harvester; **moissonneuse-batteuse** nf combine harvester.

moite [mwat] a sweaty, sticky.

moitié [mwatje] nf half (pl halves); (épouse): **sa** ~ his loving wife, his better half; **la** ~ half; **la** ~ **de** half (of), half the amount (ou number) of; **la** ~ **du temps/des gens** half the time/the people; **à la** ~ **de** halfway through; ~ **moins grand** half as tall; ~ **plus long** half as long again, longer by half; **à** ~ half (avant le verbe); half- (avant l'adjectif); **de** ~ by half; ~ ~ half-and-half.

moka [mɔka] nm mocha coffee; mocha cake.

mol [mɔl] a voir **mou**.

molaire [mɔlɛʀ] nf molar.

molécule [mɔlekyl] nf molecule.

moleskine [mɔlɛskin] nf imitation leather.

molester [mɔlɛste] vt to manhandle, maul (about).

molette [mɔlɛt] nf toothed ou cutting wheel.

molle [mɔl] af voir **mou**; ~**ment** ad softly; (péj) sluggishly; (protester) feebly; **mollesse** nf softness; flabbiness; limpness; sluggishness.

mollet [mɔlɛ] nm calf (pl calves) // am: **œuf** ~ soft-boiled egg; **molletière** af: **bande molletière** puttee.

molletonné, e [mɔltɔne] a fleece-lined, flannelette-lined.

mollir [mɔliʀ] vi to give way; to relent; to go soft.

mollusque [mɔlysk(ə)] nm (ZOOL) mollusc.

molosse [mɔlɔs] nm big ferocious dog.

môme [mom] nm/f (fam: enfant) brat; (: fille) bird.

moment [mɔmɑ̃] nm moment; **ce n'est pas le** ~ this is not the (right) time; **à un certain** ~ at some point; **pour un bon** ~ for a good while; **pour le** ~ for the moment, for the time being; **au** ~ **de** at the time of; **au** ~ **où** as; at a time when; **à tout** ~ at any time ou moment; constantly, continually; **en ce** ~ at the moment; at present; **sur le** ~ at the time; **par** ~ **s** now and then, at times; **du** ~ **où** ou **que** seeing that, since; **momentané, e** a temporary, momentary.

momie [mɔmi] nf mummy.

mon [mɔ̃], **ma** [ma], pl **mes** [me] dét my.

monacal, e, aux [mɔnakal, -o] a monastic.

monarchie [mɔnaʀʃi] nf monarchy; **monarchiste** a, nm/f monarchist.

monarque [mɔnaʀk(ə)] nm monarch.

monastère [mɔnastɛʀ] nm monastery.

monastique [mɔnastik] a monastic.

monceau, x [mɔ̃so] nm heap.

mondain, e [mɔ̃dɛ̃, -ɛn] a society cpd; social; fashionable // nm/f society man/woman, socialite // nf: **la M**~**e, la police** ~**e** ≈ the vice squad; **mondanités** nfpl society life sg; (society) small talk sg; (society) gossip column sg.

monde [mɔ̃d] nm world; (haute société): **le** ~ (high) society; (milieu): **être du même** ~ to move in the same circles; (gens): **il y a du** ~ (beaucoup de gens) there are many people; (quelques personnes) there are some people; **y a-t-il du** ~ **dans le salon?** is there anybody in the lounge?; **beaucoup/peu de** ~ many/few people; **le meilleur** etc **du** ~ the best etc in the world ou on earth; **mettre au** ~ to bring into the world; **pas le moins du** ~ not in the least; **se faire un** ~ **de qch** to make a great deal of fuss about sth; **mondial, e, aux** a (population) world cpd; (influence) world-wide; **mondialement** ad throughout the world; **mondovision** nf world coverage by satellite.

monégasque [mɔnegask(ə)] a Monegasque, of ou from Monaco.

monétaire [mɔnetɛʀ] a monetary.

mongolien, ne [mɔ̃gɔljɛ̃, -jɛn] a, nm/f mongol.

mongolisme [mɔ̃gɔlism(ə)] nm mongolism.

moniteur, trice [mɔnitœʀ, -tʀis] nm/f (SPORT) instructor/instructress; (de colonie de vacances) supervisor // nm: ~ **cardiaque** cardiac monitor; ~ **d'auto-école** driving instructor.

monnaie [mɔnɛ] nf (pièce) coin; (ÉCON, gén: moyen d'échange) currency; (petites pièces): **avoir de la** ~ to have (some) change; **faire de la** ~ to get (some) change; **avoir/faire la** ~ **de 20 F** to have change of/get change for 20 F; **faire à qn la** ~ **de 20 F** to give sb change for 20 F, change 20 F for sb; **rendre à qn la** ~ (**sur 20 F**) to give sb the change (out of ou from 20 F); **c'est** ~ **courante** it's a common occurrence; **monnayer** vt to convert into cash; (talent) to capitalize on; **monnayeur** nm voir **faux**.

monocle [mɔnɔkl(ə)] nm monocle, eyeglass.

monocorde [mɔnɔkɔʀd(ə)] a monotonous.

monoculture [mɔnɔkyltyʀ] nf single-crop farming, monoculture.

monogramme [mɔnɔgʀam] nm monogram.

monolingue [mɔnɔlɛ̃g] a monolingual.

monologue [mɔnɔlɔg] nm monologue, soliloquy; **monologuer** vi to soliloquize.

monôme [mɔnom] nm (MATH) monomial; (d'étudiants) students' rag procession.

monoplace [mɔnɔplas] a, nm, nf single-seater, one-seater.

monopole [mɔnɔpɔl] nm monopoly; **monopoliser** vt to monopolize.

monorail [mɔnɔʀaj] nm monorail, monorail train.

monosyllabe [mɔnɔsilab] nm monosyllable, word of one syllable.

monotone [mɔnɔtɔn] a monotonous; **monotonie** nf monotony.

monseigneur [mɔ̃sɛɲœʀ] nm (archevêque, évêque) Your (ou His) Grace; (cardinal) Your (ou His) Eminence; **Mgr Thomas** Bishop Thomas; Cardinal Thomas.

Monsieur [məsjø], pl **Messieurs** [mesjø] titre Mr ['mistə°]; (homme quelconque): **un/le m**~ a/the gentleman; voir aussi **Madame**.

monstre [mɔ̃stʀ(ə)] nm monster // a: **un travail** ~ a fantastic amount of work; an enormous job; **monstrueux, euse** a monstrous; **monstruosité** nf monstrosity.

mont [mɔ̃] nm: par ~s et par vaux up hill and down dale; le M~ Blanc Mont Blanc; le ~ de Vénus mons veneris.

montage [mɔ̃taʒ] nm putting up; mounting, setting; assembly; (PHOTO) photomontage; (CINÉMA) editing; ~ sonore sound editing.

montagnard, e [mɔ̃taɲaʀ, -aʀd(ə)] a mountain cpd // nm/f mountain-dweller.

montagne [mɔ̃taɲ] nf (cime) mountain; (région): la ~ the mountains pl; ~s russes big dipper sg, switchback sg.

montant, e [mɔ̃tɑ̃, -ɑ̃t] a rising; (robe, corsage) high-necked // nm (somme, total), (sum) total, (total) amount; (de fenêtre) upright; (de lit) post.

mont-de-piété [mɔ̃dpjete] nm pawnshop.

monte-charge [mɔ̃tʃaʀʒ(ə)] nm inv goods lift, hoist.

montée [mɔ̃te] nf rising, rise; ascent, climb; (chemin) way up; (côte) hill; au milieu de la ~ halfway up; le moteur chauffe dans les ~s the engine overheats going uphill.

monte-plats [mɔ̃tpla] nm inv service lift.

monter [mɔ̃te] vt (escalier, côte) to go (ou come) up; (valise, paquet) to take (ou bring) up; (cheval) to mount; (femelle) to cover, serve; (étagère) to raise; (tente, échafaudage) to put up; (machine) to assemble; (bijou) to mount, set; (COUTURE) to set in; to sew on; (CINÉMA) to edit; (THÉÂTRE) to put on, stage; (société etc) to set up // vi to go (ou come) up; (avion etc) to climb, go up; (chemin, niveau, température) to go up, rise; (passager) to get on; (à cheval): ~ bien/mal to ride well/badly; ~ à pied/en voiture to walk/drive up, go up on foot/by car; ~ dans le train/l'avion to get into the train/plane, board the train/plane; ~ sur to climb up onto; ~ à cheval to get on ou mount a horse; se ~ (s'équiper) to equip o.s., get kitted up; se ~ à (frais etc) to add up to, come to; ~ qn contre qn to set sb against sb; ~ la tête à qn to give sb ideas; **monteur, euse** nm/f (TECH) fitter; (CINÉMA) (film) editor.

monticule [mɔ̃tikyl] nm mound.

montre [mɔ̃tʀ(ə)] nf watch; (ostentation): pour la ~ for show; faire ~ de to show, display; contre la ~ (SPORT) against the clock; ~-bracelet nf wrist watch.

montrer [mɔ̃tʀe] vt to show; ~ qch à qn to show sb sth; **montreur de marionnettes** nm puppeteer.

monture [mɔ̃tyʀ] nf (bête) mount; (d'une bague) setting; (de lunettes) frame.

monument [mɔnymɑ̃] nm monument; ~ aux morts war memorial; **monumental, e, aux** a monumental.

moquer [mɔke]: se ~ de vt to make fun of, laugh at; (fam: se désintéresser de) not to care about; (tromper): se ~ de qn to take sb for a ride.

moquerie [mɔkʀi] nf mockery q.

moquette [mɔkɛt] nf fitted carpet, wall-to-wall carpeting q.

moqueur, euse [mɔkœʀ, -øz] a mocking.

moral, e, aux [mɔʀal, -o] a moral // nm morale // nf (conduite) morals pl; (règles) moral code, ethic; (valeurs) moral standards pl, morality; (science) ethics sg, moral philosophy; (conclusion: d'une fable etc) moral; au ~, sur le plan ~ morally; faire la ~ e à to lecture, preach at; ~ isateur, trice a moralizing, sanctimonious; ~ iser vt (sermonner) to lecture, preach at; ~ iste nm/f moralist // a moralistic; ~ ité nf morality; (conduite) morals pl; (conclusion, enseignement) moral.

morbide [mɔʀbid] a morbid.

morceau, x [mɔʀso] nm piece, bit; (d'une œuvre) passage, extract; (MUS) piece; (CULIN: de viande) cut; mettre en ~x to pull to pieces ou bits.

morceler [mɔʀsəle] vt to break up, divide up.

mordant, e [mɔʀdɑ̃, -ɑ̃t] a scathing, cutting; biting // nm spirit; bite, punch.

mordicus [mɔʀdikys] ad (affirmer etc) obstinately, stubbornly.

mordiller [mɔʀdije] vt to nibble at, chew at.

mordoré, e [mɔʀdɔʀe] a lustrous bronze.

mordre [mɔʀdʀ(ə)] vt to bite; (suj: lime, vis) to bite into // vi (poisson) to bite; ~ dans (fruit) to bite into; ~ sur (fig) to go over into, overlap into; ~ à l'hameçon to bite, rise to the bait.

mordu, e [mɔʀdy] pp de mordre // a (amoureux) smitten // nm/f: un ~ du jazz/de la voile a jazz/sailing fanatic ou buff.

morfondre [mɔʀfɔ̃dʀ(ə)]: se ~ vi to fret.

morgue [mɔʀg(ə)] nf (arrogance) haughtiness; (lieu: de la police) morgue; (: à l'hôpital) mortuary.

moribond, e [mɔʀibɔ̃, -ɔ̃d] a dying, moribund.

morille [mɔʀij] nf morel.

morne [mɔʀn(ə)] a dismal, dreary.

morose [mɔʀoz] a sullen, morose.

morphine [mɔʀfin] nf morphine; **morphinomane** nm/f morphine addict.

morphologie [mɔʀfɔlɔʒi] nf morphology.

mors [mɔʀ] nm bit.

morse [mɔʀs(ə)] nm (ZOOL) walrus; (TEL) Morse (code).

morsure [mɔʀsyʀ] nf bite.

mort [mɔʀ] nf death; se donner la ~ to take one's life.

mort, e [mɔʀ, mɔʀt(ə)] pp de mourir // a dead // nm/f (défunt) dead man/woman; (victime): il y a eu plusieurs ~s several people were killed, there were several killed // nm (CARTES) dummy; ~ ou vif dead or alive; ~ de peur/fatigue frightened to death/dead tired.

mortadelle [mɔʀtadɛl] nf mortadella (type of luncheon meat).

mortalité [mɔʀtalite] nf mortality, death rate.

mortel, le [mɔʀtɛl] a (poison etc) deadly, lethal; (accident, blessure) fatal; (REL) mortal; (fig) deathly; deadly boring // nm/f mortal.

morte-saison [mɔʀtəsɛzɔ̃] nf slack ou off season.

mortier [mɔʀtje] nm (gén) mortar.

mortifier [mɔrtifje] vt to mortify.

mort-né, e [mɔrne] a (enfant) stillborn ; (fig) abortive.

mortuaire [mɔrtɥɛr] a funeral cpd ; **avis ~s** death announcements, intimations ; **chapelle ~** mortuary chapel ; **couronne ~** (funeral) wreath ; **domicile ~** house of the deceased ; **drap ~** pall.

morue [mɔry] nf (ZOOL) cod inv ; (CULIN : salée) salt-cod ; **morutier** nm cod fisherman ; cod fishing boat.

morveux, euse [mɔrvø, -øz] a (fam) snotty-nosed.

mosaïque [mɔzaik] nf (ART) mosaic ; (fig) patchwork.

Moscou [mɔsku] n Moscow ; **moscovite** a of ou from Moscow // a,n/f Muscovite.

mosquée [mɔske] nf mosque.

mot [mo] nm word ; (message) line, note ; (bon mot etc) saying ; sally ; **~ à ~** a, ad word for word ; **~ pour ~** word for word, verbatim ; **prendre qn au ~** to take sb at his word ; **avoir son ~ à dire** to have a say ; **~s croisés** crossword (puzzle) sg ; **~ d'ordre** watchword ; **~ de passe** password.

motard [mɔtar] nm motorcycle cop.

motel [mɔtɛl] nm motel.

moteur, trice [mɔtœr, -tris] a (ANAT, PHYSIOL) motor ; (troubles) motory ; (TECH) driving ; (AUTO): **à 4 roues motrices** 4-wheel drive // nm engine, motor ; (fig) mover, mainspring ; **à ~** power-driven, motor cpd ; **~ à deux temps** two-stroke engine ; **~ à explosion** internal combustion engine.

motif [mɔtif] nm (cause) motive ; (décoratif) design, pattern, motif ; (d'un tableau) subject, motif ; (MUS) figure, motif ; **~s** nmpl (JUR) grounds pl ; **sans ~** a groundless.

motion [mosjɔ̃] nf motion ; **~ de censure** motion of censure, vote of no confidence.

motivation [mɔtivusjɔ̃] nf motivation.

motivé, e [mɔtive] a (acte) justified ; (personne) motivated.

motiver [mɔtive] vt (justifier) to justify, account for ; (ADMIN, JUR, PSYCH) to motivate.

moto [mɔto] nf (motor)bike ; **~-cross** nm motocross ; **~cyclette** nf motorbike, motorcycle ; **~cyclisme** nm motorcycle racing ; **~cycliste** nm/f motorcyclist.

motorisé, e [mɔtɔrize] a (troupe) motorized ; (personne) having transport ou a car.

motrice [mɔtris] a voir **moteur** ; **motricité** nf motor functions.

motte [mɔt] nf: **~ de terre** lump of earth, clod (of earth) ; **~ de gazon** turf, sod ; **~ de beurre** lump of butter.

motus [mɔtys] excl: **~ (et bouche cousue)!** mum's the word!

mou(mol), molle [mu, mɔl] a soft ; (péj) flabby ; limp ; sluggish ; feeble // nm (abats) lights pl, lungs pl ; (de la corde): **avoir du ~** to be slack.

mouchard, e [muʃar, -ard(ə)] nm/f grass // nm (appareil) control device.

mouche [muʃ] nf fly ; (ESCRIME) button ; (de taffetas) patch ; **prendre la ~** to take the huff ; **faire ~** to score a bull's-eye.

moucher [muʃe] vt (enfant) to blow the nose of ; (chandelle) to snuff (out) ; **se ~** vi to blow one's nose.

moucheron [muʃrɔ̃] nm midge.

moucheté, e [muʃte] a dappled ; flecked ; (ESCRIME) buttoned.

mouchoir [muʃwar] nm handkerchief, hanky ; **~ en papier** tissue, paper hanky.

moudre [mudr(ə)] vt to grind.

moue [mu] nf pout ; **faire la ~** to pout ; (fig) to pull a face.

mouette [mwɛt] nf (sea)gull.

moufle [mufl(ə)] nf (gant) mitt(en) ; (TECH) pulley block.

mouflon [muflɔ̃] nm mouf(f)lon.

mouillage [mujaʒ] nm (NAVIG : lieu) anchorage, moorings pl.

mouillé, e [muje] a wet.

mouiller [muje] vt (humecter) to wet, moisten ; (tremper): **~ qn/qch** to make sb/sth wet ; (couper, diluer) to water down ; (mine etc) to lay // vi (NAVIG) to lie ou be at anchor ; **se ~** to get wet ; (fam) to commit o.s. ; to get o.s. involved ; **~ l'ancre** to drop ou cast anchor ; **mouillure** nf wet q ; wet patch.

moulage [mulaʒ] nm moulding ; casting ; (objet) cast.

moule [mul] nf mussel // nm (creux, CULIN) mould ; (modèle plein) cast ; **~ à gâteaux** nm cake tin.

moulent vb voir aussi **moudre**.

mouler [mule] vt (brique) to mould ; (statue) to cast ; (visage, bas-relief) to make a cast of ; (lettre) to shape with care ; (suj : vêtement) to hug, fit closely round ; **~ qch sur** (fig) to model sth on.

moulin [mulɛ̃] nm mill ; (fam) engine ; **~ à café/à poivre** coffee/pepper mill ; **~ à légumes** (vegetable) shredder ; **~ à paroles** (fig) chatterbox ; **~ à prières** prayer wheel ; **~ à vent** windmill.

moulinet [mulinɛ] nm (de treuil) winch ; (de canne à pêche) reel ; (mouvement): **faire des ~s avec qch** to whirl sth around.

moulinette [mulinɛt] nf (vegetable) shredder.

moulu, e [muly] pp de **moudre**.

moulure [mulyr] nf (ornement) moulding.

mourant, e [murɑ̃, -ɑ̃t] a dying // nm/f dying man/woman.

mourir [murir] vi to die ; (civilisation) to die out ; **~ de froid/faim** to die of exposure/hunger ; **~ de faim/d'ennui** (fig) to be starving/be bored to death ; **~ d'envie de faire** to be dying to do.

mousquetaire [muskətɛr] nm musketeer.

mousqueton [muskətɔ̃] nm (fusil) carbine ; (anneau) snap-link, karabiner.

mousse [mus] nf (BOT) moss ; (écume : sur eau, bière) froth, foam ; (: shampooing) lather ; (CULIN) mousse // nm (NAVIG) ship's boy ; **bain de ~** bubble bath ; **bas ~** stretch stockings ; **balle ~** rubber ball ; **~ carbonique** (fire-fighting) foam ; **~ de nylon** stretch nylon ; foam ; **~ à raser** shaving foam.

mousseline [muslin] nf muslin ; chiffon ; **pommes ~** creamed potatoes.

mousser [muse] vi to foam ; to lather.

mousseux, euse [musø, -øz] a frothy // nm: (vin) ~ sparkling wine.

mousson [musɔ̃] nf monsoon.

moussu, e [musy] a mossy.

moustache [mustaʃ] nf moustache ; ~s nfpl (du chat) whiskers pl ; **moustachu, e** a wearing a moustache.

moustiquaire [mustikɛʀ] nf mosquito net (ou screen).

moustique [mustik] nm mosquito.

moutarde [mutaʀd] nf mustard.

mouton [mutɔ̃] nm (zool, péj) sheep inv ; (peau) sheepskin ; (culin) mutton ; ~s nmpl (fig) white horses ; fluffy ou fleecy clouds ; bits of fluff.

mouture [mutyʀ] nf grinding ; (péj) rehash.

mouvant, e [muvɑ̃, -ɑ̃t] a unsettled ; changing ; shifting.

mouvement [muvmɑ̃] nm (gén, aussi: mécanisme) movement ; (fig) activity ; impulse ; reaction ; gesture ; (mus: rythme) tempo (pl s) ; **en** ~ in motion ; on the move ; **mettre qch en** ~ to set sth in motion, set sth going ; ~ **d'humeur** fit ou burst of temper ; ~ **d'opinion** trend of (public) opinion ; **le** ~ **perpétuel** perpetual motion ; **mouvementé, e** a (vie, poursuite) eventful ; (réunion) turbulent.

mouvoir [muvwaʀ] vt (levier, membre) to move ; (machine) to drive ; **se** ~ to move.

moyen, ne [mwajɛ̃, -ɛn] a average ; (tailles, prix) medium ; (de grandeur moyenne) medium-sized // nm (façon) means sg, way // nf average ; (math) mean ; (scol: à l'examen) pass mark ; (auto) average speed ; ~s nmpl (capacités) means ; **au** ~ **de** by means of ; **y a-t-il** ~ **de** ...? is it possible to ...?, can one ...? ; **par quel** ~? how?, which way?, by which means? ; **par tous les** ~s by every possible means, every possible way ; **employer les grands** ~s to resort to drastic measures ; **par ses propres** ~s all by oneself ; **en** ~**ne** on (an) average ; ~ **de locomotion/d'expression** means of transport/expression ; ~ **âge** Middle Ages ; ~**ne d'âge** average age.

moyennant [mwajɛnɑ̃] prép (somme) for ; (service, conditions) in return for ; (travail, effort) with.

Moyen-Orient [mwajɛnɔʀjɑ̃] nm: **le** ~ the Middle East.

moyeu, x [mwajø] nm hub.

mû, mue [my] pp de **mouvoir**.

mucosité [mykozite] nf mucus q.

mucus [mykys] nm mucus q.

mue [my] pp voir **mouvoir** // nf moulting ; sloughing ; breaking of the voice.

muer [mɥe] vi (oiseau, mammifère) to moult ; (serpent) to slough ; (jeune garçon) : **il mue** his voice is breaking ; **se** ~ **en** to transform into.

muet, te [mɥɛ, -ɛt] a dumb ; (fig) : ~ **d'admiration** etc speechless with admiration etc ; (joie, douleur, cinéma) silent ; (ling: lettre) silent, mute ; (carte) blank // nm/f mute.

mufle [myfl(ə)] nm muzzle ; (goujat) boor // a boorish.

mugir [myʒiʀ] vi to bellow ; to low ; (fig) to howl.

muguet [mygɛ] nm lily of the valley.

mulâtre, tresse [mylɑtʀ(ə), -tʀɛs] nm/f mulatto.

mule [myl] nf (zool) (she-)mule ; ~s nfpl (pantoufles) mules.

mulet [mylɛ] nm (zool) (he-)mule ; **muletier, ière** a: **chemin muletier** mule track.

mulot [mylo] nm field mouse (pl mice).

multicolore [myltikɔlɔʀ] a multicoloured.

multinational, e, aux [myltinasjɔnal, -o] a multinational.

multiple [myltipl(ə)] a multiple, numerous ; (varié) many, manifold // nm (math) multiple.

multiplicateur [myltiplikatœʀ] nm multiplier.

multiplication [myltiplikasjɔ̃] nf multiplication.

multiplicité [myltiplisite] nf multiplicity.

multiplier [myltiplije] vt to multiply ; **se** ~ vi to multiply ; to increase in number.

multitude [myltityd] nf multitude ; mass ; **une** ~ **de** a vast number of, a multitude of.

municipal, e, aux [mynisipal, -o] a municipal ; town cpd, ≈ borough cpd.

municipalité [mynisipalite] nf (corps municipal) town council, corporation ; (commune) town, municipality.

munir [myniʀ] vt: ~ **qn/qch de** to equip sb/sth with.

munitions [mynisjɔ̃] nfpl ammunition sg.

muqueuse [mykøz] nf mucous membrane.

mur [myʀ] nm wall ; ~ **du son** sound barrier.

mûr, e [myʀ] a ripe ; (personne) mature // nf blackberry ; mulberry.

muraille [myʀaj] nf (high) wall.

mural, e, aux [myʀal, -o] a wall cpd ; mural.

mûrement [myʀmɑ̃] ad: **ayant** ~ **réfléchi** having given the matter much thought.

murène [myʀɛn] nf moray (eel).

murer [myʀe] vt (enclos) to wall (in) ; (porte, issue) to wall up ; (personne) to wall up ou in.

muret [myʀɛ] nm low wall.

mûrier [myʀje] nm blackberry bush ; mulberry tree.

mûrir [myʀiʀ] vi (fruit, blé) to ripen ; (abcès, furoncle) to come to a head ; (fig: idée, personne) to mature // vt to ripen ; to (make) mature.

murmure [myʀmyʀ] nm murmur ; ~s nmpl (plaintes) murmurings, mutterings ; **murmurer** vi to murmur ; (se plaindre) to mutter, grumble.

musaraigne [myzaʀɛɲ] nf shrew.

musarder [myzaʀde] vi to dawdle (along) ; to idle (about).

musc [mysk] nm musk.

muscade [myskad] nf nutmeg.

muscat [myska] nm muscat grape ; muscatel (wine).

muscle [myskl(ə)] nm muscle ; **musclé, e** a muscular ; **musculation** nf: **exercices de musculation** muscle-developing exercises ; **musculature** nf muscle structure, muscles pl.

museau, x [myzo] *nm* muzzle.

musée [myze] *nm* museum ; art gallery.

museler [myzle] *vt* to muzzle ; **muselière** *nf* muzzle.

musette [myzɛt] *nf* (*sac*) lunchbag // *a inv* (*orchestre etc*) accordion *cpd*.

muséum [myzeɔm] *nm* museum.

musical, e, aux [myzikal, -o] *a* musical.

music-hall [myzikol] *nm* variety theatre ; (*genre*) variety.

musicien, ne [myzisjɛ̃, -jɛn] *nm/f* musician.

musique [myzik] *nf* music ; (*fanfare*) band ; **faire de la ~** to make some music ; to play an instrument ; **~ de chambre** chamber music ; **~ de fond** background music.

musqué, e [myske] *a* musky.

musulman, e [myzylmɑ̃, -an] *a, nm/f* Moslem, Muslim.

mutation [mytɑsjɔ̃] *nf* (*ADMIN*) transfer ; (*BIO*) mutation.

muter [myte] *vt* (*ADMIN*) to transfer.

mutilation [mytilɑsjɔ̃] *nf* mutilation.

mutilé, e [mytile] *nm/f* disabled person (*through loss of limbs*).

mutiler [mytile] *vt* to mutilate, maim ; (*fig*) to mutilate, deface.

mutin, e [mytɛ̃, -in] *a* (*air, ton*) mischievous, impish // *nm/f* (*MIL, NAVIG*) mutineer.

mutiner [mytine]: **se ~** *vi* to mutiny ; **mutinerie** *nf* mutiny.

mutisme [mytism(ə)] *nm* silence.

mutuel, le [mytɥɛl] *a* mutual // *nf* mutual benefit society.

myocarde [mjɔkaRd(ə)] *nm voir* infarctus.

myope [mjɔp] *a* short-sighted ; **myopie** *nf* short-sightedness, myopia.

myosotis [mjozɔtis] *nm* forget-me-not.

myriade [miRjad] *nf* myriad.

myrtille [miRtij] *nf* bilberry, whortleberry.

mystère [mistɛR] *nm* mystery ; **mystérieux, euse** *a* mysterious.

mysticisme [mistisism(ə)] *nm* mysticism.

mystification [mistifikɑsjɔ̃] *nf* hoax ; mystification.

mystifier [mistifje] *vt* to fool ; to mystify.

mystique [mistik] *a* mystic, mystical // *nm/f* mystic.

mythe [mit] *nm* myth ; **mythique** *a* mythical.

mythologie [mitɔlɔʒi] *nf* mythology ; **mythologique** *a* mythological.

mythomane [mitɔman] *nm/f* mythomaniac.

N

n' [n] *ad voir* ne.

nacelle [nasɛl] *nf* (*de ballon*) basket.

nacre [nakR(ə)] *nf* mother of pearl ; **nacré, e** *a* pearly.

nage [naʒ] *nf* swimming ; style of swimming, stroke ; **traverser/s'éloigner à la ~** to swim across/away ; **en ~** bathed in perspiration.

nageoire [naʒwaR] *nf* fin.

nager [naʒe] *vi* to swim ; **nageur, euse** *nm/f* swimmer.

naguère [nagɛR] *ad* formerly.

naïf, ïve [naif, naiv] *a* naïve.

nain, e [nɛ̃, nɛn] *nm/f* dwarf.

naissance [nɛsɑ̃s] *nf* birth ; **donner ~ à** to give birth to ; (*fig*) to give rise to ; **aveugle de ~** born blind ; **Français de ~** French by birth ; **à la ~ des cheveux** at the roots of the hair.

naissant, e [nɛsɑ̃, -ɑ̃t] *a* budding, incipient ; dawning.

naître [nɛtR(ə)] *vi* to be born ; (*conflit, complications*): **~ de** to arise from, be born out of ; **~ à** (*amour, poésie*) to awaken to ; **il est né en 1960** he was born in 1960 ; **il naît plus de filles que de garçons** there are more girls born than boys ; **faire ~** (*fig*) to give rise to, arouse.

naïveté [naivte] *nf* naïvety.

nantir [nɑ̃tiR] *vt*: **~ qn de** to provide sb with ; **les nantis** (*péj*) the well-to-do.

napalm [napalm] *nm* napalm.

nappe [nap] *nf* tablecloth ; (*fig*) sheet ; layer ; **~-ron** *nm* table-mat.

naquit *etc vb voir* naître.

narcisse [narsis] *nm* narcissus.

narcissisme [narsisism(ə)] *nm* narcissism.

narcotique [narkɔtik] *a, nm* narcotic.

narguer [narge] *vt* to taunt.

narine [narin] *nf* nostril.

narquois, e [narkwa, -waz] *a* derisive, mocking.

narrateur, trice [naratœR, -tRis] *nm/f* narrator.

narrer [naRe] *vt* to tell the story of, recount.

nasal, e, aux [nazal, -o] *a* nasal.

naseau, x [nazo] *nm* nostril.

nasiller [nazije] *vi* to speak with a (nasal) twang.

nasse [nas] *nf* fish-trap.

natal, e [natal] *a* native.

nataliste [natalist(ə)] *a* supporting a rising birth rate.

natalité [natalite] *nf* birth rate.

natation [natɑsjɔ̃] *nf* swimming.

natif, ive [natif, -iv] *a* native.

nation [nɑsjɔ̃] *nf* nation ; **les N~s Unies** the United Nations.

national, e, aux [nasjɔnal, -o] *a* national // *nf*: (*route*) **~e** trunk road, ≈ A road ; **obsèques ~es** state funeral ; **~iser** *vt* to nationalize ; **~isme** *nm* nationalism ; **~ité** *nf* nationality.

natte [nat] *nf* (*tapis*) mat ; (*cheveux*) plait.

naturaliser [natyRalize] *vt* to naturalize.

naturaliste [natyRalist(ə)] *nm/f* naturalist.

nature [natyR] *nf* nature // *a, ad* (*CULIN*) plain, without seasoning or sweetening ; (*café, thé*) black, without sugar ; **payer en ~** to pay in kind ; **peint d'après ~** painted from life ; **~ morte** still-life ; **naturel, le** *a* (*gén, aussi: enfant*) natural // *nm* naturalness ; disposition, nature ; (*autochtone*) native ; **naturellement** *ad* naturally ; (*bien sûr*) of course ; **naturisme** *nm* naturism ; **naturiste** *nm/f* naturist.

naufrage [nofRaʒ] *nm* (ship)wreck ; (*fig*) wreck ; **faire ~** to be shipwrecked ;

naufragé, e *nm/f* shipwreck victim, castaway.

nauséabond, e [nozeabɔ̃, -ɔ̃d] *a* foul, nauseous.

nausée [noze] *nf* nausea.

nautique [notik] *a* nautical, water *cpd*.

nautisme [notism] *nm* water sports.

naval, e [naval] *a* naval.

navet [navɛ] *nm* turnip; (*péj*) third-rate film.

navette [navɛt] *nf* shuttle; (*en car etc*) shuttle (service); **faire la ~ (entre)** to go to and fro *ou* shuttle (between).

navigable [navigabl(ə)] *a* navigable.

navigateur [navigatœʀ] *nm* (*NAVIG*) seafarer, sailor; (*AVIAT*) navigator.

navigation [navigasjɔ̃] *nf* navigation, sailing; shipping.

naviguer [navige] *vi* to navigate, sail.

navire [naviʀ] *nm* ship.

navrer [navʀe] *vt* to upset, distress; **je suis navré** I'm so sorry.

N.B. *sigle* (= *nota bene*) NB.

ne, n' [n(ə)] *ad voir* **pas, plus, jamais** *etc*; (*explétif*) *non traduit*.

né, e [ne] *pp* (*voir* **naître**): **~ en 1960** born in 1960; **~e Scott** née Scott // *a*: **un comédien ~** a born comedian.

néanmoins [neɑ̃mwɛ̃] *ad* nevertheless, yet.

néant [neɑ̃] *nm* nothingness; **réduire à ~** to bring to nought; to dash.

nébuleux, euse [nebylø, -øz] *a* nebulous.

nébulosité [nebylozite] *nf* cloud cover; **~ variable** cloudy *ou* some cloud in places.

nécessaire [nesesɛʀ] *a* necessary // *nm* necessary; (*sac*) kit; **~ de couture** sewing kit; **~ de toilette** toilet bag; **nécessité** *nf* necessity; **nécessiter** *vt* to require; **nécessiteux, euse** *a* needy.

nec plus ultra [nekplysyltʀa] *nm*: **le ~ de** the last word in.

nécrologique [nekʀɔlɔʒik] *a*: **article ~** obituary; **rubrique ~** obituary column.

nécromancien, ne [nekʀɔmɑ̃sjɛ̃, -jɛn] *nm/f* necromancer.

nécrose [nekʀoz] *nf* necrosis.

néerlandais, e [neɛʀlɑ̃dɛ, -ɛz] *a* Dutch.

nef [nɛf] *nf* (*d'église*) nave.

néfaste [nefast(ə)] *a* baneful; ill-fated.

négatif, ive [negatif, iv] *a* negative // *nm* (*PHOTO*) negative.

négligé, e [negliʒe] *a* (*en désordre*) slovenly // *nm* (*tenue*) negligee.

négligence [negliʒɑ̃s] *nf* carelessness *q*; careless omission.

négligent, e [negliʒɑ̃, -ɑ̃t] *a* careless.

négliger [negliʒe] *vt* (*épouse, jardin*) to neglect; (*tenue*) to be careless about; (*avis, précautions*) to disregard; **~ de faire** to fail to do, not bother to do; **se ~** to neglect o.s.

négoce [negɔs] *nm* trade.

négociant [negɔsjɑ̃] *nm* merchant.

négociateur [negɔsjatœʀ] *nm* negotiator.

négociation [negɔsjasjɔ̃] *nf* negotiation.

négocier [negɔsje] *vi, vt* to negotiate.

nègre [nɛgʀ(ə)] *nm* Negro; hack(writer) // *a* Negro.

négresse [negʀɛs] *nf* Negro woman.

neige [nɛʒ] *nf* snow; **~ carbonique** dry ice; **neiger** *vi* to snow; **neigeux, euse** *a* snowy, snow-covered.

nénuphar [nenyfaʀ] *nm* water-lily.

néologisme [neɔlɔʒism(ə)] *nm* neologism.

néon [neɔ̃] *nm* neon.

néophyte [neɔfit] *nm/f* novice.

néo-zélandais, e [neɔzelɑ̃dɛ, -ɛz] *a* New Zealand *cpd* // *nm/f* New Zealander.

nerf [nɛʀ] *nm* nerve; (*fig*) vim, stamina; **nerveux, euse** *a* nervous; (*voiture*) nippy, responsive; (*tendineux*) sinewy; **nervosité** *nf* excitability; state of agitation; nervousness.

nervure [nɛʀvyʀ] *nf* vein; (*ARCHIT, TECH*) rib.

n'est-ce pas [nɛspa] *ad* isn't it?, won't you? *etc*, *selon le verbe qui précède*; **~ que c'est bon?** it's good, don't you think?

net, nette [nɛt] *a* (*sans équivoque, distinct*) clear; (*évident*) definite; (*propre*) neat, clean; (*COMM: prix, salaire*) net // *ad* (*refuser*) flatly; **s'arrêter ~** to stop dead; **la lame a cassé ~** the blade snapped clean through; **mettre au ~** to copy out, tidy up; **~teté** *nf* clearness.

nettoyage [nɛtwajaʒ] *nm* cleaning; **~ à sec** dry cleaning.

nettoyer [nɛtwaje] *vt* to clean; (*fig*) to clean out.

neuf [nœf] *num* nine.

neuf, neuve [nœf, nœv] *a* new // *nm*: **repeindre à ~** to redecorate; **remettre à ~** to do up (as good as new), refurbish.

neurasthénique [nøʀastenik] *a* neurasthenic.

neurologie [nøʀɔlɔʒi] *nf* neurology.

neutraliser [nøtʀalize] *vt* to neutralize.

neutralité [nøtʀalite] *nf* neutrality.

neutre [nøtʀ(ə)] *a* neutral; (*LING*) neuter // *nm* (*LING*) neuter.

neutron [nøtʀɔ̃] *nm* neutron.

neuve [nœv] *a voir* **neuf**.

neuvième [nœvjɛm] *num* ninth.

névé [neve] *nm* permanent snowpatch.

neveu, x [nəvø] *nm* nephew.

névralgie [nevʀalʒi] *nf* neuralgia.

névrite [nevʀit] *nf* neuritis.

névrose [nevʀoz] *nf* neurosis; **névrosé, e** *a, nm/f* neurotic.

nez [ne] *nm* nose; **~ à ~ avec** face to face with.

ni [ni] *cj*: **~ l'un ~ l'autre ne sont** neither one nor the other are; **il n'a rien dit ~ fait** he hasn't said or done anything.

niais, e [njɛ, -ɛz] *a* silly, thick.

niche [niʃ] *nf* (*du chien*) kennel; (*de mur*) recess, niche.

nichée [niʃe] *nf* brood, nest.

nicher [niʃe] *vi* to nest; **se ~ dans** to lodge o.s. in; to hide in.

nickel [nikɛl] *nm* nickel.

nicotine [nikɔtin] *nf* nicotine.

nid [ni] *nm* nest; **~ de poule** pothole.

nièce [njɛs] *nf* niece.

nième [ɛnjɛm] *a*: **la ~ fois** the nth time.

nier [nje] *vt* to deny.

nigaud, e [nigo, -od] *nm/f* booby, fool.

n'importe [nɛ̃pɔʀt(ə)] ad: ~ **qui/quoi/où** anybody/anything/ anywhere ; ~ **quand** any time ; ~ **quel** any ; ~ **lequel/laquelle** any (one) ; ~ **comment** (sans soin) carelessly.

nippes [nip] nfpl togs.

nippon, e [nipɔ̃, -on] a Japanese.

nique [nik] nf: **faire la** ~ **à** to thumb one's nose at (fig).

nitouche [nituʃ] nf (péj): **c'est une sainte** ~ she looks as if butter wouldn't melt in her mouth, she's a little hypocrite.

nitrate [nitʀat] nm nitrate.

nitroglycérine [nitʀogliseʀin] nf nitroglycerin(e).

niveau, x [nivo] nm level ; (des élèves, études) standard ; **de** ~ **(avec)** level (with) ; ~ **(à bulle)** spirit level ; **le** ~ **de la mer** sea level ; ~ **de vie** standard of living.

niveler [nivle] vt to level ; **nivellement** nm levelling.

nobiliaire [nɔbiljɛʀ] a voir **particule**.

noble [nɔbl(ə)] a noble // nm/f noble (man/woman) ; **noblesse** nf nobility ; (d'une action etc) nobleness.

noce [nɔs] nf wedding ; (gens) wedding party (ou guests pl) ; **faire la** ~ (fam) to go on a binge ; ~**s d'or/d'argent** golden/silver wedding.

nocif, ive [nɔsif, -iv] a harmful, noxious.

noctambule [nɔktɑ̃byl] nm night-bird, late-nighter.

nocturne [nɔktyʀn(ə)] a nocturnal // nf (SPORT) floodlit fixture.

Noël [nɔɛl] nm Christmas.

nœud [nø] nm (de corde, du bois, NAVIG) knot ; (ruban) bow ; (fig: liens) bond, tie ; ~ **coulant** noose ; ~ **papillon** bow tie.

noir, e [nwaʀ] a black ; (obscur, sombre) dark // nm/f black man/woman, Negro/Negro woman // nm: **dans le** ~ in the dark // nf (MUS) crotchet ; ~**ceur** nf blackness ; darkness ; ~**cir** vt, vi to blacken.

noise [nwaz] nf: **chercher** ~ **à** to try and pick a quarrel with.

noisetier [nwaztje] nm hazel.

noisette [nwazɛt] nf hazelnut.

noix [nwa] nf walnut ; (fam) twit ; (CULIN): **une** ~ **de beurre** a knob of butter ; **à la** ~ (fam) worthless ; ~ **de cajou** cashew nut ; ~ **de coco** coconut ; ~ **muscade** nutmeg.

nom [nɔ̃] nm name ; (LING) noun ; ~ **commun/propre** common/proper noun ; ~ **d'emprunt** assumed name ; ~ **de famille** surname ; ~ **de jeune fille** maiden name.

nomade [nɔmad] a nomadic // nm/f nomad.

nombre [nɔ̃bʀ(ə)] nm number ; **venir en** ~ to come in large numbers ; **depuis** ~ **d'années** for many years ; **ils sont au** ~ **de 3** there are 3 of them ; **au** ~ **de mes amis** among my friends ; ~ **premier/entier** prime/whole number. ~

nombreux, euse [nɔ̃bʀø, -øz] a many, numerous ; (avec nom sg: foule etc) large ; **peu** ~ few ; small.

nombril [nɔ̃bʀi] nm navel.

nomenclature [nɔmɑ̃klatyʀ] nf wordlist ; list of items.

nominal, e, aux [nɔminal, -o] a nominal.

nominatif [nɔminatif] nm nominative.

nomination [nɔminɑsjɔ̃] nf nomination.

nommément [nɔmemɑ̃] ad (désigner) by name.

nommer [nɔme] vt (baptiser) to name, give a name to ; (qualifier) to call ; (mentionner) to name, give the name of ; (élire) to appoint, nominate ; **se** ~ : **il se nomme Pascal** his name's Pascal, he's called Pascal.

non [nɔ̃] ad (réponse) no ; (avec loin, sans, seulement) not ; ~ **que** not that ; ~ **plus : moi** ~ **plus** neither do I, I don't either.

nonagénaire [nɔnaʒenɛʀ] nm/f man/woman in his/her nineties.

non-alcoolisé, e [nɔnalkɔlize] a non-alcoholic.

nonchalance [nɔ̃ʃalɑ̃s] nf nonchalance, casualness.

non-fumeur [nɔ̃fymœʀ] nm non-smoker.

non-lieu [nɔ̃ljø] nm: **il y a eu** ~ **the case was dismissed.**

nonne [nɔn] nf nun.

nonobstant [nɔnɔpstɑ̃] prép notwithstanding.

non-sens [nɔ̃sɑ̃s] nm absurdity.

nord [nɔʀ] nm North // a northern ; north ; ~**-africain, e** a, nm/f North-African ; ~**-est** nm North-East ; **nordique** a nordic, northern European ; ~**-ouest** nm North-West.

normal, e, aux [nɔʀmal, -o] a normal // nf: **la** ~**e** the norm, the average ; ~**ement** ad normally ; ~**iser** vt (COMM, TECH) to standardize ; (POL) to normalize.

normand, e [nɔʀmɑ̃, -ɑ̃d] a of Normandy.

Normandie [nɔʀmɑ̃di] nf Normandy.

norme [nɔʀm(ə)] nf norm ; (TECH) standard.

Norvège [nɔʀvɛʒ] nf Norway ; **norvégien, ne** a, nm, nf Norwegian.

nos [no] dét voir **notre**.

nostalgie [nɔstalʒi] nf nostalgia.

notable [nɔtabl(ə)] a notable, noteworthy ; (marqué) noticeable, marked // nm prominent citizen.

notaire [nɔtɛʀ] nm notary ; solicitor.

notamment [nɔtamɑ̃] ad in particular, among others.

notarié, e [nɔtaʀje] a: **acte** ~ deed drawn up by a notary.

note [nɔt] nf (écrite, MUS) note ; (SCOL) mark ; (facture) bill ; **prendre** ~ **de** to write down ; to note ; ~ **de service** memorandum.

noté, e [nɔte] a: **être bien/mal** ~ (employé etc) to have a good/bad record.

noter [nɔte] vt (écrire) to write down ; (remarquer) to note, notice.

notice [nɔtis] nf summary, short article ; (brochure) leaflet, instruction book.

notifier [nɔtifje] vt: ~ **qch à qn** to notify sb of sth, notify sth to sb.

notion [nɔsjɔ̃] nf notion, idea.

notoire [nɔtwaʀ] a widely known ; (en mal) notorious ; **le fait est** ~ **ou de notoriété publique** the fact is common knowledge.

notre, nos [nɔtR(ə), no] *dét* our.

nôtre [notR(ə)] *pronom*: le/la ~ ours; les ~s ours; (*alliés* etc) our own people; soyez des ~s join us // a ours.

nouer [nwe] *vt* to tie, knot; (*fig: alliance* etc) to strike up; **sa gorge se noua** a lump came to her throat.

noueux, euse [nwé, -éz] *a* gnarled.

nougat [nuga] *nm* nougat.

nouilles [nuj] *nfpl* noodles; pasta *sg*.

nourri, e [nuRi] *a* (*feu* etc) sustained.

nourrice [nuRis] *nf* wet-nurse.

nourrir [nuRiR] *vt* to feed; (*fig: espoir*) to harbour, nurse; **logé nourri** with board and lodging; ~ **au sein** to breast-feed; **nourrissant, e** *a* nourishing, nutritious.

nourrisson [nuRisɔ̃] *nm* (unweaned) infant.

nourriture [nuRityR] *nf* food.

nous [nu] *pronom* (*sujet*) we; (*objet*) us; ~-**mêmes** ourselves.

nouveau(nouvel), elle, x [nuvo, -ɛl] *a* new // *nm/f* new pupil (*ou* employee) // *nf* (piece of) news *sg*; (*LITTÉRATURE*) short story; de ~, à ~ again; **je suis sans nouvelles de lui** I haven't heard from him; ~ **venu, nouvelle venue** *nm/f* newcomer; **Nouvel An** New Year; ~-**né, e** *nm/f* newborn baby; **Nouvelle-Zélande** *nf* New Zealand; ~**té** *nf* novelty; (*COMM*) new film (*ou* book *ou* creation etc).

nouvel am, **nouvelle** af, nf [nuvɛl] *voir* **nouveau.**

novateur, trice [nɔvatœR, -tRis] *nm/f* innovator.

novembre [nɔvɑ̃bR(ə)] *nm* November.

novice [nɔvis] *a* inexperienced // *nm/f* novice.

noyade [nwajad] *nf* drowning *q*.

noyau, x [nwajo] *nm* (*de fruit*) stone; (*BIO, PHYSIQUE*) nucleus; (*ÉLEC, GÉO, fig: centre*) core; ~**ter** *vt* (*POL*) to infiltrate

noyé, e [nwaje] *nm/f* drowning (*ou* drowned) man/woman.

noyer [nwaje] *nm* walnut (tree); (*bois*) walnut // *vt* to drown; (*fig*) to flood; to submerge; **se** ~ to be drowned, drown; (*suicide*) to drown o.s.

nu, e [ny] *a* naked; (*membres*) naked, bare; (*chambre, fil, plaine*) bare // *nm* (*ART*) nude; **le** ~ **intégral** total nudity; ~-**pieds** barefoot; ~-**tête**, bareheaded; **à mains** ~**es** with one's bare hands; **se mettre** ~ to strip; **mettre à** ~ to bare.

nuage [nɥaʒ] *nm* cloud; **nuageux, euse** *a* cloudy.

nuance [nɥɑ̃s] *nf* (*de couleur, sens*) shade; **il y a une** ~ (**entre**) there's a slight difference (between); **une** ~ **de tristesse** a tinge of sadness; **nuancer** *vt* (*opinion*) to bring some reservations *ou* qualifications to.

nubile [nybil] *a* nubile.

nucléaire [nykleɛR] *a* nuclear.

nudisme [nydism] *nm* nudism; **nudiste** *nm/f* nudist.

nudité [nydite] *nf* nudity, nakedness; bareness.

nuée [nɥe] *nf*: **une** ~ **de** a cloud *ou* host *ou* swarm of.

nues [ny] *nfpl*: **tomber des** ~ to be taken aback; **porter qn aux** ~ to praise sb to the skies.

nuire [nɥiR] *vi* to be harmful; ~ **à** to harm, do damage to; **nuisible** *a* harmful; **animal nuisible** pest.

nuit [nɥi] *nf* night; **il fait** ~ it's dark; **cette** ~ last night; tonight; ~ **blanche** sleepless night; ~ **de noces** wedding night; **nuitamment** *ad* by night; **nuitées** *nfpl* overnight stays, beds occupied (*in statistics*).

nul, nulle [nyl] *a* (*aucun*) no; (*minime*) nil, non-existent; (*non valable*) null; (*péj*) useless, hopeless // *pronom* none, no one; **résultat** ~, **match** ~ draw; ~**le part** *ad* nowhere; ~**lement** *ad* by no means; ~**lité** *nf* nullity; hopelessness; hopeless individual, nonentity.

numéraire [nymeRɛR] *nm* cash; metal currency.

numération [nymeRasjɔ̃] *nf*: ~ **décimale/binaire** decimal/binary notation.

numérique [nymeRik] *a* numerical.

numéro [nymeRo] *nm* number; (*spectacle*) act, turn; ~**ter** *vt* to number.

numismate [nymismat] *nm/f* numismatist, coin collector.

nuptial, e, aux [nypsjal, -o] *a* nuptial; wedding *cpd*.

nuque [nyk] *nf* nape of the neck.

nutritif, ive [nytRitif, -iv] *a* nutritional; (*aliment*) nutritious.

nylon [nilɔ̃] *nm* nylon.

nymphomane [nɛ̃fɔman] *nf* nymphomaniac.

O

oasis [ɔazis] *nf* oasis (*pl* oases).

obédience [ɔbedjɑ̃s] *nf* allegiance.

obéir [ɔbeiR] *vi* to obey; ~ **à** to obey; (*suj: moteur, véhicule*) to respond to; **obéissance** *nf* obedience; **obéissant, e** *a* obedient.

obélisque [ɔbelisk(ə)] *nm* obelisk.

obèse [ɔbɛz] *a* obese; **obésité** *nf* obesity.

objecter [ɔbʒɛkte] *vt* (*prétexter*) to plead, put forward as an excuse; ~ **qch à** (*argument*) to put forward sth against; ~ (**à qn**) **que** to object (to sb) that.

objecteur [ɔbʒɛktœR] *nm*: ~ **de conscience** conscientious objector.

objectif, ive [ɔbʒɛktif, -iv] *a* objective // *nm* (*OPTIQUE, PHOTO*) lens *sg*, objective; (*MIL, fig*) objective; ~ **à focale variable** zoom lens.

objection [ɔbʒɛksjɔ̃] *nf* objection; ~ **de conscience** conscientious objection.

objectivité [ɔbʒɛktivite] *nf* objectivity.

objet [ɔbʒɛ] *nm* object; (*d'une discussion, recherche*) subject; **être** *ou* **faire l'**~ **de** (*discussion*) to be the subject of; (*soins*) to be given *ou* shown; **sans** ~ *a* purposeless; groundless; ~ **d'art** objet d'art; ~**s personnels** personal items; ~**s de toilette** toilet requisites; ~**s trouvés** lost property *sg*.

objurgations [ɔbʒyRgasjɔ̃] *nfpl* objurgations; entreaties.

obligation [ɔbligasjɔ̃] *nf* obligation; (*COMM*) bond, debenture; **être dans l'**~ **de**

faire to be obliged to do; **avoir l'~ de faire** to be under an obligation to do; **obligatoire** *a* compulsory, obligatory.

obligé, e [ɔbliʒe] *a* (*redevable*): **être très ~ à qn** to be most obliged to sb; **obligeance** *nf*: **avoir l'obligeance de** to be kind *ou* good enough to; **obligeant, e** *a* obliging; kind.

obliger [ɔbliʒe] *vt* (*contraindre*): **~ qn à faire** to force *ou* oblige sb to do; (*JUR*: *engager*) to bind; (*rendre service à*) to oblige; **je suis bien obligé** I have to.

oblique [ɔblik] *a* oblique; **regard ~** sidelong glance; **en ~** *ad* diagonally; **obliquer** *vi*: **obliquer vers** to turn off towards.

oblitération [ɔbliterɑsjɔ̃] *nf* cancelling *q*, cancellation.

oblitérer [ɔblitere] *vt* (*timbre-poste*) to cancel.

oblong, oblongue [ɔblɔ̃, -ɔ̃g] *a* oblong.

obnubiler [ɔbnybile] *vt* to obsess.

obole [ɔbɔl] *nf* offering.

obscène [ɔpsɛn] *a* obscene; **obscénité** *nf* obscenity.

obscur, e [ɔpskyʀ] *a* dark; (*fig*) obscure; vague; humble, lowly; **~cir** *vt* to darken; (*fig*) to obscure; **s'~cir** *vi* to grow dark; **~ité** *nf* darkness; **dans l'~ité** in the dark, in darkness.

obsédé, e [ɔpsede] *nm/f*: **~(e) sexuel(le)** sex maniac.

obséder [ɔpsede] *vt* to obsess, haunt.

obsèques [ɔpsɛk] *nfpl* funeral *sg*.

obséquieux, euse [ɔpsekjø, -øz] *a* obsequious.

observateur, trice [ɔpsɛʀvatœʀ, -tʀis] *a* observant, perceptive // *nm/f* observer.

observation [ɔpsɛʀvɑsjɔ̃] *nf* observation; (*d'un règlement etc*) observance; (*commentaire*) observation, remark; (*reproche*) reproof; **en ~** (*MED*) under observation.

observatoire [ɔpsɛʀvatwaʀ] *nm* observatory; (*lieu élevé*) observation post, vantage point.

observer [ɔpsɛʀve] *vt* (*regarder*) to observe, watch; (*examiner*) to examine; (*scientifiquement, aussi: règlement, jeûne etc*) to observe; (*surveiller*) to watch; (*remarquer*) to observe, notice; **faire ~ qch à qn** (*dire*) to point out sth to sb.

obsession [ɔpsesjɔ̃] *nf* obsession; **avoir l'~ de** to have an obsession with.

obstacle [ɔpstakl(ə)] *nm* obstacle; (*EQUITATION*) jump, hurdle; **faire ~ à** (*lumière*) to block out; (*projet*) to hinder, put obstacles in the path of; **~s antichars** tank defences.

obstétrique [ɔpstetʀik] *nf* obstetrics *sg*.

obstination [ɔpstinɑsjɔ̃] *nf* obstinacy.

obstiné, e [ɔpstine] *a* obstinate.

obstiner [ɔpstine]: **s'~** *vi* to insist, dig one's heels in; **s'~ à faire** to persist (obstinately) in doing; **s'~ sur qch** to keep working at sth, labour away at sth.

obstruction [ɔpstʀyksjɔ̃] *nf* obstruction, blockage; (*SPORT*) obstruction; **faire de l'~** (*fig*) to be obstructive.

obstruer [ɔpstʀye] *vt* to block, obstruct; **s'~** *vi* to become blocked.

obtempérer [ɔptɑ̃peʀe] *vi* to obey; **~ à** to obey, comply with.

obtenir [ɔptəniʀ] *vt* to obtain, get; (*total, résultat*) to arrive at, reach; to achieve, obtain; **~ de pouvoir faire** to obtain permission to do; **~ de qn qu'il fasse** to get sb to agree to do; **obtention** *nf* obtaining.

obturateur [ɔptyʀatœʀ] *nm* (*PHOTO*) shutter; **~ à rideau** focal plane shutter.

obturation [ɔptyʀɑsjɔ̃] *nf* closing (up); **~ (dentaire)** filling; **vitesse d'~** (*PHOTO*) shutter speed.

obturer [ɔptyʀe] *vt* to close (up); (*dent*) to fill.

obtus, e [ɔpty, -yz] *a* obtuse.

obus [ɔby] *nm* shell.

obvier [ɔbvje]: **~ à** *vt* to obviate.

O.C. *sigle voir* **onde**.

occasion [ɔkazjɔ̃] *nf* (*aubaine, possibilité*) opportunity; (*circonstance*) occasion; (*COMM: article non neuf*) secondhand buy; (: *acquisition avantageuse*) bargain; **à plusieurs ~s** on several occasions; **avoir l'~ de faire** to have the opportunity to do; **être l'~ de** to occasion, give rise to; **à l'~** *ad* sometimes, on occasions; some time; **d'~** *a, ad* secondhand; **occasionnel, le** *a* (*fortuit*) chance *cpd*; (*non régulier*) occasional; casual.

occasionner [ɔkazjɔne] *vt* to cause, bring about; **~ qch à qn** to cause sb sth.

occident [ɔksidɑ̃] *nm*: **l'~** the west; **occidental, e, aux** western; (*POL*) Western // *nm/f* Westerner.

occiput [ɔksipyt] *nm* back of the head, occiput.

occire [ɔksiʀ] *vt* to slay.

occitan, e [ɔksitɑ̃, -an] *a* of the langue d'oc, of Provençal French.

occlusion [ɔklyzjɔ̃] *nf*: **~ intestinale** obstruction of the bowels.

occulte [ɔkylt(ə)] *a* occult, supernatural.

occulter [ɔkylte] *vt* (*fig*) to overshadow.

occupant, e [ɔkypɑ̃, -ɑ̃t] *a* occupying // *nm/f* (*d'un appartement*) occupier, occupant // *nm* (*MIL*) occupying forces *pl*; (*POL: d'usine etc*) occupier.

occupation [ɔkypɑsjɔ̃] *nf* occupation.

occupé, e [ɔkype] *a* (*MIL, POL*) occupied; (*personne: affairé, pris*) busy; (*place, sièges*) taken; (*toilettes, ligne*) engaged.

occuper [ɔkype] *vt* to occupy; (*main-d'œuvre*) to employ; **s'~** to occupy o.s., keep o.s. busy; **s'~ de** (*être responsable de*) to be in charge of; (*se charger de: affaire*) to take charge of, deal with; (: *clients etc*) to attend to; (*s'intéresser à, pratiquer*) to be involved in; **ça occupe trop de place** it takes up too much room.

occurrence [ɔkyʀɑ̃s] *nf*: **en l'~** in this case.

océan [ɔseɑ̃] *nm* ocean; **l'~ Indien** the Indian Ocean; **l'Océanie** *nf* Oceania; **océanique** *a* oceanic; **océanographie** *nf* oceanography.

ocelot [ɔslo] *nm* ocelot; (*fourrure*) ocelot fur.

ocre [ɔkʀ(ə)] *a inv* ochre.

octane [ɔktan] *nm* octane.

octave [ɔktav] *nf* octave.

octobre [ɔktɔbR(ə)] *nm* October.

octogénaire [ɔktɔʒenɛR] *a*, *nm/f* octogenarian.

octogone [ɔktɔgɔn] *nm* octagon.

octroi [ɔktRwa] *nm* granting.

octroyer [ɔktRwaje] *vt*: ~ qch à qn to grant sth to sb, grant sb sth.

oculaire [ɔkylɛR] *a* ocular, eye *cpd* // *nm* (*de microscope*) eyepiece.

oculiste [ɔkylist(ə)] *nm/f* eye specialist, oculist.

ode [ɔd] *nf* ode.

odeur [ɔdœR] *nf* smell.

odieux, euse [ɔdjø, -øz] *a* odious, hateful.

odorant, e [ɔdɔRɑ̃, -ɑ̃t] *a* sweet-smelling, fragrant.

odorat [ɔdɔRa] *nm* (sense of) smell.

odoriférant, e [ɔdɔRiferɑ̃, -ɑ̃t] *a* sweet-smelling, fragrant.

odyssée [ɔdise] *nf* odyssey.

œcuménique [ekymenik] *a* oecumenical.

œil [œj], *pl* **yeux** [jø] *nm* eye; **à l'~** (*fam*) for free; **à l'~ nu** with the naked eye; **tenir qn à l'~** to keep an eye ou a watch on sb; **avoir l'~ à** to keep an eye on; **faire de l'~ à qn** to make eyes at sb; **à l'~ vif** with a lively expression; **fermer les yeux (sur)** (*fig*) to turn a blind eye (to); **fermer l'~** to get a moment's sleep; **~ de verre** glass eye.

œillade [œjad] *nf*: **lancer une ~ à qn** to wink at sb, give sb a wink; **faire des ~s à** to make eyes at.

œillères [œjɛR] *nfpl* blinkers.

œillet [œjɛ] *nm* (*BOT*) carnation; (*trou*) eyelet.

œnologue [enɔlɔg] *nm/f* oenologist, wine expert.

œsophage [ezɔfaʒ] *nm* oesophagus.

œuf [œf, *pl* ø] *nm* egg; **étouffer dans l'~** to nip in the bud; **~ à la coque/dur** boiled/hard-boiled egg; **~ au plat** fried egg; **~s brouillés** scrambled eggs; **~ de Pâques** Easter egg; **~ à repriser** darning egg.

œuvre [œvR(ə)] *nf* (*tâche*) task, undertaking; (*ouvrage achevé, livre, tableau etc*) work; (*ensemble de la production artistique*) works *pl*; (*organisation charitable*) charity // *nm* (*d'un artiste*) works *pl*; (*CONSTR*): **le gros ~** the shell; **être à l'~** to be at work; **mettre en ~** (*moyens*) to make use of; **~ d'art** work of art.

offense [ɔfɑ̃s] *nf* insult; (*REL*: *péché*) transgression, trespass.

offenser [ɔfɑ̃se] *vt* to offend, hurt; (*principes, Dieu*) to offend against; **s'~ de** to take offence at.

offensif, ive [ɔfɑ̃sif, -iv] *a*, *nf* offensive; **passer à l'offensive** to go into the attack ou offensive.

offert, e [ɔfɛR, -ɛRt(ə)] *pp de* **offrir**.

offertoire [ɔfɛRtwaR] *nm* offertory.

office [ɔfis] *nm* (*charge*) office; (*agence*) bureau, agency; (*REL*) service // *nm ou nf* (*pièce*) pantry; **faire ~ de** to act as; to do duty as; **d'~** *ad* automatically; **bons ~s** (*POL*) good offices; **~ du tourisme** tourist bureau.

officialiser [ɔfisjalize] *vt* to make official.

officiel, le [ɔfisjɛl] *a*, *nm/f* official.

officier [ɔfisje] *nm* officer // *vi* to officiate; **~ de l'état-civil** registrar; **~ ministériel** member of the legal profession; **~ de police** ≈ police officer.

officieux, euse [ɔfisjø, -øz] *a* unofficial.

officinal, e, aux [ɔfisinal, -o] *a*: **plantes ~es** medicinal plants.

officine [ɔfisin] *nf* (*de pharmacie*) dispensary; (*pharmacie*) pharmacy; (*gén péj*: *bureau*) agency, office.

offrande [ɔfRɑ̃d] *nf* offering.

offrant [ɔfRɑ̃] *nm*: **au plus ~** to the highest bidder.

offre [ɔfR(ə)] *nf* offer; (*aux enchères*) bid; (*ADMIN*: *soumission*) tender; (*ÉCON*): **l'~** supply; **~ d'emploi** job advertised; **'~s d'emploi'** situations vacant; **~ publique d'achat (O.P.A.)** takeover bid; **~s de service** offer of service.

offrir [ɔfRiR] *vt* to offer; (*faire cadeau de*): **~ (à qn)** to give (to sb); **s'~ vi** (*occasion, paysage*) to present itself // *vt* (*vacances, voiture*) to treat o.s. to; **~ (à qn) de faire qch** to offer to do sth (for sb); **~ à boire à qn** to offer sb a drink; **s'~ comme guide/en otage** to offer one's services as (a) guide/offer o.s. as hostage; **s'~ aux regards** (*suj*: *personne*) to expose o.s. to the public gaze.

offset [ɔfsɛt] *nm* offset (printing).

offusquer [ɔfyske] *vt* to offend; **s'~ de** to take offence at, be offended by.

ogive [ɔʒiv] *nf* (*ARCHIT*) diagonal rib; (*d'obus, de missile*) nose cone; **voûte en ~** rib vault; **arc en ~** lancet arch; **~ nucléaire** nuclear warhead.

ogre [ɔgR(ə)] *nm* ogre.

oie [wa] *nf* (*ZOOL*) goose (*pl* geese).

oignon [ɔɲɔ̃] *nm* (*BOT, CULIN*) onion; (*de tulipe etc*: *bulbe*) bulb; (*MÉD*) bunion; **petits ~s** pickling onions.

oindre [wɛ̃dR(ə)] *vt* to anoint.

oiseau, x [wazo] *nm* bird; **~ de proie** bird of prey; **~-mouche** *nm* hummingbird.

oisellerie [wazɛlRi] *nf* bird shop.

oiseux, euse [wazø, -øz] *a* pointless; trivial.

oisif, ive [wazif, -iv] *a* idle // *nm/f* (*péj*) man/woman of leisure; **oisiveté** *nf* idleness.

O.K. [ɔkɛ] *excl* O.K., all right.

oléagineux, euse [ɔleaʒinø, -øz] *a* oleaginous, oil-producing.

oléoduc [ɔleɔdyk] *nm* (oil) pipeline.

olfactif, ive [ɔlfaktif, -iv] *a* olfactory.

oligarchie [ɔligaRʃi] *nf* oligarchy.

olivâtre [ɔlivɑtR(ə)] *a* olive-greenish; (*teint*) sallow.

olive [ɔliv] *nf* (*BOT*) olive // *a inv* olive(-green); **~raie** *nf* olive grove; **olivier** *nm* olive tree; (*bois*) olive wood.

olympiade [ɔlɛ̃pjad] *nf* (*période*) Olympiad; **les ~s** (*jeux*) the Olympiad *sg*.

olympien, ne [ɔlɛ̃pjɛ̃, -jɛn] *a* Olympian, of Olympian physique.

olympique [ɔlɛ̃pik] *a* Olympic.

ombilical, e, aux [ɔ̃bilikal, -o] *a* umbilical.

ombrage [ɔ̃bʀaʒ] *nm* (*ombre*) (leafy) shade; (*fig*): **prendre ~ de** to take umbrage *ou* offence at; **ombragé, e** *a* shaded, shady; **ombrageux, euse** *a* (*cheval*) skittish, nervous; (*personne*) touchy, easily offended.

ombre [ɔ̃bʀ(ə)] *nf* (*espace non ensoleillé*) shade; (*ombre portée, tache*) shadow; **à l'~** in the shade; (*fam*) behind bars; **à l'~ de** in the shade of; (*tout près de, fig*) in the shadow of; **tu me fais de l'~** you're in my light; **ça nous donne de l'~** it gives us (some) shade; **vivre dans l'~** (*fig*) to live in obscurity; **laisser dans l'~** (*fig*) to leave in the dark; **~ à paupières** eyeshadow; **~ portée** shadow; **~s chinoises** (*spectacle*) shadow show *sg*.

ombrelle [ɔ̃bʀɛl] *nf* parasol, sunshade.

omelette [ɔmlɛt] *nf* omelette; **~ au fromage/au jambon** cheese/ham omelette; **~ aux herbes** omelette with herbs.

omettre [ɔmɛtʀ(ə)] *vt* to omit, leave out; **~ de faire** to fail *ou* omit to do; **omission** *nf* omission.

omni... [ɔmni] *préfixe*: **~bus** *nm* slow *ou* stopping train; **~potent, e** *a* omnipotent; **~scient, e** *a* omniscient; **~vore** *a* omnivorous.

omoplate [ɔmɔplat] *nf* shoulder blade.

O.M.S. *sigle f voir* **organisation**.

on [ɔ̃] *pronom* (*indéterminé*): **~ peut le faire ainsi** you *ou* one can do it like this, it can be done like this; (*quelqu'un*): **~ les a attaqués** they were attacked; (*nous*): **~ va y aller demain** we're going tomorrow; (*les gens*): **autrefois, ~ croyait aux fantômes** they used to believe in ghosts years ago; **~ vous demande au téléphone** there's a phone call for you, there's somebody on the phone for you; **~ ne peut plus** *ad*: **~ ne peut plus stupide** as stupid as can be.

oncle [ɔ̃kl(ə)] *nm* uncle.

onctueux, euse [ɔ̃ktɥø, -øz] *a* creamy, smooth; (*fig*) smooth, unctuous.

onde [ɔ̃d] *nf* (*PHYSIQUE*) wave; **sur l'~ on** the waters; **sur les ~s** on the radio; **mettre en ~s** to produce for the radio; **sur ~s courtes** (o.c.) on short wave *sg*; **moyennes/ longues ~s** medium/long wave *sg*.

ondée [ɔ̃de] *nf* shower.

on-dit [ɔ̃di] *nm inv* rumour.

ondoyer [ɔ̃dwaje] *vi* to ripple, wave.

ondulant, e [ɔ̃dylɑ̃, -ɑ̃t] *a* swaying; undulating.

ondulation [ɔ̃dylɑsjɔ̃] *nf* undulation.

onduler [ɔ̃dyle] *vi* to undulate; (*cheveux*) to wave.

onéreux, euse [ɔneʀø, -øz] *a* costly; **à titre ~** in return for payment.

ongle [ɔ̃gl(ə)] *nm* (*ANAT*) nail; **se faire les ~s** to do one's nails.

onglet [ɔ̃glɛ] *nm* (*rainure*) (thumbnail) groove; (*bande de papier*) tab.

onguent [ɔ̃gɑ̃] *nm* ointment.

onomatopée [ɔnɔmatɔpe] *nf* onomatopoeia.

ont *vb voir* **avoir**.

O.N.U. [ɔny] *sigle f voir* **organisation**.

onyx [ɔniks] *nm* onyx.

onze [ɔ̃z] *num* eleven; **onzième** *num* eleventh.

O.P.A. *sigle f voir* **offre**.

opacité [ɔpasite] *nf* opaqueness.

opale [ɔpal] *nf* opal.

opalin, e [ɔpalɛ̃, -in] *a, nf* opaline.

opaque [ɔpak] *a* opaque.

O.P.E.P. [ɔpɛp] *sigle f* (= organisation des pays exportateurs de pétrole) O.P.E.C. (organization of petroleum exporting countries).

opéra [ɔpeʀa] *nm* opera; (*édifice*) opera house; **~-comique** *nm* light opera, opéra comique.

opérateur, trice [ɔpeʀatœʀ, -tʀis] *nm/f* operator; **~ (de prise de vues)** cameraman.

opération [ɔpeʀasjɔ̃] *nf* operation; (*COMM*) dealing.

opératoire [ɔpeʀatwaʀ] *a* operating; (*choc etc*) post-operative.

opéré, e [ɔpeʀe] *nm/f* patient (*having undergone an operation*).

opérer [ɔpeʀe] *vt* (*MÉD*) to operate on; (*faire, exécuter*) to carry out, make // *vi* (*remède: faire effet*) to act, work; (*procéder*) to proceed; (*MÉD*) to operate; **s'~** *vi* (*avoir lieu*) to occur, take place; **se faire ~** to have an operation; **se faire ~ des amygdales/du cœur** to have one's tonsils out/have a heart operation.

opérette [ɔpeʀɛt] *nf* operetta, light opera.

ophtalmologie [ɔftalmɔlɔʒi] *nf* ophthalmology; **ophtalmologue** *nm/f* ophthalmologist.

opiner [ɔpine] *vi*: **~ de la tête** to nod assent.

opiniâtre [ɔpinjɑtʀ(ə)] *a* stubborn.

opinion [ɔpinjɔ̃] *nf* opinion; **l'~ (publique)** public opinion.

opium [ɔpjɔm] *nm* opium.

opportun, e [ɔpɔʀtɛ̃, -yn] *a* timely, opportune; **en temps ~** at the appropriate time; **opportunisme** *nm* opportunism; **opportuniste** *a, nm/f* opportunist; **opportunité** *nf* timeliness, opportuneness.

opposant, e [ɔpozɑ̃, -ɑ̃t] *a* opposing; **~s** *nmpl* opponents.

opposé, e [ɔpoze] *a* (*direction, rive*) opposite; (*faction*) opposing; (*couleurs*) contrasting; (*opinions, intérêts*) conflicting; (*contre*): **~ à** opposed to, against // *nm*: **l'~** the other *ou* opposite side (*ou* direction); (*contraire*) the opposite; **à l'~** (*fig*) on the other hand; **à l'~ de** on the other *ou* opposite side from; (*fig*) contrary to, unlike.

opposer [ɔpoze] *vt* (*meubles, objets*) to place opposite each other; (*personnes, armées, équipes*) to oppose; (*couleurs, termes, tons*) to contrast; **~ qch à** (*comme obstacle, défense*) to set sth against; (*comme objection*) to put sth forward against; to put up sth to; (*en contraste*) to set sth opposite; to match sth with; **s'~** (*sens réciproque*) to conflict; to clash; to face each other; to contrast; **s'~ à** (*interdire, empêcher*) to oppose; (*tenir tête à*) to rebel against; **sa religion s'y oppose**

it's against his religion; **s'~ à ce que qn fasse** to be opposed to sb's doing.

opposition [ɔpozisjɔ̃] nf opposition; **par ~ à** as opposed to, in contrast with; **entrer en ~ avec** to come into conflict with; **être en ~ avec** (idées, conduite) to be at variance with; **faire ~ à un chèque** to stop a cheque.

oppresser [ɔprese] vt to oppress; **oppresseur** nm oppressor; **oppressif, ive** a oppressive; **oppression** nf oppression; (malaise) feeling of suffocation.

opprimer [ɔprime] vt to oppress; (liberté, opinion) to suppress, stifle; (suj: chaleur etc) to suffocate, oppress.

opprobre [ɔprɔbr(ə)] nm disgrace.

opter [ɔpte] vi: **~ pour** to opt for; **~ entre** to choose between.

opticien, ne [ɔptisjɛ̃, -ɛn] nm/f optician.

optimal, e, aux [ɔptimal, -o] a optimal.

optimisme [ɔptimism(ə)] nm optimism; **optimiste** nm/f optimist.

optimum [ɔptimɔm] a optimum.

option [ɔpsjɔ̃] nf option; **matière à ~** (SCOL) optional subject; **prendre une ~ sur** to take (out) an option on.

optique [ɔptik] a (nerf) optic; (verres) optical // nf (PHOTO: lentilles etc) optics pl; (science, industrie) optics sg; (fig: manière de voir) perspective.

opulence [ɔpylɑ̃s] nf wealth, opulence.

opulent, e [ɔpylɑ̃, -ɑ̃t] a wealthy, opulent; (formes, poitrine) ample, generous.

or [ɔr] nm gold // cj now, but; **en ~** gold cpd; (fig) golden, marvellous; **d'~** (fig) golden.

oracle [ɔrɑkl(ə)] nm oracle.

orage [ɔraʒ] nm (thunder)storm; **orageux, euse** a stormy.

oraison [ɔrɛzɔ̃] nf orison, prayer; **~ funèbre** funeral oration.

oral, e, aux [ɔral, -o] a, nm oral; **~ement** ad orally.

orange [ɔrɑ̃ʒ] nf, a inv orange; **orangé, e** a orangey, orange-coloured; **orangeade** nf orangeade; **oranger** nm orange tree; **~raie** nf orange grove; **~rie** nf orangery.

orateur [ɔratœr] nm speaker; orator.

oratoire [ɔratwar] nm oratory; wayside shrine // a oratorical.

orbital, e, aux [ɔrbital, -o] a orbital.

orbite [ɔrbit] nf (ANAT) (eye-)socket; (PHYSIQUE) orbit; **mettre sur ~** to put into orbit; (fig) to launch; **dans l'~ de** (fig) within the sphere of influence of.

orchestration [ɔrkɛstrɑsjɔ̃] nf orchestration.

orchestre [ɔrkɛstr(ə)] nm orchestra; (de jazz, danse) band; (places) stalls pl; **orchestrer** vt (MUS) to orchestrate; (fig) to mount, stage-manage.

orchidée [ɔrkide] nf orchid.

ordinaire [ɔrdinɛr] a ordinary; everyday; standard // nm ordinary; (menus) everyday fare // nf (essence) ≈ two-star (petrol); **d'~** usually, normally; **à l'~** usually, ordinarily.

ordinal, e, aux [ɔrdinal, -o] a ordinal.

ordinateur [ɔrdinatœr] nm computer.

ordination [ɔrdinɑsjɔ̃] nf ordination.

ordonnance [ɔrdɔnɑ̃s] nf organization; layout; (MÉD) prescription; (JUR) order; (MIL) orderly, batman; **d'~** (MIL) regulation cpd.

ordonné, e [ɔrdɔne] a tidy, orderly; (MATH) ordered // nf (MATH) ordinate, Y-axis.

ordonner [ɔrdɔne] vt (agencer) to organize, arrange; (: meubles, appartement) to lay out, arrange; (donner un ordre): **~ à qn de faire** to order sb to do; (MATH) to (arrange in) order; (REL) to ordain; (MÉD) to prescribe; (JUR) to order.

ordre [ɔrdr(ə)] nm (gén) order; (propreté et soin) orderliness, tidiness; (nature): **d'~ pratique** of a practical nature; **~s** nmpl (REL) holy orders; **mettre en ~** to tidy (up), put in order; **avoir de l'~** to be tidy ou orderly; **mettre bon ~ à** to put to rights, sort out; **être aux ~s de qn/sous les ~s de qn** to be at sb's disposal/under sb's command; **jusqu'à nouvel ~** until further notice; **dans le même ~ d'idées** in this connection; **donnez-nous un ~ de grandeur** give us some idea as regards size (ou the amount); **de premier ~** first-rate; **~ du jour** (d'une réunion) agenda; (MIL) order of the day; **à l'~ du jour** on the agenda; (fig) topical; (MIL: citer) in dispatches; **~ de route** marching orders pl.

ordure [ɔrdyr] nf filth q; **~s** (balayures, déchets) rubbish sg, refuse sg; **~s ménagères** household refuse; **ordurier, ière** a lewd, filthy.

oreille [ɔrɛj] nf (ANAT) ear; (de marmite, tasse) handle; **avoir de l'~** to have a good ear (for music).

oreiller [ɔreje] nm pillow.

oreillette [ɔrɛjɛt] nf (ANAT) auricle.

oreillons [ɔrɛjɔ̃] nmpl mumps sg.

ores [ɔr]: **d'~ et déjà** ad already.

orfèvre [ɔrfɛvr(ə)] nm goldsmith; silversmith; **orfèvrerie** nf goldsmith's (ou silversmith's) trade; (ouvrage) gold (ou silver) plate.

orfraie [ɔrfrɛ] nm white-tailed eagle; **pousser des cris d'~** to yell at the top of one's voice.

organe [ɔrgan] nm organ; (porte-parole) representative, mouthpiece; **~s de commande** (TECH) controls; **~s de transmission** (TECH) transmission system sg.

organigramme [ɔrganigram] nm organization chart; flow chart.

organique [ɔrganik] a organic.

organisateur, trice [ɔrganizatœr, -tris] nm/f organizer.

organisation [ɔrganizɑsjɔ̃] nf organization; **O~ des Nations Unies (O.N.U.)** United Nations (Organization) (U.N., U.N.O.); **O~ mondiale de la santé (O.M.S.)** World Health Organization (W.H.O.); **O~ du traité de l'Atlantique Nord (O.T.A.N.)** North Atlantic Treaty Organization (N.A.T.O.).

organiser [ɔrganize] vt to organize; (mettre sur pied: service etc) to set up; **s'~** to get organized.

organisme [ɔrganism(ə)] nm (BIO)

organism ; (corps humain) body ; (ADMIN, POL etc) body, organism.

organiste [ɔʀɡanist(ə)] nm/f organist.

orgasme [ɔʀɡasm(ə)] nm orgasm, climax.

orge [ɔʀʒ(ə)] nf barley.

orgelet [ɔʀʒəlɛ] nm sty(e).

orgie [ɔʀʒi] nf orgy.

orgue [ɔʀɡ(ə)] nm organ ; ~s nfpl organ sg ; ~ de Barbarie barrel ou street organ.

orgueil [ɔʀɡœj] nm pride ; **orgueilleux, euse** a proud.

Orient [ɔʀjɑ̃] nm: l'~ the East, the Orient.

orientable [ɔʀjɑ̃tabl(ə)] a adjustable.

oriental, e, aux [ɔʀjɑ̃tal, -o] a oriental, eastern ; (frontière) eastern // nm/f: O~, e Oriental.

orientation [ɔʀjɑ̃tasjɔ̃] nf positioning ; adjustment ; orientation ; direction ; (d'un journal) leanings pl ; **avoir le sens de l'~** to have a (good) sense of direction ; ~ **professionnelle** careers advising ; careers advisory service.

orienté, e [ɔʀjɑ̃te] a (fig: article, journal) slanted ; **bien/mal** ~ (appartement) well/badly positioned ; ~ **au sud** facing south ou with a southern aspect.

orienter [ɔʀjɑ̃te] vt (situer) to position ; (placer, disposer: pièce mobile) to adjust, position ; (tourner) to direct, turn ; (voyageur, touriste, recherches) to direct ; (fig: élève) to orientate ; **s'~** (se repérer) to find one's bearings ; **s'~ vers** (fig) to turn towards ; **orienteur** nm (SCOL) careers adviser.

orifice [ɔʀifis] nm opening, orifice.

oriflamme [ɔʀiflam] nf banner, standard.

origan [ɔʀiɡɑ̃] nm (CULIN) oregano.

originaire [ɔʀiʒinɛʀ] a original ; **être** ~ **de** to be a native of ; (provenir de) to originate from ; to be native to.

original, e, aux [ɔʀiʒinal, -o] a original ; (bizarre) eccentric // nm/f eccentric // nm (document etc, ART) original ; (dactylographie) top copy ; ~**ité** nf originality q ; eccentricity.

origine [ɔʀiʒin] nf origin ; **d'~** of origin ; (pneus etc) original ; (bureau postal) dispatching ; **dès l'~** at ou from the outset ; **à l'~** originally ; **avoir son** ~ **dans** to have its origins in, originate in ; **originel, le** a original.

oripeaux [ɔʀipo] nmpl rags.

O.R.L. nm/f ou titre = **oto-rhino-laryngologiste**.

orme [ɔʀm(ə)] nm elm.

orné, e [ɔʀne] a ornate.

ornement [ɔʀnəmɑ̃] nm ornament ; (fig) embellishment, adornment ; ~**s sacerdotaux** vestments ; **ornemental, e, aux** a ornamental ; **ornementer** vt to ornament.

orner [ɔʀne] vt to decorate, adorn ; ~ **qch de** to decorate sth with.

ornière [ɔʀnjɛʀ] nf rut.

ornithologie [ɔʀnitɔlɔʒi] nf ornithology.

orphelin, e [ɔʀfəlɛ̃, -in] a orphan(ed) // nm/f orphan ; ~ **de père/mère** fatherless/motherless ; **orphelinat** nm orphanage.

O.R.S.E.C. [ɔʀsɛk] sigle (= organisation des secours): le plan ~ disaster contingency plan.

orteil [ɔʀtɛj] nm toe ; **gros** ~ big toe.

O.R.T.F. sigle m = Office de la radiodiffusion et télévision française (the French broadcasting corporation).

orthodoxe [ɔʀtɔdɔks(ə)] a orthodox ; **orthodoxie** nf orthodoxy.

orthographe [ɔʀtɔɡʀaf] nf spelling ; **orthographier** vt to spell ; **mal orthographié** misspelt.

orthopédie [ɔʀtɔpedi] nf orthopaedics sg ; **orthopédique** a orthopaedic ; **orthopédiste** nm/f orthopaedic specialist.

ortie [ɔʀti] nf (stinging) nettle.

os [ɔs, pl o] nm bone ; **sans** ~ (BOUCHERIE) off the bone, boned ; ~ **à moelle** marrowbone.

O.S. sigle m voir **ouvrier**.

oscillation [ɔsilasjɔ̃] nf oscillation ; ~**s** nfpl (fig) fluctuations.

osciller [ɔsile] vi (pendule) to swing ; (au vent etc) to rock ; (TECH) to oscillate ; (fig): ~ **entre** to waver ou fluctuate between.

osé, e [ɔze] a daring, bold.

oseille [ozɛj] nf sorrel.

oser [oze] vi, vt to dare ; ~ **faire** to dare (to) do.

osier [ozje] nm willow ; **d'~, en** ~ wicker(work).

ossature [ɔsatyʀ] nf (ANAT) frame, skeletal structure ; (: du visage) bone structure ; (fig) framework.

osselet [ɔslɛ] nm (ANAT) ossicle ; **jouer aux** ~**s** to play knucklebones.

ossements [ɔsmɑ̃] nmpl bones.

osseux, euse [ɔsø, -øz] a bony ; (tissu, maladie, greffe) bone cpd.

ossifier [ɔsifje]: **s'~** vi to ossify.

ossuaire [ɔsɥɛʀ] nm ossuary.

ostensible [ɔstɑ̃sibl(ə)] a conspicuous.

ostensoir [ɔstɑ̃swaʀ] nm monstrance.

ostentation [ɔstɑ̃tasjɔ̃] nf ostentation ; **faire** ~ **de** to parade, make a display of.

ostracisme [ɔstʀasism(ə)] nm ostracism ; **frapper d'**~ to ostracize.

ostréiculture [ɔstʀeikyltyʀ] nf oyster-farming.

otage [ɔtaʒ] nm hostage ; **prendre qn comme** ~ to take sb hostage.

O.T.A.N. [ɔtɑ̃] sigle f voir **organisation**.

otarie [ɔtaʀi] nf sea-lion.

ôter [ote] vt to remove ; (soustraire) to take away ; ~ **qch à qn** to take sth (away) from sb ; ~ **qch de** to remove sth from.

otite [ɔtit] nf ear infection.

oto-rhino(-laryngologiste) [ɔtɔʀino-(laʀɛ̃ɡɔlɔʒist(ə)] nm/f ear nose and throat specialist.

ou [u] cj or ; ~ ... ~ either ... or ; ~ **bien** or (else).

où [u] ad, pronom where ; (dans lequel) in which, into which ; from which, out of which ; (sur lequel) on which ; (sens de 'que'): **au train** ~ **ça va/prix** ~ **c'est** at the rate it's going/price it is ; **le jour** ~ **il est parti** the day (that) he left ; **par** ~ **passer?** which way should we go? ; **les villes par** ~ **il est passé** the towns he went through ; **le village d'**~ **je viens** the village I come from ; **la chambre** ~ **il était**

the room he was in ; **d'~ vient qu'il est parti?** how come he left?

ouate [wat] *nf* cotton wool ; *(bourre)* padding, wadding ; **ouaté, e** *a* cotton-wool ; *(doublé)* quilted ; *(fig)* cocoon-like ; muffled.

oubli [ubli] *nm (acte):* **l'~ de forgetting** ; *(étourderie)* forgetfulness *q* ; *(négligence)* omission, oversight ; *(absence de souvenirs)* oblivion ; **~ de soi** self-effacement, self-negation.

oublier [ublije] *vt (gén)* to forget ; *(ne pas voir: erreurs etc)* to miss ; *(ne pas mettre: virgule, nom)* to leave out ; *(laisser quelque part: chapeau etc)* to leave behind ; **s'~** to forget o.s.

oubliettes [ublijɛt] *nfpl* dungeon *sg*.

oublieux, euse [ublijø, -øz] *a* forgetful.

oued [wɛd] *nm* wadi.

ouest [wɛst] *nm* west // *a inv* west ; *(région)* western ; **à l'~** in the west ; **(to the) west**, westwards ; **à l'~ de** (to the) west of ; **vent d'~** westerly wind ; **~allemand, e** *a, nm/f* West German.

ouf [uf] *excl* phew!

oui [wi] *ad* yes ; **répondre (par) ~ to** answer yes.

oui-dire [widiʀ] *nm inv:* **par ~** by hearsay.

ouïe [wi] *nf* hearing ; **~s** *nfpl (de poisson)* gills ; *(de violon)* sound-hole.

ouïr [wiʀ] *vt* to hear ; **avoir ouï dire que** to have heard it said that.

ouistiti [wistiti] *nm* marmoset.

ouragan [uʀagɑ̃] *nm* hurricane ; *(fig)* storm.

ourlé, e [uʀle] *a* hemmed ; *(fig)* rimmed.

ourler [uʀle] *vt* to hem.

ourlet [uʀlɛ] *nm* hem ; *(de l'oreille)* rim.

ours [uʀs] *nm* bear ; **~ brun/blanc** brown/polar bear ; **~ mal léché** uncouth fellow ; **~ (en peluche)** teddy (bear).

ourse [uʀs(ə)] *nf (ZOOL)* she-bear ; **la Grande/Petite O~** the Great/Little Bear, Ursa Major/ Minor.

oursin [uʀsɛ̃] *nm* sea urchin.

ourson [uʀsɔ̃] *nm* (bear-)cub.

ouste [ust(ə)] *excl* hop it!

outil [uti] *nm* tool.

outillage [utijaʒ] *nm* set of tools ; *(d'atelier)* equipment *q*.

outiller [utije] *vt (ouvrier, usine)* to equip.

outrage [utʀaʒ] *nm* insult ; **faire subir les derniers ~s à** *(femme)* to ravish ; **~ aux bonnes mœurs** outrage to public decency ; **~ à magistrat** contempt of court ; **~ à la pudeur** indecent behaviour *q*.

outrageant, e [utʀaʒɑ̃, -ɑ̃t] *a* offensive.

outrager [utʀaʒe] *vt* to offend gravely ; *(fig: contrevenir à)* to outrage, insult.

outrance [utʀɑ̃s] *nf* excessiveness *q*, excess ; **à ~** *ad* excessively, to excess ; **outrancier, ière** *a* extreme.

outre [utʀ(ə)] *nf* goatskin, water skin // *prép* besides // *ad:* **passer ~ à** to disregard, take no notice of ; **en ~** besides, moreover ; **~ que** apart from the fact that ; **~ mesure** immoderately ; unduly.

outré, e [utʀe] *a* excessive, exaggerated ; outraged.

outre-Atlantique [utʀaatlɑ̃tik] *ad* across the Atlantic.

outrecuidance [utʀəkɥidɑ̃s] *nf* presumptuousness *q*.

outre-Manche [utʀəmɑ̃ʃ] *ad* across the Channel.

outremer [utʀəmɛʀ] *a* ultramarine.

outre-mer [utʀəmɛʀ] *ad* overseas.

outrepasser [utʀəpɑse] *vt* to go beyond, exceed.

outrer [utʀe] *vt* to exaggerate ; to outrage.

outsider [awtsajdœʀ] *nm* outsider.

ouvert, e [uvɛʀ, -ɛʀt(ə)] *pp de* **ouvrir** // *a* open ; *(robinet, gaz etc)* on ; **ouvertement** *ad* openly.

ouverture [uvɛʀtyʀ] *nf* opening ; *(MUS)* overture ; *(POL):* **l'~** the widening of the political spectrum ; *(PHOTO):* **~ (du diaphragme)** aperture ; **~s** *nfpl (propositions)* overtures ; **~ d'esprit** open-mindedness ; **heures d'~** *(COMM)* opening hours ; **jours d'~** *(COMM)* days of opening.

ouvrable [uvʀabl(ə)] *a:* **jour ~** working day, weekday.

ouvrage [uvʀaʒ] *nm (tâche, de tricot etc, MIL)* work *q* ; *(texte, livre)* work ; **corbeille à ~** work basket ; **~ d'art** *(GÉNIE CIVIL)* bridge or tunnel etc.

ouvragé, e [uvʀaʒe] *a* finely embroidered *(ou* worked *ou* carved).

ouvrant, e [uvʀɑ̃, -ɑ̃t] *a:* **toit ~** *(AUTO)* sunshine roof.

ouvre-boîte(s) [uvʀəbwat] *nm inv* tin *ou* can opener.

ouvre-bouteille(s) [uvʀəbutɛj] *nm inv* bottle-opener.

ouvreuse [uvʀøz] *nf* usherette.

ouvrier, ière [uvʀje, -jɛʀ] *nm/f* worker // *nf (ZOOL)* worker (bee) // *a* working-class ; industrial, labour *cpd* ; workers' ; **classe ouvrière** working class ; **~ qualifié** skilled worker ; **~ spécialisé (O.S.)** semiskilled worker ; **~ d'usine** factory worker.

ouvrir [uvʀiʀ] *vt (gén)* to open ; *(brèche, passage)* to open up ; *(commencer l'exploitation de, créer)* to open (up) ; *(eau, électricité, chauffage, robinet)* to turn on ; *(MÉD: abcès)* to open up, cut open // *vi* to open ; to open up ; **s'~** *vi* to open ; **s'~ à** *(art etc)* to open one's mind to ; **s'~ à qn (de qch)** to open one's heart to sb (about sth) ; **s'~ les veines** to slash *ou* cut one's wrists ; **~ l'appétit à qn** to whet sb's appetite.

ouvroir [uvʀwaʀ] *nm* workroom ; sewing room.

ovaire [ɔvɛʀ] *nm* ovary.

ovale [ɔval] *a* oval.

ovation [ɔvasjɔ̃] *nf* ovation ; **ovationner** *vt:* **ovationner qn** to give sb an ovation.

O.V.N.I. [ɔvni] *sigle m* (= *objet volant non identifié)* U.F.O. (unidentified flying object).

ovule [ɔvyl] *nm (PHYSIOL)* ovum *(pl* ova) ; *(MÉD)* pessary.

oxydable [ɔksidabl(ə)] *a* liable to rust.

oxyde [ɔksid] *nm* oxide ; **~ de carbone** carbon monoxide.

oxyder [ɔkside]: **s'~** *vi* to become oxidized.

oxygène [ɔksiʒɛn] nm oxygen ; (fig): cure d'~ fresh air cure.

oxygéné, e [ɔksiʒene] a: eau ~e hydrogen peroxide.

ozone [ozɔn] nm ozone.

P

pacage [pakaʒ] nm grazing, pasture.

pachyderme [paʃidɛrm(ə)] nm pachyderm ; elephant.

pacifier [pasifje] vt to pacify.

pacifique [pasifik] a (personne) peaceable ; (intentions, coexistence) peaceful // nm: le P~, l'océan P~ the Pacific (Ocean).

pacotille [pakɔtij] nf (péj) cheap goods pl ; de ~ cheap.

pacte [pakt(ə)] nm pact, treaty.

pactiser [paktize] vi: ~ avec to come to terms with.

pagaie [pagɛ] nf paddle.

pagaille [pagaj] nf mess, shambles sg.

pagayer [pageje] vi to paddle.

page [paʒ] nf page // nm page ; mettre en ~s to make up (into pages) ; à la ~ (fig) up-to-date.

pagne [paɲ] nm loincloth.

pagode [pagɔd] nf pagoda.

paie [pɛ] nf = paye.

paiement [pɛmɑ̃] nm = payement.

paien, ne [pajɛ̃, -jɛn] a, nm/f pagan, heathen.

paillard, e [pajar, -ard(ə)] a bawdy.

paillasse [pajas] nf straw mattress.

paillasson [pujasɔ̃] nm doormat.

paille [puj] nf straw ; (défaut) flaw ; ~ de fer steel wool.

pailleté, e [pajte] a sequined.

paillette [pajɛt] nf speck, flake ; ~s nfpl (décoratives) sequins, spangles ; lessive en ~s soapflakes pl.

pain [pɛ̃] nm (substance) bread ; (unité) loaf (pl loaves) (of bread) ; (morceau): ~ de cire etc bar of wax etc ; ~ bis/complet brown/ wholemeal bread ; ~ d'épice gingerbread ; ~ grillé toast ; ~ de mie sandwich loaf ; ~ de seigle rye bread ; ~ de sucre sugar loaf.

pair, e [pɛr] a (nombre) even // nm peer ; aller de ~ (avec) to go hand in hand ou together (with) ; au ~ (FINANCE) at par ; jeune fille au ~ au pair girl.

paire [pɛr] nf pair ; une ~ de lunettes/tenailles a pair of glasses/pincers.

paisible [pezibl(ə)] a peaceful, quiet.

paitre [pɛtr(ə)] vi to graze.

paix [pɛ] nf peace ; (fig) peacefulness ; peace ; faire la ~ avec to make peace with ; avoir la ~ to have peace (and quiet).

palabrer [palabre] vi to argue endlessly.

palace [palas] nm luxury hotel.

palais [palɛ] nm palace ; (ANAT) palate ; le P~ Bourbon the National Assembly buildings ; ~ des expositions exhibition hall ; le P~ de Justice the Law Courts pl.

palan [palɑ̃] nm hoist.

pale [pal] nf (d'hélice, de rame) blade ; (de roue) paddle.

pâle [pal] a pale ; bleu ~ pale blue.

paléontologie [paleɔ̃tɔlɔʒi] nf paleontology.

Palestine [palɛstin] nf: la ~ Palestine ; palestinien, ne a, nm/f Palestinian.

palet [palɛ] nm disc ; (HOCKEY) puck.

paletot [palto] nm (short) coat.

palette [palɛt] nf (de peintre) palette.

palétuvier [paletyvje] nm mangrove.

pâleur [palœr] nf paleness.

palier [palje] nm (d'escalier) landing ; (fig) level, plateau ; (TECH) bearing ; nos voisins de ~ our neighbours across the landing ; en ~ ad level ; par ~s in stages ; palière af landing cpd.

pâlir [palir] vi to turn ou go pale ; (couleur) to fade.

palissade [palisad] nf fence.

palissandre [palisɑ̃dr(ə)] nm rosewood.

palliatif [paljatif] nm palliative ; (expédient) stopgap measure.

pallier [palje] vt, ~ à vt to offset, make up for.

palmarès [palmarɛs] nm record (of achievements) ; (SCOL) prize list ; (SPORT) list of winners.

palme [palm(ə)] nf (BOT) palm leaf (pl leaves) ; (symbole) palm ; (en caoutchouc) flipper ; ~s (académiques) decoration for services to education ; palmé, e a (pattes) webbed.

palmeraie [palmərɛ] nf palm grove.

palmier [palmje] nm palm tree.

palmipède [palmiped] nm palmiped, webfooted bird.

palombe [palɔ̃b] nf woodpigeon, ringdove.

pâlot, te [palo, -ɔt] a pale, peaky.

palourde [palurd(ə)] nf clam.

palper [palpe] vt to feel, finger.

palpitant, e [palpitɑ̃, -ɑ̃t] a thrilling.

palpitation [palpitasjɔ̃] nf palpitation.

palpiter [palpite] vi (cœur, pouls) to beat ; (: plus fort) to pound, throb ; (narines, chair) to quiver.

paludisme [palydism(ə)] nm paludism, malaria.

pâmer [pame]: se ~ vi to swoon ; (fig): se ~ devant to go into raptures over ; pâmoison nf: tomber en pâmoison to swoon.

pampa [pɑ̃pa] nf pampas pl.

pamphlet [pɑ̃flɛ] nm lampoon, satirical tract.

pamplemousse [pɑ̃pləmus] nm grapefruit.

pan [pɑ̃] nm section, piece // excl bang! ; ~ de chemise shirt tail.

panacée [panase] nf panacea.

panachage [panaʃaʒ] nm blend, mix.

panache [panaʃ] nm plume ; (fig) spirit, panache.

panaché, e [panaʃe] a: œillet ~ variegated carnation ; glace ~e mixed-flavour ice cream ; salade ~e mixed salad ; bière ~e shandy.

panaris [panari] nm whitlow.

pancarte [pɑ̃kart(ə)] nf sign, notice ; (dans un défilé) placard.

pancréas [pɑ̃kʀeɑs] *nm* pancreas.
pané, e [pane] *a* fried in breadcrumbs.
panier [panje] *nm* basket; **mettre au ~** to chuck away; **~ à provisions** shopping basket; **~ à salade** Black Maria, police van; **~-repas** *nm* packed lunch.
panification [panifikɑsjɔ̃] *nf* bread-making.
panique [panik] *nf, a* panic; **paniquer** *vi* to panic.
panne [pan] *nf* (*d'un mécanisme, moteur*) breakdown; **être/tomber en ~** to have broken down/break down; **être en ~ d'essence** *ou* **sèche** to have run out of petrol; **~ d'électricité** *ou* **de courant** power *ou* electrical failure.
panneau, x [pano] *nm* (*écriteau*) sign, notice; (*de boiserie, de tapisserie etc*) panel; **tomber dans le ~** (*fig*) to walk into the trap; **~ d'affichage** notice board; **~ de signalisation** roadsign; **~-réclame** *nm* hoarding.
panonceau, x [panɔ̃so] *nm* sign.
panoplie [panɔpli] *nf* (*jouet*) outfit; (*d'armes*) display; (*fig*) array.
panorama [panɔʀama] *nm* panorama; **panoramique** *a* panoramic; (*carrosserie*) with panoramic windows.
panse [pɑ̃s] *nf* paunch.
pansement [pɑ̃smɑ̃] *nm* dressing, bandage; **~ adhésif** sticking plaster.
panser [pɑ̃se] *vt* (*plaie*) to dress, bandage; (*bras*) to put a dressing on, bandage; (*cheval*) to groom.
pantalon [pɑ̃talɔ̃] *nm* (*aussi*: **~s, paire de ~s**) trousers *pl*, pair of trousers; **~ de ski** ski pants *pl*.
pantelant, e [pɑ̃tlɑ̃, -ɑ̃t] *a* gasping for breath, panting.
panthère [pɑ̃tɛʀ] *nf* panther.
pantin [pɑ̃tɛ̃] *nm* jumping jack; (*péj*) puppet.
pantois [pɑ̃twa] *am*: **rester ~** to be flabbergasted.
pantomime [pɑ̃tɔmim] *nf* mime; (*pièce*) mime show.
pantouflard, e [pɑ̃tuflaʀ, -aʀd(ə)] *a* (*péj*) stay-at-home.
pantoufle [pɑ̃tufl(ə)] *nf* slipper.
panure [panyʀ] *nf* breadcrumbs *pl*.
paon [pɑ̃] *nm* peacock.
papa [papa] *nm* dad(dy).
papauté [papote] *nf* papacy.
pape [pap] *nm* pope.
paperasse [papʀas] *nf* (*péj*) bumf *q*, papers *pl*; forms *pl*; **~rie** *nf* (*péj*) red tape *q*; paperwork *q*.
papeterie [papetʀi] *nf* (*usine*) paper mill; (*magasin*) stationer's (shop).
papetier, ière [paptje, -jɛʀ] *nm/f* paper-maker; stationer; **~-libraire** *nm* bookseller and stationer.
papier [papje] *nm* paper; (*article*) article; **~s** *nmpl* (*aussi*: **~s d'identité**) (identity) papers; **~ couché/glacé** art/glazed paper; **~ (d')aluminium** aluminium foil, tinfoil; **~ d'Arménie** incense paper; **~ bible** India *ou* bible paper; **~ buvard** blotting paper; **~ calque** tracing paper; **~ carbone** carbon paper; **~ collant** sellotape ®, sticky tape; **~ hygiénique**

toilet paper; **~ journal** newsprint; (*pour emballer*) newspaper; **~ à lettres** writing paper, notepaper; **~ mâché** papier-mâché; **~ machine** typing paper; **~ peint** wallpaper; **~ pelure** India paper; **~ de soie** tissue paper; **~ de tournesol** litmus paper; **~ de verre** sandpaper.
papille [papij] *nf*: **~s gustatives** taste buds.
papillon [papijɔ̃] *nm* butterfly; (*fam*: *contravention*) (parking) ticket; (*TECH*: *écrou*) wing *ou* butterfly nut; **~ de nuit** moth.
papillote [papijɔt] *nf* curlpaper.
papilloter [papijɔte] *vi* to blink, flicker.
papoter [papɔte] *vi* to chatter.
paprika [papʀika] *nm* paprika.
paquebot [pakbo] *nm* liner.
pâquerette [pakʀɛt] *nf* daisy.
Pâques [pak] *nm, nfpl* Easter; **faire ses ~** to do one's Easter duties.
paquet [pakɛ] *nm* packet; (*colis*) parcel; (*fig*: *tas*): **~ de** pile *ou* heap of; **mettre le ~** (*fam*) to give one's all; **~ de mer** big wave; **paquetage** *nm* (*MIL*) kit, pack; **~-cadeau** *nm* gift-wrapped parcel.
par [paʀ] *prép* by; **finir** *etc* **~** to end *etc* with; **~ amour** out of love; **passer ~ Lyon/la côte** to go via *ou* through Lyons/along by the coast; **~ la fenêtre** (*jeter, regarder*) out of the window; **3 ~ jour/personne** 3 a *ou* per day/head; **2 ~ 2** two at a time; in twos; **~ où?** which way?; **~ ici** this way; (*dans le coin*) round here; **~-ci, ~-là** here and there.
para [paʀa] *nm* (*abr de parachutiste*) para.
parabole [paʀabɔl] *nf* (*REL*) parable; (*GÉOM*) parabola; **parabolique** *a* parabolic.
parachever [paʀaʃve] *vt* to perfect.
parachute [paʀaʃyt] *nm* parachute.
parachutiste [paʀaʃytist(ə)] *nm/f* parachutist; (*MIL*) paratrooper.
parade [paʀad] *nf* (*spectacle, défilé*) parade; (*ESCRIME, BOXE*) parry; (*ostentation*): **faire ~ de** to display, show off.
paradis [paʀadi] *nm* heaven, paradise.
paradoxal, e, aux [paʀadɔksal, -o] *a* paradoxical.
paradoxe [paʀadɔks(ə)] *nm* paradox.
parafe [paʀaf] *nm*, **parafer** [paʀafe] *vt* voir **paraphe, parapher.**
paraffine [paʀafin] *nf* paraffin; paraffin wax.
parages [paʀaʒ] *nmpl*: **dans les ~ (de)** in the area *ou* vicinity (of).
paragraphe [paʀagʀaf] *nm* paragraph.
paraître [paʀɛtʀ(ə)] *vb avec attribut* to seem, look, appear // *vi* to appear; (*être visible*) to show; (*PRESSE, ÉDITION*) to be published, come out, appear; (*briller*) to show off // *vb impersonnel*: **il paraît que** it seems *ou* appears that, they say that; **il me paraît que** it seems to me that.
parallèle [paʀalɛl] *a* parallel; (*police, marché*) unofficial // *nm* (*comparaison*): **faire un ~ entre** to draw a parallel between; (*GÉO*) parallel // *nf* parallel (line); **parallélisme** *nm* parallelism; (*AUTO*) wheel alignment; **parallélogramme** *nm* parallelogram.

paralyser [paralize] *vt* to paralyze.
paralysie [paralizi] *nf* paralysis.
paralytique [paralitik] *a, nm/f* paralytic.
paramédical, e, aux [paramedikal, -o] *a* paramedical.
paranoïaque [paranɔjak] *nm/f* paranoiac.
parapet [parapɛ] *nm* parapet.
paraphe [paraf] *nm* flourish; initials *pl*; signature; **parapher** *vt* to initial; to sign.
paraphrase [parafraz] *nf* paraphrase.
parapluie [paraplɥi] *nm* umbrella; ~ **pliant** telescopic umbrella.
parasite [parazit] *nm* parasite // *a* (BOT, BIO) parasitic(al); ~**s** (TÉL) interference *sg*.
parasol [parasɔl] *nm* parasol, sunshade.
paratonnerre [paratɔnɛr] *nm* lightning conductor.
paravent [paravã] *nm* folding screen.
parc [park] *nm* (public) park, gardens *pl*; (*de château etc*) grounds *pl*; (*pour le bétail*) pen, enclosure; (*d'enfant*) playpen; (MIL: *entrepôt*) depot; (*ensemble d'unités*) stock; fleet; ~ **automobile** (*d'un pays*) number of cars on the roads; (*d'une société*) car fleet; ~ **à huîtres** oyster bed; ~ **national** national park; ~ **de stationnement** car park.
parcelle [parsɛl] *nf* fragment, scrap; (*de terrain*) plot, parcel.
parce que [parsk(ə)] *cj* because.
parchemin [parʃəmɛ̃] *nm* parchment.
parcimonie [parsimɔni] *nf* parsimony, parsimoniousness.
parc(o)mètre [park(ɔ)mɛtr(ə)] *nm* parking meter.
parcourir [parkurir] *vt* (*trajet, distance*) to cover; (*article, livre*) to skim *ou* glance through; (*lieu*) to go all over, travel up and down; (*suj: frisson, vibration*) to run through; ~ **des yeux** to run one's eye over.
parcours [parkur] *nm* (*trajet*) journey; (*itinéraire*) route; (SPORT: *de golf etc*) course; (: *accompli par un concurrent*) round; run; lap.
par-delà [pardəla] *prép* beyond.
par-dessous [pardəsu] *prép, ad* under(neath).
pardessus [pardəsy] *nm* overcoat.
par-dessus [pardəsy] *prép* over (the top of) // *ad* over (the top); ~ **le marché** on top of all that.
par-devant [pardəvã] *prép* in the presence of, before // *ad* at the front; round the front.
pardon [pardɔ̃] *nm* forgiveness *q* // *excl* sorry; (*pour interpeller etc*) excuse me; **demander** ~ **à qn** (**de**) to apologize to sb (for); **je vous demande** ~ I'm sorry; excuse me.
pardonner [pardɔne] *vt* to forgive; ~ **qch à qn** to forgive sb for sth.
paré, e [pare] *a* ready, prepared.
pare-balles [parbal] *a inv* bulletproof.
pare-boue [parbu] *nm inv* mudguard.
pare-brise [parbriz] *nm inv* windscreen.
pare-chocs [parʃɔk] *nm inv* bumper.
pareil, le [parɛj] *a* (*identique*) the same, alike; (*similaire*) similar; (*tel*): **un courage/livre** ~ such courage/a book,

courage/a book like this; **de** ~**s livres** such books; **j'en veux un** ~ I'd like one just like it; **rien de** ~ no (*ou* any) such thing, nothing (*ou* anything) like it; **ses** ~**s** one's fellow men; one's peers; **ne pas avoir son(sa)** ~**(le)** to be second to none; ~ **à** the same as; similar to; **sans** ~ unparalleled, unequalled; ~**lement** *ad* the same, alike; in such a way; (*également*) likewise.
parement [parmã] *nm* (CONSTR) facing; (REL): ~ **d'autel** antependium.
parent, e [parã, -ãt] *nm/f*: **un/une** ~**/e** a relative *ou* relation // *a*: **être** ~ **de** to be related to; ~**s** *nmpl* (*père et mère*) parents; **parenté** *nf* (*lien*) relationship; (*personnes*) relatives *pl*, relations *pl*.
parenthèse [parãtɛz] *nf* (*ponctuation*) bracket, parenthesis; (MATH) bracket; (*digression*) parenthesis, digression; **ouvrir/fermer la** ~ to open/close the brackets; **entre** ~**s** in brackets; (*fig*) incidentally.
parer [pare] *vt* to adorn; (CULIN) to dress, trim; (*éviter*) to ward off; ~ **à** (*danger*) to ward off; (*inconvénient*) to deal with; ~ **au plus pressé** to attend to what's most urgent.
pare-soleil [parsɔlɛj] *nm inv* sun visor.
paresse [parɛs] *nf* laziness; **paresser** *vi* to laze around; **paresseux, euse** *a* lazy; (*fig*) slow, sluggish // *nm* (ZOOL) sloth.
parfaire [parfɛr] *vt* to perfect; to complete.
parfait, e [parfɛ, -ɛt] *a* perfect // *nm* (LING) perfect (tense); (CULIN) parfait // *excl* fine, excellent; **parfaitement** *ad* perfectly // *excl* (*most*) certainly.
parfois [parfwa] *ad* sometimes.
parfum [parfœ̃] *nm* (*produit*) perfume, scent; (*odeur: de fleur*) scent, fragrance; (: *de tabac, vin*) aroma; (*à choisir: de glace, milk-shake*) flavour; **parfumé, e** *a* (*fleur, fruit*) fragrant; (*papier à lettres etc*) scented; (*femme*) wearing perfume *ou* scent, perfumed; **parfumé au café** coffee-flavoured, flavoured with coffee; **parfumer** *vt* (*suj: odeur, bouquet*) to perfume; (*mouchoir*) to put scent *ou* perfume on; (*crème, gâteau*) to flavour; **se parfumer** to put on (some) perfume *ou* scent; to use perfume *ou* scent; **parfumerie** *nf* (*commerce*) perfumery; (*produits*) perfumes *pl*; (*boutique*) perfume shop.
pari [pari] *nm* bet, wager; (SPORT) bet; **P**~ **Mutuel urbain** (**P.M.U.**) (*State-controlled*) organisation for forecast betting on horse-racing.
paria [parja] *nm* outcast.
parier [parje] *vt* to bet; **parieur** *nm* (*turfiste etc*) punter.
Paris [pari] *n* Paris; **parisien, ne** *a* Parisian; (GÉO, ADMIN) Paris *cpd* // *nm/f*: **Parisien, ne** Parisian.
paritaire [pariter] *a*: **commission** ~ joint commission.
parité [parite] *nf* parity.
parjure [parʒyr] *nm* (*acte*) false oath, perjury; breach of oath, perjury // *nm/f* perjurer; **se parjurer** to forswear *ou* perjure o.s.

parking [paʀkiŋ] nm (lieu) car park.
parlant, e [paʀlɑ̃, -ɑ̃t] a (fig) graphic, vivid; eloquent; (CINÉMA) talking // ad: **généralement ~** generally speaking.
parlement [paʀləmɑ̃] nm parliament; **parlementaire** a parliamentary // nm/f member of parliament; parliamentarian; negotiator, mediator.
parlementer [paʀləmɑ̃te] vi to negotiate, parley.
parler [paʀle] nm speech; dialect // vi to speak, talk; (avouer) to talk; **~ (à qn) de** to talk ou speak (to sb) about; **~ pour qn** (intercéder) to speak for sb; **~ le/en français** to speak French/in French; **~ affaires** to talk business; **~ en dormant/du nez** to talk in one's sleep/through one's nose; **sans ~ de** (fig) not to mention, to say nothing of; **tu parles!** you must be joking!
parloir [paʀlwaʀ] nm (d'une prison, d'un hôpital) visiting room; (REL) parlour.
parmi [paʀmi] prép among(st).
parodie [paʀɔdi] nf parody; **parodier** vt (œuvre, auteur) to parody.
paroi [paʀwa] nf wall; (cloison) partition; **~ rocheuse** rock face.
paroisse [paʀwas] nf parish; **paroissial, e, aux** a parish cpd; **paroissien, ne** nm/f parishioner // nm prayer book.
parole [paʀɔl] nf (faculté): **la ~** speech; (mot, promesse) word; **~s** nfpl (MUS) words, lyrics; **tenir ~** to keep one's word; **prendre la ~** to speak; **demander la ~** to ask for permission to speak; **je le crois sur ~** I'll take his word for it.
paroxysme [paʀɔksism(ə)] nm height, paroxysm.
parpaing [paʀpɛ̃] nm bond-stone, parpen.
parquer [paʀke] vt (voiture, matériel) to park; (bestiaux) to pen (in ou up); (prisonniers) to pack in.
parquet [paʀkɛ] nm (parquet) floor; (JUR): **le ~** the Public Prosecutor's department; **parqueter** vt to lay a parquet floor in.
parrain [paʀɛ̃] nm godfather; (d'un nouvel adhérent) sponsor, proposer; **parrainer** vt (nouvel adhérent) to sponsor, propose; (entreprise) to promote, sponsor.
parricide [paʀisid] nm, nf parricide.
pars vb voir **partir**.
parsemer [paʀsəme] vt (suj: feuilles, papiers) to be scattered over; **~ qch de** to scatter sth with.
part [paʀ] nf (qui revient à qn) share; (fraction, partie) part; (FINANCE) (non-voting) share; **prendre ~ à** (débat etc) to take part in; (soucis, douleur de qn) to share in; **faire ~ de qch à qn** to announce sth to sb, inform sb of sth; **pour ma ~** as for me, as far as I'm concerned; **à ~ entière** a full; **de la ~ de** (au nom de) on behalf of; (donné par) from; **de toute(s) ~(s)** from all sides ou quarters; **de ~ et d'autre** on both sides, on either side; **de ~ en ~** right through; **d'une ~ ... d'autre ~** on the one hand ... on the other hand; **à ~** separately; (de côté) aside // prép apart from, except for // a exceptional, special; **faire la ~ des choses** to make allowances.

partage [paʀtaʒ] nm dividing up; sharing (out) q, share-out; sharing; **recevoir qch en ~** to receive sth as one's share (ou lot); **sans ~** undivided.
partagé, e [paʀtaʒe] a (opinions etc) divided.
partager [paʀtaʒe] vt to share; (distribuer, répartir) to share (out); (morceler, diviser) to divide (up); **se ~** vt (héritage etc) to share between themselves (ou ourselves).
partance [paʀtɑ̃s]: **en ~** ad outbound, due to leave; **en ~ pour** (bound) for.
partant [paʀtɑ̃] vb voir **partir** // nm (SPORT) starter; (HIPPISME) runner.
partenaire [paʀtənɛʀ] nm/f partner.
parterre [paʀtɛʀ] nm (de fleurs) (flower) bed, border; (THÉÂTRE) stalls pl.
parti [paʀti] nm (POL) party; (décision) course of action; (personne à marier) match; **tirer ~ de** to take advantage of, turn to good account; **prendre le ~ de faire** to make up one's mind to do, resolve to do; **prendre le ~ de qn** to stand up for sb, side with sb; **prendre ~ (pour/contre)** to take sides ou a stand (for/against); **prendre son ~ de** to come to terms with; **~ pris** bias.
partial, e, aux [paʀsjal, -o] a biased, partial.
participant, e [paʀtisipɑ̃, -ɑ̃t] nm/f participant; (à un concours) entrant; (d'une société) member.
participation [paʀtisipɑsjɔ̃] nf participation; sharing; (COMM) interest; **la ~ aux bénéfices** profit-sharing; **la ~ ouvrière** worker participation.
participe [paʀtisip] nm participle; **~ passé/présent** past/present participle.
participer [paʀtisipe]: **~ à** vt (course, réunion) to take part in; (profits etc) to share in; (frais etc) to contribute to; (entreprise: financièrement) to cooperate in; (chagrin, succès de qn) to share (in); **~ de** vt to partake of.
particularisme [paʀtikylaʀism(ə)] nm sense of identity; specific characteristic.
particularité [paʀtikylaʀite] nf particularity; (distinctive) characteristic, feature.
particule [paʀtikyl] nf particle; **~ (nobiliaire)** nobiliary particle.
particulier, ière [paʀtikylje, -jɛʀ] a (personnel, privé) private; (spécial) special, particular; (caractéristique) characteristic, distinctive; (spécifique) particular // nm (individu: ADMIN) private individual; '**~ vend ...**' (COMM) 'for sale privately ...'; **~ à** peculiar to; **en ~** ad (surtout) in particular, particularly; (en privé) in private; **particulièrement** ad particularly.
partie [paʀti] nf (gén) part; (profession, spécialité) field, subject; (JUR etc: protagonistes) party; (de cartes, tennis etc) game; **une ~ de campagne/de pêche** an outing in the country/a fishing party ou trip; **en ~** ad partly, in part; **faire ~ de** to belong to; (suj: chose) to be part of; **prendre qn à ~** to take sb to task; (malmener) to set on sb; **en grande ~** largely, in the main; **~ civile** (JUR) private

party associating in action with public prosecutor.

partiel, le [paʀsjɛl] a partial // nm (SCOL) class exam.

partir [paʀtiʀ] vi (gén) to go; (quitter) to go, leave; (s'éloigner) to go (ou drive etc) away ou off; (moteur) to start; (pétard) to go off; **de** (lieu: quitter) to leave; (: commencer à) to start from; (date) to run ou start from; **à ~ de** from.

partisan, e [paʀtizɑ̃, -an] nm/f partisan // a: **être ~ de qch/faire** to be in favour of sth/doing.

partitif, ive [paʀtitif, -iv] a: **article ~** article used in the partitive genitive.

partition [paʀtisjɔ̃] nf (MUS) score.

partout [paʀtu] ad everywhere; **~ où il allait** everywhere ou wherever he went; **trente ~** (TENNIS) thirty all.

paru, e pp de **paraître**.

parure [paʀyʀ] nf (toilette, bijoux) finery q; jewellery q; (assortiment) set.

parution [paʀysjɔ̃] nf publication, appearance.

parvenir [paʀvəniʀ]: **~ à** vt (atteindre) to reach; (réussir): **~ à faire** to manage to do, succeed in doing; **faire ~ qch à qn** to have sth sent to sb.

parvenu, e [paʀvəny] nm/f (péj) parvenu, upstart.

parvis [paʀvi] nm square (in front of a church).

pas [pɑ] nm voir le mot suivant // ad not; **~ de** no; **ne ... ~**: **il ne le voit ~/ne l'a ~ vu/ne le verra ~** he doesn't see it/hasn't seen it ou didn't see it/won't see it; **ils n'ont ~ de voiture/d'enfants** they haven't got a car/any children, they have no car/children; **il m'a dit de ne ~ le faire** he told me not to do it; **il n'est ~ plus grand** he isn't bigger, he's no bigger; **... lui ~ ou ~ lui** he doesn't (ou isn't etc); **non ~ que ...** not that ...; **une pomme ~ mûre** an apple which isn't ripe; **~ du tout** not at all; **~ plus tard qu'hier** only yesterday; **~ mal** a not bad, quite good (ou pretty ou nice) // ad quite well; (beaucoup) quite a lot; **~ mal de** quite a lot of.

pas [pɑ] ad voir le mot précédent // nm (allure, mesure) pace; (démarche) tread; (enjambée, DANSE) step; (bruit) (foot)step; (trace) footprint; (TECH: de vis, d'écrou) thread; **~ à ~** step by step; **au ~** at walking pace; **mettre qn au ~** to bring sb to heel; **au ~ de gymnastique/de course** at a jog trot/at a run; **à ~ de loup** stealthily; **faire les cent ~** to pace up and down; **faire les premiers ~** to make the first move; **sur le ~ de la porte** on the doorstep; **le ~ de Calais** (détroit) the Straits of Dover; **~ de porte** (COMM) key money.

pascal, e, aux [paskal, -o] a Easter cpd.

passable [pɑsabl(ə)] a (travail) passable, tolerable.

passage [pɑsaʒ] nm (fait de passer) voir **passer**; (lieu, prix de la traversée, extrait de livre etc) passage; (chemin) way; **de ~** (touristes) passing through; (amants etc) casual; **~ clouté** pedestrian crossing; '**~ interdit**' 'no entry'; **~ à niveau** level

crossing; '**~ protégé**' right of way over secondary road(s) on your right; **~ souterrain** subway, underground passage; **~ à tabac** beating-up.

passager, ère [pɑsaʒe, -ɛʀ] a passing // nm/f passenger; **~ clandestin** stowaway.

passant, e [pɑsɑ̃, -ɑ̃t] a (rue, endroit) busy // nm/f passer-by // nm (pour ceinture etc) loop.

passe [pɑs] nf (SPORT, magnétique, NAVIG) pass // nm (passe-partout) master ou skeleton key; **être en ~ de faire** to be on the way to doing.

passé, e [pɑse] a (événement, temps) past; (couleur, tapisserie) faded // prép after // nm past; (LING) past (tense); **il est ~ midi** ou **midi ~** it's gone twelve; **~ de mode** out of fashion; **~ composé** perfect (tense); **~ simple** past historic.

passe-droit [pɑsdʀwa] nm special privilege.

passéiste [pɑseist] a backward-looking.

passementerie [pɑsmɑ̃tʀi] nf trimmings pl.

passe-montagne [pɑsmɔ̃taɲ] nm balaclava.

passe-partout [pɑspaʀtu] nm inv master ou skeleton key // a inv all-purpose.

passe-passe [pɑspɑs] nm: **tour de ~** trick, sleight of hand q.

passe-plats [pɑspla] nm inv serving hatch.

passeport [pɑspɔʀ] nm passport.

passer [pɑse] vi (se rendre, aller) to go; (voiture, piétons: défiler) to pass (by), go by; (faire une halte rapide: facteur, laitier etc) to come, call; (: pour rendre visite) to call ou drop in; (courant, air, lumière, franchir un obstacle etc) to get through; (accusé, projet de loi): **~ devant** to come before; (film, émission) to be on; (temps, jours) to pass, go by; (couleur, papier) to fade; (douleur) to pass, go away; (CARTES) to pass; (SCOL) to go up (to the next class) // vt (frontière, rivière etc) to cross; (douane) to go through; (examen) to sit, take; (visite médicale etc) to have; (journée, temps) to spend; (donner): **~ qch à qn** to pass sth to sb; to give sb sth; (transmettre): **~ qch à qn** to pass sth on to sb; (enfiler: vêtement) to slip on; (faire entrer, mettre): **(faire) ~ qch dans/par** to get sth into/through; (café) to pour the water on; (thé, soupe) to strain; (film, pièce) to show, put on; (disque) to play, put on; (marché, accord) to agree on; (tolérer): **~ qch à qn** to let sb get away with sth; **se ~** vi (avoir lieu: scène, action) to take place; (se dérouler: entretien etc) to go; (arriver): **que s'est-il passé?** what happened?; (s'écouler: semaine etc) to pass, go by; **se ~ de** vt to go ou do without; **se ~ les mains sous l'eau/de l'eau sur le visage** to put one's hands under the tap/run water over one's face; **~ par** to go through; **passe devant/par ici** go in front/this way; **~ sur** vt (faute, détail inutile) to pass over; **~ avant qch/qn** (fig) to come before sth/sb; **laisser ~** (air, lumière, personne) to let through; (occasion) to let slip, miss; (erreur) to overlook; **~ à la radio/fouille** to be

X-rayed/searched ; ~ à la radio/télévision to be on the radio/on television ; ~ pour riche to be taken for a rich man ; il passait pour avoir he was said to have ; ~ à l'opposition to go over to the opposition ; passons! let's say no more (about it) ; ~ en seconde, ~ la seconde (AUTO) to change into second ; ~ qch en fraude to smuggle sth in (ou out) ; ~ la main par la portière to stick one's hand out of the door ; ~ le balai/l'aspirateur to sweep up/hoover ; je vous passe M. X (je vous mets en communication avec lui) I'm putting you through to Mr X ; (je lui passe l'appareil) here is Mr X, I'll hand you over to Mr X.

passerelle [pɑsʀɛl] nf footbridge ; (de navire, avion) gangway.

passe-temps [pɑstɑ̃] nm inv pastime.

passeur, euse [pɑsœʀ, -øz] nm/f smuggler.

passible [pɑsibl(ə)] a: ~ de liable to.

passif, ive [pasif, -iv] a passive // nm (LING) passive ; (COMM) liabilities pl.

passion [pɑsjɔ̃] nf passion ; avoir la ~ de to have a passion for ; passionné, e a passionate ; impassioned ; passionnel, le a of passion ; passionner vt (personne) to fascinate, grip ; se passionner pour to take an avid interest in ; to have a passion for.

passoire [pɑswaʀ] nf sieve ; (à légumes) colander ; (à thé) strainer.

pastel [pastɛl] nm, a inv (ART) pastel.

pastèque [pastɛk] nf watermelon.

pasteur [pastœʀ] nm (protestant) minister, pastor.

pasteuriser [pastœʀize] vt to pasteurize.

pastiche [pastiʃ] nm pastiche.

pastille [pastij] nf (à sucer) lozenge, pastille ; (de papier etc) (small) disc ; ~s pour la toux throat lozenges.

pastis [pastis] nm pastis.

patate [patat] nf spud ; ~ douce sweet potato.

patauger [patoʒe] vi (pour s'amuser) to splash about ; (avec effort) to wade about ; ~ dans (en marchant) to wade through.

pâte [pɑt] nf (à tarte) pastry ; (à pain) dough ; (à frire) batter ; (substance molle) paste ; cream ; ~s nfpl (macaroni etc) pasta sg ; fromage à ~ dure/molle hard/soft cheese ; ~ d'amandes almond paste ; ~ brisée shortcrust pastry ; ~ de fruits crystallized fruit q ; ~ à modeler modelling clay, Plasticine ® ; ~ à papier paper pulp.

pâté [pɑte] nm (charcuterie) pâté ; (tache) ink blot ; (de sable) sandcastle, sandpie ; ~ en croûte ≈ pork pie ; ~ de maisons block (of houses).

pâtée [pɑte] nf mash, feed.

patente [patɑ̃t] nf (COMM) trading licence.

patère [patɛʀ] nf (coat-)peg.

paternel, le [patɛʀnɛl] a (amour, soins) fatherly ; (ligne, autorité) paternal.

paternité [patɛʀnite] nf paternity, fatherhood.

pâteux, euse [pɑtø, -øz] a thick ; pasty.

pathétique [patetik] a moving, pathetic.

pathologie [patɔlɔʒi] nf pathology.

patibulaire [patibylɛʀ] a sinister.

patience [pasjɑ̃s] nf patience.

patient, e [pasjɑ̃, -ɑ̃t] a, nm/f patient.

patienter [pasjɑ̃te] vi to wait.

patin [patɛ̃] nm skate ; (sport) skating ; (de traineau, luge) runner ; (pièce de tissu) cloth pad (used as slippers to protect polished floor) ; ~s (à glace) (ice) skates ; ~s à roulettes roller skates.

patinage [patinaʒ] nm skating ; ~ artistique/de vitesse figure/speed skating.

patine [patin] nf sheen.

patiner [patine] vi to skate ; (embrayage) to slip ; (roue, voiture) to spin ; se ~ vi (meuble, cuir) to acquire a sheen, become polished ; patineur, euse nm/f skater ; patinoire nf skating rink, (ice) rink.

pâtir [pɑtiʀ]: ~ de vt to suffer because of.

pâtisserie [pɑtisʀi] nf (boutique) cake shop ; (métier) confectionery ; (à la maison) pastry- ou cake-making, baking ; ~s nfpl (gâteaux) pastries, cakes ; pâtissier, ière nm/f pastrycook ; confectioner.

patois [patwa] nm dialect, patois.

patriarche [patʀijaʀʃ(ə)] nm patriarch.

patrie [patʀi] nf homeland.

patrimoine [patʀimwan] nm inheritance, patrimony.

patriote [patʀijɔt] a patriotic // nm/f patriot ; patriotique a patriotic.

patron, ne [patʀɔ̃, -ɔn] nm/f (chef) boss, manager/eress ; (propriétaire) owner, proprietor/tress ; (employeur) employer ; (MED) ≈ senior consultant ; (REL) patron saint // nm (COUTURE) pattern ; ~ de thèse supervisor (of postgraduate thesis) ; patronal, e, aux a (syndicat, intérêts) employers'.

patronage [patʀɔnaʒ] nm patronage ; (parish) youth club.

patronat [patʀɔna] nm employers pl.

patronner [patʀɔne] vt to sponsor, support.

patrouille [patʀuj] nf patrol ; patrouiller vi to patrol, be on patrol.

patte [pat] nf (jambe) leg ; (pied: de chien, chat) paw ; (: d'oiseau) foot ; (languette) strap ; (: de poche) flap ; à ~s d'éléphant a bell-bottomed ; ~s d'oie (fig) crow's feet.

pattemouille [patmuj] nf damp cloth (for ironing).

pâturage [pɑtyʀaʒ] nm pasture.

pâture [pɑtyʀ] nf food.

paume [pom] nf palm.

paumer [pome] vt (fam) to lose.

paupière [popjɛʀ] nf eyelid.

paupiette [popjɛt] nf: ~s de veau veal olives.

pause [poz] nf (arrêt) break ; (en parlant, MUS) pause.

pauvre [povʀ(ə)] a poor // nm/f poor man/woman ; les ~s the poor ; ~ en calcium with a low calcium content ; ~té nf (état) poverty.

pavaner [pavane]: se ~ vi to strut about.

pavé, e [pave] a paved ; cobbled // nm (bloc) paving stone ; cobblestone ; (pavage) paving.

pavillon [pavijɔ̃] nm (de banlieue) small (detached) house; (kiosque) lodge; pavilion; (d'hôpital) ward; (MUS: de cor etc) bell; (ANAT: de l'oreille) pavilion, pinna; (drapeau) flag; ~ **de complaisance** flag of convenience.

pavoiser [pavwaze] vt to deck with flags // vi to put out flags; (fig) to rejoice, exult.

pavot [pavo] nm poppy.

payant, e [pejɑ̃, -ɑ̃t] a (spectateurs etc) paying; (fig: entreprise) profitable; **c'est** ~ you have to pay, there is a charge.

paye [pɛj] nf pay, wages pl.

payement [pɛjmɑ̃] nm payment.

payer [peje] vt (créancier, employé, loyer) to pay; (achat, réparations, fig: faute) to pay for // vi to pay; (métier) to be well-paid; (tactique etc) to pay off; **il me l'a fait** ~ **10 F** he charged me 10 F for it; ~ **qch à qn** to buy sth for sb, buy sb sth; **ils nous ont payé le voyage** they paid for our trip; ~ **de sa personne** to give of o.s.; ~ **d'audace** to act with great daring; **cela ne paie pas de mine** it doesn't look much; **se** ~ **la tête de qn** to take the mickey out of sb; to take sb for a ride.

pays [pei] nm country; land; region; village; **du** ~ a local.

paysage [peizaʒ] nm landscape; **paysagiste** nm/f landscape gardener; landscape painter.

paysan, ne [peizɑ̃, -an] nm/f countryman/woman; farmer; (péj) peasant // a country cpd; farming, farmers'.

Pays-Bas [peiba] nmpl: **les** ~ the Netherlands.

P.C.V. sigle voir **communication**.

P.D.G. sigle m voir **président**.

péage [peaʒ] nm toll; (endroit) tollgate; **pont à** ~ toll bridge.

peau, x [po] nf skin; **gants de** ~ fine leather gloves; ~ **de chamois** (chiffon) chamois leather, shammy; **P~-Rouge** nm/f Red Indian, redskin.

peccadille [pekadij] nf trifle; peccadillo.

pêche [pɛʃ] nf (sport, activité) fishing; (poissons pêchés) catch; (fruit) peach; ~ **à la ligne** (en rivière) angling.

péché [peʃe] nm sin; ~ **mignon** weakness.

pêche-abricot [pɛʃabriko] nf yellow peach.

pécher [peʃe] vi (REL) to sin; (fig) to err; to be flawed.

pêcher [peʃe] nm peach tree // vi to go fishing; (en rivière) to go angling // vt to catch, land; to fish for; ~ **au chalut** to trawl.

pécheur, eresse [peʃœr, peʃrɛs] nm/f sinner.

pêcheur [pɛʃœr] nm fisherman; angler; ~ **de perles** pearl diver.

pectoraux [pɛktɔro] nmpl pectoral muscles.

pécule [pekyl] nm savings pl, nest egg; (d'un détenu) earnings pl (paid on release).

pécuniaire [pekynjɛr] a financial.

pédagogie [pedagɔʒi] nf educational methods pl, pedagogy; **pédagogique** a educational; **formation pédagogique**

teacher training; **pédagogue** nm/f teacher; educationalist.

pédale [pedal] nf pedal; **pédaler** vi to pedal; **pédalier** nm pedal and gear mechanism.

pédalo [pedalo] nm pedalo, pedal-boat.

pédant, e [pedɑ̃, -ɑ̃t] a (péj) pedantic.

pédéraste [pederast(ə)] nm homosexual, pederast.

pédestre [pedɛstr(ə)] a: **tourisme** ~ hiking.

pédiatre [pedjatr(ə)] nm/f paediatrician, child specialist.

pédiatrie [pedjatri] nf paediatrics sg.

pédicure [pedikyr] nm/f chiropodist.

pègre [pɛgr(ə)] nf underworld.

peignais etc vb voir **peindre**.

peigne [pɛɲ] nm comb.

peigné, e [peɲe] a: **laine** ~**e** wool worsted; combed wool.

peigner [peɲe] vt to comb (the hair of); **se** ~ to comb one's hair.

peignis etc vb voir **peindre**.

peignoir [peɲwar] nm dressing gown; ~ **de bain** bathrobe.

peindre [pɛ̃dr(ə)] vt to paint; (fig) to portray, depict.

peine [pɛn] nf (affliction) sorrow, sadness q; (mal, effort) trouble q, effort; (difficulté) difficulty; (punition, châtiment) punishment; (JUR) sentence; **faire de la** ~ **à qn** to distress ou upset sb; **prendre la** ~ **de faire** to go to the trouble of doing; **se donner de la** ~ to make an effort; **ce n'est pas la** ~ **de faire** there's no point in doing, it's not worth doing; **avoir de la** ~ **à faire** to have difficulty doing; **à** ~ ad scarcely, hardly, barely; **à** ~ ... **que** hardly ... than; **sous** ~: **sous** ~ **d'être puni** for fear of being punished; **défense d'afficher sous** ~ **d'amende** billposters will be fined; **peiner** vi to work hard; to struggle; (moteur, voiture) to labour // vt to grieve, sadden.

peintre [pɛ̃tr(ə)] nm painter; ~ **en bâtiment** house painter, painter and decorator; ~ **d'enseignes** signwriter.

peinture [pɛ̃tyr] nf painting; (couche de couleur, couleur) paint; (surfaces peintes: aussi: ~**s**) paintwork; ~ **mate/brillante** matt/gloss paint; **'**~ **fraîche'** 'wet paint'.

péjoratif, ive [peʒɔratif, -iv] a pejorative, derogatory.

pelage [pəlaʒ] nm coat, fur.

pêle-mêle [pɛlmɛl] ad higgledy-piggledy.

peler [pəle] vt, vi to peel.

pèlerin [pɛlrɛ̃] nm pilgrim; **pèlerinage** nm pilgrimage; place of pilgrimage, shrine.

pélican [pelikɑ̃] nm pelican.

pelle [pɛl] nf shovel; (d'enfant, de terrassier) spade; ~ **à gâteau** cake slice; ~ **mécanique** mechanical digger; ~**ter** vt to shovel (up).

pelletier [pɛltje] nm furrier.

pellicule [pelikyl] nf film; ~**s** nfpl (MED) dandruff sg.

pelote [pəlɔt] nf (de fil, laine) ball; (d'épingles) pin cushion; ~ **basque** pelota.

peloter [pəlɔte] vt (fam) to feel (up); **se** ~ to pet.

peloton [pəlɔtɔ̃] *nm* group, squad; (CYCLISME) pack; ~ **d'exécution** firing squad.

pelotonner [pəlɔtɔne]: **se** ~ *vi* to curl (o.s.) up.

pelouse [pəluz] *nf* lawn.

peluche [pəlyʃ] *nf*: **animal en** ~ fluffy animal, soft toy; **pelucher** *vi* to become fluffy, fluff up.

pelure [pəlyʀ] *nf* peeling, peel *q*; ~ **d'oignon** onion skin.

pénal, e, aux [penal, -o] *a* penal.

pénaliser [penalize] *vt* to penalize.

pénalité [penalite] *nf* penalty.

penalty, les [penalti, -z] *nm* (SPORT) penalty (kick).

penaud, e [pəno, -od] *a* sheepish, contrite.

penchant [pɑ̃ʃɑ̃] *nm* tendency, propensity; liking, fondness.

penché, e [pɑ̃ʃe] *a* slanting.

pencher [pɑ̃ʃe] *vi* to tilt, lean over // *vt* to tilt; **se** ~ *vi* to lean over; (se baisser) to bend down; **se** ~ **sur** to bend over; (fig: problème) to look into; **se** ~ **au dehors** to lean out; ~ **pour** to be inclined to favour.

pendaison [pɑ̃dɛzɔ̃] *nf* hanging.

pendant, e [pɑ̃dɑ̃, -ɑ̃t] *a* hanging (out); (ADMIN, JUR) pending // *nm* counterpart; matching piece // *prép* during; **faire** ~ **à** to match; **to be the counterpart of**; ~**s d'oreilles** drop *ou* pendant earrings.

pendeloque [pɑ̃dlɔk] *nf* pendant.

pendentif [pɑ̃dɑ̃tif] *nm* pendant.

penderie [pɑ̃dʀi] *nf* wardrobe; (placard) walk-in cupboard.

pendre [pɑ̃dʀ(ə)] *vt, vi* to hang; **se** ~ **(à)** (se suicider) to hang o.s. (on); **se** ~ **à** (se suspendre) to hang from; ~ **à** to hang (down) from; ~ **qch à** (mur) to hang sth (up) on; (plafond) to hang sth (up) from.

pendule [pɑ̃dyl] *nf* clock // *nm* pendulum.

pendulette [pɑ̃dylɛt] *nf* small clock.

pêne [pɛn] *nm* bolt.

pénétrer [penetʀe] *vi* to come *ou* get in // *vt* to penetrate; ~ **dans** to enter; (suj: projectile) to penetrate; (: air, eau) to come into, get into; **se** ~ **de qch** to get sth firmly set in one's mind.

pénible [penibl(ə)] *a* (astreignant) hard; (affligeant) painful; (personne, caractère) tiresome; ~**ment** *ad* with difficulty.

péniche [peniʃ] *nf* barge; ~ **de débarquement** landing craft *inv*.

pénicilline [penisilin] *nf* penicillin.

péninsule [penɛ̃syl] *nf* peninsula.

pénis [penis] *nm* penis.

pénitence [penitɑ̃s] *nf* (repentir) penitence; (peine) penance.

pénitencier [penitɑ̃sje] *nm* penitentiary.

pénombre [penɔ̃bʀ(ə)] *nf* half-light; darkness.

pense-bête [pɑ̃sbɛt] *nm* aide-mémoire.

pensée [pɑ̃se] *nf* thought; (démarche, doctrine) thinking *q*; (BOT) pansy; **en** ~ in one's mind.

penser [pɑ̃se] *vi* to think // *vt* to think; (concevoir: problème, machine) to think out; ~ **à** to think of; (songer à: ami, vacances) to think of *ou* about; (réfléchir à: problème, offre) ~ **à qch** to think about

sth *ou* sth over; ~ **à faire qch** to think of doing sth; ~ **faire qch** to be thinking of doing sth, intend to do sth; **penseur** *nm* thinker; **pensif, ive** *a* pensive, thoughtful.

pension [pɑ̃sjɔ̃] *nf* (allocation) pension; (prix du logement) board and lodgings, bed and board; (maison particulière) boarding house; (hôtel) guesthouse, hotel; (école) boarding school; **prendre** ~ **chez** to take board and lodging at; **prendre qn en** ~ to take sb (in) as a lodger; **mettre en** ~ to send to boarding school; ~ **alimentaire** (d'étudiant) living allowance; (de divorcée) maintenance allowance; alimony; ~ **complète** full board; ~ **de famille** boarding house, guesthouse; **pensionnaire** *nm/f* boarder; guest; **pensionnat** *nm* boarding school.

pentagone [pɛ̃tagɔn] *nm* pentagon.

pente [pɑ̃t] *nf* slope; **en** ~ *a* sloping.

Pentecôte [pɑ̃tkot] *nf*: **la** ~ Whitsun; (dimanche) Whitsunday; **lundi de** ~ Whit Monday.

pénurie [penyʀi] *nf* shortage.

pépier [pepje] *vi* to chirp, tweet.

pépin [pepɛ̃] *nm* (BOT: graine) pip; (ennui) snag, hitch; (fam) brolly.

pépinière [pepinjɛʀ] *nf* tree nursery; (fig) nest, breeding-ground.

pépite [pepit] *nf* nugget.

perçant, e [pɛʀsɑ̃, -ɑ̃t] *a* sharp, keen; piercing, shrill.

percée [pɛʀse] *nf* (trouée) opening; (MIL) breakthrough; (SPORT) break.

perce-neige [pɛʀsənɛʒ] *nm inv* snowdrop.

percepteur [pɛʀsɛptœʀ] *nm* tax collector.

perceptible [pɛʀsɛptibl(ə)] *a* perceptible.

perception [pɛʀsɛpsjɔ̃] *nf* perception; (d'impôts etc) collection.

percer [pɛʀse] *vt* to pierce; (ouverture etc) to make; (mystère, énigme) to penetrate // *vi* to come through; to break through; ~ **une dent** to cut a tooth.

perceuse [pɛʀsøz] *nf* drill.

percevoir [pɛʀsəvwaʀ] *vt* (distinguer) to perceive, detect; (taxe, impôt) to collect; (revenu, indemnité) to receive.

perche [pɛʀʃ(ə)] *nf* (ZOOL) perch; (bâton) pole.

percher [pɛʀʃe] *vt*: ~ **qch sur** to perch sth on // *vi*, **se** ~ *vi* (oiseau) to perch; **perchoir** *nm* perch.

perclus, e [pɛʀkly, -yz] *a*: ~ **de** (rhumatismes) crippled with.

perçois etc *vb voir* **percevoir**.

percolateur [pɛʀkɔlatœʀ] *nm* percolator.

perçu, e *pp de* **percevoir**.

percussion [pɛʀkysjɔ̃] *nf* percussion.

percuter [pɛʀkyte] *vt* to strike; (suj: véhicule) to crash into.

perdant, e [pɛʀdɑ̃, -ɑ̃t] *a, nm/f* loser.

perdition [pɛʀdisjɔ̃] *nf*: **en** ~ (NAVIG) in distress; **lieu de** ~ den of vice.

perdre [pɛʀdʀ(ə)] *vt* to lose; (gaspiller: temps, argent) to waste; (personne: moralement etc) to ruin // *vi* to lose; (sur une vente etc) to lose out; (récipient) to leak; **se** ~ *vi* (s'égarer) to get lost, lose one's way; (fig) to go to waste; to disappear, vanish.

perdreau, x [pɛʀdʀo] nm (young) partridge.

perdrix [pɛʀdʀi] nf partridge.

perdu, e [pɛʀdy] pp de perdre // a (isolé) out-of-the-way, godforsaken ; (COMM: emballage) non-returnable ; (malade): il est ~ there's no hope left for him ; à vos moments ~s in your spare time.

père [pɛʀ] nm father ; ~s nmpl (ancêtres) forefathers ; de ~ en fils from father to son ; ~ de famille man with a family ; family man ; le ~ Noël Father Christmas.

péremptoire [peʀɑ̃ptwaʀ] a peremptory.

perfection [pɛʀfɛksjɔ̃] nf perfection.

perfectionné, e [pɛʀfɛksjɔne] a sophisticated.

perfectionnement [pɛʀfɛksjɔnmɑ̃] nm improvement.

perfectionner [pɛʀfɛksjɔne] vt to improve, perfect ; se ~ en anglais to improve one's English.

perfide [pɛʀfid] a perfidious, treacherous.

perforant, e [pɛʀfɔʀɑ̃, -ɑ̃t] a (balle) armour-piercing.

perforateur, trice [pɛʀfɔʀatœʀ, -tʀis] nm/f punch-card operator // nm (perceuse) borer ; drill // nf (perceuse) borer ; drill ; (pour cartes) card-punch ; (de bureau) punch.

perforation [pɛʀfɔʀasjɔ̃] nf perforation ; punching ; (trou) hole.

perforatrice [pɛʀfɔʀatʀis] nf voir perforateur.

perforer [pɛʀfɔʀe] vt to perforate ; to punch a hole (ou holes) in ; (ticket, bande, carte) to punch.

performance [pɛʀfɔʀmɑ̃s] nf performance.

perfusion [pɛʀfyzjɔ̃] nf perfusion ; faire une ~ à qn to put sb on a drip.

péricliter [peʀiklite] vi to go downhill.

péril [peʀil] nm peril ; périlleux, euse [-jo, -oz] a perilous.

périmé, e [peʀime] a (out)dated ; (ADMIN) out-of-date, expired.

périmètre [peʀimɛtʀ(ə)] nm perimeter.

période [peʀjɔd] nf period ; périodique a (phases) periodic ; (publication) periodical ; (MATH: fraction) recurring // nm periodical ; garniture ou serviette périodique sanitary towel.

péripéties [peʀipesi] nfpl events, episodes.

périphérie [peʀifeʀi] nf periphery ; (d'une ville) outskirts pl ; périphérique a (quartiers) outlying ; (ANAT, TECH) peripheral ; (station de radio) operating from outside France // nm (AUTO) ring road.

périphrase [peʀifʀaz] nf circumlocution.

périple [peʀipl(ə)] nm journey.

périr [peʀiʀ] vi to die, perish.

périscope [peʀiskɔp] nm periscope.

périssable [peʀisabl(ə)] a perishable.

péritonite [peʀitɔnit] nf peritonitis.

perle [pɛʀl(ə)] nf pearl ; (de plastique, métal, sueur) bead.

perlé, e [pɛʀle] a: grève ~e go-slow.

perler [pɛʀle] vi to form in droplets.

perlier, ière [pɛʀlje, -jɛʀ] a pearl cpd.

permanence [pɛʀmanɑ̃s] nf permanence ; (local) (duty) office ; strike headquarters ; emergency service ; assurer une ~ (service public, bureaux) to operate ou maintain a basic service ; être de ~ to be on call ou duty ; en ~ ad permanently ; continuously.

permanent, e [pɛʀmanɑ̃, -ɑ̃t] a permanent ; (spectacle) continuous // nf perm, permanent wave.

perméable [pɛʀmeabl(ə)] a (terrain) permeable ; ~ à (fig) receptive ou open to.

permettre [pɛʀmɛtʀ(ə)] vt to allow, permit ; ~ à qn de faire/qch to allow sb to do/sth.

permis [pɛʀmi] nm permit, licence ; ~ de chasse hunting permit ; ~ (de conduire) (driving) licence ; ~ de construire planning permission ; ~ d'inhumer burial certificate ; ~ poids lourds HGV (driving) licence ; ~ de séjour residence permit.

permission [pɛʀmisjɔ̃] nf permission ; (MIL) leave ; (: papier) pass ; en ~ on leave ; avoir la ~ de faire to have permission to do, be allowed to do ; permissionnaire nm soldier on leave.

permuter [pɛʀmyte] vt to change around, permutate // vi to change, swap.

pernicieux, euse [pɛʀnisjø, -øz] a pernicious.

pérorer [peʀɔʀe] vi to hold forth.

perpendiculaire [pɛʀpɑ̃dikylɛʀ] a, nf perpendicular.

perpétrer [pɛʀpetʀe] vt to perpetrate.

perpétuel, le [pɛʀpetɥɛl] a perpetual ; (ADMIN etc) permanent ; for life.

perpétuer [pɛʀpetɥe] vt to perpetuate.

perpétuité [pɛʀpetɥite] nf: à ~ a, ad for life ; être condamné à ~ to be sentenced to life imprisonment, receive a life sentence.

perplexe [pɛʀplɛks(ə)] a perplexed, puzzled.

perquisition [pɛʀkizisjɔ̃] nf (police) search ; perquisitionner vi to carry out a search.

perron [pɛʀɔ̃] nm steps pl (in front of mansion etc).

perroquet [pɛʀɔkɛ] nm parrot.

perruche [pɛʀyʃ] nf budgerigar, budgie.

perruque [pɛʀyk] nf wig.

persan, e [pɛʀsɑ̃, -an] a Persian.

persécuter [pɛʀsekyte] vt to persecute ; persécution nf persecution.

persévérant, e [pɛʀseveʀɑ̃, -ɑ̃t] a persevering.

persévérer [pɛʀseveʀe] vi to persevere.

persiennes [pɛʀsjɛn] nfpl (metal) shutters.

persiflage [pɛʀsiflaʒ] nm mockery q.

persil [pɛʀsi] nm parsley.

Persique [pɛʀsik] a: le golfe ~ the (Persian) Gulf.

persistant, e [pɛʀsistɑ̃, -ɑ̃t] a persistent ; (feuilles) evergreen ; à feuillage ~ evergreen.

persister [pɛʀsiste] vi to persist ; ~ à faire qch to persist in doing sth.

personnage [pɛʀsɔnaʒ] nm (notable) personality, figure ; (individu) character, individual ; (THÉÂTRE) character ; (PEINTURE) figure.

personnaliser [pɛRsɔnalize] vt to personalize.

personnalité [pɛRsɔnalite] nf personality.

personne [pɛRsɔn] nf person // pronom nobody, no one ; (quelqu'un) anybody, anyone ; ~s people pl ; **il n'y a ~** there's nobody in, there isn't anybody in ; **10 F par ~** 10 F per person ou a head ; ~ **âgée** elderly person ; **personnel, le** a personal // nm staff ; personnel ; **personnellement** ad personally ; **personnifier** vt to personify ; to typify.

perspective [pɛRspɛktiv] nf (ART) perspective ; (vue, coup d'œil) view ; (point de vue) viewpoint, angle ; (chose escomptée, envisagée) prospect ; **en ~** in prospect ; in the offing.

perspicace [pɛRspikas] a clear-sighted, gifted with (ou showing) insight.

persuader [pɛRsyade] vt: ~ **qn (de/de faire)** to persuade sb (of/to do) ; **persuasif, ive** a persuasive ; **persuasion** nf persuasion.

perte [pɛRt(ə)] nf loss ; (de temps) waste ; (fig: morale) ruin ; **à ~** (COMM) at a loss ; **à ~ de vue** as far as the eye can (ou could) see ; (fig) interminably ; ~ **sèche** dead loss ; ~s **blanches** (vaginal) discharge sg.

pertinent, e [pɛRtinɑ̃, -ɑ̃t] a apt, pertinent ; discerning, judicious.

perturbation [pɛRtyRbasjɔ̃] nf disruption ; perturbation ; ~ **(atmosphérique)** atmospheric disturbance.

perturber [pɛRtyRbe] vt to disrupt ; (PSYCH) to perturb, disturb.

pervenche [pɛRvɑ̃ʃ] nf periwinkle.

pervers, e [pɛRvɛR, -ɛRs(ə)] a perverted, depraved ; perverse.

perversion [pɛRvɛRsjɔ̃] nf perversion.

perverti, e [pɛRvɛRti] nm/f pervert.

pervertir [pɛRvɛRtiR] vt to pervert.

pesage [pəzaʒ] nm weighing ; (HIPPISME) weigh-in ; weighing room ; enclosure.

pesamment [pəzamɑ̃] ad heavily.

pesant, e [pəzɑ̃, -ɑ̃t] a heavy ; (fig) burdensome // nm: **valoir son ~ de** to be worth one's weight in.

pesanteur [pəzɑ̃tœR] nf gravity.

pèse-bébé [pɛzbebe] nm (baby) scales pl.

pesée [pəze] nf weighing ; (BOXE) weigh-in ; (pression) pressure.

pèse-lettre [pɛzlɛtR(ə)] nm letter scales pl.

pèse-personne [pɛzpɛRsɔn] nm (bathroom) scales pl.

peser [pəze] vt, vb avec attribut to weigh // vi to be heavy ; (fig) to carry weight ; ~ **sur** (levier, bouton) to press, push ; (fig) to lie heavy on ; to influence ; ~ **à qn** to weigh heavy on sb.

pessaire [pɛsɛR] nm pessary.

pessimisme [pesimism(ə)] nm pessimism ; **pessimiste** a pessimistic // nm/f pessimist.

peste [pɛst(ə)] nf plague.

pester [pɛste] vi: ~ **contre** to curse.

pestiféré, e [pɛstifeRe] nm/f plague victim.

pestilentiel, le [pɛstilɑ̃sjɛl] a foul.

pet [pɛ] nm (fam!) fart (!).

pétale [petal] nm petal.

pétanque [petɑ̃k] nf petanque (bowls).

pétarader [petaRade] vi to backfire.

pétard [petaR] nm banger ; cracker ; (RAIL) detonator.

péter [pete] vi (fam: casser, sauter) to burst ; to bust ; (fam!) to fart (!).

pétiller [petije] vi (flamme, bois) to crackle ; (mousse, champagne) to bubble ; (yeux) to sparkle.

petit, e [pəti, -it] a (gén) small ; (main, objet, colline, en âge: enfant) small, little (avant le nom) ; (voyage) short, little ; (bruit etc) faint, slight ; (mesquin) mean // nm (d'un animal) young pl ; **faire des ~s** to have kittens (ou puppies etc) ; **en ~** in miniature ; **mon ~** son ; little one ; **ma ~e** dear ; little one ; **pauvre ~** poor little thing ; **la classe des ~s** the infant class ; **pour ~s et grands** for children and adults ; **les tout-petits** the little ones, the tiny tots ; ~ **à ~** bit by bit, gradually ; ~/**e ami/e** boyfriend/girlfriend ; ~ **déjeuner** breakfast ; ~ **doigt** little finger, pinkie ; ~ **four** petit four ; ~**e vérole** smallpox ; ~**s pois** petit pois pl, garden pea(s) ; ~**-bourgeois**, ~**e-bourgeoise** a (péj) petit-bourgeois(e), middle-class ; ~**e-fille** nf granddaughter ; ~**-fils** nm grandson.

pétition [petisjɔ̃] nf petition.

petit-lait [pətilɛ] nm whey.

petit-nègre [ptinɛgR(ə)] nm (péj) pidgin French.

petits-enfants [pətizɑ̃fɑ̃] nmpl grandchildren.

pétrifier [petRifje] vt to petrify ; (fig) to paralyze, transfix.

pétrin [petRɛ̃] nm kneading-trough ; (fig): **dans le ~** in a jam ou fix.

pétrir [petRiR] vt to knead.

pétrole [petRɔl] nm oil ; (pour lampe, réchaud etc) paraffin (oil) ; **pétrolier, ière** a oil cpd // nm oil tanker ; **pétrolifère** a oil(-bearing).

peu [pø] ad little, tournure négative + much ; (avec adjectif) tournure négative + very // pronom few // nm little ; ~ **avant/après** shortly before/afterwards ; ~ **de** (nombre) few, négation + (very) many ; (quantité) little, négation + (very) much ; **pour ~ de temps** for (only) a short while ; **le ~ de gens qui** the few people who ; **le ~ de sable qui** what little sand, the little sand which ; **un (petit) ~** a little (bit) ; **un ~ de** a little ; **un ~ plus/moins de** slightly more/less (ou fewer) ; **de ~** (only) just ; ~ **à ~** little by little ; **à ~ près** ad just about, more or less ; **à ~ près 10 kg/10 F** approximately 10 kg/10 F ; **avant ~** before long.

peuplade [pœplad] nf (horde, tribu) tribe, people.

peuple [pœpl(ə)] nm people.

peupler [pœple] vt (pays, région) to populate ; (étang) to stock ; (suj: hommes, poissons) to inhabit ; (fig: imagination, rêves) to fill.

peuplier [pøplije] nm poplar (tree).

peur [pœR] nf fear ; **avoir ~ (de/de faire/que)** to be frightened ou afraid (of/of doing/that) ; **faire ~ à** to frighten ;

de ~ de/que for fear of/that ; ~eux, euse a fearful, timorous.

peut vb voir **pouvoir**.

peut-être [pøtɛtʀ(ə)] ad perhaps, maybe ; ~ que perhaps, maybe ; ~ bien qu'il fera/est he may well do/be.

peux etc vb voir **pouvoir**.

phalange [falɑ̃ʒ] nf (ANAT) phalanx (pl phalanges) ; (MIL) phalanx (pl es).

phallocrate [falɔkʀat] nm male chauvinist.

phallus [falys] nm phallus.

phare [faʀ] nm (en mer) lighthouse ; (d'aéroport) beacon ; (de véhicule) headlamp ; **mettre ses ~s** to put on the full beam ; ~s **de recul** reversing lights.

pharmaceutique [faʀmasøtik] a pharmaceutic(al).

pharmacie [faʀmasi] nf (science) pharmacology ; (magasin) chemist's, pharmacy ; (officine) dispensary ; (produits) pharmaceuticals pl ; **pharmacien, ne** nm/f pharmacist, chemist.

pharyngite [faʀɛ̃ʒit] nf pharyngitis q.

pharynx [faʀɛ̃ks] nm pharynx.

phase [faz] nf phase.

phénomène [fenɔmɛn] nm phenomenon (pl a) ; (monstre) freak.

philanthrope [filɑ̃tʀɔp] nm/f philanthropist.

philanthropie [filɑ̃tʀɔpi] nf philanthropy.

philatélie [filateli] nf philately, stamp collecting ; **philatéliste** nm/f philatelist, stamp collector.

philharmonique [filaʀmɔnik] a philharmonic.

philo [filo] nf abr de **philosophie**.

philosophe [filɔzɔf] nm/f philosopher // a philosophical.

philosophie [filɔzɔfi] nf philosophy ; **philosophique** a philosophical.

phobie [fɔbi] nf phobia.

phonétique [fɔnetik] a phonetic // nf phonetics sg.

phonographe [fɔnɔgʀaf] nm (wind-up) gramophone.

phoque [fɔk] nm seal ; (fourrure) sealskin.

phosphate [fɔsfat] nm phosphate.

phosphore [fɔsfɔʀ] nm phosphorus.

phosphorescent, e [fɔsfɔʀesɑ̃, -ɑ̃t] a luminous.

photo [fɔto] nf photo(graph) ; **en ~** in ou on a photograph ; **prendre en ~** to take a photo of ; **aimer la/faire de la ~** to like taking/take photos ; ~ **d'identité** passport photograph.

photo... [fɔto] préfixe: ~**copie** nf photocopying, photostatting ; photocopy, photostat (copy) ; ~**copier** vt to photocopy, photostat ; ~-**électrique** a photoelectric ; ~**génique** a photogenic ; ~**graphe** nm/f photographer ; ~**graphie** nf (procédé, technique) photography ; (cliché) photograph ; **faire de la ~graphie** to have photography as a hobby ; to be a photographer ; ~**graphier** vt to photograph, take ; ~**graphique** a photographic ; ~**maton** nm photo-booth ; **photomat** ; ~-**robot** nf identikit (picture).

phrase [fʀaz] nf (LING) sentence ; (propos, MUS) phrase ; ~s (péj) flowery language sg.

phtisie [ftizi] nf consumption.

physicien, ne [fizisjɛ̃, -ɛn] nm/f physicist.

physiologie [fizjɔlɔʒi] nf physiology ; **physiologique** a physiological.

physionomie [fizjɔnɔmi] nf face ; **physionomiste** nm/f good judge of faces ; person who has a good memory for faces.

physique [fizik] a physical // nm physique // nf physics sg ; **au ~** physically ; ~**ment** ad physically.

piaffer [pjafe] vi to stamp.

piailler [pjaje] vi to squawk.

pianiste [pjanist(ə)] nm/f pianist.

piano [pjano] nm piano.

pianoter [pjanɔte] vi to tinkle away (at the piano) ; (tapoter): ~ **sur** to drum one's fingers on.

piaule [pjol] nf (fam) pad.

piauler [pjole] vi to whimper ; to cheep.

pic [pik] nm (instrument) pick(axe) ; (montagne) peak ; (ZOOL) woodpecker ; **à ~** ad vertically ; (fig) just at the right time.

pichenette [piʃnɛt] nf flick.

pichet [piʃɛ] nm jug.

pickpocket [pikpɔkɛt] nm pickpocket.

pick-up [pikœp] nm record player.

picorer [pikɔʀe] vt to peck.

picotement [pikɔtmɑ̃] nm tickle q ; smarting q ; prickling q.

picoter [pikɔte] vt (suj: oiseau) to peck // vi (irriter) to smart, prickle.

pie [pi] nf magpie ; (fig) chatterbox.

pièce [pjɛs] nf (d'un logement) room ; (THÉÂTRE) play ; (de mécanisme, machine) part ; (de monnaie) coin ; (COUTURE) patch ; (document) document ; (de drap, fragment, de bétail, de collection) piece ; **dix francs ~ ten francs each ; vendre à la ~** to sell separately ou individually ; **travailler/payer à la ~** to do piecework/pay piece rate ; **un maillot une ~** a one-piece swimsuit ; **un deux-~s cuisine** a two-room(ed) flat with kitchen ; ~ **à conviction** exhibit ; ~ **d'eau** ornamental lake ou pond ; ~ **d'identité: avez-vous une ~ d'identité?** have you got any (means of) identification? ; ~ **montée** tiered cake ; ~s **détachées** spares, (spare) parts ; **en ~s détachées** (à monter) in kit form.

pied [pje] nm foot (pl feet) ; (de verre) stem ; (de table) leg ; (de lampe) base ; ~s **nus** barefoot ; **à ~** on foot ; **à ~ sec** without getting one's feet wet ; **au ~ de la lettre** literally ; **au ~ levé** at a moment's notice ; **de ~ en cap** from head to foot ; **en ~** (portrait) full-length ; **avoir ~** to be able to touch the bottom, not to be out of one's depth ; **avoir le ~ marin** to be a good sailor ; **perdre ~** to lose one's footing ; **sur ~** (AGR) on the stalk, uncut ; (debout, rétabli) up and about ; **mettre sur ~** (entreprise) to set up ; **mettre à ~** to dismiss ; to lay off ; **sur le ~ de guerre** ready for action ; **sur ~ d'intervention** on stand-by ; **faire du ~ à qn** to give sb a (warning) kick ; to play footsy with sb ; ~ **de lit** footboard ; ~ **de nez: faire un ~ de nez à** to thumb one's nose at ; ~ **de salade** lettuce plant ; ~ **de vigne** vine ;

~-à-terre nm inv pied-à-terre ; **~-de-biche** nm claw ; (COUTURE) presser foot ; **~-de-poule** a inv hound's-tooth.

piédestal, aux [pjedɛstal, -o] nm pedestal.

pied-noir [pjenwaʀ] nm Algerian-born Frenchman.

piège [pjɛʒ] nm trap ; **prendre au ~** to trap ; **piéger** vt (avec une mine) to booby-trap ; **lettre/voiture piégée** letter-/car-bomb.

pierraille [pjɛʀɑj] nf loose stones pl.

pierre [pjɛʀ] nf stone ; **~ à briquet** flint ; **~ fine** semiprecious stone ; **~ de taille** freestone q ; **~ de touche** touchstone ; **mur de ~s sèches** drystone wall.

pierreries [pjɛʀʀi] nfpl gems, precious stones.

piété [pjete] nf piety.

piétiner [pjetine] vi (trépigner) to stamp (one's foot) ; (marquer le pas) to stand about ; (fig) to be at a standstill // vt to trample on.

piéton, ne [pjetɔ̃, -ɔn] nm/f pedestrian ; **piétonnier, ière** a pedestrian cpd.

piètre [pjɛtʀ(ə)] a poor, mediocre.

pieu, x [pjø] nm post ; (pointu) stake.

pieuvre [pjœvʀ(ə)] nf octopus.

pieux, euse [pjø, -øz] a pious.

pigeon [piʒɔ̃] nm pigeon ; **~ voyageur** homing pigeon ; **pigeonnier** nm pigeon house.

piger [piʒe] vi, vt (fam) to understand.

pigment [pigmɑ̃] nm pigment.

pignon [piɲɔ̃] nm (de mur) gable ; (d'engrenage) cog(wheel), gearwheel ; (graine) pine kernel ; **avoir ~ sur rue** (fig) to have a prosperous business.

pile [pil] nf (tas) pile ; (ÉLEC) battery // a : **le côté ~** tails // ad (s'arrêter etc) dead ; **à deux heures ~** at two on the dot ; **jouer à ~ ou face** to toss up (for it) ; **~ ou face?** heads or tails?

piler [pile] vt to crush, pound.

pileux, euse [pilø, -øz] a : **système ~** (body) hair.

pilier [pilje] nm pillar.

pillard, e [pijaʀ, -aʀd(ə)] nm/f looter ; plunderer.

piller [pije] vt to pillage, plunder, loot.

pilon [pilɔ̃] nm pestle.

pilonner [pilɔne] vt to pound.

pilori [piloʀi] nm: **mettre ou clouer au ~** to pillory.

pilotage [pilotaʒ] nm piloting ; flying ; **~ sans visibilité** blind flying.

pilote [pilɔt] nm pilot ; (de char, voiture) driver // a pilot cpd ; **~ de ligne/d'essai/de chasse** airline/test/fighter pilot.

piloter [pilɔte] vt to pilot ; to fly ; to drive ; (fig): **~ qn** to guide sb round.

pilotis [pilɔti] nm pile ; stilt.

pilule [pilyl] nf pill ; **prendre la ~** to be on the pill.

pimbêche [pɛ̃bɛʃ] nf (péj) stuck-up girl.

piment [pimɑ̃] nm (BOT) pepper, capsicum ; (fig) spice, piquancy ; **~ rouge** (CULIN) chilli.

pimpant, e [pɛ̃pɑ̃, -ɑ̃t] a trim and fresh-looking.

pin [pɛ̃] nm pine (tree) ; (bois) pine(wood).

pince [pɛ̃s] nf (outil) pliers pl ; (de homard, crabe) pincer, claw ; (COUTURE: pli) dart ; **~ à sucre/glace** sugar/ice tongs pl ; **~ à épiler** tweezers pl ; **~ à linge** clothes peg ; **~s de cycliste** bicycle clips.

pinceau, x [pɛ̃so] nm (paint)brush.

pincé, e [pɛ̃se] a (air) stiff // nf: **une ~e de** a pinch of.

pincer [pɛ̃se] vt to pinch ; (MUS: cordes) to pluck ; (COUTURE) to put, put darts in ; (fam) to nab ; **se ~ le nez** to hold one's nose.

pince-sans-rire [pɛ̃ssɑ̃ʀiʀ] a inv deadpan.

pincettes [pɛ̃sɛt] nfpl (pour le feu) (fire) tongs.

pinède [pinɛd] nf pinewood, pine forest.

pingouin [pɛ̃gwɛ̃] nm penguin.

ping-pong [piŋpɔ̃g] nm table tennis.

pingre [pɛ̃gʀ(ə)] a niggardly.

pinson [pɛ̃sɔ̃] nm chaffinch.

pintade [pɛ̃tad] nf guinea-fowl.

pin-up [pinœp] nf inv pinup (girl).

pioche [pjɔʃ] nf pickaxe ; **piocher** vt to dig up (with a pickaxe) ; (fam) to swot at ; **piocher dans** to dig into.

piolet [pjɔlɛ] nm ice axe.

pion, ne [pjɔ̃, pjɔn] nm/f (SCOL: péj) student paid to supervise schoolchildren // nm (ÉCHECS) pawn ; (DAMES) piece, draught.

pionnier [pjɔnje] nm pioneer.

pipe [pip] nf pipe ; **~ de bruyère** briar pipe.

pipeau, x [pipo] nm (reed-)pipe.

pipe-line [pajplajn] nm pipeline.

pipi [pipi] nm (fam): **faire ~** to have a wee.

piquant, e [pikɑ̃, -ɑ̃t] a (barbe, rosier etc) prickly ; (saveur, sauce) hot, pungent ; (fig) racy ; biting // nm (épine) thorn, prickle ; (de hérisson) quill, spine ; (fig) spiciness, spice.

pique [pik] nf pike ; (fig) cutting remark // nm (CARTES: couleur) spades pl ; (: carte) spade.

piqué, e [pike] a (COUTURE) (machine-)stitched, quilted ; (fam) barmy // nm (AVIAT) dive ; (TEXTILE) piqué.

pique-assiette [pikasjɛt] nm/f inv (péj) scrounger, sponger.

pique-nique [piknik] nm picnic.

piquer [pike] vt (percer) to prick ; (planter): **~ qch dans** to stick sth into ; (fixer): **~ qch à/sur** to pin sth onto ; (MÉD) to give a jab to ; (: animal blessé) to put to sleep ; (suj: insecte, fumée, ortie) to sting ; (suj: poivre) to burn ; (: froid) to bite ; (COUTURE) to machine (stitch) ; (intérêt etc) to arouse ; (fam) to pick up ; to pinch, to nab // vi (avion) to go into a dive ; (saveur) to be pungent ; (suj: sauce) to be sour ; **~ sur** to swoop down on ; to head straight for ; **se ~ de faire** to pride o.s. on one's ability to do ; **~ du nez** (avion) to go into a nose-dive ; **~ un galop/un cent mètres** to break into a gallop/put on a sprint ; **~ une crise** to throw a fit.

piquet [pike] nm (pieu) post, stake ; (de tente) peg ; **mettre un élève au ~** to make a pupil stand in the corner ; **~ de grève** (strike-)picket ; **~ d'incendie** fire-fighting squad.

piqueté, e [pikte] a: ~ **de** dotted with.
piqûre [pikyʀ] nf (d'épingle) prick;
(d'ortie) sting; (de moustique) bite; (MÉD)
injection; (COUTURE) (straight) stitch;
straight stitching; **faire une** ~ **à qn** to
give sb an injection.
pirate [piʀat] nm, a pirate; ~ **de l'air**
hijacker.
pire [piʀ] a worse; (superlatif): **le(la)** ~
... the worst ... // nm: **le** ~ (**de**) the worst
(of).
pirogue [piʀɔg] nf dugout canoe.
pirouette [piʀwɛt] nf pirouette.
pis [pi] nm (de vache) udder; (pire): **le** ~
the worst // a, ad worse; **pis-aller** nm inv
stopgap.
pisciculture [pisikyltyʀ] nf fish farming.
piscine [pisin] nf (swimming) pool; ~
couverte indoor (swimming) pool.
pissenlit [pisɑ̃li] nm dandelion.
pisser [pise] vi (fam!) to pee (!); **pissotière**
nf (fam) public urinal.
pistache [pistaʃ] nf pistachio (nut).
piste [pist(ə)] nf (d'un animal, sentier)
track, trail; (indice) lead; (de stade, de
magnétophone) track; (de cirque) ring; (de
danse) floor; (de patinage) rink; (de ski)
run; (AVIAT) runway.
pistil [pistil] nm pistil.
pistolet [pistɔlɛ] nm (arme) pistol, gun; (à
peinture) spray gun; ~ **à bouchon/air
comprimé** popgun/ airgun; ~-
mitrailleur nm submachine gun.
piston [pistɔ̃] nm (TECH) piston; (MUS)
valve; (fig) string-pulling; **pistonner** vt
(candidat) to pull strings for.
pitance [pitɑ̃s] nf (péj) (means of)
sustenance.
piteux, euse [pitø, -øz] a pitiful, sorry
(avant le nom).
pitié [pitje] nf pity; **sans** ~ a pitiless,
merciless; **faire** ~ to inspire pity; **il me
fait** ~ I pity him, I feel sorry for him;
avoir ~ **de** (compassion) to pity, feel sorry
for; (merci) to have pity ou mercy on.
piton [pitɔ̃] nm (clou) peg, bolt; ~
rocheux rocky outcrop.
pitoyable [pitwajabl(ə)] a pitiful.
pitre [pitʀ(ə)] nm clown; **pitrerie** nf
tomfoolery q.
pittoresque [pitɔʀɛsk(ə)] a picturesque.
pivot [pivo] nm pivot; **pivoter** vi to
swivel; to revolve.
pizza [pidza] nf pizza.
P.J. sigle f voir **police**.
Pl. abr de **place**.
placage [plakaʒ] nm (bois) veneer.
placard [plakaʀ] nm (armoire) cupboard;
(affiche) poster, notice; (TYPO) galley; ~
publicitaire display advertisement;
placarder vt (affiche) to put up.
place [plas] nf (emplacement, situation,
classement) place; (de ville, village) square;
(espace libre) room, space; (de parking)
space; (siège: de train, cinéma, voiture)
seat; (emploi) job; **en** ~ (mettre) in its
place; **sur** ~ on the spot; **faire** ~ **à** to
give way to; **faire de la** ~ **à** to make room
for; **ça prend de la** ~ it takes up a lot
of room ou space; **à la** ~ **de** in place of,
instead of; **une quatre** ~**s** (AUTO) a four-

seater; **il y a 20** ~**s assises/debout** there
are 20 seats/is standing room for 20; ~
forte fortified town.
placé, e [plase] a (HIPPISME) placed; **haut**
~ (fig) high-ranking.
placement [plasmɑ̃] nm placing;
investment; **bureau de** ~ employment
agency.
placenta [plasɑ̃ta] nm placenta.
placer [plase] vt to place; (convive,
spectateur) to seat; (capital, argent) to
place, invest; (dans la conversation) to put
ou get in; ~ **qn chez** to get sb a job at
(ou with); **se** ~ **au premier rang** to go
and stand (ou sit) in the first row.
placide [plasid] a placid.
plafond [plafɔ̃] nm ceiling.
plafonner [plafɔne] vi to reach one's (ou
a) ceiling.
plage [plaʒ] nf beach; (station) (seaside)
resort; (fig) band, bracket; (de disque)
track, band; ~ **arrière** (AUTO) parcel ou
back shelf.
plagiat [plaʒja] nm plagiarism.
plagier [plaʒje] vt to plagiarize.
plaider [plede] vi (avocat) to plead;
(plaignant) to go to court, litigate // vt to
plead; ~ **pour** (fig) to speak for;
plaideur, euse nm/f litigant; **plaidoirie** nf
(JUR) speech for the defence; **plaidoyer**
nm (JUR) speech for the defence; (fig) plea.
plaie [plɛ] nf wound.
plaignant, e [plɛɲɑ̃, -ɑ̃t] nm/f plaintiff.
plaindre [plɛ̃dʀ(ə)] vt to pity, feel sorry
for; **se** ~ (gémir) to moan; (protester,
rouspéter): **se** ~ (**à qn**) (**de**) to complain
(to sb) (about); (souffrir): **se** ~ **de** to
complain of.
plaine [plɛn] nf plain.
plain-pied [plɛ̃pje]: **de** ~ ad at street-
level; (fig) straight; **de** ~ **avec** on the
same level as.
plainte [plɛ̃t] nf (gémissement) moan,
groan; (doléance) complaint; **porter** ~ to
lodge a complaint; **plaintif, ive** a plaintive.
plaire [plɛʀ] vi to be a success, be
successful; to please; ~ **à**: **cela me plaît**
I like it; **essayer de** ~ **à qn** (en étant
serviable etc) to try and please sb; **elle
plaît aux hommes** she's a success with
men, men like her; **se** ~ **quelque part**
to like being somewhere ou like it
somewhere; **se** ~ **à faire** to take pleasure
in doing; **ce qu'il vous plaira** what(ever)
you like ou wish; **s'il vous plaît** please.
plaisamment [plɛzamɑ̃] ad pleasantly.
plaisance [plɛzɑ̃s] nf (aussi: **navigation
de** ~) (pleasure) sailing, yachting;
plaisancier nm amateur sailor, yachting
enthusiast.
plaisant, e [plɛzɑ̃, -ɑ̃t] a pleasant;
(histoire, anecdote) amusing.
plaisanter [plɛzɑ̃te] vi to joke; **pour** ~
for a joke; **on ne plaisante pas avec cela**
that's no joking matter; **plaisanterie** nf
joke; joking q; **plaisantin** nm joker.
plaise etc vb voir **plaire**.
plaisir [pleziʀ] nm pleasure; **faire** ~ **à qn**
(délibérément) to be nice to sb, please sb;
(suj: cadeau, nouvelle etc): **ceci me fait** ~
I'm delighted ou very pleased with this;
prendre ~ **à/faire** to take pleasure in/in

doing ; à ~ freely ; for the sake of it ; au ~ (de vous revoir) (I hope to) see you again ; pour le ou par ~ for pleasure.

plan, e [plɑ̃, -an] a flat // nm plan ; (GÉOM) plane ; (fig) level, plane ; (CINÉMA) shot ; au premier/second ~ in the foreground/middle distance ; à l'arrière ~ in the background ; mettre qch au premier ~ (fig) to consider sth to be of primary importance ; sur le ~ sexuel sexually, as far as sex is concerned ; ~ d'eau stretch of water ; ~ de travail work programme ou schedule.

planche [plɑ̃ʃ] nf (pièce de bois) plank, (wooden) board ; (illustration) plate ; les ~s (THÉÂTRE) the stage sg, the boards ; faire la ~ (dans l'eau) to float on one's back ; ~ à dessin drawing board ; ~ à pain breadboard ; ~ à repasser ironing board ; ~ de salut (fig) sheet anchor.

plancher [plɑ̃ʃe] nm floor ; floorboards pl ; (fig) minimum level.

plancton [plɑ̃ktɔ̃] nm plankton.

planer [plane] vi to glide ; ~ sur (fig) to hang over ; to hover above.

planétaire [planetɛʀ] a planetary.

planète [planɛt] nf planet.

planeur [planœʀ] nm glider.

planification [planifikɑsjɔ̃] nf (economic) planning.

planifier [planifje] vt to plan.

planning [planiŋ] nm programme, schedule ; ~ familial family planning.

planque [plɑ̃k] nf (fam) cushy number ; hideout ; stash.

plant [plɑ̃] nm seedling, young plant.

plantaire [plɑ̃tɛʀ] a voir voûte.

plantation [plɑ̃tɑsjɔ̃] nf plantation.

plante [plɑ̃t] nf plant ; ~ d'appartement house ou pot plant ; ~ du pied sole (of the foot).

planter [plɑ̃te] vt (plante) to plant ; (enfoncer) to hammer ou drive in ; (tente) to put up, pitch ; (fam) to dump ; to ditch ; ~ qch dans to hammer ou drive sth into ; to stick sth into ; se ~ dans to sink into ; to get stuck in ; se ~ devant to plant o.s. in front of ; planteur nm planter.

planton [plɑ̃tɔ̃] nm orderly.

plantureux, euse [plɑ̃tyʀø, -øz] a copious, lavish ; buxom.

plaquage [plakaʒ] nm (RUGBY) tackle.

plaque [plak] nf plate ; (de verglas, d'eczéma) patch ; (avec inscription) plaque ; ~s (minéralogiques ou de police ou d'immatriculation) number plates ; ~ de beurre tablet of butter ; ~ chauffante hotplate ; ~ de chocolat bar of chocolate ; ~ d'identité identity disc ; ~ tournante (fig) centre.

plaqué, e [plake] a: ~ or/argent gold-/silver-plated ; ~ acajou veneered in mahogany.

plaquer [plake] vt (bijou) to plate ; (bois) to veneer ; (aplatir): ~ qch sur/contre to make sth stick ou cling to ; (RUGBY) to bring down ; (fam) to ditch ; se ~ contre to flatten o.s. against ; ~ qn contre to pin sb to.

plaquette [plakɛt] nf tablet ; bar ; (livre) small volume.

plasma [plasma] nm plasma.

plastic [plastik] nm plastic explosive.

plastifié, e [plastifje] a plastic-coated.

plastique [plastik] a plastic // nm plastic // nf plastic arts pl ; modelling.

plastiquer [plastike] vt to blow up (with a plastic bomb).

plastron [plastʀɔ̃] nm shirt front.

plastronner [plastʀɔne] vi to swagger.

plat, e [pla, -at] a flat ; (cheveux) straight ; (personne, livre) dull // nm (récipient, CULIN) dish ; (d'un repas): le premier ~ the first course ; (partie plate): le ~ de la main the flat of the hand ; à ~ ventre ad face down ; (tomber) flat on one's face ; à ~ ad, a (aussi: pneu, batterie) flat ; ~ du jour day's special (menu) ; ~ de résistance main course.

platane [platan] nm plane tree.

plateau, x [plato] nm (support) tray ; (GÉO) plateau ; (de tourne-disques) turntable ; (CINÉMA) set ; ~ à fromages cheeseboard.

plate-bande [platbɑ̃d] nf flower bed.

platée [plate] nf dish(ful).

plate-forme [platfɔʀm(ə)] nf platform ; ~ de forage/pétrolière drilling/oil rig.

platine [platin] nm platinum // nf (d'un tourne-disque) turntable.

plâtras [plɑtʀa] nm rubble q.

plâtre [plɑtʀ(ə)] nm (matériau) plaster ; (statue) plaster statue ; (MÉD) (plaster) cast ; avoir un bras dans le ~ to have an arm in plaster ; plâtrer vt to plaster ; (MÉD) to set ou put in a (plaster) cast.

plausible [plozibl(ə)] a plausible.

plébiscite [plebisit] nm plebiscite.

plein, e [plɛ̃, -ɛn] a full ; (porte, roue) solid ; (chienne, jument) big (with young) // nm: faire le ~ (d'essence) to fill up (with petrol) ; les ~s the downstrokes (in handwriting) ; ~ de full of ; à ~es mains (ramasser) in handfuls ; (empoigner) firmly ; à ~ régime at maximum revs ; (fig) full steam ; à ~ temps full-time ; en ~ air/~e mer in the open air/on the open sea ; en ~ soleil right out in the sun ; en ~e nuit/rue in the middle of the night/street ; en ~ milieu right in the middle ; en ~ jour in broad daylight ; en ~ sur right on ; ~-emploi nm full employment.

plénière [plenjɛʀ] af: assemblée ~ plenary assembly.

plénitude [plenityd] nf fullness.

pléthore [pletɔʀ] nf: ~ de overabundance ou plethora of.

pleurer [plœʀe] vi to cry ; (yeux) to water // vt to mourn (for) ; ~ sur vt to lament (over), to bemoan.

pleurésie [plœʀezi] nf pleurisy.

pleurnicher [plœʀniʃe] vi to grizzle, whine.

pleurs [plœʀ] nmpl: en ~ in tears.

pleutre [pløtʀ(ə)] a cowardly.

pleuvoir [pløvwaʀ] vb impersonnel to rain // vi (fig): ~ (sur) to shower down (upon) ; to be showered upon.

plexiglas [plɛksiɡlas] nm plexiglass.

pli [pli] nm fold ; (de jupe) pleat ; (de pantalon) crease ; (aussi: faux ~) crease ; (enveloppe) envelope ; (lettre) letter ;

(CARTES) trick ; **prendre le ~ de faire** to get into the habit of doing ; **~ d'aisance** inverted pleat.

pliage [plijaʒ] nm folding ; (ART) origami.

pliant, e [plijɑ̃, -ɑ̃t] a folding // nm folding stool, campstool.

plier [plije] vt to fold ; (pour ranger) to fold up ; (table pliante) to fold down ; (genou, bras) to bend // vi to bend ; (fig) to yield ; **se ~ à** to submit to ; **~ bagages** to pack up (and go).

plinthe [plɛ̃t] nf skirting board.

plissé, e [plise] a (GÉO) folded // nm (COUTURE) pleats pl.

plissement [plismɑ̃] nm (GÉO) fold.

plisser [plise] vt (rider, chiffonner) to crease ; (jupe) to put pleats in.

plomb [plɔ̃] nm (métal) lead ; (d'une cartouche) (lead) shot ; (PÊCHE) sinker ; (sceau) (lead) seal ; (ÉLEC) fuse ; **mettre à ~** to plumb.

plombage [plɔ̃baʒ] nm (de dent) filling.

plomber [plɔ̃be] vt (canne, ligne) to weight (with lead) ; (colis, wagon) to put a lead seal on ; (dent) to fill.

plomberie [plɔ̃bʀi] nf plumbing.

plombier [plɔ̃bje] nm plumber.

plonge [plɔ̃ʒ] nf: **faire la ~** to be a washer-up.

plongeant, e [plɔ̃ʒɑ̃, -ɑ̃t] a (vue) from above ; (tir, décolleté) plunging.

plongée [plɔ̃ʒe] nf diving q ; (de sous-marin) submersion, dive ; **en ~** (sous-marin) submerged ; (prise de vue) high angle.

plongeoir [plɔ̃ʒwaʀ] nm diving board.

plongeon [plɔ̃ʒɔ̃] nm dive.

plonger [plɔ̃ʒe] vi to dive // vt: **~ qch dans** (immerger) to plunge ou dip sth into ; (planter) to thrust sth into ; (fig) to plunge sth into ; **plongeur, euse** nm/f diver ; (de café) washer-up.

ployer [plwaje] vt to bend // vi to sag ; to bend.

plu pp de **plaire, pleuvoir.**

pluie [plɥi] nf rain ; (fig): **~ de** shower of ; **retomber en ~** to shower down ; **sous la ~** in the rain.

plume [plym] nf feather ; (pour écrire) (pen) nib ; (fig) pen.

plumeau, x [plymo] nm feather duster.

plumer [plyme] vt to pluck.

plumet [plymɛ] nm plume.

plumier [plymje] nm pencil box.

plupart [plypaʀ]: **la ~** pronom the majority, most (of them) ; **la ~ des** most, the majority of ; **la ~ du temps/d'entre nous** most of the time/of us ; **pour la ~** ad for the most part, mostly.

pluriel [plyʀjɛl] nm plural ; **au ~** in the plural.

plus vb [ply] voir **plaire** // ad [ply, plyz + voyelle] (comparatif) more, adjectif court + ...er ; (davantage) [plys] more ; (négatif): **ne ~** ... no more, tournure négative + any more ; no longer // cj [plys]: **~ 2** plus 2 ; **~ que** more than ; **~ grand que** bigger than ; **~ de 10 personnes** more than 10 people, over 10 people ; **~ de pain** more bread ; **~ il travaille, ~ il est heureux** the more he works, the happier he is ; **le**

~ intelligent/grand the most intelligent/biggest ; **3 heures/kilos de ~ que** 3 hours/kilos more than ; **de ~** what's more, moreover ; **3 kilos en ~** 3 kilos more, 3 extra kilos ; **en ~ de** in addition to ; **de ~ en ~** more and more ; **(tout) au ~** at the (very) most ; **~ ou moins** more or less ; **ni ~ ni moins** no more, no less.

plusieurs [plyzjœʀ] dét, pronom several ; **ils sont ~** there are several of them.

plus-que-parfait [plyskəpaʀfɛ] nm pluperfect, past perfect.

plus-value [plyvaly] nf appreciation ; capital gain ; surplus.

plut vb voir **plaire.**

plûtot [plyto] ad rather ; **je ferais ~ ceci** I'd rather ou sooner do this ; **fais ~ comme ça** try this way instead, you'd better try this way ; **~ que (de) faire** rather than ou instead of doing.

pluvieux, euse [plyvjø, -øz] a rainy, wet.

P.M.U. sigle m voir **pari.**

pneu, x [pnø] nm tyre ; letter sent by pneumatic tube.

pneumatique [pnømatik] a pneumatic ; rubber cpd // nm tyre.

pneumonie [pnømɔni] nf pneumonia.

P.O. sigle = petites ondes.

poche [pɔʃ] nf pocket ; (déformation): **faire une/des ~(s)** to bag ; (sous les yeux) bag, pouch // nm (abr de livre de ~) (pocket-size) paperback ; **de ~** pocket cpd.

poché, e [pɔʃe] a: **œuf ~** poached egg ; **œil ~** black eye.

poche-revolver [pɔʃʀevɔlvɛʀ] nf hip pocket.

pochette [pɔʃɛt] nf (de timbres) wallet, envelope ; (d'aiguilles etc) case ; (sur veston) breast pocket ; (mouchoir) breast pocket handkerchief ; **~ d'allumettes** book of matches ; **~ de disque** record sleeve.

pochoir [pɔʃwaʀ] nm (ART) stencil ; transfer.

podium [pɔdjɔm] nm podium (pl ia).

poêle [pwal] nm stove // nf: **~ (à frire)** frying pan.

poêlon [pwalɔ̃] nm casserole.

poème [pɔɛm] nm poem.

poésie [pɔezi] nf (poème) poem ; (art): **la ~** poetry.

poète [pɔɛt] nm poet.

poétique [pɔetik] a poetic.

pognon [pɔɲɔ̃] nm (fam) dough.

poids [pwa] nm weight ; (SPORT) shot ; **vendre au ~** to sell by weight ; **prendre du ~** to put on weight ; **~ plume/mouche/coq/ moyen** (BOXE) feather/fly/bantam/ middleweight ; **~ et haltères** nmpl weight lifting sg ; **~ lourd** (BOXE) heavyweight ; (camion) (big) lorry ; (: ADMIN) heavy goods vehicle (HGV) ; **~ mort** dead load.

poignant, e [pwaɲɑ̃, -ɑ̃t] a poignant, harrowing.

poignard [pwaɲaʀ] nm dagger ; **poignarder** vt to stab, knife.

poigne [pwaɲ] nf grip ; (fig) firm-handedness.

poignée [pwaɲe] nf (de sel etc, fig) handful; (de couvercle, porte) handle; ~ **de main** handshake.

poignet [pwaɲɛ] nm (ANAT) wrist; (de chemise) cuff.

poil [pwal] nm (ANAT) hair; (de pinceau, brosse) bristle; (de tapis) strand; (pelage) coat; (ensemble des poils): avoir du ~ sur la poitrine to have hair(s) on one's chest, have a hairy chest; à ~ a (fam) starkers; au ~ a (fam) hunky-dory; **poilu, e** a hairy.

poinçon [pwɛ̃sɔ̃] nm awl; bodkin; style; die; (marque) hallmark; **poinçonner** vt to stamp; to hallmark; (billet, ticket) to clip, punch; **poinçonneuse** nf (outil) punch.

poing [pwɛ̃] nm fist.

point [pwɛ̃] nm (marque, signe) dot; (: de ponctuation) full stop; (moment, de score etc, fig: question) point; (endroit) spot; (COUTURE, TRICOT) stitch // ad = pas; faire le ~ (NAVIG) to take a bearing; (fig) to take stock (of the situation); en tout ~ in every respect; sur le ~ de faire (just) about to do; à tel ~ que so much so that; mettre au ~ (mécanisme, procédé) to perfect; (appareil-photo) to focus; (affaire) to settle; à ~ (CULIN) medium; just right; à ~ (nommé) just at the right time; ~ (de côté) stitch (pain); ~ culminant summit; (fig) height, climax; ~ d'eau spring; water point; ~ d'exclamation exclamation mark; ~ faible weak point; ~ final full stop, period; ~ d'interrogation question mark; ~ mort (AUTO): au ~ mort in neutral; ~ noir (sur le visage) blackhead; (AUTO) accident spot; ~ de repère landmark; (dans le temps) point of reference; ~ de vente retail outlet; ~ de vue viewpoint; (fig: opinion) point of view; du ~ de vue de from the point of view of; ~s cardinaux points of the compass, cardinal points; ~s de suspension suspension points.

pointe [pwɛ̃t] nf point; (d'une île) headland; (allusion) dig; sally; (fig): une ~ d'ail/d'accent a touch ou hint of garlic/of an accent; être à la ~ de (fig) to be in the forefront of; sur la ~ des pieds on tip-toe; en ~ ad (tailler) into a point // a pointed, tapered; de ~ a (technique etc) leading; heures/jours de ~ peak hours/days; faire du 180 en ~ (AUTO) to have a top ou maximum speed of 180; faire des ~s (DANSE) to dance on points; ~ de vitesse burst of speed.

pointer [pwɛ̃te] vt (cocher) to tick off; (employés etc) to check in (ou out); (diriger: canon, longue-vue, doigt): ~ vers qch to point at sth // vi (employé) to clock in (ou out); **pointeuse** nf timeclock.

pointillé [pwɛ̃tije] nm (trait) dotted line; (ART) stippling q.

pointilleux, euse [pwɛ̃tijø, -øz] a particular, pernickety.

pointu, e [pwɛ̃ty] a pointed; (clou) sharp; (voix) shrill.

pointure [pwɛ̃tyʀ] nf size.

point-virgule [pwɛ̃viʀgyl] nm semi-colon.

poire [pwaʀ] nf pear; (fam: péj) mug; ~ à injections syringe.

poireau, x [pwaʀo] nm leek.

poirier [pwaʀje] nm pear tree.

pois [pwa] nm (BOT) pea; (sur une étoffe) dot, spot; à ~ (cravate etc) dotted, polka-dot cpd; ~ chiche chickpea; ~ de senteur sweet pea.

poison [pwazɔ̃] nm poison.

poisse [pwas] nf rotten luck.

poisseux, euse [pwasø, -øz] a sticky.

poisson [pwasɔ̃] nm fish gén inv; les P~s (signe) Pisces, the Fishes; être des P~s to be Pisces; ~ d'avril! April fool!; **poissonnerie** nf fish-shop; **poissonneux, euse** a abounding in fish; **poissonnier, ière** nm/f fishmonger.

poitrail [pwatʀaj] nm breast.

poitrine [pwatʀin] nf chest; (seins) bust, bosom; (CULIN) breast; ~ de bœuf brisket.

poivre [pwavʀ(ə)] nm pepper; ~ en grains/moulu whole/ground pepper; **poivré, e** a peppery; **poivrier** nm (BOT) pepper plant; (ustensile) pepperpot.

poivron [pwavʀɔ̃] nm pepper, capsicum; ~ vert/rouge green/red pepper.

poker [pokɛʀ] nm: le ~ poker; ~ d'as four aces.

polaire [polɛʀ] a polar.

polariser [polaʀize] vt to polarize; (fig) to attract; to focus.

pôle [pol] nm (GÉO, ÉLEC) pole; le ~ Nord/Sud the North/South Pole.

polémique [polemik] a controversial, polemic(al) // nf controversy; **polémiste** nm/f polemist, polemicist.

poli, e [poli] a polite; (lisse) smooth; polished.

police [polis] nf police; (discipline): assurer la ~ de ou dans to keep order in; peine de simple ~ sentence imposed by a magistrates ou police court; ~ d'assurance insurance policy; ~ judiciaire, P.J. ≈ Criminal Investigation Department, C.I.D.; ~ des mœurs ≈ vice squad; ~ secours ≈ emergency services pl.

polichinelle [poliʃinɛl] nm Punch; (péj) buffoon.

policier, ière [polisje, -jɛʀ] a police cpd // nm policeman; (aussi: roman ~) detective novel.

policlinique [poliklinik] nf ≈ outpatients (department).

polio(myélite) [poljo(mjelit)] nf polio(myelitis); **poliomyélitique** nm/f polio patient ou case.

polir [poliʀ] vt to polish.

polisson, ne [polisɔ̃, -ɔn] a naughty.

politesse [polites] nf politeness; ~s (exchange of) courtesies, polite gestures; rendre une ~ à qn to return sb's favour.

politicien, ne [politisjɛ̃, -ɛn] nm/f politician.

politique [politik] a political // nf (science, pratique, activité) politics sg; (mesures, méthode) policies pl; **politiser** vt to politicize; **politiser** qn to make sb politically aware.

pollen [polɛn] nm pollen.

polluer [polɥe] vt to pollute; **pollution** nf pollution.

polo [polo] nm (sport) polo; (tricot) sweat shirt.

Pologne [pɔlɔɲ] *nf*: **la ~** Poland; **polonais, e** *a*, *nm* (*langue*) Polish // *nm/f* Pole.

poltron, ne [pɔltʀɔ̃, -ɔn] *a* cowardly.

poly... [pɔli] *préfixe*: **~clinique** *nf* polyclinic; **~copier** *vt* to duplicate; **~gamie** *nf* polygamy; **~glotte** *a* polyglot; **~gone** *nm* polygon.

Polynésie [pɔlinezi] *nf*: **la ~** Polynesia.

polytechnicien, ne [pɔlitɛknisjɛ̃, -ɛn] *nm/f* student (or former student) of the *École Polytechnique*.

polyvalent, e [pɔlivalɑ̃, -ɑ̃t] *a* polyvalent; versatile, multi-purpose // *nm* ≈ tax inspector.

pommade [pɔmad] *nf* ointment, cream.

pomme [pɔm] *nf* (*BOT*) apple; (*boule décorative*) knob; (*pomme de terre*): **steak ~s** (frites) steak and chips; **tomber dans les ~s** (*fam*) to pass out; **~ d'Adam** Adam's apple; **~ d'arrosoir** (sprinkler) rose; **~ de pin** pine ou fir cone; **~ de terre** potato; **~s vapeur** boiled potatoes.

pommé, e [pɔme] *a* (*chou etc*) firm, with a good heart.

pommeau, x [pɔmo] *nm* (*boule*) knob; (*de selle*) pommel.

pommette [pɔmɛt] *nf* cheekbone.

pommier [pɔmje] *nm* apple tree.

pompe [pɔ̃p] *nf* pump; (*faste*) pomp (and ceremony); **~ de bicyclette** bicycle pump; **~ à essence** petrol pump; **~ à incendie** fire engine (*apparatus*); **~s funèbres** funeral parlour *sg*, undertaker's *sg*.

pomper [pɔ̃pe] *vt* to pump; (*évacuer*) to pump out; (*aspirer*) to pump up; (*absorber*) to soak up // *vi* to pump.

pompeux, euse [pɔ̃pø, -øz] *a* pompous.

pompier [pɔ̃pje] *nm* fireman // *am* (*style*) pretentious, pompous.

pompon [pɔ̃pɔ̃] *nm* pompom, bobble.

pomponner [pɔ̃pɔne] *vt* to titivate, dress up.

ponce [pɔ̃s] *nf*: **pierre ~** pumice stone.

poncer [pɔ̃se] *vt* to sand (down); **ponceuse** *nf* sander.

poncif [pɔ̃sif] *nm* cliché.

ponction [pɔ̃ksjɔ̃] *nf*: **~ lombaire** lumbar puncture.

ponctualité [pɔ̃ktɥalite] *nf* punctuality.

ponctuation [pɔ̃ktɥasjɔ̃] *nf* punctuation.

ponctuel, le [pɔ̃ktɥɛl] *a* (*à l'heure, aussi TECH*) punctual; (*fig: opération etc*) one-off, single; (*scrupuleux*) punctilious, meticulous.

ponctuer [pɔ̃ktɥe] *vt* to punctuate; (*MUS*) to phrase.

pondéré, e [pɔ̃deʀe] *a* level-headed, composed.

pondre [pɔ̃dʀ(ə)] *vt* to lay; (*fig*) to produce // *vi* to lay.

poney [pɔnɛ] *nm* pony.

pongiste [pɔ̃ʒist] *nm/f* table tennis player.

pont [pɔ̃] *nm* bridge; (*AUTO*): **~ arrière/avant** rear/front axle; (*NAVIG*) deck; **faire le ~** to take the extra day off; **~ aérien** airlift; **~ d'envol** flight deck; **~ de graissage** ramp (*in garage*); **~ roulant** travelling crane; **~ suspendu** suspension bridge; **~ tournant** swing bridge; **P~s et Chaussées** highways department.

ponte [pɔ̃t] *nf* laying // *nm* (*fam*) big shot.

pontife [pɔ̃tif] *nm* pontiff.

pontifier [pɔ̃tifje] *vi* to pontificate.

pont-levis [pɔ̃lvi] *nm* drawbridge.

pop [pɔp] *a inv* pop.

populace [pɔpylas] *nf* (*péj*) rabble.

populaire [pɔpylɛʀ] *a* popular; (*manifestation*) mass *cpd*, of the people; (*milieux, clientèle*) working-class; **populariser** *vt* to popularize; **popularité** *nf* popularity.

population [pɔpylasjɔ̃] *nf* population.

populeux, euse [pɔpylø, -øz] *a* densely populated.

porc [pɔʀ] *nm* (*ZOOL*) pig; (*CULIN*) pork; (*peau*) pigskin.

porcelaine [pɔʀsəlɛn] *nf* porcelain, china; piece of china(ware).

porcelet [pɔʀsəlɛ] *nm* piglet.

porc-épic [pɔʀkepik] *nm* porcupine.

porche [pɔʀʃ(ə)] *nm* porch.

porcherie [pɔʀʃəʀi] *nf* pigsty.

porcin, e [pɔʀsɛ̃, -in] *a* porcine; (*fig*) piglike.

pore [pɔʀ] *nm* pore; **poreux, euse** *a* porous.

pornographie [pɔʀnɔgʀafi] *nf* pornography; **pornographique** *a* (*abr* **porno**) pornographic.

port [pɔʀ] *nm* (*NAVIG*) harbour, port; (*ville*) port; (*de l'uniforme etc*) wearing; (*pour lettre*) postage; (*pour colis, aussi: posture*) carriage; **~ d'arme** (*JUR*) carrying of a firearm; **~ d'attache** (*NAVIG*) port of registry; **~ franc** free port.

portail [pɔʀtaj] *nm* gate; (*de cathédrale*) portal.

portant, e [pɔʀtɑ̃, -ɑ̃t] *a* (*murs*) structural, weight-bearing; **bien/ mal ~** in good/poor health.

portatif, ive [pɔʀtatif, -iv] *a* portable.

porte [pɔʀt(ə)] *nf* door; (*de ville, forteresse, SKI*) gate; **mettre à la ~** to throw out; **~ d'entrée** front door; **~ à ~** *nm* door-to-door selling.

porte... [pɔʀt(ə)] *préfixe*: **~-à-faux** *nm*: **en ~-à-faux** cantilevered; precariously balanced; **~-avions** *nm inv* aircraft carrier; **~-bagages** *nm inv* luggage rack; **~-bonheur** *nm inv* lucky charm; **~-cartes** *nm inv* card holder; map wallet; **~-cigarettes** *nm inv* cigarette case; **~-clefs** *nm inv* keyring; **~-crayon** *nm* pencil holder; **~-documents** *nm inv* attaché ou document case.

portée [pɔʀte] *nf* (*d'une arme*) range; (*fig*) impact, import; scope, capability; (*de chatte etc*) litter; (*MUS*) stave, staff (*pl* staves); **à/hors de ~ (de)** within/out of reach (of); **à ~ de (la) main** within (arm's) reach; **à ~ de voix** within earshot; **à la ~ de qn** (*fig*) at sb's level, within sb's capabilities.

porte-fenêtre [pɔʀtfənɛtʀ(ə)] *nf* French window.

portefeuille [pɔʀtəfœj] *nm* wallet; (*POL, BOURSE*) portfolio.

porte-jarretelles [pɔʀtʒaʀtɛl] *nm inv* suspender belt.

portemanteau, x [pɔrtmɑ̃to] nm coat hanger; coat rack.

porte-mine [pɔrtəmin] nm propelling pencil.

porte-monnaie [pɔrtmɔnɛ] nm inv purse.

porte-parole [pɔrtparɔl] nm inv spokesman.

porte-plume [pɔrtəplym] nm inv penholder.

porter [pɔrte] vt (charge ou sac etc, aussi: fœtus) to carry; (sur soi: vêtement, barbe, bague) to wear; (fig: responsabilité etc) to bear, carry; (inscription, marque, titre, patronyme, suj: arbre: fruits, fleurs) to bear; (apporter): ~ qch quelque part/à qn to take sth somewhere/to sb; (inscrire): ~ qch sur to put sth down on; to enter sth in // vi (voix, regard, canon) to carry; (coup, argument) to hit home; ~ sur (peser) to rest on; (accent) to fall on; (conférence etc) to concern; (heurter) to strike; se ~ vi (se sentir): se ~ bien/mal to be well/unwell; (aller): se ~ vers to go towards; **être porté à faire** to be apt ou inclined to do; **elle portait le nom de Rosalie** she was called Rosalie; ~ qn au pouvoir to bring sb to power; ~ son âge to look one's age; **se faire** ~ **malade** to report sick; ~ **la main à son chapeau** to raise one's hand to one's hat; ~ **son effort sur** to direct one's efforts towards.

porte-savon [pɔrtsavɔ̃] nm soapdish.

porte-serviettes [pɔrtsɛrvjɛt] nm inv towel rail.

porteur, euse [pɔrtœr, -øz] a: **être** ~ **de** (nouvelle) to be the bearer of // nm (de bagages) porter; (COMM: de chèque) bearer.

porte-voix [pɔrtəvwa] nm inv loudhailer.

portier [pɔrtje] nm commissionnaire, porter.

portière [pɔrtjɛr] nf door.

portillon [pɔrtijɔ̃] nm gate.

portion [pɔrsjɔ̃] nf (part) portion, share; (partie) portion, section.

portique [pɔrtik] nm (GYM) crossbar; (ARCHIT) portico; (RAIL) gantry.

porto [pɔrto] nm port (wine).

portrait [pɔrtrɛ] nm portrait; photograph; **portraitiste** nm/f portrait painter; ~-**robot** nm Identikit ou photofit picture.

portuaire [pɔrtɥɛr] a port cpd, harbour cpd.

portugais, e [pɔrtygɛ, -ɛz] a, nm, nf Portuguese.

Portugal [pɔrtygal] nm: le ~ Portugal.

pose [poz] nf laying; hanging; (attitude, d'un modèle) pose; (PHOTO) exposure.

posé, e [poze] a serious.

posemètre [pozmɛtr(ə)] nm exposure meter.

poser [poze] vt (déposer): ~ qch (sur)/qn à to put sth down (on)/drop sb at; (placer): ~ qch sur/quelque part to put sth on/somewhere; (installer: moquette, carrelage) to lay; (: rideaux, papier peint) to hang; (question) to ask; (principe, conditions) to lay ou set down; (problème) to formulate; (difficulté) to pose // vi (modèle) to pose; to sit; se ~ (oiseau, avion) to land; (question) to arise.

poseur, euse [pozœr, -øz] nm/f (péj) show-off, poseur; ~ **de parquets/ carrelages** floor/tile layer.

positif, ive [pozitif, -iv] a positive.

position [pozisjɔ̃] nf position; **prendre** ~ (fig) to take a stand.

posologie [pozɔlɔʒi] nf directions pl for use, dosage.

posséder [pɔsede] vt to own, possess; (qualité, talent) to have, possess; (bien connaître: métier, langue) to master, have a thorough knowledge of; (sexuellement, aussi: suj: colère etc) to possess; (fam: duper) to take in; **possesseur** nm owner; **possessif, ive** a, nm possessive; **possession** nf ownership q; possession; être/entrer en possession de qch to be in/take possession of sth.

possibilité [pɔsibilite] nf possibility; ~**s** nfpl (moyens) means; (potentiel) potential sg; **avoir la** ~ **de faire** to be in a position to do; to have the opportunity to do.

possible [pɔsibl(ə)] a possible; (projet, entreprise) feasible // nm: **faire son** ~ to do all one can, do one's utmost; **le plus/moins de livres** ~ as many/few books as possible; **le plus/moins d'eau** ~ as much/little water as possible; **dès que** ~ as soon as possible; **gentil** etc **au** ~ as nice etc as it is possible to be.

postal, e, aux [pɔstal, -o] a postal, post office cpd; **sac** ~ mailbag, postbag.

poste [pɔst(ə)] nf (service) post, postal service; (administration, bureau) post office // nm (fonction, MIL) post; (de radio etc) set; (de budget) item; ~**s** nfpl post office sg; **P**~**s et Télécommunications** (P.T.T.: abr de Postes, Télégraphes, Téléphones) ≈ General Post Office (G.P.O.); ~ (de radio/télévision) nm (radio/television) set; ~ **émetteur** nm transmitting set; ~ **d'essence** nm petrol ou filling station; ~ **d'incendie** nm fire point; ~ **de péage** nm tollgate; ~ **de pilotage** nm cockpit; ~ (de police) nm police station; ~ **restante** nf poste restante; ~ **de secours** nm firstaid post.

poster vt [pɔste] to post // nm [pɔstɛr] poster.

postérieur, e [pɔsterjœr] a (date) later; (partie) back // nm (fam) behind.

posteriori [pɔsterjɔri]: a ~ ad with hindsight, a posteriori.

postérité [pɔsterite] nf posterity.

posthume [pɔstym] a posthumous.

postiche [pɔstiʃ] a false // nm hairpiece.

postillonner [pɔstijɔne] vi to spl(l)utter.

post-scriptum [pɔstskriptɔm] nm inv postscript.

postulant, e [pɔstylɑ̃, -ɑ̃t] nm/f applicant.

postulat [pɔstyla] nm postulate.

postuler [pɔstyle] vt (emploi) to apply for, put in for.

posture [pɔstyr] nf posture, position; (fig) position.

pot [po] nm jar, pot; carton; (en métal) tin; **boire un** ~ (fam) to have a drink; ~ (de chambre) (chamber)pot; ~ **d'échappement** exhaust pipe; ~ **de fleurs** plant pot, flowerpot; (fleurs) pot plant; ~ **à tabac** tobacco jar.

potable [pɔtabl(ə)] *a* (*fig*) drinkable; decent; **eau** ~ drinking water.

potache [pɔtaʃ] *nm* schoolboy.

potage [pɔtaʒ] *nm* soup; soup course.

potager, ère [pɔtaʒe, -ɛʀ] *a* (*plante*) edible, vegetable *cpd*; (**jardin**) ~ kitchen *ou* vegetable garden.

potasse [pɔtas] *nf* potassium hydroxide; (*engrais*) potash.

potasser [pɔtase] *vt* (*fam*) to swot up.

pot-au-feu [pɔtofø] *nm inv* (beef) stew; (*viande*) stewing beef.

pot-de-vin [podvɛ̃] *nm* bribe.

poteau, x [pɔto] *nm* post; ~ (**d'exécution**) execution post, stake; ~ **indicateur** signpost; ~ **télégraphique** telegraph pole; ~**x** (**de but**) goal-posts.

potelé, e [pɔtle] *a* plump, chubby.

potence [pɔtɑ̃s] *nf* gallows *sg*.

potentiel, le [pɔtɑ̃sjɛl] *a*, *nm* potential.

poterie [pɔtʀi] *nf* pottery; piece of pottery.

potiche [pɔtiʃ] *nf* large vase.

potier [pɔtje] *nm* potter.

potins [pɔtɛ̃] *nmpl* gossip *sg*.

potion [posjɔ̃] *nf* potion.

potiron [pɔtiʀɔ̃] *nm* pumpkin.

pot-pourri [popuʀi] *nm* potpourri, medley.

pou, x [pu] *nm* louse (*pl* lice).

poubelle [pubɛl] *nf* (dust)bin.

pouce [pus] *nm* thumb.

poudre [pudʀ(ə)] *nf* powder; (*fard*) (face) powder; (*explosif*) gunpowder; **en** ~: **café en** ~ instant coffee; **savon en** ~ soap powder; **lait en** ~ dried *ou* powdered milk; **poudrer** *vt* to powder; ~**rie** *nf* gunpowder factory; **poudreux, euse** *a* dusty; powdery; **neige poudreuse** powder snow; **poudrier** *nm* (powder) compact; **poudrière** *nf* powder magazine; (*fig*) powder keg.

poudroyer [pudʀwaje] *vi* to rise in clouds *ou* a flurry.

pouf [puf] *nm* pouffe.

pouffer [pufe] *vi*: ~ (**de rire**) to snigger; to giggle.

pouilleux, euse [pujø, -øz] *a* flea-ridden; (*fig*) grubby; seedy.

poulailler [pulaje] *nm* henhouse; (*THÉÂTRE*): **le** ~ the gods *sg*.

poulain [pulɛ̃] *nm* foal; (*fig*) protégé.

poularde [pulaʀd(ə)] *nf* fatted chicken.

poule [pul] *nf* (*ZOOL*) hen; (*CULIN*) (boiling) fowl; (*fam*) tart; broad; ~ **d'eau** moorhen; ~ **mouillée** coward; ~ **pondeuse** layer; ~ **au riz** chicken and rice.

poulet [pulɛ] *nm* chicken; (*fam*) cop.

pouliche [puliʃ] *nf* filly.

poulie [puli] *nf* pulley; block.

poulpe [pulp(ə)] *nm* octopus.

pouls [pu] *nm* pulse; **prendre le** ~ **de qn** to feel sb's pulse.

poumon [pumɔ̃] *nm* lung; ~ **d'acier** iron lung.

poupe [pup] *nf* stern; **en** ~ astern.

poupée [pupe] *nf* doll; **jouer à la** ~ to play with one's doll *ou* dolls.

poupon [pupɔ̃] *nm* babe-in-arms; **pouponnière** *nf* crèche, day nursery.

pour [puʀ] *prép* for; ~ **faire** (so as) to do, in order to do; ~ **avoir fait** for having done; ~ **que** so that, in order that; ~ **riche qu'il soit** rich though he may be; ~ **10 F d'essence** 10 francs' worth of petrol; ~ **cent** per cent; ~ **ce qui est de** as for; **le** ~ **et le contre** the pros and cons.

pourboire [puʀbwaʀ] *nm* tip.

pourcentage [puʀsɑ̃taʒ] *nm* percentage.

pourchasser [puʀʃase] *vt* to pursue.

pourlécher [puʀleʃe]: **se** ~ *vi* to lick one's lips.

pourparlers [puʀpaʀle] *nmpl* talks, negotiations; **être en** ~ **avec** to be having talks with.

pourpre [puʀpʀ(ə)] *a* crimson.

pourquoi [puʀkwa] *ad*, *cj* why // *nm inv*: **le** ~ (**de**) the reason (for).

pourrai *etc vb voir* **pouvoir**.

pourri, e [puʀi] *a* rotten.

pourrir [puʀiʀ] *vi* to rot; (*fruit*) to go rotten *ou* bad // *vt* to rot; (*fig*) to corrupt; to spoil thoroughly; **pourriture** *nf* rot.

pourrons *etc vb voir* **pouvoir**.

poursuite [puʀsɥit] *nf* pursuit, chase; ~**s** *nfpl* (*JUR*) legal proceedings; (**course**) ~ track race; (*fig*) chase.

poursuivant, e [puʀsɥivɑ̃, -ɑ̃t] *nm/f* pursuer.

poursuivre [puʀsɥivʀ(ə)] *vt* to pursue, chase (after); (*relancer*) to hound, harry; (*obséder*) to haunt; (*JUR*) to bring proceedings against, prosecute; (: *au civil*) to sue; (*but*) to strive towards; (*voyage, études*) to carry on with, continue // *vi* to carry on, go on; **se** ~ *vi* to go on, continue.

pourtant [puʀtɑ̃] *ad* yet; **c'est** ~ **facile** (and) yet it's easy.

pourtour [puʀtuʀ] *nm* perimeter.

pourvoi [puʀvwa] *nm* appeal.

pourvoir [puʀvwaʀ] *vt*: ~ **qch/qn de** to equip sth/sb with // *vi*: ~ **à** to provide for; (*emploi*) to fill; **se** ~ (*JUR*): **se** ~ **en cassation** to take one's case to the Court of Appeal.

pourvu, e [puʀvy] *a*: ~ **de** equipped with; ~ **que** *cj* (*si*) provided that, so long as; (*espérons que*) let's hope (that).

pousse [pus] *nf* growth; (*bourgeon*) shoot.

poussé, e [puse] *a* sophisticated, advanced; (*moteur*) souped-up.

pousse-café [puskafe] *nm inv* (after-dinner) liqueur.

poussée [puse] *nf* thrust; (*coup*) push; (*MÉD*) eruption; (*fig*) upsurge.

pousse-pousse [puspus] *nm inv* rickshaw.

pousser [puse] *vt* to push; (*inciter*): ~ **qn à** to urge *ou* press sb to + *infinitif*; (*acculer*): ~ **qn à** to drive sb to; (*émettre*: *cri etc*) to give; (*stimuler*) to urge on; to drive hard; (*poursuivre*) to carry on (further) // *vi* to push; (*croître*) to grow; (*aller*): ~ **plus loin** to push on a bit further; **se** ~ *vi* to move over; **faire** ~ (*plante*) to grow.

poussette [pusɛt] *nf* (*voiture d'enfant*) push chair.

poussière [pusjɛʀ] *nf* dust ; (*grain*) speck of dust ; **et des ~s** (*fig*) and a bit ; **~ de charbon** coaldust ; **poussiéreux, euse** *a* dusty.

poussif, ive [pusif, -iv] *a* wheezy, wheezing.

poussin [pusɛ̃] *nm* chick.

poutre [putʀ(ə)] *nf* beam ; (*en fer, ciment armé*) girder ; **poutrelle** *nf* girder.

pouvoir [puvwaʀ] *nm* power ; (*POL: dirigeants*): **le ~** those in power, the government // *vb + infinitif* can ; (*suj: personne*) can, to be able to ; (*permission*) can, may ; (*probabilité, hypothèse*) may ; **il peut arriver que** it may happen that ; **il pourrait pleuvoir** it might rain ; **déçu de ne pas ~ le faire** disappointed not to be able to do it *ou* that he couldn't do it ; **il aurait pu le dire!** he could *ou* might have said! ; **il se peut que** it may be that ; **je n'en peux plus** I'm exhausted ; I can't take any more ; **~ d'achat** purchasing power ; **les ~s publics** the authorities.

prairie [pʀeʀi] *nf* meadow.

praliné, e [pʀaline] *a* sugared ; praline-flavoured.

praticable [pʀatikabl(ə)] *a* passable, practicable.

praticien, ne [pʀatisjɛ̃, -jɛn] *nm/f* practitioner.

pratiquant, e [pʀatikɑ̃, -ɑ̃t] *a* practising.

pratique [pʀatik] *nf* practice // *a* practical ; **dans la ~** in (actual) practice ; **mettre en ~** to put into practice.

pratiquement [pʀatikmɑ̃] *ad* (*pour ainsi dire*) practically, virtually.

pratiquer [pʀatike] *vt* to practise ; (*intervention, opération*) to carry out ; (*ouverture, abri*) to make // *vi* (*REL*) to be a churchgoer.

pré [pʀe] *nm* meadow.

préalable [pʀealabl(ə)] *a* preliminary ; **condition ~ (de)** precondition (for), prerequisite (for) ; **sans avis ~** without prior *ou* previous notice ; **au ~** first, beforehand.

préambule [pʀeɑ̃byl] *nm* preamble ; (*fig*) prelude ; **sans ~** straight away.

préau, x [pʀeo] *nm* playground ; inner courtyard.

préavis [pʀeavi] *nm* notice ; **~ de congé** notice ; **communication avec ~** (*TÉL*) personal *ou* person to person call.

précaire [pʀekɛʀ] *a* precarious.

précaution [pʀekosjɔ̃] *nf* precaution ; **avec ~** cautiously ; **par ~** as a precaution.

précédemment [pʀesedamɑ̃] *ad* before, previously.

précédent, e [pʀesedɑ̃, -ɑ̃t] *a* previous // *nm* precedent ; **sans ~** unprecedented ; **le jour ~** the day before, the previous day.

précéder [pʀesede] *vt* to precede ; (*marcher ou rouler devant*) to be in front of ; (*arriver avant*) to get ahead of.

précepte [pʀesɛpt(ə)] *nm* precept.

précepteur, trice [pʀesɛptœʀ, tʀis] *nm/f* (*private*) tutor.

prêcher [pʀeʃe] *vt* to preach.

précieux, euse [pʀesjø, -øz] *a* precious ; invaluable ; (*style, écrivain*) précieux, precious.

précipice [pʀesipis] *nm* drop, chasm ; (*fig*) abyss ; **au bord du ~** at the edge of the precipice.

précipitamment [pʀesipitamɑ̃] *ad* hurriedly, hastily.

précipitation [pʀesipitasjɔ̃] *nf* (*hâte*) haste ; **~s (atmosphériques)** (atmospheric) precipitation *sg*.

précipité, e [pʀesipite] *a* fast ; hurried ; hasty.

précipiter [pʀesipite] *vt* (*faire tomber*): **~ qn/qch du haut de** to throw *or* hurl sb/sth off *ou* from ; (*hâter: marche*) to quicken ; (: *départ* (*événements*) to move faster ; **se ~ sur/vers** to rush at/towards.

précis, e [pʀesi, -iz] *a* precise ; (*tir, mesures*) accurate, precise // *nm* handbook ; **précisément** *ad* precisely ; **préciser** *vt* (*expliquer*) to be more specific about, clarify ; (*spécifier*) to state, specify ; **se préciser** *vi* to become clear(er) ; **précision** *nf* precision ; accuracy ; point *ou* detail (*made clear or to be clarified*) ; **précisions** *nfpl* further details.

précoce [pʀekɔs] *a* early ; (*enfant*) precocious ; (*calvitie*) premature.

préconçu, e [pʀekɔ̃sy] *a* preconceived.

préconiser [pʀekɔnize] *vt* to advocate.

précurseur [pʀekyʀsœʀ] *am* precursory // *nm* forerunner, precursor.

prédécesseur [pʀedesesœʀ] *nm* predecessor.

prédestiner [pʀedɛstine] *vt*: **~ qn à qch/faire** to predestine sb for sth/to do.

prédicateur [pʀedikatœʀ] *nm* preacher.

prédiction [pʀediksjɔ̃] *nf* prediction.

prédilection [pʀedilɛksjɔ̃] *nf*: **avoir une ~ pour** to be partial to ; **de ~** favourite.

prédire [pʀediʀ] *vt* to predict.

prédisposer [pʀedispoze] *vt*: **~ qn à qch/faire** to predispose sb to sth/to do.

prédominer [pʀedɔmine] *vi* to predominate ; (*avis*) to prevail.

préfabriqué, e [pʀefabʀike] *a* prefabricated // *nm* prefabricated material.

préface [pʀefas] *nf* preface ; **préfacer** *vt* to write a preface for.

préfectoral, e, aux [pʀefɛktɔʀal, -o] *a* prefectorial.

préfecture [pʀefɛktyʀ] *nf* prefecture ; **~ de police** police headquarters.

préférable [pʀefeʀabl(ə)] *a* preferable.

préféré, e [pʀefeʀe] *a, nm/f* favourite.

préférence [pʀefeʀɑ̃s] *nf* preference ; **de ~ preferably** ; **à ~** in preference to, rather than ; **obtenir la ~ sur** to have preference over ; **préférentiel, le** *a* preferential.

préférer [pʀefeʀe] *vt*: **~ qn/qch (à)** to prefer sb/sth (to), like sb/sth better (than) ; **~ faire** to prefer to do ; **je préférerais du thé** I would rather have tea, I'd prefer tea.

préfet [pʀefɛ] *nm* prefect ; **~ de police** prefect of police, ≈ Metropolitan Commissioner.

préfixe [pʀefiks(ə)] *nm* prefix.

préhistoire [pʀeistwaʀ] *nf* prehistory ; **préhistorique** *a* prehistoric.

préjudice [pRe3ydis] *nm* (*matériel*) loss ; (*moral*) harm *q* ; **porter ~ à** to harm, be detrimental to ; **au ~ de** at the expense of.

préjugé [pRe3y3e] *nm* prejudice ; **avoir un ~ contre** to be prejudiced *ou* biased against.

préjuger [pRe3y3e]: **~ de** *vt* to prejudge.

prélasser [pRelase]: **se ~** *vi* to lounge.

prélat [pRela] *nm* prelate.

prélavage [pRelava3] *nm* pre-wash.

prélèvement [pRelɛvmɑ̃] *nm* deduction ; withdrawal ; **faire un ~ de sang** to take a blood sample.

prélever [pRelve] *vt* (*échantillon*) to take ; (*argent*): **~ (sur)** to deduct (from) ; (: *sur son compte*): **~ (sur)** to withdraw (from).

préliminaire [pRelimineR] *a* preliminary ; **~s** *nmpl* preliminary talks ; preliminaries.

prélude [pRelyd] *nm* prelude ; (*avant le concert*) warm-up.

prématuré, e [pRematyRe] *a* premature ; (*retraite*) early // *nm* premature baby.

préméditation [pRemeditɑsjɔ̃] *nf*: **avec ~** a premeditated // ad with intent ; **préméditer** *vt* to premeditate, plan.

premier, ière [pRəmje, -jɛR] *a* first ; (*branche, marche, grade*) bottom ; (*fig*) basic ; prime ; initial // *nf* (THÉÂTRE) first night ; (CINÉMA) première ; (*exploit*) first ; **le ~ venu** the first person to come along ; **P~ Ministre** Prime Minister ; **premièrement** ad firstly.

prémisse [pRemis] *nf* premise.

prémonition [pRemɔnisjɔ̃] *nf* premonition ; **prémonitoire** a premonitory.

prémunir [pRemyniR]: **se ~** *vi*: **se ~ contre** to protect o.s. from, guard o.s. against.

prénatal, e [pRenatal] *a* (MÉD) antenatal.

prendre [pRɑ̃dR(ə)] *vt* to take ; (*ôter*): **~ qch à** to take sth from ; (*aller chercher*) to get, fetch ; (*se procurer*) to get ; (*malfaiteur, poisson*) to catch ; (*passager*) to pick up ; (*personnel, aussi: couleur, goût*) to take on ; (*locataire*) to take in ; (*élève etc: traiter*) to handle ; (*voix, ton*) to put on ; (*coincer*): **se ~ les doigts dans** to get one's fingers caught in // *vi* (*liquide, ciment*) to set ; (*greffe, vaccin*) to take ; (*mensonge*) to be successful ; (*feu: foyer*) to go ; (: *incendie*) to start ; (*allumette*) to light ; (*se diriger*): **~ à gauche** to turn (to the) left ; **~ qn pour** to take sb for ; **se ~ pour** to think one is ; **s'en ~ à** (*agresser*) to set about ; (*critiquer*) to attack ; **se ~ d'amitié/d'affection pour** to befriend/become fond of ; **s'y ~** (*procéder*) to set about it ; **s'y ~ à l'avance** to see to it in advance ; **s'y ~ à deux fois** to try twice, make two attemps.

preneur [pRənœR] *nm*: **être/trouver ~** to be willing to buy/find a buyer.

preniez, prenne *etc vb voir* **prendre**.

prénom [pRenɔ̃] *nm* first *ou* Christian name ; **prénommer** *vt*: **elle se prénomme Claude** her (first) name is Claude.

prénuptial, e, aux [pRenypsjal, -o] *a* premarital.

préoccupation [pReɔkypasjɔ̃] *nf* (*souci*) worry, anxiety ; (*idée fixe*) preoccupation.

préoccuper [pReɔkype] *vt* to worry ; to preoccupy ; **se ~ de qch** to be concerned about sth ; to show concern about sth.

préparatifs [pRepaRatif] *nmpl* preparations.

préparation [pRepaRɑsjɔ̃] *nf* preparation ; (SCOL) piece of homework.

préparatoire [pRepaRatwaR] *a* preparatory.

préparer [pRepaRe] *vt* to prepare ; (*café*) to make ; (*examen*) to prepare for ; (*voyage, entreprise*) to plan ; **se ~** *vi* (*orage, tragédie*) to brew, be in the air ; **se ~ (à qch/faire)** to prepare (o.s.) *ou* get ready (for sth/to do) ; **~ qch à qn** (*surprise etc*) to have sth in store for sb.

prépondérant, e [pRepɔ̃deRɑ̃, -ɑ̃t] *a* major, dominating.

préposé, e [pRepoze] *a*: **~ à** in charge of // *nm/f* employee ; official ; attendant ; postman/woman.

préposition [pRepozisjɔ̃] *nf* preposition.

prérogative [pReRɔgativ] *nf* prerogative.

près [pRɛ] *ad* near, close ; **~ de** *prép* near (to), close to ; (*environ*) nearly, almost ; **de ~** *ad* closely ; **à 5 kg ~** to within about 5 kg ; **à cela ~ que** apart from the fact that.

présage [pReza3] *nm* omen.

présager [pReza3e] *vt* to foresee.

presbyte [pRɛsbit] *a* long-sighted.

presbytère [pRɛsbiteR] *nm* presbytery.

presbytérien, ne [pRɛsbiteRjɛ̃, -jɛn] *a, nm/f* Presbyterian.

prescription [pRɛskRipsjɔ̃] *nf* (*instruction*) order, instruction ; (MÉD, JUR) prescription.

prescrire [pRɛskRiR] *vt* to prescribe ; **se ~** *vi* (JUR) to lapse ; **prescrit, e** *a* (*date etc*) stipulated.

préséance [pReseɑ̃s] *nf* precedence *q*.

présence [pRezɑ̃s] *nf* presence ; (*au bureau etc*) attendance ; **en ~ de** in (the) presence of ; (*fig*) in the face of ; **~ d'esprit** presence of mind.

présent, e [pRezɑ̃, -ɑ̃t] *a, nm* present ; **à ~ (que)** now (that).

présentateur, trice [pRezɑ̃tatœR, -tRis] *nm/f* presenter.

présentation [pRezɑ̃tɑsjɔ̃] *nf* introduction ; presentation ; (*allure*) appearance.

présenter [pRezɑ̃te] *vt* to present ; (*soumettre*) to submit ; (*invité, conférencier*): **~ qn (à)** to introduce sb (to) // *vi*: **~ mal/bien** to have an unattractive/a pleasing appearance ; **se ~** *vi* (*sur convocation*) to report, come ; (*à une élection*) to stand ; (*occasion*) to arise ; **~ bien/mal** to look good/not too good ; **présentoir** *nm* display shelf (*pl* shelves).

préservatif [pRezɛRvatif] *nm* sheath, condom.

préserver [pRezɛRve] *vt*: **~ de** to protect from ; to save from.

présidence [pRezidɑ̃s] *nf* presidency ; office of President ; chairmanship.

président [pRezidɑ̃] *nm* (POL) president ; (*d'une assemblée*, COMM) chairman ; **~ directeur général (P.D.G.)** chairman and managing director ; **~ du jury** (JUR) foreman of the jury; (*d'examen*) chief examiner; **présidente** *nf* president; president's wife; chairwoman; **présidentiel, le** [-sjɛl] *a* presidential.

présider [pʀezide] *vt* to preside over; (*dîner*) to be the guest of honour at; ~ **à** *vt* to direct; to govern.

présomption [pʀezɔ̃psjɔ̃] *nf* presumption.

présomptueux, euse [pʀezɔ̃ptɥø, -øz] *a* presumptuous.

presque [pʀɛsk(ə)] *ad* almost, nearly; ~ **rien** hardly anything; ~ **pas** hardly (at all).

presqu'île [pʀɛskil] *nf* peninsula.

pressant, e [pʀɛsɑ̃, -ɑ̃t] *a* urgent.

presse [pʀɛs] *nf* press; (*affluence*): **heures de** ~ busy times; **sous** ~ *a* in press, being printed; ~ **féminine** women's magazines *pl*; ~ **d'information** quality newspapers *pl*.

pressé, e [pʀese] *a* in a hurry; (*air*) hurried; (*besogne*) urgent; **orange** ~**e** fresh orange juice.

presse-citron [pʀɛsitʀɔ̃] *nm inv* lemon squeezer.

pressentiment [pʀesɑ̃timɑ̃] *nm* foreboding, premonition.

pressentir [pʀesɑ̃tiʀ] *vt* to sense; (*prendre contact avec*) to approach.

presse-papiers [pʀɛspapje] *nm inv* paperweight.

presser [pʀese] *vt* (*fruit, éponge*) to squeeze; (*interrupteur, bouton*) to press, push; (*allure, affaire*) to speed up; (*débiteur etc*) to press; (*inciter*): ~ **qn de faire** to urge ou press sb to do // *vi* to be urgent; **rien ne presse** there's no hurry; **se** ~ (*se hâter*) to hurry (up); (*se grouper*) to crowd; **se** ~ **contre qn** to squeeze up against sb; ~ **qn entre ses bras** to hug sb (tight).

pressing [pʀesiŋ] *nm* steam-pressing; (*magasin*) dry-cleaner's.

pression [pʀesjɔ̃] *nf* pressure; **faire** ~ **sur** to put pressure on; **sous** ~ pressurized, under pressure; (*fig*) keyed up; ~ **artérielle** blood pressure.

pressoir [pʀeswaʀ] *nm* (wine ou oil etc) press.

pressurer [pʀesyʀe] *vt* (*fig*) to squeeze.

pressurisé, e [pʀesyʀize] *a* pressurized.

prestance [pʀɛstɑ̃s] *nf* presence, imposing bearing.

prestataire [pʀɛstatɛʀ] *nm/f* person receiving benefits.

prestation [pʀɛstasjɔ̃] *nf* (*allocation*) benefit; (*d'une assurance*) cover *q*; (*d'une entreprise*) service provided; (*d'un joueur, artiste*) performance; ~ **de serment** taking the oath; ~ **de service** provision of a service.

preste [pʀɛst(ə)] *a* nimble; swift; ~**ment** *ad* swiftly.

prestidigitateur, trice [pʀɛstidiʒitatœʀ, -tʀis] *nm/f* conjurer.

prestidigitation [pʀɛstidiʒitasjɔ̃] *nf* conjuring.

prestige [pʀɛstiʒ] *nm* prestige; **prestigieux, euse** *a* prestigious.

présumer [pʀezyme] *vt*: ~ **que** to presume ou assume that; ~ **de** to

overrate; ~ **qn coupable** to presume sb guilty.

prêt, e [pʀɛ, pʀɛt] *a* ready // *nm* lending *q*; loan; ~ **sur gages** pawnbroking *q*; **prêt-à-porter** *nm* ready-to-wear ou off-the-peg clothes *pl*.

prétendant [pʀetɑ̃dɑ̃] *nm* pretender; (*d'une femme*) suitor.

prétendre [pʀetɑ̃dʀ(ə)] *vt* (*affirmer*): ~ **que** to claim that; (*avoir l'intention de*): ~ **faire qch** to mean ou intend to do sth; ~ **à** *vt* (*droit, titre*) to lay claim to; **prétendu, e** *a* (*supposé*) so-called.

prétentieux, euse [pʀetɑ̃sjø, -øz] *a* pretentious.

prétention [pʀetɑ̃sjɔ̃] *nf* claim; pretentiousness.

prêter [pʀete] *vt* (*livres, argent*): ~ **qch (à)** to lend sth (to); (*supposer*): ~ **à qn** (*caractère, propos*) to attribute to sb // *vi* (*aussi*: **se** ~: *tissu, cuir*) to give; ~ **à** (*commentaires etc*) to be open to, give rise to; **se** ~ **à** to lend o.s. (ou itself) to; (*manigances etc*) to go along with; ~ **assistance à** to give help to; ~ **serment** to take the oath; ~ **l'oreille** to listen; **prêteur** *nm* moneylender; **prêteur sur gages** pawnbroker.

prétexte [pʀetɛkst(ə)] *nm* pretext, excuse; **sous aucun** ~ on no account; **prétexter** *vt* to give as a pretext ou an excuse.

prêtre [pʀɛtʀ(ə)] *nm* priest; **prêtrise** *nf* priesthood.

preuve [pʀœv] *nf* proof; (*indice*) proof, evidence *q*; **faire** ~ **de** to show; **faire ses** ~**s** to prove o.s. (ou itself).

prévaloir [pʀevalwaʀ] *vi* to prevail; **se** ~ **de** *vt* to take advantage of; to pride o.s. on.

prévenances [pʀevnɑ̃s] *nfpl* thoughtfulness *sg*, kindness *sg*.

prévenant, e [pʀevnɑ̃, -ɑ̃t] *a* thoughtful, kind.

prévenir [pʀevniʀ] *vt* (*avertir*): ~ **qn (de)** to warn sb (about); (*informer*): ~ **qn (de)** to tell ou inform sb (about); (*éviter*) to avoid, prevent; (*anticiper*) to forestall; to anticipate; (*influencer*): ~ **qn contre** to prejudice sb against.

préventif, ive [pʀevɑ̃tif, -iv] *a* preventive.

prévention [pʀevɑ̃sjɔ̃] *nf* prevention; ~ **routière** road safety.

prévenu, e [pʀevny] *nm/f* (*JUR*) defendant, accused.

prévision [pʀevizjɔ̃] *nf*: ~**s** predictions; forecast *sg*; **en** ~ **de** in anticipation of; ~**s météorologiques** ou **du temps** weather forecast *sg*.

prévoir [pʀevwaʀ] *vt* (*deviner*) to foresee; (*s'attendre à*) to expect, reckon on; (*prévenir*) to anticipate; (*organiser*) to plan; (*préparer, réserver*) to allow; **prévu pour 4 personnes** designed for 4 people; **prévu pour 10h** scheduled for 10 o'clock.

prévoyance [pʀevwajɑ̃s] *nf* foresight; **une société/caisse de** ~ a provident society/contingency fund.

prévoyant, e [pʀevwajɑ̃, -ɑ̃t] *a* gifted with (ou showing) foresight.

prier [pRije] *vi* to pray // *vt* (*Dieu*) to pray to; (*implorer*) to beg; (*demander*): ~ qn de faire to ask sb to do; se faire ~ to need coaxing *ou* persuading; je vous en prie please do; don't mention it.

prière [pRijɛR] *nf* prayer; '~ de faire ...' 'please do ...'.

primaire [pRimɛR] *a* primary; (*péj*) simple-minded; simplistic // *nm* (*SCOL*) primary education.

primauté [pRimote] *nf* (*fig*) primacy.

prime [pRim] *nf* (*bonification*) bonus; (*subside*) premium; allowance; (*COMM: cadeau*) free gift; (*ASSURANCES, BOURSE*) premium // *a*: de ~ abord at first glance; ~ de risque danger money *q*.

primer [pRime] *vt* (*l'emporter sur*) to prevail over; (*récompenser*) to award a prize to // *vi* to dominate; to prevail.

primesautier, ère [pRimsotje, -jɛR] *a* impulsive.

primeur [pRimœR] *nf*: avoir la ~ de to be the first to hear (*ou* see *etc*); ~s *nfpl* (*fruits, légumes*) early fruits and vegetables; marchand de ~s greengrocer.

primevère [pRimvɛR] *nf* primrose.

primitif, ive [pRimitif, -iv] *a* primitive; (*originel*) original // *nm/f* primitive.

primordial, e, aux [pRimɔRdjal, -o] *a* essential, primordial.

prince, esse [pRɛs, pRɛsɛs] *nm/f* prince/princess; ~ de Galles *nm inv* check cloth; ~ héritier crown prince; princier, ière *a* princely.

principal, e, aux [pRɛsipal, -o] *a* principal, main // *nm* (*SCOL*) principal, head(master) // *nf*: (*proposition*) ~e main clause.

principauté [pRɛsipote] *nf* Principality.

principe [pRɛsip] *nm* principle; partir du ~ que to work on the principle *ou* assumption that; pour le ~ on principle, for the sake of it; de ~ *a* (*accord, hostilité*) automatic; par ~ on principle; en ~ (*habituellement*) as a rule; (*théoriquement*) in principle.

printanier, ère [pRɛtanje, -jɛR] *a* spring *cpd*; spring-like.

printemps [pRɛtɑ̃] *nm* spring.

priori [pRijɔRi]: à ~ *ad* without the benefit of hindsight; a priori; initially.

prioritaire [pRijɔRitɛR] *a* having priority; (*AUTO*) having right of way.

priorité [pRijɔRite] *nf* (*AUTO*): avoir la ~ (sur) to have right of way (over); ~ à droite right of way to vehicles coming from the right; en ~ as a (matter of) priority.

pris, e [pRi, pRiz] *pp de* prendre // *a* (*place*) taken; (*journée, mains*) full; (*billets*) sold; (*personne*) busy; (*MÉD: enflammé*): avoir le nez/la gorge ~(e) to have a stuffy nose/a hoarse throat; (*saisi*): être ~ de peur/de fatigue to be stricken with fear/overcome with fatigue.

prise [pRiz] *nf* (*d'une ville*) capture; (*PÊCHE, CHASSE*) catch; (*de judo ou catch, point d'appui ou pour empoigner*) hold; (*ÉLEC: fiche*) plug; (: *femelle*) socket; (: *au mur*) point; en ~ (*AUTO*) in gear; être aux ~s avec to be grappling with; to be battling

with; lâcher ~ to let go; ~ en charge (*taxe*) pick-up charge; ~ de courant power point; ~ d'eau water (supply) point; tap; ~ multiple adaptor; ~ de sang blood test; ~ de son sound recording; ~ de tabac pinch of snuff; ~ de terre earth; ~ de vue (*photo*) shot; (*action*): ~ de vue(s) filming, shooting.

priser [pRize] *vt* (*tabac, héroïne*) to take; (*estimer*) to prize, value // *vi* to take snuff.

prisme [pRism(ə)] *nm* prism.

prison [pRizɔ̃] *nf* prison; aller/être en ~ to go to/be in prison *ou* jail; faire de la ~ to serve time; prisonnier, ière *nm/f* prisoner // *a* captive; faire qn prisonnier to take sb prisoner.

prit *vb voir* prendre.

privations [pRivɑsjɔ̃] *nfpl* privations, hardships.

privé, e [pRive] *a* private; (*dépourvu*): ~ de without, lacking; en ~ in private.

priver [pRive] *vt*: ~ qn de to deprive sb of; se ~ de to go *ou* do without; ne pas se ~ de faire not to refrain from doing.

privilège [pRivilɛʒ] *nm* privilege; privilégié, e *a* privileged.

prix [pRi] *nm* (*valeur*) price; (*récompense, SCOL*) prize; hors de ~ exorbitantly priced; à aucun ~ not at any price; à tout ~ at all costs; ~ d'achat/de vente purchasing/selling price.

probabilité [pRɔbabilite] *nf* probability.

probable [pRɔbabl(ə)] *a* likely, probable; ~ment *ad* probably.

probant, e [pRɔbɑ̃, -ɑ̃t] *a* convincing.

probité [pRɔbite] *nf* integrity, probity.

problème [pRɔblɛm] *nm* problem.

procédé [pRɔsede] *nm* (*méthode*) process; (*comportement*) behaviour *q*.

procéder [pRɔsede] *vi* to proceed; to behave; ~ à *vt* to carry out.

procédure [pRɔsedyR] *nf* (*ADMIN, JUR*) procedure.

procès [pRɔsɛ] *nm* trial; (*poursuites*) proceedings *pl*; être en ~ avec to be involved in a lawsuit with.

procession [pRɔsesjɔ̃] *nf* procession.

processus [pRɔsesys] *nm* process.

procès-verbal, aux [pRɔsevɛRbal, -o] *nm* (*constat*) statement; (*aussi*: P.V.): avoir un ~ to get a parking ticket; to be booked; (*de réunion*) minutes *pl*.

prochain, e [pRɔʃɛ̃, -ɛn] *a* next; (*proche*) impending; near // *nm* fellow man; la ~e fois/semaine ~e next time/week; prochainement *ad* soon, shortly.

proche [pRɔʃ] *a* nearby; (*dans le temps*) imminent; close at hand; (*parent, ami*) close; ~s *nmpl* close relatives, next of kin; être ~ (de) to be near, be close (to); de ~ en ~ gradually; le P~ Orient the Middle East, the Near East.

proclamation [pRɔklamɑsjɔ̃] *nf* proclamation.

proclamer [pRɔklame] *vt* to proclaim.

procréer [pRɔkRee] *vt* to procreate.

procuration [pRɔkyRɑsjɔ̃] *nf* proxy, power of attorney.

procurer [pRɔkyRe] *vt* (*fournir*): ~ qch à qn to get *ou* obtain sth for sb; (*causer*:

plaisir etc): ~ qch à qn to bring *ou* give sb sth; **se** ~ vt to get.

procureur [prɔkyrœr] *nm* public prosecutor.

prodige [prɔdiʒ] *nm* marvel, wonder; (*personne*) prodigy; **prodigieux, euse** *a* prodigious; phenomenal.

prodigue [prɔdig] *a* generous; extravagant, wasteful; **fils** ~ prodigal son.

prodiguer [prɔdige] *vt* (*argent, biens*) to be lavish with; (*soins, attentions*): ~ qch à qn to give sb sth; to lavish sth on sb.

producteur, trice [prɔdyktœr, -tris] *a*: ~ **de blé** wheat-producing // *nm/f* producer.

productif, ive [prɔdyktif, -iv] *a* productive.

production [prɔdyksjɔ̃] *nf* (*gén*) production; (*rendement*) output; (*produits*) products *pl*, goods *pl*.

productivité [prɔdyktivite] *nf* productivity.

produire [prɔdɥir] *vt* to produce; **se** ~ *vi* (*acteur*) to perform, appear; (*événement*) to happen, occur.

produit [prɔdɥi] *nm* (*gén*) product; ~**s agricoles** farm produce *sg*; ~ **d'entretien** cleaning product.

proéminent, e [prɔeminɑ̃, -ɑ̃t] *a* prominent.

profane [prɔfan] *a* (*rel*) secular // *nm/f* layman.

profaner [prɔfane] *vt* to desecrate.

proférer [prɔfere] *vt* to utter.

professer [prɔfese] *vt* (*déclarer*) to profess // *vi* to teach.

professeur [prɔfesœr] *nm* teacher; (*titulaire d'une chaire*) professor; ~ **(de faculté)** (university) lecturer.

profession [prɔfesjɔ̃] *nf* profession; **sans** ~ unemployed; **professionnel, le** *a, nm/f* professional.

professorat [prɔfesɔra] *nm*: **le** ~ the teaching profession.

profil [prɔfil] *nm* profile; (*d'une voiture*) line, contour; **de** ~ in profile; ~**er** vt to streamline; **se** ~**er** *vi* (*arbre, tour*) to stand out, be silhouetted.

profit [prɔfi] *nm* (*avantage*) benefit, advantage; (*comm, finance*) profit; **au** ~ **de** in aid of; **tirer** ~ **de** to profit from; **mettre à** ~ to take advantage of; to turn to good account.

profitable [prɔfitabl(ə)] *a* beneficial; profitable.

profiter [prɔfite] *vi*: ~ **de** to take advantage of; to make the most of; ~ **à** to be of benefit to, benefit; to be profitable to.

profond, e [prɔfɔ̃, -ɔ̃d] *a* deep; (*méditation, mépris*) profound; **profondeur** *nf* depth.

profusion [prɔfyzjɔ̃] *nf* profusion; **à** ~ in plenty.

progéniture [prɔʒenityr] *nf* offspring *inv*.

programmation [prɔgramasjɔ̃] *nf* programming.

programme [prɔgram] *nm* programme; (*tv, radio*) programmes *pl*; (*scol*) syllabus, curriculum; (*informatique*) program; **au** ~ **de ce soir** (*tv*) among tonight's

programmes; **programmer** *vt* (*tv, radio*) to put on, show; (*informatique*) to program; **programmeur, euse** *nm/f* computer programmer.

progrès [prɔgrɛ] *nm* progress *q*; **faire des/être en** ~ to make/be making progress.

progresser [prɔgrese] *vi* to progress; (*troupes etc*) to make headway *ou* progress; **progressif, ive** *a* progressive; **progression** *nf* progression; (*d'une troupe etc*) advance, progress.

prohiber [prɔibe] *vt* to prohibit, ban.

proie [prwa] *nf* prey *q*; **être la** ~ **de** to fall prey to; **être en** ~ **à** to be prey to; to be suffering.

projecteur [prɔʒɛktœr] *nm* projector; (*de théâtre, cirque*) spotlight.

projectile [prɔʒɛktil] *nm* missile; (*d'arme*) projectile, bullet (*ou* shell *etc*).

projection [prɔʒɛksjɔ̃] *nf* projection; showing; **conférence avec** ~**s** lecture with slides (*ou* a film).

projet [prɔʒɛ] *nm* plan; (*ébauche*) draft; **faire des** ~**s** to make plans; ~ **de loi** bill.

projeter [prɔʒte] *vt* (*envisager*) to plan; (*film, photos*) to project; (: *passer*) to show; (*ombre, lueur*) to throw, cast, project; (*jeter*) to throw up (*ou* off *ou* out).

prolétaire [prɔletɛr] *nm* proletarian; **prolétariat** *nm* proletariat.

proliférer [prɔlifere] *vi* to proliferate.

prolifique [prɔlifik] *a* prolific.

prolixe [prɔliks(ə)] *a* verbose.

prologue [prɔlɔg] *nm* prologue.

prolongation [prɔlɔ̃gɑsjɔ̃] *nf* prolongation; extension; ~**s** *nfpl* (*football*) extra time *sg*.

prolongement [prɔlɔ̃ʒmɑ̃] *nm* extension; ~**s** *nmpl* (*fig*) repercussions, effects; **dans le** ~ **de** running on from.

prolonger [prɔlɔ̃ʒe] *vt* (*débat, séjour*) to prolong; (*délai, billet, rue*) to extend; (*suj: chose*) to be a continuation *ou* an extension of; **se** ~ *vi* to go on.

promenade [prɔmnad] *nf* walk (*ou* drive *ou* ride); **faire une** ~ to go for a walk; **une** ~ **en voiture/à vélo** a drive/(bicycle) ride.

promener [prɔmne] *vt* (*chien*) to take out for a walk; (*fig*) to carry around; to trail round; (*doigts, regard*): ~ qch sur to run sth over; **se** ~ *vi* to go for (*ou* be out for) a walk; (*fig*): **se** ~ **sur** to wander over; **promeneur, euse** *nm/f* walker, stroller.

promesse [prɔmɛs] *nf* promise; ~ **d'achat** commitment to buy.

prometteur, euse [prɔmɛtœr, -øz] *a* promising.

promettre [prɔmɛtr(ə)] *vt* to promise // *vi* to be *ou* look promising; **se** ~ **de faire** to resolve *ou* mean to do; ~ **à qn de faire** to promise sb that one will do.

promiscuité [prɔmiskɥite] *nf* crowding; lack of privacy.

promontoire [prɔmɔ̃twar] *nm* headland.

promoteur, trice [prɔmɔtœr, -tris] *nm/f* (*instigateur*) instigator, promoter; ~ **(immobilier)** property developer.

promotion [pʀɔmosjɔ̃] nf promotion.
promouvoir [pʀɔmuvwaʀ] vt to promote.
prompt, e [pʀɔ̃, pʀɔ̃t] a swift, rapid.
promulguer [pʀɔmylge] vt to promulgate.
prôner [pʀone] vt (louer) to laud, extol ; (préconiser) to advocate, commend.
pronom [pʀɔnɔ̃] nm pronoun ; **pronominal, e, aux** a pronominal ; reflexive.
prononcé, e [pʀɔnɔ̃se] a pronounced, marked.
prononcer [pʀɔnɔ̃se] vt (son, mot, jugement) to pronounce ; (dire) to utter ; (allocution) to deliver // vi : ~ bien/mal to have a good/poor pronunciation ; se ~ vi to reach a decision, give a verdict ; se ~ sur to give an opinion on ; se ~ contre to come down against ; **prononciation** nf pronunciation.
pronostic [pʀɔnɔstik] nm (MÉD) prognosis (pl oses) ; (fig: aussi: ~s) forecast.
propagande [pʀɔpagɑ̃d] nf propaganda.
propager [pʀɔpaʒe] vt to spread ; se ~ vi to spread ; (PHYSIQUE) to be propagated.
prophète [pʀɔfɛt] nm prophet.
prophétie [pʀɔfesi] nf prophecy ; **prophétiser** vt to prophesy.
propice [pʀɔpis] a favourable.
proportion [pʀɔpɔʀsjɔ̃] nf proportion ; en ~ de in proportion to ; toute(s) ~(s) gardée(s) making due allowance(s) ; **proportionnel, le** a proportional ; **proportionner** vt : proportionner qch à to proportion ou adjust sth to.
propos [pʀɔpo] nm (paroles) talk q, remark ; (intention) intention, aim ; (sujet): à quel ~? what about?; à ~ de about, regarding ; à tout ~ for no reason at all ; à ~ ad by the way ; (opportunément) (just) at the right moment.
proposer [pʀɔpoze] vt (suggérer): ~ qch (à qn)/de faire to suggest sth (to sb)/doing, propose to do ; (offrir): ~ qch à qn/de faire to offer sb sth/to do ; (candidat) to nominate, put forward ; (loi, motion) to propose ; se ~ (pour faire) to offer one's services (to do) ; se ~ de faire to intend ou propose to do ; **proposition** nf suggestion ; proposal ; offer ; (LING) clause.
propre [pʀɔpʀ(ə)] a clean ; (net) neat, tidy ; (possessif) own ; (sens) literal ; (particulier): ~ à peculiar to, characteristic of ; (approprié): ~ à suitable ou appropriate for ; (de nature à): ~ à faire likely to do, that will do // nm: recopier au ~ to make a fair copy of ; ~ment ad cleanly ; neatly, tidily ; à ~ment parler strictly speaking ; ~té nf cleanliness, cleanness ; neatness ; tidiness.
propriétaire [pʀɔpʀijetɛʀ] nm/f owner ; (d'hôtel etc) proprietor/ tress, owner ; (pour le locataire) landlord/lady ; ~ (immobilier) house-owner ; householder ; ~ récoltant grower ; ~ (terrien) landowner.
propriété [pʀɔpʀijete] nf (droit) ownership ; (objet, immeuble etc) property gén q ; (villa) residence, property ; (terres) property gén q, land gén q ; (qualité, CHIMIE, MATH) property ; (correction) appropriateness, suitability.

propulser [pʀɔpylse] vt (missile) to propel ; (projeter) to hurl, fling.
prorata [pʀɔʀata] nm inv: au ~ de in proportion to, on the basis of.
proroger [pʀɔʀɔʒe] vt to put back, defer ; (assemblée) to adjourn, prorogue.
prosaïque [pʀozaik] a mundane, prosaic.
proscrire [pʀɔskʀiʀ] vt (bannir) to banish ; (interdire) to ban, prohibit.
prose [pʀoz] nf prose (style).
prospecter [pʀɔspɛkte] vt to prospect ; (COMM) to canvass.
prospectus [pʀɔspɛktys] nm (feuille) leaflet ; (dépliant) brochure, leaflet.
prospère [pʀɔspɛʀ] a prosperous ; (entreprise) thriving, flourishing ; **prospérer** vi to thrive ; **prospérité** nf prosperity.
prosterner [pʀɔstɛʀne]: se ~ vi to bow low, prostrate o.s.
prostituée [pʀɔstitɥe] nf prostitute.
prostitution [pʀɔstitysjɔ̃] nf prostitution.
prostré, e [pʀɔstʀe] a prostrate.
protagoniste [pʀɔtagɔnist(ə)] nm protagonist.
protecteur, trice [pʀɔtɛktœʀ, -tʀis] a protective ; (air, ton: péj) patronizing // nm/f protector.
protection [pʀɔtɛksjɔ̃] nf protection ; (d'un personnage influent: aide) patronage.
protégé, e [pʀɔteʒe] nm/f protégé/e.
protège-cahier [pʀɔtɛʒkaje] nm exercise-book cover.
protéger [pʀɔteʒe] vt to protect ; se ~ de/contre to protect o.s. from.
protéine [pʀɔtein] nf protein.
protestant, e [pʀɔtɛstɑ̃, -ɑ̃t] a, nm/f Protestant ; **protestantisme** nm Protestantism.
protestation [pʀɔtɛstasjɔ̃] nf (plainte) protest ; (déclaration) protestation, profession.
protester [pʀɔtɛste] vi : ~ (contre) to protest (against ou about) ; ~ de (son innocence, sa loyauté) to protest.
prothèse [pʀɔtɛz] nf artificial limb, prosthesis ; ~ dentaire denture ; dental engineering.
protocolaire [pʀɔtɔkɔlɛʀ] a formal ; of protocol.
protocole [pʀɔtɔkɔl] nm protocol ; (fig) etiquette ; ~ d'accord draft treaty.
prototype [pʀɔtɔtip] nm prototype.
protubérance [pʀɔtybeʀɑ̃s] nf bulge, protuberance ; **protubérant, e** a protruding, bulging, protuberant.
proue [pʀu] nf bow(s pl), prow.
prouesse [pʀuɛs] nf feat.
prouver [pʀuve] vt to prove.
provenance [pʀɔvnɑ̃s] nf origin ; (de mot, coutume) source ; avion en ~ de plane (arriving) from.
provenir [pʀɔvniʀ]: ~ de vt to come from ; (résulter de) to be due to, be the result of.
proverbe [pʀɔvɛʀb(ə)] nm proverb ; **proverbial, e, aux** a proverbial.
providence [pʀɔvidɑ̃s] nf: la ~ providence ; **providentiel, le** a providential.

province [pʀɔvɛ̃s] nf province;
provincial, e, aux a provincial.
proviseur [pʀɔvizœʀ] nm ≈
head(master).
provision [pʀɔvizjɔ̃] nf (réserve) stock,
supply; (avance: à un avocat, avoué)
retainer, retaining fee; (COMM) funds pl (in
account); reserve; **~s** nfpl (vivres)
provisions, food q; **faire ~ de** to stock
up with; **armoire à ~s** food cupboard.
provisoire [pʀɔvizwaʀ] a temporary;
(JUR) provisional; **~ment** ad temporarily,
for the time being.
provocant, e [pʀɔvɔkɑ̃, -ɑ̃t] a
provocative.
provocation [pʀɔvɔkasjɔ̃] nf provocation.
provoquer [pʀɔvɔke] vt (défier) to
provoke; (causer) to cause, bring about;
(: curiosité) to arouse, give rise to; (: aveux)
to prompt, elicit.
proxénète [pʀɔksenɛt] nm procurer.
proximité [pʀɔksimite] nf nearness,
closeness, proximity; (dans le temps)
imminence, closeness; **à ~** near ou close
by; **à ~ de** near (to), close to.
prude [pʀyd] a prudish.
prudence [pʀydɑ̃s] nf carefulness;
caution; prudence; **avec ~** carefully,
cautiously; wisely; **par (mesure de) ~**
as a precaution.
prudent, e [pʀydɑ̃, -ɑ̃t] a (pas téméraire)
careful, cautious, prudent; (: en général)
safety-conscious; (sage, conseillé) wise,
sensible; (réservé) cautious; **ce n'est pas
~** it's risky; it's not sensible; **soyez ~**
take care, be careful.
prune [pʀyn] nf plum.
pruneau, x [pʀyno] nm prune.
prunelle [pʀynɛl] nf pupil; eye.
prunier [pʀynje] nm plum tree.
psalmodier [psalmɔdje] vt to chant; (fig)
to drone out.
psaume [psom] nm psalm.
pseudonyme [psødɔnim] nm (gén)
fictitious name; (d'écrivain) pseudonym,
pen name; (de comédien) stage name.
psychanalyse [psikanaliz] nf
psychoanalysis; **psychanalyser** vt to
psychoanalyze; **se faire psychanalyser**
to undergo (psycho)analysis; **psychanalyste** nm/f psychoanalyst.
psychiatre [psikjatʀ(ə)] nm/f
psychiatrist.
psychiatrie [psikjatʀi] nf psychiatry;
psychiatrique a psychiatric; (hôpital)
mental, psychiatric.
psychique [psiʃik] a psychological.
psychologie [psikɔlɔʒi] nf psychology;
psychologique a psychological;
psychologue nm/f psychologist; **être
psychologue** (fig) to be a good
psychologist.
psychose [psikoz] nf psychosis;
obsessive fear.
Pte abr de **porte**.
P.T.T. sigle fpl voir **poste**.
pu pp de **pouvoir**.
puanteur [pɥɑ̃tœʀ] nf stink, stench.
pubère [pybɛʀ] a pubescent; **puberté** nf
puberty.

pubis [pybis] nm (bas-ventre) pubes pl;
(os) pubis.
public, ique [pyblik] a public; (école,
instruction) state cpd // nm public;
(assistance) audience; **en ~** in public.
publication [pyblikasjɔ̃] nf publication.
publiciste [pyblisist(ə)] nm/f adman.
publicitaire [pyblisitɛʀ] a advertising
cpd; (film, voiture) publicity cpd.
publicité [pyblisite] nf (méthode,
profession) advertising; (annonce)
advertisement; (révélations) publicity.
publier [pyblije] vt to publish.
publique [pyblik] af voir **public**.
puce [pys] nf flea; **~s** nfpl (marché) flea
market sg.
puceau, x [pyso] am: **être ~** to be a
virgin.
pucelle [pysɛl] af: **être ~** to be a virgin.
pudeur [pydœʀ] nf modesty.
pudibond, e [pydibɔ̃, -ɔ̃d] a prudish.
pudique [pydik] a (chaste) modest;
(discret) discreet.
puer [pɥe] (péj) vi to stink // vt to stink
of, reek of.
puéricultrice [pɥeʀikyltʀis] nf paediatric
nurse.
puériculture [pɥeʀikyltyʀ] nf paediatric
nursing; infant care.
puéril, e [pɥeʀil] a childish.
pugilat [pyʒila] nm (fist) fight.
puis [pɥi] vb voir **pouvoir** // ad then; **et
~** and (then).
puiser [pɥize] vt (eau): **~ (dans)** to draw
(from); **~ dans qch** to dip into sth.
puisque [pɥisk(ə)] cj since.
puissance [pɥisɑ̃s] nf power; **en ~** a
potential; **2 (à la) ~ 5** 2 to the power
of 5.
puissant, e [pɥisɑ̃, -ɑ̃t] a powerful.
puisse etc vb voir **pouvoir**.
puits [pɥi] nm well; **~ de mine** mine shaft.
pull(-over) [pul(ɔvœʀ)] nm sweater,
jumper.
pulluler [pylyle] vi to swarm.
pulmonaire [pylmɔnɛʀ] a lung cpd;
(artère) pulmonary.
pulpe [pylp(ə)] nf pulp.
pulsation [pylsasjɔ̃] nf beat.
pulsion [pylsjɔ̃] nf drive, urge.
pulvérisateur [pylveʀizatœʀ] nm spray.
pulvériser [pylveʀize] vt (solide) to
pulverize; (liquide) to spray; (fig) to
pulverize; to smash.
punaise [pynɛz] nf (ZOOL) bug; (clou)
drawing pin.
punch [pɔ̃ʃ] nm (boisson) punch; [pœnʃ]
(BOXE) punching ability; (fig) punch;
punching-ball nm punchball.
punir [pyniʀ] vt to punish; **punition** nf
punishment.
pupille [pypij] nf (ANAT) pupil // nm/f
(enfant) ward; **~ de l'État** child in care;
~ de la Nation war orphan.
pupitre [pypitʀ(ə)] nm (SCOL) desk; (REL)
lectern; (de chef d'orchestre) rostrum; **~
de commande** panel.
pur, e [pyʀ] a pure; (vin) undiluted;
(whisky) neat; **en ~e perte** fruitlessly, to
no avail.

purée [pyʀe] *nf*: ~ (de pommes de terre) mashed potatoes *pl*; ~ de marrons chestnut purée.

pureté [pyʀte] *nf* purity.

purgatif [pyʀgatif] *nm* purgative, purge.

purgatoire [pyʀgatwaʀ] *nm* purgatory.

purge [pyʀʒ(ə)] *nf* (*POL*) purge; (*MÉD*) purging *q*; purge.

purger [pyʀʒe] *vt* (*radiateur*) to flush (out), drain; (*circuit hydraulique*) to bleed; (*MED, POL*) to purge; (*JUR: peine*) to serve.

purifier [pyʀifje] *vt* to purify; (*TECH: métal*) to refine.

purin [pyʀɛ̃] *nm* liquid manure.

puritain, e [pyʀitɛ̃, -ɛn] *a, nm/f* Puritan; **puritanisme** *nm* Puritanism.

pur-sang [pyʀsɑ̃] *nm inv* thoroughbred, purebred.

purulent, e [pyʀylɑ̃, -ɑ̃t] *a* purulent.

pus [py] *nm* pus.

pusillanime [pyzilanim] *a* fainthearted.

putain [pytɛ̃] *nf* (*fam!*) whore(!); ce/cette ~ de ... this bloody ...(!).

putréfier [pytʀefje] *vt*, **se** ~ *vi* to putrefy, rot.

puzzle [pœzl(ə)] *nm* jigsaw (puzzle).

P.V. *sigle m* = procès-verbal.

pygmée [pigme] *nm* pygmy.

pyjama [piʒama] *nm* pyjamas *pl*, pair of pyjamas.

pylône [pilon] *nm* pylon.

pyramide [piʀamid] *nf* pyramid.

pyromane [piʀɔman] *nm/f* fire bug, arsonist.

python [pitɔ̃] *nm* python.

Q

QG [kyʒe] *voir* quartier.

QI [kyi] *voir* quotient.

quadragénaire [kadʀaʒenɛʀ] *nm/f* man/woman in his/her forties.

quadrangulaire [kwadʀɑ̃gylɛʀ] *a* quadrangular.

quadrilatère [k(w)adʀilatɛʀ] *nm* quadrilateral; four-sided area.

quadrillage [kadʀijaʒ] *nm* (*lignes etc*) square pattern, criss-cross pattern.

quadrillé, e [kadʀije] *a* (*papier*) squared.

quadriller [kadʀije] *vt* (*papier*) to mark out in squares; (*POLICE*) to keep under tight control, be positioned throughout.

quadrimoteur [k(w)adʀimɔtœʀ] *nm* four-engined plane.

quadripartite [kwadʀipaʀtit] *a* four-power; four-party.

quadriphonie [kadʀifɔni] *nf* quadraphony.

quadriréacteur [k(w)adʀiʀeaktœʀ] *nm* four-engined jet.

quadrupède [k(w)adʀypɛd] *nm* quadruped.

quadruple [k(w)adʀypl(ə)] *nm*: le ~ de four times as much as; **quadrupler** *vt, vi* to increase fourfold; **quadruplés, ées** *nm/fpl* quadruplets, quads.

quai [ke] *nm* (*de port*) quay; (*de gare*) platform; (*de cours d'eau, canal*) embankment; **être à** ~ (*navire*) to be alongside; (*train*) to be in the station.

qualificatif, ive [kalifikatif, -iv] *a* (*LING*) qualifying // *nm* (*terme*) term; (*LING*) qualifier.

qualification [kalifikasjɔ̃] *nf* qualification.

qualifier [kalifje] *vt* to qualify; (*appeler*): ~ qch/qn de to describe sth/sb as; se ~ *vi* (*SPORT*) to qualify; être qualifié pour to be qualified for.

qualité [kalite] *nf* quality; (*titre, fonction*) position; en ~ de in one's capacity as; avoir ~ pour to have authority to.

quand [kɑ̃] *cj, ad* when; ~ je serai riche when I'm rich; ~ même nevertheless; all the same; really; ~ bien même even though.

quant [kɑ̃]: ~ à *prép* as for, as to; regarding.

quant-à-soi [kɑ̃taswa] *nm*: rester sur son ~ to remain aloof.

quantième [kɑ̃tjɛm] *nm* day (of the month).

quantifier [kɑ̃tifje] *vt* to quantify.

quantitatif, ive [kɑ̃titatif, -iv] *a* quantitative.

quantité [kɑ̃tite] *nf* quantity, amount; (*SCIENCE*) quantity; (*grand nombre*): une ou des ~(s) de a great deal of; a lot of; en grande ~ in large quantities; du travail en ~ a great deal of work; ~ de many.

quarantaine [kaʀɑ̃tɛn] *nf* (*MÉD*) quarantine; **la** ~ forty, the forty mark; (*âge*) the forties *pl*; une ~ (de) forty or so, about forty; mettre en ~ to put into quarantine; (*fig*) to send to Coventry.

quarante [kaʀɑ̃t] *num* forty.

quart [kaʀ] *nm* (*fraction*) quarter; (*surveillance*) watch; (*partie*): un ~ de poulet/fromage a chicken quarter/a quarter of a cheese; un ~ de beurre a quarter kilo of butter, ≈ a half pound of butter; un ~ de vin a quarter litre of wine; une livre un ~ ou et ~ one and a quarter pounds; le ~ de a quarter of; ~ d'heure quarter of an hour; être de/prendre le ~ to keep/take the watch; ~ de tour quarter turn.

quarteron [kaʀtəʀɔ̃] *nm* (*péj*) small bunch, handful.

quartette [kwaʀtɛt] *nm* quartet(te).

quartier [kaʀtje] *nm* (*de ville*) district, area; (*de bœuf*) quarter; (*de fruit, fromage*) piece; ~s *nmpl* (*MIL, BLASON*) quarters; cinéma de ~ local cinema; avoir ~ libre (*MIL*) to have leave from barracks; ne pas faire de ~ to spare no-one, give no quarter; ~ général (QG) headquarters (HQ).

quartier-maître [kaʀtjemɛtʀ(ə)] *nm* ≈ leading seaman.

quartz [kwaʀts] *nm* quartz.

quasi [kazi] *ad* almost, nearly // *préfixe*: ~-certitude near certainty; ~ment *ad* almost, nearly.

quatorze [katɔʀz(ə)] *num* fourteen.

quatrain [katʀɛ̃] *nm* quatrain.

quatre [katʀ(ə)] *num* four; à ~ pattes on all fours; tiré à ~ épingles dressed up to the nines; faire les ~ cent coups to get a bit wild; se mettre en ~ pour qn to go out of one's way for sb; ~ à ~ (*monter, descendre*) four at a time; ~ -

vingt-dix *num* ninety; ~-vingts *num* eighty; quatrième *num* fourth.

quatuor [kwatyɔʀ] *nm* quartet(te).

que [kə] *cj* (*gén*) that; (*après comparatif*) than; as: *voir* plus, autant *etc*; il sait — tu es là he knows (that) you're here; je veux — tu acceptes I want you to accept; il a dit — oui he said he would (*ou* it was *etc*, *suivant le contexte*); si vous y allez ou — vous lui téléphoniez if you go there or (if you) phone him; quand il rentrera et qu'il aura mangé when he gets back and (when he) has eaten; qu'il le veuille ou non whether he likes it or not; tenez-le qu'il ne tombe pas hold it so (that) it doesn't fall; qu'il fasse ce qu'il voudra let him do as he pleases; *voir* avant, pour, tel *etc* // *ad*: qu'il *ou* qu'est-ce qu'il est bête/court vite he is so silly/runs so fast; — de what a lot of // *pronom*: l'homme — je vois the man (whom) I see; le livre — tu vois the book (that *ou* which) you see; un jour — j'étais a day when I was; c'est une erreur — de croire it's a mistake to believe; — fais-tu?, qu'est-ce que tu fais? what are you doing?; — préfères-tu, celui-ci ou celui-là? which do you prefer, this one or that one?

Québec [kebɛk] *nm*: le — Quebec.

quel, quelle [kɛl] *a*: — livre/ homme? what book/man?; (*parmi un certain choix*) which book/man?; — est cet homme/ce livre? who/what is this man/ book?; — est le plus grand? which is the tallest (*ou* biggest *etc*)?; —s acteurs préférez-vous? which actors do you prefer?; dans —s pays êtes-vous allé? which *ou* what countries did you go to?; —le surprise! what a surprise!; — que soit le coupable whoever is guilty; — que soit votre avis whatever your opinion; whichever is your opinion.

quelconque [kɛlkɔ̃k] *a* (*médiocre*) indifferent, poor; (*sans attrait*) ordinary, plain; (*indéfini*): un ami/ prétexte — some friend/pretext or other; un livre — suffira any book will do.

quelque [kɛlk(ə)] *dét* some; —s a few, some, *tournure interrogative* + any; les —s livres qui the few books which // *ad* (*environ*): — 100 mètres some 100 metres; — livre qu'il choisisse whatever (*ou* whichever) book he chooses; 20 kg et —(s) a bit over 20 kg; — chose something, *tournure interrogative* + anything; — chose d'autre something else; anything else; — part somewhere; — peu rather, somewhat; en — sorte as it were; quelquefois *ad* sometimes; quelques-uns, -unes [-z- œ] *pronom* some, a few.

quelqu'un, une [kɛlkœ̃, -yn] *pronom* someone, somebody, *tournure interrogative* + anyone *ou* anybody; — d'autre someone *ou* somebody else; anybody else.

quémander [kemɑ̃de] *vt* to beg for.

qu'en dira-t-on [kɑ̃diʀatɔ̃] *nm inv*: le — gossip, what people say.

quenelle [kənɛl] *nf* quenelle.

quenouille [kənuj] *nf* distaff.

querelle [kəʀɛl] *nf* quarrel.

quereller [kəʀele]: se — *vi* to quarrel; querelleur, euse *a* quarrelsome.

qu'est-ce que (*ou* qui) [kɛskə(ki)] *voir* que, qui.

question [kɛstjɔ̃] *nf* (*gén*) question; (*fig*) matter; issue; il a été — de we (*ou* they) spoke about; il est — de les emprisonner there's talk of them being jailed; de quoi est-il —? what is it about?; il n'en est pas — there's no question of it; en — in question; hors de — out of the question; remettre en — to question; poser la — de confiance (*POL*) to ask for a vote of confidence.

questionnaire [kɛstjɔnɛʀ] *nm* questionnaire; questionner *vt* to question.

quête [kɛt] *nf* collection; (*recherche*) quest, search; faire la — (*à l'église*) to take the collection; (*artiste*) to pass the hat round; en — de qch in search of sth; quêter *vi* (*à l'église*) to take the collection; (*dans la rue*) to collect money (for charity) // *vt* to seek.

quetsche [kwɛtʃ(ə)] *nf* damson.

queue [kø] *nf* tail; (*fig: du classement*) bottom; (: *de poêle*) handle; (: *de fruit, feuille*) stalk; (: *de train, colonne, file*) rear; en — (de train) at the rear of (the train); faire la — to queue (up); se mettre à la — to join the queue; à la — leu leu in single file; (*fig*) one after the other; — de cheval ponytail; — de poisson: faire une — de poisson à qn (*AUTO*) to cut in front of sb; —-de-pie *nf* (*habit*) tails *pl*, tail coat.

queux [kø] *am voir* maître.

qui [ki] *pronom* (*personne*) who, *prép* + whom; (*chose, animal*) which, that; qu'est-ce — est sur la table? what is on the table?; à — est ce sac? whose bag is this?; à — parlais-tu? who were you talking to?, to whom were you talking?; amenez — vous voulez bring who you like; — que ce soit whoever it may be.

quiche [kiʃ] *nf*: — lorraine quiche Lorraine.

quiconque [kikɔ̃k] *pronom* (*celui qui*) whoever, anyone who; (*personne*) anyone, anybody.

quidam [kɥidam] *nm* fellow.

quiétude [kjetyd] *nf* (*d'un lieu*) quiet, tranquillity; en toute — in complete peace; (*mentale*) with complete peace of mind.

quignon [kiɲɔ̃] *nm*: — de pain crust of bread; hunk of bread.

quille [kij] *nf* skittle; (jeu de) —s ninepins *sg*, skittles *sg*.

quincaillerie [kɛ̃kajʀi] *nf* (*ustensiles*) hardware, ironmongery; (*magasin*) hardware shop, ironmonger's; quincaillier, ère *nm/f* ironmonger.

quinconce [kɛ̃kɔ̃s] *nm*: en — in staggered rows.

quinine [kinin] *nf* quinine.

quinquagénaire [kɛ̃kaʒenɛʀ] *nm/f* man/woman in his/her fifties.

quinquennal, e, aux [kɛ̃kenal, -o] *a* five-year, quinquennial.

quintal, aux [kɛ̃tal, -o] *nm* quintal (*100 kg*).

quinte [kɛ̃t] *nf*: — (de toux) coughing fit.

quintette [kɛ̃tɛt] nm quintet(te).

quintuple [kɛ̃typl(ə)] nm: le ~ de five times as much as; quintupler vt, vi to increase fivefold; quintuplés, ées nm/fpl quintuplets, quins.

quinzaine [kɛ̃zɛn] nf: une ~ (de) about fifteen, fifteen or so; une ~ (de jours) a fortnight, two weeks.

quinze [kɛ̃z] num fifteen; demain en ~ a fortnight ou two weeks tomorrow; dans ~ jours in a fortnight('s time), in two weeks(' time).

quiproquo [kiprɔko] nm misunderstanding; (THÉÂTRE) (case of) mistaken identity.

quittance [kitɑ̃s] nf (reçu) receipt; (facture) bill.

quitte [kit] a: être ~ envers qn to be no longer in sb's debt; (fig) to be quits with sb; être ~ de (obligation) to be clear of; en être ~ à bon compte to get off lightly; ~ à faire even if it means doing; ~ ou double (jeu) double your money.

quitter [kite] vt to leave; (espoir, illusion) to give up; (vêtement) to take off; se ~ (couples, interlocuteurs) to part; ne quittez pas (au téléphone) hold the line.

qui-vive [kiviv] nm: être sur le ~ to be on the alert.

quoi [kwa] pronom (interrogatif) what; ~ de neuf? what's the news?; as-tu de ~ écrire? have you anything to write with?; il n'a pas de ~ se l'acheter he can't afford it, he hasn't got the money to buy it; ~ qu'il arrive whatever happens; ~ qu'il en soit be that as it may; ~ que ce soit anything at all; 'il n'y a pas de ~' '(please) don't mention it'; en ~ puis-je vous aider? how can I help you?

quoique [kwak(ə)] cj (al)though.

quolibet [kɔlibɛ] nm gibe, jeer.

quorum [kɔrɔm] nm quorum.

quota [kwɔta] nm quota.

quote-part [kɔtpar] nf share.

quotidien, ne [kɔtidjɛ̃, -ɛn] a daily; (banal) everyday // nm (journal) daily (paper).

quotient [kɔsjɑ̃] nm (MATH) quotient; ~ intellectuel (QI) intelligence quotient (IQ).

quotité [kɔtite] nf (FINANCE) quota.

R

r. abr de route, rue.

rabâcher [rabɑʃe] vt to harp on, keep on repeating.

rabais [rabɛ] nm reduction, discount; au ~ at a reduction ou discount.

rabaisser [rabese] vt (rabattre) to reduce; (dénigrer) to belittle.

rabat [raba] nm flap.

rabat-joie [rabaʒwa] nm/f inv killjoy, spoilsport.

rabatteur, euse [rabatœr, -øz] nm/f (de gibier) beater; (péj) tout.

rabattre [rabatr(ə)] vt (couvercle, siège) to pull ou close down; (col) to turn down; (gibier) to drive; (somme d'un prix) to deduct, take off; se ~ vi (bords, couvercle) to fall shut; (véhicule, coureur) to cut in; se ~ sur vt to fall back on.

rabbin [rabɛ̃] nm rabbi.

rabique [rabik] a rabies cpd.

râble [rɑbl(ə)] nm back; (CULIN) saddle.

râblé, e [rɑble] a broad-backed, stocky.

rabot [rabo] nm plane; raboter vt to plane (down).

raboteux, euse [rabotø, -øz] a uneven, rough.

rabougri, e [rabugri] a stunted.

rabrouer [rabrue] vt to snub, rebuff.

racaille [rakɑj] nf (péj) rabble, riffraff.

raccommodage [rakɔmɔdaʒ] nm mending q, repairing q; darning q.

raccommoder [rakɔmɔde] vt to mend, repair; (chaussette) to darn.

raccompagner [rakɔ̃paɲe] vt to take ou see back.

raccord [rakɔr] nm link; ~ de maçonnerie pointing q; ~ de peinture join; touch up.

raccordement [rakɔrdəmɑ̃] nm joining up.

raccorder [rakɔrde] vt to join (up), link up; (suj: pont etc) to connect, link; ~ au réseau du téléphone to connect to the telephone service.

raccourci [rakursi] nm short cut.

raccourcir [rakursir] vt to shorten // vi (vêtement) to shrink.

raccroc [rakro] nm: par ~ ad by chance.

raccrocher [rakroʃe] vt (tableau, vêtement) to hang back up; (récepteur) to put down // vi (TÉL) to hang up, ring off; se ~ à vt to cling to, hang on to.

race [ras] nf race; (d'animaux, fig: espèce) breed; (ascendance, origine) stock, race; de ~ a purebred, pedigree; racé, e a thoroughbred.

rachat [raʃa] nm buying; buying back; redemption; atonement.

racheter [raʃte] vt (article perdu) to buy another; (davantage): ~ du lait/3 œufs to buy more milk/another 3 eggs ou 3 more eggs; (après avoir vendu) to buy back; (d'occasion) to buy; (COMM: part, firme) to buy up; (: pension, rente) to redeem; (REL: pécheur) to redeem; (: péché) to atone for, expiate; (mauvaise conduite, oubli, défaut) to make up for; se ~ (REL) to redeem o.s.; (gén) to make amends, make up for it.

rachitique [raʃitik] a suffering from rickets; (fig) scraggy, scrawny.

racial, e, aux [rasjal, -o] a racial.

racine [rasin] nf root; ~ carrée/cubique square/cube root; prendre ~ (fig) to take root; to put down roots.

racisme [rasism(ə)] nm racism, racialism; raciste a, nm/f racist, racialist.

racket [rakɛt] nm racketeering q.

raclée [rɑkle] nf (fam) hiding, thrashing.

racler [rɑkle] vt (os, plat) to scrape; (tache, boue) to scrape off; (suj: chose: frotter contre) to scrape (against).

raclette [rɑklɛt] nf (CULIN) raclette (Swiss cheese dish).

racoler [rakɔle] vt (attirer: suj: prostituée) to solicit; (: parti, marchand) to tout for; (attraper) to pick up; racoleur, euse a (péj: publicité) cheap and alluring // nf streetwalker.

racontars [Rakɔ̃taR] *nmpl* stories, gossip *sg*.

raconter [Rakɔ̃te] *vt*: ~ (à qn) (*décrire*) to relate (to sb), tell (sb) about; (*dire*) to tell (sb).

racorni, e [RakɔRni] *a* hard(ened).

radar [RadaR] *nm* radar.

rade [Rad] *nf* (natural) harbour; **en ~ de Toulon** in Toulon harbour; **rester en ~** (*fig*) to be left stranded.

radeau, x [Rado] *nm* raft.

radial, e, aux [Radjal, -o] *a* radial; **pneu à carcasse ~e** radial tyre.

radiateur [RadjatœR] *nm* radiator, heater; (*AUTO*) radiator; ~ **électrique/à gaz** electric/gas heater *ou* fire.

radiation [Radjɑsjɔ̃] *nf* (*voir radier*) striking off *q*; (*PHYSIQUE*) radiation.

radical, e, aux [Radikal, -o] *a* radical // *nm* (*LING*) stem.

radier [Radje] *vt* to strike off.

radieux, euse [Radjø, -øz] *a* radiant; brilliant, glorious.

radin, e [Radɛ̃, -in] *a* (*fam*) stingy.

radio [Radjo] *nf* radio; (*MED*) X-ray // *nm* radiogram, radiotelegram; radio operator; **à la ~** on the radio; **se faire faire une ~** (*des poumons*) to have an X-ray taken (of one's lungs).

radio... [Radjo] *préfixe*: ~**actif, ive** radioactive; ~**activité** *nf* radioactivity; **radiodiffuser** *vt* to broadcast (by radio); ~**graphie** *nf* radiography; (*photo*) X-ray photograph, radiograph; ~**graphier** *vt* to X-ray; ~**logue** *nm/f* radiologist; ~**phonique** *a* radio *cpd*; ~**reportage** *nm* radio report; ~**scopie** *nf* radioscopy; ~**télégraphie** *nf* radiotelegraphy; ~**télévisé, e** *a* broadcast on radio and television.

radis [Radi] *nm* radish; ~ **noir** horseradish *q*.

radium [Radjɔm] *nm* radium.

radoter [Radɔte] *vi* to ramble on.

radoub [Radu] *nm*: **bassin de ~** dry dock.

radoucir [RadusiR]: **se ~** *vi* (*se réchauffer*) to become milder; (*se calmer*) to calm down; to soften.

rafale [Rafal] *nf* (*vent*) gust (of wind); (*tir*) burst of gunfire; ~ **de mitrailleuse** burst of machine-gun fire.

raffermir [RafɛRmiR] *vt*, **se ~** *vi* (*tissus, muscle*) to firm up; (*fig*) to strengthen.

raffinage [Rafinaʒ] *nm* refining.

raffiné, e [Rafine] *a* refined.

raffinement [Rafinmɑ̃] *nm* refinement.

raffiner [Rafine] *vt* to refine; **raffinerie** *nf* refinery.

raffoler [Rafɔle]: ~ **de** *vt* to be very keen on.

raffut [Rafy] *nm* (*fam*) row, racket.

rafistoler [Rafistɔle] *vt* (*fam*) to patch up.

rafle [Rɑfl(ə)] *nf* (*de police*) roundup, raid.

rafler [Rɑfle] *vt* (*fam*) to swipe, run off with.

rafraîchir [RafReʃiR] *vt* (*atmosphère, température*) to cool (down); (*aussi*: **mettre à ~**) to chill; (*suj: air, eau*) to freshen up; (: *boisson*) to refresh; (*fig: rénover*) to brighten up; **se ~** to grow cooler; to freshen up; to refresh o.s.;

rafraîchissant, e *a* refreshing; **rafraîchissement** *nm* cooling; (*boisson etc*) cool drink, refreshment.

ragaillardir [RagajaRdiR] *vt* (*fam*) to perk *ou* buck up.

rage [Raʒ] *nf* (*MED*): **la ~** rabies; (*fureur*) rage, fury; **faire ~** to rage; ~ **de dents** (raging) toothache; **rager** *vi* to fume (with rage); **rageur, euse** *a* snarling; ill-tempered.

raglan [Raglɑ̃] *a inv* raglan.

ragot [Rago] *nm* (*fam*) malicious gossip *q*.

ragoût [Ragu] *nm* (*plat*) stew.

rai [Rɛ] *nm*: **un ~ de soleil/lumière** a sunray/ray of light.

raid [Rɛd] *nm* (*MIL*) raid; (*SPORT*) long-distance trek.

raide [Rɛd] *a* (*tendu*) taut, tight; (*escarpé*) steep; (*droit: cheveux*) straight; (*ankylosé, dur, guindé*) stiff; (*fam*) steep, stiff; stony broke // *ad* (*en pente*) steeply; ~ **mort** stone dead; **raideur** *nf* steepness; stiffness; **raidir** *vt* (*muscles*) to stiffen; (*câble*) to pull taut, tighten; **se raidir** *vi* to stiffen; to become taut; (*personne*) to tense up; to brace o.s.; to harden.

raie [Rɛ] *nf* (*ZOOL*) skate, ray; (*rayure*) stripe; (*des cheveux*) parting.

raifort [RɛfɔR] *nm* horseradish.

rail [Rɑj] *nm* (*barre d'acier*) rail; (*chemins de fer*) railways *pl*; **les ~s** (*la voie ferrée*) the rails, the track *sg*; **par ~** by rail; ~ **conducteur** live *ou* conductor rail.

railler [Rɑje] *vt* to scoff at, jeer at.

rainure [RenyR] *nf* groove; slot.

rais [Rɛ] *nm* = **rai**.

raisin [Rezɛ̃] *nm* (*aussi*: ~**s**) grapes *pl*; (*variété*): ~ **muscat** muscat grape; ~**s secs** raisins, currants.

raison [Rezɔ̃] *nf* reason; **avoir ~** to be right; **donner ~ à qn** to agree with sb; to prove sb right; **avoir ~ de qn/qch** to get the better of sb/sth; **se faire une ~** to learn to live with it; **perdre la ~** to become insane; to take leave of one's senses; **demander ~ à qn de** (*affront etc*) to demand satisfaction from sb for; ~ **de plus** all the more reason; **à plus forte ~** all the more so; **en ~ de** because of; according to; in proportion to; **à ~ de** at the rate of; ~ **sociale** corporate name; **raisonnable** *a* reasonable, sensible.

raisonnement [Rezɔnmɑ̃] *nm* reasoning; arguing; argument.

raisonner [Rezɔne] *vi* (*penser*) to reason; (*argumenter, discuter*) to argue // *vt* (*personne*) to reason with; (*attitude: justifier*) to reason out.

rajeunir [RaʒœniR] *vt* (*suj: coiffure, robe*): ~ **qn** to make sb look younger; (*suj: cure etc*) to rejuvenate; (*fig*) to brighten up; to give a new look to; to inject new blood into // *vi* to become (*ou* look) younger.

rajouter [Raʒute] *vt*: ~ **du sel/un œuf** to add some more salt/another egg; ~ **que** to add that.

rajuster [RaʒystE] *vt* (*vêtement*) to straighten, tidy; (*salaires*) to adjust; (*machine*) to readjust; **se ~** to tidy *ou* straighten o.s. up.

râle [Rɑl] *nm* groan; ~ **d'agonie** death rattle.

ralenti [Ralãti] nm: **au ~** (AUTO): **tourner au ~** to tick over, idle; (CINÉMA) in slow motion; (fig) at a slower pace.

ralentir [Ralãtir] vt, vi, **se ~** vi to slow down.

râler [Rale] vi to groan; (fam) to grouse, moan (and groan).

ralliement [Ralimã] nm rallying.

rallier [Ralje] vt (rassembler) to rally; (rejoindre) to rejoin; (gagner à sa cause) to win over; **se ~ à** (avis) to come over ou round to.

rallonge [Ralɔ̃ʒ] nf (de table) (extra) leaf (pl leaves); (de vêtement etc) extra piece.

rallonger [Ralɔ̃ʒe] vt to lengthen.

rallumer [Ralyme] vt to light up again; (fig) to revive; **se ~** vi (lumière) to come on again.

rallye [Rali] nm rally; (POL) march.

ramages [Ramaʒ] nmpl leaf pattern sg; songs.

ramassage [Ramɑsaʒ] nm: **~ scolaire** school bus service.

ramassé, e [Ramɑse] a (trapu) squat, stocky.

ramasse-miettes [Ramɑsmjɛt] nm inv table-tidy.

ramasse-monnaie [Ramɑsmɔnɛ] nm inv change-tray.

ramasser [Ramɑse] vt (objet tombé ou par terre, fam) to pick up; (recueillir) to collect; (récolter) to gather; (: pommes de terre) to lift; **se ~** vi (sur soi-même) to huddle up; to crouch; **ramasseur, euse de balles** nm/f ballboy/girl; **ramassis** nm (péj) bunch; jumble.

rambarde [Rãbard(ə)] nf guardrail.

rame [Ram] nf (aviron) oar; (de métro) train; (de papier) ream; **~ de haricots** bean support.

rameau, x [Ramo] nm (small) branch; **les R~x** (REL) Palm Sunday sg.

ramener [Ramne] vt to bring back; (reconduire) to take back; (rabattre: couverture, visière): **~ qch sur** to pull sth back over; **~ qch à** (réduire à, aussi MATH) to reduce sth to; **se ~** vi (fam) to roll ou turn up; **se ~ à** (se réduire à) to come ou boil down to.

ramer [Rame] vi to row; **rameur, euse** nm/f rower.

ramier [Ramje] nm: **(pigeon) ~** woodpigeon.

ramification [Ramifikɑsjɔ̃] nf ramification.

ramifier [Ramifje]: **se ~** vi (tige, secte, réseau): **se ~ (en)** to branch out (into); (veines, nerfs) to ramify.

ramollir [Ramɔlir] vt to soften; **se ~** vi to go soft.

ramoner [Ramɔne] vt to sweep; **ramoneur** nm (chimney) sweep.

rampe [Rãp] nf (d'escalier) banister(s pl); (dans un garage, d'un terrain) ramp; (THÉÂTRE): **la ~** the footlights pl; **~ de lancement** launching pad.

ramper [Rãpe] vi to crawl.

rancard [Rãkar] nm (fam) date; tip.

rancart [Rãkar] nm: **mettre au ~** to scrap.

rance [Rãs] a rancid.

rancœur [Rãkœr] nf rancour, resentment.

rançon [Rãsɔ̃] nf ransom; (fig) price.

rancune [Rãkyn] nf grudge, rancour; **garder ~ à qn (de qch)** to bear sb a grudge (for sth); **sans ~!** no hard feelings!; **rancunier, ière** a vindictive, spiteful.

randonnée [Rãdɔne] nf ride; (à pied) walk, ramble; hike, hiking q.

rang [Rã] nm (rangée) row; (grade, condition sociale, classement) rank; **~s** (MIL) ranks; **se mettre en ~s/sur un ~** to get into ou form rows/a line; **sur 3 ~s** (lined up) 3 deep; **se mettre en ~s par 4** to form four rows of 4; **se mettre sur les ~s** (fig) to get into the running; **au premier ~** in the first row; (fig) ranking first; **avoir ~ de** to hold the rank of.

rangé, e [Rãʒe] a (sérieux) orderly, steady.

rangée [Rãʒe] nf row.

ranger [Rãʒe] vt (classer, grouper) to order, arrange; (mettre à sa place) to put away; (mettre de l'ordre dans) to tidy up; (arranger, disposer: en cercle etc) to arrange; (fig: classer): **~ qn/qch parmi** to rank sb/sth among; **se ~** vi (véhicule, conducteur: s'écarter) to pull over; (: s'arrêter) to pull in; (piéton) to step aside; (s'assagir) to settle down; **se ~ à** (avis) to come round to, fall in with.

ranimer [Ranime] vt (personne évanouie) to bring round; (revigorer: forces, courage) to restore; (réconforter: troupes etc) to kindle new life in; (douleur, souvenir) to revive; (feu) to rekindle.

rapace [Rapas] nm bird of prey // a (péj) rapacious, grasping.

rapatrier [Rapatrije] vt to repatriate; (capitaux) to bring (back) home.

râpe [Rɑp] nf (CULIN) grater; (à bois) rasp.

râpé, e [Rɑpe] a (tissu) threadbare; (CULIN) grated.

râper [Rɑpe] vt (CULIN) to grate; (gratter, râcler) to rasp.

rapetasser [Raptase] vt (fam) to patch up.

rapetisser [Raptise] vt: **~ qch** to shorten sth; to make sth look smaller // vi, **se ~** vi to shrink.

rapide [Rapid] a fast; (prompt) quick // nm express (train); (de cours d'eau) rapid; **~ment** ad fast; quickly; **rapidité** nf speed; quickness.

rapiécer [Rapjese] vt to patch.

rappel [Rapɛl] nm (d'un ambassadeur, MIL) recall; (THÉÂTRE) curtain call; (MÉD: vaccination) booster; (ADMIN: de salaire) back pay q; (d'une aventure, d'un nom) reminder; (TECH) return; (NAVIG) sitting out q; (ALPINISME: aussi: **~ de corde**) abseiling q, roping down q, abseil; **~ à l'ordre** call to order.

rappeler [Raple] vt (pour faire revenir, retéléphoner) to call back; (ambassadeur, MIL) to recall; (faire se souvenir): **~ qch à qn** to remind sb of sth; **se ~** vt (se souvenir de) to remember, recall; **~ qn à la vie** to bring sb back to life; **ça rappelle la Provence** it's reminiscent of Provence, it reminds you of Provence.

rappliquer [Raplike] vi (fam) to turn up.

rapport [Rapɔʀ] nm (compte rendu) report ; (profit) yield, return ; revenue ; (lien, analogie) relationship ; (proportion: MATH, TECH) ratio (pl s) ; ~s nmpl (entre personnes, pays) relations : avoir ~ à to have something to do with, concern ; être en ~ avec (idée de corrélation) to be in keeping with ; être/se mettre en ~ avec qn to have dealings with sb/get in touch with sb ; par ~ à in relation to ; with regard to ; sous le ~ de from the point of view of ; ~s (sexuels) (sexual) intercourse sg.

rapporter [Rapɔʀte] vt (rendre, ramener) to bring back ; (apporter davantage) to bring more ; (COUTURE) to sew on ; (suj: investissement) to yield ; (: activité) to bring in ; (relater) to report ; (JUR: annuler) to revoke // vi (investissement) to give a good return ou yield ; (: activité) to be very profitable ; ~ qch à (fig: rattacher) to relate sth to ; se ~ à (correspondre à) to relate to ; s'en ~ à to rely on ; rapporteur, euse nm/f (de procès, commission) reporter ; (péj) telltale // nm (GEOM) protractor.

rapproché, e [Rapʀɔʃe] a (proche) near, close at hand ; ~s (l'un de l'autre) at close intervals.

rapprochement [Rapʀɔʃmɑ̃] nm (reconciliation: de nations, familles) reconciliation ; (analogie, rapport) parallel.

rapprocher [Rapʀɔʃe] vt (chaise d'une table) : ~ qch (de) to bring sth closer (to) ; (deux tuyaux) to bring closer together ; (réunir) to bring together ; (établir une analogie entre) to establish a parallel between ; se ~ vi to draw closer ou nearer ; (fig: familles, pays) to come together ; to come closer together ; se ~ de to come closer to ; (présenter une analogie avec) to be close to.

rapt [Rapt] nm abduction.

raquette [Raket] nf (de tennis) racket ; (de ping-pong) bat ; (à neige) snowshoe.

rare [RaR] a rare ; (main-d'œuvre, denrées) scarce ; (cheveux, herbe) sparse.

raréfier [Raʀefje]: se ~ vi to grow scarce ; (air) to rarefy.

rarement [RaRmɑ̃] ad rarely, seldom.

rareté [RaRte] nf rarity ; scarcity.

ras, e [Ra, Raz] a (tête, cheveux) close-cropped ; (poil, herbe) short // ad short ; en ~e campagne in open country ; à ~ bords to the brim ; au ~ de level with ; en avoir ~ le bol (fam) to be fed up ; ~ du cou a (pull, robe) crew-neck.

rasade [Razad] nf glassful.

rasé, e [Raze] a: ~ de frais freshly shaven ; ~ de près close-shaven.

rase-mottes [Razmɔt] nm inv: faire du ~ to hedgehop.

raser [Raze] vt (barbe, cheveux) to shave off ; (menton, personne) to shave ; (fam: ennuyer) to bore ; (démolir) to raze (to the ground) ; (frôler) to graze ; to skim ; se ~ to shave ; (fam) to be bored (to tears) ; rasoir nm razor ; rasoir électrique electric shaver ou razor ; rasoir de sûreté safety razor.

rassasier [Rasazje] vt to satisfy ; être rassasié (dégoûté) to be sated ; to have had more than enough.

rassemblement [Rasɑ̃bləmɑ̃] nm (groupe) gathering ; (POL) union ; association ; (MIL): le ~ parade.

rassembler [Rasɑ̃ble] vt (réunir) to assemble, gather ; (regrouper, amasser) to gather together, collect ; se ~ vi to gather.

rasseoir [RaswaR]: se ~ vi to sit down again.

rasséréner [RaseRene]: se ~ vi to recover one's serenity.

rassis, e [Rasi, -iz] a (pain) stale.

rassurer [RasyRe] vt to reassure ; se ~ to feel reassured ; rassure-toi put your mind at rest ou at ease.

rat [Ra] nm rat ; ~ d'hôtel hotel thief (pl thieves) ; ~ musqué muskrat.

ratatiné, e [Ratatine] a shrivelled (up), wrinkled.

rate [Rat] nf spleen.

raté, e [Rate] a (tentative) unsuccessful, failed // nm/f failure // nm misfiring q.

râteau, x [Rato] nm rake.

râtelier [Ratəlje] nm rack ; (fam) false teeth pl.

rater [Rate] vi (affaire, projet etc) to go wrong, fail // vt (cible, train, occasion) to miss ; (démonstration, plat) to spoil ; (examen) to fail.

ratifier [Ratifje] vt to ratify.

ration [Rasjɔ̃] nf ration ; (fig) share.

rationnel, le [Rasjɔnɛl] a rational.

rationnement [Rasjɔnmɑ̃] nm rationing ; ticket de ~ ration coupon.

rationner [Rasjɔne] vt to ration.

ratisser [Ratise] vt (allée) to rake ; (feuiller) to rake up ; (suj: armée, police) to comb.

raton [Ratɔ̃] nm: ~ laveur raccoon.

R.A.T.P. sigle f (= Régie autonome des transports parisiens) Paris transport authority.

rattacher [Rataʃe] vt (animal, cheveux) to tie up again ; (incorporer: ADMIN etc): ~ qch à to join sth to, unite sth with ; (fig: relier): ~ qch à to link sth with, relate sth to ; (: lier): ~ qn à to bind ou tie sb to.

rattrapage [RatRapaʒ] nm (SCOL) remedial classes pl.

rattraper [RatRape] vt (fugitif) to recapture ; (retenir, empêcher de tomber) to catch (hold of) ; (atteindre, rejoindre) to catch up with ; (réparer: imprudence, erreur) to make up for ; se ~ vi to make up for lost time ; to make good one's losses ; to make up for it ; se ~ (à) (se raccrocher) to stop o.s. falling (by catching hold of).

rature [RatyR] nf deletion, erasure ; **raturer** vt to cross out, delete, erase.

rauque [Rok] a raucous ; hoarse.

ravagé, e [Ravaʒe] a (visage) harrowed.

ravager [Ravaʒe] vt to devastate, ravage.

ravages [Ravaʒ] nmpl ravages ; faire des ~ to wreak havoc.

ravaler [Ravale] vt (mur, façade) to restore ; (déprécier) to lower ; ~ sa colère/son dégoût to stifle one's anger/distaste.

ravauder [Ravode] vt to repair, mend.

rave [Rav] nf (BOT) rape.

ravi, e [Ravi] a delighted ; être ~ de/que to be delighted with/that.

ravier [Ravje] *nm* hors d'œuvre dish.
ravigote [Ravigɔt] *a*: **sauce** ~ oil and vinegar dressing with shallots.
ravigoter [Ravigɔte] *vt* (*fam*) to buck up.
ravin [Ravɛ̃] *nm* gully, ravine.
raviner [Ravine] *vt* to furrow, gully.
ravir [RaviR] *vt* (*enchanter*) to delight; (*enlever*): ~ qch à qn to rob sb of sth; **à** ~ *ad* beautifully.
raviser [Ravize]: **se** ~ *vi* to change one's mind.
ravissant, e [Ravisɑ̃, -ɑ̃t] *a* delightful; ravishing.
ravisseur, euse [RavisœR, -øz] *nm/f* abductor.
ravitaillement [Ravitɑjmɑ̃] *nm* resupplying; refuelling; (*provisions*) supplies *pl*; **aller au** ~ to go for fresh supplies.
ravitailler [Ravitɑje] *vt* to resupply; (*véhicule*) to refuel; **se** ~ *vi* to get fresh supplies.
raviver [Ravive] *vt* (*feu, douleur*) to revive; (*couleurs*) to brighten up.
ravoir [RavwaR] *vt* to get back.
rayé, e [Reje] *a* (*à rayures*) striped; (*éraflé*) scratched.
rayer [Reje] *vt* (*érafler*) to scratch; (*barrer*) to cross ou score out; (*d'une liste: radier*) to cross ou strike off.
rayon [Rɛjɔ̃] *nm* (*de soleil etc*) ray; (GEOM) radius; (*de roue*) spoke; (*étagère*) shelf (*pl* shelves); (*de grand magasin*) department; (*de ruche*) (honey)comb; **dans un** ~ **de** within a radius of; ~ **d'action** range; ~ **de soleil** sunbeam, ray of sunlight; ~**s X** X-rays.
rayonnage [Rɛjɔnaʒ] *nm* set of shelves.
rayonnement [Rɛjɔnmɑ̃] *nm* radiation; (*fig*) radiance; influence.
rayonner [Rɛjɔne] *vi* (*chaleur, énergie*) to radiate; (*fig*) to shine forth; to be radiant; (*avenues, axes etc*) to radiate; (*touriste*) to go touring (*from one base*).
rayure [RɛjyR] *nf* (*motif*) stripe; (*éraflure*) scratch; (*rainure, d'un fusil*) groove; **à** ~**s** striped.
raz-de-marée [RɑdmaRe] *nm inv* tidal wave.
razzia [Razja] *nf* raid, foray.
ré [Re] *nm* (MUS) D; (*en chantant la gamme*) re.
réacteur [ReaktœR] *nm* jet engine.
réaction [Reaksjɔ̃] *nf* reaction; **moteur à** ~ jet engine; ~ **en chaine** chain reaction; **réactionnaire** *a* reactionary.
réadapter [Readapte] *vt* to readjust; (MED) to rehabilitate; **se** ~ (**à**) to readjust (to).
réaffirmer [ReafiRme] *vt* to reaffirm, reassert.
réagir [ReaʒiR] *vi* to react.
réalisateur, trice [RealizatœR, -tRis] *nm/f* (TV, CINEMA) director.
réalisation [Realizɑsjɔ̃] *nf* carrying out; realization; fulfilment; achievement; production; (*œuvre*) production; creation; work.
réaliser [Realize] *vt* (*projet, opération*) to carry out, realize; (*rêve, souhait*) to realize, fulfil; (*exploit*) to achieve; (*achat, vente*)

to make; (*film*) to produce; (*se rendre compte de*, COMM: *bien, capital*) to realize; **se** ~ *vi* to be realized.
réaliste [Realist(ə)] *a* realistic; (*peintre, roman*) realist // *nm/f* realist.
réalité [Realite] *nf* reality; **en** ~ in (actual) fact; **dans la** ~ in reality.
réanimation [Reanimɑsjɔ̃] *nf* resuscitation; **service de** ~ intensive care unit.
réarmer [ReaRme] *vt* (*arme*) to reload // *vi* (*état*) to rearm.
réassurance [ReasyRɑ̃s] *nf* reinsurance.
rébarbatif, ive [RebaRbatif, -iv] *a* forbidding, off-putting.
rebattre [Rəbatr(ə)] *vt*: ~ **les oreilles à** qn de qch to keep harping on to sb about sth; **rebattu, e** a hackneyed.
rebelle [Rəbɛl] *nm/f* rebel // *a* (*troupes*) rebel; (*enfant*) rebellious; (*mèche etc*) unruly; ~ **à** unamenable to; unwilling to + *verbe*.
rebeller [Rəbele]: **se** ~ *vi* to rebel.
rébellion [Rebeljɔ̃] *nf* rebellion; (*rebelles*) rebel forces *pl*.
reboiser [Rəbwaze] *vt* to replant with trees, reafforest.
rebondi, e [Rəbɔ̃di] *a* rounded; chubby, well-rounded.
rebondir [Rəbɔ̃diR] *vi* (*ballon: au sol*) to bounce; (: *contre un mur*) to rebound; (*fig: procès, action, conversation*) to get moving again, be suddenly revived; **rebondissements** *nmpl* (*fig*) twists and turns, sudden revivals.
rebord [RəbɔR] *nm* edge.
rebours [RəbuR]: **à** ~ *ad* the wrong way.
rebouteux, euse [Rəbutø, -øz] *nm/f* (*péj*) bonesetter.
rebrousse-poil [RbRuspwal]: **à** ~ *ad* the wrong way.
rebrousser [RəbRuse] *vt*: ~ **chemin** to turn back.
rebuffade [Rəbyfad] *nf* rebuff.
rébus [Rebys] *nm inv* rebus.
rebut [Rəby] *nm*: **mettre au** ~ to scrap, discard.
rebuter [Rəbyte] *vt* to put off.
récalcitrant, e [RekalsitRɑ̃, -ɑ̃t] *a* refractory.
recaler [Rəkale] *vt* (SCOL) to fail.
récapituler [Rekapityle] *vt* to recapitulate; to sum up.
recel [Rəsɛl] *nm* receiving (stolen goods).
receler [Rəsəle] *vt* (*produit d'un vol*) to receive; (*malfaiteur*) to harbour; (*fig*) to conceal; **receleur, euse** *nm/f* receiver.
récemment [Resamɑ̃] *ad* recently.
recensement [Rəsɑ̃smɑ̃] *nm* census; inventory.
recenser [Rəsɑ̃se] *vt* (*population*) to take a census of; (*inventorier*) to make an inventory of; (*dénombrer*) to list.
récent, e [Resɑ̃, -ɑ̃t] *a* recent.
récépissé [Resepise] *nm* receipt.
récepteur, trice [ReseptœR, -tRis] *a* receiving // *nm* receiver; ~ (**de radio**) radio set ou receiver.
réception [Resɛpsjɔ̃] *nf* receiving q; (*accueil*) reception, welcome; (*bureau*) reception desk; (*réunion mondaine*)

reception, party; (*pièces*) reception rooms *pl*; (*SPORT*: *après un saut*) landing; (: *du ballon*) catching *q*; **jour/heures de ~** day/hours for receiving visitors (*ou* students *etc*); (*MÉD*) surgery day/hours; **réceptionnaire** *nm/f* receiving clerk; **réceptionner** *vt* (*COMM*) to take delivery of; (*SPORT*: *ballon*) to catch (and control); **réceptionniste** *nm/f* receptionist.

récession [Resesjɔ̃] *nf* recession.

recette [Rəsɛt] *nf* (*CULIN*) recipe; (*fig*) formula, recipe; (*COMM*) takings *pl*; (*ADMIN*: *bureau*) tax *ou* revenue office; **~s** *nfpl* (*COMM*: *rentrées*) receipts.

receveur, euse [RəsvœR, -øz] *nm/f* (*des contributions*) tax collector; (*des postes*) postmaster/mistress; (*d'autobus*) conductor/conductress.

recevoir [RəsvwaR] *vt* to receive; (*lettre, prime*) to receive, get; (*client, patient, représentant*) to see; (*SCOL*: *candidat*) to pass // *vi* to receive visitors; to give parties; to see patients *etc*; **se ~** *vi* (*athlète*) to land; **être reçu** (*à un examen*) to pass.

rechange [Rəʃɑ̃ʒ]: **de ~** *a* (*pièces, roue*) spare; (*fig*: *plan*) alternative; **des vêtements de ~** a change of clothes.

rechaper [Rəʃape] *vt* to remould, retread.

réchapper [Reʃape]: **~ de** *ou* **à** *vt* (*accident, maladie*) to come through.

recharge [RəʃaRʒ(ə)] *nf* refill.

recharger [RəʃaRʒe] *vt* (*camion, fusil, appareil-photo*) to reload; (*briquet, stylo*) to refill; (*batterie*) to recharge.

réchaud [Reʃo] *nm* (portable) stove; plate-warmer.

réchauffer [Reʃofe] *vt* (*plat*) to reheat; (*mains, personne*) to warm; **se ~** *vi* (*température*) to get warmer.

rêche [Rɛʃ] *a* rough.

recherche [RəʃɛRʃ(ə)] *nf* (*action*): **la ~ de** the search for; (*raffinement*) affectedness, studied elegance; (*scientifique etc*): **la ~** research; **~s** *nfpl* (*de la police*) investigations; (*scientifiques*) research *sg*; **être/se mettre à la ~ de** to be/go in search of.

recherché, e [RəʃɛRʃe] *a* (*rare, demandé*) much sought-after; (*raffiné*) studied, affected.

rechercher [RəʃɛRʃe] *vt* (*objet égaré, fugitif*) to look for, search for; (*témoins, main-d'œuvre*) to look for; (*causes d'un phénomène, nouveau procédé*) to try to find; (*bonheur etc, l'amitié de qn*) to seek.

rechigner [Rəʃiɲe] *vi*: **~ (à)** to balk (at).

rechute [Rəʃyt] *nf* (*MÉD*) relapse; (*dans le péché, le vice*) lapse; **faire une ~** to have a relapse.

récidiver [Residive] *vi* to commit a second (*ou* subsequent) offence; (*fig*) to do it again; **récidiviste** *nm/f* second (*ou* habitual) offender, recidivist.

récif [Resif] *nm* reef.

récipient [Resipjɑ̃] *nm* container.

réciproque [ResipRɔk] *a* reciprocal; **~ment** *ad* reciprocally; **et ~ment** and vice versa.

récit [Resi] *nm* story.

récital [Resital] *nm* recital.

récitation [Resitasjɔ̃] *nf* recitation.

réciter [Resite] *vt* to recite.

réclamation [Reklamasjɔ̃] *nf* complaint; **~s** (*bureau*) complaints department *sg*.

réclame [Reklam] *nf*: **la ~** advertising; **une ~** an advert(isement); **article en ~** special offer.

réclamer [Reklame] *vt* (*aide, nourriture etc*) to ask for; (*revendiquer*: *dû, part, indemnité*) to claim, demand; (*nécessiter*) to demand, require // *vi* to complain; **se ~ de** to give as one's authority; to claim filiation with.

reclasser [Rəklase] *vt* (*fig*: *fonctionnaire etc*) to regrade.

reclus, e [Rəkly, -yz] *nm/f* recluse.

réclusion [Reklyzjɔ̃] *nf* imprisonment.

recoin [Rəkwɛ̃] *nm* nook, corner; (*fig*) hidden recess.

reçois *etc* *vb* *voir* **recevoir**.

récolte [Rekɔlt(ə)] *nf* harvesting; gathering; (*produits*) harvest, crop; (*fig*) crop, collection.

récolter [Rekɔlte] *vt* to harvest, gather (in); (*fig*) to collect; to get.

recommandable [Rəkɔmɑ̃dabl(ə)] *a* commendable.

recommandation [Rəkɔmɑ̃dasjɔ̃] *nf* recommendation.

recommandé [Rəkɔmɑ̃de] *nm* (*POSTES*): **en ~** by registered mail.

recommander [Rəkɔmɑ̃de] *vt* to recommend; (*suj*: *qualités etc*) to commend; (*POSTES*) to register; **~ à qn de faire** to recommend sb to do; **se ~ à qn** to commend o.s. to sb; **se ~ de qn** to give sb's name as a reference.

recommencer [Rəkɔmɑ̃se] *vt* (*reprendre*: *lutte, séance*) to resume, start again; (*refaire*: *travail, explications*) to start afresh, start (over) again; (*récidiver*: *erreur*) to make again // *vi* to start again; (*récidiver*) to do it again.

récompense [Rekɔ̃pɑ̃s] *nf* reward; (*prix*) award; **récompenser** *vt*: **récompenser qn (de** *ou* **pour)** to reward sb for.

réconciliation [Rekɔ̃siljasjɔ̃] *nf* reconciliation.

réconcilier [Rekɔ̃silje] *vt* to reconcile; **~ qn avec qch** to reconcile sb to sth; **se ~ (avec)** to be reconciled (with).

reconduction [Rəkɔ̃dyksjɔ̃] *nf* renewal.

reconduire [Rəkɔ̃dɥiR] *vt* (*raccompagner*) to take *ou* see back; (*JUR, POL*: *renouveler*) to renew.

réconfort [Rekɔ̃fɔR] *nm* comfort.

réconforter [Rekɔ̃fɔRte] *vt* (*consoler*) to comfort; (*revigorer*) to fortify.

reconnaissance [Rəkɔnɛsɑ̃s] *nf* recognition; acknowledgement; (*gratitude*) gratitude, gratefulness; (*MIL*) reconnaissance, recce; **~ de dette** acknowledgement of a debt, IOU.

reconnaissant, e [Rəkɔnɛsɑ̃, -ɑ̃t] *a* grateful; **je vous serais ~ de bien vouloir !** I should be most grateful if you would (kindly).

reconnaître [RəkɔnɛtR(ə)] *vt* to recognize; (*MIL*: *lieu*) to reconnoitre; (*JUR*: *enfant, dette, droit*) to acknowledge; **~ que** to admit *ou* acknowledge that; **~ qn/qch**

à (*l'identifier grâce à*) to recognize sb/sth by.

reconstituant, e [Rəkɔ̃stityɑ̃, -ɑ̃t] *a* (*régime*) strength-building // *nm* tonic, pick-me-up.

reconstituer [Rəkɔ̃stitɥe] *vt* (*monument ancien*) to recreate, build a replica of; (*fresque, vase brisé*) to piece together, reconstitute; (*événement, accident*) to reconstruct; (*fortune, patrimoine*) to rebuild; (BIO: *tissus etc*) to regenerate; **reconstitution** *nf* (JUR: *d'accident etc*) reconstruction.

reconstruire [Rəkɔ̃stRɥiR] *vt* to rebuild.

record [RəkɔR] *nm, a* record.

recoupement [Rəkupmɑ̃] *nm*: par ~ by cross-checking.

recouper: **se** ~ *vi* (*témoignages*) to tie *ou* match up.

recourbé, e [RəkuRbe] *a* curved; hooked; bent.

recourir [RəkuRiR]: ~ **à** *vt* (*ami, agence*) to turn *ou* appeal to; (*force, ruse, emprunt*) to resort *ou* have recourse to.

recours [RəkuR] *nm* (JUR) appeal; **avoir** ~ **à** = **recourir à**; **en dernier** ~ as a last resort; **sans** ~ final; with no way out; ~ **en grâce** plea for clemency (*ou* pardon).

recouvrer [RəkuvRe] *vt* (*vue, santé etc*) to recover, regain; (*impôts*) to collect; (*créance*) to recover.

recouvrir [RəkuvRiR] *vt* (*couvrir à nouveau*) to re-cover; (*couvrir entièrement, aussi fig*) to cover; (*cacher, masquer*) to conceal, hide; **se** ~ (*se superposer*) to overlap.

recracher [RəkRaʃe] *vt* to spit out.

récréatif, ive [RekReatif, -iv] *a* of entertainment; recreational.

récréation [RekReɑsjɔ̃] *nf* recreation, entertainment; (SCOL) break.

récrier [RekRije]: **se** ~ *vi* to exclaim.

récriminations [RekRiminɑsjɔ̃] *nfpl* remonstrations, complaints.

recroqueviller [RəkRɔkvije]: **se** ~ *vi* (*feuilles*) to curl *ou* shrivel up; (*personne*) to huddle up.

recru, e [RəkRy] *a*: ~ **de fatigue** exhausted // *nf* recruit.

recrudescence [RəkRydesɑ̃s] *nf* fresh outbreak.

recrue [RəkRy] *a, nf voir* **recru**.

recruter [RəkRyte] *vt* to recruit.

rectal, e, aux [REktal, -o] *a*: **par voie** ~e rectally.

rectangle [REktɑ̃gl(ə)] *nm* rectangle; **rectangulaire** *a* rectangular.

recteur [REktœR] *nm* ≈ (regional) director of education.

rectificatif, ive [REktifikatif, -iv] *a* corrected // *nm* correction.

rectification [REktifikɑsjɔ̃] *nf* correction.

rectifier [REktifje] *vt* (*tracé, virage*) to straighten; (*calcul, adresse*) to correct; (*erreur, faute*) to rectify, put right.

rectiligne [REktiliɲ] *a* straight; (GÉOM) rectilinear.

rectitude [REktityd] *nf* rectitude, uprightness.

reçu, e [Rəsy] *pp de* **recevoir** // *a* (*admis, consacré*) accepted // *nm* (COMM) receipt.

recueil [Rəkœj] *nm* collection.

recueillement [Rəkœjmɑ̃] *nm* meditation, contemplation.

recueillir [RəkœjiR] *vt* to collect; (*voix, suffrages*) to win; (*accueillir: réfugiés, chat*) to take in; **se** ~ *vi* to gather one's thoughts; to meditate.

recul [Rəkyl] *nm* retreat; recession; decline; (*d'arme à feu*) recoil, kick; **avoir un mouvement de** ~ to recoil, start back; **prendre du** ~ to stand back; **avec le** ~ with the passing of time, in retrospect.

reculade [Rəkylad] *nf* (*péj*) climb-down.

reculé, e [Rəkyle] *a* remote.

reculer [Rəkyle] *vi* to move back, back away; (AUTO) to reverse, back (up); (*fig*) to (be on the) decline; to be losing ground; (: *se dérober*) to shrink back // *vt* to move back; to reverse, back (up); (*fig: possibilités, limites*) to extend; (: *date, décision*) to postpone.

reculons [Rəkylɔ̃]: **à** ~ *ad* backwards.

récupérer [RekypeRe] *vt* (*rentrer en possession de*) to recover, get back; (*recueillir: ferraille etc*) to salvage (for reprocessing); (*délinquant etc*) to rehabilitate // *vi* to recover.

récurer [RekyRe] *vt* to scour.

récuser [Rekyze] *vt* to challenge; **se** ~ to decline to give an opinion.

reçut *vb voir* **recevoir**.

recycler [Rəsikle] *vt* (SCOL) to reorientate; (*employés*) to retrain.

rédacteur, trice [RedaktœR, -tRis] *nm/f* (*journaliste*) writer; subeditor; (*d'ouvrage de référence*) editor, compiler; ~ **en chef** chief editor; ~ **publicitaire** copywriter.

rédaction [Redaksjɔ̃] *nf* writing; (*rédacteurs*) editorial staff; (*bureau*) editorial office(s); (SCOL: *devoir*) essay, composition.

reddition [Redisjɔ̃] *nf* surrender.

rédemption [Redɑ̃psjɔ̃] *nf* redemption.

redescendre [Rədesɑ̃dR(ə)] *vi* (*à nouveau*) to go back down; (*après la montée*) to go down (again) // *vt* (*pente etc*) to go down.

redevable [Rədvabl(ə)] *a*: **être** ~ **de qch à qn** (*somme*) to owe sb sth; (*fig*) to be indebted to sb for sth.

redevance [Rədvɑ̃s] *nf* (*téléphonique*) rental charge; (*radiophonique*) licence fee.

rédhibitoire [RedibitwaR] *a*: **vice** ~ (*fig*) irretrievable flaw.

rédiger [Rediʒe] *vt* to write; (*contrat*) to draw up.

redire [RədiR] *vt* to repeat; **trouver à** ~ **à** to find fault with; **redite** *nf* (needless) repetition.

redondance [Rədɔ̃dɑ̃s] *nf* redundancy.

redoublé, e [Rəduble] *a*: **à coups** ~s even harder, twice as hard.

redoubler [Rəduble] *vi* (*tempête, violence*) to intensify, get even stronger *ou* fiercer etc; (SCOL) to repeat a year; ~ **de** *vt* to be twice as + *adjectif*; **le vent redouble de violence** the wind is blowing twice as hard.

redoutable [Rədutabl(ə)] a formidable, fearsome.

redouter [Rədute] vt to fear; (appréhender) to dread.

redressement [RədRɛsmɑ̃] nm: **maison de** ~ reformatory.

redresser [RədRese] vt (arbre, mât) to set upright, right; (pièce tordue) to straighten out; (AVIAT, AUTO) to straighten up; (situation, économie) to put right; **se** ~ vi (objet penché) to right itself; to straighten up; (personne) to sit (ou stand) up; to sit (ou stand) up straight.

redresseur [RədRɛsœR] nm: ~ **de torts** righter of wrongs.

réduction [Redyksjɔ̃] nf reduction.

réduire [Redɥiʀ] vt (gén, aussi CULIN, MATH) to reduce; (prix, dépenses) to cut, reduce; (carte) to scale down, reduce; (MÉD: fracture) to set; (rebelles) to put down; **se** ~ **à** (revenir à) to boil down to; **se** ~ **en** (se transformer en) to be reduced to.

réduit [Redɥi] nm tiny room, recess.

rééducation [Reedykasjɔ̃] nf (d'un membre) re-education; (de délinquants, d'un blessé) rehabilitation; ~ **de la parole** speech therapy.

réel, le [Reɛl] a real // nm: le ~ reality.

réélection [Reelɛksjɔ̃] nf re-election.

réélire [Reeliʀ] vt to re-elect.

réellement [Reelmɑ̃] ad really.

réemploi [Reɑ̃plwa] nm = **remploi**.

réescompte [Reɛskɔ̃t] nm rediscount.

réévaluation [Reevalɥasjɔ̃] nf revaluation.

réévaluer [Reevalɥe] vt to revalue.

réexpédier [Reɛkspedje] vt (à l'envoyeur) to return, send back; (au destinataire) to send on, forward.

réf. abr de **référence**.

refaire [RəfɛR] vt (faire de nouveau, recommencer) to do again; (réparer, restaurer) to do up; **se** ~ vi (en santé) to recover; (en argent) to make up one's losses; **être refait** (fam: dupé) to be had.

réfection [Refɛksjɔ̃] nf repair.

réfectoire [RefɛktwaR] nm (de collège, couvent, caserne) refectory.

référence [RefeRɑ̃s] nf reference; ~**s** nfpl (recommandations) reference sg; **faire** ~ **à** to refer to; **ouvrage de** ~ reference work.

référendum [Refeʀɑ̃dɔm] nm referendum.

référer [RefeRe] se ~ à vt to refer to; **en** ~ **à qn** to refer the matter to sb.

refiler [Rəfile] vt (fam): ~ **qch à qn** to palm sth off on sb; to pass sth on to sb.

réfléchi, e [Reflefi] a (caractère) thoughtful, (action) well-thought-out; (LING) reflexive.

réfléchir [Reflefiʀ] vt to reflect // vi to think; ~ **à** ou **sur** to think about.

reflet [Rəflɛ] nm reflection; (sur l'eau etc) sheen q, glint.

refléter [Rəflete] vt to reflect; **se** ~ vi to be reflected.

réflex [Reflɛks] a inv (PHOTO) reflex.

réflexe [Reflɛks(ə)] nm, a reflex; **avoir de bons** ~**s** to have good reactions ou reflexes.

réflexion [Reflɛksjɔ̃] nf (de la lumière etc, pensée) reflection; (fait de penser)

thought; (remarque) remark; ~**s** nfpl (méditations) thought sg, reflection sg; **sans** ~ without thinking; ~ **faite, à la** ~ on reflection.

refluer [Rəflye] vi to flow back; (foule) to surge back.

reflux [Rəfly] nm (de la mer) ebb.

refondre [Rəfɔ̃dʀ(ə)] vt (texte) to recast.

réformateur, trice [RefɔRmatœR, -tʀis] nm/f reformer.

Réformation [RefɔRmasjɔ̃] nf: la ~ the Reformation.

réforme [RefɔRm(ə)] nf reform; (MIL) declaration of unfitness for service; discharge (on health grounds); (REL): **la R**~ the Reformation.

réformé, e [Refɔrme] a, nm/f (REL) Protestant.

réformer [Refɔrme] vt to reform; (MIL: recrue) to declare unfit for service; (: soldat) to discharge, invalid out.

réformisme [RefɔRmism(ə)] nm reformism, policy of reform.

refoulé, e [Rəfule] a (PSYCH) frustrated, repressed.

refoulement [Rəfulmɑ̃] nm (PSYCH) repression.

refouler [Rəfule] vt (envahisseurs) to drive back, repulse; (liquide) to force back; (fig) to suppress; (PSYCH) to repress.

réfractaire [RefRaktɛR] a (minerai) refractory; (brique) fire cpd; (prêtre) non-juring; **soldat** ~ draft evader; **être** ~ **à** to resist.

réfracter [RefRakte] vt to refract.

refrain [RəfRɛ̃] nm (MUS) refrain, chorus; (air, fig) tune.

refréner, réfréner [RəfRene, RefRene] vt to curb, check.

réfrigérant, e [Refriʒerɑ̃, -ɑ̃t] a refrigerant, cooling.

réfrigérer [RefriʒeRe] vt to refrigerate.

refroidir [RəfRwadiʀ] vt to cool; (fig) to have a cooling effect on // vi to cool (down); **se** ~ vi (prendre froid) to catch a chill; (temps) to get cooler ou colder; (fig) to cool (off); **refroidissement** nm cooling; (grippe etc) chill.

refuge [Rəfyʒ] nm refuge; (pour piétons) (traffic) island.

réfugié, e [Refyʒje] a, nm/f refugee.

réfugier [Refyʒje]: se ~ vi to take refuge.

refus [Rəfy] nm refusal; **ce n'est pas de** ~ I won't say no, it's welcome.

refuser [Rəfyze] vt to refuse; (SCOL: candidat) to fail; ~ **qch à qn/de faire** to refuse sb sth/to do; ~ **du monde** to have to turn customers away; **se** ~ **à qch/à faire** to refuse to do.

réfuter [Refyte] vt to refute.

regagner [Rəgaɲe] vt (argent, faveur) to win back; (lieu) to get back to; ~ **le temps perdu** to make up (for) lost time; ~ **du terrain** to regain ground.

regain [Rəgɛ̃] nm (herbe) second crop of hay; (renouveau): **un** ~ **de** renewed + nom.

régal [Regal] nm treat.

régalade [Regalad] ad: à la ~ from the bottle (held away from the lips).

régaler [Regale] vt: ~ qn to treat sb to a delicious meal; ~ qn de to treat sb to; **se ~** vi to have a delicious meal; (fig) to enjoy o.s.

regard [RəgaR] nm (coup d'œil) look, glance; (expression) look (in one's eye); **parcourir/menacer du ~** to cast an eye over/look threateningly at; **au ~ de** (loi, morale) from the point of view of; **en ~** (vis à vis) opposite; **en ~ de** in comparison with.

regardant, e [Rəgardã, -ãt] a: très/peu ~ (sur) quite fussy/very free (about); (économe) very tight-fisted/quite generous (with).

regarder [RəgaRde] vt (examiner, observer, lire) to look at; (film, télévision, match) to watch; (envisager: situation, avenir) to view; (considérer: son intérêt etc) to be concerned with; (être orienté vers): ~ (vers) to face; (concerner) to concern // vi to look; ~ à vt (dépense, qualité, détails) to be fussy with ou over; ~ à faire to hesitate to do, **dépenser sans ~** to spend freely; ~ **qn/qch comme** to regard sb/sth as; ~ (qch) **dans le dictionnaire/l'annuaire** to look (sth up) in the dictionary/directory; **cela me regarde** it concerns me, it's my business.

régate(s) [Regat] nf(pl) regatta.

régénérer [ReʒeneRe] vt to regenerate; (fig) to revive.

régent [Reʒã] nm regent.

régenter [Reʒãte] vt to rule over; to dictate to.

régie [Reʒi] nf (COMM, INDUSTRIE) state-owned company; (THÉÂTRE, CINÉMA) production; **la ~ de l'État** state control.

regimber [Rəʒɛ̃be] vi to balk, jib.

régime [Reʒim] nm (POL) régime; (ADMIN: des prisons, fiscal etc) system; (MÉD) diet; (GÉO) régime; (TECH) (engine) speed; (fig) rate, pace; (de bananes, dattes) bunch; **se mettre au/suivre un ~** to go on/be on a diet; ~ **sans sel** salt-free diet; **à bas/haut ~** (AUTO) at low/high revs; ~ **matrimonial** marriage settlement.

régiment [Reʒimã] nm (MIL: unité) regiment; (fig: fam): **un ~ de** an army of; **un copain de ~** a pal from military service ou (one's) army days.

région [Reʒjɔ̃] nf region; **la ~ parisienne** the Paris area; **régional, e, aux** a regional; **régionalisme** nm regionalism.

régir [ReʒiR] vt to govern.

régisseur [ReʒisœR] nm (d'un domaine) steward; (CINÉMA, TV) assistant director; (THÉÂTRE) stage manager.

registre [RəʒistR(ə)] nm (livre) register; logbook; ledger; (MUS, LING) register; (d'orgue) stop.

réglage [Reglaʒ] nm adjustment; tuning.

règle [Rɛgl(ə)] nf (instrument) ruler; (loi, prescription) rule; ~**s** nfpl (PHYSIOL) period sg; **en ~** (papiers d'identité) in order; **être/se mettre en ~** to be/put o.s. straight with the authorities; **en ~ générale** as a (general) rule; ~ **à calcul** slide rule.

réglé, e [Regle] a well-ordered; stable, steady; (papier) ruled; (femme): **bien ~e** whose periods are regular.

règlement [Rɛglɔmã] nm settling; (arrêté) regulation; (règles, statuts) regulations pl, rules pl; ~ **de compte(s)** settling of scores; **réglementaire** a conforming to the regulations; (tenue, uniforme) regulation cpd.

réglementation [Rɛglɔmãtɑsjɔ̃] nf regulation, control; regulations pl.

réglementer [Rɛglɔmãte] vt to regulate, control.

régler [Regle] vt (mécanisme, machine) to regulate, adjust; (moteur) to tune; (thermostat etc) to set, adjust; (emploi du temps etc) to organize, plan; (question, conflit, facture, dette) to settle; (fournisseur) to settle up with, pay; (papier) to rule; ~ **son compte à qn** to sort sb out, settle sb; ~ **un compte avec qn** to settle a score with sb.

réglisse [Reglis] nf liquorice.

règne [Rɛɲ] nm (d'un roi etc, fig) reign; (BIO): **le ~ végétal/animal** the vegetable/animal kingdom.

régner [Reɲe] vi (roi) to rule, reign; (fig) to reign.

regorger [RəgɔRʒe] vi to overflow; ~ **de** to overflow with, be bursting with.

régression [RegResjɔ̃] nf regression, decline.

regret [RəgRɛ] nm regret; **à ~** with regret; **avec ~** regretfully; **être au ~ de devoir faire** to regret having to do.

regrettable [RəgRɛtabl(ə)] a regrettable.

regretter [RəgRete] vt to regret; (personne) to miss; ~ **que** to regret that, be sorry that; **je regrette** I'm sorry.

regrouper [RəgRupe] vt (grouper) to group together; (contenir) to include, comprise; **se ~** vi to gather (together).

régulariser [Regylarize] vt (fonctionnement, trafic) to regulate; (passeport, papiers) to put in order; (sa situation) to straighten out, regularize.

régularité [RegylaRite] nf regularity.

régulateur, trice [RegylatœR, -tRis] a regulating.

régulier, ière [Regylje, -jɛR] a (gén) regular; (vitesse, qualité) steady; (répartition, pression, paysage) even; (TRANSPORTS: ligne, service) scheduled, regular; (légal, réglementaire) lawful, in order; (fam: correct) straight, on the level; **régulièrement** ad regularly; steadily; evenly; normally.

réhabiliter [Reabilite] vt to rehabilitate; (fig) to restore to favour.

rehausser [Rəose] vt to heighten, raise; (fig) to set off, enhance.

rein [Rɛ̃] nm kidney; ~**s** nmpl (dos) back sg; **avoir mal aux ~s** to have backache.

reine [Rɛn] nf queen.

reine-claude [Rɛnklod] nf greengage.

reinette [Rɛnɛt] nf rennet, pippin.

réintégrer [Reɛ̃tegRe] vt (lieu) to return to; (fonctionnaire) to reinstate.

réitérer [ReiteRe] vt to repeat, reiterate.

rejaillir [RəʒajiR] vi to splash up; ~ **sur** to splash up onto; (fig) to rebound on; to fall upon.

rejet [Rəʒɛ] nm (action, aussi MÉD)

rejection ; (POÉSIE) enjambement, rejet ; (BOT) shoot.

rejeter [rəʒte] vt (relancer) to throw back ; (vomir) to bring ou throw up ; (écarter) to reject ; (déverser) to throw out, discharge ; ~ la tête/les épaules en arrière to throw one's head/pull one's shoulders back ; ~ la responsabilité de qch sur qn to lay the responsibility for sth at sb's door.

rejeton [rəʒtɔ̃] nm offspring.

rejoindre [rəʒwɛ̃dr(ə)] vt (famille, régiment) to rejoin, return to ; (lieu) to get (back) to ; (suj: route etc) to meet, join ; (rattraper) to catch up (with) ; se ~ vi to meet ; je te rejoins au café I'll see ou meet you at the café.

réjoui, e [reʒwi] a (mine) joyous.

réjouir [reʒwir] vt to delight ; se ~ vi to be delighted ; to rejoice ; se ~ de qch/faire to be delighted about sth/to do ; **réjouissances** nfpl (joie) rejoicing sg ; (fête) festivities, merry-making sg.

relâche [rəlɑʃ]: faire ~ vi (navire) to put into port ; (CINÉMA) to be closed ; sans ~ ad without respite ou a break.

relâché, e [rəlɑʃe] a loose, lax.

relâcher [rəlɑʃe] vt (ressort, prisonnier) to release ; (étreinte, cordes) to loosen // vi (NAVIG) to put into port ; se ~ vi to loosen ; (discipline) to become slack ou lax ; (élève etc) to slacken off.

relais [rəlɛ] nm (SPORT): (course de) ~ relay (race) ; (RADIO, TV) relay ; **équipe de** ~ shift team ; relay team ; **prendre le** ~ (de) to take over (from) ; ~ **de poste** post house, coaching inn ; ~ **routier** ≈ transport café.

relance [rəlɑ̃s] nf boosting, revival.

relancer [rəlɑ̃se] vt (balle) to throw back (again) ; (moteur) to restart ; (fig) to boost, revive ; (personne): ~ qn to pester sb ; to get on to sb again.

relater [rəlate] vt to relate, recount.

relatif, ive [rəlatif, -iv] a relative.

relation [rəlasjɔ̃] nf (récit) account, report ; (rapport) relation(ship) ; ~s nfpl (rapports) relations ; relationship sg ; (connaissances) connections ; être/entrer en ~(s) to be in contact ou be dealing/get in contact with ; ~s publiques public relations.

relativement [rəlativmɑ̃] ad relatively ; ~ à in relation to.

relativité [rəlativite] nf relativity.

relax [rəlaks] a inv, **relaxe** [rəlaks(ə)] a informal, casual ; easy-going.

relaxer [rəlakse] vt to relax ; (JUR) to discharge ; se ~ vi to relax.

relayer [rəleje] vt (collaborateur, coureur etc) to relieve, take over from ; (RADIO, TV) to relay ; se ~ (dans une activité) to take it in turns.

relégation [rəlegasjɔ̃] nf (SPORT) relegation.

reléguer [rəlege] vt to relegate.

relent(s) [rəlɑ̃] nm(pl) (foul) smell.

relève [rəlɛv] nf relief ; relief team (ou troops pl) ; **prendre la** ~ to take over.

relevé, e [rəlve] a (bord de chapeau) turned-up ; (manches) rolled-up ; (virage) banked ; (fig: style) elevated ; (: sauce) highly-seasoned // nm (lecture) reading ;

(de cotes) plotting ; (liste) statement ; list ; (facture) account ; ~ **de compte** bank statement.

relever [rəlve] vt (statue, meuble) to stand up again ; (personne tombée) to help up ; (vitre, plafond, niveau de vie) to raise ; (col) to turn up ; (style, conversation) to elevate ; (plat, sauce) to season ; (sentinelle, équipe) to relieve ; (souligner: fautes, points) to pick out ; (constater: traces etc) to find, pick up ; (répliquer à: remarque) to react to, reply to ; (: défi) to accept, take up ; (noter: adresse etc) to take down, note ; (: plan) to sketch ; (: cotes etc) to plot ; (compteur) to read ; (ramasser: cahiers, copies) to collect, take in ; ~ **de** vt (maladie) to be recovering from ; (être du ressort de) to be a matter for ; (ADMIN: dépendre de) to come under ; (fig) to pertain to ; se ~ vi (se remettre debout) to get up ; ~ **qn de** (vœux) to release sb from ; (fonctions) to relieve sb of ; ~ **la tête** to look up ; to hold up one's head.

relief [rəljɛf] nm relief ; (de pneu) tread pattern ; ~**s** nmpl (restes) remains ; **en** ~ in relief ; (photographie) three-dimensional ; **mettre en** ~ (fig) to bring out, highlight.

relier [rəlje] vt to link up ; (livre) to bind ; ~ **qch à** to link sth to ; **livre relié cuir** leather-bound book ; **relieur, euse** nm/f (book)binder.

religieux, euse [rəliʒjø, -øz] a religious // nm monk // nf nun ; (gâteau) cream bun.

religion [rəliʒjɔ̃] nf religion ; (piété, dévotion) faith ; **entrer en** ~ to take one's vows.

reliquaire [rəlikɛr] nm reliquary.

reliquat [rəlika] nm balance ; remainder.

relique [rəlik] nf relic.

relire [rəlir] vt (à nouveau) to reread, read again ; (vérifier) to read over.

reliure [rəljyr] nf binding.

reluire [rəlɥir] vi to gleam ; **reluisant, e** a gleaming ; **peu reluisant** (fig) unattractive ; unsavoury.

remâcher [rəmɑʃe] vt to chew or ruminate over.

remailler [rəmaje] vt to darn ; to mend.

remaniement [rəmanimɑ̃] nm: ~ **ministériel** Cabinet reshuffle.

remanier [rəmanje] vt to reshape, recast ; (POL) to reshuffle.

remarquable [rəmarkabl(ə)] a remarkable.

remarque [rəmark(ə)] nf remark ; (écrite) note.

remarquer [rəmarke] vt (voir) to notice ; (dire): ~ **que** to remark that ; se ~ to be noticeable ; se faire ~ to draw attention to o.s. ; faire ~ (à qn) que to point out (to sb) that ; faire ~ qch (à qn) to point sth out (to sb) ; **remarquez que** mark you, mind you.

rembarrer [rɑ̃bare] vt: ~ **qn** to rebuff sb ; to put sb in his/her place.

remblai [rɑ̃blɛ] nm embankment.

remblayer [rɑ̃bleje] vt to bank up ; (fossé) to fill in.

rembourrage [rɑ̃buraʒ] nm stuffing ; padding.

rembourré, e [Rãbure] a padded.
rembourrer [Rãbure] vt to stuff; (dossier, vêtement, souliers) to pad.
remboursement [Rãbursəmã] nm repayment; **envoi contre ~** cash on delivery.
rembourser [Rãburse] vt to pay back, repay.
rembrunir [Rãbrynir]: **se ~** vi to darken; to grow sombre.
remède [Rəmɛd] nm (médicament) medicine; (traitement, fig) remedy, cure.
remédier [Rəmedje]: **~ à** vt to remedy.
remembrement [Rəmãbrəmã] nm (AGR) regrouping of lands.
remémorer [Rəmemɔre]: **se ~** vt to recall, recollect.
remerciements [Rəmɛrsimã] nmpl thanks.
remercier [Rəmɛrsje] vt to thank; (congédier) to dismiss; **~ qn de/d'avoir fait** to thank sb for/for having done; **non, je vous remercie** no thank you.
remettre [Rəmɛtr(ə)] vt (vêtement): **~ qch** to put sth back on, put sth on again; (replacer): **~ qch quelque part** to put sth back somewhere; (ajouter): **~ du sel/un sucre** to add more salt/another lump of sugar; (rétablir: personne): **~ qn** to set sb back on his/her feet; (rendre, restituer): **~ qch à qn** to give sth back to sb, return sth to sb; (donner, confier: paquet, argent): **~ qch à qn** to hand over sth to sb, deliver sth to sb; (prix, décoration): **~ qch à qn** to present sb with sth; (ajourner): **~ qch (à)** to postpone sth ou put sth off (until); **se ~** vi to get better, recover; **se ~ de** to recover from, get over; **s'en ~ à** to leave it (up) to.
remise [Rəmiz] nf delivery; presentation; (rabais) discount; (local) shed; **~ en jeu** (FOOTBALL) throw-in; **~ de peine** reduction of sentence.
rémission [Remisjɔ̃]: **sans ~** a irremediable // ad unremittingly.
remontant [Rəmɔ̃tã] nm tonic, pick-me-up.
remontée [Rəmɔ̃te] nf rising; ascent; **~s mécaniques** (SKI) towing equipment sg ou facilities.
remonte-pente [Rəmɔ̃tpãt] nm skilift, (ski) tow.
remonter [Rəmɔ̃te] vi (à nouveau) to go back up; (après une descente) to go up (again); (jupe) to pull ou ride up // vt (pente) to go up; (fleuve) to sail (ou swim etc) up; (manches, pantalon) to roll up; (col) to turn up; (rayon, limite) to raise; (fig: personne) to buck up; (moteur, meuble) to put back together, reassemble; (garde-robe etc) to renew, replenish; (montre, mécanisme) to wind up; **~ à** (dater de) to date ou go back to; **~ en voiture** to get back into the car.
remontoir [Rəmɔ̃twar] nm winding mechanism, winder.
remontrance [Rəmɔ̃trãs] nf reproof, reprimand.
remontrer [Rəmɔ̃tre] vt (fig): **en ~ à** to prove one's superiority over.
remords [Rəmɔr] nm remorse q; **avoir des ~** to feel remorse, be conscience-stricken.
remorque [Rəmɔrk(ə)] nf trailer; **prendre/être en ~** to tow/be on tow; **remorquer** vt to tow; **remorqueur** nm tug(boat).
rémoulade [Remulad] nf dressing with mustard and herbs.
rémouleur [Remulœr] nm (knife- ou scissor-)grinder.
remous [Rəmu] nm (d'un navire) (back)wash q; (de rivière) swirl, eddy // nmpl (fig) stir sg.
rempailler [Rãpuje] vt to reseat (with straw).
remparts [Rãpar] nmpl walls, ramparts.
rempiler [Rãpile] vi (MIL: fam) to join up again.
remplaçant, e [Rãplasã, -ãt] nm/f replacement, substitute, stand-in; (THÉÂTRE) understudy; (SCOL) supply teacher.
remplacement [Rãplasmã] nm replacement; (job) replacement work q; **assurer le ~ de qn** (suj: remplaçant) to stand in ou substitute for sb.
remplacer [Rãplase] vt to replace; (prendre temporairement la place de) to stand in for; (tenir lieu de) to take the place of, act as a substitute for; **~ qch/qn par** to replace sth/sb with.
rempli, e [Rãpli] a (emploi du temps) full, busy; **~ de** full of, filled with.
remplir [Rãplir] vt to fill (up); (questionnaire) to fill out ou up; (obligations, fonction, condition) to fulfil; **se ~** vi to fill up.
remplissage [Rãplisaʒ] nm (fig: péj) padding.
remploi [Rãplwa] nm re-use.
remporter [Rãpɔrte] vt (marchandise) to take away; (fig) to win, achieve.
remuant, e [Rəmɥã, -ãt] a restless.
remue-ménage [Rəmymenaʒ] nm inv commotion.
remuer [Rəmɥe] vt to move; (café, sauce) to stir // vi to move; (fig: opposants) to show signs of unrest; **se ~** vi to move; (se démener) to stir o.s.; (fam) to get a move on.
rémunération [RemyneRasjɔ̃] nf remuneration.
rémunérer [Remynere] vt to remunerate, pay.
renâcler [Rənukle] vi to snort; (fig) to grumble, balk.
renaissance [Rənɛsãs] nf rebirth, revival; **la R~** the Renaissance.
renaître [Rənɛtr(ə)] vi to be revived.
rénal, e, aux [Renal, -o] a renal, kidney cpd.
renard [Rənar] nm fox.
rencard [Rãkar] nm = rancard.
rencart [Rãkar] nm = rancart.
renchérir [Rãʃerir] vi to become more expensive; (fig): **~ (sur)** to add something (to).
rencontre [Rãkɔ̃tr(ə)] nf (entrevue, congrès, match etc) meeting; (imprévue) encounter; **faire la ~ de qn** to meet sb;

aller à la ~ de qn to go and meet sb ;
amours de ~ casual love affairs.

rencontrer [Rɑ̃kɔ̃tRe] *vt* to meet ; (*mot,
expression*) to come across ; (*difficultés*) to
meet with ; **se** ~ *vi* to meet ; (*véhicules*)
to collide.

rendement [Rɑ̃dmɑ̃] *nm* (*d'un travailleur,
d'une machine*) output ; (*d'une culture*)
yield ; (*d'un investissement*) return ; **à plein
~** at full capacity.

rendez-vous [Rɑ̃devu] *nm* (*rencontre*)
appointment ; (: *d'amoureux*) date ; (*lieu*)
meeting place ; **donner ~ à qn** to arrange
to meet sb ; **fixer un ~ à qn** to give sb
an appointment ; **avoir/prendre ~
(avec)** to have/make an appointment
(with).

rendre [Rɑ̃dR(ə)] *vt* (*livre, argent etc*) to
give back, return ; (*otages, visite etc*) to
return ; (*sang, aliments*) to bring up ; (*sons:
suj: instrument*) to produce, make ;
(*exprimer, traduire*) to render ; (*faire
devenir*): **~ qn célèbre/qch possible** to
make sb famous/sth possible ; **se** ~ *vi*
(*capituler*) to surrender, give o.s. up ;
(*aller*): **se** ~ **quelque part** to go
somewhere ; **se** ~ **à** (*arguments etc*) to bow
to ; (*ordres*) to comply with ; **~ la vue/la
santé à qn** to restore sb's sight/health ;
~ la liberté à qn to set sb free.

renégat, e [Renega, -at] *nm/f* renegade.

rênes [Rɛn] *nfpl* reins.

renfermé, e [Rɑ̃fɛRme] *a* (*fig*) withdrawn
// *nm*: **sentir le** ~ to smell stuffy.

renfermer [Rɑ̃fɛRme] *vt* to contain ; **se** ~
(**sur soi-même**) to withdraw into o.s.

renflé, e [Rɑ̃fle] *a* bulging, bulbous.

renflement [Rɑ̃fləmɑ̃] *nm* bulge.

renflouer [Rɑ̃flue] *vt* to refloat ; (*fig*) to
set back on its (*ou* his/her) feet (again).

renfoncement [Rɑ̃fɔ̃smɑ̃] *nm* recess.

renforcer [Rɑ̃fɔRse] *vt* to reinforce.

renfort [Rɑ̃fɔR] : **~s** *nmpl* reinforcements ;
en ~ as a back-up ; **à grand** ~ **de** with
a great deal of.

renfrogner [Rɑ̃fRɔɲe] : **se** ~ *vi* to scowl.

rengaine [Rɑ̃gɛn] *nf* (*péj*) old tune.

rengainer [Rɑ̃gene] *vt* (*revolver*) to put
back in its holster.

rengorger [Rɑ̃gɔRʒe] : **se** ~ *vi* (*fig*) to puff
o.s. up.

renier [Rənje] *vt* (*parents*) to disown,
repudiate ; (*foi*) to renounce.

renifler [Rənifle] *vi* to sniff // *vt* (*tabac*)
to sniff up ; (*odeur*) to sniff.

renne [Rɛn] *nm* reindeer *inv*.

renom [Rən5] *nm* reputation ; renown ;
renommé, e *a* celebrated, renowned // *nf*
fame.

renoncement [Rən5smɑ̃] *nm* abnegation,
renunciation.

renoncer [Rən5se] *vi*: **~ à** *vt* to give up ;
~ à faire to give up all idea of doing ;
to give up trying to do.

renouer [Rənwe] *vt* (*cravate etc*) to retie ;
~ avec (*tradition*) to revive ; (*habitude*) to
take up again ; **~ avec qn** to take up with
sb again.

renouveau, x [Rənuvo] *nm*: **~ de succès**
renewed success ; **le** ~ **printanier**
springtide.

renouveler [Rənuvle] *vt* to renew ;
(*exploit, méfait*) to repeat ; **se** ~ *vi*
(*incident*) to recur, happen again, be
repeated ; (*cellules etc*) to be renewed *ou*
replaced ; **renouvellement** *nm* renewal ;
recurrence.

rénovation [Renɔvasjɔ̃] *nf* renovation ;
restoration.

rénover [Renɔve] *vt* (*immeuble*) to
renovate, do up ; (*meuble*) to restore ;
(*enseignement*) to reform.

renseignement [Rɑ̃sɛɲmɑ̃] *nm*
information *q*, piece of information ;
prendre des ~s sur to make inquiries
about, ask for information about ;
(**guichet des**) **~s** information desk.

renseigner [Rɑ̃seɲe] *vt*: **~ qn (sur)** to
give information to sb (about) ; **se** ~ *vi*
to ask for information, make inquiries.

rentable [Rɑ̃table(ə)] *a* profitable.

rente [Rɑ̃t] *nf* income ; pension ;
government stock *ou* bond ; **~ viagère** life
annuity ; **rentier, ière** *nm/f* person of
private means.

rentrée [Rɑ̃tRe] *nf*: **~ (d'argent)** cash *q*
coming in ; **la** ~ **(des classes)** the start
of the new school year ; **la** ~
(parlementaire) the reopening *ou*
reassembly of parliament ; **faire sa** ~
(*artiste, acteur*) to make a comeback.

rentrer [Rɑ̃tRe] *vi* (*entrer de nouveau*) to
go (*ou* come) back in ; (*entrer*) to go (*ou*
come) in ; (*revenir chez soi*) to go (*ou* come)
(back) home ; (*air, clou: pénétrer*) to go in ;
(*revenu, argent*) to come in // *vt* (*foins*) to
bring in ; (*véhicule*) to put away ; (*chemise
dans pantalon etc*) to tuck in ; (*griffes*) to
draw in ; (*train d'atterrissage*) to raise ; (*fig:
larmes, colère etc*) to hold back ; **~ le
ventre** to pull in one's stomach ; **~ dans**
to go (*ou* come) back into ; to go (*ou* come)
into ; (*famille, patrie*) to go back *ou* return
to ; (*heurter*) to crash into ; **~ dans l'ordre**
to be back to normal ; **~ dans ses frais**
to recover one's expenses (*ou* initial
outlay).

renversant, e [Rɑ̃vɛRsɑ̃, -ɑ̃t] *a* amazing.

renverse [Rɑ̃vɛRs(ə)] : **à la** ~ *ad*
backwards.

renverser [Rɑ̃vɛRse] *vt* (*faire tomber:
chaise, verre*) to knock over, overturn ;
(*piéton*) to knock down ; (*liquide, contenu*)
to spill, upset ; (*retourner: verre, image*) to
turn upside down, invert ; (: *ordre des mots
etc*) to reverse ; (*fig: gouvernement etc*) to
overthrow ; (*stupéfier*) to bowl over,
stagger ; **se** ~ *vi* to fall over ; to overturn ;
to spill ; **~ la tête/le corps (en arrière)**
to tip one's head back/throw one's body
back.

renvoi [Rɑ̃vwa] *nm* dismissal ; return ;
reflection ; postponement ; (*référence*)
cross-reference ; (*éructation*) belch.

renvoyer [Rɑ̃vwaje] *vt* to send back ;
(*congédier*) to dismiss ; (*lumière*) to reflect ;
(*son*) to echo ; (*ajourner*): **~ qch (à)** to put
sth off *ou* postpone sth (until) ; **~ qn à**
(*fig*) to refer sb to.

réorganiser [Reɔrganize] *vt* to
reorganize.

réouverture [Reuvɛrtyr] *nf* reopening.

repaire [RəpɛR] *nm* den.

repaître [RəpɛtR(ə)] *vt* to feast ; to feed ; **se ~ de** *vt* to feed on ; to wallow *ou* revel in.

répandre [Repɑ̃dR(ə)] *vt* (*renverser*) to spill ; (*étaler, diffuser*) to spread ; (*lumière*) to shed ; (*chaleur, odeur*) to give off ; **se ~** *vi* to spill ; to spread ; **se ~ en** (*injures etc*) to pour out ; **répandu, e** *a* (*opinion, usage*) widespread.

réparation [RepaRɑsjɔ̃] *nf* repairing q, repair.

réparer [RepaRe] *vt* to repair ; (*fig: offense*) to make up for, atone for ; (: *oubli, erreur*) to put right.

repartie [Rəparti] *nf* retort ; **avoir de la ~** to be quick at repartee.

repartir [Rəpartir] *vi* to set off again ; to leave again ; (*fig*) to get going again, pick up again ; **~ à zéro** to start from scratch (again).

répartir [RepaRtiR] *vt* (*pour attribuer*) to share out ; (*pour disperser, disposer*) to divide up ; (*poids, chaleur*) to distribute ; **se ~** *vt* (*travail, rôles*) to share out between themselves ; **répartition** *nf* sharing out ; dividing up ; distribution.

repas [Rəpɑ] *nm* meal.

repasser [Rəpɑse] *vi* to come (*ou* go) back // *vt* (*vêtement, tissu*) to iron ; to retake, resit ; to show again ; (*leçon, rôle: revoir*) to go over (again).

repêchage [Rəpɛʃaʒ] *nm* (*SCOL*): **question de ~** question to give candidates a second chance.

repêcher [Rəpɛʃe] *vt* (*noyé*) to recover the body of, fish out.

repentir [Rəpɑ̃tiR] *nm* repentance ; **se ~** *vi* to repent ; **se ~ de** to repent (of).

répercussions [RepɛRkysjɔ̃] *nfpl* repercussions.

répercuter [RepɛRkyte]: **se ~** *vi* (*bruit*) to reverberate ; (*fig*): **se ~ sur** to have repercussions on.

repère [RəpɛR] *nm* mark ; (*monument etc*) landmark.

repérer [Rəpere] *vt* (*erreur, connaissance*) to spot ; (*abri, ennemi*) to locate ; **se ~** *vi* to find one's way about ; **se faire ~** to be spotted.

répertoire [RepɛRtwaR] *nm* (*liste*) (alphabetical) list ; (*carnet*) index notebook ; (*de carnet*) thumb index ; (*indicateur*) directory, index ; (*d'un théâtre, artiste*) repertoire ; **répertorier** *vt* to itemize, list.

répéter [Repete] *vt* to repeat ; (*préparer: leçon: aussi vi*) to learn, go over ; (*THÉÂTRE*) to rehearse ; **se ~** (*redire*) to repeat o.s. ; (*se reproduire*) to be repeated, recur.

répétition [Repetisjɔ̃] *nf* repetition ; rehearsal ; **~s** *nfpl* (*leçons*) private coaching *sg* ; **armes à ~** repeater weapons ; **~ générale** final dress rehearsal.

repeupler [Rəpœple] *vt* to repopulate ; to restock.

répit [Repi] *nm* respite ; **sans ~** without letting up.

replet, ète [Rəplɛ, -ɛt] *a* chubby, fat.

repli [Rəpli] *nm* (*d'une étoffe*) fold ; (*MIL. fig*) withdrawal.

replier [Rəplije] *vt* (*rabattre*) to fold down *ou* over ; **se ~** *vi* (*troupes, armée*) to withdraw, fall back.

réplique [Replik] *nf* (*repartie, fig*) reply ; (*THÉÂTRE*) line ; (*copie*) replica ; **donner la ~ à** to play opposite ; to match ; **sans ~** no-nonsense ; irrefutable.

répliquer [Replike] *vi* to reply ; (*riposter*) to retaliate.

répondre [RepɔndR(ə)] *vi* to answer, reply ; (*freins, mécanisme*) to respond ; **~ à** *vt* to reply to, answer ; (*avec impertinence*): **~ à qn** to answer sb back ; (*invitation, convocation*) to reply to ; (*affection, salut*) to return ; (*provocation, suj: mécanisme etc*) to respond to ; (*correspondre à: besoin*) to answer ; (: *conditions*) to meet ; (: *description*) to match ; **~ que** to answer *ou* reply that ; **~ de** to answer for.

réponse [Repɔns] *nf* answer, reply ; **avec ~ payée** (*POSTES*) reply-paid ; **en ~ à** in reply to.

report [RəpɔR] *nm* transfer ; postponement.

reportage [RəpɔRtaʒ] *nm* (*bref*) report ; (*écrit: documentaire*) story ; article ; (*en direct*) commentary ; (*genre, activité*): **le ~** reporting.

reporter *nm* [RəpɔRtɛR] reporter // *vt* [RəpɔRte] (*total*): **~ qch sur** to carry sth forward *ou* over to ; (*ajourner*): **~ qch (à)** to postpone sth (until) ; (*transférer*): **~ qch sur** to transfer sth to ; **se ~ à** (*époque*) to think back to ; (*document*) to refer to.

repos [Rəpo] *nm* rest ; (*fig*) peace (and quiet) ; peace of mind ; (*MIL*): **~!** stand at ease! ; **en ~** at rest ; **de tout ~** safe.

repose [Rəpoz] *nf* refitting.

reposé, e [Rəpoze] *a* fresh, rested.

reposer [Rəpoze] *vt* (*verre, livre*) to put down ; (*délasser*) to rest ; (*problème*) to reformulate // *vi* (*liquide, pâte*) to settle, rest ; **~ sur** to be built on ; (*fig*) to rest on ; **se ~** *vi* to rest ; **se ~ sur qn** to rely on sb.

repoussant, e [Rəpusɑ̃, -ɑ̃t] *a* repulsive.

repoussé, e [Rəpuse] *a* (*cuir*) embossed (by hand).

repousser [Rəpuse] *vi* to grow again // *vt* to repel, repulse ; (*offre*) to turn down, reject ; (*tiroir, personne*) to push back ; (*différer*) to put back.

répréhensible [RepReɑ̃sibl(ə)] *a* reprehensible.

reprendre [RəpRɑ̃dR(ə)] *vt* (*prisonnier, ville*) to recapture ; (*objet prêté, donné*) to take back ; (*chercher*): **je viendrai te ~ à 4h** I'll come and fetch you *ou* I'll come back for you at 4 ; (*se resservir de*): **~ du pain/un œuf** to take (*ou* eat) more bread/another egg ; (*COMM: article usagé*) to take back ; to take in part exchange ; (*firme, entreprise*) to take over ; (*travail, promenade*) to resume ; (*emprunter: argument, idée*) to take up, use ; (*refaire: article etc*) to go over again ; (*jupe etc*) to alter ; to take in (*ou* up) ; to let out (*ou* down) ; (*émission, pièce*) to put on again ; (*réprimander*) to tell off ; (*corriger*) to correct // *vi* (*classes, pluie*) to start (up) again ; (*activités, travaux, combats*) to resume, start (up) again ; (*affaires,* *industrie*) to pick up ; (*dire*): **reprit-il** he went on ; **se ~** (*se ressaisir*) to recover, pull o.s. together ; **s'y ~** to make another attempt ; **~ des forces** to recover one's strength ; **~ courage** to take new heart ; **~ ses habitudes/sa liberté** to get back into one's old habits/regain one's freedom ; **~ la route** to resume one's journey, set off again ; **~ haleine** *ou* **son souffle** to get one's breath back.

représailles [ʀəpʀezaj] *nfpl* reprisals, retaliation *sg*.

représentant, e [ʀəpʀezɑ̃tɑ̃, -ɑ̃t] *nm/f* representative.

représentatif, ive [ʀəpʀezɑ̃tatif, -iv] *a* representative.

représentation [ʀəpʀezɑ̃tasjɔ̃] *nf* representation ; performing ; (*symbole, image*) representation ; (*spectacle*) performance ; (*COMM*): **la ~** commercial travelling ; sales representation ; **frais de ~** (*d'un diplomate*) entertainment allowance.

représenter [ʀəpʀezɑ̃te] *vt* to represent ; (*donner: pièce, opéra*) to perform ; **se ~** *vt* (*se figurer*) to imagine ; to visualize.

répression [ʀepʀesjɔ̃] *nf* suppression ; repression ; (*POL*): **la ~** repression.

réprimande [ʀepʀimɑ̃d] *nf* reprimand, rebuke ; **réprimander** *vt* to reprimand, rebuke.

réprimer [ʀepʀime] *vt* to suppress, repress.

repris [ʀəpʀi] *nm*: **~ de justice** ex-prisoner, ex-convict.

reprise [ʀəpʀiz] *nf* (*TV*) repeat ; (*CINÉMA*) rerun ; (*AUTO*) acceleration *q* ; (*COMM*) trade-in, part exchange ; (*de location*) sum asked for any extras or improvements made to the property ; (*raccommodage*) darn ; mend ; **à plusieurs ~s** on several occasions, several times.

repriser [ʀəpʀize] *vt* to darn ; to mend.

réprobateur, trice [ʀepʀɔbatœʀ, -tʀis] *a* reproving.

réprobation [ʀepʀɔbasjɔ̃] *nf* reprobation.

reproche [ʀəpʀɔʃ] *nm* (*remontrance*) reproach ; **faire des ~s à qn** to reproach sb ; **sans ~(s)** beyond *ou* above reproach.

reprocher [ʀəpʀɔʃe] *vt*: **~ qch à qn** to reproach *ou* blame sb for sth ; **~ qch à** (*machine, théorie*) to have sth against.

reproducteur, trice [ʀəpʀɔdyktœʀ, -tʀis] *a* reproductive.

reproduction [ʀəpʀɔdyksjɔ̃] *nf* reproduction ; **~ interdite** all rights (of reproduction) reserved.

reproduire [ʀəpʀɔdɥiʀ] *vt* to reproduce ; **se ~** *vi* (*BIO*) to reproduce ; (*recommencer*) to recur, re-occur.

réprouvé, e [ʀepʀuve] *nm/f* reprobate.

réprouver [ʀepʀuve] *vt* to reprove.

reptation [ʀɛptasjɔ̃] *nf* crawling.

reptile [ʀɛptil] *nm* reptile.

repu, e [ʀəpy] *a* satisfied, sated.

républicain, e [ʀepyblikɛ̃, -ɛn] *a, nm/f* republican.

république [ʀepyblik] *nf* republic ; **la R~ fédérale allemande** the Federal Republic of Germany.

répudier [ʀepydje] *vt* (*femme*) to repudiate ; (*doctrine*) to renounce.

répugnance [ʀepyɲɑ̃s] *nf* repugnance, loathing.

répugnant, e [ʀepyɲɑ̃, -ɑ̃t] *a* repulsive ; loathsome.

répugner [ʀepyɲe]: **~ à** *vt*: **~ à qn** to repel *ou* disgust sb ; **~ à faire** to be loath *ou* reluctant to do.

répulsion [ʀepylsjɔ̃] *nf* repulsion.

réputation [ʀepytasjɔ̃] *nf* reputation ; **réputé, e** *a* renowned.

requérir [ʀəkeʀiʀ] *vt* (*nécessiter*) to require, call for ; (*au nom de la loi*) to call upon ; (*JUR: peine*) to call for, demand.

requête [ʀəkɛt] *nf* request, petition ; (*JUR*) petition.

requiem [ʀekɥijɛm] *nm* requiem.

requin [ʀəkɛ̃] *nm* shark.

requis, e [ʀəki, -iz] *pp de* **requérir** // *a* required.

réquisition [ʀekizisjɔ̃] *nf* requisition ; **réquisitionner** *vt* to requisition.

réquisitoire [ʀekizitwaʀ] *nm* (*JUR*) closing speech for the prosecution ; (*fig*): **~ contre** indictment of.

R.E.R. *sigle m* (= *réseau express régional*) Greater Paris high speed commuter train.

rescapé, e [ʀɛskape] *nm/f* survivor.

rescousse [ʀɛskus] *nf*: **aller à la ~ de qn** to go to sb's aid *ou* rescue ; **appeler qn à la ~** to call on sb for help.

réseau, x [ʀezo] *nm* network.

réservation [ʀezɛʀvasjɔ̃] *nf* booking, reservation.

réserve [ʀezɛʀv(ə)] *nf* (*gén*) reserve ; (*entrepôt*) storeroom ; (*restriction, aussi: d'Indiens*) reservation ; (*de pêche, chasse*) preserve ; **sous ~ de** subject to ; **sans ~** ad unreservedly ; **de ~** (*provisions etc*) in reserve.

réservé, e [ʀezɛʀve] *a* (*discret*) reserved ; (*chasse, pêche*) private ; **~ à/pour** reserved for.

réserver [ʀezɛʀve] *vt* (*gén*) to reserve ; (*retenir: par une agence, au guichet*) to book, reserve ; (*mettre de côté, garder*): **~ qch pour/à** to keep *ou* save sth for ; **~ qch à qn** to reserve (*ou* book) sth for sb ; (*fig: destiner*) to have sth in store for sb ; **se ~ le droit de faire** to reserve the right to do.

réserviste [ʀezɛʀvist(ə)] *nm* reservist.

réservoir [ʀezɛʀvwaʀ] *nm* tank ; (*plan d'eau*) reservoir.

résidence [ʀezidɑ̃s] *nf* residence ; **~ secondaire** second home ; **(en) ~ surveillée** (under) house arrest ; **résidentiel, le** *a* residential.

résider [ʀezide] *vi*: **~ à/dans/en** to reside in ; **~ dans** (*fig*) to lie in.

résidu [ʀezidy] *nm* residue *q*.

résignation [ʀeziɲasjɔ̃] *nf* resignation.

résigner [ʀeziɲe] *vt* to relinquish, resign ; **se ~** *vi*: **se ~ (à qch/faire)** to resign o.s. (to sth/to doing).

résilier [ʀezilje] *vt* to terminate.

résille [ʀezij] *nf* (*hair*)net.

résine [ʀezin] *nf* resin ; **résiné, e** *a*: **vin résiné** retsina ; **résineux, euse** *a* resinous // *nm* coniferous tree.

résistance [Rezistãs] *nf* resistance ; (*de réchaud, bouilloire:* fil) element.

résistant, e [Rezistã, -ãt] *a* (*personne*) robust, tough ; (*matériau*) strong, hard-wearing // *nm/f* (*patriote*) Resistance worker *ou* fighter.

résister [Reziste] *vi* to resist ; ~ à *vt* (*assaut, tentation*) to resist ; (*effort, souffrance*) to withstand ; (*suj: matériau, plante*) to stand up to, withstand ; (*personne: désobéir à*) to stand up to, oppose.

résolu, e [Rezɔly] *pp de* **résoudre** // *a* (*ferme*) resolute ; **être ~ à qch/faire** to be set upon sth/doing.

résolution [Rezɔlysjõ] *nf* solving ; (*fermeté, décision*) resolution.

résolve etc *vb voir* **résoudre**.

résonance [Rezɔnãs] *nf* resonance.

résonner [Rezɔne] *vi* (*cloche, pas*) to reverberate, resound ; (*salle*) to be resonant ; ~ **de** to resound with.

résorber [Rezɔrbe] : **se ~** *vi* (*MÉD*) to be resorbed ; (*fig*) to be reduced ; to be absorbed.

résoudre [RezudR(ə)] *vt* to solve ; ~ **de faire** to resolve to do ; **se ~ à faire** to bring o.s. to do.

respect [Rɛspɛ] *nm* respect ; **tenir en ~** to keep at bay.

respectable [Rɛspɛktabl(ə)] *a* respectable.

respecter [Rɛspɛkte] *vt* to respect ; **le lexicographe qui se respecte** (*fig*) any self-respecting lexicographer.

respectif, ive [Rɛspɛktif, -iv] *a* respective ; **respectivement** *ad* respectively.

respectueux, euse [Rɛspɛktɥø, -øz] *a* respectful ; ~ **de** respectful of.

respiration [Rɛspirasjõ] *nf* breathing *q* ; **faire une ~ complète** to breathe in and out ; ~ **artificielle** artificial respiration.

respirer [Rɛspire] *vi* to breathe ; (*fig*) to get one's breath, have a break ; to breathe again // *vt* to breathe (in), inhale ; (*manifester: santé, calme etc*) to exude.

resplendir [RɛsplãdiR] *vi* to shine ; (*fig*): ~ (**de**) to be radiant (with).

responsabilité [Rɛspõsabilite] *nf* responsibility ; (*légale*) liability ; **refuser la ~ de** to deny responsibility (*ou* liability) for ; **prendre ses ~s** to assume responsibility for one's actions.

responsable [Rɛspõsabl(ə)] *a* responsible // *nm/f* (*du ravitaillement etc*) person in charge ; (*de parti, syndicat*) official ; ~ **de** responsible for ; (*légalement: de dégâts etc*) liable for ; (*chargé de*) in charge of, responsible for.

resquiller [Rɛskije] *vi* (*au cinéma, au stade*) to get in on the sly ; (*dans le train*) to fiddle a free ride ; **resquilleur, euse** *nm/f* gatecrasher ; fare dodger.

ressac [Rəsak] *nm* backwash.

ressaisir [RəseziR] : **se ~** *vi* to regain one's self-control ; (*équipe sportive*) to rally.

ressasser [Rəsɑse] *vt* (*remâcher*) to keep turning over ; (*redire*) to keep trotting out.

ressemblance [Rəsãblãs] *nf* (*visuelle*) resemblance, similarity, likeness ; (: *ART*) likeness ; (*analogie, trait commun*) similarity.

ressemblant, e [Rəsãblã, -ãt] *a* (*portrait*) lifelike, true to life.

ressembler [Rəsãble] : ~ **à** *vt* to be like ; to resemble ; (*visuellement*) to look like ; **se ~** to be (*ou* look) alike.

ressemeler [Rəsəmle] *vt* to (re)sole.

ressentiment [Rəsãtimã] *nm* resentment.

ressentir [RəsãtiR] *vt* to feel ; **se ~ de** to feel (*ou* show) the effects of.

resserre [RəsɛR] *nf* shed.

resserrer [RəseRe] *vt* (*pores*) to close ; (*nœud, boulon*) to tighten (up) ; (*fig: liens*) to strengthen ; **se ~** *vi* (*route, vallée*) to narrow ; (*liens*) to strengthen ; **se ~ (autour de**) to draw closer (around) ; to close in (on).

resservir [RəsɛRviR] *vi* to do *ou* serve again // *vt*: ~ **qch (à qn**) to serve sth up again (to sb) ; ~ **de qch (à qn**) to give (sb) a second helping of sth ; ~ **qn (d'un plat**) to give sb a second helping (of a dish).

ressort [RəsɔR] *nm* (*pièce*) spring ; (*force morale*) spirit ; (*recours*): **en dernier ~** as a last resort ; (*compétence*): **être du ~ de** to fall within the competence of.

ressortir [RəsɔRtiR] *vi* to go (*ou* come) out (again) ; (*contraster*) to stand out ; ~ **de** (*résulter de*): **il ressort de ceci que** it emerges from this that ; ~ **à** (*JUR*) to come under the jurisdiction of ; (*ADMIN*) to be the concern of ; **faire ~** (*fig: souligner*) to bring out.

ressortissant, e [RəsɔRtisã, -ãt] *nm/f* national.

ressource [RəsuRs(ə)] *nf*: **avoir la ~ de** to have the possibility of ; **leur seule ~ était de** the only course open to them was to ; ~**s** *nfpl* resources ; (*fig*) possibilities.

ressusciter [Resysite] *vt* to resuscitate, restore to life ; (*fig*) to revive, bring back // *vi* to rise (from the dead).

restant, e [Rɛstã, -ãt] *a* remaining // *nm*: **le ~ (de**) the remainder (of) ; **un ~ (de trop**) some left-over ; (*fig: vestige*) a remnant *ou* last trace of.

restaurant [RɛstɔRã] *nm* restaurant ; **manger au ~** to eat out ; ~ **d'entreprise** staff canteen ; ~ **universitaire** university refectory.

restaurateur, trice [RɛstɔRatœR, -tris] *nm/f* restaurant owner, restaurateur ; (*de tableaux*) restorer.

restauration [RɛstɔRasjõ] *nf* restoration ; (*hôtellerie*) catering.

restaurer [RɛstɔRe] *vt* to restore ; **se ~** *vi* to have something to eat.

restauroute [RɛstɔRut] *nm* = **restoroute**.

reste [Rɛst(ə)] *nm* (*restant*): **le ~ (de**) the rest (of) ; (*de trop*): **un ~ (de**) some left-over ; (*vestige*): **un ~ de** a remnant *ou* last trace of ; (*MATH*) remainder ; ~**s** *nmpl* left-overs ; (*d'une cité etc, dépouille mortelle*) remains ; **avoir du temps de ~** to have time to spare ; **ne voulant pas être en ~** not wishing to be outdone ; **sans demander son ~** without waiting to hear more ; **du ~, au ~** *ad* besides, moreover.

rester [Rɛste] *vi* (*dans un lieu, un état, une position*) to stay, remain ; (*subsister*) to remain, be left ; (*durer*) to last, live on //

vb impersonnel: **il reste du pain/2 œufs** there's some bread/there are 2 eggs left (over); **il reste du temps/10 minutes** there's some time/there are 10 minutes left; **il me reste assez de temps** I have enough time left; **ce qui reste à faire** what remains to be done; **ce qui me reste à faire** what remains for me to do; **en ~ à** (*stade, menaces*) to go no further than, only go as far as; **restons-en là** let's leave it at that; **y ~: il a failli y ~** he nearly met his end.

restituer [ʀɛstitɥe] *vt* (*objet, somme*): **~ qch (à qn)** to return sth (to sb); (*TECH*) to release; to reproduce.

restoroute [ʀɛstɔʀut] *nm* motorway restaurant.

restreindre [ʀɛstʀɛdʀ(ə)] *vt* to restrict, limit; **se ~** *vi* (*champ de recherches*) to narrow.

restriction [ʀɛstʀiksjɔ̃] *nf* restriction; **~s** (*mentales*) reservations.

résultat [ʀezylta] *nm* result; (*conséquence*) outcome *q*, result; (*d'élection etc*) results *pl*; **~s sportifs** sports results.

résulter [ʀezylte]: **~ de** *vt* to result from, be the result of.

résumé [ʀezyme] *nm* summary, résumé; **en ~** *ad* in brief; to sum up.

résumer [ʀezyme] *vt* (*texte*) to summarize; (*récapituler*) to sum up; (*fig*) to epitomize, typify; **se ~ à** to come down to.

résurrection [ʀezyʀɛksjɔ̃] *nf* resurrection; (*fig*) revival.

rétablir [ʀetabliʀ] *vt* to restore, re-establish; (*personne: suj: traitement*): **~ qn** to restore sb to health, help sb recover; (*ADMIN*): **~ qn dans son emploi** to reinstate sb in his post; **se ~** *vi* (*guérir*) to recover; (*silence, calme*) to return, be restored; (*GYM etc*): **se ~ (sur)** to pull o.s. up (onto); **rétablissement** *nm* restoring; recovery; pull-up.

rétamer [ʀetame] *vt* to re-coat, re-tin.

retaper [ʀətape] *vt* (*maison, voiture etc*) to do up; (*fam: revigorer*) to buck up; (*redactylographier*) to retype.

retard [ʀətaʀ] *nm* (*d'une personne attendue*) lateness *q*; (*sur l'horaire, un programme, une échéance*) delay; (*fig: scolaire, mental etc*) backwardness; **en ~** (*de 2 heures*) (2 hours) late; **avoir un ~ de 2 km** (*SPORT*) to be 2 km behind; **avoir du ~** to be late; (*sur un programme*) to be behind (schedule); **prendre du ~** (*train, avion*) to be delayed; (*montre*) to lose (time); **sans ~** *ad* without delay; **~ à l'allumage** (*AUTO*) retarded spark.

retardataire [ʀətaʀdatɛʀ] *nm/f* latecomer.

retardement: **à ~** *a* delayed action *cpd*; **bombe à ~** time bomb.

retarder [ʀətaʀde] *vt* (*sur un horaire*): **~ qn (d'une heure)** to delay sb (an hour); (*sur un programme*): **~ qn (de 3 mois)** to set sb back *ou* delay sb (3 months); (*départ, date*): **~ qch (de 2 jours)** to put sth back (2 days), delay sth (for *ou* by 2 days) // *vi* (*montre*) to be slow; to lose (time); **je retarde (d'une heure)** I'm (an hour) slow.

retenir [ʀətniʀ] *vt* (*garder, retarder*) to keep, detain; (*maintenir: objet qui glisse, fig: colère, larmes*) to hold back; (: *objet suspendu*) to hold; (: *chaleur, odeur*) to retain; (*fig: empêcher d'agir*): **~ qn (de faire)** to hold sb back (from doing); (*se rappeler*) to remember; (*réserver*) to reserve; (*accepter*) to accept; (*prélever*): **~ qch (sur)** to deduct sth (from); **se ~** (*se raccrocher*): **se ~ à** to hold onto; (*se contenir*): **se ~ de faire** to restrain o.s. from doing; **~ son souffle** *ou* **haleine** to hold one's breath; **je pose 3 et je retiens 2** put down 3 and carry 2.

retentir [ʀətɑ̃tiʀ] *vi* to ring out; (*salle*): **~ de** to ring *ou* resound with; **~ sur** *vt* (*fig*) to have an effect upon.

retentissant, e [ʀətɑ̃tisɑ̃, -ɑ̃t] *a* resounding; (*fig*) impact-making.

retentissement [ʀətɑ̃tismɑ̃] *nm* repercussion; effect, impact; stir.

retenue [ʀətny] *nf* (*prélèvement*) deduction; (*SCOL*) detention; (*modération*) (self-)restraint; (*réserve*) reserve, reticence.

réticence [ʀetisɑ̃s] *nf* hesitation, reluctance *q*.

rétif, ive [ʀetif, -iv] *a* restive.

rétine [ʀetin] *nf* retina.

retiré, e [ʀətiʀe] *a* secluded.

retirer [ʀətiʀe] *vt* to withdraw; (*vêtement, lunettes*) to take off, remove; (*extraire*): **~ qch de** to take sth out of, remove sth from; (*reprendre: bagages, billets*) to collect, pick up; **~ des avantages de** to derive advantages from; **se ~** *vi* (*partir, reculer*) to withdraw; (*prendre sa retraite*) to retire; **se ~ de** to withraw from; to retire from.

retombées [ʀətɔ̃be] *nfpl* (*radioactives*) fallout *sg*; (*fig*) fallout; spin-offs.

retomber [ʀətɔ̃be] *vi* (*à nouveau*) to fall again; (*atterrir: après un saut etc*) to land; (*tomber, redescendre*) to fall back; (*pendre*) to fall, hang (down); (*échoir*): **~ sur qn** to fall on sb.

rétorquer [ʀetɔʀke] *vt*: **~ (à qn) que** to retort (to sb) that.

retors, e [ʀətɔʀ, -ɔʀs(ə)] *a* wily.

rétorsion [ʀetɔʀsjɔ̃] *nf*: **mesures de ~** reprisals.

retouche [ʀətuʃ] *nf* touching up *q*; alteration.

retoucher [ʀətuʃe] *vt* (*photographie, tableau*) to touch up; (*texte, vêtement*) to alter.

retour [ʀətuʀ] *nm* return; **au ~** when we (*ou they etc*) get (*ou* got) back; on the way back; **être de ~ (de)** to be back (from); **par ~ du courrier** by return of post; **~ en arrière** (*CINEMA*) flashback; (*mesure*) backward step; **~ offensif** renewed attack.

retourner [ʀətuʀne] *vt* (*dans l'autre sens: matelas, crêpe*) to turn (over); (: *caisse*) to turn upside down; (: *sac, vêtement*) to turn inside out; (*fig: argument*) to turn back; (*e remuant: terre, sol, foin*) to turn over; (*émouvoir: personne*) to shake; (*renvoyer, restituer*): **~ qch à qn** to return sth to sb // *vi* (*aller, revenir*): **~ quelque part/à** to go back *ou* return somewhere/to; **~ à**

(*état, activité*) to return to, go back to; **se ~** *vi* to turn over; (*tourner la tête*) to turn round; **se ~ contre** (*fig*) to turn against; **savoir de quoi il retourne** to know what it is all about; **~ en arrière** *ou* **sur ses pas** to turn back, retrace one's steps.

retracer [RətRase] *vt* to relate, recount.

rétracter [RetRakte] *vt*, **se ~** *vi* to retract.

retraduire [RətRaduiR] *vt* to translate again; (*dans la langue de départ*) to translate back.

retrait [RətRɛ] *nm* (*voir retirer*) withdrawal; collection; redemption; (*voir se retirer*) withdrawal; (*rétrécissement*) shrinkage; **en ~** a set back; **~ du permis (de conduire)** disqualification from driving.

retraite [RətRɛt] *nf* (*d'une armée*, REL, *refuge*) retreat; (*d'un employé*) retirement; (retirement) pension; **être/mettre à la ~** to be retired *ou* in retirement/pension off *ou* retire; **prendre sa ~** to retire; **~ anticipée** early retirement; **~ aux flambeaux** torchlight tattoo; **retraité, e** a retired // *nm/f* (old age) pensioner.

retranchement [RətRɑ̃ʃmɑ̃] *nm* entrenchment.

retrancher [RətRɑ̃ʃe] *vt* (*passage, détails*) to take out, remove; (*nombre, somme*): **~ qch de** to take *ou* deduct sth from; (*couper*) to cut off; **se ~ derrière/dans** to entrench o.s. behind/in; (*fig*) to take refuge behind/in.

retransmettre [RətRɑ̃smɛtR(ə)] *vt* (*RADIO*) to broadcast, relay; (*TV*) to show; **retransmission** *nf* broadcast; showing.

retraverser [RətRavɛRse] *vt* (*dans l'autre sens*) to cross back over.

rétrécir [RetResiR] *vt* (*vêtement*) to take in // *vi* to shrink; **se ~** *vi* to narrow.

retremper [RətRɑ̃pe] *vt*: **se ~ dans** (*fig*) to reimmerse o.s. in.

rétribuer [RetRibɥe] *vt* (*travail*) to pay for; (*personne*) to pay; **rétribution** *nf* payment.

rétro [RetRo] a *inv*: **la mode ~** the nostalgia vogue.

rétroactif, ive [RetRoaktif, -iv] a retroactive.

rétrograde [RetRogRad] a reactionary, backward-looking.

rétrograder [RetRogRade] *vi* (*élève*) to fall back; (*économie*) to regress; (*AUTO*) to change down.

rétrospective [RetRospɛktiv] *nf* retrospective exhibition; season showing old films; **~ment** *ad* in retrospect.

retrousser [RətRuse] *vt* to roll up.

retrouvailles [RətRuvɑj] *nfpl* reunion *sg*.

retrouver [RətRuve] *vt* (*fugitif, objet perdu*) to find; (*occasion*) to find again; (*calme, santé*) to regain; (*revoir*) to see again; (*rejoindre*) to meet (again), join; **se ~** *vi* to meet; (*s'orienter*) to find one's way; **se ~ quelque part** to find o.s. somewhere; to end up somewhere; **s'y ~** (*rentrer dans ses frais*) to break even.

rétroviseur [RetRovizœR] *nm* (rear-view *ou* driving) mirror.

réunion [Reynjɔ̃] *nf* bringing together; joining; (*séance*) meeting; **l'île de la R~**, **la R~** Réunion.

réunir [ReyniR] *vt* (*convoquer*) to call together; (*rassembler*) to gather together; (*cumuler*) to combine; (*rapprocher*) to bring together (again), reunite; (*rattacher*) to join (together); **se ~** *vi* (*se rencontrer*) to meet; (*s'allier*) to unite.

réussi, e [Reysi] a successful.

réussir [ReysiR] *vi* to succeed, be successful; (*à un examen*) to pass; (*plante, culture*) to thrive, do well // *vi* to make a success of; to bring off; **~ à faire** to succeed in doing; **~ à qn** to go right for sb; to agree with sb.

réussite [Reysit] *nf* success; (*CARTES*) patience.

revaloir [RəvalwaR] *vt*: **je vous revaudrai cela** I'll repay you some day; (*en mal*) I'll pay you back for this.

revaloriser [RəvalɔRize] *vt* (*monnaie*) to revalue; (*salaires, pensions*) to raise the level of; (*institution, tradition*) to reassert the value of.

revanche [Rəvɑ̃ʃ] *nf* revenge; **prendre sa ~ (sur)** to take one's revenge (on); **en ~** on the other hand.

rêvasser [Rɛvase] *vi* to daydream.

rêve [Rɛv] *nm* dream; (*activité psychique*): **le ~** dreaming; **~ éveillé** daydreaming q, daydream.

revêche [Rəvɛʃ] a surly, sour-tempered.

réveil [Revɛj] *nm* (*d'un dormeur*) waking up q; (*fig*) awakening; (*pendule*) alarm (clock); **au ~** when I (*ou* he) woke up, on waking (up); **sonner le ~** (*MIL*) to sound the reveille.

réveille-matin [Revɛjmatɛ̃] *nm inv* alarm clock.

réveiller [Reveje] *vt* (*personne*) to wake up; (*fig*) to awaken, revive; **se ~** *vi* to wake up; (*fig*) to be revived, reawaken.

réveillon [Revɛjɔ̃] *nm* Christmas Eve; (*de la Saint-Sylvestre*) New Year's Eve; Christmas Eve (*ou* New Year's Eve) party *ou* dinner; **réveillonner** *vi* to celebrate Christmas Eve (*ou* New Year's Eve).

révélateur, trice [Revelatœr, -tris] a: **~ (de qch)** revealing (sth) // *nm* (*PHOTO*) developer.

révélation [Revelɑsjɔ̃] *nf* revelation.

révéler [Revele] *vt* (*gén*) to reveal; (*divulguer*) to disclose, reveal; (*dénoter*) to reveal, show; (*faire connaître au public*): **~ qn/qch** to make sb/ sth widely known, bring sb/sth to the public's notice; **se ~** *vi* to be revealed, reveal itself // *vb avec attribut* to prove (to be).

revenant, e [Rəvnɑ̃, -ɑ̃t] *nm/f* ghost.

revendeur, euse [Rəvɑ̃dœR, -øz] *nm/f* (*détaillant*) retailer; (*d'occasions*) secondhand dealer.

revendication [Rəvɑ̃dikɑsjɔ̃] *nf* claim, demand; **journée de ~** day of action (in support of one's claims).

revendiquer [Rəvɑ̃dike] *vt* to claim, demand; (*responsabilité*) to claim // *vi* to agitate in favour of one's claims.

revendre [RəvɑdR(ə)] *vt* (*d'occasion*) to resell; (*détailler*) to sell; (*vendre davantage de*): **~ du sucre/un foulard/deux bagues** to sell more sugar/another scarf/ another two rings; **à ~** *ad* (*en abondance*) to spare, aplenty.

revenir [Rəvniʀ] vi to come back ; (CULIN):
faire ~ to brown ; (coûter): **~ cher/à 100
F** (à qn) to cost (sb) a lot/100 F ; **~ à**
(études, projet) to return to, go back to ;
(équivaloir à) to amount to ; **~ à qn**
(rumeur, nouvelle) to get back to sb, reach
sb's ears ; (part, honneur) to go to sb, be
sb's ; (souvenir, nom) to come back to sb ;
~ de (fig: maladie, étonnement) to recover
from ; **~ sur** (question, sujet) to go back
over ; (engagement) to go back on ; **~ à
la charge** to return to the attack ; **~ à
soi** to come round ; **n'en pas ~: je n'en
reviens pas** I can't get over it ; **~ sur ses
pas** to retrace one's steps ; **cela revient
à dire que** it amounts to saying that.

revente [Rəvɑ̃t] nf resale.

revenu [Rəvny] nm income ; (de l'État)
revenue ; (d'un capital) yield ; **~s** nmpl
income sg.

rêver [Reve] vi, vt to dream ; **~
qch/faire** to dream of sth/doing ; **~ à** to
dream of.

réverbération [ReveʀbeRɑsjɔ̃] nf
reflection.

réverbère [RevɛʀbɛR] nm street lamp ou
light.

réverbérer [RevɛʀbeRe] vt to reflect.

révérence [ReveRɑ̃s] nf (vénération)
reverence ; (salut) bow ; curtsey.

révérend, e [ReveRɑ̃, -ɑ̃d] a: **le ~ père
Pascal** the Reverend Father Pascal.

révérer [ReveRe] vt to revere.

rêverie [Revʀi] nf daydreaming q,
daydream.

revers [RəvɛR] nm (de feuille, main) back ;
(d'étoffe) wrong side ; (de pièce, médaille)
back, reverse ; (TENNIS, PING-PONG)
backhand ; (de veston) lapel ; (de pantalon)
turn-up ; (fig: échec) setback ; **le ~ de la
médaille** (fig) the other side of the coin ;
prendre à ~ (MIL) to take from the rear.

réversible [RevɛRsibl(ə)] a reversible.

revêtement [Rəvɛtmɑ̃] nm (de paroi)
facing ; (des sols) flooring ; (de chaussée)
surface ; (de tuyau etc: enduit) coating.

revêtir [RəvɛtiR] vt (habit) to don, put on ;
(fig) to take on ; **~ qn de** to dress sb in ;
(fig) to endow ou invest sb with ; **~ qch
de** to cover sth with ; (fig) to cloak sth
in ; **~ d'un visa** to append a visa to.

rêveur, euse [RevœR, -øz] a dreamy //
nm/f dreamer.

revient [Rəvjɛ̃] vb voir **revenir** // nm: **prix
de ~** cost price.

revigorer [RevigɔRe] vt to invigorate,
brace up ; to revive, buck up.

revirement [RəviRmɑ̃] nm change of
mind ; (d'une situation) reversal.

réviser [Revize] vt (texte, SCOL: matière) to
revise ; (comptes) to audit ; (machine,
installation, moteur) to overhaul, service ;
(JUR: procès) to review.

révision [Revizjɔ̃] nf revision ; auditing q ;
overhaul ; servicing q ; review ; **conseil de
~** (MIL) recruiting board ; **faire ses ~s**
(SCOL) to do one's revision, revise ; **la ~
des 10000 km** (AUTO) the 10,000 km
service.

revisser [Rəvise] vt to screw back again.

revivifier [Rəvivifje] vt to revitalize.

revivre [RəvivR(ə)] vi (reprendre des forces)
to come alive again ; (traditions) to be
revived // vt (épreuve, moment) to relive.

révocation [Revɔkɑsjɔ̃] nf dismissal ;
revocation.

revoir [RəvwaR] vt to see again ; (réviser)
to revise // nm: **au ~** goodbye ; **dire au
~ à qn** to say goodbye to sb.

révolte [Revɔlt(ə)] nf rebellion, revolt.

révolter [Revɔlte] vt to revolt ; to outrage,
appal ; **se ~** vi: **se ~ (contre)** to rebel
(against) ; **se ~ (à)** to be outraged (by).

révolu, e [Revɔly] a past ; (ADMIN): **âgé de
18 ans ~s** over 18 years of age ; **après
3 ans ~s** when 3 full years have passed.

révolution [Revɔlysjɔ̃] nf revolution ;
révolutionnaire a, nm/f revolutionary ;
révolutionner vt to revolutionize ; (fig) to
stir up.

revolver [RevɔlvɛR] nm gun ; (à barillet)
revolver.

révoquer [Revɔke] vt (fonctionnaire) to
dismiss, remove from office ; (arrêt,
contrat) to revoke.

revue [Rəvy] nf (inventaire, examen)
review ; (MIL: défilé) review, march-past ;
(: inspection) inspection, review ;
(périodique) review, magazine ; (pièce
satirique) revue ; (de music-hall) variety
show ; **passer en ~** to review, inspect ;
(fig) to review, survey ; to go through.

révulsé, e [Revylse] a (yeux) rolled
upwards ; (visage) contorted.

rez-de-chaussée [Redʃose] nm inv
ground floor.

RF sigle = République Française.

rhabiller [Rabije] vt: **se ~** to get dressed
again, put one's clothes on again.

rhapsodie [Rapsɔdi] nf rhapsody.

rhénan, e [Renɑ̃, -an] a Rhine cpd.

Rhénanie [Renani] nf: **la ~** the Rhineland.

rhésus [Rezys] a, nm rhesus.

rhétorique [RetɔRik] nf rhetoric.

rhéto-roman, e [RetɔRɔmɑ̃, -an] a
Rhaeto-Romanic.

Rhin [Rɛ̃] nm: **le ~** the Rhine.

rhinocéros [RinɔseRɔs] nm rhinoceros.

rhodanien, ne [Rɔdanjɛ̃, -jɛn] a Rhone
cpd.

Rhodésie [Rɔdezi] nf: **la ~** Rhodesia ;
rhodésien, ne a Rhodesian.

rhododendron [Rɔdɔdɛ̃dRɔ̃] nm
rhododendron.

Rhône [Ron] nm: **le ~** the Rhone.

rhubarbe [Rybarb(ə)] nf rhubarb.

rhum [Rɔm] nm rum.

rhumatisant, e [Rymatizɑ̃, -ɑ̃t] nm/f
rheumatic.

rhumatismal, e, aux [Rymatismal, -o] a
rheumatic.

rhumatisme [Rymatism(ə)] nm
rheumatism q.

rhume [Rym] nm cold ; **~ de cerveau**
head cold ; **le ~ des foins** hay fever.

ri [Ri] pp de rire.

riant, e [Rjɑ̃, -ɑ̃t] a smiling, cheerful.

ribambelle [Ribɑ̃bɛl] nf: **une ~ de** a herd
ou swarm of.

ricaner [Rikane] vi (avec méchanceté) to
snigger ; (bêtement, avec gêne) to giggle.

riche [Riʃ] a (gén) rich; (personne, pays) rich, wealthy; ~ en rich in; ~ de full of; rich in; **richesse** nf wealth; (fig) richness; **richesses** nfpl wealth sg; treasures; **richesse en vitamines** high vitamin content.

ricin [Risɛ̃] nm: huile de ~ castor oil.

ricocher [Rikɔʃe] vi: ~ (sur) to rebound (off); (sur l'eau) to bounce (on ou off); **faire** ~ (galet) to skim.

ricochet [Rikɔʃɛ] nm rebound; bounce; **faire des** ~s to skim pebbles; **par** ~ ad on the rebound; (fig) as an indirect result.

rictus [Riktys] nm grin; (snarling) grimace.

ride [Rid] nf wrinkle; (fig) ripple.

ridé, e [Ride] a wrinkled.

rideau, x [Rido] nm curtain; ~ **de fer** metal shutter; (POL): **le** ~ **de fer** the Iron Curtain.

ridelle [Ridɛl] nf slatted side.

rider [Ride] vt to wrinkle; (fig) to ripple; to ruffle the surface of; **se** ~ vi (avec l'âge) to become wrinkled; (de contrariété) to wrinkle.

ridicule [Ridikyl] a ridiculous // nm ridiculousness q; **le** ~ ridicule; **tourner en** ~ to ridicule; **ridiculiser** vt to ridicule; **se ridiculiser** to make a fool of o.s.

rie vb voir **rire**.

rien [Rjɛ̃] pronom nothing; (quelque chose) anything; **ne** ... ~ nothing, tournure négative + anything // nm nothing; ~ **d'autre** nothing else; ~ **du tout** nothing at all; ~ **que** just, only; nothing but; **il n'a** ~ (n'est pas blessé) he's all right; **un petit** ~ (cadeau) a little something; **des** ~s trivia pl.

rieur, euse [RjœR, -øz] a cheerful, merry.

rigide [Riʒid] a stiff; (fig) rigid; strict; **rigidité** nf stiffness; **la rigidité cadavérique** rigor mortis.

rigolade [Rigɔlad] nf: **la** ~ fun; (fig): **c'est de la** ~ it's a cinch; it's a big farce.

rigole [Rigɔl] nf (conduit) channel; (filet d'eau) rivulet.

rigoler [Rigɔle] vi (rire) to laugh; (s'amuser) to have (some) fun; (plaisanter) to be joking ou kidding.

rigolo, ote [Rigɔlo, -ɔt] a (fam) funny // nm/f comic; (péj) fraud, phoney.

rigoureux, euse [RiguRø, -øz] a (morale) rigorous, strict; (personne) stern, strict; (climat, châtiment) rigorous, harsh, severe; (interdiction, neutralité) strict; (preuves, analyse, méthode) rigorous.

rigueur [RigœR] nf rigour; strictness; harshness; '**tenue de soirée de** ~' 'evening dress (to be worn)'; **être de** ~ to be the usual thing ou the rule; **à la** ~ at a pinch; possibly; **tenir** ~ **à qn de qch** to hold sth against sb.

rillettes [Rijɛt] nfpl potted meat sg.

rime [Rim] nf rhyme; **rimer** vi: **rimer (avec)** to rhyme (with); **ne rimer à rien** not to make sense.

rinçage [Rɛ̃saʒ] nm rinsing (out); (opération) rinse.

rince-doigts [Rɛ̃sdwa] nm inv finger-bowl.

rincer [Rɛ̃se] vt to rinse; (récipient) to rinse out.

ring [Riŋ] nm (boxing) ring.

rions vb voir **rire**.

ripaille [Ripɑj] nf: **faire** ~ to feast.

ripoliné, e [Ripɔline] a enamel-painted.

riposte [Ripɔst(ə)] nf retort, riposte; (fig) counter-attack, reprisal.

riposter [Ripɔste] vi to retaliate // vt: ~ **que** to retort that; ~ **à** vt to counter; to reply to.

rire [RiR] vi to laugh; (se divertir) to have fun // nm laugh; **le** ~ laughter; ~ **de** vt to laugh at; **se** ~ **de** to make light of; **pour** ~ (pas sérieusement) for a joke ou a laugh.

ris [Ri] vb voir **rire** // nm: ~ **de veau** (calf) sweetbread.

risée [Rize] nf: **être la** ~ **de** to be the laughing stock of.

risette [Rizɛt] nf: **faire** ~ (à) to give a nice little smile (to).

risible [Rizibl(ə)] a laughable, ridiculous.

risque [Risk(ə)] nm risk; **le** ~ danger; **prendre des** ~s to take risks; **à ses** ~s **et périls** at his own risk; **au** ~ **de** at the risk of.

risqué, e [Riske] a risky; (plaisanterie) risqué, daring.

risquer [Riske] vt to risk; (allusion, question) to venture, hazard; **tu risques qu'on te renvoie** you risk being dismissed; **ça ne risque rien** it's quite safe; ~ **de**: **il risque de se tuer** he could get ou risks getting himself killed; **il a risqué de se tuer** he almost got himself killed; **ce qui risque de se produire** what might ou could well happen; **il ne risque pas de recommencer** there's no chance of him doing that again; **se** ~ **dans** (s'aventurer) to venture into; **se** ~ **à faire** (tenter) to venture ou dare to do; **risque-tout** nm/f inv daredevil.

rissoler [Risɔle] vi, vt: (faire) ~ to brown.

ristourne [RistuRn(ə)] nf rebate.

rite [Rit] nm rite; (fig) ritual.

ritournelle [RituRnɛl] nf (fig) tune.

rituel, le [Rituɛl] a, nm ritual.

rivage [Rivaʒ] nm shore.

rival, e, aux [Rival, -o] a, nm/f rival.

rivaliser [Rivalize] vi: ~ **avec** to rival, vie with; (être comparable) to hold its own against, compare with; ~ **avec qn de** (élégance etc) to vie with ou rival sb in.

rivalité [Rivalite] nf rivalry.

rive [Riv] nf shore; (de fleuve) bank.

river [Rive] vt (clou, pointe) to clinch; (plaques) to rivet together; **être rivé sur/à** to be riveted on/to.

riverain, e [RivRɛ̃, -ɛn] a riverside cpd; lakeside cpd; roadside cpd // nm/f riverside (ou lakeside) resident; local ou roadside resident.

rivet [Rivɛ] nm rivet; **riveter** vt to rivet (together).

rivière [RivjɛR] nf river; ~ **de diamants** diamond rivière.

rixe [Riks(ə)] nf brawl, scuffle.

riz [Ri] nm rice; ~ **au lait** rice pudding; **rizière** nf paddy-field.

R.N. sigle f = route nationale, voir **national**.

robe [ʀɔb] nf dress; (de juge, d'ecclésiastique) robe; (de professeur) gown; (pelage) coat; ~ **de soirée/de mariée** evening/wedding dress; ~ **de baptême** christening robe; ~ **de chambre** dressing gown; ~ **de grossesse** maternity dress.

robinet [ʀɔbinɛ] nm tap; ~ **du gaz** gas tap; ~ **mélangeur** mixer tap; **robinetterie** nf taps pl, plumbing.

roboratif, ive [ʀɔbɔʀatif, -iv] a bracing, invigorating.

robot [ʀɔbo] nm robot.

robuste [ʀɔbyst(ə)] a robust, sturdy.

roc [ʀɔk] nm rock.

rocade [ʀɔkad] nf (AUTO) by-road, bypass.

rocaille [ʀɔkɑj] nf loose stones pl; rocky ou stony ground; (jardin) rockery, rock garden // a (style) rocaille; **rocailleux, euse** a rocky, stony; (voix) harsh.

rocambolesque [ʀɔkɑbɔlɛsk(ə)] a fantastic, incredible.

roche [ʀɔʃ] nf rock.

rocher [ʀɔʃe] nm rock; (ANAT) petrosal bone.

rochet [ʀɔʃɛ] nm: **roue à** ~ rachet wheel.

rocheux, euse [ʀɔʃø, -øz] a rocky.

rock (and roll) [ʀɔk(ɛnʀɔl)] nm (musique) rock(-'n'-roll); (danse) jive.

rodage [ʀɔdaʒ] nm running in; **en** ~ (AUTO) running in.

rodéo [ʀɔdeo] nm rodeo (pl s).

roder [ʀɔde] vt (moteur, voiture) to run in.

rôder [ʀode] vi to roam ou wander about; (de façon suspecte) to lurk ou loiter (about ou around); **rôdeur, euse** nm/f prowler.

rodomontades [ʀɔdɔmɔ̃tad] nfpl bragging sg; sabre rattling sg.

rogatoire [ʀɔgatwaʀ] a: **commission** ~ letters rogatory.

rogne [ʀɔɲ] nf: **être en** ~ to be ratty ou in a temper.

rogner [ʀɔɲe] vt to trim; to clip; (fig) to whittle down; ~ **sur** (fig) to cut down ou back on.

rognons [ʀɔɲɔ̃] nmpl kidneys.

rognures [ʀɔɲyʀ] nfpl trimmings; clippings.

rogue [ʀɔg] a arrogant.

roi [ʀwa] nm king; **le jour** ou **la fête des R~s, les** ~**s** Twelfth Night.

roitelet [ʀwatlɛ] nm wren; (péj) kinglet.

rôle [ʀol] nm role; (contribution) part.

rollmops [ʀɔlmɔps] nm rollmop.

romain, e [ʀɔmɛ̃, -ɛn] a, nm/f Roman // nf (BOT) cos (lettuce).

roman, e [ʀɔmɑ̃, -an] a (ARCHIT) Romanesque; (LING) Romance, Romanic // nm novel; ~ **d'espionnage** spy novel ou story; ~ **photo** romantic picture story.

romance [ʀɔmɑ̃s] nf ballad.

romancer [ʀɔmɑ̃se] vt to make into a novel; to romanticize.

romanche [ʀɔmɑ̃ʃ] a, nm Romansh.

romancier, ière [ʀɔmɑ̃sje, -jɛʀ] nm/f novelist.

romand, e [ʀɔmɑ̃, -ɑ̃d] a of ou from French-speaking Switzerland.

romanesque [ʀɔmanɛsk(ə)] a (fantastique) fantastic; storybook cpd;

(sentimental) romantic; (LITTÉRATURE) novelistic.

roman-feuilleton [ʀɔmɑ̃fœjtɔ̃] nm serialized novel.

romanichel, le [ʀɔmaniʃɛl] nm/f gipsy.

romantique [ʀɔmɑ̃tik] a romantic.

romantisme [ʀɔmɑ̃tism(ə)] nm romanticism.

romarin [ʀɔmaʀɛ̃] nm rosemary.

Rome [ʀɔm] nf Rome.

rompre [ʀɔ̃pʀ(ə)] vt to break; (entretien, fiançailles) to break off // vi (fiancés) to break it off; **se** ~ vi to break; (MÉD) to burst, rupture; **se** ~ **les os** ou **le cou** to break one's neck; ~ **avec** to break with; **rompez (les rangs)!** (MIL) dismiss!, fall out!

rompu, e [ʀɔ̃py] a (fourbu) exhausted, worn out; ~ **à** with wide experience of; inured to.

romsteak [ʀɔmstɛk] nm rumpsteak q.

ronce [ʀɔ̃s] nf (BOT) bramble branch; (MENUISERIE): ~ **de noyer** burr walnut; ~**s** nfpl brambles, thorns.

ronchonner [ʀɔ̃ʃɔne] vi (fam) to grouse, grouch.

rond, e [ʀɔ̃, ʀɔ̃d] a round; (joues, mollets) well-rounded; (fam: ivre) tight // nm (cercle) ring; (fam: sou) **je n'ai plus un** ~ I haven't a penny left // nf (gén: de surveillance) rounds pl, patrol; (danse) round (dance); (MUS) semibreve; **en** ~ (s'asseoir, danser) in a ring; **à la** ~**e** (alentour): **à 10 km à la** ~**e** for 10 km round; (à chacun son tour): **passer qch à la** ~**e** to pass sth a(r)ound; **faire des** ~**s de jambe** to bow and scrape; ~ **de serviette** serviette ring; ~**-de-cuir** nm (péj) penpusher; **rondelet, te** a plump.

rondelle [ʀɔ̃dɛl] nf (TECH) washer; (tranche) slice, round.

rondement [ʀɔ̃dmɑ̃] ad briskly; frankly.

rondeur [ʀɔ̃dœʀ] nf (d'un bras, des formes) plumpness; (bonhomie) friendly straightforwardness; ~**s** nfpl (d'une femme) curves.

rondin [ʀɔ̃dɛ̃] nm log.

rond-point [ʀɔ̃pwɛ̃] nm roundabout.

ronéotyper [ʀɔneotipe] vt to duplicate, roneo.

ronflant, e [ʀɔ̃flɑ̃, -ɑ̃t] a (péj) high-flown, grand.

ronflement [ʀɔ̃fləmɑ̃] nm snore, snoring q.

ronfler [ʀɔ̃fle] vi to snore; (moteur, poêle) to hum; to roar.

ronger [ʀɔ̃ʒe] vt to gnaw (at); (suj: vers, rouille) to eat into; ~ **son frein** to champ (at) the bit; **se** ~ **de souci, se** ~ **les sangs** to worry o.s. sick, fret; **se** ~ **les ongles** to bite one's nails; **rongeur, euse** nm/f rodent.

ronronner [ʀɔ̃ʀɔne] vi to purr.

roque [ʀɔk] nm (ÉCHECS) castling; **roquer** vi to castle.

roquet [ʀɔkɛ] nm nasty little lap-dog.

roquette [ʀɔkɛt] nf rocket.

rosace [ʀɔzas] nf (vitrail) rose window, rosace; (motif: de plafond etc) rose.

rosaire [ʀozɛʀ] nm rosary.

rosbif [ʀɔsbif] nm: **du** ~ roasting beef; (cuit) roast beef; **un** ~ a joint of beef.

rose [Roz] *nf* rose; (*vitrail*) rose window // a pink; ~ **bonbon** a *inv* candy pink; ~ **des vents** compass card.

rosé, e [Roze] a pinkish; (*vin*) ~ rosé (wine).

roseau, x [Rozo] *nm* reed.

rosée [Roze] *nf* dew; **goutte de** ~ dewdrop.

roseraie [RozRε] *nf* rose garden; (*plantation*) rose nursery.

rosette [Rozεt] *nf* rosette (*gen of the Légion d'honneur*).

rosier [Rozje] *nm* rosebush, rose tree.

rosir [RoziR] *vi* to go pink.

rosse [Ros] *nf* (*péj: cheval*) nag // a nasty, vicious.

rosser [Rose] *vt* (*fam*) to thrash.

rossignol [Rosiɲɔl] *nm* (*ZOOL*) nightingale; (*crochet*) picklock.

rot [Ro] *nm* belch; (*de bébé*) burp.

rotatif, ive [Rotatif, -iv] a rotary // *nf* rotary press.

rotation [Rotasjɔ̃] *nf* rotation; (*fig*) rotation, swap-around; turnover; **par** ~ **on a rota basis**; ~ **des cultures** rotation of crops; ~ **des stocks** stock turnover.

roter [Rote] *vi* (*fam*) to burp, belch.

rôti [Roti] *nm*: **du** ~ roasting meat; (*cuit*) roast meat; **un** ~ **de bœuf/porc** a joint of beef/pork.

rotin [Rotε̃] *nm* rattan (cane); **fauteuil en** ~ cane (arm)chair.

rôtir [RotiR] *vt* (*aussi*: **faire** ~) to roast // *vi* to roast; **se** ~ **au soleil** to bask in the sun; **rôtisserie** *nf* steakhouse; roast meat counter (*ou* shop); **rôtissoire** *nf* (roasting) spit.

rotonde [Rotɔ̃d] *nf* (*ARCHIT*) rotunda; (*RAIL*) engine shed.

rotondité [Rotɔ̃dite] *nf* roundness.

rotor [RotɔR] *nm* rotor.

rotule [Rotyl] *nf* kneecap, patella.

roturier, ière [RotyRje, -jεR] *nm/f* commoner.

rouage [Rwaʒ] *nm* cog(wheel), gearwheel; (*de montre*) part; (*fig*) cog; ~**s** (*fig*) internal structure *sg*.

roublard, e [RublaR, -aRd(ə)] a (*péj*) crafty, wily.

rouble [Rubl(ə)] *nm* rouble.

roucouler [Rukule] *vi* to coo; (*fig: péj*) to warble.

roue [Ru] *nf* wheel; **faire la** ~ (*paon*) to spread *ou* fan its tail; (*GYM*) to do a cartwheel; **descendre en** ~ **libre** to freewheel *ou* coast down; ~ **à aubes** paddle wheel; ~ **dentée** cogwheel; ~ **de secours** spare wheel.

roué, e [Rwe] a wily.

rouer [Rwe] *vt*: ~ **qn de coups** to give sb a thrashing.

rouet [Rwε] *nm* spinning wheel.

rouge [Ruʒ] a, *nm/f* red // *nm* red; (*fard*) rouge; (*vin*) ~ red wine; **passer au** ~ (*signal*) to go red; (*automobiliste*) to go through the red lights; **porter au** ~ (*métal*) to bring to red heat; ~ (**à lèvres**) lipstick; **rougeâtre** a reddish; ~**-gorge** *nm* robin (redbreast).

rougeole [Ruʒɔl] *nf* measles *sg*.

rougeoyer [Ruʒwaje] *vi* to glow red.

rouget [Ruʒε] *nm* mullet.

rougeur [RuʒœR] *nf* redness; (*du visage*) red face; ~**s** *nfpl* (*MÉD*) red blotches.

rougir [RuʒiR] *vi* (*de honte, timidité*) to blush, flush; (*de plaisir, colère*) to flush; (*fraise, tomate*) to go *ou* turn red; (*ciel*) to redden.

rouille [Ruj] *nf* rust // a *inv* rust-coloured, rusty.

rouillé, e [Ruje] a rusty.

rouiller [Ruje] *vt* to rust // *vi* to rust, go rusty; **se** ~ *vi* to rust; (*fig*) to become rusty; to grow stiff.

roulade [Rulad] *nf* (*GYM*) roll; (*CULIN*) rolled meat *q*; (*MUS*) roulade, run.

roulant, e [Rulɑ̃, -ɑ̃t] a (*meuble*) on wheels; (*surface, trottoir*) moving; **matériel** ~ (*RAIL*) rolling stock; **personnel** ~ (*RAIL*) train crews *pl*.

rouleau, x [Rulo] *nm* (*de papier, tissu, pièces de monnaie, SPORT*) roll; (*de machine à écrire*) roller, platen; (*à mise en plis, à peinture, vague*) roller; ~ **compresseur** steamroller; ~ **à pâtisserie** rolling pin; ~ **de pellicule** roll of film.

roulement [Rulmɑ̃] *nm* (*bruit*) rumbling *q*, rumble; (*rotation*) rotation; turnover; **par** ~ **on a rota basis**; ~ (**à billes**) ball bearings *pl*; ~ **de tambour** drum roll.

rouler [Rule] *vt* to roll; (*papier, tapis*) to roll up; (*CULIN: pâte*) to roll out; (*fam*) to do, con // *vi* (*bille, boule*) to roll; (*voiture, train*) to go, run; (*automobiliste*) to drive; (*cycliste*) to ride; (*bateau*) to roll; (*tonnerre*) to rumble, roll; (*dégringoler*): ~ **en bas de** to roll down; ~ **sur** (*suj: conversation*) to turn on; **se** ~ **dans** (*boue*) to roll in; (*couverture*) to roll o.s. (up) in; ~ **les épaules/hanches** to sway one's shoulders/wiggle one's hips.

roulette [Rulεt] *nf* (*de table, fauteuil*) castor; (*de pâtissier*) pastry wheel; (*jeu*): **la** ~ roulette; **à** ~**s** on castors.

roulis [Ruli] *nm* roll(ing).

roulotte [Rulɔt] *nf* caravan.

roumain, e [Rumε̃, -εn] a, *nm/f* Romanian.

Roumanie [Rumani] *nf* Romania.

roupiller [Rupije] *vi* (*fam*) to sleep.

rouquin, e [Rukε̃, -in] *nm/f* (*péj*) redhead.

rouspéter [Ruspete] *vi* (*fam*) to moan, grouse.

rousse [Rus] a *voir* **roux**.

rousseur [RusœR] *nf*: **tache de** ~ freckle.

roussi [Rusi] *nm*: **ça sent le** ~ there's a smell of burning; (*fig*) I can smell trouble.

roussir [RusiR] *vt* to scorch // *vi* (*feuilles*) to go *ou* turn brown; (*CULIN*): **faire** ~ to brown.

route [Rut] *nf* road; (*fig: chemin*) way; (*itinéraire, parcours*) route; (*fig: voie*) road, path; **par** (**la**) ~ by road; **il y a 3h de** ~ it's a 3-hour ride *ou* journey; **en** ~ *ad* on the way; **mettre en** ~ to start up; **se mettre en** ~ to set off; **faire** ~ **vers** to head towards; **routier, ière** a road *cpd* // *nm* (*camionneur*) (long-distance) lorry *ou* truck driver; (*restaurant*) ≈ transport café; (*scout*) ≈ rover // *nf* (*voiture*) touring car.

routine [Rutin] *nf* routine ; **routinier, ière** *a* (*péj*) humdrum ; addicted to routine.

rouvrir [RUVRiR] *vt, vi* to reopen, open again ; **se ~** *vi* (*blessure*) to open up again.

roux, rousse [RU, RUS] *a* red ; (*personne*) red-haired // *nm/f* redhead // *nm* (*CULIN*) roux.

royal, e, aux [Rwajal, -o] *a* royal ; (*fig*) fit for a king, princely ; blissful ; thorough.

royaliste [Rwajalist(ə)] *a, nm/f* royalist.

royaume [Rwajom] *nm* kingdom ; (*fig*) realm ; **le R~ Uni** the United Kingdom.

royauté [Rwajote] *nf* (*dignité*) kingship ; (*régime*) monarchy.

R.S.V.P. *sigle* (= *répondez s'il vous plaît*) R.S.V.P.

Rte *abr de* **route**.

ruade [Ryad] *nf* kick.

ruban [Rybã] *nm* (*gén*) ribbon ; (*pour ourlet, couture*) binding ; (*de téléscripteur etc*) tape ; (*d'acier*) strip ; **~ adhésif** adhesive tape.

rubéole [Rybeɔl] *nf* German measles *sg*, rubella.

rubicond, e [Rybikɔ̃, -ɔ̃d] *a* rubicund, ruddy.

rubis [Rybi] *nm* ruby ; (*HORLOGERIE*) jewel.

rubrique [Rybrik] *nf* (*titre, catégorie*) heading, rubric ; (*PRESSE: article*) column.

ruche [Ryʃ] *nf* hive.

rude [Ryd] *a* (*barbe, toile*) rough ; (*métier, tâche*) hard, tough ; (*climat*) severe, harsh ; (*bourru*) harsh, rough ; (*fruste*) rugged, tough ; (*fam*) jolly good ; **~ment** *ad* (*tomber, frapper*) hard ; (*traiter, reprocher*) harshly ; (*fam: très*) terribly, jolly ; (: *beaucoup*) jolly hard.

rudimentaire [Rydimãtɛr] *a* rudimentary, basic.

rudiments [Rydimã] *nmpl* rudiments ; basic knowledge *sg* ; basic principles.

rudoyer [Rydwaje] *vt* to treat harshly.

rue [Ry] *nf* street.

ruée [Rɥe] *nf* rush.

ruelle [Rɥɛl] *nf* alley(-way).

ruer [Rɥe] *vi* (*cheval*) to kick out ; **se ~** *vi* : **se ~ sur** to pounce on ; **se ~ vers/dans/hors de** to rush *ou* dash towards/into/out of ; **~ dans les brancards** to become rebellious.

rugby [Rygbi] *nm* Rugby (football) ; **~ à treize/quinze** Rugby League/Union.

rugir [RyʒiR] *vi* to roar ; **rugissement** *nm* roar, roaring *q*.

rugosité [Rygozite] *nf* roughness ; (*aspérité*) rough patch.

rugueux, euse [Rygø, -øz] *a* rough.

ruine [Rɥin] *nf* ruin ; **~s** *nfpl* ruins.

ruiner [Rɥine] *vt* to ruin ; **ruineux, euse** *a* terribly expensive to buy (*ou* run), ruinous ; extravagant.

ruisseau, x [Rɥiso] *nm* stream, brook ; (*caniveau*) gutter ; (*fig*): **~x de** floods of, streams of.

ruisseler [Rɥisle] *vi* to stream ; **~ (d'eau)** to be streaming (with water).

rumeur [RymœR] *nf* (*bruit confus*) rumbling ; hubbub *q* ; murmur(ing) ; (*nouvelle*) rumour.

ruminer [Rymine] *vt* (*herbe*) to ruminate ; (*fig*) to ruminate on *ou* over, chew over

// *vi* (*vache*) to chew the cud, ruminate.

rumsteak [Rɔmstɛk] *nm* = **romsteak**.

rupture [RyptyR] *nf* (*de câble, digue*) breaking ; (*de tendon*) rupture, tearing ; (*de négociations etc*) breakdown ; (*de contrat*) breach ; (*séparation, désunion*) break-up, split ; **en ~ de ban** at odds with authority.

rural, e, aux [RyRal, -o] *a* rural, country *cpd* // *nmpl*: **les ruraux** country people.

ruse [Ryz] *nf*: **la ~** cunning, craftiness ; trickery ; **une ~** a trick, a ruse ; **rusé, e** *a* cunning, crafty.

russe [Rys] *a, nm, nf* Russian.

Russie [Rysi] *nf*: **la ~** Russia.

rustique [Rystik] *a* rustic.

rustre [RystR(ə)] *nm* boor.

rut [Ryt] *nm*: **être en ~** to be in *ou* on heat, be rutting.

rutabaga [Rytabaga] *nm* swede.

rutilant, e [Rytilã, -ãt] *a* gleaming.

rythme [Ritm(ə)] *nm* rhythm ; (*vitesse*) rate ; (: *de la vie*) pace, tempo ; **au ~ de 10 par jour** at the rate of 10 a day ; **rythmé, e** *a* rhythmic(al) ; **rythmique** *a* rhythmic(al) // *nf* rhythmics *sg*.

S

s' [s] *pronom voir* **se**.

sa [sa] *dét voir* **son**.

S.A. *sigle voir* **société**.

sable [sabl(ə)] *nm* sand ; **~s mouvants** quicksand(s).

sablé [sable] *nm* shortbread biscuit.

sabler [sable] *vt* to sand ; (*contre le verglas*) to grit ; **~ le champagne** to drink champagne.

sableux, euse [sablø, -øz] *a* sandy.

sablier [sablije] *nm* hourglass ; (*de cuisine*) egg timer.

sablière [sablijɛR] *nf* sand quarry.

sablonneux, euse [sablɔnø, -øz] *a* sandy.

saborder [sabɔRde] *vt* (*navire*) to scuttle ; (*fig*) to wind up, shut down.

sabot [sabo] *nm* clog ; (*de cheval, bœuf*) hoof ; **~ de frein** brake shoe.

sabotage [sabɔtaʒ] *nm* sabotage.

saboter [sabɔte] *vt* to sabotage ; **saboteur, euse** *nm/f* saboteur.

sabre [sabR(ə)] *nm* sabre.

sac [sak] *nm* bag ; (*à charbon etc*) sack ; (*pillage*) sack(ing) ; **mettre à ~** to sack ; **~ à provisions/de voyage** shopping/travelling bag ; **~ de couchage** sleeping bag ; **~ à dos** rucksack ; **~ à main** handbag.

saccade [sakad] *nf* jerk ; **par ~s** jerkily ; haltingly.

saccager [sakaʒe] *vt* (*piller*) to sack, lay waste ; (*dévaster*) to create havoc in, wreck.

saccharine [sakaRin] *nf* saccharin(e).

sacerdoce [sasɛRdɔs] *nm* priesthood ; (*fig*) calling, vocation ; **sacerdotal, e, aux** *a* priestly, sacerdotal.

sache *etc vb voir* **savoir**.

sachet [saʃɛ] *nm* (small) bag ; (*de lavande, poudre, shampooing*) sachet ; **~ de thé** tea bag.

sacoche [sakɔʃ] nf (gén) bag; (de bicyclette) saddlebag; (du facteur) (post-)bag; (d'outils) toolbag.

sacre [sakR(ə)] nm coronation; consecration.

sacré, e [sakRe] a sacred; (fam: satané) blasted; (: fameux) un ~ ... a heck of a ... ; (ANAT) sacral.

sacrement [sakRəmɑ̃] nm sacrament; les derniers ~s the last rites.

sacrer [sakRe] vt (roi) to crown; (évêque) to consecrate // vi to curse, swear.

sacrifice [sakRifis] nm sacrifice.

sacrifier [sakRifje] vt to sacrifice; ~ à vt to conform to; articles sacrifiés (COMM) items given away at knock-down prices.

sacrilège [sakRilɛʒ] nm sacrilege // a sacrilegious.

sacristain [sakRistɛ̃] nm sexton; sacristan.

sacristie [sakRisti] nf sacristy; (culte protestant) vestry.

sacro-saint, e [sakRɔsɛ̃, -sɛ̃t] a sacrosanct.

sadique [sadik] a sadistic // nm/f sadist.

sadisme [sadism(ə)] nm sadism.

safari [safaRi] nm safari; faire un ~ to go on safari; ~-photo nm photographic safari.

safran [safRɑ̃] nm saffron.

sagace [sagas] a sagacious, shrewd.

sagaie [sagɛ] nf assegai.

sage [saʒ] a wise; (enfant) good // nm wise man; sage.

sage-femme [saʒfam] nf midwife (pl wives).

sagesse [saʒɛs] nf wisdom.

Sagittaire [saʒitɛR] nm: le ~ Sagittarius, the Archer; être du ~ to be Sagittarius.

Sahara [saaRa] nm: le ~ the Sahara (desert).

saharienne [saaRjɛn] nf safari jacket.

saignant, e [sɛɲɑ̃, -ɑ̃t] a (viande) rare; (blessure, plaie) bleeding.

saignée [seɲe] nf (MÉD) bleeding q, bloodletting q; (ANAT) la ~ du bras the bend of the arm; (fig) heavy losses pl; savage cut.

saignement [sɛɲmɑ̃] nm bleeding; ~ de nez nosebleed.

saigner [seɲe] vi to bleed // vt to bleed; (animal) to kill (by bleeding); ~ du nez to have a nosebleed.

saillant, e [sajɑ̃, -ɑ̃t] a (pommettes, menton) prominent; (corniche etc) projecting; (fig) salient, outstanding.

saillie [saji] nf (sur un mur etc) projection; (trait d'esprit) witticism; (accouplement) covering, serving; faire ~ to project, stick out.

saillir [sajiR] vi to project, stick out; (veine, muscle) to bulge // vt (ELEVAGE) to cover, serve.

sain, e [sɛ̃, sɛn] a healthy; (dents, constitution) healthy, sound; (lectures) wholesome; ~ et sauf safe and sound, unharmed; ~ d'esprit sound in mind, sane.

saindoux [sɛ̃du] nm lard.

saint, e [sɛ̃, sɛ̃t] a holy; (fig) saintly // nm/f saint; le S~ Esprit the Holy Spirit ou Ghost; la S~e Vierge the Blessed Virgin; sainteté nf holiness; le S~-Père the Holy Father, the Pontiff; le S~-Siège the Holy See; la S~-Sylvestre New Year's Eve.

sais etc vb voir savoir.

saisie [sezi] nf seizure.

saisir [seziR] vt to take hold of, grab; (fig: occasion) to seize; (comprendre) to grasp; (entendre) to get, catch; (suj: émotions) to take hold of, come over; (CULIN) to fry quickly; (JUR: biens, publication) to seize; (: juridiction): ~ un tribunal d'une affaire to submit ou refer a case to a court; se ~ de vt to seize; saisissant, e a startling, striking; saisissement nm emotion.

saison [sezɔ̃] nf season; la belle ~ the summer months; en/hors ~ in/out of season; haute/morte ~ high/slack season; la ~ des pluies/des amours the rainy/ mating season; saisonnier, ière a seasonal // nm (travailleur) seasonal worker.

sait vb voir savoir.

salace [salas] a salacious.

salade [salad] nf (BOT) lettuce etc (generic term); (CULIN) (green) salad; (fam) tangle, muddle; haricots en ~ bean salad; ~ de concombres cucumber salad; ~ de fruits fruit salad; ~ russe Russian salad; saladier nm salad bowl.

salaire [salɛR] nm (annuel, mensuel) salary; (hebdomadaire, journalier) pay, wages pl; (fig) reward; ~ de base basic salary/wage; ~ minimum interprofessionnel garanti (SMIG)/de croissance (SMIC) index-linked guaranteed minimum wage.

salaison [salɛzɔ̃] nf salting; ~s nfpl salt meat sg.

salami [salami] nm salami q, salami sausage.

salant [salɑ̃] am: marais ~ salt pan.

salarial, e, aux [salaRjal, -o] a salary cpd, wage(s) cpd.

salarié, e [salaRje] a salaried; wage-earning // nm/f salaried employee; wage-earner.

salaud [salo] nm (fam!) sod (!), bastard (!).

sale [sal] a dirty, filthy.

salé, e [sale] a (liquide, saveur) salty; (CULIN) salted, salt cpd; (fig) spicy, juicy; steep, stiff.

saler [sale] vt to salt.

saleté [salte] nf (état) dirtiness; (crasse) dirt, filth; (tache etc) dirt q, something dirty; (fig) filthy trick; rubbish q; filth q; infection, bug.

salière [saljɛR] nf saltcellar.

saligaud [saligo] nm (fam!) sod (!).

salin, e [salɛ̃, -in] a saline // nf saltworks sg; salt marsh.

salinité [salinite] nf salinity, salt-content.

salir [saliR] vt to (make) dirty; (fig) to soil the reputation of; se ~ to get dirty; salissant, e a (tissu) which shows the dirt; (métier) dirty, messy.

salive [saliv] nf saliva; saliver vi to salivate.

salle [sal] nf room; (d'hôpital) ward; (de restaurant) dining room; (d'un cinéma) auditorium; (: public) audience; faire ~

comble to have a full house ; ~ **d'attente** waiting room ; ~ **de bain(s)** bathroom ; ~ **de bal** ballroom ; ~ **de cinéma** cinema ; ~ **de classe** classroom ; ~ **commune** (d'hôpital) ward ; ~ **de concert** concert hall ; ~ **de douches** shower-room ; ~ **d'eau** shower-room ; ~ **d'embarquement** (à l'aéroport) departure lounge ; ~ **des machines** engine room ; ~ **à manger** dining room ; ~ **d'opération** (d'hôpital) operating theatre ; ~ **de projection** film theatre ; ~ **de séjour** living room ; ~ **de spectacle** theatre ; cinema ; ~ **des ventes** saleroom.

salon [salɔ̃] nm lounge, sitting room ; (mobilier) lounge suite ; (exposition) exhibition, show ; (mondain, littéraire) salon ; ~ **de coiffure** hairdressing salon ; ~ **de thé** tearoom.

salopard [salɔpaʀ] nm (fam!) bastard (!).
salope [salɔp] nf (fam!) bitch(!).
saloperie [salɔpʀi] nf (fam!) filth q ; dirty trick ; rubbish q.
salopette [salɔpɛt] nf overall(s).
salpêtre [salpɛtʀ(ə)] nm saltpetre.
salsifis [salsifi] nm salsify, oyster-plant.
saltimbanque [saltɛ̃bɑ̃k] nm/f (travelling) acrobat.
salubre [salybʀ(ə)] a healthy, salubrious ; **salubrité** nf healthiness, salubrity ; **salubrité publique** public health.
saluer [salɥe] vt (pour dire bonjour, fig) to greet ; (pour dire au revoir) to take one's leave ; (MIL) to salute.
salut [saly] nm (sauvegarde) safety ; (REL) salvation ; (geste) wave ; (parole) greeting ; (MIL) salute // excl (fam) hi (there) ; (style relevé) (all) hail.
salutaire [salytɛʀ] a beneficial ; salutary.
salutations [salytɑsjɔ̃] nfpl greetings ; **recevez mes ~ distinguées** ou **respectueuses** yours faithfully.
salutiste [salytist(ə)] nm/f Salvationist.
salve [salv(ə)] nf salvo ; volley of shots.
samaritain [samaʀitɛ̃] nm: **le bon S~** the Good Samaritan.
samedi [samdi] nm Saturday.
sanatorium [sanatɔʀjɔm] nm sanatorium (pl a).
sanctifier [sɑ̃ktifje] vt to sanctify.
sanction [sɑ̃ksjɔ̃] nf sanction ; (fig) penalty ; **prendre des ~s contre** to impose sanctions on ; **sanctionner** vt (loi, usage) to sanction ; (punir) to punish.
sanctuaire [sɑ̃ktɥɛʀ] nm sanctuary.
sandale [sɑ̃dal] nf sandal.
sandalette [sɑ̃dalɛt] nf sandal.
sandwich [sɑ̃dwitʃ] nm sandwich ; **pris en ~** sandwiched.
sang [sɑ̃] nm blood ; **en ~** covered in blood ; **se faire du mauvais ~** to fret, get in a state.
sang-froid [sɑ̃fʀwa] nm calm, sangfroid ; **de ~** in cold blood.
sanglant, e [sɑ̃glɑ̃, -ɑ̃t] a bloody, covered in blood ; (combat) bloody.
sangle [sɑ̃gl(ə)] nf strap ; ~**s** (pour lit etc) webbing sg ; **sangler** vt to strap up ; (animal) to girth.
sanglier [sɑ̃glije] nm (wild) boar.

sanglot [sɑ̃glo] nm sob ; **sangloter** vi to sob.
sangsue [sɑ̃sy] nf leech.
sanguin, e [sɑ̃gɛ̃, -in] a blood cpd ; (fig) fiery // nf blood orange ; (ART) red pencil drawing.
sanguinaire [sɑ̃ginɛʀ] a bloodthirsty ; bloody.
sanguinolent, e [sɑ̃ginɔlɑ̃, -ɑ̃t] a streaked with blood.
sanitaire [sanitɛʀ] a health cpd ; **installation/appareil ~** bathroom plumbing/appliance ; ~**s** nmpl (salle de bain et w.-c.) bathroom sg.
sans [sɑ̃] prép without ; ~ **qu'il s'en aperçoive** without him ou his noticing ; ~ **scrupules** unscrupulous ; ~ **manches** sleeveless ; ~-**abri** nmpl homeless (after a flood etc) ; ~-**emploi** nmpl jobless ; ~-**façon** a inv fuss-free ; free and easy ; ~-**gêne** a inv inconsiderate ; ~-**logis** nmpl homeless (through poverty) ; ~-**travail** nmpl unemployed, jobless.
santal [sɑ̃tal] nm sandal(wood).
santé [sɑ̃te] nf health ; **en bonne ~** in good health ; **boire à la ~ de qn** to drink (to) sb's health ; **'à la ~ de'** 'here's to' ; **à ta/votre ~!** cheers!
santon [sɑ̃tɔ̃] nm ornamental figure at a Christmas crib.
saoul, e [su, sul] a = **soûl, e.**
sape [sap] nf: **travail de ~** (MIL) sap ; (fig) insidious undermining process ou work.
saper [sape] vt to undermine, sap.
sapeur [sapœʀ] nm sapper ; ~-**pompier** nm fireman.
saphir [safiʀ] nm sapphire.
sapin [sapɛ̃] nm fir (tree) ; (bois) fir ; ~ **de Noël** Christmas tree ; **sapinière** nf fir plantation ou forest.
sarabande [saʀabɑ̃d] nf saraband ; (fig) hullabaloo ; whirl.
sarbacane [saʀbakan] nf blowpipe, blowgun ; (jouet) peashooter.
sarcasme [saʀkasm(ə)] nm sarcasm q ; piece of sarcasm ; **sarcastique** a sarcastic.
sarcler [saʀkle] vt to weed ; **sarcloir** nm (weeding) hoe, spud.
sarcophage [saʀkɔfaʒ] nm sarcophagus (pl i).
Sardaigne [saʀdɛɲ] nf: **la ~** Sardinia ; **sarde** a, nm/f Sardinian.
sardine [saʀdin] nf sardine ; ~**s à l'huile** sardines in oil.
sardonique [saʀdɔnik] a sardonic.
S.A.R.L. sigle voir **société.**
sarment [saʀmɑ̃] nm: ~ **(de vigne)** vine shoot.
sarrasin [saʀazɛ̃] nm buckwheat.
sarrau [saʀo] nm smock.
Sarre [saʀ] nf: **la ~** the Saar.
sarriette [saʀjɛt] nf savory.
sarrois, e [saʀwa, -waz] a Saar cpd // nm/f: **S~, e** inhabitant ou native of the Saar.
sas [sɑ] nm (de sous-marin, d'engin spatial) airlock ; (d'écluse) lock.
satané, e [satane] a confounded.
satanique [satanik] a satanic, fiendish.
satelliser [satelize] vt (fusée) to put into orbit ; (fig: pays) to make into a satellite.

satellite [satelit] *nm* satellite ; **pays ~** satellite country ; **~-espion** *nm* spy satellite.

satiété [sasjete]: **à ~ ad** to satiety *ou* satiation ; (*répéter*) ad nauseam.

satin [satɛ̃] *nm* satin ; **satiné, e** *a* satiny ; (*peau*) satin-smooth.

satire [satiʀ] *nf* satire ; **satirique** *a* satirical ; **satiriser** *vt* to satirize.

satisfaction [satisfaksjɔ̃] *nf* satisfaction.

satisfaire [satisfɛʀ] *vt* to satisfy ; **~ à** *vt* (*engagement*) to fulfil ; (*revendications, conditions*) to satisfy, meet ; to comply with ; **satisfaisant, e** *a* satisfactory ; (*qui fait plaisir*) satisfying ; **satisfait, e** *a* satisfied ; **satisfait de** happy *ou* satisfied with ; pleased with.

saturation [satyʀɑsjɔ̃] *nf* saturation.

saturer [satyʀe] *vt* to saturate.

satyre [satiʀ] *nm* satyr ; (*péj*) lecher.

sauce [sos] *nf* sauce ; (*avec un rôti*) gravy ; **~ tomate** tomato sauce ; **saucière** *nf* sauceboat ; gravy boat.

saucisse [sosis] *nf* sausage.

saucisson [sosisɔ̃] *nm* (slicing) sausage ; **~ à l'ail** garlic sausage.

sauf [sof] *prép* except ; **~ si** (*à moins que*) unless ; **~ erreur** if I'm not mistaken ; **~ avis contraire** unless you hear to the contrary.

sauf, sauve [sof, sov] *a* unharmed, unhurt ; (*fig: honneur*) intact, saved ; **laisser la vie sauve à qn** to spare sb's life.

sauf-conduit [sofkɔ̃dɥi] *nm* safe-conduct.

sauge [soʒ] *nf* sage.

saugrenu, e [sogʀəny] *a* preposterous, ludicrous.

saule [sol] *nm* willow (tree) ; **~ pleureur** weeping willow.

saumâtre [somɑtʀ(ə)] *a* briny.

saumon [somɔ̃] *nm* salmon *inv* // *a inv* salmon (pink) ; **saumoné, e** *a*: **truite saumonée** salmon trout.

saumure [somyʀ] *nf* brine.

sauna [sona] *nm* sauna.

saupoudrer [sopudʀe] *vt*: **~ qch de** to sprinkle sth with.

saur [sɔʀ] *am*: **hareng ~** smoked *ou* red herring, kipper.

saurai *etc vb voir* **savoir**.

saut [so] *nm* jump ; (*discipline sportive*) jumping ; **faire un ~** to (make a) jump *ou* leap ; **faire un ~ chez qn** to pop over to sb's (place) ; **au ~ du lit** on getting out of bed ; **~ en hauteur/longueur** high/long jump ; **~ à la corde** skipping ; **~ à la perche** pole vaulting ; **~ périlleux** somersault.

saute [sot] *nf*: **~ de vent/température** sudden change of wind direction/in the temperature.

sauté, e [sote] *a* (*CULIN*) sauté // *nm*: **~ de veau** sauté of veal.

saute-mouton [sotmutɔ̃] *nm*: **jouer à ~** to play leapfrog.

sauter [sote] *vi* to jump, leap ; (*exploser*) to blow up, explode ; (: *fusibles*) to blow ; (*se rompre*) to snap, burst ; (*se détacher*) to pop out (*ou* off) // *vt* to jump (over), leap (over) ; (*fig: omettre*) to skip, miss

(out) ; **faire ~** to blow up ; to burst open ; (*CULIN*) to sauté ; **~ à pieds joints** to make a standing jump ; **~ en parachute** to make a parachute jump ; **~ au cou de qn** to fly into sb's arms ; **~ aux yeux** to be quite obvious.

sauterelle [sotʀɛl] *nf* grasshopper.

sauteur, euse [sotœʀ, -øz] *nm/f* (*athlète*) jumper // *nf* (*casserole*) shallow casserole ; **~ à la perche** pole vaulter ; **~ à skis** skijumper.

sautiller [sotije] *vi* to hop ; to skip.

sautoir [sotwaʀ] *nm* chain ; **~ (de perles)** string of pearls.

sauvage [sovaʒ] *a* (*gén*) wild ; (*peuplade*) savage ; (*farouche*) unsociable ; (*barbare*) wild, savage ; (*non officiel*) unauthorized, unofficial // *nm/f* savage ; (*timide*) unsociable type, recluse ; **~rie** *nf* wildness ; savagery ; unsociability.

sauve [sov] *af voir* **sauf**.

sauvegarde [sovgaʀd(ə)] *nf* safeguard ; **sous la ~ de** under the protection of ; **sauvegarder** *vt* to safeguard.

sauve-qui-peut [sovkipø] *nm inv* stampede, mad rush // *excl* run for your life!

sauver [sove] *vt* to save ; (*porter secours à*) to rescue ; (*récupérer*) to salvage, rescue ; (*fig: racheter*) to save, redeem ; **se ~ vi** (*s'enfuir*) to run away ; (*fam: partir*) to be off ; **~ la vie à qn** to save sb's life ; **sauvetage** *nm* rescue ; **sauveteur** *nm* rescuer ; **sauvette: à la sauvette** *ad* (*vendre*) without authorization ; (*se marier etc*) hastily, hurriedly ; **sauveur** *nm* saviour.

savais *etc vb voir* **savoir**.

savamment [savamɑ̃] *ad* (*avec érudition*) learnedly ; (*habilement*) skilfully, cleverly.

savane [savan] *nf* savannah.

savant, e [savɑ̃, -ɑ̃t] *a* scholarly, learned ; (*calé*) clever // *nm* scientist.

saveur [savœʀ] *nf* flavour ; (*fig*) savour.

savoir [savwaʀ] *vt* to know ; (*être capable de*): **il sait nager** he knows how to swim, he can swim // *nm* knowledge ; **se ~** (*être connu*) to be known ; **à ~** *ad* that is, namely ; **faire ~ qch à qn** to inform sb about sth, to let sb know sth ; **pas que je sache** not as far as I know ; **~-faire** *nm inv* savoir-faire, know-how.

savon [savɔ̃] *nm* (*produit*) soap ; (*morceau*) bar *ou* tablet of soap ; (*fam*): **passer un ~ à qn** to give sb a good dressing-down ; **savonner** *vt* to soap ; **savonnette** *nf* bar *ou* tablet of soap ; **savonneux, euse** *a* soapy.

savons *vb voir* **savoir**.

savourer [savuʀe] *vt* to savour.

savoureux, euse [savuʀø, -øz] *a* tasty ; (*fig*) spicy, juicy.

saxo(phone) [saksɔ(fɔn)] *nm* sax(ophone) ; **saxophoniste** *nm/f* saxophonist, sax(ophone) player.

saynète [sɛnɛt] *nf* playlet.

sbire [sbiʀ] *nm* (*péj*) henchman.

scabreux, euse [skabʀø, -øz] *a* risky ; (*indécent*) improper, shocking.

scalpel [skalpɛl] *nm* scalpel.

scalper [skalpe] vt to scalp.
scandale [skɑ̃dal] nm scandal; (*tapage*): **faire du ~** to make a scene, create a disturbance; **faire ~** to scandalize people; **scandaleux, euse** a scandalous, outrageous; **scandaliser** vt to scandalize; **se scandaliser (de)** to be scandalized (by).
scander [skɑ̃de] vt (*vers*) to scan; (*slogans*) to chant; **en scandant les mots** stressing each word.
scandinave [skɑ̃dinav] a, nm/f Scandinavian.
Scandinavie [skɑ̃dinavi] nf Scandinavia.
scaphandre [skafɑ̃dʀ(ə)] nm (*de plongeur*) diving suit; (*de cosmonaute*) space-suit; **~ autonome** aqualung.
scarabée [skaʀabe] nm beetle.
scarlatine [skaʀlatin] nf scarlet fever.
scarole [skaʀɔl] nf endive.
scatologique [skatɔlɔʒik] a scatological, lavatorial.
sceau, x [so] nm seal; (*fig*) stamp, mark.
scélérat, e [seleʀa, -at] nm/f villain, blackguard.
sceller [sele] vt to seal.
scellés [sele] nmpl seals.
scénario [senaʀjo] nm (*CINÉMA*) scenario; screenplay, script; (*fig*) pattern; scenario; **scénariste** nm/f scriptwriter.
scène [sɛn] nf (*gén*) scene; (*estrade, fig: théâtre*) stage; **entrer en ~** to come on stage; **mettre en ~** (*THÉÂTRE*) to stage; (*CINÉMA*) to direct; (*fig*) to present, introduce; **porter à la ~** to adapt for the stage; **faire une ~ (à qn)** to make a scene (with sb); **~ de ménage** domestic fight ou scene; **scénique** a theatrical; scenic.
scepticisme [sɛptisism(ə)] nm scepticism.
sceptique [sɛptik] a sceptical // nm/f sceptic.
sceptre [sɛptʀ(ə)] nm sceptre.
schéma [ʃema] nm (*diagramme*) diagram, sketch; (*fig*) outline; pattern; **schématique** a diagrammatic(al), schematic; (*fig*) oversimplified.
schisme [ʃism(ə)] nm schism; rift, split.
schiste [ʃist(ə)] nm schist.
schizophrène [skizɔfʀɛn] nm/f schizophrenic.
schizophrénie [skizɔfʀeni] nf schizophrenia.
sciatique [sjatik] a: **nerf ~** sciatic nerve // nf sciatica.
scie [si] nf saw; (*fam*) catch-tune; **~ à bois** wood saw; **~ circulaire** circular saw; **~ à découper** fretsaw; **~ à métaux** hacksaw.
sciemment [sjamɑ̃] ad knowingly, wittingly.
science [sjɑ̃s] nf science; (*savoir*) knowledge; (*savoir-faire*) art, skill; **~s naturelles** (*SCOL*) natural science sg, biology sg; **~-fiction** nf science fiction; **scientifique** a scientific // nm/f scientist; science student.
scier [sje] vt to saw; (*retrancher*) to saw off; **scierie** nf sawmill; **scieur de long** nm pit sawyer.
scinder [sɛ̃de] vt, **se ~** vi to split (up).
scintillement [sɛ̃tijmɑ̃] nm sparkling q.

scintiller [sɛ̃tije] vi to sparkle.
scission [sisjɔ̃] nf split.
sciure [sjyʀ] nf: **~ (de bois)** sawdust.
sclérose [skleʀoz] nf sclerosis; (*fig*) ossification; **~ en plaques** multiple sclerosis; **sclérosé, e** a sclerosed, sclerotic; ossified.
scolaire [skɔlɛʀ] a school cpd; (*péj*) schoolish; **scolariser** vt to provide with schooling (ou schools); **scolarité** nf schooling; **frais de scolarité** school fees.
scooter [skutɛʀ] nm (motor) scooter.
scorbut [skɔʀbyt] nm scurvy.
score [skɔʀ] nm score.
scories [skɔʀi] nfpl scoria pl.
scorpion [skɔʀpjɔ̃] nm (*signe*): **le S~** Scorpio, the Scorpion; **être du S~** to be Scorpio.
scout, e [skut] a, nm scout; **scoutisme** nm (boy) scout movement; (*activités*) scouting.
scribe [skʀib] nm scribe; (*péj*) penpusher.
script [skʀipt] nm printing; (*CINÉMA*) (shooting) script; **~-girl** [-gœʀl] nf continuity girl.
scrupule [skʀypyl] nm scruple; **scrupuleux, euse** a scrupulous.
scrutateur, trice [skʀytatœʀ, -tʀis] a searching.
scruter [skʀyte] vt to search, scrutinize; (*l'obscurité*) to peer into; (*motifs, comportement*) to examine, scrutinize.
scrutin [skʀytɛ̃] nm (*vote*) ballot; (*ensemble des opérations*) poll; **~ à deux tours** poll with two ballots ou rounds; **~ de liste** list system.
sculpter [skylte] vt to sculpt; (*suj: érosion*) to carve; **sculpteur** nm sculptor.
sculptural, e, aux [skyltyʀal, -o] a sculptural; (*fig*) statuesque.
sculpture [skyltyʀ] nf sculpture; **~ sur bois** wood carving.
S.D.E.C.E. [zdɛk] sigle m = service de documentation extérieure et de contre-espionnage, ≈ Intelligence Service.
se, s' [s(ə)] pronom (*emploi réfléchi*) oneself, m himself, f herself, sujet non humain itself; pl themselves; (: *réciproque*) one another, each other; (: *passif*): **cela se répare facilement** it is easily repaired; (: *possessif*): **~ casser la jambe/laver les mains** to break one's leg/wash one's hands; *autres emplois pronominaux: voir le verbe en question.*
séance [seɑ̃s] nf (*d'assemblée, récréative*) meeting, session; (*de tribunal*) sitting, session; (*musicale, CINÉMA, THÉÂTRE*) performance; **~ tenante** forthwith.
séant, e [seɑ̃, -ɑ̃t] a seemly, fitting // nm posterior.
seau, x [so] nm bucket, pail; **~ à glace** ice-bucket.
sec, sèche [sɛk, sɛʃ] a dry; (*raisins, figues*) dried; (*cœur, personne: insensible*) hard, cold // nm: **tenir au ~** to keep in a dry place // ad hard; **je le bois ~** I drink it straight ou neat; **à ~** a dried up.
sécateur [sekatœʀ] nm secateurs pl, shears pl, pair of shears ou secateurs.
sécession [sesesjɔ̃] nf: **faire ~** to secede; **la guerre de S~** the American Civil War.

séchage [seʃaʒ] *nm* drying; seasoning.

sèche [sɛʃ] *af voir* **sec.**

sèche-cheveux [sɛʃʃəvø] *nm inv* hair-drier.

sécher [seʃe] *vt* to dry; (*dessécher: peau, blé*) to dry (out); (: *étang*) to dry up; (*bois*) to season; (*fam: classe, cours*) to skip // *vi* to dry; to dry out; to dry up; (*fam: candidat*) to be stumped; **se ~** (*après le bain*) to dry o.s.

sécheresse [sɛʃRɛs] *nf* dryness; (*absence de pluie*) drought.

séchoir [seʃwaR] *nm* drier.

second, e [səgɔ̃, -3d] *a* second // *nm* (*assistant*) second in command; (NAVIG) first mate // *nf* second; **voyager en ~e** to travel second-class; **de ~e main** second-hand; **secondaire** *a* secondary; **seconder** *vt* to assist.

secouer [səkwe] *vt* to shake; (*passagers*) to rock; (*traumatiser*) to shake (up); **se ~** (*chien*) to shake itself; (*fam: se démener*) to shake o.s. up; **~ la poussière d'un tapis** to shake off the dust from a carpet.

secourable [səkuRabl(ə)] *a* helpful.

secourir [səkuRiR] *vt* (*aller sauver*) to (go and) rescue; (*prodiguer des soins à*) to help, assist; (*venir en aide à*) to assist, aid; **secourisme** *nm* first aid; life saving; **secouriste** *nm/f* first-aid worker.

secours [səkuR] *nm* help, aid, assistance // *nmpl* aid *sg*; **cela lui a été d'un grand ~** this was a great help to him; **au ~!** help! **appeler au ~** to shout *ou* call for help; **appeler qn à son ~** to call sb to one's assistance; **porter ~ à qn** to give sb assistance, help sb; **les premiers ~** first aid *sg*; **le ~ en montagne** mountain rescue.

secousse [səkus] *nf* jolt, bump; (*électrique*) shock; (*fig: psychologique*) jolt, shock; **~ sismique** *ou* **tellurique** earth tremor.

secret, ète [səkRɛ, -ɛt] *a* secret; (*fig: renfermé*) reticent, reserved // *nm* secret; (*discrétion absolue*) **le ~** secrecy; **en ~** in secret, secretly; **au ~** in solitary confinement; **~ de fabrication** trade secret; **~ professionnel** professional secrecy.

secrétaire [səkRetɛR] *nm/f* secretary // *nm* (*meuble*) writing desk, secretaire; **~ d'ambassade** embassy secretary; **~ de direction** private *ou* personal secretary; **~ d'État** Secretary of State; **~ général** Secretary-General; **~ de mairie** town clerk; **~ de rédaction** sub-editor; **secrétariat** *nm* (*profession*) secretarial work; (*bureau: d'entreprise, d'école*) (secretary's) office; (: *d'organisation internationale*) secretariat; (POL *etc: fonction*) secretaryship, office of Secretary.

sécréter [sekRete] *vt* to secrete; **sécrétion** [-sjɔ̃] *nf* secretion.

sectaire [sɛktɛR] *a* sectarian, bigoted.

secte [sɛkt(ə)] *nf* sect.

secteur [sɛktœR] *nm* sector; (ADMIN) district; (ÉLEC): **branché sur le ~** plugged into the mains (supply); **fonctionne sur pile et ~** battery or mains operated; **le ~ privé** the private sector; **le ~**

primaire/tertiaire   primary/tertiary industry.

section [sɛksjɔ̃] *nf* section; (*de parcours d'autobus*) fare stage; (MIL: *unité*) platoon; **tube de ~ 6,5 mm** tube with a 6.5 mm bore; **~ rythmique** rhythm section; **sectionner** *vt* to sever.

sectoriel, le [sɛktɔRjɛl] *a* sector-based.

séculaire [sekylɛR] *a* secular; (*très vieux*) age-old.

séculier, ière [sekylje, -jɛR] *a* secular.

sécuriser [sekyRize] *vt* to give (a feeling of) security to.

sécurité [sekyRite] *nf* safety; security; **impression de ~** sense of security; **la ~ internationale** international security; **système de ~** safety system; **être en ~** to be safe; **la ~ de l'emploi** job security; **la ~ routière** road safety; **la ~ sociale** ≈ (the) Social Security.

sédatif, ive [sedatif, -iv] *a, nm* sedative.

sédentaire [sedɑ̃tɛR] *a* sedentary.

sédiment [sedimɑ̃] *nm* sediment; **~s** *nmpl* (*alluvions*) sediment *sg*.

séditieux, euse [sedisjø, -øz] *a* insurgent; seditious.

sédition [sedisjɔ̃] *nf* insurrection; sedition.

séducteur, trice [sedyktœR, -tris] *a* seductive // *nm/f* seducer/seductress.

séduction [sedyksjɔ̃] *nf* seduction; (*charme, attrait*) appeal, charm.

séduire [seduiR] *vt* to charm; (*femme: abuser de*) to seduce; **séduisant, e** *a* (*femme*) seductive; (*homme, offre*) very attractive.

segment [sɛgmɑ̃] *nm* segment; (AUTO): **~ (de piston)** piston ring; **segmenter** *vt* to segment.

ségrégation [segRegasjɔ̃] *nf* segregation.

seiche [sɛʃ] *nf* cuttlefish.

séide [seid] *nm* (*péj*) henchman.

seigle [sɛgl(ə)] *nm* rye.

seigneur [sɛɲœR] *nm* lord; **le S~** the Lord; **~ial, e, aux** *a* lordly, stately.

sein [sɛ̃] *nm* breast; (*entrailles*) womb; **au ~ de** *prép* (*équipe, institution*) within; (*flots, bonheur*) in the midst of; **donner le ~ à** (*bébé*) to feed (at the breast); to breast-feed.

séisme [seism(ə)] *nm* earthquake.

séismique [seismik] *etc voir* **sismique** *etc.*

seize [sɛz] *num* sixteen; **seizième** *num* sixteenth.

séjour [seʒuR] *nm* stay; (*pièce*) living room; **~ner** *vi* to stay.

sel [sɛl] *nm* salt; (*fig*) wit; spice; **~ de cuisine/de table** cooking/table salt; **~ gemme** rock salt.

sélection [selɛksjɔ̃] *nf* selection; **~ professionnelle** professional recruitment; **sélectionner** *vt* to select.

self-service [sɛlfsɛrvis] *a, nm* self-service.

selle [sɛl] *nf* saddle; **~s** *nfpl* (MÉD) stools; **aller à la ~** (MÉD) to pass a motion; **se mettre en ~** to mount, get into the saddle; **seller** *vt* to saddle.

sellette [sɛlɛt] *nf*: **être sur la ~** to be on the carpet.

sellier [selje] *nm* saddler.

selon [səlɔ̃] *prép* according to; (*en se conformant à*) in accordance with.

semailles [səmaj] *nfpl* sowing *sg*.

semaine [səmɛn] *nf* week; **en ~** during the week, on weekdays.

sémantique [semɑ̃tik] *a* semantic // *nf* semantics *sg*.

sémaphore [semafɔr] *nm* semaphore signal.

semblable [sɑ̃blabl(ə)] *a* similar; (*de ce genre*): ` de **~s** mésaventures such mishaps // *nm* fellow creature *ou* man; **~ à** similar to, like.

semblant [sɑ̃blɑ̃] *nm*: **un ~ de vérité** a semblance of truth; **faire ~ (de faire)** to pretend (to do).

sembler [sɑ̃ble] *vb avec attribut* to seem // *vb impersonnel*: **il semble que/inutile de** it seems *ou* appears that/useless to; **il me semble que** it seems to me that; I think (that); **~ être** to seem to be; **comme bon lui semble** as he sees fit.

semelle [səmɛl] *nf* sole; (*intérieure*) insole, inner sole; **~s compensées** platform soles.

semence [səmɑ̃s] *nf* (*graine*) seed; (*clou*) tack.

semer [səme] *vt* to sow; (*fig: éparpiller*) to scatter; (: *poursuivants*) to lose, shake off; **semé de** (*difficultés*) riddled with.

semestre [səmɛstr(ə)] *nm* half-year; (*scol*) semester; **semestriel, le** *a* half-yearly; semestral.

semeur, euse [səmœr, -øz] *nm/f* sower.

sémillant, e [semijɑ̃, -ɑ̃t] *a* vivacious; dashing.

séminaire [seminɛr] *nm* seminar; (*rel*) seminary; **séminariste** *nm* seminarist.

semi-remorque [səmirəmɔrk(ə)] *nf* trailer // *nm* articulated lorry.

semis [səmi] *nm* (*terrain*) seedbed, seed plot; (*plante*) seedling.

sémite [semit] *a* Semitic.

sémitique [semitik] *a* Semitic.

semoir [səmwar] *nm* seed-bag; seeder.

semonce [səmɔ̃s] *nf* reprimand; **coup de ~** warning shot across the bows.

semoule [səmul] *nf* semolina.

sempiternel, le [sɛpitɛrnɛl] *a* eternal, never-ending.

sénat [sena] *nm* Senate; **sénateur** *nm* Senator.

sénile [senil] *a* senile; **sénilité** *nf* senility.

sens [sɑ̃s] *nm* (*physiol, instinct*) sense; (*signification*) meaning, sense; (*direction*) direction // *nmpl* (*sensualité*) senses; **reprendre ses ~** to regain consciousness; **avoir le ~ des affaires/de la mesure** to have business sense/a sense of moderation; **ça n'a pas de ~** that doesn't make (any) sense; **dans le ~ des aiguilles d'une montre** clockwise; **~ commun** common sense; **~ dessus dessous** upside down; **~ interdit, ~ unique** one-way street.

sensation [sɑ̃sasjɔ̃] *nf* sensation; **faire ~** to cause a sensation, create a stir; **à ~** (*péj*) sensational; **sensationnel, le** *a* sensational; (*fig*) terrific.

sensé, e [sɑ̃se] *a* sensible.

sensibiliser [sɑ̃sibilize] *vt*: **~ qn à** to make sb sensitive to.

sensibilité [sɑ̃sibilite] *nf* sensitivity; (*affectivité, émotivité*) sensitivity, sensibility.

sensible [sɑ̃sibl(ə)] *a* sensitive; (*aux sens*) perceptible; (*appréciable: différence, progrès*) appreciable, noticeable; **~ à** sensitive to; **~ment** *ad* (*notablement*) appreciably, noticeably; (*à peu près*): **ils ont ~ment le même poids** they weigh approximately the same; **~rie** *nf* sentimentality, mawkishness; squeamishness.

sensitif, ive [sɑ̃sitif, -iv] *a* (*nerf*) sensory; (*personne*) oversensitive.

sensoriel, le [sɑ̃sɔrjɛl] *a* sensory, sensorial.

sensualité [sɑ̃syalite] *nf* sensuality; sensuousness.

sensuel, le [sɑ̃syɛl] *a* sensual; sensuous.

sente [sɑ̃t] *nf* path.

sentence [sɑ̃tɑ̃s] *nf* (*jugement*) sentence; (*adage*) maxim; **sentencieux, euse** *a* sententious.

senteur [sɑ̃tœr] *nf* scent, perfume.

sentier [sɑ̃tje] *nm* path.

sentiment [sɑ̃timɑ̃] *nm* feeling; **recevez mes ~s respectueux** yours faithfully; **faire du ~** (*péj*) to be sentimental; **sentimental, e, aux** *a* sentimental; (*vie, aventure*) love *cpd*.

sentinelle [sɑ̃tinɛl] *nf* sentry; **en ~** on sentry duty; standing guard.

sentir [sɑ̃tir] *vt* (*par l'odorat*) to smell; (*par le goût*) to taste; (*au toucher, fig*) to feel; (*répandre une odeur de*) to smell of; (: *ressemblance*) to smell like; (*avoir la saveur de*) to taste of; to taste like; (*fig: dénoter, annoncer*) to be indicative of; to smack of; to foreshadow // *vi* to smell; **~ mauvais** to smell bad; **se ~ bien** to feel good; **se ~ mal** (*être indisposé*) to feel unwell *ou* ill; **se ~ le courage/la force de faire** to feel brave/strong enough to do; **ne plus se ~ de joie** to be beside o.s. with joy; **il ne peut pas le ~** (*fam*) he can't stand him.

seoir [swar]: **~ à** *vt* to become.

séparation [separasjɔ̃] *nf* separation; (*cloison*) division, partition; **~ de biens** division of property (*in marriage settlement*); **~ de corps** legal separation.

séparatisme [separatism(ə)] *nm* separatism.

séparé, e [separe] *a* (*appartements, pouvoirs*) separate; (*époux*) separated; **~ de** separate from; separated from; **~ment** *ad* separately.

séparer [separe] *vt* (*gén*) to separate; (*suj: divergences etc*) to divide; to drive apart; (: *différences, obstacles*) to stand between; (*détacher*): **~ qch de** to pull sth (off) from; (*dissocier*) to distinguish between; (*diviser*): **~ qch par** to divide sth (up) with; **~ une pièce en deux** to divide a room into two; **se ~** (*époux*) to separate, part; (*prendre congé: amis etc*) to part, leave each other; (*adversaires*) to separate; (*se diviser: route, tige etc*) to divide; (*se détacher*): **se ~ (de)** to split off (from); to come off; **se ~ de** (*époux*) to separate *ou* part from ; (*employé, objet personnel*) to part with.

sept [sɛt] *num* seven.

septembre [sɛptɑ̃bʀ(ə)] *nm* September.

septennat [sɛpetena] *nm* seven-year term (of office) ; seven-year reign.

septentrional, e, aux [sɛptɑ̃tʀijɔnal, -o] *a* northern.

septicémie [sɛptisemi] *nf* blood poisoning, septicaemia.

septième [sɛtjɛm] *num* seventh.

septique [sɛptik] *a*: **fosse ~** septic tank.

septuagénaire [sɛptyaʒenɛʀ] *a, nm/f* septuagenarian.

sépulcre [sepylkʀ(ə)] *nm* sepulchre.

sépulture [sepyltyʀ] *nf* burial ; burial place, grave.

séquelles [sekɛl] *nfpl* after-effects ; (*fig*) after-math *sg* ; consequences.

séquence [sekɑ̃s] *nf* sequence.

séquestre [sekɛstʀ(ə)] *nm* impoundment ; **mettre sous ~** to impound.

séquestrer [sekɛstʀe] *vt* (*personne*) to confine illegally ; (*biens*) to impound.

serai *etc vb voir* **être**.

serein, e [səʀɛ̃, -ɛn] *a* serene ; (*jugement*) dispassionate.

sérénade [seʀenad] *nf* serenade ; (*fam*) hullabaloo.

sérénité [seʀenite] *nf* serenity.

serez *vb voir* **être**.

serf, serve [sɛʀ, sɛʀv(ə)] *nm/f* serf.

serge [sɛʀʒ(ə)] *nf* serge.

sergent [sɛʀʒɑ̃] *nm* sergeant ; **~-chef** *nm* staff sergeant ; **~-major** *nm* ≈ quartermaster sergeant.

sériciculture [seʀisikyltyʀ] *nf* silkworm breeding, sericulture.

série [seʀi] *nf* (*de questions, d'accidents*) series *inv* ; (*de clés, casseroles, outils*) set ; (*catégorie: SPORT*) rank ; class ; **en ~** in quick succession ; (*COMM*) mass *cpd* ; **de ~** a standard ; **hors ~** (*COMM*) custom-built ; (*fig*) outstanding ; **~ noire** *nm* (crime) thriller ; **sérier** *vt* to classify, sort out.

sérieusement [seʀjøzmɑ̃] *ad* seriously ; reliably ; responsibly ; **~?** do you mean it?, are you talking in earnest?

sérieux, euse [seʀjø, -øz] *a* serious ; (*élève, employé*) reliable, responsible ; (*client, maison*) reliable, dependable ; (*offre, proposition*) genuine, serious ; (*grave, sévère*) serious, solemn ; (*maladie, situation*) serious, grave // *nm* seriousness ; reliability ; **garder son ~** to keep a straight face ; **manquer de ~** not to be very responsible (*ou* reliable) ; **prendre qch/qn au ~** to take sth/sb seriously.

serin [səʀɛ̃] *nm* canary.

seriner [səʀine] *vt*: **~ qch à qn** to drum sth into sb.

seringue [səʀɛ̃g] *nf* syringe.

serions *vb voir* **être**.

serment [sɛʀmɑ̃] *nm* (*juré*) oath ; (*promesse*) pledge, vow ; **faire le ~ de** to take a vow to, swear to ; **sous ~** on *ou* under oath.

sermon [sɛʀmɔ̃] *nm* sermon ; (*péj*) sermon, lecture.

serpe [sɛʀp(ə)] *nf* billhook.

serpent [sɛʀpɑ̃] *nm* snake ; **~ à sonnettes** rattlesnake.

serpenter [sɛʀpɑ̃te] *vi* to wind.

serpentin [sɛʀpɑ̃tɛ̃] *nm* (*tube*) coil ; (*ruban*) streamer.

serpillière [sɛʀpijɛʀ] *nf* floorcloth.

serrage [sɛʀaʒ] *nm* tightening ; **collier de ~** clamp.

serre [sɛʀ] *nf* (*AGR*) greenhouse ; **~s** *nfpl* (*griffes*) claws, talons ; **~ chaude** hothouse.

serré, e [seʀe] *a* (*tissu*) closely woven ; (*réseau*) dense ; (*écriture*) close ; (*habits*) tight ; (*fig: lutte, match*) tight, close-fought ; (*passagers etc*) (tightly) packed.

serre-livres [sɛʀlivʀ(ə)] *nm inv* book ends *pl*.

serrement [sɛʀmɑ̃] *nm*: **~ de main** handshake ; **~ de cœur** pang of anguish.

serrer [seʀe] *vt* (*tenir*) to grip *ou* hold tight ; (*comprimer, coincer*) to squeeze ; (*poings, mâchoires*) to clench ; (*suj: vêtement*) to be too tight for ; to fit tightly ; (*rapprocher*) to close up, move closer together ; (*ceinture, nœud, frein, vis*) to tighten // *vi*: **~ à droite** to keep to the right ; to move into the right-hand lane ; **se ~** (*se rapprocher*) to squeeze up ; **se ~ contre qn** to huddle up to sb ; **se ~ les coudes** to stick together, back one another up ; **~ la main à qn** to shake sb's hand ; **~ qn dans ses bras** to hug sb, clasp sb in one's arms ; **~ la gorge à qn** (*suj: chagrin*) to bring a lump to sb's throat ; **~ qn de près** to follow close behind sb ; **~ le trottoir** to hug the kerb ; **~ sa droite** to keep well to the right ; **~ la vis à qn** to crack down harder on sb.

serre-tête [sɛʀtɛt] *nm inv* (*bandeau*) headband ; (*bonnet*) skullcap.

serrure [seʀyʀ] *nf* lock.

serrurerie [seʀyʀʀi] *nf* (*métier*) locksmith's trade ; **~ d'art** ornamental ironwork.

serrurier [seʀyʀje] *nm* locksmith.

sert *etc vb voir* **servir**.

sertir [sɛʀtiʀ] *vt* (*pierre*) to set ; (*pièces métalliques*) to crimp.

sérum [seʀɔm] *nm* serum ; **~ antivenimeux** snakebite serum ; **~ sanguin** (blood) serum ; **~ de vérité** truth drug.

servage [sɛʀvaʒ] *nm* serfdom.

servant [sɛʀvɑ̃] *nm* server.

servante [sɛʀvɑ̃t] *nf* (maid)servant.

serve [sɛʀv] *nf voir* **serf**.

serveur, euse [sɛʀvœʀ, -øz] *nm/f* waiter/waitress.

serviable [sɛʀvjabl(ə)] *a* obliging, willing to help.

service [sɛʀvis] *nm* (*gén*) service ; (*série de repas*): **premier ~** first sitting ; (*pourboire*) service (charge) ; (*assortiment de vaisselle*) set, service ; (*bureau: de la vente etc*) department, section ; (*travail*): **pendant le ~** on duty ; **~s** *nmpl* (*travail, ÉCON*) services ; **faire le ~** to serve ; **être en ~ chez qn** (*domestique*) to be in sb's service ; **être au ~ de** (*patron, patrie*) to be in the service of ; **être au ~ de qn** (*collaborateur, voiture*) to be at sb's service ; **rendre ~**

à to help; **il aime rendre ~** he likes to help; **rendre un ~ à qn** to do sb a favour; **heures de ~** hours of duty; **être de ~** to be on duty; **avoir 25 ans de ~** to have completed 25 years' service; **être/mettre en ~** to be in/put into service ou operation; **~ à thé/café** tea/coffee set ou service; **~ après vente** after-sales service; **en ~ commandé** on an official assignment; **~ funèbre** funeral service; **~ militaire** military service; **~ d'ordre** police (ou stewards) in charge of maintaining order; **~s secrets** secret service sg.

serviette [sɛʀvjɛt] nf (de table) (table) napkin, serviette; (de toilette) towel; (porte-documents) briefcase; **~ hygiénique** sanitary towel ou pad; **~-éponge** nf terry towel.

servile [sɛʀvil] a servile.

servir [sɛʀviʀ] vt (gén) to serve; (dîneur: au restaurant) to wait on; (client: au magasin) to serve, attend to; (fig: aider): **~ qn** to aid sb; to serve sb's interests; to stand sb in good stead; (COMM: rente) to pay // vi (TENNIS) to serve; (CARTES) to deal; **se ~** (prendre d'un plat) to help o.s.; **se ~ de** (plat) to help o.s. to; (voiture, outil, relations) to use; **~ à qn** (diplôme, livre) to be of use to sb; **ça m'a servi pour faire** it was useful to me when I did; I used it to do; **~ à qch/faire** (outil etc) to be used for sth/doing; **ça peut ~** it may come in handy; **ça peut encore ~** it can still be used (ou of use); **à quoi cela sert-il** (de faire)? what's the use of (doing)?; **cela ne sert à rien** it's no use; **~ (à qn) de** to serve as (for sb); **~ la messe** to serve Mass; **~ à dîner** (à qn) to serve dinner (to sb).

serviteur [sɛʀvitœʀ] nm servant.

servitude [sɛʀvityd] nf servitude; (fig) constraint; (JUR) easement.

servo... [sɛʀvo] préfixe: **~frein** servo (-assisted) brake.

ses [se] dét voir **son**.

session [sesjɔ̃] nf session.

set [sɛt] nm set.

seuil [sœj] nm doorstep; (fig) threshold; **sur le ~ de sa maison** in the doorway of his house, on his doorstep; **au ~ de** (fig) on the threshold ou brink ou edge of.

seul, e [sœl] a (sans compagnie, en isolation) alone; (avec nuance affective: isolé) lonely; (unique): **un ~ livre** only one book, a single book; **le ~ livre** the only book; **~ ce livre, ce livre ~** this book alone, only this book // ad (vivre) alone, on one's own; **parler tout ~** to talk to oneself; **faire qch (tout) ~** to do sth (all) on one's own ou (all) by oneself // nm, nf **il en reste un(e) ~(e)** there's only one left; **à lui (tout) ~** single-handed, on his own.

seulement [sœlmɑ̃] ad (pas davantage): **~ 5, 5 ~** only 5; (exclusivement): **~ eux** only them, them alone; (pas avant): **~ hier/à 10h** only yesterday/at 10 o'clock; **non ~ ... mais aussi** ou **encore** not only ... but also

sève [sɛv] nf sap.

sévère [sevɛʀ] a severe; **sévérité** nf severity.

sévices [sevis] nmpl (physical) cruelty sg, ill treatment sg.

sévir [seviʀ] vi (punir) to use harsh measures, crack down on; (suj: fléau) to rage, be rampant; **~ contre** (abus) to deal ruthlessly with, crack down on.

sevrer [səvʀe] vt to wean; (fig): **~ qn de** to deprive sb of.

sexagénaire [sɛgzaʒenɛʀ] a, nm/f sexagenarian.

sexe [sɛks(ə)] nm sex; (organe mâle) member; **sexologue** nm/f sexologist, sex specialist.

sextant [sɛkstɑ̃] nm sextant.

sexualité [sɛksyalite] nf sexuality.

sexué, e [sɛksye] a sexual.

sexuel, le [sɛksyɛl] a sexual; **acte ~** sex act.

seyait vb voir **seoir**.

seyant, e [sɛjɑ̃, -ɑ̃t] a becoming.

shampooing [ʃɑ̃pwɛ̃] nm shampoo; **se faire un ~** to shampoo one's hair; **~ colorant** (colour) rinse.

short [ʃɔʀt] nm (pair of) shorts pl.

si [si] nm (MUS) B; (en chantant la gamme) si, se // ad (oui) yes; (tellement) so // cj if; **~ seulement** if only; (tant et) **~ bien que** so much so that; **~ rapide qu'il soit** however fast he may be, fast though he is; **je me demande ~** I wonder if ou whether.

siamois, e [sjamwa, -waz] a Siamese; **frères/sœurs siamois/es** Siamese twins.

Sicile [sisil] nf: **la ~** Sicily; **sicilien, ne** a Sicilian.

sidéré, e [sidere] a staggered.

sidérurgie [sideʀyʀʒi] nf iron and steel industry.

siècle [sjɛkl(ə)] nm century; (époque) age; (REL): **le ~** the world.

sied [sje] vb voir **seoir**.

siège [sjɛʒ] nm seat; (d'entreprise) head office; (d'organisation) headquarters pl; (MIL) siege; **mettre le ~ devant** to besiege; **présentation par le ~** (MÉD) breech presentation; **~ baquet** bucket seat; **~ social** registered office.

siéger [sjeʒe] vi to sit.

sien, ne [sjɛ̃, sjɛn] pronom: **le(la) ~(ne), les ~s(~nes)** his; hers; its; **faire des ~nes** (fam) to be up to one's (usual) tricks; **les ~s** (sa famille) one's family.

siérait etc vb voir **seoir**.

sieste [sjɛst(ə)] nf (afternoon) snooze ou nap, siesta; **faire la ~** to have a snooze ou nap.

sieur [sjœʀ] nm: **le ~ Thomas** Mr Thomas; (en plaisantant) Master Thomas.

sifflant, e [siflɑ̃, -ɑ̃t] a (bruit) whistling; (toux) wheezing; (consonne) **~e** sibilant.

sifflement [sifləmɑ̃] nm whistle, whistling q; hissing noise; whistling noise.

siffler [sifle] vi (gén) to whistle; (avec un sifflet) to blow (on) one's whistle; (en parlant, dormant) to wheeze; (serpent, vapeur) to hiss // vt (chanson) to whistle; (chien etc) to whistle for; (fille) to whistle at; (pièce, orateur) to hiss, boo; (faute) to blow one's whistle at; (fin du match, départ) to blow one's whistle for; (fam: verre, bouteille) to guzzle, knock back.

sifflet [siflɛ] *nm* whistle; **~s** *nmpl* (*de mécontentement*) whistles, boos; **coup de ~** whistle.

siffloter [siflɔte] *vi*, *vt* to whistle.

sigle [sigl(ə)] *nm* acronym, (set of) initials *pl*.

signal, aux [siɲal, -o] *nm* (*signe convenu, appareil*) signal; (*indice, écriteau*) sign; **donner le ~ de** to give the signal for; **~ d'alarme** alarm signal; **~ horaire** time signal; **signaux (lumineux)** (AUTO) traffic signals.

signalement [siɲalmɑ̃] *nm* description, particulars *pl*.

signaler [siɲale] *vt* to indicate; to announce; to report; (*faire remarquer*): **~ qch à qn/à qn** que to point out sth to sb/to sb that; **se ~ par** to distinguish o.s. by; **se ~ à l'attention de qn** to attract sb's attention.

signalétique [siɲaletik] *a*: **fiche ~** identification sheet.

signalisation [siɲalizasjɔ̃] *nf* signalling, signposting; signals *pl*, roadsigns *pl*; **panneau de ~** roadsign.

signaliser [siɲalize] *vt* to put up roadsigns on; to put signals on.

signataire [siɲatɛʀ] *nm/f* signatory.

signature [siɲatyʀ] *nf* signing; signature.

signe [siɲ] *nm* sign; (TYPO) mark; **c'est bon ~** it's a good sign; **faire un ~ de la main** to give a sign with one's hand; **faire ~ à qn** (*fig*) to get in touch with sb; **faire ~ à qn d'entrer** to motion (to) sb to come in; **en ~ de** as a sign *ou* mark of; **le ~ de la croix** the sign of the Cross; **~ de ponctuation** punctuation mark; **~ du zodiaque** sign of the zodiac.

signer [siɲe] *vt* to sign; **se ~** *vi* to cross o.s.

signet [siɲɛ] *nm* bookmark.

significatif, ive [siɲifikatif, -iv] *a* significant.

signification [siɲifikasjɔ̃] *nf* meaning.

signifier [siɲifje] *vt* (*vouloir dire*) to mean, signify; (*faire connaître*): **~ qch (à qn)** to make sth known (to sb); (JUR): **~ qch à qn** to serve notice of sth on sb.

silence [silɑ̃s] *nm* silence; (MUS) rest; **garder le ~** to keep silent, say nothing; **passer sous ~** to pass over (in silence); **réduire au ~** to silence; **silencieux, euse** *a* quiet, silent // *nm* silencer.

silex [silɛks] *nm* flint.

silhouette [silwɛt] *nf* outline, silhouette; (*lignes, contour*) outline; (*figure*) figure.

silicium [silisjɔm] *nm* silicon.

silicone [silikon] *nf* silicone.

silicose [silikoz] *nf* silicosis, dust disease.

sillage [sijaʒ] *nm* wake; (*fig*) trail.

sillon [sijɔ̃] *nm* furrow; (*de disque*) groove; **sillonner** *vt* to furrow; to cross, criss-cross.

silo [silo] *nm* silo.

simagrées [simagre] *nfpl* fuss *sg*; airs and graces.

simiesque [simjɛsk(ə)] *a* monkey-like, ape-like.

similaire [similɛʀ] *a* similar; **similarité** *nf* similarity; **simili...** *préfixe* imitation *cpd*,

artificial; **similicuir** *nm* imitation leather; **similitude** *nf* similarity.

simple [sɛ̃pl(ə)] *a* (*gén*) simple; (*non multiple*) single; **~s** *nmpl* (MÉD) medicinal plants; **~ messieurs** (TENNIS) men's singles *sg*; **un ~ particulier** an ordinary citizen; **cela varie du ~ au double** it can double, it can be double the price *etc*; **~ course** *a* single; **~ d'esprit** *nm/f* simpleton; **~ soldat** private; **simplicité** *nf* simplicity; **simplifier** *vt* to simplify; **simpliste** *a* simplistic.

simulacre [simylakʀ(ə)] *nm* enactement; (*péj*): **un ~ de** a pretence of, a sham.

simulateur, trice [simylatœʀ, -tʀis] *nm/f* shammer, pretender; (*qui se prétend malade*) malingerer // *nm*: **~ de vol** flight simulator.

simulation [simylasjɔ̃] *nf* shamming, simulation; malingering.

simuler [simyle] *vt* to sham, simulate; (*suj: substance, revêtement*) to simulate.

simultané, e [simyltane] *a* simultaneous; **~ment** *ad* simultaneously.

sincère [sɛ̃sɛʀ] *a* sincere; genuine; heartfelt; **sincérité** *nf* sincerity.

sinécure [sinekyʀ] *nf* sinecure.

sine die [sinedje] *ad* sine die, indefinitely.

sine qua non [sinekwanɔn] *a*: **condition ~** indispensable condition.

singe [sɛ̃ʒ] *nm* monkey; (*de grande taille*) ape.

singer [sɛ̃ʒe] *vt* to ape, mimic.

singeries [sɛ̃ʒʀi] *nfpl* antics; (*simagrées*) airs and graces.

singulariser [sɛ̃gylaʀize] *vt* to mark out; **se ~** to call attention to o.s.

singularité [sɛ̃gylaʀite] *nf* peculiarity.

singulier, ière [sɛ̃gylje, -jɛʀ] *a* remarkable, singular; (LING) singular // *nm* singular.

sinistre [sinistʀ(ə)] *a* sinister // *nm* (*incendie*) blaze; (*catastrophe*) disaster; (ASSURANCES) accident (*giving rise to a claim*); **sinistré, e** *a* disaster-stricken // *nm/f* disaster victim.

sino... [sino] *préfixe*: **~-indien** Sino-Indian, Chinese-Indian.

sinon [sinɔ̃] *cj* (*autrement, sans quoi*) otherwise, or else; (*sauf*) except, other than; (*si ce n'est*) if not.

sinueux, euse [sinɥø, -øz] *a* winding; (*fig*) tortuous; **sinuosités** *nfpl* winding *sg*, curves.

sinus [sinys] *nm* (ANAT) sinus; (GÉOM) sine; **sinusite** *nf* sinusitis, sinus infection.

sionisme [sjɔnism(ə)] *nm* Zionism.

siphon [sifɔ̃] *nm* (*tube, d'eau gazeuse*) siphon; (*d'évier etc*) U-bend; **siphonner** *vt* to siphon.

sire [siʀ] *nm* (*titre*): **S~** Sire; **un triste ~** an unsavoury individual.

sirène [siʀɛn] *nf* siren; **~ d'alarme** air-raid siren; fire alarm.

sirop [siʀo] *nm* (*à diluer: de fruit etc*) syrup, cordial; (*boisson*) cordial; (*pharmaceutique*) syrup, mixture; **~ de menthe** mint syrup *ou* cordial; **~ contre la toux** cough syrup *ou* mixture.

siroter [siʀɔte] *vt* to sip.

sis, e [si, siz] a: ~ **rue de la Paix** located in the rue de la Paix.
sismique [sismik] a seismic.
sismographe [sismɔgraf] nm seismograph.
sismologie [sismɔlɔʒi] nf seismology.
site [sit] nm (paysage, environnement) setting ; (d'une ville etc: emplacement) site ; ~ **(pittoresque)** beauty spot ; ~**s** **touristiques** places of interest ; ~**s** **naturels/historiques** natural/ historic sites.
sitôt [sito] ad: ~ **parti** as soon as he had left ; **pas de** ~ not for a long time.
situation [situɑsjɔ̃] nf (gén) situation ; (d'un édifice, d'une ville) situation, position ; location.
situé, e [sitɥe] a: **bien** ~ well situated, in a good location ; ~ **à/près de** situated at/near.
situer [sitɥe] vt to site, situate ; (en pensée) to set, place ; **se** ~ **vi**: **se** ~ **à/près de** to be situated at/near.
six [sis] num six ; **sixième** num sixth.
sketch [skɛtʃ] nm (variety) sketch.
ski [ski] nm (objet) ski ; (sport) skiing ; **faire du** ~ to ski ; ~ **de fond** lang-lauf ; ~ **nautique** water-skiing ; ~ **de piste** downhill skiing ; ~ **de randonnée** cross-country skiing ; **skier** vi to ski ; **skieur, euse** nm/f skier.
slalom [slalɔm] nm slalom ; **faire du** ~ **entre** to slalom between ; ~ **géant/spécial** giant/special slalom.
slave [slav] a Slav(onic), Slavic.
slip [slip] nm (sous-vêtement) pants pl, briefs pl ; (de bain: d'homme) (bathing ou swimming) trunks pl ; (: du bikini) (bikini) briefs pl.
slogan [slɔgɑ̃] nm slogan.
S.M.I.C., S.M.I.G. [smik, smig] sigle m voir **salaire**.
smoking [smɔkiŋ] nm dinner ou evening suit.
snack [snak] nm snack bar.
S.N.C.F. sigle f = société nationale des chemins de fer français, ≈ British Rail.
snob [snɔb] a snobbish // nm/f snob ; ~**isme** nm snobbery.
sobre [sɔbʀ(ə)] a temperate, abstemious ; (élégance, style) sober ; ~ **de** (gestes, compliments) sparing of ; **sobriété** nf temperance, abstemiousness ; sobriety.
sobriquet [sɔbʀikɛ] nm nickname.
soc [sɔk] nm ploughshare.
sociable [sɔsjabl(ə)] a sociable.
social, e, aux [sɔsjal, -o] a social.
socialisme [sɔsjalism(ə)] nm socialism ; **socialiste** nm/f socialist.
sociétaire [sɔsjetɛʀ] nm/f member.
société [sɔsjete] nf society ; (sportive) club ; (COMM) company ; **la bonne** ~ polite society ; **la** ~ **d'abondance/de consommation** the affluent/consumer society ; ~ **anonyme (S.A.)** ≈ limited company ; ~ **à responsabilité limitée (S.A.R.L.)** type of limited liability company (with non negotiable shares).
sociologie [sɔsjɔlɔʒi] nf sociology ; **sociologue** nm/f sociologist.

socle [sɔkl(ə)] nm (de colonne, statue) plinth, pedestal ; (de lampe) base.
socquette [sɔkɛt] nf ankle sock.
sodium [sɔdjɔm] nm sodium.
sœur [sœʀ] nf sister ; (religieuse) nun, sister ; ~ **Élisabeth** (REL) Sister Elizabeth.
soi [swa] pronom oneself ; **cela va de** ~ that ou it goes without saying, it stands to reason ; ~**-disant** a inv so-called // ad supposedly.
soie [swa] nf silk ; (de porc, sanglier: poil) bristle ; ~**rie** nf (industrie) silk trade ; (tissu) silk.
soif [swaf] nf thirst ; (fig): ~ **de** thirst ou craving for ; **avoir** ~ to be thirsty ; **donner** ~ **à qn** to make sb thirsty.
soigné, e [swaɲe] a (tenue) well-groomed, neat ; (travail) careful, meticulous ; (fam) whopping ; stiff.
soigner [swaɲe] vt (malade, maladie: suj: docteur) to treat ; (suj: infirmière, mère) to nurse, look after ; (blessé) to tend ; (travail, détails) to take care over ; (jardin, chevelure, invités) to look after ; **soigneur** nm (CYCLISME, FOOTBALL) trainer ; (BOXE) second.
soigneusement [swaɲøzmɑ̃] ad carefully.
soigneux, euse [swaɲø, -øz] a (propre) tidy, neat ; (méticuleux) painstaking, careful ; ~ **de** careful with.
soi-même [swamɛm] pronom oneself.
soin [swɛ̃] nm (application) care ; (propreté, ordre) tidiness, neatness ; (responsabilité): **le** ~ **de qch** the care of sth ; ~**s** nmpl (à un malade, blessé) treatment sg, medical attention sg ; (attentions, prévenance) care and attention sg ; (hygiène) care sg ; ~**s de** **la chevelure/de beauté** hair-/beauty care ; **les** ~**s du ménage** the care of the home ; **avoir ou prendre** ~ **de** to take care of, look after ; **avoir ou prendre** ~ **de faire** to take care to do ; **sans** ~ a careless ; untidy ; **les premiers** ~**s** first aid sg ; **aux bons** ~**s de** c/o, care of.
soir [swaʀ] nm, ad evening ; **ce** ~ this evening, tonight ; **demain** ~ tomorrow evening, tomorrow night.
soirée [swaʀe] nf evening ; (réception) party ; **donner en** ~ (film, pièce) to give an evening performance of.
soit [swa] vb voir **être** ; ~ **un triangle** ABC let ABC be a triangle // cj (à savoir) namely, to wit ; (ou): ~ ... ~ either ... or // ad so be it, very well ; ~ **que ...** ~ **que** ou **ou que** whether ... or whether.
soixantaine [swasɑ̃tɛn] nf: **une** ~ **(de)** sixty or so, about sixty.
soixante [swasɑ̃t] num sixty.
soja [sɔʒa] nm soya ; (graines) soya beans pl ; **germes de** ~ beansprouts.
sol [sɔl] nm ground ; (de logement) floor ; (revêtement) flooring q ; (territoire, AGR, GÉO) soil ; (MUS) G ; (en chantant la gamme) so(h).
solaire [sɔlɛʀ] a solar, sun cpd.
solarium [sɔlaʀjɔm] nm solarium.
soldat [sɔlda] nm soldier ; S~ **inconnu** Unknown Warrior ou Soldier ; ~ **de** **plomb** tin ou toy soldier.
solde [sɔld(ə)] nf pay // nm (COMM) balance ; ~**s** nmpl ou nfpl (COMM) sale goods ; sales ; **à la** ~ **de qn** (péj) in sb's

pay ; ~ à payer balance outstanding ; en ~ at sale price ; aux ~s at the sales.
solder [sɔlde] vt (compte) to settle ; (marchandise) to sell at sale price, sell off ; se ~ par (fig) to end in ; article soldé (à) 10 F item reduced to 10 F.
sole [sɔl] nf sole inv.
soleil [sɔlɛj] nm sun ; (lumière) sun(light) ; (temps ensoleillé) sun(shine) ; (feu d'artifice) Catherine wheel ; (acrobatie) grand circle ; (BOT) sunflower ; il y a ou il fait du ~ it's sunny ; au ~ in the sun ; le ~ de minuit the midnight sun.
solennel, le [sɔlanɛl] a solemn ; ceremonial ; solenniser vt to solemnize ; solennité nf (d'une fête) solemnity ; (fête) grand occasion.
solfège [sɔlfɛʒ] nm rudiments pl of music.
soli [sɔli] pl de solo.
solidaire [sɔlidɛʀ] a (personnes) who stand together, who show solidarity ; (pièces mécaniques) interdependent ; être ~ de (collègues) to stand by ; (mécanisme) to be bound up with, be dependent on ; se solidariser avec to show solidarity with ; solidarité nf solidarity ; interdependence ; par solidarité (avec) (cesser le travail etc) in sympathy (with).
solide [sɔlid] a solid ; (mur, maison, meuble) solid, sturdy ; (connaissances, argument) sound ; (personne, estomac) robust, sturdy // nm solid ; solidifier vt, se solidifier vi to solidify ; solidité nf solidity ; sturdiness.
soliloque [sɔlilɔk] nm soliloquy.
soliste [sɔlist(ə)] nm/f soloist.
solitaire [sɔlitɛʀ] a (sans compagnie) solitary, lonely ; (isolé) solitary, isolated, lone ; (désert) lonely // nm/f recluse ; loner // nm (diamant, jeu) solitaire.
solitude [sɔlityd] nf loneliness ; (paix) solitude.
solive [sɔliv] nf joist.
sollicitations [sɔlisitasjɔ̃] nfpl entreaties, appeals ; enticements ; promptings.
solliciter [sɔlisite] vt (personne) to appeal to ; (emploi, faveur) to seek ; (moteur) to prompt ; (suj: occupations, attractions etc): ~ qn to appeal to sb's curiosity etc ; to entice sb ; to make demands on sb's time ; ~ qn de faire to appeal to ou request sb to do.
sollicitude [sɔlisityd] nf concern.
solo [sɔlo] nm, pl soli [sɔli] (MUS) solo (pl s or soli).
solstice [sɔlstis] nm solstice.
soluble [sɔlybl(ə)] a soluble.
solution [sɔlysjɔ̃] nf solution ; ~ de continuité solution of continuity, gap ; ~ de facilité easy way out.
solvabilité [sɔlvabilite] nf solvency.
solvable [sɔlvabl(ə)] a solvent.
solvant [sɔlvɑ̃] nm solvent.
sombre [sɔ̃bʀ(ə)] a dark ; (fig) sombre, gloomy.
sombrer [sɔ̃bʀe] vi (bateau) to sink, go down ; ~ dans (misère, désespoir) to sink into.
sommaire [sɔmɛʀ] a (simple) basic ; (expéditif) summary // nm summary.
sommation [sɔmasjɔ̃] nf (JUR) summons sg ; (avant de faire feu) warning.

somme [sɔm] nf (MATH) sum ; (fig) amount ; (argent) sum, amount // nm: faire un ~ to have a (short) nap ; faire la ~ de to add up ; en ~ ad all in all ; ~ toute ad when all's said and done.
sommeil [sɔmɛj] nm sleep ; avoir ~ to be sleepy ; avoir le ~ léger to be a light sleeper ; en ~ (fig) dormant ; sommeiller vi to doze ; (fig) to lie dormant.
sommelier [sɔmǝlje] nm wine waiter.
sommer [sɔme] vt: ~ qn de faire to command ou order sb to do ; (JUR) to summon sb to do.
sommes vb voir aussi être.
sommet [sɔme] nm top ; (d'une montagne) summit, top ; (fig: de la perfection, gloire) height ; (GÉOM: d'angle) vertex (pl vertices).
sommier [sɔmje] nm: ~ (à ressorts) springing g ; (interior-sprung) divan base ; ~ métallique mesh-springing ; mesh-sprung divan base.
sommité [sɔmite] nf prominent person, leading light.
somnambule [sɔmnãbyl] nm/f sleepwalker.
somnifère [sɔmnifɛʀ] nm sleeping drug (ou pill).
somnolent, e [sɔmnɔlã, -ãt] a sleepy, drowsy.
somnoler [sɔmnɔle] vi to doze.
somptuaire [sɔptчɛʀ] a: lois ~s sumptuary laws ; dépenses ~s extravagant expenditure sg.
somptueux, euse [sɔptчø, -øz] a sumptuous ; lavish.
son [sɔ̃], sa [sa], pl ses [se] dét (antécédent humain mâle) his ; (: femelle) her ; (: valeur indéfinie) one's, his/her ; (: non humain) its ; voir note sous il.
son [sɔ̃] nm sound ; (résidu) bran.
sonate [sɔnat] nf sonata.
sondage [sɔ̃daʒ] nm (de terrain) boring, drilling ; (mer, atmosphère) sounding ; probe ; (enquête) survey, sounding out of opinion ; ~ (d'opinion) (opinion) poll.
sonde [sɔ̃d] nf (NAVIG) lead ou sounding line ; (MÉTÉOROLOGIE) sonde ; (MÉD) probe ; catheter ; feeding tube ; (TECH) borer, driller ; (pour fouiller etc) probe ; ~ à avalanche pole (for probing snow and locating victims) ; ~ spatiale probe.
sonder, e [sɔ̃de] vt (NAVIG) to sound ; (atmosphère, plaie, bagages etc) to probe ; (TECH) to bore, drill ; (fig) to sound out ; to probe.
songe [sɔ̃ʒ] nm dream.
songer [sɔ̃ʒe] vi to dream ; ~ à (rêver à) to muse over, think over ; (penser à) to think of ; (envisager) to contemplate, think of ; to consider ; ~ que to consider that ; to think that ; songerie nf reverie ; songeur, euse a pensive.
sonnailles [sɔnaj] nfpl jingle of bells.
sonnant, e [sɔnã, -ãt] a: en espèces ~es et trébuchantes in coin of the realm ; à 8 heures ~es on the stroke of 8.
sonné, e [sɔne] a (fam) cracked ; il est midi ~ it's gone twelve ; il a quarante ans bien ~s he's well into his forties.
sonner [sɔne] vi to ring // vt (cloche) to ring ; (glas, tocsin) to sound ; (portier,

infirmière) to ring for ; (*messe*) to ring the
bell for ; (*fam: suj: choc, coup*) to knock
out ; ~ **du clairon** to sound the bugle ;
~ **faux** (*instrument*) to sound out of tune ;
(*rire*) to ring false ; ~ **les heures** to strike
the hours ; **minuit vient de** ~ midnight
has just struck ; ~ **chez qn** to ring sb's
doorbell, ring at sb's door.
sonnerie [sɔnʀi] *nf* (*son*) ringing ;
(*sonnette*) bell ; (*mécanisme d'horloge*)
striking mechanism ; ~ **d'alarme** alarm
bell ; ~ **de clairon** bugle call.
sonnet [sɔnɛ] *nm* sonnet.
sonnette [sɔnɛt] *nf* bell ; ~ **d'alarme**
alarm bell ; ~ **de nuit** night-bell.
sono [sɔno] *nf abr de* **sonorisation**.
sonore [sɔnɔʀ] *a* (*voix*) sonorous, ringing ;
(*salle, métal*) resonant ; (*ondes, film, signal*)
sound *cpd* ; (*LING*) voiced.
sonorisation [sɔnɔʀizasjɔ̃] *nf*
(*installations*) public address system, P.A.
system.
sonoriser [sɔnɔʀize] *vt* (*film, spectacle*) to
add the sound track to ; (*salle*) to fit with
a public address system.
sonorité [sɔnɔʀite] *nf* (*de piano, violon*)
tone ; (*de voix, mot*) sonority ; (*d'une salle*)
resonance ; acoustics *pl*.
sont *vb voir* **être**.
sophistiqué, e [sɔfistike] *a* sophisticated.
soporifique [sɔpɔʀifik] *a* soporific.
sorbet [sɔʀbɛ] *nm* water ice, sorbet.
sorcellerie [sɔʀsɛlʀi] *nf* witchcraft *q*,
sorcery *q*.
sorcier, ière [sɔʀsje, -jɛʀ] *nm/f*
sorcerer/witch *ou* sorceress.
sordide [sɔʀdid] *a* sordid ; squalid.
sornettes [sɔʀnɛt] *nfpl* twaddle *sg*.
sort [sɔʀ] *nm* (*fortune, destinée*) fate ;
(*condition, situation*) lot ; (*magique*) curse,
spell ; **le** ~ **en est jeté** the die is cast ;
tirer au ~ to draw lots ; **tirer qch au** ~
to draw lots for sth.
sorte [sɔʀt(ə)] *nf* sort, kind ; **de la** ~ *ad*
in that way ; **de** ~ **à** so as to, in order
to ; **de (telle)** ~ **que, en** ~ **que** so that ;
so much so that.
sortie [sɔʀti] *nf* (*issue*) way out, exit ; (*MIL*)
sortie ; (*fig: verbale*) outburst ; sally ;
(*promenade*) outing ; (*le soir: au restaurant
etc*) night out ; (*COMM: somme*): ~**s** items
of expenditure ; outgoings *sans sg* ; **à sa**
~ as he went out *ou* left ; **à la** ~ **de**
l'école/l'usine   (*moment*)   after
school/work ; when school/the factory
comes out ; (*lieu*) at the school/factory
gates ; **à la** ~ **de ce nouveau modèle**
when this new model comes out, when
they bring out this new model ; ~ **de bain**
(*vêtement*) bathrobe ; **'**~ **de camions'**
'vehicle exit', 'lorries turning', ~ **de**
secours emergency exit.
sortilège [sɔʀtilɛʒ] *nm* (magic) spell.
sortir [sɔʀtiʀ] *vi* (*gén*) to come out ; (*partir,
se promener, aller au spectacle etc*) to go
out ; (*numéro gagnant*) to come up // *vt*
(*gén*) to take out ; (*produit, ouvrage,
modèle*) to bring out ; (*boniments,
incongruités*) to come out with ; (*fam:
expulser*) to throw out ; ~ **qch de** to take
sth out of ; ~ **de** (*gén*) to leave ; (*endroit*)
to go (*ou* come) out of, leave ; (*rainure etc*)

to come out of ; (*cadre, compétence*) to be
outside ; (*provenir de: famille etc*) to come
from ; **se** ~ **de** (*affaire, situation*) to get
out of ; **s'en** ~ (*malade*) to pull through ;
(*d'une difficulté etc*) to come through all
right ; to get through, be able to manage.
S.O.S. *sigle m* mayday, SOS.
sosie [sɔzi] *nm* double.
sot, sotte [so, sɔt] *a* silly, foolish // *nm/f*
fool ; **sottise** *nf* silliness, foolishness ; silly
ou foolish thing (to do *ou* say).
sou [su] *nm*: **près de ses** ~**s** tight-fisted ;
sans le ~ penniless ; **pas un** ~ **de bon**
sens not a scrap *ou* an ounce of good sense.
soubassement [subɑsmɑ̃] *nm* base.
soubresaut [subʀəso] *nm* start ; jolt.
soubrette [subʀɛt] *nf* soubrette,
maidservant.
souche [suʃ] *nf* (*d'arbre*) stump ; (*de
carnet*) counterfoil, stub ; **de vieille** ~ **of**
old stock.
souci [susi] *nm* (*inquiétude*) worry ;
(*préoccupation*) concern ; (*BOT*) marigold ;
se faire du ~ to worry ; **avoir (le)** ~ **de**
to have concern for.
soucier [susje]: **se** ~ **de** *vt* to care about.
soucieux, euse [susjø, -øz] *a* concerned,
worried ; ~ **de** concerned about ; **peu** ~
de/que caring little about/whether.
soucoupe [sukup] *nf* saucer ; ~ **volante**
flying saucer.
soudain, e [sudɛ̃, -ɛn] *a* (*douleur, mort*)
sudden // *ad* suddenly, all of a sudden ;
soudainement *ad* suddenly ; **soudaineté**
nf suddenness.
soude [sud] *nf* soda.
soudé, e [sude] *a* (*fig: pétales, organes*)
joined (together).
souder [sude] *vt* (*avec fil à souder*) to
solder ; (*par soudure autogène*) to weld ;
(*fig*) to bind *ou* knit together ; to fuse
(together).
soudoyer [sudwaje] *vt* (*péj*) to bribe, buy
over.
soudure [sudyʀ] *nf* soldering ; welding ;
(*joint*) soldered joint ; weld.
souffert, e [sufɛʀ, -ɛʀt(ə)] *pp de* **souffrir**.
souffle [sufl(ə)] *nm* (*en expirant*) breath ;
(*en soufflant*) puff, blow ; (*respiration*)
breathing ; (*d'explosion, de ventilateur*)
blast ; (*du vent*) blowing ; (*fig*) inspiration ;
avoir du/manquer de ~ to have a lot
of/be short of breath ; **être à bout de** ~
to be out of breath ; **avoir le** ~ **court** to
be short-winded ; **un** ~ **d'air ou de vent**
a breath of air, a puff of wind.
soufflé, e [sufle] *a* (*CULIN*) soufflé ; (*fam:
ahuri, stupéfié*) staggered // *nm* (*CULIN*)
soufflé.
souffler [sufle] *vi* (*gén*) to blow ; (*haleter*)
to puff (and blow) // *vt* (*feu, bougie*) to
blow out ; (*chasser: poussière etc*) to blow
away ; (*TECH: verre*) to blow ; (*suj:
explosion*) to destroy (with its blast) ;
(*dire*): ~ **qch à qn** to whisper sth to sb ;
(*fam: voler*): ~ **qch à qn** to nick sth from
sb ; ~ **son rôle à qn** to prompt sb ; **laisser**
~ **qn** (*fig*) to give sb a breather.
soufflet [suflɛ] *nm* (*instrument*) bellows
pl ; (*entre wagons*) vestibule ; (*gifle*) slap (in
the face).

souffleur, euse [suflœʀ, -øz] *nm/f* (*THÉÂTRE*) prompter.

souffrance [sufʀɑ̃s] *nf* suffering; **en ~** (*marchandise*) awaiting delivery; (*affaire*) pending.

souffrant, e [sufʀɑ̃, -ɑ̃t] *a* unwell.

souffre-douleur [sufʀədulœʀ] *nm inv* whipping boy, underdog.

souffreteux, euse [sufʀətø, -øz] *a* sickly.

souffrir [sufʀiʀ] *vi* to suffer; to be in pain // *vt* to suffer, endure; (*supporter*) to bear, stand; (*admettre: exception etc*) to allow *ou* admit of; **~ de** (*maladie, froid*) to suffer from; **~ des dents** to have trouble with one's teeth; **faire ~ qn** (*suj: personne*) to make sb suffer; (: *dents, blessure etc*) to hurt sb.

soufre [sufʀ(ə)] *nm* sulphur.

souhait [swɛ] *nm* wish; **tous nos ~s de** good wishes *ou* our best wishes for; **riche etc à ~** as rich etc as one could wish; **à vos ~s!** bless you!

souhaitable [swɛtabl(ə)] *a* desirable.

souhaiter [swete] *vt* to wish for; **~ le bonjour à qn** to bid sb good day; **~ la bonne année à qn** to wish sb a happy New Year.

souiller [suje] *vt* to dirty, soil; (*fig*) to sully, tarnish; **souillure** *nf* stain.

soûl, e [su, sul] *a* drunk // *nm*: **boire tout son ~** to drink one's fill.

soulagement [sulaʒmɑ̃] *nm* relief.

soulager [sulaʒe] *vt* to relieve.

soûler [sule] *vt*: **~ qn** to get sb drunk; (*suj: boisson*) to make sb drunk; (*fig*) to make sb's head spin ou reel; **se ~** to get drunk; **se ~ de** (*fig*) to intoxicate o.s. with; **soûlerie** *nf* (*péj*) drunken binge.

soulèvement [sulɛvmɑ̃] *nm* uprising; (*GÉO*) upthrust.

soulever [sulve] *vt* to lift; (*vagues, poussière*) to send up; (*peuple*) to stir up (to revolt); (*enthousiasme*) to arouse; (*question, débat*) to raise; **se ~** *vi* (*peuple*) to rise up; (*personne couchée*) to lift o.s. up; **cela me soulève le cœur** it makes me feel sick.

soulier [sulje] *nm* shoe; **~s plats/à talons** flat/heeled shoes.

souligner [suliɲe] *vt* to underline; (*fig*) to emphasize; to stress.

soumettre [sumɛtʀ] *vt* (*pays*) to subject, subjugate; (*rebelle*) to put down, subdue; **~ qn/qch à** to subject sb/sth to; **~ qch à qn** (*projet etc*) to submit sth to sb; **se ~ (à)** (*se rendre, obéir*) to submit (to); **se ~ à** (*formalités etc*) to submit to; (*régime etc*) to submit o.s. to.

soumis, e [sumi, -iz] *a* submissive; **revenus ~ à l'impôt** taxable income.

soumission [sumisjɔ̃] *nf* (*voir se soumettre*) submission; (*docilité*) submissiveness; (*COMM*) tender.

soupape [supap] *nf* valve; **~ de sûreté** safety valve.

soupçon [supsɔ̃] *nm* suspicion; (*petite quantité*): **un ~ de** a hint ou touch of; **soupçonner** *vt* to suspect; **soupçonneux, euse** *a* suspicious.

soupe [sup] *nf* soup; **~ au lait** *a inv* quick-tempered; **~ à l'oignon/de poisson**

onion/fish soup; **~ populaire** soup kitchen.

soupente [supɑ̃t] *nf* cupboard under the stairs.

souper [supe] *vi* to have supper // *nm* supper; **avoir soupé de** (*fam*) to be sick and tired of.

soupeser [supəze] *vt* to weigh in one's hand(s), feel the weight of; (*fig*) to weigh up.

soupière [supjɛʀ] *nf* (soup) tureen.

soupir [supiʀ] *nm* sigh; (*MUS*) crotchet rest; **rendre le dernier ~** to breathe one's last.

soupirail, aux [supiʀaj, -o] *nm* (small) basement window.

soupirant [supiʀɑ̃] *nm* (*péj*) suitor, wooer.

soupirer [supiʀe] *vi* to sigh; **~ après qch** to yearn for sth.

souple [supl(ə)] *a* supple; (*fig: règlement, caractère*) flexible; (: *démarche, taille*) lithe, supple; **souplesse** *nf* suppleness; flexibility.

source [suʀs(ə)] *nf* (*point d'eau*) spring; (*d'un cours d'eau, fig*) source; **prendre sa ~ à/dans** (*suj: cours d'eau*) to have its source at/in; **tenir qch de bonne ~/de ~ sûre** to have sth on good authority/from a reliable source; **~ thermale/d'eau minérale** hot *ou* thermal/mineral spring.

sourcier [suʀsje] *nm* water diviner.

sourcil [suʀsij] *nm* (eye)brow; **sourcilière** *af voir* **arcade**.

sourciller [suʀsije] *vi*: **sans ~** without turning a hair *ou* batting an eyelid.

sourcilleux, euse [suʀsijø, -øz] *a* pernickety.

sourd, e [suʀ, suʀd(ə)] *a* deaf; (*bruit, voix*) muffled; (*couleur*) muted; (*douleur*) dull; (*lutte*) silent, hidden; (*LING*) voiceless // *nm/f* deaf person.

sourdait *etc vb voir* **sourdre**.

sourdine [suʀdin] *nf* (*MUS*) mute; **en ~** *ad* softly, quietly; **mettre une ~ à** (*fig*) to tone down.

sourd-muet, sourde-muette [suʀmyɛ, suʀdmyɛt] *a* deaf-and-dumb // *nm/f* deaf-mute.

sourdre [suʀdʀ(ə)] *vi* to rise.

souriant, e [suʀjɑ̃, -ɑ̃t] *a* cheerful.

souricière [suʀisjɛʀ] *nf* mousetrap; (*fig*) trap.

sourire [suʀiʀ] *nm* smile // *vi* to smile; **~ à qn** to smile at sb; (*fig*) to appeal to sb; to smile on sb; **faire un ~ à qn** to give sb a smile; **garder le ~** to keep smiling.

souris [suʀi] *nf* mouse (*pl* mice).

sournois, e [suʀnwa, -waz] *a* deceitful, underhand.

sous [su] *prép* (*gén*) under; **~ la pluie/le soleil** in the rain/sunshine; **~ terre** *a, ad* underground; **~ peu** *ad* shortly, before long.

sous... [su, suz + *vowel*] *préfixe* sub-, under-; **~-catégorie** sub-category; **~-alimenté/-équipé/-développé** under-nourished/equipped/developed.

sous-bois [subwa] *nm inv* undergrowth.

sous-chef [suʃɛf] nm deputy chief clerk.
souscription [suskripsjɔ̃] nf subscription; **offert en ~** available on subscription.
souscrire [suskrir]: **~ à** vt to subscribe to.
sous-directeur, trice [sudirɛktœr, -tris] nm/f assistant manager/ manageress, sub-manager/ manageress.
sous-emploi [suzɑ̃plwa] nm underemployment.
sous-entendre [suzɑ̃tɑ̃dr(ə)] vt to imply, infer; **sous-entendu, e** a implied; (verbe, complément) understood // nm innuendo, insinuation.
sous-estimer [suzɛstime] vt to underestimate.
sous-exposer [suzɛkspoze] vt to underexpose.
sous-fifre [sufifr] nm (péj) underling.
sous-jacent, e [suzasɑ̃, -ɑ̃t] a underlying.
sous-lieutenant [suljøtnɑ̃] nm sublieutenant.
sous-locataire [suləkatɛr] nm/f subtenant.
sous-louer [sulwe] vt to sublet.
sous-main [sumɛ̃] nm inv desk blotter; **en ~** ad secretly.
sous-marin, e [sumarɛ̃, -in] a (flore, volcan) submarine; (navigation, pêche, explosif) underwater // nm submarine.
sous-officier [suzɔfisje] nm ≈ non-comissioned officer (N.C.O.).
sous-préfecture [suprefɛktyr] nf subprefecture.
sous-préfet [suprefɛ] nm sub-prefect.
sous-produit [suprɔdɥi] nm by-product; (fig: péj) pale imitation.
sous-secrétaire [susəkretɛr] nm: **~ d'État** Under-Secretary of State.
soussigné, e [susiɲe] a: **je ~** I the undersigned.
sous-sol [susɔl] nm basement; (GÉO) subsoil.
sous-titre [sutitr(ə)] nm subtitle; **sous-titré, e** a with subtitles.
soustraction [sustraksjɔ̃] nf subtraction.
soustraire [sustrɛr] vt to subtract, take away; (dérober): **~ qch à qn** to remove sth from sb; **~ qn à** (danger) to shield sb from; **se ~ à** (autorité etc) to elude, escape from.
sous-traitance [sutrɛtɑ̃s(ə)] nf subcontracting.
sous-verre [suvɛr] nm inv glass mount.
sous-vêtement [suvɛtmɑ̃] nm undergarment, item of underwear; **~s** nmpl underwear sg.
soutane [sutan] nf cassock, soutane.
soute [sut] nf hold; **~ à bagages** baggage hold.
soutenable [sutnabl(ə)] a (opinion) tenable, defensible.
soutenance [sutnɑ̃s] nf: **~ de thèse** ≈ viva voce (examination).
soutènement [sutɛnmɑ̃] nm: **mur de ~** retaining wall.
souteneur [sutnœr] nm procurer.
soutenir [sutnir] vt to support; (assaut, choc) to stand up to, withstand; (intérêt, effort) to keep up; (assurer): **~ que** to

maintain that; **se ~** (dans l'eau etc) to hold o.s. up; **~ la comparaison avec** to bear ou stand comparison with; **soutenu, e** a (efforts) sustained, unflagging; (style) elevated.
souterrain, e [sutɛrɛ̃, -ɛn] a underground // nm underground passage.
soutien [sutjɛ̃] nm support; **~ de famille** breadwinner.
soutien-gorge [sutjɛ̃gɔrʒ(ə)] nm bra.
soutirer [sutire] vt: **~ qch à qn** to squeeze ou get sth out of sb.
souvenance [suvnɑ̃s] nf: **avoir ~ de** to recollect.
souvenir [suvnir] nm (réminiscence) memory; (cadeau) souvenir, keepsake; (de voyage) souvenir // vb: **se ~ de** vt to remember; **se ~ que** to remember that; **en ~ de** in memory ou remembrance of.
souvent [suvɑ̃] ad often; **peu ~** seldom, infrequently.
souverain, e [suvrɛ̃, -ɛn] a sovereign; (fig: mépris) supreme // nm/f sovereign, monarch; **souveraineté** nf sovereignty.
soviétique [sovjetik] a Soviet // nm/f: **S~** Soviet citizen.
soyeux, euse [swajø, øz] a silky.
soyons etc vb voir **être**.
S.P.A. sigle f (= société protectrice des animaux) ≈ R.S.P.C.A.
spacieux, euse [spasjø, -øz] a spacious; roomy.
spaghettis [spageti] nmpl spaghetti sg.
sparadrap [sparadra] nm adhesive ou sticking plaster.
spartiate [sparsjat] a Spartan; **~s** nfpl (sandales) Roman sandals.
spasme [spazm(ə)] nm spasm.
spasmodique [spazmɔdik] a spasmodic.
spatial, e, aux [spasjal, -o] a (AVIAT) space cpd; (PSYCH) spatial.
spatule [spatyl] nf (ustensile) slice; spatula; (bout) tip.
speaker, ine [spikœr, -krin] nm/f announcer.
spécial, e, aux [spesjal, -o] a special; (bizarre) peculiar; **~ement** ad especially, particularly; (tout exprès) specially.
spécialisé, e [spesjalize] a specialised.
spécialiser [spesjalize] vt: **se ~** to specialize.
spécialiste [spesjalist(ə)] nm/f specialist.
spécialité [spesjalite] nf speciality; (SCOL) special field; **~ pharmaceutique** patent medicine.
spécieux, euse [spesjø, -øz] a a specious.
spécification [spesifikasjɔ̃] nf specification.
spécifier [spesifje] vt to specify, state.
spécifique [spesifik] a specific.
spécimen [spesimɛn] nm specimen; (revue etc) specimen ou sample copy.
spectacle [spɛktakl(ə)] nm (tableau, scène) sight; (représentation) show; (industrie) show business, entertainment; **se donner en ~** (péj) to make a spectacle ou an exhibition of o.s.; **spectaculaire** a spectacular.
spectateur, trice [spɛktatœr, -tris] nm/f (CINÉMA etc) member of the audience;

(SPORT) spectator; (d'un événement) onlooker, witness.

spectre [spɛktʀ(ə)] nm (fantôme, fig) spectre; (PHYSIQUE) spectrum (pl a); ~ solaire solar spectrum.

spéculateur, trice [spekylatœʀ, -tʀis] nm/f speculator.

spéculation [spekylɑsjɔ̃] nf speculation.

spéculer [spekyle] vi to speculate; ~ sur (COMM) to speculate in; (réfléchir) to speculate on; (tabler sur) to bank ou rely on.

spéléologie [speleɔlɔʒi] nf (étude) speleology; (activité) potholing; **spéléologue** nm/f speleologist; potholer.

spermatozoïde [spɛʀmatozɔid] nm sperm, spermatozoon (pl zoa).

sperme [spɛʀm(ə)] nm semen, sperm.

sphère [sfɛʀ] nf sphere; **sphérique** a spherical.

sphincter [sfɛ̃ktɛʀ] nm sphincter.

spiral, aux [spiʀal, -o] nm hairspring.

spirale [spiʀal] nf spiral; **en ~** in a spiral.

spire [spiʀ] nm (single) turn; whorl.

spiritisme [spiʀitism(ə)] nm spiritualism, spiritism.

spirituel, le [spiʀitɥɛl] a spiritual; (fin, piquant) witty; **musique ~le** sacred music; **concert ~** concert of sacred music.

spiritueux [spiʀitɥø] nm spirit.

splendeur [splɑ̃dœʀ] nf splendour.

splendide [splɑ̃did] a splendid; magnificent.

spolier [spɔlje] vt: ~ qn (de) to despoil sb (of).

spongieux, euse [spɔ̃ʒjø, -øz] a spongy.

spontané, e [spɔ̃tane] a spontaneous.

sporadique [spɔʀadik] a sporadic.

sport [spɔʀ] nm sport // a inv (vêtement) casual; **faire du ~** to do sport; **~s d'équipe/d'hiver** team/winter sports; **sportif, ive** a (journal, association, épreuve) sports cpd; (allure, démarche) athletic; (attitude, esprit) sporting.

spot [spɔt] nm (lampe) spot(light); (annonce): ~ (publicitaire) commercial (break).

sprint [spʀint] nm sprint.

square [skwaʀ] nm public garden(s).

squelette [skəlɛt] nm skeleton; **squelettique** a scrawny; (fig) skimpy.

stabilisateur, trice [stabilizatœʀ, -tʀis] a stabilizing // nm stabilizer; anti-roll device; tailplane.

stabiliser [stabilize] vt to stabilize; (terrain) to consolidate.

stabilité [stabilite] nf stability.

stable [stabl(ə)] a stable, steady.

stade [stad] nm (SPORT) stadium; (phase, niveau) stage.

stage [staʒ] nm training period; training course; (d'avocat stagiaire) articles pl; **stagiaire** nm/f, a trainee.

stagnant, e [stagnɑ̃, -ɑ̃t] a stagnant.

stalactite [stalaktit] nf stalactite.

stalagmite [stalagmit] nf stalagmite.

stalle [stal] nf stall, box.

stand [stɑ̃d] nm (d'exposition) stand; (de foire) stall; ~ **de tir** (MIL) firing range;

(à la foire, SPORT) shooting range; ~ **de ravitaillement** pit.

standard [stɑ̃daʀ] a inv standard // nm switchboard; **standardiser** vt to standardize; **standardiste** nm/f switchboard operator.

standing [stɑ̃diŋ] nm standing; **immeuble de grand ~** block of luxury flats.

star [staʀ] nf star.

starter [staʀtɛʀ] nm (AUTO) choke.

station [stɑsjɔ̃] nf station; (de bus) stop; (de villégiature) resort; (posture): **la ~ debout** standing, an upright posture; ~ **de ski** ski resort; ~ **de taxis** taxi rank.

stationnaire [stasjɔnɛʀ] a stationary.

stationnement [stasjɔnmɑ̃] nm parking; **zone de ~ interdit** no parking area; ~ **alterné** parking on alternate sides.

stationner [stasjɔne] vi to park.

station-service [stasjɔ̃sɛʀvis] nf service station.

statique [statik] a static.

statisticien, ne [statistisjɛ̃, -jɛn] nm/f statistician.

statistique [statistik] nf (science) statistics sg; (rapport, étude) statistic // a statistical; ~**s** (données) statistics pl.

statue [staty] nf statue.

statuer [statɥe] vi: ~ **sur** to rule on, give a ruling on.

statuette [statɥɛt] nf statuette.

statu quo [statykwo] nm status quo.

stature [statyʀ] nf stature.

statut [staty] nm status; ~**s** nmpl (JUR, ADMIN) statutes; **statutaire** a statutory.

Sté abr de **société**.

steak [stɛk] nm steak.

stèle [stɛl] nf stela, stele.

stellaire [stelɛʀ] a stellar.

stencil [stɛnsil] nm stencil.

sténo... [stenɔ] préfixe: ~**(dactylo)** nf shorthand typist; ~**(graphie)** nf shorthand; ~**graphier** vt to take down in shorthand.

stentor [stɑ̃tɔʀ] nm: **voix de ~** stentorian voice.

steppe [stɛp] nf steppe.

stère [stɛʀ] nm stere.

stéréo(phonie) [steʀeɔ(fɔni)] nf stereo(phony); **stéréo(phonique)** a stereo(phonic).

stéréotype [steʀeɔtip] nm stereotype; **stéréotypé, e** a stereotyped.

stérile [steʀil] a sterile; (terre) barren; (fig) fruitless, futile.

stérilet [steʀilɛ] nm coil, loop.

stériliser [steʀilize] vt to sterilize.

stérilité [steʀilite] nf sterility.

sternum [stɛʀnɔm] nm breastbone, sternum.

stéthoscope [stetɔskɔp] nm stethoscope.

stigmates [stigmat] nmpl scars, marks; (REL) stigmata pl.

stigmatiser [stigmatize] vt to denounce, stigmatize.

stimulant, e [stimylɑ̃, -ɑ̃t] a stimulating // nm (MÉD) stimulant; (fig) stimulus (pl i), incentive.

stimulation [stimylasjɔ̃] nf stimulation.

stimuler [stimyle] vt to stimulate.

stimulus, l [stimylys, -i] nm stimulus (pl i).

stipulation [stipylasjɔ̃] nf stipulation.

stipuler [stipyle] vt to stipulate, specify.

stock [stɔk] nm stock ; ~ d'or (FINANCE) gold reserves pl ; ~er vt to stock ; ~iste nm stockist.

stoïque [stɔik] a stoic, stoical.

stomacal, e, aux [stɔmakal, -o] a gastric, stomach cpd.

stop [stɔp] nm (AUTO: écriteau) stop sign ; (: signal) brake-light ; (dans un télégramme) stop // excl stop.

stoppage [stɔpaʒ] nm invisible mending.

stopper [stɔpe] vt to stop, halt ; (COUTURE) to mend // vi to stop, halt.

store [stɔʀ] nm blind ; (de magasin) shade, awning.

strabisme [stʀabism(ə)] nm squinting.

strangulation [stʀɑ̃gylasjɔ̃] nf strangulation.

strapontin [stʀapɔ̃tɛ̃] nm jump ou foldaway seat.

strass [stʀas] nm paste, strass.

stratagème [stʀataʒɛm] nm stratagem.

stratège [stʀatɛʒ] nm strategist.

stratégie [stʀateʒi] nf strategy ; stratégique [stʀateʒik] a strategic.

stratifié, e [stʀatifje] a (GÉO) stratified ; (TECH) laminated.

stratosphère [stʀatɔsfɛʀ] nf stratosphere.

strict, e [stʀikt(ə)] a strict ; (tenue, décor) severe, plain ; son droit le plus ~ his most basic right ; dans la plus ~e intimité strictly in private ; le ~ nécessaire/minimum the bare essentials/minimum.

strident, e [stʀidɑ̃, -ɑ̃t] a shrill, strident.

stridulations [stʀidylasjɔ̃] nfpl stridulations, chirrings.

strie [stʀi] nf streak ; (ANAT, GÉO) stria (pl ae).

strier [stʀije] vt to streak ; to striate.

strip-tease [stʀiptiz] nm striptease ; strip-teaseuse nf stripper, striptease artist.

striures [stʀijyʀ] nfpl streaking sg.

strophe [stʀɔf] nf verse, stanza.

structure [stʀyktyʀ] nf structure ; ~s d'accueil/touristiques reception/tourist facilities ; structurer vt to structure.

stuc [styk] nm stucco.

studieux, euse [stydjø, -øz] a studious ; devoted to study.

studio [stydjo] nm (logement) (one-roomed) flatlet ; (d'artiste, TV etc) studio (pl s).

stupéfaction [stypefaksjɔ̃] nf stupéfaction, amazement.

stupéfait, e [stypefɛ, -ɛt] a amazed.

stupéfiant, e [stypefjɑ̃, -ɑ̃t] a stunning, astounding // nm (MÉD) drug, narcotic.

stupéfier [stypefje] vt to stupefy ; (étonner) to stun, astonish.

stupeur [stypœʀ] nf (inertie, insensibilité) stupor ; (étonnement) astonishment, amazement.

stupide [stypid] a stupid ; stupidité nf stupidity ; stupid thing (to do ou say).

style [stil] nm style ; meuble de ~ period piece of furniture.

stylé, e [stile] a well-trained.

stylet [stilɛ] nm stiletto, stylet.

stylisé, e [stilize] a stylized.

styliste [stilist(ə)] nm/f designer ; stylist.

stylistique [stilistik] nf stylistics sg.

stylo [stilo] nm: ~ (à encre) (fountain) pen ; ~ bille ball-point pen ; ~-feutre nm felt-tip pen.

su, e [sy] pp de savoir // nm: au ~ de with the knowledge of.

suaire [sɥɛʀ] nm shroud.

suave [sɥav] a sweet ; suave, smooth ; mellow.

subalterne [sybaltɛʀn(ə)] a (employé, officier) junior ; (rôle) subordinate, subsidiary // nm/f subordinate, inferior.

subconscient [sypkɔ̃sjɑ̃] nm subconscious.

subdiviser [sybdivize] vt to subdivide ; subdivision nf subdivision.

subir [sybiʀ] vt (affront, dégâts, mauvais traitements) to suffer ; (influence, charme) to be under, be subjected to ; (traitement, opération, châtiment) to undergo.

subit, e [sybi, -it] a sudden ; subitement ad suddenly, all of a sudden.

subjectif, ive [sybʒɛktif, -iv] a subjective.

subjonctif [sybʒɔ̃ktif] nm subjunctive.

subjuguer [sybʒyge] vt to subjugate.

sublime [syblim] a sublime.

sublimer [syblime] vt to sublimate.

submergé, e [sybmɛʀʒe] a submerged ; (fig): ~ de snowed under with ; overwhelmed with.

submerger [sybmɛʀʒe] vt to submerge ; (suj: foule) to engulf ; (fig) to overwhelm.

submersible [sybmɛʀsibl(ə)] nm submarine.

subordination [sybɔʀdinasjɔ̃] nf subordination.

subordonné, e [sybɔʀdɔne] a, nm/f subordinate ; ~ à subordinate to ; subject to, depending on.

subordonner [sybɔʀdɔne] vt: ~ qn/qch à to subordinate sb/sth to.

subornation [sybɔʀnasjɔ̃] nf bribing.

subreptice [sybʀɛptis] a stealthy.

subrepticement [sybʀɛptismɑ̃] ad surreptitiously.

subside [sypsid] nm grant.

subsidiaire [sypsidjɛʀ] a: question ~ deciding question.

subsistance [sybzistɑ̃s] nf subsistence ; pourvoir à la ~ de qn to keep sb, provide for sb's subsistence ou keep.

subsister [sybziste] vi (rester) to remain, subsist ; (vivre) to live ; (survivre) to live on.

substance [sypstɑ̃s] nf substance.

substantiel, le [sypstɑ̃sjɛl] a substantial.

substantif [sypstɑ̃tif] nm noun, substantive ; substantiver vt to nominalize.

substituer [sypstitɥe] vt: ~ qn/qch à to substitute sb/sth for ; se ~ à qn (représenter) to substitute for sb ; (évincer) to substitute o.s. for sb.

substitut [sypstity] *nm* (*JUR*) deputy public prosecutor; (*succédané*) substitute.
substitution [sypstitysjɔ̃] *nf* substitution.
subterfuge [syptɛRfyʒ] *nm* subterfuge.
subtil, e [syptil] *a* subtle.
subtiliser [syptilize] *vt*: ~ qch (à qn) to spirit sth away (from sb).
subtilité [syptilite] *nf* subtlety.
subvenir [sybvəniR]: ~ à *vt* to meet.
subvention [sybvɑ̃sjɔ̃] *nf* subsidy, grant; **subventionner** *vt* to subsidize.
subversif, ive [sybvɛRsif, -iv] *a* subversive; **subversion** *nf* subversion.
suc [syk] *nm* (*BOT*) sap; (*de viande, fruit*) juice; ~s **gastriques** gastric *ou* stomach juices.
succédané [syksedane] *nm* substitute.
succéder [syksede]: ~ à *vt* (*directeur, roi etc*) to succeed; (*venir après: dans une série*) to follow, succeed; **se** ~ *vi* (*accidents, années*) to follow one another.
succès [syksɛ] *nm* success; **avoir du** ~ to be a success, be successful; ~ **de librairie** bestseller; ~ **(féminins)** conquests.
successeur [syksesœR] *nm* successor.
successif, ive [syksesif, -iv] *a* successive.
succession [syksesjɔ̃] *nf* (*série, POL*) succession; (*JUR: patrimoine*) estate, inheritance; **prendre la** ~ **de** (*directeur*) to succeed, take over from; (*entreprise*) to take over.
succinct, e [syksɛ̃, -ɛ̃t] *a* succinct.
succion [syksjɔ̃] *nf*: **bruit de** ~ sucking noise.
succomber [sykɔ̃be] *vi* to die, succumb; (*fig*): ~ à to give way to, succumb to.
succulent, e [sykylɑ̃, -ɑ̃t] *a* succulent.
succursale [sykyRsal] *nf* branch; **magasin à** ~s **multiples** chain *ou* multiple store.
sucer [syse] *vt* to suck.
sucette [sysɛt] *nf* (*bonbon*) lollipop.
sucre [sykR(ə)] *nm* (*substance*) sugar; (*morceau*) lump of sugar, sugar lump *ou* cube; ~ **de canne/betterave** cane/beet sugar; ~ **en morceaux/cristallisé/en poudre** lump/coarse-grained/ granulated sugar; ~ **d'orge** barley sugar; **sucré, e** *a* (*produit alimentaire*) sweetened; (*au goût*) sweet; (*péj*) sugary, honeyed; **sucrer** *vt* (*thé, café*) to sweeten, put sugar in; **sucrer qn** to put sugar in sb's tea (*ou* coffee *etc*); **se sucrer** to help o.s. to sugar, have some sugar; (*fam*) to line one's pocket(s); **sucrerie** *nf* (*usine*) sugar refinery; **sucreries** *nfpl* (*bonbons*) sweets, sweet things; **sucrier, ière** *a* sugar *cpd*; sugar-producing // *nm* (*fabricant*) sugar producer; (*récipient*) sugar bowl *ou* basin.
sud [syd] *nm*: **le** ~ the south // *a inv* south; (*côte*) south, southern; **au** ~ (*situation*) in the south; (*direction*) to the south; **au** ~ **de** (to the) south of; ~-**africain, e** *a, nm/f* South African; ~-**américain, e** *a, nm/f* South American.
sudation [sydasjɔ̃] *nf* sweating, sudation.
sud-est [sydɛst] *nm, a inv* south-east.
sud-ouest [sydwɛst] *nm, a inv* south-west.
Suède [syɛd] *nf*: **la** ~ Sweden; **suédois,**

e a Swedish // *nm/f*: **Suédois, e** Swede // *nm* (*langue*) Swedish.
suer [sɥe] *vi* to sweat; (*suinter*) to ooze // *vt* (*fig*) to exude; ~ **à grosses gouttes** to sweat profusely.
sueur [sɥœR] *nf* sweat; **en** ~ sweating, in a sweat; **avoir des** ~s **froides** to be in a cold sweat.
suffire [syfiR] *vi* (*être assez*): ~ (à qn/pour qch/pour faire) to be enough *ou* sufficient (for sb/for sth/to do); (*satisfaire*): **cela lui suffit** he's content with this, this is enough for him; ~ **à** to be self-sufficient; **cela suffit pour les irriter/qu'ils se fâchent** it's enough to annoy them/for them to get angry; **il suffit d'une négligence/qu'on oublie pour que ...** it only takes one act of carelessness/one only needs to forget for

suffisamment [syfizamɑ̃] *ad* sufficiently, enough; ~ **de** sufficient, enough.
suffisance [syfizɑ̃s] *nf* (*vanité*) self-importance, bumptiousness; (*quantité*): **en** ~ in plenty.
suffisant, e [syfizɑ̃, -ɑ̃t] *a* (*temps, ressources*) sufficient; (*résultats*) satisfactory; (*vaniteux*) self-important, bumptious.
suffixe [syfiks(ə)] *nm* suffix.
suffocation [syfɔkasjɔ̃] *nf* suffocation.
suffoquer [syfɔke] *vt* to choke, suffocate; (*stupéfier*) to stagger, astound // *vi* to choke, suffocate.
suffrage [syfRaʒ] *nm* (*POL: voix*) vote; (: *méthode*): ~ **indirect** indirect suffrage; (*du public etc*) approval *q*; ~s **exprimés** valid votes.
suggérer [syɡʒeRe] *vt* to suggest; **suggestif, ive** *a* suggestive; **suggestion** *nf* suggestion.
suicidaire [sɥisidɛR] *a* suicidal.
suicide [sɥisid] *nm* suicide.
suicidé, e [sɥiside] *nm/f* suicide.
suicider [sɥiside]: **se** ~ *vi* to commit suicide.
suie [sɥi] *nf* soot.
suif [sɥif] *nm* tallow.
suinter [sɥɛ̃te] *vi* to ooze.
suis *vb voir* **être**.
suisse [sɥis] *a, nm/f* Swiss // *nm* (*bedeau*) ≈ verger // *nf*: **la S**~ Switzerland; **la S**~ **romande/allemande** French-speaking/German-speaking Switzerland; ~ **romand, e** *a, nm/f* Swiss French; ~-**allemand, e** *a, nm/f* Swiss German; **Suissesse** *nf* Swiss (woman *ou* girl).
suite [sɥit] *nf* (*continuation: d'énumération etc*) rest, remainder; (: *de feuilleton*) continuation; (: *second film etc sur le même thème*) sequel; (*série: de maisons, succès*) **une** ~ **de** a series *ou* succession of; (*MATH*) series *sg*; (*conséquence*) result; (*ordre, liaison logique*) coherence; (*appartement, MUS*) suite; (*escorte*) retinue, suite; ~s *nfpl* (*d'une maladie etc*) effects; **prendre la** ~ **de** (*directeur etc*) to succeed, take over from; **donner** ~ **à** (*requête, projet*) to follow up; **faire** ~ **à** to follow; (*faisant*) ~ **à votre lettre du** further to your letter of the; **de** ~ *ad* (*d'affilée*) in succession; (*immédiatement*) at once; **par la** ~

afterwards, subsequently; à la ~ one after the other; à la ~ de (derrière) behind; (en conséquence de) following; par ~ de owing to, as a result of; avoir de la ~ dans les idées to show great singleness of purpose; attendre la ~ to wait and see what comes next.

suivant, e [sɥivɑ̃, ɑ̃t] a next, following; (ci-après): l'exercice ~ the following exercise // prép (selon) according to; au ~! next!

suiveur [sɥivœʀ] nm (CYCLISME) (official) follower.

suivi, e [sɥivi] a (régulier) regular; (COMM: article) in general production; (cohérent) consistent; coherent; très/peu ~ (cours) well-/poorly-attended; (feuilleton etc) widely/not widely followed.

suivre [sɥivʀ(ə)] vt (gén) to follow; (SCOL: cours) to attend; (: leçon) to follow, attend to; (: programme) to keep up with; (COMM: article) to continue to stock // vi to follow; (élève) to attend, pay attention; to keep up, follow; se ~ (accidents etc) to follow one after the other; (raisonnement) to be coherent; faire ~ (lettre) to forward; ~ son cours (suj: enquête etc) to run ou take its course; 'à ~' 'to be continued'.

sujet, te [syʒɛ, -ɛt] a: être ~ à (vertige etc) to be liable ou subject to // nm/f (d'un souverain) subject // nm subject; (raison: d'une dispute etc) cause; avoir ~ de se plaindre to have cause for complaint; au ~ de prép about; ~ à caution a questionable; ~ de conversation topic ou subject of conversation; ~ d'examen (SCOL) examination question; examination paper; ~ d'expérience (BIO etc) experimental subject.

sujétion [syʒesjɔ̃] nf subjection; (fig) constraint.

sulfater [sylfate] vt to spray with copper sulphate.

sulfureux, euse [sylfyʀø, -øz] a sulphurous.

sulfurique [sylfyʀik] a: acide ~ sulphuric acid.

summum [sɔmɔm] nm: le ~ de the height of.

superbe [sypɛʀb(ə)] a magnificent, superb.

super(carburant) [sypɛʀ(kaʀbyʀɑ̃)] nm high-octane petrol.

supercherie [sypɛʀʃəʀi] nf trick.

superfétatoire [sypɛʀfetatwaʀ] a superfluous.

superficie [sypɛʀfisi] nf (surface) area; (fig) surface.

superficiel, le [sypɛʀfisjɛl] a superficial.

superflu, e [sypɛʀfly] a superfluous.

supérieur, e [sypeʀjœʀ] a (lèvre, étages, classes) upper; (plus élevé: température, niveau): ~ (à) higher (than); (meilleur: qualité, produit): ~ (à) superior (to); (excellent, hautain) superior // nm, nf superior; Mère ~e Mother Superior; à l'étage ~ on the next floor up; ~ en nombre superior in number; supériorité nf superiority.

superlatif [sypɛʀlatif] nm superlative.

supermarché [sypɛʀmaʀʃe] nm supermarket.

superposer [sypɛʀpoze] vt to superpose; (faire chevaucher) to superimpose; se ~ vi (images, souvenirs) to be superimposed; lits superposés bunk beds.

superpréfet [sypɛʀpʀefɛ] nm prefect in charge of a region.

superproduction [sypɛʀpʀɔdyksjɔ̃] nf (film) spectacular.

superpuissance [sypɛʀpɥisɑ̃s] nf superpower.

supersonique [sypɛʀsɔnik] a supersonic.

superstitieux, euse [sypɛʀstisjø, -øz] a superstitious.

superstition [sypɛʀstisjɔ̃] nf superstition.

superstructure [sypɛʀstʀyktyʀ] nf superstructure.

superviser [sypɛʀvize] vt to supervise.

supplanter [syplɑ̃te] vt to supplant.

suppléance [sypleɑ̃s] nf supply post.

suppléant, e [sypleɑ̃, ɑ̃t] a (juge, fonctionnaire) deputy cpd; (professeur) supply cpd // nm/f deputy; supply teacher; médecin ~ locum.

suppléer [syplee] vt (ajouter: mot manquant etc) to supply, provide; (compenser: lacune) to fill in; (: défaut) to make up for; (remplacer: professeur) to stand in for; (: juge) to deputize for; ~ à vt to make up for; to substitute for.

supplément [syplemɑ̃] nm supplement; un ~ de travail extra ou additional work; un ~ de frites etc an extra portion of chips etc; un ~ de 100 F a supplement of 100 F, an extra ou additional 100 F; ceci est en ~ (au menu etc) this is extra, there is an extra charge for this; supplémentaire a additional, further; (train, bus) relief cpd, extra.

supplétif, ive [sypletif, -iv] a (MIL) auxiliary.

supplication [syplikasjɔ̃] nf (REL) supplication; ~s nfpl (adjurations) pleas, entreaties.

supplice [syplis] nm (peine corporelle) torture q; form of torture; (douleur physique, morale) torture, agony.

supplier [syplije] vt to implore, beseech.

supplique [syplik] nf petition.

support [sypɔʀ] nm support; (pour livre, outils) stand; ~ audio-visuel audio-visual aid; ~ publicitaire advertising medium.

supportable [sypɔʀtabl(ə)] a (douleur) bearable.

supporter nm [sypɔʀtɛʀ] supporter, fan // vt [sypɔʀte] (poids, poussée) to support; (conséquences, épreuve) to bear, endure; (défauts, personne) to tolerate, put up with; (suj: chose: chaleur etc) to withstand; (suj: personne: chaleur, vin) to take.

supposé, e [sypoze] a (nombre) estimated; (auteur) supposed.

supposer [sypoze] vt to suppose; (impliquer) to presuppose; à ~ que supposing (that); supposition nf supposition.

suppositoire [sypozitwaʀ] nm suppository.

suppôt [sypo] nm (péj) henchman.

suppression [sypʀesjɔ̃] nf removal; deletion; cancellation; suppression.

supprimer [sypRime] *vt* (*cloison, cause, anxiété*) to remove ; (*clause, mot*) to delete ; (*congés, service d'autobus etc*) to cancel ; (*publication, article*) to suppress ; (*emplois, privilèges, témoin gênant*) to do away with.

suppurer [sypyRe] *vi* to suppurate.

supputations [sypytasjɔ̃] *nfpl* calculations, reckonings.

supputer [sypyte] *vt* to calculate, reckon.

suprématie [sypRemasi] *nf* supremacy.

suprême [sypRɛm] *a* supreme.

sur [syR] *prep* (*gén*) on ; (*par-dessus*) over ; (*au-dessus*) above ; (*direction*) towards ; (*à propos de*) about, on ; **un ~ 10** one out of 10 ; **4m ~ 2** 4m by 2 ; **je n'ai pas d'argent ~ moi** I haven't got any money with *ou* on me ; **~ ce** *ad* hereupon.

sur, e [syR] *a* sour.

sûr, e [syR] *a* sure, certain ; (*digne de confiance*) reliable ; (*sans danger*) safe ; **peu ~** unreliable ; **~ de qch** sure *ou* certain of sth ; **être ~ de qn** to be sure of sb ; **~ de soi** self-assured, self-confident ; **le plus ~ est de** the safest thing is to.

surabonder [syRabɔ̃de] *vi* to be overabundant.

suraigu, uë [syRegy] *a* very shrill.

surajouter [syRaʒute] *vt*: **~ qch à** to add sth to.

suralimenté, e [syRalimɑ̃te] *a* overfed.

suranné, e [syRane] *a* outdated, outmoded.

surbaissé, e [syRbese] *a* lowered, low.

surcharge [syRʃaRʒ(ə)] *nf* (*de passagers, marchandises*) excess load ; (*correction*) alteration ; (*PHILATELIE*) surcharge ; **prendre des passagers en ~** to take on excess *ou* extra passengers ; **~ de bagages** excess luggage ; **~ de travail** extra work.

surcharger [syRʃaRʒe] *vt* to overload ; (*timbre-poste*) to surcharge.

surchauffé, e [syRʃofe] *a* overheated.

surchoix [syRʃwa] *a inv* top-quality.

surclasser [syRkluse] *vt* to outclass.

surcouper [syRkupe] *vt* to overtrump.

surcroît [syRkRwa] *nm*: **un ~ de** additional + *nom* ; **par** *ou* **de ~** moreover ; **en ~** in addition.

surdi-mutité [syRdimytite] *nf*: **atteint de ~** deaf and dumb.

surdité [syRdite] *nf* deafness.

sureau, x [syRo] *nm* elder (tree).

surélever [syRelve] *vt* to raise, heighten.

sûrement [syRmɑ̃] *ad* reliably ; safely, securely ; (*certainement*) certainly.

surenchère [syRɑ̃ʃɛR] *nf* (*aux enchères*) higher bid ; (*sur prix fixe*) overbid ; (*fig*) overstatement ; outbidding tactics *pl* ; **surenchérir** *vi* to bid higher ; to raise one's bid ; (*fig*) to try and outbid each other.

surent *vb voir* **savoir**.

surestimer [syRɛstime] *vt* to overestimate.

sûreté [syRte] *nf* (*voir* **sûr**) reliability ; safety ; (*JUR*) guaranty ; surety ; **mettre en ~** to put in a safe place ; **pour plus de ~** as an extra precaution ; to be on the safe side ; **la S~ (nationale)** *division of the Ministère de l'Intérieur heading all police forces except the gendarmerie and the Paris préfecture de police.*

surexcité, e [syRɛksite] *a* overexcited.

surexposer [syRɛkspoze] *vt* to overexpose.

surf [syRf] *nm* surfing.

surface [syRfas] *nf* surface ; (*superficie*) surface area ; **faire ~** to surface ; **en ~** *ad* near the surface ; (*fig*) superficially ; **la pièce fait 100m²** **de ~** the room has a surface area of 100m² ; **~ de réparation** penalty area.

surfait, e [syRfɛ, -ɛt] *a* overrated.

surfin, e [syRfɛ̃, -in] *a* superfine.

surgelé, e [syRʒəle] *a* (deep-)frozen.

surgir [syRʒiR] *vi* (*personne, véhicule*) to appear suddenly ; (*geyser etc: de terre*) to shoot up ; (*fig: problème, conflit*) to arise.

surhomme [syRɔm] *nm* superman.

surhumain, e [syRymɛ̃, -ɛn] *a* superhuman.

surimposer [syRɛ̃poze] *vt* to overtax.

surimpression [syRɛ̃pResjɔ̃] *nf* (*PHOTO*) double exposure ; **en ~** superimposed.

sur-le-champ [syRləʃɑ̃] *ad* immediately.

surlendemain [syRlɑ̃dmɛ̃] *nm*: **le ~ (soir)** two days later (in the evening) ; **le ~ de** two days after.

surmenage [syRmənaʒ] *nm* overwork ; **le ~ intellectuel** mental fatigue.

surmené, e [syRməne] *a* overworked.

surmener [syRməne] *vt*, **se ~** *vi* to overwork.

surmonter [syRmɔ̃te] *vt* (*suj: coupole etc*) to surmount, top ; (*vaincre*) to overcome, surmount.

surmultiplié, e [syRmyltiplije] *a, nf*: (*vitesse*) **~e** overdrive.

surnager [syRnaʒe] *vi* to float.

surnaturel, le [syRnatyRɛl] *a, nm* supernatural.

surnom [syRnɔ̃] *nm* nickname.

surnombre [syRnɔ̃bR(ə)] *nm*: **être en ~** to be too many (*ou* one too many).

surnommer [syRnɔme] *vt* to nickname.

surnuméraire [syRnymeRɛR] *nm/f* supernumerary.

suroît [syRwa] *nm* sou'wester.

surpasser [syRpase] *vt* to surpass.

surpeuplé, e [syRpœple] *a* overpopulated.

surplis [syRpli] *nm* surplice.

surplomb [syRplɔ̃] *nm* overhang ; **en ~** overhanging.

surplomber [syRplɔ̃be] *vi* to be overhanging // *vt* to overhang ; to tower above.

surplus [syRply] *nm* (*COMM*) surplus ; (*reste*): **~ de bois** wood left over ; **~ américains** American army surplus *sg*.

surprenant, e [syRpRənɑ̃, -ɑ̃t] *a* surprising.

surprendre [syRpRɑ̃dR(ə)] *vt* (*étonner, prendre à l'improviste*) to surprise ; (*tomber sur: intrus etc*) to catch ; (*fig*) to detect ; to chance *ou* happen upon ; to intercept ; to overhear ; **~ la vigilance/bonne foi de qn** to catch sb out/betray sb's good faith ; **se ~ à faire** to catch *ou* find o.s. doing.

surprime [syRpRim] *nf* additional premium.

surpris, e [syʀpʀi, -iz] a: ~ (de/que) surprised (at/that).

surprise [syʀpʀiz] nf surprise; **faire une ~ à qn** to give sb a surprise; **par ~** ad by surprise.

surprise-partie [syʀpʀizpaʀti] nf party.

surproduction [syʀpʀɔdyksjɔ̃] nf overproduction.

surréaliste [syʀʀealist(ə)] a surrealist.

sursaut [syʀso] nm start, jump; ~ **de** (énergie, indignation) sudden fit ou burst of; **en ~** ad with a start; **sursauter** vi to (give a) start, jump.

surseoir [syʀswaʀ]: ~ **à** vt to defer; (JUR) to stay.

sursis [syʀsi] nm (JUR: gén) suspended sentence; (à l'exécution capitale, aussi fig) reprieve; (MIL): ~ (d'appel ou d'incorporation) deferment; **condamné à 5 mois (de prison) avec ~** given a 5-month suspended (prison) sentence; **sursitaire** nm (MIL) deferred conscript.

sursois etc vb voir **surseoir**.

surtaxe [syʀtaks(ə)] nf surcharge.

surtout [syʀtu] ad (avant tout, d'abord) above all; (spécialement, particulièrement) especially; **il aime le sport, ~ le football** he likes sport, especially football; **cet été, il a ~ fait de la pêche** this summer he went fishing more than anything (else); ~, **ne dites rien!** whatever you do — don't say anything!; ~ **pas!** certainly ou definitely not!; ~ **que...** especially as ...

surveillance [syʀvɛjɑ̃s] nf watch; (POLICE, MIL) surveillance; **sous ~ médicale** under medical supervision; **la ~ du territoire** internal security (voir aussi **D.S.T.**).

surveillant, e [syʀvɛjɑ̃, -ɑ̃t] nm/f (de prison) warder; (SCOL) monitor; (de travaux) supervisor, overseer.

surveiller [syʀveje] vt (enfant, élèves, bagages) to watch, keep an eye on; (malade) to watch over; (prisonnier, suspect) to keep (a) watch on; (territoire, bâtiment) to (keep) watch over; (travaux, cuisson) to supervise; (SCOL: examen) to invigilate; **se ~** to keep a check ou watch on o.s.; ~ **son langage/sa ligne** to watch one's language/figure.

survenir [syʀvəniʀ] vi (incident, retards) to occur, arise; (événement) to take place; (personne) to appear, arrive.

survêtement [syʀvɛtmɑ̃] nm tracksuit.

survie [syʀvi] nf survival; (REL) afterlife; **une ~ de quelques mois** a few more months of life.

survivant, e [syʀvivɑ̃, -ɑ̃t] nm/f survivor.

survivre [syʀvivʀ(ə)] vi to survive; ~ **à** vt (accident etc) to survive; (personne) to outlive.

survol [syʀvɔl] nm flying over.

survoler [syʀvɔle] vt to fly over; (fig: livre) to skim through.

survolté, e [syʀvɔlte] a (ÉLEC) stepped up, boosted; (fig) worked up.

sus [sy(s)]: **en ~ de** prép in addition to, over and above; **en ~** ad in addition; ~ **à** excl: ~ **au tyran!** at the tyrant!

susceptibilité [sysɛptibilite] nf sensitiveness q.

susceptible [sysɛptibl(ə)] a touchy, sensitive; ~ **d'amélioration** ou **d'être amélioré** that can be improved, open to improvement; ~ **de faire** able to do; liable to do.

susciter [sysite] vt (admiration) to arouse; (obstacles, ennuis): ~ (à qn) to create (for sb).

susdit, e [sysdi, -dit] a foresaid.

susmentionné, e [sysmɑ̃sjɔne] a above-mentioned.

suspect, e [syspɛ(kt), -ɛkt(ə)] a suspicious; (témoignage, opinions) suspect // nm/f suspect; **peu ~ de** most unlikely to be suspected of.

suspecter [syspɛkte] vt to suspect; (honnêteté de qn) to question, have one's suspicions about; ~ **qn d'être** to suspect sb of being.

suspendre [syspɑ̃dʀ(ə)] vt (accrocher: vêtement): ~ **qch (à)** to hang sth up (on); (fixer: lustre etc): ~ **qch à** to hang sth from; (interrompre, démettre) to suspend; (remettre) to defer; **se ~ à** to hang from.

suspendu, e [syspɑ̃dy] pp de **suspendre** // a (accroché): ~ **à** hanging on (ou from); (perché): ~ **au-dessus de** suspended over; (AUTO): **bien/mal ~** with good/poor suspension.

suspens [syspɑ̃]: **en ~** ad (affaire) in abeyance; **tenir en ~** to keep in suspense.

suspense [syspɑ̃s] nm suspense.

suspension [syspɑ̃sjɔ̃] nf suspension; deferment; (AUTO) suspension; (lustre) pendent light fitting; **en ~** in suspension, suspended; ~ **d'audience** adjournment.

suspicion [syspisjɔ̃] nf suspicion.

sustenter [systɑ̃te]: **se ~** vi to take sustenance.

susurrer [sysyʀe] vt to whisper.

sut vb voir **savoir**.

suture [sytyʀ] nf: **point de ~** stitch; **suturer** vt to stitch up, suture.

svelte [svɛlt(ə)] a slender, svelte.

S.V.P. sigle (= s'il vous plaît) please.

syllabe [silab] nf syllable.

sylvestre [silvɛstʀ(ə)] a: **pin ~** Scots pine, Scotch fir.

sylviculture [silvikyltyʀ] nf forestry, sylviculture.

symbole [sɛ̃bɔl] nm symbol; **symbolique** a symbolic(al); (geste, offrande) token cpd; (salaire, dommage-intérêts) nominal; **symboliser** vt to symbolize.

symétrie [simetʀi] nf symmetry; **symétrique** a symmetrical.

sympa [sɛ̃pa] a abr de **sympathique**.

sympathie [sɛ̃pati] nf (inclination) liking; (affinité) fellow feeling; (condoléances) sympathy; **accueillir avec ~** (projet) to receive favourably; **avoir de la ~ pour qn** to like sb, have a liking for sb; **témoignages de ~** expressions of sympathy; **croyez à toute ma ~** you have my deepest sympathy.

sympathique [sɛ̃patik] a nice, friendly; likeable; pleasant.

sympathisant, e [sɛ̃patizɑ̃, -ɑ̃t] nm/f sympathizer.

sympathiser [sɛ̃patize] vi (voisins etc: s'entendre) to get on (well); (: se fréquenter) to socialize, see each other; ~ avec to get on (well) with; to see, socialize with.

symphonie [sɛfɔni] nf symphony; **symphonique** a (orchestre, concert) symphony cpd; (musique) symphonic.

symptomatique [sɛptɔmatik] a symptomatic.

symptôme [sɛptom] nm symptom.

synagogue [sinagɔg] nf synagogue.

synchronique [sɛkʀɔnik] a: tableau ~ synchronic table of events.

synchroniser [sɛkʀɔnize] vt to synchronize.

syncope [sɛkɔp] nf (MÉD) blackout; (MUS) syncopation; tomber en ~ to faint, pass out; syncopé, e a syncopated.

syndic [sɛdik] nm managing agent.

syndical, e, aux [sɛdikal, -o] a (trade-)union cpd; ~isme nm trade unionism; union(ist) activities pl; ~iste nm/f trade unionist.

syndicat [sɛdika] nm (d'ouvriers, employés) (trade) union; (autre association d'intérêts) association; ~ d'initiative tourist office ou bureau; ~ patronal employers' syndicate, federation of employers; ~ de propriétaires association of property owners.

syndiqué, e [sɛdike] a belonging to a (trade) union; non ~ non-union.

syndiquer [sɛdike]: se ~ vi to form a trade union; (adhérer) to join a trade union.

syndrome [sɛdʀom] nm syndrome.

synode [sinɔd] nm synod.

synonyme [sinɔnim] a synonymous // nm synonym; ~ de synonymous with.

synoptique [sinɔptik] a: tableau ~ synoptic table.

synovie [sinɔvi] nf synovia.

syntaxe [sɛtaks(ə)] nf syntax.

synthèse [sɛtɛz] nf synthesis (pl es); faire la ~ de to synthesize.

synthétique [sɛtetik] a synthetic.

synthétiseur [sɛtetizœʀ] nm (MUS) synthesizer.

syphilis [sifilis] nf syphilis.

Syrie [siʀi] nf: la ~ Syria; **syrien, ne** a, nm/f Syrian.

systématique [sistematik] a systematic.

systématiser [sistematize] vt to systematize.

système [sistɛm] nm system; le ~ D resourcefulness; le ~ solaire the solar system.

T

t' [t(ə)] pronom voir te.

ta [ta] dét voir ton.

tabac [taba] nm tobacco; tobacconist's (shop) // a inv: (couleur) ~ buff(-coloured); passer qn à ~ to beat sb up; ~ blond/brun light/dark tobacco; ~ gris shag; ~ à priser snuff; tabagie nf smoke den; tabatière nf snuffbox.

tabernacle [tabɛʀnakl(ə)] nm tabernacle.

table [tabl(ə)] nf table; à ~! dinner etc is ready!; se mettre à ~ to sit down to eat; (fig: fam) to come clean; mettre la ~ to lay the table; faire ~ rase de to make a clean sweep of; ~ basse coffee table; ~ d'écoute wire-tapping set; ~ d'harmonie sounding board; ~ des matières (table of) contents pl; ~ de multiplication multiplication table; ~ de nuit ou de chevet bedside table; ~ ronde (débat) round table; ~ de toilette washstand.

tableau, x [tablo] nm painting; (reproduction, fig) picture; (panneau) board; (schéma) table, chart; ~ d'affichage notice board; ~ de bord dashboard; (AVIAT) instrument panel; ~ de chasse tally; ~ noir blackboard.

tabler [table] vi: ~ sur to count ou bank on.

tablette [tablɛt] nf (planche) shelf (pl shelves); ~ de chocolat bar of chocolate.

tablier [tablije] nm apron; (de pont) roadway.

tabou [tabu] nm, a taboo.

tabouret [tabuʀɛ] nm stool.

tabulateur [tabylatœʀ] nm tabulator.

tac [tak] nm: du ~ au ~ tit for tat.

tache [taʃ] nf (saleté) stain, mark; (ART, de couleur, lumière) spot; splash, patch; faire ~ d'huile to spread, gain ground.

tâche [taʃ] nf task; travailler à la ~ to do general jobbing, work as a jobbing gardener/builder etc.

tacher [taʃe] vt to stain, mark; (fig) to sully, stain.

tâcher [taʃe] vi: ~ de faire to try ou endeavour to do.

tâcheron [taʃʀɔ] nm (fig) drudge.

tacite [tasit] a tacit.

taciturne [tasityʀn(ə)] a taciturn.

tacot [tako] nm (péj) banger.

tact [takt] nm tact; avoir du ~ to be tactful, have tact.

tactile [taktil] a tactile.

tactique [taktik] a tactical // nf (technique) tactics sg; (plan) tactic.

taie [tɛ] nf: ~ (d'oreiller) pillowslip, pillowcase.

taille [taj] nf cutting; pruning; (milieu du corps) waist; (hauteur) height; (grandeur) size; de ~ à faire capable of doing; de ~ a sizeable.

taille-crayon(s) [tajkʀɛjɔ] nm pencil sharpener.

tailler [taje] vt (pierre, diamant) to cut; (arbre, plante) to prune; (vêtement) to cut out; (crayon) to sharpen; se ~ vt (ongles, barbe) to trim, cut; (fig: réputation) to gain, win // vi (fam) to beat it; ~ dans (chair, bois) to cut into.

tailleur [tajœʀ] nm (couturier) tailor; (vêtement) suit, costume; en ~ (assis) cross-legged; ~ de diamants diamond-cutter.

taillis [taji] nm copse.

tain [tɛ] nm silvering; glace sans ~ two-way mirror.

taire [tɛʀ] vt to keep to o.s., conceal // vi: faire ~ qn to make sb be quiet; (fig) to silence sb; se ~ vi (s'arrêter de parler) to fall silent, stop talking; (ne pas parler) to be silent ou quiet; to keep quiet; tais-toi!, taisez-vous! be quiet!

talc [talk] nm talcum powder.

talé, e [tale] *a (fruit)* bruised.
talent [talɑ̃] *nm* talent ; **talentueux, euse** *a* talented.
talion [taljɔ̃] *nm:* **la loi du ~** an eye for an eye.
talisman [talismɑ̃] *nm* talisman.
talon [talɔ̃] *nm* heel ; *(de chèque, billet)* stub, counterfoil ; **~s plats/aiguilles** flat/stiletto heels.
talonner [talɔne] *vt* to follow hard behind ; *(fig)* to hound.
talonnette [talɔnɛt] *nf* heelpiece.
talquer [talke] *vt* to put talcum powder on.
talus [taly] *nm* embankment.
tambour [tɑ̃buʀ] *nm (MUS, aussi TECH)* drum ; *(musicien)* drummer ; *(porte)* revolving door(s *pl*).
tambourin [tɑ̃buʀɛ̃] *nm* tambourine.
tambouriner [tɑ̃buʀine] *vi:* **~ contre** to drum against *ou* on.
tambour-major [tɑ̃buʀmaʒɔʀ] *nm* drum major.
tamis [tami] *nm* sieve.
Tamise [tamiz] *nf:* **la ~** the Thames.
tamisé, e [tamize] *a (fig)* subdued, soft.
tamiser [tamize] *vt* to sieve, sift.
tampon [tɑ̃pɔ̃] *nm (de coton, d'ouate)* wad, pad ; *(amortisseur)* buffer ; *(bouchon)* plug, stopper ; *(cachet, timbre)* stamp ; **~ (hygiénique)** tampon ; **tamponner** *vt (timbres)* to stamp ; *(heurter)* to crash *ou* ram into ; **tamponneuse** *a:* **autos tamponneuses** dodgems.
tam-tam [tamtam] *nm* tomtom.
tandem [tɑ̃dɛm] *nm* tandem ; *(fig)* duo, pair.
tandis [tɑ̃di]: **~ que** *cj* while.
tangage [tɑ̃gaʒ] *nm* pitching (and tossing).
tangent, e [tɑ̃ʒɑ̃, -ɑ̃t] *a (MATH):* **~ à** tangential to ; *(fam)* close // *nf (MATH)* tangent.
tangible [tɑ̃ʒibl(ə)] *a* tangible, concrete.
tango [tɑ̃go] *nm* tango.
tanguer [tɑ̃ge] *vi* to pitch (and toss).
tanière [tanjɛʀ] *nf* lair, den.
tanin [tanɛ̃] *nm* tannin.
tank [tɑ̃k] *nm* tank.
tanné, e [tane] *a* weather-beaten.
tanner [tane] *vt* to tan.
tannerie [tanʀi] *nf* tannery.
tanneur [tanœʀ] *nm* tanner.
tant [tɑ̃] *ad* so much ; **~ de** *(sable, eau)* so much ; *(gens, livres)* so many ; **~ que** *cj* as long as ; **~ que** *(comparatif)* as much as ; **~ mieux** that's great ; so much the better ; **~ pis** never mind ; too bad ; **~ pis pour lui** too bad for him ; **~ soit peu** a little bit ; *(even)* remotely.
tante [tɑ̃t] *nf* aunt.
tantinet [tɑ̃tinɛ]: **un ~** *ad* a tiny bit.
tantôt [tɑ̃to] *ad (parfois):* **~ ... ~** now ... now ; *(cet après-midi)* this afternoon.
taon [tɑ̃] *nm* horsefly, gadfly.
tapage [tapaʒ] *nm* uproar, din ; **~ nocturne** *(JUR)* disturbance of the peace (at night).
tapageur, euse [tapaʒœʀ, -øz] *a* loud, flashy ; noisy.

tape [tap] *nf* slap.
tape-à-l'œil [tapalœj] *a inv* flashy, showy.
taper [tape] *vt (porte)* to bang, slam ; *(dactylographier)* to type (out) ; *(fam: emprunter):* **~ qn de 10 F** to touch sb for 10 F, cadge 10 F off sb // *vi (soleil)* to beat down ; **~ sur qn** to thump sb ; *(fig)* to run sb down ; **~ sur qch** to hit sth ; to bang on sth ; **~ à** *(porte etc)* to knock on ; **~ dans** *vt (se servir)* to dig into ; **~ des mains/pieds** to clap one's hands/stamp one's feet ; **~ (à la machine)** to type.
tapi, e [tapi] *a:* **~ dans/derrière** crouching *ou* cowering in/behind ; hidden away in/behind.
tapioca [tapjɔka] *nm* tapioca.
tapis [tapi] *nm* carpet ; *(de table)* cloth ; **mettre sur le ~** *(fig)* to bring up for discussion ; **~ roulant** conveyor belt ; **~ de sol** *(de tente)* groundsheet ; **~-brosse** *nm* doormat.
tapisser [tapise] *vt (avec du papier peint)* to paper ; *(recouvrir):* **~ qch (de)** to cover sth (with).
tapisserie [tapisʀi] *nf (tenture, broderie)* tapestry ; *(: travail)* tapestry-making ; tapestry work ; *(papier peint)* wallpaper ; **faire ~** to sit out, be a wallflower.
tapissier, ière [tapisje, -jɛʀ] *nm/f:* **~ (-décorateur)** upholsterer (and decorator).
tapoter [tapɔte] *vt* to pat, tap.
taquet [takɛ] *nm* wedge ; peg.
taquin, e [takɛ̃, -in] *a* teasing.
taquiner [takine] *vt* to tease.
tarabiscoté, e [taʀabiskɔte] *a* over-ornate, fussy.
tarabuster [taʀabyste] *vt* to bother, worry.
tarauder [taʀode] *vt (TECH)* to tap ; to thread ; *(fig)* to pierce.
tard [taʀ] *ad* late ; **au plus ~** at the latest ; **plus ~** later (on) ; **sur le ~** late in life.
tarder [taʀde] *vi (chose)* to be a long time coming ; *(personne):* **~ à faire** to delay doing ; **il me tarde d'être** I am longing to be ; **sans (plus) ~** without (further) delay.
tardif, ive [taʀdif, -iv] *a* late ; **tardivement** *ad* late.
tare [taʀ] *nf (COMM)* tare ; *(fig)* defect ; taint, blemish.
targuer [taʀge]: **se ~ de** *vt* to boast about.
tarif [taʀif] *nm (liste)* price list ; tariff ; *(barème)* rates *pl* ; fares *pl* ; tariff ; *(prix)* rate ; fare ; **~-aire** *a* tariff *cpd* ; **~er** *vt* to fix the price *ou* rate for ; **~é 10 F** priced 10 F.
tarir [taʀiʀ] *vi* to dry up, run dry // *vt* to dry up.
tarot(s) [taʀo] *nm(pl)* tarot cards.
tartare [taʀtaʀ] *a (CULIN)* tartar(e).
tarte [taʀt(ə)] *nf* tart ; **~ aux pommes/à la crème** apple/custard tart ; **~lette** *nf* tartlet.
tartine [taʀtin] *nf* slice of bread and butter *(ou* jam) ; **~ au miel** slice of bread and honey ; **tartiner** *vt* to spread ; **fromage à tartiner** cheese spread.
tartre [taʀtʀ(ə)] *nm (des dents)* tartar ; *(de chaudière)* fur, scale.

tas [tɑ] *nm* heap, pile ; (*fig*): un ~ de heaps of, lots of ; en ~ in a heap *ou* pile ; dans le ~ (*fig*) in the crowd ; among them ; formé sur le ~ trained on the job.

tasse [tɑs] *nf* cup.

tassé, e [tɑse] *a*: bien ~ (*café etc*) strong.

tasser [tɑse] *vt* (*terre, neige*) to pack down ; (*entasser*): ~ qch dans to cram sth into ; se ~ *vi* (*terrain*) to settle ; (*fig*) to sort itself out, settle down.

tâter [tɑte] *vt* to feel ; (*fig*) to try out ; to test out ; ~ de (*prison etc*) to have a taste of ; se ~ (*hésiter*) to be in two minds ; ~ le terrain (*fig*) to test the ground.

tatillon, ne [tatijɔ̃, -ɔn] *a* pernickety.

tâtonnement [tɑtɔnmɑ̃] *nm*: par ~s (*fig*) by trial and error.

tâtonner [tɑtɔne] *vi* to grope one's way along.

tâtons [tɑtɔ̃]: à ~ *ad*: chercher/avancer à ~ to grope around for/grope one's way forward.

tatouage [tatwaʒ] *nm* tattooing ; (*dessin*) tattoo.

tatouer [tatwe] *vt* to tattoo.

taudis [todi] *nm* hovel, slum.

taupe [top] *nf* mole ; **taupinière** *nf* molehill.

taureau, x [tɔro] *nm* bull ; (*signe*): le T~ Taurus, the Bull ; être du T~ to be Taurus.

tauromachie [tɔrɔmaʃi] *nf* bullfighting.

taux [to] *nm* rate ; (*d'alcool*) level ; ~ d'intérêt interest rate.

tavelé, e [tavle] *a* marbled.

taverne [tavɛrn(ə)] *nf* inn, tavern.

taxe [taks] *nf* tax ; (*douanière*) duty ; ~ de séjour tourist tax ; ~ à la valeur ajoutée (T.V.A.) value added tax (V.A.T.).

taxer [takse] *vt* (*personne*) to tax ; (*produit*) to put a tax on, tax ; (*fig*): ~ qn de to call sb + *attribut*; to accuse sb of, tax sb with.

taxi [taksi] *nm* taxi.

taximètre [taksimɛtr(ə)] *nm* (taxi)meter.

taxiphone [taksifɔn] *nm* pay phone.

T.C.F. *sigle m* = *Touring Club de France*, ≈ AA *ou* RAC.

Tchécoslovaquie [tʃekɔslɔvaki] *nf* Czechoslovakia ; **tchèque** *a, nm, nf* Czech.

te, t' [t(ə)] *pronom* you ; (*réfléchi*) yourself.

té [te] *nm* T-square.

technicien, ne [tɛknisjɛ̃, -jɛn] *nm/f* technician.

technique [tɛknik] *a* technical // *nf* technique ; ~ment *ad* technically.

technocrate [tɛknɔkrat] *nm/f* technocrat.

technocratie [tɛknɔkrasi] *nf* technocracy.

technologie [tɛknɔlɔʒi] *nf* technology ; **technologique** *a* technological.

teck [tɛk] *nm* teak.

teckel [tekɛl] *nm* dachshund.

teignais *etc vb voir* **teindre**.

teigne [tɛɲ] *nf* (*ZOOL*) moth ; (*MÉD*) ringworm.

teigneux, euse [tɛɲø, -øz] *a* (*péj*) nasty, scabby.

teindre [tɛ̃dr(ə)] *vt* to dye.

teint, e [tɛ̃, tɛ̃t] *a* dyed // *nm* (*du visage*)

complexion, colouring ; colour // *nf* shade, colour ; **grand** ~ *a inv* colourfast.

teinté, e [tɛ̃te] *a* (*verres*) tinted ; (*bois*) stained ; ~ acajou mahogany-stained ; ~ de (*fig*) tinged with.

teinter [tɛ̃te] *vt* to tint ; (*bois*) to stain ; **teinture** *nf* dyeing ; (*substance*) dye ; (*MÉD*): **teinture d'iode** tincture of iodine.

teinturerie [tɛ̃tyrri] *nf* dry cleaner's.

teinturier [tɛ̃tyrje] *nm* dry cleaner.

tel, telle [tɛl] *a* (*pareil*) such ; (*comme*): ~ un/des ... like a/ like... ; (*indéfini*) such-and-such a, a given ; (*intensif*): un ~/de ~s ... such (a)/such ... ; **rien de** ~ nothing like it, no such thing ; ~ **que** *cj* like, such as ; ~ **quel** as it is *ou* stands (*ou* was *etc*).

tél. *abr de* **téléphone**.

télé [tele] *nf* (*abr de* **télévision**) (*poste*) T.V. (set) ; **à la** ~ on the telly, on T.V.

télé... [tele] *préfixe*: ~**benne** *nf* (*benne*) telecabine, gondola // *nm* telecabine ; ~**cabine** *nf* (*benne*) telecabine, gondola // *nm* telecabine ; ~**commande** *nf* remote control ; ~**commander** *vt* to operate by remote control ; ~**communications** *nfpl* telecommunications ; ~**férique** *nm* = ~**phérique** ; ~**gramme** *nm* telegram.

télégraphe [telegraf] *nm* telegraph ; **télégraphie** *nf* telegraphy ; **télégraphier** *vt* to telegraph, cable ; **télégraphique** *a* telegraph *cpd*, telegraphic ; (*fig*) telegraphic ; **télégraphiste** *nm/f* telegraphist.

téléguider [telegide] *vt* to operate by remote control, radio-control.

téléobjectif [teleɔbʒɛktif] *nm* telephoto lens *sg*.

télépathie [telepati] *nf* telepathy.

téléphérique [teleferik] *nm* cable-car.

téléphone [telefɔn] *nm* telephone ; (*appel*) (telephone) call ; telephone conversation ; **avoir le** ~ to be on the (tele)phone ; **au** ~ on the phone ; **les** T~**s** ≈ Post Office Telecommunications ; ~ **arabe** bush telephone ; ~ **manuel** manually-operated telephone system ; **téléphoner** *vt* to telephone // *vi* to telephone, ring ; to make a phone call ; **téléphoner à** to phone up, ring up, call up ; **téléphonique** *a* telephone *cpd*, phone *cpd* ; **téléphoniste** *nm/f* telephonist, telephone operator ; (*d'entreprise*) switchboard operator.

télescope [telɛskɔp] *nm* telescope.

télescoper [telɛskɔpe] *vt* to smash up ; **se** ~ (*véhicules*) to concertina.

télescopique [telɛskɔpik] *a* telescopic.

téléscripteur [teleskriptœr] *nm* teleprinter.

télésiège [telesjɛʒ] *nm* chairlift.

téléski [teleski] *nm* ski-tow ; ~ **à archets** T-bar tow ; ~ **à perche** button lift.

téléspectateur, trice [telespɛktatœr, -tris] *nm/f* (*television*) viewer.

téléviser [televize] *vt* to televise.

téléviseur [televizœr] *nm* television set.

télévision [televizjɔ̃] *nf* television ; **avoir la** ~ to have a television ; **à la** ~ on television.

télex [telɛks] *nm* telex.

telle [tɛl] *a voir* **tel**.

tellement [tɛlmɑ̃] ad (tant) so much ; (si) so ; ~ **plus grand (que)** so much bigger (than) ; ~ **de** (sable, eau) so much ; (gens, livres) so many ; **il s'est endormi** ~ **il était fatigué** he was so tired (that) he fell asleep ; **pas** ~ not (all) that much ; not (all) that + adjectif.

tellurique [telyʀik] a: **secousse** ~ earth tremor.

téméraire [temeʀɛʀ] a reckless, rash ; **témérité** nf recklessness, rashness.

témoignage [temwaɲaʒ] nm (JUR: déclaration) testimony q, evidence q ; (: faits) evidence q ; (rapport, récit) account ; (fig: d'affection etc) token, mark ; expression.

témoigner [temwaɲe] vt (intérêt, gratitude) to show // vi (JUR) to testify, give evidence ; ~ **que** to testify that ; (fig) to reveal that, testify to the fact that ; ~ **de** vt to bear witness to, testify to.

témoin [temwɛ̃] nm witness ; (fig) testimony ; (SPORT) baton ; (CONSTR) telltale // a control cpd, test cpd ; **appartement** ~ show flat ; **être** ~ **de** to witness ; **prendre à** ~ to call to witness ; ~ **de moralité** character reference ; ~ **oculaire** eyewitness.

tempe [tɑ̃p] nf temple.

tempérament [tɑ̃peʀamɑ̃] nm temperament, disposition ; (santé) constitution ; **à** ~ (vente) on deferred (payment) terms ; (achat) by instalments, hire purchase cpd ; **avoir du** ~ to be hot-blooded.

tempérance [tɑ̃peʀɑ̃s] nf temperance.

température [tɑ̃peʀatyʀ] nf temperature ; **prendre la** ~ **de** to take the temperature of ; (fig) to gauge the feeling of ; **avoir ou faire de la** ~ to have ou be running a temperature.

tempéré, e [tɑ̃peʀe] a temperate.

tempérer [tɑ̃peʀe] vt to temper.

tempête [tɑ̃pɛt] nf storm ; ~ **de sable/neige** sand/snowstorm.

tempêter [tɑ̃pete] vi to rant and rave.

temple [tɑ̃pl(ə)] nm temple ; (protestant) church.

tempo [tɛmpo] nm tempo (pl s).

temporaire [tɑ̃pɔʀɛʀ] a temporary ; ~**ment** ad temporarily.

temporel, le [tɑ̃pɔʀɛl] a temporal.

temporiser [tɑ̃pɔʀize] vi to temporize, play for time.

temps [tɑ̃] nm (atmosphérique) weather ; (durée) time ; (époque) time, times pl ; (LING) tense ; (MUS) beat ; (TECH) stroke ; **il fait beau/mauvais** ~ the weather is fine/bad ; **avoir le** ~/**tout le** ~/**juste le** ~ to have time/plenty of time/just enough time ; **avoir fait son** ~ (fig) to have had its (ou his etc) day ; **en** ~ **de paix/guerre** in peacetime/wartime ; **en** ~ **utile** ou **voulu** in due time ou course ; **de** ~ **en** ~, **de** ~ **à autre** from time to time, now and again ; **à** ~ (partir, arriver) in time ; **à** ~ **partiel** ad, a part-time ; **dans le** ~ at one time ; **de tout** ~ always ; **du** ~ **que** at the time when, in the days when ; ~ **d'arrêt** pause, halt ; ~ **mort** (COMM) slack period.

tenable [tənabl(ə)] a bearable.

tenace [tənas] a tenacious, persistent ; **ténacité** nf tenacity, persistence.

tenailler [tənaje] (fig) vt to torment, torture.

tenailles [tənaj] nfpl pincers.

tenais etc vb voir **tenir**.

tenancier, ière [tənɑ̃sje, -jɛʀ] nm/f manager/manageress.

tenant, e [tənɑ̃, -ɑ̃t] a voir **séance** // nm/f (SPORT): ~ **du titre** title-holder // nm: **d'un seul** ~ in one piece ; **les** ~**s et les aboutissants** the ins and outs.

tendance [tɑ̃dɑ̃s] nf (opinions) leanings pl, sympathies pl ; (inclination) tendency ; (évolution) trend ; ~ **à la hausse** upward trend ; **avoir** ~ **à** to have a tendency to, tend to ; **tendancieux, euse** a tendentious.

tendeur [tɑ̃dœʀ] nm (de vélo) chain-adjuster ; (de câble) wire-strainer ; (de tente) runner ; (attache) sandow, elastic strap.

tendon [tɑ̃dɔ̃] nm tendon, sinew ; ~ **d'Achille** Achilles' tendon.

tendre [tɑ̃dʀ(ə)] a (viande, légumes) tender ; (bois, roche, couleur) soft ; (affectueux) tender, loving // vt (élastique, peau) to stretch, draw tight ; (muscle) to tense ; (donner): ~ **qch à qn** to hold sth out to sb ; to offer sb sth ; (fig: piège) to set, lay ; (tapisserie): **tendu de soie** hung with silk, with silk hangings ; **se** ~ vi (corde) to tighten ; (relations) to become strained ; ~ **à qch/à faire** to tend towards sth/to do ; ~ **l'oreille** to prick up one's ears ; ~ **la main/le bras** to hold out one's hand/stretch out one's arm ; ~**ment** ad tenderly, lovingly ; **tendresse** nf tenderness.

tendu, e [tɑ̃dy] pp de **tendre** // a tight ; tensed ; strained.

ténèbres [tenɛbʀ(ə)] nfpl darkness sg ; **ténébreux, euse** a obscure, mysterious ; (personne) saturnine.

teneur [tənœʀ] nf content, substance ; (d'une lettre) terms pl, content ; ~ **en cuivre** copper content.

ténia [tenja] nm tapeworm.

tenir [təniʀ] vt to hold ; (magasin, hôtel) to run ; (promesse) to keep // vi to hold ; (neige, gel) to last ; **se** ~ vi (avoir lieu) to be held, take place ; (être: personne) to stand ; **se** ~ **droit** to stand up (ou sit up) straight ; **bien se** ~ to behave well ; **se** ~ **à qch** to hold on to sth ; **s'en** ~ **à qch** to confine o.s. to sth ; to stick to sth ; ~ **à** vt to be attached to ; to care about ; to depend on ; to stem from ; ~ **à faire** to want to do, be keen to do ; ~ **de** vt to partake of ; to take after ; **ça ne tient qu'à lui** it is entirely up to him ; ~ **qn pour** to take sb for ; ~ **qch de qn** (histoire) to have heard ou learnt sth from sb ; (qualité, défaut) to have inherited ou got sth from sb ; ~ **les comptes** to keep the books ; ~ **un rôle** to play a part ; ~ **l'alcool** to be able to hold a drink ; ~ **le coup** to hold out ; ~ **3 jours/2 mois** (résister) to hold out ou last 3 days/2 months ; ~ **au chaud/à l'abri** to keep hot/under shelter ou cover ; **tiens/tenez, voilà le stylo!**

there's the pen! ; **tiens, Alain!** look, here's Alain! ; **tiens?** (*surprise*) really?

tennis [tenis] *nm* tennis ; (*aussi:* **court de** ~) tennis court // *nm ou fpl* (*aussi:* **chaussures de** ~) tennis *ou* gym shoes ; ~ **de table** table tennis ; ~**man** *nm* tennis player.

ténor [tenɔʀ] *nm* tenor.

tension [tɑ̃sjɔ̃] *nf* tension ; (*fig*) tension ; strain ; (*MÉD*) blood pressure ; **faire** *ou* **avoir de la** ~ to have high blood pressure.

tentaculaire [tɑ̃takylɛʀ] *a* (*fig*) sprawling.

tentacule [tɑ̃takyl] *nm* tentacle.

tentant, e [tɑ̃tɑ̃, -ɑ̃t] *a* tempting.

tentateur, trice [tɑ̃tatœʀ, -tʀis] *a* tempting // *nm* (*REL*) tempter.

tentation [tɑ̃tasjɔ̃] *nf* temptation.

tentative [tɑ̃tativ] *nf* attempt, bid ; ~ **d'évasion** escape bid.

tente [tɑ̃t] *nf* tent ; ~ **à oxygène** oxygen tent.

tenter [tɑ̃te] *vt* (*éprouver, attirer*) to tempt ; (*essayer*): **qch/de faire** to attempt *ou* try sth/to do ; **être tenté de** to be tempted to ; ~ **sa chance** to try one's luck.

tenture [tɑ̃tyʀ] *nf* hanging.

tenu, e [təny] *pp de* **tenir** // *a* (*maison, comptes*): **bien** ~ well-kept ; (*obligé*): ~ **de faire** under an obligation to do // *nf* (*action de tenir*) running ; keeping ; holding ; (*vêtements*) clothes *pl*, gear ; (*allure*) dress *q*, appearance ; (*comportement*) manners *pl*, behaviour ; **en grande** ~**e** in full dress ; **en petite** ~**e** scantily dressed *ou* clad ; **avoir de la** ~**e** to have good manners ; (*journal*) to have a high standard ; **une** ~ **de voyage/sport** travelling/sports clothes *pl ou* gear *q* ; ~**e de combat** combat gear *ou* dress ; ~**e de route** (*AUTO*) road-holding ; ~**e de soirée** evening dress.

ténu, e [teny] *a* (*indice, nuance*) tenuous, subtle ; (*fil, objet*) fine ; (*voix*) thin.

ter [tɛʀ] *a*: **16** ~ **16b** *ou* **B**.

térébenthine [teʀebɑ̃tin] *nf*: (**essence de**) ~ (oil of) turpentine.

tergiverser [tɛʀʒivɛʀse] *vi* to shilly-shally.

terme [tɛʀm(ə)] *nm* term ; (*fin*) end ; **vente/achat à** ~ (*COMM*) forward sale/purchase ; **à court/long** ~ *a* short-/long-term *ou* -range // *ad* in the short/long term ; **à** ~ (*MÉD*) a full-term // *ad* at term ; **avant** ~ (*MÉD*) a premature // *ad* prematurely ; **mettre un** ~ **à** to put an end *ou* a stop to.

terminaison [tɛʀminɛzɔ̃] *nf* (*LING*) ending.

terminal, e, aux [tɛʀminal, -o] *a* final // *nm* terminal // *nf* (*SCOL*) ≈ Upper Sixth.

terminer [tɛʀmine] *vt* to end ; (*nourriture, repas*) to finish ; **se** ~ *vi* to end ; **se** ~ **par** to end with.

terminologie [tɛʀminɔlɔʒi] *nf* terminology.

terminus [tɛʀminys] *nm* terminus (*pl* i).

termite [tɛʀmit] *nm* termite, white ant.

terne [tɛʀn(ə)] *a* dull.

ternir [tɛʀniʀ] *vt* to dull ; (*fig*) to sully, tarnish ; **se** ~ *vi* to become dull.

terrain [tɛʀɛ̃] *nm* (*sol, fig*) ground ; (*COMM*) land *q*, plot (of land) ; site ; **sur le** ~ (*fig*) on the field ; ~ **de football/rugby** football/rugby pitch ; ~ **d'aviation** airfield ; ~ **de camping** camping site ; un ~ **d'entente** an area of agreement ; ~ **de golf** golf course ; ~ **de jeu** games field ; playground ; ~ **de sport** sports ground ; ~ **vague** waste ground *q*.

terrasse [teʀas] *nf* terrace ; (*de café*) pavement area, terrasse ; **à la** ~ (*café*) outside.

terrassement [teʀasmɑ̃] *nm* earthmoving, earthworks *pl* ; embankment.

terrasser [teʀase] *vt* (*adversaire*) to floor, bring down ; (*suj: maladie etc*) to lay low.

terrassier [teʀasje] *nm* navvy, roadworker.

terre [tɛʀ] *nf* (*gén, aussi* ÉLEC) earth ; (*substance*) soil, earth ; (*opposé à mer*) land *q* ; (*contrée*) land ; ~**s** *nfpl* (*terrains*) lands, land *sg* ; **le travail de la** ~ work on the land ; **en** ~ (*pipe, poterie*) clay *cpd* ; **à** ~ *ou* **par** ~ (*mettre, être*) on the ground (*ou* floor) ; (*jeter, tomber*) to the ground, down ; ~ **cuite** earthenware ; terracotta ; **la** ~ **ferme** dry land, terra firma ; ~ **glaise** clay ; **la T**~ **Sainte** the Holy Land ; ~ **à** ~ *inv* down-to-earth, matter-of-fact.

terreau [teʀo] *nm* compost.

terre-plein [tɛʀplɛ̃] *nm* platform.

terrer [teʀe] : **se** ~ *vi* to hide away ; to go to ground.

terrestre [teʀɛstʀ(ə)] *a* (*surface*) earth's, of the earth ; (*BOT, ZOOL, MIL*) land *cpd* ; (*REL*) earthly, worldly.

terreur [teʀœʀ] *nf* terror *q*, fear.

terrible [teʀibl(ə)] *a* terrible, dreadful ; (*fam*) terrific ; ~**ment** *ad* (*très*) terribly, awfully.

terrien, ne [teʀjɛ̃, -jɛn] *nm/f* countryman/woman, man/woman of the soil ; (*non martien etc*) earthling.

terrier [teʀje] *nm* burrow, hole ; (*chien*) terrier.

terrifier [teʀifje] *vt* to terrify.

terril [teʀil] *nm* slag heap.

terrine [teʀin] *nf* (*récipient*) terrine ; (*CULIN*) pâté.

territoire [teʀitwaʀ] *nm* territory ; **territorial, e, aux** *a* territorial.

terroir [teʀwaʀ] *nm* (*AGR*) soil ; **accent du** ~ country *ou* rural accent.

terroriser [teʀɔʀize] *vt* to terrorize ; **terrorisme** *nm* terrorism ; **terroriste** *nm/f* terrorist.

tertiaire [tɛʀsjɛʀ] *a* tertiary // *nm* (*ÉCON*) tertiary sector, service industries *pl*.

tertre [tɛʀtʀ(ə)] *nm* hillock, mound.

tes [te] *dét voir* **ton**.

tesson [tesɔ̃] *nm*: ~ **de bouteille** piece of broken bottle.

test [tɛst] *nm* test.

testament [tɛstamɑ̃] *nm* (*JUR*) will ; (*REL*) Testament ; **faire son** ~ to make out one's will ; **testamentaire** *a* of a will.

tester [tɛste] *vt* to test.

testicule [tɛstikyl] *nm* testicle.

tétanos [tetanos] *nm* tetanus, lockjaw.

têtard [tɛtaʀ] *nm* tadpole.

tête [tɛt] *nf* head ; (*cheveux*) hair *q* ; (*visage*) face ; (*FOOTBALL*) header ; **de** ~ *a* (*wagon etc*) front *cpd* // *ad* (*calculer*) in one's head, mentally ; **perdre la** ~ (*fig*) to lose one's head ; to go off one's head ; **tenir ~ à qn** to stand up to ou defy sb ; **la ~ en bas** with one's head down ; **la ~ la première** (*tomber*) headfirst ; **faire une ~** (*FOOTBALL*) to head the ball ; **faire la ~** (*fig*) to sulk ; **en ~** (*SPORT*) in the lead ; at the front ou head ; **en ~ à ~** in private, alone together ; **de la ~ aux pieds** from head to toe ; **~ d'affiche** (*THÉÂTRE etc*) top of the bill ; **~ de bétail** head inv of cattle ; **~ chercheuse** homing device ; **~ de lecture** pickup head ; **~ de liste** (*POL*) chief candidate ; **~ de mort** skull and crossbones ; **~ de série** (*TENNIS*) seeded player, seed ; **~ de Turc** (*fig*) whipping boy ; **~ de veau** (*CULIN*) calf's head ; **~-à-queue** nm inv : **faire un ~-à-queue** to spin round ; **~-à-~** nm inv tête-à-tête ; **~-bêche** ad head to tail.

tétée [tete] nf (*action*) sucking ; (*repas*) feed.

téter [tete] vt : **~ (sa mère)** to suck at one's mother's breast, feed.

tétine [tetin] nf teat ; (*sucette*) dummy.

téton [tetɔ̃] nm (*fam*) breast.

têtu, e [tety] a stubborn, pigheaded.

texte [tɛkst(ə)] nm text ; **apprendre son ~** (*THÉÂTRE*) to learn one's lines.

textile [tɛkstil] a textile cpd // nm textile ; textile industry.

textuel, le [tɛkstɥɛl] a literal, word for word.

texture [tɛkstyR] nf texture.

thé [te] nm tea ; **prendre le ~** to have tea ; **faire le ~** to make the tea.

théâtral, e, aux [teatRal, -o] a theatrical.

théâtre [teatR(ə)] nm theatre ; (*techniques, genre*) drama, theatre ; (*activité*) stage, theatre ; (*œuvres*) plays pl, dramatic works pl ; (*fig: lieu*): **le ~ de** the scene of ; (*péj*) histrionics pl, playacting ; **faire du ~** to be on the stage ; to do some acting ; **~ filmé** filmed stage productions pl.

théière [tejɛR] nf teapot.

thème [tɛm] nm theme ; (*SCOL: traduction*) prose (composition).

théologie [teɔlɔʒi] nf theology ; **théologien** nm theologian ; **théologique** a theological.

théorème [teɔRɛm] nm theorem.

théoricien, ne [teɔRisjɛ̃, ·jɛn] nm/f theoretician, theorist.

théorie [teɔRi] nf theory ; **théorique** a theoretical.

thérapeutique [teRapøtik] a therapeutic // nf therapeutics sg.

thérapie [teRapi] nf therapy.

thermal, e, aux [tɛRmal, -o] a thermal ; **station ~e** spa ; **cure ~e** water cure.

thermes [tɛRm(ə)] nmpl thermal baths ; (*romains*) thermae pl.

thermique [tɛRmik] a (*énergie*) thermic ; (*unité*) thermal.

thermomètre [tɛRmɔmɛtR(ə)] nm thermometer.

thermonucléaire [tɛRmɔnykleɛR] a thermonuclear.

thermos ® [tɛRmos] nm ou nf: **(bouteille) ~** vacuum ou Thermos ® flask.

thermostat [tɛRmɔsta] nm thermostat.

thésauriser [tezɔRize] vi to hoard money.

thèse [tɛz] nf thesis (pl theses).

thon [tɔ̃] nm tuna (fish).

thoracique [tɔRasik] a thoracic.

thorax [tɔRaks] nm thorax.

thrombose [tRɔ̃boz] nf thrombosis.

thym [tɛ̃] nm thyme.

thyroïde [tiRɔid] nf thyroid (gland).

tiare [tjaR] nf tiara.

tibia [tibja] nm shinbone, tibia ; shin.

tic [tik] nm tic, (nervous) twitch ; (*de langage etc*) mannerism.

ticket [tikɛ] nm ticket ; **~ de quai** platform ticket.

tic-tac [tiktak] nm inv tick-tock ; **tictaquer** vi to tick (away).

tiède [tjɛd] a lukewarm ; tepid ; (*vent, air*) mild, warm ; **tiédir** vi to cool ; to grow warmer.

tien, tienne [tjɛ̃, tjɛn] pronom: **le ~ (la tienne), les ~s (tiennes)** yours ; **à la tienne!** cheers!

tiens [tjɛ̃] vb, excl voir **tenir**.

tierce [tjɛRs(ə)] a, nf voir **tiers**.

tiercé [tjɛRse] nm system of forecast betting giving first 3 horses.

tiers, tierce [tjɛR, tjɛRs(ə)] a third // nm (*JUR*) third party ; (*fraction*) third // nf (*MUS*) third ; (*CARTES*) tierce ; **une tierce personne** a third party ; **~ provisionnel** interim payment of tax.

tige [tiʒ] nf stem ; (*baguette*) rod.

tignasse [tiɲas] nf (*péj*) shock ou mop of hair.

tigre [tigR(ə)] nm tiger.

tigré, e [tigRe] a striped ; spotted.

tigresse [tigRɛs] nf tigress.

tilleul [tijœl] nm lime (tree), linden (tree) ; (*boisson*) lime(-blossom) tea.

timbale [tɛ̃bal] nf (*metal*) tumbler ; **~s** nfpl (*MUS*) timpani, kettledrums.

timbre [tɛ̃bR(ə)] nm (*tampon*) stamp ; (*aussi:* **~-poste**) (postage) stamp ; (*cachet de la poste*) postmark ; (*sonnette*) bell ; (*MUS: de voix, instrument*) timbre, tone.

timbrer [tɛ̃bRe] vt to stamp.

timide [timid] a shy ; timid ; (*timoré*) timid, timorous ; **timidité** nf shyness, timidity.

timonerie [timɔnRi] nf wheelhouse.

timoré, e [timɔRe] a timorous.

tins etc vb voir **tenir**.

tintamarre [tɛ̃tamaR] nm din, uproar.

tinter [tɛ̃te] vi to ring, chime ; (*argent, clefs*) to jingle.

tir [tiR] nm (*sport*) shooting ; (*fait ou manière de tirer*) firing q ; (*FOOTBALL*) shot ; (*stand*) shooting gallery ; **~ d'obus/de mitraillette** shell/machine gun fire ; **~ à l'arc** archery ; **~ au pigeon** clay pigeon shooting.

tirade [tiRad] nf tirade.

tirage [tiRaʒ] nm (*action*) printing ; (*de journal*) circulation ; (*de livre*) (print-)run ; edition ; (*de cheminée*) draught ; (*de loterie*) draw ; (*désaccord*) friction ; **~ au sort** drawing lots.

tirailler [tiRaje] vt to pull at, tug at // vi to fire at random ; **tirailleur** nm skirmisher.

tirant [tiʀɑ̃] nm: ~ d'eau draught.

tire [tiʀ] nf: vol à la ~ pickpocketing.

tiré [tiʀe] nm (COMM) drawee; ~ à part off-print.

tire-au-flanc [tiʀoflɑ̃] nm inv (péj) skiver.

tire-bouchon [tiʀbuʃɔ̃] nm corkscrew.

tire-d'aile [tiʀdɛl]: à ~ ad swiftly.

tire-fesses [tiʀfɛs] nm inv ski-tow.

tirelire [tiʀliʀ] nf moneybox.

tirer [tiʀe] vt (gén) to pull; (extraire): ~ qch de to take ou pull sth out of; to get sth out of; to extract sth from; (tracer: ligne, trait) to draw, trace; (fermer: volet, rideau) to draw, close; (choisir: carte, conclusion, aussi COMM: chèque) to draw; (en faisant feu: balle, coup) to fire; (: animal) to shoot; (journal, livre, photo) to print; (FOOTBALL: corner etc) to take // vi (faire feu) to fire; (faire du tir, FOOTBALL) to shoot; (cheminée) to draw; se ~ vi (fam) to push off; s'en ~ to pull through, get off; ~ sur to pull on ou at; to shoot ou fire at; (pipe) to draw on; (fig: avoisiner) to verge ou border on; ~ son nom de to take ou get its name from; ~ qn de (embarras etc) to help ou get sb out of; ~ à l'arc/la carabine to shoot with a bow and arrow/with a rifle.

tiret [tiʀɛ] nm dash.

tireur, euse [tiʀœʀ, -øz] nm/f gunman; (COMM) drawer; **bon** ~ good shot; ~ **d'élite** marksman; ~s **débutants** beginners at shooting.

tiroir [tiʀwaʀ] nm drawer; ~-**caisse** nm till.

tisane [tizan] nf herb tea.

tison [tizɔ̃] nm brand; **tisonner** vt to poke; **tisonnier** nm poker.

tissage [tisaʒ] nm weaving q.

tisser [tise] vt to weave; **tisserand** nm weaver.

tissu [tisy] nm fabric, material, cloth q; (ANAT, BIO) tissue; ~ **de mensonges** web of lies.

tissu, e [tisy] a: ~ **de** woven through with.

tissu-éponge [tisyepɔ̃ʒ] nm (terry) towelling q.

titane [titan] nm titanium.

titanesque [titanɛsk(ə)] a titanic.

titre [titʀ(ə)] nm (gén) title; (de journal) headline; (diplôme) qualification; (COMM) security; (CHIMIE) titre; **en** ~ (champion, responsable) official, recognised; **à juste** ~ with just cause, rightly; **à quel** ~? on what grounds?; **à aucun** ~ on no account; **au même** ~ (que) in the same way (as); **à** ~ **d'exemple** as an ou by way of an example; **à** ~ **d'information** for (your) information; **à** ~ **gracieux** free of charge; **à** ~ **d'essai** on a trial basis; **à** ~ **privé** in a private capacity; ~ **de propriété** title deed; ~ **de transport** ticket.

titré, e [titʀe] a titled.

titrer [titʀe] vt (CHIMIE) to titrate; to assay; (PRESSE) to run as a headline; (suj: vin): ~ **10°** to be 10° proof.

tituber [titybe] vi to stagger ou reel (along).

titulaire [titylɛʀ] a (ADMIN) appointed, with tenure // nm (ADMIN) incumbent; **être**

~ **de** (poste) to hold; (permis) to be the holder of.

toast [tost] nm slice ou piece of toast; (de bienvenue) (welcoming) toast; **porter un** ~ **à qn** to propose ou drink a toast to sb.

toboggan [tɔbɔgɑ̃] nm toboggan.

toc [tɔk] nm: **en** ~ imitation cpd.

tocsin [tɔksɛ̃] nm alarm (bell).

toge [tɔʒ] nf toga; (de juge) gown.

tohu-bohu [tɔybɔy] nm confusion; commotion.

toi [twa] pronom you.

toile [twal] nf (matériau) cloth q; (bâche) piece of canvas; (tableau) canvas; **grosse** ~ canvas; **tisser sa** ~ (araignée) to spin its web; ~ **d'araignée** cobweb; ~ **cirée** oilcloth; ~ **de fond** (fig) backdrop; ~ **de jute** hessian; ~ **de lin** linen.

toilette [twalɛt] nf wash; (s'habiller et se préparer) getting ready, washing and dressing; (habits) outfit; dress q; ~s nfpl (w.-c.) toilet sg; **les** ~s **des dames/messieurs** the ladies'/gents' (toilets); **faire sa** ~ to have a wash, get washed; **articles de** ~ toiletries; ~ **intime** personal hygiene.

toi-même [twamɛm] pronom yourself.

toise [twaz] nf: **passer à la** ~ to have one's height measured.

toiser [twaze] vt to eye up and down.

toison [twazɔ̃] nf (de mouton) fleece; (cheveux) mane.

toit [twa] nm roof.

toiture [twatyʀ] nf roof.

tôle [tol] nf sheet metal q; (plaque) steel ou iron sheet; ~s (carrosserie) bodywork sg; panels; ~ **d'acier** sheet steel q; ~ **ondulée** corrugated iron.

tolérable [tɔleʀabl(ə)] a tolerable, bearable.

tolérance [tɔleʀɑ̃s] nf tolerance; (hors taxe) allowance.

tolérant, e [tɔleʀɑ̃, -ɑ̃t] a tolerant.

tolérer [tɔleʀe] vt to tolerate; (ADMIN: hors taxe etc) to allow.

tôlerie [tolʀi] nf sheet metal manufacture; sheet metal workshop.

tollé [tɔle] nm: **un** ~ (de protestations) a general outcry.

T.O.M. [parfois: tɔm] sigle m(pl) = territoire(s) d'outre-mer.

tomate [tɔmat] nf tomato.

tombal, e [tɔ̃bal] a: **pierre** ~**e** tombstone, gravestone.

tombant, e [tɔ̃bɑ̃, -ɑ̃t] a (fig) drooping, sloping.

tombe [tɔ̃b] nf (sépulture) grave; (avec monument) tomb.

tombeau, x [tɔ̃bo] nm tomb.

tombée [tɔ̃be] nf: **à la** ~ **du jour** ou **de la nuit** at the close of day, at nightfall.

tomber [tɔ̃be] vi to fall // vt: ~ **la veste** to slip off one's jacket; **laisser** ~ to drop; ~ **sur** vt (rencontrer) to come across; (attaquer) to set about; ~ **de fatigue/sommeil** to drop from exhaustion/be falling asleep on one's feet; **ça tombe bien** it comes at the right time; **il est bien tombé** he's been lucky.

tombereau, x [tɔ̃bʀo] nm tipcart.

tombeur [tɔ̃bœʀ] nm (péj) Casanova.
tombola [tɔ̃bɔla] nf tombola.
tome [tɔm] nm volume.
tommette [tɔmɛt] nf hexagonal floor tile.
ton, ta, pl **tes** [tɔ̃, ta, te] dét your.
ton [tɔ̃] nm (gén) tone ; (MUS) key ; (couleur) shade, tone ; **de bon ~** in good taste.
tonal, e [tɔnal] a tonal.
tonalité [tɔnalite] nf (au téléphone) dialling tone ; (MUS) tonality ; key ; (fig) tone.
tondeuse [tɔ̃døz] nf (à gazon) (lawn)-mower ; (du coiffeur) clippers pl ; (pour la tonte) shears pl.
tondre [tɔ̃dʀ(ə)] vt (pelouse, herbe) to mow ; (haie) to cut, clip ; (mouton, toison) to shear ; (cheveux) to crop.
tonifiant, e [tɔnifjɑ̃, -ɑ̃t] a invigorating, revivifying.
tonifier [tɔnifje] vt (peau, organisme) to tone up.
tonique [tɔnik] a fortifying // nm, nf tonic.
tonitruant, e [tɔnitʀyɑ̃, -ɑ̃t] a: **voix ~e** thundering voice.
tonnage [tɔnaʒ] nm tonnage.
tonne [tɔn] nf metric ton, tonne.
tonneau, x [tɔno] nm (à vin, cidre) barrel ; (NAVIG) ton ; **faire des ~x** (voiture, avion) to roll over.
tonnelier [tɔnəlje] nm cooper.
tonnelle [tɔnɛl] nf bower, arbour.
tonner [tɔne] vi to thunder ; **il tonne** it is thundering, there's some thunder.
tonnerre [tɔnɛʀ] nm thunder ; **~ d'applaudissements** thunderous applause ; **du ~** a (fam) terrific.
tonsure [tɔ̃syʀ] nf tonsure ; bald patch.
tonte [tɔ̃t] nf shearing.
tonus [tɔnys] nm tone.
top [tɔp] nm: **au 3ème ~** at the 3rd stroke // a: **~ secret** top secret.
topaze [tɔpaz] nf topaz.
toper [tɔpe] vi: **tope-/topez-là!** it's a deal!, you're on!
topinambour [tɔpinɑ̃buʀ] nm Jerusalem artichoke.
topographie [tɔpɔgʀafi] nf topography ; **topographique** a topographical.
toponymie [tɔpɔnimi] nf study of place-names, toponymy.
toque [tɔk] nf (de fourrure) fur hat ; **~ de jockey/juge** jockey's/judge's cap ; **~ de cuisinier** chef's hat.
toqué, e [tɔke] a (fam) touched, cracked.
torche [tɔʀʃ(ə)] nf torch ; **se mettre en ~** (parachute) to candle.
torcher [tɔʀʃe] vt (fam) to wipe.
torchère [tɔʀʃɛʀ] nf flare.
torchon [tɔʀʃɔ̃] nm cloth, duster ; (à vaisselle) tea towel, dish towel.
tordre [tɔʀdʀ(ə)] vt (chiffon) to wring ; (barre, fig: visage) to twist ; **se ~** vi (barre) to bend ; (roue) to twist, buckle ; (ver, serpent) to writhe ; **se ~ le pied/bras** to twist ou sprain one's foot/arm ; **se ~ de douleur/rire** to writhe in pain/be doubled up with laughter.
tordu, e [tɔʀdy] a (fig) warped, twisted.
torero [tɔʀeʀo] nm bullfighter.
tornade [tɔʀnad] nf tornado.

torpeur [tɔʀpœʀ] nf torpor, drowsiness.
torpille [tɔʀpij] nf torpedo ; **torpiller** vt to torpedo.
torréfier [tɔʀefje] vt to roast.
torrent [tɔʀɑ̃] nm torrent, mountain stream ; (fig): **~ de** torrent ou flood of ; **il pleut à ~s** the rain is lashing down ; **torrentiel, le** a torrential.
torride [tɔʀid] a torrid.
torsade [tɔʀsad] nf twist ; (ARCHIT) cable moulding ; **torsader** vt to twist.
torse [tɔʀs(ə)] nm (ANAT) torso ; chest.
torsion [tɔʀsjɔ̃] nf twisting ; torsion.
tort [tɔʀ] nm (défaut) fault ; (préjudice) wrong q ; **~s** nmpl (JUR) fault sg ; **avoir ~** to be wrong ; **être dans son ~** to be in the wrong ; **donner ~ à qn** to lay the blame on sb ; (fig) to prove sb wrong ; **causer du ~ à** to harm ; to be harmful ou detrimental to ; **en ~** in the wrong, at fault ; **à ~** wrongly ; **à ~ et à travers** wildly.
torticolis [tɔʀtikɔli] nm stiff neck.
tortiller [tɔʀtije] vt to twist ; to twiddle ; **se ~** vi to wriggle, squirm.
tortionnaire [tɔʀsjɔnɛʀ] nm torturer.
tortue [tɔʀty] nf tortoise.
tortueux, euse [tɔʀtyø, -øz] a (rue) twisting ; (fig) tortuous.
torture [tɔʀtyʀ] nf torture ; **torturer** vt to torture ; (fig) to torment.
torve [tɔʀv(ə)] a: **regard ~** menacing ou grim look.
tôt [to] ad early ; **~ ou tard** sooner or later ; **si ~** so early ; (déjà) so soon ; **au plus ~** at the earliest, as soon as possible ; **plus ~** earlier ; **il eut ~ fait de faire** he soon did.
total, e, aux [tɔtal, -o] a, nm total ; **au ~** in total ou all ; **faire le ~** to work out the total, add up ; **~ement** ad totally, completely ; **~iser** vt total (up).
totalitaire [tɔtalitɛʀ] a totalitarian.
totalité [tɔtalite] nf: **la ~ de** all of, the total amount (ou number) of ; **the whole + sg** ; **en ~** entirely.
totem [tɔtɛm] nm totem.
toubib [tubib] nm (fam) doctor.
touchant, e [tuʃɑ̃, -ɑ̃t] a touching.
touche [tuʃ] nf (de piano, de machine à écrire) key ; (PEINTURE etc) stroke, touch ; (fig: de nostalgie) touch, hint ; (RUGBY) line-out ; (FOOTBALL: aussi: **remise en ~**) throw-in ; (: **ligne de ~**) touch-line ; (ESCRIME) hit ; **en ~** in (ou into) touch ; **avoir une drôle de ~** to look a sight.
touche-à-tout [tuʃatu] nm/f inv (péj) meddler ; dabbler.
toucher [tuʃe] nm touch // vt to touch ; (palper) to feel ; (atteindre: d'un coup de feu etc) to hit ; (affecter) to touch, affect ; (concerner) to concern, affect ; (contacter) to reach, contact ; (recevoir: récompense) to receive, get ; (: salaire) to draw, get ; **au ~** to the touch ; **se ~** (être en contact) to touch ; **~ à** to touch ; (modifier) to touch, tamper ou meddle with ; (traiter de, concerner) to touch on ; **je vais lui en ~ un mot** I'll have a word with him about it ; **~ à sa fin** to be drawing to a close.

touffe [tuf] *nf* tuft.

touffu, e [tufy] *a* thick, dense; *(fig)* complex, involved.

toujours [tuʒuʀ] *ad* always; *(encore)* still; *(constamment)* forever; ~ **plus** more and more; **pour** ~ forever; ~ **est-il que** the fact remains that; **essaie** ~ (you can) try anyway.

toupie [tupi] *nf* (spinning) top.

tour [tuʀ] *nf* tower; *(immeuble)* high-rise block, tower block; *(ÉCHECS)* castle, rook // *nm (excursion)* stroll, walk; run, ride; trip; *(SPORT: aussi:* ~ **de piste)** lap; *(d'être servi ou de jouer etc, tournure, de vis ou clef)* turn; *(de roue etc)* revolution; *(circonférence):* **de 3 m de** ~ 3 m round, with a circumference *ou* girth of 3 m; *(POL: aussi:* ~ **de scrutin)** ballot; *(ruse, de prestidigitation)* trick; *(de potier)* wheel; *(à bois, métaux)* lathe; **faire le** ~ **de** to go round; *(à pied)* to walk round; **faire un** ~ to go for a walk; *(en voiture etc)* to go for a ride; **faire 2** ~**s** to go round twice; *(hélice etc)* to turn *ou* revolve twice; **fermer à double** ~ *vi* to double-lock the door; **c'est au** ~ **de Renée** it's Renée's turn; **à** ~ **de rôle,** ~ **à** ~ in turn; ~ **de taille/tête** waist/head measurement ~ **de chant** song recital; ~ **de contrôle** *nf* control tower; ~ **de garde** spell of duty; ~ **d'horizon** *(fig)* general survey; ~ **de lit** valance; ~ **de reins** sprained back.

tourbe [tuʀb(ə)] *nf* peat; **tourbière** *nf* peat-bog.

tourbillon [tuʀbijɔ̃] *nm* whirlwind; *(d'eau)* whirlpool; *(fig)* whirl, swirl; **tourbillonner** *vi* to whirl, swirl; to whirl *ou* swirl round.

tourelle [tuʀɛl] *nf* turret.

tourisme [tuʀism(ə)] *nm* tourism; tourist industry; **agence de** ~ tourist agency; **faire du** ~ to do some sightseeing, go touring; **touriste** *nm/f* tourist; **touristique** *a* tourist *cpd*; *(région)* touristic, with tourist appeal.

tourment [tuʀmɑ̃] *nm* torment.

tourmente [tuʀmɑ̃t] *nf* storm.

tourmenté, e [tuʀmɑ̃te] *a* tormented, tortured.

tourmenter [tuʀmɑ̃te] *vt* to torment; **se** ~ *vi* to fret, worry o.s.

tournage [tuʀnaʒ] *nm (d'un film)* shooting.

tournant, e [tuʀnɑ̃, -ɑ̃t] *a: voir* **plaque, grève** // *nm (de route)* bend; *(fig)* turning point.

tournebroche [tuʀnəbʀɔʃ] *nm* roasting spit.

tourne-disque [tuʀnədisk(ə)] *nm* record player.

tournée [tuʀne] *nf (du facteur etc)* round; *(d'artiste, politicien)* tour; *(au café)* round (of drinks); ~ **musicale** concert tour.

tourner [tuʀne] *vt* to turn; *(contourner)* to get round; *(CINÉMA)* to shoot; to make // *vi* to turn; *(moteur)* to run; *(compteur)* to tick away; *(lait etc)* to turn (sour); **se** ~ *vi* to turn round; **se** ~ **vers** to turn to; to turn towards; **bien** ~ to turn out well; ~ **autour de** to go round; to revolve round; *(péj)* to hang round; ~ **à/en** to turn into; ~ **à la pluie/au rouge** to turn

rainy/red; ~ **le dos à** to turn one's back on; to have one's back to; **se** ~ **les pouces** to twiddle one's thumbs; ~ **la tête** to look away; ~ **la tête à qn** *(fig)* to go to sb's head; ~ **de l'œil** to pass out.

tournesol [tuʀnəsɔl] *nm* sunflower.

tourneur [tuʀnœʀ] *nm* turner; lathe-operator.

tournevis [tuʀnəvis] *nm* screwdriver.

tourniquet [tuʀnikɛ] *nm (pour arroser)* sprinkler; *(portillon)* turnstile; *(présentoir)* revolving stand.

tournoi [tuʀnwa] *nm* tournament.

tournoyer [tuʀnwaje] *vi* to whirl round; to swirl round.

tournure [tuʀnyʀ] *nf (LING)* turn of phrase; form; phrasing; *(évolution):* **la** ~ **de qch** the way sth is developing; *(aspect):* **la** ~ **de** the look of; ~ **d'esprit** turn *ou* cast of mind; **la** ~ **des événements** the turn of events.

tourte [tuʀt(ə)] *nf* pie.

tourteau, x [tuʀto] *nm (AGR)* oilcake, cattle-cake; *(ZOOL)* edible crab.

tourterelle [tuʀtəʀɛl] *nf* turtledove.

tous *dét* [tu], *pronom* [tus] *voir* **tout.**

Toussaint [tusɛ̃] *nf:* **la** ~ All Saints' Day.

tousser [tuse] *vi* to cough; **toussoter** *vi* to have a slight cough; to cough a little; *(pour avertir)* to give a slight cough.

tout, e, *pl* **tous, toutes** [tu, tus, tut] *dét* all; ~ **le lait** all the milk, the whole of the milk; ~**e la nuit** all night, the whole night; ~ **le livre** the whole book; ~ **un pain** a whole loaf; **tous les livres** all the books; **toutes les nuits** every night; **à** ~ **âge** at any age; **toutes les fois** every time; **toutes les 3/2 semaines** every third/other *ou* second week; **tous les 2** both *ou* each of us (*ou* them); **toutes les 3** all 3 of us (*ou* them); ~ **le temps** *ad* all the time; **the whole time;** **c'est** ~ **le contraire** it's quite the opposite; **il avait pour** ~**e nourriture** his only food was // *pronom* everything, all; **tous, toutes** all (of them); **je les vois tous** I can see them all *ou* all of them; **nous y sommes tous allés** all of us went, we all went; **en** ~ in all // *ad* quite; very; ~ **en haut** right at the top; **le** ~ **premier** the very first; **le livre** ~ **entier** the whole book; ~ **seul** all alone; ~ **droit** straight ahead; ~ **en travaillant** while working, as *ou* while he etc works // *nm* whole; **le** ~ all of it (*ou* them), the whole lot; ~ **d'abord** first of all; ~ **à coup** suddenly; ~ **à fait** absolutely; ~ **à l'heure** a short while ago; in a short while, shortly; ~ **de même** all the same; ~ **le monde** everybody; ~ **de suite** immediately, straight away; ~ **terrain** *ou* **tous terrains** *a inv* general-purpose; ~**-à-l'égout** *nm inv* mains drainage.

toutefois [tutfwa] *ad* however.

toutou [tutu] *nm (fam)* doggie.

toux [tu] *nf* cough.

toxicomane [tɔksikɔman] *nm/f* drug addict.

toxine [tɔksin] *nf* toxin.

toxique [tɔksik] *a* toxic, poisonous.

trac [tʀak] *nm* nerves *pl*; *(THÉÂTRE)* stage

fright ; **avoir le** ~ **to** get an attack of nerves ; to have stage fright.

tracas [tRaka] *nm* bother *q*, worry *q*; **tracasser** *vt* to worry, bother ; to harass ; **se tracasser** *vi* to worry o.s., fret ; **tracasserie** *nf* annoyance *q*; harassment *q*; **tracassier, ière** *a* irksome.

trace [tRas] *nf* (*empreintes*) tracks *pl*; (*marques, aussi fig*) mark ; (*restes, vestige*) trace ; (*indice*) sign ; ~**s de pas** footprints.

tracé [tRase] *nm* line ; layout.

tracer [tRase] *vt* to draw ; (*mot*) to trace ; (*piste*) to open up.

trachée(-artère) [tRaʃe(aRtɛR)] *nf* windpipe, trachea ; **trachéite** [tRakeit] *nf* tracheitis.

tract [tRakt] *nm* tract, pamphlet.

tractations [tRaktɑsjɔ̃] *nfpl* dealings, bargaining *sg*.

tracteur [tRaktœR] *nm* tractor.

traction [tRaksjɔ̃] *nf* traction ; (*GYM*) pull-up ; ~ **avant/arrière** front-wheel/rear-wheel drive ; ~ **électrique** electric(al) traction *ou* haulage.

tradition [tRadisjɔ̃] *nf* tradition ; **traditionnel, le** *a* traditional.

traducteur, trice [tRadyktœR, -tRis] *nm/f* translator.

traduction [tRadyksjɔ̃] *nf* translation.

traduire [tRadɥiR] *vt* to translate ; (*exprimer*) to render, convey ; ~ **en français** to translate into French ; ~ **en justice** to bring before the courts.

trafic [tRafik] *nm* traffic ; ~ **d'armes** arms dealing ; **trafiquant, e** *nm/f* trafficker ; dealer ; **trafiquer** *vt* (*péj*) to doctor, tamper with // *vi* to traffic, be engaged in trafficking.

tragédie [tRaʒedi] *nf* tragedy ; **tragédien, ne** *nm/f* tragedian/ tragedienne.

tragique [tRaʒik] *a* tragic ; ~**ment** *ad* tragically.

trahir [tRaiR] *vt* to betray ; (*fig*) to give away, reveal ; **trahison** *nf* betrayal ; (*MIL*) treason.

train [tRɛ̃] *nm* (*RAIL*) train ; (*allure*) pace ; (*fig: ensemble*) set ; **mettre qch en** ~ **to** get sth under way ; **mettre qn en** ~ **to** put sb in good spirits ; **se mettre en** ~ to get started ; to warm up ; **se sentir en** ~ to feel in good form ; ~ **avant/arrière** front-wheel/rear-wheel axle unit ; ~ **d'atterrissage** undercarriage ; ~ **autos-couchettes** car-sleeper train ; ~ **électrique** (*jouet*) (electric) train set ; ~ **de pneus** set of tyres ; ~ **de vie** style of living.

traînant, e [tRenɑ̃, -ɑ̃t] *a* (*voix, ton*) drawling.

traînard, e [tRenaR, -aRd(ə)] *nm/f* (*péj*) slowcoach.

traîne [tRɛn] *nf* (*de robe*) train ; **être à la** ~ to be in tow ; to lag behind.

traîneau, x [tRɛno] *nm* sleigh, sledge.

traînée [tRene] *nf* streak, trail ; (*péj*) slut.

traîner [tRene] (*remorque*) to pull ; (*enfant, chien*) to drag *ou* trail along // *vi* (*être en désordre*) to lie around ; (*marcher lentement*) to dawdle (along) ; (*vagabonder*) to hang about ; (*agir lentement*) to idle about ; (*durer*) to drag on ; **se** ~ *vi* to crawl along ; **to drag o.s. along** ; (*durer*) to drag on ; ~ **les pieds** to drag one's feet.

train-train [tRɛ̃tRɛ̃] *nm* humdrum routine.

traire [tRɛR] *vt* to milk.

trait [tRɛ] *nm* (*ligne*) line ; (*de dessin*) stroke ; (*caractéristique*) feature, trait ; (*flèche*) dart, arrow ; shaft ; ~**s** *nmpl* (*du visage*) features ; **d'un** ~ (*boire*) in one gulp ; **de** ~ *a* (*animal*) draught ; **avoir** ~ **à** to concern ; ~ **de caractère** characteristic, trait ; ~ **d'esprit** flash of wit ; ~ **d'union** hyphen ; (*fig*) link.

traitant [tRɛtɑ̃] *am*: **votre médecin** ~ your usual *ou* family doctor ; **shampooing** ~ medicated shampoo.

traite [tRɛt] *nf* (*COMM*) draft ; (*AGR*) milking ; (*trajet*) stretch ; **d'une (seule)** ~ without stopping (once) ; **la** ~ **des noirs** the slave trade.

traité [tRete] *nm* treaty.

traitement [tRɛtmɑ̃] *nm* treatment ; processing ; (*salaire*) salary.

traiter [tRete] *vt* (*gén*) to treat ; (*TECH: matériaux*) to process, treat ; (*affaire*) to deal with, handle ; (*qualifier*): ~ **qn d'idiot** to call sb a fool // *vi* to deal ; ~ **de** *vt* to deal with ; **bien/mal** ~ to treat well/ill-treat.

traiteur [tRɛtœR] *nm* caterer.

traître, esse [tRɛtR(ə), -tRɛs] *a* (*dangereux*) treacherous // *nm* traitor ; **prendre qn en** ~ to make an insidious attack on sb ; **traîtrise** *nf* treachery, treacherousness.

trajectoire [tRaʒɛktwaR] *nf* trajectory, path.

trajet [tRaʒɛ] *nm* journey ; (*itinéraire*) route ; (*fig*) path, course.

tralala [tRalala] *nm* (*péj*) fuss.

tram [tRam] *nm abr de* **tramway**.

trame [tRam] *nf* (*de tissu*) weft ; (*fig*) framework ; texture ; (*TYPO*) screen.

tramer [tRame] *vt* to plot, hatch.

tramway [tRamwɛ] *nm* tram(way) ; tram(car).

tranchant, e [tRɑ̃ʃɑ̃, -ɑ̃t] *a* sharp ; (*fig*) peremptory // *nm* (*d'un couteau*) cutting edge ; (*de la main*) edge.

tranche [tRɑ̃ʃ] *nf* (*morceau*) slice ; (*arête*) edge ; (*partie*) section ; (*série*) block ; issue ; bracket.

tranché, e [tRɑ̃ʃe] *a* (*couleurs*) distinct, sharply contrasted ; (*opinions*) clear-cut, definite // *nf* trench.

trancher [tRɑ̃ʃe] *vt* to cut, sever ; (*fig: résoudre*) to settle // *vi*: ~ **avec** to contrast sharply with.

tranchet [tRɑ̃ʃɛ] *nm* knife.

tranchoir [tRɑ̃ʃwaR] *nm* chopper.

tranquille [tRɑ̃kil] *a* calm, quiet ; (*enfant, élève*) quiet ; (*rassuré*) easy in one's mind, with one's mind at rest ; **se tenir** ~ (*enfant*) to be quiet ; **avoir la conscience** ~ to have an easy conscience ; **laisse-moi/laisse-ça** ~! leave me/it alone ; ~**ment** *ad* calmly ; **tranquillisant** *nm* tranquillizer ; **tranquilliser** *vt* to reassure ; **tranquillité** *nf* quietness ; peace (and quiet) ; **tranquillité (d'esprit)** peace of mind.

transaction [trɑ̃zaksjɔ̃] nf (COMM) transaction, deal.

transat [trɑ̃zat] nm deckchair.

transatlantique [trɑ̃zatlɑ̃tik] a transatlantic // nm transatlantic liner.

transborder [trɑ̃sbɔrde] vt to tran(s)ship.

transcendant, e [trɑ̃sɑ̃dɑ̃, -ɑ̃t] a transcendent(al).

transcription [trɑ̃skripsjɔ̃] nf transcription.

transcrire [trɑ̃skrir] vt to transcribe.

transe [trɑ̃s] nf: **entrer en** ~ to go into a trance ; ~s agony sg.

transférer [trɑ̃sfere] vt to transfer ; **transfert** nm transfer.

transfigurer [trɑ̃sfigyre] vt to transform.

transformateur [trɑ̃sfɔrmatœr] nm transformer.

transformation [trɑ̃sfɔrmɑsjɔ̃] nf transformation ; (RUGBY) conversion.

transformer [trɑ̃sfɔrme] vt to transform, alter ('alter' implique un changement moins radical) ; (matière première, appartement, RUGBY) to convert ; ~ **en** to transform into ; to turn into ; to convert into ; **se** ~ vi to be transformed ; to alter.

transfuge [trɑ̃sfyʒ] nm renegade.

transfusion [trɑ̃sfyzjɔ̃] nf: ~ **sanguine** blood transfusion.

transgresser [trɑ̃sgrese] vt to contravene, disobey.

transhumance [trɑ̃zymɑ̃s] nf transhumance, seasonal move to new pastures.

transi, e [trɑ̃zi] a numb (with cold), chilled to the bone.

transiger [trɑ̃ziʒe] vi to compromise, come to an agreement.

transistor [trɑ̃zistɔr] nm transistor.

transit [trɑ̃zit] nm transit ; ~**er** vi to pass in transit.

transitif, ive [trɑ̃zitif, -iv] a transitive.

transition [trɑ̃zisjɔ̃] nf transition ; **de** ~ transitional ; **transitoire** a transitional, provisional ; transient.

translucide [trɑ̃slysid] a translucent.

transmetteur [trɑ̃smetœr] nm transmitter.

transmettre [trɑ̃smetr(ə)] vt (passer): ~ **qch à qn** to pass sth on to sb ; (TECH, TEL, MED) to transmit ; (TV, RADIO: retransmettre) to broadcast ; **transmissible** a transmissible.

transmission [trɑ̃smisjɔ̃] nf transmission, passing on ; (AUTO) transmission ; ~**s** nfpl (MIL) ≈ signals corps ; ~ **de pensée** telepathy.

transparaître [trɑ̃sparetr(ə)] vi to show (through).

transparence [trɑ̃sparɑ̃s] nf transparence ; **par** ~ (regarder) against a source of light ; (voir) showing through.

transparent, e [trɑ̃sparɑ̃, -ɑ̃t] a transparent.

transpercer [trɑ̃sperse] vt to go through, pierce.

transpiration [trɑ̃spirɑsjɔ̃] nf perspiration.

transpirer [trɑ̃spire] vi to perspire.

transplanter [trɑ̃splɑ̃te] vt (MED, BOT) to transplant ; (personne) to uproot, move.

transport [trɑ̃spɔr] nm transport ; ~**s en commun** public transport sg.

transporter [trɑ̃spɔrte] vt to carry, move ; (COMM) to transport, convey ; (fig) to send into raptures ; ~ **qn à l'hôpital** to take sb to hospital ; **transporteur** nm haulier, haulage contractor.

transposer [trɑ̃spoze] vt to transpose ; **transposition** nf transposition.

transvaser [trɑ̃svaze] vt to decant.

transversal, e, aux [trɑ̃sversal, -o] a transverse, cross(-) ; cross-country ; running at right angles.

trapèze [trapez] nm (GEOM) trapezium ; (au cirque) trapeze ; **trapéziste** nm/f trapeze artist.

trappe [trap] nf trap door.

trappeur [trapœr] nm trapper, fur trader.

trapu, e [trapy] a squat, stocky.

traquenard [traknar] nm trap.

traquer [trake] vt to track down ; (harceler) to hound.

traumatiser [tromatize] vt to traumatize.

traumatisme [tromatism(ə)] nm traumatism.

travail, aux [travaj, -o] nm (gén) work ; (tâche, métier) work q, job ; (ECON, MED) labour // nmpl (de réparation, agricoles etc) work sg ; (sur route) roadworks sg ; (de construction) building (work) ; **être/entrer en** ~ (MED) to be in/start labour ; **être sans** ~ (employé) to be out of work ou unemployed ; ~ **noir** moonlighting ; **travaux des champs** farmwork sg ; **travaux dirigés** (SCOL) supervised practical work sg ; **travaux forcés** hard labour sg ; **travaux manuels** (SCOL) handicrafts ; **travaux ménagers** housework sg ; **travaux publics** ≈ public works sg.

travaillé, e [travaje] a (style) polished.

travailler [travaje] vi to work ; (bois) to warp // vt (bois, métal) to work ; (objet d'art, discipline, fig: influencer) to work on ; **cela le travaille** it is on his mind ; ~ **la terre** to till the land ; ~ **son piano** to do one's piano practice ; ~ **à** to work on ; (fig: contribuer à) to work towards ; **travailleur, euse** a hard-working // nm/f worker ; **travailleur de force** labourer ; **travailliste** a Labour.

travée [trave] nf row ; (ARCHIT) bay ; span.

travelling [travliŋ] nm (chariot) dolly ; (technique) tracking ; ~ **optique** zoom shots pl.

travers [traver] nm fault, failing ; **en** ~ (de) across ; **au** ~ (de) through ; **de** ~ a askew // sideways ; (fig) the wrong way ; **à** ~ through ; **regarder de** ~ (fig) to look askance at.

traverse [travers(ə)] nf (RAIL) sleeper ; **chemin de** ~ shortcut.

traversée [traverse] nf crossing.

traverser [traverse] vt (gén) to cross ; (ville, tunnel, aussi: percer, fig) to go through ; (suj: ligne, trait) to run across.

traversin [traversɛ̃] nm bolster.

travesti [tRavɛsti] *nm* (*costume*) fancy dress ; (*artiste de cabaret*) female impersonator, drag artist ; (*pervers*) transvestite.

travestir [tRavɛstiR] *vt* (*vérité*) to misrepresent ; **se** ~ to dress up ; to put on drag ; to dress as a woman.

trébucher [tRebyʃe] *vi* : ~ **(sur)** to stumble (over), trip (against).

trèfle [tRɛfl(ə)] *nm* (*BOT*) clover ; (*CARTES*: *couleur*) clubs *pl* ; (: *carte*) club ; ~ **à quatre feuilles** four-leaf clover.

treillage [tRɛjaʒ] *nm* lattice work.

treille [tRɛj] *nf* vine arbour ; climbing vine.

treillis [tReji] *nm* (*métallique*) wire-mesh ; (*toile*) canvas ; (*uniforme*) battle-dress.

treize [tRɛz] *num* thirteen ; **treizième** *num* thirteenth.

tréma [tRema] *nm* diaeresis.

tremble [tRɑ̃bl(ə)] *nm* (*BOT*) aspen.

tremblement [tRɑ̃bləmɑ̃] *nm* trembling *q*, shaking *q*, shivering *q* ; ~ **de terre** earthquake.

trembler [tRɑ̃ble] *vi* to tremble, shake ; ~ **de** (*froid, fièvre*) to shiver *ou* tremble with ; (*peur*) to shake *ou* tremble with ; ~ **pour qn** to fear for sb ; **trembloter** *vi* to tremble *ou* shake slightly.

trémolo [tRemɔlo] *nm* (*instrument*) tremolo ; (*voix*) quaver.

trémousser [tRemuse] : **se** ~ *vi* to jig about, wriggle about.

trempe [tRɑ̃p] *nf* (*fig*): **de cette/sa** ~ of this/his calibre.

trempé, e [tRɑ̃pe] *a* soaking (wet), drenched ; (*TECH*) tempered.

tremper [tRɑ̃pe] *vt* to soak, drench ; (*aussi*: **faire** ~, **mettre à** ~) to soak ; (*plonger*): ~ **qch dans** to dip sth in(to) // *vi* to soak ; (*fig*): ~ **dans** to be involved *ou* have a hand in ; **se** ~ *vi* to have a quick dip ; **se faire** ~ to get soaked *ou* drenched ; **trempette** *nf*: **faire trempette** to have a quick dip.

tremplin [tRɑ̃plɛ̃] *nm* springboard ; (*SKI*) ski-jump.

trentaine [tRɑ̃tɛn] *nf*: **une** ~ **(de)** thirty or so, about thirty.

trente [tRɑ̃t] *num* thirty ; **trentième** *num* thirtieth.

trépaner [tRepane] *vt* to trepan, trephine.

trépasser [tRepase] *vi* to pass away.

trépider [tRepide] *vi* to vibrate.

trépied [tRepje] *nm* (*d'appareil*) tripod ; (*meuble*) trivet.

trépigner [tRepiɲe] *vi* to stamp (one's feet).

très [tRɛ] *ad* very ; much + *pp*, highly + *pp* ; ~ **critiqué** much criticized ; ~ **industrialisé** highly industrialized ; **j'ai** ~ **faim** I'm very hungry.

trésor [tRezɔR] *nm* treasure ; (*ADMIN*) finances *pl* ; funds *pl* ; **T** ~ **(public)** public revenue.

trésorerie [tRezɔRRi] *nf* (*fonds*) funds *pl* ; (*gestion*) accounts *pl* ; (*bureaux*) accounts department ; (*poste*) treasurership ; **difficultés de** ~ cash problems, shortage of cash *ou* funds.

trésorier, ière [tRezɔRje, -jɛR] *nm/f* treasurer ; ~-**payeur** *nm* paymaster.

tressaillir [tRɛsajiR] *vi* to shiver, shudder ; to quiver.

tressauter [tRɛsote] *vi* to start, jump.

tresse [tRɛs] *nf* braid, plait.

tresser [tRese] *vi* (*cheveux*) to braid, plait ; (*fil, jonc*) to plait ; (*corbeille*) to weave ; (*corde*) to twist.

tréteau, x [tReto] *nm* trestle ; **les** ~**x** (*fig*) the stage.

treuil [tRœj] *nm* winch ; **treuiller** *vt* to winch up.

trêve [tRɛv] *nf* (*MIL, POL*) truce ; (*fig*) respite ; ~ **de ...** enough of this...

tri [tRi] *nm* sorting out *q* ; selection ; (*POSTES*) sorting ; sorting office.

triage [tRijaʒ] *nm* (*RAIL*) shunting ; (*gare*) marshalling yard.

triangle [tRijɑ̃gl(ə)] *nm* triangle ; ~ **rectangle** right-angled triangle.

tribal, e, aux [tRibal, -o] *a* tribal.

tribord [tRibɔR] *nm*: **à** ~ to starboard, on the starboard side.

tribu [tRiby] *nf* tribe.

tribulations [tRibylɑsjɔ̃] *nfpl* tribulations, trials.

tribunal, aux [tRibynal, -o] *nm* (*JUR*) court ; (*MIL*) tribunal ; ~ **de police/pour enfants** police/juvenile court ; ~ **d'instance** ≈ magistrates' court ; ~ **de grande instance** ≈ high court.

tribune [tRibyn] *nf* (*estrade*) platform, rostrum ; (*débat*) forum ; (*d'église, de tribunal*) gallery ; (*de stade*) stand ; ~ **libre** (*PRESSE*) opinion column.

tribut [tRiby] *nm* tribute.

tributaire [tRibytɛR] *a*: **être** ~ **de** to be dependent on ; (*GEO*) to be a tributary of.

tricher [tRiʃe] *vi* to cheat ; **tricherie** *nf* cheating *q* ; **tricheur, euse** *nm/f* cheat.

tricolore [tRikɔlɔR] *a* three-coloured ; (*français*) red, white and blue.

tricot [tRiko] *nm* (*technique, ouvrage*) knitting *q* ; (*tissu*) knitted fabric ; (*vêtement*) jersey, sweater.

tricoter [tRikɔte] *vt* to knit.

trictrac [tRiktRak] *nm* backgammon.

tricycle [tRisikl(ə)] *nm* tricycle.

triennal, e, aux [tRiɛnal, -o] *a* three-yearly ; three-year.

trier [tRije] *vt* to sort out ; (*POSTES, fruits*) to sort.

trigonométrie [tRigɔnɔmetRi] *nf* trigonometry.

trimbaler [tRɛ̃bale] *vt* to cart around, trail along.

trimer [tRime] *vi* to slave away.

trimestre [tRimɛstR(ə)] *nm* (*SCOL*) term ; (*COMM*) quarter ; **trimestriel, le** *a* quarterly ; (*SCOL*) end-of-term.

tringle [tRɛ̃gl(ə)] *nf* rod.

Trinité [tRinite] *nf* Trinity.

trinquer [tRɛ̃ke] *vi* to clink glasses ; (*fam*) to cop it ; ~ **à qch/la santé de qn** to drink to sth/sb.

trio [tRijo] *nm* trio.

triomphal, e, aux [tRijɔ̃fal, -o] *a* triumphant, triumphal.

triomphant, e [tRijɔ̃fɑ̃, -ɑ̃t] *a* triumphant.

triomphe [tRijɔ̃f] *nm* triumph ; **être reçu/porté en** ~ to be given a triumphant welcome/be carried shoulder-high in triumph.

triompher [tʀijɔ̃fe] *vi* to triumph, win ; ~ de to triumph over, overcome.

tripes [tʀip] *nfpl* (CULIN) tripe *sg* ; (*fam*) guts.

triple [tʀipl(ə)] *a* triple ; treble // *nm*: le ~ (de) (*comparaison*) three times as much (as) ; **en ~ exemplaire** in triplicate ; ~**ment** *ad* three times over ; in three ways, on three counts // *nm* trebling, threefold increase ; **tripler** *vi, vt* to triple, treble, increase threefold.

tripot [tʀipo] *nm* (*péj*) dive.

tripotage [tʀipɔtaʒ] *nm* (*péj*) jiggery-pokery.

tripoter [tʀipɔte] *vt* to fiddle with, finger.

trique [tʀik] *nf* cudgel.

triste [tʀist(ə)] *a* sad ; (*péj*): ~ **personnage/affaire** sorry individual/affair ; **tristesse** *nf* sadness.

triturer [tʀityʀe] *vt* (*pâte*) to knead ; (*objets*) to manipulate.

trivial, e, aux [tʀivjal, -o] *a* coarse, crude ; (*commun*) mundane.

troc [tʀɔk] *nm* (ECON) barter ; (*transaction*) exchange, swap.

troglodyte [tʀɔglɔdit] *nm/f* cave dweller, troglodyte.

trognon [tʀɔɲɔ̃] *nm* (*de fruit*) core ; (*de légume*) stalk.

trois [tʀwɑ] *num* three ; **troisième** *num* third ; **troisièmement** *ad* thirdly ; ~-**quarts** *nmpl*: **les** ~-**quarts de** three-quarters of.

trolleybus [tʀɔlɛbys] *nm* trolley bus.

trombe [tʀɔ̃b] *nf* waterspout ; **des** ~**s d'eau** a downpour ; **en** ~ (*arriver, passer*) like a whirlwind.

trombone [tʀɔ̃bɔn] *nm* (MUS) trombone ; (*de bureau*) paper clip ; ~ **à coulisse** slide trombone ; **tromboniste** *nm/f* trombonist.

trompe [tʀɔ̃p] *nf* (*d'éléphant*) trunk ; (MUS) trumpet, horn ; ~ **d'Eustache** Eustachian tube ; ~**s utérines** Fallopian tubes.

trompe-l'œil [tʀɔ̃plœj] *nm*: **en** ~ in trompe-l'œil style.

tromper [tʀɔ̃pe] *vt* to deceive ; (*vigilance, poursuivants*) to elude ; **se** ~ *vi* to make a mistake, be mistaken ; **se** ~ **de voiture/jour** to take the wrong car/get the day wrong ; **se** ~ **de 3 cm/20 F** to be out by 3 cm/20 F ; **tromperie** *nf* deception, trickery *q*.

trompette [tʀɔ̃pɛt] *nf* trumpet ; **en** ~ (*nez*) turned-up ; **trompettiste** *nm/f* trumpet player.

trompeur, euse [tʀɔ̃pœʀ, -øz] *a* deceptive, misleading.

tronc [tʀɔ̃] *nm* (BOT, ANAT) trunk ; (*d'église*) collection box ; ~ **d'arbre** tree trunk ; ~ **commun** (SCOL) common-core syllabus ; ~ **de cône** truncated cone.

tronche [tʀɔ̃ʃ] *nf* (*fam*) mug, face.

tronçon [tʀɔ̃sɔ̃] *nm* section.

tronçonner [tʀɔ̃sɔne] *vt* to saw up ; **tronçonneuse** *nf* chain saw.

trône [tʀon] *nm* throne.

trôner [tʀone] *vi* (*fig*) to sit in the place of honour.

tronquer [tʀɔ̃ke] *vt* to truncate ; (*fig*) to curtail.

trop [tʀo] *ad vb* + too much, too + *adjectif, adverbe* ; ~ (**nombreux**) too many ; ~ **peu (nombreux)** too few ; ~ (**souvent**) too often ; ~ (**longtemps**) (for) too long ; ~ **de** (*nombre*) too many ; (*quantité*) too much ; **de** ~, **en** ~: **des livres en** ~ a few books too many, a few extra books ; **du lait en** ~ some milk over *ou* extra, too much milk ; **3 livres/F de** ~ 3 books too many/F too much.

trophée [tʀɔfe] *nm* trophy.

tropical, e, aux [tʀɔpikal, -o] *a* tropical.

tropique [tʀɔpik] *nm* tropic ; ~**s** *nmpl* tropics.

trop-plein [tʀoplɛ̃] *nm* (*tuyau*) overflow *ou* outlet (pipe) ; (*liquide*) overflow.

troquer [tʀɔke] *vt*: ~ **qch contre** to barter *ou* trade sth for ; (*fig*) to swap sth for.

trot [tʀo] *nm* trot ; **aller au** ~ to trot along ; **partir au** ~ to set off at a trot.

trotter [tʀɔte] *vi* to trot ; (*fig*) to scamper along (*ou* about).

trotteuse [tʀɔtøz] *nf* (*de montre*) second hand.

trottiner [tʀɔtine] *vi* (*fig*) to scamper along (*ou* about).

trottinette [tʀɔtinɛt] *nf* (child's) scooter.

trottoir [tʀɔtwaʀ] *nm* pavement ; **faire le** ~ (*péj*) to walk the streets ; ~ **roulant** moving walkway, travellator.

trou [tʀu] *nm* hole ; (*fig*) gap ; ~ **d'air** air pocket ; ~ **de mémoire** blank, lapse of memory ; **le** ~ **de la serrure** the keyhole.

troublant, e [tʀublɑ̃, -ɑ̃t] *a* disturbing.

trouble [tʀubl(ə)] *a* (*liquide*) cloudy ; (*image, mémoire*) indistinct, hazy ; (*affaire*) shady, murky // *nm* (*désarroi*) distress, agitation ; (*émoi sensuel*) turmoil, agitation ; (*embarras*) confusion ; (*zizanie*) unrest, discord ; ~**s** *nmpl* (POL) disturbances, troubles, unrest *sg* ; (MED) trouble *sg*, disorders.

trouble-fête [tʀubləfɛt] *nm/f inv* spoilsport.

troubler [tʀuble] *vt* (*embarrasser*) to confuse, disconcert ; (*émouvoir*) to agitate ; to disturb ; to perturb ; (*perturber: ordre etc*) to disrupt, disturb ; (*liquide*) to make cloudy ; **se** ~ *vi* (*personne*) to become flustered *ou* confused ; ~ **l'ordre public** to cause a breach of the peace.

troué, e [tʀue] *a* with a hole (*ou* holes) in it // *nf* gap ; (MIL) breach.

trouer [tʀue] *vt* to make a hole (*ou* holes) in ; (*fig*) to pierce.

trouille [tʀuj] *nf* (*fam*): **avoir la** ~ to have the jitters, be in a funk.

troupe [tʀup] *nf* (MIL) troop ; (*groupe*) troop, group ; **la** ~ (MIL) the army ; the troops *pl* ; ~ (**de théâtre**) (theatrical) company.

troupeau, x [tʀupo] *nm* (*de moutons*) flock ; (*de vaches*) herd.

trousse [tʀus] *nf* case, kit ; (*d'écolier*) pencil case ; (*de docteur*) instrument case ; **aux** ~**s de** (*fig*) on the heels *ou* tail of ; ~ **à outils** toolkit ; ~ **de toilette** toilet *ou* sponge bag.

trousseau, x [tʀuso] nm (de jeune mariée) trousseau ; ~ de clefs bunch of keys.
trouvaille [tʀuvaj] nf find.
trouver [tʀuve] vt to find ; (rendre visite): **aller/venir ~** qn to go/come and see sb ; **je trouve que** I find ou think that ; **~ à boire/critiquer** to find something to drink/criticize ; **se ~** vi (être) to be ; (être soudain) to find o.s. ; **se ~ être/avoir** to happen to be/have ; **il se trouve que** it happens that, it turns out that ; **se ~ bien** to feel well ; **se ~ mal** to pass out.
truand [tʀyɑ̃] nm villain, crook.
truc [tʀyk] nm (astuce) way, device ; (de cinéma, prestidigitateur) trick effect ; (chose) thing ; (machin) thingumajig, whatsit ; **avoir le ~** to have the knack.
truchement [tʀyʃmɑ̃] nm: **par le ~ de** qn through (the intervention of) sb.
truculent, e [tʀykylɑ̃, -ɑ̃t] a colourful.
truelle [tʀyɛl] nf trowel.
truffe [tʀyf] nf truffle ; (nez) nose.
truffer [tʀyfe] vt (CULIN) to garnish with truffles ; **truffé de** (fig) peppered with ; bristling with.
truie [tʀyi] nf sow.
truite [tʀyit] nf trout inv.
truquage [tʀykaʒ] nm fixing ; (CINÉMA) special effects pl.
truquer [tʀyke] vt (élections, serrure, dés) to fix ; (CINÉMA) to use special effects in.
trust [tʀœst] nm (COMM) trust.
tsar [dzaʀ] nm tsar.
T.S.F. [teɛsɛf] sigle f (= télégraphie sans fil) wireless.
tsigane [tsigan] a, nm/f = **tzigane**.
T.S.V.P. sigle (= tournez s.v.p.) P.T.O. (please turn over).
T.T.C. sigle = toutes taxes comprises.
tu [ty] pronom you // nm: **employer le ~** to use the 'tu' form.
tu, e [ty] pp de **taire**.
tuba [tyba] nm (MUS) tuba ; (SPORT) snorkel.
tube [tyb] nm tube ; pipe ; (chanson, disque) hit song ou record ; **~ digestif** alimentary canal, digestive tract.
tuberculeux, euse [tybɛʀkylø, -øz] a tubercular // nm/f tuberculosis ou TB patient.
tuberculose [tybɛʀkyloz] nf tuberculosis.
tubulaire [tybylɛʀ] a tubular.
tubulure [tybylyʀ] nf pipe ; piping q ; (AUTO) manifold.
tué, e [tye] nm/f: **5 ~s** 5 killed ou dead.
tuer [tye] vt to kill ; **se ~** vi to be killed ; **se ~ au travail** (fig) to work o.s. to death ; **tuerie** nf slaughter q.
tue-tête [tytɛt]: **à ~** ad at the top of one's voice.
tueur [tyœʀ] nm killer ; **~ à gages** hired killer.
tuile [tyil] nf tile ; (fam) spot of bad luck, blow.
tulipe [tylip] nf tulip.
tuméfié, e [tymefje] a puffy, swollen.
tumeur [tymœʀ] nf growth, tumour.
tumulte [tymylt(ə)] nm commotion, hubbub.
tumultueux, euse [tymyltɥø, -øz] a stormy, turbulent.

tunique [tynik] nf tunic ; (de femme) smock, tunic.
Tunisie [tynizi] nf: **la ~** Tunisia ; **tunisien, ne** a, nm/f Tunisian.
tunnel [tynɛl] nm tunnel.
turban [tyʀbɑ̃] nm turban.
turbin [tyʀbɛ̃] nm (fam) work q.
turbine [tyʀbin] nf turbine.
turboréacteur [tyʀbɔʀeaktœʀ] nm turbojet.
turbulences [tyʀbylɑ̃s] nfpl (AVIAT) turbulence sg.
turbulent, e [tyʀbylɑ̃, -ɑ̃t] a boisterous, unruly.
turc, turque [tyʀk(ə)] a Turkish // nm/f: **T~, Turque** Turk/Turkish woman // nm (langue) Turkish ; **à la turque** ad cross-legged // a (w.-c.) seatless.
turf [tyʀf] nm racing ; **~iste** nm/f racegoer.
turpitude [tyʀpityd] nf base act, baseness q.
turque [tyʀk(ə)] a, nf voir **turc**.
Turquie [tyʀki] nf: **la ~** Turkey.
turquoise [tyʀkwaz] nf, a inv turquoise.
tus etc vb voir **taire**.
tutelle [tytɛl] nf (JUR) guardianship ; (POL) trusteeship ; **sous la ~ de** (fig) under the supervision of.
tuteur [tytœʀ] nm (JUR) guardian ; (de plante) stake, support.
tutoyer [tytwaje] vt: **~ qn** to address sb as 'tu'.
tuyau, x [tɥijo] nm pipe ; (flexible) tube ; (fam) tip ; gen q ; **~ d'arrosage** hosepipe ; **~ d'échappement** exhaust pipe ; **~té, e** a fluted ; **~terie** nf piping q.
tuyère [tɥijɛʀ] nf nozzle.
T.V.A. sigle f voir **taxe**.
tympan [tɛ̃pɑ̃] nm (ANAT) eardrum.
type [tip] nm type ; (fam) chap, bloke // a typical, standard ; **avoir le ~ nordique** to be Nordic-looking.
typhoïde [tifɔid] nf typhoid (fever).
typhon [tifɔ̃] nm typhoon.
typhus [tifys] nm typhus (fever).
typique [tipik] a typical.
typographe [tipɔgʀaf] nm/f typographer.
typographie [tipɔgʀafi] nf typography ; (procédé) letterpress (printing) ; **typographique** a typographical ; letterpress cpd.
tyran [tiʀɑ̃] nm tyrant ; **tyrannie** nf tyranny ; **tyrannique** a tyrannical ; **tyranniser** vt to tyrannize.
tzigane [dzigan] a, nm/f gipsy, tzigane // nm/f (Hungarian) gipsy, Tzigane.

U

ubiquité [ybikɥite] nf: **avoir le don d'~** to be everywhere at once ou be ubiquitous.
ulcère [ylsɛʀ] nm ulcer ; **~ à l'estomac** stomach ulcer.
ulcérer [ylseʀe] vt (MÉD) to ulcerate ; (fig) to sicken, appal.
ultérieur, e [ylteʀjœʀ] a later, subsequent ; **remis à une date ~e** postponed to a later date ; **~ement** ad later.

ultimatum [yltimatɔm] *nm* ultimatum.

ultime [yltim] *a* final.

ultra... [yltRa] *préfixe:* ~**moderne**/
-rapide ultra-modern/-fast; ~**-sensible** *a*
(*PHOTO*) high-speed; ~**-sons** *nmpl*
ultrasonics; ~**-violet, te** *a* ultraviolet.

un, une [œ̃, yn] *dét* a, an + *voyelle* //
pronom, num, a one; **l'un l'autre, les** ~**s**
les autres each other, one another; **l'**~
..., l'autre (the) one ..., the other; **les** ~**s**
..., les autres some ..., others; **l'**~ **et**
l'autre both (of them); **l'**~ **ou l'autre**
either (of them); **l'**~ **des meilleurs** one
of the best.

unanime [ynanim] *a* unanimous;
unanimité *nf* unanimity; **à l'unanimité**
unanimously.

uni, e [yni] *a* (*ton, tissu*) plain; (*surface*)
smooth, even; (*famille*) close(-knit); (*pays*)
united.

unification [ynifikasjɔ̃] *nf* uniting;
unification; standardization.

unifier [ynifje] *vt* to unite, unify;
(*systèmes*) to standardize, unify.

uniforme [ynifɔRm(ə)] *a* (*mouvement*)
regular, uniform; (*surface, ton*) even;
(*objets, maisons*) uniform // *nm* uniform;
être sous l'~ (*MIL*) to be serving;
uniformiser *vt* to make uniform;
(*systèmes*) to standardize; **uniformité** *nf*
regularity; uniformity; evenness.

unijambiste [ynizɑ̃bist(ə)] *nm/f* one-
legged man/woman.

unilatéral, e, aux [ynilateRal, -o] *a*
unilateral; **stationnement** ~ parking on
one side only.

union [ynjɔ̃] *nf* union; ~ **conjugale** union
of marriage; ~ **de consommateurs**
consumers' association; **l'U**~ **soviétique**
the Soviet Union.

unique [ynik] *a* (*seul*) only; (*le même*): **un**
prix/système ~ a single price/system;
(*exceptionnel*) unique; **ménage à salaire**
~ one-salary family; **route à voie** ~
single-lane road; **fils/fille** ~ only
son/daughter; ~ **en France** the only one
of its kind in France; ~**ment** *ad* only,
solely; (*juste*) only, merely.

unir [yniR] *vt* (*nations*) to unite; (*éléments,*
couleurs) to combine; (*en mariage*) to
unite, join together; ~ **qch à** to unite sth
with; to combine sth with; **s'**~ to unite;
(*en mariage*) to be joined together.

unisson [ynisɔ̃] à **l'**~ *ad* in unison.

unitaire [yniteR] *a* unitary; **prix** ~ price
per unit.

unité [ynite] *nf* (*harmonie, cohésion*) unity;
(*COMM, MIL, de mesure, MATH*) unit.

univers [yniveR] *nm* universe.

universel, le [yniveRsɛl] *a* universal;
(*esprit*) all-embracing.

universitaire [yniveRsiteR] *a* university
cpd; (*diplôme, études*) academic, university
cpd // *nm/f* academic.

université [yniveRsite] *nf* university.

uranium [yRanjɔm] *nm* uranium.

urbain, e [yRbɛ̃, -ɛn] *a* urban, city *cpd*,
town *cpd*; (*poli*) urbane; **urbaniser** *vt* to
urbanize; **urbanisme** *nm* town planning;
urbaniste *nm/f* town planner.

urgence [yRzɑ̃s] *nf* urgency; (*MÉD etc*)

emergency; **d'**~ *a* emergency *cpd* // *ad*
as a matter of urgency.

urgent, e [yRzɑ̃, -ɑ̃t] *a* urgent.

urinal, aux [yRinal, -o] *nm* (bed) urinal.

urine [yRin] *nf* urine; **uriner** *vi* to urinate;
urinoir *nm* (public) urinal.

urne [yRn(ə)] *nf* (*électorale*) ballot box;
(*vase*) urn; **aller aux** ~**s** (*voter*) to go to
the polls.

URSS [*parfois:* yRs] *sigle f:* **l'**~ the USSR.

urticaire [yRtikɛR] *nf* nettle rash.

us [ys] *nmpl:* ~ **et coutumes** (habits and)
customs.

U.S.A. *sigle mpl:* **les** ~ the U.S.A.

usage [yzaʒ] *nm* (*emploi, utilisation*) use;
(*coutume*) custom; (*LING*): **l'**~ usage; **faire**
~ **de** (*pouvoir, droit*) to exercise; **avoir**
l'~ **de** to have the use of; **à l'**~ *ad* with
use; **à l'**~ **de** (*pour*) for (use of); **en** ~
in use; **hors d'**~ out of service; wrecked;
à ~ **interne** to be taken; **à** ~ **externe**
for external use only.

usagé, e [yzaʒe] *a* (*usé*) worn; (*d'occasion*)
used.

usager, ère [yzaʒe, -ɛR] *nm/f* user.

usé, e [yze] *a* worn; (*banal*) hackneyed.

user [yze] *vt* (*outil*) to wear down;
(*vêtement*) to wear out; (*matière*) to wear
away; (*consommer: charbon etc*) to use;
s'~ *vi* to wear; to wear out; (*fig*) to
decline; **s'**~ **à la tâche** to wear o.s. out
with work; ~ **de** *vt* (*moyen, procédé*) to
use, employ; (*droit*) to exercise.

usine [yzin] *nf* factory; ~ **à gaz** gasworks
sg; ~ **marémotrice** tidal power station.

usiner [yzine] *vt* (*TECH*) to machine.

usité, e [yzite] *a* in common use,
common; **peu** ~ rarely used.

ustensile [ystɑ̃sil] *nm* implement; ~ **de**
cuisine kitchen utensil.

usuel, le [yzɥɛl] *a* everyday, common.

usufruit [yzyfRɥi] *nm* usufruct.

usuraire [yzyRɛR] *a* usurious.

usure [yzyR] *nf* wear; worn state; (*de*
l'usurier) usury; **avoir qn à l'**~ to wear
sb down; **usurier, ière** *nm/f* usurer.

usurper [yzyRpe] *vt* to usurp.

ut [yt] *nm* (*MUS*) C.

utérin, e [yteRɛ̃, -in] *a* uterine.

utérus [yteRys] *nm* uterus, womb.

utile [ytil] *a* useful.

utilisation [ytilizasjɔ̃] *nf* use.

utiliser [ytilize] *vt* to use.

utilitaire [ytilitɛR] *a* utilitarian; (*objets*)
practical.

utilité [ytilite] *nf* usefulness *q*; use; **jouer**
les ~**s** (*THÉÂTRE*) to play bit parts;
reconnu d'~ **publique** state-approved;
c'est d'une grande ~ it's of great use.

utopie [ytɔpi] *nf* utopian idea *ou* view;
utopia; **utopiste** *nm/f* utopian.

uvule [yvyl] *nf* uvula.

V

va *vb voir* **aller**.

vacance [vakɑ̃s] *nf* (*ADMIN*) vacancy; ~**s**
nfpl holiday(s *pl*), vacation *sg*; **prendre**
des/ses ~**s** to take a holiday/one's
holiday(s); **aller en** ~**s** to go on holiday;

vacancier, lère nm/f holiday-maker.
vacant, e [vakɑ̃, -ɑ̃t] a vacant.
vacarme [vakaʀm(ə)] nm row, din.
vaccin [vaksɛ̃] nm vaccine; (opération) vaccination; **vaccination** nf vaccination; **vacciner** vt to vaccinate; (fig) to make immune.
vache [vaʃ] nf (ZOOL) cow; (cuir) cowhide // a (fam) rotten, mean; ~ à eau (canvas) water bag; ~ à lait (péj) mug, sucker; ~ laitière dairy cow; **vachement** ad (fam) damned, hellish; **vacher, ère** nm/f cowherd; **vacherie** nf (fam) meanness q; dirty trick; nasty remark.
vaciller [vasije] vi to sway, wobble; (bougie, lumière) to flicker; (fig) to be failing, falter.
vacuité [vakɥite] nf emptiness, vacuity.
vade-mecum [vademekɔm] nm inv pocketbook.
vadrouiller [vadʀuje] vi to rove around ou about.
va-et-vient [vaevjɛ̃] nm inv (de pièce mobile) to and fro (ou up and down) movement; (de personnes, véhicules) comings and goings pl, to-ings and fro-ings pl.
vagabond, e [vagabɔ̃, -ɔ̃d] a wandering; (imagination) roaming, roving // nm (rôdeur) tramp, vagrant; (voyageur) wanderer.
vagabondage [vagabɔ̃daʒ] nm roaming, wandering; (JUR) vagrancy.
vagabonder [vagabɔ̃de] vi to roam, wander.
vagin [vaʒɛ̃] nm vagina.
vagissement [vaʒismɑ̃] nm cry (of newborn baby).
vague [vag] nf wave // a vague; (regard) faraway; (manteau, robe) loose(-fitting); (quelconque): un ~ bureau/cousin some office/cousin or other // nm: rester dans le ~ to keep things rather vague; regarder dans le ~ to gaze into space; ~ à l'âme nm vague melancholy; ~ d'assaut nf (MIL) wave of assault; ~ de chaleur nf heatwave; ~ de fond nf ground swell; ~ de froid nf cold spell; ~ment ad vaguely.
vaillant, e [vajɑ̃, -ɑ̃t] a (courageux) brave, gallant; (robuste) vigorous, hale and hearty; n'avoir plus un sou ~ to be penniless.
vaille vb voir **valoir**.
vain, e [vɛ̃, vɛn] a vain; en ~ ad in vain.
vaincre [vɛ̃kʀ(ə)] vt to defeat; (fig) to conquer, overcome; **vaincu, e** nm/f defeated party; **vainqueur** nm victor; (SPORT) winner // am victorious.
vais vb voir **aller**.
vaisseau, x [vɛso] nm (ANAT) vessel; (NAVIG) ship, vessel; ~ spatial spaceship.
vaisselier [vɛsəlje] nm dresser.
vaisselle [vɛsɛl] nf (service) crockery; (plats etc à laver) (dirty) dishes pl; (lavage) washing-up; **faire la** ~ to do the washing-up ou the dishes.
val, vaux ou **vals** [val, vo] nm valley.
valable [valabl(ə)] a valid; (acceptable) decent, worthwhile.

valent etc vb voir **valoir**.
valet [valɛ] nm valet; (CARTES) jack, knave; ~ de chambre manservant, valet; ~ de ferme farmhand; ~ de pied footman.
valeur [valœʀ] nf (gén) value; (mérite) worth, merit; (COMM: titre) security; **mettre en** ~ (bien) to exploit; (terrain, région) to develop; (fig) to highlight; to show off to advantage; **avoir de la** ~ to be valuable; **prendre de la** ~ to go up ou gain in value.
valeureux, euse [valœrø, -øz] a valorous.
valide [valid] a (en bonne santé) fit, well; (indemne) able-bodied, fit; (valable) valid; **valider** vt to validate; **validité** nf validity.
valions vb voir **valoir**.
valise [valiz] nf (suit)case; **la** ~ (diplomatique) the diplomatic bag.
vallée [vale] nf valley.
vallon [valɔ̃] nm small valley.
vallonné, e [valɔne] n undulating.
valoir [valwaʀ] vi (être valable) to hold, apply // vt (prix, valeur, effort) to be worth; (causer): ~ qch à qn to earn sb sth; **se** ~ to be of equal merit; (péj) to be two of a kind; **faire** ~ (droits, prérogatives) to assert; (domaine, capitaux) to exploit; **faire** ~ **que** to point out that; **à** ~ **sur** on account; **à** ~ **sur** to be deducted from; **vaille que vaille** somehow or other; **cela ne me dit rien qui vaille** I don't like the look of it at all; **ce climat ne me vaut rien** this climate doesn't suit me; ~ **la peine** to be worth the trouble ou worth it; ~ **mieux**: **il vaut mieux se taire** it's better to say nothing; **ça ne vaut rien** it's worthless; **que vaut ce candidat?** how good is this applicant?
valoriser [valɔʀize] vt (ÉCON) to develop (the economy of); (PSYCH) to increase the standing of.
valse [vals(ə)] nf waltz; **valser** vi to waltz; (fig): **aller valser** to go flying.
valu, e [valy] pp de **valoir**.
valve [valv(ə)] nf valve.
vandale [vɑ̃dal] nm/f vandal; **vandalisme** nm vandalism.
vanille [vanij] nf vanilla.
vanité [vanite] nf vanity; **vaniteux, euse** a vain, conceited.
vanne [van] nf gate.
vanner [vane] vt to winnow.
vannerie [vanʀi] nf basketwork.
vantail, aux [vɑ̃taj, -o] nm door, leaf (pl leaves).
vantard, e [vɑ̃taʀ, -aʀd(ə)] a boastful; **vantardise** nf boastfulness q; boast.
vanter [vɑ̃te] vt to speak highly of, vaunt; **se** ~ vi to boast, brag; **se** ~ **de** to boast of.
va-nu-pieds [vanypje] nm/f inv tramp, beggar.
vapeur [vapœʀ] nf steam; (émanation) vapour, fumes pl; ~**s** nfpl (bouffées) vapours; **à** ~ steam-powered, steam cpd; **à toute** ~ full steam ahead; (fig) at full tilt; **renverser la** ~ to reverse engines; (fig) to backtrack, backpedal; **cuit à la** ~ steamed.

vaporeux, euse [vapɔʀø, -øz] *a* (*flou*) hazy, misty; (*léger*) filmy, gossamer *cpd*.

vaporisateur [vapɔʀizatœʀ] *nm* spray.

vaporiser [vapɔʀize] *vt* (*CHIMIE*) to vaporize; (*parfum etc*) to spray.

vaquer [vake] *vi*: ~ **à ses occupations** to attend to one's affairs, go about one's business.

varappe [vaʀap] *nf* rock climbing; **varappeur, euse** *nm/f* (rock) climber.

varech [vaʀɛk] *nm* wrack, varec.

vareuse [vaʀøz] *nf* (*blouson*) pea jacket; (*d'uniforme*) tunic.

variable [vaʀjabl(ə)] *a* variable; (*temps, humeur*) changeable, variable; (*TECH: à plusieurs positions etc*) adaptable; (*LING*) inflectional; (*divers: résultats*) varied, various // *nf* (*MATH*) variable.

variante [vaʀjɑ̃t] *nf* variant.

variation [vaʀjusjɔ̃] *nf* variation; changing q, change.

varice [vaʀis] *nf* varicose vein.

varicelle [vaʀisɛl] *nf* chickenpox.

varié, e [vaʀje] *a* varied; (*divers*) various; **hors-d'œuvre** ~**s** selection of hors d'œuvres.

varier [vaʀje] *vi* to vary; (*temps, humeur*) to vary, change // *vt* to vary.

variété [vaʀjete] *nf* variety; **spectacle de** ~**s** variety show.

variole [vaʀjɔl] *nf* smallpox.

variqueux, euse [vaʀikø, -øz] *a* varicose.

vas *vb voir* **aller**.

vase [vɑz] *nm* vase // *nf* silt, mud; **en** ~ **clos** in isolation; ~ **de nuit** chamberpot; ~**s communicants** communicating vessels.

vaseline [vazlin] *nf* vaseline.

vaseux, euse [vɑzø, -øz] *a* silty, muddy; (*fig: confus*) woolly, hazy; (: *fatigué*) peaky; woozy.

vasistas [vazistɑs] *nm* fanlight.

vaste [vast(ə)] *a* vast, immense.

Vatican [vatikɑ̃] *nm*: **le** ~ the Vatican.

vaticiner [vatisine] *vi* (*péj*) to make pompous predictions.

va-tout [vatu] *nm*: **jouer son** ~ to stake one's all.

vaudeville [vodvil] *nm* vaudeville, light comedy.

vaudrai *etc vb voir* **valoir**.

vau-l'eau [volo]: **à** ~ *ad* with the current; (*fig*) adrift.

vaurien, ne [voʀjɛ̃, -ɛn] *nm/f* good-for-nothing, guttersnipe.

vautour [votuʀ] *nm* vulture.

vautrer [votʀe]: **se** ~ *vi*: **se** ~ **dans/sur** to wallow in/sprawl on.

vaux [vo] *pl de* **val** // *vb voir* **valoir**.

veau, x [vo] *nm* (*ZOOL*) calf (*pl* calves); (*CULIN*) veal; (*peau*) calfskin.

vecteur [vɛktœʀ] *nm* vector; (*MIL*) carrier.

vécu, e [veky] *pp de* **vivre** // *a* (*aventure*) real(-life).

vedette [vədɛt] *nf* (*artiste etc*) star; (*canot*) patrol boat; launch; **avoir la** ~ to top the bill, get star billing.

végétal, e, aux [veʒetal, -o] *a* vegetable // *nm* vegetable, plant.

végétarien, ne [veʒetaʀjɛ̃, -ɛn] *a, nm/f* vegetarian.

végétarisme [veʒetaʀism(ə)] *nm* vegetarianism.

végétation [veʒetɑsjɔ̃] *nf* vegetation; ~**s** *nfpl* (*MÉD*) adenoids.

végéter [veʒete] *vi* (*fig*) to vegetate; to stagnate.

véhément, e [veemɑ̃, -ɑ̃t] *a* vehement.

véhicule [veikyl] *nm* vehicle; ~ **utilitaire** commercial vehicle.

veille [vɛj] *nf* (*garde*) watch; (*PSYCH*) wakefulness; (*jour*): **la** ~ the day before, the previous day; **la** ~ **au soir** the previous evening; **la** ~ **de** the day before; **à la** ~ **de** on the eve of.

veillée [veje] *nf* (*soirée*) evening; (*réunion*) evening gathering; ~ **d'armes** night before combat; ~ (**mortuaire**) watch.

veiller [veje] *vi* to stay *ou* sit up; to be awake; to be on watch; to be watchful // *vt* (*malade, mort*) to watch over, sit up with; ~ **à** *vt* to attend to, see to; ~ **à ce que** to make sure that, see to it that; ~ **sur** *vt* to keep a watch *ou* an eye on; **veilleur de nuit** *nm* night watchman.

veilleuse [vɛjøz] *nf* (*lampe*) night light; (*AUTO*) sidelight; (*flamme*) pilot light; **en** ~ *a, ad* (*lampe*) dimmed.

veinard, e [venaʀ, -aʀd(ə)] *nm/f* (*fam*) lucky devil.

veine [vɛn] *nf* (*ANAT, du bois etc*) vein; (*filon*) vein, seam; (*fam: chance*): **avoir de la** ~ to be lucky; (*inspiration*) inspiration; **veiné, e** *a* veined; (*bois*) grained; **veineux, euse** *a* venous.

vêler [vele] *vi* to calve.

vélin [velɛ̃] *nm* vellum (paper).

velléitaire [veleitɛʀ] *a* irresolute, indecisive.

velléités [veleite] *nfpl* vague impulses.

vélo [velo] *nm* bike, cycle; **faire du** ~ to go cycling.

véloce [velɔs] *a* swift.

vélodrome [velodʀɔm] *nm* velodrome.

vélomoteur [velomɔtœʀ] *nm* light motorcycle.

velours [vəluʀ] *nm* velvet; ~ **côtelé** corduroy.

velouté, e [vəlute] *a* (*au toucher*) velvety; (*à la vue*) soft, mellow; (*au goût*) smooth, me.low // *nm*: ~ **d'asperges/de tomates** cream of asparagus/tomato (soup).

velu, e [vəly] *a* hairy.

venais *etc vb voir* **venir**.

venaison [vənɛzɔ̃] *nf* venison.

vénal, e, aux [venal, -o] *a* venal; ~**ité** *nf* venality.

venant [vənɑ̃]: **à tout** ~ *ad* to all and sundry.

vendange [vɑ̃dɑ̃ʒ] *nf* (*opération, période: aussi*: ~**s**) grape harvest; (*raisins*) grape crop, grapes *pl*.

vendanger [vɑ̃dɑ̃ʒe] *vi* to harvest the grapes; **vendangeur, euse** *nm/f* grape-picker.

vendeur, euse [vɑ̃dœʀ, -øz] *nm/f* (*de magasin*) shop assistant; sales assistant; (*COMM*) salesman/ woman // *nm* (*JUR*) vendor, seller; ~ **de journaux** newspaper seller.

vendre [vɑ̃dʀ(ə)] vt to sell; ~ qch à qn to sell sb sth; **cela se vend à la douzaine** these are sold by the dozen; **cela se vend bien** it's selling well; **'à ~'** 'for sale.'

vendredi [vɑ̃dʀədi] nm Friday; **V~ saint** Good Friday.

vénéneux, euse [venenø, -øz] a poisonous.

vénérable [venerabl(ə)] a venerable.

vénération [venerasjɔ̃] nf veneration.

vénérer [venere] vt to venerate.

vénérien, ne [venerjɛ̃, -ɛn] a venereal.

vengeance [vɑ̃ʒɑ̃s] nf vengeance q, revenge q; act of vengeance ou revenge

venger [vɑ̃ʒe] vt to avenge; **se ~** vi to avenge o.s.; (par rancune) to take revenge; **se ~ de qch** to avenge o.s. for sth; **se ~ de qn** to take one's revenge for sth; **se ~ sur** to wreak vengeance upon; to take revenge on ou through; to take it out on; **vengeur, eresse** a vengeful // nm/f avenger.

véniel, le [venjɛl] a venial.

venimeux, euse [vənimø, -øz] a poisonous, venomous; (fig: haineux) venomous, vicious.

venin [vənɛ̃] nm venom, poison.

venir [vəniʀ] vi to come; ~ **de** to come from; ~ **de faire: je viens d'y aller/de le voir** I've just been there/seen him; **s'il vient à pleuvoir** if it should rain, if it happens to rain; **j'en viens à croire que** I have come to believe that; **il en est venu à mendier** he has been reduced to begging; **faire ~** (docteur, plombier) to call (out).

vent [vɑ̃] nm wind; **il y a du ~** it's windy; **c'est du ~** it's all hot air; **au ~** to windward; **sous le ~** to leeward; **avoir le ~ debout/arrière** to head into the wind/have the wind astern; **dans le ~** (fam) trendy, with it; **prendre le ~** (fig) to see which way the wind blows; **avoir ~ de** to get wind of.

vente [vɑ̃t] nf sale; **la ~** (activité) selling; (secteur) sales pl; **mettre en ~** to put on sale; (objets personnels) to put up for sale; ~ **de charité** sale in aid of charity; ~ **aux enchères** auction sale.

venter [vɑ̃te] vb impersonnel: **il vente** the wind is blowing; **venteux, euse** a windswept, windy.

ventilateur [vɑ̃tilatœʀ] nm fan.

ventilation [vɑ̃tilasjɔ̃] nf ventilation.

ventiler [vɑ̃tile] vt to ventilate; (total, statistiques) to break down.

ventouse [vɑ̃tuz] nf (ampoule) cupping glass; (de caoutchouc) suction pad; (ZOOL) sucker.

ventre [vɑ̃tʀ(ə)] nm (ANAT) stomach; (fig) belly; **prendre du ~** to be getting a paunch; **avoir mal au ~** to have stomach ache.

ventricule [vɑ̃tʀikyl] nm ventricle.

ventriloque [vɑ̃tʀilɔk] nm/f ventriloquist.

ventripotent, e [vɑ̃tʀipɔtɑ̃, -ɑ̃t] a potbellied.

ventru, e [vɑ̃tʀy] a potbellied.

venu, e [vəny] pp de **venir** // a: **être mal ~ à ou de faire** to have no grounds for doing, be in no position to do // nf coming.

vêpres [vɛpʀ(ə)] nfpl vespers.

ver [vɛʀ] nm voir aussi **vers**; worm; (des fruits etc) maggot; (du bois) woodworm q; ~ **luisant** glow-worm; ~ **à soie** silkworm; ~ **solitaire** tapeworm; ~ **de terre** earthworm.

véracité [verasite] nf veracity.

véranda [verɑ̃da] nf veranda(h).

verbal, e, aux [vɛʀbal, -o] a verbal.

verbaliser [vɛʀbalize] vi (POLICE) to book ou report an offender.

verbe [vɛʀb(ə)] nm (LING) verb; (voix): **avoir le ~ sonore** to have a sonorous tone (of voice); (expression): **la magie du ~** the magic of language ou the word; (REL): **le V~** the Word.

verbeux, euse [vɛʀbø, -øz] a verbose, wordy.

verdâtre [vɛʀdɑtʀ(ə)] a greenish.

verdeur [vɛʀdœʀ] nf (vigueur) vigour, vitality; (crudité) forthrightness; (défaut de maturité) tartness, sharpness.

verdict [vɛʀdik(t)] nm verdict.

verdir [vɛʀdiʀ] vi, vt to turn green.

verdoyant, e [vɛʀdwajɑ̃, -ɑ̃t] a green, verdant.

verdure [vɛʀdyʀ] nf greenery, verdure.

véreux, euse [verø, -øz] a worm-eaten; (malhonnête) shady, corrupt.

verge [vɛʀʒ(ə)] nf (ANAT) penis; (baguette) stick, cane.

verger [vɛʀʒe] nm orchard.

verglacé, e [vɛʀglase] a icy, iced-over.

verglas [vɛʀgla] nm (black) ice.

vergogne [vɛʀgɔɲ]: **sans ~** ad shamelessly.

véridique [veridik] a truthful, veracious.

vérification [verifikasjɔ̃] nf checking q, check.

vérifier [verifje] vt to check; (corroborer) to confirm, bear out.

vérin [verɛ̃] nm jack.

véritable [veritabl(ə)] a real; (ami, amour) true; **un ~ désastre** an absolute disaster.

vérité [verite] nf truth; (d'un portrait romanesque) lifelikeness; (sincérité) truthfulness, sincerity.

vermeil, le [vɛʀmɛj] a bright red, ruby-red // nm (substance) vermeil.

vermicelles [vɛʀmisɛl] nmpl vermicelli sg.

vermillon [vɛʀmijɔ̃] a inv vermilion, scarlet.

vermine [vɛʀmin] nf vermin pl.

vermoulu, e [vɛʀmuly] a worm-eaten, with woodworm.

vermout(h) [vɛʀmut] nm vermouth.

verni, e [vɛʀni] a (fam) lucky; **cuir ~** patent leather.

vernir [vɛʀniʀ] vt (bois, tableau, ongles) to varnish; (poterie) to glaze.

vernis [vɛʀni] nm (enduit) varnish; glaze; (fig) veneer; ~ **à ongles** nail polish ou varnish.

vernissage [vɛʀnisaʒ] nm varnishing; glazing; (d'une exposition) preview.

vérole [verɔl] nf (variole) smallpox; (fam: syphilis) pox.

verrai etc vb voir **voir**.

verre [vɛʀ] nm glass; (de lunettes) lens sg; **boire ou prendre un ~** to have a drink;

~ **à vin/à liqueur** wine/liqueur glass ; ~ **à dents** tooth mug ; ~ **dépoli** frosted glass ; ~ **de lampe** lamp glass ou chimney ; ~ **de montre** watch glass ; ~ **à pied** stemmed glass ; ~**s de contact** contact lenses.

verrerie [vɛRRi] nf (fabrique) glassworks sg ; (activité) glass-making ; glass-working ; (objets) glassware.

verrière [vɛRjɛR] nf (grand vitrage) window ; (toit vitré) glass roof.

verrons etc vb voir **voir**.

verroterie [vɛRɔtRi] nf glass beads pl ou jewellery.

verrou [vɛRu] nm (targette) bolt ; (fig) constriction ; **mettre le** ~ **to bolt the door ; mettre qn sous les** ~**s** to put sb behind bars ; **verrouiller** vt to bolt ; (MIL: brèche) to close.

verrue [vɛRy] nf wart ; (fig) eyesore.

vers [vɛR]. nm line // nmpl (poésie) verse sg // prép (en direction de) toward(s) ; (près de) around (about) ; (temporel) about, around.

versant [vɛRsɑ̃] nm slopes pl, side.

versatile [vɛRsatil] a fickle, changeable.

verse [vɛRs(ə)]: **à** ~ ad: **il pleut à** ~ it's pouring (with rain).

versé, e [vɛRse] a: **être** ~ **dans** (science) to be (well-)versed in.

Verseau [vɛRso] nm: **le** ~ Aquarius, the water-carrier ; **être du** ~ to be Aquarius.

versement [vɛRsəmɑ̃] nm payment ; **en 3** ~**s** in 3 instalments.

verser [vɛRse] vt (liquide, grains) to pour ; (larmes, sang) to shed ; (argent) to pay ; (soldat: affecter): ~ **qn dans** to assign sb to // vi (véhicule) to overturn ; (fig): ~ **dans** to lapse into.

verset [vɛRsɛ] nm verse ; versicle.

verseur [vɛRsœR] am voir **bec**.

versifier [vɛRsifje] vt to put into verse // vi to versify, write verse.

version [vɛRsjɔ̃] nf version ; (SCOL) translation (into the mother tongue).

verso [vɛRso] nm back ; **voir au** ~ see over(leaf).

vert, e [vɛR, vɛRt(ə)] a green ; (vin) young ; (vigoureux) sprightly ; (cru) forthright // nm green ; ~ **d'eau** a inv sea-green ; ~ **pomme** a inv apple-green ; ~**-de-gris** nm verdigris // a inv grey(ish)-green.

vertébral, e, aux [vɛRtebRal, -o] a voir **colonne**.

vertèbre [vɛRtɛbR(ə)] nf vertebra (pl ae) ; **vertébré, e** a, nm/f vertebrate.

vertement [vɛRtəmɑ̃] ad (réprimander) sharply.

vertical, e, aux [vɛRtikal, -o] a, nf vertical ; **à la** ~**e** ad, ~**ement** ad vertically ; ~**ité** nf verticalness, verticality.

vertige [vɛRtiʒ] nm (peur du vide) vertigo ; (étourdissement) dizzy spell ; (fig) fever ; **vertigineux, euse** a breathtaking ; breathtakingly high (ou deep).

vertu [vɛRty] nf virtue ; **en** ~ **de** prép in accordance with ; ~**eux, euse** a virtuous.

verve [vɛRv(ə)] nf witty eloquence ; **être en** ~ to be in brilliant form.

verveine [vɛRvɛn] nf (BOT) verbena, vervain ; (infusion) verbena tea.

vésicule [vezikyl] nf vesicle ; ~ **biliaire** gall-bladder.

vespasienne [vɛspazjɛn] nf urinal.

vespéral, e, aux [vɛspeRal, -o] a vespertine, evening cpd.

vessie [vesi] nf bladder.

veste [vɛst(ə)] nf jacket ; ~ **droite/croisée** single-/double-breasted jacket.

vestiaire [vɛstjɛR] nm (au théâtre etc) cloakroom ; (de stade etc) changing-room.

vestibule [vɛstibyl] nm hall.

vestige [vɛstiʒ] nm relic ; trace ; (fig) remnant, vestige ; ~**s** nmpl remains ; remnants, relics.

vestimentaire [vɛstimɑ̃tɛR] a (dépenses) clothing ; (détail) of dress ; (élégance) sartorial.

veston [vɛstɔ̃] nm jacket.

vêtement [vɛtmɑ̃] nm garment, item of clothing ; (COMM): **le** ~ the clothing industry ; ~**s** nmpl clothes ; ~**s de sport** sportswear sg, sports clothes.

vétéran [veteRɑ̃] nm veteran.

vétérinaire [veteRinɛR] a veterinary // nm/f vet, veterinary surgeon.

vétille [vetij] nf trifle, triviality.

vétilleux, euse [vetijø, -øz] a punctilious.

vêtir [vetiR] vt to clothe, dress.

veto [veto] nm veto ; **opposer un** ~ **à** to veto.

vêtu, e [vety] pp de **vêtir** // a: ~ **de** dressed in, wearing ; **chaudement** ~ warmly dressed.

vétuste [vetyst(ə)] a ancient, timeworn.

veuf, veuve [vœf, vœv] a widowed // nm widower // nf widow.

veuille etc vb voir **vouloir**.

veule [vøl] a spineless.

veuvage [vœvaʒ] nm widowhood.

veuve [vœv] a, nf voir **veuf**.

veux vb voir **vouloir**.

vexations [vɛksɑsjɔ̃] nfpl humiliations.

vexatoire [vɛksatwaR] a: **mesures** ~**s** harassment sg.

vexer [vɛkse] vt to hurt, upset ; **se** ~ vi to be hurt, get upset.

viabiliser [vjabilize] vt to provide with services (water etc).

viabilité [vjabilite] nf viability ; (d'un chemin) practicability.

viable [vjabl(ə)] a viable.

viaduc [vjadyk] nm viaduct.

viager, ère [vjaʒe, -ɛR] a: **rente viagère** life annuity // nm: **mettre en** ~ to sell in return for a life annuity.

viande [vjɑ̃d] nf meat.

viatique [vjatik] nm (REL) viaticum ; (fig) provisions pl (ou money) for the journey.

vibraphone [vibRafɔn] nm vibraphone, vibes pl.

vibration [vibRɑsjɔ̃] nf vibration.

vibrer [vibRe] vi to vibrate ; (son, voix) to be vibrant ; (fig) to be stirred ; **faire** ~ to (cause to) vibrate ; to stir, thrill ; **vibro-masseur** nm vibrator.

vicaire [vikɛR] nm curate.

vice [vis] nm vice ; (défaut) fault ; ~ **de forme** legal flaw ou irregularity.

vice... [vis] *préfixe*: ~-consul *nm* vice-consul ; ~-président, e *nm/f* vice-président ; vice-chairman ; ~-roi *nm* viceroy.

vice-versa [visevɛrsa] *ad* vice versa.

vichy [viʃi] *nm* (*toile*) gingham ; (*eau*) Vichy water.

vicié, e [visje] *a* (*air*) polluted, tainted ; (*JUR*) invalidated.

vicieux, euse [visjø, -øz] *a* (*pervers*) dirty(-minded) ; nasty ; (*fautif*) incorrect, wrong.

vicinal, e, aux [visinal, -o] *a*: chemin ~ by-road, byway.

vicissitudes [visisityd] *nfpl* (trials and) tribulations.

vicomte [vikɔ̃t] *nm* viscount.

victime [viktim] *nf* victim ; (*d'accident*) casualty ; être (la) ~ de to be the victim of ; être ~ d'une attaque/d'un accident to suffer a stroke/be involved in an accident.

victoire [viktwar] *nf* victory ; victorieux, euse *a* victorious ; (*sourire, attitude*) triumphant.

victuailles [viktɥaj] *nfpl* provisions.

vidange [vidɑ̃ʒ] *nf* (*d'un fossé, réservoir*) emptying ; (*AUTO*) oil change ; (*de lavabo: bonde*) waste outlet ; ~s *nfpl* (*matières*) sewage *sg* ; faire la ~ (*AUTO*) to change the oil, do an oil change ; vidanger *vt* to empty.

vide [vid] *a* empty // *nm* (*PHYSIQUE*) vacuum : (*solution de continuité*) (empty) space, gap ; (*sous soi: dans une falaise etc*) drop ; (*futilité, néant*) void ; sous ~ *ad* in a vacuum ; emballé sous ~ vacuum packed ; à ~ *ad* (*sans occupants*) empty ; (*sans charge*) unladen ; (*TECH*) without gripping *ou* being in gear.

vide-ordures [vidɔrdyr] *nm inv* (rubbish) chute.

vide-poches [vidpɔʃ] *nm inv* tidy ; (*AUTO*) glove compartment.

vider [vide] *vt* to empty ; (*CULIN: volaille, poisson*) to gut, clean out ; (*régler: querelle*) to settle ; (*fatiguer*) to wear out ; (*fam: expulser*) to throw out, chuck out ; se ~ *vi* to empty ; ~ les lieux to quit *ou* vacate the premises ; videur *nm* (*de boîte de nuit*) bouncer.

vie [vi] *nf* life (*pl* lives) ; être en ~ to be alive ; sans ~ lifeless ; à ~ for life ; avoir la ~ dure to have nine lives ; to die hard ; mener la ~ dure à qn to make life a misery for sb.

vieil [vjɛj] *am voir* vieux.

vieillard [vjɛjar] *nm* old man ; les ~s old people, the elderly.

vieille [vjɛj] *a, nf voir* vieux.

vieilleries [vjɛjri] *nfpl* old things *ou* stuff *sg*.

vieillesse [vjɛjɛs] *nf* old age ; (*vieillards*): la ~ the old *pl*, the elderly *pl*.

vieillir [vjɛjir] *vi* (*prendre de l'âge*) to grow old ; (*population, vin*) to age ; (*doctrine, auteur*) to become dated // *vt* to age ; il a beaucoup vieilli he has aged a lot ; vieillissement *nm* growing old ; ageing.

vieillot, te [vjɛjo, -ɔt] *a* antiquated, quaint.

vielle [vjɛl] *nf* hurdy-gurdy.

vienne, viens *etc vb voir* venir.

vierge [vjɛrʒ(ə)] *a* virgin ; (*jeune fille*): être ~ to be a virgin // *nf* virgin ; (*signe*): la V~ Virgo, the Virgin ; être de la V~ to be Virgo ; ~ de (*sans*) free from, unsullied by.

vieux(vieil), vieille [vjø, vjɛj] *a* old // *nm/f* old man/woman // *nmpl* old people ; un petit ~ a little old man ; mon ~/ma vieille (*fam*) old man/girl ; prendre un coup de ~ to put years on ; un ~ de la vieille one of the old brigade ; ~ garçon *nm* bachelor ; ~ jeu *a inv* old-fashioned ; ~ rose *a inv* old rose ; vieil or *a inv* old gold ; vieille fille *nf* spinster.

vif, vive [vif, viv] *a* (*animé*) lively ; (*alerte*) sharp, quick ; (*brusque*) sharp, brusque ; (*aigu*) sharp ; (*lumière, couleur*) brilliant ; (*air*) crisp ; (*vent*) keen ; (*émotion*) keen, sharp ; (*fort: regret, déception*) great, deep ; (*vivant*): brûlé ~ burnt alive ; de vive voix personally ; piquer qn au ~ to cut sb to the quick ; tailler dans le ~ to cut into the living flesh ; à ~ (*plaie*) open ; avoir les nerfs à ~ to be on edge ; sur le ~ (*ART*) from life ; entrer dans le ~ du sujet to get to the very heart of the matter.

vif-argent [vifarʒɑ̃] *nm inv* quicksilver.

vigie [viʒi] *nf* look-out ; look-out post, crow's nest.

vigilance [viʒilɑ̃s] *nf* vigilance.

vigilant, e [viʒilɑ̃, -ɑ̃t] *a* vigilant.

vigne [viɲ] *nf* (*plante*) vine ; (*plantation*) vineyard ; ~ vierge Virginia creeper.

vigneron [viɲrɔ̃] *nm* wine grower.

vignette [viɲɛt] *nf* (*motif*) vignette ; (*de marque*) manufacturer's label *ou* seal ; (*ADMIN*) ≈ (road) tax disc ; price label (*on medicines for reimbursement by Social Security*).

vignoble [viɲɔbl(ə)] *nm* (*plantation*) vineyard ; (*vignes d'une région*) vineyards *pl*.

vigoureux, euse [vigurø, -øz] *a* vigorous, strong, robust.

vigueur [vigœr] *nf* vigour ; être/entrer en ~ to be in/come into force ; en ~ current.

vil, e [vil] *a* vile, base ; à ~ prix at a very low price.

vilain, e [vilɛ̃, -ɛn] *a* (*laid*) ugly ; (*affaire, blessure*) nasty ; (*pas sage: enfant*) naughty // *nm* (*paysan*) villein, villain ; ça va tourner au ~ it's going to turn nasty.

vilebrequin [vilbrəkɛ̃] *nm* (*outil*) (bit-)brace ; (*AUTO*) crankshaft.

vilenie [vilni] *nf* vileness *q*, baseness *q*.

vilipender [vilipɑ̃de] *vt* to revile, vilify.

villa [vila] *nf* (detached) house.

village [vilaʒ] *nm* village ; ~ de toile tent village ; villageois, e *a* village *cpd* // *nm/f* villager.

ville [vil] *nf* town ; (*importante*) city ; (*administration*): la ~ ≈ the Corporation ; ≈ the (town) council.

villégiature [vileʒiatyr] *nf* holiday ; (*holiday*) resort.

vin [vɛ̃] *nm* wine ; avoir le ~ gai to get happy after a few drinks ; ~ d'honneur reception (*with wine and snacks*) ; ~ de

messe mass wine; **~ ordinaire** table wine; **~ de pays** local wine.

vinaigre [vinɛgʀ(ə)] nm vinegar; **tourner au ~** (fig) to turn sour; **~ de vin/d'alcool** wine/spirit vinegar; **vinaigrette** nf vinaigrette, French dressing; **vinaigrier** nm (fabricant) vinegar-maker; (flacon) vinegar cruet ou bottle.

vinasse [vinas] nf (péj) cheap wine.

vindicatif, ive [vɛdikatif, -iv] a vindictive.

vindicte [vɛdikt(ə)] nf: **désigner qn à la ~ publique** to expose sb to public condemnation.

vineux, euse [vinø, -øz] a win(e)y.

vingt [vɛ̃, vɛ̃t + vowel and in 22 etc] num twenty; **vingtaine** nf: **une vingtaine (de)** around twenty, twenty or so; **vingtième** num twentieth.

vinicole [vinikɔl] a wine cpd, wine-growing.

vins etc vb voir **venir.**

viol [vjɔl] nm (d'une femme) rape; (d'un lieu sacré) violation.

violacé, e [vjɔlase] a purplish, mauvish.

violation [vjɔlasjɔ̃] nf desecration; violation.

violemment [vjɔlamɑ̃] ad violently.

violence [vjɔlɑ̃s] nf violence; **~s** nfpl acts of violence; **faire ~ à qn** to do violence to sb.

violent, e [vjɔlɑ̃, -ɑ̃t] a violent; (remède) drastic; (besoin, désir) intense, urgent.

violenter [vjɔlɑ̃te] vt to assault (sexually).

violer [vjɔle] vt (femme) to rape; (sépulture) to desecrate, violate; (réglement, traité) to violate.

violet, te [vjɔlɛ, -ɛt] a, nm purple, mauve // nf (fleur) violet.

violon [vjɔlɔ̃] nm violin; (fam: prison) lock-up; **premier ~** (MUS) first violin ou fiddle; **~ d'Ingres** (artistic) hobby.

violoncelle [vjɔlɔ̃sɛl] nm cello; **violoncelliste** nm/f cellist.

violoniste [vjɔlɔnist(ə)] nm/f violinist, violin-player.

vipère [vipɛʀ] nf viper, adder.

virage [viʀaʒ] nm (d'un véhicule) turn; (d'une route, piste) bend; (CHIMIE) change in colour; (de cuti-réaction) positive reaction; (PHOTO) toning; (fig: POL) change in policy; **prendre un ~** to go into a bend, take a bend; **~ sans visibilité** blind bend.

viral, e, aux [viʀal, -o] a viral.

virée [viʀe] nf (courte) run; (: à pied) walk; (longue) trip; hike, walking tour.

virement [viʀmɑ̃] nm (COMM) transfer; **~ bancaire/postal** (bank) credit/(National) Giro transfer.

virent vb voir aussi **voir.**

virer [viʀe] vt (COMM): **~ qch (sur)** to transfer sth (into); (PHOTO) to tone // vi to turn; (CHIMIE) to change colour; (cuti-réaction) to come up positive; (PHOTO) to tone; **~ au bleu** to turn blue; **~ de bord** to tack; **~ sur l'aile** to bank.

virevolte [viʀvɔlt(ə)] nf twirl; **virevolter** vi to twirl around.

virginité [viʀʒinite] nf virginity.

virgule [viʀgyl] nf comma; (MATH) point;

4 ~ 2 4 point 2; **~ flottante** floating decimal.

viril, e [viʀil] a (propre à l'homme) masculine; (énergique, courageux) manly, virile; **~ité** nf masculinity; manliness; (sexuelle) virility.

virtualité [viʀtɥalite] nf virtuality; potentiality.

virtuel, le [viʀtɥɛl] a potential; (théorique) virtual; **~lement** a potentially; (presque) virtually.

virtuose [viʀtɥoz] nm/f (MUS) virtuoso; (gén) master; **virtuosité** nf virtuosity; masterliness, masterful skills pl.

virulent, e [viʀylɑ̃, -ɑ̃t] a virulent.

virus [viʀys] nm virus.

vis vb [vi] voir **voir, vivre** // nf [vis] screw; **~ sans fin** worm, endless screw.

visa [viza] nm (sceau) stamp; (validation de passeport) visa; **~ de censure** (censor's) certificate.

visage [vizaʒ] nm face; **visagiste** nm/f beautician.

vis-à-vis [vizavi] ad face to face // nm person opposite; house etc opposite; **~ de** prép opposite; (fig) towards, vis-à-vis; **en ~** facing ou opposite each other, **sans ~** (immeuble) with an open outlook.

viscéral, e, aux [viseʀal, -o] a (fig) deep-seated, deep-rooted.

viscères [visɛʀ] nmpl intestines, entrails.

viscosité [viskozite] nf viscosity.

visée [vize] nf (avec une arme) aiming; (ARPENTAGE) sighting; **~s** nfpl (intentions) designs.

viser [vize] vi to aim // vt to aim at; (concerner) to be aimed ou directed at; (apposer un visa sur) to stamp, visa; **~ à qch/faire** to aim at sth/at doing ou to do.

viseur [vizœʀ] nm (d'arme) sights pl; (PHOTO) viewfinder.

visibilité [vizibilite] nf visibility.

visible [vizibl(ə)] a visible; (disponible): **est-il ~?** can he see me?, will he see visitors?

visière [vizjɛʀ] nf (de casquette) peak; (qui s'attache) eyeshade.

vision [vizjɔ̃] nf vision; (sens) (eye)sight, vision; (fait de voir): **la ~ de** the sight of; **première ~** (CINEMA) first showing; **visionnaire** a, nm/f visionary; **visionner** vt to view; **visionneuse** nf viewer.

visite [vizit] nf visit; (personne qui rend visite) visitor; (médicale, à domicile) visit, call; **la ~** (MÉD) (medical) consultations pl, surgery; (MIL: d'entrée) medicals pl; (: quotidienne) sick parade; **faire une ~ à qn** to call on sb, pay sb a visit; **rendre ~ à qn** to visit sb, pay sb a visit; **être en ~ (chez qn)** to be visiting (sb); **heures de ~** (hôpital, prison) visiting hours; **le droit de ~** (JUR: aux enfants) right of access, access; **~ de douane** customs inspection ou examination.

visiter [vizite] vt to visit; (musée, ville) to visit, go round; **visiteur, euse** nm/f visitor; **visiteur des douanes** customs inspector.

vison [vizɔ̃] nm mink.

visqueux, euse [viskø, -øz] a viscous; (péj) gooey; slimy.

visser [vise] vt: ~ qch (fixer, serrer) to screw sth on.

visu [vizy]: **de** ~ ad with one's own eyes.

visuel, le [vizɥɛl] a visual // nm (visual) display.

vit vb voir **voir, vivre**.

vital, e, aux [vital, -o] a vital.

vitalité [vitalite] nf vitality.

vitamine [vitamin] nf vitamin; **vitaminique** a vitamin cpd.

vite [vit] ad (rapidement) quickly, fast; (sans délai) quickly; soon; **faire** ~ to act quickly; to be quick; **viens** ~ come quick(ly).

vitesse [vitɛs] nf speed; (AUTO: dispositif) gear; **faire de la** ~ to drive fast ou at speed; **prendre qn de** ~ to outstrip sb; get ahead of sb; **prendre de la** ~ to pick up ou gather speed; **à toute** ~ at full ou top speed; ~ **acquise** momentum; ~ **du son** speed of sound.

viticole [vitikɔl] a wine cpd, wine-growing.

viticulteur [vitikyltœR] nm wine grower.

viticulture [vitikyltyR] nf wine growing.

vitrage [vitraʒ] nm (cloison) glass partition; (toit) glass roof; (rideau) net curtain.

vitrail, aux [vitRaj, -o] nm stained-glass window.

vitre [vitR(ə)] nf (window) pane; (de portière, voiture) window.

vitré, e [vitRe] a glass cpd.

vitrer [vitRe] vt to glaze.

vitreux, euse [vitRø, -øz] a vitreous; (terne) glassy.

vitrier [vitRije] nm glazier.

vitrifier [vitRifje] vt to vitrify; (parquet) to glaze.

vitrine [vitRin] nf (devanture) (shop) window; (étalage) display; (petite armoire) display cabinet; **en** ~ in the window, on display; ~ **publicitaire** display case, showcase.

vitriol [vitRijɔl] nm vitriol; **au** ~ (fig) vitriolic.

vitupérer [vitypeRe] vi to rant and rave; ~ **contre** to rail against.

vivable [vivabl(ə)] a (personne) livable-with; (endroit) fit to live in.

vivace a [vivas] (arbre, plante) hardy; (fig) indestructible, inveterate // ad [vivatʃe] (MUS) vivace.

vivacité [vivasite] nf liveliness, vivacity; sharpness; brilliance.

vivant, e [vivɑ̃, -ɑ̃t] a (qui vit) living, alive; (animé) lively; (preuve, exemple) living // nm: **du** ~ **de qn** in sb's lifetime; **les** ~**s** **et les morts** the living and the dead.

vivats [viva] nmpl cheers.

vive [viv] af voir **vif** // vb voir **vivre** // excl: ~ **le roi!** long live the king!; ~ **les vacances!** hurrah for the holidays!; ~**ment** ad vivaciously; sharply // excl: ~**ment les vacances!** I can't wait for the holidays!, roll on the holidays!

viveur [vivœR] nm (péj) high liver, pleasure-seeker.

vivier [vivje] nm fish tank; fishpond.

vivifiant, e [vivifjɑ̃, -ɑ̃t] a invigorating.

vivions vb voir **vivre**.

vivisection [vivisɛksjɔ̃] nf vivisection.

vivoter [vivɔte] vi to rub along, struggle along.

vivre [vivR(ə)] vi, vt to live // nm: **le** ~ **et le logement** board and lodging; ~**s** nmpl provisions, food supplies; **il vit encore** he is still alive; **se laisser** ~ to take life as it comes; **ne plus** ~ (être anxieux) to live on one's nerves; **il a vécu** (eu une vie aventureuse) he has seen life; **ce régime a vécu** this regime has had its day; **être facile à** ~ to be easy to get on with; **faire** ~ **qn** (pourvoir à sa subsistance) to provide (a living) for sb; ~ **mal** (chichement) to have a meagre existence; ~ **de** (salaire etc) to live on.

vlan [vlɑ̃] excl wham!, bang!

vocable [vɔkabl(ə)] nm term.

vocabulaire [vɔkabylɛR] nm vocabulary.

vocal, e, aux [vɔkal, -o] a vocal.

vocalique [vɔkalik] a vocalic, vowel cpd.

vocalise [vɔkaliz] nf singing exercise.

vocation [vɔkasjɔ̃] nf vocation, calling.

vociférations [vɔsifeRɑsjɔ̃] nfpl cries of rage, screams.

vociférer [vɔsifeRe] vi, vt to scream.

vodka [vɔdka] nf vodka.

vœu, x [vø] nm wish; (à Dieu) vow; **faire** ~ **de** to take a vow of; ~**x de bonne année** best wishes for the New Year; **avec tous nos** ~**x** with every good wish ou our best wishes.

vogue [vɔg] nf fashion, vogue.

voguer [vɔge] vi to sail.

voici [vwasi] prép (pour introduire, désigner) here is + sg, here are + pl; **et** ~ **que...** and now it (ou he)...; voir aussi **voilà**.

voie [vwa] nf way; (RAIL) track, line; (AUTO) lane; **suivre la** ~ **hiérarchique** to go through official channels; **être en bonne** ~ to be shaping ou going well; **mettre qn sur la** ~ to put sb on the right track; **être en** ~ **d'achèvement/de rénovation** to be nearing completion/in the process of renovation; **à** ~ **étroite** narrow-gauge; **route à 2/3** ~**s** 2-/3-lane road; **par la** ~ **aérienne/maritime** by air/sea; ~ **d'eau** (NAVIG) leak; ~ **ferrée** track; railway line; **par** ~ **ferrée** by rail; ~ **de garage** (RAIL) siding; **la** ~ **lactée** the Milky Way; ~ **navigable** waterway; ~ **privée** private road; **la** ~ **publique** the public highway.

voilà [vwala] prép (en désignant) there is + sg, there are + pl; **les** ~ ou **voici here ou there they are; **en** ~ ou **voici un** here's one, there's one; ~ ou **voici deux ans** two years ago; ~ ou **voici deux ans que** it's two years since; **et** ~**!** there we are!; ~ **tout** that's all; **'**~ ou **voici!'** (en offrant etc) 'there ou here you are'.

voile [vwal] nm veil; (tissu léger) net // nf sail; (sport) sailing; **prendre le** ~ to take the veil; **mettre à la** ~ to make way under sail; ~ **du palais** nm soft palate, velum; ~ **au poumon** nm shadow on the lung.

voiler [vwale] vt to veil; (fausser: roue) to buckle; (: bois) to warp; **se** ~ vi (lune, regard) to mist over; (ciel) to grow hazy; (voix) to become husky; (roue, disque) to buckle; (*planche*) to warp; **se ~ la face** to hide one's face.

voilette [vwalɛt] *nf* (hat) veil.

voilier [vwalje] *nm* sailing ship; (*de plaisance*) sailing boat.

voilure [vwalyʀ] *nf* (*de voilier*) sails *pl*; (*d'avion*) aerofoils *pl*; (*de parachute*) canopy.

voir [vwaʀ] *vi*, *vt* to see; **se ~: se ~ critiquer/transformer** to be criticized/transformed; **cela se voit** (*cela arrive*) it happens; (*c'est visible*) that's obvious, it shows; **~ venir** (*fig*) to wait and see; **faire ~ qch à qn** to show sb sth; **en faire ~ à qn** (*fig*) to give sb a hard time; **ne pas pouvoir ~ qn** (*fig*) not to be able to stand sb; **regardez ~** just look; **dites-~** tell me; **voyons!** let's see now; (*indignation etc*) come (along) now!; **avoir quelque chose à ~ avec** to have something to do with.

voire [vwaʀ] *ad* indeed; nay.

voirie [vwaʀi] *nf* highway maintenance; (*administration*) highways department; (*enlèvement des ordures*) refuse collection.

voisin, e [vwazɛ̃, -in] *a* (*proche*) neighbouring; (*contigu*) next; (*ressemblant*) connected // *nm/f* neighbour; **voisinage** *nm* (*proximité*) proximity; (*environs*) vicinity; (*quartier, voisins*) neighbourhood; **relations de bon voisinage** neighbourly terms; **voisiner** *vi*: **voisiner avec** to be side by side with.

voiture [vwatyʀ] *nf* car; (*wagon*) coach, carriage; **~ d'enfant** pram; **~ d'infirme** invalid carriage; **~ de sport** sports car; **~-lit** sleeper.

voix [vwa] *nf* voice; (*POL*) vote; **à haute ~** aloud; **à ~ basse** in a low voice; **à 2/4 ~** (*MUS*) in 2/4 parts; **avoir ~ au chapitre** to have a say in the matter; **mettre aux ~** to put to the vote.

vol [vɔl] *nm* (*mode de locomotion*) flying; (*trajet, voyage, groupe d'oiseaux*) flight; (*mode d'appropriation*) theft, stealing; (*larcin*) theft; **à ~ d'oiseau** as the crow flies; **au ~: attraper qch au ~** to catch sth as it flies past; **prendre son ~** to take flight; **en ~** in flight; **~ avec effraction** breaking and entering q, break-in; **~ libre** ou **sur aile delta** hang-gliding; **~ à main armée** armed robbery; **~ de nuit** night flight; **~ à voile** gliding.

volage [vɔlaʒ] *a* fickle.

volaille [vɔlaj] *nf* (*oiseaux*) poultry *pl*; (*viande*) poultry q; (*oiseau*) fowl; **volailler** *nm* poulterer.

volant, e [vɔlɑ̃, -ɑ̃t] *a voir* **feuille** etc // *nm* (*d'automobile*) (steering) wheel; (*de commande*) wheel; (*objet lancé*) shuttlecock; (*jeu*) battledore and shuttlecock; (*bande de tissu*) flounce; (*feuillet détachable*) tear-off portion; **les ~s** (*AVIAT*) the flight staff

volatil, e [vɔlatil] *a* volatile

volatile [vɔlatil] *nm* (*volaille*) bird; (*tout oiseau*) winged creature

volatiliser [vɔlatilize] **se ~** *vi* (*CHIMIE*) to volatilize; (*fig*) to vanish into thin air

vol-au-vent [vɔlovɑ̃] *nm inv* vol-au-vent

volcan [vɔlkɑ̃] *nm* volcano; **volcanique** *a*

volcanic; **volcanologue** *nm/f* vulcanologist.

volée [vɔle] *nf* (*groupe d'oiseaux*) flight, flock; (*TENNIS*) volley; **~ de coups/de flèches** volley of blows/arrows; **à la ~: rattraper à la ~** to catch in mid air; **lancer à la ~** to fling about; **à toute ~** (*sonner les cloches*) vigorously; (*lancer un projectile*) with full force.

voler [vɔle] *vi* (*avion, oiseau, fig*) to fly; (*voleur*) to steal // *vt* (*objet*) to steal; (*personne*) to rob; **~ qch à qn** to steal sth from sb.

volet [vɔlɛ] *nm* (*de fenêtre*) shutter; (*AVIAT*) flap; (*de feuillet, document*) section; **trié sur le ~** hand-picked.

voleter [vɔlte] *vi* to flutter (about).

voleur, euse [vɔlœʀ, -øz] *nm/f* thief (*pl* thieves) // *a* thieving.

volière [vɔljɛʀ] *nf* aviary.

volontaire [vɔlɔ̃tɛʀ] *a* voluntary; (*caractère, personne: décidé*) self-willed // *nm/f* volunteer; **volontariat** *nm* voluntary service.

volonté [vɔlɔ̃te] *nf* (*faculté de vouloir*) will; (*énergie, fermeté*) will(power); (*souhait, désir*) wish; **se servir/boire à ~** to take/drink as much as one likes; **bonne ~** goodwill, willingness; **mauvaise ~** lack of goodwill, unwillingness.

volontiers [vɔlɔ̃tje] *ad* (*de bonne grâce*) willingly; (*avec plaisir*) willingly, gladly; (*habituellement, souvent*) readily, willingly; **'~'** 'with pleasure', 'I'd be glad to'.

volt [vɔlt] *nm* volt; **~age** *nm* voltage.

volte-face [vɔltafas] *nf inv* about-turn.

voltige [vɔltiʒ] *nf* (*ÉQUITATION*) trick riding; (*au cirque*) acrobatic feat; (*AVIAT*) (aerial) acrobatics *sg*; **numéro de haute ~** acrobatic act.

voltiger [vɔltiʒe] *vi* to flutter (about).

voltigeur, euse [vɔltiʒœʀ, -øz] *nm/f* (*au cirque*) acrobat.

voltmètre [vɔltmɛtʀ(ə)] *nm* voltmeter.

volubile [vɔlybil] *a* voluble.

volume [vɔlym] *nm* volume; (*GÉOM: solide*) solid; **volumineux, euse** *a* voluminous, bulky.

volupté [vɔlypte] *nf* sensual delight ou pleasure; **voluptueux, euse** *a* voluptuous.

volute [vɔlyt] *nf* (*ARCHIT*) volute; **~ de fumée** curl of smoke.

vomi [vɔmi] *nm* vomit.

vomir [vɔmiʀ] *vi* to vomit, be sick // *vt* to vomit, bring up; (*fig*) to belch out, spew out; (*exécrer*) to loathe, abhor; **vomissement** *nm* vomiting q; **vomissure** *nf* vomit q; **vomitif** *nm* emetic.

vont [vɔ̃] *vb voir* **aller.**

vorace [vɔʀas] *a* voracious.

vos [vo] *dét voir* **votre.**

votant, e [vɔtɑ̃, -ɑ̃t] *nm/f* voter.

vote [vɔt] *nm* vote; **~ par correspondance/procuration** postal/ proxy vote.

voter [vɔte] *vi* to vote // *vt* (*loi, décision*) to vote for.

votre [vɔtʀ(ə)], *pl* **vos** [vo] *dét* your.

vôtre [votʀ(ə)] *pronom*: **le ~, la ~, les ~s** yours; **les ~s** (*fig*) your family ou folks; **à la ~** (*toast*) your (good) health!

voudrai etc vb voir **vouloir**.

voué, e [vwe] a: ~ à doomed to, destined for.

vouer [vwe] vt: ~ qch à (Dieu/un saint) to dedicate sth to; ~ **sa vie/son temps à** (étude, cause etc) to devote one's life/time to; ~ **une haine/amitié éternelle à qn** to vow undying hatred/love to sb.

vouloir [vulwaʀ] vi to show will, have willpower // vt to want // nm: **le bon ~ de qn** sb's goodwill; sb's pleasure; ~ **que qn fasse** to want sb to do; **je voudrais ceci** I would like this; **veuillez attendre** please wait; **je veux bien** (bonne volonté) I'll be happy to; (concession) fair enough, that's fine; **si on veut** (en quelque sorte) if you like; **que me veut-il?** what does he want with me?; ~ **dire (que)** (signifier) to mean (that); **sans le ~** (involontairement) without meaning to, unintentionally; **en ~ à qn** to bear sb a grudge; **en ~ à qch** (avoir des visées sur) to be after sth; **s'en ~ de** to be annoyed with o.s. for; ~ **de qch/qn** (accepter) to want sth/sb.

voulu, e [vuly] a (requis) required, requisite; (délibéré) deliberate, intentional.

vous [vu] pronom you; (objet indirect) (to) you; (réfléchi) yourself, pl yourselves; (réciproque) each other // nm: **employer le ~** (vouvoyer) to use the 'vous' form; ~-**même** yourself; ~-**mêmes** yourselves.

voûte [vut] nf vault; ~ **du palais** (ANAT) roof of the mouth; ~ **plantaire** arch (of the foot).

voûté, e [vute] a vaulted, arched; (dos, personne) bent, stooped.

voûter [vute] vt (ARCHIT) to arch, vault; **se** ~ vi (dos, personne) to become stooped.

vouvoyer [vuvwaje] vt: ~ **qn** to address sb as 'vous'.

voyage [vwajaʒ] nm journey, trip; (fait de voyager): **le** ~ travel(ling); **partir/être en** ~ to go off/be away on a journey ou trip; **faire un** ~ to go on ou make a trip ou journey; **faire bon** ~ to have a good journey; ~ **d'agrément/d'affaires** pleasure/business trip; ~ **de noces** honeymoon; ~ **organisé** package tour.

voyager [vwajaʒe] vi to travel; **voyageur, euse** nm/f traveller; (passager) passenger; **voyageur (de commerce)** commercial traveller.

voyant, e [vwajɑ̃, -ɑ̃t] a (couleur) loud, gaudy // nm (signal) (warning) light // nf clairvoyant.

voyelle [vwajɛl] nf vowel.

voyeur, euse [vwajœʀ, -øz] nm/f voyeur; peeping Tom.

voyou [vwaju] nm lout, hoodlum; (enfant) guttersnipe // a loutish.

vrac [vʀak]: **en** ~ ad higgledy-piggledy; (COMM) in bulk.

vrai, e [vʀɛ] a (véridique: récit, faits) true; (non factice, authentique) real; à ~ **dire** to tell the truth; **être dans le** ~ to be right.

vraiment [vʀɛmɑ̃] ad really.

vraisemblable [vʀɛsɑ̃blabl(ə)] a (plausible) likely, plausible; (probable) likely, probable; ~**ment** ad in all likelihood, very likely.

vraisemblance [vʀɛsɑ̃blɑ̃s] nf likelihood, plausibility; (romanesque) verisimilitude.

vrille [vʀij] nf (de plante) tendril; (outil) gimlet; (spirale) spiral; (AVIAT) spin.

vriller [vʀije] vt to bore into, pierce.

vrombir [vʀɔ̃biʀ] vi to hum.

vu [vy] prép (en raison de) in view of; ~ **que** in view of the fact that.

vu, e [vy] pp de **voir** // a: **bien/mal** ~ (fig) well/poorly thought of; good/bad form // nm: **au** ~ **et au su de tous** openly and publicly.

vue [vy] nf (fait de voir): **la** ~ **de** the sight of; (sens, faculté) (eye)sight; (panorama, image, photo) view; (spectacle) sight; ~**s** nfpl (idées) views; (dessein) designs; **perdre la** ~ to lose one's (eye)sight; **perdre de** ~ to lose sight of; **à la** ~ **de tous** in full view of everybody; **hors de** ~ out of sight; **à première** ~ at first sight; **connaître de** ~ to know by sight; **à** ~ (COMM) at sight; **tirer à** ~ to shoot on sight; **à** ~ **d'œil** ad visibly; at a quick glance; **en** ~ (visible) in sight; (COMM) in the public eye; **avoir qch en** ~ (intentions) to have one's sights on sth; **en** ~ **de** (arriver, être) within sight of; **en** ~ **de faire** with the intention of doing, with a view to doing; ~ **de l'esprit** theoretical view.

vulcaniser [vylkanize] vt to vulcanize.

vulgaire [vylgɛʀ] a (grossier) vulgar, coarse; (trivial) commonplace, mundane; (péj: quelconque): **de** ~**s touristes/chaises de cuisine** common tourists/kitchen chairs; (BOT, ZOOL: non latin) common; ~**ment** ad vulgarly, coarsely; (communément) commonly; **vulgarisation** nf: **ouvrage de vulgarisation** popularizing work, popularization; **vulgariser** vt to popularize; to coarsen; **vulgarité** nf vulgarity, coarseness.

vulnérable [vylneʀabl(ə)] a vulnerable.

vulve [vylv(ə)] nf vulva.

W X Y Z

wagon [vagɔ̃] nm (de voyageurs) carriage; (de marchandises) truck, wagon; ~-**citerne** nm tanker; ~-**lit** nm sleeper, sleeping car; ~-**poste** nm mail van; ~-**restaurant** nm restaurant ou dining car.

wallon, ne [valɔ̃, -ɔn] a Walloon.

waters [watɛʀ] nmpl toilet sg, loo sg.

watt [wat] nm watt.

w.-c. [vese] nmpl toilet sg, lavatory sg.

week-end [wikɛnd] nm weekend.

western [wɛstɛʀn] nm western.

whisky, pl whiskies [wiski] nm whisky.

x [iks] nm: **plainte contre X** (JUR) action against person or persons unknown; **l'X** the École Polytechnique.

xénophobe [ksenɔfɔb] nm/f xenophobe.

xérès [gzeʀɛs] nm sherry.

xylographie [ksilɔgʀafi] nf xylography; (image) xylograph.

xylophone [ksilɔfɔn] nm xylophone.

y [i] *ad* (*à cet endroit*) there; (*dessus*) on it (*ou* them); (*dedans*) in it (*ou* them) // *pronom* (*about ou on ou of*) it: *vérifier la syntaxe du verbe employé*; **j'~ pense** I'm thinking about it; *voir aussi* **aller, avoir.**

yacht [jɔt] *nm* yacht.

yaourt [jauʀt] *nm* yoghourt.

yeux [jø] *pl de* **œil.**

yoga [jɔga] *nm* yoga.

yoghourt [jɔguʀt] *nm* = **yaourt.**

yole [jɔl] *nf* skiff.

yougoslave [jugɔslav] *a, nm/f* Yugoslav(ian).

Yougoslavie [jugɔslavi] *nf* Yugoslavia.

youyou [juju] *nm* dinghy.

yo-yo [jojo] *nm inv* yo-yo.

zèbre [zɛbʀ(ə)] *nm* (*ZOOL*) zebra.

zébré, e [zebʀe] *a* striped, streaked; **zébrure** *nf* stripe, streak.

zélateur, trice [zelatœʀ, -tʀis] *nm/f* partisan, zealot.

zèle [zɛl] *nm* zeal; **faire du ~** (*péj*) to be over-zealous; **zélé, e** *a* zealous.

zénith [zenit] *nm* zenith.

zéro [zeʀo] *nm* zero, nought; **au-dessous de ~** below zero (Centigrade) *ou* freezing; **partir de ~** to start from scratch; **trois (buts) à ~** 3 (goals to) nil.

zeste [zɛst(ə)] *nm* peel, zest; **un ~ de citron** a piece of lemon peel.

zézayer [zezeje] *vi* to have a lisp.

zibeline [ziblin] *nf* sable.

zigzag [zigzag] *nm* zigzag; **zigzaguer** *vi* to zigzag (along).

zinc [zɛ̃g] *nm* (*CHIMIE*) zinc; (*comptoir*) bar, counter.

zizanie [zizani] *nf*: **semer la ~** to stir up ill-feeling.

zizi [zizi] *nm* (*fam*) willy.

zodiaque [zɔdjak] *nm* zodiac.

zona [zona] *nm* shingles *sg*.

zone [zon] *nf* zone, area; (*quartiers*): **la ~** the slum belt; **~ bleue** ≈ restricted parking area.

zoo [zoo] *nm* zoo.

zoologie [zɔɔlɔʒi] *nf* zoology; **zoologique** *a* zoological; **zoologiste** *nm/f* zoologist.

Z.U.P. [zyp] *sigle f* = **zone à urbaniser en priorité**, ≈ (planned) housing scheme.

zut [zyt] *excl* dash (it)!

ENGLISH-FRENCH
ANGLAIS-FRANÇAIS

A

a, an [eɪ, ə, æn, ən, n] *det* un(e); **3 a day/week** 3 par jour/semaine; **10 km an hour** 10 km à l'heure.

A [eɪ] *n* (MUS) la *m*.

A.A. *n abbr of* Automobile Association; Alcoholics Anonymous.

aback [ə'bæk] *ad*: **to be taken ~** être stupéfait(e).

abacus, *pl* **abaci** ['æbəkəs, -saɪ] *n* boulier *m*.

abandon [ə'bændən] *vt* abandonner // *n* abandon *m*.

abashed [ə'bæʃt] *a* confus(e), embarrassé(e).

abate [ə'beɪt] *vi* s'apaiser, se calmer.

abattoir ['æbətwɑ:*] *n* abattoir *m*.

abbey ['æbɪ] *n* abbaye *f*.

abbot ['æbət] *n* père supérieur.

abbreviate [ə'bri:vɪeɪt] *vt* abréger; **abbreviation** [-'eɪʃən] *n* abréviation *f*.

abdicate ['æbdɪkeɪt] *vt,vi* abdiquer; **abdication** [-'keɪʃən] *n* abdication *f*.

abdomen ['æbdəmɛn] *n* abdomen *m*; **abdominal** [æb'dɔmɪnl] *a* abdominal(e).

abduct [æb'dʌkt] *vt* enlever; **abduction** [-ʃən] *n* enlèvement *m*.

abet [ə'bɛt] *vt* encourager; aider.

abeyance [ə'beɪəns] *n*: **in ~** (*law*) en désuétude; (*matter*) en suspens.

abhor [əb'hɔ:*] *vt* abhorrer, exécrer; **~rent** *a* odieux(euse), exécrable.

abide [ə'baɪd], *pt,pp* **abode** *or* **abided** [ə'baɪd, ə'baud] *vt* souffrir, supporter; **to ~ by** *vt fus* observer, respecter.

ability [ə'bɪlɪtɪ] *n* compétence *f*; capacité *f*; talent *m*.

ablaze [ə'bleɪz] *a* en feu, en flammes; **~ with light** resplendissant de lumière.

able ['eɪbl] *a* compétent(e); **to be ~ to do sth** pouvoir faire qch, être capable de faire qch; **~-bodied** *a* robuste; **ably** *ad* avec compétence *or* talent, habilement.

abnormal [æb'nɔ:məl] *a* anormal(e); **~ity** [-'mælɪtɪ] *n* anomalie *f*.

aboard [ə'bɔ:d] *ad* à bord // *prep* à bord de.

abode [ə'baud] *pt,pp* of **abide**.

abolish [ə'bɔlɪʃ] *vt* abolir.

abolition [æbəu'lɪʃən] *n* abolition *f*.

abominable [ə'bɔmɪnəbl] *a* abominable.

aborigine [æbə'rɪdʒɪnɪ] *n* aborigène *m/f*.

abort [ə'bɔ:t] *vt* faire avorter; **~ion** [ə'bɔ:ʃən] *n* avortement *m*; **~ive** *a* manqué(e).

abound [ə'baund] *vi* abonder; **to ~ in** abonder en, regorger de.

about [ə'baut] *prep* au sujet de, à propos de // *ad* environ; (*here and there*) de côté et d'autre, çà et là; **it takes ~ 10 hours** ça prend environ *or* à peu près 10 heures; **at ~ 2 o'clock** vers 2 heures; **it's ~ here** c'est par ici, c'est dans les parages; **to walk ~ the town** se promener dans *or* à travers la ville; **to be ~ to**: **he was**

~ to cry il allait pleurer, il était sur le point de pleurer; **what** *or* **how ~ doing this?** et si nous faisions ceci?; **~ turn** *n* demi-tour *m*.

above [ə'bʌv] *ad* au-dessus // *prep* au-dessus de; **mentioned** ~ mentionné ci-dessus; **costing ~ £10** coûtant plus de 10 livres; ~ **all** par-dessus tout, surtout; **~board** *a* franc(franche), loyal(e), honnête.

abrasion [ə'breɪʒən] *n* frottement *m*; (*on skin*) écorchure *f*.

abrasive [ə'breɪzɪv] *a* abrasif(ive); (*fig*) caustique, agressif(ive).

abreast [ə'brɛst] *ad* de front; **to keep ~ of** se tenir au courant de.

abridge [ə'brɪdʒ] *vt* abréger.

abroad [ə'brɔ:d] *ad* à l'étranger.

abrupt [ə'brʌpt] *a* (*steep, blunt*) abrupt(e); (*sudden, gruff*) brusque.

abscess ['æbsɪs] *n* abcès *m*.

abscond [əb'skɔnd] *vi* disparaître, s'enfuir.

absence ['æbsəns] *n* absence *f*.

absent ['æbsənt] *a* absent(e); **~ee** [-'ti:] *n* absent/e; **~eeism** [-'ti:ɪzəm] *n* absentéisme *m*; **~-minded** *a* distrait(e); **~-mindedness** *n* distraction *f*.

absolute ['æbsəlu:t] *a* absolu(e); **~ly** [-'lu:tlɪ] *ad* absolument.

absolve [əb'zɔlv] *vt*: **to ~ sb (from)** (*sin etc*) absoudre qn (de); **to ~ sb from** (*oath*) délier qn de.

absorb [əb'zɔ:b] *vt* absorber; **to be ~ed in a book** être plongé dans un livre; **~ent** *a* absorbant(e); **~ent cotton** *n* (*US*) coton *m* hydrophile; **~ing** *a* absorbant(e).

abstain [əb'steɪn] *vi*: **to ~ (from)** s'abstenir (de).

abstemious [əb'sti:mɪəs] *a* sobre, frugal(e).

abstention [əb'stɛnʃən] *n* abstention *f*.

abstinence ['æbstɪnəns] *n* abstinence *f*.

abstract *a and n* ['æbstrækt] *a* abstrait(e) // *n* (*summary*) résumé *m* // *vt* [æb'strækt] extraire.

absurd [əb'sə:d] *a* absurde; **~ity** *n* absurdité *f*.

abundance [ə'bʌndəns] *n* abondance *f*; **abundant** *a* abondant(e).

abuse *n* [ə'bju:s] abus *m*; insultes *fpl*, injures *fpl* // *vt* [ə'bju:z] abuser de; **abusive** *a* grossier(ère), injurieux(euse).

abysmal [ə'bɪzməl] *a* exécrable; (*ignorance etc*) sans bornes.

abyss [ə'bɪs] *n* abime *m*, gouffre *m*.

academic [ækə'dɛmɪk] *a* universitaire; (*pej: issue*) oiseux(euse), purement théorique // *n* universitaire *m/f*; **~ freedom** *n* liberté *f* académique.

academy [ə'kædəmɪ] *n* (*learned body*) académie *f*; (*school*) collège *m*; **military/naval ~** école militaire/navale; **~ of music** conservatoire *m*.

accede [æk'si:d] *vi*: to ~ to (*request*, *throne*) accéder à.

accelerate [æk'sɛləreɪt] *vt,vi* accélérer; **acceleration** [-'reɪʃən] *n* accélération *f*; **accelerator** *n* accélérateur *m*.

accent ['æksənt] *n* accent *m*.

accept [ək'sɛpt] *vt* accepter; ~able *a* acceptable; ~ance *n* acceptation *f*.

access ['æksɛs] *n* accès *m*; to have ~ to (*information, library etc*) avoir accès à, pouvoir utiliser *or* consulter; (*person*) avoir accès auprès de; ~ible [æk'sɛsəbl] *a* accessible; ~ion [æk'sɛʃən] *n* accession *f*.

accessory [æk'sɛsərɪ] *n* accessoire *m*; toilet **accessories** *npl* articles *mpl* de toilette.

accident ['æksɪdənt] *n* accident *m*; (*chance*) hasard *m*; by ~ par hasard; accidentellement; ~al [-'dɛntl] *a* accidentel(le); ~ally [-'dɛntəlɪ] *ad* accidentellement; ~-prone *a* sujet(te) aux accidents.

acclaim [ə'kleɪm] *vt* acclamer // *n* acclamation *f*.

acclimatize [ə'klaɪmətaɪz] *vt*: to become ~d s'acclimater.

accommodate [ə'kɔmədeɪt] *vt* loger, recevoir; (*oblige, help*) obliger; (*adapt*): to ~ one's plans to adapter ses projets à.

accommodating [ə'kɔmədeɪtɪŋ] *a* obligeant(e), arrangeant(e).

accommodation [əkɔmə'deɪʃən] *n* logement *m*; he's found ~ il a trouvé à se loger; they have ~ for 500 ils peuvent recevoir 500 personnes, il y a de la place pour 500 personnes.

accompaniment [ə'kʌmpənɪmənt] *n* accompagnement *m*.

accompanist [ə'kʌmpənɪst] *n* accompagnateur/trice.

accompany [ə'kʌmpənɪ] *vt* accompagner.

accomplice [ə'kʌmplɪs] *n* complice *m/f*.

accomplish [ə'kʌmplɪʃ] *vt* accomplir; ~ed *a* accompli(e); ~ment *n* accomplissement *m*; réussite *f*, résultat *m*; ~ments *npl* talents *mpl*.

accord [ə'kɔ:d] *n* accord *m* // *vt* accorder; of his own ~ de son plein gré; ~ance *n*: in ~ance with conformément à; ~ing to *prep* selon; ~ingly *ad* en conséquence.

accordion [ə'kɔ:dɪən] *n* accordéon *m*.

accost [ə'kɔst] *vt* accoster, aborder.

account [ə'kaunt] *n* (COMM) compte *m*; (*report*) compte rendu; récit *m*; by all ~s au dire de tous; of little ~ de peu d'importance; on ~ en acompte; on no ~ en aucun cas; on ~ of à cause de; to take into ~, take ~ of tenir compte de; to ~ for expliquer, rendre compte de; ~able *a* responsable.

accountancy [ə'kauntənsɪ] *n* comptabilité *f*.

accountant [ə'kauntənt] *n* comptable *m/f*.

accredited [ə'krɛdɪtɪd] *a* accrédité(e); admis(e).

accretion [ə'kri:ʃən] *n* accroissement *m*.

accrue [ə'kru:] *vi* s'accroître; ~d interest intérêt couru.

accumulate [ə'kju:mjuleɪt] *vt* accumuler, amasser // *vi* s'accumuler, s'amasser; **accumulation** [-'leɪʃən] *n* accumulation *f*.

accuracy ['ækjurəsɪ] *n* exactitude *f*, précision *f*.

accurate ['ækjurɪt] *a* exact(e), précis(e); ~ly *ad* avec précision.

accusation [ækju'zeɪʃən] *n* accusation *f*.

accusative [ə'kju:zətɪv] *n* (LING) accusatif *m*.

accuse [ə'kju:z] *vt* accuser; ~d *n* accusé/e.

accustom [ə'kʌstəm] *vt* accoutumer, habituer; ~ed *a* (*usual*) habituel(le); ~ed to habitué *or* accoutumé à.

ace [eɪs] *n* as *m*; within an ~ of à deux doigts or un cheveu de.

ache [eɪk] *n* mal *m*, douleur *f* // *vi* (*be sore*) faire mal, être douloureux(euse); my head ~s j'ai mal à la tête; I'm aching all over j'ai mal partout.

achieve [ə'tʃi:v] *vt* (*aim*) atteindre; (*victory, success*) remporter, obtenir; (*task*) accomplir; ~ment *n* exploit *m*, réussite *f*.

acid ['æsɪd] *a,n* acide (*m*); ~ity [ə'sɪdɪtɪ] *n* acidité *f*.

acknowledge [ək'nɔlɪdʒ] *vt* (*letter*) accuser réception de; (*fact*) reconnaître; ~ment *n* accusé *m* de réception.

acne ['æknɪ] *n* acné *m*.

acorn ['eɪkɔ:n] *n* gland *m*.

acoustic [ə'ku:stɪk] *a* acoustique; ~s *n,npl* acoustique *f*.

acquaint [ə'kweɪnt] *vt*: to ~ sb with sth mettre qn au courant de qch; to be ~ed with (*person*) connaître; ~ance *n* connaissance *f*.

acquire [ə'kwaɪə*] *vt* acquérir.

acquisition [ækwɪ'zɪʃən] *n* acquisition *f*.

acquisitive [ə'kwɪzɪtɪv] *a* qui a l'instinct de possession or le goût de la propriété.

acquit [ə'kwɪt] *vt* acquitter; to ~ o.s. well bien se comporter, s'en tirer très honorablement; ~tal *n* acquittement *m*.

acre ['eɪkə*] *n* acre *f* (= 4047 m²); ~age *n* superficie *f*.

acrimonious [ækrɪ'məunɪəs] *a* acrimonieux(euse), aigre.

acrobat ['ækrəbæt] *n* acrobate *m/f*.

acrobatics [ækrəu'bætɪks] *n,npl* acrobatie *f*.

across [ə'krɔs] *prep* (*on the other side*) de l'autre côté de; (*crosswise*) en travers de // *ad* de l'autre côté; en travers; to walk ~ (the road) traverser (la route); to take sb ~ the road faire traverser la route à qn; a road ~ the wood une route qui traverse le bois; ~ from en face de.

act [ækt] *n* acte *m*, action *f*; (THEATRE) acte; (*in music-hall etc*) numéro *m*; (LAW) loi *f* // *vi* agir; (THEATRE) jouer; (*pretend*) jouer la comédie // *vt* (*part*) jouer, tenir; to ~ Hamlet tenir or jouer le rôle d'Hamlet; to ~ the fool faire l'idiot; to ~ as servir de; ~ing *a* suppléant(e), par intérim // *n* (*of actor*) jeu *m*; (*activity*): to do some ~ing faire du théâtre (or du cinéma).

action ['ækʃən] *n* action *f*; (MIL) combat(s) *m(pl)*; (LAW) procès *m*, action en justice; out of ~ hors de combat; hors d'usage; to take ~ agir, prendre des mesures.

activate ['æktɪveɪt] *vt* (*mechanism*)

actionner, faire fonctionner; (CHEM, PHYSICS) activer.

active ['æktɪv] a actif(ive); (volcano) en activité; ~ly ad activement.

activity [æk'tɪvɪtɪ] n activité f.

actor ['æktə*] n acteur m.

actress ['æktrɪs] n actrice f.

actual ['æktjuəl] a réel(le), véritable; ~ly ad réellement, véritablement; en fait.

acumen ['ækjumən] n perspicacité f.

acupuncture ['ækjupʌŋktʃə*] n acupuncture f.

acute [ə'kju:t] a aigu(ë); (mind, observer) pénétrant(e).

ad [æd] n abbr of **advertisement**.

A.D. ad (abbr of Anno Domini) ap. J.-C.

Adam ['ædəm] n Adam m; ~'s apple n pomme f d'Adam.

adamant ['ædəmənt] a inflexible.

adapt [ə'dæpt] vt adapter // vi: **to ~ (to)** s'adapter (à); ~**able** a (device) adaptable; (person) qui s'adapte facilement; ~**ation** [ædæp'teɪʃən] n adaptation f; ~**er** n (ELEC) adapteur m.

add [æd] vt ajouter; (figures: also: **to ~ up**) additionner // vi: **to ~ to** (increase) ajouter à, accroître.

adder ['ædə*] n vipère f.

addict ['ædɪkt] n intoxiqué m; (fig) fanatique m/f; ~**ed** [ə'dɪktɪd] a: **to be ~ed to** (drink etc) être adonné à; (fig: football etc) être un fanatique de; ~**ion** [ə'dɪkʃən] n (MED) dépendance f.

adding machine ['ædɪŋməʃi:n] n machine f à calculer.

addition [ə'dɪʃən] n addition f; **in ~** de plus; de surcroît; **in ~ to** en plus de; ~**al** a supplémentaire.

additive ['ædɪtɪv] n additif m.

addled ['ædld] a (egg) pourri(e).

address [ə'drɛs] n adresse f; (talk) discours m, allocution f // vt adresser; (speak to) s'adresser à.

adenoids ['ædɪnɔɪdz] npl végétations fpl.

adept ['ædɛpt] a: ~ **at** expert(e) à or en.

adequate ['ædɪkwɪt] a adéquat(e); suffisant(e); compétent(e); ~**ly** ad de façon adéquate.

adhere [əd'hɪə*] vi: **to ~ to** adhérer à; (fig: rule, decision) se tenir à.

adhesion [əd'hi:ʒən] n adhésion f.

adhesive [əd'hi:zɪv] a adhésif(ive) // n adhésif m.

adjacent [ə'dʒeɪsənt] a adjacent(e); ~ **to** adjacent à.

adjective ['ædʒɛktɪv] n adjectif m.

adjoining [ə'dʒɔɪnɪŋ] a voisin(e), adjacent(e), attenant(e) // prep voisin de, adjacent à.

adjourn [ə'dʒə:n] vt ajourner // vi suspendre la séance; lever la séance; clore la session; (go) se retirer.

adjust [ə'dʒʌst] vt ajuster, régler; rajuster // vi: **to ~ (to)** s'adapter (à); ~**able** a réglable; ~**ment** n ajustage m, réglage m; (of prices, wages) rajustement m; (of person) adaptation f.

adjutant ['ædʒətənt] n adjudant m.

ad-lib [æd'lɪb] vt,vi improviser // n improvisation f // ad: **ad lib** à volonté, à discrétion.

administer [əd'mɪnɪstə*] vt administrer; (justice) rendre.

administration [ədmɪnɪs'treɪʃən] n administration f.

administrative [əd'mɪnɪstrətɪv] a administratif(ive).

administrator [əd'mɪnɪstreɪtə*] n administrateur/trice.

admirable ['ædmərəbl] a admirable.

admiral ['ædmərəl] n amiral m; A~**ty** n amirauté f; ministère m de la Marine.

admiration [ædmə'reɪʃən] n admiration f.

admire [əd'maɪə*] vt admirer; ~**r** n admirateur/trice.

admission [əd'mɪʃən] n admission f; (to exhibition, night club etc) entrée f; (confession) aveu m.

admit [əd'mɪt] vt laisser entrer; admettre; (agree) reconnaître, admettre; **to ~ of** admettre, permettre; **to ~ to** reconnaître, avouer; ~**tance** n admission f, (droit m d')entrée f; ~**tedly** ad il faut en convenir.

admonish [əd'mɔnɪʃ] vt donner un avertissement à; réprimander.

ado [ə'du:] n: **without (any) more ~** sans plus de cérémonies.

adolescence [ædəu'lɛsns] n adolescence f.

adolescent [ædəu'lɛsnt] a,n adolescent(e).

adopt [ə'dɔpt] vt adopter; ~**ed** a adoptif(ive), adopté(e); ~**ion** [ə'dɔpʃən] n adoption f.

adore [ə'dɔ:*] vt adorer; **adoringly** ad avec adoration.

adorn [ə'dɔ:n] vt orner; ~**ment** n ornement m.

adrenalin [ə'drɛnəlɪn] n adrénaline f.

Adriatic (Sea) [eɪdrɪ'ætɪk(si:)] n Adriatique f.

adrift [ə'drɪft] ad à la dérive.

adroit [ə'drɔɪt] a adroit(e), habile.

adult ['ædʌlt] n adulte m/f.

adulterate [ə'dʌltəreɪt] vt frelater, falsifier.

adultery [ə'dʌltərɪ] n adultère m.

advance [əd'vɑ:ns] n avance f // vt avancer // vi s'avancer; **in ~** en avance, d'avance; ~**d** a avancé(e); (SCOL: studies) supérieur(e); ~**ment** n avancement m.

advantage [əd'vɑ:ntɪdʒ] n (also TENNIS) avantage m; **to take ~ of** profiter de; ~**ous** [ædvən'teɪdʒəs] a avantageux(euse).

advent ['ædvənt] n avènement m, venue f; A~ Avent m.

adventure [əd'vɛntʃə*] n aventure f; **adventurous** [-tʃərəs] a aventureux(euse).

adverb ['ædvə:b] n adverbe m.

adversary ['ædvəsərɪ] n adversaire m/f.

adverse ['ædvə:s] a contraire, adverse; **in ~ circumstances** dans l'adversité; ~ **to** hostile à.

adversity [əd'və:sɪtɪ] n adversité f.

advert ['ædvə:t] n abbr of **advertisement**.

advertise ['ædvətaɪz] vi(vt) faire de la publicité or de la réclame (pour); mettre une annonce (pour vendre).

advertisement [əd'və:tɪsmənt] n (COMM) réclame f, publicité f; (in classified ads) annonce f.

advertising ['ædvətaɪzɪŋ] n publicité f, réclame f.

advice [əd'vaɪs] n conseils mpl; (notification) avis m; piece of ~ conseil.

advisable [əd'vaɪzəbl] a recommandable, indiqué(e).

advise [əd'vaɪz] vt conseiller; to ~ sb of sth aviser or informer qn de qch; ~r n conseiller/ère; **advisory** [-əri] a consultatif(ive).

advocate vt ['ædvəkeɪt] recommander, prôner.

aegis ['iːdʒɪs] n: under the ~ of sous l'égide de.

aerial ['ɛərɪəl] n antenne f // a aérien(ne).

aeroplane ['ɛərəpleɪn] n avion m.

aerosol ['ɛərəsɔl] n aérosol m.

aesthetic [ɪs'θɛtɪk] a esthétique.

afar [ə'fuː] ad: from ~ de loin.

affable ['æfəbl] a affable.

affair [ə'fɛə] n affaire f; (also: love ~) liaison f; aventure f.

affect [ə'fɛkt] vt affecter; ~ation [æfɛk'teɪʃən] n affectation f; ~ed a affecté(e).

affection [ə'fɛkʃən] n affection f; ~ate a affectueux(euse); ~ately ad affectueusement.

affiliated [ə'fɪlɪeɪtɪd] a affilié(e).

affinity [ə'fɪnɪtɪ] n affinité f.

affirmation [æfə'meɪʃən] n affirmation f, assertion f.

affirmative [ə'fəːmətɪv] a affirmatif(ive) // n: in the ~ dans or par l'affirmative.

affix [ə'fɪks] vt apposer, ajouter.

afflict [ə'flɪkt] vt affliger; ~ion [ə'flɪkʃən] n affliction f, détresse f.

affluence ['æfluəns] n abondance f, opulence f.

affluent ['æfluənt] a abondant(e); opulent(e); (person) dans l'aisance, riche.

afford [ə'fɔːd] vt se permettre; avoir les moyens d'acheter or d'entretenir; (provide) fournir, procurer; I can't ~ the time je n'ai vraiment pas le temps.

affray [ə'freɪ] n échauffourée f.

affront [ə'frʌnt] n affront m; ~ed a insulté(e).

afield [ə'fiːld] ad: far ~ loin.

afloat [ə'fləut] a à flot // ad: to stay ~ surnager; to keep/get a business ~ maintenir à flot/lancer une affaire.

afoot [ə'fut] ad: there is something ~ il se prépare quelque chose.

aforesaid [ə'fɔːsɛd] a susdit(e), susmentionné(e).

afraid [ə'freɪd] a effrayé(e); to be ~ of or to avoir peur de; I am ~ that je crains que + sub.

afresh [ə'frɛʃ] ad de nouveau.

Africa ['æfrɪkə] n Afrique f; ~n a africain(e) // n Africain/e.

aft [uːft] ad à l'arrière, vers l'arrière.

after ['uːftə] prep,ad après // cj après que, après avoir or être + pp; what/who are you ~? que/qui cherchez-vous?; ask ~ him demandez de ses nouvelles; ~ all après tout; ~-effects npl répercussions fpl; (of illness) séquelles fpl, suites fpl; ~life n vie future; ~math n conséquences fpl; in the ~math of dans

les mois or années etc qui suivirent, au lendemain de; ~noon n après-midi m or f; ~-shave (lotion) n after-shave m; ~thought n: I had an ~thought il m'est venu une idée après coup; ~wards ad après.

again [ə'gɛn] ad de nouveau; to begin/see ~ recommencer/revoir; not ... ~ ne ... plus; ~ and ~ à plusieurs reprises; he's opened it ~ il l'a rouvert, il l'a de nouveau or il l'a encore ouvert.

against [ə'gɛnst] prep contre; ~ a blue background sur un fond bleu.

age [eɪdʒ] n âge m // vt,vi vieillir; it's been ~s since ça fait une éternité que; to come of ~ atteindre sa majorité; ~d a âgé(e); ~d 10 âgé de 10 ans; the ~d ['eɪdʒɪd] les personnes âgées; ~ group n tranche f d'âge; ~less a sans âge; ~ limit n limite f d'âge.

agency ['eɪdʒənsɪ] n agence f; through or by the ~ of par l'entremise or l'action de.

agenda [ə'dʒɛndə] n ordre m du jour.

agent ['eɪdʒənt] n agent m.

aggravate ['ægrəveɪt] vt aggraver; (annoy) exaspérer.

aggravation [ægrə'veɪʃən] n (of quarrel) envenimement m.

aggregate ['ægrɪgeɪt] n ensemble m, total m; on ~ (SPORT) au goal average.

aggression [ə'grɛʃən] n agression f.

aggressive [ə'grɛsɪv] a agressif(ive); ~ness n agressivité f.

aggrieved [ə'griːvd] a chagriné(e), affligé(e).

aghast [ə'guːst] a consterné(e), atterré(e).

agile ['ædʒaɪl] a agile.

agitate ['ædʒɪteɪt] vt rendre inquiet(ète) or agité(e); agiter // vi faire de l'agitation (politique); to ~ for faire campagne pour; **agitator** n agitateur/trice (politique).

ago [ə'gəu] ad: 2 days ~ il y a deux jours; not long ~ il n'y a pas longtemps.

agonizing ['ægənaɪzɪŋ] a angoissant(e); déchirant(e).

agony ['ægənɪ] n grande souffrance or angoisse; to be in ~ souffrir le martyre.

agree [ə'griː] vt (price) convenir de // vi: to ~ (with) (person) être d'accord (avec); (statements etc) concorder (avec); (LING) s'accorder (avec); to ~ to do accepter de or consentir à faire; to ~ to sth consentir à qch; to ~ that (admit) convenir or reconnaître que; they ~ on this ils sont d'accord sur ce point; they ~d on going/a price ils se mirent d'accord pour y aller/sur un prix; **garlic doesn't ~ with me** je ne supporte pas l'ail; ~able a agréable; (willing) consentant(e), d'accord; are you ~able to this? est-ce que cela vous va or convient?; ~d a (time, place) convenu(e); to be ~d être d'accord; ~ment n accord m; in ~ment d'accord.

agricultural [ægrɪ'kʌltʃərəl] a agricole.

agriculture ['ægrɪkʌltʃə] n agriculture f.

aground [ə'graund] ad: to run ~ s'échouer.

ahead [ə'hɛd] ad en avant; devant; ~ of devant; (fig: schedule etc) en avance sur; ~ of time en avance; go right or straight ~ allez tout droit; they were (right) ~

of us ils nous précédaient (de peu), ils étaient (juste) devant nous.

aid [eɪd] n aide f // vt aider ; **to ~ and abet** (LAW) se faire le complice de.

aide [eɪd] n (person) collaborateur/trice, assistant/e.

ailment ['eɪlmənt] n petite maladie, affection f.

aim [eɪm] vt: **to ~ sth at** (such as gun, camera) braquer or pointer qch sur, diriger qch contre ; (missile) lancer qch à or contre or en direction de ; (remark, blow) destiner or adresser qch à // vi (also: **to take ~**) viser // n but m ; **to ~ at** viser ; (fig) viser (à) ; avoir pour but or ambition ; **to ~ to do** avoir l'intention de faire ; **~less** a sans but ; **~lessly** ad sans but, à l'aventure.

air [ɛə*] n air m // vt aérer ; (grievances, ideas) exposer (librement) // cpd (currents, attack etc) aérien(ne) ; **~bed** n matelas m pneumatique ; **~borne** a en vol ; aeroporté(e) ; **~-conditioned** a climatisé(e), à air conditionné ; **~ conditioning** n climatisation f ; **~-cooled** a à refroidissement à air ; **~craft** n,pl inv avion m ; **~craft carrier** n porte-avions m inv ; **~ cushion** n coussin m d'air ; **A-Force** n Armée f de l'air ; **~gun** n fusil m à air comprimé ; **~ hostess** n hôtesse f de l'air ; **~ily** ad d'un air dégagé ; **~letter** n aérogramme m ; **~lift** n pont aérien ; **~line** n ligne aérienne ; compagnie f d'aviation ; **~liner** n avion m de ligne ; **~lock** n sas m ; **by ~mail** par avion ; **~port** n aéroport m ; **~ raid** n attaque aérienne ; **~sick** a qui a le mal de l'air ; **~strip** n terrain m d'atterrissage ; **~tight** a hermétique ; **~y** a bien aéré(e) ; (manners) dégagé(e).

aisle [aɪl] n (of church) allée centrale ; nef latérale.

ajar [ə'dʒɑ:*] a entrouvert(e).

alarm [ə'lɑ:m] n alarme f // vt alarmer ; **~ clock** n réveille-matin m, réveil m ; **~ist** n alarmiste m/f.

Albania [æl'beɪnɪə] n Albanie f.

album ['ælbəm] n album m ; (L.P.) 33 tours m inv.

albumen ['ælbjumɪn] n albumine f ; (of egg) albumen m.

alchemy ['ælkɪmɪ] n alchimie f.

alcohol ['ælkəhɔl] n alcool m ; **~ic** [-'hɔlɪk] a,n alcoolique (m/f) ; **~ism** n alcoolisme m.

alcove ['ælkəuv] n alcôve f.

alderman ['ɔ:ldəmən] n conseiller municipal (en Angleterre).

ale [eɪl] n bière f.

alert [ə'lə:t] a alerte, vif(vive) ; vigilant(e) // n alerte f ; **on the ~** sur le qui-vive ; (MIL) en état d'alerte.

algebra ['ældʒɪbrə] n algèbre m.

Algeria [æl'dʒɪərɪə] n Algérie f ; **~n** a algérien(ne) // n Algérien/ne.

Algiers [æl'dʒɪəz] n Alger.

alias ['eɪlɪæs] ad alias // n faux nom, nom d'emprunt.

alibi ['ælɪbaɪ] n alibi m.

alien ['eɪlɪən] n étranger/ère // a: **~ (to/from)** étranger(ère) (à) ; **~ate** vt aliéner ; s'aliéner ; **~ation** [-'neɪʃən] n aliénation f.

alight [ə'laɪt] a,ad en feu // vi mettre pied à terre ; (passenger) descendre ; (bird) se poser.

align [ə'laɪn] vt aligner ; **~ment** n alignement m.

alike [ə'laɪk] a semblable, pareil(le) // ad de même ; **to look ~** se ressembler.

alimony ['ælɪmənɪ] n (payment) pension f alimentaire.

alive [ə'laɪv] a vivant(e) ; (active) plein(e) de vie ; **~ with** grouillant(e) de ; **~ to** sensible à.

alkali ['ælkəlaɪ] n alcali m.

all [ɔ:l] a tout(e), tous(toutes) pl // pronoun tout m ; (pl) tous(toutes) // ad tout ; **~ wrong/alone** tout faux/seul ; **~ the time/his life** tout le temps/toute sa vie ; **~ five** (tous) les cinq ; **~ of them** tous, toutes ; **~ of it** tout ; **~ of us went** nous y sommes tous allés ; **not as hard etc as ~ that** pas si dur etc que ça ; **~ in ~** à tout prendre, l'un dans l'autre.

allay [ə'leɪ] vt (fears) apaiser, calmer.

allegation [ælɪ'geɪʃən] n allégation f.

allege [ə'lɛdʒ] vt alléguer, prétendre ; **~dly** [ə'lɛdʒɪdlɪ] ad à ce que l'on prétend, paraît-il.

allegiance [ə'li:dʒəns] n fidélité f, obéissance f.

allegory ['ælɪgərɪ] n allégorie f.

all-embracing ['ɔ:lɪm'breɪsɪŋ] a universel(le).

allergic [ə'lə:dʒɪk] a: **~ to** allergique à.

allergy ['ælədʒɪ] n allergie f.

alleviate [ə'li:vɪeɪt] vt soulager, adoucir.

alley ['ælɪ] n ruelle f ; (in garden) allée f.

alliance [ə'laɪəns] n alliance f.

allied ['ælaɪd] a allié(e).

alligator ['ælɪgeɪtə*] n alligator m.

all-important ['ɔ:lɪm'pɔ:tənt] a capital(e), crucial(e).

all-in ['ɔ:lɪn] a (also ad: charge) tout compris ; **~ wrestling** n catch m.

alliteration [əlɪtə'reɪʃən] n allitération f.

all-night ['ɔ:l'naɪt] a ouvert(e) or qui dure toute la nuit.

allocate ['æləkeɪt] vt (share out) répartir, distribuer ; (duties): **to ~ sth to** assigner or attribuer qch à ; (sum, time): **to ~ sth to** allouer qch à ; **to ~ sth for** affecter qch à.

allocation [æləu'keɪʃən] n: **~ (of money)** crédit(s) m(pl), somme(s) allouée(s).

allot [ə'lɔt] vt (share out) répartir, distribuer ; (time): **to ~ sth to** allouer qch à ; (duties): **to ~ sth to** assigner qch à ; **~ment** n (share) part f ; (garden) lopin m de terre (loué à la municipalité).

all-out ['ɔ:laut] a (effort etc) total(e) // ad: **all out** à fond.

allow [ə'lau] vt (practice, behaviour) permettre, autoriser ; (sum to spend etc) accorder ; allouer ; (sum, time estimated) compter, prévoir ; (concede): **to ~ that** convenir que ; **to ~ sb to do** permettre à qn de faire, autoriser qn à faire ; **to ~ for** vt fus tenir compte de ; **~ance** n (money received) allocation f ; subside m ; indemnité f ; (TAX) somme f déductible du revenu imposable, abattement m ; **to make ~ances for** tenir compte de.

alloy ['ælɔı] n alliage m.
all right ['ɔːl'raıt] ad (feel, work) bien ; (as answer) d'accord.
all-round ['ɔːl'raund] a compétent(e) dans tous les domaines ; (athlete etc) complet(ète).
all-time ['ɔːl'taım] a (record) sans précédent, absolu(e).
allude [ə'luːd] vi: **to ~ to** faire allusion à.
alluring [ə'ljuərıŋ] a séduisant(e), allèchant(e).
allusion [ə'luːʒən] n allusion f.
alluvium [ə'luːvıəm] n alluvions fpl.
ally ['ælaı] n allié m.
almighty [ɔːl'maıtı] a tout-puissant.
almond ['ɑːmənd] n amande f.
almost ['ɔːlməust] ad presque.
alms [ɑːmz] n aumône(s) f(pl).
alone [ə'ləun] a seul(e) ; **to leave sb ~** laisser qn tranquille ; **to leave sth ~** ne pas toucher à qch.
along [ə'lɔŋ] prep le long de // ad: **is he coming ~?** vient-il avec nous? ; **he was hopping/limping ~** il venait or avançait en sautillant/boitant ; **~ with** en compagnie de ; avec, en plus de ; **~side** prep le long de ; au côté de // ad bord à bord ; côte à côte.
aloof [ə'luːf] a,ad à distance, à l'écart ; **~ness** réserve (hautaine), attitude distante.
aloud [ə'laud] ad à haute voix.
alphabet ['ælfəbɛt] n alphabet m ; **~ical** [-'bɛtıkəl] a alphabétique.
alpine ['ælpaın] a alpin(e), alpestre.
Alps [ælps] npl: **the ~** les Alpes fpl.
already [ɔːl'rɛdı] ad déjà.
alright ['ɔːl'raıt] ad = **all right**.
also ['ɔːlsəu] ad aussi.
altar ['ɔltə*] n autel m.
alter ['ɔltə*] vt,vi changer, modifier ; **~ation** [ɔltə'reıʃən] n changement m, modification f.
alternate a [ɔl'təːnıt] alterné(e), alternant(e), alternatif(ive) // vi ['ɔltə:neıt] alterner ; **on ~ days** un jour sur deux, tous les deux jours ; **~ly** ad alternativement, en alternant ; **alternating** a (current) alternatif(ive).
alternative [ɔl'tə:nətıv] a (solutions) interchangeable, possible ; (solution) autre, de remplacement // n (choice) alternative f ; (other possibility) solution f de remplacement or de rechange, autre possibilité f ; **~ly** ad: **~ly one could** une autre or l'autre solution serait de.
alternator ['ɔltə:neıtə*] n (AUT) alternateur m.
although [ɔːl'ðəu] cj bien que + sub.
altitude ['æltıtjuːd] n altitude f.
alto ['æltəu] n (female) contralto m ; (male) haute-contre f.
altogether [ɔːltə'gɛðə*] ad entièrement, tout à fait ; (on the whole) tout compte fait ; (in all) en tout.
altruistic [æltru'ıstık] a altruiste.
aluminium [ælju'mınıəm], **aluminum** [ə'luːmınəm] (US) n aluminium m.
always ['ɔːlweız] ad toujours.

am [æm] vb see **be**.
a.m. ad (abbr of ante meridiem) du matin.
amalgamate [ə'mælgəmeıt] vt,vi fusionner ; **amalgamation** [-'meıʃən] n fusion f ; (COMM) fusionnement m ; amalgame m.
amass [ə'mæs] vt amasser.
amateur ['æmətə*] n amateur m // a (SPORT) amateur inv ; **~ish** a (pej) d'amateur.
amaze [ə'meız] vt stupéfier ; **~ment** n stupéfaction f, stupeur f.
ambassador [æm'bæsədə*] n ambassadeur m.
amber ['æmbə*] n ambre m ; **at ~** (AUT) à l'orange.
ambidextrous [æmbı'dɛkstrəs] a ambidextre.
ambiguity [æmbı'gjuıtı] n ambiguïté f.
ambiguous [æm'bıgjuəs] a ambigu(ë).
ambition [æm'bıʃən] n ambition f.
ambitious [æm'bıʃəs] a ambitieux(euse).
ambivalent [æm'bıvələnt] a (attitude) ambivalent(e).
amble ['æmbl] vi (gen: **to ~ along**) aller d'un pas tranquille.
ambulance ['æmbjuləns] n ambulance f.
ambush ['æmbuʃ] n embuscade f // vt tendre une embuscade à.
ameliorate [ə'miːlıəreıt] vt améliorer.
amenable [ə'miːnəbl] a: **~ to** (advice etc) disposé(e) à écouter or suivre ; **~ to the law** responsable devant la loi.
amend [ə'mɛnd] vt (law) amender ; (text) corriger ; (habits) réformer // vi s'amender, se corriger ; **to make ~s** réparer ses torts, faire amende honorable ; **~ment** n (to law) amendement m ; (to text) correction f.
amenities [ə'miːnıtız] npl aménagements mpl (prévus pour le loisir des habitants).
amenity [ə'miːnıtı] n charme m, agrément m.
America [ə'mɛrıkə] n Amérique f ; **~n** a américain(e) // n Américain/e ; **a~nize** vt américaniser.
amethyst ['æmıθıst] n améthyste f.
amiable ['eımıəbl] a aimable, affable.
amicable ['æmıkəbl] a amical(e).
amid(st) [ə'mıd(st)] prep parmi, au milieu de.
amiss [ə'mıs] a,ad: **there's something ~** il y a quelque chose qui ne va pas or qui cloche ; **to take sth ~** prendre qch mal or de travers.
ammunition [æmju'nıʃən] n munitions fpl.
amnesia [æm'niːzıə] n amnésie f.
amnesty ['æmnıstı] n amnistie f.
amok [ə'mɔk] ad: **to run ~** être pris(e) d'un accès de folie furieuse.
among(st) [ə'mʌŋ(st)] prep parmi, entre.
amoral [æ'mɔrəl] a amoral(e).
amorous ['æmərəs] a amoureux(euse).
amorphous [ə'mɔːfəs] a amorphe.
amount [ə'maunt] n somme f ; montant m ; quantité f ; nombre m // vi: **to ~ to** (total) s'élever à ; (be same as) équivaloir à, revenir à.

amp(ère) ['æmp(εə*)] n ampère m.

amphibian [æm'fɪbɪən] n batracien m.

amphibious [æm'fɪbɪəs] a amphibie.

amphitheatre ['æmfɪθɪətə*] n amphithéâtre m.

ample ['æmpl] a ample, spacieux(euse); (enough): **this is** ~ c'est largement suffisant; **to have** ~ **time/room** avoir bien assez de temps/place, avoir largement le temps/la place.

amplifier ['æmplɪfaɪə*] n amplificateur m.

amplify ['æmplɪfaɪ] vt amplifier.

amply ['æmplɪ] ad amplement, largement.

amputate ['æmpjuteɪt] vt amputer.

amuck [ə'mʌk] ad = **amok**.

amuse [ə'mju:z] vt amuser; ~**ment** n amusement m.

an [æn, ən, n] det see **a**.

anaemia [ə'ni:mɪə] n anémie f.

anaemic [ə'ni:mɪk] a anémique.

anaesthetic [ænɪs'θetɪk] a,n anesthésique (m); **under the** ~ sous anesthésie.

anaesthetist [æ'ni:sθɪtɪst] n anesthésiste m/f.

anagram ['ænəgræm] n anagramme m.

analgesic [ænæl'dʒi:sɪk] a,n analgésique (m).

analogy [ə'nælədʒɪ] n analogie f.

analyse ['ænəlaɪz] vt analyser.

analysis, pl **analyses** [ə'næləsɪs, -si:z] n analyse f.

analyst ['ænəlɪst] n (US) psychanalyste m/f.

analytic(al) [ænə'lɪtɪk(əl)] a analytique.

analyze ['ænəlaɪz] vt (US) = **analyse**.

anarchist ['ænəkɪst] a,n anarchiste (m/f).

anarchy ['ænəkɪ] n anarchie f.

anathema [ə'næθɪmə] n: **it is** ~ **to him** il a cela en abomination.

anatomical [ænə'tɔmɪkəl] a anatomique.

anatomy [ə'nætəmɪ] n anatomie f.

ancestor ['ænsɪstə*] n ancêtre m, aïeul m.

ancestral [æn'sestrəl] a ancestral(e).

ancestry ['ænsɪstrɪ] n ancêtres mpl; ascendance f.

anchor ['æŋkə*] n ancre f // vi (also: **to drop** ~) jeter l'ancre, mouiller // vt mettre à l'ancre; ~**age** n mouillage m, ancrage m.

anchovy ['æntʃəvɪ] n anchois m.

ancient ['eɪnʃənt] a ancien(ne), antique; (fig) d'un âge vénérable, antique.

and [ænd] cj et; ~ **so on** et ainsi de suite; **try** ~ **come** tâchez de venir; **come** ~ **sit here** viens t'asseoir ici; **better** ~ **better** de mieux en mieux; **more** ~ **more** de plus en plus.

Andes ['ændi:z] npl: **the** ~ les Andes fpl.

anecdote ['ænɪkdəut] n anecdote f.

anemia [ə'ni:mɪə] n = **anaemia**.

anemic [ə'ni:mɪk] a = **anaemic**.

anesthetic [ænɪs'θetɪk] a,n = **anaesthetic**.

anesthetist [æ'ni:sθɪtɪst] n = **anaesthetist**.

anew [ə'nju:] ad à nouveau.

angel ['eɪndʒəl] n ange m.

anger ['æŋgə*] n colère f // vt mettre en colère, irriter.

angina [æn'dʒaɪnə] n angine f de poitrine.

angle ['æŋgl] n angle m; **from their** ~ de leur point de vue // vi: **to** ~ **for** (trout) pêcher; (compliments) chercher, quêter; ~**r** n pêcheur/euse à la ligne.

Anglican ['æŋglɪkən] a,n anglican(e).

anglicize ['æŋglɪsaɪz] vt angliciser.

angling ['æŋglɪŋ] n pêche f à la ligne.

Anglo- ['æŋgləu] prefix anglo(-); ~**Saxon** a,n anglo-saxon(ne).

angrily ['æŋgrɪlɪ] ad avec colère.

angry ['æŋgrɪ] a en colère, furieux(euse); **to be** ~ **with sb/at sth** être furieux contre qn/de qch; **to get** ~ se fâcher, se mettre en colère; **to make sb** ~ mettre qn en colère.

anguish ['æŋgwɪʃ] n angoisse f.

angular ['æŋgjulə*] a anguleux(euse).

animal ['ænɪməl] n animal m // a animal(e); ~ **spirits** npl entrain m, vivacité f.

animate vt ['ænɪmeɪt] animer // a ['ænɪmɪt] animé(e), vivant(e); ~**d** a animé(e).

animosity [ænɪ'mɔsɪtɪ] n animosité f.

aniseed ['ænɪsi:d] n anis m.

ankle ['æŋkl] n cheville f.

annex n ['æneks] (also: **annexe**) annexe f // vt [ə'neks] annexer; ~**ation** [-'eɪʃən] n annexion f.

annihilate [ə'naɪəleɪt] vt annihiler, anéantir.

anniversary [ænɪ'və:sərɪ] n anniversaire m; ~ **dinner** n dîner commémoratif or anniversaire.

annotate ['ænəuteɪt] vt annoter.

announce [ə'nauns] vt annoncer; (birth, death) faire part de; ~**ment** n annonce f; (for births etc: in newspaper) avis m de faire-part; (:letter, card) faire-part m; ~**r** n (RADIO, TV) (between programmes) speaker/ine; (in a programme) présentateur/trice.

annoy [ə'nɔɪ] vt agacer, ennuyer, contrarier; **don't get** ~**ed!** ne vous fâchez pas!; ~**ance** n mécontentement m, contrariété f; ~**ing** a ennuyeux(euse), agaçant(e), contrariant(e).

annual ['ænjuəl] a annuel(le) // n (BOT) plante annuelle; (book) album m; ~**ly** ad annuellement.

annuity [ə'nju:ɪtɪ] n rente f; **life** ~ rente viagère.

annul [ə'nʌl] vt annuler; (law) abroger; ~**ment** n annulation f; abrogation f.

annum ['ænəm] n see **per**.

anoint [ə'nɔɪnt] vt oindre.

anomalous [ə'nɔmələs] a anormal(e).

anomaly [ə'nɔməlɪ] n anomalie f.

anonymity [ænə'nɪmɪtɪ] n anonymat m.

anonymous [ə'nɔnɪməs] a anonyme.

anorak ['ænəræk] n anorak m.

another [ə'nʌðə*] a: ~ **book** (one more) un autre livre, encore un livre, un livre de plus; (a different one) un autre livre // pronoun un(e) autre, encore un(e), un(e) de plus; see also **one**.

answer ['ɑ:nsə*] n réponse f; solution f // vi répondre // vt (reply to) répondre à; (problem) résoudre; (prayer) exaucer; **to** ~ **the phone** répondre (au téléphone);

in ~ to your letter suite à or en réponse
à votre lettre; to ~ the bell or the door
aller or venir ouvrir (la porte); to ~ back
vi répondre, répliquer; to ~ for vt fus
répondre de, se porter garant de; être
responsable de; to ~ to vt fus (description)
répondre or correspondre à; ~able a:
~able (to sb/for sth) responsable
(devant qn/de qch); I am ~able to
no-one je n'ai de comptes à rendre à
personne.
ant [ænt] n fourmi f.
antagonism [æn'tægənɪzəm] n
antagonisme m.
antagonist [æn'tægənɪst] n antagoniste
m/f, adversaire m/f; ~ic [æntægə'nɪstɪk]
a opposé(e); antagoniste.
antagonize [æn'tægənaɪz] vt éveiller
l'hostilité de, contrarier.
Antarctic [ænt'ɑ:ktɪk] n Antarctique m //
a antarctique, austral(e).
anteater ['ænti:tə*] n fourmilier m,
tamanoir m.
antecedent [æntɪ'si:dənt] n antécédent m.
antelope ['æntɪləup] n antilope f.
antenatal ['æntɪ'neɪtl] a prénatal(e); ~
clinic n service m de consultation
prénatale.
antenna, pl ~e [æn'tɛnə, -ni:] n antenne
f.
anthem ['ænθəm] n motet m; **national** ~
hymne national.
ant-hill ['ænthɪl] n fourmilière f.
anthology [æn'θɒlədʒɪ] n anthologie f.
anthropologist [ænθrə'pɒlədʒɪst] n
anthropologue m/f.
anthropology [ænθrə'pɒlədʒɪ] n
anthropologie f.
anti- ['ænti] prefix anti-.
anti-aircraft ['ænti'ɛəkrɑ:ft] a
antiaérien(ne); ~ **defence** n défense f
contre avions, DCA f.
antibiotic ['æntibaɪ'ɒtɪk] a,n antibiotique
(m).
anticipate [æn'tɪsɪpeɪt] vt s'attendre à;
prévoir; (wishes, request) aller au devant
de, devancer.
anticipation [æntɪsɪ'peɪʃən] n attente f;
thanking you in ~ en vous remerciant
d'avance, avec mes remerciements
anticipés.
anticlimax ['ænti'klaɪmæks] n réalisation
décevante d'un événement que l'on
escomptait important, intéressant etc.
anticlockwise ['ænti'klɒkwaɪz] a dans le
sens inverse des aiguilles d'une montre.
antics ['æntɪks] npl singeries fpl.
anticyclone ['ænti'saɪkləun] n
anticyclone m.
antidote ['æntɪdəut] n antidote m,
contrepoison m.
antifreeze ['ænti'fri:z] n antigel m.
antipathy [æn'tɪpəθɪ] n antipathie f.
antiquarian [æntɪ'kwɛəriən] a: ~
bookshop librairie f d'ouvrages anciens //
n expert m en objets or livres anciens;
amateur m d'antiquités.
antiquated ['æntɪkweɪtɪd] a vieilli(e),
suranné(e), vieillot(te).
antique [æn'ti:k] n objet m d'art ancien,
meuble ancien or d'époque, antiquité f //

a ancien(ne); (pre-mediaeval) antique; ~
dealer n antiquaire m/f; ~ **shop** n
magasin m d'antiquités.
antiquity [æn'tɪkwɪtɪ] n antiquité f.
antiseptic [æntɪ'sɛptɪk] a,n antiseptique
(m).
antisocial ['ænti'səuʃəl] a peu liant(e),
sauvage, insociable; (against society) anti-
social(e).
antlers ['æntləz] npl bois mpl, ramure f.
anus ['eɪnəs] n anus m.
anvil ['ænvɪl] n enclume f.
anxiety [æŋ'zaɪətɪ] n anxiété f; (keenness):
~ **to do** grand désir or impatience f de
faire.
anxious ['æŋkʃəs] a anxieux(euse), (très)
inquiet(ète); (keen): ~ **to do/that** qui
tient beaucoup à faire/à ce que;
impatient(e) de faire/que; ~ly ad
anxieusement.
any ['ɛnɪ] a (in negative and interrogative sentences = some) de, d'; du, de l', de la, des;
(no matter which) n'importe quel(le),
quelconque; (each and every) tout(e),
chaque; **I haven't ~ money/books** je
n'ai pas d'argent/de livres; **have you ~
butter/children?** avez-vous du
beurre/des enfants?; **without ~ difficulty** sans la moindre difficulté; **come
(at) ~ time** venez à n'importe quelle
heure; **at ~ moment** à tout moment, d'un
instant à l'autre; **in ~ case** de toute
façon; en tout cas; **at ~ rate** de toute
façon // pronoun n'importe
lequel(laquelle); (anybody) n'importe qui;
(in negative and interrogative sentences): **I
haven't ~** je n'en ai pas, je n'en ai aucun;
have you got ~? en avez-vous?; **can ~
of you sing?** est-ce que l'un d'entre vous
or quelqu'un parmi vous sait chanter? //
ad (in negative sentences) nullement,
aucunement; (in interrogative and conditional constructions) un peu; tant soit peu; **I
can't hear him ~ more** je ne l'entends
plus; **are you feeling ~ better?** vous
sentez-vous un peu mieux?; **do you want
~ more soup?** voulez-vous encore un peu
de soupe?; ~**body** pronoun n'importe qui;
(in interrogative sentences) quelqu'un; (in
negative sentences): **I don't see ~body** je
ne vois personne; ~**how** ad quoi qu'il en
soit; ~**one** = ~body; ~**thing** pronoun
(see anybody) n'importe quoi; quelque
chose; ne ... rien; ~**time** ad n'importe
quand; ~**way** ad de toute façon;
~**where** ad (see anybody) n'importe où;
quelque part; **I don't see him ~where**
je ne le vois nulle part.
apart [ə'pɑ:t] ad (to one side) à part; de
côté; à l'écart; (separately) séparément;
10 miles/a long way ~ à 10 milles/très
éloignés l'un de l'autre; **they are living
~** ils sont séparés; ~ **from** prep à part,
excepté.
apartheid [ə'pɑ:teɪt] n apartheid m.
apartment [ə'pɑ:tmənt] n (US)
appartement m, logement m; ~**s** npl
appartement m.
apathetic [æpə'θɛtɪk] a apathique,
indifférent(e).
apathy ['æpəθɪ] n apathie f, indifférence
f.

ape [eɪp] *n* (grand) singe // *vt* singer.
aperitif [ə'pɛrɪtɪv] *n* apéritif *m*.
aperture ['æpətʃjuə*] *n* orifice *m*, ouverture *f*; (*PHOT*) ouverture (du diaphragme).
apex ['eɪpɛks] *n* sommet *m*.
aphrodisiac [æfrəʊ'dɪzɪæk] *a,n* aphrodisiaque (*m*).
apiece [ə'piːs] *ad* (*for each person*) chacun(e), par tête; (*for each item*) chacun(e), (la) pièce.
aplomb [ə'plɔm] *n* sang-froid *m*, assurance *f*.
apocalypse [ə'pɔkəlɪps] *n* apocalypse *f*.
apolitical [eɪpə'lɪtɪkl] *a* apolitique.
apologetic [əpɔlə'dʒɛtɪk] *a* (*tone, letter*) d'excuse; **to be very ~ about** s'excuser vivement de.
apologize [ə'pɔlədʒaɪz] *vi*: **to ~ (for sth to sb)** s'excuser (de qch auprès de qn), présenter des excuses (à qn pour qch).
apology [ə'pɔlədʒɪ] *n* excuses *fpl*; **to send one's apologies** envoyer une lettre *or* un mot d'excuse, s'excuser (de ne pas pouvoir venir).
apoplexy ['æpəplɛksɪ] *n* apoplexie *f*.
apostle [ə'pɔsl] *n* apôtre *m*.
apostrophe [ə'pɔstrəfɪ] *n* apostrophe *f*.
appal [ə'pɔːl] *vt* consterner, atterrer; horrifier; **~ling** *a* épouvantable; (*stupidity*) consternant(e).
apparatus [æpə'reɪtəs] *n* appareil *m*, dispositif *m*.
apparent [ə'pærənt] *a* apparent(e); **~ly** *ad* apparemment.
apparition [æpə'rɪʃən] *n* apparition *f*.
appeal [ə'piːl] *vi* (*LAW*) faire *or* interjeter appel // *n* (*LAW*) appel *m*; (*request*) prière *f*; appel *m*; (*charm*) attrait *m*, charme *m*; **to ~ for** demander (instamment); implorer; **to ~ to** (*subj: person*) faire appel à; (*subj: thing*) plaire à; **to ~ to sb for mercy** implorer la pitié de qn, prier *or* adjurer qn d'avoir pitié; **it doesn't ~ to me** cela ne m'attire pas; **~ing** *a* (*nice*) attrayant(e); (*touching*) attendrissant(e).
appear [ə'pɪə*] *vi* apparaître, se montrer; (*LAW*) comparaître; (*publication*) paraître, sortir, être publié(e); (*seem*) paraître, sembler; **it would ~ that** il semble que; **to ~ in Hamlet** jouer dans Hamlet; **to ~ on TV** passer à la télé; **~ance** *n* apparition *f*; parution *f*; (*look, aspect*) apparence *f*, aspect *m*; **to put in** *or* **make an ~ance** faire acte de présence; (*THEATRE*): **by order of ~ance** par ordre d'entrée en scène.
appease [ə'piːz] *vt* apaiser, calmer.
appendage [ə'pɛndɪdʒ] *n* appendice *m*.
appendicitis [əpɛndɪ'saɪtɪs] *n* appendicite *f*.
appendix, *pl* **appendices** [ə'pɛndɪks, -siːz] *n* appendice *m*.
appetite ['æpɪtaɪt] *n* appétit *m*.
appetizing ['æpɪtaɪzɪŋ] *a* appétissant(e).
applaud [ə'plɔːd] *vt,vi* applaudir.
applause [ə'plɔːz] *n* applaudissements *mpl*.
apple ['æpl] *n* pomme *f*; **it's the ~ of my eye** j'y tiens comme à la prunelle de mes

yeux; **~ tree** *n* pommier *m*; **~ turnover** *n* chausson *m* aux pommes.
appliance [ə'plaɪəns] *n* appareil *m*.
applicable [ə'plɪkəbl] *a* applicable.
applicant ['æplɪkənt] *n* candidat/e (*for a post* à un poste).
application [æplɪ'keɪʃən] *n* application *f*; (*for a job, a grant etc*) demande *f*; candidature *f*; **on ~** sur demande.
applied [ə'plaɪd] *a* appliqué(e); **~ arts** *npl* arts décoratifs.
apply [ə'plaɪ] *vt* (*paint, ointment*): **to ~ (to)** appliquer (sur); (*theory, technique*): **to ~ (to)** appliquer (à) // *vi*: **to ~ to** (*ask*) s'adresser à; (*be suitable for, relevant to*) s'appliquer à; se rapporter à; être valable pour; **to ~ (for)** (*permit, grant*) faire une demande (en vue d'obtenir); (*job*) poser sa candidature (pour), faire une demande d'emploi (concernant); **to ~ the brakes** actionner les freins, freiner; **to ~ o.s. to** s'appliquer à.
appoint [ə'pɔɪnt] *vt* nommer, engager; (*date, place*) fixer, désigner; **~ment** *n* nomination *f*; rendez-vous *m*; **to make an ~ment (with)** prendre rendez-vous (avec).
apportion [ə'pɔːʃən] *vt* (*share out*) répartir, distribuer; **to ~ sth to sb** attribuer *or* assigner *or* allouer qch à qn.
appraisal [ə'preɪzl] *n* évaluation *f*.
appreciable [ə'priːʃəbl] *a* appréciable.
appreciate [ə'priːʃɪeɪt] *vt* (*like*) apprécier, faire cas de; être reconnaissant(e) de; (*assess*) évaluer; (*be aware of*) comprendre; se rendre compte de // *vi* (*FINANCE*) prendre de la valeur.
appreciation [əpriːʃɪ'eɪʃən] *n* appréciation *f*; reconnaissance *f*; (*COMM*) hausse *f*, valorisation *f*.
appreciative [ə'priːʃɪətɪv] *a* (*person*) sensible; (*comment*) élogieux(euse).
apprehend [æprɪ'hɛnd] *vt* appréhender, arrêter; (*understand*) comprendre.
apprehension [æprɪ'hɛnʃən] *n* appréhension *f*, inquiétude *f*.
apprehensive [æprɪ'hɛnsɪv] *a* inquiet-(ète), appréhensif(ive).
apprentice [ə'prɛntɪs] *n* apprenti *m*; **~ship** *n* apprentissage *m*.
approach [ə'prəʊtʃ] *vi* approcher // *vt* (*come near*) approcher de; (*ask, apply to*) s'adresser à; (*subject, passer-by*) aborder // *n* approche *f*; accès *m*, abord *m*; démarche *f* (*auprès de qn*); démarche (*intellectuelle*); **~able** *a* accessible.
approbation [æprə'beɪʃən] *n* approbation *f*.
appropriate *vt* [ə'prəʊprɪeɪt] (*take*) s'approprier; (*allot*): **to ~ sth for** affecter qch à // *a* [ə'prəʊprɪɪt] opportun(e); qui convient, approprié(e); **~ly** *ad* pertinemment, avec à-propos.
approval [ə'pruːvl] *n* approbation *f*; **on ~** (*COMM*) à l'examen.
approve [ə'pruːv] *vt* approuver; **to ~ of** *vt fus* approuver; **~d school** *n* centre *m* d'éducation surveillée; **approvingly** *ad* d'un air approbateur.
approximate *a* [ə'prɔksɪmɪt] approximatif(ive) // *vt* [ə'prɔksɪmeɪt] se rapprocher de; être proche de;

approximation [-'meɪʃən] n approximation f.

apricot ['eɪprɪkɔt] n abricot m.

April ['eɪprəl] n avril m; ~ **fool!** poisson d'avril!

apron ['eɪprən] n tablier m.

apt [æpt] a (suitable) approprié(e); (able): ~ **(at)** doué(e) (pour); apte (à); (likely): ~ **to do** susceptible de faire; ayant tendance à faire.

aptitude ['æptɪtjuːd] n aptitude f.

aqualung ['ækwəlʌŋ] n scaphandre m autonome.

aquarium [ə'kwɛərɪəm] n aquarium m.

Aquarius [ə'kwɛərɪəs] n le Verseau; **to be** ~ être du Verseau.

aquatic [ə'kwætɪk] a aquatique; (SPORT) nautique.

aqueduct ['ækwɪdʌkt] n aqueduc m.

Arab ['ærəb] n Arabe m/f.

Arabia [ə'reɪbɪə] n Arabie f; ~n a arabe.

Arabic ['ærəbɪk] a,n arabe (m).

arable ['ærəbl] a arable.

arbiter ['ɑːbɪtə*] n arbitre m.

arbitrary ['ɑːbɪtrərɪ] a arbitraire.

arbitrate ['ɑːbɪtreɪt] vi arbitrer; trancher; **arbitration** [-'treɪʃən] n arbitrage m.

arbitrator ['ɑːbɪtreɪtə*] n arbitre m, médiateur/trice.

arc [ɑːk] n arc m.

arcade [ɑː'keɪd] n arcade f; (passage with shops) passage m, galerie f.

arch [ɑːtʃ] n arche f; (of foot) cambrure f, voûte f plantaire // vt arquer, cambrer // a malicieux(euse) // prefix: ~(-) achevé(e); par excellence; **pointed.** ~ n ogive f.

archaeologist [ɑːkɪ'ɔlədʒɪst] n archéologue m/f.

archaeology [ɑːkɪ'ɔlədʒɪ] n archéologie f.

archaic [ɑː'keɪɪk] a archaïque.

archbishop [ɑːtʃ'bɪʃəp] n archevêque m.

arch-enemy ['ɑːtʃ'ɛnɪmɪ] n ennemi m de toujours or par excellence.

archeologist [ɑːkɪ'ɔlədʒɪst] n (US) = **archaeologist.**

archeology [ɑːkɪ'ɔlədʒɪ] n (US) = **archaeology.**

archer ['ɑːtʃə*] n archer m; ~y n tir m à l'arc.

archetype ['ɑːkɪtaɪp] n prototype m, archétype m.

archipelago [ɑːkɪ'pɛlɪgəu] n archipel m.

architect ['ɑːkɪtɛkt] n architecte m; ~ural [ɑːkɪ'tɛktʃərəl] a architectural(e); ~ure ['ɑːkɪtɛktʃə*] n architecture f.

archives ['ɑːkaɪvz] npl archives fpl; **archivist** ['ɑːkɪvɪst] n archiviste m/f.

archway ['ɑːtʃweɪ] n voûte f, porche voûté or cintré.

Arctic ['ɑːktɪk] a arctique // n: **the** ~ l'Arctique m.

ardent ['ɑːdənt] a fervent(e).

arduous ['ɑːdjuəs] a ardu(e).

are [ɑː*] vb see **be.**

area ['ɛərɪə] n (GEOM) superficie f; (zone) région f; (:smaller) secteur m; **dining** ~ n coin m salle à manger.

arena [ə'riːnə] n arène f.

aren't [ɑːnt] = **are not.**

Argentina [ɑːdʒən'tiːnə] n Argentine f; **Argentinian** [-'tɪnɪən] a argentin(e) // n Argentin/e.

arguable ['ɑːgjuəbl] a discutable.

argue ['ɑːgjuː] vi (quarrel) se disputer; (reason) argumenter; **to** ~ **that** objecter or alléguer que, donner comme argument que.

argument ['ɑːgjumənt] n (reasons) argument m; (quarrel) dispute f, discussion f; (debate) discussion f, controverse f; ~**ative** [ɑːgju'mɛntətɪv] a ergoteur(euse), raisonneur(euse).

arid ['ærɪd] a aride; ~**ity** [ə'rɪdɪtɪ] n aridité f.

Aries ['ɛərɪz] n le Bélier; **to be** ~ être du Bélier.

arise, pt **arose**, pp **arisen** [ə'raɪz, -'rəuz, -'rɪzn] vi survenir, se présenter; **to** ~ **from** résulter de.

aristocracy [ærɪs'tɔkrəsɪ] n aristocratie f.

aristocrat ['ærɪstəkræt] n aristocrate m/f; ~**ic** [-'krætɪk] a aristocratique.

arithmetic [ə'rɪθmətɪk] n arithmétique f.

ark [ɑːk] n: **Noah's A**~ l'Arche f de Noé.

arm [ɑːm] n bras m; (MIL: branch) arme f // vt armer; ~**s** npl (weapons, HERALDRY) armes fpl; ~ **in** ~ bras dessus bras dessous; ~**band** n brassard m; ~**chair** n fauteuil m; ~**ed** a armé(e); ~**ed robbery** n vol m à main armée; ~**ful** n brassée f.

armistice ['ɑːmɪstɪs] n armistice m.

armour ['ɑːmə*] n armure f; (also: ~**plating**) blindage m; (MIL: tanks) blindés mpl; ~**ed car** n véhicule blindé; ~**y** n arsenal m.

armpit ['ɑːmpɪt] n aisselle f.

army ['ɑːmɪ] n armée f.

aroma [ə'rəumə] n arôme m; ~**tic** [ærə'mætɪk] a aromatique.

arose [ə'rəuz] pt of **arise.**

around [ə'raund] ad (tout) autour; dans les parages // prep autour de; (fig: about) environ; vers; **is he** ~? est-il dans les parages or là?

arouse [ə'rauz] vt (sleeper) éveiller; (curiosity, passions) éveiller, susciter; exciter.

arpeggio [ɑː'pɛdʒɪəu] n arpège m.

arrange [ə'reɪndʒ] vt arranger; (programme) arrêter, convenir de; ~**ment** n arrangement m; (plans etc): ~**ments** dispositions fpl.

array [ə'reɪ] n: ~ **of** déploiement m or étalage m de.

arrears [ə'rɪəz] npl arriéré m; **to be in** ~ **with one's rent** devoir un arriéré de loyer, être en retard pour le paiement de son loyer.

arrest [ə'rɛst] vt arrêter; (sb's attention) retenir, attirer // n arrestation f; **under** ~ en état d'arrestation.

arrival [ə'raɪvəl] n arrivée f; (COMM) arrivage m; (person) arrivant/e.

arrive [ə'raɪv] vi arriver; **to** ~ **at** vt fus (fig) parvenir à.

arrogance ['ærəgəns] n arrogance f.

arrogant ['ærəgənt] a arrogant(e).

arrow ['ærəu] n flèche f.
arsenal ['ɑːsɪnl] n arsenal m.
arsenic ['ɑːsnɪk] n arsenic m.
arson ['ɑːsn] n incendie criminel.
art [ɑːt] n art m; (craft) métier m; **A~s** npl (SCOL) les lettres fpl; ~ **gallery** n musée m d'art; (small and private) galerie f de peinture.
artefact ['ɑːtɪfækt] n objet fabriqué.
artery ['ɑːtərɪ] n artère f.
artful ['ɑːtful] a rusé(e).
arthritis [ɑː'θraɪtɪs] n arthrite f.
artichoke ['ɑːtɪtʃəuk] n artichaut m.
article ['ɑːtɪkl] n article m; (LAW: training): ~**s** npl ≈ stage m.
articulate a [ɑː'tɪkjulɪt] (person) qui s'exprime clairement et aisément; (speech) bien articulé(e), prononcé(e) clairement // vi [ɑː'tɪkjuleɪt] articuler, parler distinctement; ~**d lorry** n (camion m) semi-remorque m.
artifice ['ɑːtɪfɪs] n ruse f.
artificial [ɑːtɪ'fɪʃəl] a artificiel(le); ~ **respiration** n respiration artificielle.
artillery [ɑː'tɪlərɪ] n artillerie f.
artisan ['ɑːtɪzæn] n artisan/e.
artist ['ɑːtɪst] n artiste m/f; ~**ic** [ɑː'tɪstɪk] a artistique; ~**ry** n art m, talent m.
artless ['ɑːtlɪs] a naïf(ïve), simple, ingénu(e).
as [æz, əz] cj (cause) comme, puisque; (time: moment) alors que, comme; (: duration) tandis que; (manner) comme; (in the capacity of) en tant que, en qualité de; ~ **big** ~ aussi grand que; **twice** ~ **big** ~ deux fois plus grand que; **big** ~ **it is** si grand que ce soit; ~ **she said** comme elle l'avait dit; ~ **if** or **though** comme si; ~ **for** or **to** en ce qui concerne, quant à; ~ **or so long** ~ cj à condition que, si; ~ **much/many** (~) autant (que); ~ **soon** ~ cj aussitôt que, dès que; ~ **such** ad en tant que tel(le); ~ **well** ad aussi; ~ **well** ~ cj en plus de, en même temps que; see also **so, such**.
asbestos [æz'bɛstəs] n asbeste m, amiante m.
ascend [ə'sɛnd] vt gravir; ~**ancy** n ascendant m.
ascent [ə'sɛnt] n ascension f.
ascertain [æsə'teɪn] vt s'assurer de, vérifier; établir.
ascetic [ə'sɛtɪk] a ascétique.
ascribe [ə'skraɪb] vt: to ~ **sth to** attribuer qch à; (blame) imputer qch à.
ash [æʃ] n (dust) cendre f; ~ (**tree**) frêne m.
ashamed [ə'ʃeɪmd] a honteux(euse), confus(e); **to be** ~ **of** avoir honte de; **to be** ~ (**of o.s.**) **for having done** avoir honte d'avoir fait.
ashen ['æʃn] a (pale) cendreux(euse), blême.
ashore [ə'ʃɔː*] ad à terre; **to go** ~ aller à terre, débarquer.
ashtray ['æʃtreɪ] n cendrier m.
Asia ['eɪʃə] n Asie f; ~ **Minor** n Asie Mineure; ~**n** n Asiatique m/f // a asiatique; ~**tic** [eɪsɪ'ætɪk] a asiatique.
aside [ə'saɪd] ad de côté; à l'écart // n aparte m.

ask [ɑːsk] vt demander; (invite) inviter; **to** ~ **sb sth/to do sth** demander à qn qch/de faire qch; **to** ~ **sb about sth** questionner qn au sujet de qch; se renseigner auprès de qn au sujet de qch; **to** ~ **about the price** s'informer du prix, se renseigner au sujet du prix; **to** ~ (**sb**) **a question** poser une question (à qn); **to** ~ **sb out to dinner** inviter qn au restaurant; **to** ~ **for** vt fus demander.
askance [ə'skɑːns] ad: **to look** ~ **at sb** regarder qn de travers or d'un œil désapprobateur.
askew [ə'skjuː] ad de travers, de guinguois.
asleep [ə'sliːp] a endormi(e); **to be** ~ dormir, être endormi; **to fall** ~ s'endormir.
asp [æsp] n aspic m.
asparagus [əs'pærəgəs] n asperges fpl; ~ **tips** npl pointes fpl d'asperges.
aspect ['æspɛkt] n aspect m; (direction in which a building etc faces) orientation f, exposition f.
aspersions [əs'pəːʃənz] npl **to cast** ~ **on** dénigrer.
asphalt ['æsfælt] n asphalte m.
asphyxiate [æs'fɪksɪeɪt] vt asphyxier; **asphyxiation** [-'eɪʃən] n asphyxie f.
aspirate vt ['æspəreɪt] aspirer // a ['æspərɪt] aspiré(e).
aspiration [æspə'reɪʃən] n aspiration f.
aspire [əs'paɪə*] vi: **to** ~ **to** aspirer à.
aspirin ['æsprɪn] n aspirine f.
ass [æs] n âne m; (col) imbécile m/f.
assail [ə'seɪl] vt assaillir; ~**ant** n agresseur m; assaillant m.
assassin [ə'sæsɪn] n assassin m; ~**ate** vt assassiner; ~**ation** [əsæsɪ'neɪʃən] n assassinat m.
assault [ə'sɔːlt] n (MIL) assaut m; (gen: attack) agression f; (LAW): ~ (**and battery**) voies fpl de fait, coups mpl et blessures fpl // vt attaquer; (sexually) violenter.
assemble [ə'sɛmbl] vt assembler // vi s'assembler, se rassembler.
assembly [ə'sɛmblɪ] n (meeting) rassemblement m; (construction) assemblage m; ~ **line** n chaine f de montage.
assent [ə'sɛnt] n assentiment m, consentement m // vi donner son assentiment, consentir.
assert [ə'sɜːt] vt affirmer, déclarer; établir; ~**ion** [ə'sɜːʃən] n assertion f, affirmation f; ~**ive** a assuré(e), péremptoire.
assess [ə'sɛs] vt évaluer, estimer; (tax, damages) établir or fixer le montant de; (property etc: for tax) calculer la valeur imposable de; ~**ment** n évaluation f, estimation f; ~**or** n expert m (en matière d'impôt et d'assurance).
asset ['æsɛt] n avantage m, atout m; ~**s** npl capital m; avoir(s) m(pl); actif m.
assiduous [ə'sɪdjuəs] a assidu(e).
assign [ə'saɪn] vt (date) fixer, arrêter; (task): **to** ~ **sth to** assigner qch à; (resources): **to** ~ **sth to** affecter qch à; (cause, meaning): **to** ~ **sth to** attribuer qch à; ~**ment** n tâche f, mission f.

assimilate [ə'sımıleıt] vt assimiler ; **assimilation** (-'leıʃən] n assimilation f.

assist [ə'sıst] vt aider, assister ; secourir ; **~ance** n aide f, assistance f ; secours mpl ; **~ant** n assistant/e, adjoint/e ; (also: **shop ~ant**) vendeur/euse.

assizes [ə'saızız] npl assises fpl.

associate a,n [ə'səuʃııt] associé(e) // vb [ə'səuʃıeıt] vt associer // vi: **to ~ with sb** fréquenter qn.

association [əsəusı'eıʃən] n association f ; **~ football** n football m.

assorted [ə'sɔːtıd] a assorti(e).

assortment [ə'sɔːtmənt] n assortiment m.

assume [ə'sjuːm] vt supposer ; (responsibilities etc) assumer ; (attitude, name) prendre, adopter ; **~d name** n nom m d'emprunt.

assumption [ə'sʌmpʃən] n supposition f, hypothèse f.

assurance [ə'ʃuərəns] n assurance f.

assure [ə'ʃuə*] vt assurer.

asterisk ['æstərısk] n astérisque m.

astern [ə'stəːn] ad à l'arrière.

asthma ['æsmə] n asthme m ; **~tic** [æs'mætık] a,n asthmatique (m/f).

astir [ə'stəː*] ad en émoi.

astonish [ə'stɔnıʃ] vt étonner, stupéfier ; **~ment** n étonnement m.

astound [ə'staund] vt stupéfier, sidérer.

astray [ə'streı] ad: **to go ~** s'égarer ; (fig) quitter le droit chemin.

astride [ə'straıd] ad à cheval // prep à cheval sur.

astringent [əs'trındʒənt] a astringent(e) // n astringent m.

astrologer [əs'trɔlədʒə*] n astrologue m.

astrology [əs'trɔlədʒı] n astrologie f.

astronaut ['æstrənɔːt] n astronaute m/f.

astronomer [əs'trɔnəmə*] n astronome m.

astronomical [æstrə'nɔmıkəl] a astronomique.

astronomy [əs'trɔnəmı] n astronomie f.

astute [əs'tjuːt] a astucieux(euse), malin(igne).

asunder [ə'sʌndə*] ad: **to tear ~** déchirer.

asylum [ə'saıləm] n asile m.

at [æt] prep à ; (because of: following surprised, annoyed etc) de ; par ; **~ Pierre's** chez Pierre ; **~ the baker's** chez le boulanger, à la boulangerie ; **~ times** parfois.

ate [eıt] pt of **eat**.

atheism ['eıθıızəm] n athéisme m.

atheist ['eıθııst] n athée m/f.

Athens ['æθınz] n Athènes.

athlete ['æθliːt] n athlète m/f.

athletic [æθ'letık] a athlétique ; **~s** n athlétisme m.

Atlantic [ət'læntık] a atlantique // n: **the ~ (Ocean)** l'Atlantique m, l'océan m Atlantique.

atlas ['ætləs] n atlas m.

atmosphere ['ætməsfıə*] n atmosphère f.

atmospheric [ætməs'ferık] a atmosphérique ; **~s** n (RADIO) parasites mpl.

atoll ['ætɔl] n atoll m.

atom ['ætəm] n atome m ; **~ic** [ə'tɔmık] a atomique ; **~(ic) bomb** n bombe f atomique ; **~izer** ['ætəmaızə*] n atomiseur m.

atone [ə'təun] vi: **to ~ for** expier, racheter.

atrocious [ə'trəuʃəs] a (very bad) atroce, exécrable.

atrocity [ə'trɔsıtı] n atrocité f.

atrophy ['ætrəfı] n atrophie f // vt atrophier // vi s'atrophier.

attach [ə'tætʃ] vt (gen) attacher ; (document, letter) joindre ; (MIL: troops) affecter ; **to be ~ed to sb/sth** (to like) être attaché à qn/qch ; **~é** [ə'tæʃeı] n attaché m ; **~é case** n attaché-case m ; **~ment** n (tool) accessoire m ; (love): **~ment (to)** affection f (pour), attachement m (à).

attack [ə'tæk] vt attaquer ; (task etc) s'attaquer à // n attaque f ; (also: **heart ~**) crise f cardiaque ; **~er** n attaquant m ; agresseur m.

attain [ə'teın] vt (also: **to ~ to**) parvenir à, atteindre ; acquérir ; **~ments** npl connaissances fpl, résultats mpl.

attempt [ə'tempt] n tentative f // vt essayer, tenter ; **~ed theft** etc (LAW) tentative de vol etc ; **to make an ~ on sb's life** attenter à la vie de qn.

attend [ə'tend] vt (course) suivre ; (meeting, talk) assister à ; (school, church) aller à, fréquenter ; (patient) soigner, s'occuper de ; **to ~ (up)on** servir ; être au service de ; **to ~ to** vt fus (needs, affairs etc) s'occuper de ; (customer) s'occuper de, servir ; **~ance** n (being present) présence f ; (people present) assistance f ; **~ant** n employé/e ; gardien/ne // a concomitant(e), qui accompagne or s'ensuit.

attention [ə'tenʃən] n attention f ; **~s** attentions fpl, prévenances fpl ; **~!** (MIL) garde-à-vous! ; **at ~** (MIL) au garde-à-vous ; **for the ~ of** (ADMIN) à l'attention de.

attentive [ə'tentıv] a attentif(ive) ; (kind) prévenant(e) ; **~ly** ad attentivement, avec attention.

attenuate [ə'tenjueıt] vt atténuer // vi s'atténuer.

attest [ə'test] vi: **to ~ to** témoigner de, attester (de).

attic ['ætık] n grenier m, combles mpl.

attire [ə'taıə*] n habit m, atours mpl.

attitude ['ætıtjuːd] n attitude f, manière f ; pose f, maintien m.

attorney [ə'təːnı] n (lawyer) avoué m ; (having proxy) mandataire m ; **A~ General** n (Brit) ≈ procureur général ; (US) ≈ garde m des Sceaux, ministre m de la Justice ; **power of ~** n procuration f.

attract [ə'trækt] vt attirer ; **~ion** [ə'trækʃən] n (gen pl: pleasant things) attraction f, attrait m ; (PHYSICS) attraction f ; (fig: towards sth) attirance f ; **~ive** a séduisant(e), attrayant(e).

attribute n ['ætrıbjuːt] attribut m // vt [ə'trıbjuːt]: **to ~ sth to** attribuer qch à.

attrition [ə'trıʃən] n: **war of ~** guerre f d'usure.

aubergine ['əubəʒiːn] n aubergine f.

auburn ['ɔːbən] a auburn inv, châtain roux inv.

auction ['ɔ:kʃən] n (also: **sale by ~**) vente f aux enchères // vt (also: **to sell by ~**) vendre aux enchères; (also: **to put up for ~**) mettre aux enchères; **~eer** [-'nıə*] n commissaire-priseur m.

audacious [ɔ:'deıʃəs] a impudent(e); audacieux(euse), intrépide.

audacity [ɔ:'dæsıtı] n impudence f; audace f.

audible ['ɔ:dıbl] a audible.

audience ['ɔ:dıəns] n (people) assistance f, auditoire m; auditeurs mpl; spectateurs mpl; (interview) audience f.

audio-visual [ɔ:dıəu'vızjuəl] a audio-visuel(le).

audit ['ɔ:dıt] n vérification f des comptes, apurement m // vt vérifier, apurer.

audition [ɔ:'dıʃən] n audition f.

auditor ['ɔ:dıtə*] n vérificateur m des comptes.

auditorium [ɔ:dı'tɔ:rıəm] n auditorium m, salle f de concert or de spectacle.

augment [ɔ:g'mɛnt] vt,vi augmenter.

augur ['ɔ:gə*] vt (be a sign of) présager, annoncer // vi: **it ~s well** c'est bon signe or de bon augure, cela s'annonce bien.

August ['ɔ:gəst] n août m.

august [ɔ:'gʌst] a majestueux(euse), imposant(e).

aunt [ɑ:nt] n tante f; **~ie**, **~y** n diminutive of aunt.

au pair ['əu'pɛə*] n (also: **~ girl**) jeune fille f au pair.

aura ['ɔ:rə] n atmosphère f.

auspices ['ɔ:spısız] npl: **under the ~ of** sous les auspices de.

auspicious [ɔ:s'pıʃəs] a de bon augure, propice.

austere [ɔs'tıə*] a austère.

Australia [ɔs'treılıə] n Australie f; **~n** a australien(ne) // n Australien/ne.

Austria ['ɔstrıə] n Autriche f; **~n** a autrichien(ne) // n Autrichien/ne.

authentic [ɔ:'θɛntık] a authentique; **~ate** vt établir l'authenticité de.

author ['ɔ:θə*] n auteur m.

authoritarian [ɔ:θɒrı'tɛərıən] a autoritaire.

authoritative [ɔ:'θɒrıtətıv] a (account) digne de foi; (study, treatise) qui fait autorité; (manner) autoritaire.

authority [ɔ:'θɒrıtı] n autorité f; (permission) autorisation (formelle); **the authorities** npl les autorités fpl, l'administration f.

authorize ['ɔ:θəraız] vt autoriser.

authorship ['ɔ:θəʃıp] n paternité f (littéraire etc).

autistic [ɔ:'tıstık] a autistique.

auto ['ɔ:təu] n (US) auto f, voiture f.

autobiography [ɔ:təbaı'ɒgrəfı] n autobiographie f.

autocratic [ɔ:tə'krætık] a autocratique.

autograph ['ɔ:təgrɑ:f] n autographe m // vt signer, dédicacer.

automatic [ɔ:tə'mætık] a automatique // n (gun) automatique m; **~ally** ad automatiquement.

automation [ɔ:tə'meıʃən] n automatisation f.

automaton, pl automata [ɔ:'tɒmətən, -tə] n automate m.

automobile ['ɔ:təmƏbi:l] n (US) automobile f.

autonomous [ɔ:'tɒnəməs] a autonome.

autonomy [ɔ:'tɒnəmı] n autonomie f.

autopsy ['ɔ:tɒpsı] n autopsie f.

autumn ['ɔ:təm] n automne m.

auxiliary [ɔ:g'zılıərı] a auxiliaire // n auxiliaire m/f.

Av. abbr of **avenue**.

avail [ə'veıl] vt: **to ~ o.s. of** user de; profiter de // n: **to no ~** sans résultat, en vain, en pure perte.

availability [əveılə'bılıtı] n disponibilité f.

available [ə'veıləbl] a disponible; **every ~ means** tous les moyens possibles or à sa (or notre etc) disposition.

avalanche ['ævəlɑ:nʃ] n avalanche f.

avant-garde ['ævɑ̃'gɑ:d] a d'avant-garde.

avaricious [ævə'rıʃəs] a avare.

Ave. abbr of **avenue**.

avenge [ə'vɛndʒ] vt venger.

avenue ['ævənju:] n avenue f.

average ['ævərıdʒ] n moyenne f // a moyen(ne) // vt (a certain figure) atteindre or faire etc en moyenne; **on ~** en moyenne; **above/below (the) ~** au-dessus/en-dessous de la moyenne; **to ~ out** vi: **to ~ out at** représenter en moyenne, donner une moyenne de.

averse [ə'və:s] a: **to be ~ to sth/doing** éprouver une forte répugnance envers qch/à faire; **I wouldn't be ~ to a drink** un petit verre ne serait pas de refus, je ne dirais pas non à un petit verre.

aversion [ə'və:ʃən] n aversion f, répugnance f.

avert [ə'və:t] vt prévenir, écarter; (one's eyes) détourner.

aviary ['eıvıərı] n volière f.

aviation [eıvı'eıʃən] n aviation f.

avid ['ævıd] a avide; **~ly** ad avidement, avec avidité.

avocado [ævə'kɑ:dəu] n (also: **~ pear**) avocat m.

avoid [ə'vɔıd] vt éviter; **~able** a évitable; **~ance** n le fait d'éviter.

await [ə'weıt] vt attendre; **~ing attention/delivery** (COMM) en souffrance.

awake [ə'weık] a éveillé(e); (fig) en éveil // vi (pt **awoke** [ə'wəuk], pp **awoken** [ə'wəukən] or **awaked**) vt éveiller // vi s'éveiller; **~ to** conscient de; **he was still ~** il ne dormait pas encore; **~ning** [ə'weıknıŋ] n réveil m.

award [ə'wɔ:d] n récompense f, prix m // vt (prize) décerner; (LAW: damages) accorder.

aware [ə'wɛə*] a: **~ of** (conscious) conscient(e) de; (informed) au courant de; **to become ~ of** avoir conscience de, prendre conscience de; se rendre compte de; **politically/socially ~** sensibilisé aux or ayant pris conscience des problèmes politiques/sociaux; **~ness** n le fait d'être conscient, au courant etc.

awash [ə'wɒʃ] a recouvert(e) (d'eau); **~ with** inondé(e) de.

away [ə'weɪ] *a,ad* (au) loin ; absent(e) ;
two kilometres ~ à (une distance de)
deux kilomètres, à deux kilomètres de
distance ; **two hours** ~ **by car** à deux
heures de voiture *or* de route ; **the holiday
was two weeks** ~ il restait deux
semaines jusqu'aux vacances ; ~ **from**
loin de ; **he's** ~ **for a week** il est parti
(pour) une semaine ; **to take** ~ *vt*
emporter ; **to work/pedal/laugh** *etc* ~ *la
particule indique la constance et l'énergie de
l'action*: il pédalait *etc* tant qu'il pouvait ;
to fade/wither *etc* ~ *la particule renforce
l'idée de la disparition, l'éloignement* ; ~
match *n* (SPORT) match *m* à l'extérieur.

awe [ɔ:] *n* respect mêlé de crainte, effroi
mêlé d'admiration ; ~-**inspiring**, ~**some**
a impressionnant(e) ; ~**struck** *a* frappé(e)
d'effroi.

awful ['ɔ:fəl] *a* affreux(euse) ; ~**ly** *ad*
(*very*) terriblement, vraiment.

awhile [ə'waɪl] *ad* un moment, quelque
temps.

awkward ['ɔ:kwəd] *a* (*clumsy*) gauche,
maladroit(e) ; (*inconvenient*) malaisé(e),
d'emploi malaisé, peu pratique ;
(*embarrassing*) gênant(e), délicat(e).

awl [ɔ:l] *n* alêne *f*.

awning ['ɔ:nɪŋ] *n* (*of tent*) auvent *m* ; (*of
shop*) store *m* ;(*of hotel etc*) marquise *f* (de
toile).

awoke, awoken [ə'wəuk, -kən] *pt,pp of*
awake.

awry [ə'raɪ] *ad,a* de travers ; **to go** ~ mal
tourner.

axe, ax (US) [æks] *n* hache *f* // *vt*
(*employee*) renvoyer ; (*project etc*)
abandonner ; (*jobs*) supprimer.

axiom ['æksɪəm] *n* axiome *m*.

axis, *pl* **axes** ['æksɪs, -si:z] *n* axe *m*.

axle ['æksl] *n* (*also*: ~-**tree**) essieu *m*.

ay(e) [aɪ] *excl* (*yes*) oui ; **the ayes** *npl* les
oui.

azure ['eɪʒə*] *a* azuré(e).

B

B [bi:] *n* (MUS) si *m*.

B.A. *abbr see* **bachelor**.

babble ['bæbl] *vi* babiller // *n* babillage
m.

baboon [bə'bu:n] *n* babouin *m*.

baby ['beɪbɪ] *n* bébé *m* ; ~ **carriage** *n* (US)
voiture *f* d'enfant ; ~**hood** *n* petite
enfance ; ~**ish** *a* enfantin(e), de bébé ; ~-
sit *vi* garder les enfants ; ~-**sitter** *n* baby-
sitter *m/f*.

bachelor ['bætʃələ*] *n* célibataire *m* ; **B**~
of Arts/Science (B.A./B.Sc.) ≈
licencié/e ès *or* en lettres/sciences ; **B**~
of Arts/Science degree (B.A./B.Sc.) *n*
≈ licence *f* ès *or* en lettres/ sciences ;
~**hood** *n* célibat *m*.

back [bæk] *n* (*of person, horse*) dos *m* ; (*of
hand*) dos, revers *m* ; (*of house*) derrière *m* ;
(*of car, train*) arrière *m* ; (*of chair*) dossier
m ; (*of page*) verso *m* ; (FOOTBALL) arrière *m*
// *vt* (*candidate: also*: ~ **up**) soutenir,
appuyer ; (*horse: at races*) parier *or* miser
sur ; (*car*) (faire) reculer // *vi* reculer ; (*car
etc*) faire marche arrière // *a* (*in compounds*) de derrière, à l'arrière ; ~

seats/wheels (AUT) sièges *mpl*/roues *fpl*
arrière ; ~ **payments/rent** arrière *m* de
paiements/loyer // *ad* (*not forward*) en
arrière ; (*returned*): **he's** ~ il est rentré, il
est de retour ; **he ran** ~ il est revenu en
courant ; (*restitution*): **throw the ball** ~
renvoie la balle ; **can I have it** ~? puis-
je le ravoir?, peux-tu me le rendre?;
(*again*): **he called** ~ il a rappelé ; **to** ~
down *vi* rabattre de ses prétentions ; **to**
~ **out** *vi* (*of promise*) se dédire ; ~**ache**
n maux *mpl* de reins ; ~**bencher** *n* membre
du parlement sans portefeuille ; ~**biting** *n*
médisance(s) *f(pl)* ; ~**bone** *n* colonne
vertébrale, épine dorsale ; ~**cloth** *n* toile
f de fond ; ~**date** *vt* (*letter*) antidater ;
~**dated pay rise** augmentation *f* avec
effet rétroactif ; ~**er** *n* partisan *m* ; (COMM)
commanditaire *m* ; ~**fire** *vi* (AUT)
pétarader ; (*plans*) mal tourner ;
~**gammon** *n* trictrac *m* ; ~**ground** *n*
arrière-plan *m* ; (*of events*) situation *f*, conjoncture *f* ; (*basic knowledge*) éléments *mpl*
de base ; (*experience*) formation *f* ; **family**
~**ground** milieu familial ; ~**ground noise**
n bruit *m* de fond ; ~**hand** *n* (TENNIS): *also*:
~**hand stroke**) revers *m* ; ~**handed** *a*
(*fig*) déloyal(e) ; équivoque ; ~**hander** *n*
(*bribe*) pot-de-vin *m* ; ~**ing** *n* (*fig*) soutien
m, appui *m* ; ~**lash** *n* contre-coup *m*,
répercussion *f* ; ~**log** *n* : ~**log of work**
travail *m* en retard ; ~ **number** *n* (*of
magazine etc*) vieux numéro ; ~ **pay** *n*
rappel *m* de traitement ; ~**side** *n* (*col*)
derrière *m*, postérieur *m* ; ~**stroke** *n* nage
f sur le dos ; ~**ward** *a* (*movement*) en
arrière ; (*measure*) rétrograde ; (*person,
country*) arriéré(e), attardé(e) ; (*shy*)
hésitant(e) ; ~**ward and forward movement** mouvement de va-et-vient ;
~**wards** *ad* (*move, go*) en arrière ; (*read
a list*) à l'envers, à rebours ; (*fall*) à la
renverse ; (*walk*) à reculons ; (*in time*) en
arrière, vers le passé ; ~**water** *n* (*fig*) coin
reculé ; bled perdu ; ~**yard** *n* arrière-cour
f.

bacon ['beɪkən] *n* bacon *m*, lard *m*.

bacteria [bæk'tɪərɪə] *npl* bactéries *fpl*.

bad [bæd] *a* mauvais(e) ; (*child*) vilain(e) ;
(*meat, food*) gâté(e), avarié(e) ; **his** ~ **leg**
sa jambe malade.

bade [bæd] *pt of* **bid**.

badge [bædʒ] *n* insigne *m* ; (*of policemen*)
plaque *f*.

badger ['bædʒə*] *n* blaireau *m* // *vt*
harceler.

badly ['bædlɪ] *ad* (*work, dress etc*) mal ; ~
wounded grièvement blessé ; **he needs it**
~ il en a absolument besoin ; ~ **off** *a,ad*
dans la gêne.

badminton ['bædmɪntən] *n* badminton *m*.

bad-tempered ['bæd'tempəd] *a* ayant
mauvais caractère ; de mauvaise humeur.

baffle ['bæfl] *vt* (*puzzle*) déconcerter.

bag [bæg] *n* sac *m* ; (*of hunter*) gibecière
f ; chasse *f* // *vt* (*col: take*) empocher ;
s'approprier ; (TECH) mettre en sacs ; ~**s
under the eyes** poches *fpl* sous les yeux ;
~**ful** *n* plein sac ; ~**gage** *n* bagages *mpl* ; ~
gy *a* avachi(e), qui fait des poches ;
~**pipes** *npl* cornemuse *f*.

Bahamas [bə'hɑ:məz] *npl*: **the** ~ les
Bahamas *fpl*.

bail [beɪl] *n* caution *f* // *vt* (*prisoner: gen:* **to give ~ to**) mettre en liberté sous caution; (*boat: also:* **~ out**) écoper; *see* **bale; to ~ out** *vt* (*prisoner*) payer la caution de.

bailiff ['beɪlɪf] *n* huissier *m*.

bait [beɪt] *n* appât *m* // *vt* appâter; (*fig*) tourmenter.

bake [beɪk] *vt* (faire) cuire au four // *vi* cuire (au four); faire de la pâtisserie; **~d beans** *npl* haricots blancs à la sauce tomate; **~r** *n* boulanger *m*; **~ry** *n* boulangerie *f*; boulangerie industrielle; **baking** *n* cuisson *f*; **baking powder** *n* levure *f* (chimique).

balaclava [bælə'klɑ:və] *n* (*also:* **~ helmet**) passe-montagne *m*.

balance ['bæləns] *n* équilibre *m*; (*COMM: sum*) solde *m*; (*scales*) balance *f*; (*ECON: of trade etc*) balance // *vt* mettre or faire tenir en équilibre; (*pros and cons*) peser; (*budget*) équilibrer; (*account*) balancer; (*compensate*) compenser, contrebalancer; **~ of trade/payments** balance commerciale/des comptes or paiements; **~ sheet** *n* bilan *m*; **~ wheel** *n* balancier *m*.

balcony ['bælkənɪ] *n* balcon *m*.

bald [bɔ:ld] *a* chauve; (*tree, hill*) dénudé(e); **~ness** *n* calvitie *f*.

bale [beɪl] *n* balle *f*, ballot *m*; **to ~ out** *vi* (*of a plane*) sauter en parachute.

baleful ['beɪlful] *a* funeste, maléfique.

balk [bɔ:k] *vi:* **to ~ (at)** regimber (contre); (*horse*) se dérober (devant).

ball [bɔ:l] *n* boule *f*; (*football*) ballon *m*; (*for tennis, golf*) balle *f*; (*dance*) bal *m*.

ballad ['bæləd] *n* ballade *f*.

ballast ['bæləst] *n* lest *m*.

ballerina [bælə'ri:nə] *n* ballerine *f*.

ballet ['bæleɪ] *n* ballet *m*; (*art*) danse *f* (classique).

ballistics [bə'lɪstɪks] *n* balistique *f*.

balloon [bə'lu:n] *n* ballon *m*; (*in comic strip*) bulle *f*; **~ist** *n* aéronaute *m/f*.

ballot ['bælət] *n* scrutin *m*; **~ box** *n* urne (électorale); **~ paper** *n* bulletin *m* de vote.

ball-point pen ['bɔ:lpɔɪnt'pɛn] *n* stylo *m* à bille.

ballroom ['bɔ:lrum] *n* salle *f* de bal.

balmy ['bɑ:mɪ] *a* (*breeze, air*) doux(douce); (*col*) = **barmy.**

balsam ['bɔ:lsəm] *n* baume *m*.

Baltic ['bɔ:ltɪk] *a,n:* **the ~ (Sea)** la (mer) Baltique.

bamboo [bæm'bu:] *n* bambou *m*.

bamboozle [bæm'bu:zl] *vt* (*col*) embobiner.

ban [bæn] *n* interdiction *f* // *vt* interdire.

banal [bə'nɑ:l] *a* banal(e).

banana [bə'nɑ:nə] *n* banane *f*.

band [bænd] *n* bande *f*; (*at a dance*) orchestre *m*; (*MIL*) musique *f*, fanfare *f*; **to ~ together** *vi* se liguer.

bandage ['bændɪdʒ] *n* bandage *m*, pansement *m*.

bandit ['bændɪt] *n* bandit *m*.

bandwagon ['bændwægən] *n:* **to jump on the ~** (*fig*) monter dans or prendre le train en marche.

bandy ['bændɪ] *vt* (*jokes, insults*) échanger; **to ~ about** vt employer à tout bout de champ or à tort et à travers.

bandy-legged ['bændɪ'lɛgd] *a* aux jambes arquées.

bang [bæŋ] *n* détonation *f*; (*of door*) claquement *m*; (*blow*) coup (violent) // *vt* frapper (violemment); (*door*) claquer // *vi* détoner; claquer; **to ~ at the door** cogner à la porte.

banger ['bæŋə*] *n* (*car: gen:* **old ~**) (vieux) tacot.

bangle ['bæŋgl] *n* bracelet *m*.

banish ['bænɪʃ] *vt* bannir.

banister(s) ['bænɪstə(z)] *n(pl)* rampe *f* (d'escalier).

banjo, **~es** or **~s** ['bændʒəu] *n* banjo *m*.

bank [bæŋk] *n* banque *f*; (*of river, lake*) bord *m*, rive *f*; (*of earth*) talus *m*, remblai *m* // *vi* (*AVIAT*) virer sur l'aile; (*COMM*): **they ~ with Pitt's** leur banque or banquier est Pitt's; **to ~ on** *vt fus* miser or tabler sur; **~ account** *n* compte en en banque; **~er** *n* banquier *m*; **B~ holiday** *n* jour férié (où les banques sont fermées); **~ing** *n* opérations *fpl* bancaires; profession *f* de banquier; **~ing hours** *npl* heures *fpl* d'ouverture des banques; **~note** *n* billet *m* de banque; **~ rate** *n* taux *m* de l'escompte.

bankrupt ['bæŋkrʌpt] *n* failli/e // *a* en faillite; **to go ~** faire faillite; **~cy** *n* faillite *f*.

banner ['bænə*] *n* bannière *f*.

bannister(s) ['bænɪstə(z)] *n(pl)* = **banister(s).**

banns [bænz] *npl* bans *mpl* (de mariage).

banquet ['bæŋkwɪt] *n* banquet *m*, festin *m*.

bantam-weight ['bæntəmweɪt] *n* poids *m* coq *inv.*

banter ['bæntə*] *n* badinage *m*.

baptism ['bæptɪzəm] *n* baptême *m*.

Baptist ['bæptɪst] *n* baptiste *m/f*.

baptize [bæp'taɪz] *vt* baptiser.

bar [bɑ:*] *n* barre *f*; (*of window etc*) barreau *m*; (*of chocolate*) tablette *f*, plaque *f*; (*fig*) obstacle *m*; mesure *f* d'exclusion; (*pub*) bar *m*; (*counter: in pub*) comptoir *m*, bar *m*; (*MUS*) mesure // *vt* (*road*) barrer; (*window*) munir de barreaux; (*person*) exclure; (*activity*) interdire; **~ of soap** savonnette *f*; **the B~** (*LAW*) le barreau; **~ none** sans exception.

Barbados [bɑ:'beɪdɔs] *n* Barbade *f*.

barbaric [bɑ:'bærɪk] *a* barbare.

barbarous ['bɑ:bərəs] *a* barbare, cruel(le).

barbecue ['bɑ:bɪkju:] *n* barbecue *m*.

barbed wire ['bɑ:bd'waɪə*] *n* fil *m* de fer barbelé.

barber ['bɑ:bə*] *n* coiffeur *m* (pour hommes).

barbiturate [bɑ:'bɪtjurɪt] *n* barbiturique *m*.

bare [bɛə*] *a* nu(e) // *vt* mettre à nu, dénuder; (*teeth*) montrer; **the ~ essentials** le strict nécessaire; **~back** *ad* à cru, sans selle; **~faced** *a* impudent(e), effronté(e); **~foot** *a,ad* nu-pieds, (les) pieds nus; **~headed** *a,ad* nu-tête, (la) tête nue; **~ly** *ad* à peine.

bargain ['bɑːgɪn] n (transaction) marché m; (good buy) affaire f, occasion f // vi (haggle) marchander; (trade) négocier, traiter; **into the ~** par-dessus le marché.

barge [bɑːdʒ] n péniche f; **to ~ in** vi (walk in) faire irruption; (interrupt talk) intervenir mal à propos; **to ~ into** vt fus rentrer dans.

baritone ['bærɪtəun] n baryton m.

bark [bɑːk] n (of tree) écorce f, (of dog) aboiement m // vi aboyer.

barley ['bɑːlɪ] n orge f.

barmaid ['bɑːmeɪd] n serveuse f (de bar), barmaid f.

barman ['bɑːmən] n serveur m (de bar), barman m.

barmy ['bɑːmɪ] a (col) timbré(e), cinglé(e).

barn [bɑːn] n grange f.

barnacle ['bɑːnəkl] n anatife m, bernache f.

barometer [bə'rɒmɪtə*] n baromètre m.

baron ['bærən] n baron m; **~ess** baronne f.

barracks ['bærəks] npl caserne f.

barrage ['bærɑːʒ] n (MIL) tir m de barrage; (dam) barrage m.

barrel ['bærəl] n tonneau m; (of gun) canon m; **~ organ** n orgue m de Barbarie.

barren ['bærən] a stérile; (hills) aride.

barricade [bærɪ'keɪd] n barricade f // vt barricader.

barrier ['bærɪə*] n barrière f.

barring ['bɑːrɪŋ] prep sauf.

barrister ['bærɪstə*] n avocat (plaidant).

barrow ['bærəu] n (cart) charrette f à bras.

bartender ['bɑːtɛndə*] n (US) barman m.

barter ['bɑːtə*] n échange m, troc m // vt: **to ~ sth for** échanger qch contre.

base [beɪs] n base f // vt: **to ~ sth on** baser or fonder qch sur // a vil(e), bas(se); **coffee~d** à base de café; **a Paris~d firm** une maison opérant de Paris or dont le siège est à Paris; **~ball** n base-ball m; **~ment** n sous-sol m.

bases ['beɪsiːz] npl of **basis**; ['beɪsɪz] npl of **base**.

bash [bæʃ] vt (col) frapper, cogner; **~ed in** a enfoncé(e), défoncé(e).

bashful ['bæʃful] a timide; modeste.

bashing ['bæʃɪŋ] n (col) raclée f.

basic ['beɪsɪk] a fondamental(e), de base; réduit(e) au minimum, rudimentaire; **~ally** [-lɪ] ad fondamentalement, à la base; en fait, au fond.

basil ['bæzl] n basilic m.

basin ['beɪsn] n (vessel, also GEO) cuvette f, bassin m; (for food) bol m; (also: **wash~**) lavabo m.

basis, pl **bases** ['beɪsɪs, -siːz] n base f.

bask [bɑːsk] vi: **to ~ in the sun** se chauffer au soleil.

basket ['bɑːskɪt] n corbeille f; (with handle) panier m; **~ball** n basket-ball m.

bass [beɪs] n (MUS) basse f; **~ clef** n clé f de fa.

bassoon [bə'suːn] n basson m.

bastard ['bɑːstəd] n enfant naturel(le), bâtard/e; (col!) salaud m(!).

baste [beɪst] vt (CULIN) arroser; (SEWING) bâtir, faufiler.

bastion ['bæstɪən] n bastion m.

bat [bæt] n chauve-souris f; (for baseball etc) batte f; (for table tennis) raquette f; **off one's own ~** de sa propre initiative; **he didn't ~ an eyelid** il n'a pas sourcillé or bronché.

batch [bætʃ] n (of bread) fournée f; (of papers) liasse f.

bated ['beɪtɪd] a: **with ~ breath** en retenant son souffle.

bath [bɑːθ, pl bɑːðz] n see also **baths**; bain m; (bathtub) baignoire f // vt baigner, donner un bain à; **to have a ~** prendre un bain; **~chair** n fauteuil roulant.

bathe [beɪð] vi se baigner // vt baigner; **~r** n baigneur/euse.

bathing ['beɪðɪŋ] n baignade f; **~ cap** n bonnet m de bain; **~ costume** n maillot m (de bain).

bath: ~mat n tapis m de bain; **~room** n salle f de bains; **~s** npl établissement m de bains(-douches); **~ towel** n serviette f de bain.

batman ['bætmən] n (MIL) ordonnance f.

baton ['bætən] n bâton m; (MUS) baguette f; (club) matraque f.

battalion [bə'tælɪən] n bataillon m.

batter ['bætə*] vt battre // n pâte f à frire; **~ed** a (hat, pan) cabossé(e); **~ed wife/child** épouse/enfant maltraité(e) or martyr(e); **~ing ram** n bélier m (fig).

battery ['bætərɪ] n batterie f; (of torch) pile f.

battle ['bætl] n bataille f, combat m // vi se battre, lutter; **~ dress** n tenue f de campagne or d'assaut; **~field** n champ m de bataille; **~ments** npl remparts mpl; **~ship** n cuirassé m.

baulk [bɔːlk] vi = **balk**.

bawdy ['bɔːdɪ] a paillard(e).

bawl [bɔːl] vi hurler, brailler.

bay [beɪ] n (of sea) baie f; **to hold sb at ~** tenir qn à distance or en échec.

bayonet ['beɪənɪt] n baïonnette f.

bay window ['beɪ'wɪndəu] n baie vitrée.

bazaar [bə'zɑː*] n bazar m; vente f de charité.

bazooka [bə'zuːkə] n bazooka m.

b. & b., B. & B. abbr see **bed**.

BBC n abbr of British Broadcasting Corporation (office de la radiodiffusion et télévision britannique).

B.C. ad (abbr of before Christ) av. J.-C.

BCG n (abbr of Bacillus Calmette-Guérin) BCG.

be, pt **was, were**, pp **been** [biː, wɔz, wɔː*, biːn] vi être; **how are you?** comment allez-vous?; **I am warm** j'ai chaud; **it is cold** il fait froid; **how much is it?** combien ça coûte?; **he is four (years old)** il a quatre ans; **2 and 2 are 4** 2 et 2 font 4; **where have you been?** où êtes-vous allé(s)?; où étiez-vous?.

beach [biːtʃ] n plage f // vt échouer; **~wear** n tenues fpl de plage.

beacon ['biːkən] n (lighthouse) fanal m; (marker) balise f.

bead [biːd] n perle f.

beak [biːk] n bec m.

beaker ['biːkə*] n gobelet m.

beam [biːm] n poutre f; (of light) rayon m // vi rayonner; ~ing a (sun, smile) radieux(euse).

bean [biːn] n haricot m; (of coffee) grain m.

bear [bɛə*] n ours m // vb (pt bore, pp borne [bɔː*, bɔːn]) vt porter; (endure) supporter // vi: to ~ right/left obliquer à droite/gauche, se diriger vers la droite/gauche; to ~ the responsibility of assumer la responsabilité de; to ~ comparison with soutenir la comparaison avec; ~able a supportable.

beard [biəd] n barbe f; ~ed a barbu(e).

bearer ['bɛərə*] n porteur m.

bearing ['bɛərɪŋ] n maintien m, allure f; (connection) rapport m; (ball) ~s npl roulements mpl (à billes); to take a ~ faire le point; to find one's ~s s'orienter.

beast [biːst] n bête f; (col): he's a ~ c'est une brute; ~ly a infect(e).

beat [biːt] n battement m; (MUS) temps m; mesure f; (of policeman) ronde f // vt (pt beat, pp beaten) battre; off the ~en track hors des chemins or sentiers battus; to ~ about the bush tourner autour du pot; to ~ time battre la mesure; to ~ off vt repousser; to ~ up vt (col: person) tabasser; (eggs) battre; ~er n (for eggs, cream) fouet m, batteur m; ~ing n raclée f.

beautician [bjuːˈtɪʃən] n esthéticien/ne.

beautiful ['bjuːtɪful] a beau(belle); ~ly ad admirablement.

beautify ['bjuːtɪfaɪ] vt embellir.

beauty ['bjuːtɪ] n beauté f; ~ salon n institut m de beauté; ~ spot n grain m de beauté; (TOURISM) site naturel (d'une grande beauté).

beaver ['biːvə*] n castor m.

becalmed [bɪˈkɑːmd] a immobilisé(e) par le calme plat.

became [bɪˈkeɪm] pt of become.

because [bɪˈkɔz] cj parce que; ~ of prep à cause de.

beckon ['bɛkən] vt (also: ~ to) faire signe (de venir) à.

become [bɪˈkʌm] vt (irg: like come) devenir; to ~ fat/thin grossir/maigrir; what has ~ of him? qu'est-il devenu?

becoming [bɪˈkʌmɪŋ] a (behaviour) convenable, bienséant(e); (clothes) seyant(e).

bed [bɛd] n lit m; (of flowers) parterre m; (of coal, clay) couche f; to go to ~ aller se coucher; ~ and breakfast (b. & b.) n (terms) chambre et petit déjeuner; ~clothes npl couvertures fpl et draps mpl; ~cover n couvre-lit m, dessus-de-lit m; ~ding n literie f.

bedlam ['bɛdləm] n chahut m, cirque m.

bedpost ['bɛdpəust] n colonne f de lit.

bedraggled [bɪˈdrægld] a dépenaillé(e), les vêtements en désordre.

bed: ~ridden a cloué(e) au lit; ~room n chambre f (à coucher); ~side n: at sb's ~side au chevet de qn; ~side book n livre m de chevet; ~sit(ter) n chambre meublée, studio m; ~spread n couvre-lit m, dessus-de-lit m.

bee [biː] n abeille f.

beech [biːtʃ] n hêtre m.

beef [biːf] n bœuf m.

beehive ['biːhaɪv] n ruche f.

beeline ['biːlaɪn] n: to make a ~ for se diriger tout droit vers.

been [biːn] pp of be.

beer [bɪə*] n bière f.

beetle ['biːtl] n scarabée m; coléoptère m.

beetroot ['biːtruːt] n betterave f.

befall [bɪˈfɔːl] vi(vt) (irg: like fall) advenir (à).

befit [bɪˈfɪt] vt seoir à.

before [bɪˈfɔː*] prep (of time) avant; (of space) devant // cj avant que + sub; avant de // ad avant; the week ~ la semaine précédente or d'avant; I've seen it ~ je l'ai déjà vu; I've never seen it ~ c'est la première fois que je le vois; ~hand ad au préalable, à l'avance.

befriend [bɪˈfrɛnd] vt venir en aide à; traiter en ami.

beg [bɛg] vi mendier // vt mendier; (favour) quémander, solliciter; (entreat) supplier.

began [bɪˈgæn] pt of begin.

beggar ['bɛgə*] n (also: ~man, ~woman) mendiant/e.

begin, pt began, pp begun [bɪˈgɪn, -ˈgæn, -ˈgʌn] vt, vi commencer; ~ner n débutant/e; ~ning n commencement m, début m.

begrudge [bɪˈgrʌdʒ] vt: to ~ sb sth envier qch à qn; donner qch à contrecœur or à regret à qn; I don't ~ doing it je le fais volontiers.

begun [bɪˈgʌn] pp of begin.

behalf [bɪˈhɑːf] n: on ~ of de la part de; au nom de; pour le compte de.

behave [bɪˈheɪv] vi se conduire, se comporter; (well: also: ~ o.s.) se conduire bien or comme il faut.

behaviour, behavior (US) [bɪˈheɪvjə*] n comportement m, conduite f (the latter often from a moral point of view, the former being more objective).

beheld [bɪˈhɛld] pt,pp of behold.

behind [bɪˈhaɪnd] prep derrière; (time) en retard sur // ad derrière; en retard // n derrière m; ~ the scenes dans les coulisses.

behold [bɪˈhəuld] vt (irg: like hold) apercevoir, voir.

beige [beɪʒ] a beige.

being ['biːɪŋ] n être m; to come into ~ prendre naissance.

belated [bɪˈleɪtɪd] a tardif(ive).

belch [bɛltʃ] vi avoir un renvoi, roter // vt (gen: ~ out: smoke etc) vomir, cracher.

belfry ['bɛlfrɪ] n beffroi m.

Belgian ['bɛldʒən] a belge, de Belgique // n Belge m/f.

Belgium ['bɛldʒəm] n Belgique f.

belie [bɪˈlaɪ] vt démentir.

belief [bɪˈliːf] n (opinion) conviction f; (trust, faith) foi f; (acceptance as true) croyance f.

believable [bɪˈliːvəbl] a croyable.

believe [bɪˈliːv] vt,vi croire; ~r n croyant/e.

belittle [bɪˈlɪtl] vt déprécier, rabaisser.

bell [bɛl] n cloche f; (small) clochette f, grelot m; (on door) sonnette f; (electric) sonnerie f; **~-bottomed trousers** npl pantalon m à pattes d'éléphant.

belligerent [bɪ'lɪdʒərənt] a (at war) belligérant(e); (fig) agressif(ive).

bellow ['bɛləu] vi mugir // vt (orders) hurler.

bellows ['bɛləuz] npl soufflet m.

belly ['bɛlɪ] n ventre m; **to ~ache** vi (col) ronchonner; **~button** n nombril m.

belong [bɪ'lɔŋ] vi: **to ~ to** appartenir à; (club etc) faire partie de; **this book ~s here** ce livre va ici, la place de ce livre est ici; **~ings** npl affaires fpl, possessions fpl.

beloved [bɪ'lʌvɪd] a (bien-)aimé(e), chéri(e) // n bien-aimé/e.

below [bɪ'ləu] prep sous, au-dessous de // ad en dessous; en contre-bas; **see ~** voir plus bas or plus loin or ci-dessous.

belt [bɛlt] n ceinture f; (TECH) courroie f // vt (thrash) donner une raclée à // vi (col) filer (à toutes jambes).

bench [bɛntʃ] n banc m; (in workshop) établi m; **the B~** (LAW) la magistrature, la Cour.

bend [bɛnd] vb (pt,pp bent [bɛnt]) vt courber; (leg, arm) plier // vi se courber // n (in road) virage m, tournant m; (in pipe, river) coude m; **to ~ down** vi se baisser; **to ~ over** vi se pencher.

beneath [bɪ'ni:θ] prep sous, au-dessous de; (unworthy of) indigne de // ad dessous, au-dessous, en bas.

benefactor ['bɛnɪfæktə*] n bienfaiteur m.

benefactress ['bɛnɪfæktrɪs] n bienfaitrice f.

beneficial [bɛnɪ'fɪʃəl] a salutaire; avantageux(euse).

benefit ['bɛnɪfɪt] n avantage m, profit m; (allowance of money) allocation f // vt faire du bien à, profiter à // vi: **he'll ~ from it** cela lui fera du bien, il y gagnera or s'en trouvera bien; **~ performance** n représentation f or gala m de bienfaisance.

Benelux ['bɛnɪlʌks] n Bénélux m.

benevolent [bɪ'nɛvələnt] a bienveillant(e).

bent [bɛnt] pt,pp of **bend** // n inclination f, penchant m // a (dishonest) véreux(euse); **to be ~ on** être résolu(e) à.

bequeath [bɪ'kwi:ð] vt léguer.

bequest [bɪ'kwɛst] n legs m.

bereaved [bɪ'ri:vd] n: **the ~** la famille du disparu.

bereavement [bɪ'ri:vmənt] n deuil m.

beret ['bɛreɪ] n béret m.

Bermuda [bə:'mju:də] n Bermudes fpl.

berry ['bɛrɪ] n baie f.

berserk [bə'sə:k] a: **to go ~** être pris(e) d'une rage incontrôlable; se déchaîner.

berth [bə:θ] n (bed) couchette f; (for ship) poste m d'amarrage; mouillage m // vi (in harbour) venir à quai; (at anchor) mouiller.

beseech, pt,pp besought [bɪ'si:tʃ, -'sɔ:t] vt implorer, supplier.

beset, pt,pp beset [bɪ'sɛt] vt assaillir.

beside [bɪ'saɪd] prep à côté de; **to be ~ o.s. (with anger)** être hors de soi.

besides [bɪ'saɪdz] ad en outre, de plus // prep en plus de; excepté.

besiege [bɪ'si:dʒ] vt (town) assiéger; (fig) assaillir.

besought [bɪ'sɔ:t] pt,pp of **beseech**.

bespectacled [bɪ'spɛktɪkld] a à lunettes.

best [bɛst] a meilleur(e) // ad le mieux; **the ~ part of** (quantity) le plus clair de, la plus grande partie de; **at ~** au mieux; **to make the ~ of sth** s'accommoder de qch (du mieux que l'on peut); **to the ~ of my knowledge** pour autant que je sache; **to the ~ of my ability** du mieux que je pourrai; **~ man** n garçon m d'honneur.

bestow [bɪ'stəu] vt accorder; (title) conférer.

bestseller ['bɛst'sɛlə*] n bestseller m, succès m de librairie.

bet [bɛt] n pari m // vt,vi (pt,pp bet or betted) parier.

betray [bɪ'treɪ] vt trahir; **~al** n trahison f.

better ['bɛtə*] a meilleur(e) // ad mieux // vt améliorer // n: **to get the ~ of** triompher de, l'emporter sur; **you had ~ do it** vous feriez mieux de le faire; **he thought ~ of it** il s'est ravisé; **to get ~** aller mieux; s'améliorer; **~ off** a plus à l'aise financièrement; (fig): **you'd be ~ off this way** vous vous en trouveriez mieux ainsi, ce serait mieux or plus pratique ainsi.

betting ['bɛtɪŋ] n paris mpl; **~ shop** n bureau m de paris.

between [bɪ'twi:n] prep entre // ad au milieu; dans l'intervalle.

bevel ['bɛvəl] n (also: **~ edge**) biseau m.

beverage ['bɛvərɪdʒ] n boisson f (gén sans alcool).

bevy ['bɛvɪ] n: **a ~ of** un essaim or une volée de.

beware [bɪ'wɛə*] vt,vi: **to ~ (of)** prendre garde (à).

bewildered [bɪ'wɪldəd] a dérouté(e), ahuri(e).

bewitching [bɪ'wɪtʃɪŋ] a enchanteur-(teresse).

beyond [bɪ'jɔnd] prep (in space) au-delà de; (exceeding) au-dessus de // ad au-delà; **~ doubt** hors de doute; **~ repair** irréparable.

bias ['baɪəs] n (prejudice) préjugé m, parti pris; (preference) prévention f; **~(s)ed** a partial(e), montrant un parti pris.

bib [bɪb] n bavoir m, bavette f.

Bible ['baɪbl] n Bible f.

bibliography [bɪblɪ'ɔgrəfɪ] n bibliographie f.

bicker ['bɪkə*] vi se chamailler.

bicycle ['baɪsɪkl] n bicyclette f.

bid [bɪd] n offre f; (at auction) enchère f; (attempt) tentative f // vb (pt bade [bæd] or bid, pp bidden ['bɪdn] or bid) vi faire une enchère or offre // vt faire une enchère or offre de; **to ~ sb good day** souhaiter le bonjour à qn; **~der** n: **the highest ~der** le plus offrant; **~ding** n enchères fpl.

bide [baɪd] vt: **to ~ one's time** attendre son heure.

bier [bɪə*] n bière f.

big [bɪg] a grand(e); gros(se).

bigamy ['bɪgəmɪ] n bigamie f.

bigheaded ['bɪg'hɛdɪd] a prétentieux(euse).

big-hearted ['bɪg'hɑːtɪd] a au grand cœur.

bigot ['bɪgət] n fanatique m/f, sectaire m/f; ~ed a fanatique, sectaire; ~ry n fanatisme m, sectarisme m.

bigwig ['bɪgwɪg] n (col) grosse légume, huile f.

bike [baɪk] n vélo m, bécane f.

bikini [bɪ'kiːnɪ] n bikini m.

bile [baɪl] n bile f.

bilingual [baɪ'lɪŋgwəl] a bilingue.

bilious ['bɪlɪəs] a bilieux(euse); (fig) maussade, irritable.

bill [bɪl] n note f, facture f; (POL) projet m de loi; (US: banknote) billet m (de banque); (of bird) bec m; to fit or fill the ~ (fig) faire l'affaire.

billet ['bɪlɪt] n cantonnement m (chez l'habitant).

billfold ['bɪlfəuld] n (US) portefeuille m.

billiards ['bɪlɪədz] n (jeu m de) billard m.

billion ['bɪljən] n (Brit) billion m (million de millions); (US) milliard m.

billy goat ['bɪlɪgəut] n bouc m.

bin [bɪn] n boîte f; (also: dust~) poubelle f; (for coal) coffre m; bread~ n boîte f or huche f à pain.

bind, pt,pp **bound** [baɪnd, baund] vt attacher; (book) relier; (oblige) obliger, contraindre; ~ing n (of book) reliure f // a (contract) constituant une obligation.

bingo ['bɪŋgəu] n sorte de jeu de loto pratiqué dans des établissements publics et connaissant une grande vogue en Grande-Bretagne.

binoculars [bɪ'nɔkjuləz] npl jumelles fpl.

bio... [baɪə'...] prefix: ~**chemistry** n biochimie f; ~**graphic(al)** a biographique; ~**graphy** [baɪ'ɔgrəfɪ] n biographie f; ~**logical** a biologique; ~**logist** [baɪ'ɔlədʒɪst] n biologiste m/f; ~**logy** [baɪ'ɔlədʒɪ] n biologie f.

birch [bəːtʃ] n bouleau m.

bird [bəːd] n oiseau m; (col: girl) nana f; ~'s-eye view n vue f à vol d'oiseau; (fig) vue d'ensemble or générale; ~ watcher n ornithologue m/f amateur.

birth [bəːθ] n naissance f; ~ certificate n acte m de naissance; ~ control n limitation f des naissances; méthode(s) contraceptive(s); ~day n anniversaire m; ~place n lieu m de naissance; ~ rate n (taux m de) natalité f.

biscuit ['bɪskɪt] n biscuit m.

bisect [baɪ'sɛkt] vt couper or diviser en deux.

bishop ['bɪʃəp] n évêque m.

bit [bɪt] pt of **bite** // n morceau m; (of tool) mèche f; (of horse) mors m; a ~ of un peu de; a ~ mad/dangerous un peu fou/risqué.

bitch [bɪtʃ] n (dog) chienne f; (col!) salope f (!), garce f.

bite [baɪt] vt,vi (pt **bit** [bɪt], pp **bitten** ['bɪtn]) mordre // n morsure f; (insect ~) piqûre f; (mouthful) bouchée f; let's have

a ~ (to eat) mangeons un morceau; to ~ one's nails se ronger les ongles.

biting ['baɪtɪŋ] a mordant(e).

bitten ['bɪtn] pp of **bite**.

bitter ['bɪtə*] a amer(ère); (wind, criticism) cinglant(e) // n (beer) bière f (à forte teneur en houblon); to the ~ end jusqu'au bout; ~ness n amertume f; goût amer; ~sweet a aigre-doux(douce).

bivouac ['bɪvuæk] n bivouac m.

bizarre [bɪ'zɑː*] a bizarre.

blab [blæb] vi jaser, trop parler // vt (also: ~ out) laisser échapper, aller raconter.

black [blæk] a noir(e) // n noir m // vt (shoes) cirer; (INDUSTRY) boycotter; to give sb a ~ eye pocher l'œil à qn, faire un œil au beurre noir à qn; ~ and blue a couvert(e) de bleus; ~berry n mûre f; ~bird n merle m; ~board n tableau noir; ~currant n cassis m; ~en vt noircir; ~leg n briseur m de grève, jaune m; ~list n liste noire; ~mail n chantage m // vt faire chanter, soumettre au chantage; ~mailer n maître-chanteur m; ~ market n marché noir; ~out n panne f d'électricité; (fainting) syncope f; (in wartime) black-out m; the B~ Sea n la mer Noire; ~ sheep n brebis galeuse; ~smith n forgeron m.

bladder ['blædə*] n vessie f.

blade [bleɪd] n lame f; (of oar) plat m; ~ of grass brin m d'herbe.

blame [bleɪm] n faute f, blâme m // vt: to ~ sb/sth for sth attribuer à qn/qch la responsabilité de qch; reprocher qch à qn/qch; who's to ~? qui est le fautif or coupable or responsable?; ~less a irréprochable.

bland [blænd] a affable; (taste) doux(douce), fade.

blank [blæŋk] a blanc(blanche); (look) sans expression, dénué(e) d'expression // n espace m vide, blanc m; (cartridge) cartouche f à blanc.

blanket ['blæŋkɪt] n couverture f.

blare [blɛə*] vi (brass band, horns, radio) beugler.

blarney ['blɑːnɪ] n boniment m.

blasé ['blɑːzeɪ] a blasé(e).

blasphemous ['blæsfɪməs] a (words) blasphématoire; (person) blasphémateur(trice).

blasphemy ['blæsfɪmɪ] n blasphème m.

blast [blɑːst] n souffle m; explosion f // vt faire sauter or exploser; ~-off n (SPACE) lancement m.

blatant ['bleɪtənt] a flagrant(e), criant(e).

blaze [bleɪz] n (fire) incendie m; (fig) flamboiement m // vi (fire) flamber; (fig) flamboyer, resplendir // vt: to ~ a trail (fig) montrer la voie.

blazer ['bleɪzə*] n blazer m.

bleach [bliːtʃ] n (also: household ~) eau f de Javel // vt (linen) blanchir; ~ed a (hair) oxygéné(e), décoloré(e).

bleak [bliːk] a morne, désolé(e).

bleary-eyed ['blɪərɪ'aɪd] a aux yeux pleins de sommeil.

bleat [bliːt] n bêlement m // vi bêler.

bleed, pt,pp **bled** [bliːd, blɛd] vt, vi

saigner ; my nose is ~ing je saigne du nez.

blemish ['blɛmɪʃ] n défaut m ; (on reputation) tache f.

blend [blɛnd] n mélange m // vt mélanger // vi (colours etc) se mélanger, se fondre, s'allier.

bless, pt,pp **blessed** or **blest** [blɛs, blɛst] vt bénir ; **to be ~ed with** avoir le bonheur de jouir de or d'avoir ; ~**ing** n bénédiction f ; bienfait m.

blew [blu:] pt of **blow**.

blight [blaɪt] n (of plants) rouille f // vt (hopes etc) anéantir, briser.

blimey ['blaɪmɪ] excl (col) mince alors!

blind [blaɪnd] a aveugle // n (for window) store m // vt aveugler ; **to turn a ~ eye (on** or **to)** fermer les yeux (sur) ; ~ **alley** n impasse f ; ~ **corner** n virage m sans visibilité ; ~**fold** n bandeau m // a,ad les yeux bandés // vt bander les yeux à ; ~**ly** ad aveuglément ; ~**ness** n cécité f ; (fig) aveuglement m ; ~ **spot** n (AUT etc) angle m aveugle ; (fig) angle mort.

blink [blɪŋk] vi cligner des yeux ; (light) clignoter ; ~**ers** npl œillères fpl.

blinking ['blɪŋkɪŋ] a (col): this ~... ce fichu or sacré ... .

bliss [blɪs] n félicité f, bonheur m sans mélange.

blister ['blɪstə*] n (on skin) ampoule f, cloque f ; (on paintwork) boursouflure f // vi (paint) se boursoufler, se cloquer.

blithe [blaɪð] a joyeux(euse), allègre.

blithering ['blɪðərɪŋ] a (col): this ~ **idiot** cet espèce d'idiot.

blitz [blɪts] n bombardement (aérien).

blizzard ['blɪzəd] n blizzard m, tempête f de neige.

bloated ['bləutɪd] a (face) bouffi(e) ; (stomach) gonflé(e).

blob [blɔb] n (drop) goutte f ; (stain, spot) tache f.

block [blɔk] n bloc m ; (in pipes) obstruction f ; (toy) cube m ; (of buildings) pâté m (de maisons) // vt bloquer ; ~**ade** ['-'keɪd] n blocus m // vt faire le blocus de ; ~**age** n obstruction f ; ~**head** n imbécile m/f ; ~ **of flats** n immeuble (locatif) ; ~ **letters** npl majuscules fpl.

bloke [bləuk] n (col) type m.

blonde [blɔnd] a,n blond(e).

blood [blʌd] n sang m ; ~ **donor** n donneur/euse de sang ; ~ **group** n groupe sanguin ; ~**less** a (victory) sans effusion de sang ; (pale) anémié(e) ; ~ **poisoning** n empoisonnement m du sang ; ~ **pressure** n tension f (artérielle) ; ~**shed** n effusion f de sang, carnage m ; ~**shot** a: ~**shot eyes** yeux injectés de sang ; ~**stained** a tache(e) de sang ; ~**stream** n sang m, système sanguin ; ~**thirsty** a sanguinaire ; ~ **transfusion** n transfusion f de sang ; ~**y** a sanglant(e) ; (col!): this ~**y ...** ce foutu..., ce putain de... (!) ; ~**y strong/good** (col!) vachement or sacrément fort/bon ; ~**y-minded** a (col) contrariant(e), obstiné(e).

bloom [blu:m] n fleur f ; (fig) épanouissement m // vi être en fleur ; (fig) s'épanouir ; être florissant ; ~**ing** a (col): this ~**ing...** ce fichu or sacré... .

blossom ['blɔsəm] n fleur(s) f(pl) // vi être en fleurs ; (fig) s'épanouir.

blot [blɔt] n tache f // vt tacher ; (ink) sécher ; **to ~ out** vt (memories) effacer ; (view) cacher, masquer ; (nation, city) annihiler.

blotchy ['blɔtʃɪ] a (complexion) couvert(e) de marbrures.

blotting paper ['blɔtɪŋpeɪpə*] n buvard m.

blouse [blauz] n (feminine garment) chemisier m, corsage m.

blow [bləu] n coup m // vb (pt **blew**, pp **blown** [blu:, bləun]) vi souffler // vt (glass) souffler ; (fuse) faire sauter ; **to ~ one's nose** se moucher ; **to ~ a whistle** siffler ; **to ~ away** vt chasser, faire s'envoler ; **to ~ down** vt faire tomber, renverser ; **to ~ off** vt emporter ; **to ~ off course** faire dévier ; **to ~ out** vi éclater, sauter ; **to ~ over** vi s'apaiser ; **to ~ up** vi exploser, sauter // vt faire sauter ; (tyre) gonfler ; (PHOT) agrandir ; ~**lamp** n chalumeau m ; ~**-out** n (of tyre) éclatement m.

blubber ['blʌbə*] n blanc m de baleine // vi (pej) pleurer comme un veau.

bludgeon ['blʌdʒən] n gourdin m, trique f.

blue [blu:] a bleu(e) ; ~ **film/joke** film m/histoire f pornographique ; **to have the ~s** avoir le cafard ; ~**bell** n jacinthe f des bois ; ~**bottle** n mouche f à viande ; ~**jeans** npl blue-jeans mpl ; ~**print** n (fig) projet m, plan directeur.

bluff [blʌf] vi bluffer // n bluff m // a (person) bourru(e), brusque ; **to call sb's ~** mettre qn au défi d'exécuter ses menaces.

blunder ['blʌndə*] n gaffe f, bévue f // vi faire une gaffe or une bévue.

blunt [blʌnt] a émoussé(e), peu tranchant(e) ; (person) brusque, ne mâchant pas ses mots // vt émousser ; ~**ly** ad carrément, sans prendre de gants ; ~**ness** n (of person) brusquerie f, franchise brutale.

blur [blə:*] n tache or masse floue or confuse // vt brouiller, rendre flou.

blurt [blə:t]: **to ~ out** vt (reveal) lâcher ; (say) balbutier, dire d'une voix entrecoupée.

blush [blʌʃ] vi rougir // n rougeur f.

blustering ['blʌstərɪŋ] a fanfaron(ne).

blustery ['blʌstərɪ] a (weather) à bourrasques.

B.O. n (abbr of body odour) odeurs corporelles.

boar [bɔ:*] n sanglier m.

board [bɔ:d] n planche f ; (on wall) panneau m ; (committee) conseil m, comité m ; (in firm) conseil d'administration // vt (ship) monter à bord de ; (train) monter dans ; ~ **and lodging** n chambre f avec pension ; **full ~** pension complète ; **with ~ and lodging** (job) logé nourri ; **to go by the ~** (fig): **which goes by the ~** (fig) qu'on laisse tomber, qu'on abandonne ; **to ~ up** vt (door) condamner (au moyen de planches, de tôle) ; ~**er** n pensionnaire m/f ; (SCOL) interne m/f, pensionnaire m/f ; ~**ing house** n pension f ; ~**ing school** n internat *m*, pensionnat *m* ; ~ **room** *n* salle *f* du conseil d'administration (*souvent symbole de pouvoir décisionnaire*).

boast [bəust] *vi* se vanter // *vt* s'enorgueillir de // *n* vantardise *f* ; sujet *m* d'orgueil or de fierté ; ~**ful** *a* vantard(e) ; ~**fulness** *n* vantardise *f*.

boat [bəut] *n* bateau *m* ; (*small*) canot *m* ; barque *f* ; **to be in the same** ~ (*fig*) être logé à la même enseigne ; ~**er** *n* (*hat*) canotier *m* ; ~**ing** *n* canotage *m* ; ~**swain** ['bəusn] *n* maître *m* d'équipage.

bob [bɔb] *vi* (*boat, cork on water: also:* ~ **up and down**) danser, se balancer // *n* (*col*) = **shilling** ; **to** ~ **up** *vi* surgir or apparaître brusquement.

bobbin ['bɔbɪn] *n* bobine *f* ; (*of sewing machine*) navette *f*.

bobby ['bɔbɪ] *n* (*col*) ≈ agent *m* (de police).

bobsleigh ['bɔbsleɪ] *n* bob *m*.

bodice ['bɔdɪs] *n* corsage *m*.

bodily ['bɔdɪlɪ] *a* corporel(le) // *ad* physiquement ; dans son entier or ensemble ; en personne.

body ['bɔdɪ] *n* corps *m* ; (*of car*) carrosserie *f* ; (*of plane*) fuselage *m* ; (*fig: society*) organe *m*, organisme *m* ; (*fig: quantity*) ensemble *m*, masse *f* ; (*of wine*) corps *m* ; **in a** ~ en masse, ensemble ; ~**guard** *n* garde *m* du corps ; ~ **repairs** *npl* travaux *mpl* de carrosserie ; ~**work** *n* carrosserie *f*.

bog [bɔg] *n* tourbière *f* // *vt*: **to get** ~**ged down** (*fig*) s'enliser.

boggle ['bɔgl] *vi*: **the mind** ~**s** c'est incroyable, on en reste sidéré.

bogie ['bəugɪ] *n* bogie *m*.

bogus ['bəugəs] *a* bidon *inv* ; fantôme.

boil [bɔɪl] *vt* (faire) bouillir // *vi* bouillir // *n* (*MED*) furoncle *m* ; **to come to the** ~ bouillir ; **to** ~ **down** *vi* (*fig*): **to** ~ **down to** se réduire or ramener à ; ~**er** *n* chaudière *f* ; ~**er suit** *n* bleu *m* de travail, combinaison *f* ; ~**ing hot** *a* brûlant(e), bouillant(e) ; ~**ing point** *n* point *m* d'ébullition.

boisterous ['bɔɪstərəs] *a* bruyant(e), tapageur(euse).

bold [bəuld] *a* hardi(e), audacieux(euse) ; (*pej*) effronté(e) ; (*outline, colour*) franc(franche), tranché(e), marqué(e) ; ~**ness** *n* hardiesse *f*, audace *f* ; aplomb *m*, effronterie *f* ; ~ **type** *n* caractères *mpl* gras.

Bolivia [bə'lɪvɪə] *n* Bolivie *f*.

bollard ['bɔləd] *n* (*NAUT*) bitte *f* d'amarrage ; (*AUT*) borne lumineuse or de signalisation.

bolster ['bəulstə*] *n* traversin *m* ; **to** ~ **up** *vt* soutenir.

bolt [bəult] *n* verrou *m* ; (*with nut*) boulon *m* // *vt* verrouiller ; (*food*) engloutir // *vi* se sauver, filer (comme une flèche) ; **a** ~ **from the blue** (*fig*) un coup de tonnerre dans un ciel bleu.

bomb [bɔm] *n* bombe *f* // *vt* bombarder ; ~**ard** [bɔm'bɑ:d] *vt* bombarder ; ~**ardment** [bɔm'bɑ:dmənt] *n* bombardement *m*.

bombastic [bɔm'bæstɪk] *a* grandiloquent(e), pompeux(euse).

bomb disposal ['bɔmdɪspəuzl] *n*: ~ **unit** section *f* de déminage.

bomber ['bɔmə*] *n* caporal *m* d'artillerie ; (*AVIAT*) bombardier *m*.

bombing ['bɔmɪŋ] *n* bombardement *m*.

bombshell ['bɔmʃel] *n* obus *m* ; (*fig*) bombe *f*.

bona fide ['bəunə'faɪdɪ] *a* de bonne foi ; (*offer*) sérieux(euse).

bond [bɔnd] *n* lien *m* ; (*binding promise*) engagement *m*, obligation *f* ; (*FINANCE*) obligation *f*.

bone [bəun] *n* os *m* ; (*of fish*) arête *f* // *vt* désosser ; ôter les arêtes de ; ~**-dry** *a* absolument sec(sèche) ; ~**r** *n* (*US*) gaffe *f*, bourde *f*.

bonfire ['bɔnfaɪə*] *n* feu *m* (de joie) ; (*for rubbish*) feu *m*.

bonnet ['bɔnɪt] *n* bonnet *m* ; (*Brit: of car*) capot *m*.

bonus ['bəunəs] *n* prime *f*, gratification *f*.

bony ['bəunɪ] *a* (*arm, face, MED: tissue*) osseux(euse) ; (*meat*) plein(e) d'os ; (*fish*) plein d'arêtes.

boo [bu:] *excl* hou!, peuh! // *vt* huer // *n* huée *f*.

booby trap ['bu:bɪtræp] *n* engin piégé.

book [buk] *n* livre *m* ; (*of stamps etc*) carnet *m* ; (*COMM*): ~**s** comptes *mpl*, comptabilité *f* // *vt* (*ticket*) prendre ; (*seat, room*) réserver ; (*driver*) dresser un procès-verbal à ; (*football player*) prendre le nom de ; ~**able** *a*: **seats are** ~**able** on peut réserver ses places ; ~**case** *n* bibliothèque *f* (*meuble*) ; ~ **ends** *npl* serre-livres *m inv* ; ~**ing office** *n* bureau *m* de location ; ~**keeping** *n* comptabilité *f* ; ~**let** *n* brochure *f* ; ~**maker** *n* bookmaker *m* ; ~**seller** *n* libraire *m/f* ; ~**shop** *n* librairie *f* ; ~**stall** *n* kiosque *m* à journaux ; ~**store** *n* = ~**shop**.

boom [bu:m] *n* (*noise*) grondement *m* ; (*busy period*) boom *m*, vague *f* de prospérité // *vi* gronder ; prospérer.

boomerang ['bu:məræŋ] *n* boomerang *m*.

boon [bu:n] *n* bénédiction *f*, grand avantage.

boorish ['buərɪʃ] *a* grossier(ère), rustre.

boost [bu:st] *n* stimulant *m*, remontant *m* ; (*MED: vaccine*) rappel *m* // *vt* stimuler.

boot [bu:t] *n* botte *f* ; (*for hiking*) chaussure *f* (de marche) ; (*for football etc*) soulier *m* ; (*Brit: of car*) coffre *m* ; **to** ~ (*in addition*) par-dessus le marché, en plus.

booth [bu:ð] *n* (*at fair*) baraque (foraine) ; (*of cinema, telephone etc*) cabine *f* ; (*also: voting* ~) isoloir *m*.

booty ['bu:tɪ] *n* butin *m*.

booze [bu:z] (*col*) *n* boissons *fpl* alcooliques, alcool *m* // *vi* boire, picoler.

border ['bɔ:də*] *n* bordure *f* ; bord *m* ; (*of a country*) frontière *f* ; **the B**~ la frontière entre l'Écosse et l'Angleterre ; **the B**~**s** la région frontière entre l'Écosse et l'Angleterre ; **to** ~ **on** *vt fus* être voisin(e) de, toucher à ; ~**line** *n* (*fig*) ligne *f* de démarcation ; ~**line case** *n* cas *m* limite.

bore [bɔ:*] *pt of* **bear** // *vt* (*hole*) percer ; (*person*) ennuyer, raser // *n* (*person*) raseur/euse ; (*of gun*) calibre *m* ; ~**dom** *n* ennui *m*.

boring ['bɔ:rɪŋ] a ennuyeux(euse).

born [bɔ:n] a: **to be ~** naître ; **I was ~ in 1960** je suis né en 1960 ; **~ blind** aveugle de naissance ; **a ~ comedian** un comédien-né.

borne [bɔ:n] pp of **bear**.

borough ['bʌrə] n municipalité f.

borrow ['bɔrəu] vt: **to ~ sth (from sb)** emprunter qch (à qn).

borstal ['bɔ:stl] n ≈ maison f de correction.

bosom ['buzəm] n poitrine f ; (fig) sein m ; **~ friend** n ami/e intime.

boss [bɔs] n patron/ne // vt commander ; **~y** a autoritaire.

bosun ['bəusn] n maitre m d'équipage.

botanical [bə'tænɪkl] a botanique.

botanist ['bɔtənɪst] n botaniste m/f.

botany ['bɔtənɪ] n botanique f.

botch [bɔtʃ] vt (also: **~ up**) saboter, bâcler.

both [bəuθ] a les deux, l'un(e) et l'autre // pronoun: **~** (of them) tous(toutes) (les) deux, l'un(e) et l'autre ; **~ of us went**, **we ~ went** nous y sommes allés (tous) les deux // ad: **they sell ~ the fabric and the finished curtains** ils vendent (et) le tissu et les rideaux (finis), ils vendent à la fois le tissu et les rideaux (finis).

bother ['bɔðə*] vt (worry) tracasser ; (needle, bait) importuner, ennuyer ; (disturb) déranger // vi (gen: **~ o.s.**) se tracasser, se faire du souci ; **to ~ doing** prendre la peine de faire // n: **it is a ~ to have to do** c'est vraiment ennuyeux d'avoir à faire ; **it was no ~ finding** il n'y a eu aucun problème pour or ça a été très facile de trouver.

bottle ['bɔtl] n bouteille f ; (baby's) biberon m // vt mettre en bouteille(s) ; **to ~ up** vt refouler, contenir ; **~neck** n étranglement m ; **~-opener** n ouvre-bouteille m.

bottom ['bɔtəm] n (of container, sea etc) fond m ; (buttocks) derrière m ; (of page, list) bas m ; (of chair) siège m // a du fond ; du bas ; **~less** a sans fond, insondable.

bough [bau] n branche f, rameau m.

bought [bɔ:t] pt,pp of **buy**.

boulder ['bəuldə*] n gros rocher (gén lisse, arrondi).

bounce [bauns] vi (ball) rebondir ; (cheque) être refusé (étant sans provision) ; (gen: **to ~ forward/out** etc) bondir, s'élancer // vt faire rebondir // n (rebound) rebond m.

bound [baund] pt,pp of **bind** // n (gen pl) limite f ; (leap) bond m // vt (leap) bondir ; (limit) borner // a: **to be ~ to do sth** (obliged) être obligé(e) or avoir obligation de faire qch ; **out of ~s** dont l'accès est interdit ; **he's ~ to fail** (likely) il est sûr d'échouer, son échec est inévitable or assuré ; **~ for** à destination de.

boundary ['baundrɪ] n frontière f.

boundless ['baundlɪs] a illimité(e), sans bornes.

bout [baut] n période f ; (of malaria etc) accès m, crise f, attaque f ; (BOXING etc) combat m, match m.

bow n [bəu] nœud m ; (weapon) arc m ; (MUS) archet m ; [bau] révérence f, inclination f (du buste or corps) // vi [bau] faire une révérence, s'incliner ; (yield): **to ~ to** or **before** s'incliner devant, se soumettre à.

bowels [bauəlz] npl intestins mpl ; (fig) entrailles fpl.

bowl [bəul] n (for eating) bol m ; (for washing) cuvette f ; (ball) boule f ; (of pipe) fourneau m // vi (CRICKET) lancer (la balle) ; **~s** n (jeu m de) boules fpl ; **to ~ over** vt (fig) renverser (fig).

bow-legged ['bəulɛgɪd] a aux jambes arquées.

bowler ['bəulə*] n joueur m de boules ; (CRICKET) lanceur m (de la balle) ; (also: **~ hat**) (chapeau m) melon m.

bowling ['bəulɪŋ] n (game) jeu m de boules ; **~ alley** n bowling m ; jeu m de quilles ; **~ green** n terrain m de boules (gazonné et carré).

bow tie ['bəu'taɪ] n nœud m papillon.

box [bɔks] n boîte f ; (also: **cardboard ~**) carton m ; (THEATRE) loge f // vt mettre en boîte ; (SPORT) boxer avec // vi boxer, faire de la boxe ; **~er** n (person) boxeur m ; (dog) boxer m ; **~ing** n (SPORT) boxe f ; **B~ing Day** n le lendemain de Noël ; **~ing gloves** npl gants mpl de boxe ; **~ing ring** n ring m ; **~ office** n bureau m de location ; **~ room** n débarras m ; chambrette f.

boy [bɔɪ] n garçon m ; (servant) boy m.

boycott ['bɔɪkɔt] n boycottage m // vt boycotter.

boyfriend ['bɔɪfrɛnd] n (petit) ami.

boyish ['bɔɪʃ] a d'enfant, de garçon.

B.R. abbr of **British Rail**.

bra [brɑ:] n soutien-gorge m.

brace [breɪs] n attache f, agrafe f ; (on teeth) appareil m (dentaire) ; (tool) vilbrequin m ; (TYP: also: **~ bracket**) accolade f // vt consolider, soutenir ; **~s** npl bretelles fpl ; **to ~ o.s.** (fig) se préparer mentalement.

bracelet ['breɪslɪt] n bracelet m.

bracing ['breɪsɪŋ] a tonifiant(e), tonique.

bracken ['brækən] n fougère f.

bracket ['brækɪt] n (TECH) tasseau m, support m ; (group) classe f, tranche f ; (also: **brace ~**) accolade f ; (also: **round ~**) parenthèse f ; (gen: **square ~**) crochet m // vt mettre entre parenthèse(s).

brag [bræg] vi se vanter.

braid [breɪd] n (trimming) galon m ; (of hair) tresse f, natte f.

Braille [breɪl] n braille m.

brain [breɪn] n cerveau m ; **~s** npl cervelle f ; **he's got ~s** il est intelligent ; **~less** a sans cervelle, stupide ; **~wash** vt faire subir un lavage de cerveau à ; **~wave** n idée géniale ; **~y** a intelligent(e), doué(e).

braise [breɪz] vt braiser.

brake [breɪk] n (on vehicle) frein m // vt,vi freiner.

bramble ['bræmbl] n ronces fpl.

bran [bræn] n son m.

branch [brɑ:ntʃ] n branche f ; (COMM) succursale f // vi bifurquer.

brand [brænd] n marque (commerciale) // vt (cattle) marquer (au fer rouge) ; (fig:

pej): to ~ sb a **communist** etc traiter or qualifier qn de communiste etc.

brandish ['brændɪʃ] vt brandir.

brand-new ['brænd'nju:] a tout(e) neuf(neuve), flambant neuf(neuve).

brandy ['brændɪ] n cognac m, fine f.

brash [bræʃ] a effronté(e).

brass [brɑ:s] n cuivre m (jaune), laiton m ; **the ~** (MUS) les cuivres ; **~ band** n fanfare f.

brassière ['bræsɪə*] n soutien-gorge m.

brat [bræt] n (pej) mioche m/f, môme m/f.

bravado [brə'vɑ:dəu] n bravade f.

brave [breɪv] a courageux(euse), brave // n guerrier indien // vt braver, affronter ; **~ry** n bravure f, courage m.

brawl [brɔ:l] n rixe f, bagarre f // vi se bagarrer.

brawn [brɔ:n] n muscle m ; (meat) fromage m de tête ; **~y** a musclé(e), costaud(e).

bray [breɪ] n braiement m // vi braire.

brazen ['breɪzn] a impudent(e), effronté(e) // vt: **to ~ it out** payer d'effronterie, crâner.

brazier ['breɪzɪə*] n brasero m.

Brazil [brə'zɪl] n Brésil m ; **~ian** a brésilien(ne) // n Brésilien/ne ; **~ nut** n noix f du Brésil.

breach [bri:tʃ] vt ouvrir une brèche dans // n (gap) brèche f ; (breaking): **~ of confidence** abus m de confiance ; **~ of contract** rupture f de contrat ; **~ of the peace** attentat m à l'ordre public.

bread [brɛd] n pain m ; **~ and butter** n tartines fpl (beurrées) ; (fig) subsistance f ; **~crumbs** npl miettes fpl de pain ; (CULIN) chapelure f, panure f ; **~ line** n: **to be on the ~ line** être sans le sou or dans l'indigence.

breadth [brɛtθ] n largeur f.

breadwinner ['brɛdwɪnə*] n soutien m de famille.

break [breɪk] vb (pt **broke** [brəuk], pp **broken** ['brəukən]) vt casser, briser ; (promise) rompre ; (law) violer // vi (se) casser, se briser ; (weather) tourner // n (gap) brèche f ; (fracture) cassure f ; (rest) interruption f, arrêt m ; (:short) pause f ; (:at school) récréation f ; (chance) chance f, occasion f favorable ; **to ~ one's leg** etc se casser la jambe etc ; **to ~ a record** battre un record ; **to ~ the news to sb** annoncer la nouvelle à qn ; **to ~ down** vt (figures, data) décomposer, analyser // vi s'effondrer ; (MED) faire une dépression (nerveuse) ; (AUT) tomber en panne ; **to ~ even** vi rentrer dans ses frais ; **to ~ free** or **loose** vi se dégager, s'échapper ; **to ~ in** vt (horse etc) dresser // vi (burglar) entrer par effraction ; **to ~ into** vt fus (house) s'introduire or pénétrer par effraction dans ; **to ~ off** vi (speaker) s'interrompre ; (branch) se rompre ; **to ~ open** vt (door etc) forcer, fracturer ; **to ~ out** vi éclater, se déclarer ; **to ~ out in spots** se couvrir de boutons ; **to ~ up** vi (partnership) cesser, prendre fin ; (friends) se séparer // vt fracasser, casser ; (fight etc) interrompre, faire cesser ; **~able** a cassable, fragile ; **~age** n casse f ; **~down** n (AUT) panne f ; (in communications) rupture f ; (MED: also: **nervous ~down**)

dépression (nerveuse) ; **~down lorry** n dépanneuse f ; **~down service** n service m de dépannage ; **~er** n brisant m.

breakfast ['brɛkfəst] n petit déjeuner m.

breakthrough ['breɪkθru:] n percée f.

breakwater ['breɪkwɔ:tə*] n brise-lames m inv, digue f.

breast [brɛst] n (of woman) sein m ; (chest) poitrine f ; **~-stroke** n brasse f.

breath [brɛθ] n haleine f, souffle m ; **to go out for a ~ of air** sortir prendre l'air ; **out of ~** à bout de souffle, essoufflé(e) ; **~alyser** n alcootest m.

breathe [bri:ð] vt,vi respirer ; **~r** n moment m de repos or de répit.

breathless ['brɛθlɪs] a essoufflé(e), haletant(e) ; oppressé(e).

breath-taking ['brɛθteɪkɪŋ] a stupéfiant(e), à vous couper le souffle.

breed [bri:d] vb (pt,pp **bred** [brɛd]) vt élever, faire l'élevage de // vi se reproduire // n race f, variété f ; **~er** n (person) éleveur m ; **~ing** n reproduction f ; élevage m.

breeze [bri:z] n brise f.

breezy ['bri:zɪ] a frais(fraiche) ; aéré(e) ; désinvolte, jovial(e).

brevity ['brɛvɪtɪ] n brièveté f.

brew [bru:] vt (tea) faire infuser ; (beer) brasser ; (plot) tramer, préparer // vi (tea) infuser ; (beer) fermenter ; (fig) se préparer, couver ; **~er** n brasseur m ; **~ery** n brasserie f (fabrique).

bribe [braɪb] n pot-de-vin m // vt acheter ; soudoyer ; **~ry** n corruption f.

brick [brɪk] n brique f ; **~layer** n maçon m ; **~work** n briquetage m, maçonnerie f ; **~works** n briqueterie f.

bridal ['braɪdl] a nuptial(e) ; **~ party** n noce f.

bride [braɪd] n mariée f, épouse f ; **~groom** n marié m, époux m ; **~smaid** n demoiselle f d'honneur.

bridge [brɪdʒ] n pont m ; (NAUT) passerelle f (de commandement) ; (of nose) arête f ; (CARDS, DENTISTRY) bridge m // vt (river) construire un pont sur ; (gap) combler ; **bridging loan** n prêt m de raccord.

bridle ['braɪdl] n bride f // vt refréner, mettre la bride à ; (horse) brider ; **~ path** n piste or allée cavalière.

brief [bri:f] a bref(brève) // n (LAW) dossier m, cause f // vt donner des instructions à ; **~s** npl slip m ; **~case** n serviette f ; porte-documents m inv ; **~ing** n instructions fpl ; **~ly** ad brièvement ; **~ness** n brièveté f.

brigade [brɪ'geɪd] n (MIL) brigade f.

brigadier [brɪgə'dɪə*] n brigadier général.

bright [braɪt] a brillant(e) ; (room, weather) clair(e) ; (person) intelligent(e), doué(e) ; (colour) vif(vive) ; **~en** vt (room) éclaircir ; égayer // vi s'éclaircir ; (person: gen: **~en up**) retrouver un peu de sa gaieté ; **~ly** ad brillamment.

brilliance ['brɪljəns] n éclat m.

brilliant ['brɪljənt] a brillant(e).

brim [brɪm] n bord m ; **~ful** a plein(e) à ras bord ; (fig) débordant(e).

brine [braɪn] n eau salée ; (CULIN) saumure f.

bring, *pt,pp* **brought** [brɪŋ, brɔːt] *vt*
(*thing*) apporter ; (*person*) amener ; to ~
about *vt* provoquer, entraîner ; to ~ **back**
vt rapporter ; ramener ; to ~ **down** *vt*
abaisser ; faire s'effondrer ; to ~ **forward**
vt avancer ; to ~ **off** *vt* (*task, plan*) réussir,
mener à bien ; to ~ **out** *vt* (*meaning*) faire
ressortir, mettre en relief ; to ~ **round** *or*
to *vt* (*unconscious person*) ranimer ; to ~
up *vt* élever ; (*question*) soulever.

brink [brɪŋk] *n* bord *m*.

brisk [brɪsk] *a* vif(vive), alerte.

bristle ['brɪsl] *n* poil *m* // *vi* se hérisser ;
bristling with hérissé(e) de.

Britain ['brɪtən] *n* Grande-Bretagne *f*.

British ['brɪtɪʃ] *a* britannique ; **the ~** *npl*
les Britanniques *mpl* ; **the ~ Isles** *npl* les
Îles *fpl* Britanniques.

Briton ['brɪtən] *n* Britannique *m/f*.

Brittany ['brɪtənɪ] *n* Bretagne *f*.

brittle ['brɪtl] *a* cassant(e), fragile.

broach [brəutʃ] *vt* (*subject*) aborder.

broad [brɔːd] *a* large ; (*distinction*)
général(e) ; (*accent*) prononcé(e) ; **in ~**
daylight en plein jour ; ~ **hint** *n* allusion
transparente ; ~**cast** *n* émission *f* // *vb*
(*pt,pp* **broadcast**) *vt* radiodiffuser ;
téléviser // *vi* émettre ; ~**casting** *n*
radiodiffusion *f* ; télévision *f* ; ~**en** *vt*
élargir // *vi* s'élargir ; ~**ly** *ad* en gros,
généralement ; ~**minded** *a* large d'esprit.

brochure ['brəuʃjuə*] *n* prospectus *m*,
dépliant *m*.

broil [brɔɪl] *vt* rôtir ; ~**er** *n* (*fowl*) poulet
m (à rôtir).

broke [brəuk] *pt of* **break** // *a* (*col*)
fauché(e) ; ~**n** *pp of* **break** // *a*: ~**n leg**
etc jambe *etc* cassée ; **in** ~**n**
French/English dans un français/anglais
approximatif *or* hésitant ; ~**n-hearted** *a*
(ayant) le cœur brisé.

broker ['brəukə*] *n* courtier *m*.

bronchitis [brɔŋ'kaɪtɪs] *n* bronchite *f*.

bronze [brɔnz] *n* bronze *m* ; ~**d** *a*
bronzé(e), hâlé(e).

brooch [brəutʃ] *n* broche *f*.

brood [bruːd] *n* couvée *f* // *vi* (*hen, storm*)
couver ; (*person*) méditer (sombrement),
ruminer ; ~**y** *a* (*fig*) taciturne,
mélancolique.

brook [bruk] *n* ruisseau *m*.

broom [brum] *n* balai *m* ; ~**stick** *n*
manche *m* à balai.

Bros. *abbr of* **Brothers**.

broth [brɔθ] *n* bouillon *m* de viande et de
légumes.

brothel ['brɔθl] *n* maison close, bordel *m*.

brother ['brʌðə*] *n* frère *m* ; ~**hood** *n*
fraternité *f* ; ~**in-law** *n* beau-frère *m* ;
~**ly** *a* fraternel(le).

brought [brɔːt] *pt,pp of* **bring**.

brow [brau] *n* front *m* ; (*rare, gen*: **eye**~)
sourcil *m* ; (*of hill*) sommet *m* ; ~**beat** *vt*
intimider, brusquer.

brown [braun] *a* brun(e) // *n* (*colour*) brun
m // *vt* brunir ; (*CULIN*) faire dorer, faire
roussir ; ~**ie** *n* jeannette *f*, éclaireuse
(cadette).

browse [brauz] *vi* (*among books*)
bouquiner, feuilleter les livres.

bruise [bruːz] *n* bleu *m*, ecchymose *f*,
contusion *f* // *vt* contusionner, meurtrir //
vi (*fruit*) se taler, se meurtrir ; to ~ **one's**
arm se faire un bleu au bras.

brunette [bruː'nɛt] *n* (femme) brune.

brunt [brʌnt] *n*: **the ~ of** (*attack, criticism*
etc) le plus gros de.

brush [brʌʃ] *n* brosse *f* ; (*quarrel*)
accrochage *m*, prise *f* de bec // *vt* brosser ;
(*gen*: ~ **past**, ~ **against**) effleurer, frôler ;
to ~ **aside** *vt* écarter, balayer ; to ~ **up**
vt (*knowledge*) rafraîchir, réviser ; ~**off** *n*:
to give sb the ~off envoyer qn
promener ; ~**wood** *n* broussailles *fpl*,
taillis *m*.

Brussels ['brʌslz] *n* Bruxelles ; ~ **sprout**
n chou *m* de Bruxelles.

brutal ['bruːtl] *a* brutal(e) ; ~**ity**
[bruː'tælɪtɪ] *n* brutalité *f*.

brute [bruːt] *n* brute *f*.

brutish ['bruːtɪʃ] *a* grossier(ère), brutal(e).

B.Sc. *abbr see* **bachelor**.

bubble ['bʌbl] *n* bulle *f* // *vi* bouillonner,
faire des bulles ; (*sparkle, fig*) pétiller.

buck [bʌk] *n* mâle *m* (*d'un lapin, lièvre, daim*
etc) ; (*US: col*) dollar *m* // *vi* ruer, lancer
une ruade ; **to pass the ~ (to sb)** se
décharger de la responsabilité (sur qn) ; to
~ **up** *vi* (*cheer up*) reprendre du poil de
la bête, se remonter.

bucket ['bʌkɪt] *n* seau *m*.

buckle ['bʌkl] *n* boucle *f* // *vt* boucler,
attacher ; (*warp*) tordre, gauchir ; (: *wheel*)
voiler.

bud [bʌd] *n* bourgeon *m* ; (*of flower*) bouton
m // *vi* bourgeonner ; (*flower*) éclore.

Buddha ['budə] *n* Bouddha *m* ; **Buddhism**
n bouddhisme *m* ; **Buddhist** *a* bouddhiste
// *n* Bouddhiste *m/f*.

budding ['bʌdɪŋ] *a* (*flower*) en bouton ;
(*poet etc*) en herbe ; (*passion etc*)
naissant(e).

buddy ['bʌdɪ] *n* (*US*) copain *m*.

budge [bʌdʒ] *vt* faire bouger // *vi* bouger.

budgerigar ['bʌdʒərɪgɑː*] *n* perruche *f*.

budget ['bʌdʒɪt] *n* budget *m* // *vi*: **to ~**
for sth inscrire qch au budget.

budgie ['bʌdʒɪ] *n* = **budgerigar**.

buff [bʌf] *a* (couleur *f*) chamois *m* // *n*
(*enthusiast*) mordu/e.

buffalo, *pl* ~ *or* ~**es** ['bʌfələu] *n* buffle
m ; (*US*) bison *m*.

buffer ['bʌfə*] *n* tampon *m* ; ~ **state** *n* état
m tampon.

buffet *n* ['bufeɪ] (*bar, food*) buffet *m* // *vt*
['bʌfɪt] gifler, frapper ; secouer, ébranler.

buffoon [bə'fuːn] *n* buffon *m*, pitre *m*.

bug [bʌg] *n* (*insect*) punaise *f* ; (: *gen*)
insecte *m*, bestiole *f* ; (: *fig: germ*) virus *m*,
microbe *m* ; (*spy device*) dispositif *m*
d'écoute (électronique), micro clandestin
// *vt* garnir de dispositifs d'écoute ;
~**bear** *n* cauchemar *m*, bête noire.

bugle ['bjuːgl] *n* clairon *m*.

build [bɪld] *n* (*of person*) carrure *f*,
charpente *f* // *vt* (*pt,pp* **built** [bɪlt])
construire, bâtir ; ~**er** *n* entrepreneur *m* ;
~**ing** *n* construction *f* ; bâtiment *m*, construction *f* ; (*habitation, offices*) immeuble
m ; ~**ing society** *n* société *f* de crédit
immobilier ; **to** ~ **up** *vt* accumuler,

amasser ; accroître ; **~-up** n (of gas etc) accumulation f.

built [bɪlt] pt,pp of **build**; **well-~** a (person) bien bâti(e); **~-in** a (cupboard) encastré(e); (device) incorporé(e); intégré(e); **-up area** n agglomération (urbaine); zone urbanisée.

bulb [bʌlb] n (BOT) bulbe m, oignon m; (ELEC) ampoule f; **~ous** a bulbeux(euse).

Bulgaria [bʌl'gɛərɪə] n Bulgarie f; **~n** a bulgare // n Bulgare m/f; (LING) bulgare m.

bulge [bʌldʒ] n renflement m, gonflement m // vi faire saillie; présenter un renflement; **to be bulging with** être plein(e) à craquer de.

bulk [bʌlk] n masse f, volume m; **in ~** (COMM) en vrac; **the ~ of** la plus grande or grosse partie de; **~head** n cloison f (étanche); **~y** a volumineux(euse), encombrant(e).

bull [bul] n taureau m; **~dog** n bouledogue m.

bulldoze ['buldəuz] vt passer or raser au bulldozer; **~r** n bulldozer m.

bullet ['bulɪt] n balle f (de fusil etc).

bulletin ['bulɪtɪn] n bulletin m, communiqué m.

bullfight ['bulfaɪt] n corrida f, course f de taureaux; **~er** n torero m; **~ing** n tauromachie f.

bullion ['buljən] n or m or argent m en lingots.

bullock ['bulək] n bœuf m.

bull's-eye ['bulzaɪ] n centre m (de la cible).

bully ['bulɪ] n brute f, tyran m // vt tyranniser, rudoyer; (frighten) intimider; **~ing** n brimades fpl.

bum [bʌm] n (col: backside) derrière m; (tramp) vagabond/e, traîne-savates m/f inv; **to ~ around** vi vagabonder.

bumblebee ['bʌmblbi:] n (ZOOL) bourdon m.

bump [bʌmp] n (blow) coup m, choc m; (jolt) cahot m; (on road etc, on head) bosse f // vt heurter, cogner; **to ~ along** vi avancer en cahotant; **to ~ into** vt fus rentrer dans, tamponner; **~er** n (Brit) pare-chocs m inv // a: **~er crop/harvest** récolte/moisson exceptionnelle.

bumptious ['bʌmpʃəs] a suffisant(e), prétentieux(euse).

bumpy ['bʌmpɪ] a cahoteux(euse).

bun [bʌn] n petit pain au lait; (of hair) chignon m.

bunch [bʌntʃ] n (of flowers) bouquet m; (of keys) trousseau m; (of bananas) régime m; (of people) groupe m; **~ of grapes** grappe f de raisin.

bundle ['bʌndl] n paquet m // vt (also: **~ up**) faire un paquet de; (put): **to ~ sth/sb into** fourrer or enfourner qch/qn dans; **to ~ off** vt (person) faire sortir (en toute hâte); expédier; **to ~ out** vt éjecter, sortir (sans ménagements).

bung [bʌŋ] n bonde f, bouchon m // vt (throw: gen: **~ into**) flanquer.

bungalow ['bʌŋgələu] n bungalow m.

bungle ['bʌŋgl] vt bâcler, gâcher.

bunion ['bʌnjən] n oignon m (au pied).

bunk [bʌŋk] n couchette f; **~ beds** npl lits superposés.

bunker ['bʌŋkə*] n (coal store) soute f à charbon; (MIL, GOLF) bunker m.

bunny ['bʌnɪ] n (also: **~ rabbit**) Jeannot m lapin; **~ girl** n hôtesse de cabaret.

bunting ['bʌntɪŋ] n pavoisement m, drapeaux mpl.

buoy [bɔɪ] n bouée f; **to ~ up** vt faire flotter; (fig) soutenir, épauler; **~ancy** n (of ship) flottabilité f; **~ant** a gai(e), plein(e) d'entrain.

burden ['bə:dn] n fardeau m, charge f // vt charger; (oppress) accabler, surcharger.

bureau, pl **~x** [bjuə'rəu, -z] n (furniture) bureau m, secrétaire m; (office) bureau m, office m.

bureaucracy [bjuə'rɔkrəsɪ] n bureaucratie f.

bureaucrat ['bjuərəkræt] n bureaucrate m/f, rond-de-cuir m; **~ic** [-'krætɪk] a bureaucratique.

burglar ['bə:glə*] n cambrioleur m; **~ alarm** n sonnerie f d'alarme; **~ize** vt (US) cambrioler; **~y** n cambriolage m.

burgle ['bə:gl] vt cambrioler.

Burgundy ['bə:gəndɪ] n Bourgogne f.

burial ['bɛrɪəl] n enterrement m; **~ ground** n cimetière m.

burlesque [bə:'lɛsk] n caricature f, parodie f.

burly ['bə:lɪ] a de forte carrure, costaud(e).

Burma ['bə:mə] n Birmanie f; **Burmese** [-'mi:z] a birman(e), de Birmanie // n, pl inv Birman/e; (LING) birman m.

burn [bə:n] vt,vi (pt,pp **burned** or **burnt** [bə:nt]) brûler // n brûlure f; **to ~ down** vt incendier, détruire par le feu; **~er** n brûleur m; **~ing question** n question brûlante.

burnish ['bə:nɪʃ] vt polir.

burnt [bə:nt] pt,pp of **burn**; **~ sugar** n caramel m.

burp [bə:p] (col) n rot m // vi roter.

burrow ['bʌrəu] n terrier m // vt creuser.

bursar ['bə:sə*] n économe m/f; (student) boursier/ère; **~y** n bourse f (d'études).

burst [bə:st] vb (pt,pp **burst**) vt crever; faire éclater // vi éclater; (tyre) crever // n explosion f; (also: **~ pipe**) rupture f, fuite f; **~ of energy** déploiement soudain d'énergie, activité soudaine; **~ of laughter** éclat m de rire; **~ blood vessel** rupture f de vaisseau sanguin; **to ~ into flames** s'enflammer soudainement; **to ~ into laughter** éclater de rire; **to ~ into tears** fondre en larmes; **to be ~ing with** être plein (à craquer) de; regorger de; **to ~ into** vt fus (room etc) faire irruption dans; **to ~ open** vi s'ouvrir violemment or soudainement; **to ~ out of** vt fus sortir précipitamment de.

bury ['bɛrɪ] vt enterrer; **to ~ one's face in one's hands** se couvrir le visage de ses mains; **to ~ one's head in the sand** (fig) pratiquer la politique de l'autruche; **to ~ the hatchet** enterrer la hache de guerre.

bus, **~es** [bʌs, 'bʌsɪz] n autobus m.

bush [buʃ] n buisson m; (scrub land) brousse f.

bushel ['buʃl] n boisseau m.
bushy ['buʃi] a broussailleux(euse), touffu(e).
busily ['bizili] ad activement.
business ['biznis] n (matter, firm) affaire f; (trading) affaires fpl; (job, duty) travail m; **to be away on ~** être en déplacement d'affaires; **it's none of my ~** cela ne me regarde pas, ce ne sont pas mes affaires; **he means ~** il ne plaisante pas, il est sérieux; **~like** a sérieux(euse); efficace; **~man** n homme m d'affaires.
bus-stop ['bʌsstɔp] n arrêt m d'autobus.
bust [bʌst] n buste m // a (broken) fichu(e), fini(e); **to go ~** faire faillite.
bustle ['bʌsl] n remue-ménage m, affairement m // vi s'affairer, se démener; **bustling** a (person) affairé(e); (town) très animé(e).
bust-up ['bʌstʌp] n (col) engueulade f.
busy ['bizi] a occupé(e); (shop, street) très fréquenté(e) // vt: **to ~ o.s.** s'occuper; **~body** n mouche f du coche, âme f charitable.
but [bʌt] cj mais // prep excepté, sauf; **nothing ~** rien d'autre que; **~ for** sans, si ce n'était pour; **all ~ finished** pratiquement fini; **anything ~ finished** tout sauf fini, très loin d'être fini.
butane ['bju:tein] n butane m.
butcher ['butʃə*] n boucher m // vt massacrer; (cattle etc for meat) tuer.
butler ['bʌtlə*] n maître m d'hôtel.
butt [bʌt] n (cask) gros tonneau; (thick end) (gros) bout; (of gun) crosse f; (of cigarette) mégot m; (fig: target) cible f // vt donner un coup de tête à.
butter ['bʌtə*] n beurre m // vt beurrer; **~ dish** n beurrier m.
butterfly ['bʌtəflai] n papillon m.
buttocks ['bʌtəks] npl fesses fpl.
button ['bʌtn] n bouton m // vt boutonner // vi se boutonner; **~hole** n boutonnière f // vt accrocher, arrêter, retenir.
buttress ['bʌtris] n contrefort m.
buxom ['bʌksəm] a aux formes avantageuses or épanouies, bien galbé(e).
buy [bai] vb (pt,pp **bought** [bɔ:t]) vt acheter; **to ~ sb sth/sth from sb** acheter qch à qn; **to ~ sb a drink** offrir un verre or à boire à qn; **to ~ up** vt acheter en bloc, rafler; **~er** n acheteur/euse.
buzz [bʌz] n bourdonnement m; (col: phone call) coup m de fil // vi bourdonner.
buzzard ['bʌzəd] n buse f.
buzzer ['bʌzə*] n timbre m électrique.
by [bai] prep par; (beside) à côté de; au bord de; (before): **~ 4 o'clock** avant 4 heures, d'ici 4 heures // ad see **pass, go** etc; **~ bus/car** en autobus/voiture; **paid ~ the hour** payé à l'heure; **to increase** etc **~ the hour** augmenter etc d'heure en heure; (all) **~ oneself** tout(e) seul(e); **~ the way** à propos; **~ and large** dans l'ensemble; **~ and ~** bientôt.
bye(-bye) ['bai('bai)] excl au revoir!, salut!
by(e)-law ['bailɔ:] n arrêté municipal.
by-election ['baiilekʃən] n élection (législative) partielle.
bygone ['baigɔn] a passé(e) // n: let **~s** be **~s** passons l'éponge, oublions le passé.

bypass ['baipɑ:s] n (route f de) contournement m // vt éviter.
by-product ['baiprɔdʌkt] n sous-produit m, dérivé m; (fig) conséquence f secondaire, retombée f.
byre ['baiə*] n étable f (à vaches).
bystander ['baistændə*] n spectateur/-trice, badaud/e.
byword ['baiwə:d] n: **to be a ~ for** être synonyme de (fig).

C

C [si:] n (MUS) do m.
C. abbr of **centigrade**.
C.A. abbr of **chartered accountant**.
cab [kæb] n taxi m; (of train, truck) cabine f; (horse-drawn) fiacre m.
cabaret ['kæbərei] n attractions fpl, spectacle m de cabaret.
cabbage ['kæbidʒ] n chou m.
cabin ['kæbin] n cabane f, hutte f; (on ship) cabine f; **~ cruiser** n yacht m (à moteur).
cabinet ['kæbinit] n (POL) cabinet m; (furniture) petit meuble à tiroirs et rayons; (also: **display ~**) vitrine f, petite armoire vitrée; **cocktail ~** n meuble-bar m; **medicine ~** n armoire f à pharmacie; **~-maker** n ébéniste m.
cable ['keibl] n câble m // vt câbler, télégraphier; **~-car** n téléphérique m; **~-gram** n câblogramme m; **~ railway** n funiculaire m.
cache [kæʃ] n cachette f; **a ~ of food** etc un dépôt secret de provisions etc, une cachette contenant des provisions etc.
cackle ['kækl] vi caqueter.
cactus, pl **cacti** ['kæktəs, -tai] n cactus m.
caddie ['kædi] n caddie m.
cadet [kə'dɛt] n (MIL) élève m officier.
cadge [kædʒ] vt se faire donner; **to ~ a meal (off sb)** se faire inviter à manger (par qn); **~r** n pique-assiette m/f inv, tapeur/euse.
Caesarean [si:'zɛəriən] a: **~ (section)** césarienne f.
café ['kæfei] n ≈ café(-restaurant) m (sans alcool); **cafeteria** [kæfi'tiəriə] n cafeteria f.
caffein(e) ['kæfi:n] n caféine f.
cage [keidʒ] n cage f // vt mettre en cage.
cagey ['keidʒi] a (col) réticent(e); méfiant(e).
Cairo ['kaiərəu] n le Caire.
cajole [kə'dʒəul] vt couvrir de flatteries or de gentillesses.
cake [keik] n gâteau m; **~ of soap** savonnette f; **~d** a: **~d with** raidi(e) par, couvert(e) d'une croûte de.
calamitous [kə'læmitəs] a catastrophique, désastreux(euse).
calamity [kə'læmiti] n calamité f, désastre m.
calcium ['kælsiəm] n calcium m.
calculate ['kælkjuleit] vt calculer; **calculating** a calculateur(trice); **calculation** [-'leiʃən] n calcul m; **calculator** n machine f à calculer, calculatrice f.

calculus ['kælkjuləs] *n* analyse *f* (mathématique), calcul infinitésimal; **integral/differential** ~ calcul intégral/différentiel.

calendar ['kæləndə*] *n* calendrier *m*; ~ **month** *n* mois *m* (de calendrier); ~ **year** *n* année civile.

calf, calves [kɑːf, kɑːvz] *n* (*of cow*) veau *m*; (*of other animals*) petit *m*; (*also:* ~**skin**) veau *m*, vachette *f*; (ANAT) mollet *m*.

calibre, caliber (US) ['kælɪbə*] *n* calibre *m*.

call [kɔːl] *vt* (*gen, also* TEL) appeler // *vi* appeler; (*visit: also:* ~ **in**, ~ **round**): to ~ **(for)** passer (prendre) // *n* (*shout*) appel *m*, cri *m*; (*visit*) visite *f*; (*also:* **telephone** ~) coup *m* de téléphone; communication *f*; **she's** ~**ed Suzanne** elle s'appelle Suzanne; **to be on** ~ être de permanence; **to** ~ **for** *vt fus* demander; **to** ~ **off** *vt* annuler; **to** ~ **on** *vt fus* (*visit*) rendre visite à, passer voir; (*request*): **to** ~ **on sb to do** inviter qn à faire; **to** ~ **up** *vt* (MIL) appeler, mobiliser; ~ **box** *n* cabine *f* téléphonique; ~**er** *n* personne *f* qui appelle; visiteur *m*; ~ **girl** *n* call-girl *f*; ~**ing** *n* vocation *f*; (*trade, occupation*) état *m*; ~**ing card** *n* (US) carte *f* de visite.

callous ['kæləs] *a* dur(e), insensible; ~**ness** *n* dureté *f*, manque *m* de cœur, insensibilité *f*.

callow ['kæləu] *a* sans expérience (de la vie).

calm [kɑːm] *n* calme *m* // *vt* calmer, apaiser // *a* calme; ~**ly** *ad* calmement, avec calme; ~**ness** *n* calme *m*; **to** ~ **down** *vi* se calmer, s'apaiser // *vt* calmer, apaiser.

calorie ['kælərɪ] *n* calorie *f*.

calve [kɑːv] *vi* vêler, mettre bas.

calves [kɑːvz] *npl of* **calf**.

camber ['kæmbə*] *n* (*of road*) bombement *m*.

Cambodia [kæm'bəudjə] *n* Cambodge *m*.

came [keɪm] *pt of* **come**.

camel ['kæməl] *n* chameau *m*.

cameo ['kæmɪəu] *n* camée *m*.

camera ['kæmərə] *n* appareil-photo *m*; (*also:* **cine-**~, **movie** ~) caméra *f*; **35mm** ~ appareil 24 x 36 *or* petit format; **in** ~ à huis clos, en privé; ~**man** *n* caméraman *m*.

camouflage ['kæməflɑːʒ] *n* camouflage *m* // *vt* camoufler.

camp [kæmp] *n* camp *m* //, *vi* camper.

campaign [kæm'peɪn] *n* (MIL, POL *etc*) campagne *f* // *vi* (*also fig*) faire campagne.

campbed ['kæmp'bɛd] *n* lit *m* de camp.

camper ['kæmpə*] *n* campeur/euse.

camping ['kæmpɪŋ] *n* camping *m*; ~ **site** *n* (terrain *m* de) camping.

campsite ['kæmpsaɪt] *n* campement *m*.

campus ['kæmpəs] *n* campus *m*.

can [kæn] *auxiliary vb* (*gen*) pouvoir; (*know how to*) savoir; **I** ~ **swim** *etc* je sais nager *etc*; **I** ~ **speak French** je parle français // *n* (*of milk, oil, water*) bidon *m*; (US: *tin*) boîte *f* (de conserve) // *vt* mettre en conserve.

Canada ['kænədə] *n* Canada *m*.

Canadian [kə'neɪdɪən] *a* canadien(ne) // *n* Canadien/ne.

canal [kə'næl] *n* canal *m*.

canary [kə'nɛərɪ] *n* canari *m*, serin *m*.

cancel ['kænsəl] *vt* annuler; (*train*) supprimer; (*party, appointment*) décommander; (*cross out*) barrer, rayer; (*stamp*) oblitérer; ~**lation** [-'leɪʃən] *n* annulation *f*; suppression *f*; oblitération *f*; (TOURISM) réservation annulée, client *etc* qui s'est décommandé.

cancer ['kænsə*] *n* cancer *m*; **C**~ (*sign*) le Cancer; **to be C**~ être du Cancer.

candid ['kændɪd] *a* (très) franc(franche), sincère.

candidate ['kændɪdeɪt] *n* candidat/e.

candle ['kændl] *n* bougie *f*; (*of tallow*) chandelle *f*; (*in church*) cierge *m*; **by** ~**light** à la lumière d'une bougie; (*dinner*) aux chandelles; ~**stick** *n* (*also:* ~ **holder**) bougeoir *m*; (*bigger, ornate*) chandelier *m*.

candour ['kændə*] *n* (grande) franchise *or* sincérité.

candy ['kændɪ] *n* sucre candi; (US) bonbon *m*; ~-**floss** *n* barbe *f* à papa.

cane [keɪn] *n* canne *f* // *vt* (SCOL) administrer des coups de bâton à.

canine ['kænaɪn] *a* canin(e).

canister ['kænɪstə*] *n* boîte *f* (*gén en métal*).

cannabis ['kænəbɪs] *n* (*drug*) cannabis *m*; (*also:* ~ **plant**) chanvre indien.

canned ['kænd] *a* (*food*) en boîte, en conserve.

cannibal ['kænɪbəl] *n* cannibale *m/f*, anthropophage *m/f*; ~**ism** *n* cannibalisme *m*, anthropophagie *f*.

cannon, *pl* ~ *or* ~**s** ['kænən] *n* (*gun*) canon *m*; ~-**ball** *n* boulet *m* de canon.

cannot ['kænɔt] = **can not**.

canny ['kænɪ] *a* madré(e), finaud(e).

canoe [kə'nuː] *n* pirogue *f*; (SPORT) canoë *m*; ~**ing** *n* (SPORT) canoë *m*; ~**ist** *n* canoëiste *m/f*.

canon ['kænən] *n* (*clergyman*) chanoine *m*; (*standard*) canon *m*.

canonize ['kænənaɪz] *vt* canoniser.

can opener ['kænəupnə*] *n* ouvre-boîte *m*.

canopy ['kænəpɪ] *n* baldaquin *m*; dais *m*.

cant [kænt] *n* jargon *m* // *vt, vi* pencher.

can't [kænt] = **can not**.

cantankerous [kæn'tæŋkərəs] *a* querelleur(euse), acariâtre.

canteen [kæn'tiːn] *n* cantine *f*; (*of cutlery*) ménagère *f*.

canter ['kæntə*] *n* petit galop // *vi* aller au petit galop.

cantilever ['kæntɪliːvə*] *n* porte-à-faux *m inv*.

canvas ['kænvəs] *n* (*gen*) toile *f*; **under** ~ (*camping*) sous la tente; (NAUT) toutes voiles dehors.

canvass ['kænvəs] *vt*: ~**ing** (POL) prospection électorale, démarchage électoral; (COMM) démarchage, prospection.

canyon ['kænjən] *n* cañon *m*, gorge *f* (profonde).

cap [kæp] *n* casquette *f*; (*of pen*) capuchon *m*; (*of bottle*) capsule *f*; (*also:* **Dutch** ~)

diaphragme m; (FOOTBALL) sélection f pour l'équipe nationale // vt capsuler; (outdo) surpasser; ~ped with coiffé(e) de.

capability [keɪpə'bɪlɪtɪ] n aptitude f, capacité f.

capable ['keɪpəbl] a capable; ~ of capable de; susceptible de.

capacity [kə'pæsɪtɪ] n capacité f, contenance f; aptitude f; in his ~ as en sa qualité de; to work at full ~ travailler à plein rendement.

cape [keɪp] n (garment) cape f; (GEO) cap m.

caper ['keɪpə*] n (CULIN: gen: ~s) câpre f.

capital ['kæpɪtl] n (also: ~ city) capitale f; (money) capital m; (also: ~ letter) majuscule f; ~ gains npl plus-values fpl; ~ism n capitalisme m; ~ist a capitaliste; ~ punishment n peine capitale.

capitulate [kə'pɪtjuleɪt] vi capituler; **capitulation** [-'leɪʃən] n capitulation f.

capricious [kə'prɪʃəs] a capricieux(euse), fantasque.

Capricorn ['kæprɪkɔːn] n le Capricorne; to be ~ être du Capricorne.

capsize [kæp'saɪz] vt faire chavirer // vi chavirer.

capstan ['kæpstən] n cabestan m.

capsule ['kæpsjuːl] n capsule f.

captain ['kæptɪn] n capitaine m // vt commander, être le capitaine de.

caption ['kæpʃən] n légende f.

captivate ['kæptɪveɪt] vt captiver, fasciner.

captive ['kæptɪv] a, n captif(ive).

captivity [kæp'tɪvɪtɪ] n captivité f.

capture ['kæptʃə*] vt capturer, prendre; (attention) capter // n capture f.

car [kɑː*] n voiture f, auto f.

carafe [kə'ræf] n carafe f; (in restaurant: ~ wine) ≈ vin ouvert.

caramel ['kærəməl] n caramel m.

carat ['kærət] n carat m.

caravan ['kærəvæn] n caravane f.

caraway ['kærəweɪ] n: ~ seed graine f de cumin, cumin m.

carbohydrates [kɑːbəu'haɪdreɪts] npl (foods) aliments mpl riches en hydrate de carbone.

carbon ['kɑːbən] n carbone m; ~ copy n carbone m; ~ paper n papier m carbone.

carburettor [kɑːbju'rɛtə*] n carburateur m.

carcass ['kɑːkəs] n carcasse f.

card [kɑːd] n carte f; ~board n carton m; ~ game n jeu m de cartes.

cardiac ['kɑːdɪæk] a cardiaque.

cardigan ['kɑːdɪgən] n cardigan m.

cardinal ['kɑːdɪnl] a cardinal(e) // n cardinal m.

card index ['kɑːdɪndɛks] n fichier m (alphabétique).

care [kɛə*] n soin m, attention f; (worry) souci m // vi: to ~ about se soucier de, s'intéresser à; would you ~ to/for .. ? voulez-vous ...?; I wouldn't ~ to do it je n'aimerais pas le faire; in sb's ~ à la garde de qn, confié à qn; to take ~ faire attention, prendre garde; to take ~ of vt s'occuper de, prendre soin de; to ~

for vt fus s'occuper de; (like) aimer; I don't ~ ça m'est bien égal, peu m'importe; I couldn't ~ less cela m'est complètement égal, je m'en fiche complètement.

career [kə'rɪə*] n carrière f // vi (also: ~ along) aller à toute allure.

carefree ['kɛəfriː] a sans souci, insouciant(e).

careful ['kɛəful] a soigneux(euse); (cautious) prudent(e); (be) ~! (fais) attention!; ~ly ad avec soin, soigneusement; prudemment.

careless ['kɛəlɪs] a négligent(e); (heedless) insouciant(e); ~ly ad négligemment; avec insouciance; ~ness n manque m de soin, négligence f; insouciance f.

caress [kə'rɛs] n caresse f // vt caresser.

caretaker ['kɛəteɪkə*] n gardien/ne, concierge m/f.

car-ferry ['kɑːfɛrɪ] n (on sea) ferry (-boat) m; (on river) bac m.

cargo, ~es ['kɑːgəu] n cargaison f, chargement m.

Caribbean [kærɪ'biːən] a: the ~ (Sea) la mer des Antilles ou Caraïbes.

caricature ['kærɪkətjuə*] n caricature f.

carnal ['kɑːnl] a charnel(le).

carnation [kɑː'neɪʃən] n œillet m.

carnival ['kɑːnɪvəl] n (public celebration) carnaval m.

carol ['kærəl] n: (Christmas) ~ chant m de Noël.

carp [kɑːp] n (fish) carpe f; to ~ at vt fus critiquer.

car park ['kɑːpɑːk] n parking m, parc m de stationnement.

carpenter ['kɑːpɪntə*] n charpentier m.

carpentry ['kɑːpɪntrɪ] n charpenterie f, métier m de charpentier; (woodwork: at school etc) menuiserie f.

carpet ['kɑːpɪt] n tapis m // vt recouvrir (d'un tapis).

carriage ['kærɪdʒ] n voiture f; (of goods) transport m; (: taxe) port m; (of typewriter) chariot m; (bearing) maintien m, port m; ~way n (part of road) chaussée f.

carrier ['kærɪə*] n transporteur m, camionneur m; ~ bag n sac m en papier ou en plastique; ~ pigeon n pigeon voyageur.

carrot ['kærət] n carotte f.

carry ['kærɪ] vt (subj: person) porter, (: vehicle) transporter; (a motion, bill) voter, adopter; (involve: responsibilities etc) comporter, impliquer // vi (sound) porter; to be carried away (fig) s'emballer, s'enthousiasmer; to ~ on vi: to ~ on with sth/doing continuer qch/à faire // vt entretenir, poursuivre; to ~ out vt (orders) exécuter; (investigation) effectuer; ~cot n porte-bébé m.

cart [kɑːt] n charrette f // vt transporter.

cartilage ['kɑːtɪlɪdʒ] n cartilage m.

cartographer [kɑː'tɔgrəfə*] n cartographe m/f.

carton ['kɑːtən] n (box) carton m; (of yogurt) pot m (en carton); (of cigarettes) cartouche f.

cartoon [kɑ:'tu:n] *n* (PRESS) dessin *m* (humoristique); (*satirical*) caricature *f*; (*comic strip*) bande dessinée; (CINEMA) dessin animé; ~**ist** *n* dessinateur/trice humoristique; caricaturiste *m/f*; auteur *m* de dessins animés; auteur de bandes dessinées.

cartridge ['kɑ:trɪdʒ] *n* (*for gun, pen*) cartouche *f*; (*for camera*) chargeur *m*; (*music tape*) cassette *f*; (*of record player*) cellule *f*.

carve [kɑ:v] *vt* (*meat*) découper; (*wood, stone*) tailler, sculpter; **carving** *n* (*in wood etc*) sculpture *f*; **carving knife** *n* couteau *m* à découper.

car wash ['kɑ:wɔʃ] *n* station *f* de lavage (de voitures).

cascade [kæs'keɪd] *n* cascade *f* // *vi* tomber en cascade.

case [keɪs] *n* cas *m*; (LAW) affaire *f*, procès *m*; (*box*) caisse *f*, boîte *f*, étui *m*; (*also*: suit~) valise *f*; **he hasn't put forward his** ~ **very well** ses arguments ne sont guère convaincants; **in** ~ **of** en cas de; **in** ~ **he** au cas où il; **just in** ~ à tout hasard.

cash [kæʃ] *n* argent *m*; (COMM) argent liquide, numéraire *m*; liquidités *fpl*; (COMM: *in payment*) argent comptant, espèces *fpl* // *vt* encaisser; **to pay (in)** ~ payer (en argent) comptant; ~ **with order/ on delivery** (COMM) payable or paiement à la commande/livraison; ~**book** *n* livre *m* de caisse; ~**desk** *n* caisse *f*.

cashew [kæ'ʃu:] *n* (*also*: ~ **nut**) noix *f* de cajou.

cashier [kæ'ʃɪə*] *n* caissier/ère.

cashmere [kæʃ'mɪə*] *n* cachemire *m*.

cash payment ['kæʃ'peɪmənt] *n* paiement comptant, versement *m* en espèces.

cash register ['kæʃrɛdʒɪstə*] *n* caisse enregistreuse.

casing ['keɪsɪŋ] *n* revêtement (protecteur), enveloppe (protectrice).

casino [kə'si:nəu] *n* casino *m*.

cask [kɑ:sk] *n* tonneau *m*.

casket ['kɑ:skɪt] *n* coffret *m*; (US: *coffin*) cercueil *m*.

casserole ['kæsərəul] *n* cocotte *f*; (*food*) ragoût *m* (en cocotte).

cassette [kæ'sɛt] *n* cassette *f*, musicassette *f*; ~**player** lecteur *m* de cassettes; ~**recorder** magnétophone *m* à cassettes.

cast [kɑ:st] *vt* (*pt, pp* **cast**) (*throw*) jeter; (*shed*) perdre; se dépouiller de; (*metal*) couler, fondre // *n* (THEATRE) distribution *f*; (*mould*) moule *m*; (*also*: **plaster** ~) plâtre *m*; (TECH): **to** ~ **sb as Hamlet** attribuer à qn le rôle d'Hamlet; **to** ~ **one's vote** voter, exprimer son suffrage; **to** ~ **off** *vi* (NAUT) larguer les amarres.

castanets [kæstə'nɛts] *npl* castagnettes *fpl*.

castaway ['kɑ:stəwəɪ] *n* naufragé/e.

caste [kɑ:st] *n* caste *f*, classe sociale.

casting ['kɑ:stɪŋ] *a*: ~ **vote** voix prépondérante (*pour départager*).

cast iron ['kɑ:st'aɪən] *n* fonte *f*.

castle ['kɑ:sl] *n* château-fort *m*; (*manor*) château *m*.

castor ['kɑ:stə*] *n* (*wheel*) roulette *f*; ~ **oil** *n* huile *f* de ricin; ~ **sugar** *n* sucre *m* semoule.

castrate [kæs'treɪt] *vt* châtrer.

casual ['kæʒjul] *a* (*by chance*) de hasard, fait(e) au hasard, fortuit(e); (*irregular*: work etc) temporaire; (*unconcerned*) désinvolte; ~ **wear** *n* vêtements *mpl* sport inv; ~ **labour** *n* main-d'œuvre *f* temporaire; ~**ly** *ad* avec désinvolture, négligemment; fortuitement.

casualty ['kæʒjultɪ] *n* accidenté/e, blessé/e; (*dead*) victime *f*, mort/e; **heavy casualties** *npl* lourdes pertes.

cat [kæt] *n* chat *m*.

catalogue, catalog (US) ['kætəlɔg] *n* catalogue *m* // *vt* cataloguer.

catalyst ['kætəlɪst] *n* catalyseur *m*.

catapult ['kætəpʌlt] *n* lance-pierres *m inv*, fronde *f*; (AVIAT, HISTORY) catapulte *f*.

cataract ['kætərækt] *n* (*also* MED) cataracte *f*.

catarrh [kə'tɑ:*] *n* rhume *m* chronique, catarrhe *f*.

catastrophe [kə'tæstrəfɪ] *n* catastrophe *f*; **catastrophic** [kætə'strɔfɪk] *a* catastrophique.

catch [kætʃ] *vb* (*pt,pp* **caught** [cɔ:t]) *vt* (*ball, train, thief, cold*) attraper; (*person: by surprise*) prendre, surprendre; (*understand*) saisir; (*get entangled*) accrocher // *vi* (*fire*) prendre // *n* (*fish etc caught*) prise *f*; (*thief etc caught*) capture *f*; (*trick*) attrape *f*; (TECH) loquet *m*; cliquet *m*; **to** ~ **sb's attention** *or* **eye** attirer l'attention de qn; **to** ~ **fire** prendre feu; **to** ~ **sight of** apercevoir; **to** ~ **up** *vi* se rattraper, combler son retard // *vt* (*also*: ~ **up with**) rattraper.

catching ['kætʃɪŋ] *a* (MED) contagieux(euse).

catchment area ['kætʃmənt'ɛərɪə] *n* (SCOL) aire *f* de recrutement; (GEO) bassin *m* hydrographique.

catch phrase ['kætʃfreɪz] *n* slogan *m*; expression toute faite.

catchy ['kætʃɪ] *a* (*tune*) facile à retenir.

catechism ['kætɪkɪzəm] *n* (REL) catéchisme *m*.

categoric(al) [kætɪ'gɔrɪk(əl)] *a* catégorique.

categorize ['kætɪgəraɪz] *vt* classer par catégories.

category ['kætɪgərɪ] *n* catégorie *f*.

cater ['keɪtə*] *vi* (*gen*: ~ **for sb**) préparer des repas, se charger de la restauration; **to** ~ **for** *vt fus* (*needs*) satisfaire, pourvoir à; (*readers, consumers*) s'adresser à, pourvoir aux besoins de; ~**er** *n* traiteur *m*; fournisseur *m*; ~**ing** *n* restauration *f*; approvisionnement *m*, ravitaillement *m*; ~**ing (trade)** restauration *f*.

caterpillar ['kætəpɪlə*] *n* chenille *f*; ~ **track** *n* chenille *f*; ~ **vehicle** *n* véhicule *m* à chenille.

cathedral [kə'θi:drəl] *n* cathédrale *f*.

catholic ['kæθəlɪk] *a* éclectique; universel(le); libéral(e); **C**~ *a,n* (REL) catholique (*m/f*).

cattle ['kætl] *npl* bétail *m*, bestiaux *mpl*.

catty ['kætɪ] a méchant(e).
Caucasus ['kɔ:kəsəs] n Caucase m.
caught [kɔ:t] pt,pp of **catch**.
cauliflower ['kɔlɪflauə*] n chou-fleur m.
cause [kɔ:z] n cause f // vt causer; **there is no ~ for concern** il n'y a pas lieu de s'inquiéter.
causeway ['kɔ:zweɪ] n chaussée (surélevée).
caustic ['kɔ:stɪk] a caustique.
caution ['kɔ:ʃən] n prudence f; (warning) avertissement m // vt avertir, donner un avertissement à.
cautious ['kɔ:ʃəs] a prudent(e); **~ly** ad prudemment, avec prudence; **~ness** n prudence f.
cavalier [kævə'lɪə*] a cavalier(ère), désinvolte.
cavalry ['kævəlrɪ] n cavalerie f.
cave [keɪv] n caverne f, grotte f; **to ~ in** vi (roof etc) s'effondrer; **~man** n homme m des cavernes.
cavern ['kævən] n caverne f.
caviar(e) ['kævɪɑ:*] n caviar m.
cavity ['kævɪtɪ] n cavité f.
cavort [kə'vɔ:t] vi cabrioler, faire des cabrioles.
CBI n abbr of Confederation of British Industries (groupement du patronat).
cc abbr of cubic centimetres; carbon copy.
cease [si:s] vt,vi cesser; **~fire** n cessez-le-feu m; **~less** a incessant(e), continuel(le).
cedar ['si:də*] n cèdre m.
cede [si:d] vt céder.
cedilla [sɪ'dɪlə] n cédille f.
ceiling ['si:lɪŋ] n plafond m.
celebrate ['sɛlɪbreɪt] vt,vi célébrer; **~d** a célèbre; **celebration** [-'breɪʃən] n célébration f.
celebrity [sɪ'lɛbrɪtɪ] n célébrité f.
celery ['sɛlərɪ] n céleri m (en branches).
celestial [sɪ'lɛstɪəl] a céleste.
celibacy ['sɛlɪbəsɪ] n célibat m.
cell [sɛl] n (gen) cellule f; (ELEC) élément m (de pile).
cellar ['sɛlə*] n cave f.
'cellist ['tʃɛlɪst] n violoncelliste m/f.
'cello ['tʃɛləu] n violoncelle m.
cellophane ['sɛləfeɪn] n ® cellophane f ®.
cellular ['sɛljulə*] a cellulaire.
cellulose ['sɛljuləus] n cellulose f.
Celtic ['kɛltɪk, 'sɛltɪk] a celte.
cement [sə'mɛnt] n ciment m // vt cimenter.
cemetery ['sɛmɪtrɪ] n cimetière m.
cenotaph ['sɛnətɑ:f] n cénotaphe m.
censor ['sɛnsə*] n censeur m; **~ship** n censure f.
censure ['sɛnʃə*] vt blâmer, critiquer.
census ['sɛnsəs] n recensement m.
cent [sɛnt] n (US: coin) cent m, = 1:100 du dollar; see also **per**.
centenary [sɛn'ti:nərɪ] n centenaire m.
center ['sɛntə*] n (US) = **centre**.
centi... ['sɛntɪ] prefix: **~grade** a centigrade; **~litre** n centilitre m; **~metre** n centimètre m.
centipede ['sɛntɪpi:d] n mille-pattes m inv.

central ['sɛntrəl] a central(e); **~ heating** n chauffage central; **~ize** vt centraliser.
centre ['sɛntə*] n centre m; **~forward** n (SPORT) avant-centre m // vt centrer; (PHOT) cadrer **~half** n (SPORT) demi-centre m.
centrifugal [sɛn'trɪfjugəl] a centrifuge.
century ['sɛntjurɪ] n siècle m.
ceramic [sɪ'ræmɪk] a céramique.
cereal ['si:rɪəl] n céréale f.
ceremony ['sɛrɪmənɪ] n cérémonie f; **to stand on ~** faire des façons.
certain ['sə:tən] a certain(e); **to make ~ of** s'assurer de; **for ~** certainement, sûrement; **~ly** ad certainement; **~ty** n certitude f.
certificate [sə'tɪfɪkɪt] n certificat m.
certify ['sə:tɪfaɪ] vt certifier // vi: **to ~ to** attester.
cervix ['sə:vɪks] n col m de l'utérus.
cessation [sə'seɪʃən] n cessation f, arrêt m.
cesspool ['sɛspu:l] n fosse f d'aisance.
Ceylon [sɪ'lɔn] n Ceylan m.
cf. (abbr = compare) cf., voir.
chafe [tʃeɪf] vt irriter, frotter contre.
chaffinch ['tʃæfɪntʃ] n pinson m.
chagrin ['ʃægrɪn] n contrariété f, déception f.
chain [tʃeɪn] n (gen) chaîne f // vt (also: **~ up**) enchaîner, attacher (avec une chaîne); **~ reaction** n réaction f en chaîne; **to ~ smoke** vi fumer cigarette sur cigarette; **~ store** n magasin m à succursales multiples.
chair [tʃɛə*] n chaise f; (armchair) fauteuil m; (of university) chaire f // vt (meeting) présider; **~lift** n télésiège m; **~man** n président m.
chalet ['ʃæleɪ] n chalet m.
chalice ['tʃælɪs] n calice m.
chalk [tʃɔ:k] n craie f.
challenge ['tʃælɪndʒ] n défi m // vt défier; (statement, right) mettre en question, contester; **to ~ sb to a fight/game** inviter qn à se battre/à jouer (sous forme d'un défi); **to ~ sb to do** mettre qn au défi de faire; **~r** n (SPORT) challenger m; **challenging** a de défi, provocateur(trice).
chamber ['tʃeɪmbə*] n chambre f; **~ of commerce** chambre f de commerce; **~maid** n femme f de chambre; **~ music** n musique f de chambre; **~pot** n pot m de chambre.
chamois ['ʃæmwɑ:] n chamois m; **~ leather** ['ʃæmɪlɛðə*] n peau f de chamois.
champagne [ʃæm'peɪn] n champagne m.
champion ['tʃæmpɪən] n champion/ne m; **~ship** n championnat m.
chance [tʃɑ:ns] n hasard m; (opportunity) occasion f, possibilité f; (hope, likelihood) chance f // vt: **to ~ it** risquer (le coup), essayer // a fortuit(e), de hasard; **there is little ~ of his coming** il est peu probable or il y a peu de chances qu'il vienne; **to take a ~** prendre un risque; **by ~** par hasard.
chancel ['tʃɑ:nsəl] n chœur m.
chancellor ['tʃɑ:nsələ*] n chancelier m;

C~ of the Exchequer n chancelier m de l'Échiquier.

chandelier [ʃændə'liə*] n lustre m.

change [tʃeindʒ] vt (alter, replace, COMM: money) changer; (switch, substitute: gear, hands, trains, clothes, one's name etc) changer de; (transform): to ~ sb into changer or transformer qn en // vi (gen) changer; (change clothes) se changer; (be transformed): to ~ into se changer or transformer en // n changement m; (money) monnaie f; to ~ one's mind changer d'avis; a ~ of clothes des vêtements de rechange; for a ~ pour changer; small ~ petite monnaie; to give sb ~ for or of £10 faire à qn la monnaie de 10 livres; ~able a (weather) variable; ~over n (to new system) changement m, passage m.

changing ['tʃeindʒiŋ] a changeant(e); ~ room n (in shop) salon m d'essayage; (SPORT) vestiaire m.

channel ['tʃænl] n (TV) chaîne f; (waveband, groove, fig: medium) canal m; (of river, sea) chenal m // vt canaliser; through the usual ~s en suivant la filière habituelle; the (English) C~ la Manche; the C~ Islands les îles de la Manche, les îles anglo-normandes.

chant [tʃɑ:nt] n chant m; mélopée f; psalmodie f // vt chanter, scander; psalmodier.

chaos ['keiɔs] n chaos m.

chaotic [kei'ɔtik] a chaotique.

chap [tʃæp] n (col: man) type m // vt (skin) gercer, crevasser.

chapel ['tʃæpəl] n chapelle f.

chaperon ['ʃæpərəun] n chaperon m // vt chaperonner.

chaplain ['tʃæplin] n aumônier m.

chapter ['tʃæptə*] n chapitre m.

char [tʃɑ:*] vt (burn) carboniser // vi (cleaner) faire des ménages // n = charlady.

character ['kæriktə*] n caractère m; (in novel, film) personnage m; (eccentric) numéro m, phénomène m; ~istic [-'ristik] a,n caractéristique (f); ~ize vt caractériser.

charade [ʃə'rɑ:d] n charade f.

charcoal ['tʃɑ:kəul] n charbon m de bois.

charge [tʃɑ:dʒ] n accusation f; (LAW) inculpation f; (cost) prix (demandé); (of gun, battery, MIL: attack) charge f // vt (LAW): to ~sb (with) inculper qn (de); (gun, battery, MIL: enemy) charger; (customer, sum) faire payer // vi (gen with: up, along etc) foncer; ~s npl: bank/labour ~s frais mpl de banque/main-d'œuvre; to ~ in/out entrer/sortir en trombe; to ~ down/up dévaler/grimper à toute allure; is there a ~? doit-on payer?; there's no ~ c'est gratuit, on ne fait pas payer; to take ~ of se charger de; to be in ~ of être responsable de, s'occuper de; to have ~ of sb avoir la charge de qn; they ~d us £10 for the meal ils nous ont fait payer le repas 10 livres, ils nous ont compté 10 livres pour le repas; how much do you ~ for this repair? combien demandez-vous pour cette réparation?; to ~ an

expense (up) to sb mettre une dépense sur le compte de qn.

charitable ['tʃæritəbl] a charitable.

charity ['tʃæriti] n charité f; institution f charitable or de bienfaisance, œuvre f (de charité).

charlady ['tʃɑ:leidi] n femme f de ménage.

charm [tʃɑ:m] n charme m // vt charmer, enchanter; ~ing a charmant(e).

chart [tʃɑ:t] n tableau m, diagramme m; graphique m; (map) carte marine // vt dresser or établir la carte de.

charter ['tʃɑ:tə*] vt (plane) affréter // n (document) charte f; ~ed accountant n expert-comptable m; ~ flight n charter m.

charwoman ['tʃɑ:wumən] n = charlady.

chase [tʃeis] vt poursuivre, pourchasser // n poursuite f, chasse f.

chasm ['kæzəm] n gouffre m, abîme m.

chassis ['ʃæsi] n châssis m.

chastity ['tʃæstiti] n chasteté f.

chat [tʃæt] vi (also: have a ~) bavarder, causer // n conversation f.

chatter ['tʃætə*] vi (person) bavarder, papoter // n bavardage m, papotage m; my teeth are ~ing je claque des dents; ~box n moulin m à paroles, babillard/e.

chatty ['tʃæti] a (style) familier(ère); (person) enclin(e) à bavarder or au papotage.

chauffeur ['ʃəufə*] n chauffeur m (de maître).

cheap [tʃi:p] a bon marché inv, pas cher(chère); (joke) facile, d'un goût douteux; (poor quality) à bon marché, de qualité médiocre // ad à bon marché, pour pas cher; ~en vt rabaisser, déprécier; ~ly ad à bon marché, à bon compte.

cheat [tʃi:t] vi tricher // vt tromper, duper; (rob) escroquer // n tricheur/euse; escroc m; (trick) duperie f, tromperie f; ~ing n tricherie f.

check [tʃek] vt vérifier; (passport, ticket) contrôler; (halt) enrayer; (restrain) maîtriser // n vérification f; contrôle m; (curb) frein m; (bill) addition f; (pattern: gen pl) carreaux mpl; (US) = cheque; to ~ in vi (in hotel) remplir sa fiche (d'hôtel); (at airport) se présenter à l'enregistrement // vt (luggage) (faire) enregistrer; to ~ off vt cocher; to ~ out vi (in hotel) régler sa note // vt (luggage) retirer; to ~ up vi: to ~ up (on sth) vérifier (qch); to ~ up on sb se renseigner sur le compte de qn; ~ers n (US) jeu m de dames; ~mate n échec et mat m; ~point n contrôle m; ~up n (MED) examen médical, check-up m.

cheek [tʃi:k] n joue f; (impudence) toupet m, culot m; ~bone n pommette f; ~y a effronté(e), culotté(e).

cheer [tʃiə*] vt acclamer, applaudir; (gladden) réjouir, réconforter // vi applaudir // n (gen pl) acclamations fpl, applaudissements mpl; bravos mpl, hourras mpl; ~s! (à votre) santé!; to ~ up vi se dérider, reprendre courage // vt remonter le moral à or de, dérider, égayer; ~ful a gai(e), joyeux(euse); ~fulness n gaieté f, bonne humeur; ~io excl salut!, au revoir!; ~less a sombre, triste.

cheese [tʃiːz] n fromage m; **~board** n plateau m à fromages.

chef [ʃef] n chef (cuisinier).

chemical ['kemɪkəl] a chimique // n produit m chimique.

chemist ['kemɪst] n pharmacien/ne; (scientist) chimiste m/f; **~ry** n chimie f; **~'s (shop)** n pharmacie f.

cheque [tʃek] n chèque m; **~book** n chéquier m, carnet m de chèques.

chequered ['tʃekəd] a (fig) varié(e).

cherish ['tʃerɪʃ] vt chérir; (hope etc) entretenir.

cheroot [ʃə'ruːt] n cigare m de Manille.

cherry ['tʃerɪ] n cerise f.

chess [tʃes] n échecs mpl; **~board** n échiquier m; **~man** n pièce f (de jeu d'échecs); **~player** n joueur/euse d'échecs.

chest [tʃest] n poitrine f; (box) coffre m, caisse f; **~ of drawers** n commode f.

chestnut ['tʃesnʌt] n châtaigne f; **~ (tree)** n châtaignier m.

chew [tʃuː] vt mâcher; **~ing gum** n chewing-gum m.

chic [ʃiːk] a chic inv, élégant(e).

chick [tʃɪk] n poussin m.

chicken ['tʃɪkɪn] n poulet m; **~ feed** n (fig) broutilles fpl, bagatelle f; **~ pox** n varicelle f.

chick pea ['tʃɪkpiː] n pois m chiche.

chicory ['tʃɪkərɪ] n (for coffee) chicorée f; (salad) endive f.

chief [tʃiːf] n chef m // a principal(e); **~ly** ad principalement, surtout.

chiffon ['ʃɪfɔn] n mousseline f de soie.

chilblain ['tʃɪlbleɪn] n engelure f.

child, pl **~ren** [tʃaɪld, 'tʃɪldrən] n enfant m/f; **~birth** n accouchement m; **~hood** n enfance f; **~ish** a puéril(e), enfantin(e); **~like a** innocent(e), pur(e); **~ minder** n garde f d'enfants.

Chile ['tʃɪlɪ] n Chili m; **~an** a chilien(ne) // n Chilien/ne.

chill [tʃɪl] n froid m; (MED) refroidissement m, coup m de froid // a froid(e), glacial(e) // vt faire frissonner; refroidir; (CULIN) mettre au frais, rafraîchir; **serve ~ed à** servir frais; **~y** a froid(e), glacé(e); (sensitive to cold) frileux(euse); **to feel ~y** avoir froid.

chime [tʃaɪm] n carillon m // vi carillonner, sonner.

chimney ['tʃɪmnɪ] n cheminée f.

chimpanzee [tʃɪmpæn'ziː] n chimpanzé m.

chin [tʃɪn] n menton m.

china ['tʃaɪnə] n porcelaine f; (vaisselle f en) porcelaine.

China ['tʃaɪnə] n Chine f.

Chinese [tʃaɪ'niːz] a chinois(e) // n Chinois/e; (LING) chinois m.

chink [tʃɪŋk] n (opening) fente f, fissure f; (noise) tintement m.

chip [tʃɪp] n (gen pl: CULIN) frite f; (of wood) copeau m; (of glass, stone) éclat m // vt (cup, plate) ébrécher; **~board n** aggloméré m; **~pings npl: loose ~pings** gravillons mpl.

chiropodist [kɪ'rɔpədɪst] n pédicure m/f.

chirp [tʃəːp] n pépiement m, gazouillis m // vi pépier, gazouiller.

chisel ['tʃɪzl] n ciseau m.

chit [tʃɪt] n mot m, note f.

chitchat ['tʃɪttʃæt] n bavardage m, papotage m.

chivalrous ['ʃɪvəlrəs] a chevaleresque.

chivalry ['ʃɪvəlrɪ] n chevalerie f; esprit m chevaleresque.

chives [tʃaɪvz] npl ciboulette f, civette f.

chloride ['klɔːraɪd] n chlorure m.

chlorine ['klɔːriːn] n chlore m.

chock [tʃɔk] n cale f; **~-a-block, ~-full a** plein(e) à craquer.

chocolate ['tʃɔklɪt] n chocolat m.

choice [tʃɔɪs] n choix m // a de choix.

choir ['kwaɪə*] n chœur m, chorale f; **~boy** n jeune choriste m, petit chanteur.

choke [tʃəuk] vi étouffer // vt étrangler; étouffer; (block) boucher, obstruer // n (AUT) starter m.

cholera ['kɔlərə] n choléra m.

choose, pt **chose**, pp **chosen** [tʃuːz, tʃəuz, 'tʃəuzn] vt choisir; **to ~ to do** décider de faire, juger bon de faire.

chop [tʃɔp] vt (wood) couper (à la hache); (CULIN: also: **~ up**) couper (fin), émincer, hacher (en morceaux) // n coup m (de hache, du tranchant de la main); (CULIN) côtelette f; **~s npl (jaws) mâchoires fpl; babines fpl; to ~ down** vt (tree) abattre; **~py a** (sea) un peu agité(e); **~sticks** npl baguettes fpl.

choral ['kɔːrəl] a choral(e), chanté(e) en chœur.

chord [kɔːd] n (MUS) accord m.

chore [tʃɔː*] n travail m de routine; **household ~s** travaux mpl du ménage.

choreographer [kɔrɪ'ɔgrəfə*] n chorégraphe m/f.

chorister ['kɔrɪstə*] n choriste m/f.

chortle ['tʃɔːtl] vi glousser.

chorus ['kɔːrəs] n chœur m; (repeated part of song, also fig) refrain m.

chose [tʃəuz] pt of **choose**.

chosen ['tʃəuzn] pp of **choose**.

chow [tʃau] n (dog) chow-chow m.

Christ [kraɪst] n Christ m.

christen ['krɪsn] vt baptiser; **~ing** n baptême m.

Christian ['krɪstɪən] a,n chrétien(ne); **~ity** [-'ænɪtɪ] n christianisme m; chrétienté f; **~ name** n prénom m.

Christmas ['krɪsməs] n Noël m or f; **~ card** n carte f de Noël; **~ Eve** n la veille de Noël; la nuit de Noël; **~ tree** n arbre m de Noël.

chrome [krəum] n = **chromium**.

chromium ['krəumɪəm] n chrome m; (also: **~ plating**) chromage m.

chromosome ['krəuməsəum] n chromosome m.

chronic ['krɔnɪk] a chronique.

chronicle ['krɔnɪkl] n chronique f.

chronological [krɔnə'lɔdʒɪkəl] a chronologique.

chrysanthemum [krɪ'sænθəməm] n chrysanthème m.

chubby ['tʃʌbɪ] a potelé(e), rondelet(te).

chuck [tʃʌk] vt lancer, jeter; **to ~ out** vt flanquer dehors or à la porte; **to ~ (up)** vt lâcher, plaquer.

chuckle ['tʃʌkl] vi glousser.

chum [tʃʌm] n copain/copine.

chunk [tʃʌŋk] n gros morceau; (of bread) quignon m.

church [tʃəːtʃ] n église f; **~yard** n cimetière m.

churlish ['tʃəːlɪʃ] a grossier(ère); hargneux(euse).

churn [tʃəːn] n (for butter) baratte f; (for transport: milk ~) (grand) bidon à lait.

chute [ʃuːt] n glissoire f; (also: rubbish ~) vide-ordures m inv; (children's slide) toboggan m.

chutney ['tʃʌtnɪ] n condiment m à base de fruits.

CID n (abbr of Criminal Investigation Department) ≈ Police f judiciaire (P.J.).

cider ['saɪdə*] n cidre m.

cigar [sɪ'gaː*] n cigare m.

cigarette [sɪgə'rɛt] n cigarette f; **~ case** n étui m à cigarettes; **~ end** n mégot m; **~ holder** n fume-cigarettes m inv.

cinch [sɪntʃ] n (col): **it's a ~** c'est du gâteau, c'est l'enfance de l'art.

cinder ['sɪndə*] n cendre f.

cine ['sɪnɪ]: **~-camera** n caméra f; **~-film** n film m.

cinema ['sɪnəmə] n cinéma m.

cine-projector [sɪnɪprə'dʒɛktə*] n projecteur m de cinéma.

cinnamon ['sɪnəmən] n cannelle f.

cipher ['saɪfə*] n code secret; (fig: faceless employee etc) numéro m.

circle ['səːkl] n cercle m; (in cinema) balcon m // vi faire or décrire des cercles // vt (surround) entourer, encercler; (move round) faire le tour de, tourner autour de.

circuit ['səːkɪt] n circuit m; **~ous** [səː'kjuːtəs] a indirect(e), qui fait un détour.

circular ['səːkjulə*] a circulaire // n circulaire f.

circulate ['səːkjuleɪt] vi circuler // vt faire circuler; **circulation** [-'leɪʃən] n circulation f; (of newspaper) tirage m.

circumcise ['səːkəmsaɪz] vt circoncire.

circumference [sə'kʌmfərəns] n circonférence f.

circumspect ['səːkəmspɛkt] a circonspect(e).

circumstances ['səːkəmstənsɪz] npl circonstances fpl; (financial condition) moyens mpl, situation financière.

circus ['səːkəs] n cirque m.

cistern ['sɪstən] n réservoir m (d'eau); (in toilet) réservoir de la chasse d'eau.

cite [saɪt] vt citer.

citizen ['sɪtɪzn] n (POL) citoyen/ne; (resident): **the ~s of this town** les habitants de cette ville; **~ship** n citoyenneté f.

citrus fruit ['sɪtrəs'fruːt] n agrume m.

city ['sɪtɪ] n ville f, cité f; **the C~** la Cité de Londres (centre des affaires).

civic ['sɪvɪk] a civique.

civil ['sɪvɪl] a civil(e); poli(e), civil; **~ engineer** n ingénieur civil; **~ engineering** n génie civil, travaux publics; **~ian** [sɪ'vɪlɪən] a,n civil(e).

civilization [sɪvɪlaɪ'zeɪʃən] n civilisation f.

civilized ['sɪvɪlaɪzd] a civilisé(e); (fig) où règnent les bonnes manières, empreint(e) d'une courtoisie de bon ton.

civil: **~ law** n code civil; (study) droit civil; **~ servant** n fonctionnaire m/f; **C~ Service** n fonction publique, administration f; **~ war** n guerre civile.

claim [kleɪm] vt revendiquer; demander, prétendre à; déclarer, prétendre // vi (for insurance) faire une déclaration de sinistre // n revendication f; demande f; prétention f, déclaration f; (right) droit m, titre m; **(insurance) ~** demande f d'indemnisation, déclaration f de sinistre; **~ant** n (ADMIN, LAW) requérant/e.

clam [klæm] n palourde f.

clamber ['klæmbə*] vi grimper, se hisser.

clammy ['klæmɪ] a humide et froid(e) (au toucher), moite.

clamp [klæmp] n étau m à main; agrafe f, crampon m // vt serrer; cramponner; **to ~ down on** vt fus sévir contre, prendre des mesures draconiennes à l'égard de.

clan [klæn] n clan m.

clang [klæŋ] n bruit m or fracas m métallique.

clap [klæp] vi applaudir // vt: **to ~ (one's hands)** battre des mains // n claquement m; tape f; **~ping** n applaudissements mpl.

claret ['klærət] n (vin m de) bordeaux m (rouge).

clarification [klærɪfɪ'keɪʃən] n (fig) clarification f, éclaircissement m.

clarify ['klærɪfaɪ] vt clarifier.

clarinet [klærɪ'nɛt] n clarinette f.

clarity ['klærɪtɪ] n clarté f.

clash [klæʃ] n choc m; (fig) conflit m // vi se heurter; être or entrer en conflit.

clasp [klaːsp] n fermoir m // vt serrer, étreindre.

class [klaːs] n (gen) classe f // vt classer, classifier.

classic ['klæsɪk] a classique // n (author) classique m; (race etc) classique f; **~al** a classique.

classification [klæsɪfɪ'keɪʃən] n classification f.

classified ['klæsɪfaɪd] a (information) secret(ète); **~ ads** petites annonces.

classify ['klæsɪfaɪ] vt classifier, classer.

classmate ['klaːsmeɪt] n camarade m/f de classe.

classroom ['klaːsrum] n (salle f de) classe f.

clatter ['klætə*] n cliquetis m; caquetage m // vi cliqueter; (talk) caqueter, jacasser.

clause [klɔːz] n clause f; (LING) proposition f.

claustrophobia [klɔːstrə'fəubɪə] n claustrophobie f.

claw [klɔː] n griffe f; (of bird of prey) serre f; (of lobster) pince f // vt griffer; déchirer.

clay [kleɪ] n argile f.

clean [kliːn] a propre; (clear, smooth) net(te) // vt nettoyer; **to ~** vt nettoyer (à fond); **to ~ up** vt nettoyer; (fig) remettre de l'ordre dans; **~er** n (person) nettoyeur/euse, femme f de ménage; (also: **dry ~er**) teinturier/ière; (product) détachant m; **~ing** n nettoyage m; ~**liness** ['klɛnlınıs] n propreté f; ~**ly** ad proprement; nettement.

cleanse [klɛnz] vt nettoyer; purifier; ~**r** n détergent m; (for face) démaquillant m; **cleansing department** n service m de voirie.

clean-shaven ['kli:n'ʃeıvn] a rasé(e) de près.

clean-up ['kli:n'ʌp] n nettoyage m.

clear [klıə*] a clair(e); (road, way) libre, dégagé(e) // vt dégager, déblayer, débarrasser; faire évacuer; (COMM: goods) liquider; (LAW suspect) innocenter; (obstacle) franchir or sauter sans heurter // vi (weather) s'éclaircir; (fog) se dissiper // ad: ~ of à distance de, à l'écart de; to ~ one's throat s'éclaircir la gorge; to ~ up vi s'éclaircir, se dissiper // vt ranger, mettre en ordre; (mystery) éclaircir, résoudre; ~**ance** n (removal) déblayage m; (free space) dégagement m; (permission) autorisation f; ~**ance sale** n liquidation f; ~**cut** a précise(e), nettement défini(e); ~**ing** n clairière f; (BANKING) compensation f, clearing m; ~**ly** ad clairement; de toute évidence; ~**way** n (Brit) route f à stationnement interdit.

cleavage ['kli:vıdʒ] n (of dress) décolleté m.

clef [klɛf] n (MUS) clé f.

clench [klɛntʃ] vt serrer.

clergy ['klə:dʒı] n clergé m; ~**man** n ecclésiastique m.

clerical ['klɛrıkəl] a de bureau, d'employé de bureau; (REL) clérical(e), du clergé.

clerk [klɑ:k, (US) klə:rk] n employé/e de bureau; (US: salesman/woman) vendeur/-euse.

clever ['klɛvə*] a (mentally) intelligent(e); (deft, crafty) habile, adroit(e); (device, arrangement) ingénieux(euse), astucieux-(euse).

cliché ['kli:ʃeı] n cliché m.

click [klık] vi faire un bruit sec or un déclic.

client ['klaıənt] n client/e; ~**ele** [kli:ɑ̃:n'tɛl] n clientèle f.

cliff [klıf] n falaise f.

climate ['klaımıt] n climat m.

climax ['klaımæks] n apogée m, point culminant; (sexual) orgasme m.

climb [klaım] vi grimper, monter // vt gravir, escalader, monter sur // n montée f, escalade f; to ~ down vi (re)descendre; ~**er** n (also: rock ~er) grimpeur/euse, varappeur/ euse; ~**ing** n (also: rock ~ing) escalade f, varappe f.

clinch [klıntʃ] vt (deal) conclure, sceller.

cling, pt, pp **clung** [klıŋ, klʌŋ] vi: to ~ (to) se cramponner (à), s'accrocher (à); (of clothes) coller (à).

clinic ['klınık] n centre médical; ~**al** a clinique.

clink [klıŋk] vi tinter, cliqueter.

clip [klıp] n (for hair) barrette f; (also: **paper** ~) trombone m; (also: **bulldog** ~) pince f de bureau; (holding hose etc) collier m or bague f (métallique) de serrage // vt (also: ~ **together** papers) attacher; (hair, nails) couper; (hedge) tailler; ~**pers** npl tondeuse f; (also: nail ~**pers**) coupe-ongles m inv.

clique [kli:k] n clique f, coterie f.

cloak [kləuk] n grande cape; ~**room** n (for coats etc) vestiaire m; (W.C.) toilettes fpl.

clock [klɔk] n (large) horloge f; (small) pendule f; ~**wise** ad dans le sens des aiguilles d'une montre; ~**work** n mouvement m (d'horlogerie); rouages mpl, mécanisme m.

clog [klɔg] n sabot m // vt boucher, encrasser // vi se boucher, s'encrasser.

cloister ['klɔıstə*] n cloître m.

close a, ad and derivatives [kləus] a près, proche; (writing, texture) serré(e); (watch) étroit(e), strict(e); (examination) atten-tif(ive); (weather) lourd(e), étouffant(e); (room) mal aéré(e) // ad près, à proximité; a ~ **friend** un ami intime; to **have a** ~ **shave** (fig) l'échapper belle // vb and derivatives [kləuz] vt fermer // vi (shop etc) fermer; (lid, door etc) se fermer; (end) se terminer, se conclure // n (end) conclusion f; to ~ **down** vt, vi fermer (définitivement); ~**d** a (shop etc) fermé(e); (road) fermé à la circulation; ~**d shop** n organisation f qui n'admet que des travailleurs syndiqués; ~**ly** ad (examine, watch) de près.

closet ['klɔzıt] n (cupboard) placard m, réduit m.

close-up ['kləusʌp] n gros plan.

closure ['kləuʒə*] n fermeture f.

clot [klɔt] n (gen: blood ~) caillot m // vi (blood) former des caillots; (: external bleeding) se coaguler; ~**ted cream** n crème caillée.

cloth [klɔθ] n (material) tissu m, étoffe f; (also: tea~) torchon m; lavette f.

clothe [kləuð] vt habiller, vêtir; ~**s** npl vêtements mpl, habits mpl; ~**s brush** n brosse f à habits; ~**s line** n corde f (à linge); ~**s peg** n pince f à linge.

clothing ['kləuðıŋ] n = **clothes**.

cloud [klaud] n nuage m; ~**burst** n violente averse; ~**y** a nuageux(euse), couvert(e); (liquid) trouble.

clout [klaut] n (blow) taloche f // vt flanquer une taloche à.

clove [kləuv] n clou m de girofle; ~ **of garlic** gousse f d'ail.

clover ['kləuvə*] n trèfle m; ~**leaf** n feuille f de trèfle; ~**leaf junction** (AUT) n croisement m en trèfle.

clown [klaun] n clown m // vi (also: ~ **about**, ~ **around**) faire le clown.

club [klʌb] n (society) club m; (weapon) massue f, matraque f; (also: golf ~) club // vt matraquer // vi: to ~ **together** s'associer; ~**s** npl (CARDS) trèfle m; ~**house** n pavillon m.

cluck [klʌk] vi glousser.

clue [klu:] n indice m; (in crosswords) définition f; I haven't a ~ je n'en ai pas la moindre idée.

clump [klʌmp] n: ~ **of trees** bouquet m d'arbres.

clumsy ['klʌmzı] a (person) gauche, maladroit(e); (object) malcommode, peu maniable.

clung [klʌŋ] pt, pp of **cling**.

cluster ['klʌstə*] n (petit) groupe // vi se rassembler.

clutch [klʌtʃ] n (grip, grasp) étreinte f, prise f; (AUT) embrayage m // vt agripper, serrer fort; **to ~ at** se cramponner à.
clutter ['klʌtə*] vt encombrer.
Co. abbr of **county**; **company**.
c/o (abbr of **care of**) c/o, aux bons soins de.
coach [kəutʃ] n (bus) autocar m; (horse-drawn) diligence f; (of train) voiture f, wagon m; (SPORT: trainer) entraîneur/euse; (school: tutor) répétiteur/trice // vt entraîner; donner des leçons particulières à.
coagulate [kəu'ægjuleɪt] vt coaguler // vi se coaguler.
coal [kəul] n charbon m; ~ **face** n front m de taille; (~) **face workers** npl mineurs mpl de fond; ~**field** n bassin houiller.
coalition [kəuə'lɪʃən] n coalition f.
coalman, coal merchant ['kəulmən, 'kəulmə:tʃənt] n charbonnier m, marchand m de charbon.
coalmine ['kəulmaɪn] n mine f de charbon.
coarse [kɔ:s] a grossier(ère), rude.
coast [kəust] n côte f // vi (with cycle etc) descendre en roue libre; ~**al** a côtier(ère); ~**er** n caboteur m; ~**guard** n garde-côte m; ~**line** n côte f, littoral m.
coat [kəut] n manteau m; (of animal) pelage m, poil m; (of paint) couche f // vt couvrir, enduire; ~ **of arms** n blason m, armoiries fpl; ~ **hanger** n cintre m; ~**ing** n couche f, enduit m.
coax [kəuks] vt persuader par des cajoleries.
cob [kɔb] n see **corn**.
cobbles, cobblestones ['kɔblz, 'kɔblstəunz] npl pavés (ronds).
cobra ['kəubrə] n cobra m.
cobweb ['kɔbwɛb] n toile f d'araignée.
cocaine [kə'keɪn] n cocaïne f.
cock [kɔk] n (rooster) coq m; (male bird) mâle m // vt (gun) armer; **to ~ one's ears** (fig) dresser l'oreille; ~**erel** n jeune coq m; ~**-eyed** a (fig) de travers; qui louche; qui ne tient pas debout (fig).
cockle ['kɔkl] n coque f.
cockney ['kɔknɪ] n cockney m/f (habitant des quartiers populaires de l'East End de Londres), ≈ faubourien/ne.
cockpit ['kɔkpɪt] n (in aircraft) poste m de pilotage, cockpit m.
cockroach ['kɔkrəutʃ] n cafard m, cancrelat m.
cocktail ['kɔkteɪl] n cocktail m; ~ **cabinet** n (meuble-)bar m; ~ **party** n cocktail m; ~ **shaker** n shaker m.
cocoa ['kəukəu] n cacao m.
coconut ['kəukənʌt] n noix f de coco.
cocoon [kə'ku:n] n cocon m.
cod [kɔd] n morue (fraîche), cabillaud m.
code [kəud] n code m.
codify ['kəudɪfaɪ] vt codifier.
coeducational ['kəuɛdju'keɪʃənl] a mixte.
coerce [kəu'ə:s] vt contraindre; **coercion** [-'ə:ʃən] n contrainte f.
coexistence ['kəuɪg'zɪstəns] n coexistence f.
coffee ['kɔfɪ] n café m; ~ **grounds** npl marc m de café; ~**pot** n cafetière f; ~ **table** n (petite) table basse.

coffin ['kɔfɪn] n cercueil m.
cog [kɔg] n dent f (d'engrenage); ~**wheel** n roue dentée.
cogent ['kəudʒənt] a puissant(e), convaincant(e).
cognac ['kɔnjæk] n cognac m.
coherent [kəu'hɪərənt] a cohérent(e).
coil [kɔɪl] n rouleau m, bobine f; (one loop) anneau m, spire f; (contraceptive) stérilet m // vt enrouler.
coin [kɔɪn] n pièce f de monnaie // vt (word) inventer; ~**age** n monnaie f, système m monétaire; ~**-box** n cabine f téléphonique.
coincide [kəuɪn'saɪd] vi coïncider; ~**nce** [kəu'ɪnsɪdəns] n coïncidence f.
coke [kəuk] n coke m.
colander ['kɔləndə*] n passoire f (à légumes).
cold [kəuld] a froid(e) // n froid m; (MED) rhume m; **it's ~** il fait froid; **to be ~** avoir froid; **to have ~ feet** avoir froid aux pieds; (fig) avoir la frousse or la trouille; **to give sb the ~ shoulder** battre froid à qn; ~**ly** a froidement; ~ **sore** n herpès m.
coleslaw ['kəulslɔ:] n sorte de salade de chou cru.
colic ['kɔlɪk] n colique(s) f(pl).
collaborate [kə'læbəreɪt] vi collaborer; **collaboration** [-'reɪʃən] n collaboration f; **collaborator** n collaborateur/trice.
collage [kɔ'lɑ:ʒ] n (ART) collage m.
collapse [kə'læps] vi s'effondrer, s'écrouler // n effondrement m, écroulement m.
collapsible [kə'læpsəbl] a pliant(e); télescopique.
collar ['kɔlə*] n (of coat, shirt) col m; ~**bone** n clavicule f.
collate [kɔ'leɪt] vt collationner.
colleague ['kɔli:g] n collègue m/f.
collect [kə'lɛkt] vt rassembler; ramasser; (as a hobby) collectionner; (call and pick up) (passer) prendre; (mail) faire la levée de, ramasser; (money owed) encaisser; (donations, subscriptions) recueillir // vi se rassembler; s'amasser; ~**ed** a: ~**ed works** œuvres complètes; ~**ion** [kə'lɛkʃən] n collection f; levée f; (for money) collecte f, quête f.
collective [kə'lɛktɪv] a collectif(ive).
collector [kə'lɛktə*] n collectionneur m; (of taxes) percepteur m; (of rent, cash) encaisseur m.
college ['kɔlɪdʒ] n collège m; ~ **of education** ≈ école normale.
collide [kə'laɪd] vi: **to ~ (with)** entrer en collision (avec); (fig) entrer en conflit (avec), se heurter (à).
colliery ['kɔlɪərɪ] n mine f de charbon, houillère f.
collision [kə'lɪʒən] n collision f, heurt m; (fig) conflit m.
colloquial [kə'ləukwɪəl] a familier(ère).
colon ['kəulən] n (sign) deux-points mpl; (MED) côlon m.
colonel ['kə:nl] n colonel m.
colonial [kə'ləunɪəl] a colonial(e).
colonize ['kɔlənaɪz] vt coloniser.

colony ['kɔlənı] n colonie f.
color ['kʌlə*] n,vt (US) = **colour**.
Colorado [kɔləˈrɑːdəu]: ~ **beetle** n
doryphore m.
colossal [kəˈlɔsl] a colossal(e).
colour, color (US) ['kʌlə*] n couleur f //
vt colorer; peindre; (with crayons)
colorier; (news) fausser, exagérer; ~s npl
(of party, club) couleurs fpl; ~ **bar** n
discrimination raciale (dans un
établissement etc); ~-**blind** a
daltonien(ne); ~**ed** a coloré(e); (photo) en
couleur // n: ~**eds** personnes fpl de
couleur; ~ **film** n (for camera) pellicule
f (en) couleur; ~**ful** a coloré(e), vif(vive);
(personality) pittoresque, haut(e) en
couleurs; ~ **scheme** n combinaison f
de(s) couleurs; ~ **television** n télévision
f en couleur
colt [kəult] n poulain m.
column ['kɔləm] n colonne f; ~**ist**
['kɔləmnıst] n rédacteur/trice d'une
rubrique.
coma ['kəumə] n coma m.
comb [kəum] n peigne m // vt (hair)
peigner; (area) ratisser, passer au peigne
fin.
combat ['kɔmbæt] n combat m // vt
combattre, lutter contre.
combination [kɔmbıˈneıʃən] n (gen)
combinaison f.
combine vb [kəmˈbaın] vt combiner; (one
quality with another) joindre (à), allier (à)
// vi s'associer; (CHEM) se combiner // n
['kɔmbaın] association f; (ECON) trust m;
~ (**harvester**) n moissonneuse-batteuse(-
lieuse) f.
combustible [kəmˈbʌstıbl] a combustible.
combustion [kəmˈbʌstʃən] n combustion
f.
come, pt **came**, pp **come** [kʌm, keım]
vi venir; arriver; **to** ~ **into sight** or **view**
apparaître; **to** ~ **to** (decision etc) parvenir
or arriver à; **to** ~ **undone/loose** se
défaire/desserrer; **to** ~ **about** vi se
produire, arriver; **to** ~ **across** vt fus
rencontrer par hasard, tomber sur; **to** ~
along vi = **to come on**; **to** ~ **apart** vi
s'en aller en morceaux; se détacher; **to**
~ **away** vi partir, s'en aller; se détacher;
to ~ **back** vi revenir; **to** ~ **by** vt fus
(acquire) obtenir, se procurer; **to** ~ **down**
vi descendre; (prices) baisser; (buildings)
s'écrouler; être démoli(e); **to** ~ **forward**
vi s'avancer; se présenter, s'annoncer; **to**
~ **from** vi être originaire de; venir de;
to ~ **in** vi entrer; **to** ~ **in for** vt fus
(criticism etc) être l'objet de; **to** ~ **into**
vt fus (money) hériter de; **to** ~ **off** vi
(button) se détacher; (stain) s'enlever;
(attempt) réussir; **to** ~ **on** vi (pupil,
undertaking) faire des progrès, avancer; ~
on! viens!; allons!, allez!; **to** ~ **out** vi
sortir; (book) paraître; (strike) cesser le
travail, se mettre en grève; **to** ~ **to** vi
revenir à soi; **to** ~ **up** vi monter; **to** ~
up against vt fus (resistance, difficulties)
rencontrer; **to** ~ **up with** vt fus: **he came
up with an idea** il a eu une idée, il a
proposé quelque chose; **to** ~ **upon** vt fus
tomber sur; ~**back** n (THEATRE etc) rentrée
f.

comedian [kəˈmiːdıən] n (in music hall etc)
comique m; (THEATRE) comédien m.
comedienne [kəmiːdıˈɛn] n comédienne f.
comedown ['kʌmdaun] n déchéance f.
comedy ['kɔmıdı] n comédie f.
comet ['kɔmıt] n comète f.
comfort ['kʌmfət] n confort m, bien-être
m; (solace) consolation f, réconfort m //
vt consoler, réconforter; ~**s** npl aises fpl;
~**able** a confortable; ~ **station** n (US)
toilettes fpl.
comic ['kɔmık] a (also: ~**al**) comique //
n comique m; (magazine) illustré m; ~
strip n bande dessinée.
coming ['kʌmıŋ] n arrivée f; ~(**s**) **and
going(s)** n(pl) va-et-vient m inv.
comma ['kɔmə] n virgule f.
command [kəˈmɑːnd] n ordre m,
commandement m; (MIL: authority)
commandement m; (mastery) maîtrise f // vt
(troops) commander; (be able to get)
(pouvoir) disposer de, avoir à sa
disposition; (deserve) avoir droit à; **to** ~
sb to do donner l'ordre or commander à
qn de faire; ~**eer** [kɔmənˈdıə*] vt
réquisitionner (par la force); ~**er** n chef
m; (MIL) commandant m; ~**ing officer** n
commandant m.
commando [kəˈmɑːndəu] n commando
m; membre m d'un commando.
commemorate [kəˈmɛməreıt] vt commémorer; **commemoration** [-ˈreıʃən] n commémoration f.
commemorative [kəˈmɛmərətıv] a com-
mémoratif(ive).
commence [kəˈmɛns] vt,vi commencer.
commend [kəˈmɛnd] vt louer; recommander; ~**able** a louable; ~**ation** [kɔmɛn-
ˈdeıʃən] n éloge m; recommandation f.
commensurate [kəˈmɛnʃərıt] a: ~ **with**
en proportion de, proportionné(e) à.
comment ['kɔmɛnt] n commentaire m //
vi faire des remarques or commentaires;
~**ary** ['kɔməntərı] n commentaire m;
(SPORT) reportage m (en direct); ~**ator**
['kɔmənteıtə*] n commentateur m;
reporter m.
commerce ['kɔməːs] n commerce m.
commercial [kəˈməːʃəl] a commercial(e)
// n (TV: also: ~ **break**) annonce f
publicitaire, spot m (publicitaire); ~
college n école f de commerce; ~**ize** vt
commercialiser; ~ **television** n la
publicité à la télévision, les chaînes
indépendantes; ~ **traveller** n voyageur m
de commerce; ~ **vehicle** n véhicule m
utilitaire.
commiserate [kəˈmızəreıt] vi: **to** ~ **with**
compatir à.
commission [kəˈmıʃən] n (committee, fee)
commission f; (order for work of art etc)
commande f // vt (MIL) nommer (à un
commandement); (work of art)
commander, charger un artiste de
l'exécution de; **out of** ~ (NAUT) hors de
service; ~**aire** [kəmıʃəˈnɛə*] n (at shop,
cinema etc) portier m (en uniforme); ~**er**
n membre m d'une commission; (POLICE)
préfet m (de police).
commit [kəˈmıt] vt (act) commettre; (to
sb's care) confier (à); **to** ~ **o.s. (to do)**
s'engager (à faire); **to** ~ **suicide** se

suicider; **to ~ to writing** coucher par
écrit; **~ment** n engagement m,
responsabilité(s) f(pl).
committee [kə'mıtı] n comité m.
commodity [kə'mɒdıtı] n produit m,
marchandise f, article m; (food) denrée f.
common ['kɒmən] a (gen, also pej)
commun(e); (usual) courant(e) // n
terrain communal; **the C~s** npl la
chambre des Communes; **in ~** en
commun; **it's ~ knowledge that** il est
bien connu or notoire que; **to the ~ good**
pour le bien de tous, dans l'intérêt
général; **~er** n roturier/ière; **~ ground**
n (fig) terrain m d'entente; **~ law** n droit
coutumier; **~ly** ad communément,
généralement; couramment; **C~ Market**
n Marché commun; **~place** a banal(e),
ordinaire; **~room** n salle commune;
(SCOL) salle des professeurs; **~ sense** n
bon sens; **the C~wealth** n le
Commonwealth.
commotion [kə'məʊʃən] n désordre m,
tumulte m.
communal ['kɒmju:nl] a (life)
communautaire; (for common use)
commun(e).
commune n ['kɒmju:n] (group)
communauté f // vi [kə'mju:n]: **to ~ with**
converser intimement avec; communier
avec.
communicate [kə'mju:nıkeıt] vt
communiquer, transmettre // vi: **to ~
(with)** communiquer (avec).
communication [kəmju:nı'keıʃən] n
communication f; **~ cord** n sonnette f
d'alarme.
communion [kə'mju:nıən] n (also: **Holy
C~**) communion f.
communiqué [kə'mju:nıkeı] n communiqué m.
communism ['kɒmjunızəm] n communisme m; **communist** a,n communiste
(m/f).
community [kə'mju:nıtı] n communauté
f; **~ centre** n foyer socio-éducatif, centre
m de loisirs; **~ chest** n (US) fonds
commun.
commutation ticket [kɒmju:teıʃəntıkıt]
n (US) carte f d'abonnement.
commute [kə'mju:t] vi faire le trajet
journalier (de son domicile à un lieu de
travail assez éloigné) // vt (LAW)
commuer; (MATH: terms etc) opérer la
commutation de; **~r** n banlieusard/e (qui
... see vi).
compact a [kəm'pækt] compact(e) // n
['kɒmpækt] contrat m, entente f; (also:
powder ~) poudrier m.
companion [kəm'pænıən] n compagnon/-
compagne; **~ship** n camaraderie f.
company ['kʌmpənı] n (also COMM, MIL,
THEATRE) compagnie f; **he's good ~** il est
d'une compagnie agréable; **we have ~**
nous avons de la visite; **to keep sb ~**
tenir compagnie à qn; **to part ~ with** se
séparer de; **~ secretary** n (COMM)
secrétaire général (d'une société).
comparable ['kɒmpərəbl] a comparable.
comparative [kəm'pærətıv] a
comparatif(ive); (relative) relatif(ive).

compare [kəm'pɛə*] vt: **to ~ sth/sb
with/to** comparer qch/qn avec or et/à //
vi: **to ~ (with)** se comparer (à); être
comparable (à); **comparison** [-'pærısn] n
comparaison f; **in comparison (with)** en
comparaison (de).
compartment [kəm'pɑ:tmənt] n (also
RAIL) compartiment m.
compass ['kʌmpəs] n boussole f; **~es** npl
compas m.
compassion [kəm'pæʃən] n compassion
f, humanité f; **~ate** a accessible à la
compassion, au cœur charitable et
bienveillant; **on ~ate grounds** pour
raisons personnelles or de famille.
compatible [kəm'pætıbl] a compatible.
compel [kəm'pel] vt contraindre, obliger;
~ling a (fig: argument) irrésistible.
compendium [kəm'pendıəm] n abrégé m.
compensate ['kɒmpənseıt] vt indemniser,
dédommager // vi: **to ~ for** compenser;
compensation [-'seıʃən] n compensation
f; (money) dédommagement m, indemnité
f.
compère ['kɒmpɛə*] n présentateur/trice,
animateur/trice.
compete [kəm'pi:t] vi (take part)
concourir; (vie): **to ~ (with)** rivaliser
(avec), faire concurrence (à).
competence ['kɒmpıtəns] n compétence
f, aptitude f.
competent ['kɒmpıtənt] a compétent(e),
capable.
competition [kɒmpı'tıʃən] n compétition
f, concours m; (ECON) concurrence f.
competitive [kəm'petıtıv] a (ECON)
concurrentiel(le); **~ examination** n (SCOL)
concours m.
competitor [kəm'petıtə*] n concurrent/e.
compile [kəm'paıl] vt compiler.
complacency [kəm'pleısnsı] n contentement de soi, vaine complaisance.
complacent [kəm'pleısənt] a (trop)
content(e) de soi; suffisant(e).
complain [kəm'pleın] vi: **to ~ (about)** se
plaindre (de); (in shop etc) réclamer (au
sujet de); **to ~ of** (MED) se plaindre
de; **~t** n plainte f; réclamation f; (MED)
affection f.
complement ['kɒmplımənt] n
complément m; (especially of ship's crew
etc) effectif complet; **~ary**
[kɒmplı'mentərı] a complémentaire.
complete [kəm'pli:t] a complet(ète) // vt
achever, parachever; (a form) remplir;
~ly ad complètement; **completion** n
achèvement m.
complex ['kɒmpleks] a complexe // n
(PSYCH, buildings etc) complexe m.
complexion [kəm'plekʃən] n (of face)
teint m; (of event etc) aspect m, caractère
m.
complexity [kəm'pleksıtı] n complexité f.
compliance [kəm'plaıəns] n (see
compliant) docilité f; (see comply): **~ with**
le fait de se conformer à; **in ~ with** en
conformité avec, conformément à.
compliant [kəm'plaıənt] a docile, très
accommodant(e).
complicate ['kɒmplıkeıt] vt compliquer;

~d *a* compliqué(e); **complication** [-'keɪʃən] *n* complication *f*.
compliment *n* ['kɔmplɪmənt] compliment *m* // *vt* ['kɔmplɪmɛnt] complimenter; **~s** *npl* compliments *mpl*, hommages *mpl*; vœux *mpl*; **~ary** [-'mɛntərɪ] *a* flatteur(euse); (*free*) à titre gracieux; **~ary ticket** *n* billet *m* de faveur.
comply [kəm'plaɪ] *vi*: **to ~ with** se soumettre à, se conformer à.
component [kəm'pəunənt] *a* composant(e), constituant(e) // *n* composant *m*, élément *m*.
compose [kəm'pəuz] *vt* composer; **to ~ o.s.** se calmer, se maîtriser; prendre une contenance; **~d** *a* calme, posé(e); **~r** *n* (*MUS*) compositeur *m*.
composite ['kɔmpəzɪt] *a* composite; (*BOT, MATH*) composé(e).
composition [kɔmpə'zɪʃən] *n* composition *f*.
compost ['kɔmpɔst] *n* compost *m*.
composure [kəm'pəuʒə*] *n* calme *m*, maîtrise *f* de soi.
compound ['kɔmpaund] *n* (*CHEM, LING*) composé *m*; (*enclosure*) enclos *m*, enceinte *f* // *a* composé(e); **~ fracture** *n* fracture compliquée; **~ interest** *n* intérêt composé.
comprehend [kɔmprɪ'hɛnd] *vt* comprendre; **comprehension** [-'hɛnʃən] *n* compréhension *f*.
comprehensive [kɔmprɪ'hɛnsɪv] *a* (très) complet(ète); **~ policy** *n* (*INSURANCE*) assurance *f* tous risques; **~ (school)** *n* école secondaire non sélective, avec libre circulation d'une section à l'autre, ≈ C.E.S. *m*.
compress *vt* [kəm'prɛs] comprimer // *n* ['kɔmprɛs] (*MED*) compresse *f*; **~ion** [-'prɛʃən] *n* compression *f*.
comprise [kəm'praɪz] *vt* (*also*: **be ~d of**) comprendre.
compromise ['kɔmprəmaɪz] *n* compromis *m* // *vt* compromettre // *vi* transiger, accepter un compromis.
compulsion [kəm'pʌlʃən] *n* contrainte *f*, force *f*.
compulsive [kəm'pʌlsɪv] *a* (*reason, demand*) coercitif(ive); (*PSYCH*) compulsif(ive): **he's a ~ smoker** c'est un fumeur invétéré.
compulsory [kəm'pʌlsərɪ] *a* obligatoire.
computer [kəm'pju:tə*] *n* ordinateur *m*; (*mechanical*) calculatrice *f*; **~ize** *vt* traiter or automatiser par ordinateur; **~language** *n* langage *m* machine *or* de programmation; **~ programming** *n* programmation *f*; **~ science** *n* informatique *f*; **~ scientist** *n* informaticien/ne.
comrade ['kɔmrɪd] *n* camarade *m/f*; **~ship** *n* camaraderie *f*.
con [kɔn] *vt* duper; escroquer.
concave ['kɔn'keɪv] *a* concave.
conceal [kən'si:l] *vt* cacher, dissimuler.
concede [kən'si:d] *vt* concéder // *vi* céder.
conceit [kən'si:t] *n* vanité *f*, suffisance *f*, prétention *f*; **~ed** *a* vaniteux(euse), suffisant(e).
conceivable [kən'si:vəbl] *a* concevable, imaginable.

conceive [kən'si:v] *vt* concevoir.
concentrate ['kɔnsəntreɪt] *vi* se concentrer // *vt* concentrer.
concentration [kɔnsən'treɪʃən] *n* concentration *f*; **~ camp** *n* camp *m* de concentration.
concentric [kɔn'sɛntrɪk] *a* concentrique.
concept ['kɔnsɛpt] *n* concept *m*.
conception [kən'sɛpʃən] *n* conception *f*.
concern [kən'sə:n] *n* affaire *f*; (*COMM*) entreprise *f*, firme *f*; (*anxiety*) inquiétude *f*, souci *m* // *vt* concerner; **to be ~ed (about)** s'inquiéter (de), être inquiet (au sujet de); **~ing** *prep* en ce qui concerne, à propos de.
concert ['kɔnsət] *n* concert *m*; **in ~** à l'unisson, en chœur; ensemble; **~ed** [kən'sə:tɪd] *a* concerté(e); **~ hall** *n* salle *f* de concert.
concertina [kɔnsə'ti:nə] *n* concertina *m* // *vi* se télescoper, se caramboler.
concerto [kən'tʃə:təu] *n* concerto *m*.
concession [kən'sɛʃən] *n* concession *f*.
conciliation [kənsɪlɪ'eɪʃən] *n* conciliation *f*, apaisement *m*.
conciliatory [kən'sɪlɪətrɪ] *a* conciliateur(trice); conciliant(e).
concise [kən'saɪs] *a* concis(e).
conclave ['kɔnkleɪv] *n* assemblée secrète; (*REL*) conclave *m*.
conclude [kən'klu:d] *vt* conclure; **conclusion** [-'klu:ʒən] *n* conclusion *f*; **conclusive** [-'klu:sɪv] *a* concluant(e), définitif(ive).
concoct [kən'kɔkt] *vt* confectionner, composer.
concourse ['kɔnkɔ:s] *n* (*hall*) hall *m*, salle *f* des pas perdus; (*crowd*) affluence *f*; multitude *f*.
concrete ['kɔnkri:t] *n* béton *m* // *a* concret(ète); en béton.
concur [kən'kə:*] *vi* être d'accord.
concurrently [kən'kʌrntlɪ] *ad* simultanément.
concussion [kən'kʌʃən] *n* ébranlement *m*, secousse *f*; (*MED*) commotion (cérébrale).
condemn [kən'dɛm] *vt* condamner; **~ation** [kɔndɛm'neɪʃən] *n* condamnation *f*.
condensation [kɔndɛn'seɪʃən] *n* condensation *f*.
condense [kən'dɛns] *vi* se condenser // *vt* condenser; **~d milk** *n* lait condensé (sucré).
condescend [kɔndɪ'sɛnd] *vi* condescendre, s'abaisser; **~ing** *a* condescendant(e).
condition [kən'dɪʃən] *n* condition *f* // *vt* déterminer, conditionner; **on ~ that** à condition que + *sub*, à condition de; **~al** *a* conditionnel(le); **to be ~al upon** dépendre de.
condolences [kən'dəulənsɪz] *npl* condoléances *fpl*.
condone [kən'dəun] *vt* fermer les yeux sur, approuver (tacitement).
conducive [kən'dju:sɪv] *a*: **~ to** favorable à, qui contribue à.
conduct *n* ['kɔndʌkt] conduite *f* // *vt* [kən'dʌkt] conduire; (*manage*) mener, diriger; (*MUS*) diriger; **to ~ o.s.** se

conduire, se comporter; **~ed tour** n voyage organisé, visite guidée; **~or** n (of orchestra) chef m d'orchestre; (on bus) receveur m; (ELEC) conducteur m; **~ress** n (on bus) receveuse f.

conduit ['kɔndɪt] n conduit m, tuyau m; tube m.

cone [kəun] n cône m; (for ice-cream) cornet m; (BOT) pomme f de pin, cône.

confectioner [kən'fɛkʃənə*] n (of cakes) pâtissier/ière; (of sweets) confiseur/euse; **~y** n pâtisserie f; confiserie f.

confederation [kənfɛdə'reɪʃən] n confédération f.

confer [kən'fə:*] vt: to ~ sth on conférer qch à // vi conférer, s'entretenir.

conference ['kɔnfərns] n conférence f.

confess [kən'fɛs] vt confesser, avouer // vi se confesser; **~ion** [-'fɛʃən] n confession f; **~ional** [-'fɛʃənl] n confessional m; **~or** n confesseur m.

confetti [kən'fɛtɪ] n confettis mpl.

confide [kən'faɪd] vi: to ~ in s'ouvrir à, se confier à.

confidence ['kɔnfɪdns] n confiance f; (also: self-~) assurance f, confiance en soi; (secret) confidence f; ~ trick n escroquerie f; **confident** a sûr(e), assuré(e); **confidential** [kɔnfɪ'dɛnʃəl] a confidentiel(le).

confine [kən'faɪn] vt limiter, borner; (shut up) confiner, enfermer; **~s** ['kɔnfaɪnz] npl confins mpl, bornes fpl; **~d** a (space) restreint(e), réduit(e); **~ment** n emprisonnement m, détention f; (MIL) consigne f (au quartier); (MED) accouchement m.

confirm [kən'fə:m] vt (report) confirmer; (appointment) ratifier; **~ation** [kɔnfə'meɪʃən] n confirmation f; **~ed** a invétéré(e), incorrigible.

confiscate ['kɔnfɪskeɪt] vt confisquer; **confiscation** [-'keɪʃən] n confiscation f.

conflagration [kɔnflə'greɪʃən] n incendie m.

conflict n ['kɔnflɪkt] conflit m, lutte f // vi [kən'flɪkt] être or entrer en conflit; (opinions) s'opposer, se heurter; **~ing** a contradictoire.

conform [kən'fɔ:m] vi: to ~ (to) se conformer (à); **~ist** n conformiste m/f.

confound [kən'faund] vt confondre; **~ed** a maudit(e), sacré(e).

confront [kən'frʌnt] vt confronter, mettre en présence; (enemy, danger) affronter, faire face à; **~ation** [kɔnfrən'teɪʃən] n confrontation f.

confuse [kən'fju:z] vt embrouiller; (one thing with another) confondre; **confusing** a peu clair(e), déroutant(e); **confusion** [-'fju:ʒən] n confusion f.

congeal [kən'dʒi:l] vi (oil) se figer; (blood) se coaguler.

congenial [kən'dʒi:nɪəl] a sympathique, agréable.

congenital [kən'dʒɛnɪtl] a congénital(e).

conger eel ['kɔngəri:l] n congre m.

congested [kən'dʒɛstɪd] a (MED) congestionné(e); (fig) surpeuplé(e); congestionné; bloqué(e).

congestion [kən'dʒɛstʃən] n congestion f; (fig) encombrement m.

conglomeration [kənglɔmə'reɪʃən] n groupement m; agglomération f.

congratulate [kən'grætjuleɪt] vt: to ~ sb (on) féliciter qn (de); **congratulations** [-'leɪʃənz] npl félicitations fpl.

congregate ['kɔngrɪgeɪt] vi se rassembler, se réunir.

congregation [kɔngrɪ'geɪʃən] n assemblée f (des fidèles).

congress ['kɔngrɛs] n congrès m; **~man** n (US) membre m du Congrès.

conical ['kɔnɪkl] a (de forme) conique.

conifer ['kɔnɪfə*] n conifère m; **~ous** [kə'nɪfərəs] a (forest) de conifères.

conjecture [kən'dʒɛktjə*] n conjecture f // vi, vi conjecturer.

conjugal ['kɔndʒugl] a conjugal(e).

conjugate ['kɔndʒugeɪt] vt conjuguer; **conjugation** [-'geɪʃən] n conjugaison f.

conjunction [kən'dʒʌŋkʃən] n conjonction f.

conjunctivitis [kəndʒʌŋktɪ'vaɪtɪs] n conjonctivite f.

conjure ['kʌndʒə*] vt faire apparaître (par la prestidigitation); [kən'dʒuə*] conjurer, supplier; to ~ up vt (ghost, spirit) faire apparaître; (memories) évoquer; **~r** n prestidigitateur m, illusionniste m/f; **conjuring trick** n tour m de prestidigitation.

conk [kɔŋk]: to ~ out vi (col) tomber or rester en panne.

conman ['kɔnmæn] n escroc m.

connect [kə'nɛkt] vt joindre, relier; (ELEC) connecter; (fig) établir un rapport entre, faire un rapprochement entre // vi (train): to ~ with assurer la correspondance avec; to be ~ed with avoir un rapport avec; avoir des rapports avec, être en relation avec; **~ion** [-ʃən] n relation f, lien m; (ELEC) connexion f; (TEL) communication f; in ~ion with à propos de.

connexion [kə'nɛkʃən] n = **connection**.

conning tower ['kɔnɪŋtauə*] n kiosque m (de sous-marin).

connive [kə'naɪv] vi: to ~ at se faire le complice de.

connoisseur [kɔnɪ'sə*] n connaisseur m.

connotation [kɔnə'teɪʃən] n connotation f, implication f.

connubial [kɔ'nju:bɪəl] a conjugal(e).

conquer ['kɔŋkə*] vt conquérir; (feelings) vaincre, surmonter; **~or** n conquérant m, vainqueur m.

conquest ['kɔŋkwɛst] n conquête f.

cons [kɔnz] npl see **pro**, **convenience**.

conscience ['kɔnʃəns] n conscience f.

conscientious [kɔnʃɪ'ɛnʃəs] a consciencieux(euse); (scruple, objection) de conscience; **~ objector** n objecteur m de conscience.

conscious ['kɔnʃəs] a conscient(e); **~ness** n conscience f; (MED) connaissance f; to lose/regain **~ness** perdre/reprendre connaissance.

conscript ['kɔnskrɪpt] n conscrit m; **~ion** [kən'skrɪpʃən] n conscription f.

consecrate ['kɔnsɪkreɪt] vt consacrer.
consecutive [kən'sɛkjutɪv] a consécutif(ive).
consensus [kən'sɛnsəs] n consensus m.
consent [kən'sɛnt] n consentement m // vi: **to ~ (to)** consentir (à); **age of ~** âge nubile (légal).
consequence ['kɔnsɪkwəns] n suites fpl, conséquence f; importance f.
consequently ['kɔnsɪkwəntlɪ] ad par conséquent, donc.
conservation [kɔnsə:'veɪʃən] n préservation f, protection f.
conservative [kən'sə:vətɪv] a conservateur(trice); (cautious) prudent(e); **C~** a,n conservateur(trice).
conservatory [kən'sə:vətrɪ] n (greenhouse) serre f.
conserve [kən'sə:v] vt conserver, préserver.
consider [kən'sɪdə*] vt considérer, réfléchir à; (take into account) penser à, prendre en considération; (regard, judge) considérer, estimer.
considerable [kən'sɪdərəbl] a considérable.
considerate [kən'sɪdərɪt] a prévenant(e), plein(e) d'égards.
consideration [kənsɪdə'reɪʃən] n considération f; (reward) rétribution f, rémunération f; **out of ~ for** par égard pour; **under ~** à l'étude.
considering [kən'sɪdərɪŋ] prep étant donné.
consign [kən'saɪn] vt expédier, livrer; **~ment** n arrivage m, envoi m.
consist [kən'sɪst] vi: **to ~ of** consister en, se composer de.
consistency [kən'sɪstənsɪ] n consistance f, (fig) cohérence f.
consistent [kən'sɪstənt] a logique, cohérent(e), **~ with** compatible avec, en accord avec.
consolation [kɔnsə'leɪʃən] n consolation f
console vt [kən'səul] consoler // n ['kɔnsəul] console f.
consolidate [kən'sɔlɪdeɪt] vt consolider.
consommé [kən'sɔmeɪ] n consommé m.
consonant ['kɔnsənənt] n consonne f.
consortium [kən'sɔ:tɪəm] n consortium m, comptoir m.
conspicuous [kən'spɪkjuəs] a voyant(e), qui attire la vue or l'attention.
conspiracy [kən'spɪrəsɪ] n conspiration f, complot m.
conspire [kən'spaɪə*] vi conspirer, comploter.
constable ['kʌnstəbl] n ≈ agent m de police, gendarme m; **chief ~** n ≈ préfet m de police.
constabulary [kən'stæbjulərɪ] n ≈ police f, gendarmerie f.
constant ['kɔnstənt] a constant(e); incessant(e); **~ly** ad constamment, sans cesse.
constellation [kɔnstə'leɪʃən] n constellation f.
consternation [kɔnstə'neɪʃən] n consternation f.

constipated ['kɔnstɪpeɪtəd] a constipé(e).
constipation [kɔnstɪ'peɪʃən] n constipation f.
constituency [kən'stɪtjuənsɪ] n circonscription électorale.
constituent [kən'stɪtjuənt] n électeur/-trice; (part) élément constitutif, composant m.
constitute ['kɔnstɪtju:t] vt constituer.
constitution [kɔnstɪ'tju:ʃən] n constitution f; **~al** a constitutionnel(le).
constrain [kən'streɪn] vt contraindre, forcer; **~ed** a contraint(e), gêné(e); **~t** n contrainte f.
constrict [kən'strɪkt] vt rétrécir, resserrer; gêner, limiter.
construct [kən'strʌkt] vt construire; **~ion** [-ʃən] n construction f; **~ive** a constructif(ive).
construe [kən'stru:] vt analyser, expliquer.
consul ['kɔnsl] n consul m; **~ate** ['kɔnsjulɪt] n consulat m.
consult [kən'sʌlt] vt consulter; **~ancy** n: **~ancy fee** honoraires mpl d'expert; **~ant** n (MED) médecin consultant; (other specialist) consultant m, (expert-)conseil m // a: **~ant engineer** ingénieur-conseil m; **legal/management ~ant** conseiller en juridique/en gestion; **~ation** [kɔnsəl'teɪʃən] n consultation f; **~ing room** n cabinet m de consultation.
consume [kən'sju:m] vt consommer; **~r** n consommateur/ trice; **consumerism** n mouvement m pour la protection des consommateurs; **~r society** n société f de consommation.
consummate ['kɔnsʌmeɪt] vt consommer.
consumption [kən'sʌmpʃən] n consommation f; (MED) consomption f (pulmonaire).
cont. abbr of continued.
contact ['kɔntækt] n contact m; (person) connaissance f, relation f // vt se mettre en contact or en rapport avec; **~ lenses** npl verres mpl de contact.
contagious [kən'teɪdʒəs] a contagieux(euse).
contain [kən'teɪn] vt contenir; **to ~ o.s.** se contenir, se maîtriser; **~er** n récipient m; (for shipping etc) container m.
contaminate [kən'tæmɪneɪt] vt contaminer; **contamination** [-'neɪʃən] n contamination f.
cont'd abbr of continued.
contemplate ['kɔntəmpleɪt] vt contempler; (consider) envisager; **contemplation** [-'pleɪʃən] n contemplation f.
contemporary [kən'tɛmpərərɪ] a contemporain(e); (design, wallpaper) moderne // n contemporain/e.
contempt [kən'tɛmpt] n mépris m, dédain m; **~ible** a méprisable, vil(e); **~uous** a dédaigneux(euse), méprisant(e).
contend [kən'tɛnd] vt: **to ~ that** soutenir or prétendre que // vi: **to ~ with** rivaliser avec, lutter avec; **~er** n prétendant/e; adversaire m/f.
content [kən'tɛnt] a content(e), satisfait(e) // vt contenter, satisfaire // n ['kɔntɛnt] contenu m; teneur f; **~s** npl

contenu ; (of barrel etc: capacity) contenance f ; (table of) ~s table f des matières ; to be ~ with se contenter de ; ~ed a content(e), satisfait(e).

contention [kən'tɛnʃən] n dispute f, contestation f ; (argument) assertion f, affirmation f ; **contentious** a querelleur(euse) ; litigieux(euse).

contentment [kən'tɛntmənt] n contentement m, satisfaction f.

contest n ['kɔntɛst] combat m, lutte f ; (competition) concours m // vt [kən'tɛst] contester, discuter ; (compete for) disputer ; ~ant [kən'tɛstənt] n concurrent/e ; (in fight) adversaire m/f.

context ['kɔntɛkst] n contexte m.

continent ['kɔntɪnənt] n continent m ; the C~ l'Europe continentale ; ~al [-'nɛntl] a continental(e) // n Européen/ne (continental(e)).

contingency [kən'tɪndʒənsɪ] n éventualité f, événement imprévu ; ~ plan n plan m d'urgence.

contingent [kən'tɪndʒənt] a contingent(e) // n contingent m ; to be ~ upon dépendre de.

continual [kən'tɪnjuəl] a continuel(le) ; ~ly ad continuellement, sans cesse.

continuation [kəntɪnju'eɪʃən] n continuation f ; (after interruption) reprise f ; (of story) suite f.

continue [kən'tɪnju:] vi continuer // vt continuer ; (start again) reprendre ; to be ~d (story) à suivre.

continuity [kɔntɪ'njuɪtɪ] n continuité f ; ~ girl n (CINEMA) script-girl f.

continuous [kən'tɪnjuəs] a continu(e), permanent(e).

contort [kən'tɔ:t] vt tordre, crisper ; ~ion [-'tɔ:ʃən] n crispation f, torsion f ; (of acrobat) contorsion f ; ~ionist [-'tɔ:ʃənɪst] n contorsionniste m/f.

contour ['kɔntuə*] n contour m, profil m ; (also: ~ line) courbe f de niveau.

contraband ['kɔntrəbænd] n contrebande f.

contraception [kɔntrə'sɛpʃən] n contraception f.

contraceptive [kɔntrə'sɛptɪv] a contraceptif(ive), anticonceptionnel(le) // n contraceptif m.

contract n ['kɔntrækt] contrat m // vb [kən'trækt] vi (COMM): to ~ to do sth s'engager (par contrat) à faire qch ; (become smaller) se contracter, se resserrer // vt contracter ; ~ion [-'ʃən] n contraction f ; (LING) forme contractée ; ~or n entrepreneur m.

contradict [kɔntrə'dɪkt] vt contredire ; (be contrary to) démentir, être en contradiction avec ; ~ion [-'ʃən] n contradiction f.

contralto [kən'træltəu] n contralto m.

contraption [kən'træpʃən] n (pej) machin m, truc m.

contrary ['kɔntrərɪ] a contraire, opposé(e) ; [kən'trɛərɪ] (perverse) contrariant(e), entêté(e) // n contraire m ; on the ~ au contraire ; unless you hear to the ~ sauf avis contraire.

contrast n ['kɔntrɑ:st] contraste m // vt [kən'trɑ:st] mettre en contraste,

contraster ; ~ing a opposé(e), contrasté(e).

contravene [kɔntrə'vi:n] vt enfreindre, violer, contrevenir à.

contribute [kən'trɪbju:t] vi contribuer // vt: to ~ £10/an article to donner 10 livres/un article à ; to ~ to (gen) contribuer à ; (newspaper) collaborer à ; **contribution** [kɔntrɪ'bju:ʃən] n contribution f ; **contributor** n (to newspaper) collaborateur/trice.

contrite ['kɔntraɪt] a contrit(e).

contrivance [kən'traɪvəns] n invention f, combinaison f ; mécanisme m, dispositif m.

contrive [kən'traɪv] vt combiner, inventer // vi: to ~ to do s'arranger pour faire, trouver le moyen de faire.

control [kən'trəul] vt maîtriser ; (check) contrôler // n contrôle m, autorité f ; maîtrise f ; ~s npl commandes fpl ; to be in ~ of être maître de, maîtriser ; être responsable de ; **circumstances beyond our** ~ circonstances indépendantes de notre volonté ; ~ point n (poste m de) contrôle ; ~ tower n (AVIAT) tour f de contrôle.

controversial [kɔntrə'və:ʃl] a discutable, controversé(e).

controversy ['kɔntrəvə:sɪ] n controverse f, polémique f.

convalesce [kɔnvə'lɛs] vi relever de maladie, se remettre (d'une maladie).

convalescence [kɔnvə'lɛsns] n convalescence f.

convalescent [kɔnvə'lɛsnt] a, n convalescent(e).

convector [kən'vɛktə*] n radiateur m à convection, appareil m de chauffage par convection.

convene [kən'vi:n] vt convoquer, assembler // vi se réunir, s'assembler.

convenience [kən'vi:nɪəns] n commodité f ; at your ~ quand or comme cela vous convient ; all modern ~, all mod cons avec tout le confort moderne, tout confort.

convenient [kən'vi:nɪənt] a commode.

convent ['kɔnvənt] n couvent m ; ~ school n couvent m.

convention [kən'vɛnʃən] n convention f ; ~al a conventionnel(le).

converge [kən'və:dʒ] vi converger.

conversant [kən'və:snt] a: to be ~ with s'y connaître en ; être au courant de.

conversation [kɔnvə'seɪʃən] n conversation f ; ~al a de la conversation ; ~alist n brillant/e causeur/euse.

converse n ['kɔnvə:s] contraire m, inverse m ; ~ly [-'və:slɪ] ad inversement, réciproquement.

conversion [kən'və:ʃən] n conversion f ; ~ table n table f de conversion.

convert vt [kən'və:t] (REL, COMM) convertir ; (alter) transformer, aménager ; (RUGBY) transformer // n ['kɔnvə:t] converti/e ; ~ible n (voiture f) décapotable f.

convex [kɔn'vɛks] a convexe.

convey [kən'veɪ] vt transporter ; (thanks) transmettre ; (idea) communiquer ; ~or belt n convoyeur m, tapis roulant.

convict vt [kən'vɪkt] déclarer (or reconnaître) coupable // n ['kɔnvɪkt] forçat m, convict m; ~**ion** [-ʃən] n condamnation f; (belief) conviction f.

convince [kən'vɪns] vt convaincre, persuader; **convincing** a persuasif(ive), convaincant(e).

convivial [kən'vɪvɪəl] a joyeux(euse), plein(e) d'entrain.

convoy ['kɔnvɔɪ] n convoi m.

convulse [kən'vʌls] vt ébranler; to be ~d with laughter se tordre de rire.

convulsion [kən'vʌlʃən] n convulsion f.

coo [ku:] vi roucouler.

cook [kuk] vt (faire) cuire // vi cuire; (person) faire la cuisine // n cuisinier/ière; ~**book** n = ~**ery book**; ~**er** n cuisinière f; ~**ery** n cuisine f; ~**ery book** n livre m de cuisine; ~**ie** n (US) biscuit m, petit gâteau sec; ~**ing** n cuisine f.

cool [ku:l] a frais(fraîche); (not afraid) calme; (unfriendly) froid(e); (impertinent) effronté(e) // vt, vi rafraîchir, refroidir; ~**ing tower** n refroidisseur m; ~**ness** n fraîcheur f; sang-froid m, calme m.

coop [ku:p] n poulailler m // vt: to ~ up (fig) cloîtrer, enfermer.

co-op ['kəuɔp] n abbr of Cooperative (Society).

cooperate [kəu'ɔpəreɪt] vi coopérer, collaborer; **cooperation** [-'reɪʃən] n coopération f, collaboration f.

cooperative [kəu'ɔpərətɪv] a coopératif(ive) // n coopérative f.

coordinate [kəu'ɔːdɪneɪt] vt coordonner; **coordination** [-'neɪʃən] n coordination f.

coot [ku:t] n foulque f.

cop [kɔp] n (col) flic m.

cope [kəup] vi se débrouiller; to ~ with faire face à; s'occuper de.

co-pilot ['kəu'paɪlət] n copilote m.

copious ['kəupɪəs] a copieux(euse), abondant(e).

copper ['kɔpə*] n cuivre m; (col: policeman) flic m; ~s npl petite monnaie.

coppice ['kɔpɪs] n taillis m.

copse [kɔps] n = **coppice**.

copulate ['kɔpjuleɪt] vi copuler.

copy ['kɔpɪ] n copie f; (book etc) exemplaire m // vt copier; ~**cat** n (pej) copieur/euse; ~**right** n droit m d'auteur, copyright m; ~**right reserved** tous droits (de reproduction) réservés; ~**writer** n rédacteur/trice publicitaire.

coral ['kɔrəl] n corail m; ~ **reef** n récif m de corail.

cord [kɔːd] n corde f; (fabric) velours côtelé; whipcord m; corde f.

cordial ['kɔːdɪəl] a cordial(e), chaleureux(euse) // n sirop; cordial m.

cordon ['kɔːdn] n cordon m; to ~ off vt boucler (par cordon de police).

corduroy ['kɔːdərɔɪ] n velours côtelé.

core [kɔː*] n (of fruit) trognon m, cœur m; (TECH) noyau m // vt enlever le trognon or le cœur de.

coriander [kɔrɪ'ændə*] n coriandre f.

cork [kɔːk] n liège m; (of bottle) bouchon m; ~**age** n droit payé par le client qui apporte sa propre bouteille de vin; ~**screw** n tire-bouchon m.

corm [kɔːm] n bulbe m.

cormorant ['kɔːmərnt] n cormorant m.

corn [kɔːn] n blé m; (US: maize) maïs m; (on foot) cor m; ~ **on the cob** (CULIN) épi m de maïs au naturel.

cornea ['kɔːnɪə] n cornée f.

corned beef ['kɔːnd'biːf] n corned-beef m.

corner ['kɔːnə*] n coin m; (AUT) tournant m, virage m // vt acculer, mettre au pied du mur; coincer; (COMM: market) accaparer // vi prendre un virage; ~ **flag** n (FOOTBALL) piquet m de coin; ~ **kick** n corner m; ~**stone** n pierre f angulaire.

cornet ['kɔːnɪt] n (MUS) cornet m à pistons; (of ice-cream) cornet (de glace).

cornflour ['kɔːnflauə*] n farine f de maïs, maïzena f.

cornice ['kɔːnɪs] n corniche f.

Cornish ['kɔːnɪʃ] a de Cornouailles, cornouaillais(e).

cornucopia [kɔːnju'kəupɪə] n corne f d'abondance.

Cornwall ['kɔːnwəl] n Cornouailles f.

corny ['kɔːnɪ] a (col) rebattu(e), galvaudé(e).

corollary [kə'rɔlərɪ] n corollaire m.

coronary ['kɔrənərɪ] n: ~ (thrombosis) infarctus m (du myocarde), thrombose f coronaire.

coronation [kɔrə'neɪʃən] n couronnement m.

coroner ['kɔrənə*] n coroner m.

coronet ['kɔrənɪt] n couronne f.

corporal ['kɔːpərl] n caporal m, brigadier m // a: ~ **punishment** châtiment corporel.

corporate ['kɔːpərɪt] a en commun; constitué(e) (en corporation).

corporation [kɔːpə'reɪʃən] n (of town) municipalité f, conseil municipal; (COMM) société f; ~ **tax** n ≈ impôt m sur les bénéfices.

corps [kɔː*], pl **corps** [kɔːz] n corps m.

corpse [kɔːps] n cadavre m.

corpuscle ['kɔːpʌsl] n corpuscule m.

corral [kə'rɑːl] n corral m.

correct [kə'rɛkt] a (accurate) correct(e), exact(e); (proper) correct(e), convenable // vt corriger; ~**ion** [-ʃən] n correction f.

correlate ['kɔrɪleɪt] vt mettre en corrélation.

correspond [kɔrɪs'pɔnd] vi correspondre; ~**ence** n correspondance f; ~**ence course** n cours m par correspondance; ~**ent** n correspondant/e.

corridor ['kɔrɪdɔː*] n couloir m, corridor m.

corroborate [kə'rɔbəreɪt] vt corroborer, confirmer.

corrode [kə'rəud] vt corroder, ronger // vi se corroder; **corrosion** [-'rəuʒən] n corrosion f.

corrugated ['kɔrəgeɪtɪd] a plissé(e); cannelé(e); ondulé(e); ~ **cardboard** n carton ondulé; ~ **iron** n tôle ondulée.

corrupt [kə'rʌpt] a corrompu(e) // vt corrompre; ~**ion** [-ʃən] n corruption f.

corset ['kɔːsɪt] n corset m.

Corsica ['kɔːsɪkə] n Corse f.

cortège [kɔːˈteːʒ] n cortège m (gén funèbre).

coruscating ['kɔrəskeɪtɪŋ] a scintillant(e).

cosh [kɔʃ] n matraque f.

cosignatory ['kəʊˈsɪgnətərɪ] n cosignataire m/f.

cosiness ['kəʊzɪnɪs] n atmosphère douillette, confort m.

cos lettuce [kɔsˈlɛtɪs] n (laitue f) romaine f.

cosmetic [kɔzˈmɛtɪk] n produit m de beauté, cosmétique m.

cosmic ['kɔzmɪk] a cosmique.

cosmonaut ['kɔzmənɔːt] n cosmonaute m/f.

cosmopolitan [kɔzməˈpɔlɪtn] a cosmopolite.

cosmos ['kɔzmɔs] n cosmos m.

cosset ['kɔsɪt] vt choyer, dorloter.

cost [kɔst] n coût m // vb (pt, pp cost) vi coûter // vt établir or calculer le prix de revient de; it ~s £5/too much cela coûte cinq livres/trop cher; it ~ him his life/job ça lui a coûté la vie/son emploi; at all ~s coûte que coûte, à tout prix.

co-star ['kəʊstɑː*] n partenaire m/f.

costly ['kɔstlɪ] a coûteux(euse).

cost price ['kɔstˈpraɪs] n prix coûtant or de revient.

costume ['kɔstjuːm] n costume m; (lady's suit) tailleur m; (also: swimming ~) maillot m (de bain); ~ jewellery n bijoux mpl de fantaisie.

cosy ['kəʊzɪ] a douillet(te).

cot [kɔt] n (child's) lit m d'enfant, petit lit.

cottage ['kɔtɪdʒ] n petite maison (à la campagne), cottage m; ~ cheese n fromage blanc (maigre).

cotton ['kɔtn] n coton m; ~ dress etc robe etc en or de coton; ~ wool n ouate f, coton m hydrophile.

couch [kaʊtʃ] n canapé m; divan m // vt formuler, exprimer.

cough [kɔf] vi tousser // n toux f; ~ drop n pastille f pour or contre la toux.

could [kʊd] pt of can; ~n't = could not.

council ['kaʊnsl] n conseil m; city or town ~ conseil municipal; ~ estate n (quartier m or zone f de) logements loués à/par la municipalité; ~ house n maison f (à loyer modéré) louée par la municipalité; ~lor n conseiller/ère.

counsel ['kaʊnsl] n avocat/e; consultation f, délibération f; ~lor n conseiller/ère.

count [kaʊnt] vt, vi compter // n compte m; (nobleman) comte m; to ~ on vt fus compter sur; to ~ up vt compter, additionner; ~down n compte m à rebours.

countenance ['kaʊntɪnəns] n expression f // vt approuver.

counter ['kaʊntə*] n comptoir m; (machine) compteur m // vt aller à l'encontre de, opposer; (blow) parer // ad: ~ to à l'encontre de; contrairement à; ~act vt neutraliser, contrebalancer; ~attack n contre-attaque f // vi contre-attaquer; ~balance vt contrebalancer,

faire contrepoids à; ~-clockwise ad en sens inverse des aiguilles d'une montre; ~-espionage n contre-espionnage m.

counterfeit ['kaʊntəfɪt] n faux m, contrefaçon f // vt contrefaire // a faux(fausse).

counterfoil ['kaʊntəfɔɪl] n talon m, souche f.

counterpart ['kaʊntəpɑːt] n (of document etc) double m; (of person) homologue m/f.

countersink ['kaʊntəsɪŋk] vt (hole) fraiser.

countess ['kaʊntɪs] n comtesse f.

countless ['kaʊntlɪs] a innombrable.

countrified ['kʌntrɪfaɪd] a rustique, à l'air campagnard.

country ['kʌntrɪ] n pays m; (native land) patrie f; (as opposed to town) campagne f; (region) région f, pays m; ~ dancing n danse f folklorique; ~ house n manoir m, (petit) château; ~man n (national) compatriote m; (rural) habitant m de la campagne, campagnard m; ~side n campagne f.

county ['kaʊntɪ] n comté m; ~ town n chef-lieu m.

coup, ~s [kuː, -z] n beau coup m; (also: ~ d'état) coup d'État.

coupé [kuːˈpeɪ] n coupé m.

couple ['kʌpl] n couple m // vt (carriages) atteler; (TECH) coupler; (ideas, names) associer; a ~ of deux.

couplet ['kʌplɪt] n distique m.

coupling ['kʌplɪŋ] n (RAIL) attelage m.

coupon ['kuːpɔn] n coupon m, bon-prime m, bon-réclame m; (COMM) coupon m.

courage ['kʌrɪdʒ] n courage m; ~ous [kəˈreɪdʒəs] a courageux(euse).

courier ['kʊrɪə*] n messager m, courrier m; (for tourists) accompagnateur/trice.

course [kɔːs] n cours m; (of ship) route f; (CONSTR) assise f; (for golf) terrain m; (part of meal) plat m; first ~ entrée f; of ~ ad bien sûr; in due ~ en temps utile or voulu; ~ of action parti m, ligne f de conduite; ~ of lectures série f de conférences; ~ of treatment (MED) traitement m.

court [kɔːt] n cour f; (LAW) cour, tribunal m; (TENNIS) court m // vt (woman) courtiser, faire la cour à; out of ~ (LAW: settle) à l'amiable; to take to ~ actionner or poursuivre en justice.

courteous ['kɜːtɪəs] a courtois(e), poli(e).

courtesan [kɔːtɪˈzæn] n courtisane f.

courtesy ['kɜːtəsɪ] n courtoisie f, politesse f.

court-house ['kɔːthaʊs] n (US) palais m de justice.

courtier ['kɔːtɪə*] n courtisan m, dame f de cour.

court-martial, pl courts-martial ['kɔːtˈmɑːʃəl] n cour martiale, conseil m de guerre.

courtroom ['kɔːtrum] n salle f de tribunal.

courtyard ['kɔːtjɑːd] n cour f.

cousin ['kʌzn] n cousin/e.

cove [kəʊv] n petite baie, anse f.

covenant ['kʌvənənt] n contrat m, engagement m.

cover ['kʌvə*] vt couvrir // n (for bed, of book, COMM) couverture f; (of pan) couvercle m; (over furniture) housse f; (shelter) abri m; under ~ à l'abri; ~age n reportage m; (INSURANCE) couverture f; ~ charge n couvert m (supplément à payer); ~ing n couverture f, enveloppe f; ~ing letter n lettre explicative.

covet ['kʌvɪt] vt convoiter.

cow [kau] n vache f // cpd femelle.

coward ['kauəd] n lâche m/f; ~ice [-ɪs] n lâcheté f; ~ly a lâche.

cowboy ['kaubɔɪ] n cow-boy m.

cower ['kauə*] vi se recroqueviller; trembler.

cowshed ['kauʃed] n étable f.

coxswain ['kɔksn] n (abbr: cox) barreur m; (of ship) patron m.

coy [kɔɪ] a faussement effarouché(e) or timide.

coyote [kɔɪ'əutɪ] n coyote m.

crab [kræb] n crabe m; ~ apple n pomme f sauvage.

crack [kræk] n fente f, fissure f; fêlure f; lézarde f; (noise) craquement m, coup (sec) // vt fendre, fissurer; fêler; lézarder; (whip) faire claquer; (nut) casser // a (athlete) de première classe, d'élite; to ~ up vi être au bout de son rouleau, flancher; ~ed a (col) toqué(e); timbré(e); ~er n pétard m; biscuit (salé), craquelin m.

crackle ['krækl] vi crépiter, grésiller // n (of china) craquelure f; **crackling** n crépitement m, grésillement m; (of pork) couenne f.

cradle ['kreɪdl] n berceau m.

craft [krɑːft] n métier (artisanal); (cunning) ruse f, astuce f; (boat) embarcation f, barque f; ~sman n artisan m, ouvrier (qualifié); ~smanship n métier m, habileté f; ~y a rusé(e), malin(igne), astucieux(euse).

crag [kræg] n rocher escarpé; ~gy a escarpé(e), rocheux(euse).

cram [kræm] vt (fill): to ~ sth with bourrer qch de; (put): to ~ sth into fourrer qch dans, ~ming n (fig: pej) bachotage m.

cramp [kræmp] n crampe f // vt gêner, entraver; ~ed a à l'étroit, très serré(e).

crampon ['kræmpən] n crampon m.

cranberry ['krænbərɪ] n canneberge f.

crane [kreɪn] n grue f.

cranium, pl **crania** ['kreɪnɪəm, 'kreɪnɪə] n boîte crânienne.

crank [kræŋk] n manivelle f; (person) excentrique m/f; ~shaft n vilebrequin m.

cranky ['kræŋkɪ] a excentrique, loufoque; (bad-tempered) grincheux(euse), revêche.

cranny ['krænɪ] n see **nook**.

crash [kræʃ] n fracas m; (of car, plane) collision f // vt (plane) écraser // vi (plane) s'écraser; (two cars) se percuter, s'emboutir; (fig) s'effondrer; to ~ into se jeter or se fracasser contre; ~ course n cours intensif; ~ helmet n casque (protecteur); ~ landing n atterrissage forcé or en catastrophe.

crate [kreɪt] n cageot m.

crater ['kreɪtə*] n cratère m.

cravat(e) [krə'væt] n foulard (noué autour du cou).

crave [kreɪv] vt: to ~ for désirer violemment, avoir un besoin physiologique de, avoir une envie irrésistible de.

crawl [krɔːl] vi ramper; (vehicle) avancer au pas // n (SWIMMING) crawl m.

crayfish ['kreɪfɪʃ] n, pl inv écrevisse f; langoustine f.

crayon ['kreɪən] n crayon m (de couleur).

craze [kreɪz] n engouement m.

crazy ['kreɪzɪ] a fou(folle); ~ paving n dallage irrégulier (en pierres plates).

creak [kriːk] vi grincer; craquer.

cream [kriːm] n crème f // a (colour) crème inv; ~ cake n (petit) gâteau à la crème; ~ cheese n fromage m à la crème, fromage blanc; ~ery n (shop) crèmerie f; (factory) laiterie f; ~y a crèmeux(euse).

crease [kriːs] n pli m // vt froisser, chiffonner // vi se froisser, se chiffonner.

create [kriː'eɪt] vt créer; **creation** [-ʃən] n création f; **creative** a créateur(trice); **creator** n créateur/trice.

creature ['kriːtʃə*] n créature f.

credence ['kriːdns] n croyance f, foi f.

crèche, creche [krɛʃ] n garderie f, crèche f.

credentials [krɪ'denʃlz] npl (papers) références fpl.

credibility [kredɪ'bɪlɪtɪ] n crédibilité f.

credible ['kredɪbl] a digne de foi, crédible.

credit ['kredɪt] n crédit m // vt (COMM) créditer; (believe: also: give ~ to) ajouter foi à, croire; ~s npl (CINEMA) générique m; to ~ sb with (fig) prêter or attribuer à qn; to ~ £5 to sb créditer (le compte de) qn de 5 livres; to one's ~ à son honneur; à son actif; to take the ~ for s'attribuer le mérite de; it does him ~ cela lui fait honneur; ~able a honorable, estimable; ~ card n carte f de crédit; ~or n créancier/ière.

credulity [krɪ'djuːlɪtɪ] n crédulité f.

creed [kriːd] n croyance f; credo m, principes mpl.

creek [kriːk] n crique f, anse f; (US) ruisseau m, petit cours d'eau.

creep, pt, pp **crept** [kriːp, krept] vi ramper; (fig) se faufiler, se glisser; (plant) grimper; ~er n plante grimpante; ~y a (frightening) qui fait frissonner, qui donne la chair de poule.

cremate [krɪ'meɪt] vt incinérer; **cremation** [-ʃən] n incinération f.

crematorium, pl **crematoria** [kremə'tɔːrɪəm, -'tɔːrɪə] n four m crématoire.

creosote ['krɪəsəut] n créosote f.

crêpe [kreɪp] n crêpe m; ~ bandage n bande f Velpeau ®

crept [krept] pt, pp of **creep**.

crescendo [krɪ'ʃendəu] n crescendo m.

crescent ['kresnt] n croissant m; rue f (en arc de cercle).

cress [kres] n cresson m.

crest [krest] n crête f; (of helmet) cimier m; (of coat of arms) timbre m; ~fallen a déconfit(e), découragé(e).

Crete ['kriːt] n Crète f.

crevasse [krɪ'væs] n crevasse f.
crevice ['krɛvɪs] n fissure f, lézarde f, fente f.
crew [kru:] n équipage m; to have a ~-cut avoir les cheveux en brosse; ~-neck n col ras.
crib [krɪb] n lit m d'enfant // vt (col) copier.
cribbage ['krɪbɪdʒ] n sorte de jeu de cartes.
crick [krɪk] n crampe f.
cricket ['krɪkɪt] n (insect) grillon m, cri-cri m inv; (game) cricket m; ~er n joueur m de cricket.
crime [kraɪm] n crime m; criminal ['krɪmɪnl] a, n criminel(le); the Criminal Investigation Department (C.I.D.) ≈ la police judiciaire (P.J.).
crimp [krɪmp] vt friser, frisotter.
crimson ['krɪmzn] a cramoisi(e).
cringe [krɪndʒ] vi avoir un mouvement de recul; (fig) s'humilier, ramper.
crinkle ['krɪŋkl] vt froisser, chiffonner.
cripple ['krɪpl] n boiteux/euse, infirme m/f // vt estropier, paralyser.
crisis, pl crises ['kraɪsɪs, -sɪːz] n crise f.
crisp [krɪsp] a croquant(e); (fig) vif(vive); brusque; ~s npl (pommes) chips fpl.
criss-cross ['krɪskrɔs] a entrecroisé(e).
criterion, pl criteria [kraɪ'tɪərɪən, -'tɪərɪə] n critère m.
critic ['krɪtɪk] n critique m/f; ~al a critique; ~ally ad d'un œil critique; ~ally ill gravement malade; ~ism ['krɪtɪsɪzm] n critique f; ~ize ['krɪtɪsaɪz] vt critiquer.
croak [krəʊk] vi (frog) coasser; (raven) croasser.
crochet ['krəʊʃeɪ] n travail m au crochet.
crockery ['krɔkərɪ] n vaisselle f.
crocodile ['krɔkədaɪl] n crocodile m.
crocus ['krəʊkəs] n crocus m.
croft [krɔft] n petite ferme; ~er n fermier m.
crony ['krəʊnɪ] n copain/copine.
crook [kruk] n escroc m; (of shepherd) houlette f; ~ed ['krukɪd] a courbé(e), tordu(e); (action) malhonnête.
crop [krɔp] n récolte f; culture f; to ~ up vi surgir, se présenter, survenir.
cropper ['krɔpə*] n: to come a ~ (col) faire la culbute, s'étaler.
croquet ['krəʊkeɪ] n croquet m.
croquette [krə'kɛt] n croquette f.
cross [krɔs] n croix f; (BIOL) croisement m // vt (street etc) traverser; (arms, legs, BIOL) croiser; (cheque) barrer // a en colère, fâché(e); to ~ out vt barrer, biffer; to ~ over vi traverser; ~bar n barre transversale; ~breed n hybride m, métis/se; ~country (race) n cross(-country) m; ~-examination n examen m contradictoire (d'un témoin); ~-examine vt (LAW) faire subir un examen contradictoire à; ~-eyed a qui louche; ~ing n croisement m, carrefour m; (sea-passage) traversée f; (also: pedestrian ~ing) passage clouté; ~-reference n renvoi m, référence f; ~roads n carrefour m; ~section n (BIOL) coupe transversale; (in population) échantillon m; ~wind n vent m de travers; ~wise ad en travers; ~word n mots croisés mpl.

crotch [krɔtʃ] n (of garment) entre-jambes m inv.
crotchet ['krɔtʃɪt] n (MUS) noire f.
crotchety ['krɔtʃɪtɪ] a (person) grognon(ne), grincheux(euse).
crouch [krautʃ] vi s'accroupir; se tapir, se ramasser.
crouton ['kru:tɔn] n croûton m.
crow [krəʊ] n (bird) corneille f; (of cock) chant m du coq, cocorico m // vi (cock) chanter; (fig) pavoiser, chanter victoire.
crowbar ['krəʊbɑː*] n levier m.
crowd [kraud] n foule f // vt bourrer, remplir // vi affluer, s'attrouper, s'entasser; ~ed a bondé(e), plein(e); ~ed with plein(e) de.
crown [kraun] n couronne f; (of head) sommet m de la tête, calotte crânienne; (of hat) fond m; (of hill) sommet m // vt couronner; C~ court n ≈ Cour f d'assises; ~ jewels npl joyaux mpl de la Couronne; ~ prince n prince héritier.
crow's-nest ['krəʊznɛst] n (on sailing-ship) nid m de pie.
crucial ['kru:ʃl] a crucial(e), décisif(ive).
crucifix ['kru:sɪfɪks] n crucifix m; ~ion [-'fɪkʃən] n crucifiement m, crucifixion f.
crucify ['kru:sɪfaɪ] vt crucifier, mettre en croix.
crude [kru:d] a (materials) brut(e); non raffiné(e); (fig: basic) rudimentaire, sommaire; (: vulgar) cru(e), grossier(ère); ~ (oil) n (pétrole) brut m.
cruel ['kruəl] a cruel(le); ~ty n cruauté f.
cruet ['kru:ɪt] huilier m; vinaigrier m.
cruise [kru:z] n croisière f // vi (ship) croiser; (car) rouler; (aircraft) voler; (taxi) être en maraude; ~r n croiseur m; cruising speed n vitesse f de croisière.
crumb [krʌm] n miette f.
crumble ['krʌmbl] vt émietter // vi s'émietter; (plaster etc) s'effriter; (land, earth) s'ébouler; (building) s'écrouler, crouler; (fig) s'effondrer; crumbly a friable.
crumpet ['krʌmpɪt] n petite crêpe (épaisse).
crumple ['krʌmpl] vt froisser, friper.
crunch [krʌntʃ] vt croquer; (underfoot) faire craquer, écraser; faire crisser // n (fig) instant m or moment m critique, moment de vérité; ~y a croquant(e), croustillant(e).
crusade [kru:'seɪd] n croisade f; ~r n croisé m.
crush [krʌʃ] n foule f, cohue f; (love): to have a ~ on sb avoir le béguin pour qn; (drink): lemon ~ citron pressé // vt écraser; (crumple) froisser; ~ing a écrasant(e).
crust [krʌst] n croûte f.
crutch [krʌtʃ] n béquille f; (TECH) support m.
crux [krʌks] n point crucial.
cry [kraɪ] vi pleurer; (shout) crier // n cri m; to ~ off vi se dédire; se décommander; ~ing a (fig) criant(e), flagrant(e).
crypt [krɪpt] n crypte f.

cryptic ['krɪptɪk] a énigmatique.
crystal ['krɪstl] n cristal m; ~**-clear** a clair(e) comme de l'eau de roche; **crystallize** vt cristalliser // vi (se) cristalliser.
cu. abbr: ~ **ft.** = cubic feet; ~ **in.** = cubic inches.
cub [kʌb] n petit m (d'un animal).
Cuba ['kju:bə] n Cuba m; ~**n** a cubain(e) // n Cubain/e.
cubbyhole ['kʌbɪhəul] n cagibi m.
cube [kju:b] n cube m // vt (MATH) élever au cube; ~ **root** n racine f cubique; **cubic** a cubique; **cubic metre** etc mètre m cube etc.
cubicle ['kju:bɪkl] n box m, cabine f.
cuckoo ['kuku:] n coucou m; ~ **clock** n (pendule f à) coucou m.
cucumber ['kju:kʌmbə*] n concombre m.
cud [kʌd] n: **to chew the** ~ ruminer.
cuddle ['kʌdl] vt câliner, caresser // vi se blottir l'un contre l'autre; **cuddly** a câlin(e).
cudgel ['kʌdʒl] n gourdin m.
cue [kju:] n queue f de billard; (THEATRE etc) signal m.
cuff [kʌf] n (of shirt, coat etc) poignet m, manchette f; (US) = **turn-up**; **off the** ~ ad de chic, à l'improviste; ~**link** n bouton m de manchette.
cuisine [kwɪ'zi:n] n cuisine f, art m culinaire.
cul-de-sac ['kʌldəsæk] n cul-de-sac m, impasse f.
culinary ['kʌlɪnərɪ] a culinaire.
cull [kʌl] vt sélectionner.
culminate ['kʌlmɪneɪt] vi culminer; **culmination** [-'neɪʃən] n point culminant.
culpable ['kʌlpəbl] a coupable.
culprit ['kʌlprɪt] n coupable m/f.
cult [kʌlt] n culte m.
cultivate ['kʌltɪveɪt] vt (also fig) cultiver; **cultivation** [-'veɪʃən] n culture f.
cultural ['kʌltʃərəl] a culturel(le).
culture ['kʌltʃə*] n (also fig) culture f; ~**d** a cultivé(e) (fig).
cumbersome ['kʌmbəsəm] a encombrant(e), embarrassant(e).
cumulative ['kju:mjulətɪv] a cumulatif(ive).
cunning ['kʌnɪŋ] n ruse f, astuce f // a rusé(e), malin(igne).
cup [kʌp] n tasse f; (prize, event) coupe f; (of bra) bonnet m.
cupboard ['kʌbəd] n placard m.
Cupid ['kju:pɪd] n Cupidon m; (figurine) amour m.
cupidity [kju:'pɪdɪtɪ] n cupidité f.
cupola ['kju:pələ] n coupole f.
cup-tie ['kʌptaɪ] n match m de coupe.
curable ['kjuərəbl] a guérissable, curable.
curate ['kjuərɪt] n vicaire m.
curator [kjuə'reɪtə*] n conservateur m (d'un musée etc).
curb [kə:b] vt refréner, mettre un frein à // n frein m (fig); (US) = **kerb**.
curdle ['kə:dl] vi (se) cailler.
curds [kə:dz] npl lait caillé.
cure [kjuə*] vt guérir; (CULIN) saler; fumer; sécher // n remède m.

curfew ['kə:fju:] n couvre-feu m.
curio ['kjuərɪəu] n bibelot m, curiosité f.
curiosity [kjuərɪ'ɒsɪtɪ] n curiosité f.
curious ['kjuərɪəs] a curieux(euse); ~**ly** ad curieusement.
curl [kə:l] n boucle f (de cheveux) // vt, vi boucler; (tightly) friser; **to** ~ **up** vi s'enrouler; se pelotonner; ~**er** n bigoudi m, rouleau m; (SPORT) joueur/euse de curling.
curling ['kə:lɪŋ] n (SPORT) curling m.
curly ['kə:lɪ] a bouclé(e); frisé(e).
currant ['kʌrnt] n raisin m de Corinthe, raisin sec.
currency ['kʌrnsɪ] n monnaie f; **foreign** ~ devises étrangères, monnaie étrangère; **to gain** ~ (fig) s'accréditer.
current ['kʌrnt] n courant m // a courant(e); ~ **account** n compte courant; ~ **affairs** npl (questions fpl d')actualité f; ~**ly** ad actuellement.
curriculum, pl ~**s** or **curricula** [kə'rɪkjuləm, -lə] n programme m d'études; ~ **vitae** n curriculum vitae (C.V.) m.
curry ['kʌrɪ] n curry m // vt: **to** ~ **favour with** chercher à gagner la faveur or à s'attirer les bonnes grâces de; **chicken** ~ curry de poulet, poulet m au curry; ~ **powder** n poudre f de curry.
curse [kə:s] vi jurer, blasphémer // vt maudire // n malédiction f; fléau m; (swearword) juron m.
cursory ['kə:sərɪ] a superficiel(le), hâtif(ive).
curt [kə:t] a brusque, sec(sèche).
curtail [kə:'teɪl] vt (visit etc) écourter; (expenses etc) réduire.
curtain ['kə:tn] n rideau m.
curts(e)y [kə:tsɪ] n révérence f // vi faire une révérence.
curve [kə:v] n courbe f; (in the road) tournant m, virage m // vt courber // vi se courber; (road) faire une courbe.
cushion ['kuʃən] n coussin m // vt (seat) rembourrer; (shock) amortir.
custard ['kʌstəd] n (for pouring) crème anglaise.
custodian [kʌs'təudɪən] n gardien/ne; (of collection etc) conservateur/trice.
custody ['kʌstədɪ] n (of child) garde f; (for offenders) détention préventive.
custom ['kʌstəm] n coutume f, usage m; (LAW) droit coutumier, coutume; (COMM) clientèle f; ~**ary** a habituel(le).
customer ['kʌstəmə*] n client/e.
custom-made ['kʌstəm'meɪd] a (clothes) fait(e) sur mesure; (other goods) hors série, fait(e) sur commande.
customs ['kʌstəmz] npl douane f; ~ **duty** n droits mpl de douane; ~ **officer** n douanier m.
cut [kʌt] vb (pt, pp cut) vt couper; (meat) découper; (shape, make) tailler; couper; creuser; graver; (reduce) réduire // vi couper; (intersect) se couper // n (gen) coupure f; (of clothes) coupe f; (of jewel) taille f; (in salary etc) réduction f; (of meat) morceau m; ~ **power** ~ coupure de courant; **to** ~ **teeth** (baby) faire ses dents; **to** ~ **a tooth** percer une dent; **to** ~ **down (on)** vt fus réduire; **to** ~ **off** vt

couper; (fig) isoler; to ~ out vt ôter; découper; tailler; ~away a, n: ~away (drawing) écorché m; ~back n réductions fpl.

cute [kju:t] a mignon(ne), adorable; (clever) rusé(e), astucieux(euse).

cut glass [kʌt'glɑ:s] n cristal taillé.

cuticle ['kju:tɪkl] n (on nail): ~ remover n repousse-peaux m inv.

cutlery ['kʌtlərɪ] n couverts mpl; (trade) coutellerie f.

cutlet ['kʌtlɪt] n côtelette f.

cut: ~off switch n interrupteur m; ~out n coupe-circuit m inv; ~-price a au rabais, à prix réduit; ~ throat n assassin m.

cutting ['kʌtɪŋ] a tranchant(e), coupant(e); (fig) cinglant(e), mordant(e) // n (PRESS) coupure f (de journal); (RAIL) tranchée f.

cuttlefish ['kʌtlfɪʃ] n seiche f.

cut-up ['kʌtʌp] a affecté(e), démoralisé(e).

cwt abbr of hundredweight(s).

cyanide ['saɪənaɪd] n cyanure m.

cybernetics [saɪbə'nɛtɪks] n cybernétique f.

cyclamen ['sɪkləmən] n cyclamen m.

cycle ['saɪkl] n cycle m // vi faire de la bicyclette.

cycling ['saɪklɪŋ] n cyclisme m.

cyclist ['saɪklɪst] n cycliste m/f.

cyclone ['saɪkləun] n cyclone m.

cygnet ['sɪgnɪt] n jeune cygne m.

cylinder ['sɪlɪndə*] n cylindre m; ~ block n bloc-cylindres m; ~ capacity n cylindrée f; ~ head n culasse f; ~-head gasket n joint m de culasse.

cymbals ['sɪmblz] npl cymbales fpl.

cynic ['sɪnɪk] n cynique m/f; ~al a cynique; ~ism ['sɪnɪsɪzəm] n cynisme m.

cypress ['saɪprɪs] n cyprès m.

Cypriot ['sɪprɪət] a cypriote, chypriote // n Cypriote m/f, Chypriote m/f.

Cyprus ['saɪprəs] n Chypre f.

cyst [sɪst] n kyste m.

cystitis [sɪs'taɪtɪs] cystite f.

czar [zɑ:*] n tsar m.

Czech [tʃɛk] a tchèque // n Tchèque m/f; (LING) tchèque m.

Czechoslovakia [tʃɛkəslə'vækɪə] n la Tchécoslovaquie; ~n a tchécoslovaque // n Tchécoslovaque m/f.

D

D [di:] n (MUS) ré m; ~-day n le jour J.

dab [dæb] vt (eyes, wound) tamponner; (paint, cream) appliquer (par petites touches or rapidement); a ~ of paint un petit coup de peinture.

dabble ['dæbl] vi: to ~ in faire or se mêler or s'occuper un peu de.

dad, daddy [dæd, 'dædɪ] n papa m; daddy-long-legs n tipule f; faucheux m.

daffodil ['dæfədɪl] n jonquille f.

daft [dɑ:ft] a idiot(e), stupide; to be ~ about être toqué or mordu de.

dagger ['dægə*] n poignard m; to be at ~s drawn with sb être à couteaux tirés

avec qn; to look ~s at sb foudroyer qn du regard.

daily ['deɪlɪ] a quotidien(ne), journalier-(ère) // n quotidien m // ad tous les jours.

dainty ['deɪntɪ] a délicat(e), mignon(ne).

dairy ['dɛərɪ] n (shop) crémerie f, laiterie f; (on farm) laiterie // a laitier(ère).

daisy ['deɪzɪ] n pâquerette f.

dale [deɪl] n vallon m.

dally ['dælɪ] vi musarder, flâner.

dam [dæm] n barrage m // vt endiguer.

damage ['dæmɪdʒ] n dégâts mpl, dommages mpl; (fig) tort m // vt endommager, abimer; (fig) faire du tort à; ~s npl (LAW) dommages-intérêts mpl.

damn [dæm] vt condamner; (curse) maudire // n (col): I don't give a ~ je m'en fous // a (col): this ~ ... ce sacré or foutu ... ; ~ (it)! zut! ; ~ing a (evidence) accablant(e).

damp [dæmp] a humide // n humidité f // vt (also: ~en) (cloth, rag) humecter; (enthusiasm etc) refroidir; ~ness n humidité f.

damson ['dæmzən] n prune f de Damas.

dance [dɑ:ns] n danse f; (ball) bal m // vi danser; ~ hall n salle f de bal, dancing m; ~r n danseur/euse.

dancing ['dɑ:nsɪŋ] n danse f.

dandelion ['dændɪlaɪən] n pissenlit m.

dandruff ['dændrəf] n pellicules fpl.

Dane [deɪn] n Danois/e.

danger ['deɪndʒə*] n danger m; there is a ~ of fire il y a (un) risque d'incendie; in ~ en danger; he was in ~ of falling il risquait de tomber; ~ous a dangereux(euse); ~ously ad dangereusement.

dangle ['dæŋgl] vt balancer; (fig) faire miroiter // vi pendre, se balancer.

Danish ['deɪnɪʃ] a danois(e) // n (LING) danois m.

dapper ['dæpə*] a pimpant(e).

dare [dɛə*] vt: to ~ sb to do défier qn or mettre qn au défi de faire // vi: to ~ (to) do sth oser faire qch; ~devil n casse-cou m inv; daring a hardi(e), audacieux(euse).

dark [dɑ:k] a (night, room) obscur(e), sombre; (colour, complexion) foncé(e), sombre; (fig) sombre // n: in the ~ dans le noir; in the ~ about (fig) ignorant tout de; after ~ après la tombée de la nuit; ~en vt obscurcir, assombrir // vi s'obscurcir, s'assombrir; ~ glasses npl lunettes noires; ~ness n obscurité f; ~ room n chambre noire.

darling ['dɑ:lɪŋ] a, n chéri(e).

darn [dɑ:n] vt repriser.

dart [dɑ:t] n fléchette f // vi: to ~ towards (also: make a ~ towards) se précipiter or s'élancer vers; to ~ away/along partir/passer comme une flèche; ~s n jeu m de fléchettes; ~board n cible f (de jeu de fléchettes).

dash [dæʃ] n (sign) tiret m // vt (missile) jeter or lancer violemment; (hopes) anéantir // vi: to ~ towards (also: make a ~ towards) se précipiter or se ruer vers; to ~ away vi partir à toute allure;

~board n tableau m de bord ; **~ing** a fringant(e).
data ['deɪtə] npl données fpl ; **~ processing** n traitement m (électronique) de l'information.
date [deɪt] n date f; rendez-vous m ; (fruit) datte f // vt dater ; **to ~** ad à ce jour; **out of ~** périmé(e) ; **up to ~** à la page; mis(e) à jour ; moderne ; **~d the 13th** daté du 13 ; **~d** a démodé(e) ; **~line** n ligne f de changement de date.
daub [dɔːb] vt barbouiller.
daughter ['dɔːtə*] n fille f; **~-in-law** n belle-fille f, bru f.
daunt [dɔːnt] vt intimider, décourager ; **~less** a intrépide.
dawdle ['dɔːdl] vi traîner, lambiner.
dawn [dɔːn] n aube f, aurore f // vi (day) se lever, poindre ; (fig) naître, se faire jour.
day [deɪ] n jour m ; (as duration) journée f; (period of time, age) époque f, temps m ; **the ~ before** la veille, le jour précédent ; **the following ~** le lendemain, le jour suivant ; **by ~** de jour ; **~boy/girl** n (SCOL) externe m/f; **~break** n point m du jour ; **~dream** n rêverie f // vi rêver (tout éveillé); **~light** n (lumière f du) jour m ; **~time** n jour m, journée f.
daze [deɪz] vt (subject: drug) hébéter ; (: blow) étourdir // n: **in a ~** hébété(e); étourdi(e).
dazzle ['dæzl] vt éblouir, aveugler.
dead [dɛd] a mort(e) ; (numb) engourdi(e), insensible // ad absolument, complètement ; **he was shot ~** il a été tué d'un coup de revolver ; **~ on time** à l'heure pile ; **~ tired** éreinté, complètement fourbu; **to stop ~** s'arrêter pile or net ; **the ~** les morts ; **~en** vt (blow, sound) amortir ; (make numb) endormir, rendre insensible ; **~ end** n impasse f; **~heat** n (SPORT): **to finish in a ~ heat** terminer ex-æquo ; **~line** n date f or heure f limite ; **~lock** n impasse f (fig) ; **~ly** a mortel(le) ; (weapon) meurtrier(ère) ; **~pan** a impassible ; (humour) pince-sans-rire inv.
deaf [dɛf] a sourd(e) ; **~-aid** n appareil auditif ; **~en** vt rendre sourd; (fig) assourdir ; **~ening** a assourdissant(e) ; **~ness** n surdité f; **~-mute** n sourd/e-muet/te.
deal [diːl] n affaire f, marché m // vt (pt, pp **dealt** [dɛlt]) (blow) porter ; (cards) donner, distribuer ; **a great ~ (of)** beaucoup (de) ; **to ~ in** faire le commerce de ; **to ~ with** vt fus (COMM) traiter avec ; (handle) s'occuper or se charger de ; (be about: book etc) traiter de ; **~er** n marchand m ; **~ings** npl (COMM) transactions fpl ; (relations) relations fpl, rapports mpl.
dean [diːn] n (SCOL) doyen m.
dear [dɪə*] a cher(chère) ; (expensive) cher, coûteux(euse) // n: **my ~** mon cher/ma chère ; **~ me!** mon Dieu! ; **D~ Sir/Madam** (in letter) Monsieur/Madame ; **D~ Mr/Mrs X** Cher Monsieur/Chère Madame X ; **~ly** ad (love) tendrement ; (pay) cher.
dearth [dəːθ] n disette f, pénurie f.

death [dɛθ] n mort f; (ADMIN) décès m; **~bed** n lit m de mort; **~ certificate** n acte m de décès ; **~ duties** npl (Brit) droits mpl de succession ; **~ly** a de mort ; **~penalty** n peine f de mort ; **~ rate** n (taux m de) mortalité f.
debar [dɪ'bɑː*] vt: **to ~ sb from a club** etc exclure qn d'un club etc ; **to ~ sb from doing** interdire à qn de faire.
debase [dɪ'beɪs] vt (currency) déprécier, dévaloriser ; (person) abaisser, avilir.
debatable [dɪ'beɪtəbl] a discutable, contestable.
debate [dɪ'beɪt] n discussion f, débat m // vt discuter, débattre // vi (consider): **to ~ whether** se demander si.
debauchery [dɪ'bɔːtʃərɪ] n débauche f.
debit ['dɛbɪt] n débit m // vt: **to ~ a sum to sb** or **to sb's account** porter une somme au débit de qn, débiter qn d'une somme.
debris ['dɛbriː] n débris mpl, décombres mpl.
debt [dɛt] n dette f; **to be in ~** avoir des dettes, être endetté(e) ; **~or** n débiteur/trice.
début ['deɪbjuː] n début(s) m(pl).
decade ['dɛkeɪd] n décennie f, décade f.
decadence ['dɛkədəns] n décadence f.
decanter [dɪ'kæntə*] n carafe f.
decarbonize [diː'kɑːbənaɪz] vt (AUT) décalaminer.
decay [dɪ'keɪ] n décomposition f, pourrissement m ; (fig) déclin m, délabrement m ; (also: **tooth ~**) carie f (dentaire) // vi (rot) se décomposer, pourrir ; (fig) se délabrer ; décliner ; se détériorer.
decease [dɪ'siːs] n décès m ; **~d** n défunt/e.
deceit [dɪ'siːt] n tromperie f, supercherie f; **~ful** a trompeur(euse).
deceive [dɪ'siːv] vt tromper ; **to ~ o.s.** s'abuser.
decelerate [diː'sɛləreɪt] vt,vi ralentir.
December [dɪ'sɛmbə*] n décembre m.
decency ['diːsənsɪ] n décence f.
decent ['diːsənt] a décent(e), convenable ; **they were very ~ about it** ils se sont montrés très chics.
decentralize [diː'sɛntrəlaɪz] vt décentraliser.
deception [dɪ'sɛpʃən] n tromperie f.
deceptive [dɪ'sɛptɪv] a trompeur(euse).
decibel ['dɛsɪbɛl] n décibel m.
decide [dɪ'saɪd] vt (person) décider, (question, argument) trancher, régler // vi se décider, décider ; **to ~ to do/that** décider de faire/que ; **to ~ on** décider de, se décider pour ; **to ~ on doing** décider de faire ; **~d** a (resolute) résolu(e), décidé(e) ; (clear, definite) net(te), marqué(e) ; **~dly** [-dɪdlɪ] ad résolument ; incontestablement, nettement.
deciduous [dɪ'sɪdjuəs] a à feuilles caduques.
decimal ['dɛsɪməl] a décimal(e) // n décimale f; **~ point** n ≈ virgule f.
decimate ['dɛsɪmeɪt] vt décimer.
decipher [dɪ'saɪfə*] vt déchiffrer.

decision [dɪ'sɪʒən] n décision f.

decisive [dɪ'saɪsɪv] a décisif(ive).

deck [dɛk] n (NAUT) pont m; (of bus): **top ~** impériale f; (of cards) jeu m; **~chair** n chaise longue; **~ hand** n matelot m.

declaration [dɛklə'reɪʃən] n déclaration f.

declare [dɪ'klɛə*] vt déclarer.

decline [dɪ'klaɪn] n (decay) déclin m; (lessening) baisse f // vt refuser, décliner // vi décliner; être en baisse, baisser.

declutch ['diː'klʌtʃ] vi débrayer.

decode ['diː'kəud] vt décoder.

decompose [diːkəm'pəuz] vi se décomposer; **decomposition** [diːkɔmpə'zɪʃən] n décomposition f.

decontaminate [diːkən'tæmɪneɪt] vt décontaminer.

décor ['deɪkɔː*] n décor m.

decorate ['dɛkəreɪt] vt (adorn, give a medal to) décorer; (paint and paper) peindre et tapisser; **decoration** [-'reɪʃən] n (medal etc, adornment) décoration f; **decorative** ['dɛkərətɪv] a décoratif(ive); **decorator** n peintre m en bâtiment.

decoy ['diːkɔɪ] n piège m; **they used him as a ~ for the enemy** ils se sont servis de lui pour attirer l'ennemi.

decrease n ['diːkriːs] diminution f // vt, vi [diː'kriːs] diminuer.

decree [dɪ'kriː] n (POL, REL) décret m; (LAW: of tribunal) arrêt m, jugement m; **~ nisi** n jugement m provisoire de divorce.

decrepit [dɪ'krɛpɪt] a décrépit(e); délabré(e).

dedicate ['dɛdɪkeɪt] vt consacrer; (book etc) dédier.

dedication [dɛdɪ'keɪʃən] n (devotion) dévouement m.

deduce [dɪ'djuːs] vt déduire, conclure.

deduct [dɪ'dʌkt] vt: **to ~ sth (from)** déduire qch (de), retrancher qch (de); (from wage etc) prélever qch (sur), retenir qch (sur); **~ion** [dɪ'dʌkʃən] n (deducting) déduction f; (from wage etc) prélèvement m, retenue f; (deducing) déduction, conclusion f.

deed [diːd] n action f, acte m; (LAW) acte notarié, contrat m.

deep [diːp] a (water, sigh, sorrow, thoughts) profond(e); (voice) grave; **he took a ~ breath** il inspira profondément, il prit son souffle; **4 metres ~** de 4 mètres de profondeur // ad: **~ in snow** recouvert(e) d'une épaisse couche de neige; **spectators stood 20 ~** il y avait 20 rangs de spectateurs; **knee-~ in water** dans l'eau jusqu'aux genoux; **~en** vt (hole) approfondir // vi s'approfondir; (darkness) s'épaissir; **~-freeze** n congélateur m // vt surgeler; **~-fry** vt faire frire (en friteuse); **~-sea** a: **~-sea diving** n plongée sous-marine; **~-sea fishing** n pêche hauturière; **~-seated** a (beliefs) profondément enraciné(e); **~-set** a (eyes) enfoncé(e).

deer [dɪə*] n, pl inv: **the ~** les cervidés mpl (ZOOL); **(red) ~** cerf m; **(fallow) ~** daim m; **(roe) ~** chevreuil m; **~skin** n peau f de daim.

deface [dɪ'feɪs] vt dégrader; barbouiller; rendre illisible.

defamation [dɛfə'meɪʃən] n diffamation f.

default [dɪ'fɔːlt] vi (LAW) faire défaut; (gen) manquer à ses engagements // n: **by ~** (LAW) par défaut, par contumace; (SPORT) par forfait; **~er** n (in debt) débiteur défaillant.

defeat [dɪ'fiːt] n défaite f // vt (team, opponents) battre; (fig: plans, efforts) faire échouer; **~ist** a,n défaitiste (m/f).

defect n ['diːfɛkt] défaut m // vi [dɪ'fɛkt]: **to ~ to the enemy/the West** passer à l'ennemi/l'Ouest; **~ive** [dɪ'fɛktɪv] a défectueux(euse).

defence [dɪ'fɛns] n défense f; **in ~ of** pour défendre; **~less** a sans défense.

defend [dɪ'fɛnd] vt défendre; **~ant** n défendeur/deresse; (in criminal case) accusé/e, prévenu/e; **~er** n défenseur m.

defense [dɪ'fɛns] n (US) = **defence**.

defensive [dɪ'fɛnsɪv] a défensif(ive).

defer [dɪ'fɜː*] vt (postpone) différer, ajourner.

deference ['dɛfərəns] n déférence f; égards mpl.

defiance [dɪ'faɪəns] n défi m; **in ~ of** au mépris de.

defiant [dɪ'faɪənt] a provocant(e), de défi.

deficiency [dɪ'fɪʃənsɪ] n insuffisance f, déficience f; carence f; **~ disease** n maladie f de carence.

deficient [dɪ'fɪʃənt] a insuffisant(e); défectueux(euse); déficient(e); **~ in** manquant de.

deficit ['dɛfɪsɪt] n déficit m.

defile vb [dɪ'faɪl] vt souiller // vi défiler // n ['diːfaɪl] défilé m.

define [dɪ'faɪn] vt définir.

definite ['dɛfɪnɪt] a (fixed) défini(e), (bien) déterminé(e); (clear, obvious) net(te), manifeste; (LING) défini(e); **he was ~ about it** il a été catégorique; il était sûr de son fait; **~ly** ad sans aucun doute.

definition [dɛfɪ'nɪʃən] n définition f.

definitive [dɪ'fɪnɪtɪv] a définitif(ive).

deflate [diː'fleɪt] vt dégonfler.

deflation [diː'fleɪʃən] n (COMM) déflation f.

deflect [dɪ'flɛkt] vt détourner, faire dévier.

deform [dɪ'fɔːm] vt déformer; **~ed** a difforme; **~ity** n difformité f.

defraud [dɪ'frɔːd] vt frauder; **to ~ sb of sth** soutirer qch malhonnêtement à qn; escroquer qch à qn; frustrer qn de qch.

defray [dɪ'freɪ] vt: **to ~ sb's expenses** défrayer qn (de ses frais), rembourser or payer à qn ses frais.

defrost [diː'frɔst] vt (fridge) dégivrer.

deft [dɛft] a adroit(e), preste.

defunct [dɪ'fʌŋkt] a défunt(e).

defuse [diː'fjuːz] vt désamorcer.

defy [dɪ'faɪ] vt défier; (efforts etc) résister à.

degenerate vi [dɪ'dʒɛnəreɪt] dégénérer // a [dɪ'dʒɛnərɪt] dégénéré(e).

degradation [dɛgrə'deɪʃən] n dégradation f.

degrading [dɪ'greɪdɪŋ] a dégradant(e).

degree [dɪ'griː] n degré m; grade m (universitaire); **a (first) ~ in maths** une licence en maths.

dehydrated [diːhaɪ'dreɪtɪd] a déshydraté(e); (milk, eggs) en poudre.

de-ice [di:'aɪs] vt (windscreen) dégivrer.

deign [deɪn] vi: to ~ to do daigner faire.

deity ['di:ɪtɪ] n divinité f; dieu m, déesse f.

dejected [dɪ'dʒɛktɪd] a abattu(e), déprimé(e).

dejection [dɪ'dʒɛkʃən] n abattement m, découragement m.

delay [dɪ'leɪ] vt (journey, operation) retarder, différer; (travellers, trains) retarder // n délai m, retard m; without ~ sans délai; sans tarder; ~ed-action a à retardement.

delegate n ['dɛlɪgɪt] délégué/e // vt ['dɛlɪgeɪt] déléguer.

delegation [dɛlɪ'geɪʃən] n délégation f.

delete [dɪ'li:t] vt rayer, supprimer.

deliberate a [dɪ'lɪbərɪt] (intentional) délibéré(e); (slow) mesuré(e) // vi [dɪ'lɪbəreɪt] délibérer, réfléchir; ~ly ad (on purpose) exprès, délibérément.

delicacy ['dɛlɪkəsɪ] n délicatesse f; (choice food) mets fin or délicat, friandise f.

delicate ['dɛlɪkɪt] a délicat(e).

delicatessen [dɛlɪkə'tɛsn] n épicerie fine.

delicious [dɪ'lɪʃəs] a délicieux(euse), exquis(e).

delight [dɪ'laɪt] n (grande) joie, grand plaisir // vt enchanter; a ~ to the eyes un régal or plaisir pour les yeux; to take ~ in prendre grand plaisir à; to be the ~ of faire les délices or la joie de; ~ful a adorable; merveilleux(euse); délicieux(euse).

delinquency [dɪ'lɪŋkwənsɪ] n délinquance f.

delinquent [dɪ'lɪŋkwənt] a,n délinquant(e).

delirium [dɪ'lɪrɪəm] n délire m.

deliver [dɪ'lɪvə*] vt (mail) distribuer; (goods) livrer; (message) remettre; (speech) prononcer; (warning, ultimatum) lancer; (free) délivrer; (MED) accoucher; to ~ the goods (fig) tenir ses promesses; ~y n distribution f; livraison f; (of speaker) élocution f; (MED) accouchement m; to take ~y of prendre livraison de.

delouse [di:'laus] vt épouiller, débarrasser de sa (or leur etc) vermine.

delta ['dɛltə] n delta m.

delude [dɪ'lu:d] vt tromper, leurrer; to ~ o.s. se leurrer, se faire des illusions.

deluge ['dɛlju:dʒ] n déluge m.

delusion [dɪ'lu:ʒən] n illusion f.

delve [dɛlv] vi: to ~ into fouiller dans.

demagogue ['dɛməgɔg] n démagogue m/f.

demand [dɪ'mɑ:nd] vt réclamer, exiger // n exigence f; (claim) revendication f; (ECON) demande f; in ~ demandé(e), recherché(e); on ~ sur demande; ~ing a (boss) exigeant(e); (work) astreignant(e).

demarcation [di:mɑ:'keɪʃən] n démarcation f.

demean [dɪ'mi:n] vt: to ~ o.s. s'abaisser.

demeanour [dɪ'mi:nə*] n comportement m; maintien m.

demented [dɪ'mɛntɪd] a dément(e), fou(folle).

demise [dɪ'maɪz] n décès m.

demister [di:'mɪstə*] n (AUT) dispositif m anti-buée inv.

demobilize [di:'məubɪlaɪz] vt démobiliser.

democracy [dɪ'mɔkrəsɪ] n démocratie f.

democrat ['dɛməkræt] n démocrate m/f; ~ic [dɛmə'krætɪk] a démocratique.

demography [dɪ'mɔgrəfɪ] n démographie f.

demolish [dɪ'mɔlɪʃ] démolir.

demolition [dɛmə'lɪʃən] n démolition f.

demonstrate ['dɛmənstreɪt] vt démontrer, prouver.

demonstration [dɛmən'streɪʃən] n démonstration f, manifestation f.

demonstrative [dɪ'mɔnstrətɪv] a démonstratif(ive).

demonstrator ['dɛmənstreɪtə*] n (POL) manifestant/e.

demoralize [dɪ'mɔrəlaɪz] vt démoraliser.

demote [dɪ'məut] vt rétrograder.

demur [dɪ'mə:*] vi protester; hésiter.

demure [dɪ'mjuə*] a sage, réservé(e); d'une modestie affectée.

den [dɛn] n tanière f, antre m.

denial [dɪ'naɪəl] n démenti m; dénégation f.

denigrate ['dɛnɪgreɪt] vt dénigrer.

denim ['dɛnɪm] n coton émerisé; ~s npl (blue-)jeans mpl.

Denmark ['dɛnmɑ:k] n Danemark m.

denomination [dɪnɔmɪ'neɪʃən] n (money) valeur f; (REL) confession f; culte m.

denominator [dɪ'nɔmɪneɪtə*] n dénominateur m.

denote [dɪ'nəut] vt dénoter.

denounce [dɪ'nauns] vt dénoncer.

dense [dɛns] a dense; (stupid) obtus(e), dur(e) or lent(e) à la comprenette; ~ly ad: ~ly wooded couvert d'épaisses forêts; ~ly populated à forte densité (de population), très peuplé.

density ['dɛnsɪtɪ] n densité f.

dent [dɛnt] n bosse f // vt (also: make a ~ in) cabosser; to make a ~ in (fig) entamer.

dental ['dɛntl] a dentaire; ~ surgeon n (chirurgien/ne) dentiste.

dentifrice ['dɛntɪfrɪs] n dentifrice m.

dentist ['dɛntɪst] n dentiste m/f; ~ry n art m dentaire.

denture ['dɛntʃə*] n dentier m.

deny [dɪ'naɪ] vt nier; (refuse) refuser; (disown) renier.

deodorant [di:'əudərənt] n désodorisant m, déodorant m.

depart [dɪ'pɑ:t] vi partir; to ~ from (leave) quitter, partir de; (fig: differ from) s'écarter de.

department [dɪ'pɑ:tmənt] n (COMM) rayon m; (SCOL) section f; (POL) ministère m, département m; ~ store n grand magasin.

departure [dɪ'pɑ:tʃə*] n départ m; (fig): ~ from écart m par rapport à.

depend [dɪ'pɛnd] vi: to ~ on dépendre de; (rely on) compter sur; it ~s cela dépend; ~able a sûr(e), digne de confiance; ~ence n dépendance f; ~ant, ~ent n personne f à charge.

depict [dɪ'pɪkt] vt (in picture) représenter; (in words) (dé)peindre, décrire.

depleted [dɪ'pli:td] a (considérablement) réduit(e) or diminué(e).

deplorable [dɪ'plɔːrəbl] *a* déplorable, lamentable.

deplore [dɪ'plɔː*] *vt* déplorer.

deploy [dɪ'plɔɪ] *vt* déployer.

depopulation ['diːpɔpju'leɪʃən] *n* dépopulation *f*, dépeuplement *m*.

deport [dɪ'pɔːt] *vt* déporter; expulser; ~**ation** [diːpɔː'teɪʃən] *n* déportation *f*, expulsion *f*; ~**ment** *n* maintien *m*, tenue *f*.

depose [dɪ'pəuz] *vt* déposer.

deposit [dɪ'pɔzɪt] *n* (CHEM, COMM, GEO) dépôt *m*; (of ore, oil) gisement *m*; (part payment) arrhes *fpl*, acompte *m*; (on bottle etc) consigne *f*; (for hired goods etc) cautionnement *m*, garantie *f* // *vt* déposer; mettre or laisser en dépôt; fournir or donner en acompte; laisser en garantie; ~ **account** *n* compte *m* de dépôt; ~**or** *n* déposant/e.

depot ['dɛpəu] *n* dépôt *m*.

deprave [dɪ'preɪv] *vt* dépraver, corrompre, pervertir.

depravity [dɪ'prævɪtɪ] *n* dépravation *f*.

deprecate ['dɛprɪkeɪt] *vt* désapprouver.

depreciate [dɪ'priːʃieɪt] *vt* déprécier // *vi* se déprécier, se dévaloriser; **depreciation** [-'eɪʃən] *n* dépréciation *f*.

depress [dɪ'prɛs] *vt* déprimer; (press down) appuyer sur, abaisser; ~**ed** *a* (person) déprimé(e), abattu(e); (area) en déclin, touché(e) par le sous-emploi; ~**ing** *a* déprimant(e); ~**ion** [dɪ'prɛʃən] *n* dépression *f*.

deprivation [dɛprɪ'veɪʃən] *n* privation *f*; (loss) perte *f*.

deprive [dɪ'praɪv] *vt*: to ~ **sb of** priver qn de; enlever à qn; ~**d** *a* déshérité(e).

depth [dɛpθ] *n* profondeur *f*; **in the** ~**s of** au fond de; au cœur de; au plus profond de; ~ **charge** *n* grenade sous-marine.

deputation [dɛpju'teɪʃən] *n* députation *f*, délégation *f*.

deputize ['dɛpjutaɪz] *vi*: to ~ **for** assurer l'intérim de.

deputy ['dɛpjutɪ] *a*: ~ **chairman** vice-président *m*; ~ **head** directeur adjoint, sous-directeur *m* // *n* (replacement) suppléant/e, intérimaire *m/f*; (second in command) adjoint/e.

derail [dɪ'reɪl] *vt* faire dérailler; **to be** ~**ed** dérailler; ~**ment** *n* déraillement *m*.

deranged [dɪ'reɪndʒd] *a* (machine) déréglé(e); **to be (mentally)** ~ avoir le cerveau dérangé.

derelict ['dɛrɪlɪkt] *a* abandonné(e), à l'abandon.

deride [dɪ'raɪd] *vt* railler.

derision [dɪ'rɪʒən] *n* dérision *f*.

derisive [dɪ'raɪsɪv] *a* moqueur (euse), railleur(euse).

derisory [dɪ'raɪsərɪ] *a* (sum) dérisoire; (smile, person) moqueur(euse), railleur(euse).

derivation [dɛrɪ'veɪʃən] *n* dérivation *f*.

derivative [dɪ'rɪvətɪv] *n* dérivé *m* // *a* dérivé(e).

derive [dɪ'raɪv] *vt*: to ~ **sth from** tirer qch de; trouver qch dans // *vi*: to ~ **from** provenir de, dériver de.

dermatology [də:mə'tɔlədʒɪ] *n* dermatologie *f*.

derogatory [dɪ'rɔgətərɪ] *a* désobligeant(e); péjoratif(ive).

derrick ['dɛrɪk] *n* mât *m* de charge; derrick *m*.

desalination [diːsælɪ'neɪʃən] *n* dessalement *m*, dessalage *m*.

descend [dɪ'sɛnd] *vt*, *vi* descendre; **to** ~ **from** descendre de, être issu de; ~**ant** *n* descendant/e.

descent [dɪ'sɛnt] *n* descente *f*; (origin) origine *f*.

describe [dɪs'kraɪb] *vt* décrire; **description** [-'krɪpʃən] *n* description *f*; (sort) sorte *f*, espèce *f*; **descriptive** [-'krɪptɪv] *a* descriptif(ive).

desecrate ['dɛsɪkreɪt] *vt* profaner.

desert *n* ['dɛzət] désert *m* // *vb* [dɪ'zə:t] *vt* déserter, abandonner // *vi* (MIL) déserter; ~**er** *n* déserteur *m*; ~**ion** [dɪ'zə:ʃən] *n* désertion *f*.

deserve [dɪ'zə:v] *vt* mériter; **deserving** *a* (person) méritant(e); (action, cause) méritoire.

design [dɪ'zaɪn] *n* (sketch) plan *m*, dessin *m*; (layout, shape) conception *f*, ligne *f*; (pattern) dessin *m*, motif(s) *m(pl)*; (COMM) esthétique industrielle; (intention) dessein *m* // *vt* dessiner; concevoir; **to have** ~**s on** avoir des visées sur; **well-**~**ed** *a* bien conçu(e).

designate *vt* ['dɛzɪgneɪt] désigner // *a* ['dɛzɪgnɪt] désigné(e); **designation** [-'neɪʃən] *n* désignation *f*.

designer [dɪ'zaɪnə*] *n* (ART, TECH) dessinateur/trice; (fashion) modéliste *m/f*.

desirability [dɪzaɪərə'bɪlɪtɪ] *n* avantage *m*; attrait *m*.

desirable [dɪ'zaɪərəbl] *a* désirable.

desire [dɪ'zaɪə*] *n* désir *m* // *vt* désirer, vouloir.

desirous [dɪ'zaɪərəs] *a*: ~ **of** désireux-(euse) de.

desk [dɛsk] *n* (in office) bureau *m*; (for pupil) pupitre *m*; (in shop, restaurant) caisse *f*; (in hotel, at airport) réception *f*.

desolate ['dɛsəlɪt] *a* désolé(e).

desolation [dɛsə'leɪʃən] *n* désolation *f*.

despair [dɪs'pɛə*] *n* désespoir *m* // *vi*: to ~ **of** désespérer de.

despatch [dɪs'pætʃ] *n*, *vt* = **dispatch**.

desperate ['dɛspərɪt] *a* désespéré(e); (fugitive) prêt(e) à tout; ~**ly** *ad* désespérément; (very) terriblement, extrêmement.

desperation [dɛspə'reɪʃən] *n* désespoir *m*; **in** ~ à bout de nerf; en désespoir de cause.

despicable [dɪs'pɪkəbl] *a* méprisable.

despise [dɪs'paɪz] *vt* mépriser, dédaigner.

despite [dɪs'paɪt] *prep* malgré, en dépit de.

despondent [dɪs'pɔndənt] *a* découragé(e), abattu(e).

dessert [dɪ'zə:t] *n* dessert *m*; ~**spoon** *n* cuiller *f* à dessert.

destination [dɛstɪ'neɪʃən] *n* destination *f*.

destine ['dɛstɪn] *vt* destiner.

destiny ['dɛstɪnɪ] *n* destinée *f*, destin *m*.

destitute ['dɛstɪtjuːt] *a* indigent(e), dans

le dénuement ; ~ of dépourvu or dénué de.

destroy [dis'trɔi] vt détruire ; ~er n (NAUT) contre-torpilleur m.

destruction [dis'trʌkʃən] n destruction f.

destructive [dis'trʌktiv] a destructeur(trice).

detach [di'tætʃ] vt détacher ; ~able a amovible, détachable ; ~ed a (attitude) détaché(e) ; ~ed house n pavillon m, maison(nette) (individuelle) ; ~ment n (MIL) détachement m ; (fig) détachement m, indifférence f.

detail ['di:teil] n détail m // vt raconter en détail, énumérer ; (MIL): to ~ sb (for) affecter qn (à), détacher qn (pour) ; in ~ en détail ; ~ed a détaillé(e).

detain [di'tein] vt retenir ; (in captivity) détenir ; (in hospital) hospitaliser.

detect [di'tɛkt] vt déceler, percevoir ; (MED, POLICE) dépister ; (MIL, RADAR, TECH) détecter ; ~ion [di'tɛkʃən] n découverte f ; dépistage m ; détection f ; to escape ~ion échapper aux recherches, éviter d'être découvert ; crime ~ion le dépistage des criminels ; ~ive n agent m de la sûreté, policier m ; private ~ive détective privé ; ~ive story n roman policier ; ~or n détecteur m.

detention [di'tɛnʃən] n détention f ; (SCOL) retenue f, consigne f.

deter [di'tə:*] vt dissuader.

detergent [di'tə:dʒənt] n détersif m, détergent m.

deteriorate [di'tiəriəreit] vi se détériorer, se dégrader ; **deterioration** [-'reiʃən] n détérioration f.

determination [ditə:mi'neiʃən] n détermination f.

determine [di'tə:min] vt déterminer ; to ~ to do résoudre de faire, se déterminer à faire ; ~d a (person) déterminé(e), décidé(e) ; (quantity) déterminé, établi(e).

deterrent [di'tɛrənt] n effet m de dissuasion ; force f de dissuasion.

detest [di'tɛst] vt détester, avoir horreur de ; ~able a détestable, odieux(euse).

detonate ['dɛtəneit] vi exploser ; détoner // vt faire exploser or détoner ; **detonator** n détonateur m.

detour ['di:tuə*] n détour m.

detract [di'trækt] vt: to ~ from (quality, pleasure) diminuer ; (reputation) porter atteinte à.

detriment ['dɛtrimənt] n: to the ~ of au détriment de, au préjudice de ; ~al [dɛtri'mɛntl] a: ~al to préjudiciable or nuisible à.

devaluation [divælju'eiʃən] n dévaluation f.

devalue [di:'vælju:] vt dévaluer.

devastate ['dɛvəsteit] vt dévaster.

devastating ['dɛvəsteitiŋ] a dévastateur(trice).

develop [di'vɛləp] vt (gen) développer ; (habit) contracter ; (resources) mettre en valeur, exploiter // vi se développer ; (situation, disease; evolve) évoluer ; (facts, symptoms; appear) se manifester, se produire ; ~er n (PHOT) révélateur m ; (of land) promoteur m ; ~ing country pays m en voie de développement ; ~ment n développement m ; (of affair, case)

rebondissement m, fait(s) nouveau(x).

deviate ['di:vieit] vi dévier.

deviation [di:vi'eiʃən] n déviation f.

device [di'vais] n (scheme) moyen m, expédient m ; (apparatus) engin m, dispositif m.

devil ['dɛvl] n diable m ; démon m ; ~ish a diabolique.

devious ['di:viəs] a (means) détourné(e) ; (person) sournois(e), dissimulé(e).

devise [di'vaiz] vt imaginer, concevoir.

devoid [di'vɔid] a: ~ of dépourvu(e) de, dénué(e) de.

devote [di'vaut] vt: to ~ sth to consacrer qch à ; ~d a dévoué(e) ; to be ~d to être dévoué or très attaché à ; ~e [dɛvəu'ti:] n (REL) adepte m/f ; (MUS, SPORT) fervent/e.

devotion [di'vauʃən] n dévouement m, attachement m ; (REL) dévotion f, piété f.

devour [di'vauə*] vt dévorer.

devout [di'vaut] a pieux(euse), dévot(e).

dew [dju:] n rosée f.

dexterity [dɛks'tɛriti] n dextérité f, adresse f.

diabetes [daiə'bi:ti:z] n diabète m ; **diabetic** [-'bɛtik] a, n diabétique (m/f).

diaeresis [dai'ɛrisis] n tréma m.

diagnose [daiəg'nəuz] vt diagnostiquer.

diagnosis, pl diagnoses [daiəg'nəusis, -si:z] n diagnostic m.

diagonal [dai'ægənl] a diagonal(e) // n diagonale f.

diagram ['daiəgræm] n diagramme m, schéma m ; graphique m.

dial ['daiəl] n cadran m // vt (number) faire, composer ; ~ling tone n tonalité f.

dialect ['daiəlɛkt] n dialecte m.

dialogue ['daiəlɔg] n dialogue m.

diameter [dai'æmitə*] n diamètre m.

diamond ['daiəmənd] n diamant m ; (shape) losange m ; ~s npl (CARDS) carreau m.

diaper ['daiəpə*] n (US) couche f.

diaphragm ['daiəfræm] n diaphragme m.

diarrhoea, diarrhea (US) [daiə'ri:ə] n diarrhée f.

diary ['daiəri] n (daily account) journal m ; (book) agenda m.

dice [dais] n, pl inv dé m // vt (CULIN) couper en dés or en cubes.

dictate vt [dik'teit] dicter // n ['dikteit] injonction f.

dictation [dik'teiʃən] n dictée f.

dictator [dik'teitə*] n dictateur m ; ~ship n dictature f.

diction ['dikʃən] n diction f, élocution f.

dictionary ['dikʃənri] n dictionnaire m.

did [did] pt of do.

die [dai] n (pl: dice) dé m ; (pl: dies) coin m ; matrice f ; étampe f // vi mourir ; to ~ away vi s'éteindre ; to ~ down vi se calmer, s'apaiser ; to ~ out vi disparaître, s'éteindre.

Diesel ['di:zəl]: ~ engine n moteur m diesel.

diet ['daiət] n alimentation f ; (restricted food) régime m // vi (also: be on a ~) suivre un régime.

differ ['difə*] vi: to ~ from sth être différent de ; différer de ; to ~ from sb

over sth ne pas être d'accord avec qn au sujet de qch ; **~ence** n différence f ; (quarrel) différend m, désaccord m ; **~ent** a différent(e) ; **~ential** [-'rɛnʃəl] n (AUT. wages) différentiel m ; **~entiate** [-'rɛnʃieit] vt différencier // vi se différencier ; **to ~entiate between** faire une différence entre ; **~ently** ad différemment.

difficult ['dɪfɪkəlt] a difficile ; **~y** n difficulté f.

diffidence ['dɪfɪdəns] n manque m de confiance en soi, manque d'assurance.

diffident ['dɪfɪdənt] a qui manque de confiance or d'assurance, peu sûr(e) de soi.

diffuse a [dɪ'fju:s] diffus(e) // vt [dɪ'fju:z] diffuser, répandre.

dig [dɪg] vt (pt, pp dug [dʌg]) (hole) creuser ; (garden) bêcher // n (prod) coup m de coude ; (fig) coup de griffe or de patte ; **to ~ into** (snow, soil) creuser ; **to ~ one's nails into** enfoncer ses ongles dans ; **to ~ up** vt déterrer.

digest vt [daɪ'dʒɛst] digérer // n ['daɪdʒɛst] sommaire m, résumé m ; **~ible** [dɪ'dʒɛstəbl] a digestible ; **~ion** [dɪ'dʒɛstʃən] n digestion f.

digit ['dɪdʒɪt] n chiffre m (de 0 à 9) ; (finger) doigt m ; **~al** a digital(e) ; à affichage numérique or digital.

dignified ['dɪgnɪfaɪd] a digne.

dignitary ['dɪgnɪtərɪ] n dignitaire m.

dignity ['dɪgnɪtɪ] n dignité f.

digress [daɪ'grɛs] vi: **to ~ from** s'écarter de, s'éloigner de ; **~ion** [daɪ'grɛʃən] n digression f.

digs [dɪgz] npl (Brit: col) piaule f, chambre meublée.

dilapidated [dɪ'læpɪdeɪtd] a délabré(e).

dilate [daɪ'leɪt] vt dilater // vi se dilater.

dilatory ['dɪlətərɪ] a dilatoire.

dilemma [daɪ'lɛmə] n dilemme m.

diligent ['dɪlɪdʒənt] a appliqué(e), assidu(e).

dilute [daɪ'lu:t] vt diluer // a dilué(e).

dim [dɪm] a (light, eyesight) faible ; (memory, outline) vague, indécis(e) ; (stupid) borné(e), obtus(e) // vt (light) réduire, baisser.

dime [daɪm] n (US) = 10 cents.

dimension [dɪ'mɛnʃən] n dimension f.

diminish [dɪ'mɪnɪʃ] vt,vi diminuer.

diminutive [dɪ'mɪnjutɪv] a minuscule, tout(e) petit(e) // n (LING) diminutif m.

dimly ['dɪmlɪ] ad faiblement ; vaguement.

dimple ['dɪmpl] n fossette f.

dim-witted ['dɪm'wɪtɪd] a (col) stupide, borné(e).

din [dɪn] n vacarme m.

dine [daɪn] vi dîner ; **~r** n (person) dîneur/euse ; (RAIL) = **dining car**.

dinghy ['dɪŋgɪ] n youyou m ; canot m pneumatique ; (also: **sailing ~**) voilier m, dériveur m.

dingy ['dɪndʒɪ] a miteux(euse), minable.

dining ['daɪnɪŋ] cpd : **~ car** n wagon-restaurant m ; **~ room** n salle f à manger.

dinner ['dɪnə*] n dîner m ; (public) banquet m ; **~ jacket** n smoking m ; **~ party** n dîner m ; **~ time** n heure f du dîner.

diocese ['daɪəsɪs] n diocèse m.

dip [dɪp] n déclivité f ; (in sea) baignade f, bain m // vt tremper, plonger ; (AUT: lights) mettre en code, baisser // vi plonger.

diphtheria [dɪf'θɪərɪə] n diphtérie f.

diphthong ['dɪfθɒŋ] n diphtongue f.

diploma [dɪ'pləumə] n diplôme m.

diplomacy [dɪ'pləuməsɪ] n diplomatie f.

diplomat ['dɪpləmæt] n diplomate m ; **~ic** [dɪplə'mætɪk] a diplomatique ; **~ic corps** n corps m diplomatique.

dipstick ['dɪpstɪk] n (AUT) jauge f de niveau d'huile.

dire [daɪə*] a terrible, extrême, affreux(euse).

direct [daɪ'rɛkt] a direct(e) // vt diriger, orienter ; **can you ~ me to ...?** pouvez-vous m'indiquer le chemin de ...? ; **~ current** n courant continu ; **~ hit** n coup m au but, touché m.

direction [dɪ'rɛkʃən] n direction f ; **sense of ~** sens m de l'orientation ; **~s** npl (advice) indications fpl ; **~s for use** mode m d'emploi.

directly [dɪ'rɛktlɪ] ad (in straight line) directement, tout droit ; (at once) tout de suite, immédiatement.

director [dɪ'rɛktə*] n directeur m ; administrateur m ; (THEATRE) metteur m en scène ; (CINEMA, TV) réalisateur/trice.

directory [dɪ'rɛktərɪ] n annuaire m.

dirt [də:t] n saleté f ; crasse f ; **~-cheap** a (ne) coûtant presque rien ; **~ road** n (US) chemin non macadamisé or non revêtu ; **~-y** a sale // vt salir ; **~y story** n histoire cochonne ; **~y trick** n coup tordu.

disability [dɪsə'bɪlɪtɪ] n invalidité f, infirmité f.

disabled [dɪs'eɪbld] a infirme, invalide ; (maimed) mutilé(e) ; (through illness, old age) impotent(e).

disadvantage [dɪsəd'vɑ:ntɪdʒ] n désavantage m, inconvénient m ; **~ous** [dɪsædvɑ:n'teɪdʒəs] a désavantageux-(euse).

disagree [dɪsə'gri:] vi (differ) ne pas concorder ; (be against, think otherwise): **to ~ (with)** ne pas être d'accord (avec) ; **garlic ~s with me** l'ail ne me convient pas, je ne supporte pas l'ail ; **~able** a désagréable ; **~ment** n désaccord m, différend m.

disallow ['dɪsə'lau] vt rejeter, désavouer.

disappear [dɪsə'pɪə*] vi disparaître ; **~ance** n disparition f.

disappoint [dɪsə'pɔint] vt décevoir ; **~ment** n déception f.

disapproval [dɪsə'pru:vəl] n désapprobation f.

disapprove [dɪsə'pru:v] vi: **to ~ of** désapprouver.

disarm [dɪs'ɑ:m] vt désarmer ; **~ament** n désarmement m.

disarray [dɪsə'reɪ] n désordre m, confusion f.

disaster [dɪ'zɑ:stə*] n catastrophe f, désastre m ; **disastrous** a désastreux-(euse).

disband [dɪs'bænd] vt démobiliser; disperser // vi se séparer; se disperser.

disbelief ['dɪsbə'li:f] n incrédulité f.

disc [dɪsk] n disque m.

discard [dɪs'kɑ:d] vt (old things) se défaire de, mettre au rencart or au rebut; (fig) écarter, renoncer à.

disc brake ['dɪskbreɪk] n frein m à disque.

discern [dɪ'sə:n] vt discerner, distinguer; ~ing a judicieux(euse), perspicace.

discharge vt [dɪs'tʃɑ:dʒ] (duties) s'acquitter de; (waste etc) déverser; décharger; (ELEC, MED) émettre; (patient) renvoyer (chez lui); (employee, soldier) congédier, licencier; (defendant) relaxer, élargir // n ['dɪstʃɑ:dʒ] (ELEC, MED) émission f; (dismissal) renvoi m; licenciement m; élargissement m; to ~ one's gun faire feu.

disciple [dɪ'saɪpl] n disciple m.

disciplinary ['dɪsɪplɪnərɪ] a disciplinaire.

discipline ['dɪsɪplɪn] n discipline f // vt discipliner; (punish) punir.

disc jockey ['dɪskdʒɔkɪ] n disque-jockey m.

disclaim [dɪs'kleɪm] vt désavouer, dénier.

disclose [dɪs'kləuz] vt révéler, divulguer; disclosure [-'kləuʒə*] n révélation f, divulgation f.

disco ['dɪskəu] n abbr of discothèque.

discoloured [dɪs'kʌləd] a décoloré(e); jauni(e).

discomfort [dɪs'kʌmfət] n malaise m, gêne f; (lack of comfort) manque m de confort.

disconcert [dɪskən'sə:t] vt déconcerter, décontenancer.

disconnect [dɪskə'nɛkt] vt détacher; (ELEC, RADIO) débrancher; (gas, water) couper; ~ed a (speech, thought) décousu(e), peu cohérent(e).

disconsolate [dɪs'kɔnsəlɪt] a inconsolable.

discontent [dɪskən'tɛnt] n mécontentement m; ~ed a mécontent(e).

discontinue [dɪskən'tɪnju:] vt cesser, interrompre; '~d' (COMM) 'fin de série'.

discord [dɪs'kɔ:d] n discorde f, dissension f; (MUS) dissonance f; ~ant [dɪs'kɔ:dənt] a discordant(e), dissonant(e).

discothèque ['dɪskəutɛk] n discothèque f.

discount n ['dɪskaunt] remise f, rabais m // vt [dɪs'kaunt] ne pas tenir compte de.

discourage [dɪs'kʌrɪdʒ] vt décourager; discouraging a décourageant(e).

discourteous [dɪs'kə:tɪəs] a incivil(e), discourtois(e).

discover [dɪs'kʌvə*] vt découvrir; ~y n découverte f.

discredit [dɪs'krɛdɪt] vt mettre en doute; discréditer.

discreet [dɪ'skri:t] a discret(ète); ~ly ad discrètement.

discrepancy [dɪ'skrɛpənsɪ] n divergence f, contradiction f.

discretion [dɪ'skrɛʃən] n discrétion f.

discriminate [dɪ'skrɪmɪneɪt] vi: to ~ between établir une distinction entre, faire la différence entre; to ~ against pratiquer une discrimination contre; discriminating a qui a du discernement;

discrimination [-'neɪʃən] n discrimination f; (judgment) discernement m.

discus ['dɪskəs] n disque m.

discuss [dɪ'skʌs] vt discuter de; (debate) discuter; ~ion [dɪ'skʌʃən] n discussion f.

disdain [dɪs'deɪn] n dédain m.

disease [dɪ'zi:z] n maladie f.

disembark [dɪsɪm'bɑ:k] vt, vi débarquer.

disembodied [dɪsɪm'bɔdɪd] a désincarné(e).

disembowel [dɪsɪm'bauəl] vt éviscérer, étriper.

disenchanted [dɪsɪn'tʃɑ:ntɪd] a désenchanté(e), désabusé(e).

disengage [dɪsɪn'geɪdʒ] vt dégager; (TECH) déclencher; to ~ the clutch (AUT) débrayer; ~ment n (POL) désengagement m.

disentangle [dɪsɪn'tæŋgl] vt démêler.

disfavour [dɪs'feɪvə*] n défaveur f; disgrâce f // vt voir d'un mauvais œil, désapprouver.

disfigure [dɪs'fɪgə*] vt défigurer.

disgorge [dɪs'gɔ:dʒ] vt déverser.

disgrace [dɪs'greɪs] n honte f; (disfavour) disgrâce f // vt déshonorer, couvrir de honte; ~ful a scandaleux(euse), honteux(euse).

disgruntled [dɪs'grʌntld] a mécontent(e).

disguise [dɪs'gaɪz] n déguisement m // vt déguiser; in ~ déguisé(e).

disgust [dɪs'gʌst] n dégoût m, aversion f // vt dégoûter, écœurer; ~ing a dégoûtant(e); révoltant(e).

dish [dɪʃ] n plat m; to do or wash the ~es faire la vaisselle; to ~ up vt servir; (facts, statistics) sortir, débiter; ~cloth n (for drying) torchon m; (for washing) lavette f.

dishearten [dɪs'hɑ:tn] vt décourager.

dishevelled [dɪ'ʃevəld] a ébouriffé(e); décoiffé(e); débraillé(e).

dishonest [dɪs'ɔnɪst] a malhonnête; ~y n malhonnêteté f.

dishonour [dɪs'ɔnə*] n déshonneur m; ~able a déshonorant(e).

dishwasher ['dɪʃwɔʃə*] n lave-vaisselle m; (person) plongeur/euse.

disillusion [dɪsɪ'lu:ʒən] vt désabuser, désenchanter // n désenchantement m.

disinfect [dɪsɪn'fɛkt] vt désinfecter; ~ant n désinfectant m.

disintegrate [dɪs'ɪntɪgreɪt] vi se désintégrer.

disinterested [dɪs'ɪntrəstɪd] a désintéressé(e).

disjointed [dɪs'dʒɔɪntɪd] a décousu(e), incohérent(e).

disk [dɪsk] n = disc.

dislike [dɪs'laɪk] n aversion f, antipathie f // vt ne pas aimer.

dislocate ['dɪsləkeɪt] vt disloquer; déboîter; désorganiser.

dislodge [dɪs'lɔdʒ] vt déplacer, faire bouger; (enemy) déloger.

disloyal [dɪs'lɔɪəl] a déloyal(e).

dismal ['dɪzml] a lugubre, maussade.

dismantle [dɪs'mæntl] vt démonter; (fort, warship) démanteler.

dismast [dɪs'mɑ:st] vt démâter.

dismay [dıs'meı] n consternation f // vt consterner.

dismiss [dıs'mıs] vt congédier, renvoyer ; (idea) écarter ; (LAW) rejeter ; **~al** n renvoi m.

dismount [dıs'maunt] vi mettre pied à terre.

disobedience [dısə'bi:dıəns] n désobéissance f ; insoumission f.

disobedient [dısə'bi:dıənt] a désobéissant(e) ; (soldier) indiscipliné(e).

disobey [dısə'beı] vt désobéir à.

disorder [dıs'ɔ:də*] n désordre m ; (rioting) désordres mpl ; (MED) troubles mpl ; **~ly** a en désordre ; désordonné(e).

disorganize [dıs'ɔ:gənaız] vt désorganiser.

disorientate [dıs'ɔ:rıənteıt] vt désorienter.

disown [dıs'əun] vt renier.

disparaging [dıs'pærıdʒıŋ] a désobligeant(e).

disparity [dıs'pærıtı] n disparité f.

dispassionate [dıs'pæʃənət] a calme, froid(e) ; impartial(e), objectif(ive).

dispatch [dıs'pætʃ] vt expédier, envoyer // n envoi m, expédition f ; (MIL, PRESS) dépêche f.

dispel [dıs'pɛl] vt dissiper, chasser.

dispensary [dıs'pɛnsərı] n pharmacie f ; (in chemist's) officine f.

dispense [dıs'pɛns] vt distribuer, administrer ; **to ~ sb from** dispenser qn de ; **to ~ with** vt fus se passer de ; **~r** n (container) distributeur m ; **dispensing chemist** n pharmacie f.

dispersal [dıs'pə:sl] n dispersion f ; (ADMIN) déconcentration f.

disperse [dıs'pə:s] vt disperser ; (knowledge) disséminer // vi se disperser.

dispirited [dıs'pırıtıd] a découragé(e), déprimé(e).

displace [dıs'pleıs] vt déplacer ; **~d person** n (POL) personne déplacée ; **~ment** n déplacement m.

display [dıs'pleı] n étalage m ; déploiement m ; affichage m ; (screen) écran m de visualisation, visuel m ; (of feeling) manifestation f ; (pej) ostentation f // vt montrer ; (goods) mettre à l'étalage, exposer ; (results, departure times) afficher ; (troops) déployer ; (pej) faire étalage de.

displease [dıs'pli:z] vt mécontenter, contrarier ; **~d with** mécontent(e) de ; **displeasure** [-'plɛʒə*] n mécontentement m.

disposable [dıs'pəuzəbl] a (pack etc) à jeter ; (income) disponible.

disposal [dıs'pəuzl] n (availability, arrangement) disposition f ; (of property) disposition f, cession f ; (of rubbish) évacuation f, destruction f ; **at one's ~** à sa disposition.

dispose [dıs'pəuz] vt disposer ; **to ~ of** vt (time, money) disposer de ; (unwanted goods) se débarrasser de, se défaire de ; (problem) expédier ; **~d a** : **~d to do** disposé(e) à faire ; **disposition** [-'zıʃən] n disposition f ; (temperament) naturel m.

disproportionate [dısprə'pɔ:ʃənət] a disproportionné(e).

disprove [dıs'pru:v] vt réfuter.

dispute [dıs'pju:t] n discussion f ; (also: **industrial ~**) conflit m // vt contester ; (matter) discuter ; (victory) disputer.

disqualification [dıskwɔlıfı'keıʃən] n disqualification f ; **~ (from driving)** retrait m du permis (de conduire).

disqualify [dıs'kwɔlıfaı] vt (SPORT) disqualifier ; **to ~ sb for sth/from doing** rendre qn inapte à qch/à faire ; signifier à qn l'interdiction de faire ; mettre qn dans l'impossibilité de faire ; **to ~ sb (from driving) for speeding** retirer à qn son permis (de conduire) pour excès de vitesse.

disquiet [dıs'kwaıət] n inquiétude f, trouble m.

disregard [dısrı'gɑ:d] vt ne pas tenir compte de.

disrepair [dısrı'pɛə*] n mauvais état.

disreputable [dıs'rɛpjutəbl] a (person) de mauvaise réputation, peu recommandable ; (behaviour) déshonorant(e).

disrespectful [dısrı'spɛktful] a irrespectueux(euse).

disrupt [dıs'rʌpt] vt (plans) déranger ; (conversation) interrompre ; **~ion** [-'rʌpʃən] n dérangement m ; interruption f.

dissatisfaction [dıssætıs'fækʃən] n mécontentement m, insatisfaction f.

dissatisfied [dıs'sætısfaıd] a: **~ (with)** mécontent(e) or insatisfait(e) (de).

dissect [dı'sɛkt] vt disséquer.

disseminate [dı'sɛmıneıt] vt disséminer.

dissent [dı'sɛnt] n dissentiment m, différence f d'opinion.

disservice [dıs'sə:vıs] n: **to do sb a ~** rendre un mauvais service à qn ; desservir qn.

dissident ['dısıdnt] a dissident(e).

dissimilar [dı'sımılə*] a: **~ (to)** dissemblable (à), différent(e) (de).

dissipate ['dısıpeıt] vt dissiper ; (energy, efforts) disperser ; **~d** a dissolu(e) ; débauché(e).

dissociate [dı'səuʃıeıt] vt dissocier.

dissolute ['dısəlu:t] a débauché(e), dissolu(e).

dissolve [dı'zɔlv] vt dissoudre // vi se dissoudre, fondre ; (fig) disparaître.

dissuade [dı'sweıd] vt: **to ~ sb (from)** dissuader qn (de).

distance ['dıstns] n distance f ; **in the ~** au loin.

distant ['dıstnt] a lointain(e), éloigné(e) ; (manner) distant(e), froid(e).

distaste [dıs'teıst] n dégoût m ; **~ful a** déplaisant(e), désagréable.

distemper [dıs'tɛmpə*] n (paint) détrempe f, badigeon m.

distend [dıs'tɛnd] vt distendre // vi se distendre, se ballonner.

distil [dıs'tıl] vt distiller ; **~lery** n distillerie f.

distinct [dıs'tıŋkt] a distinct(e) ; (preference, progress) marqué(e) ; **~ion** [dıs'tıŋkʃən] n distinction f ; (in exam) mention f très bien ; **~ive a** distinctif(ive) ; **~ly** ad distinctement ; expressément.

distinguish [dɪs'tɪŋgwɪʃ] vt distinguer ; différencier ; **~ed** a (eminent) distingué(e) ; **~ing** a (feature) distinctif(ive), caractéristique.

distort [dɪs'tɔ:t] vt déformer ; **~ion** [dɪs'tɔ:ʃən] n déformation f.

distract [dɪs'trækt] vt distraire, déranger ; **~ed** a éperdu(e), égaré(e) ; **~ion** [dɪs'trækʃən] n distraction f ; égarement m ; **to drive sb to ~ion** rendre qn fou(folle).

distraught [dɪs'trɔ:t] a éperdu(e).

distress [dɪs'trɛs] n détresse f ; (pain) douleur f // vt affliger ; **~ed area** n zone sinistrée ; **~ing** a douloureux(euse), pénible ; **~ signal** n signal m de détresse.

distribute [dɪs'trɪbju:t] vt distribuer ; **distribution** [-'bju:ʃən] n distribution f ; **distributor** n distributeur m.

district ['dɪstrɪkt] n (of country) région f ; (of town) quartier m ; (ADMIN) district m ; **~ attorney** n (US) ≈ procureur m de la République ; **~ nurse** n (Brit) infirmière visiteuse.

distrust [dɪs'trʌst] n méfiance f, doute m // vt se méfier de.

disturb [dɪs'tə:b] vt troubler ; (inconvenience) déranger ; **~ance** n dérangement m ; (political etc) troubles mpl ; (by drunks etc) tapage m ; **~ing** a troublant(e), inquiétant(e).

disuse [dɪs'ju:s] n: **to fall into ~** tomber en désuétude f.

disused [dɪs'ju:zd] a désaffecté(e).

ditch [dɪtʃ] n fossé m // vt (col) abandonner.

dither ['dɪðə*] vi hésiter.

ditto ['dɪtəu] ad idem.

divan [dɪ'væn] n divan m.

dive [daɪv] n plongeon m ; (of submarine) plongée f ; (AVIAT) piqué m ; (pej) bouge m // vi plonger ; **~r** n plongeur m.

diverge [daɪ'və:dʒ] vi diverger.

diverse [daɪ'və:s] a divers(e).

diversify [daɪ'və:sɪfaɪ] vt diversifier.

diversion [daɪ'və:ʃən] n (AUT) déviation f ; (distraction, MIL) diversion f.

diversity [daɪ'və:sɪtɪ] n diversité f, variété f.

divert [daɪ'və:t] vt (traffic) dévier ; (river) détourner ; (amuse) divertir.

divest [daɪ'vɛst] vt: **to ~ sb of** dépouiller qn de.

divide [dɪ'vaɪd] vt diviser ; (separate) séparer // vi se diviser ; **~d skirt** n jupe-culotte f.

dividend ['dɪvɪdɛnd] n dividende m.

divine [dɪ'vaɪn] a divin(e).

diving ['daɪvɪŋ] n plongée (sous-marine) ; **~ board** n plongeoir m ; **~ suit** n scaphandre m.

divinity [dɪ'vɪnɪtɪ] n divinité f ; théologie f.

division [dɪ'vɪʒən] n division f ; séparation f ; (Brit POL) vote m.

divorce [dɪ'vɔ:s] n divorce m // vt divorcer d'avec ; **~d** a divorcé(e) ; **~e** [-'si:] n divorcé/e.

divulge [daɪ'vʌldʒ] vt divulguer, révéler.

D.I.Y. a,n abbr of **do-it-yourself**.

dizziness ['dɪzɪnɪs] n vertige m, étourdissement m.

dizzy ['dɪzɪ] a (height) vertigineux(euse) ; **to make sb ~** donner le vertige à qn ; **to feel ~** avoir la tête qui tourne.

DJ n abbr of **disc jockey**.

do, pt **did**, pp **done** [du:, dɪd, dʌn] vt, vi faire ; **he didn't laugh** il n'a pas ri ; **~ you want any?** en voulez-vous?, est-ce que vous en voulez?; **she swims better than I ~** elle nage mieux que moi ; **he laughed, didn't he?** il a ri, n'est-ce pas?; **~ they?** ah oui?, vraiment?; **who broke it? - I did** qui l'a cassé? - (c'est) moi ; **~ you agree?** - **I ~** êtes-vous d'accord? - oui ; **to ~ one's nails/teeth** se faire les ongles/brosser les dents ; **will it ~?** est-ce que ça ira?; **to ~ without sth** se passer de qch ; **what did he ~ with the cat?** qu'a-t-il fait du chat?; **to ~ away with** vt fus supprimer, abolir ; **to ~ up** vt remettre à neuf.

docile ['dəusaɪl] a docile.

dock [dɔk] n dock m ; (LAW) banc m des accusés // vi se mettre à quai ; **~er** n docker m.

docket ['dɔkɪt] n bordereau m.

dockyard ['dɔkjɑ:d] n chantier m de construction navale.

doctor ['dɔktə*] n médecin m, docteur m ; (Ph.D. etc) docteur // vt (cat) couper ; (fig) falsifier.

doctrine ['dɔktrɪn] n doctrine f.

document ['dɔkjumənt] n document m ; **~ary** [-'mɛntərɪ] a, n documentaire (m) ; **~ation** [-'teɪʃən] n documentation f.

doddering ['dɔdərɪŋ] a (senile) gâteux(euse).

dodge [dɔdʒ] n truc m ; combine f // vt esquiver, éviter.

dodgems ['dɔdʒəmz] npl autos tamponneuses.

dog [dɔg] n chien/ne ; **~ biscuits** npl biscuits mpl pour chien ; **~ collar** n collier m de chien ; (fig) faux-col m d'ecclésiastique ; **~-eared** a corné(e).

dogged ['dɔgɪd] a obstiné(e), opiniâtre.

dogma ['dɔgmə] n dogme m ; **~tic** [-'mætɪk] a dogmatique.

doings ['duɪŋz] npl activités fpl.

do-it-yourself [du:ɪtjɔ:'sɛlf] n bricolage m.

doldrums ['dɔldrəmz] npl: **to be in the ~** avoir le cafard ; être dans le marasme.

dole [dəul] n (Brit) allocation f de chômage ; **on the ~** au chômage ; **to ~ out** vt donner au compte-goutte.

doleful ['dəulful] a triste, lugubre.

doll [dɔl] n poupée f ; **to ~ o.s. up** se faire beau(belle).

dollar ['dɔlə*] n dollar m.

dolphin ['dɔlfɪn] n dauphin m.

domain [də'meɪn] n domaine m.

dome [dəum] n dôme m.

domestic [də'mɛstɪk] a (duty, happiness) familial(e) ; (policy, affairs, flights) intérieur(e) ; (animal) domestique ; **~ated** a domestiqué(e) ; (pej) d'intérieur.

domicile ['dɔmɪsaɪl] n domicile m.

dominant ['dɔmɪnənt] a dominant(e).

dominate ['dɔmɪneɪt] vt dominer ; **domination** [-'neɪʃən] n domination f ;

domineering [-'nɪərɪŋ] *a* dominateur(trice), autoritaire.

dominion [də'mɪnɪən] *n* domination *f*; territoire *m*; dominion *m*.

domino, ~**es** ['dɒmɪnəu] *n* domino *m*; ~**es** *n* (*game*) dominos *mpl*.

don [dɒn] *n* professeur *m* d'université // *vt* revêtir.

donate [də'neɪt] *vt* faire don de, donner; **donation** [də'neɪʃən] *n* donation *f*, don *m*.

done [dʌn] *pp* of **do**.

donkey ['dɒŋkɪ] *n* âne *m*.

donor ['dəunə*] *n* (*of blood etc*) donneur/euse; (*to charity*) donateur/trice.

don't [dəunt] *vb* = **do not**.

doom [du:m] *n* destin *m*; ruine *f* // *vt*: to be ~**ed** (**to failure**) être voué(e) à l'échec; ~**sday** *n* le Jugement dernier.

door [dɔ:*] *n* porte *f*; ~**bell** *n* sonnette *f*; ~ **handle** *n* poignée *f* de porte; ~**man** *n* (*in hotel*) portier *m*; (*in block of flats*) concierge *m*; ~**mat** *n* paillasson *m*; ~**post** *n* montant *m* de porte; ~**step** *n* pas *m* de (la) porte, seuil *m*.

dope [dəup] *n* (*col*) drogue *f* // *vt* (*horse etc*) doper.

dopey ['dəupɪ] *a* (*col*) à moitié endormi(e).

dormant ['dɔ:mənt] *a* assoupi(e), en veilleuse; (*rule, law*) inappliqué(e).

dormice ['dɔ:maɪs] *npl* of **dormouse**.

dormitory ['dɔ:mɪtrɪ] *n* dortoir *m*.

dormouse, *pl* **dormice** ['dɔ:maus, -maɪs] *n* loir *m*.

dosage ['dəusɪdʒ] *n* dose *f*; dosage *m*; (*on label*) posologie *f*.

dose [dəus] *n* dose *f*; (*bout*) attaque *f* // *vt*: to ~ o.s. se bourrer de médicaments.

doss house ['dɒshaus] *n* asile *m* de nuit.

dot [dɒt] *n* point *m* // *vt*: ~**ted with** parsemé(e) de; **on the** ~ à l'heure tapante.

dote [dəut]: **to** ~ **on** *vt fus* être fou(folle) de.

dotted line [dɒtɪd'laɪn] *n* ligne pointillée; (AUT) ligne discontinue.

double ['dʌbl] *a* double // *ad* (*fold*) en deux; (*twice*): **to cost** ~ (**sth**) coûter le double (de qch) *or* deux fois plus (que qch) // *n* double *m*; (CINEMA) doublure *f* // *vt* doubler; (*fold*) plier en deux // *vi* doubler; **at the** ~ au pas de course; ~**s** *n* (TENNIS) double *m*; ~ **bass** *n* contrebasse *f*; ~ **bed** *n* grand lit; ~ **bend** *n* virage *m* en S; ~-**breasted** *a* croisé(e); ~-**cross** *vt* doubler, trahir; ~-**decker** *n* autobus *m* à impériale; ~ **declutch** *vi* faire un double débrayage; ~ **exposure** *n* surimpression *f*; ~ **parking** *n* stationnement *m* en double file; ~ **room** *n* chambre *f* pour deux; **doubly** *ad* doublement, deux fois plus.

doubt [daut] *n* doute *m* // *vt* douter de; **to** ~ **that** douter que; ~**ful** *a* douteux(euse); (*person*) incertain(e); ~**less** *ad* sans doute, sûrement.

dough [dəu] *n* pâte *f*; ~**nut** *n* beignet *m*.

dour [duə*] *a* austère.

dove [dʌv] *n* colombe *f*.

Dover ['dəuvə*] *n* Douvres *m*.

dovetail ['dʌvteɪl] *n*: ~ **joint** *n* assemblage *m* à queue d'aronde // *vi* (*fig*) concorder.

dowdy ['daudɪ] *a* démodé(e); mal fagoté(e).

down [daun] *n* (*fluff*) duvet *m* // *ad* en bas // *prep* en bas de // *vt* (*enemy*) abattre; (*col: drink*) vider; **the D**~**s** *collines crayeuses du S.-E. de l'Angleterre*; ~ **with X!** à bas X!; ~**at-heel** *a* éculé(e); (*fig*) miteux(euse); ~**cast** *a* démoralisé(e); ~**fall** *n* chute *f*; ruine *f*; ~**hearted** *a* découragé(e); ~**hill** *ad*: to go ~**hill** descendre; ~ **payment** *n* acompte *m*; ~**pour** *n* pluie torrentielle, déluge *m*; ~**right** *a* franc(franche); (*refusal*) catégorique; ~**stairs** *ad* au rez-de-chaussée; à l'étage inférieur; ~**stream** *ad* en aval; ~-**to-earth** *a* terre à terre *inv*; ~**town** *ad* en ville // *a* (US): ~**town Chicago** le centre commerçant de Chicago; ~**ward** ['daunwəd] *a,ad*, ~**wards** ['daunwədz] *ad* vers le bas.

dowry ['daurɪ] *n* dot *f*.

doz. *abbr of* **dozen**.

doze [dəuz] *vi* sommeiller; **to** ~ **off** *vi* s'assoupir.

dozen ['dʌzn] *n* douzaine *f*; **a** ~ **books** une douzaine de livres.

Dr. *abbr of* **doctor**; **drive** (*n*).

drab [dræb] *a* terne, morne.

draft [drɑ:ft] *n* brouillon *m*; (COMM) traite *f*; (US: MIL) contingent *m*; (: *call-up*) conscription *f* // *vt* faire le brouillon de; *see also* **draught**.

drag [dræg] *vt* traîner; (*river*) draguer // *vi* traîner // *n* (*col*) raseur/euse; corvée *f*; **to** ~ **on** *vi* s'éterniser.

dragonfly ['drægənflaɪ] *n* libellule *f*.

drain [dreɪn] *n* égout *m*; (*on resources*) saignée *f* // *vt* (*land, marshes*) drainer, assécher; (*vegetables*) égoutter; (*reservoir etc*) vider // *vi* (*water*) s'écouler; ~**age** *n* système *m* d'égouts; ~**ing board**, ~**board** (US) *n* égouttoir *m*; ~**pipe** *n* tuyau *m* d'écoulement.

dram [dræm] *n* petit verre.

drama ['drɑ:mə] *n* (*art*) théâtre *m*, art *m* dramatique; (*play*) pièce *f*; (*event*) drame *m*; ~**tic** [drə'mætɪk] *a* dramatique; spectaculaire; ~**tist** ['dræmətɪst] *n* auteur *m* dramatique.

drank [dræŋk] *pt* of **drink**.

drape [dreɪp] *vt* draper; ~**s** *npl* (US) rideaux *mpl*; ~**r** *n* marchand/e de nouveautés.

drastic ['dræstɪk] *a* sévère; énergique.

draught [drɑ:ft] *n* courant *m* d'air; (*of chimney*) tirage *m*; (NAUT) tirant *m* d'eau; ~**s** *n* (*jeu m de*) dames *fpl*; **on** ~ (*beer*) à la pression; ~**board** *n* damier *m*.

draughtsman ['drɑ:ftsmən] *n* dessinateur/trice (industriel/le).

draw [drɔ:] *vb* (*pt* **drew**, *pp* **drawn** [dru:, drɔ:n]) *vt* tirer; (*attract*) attirer; (*picture*) dessiner; (*line, circle*) tracer; (*money*) retirer // *vi* (SPORT) faire match nul // *n* match nul; tirage *m* au sort; loterie *f*; **to** ~ **to a close** toucher à *or* tirer à sa fin; **to** ~ **near** s'approcher; approcher; **to** ~ **out** *vi* (*lengthen*) s'allonger // *vt* (*money*) retirer; **to** ~ **up** *vi* (*stop*) s'arrêter // *vt* (*document*) établir, dresser; ~**back** *n* inconvénient *m*, désavantage *m*; ~**bridge** *n* pont-levis *m*.

drawer [drɔːʳ] n tiroir m.

drawing ['drɔːɪŋ] n dessin m ; ~ **board** n planche f à dessin ; ~ **pin** n punaise f ; ~ **room** n salon m.

drawl [drɔːl] n accent traînant.

drawn [drɔːn] pp of **draw**.

dread [drɛd] n épouvante f, effroi m // vt redouter, appréhender ; ~**ful** a épouvantable, affreux(euse).

dream [driːm] n rêve m // vt, vi (pt, pp **dreamed** or **dreamt** [drɛmt]) rêver ; ~**er** n rêveur/euse ; ~ **world** n monde m imaginaire ; ~**y** a rêveur(euse).

dreary ['drɪərɪ] a triste ; monotone.

dredge [drɛdʒ] vt draguer ; ~**r** n (ship) dragueur m ; (machine) drague f ; (also: sugar ~**r**) saupoudreuse f.

dregs [drɛgz] npl lie f.

drench [drɛntʃ] vt tremper.

dress [drɛs] n robe f ; (clothing) habillement m, tenue f // vt habiller ; (wound) panser ; (food) préparer ; **to ~ up** vi s'habiller ; (in fancy dress) se déguiser ; ~ **circle** n premier balcon ; ~ **designer** n modéliste m/f ; ~**er** n (THEATRE) habilleur/euse ; (also: **window** ~**er**) étalagiste m/f ; (furniture) buffet m ; ~**ing** n (MED) pansement m ; (CULIN) sauce f, assaisonnement m ; ~**ing gown** n robe f de chambre ; ~**ing room** n (THEATRE) loge f ; (SPORT) vestiaire m ; ~**ing table** n coiffeuse f ; ~**maker** n couturière f ; ~**making** n couture f ; travaux mpl de couture ; ~ **rehearsal** n (répétition) générale ; ~ **shirt** n chemise f à plastron.

drew [druː] pt of **draw**.

dribble ['drɪbl] vi tomber goutte à goutte ; (baby) baver // vt (ball) dribbler.

dried [draɪd] a (fruit, beans) sec(sèche) ; (eggs, milk) en poudre.

drift [drɪft] n (of current etc) force f ; direction f ; (of sand etc) amoncellement m ; (of snow) rafale f ; coulée f ; (: on ground) congère f ; (general meaning) sens général m // vi (boat) aller à la dérive, dériver ; (sand, snow) s'amonceler, s'entasser ; ~**wood** n bois flotté.

drill [drɪl] n perceuse f ; (bit) foret m ; (of dentist) roulette f, fraise f ; (MIL) exercice m // vt percer // vi (for oil) faire un or des forage(s).

drink [drɪŋk] n boisson f // vt, vi (pt drank, pp drunk [dræŋk, drʌŋk]) boire ; **to have a** ~ boire quelque chose, boire un verre ; prendre l'apéritif ; ~**er** n buveur/euse ; ~**ing water** n eau f potable.

drip [drɪp] n bruit m d'égouttement ; goutte f ; (MED) goutte-à-goutte m inv ; perfusion f // vi tomber goutte à goutte ; (washing) s'égoutter ; (wall) suinter ; ~-**dry** a (shirt) sans repassage ; ~-**feed** vt alimenter au goutte-à-goutte or par perfusion ; ~**ping** n graisse f de rôti ; ~**ping wet** a trempé(e).

drive [draɪv] n promenade f or trajet m en voiture ; (also: ~**way**) allée f ; (energy) dynamisme m, énergie f ; (PSYCH) besoin m ; pulsion f ; (push) effort (concerté) ; campagne f ; (SPORT) drive m ; (TECH) entraînement m ; traction f ; transmission f // vb (pt drove, pp driven ['drəuv, 'drɪvn]) vt conduire ; (nail) enfoncer ; (push) chasser, pousser ; (TECH: motor) actionner ; entraîner // vi (AUT: at controls) conduire ; (: travel) aller en voiture ; **left-/right-hand** ~ conduite f à gauche/droite.

driver ['draɪvəʳ] n conducteur/trice ; (of taxi, bus) chauffeur m ; ~'s **license** n (US) permis m de conduire.

driving ['draɪvɪŋ] a: ~ **rain** n pluie battante // n conduite f ; ~ **belt** n courroie f de transmission ; ~ **instructor** n moniteur m d'auto-école ; ~ **lesson** n leçon f de conduite ; ~ **licence** n (Brit) permis m de conduire ; ~ **school** n auto-école f ; ~ **test** n examen m du permis de conduire.

drizzle ['drɪzl] n bruine f, crachin m // vi bruiner.

droll [drəul] a drôle.

dromedary ['drɒmədərɪ] n dromadaire m.

drone [drəun] n bourdonnement m ; (male bee) faux-bourdon m.

drool [druːl] vi baver.

droop [druːp] vi s'affaisser ; tomber.

drop [drɒp] n goutte f ; (fall) baisse f ; (also: parachute ~) saut m ; (of cliff) dénivellation f ; à-pic m // vt laisser tomber ; (voice, eyes, price) baisser ; (set down from car) déposer // vi tomber ; **to ~ off** vi (sleep) s'assoupir ; **to ~ out** vi (withdraw) se retirer ; (student etc) abandonner, décrocher ; ~**pings** npl crottes fpl.

dross [drɒs] n déchets mpl ; rebut m.

drought [draut] n sécheresse f.

drove [drəuv] pt of **drive** // n: ~**s of people** une foule de gens.

drown [draun] vt noyer // vi se noyer.

drowsy ['drauzɪ] a somnolent(e).

drudge [drʌdʒ] n bête f de somme (fig) ; ~**ry** ['drʌdʒərɪ] n corvée f.

drug [drʌg] n médicament m ; (narcotic) drogue f // vt droguer ; ~ **addict** n toxicomane m/f ; ~**gist** n (US) pharmacien/ne-droguiste ; ~**store** n (US) pharmacie-droguerie f, drugstore m.

drum [drʌm] n tambour m ; (for oil, petrol) bidon m ; ~**mer** n (joueur m de) tambour m ; ~ **roll** n roulement de tambour ; ~**stick** n (MUS) baguette f de tambour ; (of chicken) pilon m.

drunk [drʌŋk] pp of **drink** // a ivre, soûl(e) // n soûlard/e ; homme/femme soûl(e) ; ~**ard** ['drʌŋkəd] n ivrogne m/f ; ~**en** a ivre, soûl(e) ; ivrogne, d'ivrogne ; ~**enness** n ivresse f ; ivrognerie f.

dry [draɪ] a sec(sèche) ; (day) sans pluie // vt sécher ; (clothes) faire sécher // vi sécher ; **to ~ up** vi se tarir ; ~-**cleaner** n teinturier m ; ~-**cleaner's** n teinturerie f ; ~-**cleaning** n nettoyage m à sec ; ~**er** n séchoir m ; ~**ness** n sécheresse f ; ~ **rot** n pourriture sèche (du bois).

dual ['djuəl] a double ; ~ **carriageway** n route f à quatre voies ; ~-**control** a à doubles commandes ; ~ **nationality** n double nationalité f ; ~-**purpose** a à double emploi.

dubbed [dʌbd] a (CINEMA) doublé(e) ; (nicknamed) surnommé(e).

dubious ['djuːbɪəs] a hésitant(e), incertain(e) ; (reputation, company) douteux(euse).

duchess ['dʌtʃɪs] n duchesse f.

duck [dʌk] n canard m // vi se baisser vivement, baisser subitement la tête; ~**ling** n caneton m.

duct [dʌkt] n conduite f, canalisation f; (ANAT) conduit m.

dud [dʌd] n (shell) obus non éclaté; (object, tool): it's a ~ c'est de la camelote, ça ne marche pas // a (cheque) sans provision; (note, coin) faux(fausse).

due [djuː] a dû(due); (expected) attendu(e); (fitting) qui convient // n dû m // ad: ~ north droit vers le nord; ~s npl (for club, union) cotisation f; (in harbour) droits mpl (de port); in ~ course en temps utile or voulu; finalement; ~ to dû(due) à; causé(e) par.

duel ['djuəl] n duel m.

duet [djuːˈɛt] n duo m.

dug [dʌg] pt, pp of **dig**.

duke [djuːk] n duc m.

dull [dʌl] a ennuyeux(euse); terne; (sound, pain) sourd(e); (weather, day) gris(e), maussade; (blade) émoussé(e) // vt (pain, grief) atténuer; (mind, senses) engourdir.

duly ['djuːlɪ] ad (on time) en temps voulu; (as expected) comme il se doit.

dumb [dʌm] a muet(te); (stupid) bête; **dumbfounded** [dʌm'faundɪd] a sidéré(e).

dummy ['dʌmɪ] n (tailor's model) mannequin m; (SPORT) feinte f; (for baby) tétine f // a faux(fausse), factice.

dump [dʌmp] n tas m d'ordures; (place) décharge (publique); (MIL) dépôt m // vt (put down) déposer; déverser; (get rid of) se débarrasser de; ~**ing** n (ECON) dumping m; (of rubbish): 'no ~**ing**' 'décharge interdite'.

dumpling ['dʌmplɪŋ] n boulette f (de pâte).

dunce [dʌns] n âne m, cancre m.

dune [djuːn] n dune f.

dung [dʌŋ] n fumier m.

dungarees [dʌŋgəˈriːz] npl bleu(s) m(pl); salopette f.

dungeon ['dʌndʒən] n cachot m.

Dunkirk [dʌnˈkəːk] n Dunkerque.

dupe [djuːp] n dupe f // vt duper, tromper.

duplicate n ['djuːplɪkət] double m, copie exacte // vt ['djuːplɪkeɪt] faire un double de; (on machine) polycopier; in ~ en deux exemplaires, en double; **duplicator** n duplicateur m.

durable ['djuərəbl] a durable; (clothes, metal) résistant(e), solide.

duration [djuəˈreɪʃən] n durée f.

duress [djuəˈrɛs] n: under ~ sous la contrainte.

during ['djuərɪŋ] prep pendant, au cours de.

dusk [dʌsk] n crépuscule m; ~**y** a sombre.

dust [dʌst] n poussière f // vt (furniture) essuyer, épousseter; (cake etc) to ~ with saupoudrer de; ~**bin** n (Brit) poubelle f; ~**er** n chiffon m; ~**jacket** n jaquette f; ~**man** n (Brit) boueux m, éboueur m; ~**y** a poussiéreux(euse).

Dutch [dʌtʃ] a hollandais(e), néerlandais(e) // (LING) hollandais m; the ~ les Hollandais; ~**man/woman** n Hollandais/e.

dutiable ['djuːtɪəbl] a taxable; soumis(e) à des droits de douane.

duty ['djuːtɪ] n devoir m; (tax) droit m, taxe f; **duties** npl fonctions fpl; on ~ de service; (at night etc) de garde; off ~ libre, pas de service or de garde; ~**-free** a exempté(e) de douane, hors-taxe.

dwarf [dwɔːf] n nain/e // vt écraser.

dwell, pt, pp **dwelt** [dwɛl, dwɛlt] vi demeurer; to ~ on vt fus s'étendre sur; ~**ing** n habitation f, demeure f.

dwindle ['dwɪndl] vi diminuer, décroître.

dye [daɪ] n teinture f // vt teindre; ~**stuffs** npl colorants mpl.

dying ['daɪɪŋ] a mourant(e), agonisant(e).

dyke [daɪk] n digue f.

dynamic [daɪˈnæmɪk] a dynamique; ~**s** n or npl dynamique f.

dynamite ['daɪnəmaɪt] n dynamite f.

dynamo ['daɪnəməu] n dynamo f.

dynasty ['dɪnəstɪ] n dynastie f.

dysentery ['dɪsntrɪ] n dysenterie f.

E

E [iː] n (MUS) mi m.

each [iːtʃ] det chaque // pronoun chacun(e); ~ one chacun(e); ~ other se (or nous etc); they hate ~ other ils se détestent (mutuellement); you are jealous of ~ other vous êtes jaloux l'un de l'autre.

eager ['iːgə*] a impatient(e); avide; ardent(e), passionné(e); to be ~ to do sth être impatient de faire qch, brûler de faire qch; désirer vivement faire qch; to be ~ for désirer vivement, être avide de.

eagle ['iːgl] n aigle m.

ear [ɪə*] n oreille f; (of corn) épi m; ~**ache** n douleurs fpl aux oreilles; ~**drum** n tympan m; ~ **nose and throat specialist** n oto-rhino-laryngologiste m/f.

earl [əːl] n comte m.

earlier ['əːlɪə] a (date etc) plus rapproché(e); (edition etc) plus ancien(ne), antérieur(e) // ad plus tôt.

early ['əːlɪ] ad tôt, de bonne heure; (ahead of time) en avance // a précoce; anticipé(e); qui se manifeste (or se fait) tôt or de bonne heure; **have an ~ night/start** couchez-vous/partez tôt or de bonne heure; **take the ~ train/plane** prenez le premier train/vol; **in the ~ or ~ in the spring/19th century** au début or commencement du printemps/ 19ème siècle; ~ **retirement** n retraite anticipée.

earmark ['ɪəmɑːk] vt: to ~ sth for réserver or destiner qch à.

earn [əːn] vt gagner; (COMM: yield) rapporter; this ~ed him much praise, he ~ed much praise for this ceci lui a valu de nombreux éloges; he's ~ed his rest/reward il mérite or a bien mérité or a bien gagné son repos/sa récompense.

earnest ['əːnɪst] a sérieux(euse); in ~ ad sérieusement, pour de bon.

earnings ['əːnɪŋz] npl salaire m; gains mpl.

earphones ['ɪəfəunz] npl écouteurs mpl.

earring ['ɪərɪŋ] n boucle f d'oreille.

earshot ['ɪəʃɒt] n: out of/within ~ hors de portée/à portée de la voix.

earth [ə:θ] n (gen, also ELEC) terre f; (of fox etc) terrier m // vt (ELEC) relier à la terre; **~enware** n poterie f; faïence f // a de or en faïence; **~quake** n tremblement m de terre, séisme m; **~ tremor** n secousse f sismique; **~works** npl travaux mpl de terrassement; **~y** a (fig) terre à terre inv; truculent(e).

earwax ['ɪəwæks] n cérumen m.

earwig ['ɪəwɪg] n perce-oreille m.

ease [i:z] n facilité f, aisance f // vt (soothe) calmer; (loosen) relâcher, détendre; (help pass): **to ~ sth in/out** faire pénétrer/sortir qch délicatement or avec douceur; faciliter la pénétration/la sortie de qch; **life of ~** vie oisive; **at ~** à l'aise; (MIL) au repos; **to ~ off or up** vi diminuer; ralentir; se détendre.

easel ['i:zl] n chevalet m.

easily ['i:zɪlɪ] ad facilement.

east [i:st] n est m // a d'est // ad à l'est, vers l'est; **the E~** l'Orient m.

Easter ['i:stə*] n Pâques fpl.

easterly ['i:stəlɪ] a d'est.

eastern ['i:stən] a de l'est, oriental(e).

East Germany [i:st'dʒə:mənɪ] n Allemagne f de l'Est.

eastward(s) ['i:stwəd(z)] ad vers l'est, à l'est.

easy ['i:zɪ] a facile; (manner) aisé(e) // ad: **to take it or things ~** ne pas se fatiguer; ne pas (trop) s'en faire; **~ chair** n fauteuil m; **~ going** a accommodant(e), facile à vivre.

eat, pt **ate**, pp **eaten** [i:t, eɪt, 'i:tn] vt manger; **to ~ into**, **to ~ away at** vt fus ronger, attaquer; **~able** a mangeable; (safe to eat) comestible.

eaves [i:vz] npl avant-toit m.

eavesdrop ['i:vzdrɔp] vi: **to ~ (on a conversation)** écouter (une conversation) de façon indiscrète.

ebb [ɛb] n reflux m // vi refluer; (fig: also: **~ away**) décliner.

ebony ['ɛbənɪ] n ébène f.

ebullient [ɪ'bʌlɪənt] a exubérant(e).

eccentric [ɪk'sɛntrɪk] a,n excentrique (m/f).

ecclesiastic [ɪkli:zɪ'æstɪk] n ecclésiastique m; **~al** a ecclésiastique.

echo, **~es** ['ɛkəu] n écho m // vt répéter; faire chorus avec // vi résonner; faire écho.

eclipse [ɪ'klɪps] n éclipse f // vt éclipser.

ecology [ɪ'kɔlədʒɪ] n écologie f.

economic [i:kə'nɔmɪk] a économique; (business etc) rentable; **~al** a économique; (person) économe; **~s** n économie f politique.

economist [ɪ'kɔnəmɪst] n économiste m/f.

economize [ɪ'kɔnəmaɪz] vi économiser, faire des économies.

economy [ɪ'kɔnəmɪ] n économie f.

ecstasy ['ɛkstəsɪ] n extase f; **to go into ecstasies over** s'extasier sur; **ecstatic** [-'tætɪk] a extatique, en extase.

ecumenical [i:kju'mɛnɪkl] a œcuménique.

eczema ['ɛksɪmə] n eczéma m.

eddy ['ɛdɪ] n tourbillon m.

edge [ɛdʒ] n bord m; (of knife etc) tranchant m, fil m // vt border; **on ~** (fig)

= **edgy**; **to have the ~ on** l'emporter (de justesse) sur, être légèrement meilleur que; **to ~ away from** s'éloigner furtivement de; **~ways** ad latéralement; **he couldn't get a word in ~ways** il ne pouvait pas placer un mot; **edging** n bordure f.

edgy ['ɛdʒɪ] a crispé(e), tendu(e).

edible ['ɛdɪbl] a comestible; (meal) mangeable.

edict ['i:dɪkt] n décret m.

edifice ['ɛdɪfɪs] n édifice m.

edit ['ɛdɪt] vt éditer; **~ion** [ɪ'dɪʃən] n édition f; **~or** n (in newspaper) rédacteur/trice; rédacteur/trice en chef; (of sb's work) éditeur/trice; **~orial** [-'tɔ:rɪəl] a de la rédaction, éditorial(e) // n éditorial m.

educate ['ɛdjukeɪt] vt instruire; éduquer.

education [ɛdju'keɪʃən] n éducation f; (schooling) enseignement m, instruction f; **~al** a pédagogique; scolaire; instructif(ive).

EEC n (abbr of European Economic Community) C.E.E. (Communauté économique européenne).

eel [i:l] n anguille f.

eerie ['ɪərɪ] a inquiétant(e), spectral(e), surnaturel(le).

effect [ɪ'fɛkt] n effet m // vt effectuer; **~s** npl (THEATRE) effets mpl; **to take ~** (law) entrer en vigueur, prendre effet; (drug) agir, faire son effet; **in ~** en fait; **~ive** a efficace; **~iveness** n efficacité f.

effeminate [ɪ'fɛmɪnɪt] a efféminé(e).

effervescent [ɛfə'vɛsnt] a effervescent(e).

efficacy ['ɛfɪkəsɪ] n efficacité f.

efficiency [ɪ'fɪʃənsɪ] n efficacité f; rendement m.

efficient [ɪ'fɪʃənt] a efficace; **~ly** ad efficacement.

effigy ['ɛfɪdʒɪ] n effigie f.

effort ['ɛfət] n effort m; **~less** a sans effort, aisé(e).

effrontery [ɪ'frʌntərɪ] n effronterie f.

e.g. ad (abbr of exempli gratia) par exemple, p. ex.

egalitarian [ɪgælɪ'tɛərɪən] a égalitaire.

egg [ɛg] n œuf m; **to ~ on** vt pousser; **~cup** n coquetier m; **~plant** n aubergine f; **~shell** n coquille f d'œuf // a (colour) blanc cassé inv.

ego ['i:gəu] n moi m.

egoist ['ɛgəuɪst] n égoïste m/f.

egotist ['ɛgəutɪst] n égocentrique m/f.

Egypt ['i:dʒɪpt] n Égypte f; **~ian** [ɪ'dʒɪpʃən] a égyptien(ne) // n Égyptien/ne.

eiderdown ['aɪdədaun] n édredon m.

eight [eɪt] num huit; **~een** num dix-huit; **~h** num huitième; **~y** num quatre-vingt(s).

Eire ['ɛərə] n République f d'Irlande.

either ['aɪðə*] det l'un ou l'autre; (both, each) chaque; **on ~ side** de chaque côté // pronoun: **~ (of them)** l'un ou l'autre; **I don't like ~** je n'aime ni l'un ni l'autre // ad non plus; **no, I don't ~** moi non plus // cj: **~ good or bad** ou bon ou mauvais, soit bon soit mauvais; **I haven't**

seen ~ one or the other je n'ai vu ni l'un ni l'autre.

ejaculation [ɪdʒækju'leɪʃən] n (PHYSIOL) éjaculation f.

eject [ɪ'dʒɛkt] vt expulser; éjecter; ~or seat n siège m éjectable.

eke [iːk]: to ~ out vt faire durer; augmenter.

elaborate a [ɪ'læbərɪt] compliqué(e), recherché(e), minutieux (euse) // vb [ɪ'læbəreɪt] vt élaborer // vi entrer dans les détails.

elapse [ɪ'læps] vi s'écouler, passer.

elastic [ɪ'læstɪk] a, n élastique (m); ~ band n élastique m; ~ity [-'tɪsɪti] n élasticité f.

elated [ɪ'leɪtɪd] a transporté(e) de joie.

elation [ɪ'leɪʃən] n (grande) joie, allégresse f.

elbow ['ɛlbəu] n coude m.

elder ['ɛldə*] a aîné(e) // n (tree) sureau m; one's ~s ses aînés; ~ly a âgé(e) // n: the ~ly les personnes âgées.

eldest ['ɛldɪst] a,n: the ~ (child) l'aîné(e) (des enfants).

elect [ɪ'lɛkt] vt élire; to ~ to do choisir de faire // a: the president ~ le président désigné; ~ion [ɪ'lɛkʃən] n élection f; ~ioneering [ɪlɛkʃə'nɪərɪŋ] n propagande électorale, manœuvres électorales; ~or n électeur/trice; ~oral a électoral(e); ~orate n électorat m.

electric [ɪ'lɛktrɪk] a électrique; ~al a électrique; ~ blanket n couverture chauffante; ~ chair n chaise f électrique; ~ cooker n cuisinière f électrique; ~ current n courant m électrique; ~ fire n radiateur m électrique.

electrician [ɪlɛk'trɪʃən] n électricien m.

electricity [ɪlɛk'trɪsɪti] n électricité f.

electrify [ɪ'lɛktrɪfaɪ] vt (RAIL) électrifier; (audience) électriser.

electro... [ɪ'lɛktrəu] prefix: **electrocute** [-kjuːt] vt électrocuter; **electrode** [ɪ'lɛktrəud] n électrode f; **electrolysis** [ɪlɛk'trɔlɪsɪs] n électrolyse f.

electron [ɪ'lɛktrɔn] n électron m.

electronic [ɪlɛk'trɔnɪk] a électronique; ~s n électronique f.

elegance ['ɛlɪgəns] n élégance f.

elegant ['ɛlɪgənt] a élégant(e).

element ['ɛlɪmənt] n (gen) élément m; (of heater, kettle etc) résistance f; ~ary [-'mɛntəri] a élémentaire; (school, education) primaire.

elephant ['ɛlɪfənt] n éléphant m.

elevate ['ɛlɪveɪt] vt élever; ~d railway n métro aérien.

elevation [ɛlɪ'veɪʃən] n élévation f; (height) altitude f.

elevator ['ɛlɪveɪtə*] n élévateur m, monte-charge m inv; (US: lift) ascenseur m.

eleven [ɪ'lɛvn] num onze; ~ses npl ≈ pause-café f; ~th a onzième.

elf, elves [ɛlf, ɛlvz] n lutin m.

elicit [ɪ'lɪsɪt] vt: to ~ (from) obtenir (de), arracher (à).

eligible ['ɛlɪdʒəbl] a éligible; (for membership) admissible; ~ for a pension ayant droit à la retraite.

eliminate [ɪ'lɪmɪneɪt] vt éliminer; **elimination** n élimination f.

élite [eɪ'liːt] n élite f.

ellipse [ɪ'lɪps] n ellipse f.

elliptical [ɪ'lɪptɪkl] a elliptique.

elm [ɛlm] n orme m.

elocution [ɛlə'kjuːʃən] n élocution f.

elongated ['iːlɔŋgeɪtɪd] a étiré(e), allongé(e).

elope [ɪ'ləup] vi (lovers) s'enfuir (ensemble); ~ment n fugue amoureuse.

eloquence ['ɛləkwəns] n éloquence f.

eloquent ['ɛləkwənt] a éloquent(e).

else [ɛls] ad d'autre; **something** ~ quelque chose d'autre, autre chose; **somewhere** ~ ailleurs, autre part; everywhere ~ partout ailleurs; **where** ~? à quel autre endroit?; **little** ~ pas grand-chose d'autre; ~**where** ad ailleurs, autre part.

elucidate [ɪ'luːsɪdeɪt] vt élucider.

elude [ɪ'luːd] vt échapper à; (question) éluder.

elusive [ɪ'luːsɪv] a insaisissable; (answer) évasif(ive).

elves [ɛlvz] npl of elf.

emaciated [ɪ'meɪsɪeɪtɪd] a émacié(e), décharné(e).

emanate ['ɛməneɪt] vi: to ~ from émaner de.

emancipate [ɪ'mænsɪpeɪt] vt émanciper; **emancipation** [-'peɪʃən] n émancipation f.

embalm [ɪm'bɑːm] vt embaumer.

embankment [ɪm'bæŋkmənt] n (of road, railway) remblai m, talus m; (riverside) berge f, quai m; (dyke) digue f.

embargo, ~**es** [ɪm'bɑːgəu] n embargo m // vt frapper d'embargo, mettre l'embargo sur.

embark [ɪm'bɑːk] vi: to ~ (on) (s')embarquer (à bord de or sur) // vt embarquer; to ~ on (fig) se lancer or s'embarquer dans; ~ation [ɛmbɑː'keɪʃən] n embarquement m.

embarrass [ɪm'bærəs] vt embarrasser, gêner; ~**ing** a gênant(e), embarrassant(e); ~**ment** n embarras m, gêne f.

embassy ['ɛmbəsi] n ambassade f.

embed [ɪm'bɛd] vt enfoncer, ficher, sceller.

embellish [ɪm'bɛlɪʃ] vt embellir; enjoliver.

embers ['ɛmbəz] npl braise f.

embezzle [ɪm'bɛzl] vt détourner; ~**ment** n détournement m (de fonds).

embitter [ɪm'bɪtə*] vt aigrir; envenimer.

emblem ['ɛmbləm] n emblème m.

embodiment [ɪm'bɔdɪmənt] n personification f, incarnation f.

embody [ɪm'bɔdi] vt (features) réunir, comprendre; (ideas) formuler, exprimer.

embossed [ɪm'bɔst] a repoussé(e); gaufré(e); ~ with où figure(nt) en relief.

embrace [ɪm'breɪs] vt embrasser, étreindre; (include) embrasser, couvrir // n étreinte f.

embroider [ɪm'brɔɪdə*] vt broder; (fig: story) enjoliver; ~y n broderie f.

embryo ['ɛmbrɪəu] n (also fig) embryon m.

emerald ['ɛmərəld] n émeraude f.

emerge [ɪ'məːdʒ] vi apparaître, surgir.

emergence [ɪ'məːdʒəns] n apparition f.

emergency [ɪ'məːdʒənsɪ] n urgence f; **in an ~** en cas d'urgence; **state of ~** état m d'urgence; **~ exit** n sortie f de secours.

emergent [ɪ'məːdʒənt] a: **~ nation** pays m en voie de développement.

emery ['ɛmərɪ] n: **~ board** n lime f à ongles (en carton émerisé); **~ paper** n papier m (d')émeri.

emetic [ɪ'mɛtɪk] n vomitif m, émétique m.

emigrant ['ɛmɪɡrənt] n émigrant/e.

emigrate ['ɛmɪɡreɪt] vi émigrer; **emigration** [-'ɡreɪʃən] n émigration f.

eminence ['ɛmɪnəns] n éminence f.

eminent ['ɛmɪnənt] a éminent(e).

emission [ɪ'mɪʃən] n émission f.

emit [ɪ'mɪt] vt émettre.

emotion [ɪ'məʊʃən] n émotion f; **~al** a (person) émotif(ive), très sensible; (scene) émouvant(e); (tone, speech) qui fait appel aux sentiments; **~ally** ad: **~ally disturbed** qui souffre de troubles de l'affectivité.

emotive [ɪ'məʊtɪv] a émotif(ive); **~ power** n capacité f d'émouvoir or de toucher.

emperor ['ɛmpərə*] n empereur m.

emphasis, pl **ases** ['ɛmfəsɪs, -siːz] n accent m; force f, insistance f.

emphasize ['ɛmfəsaɪz] vt (syllable, word, point) appuyer or insister sur; (feature) souligner, accentuer.

emphatic [ɛm'fætɪk] a (strong) énergique, vigoureux(euse); (unambiguous, clear) catégorique; **~ally** ad avec vigueur et énergie; catégoriquement.

empire ['ɛmpaɪə*] n empire m.

empirical [ɛm'pɪrɪkl] a empirique.

employ [ɪm'plɔɪ] vt employer; **~ee** [-'iː] n employé/e; **~er** n employeur/euse; **~ment** n emploi m; **~ment agency** n agence f or bureau m de placement; **~ment exchange** n bourse f du travail.

empower [ɪm'paʊə*] vt: **to ~ sb to do** autoriser or habiliter qn à faire.

empress ['ɛmprɪs] n impératrice f.

emptiness ['ɛmptɪnɪs] n vide m.

empty ['ɛmptɪ] a vide; (threat, promise) en l'air, vain(e) // vt vider // vi se vider; (liquid) s'écouler; **on an ~ stomach** à jeun; **~-handed** a les mains vides.

emulate ['ɛmjuleɪt] vt rivaliser avec, imiter.

emulsion [ɪ'mʌlʃən] n émulsion f; **~ (paint)** n peinture mate.

enable [ɪ'neɪbl] vt: **to ~ sb to do** permettre à qn de faire, donner à qn la possibilité de faire.

enamel [ɪ'næməl] n émail m.

enamoured [ɪ'næməd] a: **~ of** amoureux(euse) de; (idea) enchanté(e) par.

encased [ɪn'keɪst] a: **~ in** enfermé(e) dans, recouvert(e) de.

enchant [ɪn'tʃuːnt] vt enchanter; (subject: magic spell) ensorceler; **~ing** a ravissant(e), enchanteur(eresse).

encircle [ɪn'səːkl] vt entourer, encercler.

encl. (abbr of enclosed) annexe(s).

enclose [ɪn'kləuz] vt (land) clôturer; (letter etc): **to ~ (with)** joindre (à); **please find ~d** veuillez trouver ci-joint.

enclosure [ɪn'kləuʒə*] n enceinte f; (COMM) annexe f.

encore [ɔŋ'kɔː*] excl, n bis (m).

encounter [ɪn'kauntə*] n rencontre f // vt rencontrer.

encourage [ɪn'kʌrɪdʒ] vt encourager; **~ment** n encouragement m.

encroach [ɪn'krəutʃ] vi: **to ~ (up)on** empiéter sur.

encyclop(a)edia [ɛnsaɪkləu'piːdɪə] n encyclopédie f.

end [ɛnd] n (gen, also: aim) fin f; (of table, street etc) bout m, extrémité f // vt terminer; (also: **bring to an ~**, **put an ~ to**) mettre fin à // vi se terminer, finir; **to come to an ~** prendre fin; **in the ~** finalement; **on ~** (object) debout, dressé(e); **for 5 hours on ~** durant 5 heures d'affilée or de suite; **for hours on ~** pendant des heures (et des heures); **to ~ up** vi: **to ~ up in** finir par; (place) finir or aboutir à.

endanger [ɪn'deɪndʒə*] vt mettre en danger.

endearing [ɪn'dɪərɪŋ] a attachant(e).

endeavour [ɪn'devə*] n tentative f, effort m // vi: **to ~ to do** tenter or s'efforcer de faire.

ending ['ɛndɪŋ] n dénouement m, conclusion f; (LING) terminaison f.

endive ['ɛndaɪv] n chicorée f.

endless ['ɛndlɪs] a sans fin, interminable; (patience, resources) inépuisable, sans limites.

endorse [ɪn'dɔːs] vt (cheque) endosser; (approve) appuyer, approuver, sanctionner; **~ment** n (on driving licence) contravention portée au permis de conduire.

endow [ɪn'dau] vt (provide with money) faire une donation à, doter; (equip): **to ~ with** gratifier de, doter de.

end product ['ɛndprɔdʌkt] n produit fini; (fig) résultat m.

endurable [ɪn'djuərəbl] a supportable.

endurance [ɪn'djuərəns] n endurance f, résistance f; patience f.

endure [ɪn'djuə*] vt supporter, endurer // vi durer.

enemy ['ɛnəmɪ] a,n ennemi(e).

energetic [ɛnə'dʒɛtɪk] a énergique; actif(ive); qui fait se dispenser (physiquement).

energy ['ɛnədʒɪ] n énergie f.

enervating ['ɛnəːveɪtɪŋ] a débilitant(e), affaiblissant(e).

enforce [ɪn'fɔːs] vt (LAW) appliquer, faire respecter; **~d** a forcé(e).

engage [ɪn'ɡeɪdʒ] vt engager; (MIL) engager le combat avec // vi (TECH) s'enclencher, s'engrener; **to ~ in** se lancer dans; **~d** a (busy, in use) occupé(e); (betrothed) fiancé(e); **to get ~d** se fiancer; **he is ~d in research/a survey** il fait de la recherche/une enquête; **~ment** n obligation f, engagement m; rendez-vous m inv; (to marry) fiançailles fpl; (MIL) combat m; **~ment ring** n bague f de fiançailles.

engaging [ɪn'geɪdʒɪŋ] a engageant(e), attirant(e).
engender [ɪn'dʒɛndə*] vt produire, causer.
engine ['ɛndʒɪn] n (AUT) moteur m; (RAIL) locomotive f; ~ **failure** n panne f; ~ **trouble** n ennuis mpl mécaniques.
engineer [ɛndʒɪ'nɪə*] n ingénieur m; (US: RAIL) mécanicien m; ~**ing** n engineering m, ingénierie f; (of bridges, ships) génie m; (of machine) mécanique f.
England ['ɪŋglənd] n Angleterre f.
English ['ɪŋglɪʃ] a anglais(e) // n (LING) anglais m; **the** ~ les Anglais; ~**man/woman** n Anglais/e.
engrave [ɪn'greɪv] vt graver.
engraving [ɪn'greɪvɪŋ] n gravure f.
engrossed [ɪn'grəust] a: ~ **in** absorbé(e) par, plongé(e) dans.
engulf [ɪn'gʌlf] vt engloutir.
enhance [ɪn'hɑːns] vt rehausser, mettre en valeur.
enigma [ɪ'nɪgmə] n énigme f; ~**tic** [ɛnɪg'mætɪk] a énigmatique.
enjoy [ɪn'dʒɔɪ] vt aimer, prendre plaisir à; (have: health, fortune) jouir de; (: success) connaître; **to** ~ **oneself** s'amuser; ~**able** a agréable; ~**ment** n plaisir m.
enlarge [ɪn'lɑːdʒ] vt accroître; (PHOT) agrandir // vi: **to** ~ **on** (subject) s'étendre sur; ~**ment** n (PHOT) agrandissement m.
enlighten [ɪn'laɪtn] vt éclairer; ~**ed** a éclairé(e); ~**ment** n édification f; vues éclairées; éclaircissements mpl; (HISTORY): **the E**~**ment** ≈ le Siècle des lumières.
enlist [ɪn'lɪst] vt recruter; (support) s'assurer // vi s'engager.
enmity ['ɛnmɪtɪ] n inimitié f.
enormity [ɪ'nɔːmɪtɪ] n énormité f.
enormous [ɪ'nɔːməs] a énorme.
enough [ɪ'nʌf] a, n: ~ **time/books** assez or suffisamment de temps/livres; **have you got** ~? (en) avez-vous assez? // ad: **big** ~ assez or suffisamment grand; **he has not worked** ~ il n'a pas assez or suffisamment travaillé, il n'a pas travaillé assez or suffisamment; ~! assez!, ça suffit!; **it's hot** ~ **(as it is)!** il fait assez chaud comme ça!; ... **which, funnily** ~ ... qui, chose curieuse.
enquire [ɪn'kwaɪə*] vt,vi = **inquire**.
enrich [ɪn'rɪtʃ] vt enrichir.
enrol [ɪn'rəul] vt inscrire // vi s'inscrire; ~**ment** n inscription f.
ensconced [ɪn'skɔnst] a: ~ **in** bien calé(e) dans; plongé(e) dans.
ensign n (NAUT) ['ɛnsən] enseigne f, pavillon m; (MIL) ['ɛnsaɪn] porte-étendard m.
enslave [ɪn'sleɪv] vt asservir.
ensue [ɪn'sjuː] vi s'ensuivre, résulter.
ensure [ɪn'ʃuə*] vt assurer; garantir; **to** ~ **that** s'assurer que.
entail [ɪn'teɪl] vt entraîner, nécessiter.
entangle [ɪn'tæŋgl] vt emmêler, embrouiller.
enter ['ɛntə*] vt (room) entrer dans, pénétrer dans; (club, army) entrer à; (competition) s'inscrire à or pour; (sb for a competition) (faire) inscrire; (write down) inscrire, noter; **to** ~ **for** vt fus s'inscrire à, se présenter pour or à; **to** ~ **into** vt

fus (exploration) se lancer dans; (debate) prendre part à; (agreement) conclure; **to** ~ **up** vt inscrire; **to** ~ **(up)on** vt fus commencer.
enterprise ['ɛntəpraɪz] n entreprise f; (esprit m d')initiative f.
enterprising ['ɛntəpraɪzɪŋ] a entreprenant(e), dynamique.
entertain [ɛntə'teɪn] vt amuser, distraire; (invite) recevoir (à dîner); (idea, plan) envisager; ~**er** n artiste m/f de variétés; ~**ing** a amusant(e), distrayant(e); ~**ment** n (amusement) distraction f, divertissement m, amusement m; (show) spectacle m.
enthralled [ɪn'θrɔːld] a captivé(e).
enthusiasm [ɪn'θuːzɪæzəm] n enthousiasme m.
enthusiast [ɪn'θuːzɪæst] n enthousiaste m/f; **a jazz etc** ~ un fervent or passionné du jazz etc; ~**ic** [-'æstɪk] a enthousiaste.
entice [ɪn'taɪs] vt attirer, séduire.
entire [ɪn'taɪə*] a (tout) entier(ère); ~**ly** ad entièrement, complètement; ~**ty** [ɪn'taɪərətɪ] n: **in its** ~**ty** dans sa totalité.
entitle [ɪn'taɪtl] vt (allow): **to** ~ **sb to do** donner (le) droit à qn de faire; **to** ~ **sb to sth** donner droit à qch à qn; ~**d** a (book) intitulé(e); **to be** ~**d to do** avoir le droit de or être habilité à faire.
entrance n ['ɛntrns] entrée f // vt [ɪn'trɑːns] enchanter, ravir; **to gain** ~ **to** (university etc) être admis à; ~ **examination** n examen m d'entrée; ~ **fee** n droit m d'inscription; (to museum etc) prix m d'entrée.
entrant ['ɛntrnt] n participant/e; concurrent/e.
entreat [ɛn'triːt] vt supplier; ~**y** n supplication f, prière f.
entrée ['ɔntreɪ] n (CULIN) entrée f.
entrenched [ɛn'trɛntʃd] a retranché(e).
entrust [ɪn'trʌst] vt: **to** ~ **sth to** confier qch à.
entry ['ɛntrɪ] n entrée f; (in register) inscription f; ~ **form** n feuille f d'inscription.
entwine [ɪn'twaɪn] vt entrelacer.
enumerate [ɪ'njuːməreɪt] vt énumérer.
enunciate [ɪ'nʌnsɪeɪt] vt énoncer; prononcer.
envelop [ɪn'vɛləp] vt envelopper.
envelope ['ɛnvələup] n enveloppe f.
envious ['ɛnvɪəs] a envieux(euse).
environment [ɪn'vaɪərnmənt] n milieu m; environnement m; ~**al** [-'mɛntl] a écologique; du milieu.
envisage [ɪn'vɪzɪdʒ] vt envisager; prévoir.
envoy ['ɛnvɔɪ] n envoyé/e.
envy ['ɛnvɪ] n envie f // vt envier.
enzyme ['ɛnzaɪm] n enzyme m.
ephemeral [ɪ'fɛmərl] a éphémère.
epic ['ɛpɪk] n épopée f // a épique.
epidemic [ɛpɪ'dɛmɪk] n épidémie f.
epilepsy ['ɛpɪlɛpsɪ] n épilepsie f; **epileptic** [-'lɛptɪk] a,n épileptique (m/f).
epilogue ['ɛpɪlɔg] n épilogue m.
episode ['ɛpɪsəud] n épisode m.
epistle [ɪ'pɪsl] n épître f.
epitaph ['ɛpɪtɑːf] n épitaphe f.
epitome [ɪ'pɪtəmɪ] n résumé m;

quintessence f, type m; **epitomize** vt résumer; illustrer, incarner.

epoch ['i:pɔk] n époque f, ère f; ~-**making** a qui fait époque.

equable ['ɛkwəbl] a égal(e); de tempérament égal.

equal ['i:kwl] a égal(e) // n égal/e // vt égaler; ~ **to** (task) à la hauteur de; ~ **to doing** de taille à or capable de faire; ~**ity** [i:'kwɔliti] n égalité f; ~**ize** vt,vi égaliser; ~**izer** n but égalisateur; ~**ly** ad également; (just as) tout aussi; ~(s) **sign** n signe m d'égalité.

equanimity [ɛkwə'nimiti] n égalité f d'humeur.

equate [i'kweit] vt: **to** ~ **sth with** comparer qch à; assimiler qch à; **to** ~ **sth to** mettre qch en équation avec; égaler qch à; **equation** [i'kweifən] n (MATH) équation f.

equator [i'kweitə*] n équateur m; ~**ial** [ɛkwə'tɔ:riəl] a équatorial(e).

equilibrium [i:kwi'libriəm] n équilibre m.

equinox ['i:kwinɔks] n équinoxe m.

equip [i'kwip] vt équiper; **to** ~ **sb/sth with** équiper or munir qn/qch de; ~**ment** n équipement m; (electrical etc) appareillage m, installation f.

equitable ['ɛkwitəbl] a équitable.

equity ['ɛkwiti] n équité f; **equities** npl (COMM) actions cotées en Bourse.

equivalent [i'kwivəlnt] a équivalent(e) // n équivalent m.

equivocal [i'kwivəkl] a équivoque; (open to suspicion) douteux(euse).

era ['iərə] n ère f, époque f.

eradicate [i'rædikeit] vt éliminer.

erase [i'reiz] vt effacer; ~**r** n gomme f.

erect [i'rɛkt] a droit(e) // vt construire; (monument) ériger; élever; (tent etc) dresser.

erection [i'rɛkfən] n érection f.

ermine ['ə:min] n hermine f.

erode [i'rəud] vt éroder; (metal) ronger; **erosion** [i'rəuʒən] n érosion f.

erotic [i'rɔtik] a érotique; ~**ism** [i'rɔtisizm] n érotisme m.

err [ə:*] vi se tromper; (REL) pécher.

errand ['ɛrnd] n course f, commission f; ~ **boy** n garçon m de courses.

erratic [i'rætik] a irrégulier(ère); inconstant(e).

erroneous [i'rəuniəs] a erroné(e).

error ['ɛrə*] n erreur f.

erudite ['ɛrjudait] a savant(e).

erupt [i'rʌpt] vi entrer en éruption; (fig) éclater; ~**ion** [i'rʌpfən] n éruption f.

escalate ['ɛskəleit] vi s'intensifier; **escalation** [-'leifən] n escalade f.

escalator ['ɛskəleitə*] n escalier roulant.

escapade [ɛskə'peid] n fredaine f; équipée f.

escape [i'skeip] n évasion f; fuite f; (of gas etc) échappement m; fuite // vi s'échapper, fuir; (from jail) s'évader; (fig) s'en tirer; (leak) s'échapper; fuir // vt échapper à; **to** ~ **from sb** échapper à qn; **to** ~ **from** (place) s'échapper de; (fig) fuir; **escapism** n évasion f (fig).

escort n ['ɛskɔ:t] escorte f // vt [i'skɔ:t] escorter; ~ **agency** n bureau m d'hôtesses.

Eskimo ['ɛskiməu] n Esquimau/de.

especially [i'spɛfli] ad particulièrement; surtout; exprès.

espionage ['ɛspiəna:ʒ] n espionnage m.

esplanade [ɛspla'neid] n esplanade f.

Esquire [i'skwaiə*] n (abbr Esq.): J. Brown, ~ Monsieur J. Brown.

essay ['ɛsei] n (SCOL) dissertation f; (LITERATURE) essai m; (attempt) tentative f.

essence ['ɛsns] n essence f.

essential [i'sɛnfl] a essentiel(le); (basic) fondamental(e); ~**ly** ad essentiellement.

establish [i'stæblif] vt établir; (business) fonder, créer; (one's power etc) asseoir, affermir; ~**ment** n établissement m; **the E**~**ment** les pouvoirs établis; l'ordre établi; les milieux dirigeants.

estate [i'steit] n domaine m, propriété f; biens mpl, succession f; ~ **agent** n agent immobilier; ~ **car** n (Brit) break m.

esteem [i'sti:m] n estime f.

esthetic [is'θɛtik] a (US) = aesthetic.

estimate n ['ɛstimət] estimation f; (COMM) devis m // vt ['ɛstimeit] estimer; **estimation** [-'meifən] n opinion f; estime f.

estuary ['ɛstjuəri] n estuaire m.

etching ['ɛtfiŋ] n eau-forte f.

eternal [i'tə:nl] a éternel(le).

eternity [i'tə:niti] n éternité f.

ether ['i:θə*] n éther m.

ethical ['ɛθikl] a moral(e).

ethics ['ɛθiks] n éthique f // npl moralité f.

ethnic ['ɛθnik] a ethnique.

ethnology [ɛθ'nɔlədʒi] n ethnologie f.

etiquette ['ɛtikɛt] n convenances fpl, étiquette f.

etymology [ɛti'mɔlədʒi] n étymologie f.

eulogy ['ju:lədʒi] n éloge m.

euphemism ['ju:fəmizm] n euphémisme m.

euphoria [ju:'fɔ:riə] n euphorie f.

Europe ['juərəp] n Europe f; ~**an** [-'pi:ən] a européen(ne) // n Européen/ne.

euthanasia [ju:θə'neiziə] n euthanasie f.

evacuate [i'vækjueit] vt évacuer; **evacuation** [-'eifən] n évacuation f.

evade [i'veid] vt échapper à; (question etc) éluder; (duties) se dérober à.

evaluate [i'væljueit] vt évaluer.

evangelist [i'vændʒəlist] n évangéliste m.

evangelize [i'vændʒəlaiz] vt évangéliser, prêcher l'Évangile à.

evaporate [i'væpəreit] vi s'évaporer // vt faire évaporer; ~**d milk** n lait concentré; **evaporation** [-'reifən] n évaporation f.

evasion [i'veiʒən] n dérobade f; faux-fuyant m.

evasive [i'veisiv] a évasif(ive).

eve [i:v] n: **on the** ~ **of** à la veille de.

even ['i:vn] a régulier(ère), égal(e); (number) pair(e) // ad même; ~ **more** encore plus; ~ **so** quand même; **to** ~ **out** vi s'égaliser; **to get** ~ **with sb** prendre sa revanche sur qn.

evening ['i:vniŋ] n soir m; (as duration, event) soirée f; **in the** ~ le soir; ~ **class**

n cours *m* du soir ; ~ **dress** *n* (*man's*) habit *m* de soirée, smoking *m* ; (*woman's*) robe *f* de soirée.

evensong ['i:vnsɔŋ] *n* office *m* du soir.

event [ı'vɛnt] *n* évènement *m* ; (*SPORT*) épreuve *f* ; **in the** ~ **of** en cas de ; ~**ful** *a* mouvementé(e).

eventual [ı'vɛntʃuəl] *a* final(e) ; ~**ity** [-'ælıtı] *n* possibilité *f*, éventualité *f* ; ~**ly** *ad* finalement.

ever ['ɛvə*] *ad* jamais ; (*at all times*) toujours ; **the best** ~ le meilleur qu'on ait jamais vu ; **have you** ~ **seen it?** l'as-tu déjà vu?, as-tu eu l'occasion *or* t'est-il arrivé de le voir? ; **hardly** ~ ne ... presque jamais ; ~ **since** *ad* depuis // *cj* depuis que ; ~ **so pretty** si joli ; ~**green** *n* arbre *m* à feuilles persistantes ; ~**lasting** *a* éternel(le).

every ['ɛvrı] *det* chaque ; ~ **day** tous les jours, chaque jour ; ~ **other/third day** tous les deux/trois jours ; ~ **other car** une voiture sur deux ; ~ **now and then** de temps en temps ; ~**body** *pronoun* tout le monde, tous *pl* ; ~**day** *a* quotidien(ne) ; de tous les jours ; ~**one** = ~**body** ; ~**thing** *pronoun* tout ; ~**where** *ad* partout.

evict [ı'vıkt] *vt* expulser ; ~**ion** [ı'vıkʃən] *n* expulsion *f*.

evidence ['ɛvıdns] *n* (*proof*) preuve(s) *f(pl)* ; (*of witness*) témoignage *m* ; (*sign*): **to show** ~ **of** donner des signes de ; **to give** ~ témoigner, déposer ; **in** ~ (*obvious*) en évidence ; en vue.

evident ['ɛvıdnt] *a* évident(e) ; ~**ly** *ad* de toute évidence.

evil ['i:vl] *a* mauvais(e) // *n* mal *m*.

evocative [ı'vɔkətıv] *a* évocateur(trice).

evoke [ı'vəuk] *vt* évoquer.

evolution [i:və'lu:ʃən] *n* évolution *f*.

evolve [ı'vɔlv] *vt* élaborer // *vi* évoluer, se transformer.

ewe [ju:] *n* brebis *f*.

ewer ['ju:ə*] *n* broc *m*.

ex- [ɛks] *prefix* ex-.

exact [ıg'zækt] *a* exact(e) // *vt*: **to** ~ **sth (from)** extorquer qch (à) ; exiger qch (de) ; ~**ing** *a* exigeant(e) ; (*work*) fatigant(e) ; ~**itude** *n* exactitude *f*, précision *f* ; ~**ly** *ad* exactement.

exaggerate [ıg'zædʒəreıt] *vt,vi* exagérer ; **exaggeration** [-'reıʃən] *n* exagération *f*.

exalt [ıg'zɔ:lt] *vt* exalter ; élever.

exam [ıg'zæm] *n abbr of* **examination.**

examination [ıgzæmı'neıʃən] *n* (*SCOL, MED*) examen *m*.

examine [ıg'zæmın] *vt* (*gen*) examiner ; (*SCOL, LAW: person*) interroger ; (*at customs: luggage*) inspecter ; ~**r** *n* examinateur/trice.

example [ıg'zɑ:mpl] *n* exemple *m* ; **for** ~ par exemple.

exasperate [ıg'zɑ:spəreıt] *vt* exaspérer, agacer.

excavate ['ɛkskəveıt] *vt* excaver ; (*object*) mettre au jour ; **excavation** [-'veıʃən] *n* excavation *f* ; **excavator** *n* excavateur *m*, excavatrice *f*.

exceed [ık'si:d] *vt* dépasser ; (*one's powers*) outrepasser ; ~**ingly** *ad* excessivement.

excel [ık'sɛl] *vi* exceller // *vt* surpasser.

excellence ['ɛksələns] *n* excellence *f*.

Excellency ['ɛksələnsı] *n*: **His** ~ son Excellence *f*.

excellent ['ɛksələnt] *a* excellent(e).

except [ık'sɛpt] *prep* (*also*: ~ **for**, ~**ing**) sauf, excepté, à l'exception de // *vt* excepter ; ~ **if/when** sauf si/quand ; ~ **that** excepté que, si ce n'est que ; ~**ion** [ık'sɛpʃən] *n* exception *f* ; **to take** ~**ion to** s'offusquer de ; ~**ional** [ık'sɛpʃənl] *a* exceptionnel(le).

excerpt ['ɛksə:pt] *n* extrait *m*.

excess [ık'sɛs] *n* excès *m* ; ~ **fare** *n* supplément *m* ; ~ **baggage** *n* excédent *m* de bagages ; ~**ive** *a* excessif(ive).

exchange [ıks'tʃeındʒ] *n* échange *m* ; (*also*: **telephone** ~) central *m* // *vt* échanger ; ~ **market** *n* marché *m* des changes.

exchequer [ıks'tʃɛkə*] *n* Échiquier *m*, ≈ ministère *m* des Finances.

excisable [ık'saızəbl] *a* taxable.

excise *n* ['ɛksaız] taxe *f* // *vt* [ɛk'saız] exciser ; ~ **duties** *npl* impôts indirects.

excite [ık'saıt] *vt* exciter ; **to get** ~**d** s'exciter ; ~**ment** *n* excitation *f* ; **exciting** *a* passionnant(e).

exclaim [ık'skleım] *vi* s'exclamer ; **exclamation** [ɛksklə'meıʃən] *n* exclamation *f* ; **exclamation mark** *n* point *m* d'exclamation.

exclude [ık'sklu:d] *vt* exclure ; **exclusion** [ık'sklu:ʒən] *n* exclusion *f*.

exclusive [ık'sklu:sıv] *a* exclusif(ive) ; (*club, district*) sélect(e) ; (*item of news*) en exclusivité // *ad* (*COMM*) exclusivement, non inclus ; ~ **of VAT** TVA non comprise ; ~**ly** *ad* exclusivement ; ~ **rights** *npl* (*COMM*) exclusivité *f*.

excommunicate [ɛkskə'mju:nıkeıt] *vt* excommunier.

excrement ['ɛkskrəmənt] *n* excrément *m*.

excruciating [ık'skru:ʃıeıtıŋ] *a* atroce, déchirant(e).

excursion [ık'skə:ʃən] *n* excursion *f*.

excusable [ık'skju:zəbl] *a* excusable.

excuse *n* [ık'skju:s] excuse *f* // *vt* [ık'skju:z] excuser ; **to** ~ **sb from** (*activity*) dispenser qn de ; ~ **me!** excusez-moi!, pardon!

execute ['ɛksıkju:t] *vt* exécuter.

execution [ɛksı'kju:ʃən] *n* exécution *f* ; ~**er** *n* bourreau *m*.

executive [ıg'zɛkjutıv] *n* (*COMM*) cadre *m* ; (*POL*) exécutif *m* // *a* exécutif(ive).

executor [ıg'zɛkjutə*] *n* exécuteur/trice testamentaire.

exemplary [ıg'zɛmplərı] *a* exemplaire.

exemplify [ıg'zɛmplıfaı] *vt* illustrer.

exempt [ıg'zɛmpt] *a*: ~ **from** exempté(e) *or* dispensé(e) de // *vt*: **to** ~ **sb from** exempter *or* dispenser qn de ; ~**ion** [ıg'zɛmpʃən] *n* exemption *f*, dispense *f*.

exercise ['ɛksəsaız] *n* exercice *m* // *vt* exercer ; (*patience, clemency*) faire preuve de ; (*dog*) promener ; **to take** ~ prendre de l'exercice ; ~ **book** *n* cahier *m*.

exert [ıg'zə:t] *vt* exercer, employer ; **to** ~ **o.s.** se dépenser.

exhaust [ig'zɔ:st] n (also: ~ fumes) gaz mpl d'échappement ; (also: ~ pipe) tuyau m d'échappement // vt épuiser ; ~ed a épuisé(e) ; ~ion [ig'zɔ:stʃən] n épuisement m ; ~ive a très complet(ète).

exhibit [ig'zibit] n (ART) pièce f or objet m exposé(e) ; (LAW) pièce à conviction // vt exposer ; (courage, skill) faire preuve de ; ~ion [ɛksɪ'bɪʃən] n exposition f ; ~ion of temper n manifestation f de colère ; ~ionist [ɛksɪ'bɪʃənɪst] n exhibitionniste m/f ; ~or n exposant/e.

exhilarating [ig'zɪləreitɪŋ] a grisant(e) ; stimulant(e).

exhort [ig'zɔ:t] vt exhorter.

exile ['ɛksaɪl] n exil m ; exilé/e // vt exiler ; in ~ en exil.

exist [ig'zɪst] vi exister ; ~ence n existence f ; to be in ~ence exister.

exit ['ɛksɪt] n sortie f.

exonerate [ig'zɔnəreit] vt: to ~ from disculper de ; (free) exempter de.

exorcize ['ɛksɔ:saɪz] vt exorciser.

exotic [ig'zɔtɪk] a exotique.

expand [ik'spænd] vt agrandir ; accroître, étendre // vi (trade etc) se développer, s'accroître ; s'étendre ; (gas, metal) se dilater.

expanse [ik'spæns] n étendue f.

expansion [ik'spænʃən] n développement m, accroissement m ; dilatation f.

expatriate n [ɛks'pætrɪət] expatrié/e // vt [ɛks'pætrɪeɪt] expatrier, exiler.

expect [ik'spɛkt] vt (anticipate) s'attendre à, s'attendre à ce que + sub ; (count on) compter sur, escompter ; (hope for) espérer ; (require) demander, exiger ; (suppose) supposer ; (await, also baby) attendre // vi: to be ~ing être enceinte ; to ~ sb to do s'attendre à ce que qn fasse ; attendre de qn qu'il fasse ; ~ant a qui attend (quelque chose) ; ~ant mother n future maman ; ~ation [ɛkspɛk'teɪʃən] n attente f, prévisions fpl ; espérance(s) f(pl).

expedience, expediency [ɛk'spi:dɪəns, ɛk'spi:dɪənsɪ] n: for the sake of ~ parce que c'est plus commode.

expedient [ik'spi:dɪənt] a indiqué(e), opportun(e) ; commode // n expédient m.

expedite ['ɛkspədaɪt] vt hâter ; expédier.

expedition [ɛkspə'dɪʃən] n expédition f.

expeditious [ɛkspə'dɪʃəs] a expéditif(ive), prompt(e).

expel [ik'spɛl] vt chasser, expulser ; (SCOL) renvoyer, exclure.

expend [ik'spɛnd] vt consacrer ; (use up) dépenser ; ~able a remplaçable ; ~iture [ik'spɛndɪtʃə*] n dépense f ; dépenses fpl.

expense [ik'spɛns] n dépense f ; frais mpl ; (high cost) coût m ; ~s npl (COMM) frais mpl ; at great/little ~ à grands/peu de frais ; at the ~ of aux dépens de ; ~ account n (note f de) frais mpl.

expensive [ik'spɛnsɪv] a cher(chère), coûteux(euse) ; to be ~ coûter cher ; ~ tastes npl goûts mpl de luxe.

experience [ik'spɪərɪəns] n expérience f // vt connaître ; éprouver ; ~d a expérimenté(e).

experiment [ik'spɛrɪmənt] n expérience f // vi faire une expérience ; to ~ with expérimenter ; ~al [-'mɛntl] a expérimental(e).

expert ['ɛkspə:t] a expert(e) // n expert m ; ~ise [-'ti:z] n (grande) compétence.

expire [ik'spaɪə*] vi expirer ; expiry n expiration f.

explain [ik'spleɪn] vt expliquer ; explanation [ɛksplə'neɪʃən] n explication f ; explanatory [ik'splænətrɪ] a explicatif(ive).

explicit [ik'splɪsɪt] a explicite ; (definite) formel(le).

explode [ik'spləud] vi exploser // vt faire exploser.

exploit n ['ɛksplɔɪt] exploit m // vt [ik'splɔɪt] exploiter ; ~ation [-'teɪʃən] n exploitation f.

exploration [ɛksplə'reɪʃən] n exploration f.

exploratory [ik'splɔrətrɪ] a (fig: talks) préliminaire.

explore [ik'splɔ:*] vt explorer ; (possibilities) étudier, examiner ; ~r n explorateur/trice.

explosion [ik'spləuʒən] n explosion f.

explosive [ik'spləusɪv] a explosif(ive) // n explosif(ive).

exponent [ik'spəunənt] n (of school of thought etc) interprète m, représentant m ; (MATH) exposant m.

export vt [ɛk'spɔ:t] exporter // n ['ɛkspɔ:t] exportation f // cpd d'exportation ; ~ation [-'teɪʃən] n exportation f ; ~er n exportateur m.

expose [ik'spəuz] vt exposer ; (unmask) démasquer, dévoiler ; to ~ o.s. (LAW) commettre un outrage à la pudeur.

exposure [ik'spəuʒə*] n exposition f ; (PHOT) (temps m de) pose f ; (: shot) pose f ; suffering from ~ (MED) souffrant des effets du froid et de l'épuisement ; ~ meter n posemètre m.

expound [ik'spaund] vt exposer, expliquer.

express [ik'sprɛs] a (definite) formel(le), exprès(esse) ; (letter etc) exprès inv // n (train) rapide m // ad (send) exprès // vt exprimer ; ~ion [ik'sprɛʃən] n expression f ; ~ive a expressif(ive) ; ~ly ad expressément, formellement.

expropriate [ɛks'prəuprɪeɪt] vt exproprier.

expulsion [ik'spʌlʃən] n expulsion f ; renvoi m.

exquisite [ɛk'skwɪzɪt] a exquis(e).

extend [ik'stɛnd] vt (visit, street) prolonger ; (building) agrandir ; (offer) présenter, offrir // vi (land) s'étendre.

extension [ik'stɛnʃən] n prolongation f ; agrandissement m ; (building) annexe f ; (to wire, table) rallonge f ; (telephone: in offices) poste m ; (: in private house) téléphone m supplémentaire.

extensive [ik'stɛnsɪv] a étendu(e), vaste ; (damage, alterations) considérable ; (inquires) approfondi(e) ; (use) largement répandu(e) ; he's travelled ~ly il a beaucoup voyagé ; ~ travelling déplacements fréquents et prolongés.

extent [ik'stənt] n étendue f; **to some ~** dans une certaine mesure; **to what ~?** dans quelle mesure?, jusqu'à quel point?

exterior [ɛk'stɪərɪə*] a extérieur(e), du dehors // n extérieur m; dehors m.

exterminate [ik'stə:mneɪt] vt exterminer; **extermination** [-'neɪʃən] n extermination f.

external [ɛk'stə:nl] a externe; **~ly** ad extérieurement.

extinct [ik'stɪŋkt] a éteint(e); **~ion** [ik'stɪŋkʃən] n extinction f.

extinguish [ik'stɪŋgwɪʃ] vt éteindre; **~er** n extincteur m.

extol [ik'stəul] vt porter aux nues, chanter les louanges de.

extort [ik'stɔ:t] vt: **to ~ sth (from)** extorquer qch (à); **~ion** [ik'stɔ:ʃən] n extorsion f; **~ionate** [ik'stɔ:ʃnət] a exorbitant(e).

extra ['ɛkstrə] a supplémentaire, de plus // ad (in addition) en plus // n supplément m; (THEATRE) figurant/e.

extra... ['ɛkstrə] prefix extra... .

extract vt [ik'strækt] extraire; (tooth) arracher; (money, promise) soutirer // n ['ɛkstrækt] extrait m; **~ion** [ik'strækʃən] n (also descent) extraction f.

extradite ['ɛkstrədaɪt] vt extrader; **extradition** [-'dɪʃən] n extradition f.

extramarital [ɛkstrə'mærɪtl] a extra-conjugal(e).

extramural [ɛkstrə'mjuərl] a hors-faculté inv.

extraneous [ɛk'streɪnɪəs] a: **~ to** étranger(ère) à.

extraordinary [ik'strɔ:dnrɪ] a extraordinaire.

extra time [ɛkstrə'taɪm] n (FOOTBALL) prolongations fpl.

extravagant [ik'strævəgənt] a extravagant(e); (in spending) prodigue, dépensier(ère); (wasteful) dispendieux(euse).

extreme [ik'stri:m] a,n extrême (m); **~ly** ad extrêmement; **extremist** a,n extrémiste (m/f).

extremity [ik'strɛmətɪ] n extrémité f.

extricate ['ɛkstrɪkeɪt] vt: **to ~ sth (from)** dégager qch (de).

extrovert ['ɛkstrəvə:t] n extraverti/e.

exuberant [ig'zju:bərnt] a exubérant(e).

exude [ig'zju:d] vt exsuder; (fig) respirer; **the charm etc he ~s** le charme etc qui émane de lui.

exult [ig'zʌlt] vi exulter, jubiler.

eye [aɪ] n œil m (pl yeux); (of needle) trou m, chas m // vt examiner; **to keep an ~ on** surveiller; **in the public ~** en vue; **~ball** n globe m oculaire; **~bath** n œillère f (pour bains d'œil); **~brow** n sourcil m; **~-catching** a voyant(e), accrocheur(euse); **~drops** npl gouttes fpl pour les yeux; **~glass** n monocle m; **~lash** n cil m; **~let** ['aɪlɪt] n œillet m; **~lid** n paupière f; **~-opener** n révélation f; **~shadow** n ombre f à paupières; **~sight** n vue f; **~sore** n horreur f, chose f qui dépare or enlaidit; **~wash** n bain m d'œil; (fig) frime f; **~ witness** n témoin m oculaire.

eyrie ['ɪərɪ] n aire f.

F [ɛf] n (MUS) fa m.

F. abbr of Fahrenheit.

fable ['feɪbl] n fable f.

fabric ['fæbrɪk] n tissu m.

fabrication [fæbrɪ'keɪʃən] n invention(s) f(pl), fabulation f; fait m (or preuve f) forgé(e) de toutes pièces.

fabulous ['fæbjuləs] a fabuleux(euse); (col: super) formidable, sensationnel(le).

façade [fə'sɑ:d] n façade f.

face [feɪs] n visage m, figure f; expression f; grimace f; (of clock) cadran m; (of building) façade f; (side, surface) face f // vt faire face à; **to lose ~** perdre la face; **to pull a ~** faire une grimace; **in the ~ of** (difficulties etc) face à, devant; **on the ~ of it** à première vue; **to ~ up to** vt fus faire face à, affronter; **~ cloth** n gant m de toilette; **~ cream** n crème f pour le visage; **~ lift** n lifting m; (of façade etc) ravalement m, retapage m; **~ powder** n poudre f (pour le visage).

facet ['fæsɪt] n facette f.

facetious [fə'si:ʃəs] a facétieux(euse).

face-to-face ['feɪstə'feɪs] ad face à face.

face value ['feɪs'vælju:] n (of coin) valeur nominale; **to take sth at ~** (fig) prendre qch pour argent comptant.

facia ['feɪʃə] n = **fascia**.

facial ['feɪʃəl] a facial(e).

facile ['fæsaɪl] a facile.

facilitate [fə'sɪlɪteɪt] vt faciliter.

facility [fə'sɪlɪtɪ] n facilité f; **facilities** npl installations fpl, équipement m.

facing ['feɪsɪŋ] n (of wall etc) revêtement m; (SEWING) revers m.

facsimile [fæk'sɪmɪlɪ] n fac-similé m.

fact [fækt] n fait m; **in ~** en fait.

faction ['fækʃən] n faction f.

factor ['fæktə*] n facteur m.

factory ['fæktərɪ] n usine f, fabrique f.

factual ['fæktjuəl] a basé(e) sur les faits.

faculty ['fækəltɪ] n faculté f; (US: teaching staff) corps enseignant.

fad [fæd] n manie f; engouement m.

fade [feɪd] vi se décolorer, passer; (light, sound, hope) s'affaiblir, disparaître; (flower) se faner.

fag [fæg] n (col: cigarette) sèche f; (: chore): **what a ~!** quelle corvée!; **~ end** n mégot m; **~ged out** a (col) crevé(e).

fail [feɪl] vt (exam) échouer à; (candidate) recaler; (subj: courage, memory) faire défaut à // vi échouer; (supplies) manquer; (eyesight, health, light) baisser, s'affaiblir; **to ~ to do sth** (neglect) négliger de faire qch; (be unable) ne pas arriver or parvenir à faire qch; **without ~** à coup sûr; sans faute; **~ing** n défaut m // prep faute de; **~ure** ['feɪljə*] n échec m; (person) raté/e; (mechanical etc) défaillance f.

faint [feɪnt] a faible; (recollection) vague; (mark) à peine visible // n évanouissement m // vi s'évanouir; **to feel ~** défaillir; **~-hearted** a pusillanime; **~ly** ad faiblement; vaguement; **~ness** *n* faiblesse *f*.

fair [fɛə*] *a* blond(e); équitable, juste, impartial(e); (*skin, complexion*) pâle, blanc(blanche); (*weather*) beau(belle); (*good enough*) assez bon(ne); (*sizeable*) considérable // *ad* (*play*) franc-jeu // *n* foire *f*; **~ copy** *n* copie *f* au propre; corrigé *m*; **~ly** *ad* équitablement; (*quite*) assez; **~ness** *n* justice *f*, équité *f*, impartialité *f*.

fairy ['fɛərɪ] *n* fée *f*; **~ tale** *n* conte *m* de fées.

faith [feɪθ] *n* foi *f*; (*trust*) confiance *f*; (*sect*) culte *m*, religion *f*; **~ful** *a* fidèle; **~fully** *ad* fidèlement.

fake [feɪk] *n* (*painting etc*) faux *m*; (*photo*) trucage *m*; (*person*) imposteur *m* // *a* faux(fausse); simulé(e) // *vt* simuler; (*photo*) truquer; (*story*) fabriquer; **his illness is a ~** sa maladie est une comédie *or* de la simulation.

falcon ['fɔ:lkən] *n* faucon *m*.

fall [fɔ:l] *n* chute *f*; (*US: autumn*) automne *m* // *vi* (*pt* fell, *pp* fallen [fɛl, 'fɔ:lən]) tomber; **~s** *npl* (*waterfall*) chute *f* d'eau, cascade *f*; **to ~ flat** *vi* (*on one's face*) tomber de tout son long, s'étaler; (*joke*) tomber à plat; (*plan*) échouer; **to ~ back** *vt fus* se rabattre sur; **to ~ behind** *vi* prendre du retard; **to ~ down** *vi* (*person*) tomber; (*building, hopes*) s'effondrer, s'écrouler; **to ~ for** *vt fus* (*trick*) se laisser prendre à; (*person*) tomber amoureux . de; **to ~ in** *vi* s'effondrer; (*MIL*) se mettre en rangs; **to ~ off** *vi* tomber; (*diminish*) baisser, diminuer; **to ~ out** *vi* (*friends etc*) se brouiller; **to ~ through** *vi* (*plan, project*) tomber à l'eau.

fallacy ['fæləsɪ] *n* erreur *f*, illusion *f*.

fallen ['fɔ:lən] *pp of* fall.

fallible ['fæləbl] *a* faillible.

fallout ['fɔ:laut] *n* retombées (radioactives).

fallow ['fæləu] *a* en jachère; en friche.

false [fɔ:ls] *a* faux(fausse); **under ~ pretences** sous un faux prétexte; **~ alarm** *n* fausse alerte; **~hood** *n* mensonge *m*; **~ly** *ad* (*accuse*) à tort; **~ teeth** *npl* fausses dents.

falter ['fɔ:ltə*] *vi* chanceler, vaciller.

fame [feɪm] *n* renommée *f*, renom *m*.

familiar [fə'mɪlɪə*] *a* familier(ère); **to be ~ with** (*subject*) connaître; **~ity** [fəmɪlɪ'ærɪtɪ] *n* familiarité *f*; **~ize** [fə'mɪljəraɪz] *vt* familiariser.

family ['fæmɪlɪ] *n* famille *f*; **~ allowance** *n* allocations familiales; **~ business** *n* entreprise familiale; **~ doctor** *n* médecin *m* de famille; **~ life** *n* vie *f* de famille.

famine ['fæmɪn] *n* famine *f*.

famished ['fæmɪʃt] *a* affamé(e).

famous ['feɪməs] *a* célèbre; **~ly** *ad* (*get on*) fameusement, à merveille.

fan [fæn] *n* (*folding*) éventail *m*; (*ELEC*) ventilateur *m*; (*person*) fan *m*, admirateur/trice; supporter *m/f* // *vt* éventer; (*fire, quarrel*) attiser; **to ~ out** *vi* se déployer (en éventail).

fanatic [fə'nætɪk] *n* fanatique *m/f*; **~al** *a* fanatique.

fan belt ['fænbɛlt] *n* courroie *f* de ventilateur.

fancied ['fænsɪd] *a* imaginaire.

fanciful ['fænsɪful] *a* fantaisiste.

fancy ['fænsɪ] *n* fantaisie *f*, envie *f*; imagination *f* // *cpd* (de) fantaisie *inv* // *vt* (*feel like, want*) avoir envie de; **to take a ~ to** se prendre d'affection pour; s'enticher de; **it took** *or* **caught my ~** ça m'a plu; **to ~ that ... se figurer** *or* s'imaginer que ...; **he fancies her** elle lui plaît; **~ dress** *n* déguisement *m*, travesti *m*; **~-dress ball** *n* bal masqué *or* costumé.

fang [fæŋ] *n* croc *m*; (*of snake*) crochet *m*.

fanlight ['fænlaɪt] *n* imposte *f*.

fantastic [fæn'tæstɪk] *a* fantastique.

fantasy ['fæntəzɪ] *n* imagination *f*, fantaisie *f*; fantasme *m*; chimère *f*.

far [fɑ:*] *a*: **the ~ side/end** l'autre côté/bout // *ad* loin; **~ away, ~ off** au loin, dans le lointain; **~ better** beaucoup mieux; **~ from** loin de; **by ~** de loin, de beaucoup; **go as ~ as the farm** allez jusqu'à la ferme; **as ~ as I know** pour autant que je sache; **as ~ as possible** dans la mesure du possible; **~away** *a* lointain(e).

farce [fɑ:s] *n* farce *f*.

farcical ['fɑ:sɪkəl] *a* grotesque.

fare [fɛə*] *n* (*on trains, buses*) prix *m* du billet; (*in taxi*) prix de la course; (*passenger in taxi*) client *m*; (*food*) table *f*, chère *f* // *vi* se débrouiller.

Far East [fɑ:r'i:st] *n*: **the ~** l'Extrême-Orient *m*.

farewell [fɛə'wɛl] *excl, n* adieu *m*; **~ party** *n* soirée *f* d'adieux.

far-fetched ['fɑ:'fɛtʃt] *a* exagéré(e), poussé(e).

farm [fɑ:m] *n* ferme *f* // *vt* cultiver; **~er** *n* fermier/ère; cultivateur/trice; **~hand** *n* ouvrier/ère agricole; **~house** *n* (maison *f* de) ferme *f*; **~ing** *n* agriculture *f*; **intensive ~ing** culture intensive; **~land** *n* terres cultivées *or* arables; **~ worker** *n* = **~hand**; **~yard** *n* cour *f* de ferme.

far-reaching ['fɑ:'ri:tʃɪŋ] *a* d'une grande portée.

far-sighted ['fɑ:'saɪtɪd] *a* presbyte; (*fig*) prévoyant(e), qui voit loin.

fart [fɑ:t] (*col!*) *n* pet *m* // *vi* péter.

farther ['fɑ:ðə*] *ad* plus loin.

farthest ['fɑ:ðɪst] *superlative of* far.

fascia ['feɪʃə] *n* (*AUT*) (garniture *f* du) tableau *m* de bord.

fascinate ['fæsɪneɪt] *vt* fasciner, captiver; **fascination** [-'neɪʃən] *n* fascination *f*.

fascism ['fæʃɪzəm] *n* fascisme *m*.

fascist ['fæʃɪst] *a,n* fasciste (*m/f*).

fashion ['fæʃən] *n* mode *f*; (*manner*) façon *f*, manière *f* // *vt* façonner; **in ~** à la mode; **out of ~** démodé(e); **~able** *a* à la mode; **~ show** *n* défilé *m* de mannequins *or* de mode.

fast [fɑ:st] *a* rapide; (*clock*): **to be ~** avancer; (*dye, colour*) grand *or* bon teint *inv* // *ad* vite, rapidement; (*stuck, held*) solidement // *n* jeûne *m* // *vi* jeûner; **~ asleep** profondément endormi.

fasten ['fɑ:sn]. vt attacher, fixer; (coat) attacher, fermer // vi se fermer, s'attacher; ~er, ~ing n fermeture f, attache f.

fastidious [fæs'tɪdɪəs] a exigeant(e), difficile.

fat [fæt] a gros(se) // n graisse f; (on meat) gras m.

fatal ['feɪtl] a mortel(le); fatal(e); désastreux(euse); ~ism n fatalisme m; ~ity [fə'tælɪtɪ] n (road death etc) victime f, décès m; ~ly ad mortellement.

fate [feɪt] n destin m; (of person) sort m; to meet one's ~ trouver la mort; ~ful a fatidique.

father ['fɑ:ðə*] n père m; ~-in-law n beau-père m; ~ly a paternel(le).

fathom ['fæðəm] n brasse f (= 1828 mm) // vt (mystery) sonder, pénétrer.

fatigue [fəti:g] n fatigue f; (MIL) corvée f.

fatness ['fætnɪs] n corpulence f, grosseur f.

fatten ['fætn] vt, vi engraisser.

fatty ['fætɪ] a (food) gras(se).

fatuous ['fætjuəs] a stupide.

faucet ['fɔ:sɪt] n (US) robinet m.

fault [fɔ:lt] n faute f; (defect) défaut m; (GEO) faille f // vt trouver des défauts à, prendre en défaut; it's my ~ c'est de ma faute; to find ~ with trouver à redire or à critiquer à; at ~ fautif(ive), coupable; to a ~ à l'excès; ~less a sans faute, impeccable; irréprochable; ~y a défectueux(euse).

fauna ['fɔ:nə] n faune f.

favour, favor (US) ['feɪvə*] n faveur f; (help) service m // vt (proposition) être en faveur de; (pupil etc) favoriser; (team, horse) donner gagnant; to do ab a ~ rendre un service à qn; in ~ of en faveur de; ~able a favorable; (price) avantageux(euse); ~ably ad favorablement; ~ite [-rɪt] a,n favori(te); ~itism n favoritisme m.

fawn [fɔ:n] n faon m // a (also: ~-coloured) fauve // vi: to ~ (up)on flatter servilement.

fear [fɪə*] n crainte f, peur f // vt craindre; for ~ of de peur que + sub or de + infinitive; ~ful a craintif(ive); (sight, noise) affreux(euse), épouvantable; ~less a intrépide, sans peur.

feasibility [fi:zə'bɪlɪtɪ] n (of plan) possibilité f de réalisation.

feasible ['fi:zəbl] a faisable, réalisable.

feast [fi:st] n festin m, banquet m; (REL: also: ~ day) fête f // vi festoyer; to ~ on se régaler de.

feat [fi:t] n exploit m, prouesse f.

feather ['feðə*] n plume f; ~-weight n poids m plume inv.

feature ['fi:tʃə*] n caractéristique f; (article) chronique f, rubrique f // vt (subj: film) avoir pour vedette(s) // vi figurer (en bonne place); ~s npl (of face) traits mpl; ~ film n film principal m; ~less a anonyme, sans traits distinctifs.

February ['februərɪ] n février m.

fed [fed] pt, pp of feed; to be ~ up en avoir marre or plein le dos.

federal ['fedərəl] a fédéral(e).

federation [fedə'reɪʃən] n fédération f.

fee [fi:] n rémunération f; (of doctor, lawyer) honoraires mpl; (of school, college etc) frais mpl de scolarité; (for examination) droits mpl.

feeble ['fi:bl] a faible; ~-minded a faible d'esprit.

feed [fi:d] n (of baby) tétée f // vt (pt, pp fed [fed]) nourrir; (horse etc) donner à manger à; (machine) alimenter; (data, information): to ~ into fournir à; to ~ on vt se nourrir de; ~-back n feedback m; ~ing bottle n biberon m.

feel [fi:l] n sensation f // vt (pt, pp felt [felt]) toucher; tâter, palper; (cold, pain) sentir; (grief, anger) ressentir, éprouver; (think, believe): to ~ (that) trouver que; to ~ hungry/cold avoir faim/froid; to ~ lonely/better se sentir seul/mieux; to ~ sorry for avoir pitié de; it ~s soft c'est doux au toucher; it ~s like velvet on dirait du velours, ça ressemble au velours; to ~ like (want) avoir envie de; to ~ about or around fouiller, tâtonner; ~er n (of insect) antenne f; to put out a ~er tâter le terrain; ~ing n sensation f; sentiment m; my ~ing is that... j'estime que...

feet [fi:t] npl of foot.

feign [feɪn] vt feindre, simuler.

felicitous [fɪ'lɪsɪtəs] a heureux(euse).

fell [fel] pt of fall // vt (tree) abattre; (person) assommer; ~-walking n randonnée f en montagne.

fellow ['feləu] n type m; compagnon m; (of learned society) membre m; their ~ prisoners/students leurs camarades prisonniers/étudiants; ~ citizen n concitoyen/ne; ~ countryman n compatriote m; ~ men npl semblables mpl; ~ship n association f; amitié f, camaraderie f; sorte de bourse universitaire.

felony ['felənɪ] n crime m, forfait m.

felt [felt] pt, pp of feel // n feutre m; ~-tip pen n stylo-feutre m.

female ['fi:meɪl] n (ZOOL) femelle f; (pej: woman) bonne femme // a (BIOL, ELEC) femelle; (sex, character) féminin(e); (vote etc) des femmes; (child etc) du sexe féminin; male and ~ students étudiants et étudiantes; ~ impersonator n travesti m.

feminine ['femɪnɪn] a féminin(e) // n féminin m.

feminist ['femɪnɪst] n féministe m/f.

fence [fens] n barrière f; (col: person) receleur/euse // vt (also: ~ in) clôturer // vi faire de l'escrime; **fencing** n escrime m.

fend [fend] vi: to ~ for o.s. se débrouiller (tout seul).

fender ['fendə*] n garde-feu m inv; (US) gardeboue m inv; pare-chocs m inv.

ferment vi [fə'ment] fermenter // n ['fə:ment] agitation f, effervescence f; ~ation [-'teɪʃən] n fermentation f.

fern [fə:n] n fougère f.

ferocious [fə'rəuʃəs] a féroce.

ferocity [fə'rɔsɪtɪ] n férocité f.

ferry ['ferɪ] n (small) bac m; (large: also: ~-boat) ferry(-boat) m // vt transporter.

fertile ['fə:taɪl] a fertile; (BIOL) fécond(e);
~ **period** n période f de fécondité;
fertility [fə'tɪlɪtɪ] n fertilité f; fécondité f;
fertilize ['fə:tɪlaɪz] vt fertiliser; féconder;
fertilizer n engrais m.
fervent ['fə:vənt] a fervent(e), ardent(e).
fester ['fɛstə*] vi suppurer.
festival ['fɛstɪvəl] n (REL) fête f; (ART, MUS)
festival m.
festive ['fɛstɪv] a de fête; **the ~ season**
(Christmas) la période des fêtes.
festivities [fɛs'tɪvɪtɪz] npl réjouissances
fpl.
fetch [fɛtʃ] vt aller chercher; (sell for) se
vendre.
fetching ['fɛtʃɪŋ] a charmant(e).
fête [feɪt] n fête f, kermesse f.
fetish ['fɛtɪʃ] n fétiche m.
fetters ['fɛtəz] npl chaînes fpl.
fetus ['fi:təs] n (US) = **foetus.**
feud [fju:d] n dispute f, dissension f // vi
se disputer, se quereller; ~**al** a féodal(e);
~**alism** n féodalité f.
fever ['fi:və*] n fièvre f; ~**ish** a
fièvreux(euse), fébrile.
few [fju:] a peu de; **they were ~** ils
étaient peu (nombreux); **a ~** a quelques
// pronoun quelques-uns; ~**er** a moins
de; moins (nombreux); ~**est** a le moins
nombreux.
fiancé [fɪ'ɑ̃:ŋseɪ] n fiancé m; ~**e** n fiancée
f.
fiasco [fɪ'æskəu] n fiasco m.
fib [fɪb] n bobard m.
fibre, fiber (US) ['faɪbə*] n fibre f; ~-
glass n fibre de verre.
fickle ['fɪkl] a inconstant(e), volage,
capricieux(euse).
fiction ['fɪkʃən] n romans mpl, littérature
f romanesque; fiction f; ~**al** a fictif(ive).
fictitious [fɪk'tɪʃəs] a fictif(ive),
imaginaire.
fiddle ['fɪdl] n (MUS) violon m; (cheating)
combine f; escroquerie f // vt (accounts)
falsifier, maquiller; **to ~ with** vt fus
tripoter; ~**r** n violoniste m/f.
fidelity [fɪ'dɛlɪtɪ] n fidélité f.
fidget ['fɪdʒɪt] vi se trémousser, remuer;
~**y** a agité(e), qui a la bougeotte.
field [fi:ld] n champ m; (fig) domaine m,
champ m; (SPORT: ground) terrain m; ~
glasses npl jumelles fpl; ~ **marshal** n
maréchal m; ~**work** n travaux mpl
pratiques (sur le terrain).
fiend [fi:nd] n démon m; ~**ish** a
diabolique.
fierce [fɪəs] a (look) féroce, sauvage;
(wind, attack) (très) violent(e); (fighting,
enemy) acharné(e).
fiery ['faɪərɪ] a ardent(e), brûlant(e);
fougueux(euse).
fifteen [fɪf'ti:n] num quinze.
fifth [fɪfθ] num cinquième.
fiftieth ['fɪftɪɪθ] num cinquantième.
fifty ['fɪftɪ] num cinquante.
fig [fɪg] n figue f.
fight [faɪt] n bagarre f; (MIL) combat m;
(against cancer etc) lutte f // vb (pt, pp
fought [fɔ:t]) vt se battre contre; (cancer,
alcoholism) combattre, lutter contre // vi

se battre; ~**er** n lutteur m (fig); (plane)
chasseur m; ~**ing** n combats mpl.
figment ['fɪgmənt] n: **a ~ of the
imagination** une invention.
figurative ['fɪgjurətɪv] a figuré(e).
figure ['fɪgə*] n (DRAWING, GEOM) figure f;
(number, cipher) chiffre m; (body, outline)
silhouette f, ligne f, formes fpl // vt (US)
supposer // vi (appear) figurer; (US: make
sense) s'expliquer; **to ~ out** vt arriver à
comprendre; calculer; ~**head** n (NAUT)
figure f de proue; (pej) prête-nom m;
figure skating n figures imposées (en
patinage).
filament ['fɪləmənt] n filament m.
file [faɪl] n (tool) lime f; (dossier) dossier
m; (folder) classeur m; (row) file f // vt
(nails, wood) limer; (papers) classer; (LAW:
claim) faire enregistrer; déposer; **to ~
in/out** vi entrer/sortir l'un derrière
l'autre; **to ~ past** vt fus défiler devant.
filing ['faɪlɪŋ] n (travaux mpl de)
classement m; ~**s** npl limaille f; ~
cabinet n classeur m (meuble).
fill [fɪl] vt remplir // n: **to eat one's ~**
manger à sa faim; **to ~ in** vt (hole)
boucher; (form) remplir; **to ~ up** vt
remplir // vi (AUT) faire le plein; ~ **it up,
please** (AUT) le plein, s'il vous plaît.
fillet ['fɪlɪt] n filet m // vt préparer en filets.
filling ['fɪlɪŋ] n (CULIN) garniture f, farce f;
(for tooth) plombage m; ~ **station** n
station f d'essence.
fillip ['fɪlɪp] n coup m de fouet (fig).
film [fɪlm] n film m; (PHOT) pellicule f, film
m // vt (scene) filmer; ~ **star** n vedette
f de cinéma; ~**strip** n (film m pour)
projection f fixe.
filter ['fɪltə*] n filtre m // vt filtrer; ~ **lane**
n (AUT) voie f de sortie; ~ **tip** n bout m
filtre.
filth [fɪlθ] n saleté f; ~**y** a sale,
dégoûtant(e); (language) ordurier (ère),
grossier(ère).
fin [fɪn] n (of fish) nageoire f.
final ['faɪnl] a final(e), dernier(ère);
définitif(ive) // n (SPORT) finale f; ~**s** npl
(SCOL) examens mpl de dernière année; ~**e**
[fɪ'nɑ:lɪ] n finale m; ~**ist** n (SPORT) finaliste
m/f; ~**ize** vt mettre au point; ~**ly** ad
(lastly) en dernier lieu; (eventually) enfin,
finalement; (irrevocably) définitivement.
finance [faɪ'næns] n finance f; ~**s** npl
finances fpl // vt financer.
financial [faɪ'nænʃəl] a financier (ère);
~**ly** ad financièrement; ~ **year** n année
f budgétaire.
financier [faɪ'nænsɪə*] n financier m.
find [faɪnd] vt (pt, pp **found** [faund])
trouver; (lost object) retrouver // n
trouvaille f, découverte f; **to ~ sb guilty**
(LAW) déclarer qn coupable; **to ~ out** vt
se renseigner sur; (truth, secret)
découvrir; (person) démasquer; **to ~ out
about** se renseigner sur; (by chance)
apprendre; ~**ings** npl (LAW) conclusions
fpl, verdict m; (of report) constatations fpl.
fine [faɪn] n a beau(belle); excellent(e);
fin(e) // ad (well) très bien; (small) fin,
finement // n (LAW) amende f;
contravention f // vt (LAW) condamner à

une amende ; donner une contravention à ; ~ **arts** npl beaux-arts mpl.

finery ['faɪnərɪ] n parure f.

finesse [fɪ'nɛs] n finesse f.

finger ['fɪŋgə*] n doigt m // vt palper, toucher ; ~**nail** n ongle m (de la main) ; ~**print** n empreinte digitale ; ~**stall** n doigtier m ; ~**tip** n bout m du doigt.

finicky ['fɪnɪkɪ] a tatillon(ne), méticuleux(euse) ; minutieux(euse).

finish ['fɪnɪʃ] n fin f ; (SPORT) arrivée f ; (polish etc) finition f // vt finir, terminer // vi finir, se terminer ; (session) s'achever ; **to** ~ **off** vt finir, terminer ; (kill) achever ; **to** ~ **up** vi,vt finir ; ~**ing line** n ligne f d'arrivée ; ~**ing school** n institution privée (pour jeunes filles).

finite ['faɪnaɪt] a fini(e) ; (verb) conjugué(e).

Finland ['fɪnlənd] n Finlande f.

Finn [fɪn] n Finnois/e ; Finlandais/e ; ~**ish** a finnois(e) ; finlandais(e) // n (LING) finnois m.

fiord [fjɔ:d] n fjord m.

fir [fə:*] n sapin m.

fire ['faɪə*] n feu m ; incendie m // vt (discharge): **to** ~ **a gun** tirer un coup de feu ; (fig) enflammer, animer ; (dismiss) mettre à la porte, renvoyer // vi tirer, faire feu ; **on** ~ en feu ; ~ **alarm** n avertisseur m d'incendie ; ~**arm** n arme f à feu ; ~ **brigade** n (régiment m de sapeurs-)pompiers mpl ; ~ **engine** n pompe f à incendie ; ~ **escape** n escalier m de secours ; ~ **extinguisher** n extincteur m ; ~**man** n pompier m ; ~**master** n capitaine m des pompiers ; ~**place** n cheminée f ; ~**proof** a ignifuge ; ~**side** n foyer m, coin m du feu ; ~ **station** n caserne f de pompiers ; ~**wood** n bois m de chauffage ; ~**work** n feu m d'artifice ; ~**works** npl (display) feu(x) d'artifice.

firing ['faɪərɪŋ] n (MIL) feu m, tir m ; ~ **squad** n peloton m d'exécution.

firm [fə:m] a ferme // n compagnie f, firme f ; ~**ly** ad fermement ; ~**ness** n fermeté f.

first [fə:st] a premier(ère) // ad (before others) le premier, la première ; (before other things) en premier, d'abord ; (when listing reasons etc) en premier lieu, premièrement // n (person: in race) premier/ère ; (SCOL) mention f très bien ; (AUT) première f ; **at** ~ au commencement, au début ; ~ **of all** tout d'abord, pour commencer ; ~ **aid** premiers secours or soins ; ~-**aid kit** n trousse f à pharmacie ; ~-**class** a de première classe ; ~-**hand** a de première main ; ~ **lady** n (US) femme f du président ; ~**ly** ad premièrement, en premier lieu ; ~ **name** n prénom m ; ~ **night** n (THEATRE) première f ; ~-**rate** a excellent(e).

fir tree ['fə:tri:] n sapin m.

fiscal ['fɪskəl] a fiscal(e).

fish [fɪʃ] n,pl inv poisson m ; poissons mpl // vt,vi pêcher ; **to** ~ **a river** pêcher dans une rivière ; **to go** ~**ing** aller à la pêche ; ~**erman** n pêcheur m ; ~**ery** n pêcherie f ; ~ **fingers** npl bâtonnets de poisson (congelés) ; ~ **hook** n hameçon m ; ~**ing**

boat n barque f de pêche ; ~**ing line** n ligne f (de pêche) ; ~**ing rod** n canne f à pêche ; ~**ing tackle** n attirail m de pêche ; ~ **market** n marché m au poisson ; ~**monger** n marchand m de poisson ; ~**slice** n pelle f à poisson ; ~**y** a (fig) suspect(e), louche.

fission ['fɪʃən] n fission f.

fissure ['fɪʃə*] n fissure f.

fist [fɪst] n poing m.

fit [fɪt] a (MED, SPORT) en (bonne) forme ; (proper) convenable ; approprié(e) // vt (subj: clothes) aller à ; (adjust) ajuster ; (put in, attach) installer, poser ; adapter ; (equip) équiper, garnir, munir // vi (clothes) aller ; (parts) s'adapter ; (in space, gap) entrer, s'adapter // n (MED) accès m, crise f ; (of coughing) quinte f ; ~ **to** en état de ; ~ **for** digne de ; apte à ; **this dress is a tight/good** ~ cette robe est un peu juste/(me) va très bien ; **by** ~**s and starts** par à-coups ; **to** ~ **in** vi s'accorder ; s'adapter ; **to** ~ **out** (also: ~ up) vt équiper ; ~**ful** a intermittent(e) ; ~**ment** n meuble encastré, élément m ; ~**ness** n (MED) forme f physique ; (of remark) à-propos m, justesse f ; ~**ter** n monteur m ; (DRESSMAKING) essayeur/euse ; ~**ting** a approprié(e) // n (of dress) essayage m ; (of piece of equipment) pose f, installation f ; ~**tings** npl installations fpl.

five [faɪv] num cinq ; ~**r** n (Brit: col) billet m de cinq livres.

fix [fɪks] vt fixer ; arranger ; (mend) réparer // n: **to be in a** ~ être dans le pétrin ; ~**ed** [fɪkst] a (prices etc) fixe ; ~**ture** ['fɪkstʃə*] n installation f (fixe) ; (SPORT) rencontre f (au programme).

fizz [fɪz] vi pétiller.

fizzle ['fɪzl] vi pétiller ; **to** ~ **out** vi rater.

fizzy ['fɪzɪ] a pétillant(e) ; gazeux(euse).

fjord [fjɔ:d] n = **fiord**.

flabbergasted ['flæbəga:stɪd] a sidéré(e), ahuri(e).

flabby ['flæbɪ] a mou(molle).

flag [flæg] n drapeau m ; (also: ~**stone**) dalle f // vi faiblir ; fléchir ; **to** ~ **down** vt héler, faire signe (de s'arrêter) à ; ~ **of convenience** n pavillon m de complaisance.

flagon ['flægən] n bonbonne f.

flagpole ['flægpəul] n mât m.

flagrant ['fleɪgrənt] a flagrant(e).

flair [flɛə*] n flair m.

flake [fleɪk] n (of rust, paint) écaille f ; (of snow, soap powder) flocon m // vi (also: ~ off) s'écailler.

flamboyant [flæm'bɔɪənt] a flamboyant(e), éclatant(e) ; (person) haut(e) en couleur.

flame [fleɪm] n flamme f.

flamingo [flə'mɪŋgəu] n flamant m (rose).

flammable ['flæməbl] a inflammable.

flan [flæn] n tarte f.

Flanders ['flɑ:ndəz] n Flandre(s) f(pl).

flange [flændʒ] n boudin m ; collerette f.

flank [flæŋk] n flanc m // vt flanquer.

flannel ['flænl] n (also: **face** ~) gant m de toilette ; (fabric) flanelle f ; (col) baratin m ; ~**s** npl pantalon m de flanelle.

flap [flæp] n (of pocket, envelope) rabat m // vt (wings) battre (de) // vi (sail, flag) claquer; (col: also: be in a ~) paniquer.

flare [flɛə*] n fusée éclairante; (in skirt etc) évasement m; to ~ up vi s'embraser; (fig: person) se mettre en colère, s'emporter; (: revolt) éclater; ~d a (trousers) à jambes évasées.

flash [flæʃ] n éclair m; (also: news ~) flash m (d'information); (PHOT) flash m // vt (switch on) allumer (brièvement); (direct): to ~ sth at braquer qch sur; (display) étaler, exhiber; (send: message) câbler // vi briller; jeter des éclairs; (light on ambulance etc) clignoter; in a ~ en un clin d'œil; to ~ one's headlights faire un appel de phares; he ~ed by or past il passa (devant nous) comme un éclair; ~back n flashback m, retour m en arrière; ~ bulb n ampoule f de flash; ~er n (AUT) clignotant m.

flashy ['flæʃi] a (pej) tape-à-l'œil inv, tapageur(euse).

flask [flɑ:sk] n flacon m, bouteille f; (CHEM) ballon m; (also: vacuum ~) bouteille f thermos ®.

flat [flæt] a plat(e); (tyre) dégonflé(e), à plat; (denial) catégorique; (MUS) bémolisé(e) // n (rooms) appartement m; (MUS) bémol m; (AUT) crevaison f, pneu crevé; to be ~-footed avoir les pieds plats; ~ly ad catégoriquement; ~ness n (of land) absence f de relief, aspect plat; ~ten vt (also: ~ten out) aplatir.

flatter ['flætə*] vt flatter; ~er n flatteur m; ~ing a flatteur(euse); ~y n flatterie f.

flatulence ['flætjuləns] n flatulence f.

flaunt [flɔ:nt] vt faire étalage de.

flavour, flavor (US) ['fleivə*] n goût m, saveur f; (of ice cream etc) parfum m // vt parfumer, aromatiser; (send: message) vanilla~ed à l'arôme de vanille, vanillé(e); to give or add ~ to donner du goût à, relever; ~ing n arôme m (synthétique).

flaw [flɔ:] n défaut m; ~less a sans défaut.

flax [flæks] n lin m; ~en a blond(e).

flea [fli:] n puce f.

fledg(e)ling ['fledʒliŋ] n oisillon m.

flee, pt, pp **fled** [fli:, fled] vt fuir, s'enfuir de // vi fuir, s'enfuir.

fleece [fli:s] n toison f // vt (col) voler, filouter.

fleet [fli:t] n flotte f; (of lorries etc) parc m; convoi m.

fleeting ['fli:tiŋ] a fugace, fugitif(ive); (visit) très bref(brève).

Flemish ['flemiʃ] a flamand(e) // n (LING) flamand m; the ~ les Flamands.

flesh [fleʃ] n chair f; ~ wound n blessure superficielle.

flew [flu:] pt of **fly**.

flex [fleks] n fil m or câble m électrique (souple) // vt fléchir; (muscles) tendre; ~ibility [-'biliti] n flexibilité f; ~ible a flexible.

flick [flik] n petite tape; chiquenaude f; sursaut m; ~ knife n couteau m à cran d'arrêt; to ~ through vt fus feuilleter.

flicker ['flikə*] vi vaciller // n vacillement m; a ~ of light une brève lueur.

flier ['flaiə*] n aviateur m.

flight [flait] n vol m; (escape) fuite f; (also: ~ of steps) escalier m; to take ~ prendre la fuite; to put to ~ mettre en fuite; ~ deck n (AVIAT) poste m de pilotage; (NAUT) pont m d'envol.

flimsy ['flimzi] a (partition, fabric) peu solide, mince; (excuse) pauvre, mince.

flinch [flintʃ] vi tressaillir; to ~ from se dérober à, reculer devant.

fling, pt, pp **flung** [fliŋ, flʌŋ] vt jeter, lancer.

flint [flint] n silex m; (in lighter) pierre f (à briquet).

flip [flip] n chiquenaude f.

flippant ['flipənt] a désinvolte, irrévérencieux(euse).

flirt [flə:t] vi flirter // n flirteuse f; ~ation [-'teiʃən] n flirt m.

flit [flit] vi voleter.

float [fləut] n flotteur m; (in procession) char m // vi flotter // vt faire flotter; (loan, business) lancer; ~ing a flottant(e).

flock [flɔk] n troupeau m; (of people) foule f.

flog [flɔg] vt fouetter.

flood [flʌd] n inondation f; (of words, tears etc) flot m, torrent m // vt inonder; in ~ en crue; ~ing n inondation f; ~light n projecteur m // vt éclairer aux projecteurs, illuminer.

floor [flɔ:*] n sol m; (storey) étage m; (fig: at meeting): the ~ l'assemblée f, les membres mpl de l'assemblée // vt terrasser; on the ~ par terre; ground ~ (Brit), first ~ (US) rez-de-chaussée m; first ~ (Brit), second ~ (US) premier étage m; ~board n planche f (du plancher); ~ show n spectacle m de variétés.

flop [flɔp] n fiasco m // vi (fail) faire fiasco.

floppy ['flɔpi] a lâche, flottant(e); ~ hat n chapeau m à bords flottants.

flora ['flɔ:rə] n flore f.

floral ['flɔ:rl] a floral(e).

florid ['flɔrid] a (complexion) fleuri(e); (style) plein(e) de fioritures.

florist ['flɔrist] n fleuriste m/f.

flounce [flauns] n volant m; to ~ out vi sortir dans un mouvement d'humeur.

flounder ['flaundə*] vi patauger.

flour ['flauə*] n farine f.

flourish ['flʌriʃ] vi prospérer // vt brandir // n fioriture f; (of trumpets) fanfare f; ~ing a prospère, florissant(e).

flout [flaut] vt se moquer de, faire fi de.

flow [fləu] n flot m; courant m; circulation f; (tide) flux m // vi couler; (traffic) s'écouler; (robes, hair) flotter; ~ chart n organigramme m.

flower ['flauə*] n fleur f // vi fleurir; ~ bed n plate-bande f; ~pot n pot m (à fleurs); ~y a fleuri(e).

flown [fləun] pp of **fly**.

flu [flu:] n grippe f.

fluctuate ['flʌktjueit] vi varier, fluctuer; **fluctuation** [-'eiʃən] n fluctuation f, variation f.

fluency ['flu:ənsi] n facilité f, aisance f.

fluent ['flu:ənt] a (speech) coulant(e), aisé(e); he speaks ~ French, he's ~ in French il parle le français couramment;

~ly *ad* couramment; avec aisance *or* facilité.

fluff [flʌf] *n* duvet *m*; peluche *f*; **~y** *a* duveteux(euse); pelucheux (euse); **~y toy** *n* jouet *m* en peluche.

fluid ['fluːɪd] *a,n* fluide (*m*); **~ ounce** *n* = 0.028 l; 0.05 pints.

fluke [fluːk] *n* (*col*) coup *m* de veine *or* de chance.

flung [flʌŋ] *pt,pp* of **fling**.

fluorescent [fluə'rɛsnt] *a* fluorescent(e).

fluoride ['fluəraɪd] *n* fluor *m*.

fluorine ['fluəriːn] *n* fluor *m*.

flurry ['flʌrɪ] *n* (*of snow*) rafale *f*, bourrasque *f*; **~ of activity/excitement** affairement *m*/excitation *f* soudain(e).

flush [flʌʃ] *n* rougeur *f*; excitation *f* // *vt* nettoyer à grande eau // *vi* rougir // *a*: **~ with** au ras de, de niveau avec; **~ against** tout contre; **to ~ the toilet** tirer la chasse (d'eau); **~ed** *a* (tout(e)) rouge.

fluster ['flʌstə*] *n* agitation *f*, trouble *m*; **~ed** *a* énervé(e).

flute [fluːt] *n* flûte *f*.

fluted ['fluːtɪd] *a* cannelé(e).

flutter ['flʌtə*] *n* agitation *f*; (*of wings*) battement *m* // *vi* battre des ailes, voleter; (*person*) aller et venir dans une grande agitation.

flux [flʌks] *n*: **in a state of ~** fluctuant sans cesse.

fly [flaɪ] *n* (*insect*) mouche *f*; (*on trousers*: *also*: **flies**) braguette *f* // *vb* (*pt* **flew**, *pp* **flown** [fluː, fləun]) *vt* piloter; (*passengers, cargo*) transporter (par avion); (*distances*) parcourir // *vi* voler; (*passengers*) aller en avion; (*escape*) s'enfuir, fuir; (*flag*) se déployer; **to ~ open** *vi* s'ouvrir brusquement; **~ing** *n* (*activity*) aviation *f* // *a*: **~ing visit** visite *f* éclair *inv*; **with ~ing colours** haut la main; **~ing buttress** *n* arc-boutant *m*; **~ing saucer** *n* soucoupe volante; **~ing start** *n*: **to get off to a ~ing start** faire un excellent départ; **~over** *n* (*Brit*: *bridge*) saut-de-mouton *m*; **~past** *n* défilé aérien; **~sheet** *n* (*for tent*) double toit *m*; **~wheel** *n* volant *m* (de commande).

F.M. (*abbr of frequency modulation*) F.M., M.F. (modulation *f* de fréquence).

foal [fəul] *n* poulain *m*.

foam [fəum] *n* écume *f*; (*on beer*) mousse *f*; (*also*: **plastic ~**) mousse cellulaire *or* de plastique // *vi* écumer; (*soapy water*) mousser; **~ rubber** *n* caoutchouc *m* mousse.

fob [fɔb] *vt*: **to ~ sb off with** refiler à qn; se débarrasser de qn avec.

focal ['fəukəl] *a* focal(e).

focus ['fəukəs] *n* (*pl*: **~es**) foyer *m*; (*of interest*) centre *m* // *vt* (*field glasses etc*) mettre au point; (*light rays*) faire converger; **in ~** au point; **out of ~** pas au point.

fodder ['fɔdə*] *n* fourrage *m*.

foe [fəu] *n* ennemi *m*.

foetus ['fiːtəs] *n* fœtus *m*.

fog [fɔg] *n* brouillard *m*; **~gy** *a*: **it's ~gy** il y a du brouillard.

foible ['fɔɪbl] *n* faiblesse *f*.

foil [fɔɪl] *vt* déjouer, contrecarrer // *n* feuille *f* de métal; (*also*: **kitchen ~**) papier *m* d'alu(minium); (*FENCING*) fleuret *m*; **to act as a ~ to** (*fig*) servir de repoussoir *or* de faire-valoir à.

fold [fəuld] *n* (*bend, crease*) pli *m*; (*AGR*) parc *m* à moutons; (*fig*) bercail *m* // *vt* plier; **to ~ up** *vi* (*map etc*) se plier, se replier; (*business*) fermer boutique // *vt* (*map etc*) plier, replier; **~er** *n* (*for papers*) chemise *f*; classeur *m*; (*brochure*) dépliant *m*; **~ing** *a* (*chair, bed*) pliant(e).

foliage ['fəulɪɪdʒ] *n* feuillage *m*.

folk [fəuk] *npl* gens *mpl* // *a* folklorique; **~s** *npl* famille *f*, parents *mpl*; **~lore** ['fəuklɔː°] *n* folklore *m*; **~song** *n* chanson *f* folklorique (*gén de l'Ouest américain*).

follow ['fɔləu] *vt* suivre // *vi* suivre; (*result*) s'ensuivre; **he ~ed suit** il fit de même; **to ~ up** *vt* (*victory*) tirer parti de; (*letter, offer*) donner suite à; (*case*) suivre; **~er** *n* disciple *m/f*, partisan/e; **~ing** *a* suivant(e) // *n* partisans *mpl*, disciples *mpl*.

folly ['fɔlɪ] *n* inconscience *f*; sottise *f*; (*building*) folie *f*.

fond [fɔnd] *a* (*memory, look*) tendre, affectueux(euse); **to be ~ of** aimer beaucoup.

fondle ['fɔndl] *vt* caresser.

fondness ['fɔndnɪs] *n* (*for things*) attachement *m*; (*for people*) sentiments affectueux; **a special ~ for** une prédilection pour.

font [fɔnt] *n* fonts baptismaux.

food [fuːd] *n* nourriture *f*; **~ mixer** *n* mixeur *m*; **~ poisoning** *n* intoxication *f* alimentaire; **~stuffs** *npl* denrées *fpl* alimentaires.

fool [fuːl] *n* idiot/e; (*HISTORY*: *of king*) bouffon *m*, fou *m*; (*CULIN*) purée *f* de fruits à la crème // *vt* berner, duper // *vi* (*gen*: **~ around**) faire l'idiot *or* l'imbécile; **~hardy** *a* téméraire, imprudent(e); **~ish** *a* idiot(e), stupide; imprudent(e); écervelé(e); **~proof** *a* (*plan etc*) infaillible.

foot [fut] *n* (*pl*: **feet** [fiːt]) pied *m*; (*measure*) pied (= 304 mm; 12 inches); (*of animal*) patte *f* // *vt* (*bill*) casquer, payer; **on ~** à pied; **~ and mouth (disease)** *n* fièvre aphteuse; **~ball** *n* ballon *m* (de football); (*sport*) football *m*; **~baller** *n* footballeur *m*; **~brake** *n* frein *m* à pied; **~bridge** *n* passerelle *f*; **~hills** *npl* contreforts *mpl*; **~hold** *n* prise *f* (de pied); **~ing** *n* (*fig*) position *f*; **to lose one's ~ing** perdre pied; **on an equal ~ing** sur pied d'égalité; **~lights** *npl* rampe *f*; **~man** *n* laquais *m*; **~note** *n* note *f* (en bas de page); **~path** *n* sentier *m*; (*in street*) trottoir *m*; **~rest** *n* marchepied *m*; **~sore** *a* aux pieds endoloris; **~step** *n* pas *m*; **~wear** *n* chaussure(s) *f(pl)* (*terme générique en anglais*).

for [fɔː°] *prep* pour; (*during*) pendant; (*in spite of*) malgré // *cj* car; **I haven't seen him ~ a week** je ne l'ai vu depuis une semaine, cela fait une semaine que je ne l'ai pas vu; **he went down ~ the paper** il est descendu chercher le journal; **~ sale** à vendre.

forage ['fɔrɪdʒ] *n* fourrage *m* // *vi* fourrager, fouiller; **~ cap** *n* calot *m*.

foray ['fɔreɪ] n incursion f.

forbad(e) [fə'bæd] pt of **forbid**.

forbearing /fɔ:'bɛərɪŋ] a patient(e), tolérant(e).

forbid, pt **forbad(e)**, pp **forbidden** [fə'bɪd, -'bæd, -'bɪdn] vt défendre, interdire; ~**den** a défendu(e); ~**ding** a d'aspect d'allure sévère or sombre.

force [fɔ:s] n force f // vt forcer; **the F~s** npl l'armée f; **in** ~ en force; **to come into** ~ entrer en vigueur; ~**d** [fɔ:st] a forcé(e); ~**ful** a énergique, volontaire.

forceps ['fɔ:sɛps] npl forceps m.

forcibly ['fɔ:səblɪ] ad par la force, de force; (vigorously) énergiquement.

ford [fɔ:d] n gué m // vt passer à gué.

fore [fɔ:*] n: **to the** ~ en évidence.

forearm ['fɔ:rɑ:m] n avant-bras m inv.

foreboding [fɔ:'bəudɪŋ] n pressentiment m (néfaste).

forecast ['fɔ:kɑ:st] n prévision f // vt (irg: like **cast**) prévoir.

forecourt ['fɔ:kɔ:t] n (of garage) devant m.

forefathers ['fɔ:fɑ:ðəz] npl ancêtres mpl.

forefinger ['fɔ:fɪŋgə*] n index m.

forego, pt **forewent**, pp **foregone** [fɔ:'gəu, -'wɛnt, -'gɔn] vt = **forgo**.

foregone ['fɔ:gɔn] a: **it's a** ~ **conclusion** c'est à prévoir, c'est couru d'avance.

foreground ['fɔ:graund] n premier plan.

forehead ['fɔrɪd] n front m.

foreign ['fɔrɪn] a étranger(ère); (trade) extérieur(e); ~ **body** n corps étranger; ~**er** n étranger/ère; ~ **exchange market** n marché m des devises; ~ **exchange rate** n cours m des devises; ~ **minister** n ministre m des Affaires étrangères.

foreleg ['fɔ:lɛg] n patte f de devant; jambe antérieure.

foreman ['fɔ:mən] n contremaître m.

foremost ['fɔ:məust] a le(la) plus en vue; premier(ère).

forensic [fə'rɛnsɪk] a: ~ **medicine** médecine légale; ~ **expert** expert m de la police, expert légiste.

forerunner ['fɔ:rʌnə*] n précurseur m.

foresee, pt **foresaw**, pp **foreseen** [fɔ:'si:, -'sɔ:, -'si:n] vt prévoir; ~**able** a prévisible.

foresight ['fɔ:saɪt] n prévoyance f.

forest ['fɔrɪst] n forêt f.

forestall [fɔ:'stɔ:l] vt devancer.

forestry ['fɔrɪstrɪ] n sylviculture f.

foretaste ['fɔ:teɪst] n avant-goût m.

foretell, pt,pp **foretold** [fɔ:'tɛl, -'təuld] vt prédire.

forever [fə'rɛvə*] ad pour toujours; (fig) continuellement.

forewent [fɔ:'wɛnt] pt of **forego**.

foreword ['fɔ:wə:d] n avant-propos m inv.

forfeit ['fɔ:fɪt] n prix m, rançon f // vt perdre; (one's life, health) payer de.

forgave [fə'geɪv] pt of **forgive**.

forge [fɔ:dʒ] n forge f // vt (signature) contrefaire; (wrought iron) forger; **to** ~ **documents/a will** fabriquer de faux papiers/un faux testament; **to** ~ **money** fabriquer de la fausse monnaie; **to** ~ **ahead** vi pousser de l'avant, prendre de l'avance; ~**r** n faussaire m; ~**ry** n faux m, contrefaçon f.

forget, pt **forgot**, pp **forgotten** [fə'gɛt, -'gɔt, -'gɔtn] vt,vi oublier; ~**ful** a distrait(e), étourdi(e); ~**ful** of oublieux(euse) de; ~**fulness** n tendance f aux oublis; (oblivion) oubli m.

forgive, pt **forgave**, pp **forgiven** [fə'gɪv, -'geɪv, -'gɪvn] vt pardonner; ~**ness** n pardon m.

forgo, pt **forwent**, pp **forgone** [fɔ:'gəu, -'wɛnt, -'gɔn] vt renoncer à.

forgot [fə'gɔt] pt of **forget**.

forgotten [fə'gɔtn] pp of **forget**.

fork [fɔ:k] n (for eating) fourchette f; (for gardening) fourche f; (of roads) bifurcation f; (of railways) embranchement m // vi (road) bifurquer; **to** ~ **out** (col: pay) vt allonger, se fendre de // vi casquer; ~**ed** [fɔ:kt] a (lightning) en zigzags, ramifié(e); ~**-lift truck** n chariot élévateur.

form [fɔ:m] n forme f; (SCOL) classe f; (questionnaire) formulaire m // vt former; **in top** ~ en pleine forme.

formal ['fɔ:məl] a (offer, receipt) en bonne et due forme; (person) cérémonieux(euse), à cheval sur les convenances; (occasion, dinner) officiel(le); (ART, PHILOSOPHY) formel(le); ~**ly** ad officiellement; formellement; cérémonieusement.

format ['fɔ:mæt] n format m.

formation [fɔ:'meɪʃən] n formation f.

formative ['fɔ:mətɪv] a: ~ **years** années fpl d'apprentissage (fig) or de formation (d'un enfant, d'un adolescent).

former ['fɔ:mə*] a ancien(ne) (before n), précédent(e); **the** ~ ... **the latter** le premier ... le second, celui-là ... celui-ci; ~**ly** ad autrefois.

formidable ['fɔ:mɪdəbl] a redoutable.

formula ['fɔ:mjulə] n formule f.

formulate ['fɔ:mjuleɪt] vt formuler.

forsake, pt **forsook**, pp **forsaken** [fə'seɪk, -'suk, -'seɪkən] vt abandonner.

fort [fɔ:t] n fort m.

forte ['fɔ:tɪ] n (point) fort m.

forth [fɔ:θ] ad en avant; **to go back and** ~ aller et venir; **and so** ~ et ainsi de suite; ~**coming** a qui va paraître or avoir lieu prochainement; (character) ouvert(e), communicatif(ive); ~**right** a franc(franche), direct(e).

fortieth ['fɔ:tɪɪθ] num quarantième.

fortification [fɔ:tɪfɪ'keɪʃən] n fortification f.

fortify ['fɔ:tɪfaɪ] vt fortifier; **fortified wine** n vin liquoreux or de liqueur.

fortitude ['fɔ:tɪtju:d] n courage m, force f d'âme.

fortnight ['fɔ:tnaɪt] n quinzaine f, quinze jours mpl; ~**ly** a bimensuel(le) // ad tous les quinze jours.

fortress ['fɔ:trɪs] n forteresse f.

fortuitous [fɔ:'tju:ɪtəs] a fortuit(e).

fortunate ['fɔ:tʃənɪt] a: **to be** ~ avoir de la chance; **it is** ~ **that** c'est une chance que, il est heureux que; ~**ly** ad heureusement, par bonheur.

fortune ['fɔ:tʃən] n chance f; (wealth) fortune f; ~**teller** n diseuse f de bonne aventure.

forty ['fɔ:tɪ] *num* quarante.

forum ['fɔ:rəm] *n* forum *m*, tribune *f*.

forward ['fɔ:wəd] *a* (*ahead of schedule*) en avance ; (*movement, position*) en avant, vers l'avant ; (*not shy*) ouvert(e) ; direct(e) ; effronté(e) // *ad* en avant // *n* (SPORT) avant *m* // *vt* (*letter*) faire suivre ; (*parcel, goods*) expédier ; (*fig*) promouvoir, contribuer au développement *or* à l'avancement de ; to move ~ avancer ; ~s *ad* en avant.

forwent [fɔ:'wɛnt] *pt of* forgo.

fossil ['fɔsl] *a,n* fossile (*m*).

foster ['fɔstə*] *vt* encourager, favoriser ; ~ brother *n* frère adoptif ; frère de lait ; ~ child *n* enfant adopté ; ~ mother *n* mère adoptive ; mère nourricière.

fought [fɔ:t] *pt, pp of* fight.

foul [faul] *a* (*weather, smell, food*) infect(e) ; (*language*) ordurier(ère) ; (*deed*) infâme ! *n* (FOOTBALL) faute *f* // *vt* salir, encrasser ; (*football player*) commettre une faute sur ; ~ play *n* (SPORT) jeu déloyal ; ~ play is not suspected la mort (*or* l'incendie *etc*) n'a pas de causes suspectes, on écarte l'hypothèse d'un meurtre (*or* d'un acte criminel).

found [faund] *pt, pp of* find // *vt* (*establish*) fonder ; ~ation [-'deɪʃən] *n* (*act*) fondation *f* ; (*base*) fondement *m* ; (*also*: ~ation cream) fond *m* de teint ; ~ations *npl* (*of building*) fondations *fpl*.

founder ['faundə*] *n* fondateur *m* // *vi* couler, sombrer.

foundry ['faundrɪ] *n* fonderie *f*.

fount [faunt] *n* source *f* ; ~ain ['fauntɪn] *n* fontaine *f* ; ~ain pen *n* stylo *m* (à encre).

four [fɔ:*] *num* quatre ; on all ~s à quatre pattes ; ~some ['fɔ:səm] *n* partie *f* à quatre ; sortie *f* à quatre ; ~teen *num* quatorze ; ~teenth *num* quatorzième ; ~th *num* quatrième.

fowl [faul] *n* volaille *f*.

fox [fɔks] *n* renard *m* // *vt* mystifier.

foyer ['fɔɪeɪ] *n* vestibule *m* ; (THEATRE) foyer *m*.

fraction ['frækʃən] *n* fraction *f*.

fracture ['fræktʃə*] *n* fracture *f* // *vt* fracturer.

fragile ['frædʒaɪl] *a* fragile.

fragment ['frægmənt] *n* fragment *m* ; ~ary *a* fragmentaire.

fragrance ['freɪgrəns] *n* parfum *m*.

fragrant ['freɪgrənt] *a* parfumé(e), odorant(e).

frail [freɪl] *a* fragile, délicat(e).

frame [freɪm] *n* (*of building*) charpente *f* ; (*of human, animal*) charpente, ossature *f* ; (*of picture*) cadre *m* ; (*of door, window*) encadrement *m*, chambranle *m* ; (*of spectacles: also*: ~s) monture *f* // *vt* encadrer ; (*theory, plan*) construire, élaborer ; ~ of mind *n* disposition *f* d'esprit ; ~work *n* structure *f*.

France [frɑ:ns] *n* France *f*.

franchise ['fræntʃaɪz] *n* (POL) droit *m* de vote.

frank [fræŋk] *a* franc(franche) // *vt* (*letter*) affranchir ; ~ly *ad* franchement ; ~ness *n* franchise *f*.

frantic ['fræntɪk] *a* frénétique ; ~ally *ad* frénétiquement.

fraternal [frə'tə:nl] *a* fraternel(le).

fraternity [frə'tə:nɪtɪ] *n* (*club*) communauté *f*, confrérie *f* ; (*spirit*) fraternité *f*.

fraternize ['frætənaɪz] *vi* fraterniser.

fraud [frɔ:d] *n* supercherie *f*, fraude *f*, tromperie *f* ; imposteur *m*.

fraudulent ['frɔ:djulənt] *a* frauduleux(euse).

fraught [frɔ:t] *a*: ~ with chargé(e) de, plein(e) de.

fray [freɪ] *n* bagarre *f* // *vt* effilocher // *vi* s'effilocher ; tempers were ~ed les gens commençaient à s'énerver *or* perdre patience ; her nerves were ~ed elle était à bout de nerfs.

freak [fri:k] *n* (*also cpd*) phénomène *m*, créature *ou* événement exceptionnel par sa rareté, son caractère d'anomalie.

freckle ['frɛkl] *n* tache *f* de rousseur.

free [fri:] *a* libre ; (*gratis*) gratuit(e) ; (*liberal*) généreux(euse), large // *vt* (*prisoner etc*) libérer ; (*jammed object or person*) dégager ; ~ (*of charge*) *ad* gratuitement ; ~dom ['fri:dəm] *n* liberté *f* ; ~-for-all *n* mêlée générale ; ~ kick *n* coup franc ; ~lance *a* indépendant(e) ; ~ly *ad* librement ; (*liberally*) libéralement ; ~mason *n* franc-maçon *m* ; ~masonry *n* franc-maçonnerie *f* ; ~ trade *n* libre-échange *m* ; ~way *n* (US) autoroute *f* ; ~wheel *vi* descendre en roue libre ; ~ will *n* libre arbitre *m* ; of one's own ~ will de son plein gré.

freeze [fri:z] *vb* (*pt* froze, *pp* frozen [frəuz, 'frəuzn]) *vi* geler // *vt* geler ; (*food*) congeler ; (*prices, salaries*) bloquer, geler // *n* gel *m* ; blocage *m* ; ~-dried *a* lyophilisé(e) ; ~r *n* congélateur *m*.

freezing ['fri:zɪŋ] *a*: ~ cold *a* glacial(e) ; ~ point *n* point *m* de congélation ; 3 degrees below ~ 3 degrés au-dessous de zéro.

freight [freɪt] *n* (*goods*) fret *m*, cargaison *f* ; (*money charged*) fret, prix *m* du transport ; ~ car *n* (US) wagon *m* de marchandises ; ~er *n* (NAUT) cargo *m*.

French [frɛntʃ] *a* français(e) // *n* (LING) français *m* ; the ~ les Français ; ~ fried (potatoes) *npl* (pommes de terre *fpl*) frites *fpl* ; ~man *n* Français *m* ; ~ window *n* porte-fenêtre *f* ; ~woman *n* Française *f*.

frenzy ['frɛnzɪ] *n* frénésie *f*.

frequency ['fri:kwənsɪ] *n* fréquence *f*.

frequent *a* ['fri:kwənt] fréquent(e) // *vt* [frɪ'kwɛnt] fréquenter ; ~ly *ad* fréquemment.

fresco ['frɛskəu] *n* fresque *f*.

fresh [frɛʃ] *a* frais(fraîche) ; (*new*) nouveau(nouvelle) ; (*cheeky*) familier(ère), culotté(e) ; ~en *vi* (*wind, air*) fraichir ; to ~en up *vi* faire un brin de toilette ; ~ly *ad* nouvellement, récemment ; ~ness *n* fraicheur *f* ; ~water *a* (*fish*) d'eau douce.

fret [frɛt] *vi* s'agiter, se tracasser.

friar ['fraɪə*] *n* moine *m*, frère *m*.

friction ['frɪkʃən] *n* friction *f*, frottement *m*.

Friday ['fraɪdɪ] *n* vendredi *m*.

fridge [frɪdʒ] n frigo m, frigidaire m ®.
fried [fraɪd] pt, pp of **fry** // a frit(e).
friend [frɛnd] n ami/e ; **to make ~s with**
se lier (d'amitié) avec ; ~**liness** n attitude
amicale ; ~**ly** a amical(e) ; gentil(le) ; **to
be ~ly with** être ami(e) avec ; ~**ship** n
amitié f.
frieze [fri:z] n frise f, bordure f.
frigate ['frɪgɪt] n (NAUT: modern) frégate f.
fright [fraɪt] n peur f, effroi m ; **she looks
a ~** elle a l'air d'un épouvantail ; **to ~**
effrayer, faire peur à ; ~**ened** a: **to be
~ened (of)** avoir peur (de) ; ~**ening** a
effrayant(e) ; ~**ful** a affreux(euse) ;
~**fully** ad affreusement.
frigid ['frɪdʒɪd] a (woman) frigide ; ~**ity**
[frɪ'dʒɪdɪtɪ] n frigidité f.
frill [frɪl] n (of dress) volant m ; (of shirt)
jabot m.
fringe [frɪndʒ] n frange f ; (edge: of forest
etc) bordure f, (fig): **on the ~** en marge ;
~ **benefits** npl avantages sociaux or en
nature.
frisk [frɪsk] vt fouiller.
frisky ['frɪskɪ] a vif(vive), sémillant(e).
fritter ['frɪtə*] n beignet m ; **to ~ away**
vt gaspiller.
frivolity [frɪ'vɔlɪtɪ] n frivolité f.
frivolous ['frɪvələs] a frivole.
frizzy ['frɪzɪ] a crépu(e).
fro [frəu] see **to**.
frock [frɔk] n robe f.
frog [frɔg] n grenouille f ; ~**man** n homme-
grenouille m.
frolic ['frɔlɪk] n ébats mpl // vi folâtrer,
batifoler.
from [frɔm] prep de ; ~ **a pound/January**
à partir d'une livre/de janvier ; ~ **what**
he says d'après ce qu'il dit.
front [frʌnt] n (of house, dress) devant m ;
(of coach, train) avant m ; (of book)
couverture f ; (promenade: also: **sea ~**)
bord m de mer ; (MIL, POL, METEOROLOGY) front
m ; (fig: appearances) contenance f, façade
f // a de devant ; premier(ère) ; **in ~ (of)**
devant ; ~**age** ['frʌntɪdʒ] n façade f ; ~**al**
a frontal(e) ; ~ **door** n porte f d'entrée ;
(of car) portière f avant ; ~**ier** ['frʌntɪə*]
n frontière f ; ~ **page** n première page ;
~ **room** n (Brit) pièce f de devant, salon
m ; ~**-wheel drive** n traction f avant.
frost [frɔst] n gel m, gelée f ; ~**bite** n
gelures fpl ; ~**ed** a (glass) dépoli(e) ; ~**y**
a (window) couvert(e) de givre ; (welcome)
glacial(e).
froth ['frɔθ] n mousse f ; écume f.
frown [fraun] n froncement m de sourcils
// vi froncer les sourcils.
froze [frəuz] pt of **freeze** ; ~**n** pp of **freeze**
// a (food) congelé(e).
frugal ['fru:gəl] a frugal(e).
fruit [fru:t] n, pl inv fruit m ; ~**erer** n
fruitier m, marchand/e de fruits ; ~**ful** a
fructueux(euse) ; (plant, soil) fécond(e) ;
~**ion** [fru:'ɪʃən] n: **to come to ~ion** se
réaliser ; ~ **machine** n machine f à sous ;
~ **salad** n salade f de fruits.
frustrate [frʌs'treɪt] vt frustrer ; (plot,
plans) faire échouer ; ~**d** a frustré(e) ;
frustration [-'treɪʃən] n frustration f.

fry, pt, pp **fried** [fraɪ, -d] vt (faire) frire ;
the small ~ le menu fretin ; ~**ing pan**
n poêle f (à frire).
ft. abbr of **foot, feet.**
fuchsia ['fju:ʃə] n fuchsia m.
fuddy-duddy ['fʌdɪdʌdɪ] n (pej) vieux
schnock.
fudge [fʌdʒ] n (CULIN) sorte de confiserie à
base de sucre, de beurre et de lait.
fuel [fjuəl] n (for heating) combustible m ;
(for propelling) carburant m ; ~ **oil** n
mazout m ; ~ **tank** n cuve f à mazout,
citerne f ; (on vehicle) réservoir m de or à
carburant.
fugitive ['fju:dʒɪtɪv] n fugitif/ive.
fulfil [ful'fɪl] vt (function) remplir ; (order)
exécuter ; (wish, desire) satisfaire, réaliser ;
~**ment** n (of wishes) réalisation f.
full [ful] a plein(e) ; (details, information)
complet(ète) ; (skirt) ample, large // ad: **to
know ~ well that** savoir fort bien que ;
I'm ~ j'ai bien mangé ; ~ **employ-
ment/fare** plein emploi/tarif ; **a ~ two
hours** deux bonnes heures ; **at ~ speed**
à toute vitesse ; **in ~** (reproduce, quote)
intégralement ; (write name etc) en toutes
lettres ; ~**back** n (RUGBY, FOOTBALL) arrière
m ; ~**-length** a (portrait) en pied ; ~ **moon**
n pleine lune ; ~**-sized** a (portrait etc)
grandeur nature inv ; ~ **stop** n point m ;
~**-time** a (work) à plein temps // n (SPORT)
fin f du match ; ~**y** ad entièrement,
complètement ; ~**y-fledged** a (teacher,
barrister) diplômé(e) ; (citizen, member) à
part entière.
fumble ['fʌmbl] vi fouiller, tâtonner // vt
(ball) mal réceptionner, cafouiller ; **to ~
with** vt fus tripoter.
fume [fju:m] vi rager ; ~**s** npl vapeurs fpl,
émanations fpl, gaz mpl.
fumigate ['fju:mɪgeɪt] vt désinfecter (par
fumigation).
fun [fʌn] n amusement m, divertissement
m ; **to have ~** s'amuser ; **for ~** pour rire ;
it's not much ~ ce n'est pas très drôle
or amusant ; **to make ~ of** vt fus se
moquer de.
function ['fʌŋkʃən] n fonction f ;
cérémonie f, soirée officielle // vi
fonctionner ; ~**al** a fonctionnel(le).
fund [fʌnd] n caisse f, fonds m ; (source,
store) source f, mine f ; ~**s** npl fonds mpl.
fundamental [fʌndə'mɛntl] a
fondamental(e) ; ~**s** npl principes mpl de
base ; ~**ly** ad fondamentalement.
funeral ['fju:nərəl] n enterrement m,
obsèques fpl (more formal occasion) ; ~
director n entrepreneur m des pompes
funèbres ; ~ **service** n service m funèbre.
funereal [fju:'nɪərɪəl] a lugubre, funèbre.
fun fair ['fʌnfɛə*] n fête (foraine).
fungus, pl **fungi** ['fʌŋgəs, -gaɪ] n
champignon m ; (mould) moisissure f.
funnel ['fʌnl] n entonnoir m ; (of ship)
cheminée f.
funnily ['fʌnɪlɪ] ad drôlement ;
curieusement.
funny ['fʌnɪ] a amusant(e), drôle ; (strange)
curieux(euse), bizarre.
fur [fə:*] n fourrure f ; (in kettle etc) (dépôt
m de) tartre m ; ~ **coat** n manteau m de
fourrure.

furious ['fjuərɪəs] a furieux(euse); (*effort*) acharné(e); ~**ly** *ad* furieusement; avec acharnement.

furl [fə:l] *vt* rouler; (*NAUT*) ferler.

furlong ['fə:lɔŋ] *n* = 201.17 m (*terme d'hippisme*).

furlough ['fə:ləu] *n* (*US*) permission *f*, congé *m*.

furnace ['fə:nɪs] *n* fourneau *m*.

furnish ['fə:nɪʃ] *vt* meubler; (*supply*) fournir; ~**ings** *npl* mobilier *m*, articles *mpl* d'ameublement.

furniture ['fə:nɪtʃə*] *n* meubles *mpl*, mobilier *m*; **piece of** ~ meuble *m*; ~ **polish** *n* encaustique *f*.

furrier ['fʌrɪə*] *n* fourreur *m*.

furrow ['fʌrəu] *n* sillon *m*.

furry ['fə:rɪ] a (*animal*) à fourrure; (*toy*) en peluche.

further ['fə:ðə*] a supplémentaire, autre; nouveau(nouvelle); plus loin // *ad* plus loin; (*more*) davantage; (*moreover*) de plus // *vt* faire avancer *or* progresser, promouvoir; **until** ~ **notice** jusqu'à nouvel ordre *or* avis; ~ **education** *n* enseignement *m* post-scolaire (*recyclage, formation professionnelle*); ~**more** [fə:ðə'mɔ:*] *ad* de plus, en outre.

furthest ['fə:ðist] *superlative of* **far**.

furtive ['fə:tɪv] a furtif(ive); ~**ly** *ad* furtivement.

fury ['fjuərɪ] *n* fureur *f*.

fuse, fuze (*US*) [fju:z] *n* fusible *m*; (*for bomb etc*) amorce *f*, détonateur *m* // *vt,vi* (*metal*) fondre; (*fig*) fusionner; (*ELEC*): **to** ~ **the lights** faire sauter les fusibles *or* les plombs; ~ **box** *n* boîte *f* à fusibles.

fuselage ['fju:zəla:ʒ] *n* fuselage *m*.

fusion ['fju:ʒən] *n* fusion *f*.

fuss [fʌs] *n* chichis *mpl*, façons *fpl*; embarras *mpl*; (*complaining*) histoire(s) *f(pl)*; **to make a** ~ faire des façons *etc*; ~**y** a (*person*) tatillon(ne), difficile; chichiteux(euse); (*dress, style*) tarabiscoté(e).

futile ['fju:taɪl] a futile.

futility [fju:'tɪlɪtɪ] *n* futilité *f*.

future ['fju:tʃə*] a futur(e) // *n* avenir *m*; (*LING*) futur *m*; **in** (**the**) ~ à l'avenir; **futuristic** [-'rɪstɪk] a futuriste.

fuze [fju:z] *n*, *vt*, *vi* (*US*) = **fuse**.

fuzzy ['fʌzɪ] a (*PHOT*) flou(e); (*hair*) crépu(e).

G

g. *abbr of* **gram(s)**.

G [dʒi:] *n* (*MUS*) sol *m*.

gabble ['gæbl] *vi* bredouiller; jacasser.

gable ['geɪbl] *n* pignon *m*.

gadget ['gædʒɪt] *n* gadget *m*.

Gaelic ['geɪlɪk] *n* (*LING*) gaélique *m*.

gag [gæg] *n* bâillon *m*; (*joke*) gag *m* // *vt* bâillonner.

gaiety ['geɪtɪ] *n* gaieté *f*.

gaily ['geɪlɪ] *ad* gaiement.

gain [geɪn] *n* gain *m*, profit *m* // *vt* gagner // *vi* (*watch*) avancer; **to** ~ **in/by** gagner en/à; **to** ~ **3lbs** (**in weight**) prendre 3 livres; ~**ful** a profitable, lucratif(ive).

gainsay [geɪn'seɪ] *vt irg* (*like say*) contredire; nier.

gait [geɪt] *n* démarche *f*.

gal. *abbr of* **gallon**.

gala ['gɑ:lə] *n* gala *m*.

galaxy ['gæləksɪ] *n* galaxie *f*.

gale [geɪl] *n* rafale *f* de vent; coup *m* de vent.

gallant ['gælənt] a vaillant(e), brave; (*towards ladies*) empressé(e), galant(e); ~**ry** *n* bravoure *f*, vaillance *f*; empressement *m*, galanterie *f*.

gall-bladder ['gɔ:lblædə*] *n* vésicule *f* biliaire.

gallery ['gælərɪ] *n* galerie *f*; (*also*: **art** ~) musée *m*; (*: private*) galerie.

galley ['gælɪ] *n* (*ship's kitchen*) cambuse *f*; (*ship*) galère *f*; (*TYP*) placard *m*, galée *f*.

gallon ['gæln] *n* gallon *m* (= 4.543 *l*; 8 pints).

gallop ['gæləp] *n* galop *m* // *vi* galoper.

gallows ['gæləuz] *n* potence *f*.

gallstone ['gɔ:lstəun] *n* calcul *m* (biliaire).

gambit ['gæmbɪt] *n* (*fig*): (**opening**) ~ manœuvre *f* stratégique.

gamble ['gæmbl] *n* pari *m*, risque calculé // *vt, vi* jouer; **to** ~ **on** (*fig*) miser sur; ~**r** *n* joueur *m*; **gambling** *n* jeu *m*.

game [geɪm] *n* jeu *m*; (*event*) match *m*; (*HUNTING*) gibier *m* // a brave; (*ready*): **to be** ~ (**for sth/to do**) être prêt(e) (à qch/à faire), se sentir de taille (à faire); **a** ~ **of football/tennis** une partie de football/tennis; **big** ~ *n* gros gibier; ~**keeper** *n* garde-chasse *m*.

gammon ['gæmən] *n* (*bacon*) quartier *m* de lard fumé; (*ham*) jambon fumé.

gamut ['gæmət] *n* gamme *f*.

gang [gæŋ] *n* bande *f*, groupe *m* // *vi*: **to** ~ **up on sb** se liguer contre qn.

gangrene ['gæŋgri:n] *n* gangrène *f*.

gangster ['gæŋstə*] *n* gangster *m*, bandit *m*.

gangway ['gæŋweɪ] *n* passerelle *f*; (*of bus*) couloir central; (*THEATRE, CINEMA*) allée *f*.

gantry ['gæntrɪ] *n* portique *m*.

gaol [dʒeɪl] *n*, *vt* = **jail**.

gap [gæp] *n* trou *m*; (*in time*) intervalle *f*; (*fig*) lacune *f*; vide *m*.

gape [geɪp] *vi* être *or* rester bouche bée; **gaping** a (*hole*) béant(e).

garage ['gærɑ:ʒ] *n* garage *m*.

garb [gɑ:b] *n* tenue *f*, costume *m*.

garbage ['gɑ:bɪdʒ] *n* ordures *fpl*, détritus *mpl*; ~ **can** *n* (*US*) poubelle *f*, boîte *f* à ordures.

garbled ['gɑ:bld] a déformé(e); faussé(e).

garden ['gɑ:dn] *n* jardin *m* // *vi* jardiner; ~**er** *n* jardinier *m*; ~**ing** jardinage *m*.

gargle ['gɑ:gl] *vi* se gargariser // *n* gargarisme *m*.

gargoyle ['gɑ:gɔɪl] *n* gargouille *f*.

garish ['gɛərɪʃ] a criard(e), voyant(e).

garland ['gɑ:lənd] *n* guirlande *f*; couronne *f*.

garlic ['gɑ:lɪk] *n* ail *m*.

garment ['gɑ:mənt] *n* vêtement *m*.

garnish ['gɑ:nɪʃ] *vt* garnir.

garret ['gærɪt] *n* mansarde *f*.

garrison ['gærɪsn] *n* garnison *f* // *vt* mettre en garnison, stationner.

garrulous ['gærjuləs] a volubile, loquace.

garter ['gɑːtə*] n jarretière f.

gas [gæs] n gaz m; (used as anaesthetic): to be given ~ se faire endormir; (US: gasoline) essence f // vt asphyxier; (MIL) gazer; ~ **cooker** n cuisinière f à gaz; ~ **cylinder** n bouteille f de gaz; ~ **fire** n radiateur m à gaz.

gash [gæʃ] n entaille f; (on face) balafre f // vt taillader; balafrer.

gasket ['gæskɪt] n (AUT) joint m de culasse.

gasmask ['gæsmɑːsk] n masque m à gaz.

gas meter ['gæsmiːtə*] n compteur m à gaz.

gasoline ['gæsəliːn] n (US) essence f.

gasp [gɑːsp] vi haleter; (fig) avoir le souffle coupé.

gas ring ['gæsrɪŋ] n brûleur m.

gas stove ['gæsstəuv] n réchaud m à gaz; (cooker) cuisinière f à gaz.

gassy ['gæsɪ] a gazeux(euse).

gastric ['gæstrɪk] a gastrique; ~ **ulcer** n ulcère m de l'estomac.

gastronomy [gæs'trɒnəmɪ] n gastronomie f.

gasworks ['gæswəːks] n usine f à gaz.

gate [geɪt] n (of garden) portail m; (of farm) barrière f; (of building) porte f; (of lock) vanne f; ~**crash** vt s'introduire sans invitation dans; ~**way** n porte f.

gather ['gæðə*] vt (flowers, fruit) cueillir; (pick up) ramasser; (assemble) rassembler, réunir; recueillir; (understand) comprendre // vi (assemble) se rassembler; to ~ speed prendre de la vitesse; ~**ing** n rassemblement m.

gauche [gəuʃ] a gauche, maladroit(e).

gaudy ['gɔːdɪ] a voyant(e).

gauge [geɪdʒ] n (standard measure) calibre m; (RAIL) écartement m; (instrument) jauge f // vt jauger.

gaunt [gɔːnt] a décharné(e); (grim, desolate) désolé(e).

gauntlet ['gɔːntlɪt] n (fig): to run the ~ through an angry crowd se frayer un passage à travers une foule hostile or entre deux haies de manifestants etc hostiles.

gauze [gɔːz] n gaze f.

gave [geɪv] pt of **give**.

gavel ['gævl] n marteau m.

gawp [gɔːp] vi: to ~ at regarder bouche bée.

gay [geɪ] a (person) gai(e), réjoui(e); (colour) gai, vif(vive); (col) homosexuel(le).

gaze [geɪz] n regard m fixe; to ~ **at** vt fixer du regard.

gazelle [gə'zɛl] n gazelle f.

gazetteer [gæzə'tɪə*] n dictionnaire m géographique.

gazumping [gə'zʌmpɪŋ] n le fait de revenir sur une promesse de vente pour accepter un prix plus élevé.

G.B. abbr of **Great Britain**.

G.C.E. n (abbr of General Certificate of Education) ≈ baccalauréat m.

Gdns. abbr of **gardens**.

gear [gɪə*] n matériel m, équipement m; attirail m; (TECH) engrenage m; (AUT) vitesse f; top/low/bottom ~ quatrième (or cinquième/deuxième/première vi-

tesse; in ~ en prise; out of ~ au point mort; ~ **box** n boîte f de vitesse; ~ **lever**, ~ **shift** (US) n levier m de vitesse.

geese [giːs] npl of **goose**.

gelatin(e) ['dʒɛlətiːn] n gélatine f.

gelignite ['dʒɛlɪgnaɪt] n plastic m.

gem [dʒɛm] n pierre précieuse.

Gemini ['dʒɛmɪnaɪ] n les Gémeaux mpl; to be ~ être des Gémeaux.

gender ['dʒɛndə*] n genre m.

general ['dʒɛnərl] n général m // a général(e); in ~ en général; ~ **election** n élection(s) législative(s); ~**ization** [-'zeɪʃən] n généralisation f; ~**ize** vi généraliser; ~**ly** ad généralement; **G~ Post Office (GPO)** n Postes et Télécommunications fpl (PTT); ~ **practitioner (G.P.)** n généraliste m/f; who's your G.P.? qui est votre médecin traitant?

generate ['dʒɛnəreɪt] vt engendrer; (electricity) produire.

generation [dʒɛnə'reɪʃən] n génération f.

generator ['dʒɛnəreɪtə*] n générateur m.

generosity [dʒɛnə'rɒsɪtɪ] n générosité f.

generous ['dʒɛnərəs] a généreux (euse); (copious) copieux(euse).

genetics [dʒɪ'nɛtɪks] n génétique f.

Geneva [dʒɪ'niːvə] n Genève.

genial ['dʒiːnɪəl] a cordial(e), chaleureux(euse); (climate) clément(e).

genitals ['dʒɛnɪtlz] npl organes génitaux.

genitive ['dʒɛnɪtɪv] n génitif m.

genius ['dʒiːnɪəs] n génie m.

gent [dʒɛnt] n abbr of **gentleman**.

genteel [dʒɛn'tiːl] a de bon ton, distingué(e).

gentle ['dʒɛntl] a doux(douce).

gentleman ['dʒɛntlmən] n monsieur m; (well-bred man) gentleman m.

gentleness ['dʒɛntlnɪs] n douceur f.

gently ['dʒɛntlɪ] ad doucement.

gentry ['dʒɛntrɪ] n petite noblesse.

gents [dʒɛnts] n W.-C. mpl (pour hommes).

genuine ['dʒɛnjuɪn] a véritable, authentique; sincère.

geographer [dʒɪ'ɔgrəfə*] n géographe m/f.

geographic(al) [dʒɪə'græfɪk(l)] a géographique.

geography [dʒɪ'ɔgrəfɪ] n géographie f.

geological [dʒɪə'lɔdʒɪkl] a géologique.

geologist [dʒɪ'ɔlədʒɪst] n géologue m/f.

geology [dʒɪ'ɔlədʒɪ] n géologie f.

geometric(al) [dʒɪə'mɛtrɪk(l)] a géométrique.

geometry [dʒɪ'ɔmətrɪ] n géométrie f.

geranium [dʒɪ'reɪnjəm] n géranium m.

germ [dʒəːm] n (MED) microbe m; (BIO, fig) germe m.

German ['dʒəːmən] a allemand(e) // n Allemand/e; (LING) allemand m; ~ **measles** n rubéole f.

Germany ['dʒəːmənɪ] n Allemagne f.

germination [dʒəːmɪ'neɪʃən] n germination f.

gerrymandering ['dʒɛrɪmændərɪŋ] n tripotage m du découpage électoral.

gestation [dʒɛs'teɪʃən] n gestation f.

gesticulate [dʒɛsˈtɪkjuleɪt] vi gesticuler.
gesture [ˈdʒɛstjəʳ] n geste m.

get, pt, pp **got**, pp **gotten** (US) [gɛt, gɔt, ˈgɔtn] vt (obtain) avoir, obtenir; (receive) recevoir; (find) trouver, acheter; (catch) attraper; (fetch) aller chercher; (understand) comprendre, saisir; (have): to **have got** avoir; (become): to ~ **rich/old** s'enrichir/vieillir // vi: to ~ **to** (place) aller à; arriver à; parvenir à; **he got across the bridge/under the fence** il a traversé le pont/est passé par-dessous la barrière; to ~ **ready/washed/shaved** etc se préparer/laver/raser etc; to ~ **sb to do sth** faire faire qch à qn; to ~ **sth through/out** of faire passer qch par/sortir qch de; to ~ **about** vi se déplacer; (news) se répandre; to ~ **along** vi (agree) s'entendre; (depart) s'en aller; (manage) = to **get by**; to ~ **at** vt fus (attack) s'en prendre à; (reach) atteindre; to ~ **away** vi partir, s'en aller; (escape) s'échapper; to ~ **away with** vt fus en être quitte pour; se faire passer or pardonner; to ~ **back** vi (return) rentrer // vt récupérer, recouvrer; to ~ **by** vi (pass) passer; (manage) se débrouiller; to ~ **down** vi, vt fus descendre // vt descendre; (depress) déprimer; to ~ **down to** vt fus (work) se mettre à (faire); to ~ **in** vi entrer; (train) arriver; (arrive home) rentrer; to ~ **into** vt fus entrer dans; to ~ **into bed/a rage** se mettre au lit/en colère; to ~ **off** vi (from train etc) descendre; (depart: person, car) s'en aller; (escape) s'en tirer // vt (remove: clothes, stain) enlever // vt fus (train, bus) descendre; to ~ **on** vi (at exam etc) se débrouiller; (agree): to ~ **on** (with) s'entendre (avec) // vt fus monter dans; (horse) monter sur; to ~ **out** vi sortir; (of vehicle) descendre // vt sortir; to ~ **out of** vt fus sortir de; (duty etc) échapper à, se soustraire à; to ~ **over** vt fus (illness) se remettre de; to ~ **round** vt fus contourner; (fig: person) entortiller; to ~ **through** vi (TEL) avoir la communication; to ~ **through to** vt fus (TEL) atteindre; to ~ **together** vi se réunir // vt assembler; to ~ **up** vi (rise) se lever // vt fus monter; to ~ **up to** vt fus (reach) arriver à; (prank etc) faire; **~away** n fuite f.

geyser [ˈgiːzəʳ] n chauffe-eau m inv; (GEO) geyser m.

Ghana [ˈgɑːnə] n Ghana m; **~ian** [-ˈneɪən] a ghanéen(ne) // n Ghanéen/ne.

ghastly [ˈgɑːstlɪ] a atroce, horrible; (pale) livide, blème.

gherkin [ˈgəːkɪn] n cornichon m.

ghetto [ˈgɛtəu] n ghetto m.

ghost [gəust] n fantôme m, revenant m; **~ly** a fantomatique.

giant [ˈdʒaɪənt] n géant/e // a géant(e), énorme.

gibberish [ˈdʒɪbərɪʃ] n charabia m.

gibe [dʒaɪb] n sarcasme m // vi: to ~ **at** railler.

giblets [ˈdʒɪblɪts] npl abats mpl.

giddiness [ˈgɪdɪnɪs] n vertige m.

giddy [ˈgɪdɪ] a (dizzy): to be ~ avoir le

vertige; (height) vertigineux(euse); (thoughtless) sot(te), étourdi(e).

gift [gɪft] n cadeau m, présent m; (donation, ability) don m; **~ed** a doué(e).

gigantic [dʒaɪˈgæntɪk] a gigantesque.

giggle [ˈgɪgl] vi pouffer, ricaner sottement // n petit rire sot, ricanement m.

gild [gɪld] vt dorer.

gill n [dʒɪl] (measure) = 0.14 l; 0.25 pints; **~s** [gɪlz] npl (of fish) ouïes fpl, branchies fpl.

gilt [gɪlt] n dorure f // a doré(e).

gimlet [ˈgɪmlɪt] n vrille f.

gimmick [ˈgɪmɪk] n truc m.

gin [dʒɪn] n (liquor) gin m.

ginger [ˈdʒɪndʒəʳ] n gingembre m; to ~ **up** vt secouer; animer; **~ ale**, **~ beer** n boisson gazeuse au gingembre; **~bread** n pain m d'épices; **~ group** n groupe m de pression; **~haired** a roux(rousse).

gingerly [ˈdʒɪndʒəlɪ] ad avec précaution.

gingham [ˈgɪŋəm] n vichy m.

gipsy [ˈdʒɪpsɪ] n gitan/e, bohémien/ne.

giraffe [dʒɪˈrɑːf] n girafe f.

girder [ˈgəːdəʳ] n poutrelle f.

girdle [ˈgəːdl] n (corset) gaine f // vt ceindre.

girl [gəːl] n fille f, fillette f; (young unmarried woman) jeune fille; (daughter) fille; **an English ~** une jeune Anglaise; **a little English ~** une petite Anglaise; **~friend** n (of girl) amie f; (of boy) petite amie; **~ish** a de jeune fille.

Giro [ˈdʒaɪrəu] n: **the National ~** ≈ les comptes chèques postaux.

girth [gəːθ] n circonférence f; (of horse) sangle f.

gist [dʒɪst] n essentiel m.

give [gɪv] n (of fabric) élasticité f // vb (pt **gave**, pp **given** [geɪv, ˈgɪvn]) vt donner // vi (break) céder; (stretch: fabric) se prêter; to ~ **sb sth**, ~ **sth to sb** donner qch à qn; to ~ **a cry/sigh** pousser un cri/un soupir; to ~ **away** vt donner; (give free) faire cadeau de; (betray) donner, trahir; (disclose) révéler; (bride) conduire à l'autel; to ~ **back** vt rendre; to ~ **in** vi céder // vt donner; to ~ **off** vt dégager; to ~ **out** vt distribuer; annoncer; to ~ **up** vi renoncer // vt renoncer à; to ~ **up smoking** arrêter de fumer; to ~ **o.s. up** se rendre; to ~ **way** vi céder; (AUT) donner la priorité.

glacier [ˈglæsɪəʳ] n glacier m.

glad [glæd] a content(e); **~den** vt réjouir.

gladioli [glædɪˈəulaɪ] npl glaïeuls mpl.

gladly [ˈglædlɪ] ad volontiers.

glamorous [ˈglæmərəs] a séduisant(e).

glamour [ˈglæməʳ] n éclat m, prestige m.

glance [glɑːns] n coup m d'œil // vi: to ~ **at** jeter un coup d'œil à; to ~ **off** (bullet) ricocher sur; **glancing** a (blow) oblique.

gland [glænd] n glande f.

glandular [ˈglændjuləʳ] a: ~ **fever** n mononucléose infectieuse.

glare [glɛəʳ] n lumière éblouissante // vi briller d'un éclat aveuglant; to ~ **at** lancer un or des regard(s) furieux à; **glaring** a (mistake) criant(e), qui saute aux yeux.

glass [glɑ:s] n verre m; (also: looking ~) miroir m; ~es npl lunettes fpl; ~house n serre f; ~ware n verrerie f; ~y a (eyes) vitreux(euse).

glaze [gleɪz] vt (door) vitrer; (pottery) vernir // n vernis m; ~d a (eye) vitreux(euse); (pottery) verni(e); (tiles) vitrifié(e).

glazier ['gleɪzɪə*] n vitrier m.

gleam [gli:m] n lueur f; rayon m // vi luire, briller; ~ing a luisant(e).

glee [gli:] n joie f; ~ful a joyeux(euse).

glen [glɛn] n vallée f.

glib [glɪb] a qui a du bagou; facile.

glide [glaɪd] vi glisser; (AVIAT, birds) planer // n glissement m; vol plané; ~r n (AVIAT) planeur m; **gliding** n (AVIAT) vol m à voile.

glimmer ['glɪmə*] vi luire // n lueur f.

glimpse [glɪmps] n vision passagère, aperçu m // vt entrevoir, apercevoir.

glint [glɪnt] n éclair m // vi étinceler.

glisten ['glɪsn] vi briller, luire.

glitter ['glɪtə*] vi scintiller, briller // n scintillement m.

gloat [gləʊt] vi: to ~ (over) jubiler (à propos de).

global ['gləʊbl] a mondial(e).

globe [gləʊb] n globe m.

gloom [glu:m] n obscurité f; (sadness) tristesse f, mélancolie f; ~y a sombre, triste, mélancolique.

glorification [glɔ:rɪfɪ'keɪʃən] n glorification f.

glorify ['glɔ:rɪfaɪ] vt glorifier.

glorious ['glɔ:rɪəs] a glorieux (euse); splendide.

glory ['glɔ:rɪ] n gloire f; splendeur f; to ~ in se glorifier de.

gloss [glɔs] n (shine) brillant m, vernis m; to ~ over vt fus glisser sur.

glossary ['glɔsərɪ] n glossaire m, lexique m.

gloss paint ['glɔspeɪnt] n peinture brillante.

glossy ['glɔsɪ] a brillant(e), luisant(e); ~ (magazine) n revue f de luxe.

glove [glʌv] n gant m; ~ compartment n (AUT) boîte f à gants, vide-poches m inv.

glow [gləʊ] vi rougeoyer; (face) rayonner // n rougeoiement m.

glower ['glaʊə*] vi lancer des regards mauvais.

glucose ['glu:kəʊs] n glucose m.

glue [glu:] n colle f // vt coller.

glum [glʌm] a maussade, morose.

glut [glʌt] n surabondance f // vt rassasier; (market) encombrer.

glutton ['glʌtn] n glouton/ne; a ~ for work un bourreau de travail; ~ous a glouton(ne); ~y n gloutonnerie f; (sin) gourmandise f.

glycerin(e) ['glɪsəri:n] n glycérine f.

gm, gms abbr of **gram(s)**.

gnarled [nɑ:ld] a noueux(euse).

gnat [næt] n moucheron m.

gnaw [nɔ:] vt ronger.

gnome [nəʊm] n gnome m, lutin m.

go [gəʊ] vb (pt went, pp gone [wɛnt, gɔn]) vi aller; (depart) partir, s'en aller; (work) marcher; (be sold): to ~ for £10 se vendre 10 livres; (fit, suit): to ~ with aller avec; (become): to ~ pale/mouldy pâlir/moisir; (break etc) céder // n (pl: ~es): to have a ~ (at) essayer (de faire); to be on the ~ être en mouvement; whose ~ is it? à qui est-ce de jouer?; he's going to do it il va faire, il est sur le point de faire; to ~ for a walk aller se promener; to ~ dancing/shopping aller danser/faire les courses; how is it ~ing? comment ça marche?; how did it ~? comment est-ce que ça s'est passé?; to ~ round the back/by the shop passer par derrière/devant le magasin; to ~ about vi (rumour) se répandre // vt fus: how do I ~ about this? comment dois-je m'y prendre (pour faire ceci)?; to ~ ahead vi (make progress) avancer; (get going) y aller; to ~ along vi aller, avancer // vt fus longer, parcourir; as you ~ along (with your work) au fur et à mesure de votre travail); to ~ away vi partir, s'en aller; to ~ back vi rentrer, revenir; (go again) retourner; to ~ back on vi fus (promise) revenir sur; to ~ by (years, time) passer, s'écouler // vt fus s'en tenir à; en croire; to ~ down vi descendre; (ship) couler; (sun) se coucher // vt fus descendre; to ~ for vt fus (fetch) aller chercher; (like) aimer; (attack) s'en prendre à; attaquer; to ~ in vi entrer; to ~ in for vt fus (competition) se présenter à; (like) aimer; to ~ into vt fus entrer dans; (investigate) étudier, examiner; (embark on) se lancer dans; to ~ off vi partir, s'en aller; (food) se gâter; (explode) sauter; (event) se dérouler // vt fus ne plus aimer, ne plus avoir envie de; the gun went off le coup est parti; to ~ off to sleep s'endormir; to ~ on vi continuer; (happen) se passer; to ~ on doing continuer à faire; to ~ on with vt fus poursuivre, continuer; to ~ out vi sortir; (fire, light) s'éteindre; to ~ over vi (ship) chavirer // vt fus (check) revoir, vérifier; to ~ through vt fus (town etc) traverser; to ~ up vi monter; (price) augmenter // vt fus gravir; to ~ without vt fus se passer de.

goad [gəʊd] vt aiguillonner.

go-ahead ['gəʊəhɛd] a dynamique, entreprenant(e) // n feu vert.

goal [gəʊl] n but m; ~keeper n gardien m de but; ~post n poteau m de but.

goat [gəʊt] n chèvre f.

gobble ['gɔbl] vt (also: ~ down, ~ up) engloutir.

go-between ['gəʊbɪtwi:n] n médiateur m.

goblet ['gɔblɪt] n goblet m.

goblin ['gɔblɪn] n lutin m.

go-cart ['gəʊkɑ:t] n kart m; ~ racing n karting m.

god [gɔd] n dieu m; G~ n Dieu m; ~child n filleul/e; ~dess n déesse f; ~father n parrain m; ~forsaken a maudit(e); ~mother n marraine f; ~send n aubaine f; ~son n filleul m.

goggle ['gɔgl] vi: to ~ at regarder avec des yeux ronds; ~s npl lunettes fpl (protectrices: de motocycliste etc).

going ['gəʊɪŋ] n (conditions) état m du terrain // a: the ~ rate le tarif (en

vigueur); **a ~ concern** une affaire prospère.
go-kart ['gəukɑːt] n = **go-cart**.
gold [gəuld] n or m // a en or; **~en** a (made of gold) en or; (gold in colour) doré(e); **~en rule/age** règle/âge d'or; **~fish** n poisson m rouge; **~mine** n mine f d'or.
golf [gɔlf] n golf m; **~ club** n club m de golf; (stick) club m, crosse f de golf; **~ course** n terrain m de golf; **~er** n joueur/euse de golf.
gondola ['gɔndələ] n gondole f.
gone [gɔn] pp of **go** // a parti(e).
gong [gɔŋ] n gong m.
good [gud] a bon(ne); (kind) gentil(le); (child) sage // n bien m; **~s** npl marchandise f; articles mpl; **she is ~ with children/her hands** elle sait bien s'occuper des enfants/sait se servir de ses mains; **would you be ~ enough to ...?** auriez-vous la bonté or l'amabilité de ...?; **a ~ deal (of)** beaucoup (de); **a ~ many** beaucoup (de); **~ morning/afternoon!** bonjour!; **~ evening!** bonsoir!; **~ night!** bonsoir!; (on going to bed) bonne nuit!; **~bye!** au revoir!; **G~ Friday** n Vendredi saint; **~-looking** a bien inv; **~ness** n (of person) bonté f; **for ~ness sake!** je vous en prie!; **~ness gracious!** mon Dieu!; **~will** n bonne volonté f; (COMM) réputation f (auprès de la clientèle).
goose, pl **geese** [guːs, giːs] n oie f.
gooseberry ['guzbəri] n groseille f à maquereau; **to play ~** tenir la chandelle.
gooseflesh ['guːsfleʃ] n chair f de poule.
gore [gɔː*] vt encorner // n sang m.
gorge [gɔːdʒ] n gorge f // vt: **to ~ o.s. (on)** se gorger (de).
gorgeous ['gɔːdʒəs] a splendide, superbe.
gorilla [gə'rilə] n gorille m.
gorse [gɔːs] n ajoncs mpl.
gory ['gɔːri] a sanglant(e).
go-slow ['gəu'sləu] n grève perlée.
gospel ['gɔspl] n évangile m.
gossamer ['gɔsəmə*] n (cobweb) fils mpl de la vierge; (light fabric) étoffe très légère.
gossip ['gɔsip] n bavardages mpl; commérage m, cancans mpl; (person) commère f // vi bavarder; (maliciously) cancaner, faire des commérages.
got [gɔt] pt,pp of **get**; **~ten** (US) pp of **get**.
gout [gaut] n goutte f.
govern ['gʌvən] vt (gen, LING) gouverner.
governess ['gʌvənis] n gouvernante f.
government ['gʌvnmənt] n gouvernement m; (ministers) ministère m // cpd de l'État; **~al** [-'mentl] a gouvernemental(e).
governor ['gʌvənə*] n (of state, bank) gouverneur m; (of school, hospital) administrateur m.
Govt abbr of **government**.
gown [gaun] n robe f; (of teacher, judge) toge f.
G.P. n abbr see **general**.
GPO n abbr see **general**.
grab [græb] vt saisir, empoigner; (property, power) se saisir de.
grace [greis] n grâce f // vt honorer; **5 days' ~** répit m de 5 jours; **to say ~**

dire le bénédicité; (after meal) dire les grâces; **~ful** a gracieux(euse), élégant(e); **gracious** ['greiʃəs] a bienveillant(e); de bonne grâce; miséricordieux(euse).
gradation [grə'deiʃən] n gradation f.
grade [greid] n (COMM) qualité f; calibre m; catégorie f; (in hierarchy) grade m, échelon m; (US: SCOL) classe f // vt classer; calibrer; graduer; **~ crossing** n (US) passage m à niveau.
gradient ['greidiənt] n inclinaison f, pente f; (GEOM) gradient m.
gradual ['grædjuəl] a graduel(le), progressif(ive); **~ly** ad peu à peu, graduellement.
graduate n ['grædjuit] diplômé/e d'université // vi ['grædjueit] obtenir un diplôme d'université; **graduation** [-'eiʃən] n cérémonie f de remise des diplômes.
graft [grɑːft] n (AGR, MED) greffe f; (bribery) corruption f // vt greffer; **hard ~** n (col) boulot acharné.
grain [grein] n grain m; **it goes against the ~** cela va à l'encontre de sa (or ma) nature.
gram [græm] n gramme m.
grammar ['græmə*] n grammaire f.
grammatical [grə'mætikl] a grammatical(e).
gramme [græm] n = **gram**.
gramophone ['græməfəun] n gramophone m.
granary ['grænəri] n grenier m.
grand [grænd] a magnifique, splendide, noble; **~children** npl petits-enfants mpl; **~dad** n grand-papa m; **~daughter** n petite-fille f; **~eur** ['grændjə*] n grandeur f, noblesse f; **~father** n grand-père m; **~iose** ['grændiəuz] a grandiose; (pej) pompeux(euse); **~ma** n grand-maman f; **~mother** n grand-mère f; **~pa** n = **~dad**; **~ piano** n piano m à queue; **~son** n petit-fils m; **~stand** n (SPORT) tribune f.
granite ['grænit] n granit m.
granny ['græni] n grand-maman f.
grant [grɑːnt] vt accorder; (a request) accéder à; (admit) concéder // n (SCOL) bourse f; (ADMIN) subside m, subvention f; **to take sth for ~ed** considérer qch comme acquis or allant de soi.
granulated ['grænjuleitid] a: **~ sugar** n sucre m en poudre.
granule ['grænjuːl] n granule m.
grape [greip] n raisin m.
grapefruit ['greipfruːt] n pamplemousse m.
graph [grɑːf] n graphique m, courbe f; **~ic** a graphique; (vivid) vivant(e).
grapple ['græpl] vi: **to ~ with** être aux prises avec.
grasp [grɑːsp] vt saisir, empoigner; (understand) saisir, comprendre // n (grip) prise f; (fig) emprise f, pouvoir m; compréhension f, connaissance f; **~ing** a avide.
grass [grɑːs] n herbe f; gazon m; **~hopper** n sauterelle f; **~land** n prairie f; **~ snake** n couleuvre f; **~y** a herbeux(euse).
grate [greit] n grille f de cheminée // vi grincer // vt (CULIN) râper.

grateful ['greɪtful] a reconnaissant(e); **~ly** ad avec reconnaissance.

grater ['greɪtə*] n râpe f.

gratify ['grætɪfaɪ] vt faire plaisir à; (whim) satisfaire; **~ing** a agréable; satisfaisant(e).

grating ['greɪtɪŋ] n (iron bars) grille f // a (noise) grinçant(e).

gratitude ['grætɪtjuːd] n gratitude f.

gratuitous [grə'tjuːɪtəs] a gratuit(e).

gratuity [grə'tjuːɪtɪ] n pourboire m.

grave [greɪv] n tombe f // a grave, sérieux(euse); **~digger** n fossoyeur m.

gravel ['grævl] n gravier m.

gravestone ['greɪvstəun] n pierre tombale.

graveyard ['greɪvjɑːd] n cimetière m.

gravitate ['grævɪteɪt] vi graviter.

gravity ['grævɪtɪ] n (PHYSICS) gravité f; pesanteur f; (seriousness) gravité f, sérieux m.

gravy ['greɪvɪ] n jus m (de viande); sauce f.

gray [greɪ] a = grey.

graze [greɪz] vi paître, brouter // vt (touch lightly) frôler, effleurer; (scrape) écorcher // n (MED) écorchure f.

grease [griːs] n (fat) graisse f; (lubricant) lubrifiant m // vt graisser; lubrifier; **~gun** n graisseur m; **~proof paper** n papier sulfurisé; **greasy** a gras(se), graisseux(euse).

great [greɪt] a grand(e); (col) formidable; **G~ Britain** n Grande-Bretagne f; **~grandfather** n arrière-grand-père m; **~grandmother** n arrière-grand-mère f; **~ly** ad très, grandement; (with verbs) beaucoup; **~ness** n grandeur f.

Grecian ['griːʃən] a grec(grecque).

Greece [griːs] n Grèce f.

greed [griːd] n (also: **~iness**) avidité f; (for food) gourmandise f; **~ily** ad avidement; avec gourmandise; **~y** a avide; gourmand(e).

Greek [griːk] a grec(grecque) // n Grec/Grecque f; (LING) grec m.

green [griːn] a vert(e); (inexperienced) (bien) jeune, naïf(ïve) // n vert m; (stretch of grass) pelouse f; (also: **village ~**) ≈ place f du village; **~s** npl légumes verts; **~gage** n reine-claude f; **~grocer** n marchand m de fruits et légumes; **~house** n serre f; **~ish** a verdâtre.

Greenland ['griːnlənd] n Groenland m.

greet [griːt] vt accueillir; **~ing** n salutation f; **Christmas/birthday ~ings** souhaits mpl de Noël/de bon anniversaire; **~ing(s) card** n carte f de vœux.

gregarious [grə'gɛərɪəs] a grégaire; sociable.

grenade [grə'neɪd] n grenade f.

grew [gruː] pt of grow.

grey [greɪ] a gris(e); (dismal) sombre; **~haired** a aux cheveux gris; **~hound** n lévrier m.

grid [grɪd] n grille f; (ELEC) réseau m; **~iron** n gril m.

grief [griːf] n chagrin m, douleur f.

grievance ['griːvəns] n doléance f, grief m.

grieve [griːv] vi avoir du chagrin; se désoler // vt faire de la peine à, affliger; **to ~ at** se désoler de; pleurer.

grievous ['griːvəs] a grave, cruel(le).

grill [grɪl] n (on cooker) gril m // vt griller; (question) interroger longuement, cuisiner.

grille [grɪl] n grillage m; (AUT) calandre f.

grill(room) ['grɪl(rum)] n rôtisserie f.

grim [grɪm] a sinistre, lugubre.

grimace [grɪ'meɪs] n grimace f // vi grimacer, faire une grimace.

grime [graɪm] n crasse f.

grimy ['graɪmɪ] a crasseux(euse).

grin [grɪn] n large sourire m // vi sourire.

grind [graɪnd] vt (pt, pp ground [graund]) écraser; (coffee, pepper etc) moudre; (make sharp) aiguiser // n (work) corvée f; **to ~ one's teeth** grincer des dents.

grip [grɪp] n étreinte f, poigne f; prise f; (handle) poignée f; (holdall) sac m de voyage // vt saisir, empoigner; étreindre; **to come to ~s with** en venir aux prises avec; **to ~ the road** (AUT) adhérer à la route.

gripe(s) [graɪp(s)] n(pl) coliques fpl.

gripping ['grɪpɪŋ] a prenant(e), palpitant(e).

grisly ['grɪzlɪ] a sinistre, macabre.

gristle ['grɪsl] n cartilage m (de poulet etc).

grit [grɪt] n gravillon m; (courage) cran m // vt (road) sabler; **to ~ one's teeth** serrer les dents.

grizzle ['grɪzl] vi pleurnicher.

groan [grəun] n gémissement m; grognement m // vi gémir; grogner.

grocer ['grəusə*] n épicier m; **at the ~'s** à l'épicerie, chez l'épicier; **~ies** npl provisions fpl.

grog [grɔg] n grog m.

groggy ['grɔgɪ] a groggy inv.

groin [grɔɪn] n aine f.

groom [gruːm] n palefrenier m; (also: **bride~**) marié m // vt (horse) panser; (fig): **to ~ sb for** former qn pour.

groove [gruːv] n sillon m, rainure f.

grope [grəup] vi tâtonner; **to ~ for** vt fus chercher à tâtons.

gross [grəus] a grossier(ère); (COMM) brut(e); **~ly** ad (greatly) très, grandement.

grotesque [grə'tɛsk] a grotesque.

grotto ['grɔtəu] n grotte f.

ground [graund] pt, pp of grind // n sol m, terre f; (land) terrain m, terres fpl; (SPORT) terrain m; (reason: gen pl) raison f // vt (plane) empêcher de décoller, retenir au sol // vi (ship) s'échouer; **~s** npl (of coffee etc) marc m; (gardens etc) parc m, domaine m; **on the ~, to the ~** par terre; **~ floor** n rez-de-chaussée m; **~ing** n (in education) connaissances fpl de base; **~less** a sans fondement; **~sheet** n tapis m de sol; **~staff** n équipage m au sol; **~work** n préparation f.

group [gruːp] n groupe m // vt (also: **~ together**) grouper // vi (also: **~ together**) se grouper.

grouse [graus] n, pl inv (bird) grouse f (sorte de coq de bruyère) // vi (complain) rouspéter, râler.

grove [grəuv] n bosquet m.

grovel ['grɔvl] *vi* (*fig*): **to ~ (before)** ramper (devant).

grow, *pt* **grew,** *pp* **grown** [grəu, gru:, grəun] *vi* (*plant*) pousser, croître; (*person*) grandir; (*increase*) augmenter, se développer; (*become*): **to ~ rich/weak** s'enrichir/s'affaiblir // *vt* cultiver, faire pousser; **to ~ up** *vi* grandir; **~er** *n* producteur *m*; **~ing** *a* (*fear, amount*) croissant(e), grandissant(e).

growl [graul] *vi* grogner.

grown [grəun] *pp of* **grow** // *a* adulte; **~-up** *n* adulte *m/f*, grande personne.

growth [grəuθ] *n* croissance *f*, développement *m*; (*what has grown*) pousse *f*; poussée *f*; (*MED*) grosseur *f*, tumeur *f*.

grub [grʌb] *n* larve *f*; (*col: food*) bouffe *f*.

grubby ['grʌbɪ] *a* crasseux(euse).

grudge [grʌdʒ] *n* rancune *f* // *vt*: **to ~ sb sth** donner qch à qn à contre-cœur; reprocher qch à qn; **to bear sb a ~ (for)** garder rancune *or* en vouloir à qn (de); **he ~s spending** il rechigne à dépenser; **grudgingly** *ad* à contre-cœur, de mauvaise grâce.

gruelling ['gruəlɪŋ] *a* exténuant(e).

gruesome ['gru:səm] *a* horrible.

gruff [grʌf] *a* bourru(e).

grumble ['grʌmbl] *vi* rouspéter, ronchonner.

grumpy ['grʌmpɪ] *a* grincheux(euse).

grunt [grʌnt] *vi* grogner // *n* grognement *m*.

G-string ['dʒi:strɪŋ] *n* (*garment*) cache-sexe *m inv*.

guarantee [gærən'ti:] *n* garantie *f* // *vt* garantir.

guarantor [gærən'tɔ:*] *n* garant/e.

guard [gɑ:d] *n* garde *f*, surveillance *f*; (*squad, BOXING, FENCING*) garde *f*; (*one man*) garde *m*; (*RAIL*) chef *m* de train // *vt* garder, surveiller; **~ed** *a* (*fig*) prudent(e); **~ian** *n* gardien/ne; (*of minor*) tuteur/trice; **~'s van** *n* (*RAIL*) fourgon *m*.

guerrilla [gə'rɪlə] *n* guérillero *m*; **~ warfare** *n* guérilla *f*.

guess [gɛs] *vi* deviner // *vt* deviner; (*US*) croire, penser // *n* supposition *f*, hypothèse *f*; **to take/have a ~** essayer de deviner; **~work** *n* hypothèse *f*.

guest [gɛst] *n* invité/e; (*in hotel*) client/e; **~-house** *n* pension *f*; **~ room** *n* chambre *f* d'amis.

guffaw [gʌ'fɔ:] *n* gros rire // *vi* pouffer de rire.

guidance ['gaɪdəns] *n* conseils *mpl*; **under the ~ of** conseillé(e) *or* encadré(e) par, sous la conduite de.

guide [gaɪd] *n* (*person, book etc*) guide *m* // *vt* guider; **~book** *n* guide *m*; **~d missile** *n* missile téléguidé; **~ dog** *n* chien *m* d'aveugle; **~ lines** *npl* (*fig*) instructions générales, conseils *mpl*.

guild [gɪld] *n* corporation *f*; cercle *m*, association *f*; **~hall** *n* (*Brit*) hôtel *m* de ville.

guile [gaɪl] *n* astuce *f*; **~less** *a* candide.

guillotine ['gɪləti:n] *n* guillotine *f*; (*for paper*) massicot *m*.

guilt [gɪlt] *n* culpabilité *f*; **~y** *a* coupable.

guinea ['gɪnɪ] *n* (*Brit*) guinée *f* (= 21 shillings: *cette monnaie de compte ne s'emploie plus*).

guinea pig ['gɪnɪpɪg] *n* cobaye *m*.

guise [gaɪz] *n* aspect *m*, apparence *f*.

guitar [gɪ'tɑ:*] *n* guitare *f*; **~ist** *n* guitariste *m/f*.

gulf [gʌlf] *n* golfe *m*; (*abyss*) gouffre *m*.

gull [gʌl] *n* mouette *f*.

gullet ['gʌlɪt] *n* gosier *m*.

gullible ['gʌlɪbl] *a* crédule.

gully ['gʌlɪ] *n* ravin *m*; ravine *f*; couloir *m*.

gulp [gʌlp] *vi* avaler sa salive; (*from emotion*) avoir la gorge serrée, s'étrangler // *vt* (*also: ~ down*) avaler // *n*: **at one ~ d'un seul coup.**

gum [gʌm] *n* (*ANAT*) gencive *f*; (*glue*) colle *f*; (*sweet*) boule *f* de gomme; (*also: chewing-~*) chewing-gum *m* // *vt* coller; **~boil** *n* abcès *m* dentaire; **~boots** *npl* bottes *fpl* en caoutchouc.

gumption ['gʌmpʃən] *n* bon sens, jugeote *f*.

gun [gʌn] *n* (*small*) revolver *m*, pistolet *m*; (*rifle*) fusil *m*, carabine *f*; (*cannon*) canon *m*; **~boat** *n* canonnière *f*; **~fire** *n* fusillade *f*; **~man** *n* bandit armé; **~ner** *n* artilleur *m*; **at ~point** sous la menace du pistolet (*or* fusil); **~powder** *n* poudre *f* à canon; **~shot** *n* coup *m* de feu; **within ~shot** à portée de fusil; **~smith** *n* armurier *m*.

gurgle ['gə:gl] *n* gargouillis *m* // *vi* gargouiller.

gush [gʌʃ] *n* jaillissement *m*, jet *m* // *vi* jaillir; (*fig*) se répandre en effusions.

gusset ['gʌsɪt] *n* gousset *m*, soufflet *m*.

gust [gʌst] *n* (*of wind*) rafale *f*; (*of smoke*) bouffée *f*.

gusto ['gʌstəu] *n* enthousiasme *m*.

gut [gʌt] *n* intestin *m*, boyau *m*; (*MUS etc*) boyau *m*; **~s** *npl* (*courage*) cran *m*.

gutter ['gʌtə*] *n* (*of roof*) gouttière *f*; (*in street*) caniveau *m*; (*fig*) ruisseau *m*.

guttural ['gʌtərl] *a* guttural(e).

guy [gaɪ] *n* (*also: ~rope*) corde *f*; (*col: man*) type *m*; (*figure*) effigie *de Guy Fawkes*.

guzzle ['gʌzl] *vi* s'empiffrer // *vt* avaler gloutonnement.

gym [dʒɪm] *n* (*also: gymnasium*) gymnase *m*; (*also: gymnastics*) gym *f*; **~ shoes** *npl* chaussures *fpl* de gym(nastique); **~ slip** *n* tunique *f* d'écolière).

gymnast ['dʒɪmnæst] *n* gymnaste *m/f*; **~ics** ['næstɪks] *n, npl* gymnastique *f*.

gynaecologist, gynecologist (*US*) [gaɪnɪ'kɔlədʒɪst] *n* gynécologue *m/f*.

gynaecology, gynecology (*US*) [gaɪnə'kɔlədʒɪ] *n* gynécologie *f*.

gypsy ['dʒɪpsɪ] *n* = **gipsy.**

gyrate [dʒaɪ'reɪt] *vi* tournoyer.

H

haberdashery ['hæbə'dæʃərɪ] *n* mercerie *f*.

habit ['hæbɪt] *n* habitude *f*; (*costume*) habit *m*, tenue *f*.

habitable ['hæbɪtəbl] a habitable.

habitation [hæbɪ'teɪʃən] n habitation f.

habitual [hə'bɪtjuəl] a habituel(le); (drinker, liar); invétéré(e); ~ly ad habituellement, d'habitude.

hack [hæk] vt hacher, tailler // n (cut) entaille f; (blow) coup m; (pej: writer) nègre m.

hackney cab ['hæknɪ'kæb] n fiacre m.

hackneyed ['hæknɪd] a usé(e), rebattu(e).

had [hæd] pt, pp of **have**.

haddock, pl ~ or ~s ['hædək] n églefin m; **smoked** ~ haddock m.

hadn't ['hædnt] = **had not**.

haemorrhage, **hemorrhage** (US) ['hemərɪdʒ] n hémorragie f.

haemorrhoids, **hemorrhoids** (US) ['hemərɔɪdz] npl hémorroïdes fpl.

haggard ['hægəd] a hagard(e), égaré(e).

haggle ['hægl] vi marchander; **to** ~ **over** chicaner sur; **haggling** n marchandage m.

Hague [heɪg] n: **The** ~ La Haye.

hail [heɪl] n grêle f // vt (call) héler; (greet) acclamer // vi grêler; ~**stone** n grêlon m.

hair [hɛə*] n cheveux mpl; (single hair: on head) cheveu m; (: on body) poil m; **to do one's** ~ se coiffer; ~**brush** n brosse f à cheveux; ~**cut** n coupe f (de cheveux); ~**do** ['hɛədu:] n coiffure f; ~**dresser** n coiffeur/euse; ~**drier** n sèche-cheveux m; ~**net** n résille f; ~**oil** n huile f capillaire; ~**piece** n postiche m; ~**pin** n épingle f à cheveux; ~**pin bend** n virage m en épingle à cheveux; ~**raising** a à (vous) faire dresser les cheveux sur la tête; ~**remover** n dépilateur m; ~**spray** n laque f (pour les cheveux); ~**style** n coiffure f; ~**y** a poilu(e); chevelu(e); (fig) effrayant(e).

hake [heɪk] n colin m, merlu m.

half [hɑ:f] n (pl: **halves** [hɑ:vz]) moitié f // a demi(e) // ad (à) moitié, à demi; ~-**an-hour** une demi-heure; **two and a** ~ deux et demi; **a week and a** ~ une semaine et demie; ~ (**of it**) la moitié; ~ (**of**) la moitié de; ~ **the amount of** la moitié de; **to cut sth in** ~ couper qch en deux; ~-**back** n (SPORT) demi m; ~-**breed**, ~-**caste** n métis/se; ~-**hearted** a tiède, sans enthousiasme; ~-**hour** n demi-heure f; ~-**penny** ['heɪpnɪ] n demi-penny m; (**at**) ~-**price** à moitié prix; ~-**time** n mi-temps f; ~-**way** ad à mi-chemin.

halibut ['hælɪbət] n, pl inv flétan m.

hall [hɔ:l] n salle f; (entrance way) hall m, entrée f; (corridor) couloir m; (mansion) château m, manoir m; ~ **of residence** n pavillon m or résidence f universitaire.

hallmark ['hɔ:lmɑ:k] n poinçon m; (fig) marque f.

hallo [hə'ləu] excl = **hello**.

hallucination [həlu:sɪ'neɪʃən] n hallucination f.

halo ['heɪləu] n (of saint etc) auréole f; (of sun) halo m.

halt [hɔ:lt] n halte f, arrêt m // vt faire arrêter // vi faire halte, s'arrêter.

halve [hɑ:v] vt (apple etc) partager or diviser en deux; (expense) réduire de moitié.

halves [hɑ:vz] npl of **half**.

ham [hæm] n jambon m.

hamburger ['hæmbə:gə*] n hamburger m.

hamstring ['hæmstrɪŋ] n (ANAT) tendon m du jarret.

hamlet ['hæmlɪt] n hameau m.

hammer ['hæmə*] n marteau m // vt (fig) éreinter, démolir.

hammock ['hæmək] n hamac m.

hamper ['hæmpə*] vt gêner // n panier m (d'osier).

hand [hænd] n main f; (of clock) aiguille f; (handwriting) écriture f; (at cards) jeu m; (worker) ouvrier/ère // vt passer, donner; **to give sb a** ~ donner un coup de main à qn; **at** ~ à portée de la main; **in** ~ en main; (work) en cours; **on the one** ~ ..., **on the other** ~ d'une part ..., d'autre part; **to** ~ **in** vt remettre; **to** ~ **out** vt distribuer; **to** ~ **over** vt transmettre; céder; ~**bag** n sac m à main; ~**ball** n handball m; ~**basin** n lavabo m; ~**book** n manuel m; ~**brake** n frein m à main; ~ **cream** n crème f pour les mains; ~**cuffs** npl menottes fpl; ~**ful** n poignée f.

handicap ['hændɪkæp] n handicap m // vt handicaper.

handicraft ['hændɪkrɑ:ft] n travail m d'artisanat, technique artisanale.

handkerchief ['hæŋkətʃɪf] n mouchoir m.

handle ['hændl] n (of door etc) poignée f; (of cup etc) anse f; (of knife etc) manche m; (of saucepan) queue f; (for winding) manivelle f // vt toucher, manier; (deal with) s'occuper de; (treat: people) prendre; '~ **with care**' 'fragile'; ~**bar(s)** n(pl) guidon m.

hand-luggage ['hændlʌgɪdʒ] n bagages mpl à main.

handmade ['hændmeɪd] a fait(e) à la main.

handout ['hændaut] n documentation f, prospectus m.

handshake ['hændʃeɪk] n poignée f de main.

handsome ['hænsəm] a beau(belle); généreux(euse); considérable.

handwriting ['hændraɪtɪŋ] n écriture f.

handwritten ['hændrɪtn] a manuscrit(e), écrit(e) à la main.

handy ['hændɪ] a (person) adroit(e); (close at hand) sous la main; (convenient) pratique; **handyman** n bricoleur m; (servant) homme m à tout faire.

hang, pt, pp **hung** [hæŋ, hʌŋ] vt accrocher; (criminal: pt,pp **hanged**) pendre // vi pendre; (hair, drapery) tomber; **to** ~ **about** vi flâner, traîner; **to** ~ **on** vi (wait) attendre; **to** ~ **up** vi (TEL) raccrocher // vt accrocher, suspendre.

hangar ['hæŋə*] n hangar m.

hanger ['hæŋə*] n cintre m, portemanteau m.

hanger-on [hæŋər'ɔn] n parasite m.

hang-gliding ['hæŋglaɪdɪŋ] n vol m libre or sur aile delta.

hangover ['hæŋəuvə*] n (after drinking) gueule f de bois.

hang-up ['hæŋʌp] n complexe m.

hank [hæŋk] n écheveau m.

hanker ['hæŋkə°] vi: to ~ after avoir envie de.

hankie, hanky ['hæŋkı] n abbr of handkerchief.

haphazard [hæp'hæzəd] a fait(e) au hasard, fait(e) au petit bonheur.

happen ['hæpən] vi arriver; se passer, se produire; as it ~s justement; ~ing n événement m.

happily ['hæpılı] ad heureusement.

happiness ['hæpınıs] n bonheur m.

happy ['hæpı] a heureux(euse); ~ with (arrangements etc) satisfait(e) de; ~-go-lucky a insouciant(e).

harass ['hærəs] vt accabler, tourmenter; ~ment n tracasseries fpl.

harbour, harbor (US) ['ha:bə°] port m // vt héberger, abriter; ~ master n capitaine m du port.

hard [ha:d] a dur(e) // ad (work) dur; (think, try) sérieusement; to drink ~ boire sec; ~ luck! pas de veine!; no ~ feelings! sans rancune!; to be ~ of hearing être dur(e) d'oreille; to be ~ done by être traité(e) injustement; ~back n livre relié; ~board n Isorel m ®; ~-boiled egg n œuf dur; ~ cash n espèces fpl; ~en vt durcir; (fig) endurcir // vi durcir; ~ening n durcissement m; ~-headed a réaliste; décidé(e); ~ labour n travaux forcés.

hardly ['ha:dlı] ad (scarcely) à peine; it's ~ the case ce n'est guère le cas; ~ anywhere presque nulle part.

hardness ['ha:dnıs] n dureté f.

hard sell ['ha:d'sel] n (COMM) promotion de ventes agressive.

hardship ['ha:dʃıp] n épreuves fpl; privations fpl.

hard-up [ha:d'ʌp] a (col) fauché(e).

hardware ['ha:dwɛə°] n quincaillerie f; (COMPUTERS) matériel m; ~ shop n quincaillerie f.

hard-wearing [ha:d'wɛərıŋ] a solide.

hard-working [ha:d'wə:kıŋ] a travailleur(euse).

hardy ['ha:dı] a robuste; (plant) résistant(e) au gel.

hare [hɛə°] n lièvre m; ~-brained a farfelu(e); écervelé(e); ~lip n (MED) bec-de-lièvre m.

harem [ha:'ri:m] n harem m.

harm [ha:m] n mal m; (wrong) tort m // vt (person) faire du mal ou du tort à; (thing) endommager; to mean no ~ ne pas avoir de mauvaises intentions; out of ~'s way à l'abri du danger, en lieu sûr; ~ful a nuisible; ~less a inoffensif(ive); sans méchanceté.

harmonic [ha:'mɔnık] a harmonique.

harmonica [ha:'mɔnıkə] n harmonica m.

harmonics [ha:'mɔnıks] npl harmoniques mpl ou fpl.

harmonious [ha:'məunıəs] a harmonieux-(euse).

harmonium [ha:'məunıəm] n harmonium m.

harmonize ['ha:mənaız] vt harmoniser // vi s'harmoniser.

harmony ['ha:mənı] n harmonie f.

harness ['ha:nıs] n harnais m // vt (horse) harnacher; (resources) exploiter.

harp [ha:p] n harpe f // vi: to ~ on about parler tout le temps de; ~ist n harpiste m/f.

harpoon [ha:'pu:n] n harpon m.

harpsichord ['ha:psıkɔ:d] n clavecin m.

harrow ['hærəu] n (AGR) herse f.

harrowing ['hærəuıŋ] a déchirant(e).

harsh [ha:ʃ] a (hard) dur(e); (severe) sévère; (rough: surface) rugueux(euse); (unpleasant: sound) discordant(e); (: colour) criard(e); cru(e); (: wine) âpre; ~ly ad durement; sévèrement; ~ness n dureté f; sévérité f.

harvest ['ha:vıst] n (of corn) moisson f; (of fruit) récolte f; (of grapes) vendange f // vi moissonner; récolter; vendanger; ~er n (machine) moissonneuse f.

has [hæz] see have.

hash [hæʃ] n (CULIN) hachis m; (fig: mess) gâchis m; also abbr of hashish.

hashish ['hæʃıʃ] n haschisch m.

hassle ['hæsl] n chamaillerie f.

haste [heıst] n hâte f; précipitation f; ~n ['heısn] vt hâter, accélérer // vi se hâter, s'empresser; hastily ad à la hâte; précipitamment; hasty a hâtif(ive); précipité(e).

hat [hæt] n chapeau m; ~box n carton m à chapeau.

hatch [hætʃ] n (NAUT: also: ~way) écoutille f; (also: service ~) passe-plats m inv // vi éclore // vt faire éclore; (plot) tramer.

hatchback ['hætʃbæk] n (AUT) modèle m avec hayon arrière.

hatchet ['hætʃıt] n hachette f.

hate [heıt] vt haïr, détester // n haine f; to ~ to do or doing détester faire; ~ful a odieux(euse), détestable.

hatred ['heıtrıd] n haine f.

hat trick ['hættrık] n (SPORT, also fig) triplé m (3 buts réussis au cours du même match etc).

haughty ['hɔ:tı] a hautain(e), arrogant(e).

haul [hɔ:l] vt traîner, tirer; (by lorry) camionner; (NAUT) haler // n (of fish) prise f; (of stolen goods etc) butin m; ~age n halage m; camionnage m; ~ier n transporteur (routier), camionneur m.

haunch [hɔ:ntʃ] n hanche f; ~ of venison n cuissot m de chevreuil.

haunt [hɔ:nt] vt (subj: ghost, fear) hanter; (: person) fréquenter // n repaire m.

have pt,pp had [hæv, hæd] vt avoir; (meal, shower) prendre; to ~ sth done faire faire qch; he had a suit made il s'est fait faire un costume; she has to do it il faut qu'elle le fasse, elle doit le faire; I had better leave je ferais mieux de partir; to ~ it out with sb s'expliquer (franchement) avec qn; I won't ~ it cela ne se passera pas ainsi; he's been had (col) il s'est fait avoir ou rouler.

haven ['heıvn] n port m; (fig) havre m.

haversack ['hævəsæk] n sac m à dos.

havoc ['hævək] n ravages mpl; to play ~ with (fig) désorganiser; détraquer.

hawk [hɔːk] *n* faucon *m*.

hawker ['hɔːkə*] *n* colporteur *m*.

hay [heɪ] *n* foin *m*; ~ **fever** *n* rhume *m* des foins; **~stack** *n* meule *f* de foin.

haywire ['heɪwaɪə*] *a* (col): **to go** ~ perdre la tête; mal tourner.

hazard ['hæzəd] *n* hasard *m*, chance *f*; danger *m*, risque *m* // *vt* risquer, hasarder; **~ous** *a* hasardeux(euse), risqué(e).

haze [heɪz] *n* brume *f*.

hazelnut ['heɪzlnʌt] *n* noisette *f*.

hazy ['heɪzɪ] *a* brumeux(euse); (*idea*) vague; (*photograph*) flou(e).

he [hiː] *pronoun* il; **it is** ~ **who ...** c'est lui qui ...; **here** ~ **is** le voici; **~-bear** *n* ours *m* mâle.

head [hɛd] *n* tête *f*; (*leader*) chef *m* // *vt* (*list*) être en tête de; (*group*) être à la tête de; **~s (on coin)** (le côté) face; **~s or tails** pile ou face; **to** ~ **the ball** faire une tête; **to** ~ **for** *vt fus* se diriger vers; **~ache** *n* mal *m* de tête; ~ **cold** *n* rhume *m* de cerveau; **~ing** *n* titre *m*; rubrique *f*; **~lamp** *n* phare *m*; **~land** *n* promontoire *m*, cap *m*; **~light** = **~lamp**; **~line** *n* titre *m*; **~long** *ad* (*fall*) la tête la première; (*rush*) tête baissée; **~master** *n* directeur *m*, proviseur *m*; **~mistress** *n* directrice *f*; ~ **office** *n* bureau central; **~-on** (*collision*) de plein fouet; **~phones** *npl* casque *m* (à écouteurs); **~quarters (HQ)** *npl* bureau *or* siège central; (MIL) quartier général; **~-rest** *n* appui-tête *m*; **~room** *n* (*in car*) hauteur *f* de plafond; (*under bridge*) hauteur limite; dégagement *m*; **~scarf** *n* foulard *m*; **~strong** *a* têtu(e), entêté(e); ~ **waiter** *n* maître *m* d'hôtel; **~way** *n* avance *f*, progrès *m*; **~wind** *n* vent *m* contraire; **~y** *a* capiteux(euse); enivrant(e).

heal [hiːl] *vt,vi* guérir.

health [hɛlθ] *n* santé *f*; ~ **food shop** *n* magasin *m* diététique; **the H~ Service** ≈ la Sécurité Sociale; **~y** *a* (*person*) en bonne santé; (*climate, food, attitude etc*) sain(e).

heap [hiːp] *n* tas *m*, monceau *m* // *vt* entasser, amonceler.

hear, *pt, pp* **heard** [hɪə*, həːd] *vt* entendre; (*news*) apprendre; (*lecture*) assister à, écouter // *vi* entendre; **to** ~ **about** avoir des nouvelles de; entendre parler de; **did you** ~ **about the move?** tu es au courant du déménagement?; **to** ~ **from sb** recevoir des nouvelles de qn; **~ing** *n* (*sense*) ouïe *f*; (*of witnesses*) audition *f*; (*of a case*) audience *f*; (*of committee*) séance *f*; **~ing aid** *n* appareil *m* acoustique; **by ~say** *ad* par ouï-dire *m*.

hearse [həːs] *n* corbillard *m*.

heart [hɑːt] *n* cœur *m*; **~s** *npl* (CARDS) cœur *m*; **at** ~ au fond; **by** ~ (*learn, know*) par cœur; **to lose** ~ perdre courage, se décourager; ~ **attack** *n* crise *f* cardiaque; **~beat** *n* battement *m* de cœur; **~breaking** *a* navrant(e), déchirant(e); **to be ~broken** avoir beaucoup de chagrin; **~burn** *n* brûlures *fpl* d'estomac; **~failure** *n* arrêt *m* du cœur; **~felt** *a* sincère.

hearth [hɑːθ] *n* foyer *m*, cheminée *f*.

heartily ['hɑːtɪlɪ] *ad* chaleureusement; (*laugh*) de bon cœur; (*eat*) de bon appétit; **to agree** ~ être entièrement d'accord.

heartless ['hɑːtlɪs] *a* sans cœur, insensible; cruel(le).

heartwarming ['hɑːtwɔːmɪŋ] *a* réconfortant(e).

hearty ['hɑːtɪ] *a* chaleureux(euse); robuste; vigoureux(euse).

heat [hiːt] *n* chaleur *f*; (*fig*) ardeur *f*; feu *m*; (SPORT: *also*: **qualifying** ~) éliminatoire *f* // *vt* chauffer; **to** ~ **up** *vi* (*liquids*) chauffer; (*room*) se réchauffer // *vt* réchauffer; **~ed** *a* chauffé(e); (*fig*) passionné(e); échauffé(e), excité(e); **~er** *n* appareil *m* de chauffage; radiateur *m*.

heath [hiːθ] *n* (*Brit*) lande *f*.

heathen ['hiːðn] *a, n* païen(ne).

heather ['hɛðə*] *n* bruyère *f*.

heating ['hiːtɪŋ] *n* chauffage *m*.

heatstroke ['hiːtstrəuk] *n* coup *m* de chaleur.

heatwave ['hiːtweɪv] *n* vague *f* de chaleur.

heave [hiːv] *vt* soulever (avec effort) // *vi* se soulever // *n* nausée *f*, haut-le-cœur *m*; (*push*) poussée *f*.

heaven ['hɛvn] *n* ciel *m*, paradis *m*; ~ **forbid!** surtout pas!; **~ly** *a* céleste, divin(e).

heavily ['hɛvɪlɪ] *ad* lourdement; (*drink, smoke*) beaucoup; (*sleep, sigh*) profondément.

heavy ['hɛvɪ] *a* lourd(e); (*work, sea, rain, eater*) gros(se); (*drinker, smoker*) grand(e); **it's** ~ **going** ça va pas tout seul, c'est pénible; **~weight** *n* (SPORT) poids lourd.

Hebrew ['hiːbruː] *a* hébraïque // *n* (LING) hébreu *m*.

heckle ['hɛkl] *vt* interpeller (*un orateur*).

hectare ['hɛktɑː*] *n* hectare *m*.

hectic ['hɛktɪk] *a* agité(e), trépidant(e).

he'd [hiːd] = **he would**, **he had**.

hedge [hɛdʒ] *n* haie *f* // *vi* se défiler; **to** ~ **one's bets** (*fig*) se couvrir; **to** ~ **in** *vt* entourer d'une haie.

hedgehog ['hɛdʒhɔg] *n* hérisson *m*.

heed [hiːd] *vt* (*also*: **take** ~ **of**) tenir compte de, prendre garde à; **~less** *a* insouciant(e).

heel [hiːl] *n* talon *m* // *vt* (*shoe*) retalonner; **to bring sb to** ~ rappeler qn à l'ordre.

hefty ['hɛftɪ] *a* (*person*) costaud(e); (*parcel*) lourd(e); (*piece, price*) gros(se).

heifer ['hɛfə*] *n* génisse *f*.

height [haɪt] *n* (*of person*) taille *f*, grandeur *f*; (*of object*) hauteur *f*; (*of plane, mountain*) altitude *f*; (*high ground*) hauteur, éminence *f*; (*fig: of glory*) sommet *m*; (: *of stupidity*) comble *m*; **~en** *vt* hausser, surélever; (*fig*) augmenter.

heir [ɛə*] *n* héritier *m*; **~ess** *n* héritière *f*; **~loom** *n* meuble *m* (*or* bijou *m or* tableau *m*) de famille.

held [hɛld] *pt, pp of* **hold**.

helicopter ['hɛlɪkɔptə*] *n* hélicoptère *m*.

helium ['hiːlɪəm] *n* hélium *m*.

hell [hɛl] *n* enfer *m*; **a** ~ **of a...** (*col*) un(e) sacré(e)... .

he'll [hiːl] = **he will**, **he shall**.

hellish ['hɛlıʃ] a infernal(e).

hello [hə'ləu] excl bonjour! ; salut! (to sb one addresses as 'tu') ; (surprise) tiens!

helm [hɛlm] n (NAUT) barre f.

helmet ['hɛlmıt] n casque m.

helmsman ['hɛlmzmən] n timonier m.

help [hɛlp] n aide f ; (charwoman) femme f de ménage ; (assistant etc) employé/e // vt aider ; ~! au secours! ; ~ yourself (to bread) servez-vous (de pain) ; I can't ~ saying je ne peux pas m'empêcher de dire ; he can't ~ it il n'y peut rien ; ~er n aide m/f, assistant/e ; ~ful a serviable, obligeant(e) ; (useful) utile ; ~ing n portion f ; ~less a impuissant(e) ; faible.

hem [hɛm] n ourlet m // vt ourler ; to ~ in vt cerner.

hemisphere ['hɛmısfıə*] n hémisphère m.

hemorrhage ['hɛmərıdʒ] n (US) = haemorrhage.

hemorrhoids ['hɛmərɔıdz] npl (US) = haemorrhoids.

hemp [hɛmp] n chanvre m.

hen [hɛn] n poule f.

hence [hɛns] ad (therefore) d'où, de là ; 2 years ~ d'ici 2 ans ; ~forth ad dorénavant.

henchman ['hɛntʃmən] n (pej) acolyte m, séide m.

henpecked ['hɛnpɛkt] a dominé par sa femme.

her [hə:*] pronoun (direct) la, l' + vowel or h mute ; (indirect) lui ; (stressed, after prep) elle ; see note at **she** // a son(sa), ses pl ; I see ~ je la vois ; give ~ a book donne-lui un livre ; after ~ après elle.

herald ['hɛrəld] n héraut m // vt annoncer.

heraldry ['hɛrəldrı] n héraldique f.

herb [hə:b] n herbe f ; ~s npl (CULIN) fines herbes.

herd [hə:d] n troupeau m // vt: ~ed together parqués (comme du bétail).

here [hıə*] ad ici // excl tiens!, tenez! ; ~! présent! ; ~'s my sister voici ma sœur ; ~ she is la voici ; ~ she comes la voici qui vient ; ~after ad après, plus tard ; ci-après // n: the ~after l'au-delà m ; ~by ad (in letter) par la présente.

hereditary [hı'rɛdıtrı] a héréditaire.

heredity [hı'rɛdıtı] n hérédité f.

heresy ['hɛrəsı] n hérésie f.

heretic ['hɛrətık] n hérétique m/f ; ~al [hı'rɛtıkl] a hérétique.

herewith [hıə'wıð] ad avec ceci, ci-joint.

heritage ['hɛrıtıdʒ] n héritage m.

hermetically [hə:'mɛtıklı] ad hermétiquement.

hermit ['hə:mıt] n ermite m.

hernia ['hə:nıə] n hernie f.

hero, ~es ['hıərəu] n héros m ; ~ic [hı'rəuık] a héroïque.

heroin ['hɛrəuın] n héroïne f.

heroine ['hɛrəuın] n héroïne f.

heroism ['hɛrəuızm] n héroïsme m.

heron ['hɛrən] n héron m.

herring ['hɛrıŋ] n hareng m.

hers [hə:z] pronoun le(la) sien(ne), les siens(siennes).

herself [hə:'sɛlf] pronoun (reflexive) se ; (emphatic) elle-même ; (after prep) elle.

he's [hi:z] = he is, he has.

hesitant ['hɛzıtənt] a hésitant(e), indécis(e).

hesitate ['hɛzıteıt] vi: to ~ (about/to do) hésiter (sur/à faire) ; **hesitation** ['-teıʃən] n hésitation f.

hessian ['hɛsıən] n toile f de jute.

het up [hɛt'ʌp] a agité(e), excité(e).

hew [hju:] vt tailler (à la hache).

hexagon ['hɛksəgən] n hexagone m ; ~al [-'sægənl] a hexagonal(e).

heyday ['heıdeı] n: the ~ of l'âge m d'or de, les beaux jours de.

hi [haı] excl salut!

hibernate ['haıbəneıt] vi hiberner.

hiccough, hiccup ['hıkʌp] vi hoqueter // n hoquet m ; to have (the) ~s avoir le hoquet.

hid [hıd] pt of hide.

hidden ['hıdn] pp of hide.

hide [haıd] n (skin) peau f // vb (pt hid, pp hidden [hıd, 'hıdn]) vt: to ~ sth (from sb) cacher qch (à qn) // vi: to ~ (from sb) se cacher de qn ; ~-and-seek n cache-cache m ; ~away n cachette f.

hideous ['hıdıəs] a hideux(euse) ; atroce.

hiding ['haıdıŋ] n (beating) correction f, volée f de coups ; to be in ~ (concealed) se tenir caché(e) ; ~ place n cachette f.

hierarchy ['haıərɑ:kı] n hiérarchie f.

high [haı] a haut(e) ; (speed, respect, number) grand(e) ; (price) élevé(e) ; (wind) fort(e), violent(e) ; (voice) aigu(aiguë) // ad haut, en haut ; 20 m ~ haut(e) de 20 m ; ~brow a,n intellectuel(le) ; ~chair n chaise haute (pour enfant) ; ~-flying a (fig) ambitieux(euse) ; ~-handed a très autoritaire ; très cavalier(ère) ; ~-heeled a à hauts talons ; ~jack = hijack ; ~ jump n (SPORT) saut m en hauteur ; ~light n (fig: of event) point culminant // vt faire ressortir, souligner ; ~ly ad très, fort, hautement ; ~ly strung a nerveux(euse), toujours tendu(e) ; H~ Mass n grand-messe f ; ~ness n hauteur f ; Her H~ness son Altesse f ; ~-pitched a aigu(aiguë) ; ~-rise block n tour f (d'habitation).

high school ['haısku:l] n lycée m ; (US) établissement m d'enseignement supérieur.

high street ['haıstri:t] n grand-rue f.

highway ['haıweı] n grand'route f, route nationale.

hijack ['haıdʒæk] vt détourner (par la force) ; ~er n auteur m d'un détournement d'avion, pirate m de l'air.

hike [haık] vi aller à pied // n excursion f à pied, randonnée f ; ~r n promeneur/euse, excursionniste m/f ; **hiking** n excursions fpl à pied, randonnée f.

hilarious [hı'lɛərıəs] a (behaviour, event) désopilant(e).

hilarity [hı'lærıtı] n hilarité f.

hill [hıl] n colline f ; (fairly high) montagne f ; (on road) côte f ; ~side n (flanc m de) coteau m ; ~ start n (AUT) démarrage m en côte ; ~y a vallonné(e) ; montagneux(euse) ; (road) à fortes côtes.

hilt [hılt] n (of sword) garde f.

him [hım] pronoun (direct) le, l' + vowel or h mute ; (stressed, indirect, after prep) lui ;

I see ~ je le vois; give ~ a book donne-lui un livre; after ~ après lui; ~self pronoun (reflexive) se; (emphatic) lui-même; (after prep) lui.

hind [haɪnd] a de derrière // n biche f.

hinder ['hɪndə*] vt gêner; (delay) retarder; (prevent): to ~ sb from doing empêcher qn de faire; **hindrance** ['hɪndrəns] n gêne f, obstacle m.

Hindu ['hɪnduː] n Hindou/e.

hinge [hɪndʒ] n charnière // vi (fig): to ~ on dépendre de.

hint [hɪnt] n allusion f; (advice) conseil m // vt: to ~ that insinuer que // vi: to ~ at faire une allusion à.

hip [hɪp] n hanche f; ~ **pocket** n poche f revolver.

hippopotamus, pl ~es or **hippopotami** ['hɪpə'pɒtəməs, -'pɒtəmaɪ] n hippopotame m.

hire ['haɪə*] vt (car, equipment) louer; (worker) embaucher, engager // n location f; **for** ~ à louer; (taxi) libre; ~ **purchase** (H.P.) n achat m (or vente f) à tempérament or crédit.

his [hɪz] pronoun le(la) sien(ne), les siens(siennes) // a son(sa), ses pl.

hiss [hɪs] vi siffler // n sifflement m.

historian [hɪ'stɔːrɪən] n historien/ne.

historic(al) [hɪ'stɒrɪk(l)] a historique.

history ['hɪstərɪ] n histoire f.

hit [hɪt] vt (pt, pp hit) frapper; (knock against) cogner; (reach: target) atteindre, toucher; (collide with: car) entrer en collision avec, heurter; (fig: affect) toucher; (find) tomber sur // n coup m; (success) coup réussi; succès m; (song) chanson f à succès, tube m; to ~ it off with sb bien s'entendre avec qn; ~-**and-run driver** n chauffard m; ~-**or-miss** a fait(e) au petit bonheur.

hitch [hɪtʃ] vt (fasten) accrocher, attacher; (also: ~ up) remonter d'une saccade // n (knot) nœud m; (difficulty) anicroche f, contretemps m; to ~ a lift faire du stop.

hitch-hike ['hɪtʃhaɪk] vi faire de l'auto-stop; ~r n auto-stoppeur/euse.

hive [haɪv] n ruche f.

H.M.S. abbr of His(Her) Majesty's Ship.

hoard [hɔːd] n (of food) provisions fpl, réserves fpl; (of money) trésor m // vt amasser.

hoarding ['hɔːdɪŋ] n panneau m d'affichage or publicitaire.

hoarfrost ['hɔːfrɒst] n givre m.

hoarse [hɔːs] a enroué(e).

hoax [həʊks] n canular m.

hob [hɒb] n plaque chauffante.

hobble ['hɒbl] vi boitiller.

hobby ['hɒbɪ] n passe-temps favori; ~-**horse** n cheval m à bascule; (fig) dada m.

hobo ['həʊbəʊ] n (US) vagabond m.

hock [hɒk] n vin m du Rhin.

hockey ['hɒkɪ] n hockey m.

hoe [həʊ] n houe f, binette f // vt biner, sarcler.

hog [hɒg] n sanglier m // vt (fig) accaparer; **to go the whole** ~ aller jusqu'au bout.

hoist [hɔɪst] n palan m // vt hisser.

hold [həʊld] vb (pt, pp held [hɛld]) vt tenir; (contain) contenir; (keep back) retenir; (believe) maintenir; considérer; (possess) avoir; détenir // vi (withstand pressure) tenir (bon); (be valid) valoir // n prise f; (fig) influence f; (NAUT) cale f; ~ **the line!** (TEL) ne quittez pas!; to ~ **one's own** (fig) (bien) se défendre; to **catch** or **get** (a) ~ **of** saisir; to **get** ~ **of** (fig) trouver; to **get** ~ **of o.s.** se contrôler; to ~ **back** vt retenir; (secret) cacher; to ~ **down** vt (person) maintenir à terre; (job) occuper; to ~ **off** vt tenir à distance; to ~ **on** vi tenir bon; (wait) attendre; ~ **on!** (TEL) ne quittez pas!; to ~ **on to** vt fus se cramponner à; (keep) conserver, garder; to ~ **out** vt offrir // vi (resist) tenir bon; to ~ **up** vt (raise) lever; (support) soutenir; (delay) retarder; ~**all** n fourre-tout m inv; ~**er** n (of ticket, record) détenteur/trice; (of office, title etc) titulaire m/f; ~**ing** n (share) intérêts mpl; (farm) ferme f; ~**ing company** n holding m; ~**up** n (robbery) hold-up m; (delay) retard m; (in traffic) embouteillage m.

hole [həʊl] n trou m // vt trouer, faire un trou dans.

holiday ['hɒlɪdɪ] n vacances fpl; (day off) jour m de congé; (public) jour férié; ~-**maker** n vacancier/ère; ~ **resort** n centre m de villégiature or de vacances.

holiness ['həʊlɪnɪs] n sainteté f.

Holland ['hɒlənd] n Hollande f.

hollow ['hɒləʊ] a creux(euse); (fig) faux(fausse) // n creux m; (in land) dépression f (de terrain), cuvette f // vt: to ~ **out** creuser, évider.

holly ['hɒlɪ] n houx m; ~**hock** n rose trémière.

holster ['həʊlstə*] n étui m de revolver.

holy ['həʊlɪ] a saint(e); (bread, water) bénit(e); (ground) sacré(e); H~ **Ghost** or **Spirit** n Saint-Esprit m; ~ **orders** npl ordres (majeurs).

homage ['hɒmɪdʒ] n hommage m; to **pay** ~ to rendre hommage à.

home [həʊm] n foyer m, maison f; (country) pays natal, patrie f; (institution) maison f // a de famille; (ECON, POL) national(e), intérieur(e) // ad chez soi, à la maison; au pays natal; (right in: nail etc) à fond; at ~ chez soi, à la maison; to **go** (or **come**) ~ rentrer (chez soi), rentrer à la maison (or au pays); **make yourself at** ~ faites comme chez vous; **near my** ~ près de chez moi; ~ **address** n domicile permanent; ~**land** n patrie f; ~**less** a sans foyer; sans abri; ~**ly** simple, sans prétention; accueillant(e); ~-**made** a fait(e) à la maison; ~ **rule** n autonomie f; H~ **Secretary** n (Brit) ministre m de l'Intérieur; ~**sick** a: **to be** ~**sick** avoir le mal du pays; s'ennuyer de sa famille; ~ **town** n ville natale; ~**ward** ['həʊmwəd] a (journey) du retour; ~**work** n devoirs mpl.

homicide ['hɒmɪsaɪd] n (US) homicide m

homoeopathy [həʊmɪ'ɒpəθɪ] n homéopathie f.

homogeneous [hɒməʊ'dʒiːnɪəs] a homogène.

homosexual [hɔməu'sɛksjuəl] a,n homo-sexuel(le).

hone [həun] n pierre f à aiguiser // vt affûter, aiguiser.

honest ['ɔnɪst] a honnête; (sincere) franc(franche); ~ly ad honnêtement; franchement; ~y n honnêteté f.

honey ['hʌnɪ] n miel m; ~comb n rayon m de miel; (pattern) nid m d'abeilles, motif alvéolé; ~moon n lune f de miel; (trip) voyage m de noces.

honk [hɔŋk] n (AUT) coup m de klaxon // vi klaxonner.

honorary ['ɔnərərɪ] a honoraire; (duty, title) honorifique.

honour, honor (US) ['ɔnə*] vt honorer // n honneur m; ~able a honorable; ~s degree n (SCOL) licence avec mention.

hood [hud] n capuchon m; (Brit: AUT) capote f; (US: AUT) capot m; ~wink vt tromper.

hoof, ~s or hooves [hu:f, hu:vz] n sabot m.

hook [huk] n crochet m; (on dress) agrafe f; (for fishing) hameçon m // vt accrocher; (dress) agrafer.

hooligan ['hu:lɪgən] n voyou m.

hoop [hu:p] n cerceau m; (of barrel) cercle m.

hoot [hu:t] vi (AUT) klaxonner; (siren) mugir // vt (jeer at) huer // n huée f; coup m de klaxon; mugissement m; to ~ with laughter rire aux éclats; ~er n (AUT) klaxon m; (NAUT) sirène f.

hooves [hu:vz] npl of hoof.

hop [hɔp] vi sauter; (on one foot) sauter à cloche-pied // n saut m.

hope [həup] vt,vi espérer // n espoir m; I ~ so je l'espère; I ~ not j'espère que non; ~ful a (person) plein(e) d'espoir; (situation) prometteur(euse), encourageant(e); ~fully ad avec espoir, avec optimisme; ~less a désespéré(e); (useless) nul(le).

hops [hɔps] npl houblon m.

horde [hɔ:d] n horde f.

horizon [hə'raɪzn] n horizon m; ~tal [hɔrɪ'zɔntl] a horizontal(e).

hormone ['hɔ:məun] n hormone f.

horn [hɔ:n] n corne f; (MUS) cor m; (AUT) klaxon m; ~ed a (animal) à cornes.

hornet ['hɔ:nɪt] n frelon m.

horny ['hɔ:nɪ] a corné(e); (hands) calleux(euse).

horoscope ['hɔrəskəup] n horoscope m.

horrible ['hɔrɪbl] a horrible, affreux(euse).

horrid ['hɔrɪd] a méchant(e), désagréable.

horrify ['hɔrɪfaɪ] vt horrifier.

horror ['hɔrə*] n horreur f; ~ film n film m d'épouvante.

hors d'œuvre [ɔ:'də:vrə] n hors d'œuvre m.

horse [hɔ:s] n cheval m; on ~back à cheval; ~ chestnut n marron m (d'Inde); ~-drawn a tiré(e) par des chevaux; ~man n cavalier m; ~power (h.p.) n puissance f (en chevaux); ~-racing n courses fpl de chevaux; ~radish n raifort m; ~shoe n fer m à cheval.

horsy ['hɔ:sɪ] a féru(e) d'équitation or de cheval; chevalin(e).

horticulture ['hɔ:tɪkʌltʃə*] n horticulture f.

hose [həuz] n (also: ~pipe) tuyau m; (also: garden ~) tuyau d'arrosage.

hosiery ['həuzɪərɪ] n (in shop) (rayon m des) bas mpl.

hospitable ['hɔspɪtəbl] a hospitalier(ère).

hospital ['hɔspɪtl] n hôpital m; in ~ à l'hôpital.

hospitality [hɔspɪ'tælɪtɪ] n hospitalité f.

host [həust] n hôte m; (large number): a ~ of une foule de; (REL) hostie f.

hostage ['hɔstɪdʒ] n otage m.

hostel ['hɔstl] n foyer m; (youth) ~ n auberge f de jeunesse.

hostess ['həustɪs] n hôtesse f.

hostile ['hɔstaɪl] a hostile.

hostility [hɔ'stɪlɪtɪ] n hostilité f.

hot [hɔt] a chaud(e); (as opposed to only warm) très chaud; (spicy) fort(e); (fig) acharné(e), brûlant(e), violent(e), passionné(e); ~ dog n hot-dog m.

hotel [həu'tɛl] n hôtel m; ~ier n hôtelier/ère.

hot: ~-headed a impétueux(euse); ~house n serre chaude; ~ly ad passionnément, violemment; ~-water bottle n bouillotte f.

hound [haund] vt poursuivre avec acharnement // n chien courant; the ~s la meute.

hour ['auə*] n heure f; ~ly a toutes les heures; ~ly paid a payé(e) à l'heure.

house [haus] (pl: ~s ['hauzɪz]) (also: firm) maison f; (POL) chambre f; (THEATRE) salle f; auditoire m // vt [hauz] (person) loger, héberger; the H~ (of Commons) la Chambre des communes; on the ~ (fig) aux frais de la maison; ~ arrest n assignation f à domicile; ~boat n bateau (aménagé en habitation); ~breaking n cambriolage m (avec effraction); ~hold n famille f, maisonnée f; ménage m; ~keeper n gouvernante f; ~keeping n (work) ménage m; ~-warming party n pendaison f de crémaillère; ~wife n ménagère f; ~work n (travaux mpl du) ménage m.

housing ['hauzɪŋ] n logement m; ~ estate n cité f, lotissement m; ~ shortage n crise f du logement.

hovel ['hɔvl] n taudis m.

hover ['hɔvə*] vi planer; to ~ round sb rôder or tourner autour de qn; ~craft n aéroglisseur m.

how [hau] ad comment; ~ are you? comment allez-vous?; ~ long have you been here? depuis combien de temps êtes-vous là?; ~ lovely! que or comme c'est joli!; ~ many/much? combien?; ~ many people/much milk combien de gens/lait; ~ old are you? quel âge avez-vous?; ~ is it that ...? comment se fait-il que ...? + sub; ~ever ad de quelque façon or manière que + sub; (+ adjective) quelque or si ... que + sub; (in questions) comment // cj pourtant, cependant.

howl [haul] n hurlement m // vi hurler.

howler ['haulə*] n gaffe f, bourde f.

h.p., H.P. see hire; horse.

HQ *abbr of* **headquarters.**

hr(s) *abbr of* **hour(s).**

hub [hʌb] *n (of wheel)* moyeu *m* ; *(fig)* centre *m*, foyer *m*.

hubbub ['hʌbʌb] *n* brouhaha *m*.

hub cap ['hʌbkæp] *n* enjoliveur *m*.

huddle ['hʌdl] *vi:* **to ~ together** se blottir les uns contre les autres.

hue [hju:] *n* teinte *f*, nuance *f* ; **~ and cry** *n* tollé (général), clameur *f*.

huff [hʌf] *n:* **in a ~** fâché(e) ; **to take the ~** prendre la mouche.

hug [hʌg] *vt* serrer dans ses bras ; *(shore, kerb)* serrer // *n* étreinte *f* ; **to give sb a ~** serrer qn dans ses bras.

huge [hju:dʒ] *a* énorme, immense.

hulk [hʌlk] *n (ship)* vieux rafiot ; *(car etc)* carcasse *f* ; **~ing** *a* balourd(e).

hull [hʌl] *n (of ship, nuts)* coque *f* ; *(of peas)* cosse *f*.

hullo [hə'ləu] *excl* = **hello.**

hum [hʌm] *vt (tune)* fredonner // *vi* fredonner ; *(insect)* bourdonner ; *(plane, tool)* vrombir // *n* fredonnement *m* ; bourdonnement *m* ; vrombissement *m*.

human ['hju:mən] *a* humain(e) // *n* être humain.

humane [hju:'meɪn] *a* humain(e), humanitaire.

humanity [hju:'mænɪtɪ] *n* humanité *f*.

humble ['hʌmbl] *a* humble, modeste // *vt* humilier ; **humbly** *ad* humblement, modestement.

humbug ['hʌmbʌg] *n* fumisterie *f* ; *(sweet)* sorte de bonbon à la menthe.

humdrum ['hʌmdrʌm] *a* monotone, routinier(ère).

humid ['hju:mɪd] *a* humide ; **~ity** [-'mɪdɪtɪ] *n* humidité *f*.

humiliate [hju:'mɪlɪeɪt] *vt* humilier ; **humiliation** [-'eɪʃən] *n* humiliation *f*.

humility [hju:'mɪlɪtɪ] *n* humilité *f*.

humorist ['hju:mərɪst] *n* humoriste *m/f*.

humorous ['hju:mərəs] *a* humoristique ; *(person)* plein(e) d'humour.

humour, humor *(US)* ['hju:mə*] *n* humour *m* ; *(mood)* humeur *f* // *vt (person)* faire plaisir à ; se prêter aux caprices de.

hump [hʌmp] *n* bosse *f* ; **~back** *n* dos-d'âne *m*.

hunch [hʌntʃ] *n* bosse *f* ; *(premonition)* intuition *f* ; **~back** *n* bossu/e ; **~ed** *a* arrondi(e), voûté(e).

hundred ['hʌndrəd] *num* cent ; **~weight** *n (Brit)* = 50.8 *kg* ; 112 *lb* ; *(US)* = 45.3 *kg* ; 100 *lb*.

hung [hʌŋ] *pt, pp of* **hang.**

Hungarian [hʌŋ'gɛərɪən] *a* hongrois(e) // *n* Hongrois/e ; *(LING)* hongrois *m*.

Hungary ['hʌŋgərɪ] *n* Hongrie *f*.

hunger ['hʌŋgə*] *n* faim *f* // *vi:* **to ~ for** avoir faim de, désirer ardemment.

hungrily ['hʌŋgrəlɪ] *ad* voracement ; *(fig)* avidement.

hungry ['hʌŋgrɪ] *a* affamé(e) ; **to be ~** avoir faim.

hunt [hʌnt] *vt (seek)* chercher ; *(SPORT)* chasser // *vi* chasser // *n* chasse *f* ; **~er** *n* chasseur *m* ; **~ing** *n* chasse *f*.

hurdle ['hə:dl] *n (for fences)* claie *f* ; *(SPORT)* haie *f* ; *(fig)* obstacle *m*.

hurl [hə:l] *vt* lancer (avec violence).

hurrah, hurray [hu'rɑ:, hu'reɪ] *n* hourra *m*.

hurricane ['hʌrɪkən] *n* ouragan *m*.

hurried ['hʌrɪd] *a* pressé(e), précipité(e) ; *(work)* fait(e) à la hâte ; **~ly** *ad* précipitamment, à la hâte.

hurry ['hʌrɪ] *n* hâte *f*, précipitation *f* // *vi* se presser, se dépêcher // *vt (person)* faire presser, faire se dépêcher ; *(work)* presser ; **to be in a ~** être pressé(e) ; **to do sth in a ~** faire qch en vitesse ; **to ~ in/out** entrer/sortir précipitamment.

hurt [hə:t] *vb (pt, pp* **hurt)** *vt (cause pain to)* faire mal à ; *(injure, fig)* blesser // *vi* faire mal // *a* blessé(e) ; **~ful** *a (remark)* blessant(e).

hurtle ['hə:tl] *vt* lancer (de toutes ses forces) // *vi:* **to ~** passer en trombe ; **to ~ down** dégringoler.

husband ['hʌzbənd] *n* mari *m*.

hush [hʌʃ] *n* calme *m*, silence *m* // *vt* faire taire ; **~!** chut!

husk [hʌsk] *n (of wheat)* balle *f* ; *(of rice, maize)* enveloppe *f* ; *(of peas)* cosse *f*.

husky ['hʌskɪ] *a* rauque ; *(burly)* costaud(e) // *n* chien *m* esquimau *or* de traineau.

hustle ['hʌsl] *vt* pousser, bousculer // *n* bousculade *f* ; **~ and bustle** *n* tourbillon *m* (d'activité).

hut [hʌt] *n* hutte *f* ; *(shed)* cabane *f* ; *(MIL)* baraquement *m*.

hutch [hʌtʃ] *n* clapier *m*.

hyacinth ['haɪəsɪnθ] *n* jacinthe *f*.

hybrid ['haɪbrɪd] *a, n* hybride *(m)*.

hydrant ['haɪdrənt] *n* prise *f* d'eau ; *(also:* **fire ~)** bouche *f* d'incendie.

hydraulic [haɪ'drɔ:lɪk] *a* hydraulique.

hydroelectric [haɪdrəu'ɪsktrɪk] *a* hydro-électrique.

hydrogen ['haɪdrədʒən] *n* hydrogène *m*.

hyena [haɪ'i:nə] *n* hyène *f*.

hygiene ['haɪdʒi:n] *n* hygiène *f*.

hygienic [haɪ'dʒi:nɪk] *a* hygiénique.

hymn [hɪm] *n* hymne *m* ; cantique *m*.

hyphen ['haɪfn] *n* trait *m* d'union.

hypnosis [hɪp'nəusɪs] *n* hypnose *f*.

hypnotism ['hɪpnətɪzm] *n* hypnotisme *m*.

hypnotist ['hɪpnətɪst] *n* hypnotiseur/euse.

hypnotize ['hɪpnətaɪz] *vt* hypnotiser.

hypocrisy [hɪ'pɔkrɪsɪ] *n* hypocrisie *f*.

hypocrite ['hɪpəkrɪt] *n* hypocrite *m/f* ; **hypocritical** [-'krɪtɪkl] *a* hypocrite.

hypothesis, *pl* **hypotheses** [haɪ'pɔθɪsɪs, -sɪːz] *n* hypothèse *f*.

hypothetic(al) [haɪpəu'θɛtɪk(l)] *a* hypothétique.

hysteria [hɪ'stɪərɪə] *n* hystérie *f*.

hysterical [hɪ'stɛrɪkl] *a* hystérique ; **to become ~** avoir une crise de nerfs.

hysterics [hɪ'stɛrɪks] *npl* (violente) crise de nerfs ; *(laughter)* crise de rire.

I

I [aɪ] *pronoun* je ; *(before vowel)* j' ; *(stressed)* moi.

ice [aɪs] *n* glace *f* ; *(on road)* verglas *m* // *vt (cake)* glacer ; *(drink)* faire rafraîchir //

vi (*also:* ~ **over**) geler ; (*also:* ~ **up**) se givrer ; ~ **axe** *n* piolet *m* ; ~**berg** *n* iceberg *m* ; ~**box** *n* (*US*) réfrigérateur *m* ; (*Brit*) compartiment *m* à glace ; (*insulated box*) glacière *f* ; ~**-cold** *a* glacé(e) ; ~ **cream** *n* glace *f* ; ~ **cube** *n* glaçon *m* ; ~ **hockey** *n* hockey *m* sur glace.

Iceland ['aisland] *n* Islande *f* ; ~**er** *n* Islandais/e ; ~**ic** [-'lændik] *a* islandais(e) // *n* (*LING*) islandais *m*.

ice rink ['aisriŋk] *n* patinoire *f*.

icicle ['aisikl] *n* glaçon *m* (*naturel*).

icing ['aisiŋ] *n* (*AVIAT etc*) givrage *m* ; (*CULIN*) glaçage *m* ; ~ **sugar** *n* sucre *m* glace.

icon ['aikən] *n* icône *f*.

icy ['aisi] *a* glacé(e) ; (*road*) verglacé(e) ; (*weather, temperature*) glacial(e).

I'd [aid] = **I would, I had**.

idea [ai'diə] *n* idée *f*.

ideal [ai'diəl] *n* idéal *m* // *a* idéal(e) ; ~**ist** *n* idéaliste *m/f*.

identical [ai'dentikl] *a* identique.

identification [aidentıfı'keıʃən] *n* identification *f* ; **means of** ~ pièce *f* d'identité.

identify [ai'dentifai] *vt* identifier.

identity [ai'dentiti] *n* identité *f*.

ideology [aidi'ɔlədʒi] *n* idéologie *f*.

idiocy ['idiəsi] *n* idiotie *f*, stupidité *f*.

idiom ['idiəm] *n* langue *f*, idiome *m* ; (*phrase*) expression *f* idiomatique.

idiosyncrasy [idiəu'siŋkrəsi] *n* particularité *f*, caractéristique *f*.

idiot ['idiət] *n* idiot/e, imbécile *m/f* ; ~**ic** [-'ɔtik] *a* idiot(e), bête, stupide.

idle ['aidl] *a* sans occupation, désœuvré(e) ; (*lazy*) oisif(ive), paresseux(euse) ; (*unemployed*) au chômage ; (*machinery*) au repos ; (*question, pleasures*) vain(e), futile ; **to lie** ~ être arrêté, ne pas fonctionner ; ~**ness** *n* désœuvrement *m* ; oisiveté *f* ; ~**r** *n* désœuvré/e ; oisif/ive.

idol ['aidl] *n* idole *f* ; ~**ize** *vt* idolâtrer, adorer.

idyllic [i'dilik] *a* idyllique.

i.e. *ad* (*abbr of id est*) c'est-à-dire.

if [if] *cj* si.

igloo ['iglu:] *n* igloo *m*.

ignite [ig'nait] *vt* mettre le feu à, enflammer // *vi* s'enflammer.

ignition [ig'niʃən] *n* (*AUT*) allumage *m* ; **to switch on/off the** ~ mettre/couper le contact ; ~ **key** *n* (*AUT*) clé *f* de contact.

ignoramus [ignə'reiməs] *n* personne *f* ignare.

ignorance ['ignərəns] *n* ignorance *f*.

ignorant ['ignərənt] *a* ignorant(e).

ignore [ig'nɔ:*] *vt* ne tenir aucun compte de, ne pas relever ; (*person*) faire semblant de ne pas reconnaître, ignorer ; (*fact*) méconnaître.

ikon ['aikɔn] *n* = **icon**.

I'll [ail] = **I will, I shall**.

ill [il] *a* (*sick*) malade ; (*bad*) mauvais(e) // *n* mal *m* ; **to take** *or* **be taken** ~ tomber malade ; ~**-advised** *a* (*decision*) peu judicieux(euse) ; (*person*) malavisé(e) ; ~**-at-ease** *a* mal à l'aise.

illegal [i'li:gl] *a* illégal(e) ; ~**ly** *ad* illégalement.

illegible [i'ledʒibl] *a* illisible.

illegitimate [ili'dʒitimət] *a* illégitime.

ill-fated [il'feitid] *a* malheureux(euse) ; (*day*) néfaste.

ill feeling [il'fi:liŋ] *n* ressentiment *m*, rancune *f*.

illicit [i'lisit] *a* illicite.

illiterate [i'litərət] *a* illettré(e) ; (*letter*) plein(e) de fautes.

ill-mannered [il'mænəd] *a* impoli(e), grossier(ère).

illness ['ilnis] *n* maladie *f*.

illogical [i'lɔdʒikl] *a* illogique.

ill-treat [il'tri:t] *vt* maltraiter.

illuminate [i'lu:mineit] *vt* (*room, street*) éclairer ; (*building*) illuminer ; ~**d sign** *n* enseigne lumineuse ; **illumination** [-'neiʃən] *n* éclairage *m* ; illumination *f*.

illusion [i'lu:ʒən] *n* illusion *f* ; **to be under the** ~ **that** s'imaginer *or* croire que.

illusive, illusory [i'lu:siv, i'lu:səri] *a* illusoire.

illustrate ['iləstreit] *vt* illustrer ; **illustration** [-'streiʃən] *n* illustration *f*.

illustrious [i'lʌstriəs] *a* illustre.

ill will [il'wil] *n* malveillance *f*.

I'm [aim] = **I am**.

image ['imidʒ] *n* image *f* ; (*public face*) image de marque ; ~**ry** *n* images *fpl*.

imaginary [i'mædʒinəri] *a* imaginaire.

imagination [imædʒi'neiʃən] *n* imagination *f*.

imaginative [i'mædʒinətiv] *a* imaginatif(ive) ; plein(e) d'imagination.

imagine [i'mædʒin] *vt* s'imaginer ; (*suppose*) imaginer, supposer.

imbalance [im'bæləns] *n* déséquilibre *m*.

imbecile ['imbəsi:l] *n* imbécile *m/f*.

imbue [im'bju:] *vt*: **to** ~ **sth with** imprégner qch de.

imitate ['imiteit] *vt* imiter ; **imitation** [-'teiʃən] *n* imitation *f* ; **imitator** *n* imitateur/trice.

immaculate [i'mækjulət] *a* impeccable ; (*REL*) immaculé(e).

immaterial [imə'tiəriəl] *a* sans importance, insignifiant(e).

immature [imə'tjuə*] *a* (*fruit*) qui n'est pas mûr(e) ; (*person*) qui manque de maturité.

immediate [i'mi:diət] *a* immédiat(e) ; ~**ly** *ad* (*at once*) immédiatement ; ~**ly next to** juste à côté de.

immense [i'mens] *a* immense ; énorme.

immerse [i'mə:s] *vt* immerger, plonger ; **to** ~ **sth in** plonger qch dans.

immersion heater [i'mə:ʃnhi:tə*] *n* chauffe-eau *m* électrique.

immigrant ['imigrənt] *n* immigrant/e ; immigré/e.

immigration [imi'greiʃən] *n* immigration *f*.

imminent ['iminənt] *a* imminent(e).

immobilize [i'məubilaiz] *vt* immobiliser.

immoderate [i'mɔdərət] *a* immodéré(e), démesuré(e).

immoral [i'mɔrl] *a* immoral(e) ; ~**ity** [-'ræliti] *n* immoralité *f*.

immortal [i'mɔ:tl] *a, n* immortel(le) ; ~**ize** *vt* immortaliser.

immune [ɪˈmjuːn] *a*: ~ (to) immunisé(e) (contre).

immunization [ˌɪmjunaɪˈzeɪʃən] *n* immunisation *f*.

immunize [ˈɪmjunaɪz] *vt* immuniser.

impact [ˈɪmpækt] *n* choc *m*, impact *m*; (*fig*) impact.

impair [ɪmˈpɛə*] *vt* détériorer, diminuer.

impale [ɪmˈpeɪl] *vt* empaler.

impartial [ɪmˈpɑːʃl] *a* impartial(e); ~ity [ɪmˌpɑːʃiˈælɪtɪ] *n* impartialité *f*.

impassable [ɪmˈpɑːsəbl] *a* infranchissable; (*road*) impraticable.

impassioned [ɪmˈpæʃənd] *a* passionné(e).

impatience [ɪmˈpeɪʃəns] *n* impatience *f*.

impatient [ɪmˈpeɪʃənt] *a* impatient(e).

impeach [ɪmˈpiːtʃ] *vt* accuser, attaquer; (*public official*) mettre en accusation.

impeccable [ɪmˈpɛkəbl] *a* impeccable, parfait(e).

impede [ɪmˈpiːd] *vt* gêner.

impediment [ɪmˈpɛdɪmənt] *n* obstacle *m*; (*also: speech ~*) défaut *m* d'élocution.

impending [ɪmˈpɛndɪŋ] *a* imminent(e).

impenetrable [ɪmˈpɛnɪtrəbl] *a* impénétrable.

imperative [ɪmˈpɛrətɪv] *a* nécessaire; urgent(e); pressant(e); (*voice*) impérieux(euse) // *n* (*LING*) impératif *m*.

imperceptible [ɪmpəˈsɛptɪbl] *a* imperceptible.

imperfect [ɪmˈpəːfɪkt] *a* imparfait(e); (*goods etc*) défectueux(euse) // *n* (*LING*: *also*: ~ **tense**) imparfait *m*; ~**ion** [-ˈfɛkʃən] *n* imperfection *f*, défectuosité *f*.

imperial [ɪmˈpɪərɪəl] *a* impérial(e); (*measure*) légal(e); ~**ism** *n* impérialisme *m*.

imperil [ɪmˈpɛrɪl] *vt* mettre en péril.

impersonal [ɪmˈpəːsənl] *a* impersonnel(le).

impersonate [ɪmˈpəːsəneɪt] *vt* se faire passer pour; (*THEATRE*) imiter; **impersonation** [-ˈneɪʃən] *n* (*LAW*) usurpation *f* d'identité; (*THEATRE*) imitation *f*.

impertinent [ɪmˈpəːtɪnənt] *a* impertinent(e), insolent(e).

impervious [ɪmˈpəːvɪəs] *a* imperméable; (*fig*): ~ **to** insensible à; inaccessible à.

impetuous [ɪmˈpɛtjuəs] *a* impétueux(euse), fougueux(euse).

impetus [ˈɪmpətəs] *n* impulsion *f*; (*of runner*) élan *m*.

impinge [ɪmˈpɪndʒ]: **to ~ on** *vt fus* (*person*) affecter, toucher; (*rights*) empiéter sur.

implausible [ɪmˈplɔːzɪbl] *a* peu plausible.

implement *n* [ˈɪmplɪmənt] outil *m*, instrument *m*; (*for cooking*) ustensile *m* // *vt* [ˈɪmplɪmənt] exécuter, mettre à effet.

implicate [ˈɪmplɪkeɪt] *vt* impliquer, compromettre; **implication** [-ˈkeɪʃən] *n* implication *f*.

implicit [ɪmˈplɪsɪt] *a* implicite; (*complete*) absolu(e), sans réserve.

implore [ɪmˈplɔː*] *vt* implorer, supplier.

imply [ɪmˈplaɪ] *vt* suggérer, laisser entendre; indiquer, supposer.

impolite [ɪmpəˈlaɪt] *a* impoli(e).

imponderable [ɪmˈpɒndərəbl] *a* impondérable.

import *vt* [ɪmˈpɔːt] importer // *n* [ˈɪmpɔːt] (*COMM*) importation *f*; (*meaning*) portée *f*, signification *f*.

importance [ɪmˈpɔːtns] *n* importance *f*.

important [ɪmˈpɔːtnt] *a* important(e).

importation [ɪmpɔːˈteɪʃən] *n* importation *f*.

imported [ɪmˈpɔːtɪd] *a* importé(e), d'importation.

importer [ɪmˈpɔːtə*] *n* importateur/trice.

impose [ɪmˈpəuz] *vt* imposer // *vi*: **to ~ on sb** abuser de la gentillesse (*or* crédulité) de qn.

imposing [ɪmˈpəuzɪŋ] *a* imposant(e), impressionnant(e).

impossibility [ɪmpɒsəˈbɪlɪtɪ] *n* impossibilité *f*.

impossible [ɪmˈpɒsɪbl] *a* impossible.

impostor [ɪmˈpɒstə*] *n* imposteur *m*.

impotence [ˈɪmpətns] *n* impuissance *f*.

impotent [ˈɪmpətnt] *a* impuissant(e).

impound [ɪmˈpaund] *vt* confisquer, saisir.

impoverished [ɪmˈpɒvərɪʃt] *a* pauvre, appauvri(e).

impracticable [ɪmˈpræktɪkəbl] *a* impraticable.

impractical [ɪmˈpræktɪkl] *a* pas pratique; (*person*) qui manque d'esprit pratique.

imprecise [ɪmprɪˈsaɪs] *a* imprécis(e).

impregnable [ɪmˈprɛgnəbl] *a* (*fortress*) imprenable; (*fig*) inattaquable; irréfutable.

impregnate [ˈɪmprɛgneɪt] *vt* imprégner; (*fertilize*) féconder.

impresario [ɪmprɪˈsɑːrɪəu] *n* impresario *m*.

impress [ɪmˈprɛs] *vt* impressionner, faire impression sur; (*mark*) imprimer, marquer; **to ~ sth on sb** faire bien comprendre qch à qn.

impression [ɪmˈprɛʃən] *n* impression *f*; (*of stamp, seal*) empreinte *f*; **to be under the ~ that** avoir l'impression que; ~**able** *a* impressionnable, sensible; ~**ist** *n* impressionniste *m/f*.

impressive [ɪmˈprɛsɪv] *a* impressionnant(e).

imprinted [ɪmˈprɪntɪd] *a*: ~ **on** imprimé(e) sur; (*fig*) imprimé(e) *or* gravé(e) dans.

imprison [ɪmˈprɪzn] *vt* emprisonner, mettre en prison; ~**ment** *n* emprisonnement *m*.

improbable [ɪmˈprɒbəbl] *a* improbable; (*excuse*) peu plausible.

impromptu [ɪmˈprɒmptjuː] *a* impromptu(e).

improper [ɪmˈprɒpə*] *a* incorrect(e); (*unsuitable*) déplacé(e), de mauvais goût; indécent(e); **impropriety** [ɪmprəˈpraɪətɪ] *n* inconvenance *f*; (*of expression*) impropriété *f*.

improve [ɪmˈpruːv] *vt* améliorer // *vi* s'améliorer; (*pupil etc*) faire des progrès; ~**ment** *n* amélioration *f*; progrès *m*.

improvisation [ɪmprəvaɪˈzeɪʃən] *n* improvisation *f*.

improvise [ˈɪmprəvaɪz] *vt,vi* improviser.

imprudence [ɪmˈpruːdns] *n* imprudence *f*.

imprudent [ɪmˈpruːdnt] *a* imprudent(e).

impudent ['ɪmpjudnt] a impudent(e).

impulse ['ɪmpʌls] n impulsion f.

impulsive [ɪm'pʌlsɪv] a impulsif(ive).

impunity [ɪm'pju:nɪtɪ] n impunité f.

impure [ɪm'pjuə*] a impur(e).

impurity [ɪm'pjuərɪtɪ] n impureté f.

in [ɪn] prep dans ; (with time: during, within): ~ May/2 days en mai/2 jours ; (: after): ~ 2 weeks dans 2 semaines ; (with substance) en ; (with town) à ; (with country): it's ~ **France/Portugal** c'est en France/au Portugal // ad dedans, à l'intérieur ; (fashionable) à la mode ; **is he ~?** est-il là? ; ~ **the country** à la campagne ; ~ **town** en ville ; ~ **the sun** au soleil ; ~ **the rain** sous la pluie ; ~ **French** en français ; **a man** ~ **10** un homme sur 10 ; ~ **hundreds** par centaines ; **the best pupil** ~ **the class** le meilleur élève de la classe ; ~ **saying this** en disant ceci ; **their party is** ~ leur parti est au pouvoir ; **to ask sb** ~ inviter qn à entrer ; **to run/limp** etc ~ entrer en courant/boitant etc ; **the** ~**s and outs of** les tenants et aboutissants de.

in., ins abbr of **inch(es)**.

inability [ɪnə'bɪlɪtɪ] n incapacité f.

inaccessible [ɪnæk'sɛsɪbl] a inaccessible.

inaccuracy [ɪn'ækjurəsɪ] n inexactitude f ; manque m de précision.

inaccurate [ɪn'ækjurət] a inexact(e) ; (person) qui manque de précision.

inaction [ɪn'ækʃən] n inaction f, inactivité f.

inactivity [ɪnæk'tɪvɪtɪ] n inactivité f.

inadequacy [ɪn'ædɪkwəsɪ] n insuffisance f.

inadequate [ɪn'ædɪkwət] a insuffisant(e), inadéquat(e).

inadvertently [ɪnəd'və:tntlɪ] ad par mégarde.

inadvisable [ɪnəd'vaɪzəbl] a à déconseiller ; **it is** ~ **to** il est déconseillé de.

inane [ɪ'neɪn] a inepte, stupide.

inanimate [ɪn'ænɪmət] a inanimé(e).

inappropriate [ɪnə'prəuprɪət] a inopportun(e), mal à propos ; (word, expression) impropre.

inapt [ɪn'æpt] a inapte ; peu approprié(e) ; ~**itude** n inaptitude f.

inarticulate [ɪnɑ:'tɪkjulət] a (person) qui s'exprime mal ; (speech) indistinct(e).

inasmuch as [ɪnəz'mʌtʃæz] ad dans la mesure où ; (seeing that) attendu que.

inattention [ɪnə'tɛnʃən] n manque m d'attention.

inattentive [ɪnə'tɛntɪv] a inattentif(ive), distrait(e) ; négligent(e).

inaudible [ɪn'ɔ:dɪbl] a inaudible.

inaugural [ɪ'nɔ:gjurəl] a inaugural(e).

inaugurate [ɪ'nɔ:gjureɪt] vt inaugurer ; (president, official) investir de ses fonctions ; **inauguration** [-'reɪʃən] n inauguration f ; investiture f.

in-between [ɪnbɪ'twi:n] a entre les deux.

inborn [ɪn'bɔ:n] a (feeling) inné(e) ; (defect) congénital(e).

inbred [ɪn'brɛd] a inné(e), naturel(le) ; (family) consanguin(e).

inbreeding [ɪn'bri:dɪŋ] n croisement m d'animaux de même souche ; unions consanguines.

Inc. abbr see **incorporated**.

incalculable [ɪn'kælkjuləbl] a incalculable.

incapability [ɪnkeɪpə'bɪlɪtɪ] n incapacité f.

incapable [ɪn'keɪpəbl] a incapable.

incapacitate [ɪnkə'pæsɪteɪt] vt: **to** ~ **sb from doing** rendre qn incapable de faire ; ~**d** a (LAW) frappé(e) d'incapacité.

incapacity [ɪnkə'pæsɪtɪ] n incapacité f.

incarcerate [ɪn'kɑ:səreɪt] vt incarcérer.

incarnate a [ɪn'kɑ:nɪt] incarné(e) // vt ['ɪnkɑ:neɪt] incarner ; **incarnation** [-'neɪʃən] n incarnation f.

incendiary [ɪn'sɛndɪərɪ] a incendiaire.

incense n ['ɪnsɛns] encens m // vt [ɪn'sɛns] (anger) mettre en colère ; ~ **burner** n encensoir m.

incentive [ɪn'sɛntɪv] n encouragement m, raison f de se donner de la peine ; ~ **bonus** n prime f d'encouragement.

incessant [ɪn'sɛsnt] a incessant(e) ; ~**ly** ad sans cesse, constamment.

incest ['ɪnsɛst] n inceste m.

inch [ɪntʃ] n pouce m (= 25 mm ; 12 in a foot) ; **within an** ~ **of** à deux doigts de ; ~ **tape** n centimètre m (de couturière).

incidence ['ɪnsɪdns] n (of crime, disease) fréquence f.

incident ['ɪnsɪdnt] n incident m ; (in book) péripétie f.

incidental [ɪnsɪ'dɛntl] a accessoire ; (unplanned) accidentel(le) ; ~ **to** qui accompagne ; ~ **expenses** npl faux frais mpl ; ~**ly** [-'dɛntəlɪ] ad (by the way) à propos.

incinerator [ɪn'sɪnəreɪtə*] n incinérateur m.

incipient [ɪn'sɪpɪənt] a naissant(e).

incision [ɪn'sɪʒən] n incision f.

incisive [ɪn'saɪsɪv] a incisif(ive) ; mordant(e).

incite [ɪn'saɪt] vt inciter, pousser.

inclement [ɪn'klɛmənt] a inclément(e), rigoureux(euse).

inclination [ɪnklɪ'neɪʃən] n inclination f.

incline n ['ɪnklaɪn] pente f, plan incliné // vb [ɪn'klaɪn] vt incliner // vi: **to** ~ **to** avoir tendance à ; **to be** ~**d to do** être enclin(e) à faire ; avoir tendance à faire ; **to be well** ~**d towards sb** être bien disposé(e) à l'égard de qn.

include [ɪn'klu:d] vt inclure, comprendre ; **including** prep y compris.

inclusion [ɪn'klu:ʒən] n inclusion f.

inclusive [ɪn'klu:sɪv] a inclus(e), compris(e) ; ~ **terms** npl prix tout compris.

incognito [ɪnkɒg'ni:təu] ad incognito.

incoherent [ɪnkəu'hɪərənt] a incohérent(e).

income ['ɪŋkʌm] n revenu m ; ~ **tax** n impôt m sur le revenu ; ~ **tax inspector** n inspecteur m des contributions directes ; ~ **tax return** n déclaration f des revenus.

incoming ['ɪnkʌmɪŋ] a: ~ **tide** n marée montante.

incompatible [ɪnkəm'pætɪbl] a incompatible.

incompetence [ɪnˈkɔmpɪtns] *n* incompétence *f*, incapacité *f*.

incompetent [ɪnˈkɔmpɪtnt] *a* incompétent(e), incapable.

incomplete [ɪnkəmˈpliːt] *a* incomplet(ète).

incomprehensible [ɪnkɔmprɪˈhɛnsɪbl] *a* incompréhensible.

inconclusive [ɪnkənˈkluːsɪv] *a* peu concluant(e); (*argument*) peu convaincant(e).

incongruous [ɪnˈkɔŋɡruəs] *a* peu approprié(e); (*remark, act*) incongru(e), déplacé(e).

inconsequential [ɪnkɔnsɪˈkwɛnʃl] *a* sans importance.

inconsiderate [ɪnkənˈsɪdərət] *a* (*action*) inconsidéré(e); (*person*) qui manque d'égards.

inconsistent [ɪnkənˈsɪstnt] *a* sans cohérence; peu logique; qui présente des contradictions; ~ **with** en contradiction avec.

inconspicuous [ɪnkənˈspɪkjuəs] *a* qui passe inaperçu(e); (*colour, dress*) discret(ète); **to make o.s.** ~ ne pas se faire remarquer.

inconstant [ɪnˈkɔnstnt] *a* inconstant(e); variable.

incontinence [ɪnˈkɔntɪnəns] *n* incontinence *f*.

incontinent [ɪnˈkɔntɪnənt] *a* incontinent(e).

inconvenience [ɪnkənˈviːnjəns] *n* inconvénient *m*; (*trouble*) dérangement *m* // *vt* déranger.

inconvenient [ɪnkənˈviːnjənt] *a* malcommode; (*time, place*) mal choisi(e), qui ne convient pas.

incorporate [ɪnˈkɔːpəreɪt] *vt* incorporer; (*contain*) contenir // *vi* fusionner; (*two firms*) se constituer en société; ~**d** *a*: ~**d company** (*US, abbr* Inc.) société *f* anonyme (S.A.).

incorrect [ɪnkəˈrɛkt] *a* incorrect(e); (*opinion, statement*) inexact(e).

incorruptible [ɪnkəˈrʌptɪbl] *a* incorruptible.

increase *n* [ˈɪnkriːs] augmentation *f* // *vi, vt* [ɪnˈkriːs] augmenter.

increasing [ɪnˈkriːsɪŋ] *a* (*number*) croissant(e); ~**ly** *ad* de plus en plus.

incredible [ɪnˈkrɛdɪbl] *a* incroyable.

incredulous [ɪnˈkrɛdjuləs] *a* incrédule.

increment [ˈɪnkrɪmənt] *n* augmentation *f*.

incriminate [ɪnˈkrɪmɪneɪt] *vt* incriminer, compromettre.

incubation [ɪnkjuˈbeɪʃən] *n* incubation *f*.

incubator [ˈɪnkjubeɪtə*] *n* incubateur *m*; (*for babies*) couveuse *f*.

incur [ɪnˈkəː*] *vt* (*expenses*) encourir; (*anger, risk*) s'exposer à; (*debt*) contracter; (*loss*) subir.

incurable [ɪnˈkjuərəbl] *a* incurable.

incursion [ɪnˈkəːʃən] *n* incursion *f*.

indebted [ɪnˈdɛtɪd] *a*: **to be** ~ **to sb** (**for**) être redevable à qn (de).

indecent [ɪnˈdiːsnt] *a* indécent(e), inconvenant(e); ~ **assault** *n* attentat *m* à la pudeur; ~ **exposure** *n* outrage *m* (public) à la pudeur.

indecision [ɪndɪˈsɪʒən] *n* indécision *f*.

indecisive [ɪndɪˈsaɪsɪv] *a* indécis(e); (*discussion*) peu concluant(e).

indeed [ɪnˈdiːd] *ad* en effet; vraiment; **yes** ~! certainement!

indefinable [ɪndɪˈfaɪnəbl] *a* indéfinissable.

indefinite [ɪnˈdɛfɪnɪt] *a* indéfini(e); (*answer*) vague; (*period, number*) indéterminé(e); ~**ly** *ad* (*wait*) indéfiniment; (*speak*) vaguement, avec imprécision.

indelible [ɪnˈdɛlɪbl] *a* indélébile.

indemnify [ɪnˈdɛmnɪfaɪ] *vt* indemniser, dédommager.

indentation [ɪndɛnˈteɪʃən] *n* découpure *f*; (*TYP*) alinéa *m*; (*on metal*) bosse *f*.

independence [ɪndɪˈpɛndns] *n* indépendance *f*.

independent [ɪndɪˈpɛndnt] *a* indépendant(e); ~**ly** *ad* de façon indépendante; ~**ly of** indépendamment de.

indescribable [ɪndɪˈskraɪbəbl] *a* indescriptible.

index [ˈɪndɛks] *n* (*pl*: ~**es**: *in book*) index *m*; (: *in library etc*) catalogue *m*; (*pl*: **indices** [ˈɪndɪsiːz]: *ratio, sign*) indice *m*; ~ **card** *n* fiche *f*; ~ **finger** *n* index *m*; ~**linked** *a* indexé(e) (sur le coût de la vie etc).

India [ˈɪndɪə] *n* Inde *f*; ~**n** *a* indien(ne) // *n* Indien/ne; ~**n ink** *n* encre *f* de Chine; ~**n Ocean** *n* océan Indien; ~ **paper** *n* papier *m* bible.

indicate [ˈɪndɪkeɪt] *vt* indiquer; **indication** [-ˈkeɪʃən] *n* indication *f*, signe *m*.

indicative [ɪnˈdɪkətɪv] *a* indicatif(ive) // *n* (*LING*) indicatif *m*.

indicator [ˈɪndɪkeɪtə*] *n* (*sign*) indicateur *m*; (*AUT*) clignotant *m*.

indices [ˈɪndɪsiːz] *npl of* **index**.

indict [ɪnˈdaɪt] *vt* accuser; ~**able** *a* (*person*) passible de poursuites; ~**able offence** *n* délit pénal; ~**ment** *n* accusation *f*.

indifference [ɪnˈdɪfrəns] *n* indifférence *f*.

indifferent [ɪnˈdɪfrənt] *a* indifférent(e); (*poor*) médiocre, quelconque.

indigenous [ɪnˈdɪdʒɪnəs] *a* indigène.

indigestible [ɪndɪˈdʒɛstɪbl] *a* indigeste.

indigestion [ɪndɪˈdʒɛstʃən] *n* indigestion *f*, mauvaise digestion.

indignant [ɪnˈdɪɡnənt] *a*: ~ (**at sth/with sb**) indigné(e) (de qch/contre qn).

indignation [ɪndɪɡˈneɪʃən] *n* indignation *f*.

indignity [ɪnˈdɪɡnɪtɪ] *n* indignité *f*, affront *m*.

indigo [ˈɪndɪɡəu] *a* indigo *inv* // *n* indigo *m*.

indirect [ɪndɪˈrɛkt] *a* indirect(e); ~**ly** *ad* indirectement.

indiscreet [ɪndɪˈskriːt] *a* indiscret(ète); (*rash*) imprudent(e).

indiscretion [ɪndɪˈskrɛʃən] *n* indiscrétion *f*; imprudence *f*.

indiscriminate [ɪndɪˈskrɪmɪnət] *a* (*person*) qui manque de discernement; (*admiration*) aveugle; (*killings*) commis(e) au hasard.

indispensable [ɪndɪˈspɛnsəbl] *a* indispensable.

indisposed [ɪndɪˈspəuzd] *a* (*unwell*) indisposé(e), souffrant(e).

indisposition [ɪndɪspə'zɪʃən] n (illness) indisposition f, malaise m.

indisputable [ɪndɪ'spjuːtəbl] a incontestable, indiscutable.

indistinct [ɪndɪ'stɪŋkt] a indistinct(e); (memory, noise) vague.

individual [ɪndɪ'vɪdjuəl] n individu m // a individuel(le); (characteristic) particulier(ère), original(e); ~ist n individualiste m/f; ~ity [-'ælɪtɪ] n individualité f; ~ly ad individuellement.

indoctrinate [ɪn'dɔktrɪneɪt] vt endoctriner; **indoctrination** [-'neɪʃən] n endoctrinement m.

indolent ['ɪndələnt] a indolent(e), nonchalant(e).

indoor ['ɪndɔː] a d'intérieur; (plant) d'appartement; (swimming-pool) couvert(e); (sport, games) pratiqué(e) en salle; ~s [ɪn'dɔːz] ad à l'intérieur; (at home) à la maison.

indubitable [ɪn'djuːbɪtəbl] a indubitable, incontestable.

induce [ɪn'djuːs] vt persuader; (bring about) provoquer; ~ment n incitation f; (incentive) but m; (pej: bribe) pot-de-vin m.

induct [ɪn'dʌkt] vt établir dans ses fonctions; (fig) initier.

induction [ɪn'dʌkʃən] n (MED: of birth) accouchement provoqué; ~ course n stage m de mise au courant.

indulge [ɪn'dʌldʒ] vt (whim) céder à, satisfaire; (child) gâter // vi: to ~ in sth s'offrir qch, se permettre qch; se livrer à qch; ~nce n fantaisie f (que l'on s'offre); (leniency) indulgence f; ~nt a indulgent(e).

industrial [ɪn'dʌstrɪəl] a industriel(le); (injury) du travail; (dispute) ouvrier(ère); ~ action n action revendicative; ~ estate n zone industrielle; ~ist n industriel m; ~ize vt industrialiser.

industrious [ɪn'dʌstrɪəs] a travailleur(euse).

industry ['ɪndəstrɪ] n industrie f; (diligence) zèle m, application f.

inebriated [ɪ'niːbrɪeɪtɪd] a ivre.

inedible [ɪn'ɛdɪbl] a immangeable; (plant etc) non comestible.

ineffective [ɪnɪ'fɛktɪv] a inefficace.

ineffectual [ɪnɪ'fɛktʃuəl] a inefficace; incompétent(e).

inefficiency [ɪnɪ'fɪʃənsɪ] n inefficacité f.

inefficient [ɪnɪ'fɪʃənt] a inefficace.

inelegant [ɪn'ɛlɪgənt] a peu élégant(e).

ineligible [ɪn'ɛlɪdʒɪbl] a (candidate) inéligible; to be ~ for sth ne pas avoir droit à qch.

inept [ɪ'nɛpt] a inepte.

inequality [ɪnɪ'kwɔlɪtɪ] n inégalité f.

ineradicable [ɪnɪ'rædɪkəbl] a indéracinable, tenace.

inert [ɪ'nəːt] a inerte.

inertia [ɪ'nəːʃə] n inertie f; ~ reel seat belt n ceinture f de sécurité à enrouleur.

inescapable [ɪnɪ'skeɪpəbl] a inéluctable, inévitable.

inessential [ɪnɪ'sɛnʃl] a superflu(e).

inestimable [ɪn'ɛstɪməbl] a inestimable, incalculable.

inevitable [ɪn'ɛvɪtəbl] a inévitable.

inexact [ɪnɪg'zækt] a inexact(e).

inexhaustible [ɪnɪg'zɔːstɪbl] a inépuisable.

inexorable [ɪn'ɛksərəbl] a inexorable.

inexpensive [ɪnɪk'spɛnsɪv] a bon marché inv.

inexperience [ɪnɪk'spɪərɪəns] n inexpérience f, manque m d'expérience; ~d a inexpérimenté(e).

inexplicable [ɪnɪk'splɪkəbl] a inexplicable.

inexpressible [ɪnɪk'sprɛsɪbl] a inexprimable.

inextricable [ɪnɪk'strɪkəbl] a inextricable.

infallibility [ɪnfælə'bɪlɪtɪ] n infaillibilité f.

infallible [ɪn'fælɪbl] a infaillible.

infamous ['ɪnfəməs] a infâme, abominable.

infamy ['ɪnfəmɪ] n infamie f.

infancy ['ɪnfənsɪ] n petite enfance, bas âge; (fig) enfance f, débuts mpl.

infant ['ɪnfənt] n (baby) nourrisson m; (young child) petit(e) enfant; ~ile a infantile; ~ school n classes fpl préparatoires (entre 5 et 7 ans).

infantry ['ɪnfəntrɪ] n infanterie f; ~man n fantassin m.

infatuated [ɪn'fætjuertɪd] a: ~ with entiché(e) de.

infatuation [ɪnfætju'eɪʃən] n toquade f; engouement m.

infect [ɪn'fɛkt] vt infecter, contaminer; (fig: pej) corrompre; ~ed with (illness) atteint(e) de; ~ion [ɪn'fɛkʃən] n infection f; contagion f; ~ious [ɪn'fɛkʃəs] a infectieux(euse); (also: fig) contagieux(euse).

infer [ɪn'fəː] vt conclure, déduire; ~ence ['ɪnfərəns] n conclusion f; déduction f.

inferior [ɪn'fɪərɪə] a inférieur(e); (goods) de qualité inférieure // n inférieur(e); (in rank) subalterne m/f; ~ity [ɪnfɪərɪ'ɔrɪtɪ] n infériorité f; ~ity complex n complexe m d'infériorité.

infernal [ɪn'fəːnl] a infernal(e); ~ly ad abominablement.

inferno [ɪn'fəːnəu] n enfer m; brasier m.

infertile [ɪn'fəːtaɪl] a stérile; **infertility** [-'tɪltɪ] n infertilité f, stérilité f.

infested [ɪn'fɛstɪd] a: ~ (with) infesté(e) (de).

infidelity [ɪnfɪ'dɛlɪtɪ] n infidélité f.

in-fighting ['ɪnfaɪtɪŋ] n querelles fpl internes.

infiltrate ['ɪnfɪltreɪt] vt (troops etc) faire s'infiltrer; (enemy line etc) s'infiltrer dans // vi s'infiltrer.

infinite ['ɪnfɪnɪt] a infini(e).

infinitive [ɪn'fɪnɪtɪv] n infinitif m.

infinity [ɪn'fɪnɪtɪ] n infinité f; (also MATH) infini m.

infirm [ɪn'fəːm] a infirme.

infirmary [ɪn'fəːmərɪ] n hôpital m; (in school, factory) infirmerie f.

infirmity [ɪn'fəːmɪtɪ] n infirmité f.

inflame [ɪn'fleɪm] vt enflammer.

inflammable [ɪn'flæməbl] a inflammable.

inflammation [ɪnflə'meɪʃən] n inflammation f.

inflate [ɪn'fleɪt] vt (tyre, balloon) gonfler; (fig) grossir; gonfler; faire monter; to ~ the currency avoir recours à l'inflation;

~d a (*style*) enflé(e) ; (*value*) exagéré(e) ; **inflation** [ɪnˈfleɪʃən] n (ECON) inflation f.

inflexible [ɪnˈflɛksɪbl] a inflexible, rigide.

inflict [ɪnˈflɪkt] vt: to ~ on infliger à ; ~ion [ɪnˈflɪkʃən] n infliction f; affliction f.

inflow [ˈɪnfləʊ] n afflux m.

influence [ˈɪnfluəns] n influence f // vt influencer ; **under the ~ of** sous l'effet de ; **under the ~ of** drink en état d'ébriété.

influential [ɪnfluˈɛnʃl] a influent(e).

influenza [ɪnfluˈɛnzə] n grippe f.

influx [ˈɪnflʌks] n afflux m.

inform [ɪnˈfɔːm] vt: to ~ sb (of) informer or avertir qn (de) ; to ~ sb about renseigner qn sur, mettre qn au courant de.

informal [ɪnˈfɔːml] a (*person, manner*) simple, sans façon ; (*visit, discussion*) dénué(e) de formalités ; (*announcement, invitation*) non-officiel(le) ; 'dress ~' 'tenue de ville' ; ~ity [-ˈmælɪtɪ] n simplicité f, absence f de cérémonie ; caractère non-officiel ; ~ language n langage m de la conversation.

information [ɪnfəˈmeɪʃən] n information f; renseignements mpl ; (*knowledge*) connaissances fpl ; a piece of ~ un renseignement.

informative [ɪnˈfɔːmətɪv] a instructif(ive).

informer [ɪnˈfɔːmə*] n dénonciateur/- trice ; (*also*: police ~) indicateur/trice.

infra-red [ɪnfrəˈrɛd] a infrarouge.

infrequent [ɪnˈfriːkwənt] a peu fréquent(e), rare.

infringe [ɪnˈfrɪndʒ] vt enfreindre // vi: to ~ on empiéter sur ; ~ment n: ~ment (of) infraction f (à).

infuriate [ɪnˈfjʊərɪeɪt] vt mettre en fureur ; **infuriating** a exaspérant(e).

ingenious [ɪnˈdʒiːnjəs] a ingénieux(euse).

ingenuity [ɪndʒɪˈnjuːɪtɪ] n ingéniosité f.

ingenuous [ɪnˈdʒɛnjuəs] a naïf(ïve), ingénu(e).

ingot [ˈɪŋgət] n lingot m.

ingrained [ɪnˈgreɪnd] a enraciné(e).

ingratiate [ɪnˈgreɪʃɪeɪt] vt: to ~ o.s. with s'insinuer dans les bonnes grâces de, se faire bien voir de.

ingratitude [ɪnˈgrætɪtjuːd] n ingratitude f.

ingredient [ɪnˈgriːdɪənt] n ingrédient m ; élément m.

ingrown [ˈɪngrəʊn] a: ~ toenail ongle incarné.

inhabit [ɪnˈhæbɪt] vt habiter.

inhabitant [ɪnˈhæbɪtnt] n habitant/e.

inhale [ɪnˈheɪl] vt inhaler ; (*perfume*) respirer // vi (in smoking) avaler la fumée.

inherent [ɪnˈhɪərənt] a: ~ (in or to) inhérent(e) (à).

inherit [ɪnˈhɛrɪt] vt hériter (de) ; ~ance n héritage m ; law of ~ance n droit m de la succession.

inhibit [ɪnˈhɪbɪt] vt (PSYCH) inhiber ; to ~ sb from doing empêcher or retenir qn de faire ; ~ing a gênant(e) ; ~ion [-ˈbɪʃən] n inhibition f.

inhospitable [ɪnhɔsˈpɪtəbl] a inhospitalier(ère).

inhuman [ɪnˈhjuːmən] a inhumain(e).

inimitable [ɪˈnɪmɪtəbl] a inimitable.

iniquity [ɪˈnɪkwɪtɪ] n iniquité f.

initial [ɪˈnɪʃl] a initial(e) // n initiale f // vt parafer ; ~s npl initiales fpl ; (as signature) parafe m ; ~ly ad initialement, au début.

initiate [ɪˈnɪʃɪeɪt] vt (start) entreprendre ; amorcer ; lancer ; (person) initier ; to ~ sb into a secret initier qn à un secret ; to ~ proceedings against sb (LAW) intenter une action à qn ; **initiation** [-ˈeɪʃən] n (into secret etc) initiation f.

initiative [ɪˈnɪʃətɪv] n initiative f.

inject [ɪnˈdʒɛkt] vt (liquid) injecter ; (person) faire une piqûre à ; ~ion [ɪnˈdʒɛkʃən] n injection f, piqûre f.

injure [ˈɪndʒə*] vt blesser ; (wrong) faire du tort à ; (damage: reputation etc) compromettre.

injury [ˈɪndʒərɪ] n blessure f; (wrong) tort m ; ~ time n (SPORT) arrêts mpl de jeu.

injustice [ɪnˈdʒʌstɪs] n injustice f.

ink [ɪŋk] n encre f.

inkling [ˈɪŋklɪŋ] n soupçon m, vague idée f.

inky [ˈɪŋkɪ] a taché(e) d'encre.

inlaid [ˈɪnleɪd] a incrusté(e) ; (table etc) marqueté(e).

inland a [ˈɪnlənd] intérieur(e) // ad [ɪnˈlænd] à l'intérieur, dans les terres ; I~ Revenue n (Brit) fisc m, contributions directes ; ~ waterways npl canaux mpl et rivières fpl.

in-laws [ˈɪnlɔːz] npl beaux-parents mpl ; belle famille.

inlet [ˈɪnlɛt] n (GEO) crique f; ~ pipe n (TECH) tuyau m d'arrivée.

inmate [ˈɪnmeɪt] n (in prison) détenu/e ; (in asylum) interné/e.

inn [ɪn] n auberge f.

innate [ɪˈneɪt] a inné(e).

inner [ˈɪnə*] a intérieur(e) ; ~ city n centre m de zone urbaine ; ~ tube n (of tyre) chambre f à air.

innocence [ˈɪnəsns] n innocence f.

innocent [ˈɪnəsnt] a innocent(e).

innocuous [ɪˈnɔkjuəs] a inoffensif(ive).

innovation [ɪnəuˈveɪʃən] n innovation f.

innuendo, ~es [ɪnjuˈɛndəu] n insinuation f, allusion (malveillante).

innumerable [ɪˈnjuːmrəbl] a innombrable.

inoculation [ɪnɔkjuˈleɪʃən] n inoculation f.

inopportune [ɪnˈɔpətjuːn] a inopportun(e).

inordinately [ɪˈnɔːdɪnətlɪ] ad démesurément.

inorganic [ɪnɔːˈgænɪk] a inorganique.

in-patient [ˈɪnpeɪʃənt] n malade hospitalisé(e).

input [ˈɪnput] n (ELEC) énergie f, puissance f; (of machine) consommation f; (of computer) information fournie.

inquest [ˈɪnkwɛst] n enquête (criminelle).

inquire [ɪnˈkwaɪə*] vi demander // vt demander, s'informer de ; to ~ about vt fus s'informer de, se renseigner sur ; to ~ after vt fus demander des nouvelles de ; to ~ into vt fus faire une enquête sur ; **inquiring** a (mind) curieux(euse), investigateur(trice) ; **inquiry** n demande f de renseignements ; (LAW) enquête f,

investigation f; **inquiry office** n bureau m de renseignements.
inquisitive [ɪnˈkwɪzɪtɪv] a curieux(euse).
inroad [ˈɪnrəud] n incursion f.
insane [ɪnˈseɪn] a fou(folle); (MED) aliéné(e).
insanitary [ɪnˈsænɪtərɪ] a insalubre.
insanity [ɪnˈsænɪtɪ] n folie f; (MED) aliénation (mentale).
insatiable [ɪnˈseɪʃəbl] a insatiable.
inscribe [ɪnˈskraɪb] vt inscrire; (book etc): to ~ (to sb) dédicacer (à qn).
inscription [ɪnˈskrɪpʃən] n inscription f; dédicace f.
inscrutable [ɪnˈskruːtəbl] a impénétrable.
insect [ˈɪnsɛkt] n insecte m; ~icide [ɪnˈsɛktɪsaɪd] n insecticide m.
insecure [ɪnsɪˈkjuə*] a peu solide; peu sûr(e); (person) anxieux (euse); **insecurity** n insécurité f.
insensible [ɪnˈsɛnsɪbl] a insensible; (unconscious) sans connaissance.
insensitive [ɪnˈsɛnsɪtɪv] a insensible.
inseparable [ɪnˈsɛprəbl] a inséparable.
insert vt [ɪnˈsəːt] insérer // n [ˈɪnsəːt] insertion f; ~ion [ɪnˈsəːʃən] n insertion f.
inshore [ɪnˈʃɔː*] a côtier(ère) // ad près de la côte; vers la côte.
inside [ˈɪnsaɪd] n intérieur m // a intérieur(e) // ad à l'intérieur, dedans // prep à l'intérieur de; (of time): ~ 10 **minutes** en moins de 10 minutes; ~s npl (col) intestins mpl; ~ **forward** n (SPORT) intérieur m; ~ **lane** n (AUT: in Britain) voie f de gauche; ~ **out** ad à l'envers; (know) à fond; **to turn** ~ **out** retourner.
insidious [ɪnˈsɪdɪəs] a insidieux(euse).
insight [ˈɪnsaɪt] n perspicacité f; (glimpse, idea) aperçu m.
insignificant [ɪnsɪgˈnɪfɪkənt] a insignifiant(e).
insincere [ɪnsɪnˈsɪə*] a hypocrite; **insincerity** [-ˈsɛrɪtɪ] n manque m de sincérité, hypocrisie f.
insinuate [ɪnˈsɪnjueɪt] vt insinuer; **insinuation** [-ˈeɪʃən] n insinuation f.
insipid [ɪnˈsɪpɪd] a insipide, fade.
insist [ɪnˈsɪst] vi insister; to ~ **on doing** insister pour faire; **to** ~ **that** insister pour que; (claim) maintenir or soutenir que; ~**ence** n insistance f; ~**ent** a insistant(e), pressant(e).
insolence [ˈɪnsələns] n insolence f.
insolent [ˈɪnsələnt] a insolent(e).
insoluble [ɪnˈsɔljubl] a insoluble.
insolvent [ɪnˈsɔlvənt] a insolvable; en faillite.
insomnia [ɪnˈsɔmnɪə] n insomnie f.
inspect [ɪnˈspɛkt] vt inspecter; (ticket) contrôler; ~**ion** [ɪnˈspɛkʃən] n inspection f; contrôle m; ~**or** n inspecteur/trice; contrôleur/euse.
inspiration [ɪnspəˈreɪʃən] n inspiration f.
inspire [ɪnˈspaɪə*] vt inspirer; **inspiring** a inspirant(e).
instability [ɪnstəˈbɪlɪtɪ] n instabilité f.
install [ɪnˈstɔːl] vt installer; ~**ation** [ɪnstəˈleɪʃən] n installation f.
instalment, **installment** (US) [ɪnˈstɔːlmənt] n acompte m, versement partiel; (of TV serial etc) épisode m.

instance [ˈɪnstəns] n exemple m; **for** ~ par exemple; **in many** ~**s** dans bien des cas.
instant [ˈɪnstənt] n instant m // a immédiat(e); urgent(e); (coffee, food) instantané(e), en poudre; **the 10th** ~ le 10 courant; ~**ly** ad immédiatement, tout de suite.
instead [ɪnˈstɛd] ad au lieu de cela; ~ **of** au lieu de; ~ **of sb** à la place de qn.
instep [ˈɪnstɛp] n cou-de-pied m; (of shoe) cambrure f.
instigation [ɪnstɪˈgeɪʃən] n instigation f.
instil [ɪnˈstɪl] vt: to ~ (into) inculquer (à); (courage) insuffler (à).
instinct [ˈɪnstɪŋkt] n instinct m.
instinctive [ɪnˈstɪŋktɪv] a instinctif(ive); ~**ly** ad instinctivement.
institute [ˈɪnstɪtjuːt] n institut m // vt instituer, établir; (inquiry) ouvrir; (proceedings) entamer.
institution [ɪnstɪˈtjuːʃən] n institution f; établissement m (scolaire); établissement (psychiatrique).
instruct [ɪnˈstrʌkt] vt instruire, former; **to** ~ **sb in sth** enseigner qch à qn; **to** ~ **sb to do** charger qn or ordonner à qn de faire; ~**ion** [ɪnˈstrʌkʃən] n instruction f; ~**ions** npl directives fpl; ~**ions** (for use) mode m d'emploi; ~**ive** a instructif(ive); ~**or** n professeur m; (for skiing, driving) moniteur m.
instrument [ˈɪnstrumənt] n instrument m; ~**al** [-ˈmɛntl] a (MUS) instrumental(e); **to be** ~**al in** contribuer à; ~**alist** [-ˈmɛntəlɪst] n instrumentiste m/f; ~ **panel** n tableau m de bord.
insubordinate [ɪnsəˈbɔːdənɪt] a insubordonné(e); **insubordination** [-ˈneɪʃən] n insubordination f.
insufferable [ɪnˈsʌfrəbl] a insupportable.
insufficient [ɪnsəˈfɪʃənt] a insuffisant(e); ~**ly** ad insuffisamment.
insular [ˈɪnsjulə*] a insulaire; (outlook) étroit(e); (person) aux vues étroites.
insulate [ˈɪnsjuleɪt] vt isoler; (against sound) insonoriser; **insulating tape** n ruban isolant; **insulation** [-ˈleɪʃən] n isolation f; insonorisation f.
insulin [ˈɪnsjulɪn] n insuline f.
insult n [ˈɪnsʌlt] insulte f, affront m // vt [ɪnˈsʌlt] insulter, faire un affront à; ~**ing** a insultant(e), injurieux(euse).
insuperable [ɪnˈsjuːprəbl] a insurmontable.
insurance [ɪnˈʃuərəns] n assurance f; **fire/life** ~ assurance-incendie/-vie; ~ **agent** n agent m d'assurances; ~ **policy** n police f d'assurance.
insure [ɪnˈʃuə*] vt assurer.
insurrection [ɪnsəˈrɛkʃən] n insurrection f.
intact [ɪnˈtækt] a intact(e).
intake [ˈɪnteɪk] n (TECH) admission f; adduction f; (of food) consommation f; (SCOL): **an** ~ **of 200 a year** 200 admissions fpl par an.
intangible [ɪnˈtændʒɪbl] a intangible; (assets) immatériel(le).
integral [ˈɪntɪgrəl] a intégral(e); (part) intégrant(e).

integrate ['ɪntɪgreɪt] vt intégrer // vi s'intégrer.

integrity [ɪn'tɛgrɪtɪ] n intégrité f.

intellect ['ɪntəlɛkt] n intelligence f; ~ual [-'lɛktjuəl] a, n intellectuel(le).

intelligence [ɪn'tɛlɪdʒəns] n intelligence f; (MIL etc) informations fpl, renseignements mpl; I~ **Service** n services mpl de renseignements.

intelligent [ɪn'tɛlɪdʒənt] a intelligent(e); ~ly ad intelligemment.

intelligible [ɪn'tɛlɪdʒɪbl] a intelligible.

intemperate [ɪn'tɛmpərət] a immodéré(e); (drinking too much) adonné(e) à la boisson.

intend [ɪn'tɛnd] vt (gift etc): to ~ sth for destiner qch à; to ~ to do avoir l'intention de faire; ~ed a (insult) intentionnel(le); (journey) projeté(e); (effect) voulu(e).

intense [ɪn'tɛns] a intense; (person) véhément(e); ~ly ad intensément; profondément.

intensify [ɪn'tɛnsɪfaɪ] vt intensifier.

intensity [ɪn'tɛnsɪtɪ] n intensité f.

intensive [ɪn'tɛnsɪv] a intensif(ive); ~ **care unit** n service m de réanimation.

intent [ɪn'tɛnt] n intention f // a attentif(ive), absorbé(e); to all ~s and purposes en fait, pratiquement; to be ~ on doing sth être (bien) décidé à faire qch.

intention [ɪn'tɛnʃən] n intention f; ~al a intentionnel(le), délibéré(e).

intently [ɪn'tɛntlɪ] ad attentivement.

inter [ɪn'tɜ:*] vt enterrer.

interact [ɪntər'ækt] vi avoir une action réciproque; ~ion [-'ækʃən] n interaction f.

intercede [ɪntə'si:d] vi: to ~ (with) intercéder (auprès de).

intercept [ɪntə'sɛpt] vt intercepter; (person) arrêter au passage; ~ion [-'sɛpʃən] n interception f.

interchange n ['ɪntətʃeɪndʒ] (exchange) échange m; (on motorway) échangeur m // vt [ɪntə'tʃeɪndʒ] échanger; mettre à la place l'un(e) de l'autre; ~able a interchangeable.

intercom ['ɪntəkɔm] n interphone m.

interconnect [ɪntəkə'nɛkt] vi (rooms) communiquer.

intercourse ['ɪntəkɔ:s] n rapports mpl.

interest ['ɪntrɪst] n intérêt m; (COMM: stake, share) intérêts mpl // vt intéresser; ~ed a intéressé(e); to be ~ed in s'intéresser à; ~ing a intéressant(e).

interfere [ɪntə'fɪə*] vi: to ~ in (quarrel, other people's business) se mêler à; to ~ with (object) tripoter, toucher à; (plans) contrecarrer; (duty) être en conflit avec; **don't ~** mêlez-vous de vos affaires.

interference [ɪntə'fɪərəns] n (gen) intrusion f; (PHYSICS) interférence f; (RADIO, TV) parasites mpl.

interim ['ɪntərɪm] a provisoire; (post) intérimaire // n: **in the ~** dans l'intérim.

interior [ɪn'tɪərɪə*] n intérieur m // a intérieur(e).

interjection [ɪntə'dʒɛkʃən] n interjection f.

interlock [ɪntə'lɔk] vi s'enclencher // vt enclencher.

interloper ['ɪntələupə*] n intrus/e.

interlude ['ɪntəlu:d] n intervalle m; (THEATRE) intermède m.

intermarry [ɪntə'mærɪ] vi former des alliances entre familles (or tribus); former des unions consanguines.

intermediary [ɪntə'mi:dɪərɪ] n intermédiaire m/f.

intermediate [ɪntə'mi:dɪət] a intermédiaire; (SCOL: course, level) moyen(ne).

intermission [ɪntə'mɪʃən] n pause f; (THEATRE, CINEMA) entracte m.

intermittent [ɪntə'mɪtnt] a intermittent(e); ~ly ad par intermittence, par intervalles.

intern vt [ɪn'tə:n] interner // n ['ɪntə:n] (US) interne m/f.

internal [ɪn'tə:nl] a interne; (dispute, reform etc) intérieur(e); ~ly ad intérieurement; 'not to be taken ~ly' 'pour usage externe'; ~ **revenue** n (US) fisc m.

international [ɪntə'næʃənl] a international(e) // n (SPORT) international m.

internment [ɪn'tə:nmənt] n internement m.

interplay ['ɪntəpleɪ] n effet m réciproque, jeu m.

interpret [ɪn'tə:prɪt] vt interpréter // vi servir d'interprète; ~ation [-'teɪʃən] n interprétation f; ~er n interprète m/f; ~ing n (profession) interprétariat m.

interrelated [ɪntərɪ'leɪtɪd] a en corrélation, en rapport étroit.

interrogate [ɪn'tɛrəugeɪt] vt interroger; (suspect etc) soumettre à un interrogatoire; **interrogation** [-'geɪʃən] n interrogation f; interrogatoire m; **interrogative** [ɪntə'rɔgətɪv] a interrogateur(trice) // n (LING) interrogatif m; **interrogator** n interrogateur/trice.

interrupt [ɪntə'rʌpt] vt interrompre; ~ion [-'rʌpʃən] n interruption f.

intersect [ɪntə'sɛkt] vt couper, croiser // vi (roads) se croiser, se couper; ~ion [-'sɛkʃən] n intersection f; (of roads) croisement m.

intersperse [ɪntə'spə:s] vt: to ~ with parsemer de.

intertwine [ɪntə'twaɪn] vt entrelacer // vi s'entrelacer.

interval ['ɪntəvl] n intervalle m; (SCOL) récréation f; (THEATRE) entracte m; (SPORT) mi-temps f; **bright ~s** (in weather) éclaircies fpl; **at ~s** par intervalles.

intervene [ɪntə'vi:n] vi (time) s'écouler (entre-temps); (event) survenir; (person) intervenir; **intervention** [-'vɛnʃən] n intervention f.

interview ['ɪntəvju:] n (RADIO, TV etc) interview f; (for job) entrevue f // vt interviewer; avoir une entrevue avec; ~er n interviewer m.

intestate [ɪn'tɛsteɪt] a intestat.

intestinal [ɪn'tɛstɪnl] a intestinal(e).

intestine [ɪn'tɛstɪn] n intestin m.

intimacy ['ɪntɪməsɪ] n intimité f.

intimate a ['ɪntɪmət] intime; (knowledge) approfondi(e) // vt ['ɪntɪmeɪt] suggérer, laisser entendre ; (*announce*) faire savoir ; ~ly *ad* intimement.

intimation [ɪntɪˈmeɪʃən] *n* annonce *f*.

intimidate [ɪnˈtɪmɪdeɪt] *vt* intimider ; **intimidation** [-ˈdeɪʃən] *n* intimidation *f*.

into [ˈɪntu] *prep* dans ; ~ 3 pieces/French en 3 morceaux/français.

intolerable [ɪnˈtɔlərəbl] *a* intolérable.

intolerance [ɪnˈtɔlərns] *n* intolérance *f*.

intolerant [ɪnˈtɔlərnt] *a* intolérant(e).

intonation [ɪntəuˈneɪʃən] *n* intonation *f*.

intoxicate [ɪnˈtɔksɪkeɪt] *vt* enivrer ; ~d *a* ivre ; **intoxication** [-ˈkeɪʃən] *n* ivresse *f*.

intractable [ɪnˈtræktəbl] *a* (*child*, *temper*) indocile, insoumis(e) ; (*problem*) insoluble.

intransigent [ɪnˈtrænsɪdʒənt] *a* intransigeant(e).

intransitive [ɪnˈtrænsɪtɪv] *a* intransitif(ive).

intra-uterine [ɪntrəˈjuːtəraɪn] *a* intra-utérin(e) ; ~ device (I.U.D.) *n* moyen de contraception intra-utérin.

intravenous [ɪntrəˈviːnəs] *a* intraveineux(euse).

intrepid [ɪnˈtrepɪd] *a* intrépide.

intricacy [ˈɪntrɪkəsɪ] *n* complexité *f*.

intricate [ˈɪntrɪkət] *a* complexe, compliqué(e).

intrigue [ɪnˈtriːg] *n* intrigue *f* // *vt* intriguer ; **intriguing** *a* fascinant(e).

intrinsic [ɪnˈtrɪnsɪk] *a* intrinsèque.

introduce [ɪntrəˈdjuːs] *vt* introduire ; to ~ sb (to sb) présenter qn (à qn) ; to ~ sb to (*pastime*, *technique*) initier qn à ; **introduction** [-ˈdʌkʃən] *n* introduction *f* ; (*of person*) présentation *f* ; **introductory** *a* préliminaire, d'introduction.

introspective [ɪntrəuˈspektɪv] *a* introspectif(ive).

introvert [ˈɪntrəuvəːt] *a,n* introverti(e).

intrude [ɪnˈtruːd] *vi* (*person*) être importun(e) ; to ~ on or into s'immiscer dans ; am I intruding? est-ce que je vous dérange? ; ~r *n* intrus/e ; **intrusion** [-ʒən] *n* intrusion *f* ; **intrusive** *a* importun(e), gênant(e)

intuition [ɪntjuːˈɪʃən] *n* intuition *f*.

intuitive [ɪnˈtjuːɪtɪv] *a* intuitif(ive).

inundate [ˈɪnʌndeɪt] *vt*: to ~ with inonder de.

invade [ɪnˈveɪd] *vt* envahir ; ~r *n* envahisseur *m*.

invalid *n* [ˈɪnvəlɪd] malade *m/f* ; (*with disability*) invalide *m/f* // *a* [ɪnˈvælɪd] (*not valid*) invalide, non valide ; ~ate [ɪnˈvælɪdeɪt] *vt* invalider, annuler.

invaluable [ɪnˈvæljuəbl] *a* inestimable, inappréciable.

invariable [ɪnˈvɛərɪəbl] *a* invariable ; (*fig*) immanquable.

invasion [ɪnˈveɪʒən] *n* invasion *f*.

invective [ɪnˈvektɪv] *n* invective *f*.

invent [ɪnˈvent] *vt* inventer ; ~ion [ɪnˈvenʃən] *n* invention *f* ; ~ive *a* inventif(ive) ; ~iveness *n* esprit inventif or d'invention ; ~or *n* inventeur/trice.

inventory [ˈɪnvəntrɪ] *n* inventaire *m*.

inverse [ɪnˈvəːs] *a* inverse // *n* inverse *m*, contraire *m* ; ~ly *ad* inversement.

invert [ɪnˈvəːt] *vt* intervertir ; (*cup*, *object*) retourner ; ~ed commas *npl* guillemets *mpl*.

invertebrate [ɪnˈvəːtɪbrət] *n* invertébré *m*.

invest [ɪnˈvest] *vt* investir // *vi* faire un investissement.

investigate [ɪnˈvestɪgeɪt] *vt* étudier, examiner ; (*crime*) faire une enquête sur ; **investigation** [-ˈgeɪʃən] *n* examen *m* ; (*of crime*) enquête *f*, investigation *f* ; **investigator** *n* investigateur/trice.

investiture [ɪnˈvestɪtʃə*] *n* investiture *f*.

investment [ɪnˈvestmənt] *n* investissement *m*, placement *m*.

investor [ɪnˈvestə*] *n* épargnant/e ; actionnaire *m/f*.

inveterate [ɪnˈvetərət] *a* invétéré(e).

invidious [ɪnˈvɪdɪəs] *a* injuste ; (*task*) déplaisant(e).

invigorating [ɪnˈvɪgəreɪtɪŋ] *a* vivifiant(e) ; stimulant(e).

invincible [ɪnˈvɪnsɪbl] *a* invincible.

inviolate [ɪnˈvaɪələt] *a* inviolé(e).

invisible [ɪnˈvɪzɪbl] *a* invisible ; ~ ink *n* encre *f* sympathique ; ~ mending *n* stoppage *m*.

invitation [ɪnvɪˈteɪʃən] *n* invitation *f*.

invite [ɪnˈvaɪt] *vt* inviter ; (*opinions etc*) demander ; (*trouble*) chercher ; **inviting** *a* engageant(e), attrayant(e) ; (*gesture*) encourageant(e).

invoice [ˈɪnvɔɪs] *n* facture *f* // *vt* facturer.

invoke [ɪnˈvəuk] *vt* invoquer.

involuntary [ɪnˈvɔləntrɪ] *a* involontaire.

involve [ɪnˈvɔlv] *vt* (*entail*) entrainer, nécessiter ; (*associate*): to ~ sb (in) impliquer qn (dans), mêler qn à ; faire participer qn (à) ; ~d *a* complexe ; to feel ~d se sentir concerné(e) ; ~ment *n* mise *f* en jeu ; implication *f* ; ~ment (in) participation *f* (à) ; rôle *m* (dans).

invulnerable [ɪnˈvʌlnərəbl] *a* invulnérable.

inward [ˈɪnwəd] *a* (*movement*) vers l'intérieur ; (*thought*, *feeling*) profond(e), intime ; ~ly *ad* (*feel*, *think etc*) secrètement, en son for intérieur ; ~(s) *ad* vers l'intérieur.

iodine [ˈaɪəudiːn] *n* iode *m*.

iota [aɪˈəutə] *n* (*fig*) brin *m*, grain *m*.

IOU *n* (*abbr of I owe you*) reconnaissance *f* de dette.

IQ *n* (*abbr of intelligence quotient*) Q.I. *m* (quotient intellectuel).

Iran [ɪˈrɑːn] *n* Iran *m* ; ~ian [ɪˈreɪnɪən] *a* iranien(ne) // *n* Iranien/ne ; (*LING*) iranien *m*.

Iraq [ɪˈrɑːk] *n* Irak *m* ; ~i *a* irakien(ne) // *n* Irakien/ne ; (*LING*) irakien *m*.

irascible [ɪˈræsɪbl] *a* irascible.

irate [aɪˈreɪt] *a* courroucé(e).

Ireland [ˈaɪələnd] *n* Irlande *f*.

iris, ~es [ˈaɪrɪs, -ɪz] *n* iris *m*.

Irish [ˈaɪrɪʃ] *a* irlandais(e) // *npl*: the ~ les Irlandais ; ~man *n* Irlandais *m* ; ~ Sea *n* mer *f* d'Irlande ; ~woman *n* Irlandaise *f*.

irk [əːk] *vt* ennuyer ; ~some *a* ennuyeux(euse).

iron [ˈaɪən] *n* fer *m* ; (*for clothes*) fer *m* à repasser // *a* de or en fer // *vt* (*clothes*) repasser ; ~s *npl* (*chains*) fers *mpl*, chaînes *fpl*; **to ~ out** *vt* (*crease*) faire disparaître au feu; (*fig*) aplanir; faire disparaître; **the ~ curtain** *n* le rideau de fer.

ironic(al) [aɪˈrɔnɪk(l)] *a* ironique.

ironing [ˈaɪənɪŋ] *n* repassage *m*; **~ board** *n* planche *f* à repasser.

ironmonger [ˈaɪənmʌŋɡə°] *n* quincailler *m*; **~'s** (*shop*) *n* quincaillerie *f.*

iron ore [ˈaɪənɔːˑ°] *n* minerai *m* de fer.

ironworks [ˈaɪənwəːks] *n* usine *f* sidérurgique.

irony [ˈaɪrənɪ] *n* ironie *f.*

irrational [ɪˈræʃənl] *a* irrationnel(le); déraisonnable; qui manque de logique.

irreconcilable [ɪrɛkənˈsaɪləbl] *a* irréconciliable; (*opinion*): **~ with** inconciliable avec.

irredeemable [ɪrɪˈdiːməbl] *a* (*COMM*) non remboursable.

irrefutable [ɪrɪˈfjuːtəbl] *a* irréfutable.

irregular [ɪˈrɛɡjulə°] *a* irrégulier(ère); **~ity** [-ˈlærɪtɪ] *n* irrégularité *f.*

irrelevance [ɪˈrɛləvəns] *n* manque *m* de rapport *or* d'à-propos.

irrelevant [ɪˈrɛləvənt] *a* sans rapport, hors de propos.

irreligious [ɪrɪˈlɪdʒəs] *a* irréligieux(euse).

irreparable [ɪˈrɛprəbl] *a* irréparable.

irreplaceable [ɪrɪˈpleɪsəbl] *a* irremplaçable.

irrepressible [ɪrɪˈprɛsəbl] *a* irrépressible.

irreproachable [ɪrɪˈprəutʃəbl] *a* irréprochable.

irresistible [ɪrɪˈzɪstɪbl] *a* irrésistible.

irresolute [ɪˈrɛzəluːt] *a* irrésolu(e), indécis(e).

irrespective [ɪrɪˈspɛktɪv]: **~ of** *prep* sans tenir compte de.

irresponsible [ɪrɪˈspɔnsɪbl] *a* (*act*) irréfléchi(e); (*person*) qui n'a pas le sens des responsabilités.

irretrievable [ɪrɪˈtriːvəbl] *a* irréparable, irrémédiable.

irreverent [ɪˈrɛvərnt] *a* irrévérencieux(euse).

irrevocable [ɪˈrɛvəkəbl] *a* irrévocable.

irrigate [ˈɪrɪɡeɪt] *vt* irriguer; **irrigation** [-ˈɡeɪʃən] *n* irrigation *f.*

irritable [ˈɪrɪtəbl] *a* irritable.

irritate [ˈɪrɪteɪt] *vt* irriter; **irritation** [-ˈteɪʃən] *n* irritation *f.*

is [ɪz] *vb see* be.

Islam [ˈɪzlɑːm] *n* Islam *m.*

island [ˈaɪlənd] *n* île *f*; (*also*: **traffic ~**) refuge *m* (pour piétons); **~er** *n* habitant/e d'une île, insulaire *m/f.*

isle [aɪl] *n* île *f.*

isn't [ˈɪznt] = **is not.**

isolate [ˈaɪsəleɪt] *vt* isoler; **~d** *a* isolé(e); **isolation** [-ˈleɪʃən] *n* isolement *m*; **isolationism** [-ˈleɪʃənɪzm] *n* isolationnisme *m.*

isotope [ˈaɪsəutəup] *n* isotope *m.*

Israel [ˈɪzreɪl] *n* Israël *m*; **~i** [ɪzˈreɪlɪ] *a* israélien(ne) // *n* Israélien/ne.

issue [ˈɪsjuː] *n* question *f*, problème *m*; (*outcome*) résultat *m*, issue *f*; (*of banknotes etc*) émission *f*; (*of newspaper etc*) numéro *m*; (*offspring*) descendance *f* // *vt* (*rations, equipment*) distribuer; (*orders*) donner;

(*book*) faire paraître, publier; (*banknotes, cheques, stamps*) émettre, mettre en circulation; **at ~** en jeu, en cause.

isthmus [ˈɪsməs] *n* isthme *m.*

it [ɪt] *pronoun* (*subject*) il(elle); (*direct object*) le(la), l'; (*indirect object*) lui; (*impersonal*) il; ce, cela, ça; **~'s raining** il pleut; **I've come from ~** j'en viens; **it's on ~** c'est dessus; **he's proud of ~** il en est fier; **he agreed to ~** il y a consenti.

Italian [ɪˈtæljən] *a* italien(ne) // *n* Italien/ne; (*LING*) italien *m.*

italic [ɪˈtælɪk] *a* italique; **~s** *npl* italique *m.*

Italy [ˈɪtəlɪ] *n* Italie *f.*

itch [ɪtʃ] *n* démangeaison *f* // *vi* (*person*) éprouver des démangeaisons; (*part of body*) démanger; **I'm ~ing to do it** j'ai envie me démange de faire; **~ing** *n* démangeaison *f*; **~y** *a* qui démange.

it'd [ˈɪtd] = **it would; it had.**

item [ˈaɪtəm] *n* (*gen*) article *m*; (*on agenda*) question *f*, point *m*; (*in programme*) numéro *m*; (*also*: **news ~**) nouvelle *f*; **~ize** *vt* détailler, spécifier.

itinerant [ɪˈtɪnərənt] *a* itinérant(e); (*musician*) ambulant(e).

itinerary [aɪˈtɪnərərɪ] *n* itinéraire *m.*

it'll [ˈɪtl] = **it will, it shall.**

its [ɪts] *a* son(sa), ses *pl* // *pronoun* le(la) sien(ne), les siens(siennes).

it's [ɪts] = **it is; it has.**

itself [ɪtˈsɛlf] *pronoun* (*emphatic*) lui-même(elle-même); (*reflexive*) se.

ITV *n abbr of Independent Television* (chaîne fonctionnant en concurrence avec la BBC).

I.U.D. *n abbr see* **intra-uterine.**

I've [aɪv] = **I have.**

ivory [ˈaɪvərɪ] *n* ivoire *m*; **~ tower** *n* (*fig*) tour *f* d'ivoire.

ivy [ˈaɪvɪ] *n* lierre *m.*

J

jab [dʒæb] *vt*: **to ~ sth into** enfoncer *or* planter qch dans // *n* coup *m*; (*MED: col*) piqûre *f.*

jabber [ˈdʒæbə°] *vt,vi* bredouiller, baragouiner.

jack [dʒæk] *n* (*AUT*) cric *m*; (*BOWLS*) cochonnet *m*; (*CARDS*) valet *m*; **to ~ up** *vt* soulever (au cric).

jacket [ˈdʒækɪt] *n* veste *f*, veston *m*; (*of boiler etc*) enveloppe *f*; (*of book*) couverture *f*, jaquette *f*; **potatoes in their ~s** pommes de terre en robe des champs.

jack-knife [ˈdʒæknaɪf] *n* couteau *m* de poche // *vi*: **the lorry ~d** la remorque (du camion) s'est mise en travers.

jackpot [ˈdʒækpɔt] *n* gros lot.

jade [dʒeɪd] *n* (*stone*) jade *m.*

jaded [ˈdʒeɪdɪd] *a* éreinté(e), fatigué(e).

jagged [ˈdʒæɡɪd] *a* dentelé(e).

jail [dʒeɪl] *n* prison *f*; **~break** *n* évasion *f*; **~er** *n* geôlier/ière.

jam [dʒæm] *n* confiture *f*; (*of shoppers etc*) cohue *f*; (*also*: **traffic ~**) embouteillage *m* // *vt* (*passage etc*) encombrer, obstruer; (*mechanism, drawer etc*) bloquer, coincer; (*RADIO*) brouiller // *vi* (*mechanism, sliding* part) se coincer, se bloquer; (gun) s'enrayer; to ~ sth into entasser or comprimer qch dans; enfoncer qch dans.

Jamaica [dʒə'meɪkə] n Jamaïque f.

jangle ['dʒæŋgl] vi cliqueter.

janitor ['dʒænɪtə*] n (caretaker) huissier m; concierge m.

January ['dʒænjuərɪ] n janvier m.

Japan [dʒə'pæn] n Japon m; ~ese [dʒæpə'niːz] a japonais(e) // n, pl inv Japonais/e; (LING) japonais m.

jar [dʒɑː*] n (glass) pot m, bocal m // vi (sound:) produire un son grinçant or discordant; (colours etc) détonner, jurer // vt (subject: shock) ébranler, secouer.

jargon ['dʒɑːgən] n jargon m.

jasmin(e) ['dʒæzmɪn] n jasmin m.

jaundice ['dʒɔːndɪs] n jaunisse f; ~d a (fig) envieux(euse), désapprobateur(trice).

jaunt [dʒɔːnt] n balade f; ~y a enjoué(e); désinvolte.

javelin ['dʒævlɪn] n javelot m.

jaw [dʒɔː] n mâchoire f.

jaywalker ['dʒeɪwɔːkə*] n piéton indiscipliné.

jazz [dʒæz] n jazz m; to ~ up vt animer, égayer; ~ band n orchestre m or groupe m de jazz; ~y a bariolé(e), tapageur(euse).

jealous ['dʒeləs] a jaloux(ouse); ~y n jalousie f.

jeans [dʒiːnz] npl (blue-)jean m.

jeep [dʒiːp] n jeep f.

jeer [dʒɪə*] vi: to ~ (at) huer; se moquer cruellement (de), railler; ~s npl huées fpl; sarcasmes mpl.

jelly ['dʒelɪ] n gelée f; ~fish n méduse f.

jeopardize ['dʒepədaɪz] vt mettre en danger or péril.

jeopardy ['dʒepədɪ] n: in ~ en danger or péril.

jerk [dʒəːk] n secousse f; saccade f; sursaut m, spasme m // vt donner une secousse à // vi (vehicles) cahoter.

jerkin ['dʒəːkɪn] n blouson m.

jerky ['dʒəːkɪ] a saccadé(e); cahotant(e).

jersey ['dʒəːzɪ] n tricot m.

jest [dʒest] n plaisanterie f; in ~ en plaisantant.

jet [dʒet] n (gas, liquid) jet m; (AUT) gicleur m; (AVIAT) avion m à réaction, jet m; ~-black a (d'un noir) de jais; ~ engine n moteur m à réaction.

jetsam ['dʒetsəm] n objets jetés à la mer (et rejetés sur la côte).

jettison ['dʒetɪsn] vt jeter par-dessus bord.

jetty ['dʒetɪ] n jetée f, digue f.

Jew [dʒuː] n Juif m.

jewel ['dʒuːəl] n bijou m, joyau m; ~ler n bijoutier/ère, joaillier m; ~ler's (shop) n bijouterie f, joaillerie f; ~lery n bijoux mpl.

Jewess ['dʒuːɪs] n Juive f.

Jewish ['dʒuːɪʃ] a juif(juive).

jib [dʒɪb] n (NAUT) foc m; (of crane) flèche f // vi: to ~ (at) renâcler or regimber (devant).

jibe [dʒaɪb] n sarcasme m.

jiffy ['dʒɪfɪ] n (col): in a ~ en un clin d'œil.

jigsaw ['dʒɪgsɔː] n (also: ~ puzzle) puzzle m.

jilt [dʒɪlt] vt laisser tomber, plaquer.

jingle ['dʒɪŋgl] n (advert) couplet m publicitaire // vi cliqueter, tinter.

jinx [dʒɪŋks] n (col) (mauvais) sort.

jitters ['dʒɪtəz] npl (col): to get the ~ avoir la trouille or la frousse.

jiujitsu [dʒuː'dʒɪtsuː] n jiu-jitsu m.

job [dʒɔb] n travail m; (employment) emploi m, poste m, place f; ~bing a (workman) à la tâche, à la journée; ~less a sans travail, au chômage.

jockey ['dʒɔkɪ] n jockey m // vi: to ~ for position manœuvrer pour être bien placé.

jocular ['dʒɔkjulə*] a jovial(e), enjoué(e); facétieux(euse).

jog [dʒɔg] vt secouer // vi: to ~ along cahoter; trotter; to ~ sb's memory rafraîchir la mémoire de qn.

join [dʒɔɪn] vt unir, assembler; (become member of) s'inscrire à; (meet) rejoindre, retrouver; se joindre à // vi (roads, rivers) se rejoindre, se rencontrer // n raccord m; to ~ up vi s'engager.

joiner ['dʒɔɪnə*] n menuisier m; ~y n menuiserie f.

joint [dʒɔɪnt] n (TECH) jointure f; joint m; (ANAT) articulation f, jointure; (CULIN) rôti m; (col: place) boîte f // a commun(e); ~ly ad ensemble, en commun.

joist [dʒɔɪst] n solive f.

joke [dʒəuk] n plaisanterie f; (also: practical ~) farce f // vi plaisanter; to play a ~ on jouer un tour à, faire une farce à; ~r n plaisantin m, blagueur/euse; (CARDS) joker m.

jollity ['dʒɔlɪtɪ] n réjouissances fpl, gaieté f.

jolly ['dʒɔlɪ] a gai(e), enjoué(e) // ad (col) rudement, drôlement.

jolt [dʒəult] n cahot m, secousse f // vt cahoter, secouer.

Jordan ['dʒɔːdən] n Jordanie f.

jostle ['dʒɔsl] vt bousculer, pousser // vi jouer des coudes.

jot [dʒɔt] n: not one ~ pas un brin; to ~ down vt inscrire rapidement, noter; ~ter n cahier m (de brouillon); bloc-notes m.

journal ['dʒəːnl] n journal m; ~ese [-'liːz] n (pej) style m journalistique; ~ism n journalisme m; ~ist n journaliste m/f.

journey ['dʒəːnɪ] n voyage m; (distance covered) trajet m.

jowl [dʒaul] n mâchoire f (inférieure); bajoue f.

joy [dʒɔɪ] n joie f; ~ful, ~ous a joyeux(euse); ~ ride n virée f (gén avec une voiture volée).

J.P. n abbr see justice.

Jr, Jun., Junr abbr of junior.

jubilant ['dʒuːbɪlnt] a triomphant(e); réjoui(e).

jubilation [dʒuːbɪ'leɪʃən] n jubilation f.

jubilee ['dʒuːbɪliː] n jubilé m.

judge [dʒʌdʒ] n juge m // vt juger; judg(e)ment n jugement m; (punishment) châtiment m; in my judg(e)ment à mon avis, selon mon opinion.

judicial [dʒuː'dɪʃl] a judiciaire; (fair) impartial(e).

judicious [dʒu:'dɪʃəs] a judicieux(euse).
judo ['dʒu:dəu] n judo m.
jug [dʒʌg] n pot m, cruche f.
juggernaut ['dʒʌgənɔ:t] n (huge truck) mastodonte m.
juggle ['dʒʌgl] vi jongler; ~r n jongleur m.
Jugoslav ['ju:gəu'slɑ:v] a,n = **Yugoslav**.
juice [dʒu:s] n jus m.
juicy ['dʒu:sɪ] a juteux(euse).
jukebox ['dʒu:kbɔks] n juke-box m.
July [dʒu:'laɪ] n juillet m.
jumble ['dʒʌmbl] n fouillis m // vt (also: ~ up) mélanger, brouiller; ~ sale n (Brit) vente f de charité.
jumbo ['dʒʌmbəu] a: ~ jet avion géant, gros porteur (à réaction).
jump [dʒʌmp] vi sauter, bondir; (start) sursauter; (increase) monter en flèche // vt sauter, franchir // n saut m, bond m; sursaut m; to ~ the queue passer avant son tour.
jumper ['dʒʌmpə*] n pull-over m.
jumpy ['dʒʌmpɪ] a nerveux(euse), agité(e).
junction ['dʒʌŋkʃən] n (of roads) carrefour m; (of rails) embranchement n.
juncture ['dʒʌŋktʃə*] n: at this ~ à ce moment-là, sur ces entrefaites.
June [dʒu:n] n juin m.
jungle ['dʒʌŋgl] n jungle f.
junior ['dʒu:nɪə*] a, n: he's ~ to me (by 2 years), he's my ~ (by 2 years) il est mon cadet (de 2 ans), il est plus jeune que moi (de 2 ans); he's ~ to me (seniority) il est en dessous de moi (dans la hiérarchie), j'ai plus d'ancienneté que lui; ~ executive n jeune cadre m; ~ minister n ministre m sous tutelle; ~ partner n associé(-adjoint) m; ~ school n école f primaire, cours moyen; ~ sizes npl (COMM) tailles fpl fillettes/garçonnets.
juniper ['dʒu:nɪpə*] n: ~ berry baie f de genièvre.
junk [dʒʌŋk] n (rubbish) bric-à-brac m inv; (ship) jonque f; ~shop n (boutique f de) brocanteur m.
junta ['dʒʌntə] n junte f.
jurisdiction [dʒuərɪs'dɪkʃən] n juridiction f.
jurisprudence [dʒuərɪs'pru:dəns] n jurisprudence f.
juror ['dʒuərə*] n juré m.
jury ['dʒuərɪ] n jury m; ~man n = **juror**.
just [dʒʌst] a juste // ad: he's ~ done it/left il vient de le faire/partir; ~ as I expected exactement or précisément comme je m'y attendais; ~ right/two o'clock exactement or juste ce qu'il faut/deux heures; ~ as he was leaving au moment or à l'instant précis où il partait; ~ before/enough/here juste avant/assez/là; it's ~ me/a mistake ce n'est que moi/(rien) qu'une erreur; ~ missed/caught manqué/attrapé de justesse; ~ listen to this! écoutez un peu ça!
justice ['dʒʌstɪs] n justice f; Lord Chief J~ premier président de la cour d'appel; J~ of the Peace (J.P.) n juge m de paix.
justifiable [dʒʌstɪ'faɪəbl] a justifiable.

justifiably [dʒʌstɪ'faɪəblɪ] ad légitimement.
justification [dʒʌstɪfɪ'keɪʃən] n justification f.
justify ['dʒʌstɪfaɪ] vt justifier.
justly ['dʒʌstlɪ] ad avec raison, justement.
justness ['dʒʌstnɪs] n justesse f.
jut [dʒʌt] vi (also: ~ out) dépasser, faire saillie.
juvenile ['dʒu:vənaɪl] a juvénile; (court, books) pour enfants // n adolescent/e.
juxtapose ['dʒʌkstəpəuz] vt juxtaposer.

K

kaleidoscope [kə'laɪdəskəup] n kaléidoscope m.
kangaroo [kæŋgə'ru:] n kangourou m.
keel [ki:l] n quille f; on an even ~ (fig) à flot.
keen [ki:n] a (interest, desire) vif(vive); (eye, intelligence) pénétrant(e); (competition) vif, âpre; (edge) effilé(e); (eager) plein(e) d'enthousiasme; to be ~ to do or on doing sth désirer vivement faire qch, tenir beaucoup à faire qch; to be ~ on sth/sb aimer beaucoup qch/qn; ~ness n (eagerness) enthousiasme m; ~ness to do vif désir de faire.
keep [ki:p] vb (pt,pp kept [kept]) vt (retain, preserve) garder; (hold back) retenir; (a shop, the books, a diary) tenir; (feed: one's family etc) entretenir, assurer la subsistance de; (a promise) tenir; (chickens, bees, pigs etc) élever // vi (food) se conserver; (remain: in a certain state or place) rester // n (of castle) donjon m; (food etc): enough for his ~ assez pour (assurer) sa subsistance; to ~ doing sth continuer à faire qch; faire qch continuellement; to ~ sb from doing/sth from happening empêcher qn de faire or que qn (ne) fasse/que qch (n')arrive; to ~ sb happy/a place tidy faire que qn soit content/qu'un endroit reste propre; to ~ sth to o.s. garder qch pour soi, tenir qch secret; to ~ sth (back) from sb cacher qch à qn; to ~ time (clock) être à l'heure, ne pas retarder; to ~ on vi continuer; to ~ on doing continuer à faire; to ~ out vt empêcher d'entrer; '~ out' 'défense d'entrer'; to ~ up vi se maintenir // vt continuer, maintenir; to ~ up with se maintenir au niveau de; ~er n gardien/ne; ~ing n (care) garde f; in ~ing with à l'avenant de; en accord avec; ~sake n souvenir m.
keg [keg] n barrique f, tonnelet m.
kennel ['kenl] n niche f; ~s npl chenil m.
Kenya ['kenjə] n Kenya m.
kept [kept] pt,pp de **keep**.
kerb [kə:b] n bordure f du trottoir.
kernel ['kə:nl] n amande f; (fig) noyau m.
kerosene ['kerəsi:n] n kérosène m.
ketchup ['ketʃəp] n ketchup m.
kettle ['ketl] n bouilloire f.
kettle drums ['ketldrʌmz] npl timbales fpl.
key [ki:] n (gen, MUS) clé f; (of piano, typewriter) touche f // cpd (-)clé; ~board n clavier m; ~hole n trou m de la serrure;

~**note** n (MUS) tonique f; (fig) note dominante; ~ **ring** n porte-clés m.
khaki ['ka:kı] a,n kaki (m).
kibbutz [kı'bu:ts] n kibboutz m.
kick [kık] vt donner un coup de pied à // vi (horse) ruer // n coup m de pied; (of rifle) recul m; (thrill): **he does it for** ~**s** il le fait parce que ça l'excite, il le fait pour le plaisir; **to** ~ **around** vi (col) traîner; **to** ~ **off** vi (SPORT) donner le coup d'envoi; ~**off** n (SPORT) coup m d'envoi.
kid [kıd] n gamin/e, gosse m/f; (animal, leather) chevreau m // vi (col) plaisanter, blaguer.
kidnap ['kıdnæp] vt enlever, kidnapper; ~**per** n ravisseur/euse; ~**ping** n enlèvement m.
kidney ['kıdnı] n (ANAT) rein m; (CULIN) rognon m.
kill [kıl] vt tuer; (fig) faire échouer; détruire; supprimer // n mise f à mort; ~**er** n tueur/euse; meurtrier/ère; ~**ing** n meurtre m; tuerie f, massacre m; (col): **to make a** ~**ing** se remplir les poches, réussir un beau coup // a (col) tordant(e).
kiln [kıln] n four m.
kilo ['ki:ləu] n kilo m; ~**gram(me)** ['kıləugræm] n kilogramme m; ~**metre**, ~**meter** (US) ['kıləmi:tə*] n kilomètre m; ~**watt** ['kıləuwɔt] n kilowatt m.
kilt [kılt] n kilt m.
kimono [kı'məunəu] n kimono m.
kin [kın] n see next, kith.
kind [kaınd] a gentil(le), aimable // n sorte f, espèce f; (species) genre m; **in** ~ (COMM) en nature; (fig): **to repay sb in** ~ rendre la pareille à qn.
kindergarten ['kındəgɑ:tn] n jardin m d'enfants.
kind-hearted [kaınd'hɑ:tıd] a bon (bonne).
kindle ['kındl] vt allumer, enflammer.
kindly ['kaındlı] a bienveillant(e), plein(e) de gentillesse // ad avec bonté; **will you** ~... auriez-vous la bonté or l'obligeance de...; **he didn't take it** ~ il l'a mal pris.
kindness ['kaındnıs] n bonté f, gentillesse f.
kindred ['kındrıd] a apparenté(e); ~ **spirit** n âme f sœur.
kinetic [kı'nɛtık] a cinétique.
king [kıŋ] n roi m; ~**dom** n royaume m; ~**fisher** n martin-pêcheur m; ~**pin** n cheville ouvrière; ~-**size** a long format inv; format géant inv.
kink [kıŋk] n (of rope) entortillement m.
kinky ['kıŋkı] a (fig) excentrique; aux goûts spéciaux.
kiosk ['ki:ɔsk] n kiosque m; cabine f (téléphonique).
kipper ['kıpə*] n hareng fumé et salé.
kiss [kıs] n baiser m // vt embrasser; **to** ~ **(each other)** s'embrasser.
kit [kıt] n équipement m, matériel m; (set of tools etc) trousse f; (for assembly) kit m; ~**bag** n sac m de voyage or de marin.
kitchen ['kıtʃın] n cuisine f; ~ **garden** n jardin m potager; ~ **sink** n évier m; ~**ware** n vaisselle f; ustensiles mpl de cuisine.

kite [kaıt] n (toy) cerf-volant m; (ZOOL) milan m.
kith [kıθ] n: ~ **and kin** parents et amis mpl.
kitten ['kıtn] n petit chat, chaton m.
kitty ['kıtı] n (pool of money) cagnotte f.
kleptomaniac [klɛptəu'meınıæk] n kleptomane m/f.
knack [næk] n: **to have the** ~ **(for doing)** avoir le coup (pour faire); **there's a** ~ il y a un coup à prendre or une combine.
knapsack ['næpsæk] n musette f.
knave [neıv] n (CARDS) valet m.
knead [ni:d] vt pétrir.
knee [ni:] n genou m; ~**cap** n rotule f.
kneel [ni:l] vi (pt,pp **knelt** [nɛlt]) s'agenouiller.
knell [nɛl] n glas m.
knelt [nɛlt] pt,pp of **kneel**.
knew [nju:] pt of **know**.
knickers ['nıkəz] npl culotte f (de femme).
knife, knives [naıf, naıvz] n couteau m // vt poignarder, frapper d'un coup de couteau.
knight [naıt] n chevalier m; (CHESS) cavalier m; ~**hood** n chevalerie f; (title): **to get a** ~**hood** être fait chevalier.
knit [nıt] vt tricoter; (fig): **to** ~ **together** unir // vi (broken bones) se ressouder; ~**ting** n tricot m; ~**ting machine** n machine f à tricoter; ~**ting needle** n aiguille f à tricoter; ~**wear** n tricots mpl, lainages mpl.
knives [naıvz] npl of **knife**.
knob [nɔb] n bouton m; (fig): **a** ~ **of butter** une noix de beurre.
knock [nɔk] vt frapper; heurter; (fig: col) dénigrer // vi (engine) cogner; (at door etc): **to** ~ **at/on** frapper à/sur // n coup m; **to** ~ **down** vt renverser; **to** ~ **off** vi (col: finish) s'arrêter (de travailler); **to** ~ **out** vt assommer; (BOXING) mettre k.-o.; ~**er** n (on door) heurtoir m; ~-**kneed** a aux genoux cagneux; ~**out** n (BOXING) knock-out m, K.-O. m; ~**out competition** n compétition f avec épreuves éliminatoires.
knot [nɔt] n (gen) nœud m // vt nouer; ~**ty** a (fig) épineux(euse).
know [nəu] vt (pt **knew**, pp **known** [nju:, nəun]) savoir; (person, author, place) connaître; **to** ~ **that...** savoir que...; **to** ~ **how to do** savoir comment faire; ~-**how** n savoir-faire m, technique f, compétence f; ~**ing** a (look etc) entendu(e); ~**ingly** ad sciemment; d'un air entendu.
knowledge ['nɔlıdʒ] n connaissance f; (learning) connaissances, savoir m; ~**able** a bien informé(e).
known [nəun] pp of **know**.
knuckle ['nʌkl] n articulation f (des phalanges), jointure f.
K.O. n (abbr of knockout) K.-O. m // vt mettre K.-O.
Koran [kɔ'rɑ:n] n Coran m.
kudos ['kju:dɔs] n gloire f, lauriers mpl.
kw abbr of **kilowatt(s)**.

L

l. *abbr of* **litre**.

lab [læb] n (*abbr of* **laboratory**) labo m.

label ['leɪbl] n étiquette f; (*brand: of record*) marque f // vt étiqueter; **to ~ sb a...** qualifier qn de...

laboratory [ləˈbɔrətərɪ] n laboratoire m.

laborious [ləˈbɔːrɪəs] a laborieux(euse).

labour ['leɪbə*] n (*task*) travail m; (*workmen*) main-d'œuvre f; (*MED*) travail, accouchement m // vi: **to ~ (at)** travailler dur (à), peiner (sur); **in ~** (*MED*) en travail; **L~**, **the L~ party** le parti travailliste, les travaillistes mpl; **~ camp** n camp m de travaux forcés; **~ed** a lourd(e), laborieux(euse); **~er** n manœuvre m; (*on farm*) ouvrier m agricole; **~ force** n main-d'œuvre f; **~ pains** npl douleurs fpl de l'accouchement.

labyrinth ['læbɪrɪnθ] n labyrinthe m, dédale m.

lace [leɪs] n dentelle f; (*of shoe etc*) lacet m // vt (*shoe*) lacer.

lack [læk] n manque m // vt manquer de; **through** or **for ~ of** faute de, par manque de; **to be ~ing** manquer, faire défaut; **to be ~ing in** manquer de.

lackadaisical [lækəˈdeɪzɪkl] a nonchalant(e), indolent(e).

laconic [ləˈkɔnɪk] a laconique.

lacquer ['lækə*] n laque f.

lad [læd] n garçon m, gars m.

ladder ['lædə*] n échelle f; (*in tights*) maille filée // vt, vi (*tights*) filer.

laden ['leɪdn] a: **~ (with)** chargé(e) (de).

ladle ['leɪdl] n louche f.

lady ['leɪdɪ] n dame f; dame (du monde); **L~ Smith** lady Smith; **the ladies' (toilets)** les toilettes fpl des dames; **~bird**, **~bug** (*US*) n coccinelle f; **~-in-waiting** n dame f d'honneur; **~like** a distingué(e).

lag [læg] n = **time ~** // vi (*also*: **~ behind**) rester en arrière, traîner // vt (*pipes*) calorifuger.

lager ['lɑːgə*] n bière blonde.

lagging ['lægɪŋ] n enveloppe isolante, calorifuge m.

lagoon [ləˈguːn] n lagune f.

laid [leɪd] pt, pp de **lay**.

lain [leɪn] pp of **lie**.

lair [lɛə*] n tanière f, gîte m.

laity ['leɪətɪ] n laïques mpl.

lake [leɪk] n lac m.

lamb [læm] n agneau m; **~ chop** n côtelette f d'agneau; **~skin** n (peau f d')agneau m; **~swool** n laine f d'agneau.

lame [leɪm] a boiteux(euse).

lament [ləˈmɛnt] n lamentation f // vt pleurer, se lamenter sur; **~able** ['læməntəbl] a déplorable, lamentable.

laminated ['læmɪneɪtɪd] a laminé(e); (*windscreen*) (en verre) feuilleté.

lamp [læmp] n lampe f.

lampoon [læmˈpuːn] n pamphlet m.

lamp: **~post** n réverbère m; **~shade** n abat-jour m inv.

lance [lɑːns] n lance f // vt (*MED*) inciser; **~ corporal** n (soldat m de) première classe m.

lancet ['lɑːnsɪt] n bistouri m.

land [lænd] n (*as opposed to sea*) terre f (ferme); (*country*) pays m; (*soil*) terre; terrain m; (*estate*) terre(s), domaine(s) m(pl) // vi (*from ship*) débarquer; (*AVIAT*) atterrir; (*fig: fall*) (re)tomber // vt (*obtain*) décrocher; (*passengers, goods*) débarquer; **to ~ up** vi atterrir, (finir par) se retrouver; **~ed gentry** n propriétaires terriens or fonciers; **~ing** n débarquement m; atterrissage m; (*of staircase*) palier m; **~ing craft** n chaland m de débarquement; **~ing stage** n débarcadère m, embarcadère m; **~ing strip** n piste f d'atterrissage; **~lady** n propriétaire f, logeuse f; **~locked** a entouré(e) de terre(s), sans accès à la mer; **~lord** n propriétaire m, logeur m; (*of pub etc*) patron m; **~lubber** n terrien/ne; **~mark** n (point m de) repère m; **~owner** n propriétaire foncier or terrien.

landscape ['lænskeɪp] n paysage m; **~d** a aménagé(e) (par un paysagiste).

landslide ['lændslaɪd] n (*GEO*) glissement m (de terrain); (*fig: POL*) raz-de-marée (électoral).

lane [leɪn] n (*in country*) chemin m; (*in town*) ruelle f; (*AUT*) voie f; file f; (*in race*) couloir m.

language ['læŋgwɪdʒ] n langue f; (*way one speaks*) langage m; **bad ~** grossièretés fpl, langage grossier.

languid ['læŋgwɪd] a languissant(e); langoureux(euse).

languish ['læŋgwɪʃ] vi languir.

lank [læŋk] a (*hair*) raide et terne.

lanky ['læŋkɪ] a grand(e) et maigre, efflanqué(e).

lantern ['læntn] n lanterne f.

lap [læp] n (*of track*) tour m (de piste); (*of body*): **in** or **on one's ~** sur les genoux // vt (*also*: **~ up**) laper // vi (*waves*) clapoter; **~dog** n chien m d'appartement.

lapel [ləˈpɛl] n revers m.

Lapland ['læplænd] n Laponie f.

Lapp [læp] a lapon(ne) // n Lapon/ne; (*LING*) lapon m.

lapse [læps] n défaillance f // vi (*LAW*) cesser d'être en vigueur; se périmer; **to ~ into bad habits** prendre de mauvaises habitudes; **~ of time** laps m de temps, intervalle m.

larceny ['lɑːsənɪ] n vol m.

lard [lɑːd] n saindoux m.

larder ['lɑːdə*] n garde-manger m inv.

large [lɑːdʒ] a grand(e); (*person, animal*) gros(grosse); **at ~** (*free*) en liberté; (*generally*) en général; pour la plupart; **~ly** ad en grande partie; **~-scale** a (*map*) à grande échelle; (*fig*) important(e).

lark [lɑːk] n (*bird*) alouette f; (*joke*) blague f, farce f; **to ~ about** vi faire l'idiot, rigoler.

larva, pl **larvae** ['lɑːvə, -iː] n larve f.

laryngitis [lærɪnˈdʒaɪtɪs] n laryngite f.

larynx ['lærɪŋks] n larynx m.

lascivious [ləˈsɪvɪəs] a lascif(ive).

laser ['leɪzə*] n laser m.

lash [læʃ] n coup m de fouet; (gen: eyelash) cil m // vt fouetter; (tie) attacher; to ~ out vi: to ~ out (at or against sb/sth) attaquer violemment (qn/qch); to ~ out (on sth) (col: spend) se fendre (de qch).

lass [læs] n (jeune) fille f.

lasso [læ'su:] n lasso m // vt prendre au lasso.

last [lɑ:st] a dernier(ère) // ad en dernier // vi durer; ~ week la semaine dernière; ~ night hier soir, la nuit dernière; at ~ enfin; ~ but one avant-dernier(ère); ~ing a durable; ~-minute a de dernière minute.

latch [lætʃ] n loquet m; ~key n clé f (de la porte d'entrée).

late [leɪt] a (not on time) en retard; (far on in day etc) dernier(ère); tardif(ive); (recent) récent(e), dernier; (former) ancien(ne); (dead) défunt(e) // ad tard; (behind time, schedule) en retard; of ~ dernièrement; in ~ May vers la fin (du mois) de mai, fin mai; the ~ Mr X feu M. X; ~comer n retardataire m/f; ~ly ad récemment; ~ness n (of person) retard m; (of event) heure tardive.

latent ['leɪtnt] a latent(e).

later ['leɪtə*] a (date etc) ultérieur(e); (version etc) plus récent(e) // ad plus tard.

lateral ['lætərl] a latéral(e).

latest ['leɪtɪst] a tout(e) dernier(ère); at the ~ au plus tard.

latex ['leɪtɛks] n latex m.

lath, ~s [læθ, læðz] n latte f.

lathe [leɪð] n tour m; ~ operator n tourneur m (en usine).

lather ['lɑ:ðə*] n mousse f (de savon) // vt savonner // vi mousser.

Latin ['lætɪn] n latin m // a latin(e); ~ America n Amérique latine; ~-American a d'Amérique latine.

latitude ['lætɪtju:d] n latitude f.

latrine [lə'tri:n] n latrines fpl.

latter ['lætə*] a deuxième, dernier(ère) // n: the ~ ce dernier, celui-ci; ~ly ad dernièrement, récemment.

lattice ['lætɪs] n treillis m; treillage m.

laudable ['lɔ:dəbl] a louable.

laudatory ['lɔ:dətrɪ] a élogieux(euse).

laugh [lɑ:f] n rire m // vi rire; to ~ at vt fus se moquer de; to ~ off vt écarter or rejeter par une plaisanterie or par une boutade; ~able a risible, ridicule; ~ing a (face) rieur(euse); the ~ing stock of la risée de; ~ter n rire m; rires mpl.

launch [lɔ:ntʃ] n lancement m; (boat) chaloupe f; (also: motor ~) vedette f // vt (ship, rocket, plan) lancer; ~ing n lancement m; ~(ing) pad n rampe f de lancement.

launder ['lɔ:ndə*] vt blanchir.

launderette [lɔ:n'drɛt] n laverie f (automatique).

laundry ['lɔ:ndrɪ] n blanchisserie f; (clothes) linge m; to do the ~ faire la lessive.

laureate ['lɔ:rɪət] a see poet.

laurel ['lɔrl] n laurier m.

lava ['lɑ:və] n lave f.

lavatory ['lævətərɪ] n toilettes fpl.

lavender ['lævəndə*] n lavande f.

lavish ['lævɪʃ] a copieux(euse); somptueux(euse); (giving freely): ~ with prodigue de // vt: to ~ on sb/sth (care) prodiguer à qn/qch; (money) dépenser sans compter pour qn/qch.

law [lɔ:] n loi f; (science) droit m; ~-abiding a respectueux(euse) des lois; ~ and order n l'ordre public; ~breaker n personne f qui transgresse la loi; ~ court n tribunal m, cour f de justice; ~ful a légal(e); permis(e); ~fully ad légalement; ~less a sans loi.

lawn [lɔ:n] n pelouse f; ~mower n tondeuse f à gazon; ~ tennis [-'tɛnɪs] n tennis m.

law: ~ school n faculté f de droit; ~ student n étudiant/e en droit.

lawsuit ['lɔ:su:t] n procès m.

lawyer ['lɔ:jə*] n (consultant, with company) juriste m; (for sales, wills etc) ≈ notaire m; (partner, in court) ≈ avocat m.

lax [læks] a relâché(e).

laxative ['læksətɪv] n laxatif m.

laxity ['læksɪtɪ] n relâchement m.

lay [leɪ] pt of lie // a laïque: profane // vt (pt, pp laid [leɪd]) poser, mettre; (eggs) pondre; (trap) tendre; (plans) élaborer; to ~ the table mettre la table; to ~ aside or by vt mettre de côté; to ~ down vt poser; to ~ down the law faire la loi; to ~ off vt (workers) licencier; to ~ on vt (water, gas) mettre, installer; (provide) fournir; (paint) étaler; to ~ out vt (design) dessiner, concevoir; (display) disposer; (spend) dépenser; to ~ up vt (to store) amasser; (car) remiser; (ship) désarmer; (subj: illness) forcer à s'aliter; ~about n fainéant/e; ~-by n aire f de stationnement (sur le bas-côté).

layer ['leɪə*] n couche f.

layette [leɪ'ɛt] n layette f.

layman ['leɪmən] n laïque m; profane m.

layout ['leɪaut] n disposition f, plan m, agencement m; (PRESS) mise f en page.

laze [leɪz] vi paresser.

laziness ['leɪzɪnɪs] n paresse f.

lazy ['leɪzɪ] a paresseux(euse).

lb. abbr of pound (weight).

lead [li:d] see also next headword; n (front position) tête f; (distance, time ahead) avance f; (clue) piste f; (in battery) raccord m; (ELEC) fil m; (for dog) laisse f; (THEATRE) rôle principal // vb (pt,pp led [lɛd]) mener, conduire; (induce) amener; (be leader of) être à la tête de; (SPORT) être en tête de // vi mener, être en tête; to ~ to mener à; conduire à; aboutir à; to ~ astray vt détourner du droit chemin; to ~ away vt emmener; to ~ back ramener à; to ~ on vt (tease) faire marcher; to ~ on to vt (induce) amener à; to ~ up to conduire à.

lead [lɛd] see also previous headword; n plomb m; (in pencil) mine f; ~en a de or en plomb.

leader ['li:də*] n chef m; dirigeant/e, leader m; (of newspaper) éditorial m; ~ship n direction f; qualités fpl de chef.

leading ['li:dɪŋ] a de premier plan; principal(e); ~ lady n (THEATRE) vedette (féminine); ~ **light** n (person) vedette f, sommité f; ~ **man** n (THEATRE) vedette (masculine).

leaf, leaves [li:f, li:vz] n feuille f; (of table) rallonge f.

leaflet ['li:flɪt] prospectus m, brochure f; (POL REL) tract m.

leafy ['li:fɪ] a feuillu(e).

league [li:g] n ligue f; (FOOTBALL) championnat m; (measure) lieue f; to be in ~ with avoir partie liée avec, être de mèche avec.

leak [li:k] n (out, also fig) fuite f; (in) infiltration f // vi (pipe, liquid etc) fuir; (shoes) prendre l'eau // vt (liquid) répandre; (information) divulguer; to ~ out vi fuir; être divulgué(e).

lean [li:n] a maigre // n (of meat) maigre m // vb (pt,pp leaned or leant [lɛnt]) vt: to ~ sth on appuyer qch sur // vi (slope) pencher; (rest): to ~ against s'appuyer contre; être appuyé(e) contre; to ~ on s'appuyer sur; to ~ back/forward vi se pencher en arrière/avant; to ~ over vi se pencher; ~ing a penché(e) // n: ~ing (towards) penchant m (pour); ~-to n appentis m.

leap [li:p] n bond m, saut m // vi (pt,pp leaped or leapt [lɛpt]) bondir, sauter; ~frog n jeu m de saute-mouton; ~ year n année f bissextile.

learn, pt,pp **learned** or **learnt** [lə:n, -t] vt,vi apprendre; ~ed ['lə:nɪd] a érudit(e), savant(e); ~er n débutant/e; ~ing n savoir m.

lease [li:s] n bail m // vt louer à bail.

leash [li:ʃ] n laisse f.

least [li:st] ad le moins // a: the ~ + noun le (la) plus petit(e), le (la) moindre; (smallest amount of) le moins de; the ~ + adjective le moins; the ~ money le moins d'argent; the ~ expensive le moins cher; at ~ au moins; not in the ~ pas le moins du monde.

leather ['lɛðə*] n cuir m // cpd en or de cuir.

leave [li:v] vb (pt,pp left [lɛft]) vt laisser; (go away from) quitter // vi partir, s'en aller n (time off) congé m; (MIL, also: consent) permission f; to be left rester; there's some milk left over il reste du lait; on ~ en permission; to take one's ~ of prendre congé de; to ~ out vt oublier, omettre.

leaves [li:vz] npl of **leaf**.

Lebanon ['lɛbənən] n Liban m.

lecherous ['lɛtʃərəs] a lubrique.

lectern ['lɛktə:n] n lutrin m, pupitre m.

lecture ['lɛktʃə*] n conférence f; (SCOL) cours (magistral) // vi donner des cours; enseigner; to ~ on faire un cours (or son cours) sur.

lecturer ['lɛktʃərə*] n (speaker) conférencier/ère; (at university) professeur m (d'université); ≈ maître assistant, ≈ maître de conférences; assistant ~ n ≈ assistant/e; senior ~ n ≈ chargé d'enseignement.

led [lɛd] pt,pp of **lead**.

ledge [lɛdʒ] n (of window, on wall) rebord m; (of mountain) saillie f, corniche f.

ledger ['lɛdʒə*] n registre m, grand livre.

lee [li:] n côté m sous le vent.

leech [li:tʃ] n sangsue f.

leek [li:k] n poireau m.

leer [lɪə*] vi: to ~ at sb regarder qn d'un air mauvais or concupiscent, lorgner qn.

leeway ['li:weɪ] n (fig): to make up ~ rattraper son retard; to have some ~ avoir une certaine liberté d'action.

left [lɛft] pt,pp of **leave** // a gauche // ad à gauche // n gauche f; the L~ (POL) la gauche; ~-handed a gaucher(ère); ~-hand side n gauche f, côté m gauche; ~-luggage (office) n consigne f; ~-overs npl restes mpl; ~ wing n (MIL, SPORT) aile f gauche; (POL) gauche f; ~-wing a (POL) de gauche.

leg [lɛg] n jambe f; (of animal) patte f; (of furniture) pied m; (CULIN: of chicken) cuisse f; 1st/2nd ~ (SPORT) match m aller/retour; (of journey) 1ère/2ème étape; ~ of lamb n (CULIN) gigot m d'agneau.

legacy ['lɛgəsɪ] n héritage m, legs m.

legal ['li:gl] a légal(e); ~ize vt légaliser; ~ly ad légalement; ~ tender n monnaie légale.

legation [lɪ'geɪʃən] n légation f.

legend ['lɛdʒənd] n légende f; ~ary a légendaire.

-legged ['lɛgɪd] suffix: two~ à deux pattes (or jambes or pieds).

leggings ['lɛgɪŋz] npl jambières fpl, guêtres fpl.

legibility [lɛdʒɪ'bɪlɪtɪ] n lisibilité f.

legible ['lɛdʒəbl] a lisible.

legibly ['lɛdʒəblɪ] ad lisiblement.

legion ['li:dʒən] n légion f.

legislate ['lɛdʒɪsleɪt] vi légiférer; **legislation** [-'leɪʃən] n législation f; **legislative** ['lɛdʒɪslətɪv] a législatif(ive); **legislator** n législateur/trice; **legislature** ['lɛdʒɪslətʃə*] n corps législatif.

legitimacy [lɪ'dʒɪtɪməsɪ] n légitimité f.

legitimate [lɪ'dʒɪtɪmət] a légitime.

leg-room ['lɛgru:m] n place f pour les jambes.

leisure ['lɛʒə*] n loisir m, temps m libre; loisirs mpl; at ~ (tout) à loisir; à tête reposée; ~ centre n centre m de loisirs; ~ly a tranquille; fait(e) sans se presser.

lemon ['lɛmən] n citron m; ~ade n [-'neɪd] limonade f; ~ squeezer n presse-citron m inv.

lend, pt,pp **lent** [lɛnd, lɛnt] vt: to ~ sth (to sb) prêter qch (à qn); ~er n prêteur/euse; ~ing library n bibliothèque f de prêt.

length [lɛŋθ] n longueur f; (section: of road, pipe etc) morceau m, bout m; ~ of time durée f; at ~ (at last) enfin, à la fin; (lengthily) longuement; ~en vt allonger, prolonger // vi s'allonger; ~ways ad dans le sens de la longueur, en long; ~y a (très) long(longue).

leniency ['li:nɪənsɪ] n indulgence f, clémence f.

lenient ['li:nɪənt] a indulgent(e), clément(e); ~ly ad avec indulgence or clémence.

lens [lɛnz] n lentille f; (of spectacles) verre m; (of camera) objectif m.

lent [lɛnt] pt,pp of **lend**.

Lent [lɛnt] n Carême m.

lentil [ˈlɛntl] n lentille f.

Leo [ˈliːəu] n le Lion; **to be** ∼ être du Lion.

leopard [ˈlɛpəd] n léopard m.

leotard [ˈliːətɑːd] n collant m (de danseur etc).

leper [ˈlɛpə*] n lépreux/euse.

leprosy [ˈlɛprəsɪ] n lèpre f.

lesbian [ˈlɛzbɪən] n lesbienne f.

less [lɛs] det moins de // pronoun, ad moins; ∼ **than that/you** moins que cela/vous; ∼ **than half** moins de la moitié; ∼ **and** ∼ de moins en moins; **the** ∼ **he works...** moins il travaille...

lessen [ˈlɛsn] vi diminuer, s'amoindrir, s'atténuer // vt diminuer, réduire, atténuer.

lesson [ˈlɛsn] n leçon f; **a maths** ∼ une leçon or un cours de maths.

lest [lɛst] cj de peur de + infinitive, de peur que + sub.

let, pt,pp **let** [lɛt] vt laisser; (lease) louer; **he** ∼ **me go** il m'a laissé partir; ∼ **the water boil and...** faites bouillir l'eau et...; ∼**'s go** allons-y; ∼ **him come** qu'il vienne; **'to** ∼' 'à louer'; **to** ∼ **down** vt (lower) baisser; (dress) rallonger; (hair) défaire; (disappoint) décevoir; **to** ∼ **go** vi lâcher prise // vt lâcher; **to** ∼ **in** vt laisser entrer; (visitor etc) faire entrer; **to** ∼ **off** vt laisser partir; (firework etc) faire partir; (smell etc) dégager; **to** ∼ **out** vt laisser sortir; (dress) élargir; (scream) laisser échapper; **to** ∼ **up** vi diminuer, s'arrêter.

lethal [ˈliːθl] a mortel(le), fatal(e).

lethargic [lɛˈθɑːdʒɪk] a léthargique.

lethargy [ˈlɛθədʒɪ] n léthargie f.

letter [ˈlɛtə*] n lettre f; ∼**s** npl (LITERATURE) lettres; ∼ **bomb** n lettre piégée; ∼**box** n boîte f aux or à lettres; ∼**ing** n lettres fpl; caractères mpl.

lettuce [ˈlɛtɪs] n laitue f, salade f.

let-up [ˈlɛtʌp] n répit m, détente f.

leukaemia, leukemia (US) [luːˈkiːmɪə] n leucémie f.

level [ˈlɛvl] a plat(e), plan(e), uni(e); horizontal(e) // n niveau m; (flat place) terrain plat; (also: **spirit** ∼) niveau à bulle // vt niveler, aplanir; **to be** ∼ **with** être au même niveau que; **'A'** ∼**s** npl ≈ baccalauréat m; **'O'** ∼**s** npl ≈ B.E.P.C.; **on the** ∼ à l'horizontale; (fig: honest) régulier(ère); **to** ∼ **off** or **out** vi (prices etc) se stabiliser; ∼ **crossing** n passage m à niveau; ∼**-headed** a équilibré(e).

lever [ˈliːvə*] n levier m // vt: **to** ∼ **up/out** soulever/extraire au moyen d'un levier; ∼**age** n: ∼**age** (on or **with**) prise f (sur).

levity [ˈlɛvɪtɪ] n manque m de sérieux, légèreté f.

levy [ˈlɛvɪ] n taxe f, impôt m // vt prélever, imposer; percevoir.

lewd [luːd] a obscène, lubrique.

liability [laɪəˈbɪlətɪ] n responsabilité f; (handicap) handicap m; **liabilities** npl obligations fpl, engagements mpl; (on balance sheet) passif m.

liable [ˈlaɪəbl] a (subject): ∼ **to** sujet(te) à; passible de; (responsible): ∼ **(for)** responsable (de); (likely): ∼ **to do** susceptible de faire.

liaison [liːˈeɪzɔn] n liaison f.

liar [ˈlaɪə*] n menteur/euse.

libel [ˈlaɪbl] n écrit m diffamatoire; diffamation f // vt diffamer.

liberal [ˈlɪbərl] a libéral(e); (generous): ∼ **with** prodigue de, généreux(euse) avec.

liberate [ˈlɪbəreɪt] vt libérer; **liberation** [-ˈreɪʃən] n libération f.

liberty [ˈlɪbətɪ] n liberté f; **at** ∼ **to do** libre de faire; **to take the** ∼ **of** prendre la liberté de, se permettre de.

Libra [ˈliːbrə] n la Balance; **to be** ∼ être de la Balance.

librarian [laɪˈbrɛərɪən] n bibliothécaire m/f.

library [ˈlaɪbrərɪ] n bibliothèque f.

libretto [lɪˈbrɛtəu] n livret m.

Libya [ˈlɪbɪə] n Libye f; ∼**n** a lybien(ne), de Lybie // n Lybien/ne.

lice [laɪs] npl of **louse**.

licence, license (US) [ˈlaɪsns] n autorisation f, permis m; (COMM) licence f; (RADIO, TV) redevance f; (also: **driving** ∼) permis m (de conduire); (excessive freedom) licence; ∼ **plate** n plaque f minéralogique.

license [ˈlaɪsns] n (US) = **licence** // vt donner une licence à; ∼**d** a (for alcohol) patenté(e) pour la vente des spiritueux, qui a une patente de débit de boissons.

licensee [laɪsənˈsiː] n (in a pub) patron/ne, gérant/e.

licentious [laɪˈsɛnʃəs] a licentieux(euse).

lichen [ˈlaɪkən] n lichen m.

lick [lɪk] vt lécher // n coup m de langue; **a** ∼ **of paint** un petit coup de peinture.

licorice [ˈlɪkərɪs] n = **liquorice**.

lid [lɪd] n couvercle m.

lido [ˈlaɪdəu] n piscine f en plein air.

lie [laɪ] n mensonge m // vi mentir; (pt **lay,** pp **lain** [leɪ, leɪn]) (rest) être étendu(e) or allongé(e) or couché(e); (in grave) être enterré(e), reposer; (of object: be situated) se trouver, être; **to** ∼ **low** (fig) se cacher, rester caché(e); **to** ∼ **about** vi traîner; **to have a** ∼**-down** s'allonger, se reposer; **to have a** ∼**-in** faire la grasse matinée.

lieu [luː]: **in** ∼ **of** prep au lieu de.

lieutenant [lɛfˈtɛnənt] n lieutenant m.

life, lives [laɪf, laɪvz] n vie f // cpd de vie; **de la vie**; **à vie**; ∼ **assurance** n assurance-vie f; ∼**belt** n bouée f de sauvetage; ∼**boat** n canot m or chaloupe f de sauvetage; ∼**buoy** n bouée f de sauvetage; ∼ **expectancy** n espérance f de vie; ∼**guard** n surveillant m de baignade; ∼ **jacket** n gilet m or ceinture f de sauvetage; ∼**less** a sans vie, inanimé(e); (dull) qui manque de vie or de vigueur; ∼**like** a qui semble vrai(e) or vivant(e); ressemblant(e); ∼**line** n corde f de sauvetage; ∼**long** a de toute une vie, de toujours; ∼ **preserver** n (US) gilet m or ceinture f de sauvetage; (Brit: col) matraque f; ∼**-raft** n radeau m de sauvetage; ∼**-saver** n surveillant m de baignade; ∼ **sentence** n condamnation f à vie *or* à perpétuité ; **~-sized** *a* grandeur nature *inv* ; **~ span** *n* (durée *f* de) vie *f* ; **~ support system** *n* (MED) respirateur artificiel ; **~time** *n*: in his **~time** de son vivant ; in a **~time** au cours d'une vie entière ; dans sa vie.

lift [lɪft] *vt* soulever, lever ; (*steal*) prendre, voler // *vi* (*fog*) se lever // *n* (*elevator*) ascenseur *m* ; to **give** sb a **~** emmener *or* prendre qn en voiture ; **~-off** *n* décollage *m*.

ligament ['lɪgəmənt] *n* ligament *m*.

light [laɪt] *n* lumière *f* ; (*daylight*) lumière, jour *m* ; (*lamp*) lampe *f* ; (ALT. traffic **~**, rear **~**) feu *m* ; (: *headlamp*) phare *m* ; (*for cigarette etc*): **have you got a ~?** avez-vous du feu ? // *vt* (*pt*, *pp* **lighted** *or* **lit** [lɪt]) (*candle, cigarette, fire*) allumer ; (*room*) éclairer // *a* (*room, colour*) clair(e) ; (*not heavy, also fig*) léger(ère) ; to **~ up** *vi* s'allumer ; (*face*) s'éclairer // *vt* (*illuminate*) éclairer, illuminer ; **~ bulb** *n* ampoule *f* ; **~en** *vi* s'éclairer // *vt* (*give light to*) éclairer ; (*make lighter*) éclaircir ; (*make less heavy*) alléger ; **~er** *n* (*also*: **cigarette ~**) briquet *m* ; (: *in car*) allume-cigare *m inv* ; (*boat*) péniche *f* ; **~-headed** *a* étourdi(e), écervelé(e) ; **~-hearted** *a* gai(e), joyeux(euse), enjoué(e) ; **~-house** *n* phare *m* ; **~ing** *n* (*on road*) éclairage *m* ; (*in theatre*) éclairages ; **~ing-up time** *n* heure officielle de la tombée du jour ; **~ly** *ad* légèrement ; **~ meter** *n* (PHOT) photomètre *m*, cellule *f* ; **~ness** *n* clarté *f* ; (*in weight*) légèreté *f*.

lightning ['laɪtnɪŋ] *n* éclair *m*, foudre *f* ; **~ conductor** *n* paratonnerre *m*.

lightship ['laɪtʃɪp] *n* bateau-phare *m*.

lightweight ['laɪtweɪt] *a* (*suit*) léger(ère) ; (*boxer*) poids léger *inv*.

light year ['laɪtjɪə*] *n* année-lumière *f*.

lignite ['lɪgnaɪt] *n* lignite *m*.

like [laɪk] *vt* aimer (bien) // *prep* comme // *a* semblable, pareil(le) // *n*: **the ~** un(e) pareil(le) *or* semblable ; le(la) pareil(le) ; (*pej*) (d')autres du même genre *or* acabit ; **his ~s and dislikes** ses goûts *mpl or* préférences *fpl* ; **I would ~**, **I'd ~** je voudrais, j'aimerais ; to **be/look ~ sb/sth** ressembler à qn/qch ; **that's just ~ him** c'est bien de lui, ça lui ressemble ; **nothing ~...** rien de tel que... ; **~able** *a* sympathique, agréable.

likelihood ['laɪklɪhud] *n* probabilité *f*.

likely ['laɪklɪ] *a* probable ; plausible ; **he's ~ to leave** il va sûrement partir, il risque fort de partir.

like-minded [laɪk'maɪndɪd] *a* de même opinion.

liken ['laɪkən] *vt*: to **~ sth to** comparer qch à.

likewise ['laɪkwaɪz] *ad* de même, pareillement.

liking ['laɪkɪŋ] *n*: **~ (for)** affection *f* (pour), penchant *m* (pour) ; goût *m* (pour).

lilac ['laɪlək] *n* lilas *m* // *a* lilas *inv*.

lilting ['lɪltɪŋ] *a* aux cadences mélodieuses ; chantant(e).

lily ['lɪlɪ] *n* lis *m* ; **~ of the valley** *n* muguet *m*.

limb [lɪm] *n* membre *m*.

limber ['lɪmbə*]: to **~ up** *vi* se dégourdir, se mettre en train.

limbo ['lɪmbəu] *n*: to **be in ~** (*fig*) être tombé(e) dans l'oubli.

lime [laɪm] *n* (*tree*) tilleul *m* ; (*fruit*) lime *f* ; (GEO) chaux *f* ; **~ juice** *n* jus *m* de citron vert.

limelight ['laɪmlaɪt] *n*: **in the ~** (*fig*) en vedette, au premier plan.

limerick ['lɪmərɪk] *n* poème *m* humoristique (de 5 vers).

limestone ['laɪmstəun] *n* pierre *f* à chaux ; (GEO) calcaire *m*.

limit ['lɪmɪt] *n* limite *f* // *vt* limiter ; **~ation** [-'teɪʃən] *n* limitation *f*, restriction *f* ; **~ed** *a* limité(e), restreint(e) ; **~ed (liability) company (Ltd)** *n* ≈ société *f* anonyme (S.A.).

limousine ['lɪməzi:n] *n* limousine *f*.

limp [lɪmp] *n*: to **have a ~** boiter // *vi* boiter // *a* mou(molle).

limpet ['lɪmpɪt] *n* patelle *f* ; **like a ~** (*fig*) comme une ventouse.

line [laɪn] *n* (*gen*) ligne *f* ; (*rope*) corde *f* ; (*wire*) fil *m* ; (*of poem*) vers *m* ; (*row, series*) rangée *f* ; file *f*, queue *f* ; (COMM: *series of goods*) article(s) *m(pl)* // *vt* (*clothes*): to **~ (with)** doubler (de) ; (*box*): to **~ (with)** garnir *or* tapisser (de) ; (*subj: trees, crowd*) border ; **in his ~ of business** dans sa partie, dans son rayon ; **in ~ with** en accord avec ; to **~ up** *vi* s'aligner, se mettre en rang(s) // *vt* aligner.

linear ['lɪnɪə*] *a* linéaire.

linen ['lɪnɪn] *n* linge *m* (de corps *or* de maison) ; (*cloth*) lin *m*.

liner ['laɪnə*] *n* paquebot *m* de ligne.

linesman ['laɪnzmən] *n* (TENNIS) juge *m* de ligne ; (FOOTBALL) juge de touche.

line-up ['laɪnʌp] *n* file *f* ; (SPORT) (composition *f* de l')équipe *f*.

linger ['lɪŋgə*] *vi* s'attarder ; traîner ; (*smell, tradition*) persister ; **~ing** *a* persistant(e) ; qui subsiste ; (*death*) lent(e).

lingo, **~es** ['lɪŋgəu] *n* (*pej*) jargon *m*.

linguist ['lɪŋgwɪst] *n* linguiste *m/f* ; personne douée pour les langues ; **~ic** *a* linguistique ; **~ics** *n* linguistique *f*.

lining ['laɪnɪŋ] *n* doublure *f*.

link [lɪŋk] *n* (*of a chain*) maillon *m* ; (*connection*) lien *m*, rapport *m* // *vt* relier, lier, unir ; **~s** *npl* (*terrain m de*) golf *m* ; to **~ up** *vt* relier // *vi* se rejoindre ; s'associer ; **~-up** *n* liaison *f*.

linoleum [lɪ'nəuliəm] *n* linoléum *m*.

linseed oil ['lɪnsi:d'ɔɪl] *n* huile *f* de lin.

lint [lɪnt] *n* tissu ouaté (*pour pansements*).

lintel ['lɪntl] *n* linteau *m*.

lion ['laɪən] *n* lion *m* ; **~ cub** *n* lionceau *m* ; **~ess** *n* lionne *f*.

lip [lɪp] *n* lèvre *f* ; (*of cup etc*) rebord *m* ; (*insolence*) insolences *fpl* ; **~-read** *vi* lire sur les lèvres ; to **pay ~-service to sth** ne reconnaître le mérite de qch que pour la forme *or* qu'en paroles ; **~stick** *n* rouge *m* à lèvres.

liquefy ['lɪkwɪfaɪ] *vt* liquéfier.

liqueur [lɪ'kjuə*] *n* liqueur *f*.

liquid ['lɪkwɪd] *n* liquide *m* // *a* liquide ; **~ assets** *npl* liquidités *fpl*, disponibilités *fpl*.

liquidate [ˈlɪkwɪdeɪt] vt liquider; **liquidation** [-ˈdeɪʃən] n liquidation f; **liquidator** n liquidateur m.

liquidize [ˈlɪkwɪdaɪz] vt (CULIN) passer au mixeur.

liquor [ˈlɪkə*] n spiritueux m, alcool m.

liquorice [ˈlɪkərɪs] n réglisse m.

lisp [lɪsp] n zézaiement m.

list [lɪst] n liste f; (of ship) inclinaison f // vt (write down) inscrire; faire la liste de; (enumerate) énumérer // vi (ship) giter, donner de la bande.

listen [ˈlɪsn] vi écouter; **to ~ to** écouter; **~er** n auditeur/trice.

listless [ˈlɪstlɪs] a indolent(e), apathique; **~ly** ad avec indolence or apathie.

lit [lɪt] pt, pp of **light**.

litany [ˈlɪtənɪ] n litanie f.

literacy [ˈlɪtərəsɪ] n degré m d'alphabétisation, fait m de savoir lire et écrire.

literal [ˈlɪtərl] a littéral(e); (unimaginative) prosaïque, sans imagination; **~ly** ad littéralement.

literary [ˈlɪtərərɪ] a littéraire.

literate [ˈlɪtərət] a qui sait lire et écrire, instruit(e).

literature [ˈlɪtrɪtʃə*] n littérature f; (brochures etc) copie f publicitaire, prospectus mpl.

lithe [laɪð] a agile, souple.

lithography [lɪˈθɔɡrəfɪ] n lithographie f.

litigate [ˈlɪtɪɡeɪt] vt mettre en litige // vi plaider; **litigation** [-ˈɡeɪʃən] n litige m; contentieux m.

litmus [ˈlɪtməs] n: **~ paper** papier m de tournesol.

litre, liter (US) [ˈliːtə*] n litre m.

litter [ˈlɪtə*] n (rubbish) détritus mpl, ordures fpl; (young animals) portée f // vt éparpiller; laisser des détritus dans // vi (ZOOL) mettre bas; **~ bin** n boîte f à ordures, poubelle f; **~ed with** jonché(e) de, couvert(e) de.

little [ˈlɪtl] a (small) petit(e); (not much): **it's ~** c'est peu; **~ milk** peu de lait // ad peu; **a ~** un peu (de); **a ~ milk** un peu de lait; **~ by ~** petit à petit, peu à peu; **to make ~ of** faire peu de cas de.

liturgy [ˈlɪtədʒɪ] n liturgie f.

live vi [lɪv] vivre; (reside) vivre, habiter // a [laɪv] (animal) vivant(e), en vie; (wire) sous tension; (broadcast) (transmis(e)) en direct; **to ~ down** vt faire oublier (avec le temps); **to ~ in** vi être logé(e) et nourri(e); être interne; **to ~ on** vt fus (food) vivre de // vi survivre, subsister; **to ~ up to** vt fus se montrer à la hauteur de.

livelihood [ˈlaɪvlɪhud] n moyens mpl d'existence.

liveliness [ˈlaɪvlɪnəs] n vivacité f, entrain m.

lively [ˈlaɪvlɪ] a vif(vive), plein(e) d'entrain.

liver [ˈlɪvə*] n (ANAT) foie m; **~ish** a qui a mal au foie; (fig) grincheux(euse).

livery [ˈlɪvərɪ] n livrée f.

lives [laɪvz] npl of **life**.

livestock [ˈlaɪvstɔk] n cheptel m, bétail m.

livid [ˈlɪvɪd] a livide, blafard(e); (furious) furieux(euse), furibond(e).

living [ˈlɪvɪŋ] a vivant(e), en vie // n: **to earn or make a ~** gagner sa vie; **~ room** n salle f de séjour; **~ standards** npl niveau m de vie; **~ wage** n salaire m permettant de vivre (décemment).

lizard [ˈlɪzəd] n lézard m.

llama [ˈlɑːmə] n lama m.

load [ləud] n (weight) poids m; (thing carried) chargement m, charge f; (ELEC, TECH) charge f // vt: **to ~ (with)** (lorry, ship) charger (de); (gun, camera) charger (avec); **a ~ of, ~s of** (fig) un or des tas de, des masses de; **a ~ed** a (dice) pipé(e); (question, word) insidieux(euse); (col: rich) bourré(e) de fric; (: drunk) bourré.

loaf, loaves [ləuf, ləuvz] n pain m, miche f // vi (also: **~ about, ~ around**) fainéanter, traîner.

loam [ləum] n terreau m.

loan [ləun] n prêt m // vt prêter; **on ~** prêté(e), en prêt; **public ~** emprunt public.

loath [ləuθ] a: **to be ~ to do** répugner à faire.

loathe [ləuð] vt détester, avoir en horreur; **loathing** n dégoût m, répugnance f.

loaves [ləuvz] npl of **loaf**.

lobby [ˈlɔbɪ] n hall m, entrée f; (POL: pressure group) groupe m de pression, lobby m // vt faire pression sur.

lobe [ləub] n lobe m.

lobster [ˈlɔbstə*] n homard m.

local [ˈləukl] a local(e) // n (pub) pub m or café m du coin; **the ~s** npl les gens mpl du pays or du coin; **~ call** n communication urbaine; **~ government** n administration locale or municipale.

locality [ləuˈkælɪtɪ] n région f, environs mpl; (position) lieu m.

locally [ˈləukəlɪ] ad localement; dans les environs or la région.

locate [ləuˈkeɪt] vt (find) trouver, repérer; (situate) situer.

location [ləuˈkeɪʃən] n emplacement m; **on ~** (CINEMA) en extérieur.

loch [lɔx] n lac m, loch m.

lock [lɔk] n (of door, box) serrure f; (of canal) écluse f; (of hair) mèche f, boucle f // vt (with key) fermer à clé; (immobilize) bloquer // vi (door etc) fermer à clé; (wheels) se bloquer.

locker [ˈlɔkə*] n casier m.

locket [ˈlɔkɪt] n médaillon m.

lockjaw [ˈlɔkdʒɔː] n tétanos m.

locomotive [ləukəˈməutɪv] n locomotive f.

locust [ˈləukəst] n locuste f, sauterelle f.

lodge [lɔdʒ] n pavillon m (de gardien); (FREEMASONRY) loge f // vi (person): **to ~ (with)** être logé(e) (chez), être en pension (chez) // vt (appeal etc) présenter; déposer; **to ~ a complaint** porter plainte; **to ~ (itself) in/between** se loger dans/entre; **~r** n locataire m/f; (with room and meals) pensionnaire m/f.

lodgings [ˈlɔdʒɪŋz] npl chambre f; meublé m.

loft [lɔft] n grenier m.

lofty [ˈlɔftɪ] a élevé(e); (haughty) hautain(e).

log [lɔɡ] n (of wood) bûche f; (book) = **logbook**.

logarithm ['lɔgərɪðəm] n logarithme m.

logbook ['lɔgbuk] n (NAUT) livre m or journal m de bord; (AVIAT) carnet m de vol; (of lorry-driver) carnet m de route; (of events, movement of goods etc) registre m; (of car) ≈ carte grise.

loggerheads ['lɔgəhɛdz] npl: at ~ (with) à couteaux tirés (avec).

logic ['lɔdʒɪk] n logique f; ~al a logique; ~ally ad logiquement.

logistics [lɔ'dʒɪstɪks] n logistique f.

loin [lɔɪn] n (CULIN) filet m, longe f; ~s npl reins mpl.

loiter ['lɔɪtə*] vi s'attarder; to ~ (about) traîner, musarder; (pej) rôder.

loll [lɔl] vi (also: ~ about) se prélasser, fainéanter.

lollipop ['lɔlɪpɔp] n sucette f; ~ man/lady n contractuel/le qui fait traverser la rue aux enfants.

London ['lʌndən] n Londres m; ~er n Londonien/ne.

lone [ləun] a solitaire.

loneliness ['ləunlɪnɪs] n solitude f, isolement m.

lonely ['ləunlɪ] a seul(e); solitaire, isolé(e); to feel ~ se sentir seul.

loner ['ləunə*] n solitaire m/f.

long [lɔŋ] a long(longue) // ad longtemps // vi: to ~ for sth/to do avoir très envie de qch/de faire; attendre qch avec impatience/impatience de faire; he had ~ understood that... il avait compris depuis longtemps que...; how ~ is this river/course? quelle est la longueur de ce fleuve/la durée de ce cours?; 6 metres ~ (long) de 6 mètres; 6 months ~ qui dure 6 mois, de 6 mois; all night ~ toute la nuit; ~ before longtemps avant; before ~ (+ future) avant peu, dans peu de temps; (+ past) peu de temps après; at ~ last enfin; no ~er, any ~er ne...plus; ~-distance a (race) de fond; (call) interurbain(e); ~-haired a (person) aux cheveux longs; (animal) aux longs poils; ~-hand n écriture normale or courante; ~ing n désir m, envie f, nostalgie f // a plein(e) d'envie or de nostalgie.

longitude ['lɔŋgɪtjuːd] n longitude f.

long: ~ jump n saut m en longueur; ~-lost a perdu(e) depuis longtemps; ~-playing a: ~-playing record (L.P.) n (disque m) 33 tours m inv; ~-range a à longue portée; ~-sighted a presbyte; (fig) prévoyant(e); ~-standing a de longue date; ~-suffering a empreint(e) d'une patience résignée; extrêmement patient(e); ~-term a à long terme; ~-wave n grandes ondes; ~-winded a intarissable, interminable

loo [luː] n (col) w.-c. mpl, petit coin.

loofah ['luːfə] n sorte d'éponge végétale.

look [luk] vi regarder; (seem) sembler, paraître, avoir l'air; (building etc) to ~ south/on to the sea donner au sud/sur la mer // n regard m; (appearance) air m, allure f; aspect m; ~s npl mine f; physique m; beauté f; to ~ like ressembler à; it ~s like him on dirait que c'est lui; to ~ after vt fus s'occuper de, prendre soin de; garder, surveiller; to ~ at vt fus regarder; to ~ down on vt fus

(fig) regarder de haut, dédaigner; to ~ for vt fus chercher; to ~ forward to vt fus attendre avec impatience; to ~ on vi regarder (en spectateur); to ~ out vi (beware): to ~ out (for) prendre garde (à), faire attention (à); to ~ out for vt fus être à la recherche de; guetter; to ~ to vt fus veiller à; (rely on) compter sur; to ~ up vi lever les yeux; (improve) s'améliorer // vt (word) chercher; (friend) passer voir; to ~ up to vt fus avoir du respect pour; ~-out n poste m de guet; guetteur m; to be on the ~-out (for) guetter.

loom [luːm] n métier m à tisser // vi surgir; (fig) menacer, paraître imminent(e).

loop [luːp] n boucle f; (contraceptive) stérilet m; ~hole n porte f de sortie (fig); échappatoire f.

loose [luːs] a (knot, screw) desserré(e); (stone) branlant(e); (clothes) vague, ample, lâche; (animal) en liberté, échappé(e); (life) dissolu(e); (morals, discipline) relâché(e); (thinking) peu rigoureux(euse), vague; (translation) approximatif(ive); to be at a ~ end ne pas trop savoir quoi faire; ~ly ad sans serrer; approximativement; ~n vt desserrer, relâcher, défaire.

loot [luːt] n butin m // vt piller; ~ing n pillage m.

lop [lɔp] : to ~ off vt couper, trancher.

lop-sided ['lɔp'saɪdɪd] a de travers, asymétrique.

lord [lɔːd] n seigneur m; L~ Smith lord Smith; the L~ le Seigneur; the (House of) L~s la Chambre des Lords; ~ly a noble, majestueux(euse); (arrogant) hautain(e); ~ship n: your L~ship Monsieur le comte (or le baron or le Juge).

lore [lɔː*] n tradition(s) f(pl).

lorry ['lɔrɪ] n camion m; ~ driver n camionneur m, routier m.

lose, pt,pp **lost** [luːz, lɔst] vt perdre; (opportunity) manquer, perdre; (pursuers) distancer, semer // vi perdre; to ~ (time) (clock) retarder; to get lost vi se perdre; ~r n perdant/e.

loss [lɔs] n perte f; to be at a ~ être perplexe or embarrassé(e); to be at a ~ to do se trouver incapable de faire.

lost [lɔst] pt,pp of **lose** // a perdu(e); ~ property n objets trouvés.

lot [lɔt] n (at auctions) lot m; (destiny) sort m, destinée f; the ~ le tout; tous mpl, toutes fpl; a ~ beaucoup; a ~ of beaucoup de; ~s of des tas de; to draw ~s (for sth) tirer (qch) au sort.

lotion ['ləuʃən] n lotion f.

lottery ['lɔtərɪ] n loterie f.

loud [laud] a bruyant(e), sonore, fort(e); (gaudy) voyant(e), tapageur(euse) // ad (speak etc) fort; ~-hailer n porte-voix m inv; ~ly ad fort, bruyamment; ~speaker n haut-parleur m.

lounge [laundʒ] n salon m // vi se prélasser, paresser; ~ suit n complet m, 'tenue de ville'.

louse, pl **lice** [laus, laɪs] n pou m.

lousy ['lauzɪ] a (fig) infect(e), moche.

lout [laut] *n* rustre *m*, butor *m*.

lovable ['lʌvəbl] *a* très sympathique; adorable.

love [lʌv] *n* amour *m* // *vt* aimer; aimer beaucoup; **to** ~ **to do** aimer beaucoup *or* adorer faire; **to be in** ~ **with** être amoureux(euse) de; **to make** ~ faire l'amour; '**15** ~ ' (*TENNIS*) '15 à rien *or* zéro'; ~ **at first sight** le coup de foudre; ~ **affair** *n* liaison (amoureuse); ~ **letter** *n* lettre *f* d'amour; ~ **life** *n* vie sentimentale.

lovely ['lʌvlɪ] *a* (très) joli(e); ravissant(e), charmant(e); agréable.

lover ['lʌvə*] *n* amant *m*; (*amateur*): **a** ~ **of** un(e) ami(e) de; un(e) amoureux(euse) de.

lovesong ['lʌvsɔŋ] *n* chanson *f* d'amour.

loving ['lʌvɪŋ] *a* affectueux(euse), tendre, aimant(e).

low [ləu] *a* bas(basse) // *ad* bas // *n* (*METEOROLOGY*) dépression *f* // *vi* (*cow*) mugir; **to feel** ~ se sentir déprimé(e); **he's very** ~ (*ill*) il est bien bas *or* très affaibli; **to turn (down)** ~ *vt* baisser; ~-**cut** *a* (*dress*) décolleté(e); ~-**er** *vt* abaisser, baisser; ~-**ly** *a* humble, modeste; ~-**lying** *a* à faible altitude; ~-**paid** *a* mal payé(e), aux salaires bas.

loyal ['lɔɪəl] *a* loyal(e), fidèle; ~**ty** *n* loyauté *f*, fidélité *f*.

lozenge ['lɔzɪndʒ] *n* (*MED*) pastille *f*; (*GEOM*) losange *m*.

L.P. *n abbr see* **long-playing**.

L-plates ['ɛlpleɪts] *npl* plaques *fpl* d'apprenti conducteur.

Ltd *abbr see* **limited**.

lubricant ['lu:brɪkənt] *n* lubrifiant *m*.

lubricate ['lu:brɪkeɪt] *vt* lubrifier, graisser.

lucid ['lu:sɪd] *a* lucide; ~**ity** [-'sɪdɪtɪ] *n* lucidité *f*.

luck [lʌk] *n* chance *f*; **bad** ~ malchance *f*, malheur *m*; **good** ~! bonne chance! ~**ily** *ad* heureusement, par bonheur; ~**y** *a* (*person*) qui a de la chance; (*coincidence*) heureux(euse); (*number etc*) qui porte bonheur.

lucrative ['lu:krətɪv] *a* lucratif(ive), rentable, qui rapporte.

ludicrous ['lu:dɪkrəs] *a* ridicule, absurde.

ludo ['lu:dəu] *n* jeu *m* des petits chevaux.

lug [lʌg] *vt* traîner, tirer.

luggage ['lʌgɪdʒ] *n* bagages *mpl*; ~ **rack** *n* (*in train*) porte-bagages *m inv*; (: *made of string*) filet *m* à bagages; (*on car*) galerie *f*.

lugubrious [lu'gu:brɪəs] *a* lugubre.

lukewarm ['lu:kwɔ:m] *a* tiède.

lull [lʌl] *n* accalmie *f* // *vt* (*child*) bercer; (*person, fear*) apaiser, calmer.

lullaby ['lʌləbaɪ] *n* berceuse *f*.

lumbago [lʌm'beɪgəu] *n* lumbago *m*.

lumber ['lʌmbə*] *n* bric-à-brac *m inv*; ~**jack** *n* bûcheron *m*.

luminous ['lu:mɪnəs] *a* lumineux(euse).

lump [lʌmp] *n* morceau *m*; (*in sauce*) grumeau *m*; (*swelling*) grosseur *f* // *vt* (*also*: ~ **together**) réunir, mettre en tas; **a** ~ **sum** une somme globale *or* forfaitaire; ~**y** *a* (*sauce*) qui a des grumeaux.

lunacy ['lu:nəsɪ] *n* démence *f*, folie *f*.

lunar ['lu:nə*] *a* lunaire.

lunatic ['lu:nətɪk] *n* fou/folle, dément/e // *a* fou(folle), dément(e).

lunch [lʌntʃ] *n* déjeuner *m*; **it is his** ~ **hour** c'est l'heure où il déjeune; **it is** ~**time** c'est l'heure du déjeuner.

luncheon ['lʌntʃən] *n* déjeuner *m*; ~ **meat** *n* sorte de saucisson; ~ **voucher** *n* chèque-déjeuner *m*.

lung [lʌŋ] *n* poumon *m*; ~ **cancer** *n* cancer *m* du poumon.

lunge [lʌndʒ] *vi* (*also*: ~ **forward**) faire un mouvement brusque en avant.

lupin ['lu:pɪn] *n* lupin *m*.

lurch [lə:tʃ] *vi* vaciller, tituber // *n* écart *m* brusque, embardée *f*.

lure [luə*] *n* appât *m*, leurre *m* // *vt* attirer *or* persuader par la ruse.

lurid ['luərɪd] *a* affreux(euse), atroce.

lurk [lə:k] *vi* se tapir, se cacher.

luscious ['lʌʃəs] *a* succulent(e); appétissant(e).

lush [lʌʃ] *a* luxuriant(e).

lust [lʌst] *n* luxure *f*; lubricité *f*; désir *m*; (*fig*): ~ **for** soif *f* de; **to** ~ **after** *vt fus* convoiter, désirer; ~**ful** *a* lascif(ive).

lustre, luster (*US*) ['lʌstə*] *n* lustre *m*, brillant *m*.

lusty ['lʌstɪ] *a* vigoureux(euse), robuste.

lute [lu:t] *n* luth *m*.

Luxembourg ['lʌksəmbə:g] *n* Luxembourg *m*.

luxuriant [lʌg'zjuərɪənt] *a* luxuriant(e).

luxurious [lʌg'zjuərɪəs] *a* luxueux(euse).

luxury ['lʌkʃərɪ] *n* luxe *m* // *cpd* de luxe.

lying ['laɪɪŋ] *n* mensonge(s) *m(pl)*.

lynch [lɪntʃ] *vt* lyncher.

lynx [lɪŋks] *n* lynx *m inv*.

lyre ['laɪə*] *n* lyre *f*.

lyric ['lɪrɪk] *a* lyrique; ~**s** *npl* (*of song*) paroles *fpl*; ~**al** *a* lyrique; ~**ism** ['lɪrɪsɪzəm] *n* lyrisme *m*.

M

m. *abbr of* **metre, mile, million**.

M.A. *abbr see* **master**.

mac [mæk] *n* imper(méable) *m*.

macaroni [mækə'rəunɪ] *n* macaronis *mpl*.

macaroon [mækə'ru:n] *n* macaron *m*.

mace [meɪs] *n* masse *f*; (*spice*) macis *m*.

machine [mə'ʃi:n] *n* machine *f* // *vt* (*dress etc*) coudre à la machine; ~ **gun** *n* mitrailleuse *f*; ~**ry** *n* machinerie *f*, machines *fpl*; (*fig*) mécanisme(s) *m(pl)*; ~ **tool** *n* machine-outil *f*; **machinist** *n* machiniste *m/f*.

mackerel ['mækrl] *n*, *pl inv* maquereau *m*.

mackintosh ['mækɪntɔʃ] *n* imperméable *m*.

mad [mæd] *a* fou(folle); (*foolish*) insensé(e); (*angry*) furieux(euse).

madam ['mædəm] *n* madame *f*; **yes** ~ oui Madame.

madden ['mædn] *vt* exaspérer.

made [meɪd] *pt*, *pp of* **make**; ~-**to-measure** *a* fait(e) sur mesure.

madly ['mædlɪ] *ad* follement.

madman ['mædmən] n fou m, aliéné m.
madness ['mædnɪs] n folie f.
magazine [mægə'ziːn] n (PRESS) magazine m, revue f; (MIL: store) dépôt m, arsenal m; (of firearm) magasin m.
maggot ['mægət] n ver m, asticot m.
magic ['mædʒɪk] n magie f // a magique; ~al a magique; ~ian [mə'dʒɪʃən] n magicien/ne.
magistrate ['mædʒɪstreɪt] n magistrat m; juge m.
magnanimous [mæg'nænɪməs] a magnanime.
magnate ['mægneɪt] n magnat m.
magnesium [mæg'niːzɪəm] n magnésium m.
magnet ['mægnɪt] n aimant m; ~ic [-'netɪk] a magnétique; ~ism n magnétisme m.
magnification [mægnɪfɪ'keɪʃən] n grossissement m.
magnificence [mæg'nɪfɪsns] n magnificence f.
magnificent [mæg'nɪfɪsnt] a superbe, magnifique.
magnify ['mægnɪfaɪ] vt grossir; (sound) amplifier; ~ing glass n loupe f.
magnitude ['mægnɪtjuːd] n ampleur f.
magnolia [mæg'nəʊlɪə] n magnolia m.
magpie ['mægpaɪ] n pie f.
mahogany [mə'hɒgənɪ] n acajou m // cpd en (bois d')acajou.
maid [meɪd] n bonne f; old ~ (pej) vieille fille.
maiden ['meɪdn] n jeune fille f // a (aunt etc) non mariée; (speech, voyage) inaugural(e); ~ name n nom m de jeune fille.
mail [meɪl] n poste f; (letters) courrier m // vt envoyer (par la poste); ~box n (US) boîte f aux lettres; ~ing list n liste f d'adresses; ~-order n vente f or achat m par correspondance.
maim [meɪm] vt mutiler.
main [meɪn] a principal(e) // n (pipe) conduite principale, canalisation f; the ~s (ELEC) le secteur; in the ~ dans l'ensemble; ~land n continent m; ~stay n (fig) pilier m.
maintain [meɪn'teɪn] vt entretenir; (continue) maintenir, préserver; (affirm) soutenir; **maintenance** ['meɪntənəns] n entretien m.
maisonette [meɪzə'nɛt] n appartement m en duplex.
maize [meɪz] n maïs m.
majestic [mə'dʒɛstɪk] a majestueux(euse).
majesty ['mædʒɪstɪ] n majesté f.
major ['meɪdʒə*] n (MIL) commandant m // a important(e), principal(e); (MUS) majeur(e).
majority [mə'dʒɒrɪtɪ] n majorité f.
make [meɪk] vt (pt, pp made [meɪd]) faire; (manufacture) faire, fabriquer; (cause to be): to ~ sb sad etc rendre qn triste etc; (force): to ~ sb do sth obliger qn à faire qch, faire faire qch à qn; (equal): 2 and 2 ~ 4 2 et 2 font 4 // n fabrication f; (brand) marque f; to ~ do with se contenter de; se débrouiller avec; to ~ for vt fus (place) se diriger vers; to ~ out

vt (write out) écrire; (understand) comprendre; (see) distinguer; to ~ up vt (invent) inventer, imaginer; (parcel) faire // vi se réconcilier; (with cosmetics) se maquiller, se farder; to ~ up for vt fus compenser; racheter; ~-believe a feint(e), de fantaisie; ~r n fabricant m; ~shift a provisoire, improvisé(e); ~-up n maquillage m.
making ['meɪkɪŋ] n (fig): in the ~ en formation or gestation.
maladjusted [mælə'dʒʌstɪd] a inadapté(e).
malaise [mæ'leɪz] n malaise m.
malaria [mə'lɛərɪə] n malaria f, paludisme m.
Malay [mə'leɪ] a malais(e) // n (person) Malais/e; (language) malais m.
Malaysia [mə'leɪzɪə] n Malaisie f.
male [meɪl] n (BIOL, ELEC) mâle m // a (sex, attitude) masculin(e); mâle; (child etc) du sexe masculin; ~ and female students étudiants et étudiantes.
malevolence [mə'lɛvələns] n malveillance f.
malevolent [mə'lɛvələnt] a malveillant(e).
malfunction [mæl'fʌŋkʃən] n fonctionnement défectueux.
malice ['mælɪs] n méchanceté f, malveillance f; **malicious** [mə'lɪʃəs] a méchant(e), malveillant(e); (LAW) avec intention criminelle.
malign [mə'laɪn] vt diffamer, calomnier.
malignant [mə'lɪgnənt] a (MED) malin(igne).
malingerer [mə'lɪŋgərə*] n simulateur/trice.
malleable ['mælɪəbl] a malléable.
mallet ['mælɪt] n maillet m.
malnutrition [mælnjuː'trɪʃən] n malnutrition f.
malpractice [mæl'præktɪs] n faute professionnelle; négligence f.
malt [mɔːlt] n malt m // cpd (whisky) pur malt.
Malta ['mɔːltə] n Malte f; **Maltese** [-'tiːz] a maltais(e) // n, pl inv Maltais/e.
maltreat [mæl'triːt] vt maltraiter.
mammal ['mæml] n mammifère m.
mammoth ['mæməθ] n mammouth m // a géant(e), monstre.
man, pl **men** [mæn, mɛn] n homme m; (CHESS) pièce f; (DRAUGHTS) pion m // vt garnir d'hommes; servir, assurer le fonctionnement de; être de service à; an old ~ un vieillard.
manage ['mænɪdʒ] vi se débrouiller // vt (be in charge of) s'occuper de; gérer; to ~ to do se débrouiller pour faire; réussir à faire; ~able a maniable; faisable; ~ment n administration f, direction f; ~r n directeur m; administrateur m; (of hotel etc) gérant m; (of artist) impresario m; ~ress [-ə'rɛs] n directrice f; gérante f; ~rial [-ə'dʒɪərɪəl] a directorial(e); ~rial staff n cadres mpl; **managing** a: managing director directeur général.
mandarin ['mændərɪn] n (also: ~ orange) mandarine f; (person) mandarin m.

mandate ['mændeɪt] n mandat m.
mandatory ['mændətərɪ] a obligatoire; (powers etc) mandataire.
mandolin(e) ['mændəlɪn] n mandoline f.
mane [meɪn] n crinière f.
maneuver [mə'nu:və*] etc (US) = **manoeuvre** etc.
manful ['mænful] a courageux(euse), vaillant(e).
manganese [mæŋgə'ni:z] n manganèse m.
mangle ['mæŋgl] vt déchiqueter; mutiler // n essoreuse f; calandre f.
mango, ~es ['mæŋgəu] n mangue f.
mangrove ['mæŋgrəuv] n palétuvier m.
mangy ['meɪndʒɪ] a galeux(euse).
manhandle ['mænhændl] vt malmener.
manhole ['mænhəul] n trou m d'homme.
manhood ['mænhud] n âge m d'homme; virilité f.
manhunt ['mænhʌnt] n chasse f à l'homme.
mania ['meɪnɪə] n manie f; ~c ['meɪnɪæk] n maniaque m/f.
manicure ['mænɪkjuə*] n manucure f // vt (person) faire les mains à; ~ set n trousse f à ongles.
manifest ['mænɪfɛst] vt manifester // a manifeste, évident(e); ~ation [-'teɪʃən] n manifestation f.
manifesto [mænɪ'fɛstəu] n manifeste m.
manipulate [mə'nɪpjuleɪt] vt manipuler.
mankind [mæn'kaɪnd] n humanité f, genre humain.
manly ['mænlɪ] a viril(e); courageux(euse).
man-made ['mæn'meɪd] a artificiel(le).
manner ['mænə*] n manière f, façon f; ~s npl manières; ~ism n particularité f de langage (or de comportement), tic m.
manoeuvre, **maneuver** (US) [mə'nu:və*] vt,vi manœuvrer // n manœuvre f.
manor ['mænə*] n (also: ~ house) manoir m.
manpower ['mænpauə*] n main-d'œuvre f.
manservant, pl **menservants** ['mænsə:vənt, 'mɛn-] n domestique m.
mansion ['mænʃən] n château m, manoir m.
manslaughter ['mænslɔ:tə*] n homicide m involontaire.
mantelpiece ['mæntlpi:s] n cheminée f.
mantle ['mæntl] n cape f; (fig) manteau m.
manual ['mænjuəl] a manuel(le) // n manuel m.
manufacture [mænju'fæktʃə*] vt fabriquer // n fabrication f; ~r n fabricant m.
manure [mə'njuə*] n fumier m; (artificial) engrais m.
manuscript ['mænjuskrɪpt] n manuscrit m.
many ['mɛnɪ] det beaucoup de, de nombreux(euses) // pronoun beaucoup, un grand nombre; a great ~ un grand nombre (de); ~ a... bien des... , plus d'un(e)... .

map [mæp] n carte f // vt dresser la carte de; to ~ out vt tracer.
maple ['meɪpl] n érable m.
mar [mɑ:*] vt gâcher, gâter.
marathon ['mærəθən] n marathon m.
marauder [mə'rɔ:də*] n maraudeur/euse.
marble ['mɑ:bl] n marbre m; (toy) bille f; ~s n (game) billes.
March [mɑ:tʃ] n mars m.
march [mɑ:tʃ] vi marcher au pas; défiler // n marche f; (demonstration) rallye m; ~-past n défilé m.
mare [mɛə*] n jument f.
margarine [mɑ:dʒə'ri:n] n margarine f.
margin [mɑ:dʒɪn] n marge f; ~al a marginal(e).
marigold ['mærɪgəuld] n souci m.
marijuana [mærɪ'wɑ:nə] n marijuana f.
marina [mə'ri:nə] n marina f.
marine [mə'ri:n] a marin(e) // n fusilier marin; (US) marine m.
marital ['mærɪtl] a matrimonial(e).
maritime ['mærɪtaɪm] a maritime.
marjoram ['mɑ:dʒərəm] n marjolaine f.
mark [mɑ:k] n marque f; (of skid etc) trace f; (SCOL) note f; (SPORT) cible f; (currency) mark m // vt (stain) tacher; (SCOL) noter; corriger; to ~ time marquer le pas; to ~ out vt désigner; ~ed a marqué(e), net(te); ~er n (sign) jalon m; (bookmark) signet m.
market ['mɑ:kɪt] n marché m // vt (COMM) commercialiser; ~ day n jour m de marché; ~ garden n (Brit) jardin maraîcher; ~ing n marketing m; ~ place n place f du marché.
marksman ['mɑ:ksmən] n tireur m d'élite; ~ship n adresse f au tir.
marmalade ['mɑ:məleɪd] n confiture f d'oranges.
maroon [mə'ru:n] vt (fig): to be ~ed (in or at) être bloqué(e) (à) // a bordeaux inv.
marquee [mɑ:'ki:] n chapiteau m.
marquess, **marquis** ['mɑ:kwɪs] n marquis m.
marriage ['mærɪdʒ] n mariage m; ~ bureau n agence matrimoniale.
married ['mærɪd] a marié(e); (life, love) conjugal(e).
marrow ['mærəu] n moelle f; (vegetable) courge f.
marry ['mærɪ] vt épouser, se marier avec; (subj: father, priest etc) marier // vi (also: get married) se marier.
Mars [mɑ:z] n (planet) Mars f.
marsh [mɑ:ʃ] n marais m, marécage m.
marshal ['mɑ:ʃl] n maréchal m; (US: fire, police) ≈ capitaine m // vt rassembler; ~ing yard n gare f de triage.
marshy ['mɑ:ʃɪ] a marécageux(euse).
martial ['mɑ:ʃl] a martial(e); ~ law n loi martiale.
Martian ['mɑ:ʃɪən] Martien/ne.
martyr ['mɑ:tə*] n martyr/e // vt martyriser; ~dom n martyre m.
marvel ['mɑ:vl] n merveille f // vi: to ~ (at) s'émerveiller (de); ~lous, ~ous (US) a merveilleux(euse).
Marxism ['mɑ:ksɪzəm] n marxisme m.

Marxist ['mɑ:ksɪst] a,n marxiste (m/f).
marzipan ['mɑ:zɪpæn] n pâte f d'amandes.
mascara [mæs'kɑ:rə] n mascara m.
mascot ['mæskət] n mascotte f.
masculine ['mæskjulɪn] a masculin(e) // n masculin m; **masculinity** [-'lɪnɪtɪ] n masculinité f.
mashed [mæʃt] a: ~ **potatoes** purée f de pommes de terre.
mask [mɑ:sk] n masque m // vt masquer.
masochist ['mæsəukɪst] n masochiste m/f.
mason ['meɪsn] n (also: **stone**~) maçon m; (also: **free**~) franc-maçon m; ~**ic** [mə'sɔnɪk] a maçonnique; ~**ry** n maçonnerie f.
masquerade [mæskə'reɪd] n bal masqué; (fig) mascarade f // vi: to ~ **as** se faire passer pour.
mass [mæs] n multitude f, masse f; (PHYSICS) masse; (REL) messe f // vi se masser; the ~**es** les masses.
massacre ['mæsəkə*] n massacre m // vt massacrer.
massage ['mæsɑ:ʒ] n massage m // vt masser.
masseur [mæ'sə:*] n masseur m; **masseuse** [-'sə:z] n masseuse f.
massive ['mæsɪv] a énorme, massif(ive).
mass media ['mæs'mi:dɪə] npl mass-media mpl.
mass-produce ['mæsprə'dju:s] vt fabriquer en série.
mast [mɑ:st] n mât m.
master ['mɑ:stə*] n maître m; (in secondary school) professeur m; (title for boys): M~ X Monsieur X // vt maîtriser; (learn) apprendre à fond; (understand) posséder parfaitement or à fond; M~'s degree n ≈ maîtrise f; ~ **key** n passe-partout m inv; ~**ly** a magistral(e); ~**mind** n esprit supérieur // vt diriger, être le cerveau de; M~ **of Arts/Science** (M.A./M.Sc.) n ≈ titulaire m/f d'une maîtrise (en lettres/science); M~ **of Arts/Science degree** (M.A./M.Sc.) n ≈ maîtrise f; ~**piece** n chef-d'œuvre m; ~ **plan** n stratégie f d'ensemble; ~ **stroke** n coup m de maître; ~**y** n maîtrise f; connaissance parfaite.
masturbate ['mæstəbeɪt] vi se masturber; **masturbation** [-'beɪʃən] n masturbation f.
mat [mæt] n petit tapis; (also: **door**~) paillasson m // a = **matt**.
match [mætʃ] n allumette f; (game) match m, partie f; (fig) égal/e; mariage m; parti m // vt assortir; (go well with) aller bien avec, s'assortir à; (equal) égaler, valoir // vi être assorti(e); to be a good ~ être bien assorti(e); to ~ **up** vt assortir; ~**box** n boîte f d'allumettes; ~**ing** a assorti(e); ~**less** a sans égal.
mate [meɪt] n camarade m/f de travail; (col) copain/copine; (animal) partenaire m/f, mâle/femelle; (in merchant navy) second m // vi s'accoupler // vt accoupler.
material [mə'tɪərɪəl] n (substance) matière f, matériau m; (cloth) tissu m, étoffe f // a matériel(le); (important) essentiel(le); ~**s** npl matériaux mpl; ~**istic** [-ə'lɪstɪk] a

materialiste; ~**ize** vi se matérialiser, se réaliser; ~**ly** ad matériellement.
maternal [mə'tə:nl] a maternel(le).
maternity [mə'tə:nɪtɪ] n maternité f // cpd de maternité, de grossesse; ~ **hospital** n maternité f.
matey ['meɪtɪ] a (col) copain-copain inv.
mathematical [mæθə'mætɪkl] a mathématique.
mathematician [mæθəmə'tɪʃən] n mathématicien/ne.
mathematics [mæθə'mætɪks] n mathématiques fpl.
maths [mæθs] n math(s) fpl.
matinée ['mætɪneɪ] n matinée f.
mating ['meɪtɪŋ] n accouplement m; ~ **call** n appel m du mâle; ~ **season** n saison f des amours.
matriarchal [meɪtrɪ'ɑ:kl] a matriarcal(e).
matrices ['meɪtrɪsi:z] npl of **matrix**.
matriculation [mətrɪkju'leɪʃən] n inscription f.
matrimonial [mætrɪ'məunɪəl] a matrimonial(e), conjugal(e).
matrimony ['mætrɪmənɪ] n mariage m.
matrix, pl **matrices** ['meɪtrɪks, 'meɪtrɪsi:z] n matrice f.
matron ['meɪtrən] n (in hospital) infirmière-chef f; (in school) infirmière; ~**ly** a de matrone; imposant(e).
matt [mæt] a mat(e).
matted ['mætɪd] a emmêlé(e).
matter ['mætə*] n question f; (PHYSICS) matière f, substance f; (content) contenu m, fond m; (MED: pus) pus m // vi importer; **it doesn't** ~ cela n'a pas d'importance; (I don't mind) cela ne fait rien; **what's the** ~? qu'est-ce qu'il y a?, qu'est-ce qui ne va pas?; **no** ~ **what** quoiqu'il arrive; **that's another** ~ c'est une autre affaire; **as a** ~ **of course** tout naturellement; **as a** ~ **of fact** en fait; **it's a** ~ **of habit** c'est une question d'habitude; ~**-of-fact** a terre à terre, neutre.
matting ['mætɪŋ] n natte f.
mattress ['mætrɪs] n matelas m.
mature [mə'tjuə*] a mûr(e); (cheese) fait(e) // vi mûrir; se faire; **maturity** n maturité f.
maudlin ['mɔ:dlɪn] a larmoyant(e).
maul [mɔ:l] vt lacérer.
Mauritius [mə'rɪʃəs] n l'île f Maurice.
mausoleum [mɔ:sə'lɪəm] n mausolée m.
mauve [məuv] a mauve.
mawkish ['mɔ:kɪʃ] a mièvre; fade.
max. abbr of **maximum**.
maxim ['mæksɪm] n maxime f.
maxima ['mæksɪmə] npl of **maximum**.
maximum ['mæksɪməm] a maximum // n (pl **maxima** ['mæksɪmə]) maximum m.
May [meɪ] n mai m.
may [meɪ] vi (conditional: **might**) (indicating possibility): **he** ~ **come** il se peut qu'il vienne; (be allowed to): ~ **I smoke?** puis-je fumer?; (wishes): ~ **God bless you!** (que) Dieu vous bénisse!; **he might be there** il pourrait bien y être, il se pourrait qu'il y soit; **I might as well go** je ferais aussi bien d'y aller, autant y

aller ; **you might like to try** vous pourriez (peut-être) essayer.

maybe ['meɪbi:] ad peut-être ; ~ **he'll...** peut-être qu'il... .

mayday ['meɪdeɪ] n S.O.S. m.

May Day ['meɪdeɪ] n le Premier mai.

mayhem ['meɪhɛm] n grabuge m.

mayonnaise [meɪə'neɪz] n mayonnaise f.

mayor [mɛə°] n maire m ; **~ess** n maire m ; épouse f du maire.

maypole ['meɪpəul] n mât enrubanné (autour duquel on danse).

maze [meɪz] n labyrinthe m, dédale m.

M.D. abbr = Doctor of Medicine.

me [mi:] pronoun me, m' + vowel ; (stressed, after prep) moi.

meadow ['mɛdəu] n prairie f, pré m.

meagre, meager (US) ['mi:gə°] a maigre.

meal [mi:l] n repas m ; (flour) farine f ; ~**time** n l'heure f du repas ; ~**y-mouthed** a mielleux(euse).

mean [mi:n] a (with money) avare, radin(e) ; (unkind) mesquin(e), méchant(e) ; (average) moyen(ne) // vt (pt, pp **meant** [mɛnt]) (signify) signifier, vouloir dire ; (intend): to ~ to do avoir l'intention de faire // n moyenne f ; ~**s** npl moyens mpl ; **by ~s of** par l'intermédiaire de ; au moyen de ; **by all ~s** je vous en prie ; **to be meant for** être destiné(e) à ; **what do you ~?** que voulez-vous dire?

meander [mɪ'ændə°] vi faire des méandres ; (fig) flâner.

meaning ['mi:nɪŋ] n signification f, sens m ; ~**ful** a significatif(ive) ; ~**less** a dénué(e) de sens.

meanness ['mi:nnɪs] n avarice f ; mesquinerie f.

meant [mɛnt] pt, pp of mean.

meantime ['mi:ntaɪm] ad, **meanwhile** ['mi:nwaɪl] ad (also: **in the ~**) pendant ce temps.

measles ['mi:zlz] n rougeole f.

measly ['mi:zlɪ] a (col) minable.

measurable ['mɛʒərəbl] a mesurable.

measure ['mɛʒə°] vt, vi mesurer // n mesure f ; (ruler) règle (graduée) ; ~**d** a mesuré(e) ; ~**ments** npl mesures fpl ; **chest/hip ~ment** tour m de poitrine/hanches.

meat [mi:t] n viande f ; ~ **pie** n pâté m en croûte ; ~**y** a qui a le goût de la viande ; (fig) substantiel(le).

Mecca ['mɛkə] n la Mecque.

mechanic [mɪ'kænɪk] n mécanicien m ; ~**s** n mécanique f // npl mécanisme m ; ~**al** a mécanique.

mechanism ['mɛkənɪzəm] n mécanisme m.

mechanization [mɛkənaɪ'zeɪʃən] n mécanisation f.

medal ['mɛdl] n médaille f ; ~**lion** [mɪ'dælɪən] n médaillon m ; ~**list, ~ist** (US) n (SPORT) médaillé/e.

meddle ['mɛdl] vi: to ~ **in** se mêler de, s'occuper de ; to ~ **with** toucher à ; ~**some** a indiscret(ète).

media ['mi:dɪə] npl media mpl.

mediaeval [mɛdɪ'i:vl] a = medieval.

mediate ['mi:dɪeɪt] vi s'interposer ; servir d'intermédiaire ; **mediation** [-'eɪʃən] n médiation f ; **mediator** n médiateur/trice.

medical ['mɛdɪkl] a médical(e) ; ~ **student** n étudiant/e en médecine.

medicated ['mɛdɪkeɪtɪd] a traitant(e), médicamenteux(euse).

medicinal [mɛ'dɪsɪnl] a médicinal(e).

medicine ['mɛdsɪn] n médecine f ; (drug) médicament m ; ~ **chest** n pharmacie f (murale ou portative).

medieval [mɛdɪ'i:vl] a médiéval(e).

mediocre [mi:dɪ'əukə°] a médiocre ; **mediocrity** [-'ɔkrɪtɪ] n médiocrité f.

meditate ['mɛdɪteɪt] vi: to ~ (on) méditer (sur) ; **meditation** [-'teɪʃən] n méditation f.

Mediterranean [mɛdɪtə'reɪnɪən] a méditerranéen(ne) ; **the ~ (Sea)** la (mer) Méditerranée.

medium ['mi:dɪəm] a moyen(ne) // n (pl media: means) moyen m ; (pl mediums: person) médium m ; **the happy ~** le juste milieu.

medley ['mɛdlɪ] n mélange m.

meek [mi:k] a doux(douce), humble.

meet, pt,pp **met** [mi:t, mɛt] vt rencontrer ; (by arrangement) retrouver, rejoindre ; (for the first time) faire la connaissance de ; (go and fetch): **I'll ~ you at the station** j'irai te chercher à la gare ; (fig) faire face à ; satisfaire à ; se joindre à // vi se rencontrer ; se retrouver ; (in session) se réunir ; (join: objects) se joindre ; to ~ **with** vt fus rencontrer ; ~**ing** n rencontre f ; (session: of club etc) réunion f ; (interview) entrevue f ; **she's at a ~ing** (COMM) elle est en conférence.

megaphone ['mɛgəfəun] n porte-voix m inv.

melancholy ['mɛlənkəlɪ] n mélancolie f // a mélancolique.

mellow ['mɛləu] a velouté(e) ; doux(douce) ; (colour) riche et profond(e) ; (fruit) mûr(e) // vi (person) s'adoucir.

melodious [mɪ'ləudɪəs] a mélodieux(euse).

melodrama ['mɛləudrɑ:mə] n mélodrame m.

melody ['mɛlədɪ] n mélodie f.

melon ['mɛlən] n melon m.

melt [mɛlt] vi fondre ; (become soft) s'amollir ; (fig) s'attendrir // vt faire fondre ; (person) attendrir ; to ~ **away** vi fondre complètement ; to ~ **down** vt fondre ; ~**ing point** n point m de fusion ; ~**ing pot** n (fig) creuset m.

member ['mɛmbə°] n membre m ; ~ **country/state** n pays m/état m member ; **M~ of Parliament (M.P.)** député m ; ~**ship** n adhésion f ; statut m de membre ; (nombre m de) membres mpl, adhérents mpl.

membrane ['mɛmbreɪn] n membrane f.

memento [mə'mɛntəu] n souvenir m.

memo ['mɛməu] n note f (de service).

memoir ['mɛmwɑ:°] n mémoire m, étude f ; ~**s** npl mémoires.

memorable ['mɛmərəbl] a mémorable.

memorandum, pl **memoranda** [mɛmə'rændəm, -də] n note f (de service) ; (DIPLOMACY) mémorandum m.

memorial [mɪˈmɔːrɪəl] n mémorial m // a commémoratif(ive).

memorize [ˈmɛməraɪz] vt apprendre or retenir par cœur.

memory [ˈmɛməri] n mémoire f; (recollection) souvenir m; **in ~ of** à la mémoire de.

men [mɛn] npl of **man**.

menace [ˈmɛnəs] n menace f // vt menacer; **menacing** a menaçant(e).

menagerie [mɪˈnædʒəri] n ménagerie f.

mend [mɛnd] vt réparer; (darn) raccommoder, repriser // n reprise f; **on the ~** en voie de guérison; **~ing** n raccommodages mpl.

menial [ˈmiːnɪəl] a de domestique, inférieur(e); subalterne.

meningitis [mɛnɪnˈdʒaɪtɪs] n méningite f.

menopause [ˈmɛnəupɔːz] n ménopause f.

menservants npl of **manservant**.

menstruate [ˈmɛnstrueɪt] vi avoir ses règles; **menstruation** [-ˈeɪʃən] n menstruation f.

mental [ˈmɛntl] a mental(e).

mentality [mɛnˈtælɪti] n mentalité f.

mention [ˈmɛnʃən] n mention f // vt mentionner, faire mention de; **don't ~ it!** je vous en prie, il n'y a pas de quoi!

menu [ˈmɛnjuː] n (set ~) menu m; (printed) carte f.

mercantile [ˈmɜːkəntaɪl] a marchand(e); (law) commercial(e).

mercenary [ˈmɜːsɪnəri] a mercantile // n mercenaire m.

merchandise [ˈmɜːtʃəndaɪz] n marchandises fpl.

merchant [ˈmɜːtʃənt] n négociant m, marchand m; **timber/wine ~** négociant en bois/vins, marchand de bois/vins; **~ bank** n banque f d'affaires; **~ navy** n marine marchande.

merciful [ˈmɜːsɪful] a miséricordieux(euse), clément(e).

merciless [ˈmɜːsɪlɪs] a impitoyable, sans pitié.

mercurial [mɜːˈkjuərɪəl] a changeant(e); (lively) vif(vive).

mercury [ˈmɜːkjuri] n mercure m.

mercy [ˈmɜːsi] n pitié f, merci f; (REL) miséricorde f; **to have ~ on sb** avoir pitié de qn; **at the ~ of** à la merci de.

mere [mɪə*] a simple; **~ly** ad simplement, purement.

merge [mɜːdʒ] vt unir // vi se fondre; (COMM) fusionner; **~r** n (COMM) fusion f.

meridian [məˈrɪdɪən] n méridien m.

meringue [məˈræŋ] n meringue f.

merit [ˈmɛrɪt] n mérite m, valeur f // vt mériter.

mermaid [ˈmɜːmeɪd] n sirène f.

merrily [ˈmɛrɪli] ad joyeusement, gaiement.

merriment [ˈmɛrɪmənt] n gaieté f.

merry [ˈmɛri] a gai(e); **~-go-round** n manège m.

mesh [mɛʃ] n maille f; filet m // vi (gears) s'engrener.

mesmerize [ˈmɛzməraɪz] vt hypnotiser; fasciner.

mess [mɛs] n désordre m, fouillis m, pagaille f; (MIL) mess m, cantine f; **to ~**

about vi (col) perdre son temps; **to ~ about with** vt fus (col) chambarder, tripoter; **to ~ up** vt salir; chambarder; gâcher.

message [ˈmɛsɪdʒ] n message m.

messenger [ˈmɛsɪndʒə*] n messager m.

messy [ˈmɛsi] a sale; en désordre.

met [mɛt] pt, pp of **meet**.

metabolism [mɛˈtæbəlɪzəm] n métabolisme m.

metal [ˈmɛtl] n métal m // vt empierrer; **~lic** [-ˈtælɪk] a métallique; **~lurgy** [-ˈtælədʒi] n métallurgie f.

metamorphosis, pl **phoses** [mɛtəˈmɔːfəsɪs, -iːz] n métamorphose f.

metaphor [ˈmɛtəfə*] n métaphore f.

metaphysics [mɛtəˈfɪzɪks] n métaphysique f.

mete [miːt]: **to ~ out** vt fus infliger.

meteor [ˈmiːtɪə*] n météore m.

meteorological [miːtɪərəˈlɒdʒɪkl] a météorologique.

meteorology [miːtɪəˈrɒlədʒi] n météorologie f.

meter [ˈmiːtə*] n (instrument) compteur m; (US) = **metre**.

method [ˈmɛθəd] n méthode f; **~ical** [mɪˈθɒdɪkl] a méthodique.

Methodist [ˈmɛθədɪst] a,n méthodiste (m/f).

methylated spirit [ˈmɛθɪleɪtɪdˈspɪrɪt] n (also: **meths**) alcool m à brûler.

meticulous [mɛˈtɪkjuləs] a méticuleux(euse).

metre, meter (US) [ˈmiːtə*] n mètre m.

metric [ˈmɛtrɪk] a métrique; **~al** a métrique; **~ation** [-ˈkeɪʃən] n conversion f au système métrique.

metronome [ˈmɛtrənəum] n métronome m.

metropolis [mɪˈtrɒpəlɪs] n métropole f.

mettle [ˈmɛtl] n courage m.

mew [mjuː] vi (cat) miauler.

mews [mjuːz] n: **~ cottage** maisonnette aménagée dans les anciennes écuries d'un hôtel particulier.

Mexican [ˈmɛksɪkən] a mexicain(e) // n Mexicain/e.

Mexico [ˈmɛksɪkəu] n Mexique m; **~ City** Mexico.

mezzanine [ˈmɛtsəniːn] n mezzanine f; (of shops, offices) entresol m.

miaow [miːˈau] vi miauler.

mice [maɪs] npl of **mouse**.

microbe [ˈmaɪkrəub] n microbe m.

microfilm [ˈmaɪkrəufɪlm] n microfilm m // vt microfilmer.

microphone [ˈmaɪkrəfəun] n microphone m.

microscope [ˈmaɪkrəskəup] n microscope m; **microscopic** [-ˈskɒpɪk] a microscopique.

mid [mɪd] a: **~ May** la mi-mai; **~ afternoon** le milieu de l'après-midi; **in ~ air** en plein ciel; **~day** midi m.

middle [ˈmɪdl] n milieu m; (waist) ceinture f, taille f // a du milieu; **~-aged** a d'un certain âge; **the M~ Ages** npl le moyen âge; **~-class** a ≈ bourgeois(e); **the ~ class(es)** ≈ les classes moyennes; **M~ East** n Proche-Orient m, Moyen-Orient m;

~man n intermédiaire m; ~ name n
deuxième nom m.

middling ['mɪdlɪŋ] a moyen(ne).

midge [mɪdʒ] n moucheron m.

midget ['mɪdʒɪt] n nain/e // a minuscule.

Midlands ['mɪdləndz] npl comtés du centre
de l'Angleterre.

midnight ['mɪdnaɪt] n minuit m.

midriff ['mɪdrɪf] n estomac m, taille f.

midst [mɪdst] n: in the ~ of au milieu
de.

midsummer [mɪd'sʌmə°] n milieu m de
l'été.

midway [mɪd'weɪ] a, ad: ~ (between) à
mi-chemin (entre).

midweek [mɪd'wi:k] n milieu m de la
semaine.

midwife, midwives ['mɪdwaɪf, -vz] n
sage-femme f; ~ry [-wɪfərɪ] n obstétrique
f.

midwinter [mɪd'wɪntə°] n milieu m de
l'hiver.

might [maɪt] vb see **may** // n puissance
f, force f; ~y a puissant(e) // ad (col)
rudement.

migraine ['mi:greɪn] n migraine f.

migrant ['maɪgrənt] n (bird, animal)
migrateur m; (person) migrant/e; nomade
m/f // a migrateur(trice); migrant(e);
nomade; (worker) saisonnier(ère).

migrate [maɪ'greɪt] vi émigrer; **migration**
['greɪʃən] n migration f.

mike [maɪk] n (abbr of microphone) micro
m.

mild [maɪld] a doux(douce); (reproach)
léger(ère); (illness) bénin(bénigne) // n
bière légère.

mildew ['mɪldju:] n mildiou m.

mildly ['maɪldlɪ] ad doucement;
légèrement.

mildness ['maɪldnɪs] n douceur f.

mile [maɪl] n mil(l)e m (= 1609 m); ~age
n distance f en milles, ≈ kilométrage m;
~ometer n = **milometer**; ~stone n
borne f; (fig) jalon m.

milieu ['mi:ljə:] n milieu m.

militant ['mɪlɪtnt] a,n militant(e).

military ['mɪlɪtərɪ] a militaire // n: the ~
l'armée f, les militaires mpl.

militate ['mɪlɪteɪt] vi: to ~ against militer
contre.

militia [mɪ'lɪʃə] n milice f.

milk [mɪlk] n lait m // vt (cow) traire; (fig)
dépouiller, plumer; ~ chocolate n
chocolat m au lait; ~ing n traite f; ~man
n laitier m; ~ shake n milk-shake m; ~y
a lacté(e); (colour) laiteux(euse); M~y
Way n Voie lactée.

mill [mɪl] n moulin m; (factory) usine f,
fabrique f; (spinning ~) filature f; (flour
~) minoterie f // vt moudre, broyer // vi
(also: ~ about) grouiller.

millennium, pl ~s or **millennia**
[mɪ'lenɪəm, -'lenɪə] n millénaire m.

miller ['mɪlə°] n meunier m.

millet ['mɪlɪt] n millet m.

milli... ['mɪlɪ] prefix: ~gram(me) n
milligramme m; ~litre n millilitre m;
~metre n millimètre m.

milliner ['mɪlɪnə°] n modiste f; ~y n
modes fpl.

million ['mɪljən] n million m; ~aire n
millionnaire m.

millstone ['mɪlstəun] n meule f.

millwheel ['mɪlwi:l] n roue f de moulin.

milometer [maɪ'lɔmɪtə°] n ≈ compteur m
kilométrique.

mime [maɪm] n mime m // vt, vi mimer.

mimic ['mɪmɪk] n imitateur/trice // vt, vi
imiter, contrefaire; ~ry n imitation f;
(zool) mimétisme m.

min. abbr of minute(s), minimum.

minaret [mɪnə'rɛt] n minaret m.

mince [mɪns] vt hacher // vi (in walking)
marcher à petits pas maniérés // n (culin)
viande hachée, hachis m; he does not ~
(his) words il ne mâche pas ses mots;
~meat n hachis de fruits secs utilisés en
pâtisserie; ~ pie n sorte de tarte aux fruits
secs; ~r n hachoir m.

mincing ['mɪnsɪŋ] a affecté(e).

mind [maɪnd] n esprit m // vt (attend to,
look after) s'occuper de; (be careful) faire
attention à; (object to): I don't ~ the
noise je ne crains pas le bruit, le bruit ne
me dérange pas; do you ~ if ...? est-ce
que cela vous gêne si ...?; I don't ~ cela
ne me dérange pas; it is on my ~ cela
me préoccupe; to my ~ à mon avis or
sens; to be out of one's ~ ne plus avoir
toute sa raison; never ~ peu importe, ça
ne fait rien; to keep sth in ~ ne pas
oublier qch; to bear sth in ~ tenir
compte de qch; to make up one's ~ se
décider; '~ the step' 'attention à la
marche'; to have in ~ to do avoir
l'intention de faire; ~ful a: ~ful of
attentif(ive) à, soucieux(euse) de; ~less
a irréfléchi(e).

mine [maɪn] pronoun le(la) mien(ne), pl les
miens(miennes) // a: this book is ~ ce
livre est à moi or c'est à moi // n mine f // vt (coal)
extraire; (ship, beach) miner; ~ detector
n détecteur m de mines; ~field n champ
m de mines; ~r n mineur m.

mineral ['mɪnərəl] a minéral(e) // n
minéral m; ~s npl (soft drinks) boissons
gazeuses (sucrées); ~ogy [-'rælədʒɪ] n
minéralogie f; ~ water n eau minérale.

minesweeper ['maɪnswi:pə°] n dragueur
m de mines.

mingle ['mɪŋgl] vt mêler, mélanger // vi:
to ~ with se mêler à.

mingy ['mɪndʒɪ] a (col) radin(e).

miniature ['mɪnətʃə°] a (en) miniature // n miniature f.

minibus ['mɪnɪbʌs] n minibus m.

minicab ['mɪnɪkæb] n minitaxi m.

minim ['mɪnɪm] n (mus) blanche f.

minima ['mɪnɪmə] npl of **minimum**.

minimal ['mɪnɪml] a minimal(e).

minimize ['mɪnɪmaɪz] vt minimiser.

minimum ['mɪnɪməm] n (pl: **minima**
['mɪnɪmə]) minimum m // a minimum.

mining ['maɪnɪŋ] n exploitation minière // a minier(ère); de mineurs.

minion ['mɪnjən] n (pej) laquais m;
favori/te.

miniskirt ['mɪnɪskə:t] n mini-jupe f.

minister ['mɪnɪstə°] n (pol) ministre m;
(rel) pasteur m; ~ial [-'tɪərɪəl] a (pol)
ministériel(le).

ministry ['mɪnɪstrɪ] n ministère m; (REL): to go into the ~ devenir pasteur.

mink [mɪŋk] n vison m; ~ coat n manteau m de vison.

minnow ['mɪnəʊ] n vairon m.

minor ['maɪnə*] a petit(e), de peu d'importance; (MUS) mineur(e) // n (LAW) mineur/e.

minority [maɪ'nɔrɪtɪ] n minorité f.

minster ['mɪnstə*] n église abbatiale.

minstrel ['mɪnstrəl] n trouvère m, ménestrel m.

mint [mɪnt] n (plant) menthe f; (sweet) bonbon m à la menthe // vt (coins) battre; the (Royal) M~ ≈ l'hôtel m de la Monnaie; in ~ condition à l'état de neuf; ~ sauce n sauce f à la menthe.

minuet [mɪnju'ɛt] n menuet m.

minus ['maɪnəs] n (also: ~ sign) signe m moins // prep moins.

minute a [maɪ'njuːt] minuscule; (detail) minutieux(euse) // n ['mɪnɪt] minute f; (official record) procès-verbal m, compte rendu; ~s npl procès-verbal.

miracle ['mɪrəkl] n miracle m; **miraculous** [mɪ'rækjʊləs] a miraculeux(euse).

mirage ['mɪrɑːʒ] n mirage m.

mirror ['mɪrə*] n miroir m, glace f // vt refléter.

mirth [məːθ] n gaieté f.

misadventure [mɪsəd'vɛntʃə*] n mésaventure f; death by ~ décès accidentel.

misanthropist [mɪ'zænθrəpɪst] n misanthrope m/f.

misapprehension ['mɪsæprɪ'hɛnʃən] n malentendu m, méprise f.

misappropriate [mɪsə'prəʊprɪeɪt] vt détourner.

misbehave [mɪsbɪ'heɪv] vi se conduire mal; misbehaviour n mauvaise conduite.

miscalculate [mɪs'kælkjʊleɪt] vt mal calculer; **miscalculation** [-'leɪʃən] n erreur f de calcul.

miscarriage ['mɪskærɪdʒ] n (MED) fausse couche; ~ of justice erreur f judiciaire.

miscellaneous [mɪsɪ'leɪnɪəs] a (items) divers(es); (selection) varié(e).

miscellany [mɪ'sɛlənɪ] n recueil m.

mischance [mɪs'tʃɑːns] n malchance f.

mischief ['mɪstʃɪf] n (naughtiness) sottises fpl; (harm) mal m, dommage m; (maliciousness) méchanceté f; **mischievous** a (naughty) coquin(e), espiègle; (harmful) méchant(e).

misconception ['mɪskən'sɛpʃən] n idée fausse.

misconduct [mɪs'kɔndʌkt] n inconduite f; professional ~ faute professionnelle.

misconstrue [mɪskən'struː] vt mal interpréter.

miscount [mɪs'kaʊnt] vt,vi mal compter.

misdemeanour, misdemeanor (US) [mɪsdɪ'miːnə*] n écart m de conduite; infraction f.

misdirect [mɪsdɪ'rɛkt] vt (person) mal renseigner; (letter) mal adresser.

miser ['maɪzə*] n avare m/f.

miserable ['mɪzərəbl] a malheureux(euse); (wretched) misérable.

miserly ['maɪzəlɪ] a avare.

misery ['mɪzərɪ] n (unhappiness) tristesse f; (pain) souffrances fpl; (wretchedness) misère f.

misfire [mɪs'faɪə*] vi rater; (car engine) avoir des ratés.

misfit ['mɪsfɪt] n (person) inadapté/e.

misfortune [mɪs'fɔːtʃən] n malchance f, malheur m.

misgiving(s) [mɪs'gɪvɪŋ(z)] n(pl) craintes fpl, soupçons mpl.

misguided [mɪs'gaɪdɪd] a malavisé(e).

mishandle [mɪs'hændl] vt (treat roughly) malmener; (mismanage) mal s'y prendre pour faire or résoudre etc.

mishap ['mɪshæp] n mésaventure f.

mishear [mɪs'hɪə*] vt irg mal entendre.

misinform [mɪsɪn'fɔːm] vt mal renseigner.

misinterpret [mɪsɪn'təːprɪt] vt mal interpréter; ~ation [-'teɪʃən] n interprétation erronée, contresens m.

misjudge [mɪs'dʒʌdʒ] vt méjuger, se méprendre sur le compte de.

mislay [mɪs'leɪ] vt irg égarer.

mislead [mɪs'liːd] vt irg induire en erreur; ~ing a trompeur(euse).

mismanage [mɪs'mænɪdʒ] vt mal gérer; mal s'y prendre pour faire or résoudre etc; ~ment n mauvaise gestion.

misnomer [mɪs'nəʊmə*] n terme or qualificatif trompeur or peu approprié.

misogynist [mɪ'sɔdʒɪnɪst] n misogyne m/f.

misplace [mɪs'pleɪs] vt égarer.

misprint ['mɪsprɪnt] n faute f d'impression.

mispronounce [mɪsprə'naʊns] vt mal prononcer.

misread [mɪs'riːd] vt irg mal lire.

misrepresent [mɪsrɛprɪ'zɛnt] vt présenter sous un faux jour.

miss [mɪs] vt (fail to get) manquer, rater; (regret the absence of): I ~ him/it il/cela me manque // vi manquer // n (shot) coup manqué; (fig): that was a near ~ il s'en est fallu de peu; to ~ out vt oublier.

Miss [mɪs] n Mademoiselle.

missal ['mɪsl] n missel m.

misshapen [mɪs'ʃeɪpən] a difforme.

missile ['mɪsaɪl] n (AVIAT) missile m; (object thrown) projectile m.

missing ['mɪsɪŋ] a manquant(e); (after escape, disaster: person) disparu(e); to go ~ disparaître.

mission ['mɪʃən] n mission f; ~ary n missionnaire m/f.

missive ['mɪsɪv] n missive f.

misspent ['mɪs'spɛnt] a: his ~ youth sa folle jeunesse.

mist [mɪst] n brume f, brouillard m // vi (also: ~ over, ~ up) devenir brumeux(euse); (windows) s'embuer.

mistake [mɪs'teɪk] n erreur f, faute f // vt (irg: like take) mal comprendre; se méprendre sur; to make a ~ se tromper, faire une erreur; to ~ for prendre pour; ~ n a (idea etc) erroné(e); to be ~n faire erreur, se tromper; ~n identity n erreur f d'identité.

mister ['mɪstə*] n (col) Monsieur m; see Mr.

mistletoe ['mɪsltəu] n gui m.
mistook [mɪs'tuk] pt of **mistake**.
mistranslation [mɪstræns'leɪʃən] n erreur f de traduction, contresens m.
mistreat [mɪs'triːt] vt maltraiter.
mistress ['mɪstrɪs] n (also: lover) maîtresse f; (in primary school) institutrice f; see **Mrs**.
mistrust [mɪs'trʌst] vt se méfier de.
misty ['mɪstɪ] a brumeux(euse).
misunderstand [mɪsʌndə'stænd] vt, vi irg mal comprendre; ~ing n méprise f, malentendu m.
misuse n [mɪs'juːs] mauvais emploi; (of power) abus m // vt [mɪs'juːz] mal employer; abuser de.
mitigate ['mɪtɪgeɪt] vt atténuer.
mitre, miter (US) ['maɪtə*] n mitre f; (CARPENTRY) onglet m.
mitt(en) ['mɪt(n)] n mitaine f; moufle f.
mix [mɪks] vt mélanger // vi se mélanger // n mélange m; dosage m; to ~ up vt mélanger; (confuse) confondre; ~ed a (assorted) assortis(ies); (school etc) mixte; ~ed grill n assortiment m de grillades; ~ed-up a (confused) désorienté(e), embrouillé(e); ~er n (for food) batteur m, mixeur m; (person): he is a good ~er il est très liant; ~ture n assortiment m, mélange m; (MED) préparation f; ~-up n confusion f.
moan [məun] n gémissement m // vi gémir; (col: complain): to ~ (about) se plaindre (de); ~ing n gémissements mpl.
moat [məut] n fossé m, douves fpl.
mob [mɔb] n foule f; (disorderly) cohue f; (pej): the ~ la populace // vt assaillir.
mobile ['məubaɪl] a mobile // n mobile m; ~ home n caravane f.
mobility [məu'bɪlɪtɪ] n mobilité f.
moccasin ['mɔkəsɪn] n mocassin m.
mock [mɔk] vt ridiculiser, se moquer de // a faux(fausse); ~ery n moquerie f, raillerie f; ~ing a moqueur(euse); ~ingbird n moqueur m; ~-up n maquette f.
mod [mɔd] a see **convenience**.
mode [məud] n mode m.
model ['mɔdl] n modèle m; (person: for fashion) mannequin m; (: for artist) modèle // vt modeler // vi travailler comme mannequin // a (railway: toy) modèle réduit inv; (child, factory) modèle; to ~ clothes présenter des vêtements; ~ler, ~er (US) n modeleur m; (~ maker) maquettiste m/f; fabricant m de modèles réduits.
moderate a,n ['mɔdərət] a modéré(e) // n (POL) modéré/e // vb ['mɔdəreɪt] vi se modérer, se calmer // vt modérer; **moderation** [-'reɪʃən] n modération f, mesure f; **in moderation** à dose raisonnable, pris(e) or pratiqué(e) modérément.
modern ['mɔdən] a moderne; ~ize vt moderniser.
modest ['mɔdɪst] a modeste; ~y n modestie f.
modicum ['mɔdɪkəm] n: a ~ of un minimum de.

modification [mɔdɪfɪ'keɪʃən] n modification f.
modify ['mɔdɪfaɪ] vt modifier.
modulation [mɔdju'leɪʃən] n modulation f.
module ['mɔdjuːl] n module m.
mohair ['məuhɛə*] n mohair m.
moist [mɔɪst] a humide, moite; ~en ['mɔɪsn] vt humecter, mouiller légèrement; ~ure ['mɔɪstʃə*] n humidité f; (on glass) buée f; ~urizer ['mɔɪstʃəraɪzə*] n produit hydratant.
molar ['məulə*] n molaire f.
molasses [məu'læsɪz] n mélasse f.
mold [məuld] n, vt (US) = **mould**.
mole [məul] n (animal) taupe f; (spot) grain m de beauté.
molecule ['mɔlɪkjuːl] n molécule f.
molehill ['məulhɪl] n taupinière f.
molest [məu'lɛst] vt tracasser; molester.
mollusc ['mɔləsk] n mollusque m.
mollycoddle ['mɔlɪkɔdl] vt chouchouter, couver. ·
molt [məult] vi (US) = **moult**.
molten ['məultən] a fondu(e).
moment ['məumənt] n moment m, instant m; importance f; ~ary a momentané(e), passager(ère); ~ous [-'mɛntəs] a important(e), capital(e).
momentum [məu'mɛntəm] n élan m, vitesse acquise; to gather ~ prendre de la vitesse.
monarch ['mɔnək] n monarque m; ~ist n monarchiste m/f; ~y n monarchie f.
monastery ['mɔnəstərɪ] n monastère m.
monastic [mə'næstɪk] a monastique.
Monday ['mʌndɪ] n lundi m.
monetary ['mʌnɪtərɪ] a monétaire.
money ['mʌnɪ] n argent m; to make ~ gagner de l'argent; faire des bénéfices; rapporter; danger ~ prime f de risque; ~ed a riche; ~lender n prêteur/euse; ~ order n mandat m.
mongol ['mɔngəl] a,n (MED) mongolien(ne).
mongoose ['mɔnguːs] n mangouste f.
mongrel ['mʌngrəl] n (dog) bâtard m.
monitor ['mɔnɪtə*] n (SCOL) chef m de classe; (also: television ~) moniteur m // vt contrôler.
monk [mʌnk] n moine m.
monkey ['mʌnkɪ] n singe m; ~ nut n cacahuète f; ~ wrench n clé f à molette.
mono... ['mɔnəu] prefix: ~chrome a monochrome.
monocle ['mɔnəkl] n monocle m.
monogram ['mɔnəgræm] n monogramme m.
monologue ['mɔnəlɔg] n monologue m.
monopolize [mə'nɔpəlaɪz] vt monopoliser.
monopoly [mə'nɔpəlɪ] n monopole m.
monorail ['mɔnəureɪl] n monorail m.
monosyllabic [mɔnəusɪ'læbɪk] a monosyllabique; (person) laconique.
monotone ['mɔnətəun] n ton m (or voix f) monocorde.
monotonous [mə'nɔtənəs] a monotone.
monotony [mə'nɔtənɪ] n monotonie f.
monsoon [mɔn'suːn] n mousson f.
monster ['mɔnstə*] n monstre m.

monstrosity [mɔns'trɔsɪtɪ] n monstruosité f, atrocité f.

monstrous ['mɔnstrəs] a (huge) gigantesque; (atrocious) monstrueux(euse); atroce.

montage [mɔn'tu:ʒ] n montage m.

month [mʌnθ] n mois m; ~ly a mensuel(le) // ad mensuellement // n (magazine) mensuel m, publication mensuelle.

monument ['mɔnjumənt] n monument m; ~al [-'mɛntl] a monumental(e); ~al mason n marbrier m.

moo [mu:] vi meugler, beugler.

mood [mu:d] n humeur f, disposition f; to be in a good/bad ~ être de bonne/mauvaise humeur; to be in the ~ for être d'humeur à, avoir envie de; ~y a (variable) d'humeur changeante, lunatique; (sullen) morose, maussade.

moon [mu:n] n lune f; ~beam n rayon m de lune; ~light n clair m de lune; ~lit a éclairé(e) par la lune.

moor [muə*] n lande f // vt (ship) amarrer // vi mouiller.

Moor [muə*] n Maure/Mauresque.

moorings ['muərɪŋz] npl (chains) amarres fpl; (place) mouillage m.

Moorish ['muərɪʃ] a maure (mauresque).

moorland ['muələnd] n lande f.

moose [mu:s] n, pl inv élan m.

moot [mu:t] vt soulever // a: ~ point point m discutable.

mop [mɔp] n balai m à laver // vt éponger, essuyer; to ~ up vt éponger; ~ of hair n tignasse f.

mope [məup] vi avoir le cafard, se morfondre.

moped ['məupɛd] n (Brit) cyclomoteur m.

moquette [mɔ'kɛt] n moquette f.

moral ['mɔrl] a moral(e) // n morale f; ~s npl moralité f.

morale [mɔ'ru:l] n moral m.

morality [mə'rælɪtɪ] n moralité f.

morally ['mɔrəlɪ] ad moralement.

morass [mə'ræs] n marais m, marécage m.

morbid ['mɔ:bɪd] a morbide.

more [mɔ:*] det plus de, davantage de // ad plus; ~ people plus de gens; I want ~ j'en veux plus or davantage; ~ dangerous than plus dangereux que; ~ or less plus ou moins; ~ than ever plus que jamais.

moreover [mɔ:'rəuvə*] ad de plus.

morgue [mɔ:g] n morgue f.

moribund ['mɔrɪbʌnd] a moribond(e).

morning ['mɔ:nɪŋ] n matin m; matinée f; in the ~ le matin; 7 o'clock in the ~ 7 heures du matin; ~ sickness n nausées matinales.

Moroccan [mə'rɔkən] a marocain(e) // n Marocain/e.

Morocco [mə'rɔkəu] n Maroc m.

moron ['mɔ:rɔn] n idiot/e, minus m/f; ~ic [mə'rɔnɪk] a idiot(e), imbécile.

morose [mə'rəus] a morose, maussade.

morphine ['mɔ:fi:n] n morphine f.

Morse [mɔ:s] n (also: ~ code) morse m.

morsel ['mɔ:sl] n bouchée f.

mortal ['mɔ:tl] a, n mortel(le); ~ity [-'tælɪtɪ] n mortalité f.

mortar ['mɔ:tə*] n mortier m.

mortgage ['mɔ:gɪdʒ] n hypothèque f; (loan) prêt m (or crédit m) hypothécaire // vt hypothéquer.

mortified ['mɔ:tɪfaɪd] a mortifié(e).

mortuary ['mɔ:tjuərɪ] n morgue f.

mosaic [məu'zeɪɪk] n mosaïque f.

Moscow ['mɔskəu] n Moscou.

Moslem ['mɔzləm] a, n = **Muslim**.

mosque [mɔsk] n mosquée f.

mosquito, ~es [mɔs'ki:təu] n moustique m; ~ net n moustiquaire f.

moss [mɔs] n mousse f; ~y a moussu(e).

most [məust] det la plupart de; le plus de // pronoun la plupart // ad le plus; (very) très, extrêmement; the ~ (also: + adjective) le plus; ~ fish la plupart des poissons; ~ of la plus grande partie de; I saw ~ j'en ai vu la plupart; c'est moi qui en ai vu le plus; at the (very) ~ au plus; to make the ~ of profiter au maximum de; ~ly ad surtout, principalement.

MOT n (abbr of Ministry of Transport): the ~ (test) la visite technique (annuelle) obligatoire des véhicules à moteur.

motel [məu'tɛl] n motel m.

moth [mɔθ] n papillon m de nuit; mite f; ~ball n boule f de naphtaline; ~-eaten a mité(e).

mother ['mʌðə*] n mère f // vt (care for) dorloter; ~hood n maternité f; ~-in-law n belle-mère f; ~ly a maternel(le); ~-of-pearl n nacre f; ~-to-be n future maman; ~ tongue n langue maternelle.

mothproof ['mɔθpru:f] a traité(e) à l'antimite.

motif [məu'ti:f] n motif m.

motion ['məuʃən] n mouvement m; (gesture) geste m; (at meeting) motion f // vt, vi: to ~ (to) sb to do faire signe à qn de faire; ~less a immobile, sans mouvement; ~ picture n film m.

motivated ['məutɪveɪtɪd] a motivé(e).

motivation [məutɪ'veɪʃən] n motivation f.

motive ['məutɪv] n motif m, mobile m // a moteur(trice).

motley ['mɔtlɪ] a hétéroclite; bigarré(e), bariolé(e).

motor ['məutə*] n moteur m; (col: vehicle) auto f // a moteur(trice); ~bike n moto f; ~boat n bateau m à moteur; ~car n automobile f; ~cycle n vélomoteur m; ~cyclist n motocycliste m/f; ~ing n tourisme m automobile // a: ~ing accident n accident m de voiture; ~ing holiday n vacances fpl en voiture; ~ist n automobiliste m/f; ~ oil n huile f de graissage; ~ racing n course f automobile; ~ scooter n scooter m; ~ vehicle n véhicule m automobile; ~way n (Brit) autoroute f.

mottled ['mɔtld] a tacheté(e), marbré(e).

motto, ~es ['mɔtəu] n devise f.

mould, mold (US) [məuld] n moule m; (mildew) moisissure f // vt mouler, modeler; (fig) façonner; ~er vi (decay) moisir; ~ing n (in plaster) moulage m,

moulure f; (in wood) moulure; ~y a
moisi(e).
moult, molt (US) [məult] vi muer.
mound [maund] n monticule m, tertre m.
mount [maunt] n mont m, montagne f;
(horse) monture f; (for jewel etc) monture
// vt monter // vi (also: ~ up) s'élever,
monter.
mountain ['mauntɪn] n montagne f // cpd
de (la) montagne; ~eer [-'nɪə°] n alpiniste
m/f; ~eering [-'nɪərɪŋ] n alpinisme m; to
go ~eering faire de l'alpinisme; ~ous a
montagneux(euse);　　　　(very　　　big)
gigantesque; ~ side n flanc m or versant
m de la montagne.
mourn [mɔ:n] vt pleurer // vi: to ~ (for)
se lamenter (sur); ~er n parent/e or
ami/e du défunt; personne f en deuil or
venue rendre hommage au défunt; ~ful
a triste, lugubre; ~ing n deuil m // cpd
(dress) de deuil; in ~ing en deuil.
mouse, pl mice [maus, maɪs] n souris f;
~trap n souricière f.
moustache [məs'tɑ:ʃ] n moustache(s)
f(pl).
mousy ['mausɪ] a (person) effacé(e); (hair)
d'un châtain terne.
mouth, ~s [mauθ, -ðz] n bouche f; (of
dog, cat) gueule f; (of river) embouchure
f; (of bottle) goulot m; (opening) orifice m;
~ful n bouchée f; ~ organ n harmonica
m; ~piece n (of musical instrument)
embouchure f; (spokesman) porte-parole
m inv; ~wash n bain m de bouche; ~-
watering a qui met l'eau à la bouche.
movable ['mu:vəbl] a mobile.
move [mu:v] n (movement) mouvement m;
(in game) coup m; (: turn to play) tour m;
(change of house) déménagement m // vt
déplacer, bouger; (emotionally) émouvoir;
(POL: resolution etc) proposer // vi (gen)
bouger, remuer; (traffic) circuler; (also:
house) déménager; to ~ towards se
diriger vers; to ~ sb to do sth pousser
or inciter qn à faire qch; to get a ~ on
se dépêcher, se remuer; to ~ about vi
(fidget) remuer; (travel) voyager, se
déplacer; to ~ along vi se pousser; to
~ away vi s'en aller, s'éloigner; to ~
back vi revenir, retourner; to ~ forward
vi avancer // vt avancer; (people) faire
avancer; to ~ in vi (to a house)
emménager; to ~ on vi se remettre en
route // vt (onlookers) faire circuler; to
~ out vi (of house) déménager; to ~ up
vi avancer; (employee) avoir de
l'avancement.
movement ['mu:vmənt] n mouvement m.
movie ['mu:vɪ] n film m; the ~s le
cinéma; ~ camera n caméra f.
moving ['mu:vɪŋ] a en mouvement;
émouvant(e).
mow, pt mowed, pp mowed or mown
[məu, -n] vt faucher; (lawn) tondre; to ~
down vt faucher; ~er n faucheur/euse.
M.P. n abbr see member.
m.p.g. abbr = miles per gallon (30 m.p.g.
= 29.5 l. aux 100 km).
m.p.h. abbr = miles per hour (60 m.p.h. =
96 km/h).
Mr ['mɪstə°] n: ~ X Monsieur X, M. X.

Mrs ['mɪsɪz] n: ~ X Madame X, Mme X.
Ms [mɪz] n (= Miss or Mrs): ~ X ≈
Madame X, Mme X.
M.Sc. abbr see master.
much [mʌtʃ] det beaucoup de // ad, n or
pronoun beaucoup; ~ milk beaucoup de
lait; how ~ is it? combien est-ce que ça
coûte?; it's not ~ ce n'est pas beaucoup.
muck [mʌk] n (mud) boue f; (dirt) ordures
fpl; to ~ about vi (col) faire l'imbécile;
(waste time) traînasser; to ~ up vt (col:
ruin) gâcher, esquinter; ~y a (dirty)
boueux(euse), sale.
mucus ['mju:kəs] n mucus m.
mud [mʌd] n boue f.
muddle ['mʌdl] n pagaille f; désordre m,
fouillis m // vt (also: ~ up) brouiller,
embrouiller; to be in a ~ (person) ne plus
savoir où l'on en est; to get in a ~ (while
explaining etc) s'embrouiller; to ~
through vi se débrouiller.
mud: ~dy a boueux(euse); ~ flats npl
plage f de vase; ~guard n garde-boue m
inv; ~pack n masque m de beauté; ~-
slinging n médisance f, dénigrement m.
muff [mʌf] n manchon m.
muffin ['mʌfɪn] n petit pain rond et plat.
muffle ['mʌfl] vt (sound) assourdir,
étouffer; (against cold) emmitoufler; ~d
a étouffé(e), voilé(e).
mufti ['mʌftɪ] n: in ~ en civil.
mug [mʌg] n (cup) tasse f (sans soucoupe)
(: for beer) chope f; (col: face) bouille f;
(: fool) poire f // vt (assault) agresser;
~ging n agression f.
muggy ['mʌgɪ] a lourd(e), moite.
mulatto, ~es [mju:'lætəu] n mulâtre/sse.
mule [mju:l] n mule f.
mull [mʌl]: to ~ over vt réfléchir à,
ruminer.
mulled [mʌld] a: ~ wine vin chaud.
multi... ['mʌltɪ] prefix multi...;
~coloured, ~colored (US) a multicolore.
multifarious [mʌltɪ'fɛərɪəs] a divers(es);
varié(e).
multiple ['mʌltɪpl] a, n multiple (m); ~
crash n carambolage m; ~ sclerosis n
sclérose f en plaques; ~ store n grand
magasin (à succursales multiples).
multiplication [mʌltɪplɪ'keɪʃən] n
multiplication f.
multiply ['mʌltɪplaɪ] vt multiplier // vi se
multiplier.
multitude ['mʌltɪtju:d] n multitude f.
mum [mʌm] n maman f // a: to keep ~
ne pas souffler mot; ~'s the word! motus
et bouche cousue!
mumble ['mʌmbl] vt, vi marmotter,
marmonner.
mummy ['mʌmɪ] n (mother) maman f;
(embalmed) momie f.
mumps [mʌmps] n oreillons mpl.
munch [mʌntʃ] vt, vi mâcher.
mundane [mʌn'deɪn] a banal(e), terre à
terre inv.
municipal [mju:'nɪsɪpl] a municipal(e);
~ity [-'pælɪtɪ] n municipalité f.
munitions [mju:'nɪʃənz] npl munitions fpl.
mural ['mjuərəl] n peinture murale.
murder ['mə:də°] n meurtre m, assassinat
m // vt assassiner; ~er n meurtrier m,

assassin *m*; ~**ess** *n* meurtrière *f*; ~**ous** *a* meurtrier(ère).

murk [mə:k] *n* obscurité *f*; ~**y** *a* sombre, ténébreux(euse).

murmur ['mə:mə*] *n* murmure *m* // *vt*, *vi* murmurer.

muscle ['mʌsl] *n* muscle *m*; **to** ~ **in** *vi* s'imposer, s'immiscer.

muscular ['mʌskjulə*] *a* musculaire; (*person*, *arm*) musclé(e).

muse [mju:z] *vi* méditer, songer // *n* muse *f*.

museum [mju:'ziəm] *n* musée *m*.

mushroom ['mʌʃrum] *n* champignon *m* // *vi* (*fig*) pousser comme un (*or* des) champignon(s).

mushy ['mʌʃi] *a* en bouillie; (*pej*) à l'eau de rose.

music ['mju:zik] *n* musique *f*; ~**al** *a* musical(e); (*person*) musicien(ne) // *n* (*show*) comédie musicale; ~**al box** *n* boîte *f* à musique; ~**al instrument** *n* instrument *m* de musique; ~ **hall** *n* music-hall *m*; ~**ian** [-'ziʃən] *n* musicien/ne; ~ **stand** *n* pupitre *m* à musique.

musket ['mʌskit] *n* mousquet *m*.

Muslim ['mʌzlim] *a*, *n* musulman(e).

muslin ['mʌzlin] *n* mousseline *f*.

musquash ['mʌskwɔʃ] *n* loutre *f*.

mussel ['mʌsl] *n* moule *f*.

must [mʌst] *auxiliary vb* (*obligation*): **I** ~ **do it** je dois le faire, il faut que je le fasse; (*probability*): **he** ~ **be there by now** il doit y être maintenant, il y est probablement maintenant, **I** ~ **have made a mistake** j'ai dû me tromper // *n* nécessité *f*, impératif *m*.

mustard ['mʌstəd] *n* moutarde *f*.

muster ['mʌstə*] *vt* rassembler.

mustn't ['mʌsnt] = **must not**.

musty ['mʌsti] *a* qui sent le moisi *or* le renfermé.

mute [mju:t] *a*,*n* muet(te).

muted ['mju:tid] *a* assourdi(e); voilé(e); (*MUS*) en sourdine; (: *trumpet*) bouché(e).

mutilate ['mju:tileit] *vt* mutiler; **mutilation** [-'leiʃən] *n* mutilation *f*.

mutinous ['mju:tinəs] *a* (*troops*) mutiné(e); (*attitude*) rebelle.

mutiny ['mju:tini] *n* mutinerie *f* // *vi* se mutiner.

mutter ['mʌtə*] *vt*,*vi* marmonner, marmotter.

mutton ['mʌtn] *n* mouton *m*.

mutual ['mju:tʃuəl] *a* mutuel(le), réciproque; ~**ly** *ad* mutuellement, réciproquement.

muzzle ['mʌzl] *n* museau *m*; (*protective device*) muselière *f*; (*of gun*) gueule *f* // *vt* museler.

my [mai] *a* mon(ma), mes *pl*.

myopic [mai'ɔpik] *a* myope.

myself [mai'self] *pronoun* (*reflexive*) me; (*emphatic*) moi-même; (*after prep*) moi.

mysterious [mis'tiəriəs] *a* mystérieux(euse).

mystery ['mistəri] *n* mystère *m*; ~ **story** *n* roman *m* à suspense.

mystic ['mistik] *n* mystique *m*/*f* // *a* (*mysterious*) ésotérique; ~**al** *a* mystique.

mystify ['mistifai] *vt* mystifier; (*puzzle*) ébahir.

mystique [mis'ti:k] *n* mystique *f*.

myth [miθ] *n* mythe *m*; ~**ical** *a* mythique; ~**ological** [miθə'lɔdʒikl] *a* mythologique; ~**ology** [mi'θɔlədʒi] *n* mythologie *f*.

N

nab [næb] *vt* pincer, attraper.

nag [næg] *n* (*pej*: *horse*) canasson *m* // *vt* (*person*) être toujours après, reprendre sans arrêt; ~**ging** *a* (*doubt*, *pain*) persistant(e) // *n* remarques continuelles.

nail [neil] *n* (*human*) ongle *m*; (*metal*) clou *m* // *vt* clouer; **to** ~ **sb down to a date/price** contraindre qn à accepter or donner une date/un prix; ~**brush** *n* brosse *f* à ongles; ~**file** *n* lime *f* à ongles; ~ **polish** *n* vernis *m* à ongles; ~ **scissors** *npl* ciseaux *mpl* à ongles.

naïve [nai'i:v] *a* naïf(ïve).

naked ['neikid] *a* nu(e); ~**ness** *n* nudité *f*.

name [neim] *n* nom *m*; réputation *f* // *vt* nommer; citer; (*price*, *date*) fixer, donner; **in the** ~ **of** au nom de; ~ **dropping** *n* mention *f* (pour se faire valoir) du nom de personnalités qu'on connaît (ou prétend connaître); ~**less** *a* sans nom; (*witness*, *contributor*) anonyme; ~**ly** *ad* à savoir; ~**sake** *n* homonyme *m*.

nanny ['næni] *n* bonne *f* d'enfants; ~ **goat** *n* chèvre *f*.

nap [næp] *n* (*sleep*) (petit) somme; **to be caught** ~**ping** être pris à l'improviste or en défaut.

napalm ['neipɑ:m] *n* napalm *m*.

nape [neip] *n*: ~ **of the neck** nuque *f*.

napkin ['næpkin] *n* serviette *f* (de table); (*Brit*: *for baby*) couche *f* (*gen pl*).

nappy ['næpi] *n* couche *f* (*gen pl*).

narcissus, *pl* **narcissi** [nɑ:'sisəs, -sai] *n* narcisse *m*.

narcotic [nɑ:'kɔtik] *n* (*drug*) stupéfiant *m*; (*MED*) narcotique *m*.

nark [nɑ:k] *vt* mettre en rogne.

narrate [nə'reit] *vt* raconter, narrer.

narrative ['nærətiv] *n* récit *m* // *a* narratif(ive).

narrator [nə'reitə*] *n* narrateur/trice.

narrow ['nærəu] *a* étroit(e); (*fig*) restreint(e), limité(e) // *vi* devenir plus étroit, se rétrécir; **to have a** ~ **escape** l'échapper belle; **to** ~ **sth down to** réduire qch à; ~ **gauge** *a* à voie étroite; ~**ly** *ad*: **he** ~**ly missed injury/the tree** il a failli se blesser/rentrer dans l'arbre; **he only** ~**ly missed the target** il a manqué la cible de peu *or* de justesse; ~-**minded** *a* à l'esprit étroit, borné(e).

nasal ['neizl] *a* nasal(e).

nastily ['nɑ:stili] *ad* (*say*, *act*) méchamment.

nastiness ['nɑ:stinis] *n* (*of remark*) méchanceté *f*.

nasty ['nɑ:sti] *a* (*person*) méchant(e); très désagréable; (*smell*) dégoûtant(e); (*wound*, *situation*) mauvais(e), vilain(e); **it's a** ~ **business** c'est une sale affaire.

nation ['neɪʃən] n nation f.

national ['næʃənl] a national(e) // n (abroad) ressortissant/e ; (when home) national/e ; ~ **dress** n costume national ; ~**ism** n nationalisme m ; ~**ist** a,n nationaliste (m/f) ; ~**ity** [-'nælɪtɪ] n nationalité f ; ~**ization** [-aɪ'zeɪʃən] n nationalisation f ; ~**ize** vt nationaliser ; ~**ly** ad du point de vue national ; dans le pays entier ; ~ **park** n parc national.

nation-wide ['neɪʃənwaɪd] a s'étendant à l'ensemble du pays ; (problem) à l'échelle du pays entier // ad à travers or dans tout le pays.

native ['neɪtɪv] n habitant/e du pays, autochtone m/f ; (in colonies) indigène m/f // a du pays, indigène ; (country) natal(e) ; (language) maternel(le) ; (ability) inné(e) ; a ~ **of Russia** une personne originaire de Russie ; a ~ **speaker of French** une personne de langue maternelle française.

NATO ['neɪtəu] n (abbr of North Atlantic Treaty Organization) O.T.A.N.

natter ['nætə*] vi bavarder.

natural ['nætʃrəl] a naturel(le) ; ~ **gas** n gaz naturel ; ~**ist** n naturaliste m/f ; ~**ize** vt naturaliser ; (plant) acclimater ; ~**ly** ad naturellement ; ~**ness** n naturel m.

nature ['neɪtʃə*] n nature f ; by ~ par tempérament, de nature.

naught [nɔ:t] n zéro m.

naughty ['nɔ:tɪ] a (child) vilain(e), pas sage ; (story, film) polisson(ne).

nausea ['nɔ:sɪə] n nausée f ; ~**te** ['nɔ:sɪeɪt] vt écœurer, donner la nausée à.

nautical ['nɔ:tɪkl] a nautique ; ~ **mile** n mille marin (= 1853 m).

naval ['neɪvl] a naval(e) ; ~ **officer** n officier m de marine.

nave [neɪv] n nef f.

navel ['neɪvl] n nombril m.

navigable ['nævɪgəbl] a navigable.

navigate ['nævɪgeɪt] vt diriger, piloter // vi naviguer ; **navigation** [-'geɪʃən] n navigation f ; **navigator** n navigateur m.

navvy ['nævɪ] n terrassier m.

navy ['neɪvɪ] n marine f ; ~**-(blue)** a bleu marine inv.

neap [ni:p] n (also: ~**tide**) mortes- eaux fpl.

near [nɪə*] a proche // ad près // prep (also: ~ **to**) près de // vt approcher de ; **to come** ~ vi s'approcher ; ~**by** [nɪə'baɪ] a proche // ad tout près, à proximité ; **N~ East** n Proche-Orient m ; ~**er** a plus proche // ad plus près ; ~**ly** ad presque ; **I** ~**ly fell** j'ai failli tomber ; ~ **miss** n collision évitée de justesse ; (when aiming) coup manqué de peu or de justesse ; ~**ness** n proximité f ; ~**side** n (AUT: right-hand drive) côté m gauche ; ~**sighted** a myope.

neat [ni:t] a (person, work) soigné(e) ; (room etc) bien tenu(e) or rangé(e) ; (solution, plan) habile ; (spirits) pur(e) ; **I drink it** ~ je le bois sec or sans eau ; ~**ly** ad avec soin or ordre ; habilement.

nebulous ['nɛbjuləs] a nébuleux(euse).

necessarily ['nɛsɪsrɪlɪ] ad nécessairement.

necessary ['nɛsɪsrɪ] a nécessaire.

necessitate [nɪ'sɛsɪteɪt] vt nécessiter.

necessity [nɪ'sɛsɪtɪ] n nécessité f ; chose nécessaire or essentielle.

neck [nɛk] n cou m ; (of horse, garment) encolure f ; (of bottle) goulot m ; ~ **and** ~ à égalité.

necklace ['nɛklɪs] n collier m.

neckline ['nɛklaɪn] n encolure f.

necktie ['nɛktaɪ] n cravate f.

née [neɪ] a : ~ **Scott** née Scott.

need [ni:d] n besoin m // vt avoir besoin de ; **to** ~ **to do** devoir faire ; avoir besoin de faire.

needle ['ni:dl] n aiguille f // vt asticoter, tourmenter ; ~**cord** n velours m milleraies.

needless ['ni:dlɪs] a inutile ; ~**ly** ad inutilement.

needlework ['ni:dlwə:k] n (activity) travaux mpl d'aiguille ; (object) ouvrage m.

needy ['ni:dɪ] a nécessiteux(euse) ; **in** ~ **circumstances** dans le besoin.

negation [nɪ'geɪʃən] n négation f.

negative ['nɛgətɪv] n (PHOT, ELEC) négatif m ; (LING) terme m de négation // a négatif(ive) ; **to answer in the** ~ répondre par la négative.

neglect [nɪ'glɛkt] vt négliger // n (of person, duty, garden) le fait de négliger ; (state of) ~ abandon m.

negligee ['nɛglɪʒeɪ] n déshabillé m.

negligence ['nɛglɪdʒəns] n négligence f.

negligent ['nɛglɪdʒənt] a négligent(e) ; ~**ly** ad par négligence ; (offhandedly) négligemment.

negligible ['nɛglɪdʒɪbl] a négligeable.

negotiable [nɪ'gəuʃɪəbl] a négociable.

negotiate [nɪ'gəuʃɪeɪt] vi négocier // vt (COMM) négocier ; (obstacle) franchir, négocier ; **negotiation** [-'eɪʃən] n négociation f, pourparlers mpl ; **negotiator** n négociateur/trice.

Negress ['ni:grɪs] n négresse f.

Negro ['ni:grəu] a (gen) noir(e) ; (music, arts) nègre, noir // n (pl: ~**es**) Noir/e.

neighbour, neighbor (US) ['neɪbə*] n voisin/e ; ~**hood** n quartier m ; voisinage m ; ~**ing** a voisin(e), avoisinant(e) ; ~**ly** a obligeant(e) ; (relations) de bon voisinage.

neither ['naɪðə*] a, pronoun aucun(e) (des deux), ni l'un(e) ni l'autre // cj : **I didn't move and** ~ **did Claude** je n'ai pas bougé, (et) Claude non plus ; ..., ~ **did I refuse** ..., (et or mais) je n'ai pas non plus refusé ... // ad : ~ **good nor bad** ni bon ni mauvais.

neo... ['ni:əu] prefix néo-.

neon ['ni:ɔn] n néon m ; ~ **light** n lampe f au néon ; ~ **sign** n enseigne (lumineuse) au néon.

nephew ['nɛvju:] n neveu m.

nerve [nə:v] n nerf m ; (fig) sang-froid m, courage m ; aplomb m, toupet m ; **he gets on my** ~**s** il m'énerve ; ~**-racking** a éprouvant (pour les nerfs).

nervous ['nə:vəs] a nerveux(euse) ; inquiet(ète), plein(e) d'appréhension ; ~ **breakdown** n dépression nerveuse ; ~**ly** ad nerveusement ; ~**ness** n nervosité f, inquiétude f, appréhension f.

nest [nɛst] n nid m ; ~ **of tables** n table f gigogne.

nestle ['nɛsl] vi se blottir.

net [nɛt] n filet m // a net(te); ~**ball** n netball m.

Netherlands ['nɛðələndz] npl: the ~ les Pays-Bas mpl.

nett [nɛt] a = net.

netting ['nɛtɪŋ] n (for fence etc) treillis m, grillage m.

nettle ['nɛtl] n ortie f.

network ['nɛtwəːk] n réseau m.

neurosis, pl **neuroses** [njuə'rəusɪs, -siːz] n névrose f.

neurotic [njuə'rɔtɪk] a, n névrosé(e).

neuter ['njuːtə*] a, n neutre (m) // vt (cat etc) châtrer, couper.

neutral ['njuːtrəl] a neutre // n (AUT) point mort; ~**ity** [-'trælɪtɪ] n neutralité f.

never ['nɛvə*] ad (ne ...) jamais; ~ **again** plus jamais; ~**-ending** a interminable; ~**theless** [nɛvəðə'lɛs] ad néanmoins, malgré tout.

new [njuː] a nouveau(nouvelle); (brand new) neuf(neuve); ~**born** a nouveau-né(e); ~**comer** ['njuːkʌmə*] n nouveau venu/nouvelle venue; ~**ly** ad nouvellement, récemment; ~ **moon** n nouvelle lune; ~**ness** n nouveauté f.

news [njuːz] n nouvelle(s) f(pl); (RADIO, TV) informations fpl; a **piece of** ~ une nouvelle; ~ **agency** n agence f de presse; ~**agent** n marchand m de journaux; ~ **flash** n flash m d'information; ~**letter** n bulletin m; ~**paper** n journal m; ~**reel** n actualités (filmées); ~ **stand** n kiosque m à journaux.

New Year ['njuː'jɪə*] n Nouvel An; ~'s **Day** n le jour de l'An; ~'s **Eve** n la Saint-Sylvestre.

New Zealand [njuː'ziːlənd] n la Nouvelle-Zélande.

next [nɛkst] a (seat, room) voisin(e), d'à côté; (meeting, bus stop) suivant(e); prochain(e) // ad la fois suivante; la prochaine fois; (afterwards) ensuite; **when do we meet** ~? quand nous revoyons-nous?; ~ **door** ad à côté; ~-**of-kin** n parent m le plus proche; ~ **time** ad la prochaine fois; ~ **to** prep à côté de; ~ **to nothing** presque rien.

N.H.S. n abbr of National Health Service.

nib [nɪb] n (of pen) (bec m de) plume f.

nibble ['nɪbl] vt grignoter.

nice [naɪs] a (holiday, trip) agréable; (flat, picture) joli(e); (person) gentil(le); (distinction, point) subtil(e); ~-**looking** a joli(e); ~**ly** ad agréablement; joliment; gentiment; subtilement.

niceties ['naɪsɪtɪz] npl subtilités fpl.

nick [nɪk] n encoche f // vt (col) faucher, piquer; **in the** ~ **of time** juste à temps.

nickel ['nɪkl] n nickel m; (US) pièce f de 5 cents.

nickname ['nɪkneɪm] n surnom m // vt surnommer.

nicotine ['nɪkətiːn] n nicotine f.

niece [niːs] n nièce f.

Nigeria [naɪ'dʒɪərɪə] n Nigéria m or f; ~n a nigérien(ne) // n Nigérien/ne.

niggardly ['nɪgədlɪ] a pingre.

niggling ['nɪglɪŋ] a tatillon(ne).

night [naɪt] n nuit f; (evening) soir m; **at** ~ **la nuit**; **by** ~ de nuit; ~**cap** n boisson prise avant le coucher; ~ **club** n boîte f de nuit; ~**dress** n chemise f de nuit; ~**fall** n tombée f de la nuit; ~**ie** ['naɪtɪ] n chemise f de nuit.

nightingale ['naɪtɪŋgeɪl] n rossignol m.

night life ['naɪtlaɪf] n vie f nocturne.

nightly ['naɪtlɪ] a de chaque nuit or soir; (by night) nocturne // ad chaque nuit or soir; nuitamment.

nightmare ['naɪtmɛə*] n cauchemar m.

night school ['naɪtskuːl] n cours mpl du soir.

night-time ['naɪttaɪm] n nuit f.

night watchman ['naɪt'wɔtʃmən] n veilleur m de nuit.

nil [nɪl] n rien m; (SPORT) zéro m.

nimble ['nɪmbl] a agile.

nine [naɪn] num neuf; ~**teen** num dix-neuf; ~**ty** num quatre-vingt-dix.

ninth [naɪnθ] a neuvième.

nip [nɪp] vt pincer // n pincement m.

nipple ['nɪpl] n (ANAT) mamelon m, bout m du sein.

nippy ['nɪpɪ] a (person) alerte, leste.

nitrogen ['naɪtrədʒən] n azote m.

no [nəu] det pas de, aucun(e) + sg // ad, n non (m); ~ **entry** défense d'entrer, entrée interdite; ~ **dogs** les chiens ne sont pas admis.

nobility [nəu'bɪlɪtɪ] n noblesse f.

noble ['nəubl] a noble; ~**man** n noble m; **nobly** ad noblement.

nobody ['nəubədɪ] pronoun personne (with negative).

nod [nɔd] vi faire un signe de (la) tête (affirmatif ou amical); (sleep) somnoler // n signe m de (la) tête; **to** ~ **off** vi s'assoupir.

noise [nɔɪz] n bruit m; ~**less** a silencieux(euse); **noisily** ad bruyamment; **noisy** a bruyant(e).

nomad ['nəumæd] n nomade m/f; ~**ic** [-'mædɪk] a nomade.

no man's land ['nəumænzlænd] n no man's land m.

nominal ['nɔmɪnl] a (rent, fee) symbolique; (value) nominal(e).

nominate ['nɔmɪneɪt] vt (propose) proposer; (elect) nommer.

nomination [nɔmɪ'neɪʃən] n nomination f.

nominee [nɔmɪ'niː] n candidat agréé; personne nommée.

non... [nɔn] prefix non-; ~**alcoholic** a non-alcoolisé(e); ~**breakable** a incassable; ~**committal** ['nɔnkə'mɪtl] a évasif(ive); ~**descript** ['nɔndɪskrɪpt] a quelconque, indéfinissable.

none [nʌn] pronoun aucun/e; **he's** ~ **the worse for it** il ne s'en porte pas plus mal.

nonentity [nɔ'nɛntɪtɪ] n personne insignifiante.

non: ~-**fiction** n littérature f non-romanesque; ~-**flammable** a ininflammable.

nonplussed [nɔn'plʌst] a perplexe.

nonsense ['nɔnsəns] n absurdités fpl, idioties fpl.

non: ~-**smoker** n non-fumeur m; ~-**stick** a qui n'attache pas; ~-**stop** a direct(e), sans arrêt (or escale) // ad sans arrêt.

noodles ['nu:dlz] npl nouilles fpl.

nook [nuk] n: ~s and crannies recoins mpl.

noon [nu:n] n midi m.

no one ['nəuwʌn] pronoun = **nobody**.

nor [nɔ:º] cj = **neither** // ad see **neither**.

norm [nɔ:m] n norme f.

normal ['nɔ:ml] a normal(e); ~ly ad normalement.

Normandy ['nɔ:məndɪ] n Normandie f.

north [nɔ:θ] n nord m // a du nord, nord (inv) // ad au or vers le nord; N~ **America** n Amérique f du Nord; ~-**east** n nord-est m; ~**ern** ['nɔ:ðən] a du nord, septentrional(e); N~**ern Ireland** n Irlande f du Nord; N~ **Pole** n pôle m Nord; N~ **Sea** n mer f du Nord; ~**ward(s)** ['nɔ:θwəd(z)] ad vers le nord; ~-**west** n nord-ouest m.

Norway ['nɔ:weɪ] n Norvège f.

Norwegian [nɔ:'wi:dʒən] a norvégien(ne) // n Norvégien/ne; (LING) norvégien m.

nose [nəuz] n nez m; (fig) flair m; ~**bleed** n saignement m de nez; ~**dive** n (descente f en) piqué m; ~**y** a curieux(euse).

nostalgia [nɔs'tældʒɪə] n nostalgie f; **nostalgic** a nostalgique.

nostril ['nɔstrɪl] n narine f; (of horse) naseau m.

nosy ['nəuzɪ] a = **nosey**.

not [nɔt] ad (ne ...) pas; ~ **at all** pas du tout; **you must** ~ or **mustn't do this** tu ne dois pas faire ça; **he isn't...** il n'est pas...

notable ['nəutəbl] a notable.

notably ['nəutəblɪ] ad en particulier.

notch [nɔtʃ] n encoche f.

note [nəut] n note f; (letter) mot m; (banknote) billet m // vt (also: ~ **down**) noter; (notice) constater; ~**book** n carnet m; ~-**case** n porte-feuille m; ~**d** ['nəutɪd] a réputé(e); ~**paper** n papier m à lettres.

nothing ['nʌθɪŋ] n rien m; ~ **new** rien de nouveau; **for** ~ (free) pour rien, gratuitement.

notice ['nəutɪs] n avis m; (of leaving) congé m // vt remarquer, s'apercevoir de; **to take** ~ **of** prêter attention à; **to bring sth to sb's** ~ porter qch à la connaissance de qn; **to avoid** ~ éviter de se faire remarquer; ~**able** a visible; ~ **board** n (Brit) panneau m d'affichage.

notify ['nəutɪfaɪ] vt: **to** ~ **sth to sb** notifier qch à qn; **to** ~ **sb of sth** avertir qn de qch.

notion ['nəuʃən] n idée f; (concept) notion f.

notorious [nəu'tɔ:rɪəs] a notoire (souvent en mal).

notwithstanding [nɔtwɪθ'stændɪŋ] ad néanmoins // prep en dépit de.

nougat ['nu:ga:] n nougat m.

nought [nɔ:t] n zéro m.

noun [naun] n nom m.

nourish ['nʌrɪʃ] vt nourrir; ~**ing** a nourrissant(e); ~**ment** n nourriture f.

novel ['nɔvl] n roman m // a

nouveau(nouvelle), original(e); ~**ist** n romancier m; ~**ty** n nouveauté f.

November [nəu'vɛmbəº] n novembre m.

novice ['nɔvɪs] n novice m/f.

now [nau] ad maintenant; ~ **and then**, ~ **and again** de temps en temps; **from** ~ **on** dorénavant; ~**adays** ['nauədeɪz] ad de nos jours.

nowhere ['nəuwɛəº] ad nulle part.

nozzle ['nɔzl] n (of hose) jet m, lance f.

nuance ['nju:ɑ:ns] n nuance f.

nuclear ['nju:klɪəº] a nucléaire.

nucleus, pl nuclei ['nju:klɪəs, 'nju:klɪaɪ] n noyau m.

nude [nju:d] a nu(e) // n (ART) nu m; **in the** ~ (tout(e)) nu(e).

nudge [nʌdʒ] vt donner un (petit) coup de coude à.

nudist ['nju:dɪst] n nudiste m/f.

nudity ['nju:dɪtɪ] n nudité f.

nuisance ['nju:sns] n: **it's a** ~ c'est (très) ennuyeux or gênant; **he's a** ~ il est assommant or casse-pieds.

null [nʌl] a: ~ **and void** nul(le) et non avenu(e); ~**ify** ['nʌlɪfaɪ] vt invalider.

numb [nʌm] a engourdi(e) // vt engourdir.

number ['nʌmbəº] n nombre m; (numeral) chiffre m; (of house, car, telephone, newspaper) numéro m // vt numéroter; (include) compter; **a** ~ **of** un certain nombre de; **the staff** ~**s 20** le nombre d'employés s'élève à or est de 20; ~ **plate** n plaque f minéralogique or d'immatriculation.

numbness ['nʌmnɪs] n engourdissement m.

numeral ['nju:mərəl] n chiffre m.

numerical ['nju:'mɛrɪkl] a numérique.

numerous ['nju:mərəs] a nombreux(euse).

nun [nʌn] n religieuse f, sœur f.

nurse [nə:s] n infirmière f // vt (patient, cold) soigner; (hope) nourrir; ~(**maid**) n bonne f d'enfants.

nursery ['nə:sərɪ] n (room) nursery f; (institution) pouponnière f; (for plants) pépi ère f; ~ **rhyme** n comptine f, chansonnette f pour enfants; ~ **school** n école maternelle; ~ **slope** n (SKI) piste f pour débutants.

nursing ['nə:sɪŋ] n (profession) profession f d'infirmière; ~ **home** n clinique f; maison f de convalescence.

nut [nʌt] n (of metal) écrou m; (fruit) noix f, noisette f, cacahuète f (terme générique en anglais); **he's** ~**s** (col) il est dingue; ~-**case** n (col) dingue m/f; ~-**crackers** npl casse-noix m inv, casse-noisette(s) m; ~**meg** ['nʌtmɛg] n (noix f) muscade f.

nutrient ['nju:trɪənt] n substance nutritive.

nutrition [nju:'trɪʃən] n nutrition f, alimentation f.

nutritious [nju:'trɪʃəs] a nutritif(ive), nourrissant(e).

nutshell ['nʌtʃɛl] n coquille f de noix; **in a** ~ en un mot.

nylon ['naɪlɔn] n nylon m; ~**s** npl bas mpl nylon.

O

oaf [əuf] n balourd m.

oak [əuk] n chêne m.

O.A.P. abbr see old.

oar [ɔ:*] n aviron m, rame f; ~sman/woman rameur/euse.

oasis, pl oases [əu'eisis, əu'eisi:z] n oasis f.

oath [əuθ] n serment m; (swear word) juron m; to take the ~ prêter serment; on ~ sous serment; assermenté(e).

oatmeal ['əutmi:l] n flocons mpl d'avoine.

oats [əuts] n avoine f.

obedience [ə'bi:diəns] n obéissance f; in ~ to conformément à.

obedient [ə'bi:diənt] a obéissant(e).

obelisk ['ɔbilisk] n obélisque m.

obesity [əu'bi:siti] n obésité f.

obey [ə'bei] vt obéir à; (instructions, regulations) se conformer à // vi obéir.

obituary [ə'bitjuəri] n nécrologie f.

object n ['ɔbdʒikt] objet m; (purpose) but m, objet m; (LING) complément m d'objet // vi [əb'dʒekt]: to ~ to (attitude) désapprouver; (proposal) protester contre, élever une objection contre; I ~! je proteste!; he ~ed that ... il a fait valoir or a objecté que ...; ~ion [əb'dʒekʃən] n objection f; (drawback) inconvénient m; if you have no ~ion si vous n'y voyez pas d'inconvénient; ~ionable [əb'dʒekʃənəbl] a très désagréable; choquant(e); ~ive n objectif m // a objectif(ive); ~ivity [ɔbdʒik'tiviti] n objectivité f; ~or n opposant/e.

obligation [ɔbli'geiʃən] n obligation f, devoir m; (debt) dette f (de reconnaissance).

obligatory [ə'bligətəri] a obligatoire.

oblige [ə'blaidʒ] vt (force): to ~ sb to do obliger or forcer qn à faire; (do a favour) rendre service à, obliger; to be ~d to sb for sth être obligé(e) à qn de qch; obliging a obligeant(e), serviable.

oblique [ə'bli:k] a oblique; (allusion) indirect(e).

obliterate [ə'blitəreit] vt effacer.

oblivion [ə'bliviən] n oubli m.

oblivious [ə'bliviəs] a: ~ of oublieux(euse) de.

oblong ['ɔblɔŋ] a oblong(ue) // n rectangle m.

obnoxious [əb'nɔkʃəs] a odieux (euse); (smell) nauséabond(e).

oboe ['əubəu] n hautbois m.

obscene [əb'si:n] a obscène.

obscenity [əb'seniti] n obscénité f.

obscure [əb'skjuə*] a obscur(e) // vt obscurcir; (hide: sun) cacher; obscurity n obscurité f.

obsequious [əb'si:kwiəs] a obséquieux(euse).

observable [əb'zə:vəbl] a observable; (appreciable) notable.

observance [əb'zə:vns] n observance f, observation f.

observant [əb'zə:vnt] a observateur(trice).

observation [ɔbzə'veiʃən] n observation f; (by police etc) surveillance f.

observatory [əb'zə:vətri] n observatoire m.

observe [əb'zə:v] vt observer; (remark) faire observer or remarquer; ~r n observateur/trice.

obsess [əb'ses] vt obséder; ~ion [əb'seʃən] n obsession f; ~ive a obsédant(e).

obsolescence [ɔbsə'lesns] n vieillissement m; built-in or planned ~ (COMM) désuétude calculée.

obsolete ['ɔbsəli:t] a dépassé(e); démodé(e).

obstacle ['ɔbstəkl] n obstacle m; ~ race n course f d'obstacles.

obstetrics [ɔb'stetriks] n obstétrique f.

obstinacy ['ɔbstinəsi] n obstination f.

obstinate ['ɔbstinit] a obstiné(e); (pain, cold) persistant(e).

obstreperous [əb'strepərəs] a turbulent(e).

obstruct [əb'strʌkt] vt (block) boucher, obstruer; (halt) arrêter; (hinder) entraver; ~ion [əb'strʌkʃən] n obstruction f; obstacle m; ~ive a obstructionniste.

obtain [əb'tein] vt obtenir // vi avoir cours; ~able a qu'on peut obtenir.

obtrusive [əb'tru:siv] a (person) importun(e); (smell) pénétrant(e); (building etc) trop en évidence.

obtuse [əb'tju:s] a obtus(e).

obviate ['ɔbvieit] vt parer à, obvier à.

obvious ['ɔbviəs] a évident(e), manifeste; ~ly ad manifestement; bien sûr.

occasion [ə'keiʒən] n occasion f; (event) événement m // vt occasionner, causer; ~al a pris(e) or fait(e) etc de temps en temps; occasionnel(le); ~al table n table décorative.

occupation [ɔkju'peiʃən] n occupation f; (job) métier m, profession f; unfit for ~al (house) impropre à l'habitation; ~al disease n maladie f du travail; ~al hazard n risque m du métier.

occupier ['ɔkjupaiə*] n occupant/e.

occupy ['ɔkjupai] vt occuper; to ~ o.s. with or by doing s'occuper à faire.

occur [ə'kə:*] vi se produire; (difficulty, opportunity) se présenter; (phenomenon, error) se rencontrer; to ~ to sb venir à l'esprit de qn; ~rence n présence f, existence f; cas m, fait m.

ocean ['əuʃən] n océan m; ~-going a de haute mer; ~ liner n paquebot m.

ochre ['əukə*] a ocre.

o'clock [ə'klɔk] ad: it is 5 ~ il est 5 heures.

octagonal [ɔk'tægənl] a octogonal(e).

octane ['ɔktein] n octane m.

octave ['ɔktiv] n octave f.

October [ɔk'təubə*] n octobre m.

octopus ['ɔktəpəs] n pieuvre f.

odd [ɔd] a (strange) bizarre, curieux(euse); (number) impair(e); (left over) qui reste, en plus; (not of a set) dépareillé(e); 60 ~ 60 et quelques; at ~ times de temps en temps; the ~ one out l'exception f; ~ity n bizarrerie f; (person) excentrique m/f; ~-job man n homme m à tout faire; ~ jobs npl petits travaux divers; ~ly ad bizarrement, curieusement; ~ments npl (COMM) fins fpl de série; ~s npl (in betting) cote f; the ~s are against his coming il y a peu de chances qu'il vienne; it

makes no ~s cela n'a pas d'importance ;
at ~s en désaccord.
ode [əud] *n* ode *f*.
odious ['əudiəs] *a* odieux(euse), détestable.
odour, odor (*US*) ['əudə*] *n* odeur *f*;
~**less** *a* inodore.
of [ɔv, əv] *prep* de ; **a friend** ~ **ours** un
de nos amis ; **3** ~ **them** went 3 d'entre
eux y sont allés ; **the 5th** ~ **July** le 5 juillet ; **a boy** ~ **10** un garçon de 10 ans.
off [ɔf] *a,ad* (*engine*) coupé(e) ; (*tap*)
fermé(e) ; (*food: bad*) mauvais(e),
avancé(e) ; (*milk*) tourné(e) ; (*absent*)
absent(e) ; (*cancelled*) annulé(e) // *prep*
de ; sur ; **to be** ~ (*to leave*) partir, s'en
aller ; **to be** ~ **sick** être absent(e) pour
cause de maladie ; **a day** ~ un jour de
congé ; **to have an** ~ **day** n'être pas en
forme ; **he had his coat** ~ il avait enlevé
son manteau ; **the hook is** ~ le crochet
s'est détaché ; le crochet n'est pas mis ;
10% ~ (*COMM*) 10% de rabais ; **5 km** ~
(*the road*) à 5 km (de la route) ; ~ **the
coast** au large de la côte ; **a house** ~ **the
main road** une maison à l'écart de la
grand-route ; **I'm** ~ **meat** je ne mange
plus de viande ; je n'aime plus la viande ;
on the ~ **chance** à tout hasard.
offal ['ɔfl] *n* (*CULIN*) abats *mpl*.
offbeat ['ɔfbi:t] *a* excentrique.
off-colour ['ɔf'kʌlə*] *a* (*ill*) malade, mal
fichu(e).
offence, offense (*US*) [ə'fɛns] *n* (*crime*)
délit *m*, infraction *f*; **to give** ~ **to** blesser, offenser ; **to take** ~ **at** se vexer de,
s'offenser de.
offend [ə'fɛnd] *vt* (*person*) offenser, blesser ; ~**er** *n* délinquant/e ; (*against regulations*) contrevenant/e.
offensive [ə'fɛnsɪv] *a* offensant(e),
choquant(e) ; (*smell etc*) très
déplaisant(e) ; (*weapon*) offensif(ive) // *n*
(*MIL*) offensive *f*.
offer ['ɔfə*] *n* offre *f*, proposition *f* // *vt*
offrir, proposer ; **'on** ~**'** (*COMM*) 'en promotion' ; ~**ing** *n* offrande *f*.
offhand [ɔf'hænd] *a* désinvolte // *ad*
spontanément.
office ['ɔfɪs] *n* (*place*) bureau *m*; (*position*)
charge *f*, fonction *f*; **to take** ~ entrer en
fonctions ; ~ **block** *n* immeuble *m* de
bureaux ; ~ **boy** *n* garçon *m* de bureau ;
~**r** *n* (*MIL etc*) officier *m*; (*of organization*)
membre *m* du bureau directeur ; (*also*:
police ~**r**) agent *m* (de police) ~ **work**
n travail *m* de bureau ; ~ **worker** *n*
employé/e de bureau.
official [ə'fɪʃl] *a* (*authorized*) officiel(le) //
n officiel *m*; (*civil servant*) fonctionnaire
m/f; employé/e ; ~**ly** *ad* officiellement.
officious [ə'fɪʃəs] *a* trop empressé(e).
offing ['ɔfɪŋ] *n*: **in the** ~ (*fig*) en perspective.
off: ~**-licence** *n* (*Brit: shop*) débit *m* de
vins et de spiritueux ; ~**-peak** *a* aux
heures creuses ; ~**-putting** *a*
rébarbatif(ive) ; rebutant(e), peu
engageant(e) ; ~**-season** *a, ad* hors-saison.
offset ['ɔfsɛt] *vt irg* (*counteract*) contrebalancer, compenser // *n* (*also*: ~
printing) offset *m*.

offshore [ɔf'ʃɔ:*] *a* (*breeze*) de terre ;
(*island*) proche du littoral ; (*fishing*)
côtier(ère).
offside ['ɔf'saɪd] *a* (*SPORT*) hors jeu // *n*
(*AUT: with right-hand drive*) côté droit.
offspring ['ɔfsprɪŋ] *n* progéniture *f*.
off: ~**-stage** *ad* dans les coulisses ; ~**-the-
cuff** *ad* au pied levé ; de chic ; ~**-the-peg**
ad en prêt-à-porter ; ~**-white** *a* blanc
cassé *inv*.
often ['ɔfn] *ad* souvent ; **as** ~ **as not** la
plupart du temps.
ogle ['əugl] *vt* lorgner.
oil [ɔɪl] *n* huile *f*; (*petroleum*) pétrole *m*;
(*for central heating*) mazout *m* // *vt*
(*machine*) graisser ; ~**can** *n* burette *f* de
graissage ; (*for storing*) bidon *m* à huile ;
~ **change** *n* vidange *f*; ~**field** *n* gisement
m de pétrole ; ~**-fired** *a* au mazout ; ~
level *n* niveau *m* d'huile ; ~ **painting** *n*
peinture *f* à l'huile ; ~ **refinery** *n* raffinerie
f de pétrole ; ~ **rig** *n* derrick *m*; (*at sea*)
plate-forme pétrolière ; ~**skins** *npl* ciré *m*;
~ **slick** *n* nappe *f* de mazout ; ~ **tanker**
n pétrolier *m*; ~ **well** *n* puits *m* de pétrole ; ~**y** *a* huileux(euse) ; (*food*) gras(se).
ointment ['ɔɪntmənt] *n* onguent *m*.
O.K., okay ['əu'keɪ] *excl* d'accord! // *a*
bien ; en règle ; en bon état ; pas mal //
vt approuver, donner son accord à ; **is it**
~**?, are you** ~**?** ça va?
old [əuld] *a* vieux(vieille) ; (*person*) vieux,
âgé(e) ; (*former*) ancien(ne), vieux ; **how** ~
are you? quel âge avez-vous? ; **he's 10
years** ~ il a 10 ans, il est âgé de 10 ans ;
~ **age** *n* vieillesse *f*; ~**-age pensioner**
(*O.A.P.*) *n* retraité/e ; ~**er brother/sis-
ter** frère/sœur aîné(e) ; ~**-fashioned** *a*
démodé(e) ; (*person*) vieux jeu *inv*; ~
people's home *n* maison *f* de retraite.
olive ['ɔlɪv] *n* (*fruit*) olive *f*; (*tree*) olivier
m // *a* (*also*: ~**-green**) (vert) olive *inv*;
~ **oil** *n* huile *f* d'olive.
Olympic [əu'lɪmpɪk] *a* olympique ; **the** ~
Games, the ~**s** les Jeux *mpl* olympiques.
omelet(te) ['ɔmlɪt] *n* omelette *f*;
ham/cheese ~ omelette au
jambon/fromage.
omen ['əumən] *n* présage *m*.
ominous ['ɔmɪnəs] *a* menaçant(e),
inquiétant(e) ; (*event*) de mauvais augure.
omission [əu'mɪʃən] *n* omission *f*.
omit [əu'mɪt] *vt* omettre.
on [ɔn] *prep* sur // *ad* (*machine*) en marche ;
(*light, radio*) allumé(e) ; (*tap*) ouvert(e) ; **is
the meeting still** ~**?** est-ce que la réunion
a bien lieu? ; **la réunion dure-t-elle
encore?** ; **when is this film** ~**?** quand
passe or passe-t-on ce film? ; ~ **the train**
dans le train ; ~ **the wall** sur le or au mur ;
~ **television** à la télévision ; ~ **learning
this** en apprenant cela ; ~ **arrival** à
l'arrivée ; ~ **the left** à gauche ; ~ **Friday**
vendredi ; ~ **Fridays** le vendredi ; **a week**
~ **Friday** vendredi en huit ; **to have one's
coat** ~ avoir (mis) son manteau ; **to walk**
etc ~ continuer à marcher *etc*; **it's not**
~**!** pas question! ; ~ **and off** de temps à
autre.
once [wʌns] *ad* une fois ; (*formerly*) autrefois // *cj* une fois que ; **at** ~ tout de suite ;
immédiatement ; (*simultaneously*) à la fois ;

all at ~ ad tout d'un coup ; **~ a week** une fois par semaine ; **~ more encore une fois** ; **~ and for all** une fois pour toutes.

oncoming ['ɒnkʌmɪŋ] a (traffic) venant en sens inverse.

one [wʌn] det, num un(e) // pronoun un(e) ; (impersonal) on ; **this ~** celui-ci/celle-ci ; **that ~** celui-là/celle-là ; **the ~ book which...** l'unique livre que... ; **~ by ~** un(e) par un(e) ; **~ never knows** on ne sait jamais ; **~ another** l'un(e) l'autre ; **~-man** a (business) dirigé(e) etc par un seul homme ; **~-man band** n homme-orchestre m ; **~self** pronoun se ; (after prep, also emphatic) soi-même ; **~-way** a (street, traffic) à sens unique.

ongoing ['ɒngəʊɪŋ] a en cours ; suivi(e).

onion ['ʌnjən] n oignon m.

onlooker ['ɒnlʊkə*] n spectateur/trice.

only ['əʊnlɪ] ad seulement // a seul(e), unique // cj seulement, mais ; **an ~ child** un enfant unique ; **not ~** non seulement ; **I ~ took one** j'en ai seulement pris un, je n'en ai pris qu'un.

onset ['ɒnsɛt] n début m ; (of winter, old age) approche f.

onshore ['ɒnʃɔ:*] a (wind) du large.

onslaught ['ɒnslɔ:t] n attaque f, assaut m.

onto ['ɒntʊ] prep = on to.

onus ['əʊnəs] n responsabilité f.

onward(s) ['ɒnwəd(z)] ad (move) en avant ; **from this time ~** dorénavant.

onyx ['ɒnɪks] n onyx m.

ooze [u:z] vi suinter.

opacity [əʊ'pæsɪtɪ] n (of substance) opacité f.

opal ['əʊpl] n opale f.

opaque [əʊ'peɪk] a opaque.

OPEC ['əʊpɛk] n (abbr of Organization of petroleum exporting countries) O.P.E.P. (Organisation des pays exportateurs de pétrole).

open ['əʊpn] a ouvert(e) ; (car) découvert(e) ; (road, view) dégagé(e) ; (meeting) public(ique) ; (admiration) manifeste ; (question) non résolu(e) ; (enemy) déclaré(e) // vt ouvrir // vi (flower, eyes, door, debate) s'ouvrir ; (shop, bank, museum) ouvrir ;. (book etc: commence) commencer, débuter ; **to ~ on to** vt fus (subj: room, door) donner sur ; **to ~ out** vt ouvrir // vi s'ouvrir ; **to ~ up** vt ouvrir ; (blocked road) dégager // vi s'ouvrir ; **in the ~ (air)** en plein air ; **~-air** a en plein air ; **~ing** n ouverture f ; (opportunity) occasion f ; débouché m ; (job) poste vacant ; **~ly** ad ouvertement ; **~-minded** a à l'esprit ouvert ; **~-necked** a à col ouvert ; **~ sandwich** n canapé m ; **the ~ sea** n le large.

opera ['ɒpərə] n opéra m ; **~ glasses** npl jumelles fpl de théâtre ; **~ house** n opéra m.

operate ['ɒpəreɪt] vt (machine) faire marcher, faire fonctionner ; (system) pratiquer // vi fonctionner ; (drug) faire effet ; **to ~ on sb (for)** (MED) opérer qn (de).

operatic [ɒpə'rætɪk] a d'opéra.

operating ['ɒpəreɪtɪŋ] a : **~ table/theatre** table f/salle f d'opération.

operation [ɒpə'reɪʃən] n opération f ; **to be in ~** (machine) être en service ;

(system) être en vigueur ; **~al** a opérationnel(le).

operative ['ɒpərətɪv] a (measure) en vigueur // n (in factory) ouvrier/ère.

operator ['ɒpəreɪtə*] n (of machine) opérateur/trice ; (TEL) téléphoniste m/f.

operetta [ɒpə'rɛtə] n opérette f.

opinion [ə'pɪnɪən] n opinion f, avis m ; **in my ~** à mon avis ; **~ated** a aux idées bien arrêtées ; **~ poll** n sondage m (d'opinion).

opium ['əʊpɪəm] n opium m.

opponent [ə'pəʊnənt] n adversaire m/f.

opportune ['ɒpətju:n] a opportun(e) ; **opportunist** [-'tju:nɪst] n opportuniste m/f.

opportunity [ɒpə'tju:nɪtɪ] n occasion f ; **to take the ~ of doing** profiter de l'occasion pour faire.

oppose [ə'pəʊz] vt s'opposer à ; **~d to a** opposé(e) à ; **as ~d to** par opposition à ; **opposing** a (side) opposé(e).

opposite ['ɒpəzɪt] a opposé(e) ; (house etc) d'en face // ad en face // prep en face de // n opposé m, contraire m ; (of word) contraire m ; **'see ~ page'** 'voir ci-contre' ; **his ~ number** son homologue m/f.

opposition [ɒpə'zɪʃən] n opposition f.

oppress [ə'prɛs] vt opprimer ; **~ion** [ə'prɛʃən] n oppression f ; **~ive** a oppressif(ive).

opt [ɒpt] vi : **to ~ for** opter pour ; **to ~ to do** choisir de faire ; **to ~ out of** choisir de quitter.

optical ['ɒptɪkl] a optique ; (instrument) 'optique.

optician [ɒp'tɪʃən] n opticien/ne.

optimism ['ɒptɪmɪzəm] n optimisme m.

optimist ['ɒptɪmɪst] n optimiste m/f ; **~ic** [-'mɪstɪk] a optimiste.

optimum ['ɒptɪməm] a optimum.

option ['ɒpʃən] n choix m, option f ; (SCOL) matière f à option ; (COMM) option ; **to keep one's ~s open** (fig) ne pas s'engager ; **~al** a facultatif(ive) ; (COMM) en option.

opulence ['ɒpjʊləns] n opulence f ; abondance f.

opulent ['ɒpjʊlənt] a opulent(e) ; abondant(e).

or [ɔ:*] cj ou ; (with negative): **he hasn't seen ~ heard anything** il n'a rien vu ni entendu ; **~ else** sinon ; ou bien.

oracle ['ɒrəkl] n oracle m.

oral ['ɔ:rəl] a oral(e) // n oral m.

orange ['ɒrɪndʒ] n (fruit) orange f // a orange inv.

oration [ɔ:'reɪʃən] n discours solennel.

orator ['ɒrətə*] n orateur/trice.

oratorio [ɒrə'tɔ:rɪəʊ] n oratorio m.

orb [ɔ:b] n orbe m.

orbit ['ɔ:bɪt] n orbite f // vt décrire une or des orbite(s) autour de.

orchard ['ɔ:tʃəd] n verger m.

orchestra ['ɔ:kɪstrə] n orchestre m ; **~l** [-'kɛstrəl] a orchestral(e) ; (concert) symphonique.

orchid ['ɔ:kɪd] n orchidée f.

ordain [ɔ:'deɪn] vt (REL) ordonner ; (decide) décréter.

ordeal [ɔ:'di:l] n épreuve f.

order ['ɔ:də*] n ordre m ; (COMM) commande f // vt ordonner ; (COMM) commander ; **in ~** en ordre ; (of document) en

règle ; in ~ of size par ordre de grandeur ;
in ~ to do/that pour faire/que + sub ;
to ~ sb to do ordonner à qn de faire ;
the lower ~s (pej) les classes inférieures ;
~ form n bon m de commande ; ~ly n
(MIL) ordonnance f // a (room) en ordre ;
(mind) méthodique ; (person) qui a de
l'ordre.

ordinal ['ɔ:dɪnl] a (number) ordinal(e).

ordinary ['ɔ:dnrɪ] a ordinaire, normal(e) ;
(pej) ordinaire, quelconque.

ordination [ɔ:dɪ'neɪʃən] n ordination f.

ordnance ['ɔ:dnəns] n (MIL: unit) service
m du matériel ; O~ Survey map n ≈
carte f d'État-major.

ore [ɔ:*] n minerai m.

organ ['ɔ:gən] n organe m ; (MUS) orgue m,
orgues fpl ; ~ic [ɔ:'gænɪk] a organique.

organism ['ɔ:gənɪzəm] n organisme m.

organist ['ɔ:gənɪst] n organiste m/f.

organization [ɔ:gənaɪ'zeɪʃən] n organisation f.

organize ['ɔ:gənaɪz] vt organiser ; ~d labour n main-d'œuvre syndiquée ; ~r n
organisateur/trice.

orgasm ['ɔ:gæzəm] n orgasme m.

orgy ['ɔ:dʒɪ] n orgie f.

Orient ['ɔ:rɪənt] n: the ~ l'Orient m ;
oriental [-'ɛntl] a oriental(e) // n
Oriental/e.

orientate ['ɔ:rɪəntɛɪt] vt orienter.

orifice ['ɔrɪfɪs] n orifice m.

origin ['ɔrɪdʒɪn] n origine f.

original [ə'rɪdʒɪnl] a original(e) ; (earliest)
originel(le) // n original m ; ~ity [-'nælɪtɪ]
n originalité f ; ~ly ad (at first) à l'origine.

originate [ə'rɪdʒɪnɛɪt] vi: to ~ from être
originaire de ; (suggestion) provenir de ; to
~ in prendre naissance dans ; avoir son
origine dans ; originator n auteur m.

ornament ['ɔ:nəmənt] n ornement m ;
(trinket) bibelot m ; ~al [-'mɛntl] a
décoratif(ive) ; (garden) d'agrément ;
~ation [-'teɪʃən] n ornementation f.

ornate [ɔ:'neɪt] a très orné(e).

ornithologist [ɔ:nɪ'θɔlədʒɪst] n ornithologue m/f.

ornithology [ɔ:nɪ'θɔlədʒɪ] n ornithologie f.

orphan ['ɔ:fn] n orphelin/e // vt: to be
~ed devenir orphelin ; ~age n orphelinat
m.

orthodox ['ɔ:θədɔks] a orthodoxe.

orthopaedic, orthopedic (US)
[ɔ:θə'pi:dɪk] a orthopédique.

oscillate ['ɔsɪlɛɪt] vi osciller.

ostensible [ɔs'tɛnsɪbl] a prétendu(e) ;
apparent(e) ; ostensibly ad en apparence.

ostentation [ɔstɛn'teɪʃən] n ostentation f.

ostentatious [ɔstɛn'teɪʃəs] a préten-
tieux(euse) ; ostentatoire.

osteopath ['ɔstɪəpæθ] n ostéopathe m/f.

ostracize ['ɔstrəsaɪz] vt frapper
d'ostracisme.

ostrich ['ɔstrɪtʃ] n autruche f.

other ['ʌðə*] a autre ; ~ than autrement
que ; à part ; ~wise ad,cj autrement.

otter ['ɔtə*] n loutre f.

ought, pt ought [ɔ:t] auxiliary vb: I ~ to
do it je devrais le faire, il faudrait que je
le fasse ; this ~ to have been corrected

cela aurait dû être corrigé ; he ~ to win
il devrait gagner.

ounce [auns] n once f (= 28.35 g ; 16 in
a pound).

our ['auə*] a notre, pl nos ; ~s pronoun
le(la) nôtre, les nôtres ; ~selves pronoun
pl (reflexive, after preposition) nous ; (emphatic) nous-mêmes.

oust [aust] vt évincer.

out [aut] ad dehors ; (published, not at home
etc) sorti(e) ; (light, fire) éteint(e) ; ~ here
ici ; ~ there là-bas ; he's ~ (absent), il
est sorti ; (unconscious) il est sans connaissance ; to be ~ in one's calculations
s'être trompé dans ses calculs ; to
run/back etc ~ sortir en courant/en
reculant etc ; ~ loud ad à haute voix ; ~
of (outside) en dehors de ; (because of:
anger etc) par ; (from among): ~ of 10 sur
10 ; (without): ~ of petrol sans essence,
à court d'essence ; made ~ of wood en
or de bois ; ~ of order (machine) en
panne ; (TEL: line) en dérangement ; ~-
of-the-way écarté(e) ; (fig) insolite.

outback ['autbæk] n campagne isolée ; (in
Australia) intérieur m.

outboard ['autbɔ:d] n: ~ (motor)
(moteur m) hors-bord m.

outbreak ['autbreɪk] n accès m ; début m ;
éruption f.

outbuilding ['autbɪldɪŋ] n dépendance f.

outburst ['autbə:st] n explosion f, accès
m.

outcast ['autkɑ:st] n exilé/e ; (socially)
paria m.

outclass [aut'klɑ:s] vt surclasser.

outcome ['autkʌm] n issue f, résultat m.

outcry ['autkraɪ] n tollé m (général).

outdated [aut'deɪtɪd] a démodé(e).

outdo [aut'du:] vt irg surpasser.

outdoor [aut'dɔ:*] a de or en plein air ;
~s ad dehors ; au grand air.

outer ['autə*] a extérieur(e) ; ~ space n
espace m cosmique ; ~ suburbs npl
grande banlieue.

outfit ['autfɪt] n équipement m ; (clothes)
tenue f ; '~ter's' 'confection pour
hommes'.

outgoings ['autgəuɪŋz] npl (expenses)
dépenses fpl.

outgrow [aut'grəu] vt irg (clothes) devenir
trop grand(e) pour.

outing ['autɪŋ] n sortie f ; excursion f.

outlandish [aut'lændɪʃ] a étrange.

outlaw ['autlɔ:] n hors-la-loi m inv // vt
(person) mettre hors la loi ; (practice) proscrire.

outlay ['autleɪ] n dépenses fpl ; (investment) mise f de fonds.

outlet ['autlɛt] n (for liquid etc) issue f,
sortie f ; (for emotion) exutoire m ; (for
goods) débouché m ; (also: retail ~) point
m de vente.

outline ['autlaɪn] n (shape) contour m ;
(summary) esquisse f, grandes lignes.

outlive [aut'lɪv] vt survivre à.

outlook ['autluk] n perspective f.

outlying ['autlaɪɪŋ] a écarté(e).

outmoded [aut'məudɪd] a démodé(e) ;
dépassé(e).

outnumber [aut'nʌmbə*] vt surpasser en nombre.

outpatient ['autpeiʃənt] n malade m/f en consultation externe.

outpost ['autpəust] n avant-poste m.

output ['autput] n rendement m, production f.

outrage ['autreidʒ] n atrocité f, acte m de violence; scandale m // vt outrager; **~ous** [-'reidʒəs] a atroce; scandaleux(euse).

outrider ['autraidə*] n (on motorcycle) motard m.

outright ad [aut'rait] complètement; catégoriquement; carrément; sur le coup // a ['autrait] complet(ète); catégorique.

outset ['autsɛt] n début m.

outside [aut'said] n extérieur m // a extérieur(e) // ad (au) dehors, à l'extérieur // prep hors de, à l'extérieur de; at the ~ (fig) au plus or maximum; ~ lane n (AUT: in Britain) voie f de droite; ~-left/-right (FOOTBALL) ailier gauche/droit; ~r n (in race etc) outsider m; (stranger) étranger/ère.

outsize ['autsaiz] a énorme; (clothes) grande taille inv.

outskirts ['autskə:ts] npl faubourgs mpl.

outspoken [aut'spəukən] a très franc(he).

outstanding [aut'stændiŋ] a remarquable, exceptionnel(le); (unfinished) en suspens; en souffrance; non réglé(e).

outstay [aut'stei] vt: to ~ one's welcome abuser de l'hospitalité de son hôte.

outstretched [aut'strɛtʃt] a (hand) tendu(e); (body) étendu(e).

outward [autwəd] a (sign, appearances) extérieur(e); (journey) (d')aller; ~ly ad extérieurement; en apparence.

outweigh [aut'wei] vt l'emporter sur.

outwit [aut'wit] vt se montrer plus malin que.

oval ['əuvl] a,n ovale (m).

ovary ['əuvəri] n ovaire m.

ovation [əu'veiʃən] n ovation f.

oven ['ʌvn] n four m; ~proof a allant au four.

over ['əuvə*] ad (par-)dessus // a (or ad) (finished) fini(e), terminé(e); (too much) en plus // prep sur; par-dessus; (above) au-dessus de; (on the other side of) de l'autre côté de; (more than) plus de; (during) pendant; ~ here ici; ~ there là-bas; all ~ (everywhere) partout; (finished) fini(e); ~ and ~ (again) à plusieurs reprises; ~ and above en plus de; to ask sb ~ inviter qn (à passer); to go ~ to sb's passer chez qn.

over... ['əuvə*] prefix: ~abundant surabondant(e).

overact [əuvər'ækt] vi (THEATRE) outrer son rôle.

overall a,n ['əuvərɔ:l] a (length) total(e); (study) d'ensemble // n (Brit) blouse f // ad [əuvər'ɔ:l] dans l'ensemble, en général // ~s npl bleus mpl (de travail).

overawe [əuvər'ɔ:] vt impressionner.

overbalance [əuvə'bæləns] vi basculer.

overbearing [əuvə'bɛəriŋ] a impérieux(euse), autoritaire.

overboard ['əuvəbɔ:d] ad (NAUT) par-dessus bord.

overcast ['əuvəkɑ:st] a couvert(e).

overcharge [əuvə'tʃɑ:dʒ] vt: to ~ sb for sth faire payer qch trop cher à qn.

overcoat ['əuvəkəut] n pardessus m.

overcome [əuvə'kʌm] vt irg triompher de; surmonter; to be ~ by être saisi(e) de; succomber à; être victime de; ~ with grief accablé(e) de douleur.

overcrowded [əuvə'kraudid] a bondé(e).

overcrowding [əuvə'kraudiŋ] n surpeuplement m; (in bus) encombrement m.

overdo [əuvə'du:] vt irg exagérer; (overcook) trop cuire.

overdose ['əuvədəus] n dose excessive.

overdraft ['əuvədrɑ:ft] n découvert m.

overdrawn [əuvə'drɔ:n] a (account) à découvert.

overdrive ['əuvədraiv] n (AUT) (vitesse) surmultipliée f.

overdue [əuvə'dju:] a en retard; (recognition) t~ 'if(ive).

overes...mate [əuvər'ɛstimeit] vt surestimer.

overexcited [əuvərik'saitid] a surexcité(e).

overexertion [əuvərig'zə:ʃən] n surmenage m (physique).

overexpose [əuvərik'spəuz] vt (PHOT) surexposer.

overflow vi [əuvə'fləu] déborder // n ['əuvəfləu] trop-plein m; (also: ~ pipe) tuyau m d'écoulement, trop-plein m.

overgrown [əuvə'grəun] a (garden) envahi(e) par la végétation.

overhaul vt [əuvə'hɔ:l] réviser // n ['əuvəhɔ:l] révision f.

overhead ad [əuvə'hɛd] au-dessus // a ['əuvəhɛd] aérien(ne); (lighting) vertical(e); ~s npl frais généraux.

overhear [əuvə'hiə*] vt irg entendre (par hasard).

overjoyed [əuvə'dʒɔid] a ravi(e), enchanté(e).

overland ['əuvəlænd] a, ad par voie de terre.

overlap vi [əuvə'læp] se chevaucher // n ['əuvəlæp] chevauchement m.

overleaf [əuvə'li:f] ad au verso.

overload [əuvə'ləud] vt surcharger.

overlook [əuvə'luk] vt (have view on) donner sur; (miss) oublier, négliger; (forgive) fermer les yeux sur.

overlord ['əuvəlɔ:d] n chef m suprême.

overnight [əuvə'nait] ad (happen) durant la nuit; (fig) soudain // a d'une (or de) nuit; soudain(e); he stayed there ~ il y a passé la nuit; if you travel ~... si tu fais le voyage de nuit...; he'll be away ~ il ne rentrera pas ce soir.

overpass ['əuvəpɑ:s] n pont autoroutier.

overpower [əuvə'pauə*] vt vaincre; (fig) accabler; ~ing a irrésistible; (heat, stench) suffocant(e).

overrate [əuvə'reit] vt surestimer.

overreact [əuvəri:'ækt] vi réagir de façon excessive.

override [əuvə'raid] vt (irg: like ride) (order, objection) passer outre à; (decision)

annuler; **overriding** a prépondérant(e).
overrule [əuvə'ru:l] vt (decision) annuler; (claim) rejeter.
overseas [əuvə'si:z] ad outre-mer; (abroad) à l'étranger // a (trade) extérieur(e); (visitor) étranger(ère).
overseer ['əuvəsɪə*] n (in factory) contremaître m.
overshadow [əuvə'ʃædəu] vt (fig) éclipser.
overshoot [əuvə'ʃu:t] vt irg dépasser.
oversight ['əuvəsaɪt] n omission f, oubli m.
oversimplify [əuvə'sɪmplɪfaɪ] vt simplifier à l'excès.
oversleep [əuvə'sli:p] vi irg se réveiller (trop) tard.
overspill ['əuvəspɪl] n excédent m de population.
overstate [əuvə'steɪt] vt exagérer; **~ment** n exagération f.
overt [əu'və:t] a non dissimulé(e).
overtake [əuvə'teɪk] vt irg dépasser; (AUT) dépasser, doubler; **overtaking** n (AUT) dépassement m.
overthrow [əuvə'θrəu] vt irg (government) renverser.
overtime ['əuvətaɪm] n heures fpl supplémentaires.
overtone ['əuvətəun] n (also: ~s) note f, sous-entendus mpl.
overture ['əuvətʃuə*] n (MUS, fig) ouverture f.
overturn [əuvə'tə:n] vt renverser // vi se retourner.
overweight [əuvə'weɪt] a (person) trop gros(se); (luggage) trop lourd(e).
overwhelm [əuvə'wɛlm] vt accabler; submerger; écraser; **~ing** a (victory, defeat) écrasant(e); (desire) irrésistible.
overwork [əuvə'wə:k] n surmenage m // vt surmener // vi se surmener.
overwrought [əuvə'rɔ:t] a excédé(e).
owe [əu] vt devoir; to ~ sb sth, to ~ sth to sb devoir qch à qn.
owing to ['əuɪŋtu:] prep à cause de, en raison de.
owl [aul] n hibou m.
own [əun] vt posséder // a propre; a room of my ~ une chambre à moi, ma propre chambre; to get one's ~ back prendre sa revanche; on one's ~ tout(e) seul(e); to ~ up vi avouer; **~er** n propriétaire m/f; **~ership** n possession f.
ox, pl **oxen** [ɔks, 'ɔksn] n bœuf m.
oxide ['ɔksaɪd] n oxyde m.
oxtail ['ɔksteɪl] n: ~ **soup** soupe f à la queue de bœuf.
oxygen ['ɔksɪdʒən] n oxygène m; ~ **mask/tent** n masque m/tente f à oxygène.
oyster ['ɔɪstə*] n huître f.
oz. abbr of **ounce(s)**.
ozone ['əuzəun] n ozone m.

P

p [pi:] abbr of **penny, pence**.
p.a. abbr of **per annum**.
P.A. see **public, personal**.

pa [pɑ:] n (col) papa m.
pace [peɪs] n pas m; (speed) allure f; vitesse f // vi: to ~ **up and down** faire les cent pas; to keep ~ **with** aller à la même vitesse que; (events) se tenir au courant de; **~maker** n (MED) stimulateur m cardiaque.
pacification [pæsɪfɪ'keɪʃən] n pacification f.
pacific [pə'sɪfɪk] a pacifique // n: the P~ (Ocean) le Pacifique, l'océan m Pacifique.
pacifist ['pæsɪfɪst] n pacifiste m/f.
pacify ['pæsɪfaɪ] vt pacifier; (soothe) calmer.
pack [pæk] n paquet m; ballot m; (of hounds) meute f; (of thieves etc) bande f; (of cards) jeu m // vt (goods) empaqueter, emballer; (in suitcase etc) emballer; (box) remplir; (cram) entasser; (press down) tasser; damer; to ~ (one's bags) faire ses bagages; to ~ one's case faire sa valise.
package ['pækɪdʒ] n paquet m; ballot m; (also: ~ deal) marché global; forfait m; ~ **tou.** n voyage organisé.
packet ['pækɪt] n paquet m.
pack ice [pækaɪs] n banquise f.
packing ['pækɪŋ] n emballage m; ~ **case** n caisse f (d'emballage).
pact [pækt] n pacte m; traité m.
pad [pæd] n bloc(-notes) m; (for inking) tampon encreur; (col: flat) piaule f // vt rembourrer; **~ding** n rembourrage m; (fig) délayage m.
paddle ['pædl] n (oar) pagaie f // vi barboter, faire trempette; ~ **steamer** n bateau m à aubes; **paddling pool** n petit bassin.
paddock ['pædək] n enclos m; paddock m.
paddy ['pædɪ] n: ~ **field** n rizière f.
padlock ['pædlɔk] n cadenas m // vt cadenasser.
padre ['pɑ:drɪ] n aumônier m.
paediatrics, pediatrics (US) [pi:dɪ'ætrɪks] n pédiatrie f.
pagan ['peɪgən] a,n païen(ne).
page [peɪdʒ] n (of book) page f; (also: ~ boy) groom m, chasseur m; (at wedding) garçon m d'honneur // vt (in hotel etc) (fair~) appeler.
pageant ['pædʒənt] n spectacle m historique; grande cérémonie; **~ry** n apparat m, pompe f.
pagoda [pə'gəudə] n pagode f.
paid [peɪd] pt, pp of **pay** // a (work, official) rémunéré(e); to put ~ to mettre fin à, régler.
pail [peɪl] n seau m.
pain [peɪn] n douleur f; to be in ~ souffrir, avoir mal; to have a ~ in avoir mal à or une douleur à or dans; to take ~s to do se donner du mal pour faire; **~ed** a peiné(e), chagrin(e); **~ful** a douloureux(euse); difficile, pénible; **~fully** ad (fig: very) terriblement; **~killer** n calmant m; **~less** a indolore; **~staking** ['peɪnzteɪkɪŋ] a (person) soigneux(euse); (work) soigné(e).
paint [peɪnt] n peinture f // vt peindre; (fig) dépeindre; to ~ the door blue

peindre la porte en bleu ; to ~ **in oils** faire de la peinture à l'huile ; ~**brush** n pinceau m ; ~**er** n peintre m ; ~**ing** n peinture f ; (picture) tableau m ; ~**-stripper** n décapant m.

pair [peə*] n (of shoes, gloves etc) paire f ; (of people) couple m ; duo m ; paire ; ~ **of scissors** (paire de) ciseaux mpl ; ~ **of trousers** pantalon m.

pajamas [pɪ'dʒɑ:məz] npl (US) pyjama(s) m(pl).

Pakistan [pu:kɪ'stɑ:n] n Pakistan m ; ~**i** a pakistanais(e) // n Pakistanais/e.

pal [pæl] n (col) copain/copine.

palace ['pæləs] n palais m.

palatable ['pælɪtəbl] a bon(bonne), agréable au goût.

palate ['pælɪt] n palais m.

palaver [pə'lɑ:və*] n palabres fpl or mpl ; histoire(s) f(pl).

pale [peɪl] a pâle ; **to grow** ~ pâlir ; ~ **blue** a bleu pâle inv ; ~**ness** n pâleur f.

Palestine ['pælɪstaɪn] n Palestine f ; **Palestinian** [-'tɪnɪən] a palestinien(ne) // n Palestinien/ne.

palette ['pælɪt] n palette f.

palisade [pælɪ'seɪd] n palissade f.

pall [pɔ:l] n (of smoke) voile m // vi: **to** ~ **(on)** devenir lassant (pour).

pallid ['pælɪd] a blême.

pally ['pælɪ] a (col) copain(copine).

palm [pɑ:m] n (ANAT) paume f ; (also: ~ **tree**) palmier m ; (leaf, symbol) palme f // vt: **to** ~ **sth off on sb** (col) refiler qch à qn ; ~**ist** n chiromancien/ne ; **P**~ **Sunday** n le dimanche des Rameaux.

palpable ['pælpəbl] a évident(e), manifeste.

palpitation [pælpɪ'teɪʃən] n palpitation(s) f(pl).

paltry ['pɔ:ltrɪ] a dérisoire ; piètre.

pamper ['pæmpə*] vt gâter, dorloter.

pamphlet ['pæmflət] n brochure f.

pan [pæn] n (also: **sauce**~) casserole f ; (also: **frying** ~) poêle f ; (of lavatory) cuvette f // vi (CINEMA) faire un panoramique.

panacea [pænə'sɪə] n panacée f.

Panama ['pænəmɑ:] n Panama m ; ~ **canal** n canal m de Panama.

pancake ['pænkeɪk] n crêpe f.

panda ['pændə] n panda m ; ~ **car** n ≈ voiture f pie inv.

pandemonium [pændɪ'məunɪəm] n tohu-bohu m.

pander ['pændə*] vi: **to** ~ **to** flatter bassement ; obéir servilement à.

pane [peɪn] n carreau m (de fenêtre).

panel ['pænl] n (of wood, cloth etc) panneau m ; (RADIO, TV) panel m ; invités mpl, experts mpl ; ~**ling**, ~**ing** (US) n boiseries fpl.

pang [pæŋ] n: ~**s of remorse** pincements mpl de remords ; ~**s of hunger/conscience** tiraillements mpl d'estomac/de la conscience.

panic ['pænɪk] n panique f, affolement m // vi s'affoler, paniquer ; ~**ky** a (person) qui panique or s'affole facilement.

pannier ['pænɪə*] n (on animal) bât m ; (on bicycle) sacoche f.

panorama [pænə'rɑ:mə] n panorama m ; **panoramic** a panoramique.

pansy ['pænzɪ] n (BOT) pensée f ; (col) tapette f, pédé m.

pant [pænt] vi haleter // n: see **pants**.

pantechnicon [pæn'teknɪkən] n (grand) camion de déménagement.

panther ['pænθə*] n panthère f.

panties ['pæntɪz] npl slip m, culotte f.

pantomime ['pæntəmaɪm] n spectacle m de Noël.

pantry ['pæntrɪ] n garde-manger m inv ; (room) office f or m.

pants [pænts] n (woman's) culotte f, slip m ; (man's) slip m, caleçon m ; (US: trousers) pantalon m.

papacy ['peɪpəsɪ] n papauté f.

papal ['peɪpəl] a papal(e), pontifical(e).

paper ['peɪpə*] n papier m ; (also: **wall**~) papier peint ; (also: **news**~) journal m ; (study, article) article m ; (exam) épreuve écrite // a en or de papier // vt tapisser (de papier peint) ; (**identity**) ~**s** npl papiers (d'identité) ; ~**back** n livre m de poche ; livre broché or non relié // a: ~**back edition** édition brochée ; ~ **bag** n sac m en papier ; ~ **clip** n trombone m ; ~ **hankie** n mouchoir m en papier ; ~ **mill** n papeterie f ; ~**weight** n presse-papiers m inv ; ~**work** n paperasserie f.

papier-mâché ['pæpɪeɪ'mæʃeɪ] n papier mâché.

paprika ['pæprɪkə] n paprika m.

par [pɑ:*] n pair m ; (GOLF) normale f du parcours ; **on a** ~ **with** à égalité avec, au même niveau que.

parable ['pærəbl] n·parabole f (REL).

parabola [pə'ræbələ] n parabole f (MATH).

parachute ['pærəʃu:t] n parachute m // vi sauter en parachute ; ~ **jump** n saut m en parachute.

parade [pə'reɪd] n défilé m ; (inspection) revue f ; (street) boulevard m // vt (fig) faire ·alage de // vi défiler.

paradise ['pærədaɪs] n paradis m.

paradox ['pærədɔks] n paradoxe m ; ~**ical** [-'dɔksɪkl] a paradoxal(e).

paraffin ['pærəfɪn] n: ~ **(oil)** pétrole (lampant) ; **liquid** ~ huile f de paraffine.

paragraph ['pærəgrɑ:f] n paragraphe m.

parallel ['pærəlɛl] a parallèle ; (fig) analogue // n (line) parallèle f ; (fig, GEO) parallèle m.

paralysis [pə'rælɪsɪs] n paralysie f.

paralytic [pærə'lɪtɪk] a paralysé(e) ; paralysant(e).

paralyze ['pærəlaɪz] vt paralyser.

paramount ['pærəmaunt] a: **of** ~ **importance** de la plus haute or grande importance.

paranoia [pærə'nɔɪə] n paranoïa f.

paraphernalia [pærəfə'neɪlɪə] n attirail m, affaires fpl.

paraphrase ['pærəfreɪz] vt paraphraser.

paraplegic [pærə'pli:dʒɪk] n paraplégique m/f.

parasite ['pærəsaɪt] n parasite m.

paratrooper ['pærətru:pə*] n parachutiste m (soldat).

parcel ['pɑ:sl] n paquet m, colis m // vt

(also: ~ up) empaqueter; ~ **post** n
service m de colis postaux.
parch [pɑːʃ] vt dessécher; ~**ed** a (person)
asoiffé(e).
parchment ['pɑːtʃmənt] n parchemin m.
pardon ['pɑːdn] n pardon m; grâce f //
vt pardonner à; (LAW) gracier; ~!
pardon!; ~ me! excusez-moi!; I beg your
~! pardon!, je suis désolé!; I beg your
~? pardon?
parent ['pɛərənt] n père m or mère f; ~s
npl parents mpl; ~al [pə'rɛntl] a
parental(e), des parents.
parenthesis, pl **parentheses**
[pə'rɛnθɪsɪs, -siːz] n parenthèse f.
Paris ['pærɪs] n Paris.
parish ['pærɪʃ] n paroisse f; (civil) ≈
commune f // a paroissial(e); ~ioner
[pə'rɪʃənə*] n paroissien/ne.
Parisian [pə'rɪzɪən] a parisien(ne) // n
Parisien/ne.
parity ['pærɪtɪ] n parité f.
park [pɑːk] n parc m, jardin public // vt
garer // vi se garer; ~ing n
stationnement m; ~ing lot n (US) parking
m, parc m de stationnement; ~ing meter
n parcomètre m; ~ing place n place f de
stationnement.
parliament ['pɑːləmənt] n parlement m;
~ary [-'mɛntərɪ] parlementaire.
parlour, parlor (US) ['pɑːlə*] n salon m.
parochial [pə'rəukɪəl] a paroissial(e);
(pej) à l'esprit de clocher.
parody ['pærədɪ] n parodie f.
parole [pə'rəul] n: on ~ en liberté
conditionnelle.
parquet ['pɑːkeɪ] n: ~ floor(ing) parquet
m.
parrot ['pærət] n perroquet m; ~ fashion
ad comme un perroquet.
parry ['pærɪ] vt esquiver, parer à.
parsimonious [pɑːsɪ'məunɪəs] a
parcimonieux(euse).
parsley ['pɑːslɪ] n persil m.
parsnip ['pɑːsnɪp] n panais m.
parson ['pɑːsn] n ecclésiastique m;
(Church of England) pasteur m.
part [pɑːt] n partie f; (of machine) pièce
f; (THEATRE etc) rôle m; (MUS) voix f; partie
// a partiel(le) // ad = partly // vt
séparer // vi (people) se séparer; (roads)
se diviser; to take ~ in participer à,
prendre part à; on his ~ de sa part; for
my ~ en ce qui me concerne; for the
most ~ en grande partie; dans la plupart
des cas; to ~ with vt fus se séparer de;
se défaire de; (take leave) quitter, prendre
congé de; in ~ exchange en reprise.
partial ['pɑːʃl] a partiel(le); (unjust)
partial(e); to be ~ to aimer, avoir un
faible pour; ~ly ad en partie,
partiellement; partialement.
participate [pɑː'tɪsɪpeɪt] vi: to ~ (in)
participer (à), prendre part (à);
participation [-'peɪʃən] n participation f.
participle ['pɑːtɪsɪpl] n participe m.
particle ['pɑːtɪkl] n particule f.
particular [pə'tɪkjulə*] a particulier(ère);
spécial(e); (detailed) détaillé(e); (fussy)
difficile; méticuleux(euse); ~s npl détails
mpl; (information) renseignements mpl;

~ly ad particulièrement; en particulier.
parting ['pɑːtɪŋ] n séparation f; (in hair)
raie f // a d'adieu.
partisan [pɑːtɪ'zæn] n partisan/e // a
partisan(e); de parti.
partition [pɑː'tɪʃən] n (POL) partition f,
division f; (wall) cloison f.
partly ['pɑːtlɪ] ad en partie, partiellement.
partner ['pɑːtnə*] n (COMM) associé/e;
(SPORT) partenaire m/f; (at dance)
cavalier/ère // vt être l'associé or le
partenaire or le cavalier de; ~ship n
association f.
partridge ['pɑːtrɪdʒ] n perdrix f.
part-time ['pɑːt'taɪm] a,ad à mi-temps, à
temps partiel.
party ['pɑːtɪ] n (POL) parti m; (team) équipe
f; groupe m; (LAW) partie f; (celebration)
réception f; soirée f; fête f.
pass [pɑːs] vt (time, object) passer; (place)
passer devant; (car, friend) croiser; (exam)
être reçu(e) à, réussir; (candidate)
admettre; (overtake, surpass) dépasser;
(approve) approuver, accepter // vi
passer; (SCOL) être reçu(e) or admis(e),
réussir // n (permit) laissez-passer m inv;
carte f d'accès or d'abonnement; (in
mountains) col m; (SPORT) passe f; (SCOL:
also: ~ mark): to get a ~ être reçu(e)
(sans mention); to ~ sth through a ring
etc (faire) passer qch dans un anneau etc;
could you ~ the vegetables round?
pourriez-vous faire passer les légumes?;
to ~ away vi mourir; to ~ by vi passer
/ vt négliger; to ~ for passer pour; to
~ out vi s'évanouir; ~able a (road)
praticable; (work) acceptable.
passage ['pæsɪdʒ] n (also: ~way) couloir
m; (gen, in book) passage m; (by boat)
traversée f.
passenger ['pæsɪndʒə*] n passager/ère.
passer-by [pɑːsə'baɪ] n passant/e.
passing ['pɑːsɪŋ] a (fig) passager(ère); in
~ en passant.
passion ['pæʃən] n passion f; amour m;
to have a ~ for sth avoir la passion de
qch; ~ate a passionné(e).
passive ['pæsɪv] a (also LING) passif(ive).
Passover ['pɑːsəuvə*] n Pâque (juive).
passport ['pɑːspɔːt] n passeport m.
password ['pɑːswɜːd] n mot m de passe.
past [pɑːst] prep (further than) au delà de,
plus loin que; après; (later than) après //
a passé(e); (president etc) ancien(ne) // n
passé m; he's ~ forty il a dépassé la
quarantaine, il a plus de or passé quarante
ans; it's ~ midnight il est plus de minuit,
il est passé minuit; for the ~ few/3 days
depuis quelques/3 jours; ces derniers/3
derniers jours; to run ~ passer en
courant; he ran ~ me il m'a dépassé en
courant; il a passé devant moi en courant.
pasta ['pæstə] n pâtes fpl.
paste [peɪst] n (glue) colle f (de pâte);
(jewellery) strass m; (CULIN) pâté m (à
tartiner); pâté f // vt coller.
pastel ['pæstl] a pastel inv.
pasteurized ['pæstəraɪzd] a pasteurisé(e).
pastille ['pæstl] n pastille f.
pastime ['pɑːstaɪm] n passe-temps m inv,
distraction f.

pastoral ['pɑ:stərl] a pastoral(e).

pastry ['peɪstrɪ] n pâte f; (cake) pâtisserie f.

pasture ['pɑ:stʃə*] n pâturage m.

pasty n ['pæstɪ] petit pâté (en croûte) // a ['peɪstɪ] pâteux(euse); (complexion) terreux(euse).

pat [pæt] vt donner une petite tape à // n: a ~ of butter une noisette de beurre.

patch [pætʃ] n (of material) pièce f; (spot) tache f; (of land) parcelle f // vt (clothes) rapiécer; a bad ~ une période difficile; to ~ up vt réparer; ~work n patchwork m; ~y a inégal(e).

pate [peɪt] n: a bald ~ un crâne chauve or dégarni.

pâté ['pæteɪ] n pâté m, terrine f.

patent ['peɪtnt] n brevet m (d'invention) // vt faire breveter // a patent(e), manifeste; ~ leather n cuir verni; ~ medicine n spécialité f pharmaceutique.

paternal [pə'tə:nl] a paternel(le).

paternity [pə'tə:nɪtɪ] n paternité f.

path [pɑ:θ] n chemin m, sentier m; allée f; (of planet) course f; (of missile) trajectoire f.

pathetic [pə'θetɪk] a (pitiful) pitoyable; (very bad) lamentable, minable; (moving) pathétique.

pathologist [pə'θɔlədʒɪst] n pathologiste m/f.

pathology [pə'θɔlədʒɪ] n pathologie f.

pathos ['peɪθɔs] n pathétique m.

pathway ['pɑ:θweɪ] n chemin m, sentier m.

patience ['peɪʃns] n patience f; (CARDS) réussite f.

patient ['peɪʃnt] n patient/e; malade m/f // a patient(e) // ~ly ad patiemment.

patio ['pætɪəu] n patio m.

patriotic [pætrɪ'ɔtɪk] a patriotique; (person) patriote.

patrol [pə'trəul] n patrouille f // vt patrouiller dans; ~ car n voiture f de police; ~man n (US) agent m de police.

patron ['peɪtrən] n (in shop) client/e; (of charity) patron/ne; ~ of the arts mécène m; ~age ['pætrənɪdʒ] n patronage m, appui m; ~ize ['pætrənaɪz] vt être (un) client or un habitué de; (fig) traiter avec condescendance; ~ saint n saint(e) patron(ne).

patter ['pætə*] n crépitement m, tapotement m; (sales talk) boniment m // vi crépiter, tapoter.

pattern ['pætən] n modèle m; (SEWING) patron m; (design) motif m; (sample) échantillon m.

paunch [pɔ:ntʃ] n gros ventre, bedaine f.

pauper ['pɔ:pə*] n indigent/e; ~'s grave n fosse commune.

pause [pɔ:z] n pause f, arrêt m; (MUS) silence m // vi faire une pause, s'arrêter.

pave [peɪv] vt paver, daller; to ~ the way for ouvrir la voie à.

pavement ['peɪvmənt] n (Brit) trottoir m.

pavilion [pə'vɪlɪən] n pavillon m; tente f.

paving ['peɪvɪŋ] n pavage m, dallage m; ~ stone n pavé m.

paw [pɔ:] n patte f // vt donner un coup de patte à; (subj: person: pej) tripoter.

pawn [pɔ:n] n gage m; (CHESS, also fig) pion m // vt mettre en gage; ~broker n prêteur m sur gages; ~shop n mont-de-piété m.

pay [peɪ] n salaire m; paie f // vb (pt,pp paid [peɪd]) vt payer // vi payer; (be profitable) être rentable; to ~ attention (to) prêter attention (à); to ~ back vt rembourser; to ~ for vt payer; to ~ in vt verser; to ~ up vt régler; ~able a payable; ~ day n jour m de paie; ~ee n bénéficiaire m/f; ~ing a payant(e); ~ment n paiement m; règlement m; versement m; ~ packet n paie f; ~roll n registre m du personnel; ~ slip n bulletin m de paie.

p.c. abbr of per cent.

pea [pi:] n (petit) pois.

peace [pi:s] n paix f; (calm) calme m, tranquillité f; ~able a paisible; ~ful a paisible, calme; ~keeping n maintien m de la paix; ~ offering n gage m de réconciliation.

peach [pi:tʃ] n pêche f.

peacock ['pi:kɔk] n paon m.

peak [pi:k] n (mountain) pic m, cime f; (fig: highest level) maximum m; (: of career, fame) apogée m; ~ period n période f de pointe.

peal [pi:l] n (of bells) carillon m; ~s of laughter éclats mpl de rire.

peanut ['pi:nʌt] n arachide f, cacahuète f; ~ butter n beurre m de cacahuète.

pear [pɛə*] n poire f.

pearl [pə:l] n perle f.

peasant ['peznt] n paysan/ne.

peat [pi:t] n tourbe f.

pebble ['pebl] n galet m, caillou m.

peck [pek] vt (also: ~ at) donner un coup de bec à; (food) picorer // n coup m de bec; (kiss) bécot m; ~ing order n ordre m des préséances; ~ish a (col): I feel ~ish ie mangerais bien quelque chose, j'ai la dent.

peculiar [pɪ'kju:lɪə*] a étrange, bizarre, curieux(euse); particulier(ère); ~ to particulier à; ~ity [pɪkju:lɪ'ærɪtɪ] n particularité f; (oddity) bizarrerie f.

pecuniary [pɪ'kju:nɪərɪ] a pécuniaire.

pedal ['pedl] n pédale f // vi pédaler.

pedantic [pɪ'dæntɪk] a pédant(e).

peddle ['pedl] vt colporter.

pedestal ['pedəstl] n piédestal m.

pedestrian [pɪ'destrɪən] n piéton m // a piétonnier(ère); (fig) prosaïque, terre à terre inv; ~ crossing n passage clouté m.

pediatrics [pi:dɪ'ætrɪks] n (US) = paediatrics.

pedigree ['pedɪgri:] n ascendance f; (of animal) pedigree m // cpd (animal) de race.

peek [pi:k] vi jeter un coup d'œil (furtif).

peel [pi:l] n pelure f, épluchure f; (of orange, lemon) écorce f // vt peler, éplucher // vi (paint etc) s'écailler; (wallpaper) se décoller; ~ings npl pelures fpl, épluchures fpl.

peep [pi:p] n (look) coup d'œil furtif; (sound) pépiement m // vi jeter un coup d'œil (furtif); to ~ out vi se montrer (furtivement); ~hole n judas m.

peer [pɪə*] vi: to ~ at regarder attentivement, scruter // n (noble) pair m; (equal) pair m, égal/e; ~age n pairie f; ~less n incomparable, sans égal.

peeved [pi:vd] a irrité(e), ennuyé(e).

peevish ['pi:vɪʃ] a grincheux(euse), maussade.

peg [pɛg] n cheville f; (for coat etc) patère f; (also: clothes ~) pince f à linge; off the ~ ad en prêt-à-porter.

pejorative [prɪ'dʒɔrətɪv] a péjoratif(ive).

pekingese [pi:kɪ'ni:z] n pékinois m.

pelican ['pɛlɪkən] n pélican m.

pellet ['pɛlɪt] n boulette f; (of lead) plomb m.

pelmet ['pɛlmɪt] n cantonnière f; lambrequin m.

pelt [pɛlt] vt: to ~ sb (with) bombarder qn (de) // vi (rain) tomber à seaux // n peau f.

pelvis ['pɛlvɪs] n bassin m.

pen [pɛn] n (for writing) stylo m; (for sheep) parc m.

penal ['pi:nl] a pénal(e); ~ize vt pénaliser; (fig) désavantager; ~ servitude n travaux forcés.

penalty ['pɛnltɪ] n pénalité f; sanction f; (fine) amende f; (SPORT) pénalisation f; ~ (kick) n (FOOTBALL) penalty m.

penance ['pɛnəns] n pénitence f.

pence [pɛns] npl of penny.

pencil ['pɛnsl] n crayon m // vt: to ~ sth in noter qch au crayon; ~ sharpener n taille-crayon(s) m inv.

pendant ['pɛndnt] n pendentif m.

pending ['pɛndɪŋ] prep en attendant // a en suspens.

pendulum ['pɛndjuləm] n pendule m; (of clock) balancier m.

penetrate ['pɛnɪtreɪt] vt pénétrer dans; pénétrer; **penetrating** a pénétrant(e); **penetration** [-'treɪʃən] n pénétration f.

penfriend ['pɛnfrɛnd] n correspondant/e.

penguin ['pɛŋgwɪn] n pingouin m.

penicillin [pɛnɪ'sɪlɪn] n pénicilline f.

peninsula [pə'nɪnsjulə] n péninsule f.

penis ['pi:nɪs] n pénis m, verge f.

penitence ['pɛnɪtns] n repentir m.

penitent ['pɛnɪtnt] a repentant(e).

penitentiary [pɛnɪ'tɛnʃərɪ] n (US) prison f.

penknife ['pɛnnaɪf] n canif m.

pennant ['pɛnənt] n flamme f, banderole f.

penniless ['pɛnɪlɪs] a sans le sou.

penny, pl **pennies** or **pence** ['pɛnɪ, 'pɛnɪz, pɛns] n penny m (pl pennies) (new: 100 in a pound; old: 12 in a shilling; on tend à employer 'pennies' ou 'two-pence piece' etc pour les pièces, 'pence' pour la valeur).

pension ['pɛnʃən] n retraite f; (MIL) pension f; ~able a qui a droit à une retraite; ~er n retraité/e; ~ fund n caisse f de retraite.

pensive ['pɛnsɪv] a pensif(ive).

pentagon ['pɛntəgən] n pentagone m.

Pentecost ['pɛntɪkɔst] n Pentecôte f.

penthouse ['pɛnthaus] n appartement m (de luxe) en attique.

pent-up ['pɛntʌp] a (feelings) refoulé(e).

penultimate [pɛ'nʌltɪmət] a pénultième, avant-dernier(ère).

people ['pi:pl] npl gens mpl; personnes fpl; (citizens) peuple m // n (nation, race) peuple m // vt peupler; 4/several ~ came 4/plusieurs personnes sont venues; the room was full of ~ la salle était pleine de monde or de gens; ~ say that... on dit or les gens disent que.

pep [pɛp] n (col) entrain m, dynamisme m; to ~ up vt remonter.

pepper ['pɛpə*] n poivre m; (vegetable) poivron m // vt poivrer; ~mint n (plant) menthe poivrée; (sweet) pastille f de menthe.

peptalk ['pɛptɔ:k] n (col) (petit) discours d'encouragement.

per [pə:*] prep par; ~ hour (miles etc) à l'heure; (fee) (de) l'heure; ~ kilo etc le kilo etc; ~ day/person par jour/personne; ~ cent pour cent; ~ annum par an.

perceive [pə'si:v] vt percevoir; (notice) remarquer, s'apercevoir de.

percentage [pə'sɛntɪdʒ] n pourcentage m.

perceptible [pə'sɛptɪbl] a perceptible.

perception [pə'sɛpʃən] n perception f; sensibilité f; perspicacité f.

perceptive [pə'sɛptɪv] a pénétrant(e); perspicace.

perch [pə:tʃ] n (fish) perche f; (for bird) perchoir m // vi vt (se) percher.

percolator ['pə:kəleɪtə*] n percolateur m; cafetière f électrique.

percussion [pə'kʌʃən] n percussion f.

peremptory [pə'rɛmptərɪ] a péremptoire.

perennial [pə'rɛnɪəl] a perpétuel(le); (BOT) vivace // n plante f vivace.

perfect a,n ['pə:fɪkt] a parfait(e) // n (also: ~ tense) parfait m // vt [pə'fɛkt] parfaire; mettre au point; ~ion [-'fɛkʃən] n perfection f; ~ionist n perfectionniste m/f; ~ly ad parfaitement.

perforate ['pə:fərɛt] vt perforer, percer; **perforation** [-'reɪʃən] n perforation f; (line of holes) pointillé m.

perform [pə'fɔ:m] vt (carry out) exécuter, rem. 'ir; (concert etc) jouer, donner // vi jouer; ~ance n représentation f, spectacle m; (of an artist) interprétation f; (of player etc) prestation f; (of car, engine) performance f; ~er n artiste m/f; ~ing a (animal) savant(e).

perfume ['pə:fju:m] n parfum m // vt parfumer.

perfunctory [pə'fʌŋktərɪ] a négligent(e), pour la forme.

perhaps [pə'hæps] ad peut-être; ~ he'll... peut-être qu'il... .

peril ['pɛrɪl] n péril m; ~ous a périlleux(euse).

perimeter [pə'rɪmɪtə*] n périmètre m; ~ wall n mur m d'enceinte.

period ['pɪərɪəd] n période f; (HISTORY) époque f; (SCOL) cours m; (full stop) point m; (MED) règles fpl // a (costume, furniture) d'époque; ~ic [-'ɔdɪk] a périodique; ~ical [-'ɔdɪkl] a périodique // n périodique m; ~ically [-'ɔdɪklɪ] ad périodiquement.

peripheral [pə'rɪfərəl] a périphérique.

periphery [pə'rɪfərɪ] n périphérie f.

periscope ['pərɪskəup] n périscope m.

perish ['pɛrɪʃ] vi périr, mourir ; (decay) se détériorer ; ~able a périssable ; ~ing a (col: cold) glacial(e).

perjure ['pə:dʒə*] vt: to ~ o.s. se parjurer ; **perjury** n (LAW: in court) faux témoignage ; (breach of oath) parjure m.

perk [pə:k] n avantage m, à-côté m ; to ~ up vi (cheer up) se ragaillardir ; ~y a (cheerful) guilleret(te), gai(e).

perm [pə:m] n (for hair) permanente f.

permanence ['pə:mənəns] n permanence f.

permanent ['pə:mənənt] a permanent(e) ; ~ly ad de façon permanente.

permeable ['pə:mɪəbl] a perméable.

permeate ['pə:mɪeɪt] vi s'infiltrer // vt s'infiltrer dans ; pénétrer.

permissible [pə'mɪsɪbl] a permis(e), acceptable.

permission [pə'mɪʃən] n permission f, autorisation f.

permissive [pə'mɪsɪv] a tolérant(e) ; the ~ society la société de tolérance.

permit n ['pə:mɪt] permis m // vt [pə'mɪt] permettre ; to ~ sb to do autoriser qn à faire, permettre à qn de faire.

permutation [pə:mju'teɪʃən] n permutation f.

pernicious [pə:'nɪʃəs] a pernicieux(euse), nocif(ive).

pernickety [pə'nɪkɪtɪ] a pointilleux(euse), tatillon(ne).

perpendicular [pə:pən'dɪkjulə*] a,n perpendiculaire (f).

perpetrate ['pə:pɪtreɪt] vt perpétrer, commettre.

perpetual [pə'pɛtjuəl] a perpétuel(le).

perpetuate [pə'pɛtjueɪt] vt perpétuer.

perpetuity [pə:pɪ'tju:ɪtɪ] n: in ~ à perpétuité.

perplex [pə'plɛks] vt rendre perplexe ; (complicate) embrouiller.

persecute ['pə:sɪkju:t] vt persécuter ; persecution [-'kju:ʃən] n persécution f.

persevere [pə:sɪ'vɪə*] vi persévérer.

Persian ['pə:ʃən] a persan(e) // n (LING) persan m ; the (~) Gulf n le golfe Persique.

persist [pə'sɪst] vi: to ~ (in doing) persister (à faire), s'obstiner (à faire) ; ~ence n persistance f, obstination f ; opiniâtreté f ; ~ent a persistant(e), tenace.

person ['pə:sn] personne f ; ~able a de belle prestance, au physique attrayant ; ~al a personnel(le) ; individuel(le) ; ~al assistant (P.A.) n secrétaire privé/e ; ~al call (TEL) communication f avec préavis ; ~ality [-'nælɪtɪ] n personnalité f ; ~ally ad personnellement ; ~ify [-'sɔnɪfaɪ] vt personnifier.

personnel [pə:sə'nɛl] n personnel m ; ~ manager n chef m du personnel.

perspective [pə'spɛktɪv] n perspective f.

perspex ['pə:spɛks] n sorte de plexiglas.

perspicacity [pə:spɪ'kæsɪtɪ] n perspicacité f.

perspiration [pə:spɪ'reɪʃən] n transpiration f.

perspire [pə'spaɪə*] vi transpirer.

persuade [pə'sweɪd] vt persuader.

persuasion [pə'sweɪʒən] n persuasion f.

persuasive [pə'sweɪsɪv] a persuasif(ive).

pert [pə:t] a (brisk) sec(sèche), brusque ; (bold) effronté(e), impertinent(e).

pertaining [pə:'teɪnɪŋ]: ~ to prep relatif(ive) à.

pertinent ['pə:tɪnənt] a pertinent(e).

perturb [pə'tə:b] vt perturber ; inquiéter.

Peru [pə'ru:] n Pérou m.

perusal [pə'ru:zl] n lecture (attentive).

Peruvian [pə'ru:vjən] a péruvien(ne) // n Péruvien/ne.

pervade [pə'veɪd] vt se répandre dans, envahir.

perverse [pə'və:s] a pervers(e) ; (stubborn) entêté(e), contrariant(e).

perversion [pə'və:ʃn] n perversion f.

perversity [pə'və:sɪtɪ] n perversité f.

pervert n ['pə:və:t] perverti/e // vt [pə'və:t] pervertir.

pessimism ['pɛsɪmɪzəm] n pessimisme m.

pessimist ['pɛsɪmɪst] n pessimiste m/f ; ~ic [-'mɪstɪk] a pessimiste.

pest [pɛst] n animal m (or insecte m) nuisible ; (fig) fléau m.

pester ['pɛstə*] vt importuner, harceler.

pesticide ['pɛstɪsaɪd] n pesticide m.

pestle ['pɛsl] n pilon m.

pet [pɛt] n animal familier ; (favourite) chouchou m // vt choyer // vi (col) se peloter ; ~ lion n lion apprivoisé.

petal ['pɛtl] n pétale m.

peter ['pi:tə*]: to ~ out vi s'épuiser ; s'affaiblir.

petite [pə'ti:t] a menu(e).

petition [pə'tɪʃən] n pétition f // vt adresser une pétition à.

petrified ['pɛtrɪfaɪd] a (fig) mort(e) de peur.

petrify ['pɛtrɪfaɪ] vt pétrifier.

petrol ['pɛtrəl] n (Brit) essence f ; ~ engine n moteur m à essence.

petroleum [pə'trəulɪəm] n pétrole m.

petrol: ~ pump n (in car, at garage) pompe f à essence ; ~ station n station-service f ; ~ tank n réservoir m d'essence.

petticoat ['pɛtɪkəut] n jupon m.

pettifogging ['pɛtɪfɔgɪŋ] a chicanier(ère).

pettiness ['pɛtɪnɪs] n mesquinerie f.

petty ['pɛtɪ] a (mean) mesquin(e) ; (unimportant) insignifiant(e), sans importance ; ~ cash n menue monnaie ; ~ officer n second-maître m.

petulant ['pɛtjulənt] a irritable.

pew [pju:] n banc m (d'église).

pewter ['pju:tə*] n étain m.

phallic ['fælɪk] a phallique.

phantom ['fæntəm] n fantôme m ; (vision) fantasme m.

Pharaoh ['fɛərəu] n pharaon m.

pharmacist ['fɑ:məsɪst] n pharmacien/ne.

pharmacy ['fɑ:məsɪ] n pharmacie f.

phase [feɪz] n phase f, période f // vt: to ~ sth in/out introduire/supprimer qch progressivement.

Ph.D. (abbr = Doctor of Philosophy) title ≈ Docteur m en Droit ou Lettres etc // n ≈ doctorat m ; titulaire m d'un doctorat.

pheasant ['fɛznt] *n* faisan *m*.

phenomenon, *pl* **phenomena** [fə'nɔmɪnən, -nə] *n* phénomène *m*.

phew [fju:] *excl* ouf!

phial ['faɪəl] *n* fiole *f*.

philanderer [fɪ'lændərə*] *n* don Juan *m*.

philanthropic [fɪlən'θrɔpɪk] *a* philanthropique.

philanthropist [fɪ'lænθrəpɪst] *n* philanthrope *m/f*.

philatelist [fɪ'lætəlɪst] *n* philatéliste *m/f*.

philately [fɪ'lætəlɪ] *n* philatélie *f*.

Philippines ['fɪlɪpi:nz] *npl* (*also*: **Philippine Islands**) Philippines *fpl*.

philosopher [fɪ'lɔsəfə*] *n* philosophe *m*.

philosophical [fɪlə'sɔfɪkl] *a* philosophique.

philosophy [fɪ'lɔsəfɪ] *n* philosophie *f*.

phlegm [flɛm] *n* flegme *m*; ~**atic** [flɛg'mætɪk] *a* flegmatique.

phobia ['fəubjə] *n* phobie *f*.

phone [fəun] *n* téléphone *m* // *vt* téléphoner; **to be on the** ~ avoir le téléphone; (*be calling*) être au téléphone; **to** ~ **back** *vt,vi* rappeler.

phonetics [fə'nɛtɪks] *n* phonétique *f*.

phoney ['fəunɪ] *a* faux(fausse), factice // *n* (*person*) charlatan *m*; fumiste *m/f*.

phonograph ['fəunəgrɑ:f] *n* (*US*) électrophone *m*.

phony ['fəunɪ] *a,n* = **phoney**.

phosphate ['fɔsfeɪt] *n* phosphate *m*.

phosphorus ['fɔsfərəs] *n* phosphore *m*.

photo ['fəutəu] *n* photo *f*.

photo... ['fəutəu] *prefix*: ~**copier** *n* machine *f* à photocopier; ~**copy** *n* photocopie *f* // *vt* photocopier; ~**electric** *a* photoélectrique; ~**genic** [-'dʒɛnɪk] *a* photogénique; ~**graph** *n* photographie *f* // *vt* photographier; ~**grapher** [fə'tɔgrəfə*] *n* photographe *m/f*; ~**graphic** [-'græfɪk] *a* photographique; ~**graphy** [fə'tɔgrəfɪ] *n* photographie *f*; ~**stat** ['fəutəustæt] *n* photocopie *f*, photostat *m*.

phrase [freɪz] *n* expression *f*; (*LING*) locution *f* // *vt* exprimer; ~**book** *n* recueil *m* d'expressions (pour touristes).

physical ['fɪzɪkl] *a* physique; ~**ly** *ad* physiquement.

physician [fɪ'zɪʃən] *n* médecin *m*.

physicist ['fɪzɪsɪst] *n* physicien/ne.

physics ['fɪzɪks] *n* physique *f*.

physiology [fɪzɪ'ɔlədʒɪ] *n* physiologie *f*.

physiotherapist [fɪzɪəu'θɛrəpɪst] *n* kinésithérapeute *m/f*.

physiotherapy [fɪzɪəu'θɛrəpɪ] *n* kinésithérapie *f*.

physique [fɪ'zi:k] *n* physique *m*; constitution *f*.

pianist ['pi:ənɪst] *n* pianiste *m/f*.

piano [pɪ'ænəu] *n* piano *m*.

piccolo ['pɪkələu] *n* piccolo *m*.

pick [pɪk] *n* (*tool*: *also*: ~**-axe**) pic *m*, pioche *f* // *vt* choisir; (*gather*) cueillir; **take your** ~ faites votre choix; **the** ~ **of le(la)** meilleur(e) de; **to** ~ **a bone** ronger un os; **to** ~ **one's teeth** se curer les dents; **to** ~ **pockets** pratiquer le vol à la tire; **to** ~ **on** *vt fus* (*person*) harceler; **to** ~ **out** *vt* choisir; (*distinguish*)

distinguer; **to** ~ **up** *vi* (*improve*) remonter, s'améliorer // *vt* ramasser; (*telephone*) décrocher; (*collect*) passer prendre; (*learn*) apprendre; **to** ~ **up speed** prendre de la vitesse; **to** ~ **o.s. up** se relever.

picket ['pɪkɪt] *n* (*in strike*) gréviste *m/f* participant à un piquet de grève; piquet *m* de grève // *vt* mettre un piquet de grève devant; ~ **line** *n* piquet *m* de grève.

pickle ['pɪkl] *n* (*also*: ~**s**: *as condiment*) pickles *mpl* // *vt* conserver dans du vinaigre *or* dans de la saumure.

pick-me-up ['pɪkmi:ʌp] *n* remontant *m*.

pickpocket ['pɪkpɔkɪt] *n* pickpocket *m*.

pickup ['pɪkʌp] *n* (*on record player*) bras *m* pick-up; (*small truck*) pick-up *m inv*.

picnic ['pɪknɪk] *n* pique-nique *m* // *vi* pique-niquer; ~**ker** *n* pique-niqueur/euse.

pictorial [pɪk'tɔ:rɪəl] *a* illustré(e).

picture ['pɪktʃə*] *n* image *f*; (*painting*) peinture *f*, tableau *m*; (*photograph*) photo(graphie) *f*; (*drawing*) dessin *m*; (*film*) film *m* // *vt* se représenter; (*describe*) dépeindre, représenter; **the** ~**s** le cinéma *m*; ~ **book** *n* livre *m* d'images.

picturesque [pɪktʃə'rɛsk] *a* pittoresque.

picture window ['pɪktʃəwɪndəu] *n* baie vitrée, fenêtre *f* panoramique.

piddling ['pɪdlɪŋ] *a* (*col*) insignifiant(e).

pidgin ['pɪdʒɪn] *a*: ~ **English** *n* pidgin *m*.

pie [paɪ] *n* tourte *f*; (*of meat*) pâté *m* en croûte.

piebald ['paɪbɔ:ld] *a* pie *inv*.

piece [pi:s] *n* morceau *m*; (*of land*) parcelle *f*; (*item*): **a** ~ **of furniture/advice** un meuble/conseil // *vt*: **to** ~ **together** rassembler; **in** ~**s** (*broken*) en morceaux, en miettes; (*not yet assembled*) en pièces détachées; **to take to** ~**s** démonter; ~**meal** *ad* par bouts; ~**work** *n* travail *m* aux pièces.

pier [pɪə*] *n* jetée *f*; (*of bridge etc*) pile *f*.

pierce [pɪəs] *vt* percer, transpercer.

piercing ['pɪəsɪŋ] *a* (*cry*) perçant(e).

piety ['paɪətɪ] *n* piété *f*.

piffling ['pɪflɪŋ] *a* insignifiant(e).

pig [pɪg] *n* cochon *m*, porc *m*.

pigeon ['pɪdʒən] *n* pigeon *m*; ~**hole** *n* casier *m*; ~**-toed** *a* marchant les pieds en dedans.

piggy bank ['pɪgɪbæŋk] *n* tirelire *f*.

pigheaded ['pɪg'hɛdɪd] *a* entêté(e), têtu(e).

piglet ['pɪglɪt] *n* petit cochon, porcelet *m*.

pigment ['pɪgmənt] *n* pigment *m*; ~**ation** [-'teɪʃən] *n* pigmentation *f*.

pigmy ['pɪgmɪ] *n* = **pygmy**.

pigsty ['pɪgstaɪ] *n* porcherie *f*.

pigtail ['pɪgteɪl] *n* natte *f*, tresse *f*.

pike [paɪk] *n* (*spear*) pique *f*; (*fish*) brochet *m*.

pilchard ['pɪltʃəd] *n* pilchard *m* (*sorte de sardine*).

pile [paɪl] *n* (*pillar, of books*) pile *f*; (*heap*) tas *m*; (*of carpet*) épaisseur *f* // *vb* (*also*: ~ **up**) *vt* empiler, entasser // *vi* s'entasser.

piles [paɪlz] *n* hémorroïdes *fpl*.

pileup ['paɪlʌp] *n* (*AUT*) télescopage *m*, collision *f* en série.

pilfer ['pɪlfə*] *vt* chaparder; ~**ing** *n* chapardage *m*.

pilgrim ['pɪlgrɪm] n pèlerin m; ~age n pèlerinage m.

pill [pɪl] n pilule f; the ~ la pilule.

pillage ['pɪlɪdʒ] vt piller.

pillar ['pɪlə*] n pilier m; ~ box n (Brit) boîte f aux lettres.

pillion ['pɪljən] n (of motor cycle) siège m arrière; to ride ~ être derrière; (on horse) être en croupe.

pillory ['pɪlərɪ] n pilori m // vt mettre au pilori.

pillow ['pɪləu] n oreiller m; ~case n taie f d'oreiller.

pilot ['paɪlət] n pilote m // cpd (scheme etc) pilote, expérimental(e) // vt piloter; ~ boat n bateau-pilote m; ~ light n veilleuse f.

pimp [pɪmp] n souteneur m, maquereau m.

pimple ['pɪmpl] n bouton m; **pimply** a boutonneux(euse).

pin [pɪn] n épingle f; (TECH) cheville f // vt épingler; ~s and needles fourmis fpl; to ~ sb against/to clouer qn contre/à; to ~ sb down (fig) obliger qn à répondre.

pinafore ['pɪnəfɔ:*] n tablier m; ~ dress n robe-chasuble f.

pincers ['pɪnsəz] npl tenailles fpl.

pinch [pɪntʃ] n pincement m; (of salt etc) pincée f // vt pincer; (col: steal) piquer, chiper; vi (shoe) serrer; at a ~ à la rigueur.

pincushion ['pɪnkuʃən] n pelote f à épingles.

pine [paɪn] n (also: ~ tree) pin m // vi: to ~ for aspirer à, désirer ardemment; to ~ away vi dépérir.

pineapple ['paɪnæpl] n ananas m.

ping [pɪŋ] n (noise) tintement m; ~-pong n ® ping-pong m ®.

pink [pɪŋk] a rose // n (colour) rose m; (BOT) œillet m, mignardise f.

pin money ['pɪnmʌnɪ] n argent m de poche.

pinnacle ['pɪnəkl] n pinacle m.

pinpoint ['pɪnpɔɪnt] n pointe f d'épingle // vt indiquer (avec précision).

pinstripe ['pɪnstraɪp] n rayure très fine.

pint [paɪnt] n pinte f (= 0.56 l).

pinup ['pɪnʌp] n pin-up f inv.

pioneer [paɪə'nɪə*] n explorateur/trice, (early settler) pionnier m; (fig) pionnier m, précurseur m.

pious ['paɪəs] a pieux(euse).

pip [pɪp] n (seed) pépin m; (time signal on radio) top m.

pipe [paɪp] n tuyau m, conduite f; (for smoking) pipe f; (MUS) pipeau m // vt amener par tuyau; ~s npl (also: bag~s) cornemuse f; to ~ down vi (col) se taire; ~ dream n chimère f, utopie f; ~line n pipe-line m; ~r n joueur/euse de pipeau (or de cornemuse); ~ tobacco n tabac m pour la pipe.

piping ['paɪpɪŋ] ad: ~ hot très chaud(e).

piquant ['pi:kənt] a piquant(e).

pique [pi:k] n dépit m.

piracy ['paɪərəsɪ] n piraterie f.

pirate ['paɪərət] n pirate m; ~ radio n radio f pirate.

pirouette [pɪru'ɛt] n pirouette f // vi faire une or des pirouette(s).

Pisces ['paɪsi:z] n les Poissons mpl; to be ~ être des Poissons.

pistol ['pɪstl] n pistolet m.

piston ['pɪstən] n piston m.

pit [pɪt] n trou m, fosse f; (also: coal ~) puits m de mine; (also: orchestra ~) fosse f d'orchestre // vt: to ~ sb against sb opposer qn à qn; ~s npl (AUT) aire f de service; to ~ o.s. against se mesurer à.

pitch [pɪtʃ] n (throw) lancement m; (MUS) ton m; (of voice) hauteur f; (SPORT) terrain m; (NAUT) tangage m; (tar) poix f // vt (throw) lancer // vi (fall) tomber; (NAUT) tanguer; to ~ a tent dresser une tente; to be ~ed forward être projeté en avant; ~-black a noir(e) comme poix; ~ed battle n bataille rangée.

pitcher ['pɪtʃə*] n cruche f.

pitchfork ['pɪtfɔ:k] n fourche f.

piteous ['pɪtɪəs] a pitoyable.

pitfall ['pɪtfɔ:l] n trappe f, piège m.

pith [pɪθ] n (of plant) moelle f; (of orange) intérieur m de l'écorce; (fig) essence f; vigueur f.

pithead ['pɪthɛd] n bouche f de puits.

pithy ['pɪθɪ] a piquant(e); vigoureux(euse).

pitiable ['pɪtɪəbl] a pitoyable.

pitiful ['pɪtɪful] a (touching) pitoyable; (contemptible) lamentable.

pitiless ['pɪtɪlɪs] a impitoyable.

pittance ['pɪtns] n salaire m de misère.

pity ['pɪtɪ] n pitié f // vt plaindre; what a ~! quel dommage!; ~ing a compatissant(e).

pivot ['pɪvət] n pivot m // vi pivoter.

pixie ['pɪksɪ] n lutin m.

placard ['plækɑ:d] n affiche f.

placate [plə'keɪt] vt apaiser, calmer.

place [pleɪs] n endroit m, lieu m; (proper position, rank, seat) place f; (house) maison f, logement m; (home): at/to his ~ chez lui // vt (object) placer, mettre; (identify) situer; reconnaître; to take ~ avoir lieu; se passer; to ~ an order passer une commande; to be ~d (in race, exam) se placer; out of ~ (not suitable) déplacé(e), inopportun(e); in the first ~ d'abord, en premier; ~ mat n set m de table.

placid ['plæsɪd] a placide; ~ity [plə'sɪdɪtɪ] n placidité f.

plagiarism ['pleɪdʒjərɪzm] n plagiat m.

plagiarize ['pleɪdʒjəraɪz] vt plagier.

plague [pleɪg] n fléau m; (MED) peste f.

plaice [pleɪs] n, pl inv carrelet m.

plaid [plæd] n tissu écossais.

plain [pleɪn] n (clear) clair(e), évident(e); (simple) simple, ordinaire; (frank) franc(franche); (not handsome) quelconque, ordinaire; (cigarette) sans filtre; (without seasoning etc) nature inv; (in one colour) uni(e) // ad franchement, carrément // n plaine f; in ~ clothes (police) en civil; ~ly ad clairement; (frankly) carrément, sans détours; ~ness n simplicité f.

plaintiff ['pleɪntɪf] n plaignant/e.

plait [plæt] n tresse f, natte f // vt tresser, natter.

plan [plæn] n plan m; (scheme) projet m // vt (think in advance) projeter; (prepare)

organiser // vi faire des projets ; **to ~ to
do** projeter de faire.
plane [pleɪn] n (AVIAT) avion m ; (tree)
platane m ; (tool) rabot m ; (ART, MATH etc)
plan m // a plan(e), plat(e) // vt (with tool)
raboter.
planet ['plænɪt] n planète f.
planetarium　　　[plænɪ'tɛərɪəm]　　n
planétarium m.
plank [plæŋk] n planche f ; (POL) point m
d'un programme.
plankton ['plæŋktən] n plancton m.
planner ['plænə*] n planificateur/trice.
planning ['plænɪŋ] n planification f ;
family ~ planning familial.
plant [plɑ:nt] n plante f ; (machinery)
matériel m ; (factory) usine f // vt planter ;
(colony) établir ; (bomb) déposer, poser.
plantation [plæn'teɪʃən] n plantation f.
plant pot ['plɑ:ntpɔt] n pot m (de fleurs).
plaque [plæk] n plaque f.
plasma ['plæzmə] n plasma m.
plaster ['plɑ:stə*] n plâtre m ; (also:
sticking ~) pansement adhésif // vt
plâtrer ; (cover): **to ~ with** couvrir de ; **in
~** (leg etc) dans le plâtre ; **~ed** a (col)
soûl(e) ; **~er** n plâtrier m.
plastic ['plæstɪk] n plastique m // a (made
of plastic) en plastique ; (flexible) plastique,
malléable ; (art) plastique.
plasticine ['plæstɪsi:n] n ® pâte f à
modeler.
plastic surgery ['plæstɪk'sə:dʒərɪ] n
chirurgie f esthétique.
plate [pleɪt] n (dish) assiette f ; (sheet of
metal, PHOT) plaque f ; (in book) gravure f ;
gold/silver ~ (dishes) vaisselle f
d'or/d'argent.
plateau, ~s or **~x** ['plætəʊ, -z] n plateau
m.
plateful ['pleɪtful] n assiette f, assiettée f.
plate glass [pleɪt'glɑ:s] n verre m (de
vitrine).
platelayer ['pleɪtleɪə*] n (RAIL) poseur m
de rails.
platform ['plætfɔ:m] n (at meeting)
tribune f ; (stage) estrade f ; (RAIL) quai m ;
~ ticket n billet m de quai.
platinum ['plætɪnəm] n platine m.
platitude ['plætɪtju:d] n platitude f, lieu
commun.
platoon [plə'tu:n] n peloton m.
platter ['plætə*] n plat m.
plausible ['plɔ:zɪbl] a plausible ; (person)
convaincant(e).
play [pleɪ] n jeu m ; (THEATRE) pièce f (de
théâtre) // vt (game) jouer à ; (team,
opponent) jouer contre ; (instrument) jouer
de ; (play, part, piece of music, note) jouer
// vi jouer ; **to ~ down** vt minimiser ; **to
~ up** vi (cause trouble) faire des siennes ;
to ~act vi jouer la comédie ; **~ed-out** a
épuisé(e) ; **~er** n joueur/euse ; (THEATRE)
acteur/trice ; (MUS) musicien/ne ; **~ful** a
enjoué(e) ; **~goer** n amateur/trice de
théâtre, habitué/e des théâtres ; **~ground**
n cour f de récréation ; **~group** n garderie
f ; **~ing card** n carte f à jouer ; **~ing field**
n terrain m de sport ; **~mate** n camarade
m/f, copain/copine ; **~-off** n (SPORT) belle
f ; **~ on words** n jeu m de mots ; **~pen**

n parc m (pour bébé) ; **~thing** n jouet m ;
~wright n dramaturge m.
plea [pli:] n (request) appel m ; (excuse)
excuse f ; (LAW) défense f.
plead [pli:d] vt plaider ; (give as excuse)
invoquer // vi (LAW) plaider ; (beg): **to ~
with sb** implorer qn.
pleasant ['plɛznt] a agréable ; **~ly** ad
agréablement ; **~ness** n (of person)
amabilité f ; (of place) agrément m ; **~ry**
n (joke) plaisanterie f ; **~ries** npl (polite
remarks) civilités fpl.
please [pli:z] vt plaire à // vi (think fit):
do as you ~ faites comme il vous plaira ;
~! s'il te (or vous) plaît ; **my bill, ~**
l'addition, s'il vous plaît ; **~ yourself!** à
ta (or votre) guise! ; **~d** a: **~d (with)**
content(e) (de) ; **~d to meet you**
enchanté (de faire votre connaissance) ;
pleasing a plaisant(e), qui fait plaisir.
pleasurable ['plɛʒərəbl] a très agréable.
pleasure ['plɛʒə*] n plaisir m ; **'it's a ~'**
'je vous en prie' ; **~ steamer** n vapeur m
de plaisance.
pleat [pli:t] n pli m.
plebiscite ['plɛbɪsɪt] n plébiscite m.
plebs [plɛbz] npl (pej) bas peuple.
plectrum ['plɛktrəm] n plectre m.
pledge [plɛdʒ] n gage m ; (promise)
promesse f // vt engager ; promettre.
plentiful ['plɛntɪful] a abondant(e),
copieux(euse).
plenty ['plɛntɪ] n abondance f ; **~ of**
beaucoup de ; (bien) assez de.
pleurisy ['plʊərɪsɪ] n pleurésie f.
pliable ['plaɪəbl] a flexible ; (person)
malléable.
pliers ['plaɪəz] npl pinces fpl.
plight [plaɪt] n situation f critique.
plimsolls ['plɪmsəlz] npl (chaussures fpl)
tennis fpl.
plinth [plɪnθ] n socle m.
plod [plɒd] vi avancer péniblement ; (fig)
peiner ; **~der** n bûcheur/euse ; **~ding** a
pesant(e).
plonk [plɒŋk] (col) n (wine) pinard m,
piquette f // vt: **to ~ sth down** poser
brusquement qch.
plot [plɒt] n complot m, conspiration f ; (of
story, play) intrigue f ; (of land) lot m de
terrain, lopin m // vt (mark out) pointer ;
relever ; (conspire) comploter // vi
comploter ; **~ter** n conspirateur/trice.
plough, plow (US) [plaʊ] n charrue f //
vt (earth) labourer ; **to ~ back** vt (COMM)
réinvestir ; **to ~ through** vt fus (snow etc)
avancer péniblement dans ; **~ing** n
labourage m.
ploy [plɔɪ] n stratagème m.
pluck [plʌk] vt (fruit) cueillir ; (musical
instrument) pincer ; (bird) plumer // n
courage m, cran m ; **to ~ one's eyebrows**
s'épiler les sourcils ; **to ~ up courage**
prendre son courage à deux mains ; **~y**
a courageux(euse).
plug [plʌg] n bouchon m, bonde f ; (ELEC)
prise f de courant ; (AUT: also: **sparking ~**)
bougie f // vt (hole) boucher ; (col:
advertise) faire du battage pour,
matraquer ; **to ~ in** vt (ELEC) brancher.

plum [plʌm] n (*fruit*) prune f // a: ~ **job** n (*col*) travail m en or.
plumb [plʌm] a vertical(e) // n plomb m // ad (*exactly*) en plein // vt sonder.
plumber ['plʌməª] n plombier m.
plumbing ['plʌmɪŋ] n (*trade*) plomberie f; (*piping*) tuyauterie f.
plumbline ['plʌmlaɪn] n fil m à plomb.
plume [pluːm] n plume f, plumet m.
plummet ['plʌmɪt] vi plonger, dégringoler.
plump [plʌmp] a rondelet(te), dodu(e), bien en chair // vt: to ~ sth (**down**) on laisser tomber qch lourdement sur; to ~ for (*col: choose*) se décider pour.
plunder ['plʌndəª] n pillage m // vt piller.
plunge [plʌndʒ] n plongeon m // vt plonger // vi (*fall*) tomber, dégringoler; to take the ~ se jeter à l'eau; **plunging** a (*neckline*) plongeant(e).
pluperfect [pluː'pəːfɪkt] n plus-que-parfait m.
plural ['pluərl] a pluriel(le) // n pluriel m.
plus [plʌs] n (*also*: ~ **sign**) signe m plus // prep plus; ten/twenty ~ plus de dix/vingt; it's a ~ c'est un atout; ~ **fours** npl pantalon m (de) golf.
plush [plʌʃ] a somptueux(euse) // n peluche f.
ply [plaɪ] n (*of wool*) fil m; (*of wood*) feuille f, épaisseur f // vt (*tool*) manier; (*a trade*) exercer // vi (*ship*) faire la navette; **three** ~ (*wool*) n laine f trois fils; to ~ **sb with drink** donner continuellement à boire à qn; ~**wood** n contre-plaqué m.
P.M. abbr see **prime**.
p.m. ad (*abbr of post meridiem*) de l'après-midi.
pneumatic [njuːˈmætɪk] a pneumatique.
pneumonia [njuːˈməʊnɪə] n pneumonie f.
P.O. abbr see **post office**.
poach [pəʊtʃ] vt (*cook*) pocher; (*steal*) pêcher (*or* chasser) sans permis // vi braconner; ~**ed** a (*egg*) poché(e); ~**er** n braconnier m; ~**ing** n braconnage m.
pocket ['pɒkɪt] n poche f // vt empocher; to be out of ~ en être de sa poche; ~**book** n (*wallet*) portefeuille m; (*notebook*) carnet m; ~ **knife** n canif m; ~ **money** n argent m de poche.
pockmarked ['pɒkmɑːkt] a (*face*) grêlé(e).
pod [pɒd] n cosse f // vt écosser.
podgy ['pɒdʒɪ] a rondelet(te).
poem ['pəʊɪm] n poème m.
poet ['pəʊɪt] n poète m; ~**ic** [-'ɛtɪk] a poétique; ~ **laureate** n poète lauréat (*nommé et appointé par la Cour royale*); ~**ry** n poésie f.
poignant ['pɔɪnjənt] a poignant(e); (*sharp*) vif(vive).
point [pɔɪnt] n (*tip*) pointe f; (*in time*) moment m; (*in space*) endroit m; (GEOM, SCOL, SPORT, *on scale*) point m; (*subject, idea*) point m, sujet m; (*also*: **decimal** ~): **2 ~ 3 (2.3)** 2 virgule 3 (2,3) // vt (*show*) indiquer; (*wall, window*) jointoyer; (*gun etc*): to ~ sth at braquer or diriger qch sur // vi montrer du doigt; ~**s** npl (AUT) vis platinées; (RAIL) aiguillage m; to make a ~ faire une remarque; to make one's ~ se faire comprendre; to get the ~ comprendre, saisir; to come to the ~ en

venir au fait; there's no ~ (**in doing**) cela ne sert à rien (de faire); **good** ~**s** qualités fpl; to ~ **out** vt faire remarquer, souligner; to ~ **to** montrer du doigt; (*fig*) signaler; ~**blank** ad (*also*: at ~**blank range**) à bout portant; (*fig*) catégorique; ~**ed** a (*shape*) pointu(e); (*remark*) plein(e) de sous-entendus; ~**edly** ad d'une manière significative; ~**er** n (*stick*) baguette f; (*needle*) aiguille f; (*dog*) chien m d'arrêt; ~**less** a inutile, vain(e); ~ **of view** n point m de vue.
poise [pɔɪz] n (*balance*) équilibre m; (*of head, body*) port m; (*calmness*) calme m // vt placer en équilibre; to be ~**d for** (*fig*) être prêt à.
poison ['pɔɪzn] n poison m // vt empoisonner; ~**ing** n empoisonnement m; ~**ous** a (*snake*) venimeux(euse); (*substance etc*) vénéneux(euse).
poke [pəʊk] vt (*fire*) tisonner; (*jab with finger, stick etc*) piquer; pousser du doigt; (*put*): to ~ sth **in**(to) fourrer or enfoncer qch dans // n (*to fire*) coup m de tisonnier; to ~ **about** vi fureter.
poker ['pəʊkəª] n tisonnier m; (CARDS) poker m; ~-**faced** a au visage impassible.
poky ['pəʊkɪ] a exigu(ë).
Poland ['pəʊlənd] n Pologne f.
polar ['pəʊləª] a polaire; ~ **bear** n ours blanc.
polarize ['pəʊləraɪz] vt polariser.
pole [pəʊl] n (*of wood*) mât m, perche f; (ELEC) poteau m; (GEO) pôle m.
Pole [pəʊl] n Polonais/e.
polecat ['pəʊlkæt] n (US) putois m.
polemic [pɒ'lɛmɪk] n polémique f.
pole star ['pəʊlstɑːª] n étoile polaire f.
pole vault ['pəʊlvɔːlt] n saut m à la perche.
police [pə'liːs] n police f, (*man: pl inv*) policier m, homme m; // vt maintenir l'ordre dans; ~ **car** n voiture f de police; ~**man** n agent m de police, policier m; ~ **record** n casier m judiciaire; ~ **state** n état policier; ~ **station** n commissariat m de police; ~**woman** n femme-agent f.
policy ['pɒlɪsɪ] n politique f; (*also*: **insurance** ~) police f (d'assurance).
polio ['pəʊlɪəʊ] n polio f.
Polish ['pəʊlɪʃ] a polonais(e) // n (LING) polonais m.
polish ['pɒlɪʃ] n (*for shoes*) cirage m; (*for floor*) cire f, encaustique f; (*for nails*) vernis m; (*shine*) éclat m, poli m; (*fig: refinement*) raffinement m // vt (*put polish on shoes, wood*) cirer; (*make shiny*) astiquer, faire briller; (*fig: improve*) perfectionner; to ~ **off** vt (*work*) expédier; (*food*) liquider; ~**ed** a (*fig*) raffiné(e).
polite [pə'laɪt] a poli(e); ~**ly** ad poliment; ~**ness** n politesse f.
politic ['pɒlɪtɪk] a diplomatique; ~**al** [pə'lɪtɪkl] a politique; ~**ian** [-'tɪʃən] n homme m politique, politicien m; ~**s** npl politique f.
polka ['pɒlkə] n polka f; ~ **dot** n pois m.
poll [pəʊl] n scrutin m, vote m; (*also*: **opinion** ~) sondage m (d'opinion) // vt obtenir.
pollen ['pɒlən] n pollen m; ~ **count** n taux m de pollen.

pollination [pɔlɪˈneɪʃən] n pollinisation f.
polling booth [ˈpəʊlɪŋbuːð] n isoloir m.
polling day [ˈpəʊlɪŋdeɪ] n jour m des élections.
polling station [ˈpəʊlɪŋsteɪʃən] n bureau m de vote.
pollute [pəˈluːt] vt polluer.
pollution [pəˈluːʃən] n pollution f.
polo [ˈpəʊləʊ] n polo m; **~-neck** a à col roulé.
polyester [pɔlɪˈestə*] n polyester m.
polygamy [pəˈlɪgəmɪ] n polygamie f.
Polynesia [pɔlɪˈniːzɪə] n Polynésie f.
polytechnic [pɔlɪˈteknɪk] n (college) I.U.T. m, Institut m Universitaire de Technologie.
polythene [ˈpɔlɪθiːn] n polyéthylène m; **~ bag** n sac m en plastique.
pomegranate [ˈpɔmɪgrænɪt] n grenade f.
pommel [ˈpɔml] n pommeau m.
pomp [pɔmp] n pompe f, faste f, apparat m.
pompous [ˈpɔmpəs] a pompeux(euse).
pond [pɔnd] n étang m; mare f.
ponder [ˈpɔndə*] vi réfléchir // vt considérer, peser; **~ous** a pesant(e), lourd(e).
pontiff [ˈpɔntɪf] n pontife m.
pontificate [pɔnˈtɪfɪkeɪt] vi (fig): to **~** (about) pontifier (sur).
pontoon [pɔnˈtuːn] n ponton m.
pony [ˈpəʊnɪ] n poney m; **~tail** n queue f de cheval; **~ trekking** n randonnée f à cheval.
poodle [ˈpuːdl] n caniche m.
pooh-pooh [puːˈpuː] vt dédaigner.
pool [puːl] n (of rain) flaque f; (pond) mare f; (artificial) bassin m; (also: **swimming ~**) piscine f; (sth shared) fonds commun; (money at cards) cagnotte f; (billiards) poule f // vt mettre en commun.
poor [puə*] a pauvre; (mediocre) médiocre, faible, mauvais(e) // npl: the **~** les pauvres mpl; **~ly** ad pauvrement; médiocrement // a souffrant(e), malade.
pop [pɔp] n (noise) bruit sec; (MUS) musique f pop; (US: col: father) papa m // vt (put) fourrer, mettre (rapidement) // vi éclater; (cork) sauter; to **~ in** vi entrer en passant; to **~ out** vi sortir; to **~ up** vi apparaître, surgir; **~concert** n concert m pop; **~corn** n pop-corn m.
pope [pəʊp] n pape m.
poplar [ˈpɔplə*] n peuplier m.
poplin [ˈpɔplɪn] n popeline f.
poppy [ˈpɔpɪ] n coquelicot m; pavot m.
populace [ˈpɔpjuləs] n peuple m.
popular [ˈpɔpjulə*] a populaire; (fashionable) à la mode; **~ity** [-ˈlærɪtɪ] n popularité f; **~ize** vt populariser; (science) vulgariser.
populate [ˈpɔpjuleɪt] vt peupler.
population [pɔpjuˈleɪʃən] n population f.
populous [ˈpɔpjuləs] a populeux(euse).
porcelain [ˈpɔːslɪn] n porcelaine f.
porch [pɔːtʃ] n porche m.
porcupine [ˈpɔːkjupaɪn] n porc-épic m.
pore [pɔː*] n pore m // vi: to **~ over** s'absorber dans, être plongé(e) dans.
pork [pɔːk] n porc m.

pornographic [pɔːnəˈɡræfɪk] a pornographique.
pornography [pɔːˈnɔɡrəfɪ] n pornographie f.
porous [ˈpɔːrəs] a poreux(euse).
porpoise [ˈpɔːpəs] n marsouin m.
porridge [ˈpɔrɪdʒ] n porridge m.
port [pɔːt] n (harbour) port m; (opening in ship) sabord m; (NAUT: left side) bâbord m; (wine) porto m; to **~** (NAUT) à bâbord.
portable [ˈpɔːtəbl] a portatif(ive).
portal [ˈpɔːtl] n portail m.
portcullis [pɔːtˈkʌlɪs] n herse f.
portend [pɔːˈtend] vt présager, annoncer.
portent [ˈpɔːtent] n présage m.
porter [ˈpɔːtə*] n (for luggage) porteur m; (doorkeeper) gardien/ne; portier m.
porthole [ˈpɔːthəʊl] n hublot m.
portico [ˈpɔːtɪkəʊ] n portique m.
portion [ˈpɔːʃən] n portion f, part f.
portly [ˈpɔːtlɪ] a corpulent(e).
portrait [ˈpɔːtreɪt] n portrait m.
portray [pɔːˈtreɪ] vt faire le portrait de; (in writing) dépeindre, représenter; **~al** n portrait m, représentation f.
Portugal [ˈpɔːtjuɡl] n Portugal m.
Portuguese [pɔːtjuˈɡiːz] a portugais(e) // n, pl inv Portugais/e; (LING) portugais m.
pose [pəʊz] n pose f; (pej) affectation f // vi poser; (pretend): to **~ as** se poser en // vt poser, créer; **~r** n question embarrassante.
posh [pɔʃ] a (col) chic inv.
position [pəˈzɪʃən] n position f; (job) situation f // vt mettre en place or en position.
positive [ˈpɔzɪtɪv] a positif(ive); (certain) sûr(e), certain(e); (definite) formel(le), catégorique; indéniable, réel(le).
posse [ˈpɔsɪ] n (US) détachement m.
possess [pəˈzes] vt posséder; **~ion** [pəˈzeʃən] n possession f; **~ive** a possessif(ive); **~ively** ad d'une façon possessive; **~or** n possesseur m.
possibility [pɔsɪˈbɪlɪtɪ] n possibilité f; éventualité f.
possible [ˈpɔsɪbl] a possible; **if ~** si possible; **as big as ~** aussi gros que possible.
possibly [ˈpɔsɪblɪ] ad (perhaps) peut-être; **if you ~ can** si cela vous est possible; **I cannot ~ come** il m'est impossible de venir.
post [pəʊst] n poste f; (collection) levée f; (letters, delivery) courrier m; (job, situation) poste m; (pole) poteau m // vt (send by post, MIL) poster; (appoint): to **~ to** affecter à; (notice) afficher; **~age** n affranchissement m; **~al** a postal(e); **~al order** n mandat(-poste) m; **~box** n boite f aux lettres; **~card** n carte postale.
postdate [pəʊstˈdeɪt] vt (cheque) postdater.
poster [ˈpəʊstə*] n affiche f.
poste restante [pəʊstˈrestɑːnt] n poste restante.
posterior [pɔsˈtɪərɪə*] n (col) postérieur m, derrière m.
posterity [pɔsˈterɪtɪ] n postérité f.
postgraduate [ˈpəʊstˈɡrædjuət] n ≈ étudiant/e de troisième cycle.

posthumous ['pɔstjuməs] a posthume;
~ly ad après la mort de l'auteur, à titre
posthume.

postman ['pəustmən] n facteur m.

postmark ['pəustmɑ:k] n cachet m (de la
poste).

postmaster ['pəustmɑ:stə*] n receveur m
des postes.

post-mortem [pəust'mɔ:təm] n autopsie
f.

post office ['pəustɔfıs] n (building) poste
f; (organization) postes fpl; ~ box (P.O.
box) n boîte postale (B.P.).

postpone [pəs'pəun] vt remettre (à plus
tard), reculer; ~ment n ajournement m,
renvoi m.

postscript ['pəustskrıpt] n post-scriptum
m.

postulate ['pɔstjuleıt] vt postuler.

posture ['pɔstʃə*] n posture f, attitude f
// vi poser.

postwar [pəust'wɔ:*] a d'après-guerre.

posy ['pəuzı] n petit bouquet.

pot [pɔt] n (for cooking) marmite f;
casserole f; (for plants, jam) pot m; (col:
marijuana) herbe f // vt (plant) mettre en
pot; to go to ~ aller à vau-l'eau.

potash ['pɔtæʃ] n potasse f.

potato, ~es [pə'teɪtəu] n pomme f de
terre; ~ flour n fécule f.

potency ['pəutnsı] n puissance f, force f;
(of drink) degré m d'alcool.

potent ['pəutnt] a puissant(e); (drink)
fort(e), très alcoolisé(e).

potentate ['pəutnteıt] n potentat m.

potential [pə'tɛnʃl] a potentiel(le) // n
potentiel m; ~ly ad en puissance.

pothole ['pɔthəul] n (in road) nid m de
poule; (underground) gouffre m, caverne f;
~r n spéléologue m/f; potholing n: to go
potholing faire de la spéléologie.

potion ['pəuʃən] n potion f.

potluck [pɔt'lʌk] n: to take ~ tenter sa
chance.

potpourri [pəu'puri:] n pot-pourri m.

potshot ['pɔtʃɔt] n: to take ~s at
canarder.

potted ['pɔtıd] a (food) en conserve;
(plant) en pot.

potter ['pɔtə*] n potier m // vt: to ~
around, ~ about bricoler; ~y n poterie
f.

potty ['pɔtı] a (col: mad) dingue // n
(child's) pot m; ~-training n
apprentissage m de la propreté.

pouch [pautʃ] n (zool) poche f; (for
tobacco) blague f.

pouf(fe) [pu:f] n (stool) pouf m.

poultice ['pəultıs] n cataplasme m.

poultry ['pəultrı] n volaille f; ~ farm n
élevage m de volaille.

pounce [pauns] vi: to ~ (on) bondir (sur),
fondre sur // n bond m, attaque f.

pound [paund] n livre f (weight = 453g,
16 ounces; money = 100 new pence, 20
shillings); (for dogs, cars) fourrière f // vt
(beat) bourrer de coups, marteler; (crush)
piler, pulvériser; (with guns) pilonner //
vi (beat) battre violemment, taper; ~
sterling n livre f sterling.

pour [pɔ:*] vt verser // vi couler à flots;
(rain) pleuvoir à verse; to ~ away or off
vt vider; to ~ in vi (people) affluer, se
précipiter; to ~ out vi (people) sortir en
masse // vt vider; déverser; (serve: a
drink) verser; ~ing a: ~ing rain pluie
torrentielle.

pout [paut] n moue f // vi faire la moue.

poverty ['pɔvətı] n pauvreté f, misère f;
~-stricken a pauvre, déshérité(e).

powder ['paudə*] n poudre f // vt
poudrer; ~ room n toilettes fpl (pour
dames); ~y a poudreux(euse).

power ['pauə*] n (strength) puissance f,
force f; (ability, POL: of party, leader)
pouvoir m; (MATH) puissance f; (mental)
facultés mentales; (ELEC) courant m // vt
faire marcher; ~ cut n coupure f de
courant; ~ed by: ~ed by actionné(e) par,
fonctionnant à, ~ful a puissant(e); ~less
a impuissant(e); ~ line n ligne f
électrique; ~ point n prise f de courant;
~ station n centrale f électrique.

powwow ['pauwau] n assemblée f.

pox [pɔks] n see chicken.

p.p. abbr (= per procurationem): ~ J.
Smith pour M. J. Smith.

P.R. abbr of public relations.

practicability [præktıkə'bılıtı] n
possibilité f de réalisation.

practicable ['præktıkəbl] a (scheme)
réalisable.

practical ['præktıkl] a pratique; ~ joke
n farce // ~ly ad (almost) pratiquement.

practice ['præktıs] n pratique f; (of
profession) exercice m; (at football etc)
entraînement m; (business) cabinet m;
clientèle f // vt,vi (US) = practise; in ~
(in reality) en pratique; out of ~
rouillé(e); 2 hours' piano ~ 2 heures de
travail or d'exercices au piano; ~ match
n match m d'entraînement.

practise, (US) practice ['præktıs] vt
(work at: piano, one's backhand etc)
s'exercer à, travailler; (train for: skiing,
running etc) s'entraîner à; (a sport, religion,
method) pratiquer; (profession) exercer //
vi s'exercer, travailler; (train) s'entraîner;
to ~ for a match s'entraîner pour un
mat... ; practising a (Christian etc)
pratiquant(e); (lawyer) en exercice.

practitioner [præk'tıʃənə*] n
praticien/ne.

pragmatic [præg'mætık] a pragmatique.

prairie ['prɛərı] n savane f; (US): the ~s
la Prairie.

praise [preız] n éloge(s) m(pl), louange(s)
f(pl) // vt louer, faire l'éloge de; ~worthy
a digne de louanges.

pram [præm] n landau m, voiture f
d'enfant.

prance [prɑ:ns] vi (horse) caracoler.

prank [præŋk] n farce f.

prattle ['prætl] vi jacasser.

prawn [prɔ:n] n crevette f (rose).

pray [preı] vi prier.

prayer [prɛə*] n prière f; ~ book n livre
m de prières.

preach [pri:tʃ] vt,vi prêcher; to ~ at sb
faire la morale à qn; ~er n prédicateur
m.

preamble [prɪ'æmbl] n préambule m.
prearranged [priːə'reɪndʒd] a organisé(e) or fixé(e) à l'avance.
precarious [prɪ'kɛərɪəs] a précaire.
precaution [prɪ'kɔːʃən] n précaution f; ~ary a (measure) de précaution.
precede [prɪ'siːd] vt, vi précéder.
precedence ['prɛsɪdəns] n préséance f.
precedent ['prɛsɪdənt] n précédent m.
preceding [prɪ'siːdɪŋ] a qui précède (or précédait).
precept ['priːsɛpt] n précepte m.
precinct ['priːsɪŋkt] n (round cathedral) pourtour m, enceinte f; **pedestrian** ~ n zone piétonnière; **shopping** ~ n centre commerical.
precious ['prɛʃəs] a précieux(euse).
precipice ['prɛsɪpɪs] n précipice m.
precipitate a [prɪ'sɪpɪtɪt] (hasty) précipité(e) // vt [prɪ'sɪpɪteɪt] précipiter; **precipitation** [-'teɪʃən] n précipitation f.
precipitous [prɪ'sɪpɪtəs] a (steep) abrupt(e), à pic.
précis, pl **précis** ['preɪsiː, -z] n résumé m.
precise [prɪ'saɪs] a précis(e); ~ly ad précisément.
preclude [prɪ'kluːd] vt exclure, empêcher; to ~ sb from doing empêcher qn de faire.
precocious [prɪ'kəuʃəs] a précoce.
preconceived [priːkən'siːvd] a (idea) préconçu(e).
precondition [priːkən'dɪʃən] n condition f nécessaire.
precursor [priː'kəːsə*] n précurseur m.
predator ['prɛdətə*] n prédateur m, rapace m; ~y a rapace.
predecessor ['priːdɪsɛsə*] n prédécesseur m.
predestination [priːdɛstɪ'neɪʃən] n prédestination f.
predetermine [priːdɪ'təːmɪn] vt déterminer à l'avance.
predicament [prɪ'dɪkəmənt] n situation f difficile.
predicate ['prɛdɪkɪt] n (LING) prédicat m.
predict [prɪ'dɪkt] vt prédire; ~ion [-'dɪkʃən] n prédiction f.
predominance [prɪ'dɔmɪnəns] n prédominance f.
predominant [prɪ'dɔmɪnənt] a prédominant(e); ~ly ad en majeure partie; surtout.
predominate [prɪ'dɔmɪneɪt] vi prédominer.
pre-eminent [priː'ɛmɪnənt] a prééminent(e).
pre-empt [priː'ɛmt] vt acquérir par droit de préemption; (fig): **to ~ the issue** conclure avant même d'ouvrir les débats.
preen [priːn] vt: **to ~ itself** (bird) se lisser les plumes; **to ~ o.s.** s'admirer.
prefab ['priːfæb] n bâtiment préfabriqué.
prefabricated [priː'fæbrikeitɪd] a préfabriqué(e).
preface ['prɛfəs] n préface f.
prefect ['priːfɛkt] n (Brit: in school) élève chargé(e) de certaines fonctions de discipline; (in France) préfet m.
prefer [prɪ'fəː*] vt préférer; ~able ['prɛfrəbl] a préférable; ~ably ['prɛfrəbli]

ad de préférence; ~ence ['prɛfrəns] n préférence f; ~ential [prɛfə'rɛnʃəl] a préférentiel(le) ~ential **treatment** traitement m de faveur.
prefix ['priːfɪks] n préfixe m.
pregnancy ['prɛgnənsɪ] n grossesse f.
pregnant ['prɛgnənt] a enceinte af.
prehistoric ['priːhɪs'tɔrɪk] a préhistorique.
prehistory [priː'hɪstərɪ] n préhistoire f.
prejudge [priː'dʒʌdʒ] vt préjuger de.
prejudice ['prɛdʒudɪs] n préjugé m; (harm) tort m, préjudice m // vt porter préjudice à; ~d a (person) plein(e) de préjugés; (view) préconçu(e), partial(e).
prelate ['prɛlət] n prélat m.
preliminary [prɪ'lɪmɪnərɪ] a préliminaire; **preliminaries** npl préliminaires mpl.
prelude ['prɛljuːd] n prélude m.
premarital ['priː'mærɪtl] a avant le mariage.
premature ['prɛmətʃuə*] a prématuré(e).
premeditated [priː'mɛdɪteɪtɪd] a prémédité(e).
premeditation [priːmɛdɪ'teɪʃən] n préméditation f.
premier ['prɛmɪə*] a premier(ère), capital(e), primordial(e) // n (POL) premier ministre.
première ['prɛmɪɛə*] n première f.
premise ['prɛmɪs] n prémisse f; ~s npl locaux mpl; **on the ~s** sur les lieux; sur place.
premium ['priːmɪəm] n prime f.
premonition [prɛmə'nɪʃən] n prémonition f.
preoccupation [priːɔkju'peɪʃən] n préoccupation f.
preoccupied [priː'ɔkjupaɪd] a préoccupé(e).
prep [prɛp] n (SCOL: study) étude f; ~ **school** n = **preparatory school**.
prepackaged [priː'pækɪdʒd] a préemballé(e), préempaqueté(e).
prepaid [priː'peɪd] a payé(e) d'avance.
preparation [prɛpə'reɪʃən] n préparation f; ~s npl (for trip, war) préparatifs mpl.
preparatory [prɪ'pærətərɪ] a préparatoire; ~ **school** n école primaire privée.
prepare [prɪ'pɛə*] vt préparer // vi: **to ~ for** se préparer à; ~d **for** preparé(e) à; ~d **to** prêt(e) à.
preponderance [prɪ'pɔndərns] n prépondérance f.
preposition [prɛpə'zɪʃən] n préposition f.
preposterous [prɪ'pɔstərəs] a absurde.
prerequisite [priː'rɛkwɪzɪt] n condition f préalable.
prerogative [prɪ'rɔgətɪv] n prérogative f.
presbyterian [prɛzbɪ'tɪərɪən] a,n presbytérien(ne).
presbytery ['prɛzbɪtərɪ] n presbytère m.
preschool ['priː'skuːl] a préscolaire.
prescribe [prɪ'skraɪb] vt prescrire.
prescription [prɪ'skrɪpʃən] n prescription f; (MED) ordonnance f.
prescriptive [prɪ'skrɪptɪv] a normatif(ive).
presence ['prɛzns] n présence f; ~ **of mind** n présence d'esprit.
present ['prɛznt] a présent(e) // n cadeau m; (also: ~ **tense**) présent m // vt

[prɪ'zɛnt] présenter ; (*give*): to ~ sb with sth offrir qch à qn ; at ~ en ce moment ; ~able [prɪ'zɛntəbl] a présentable ; ~ation [-'teɪʃən] n présentation f ; (*gift*) cadeau m, présent m ; (*ceremony*) remise f du cadeau ; ~day a contemporain(e), actuel(le) ; ~ly ad (*soon*) tout à l'heure, bientôt ; (*at present*) en ce moment.

preservation [prɛzə'veɪʃən] n préservation f, conservation f.

preservative [prɪ'zə:vətɪv] n agent m de conservation.

preserve [prɪ'zə:v] vt (*keep safe*) préserver, protéger ; (*maintain*) conserver, garder ; (*food*) mettre en conserve // n (*for game, fish*) réserve f ; (*often pl: jam*) confiture f ; (: *fruit*) fruits mpl en conserve.

preside [prɪ'zaɪd] vi présider.

presidency ['prɛzɪdənsɪ] n présidence f.

president ['prɛzɪdənt] n président/e ; ~ial [dɛn'ʃl] a présidentiel(le).

press [prɛs] n (*tool, machine, newspapers*) presse f ; (*for wine*) pressoir m ; (*crowd*) cohue f, foule f // vt (*push*) appuyer sur ; (*squeeze*) presser, serrer ; (*clothes: iron*) repasser ; (*pursue*) talonner ; (*insist*): to ~ sth on sb presser qn d'accepter qch // vi appuyer, peser ; se presser ; we are ~ed for time le temps nous manque ; to ~ for sth faire pression pour obtenir qch ; to ~ on vi continuer ; ~ agency n agence f de presse ; ~ conference n conférence f de presse ; ~ cutting n coupure f de presse ; ~gang n recruteurs de la marine (jusqu'au 19ème siècle) ; ~ing a urgent(e), pressant(e) // n repassage m ; ~ stud n bouton-pression m.

pressure ['prɛʃə*] n pression f ; (*stress*) tension f ; ~ cooker n cocotte-minute f ; ~ gauge n manomètre m ; ~ group n groupe m de pression ; **pressurized** a pressurisé(e).

prestige [prɛs'ti:ʒ] n prestige m.

prestigious [prɛs'tɪdʒəs] a prestigieux(euse).

presumably [prɪ'zju:məblɪ] ad vraisemblablement.

presume [prɪ'zju:m] vt présumer, supposer ; to ~ to do (*dare*) se permettre de faire.

presumption [prɪ'zʌmpʃən] n supposition f, présomption f ; (*boldness*) audace f.

presumptuous [prɪ'zʌmpʃəs] a présomptueux(euse).

presuppose [pri:sə'pəuz] vt présupposer.

pretence, pretense (*US*) [prɪ'tɛns] n (*claim*) prétention f ; to make a ~ of doing faire semblant de faire ; on the ~ of sous le prétexte de.

pretend [prɪ'tɛnd] vt (*feign*) feindre, simuler // vi (*feign*) faire semblant ; (*claim*): to ~ to sth prétendre à qch ; to ~ to do faire semblant de faire.

pretense [prɪ'tɛns] n (*US*) = pretence.

pretentious [prɪ'tɛnʃəs] a prétentieux(euse).

preterite ['prɛtərɪt] n prétérit m.

pretext ['pri:tɛkst] n prétexte m.

pretty ['prɪtɪ] a joli(e) // ad assez.

prevail [prɪ'veɪl] vi (*win*) l'emporter, prévaloir ; (*be usual*) avoir cours ; (*persuade*): to ~ (up)on sb to do

persuader qn de faire ; ~ing a dominant(e).

prevalent ['prɛvələnt] a répandu(e), courant(e).

prevarication [prɪværɪ'keɪʃən] n (*usage m de*) faux-fuyants mpl.

prevent [prɪ'vɛnt] vt: to ~ (from doing) empêcher (de faire) ; ~able a évitable ; ~ative a préventif(ive) ; ~ion [-'vɛnʃən] n prévention f ; ~ive a préventif(ive).

preview ['pri:vju:] n (*of film*) avant-première f ; (*fig*) aperçu m.

previous ['pri:vɪəs] a précédent(e) ; antérieur(e) ; ~ to doing avant de faire ; ~ly ad précédemment, auparavant.

prewar [pri:'wɔ:*] a d'avant-guerre.

prey [preɪ] n proie f // vi: to ~ on s'attaquer à ; it was ~ing on his mind ça le rongeait or minait.

price [praɪs] n prix m // vt (*goods*) fixer le prix de ; tarifer ; ~less a sans prix, inestimable ; ~ list n liste f des prix, tarif m.

prick [prɪk] n piqûre f // vt piquer ; to ~ up one's ears dresser or tendre l'oreille.

prickle ['prɪkl] n (*of plant*) épine f ; (*sensation*) picotement m.

prickly ['prɪklɪ] a piquant(e), épineux(euse) ; (*fig: person*) irritable ; ~ heat n fièvre f miliaire ; ~ pear n figue f de Barbarie.

pride [praɪd] n orgueil m ; fierté f // vt: to ~ o.s. on se flatter de ; s'enorgueillir e.

priest [pri:st] n prêtre m ; ~ess n prêtresse f ; ~hood n prêtrise f, sacerdoce m.

prig [prɪg] n poseur/euse, fat m.

prim [prɪm] a collet monté inv, guindé(e).

primarily ['praɪmərɪlɪ] ad principalement, essentiellement.

primary ['praɪmərɪ] a primaire ; (*first in importance*) premier(ère), primordial(e) ; ~ colour n couleur fondamentale ; ~ school n école primaire f.

primate n (*REL*) ['praɪmɪt] primat m ; (*ZOOL*) ['praɪmeɪt] primate m.

prime [praɪm] a primordial(e), fondamental(e) ; (*excellent*) excellent(e) // vt (*gun, pump*) amorcer ; (*fig*) mettre au courant ; in the ~ of life dans la fleur de l'âge ; ~ minister (P.M.) n premier ministre ; ~r n (*book*) premier livre, manuel m élémentaire ; (*paint*) apprêt m ; (*of gun*) amorce f.

primeval [praɪ'mi:vl] a primitif(ive).

primitive ['prɪmɪtɪv] a primitif(ive).

primrose ['prɪmrəuz] n primevère f.

primus (stove) ['praɪməs(stəuv)] n ⊛ réchaud m de camping.

prince [prɪns] n prince m.

princess [prɪn'sɛs] n princesse f.

principal ['prɪnsɪpl] a principal(e) // n (*headmaster*) directeur m, principal m ; (*money*) capital m, principal m.

principality [prɪnsɪ'pælɪtɪ] n principauté f.

principally ['prɪnsɪplɪ] ad principalement.

principle ['prɪnsɪpl] n principe m.

print [prɪnt] n (*mark*) empreinte f ; (*letters*) caractères mpl ; (*fabric*) imprimé m ; (*ART*)

gravure f, estampe f; (PHOT) épreuve f //
vt imprimer; (*publish*) publier; (*write in
capitals*) écrire en majuscules; out of ~
épuisé(e); ~ed matter n imprimés mpl;
~er n imprimeur m; ~ing n impression
f; ~ing press n presse f typographique;
~-out n listage m.
prior ['praɪəʳ] a antérieur(e), précédent(e)
// n prieur m; ~ to doing avant de faire.
priority [praɪ'ɔrɪtɪ] n priorité f.
priory ['praɪərɪ] n prieuré m.
prise [praɪz] vt: to ~ open forcer.
prism ['prɪzəm] n prisme m.
prison ['prɪzn] n prison f; ~er n
prisonnier/ère.
prissy ['prɪsɪ] a bégueule.
pristine ['prɪstiːn] a virginal(e).
privacy ['prɪvəsɪ] n intimité f, solitude f.
private ['praɪvɪt] a privé(e);
personnel(le); (*house, car, lesson*)
particulier(ère) // n soldat m de deuxième
classe; '~' (*on envelope*) 'personnelle'; in
~ en privé; ~ eye n détective privé; ~ly
ad en privé; (*within oneself*)
intérieurement.
privet ['prɪvɪt] n troène m.
privilege ['prɪvɪlɪdʒ] n privilège m; ~d a
privilégié(e).
privy ['prɪvɪ] a: to be ~ to être au courant
de; P~ council n conseil privé.
prize [praɪz] n prix m // a (*example, idiot*)
parfait(e); (*bull, novel*) primé(e) // vt
priser, faire grand cas de; ~ fight n
combat professionnel; ~ giving n
distribution f des prix; ~winner n
gagnant/e.
pro [prəu] n (SPORT) professionnel/le; the
~s and cons n pour et le contre.
probability [prɔbə'bɪlɪtɪ] n probabilité f.
probable ['prɔbəbl] a probable; **probably**
ad probablement.
probation [prə'beɪʃən] n (*in employment*)
essai m; (LAW) liberté surveillée; (REL)
noviciat m, probation f; on ~ (*employee*)
à l'essai; (LAW) en liberté surveillée; ~ary
a (*period*) d'essai.
probe [prəub] n (MED, SPACE) sonde f;
(*enquiry*) enquête f, investigation f // vt
sonder, explorer.
probity ['prəubɪtɪ] n probité f.
problem ['prɔbləm] n problème m; ~atic
[-'mætɪk] a problématique.
procedure [prə'siːdʒəʳ] n (ADMIN, LAW)
procédure f; (*method*) marche f à suivre,
façon f de procéder.
proceed [prə'siːd] vi (*go forward*) avancer;
(*go about it*) procéder; (*continue*): to ~
(with) continuer, poursuivre; to ~ to
aller à; passer à; to ~ to do se mettre
à faire; ~ing n procédé m, façon d'agir
f; ~ings npl mesures fpl; (LAW) poursuites
fpl; (*meeting*) réunion f, séance f; (*records*)
compte rendu; actes mpl; ~s ['prəusiːdz]
npl produit m, recette f.
process ['prəusɛs] n processus m;
(*method*) procédé m // vt traiter; ~ed
cheese fromage fondu; in ~ en cours;
~ing n traitement m.
procession [prə'sɛʃən] n défilé m, cortège
m; (REL) procession f.

proclaim [prə'kleɪm] vt déclarer,
proclamer.
proclamation [prɔklə'meɪʃən] n
proclamation f.
proclivity [prə'klɪvɪtɪ] n inclination f.
procrastination [prəukræstɪ'neɪʃən] n
procrastination f.
procreation [prəukrɪ'eɪʃən] n procréation
f.
procure [prə'kjuəʳ] vt (*for o.s.*) se
procurer; (*for sb*) procurer.
prod [prɔd] vt pousser // n (*push, jab*) petit
coup, poussée f.
prodigal ['prɔdɪgl] a prodigue.
prodigious ['prə'dɪdʒəs] a prodi-
gieux(euse).
prodigy ['prɔdɪdʒɪ] n prodige m.
produce n ['prɔdjuːs] (AGR) produits mpl
// vt [prə'djuːs] produire; (*to show*)
présenter; (*cause*) provoquer, causer;
(THEATRE) monter, mettre en scène; ~r n
(THEATRE) metteur m en scène; (AGR, CINEMA)
producteur m.
product ['prɔdʌkt] n produit m.
production [prə'dʌkʃən] n production f;
(THEATRE) mise f en scène; ~ line n chaîne
f (de fabrication).
productive [prə'dʌktɪv] a productif(ive).
productivity [prɔdʌk'tɪvɪtɪ] n
productivité f.
profane [prə'feɪn] a sacrilège; (*lay*)
profane.
profess [prə'fɛs] vt professer.
profession [prə'fɛʃən] n profession f;
~al n (SPORT) professionnel/le // a
professionnel(le); (*work*) de
professionnel; he's a ~al man il exerce
une profession libérale; ~alism n
professionnalisme m.
professor [prə'fɛsəʳ] n professeur m
(*titulaire d'une chaire*).
proficiency [prə'fɪʃənsɪ] n compétence f,
aptitude f.
proficient [prə'fɪʃənt] a compétent(e),
capable.
profile ['prəufaɪl] n profil m.
profit ['prɔfɪt] n bénéfice m; profit m //
vi: to ~ (by or from) profiter (de);
~ability [-'bɪlɪtɪ] n rentabilité f; ~able a
lucratif(ive), rentable.
profiteering [prɔfɪ'tɪərɪŋ] n (*pej*)
mercantilisme m.
profound [prə'faund] a profond(e).
profuse [prə'fjuːs] a abondant(e); (*with
money*) prodigue; ~ly ad en abondance,
profusion; **profusion** [-'fjuːʒən] n
profusion f, abondance f.
progeny ['prɔdʒɪnɪ] n progéniture f;
descendants mpl.
programme, program (US)
['prəugræm] n programme m; (RADIO, TV)
émission f // vt programmer;
programming, programing (US) n
programmation f.
progress n ['prəugrɛs] progrès m // vi
[prə'grɛs] progresser, avancer; in ~ en
cours; to make ~ progresser, faire des
progrès, être en progrès; ~ion [-'grɛʃən]
n progression f; ~ive [-'grɛsɪv] a
progressif(ive); (*person*) progressiste;
~ively [-'grɛsɪvlɪ] ad progressivement.

prohibit [prə'hɪbɪt] vt interdire, défendre ;
to ~ sb from doing défendre or interdire
à qn de faire ; ~ion [prəʊɪ'bɪʃən] n (US)
prohibition f ; ~ive a (price etc)
prohibitif(ive).

project n ['prɒdʒɛkt] (plan) projet m, plan
m ; (venture) opération f, entreprise f ; (gen
scol: research) étude f, dossier m // vb
[prə'dʒɛkt] vt projeter // vi (stick out) faire
saillie, s'avancer.

projectile [prə'dʒɛktaɪl] n projectile m.

projection [prə'dʒɛkʃən] n projection f ;
saillie f.

projector [prə'dʒɛktə*] n projecteur m.

proletarian [prəʊlɪ'tɛərɪən] a
prolétarien(ne) // n prolétaire m/f.

proletariat [prəʊlɪ'tɛərɪət] n prolétariat m.

proliferate [prə'lɪfəreɪt] vi proliférer ;
proliferation [-'reɪʃən] n prolifération f.

prolific [prə'lɪfɪk] a prolifique.

prologue ['prəʊlɒg] n prologue m.

prolong [prə'lɒŋ] vt prolonger.

prom [prɒm] n abbr of promenade ; (US:
ball) bal m d'étudiants.

promenade [prɒmə'nɑːd] n (by sea)
esplanade f, promenade f ; ~ concert n
concert m (de musique classique) ; ~ deck
n pont m promenade.

prominence ['prɒmɪnəns] n proéminence
f ; importance f.

prominent ['prɒmɪnənt] a (standing out)
proéminent(e) ; (important) important(e).

promiscuity [prɒmɪs'kjuːɪtɪ] n (sexual)
légèreté f de mœurs.

promiscuous [prə'mɪskjuəs] a (sexually)
de mœurs légères.

promise ['prɒmɪs] n promesse f // vt,vi
promettre ; **promising** a prometteur(euse).

promontory ['prɒməntrɪ] n promontoire
m.

promote [prə'məʊt] vt promouvoir ;
(venture, event) organiser, mettre sur pied ;
(new product) lancer ; ~r n (of sporting
event) organisateur/trice ; **promotion**
[-'məʊʃən] n promotion f.

prompt [prɒmpt] a rapide // ad
(punctually) à l'heure // vt inciter ;
provoquer ; (THEATRE) souffler (son rôle or
ses répliques) à ; to ~ sb to do inciter
or pousser qn à faire ; ~er n (THEATRE)
souffleur m ; ~ly ad rapidement, sans
délai ; ponctuellement ; ~ness n rapidité
f ; promptitude f ; ponctualité f.

promulgate ['prɒmʌlgeɪt] vt promulguer.

prone [prəʊn] a (lying) couché(e) (face
contre terre) ; ~ to enclin(e) à.

prong [prɒŋ] n pointe f ; (of fork) dent f.

pronoun ['prəʊnaʊn] n pronom m.

pronounce [prə'naʊns] vt prononcer //
vi: to ~ (up)on se prononcer sur ; ~d a
(marked) prononcé(e) ; ~ment n
déclaration f.

pronunciation [prənʌnsɪ'eɪʃən] n
prononciation f.

proof [pruːf] n preuve f ; (test, of book,
PHOT) épreuve f ; (of alcohol) degré m //
a: ~ against à l'épreuve de ; to be 70°
~ ≈ titrer 40 degrés ; ~reader n
correcteur/trice (d'épreuves).

prop [prɒp] n support m, étai m // vt (also:

~ up) étayer, soutenir ; (lean): to ~ sth
against appuyer qch contre or à.

propaganda [prɒpə'gændə] n propagande
f.

propagation [prɒpə'geɪʃən] n propagation f.

propel [prə'pɛl] vt propulser, faire
avancer ; ~ler n hélice f ; ~ling pencil n
porte-mine m inv.

propensity [prə'pɛnsɪtɪ] n propension f.

proper ['prɒpə*] a (suited, right)
approprié(e), bon(bonne) ; (seemly)
correct(e), convenable ; (authentic) vrai(e),
véritable ; (col: real) n + fini(e), vrai(e) ;
~ly ad correctement, convenablement ;
bel et bien ; ~ noun n nom m propre.

property ['prɒpətɪ] n (things owned) biens
mpl ; propriété(s) f(pl) ; immeuble m ;
terres fpl, domaine m ; (CHEM etc: quality)
propriété f ; it's their ~ cela leur
appartient, c'est leur propriété ; ~ owner
n propriétaire m.

prophecy ['prɒfɪsɪ] n prophétie f.

prophesy ['prɒfɪsaɪ] vt prédire // vi
prophétiser.

prophet ['prɒfɪt] n prophète m ; ~ic
[prə'fɛtɪk] a prophétique.

proportion [prə'pɔːʃən] n proportion f ;
(share) part f ; partie f // vt proportionner ;
~al, ~ate a proportionnel(le).

proposal [prə'pəʊzl] n proposition f, offre
f ; (plan) projet m ; (of marriage) demande
f en mariage.

propose [prə'pəʊz] vt proposer, suggérer
// vi faire sa demande en mariage ; to ~
to do avoir l'intention de faire ; ~r n (of
motion etc) auteur m.

proposition [prɒpə'zɪʃən] n proposition f.

propound [prə'paʊnd] vt proposer,
soumettre.

proprietary [prə'praɪətərɪ] a de marque
déposée.

proprietor [prə'praɪətə*] n propriétaire
m/f.

propulsion [prə'pʌlʃən] n propulsion f.

pro rata [prəʊ'rɑːtə] ad au prorata.

prosaic [prəʊ'zeɪɪk] a prosaïque.

prose [prəʊz] n prose f ; (SCOL: translation)
thème m.

prosecute ['prɒsɪkjuːt] vt poursuivre ;
prosecution [-'kjuːʃən] n poursuites fpl
judiciaires ; (accusing side) accusation f ;
prosecutor n procureur m ; (also: public
~) ministère public.

prospect n ['prɒspɛkt] perspective f ;
(hope) espoir m, chances fpl // vt,vi
[prə'spɛkt] prospecter ; ~s npl (for work
etc) possibilités fpl d'avenir, débouchés
mpl ; **prospecting** n prospection f ;
prospective a (possible) éventuel(le) ;
(certain) futur(e) ; **prospector** n
prospecteur m.

prospectus [prə'spɛktəs] n prospectus m.

prosper ['prɒspə*] vi prospérer ; ~ity
[-'spɛrɪtɪ] n prospérité f ; ~ous a prospère.

prostitute ['prɒstɪtjuːt] n prostituée f.

prostrate ['prɒstreɪt] a prosterné(e) ; (fig)
prostré(e).

protagonist [prə'tægənɪst] n protagoniste
m.

protect [prə'tɛkt] vt protéger; ~**ion** n protection f; ~**ive** a protecteur(trice); ~**or** n protecteur/trice.

protégé ['prəutɛʒeɪ] n protégé m; ~**e** n protégée f.

protein ['prəuti:n] n protéine f.

protest n ['prəutɛst] protestation f // vi [prə'tɛst] protester.

Protestant ['prɔtɪstənt] a,n protestant(e).

protocol ['prəutəkɔl] n protocole m.

prototype ['prəutətaɪp] n prototype m.

protracted [prə'træktɪd] a prolongé(e).

protractor [prə'træktə°] n rapporteur m.

protrude [prə'tru:d] vi avancer, dépasser.

protuberance [prə'tju:bərəns] n protubérance f.

proud [praud] a fier(ère); (pej) orgueilleux(euse); ~**ly** ad fièrement.

prove [pru:v] vt prouver, démontrer // vi: to ~ **correct** etc s'avérer juste etc; to ~ o.s. montrer ce dont on est capable; to ~ **o.s./itself** (to be) **useful** etc se montrer or se révéler utile etc.

proverb ['prɔvə:b] n proverbe m; ~**ial** [prə'və:biəl] a proverbial(e).

provide [prə'vaɪd] vt fournir; to ~ **sb with sth** fournir qch à qn; to ~ **for** vt (person) subvenir aux besoins de; (emergency) prévoir; ~**d** (that) cj à condition que + sub.

Providence ['prɔvɪdəns] n Providence f.

providing [prə'vaɪdɪŋ] cj à condition que + sub.

province ['prɔvɪns] n province f; **provincial** [prə'vɪnʃəl] a provincial(e).

provision [prə'vɪʒən] n (supply) provision f; (supplying) fourniture f; approvisionnement m; (stipulation) disposition f; ~**s** npl (food) provisions fpl; ~**al** a provisoire; ~**ally** ad provisoirement.

proviso [prə'vaɪzəu] n condition f.

provocation [prɔvə'keɪʃən] n provocation f.

provocative [prə'vɔkətɪv] a provocateur(trice), provocant(e).

provoke [prə'vəuk] vt provoquer; inciter.

prow [prau] n proue f.

prowess ['prauɪs] n prouesse f.

prowl [praul] vi (also: ~ **about**, ~ **around**) rôder // n: **on the** ~ à l'affût; ~**er** n rôdeur/euse.

proximity [prɔk'sɪmɪtɪ] n proximité f.

proxy ['prɔksɪ] n procuration f; **by** ~ par procuration.

prudence ['pru:dns] n prudence f.

prudent ['pru:dnt] a prudent(e).

prudish ['pru:dɪʃ] a prude, pudibond(e).

prune [pru:n] n pruneau m // vt élaguer.

pry [praɪ] vi: to ~ **into** fourrer son nez dans.

psalm [sɑ:m] n psaume m.

pseudo- ['sju:dəu] prefix pseudo-; ~**nym** n pseudonyme m.

psyche ['saɪkɪ] n psychisme m.

psychiatric [saɪk'ætrɪk] a psychiatrique.

psychiatrist [saɪ'kaɪətrɪst] n psychiatre m/f.

psychiatry [saɪ'kaɪətrɪ] n psychiatrie f.

psychic ['saɪkɪk] a (also: ~**al**) (méta)psychique; (person) doué(e) de télépathie or d'un sixième sens.

psychoanalyse [saɪkəu'ænəlaɪz] vt psychanalyser.

psychoanalysis, pl **lyses** [saɪkəuə'næləsɪs, -si:z] n psychanalyse f.

psychoanalyst [saɪkəu'ænəlɪst] n psychanalyste m/f.

psychological [saɪkə'lɔdʒɪkl] a psychologique.

psychologist [saɪ'kɔlədʒɪst] n psychologue m/f.

psychology [saɪ'kɔlədʒɪ] n psychologie f.

psychopath ['saɪkəupæθ] n psychopathe m/f.

psychosomatic ['saɪkəusə'mætɪk] a psychosomatique.

psychotic [saɪ'kɔtɪk] a,n psychotique (m/f).

P.T.O. abbr (= please turn over) T.S.V.P. (tournez s'il vous plaît).

pub [pʌb] n (abbr of public house) pub m.

puberty ['pju:bətɪ] n puberté f.

public ['pʌblɪk] a public(ique) // n public m; **the general** ~ le grand public; ~ **address system (P.A.)** sonorisation f; **hauts-parleurs** mpl.

publican ['pʌblɪkən] n patron m de pub.

publication [pʌblɪ'keɪʃən] n publication f.

public: ~ **company** n société f anonyme (cotée en bourse); ~ **convenience** n toilettes fpl; ~ **house** n pub m.

publicity [pʌb'lɪsɪtɪ] n publicité f.

publicly ['pʌblɪklɪ] ad publiquement.

public: ~ **opinion** n opinion publique; ~ **relations (PR)** n relations publiques; ~ **school** n (Brit) école privée; ~**-spirited** a qui fait preuve de civisme.

publish ['pʌblɪʃ] vt publier; ~**er** n éditeur m; ~**ing** n (industry) édition f; (of a book) publication f.

puce [pju:s] a puce.

puck [pʌk] n (elf) lutin m; (ICE HOCKEY) palet m.

pucker ['pʌkə°] vt plisser.

pudding ['pudɪŋ] n dessert m, entremets m; (sausage) boudin m.

puddle ['pʌdl] n flaque f d'eau.

puerile ['pjuəraɪl] a puéril(e).

puff [pʌf] n bouffée f; (also: **powder** ~) **houppe, houppette** f // vt: to ~ **one's pipe** tirer sur sa pipe // vi sortir par bouffées; (pant) haleter; to ~ **out smoke** envoyer des bouffées de fumée; ~**ed** a (col: out of breath) tout(e) essoufflé(e).

puffin ['pʌfɪn] n macareux m.

puff pastry ['pʌf'peɪstrɪ] n pâte feuilletée.

puffy ['pʌfɪ] a bouffi(e), boursouflé(e).

pugnacious [pʌg'neɪʃəs] a pugnace, batailleur(euse).

pull [pul] n (tug): **to give sth a** ~ tirer sur qch; (fig) influence f // vt tirer; (muscle) se claquer // vi tirer; to ~ **a face** faire une grimace; to ~ **to pieces** mettre en morceaux; to ~ **one's punches** ménager son adversaire; to ~ **one's weight** y mettre du sien; to ~ **o.s. together** se ressaisir; to ~ **sb's leg** faire marcher qn; to ~ **apart** vt séparer; (break) mettre en pièces, démantibuler; to

~ **down** vt baisser, abaisser; (house) démolir; (tree) abattre; to ~ **in** vi (AUT: at the kerb) se ranger; (RAIL) entrer en gare; to ~ **off** vt enlever, ôter; (deal etc) conclure; to ~ **out** vi démarrer, partir; se retirer; (AUT: come out of line) déboîter // vt sortir; (withdraw) retirer; to ~ **round** vi (unconscious person) revenir à soi; (sick person) se rétablir; to ~ **through** vi s'en sortir; to ~ **up** vi (stop) s'arrêter // vt remonter; (uproot) déraciner, arracher; (stop) arrêter.

pulley ['pulɪ] n poulie f.

pull-in ['pulɪn] n (AUT) parking m.

pullover ['puləuvə*] n pull-over m, tricot m.

pulp [pʌlp] n (of fruit) pulpe f; (for paper) pâte f à papier.

pulpit ['pulpɪt] n chaire f.

pulsate [pʌl'seɪt] vi battre, palpiter; (music) vibrer.

pulse [pʌls] n (of blood) pouls m; (of heart) battement m; (of music, engine) vibrations fpl.

pulverize ['pʌlvəraɪz] vt pulvériser.

puma ['pjuːmə] n puma m.

pummel ['pʌml] vt rouer de coups.

pump [pʌmp] n pompe f; (shoe) escarpin m // vt pomper; (fig: col) faire parler; to ~ **up** vt gonfler.

pumpkin ['pʌmpkɪn] n potiron m, citrouille f.

pun [pʌn] n jeu m de mots, calembour m.

punch [pʌntʃ] n (blow) coup m de poing; (fig: force) vivacité f, mordant m; (tool) poinçon m; (drink) punch m // vt (hit): to ~ **sb/sth** donner un coup de poing à qn/sur qch; (make a hole) poinçonner, perforer; to ~ **a hole** (in) faire un trou (dans); ~-**drunk** a sonné(e); ~-**up** n (col) bagarre f.

punctual ['pʌŋktjuəl] a ponctuel(le); ~**ity** [-'ælɪtɪ] n ponctualité f.

punctuate ['pʌŋktjueɪt] vt ponctuer; **punctuation** [-'eɪʃən] n ponctuation f.

puncture ['pʌŋktʃə*] n crevaison f // vt crever.

pundit ['pʌndɪt] n individu m qui pontifie, pontife m.

pungent ['pʌndʒənt] a piquant(e); (fig) mordant(e), caustique.

punish ['pʌnɪʃ] vt punir; ~**able** a punissable; ~**ment** n punition f, châtiment m.

punt [pʌnt] n (boat) bachot m; (FOOTBALL) coup m de volée.

punter ['pʌntə*] n (gambler) parieur/euse.

puny ['pjuːnɪ] a chétif(ive).

pup [pʌp] n chiot m.

pupil ['pjuːpl] n élève m/f.

puppet ['pʌpɪt] n marionnette f, pantin m.

puppy ['pʌpɪ] n chiot m, petit chien.

purchase ['pəːtʃɪs] n achat m // vt acheter; ~**r** n acheteur/euse.

pure [pjuə*] a pur(e).

purée ['pjuəreɪ] n purée f.

purge [pəːdʒ] n (MED) purge f; (POL) épuration f, purge // vt purger; (fig) épurer, purger.

purification [pjuərɪfɪ'keɪʃən] n purification f.

purify ['pjuərɪfaɪ] vt purifier, épurer.

purist ['pjuərɪst] n puriste m/f.

puritan ['pjuərɪtən] n puritain/e; ~**ical** [-'tænɪkl] a puritain(e).

purity ['pjuərɪtɪ] n pureté f.

purl [pəːl] n maille f à l'envers // vt tricoter à l'envers.

purple ['pəːpl] a violet(te); cramoisi(e).

purport [pəː'pɔːt] vi: to ~ **to be/do** prétendre être/faire.

purpose ['pəːpəs] n intention f, but m; on ~ exprès; ~**ful** a déterminé(e), résolu(e); ~**ly** ad exprès.

purr [pəː*] n ronronnement m // vi ronronner.

purse [pəːs] n porte-monnaie m inv, bourse f // vt serrer, pincer.

purser ['pəːsə*] n (NAUT) commissaire m du bord.

pursue [pə'sjuː] vt poursuivre; ~**r** n poursuivant/e.

pursuit [pə'sjuːt] n poursuite f; (occupation) occupation f, activité f; **scientific** ~**s** recherches fpl scientifiques.

purveyor [pə'veɪə*] n fournisseur m.

pus [pʌs] n pus m.

push [puʃ] n poussée f; (effort) gros effort; (drive) énergie f // vt pousser; (button) appuyer sur; (thrust): to ~ **sth** (**into**) enfoncer qch (dans); (fig) mettre en avant, faire de la publicité pour // vi pousser; appuyer; to ~ **aside** vt écarter; to ~ **off** vi (col) filer, ficher le camp; to ~ **on** vi (continue) continuer; to ~ **over** vt renverser; to ~ **through** vt (measure) faire voter; to ~ **up** vt (total, prices) faire monter; ~**chair** n poussette f; ~**ing** a dynamique; ~**over** n (col): it's a ~**over** c'est un jeu d'enfant; ~ (a pej) arriviste.

puss, pussy(-cat) [pus, 'pusɪ(kæt)] n minet m.

put, pt, pp **put** [put] vt mettre, poser, placer; (say) dire, exprimer; (a question) pose-- (estimate) estimer; to ~ **about** vi (NAUT) virer de bord // vt (rumour) faire courir; to ~ **across** vt (ideas etc) communiquer; faire comprendre; to ~ **away** vt (store) ranger; to ~ **back** vt (replace) remettre, replacer; (postpone) remettre; (delay) retarder; to ~ **by** vt (money) mettre de côté, économiser; to ~ **down** vt (parcel etc) poser, déposer; (pay) verser; (in writing) mettre par écrit, inscrire; (suppress: revolt etc) réprimer, faire cesser; (attribute) attribuer; to ~ **forward** vt (ideas) avancer, proposer; (date) avancer; to ~ **in** vt (gas, electricity) installer; (application, complaint) soumettre; to ~ **off** vt (light etc) éteindre; (postpone) remettre à plus tard, ajourner; (discourage) dissuader; to ~ **on** vt (clothes, lipstick etc) mettre; (light etc) allumer; (play etc) monter; (food, meal) servir; (gain: weight) prendre; (brake) mettre; to ~ **on the brakes** freiner; to ~ **out** vt mettre dehors; (one's hand) tendre; (news, rumour) faire courir, répandre; (light etc) éteindre; (person: inconvenience) déranger, gêner; to ~ **up** vt (raise) lever, relever, remonter; (pin up) afficher; (hang) accrocher; (build) construire, ériger; (a tent) monter; (increase) augmenter;

(*accommodate*) loger ; to ~ up with *vt fus* supporter.
putrid ['pju:trɪd] *a* putride.
putt [pʌt] *vt* poter (la balle) // *n* coup roulé ; ~er *n* (GOLF) putter *m* ; ~ing green *n* green *m*.
putty ['pʌtɪ] *n* mastic *m*.
put-up ['putʌp] *a*: ~ job *n* affaire montée.
puzzle ['pʌzl] *n* énigme *f*, mystère *m*; (*jigsaw*) puzzle *m*; (*also*: crossword ~) problème *m* de mots croisés // *vt* intriguer, rendre perplexe // *vi* se creuser la tête; **puzzling** *a* déconcertant(e), inexplicable.
PVC *abbr of* polyvinyl chloride.
pygmy ['pɪgmɪ] *n* pygmée *m/f*.
pyjamas [pɪ'dʒɑ:məz] *npl* pyjama *m*.
pylon ['paɪlən] *n* pylône *m*.
pyramid ['pɪrəmɪd] *n* pyramide *f*.
python ['paɪθən] *n* python *m*.

Q

quack [kwæk] *n* (*of duck*) coin-coin *m inv*; (*pej: doctor*) charlatan *m*.
quad [kwɔd] *abbr of* quadrangle, quadruplet.
quadrangle ['kwɔdræŋgl] *n* (MATH) quadrilatère *m*; (*courtyard: abbr*: quad) cour *f*.
quadruped ['kwɔdruped] *n* quadrupède *m*.
quadruple [kwɔ'drupl] *a,n* quadruple (*m*) // *vt, vi* quadrupler ; ~t [-'dru:plɪt] *n* quadruplé/e.
quagmire ['kwægmaɪə*] *n* bourbier *m*.
quail [kweɪl] *n* (ZOOL) caille *f*.
quaint [kweɪnt] *a* bizarre ; (*old-fashioned*) désuet(ète) ; au charme vieillot, pittoresque.
quake [kweɪk] *vi* trembler // *n abbr of* **earthquake**.
Quaker ['kweɪkə*] *n* quaker/esse *n*.
qualification [kwɔlɪfɪ'keɪʃən] *n* (*degree etc*) diplôme *m*; (*ability*) compétence *f*, qualification *f*; (*limitation*) réserve *f*, restriction *f*.
qualified ['kwɔlɪfaɪd] *a* diplômé(e) ; (*able*) compétent(e), qualifié(e) ; (*limited*) conditionnel(le).
qualify ['kwɔlɪfaɪ] *vt* qualifier ; (*limit: statement*) apporter des réserves à // *vi*: to ~ (as) obtenir son diplôme (de) ; to ~ (for) remplir les conditions requises (pour) ; (SPORT) se qualifier (pour).
qualitative ['kwɔlɪtətɪv] *a* qualitatif(ive).
quality ['kwɔlɪtɪ] *n* qualité *f* // *cpd* de qualité ; the ~ papers la presse d'information.
qualm [kwɑ:m] *n* doute *m*; scrupule *m*.
quandary ['kwɔndrɪ] *n*: in a ~ devant un dilemme, dans l'embarras.
quantitative ['kwɔntɪtətɪv] *a* quantitatif(ive).
quantity ['kwɔntɪtɪ] *n* quantité *f*; ~ surveyor *n* métreur *m* vérificateur.
quarantine ['kwɔrəntiːn] *n* quarantaine *f*.
quarrel ['kwɔrl] *n* querelle *f*, dispute *f* // *vi* se disputer, se quereller ; ~some *a* querelleur(euse).
quarry ['kwɔrɪ] *n* (*for stone*) carrière *f*;

(*animal*) proie *f*, gibier *m* // *vt* (*marble etc*) extraire.
quart [kwɔ:t] *n* ≈ litre *m* (= 2 *pints*).
quarter ['kwɔ:tə*] *n* quart *m*; (*of year*) trimestre *m*; (*district*) quartier *m* // *vt* partager en quartiers *or* en quatre ; (MIL) caserner, cantonner ; ~s *npl* logement *m*; (MIL) quartiers *mpl*, cantonnement *m*; a ~ of an hour un quart d'heure ; ~-deck *n* (NAUT) plage *f* arrière ; ~ final *n* quart *m* de finale ; ~ly *a* trimestriel(le) // *ad* tous les trois mois ; ~master *n* (MIL) intendant *m* militaire de troisième classe ; (NAUT) maître *m* de manœuvre.
quartet(te) [kwɔ:'tɛt] *n* quatuor *m*; (*jazz players*) quartette *m*.
quartz [kwɔ:ts] *n* quartz *m*; ~ watch *n* montre *f* à quartz.
quash [kwɔʃ] *vt* (*verdict*) annuler, casser.
quasi- ['kweɪzaɪ] *prefix* quasi- + *noun*; quasi, presque + *adjective*.
quaver ['kweɪvə*] *n* (MUS) croche *f* // *vi* trembler.
quay [ki:] *n* (*also*: ~side) quai *m*.
queasy ['kwi:zɪ] *a* (*stomach*) délicat(e) ; to feel ~ avoir mal au cœur.
queen [kwi:n] *n* (*gen*) reine *f*; (CARDS *etc*) dame *f*; ~ mother *n* reine mère *f*.
queer [kwɪə*] *a* étrange, curieux(euse) ; (*suspicious*) louche ; (*sick*): I feel ~ je ne me sens pas bien // *n* (*col*) homosexuel *m*.
quell [kwɛl] *vt* réprimer, étouffer.
quench [kwɛntʃ] *vt* (*flames*) éteindre ; to ~ one's thirst se désaltérer.
query ['kwɪərɪ] *n* question *f*; (*doubt*) doute *m*; (*question mark*) point *m* d'interrogation // *vt* mettre en question *or* en doute.
quest [kwɛst] *n* recherche *f*, quête *f*.
question ['kwɛstʃən] *n* question *f* // *vt* (*person*) interroger ; (*plan, idea*) mettre en question *or* en doute ; it's a ~ of doing il s'agit de faire ; there's some ~ of doing il est question de faire ; beyond ~ *ad* sans aucun doute ; out of the ~ hors de question ; ~able *a* discutable ; ~ing *a* interrogateur(trice) // *n* interrogatoire *m*; ~ mark *n* point *m* d'interrogation.
questionnaire [kwɛstʃə'nɛə*] *n* questionnaire *m*.
queue [kju:] *n* queue *f*, file *f* // *vi* faire la queue.
quibble ['kwɪbl] *vi* ergoter, chicaner.
quick [kwɪk] *a* rapide ; (*reply*) prompt(e), rapide ; (*mind*) vif(vive) // *ad* vite, rapidement // *n*: cut to the ~ (*fig*) touché(e) au vif ; be ~! dépêche-toi! ; ~en *vt* accélérer, presser ; (*rouse*) stimuler // *vi* s'accélérer, devenir plus rapide ; ~lime *n* chaux vive ; ~ly *ad* vite, rapidement ; ~ness *n* rapidité *f*; promptitude *f*; vivacité *f*; ~sand *n* sables mouvants ; ~step *n* (*dance*) fox-trot *m*; ~-witted *a* à l'esprit vif.
quid [kwɪd] *n*, *pl inv* (*Brit: col*) livre *f*.
quiet ['kwaɪət] *a* tranquille, calme ; (*ceremony, colour*) discret(ète) // *n* tranquillité *f*, calme *m*; keep ~! tais-toi! ; on the ~ en secret, en cachette ; ~en (*also*: ~en down) *vi* se calmer, s'apaiser // *vt* calmer, apaiser ; ~ly *ad* tranquillement, calmement ;

discrètement; ~**ness** n tranquillité f, calme m; silence m.

quill [kwɪl] n plume f (d'oie).

quilt [kwɪlt] n édredon m; (**continental**) ~ n couverture f édredon; ~**ing** n ouatine f; molletonnage m.

quin [kwɪn] abbr of **quintuplet**.

quince [kwɪns] n coing m; (tree) cognassier m.

quinine [kwɪˈniːn] n quinine f.

quintet(te) [kwɪnˈtɛt] n quintette m.

quintuplet [kwɪnˈtjuːplɪt] n quintuplé/e.

quip [kwɪp] n remarque piquante or spirituelle, pointe f // vt: ... he ~**ped** ... lança-t-il.

quirk [kwəːk] n bizarrerie f.

quit, pt, pp **quit** or **quitted** [kwɪt] vt quitter // vi (give up) abandonner, renoncer; (resign) démissionner; to ~ **doing** arrêter de faire; **notice to** ~ congé m (signifié au locataire).

quite [kwaɪt] ad (rather) assez, plutôt; (entirely) complètement, tout à fait; **I** ~ **understand** je comprends très bien; ~ **a few of them** un assez grand nombre d'entre eux; ~ (**so**)! exactement!

quits [kwɪts] a: ~ (**with**) quitte (envers).

quiver [ˈkwɪvəˈ] vi trembler, frémir // n (for arrows) carquois m.

quiz [kwɪz] n (game) jeu-concours m; test m de connaissances // vt interroger; ~**zical** a narquois(e).

quoits [kwɔɪts] npl jeu m du palet.

quorum [ˈkwɔːrəm] n quorum m.

quota [ˈkwəʊtə] n quota m.

quotation [kwəʊˈteɪʃən] n citation f; (of shares etc) cote f, cours m; (estimate) devis m; ~ **marks** npl guillemets mpl.

quote [kwəʊt] n citation f // vi (sentence) citer; (price) donner, fixer; (shares) coter // vi: **to** ~ **from** citer; **to** ~ **for a job** établir un devis pour des travaux.

quotient [ˈkwəʊʃənt] n quotient m.

R

rabbi [ˈræbaɪ] n rabbin m.

rabbit [ˈræbɪt] n lapin m; ~ **hole** n terrier m (de lapin); ~ **hutch** n clapier m.

rabble [ˈræbl] n (pej) populace f.

rabid [ˈræbɪd] a enragé(e).

rabies [ˈreɪbiːz] n rage f.

RAC n abbr of Royal Automobile Club.

raccoon [rəˈkuːn] n raton m laveur.

race [reɪs] n race f; (competition, rush) course f // vt (person) faire la course avec; (horse) faire courir; (engine) emballer // vi courir; ~**course** n champ m de courses; ~**horse** n cheval m de course; ~ **relations** npl rapports mpl entre les races; ~**track** n piste f.

racial [ˈreɪʃl] a racial(e); ~ **discrimination** n discrimination raciale; ~**ism** n racisme m; ~**ist** a, n raciste m/f.

racing [ˈreɪsɪŋ] n courses fpl; ~ **car** n voiture f de course; ~ **driver** n pilote m de course.

racist [ˈreɪsɪst] a,n (pej) raciste (m/f).

rack [ræk] n (also: **luggage** ~) filet m à bagages; (also: **roof** ~) galerie f // vt tourmenter; **magazine** ~ n porte-revues

m inv; **shoe** ~ n étagère f à chaussures; **toast** ~ n porte-toast m.

racket [ˈrækɪt] n (for tennis) raquette f; (noise) tapage m; vacarme m; (swindle) escroquerie f; (organized crime) racket m.

racoon [rəˈkuːn] n = **raccoon**.

racquet [ˈrækɪt] n raquette f.

racy [ˈreɪsɪ] a plein(e) de verve; osé(e).

radar [ˈreɪdɑːˈ] n radar m // cpd radar inv.

radiance [ˈreɪdɪəns] n éclat m, rayonnement m.

radiant [ˈreɪdɪənt] a rayonnant(e); (PHYSICS) radiant(e).

radiate [ˈreɪdɪeɪt] vt (heat) émettre, dégager // vi (lines) rayonner.

radiation [reɪdɪˈeɪʃən] n rayonnement m; (radioactive) radiation f.

radiator [ˈreɪdɪeɪtəˈ] n radiateur m; ~ **cap** n bouchon m de radiateur.

radical [ˈrædɪkl] a radical(e).

radii [ˈreɪdɪaɪ] npl of **radius**.

radio [ˈreɪdɪəʊ] n radio f; **on the** ~ à la radio; ~ **station** station f de radio.

radio... [ˈreɪdɪəʊ] prefix: ~**active** a radioactif(ive); ~**activity** n radioactivité f; ~**grapher** [-ˈɒɡrəfəˈ] n radiologue m/f (technicien); ~**graphy** [-ˈɒɡrəfɪ] n radiographie f; ~**logy** [-ˈɒlədʒɪ] n radiologie f; ~**therapist** n radiothérapeute m/f.

radish [ˈrædɪʃ] n radis m.

radium [ˈreɪdɪəm] n radium m.

radius, pl **radii** [ˈreɪdɪəs, -ɪaɪ] n rayon m; (ANAT) radius m.

raffia [ˈræfɪə] n raphia m.

raffish [ˈræfɪʃ] a dissolu(e); canaille.

raffle [ˈræfl] n tombola f.

raft [rɑːft] n (also: **life** ~) radeau m; (logs) train m de flottage.

rafter [ˈrɑːftəˈ] n chevron m.

rag [ræg] n chiffon m; (pej: newspaper) feuille f, torchon m; (for charity) attractions organisées par les étudiants au profit d'œuv...es de charité // vt chahuter, mettre en boîte; ~**s** npl haillons mpl; ~**-and-bone man** n chiffonnier m; ~**bag** n (fig) ramassis m.

rage [reɪdʒ] n (fury) rage f, fureur f // vi (person) être fou(folle) de rage; (storm) faire rage, être déchaîné(e); **it's all the** ~ cela fait fureur.

ragged [ˈrægɪd] a (edge) inégal(e), qui accroche; (cuff) effiloché(e); (appearance) déguenillé(e).

raid [reɪd] n (MIL) raid m; (criminal) hold-up m inv; (by police) descente f, rafle f // vt faire un raid sur or un hold-up dans or une descente dans; ~**er** n malfaiteur m; (plane) bombardier m.

rail [reɪl] n (on stair) rampe f; (on bridge, balcony) balustrade f; (of ship) bastingage m; (for train) rail m; ~**s** npl rails mpl, voie ferrée; **by** ~ par chemin de fer; ~**ing(s)** n(pl) grille f; ~**road** n (US), ~**way** n chemin m de fer; ~**wayman** n cheminot m; ~**way station** n gare f.

rain [reɪn] n pluie f // vi pleuvoir; **in the** ~ sous la pluie; ~**bow** n arc-en-ciel m; ~**coat** n imperméable m; ~**drop** n goutte f de pluie; ~**fall** n chute f de pluie; (measurement) hauteur f des précipitations;

~proof *a* imperméable; ~storm *n* pluie torrentielle; ~y *a* pluvieux(euse).
raise [reɪz] *n* augmentation *f* // *vt* (*lift*) lever; hausser; (*build*) ériger; (*increase*) augmenter; (*a protest, doubt*) provoquer, causer; (*a question*) soulever; (*cattle, family*) élever; (*crop*) faire pousser; (*army, funds*) rassembler; (*loan*) obtenir; to ~ one's voice élever la voix.
raisin [ˈreɪzn] *n* raisin sec.
raj [rɑːdʒ] *n* empire *m* (*aux Indes*).
rajah [ˈrɑːdʒə] *n* radja(h) *m*.
rake [reɪk] *n* (*tool*) râteau *m*; (*person*) débauché *m* // *vt* (*garden*) ratisser; (*fire*) tisonner; (*with machine gun*) balayer; to ~ **through** (*fig: search*) fouiller (dans).
rakish [ˈreɪkɪʃ] *a* dissolu(e); cavalier(ère).
rally [ˈrælɪ] *n* (*POL etc*) meeting *m*, rassemblement *m*; (*AUT*) rallye *m*; (*TENNIS*) échange *m* // *vt* rassembler, rallier // *vi* se rallier; (*sick person*) aller mieux; (*Stock Exchange*) reprendre; to ~ **round** *vt fus* se rallier à; venir en aide à.
ram [ræm] *n* bélier *m* // *vt* enfoncer; (*soil*) tasser; (*crash into*) emboutir; percuter; éperonner.
ramble [ˈræmbl] *n* randonnée *f* // *vi* (*pej: also*: ~ **on**) discourir, pérorer; ~**r** *n* promeneur/euse, randonneur/euse; (*BOT*) rosier grimpant; **rambling** *a* (*speech*) décousu(e); (*BOT*) grimpant(e).
ramification [ræmɪfɪˈkeɪʃən] *n* ramification *f*.
ramp [ræmp] *n* (*incline*) rampe *f*; dénivellation *f*; (*in garage*) pont *m*.
rampage [ræmˈpeɪdʒ] *n*: to be on the ~ se déchaîner // *vi*: **they went rampaging through the town** ils ont envahi les rues et ont tout saccagé sur leur passage.
rampant [ˈræmpənt] *a* (*disease etc*) qui sévit.
rampart [ˈræmpɑːt] *n* rempart *m*.
ramshackle [ˈræmʃækl] *a* (*house*) délabré(e); (*car etc*) déglingué(e).
ran [ræn] *pt of* run.
ranch [rɑːntʃ] *n* ranch *m*; ~**er** *n* propriétaire *m* de ranch; cowboy *m*.
rancid [ˈrænsɪd] *a* rance.
rancour, rancor (*US*) [ˈræŋkə*] *n* rancune *f*.
random [ˈrændəm] *a* fait(e) or établi(e) au hasard // *n*: at ~ au hasard.
randy [ˈrændɪ] *a* (*col*) excité(e); lubrique.
rang [ræŋ] *pt of* ring.
range [reɪndʒ] *n* (*of mountains*) chaîne *f*; (*of missile, voice*) portée *f*; (*of products*) choix *m*, gamme *f*; (*MIL: also*: **shooting** ~) champ *m* de tir; (*also*: **kitchen** ~) fourneau *m* (de cuisine) // *vt* (*place*) mettre en rang, placer; (*roam*) parcourir // *vi*: to ~ **over** couvrir; to ~ **from ... to** aller de ... à; ~**r** *n* garde *m* forestier.
rank [ræŋk] *n* rang *m*; (*MIL*) grade *m*; (*also*: **taxi** ~) station *f* de taxis // *vi*: to ~ **among** compter or se classer parmi // *a* (qui sent) fort(e); extrême; **the** ~**s** (*MIL*) la troupe; **the** ~ **and file** (*fig*) la masse, la base.
rankle [ˈræŋkl] *vi* (*insult*) rester sur le cœur.

ransack [ˈrænsæk] *vt* fouiller (à fond); (*plunder*) piller.
ransom [ˈrænsəm] *n* rançon *f*; to **hold sb** to ~ (*fig*) exercer un chantage sur qn.
rant [rænt] *vi* fulminer; ~**ing** *n* invectives *fpl*.
rap [ræp] *n* petit coup sec; tape *f* // *vt* frapper sur or à; taper sur.
rape [reɪp] *n* viol *m* // *vt* violer.
rapid [ˈræpɪd] *a* rapide; ~**s** *npl* (*GEO*) rapides *mpl*; ~**ity** [rəˈpɪdɪtɪ] *n* rapidité *f*.
rapist [ˈreɪpɪst] *n* auteur *m* d'un viol.
rapport [ræˈpɔː*] *n* entente *f*.
rapture [ˈræptʃə*] *n* extase *f*, ravissement *m*; to **go into** ~**s over** s'extasier sur; **rapturous** *a* extasié(e); frénétique.
rare [reə*] *a* rare; (*CULIN: steak*) saignant(e).
rarebit [ˈreəbɪt] *n see* Welsh.
rarefied [ˈreərɪfaɪd] *a* (*air, atmosphere*) raréfié(e).
rarely [ˈreəlɪ] *ad* rarement.
rarity [ˈreərɪtɪ] *n* rareté *f*.
rascal [ˈrɑːskl] *n* vaurien *m*.
rash [ræʃ] *a* imprudent(e), irréfléchi(e) // *n* (*MED*) rougeur *f*, éruption *f*.
rasher [ˈræʃə*] *n* fine tranche (de lard).
rasp [rɑːsp] *n* (*tool*) lime *f*.
raspberry [ˈrɑːzbərɪ] *n* framboise *f*; ~**bush** *n* framboisier *m*.
rasping [ˈrɑːspɪŋ] *a*: ~ **noise** grincement *m*.
rat [ræt] *n* rat *m*.
ratable [ˈreɪtəbl] *a* = rateable.
ratchet [ˈrætʃɪt] *n*: ~ **wheel** roue *f* à rochet.
rate [reɪt] *n* (*ratio*) taux *m*, pourcentage *m*; (*speed*) vitesse *f*, rythme *m*; (*price*) tarif *m* // *vt* classer; évaluer; to ~ **sb/sth as** considérer qn/qch comme; to ~ **sb/sth among** classer qn/qch parmi; ~**s** *npl* (*Brit*) impôts locaux; (*fees*) tarifs *mpl*; ~**able value** *n* valeur locative imposable; ~ **of exchange** *n* taux *m* or cours *m* du change; ~ **of flow** *n* débit *m*; ~**payer** *n* contribuable *m/f* (*payant les impôts locaux*).
rather [ˈrɑːðə*] *ad* plutôt; **it's** ~ **expensive** c'est assez cher; (*too much*) c'est un peu cher; **I would** or **I'd** ~ **go** j'aimerais mieux or je préférerais partir; **I had** ~ **go** il vaudrait mieux que je parte.
ratification [rætɪfɪˈkeɪʃən] *n* ratification *f*.
ratify [ˈrætɪfaɪ] *vt* ratifier.
rating [ˈreɪtɪŋ] *n* classement *m*; cote *f*; (*NAUT: category*) classe *f*; (: *sailor*) matelot *m*.
ratio [ˈreɪʃɪəu] *n* proportion *f*; **in the** ~ **of 100 to 1** dans la proportion de 100 contre 1.
ration [ˈræʃən] *n* (*gen pl*) ration(s) *f(pl)* // *vt* rationner.
rational [ˈræʃənl] *a* raisonnable, sensé(e); (*solution, reasoning*) logique; (*MED*) lucide; ~**e** [-ˈnɑːl] *n* raisonnement *m*; justification *f*; ~**ize** *vt* rationaliser; (*conduct*) essayer d'expliquer or de motiver; ~**ly** *ad* raisonnablement; logiquement.
rationing [ˈræʃnɪŋ] *n* rationnement *m*.
rat poison [ˈrætpɔɪzn] *n* mort-aux-rats *f inv*.

rat race ['rætreɪs] n foire f d'empoigne.

rattle ['rætl] n cliquetis m; (louder) bruit m de ferraille; (object: of baby) hochet m; (: of sports fan) crécelle f // vi cliqueter; faire un bruit de ferraille or du bruit // vt agiter (bruyamment); ~snake n serpent m à sonnettes.

raucous ['rɔːkəs] a rauque; ~ly ad d'une voix rauque.

ravage ['rævɪdʒ] vt ravager; ~s npl ravages mpl.

rave [reɪv] vi (in anger) s'emporter; (with enthusiasm) s'extasier; (MED) délirer.

raven ['reɪvən] n corbeau m.

ravenous ['rævənəs] a affamé(e).

ravine [rə'viːn] n ravin m.

raving ['reɪvɪŋ] a: ~ lunatic n fou furieux/folle furieuse.

ravioli [rævɪ'əulɪ] n ravioli mpl.

ravish ['rævɪʃ] vt ravir; ~ing a enchanteur(eresse).

raw [rɔː] a (uncooked) cru(e); (not processed) brut(e); (sore) à vif, irrité(e); (inexperienced) inexpérimenté(e); ~ material n matière première.

ray [reɪ] n rayon m; ~ of hope n lueur f d'espoir.

rayon ['reɪɔn] n rayonne f.

raze [reɪz] vt raser, détruire.

razor ['reɪzə*] n rasoir m; ~ blade n lame f de rasoir.

Rd abbr of road.

re [riː] prep concernant.

reach [riːtʃ] n portée f, atteinte f; (of river etc) étendue f // vt atteindre; parvenir à // vi s'étendre; out of/within ~ (object) hors de/à portée; within easy ~ (of) (place) à proximité (de), proche (de); to ~ out vi: to ~ out for allonger le bras pour prendre.

react [riː'ækt] vi réagir; ~ion [-'ækʃən] n réaction f; ~ionary [-'ækʃənrɪ] a,n réactionnaire (m/f).

reactor [riː'æktə*] n réacteur m.

read, pt,pp read [riːd, rɛd] vi lire // vt lire; (understand) comprendre, interpréter; (study) étudier; (subj: instrument etc) indiquer, marquer; to ~ out vt lire à haute voix; ~able a facile or agréable à lire; ~er n lecteur/trice; (book) livre m de lecture; (at university) maître m de conférences; ~ership n (of paper etc) (nombre m de) lecteurs mpl.

readily ['rɛdɪlɪ] ad volontiers, avec empressement; (easily) facilement.

readiness ['rɛdɪnɪs] n empressement m; in ~ (prepared) prêt(e).

reading ['riːdɪŋ] n lecture f; (understanding) interprétation f; (on instrument) indications fpl; ~ lamp n lampe f de bureau; ~ room n salle f de lecture.

readjust [riːə'dʒʌst] vt rajuster; (instrument) régler de nouveau // vi (person): to ~ (to) se réadapter (à).

ready ['rɛdɪ] a prêt(e); (willing) prêt, disposé(e); (quick) prompt(e); (available) disponible // ad: ~-cooked tout(e) cuit(e) (d'avance) // n: at the ~ (MIL) prêt à faire feu; (fig) tout(e) prêt(e); ~ cash n argent m) liquide m; ~-made a tout(e) fait(e); ~-mix n (for cakes etc) préparation f en

sachet; ~ reckoner n barème m; ~-to-wear a en prêt-à-porter.

real [rɪəl] a réel(le); véritable; in ~ terms dans la réalité; ~ estate n biens fonciers or immobiliers; ~ism n (also ART) réalisme m; ~ist n réaliste m/f; ~istic [-'lɪstɪk] a réaliste.

reality [riː'ælɪtɪ] n réalité f; in ~ en réalité, en fait.

realization [rɪəlaɪ'zeɪʃən] n prise f de conscience; réalisation f.

realize ['rɪəlaɪz] vt (understand) se rendre compte de; (a project, COMM: asset) réaliser.

really ['rɪəlɪ] ad vraiment.

realm [rɛlm] n royaume m.

ream [riːm] n rame f (de papier).

reap [riːp] vt moissonner; (fig) récolter; ~er n (machine) moissonneuse f.

reappear [riːə'pɪə*] vi réapparaître, reparaître; ~ance n réapparition f.

reapply [riːə'plaɪ] vi: to ~ for faire une nouvelle demande d'emploi concernant; reposer sa candidature à.

rear [rɪə*] a de derrière, arrière inv; (AUT: wheel etc) arrière // n arrière m, derrière m // vt (cattle, family) élever // vi (also: ~ up) (animal) se cabrer; ~-engined a (AUT) avec moteur à l'arrière; ~guard n arrière-garde f.

rearm [riː'ɑːm] vt, vi réarmer; ~ament n réarmement m.

rearrange [riːə'reɪndʒ] vt réarranger.

rear-view ['rɪəvjuː] a: ~ mirror n (AUT) rétroviseur m.

reason ['riːzn] n raison f // vi: to ~ with sb raisonner qn, faire entendre raison à qn; to have ~ to think avoir lieu de penser; it stands to ~ that il va sans dire que; ~able a raisonnable; (not bad) acceptable; ~ably ad raisonnablement; one can ~ably assume that ... on est fondé à or il est permis de supposer que ...; ~ed a (argument) raisonné(e); ~ing n raisonnement m.

reassemble [riːə'sɛmbl] vt rassembler; (machine) remonter.

reassert [riːə'səːt] vt réaffirmer.

reassure [riːə'ʃuə*] vt rassurer; to ~ sb of donner à qn l'assurance répétée de; reassuring a rassurant(e).

reawakening [riːə'weɪknɪŋ] n réveil m.

rebate ['riːbeɪt] n (on product) rabais m; (on tax etc) dégrèvement m; (repayment) remboursement m.

rebel n ['rɛbl] rebelle m/f // vi [rɪ'bɛl] se rebeller, se révolter; ~lion n rébellion f, révolte f; ~lious a rebelle.

rebirth [riː'bəːθ] n renaissance f.

rebound vi [rɪ'baund] (ball) rebondir; (bullet) ricocher // n ['riːbaund] rebond m; ricochet m.

rebuff [rɪ'bʌf] n rebuffade f // vt repousser.

rebuild [riː'bɪld] vt irg reconstruire.

rebuke [rɪ'bjuːk] n réprimande f, reproche m // vt réprimander.

rebut [rɪ'bʌt] vt réfuter; ~tal n réfutation f.

recall [rɪ'kɔːl] vt rappeler; (remember) se rappeler, se souvenir de // n rappel m; beyond ~ a irrévocable.

recant [rɪ'kænt] vi se rétracter; (REL) abjurer.

recap ['riːkæp] n récapitulation f // vt, vi récapituler.

recapture [riː'kæptʃə°] vt reprendre; (atmosphere) recréer.

recede [rɪ'siːd] vi s'éloigner; reculer; redescendre; **receding** a (forehead, chin) fuyant(e); **receding hairline** n front dégarni.

receipt [rɪ'siːt] n (document) reçu m; (for parcel etc) accusé m de réception; (act of receiving) réception f; **~s** npl (COMM) recettes fpl.

receive [rɪ'siːv] vt recevoir; (guest) recevoir, accueillir.

receiver [rɪ'siːvə°] n (TEL) récepteur m, combiné m; (of stolen goods) receleur m; (COMM) administrateur m judiciaire.

recent ['riːsnt] a récent(e); **~ly** ad récemment; **as ~ly as** pas plus tard que.

receptacle [rɪ'sɛptɪkl] n récipient m.

reception [rɪ'sɛpʃən] n réception f; (welcome) accueil m, réception; **~ desk** n réception; **~ist** n réceptionniste m/f.

receptive [rɪ'sɛptɪv] a réceptif(ive).

recess [rɪ'sɛs] n (in room) renfoncement m; (for bed) alcôve f; (secret place) recoin m; (POL etc: holiday) vacances fpl.

recharge [riː'tʃɑːdʒ] vt (battery) recharger.

recipe ['rɛsɪpɪ] n recette f.

recipient [rɪ'sɪpɪənt] n bénéficiaire m/f; (of letter) destinataire m/f.

reciprocal [rɪ'sɪprəkl] a réciproque.

reciprocate [rɪ'sɪprəkeɪt] vt retourner, offrir en retour.

recital [rɪ'saɪtl] n récital m.

recite [rɪ'saɪt] vt (poem) réciter; (complaints etc) énumérer.

reckless ['rɛkləs] a (driver etc) imprudent(e); (spender etc) insouciant(e); **~ly** ad imprudemment; avec insouciance.

reckon ['rɛkən] vt (count) calculer, compter; (consider) considérer, estimer; (think): **I ~ that ...** je pense que ...; **to ~ on** vt fus compter sur, s'attendre à; **~ing** n compte m, calcul m; **estimation** f; **the day of ~ing** le jour du Jugement.

reclaim [rɪ'kleɪm] vt (land) amender; (: from sea) assécher; (: from forest) défricher; (demand back) réclamer (le remboursement or la restitution de); **reclamation** [rɛklə'meɪʃən] n amendement m; assèchement m; défrichement m.

recline [rɪ'klaɪn] vi être allongé(e) or étendu(e); **reclining** a (seat) à dossier réglable.

recluse [rɪ'kluːs] n reclus/e, ermite m.

recognition [rɛkəg'nɪʃən] n reconnaissance f; **to gain ~** être reconnu(e); **transformed beyond ~** méconnaissable.

recognizable ['rɛkəgnaɪzəbl] a: **~ (by)** reconnaissable (à).

recognize ['rɛkəgnaɪz] vt: **to ~ (by/as)** reconnaître (à/comme étant).

recoil [rɪ'kɔɪl] vi (gun) reculer; (spring) se détendre; (person): **to ~ (from)** reculer (devant) // n recul m; détente f.

recollect [rɛkə'lɛkt] vt se rappeler, se souvenir de; **~ion** [-'lɛkʃən] n souvenir m.

recommend [rɛkə'mɛnd] vt recommander; **~ation** [-'deɪʃən] n recommandation f.

recompense ['rɛkəmpɛns] vt récompenser; (compensate) dédommager.

reconcilable ['rɛkənsaɪləbl] a (ideas) conciliable.

reconcile ['rɛkənsaɪl] vt (two people) réconcilier; (two facts) concilier, accorder; **to ~ o.s. to** se résigner à; **reconciliation** [-sɪlɪ'eɪʃən] n réconciliation f; conciliation f.

recondition [riːkən'dɪʃən] vt remettre à neuf; réviser entièrement.

reconnaissance [rɪ'kɒnɪsns] n (MIL) reconnaissance f.

reconnoitre, reconnoiter (US) [rɛkə'nɔɪtə°] (MIL) vt reconnaître // vi faire une reconnaissance.

reconsider [riːkən'sɪdə°] vt reconsidérer.

reconstitute [riː'kɒnstɪtjuːt] vt reconstituer.

reconstruct [riːkən'strʌkt] vt (building) reconstruire; (crime) reconstituer; **~ion** [-kʃən] n reconstruction f; reconstitution f.

record n ['rɛkɔːd] rapport m, récit m; (of meeting etc) procès-verbal m; (register) registre m; (file) dossier m; (also: police ~) casier m judiciaire; (MUS: disc) disque m; (SPORT) record m // vt [rɪ'kɔːd] (set down) noter; (relate) rapporter; (MUS: song etc) enregistrer; **in ~ time** dans un temps record inv; **to keep a ~ of** noter; **off the ~ a** officieux(euse); **to keep the ~ straight** (fig) mettre les choses au point; **~ card** n (in file) fiche f; **~er** n (LAW) avocat nommé à la fonction de juge; (MUS) flûte f à bec; **~ holder** n (SPORT) détenteur/trice du record; **~ing** n (MUS) enregistrement m; **~ library** n discothèque f; **~ player** n électrophone m.

recount [rɪ'kaʊnt] vt raconter.

re-count n ['riːkaʊnt] (POL: of votes) pointage m // vt [riː'kaʊnt] recompter.

recoup [rɪ'kuːp] vt: **to ~ one's losses** récupérer ce qu'on a perdu, se refaire.

recourse [rɪ'kɔːs] n recours m; expédient m; **to have ~ to** recourir à, avoir recours à.

recover [rɪ'kʌvə°] vt récupérer // vi (from illness) se rétablir; (from shock) se remettre; (country) se redresser.

re-cover [riː'kʌvə°] vt (chair etc) recouvrir.

recovery [rɪ'kʌvərɪ] n récupération f; rétablissement m; redressement m.

recreate [riːkrɪ'eɪt] vt recréer.

recreation [rɛkrɪ'eɪʃən] n récréation f; détente f; **~al** a pour la détente, récréatif(ive).

recrimination [rɪkrɪmɪ'neɪʃən] n récrimination f.

recruit [rɪ'kruːt] n recrue f // vt recruter; **~ing office** n bureau m de recrutement; **~ment** n recrutement m.

rectangle ['rɛktæŋgl] n rectangle m; **rectangular** [-'tæŋgjulə°] a rectangulaire.

rectify ['rɛktɪfaɪ] vt (error) rectifier, corriger; (omission) réparer.

rector ['rɛktə°] n (REL) pasteur m; **rectory** n presbytère m.

recuperate [rɪ'kjuːpəreɪt] *vi* récupérer; (*from illness*) se rétablir.

recur [rɪ'kəː*] *vi* se reproduire; (*idea, opportunity*) se retrouver; (*symptoms*) réapparaître; ~**rence** *n* répétition *f*; réapparition *f*; ~**rent** *a* périodique, fréquent(e); ~**ring** *a* (*MATH*) périodique.

red [rɛd] *n* rouge *m*; (*POL: pej*) rouge *m/f* // a rouge; in the ~ (*account*) à découvert; (*business*) en déficit; ~ **carpet treatment** *n* réception *f* en grande pompe; R~ **Cross** *n* Croix-Rouge *f*; ~ **currant** *n* groseille *f* (rouge); ~**den** *vt,vi* rougir; ~**dish** *a* rougeâtre; (*hair*) plutôt roux(rousse).

redecorate [riː'dɛkəreɪt] *vt* refaire à neuf, repeindre et retapisser; **redecoration** [-'reɪʃən] *n* remise *f* à neuf.

redeem [rɪ'diːm] *vt* (*debt*) rembourser; (*sth in pawn*) dégager; (*fig, also REL*) racheter; ~**ing** *a* (*feature*) qui sauve, qui rachète (le reste).

redeploy [riːdɪ'plɔɪ] *vt* (*resources*) réorganiser.

red-haired [rɛd'hɛəd] *a* roux(rousse).

red-handed [rɛd'hændɪd] *a*: to be caught ~ être pris(e) en flagrant délit *or* la main dans le sac.

redhead ['rɛdhɛd] *n* roux/rousse.

red herring ['rɛd'hɛrɪŋ] *n* (*fig*) diversion *f*, fausse piste.

red-hot [rɛd'hɔt] *a* chauffé(e) au rouge, brûlant(e).

redirect [riːdaɪ'rɛkt] *vt* (*mail*) faire suivre.

redistribute [riːdɪ'strɪbjuːt] *vt* redistribuer.

red-letter day ['rɛdlɛtə'deɪ] *n* grand jour, jour mémorable.

red light ['rɛd'laɪt] *n*: to go through a ~ (*AUT*) brûler un feu rouge; **red-light district** *n* quartier réservé.

redness ['rɛdnɪs] *n* rougeur *f*; (*of hair*) rousseur *f*.

redo [riː'duː] *vt irg* refaire.

redolent ['rɛdəulnt] *a*: ~ of qui sent; (*fig*) qui évoque.

redouble [riː'dʌbl] *vt*: to ~ one's efforts redoubler d'efforts.

redress [rɪ'drɛs] *n* réparation *f*.

red tape ['rɛd'teɪp] *n* (*fig*) paperasserie *f* (administrative).

reduce [rɪ'djuːs] *vt* réduire; (*lower*) abaisser; '~ **speed now**' (*AUT*) 'ralentir'; at a ~**d price** (*of goods*) au rabais, en solde; (*of ticket etc*) à prix réduit; **reduction** [rɪ'dʌkʃən] *n* réduction *f*; (*of price*) baisse *f*; (*discount*) rabais *m*; réduction.

redundancy [rɪ'dʌndənsɪ] *n* licenciement *m*, mise *f* au chômage.

redundant [rɪ'dʌndnt] *a* (*worker*) mis(e) au chômage, licencié(e); (*detail, object*) superflu(e); to make ~ licencier, mettre au chômage.

reed [riːd] *n* (*BOT*) roseau *m*; (*MUS: of clarinet etc*) anche *f*.

reef [riːf] *n* (*at sea*) récif *m*, écueil *m*.

reek [riːk] *vi*: to ~ (of) puer, empester.

reel [riːl] *n* bobine *f*; (*TECH*) dévidoir *m*; (*FISHING*) moulinet *m*; (*CINEMA*) bande *f* // *vt* (*TECH*) bobiner; (*also*: ~ **up**) enrouler // *vi* (*sway*) chanceler.

re-election [riːɪ'lɛkʃən] *n* réélection *f*.

re-engage [riːɪn'geɪdʒ] *vt* (*worker*) réembaucher.

re-enter [riː'ɛntə*] *vt* rentrer dans; **re-entry** *n* rentrée *f*.

ref [rɛf] *n* (*col: abbr of referee*) arbitre *m*.

refectory [rɪ'fɛktərɪ] *n* réfectoire *m*.

refer [rɪ'fəː*] *vt*: to ~ sb (or sth) to (*dispute, decision*) soumettre qch à; (*inquirer: for information*) adresser *or* envoyer qn à; (*reader: to text*) renvoyer qn à; to ~ to *vt fus* (*allude to*) parler de, faire allusion à; (*apply to*) s'appliquer à; (*consult*) se reporter à; ~**ring to your letter** (*COMM*) en réponse à votre lettre.

referee [rɛfə'riː] *n* arbitre *m*; (*for job application*) répondant/e // *vt* arbitrer.

reference ['rɛfrəns] *n* référence *f*, renvoi *m*; (*mention*) allusion *f*, mention *f*; (*for job application: letter*) références; lettre *f* de recommandation; (: *person*) répondant/e; **with** ~ **to** en ce qui concerne; (*COMM: in letter*) me référant à; '**please quote this** ~' (*COMM*) 'prière de rappeler cette référence'; ~ **book** *n* ouvrage *m* de référence.

referendum, *pl* **referenda** [rɛfə'rɛndəm, -də] *n* référendum *m*.

refill *vt* [riː'fɪl] remplir à nouveau; (*pen, lighter etc*) recharger // *n* ['riːfɪl] (*for pen etc*) recharge *f*.

refine [rɪ'faɪn] *vt* (*sugar, oil*) raffiner; (*taste*) affiner; ~**d** *a* (*person, taste*) raffiné(e); ~**ment** *n* (*of person*) raffinement *m*; ~**ry** *n* raffinerie *f*.

reflect [rɪ'flɛkt] *vt* (*light, image*) réfléchir, refléter; (*fig*) refléter // *vi* (*think*) réfléchir, méditer; to ~ on *vt fus* (*discredit*) porter atteinte à, faire tort à; ~**ion** [-'flɛkʃən] *n* réflexion *f*; (*image*) reflet *m*; (*criticism*): ~**ion on** critique *f* de; atteinte *f* à; on ~**ion** réflexion faite; ~**or** *n* (*also AUT*) réflecteur *m*.

reflex ['riːflɛks] *a, n* réflexe (*m*); ~**ive** [rɪ'flɛksɪv] *a* (*LING*) réfléchi(e).

reform [rɪ'fɔːm] *n* réforme *f* // *vt* réformer; **the R~ation** [rɛfə'meɪʃən] *n* la Réforme; ~**ed** *a* amendé(e), assagi(e); ~**er** *n* réformateur/trice.

refrain [rɪ'freɪn] *vi*: to ~ **from doing** s'abstenir de faire // *n* refrain *m*.

refresh [rɪ'frɛʃ] *vt* rafraîchir; (*subj: food*) redonner des forces à; (: *sleep*) reposer; ~**er course** *n* cours *m* de recyclage; ~**ment room** *n* buffet *m*; ~**ments** *npl* rafraîchissements *mpl*.

refrigeration [rɪfrɪdʒə'reɪʃən] *n* réfrigération *f*.

refrigerator [rɪ'frɪdʒəreɪtə*] *n* réfrigérateur *m*, frigidaire *m*.

refuel [riː'fjuəl] *vt* ravitailler en carburant // *vi* se ravitailler en carburant.

refuge ['rɛfjuːdʒ] *n* refuge *m*; to take ~ in se réfugier dans.

refugee [rɛfju'dʒiː] *n* réfugié/e.

refund *n* ['riːfʌnd] remboursement *m* // *vt* [rɪ'fʌnd] rembourser.

refurbish [riː'fəːbɪʃ] *vt* remettre à neuf.

refurnish [riː'fəːnɪʃ] *vt* remeubler.

refusal [rɪ'fjuːzəl] *n* refus *m*.

refuse n ['rɛfjuːs] ordures fpl, détritus mpl // vt, vi [rɪ'fjuːz] refuser ; ~ **collection** n ramassage m d'ordures ; ~ **collector** n éboueur m.

refute [rɪ'fjuːt] vt réfuter.

regain [rɪ'geɪn] vt regagner ; retrouver.

regal ['riːɡl] a royal(e) ; ~**ia** [rɪ'ɡeɪlɪə] n insignes mpl de la royauté.

regard [rɪ'ɡaːd] n respect m, estime f, considération f // vt considérer ; to give one's ~s to faire ses amitiés à ; 'with kindest ~s' 'bien amicalement' ; ~**ing**, as ~s, with ~ to en ce qui concerne ; ~**less** ad quand même ; ~**less of** sans se soucier de.

regatta [rɪ'ɡætə] n régate f.

regency ['riːdʒənsɪ] n régence f.

regent ['riːdʒənt] n régent/e.

régime [reɪ'ʒiːm] n régime m.

regiment ['rɛdʒɪmənt] n régiment m ; ~**al** [-'mɛntl] a d'un or du régiment ; ~**ation** [-'teɪʃən] n réglementation excessive.

region ['riːdʒən] n région f ; **in the** ~ **of** (fig) aux alentours de ; ~**al** a régional(e) ; ~**al development** n aménagement m du territoire.

register ['rɛdʒɪstə*] n registre m ; (also: **electoral** ~) liste électorale // vt en- registrer, inscrire ; (birth) déclarer ; (vehicle) immatriculer ; (luggage) enregistrer ; (letter) envoyer en recommandé ; (subj: instrument) marquer // vi se faire inscrire ; (at hotel) signer le registre ; (make impression) être (bien) com- pris(e) ; ~**ed** a (design) déposé(e) ; (letter) recommandé(e).

registrar ['rɛdʒɪstraː*] n officier m de l'état civil ; secrétaire (général).

registration [rɛdʒɪs'treɪʃən] n (act) en- registrement m ; inscription f ; (AUT: also: ~ **number**) numéro m d'immatriculation.

registry ['rɛdʒɪstrɪ] n bureau m de l'enregistrement f, ~ **office** n bureau m de l'état civil ; **to get married in a** ~ **office** ≈ se marier à la mairie.

regret [rɪ'ɡrɛt] n regret m // vt regretter ; **to** ~ **that** regretter que + sub ; ~**fully** ad à or avec regret ; ~**table** a regrettable.

regroup [riː'ɡruːp] vt regrouper // vi se regrouper.

regular ['rɛɡjulə*] a régulier(ère) ; (usual) habituel(le), normal(e) ; (soldier) de métier ; (COMM: size) ordinaire // n (client etc) habitué/e ; ~**ity** [-'lærɪtɪ] n régularité f ; ~**ly** ad régulièrement.

regulate ['rɛɡjuleɪt] vt régler ; **regulation** [-'leɪʃən] n (rule) règlement m ; (adjust- ment) réglage m // cpd réglementaire.

rehabilitation ['riːhəbɪlɪ'teɪʃən] n (of offender) réhabilitation f ; (of disabled) rééducation f, réadaptation f.

rehash [riː'hæʃ] vt (col) remanier.

rehearsal [rɪ'həːsəl] n répétition f.

rehearse [rɪ'həːs] vt répéter.

reign [reɪn] n règne m // vi régner ; ~**ing** a (monarch) régnant(e) ; (champion) ac- tuel(le).

reimburse [riːɪm'bəːs] vt rembourser.

rein [reɪn] n (for horse) rêne f.

reincarnation [riːɪnkɑː'neɪʃən] n réincar- nation f.

reindeer ['reɪndɪə*] n (pl inv) renne m.

reinforce [riːɪn'fɔːs] vt renforcer ; ~**d con- crete** n béton armé ; ~**ment** n (action) ren- forcement m ; ~**ments** npl (MIL) renfort(s) m(pl).

reinstate [riːɪn'steɪt] vt rétablir, réintégrer.

reissue [riː'ɪʃuː] vt (book) rééditer ; (film) ressortir.

reiterate [riː'ɪtəreɪt] vt réitérer, répéter.

reject n ['riːdʒɛkt] article m de rebut // vt [rɪ'dʒɛkt] refuser ; (COMM goods) mettre au rebut ; (idea) rejeter ; ~**ion** [rɪ'dʒɛkʃən] n rejet m, refus m.

rejoice [rɪ'dʒɔɪs] vi: **to** ~ (at or over) se réjouir (de).

rejuvenate [rɪ'dʒuːvəneɪt] vt rajeunir.

rekindle [riː'kɪndl] vt rallumer ; (fig) raviver.

relapse [rɪ'læps] n (MED) rechute f.

relate [rɪ'leɪt] vt (tell) raconter ; (connect) établir un rapport entre ; ~**d** a apparenté(e) ; ~**d to** apparenté à ; **relating: relating to** prep concernant.

relation [rɪ'leɪʃən] n (person) parent/e ; (link) rapport m, lien m ; ~**ship** n rapport m, lien m ; (personal ties) relations fpl, rap- ports ; (also: **family** ~**ship**) lien m de parenté ; (affair) liaison f.

relative ['rɛlətɪv] n parent/e // a relatif(ive) ; (respective) respectif(ive) ; **all her** ~**s** toute sa famille ; ~**ly** ad relative- ment.

relax [rɪ'læks] vi se relâcher ; (person: unwind) se détendre // vt relâcher ; (mind, person) détendre ; ~**ation** [riːlæk'seɪʃən] n relâchement m ; détente f ; (entertainment) distraction f ; ~**ed** a relâché(e) ; détendu(e) ; ~**ing** a délassant(e).

relay ['riːleɪ] n (SPORT) course f de relais // vt (message) retransmettre, relayer.

release [rɪ'liːs] n (from prison, obligation) libération f ; (of gas etc) émission f ; (of film etc) sortie f ; (record) disque m ; (device) déclencheur m // vt (prisoner) libérer ; (book, film) sortir ; (report, news) rendre publ.., publier ; (gas etc) émettre, dégager ; (free: from wreckage etc) dégager ; (TECH: catch, spring etc) déclencher ; (let go) relâcher ; lâcher ; desserrer ; **to** ~ **one's grip** or **hold** lâcher prise ; **to** ~ **the clutch** (AUT) débrayer.

relegate ['rɛləɡeɪt] vt reléguer.

relent [rɪ'lɛnt] vi se laisser fléchir ; ~**less** a implacable.

relevance ['rɛləvəns] n pertinence f ; ~ **of sth to sth** rapport m entre qch et qch.

relevant ['rɛləvənt] a approprié(e) ; (fact) significatif(ive) ; (information) utile, perti- nent(e) ; ~ **to** ayant rapport à, approprié à.

reliability [rɪlaɪə'bɪlɪtɪ] n sérieux m ; solidité f.

reliable [rɪ'laɪəbl] a (person, firm) sérieux(euse) ; (method) sûr(e) ; (machine) solide ; **reliably** ad: **to be reliably in- formed** savoir de source sûre.

reliance [rɪ'laɪəns] n: ~ (on) confiance f (en) ; besoin m (de), dépendance f (de).

relic ['rɛlɪk] n (REL) relique f ; (of the past) vestige m.

relief [rɪ'liːf] n (from pain, anxiety) soulage- ment m ; (help, supplies) secours m(pl) ; (of guard) relève f; (ART, GEO) relief m; ~ road n route f de délestage; ~ valve n soupape f de sûreté.

relieve [rɪ'li:v] vt (pain, patient) soulager; (bring help) secourir; (take over from: gen) relayer; (: guard) relever; to ~ sb of sth débarrasser qn de qch.

religion [rɪ'lɪdʒən] n religion f; religious a religieux(euse); (book) de piété.

reline [ri:'laɪn] vt (brakes) refaire la garniture de.

relinquish [rɪ'lɪŋkwɪʃ] vt abandonner; (plan, habit) renoncer à.

relish ['relɪʃ] n (CULIN) condiment m; (enjoyment) délectation f // vt (food etc) savourer; to ~ doing se délecter à faire.

relive [ri:'lɪv] vt revivre.

reload [ri:'ləud] vt recharger.

reluctance [rɪ'lʌktəns] n répugnance f.

reluctant [rɪ'lʌktənt] a peu disposé(e), qui hésite; ~ly ad à contrecœur, sans enthousiasme.

rely [rɪ'laɪ]: to ~ on vt fus compter sur; (be dependent) dépendre de.

remain [rɪ'meɪn] vi rester; ~der n reste m; (COMM) fin f de série; ~ing a qui reste; ~s npl restes mpl.

remand [rɪ'mɑ:nd] n: on ~ en détention préventive // vt: to ~ in custody écrouer; renvoyer en détention provisoire; ~ home n maison f d'arrêt.

remark [rɪ'mɑ:k] n remarque f, observation f // vt (faire) remarquer, dire; (notice) remarquer; ~able a remarquable.

remarry [ri:'mærɪ] vi se remarier.

remedial [rɪ'mi:dɪəl] a (tuition, classes) de rattrapage.

remedy ['remədɪ] n: ~ (for) remède m (contre or à) // vt remédier à.

remember [rɪ'membə*] vt se rappeler, se souvenir de; ~ me to (in letter) rappelez-moi au bon souvenir de; remembrance n souvenir m; mémoire f.

remind [rɪ'maɪnd] vt: to ~ sb of sth rappeler qch à qn; to ~ sb to do faire penser à qn à faire, rappeler à qn qu'il doit faire; ~er n rappel m; (note etc) pense-bête m.

reminisce [remɪ'nɪs] vi: to ~ (about) évoquer ses souvenirs (de).

reminiscences [remɪ'nɪsnsɪz] npl réminiscences fpl, souvenirs mpl.

reminiscent [remɪ'nɪsnt] a: ~ of qui rappelle, qui fait penser à.

remission [rɪ'mɪʃən] n rémission f; (of debt, sentence) remise f; (of fee) exemption f.

remit [rɪ'mɪt] vt (send: money) envoyer; ~tance n envoi m, paiement m.

remnant ['remnənt] n reste m, restant m; ~s npl (COMM) coupons mpl; fins fpl de série.

remorse [rɪ'mɔ:s] n remords m; ~ful a plein(e) de remords; ~less a (fig) impitoyable.

remote [rɪ'məut] a éloigné(e), lointain(e); (person) distant(e); ~ control n télécommande f; ~ly ad au loin; (slightly) très vaguement; ~ness n éloignement m.

remould ['ri:məuld] n (tyre) pneu rechapé.

removable [rɪ'mu:vəbl] a (detachable) amovible.

removal [rɪ'mu:vəl] n (taking away) enlèvement m; suppression f; (from house) déménagement m; (from office: sacking) renvoi m; (MED) ablation f; ~ man n déménageur m; ~ van n camion m de déménagement.

remove [rɪ'mu:v] vt enlever, retirer; (employee) renvoyer; (stain) faire partir; (doubt, abuse) supprimer; ~r (for paint) décapant m; (for varnish) dissolvant m; ~rs npl (company) entreprise f de déménagement.

remuneration [rɪmju:nə'reɪʃən] n rémunération f.

rename [ri:'neɪm] vt rebaptiser.

rend, pt, pp rent [rend, rent] vt déchirer.

render ['rendə*] vt rendre; (CULIN: fat) clarifier; ~ing n (MUS etc) interprétation f.

rendez-vous ['rɔndɪvu:] n rendez-vous m inv // vi opérer une jonction, se rejoindre.

renegade ['renɪgeɪd] n rénégat/e.

renew [rɪ'nju:] vt renouveler; (negotiations) reprendre; (acquaintance) renouer; ~al n renouvellement m; reprise f.

renounce [rɪ'nauns] vt renoncer à; (disown) renier.

renovate ['renəveɪt] vt rénover; (art work) restaurer; renovation [-'veɪʃən] n rénovation f; restauration f.

renown [rɪ'naun] n renommée f; ~ed a renommé(e).

rent [rent] pt, pp of rend // n loyer m // vt louer; ~al n (for television, car) (prix m de) location f.

renunciation [rɪnʌnsɪ'eɪʃən] n renonciation f; (self-denial) renoncement m.

reopen [ri:'əupən] vt rouvrir; ~ing n réouverture f.

reorder [ri:'ɔ:də*] vt commander de nouveau; (rearrange) réorganiser.

reorganize [ri:'ɔ:gənaɪz] vt réorganiser.

rep [rep] n (COMM: abbr of representative) représentant m (de commerce); (THEATRE: abbr of repertory) théâtre m de répertoire.

repair [rɪ'peə*] n réparation f // vt réparer; in good/bad ~ en bon/mauvais état; ~ kit n trousse f de réparations; ~ man n réparateur m; ~ shop n (AUT etc) atelier m de réparations.

repartee [repɑ:'ti:] n repartie f.

repay [ri:'peɪ] vt irg (money, creditor) rembourser; (sb's efforts) récompenser; ~ment n remboursement m; récompense f.

repeal [rɪ'pi:l] n (of law) abrogation f; (of sentence) annulation f // vt abroger; annuler.

repeat [rɪ'pi:t] n (RADIO, TV) reprise f // vt répéter; (pattern) reproduire; (promise, attack, also COMM: order) renouveler; (SCOL: a class) redoubler; ~edly ad souvent, à plusieurs reprises.

repel [rɪ'pel] vt (lit, fig) repousser; ~lent a repoussant(e) // n: insect ~lent insectifuge m; moth ~lent produit m antimite(s).

repent [rɪ'pent] vi: to ~ (of) se repentir (de); ~ance n repentir m.

repercussion [ri:pə'kʌʃən] n (consequence) répercussion f.

repertoire ['rɛpətwaː*] n répertoire m.

repertory ['rɛpətərɪ] n (also: ~ **theatre**) théâtre m de répertoire.

repetition [rɛpɪ'tɪʃən] n répétition f; (of promise, COMM: order etc) renouvellement m.

repetitive [rɪ'pɛtɪtɪv] a (movement, work) répétitif(ive); (speech) plein(e) de redites.

replace [rɪ'pleɪs] vt (put back) remettre, replacer; (take the place of) remplacer; (TEL): '~ **the receiver**' 'raccrochez'; ~ment n replacement m; remplacement m; (person) remplaçant/e; ~ment part n pièce f de rechange.

replenish [rɪ'plɛnɪʃ] vt (glass) remplir (de nouveau); (stock etc) réapprovisionner.

replete [rɪ'pliːt] a rempli(e); (well-fed) rassasié(e).

replica ['rɛplɪkə] n réplique f, copie exacte.

reply [rɪ'plaɪ] n réponse f // vi répondre.

report [rɪ'pɔːt] n rapport m; (PRESS etc) reportage m; (also: **school** ~) bulletin m (scolaire); (of gun) détonation f // vt rapporter, faire un compte rendu de; (PRESS etc) faire un reportage sur; (bring to notice: occurrence) signaler; (: person) dénoncer // vi (make a report) faire un rapport (or un reportage); (present o.s.): to ~ (to sb) se présenter (chez qn); **it is** ~ed that on dit or annonce que; ~ed speech n (LING) discours indirect; ~er n reporter m.

reprehensible [rɛprɪ'hɛnsɪbl] a répréhensible.

represent [rɛprɪ'zɛnt] vt représenter; (explain): to ~ to sb that expliquer à qn que; ~ation [-'teɪʃən] n représentation f; ~ations npl (protest) démarche f; ~ative n représentant/e; (US: POL) député m // a représentatif(ive), caractéristique.

repress [rɪ'prɛs] vt réprimer; ~ion [-'prɛʃən] n répression f; ~ive a répressif(ive).

reprieve [rɪ'priːv] n (LAW) grâce f; (fig) sursis m, délai m // vt gracier; accorder un sursis or un délai à.

reprimand ['rɛprɪmɑːnd] n réprimande f // vt réprimander.

reprint n ['riːprɪnt] réimpression f // vt [riː'prɪnt] réimprimer.

reprisal [rɪ'praɪzl] n représailles fpl.

reproach [rɪ'prəʊtʃ] n reproche m // vt: to ~ sb with sth reprocher qch à qn; **beyond** ~ irréprochable; ~ful a de reproche.

reproduce [riːprə'djuːs] vt reproduire // vi se reproduire; **reproduction** [-'dʌkʃən] n reproduction f; **reproductive** [-'dʌktɪv] a reproducteur(trice).

reprove [rɪ'pruːv] vt (action) réprouver; (person): to ~ (for) blâmer (de); **reproving** a réprobateur(trice).

reptile ['rɛptaɪl] n reptile m.

republic [rɪ'pʌblɪk] n république f; ~an a,n républicain(e).

repudiate [rɪ'pjuːdɪeɪt] vt (wife, accusation) répudier; (friend) renier.

repugnant [rɪ'pʌgnənt] a répugnant(e).

repulse [rɪ'pʌls] vt repousser.

repulsion [rɪ'pʌlʃən] n répulsion f.

repulsive [rɪ'pʌlsɪv] a repoussant(e), répulsif(ive).

reputable ['rɛpjutəbl] a de bonne réputation; (occupation) honorable.

reputation [rɛpju'teɪʃən] n réputation f; to have a ~ for être réputé(e) pour.

repute [rɪ'pjuːt] n (bonne) réputation; ~dly ad d'après ce qu'on dit.

request [rɪ'kwɛst] n demande f; (formal) requête f // vt: to ~ (of or from sb) demander (à qn); ~ **stop** n (for bus) arrêt facultatif.

requiem ['rɛkwɪəm] n requiem m.

require [rɪ'kwaɪə*] vt (need: subj: person) avoir besoin de; (: thing, situation) demander; (want) vouloir; exiger; (order) obliger; ~d a requis(e), voulu(e); if ~d s'il le faut; ~ment n exigence f; besoin m; condition requise.

requisite ['rɛkwɪzɪt] n chose nécessaire // a requis(e), nécessaire; **toilet** ~s accessoires mpl de toilette.

requisition [rɛkwɪ'zɪʃən] n: ~ **(for)** demande f (de) // vt (MIL) réquisitionner.

reroute [riː'ruːt] vt (train etc) dérouter.

resale ['riːseɪl] n revente f.

rescind [rɪ'sɪnd] vt annuler; (law) abroger; (judgment) honorable.

rescue ['rɛskjuː] n sauvetage m; (help) secours mpl // vt sauver; ~ **party** n équipe f de sauvetage; ~r n sauveteur m.

research [rɪ'sɜːtʃ] n recherche(s) f(pl) // vt faire des recherches sur; ~er n chercheur/euse; ~ **work** n recherches fpl; ~ **worker** n chercheur/euse.

resell [riː'sɛl] vt irg revendre.

resemblance [rɪ'zɛmbləns] n ressemblance f.

resemble [rɪ'zɛmbl] vt ressembler à.

resent [rɪ'zɛnt] vt éprouver du ressentiment de, être contrarié(e) par; ~ful a irrité(e), plein(e) de ressentiment; ~ment n ressentiment m.

reservation [rɛzə'veɪʃən] n (booking) réservation f; (doubt) réserve f; (protected area) réserve; (on road: also: **central** ~) banc f médiane; to **make a** ~ **(in** a hotel/a restaurant/a plane) réserver or retenir une chambre/une table/une place.

reserve [rɪ'zɜːv] n réserve f; (SPORT) remplaçant/e // vt (seats etc) réserver, retenir; ~s npl (MIL) réservistes mpl; **in** ~ en réserve; ~d a réservé(e); **reservist** n (MIL) réserviste m.

reservoir ['rɛzəvwaː*] n réservoir m.

reshape [riː'ʃeɪp] vt (policy) réorganiser.

reshuffle [riː'ʃʌfl] n: **Cabinet** ~ (POL) remaniement ministériel.

reside [rɪ'zaɪd] vi résider.

residence ['rɛzɪdəns] n résidence f; ~ **permit** n permis m de séjour.

resident ['rɛzɪdənt] n résident/e // a résident(e).

residential [rɛzɪ'dɛnʃəl] a de résidence; (area) résidentiel(le).

residue ['rɛzɪdjuː] n reste m; (CHEM, PHYSICS) résidu m.

resign [rɪ'zaɪn] vt (one's post) se démettre de // vi démissionner; to ~ o.s. to (endure) se résigner à; ~ation [rɛzɪg'neɪʃən] n démission f; résignation f; ~ed a résigné(e).

resilience [rɪ'zɪlɪəns] n (of material) élasticité f; (of person) ressort m.

resilient [rɪ'zɪlɪənt] a (person) qui réagit, qui a du ressort.

resin ['rezɪn] n résine f.

resist [rɪ'zɪst] vt résister à; ~ance n résistance f.

resolute ['rezəlu:t] a résolu(e).

resolution [rezə'lu:ʃən] n résolution f.

resolve [rɪ'zɔlv] n résolution f // vt (decide): to ~ to do résoudre or décider de faire; (problem) résoudre; ~d a résolu(e).

resonant ['rezənənt] a résonnant(e).

resort [rɪ'zɔ:t] n (town) station f; (recourse) recours m // vi: to ~ to avoir recours à; in the last ~ en dernier ressort.

resound [rɪ'zaund] vi: to ~ (with) retentir (de); ~ing a retentissant(e).

resource [rɪ'sɔ:s] n ressource f; ~s npl ressources; ~ful a plein(e) de ressource, débrouillard(e); ~fulness n ressource f.

respect [rɪs'pekt] n respect m // vt respecter; with ~ to en ce qui concerne; in ~ of sous le rapport de, quant à; in this ~ sous ce rapport, à cet égard; ~ability [-ə'bɪlɪtɪ] n respectabilité f; ~able a respectable; ~ful a respectueux(euse).

respective [rɪs'pektɪv] a respectif(ive); ~ly ad respectivement.

respiration [respɪ'reɪʃən] n respiration f.

respirator ['respɪreɪtə*] n respirateur m.

respiratory [res'pɪrətərɪ] a respiratoire.

respite ['respaɪt] n répit m.

resplendent [rɪs'plendənt] a resplendissant(e).

respond [rɪs'pɔnd] vi répondre; (to treatment) réagir.

response [rɪs'pɔns] n réponse f; (to treatment) réaction f.

responsibility [rɪspɔnsɪ'bɪlɪtɪ] n responsabilité f.

responsible [rɪs'pɔnsɪbl] a (liable): ~ (for) responsable (de); (character) digne de confiance; (job) qui comporte des responsabilités; **responsibly** ad avec sérieux.

responsive [rɪs'pɔnsɪv] a qui n'est pas réservé(e) or indifférent(e).

rest [rest] n repos m; (stop) arrêt m, pause f; (MUS) silence m; (support) support m, appui m; (remainder) reste m, restant m // vi se reposer; (be supported): to ~ on appuyer or reposer sur; (remain) rester // vt (lean): to ~ sth on/against appuyer qch sur/contre; the ~ of them les autres; it ~s with him to c'est à lui de.

restart [ri:'stɑ:t] vt (engine) remettre en marche; (work) reprendre.

restaurant ['restərɔŋ] n restaurant m; ~ car n wagon-restaurant m.

rest cure ['restkjuə*] n cure f de repos.

restful ['restful] a reposant(e).

rest home ['resthəum] n maison f de repos.

restitution [restɪ'tju:ʃən] n (act) restitution f; (reparation) réparation f.

restive ['restɪv] a agité(e), impatient(e); (horse) rétif(ive).

restless ['restlɪs] a agité(e); ~ly ad avec agitation.

restock [ri:'stɔk] vt réapprovisionner.

restoration [restə'reɪʃən] n restauration f; restitution f.

restore [rɪ'stɔ:*] vt (building) restaurer; (sth stolen) restituer; (peace, health) rétablir.

restrain [rɪs'treɪn] vt (feeling) contenir; (person): to ~ (from doing) retenir (de faire); ~ed a (style) sobre; (manner) mesuré(e); ~t n (restriction) contrainte f; (moderation) retenue f; (of style) sobriété f.

restrict [rɪs'trɪkt] vt restreindre, limiter; ~ed area n (AUT) zone f à vitesse limitée; ~ion [-kʃən] n restriction f, limitation f; ~ive a restrictif(ive).

rest room ['restrum] n (US) toilettes fpl.

result [rɪ'zʌlt] n résultat m // vi: to ~ in aboutir à, se terminer par.

resume [rɪ'zju:m] vt, vi (work, journey) reprendre.

resumption [rɪ'zʌmpʃən] n reprise f.

resurgence [rɪ'sə:dʒəns] n réapparition f.

resurrection [rezə'rekʃən] n résurrection f.

resuscitate [rɪ'sʌsɪteɪt] vt (MED) réanimer; **resuscitation** [-'teɪʃn] n réanimation f.

retail ['ri:teɪl] n (vente f au) détail m // cpd de or au détail // vt vendre au détail; ~er n détaillant/e; ~ price n prix m de détail.

retain [rɪ'teɪn] vt (keep) garder, conserver; (employ) engager; ~er n (servant) serviteur m; (fee) acompte m, provision f.

retaliate [rɪ'tælɪeɪt] vi: to ~ (against) se venger (de); to ~ (on sb) rendre la pareille (à qn); **retaliation** [-'eɪʃən] n représailles fpl, vengeance f.

retarded [rɪ'tɑ:dɪd] a retardé(e).

retch [retʃ] vi avoir des haut-le-coeur.

retentive [rɪ'tentɪv] a: ~ memory excellente mémoire.

rethink ['ri:'θɪŋk] vt repenser.

reticence ['retɪsns] n réticence f.

reticent ['retɪsnt] a réticent(e).

retina ['retɪnə] n rétine f.

retinue ['retɪnju:] n suite f, cortège m.

retire [rɪ'taɪə*] vi (give up work) prendre sa retraite; (withdraw) se retirer, partir; (go to bed) (aller) se coucher; ~d a (person) retraité(e); ~ment n retraite f; **retiring** a (person) réservé(e); **retiring age** n âge m de la retraite.

retort [rɪ'tɔ:t] n (reply) riposte f; (container) cornue f // vi riposter.

retrace [ri:'treɪs] vt reconstituer; to ~ one's steps revenir sur ses pas.

retract [rɪ'trækt] vt (statement, claws) rétracter; (undercarriage, aerial) rentrer, escamoter // vi se rétracter; rentrer; ~able a escamotable.

retrain [ri:'treɪn] vt (worker) recycler; ~ing n recyclage m.

retread [ri:'tred] vt (AUT: tyre) rechaper.

retreat [rɪ'tri:t] n retraite f // vi battre en retraite; (flood) reculer.

retrial [ri:'traɪəl] n nouveau procès.

retribution [retrɪ'bjuːʃən] n châtiment m.

retrieval [rɪ'triːvəl] n récupération f; réparation f; recherche f et extraction f.

retrieve [rɪ'triːv] vt (sth lost) récupérer; (situation, honour) sauver; (error, loss) réparer; (COMPUTERS) rechercher; ~r n chien m d'arrêt.

retrospect ['retrəspekt] n: **in** ~ rétrospectivement, après coup; ~**ive** [-'spektɪv] a (law) rétroactif(ive).

return [rɪ'təːn] n (going or coming back) retour m; (of sth stolen etc) restitution f; (recompense) récompense f; (FINANCE: from land, shares) rapport m; (report) relevé m, rapport // cpd (journey) de retour; (ticket) aller et retour; (match) retour // vi (person etc: come back) revenir; (: go back) retourner // vt rendre; (bring back) rapporter; (send back) renvoyer; (put back) remettre; (POL: candidate) élire; ~**s** npl (COMM) recettes fpl; bénéfices mpl; **many happy** ~**s (of the day)!** bon anniversaire!; ~**able** a (bottle etc) consigné(e).

reunion [riː'juːnɪən] n réunion f.

reunite [riːjuː'naɪt] vt réunir.

rev [rev] n (abbr of **revolution**: AUT) tour m // vb (also: ~ up) vt emballer // vi s'emballer.

revamp ['riː'væmp] vt (house) retaper; (firm) réorganiser.

reveal [rɪ'viːl] vt (make known) révéler; (display) laisser voir; ~**ing** a révélateur(trice); (dress) au décolleté généreux or suggestif.

reveille [rɪ'vælɪ] n (MIL) réveil m.

revel ['revl] vi: **to** ~ **in sth/in doing** se délecter de qch/à faire.

revelation [revə'leɪʃən] n révélation f.

reveller ['revlə*] n fêtard m.

revelry ['revlrɪ] n festivités fpl.

revenge [rɪ'vendʒ] n vengeance f; (in game etc) revanche f // vt venger; **to take** ~ se venger; ~**ful** a vengeur(eresse); vindicatif(ive).

revenue ['revənjuː] n revenu m.

reverberate [rɪ'vəːbəreɪt] vi (sound) retentir, se répercuter; (light) se réverbérer; **reverberation** [-'reɪʃən] n répercussion f; réverbération f.

revere [rɪ'vɪə*] vt vénérer, révérer.

reverence ['revərəns] n vénération f, révérence f.

reverent ['revərənt] a respectueux(euse).

reverie ['revərɪ] n rêverie f.

reversal [rɪ'vəːsl] n (of opinion) revirement m.

reverse [rɪ'vəːs] n contraire m, opposé m; (back) dos m, envers m; (AUT: also: ~ **gear**) marche f arrière // a (order, direction) opposé(e), inverse // vt (turn) renverser, retourner; (change) renverser, changer complètement; (LAW: judgment) réformer // vi (AUT) faire marche arrière; ~**d charge call** n (TEL) communication f en PCV.

reversion [rɪ'vəːʃən] n retour m.

revert [rɪ'vəːt] vi: **to** ~ **to** revenir à, retourner à.

review [rɪ'vjuː] n revue f; (of book, film) critique f // vt passer en revue; faire la critique de; ~**er** n critique m.

revise [rɪ'vaɪz] vt (manuscript) revoir, corriger; (opinion) réviser, modifier; (study: subject, notes) réviser; **revision** [rɪ'vɪʒən] n révision f.

revitalize [riː'vaɪtəlaɪz] vt revitaliser.

revival [rɪ'vaɪvəl] n reprise f; rétablissement m; (of faith) renouveau m.

revive [rɪ'vaɪv] vt (person) ranimer; (custom) rétablir; (hope, courage) redonner; (play, fashion) reprendre // vi (person) reprendre connaissance; (hope) renaître; (activity) reprendre.

revoke [rɪ'vəuk] vt révoquer; (promise, decision) revenir sur.

revolt [rɪ'vəult] n révolte f // vi se révolter, se rebeller; ~**ing** a dégoûtant(e).

revolution [revə'luːʃən] n révolution f; (of wheel etc) tour m, révolution; ~**ary** a, n révolutionnaire (m/f); **rev(olution) counter** n compte-tours m inv; ~**ize** vt révolutionner.

revolve [rɪ'vɔlv] vi tourner.

revolver [rɪ'vɔlvə*] n revolver m.

revolving [rɪ'vɔlvɪŋ] a (chair) pivotant(e); (light) tournant(e); ~ **door** n (porte f à) tambour m.

revue [rɪ'vjuː] n (THEATRE) revue f.

revulsion [rɪ'vʌlʃən] n dégoût m, répugnance f.

reward [rɪ'wɔːd] n récompense f // vt: **to** ~ **(for)** récompenser (de); ~**ing** a (fig) qui en vaut la peine.

rewind [riː'waɪnd] vt irg (watch) remonter; (ribbon etc) réembobiner.

rewire [riː'waɪə*] vt (house) refaire l'installation électrique de.

reword [riː'wəːd] vt formuler or exprimer différemment.

rewrite [riː'raɪt] vt irg récrire.

rhapsody ['ræpsədɪ] n (MUS) rhapsodie f; (fig) éloge délirant.

rhetoric ['retərɪk] n rhétorique f; ~**al** [rɪ'tɔrɪkl] a rhétorique.

rheumatic [ruː'mætɪk] a rhumatismal(e).

rheumatism ['ruːmətɪzəm] n rhumatisme m.

Rhine [raɪn] n: **the** ~ le Rhin.

rhinoceros [raɪ'nɔsərəs] n rhinocéros m.

Rhodesia [rəu'diːʒə] n Rhodésie f; ~**n** a rhodésien(ne) // n Rhodésien/ne.

rhododendron [rəudə'dendrn] n rhododendron m.

Rhone [rəun] n: **the** ~ le Rhône.

rhubarb ['ruːbɑːb] n rhubarbe f.

rhyme [raɪm] n rime f; (verse) vers mpl.

rhythm ['rɪðm] n rythme m; ~**ic(al)** a rythmique; ~**ically** ad avec rythme.

rib [rɪb] n (ANAT) côte f // vt (mock) taquiner.

ribald ['rɪbəld] a paillard(e).

ribbed [rɪbd] a (knitting) à côtes; (shell) strié(e).

ribbon ['rɪbən] n ruban m; **in** ~**s** (torn) en lambeaux.

rice [raɪs] n riz m; ~**field** n rizière f; ~ **pudding** n riz m au lait.

rich [rɪtʃ] a riche; (gift, clothes) somptueux(euse); **the** ~ les riches mpl; ~**es** npl richesses fpl; ~**ness** n richesse f.

rickets ['rɪkɪts] n rachitisme m.

rickety ['rɪkɪtɪ] a branlant(e).

rickshaw ['rɪkʃɔ:] n pousse(-pousse) m inv.

ricochet ['rɪkəʃeɪ] n ricochet m // vi ricocher.

rid, pt, pp **rid** [rɪd] vt: to ~ sb of débarrasser qn de; to get ~ of se débarrasser de; **good riddance!** bon débarras!

ridden ['rɪdn] pp of **ride**.

riddle ['rɪdl] n (puzzle) énigme f // vt: to be ~d with être criblé(e) de.

ride [raɪd] n promenade f, tour m; (distance covered) trajet m // vb (pt **rode**, pp **ridden** [rəud, 'rɪdn]) vi (as sport) monter (à cheval), faire du cheval; (go somewhere: on horse, bicycle) aller (à cheval or bicyclette etc); (journey: on bicycle, motor cycle, bus) rouler // vt (a certain horse) monter; (distance) parcourir, faire; **we rode all day/all the way** nous sommes restés toute la journée en selle/avons fait tout le chemin en selle or à cheval; to ~ a horse/bicycle/camel monter à cheval/à bicyclette/à dos de chameau; to ~ at anchor (NAUT) être à l'ancre; **horse/car** ~ promenade or tour à cheval/en voiture; to take sb for a ~ (fig) faire marcher qn; rouler qn; ~r n cavalier/ère; (in race) jockey m; (on bicycle) cycliste m/f; (on motorcycle) motocycliste m/f; (in document) annexe f, clause additionnelle.

ridge [rɪdʒ] n (of hill) faîte m; (of roof, mountain) arête f; (on object) strie f.

ridicule ['rɪdɪkjuːl] n ridicule m; dérision f // vt ridiculiser, tourner en dérision.

ridiculous [rɪ'dɪkjuləs] a ridicule.

riding ['raɪdɪŋ] n équitation f; ~ **school** n manège m, école f d'équitation.

rife [raɪf] a répandu(e); ~ **with** abondant(e) en.

riffraff ['rɪfræf] n racaille f.

rifle ['raɪfl] n fusil m (à canon rayé) // vt vider, dévaliser; ~ **range** n champ m de tir; (indoor) stand m de tir.

rift [rɪft] n fente f, fissure f; (fig: disagreement) désaccord m.

rig [rɪg] n (also: **oil** ~: on land) derrick m; (: at sea) plate-forme pétrolière // vt (election etc) truquer; to ~ **out** vt habiller; (pej) fringuer, attifer; to ~ **up** vt arranger, faire avec des moyens de fortune; ~**ging** n (NAUT) gréement m.

right [raɪt] a (true) juste, exact(e); (correctly chosen: answer, road etc) bon(bonne); (suitable) approprié(e), convenable; (just) juste, équitable; (morally good) bien inv; (not left) droit(e) // n (title, claim) droit m; (not left) droite f // ad (answer) correctement; (not on the left) à droite // vt redresser // excl bon!; to be ~ (person) avoir raison; (answer) être juste or correct(e); ~ **now** en ce moment même; tout de suite; ~ **against the wall** tout contre le mur; ~ **ahead** tout droit; droit devant; ~ **in the middle** en plein milieu; ~ **away** immédiatement; by ~s en toute justice; on the ~ à droite; ~ **angle** n angle droit; ~**eous** ['raɪtʃəs] a droit(e), vertueux(euse); (anger) justifié(e); ~**eousness** ['raɪtʃəsnɪs] n droiture f, vertu f; ~**ful** a (heir) légitime;

~**fully** ad à juste titre, légitimement; ~**handed** a (person) droitier(ère); ~**hand man** n bras droit (fig); the ~**hand side** le côté droit; ~**ly** ad bien, correctement; (with reason) à juste titre; ~**minded** a sensé(e), sain(e) d'esprit; ~ **of way** n droit m de passage; (AUT) priorité f; ~**wing** n (MIL, SPORT) aile droite; (POL) droite f; ~**wing** a (POL) de droite.

rigid ['rɪdʒɪd] a rigide; (principle) strict(e); ~**ity** [rɪ'dʒɪdɪtɪ] n rigidité f; ~**ly** ad rigidement; (behave) inflexiblement.

rigmarole ['rɪgmərəul] n galimatias m; comédie f.

rigor mortis ['rɪgə'mɔ:tɪs] n rigidité f cadavérique.

rigorous ['rɪgərəs] a rigoureux (euse); ~**ly** ad rigoureusement.

rigour, **rigor** (US) ['rɪgə°] n rigueur f.

rig-out ['rɪgaut] n (col) tenue f.

rile [raɪl] vt agacer.

rim [rɪm] n bord m; (of spectacles) monture f; (of wheel) jante f; ~**less** a (spectacles) à monture invisible; ~**med** a bordé(e); janté(e).

rind [raɪnd] n (of bacon) couenne f; (of lemon etc) écorce f.

ring [rɪŋ] n anneau m; (on finger) bague f; (also: **wedding** ~) alliance f; (for napkin) rond m; (of people, objects) cercle m; (of spies) réseau m; (of smoke etc) rond m; (arena) piste f, arène f; (for boxing) ring m; (sound of bell) sonnerie f; (telephone call) coup m de téléphone // vb (pt **rang**, pp **rung** [ræŋ, rʌŋ]) vi (person, bell) sonner; (also: ~ **out**: voice, words) retentir; (TEL) téléphoner // vt (TEL: also: ~ **up**) téléphoner à; to ~ **the bell** sonner; to ~ **back** vt, vi (TEL) rappeler; to ~ **off** vi (TEL) raccrocher; ~ **binder** n classeur m à anneaux; ~**leader** n (of gang) chef m, meneur m.

ringlets ['rɪŋlɪts] npl anglaises fpl.

ring road ['rɪŋrəud] n route f de ceinture.

rink [rɪŋk] n (also: **ice** ~) patinoire f.

rinse [rɪns] n rinçage m // vt rincer.

riot ['raɪət] n émeute f, bagarres fpl // vi faire une émeute, manifester avec violence; a ~ **of colours** une débauche or orgie de couleurs; to run ~ se déchaîner; ~**er** n émeutier/ère, manifestant/e; ~**ous** a tapageur(euse); tordant(e); ~**ously funny** tordant(e).

rip [rɪp] n déchirure f // vt déchirer // vi se déchirer; ~**cord** n poignée f d'ouverture.

ripe [raɪp] a (fruit) mûr(e); (cheese) fait(e); ~**n** vt mûrir // vi mûrir; se faire; ~**ness** n maturité f.

riposte [rɪ'pɔst] n riposte f.

ripple ['rɪpl] n ride f, ondulation f; égrènement m, cascade f // vi se rider, onduler // vt rider, faire onduler.

rise [raɪz] n (slope) côte f, pente f; (hill) élévation f; (increase: in wages) augmentation f; (: in prices, temperature) hausse f, augmentation f; (fig: to power etc) essor m, ascension f // vi (pt **rose**, pp **risen** [rəuz, 'rɪzn]) s'élever, monter; (prices) augmenter, monter; (waters, river) monter; (sun, wind, person: from chair, bed) se lever; (also: ~ **up**: rebel) se révolter;

se rebeller; **to give ~ to** donner lieu à; **to ~ to the occasion** se montrer à la hauteur.

risk [rɪsk] n risque m; danger m // vt risquer; **to take** or **run the ~ of doing** courir le risque de faire; **at ~** en danger; **at one's own ~** à ses risques et périls; **~y** a risqué(e).

risqué ['ri:skeɪ] a (joke) risqué(e).

rissole ['rɪsəul] n croquette f.

rite [raɪt] n rite m.

ritual ['rɪtjuəl] a rituel(le) // n rituel m.

rival ['raɪvl] n rival/e; (in business) concurrent/e // a rival(e); qui fait concurrence // vt être en concurrence avec; **to ~ sb/sth in** rivaliser avec qn/qch de; **~ry** n rivalité f; concurrence f.

river ['rɪvə*] n rivière f; (major, also fig) fleuve m; **~bank** n rive f, berge f; **~bed** n lit m (de rivière or de fleuve); **~side** n bord m de la rivière or du fleuve // cpd (port, traffic) fluvial(e).

rivet ['rɪvɪt] n rivet m // vt riveter; (fig) river, fixer.

Riviera [rɪvɪ'ɛərə] n: **the (French) ~** la Côte d'Azur.

RN abbr of Royal Navy.

road [rəud] n route f; (small) chemin m; (in town) rue f; (fig) chemin, voie f; '**~ up**' 'attention travaux'; **~block** n barrage routier; **~hog** n chauffard m; **~ map** n carte routière; **~side** n bord m de la route, bas-côté m // cpd (situé(e) etc) au bord de la route; **~sign** n panneau m de signalisation; **~ user** n usager m de la route; **~way** n chaussée f; **~worthy** a en bon état de marche.

roam [rəum] vi errer, vagabonder // vt parcourir, errer par.

roar [rɔ:*] n rugissement m; (of crowd) hurlements mpl; (of vehicle, thunder, storm) grondement m // vi rugir; hurler; gronder; **to ~ with laughter** éclater de rire; **a ~ing fire** une belle flambée; **to do a ~ing trade** faire des affaires d'or.

roast [rəust] n rôti m // vt (meat) (faire) rôtir.

rob [rɔb] vt (person) voler; (bank) dévaliser; **to ~ sb of sth** voler or dérober qch à qn; (fig: deprive) priver qn de qch; **~ber** n bandit m, voleur m; **~bery** n vol m.

robe [rəub] n (for ceremony etc) robe f; (also: **bath ~**) peignoir m // vt revêtir (d'une robe).

robin ['rɔbɪn] n rouge-gorge m.

robot ['rəubɔt] n robot m.

robust [rəu'bʌst] a robuste; (material, appetite) solide.

rock [rɔk] n (substance) roche f, roc m; (boulder) rocher m; roche; (sweet) ≈ sucre m d'orge (swing gently: cradle) balancer; (: child) bercer; (shake) ébranler, secouer // vi (se) balancer; être ébranlé(e) or secoué(e); **on the ~s** (drink) avec des glaçons; (ship) sur les écueils; (marriage etc) en train de craquer; **to ~ the boat** (fig) jouer les trouble-fête; **~-bottom** n (fig) niveau le plus bas; **~ery** n (jardin m de) rocaille f.

rocket ['rɔkɪt] n fusée f; (MIL) fusée, roquette f.

rock face ['rɔkfeɪs] n paroi rocheuse.

rock fall ['rɔkfɔ:l] n chute f de pierres.

rocking chair ['rɔkɪŋtʃɛə*] n fauteuil m à bascule.

rocking horse ['rɔkɪŋhɔ:s] n cheval m à bascule.

rocky ['rɔkɪ] a (hill) rocheux(euse); (path) rocailleux(euse); (unsteady: table) branlant(e).

rod [rɔd] n (metallic) tringle f; (TECH) tige f; (wooden) baguette f; (also: **fishing ~**) canne f à pêche.

rode [rəud] pt of **ride**.

rodent ['rəudnt] n rongeur m.

rodeo ['rəudɪəu] n rodéo m.

roe [rəu] n (species: also: **~ deer**) chevreuil m; (of fish) œufs mpl de poisson; **soft ~** laitance f; **~ deer** n chevreuil m; chevreuil femelle.

rogue [rəug] n coquin/e; **roguish** a coquin(e).

role [rəul] n rôle m.

roll [rəul] n rouleau m; (of banknotes) liasse f; (also: **bread ~**) petit pain; (register) liste f; (sound: of drums etc) roulement m; (movement: of ship) roulis m // vt rouler; (also: **~ up:** string) enrouler; (also: **~ out:** pastry) étendre au rouleau // vi rouler; (wheel) tourner; (sway: person) se balancer; **to ~ by** vi (time) s'écouler, passer; **to ~ in** vi (mail, cash) affluer; **to ~ over** vi se retourner; **to ~ up** vi (col: arrive) arriver, s'amener // vt (carpet) rouler; **~ call** n appel m; **~ed gold** a plaqué or inv; **~er** n rouleau m; (wheel) roulette f; **~er skates** npl patins mpl à roulettes.

rollicking ['rɔlɪkɪŋ] a bruyant(e) et joyeux(euse); (play) bouffon(ne); **to have a ~ time** s'amuser follement.

rolling ['rəulɪŋ] a (landscape) onduleux(euse); **~ pin** n rouleau m à pâtisserie; **~ stock** n (RAIL) matériel roulant.

roll-on-roll-off ['rəulɔn'rəulɔf] a (ferry) transroulier(ère).

roly-poly ['rəulɪ'pəulɪ] n (CULIN) roulé m à la confiture.

Roman ['rəumən] a romain(e) // n Romain/e; **~ Catholic** a, n catholique (m/f).

romance [rə'mæns] n histoire f (or film m or aventure f) romanesque; (charm) poésie f; (love affair) idylle f // vi enjoliver (à plaisir), exagérer.

Romanesque [rəumə'nɛsk] a roman(e).

Romania [rəu'meɪnɪə] n Roumanie f; **~n** a roumain(e) // n Roumain/e.

romantic [rə'mæntɪk] a romantique; sentimental(e).

romanticism [rə'mæntɪsɪzəm] n romantisme m.

romp [rɔmp] n jeux bruyants // vi (also: **~ about**) s'ébattre, jouer bruyamment.

rompers ['rɔmpəz] npl barboteuse f.

rondo ['rɔndəu] n (MUS) rondeau m.

roof [ru:f] n toit m; (of tunnel, cave) plafond m // vt couvrir (d'un toit); **the ~ of the mouth** la voûte du palais; **~ garden** n toit-terrasse m; **~ing** n toiture f; **~ rack** n (AUT) galerie f.

rook [ruk] n (*bird*) freux m; (*CHESS*) tour f // vt (*cheat*) rouler, escroquer.

room [ru:m] n (*in house*) pièce f; (*also:* **bed~**) chambre f (à coucher); (*in school etc*) salle f; (*space*) place f; **~s** npl (*lodging*) meublé m; '**~s** to let' 'chambres à louer'; **~ing house** n (*US*) maison f de rapport; **~mate** n camarade m/f de chambre; **~ service** n service m des chambres (*dans un hôtel*); **~y** a spacieux(euse); (*garment*) ample.

roost [ru:st] n juchoir m // vi se jucher.

rooster ['ru:stə*] n coq m.

root [ru:t] n (*BOT, MATH*) racine f; (*fig: of problem*) origine f, fond m // vt (*plant, belief*) enraciner; **to ~ about** vi (*fig*) fouiller; **to ~ for** vt fus applaudir; **to ~ out** vt extirper.

rope [rəup] n corde f; (*NAUT*) cordage m // vt (*box*) corder; (*climbers*) encorder; **to ~ sb in** (*fig*) embringuer qn; **to know the ~s** (*fig*) être au courant, connaître les ficelles; **~ ladder** n échelle f de corde.

rosary ['rəuzəri] n chapelet m; rosaire m.

rose [rəuz] pt of **rise** // n rose f; (*also:* **~bush**) rosier m; (*on watering can*) pomme f // a rose!.

rosé ['rəuzei] n rosé m.

rose: **~bed** n massif m de rosiers; **~bud** n bouton m de rose; **~bush** n rosier m.

rosemary ['rəuzməri] n romarin m.

rosette [rəu'zεt] n rosette f; (*larger*) cocarde f.

roster ['rɔstə*] n: **duty ~** tableau m de service.

rostrum ['rɔstrəm] n tribune f (*pour un orateur etc*).

rosy ['rəuzi] a rose; **a ~ future** un bel avenir.

rot [rɔt] n (*decay*) pourriture f; (*fig: pej*) idioties fpl, balivernes fpl // vt, vi pourrir.

rota ['rəutə] n liste f, tableau m de service; **on a ~ basis** par roulement.

rotary ['rəutəri] a rotatif(ive).

rotate [rəu'teit] vt (*revolve*) faire tourner; (*change round: crops*) alterner; (*:jobs*) faire à tour de rôle // vi (*revolve*) tourner; **rotating** a (*movement*) tournant(e); **rotation** [-'teiʃən] n rotation f; **in rotation** à tour de rôle.

rotor ['rəutə*] n rotor m.

rotten ['rɔtn] a (*decayed*) pourri(e); (*dishonest*) corrompu(e); (*col: bad*) mauvais(e), moche; **to feel ~** (*ill*) être mal fichu(e).

rotting ['rɔtiŋ] a pourrissant(e).

rotund [rəu'tʌnd] a rondelet(te); arrondi(e).

rouble, ruble (*US*) ['ru:bl] n rouble m.

rouge [ru:ʒ] n rouge m (à joues).

rough [rʌf] a (*cloth, skin*) rêche, rugueux(euse); (*terrain*) accidenté(e); (*path*) rocailleux(euse); (*voice*) rauque, rude; (*person, manner: coarse*) rude, fruste; (*: violent*) brutal(e); (*district, weather*) mauvais(e); (*plan*) ébauché(e); (*guess*) approximatif(ive) // n (*GOLF*) rough m; (*person*) voyou m; **to ~ it** vivre à la dure; **to play ~** jouer avec brutalité; **to sleep ~** coucher à la dure; **to feel ~** être mal fichu(e); **to ~ out** vt (*draft*) ébaucher; **~en** vt (*a surface*) rendre rude or rugueux(euse); **~ justice** n justice f sommaire; **~ly** ad (*handle*) rudement, brutalement; (*make*) grossièrement; (*approximately*) à peu près, en gros; **~ness** n rugosité f; rudesse f; brutalité f; **~ work** n (*at school etc*) brouillon m.

roulette [ru:'lεt] n roulette f.

Roumania [ru:'meiniə] n = **Romania**.

round [raund] a rond(e) // n rond m, cercle m; (*of toast*) tranche f; (*duty: of policeman, milkman etc*) tournée f; (*: of doctor*) visites fpl; (*game: of cards, in competition*) partie f; (*BOXING*) round m; (*of talks*) série f // vt (*corner*) tourner; (*bend*) prendre; (*cape*) doubler // ad: **right ~, all ~** tout autour; **the long way ~** (par) le chemin le plus long; **all the year ~** toute l'année; **it's just ~ the corner** c'est juste après le coin; (*fig*) c'est tout près; **to go ~** faire le tour or un détour; **to go ~ to sb's (house)** aller chez qn; **to go ~ an obstacle** contourner un obstacle; **go ~ the back** passe par derriè···; **to go ~ a house** visiter une maison, faire le tour d'une maison; **to go the ~s** (*disease, story*) circuler; **to ~ off** vt (*speech etc*) terminer; **to ~ up** vt rassembler; (*criminals*) effectuer une rafle de; (*prices*) arrondir (au chiffre supérieur); **~about** n (*AUT*) rond-point m (à sens giratoire); (*at fair*) manège m (de chevaux de bois) // a (*route, means*) détourné(e); **~ of ammunition** n cartouche f; **~ of applause** n ban m, applaudissements mpl; **~ of drinks** n tournée f; **~ of sandwiches** n sandwich m; **~ed** a arrondi(e); (*style*) harmonieux(euse); **~ly** ad (*fig*) tout net, carrément; **~-shouldered** a au dos rond; **~sman** n livreur m; **~ trip** n (voyage m) aller et retour m; **~up** n rassemblement m; (*of criminals*) rafle f.

rouse [rauz] vt (*wake up*) réveiller; (*stir up*) susciter; provoquer; éveiller; **rousing** a (*welcome*) enthousiaste.

rout [raut] n (*MIL*) déroute f // vt mettre en déroute.

route [ru:t] n itinéraire m; (*of bus*) parcours m; (*of trade, shipping*) route f; '**all ~s**' (*AUT*) 'toutes directions'; **~ map** n (*for journey*) croquis m d'itinéraire; (*for trains etc*) carte f du réseau.

routine [ru:'ti:n] a (*work*) ordinaire, courant(e); (*procedure*) d'usage // n (*pej*) routine f; (*THEATRE*) numéro m; **daily ~** occupations journalières.

roving ['rəuviŋ] a (*life*) vagabond(e); **~ reporter** n reporter volant.

row [rəu] n (*line*) rangée f; (*of people, seats, KNITTING*) rang m; (*behind one another: of cars, people*) file f // vi (*in boat*) ramer; (*as sport*) faire de l'aviron // vt (*boat*) faire aller à la rame or à l'aviron; **in a ~** (*fig*) d'affilée.

row [rau] n (*noise*) vacarme m; (*dispute*) dispute f, querelle f; (*scolding*) réprimande f, savon m // vi se disputer, se quereller.

rowdiness ['raudinis] n tapage m, chahut m; (*fighting*) bagarre f.

rowdy ['raudi] a chahuteur(euse); bagarreur(euse) // n voyou m.

rowing ['rəuɪŋ] n canotage m; (as sport) aviron m; ~ **boat** n canot m (à rames).

rowlock ['rɔlək] n dame f de nage, tolet m.

royal ['rɔɪəl] a royal(e); ~**ist** a, n royaliste (m/f).

royalty ['rɔɪəltɪ] n (royal persons) (membres mpl de la) famille royale; (payment: to author) droits mpl d'auteur; (: to inventor) royalties fpl.

r.p.m. abbr (AUT: = revs per minute) tr/mn (tours/minute).

R.S.P.C.A. n (abbr of Royal Society for the Prevention of Cruelty to Animals), ≈ S.P.A..

R.S.V.P. abbr (= répondez s'il vous plaît) R.S.V.P.

Rt Hon. abbr (= Right Honourable) titre donné aux députés de la Chambre des communes.

rub [rʌb] n (with cloth) coup m de chiffon or de torchon; (on person) friction f // vt frotter; frictionner; to ~ **sb up the wrong way** prendre qn à rebrousse-poil; to ~ **off** vi partir; to ~ **off on** déteindre sur.

rubber ['rʌbə*] n caoutchouc m; (Brit: eraser) gomme f (à effacer); ~ **band** élastique m; ~ **plant** n caoutchouc m (plante verte); ~ **stamp** m tampon m; ~-**stamp** vt (fig) approuver sans discussion; ~**y** a caoutchouteux(euse).

rubbish ['rʌbɪʃ] n (from household) ordures fpl; (fig:pej) choses fpl sans valeur; camelote f; bêtises fpl, idioties fpl; ~ **bin** n boîte f à ordures, poubelle f; ~ **dump** n (in town) décharge publique, dépotoir m.

rubble ['rʌbl] n décombres mpl; (smaller) gravats mpl.

ruble ['ru:bl] n (US) = **rouble**.

ruby ['ru:bɪ] n rubis m.

rucksack ['rʌksæk] n sac m à dos.

ructions ['rʌkʃənz] npl grabuge m.

rudder ['rʌdə*] n gouvernail m.

ruddy ['rʌdɪ] a (face) coloré(e); (sky) rougeoyant(e); (col: damned) sacré(e), fichu(e).

rude [ru:d] a (impolite: person) impoli(e); (: word, manners) grossier(ère); (shocking) indécent(e), inconvenant(e); ~**ly** ad impoliment; grossièrement; ~**ness** n impolitesse f; grossièreté f.

rudiment ['ru:dɪmənt] n rudiment m; ~**ary** [-'mɛntərɪ] a rudimentaire.

rueful ['ru:ful] a triste.

ruff [rʌf] n fraise f, collerette f.

ruffian ['rʌfɪən] n brute f, voyou m.

ruffle ['rʌfl] vt (hair) ébouriffer; (clothes) chiffonner; (water) agiter; (fig: person) émouvoir, faire perdre son flegme à.

rug [rʌg] n petit tapis; (for knees) couverture f.

rugby ['rʌgbɪ] n (also: ~ **football**) rugby m.

rugged ['rʌgɪd] a (landscape) accidenté(e); (tree bark) rugueux(euse); (features, kindness, character) rude; (determination) farouche.

rugger ['rʌgə*] n (col) rugby m.

ruin ['ru:ɪn] n ruine f // vt ruiner; (spoil: clothes) abimer; ~**s** npl ruine(s); ~**ation** [-'neɪʃən] n ruine f; ~**ous** a ruineux(euse).

rule [ru:l] n règle f; (regulation) règlement m; (government) autorité f, gouvernement m // vt (country) gouverner; (person) dominer; (decide) décider; (draw: lines) tirer à la règle // vi commander; décider; (LAW) statuer; **as a** ~ normalement, en règle générale; ~**d** a (paper) réglé(e); ~**r** n (sovereign) souverain/e; (leader) chef m (d'État); (for measuring) règle f; **ruling** a (party) au pouvoir; (class) dirigeant(e) // n (LAW) décision f.

rum [rʌm] n rhum m // a (col) bizarre.

Rumania [ru:'meɪnɪə] n = **Romania**.

rumble ['rʌmbl] n grondement m; gargouillement m // vi gronder; (stomach, pipe) gargouiller.

rummage ['rʌmɪdʒ] vi fouiller.

rumour, rumor (US) ['ru:mə*] n rumeur f, bruit m (qui court) // vt: **it is** ~**ed that** le bruit court que.

rump [rʌmp] n (of animal) croupe f; ~**steak** n rumsteck m.

rumpus ['rʌmpəs] n (col) tapage m, chahut m; (quarrel) prise f de bec.

run [rʌn] n (pas m de) course f; (outing) tour m or promenade f (en voiture); parcours m, trajet m; (series) suite f, série f; (THEATRE) série de représentations; (SKI) piste f // vb (pt ran, pp run [ræn, rʌn]) vt (operate: business) diriger; (: competition, course) organiser; (: hotel, house) tenir; (force through: rope, pipe): to ~ **sth through** faire passer qch à travers; (to pass: hand, finger): to ~ **sth over** promener or passer qch sur; (water, bath) faire couler // vi courir; (pass: road etc) passer; (work: machine, factory) marcher; (bus, train: operate) être en service; (: travel) circuler; (continue: play) se jouer; (: contract) être valide; (slide: drawer etc) glisser; (flow: river, bath) couler; (colours, washing) déteindre; (in election) être candidat, se présenter; **there was a** ~ **on** (meat, tickets) les gens se sont rués sur; **to break into a** ~ se mettre à courir; **in the long** ~ à longue échéance; à la longue; **en fin de compte; in the short** ~ à brève échéance, à court terme; **on the** ~ en fuite; **I'll** ~ **you to the station** je vais vous emmener or conduire à la gare; **to** ~ **a risk** courir un risque; **to** ~ **about** vi (children) courir çà et là; **to** ~ **across** vt fus (find) trouver par hasard; **to** ~ **away** vi s'enfuir; **to** ~ **down** vi (clock) s'arrêter (faute d'avoir été remonté) // vt (AUT) renverser; (criticize) critiquer, dénigrer; **to be** ~ **down** être fatigué(e) or à plat; **to** ~ **off** vi s'enfuir; **to** ~ **out** vi (person) sortir en courant; (liquid) couler; (lease) expirer; (money) être épuisé(e); **to** ~ **out of** vt fus se trouver à court de; **to** ~ **over** vt sep (AUT) écraser // vt fus (revise) revoir, reprendre; **to** ~ **through** vt fus (instructions) reprendre, revoir; **to** ~ **up** vt (debt) laisser accumuler; **to** ~ **up against** (difficulties) se heurter à; ~-**away** a (horse) emballé(e); (truck) fou(folle); (inflation) galopant(e).

rung [rʌŋ] pp of **ring** // n (of ladder) barreau m.

runner ['rʌnə*] n (in race: person) coureur/euse; (: horse) partant m; (on sledge) patin m; (on curtain) suspenseur m; (for drawer etc) coulisseau m; (carpet: in hall etc) chemin m; ~ bean n (BOT) haricot m (à rames); ~-up n second/e.

running ['rʌnɪŋ] n course f; direction f; organisation f; marche f, fonctionnement m // a (water) courant(e); (commentary) suivi(e); **6 days** ~ 6 jours de suite.

runny ['rʌnɪ] a qui coule.

run-of-the-mill ['rʌnəvðə'mɪl] a ordinaire, banal(e).

runt [rʌnt] n (also: pej) avorton m.

run-through ['rʌnθru:] n répétition f, essai m.

runway ['rʌnweɪ] n (AVIAT) piste f (d'envol ou d'atterrissage).

rupee [ru:'pi:] n roupie f.

rupture ['rʌptʃə*] n (MED) hernie f // vt: to ~ o.s. se donner une hernie.

rural ['ruərl] a rural(e).

ruse [ru:z] n ruse f.

rush [rʌʃ] n course précipitée; (of crowd) ruée f, bousculade f; (hurry) hâte f, bousculade; (current) flot m // vt transporter or envoyer d'urgence; (attack: town etc) prendre d'assaut; (col: overcharge) estamper; faire payer // vi se précipiter; **don't ~ me!** laissez-moi le temps de souffler!; ~**es** npl (BOT) jonc m; ~ **hour** n heures fpl de pointe or d'affluence.

rusk [rʌsk] n biscotte f.

Russia ['rʌʃə] n Russie f; ~**n** a russe // n Russe m/f; (LING) russe m.

rust [rʌst] n rouille f // vi rouiller.

rustic ['rʌstɪk] a rustique // n (pej) rustaud/e.

rustle ['rʌsl] vi bruire, produire un bruissement // vt (paper) froisser; (US: cattle) voler.

rustproof ['rʌstpru:f] a inoxydable; ~**ing** n traitement m antirouille.

rusty ['rʌstɪ] a rouillé(e).

rut [rʌt] n ornière f; (ZOOL) rut m.

ruthless ['ru:θlɪs] a sans pitié, impitoyable; ~**ness** n dureté f, cruauté f.

rye [raɪ] n seigle m; ~ **bread** n pain m de seigle.

S

sabbath ['sæbəθ] n sabbat m.

sabbatical [sə'bætɪkl] a: ~ **year** n année f sabbatique.

sabotage ['sæbətɑ:ʒ] n sabotage m // vt saboter.

saccharin(e) ['sækərɪn] n saccharine f.

sack [sæk] n (bag) sac m // vt (dismiss) renvoyer, mettre à la porte; (plunder) piller, mettre à sac; **to get the** ~ être renvoyé or mis à la porte; **a** ~**ful of** un (plein) sac de; ~**ing** n toile f à sac; renvoi m.

sacrament ['sækrəmənt] n sacrement m.

sacred ['seɪkrɪd] a sacré(e).

sacrifice ['sækrɪfaɪs] n sacrifice m // vt sacrifier.

sacrilege ['sækrɪlɪdʒ] n sacrilège m.

sacrosanct ['sækrəusæŋkt] a sacrosaint(e).

sad [sæd] a (unhappy) triste; (deplorable) triste, fâcheux(euse); ~**den** vt attrister, affliger.

saddle ['sædl] n selle f // vt (horse) seller; **to be ~d with sth** (col) avoir qch sur les bras; ~**bag** n sacoche f.

sadism ['seɪdɪzm] n sadisme m; **sadist** n sadique m/f; **sadistic** [sə'dɪstɪk] a sadique.

sadly ['sædlɪ] ad tristement; fâcheusement.

sadness ['sædnɪs] n tristesse f.

safari [sə'fɑ:rɪ] n safari m.

safe [seɪf] a (out of danger) hors de danger, en sécurité; (not dangerous) sans danger, (cautious) prudent(e); (sure: bet etc) assuré(e) // n coffre-fort m; ~ **from** à l'abri de; ~ **and sound** sain(e) et sauf(sauve); (just) **to be on the** ~ **side** pour plus de sûreté, par précaution; ~**guard** n sauvegarde f, protection f // vt sauvegarder, protéger; ~**keeping** n bonne garde; ~**ly** ad sans danger, sans risque; (without mishap) sans accident.

safety ['seɪftɪ] n sécurité f; ~ **belt** n ceinture f de sécurité; ~ **curtain** n rideau m de fer; ~ **first!** la sécurité d'abord!; ~ **pin** n épingle f de sûreté or de nourrice.

saffron ['sæfrən] n safran m.

sag [sæg] vi s'affaisser, fléchir; pendre.

sage [seɪdʒ] n (herb) sauge f; (man) sage m.

Sagittarius [sædʒɪ'tɛərɪəs] n le Sagittaire; **to be** ~ être du Sagittaire.

sago ['seɪgəu] n sagou m.

said [sɛd] pt, pp of **say**.

sail [seɪl] n (on boat) voile f; (trip): **to go for a** ~ faire un tour en bateau // vt (boat) manœuvrer, piloter // vi (travel: ship) avancer, naviguer; (: passenger) aller or se rendre (en bateau); (set off) partir, prendre la mer; (SPORT) faire de la voile; **they ~ed into Le Havre** ils sont entrés dans le port du Havre; **to ~ through** vi, vt fus (fig) réussir haut la main; ~**boat** n (US) bateau m à voiles, voilier m; ~**ing** n (SPORT) voile f; **to go ~ing** faire de la voile. ~**ing boat** n bateau m à voiles, voilier m; ~**ing ship** n grand voilier; ~**or** n marin m, matelot m.

saint [seɪnt] n saint/e; ~**ly** a saint(e), plein(e) de bonté.

sake [seɪk] n: **for the** ~ **of** pour (l'amour de), dans l'intérêt de; par égard pour; **for pity's** ~ par pitié.

salad ['sæləd] n salade f; ~ **bowl** n saladier m; ~ **cream** n (sorte f de) mayonnaise f; ~ **dressing** n vinaigrette f; ~ **oil** n huile f de table.

salaried ['sælərɪd] a (staff) salarié(e), qui touche un traitement.

salary ['sælərɪ] n salaire m, traitement m.

sale [seɪl] n vente f; (at reduced prices) soldes mpl; **'for ~'** 'à vendre'; **on** ~ en vente; **on** ~ **or return** vendu(e) avec faculté de retour; ~**room** n salle f des ventes; ~**sman** n vendeur m; (representative) représentant m de commerce; ~**smanship** n art m de la vente; ~**swoman** n vendeuse f.

salient ['seɪlɪənt] a saillant(e).

saliva [sə'laɪvə] n salive f.

sallow ['sæləu] a cireux(euse).

salmon ['sæmən] n, pl inv saumon m; ~ **trout** n truite saumonée.

saloon [sə'lu:n] n (US) bar m; (AUT) berline f; (ship's lounge) salon m.

salt [sɔlt] n sel m // vt saler // cpd de sel; (CULIN) salé(e); ~ cellar n salière f; ~-free a sans sel; ~y a salé.

salutary ['sæljutərɪ] a salutaire.

salute [sə'lu:t] n salut m // vt saluer.

salvage ['sælvɪdʒ] n (saving) sauvetage m; (things saved) biens sauvés or récupérés // vt sauver, récupérer.

salvation [sæl'veɪʃən] n salut m; S~ Army n Armée f du Salut.

salver ['sælvə*] n plateau m de métal.

salvo ['sælvəu] n salve f.

same [seɪm] a même // pronoun: the ~ le(la) même, les mêmes; the ~ book as le même livre que; all or just the ~ tout de même, quand même; to do the ~ faire de même, en faire autant; to do the ~ as sb faire comme qn; the ~ again! (in bar etc) la même chose!

sample ['sɑ:mpl] n échantillon m; (MED) prélèvement m // vt (food, wine) goûter.

sanatorium, pl **sanatoria** [sænə-'tɔ:rɪəm, -rɪə] n sanatorium m.

sanctify ['sæŋktɪfaɪ] vt sanctifier.

sanctimonious [sæŋktɪ'məunɪəs] a moralisateur(trice).

sanction ['sæŋkʃən] n sanction f // vt cautionner, sanctionner.

sanctity ['sæŋktɪtɪ] n sainteté f, caractère sacré.

sanctuary ['sæŋktjuərɪ] n (holy place) sanctuaire m; (refuge) asile m; (for wild life) réserve f.

sand [sænd] n sable m // vt sabler; ~s npl plage f (de sable).

sandal ['sændl] n sandale f.

sandbag ['sændbæg] n sac m de sable.

sandcastle ['sændkɑ:sl] n château m de sable.

sand dune ['sænddju:n] n dune f de sable.

sandpaper ['sændpeɪpə*] n papier m de verre.

sandpit ['sændpɪt] n (for children) tas m de sable.

sandstone ['sændstəun] n grès m.

sandwich ['sændwɪtʃ] n sandwich m // vt (also: ~ in) intercaler; ~ed between pris en sandwich entre; cheese/ham ~ sandwich au fromage/jambon; ~ course n cours m de formation professionnelle.

sandy ['sændɪ] a sablonneux(euse); couvert(e) de sable; (colour) sable inv, blond roux inv.

sane [seɪn] a (person) sain(e) d'esprit; (outlook) sensé(e), sain(e).

sang [sæŋ] pt of sing.

sanguine ['sæŋgwɪn] a optimiste.

sanitarium, pl **sanitaria** [sænɪ'tɛərɪəm, -rɪə] n (US) = sanatorium.

sanitary ['sænɪtərɪ] a (system, arrangements) sanitaire; (clean) hygiénique; ~ towel, ~ napkin (US) n serviette f hygiénique.

sanitation [sænɪ'teɪʃən] n (in house) installations fpl sanitaires; (in town) système m sanitaire.

sanity ['sænɪtɪ] n santé mentale; (common sense) bon sens.

sank [sæŋk] pt of sink.

Santa Claus [sæntə'klɔ:z] n le Père Noël.

sap [sæp] n (of plants) sève f // vt (strength) saper, miner.

sapling ['sæplɪŋ] n jeune arbre m.

sapphire ['sæfaɪə*] n saphir m.

sarcasm ['sɑ:kæzm] n sarcasme m, raillerie f.

sarcastic [sɑ:'kæstɪk] a sarcastique.

sarcophagus, pl **sarcophagi** [sɑ:'kɔ-fəgəs, -gaɪ] n sarcophage m.

sardine [sɑ:'di:n] n sardine f.

Sardinia [sɑ:'dɪnɪə] n Sardaigne f.

sardonic [sɑ:'dɔnɪk] a sardonique.

sartorial [sɑ:'tɔ:rɪəl] a vestimentaire.

sash [sæʃ] n écharpe f; ~ window n fenêtre f à guillotine.

sat [sæt] pt,pp of sit.

satanic [sə'tænɪk] a satanique, démoniaque.

satchel ['sætʃl] n cartable m.

satellite ['sætəlaɪt] a, n satellite (m).

satin [... ɪn] n satin m // a en or de satin, satiné(e).

satire ['sætaɪə*] n satire f; **satirical** [sə'tɪrɪkl] a satirique; **satirize** ['sætɪraɪz] vt faire la satire de, satiriser.

satisfaction [sætɪs'fækʃən] n satisfaction f.

satisfactory [sætɪs'fæktərɪ] a satisfaisant(e).

satisfy ['sætɪsfaɪ] vt satisfaire, contenter; (convince) convaincre, persuader; ~ing a satisfaisant(e).

saturate ['sætʃəreɪt] vt: to ~ (with) saturer (de); **saturation** [-'reɪʃən] n saturation f.

Saturday ['sætədɪ] n samedi m.

sauce [sɔ:s] n sauce f; ~pan n casserole f.

saucer ['sɔ:sə*] n soucoupe f.

saucy ['sɔ:sɪ] a impertinent(e).

sauna ['sɔ:nə] n sauna m.

saunter ['sɔ:ntə*] vi: to ~ to aller en flânant or se balader jusqu'à.

sausage ['sɔsɪdʒ] n saucisse f; ~ roll n friand m.

savage ['sævɪdʒ] a (cruel, fierce) brutal(e), féroce; (primitive) primitif(ive), sauvage // n sauvage m/f // vt attaquer férocement; ~ry n sauvagerie f, brutalité f, férocité f.

save [seɪv] vt (person, belongings) sauver; (money) mettre de côté, économiser; (time) (faire) gagner; (food) garder; (avoid: trouble) éviter // vi (also: ~ up) mettre de l'argent de côté // n (SPORT) arrêt m (du ballon) // prep sauf, à l'exception de.

saving ['seɪvɪŋ] n économie f // a: the ~ grace of ce qui rachète; ~s npl économies fpl; ~s bank n caisse f d'épargne.

saviour ['seɪvjə*] n sauveur m.

savour, savor (US) ['seɪvə*] n saveur f, goût m // vt savourer; ~y a savoureux(euse); (dish: not sweet) salé(e).

savvy ['sævɪ] n (col) jugeote f.

saw [sɔ:] pt of saw // n (tool) scie f // vt (pt sawed, pp sawed or sawn [sɔ:n]) scier; ~dust n sciure f; ~mill n scierie f.

saxophone ['sæksəfəun] n saxophone m.

say [seɪ] n: to have one's ~ dire ce qu'on a à dire; to have a ~ avoir voix au chapitre // vt (pt, pp **said** [sɛd]) dire; **could you ~ that again?** pourriez-vous répéter ceci?; **that is to ~** c'est-à-dire; **to ~ nothing of** sans compter; ~ **that** ... mettons or disons que ...; **that goes without** ~**ing** cela va sans dire, cela va de soi; ~**ing** n dicton m, proverbe m.

scab [skæb] n croûte f; (pej) jaune m; ~**by** a croûteux(euse).

scaffold ['skæfəuld] n échafaud m; ~**ing** n échafaudage m.

scald [skɔːld] n brûlure f // vt ébouillanter; ~**ing** a (hot) brûlant(e), bouillant(e).

scale [skeɪl] n (of fish) écaille f; (MUS) gamme f; (of ruler, thermometer etc) graduation f, échelle (graduée); (of salaries, fees etc) barème m; (of map, also size, extent) échelle f // vt (mountain) escalader; (fish) écailler; ~**s** npl balance f, (larger) bascule f; **on a large ~** sur une grande échelle, en grand; ~ **drawing** n dessin m à l'échelle; ~ **model** n modèle m à l'échelle; **small-~ model** modèle réduit.

scallop ['skɔləp] n coquille f Saint-Jacques.

scalp [skælp] n cuir chevelu // vt scalper.

scalpel ['skælpl] n scalpel m.

scamp [skæmp] vt bâcler.

scamper ['skæmpə*] vi: to ~ **away**, ~ **off** détaler.

scan [skæn] vt scruter, examiner; (glance at quickly) parcourir; (poetry) scander; (TV, RADAR) balayer.

scandal ['skændl] n scandale m; (gossip) ragots mpl; ~**ize** vt scandaliser, indigner; ~**ous** a scandaleux(euse).

Scandinavia [skændɪ'neɪvɪə] n Scandinavie f; ~**n** a scandinave // n Scandinave m/f.

scant [skænt] a insuffisant(e); ~**y** a peu abondant(e), insuffisant(e), maigre.

scapegoat ['skeɪpgəut] n bouc m émissaire.

scar [skɑː] n cicatrice f // vt laisser une cicatrice or une marque à.

scarce [skɛəs] a rare, peu abondant(e); ~**ly** ad à peine, presque pas; **scarcity** n rareté f, manque m, pénurie f.

scare [skɛə*] n peur f; panique f // vt effrayer, faire peur à; **to ~ sb stiff** faire une peur bleue à qn; **bomb ~** alerte f à la bombe; ~**crow** n épouvantail m; ~**d** a: **to be ~d** avoir peur; ~**monger** n alarmiste m/f.

scarf, scarves [skɑːf, skɑːvz] n (long) écharpe f; (square) foulard m.

scarlet ['skɑːlɪt] a écarlate; ~ **fever** n scarlatine f.

scarves [skɑːvz] npl of **scarf**.

scary ['skɛərɪ] a (col) qui fiche la frousse.

scathing ['skeɪðɪŋ] a cinglant(e), acerbe.

scatter ['skætə*] vt éparpiller, répandre; (crowd) disperser // vi se disperser; ~**brained** a écervelé(e), étourdi(e); ~**ed** a épars(e), dispersé(e).

scatty ['skætɪ] a (col) loufoque.

scavenger ['skævəndʒə*] n éboueur m.

scene [siːn] n (THEATRE, fig etc) scène f; (of crime, accident) lieu(x) m(pl), endroit m; (sight, view) spectacle m, vue f; **to appear on the ~** faire son apparition; ~**ry** n (THEATRE) décor(s) m(pl); (landscape) paysage m; **scenic** a scénique; offrant de beaux paysages or panoramas.

scent [sɛnt] n parfum m, odeur f; (fig: track) piste f; (sense of smell) odorat m // vt parfumer; (smell, also fig) flairer.

sceptic, skeptic (US) ['skɛptɪk] n sceptique m/f; ~**al** a sceptique; ~**ism** ['skɛptɪsɪzm] n scepticisme m.

sceptre, scepter (US) ['sɛptə*] n sceptre m.

schedule ['ʃɛdjuːl] n programme m, plan m; (of trains) horaire m; (of prices etc) barème m, tarif m // vt prévoir; **as ~d** comme prévu; **on ~** à l'heure (prévue); à la date prévue; **to be ahead of/behind ~** avoir de l'avance/du retard.

scheme [skiːm] n plan m, projet m; (method) procédé m; (dishonest plan, plot) complot m, combine f; (arrangement) arrangement m, classification f // vt,vi comploter, manigancer; **scheming** a rusé(e), intrigant(e) // n manigances fpl, intrigues fpl.

schism ['skɪzəm] n schisme m.

schizophrenic [skɪtsə'frɛnɪk] a schizophrène.

scholar ['skɔlə*] n érudit/e; ~**ly** a érudit(e), savant(e); ~**ship** n érudition f; (grant) bourse f (d'études).

school [skuːl] n (gen) école f; (in university) faculté f; (secondary school) collège m, lycée m // cpd scolaire // vt (animal) dresser; ~**book** n livre m scolaire or de classe; ~**boy** n écolier m; collégien m, lycéen m; ~**days** npl années fpl de scolarité; ~**girl** n écolière f; collégienne f, lycéenne f; ~**ing** n instruction f, études fpl; ~**-leaving age** n âge m de fin de scolarité; ~**master** n (primary) instituteur m; (secondary) professeur m; ~**mistress** n institutrice f; professeur m; ~ **report** n bulletin m (scolaire); ~**room** n (salle f de) classe f; ~**teacher** n instituteur/trice; professeur m.

schooner ['skuːnə*] n (ship) schooner m, goélette f; (glass) grand verre (à xérès).

sciatica [saɪ'ætɪkə] n sciatique f.

science ['saɪəns] n science f; ~ **fiction** n science-fiction f; **scientific** [-'tɪfɪk] a scientifique; **scientist** n scientifique m/f; (eminent) savant m.

scintillating ['sɪntɪleɪtɪŋ] a scintillant(e), étincelant(e).

scissors ['sɪzəz] npl ciseaux mpl; **a pair of** ~ une paire de ciseaux.

sclerosis [sklɪ'rəusɪs] n sclérose f.

scoff [skɔf] vt (col: eat) avaler, bouffer // vi: to ~ **(at)** (mock) se moquer (de).

scold [skəuld] vt gronder, attraper, réprimander.

scone [skɔn] n sorte de petit pain rond au lait.

scoop [skuːp] n pelle f (à main); (for ice cream) boule f à glace; (PRESS) reportage exclusif or à sensation; ~ **out** vt évider, creuser; ~ **up** vt ramasser.

scooter ['skuːtə*] n (motor cycle) scooter m; (toy) trottinette f.

scope [skəup] n (capacity: of plan, undertaking) portée f, envergure f; (: of person) compétence f, capacités fpl; (opportunity) possibilités fpl; **within the ~ of** dans les limites de.

scorch [skɔ:tʃ] vt (clothes) brûler (légèrement), roussir; (earth, grass) dessécher, brûler; **~ed earth policy** n politique f de la terre brûlée; **~er** n (col: hot day) journée f torride; **~ing** a torride, brûlant(e).

score [skɔ:*] n score m, décompte m des points; (MUS) partition f; (twenty) vingt // vt (goal, point) marquer; (success) remporter // vi marquer des points; (FOOTBALL) marquer un but; (keep score) compter les points; **on that ~** sur ce chapitre, à cet égard; **to ~ well/6 out of 10** obtenir un bon résultat/6 sur 10; **~board** n tableau m; **~card** n (SPORT) carton m; feuille f de marque; **~r** n auteur m du but; marqueur m de buts; (keeping score) marqueur m.

scorn [skɔ:n] n mépris m, dédain m // vt mépriser, dédaigner; **~ful** a méprisant(e), dédaigneux(euse).

Scorpio ['skɔ:pɪəu] n le Scorpion; **to be ~** être du Scorpion.

scorpion ['skɔ:pɪən] n scorpion m.

Scot [skɔt] n Écossais/e.

scotch [skɔtʃ] vt faire échouer; enrayer; étouffer; **S~** n whisky m, scotch m.

scot-free ['skɔt'fri:] a sans être puni(e); sans payer.

Scotland ['skɔtlənd] n Écosse f.

Scots [skɔts] a écossais(e); **~man/woman** Écossais/e.

Scottish ['skɔtɪʃ] a écossais(e).

scoundrel ['skaundrl] n vaurien m; (child) coquin m.

scour ['skauə*] vt (clean) récurer; frotter; décaper; (search) battre, parcourir; **~er** n tampon abrasif or à récurer.

scourge [skə:dʒ] n fléau m.

scout [skaut] n (MIL) éclaireur m; (also: **boy ~**) scout m; **to ~ around** explorer, chercher.

scowl [skaul] vi se renfrogner, avoir l'air maussade; **to ~ at** regarder de travers.

scraggy ['skrægɪ] a décharné(e), efflanqué(e), famélique.

scram [skræm] vi (col) ficher le camp.

scramble ['skræmbl] n bousculade f, ruée f // vi avancer tant bien que mal (à quatre pattes or en grimpant); **to ~ for** se bousculer or se disputer pour (avoir); **~d eggs** npl œufs brouillés.

scrap [skræp] n bout m, morceau m; (fight) bagarre f; (also: **~ iron**) ferraille f // vt jeter, mettre au rebut; (fig) abandonner, laisser tomber; **~s** npl (waste) déchets mpl; **~book** n album m.

scrape [skreip] vt, vi gratter, racler // n: **to get into a ~** s'attirer des ennuis; **~r** n grattoir m, racloir m.

scrap: **~ heap** n tas m de ferraille; (fig): **on the ~ heap** au rancart or rebut; **~ merchant** n marchand m de ferraille; **~ paper** n papier m brouillon; **~py** a fragmentaire, décousu(e).

scratch [skrætʃ] n égratignure f, rayure f; éraflure f; (from claw) coup m de griffe // a: **~ team** n équipe de fortune or improvisé(e) // vt (record) rayer; (paint etc) érafler; (with claw, nail) griffer // vi (se) gratter; **to start from ~** partir de zéro; **to be up to ~** être à la hauteur.

scrawl [skrɔ:l] n gribouillage m // vi gribouiller.

scrawny ['skrɔ:nɪ] a décharné(e).

scream [skri:m] n cri perçant, hurlement m // vi crier, hurler; **to be a ~** être impayable.

scree [skri:] n éboulis m.

screech [skri:tʃ] n cri strident, hurlement m; (of tyres, brakes) crissement m, grincement m // vi hurler; crisser, grincer.

screen [skri:n] n écran m, paravent m; (CINEMA, TV) écran m; (fig) écran, rideau m // vt masquer, cacher; (from the wind etc) abriter, protéger; (film) projeter; (book) porter à l'écran; (candidates etc) filtrer; **~ing** n (MED) test m (or tests) de dépistage.

screw [skru:] n vis f; (propeller) hélice f // vt visser; **to have one's head ~ed on** avoir la tête sur les épaules; **~driver** n tournevis m; **~y** a (col) dingue, cinglé(e).

scribble ['skrɪbl] n gribouillage m // vt gribouiller, griffonner.

scribe [skraib] n scribe m.

script [skrɪpt] n (CINEMA etc) scénario m, texte m; (in exam) copie f.

Scripture ['skrɪptʃə*] n Écriture Sainte.

scriptwriter ['skrɪptraɪtə*] n scénariste m/f, dialoguiste m/f.

scroll [skrəul] n rouleau m.

scrounge [skraundʒ] vt (col): **to ~ sth (off or from sb)** se faire payer qch (par qn), emprunter qch (à qn) // vi: **to ~ on sb** vivre aux crochets de qn; **~r** n parasite m.

scrub [skrʌb] n (clean) nettoyage m (à la brosse); (land) broussailles fpl // vt (floor) nettoyer à la brosse; (pan) récurer; (washing) frotter; (reject) annuler.

scruff [skrʌf] n: **by the ~ of the neck** par la peau du cou.

scruffy ['skrʌfɪ] a débraillé(e).

scrum(mage) ['skrʌm(ɪdʒ)] n mêlée f.

scruple ['skru:pl] n scrupule m.

scrupulous ['skru:pjuləs] a scrupuleux(euse).

scrutinize ['skru:tɪnaɪz] vt scruter, examiner minutieusement.

scrutiny ['skru:tɪnɪ] n examen minutieux.

scuff [skʌf] vt érafler.

scuffle ['skʌfl] n échauffourée f, rixe f.

scull [skʌl] n aviron m.

scullery ['skʌlərɪ] n arrière-cuisine f.

sculptor ['skʌlptə*] n sculpteur m.

sculpture ['skʌlptʃə*] n sculpture f.

scum [skʌm] n écume f, mousse f; (pej: people) rebut m, lie f.

scurrilous ['skʌrɪləs] a haineux(euse), virulent(e); calomnieux(euse).

scurry ['skʌrɪ] vi filer à toute allure.

scurvy ['skə:vɪ] n scorbut m.

scuttle ['skʌtl] n (NAUT) écoutille f; (also: **coal ~**) seau m (à charbon) // vt (ship) saborder // vi (scamper): **to ~ away, ~ off** détaler.

scythe [saɪð] n faux f.

sea [si:] n mer f // cpd marin(e), de (la) mer, maritime; **on the ~** (boat) en mer;

(*town*) au bord de la mer ; **to be all at ~** (*fig*) nager complètement ; **~ bird** *n* oiseau *m* de mer ; **~board** *n* côte *f* ; **~ breeze** *n* brise *f* de mer ; **~farer** *n* marin *m* ; **~food** *n* fruits *mpl* de mer ; **~ front** *n* bord *m* de mer ; **~going** *a* (*ship*) de haute mer ; **~gull** *n* mouette *f*.

seal [si:l] *n* (*animal*) phoque *m* ; (*stamp*) sceau *m*, cachet *m* ; (*impression*) cachet, estampille *f* // *vt* sceller ; (*envelope*) coller ; (: *with seal*) cacheter.

sea level ['si:lɛvl] *n* niveau *m* de la mer.

sealing wax ['si:lɪŋwæks] *n* cire *f* à cacheter.

sea lion ['si:laɪən] *n* lion *m* de mer.

seam [si:m] *n* couture *f* ; (*of coal*) veine *f*, filon *m*.

seaman ['si:mən] *n* marin *m*.

seamless ['si:mlɪs] *a* sans couture(s).

seamy ['si:mɪ] *a* louche, mal famé(e).

seance ['seɪɔns] *n* séance *f* de spiritisme.

seaplane ['si:pleɪn] *n* hydravion *m*.

seaport ['si:pɔ:t] *n* port *m* de mer.

search [sə:tʃ] *n* (*for person, thing*) recherche(s) *f(pl)* ; (*of drawer, pockets*) fouille *f* ; (*LAW: at sb's home*) perquisition *f* // *vt* fouiller ; (*examine*) examiner minutieusement ; scruter // *vi*: **to ~ for** chercher ; **to ~ through** *vt fus* fouiller ; **in ~ of** à la recherche de ; **~ing** *a* pénétrant(e) ; minutieux(euse) ; **~light** *n* projecteur *m* ; **~ party** *n* expédition *f* de secours ; **~ warrant** *n* mandat *m* de perquisition.

seashore ['si:ʃɔ:*] *n* rivage *m*, plage *f*, bord *m* de (la) mer.

seasick ['si:sɪk] *a* qui a le mal de mer.

seaside ['si:saɪd] *n* bord *m* de la mer ; **~ resort** *n* station *f* balnéaire.

season ['si:zn] *n* saison *f* // *vt* assaisonner, relever ; **~al** *a* saisonnier(ère) ; **~ing** *n* assaisonnement *m* ; **~ ticket** *n* carte *f* d'abonnement.

seat [si:t] *n* siège *m* ; (*in bus, train: place*) place *f* ; (*PARLIAMENT*) siège ; (*buttocks*) postérieur *m* ; (*of trousers*) fond *m* // *vt* faire asseoir, placer ; (*have room for*) avoir des places assises pour, pouvoir accueillir ; **~ belt** *n* ceinture *f* de sécurité ; **~ing room** *n* places assises.

sea water ['si:wɔ:tə*] *n* eau *f* de mer.

seaweed ['si:wi:d] *n* algues *fpl*.

seaworthy ['si:wə:ðɪ] *a* en état de naviguer.

sec. *abbr of* **second(s)**.

secede [sɪ'si:d] *vi* faire sécession.

secluded [sɪ'klu:dɪd] *a* retiré(e), à l'écart.

seclusion [sɪ'klu:ʒən] *n* solitude *f*.

second ['sɛkənd] *num* deuxième, second(e) // *ad* (*in race etc*) en seconde position ; (*RAIL*) en seconde // *n* (*unit of time*) seconde *f* ; (*in series, position*) deuxième *m/f*, second/e ; (*SCOL*) ≈ licence *f* avec mention bien *or* assez bien ; (*AUT: also*: **~ gear**) seconde *f* ; (*COMM: imperfect*) article *m* de second choix // *vt* (*motion*) appuyer ; **~ary** *a* secondaire ; **~ary school** *n* collège *m*, lycée *m* ; **~- class** *a* de deuxième classe ; **~er** *n* personne *f* qui appuie une motion ; **~hand** *a* d'occasion ; de seconde main ; **~ hand** *n* (*on clock*) trot-

teuse *f* ; **~ly** *ad* deuxièmement ; **~ment** [sɪ'kɔndmənt] *n* détachement *m* ; **~-rate** *a* de deuxième ordre, de qualité inférieure ; **~ thoughts** *npl* doutes *mpl* ; **on ~ thoughts** à la réflexion.

secrecy ['si:krəsɪ] *n* secret *m* ; **in ~** en secret, dans le secret.

secret ['si:krɪt] *a* secret(ète) // *n* secret *m*.

secretarial [sɛkrɪ'tɛərɪəl] *a* de secrétaire, de secrétariat.

secretariat [sɛkrɪ'tɛərɪət] *n* secrétariat *m*.

secretary ['sɛkrətərɪ] *n* secrétaire *m/f* ; (*COMM*) secrétaire général ; **S~ of State** (*for*) (*Brit*: *POL*) ministre *m* (de).

secretive ['si:krətɪv] *a* réservé(e) ; (*pej*) cachottier(ère), dissimulé(e).

sect [sɛkt] *n* secte *f* ; **~arian** [-'tɛərɪən] *a* sectaire.

section ['sɛkʃən] *n* coupe *f*, section *f* ; (*department*) section ; (*COMM*) rayon *m* ; (*of document*) section, article *m*, paragraphe *m* // *vt* sectionner ; **~al** *a* (*drawing*) en coupe.

sector ['sɛktə*] *n* secteur *m*.

secular ['sɛkjulə*] *a* profane ; laïque ; séculier(ère).

secure [sɪ'kjuə*] *a* (*free from anxiety*) sans inquiétude, sécurisé(e) ; (*firmly fixed*) solide, bien attaché(e) (*or* fermé(e) *etc*) ; (*in safe place*) en lieu sûr, en sûreté // *vt* (*fix*) fixer, attacher ; (*get*) obtenir, se procurer.

security [sɪ'kjurɪtɪ] *n* sécurité *f* ; mesures *fpl* de sécurité ; (*for loan*) caution *f*, garantie *f*.

sedate [sɪ'deɪt] *a* calme ; posé(e) // *vt* donner des sédatifs à.

sedation [sɪ'deɪʃən] *n* (*MED*) sédation *f*.

sedative ['sɛdɪtɪv] *n* calmant *m*, sédatif *m*.

sedentary ['sɛdntrɪ] *a* sédentaire.

sediment ['sɛdɪmənt] *n* sédiment *m*, dépôt *m*.

seduce [sɪ'dju:s] *vt* (*gen*) séduire ; **seduction** [-'dʌkʃən] *n* séduction *f* ; **seductive** [-'dʌktɪv] *a* séduisant(e), séducteur(trice).

see [.. .] *vb* (*pt* **saw**, *pp* **seen** [sɔ:, si:n]) *vt* (*gen*) voir ; (*accompany*): **to ~ sb to the door** reconduire *or* raccompagner qn jusqu'à la porte // *vi* voir // *n* évêché *m* ; **to ~ that** (*ensure*) veiller à ce que + *sub*, faire en sorte que + *sub*, s'assurer que ; **to ~ off** *vt* accompagner (à la gare *or* à l'aéroport *etc*) ; **to ~ through** *vt* mener à bonne fin // *vt fus* voir clair dans ; **to ~ to** *vt fus* s'occuper de, se charger de ; **~ you!** au revoir!, à bientôt!

seed [si:d] *n* graine *f* ; (*fig*) germe *m* ; (*TENNIS*) tête *f* de série ; **to go to ~** monter en graine ; (*fig*) se laisser aller ; **~ling** *n* jeune plant *m*, semis *m* ; **~y** *a* (*shabby*) minable, miteux(euse).

seeing ['si:ɪŋ] *cj*: **~ (that)** vu que, étant donné que.

seek, *pt,pp* **sought** [si:k, sɔ:t] *vt* chercher, rechercher.

seem [si:m] *vi* sembler, paraître ; **there seems to be ...** il semble qu'il y a ... ; on dirait qu'il y a ... ; **~ingly** *ad* apparemment.

seen [si:n] *pp of* **see**.

seep [si:p] *vi* suinter, filtrer.

seer [sɪə*] *n* prophète/prophétesse, voyant/e.

seersucker [sɪəsʌkə*] *n* cloqué *m*, étoffe cloquée.

seesaw ['si:sɔ:] *n* (jeu *m* de) bascule *f*.

seethe [si:ð] *vi* être en effervescence; to ~ **with anger** bouillir de colère.

see-through ['si:θru:] *a* transparent(e).

segment ['sɛgmənt] *n* segment *m*.

segregate ['sɛgrɪgeɪt] *vt* séparer, isoler; **segregation** [-'geɪʃən] *n* ségrégation *f*.

seismic ['saɪzmɪk] *a* sismique.

seize [si:z] *vt* (grasp) saisir, attraper; (take possession of) s'emparer de; (LAW) saisir; to ~ (up)on *vt fus* saisir, sauter sur; to ~ up *vi* (TECH) se gripper.

seizure ['si:ʒə*] *n* (MED) crise *f*, attaque *f*; (LAW) saisie *f*.

seldom ['sɛldəm] *ad* rarement.

select [sɪ'lɛkt] *a* choisi(e), d'élite; **select** *inv* // *vt* sélectionner, choisir; ~**ion** [-'lɛkʃən] *n* sélection *f*, choix *m*; ~**ive** *a* sélectif(ive); (school) à recrutement sélectif; ~**or** (person) sélectionneur/euse, (TECH) sélecteur *m*.

self [sɛlf] *n* (pl **selves** [sɛlvz]): **the** ~ **le** moi *inv* // *prefix* auto-; ~**-adhesive** *a* auto-collant(e); ~**-assertive** *a* autoritaire; ~**-assured** *a* sûr(e) de soi, plein(e) d'assurace; ~**-catering** *a* avec cuisine, où l'on peut faire sa cuisine; ~**-centred** *a* égocentrique; ~**-coloured** *a* uni(e); ~**-confidence** *n* confiance *f* en soi; ~**-conscious** *a* timide, qui manque d'assurance; ~**-contained** *a* (flat) avec entrée particulière, indépendant(e); ~**-control** *n* maîtrise *f* de soi; ~**-defeating** *a* qui a un effet contraire à l'effet recherché; ~**-defence** *n* légitime défense *f*; ~**-discipline** *n* discipline personnelle; ~**-employed** *a* qui travaille à son compte; ~**-evident** *a* évident(e), qui va de soi; ~**-explanatory** *a* qui se passe d'explication; ~**-indulgent** *a* qui ne se refuse rien; ~**-interest** *n* intérêt personnel; ~**-ish** *a* égoïste; ~**-ishness** *n* égoïsme *m*; ~**-lessly** *ad* sans penser à soi; ~**-pity** *n* apitoiement *m* sur soi-même; ~**-portrait** *n* autoportrait *m*; ~**-possessed** *a* assuré(e); ~**-preservation** *n* instinct *m* de conservation; ~**-reliant** *a* indépendant(e); ~**-respect** *n* respect *m* de soi, amour-propre *m*; ~**-respecting** *a* qui se respecte; ~**-righteous** *a* satisfait(e) de soi, pharisaïque; ~**-sacrifice** *n* abnégation *f*; ~**-satisfied** *a* content(e) de soi, suffisant(e); ~**-seal** *a* (envelope) auto-collant(e); ~**-service** *n* libre-service *m*, self-service *m*; ~**-sufficient** *a* indépendant(e); ~**-supporting** *a* financièrement indépendant(e); ~**-taught** *a* autodidacte.

sell [sɛl], *pt,pp* **sold** [sɛl, səuld] *vt* vendre // *vi* se vendre; to ~ **at** or **for 10F** se vendre 10F; to ~ **off** *vt* liquider; ~**er** *n* vendeur/euse, marchand/e; ~**ing price** *n* prix *m* de vente.

sellotape ['sɛləuteɪp] *n* ® papier collant, scotch *m* ®.

sellout ['sɛlaut] *n* trahison *f*, capitulation *f*; (of tickets): it was a ~ tous les billets ont été vendus.

selves [sɛlvz] *npl of* **self**.

semantic [sɪ'mæntɪk] *a* sémantique; ~**s** *n* sémantique *f*.

semaphore ['sɛməfɔ:*] *n* signaux *mpl* à bras; (RAIL) sémaphore *m*.

semen ['si:mən] *n* sperme *m*.

semi ['sɛmɪ] *prefix* semi-, demi-; à demi, à moitié; ~**-breve** *n* ronde *f*; ~**-circle** *n* demi-cercle *m*; ~**-colon** *n* point-virgule *m*; ~**-conscious** *a* à demi conscient(e); ~**-detached** (house) *n* maison jumelée or jumelle; ~**-final** *n* demi-finale *f*.

seminar ['sɛmɪnɑ:*] *n* séminaire *m*.

semiquaver ['sɛmɪkweɪvə*] *n* double croche *f*.

semiskilled ['sɛmɪ'skɪld] *a*: ~ **worker** *n* ouvrier/ère spécialisé/e.

semitone ['sɛmɪtəun] *n* (MUS) demi-ton *m*.

semolina [sɛmə'li:nə] *n* semoule *f*.

senate ['sɛnɪt] *n* sénat *m*; **senator** *n* sénateur *m*.

send [sɛnd], *pt,pp* **sent** [sɛnd, sɛnt] *vt* envoyer; to ~ **sb to Coventry** mettre qn en quarantaine; to ~ **away** *vt* (letter, goods) envoyer, expédier; to ~ **away for** *vt fus* commander par correspondance; to ~ **back** *vt* renvoyer; to ~ **for** *vt fus* envoyer chercher; faire venir; to ~ **off** *vt* (goods) envoyer, expédier; (SPORT: player) expulser or renvoyer du terrain; to ~ **out** *vt* (invitation) envoyer (par la poste); to ~ **up** *vt* (person, price) faire monter; (parody) mettre en boîte, parodier; (blow up) faire sauter; ~**er** *n* expéditeur/trice; ~**-off** *n*: a good ~**-off** des adieux chaleureux.

senile ['si:naɪl] *a* sénile.

senility [sɪ'nɪlɪtɪ] *n* sénilité *f*.

senior ['si:nɪə*] *a* (older) aîné(e), plus âgé(e); (of higher rank) supérieur(e) // *n* aîné/e; (in service) personne *f* qui a plus d'ancienneté; ~**ity** [-'ɔrɪtɪ] *n* priorité *f* d'âge, ancienneté *f*.

sensation [sɛn'seɪʃən] *n* sensation *f*; to **create a** ~ faire sensation; ~**al** *a* qui fait sensation; (marvellous) sensationnel(le).

sense [sɛns] *n* sens *m*; (feeling) sentiment *m*; (meaning) signification *f*; (wisdom) bon sens // *vt* sentir, pressentir; **it makes** ~ c'est logique; ~**s** *npl* raison *f*; ~**less** *a* insensé(e), stupide; (unconscious) sans connaissance; **anyone in his** ~**s** tout homme sensé.

sensibility [sɛnsɪ'bɪlɪtɪ] *n* sensibilité *f*; **sensibilities** *npl* susceptibilité *f*.

sensible ['sɛnsɪbl] *a* sensé(e), raisonnable; sage; pratique.

sensitive ['sɛnsɪtɪv] *a*: ~ **(to)** sensible (à); **sensitivity** [-'tɪvɪtɪ] *n* sensibilité *f*.

sensual ['sɛnsjuəl] *a* sensuel(le).

sensuous ['sɛnsjuəs] *a* voluptueux(euse), sensuel(le).

sent [sɛnt] *pt,pp of* **send**.

sentence ['sɛntns] *n* (LING) phrase *f*; (LAW: judgment) condamnation *f*, sentence *f*; (: punishment) peine *f* // *vt*: to ~ **sb to death**/**to 5 years** condamner qn à mort/à 5 ans.

sentiment ['sɛntɪmənt] *n* sentiment *m*; (opinion) opinion *f*, avis *m*; ~**al** [-'mɛntl] *a* sentimental(e); ~**ality** [-'tælɪtɪ] *n* sentimentalité *f*, sensiblerie *f*.

sentry ['sɛntrɪ] n sentinelle f, factionnaire m.

separable ['sɛprəbl] a séparable.

separate a ['sɛprɪt] séparé(e), indépendant(e), différent(e) // vb ['sɛpəreɪt] vt séparer // vi se séparer; **~ly** ad séparément; **~s** npl (clothes) coordonnés mpl; **separation** [-'reɪʃən] n séparation f.

September [sɛp'tɛmbə*] n septembre m.

septic ['sɛptɪk] a septique; (wound) infecté(e).

sequel ['siːkwl] n conséquence f; séquelles fpl; (of story) suite f.

sequence ['siːkwəns] n ordre m, suite f; **~ of tenses** concordance f des temps.

sequin ['siːkwɪn] n paillette f.

serenade [sɛrə'neɪd] n sérénade f // vt donner une sérénade à.

serene [sɪ'riːn] a serein(e), calme, paisible; **serenity** [sə'rɛnɪtɪ] n sérénité f, calme m.

sergeant ['saːdʒənt] n sergent m; (POLICE) brigadier m.

serial ['sɪərɪəl] n feuilleton m // a (number) de série; **~ize** vt publier (or adapter) en feuilleton.

series ['sɪəriːs] n série f; (PUBLISHING) collection f.

serious ['sɪərɪəs] a sérieux(euse), réfléchi(e); grave; **~ly** ad sérieusement, gravement; **~ness** n sérieux m, gravité f.

sermon ['səːmən] n sermon m.

serrated [sɪ'reɪtɪd] a en dents de scie.

serum ['sɪərəm] n sérum m.

servant ['səːvənt] n domestique m/f; (fig) serviteur/servante.

serve [səːv] vt (employer etc) servir, être au service de; (purpose) servir à; (customer, food, meal) servir; (apprenticeship) faire, accomplir; (prison term) faire; purger // vi (also TENNIS) servir; (be useful): **to ~ as/for/to do** servir de/à/faire // n (TENNIS) service m; **it ~s him right** c'est bien fait pour lui; **to ~ out, ~ up** vt (food) servir.

service ['səːvɪs] n (gen) service m; (AUT: maintenance) révision f // vt (car, washing machine) réviser; **the S~s** les forces armées; **to be of ~ to sb, to do sb a ~** rendre service à qn; **to put one's car in for (a) ~** donner sa voiture à réviser; **dinner ~** n service m de table; **~able** a pratique, commode; **~ area** n (on motorway) aire f de services; **~man** n militaire m; **~ station** n station-service f.

serviette [səːvɪ'ɛt] n serviette f (de table).

servile ['səːvaɪl] a servile.

session ['sɛʃən] n (sitting) séance f; (SCOL) année f scolaire (or universitaire); **to be in ~** siéger, être en session or en séance.

set [sɛt] n série f, assortiment m; (of tools etc) jeu m; (RADIO, TV) poste m; (TENNIS) set m; (group of people) cercle m, milieu m; (CINEMA) plateau m; (THEATRE: stage) scène f; (: scenery) décor m; (MATH) ensemble m; (HAIRDRESSING) mise f en plis // a (fixed) fixe, déterminé(e); (ready) prêt(e) // vb (pt, pp set) (place) mettre, poser, placer; (fix) fixer; (adjust) régler; (decide: rules etc) fixer, choisir; (TYP) composer // vi (sun) se coucher; (jam, jelly, concrete) prendre; **to be ~ on doing**

être résolu à faire; **to be (dead) ~ against** être (totalement) opposé à; **to ~ (to music)** mettre en musique; **to ~ on fire** mettre le feu à; **to ~ free** libérer; **to ~ sth going** déclencher qch; **to ~ sail** partir, prendre la mer; **to ~ about** vt fus (task) entreprendre, se mettre à; **to ~ aside** vt mettre de côté; **to ~ back** vt (in time): **to ~ back (by)** retarder (de); **to ~ off** vi se mettre en route, partir // vt (bomb) faire exploser; (cause to start) déclencher; (show up well) mettre en valeur, faire valoir; **to ~ out** vi: **to ~ out to do** entreprendre de; avoir pour but or intention de // vt (arrange) disposer; (state) présenter, exposer; **to ~ up** vt (organization) fonder, constituer; (record) établir; (monument) ériger; **to ~ up shop** (fig) s'établir, s'installer; **~back** n (hitch) revers m, contretemps m.

settee [sɛ'tiː] n canapé m.

setting ['sɛtɪŋ] n cadre m; (of jewel) monture f.

settle ['sɛtl] vt (argument, matter) régler; (problem) résoudre; (MED: calm) calmer // vi (bird, dust etc) se poser; (sediment) se déposer; (also: ~ down) s'installer, se fixer; se calmer; se ranger; **to ~ to sth** se mettre sérieusement à qch; **to ~ for sth** accepter qch, se contenter de qch; **to ~ in** vi s'installer; **to ~ on sth** opter or se décider pour qch; **to ~ up with sb** régler (ce que l'on doit à) qn; **~ment** n (payment) règlement m; (agreement) accord m; (colony) colonie f; (village etc) établissement m; hameau m; **~r** n colon m.

setup ['sɛtʌp] n (arrangement) manière f dont les choses sont organisées; (situation) situation f, allure f des choses.

seven ['sɛvn] num sept; **~teen** num dix-sept; **~th** num septième; **~ty** num soixante-dix.

sever ['sɛvə*] vt couper, trancher; (relations) rompre.

several ['sɛvərl] a,pronoun plusieurs (m/fpl); **~ of us** plusieurs d'entre nous.

severance ['sɛvərəns] n (of relations) rupture f; **~ pay** n indemnité f de licenciement.

severe [sɪ'vɪə*] a sévère, strict(e); (serious) grave, sérieux(euse); (hard) rigoureux(euse), dur(e); (plain) sévère, austère; **severity** [sɪ'vɛrɪtɪ] n sévérité f; gravité f; rigueur f.

sew, pt **sewed**, pp **sewn** [səu, səud, səun] vt,vi coudre; **to ~ up** vt (re)coudre; **it is all sewn up** (fig) c'est dans le sac or dans la poche.

sewage ['suːɪdʒ] n vidange(s) f(pl).

sewer ['suːə*] n égout m.

sewing ['səuɪŋ] n couture f; **~ machine** n machine f à coudre.

sewn [səun] pp of **sew**.

sex [sɛks] n sexe m; **to have ~ with** avoir des rapports (sexuels) avec; **~ act** n acte sexuel.

sextet [sɛks'tɛt] n sextuor m.

sexual ['sɛksjuəl] a sexuel(le).

sexy ['sɛksɪ] a sexy inv.

shabby ['ʃæbɪ] a miteux(euse); (behaviour) mesquin(e), méprisable.

shack [ʃæk] n cabane f, hutte f.
shackles ['ʃæklz] npl chaînes fpl, entraves fpl.
shade [ʃeɪd] n ombre f; (for lamp) abat-jour m inv; (of colour) nuance f, ton m; (small quantity): a ~ of un soupçon de // vt abriter du soleil, ombrager; in the ~ à l'ombre; a ~ smaller un tout petit peu plus petit.
shadow ['ʃædəu] n ombre f // vt (follow) filer; ~ cabinet n (POL) cabinet parallèle formé par le parti qui n'est pas au pouvoir; ~y a ombragé(e); (dim) vague, indistinct(e).
shady ['ʃeɪdɪ] a ombragé(e); (fig: dishonest) louche, véreux(euse).
shaft [ʃɑ:ft] n (of arrow, spear) hampe f; (AUT, TECH) arbre m; (of mine) puits m; (of lift) cage f; (of light) rayon m, trait m.
shaggy ['ʃægɪ] a hirsute; en broussaille.
shake [ʃeɪk] vb (pt shook, pp shaken [ʃuk, 'ʃeɪkn]) vt secouer; (bottle, cocktail) agiter; (house, confidence) ébranler // vi trembler // n secousse f; to ~ hands with sb serrer la main à qn; to ~ off vt secouer; (fig) se débarrasser de; to ~ up vt secouer; ~-up n grand remaniement; **shaky** a (hand, voice) tremblant(e); (building) branlant(e), peu solide.
shale [ʃeɪl] n schiste argileux.
shall [ʃæl] auxiliary vb: I ~ go j'irai.
shallot [ʃə'lɔt] n échalote f.
shallow ['ʃæləu] a peu profond(e); (fig) superficiel(le), qui manque de profondeur.
sham [ʃæm] n frime f; (jewellery, furniture) imitation f // a feint(e), simulé(e) // vt feindre, simuler.
shambles ['ʃæmblz] n confusion f, pagaïe f, fouillis m.
shame [ʃeɪm] n honte f // vt faire honte à; it is a ~ (that/to do) c'est dommage (que + sub/de faire); what a ~! quel dommage!; ~-faced a honteux(euse), penaud(e); ~ful a honteux(euse), scandaleux(euse); ~less a éhonté(e), effronté(e); (immodest) impudique.
shampoo [ʃæm'pu:] n shampooing m // vt faire un shampooing à.
shamrock ['ʃæmrɔk] n trèfle m (emblème national de l'Irlande).
shandy ['ʃændɪ] n bière panachée.
shan't [ʃɑ:nt] = shall not.
shanty ['ʃæntɪ] n cabane f, baraque f; ~town n bidonville m.
shape [ʃeɪp] n forme f // vt façonner, modeler; (statement) formuler; (sb's ideas) former; (sb's life) déterminer // vi (also: ~ up) (events) prendre tournure; (person) faire des progrès, s'en sortir; to take ~ prendre forme or tournure; -shaped suffix: heart-shaped en forme de cœur; ~less a informe, sans forme; ~ly a bien proportionné(e), beau(belle).
share [ʃɛə*] n (thing received, contribution) part f; (COMM) action f // vt partager; (have in common) avoir en commun; to ~ out (among or between) partager (entre); ~holder n actionnaire m/f.
shark [ʃɑ:k] n requin m.
sharp [ʃɑ:p] a (razor, knife) tranchant(e), bien aiguisé(e); (point) aigu(guë); (nose, chin) pointu(e); (outline) net(te); (cold, pain) vif(vive); (MUS) dièse; (voice) coupant(e); (person: quick-witted) vif(vive), éveillé(e); (: unscrupulous) malhonnête // a (MUS) dièse m // ad: at 2 o'clock ~ à 2 heures pile or tapantes; look ~! dépêche-toi!; ~en vt aiguiser; (pencil) tailler; (fig) aviver; ~ener n (also: pencil ~ener) taille-crayon(s) m inv; (also: knife ~ener) aiguisoir m; ~-eyed a à qui rien n'échappe; ~-witted a à l'esprit vif, malin(igne).
shatter ['ʃætə*] vt fracasser, briser, faire voler en éclats; (fig: upset) bouleverser; (: ruin) briser, ruiner // vi voler en éclats, se briser, se fracasser.
shave [ʃeɪv] vt raser // vi se raser // n: to have a ~ se raser; ~n a (head) rasé(e); ~r n (also: electric ~) rasoir m électrique.
shaving ['ʃeɪvɪŋ] n (action) rasage m; ~s npl (of wood etc) copeaux mpl; ~ brush n blaireau m; ~ cream n crème f à raser; ~ soap n savon m à barbe.
shawl [ʃɔ:l] n châle m.
she [ʃi:] pronoun elle // cpd: ~- femelle; ~-cat n chatte f; ~-elephant n éléphant m femelle; NB: for ships, countries follow the gender of your translation.
sheaf, sheaves [ʃi:f, ʃi:vz] n gerbe f.
shear [ʃɪə*] vt (pt ~ed, pp ~ed or shorn [ʃɔ:n]) (sheep) tondre; to ~ off vt tondre; (branch) élaguer; ~s npl (for hedge) cisaille(s) f(pl).
sheath [ʃi:θ] n gaine f, fourreau m, étui m; (contraceptive) préservatif m; ~e [ʃi:ð] vt gainer; (sword) rengainer.
sheaves [ʃi:vz] npl of sheaf.
shed [ʃed] n remise f, resserre f // vt (pt,pp shed) (leaves, fur etc) perdre; (tears) verser, répandre.
she'd [ʃi:d] = she had; she would.
sheep [ʃi:p] n, pl inv mouton m; ~dog n chien m de berger; ~ish a penaud(e), timide; ~skin n peau f de mouton.
sheer [ʃɪə*] a (utter) pur(e), pur et simple; (steep) à pic, abrupt(e); (almost transparent) extrêmement fin(e) // ad à pic, abruptement.
sheet [ʃi:t] n (on bed) drap m; (of paper) feuille f; (of glass, metal) feuille, plaque f; ~ lightning n éclair m en nappe(s); ~ metal n tôle f.
sheik(h) [ʃeɪk] n cheik m.
shelf, shelves [ʃelf, ʃelvz] n étagère f, rayon m; set of shelves rayonnage m.
shell [ʃel] n (on beach) coquillage m; (of egg, nut etc) coquille f; (explosive) obus m; (of building) carcasse f // vt (crab, prawn etc) décortiquer; (peas) écosser; (MIL) bombarder (d'obus).
she'll [ʃi:l] = she will; she shall.
shellfish ['ʃelfɪʃ] n, pl inv (crab etc) crustacé m; (scallop etc) coquillage m; (pl: as food) crustacés; coquillages.
shelter ['ʃeltə*] n abri m, refuge m // vt abriter, protéger; (give lodging to) donner asile à // vi s'abriter, se mettre à l'abri; ~ed a (life) retiré(e), à l'abri des soucis; (spot) abrité(e).
shelve [ʃelv] vt (fig) mettre en suspens or en sommeil; ~s npl of shelf.

shepherd ['ʃɛpəd] n berger m // vt (guide) guider, escorter ; **~ess** n bergère f ; **~'s pie** n ≈ hachis m Parmentier.

sheriff ['ʃɛrɪf] n shérif m.

sherry ['ʃɛrɪ] n xèrès m, sherry m.

she's [ʃiːz] = she is ; she has.

shield [ʃiːld] n bouclier m // vt: to ~ (from) protéger (de or contre).

shift [ʃɪft] n (change) changement m ; (of workers) équipe f, poste m // vt déplacer, changer de place ; (remove) enlever // vi changer de place, bouger ; ~ **work** n travail m en équipe or par relais or par roulement ; **~y** a sournois(e) ; (eyes) fuyant(e).

shilling ['ʃɪlɪŋ] n shilling m (= 12 old pence ; 20 in a pound).

shilly-shally ['ʃɪlɪʃælɪ] vi tergiverser, atermoyer.

shimmer ['ʃɪmə*] n miroitement m, chatoiement m // vi miroiter, chatoyer.

shin [ʃɪn] n tibia m.

shine [ʃaɪn] n éclat m, brillant m // vb (pt,pp shone [ʃɔn]) vi briller // vt faire briller or reluire ; (torch): to ~ sth on braquer qch sur.

shingle ['ʃɪŋgl] n (on beach) galets mpl ; (on roof) bardeau m ; **~s** n (MED) zona m.

shiny ['ʃaɪnɪ] a brillant(e).

ship [ʃɪp] n bateau m ; (large) navire m // vt transporter (par mer) ; (send) expédier (par mer) ; (load) charger, embarquer ; **~building** n construction navale ; ~ **canal** n canal m maritime or de navigation ; **~ment** n cargaison f ; **~per** n affréteur m, expéditeur m ; **~ping** n (ships) navires mpl ; (traffic) navigation f ; **~shape** a en ordre impeccable ; **~wreck** n épave f ; (event) naufrage m ; **~yard** n chantier naval.

shire ['ʃaɪə*] n comté m.

shirk [ʃəːk] vt esquiver, se dérober à.

shirt [ʃəːt] n (man's) chemise f ; in ~ sleeves en bras de chemise ; **~y** a (col) de mauvais poil.

shiver ['ʃɪvə*] n frisson m // vi frissonner.

shoal [ʃəul] n (of fish) banc m.

shock [ʃɔk] n (impact) choc m, heurt m ; (ELEC) secousse f ; (emotional) choc, secousse f ; (MED) commotion f, choc // vt choquer, scandaliser ; bouleverser ; ~ **absorber** n amortisseur m ; **~ing** a choquant(e), scandaleux(euse) ; épouvantable ; révoltant(e) ; **~proof** a anti-choc inv.

shod [ʃɔd] pt,pp of shoe ; well-~ a bien chaussé(e).

shoddy ['ʃɔdɪ] a de mauvaise qualité, mal fait(e).

shoe [ʃuː] n chaussure f, soulier m ; (also: horse~) fer m à cheval // vt (pt,pp shod [ʃɔd]) (horse) ferrer ; **~brush** n brosse f à chaussures ; **~horn** n chausse-pied m ; **~lace** n lacet m (de soulier) ; ~ **polish** n cirage m ; **~shop** n magasin m de chaussures ; **~tree** n embauchoir m.

shone [ʃɔn] pt,pp of shine.

shook [ʃuk] pt of shake.

shoot [ʃuːt] n (on branch, seedling) pousse f // vb (pt,pp shot [ʃɔt]) vt (game) chasser ; tirer ; abattre ; (person) blesser (or tuer)

d'un coup de fusil (or de revolver) ; (execute) fusiller ; (film) tourner // vi (with gun, bow): to ~ (at) tirer (sur) ; (FOOTBALL) shooter, tirer ; to ~ **down** vt (plane) abattre ; to ~ **in/out** vi entrer/sortir comme une flèche ; to ~ **up** vi (fig) monter en flèche ; **~ing** n (shots) coups mpl de feu, fusillade f ; (HUNTING) chasse f ; **~ing range** n stand m de tir ; **~ing star** n étoile filante.

shop [ʃɔp] n magasin m ; (workshop) atelier m // vi (also: go ~ping) faire ses courses or ses achats ; ~ **assistant** n vendeur/euse ; ~ **floor** n ateliers mpl ; (fig) ouvriers mpl ; **~keeper** n marchand/e, commerçant/e ; **~lifter** n voleur/euse à l'étalage ; **~lifting** n vol m à l'étalage ; **~per** n personne f qui fait ses courses, acheteur/euse ; **~ping** n (goods) achats mpl, provisions fpl ; **~ping bag** n sac m (à provisions) ; **~ping centre**, **~ping center** (US) n centre commercial ; **~soiled** a défraîchi(e), qui a fait la vitrine ; ~ **steward** n (INDUSTRY) délégué/e syndical(e) ; ~ **window** n vitrine f.

shore [ʃɔː*] n (of sea, lake) rivage m, rive f // vt: to ~ **up** étayer.

shorn [ʃɔːn] pp of shear ; ~ **of** dépouillé(e) de.

short [ʃɔːt] a (not long) court(e) ; (soon finished) court, bref(brève) ; (person, step) petit(e) ; (curt) brusque, sec(sèche) ; (insufficient) insuffisant(e) // n (also: ~ film) court métrage ; (a pair of) **~s** un short ; to be ~ of sth être à court de or manquer de qch ; I'm 3 ~ il m'en manque 3 ; in ~ bref ; en bref ; ~ **of doing** à moins de faire ; everything ~ **of** tout sauf ; it is ~ **for** c'est l'abréviation or le diminutif de ; to cut ~ (speech, visit) abréger, écourter ; (person) couper la parole à ; to fall ~ **of** ne pas être à la hauteur de ; to stop ~ s'arrêter net ; to stop ~ **of** ne pas aller jusqu'à ; **~age** n manque m, pénurie f ; **~bread** n ≈ sablé m ; **~circuit** n court-circuit m // vt court-circuiter // vi se mettre en court-circuit ; **~coming** n défaut m ; **~(crust) pastry** n pâte brisée ; **~cut** n raccourci m ; **~en** vt raccourcir ; (text, visit) abréger ; **~ening** n (CULIN) matière grasse ; **~hand** n sténo(graphie) f ; ~ **hand typist** n sténodactylo m/f ; **~list** a (for job) liste f des candidats sélectionnés ; **~lived** a de courte durée ; **~ly** ad bientôt, sous peu ; **~ness** n brièveté f ; **~sighted** a myope ; (fig) qui manque de clairvoyance ; **~story** n nouvelle f ; **~tempered** a qui s'emporte facilement ; **~term** a (effect) à court terme ; **~wave** n (RADIO) ondes courtes.

shot [ʃɔt] pt,pp of shoot // n coup m (de feu) ; (person) tireur m ; (try) coup, essai m ; (injection) piqûre f ; (PHOT) photo f ; like a ~ comme une flèche ; (very readily) sans hésiter ; **~gun** n fusil m de chasse.

should [ʃud] auxiliary vb: I ~ go now je devrais partir maintenant ; he ~ be there now il devrait être arrivé maintenant ; I ~ go if I were you si j'étais vous j'irais ; I ~ like to j'aimerais bien, volontiers.

shoulder ['ʃəuldə*] n épaule f ; (of road): hard ~ accotement m // vt (fig) endosser, se charger de ; ~ **bag** n sac m à

bandoulière ; ~ **blade** n omoplate f ; ~ **strap** n bretelle f.
shouldn't ['ʃudnt] = **should not**.
shout [ʃaut] n cri m // vt crier // vi crier, pousser des cris ; to **give sb a ~** appeler qn ; to ~ **down** vt huer ; ~**ing** n cris mpl.
shove [ʃʌv] vt pousser ; (col: put): to ~ **sth in** fourrer or ficher qch dans ; to ~ **off** vi (NAUT) pousser au large ; (fig: col) ficher le camp.
shovel ['ʃʌvl] n pelle f // vt pelleter, enlever (or enfourner) à la pelle.
show [ʃəu] n (of emotion) manifestation f, démonstration f ; (semblance) semblant m, apparence f ; (exhibition) exposition f ; salon m ; (THEATRE) spectacle m, représentation f ; (CINEMA) séance f // vb (pt ~ed, pp shown [ʃəun]) vt montrer ; (courage etc) faire preuve de, manifester ; (exhibit) exposer // vi se voir, être visible ; to ~ **sb in** faire entrer qn ; to ~ **off** vi (pej) crâner // vt (display) faire valoir ; (pej) faire étalage de ; to ~ **sb out** reconduire qn (jusqu'à la porte) ; to ~ **up** vi (stand out) ressortir ; (col: turn up) se montrer // vt démontrer ; (unmask) démasquer, dénoncer ; ~ **business** n le monde du spectacle ; ~**down** n épreuve f de force.
shower ['ʃauə*] n (rain) averse f ; (of stones etc) pluie f, grêle f ; (also: ~**bath**) douche f // vi prendre une douche, se doucher // vt: to ~ **sb with** (gifts etc) combler qn de ; (abuse etc) accabler qn de ; (missiles) bombarder qn de ; ~**proof** a imperméable ; ~**y** a (weather) pluvieux(euse).
showground ['ʃəugraund] n champ m de foire.
showing ['ʃəuŋ] n (of film) projection f.
show jumping ['ʃəudʒʌmpɪŋ] n concours m hippique.
showmanship ['ʃəumənʃɪp] n art m de la mise en scène.
shown [ʃəun] pp of **show**.
show-off ['ʃəuɔf] n (col: person) crâneur/euse, m'as-tu-vu/e.
showpiece ['ʃəupi:s] n (of exhibition etc) joyau m, clou m.
showroom ['ʃəurum] n magasin m or salle f d'exposition.
shrank [ʃræŋk] pt of **shrink**.
shrapnel ['ʃræpnl] n éclats mpl d'obus.
shred [ʃred] n (gen pl) lambeau m, petit morceau // vt mettre en lambeaux, déchirer ; (CULIN) râper ; couper en lanières.
shrewd [ʃru:d] a astucieux(euse), perspicace ; ~**ness** n perspicacité f.
shriek [ʃri:k] n cri perçant or aigu, hurlement m // vt,vi hurler, crier.
shrift [ʃrɪft] n: to **give sb short ~** expédier qn sans ménagements.
shrill [ʃrɪl] a perçant(e), aigu(guë), strident(e).
shrimp [ʃrɪmp] n crevette grise.
shrine [ʃraɪn] n châsse f ; (place) lieu m de pèlerinage.
shrink, pt shrank, pp shrunk [ʃrɪŋk, ʃræŋk, ʃrʌŋk] vi rétrécir ; (fig) se réduire ; se contracter ; to ~ (from) (faire) rétrécir // n (col: pej) psychanalyste ; ~**age** n rétrécissement m.

shrivel ['ʃrɪvl] (also: ~ **up**) vt ratatiner, flétrir // vi se ratatiner, se flétrir.
shroud [ʃraud] n linceul m // vt: ~**ed in mystery** enveloppé(e) de mystère.
Shrove Tuesday ['ʃrəuv'tju:zdɪ] n (le) Mardi gras.
shrub [ʃrʌb] n arbuste m ; ~**bery** n massif m d'arbustes.
shrug [ʃrʌg] n haussement m d'épaules // vt,vi: to ~ (one's shoulders) hausser les épaules ; to ~ **off** vt faire fi de.
shrunk [ʃrʌŋk] pp of **shrink** ; ~**en** a ratatiné(e).
shudder ['ʃʌdə*] n frisson m, frémissement m // vi frissonner, frémir.
shuffle ['ʃʌfl] vt (cards) battre ; to ~ (one's feet) traîner les pieds.
shun [ʃʌn] vt éviter, fuir.
shunt [ʃʌnt] vt (RAIL: direct) aiguiller ; (: divert) détourner // vi: to ~ (to and fro) faire la navette ; ~**ing** n (RAIL) triage m.
shush [ʃuʃ] excl chut!
shut, pt, pp shut [ʃʌt] vt fermer // vi (se) fermer ; to ~ **down** vt, vi fermer définitivement ; to ~ **off** vt couper, arrêter ; to ~ **up** vi (col: keep quiet) se taire // vt (close) fermer ; (silence) faire taire ; ~**ter** n volet m ; (PHOT) obturateur m.
shuttle ['ʃʌtl] n navette f ; (also: ~ **service**) (service m'de) navette f.
shuttlecock ['ʃʌtlkɔk] n volant m (de badminton).
shy [ʃaɪ] a timide ; to **fight ~ of** se dérober devant ; ~**ness** n timidité f.
Siamese [saɪə'mi:z] a: ~ **cat** chat siamois.
Sicily ['sɪsɪlɪ] n Sicile f.
sick [sɪk] a (ill) malade ; (vomiting): to be ~ vomir ; (humour) noir(e), macabre ; to **feel ~** avoir envie de vomir, avoir mal au cœur ; to be ~ **of** (fig) en avoir assez de ; ~ **bay** n infirmerie f ; ~**en** vt écœurer ; ~**ening** a (fig) écœurant(e), révoltant(e), répugnant(e).
sickle ['sɪkl] n faucille f.
sick: ~ leave n congé m de maladie ; ~**ly** a maladif(ive), souffreteux(euse) ; (causing nausea) écœurant(e) ; ~**ness** n maladie f ; (vomiting) vomissement(s) m(pl) ; ~ **pay** n indemnité f de maladie.
side [saɪd] n côté m ; (of lake, road) bord m // cpd (door, entrance) latéral(e) // vi: to ~ **with sb** prendre le parti de qn, se ranger du côté de qn ; by the ~ of au bord de ; ~ **by** ~ côte à côte ; from all ~s de tous côtés ; to take ~s (with) prendre parti (pour) ; ~**board** n buffet m ; ~**boards**, ~**burns** npl (whiskers) pattes fpl ; ~ **effect** n (MED) effet m secondaire ; ~**light** n (AUT) veilleuse f ; ~**line** n (SPORT) (ligne f de) touche f ; (fig) activité f secondaire ; ~**long** a oblique, de coin ; ~ **road** n petite route, route transversale ; ~**saddle** ad en amazone ; ~ **show** n attraction f ; ~**track** vt (fig) faire dévier de son sujet ; ~**walk** n (US) trottoir m ; ~**ways** ad de côté.
siding ['saɪdɪŋ] n (RAIL) voie f de garage.
sidle ['saɪdl] vi: to ~ **up (to)** s'approcher furtivement (de).
siege [si:dʒ] n siège m.

sieve [sɪv] n tamis m, passoire f // vt tamiser, passer (au tamis).

sift [sɪft] vt passer au tamis or au crible; (fig) passer au crible.

sigh [saɪ] n soupir m // vi soupirer, pousser un soupir.

sight [saɪt] n (faculty) vue f; (spectacle) spectacle m; (on gun) mire f // vt apercevoir; **in** ~ visible; (fig) en vue; **out of** ~ hors de vue; ~**seeing** n tourisme m; **to go** ~**seeing** faire du tourisme; ~**seer** n touriste m/f.

sign [saɪn] n (gen) signe m; (with hand etc) signe, geste m; (notice) panneau m, écriteau m // vt signer; **to** ~ **in/out** signer le registre (en arrivant/partant); **to** ~ **up** (MIL) vt engager // vi s'engager.

signal ['sɪgnl] n signal m // vt (person) faire signe à; (message) communiquer par signaux.

signature ['sɪgnətʃə*] n signature f; ~ **tune** n indicatif musical.

signet ring ['sɪgnətrɪŋ] n chevalière f.

significance [sɪg'nɪfɪkəns] n signification f; importance f.

significant [sɪg'nɪfɪkənt] a significatif(ive); (important) important(e), considérable.

signify ['sɪgnɪfaɪ] vt signifier.

sign language ['saɪnlæŋgwɪdʒ] n langage m par signes.

signpost ['saɪnpəʊst] n poteau indicateur.

silence ['saɪləns] n silence m // vt faire taire, réduire au silence; ~**r** n (on gun, AUT) silencieux m.

silent ['saɪlnt] a silencieux(euse); (film) muet(te); ~**ly** ad silencieusement.

silhouette [sɪluː'ɛt] n silhouette f // vt: **~d against** se profilant sur, se découpant contre.

silicon chip ['sɪlɪkəntʃɪp] n plaquette f de silicium.

silk [sɪlk] n soie f // cpd de or en soie; ~**y** a soyeux(euse).

silly ['sɪlɪ] a stupide, sot(te), bête.

silt [sɪlt] n vase f; limon m.

silver ['sɪlvə*] n argent m; (money) monnaie f (en pièces d'argent); (also: ~**ware**) argenterie f // cpd d'argent, en argent; ~ **paper** n papier m d'argent or d'étain; ~**-plated** a plaqué(e) argent; ~**smith** n orfèvre m/f; ~**y** a argenté(e).

similar ['sɪmɪlə*] a: ~ **(to)** semblable (à); ~**ity** [·'lærɪtɪ] n ressemblance f, similarité f; ~**ly** ad de la même façon, de même.

simile ['sɪmɪlɪ] n comparaison f.

simmer ['sɪmə*] vi cuire à feu doux, mijoter.

simple ['sɪmpl] a simple; ~**-minded** a simplet(te), simple d'esprit; **simplicity** [·'plɪsɪtɪ] n simplicité f; **simplification** [·keɪʃən] n simplification f; **simplify** ['sɪmplɪfaɪ] vt simplifier; **simply** ad simplement; avec simplicité.

simulate ['sɪmjʊleɪt] vt simuler, feindre; **simulation** [·'leɪʃən] n simulation f.

simultaneous [sɪməl'teɪnɪəs] a simultané(e); ~**ly** ad simultanément.

sin [sɪn] n péché m // vi pécher.

since [sɪns] ad,prep depuis // cj (time) depuis que; (because) puisque, étant donné que, comme; ~ **then** depuis ce moment-là.

sincere [sɪn'sɪə*] a sincère; **sincerity** [·'sɛrɪtɪ] n sincérité f.

sine [saɪn] n (MATH) sinus m.

sinew ['sɪnjuː] n tendon m; ~**s** npl muscles mpl.

sinful ['sɪnful] a coupable.

sing, pt **sang,** pp **sung** [sɪŋ, sæŋ, sʌŋ] vt,vi chanter.

singe [sɪndʒ] vt brûler légèrement; (clothes) roussir.

singer ['sɪŋə*] n chanteur/euse.

singing ['sɪŋɪŋ] n chant m.

single ['sɪŋgl] a seul(e), unique; (unmarried) célibataire; (not double) simple // n (also: ~ **ticket**) aller m (simple); (record) 45 tours m; ~**s** npl (TENNIS) simple m; **to** ~ **out** vt choisir; distinguer; ~ **bed** n lit à une place; ~**-breasted** a droit(e); **in** ~ **file** en file indienne; ~**-handed** ad tout(e) seul(e), sans (aucune) aide; ~**-minded** a résolu(e), tenace; ~ **room** n chambre f à un lit or pour une personne.

singlet ['sɪŋglɪt] n tricot m de corps.

singly ['sɪŋglɪ] ad séparément.

singular ['sɪŋgjʊlə*] a singulier(ère), étrange; remarquable; (LING) (au) singulier, du singulier // n (LING) singulier m; ~**ly** ad singulièrement; remarquablement; étrangement.

sinister ['sɪnɪstə*] a sinistre.

sink [sɪŋk] n évier m // vb (pt **sank,** pp **sunk** [sæŋk, sʌŋk]) vt (ship) (faire) couler, faire sombrer; (foundations) creuser; (piles etc): **to** ~ **sth into** enfoncer qch dans // vi couler, sombrer; (ground etc) s'affaisser; **to** ~ **in** s'enfoncer, pénétrer; **a** ~**ing feeling** un serrement de cœur.

sinner ['sɪnə*] n pécheur/eresse.

Sino- ['saɪnəʊ] prefix sino-.

sinuous ['sɪnjʊəs] a sinueux(euse).

sinus ['saɪnəs] n (ANAT) sinus m inv.

sip [sɪp] n petite gorgée // vt boire à petites gorgées.

siphon ['saɪfən] n siphon m; **to** ~ **off** vt siphonner.

sir [·ə*] n monsieur m; **S~ John Smith** sir John Smith; **yes** ~ oui Monsieur.

siren ['saɪərn] n sirène f.

sirloin ['sə:lɔɪn] n aloyau m.

sirocco [sɪ'rɔkəʊ] n sirocco m.

sissy ['sɪsɪ] n (col: coward) poule mouillée.

sister ['sɪstə*] n sœur f; (nun) religieuse f, (bonne) sœur; (nurse) infirmière f en chef; ~**-in-law** n belle-sœur f.

sit, pt,pp **sat** [sɪt, sæt] vi s'asseoir; (assembly) être en séance, siéger; (for painter) poser // vt (exam) passer, se présenter à; **to** ~ **tight** ne pas bouger; **to** ~ **down** vi s'asseoir; **to** ~ **up** vi s'asseoir; (not go to bed) rester debout, ne pas se coucher.

sitcom ['sɪtkɔm] n (abbr of **situation comedy**) comédie f de situation.

site [saɪt] n emplacement m, site m; (also: **building** ~) chantier m // vt placer.

sit-in ['sɪtɪn] n (demonstration) sit-in m inv, occupation f de locaux.

siting ['saitiŋ] n (location) emplacement m.
sitter ['sitə] n (for painter) modèle m.
sitting ['sitiŋ] n (of assembly etc) séance f; (in canteen) service m; ~ **room** n salon m.
situated ['sitjueitid] a situé(e).
situation [sitju'eiʃən] n situation f; '~s vacant/wanted' 'offres/demandes d'emploi'.
six [siks] num six; ~**teen** num seize; ~**th** a sixième; ~**ty** num soixante.
size [saiz] n taille; (of dimensions fpl; (of clothing) taille; (of shoes) pointure f; (glue) colle f; **to** ~ **up** vt juger, jauger; ~**able** a assez grand(e) or gros(se); assez important(e).
sizzle ['sizl] vi grésiller.
skate [skeit] n patin m; (fish: pl inv) raie f // vi patiner; ~**board** n skateboard m, planche f à roulettes; ~**r** n patineur/euse; **skating** n patinage m; **skating rink** n patinoire f.
skeleton ['skɛlitn] n squelette m; (outline) schéma m; ~ **staff** n effectifs réduits.
skeptic ['skɛptik] n (US) = **sceptic**.
sketch [skɛtʃ] n (drawing) croquis m, esquisse f; (THEATRE) sketch m, saynète f // vt esquisser, faire un croquis or une esquisse de; ~ **book** n carnet m à dessin; ~ **pad** n bloc m à dessin; ~**y** a incomplet(ète), fragmentaire.
skew [skju:] n: **on the** ~ de travers, en biais.
skewer ['skju:ə*] n brochette f.
ski [ski:] n ski m // vi skier, faire du ski; ~ **boot** n chaussure f de ski.
skid [skid] n dérapage m // vi déraper; ~**mark** n trace f de dérapage.
skier ['ski:ə*] n skieur/euse.
skiing ['ski:iŋ] n ski m.
ski jump ['ski:dʒʌmp] n saut m à skis.
skilful ['skilful] a habile, adroit(e).
ski lift ['ski:lift] n remonte-pente m inv.
skill [skil] n habileté f, adresse f, talent m; ~**ed** a habile, adroit(e); (worker) qualifié(e).
skim [skim] vt (milk) écrémer; (soup) écumer; (glide over) raser, effleurer // vi: **to** ~ **through** (fig) parcourir.
skimp [skimp] vt (work) bâcler, faire à la va-vite; (cloth etc) lésiner sur; ~**y** a étriqué(e); maigre.
skin [skin] n peau f // vt (fruit etc) éplucher; (animal) écorcher; ~**-deep** a superficiel(le); ~ **diving** n plongée sous-marine; ~ **graft** n greffe f de peau; ~**ny** a maigre, maigrichon(ne); ~ **test** n cuti(-réaction) f; ~**tight** a (dress etc) collant(e), ajusté(e).
skip [skip] n petit bond or saut; (container) benne f // vi gambader, sautiller; (with rope) sauter à la corde // vt (pass over) sauter.
ski pants ['ski:pænts] npl fuseau m (de ski).
skipper ['skipə*] n (NAUT. SPORT) capitaine m // vt (boat) commander; (team) être le chef de.
skipping rope ['skipiŋrəup] n corde f à sauter.

skirmish ['skə:miʃ] n escarmouche f, accrochage m.
skirt [skə:t] n jupe f // vt longer, contourner; ~**ing board** n plinthe f.
skit [skit] n sketch m satirique.
ski tow ['ski:təu] n = **ski lift**.
skittle ['skitl] n quille f; ~**s** n (game) (jeu m de) quilles.
skive [skaiv] (Brit) vi (col) tirer au flanc.
skulk [skʌlk] vi rôder furtivement.
skull [skʌl] n crâne m.
skunk [skʌŋk] n mouffette f; (fur) sconse m.
sky [skai] n ciel m; ~**-blue** a bleu ciel inv; ~**light** n lucarne f; ~**scraper** n gratte-ciel m inv.
slab [slæb] n plaque f; dalle f.
slack [slæk] a (loose) lâche, desserré(e); (slow) stagnant(e); (careless) négligent(e), peu sérieux(euse) or consciencieux(euse) // n (in rope etc) mou m; ~**s** npl pantalon m; ~**en** (also: ~**en off**) vi ralentir, diminuer; (in one's work, attention) se relâcher // vt relâcher.
slag [slæg] n scories fpl; ~ **heap** n crassier m.
slam [slæm] vt (door) (faire) claquer; (throw) jeter violemment, flanquer; (criticize) éreinter, démolir // vi claquer.
slander ['slɑ:ndə*] n calomnie f; diffamation f // vt calomnier; diffamer; ~**ous** a calomnieux(euse); diffamatoire.
slang [slæŋ] n argot m.
slant [slɑ:nt] n inclinaison f; (fig) angle m, point m de vue; ~**ed** a tendancieux(euse); ~**ing** a en pente, incliné(e); couché(e).
slap [slæp] n claque f, gifle f; tape f // vt donner une claque or une gifle or une tape à // ad (directly) tout droit, en plein; ~**dash** a fait(e) sans soin or à la va-vite; ~**stick** n (comedy) grosse farce, style m tarte à la crème; **a** ~**-up meal** un repas extra or fameux.
slash [slæʃ] vt entailler, taillader; (fig: prices) casser.
slate [sleit] n ardoise f // vt (fig: criticize) éreinter, démolir.
slaughter ['slɔ:tə*] n carnage m, massacre m // vt (animal) abattre; (people) massacrer; ~**house** n abattoir m.
Slav [slɑ:v] a slave.
slave [sleiv] n esclave m/f // vi (also: ~ away) trimer, travailler comme un forçat; ~**ry** n esclavage m.
Slavic ['slævik] a slave.
slavish ['sleiviʃ] a servile.
Slavonic [slə'vɔnik] a slave.
sleazy ['sli:zi] a miteux(euse), minable.
sledge [slɛdʒ] n luge f; ~**hammer** n marteau m de forgeron.
sleek [sli:k] a (hair, fur) brillant(e), luisant(e); (car, boat) aux lignes pures or élégantes.
sleep [sli:p] n sommeil m // vi (pt, pp **slept** [slɛpt]) dormir; (spend night) dormir, coucher; **to go to** ~ s'endormir; **to** ~ **in** vi (lie late) faire la grasse matinée; (oversleep) se réveiller trop tard; ~**er** n (person) dormeur/euse; (RAIL: on track) traverse f; (: train) train m de voitures-lits; ~**ily** ad d'un air endormi; ~**ing a**

qui dort, endormi(e); ~ing bag n sac m de couchage; ~ing car n wagon-lits m, voiture-lits f; ~ing pill n somnifère m; ~lessness n insomnie f; a ~less night une nuit blanche; ~walker n somnambule m/f; ~y a qui a envie de dormir; (fig) endormi(e).

sleet [sli:t] n neige fondue.

sleeve [sli:v] n manche f; ~less a (garment) sans manches.

sleigh [slei] n traineau m.

sleight [slait] n: ~ of hand tour m de passe-passe.

slender ['slɛndə*] a svelte, mince; faible, ténu(e).

slept [slɛpt] pt,pp of **sleep**.

slice [slais] n tranche f; (round) rondelle f // vt couper en tranches (or en rondelles).

slick [slik] a brillant(e) en apparence; mielleux(euse) // n (also: oil ~) nappe f de pétrole, marée noire.

slid [slid] pt,pp of **slide**.

slide [slaid] n (in playground) toboggan m; (PHOT) diapositive f; (also: hair ~) barrette f; (in prices) chute f, baisse f // vb (pt,pp **slid** [slid]) vt (faire) glisser // vi glisser; ~ rule n règle f à calcul; **sliding** a (door) coulissant(e); **sliding scale** n échelle f mobile.

slight [slait] a (slim) mince, menu(e); (frail) frêle; (trivial) faible, insignifiant(e); (small) petit(e), léger(ère) (before n) // n offense f, affront m // vt (offend) blesser, offenser; the ~est le (or la) moindre; not in the ~est pas le moins du monde, pas du tout; ~ly ad légèrement, un peu.

slim [slim] a mince // vi maigrir, suivre un régime amaigrissant.

slime [slaim] n vase f; substance visqueuse; **slimy** a visqueux(euse), gluant(e).

sling [sliŋ] n (MED) écharpe f // vt (pt,pp **slung** [slʌŋ]) lancer, jeter.

slip [slip] n faux pas; (mistake) erreur f; étourderie f; bévue f; (underskirt) combinaison f; (of paper) petite feuille, fiche f // vt (slide) glisser // vi (slide) glisser; (move smoothly): to ~ into/out of se glisser or se faufiler dans/hors de; (decline) baisser; to give sb the ~ fausser compagnie à qn; a ~ of the tongue un lapsus; to ~ away vi s'esquiver; to ~ in vt glisser; to ~ out vi sortir; ~ped disc n déplacement m de vertèbres.

slipper ['slipə*] n pantoufle f.

slippery ['slipəri] a glissant(e); insaisissable.

slip road ['slipraud] n (to motorway) bretelle f d'accès.

slipshod ['slipʃɔd] a négligé(e), peu soigné(e).

slip-up ['slipʌp] n bévue f.

slipway ['slipwei] n cale f (de construction or de lancement).

slit [slit] n fente f; (cut) incision f; (tear) déchirure f // vt (pt,pp **slit**) fendre; couper; inciser; déchirer.

slither ['sliðə*] vi glisser, déraper.

slob [slɔb] n (col) rustaud/e.

slog [slɔg] n gros effort; tâche fastidieuse // vi travailler très dur.

slogan ['slaugan] n slogan m.

slop [slɔp] vi (also: ~ over) se renverser; déborder // vt répandre; renverser.

slope [slaup] n pente f, côte f; (side of mountain) versant m; (slant) inclinaison f // vi: to ~ down être or descendre en pente; to ~ up monter; **sloping** a en pente, incliné(e); (handwriting) penché(e).

sloppy ['slɔpi] a (work) peu soigné(e), bâclé(e); (appearance) négligé(e), débraillé(e); (film etc) sentimental(e).

slot [slɔt] n fente f // vt: to ~ into encastrer or insérer dans; ~ machine n distributeur m (automatique), machine f à sous.

slouch [slautʃ] vi avoir le dos rond, être voûté(e).

slovenly ['slʌvənli] a sale, débraillé(e), négligé(e).

slow [slau] a lent(e); (watch): to be ~ retarder // ad lentement // vt,vi (also: ~ down, ~ up) ralentir; ' ~ ' (road sign) 'ralent' ~ly ad lentement; in ~ motion au ralenti; ~ness n lenteur f.

sludge [slʌdʒ] n boue f.

slug [slʌg] n limace f; (bullet) balle f; ~gish a mou(molle), lent(e).

sluice [slu:s] n vanne f; écluse f.

slum [slʌm] n taudis m.

slumber ['slʌmbə*] n sommeil m.

slump [slʌmp] n baisse soudaine, effondrement m; crise f // vi s'effondrer, s'affaisser.

slung [slʌŋ] pt,pp of **sling**.

slur [slə:*] n bredouillement m; (smear): ~ (on) atteinte f (à); insinuation f (contre); (MUS) liaison f // vt mal articuler; to be a ~ on porter atteinte à.

slush [slʌʃ] n neige fondue; ~y a (snow) fondu(e); (street) couvert(e) de neige fondue; (fig) sentimental(e).

slut [slʌt] n souillon f.

sly [slai] a rusé(e); sournois(e); on the ~ en cachette.

smack [smæk] n (slap) tape f; (on face) gifle f // vt donner une tape à, gifler; (child) donner la fessée à // vi: to ~ of avoir des relents de, sentir; to ~ one's lips se lécher les babines.

small [smɔ:l] a petit(e); ~ ads npl petites annonces; ~holder n petit cultivateur; in the ~ hours au petit matin; ~ish a plutôt or assez petit; ~pox n variole f; ~ talk n menus propos.

smarmy ['smɑːmi] a (col) flagorneur(euse), lécheur(euse).

smart [smɑːt] a élégant(e), chic inv; (clever) intelligent(e), astucieux(euse), futé(e); (quick) rapide, vif(vive), prompt(e) // vi faire mal, brûler; to ~en up vi devenir plus élégant(e), se faire beau(belle) // vt rendre plus élégant(e).

smash [smæʃ] n (also: ~-up) collision f, accident m // vt casser, briser, fracasser; (opponent) écraser; (hopes) ruiner, détruire; (SPORT: record) pulvériser // vi se briser, se fracasser; s'écraser; ~ing a (col) formidable.

smattering ['smætəriŋ] n: a ~ of quelques notions de.

smear [smɪə*] n tache f, salissure f; trace f; (MED) frottis m // vt enduire; (fig) porter atteinte à.

smell [smɛl] n odeur f; (sense) odorat m // vb (pt,pp smelt or smelled [smɛlt, smɛld]) vt sentir // vi (food etc): to ~ (of) sentir; (pej) sentir mauvais; ~y a qui sent mauvais, malodorant(e).

smile [smaɪl] n sourire m // vi sourire; smiling a souriant(e).

smirk [smə:k] n petit sourire suffisant or affecté.

smith [smɪθ] n maréchal-ferrant m; forgeron m; ~y n forge f.

smitten ['smɪtn] a: ~ with pris(e) de; frappé(e) de.

smock [smɔk] n blouse f, sarrau m.

smog [smɔg] n brouillard mêlé de fumée.

smoke [sməuk] n fumée f // vt, vi fumer; to have a ~ fumer une cigarette; ~d a (bacon, glass) fumé(e); ~r n (person) fumeur/euse; (RAIL) wagon m fumeurs; smoking n: 'no smoking' (sign) 'défense de fumer'; smoking room n fumoir m; smoky a enfumé(e); (surface) noirci(e) par la fumée.

smolder ['sməuldə*] vi (US) = smoulder.

smooth [smu:ð] a lisse; (sauce) onctueux(euse); (flavour, whisky) moelleux(euse); (movement) régulier(ère), sans à-coups or heurts; (person) doucereux(euse), mielleux(euse) // vt lisser, défroisser; (also: ~ out) (creases, difficulties) faire disparaître.

smother ['smʌðə*] vt étouffer.

smoulder ['sməuldə*] vi couver.

smudge [smʌdʒ] n tache f, bavure f // vt salir, maculer.

smug [smʌg] a suffisant(e), content(e) de soi.

smuggle ['smʌgl] vt passer en contrebande or en fraude; ~r n contrebandier/ère; smuggling n contrebande f.

smutty ['smʌtɪ] a (fig) grossier(ère), obscène.

snack [snæk] n casse-croûte m inv; ~ bar n snack(-bar) m.

snag [snæg] n inconvénient m, difficulté f.

snail [sneɪl] n escargot m.

snake [sneɪk] n serpent m.

snap [snæp] n (sound) claquement m, bruit sec; (photograph) photo f, instantané m; (game) sorte f de jeu de bataille // a subit(e); fait(e) sans réfléchir // vt faire claquer; (break) casser net; (photograph) prendre un instantané de // vi se casser net or avec un bruit sec; to ~ open/shut s'ouvrir/se refermer brusquement; to ~ at vt fus (subj: dog) essayer de mordre; to ~ off vt (break) casser net; to ~ up vt sauter sur, saisir; ~ fastener n bouton-pression m; ~py a prompt(e); ~shot n photo f, instantané m.

snare [snɛə*] n piège m // vt attraper, prendre au piège.

snarl [snɑ:l] n grondement m or grognement m féroce // vi gronder.

snatch [snætʃ] n (fig) vol m; (small amount): ~es of des fragments mpl or

bribes fpl de // vt saisir (d'un geste vif); (steal) voler.

sneak [sni:k] vi: to ~ in/out entrer/sortir furtivement or à la dérobée; ~y a sournois(e).

sneer [snɪə*] n ricanement m // vi ricaner, sourire d'un air sarcastique.

sneeze [sni:z] n éternuement m // vi éternuer.

snide [snaɪd] a sarcastique, narquois(e).

sniff [snɪf] n reniflement m // vi renifler // vt renifler, flairer.

snigger ['snɪgə*] n ricanement m; rire moqueur // vi ricaner; pouffer de rire.

snip [snɪp] n petit bout; (bargain) (bonne) occasion or affaire // vt couper.

sniper ['snaɪpə*] n (marksman) tireur embusqué.

snippet ['snɪpɪt] n bribes fpl.

snivelling ['snɪvlɪŋ] a (whimpering) larmoyant(e), pleurnicheur(euse).

snob [snɔb] n snob m/f; ~bery n snobisme m; ~bish a snob inv.

snooker ['snu:kə*] n sorte de jeu de billard.

snoop ['snu:p] vi: to ~ on sb espionner qn.

snooty ['snu:tɪ] a snob inv, prétentieux(euse).

snooze [snu:z] n petit somme // vi faire un petit somme.

snore [snɔ:*] vi ronfler; snoring n ronflement(s) m(pl).

snorkel ['snɔ:kl] n (of swimmer) tuba m.

snort [snɔ:t] n grognement m // vi grogner; (horse) renâcler.

snotty ['snɔtɪ] a morveux(euse).

snout [snaut] n museau m.

snow [snəu] n neige f // vi neiger; ~ball n boule f de neige; ~bound a enneigé(e), bloqué(e) par la neige; ~drift n congère f; ~drop n perce-neige m; ~fall n chute f de neige; ~flake n flocon m de neige; ~m... n bonhomme m de neige; ~plough, ~plow (US) n chasse-neige m inv; ~storm n tempête f de neige.

snub [snʌb] vt repousser, snober // n rebuffade f; ~-nosed a au nez retroussé.

snuff [snʌf] n tabac m à priser.

snug [snʌg] a douillet(te), confortable.

so [səu] ad (degree) si, tellement; (manner: thus) ainsi, de cette façon // cj donc, par conséquent; ~ as to do afin de or pour faire; ~ that (purpose) afin de + infinitive, pour que or afin que +sub; (result) si bien que, de (telle) sorte que; ~ do I, ~ am I etc moi etc aussi; if ~ si oui; I hope ~ je l'espère; 10 or ~ 10 à peu près or environ; ~ far jusqu'ici, jusqu'à maintenant; (in past) jusque-là; ~ long! (col) à bientôt!, au revoir!; ~ many tant de; ~ much ad tant // det tant de; ~ and ~ n un tel(une telle).

soak [səuk] vt faire or laisser tremper // vi tremper; to be ~ed through être trempé jusqu'aux os; to ~ in vi pénétrer, être absorbé(e) // ; to ~ up vt absorber.

soap [səup] n savon m; ~flakes npl paillettes fpl de savon; ~ powder n lessive f, détergent m; ~y a savonneux(euse).

soar [sɔ:*] vi monter (en flèche), s'élancer.

sob [sɔb] n sanglot m // vi sangloter.

sober ['səubə*] a qui n'est pas (or plus) ivre; (sedate) sérieux(euse), sensé(e); (moderate) mesuré(e); (colour, style) sobre, discret(ète); to ~ up vt dégriser // vi se dégriser.

Soc. abbr of **society**.

so-called ['səu'kɔ:ld] a soi-disant inv.

soccer ['sɔkə*] n football m.

sociable ['səuʃəbl] a sociable.

social ['səuʃl] a social(e) // n (petite) fête; ~ club n amicale f, foyer m; ~ism n socialisme m; ~ist a,n socialiste (m/f); ~ly ad socialement, en société; ~ science n sciences humaines; ~ security n aide sociale; ~ welfare n sécurité sociale; ~ work n assistance sociale; ~ worker n assistant/e social/e.

society [sə'saiəti] n société f; (club) société, association f; (also: high ~) (haute) société, grand monde.

sociological [səusiə'lɔdʒikl] a sociologique.

sociologist [səusi'ɔlədʒist] n sociologue m/f.

sociology [səusi'ɔlədʒi] n sociologie f.

sock [sɔk] n chaussette f // vt (hit) flanquer un coup à.

socket ['sɔkit] n cavité f; (ELEC: also: wall ~) prise f de courant; (: for light bulb) douille f.

sod [sɔd] n (of earth) motte f; (col!) con m (!); salaud m (!).

soda ['səudə] n (CHEM) soude f; (also: ~ water) eau f de Seltz.

sodden ['sɔdn] a trempé(e); détrempé(e).

sodium ['səudiəm] n sodium m.

sofa ['səufə] n sofa m; canapé m.

soft [sɔft] a (not rough) doux/(douce); (not hard) doux; mou(molle); (not loud) doux, léger(ère); (kind) doux, gentil(le); (weak) indulgent(e); (stupid) stupide, débile; ~ drink n boisson non alcoolisée; ~en ['sɔfn] vt (r)amollir; adoucir; atténuer // vi se ramollir; s'adoucir; s'atténuer; ~-hearted a au cœur tendre; ~ly ad doucement; gentiment; ~ness n douceur f; ~ware n logiciel m, software m.

soggy ['sɔgi] a trempé(e); détrempé(e).

soil [sɔil] n (earth) sol m, terre f // vt salir; (fig) souiller; ~ed a sale; (COMM) défraîchi(e).

solar ['səulə*] a solaire.

sold [səuld] pt,pp of **sell**; ~ out a (COMM) épuisé(e).

solder ['səuldə*] vt souder (au fil à souder) // n soudure f.

soldier ['səuldʒə*] n soldat m, militaire m.

sole [səul] n (of foot) plante f; (of shoe) semelle f; (fish: pl inv) sole f // a seul(e), unique; ~ly ad seulement, uniquement.

solemn ['sɔləm] a solennel(le); sérieux(euse), grave.

solicitor [sə'lisitə*] n (for wills etc) ≈ notaire m; (in court) ≈ avocat m.

solid ['sɔlid] a (not hollow) plein(e), compact(e), massif(ive); (strong, sound, reliable, not liquid) solide; (meal) consistant(e), substantiel(le) // n solide m.

solidarity [sɔli'dæriti] n solidarité f.

solidify [sə'lidifai] vi se solidifier // vt solidifier.

solidity [sə'liditi] n solidité f.

soliloquy [sə'liləkwi] n monologue m.

solitaire [sɔli'tɛə*] n (game, gem) solitaire m.

solitary ['sɔlitəri] a solitaire; ~ confinement n (LAW) isolement m.

solitude ['sɔlitju:d] n solitude f.

solo ['səuləu] n solo m; ~ist n soliste m/f.

solstice ['sɔlstis] n solstice m.

soluble ['sɔljubl] a soluble.

solution [sə'lu:ʃən] n solution f.

solve [sɔlv] vt résoudre.

solvent ['sɔlvənt] a (COMM) solvable // n (CHEM) (dis)solvant m.

sombre, somber (US) ['sɔmbə*] a sombre, morne.

some [sʌm] det (a few) quelques; (certain) certains(certaines); (a certain number or amount) see phrases below; (unspecified) un(e)... (quelconque) // pronoun quelques uns(un ; un peu // ad: ~ 10 people quelque 10 personnes, 10 personnes environ; ~ children came des enfants sont venus; have ~ tea/ice-cream/water prends du thé/de la glace/de l'eau; there's ~ milk in the fridge il y a un peu de lait or du lait dans le frigo; ~ (of it) was left il en est resté un peu; I've got ~ (i.e. books etc) j'en ai (quelques uns); (i.e. milk, money etc) j'en ai (un peu); ~body pronoun quelqu'un; ~ day ad un de ces jours, un jour ou l'autre; ~how ad d'une façon ou d'une autre; (for some reason) pour une raison ou une autre; ~one pronoun = somebody; ~place ad (US) = somewhere.

somersault ['sʌməsɔ:lt] n culbute f, saut périlleux // vi faire la culbute or un saut périlleux; (car) faire un tonneau.

something ['sʌmθiŋ] pronoun quelque chose m; ~ interesting quelque chose d'intéressant.

sometime ['sʌmtaim] ad (in future) un de ces jours, un jour ou l'autre; (in past): ~ last month au cours du mois dernier.

sometimes ['sʌmtaimz] ad quelquefois, parfois.

somewhat ['sʌmwɔt] ad quelque peu, un peu.

somewhere ['sʌmwɛə*] ad quelque part.

son [sʌn] n fils m.

sonata [sə'nɑ:tə] n sonate f.

song [sɔŋ] n chanson f; ~book n chansonnier m; ~writer n auteur-compositeur m.

sonic ['sɔnik] a (boom) supersonique.

son-in-law ['sʌninlɔ:] n gendre m, beau-fils m.

sonnet ['sɔnit] n sonnet m.

sonny ['sʌni] n (col) fiston m.

soon [su:n] ad bientôt; (early) tôt; ~ afterwards peu après; see also as; ~er ad (time) plus tôt; (preference): I would ~er do j'aimerais autant or je préférerais faire; ~er or later tôt ou tard.

soot [sut] n suie f.

soothe [su:ð] vt calmer, apaiser.

sop [sɔp] n: that's only a ~ c'est pour nous (or les etc) amadouer.

sophisticated [sə'fɪstɪkeɪtɪd] a raffiné(e), sophistiqué(e), hautement perfectionné(e), très complexe.

sophomore ['sɔfəmɔ:*] n (US) étudiant/e de seconde année.

soporific [sɔpə'rɪfɪk] a soporifique // n somnifère m.

sopping ['sɔpɪŋ] a (also: ~ wet) tout(e) trempé(e).

soppy ['sɔpɪ] a (pej) sentimental(e).

soprano [sə'prɑ:nəu] n (voice) soprano m; (singer) soprano m/f.

sorcerer ['sɔ:sərə*] n sorcier m.

sordid ['sɔ:dɪd] a sordide.

sore [sɔ:*] a (painful) douloureux(euse), sensible; (offended) contrarié(e), vexé(e) // n plaie f; ~ly ad (tempted) fortement.

sorrel ['sɔrəl] n oseille f.

sorrow ['sɔrəu] n peine f, chagrin m; ~ful a triste.

sorry ['sɔrɪ] a désolé(e); (condition, excuse) triste, déplorable; ~! pardon!, excusez-moi!; to feel ~ for sb plaindre qn.

sort [sɔ:t] n genre m, espèce f, sorte f // vt (also: ~ out: papers) trier; classer; ranger; (: letters etc) trier; (: problems) résoudre, régler; ~ing office n bureau m de tri.

SOS n (abbr of save our souls) S.O.S. m.

so-so ['səusəu] ad comme ci comme ça.

soufflé ['su:fleɪ] n soufflé m.

sought [sɔ:t] pt,pp of seek.

soul [səul] n âme f; ~-destroying a démoralisant(e); ~ful a plein(e) de sentiment; ~less a sans cœur, inhumain(e).

sound [saund] a (healthy) en bonne santé, sain(e); (safe, not damaged) solide, en bon état; (reliable, not superficial) sérieux(euse), solide; (sensible) sensé(e) // ad: ~ asleep dormant d'un profond sommeil // n (noise) son m; bruit m; (GEO) détroit m, bras m de mer // vt (alarm) sonner; (also: ~ out: opinions) sonder // vi sonner, retentir; (fig: seem) sembler (être); to ~ one's horn (AUT) actionner son avertisseur; to ~ like ressembler à; ~ barrier n mur m du son; ~ effects npl bruitage m; ~ing n (NAUT etc) sondage m; ~ly ad (sleep) profondément; (beat) complètement, à plate couture; ~proof vt insonoriser // a insonorisé(e); ~track n (of film) bande f sonore.

soup [su:p] n soupe f, potage m; in the ~ (fig) dans le pétrin; ~ course n potage m; ~spoon n cuiller f à soupe.

sour ['sauə*] a aigre, acide; (milk) tourné(e), aigre; (fig) acerbe, aigre, revêche; it's ~ grapes c'est du dépit.

source [sɔ:s] n source f.

south [sauθ] n sud m // a sud inv, du sud // ad au sud, vers le sud; S~ Africa n Afrique f du Sud; S~ African a sud-africain(e) // n Sud-Africain/e; S~ America n Amérique f du Sud; S~ American a sud-américain(e) // n Sud-Américain/e; ~-east n sud-est m; ~erly ['sʌðəlɪ] a du sud; au sud; ~ern ['sʌðən] a (du) sud; méridional(e); exposé(e) au

sud; S~ Pole n Pôle m Sud; ~ward(s) ad vers le sud; ~-west n sud-ouest m.

souvenir [su:və'nɪə*] n souvenir m (objet).

sovereign ['sɔvrɪn] a,n souverain(e); ~ty n souveraineté f.

soviet ['səuvɪət] a soviétique; the S~ Union l'Union f soviétique.

sow n [sau] truie f // vt [səu] (pt ~ed, pp sown [səun]) semer.

soy [sɔɪ] n (also: ~ sauce) sauce f de soja.

soya bean ['sɔɪəbi:n] n graine f de soja.

spa [spɑ:] n (spring) source minérale; (town) station thermale.

space [speɪs] n (gen) espace m; (room) place f; espace; (length of time) laps m de temps // cpd spatial(e) // vt (also: ~ out) espacer; ~craft n engin spatial; ~man/woman n astronaute m/f, cosmonaute m/f; ~ing n espacement m; single/double spacing interligne m simple/double.

spacious ['speɪʃəs] a spacieux(euse), grand(e).

spade [speɪd] n (tool) bêche f, pelle f; (child's) pelle; ~s npl (CARDS) pique m; ~work n (fig) gros m du travail.

spaghetti [spə'getɪ] n spaghetti mpl.

Spain [speɪn] n Espagne f.

span [spæn] pt of spin // n (of bird, plane) envergure f; (of arch) portée f; (in time) espace m de temps, durée f // vt enjamber, franchir; (fig) couvrir, embrasser.

Spaniard ['spænjəd] n Espagnol/e.

spaniel ['spænjəl] n épagneul m.

Spanish ['spænɪʃ] a espagnol(e), d'Espagne // n (LING) espagnol m.

spank [spæŋk] vt donner une fessée à.

spanner ['spænə*] n clé f (de mécanicien).

spare [spɛə*] a de réserve, de rechange; (surplus) de or en trop, de reste // n (part) pièce f de rechange, pièce détachée // vt (do without) se passer de; (afford to give) donner, accorder, passer; (refrain from hurting) épargner; (refrain from using) ménager; to ~ (surplus) en surplus, de trop; ~ part n pièce f de rechange, pièce détachée; ~ time n moments mpl de loisir.

sparing ['spɛərɪŋ] a modéré(e), restreint(e); ~ of chiche de; ~ly ad avec modération.

spark [spɑ:k] n étincelle f; (fig) étincelle, lueur f; ~(ing) plug n bougie f.

sparkle ['spɑ:kl] n scintillement m, étincellement m, éclat m // vi étinceler, scintiller; (bubble) pétiller; sparkling a étincelant(e), scintillant(e); (wine) mousseux (euse), pétillant(e).

sparrow ['spærəu] n moineau m.

sparse [spɑ:s] a clairsemé(e).

spasm ['spæzəm] n (MED) spasme m; (fig) accès m; ~odic [-'mɔdɪk] a spasmodique; (fig) intermittent(e).

spastic ['spæstɪk] n handicapé/e moteur.

spat [spæt] pt,pp of spit.

spate [speɪt] n (fig): ~ of avalanche f or torrent m de; in ~ (river) en crue.

spatter ['spætə*] n éclaboussure(s) f(pl) // vt éclabousser // vi gicler.

spatula ['spætjulə] n spatule f.

spawn [spɔ:n] vt pondre // vi frayer // n frai m.

speak, *pt* **spoke**, *pp* **spoken** [spi:k, spəuk, spəukn] *vt* (*language*) parler; (*truth*) dire // *vi* parler; (*make a speech*) prendre la parole; **to ~ to** sb/**of** *or* **about** sth parler à qn/de qch; **it ~s for itself** c'est évident; **~ up!** parle plus fort!; **~er** *n* (*in public*) orateur *m*; (*also:* loud**~er**) haut-parleur *m*; (*POL*): **the S~er** le *président de la chambre des Communes*; **to be on ~ing terms** se parler.

spear [spɪə*] *n* lance *f* // *vt* transpercer.

spec [spɛk] *n* (*col*): **on ~** à tout hasard.

special [ˈspɛʃl] *a* spécial(e); **take ~ care** soyez particulièrement prudents; **today's ~** (*at restaurant*) le menu; **~ist** *n* spécialiste *m/f*; **~ity** [spɛʃiˈælɪtɪ] *n* spécialité *f*; **~ize** *vi*: **to ~ize (in)** se spécialiser (dans); **~ly** *ad* spécialement, particulièrement.

species [ˈspiːʃiːz] *n* espèce *f*.

specific [spəˈsɪfɪk] *a* précis(e); particulier(ère); (*BOT, CHEM etc*) spécifique; **~ally** *ad* expressément, explicitement; **~ation** [spɛsɪfɪˈkeɪʃn] *n* spécification *f*; stipulation *f*.

specify [ˈspɛsɪfaɪ] *vt* spécifier, préciser.

specimen [ˈspɛsɪmən] *n* spécimen *m*, échantillon *m*; (*MED*) prélèvement *m*.

speck [spɛk] *n* petite tache, petit point; (*particle*) grain *m*.

speckled [ˈspɛkld] *a* tacheté(e), moucheté(e).

specs [spɛks] *npl* (*col*) lunettes *fpl*.

spectacle [ˈspɛktəkl] *n* spectacle *m*; **~s** *npl* lunettes *fpl*; **spectacular** [-ˈtækjulə*] *a* spectaculaire // *n* (*CINEMA etc*) superproduction *f*.

spectator [spɛkˈteɪtə*] *n* spectateur/trice.

spectra [ˈspɛktrə] *npl of* **spectrum**.

spectre, **specter** (*US*) [ˈspɛktə*] *n* spectre *m*, fantôme *m*.

spectrum, *pl* **spectra** [ˈspɛktrəm, -rə] *n* spectre *m*; (*fig*) gamme *f*.

speculate [ˈspɛkjuleɪt] *vi* spéculer; (*try to guess*): **to ~ about** s'interroger sur; **speculation** [-ˈleɪʃən] *n* spéculation *f*; conjectures *fpl*; **speculative** *a* spéculatif(ive).

speech [spiːtʃ] *n* (*faculty*) parole *f*; (*talk*) discours *m*, allocution *f*; (*manner of speaking*) façon *f* de parler, langage *m*; (*enunciation*) élocution *f*; **~ day** *n* (*SCOL*) distribution *f* des prix; **~less** *a* muet(te); **~ therapy** *n* orthophonie *f*.

speed [spiːd] *n* vitesse *f*; (*promptness*) rapidité *f*; **at full** *or* **top ~** à toute vitesse *or* allure; **to ~ up** *vi* aller plus vite, accélérer // *vt* accélérer; **~boat** *n* vedette *f*; hors-bord *m inv*; **~ily** *ad* rapidement, promptement; **~ing** *n* (*AUT*) excès *m* de vitesse; **~ limit** *n* limitation *f* de vitesse, vitesse maximale permise; **~ometer** [spɪˈdɔmɪtə*] *n* compteur *m* (de vitesse); **~way** *n* (*SPORT*) piste *f* de vitesse pour motos; **~y** *a* rapide, prompt(e).

speleologist [spɛlɪˈɔlədʒɪst] *n* spéléologue *m/f*.

spell [spɛl] *n* (*also:* **magic ~**) sortilège *m*, charme *m*; (*period of time*) (courte) période // *vt* (*pt,pp* **spelt** *or* **~ed** [spɛlt, spɛld]) (*in writing*) écrire, orthographier; (*aloud*) épeler; (*fig*) signifier; **to cast a ~ on** sb jeter un sort à qn; **he can't ~** il fait des fautes d'orthographe; **~bound** *a* envoûté(e), subjugué(e); **~ing** *n* orthographe *f*.

spelt [spɛlt] *pt,pp of* **spell**.

spend, *pt,pp* **spent** [spɛnd, spɛnt] *vt* (*money*) dépenser; (*time, life*) passer; consacrer; **~ing money** *n* argent *m* de poche; **~thrift** *n* dépensier/ère.

spent [spɛnt] *pt,pp of* **spend** // *a* (*patience*) épuisé(e), à bout.

sperm [spə:m] *n* spermatozoïde *m*; (*semen*) sperme *m*; **~ whale** *n* cachalot *m*.

spew [spju:] *vt* vomir.

sphere [sfɪə*] *n* sphère *f*; (*fig*) sphère, domaine *m*; **spherical** [ˈsfɛrɪkl] *a* sphérique.

sphinx [sfɪŋks] *n* sphinx *m*.

spice [spaɪs] *n* épice *f* // *vt* épicer.

spick-and-span [ˈspɪkənˈspæn] *a* impeccable.

spicy [ˈspaɪsɪ] *a* épicé(e), relevé(e); (*fig*) piquant(e).

spider [ˈspaɪdə*] *n* araignée *f*.

spiel [spiːl] *n* laïus *m inv*.

spike [spaɪk] *n* pointe *f*.

spill, *pt,pp* **spilt** *or* **~ed** [spɪl, -t, -d] *vt* renverser; répandre // *vi* se répandre.

spin [spɪn] *n* (*revolution of wheel*) tour *m*; (*AVIAT*) (chute *f* en) vrille *f*; (*trip in car*) petit tour, balade *f* // *vb* (*pt* **spun**, **span**, *pp* **spun** [spʌn, spæn]) *vt* (*wool etc*) filer; (*wheel*) faire tourner // *vi* tourner, tournoyer; **to ~ a yarn** débiter une longue histoire; **to ~ a coin** jouer à pile ou face; **to ~ out** *vt* faire durer.

spinach [ˈspɪnɪtʃ] *n* épinard *m*; (*as food*) épinards.

spinal [ˈspaɪnl] *a* vertébral(e), spinal(e); **~ cord** *n* moelle épinière.

spindly [ˈspɪndlɪ] *a* grêle, filiforme.

spin-drier [spɪnˈdraɪə*] *n* essoreuse *f*.

spine [spaɪn] *n* colonne vertébrale; (*thorn*) épine *f*, piquant *m*; **~less** *a* invertébré(e); (*fig*) mou(molle), sans caractère.

spinner [ˈspɪnə*] *n* (*of thread*) fileur/euse.

spinning [ˈspɪnɪŋ] *n* (*of thread*) filage *m*; (*by machine*) filature *f*; **~ top** *n* toupie *f*; **~ wheel** *n* rouet *m*.

spinster [ˈspɪnstə*] *n* célibataire *f*; vieille fille.

spiral [ˈspaɪərl] *n* spirale *f* // *a* en spirale // *vi* (*fig*) monter en flèche; **~ staircase** *n* escalier *m* en colimaçon.

spire [ˈspaɪə*] *n* flèche *f*, aiguille *f*.

spirit [ˈspɪrɪt] *n* (*soul*) esprit *m*, âme *f*; (*ghost*) esprit, revenant *m*; (*mood*) esprit, état *m* d'esprit; (*courage*) courage *m*, énergie *f*; **~s** *npl* (*drink*) spiritueux *mpl*, alcool *m*; **in good ~s** de bonne humeur; **in low ~s** démoralisé(e); **~ed** *a* vif(vive), fougueux(euse), plein(e) d'allant; **~ level** *n* niveau *m* à bulle.

spiritual [ˈspɪrɪtjuəl] *a* spirituel(le); religieux(euse) // *n* (*also:* **Negro ~**) spiritual *m*; **~ism** *n* spiritisme *m*.

spit [spɪt] *n* (*for roasting*) broche *f* // *vi* (*pt, pp* **spat** [spæt]) cracher; (*sound*) crépiter.

spite [spaɪt] n rancune f, dépit m // vt contrarier, vexer; **in ~ of** en dépit de, malgré; **~ful** a malveillant(e), rancunier(ère).

spitroast ['spɪt'rəust] vt faire rôtir à la broche.

spittle ['spɪtl] n salive f; bave f; crachat m.

spiv [spɪv] n (col) chevalier m d'industrie, aigrefin m.

splash [splæʃ] n éclaboussement m; (sound) plouf; (of colour) tache f // vt éclabousser; vi (also: ~ **about**) barboter, patauger.

splay [spleɪ] a: **~footed** marchant les pieds en dehors.

spleen [spliːn] n (ANAT) rate f.

splendid ['splɛndɪd] a splendide, superbe, magnifique.

splendour, splendor (US) ['splɛndə*] n splendeur f, magnificence f.

splice [splaɪs] vt épisser.

splint [splɪnt] n attelle f, éclisse f.

splinter ['splɪntə*] n (wood) écharde f; (metal) éclat m // vi se fragmenter.

split [splɪt] n fente f, déchirure f; (fig: POL) scission f // vb (pt,pp **split**) vt fendre, déchirer; (party) diviser; (work, profits) partager, répartir // vi (divide) se diviser; **to ~ up** (couple) se séparer, rompre; (meeting) se disperser; **~ting headache** n mal m de tête atroce.

splutter ['splʌtə*] vi bafouiller; postillonner.

spoil, pt,pp **spoilt** or **~ed** [spɔɪl, -t, -d] vt (damage) abîmer; (mar) gâcher; (child) gâter; **~s** npl butin m; **~sport** n trouble-fête m, rabat-joie m.

spoke [spəuk] pt of **speak** // n rayon m.

spoken ['spəukn] pp of **speak**.

spokesman ['spəuksmən] n porteparole m inv.

sponge [spʌndʒ] n éponge f // vt éponger // vi: **to ~ on** vivre aux crochets de; **~ bag** n sac m de toilette; **~ cake** n ≈ gâteau m de Savoie; **~r** n (pej) parasite m; **spongy** a spongieux(euse).

sponsor ['spɔnsə*] n (RADIO, TV) personne f (or organisme m) qui assure le patronage // vt patronner; parrainer; **~ship** n patronage m; parrainage m.

spontaneity [spɔntə'neɪtɪ] n spontanéité f.

spontaneous [spɔn'teɪnɪəs] a spontané(e).

spooky ['spuːkɪ] a qui donne la chair de poule.

spool [spuːl] n bobine f.

spoon [spuːn] n cuiller f; **~-feed** vt nourrir à la cuiller; (fig) mâcher le travail à; **~ful** n cuillerée f.

sporadic [spə'rædɪk] a sporadique.

sport [spɔːt] n sport m; (person) chic type/chic fille f // vt arborer; **~ing** a sportif(ive); du sponae **to give sb a ~ing chance** donner sa chance à qn; **~s car** n voiture f de sport; **~s jacket** n veste f de sport; **~sman** n sportif m; **~smanship** n esprit sportif, sportivité f; **~s page** n page f des sports; **~swear** n vêtements mpl de sport; **~swoman** n sportive f; **~y** a sportif(ive).

spot [spɔt] n tache f; (dot: on pattern) pois m; (pimple) bouton m; (place) endroit m, coin m; (small amount): **a ~ of** un peu de // vt (notice) apercevoir, repérer; **on the ~** sur place, sur les lieux; **to come out in ~s** se couvrir de boutons, avoir une éruption de boutons; **~ check** n sondage m, vérification ponctuelle; **~less** a immaculé(e); **~light** n projecteur m; (AUT) phare m auxiliaire; **~ted** a tacheté(e), moucheté(e); à pois; **~ted with** tacheté(e) de; **~ty** a (face) boutonneux(euse).

spouse [spauz] n époux/épouse.

spout [spaut] n (of jug) bec m; (of liquid) jet m // vi jaillir.

sprain [spreɪn] n entorse f, foulure f // vt: **to ~ one's ankle** se fouler or se tordre la cheville.

sprang [spræŋ] pt of **spring**.

sprawl [sprɔːl] vi s'étaler.

spray [spreɪ] n jet m (en fines gouttelettes); (container) vaporisateur m, bombe f; (of flowers) petit bouquet // vt vaporiser, pulvériser; (crops) traiter.

spread [sprɛd] n propagation f; (distribution) répartition f; (CULIN) pâte f à tartiner // vb (pt,pp **spread**) vt étendre, étaler; répandre; propager // vi s'étendre; se répandre; se propager.

spree [spriː] n: **to go on a ~** faire la fête.

sprig [sprɪg] n rameau m.

sprightly ['spraɪtlɪ] a alerte.

spring [sprɪŋ] n (leap) bond m, saut m; (coiled metal) ressort m; (season) printemps m; (of water) source f // vi (pt **sprang**, pp **sprung** [spræŋ, sprʌŋ]) bondir, sauter; **to ~ from** provenir de; **to ~ up** vi (problem) se présenter, surgir; **~board** n tremplin m; **~-clean** n (also: **~-cleaning**) grand nettoyage de printemps; **~time** n printemps m; **~y** a élastique, souple.

sprinkle ['sprɪŋkl] vt (pour) répandre; verser; **to ~ water etc on, ~ with water** etc asperger d'eau etc; **to ~ sugar etc on, ~ with sugar** etc saupoudrer de sucre etc; **~d with** (fig) parsemé(e) de.

sprint [sprɪnt] n sprint m // vi sprinter; **~er** n sprinteur/euse.

sprite [spraɪt] n lutin m.

sprout [spraut] vi germer, pousser; (Brussels) **~s** npl choux mpl de Bruxelles.

spruce [spruːs] n épicéa m // a net(te), pimpant(e).

sprung [sprʌŋ] pp of **spring**.

spry [spraɪ] a alerte, vif(vive).

spud [spʌd] n (col: potato) patate f.

spun [spʌn] pt, pp of **spin**.

spur [spəː*] n éperon m; (fig) aiguillon m // vt (also: ~ **on**) éperonner; aiguillonner; **on the ~ of the moment** sous l'impulsion du moment.

spurious ['spjuərɪəs] a faux(fausse).

spurn [spəːn] vt repousser avec mépris.

spurt [spəːt] n jet m; (of energy) sursaut m // vi jaillir, gicler.

spy [spaɪ] n espion/ne // vi: **to ~ on** espionner, épier // vt (see) apercevoir; **~ing** n espionnage m.

sq. (MATH), **Sq.** (in address) abbr of **square**.
squabble ['skwɔbl] n querelle f, chamaillerie f // vi se chamailler.
squad [skwɔd] n (MIL, POLICE) escouade f, groupe m; (FOOTBALL) contingent m.
squadron ['skwɔdrn] n (MIL) escadron m; (AVIAT, NAUT) escadrille f.
squalid ['skwɔlid] a sordide, ignoble.
squall [skwɔ:l] n rafale f, bourrasque f.
squalor ['skwɔlə*] n conditions fpl sordides.
squander ['skwɔndə*] vt gaspiller, dilapider.
square [skwɛə*] n carré m; (in town) place f; (instrument) équerre f // a carré(e); (honest) honnête, régulier(ère); (col: ideas, tastes) vieux jeu inv, qui retarde // vt (arrange) régler; arranger; (MATH) élever au carré // vi (agree) cadrer, s'accorder; **all** ~ quitte; à égalité; **a** ~ **meal** un repas convenable; **2 metres** ~ (de) 2 mètres sur 2; **1** ~ **metre** 1 mètre carré; **~ly** ad carrément.
squash [skwɔʃ] n (drink): lemon/orange ~ citronnade f/ orangeade f; (SPORT) squash m // vt écraser.
squat [skwɔt] a petit(e) et épais(se), ramassé(e) // vi s'accroupir; ~**ter** n squatter m.
squawk [skwɔ:k] vi pousser un or des gloussement(s).
squeak [skwi:k] n grincement m; petit cri // vi grincer, crier.
squeal [skwi:l] vi pousser un or des cri(s) aigu(s) or perçant(s).
squeamish ['skwi:miʃ] a facilement dégoûté(e); facilement scandalisé(e).
squeeze [skwi:z] n pression f; restrictions fpl de crédit // vt presser; (hand, arm) serrer; **to** ~ **out** vt exprimer; (fig) soutirer.
squelch [skwɛltʃ] vi faire un bruit de succion; patauger.
squib [skwib] n pétard m.
squid [skwid] n calmar m.
squint [skwint] vi loucher // n: **he has a** ~ il louche, il souffre de strabisme.
squire ['skwaiə*] n propriétaire terrien.
squirm [skwə:m] vi se tortiller.
squirrel ['skwirəl] n écureuil m.
squirt [skwə:t] n jet m // vi jaillir, gicler.
Sr abbr of **senior**.
St abbr of **saint**, **street**.
stab [stæb] n (with knife etc) coup m (de couteau etc); (col: try): **to have a** ~ **at** (doing) sth s'essayer à (faire) qch // vt poignarder.
stability [stə'biliti] n stabilité f.
stabilize ['steibəlaiz] vt stabiliser; ~**r** n stabilisateur m.
stable ['steibl] n écurie f // a stable.
stack [stæk] n tas m, pile f // vt empiler, entasser.
stadium ['steidiəm] n stade m.
staff [stɑ:f] n (work force) personnel m; (: SCOL) professeurs mpl; (: servants) domestiques mpl; (MIL) état-major m; (stick) perche f, bâton m // vt pourvoir en personnel.
stag [stæg] n cerf m.

stage [steidʒ] n scène f; (profession): **the** ~ le théâtre; (point) étape f, stade m; (platform) estrade f // vt (play) monter, mettre en scène; (demonstration) organiser; (fig: perform: recovery etc) effectuer; **in** ~**s** par étapes, par degrés; ~**coach** n diligence f; ~ **door** n entrée f des artistes; ~ **fright** n trac m; ~ **manager** n régisseur m.
stagger ['stægə*] vi chanceler, tituber // vt (person) stupéfier; bouleverser; (hours, holidays) étaler, échelonner; ~**ing** a (amazing) stupéfiant(e), renversant(e).
stagnant ['stægnənt] a stagnant(e).
stagnate [stæg'neit] vi stagner, croupir.
stag party ['stægpɑ:ti] n enterrement m de vie de garçon.
staid [steid] a posé(e), rassis(e).
stain [stein] n tache f; (colouring) colorant m // vt tacher; (wood) teindre; ~**ed glass window** n vitrail m; ~**less** a (steel) inoxydable; ~ **remover** n détachant m.
stair [stɛə*] n (step) marche f; ~**s** npl escalier m; **on the** ~**s** dans l'escalier; ~**case**, ~**way** n escalier m.
stake [steik] n pieu m, poteau m; (BETTING) enjeu m // vt risquer, jouer; **to be at** ~ être en jeu.
stalactite ['stæləktait] n stalactite f.
stalagmite ['stæləgmait] n stalagmite m.
stale [steil] a (bread) rassis(e); (beer) éventé(e); (smell) de renfermé.
stalemate ['steilmeit] n pat m; (fig) impasse f.
stalk [stɔ:k] n tige f // vt traquer // vi marcher avec raideur.
stall [stɔ:l] n éventaire m, étal m; (in stable) stalle f // vt (AUT) caler // vi (AUT) caler; (fig) essayer de gagner du temps; ~**s** npl (in cinema, theatre) orchestre m.
stalwart ['stɔ:lwət] n partisan m fidèle.
stamina ['stæminə] n vigueur f, endurance f.
stammer ['stæmə*] n bégaiement m // vi bégayer.
stamp [stæmp] n timbre m; (mark, also fig) empreinte f; (on document) cachet m // vi taper du pied // vt tamponner, estamper; (letter) timbrer; ~ **album** n album m de timbres(-poste); ~ **collecting** n philatélie f.
stampede [stæm'pi:d] n ruée f.
stance [stæns] n position f.
stand [stænd] n (position) position f; (MIL) résistance f; (structure) guéridon m; support m; (COMM) étalage m, stand m; (SPORT) tribune f // vb (pt,pp stood [stud]) vi être or se tenir (debout); (rise) se lever, se mettre debout; (be placed) se trouver // vt (place) mettre, poser; (tolerate, withstand) supporter; **to make a** ~ prendre position; **to** ~ **for parliament** se présenter aux élections (comme candidat à la députation); **it** ~**s to reason** c'est logique; cela va de soi; **to** ~ **by** vi (be ready) se tenir prêt // vt fus (opinion) s'en tenir à; **to** ~ **for** vt fus (defend) défendre, être pour; (signify) représenter, signifier; **to** ~ **in for** vt fus remplacer; **to** ~ **out** vi (be prominent) ressortir; **to** ~ **up** vi (rise) se lever, se mettre debout; **to** ~ **up for** vt

fus défendre ; **to ~ up to** *vt fus* tenir tête à, résister à.

standard ['stændəd] *n* niveau voulu ; *(flag)* étendard *m* // *a (size etc)* ordinaire, normal(e) ; courant(e) ; **~s** *npl (morals)* morale *f*, principes *mpl* ; **~ization** [-'zeɪʃən] *n* standardisation *f* ; **~ize** *vt* standardiser ; **~ lamp** *n* lampadaire *m* ; **~ of living** *n* niveau *m* de vie.

stand-by ['stændbaɪ] *n* remplaçant/e ; **~ ticket** *n* (AVIAT) billet *m* sans garantie.

stand-in ['stændɪn] *n* remplaçant/e ; *(CINEMA)* doublure *f*.

standing ['stændɪŋ] *a* debout *inv* // *n* réputation *f*, rang *m*, standing *m* ; **of many years' ~** qui dure or existe depuis longtemps ; **~ committee** *n* commission permanente ; **~ order** *n (at bank)* virement *m* automatique, prélèvement *m* bancaire ; **~ orders** *npl* (MIL) règlement *m* ; **~ room** places *fpl* debout.

stand-offish [stænd'ɔfɪʃ] *a* distant(e), froid(e).

standpoint ['stændpɔɪnt] *n* point *m* de vue.

standstill ['stændstɪl] *n*: **at a ~** à l'arrêt ; *(fig)* au point mort ; **to come to a ~** s'immobiliser, s'arrêter.

stank [stæŋk] *pt of* **stink**.

stanza ['stænzə] *n* strophe *f* ; couplet *m*.

staple ['steɪpl] *n (for papers)* agrafe *f* // *a (food etc)* de base, principal(e) // *vt* agrafer ; **~r** *n* agrafeuse *f*.

star [sta:*] *n* étoile *f* ; *(celebrity)* vedette *f* // *vi*: **to ~ (in)** être la vedette (de) // *vt (CINEMA)* avoir pour vedette.

starboard ['sta:bəd] *n* tribord *m* ; **to ~** à tribord.

starch [sta:tʃ] *n* amidon *m* ; **~ed** *a (collar)* amidonné(e), empesé(e) ; **~y** *a* riche en féculents ; *(person)* guindé(e).

stardom ['sta:dəm] *n* célébrité *f*.

stare [stɛə*] *n* regard *m* fixe // *vt*: **to ~ at** regarder fixement.

starfish ['sta:fɪʃ] *n* étoile *f* de mer.

stark [sta:k] *a (bleak)* désolé(e), morne // *ad*: **~ naked** complètement nu(e).

starlight ['sta:laɪt] *n*: **by ~** à la lumière des étoiles.

starling ['sta:lɪŋ] *n* étourneau *m*.

starlit ['sta:lɪt] *a* étoilé(e) ; illuminé(e) par les étoiles.

starry ['sta:rɪ] *a* étoilé(e) ; **~-eyed** *a (innocent)* ingénu(e).

start [sta:t] *n* commencement *m*, début *m* ; *(of race)* départ *m* ; *(sudden movement)* sursaut *m* // *vt* commencer // *vi* partir, se mettre en route ; *(jump)* sursauter ; **to ~ doing sth** se mettre à faire qch ; **to ~ off** *vi* commencer ; *(leave)* partir ; **to ~ up** *vi* commencer ; *(car)* démarrer // *vt* déclencher ; *(car)* mettre en marche ; **~er** *n* (AUT) démarreur *m* ; *(SPORT: official)* starter *m* ; *(: runner, horse)* partant *m* ; *(CULIN)* entrée *f* ; **~ing handle** *n* manivelle *f* ; **~ing point** *n* point *m* de départ.

startle ['sta:tl] *vt* faire sursauter ; donner un choc à ; **startling** *a* surprenant(e), saisissant(e).

starvation [sta:'veɪʃən] *n* faim *f*, famine *f* ; **to die of ~** mourir de faim or d'inanition.

starve [sta:v] *vi* mourir de faim ; être affamé(e) // *vt* affamer ; **I'm starving** je meurs de faim.

state [steɪt] *n* état *m* // *vt* déclarer, affirmer ; formuler ; **the S~s** les États-Unis *mpl* ; **to be in a ~** être dans tous ses états ; **~ control** *n* contrôle *m* de l'État ; **~d** *a* fixé(e), prescrit(e) ; **~ly** *a* majestueux(euse), imposant(e) ; **~ment** *n* déclaration *f* ; *(LAW)* déposition *f* ; **~ secret** *n* secret *m* d'État ; **~sman** *n* homme *m* d'État.

static ['stætɪk] *n* (RADIO) parasites *mpl* // *a* statique ; **~ electricity** *n* électricité *f* statique.

station ['steɪʃən] *n* gare *f* ; poste *m* *(militaire or de police etc)* ; *(rank)* condition *f*, rang *m* // *vt* placer, poster.

stationary ['steɪʃnərɪ] *a* à l'arrêt, immobile.

stationer ['steɪʃənə*] *n* papetier/ère ; **~'s (shop)** *n* papeterie *f* ; **~y** *n* papier *m* à lettres, petit matériel de bureau.

station master ['steɪʃənma:stə*] *n* (RAIL) chef *m* de gare.

station wagon ['steɪʃənwægən] *n* (US) break *m*.

statistic [stə'tɪstɪk] *n* statistique *f* ; **~s** *npl* *(science)* statistique *f* ; **~al** *a* statistique.

statue ['stætju:] *n* statue *f* ; **statuesque** [-'ɛsk] *a* sculptural(e).

stature ['stætʃə*] *n* stature *f* ; *(fig)* envergure *f*.

status ['steɪtəs] *n* position *f*, situation *f* ; prestige *m* ; statut *m* ; **the ~ quo** le statu quo ; **~ symbol** *n* marque *f* de standing, signe extérieur de richesse.

statute ['stætju:t] *n* loi *f* ; **~s** *npl (of club etc)* statuts *mpl* ; **statutory** *a* statutaire, prévu(e) par un article de loi.

staunch [stɔ:ntʃ] *a* sûr(e), loyal(e).

stave [steɪv] *n* (MUS) portée *f* // *vt*: **to ~ off** *(attack)* parer ; *(threat)* conjurer.

stay [steɪ] *n (period of time)* séjour *m* // *vi* rester ; *(reside)* loger ; *(spend some time)* séjourner ; **to ~ put** ne pas bouger ; **to ~ with friends** loger chez des amis ; **to ~ the night** passer la nuit ; **to ~ behind** *vi* rester en arrière ; **to ~ in** *vi (at home)* rester à la maison ; **to ~ on** *vi* rester ; **to ~ out** *vi (of house)* ne pas rentrer ; **to ~ up** *vi (at night)* ne pas se coucher.

STD *n (abbr of Subscriber Trunk Dialling)* l'automatique *m*.

steadfast ['stedfa:st] *a* ferme, résolu(e).

steadily ['stedɪlɪ] *ad* progressivement ; sans arrêt ; *(walk)* d'un pas ferme.

steady ['stedɪ] *a* stable, solide, ferme ; *(regular)* constant(e), régulier(ère) ; *(person)* calme, pondéré(e) // *vt* stabiliser ; assujettir ; calmer ; **to ~ oneself** reprendre son aplomb.

steak [steɪk] *n (meat)* bifteck *m*, steak *m* ; *(fish)* tranche *f* ; **~house** *n* ≈ grill-room *m*.

steal [sti:l], *pt* **stole**, *pp* **stolen** [sti:l, stəul, 'stəuln] *vt,vi* voler.

stealth [stelθ] *n*: **by ~** furtivement ; **~y** *a* furtif(ive).

steam [sti:m] *n* vapeur *f* // *vt* passer à la vapeur ; *(CULIN)* cuire à la vapeur // *vi* fumer ; *(ship)*: **to ~ along** filer ; **~ engine**

n locomotive f à vapeur ; ~er n (bateau m à) vapeur m ; ~roller n rouleau compresseur ; ~y a embué(e), humide.
steed [sti:d] n coursier m.
steel [sti:l] n acier m // cpd d'acier ; ~works n aciérie f.
steep [sti:p] a raide, escarpé(e) ; (price) très élevé(e), excessif(ive) // vt (faire) tremper.
steeple ['sti:pl] n clocher m ; ~chase n steeple(-chase) f ; ~jack n réparateur n de clochers et de hautes cheminées.
steeply ['sti:plɪ] ad en pente raide.
steer [stɪə*] n bœuf m // vt diriger, gouverner ; guider // vi tenir le gouvernail ; ~ing n (AUT) conduite f ; ~ing column n colonne f de direction ; ~ing wheel n volant m.
stellar ['stɛlə*] a stellaire.
stem [stɛm] n tige f ; queue f ; (NAUT) avant m, proue f // vt contenir, endiguer, juguler ; to ~ from vt fus provenir de, découler de.
stench [stɛntʃ] n puanteur f.
stencil ['stɛnsl] n stencil m ; pochoir m // vt polycopier.
step [stɛp] n pas m ; (stair) marche f ; (action) mesure f, disposition f // vi: to ~ forward faire un pas en avant, avancer ; ~s npl = **stepladder**; to ~ down vi (fig) se retirer, se désister ; to ~ off vt fus descendre de ; to ~ over vt fus marcher sur ; to ~ up vt augmenter, intensifier ; ~brother n demi-frère m ; ~child n beau-fils/belle-fille ; ~father n beau-père m ; ~ladder n escabeau m ; ~mother n belle-mère f ; **stepping stone** n pierre f de gué ; (fig) tremplin m ; ~sister n demi-sœur f.
stereo ['stɛrɪəʊ] n (system) stéréo f ; (record player) chaine f stéréo // a (also: ~phonic) a stéréophonique.
stereotype ['stɪərɪətaɪp] n stéréotype m // vt stéréotyper.
sterile ['stɛraɪl] a stérile ; **sterility** [-'rɪlɪtɪ] n stérilité f ; **sterilization** [-'zeɪʃən] n stérilisation f ; **sterilize** ['stɛrɪlaɪz] vt stériliser.
sterling ['stɜːlɪŋ] a sterling inv ; (silver) de bon aloi, fin(e) ; (fig) à toute épreuve, excellent(e) ; ~ area n zone f sterling inv.
stern [stɜːn] a sévère // n (NAUT) arrière m, poupe f.
stethoscope ['stɛθəskəʊp] n stéthoscope m.
stevedore ['sti:vədɔ:*] n docker m, débardeur m.
stew [stju:] n ragoût m // vt, vi cuire à la casserole ; ~ed tea thé trop infusé.
steward ['stju:əd] n (AVIAT, NAUT, RAIL) steward m ; (in club etc) intendant m ; ~ess n hôtesse f.
stick [stɪk] n bâton m ; morceau m // vb (pt, pp **stuck** [stʌk]) vt (glue) coller ; (thrust): to ~ sth into piquer or planter or enfoncer qch dans ; (col: put) mettre, fourrer ; (col: tolerate) supporter // vi se planter ; tenir ; (remain) rester ; to ~ out, to ~ up vi dépasser, sortir ; to ~ up for vt fus défendre ; ~er n auto-collant m.
stickleback ['stɪklbæk] n épinoche f.

stickler ['stɪklə*] n: to be a ~ for être pointilleux(euse) sur.
sticky ['stɪkɪ] a poisseux(euse) ; (label) adhésif(ive).
stiff [stɪf] a raide ; rigide ; dur(e) ; (difficult) difficile, ardu(e) ; (cold) froid(e), distant(e) ; (strong, high) fort(e), élevé(e) ; ~en vt raidir, renforcer // vi se raidir ; se durcir ; ~ neck n torticolis m ; ~ness n raideur f.
stifle ['staɪfl] vt étouffer, réprimer ; **stifling** a (heat) suffocant(e).
stigma, pl (BOT, MED, REL) ~**ta**, (fig) ~**s** ['stɪgmə, stɪg'mɑːtə] n stigmate m.
stile [staɪl] n échalier m.
stiletto [stɪ'lɛtəʊ] n (also: ~ **heel**) talon m aiguille.
still [stɪl] a immobile ; calme, tranquille // ad (up to this time) encore, toujours ; (even) encore ; (nonetheless) quand même, tout de même ; ~born a mort-né(e) ; ~ life n nature morte.
stilt [stɪlt] n échasse f ; (pile) pilotis m.
stilted ['stɪltɪd] a guindé(e), emprunté(e).
stimulant ['stɪmjʊlənt] n stimulant m.
stimulate ['stɪmjʊleɪt] vt stimuler ; **stimulating** a stimulant(e) ; **stimulation** [-'leɪʃən] n stimulation f.
stimulus, pl **stimuli** ['stɪmjʊləs, 'stɪmjʊlaɪ] n stimulant m ; (BIOL, PSYCH) stimulus m.
sting [stɪŋ] n piqûre f ; (organ) dard m // vt (pt, pp **stung** [stʌŋ]) piquer.
stingy ['stɪndʒɪ] a avare ; pingre, chiche.
stink [stɪŋk] n puanteur f // vi (pt **stank**, pp **stunk** [stæŋk, stʌŋk]) puer, empester ; ~er n (col) vacherie f ; dégueulasse m/f ; ~ing a (col): a ~ing... un(e) vache de..., un(e) foutu(e)...
stint [stɪnt] n part f de travail // vi: to ~ on lésiner sur, être chiche de.
stipend ['staɪpɛnd] n (of vicar etc) traitement m.
stipulate ['stɪpjʊleɪt] vt stipuler ; **stipulation** [-'leɪʃən] n stipulation f, condition f.
stir [stɜː*] n agitation f, sensation f // vt remuer // vi remuer, bouger ; to ~ up vt exciter ; ~ring a excitant(e) ; émouvant(e).
stirrup ['stɪrəp] n étrier m.
stitch [stɪtʃ] n (SEWING) point m ; (KNITTING) maille f ; (MED) point de suture ; (pain) point de côté // vt coudre, piquer ; suturer.
stoat [stəʊt] n hermine f (avec son pelage d'été).
stock [stɒk] n réserve f, provision f ; (COMM) stock m ; (AGR) cheptel m, bétail m ; (CULIN) bouillon m ; (FINANCE) valeurs fpl, titres mpl // a (fig: reply etc) courant(e) ; classique // vt (have in stock) avoir, vendre ; **well-~ed** bien approvisionné(e) or fourni(e) ; to take ~ (fig) faire le point ; to ~ up vt remplir, garnir // vi: to ~ up (with) s'approvisionner (en).
stockade [stɔ'keɪd] n palissade f.
stockbroker ['stɒkbrəʊkə*] n agent m de change.
stock exchange ['stɔkɪkstʃeɪndʒ] n Bourse f (des valeurs).
stocking ['stɔkɪŋ] n bas m.

stockist ['stɔkɪst] n stockiste m.

stock market ['stɔkmɑːkɪt] n Bourse f, marché financier.

stock phrase ['stɔk'freɪz] n cliché m.

stockpile ['stɔkpaɪl] n stock m, réserve f // vt stocker, accumuler.

stocktaking ['stɔkteɪkɪŋ] n (COMM) inventaire m.

stocky ['stɔkɪ] a trapu(e), râblé(e).

stodgy ['stɔdʒɪ] a bourratif(ive), lourd(e).

stoic ['stəuɪk] n stoïque m/f; ~al a stoïque.

stoke [stəuk] vt garnir, entretenir; chauffer; ~r n chauffeur m.

stole [stəul] pt of steal // n étole f.

stolen ['stəuln] pp of steal.

stolid ['stɔlɪd] a impassible, flegmatique.

stomach ['stʌmək] n estomac m; (abdomen) ventre m // vt supporter, digérer; ~ ache n mal m à l'estomac or au ventre.

stone [stəun] n pierre f; (pebble) caillou m, galet m; (in fruit) noyau m; (MED) calcul m; (weight) mesure de poids = 6.348 kg.; 14 pounds // cpd de or en pierre // vt dénoyauter; ~-cold a complètement froid(e); ~-deaf a sourd(e) comme un pot; ~mason n tailleur m de pierre(s); ~work n maçonnerie f; stony n pierreux(euse), rocailleux(euse).

stood [stud] pt,pp of stand.

stool [stuːl] n tabouret m.

stoop [stuːp] vi (also: have a ~) être voûté(e); (bend) se baisser, se courber.

stop [stɔp] n arrêt m; halte f; (in punctuation) point m // vt arrêter; (break off) interrompre; (also: put a ~ to) mettre fin à // vi s'arrêter; (rain, noise etc) cesser, s'arrêter; to ~ doing sth cesser or arrêter de faire qch; to ~ dead vi s'arrêter net; to ~ off vi faire une courte halte; to ~ up vt (hole) boucher; ~lights npl (AUT) signaux mpl de stop, feux mpl arrière; ~over n halte f; (AVIAT) escale f.

stoppage ['stɔpɪdʒ] n arrêt m; (of pay) retenue f; (strike) arrêt de travail.

stopper ['stɔpə*] n bouchon m.

stop-press ['stɔp'pres] n nouvelles fpl de dernière heure.

stopwatch ['stɔpwɔtʃ] n chronomètre m.

storage ['stɔːrɪdʒ] n emmagasinage m; (COMPUTERS) mise f en mémoire or réserve.

store [stɔː*] n provision f, réserve f; (depot) entrepôt m; (large shop) grand magasin // vt emmagasiner; to ~ up vt mettre en réserve, emmagasiner; ~room n réserve f, magasin m.

storey, story (US) ['stɔːrɪ] n étage m.

stork [stɔːk] n cigogne f.

storm [stɔːm] n orage m, tempête f; ouragan m // vi (fig) fulminer // vt prendre d'assaut; ~ cloud n nuage m d'orage; ~y a orageux(euse).

story ['stɔːrɪ] n histoire f; récit m; (US) = storey; ~book n livre m d'histoires or de contes; ~teller n conteur/euse.

stout [staut] a solide; (brave) intrépide; (fat) gros(se), corpulent(e) // n bière brune.

stove [stəuv] n (for cooking) fourneau m; (: small) réchaud m; (for heating) poêle m.

stow [stəu] vt ranger; cacher; ~away n passager/ère clandestin(e).

straddle ['strædl] vt enjamber, être à cheval sur.

strafe [strɑːf] vt mitrailler.

straggle ['strægl] vi être (or marcher) en désordre; ~d along the coast disséminé(e) tout au long de la côte; ~r n traînard/e; **straggling, straggly** a (hair) en désordre.

straight [streɪt] a droit(e); (frank) honnête, franc(he) // ad (tout) droit; (drink) sec, sans eau // n: the ~ la ligne droite; to put or get ~ mettre en ordre, mettre de l'ordre dans; ~ away, ~off (at once) tout de suite; ~ off, ~ out sans hésiter; ~en vt (also: ~en out) redresser; ~forward a simple; honnête, direct(e).

strain [streɪn] n (TECH) tension f; pression f; (physical) effort m; (mental) tension (nerveuse); (MED) entorse f; (streak, trace) tendance f; élément m // vt tendre fortement; mettre à l'épreuve; (filter) passer, filtrer // vi peiner, fournir un gros effort; ~s npl (MUS) accords mpl, accents mpl; ~ed a (laugh etc) forcé(e), contraint(e); (relations) tendu(e); ~er n passoire f.

strait [streɪt] n (GEO) détroit m; ~ jacket n camisole f de force; ~-laced a collet monté inv.

strand [strænd] n (of thread) fil m, brin m // vt (boat) échouer; ~ed a en rade, en plan.

strange [streɪndʒ] a (not known) inconnu(e); (odd) étrange, bizarre; ~ly ad étrangement, bizarrement; ~r n inconnu/e; étranger/ère.

strangle ['stræŋgl] vt étrangler; ~hold n (fig) emprise totale, mainmise f; **strangulation** [-'leɪʃən] n strangulation f.

strap [stræp] n lanière f, courroie f, sangle f; (of slip, dress) bretelle f // vt attacher (avec une courroie etc); (child etc) administrer une correction à.

strapping ['stræpɪŋ] a bien découplé(e), costaud(e).

strata ['strɑːtə] npl of stratum.

stratagem ['strætɪdʒəm] n stratagème m.

strategic [strə'tiːdʒɪk] a stratégique.

strategist ['strætɪdʒɪst] n stratège m.

strategy ['strætɪdʒɪ] n stratégie f.

stratosphere ['strætəsfɪə*] n stratosphère f.

stratum, pl strata ['strɑːtəm, 'struːtə] n strate f, couche f.

straw [strɔː] n paille f.

strawberry ['strɔːbərɪ] n fraise f; (plant) fraisier m.

stray [streɪ] a (animal) perdu(e), errant(e) // vi s'égarer; ~ bullet n balle perdue.

streak [striːk] n raie f, bande f, filet m; (fig: of madness etc): a ~ of une or des tendance(s) à // vt zébrer, strier // vi: to ~ past passer à toute allure; ~y a zébré(e), strié(e); ~y bacon n ≈ lard m (maigre).

stream [striːm] n ruisseau m; courant m, flot m; (of people) défilé ininterrompu, flot // vt (SCOL) répartir par niveau // vi

ruisseler ; to ~ in/out entrer/sortir à flots.
streamer ['stri:mə*] n serpentin m, banderole f.
streamlined ['stri:mlaɪnd] a (AVIAT) fuselé(e), profilé(e) ; (AUT) aérodynamique ; (fig) rationalisé(e).
street [stri:t] n rue f ; ~car n (US) tramway m ; ~ lamp n réverbère m.
strength [strɛŋθ] n force f ; (of girder, knot etc) solidité f ; ~en vt fortifier ; renforcer ; consolider.
strenuous ['strɛnjuəs] a vigoureux(euse), énergique ; (tiring) ardu(e), fatigant(e).
stress [strɛs] n (force, pressure) pression f ; (mental strain) tension (nerveuse) ; (accent) accent m // vt insister sur, souligner.
stretch [strɛtʃ] n (of sand etc) étendue f // vi s'étirer ; (extend): to ~ to/as far as s'étendre jusqu'à // vt tendre, étirer ; (spread) étendre ; (fig) pousser (au maximum) ; at a ~ sans discontinuer, sans interruption ; to ~ a muscle se distendre un muscle ; to ~ out vi s'étendre // vt (arm etc) allonger, tendre ; (to spread) étendre ; to ~ out for something allonger la main pour prendre qch.
stretcher ['strɛtʃə*] n brancard m, civière f.
strewn [stru:n] a: ~ with jonché(e) de.
stricken ['strɪkən] a très éprouvé(e) ; dévasté(e) ; ~ with frappé(e) or atteint(e) de.
strict [strɪkt] a strict(e) ; ~ly ad strictement ; ~ness n sévérité f.
stride [straɪd] n grand pas, enjambée f // vi (pt strode, pp stridden [strəud, 'strɪdn]) marcher à grands pas.
strident ['straɪdnt] a strident(e).
strife [straɪf] n conflit m, dissensions fpl.
strike [straɪk] n grève f ; (of oil etc) découverte f ; (attack) raid m // vb (pt,pp struck [strʌk]) vt frapper ; (oil etc) trouver, découvrir // vi faire grève ; (attack) attaquer ; (clock) sonner ; to ~ a match frotter une allumette ; to ~ down vt (fig) terrasser ; to ~ out vt rayer ; to ~ up vt (MUS) se mettre à jouer ; to ~ up a friendship with se lier d'amitié avec ; ~breaker n briseur m de grève ; ~r n gréviste m/f ; (SPORT) buteur m ; **striking** a frappant(e), saisissant(e).
string [strɪŋ] n ficelle f, fil m ; (row) rang m ; chapelet m ; file f ; (MUS) corde f // vt (pt,pp strung [strʌŋ]): to ~ out échelonner ; the ~s npl (MUS) les instruments mpl à corde ; ~ bean n haricot vert ; ~(ed) instrument n (MUS) instrument m à cordes.
stringent ['strɪndʒənt] a rigoureux(euse) ; (need) impérieux(euse).
strip [strɪp] n bande f // vt déshabiller ; dégarnir, dépouiller ; (also: ~ down: machine) démonter // vi se déshabiller ; ~ cartoon n bande dessinée.
stripe [straɪp] n raie f, rayure f ; ~d a rayé(e), à rayures.
strip light ['strɪplaɪt] n (tube m au) néon m.
stripper ['strɪpə*] n strip-teaseuse f.

striptease ['strɪpti:z] n strip-tease m.
strive, pt **strove,** pp **striven** [straɪv, strəuv, 'strɪvn] vi: to ~ to do s'efforcer de faire.
strode [strəud] pt of **stride.**
stroke [strəuk] n coup m ; (MED) attaque f ; (caress) caresse f // vt caresser ; at a ~ d'un (seul) coup ; on the ~ of 5 à 5 heures sonnantes ; a 2-~ engine un moteur à 2 temps.
stroll [strəul] n petite promenade // vi flâner, se promener nonchalamment.
strong [strɔŋ] a fort(e) ; vigoureux(euse) ; solide ; vif(vive) ; they are 50 ~ ils sont au nombre de 50 ; ~hold n bastion m ; ~ly ad fortement, avec force ; vigoureusement ; solidement ; ~room n chambre forte.
strove [strəuv] pt of **strive.**
struck [strʌk] pt,pp of **strike.**
structural ['strʌktʃərəl] a structural(e) ; (CONSTR) de construction ; affectant les parties portantes ; ~ly ad du point de vue de la construction.
structure ['strʌktʃə*] n structure f ; (building) construction f ; édifice m.
struggle ['strʌgl] n lutte f // vi lutter, se battre.
strum [strʌm] vt (guitar) gratter de.
strung [strʌŋ] pt,pp of **string.**
strut [strʌt] n étai m, support m // vi se pavaner.
stub [stʌb] n bout m ; (of ticket etc) talon m ; to ~ out vt écraser.
stubble ['stʌbl] n chaume m ; (on chin) barbe f de plusieurs jours.
stubborn ['stʌbən] a têtu(e), obstiné(e), opiniâtre.
stubby ['stʌbɪ] a trapu(e) ; gros(se) et court(e).
stuck [stʌk] pt,pp of **stick** // a (jammed) bloqué(e), coincé(e) ; ~-up a prétentieux(euse).
stud [stʌd] n clou m (à grosse tête) ; bout.. n m de col ; (of horses) écurie f, haras m ; (also: ~ horse) étalon m // vt (fig): ~ded with parsemé(e) or criblé(e) de.
student ['stju:dənt] n étudiant/e // cpd estudiantin(e) ; universitaire ; d'étudiant.
studied ['stʌdɪd] a étudié(e), calculé(e).
studio ['stju:dɪəu] n studio m, atelier m.
studious ['stju:dɪəs] a studieux(euse), appliqué(e) ; (studied) étudié(e) ; ~ly ad (carefully) soigneusement.
study ['stʌdɪ] n étude f ; (room) bureau m // vt étudier ; examiner // vi étudier, faire ses études.
stuff [stʌf] n chose(s) f(pl), truc m ; affaires fpl ; (substance) substance f // vt rembourrer ; (CULIN) farcir ; ~ing n bourre f, rembourrage m ; (CULIN) farce f ; ~y a (room) mal ventilé(e) or aéré(e) ; (ideas) vieux jeu inv.
stumble ['stʌmbl] vi trébucher ; to ~ across (fig) tomber sur ; **stumbling block** n pierre f d'achoppement.
stump [stʌmp] n souche f ; (of limb) moignon m // vt: to be ~ed sécher, ne pas savoir que répondre.
stun [stʌn] vt étourdir ; abasourdir.

stung [stʌŋ] *pt, pp of* **sting**.

stunk [stʌŋk] *pp of* **stink**.

stunning ['stʌnɪŋ] *a* étourdissant(e), stupéfiant(e).

stunt [stʌnt] *n* tour *m* de force; truc *m* publicitaire; (*AVIAT*) acrobatie *f* // *vt* retarder, arrêter; ~**ed** *a* rabougri(e); ~**man** *n* cascadeur *m*.

stupefy ['stju:pɪfaɪ] *vt* étourdir; abrutir; (*fig*) stupéfier.

stupendous [stju:'pɛndəs] *a* prodigieux(euse), fantastique.

stupid ['stju:pɪd] *a* stupide, bête; ~**ity** [-'pɪdɪtɪ] *n* stupidité *f*, bêtise *f*; ~**ly** *ad* stupidement, bêtement.

stupor ['stju:pə*] *n* stupeur *f*.

sturdy ['stə:dɪ] *a* robuste, vigoureux(euse); solide.

sturgeon ['stə:dʒən] *n* esturgeon *m*.

stutter ['stʌtə*] *n* bégaiement *m* // *vi* bégayer.

sty [staɪ] *n* (*of pigs*) porcherie *f*.

stye [staɪ] *n* (*MED*) orgelet *m*.

style [staɪl] *n* style *m*; (*distinction*) allure *f*, cachet *m*, style *m*; **stylish** *a* élégant(e), chic *inv*.

stylized ['staɪlaɪzd] *a* stylisé(e).

stylus ['staɪləs] *n* (*of record player*) pointe *f* de lecture.

suave [swɑ:v] *a* doucereux(euse), onctueux(euse).

sub... [sʌb] *prefix* sub..., sous-; **subconscious** *a* subconscient(e) // *n* subconscient *m*; **subdivide** *vt* subdiviser; **subdivision** *n* subdivision *f*.

subdue [səb'dju:] *vt* subjuguer, soumettre; ~**d** *a* contenu(e), atténué(e); (*light*) tamisé(e); (*person*) qui a perdu de son entrain.

subject *n* ['sʌbdʒɪkt] sujet *m*; (*SCOL*) matière *f* // *vt* [səb'dʒɛkt]: to ~ to soumettre à; exposer à; to be ~ to (*law*) être soumis(e) à; (*disease*) être sujet(te) à; ~**ion** [-'dʒɛkʃən] soumission *f*, sujétion *f*; ~**ive** *a* subjectif(ive); (*LING*) sujet(te); ~ **matter** *n* sujet *m*; contenu *m*.

sub judice [sʌb'dju:dɪsɪ] *a* devant les tribunaux.

subjunctive [səb'dʒʌŋktɪv] *a* subjonctif(ive) // *n* subjonctif *m*.

sublet [sʌb'lɛt] *vt* sous-louer.

sublime [sə'blaɪm] *a* sublime.

submachine gun ['sʌbmə'ʃi:ŋgʌn] *n* fusil-mitrailleur *m*.

submarine [sʌbmə'ri:n] *n* sous-marin *m*.

submerge [səb'mə:dʒ] *vt* submerger; immerger // *vi* plonger.

submission [səb'mɪʃən] *n* soumission *f*.

submissive [səb'mɪsɪv] *a* soumis(e).

submit [səb'mɪt] *vt* soumettre // *vi* se soumettre.

subordinate [sə'bɔ:dɪnət] *a,n* subordonné(e).

subpoena [səb'pi:nə] (*LAW*) *n* citation *f*, assignation *f* // *vt* citer *or* assigner (à comparaître).

subscribe [səb'skraɪb] *vi* cotiser; to ~ to (*opinion, fund*) souscrire à; (*newspaper*) s'abonner à; être abonné(e) à; ~**r** *n* (*to periodical, telephone*) abonné/e *f*.

subscription [səb'skrɪpʃən] *n* souscription *f*; abonnement *m*.

subsequent ['sʌbsɪkwənt] *a* ultérieur(e), suivant(e); consécutif(ive); ~**ly** *ad* par la suite.

subside [səb'saɪd] *vi* s'affaisser; (*flood*) baisser; (*wind*) tomber; ~**nce** [-'saɪdns] *n* affaissement *m*.

subsidiary [səb'sɪdɪərɪ] *a* subsidiaire, accessoire // *n* filiale *f*.

subsidize ['sʌbsɪdaɪz] *vt* subventionner.

subsidy ['sʌbsɪdɪ] *n* subvention *f*.

subsistence [səb'sɪstəns] *n* existence *f*, subsistance *f*.

substance ['sʌbstəns] *n* substance *f*; (*fig*) essentiel *m*; a man of ~ un homme jouissant d'une certaine fortune.

substandard [sʌb'stændəd] *a* de qualité inférieure.

substantial [səb'stænʃl] *a* substantiel(le); (*fig*) important(e); ~**ly** *ad* considérablement; en grande partie.

substantiate [səb'stænʃɪeɪt] *vt* étayer, fournir des preuves à l'appui de.

substitute ['sʌbstɪtju:t] *n* (*person*) remplaçant/e; (*thing*) succédané *m* // *vt*: to ~ sth/sb for substituer qch/qn à, remplacer par qch/qn; **substitution** [-'tju:ʃən] *n* substitution *f*.

subterfuge ['sʌbtəfju:dʒ] *n* subterfuge *m*.

subterranean [sʌbtə'reɪnɪən] *a* souterrain(e).

subtitle ['sʌbtaɪtl] *n* (*CINEMA*) sous-titre *m*.

subtle ['sʌtl] *a* subtil(e); ~**ty** *n* subtilité *f*.

subtract [səb'trækt] *vt* soustraire, retrancher; ~**ion** [-'trækʃən] *n* soustraction *f*.

subtropical [sʌb'trɒpɪkl] *a* subtropical(e).

suburb ['sʌbə:b] *n* faubourg *m*; the ~**s** la banlieue; ~**an** [sə'bə:bən] *a* de banlieue; suburbain(e).

subvention [səb'vɛnʃən] *n* (*US: subsidy*) subvention *f*.

subversive [səb'və:sɪv] *a* subversif(ive).

subway ['sʌbweɪ] *n* (*US*) métro *m*; (*Brit*) passage souterrain.

sub-zero [sʌb'zɪərəu] *a* au-dessous de zéro.

succeed [sək'si:d] *vi* réussir; avoir du succès // *vt* succéder à; to ~ in doing réussir à faire; ~**ing** *a* (*following*) suivant(e).

success [sək'sɛs] *n* succès *m*; réussite *f*; ~**ful** *a* (*venture*) couronné(e) de succès; to be ~**ful** (*in doing*) réussir (à faire); ~**fully** *ad* avec succès.

succession [sək'sɛʃən] *n* succession *f*.

successive [sək'sɛsɪv] *a* successif(ive); consécutif(ive).

successor [sək'sɛsə*] *n* successeur *m*.

succinct [sək'sɪŋkt] *a* succinct(e), bref(brève).

succulent ['sʌkjulənt] *a* succulent(e).

succumb [sə'kʌm] *vi* succomber.

such [sʌtʃ] *a, det* tel(telle); (*of that kind*): ~ a book un livre de ce genre *or* pareil, un tel livre; ~ books des livres de ce genre *or* pareils, de tels livres; (*so much*): ~ courage un tel courage; ~ a long trip un si long voyage; ~ good books de si bons livres; ~ **a long trip that** un voyage si or tellement long que; ~ **a lot of** tellement or tant de; **making** ~ **a noise that** faisant un tel bruit que or tellement de bruit que; ~ **as** (like) tel(telle) que, comme; **a noise** ~ **as to** un bruit de nature à; **as** ~ **ad** en tant que tel(telle), à proprement parler; ~**-and-**~ det tel(telle) ou tel(telle).

suck [sʌk] vt sucer; (breast, bottle) téter; ~**er** n (BOT, ZOOL, TECH) ventouse f; (col) naïf/ïve, poire f.

suckle [sʌkl] vt allaiter.

suction [sʌkʃən] n succion f.

sudden [sʌdn] a soudain(e), subit(e); **all of a** ~ soudain, tout à coup; ~**ly** ad brusquement, tout à coup, soudain.

suds [sʌdz] npl eau savonneuse.

sue [su:] vt poursuivre en justice, intenter un procès à.

suede [sweɪd] n daim m, cuir suédé // cpd de daim.

suet [suɪt] n graisse f de rognon or de bœuf.

Suez Canal [su:ɪzkə'næl] n canal m de Suez.

suffer [sʌfə*] vt souffrir, subir; (bear) tolérer, supporter // vi souffrir; ~**er** n malade m/f; victime m/f; ~**ing** n souffrance(s) f(pl).

suffice [sə'faɪs] vi suffire.

sufficient [sə'fɪʃənt] a suffisant(e); ~ **money** suffisamment d'argent; ~**ly** ad suffisamment, assez.

suffix [sʌfɪks] n suffixe m.

suffocate [sʌfəkeɪt] vi suffoquer; étouffer; **suffocation** [-'keɪʃən] n suffocation f; (MED) asphyxie f.

sugar [sugə*] n sucre m // vt sucrer; ~ **beet** n betterave sucrière; ~ **cane** n canne f à sucre; ~**y** a sucré(e).

suggest [sə'dʒɛst] vt suggérer, proposer; dénoter; ~**ion** [-'dʒɛstʃən] n suggestion f; ~**ive** a suggestif(ive).

suicidal [suɪ'saɪdl] a suicidaire.

suicide [suɪsaɪd] n suicide m.

suit [su:t] n (man's) costume m, complet m; (woman's) tailleur m, ensemble m; (CARDS) couleur f // vt aller à; convenir à; (adapt): **to** ~ **sth to** adapter or approprier qch à; ~**able** a qui convient; approprié(e); ~**ably** ad comme il se doit (or se devait etc), convenablement.

suitcase [su:tkeɪs] n valise f.

suite [swi:t] n (of rooms, also MUS) suite f; (furniture): **bedroom/dining room** ~ (ensemble m de) chambre f à coucher/salle f à manger.

sulfur [sʌlfə*] etc (US) = **sulphur** etc.

sulk [sʌlk] vi bouder; ~**y** a boudeur(euse), maussade.

sullen [sʌlən] a renfrogné(e), maussade; morne.

sulphur, sulfur (US) [sʌlfə*] n soufre m; ~**ic** [-'fjuərɪk] a: ~**ic acid** acide m sulfurique.

sultan [sʌltən] n sultan m.

sultana [sʌl'tɑ:nə] n (fruit) raisin sec de Smyrne.

sultry [sʌltrɪ] a étouffant(e).

sum [sʌm] n somme f; (SCOL etc) calcul m; f; **to** ~ **up** vt,vi résumer.

summarize [sʌməraɪz] vt résumer.

summary [sʌmərɪ] n résumé m // a (justice) sommaire.

summer [sʌmə*] n été m // cpd d'été, estival(e); ~**house** n (in garden) pavillon m; ~**time** n (season) été m; ~ **time** n (by clock) heure f d'été.

summit [sʌmɪt] n sommet m; ~ (conference) n (conférence f au) sommet m.

summon [sʌmən] vt appeler, convoquer; **to** ~ **up** vt rassembler, faire appel à; ~**s** n citation f, assignation f // vt citer, assigner.

sump [sʌmp] n (AUT) carter m.

sumptuous [sʌmptjuəs] a somptueux(euse).

sun [sʌn] n soleil m; **in the** ~ au soleil; ~**bathe** vi prendre un bain de soleil; ~**burnt** a bronzé(e), hâlé(e); (painfully) brûlé(e) par le soleil; ~ **cream** n crème f (anti-)solaire.

Sunday [sʌndɪ] n dimanche m.

sundial [sʌndaɪəl] n cadran m solaire.

sundry [sʌndrɪ] a divers(e), différent(e); **all and** ~ tout le monde, n'importe qui; **sundries** npl articles divers.

sunflower [sʌnflauə*] n tournesol m.

sung [sʌŋ] pp of **sing**.

sunglasses [sʌnglɑ:sɪz] npl lunettes fpl de soleil.

sunk [sʌŋk] pp of **sink**; ~**en** a submergé(e); creux(euse).

sun: ~**light** n (lumière f du) soleil m; ~**lit** a ensoleillé(e); ~**ny** a ensoleillé(e); (fig) épanoui(e), radieux(euse); ~**rise** n lever m du soleil; ~**set** n coucher m du soleil; ~**shade** n (over table) parasol m; ~**shine** n (lumière f du) soleil m; ~**spot** n tache f solaire; ~**stroke** n insolation f, coup m de soleil; ~**tan** n bronzage m; ~**tan oil** n huile f solaire; ~**trap** n coin très ensoleillé.

super [su:pə*] a (col) formidable.

superannuation [su:pərænju'eɪʃən] n cotisations fpl pour la pension.

superb [su:'pə:b] a superbe, magnifique.

supercilious [su:pə'sɪlɪəs] a hautain(e), dédaigneux(euse).

superficial [su:pə'fɪʃəl] a superficiel(le); ~**ly** ad superficiellement.

superfluous [su'pə:fluəs] a superflu(e).

superhuman [su:pə'hju:mən] a surhumain(e).

superimpose [su:pərɪm'pəuz] vt superposer.

superintendent [su:prɪn'tɛndənt] n directeur/trice; (POLICE) ≈ commissaire m.

superior [su'pɪərɪə*] a,n supérieur(e); ~**ity** [-'ɔrɪtɪ] n supériorité f.

superlative [su'pə:lətɪv] a sans pareil(le), suprême n // a (LING) superlatif m.

superman [su:pəmæn] n surhomme m.

supermarket [su:pəmɑ:kɪt] n supermarché m.

supernatural [su:pə'nætʃərəl] a surnaturel(le).

superpower [su:pəpauə*] n (POL) grande puissance.

supersede [su:pə'si:d] vt remplacer, supplanter.

supersonic ['suːpə'sɔnɪk] a supersonique.
superstition [suːpə'stɪʃən] n superstition f.
superstitious [suːpə'stɪʃəs] a superstitieux(euse).
supertanker ['suːpətæŋkə*] n pétrolier géant, superpétrolier m.
supervise ['suːpəvaɪz] vt surveiller; diriger; **supervision** [-'vɪʒən] n surveillance f; contrôle m; **supervisor** n surveillant/e; (in shop) chef m de rayon; **supervisory** a de surveillance.
supper ['sʌpə*] n dîner m; (late) souper m.
supple ['sʌpl] a souple.
supplement n ['sʌplɪmənt] supplément m // vt [sʌplɪ'mɛnt] ajouter à, compléter; **~ary** [-'mɛntərɪ] a supplémentaire.
supplier [sə'plaɪə*] n fournisseur m.
supply [sə'plaɪ] vt (provide) fournir; (equip): **to ~ (with)** approvisionner or ravitailler (en); fournir (en); alimenter (en) // n provision f, réserve f; (supplying) approvisionnement m; (TECH) alimentation f // cpd (teacher etc) suppléant(e); **supplies** npl (food) vivres mpl; (MIL) subsistances fpl; **~ and demand** l'offre f et la demande.
support [sə'pɔːt] n (moral, financial etc) soutien m, appui m; (TECH) support m, soutien // vt soutenir, supporter; (financially) subvenir aux besoins de; (uphold) être pour, être partisan de, appuyer; (endure) supporter, tolérer; **~er** n (POL etc) partisan/e; (SPORT) supporter m.
suppose [sə'pəuz] vt, vi supposer; imaginer; **to be ~d to do** être censé(e) faire; **~dly** [sə'pəuzɪdlɪ] ad soi-disant; **supposing** cj si, à supposer que + sub; **supposition** [sʌpə'zɪʃən] n supposition f, hypothèse f.
suppress [sə'prɛs] vt réprimer; supprimer; étouffer; refouler; **~ion** [sə'prɛʃən] n suppression f, répression f; **~or** n (ELEC etc) dispositif m antiparasite.
supremacy [su'prɛməsɪ] n suprématie f.
supreme [su'priːm] a suprême.
surcharge ['səːtʃɑːdʒ] n surcharge f; (extra tax) surtaxe f.
sure [ʃuə*] a (gen) sûr(e); (definite, convinced) sûr(e), certain(e); **~!** (of course) bien sûr!; **~ enough** effectivement; **to make ~ of** s'assurer de; vérifier; **~-footed** a au pied sûr; **~ly** ad sûrement; certainement.
surety ['ʃuərətɪ] n caution f.
surf [səːf] n ressac m.
surface ['səːfɪs] n surface f // vt (road) poser le revêtement de // vi remonter à la surface; faire surface; **~ mail** n courrier m par voie de terre (or maritime).
surfboard ['səːfbɔːd] n planche f de surf.
surfeit ['səːfɪt] n: **a ~ of** un excès de; une indigestion de.
surfing ['səːfɪŋ] n surf m.
surge [səːdʒ] n vague f, montée f // vi déferler.
surgeon ['səːdʒən] n chirurgien m.
surgery ['səːdʒərɪ] n chirurgie f; (room) cabinet m (de consultation); **to undergo**

~ être opéré(e); **~ hours** npl heures fpl de consultation.
surgical ['səːdʒɪkl] a chirurgical(e); **~ spirit** n alcool m à 90s.
surly ['səːlɪ] a revêche, maussade.
surmise [səː'maɪz] vt présumer, conjecturer.
surmount [səː'maunt] vt surmonter.
surname ['səːneɪm] n nom m de famille.
surpass [səː'pɑːs] vt surpasser, dépasser.
surplus ['səːpləs] n surplus m, excédent m // a en surplus, de trop.
surprise [sə'praɪz] n (gen) surprise f; (astonishment) étonnement m // vt surprendre; étonner; **surprising** a surprenant(e), étonnant(e).
surrealist [sə'rɪəlɪst] a surréaliste.
surrender [sə'rɛndə*] n reddition f, capitulation f // vi se rendre, capituler.
surreptitious [sʌrəp'tɪʃəs] a subreptice, furtif(ive).
surround [sə'raund] vt entourer; (MIL etc) encercler; **~ing** a environnant(e); **~ings** npl environs mpl, alentours mpl.
surveillance [səː'veɪləns] n surveillance f.
survey n ['səːveɪ] enquête f, étude f; (in housebuying etc) inspection f, (rapport m d')expertise f; (of land) levé m // vt [səː'veɪ] passer en revue; enquêter sur; inspecter; **~ing** n (of land) arpentage m; **~or** n expert m; (arpenteur m) géomètre m.
survival [sə'vaɪvl] n survie f; (relic) vestige m.
survive [sə'vaɪv] vi survivre; (custom etc) subsister // vt survivre à, réchapper de; (person) survivre à; **survivor** n survivant/e.
susceptible [sə'sɛptəbl] a: **~ (to)** sensible (à); (disease) prédisposé(e) (à).
suspect a, n ['sʌspɛkt] suspect(e) // vt [səs'pɛkt] soupçonner, suspecter.
suspend [səs'pɛnd] vt suspendre; **~ed sentence** n condamnation f avec sursis; **~er belt** n porte-jarretelles m inv; **~ers** npl jarretelles fpl; (US) bretelles fpl.
suspense [səs'pɛns] n attente f; (in film etc) suspense m.
suspension [səs'pɛnʃən] n (gen AUT) suspension f; (of driving licence) retrait m provisoire; **~ bridge** n pont suspendu.
suspicion [səs'pɪʃən] n soupçon(s) m(pl).
suspicious [səs'pɪʃəs] a (suspecting) soupçonneux(euse), méfiant(e); (causing suspicion) suspect(e).
sustain [səs'teɪn] vt supporter; soutenir; corroborer; (suffer) subir; recevoir; **~ed** a (effort) soutenu(e), prolongé(e).
sustenance ['sʌstɪnəns] n nourriture f; moyens mpl de subsistance.
swab [swɔb] n (MED) tampon m; prélèvement m.
swagger ['swægə*] vi plastronner, parader.
swallow ['swɔləu] n (bird) hirondelle f; (of food etc) gorgée f // vt avaler; (fig) gober; **to ~ up** vt engloutir.
swam [swæm] pt de **swim**.
swamp [swɔmp] n marais m, marécage m // vt submerger; **~y** a marécageux(euse).

swan [swɔn] n cygne m.

swap [swɔp] n échange m, troc m // vt: to ~ (for) échanger (contre), troquer (contre).

swarm [swɔ:m] n essaim m // vi fourmiller, grouiller.

swarthy ['swɔ:ðɪ] a basané(e), bistré(e).

swastika ['swɔstɪkə] n croix gammée.

swat [swɔt] vt écraser.

sway [sweɪ] vi se balancer, osciller; tanguer // vt (influence) influencer.

swear, pt **swore**, pp **sworn** [swɛə*, swɔ:*, swɔ:n] vi jurer; to ~ to sth jurer de qch; ~word n gros mot, juron m.

sweat [swɛt] n sueur f, transpiration f // vi suer; **in a** ~ en sueur.

sweater ['swɛtə*] n tricot m, pull m.

sweaty ['swɛtɪ] a en sueur, moite or mouillé(e) de sueur.

swede [swi:d] n rutabaga m.

Swede [swi:d] n Suédois/e.

Sweden ['swi:dn] n Suède f.

Swedish ['swi:dɪʃ] a suédois(e) // n (LING) suédois m.

sweep [swi:p] n coup m de balai; (curve) grande courbe; (range) champ m; (also: **chimney** ~) ramoneur m // vb (pt, pp **swept** [swɛpt]) vt balayer // vi avancer majestueusement or rapidement; s'élancer; s'étendre; **to** ~ **away** vt balayer; entraîner; emporter; **to** ~ **past** vi passer majestueusement or rapidement; **to** ~ **up** vt, vi balayer; ~**ing** a (gesture) large; circulaire; **a** ~**ing statement** une généralisation hâtive.

sweet [swi:t] n dessert m; (candy) bonbon m // a doux(douce); (not savoury) sucré(e); (fresh) frais(fraîche), pur(e); (fig) agréable, doux; gentil(le); mignon(ne); ~**bread** n ris m de veau; ~**corn** n maïs sucré; ~**en** vt sucrer; adoucir; ~**heart** n amoureux/euse; ~**ly** ad gentiment; mélodieusement; ~**ness** n goût sucré; douceur f; ~ **pea** n pois m de senteur; **to have a** ~ **tooth** aimer les sucreries.

swell [swɛl] n (of sea) houle f // a (col: excellent) chouette // vb (pt ~**ed**, pp **swollen**, ~**ed** ['swəulən]) vt augmenter; grossir // vi grossir, augmenter; (sound) s'enfler; (MED) enfler; ~**ing** n (MED) enflure f; grosseur f.

sweltering ['swɛltərɪŋ] a étouffant(e), oppressant(e).

swept [swɛpt] pt,pp of **sweep**.

swerve [swə:v] vi faire une embardée or un écart; dévier.

swift [swɪft] n (bird) martinet m // a rapide, prompt(e); ~**ness** n rapidité f.

swig [swɪg] n (col: drink) lampée f.

swill [swɪl] n pâtée f // vt (also: ~ out, ~ down) laver à grande eau.

swim [swɪm] n: **to go for a** ~ aller nager or se baigner // vb (pt **swam**, pp **swum** [swæm, swʌm]) vi nager; (SPORT) faire de la natation; (head, room) tourner // vt traverser (à la nage); faire (à la nage); ~**mer** n nageur/euse; ~**ming** n nage f, natation f; ~**ming baths** npl piscine f; ~**ming cap** n bonnet m de bain; ~**ming costume** n maillot m (de bain); ~**ming**

pool n piscine f; ~**suit** n maillot m (de bain).

swindle ['swɪndl] n escroquerie f // vt escroquer; ~**r** n escroc m.

swine [swaɪn] n, pl inv pourceau m, porc m; (col!) salaud m (!).

swing [swɪŋ] n balançoire f; (movement) balancement m, oscillations fpl; (MUS) swing m; rythme m // vb (pt, pp **swung** [swʌŋ]) vt balancer, faire osciller; (also: ~ **round**) tourner, faire virer // vi se balancer, osciller; (also: ~ **round**) virer, tourner; **to be in full** ~ battre son plein; ~ **bridge** n pont tournant; ~ **door** n porte battante.

swingeing ['swɪndʒɪŋ] a écrasant(e); considérable.

swinging ['swɪŋɪŋ] a rythmé(e); entraînant(e).

swipe [swaɪp] n grand coup; gifle f // vt (hit) frapper à toute volée; gifler; (col: steal) piquer.

swirl [swə:l] n tourbillon m // vi tourbillonner, tournoyer.

swish [swɪʃ] a (col: smart) rupin(e) // vi siffler.

Swiss [swɪs] a suisse // n, pl inv Suisse/esse; ~ **German** a suisse-allemand(e).

switch [swɪtʃ] n (for light, radio etc) bouton m; (change) changement m, revirement m // vt (change) changer; intervertir; **to** ~ **off** vt éteindre; (engine) arrêter; **to** ~ **on** vt allumer; (engine, machine) mettre en marche; ~**back** n montagnes fpl russes; ~**board** n (TEL) standard m; ~**board operator** standardiste m/f.

Switzerland ['swɪtsələnd] n Suisse f.

swivel ['swɪvl] vi (also: ~ **round**) pivoter, tourner.

swollen ['swəulən] pp of **swell** // a (ankle etc) enflé(e).

swoon [swu:n] vi se pâmer.

swoop [swu:p] n (by police etc) rafle f, descente f // vi (also: ~ **down**) descendre en piqué, piquer.

swop [swɔp] n, vt = **swap**.

sword [sɔ:d] n épée f; ~**fish** n espadon m.

swore [swɔ:*] pt of **swear**.

sworn [swɔ:n] pp of **swear**.

swot [swɔt] vt, vi bûcher, potasser.

swum [swʌm] pp of **swim**.

swung [swʌŋ] pt, pp of **swing**.

sycamore ['sɪkəmɔ:*] n sycomore m.

sycophantic [sɪkə'fæntɪk] a flagorneur(euse).

syllable ['sɪləbl] n syllabe f.

syllabus ['sɪləbəs] n programme m.

symbol ['sɪmbl] n symbole m; ~**ic(al)** [-'bɔlɪk(l)] a symbolique; ~**ism** n symbolisme m; ~**ize** vt symboliser.

symmetrical [sɪ'mɛtrɪkl] a symétrique.

symmetry ['sɪmɪtrɪ] n symétrie f.

sympathetic [sɪmpə'θɛtɪk] a compatissant(e); bienveillant(e), compréhensif(ive); ~ **towards** bien disposé(e) envers; ~**ally** ad avec compassion (or bienveillance).

sympathize ['sɪmpəθaɪz] vi: **to** ~ **with**

sb plaindre qn ; s'associer à la douleur de qn ; ~r n (POL) sympathisant/e.

sympathy ['sɪmpəθɪ] n compassion f; **in ~ with** en accord avec ; (strike) en or par solidarité avec ; **with our deepest ~** en vous priant d'accepter nos sincères condoléances.

symphonic [sɪm'fɔnɪk] a symphonique.

symphony ['sɪmfənɪ] n symphonie f; ~ **orchestra** n orchestre m symphonique.

symposium [sɪm'pəuzɪəm] n symposium m.

symptom ['sɪmptəm] n symptôme m; indice m; ~**atic** [-'mætɪk] a symptomatique.

synagogue ['sɪnəgɔg] n synagogue f.

synchromesh [sɪŋkrəu'mɛʃ] n synchronisation f.

synchronize ['sɪŋkrənaɪz] vt synchroniser // vi: **to ~ with** se produire en même temps que.

syncopated ['sɪŋkəpeɪtɪd] a syncopé(e).

syndicate ['sɪndɪkɪt] n syndicat m, coopérative f.

syndrome ['sɪndrəum] n syndrome m.

synonym ['sɪnənɪm] n synonyme m; ~**ous** [sɪ'nɔnɪməs] a: ~**ous (with)** synonyme (de).

synopsis, pl **synopses** [sɪ'nɔpsɪs, -si:z] n résumé m, synopsis m or f.

syntax ['sɪntæks] n syntaxe f.

synthesis, pl **syntheses** ['sɪnθəsɪs, -si:z] n synthèse f.

synthetic [sɪn'θɛtɪk] a synthétique ; ~**s** npl textiles artificiels.

syphilis ['sɪfɪlɪs] n syphilis f.

syphon ['saɪfən] n, vb = **siphon.**

Syria ['sɪrɪə] n Syrie f; ~**n** a syrien(ne) // n Syrien/ne.

syringe [sɪ'rɪndʒ] n seringue f.

syrup ['sɪrəp] n sirop m; (also: **golden** ~) mélasse raffinée ; ~**y** a sirupeux(euse).

system ['sɪstəm] n système m; (order) méthode f; (ANAT) organisme m; ~**atic** [-'mætɪk] a systématique ; méthodique ; ~**s analyst** n analyste-programmeur m/f.

T

ta [tɑ:] excl (Brit: col) merci!

tab [tæb] n (loop on coat etc) attache f; (label) étiquette f; **to keep ~s on** (fig) surveiller.

tabby ['tæbɪ] n (also: ~ **cat**) chat/te tigré(e).

tabernacle ['tæbənækl] n tabernacle m.

table ['teɪbl] n table f // vt (motion etc) présenter ; **to lay** or **set the ~** mettre le couvert or la table ; ~ **of contents** n table f des matières ; ~**cloth** n nappe f; ~ **d'hôte** [tɑ:bl'dəut] a (meal) à prix fixe ; ~ **lamp** n lampe f décorative ; ~**mat** n (for plate) napperon m, set m ; (for hot dish) dessous-de-plat m inv ; ~ **salt** n sel fin or de table ; ~**spoon** n cuiller f de service ; (also: ~**spoonful**: as measurement) cuillerée f à soupe.

tablet ['tæblɪt] n (MED) comprimé m ; (: for sucking) pastille f; (for writing) bloc m ; (of stone) plaque f.

table: ~ **tennis** n ping-pong m, tennis m de table ; ~ **wine** n vin m de table.

taboo [tə'bu:] a, n tabou (m).

tabulate ['tæbjuleɪt] vt (data, figures) mettre sous forme de table(s) ; **tabulator** n tabulateur m.

tacit ['tæsɪt] a tacite.

taciturn ['tæsɪtə:n] a taciturne.

tack [tæk] n (nail) petit clou ; (stitch) point m de bâti ; (NAUT) bord m, bordée f // vt clouer ; bâtir // vi tirer un or des bord(s) ; **to change ~** virer de bord ; **on the wrong ~** (fig) sur la mauvaise voie.

tackle ['tækl] n matériel m, équipement m ; (for lifting) appareil m de levage ; (RUGBY) plaquage m // vt (difficulty) s'attaquer à ; (RUGBY) plaquer.

tacky ['tækɪ] a collant(e) ; pas sec(sèche).

tact [tækt] n tact m ; ~**ful** a plein(e) de tact ; ~**fully** ad avec tact.

tactical ['tæktɪkl] a tactique ; ~ **error** n erreur f de tactique.

tactics ['tæktɪks] n,npl tactique f.

tactless ['tæktlɪs] a qui manque de tact ; ~**ly** ad sans tact.

tadpole ['tædpəul] n têtard m.

taffy ['tæfɪ] n (US) (bonbon m au) caramel m.

tag [tæg] n étiquette f; **to ~ along** vi suivre.

tail [teɪl] n queue f; (of shirt) pan m // vt (follow) suivre, filer ; ~**s** (on coin) (le côté) pile ; **to ~ away**, ~ **off** vi (in size, quality etc) baisser peu à peu ; ~**back** n bouchon m ; ~ **coat** n habit m ; ~ **end** n bout m, fin f; ~**gate** n hayon m (arrière).

tailor ['teɪlə*] n tailleur m (artisan) ; ~**ing** n (cut) coupe f; ~**-made** a fait(e) sur mesure ; (fig) conçu(e) spécialement.

tailwind ['teɪlwɪnd] n vent m arrière inv.

tainted ['teɪntɪd] a (food) gâté(e) ; (water, air) infecté(e) ; (fig) souillé(e).

take, pt took, pp taken [teɪk, tuk, 'teɪkn] vt prendre ; (gain: prize) remporter ; (require: effort, courage) demander ; (tolerate) accepter, supporter ; (hold: passengers etc) contenir ; (accompany) emmener, accompagner ; (bring, carry) apporter, emporter ; (exam) passer, se présenter à ; **to ~ sth from** (drawer etc) prendre qch dans ; (person) prendre qch à ; **I ~ it that** je suppose que ; **to ~ for a walk** (child, dog) emmener promener ; **to ~ after** vt fus ressembler à ; **to ~ apart** vt démonter ; **to ~ away** vt emporter ; enlever ; **to ~ back** vt (return) rendre, rapporter ; (one's words) retirer ; **to ~ down** vt (building) démolir ; (letter etc) prendre, écrire ; **to ~ in** vt (deceive) tromper, rouler ; (understand) comprendre, saisir ; (include) couvrir, inclure ; (lodger) prendre ; **to ~ off** vi (AVIAT) décoller // vt (remove) enlever ; (imitate) imiter, pasticher ; **to ~ on** vt (work) accepter, se charger de ; (employee) prendre, embaucher ; (opponent) accepter de se battre contre ; **to ~ out** vt sortir ; (remove) enlever ; (licence) prendre, se procurer ; **to ~ sth out of** enlever qch de ; prendre qch dans ; **to ~ over** vt (business) reprendre // vi: **to ~ over from sb** prendre la relève de qn ; **to ~ to** vt fus (person) se prendre d'amitié pour ; (activity) prendre goût à ; to ~ up vt (one's story, a dress) reprendre ; (occupy: time, space) prendre, occuper ; (engage in: hobby etc) se mettre à ; ~away a (food) à emporter ; ~-home pay n salaire net ; ~off n (AVIAT) décollage m ; ~over n (COMM) rachat m ; ~over bid n offre publique d'achat.

takings ['teɪkɪŋz] npl (COMM) recette f.

talc [tælk] n (also: ~um powder) talc m.

tale [teɪl] n (story) conte m, histoire f ; (account) récit m ; (pej) histoire.

talent ['tælnt] n talent m, don m ; ~ed a doué(e), plein(e) de talent.

talk [tɔːk] n propos mpl ; (gossip) racontars mpl (pej) ; (conversation) discussion f ; (interview) entretien m ; (a speech) causerie f, exposé m // vi (chatter) bavarder ; to ~ about parler de ; (converse) s'entretenir or parler de ; to ~ sb out of/into doing persuader qn de ne pas faire/de faire ; to ~ shop parler métier or affaires ; to ~ over vt discuter (de) ; ~ative a bavard(e) ; ~er n causeur/euse ; (pej) bavard/e.

tall [tɔːl] a (person) grand(e) ; (building, tree) haut(e) ; to be 6 feet ~ ≈ mesurer 1 mètre 80 ; ~boy n grande commode ; ~ness n grande taille ; hauteur f ; ~ story n histoire f invraisemblable.

tally ['tælɪ] n compte m // vi: to ~ (with) correspondre (à).

tambourine [tæmbə'riːn] n tambourin m.

tame [teɪm] a apprivoisé(e) ; (fig: story, style) insipide.

tamper ['tæmpə*] vi: to ~ with toucher à (en cachette ou sans permission).

tampon ['tæmpən] n tampon m hygiénique or périodique.

tan [tæn] n (also: sun~) bronzage m // vt,vi bronzer, brunir // a (colour) brun roux inv.

tandem ['tændəm] n tandem m.

tang [tæŋ] n odeur (or saveur) piquante.

tangent ['tændʒənt] n (MATH) tangente f.

tangerine [tændʒə'riːn] n mandarine f.

tangible ['tændʒəbl] a tangible.

tangle ['tæŋgl] n enchevêtrement m // vt enchevêtrer ; to get in(to) a ~ s'emmêler.

tango ['tæŋgəu] n tango m.

tank [tæŋk] n réservoir m ; (for processing) cuve f ; (for fish) aquarium m ; (MIL) char m d'assaut, tank m.

tankard ['tæŋkəd] n chope f.

tanker ['tæŋkə*] n (ship) pétrolier m, tanker m ; (truck) camion-citerne m.

tanned [tænd] a (skin) bronzé(e).

tantalizing ['tæntəlaɪzɪŋ] a (smell) extrêmement appétissant(e) ; (offer) terriblement tentant(e).

tantamount ['tæntəmaunt] a: ~ to qui équivaut à.

tantrum ['tæntrəm] n accès m de colère.

tap [tæp] n (on sink etc) robinet m ; (gentle blow) petite tape f // vt frapper or taper légèrement ; (resources) exploiter, utiliser ; ~-dancing n claquettes fpl.

tape [teɪp] n ruban m ; (also: magnetic ~) bande f (magnétique) // vt (record) enregistrer (sur bande) ; ~ measure n mètre m à ruban.

taper ['teɪpə*] n cierge m // vi s'effiler.

tape recorder ['teɪprɪkɔːdə*] n magnétophone m.

tapered ['teɪpəd], tapering ['teɪpərɪŋ] a fuselé(e), effilé(e).

tapestry ['tæpɪstrɪ] n tapisserie f.

tapioca [tæpɪ'əukə] n tapioca m.

tappet ['tæpɪt] n (AUT) poussoir m (de soupape).

tar [tɑː] n goudron m.

tarantula [tə'ræntjulə] n tarentule f.

tardy ['tɑːdɪ] a tardif(ive).

target ['tɑːgɪt] n cible f ; (fig: objective) objectif m ; ~ practice n exercices mpl de tir (à la cible).

tariff ['tærɪf] n (COMM) tarif m ; (taxes) tarif douanier.

tarmac ['tɑːmæk] n macadam m ; (AVIAT) aire f d'envol // vt goudronner.

tarnish ['tɑːnɪʃ] vt ternir.

tarpaulin [tɑː'pɔːlɪn] n bâche goudronnée.

tarragon ['tærəgən] n estragon m.

tart [tɑːt] n (CULIN) tarte f ; (col: pej: woman) poule f // a (flavour) âpre, aigrelet(te).

tartan ['tɑːtn] n tartan m // a écossais(e).

tartar ['tɑːtə*] n (on teeth) tartre m ; ~ sauce n sauce f tartare.

task [tɑːsk] n tâche f ; to take to ~ prendre à partie ; ~ force n (MIL, POLICE) détachement spécial.

Tasmania [tæz'meɪnɪə] n Tasmanie f.

tassel ['tæsl] n gland m ; pompon m.

taste [teɪst] n goût m ; (fig: glimpse, idea) idée f, aperçu m // vt goûter // vi: to ~ of (fish etc) avoir le or un goût de ; it ~s like fish ça a un or le goût de poisson, on dirait du poisson ; what does it ~ like? quel goût ça a? ; you can ~ the garlic (in it) on sent bien l'ail ; can I have a ~ of this wine? puis-je goûter un peu de ce vin? ; to have a ~ of sth goûter (à) qch ; to have a ~ for sth aimer qch, avoir un penchant pour qch ; ~ful a de bon goût ; ~fully ad avec goût ; ~less a (food) qui n'a aucun goût ; (remark) de mauvais goût ; tasty a savoureux(euse), délicieux(euse).

tattered ['tætəd] a see tatters.

tatters ['tætəz] mpl: in ~ (also: tattered) en lambeaux.

tattoo [tə'tuː] n tatouage m ; (spectacle) parade f militaire // vt tatouer.

tatty ['tætɪ] a (col) défraîchi(e), en piteux état.

taught [tɔːt] pt,pp of teach.

taunt [tɔːnt] n raillerie f // vt railler.

Taurus ['tɔːrəs] n le Taureau ; to be ~ être du Taureau.

taut [tɔːt] a tendu(e).

tavern ['tævən] n taverne f.

tawdry ['tɔːdrɪ] a (d'un mauvais goût) criard.

tawny ['tɔːnɪ] a fauve (couleur).

tax [tæks] n (on goods etc) taxe f ; (on income) impôts mpl, contributions fpl // vt taxer ; imposer ; (fig: strain: patience etc) mettre à l'épreuve ; ~ation [-'seɪʃən] n taxation f ; impôts mpl, contributions fpl ; ~ avoidance n évasion fiscale ; ~ collector n percepteur m ; ~ evasion n fraude fiscale ; ~ **exile** n personne qui s'expatrie pour fuir une fiscalité excessive ; ~-**free** a exempt(e) d'impôts.

taxi ['tæksɪ] n taxi m // vi (AVIAT) rouler (lentement) au sol.

taxidermist ['tæksɪdə:mɪst] n empailleur/euse (d'animaux).

taxi: ~ **driver** n chauffeur m de taxi ; ~ **rank**, ~ **stand** n station f de taxis.

tax: ~ **payer** n contribuable m/f ; ~ **return** n déclaration f d'impôts or de revenus.

TB abbr of tuberculosis.

tea [ti:] n thé m ; (snack: for children) goûter m ; **high** ~ collation combinant goûter et dîner ; ~ **bag** n sachet m de thé ; ~ **break** n pause-thé f ; ~**cake** n petit pain brioché.

teach, pt, pp **taught** [ti:tʃ, tɔ:t] vt: to ~ sb sth, ~ sth to sb apprendre qch à qn ; (in school etc) enseigner qch à qn // vi enseigner ; ~**er** n (in secondary school) professeur m ; (in primary school) instituteur/trice ; ~**ing** n enseignement m ; ~**ing staff** n enseignants mpl.

tea cosy ['ti:kəuzɪ] n couvre-théière m.

teacup ['ti:kʌp] n tasse f à thé.

teak [ti:k] n teck m // a en or de teck.

tea leaves ['ti:li:vz] npl feuilles fpl de thé.

team [ti:m] n équipe f ; (of animals) attelage m ; ~ **games/work** jeux mpl/travail m d'équipe.

tea party ['ti:pɑ:tɪ] n thé m (réception).

teapot ['ti:pɔt] n théière f.

tear n [tɛə*] déchirure f ; [tɪə*] larme f // vb [tɛə*] (pt **tore**, pp **torn** [tɔ:*, tɔ:n]) vt déchirer // vi se déchirer ; **in** ~**s** en larmes ; **to burst into** ~**s** fondre en larmes ; **to** ~ **along** vi (rush) aller à toute vitesse ; ~**ful** a larmoyant(e) ; ~ **gas** n gaz m lacrymogène.

tearoom ['ti:ru:m] n salon m de thé.

tease [ti:z] n taquin/e // vt taquiner ; (unkindly) tourmenter.

tea set ['ti:sɛt] n service m à thé.

teashop ['ti:ʃɔp] n pâtisserie-salon de thé f.

teaspoon ['ti:spu:n] n petite cuiller ; (also: ~**ful**: as measurement) ≈ cuillerée f à café.

tea strainer ['ti:streɪnə*] n passoire f (à thé).

teat [ti:t] n tétine f.

teatime ['ti:taɪm] n l'heure f du thé.

tea towel ['ti:tauəl] n torchon m (à vaisselle).

tea urn ['ti:ə:n] n fontaine f à thé.

technical ['tɛknɪkl] a technique ; ~**ity** [-'kælɪtɪ] n technicité f ; (detail) détail m technique ; ~**ly** ad techniquement.

technician [tɛk'nɪʃn] n technicien/ne.

technique [tɛk'ni:k] n technique f.

technological [tɛknə'lɔdʒɪkl] a technologique.

technologist [tɛk'nɔlədʒɪst] n technologue m/f.

technology [tɛk'nɔlədʒɪ] n technologie f.

teddy (bear) ['tɛdɪ(bɛə*)] n ours m (en peluche).

tedious ['ti:dɪəs] a fastidieux(euse).

tedium ['ti:dɪəm] n ennui m.

tee [ti:] n (GOLF) tee m.

teem [ti:m] vi grouiller, abonder ; **to** ~ **with** grouiller de ; **it is** ~**ing (with rain)** il pleut à torrents.

teenage ['ti:neɪdʒ] a (fashions etc) pour jeunes, pour adolescents ; ~**r** n jeune m/f, adolescent/e.

teens [ti:nz] npl: **to be in one's** ~ être adolescent(e).

tee-shirt ['ti:ʃə:t] n = T-shirt.

teeter ['ti:tə*] vi chanceler, vaciller.

teeth [ti:θ] npl of tooth.

teethe [ti:ð] vi percer ses dents.

teething ['ti:ðɪŋ] a: ~ **ring** n anneau m (pour bébé qui perce ses dents) ; ~ **troubles** npl (fig) difficultés initiales.

teetotal ['ti:'təutl] a (person) qui ne boit jamais d'alcool.

telecommunications ['tɛlɪkəmju:nɪ'keɪʃənz] n télécommunications fpl.

telegram ['tɛlɪgræm] n télégramme m.

telegraph ['tɛlɪgrɑ:f] n télégraphe m ; ~**ic** [-'græfɪk] a télégraphique ; ~ **pole** n poteau m télégraphique.

telepathic [tɛlɪ'pæθɪk] a télépathique.

telepathy [tə'lɛpəθɪ] n télépathie f.

telephone ['tɛlɪfəun] n téléphone m // vt (person) téléphoner à ; (message) téléphoner ; ~ **booth**, ~ **box** n cabine f téléphonique ; ~ **call** n coup m de téléphone, appel m téléphonique ; communication f téléphonique ; ~ **directory** n annuaire m (du téléphone) ; ~ **exchange** n central m (téléphonique) ; ~ **number** n numéro m de téléphone ; ~ **operator** téléphoniste m/f, standardiste m/f ; **telephonist** [tə'lɛfənɪst] n téléphoniste m/f.

telephoto ['tɛlɪ'fəutəu] a: ~ **lens** n téléobjectif m.

teleprinter ['tɛlɪprɪntə*] n téléscripteur m.

telescope ['tɛlɪskəup] n télescope m // vt télescoper ; **telescopic** [-'skɔpɪk] a télescopique.

televiewer ['tɛlɪvju:ə*] n téléspectateur/trice.

televise ['tɛlɪvaɪz] vt téléviser.

television ['tɛlɪvɪʒən] n télévision f ; ~ **programme** n émission f de télévision ; ~ **set** n poste m de télévision.

tell, pt, pp **told** [tɛl, təuld] vt dire ; (relate: story) raconter ; (distinguish): **to** ~ **sth from** distinguer qch de // vi (have effect) se faire sentir, se voir ; **to** ~ **sb to do** dire à qn de faire ; **to** ~ **on** vt fus (inform against) dénoncer, rapporter contre ; **to** ~ **off** vt réprimander, gronder ; ~**er** n (in bank) caissier/ère ; ~**ing** a (remark, detail) révélateur(trice) ; ~**tale** a (sign) éloquent(e), révélateur(trice) // n (CONSTR) témoin m.

telly ['tɛlɪ] n (col: abbr of television) télé f.

temerity [tə'mɛrɪtɪ] n témérité f.

temp [tɛmp] n (abbr of temporary) (secrétaire f) intérimaire f.

temper ['tɛmpə*] n (nature) caractère m ; (mood) humeur f ; (fit of anger) colère f // vt (moderate) tempérer, adoucir ; **to be in a** ~ être en colère ; **to lose one's** ~ se mettre en colère.

temperament ['tɛmprəmənt] n (nature) tempérament m; ~al [-'mɛntl] a capricieux(euse).

temperance ['tɛmpərns] n modération f; (in drinking) tempérance f.

temperate ['tɛmprət] a modéré(e); (climate) tempéré(e).

temperature ['tɛmprətʃə*] n température f; to have or run a ~ avoir de la fièvre; ~ chart n (MED) feuille f de température.

tempered ['tɛmpəd] a (steel) trempé(e).

tempest ['tɛmpɪst] n tempête f.

tempi ['tɛmpi:] npl of tempo.

template ['tɛmplɪt] n patron m.

temple ['tɛmpl] n (building) temple m; (ANAT) tempe f.

tempo, ~s or tempi ['tɛmpəu, 'tɛmpi:] n tempo m; (fig: of life etc) rythme m.

temporal ['tɛmpərl] a temporel(le).

temporarily ['tɛmpərərɪlɪ] ad temporairement; provisoirement.

temporary ['tɛmpərərɪ] a temporaire, provisoire; (job, worker) temporaire; ~ secretary n (secrétaire f) intérimaire f.

temporize ['tɛmpəraɪz] vi atermoyer; transiger.

tempt [tɛmpt] vt tenter; to ~ sb into doing induire qn à faire; ~ation [-'teɪʃən] n tentation f; ~ing a tentant(e).

ten [tɛn] num dix.

tenable ['tɛnəbl] a défendable.

tenacious [tə'neɪʃəs] a tenace.

tenacity [tə'næsɪtɪ] n ténacité f.

tenancy ['tɛnənsɪ] n location f; état m de locataire.

tenant ['tɛnənt] n locataire m/f.

tend [tɛnd] vt s'occuper de // vi: to ~ to do avoir une tendance à faire; (colour): to ~ to tirer sur.

tendency ['tɛndənsɪ] n tendance f.

tender ['tɛndə*] a tendre; (delicate) délicat(e); (sore) sensible; (affectionate) tendre, doux(douce) // n (COMM: offer) soumission f; (money): legal ~ cours légal // vt offrir; ~ize vt (CULIN) attendrir; ~ly ad tendrement; ~ness n tendresse f; (of meat) tendreté f.

tendon ['tɛndən] n tendon m.

tenement ['tɛnəmənt] n immeuble m (de rapport).

tenet ['tɛnət] n principe m.

tennis ['tɛnɪs] n tennis m; ~ ball n balle f de tennis; ~ court n (court m de) tennis; ~ racket n raquette f de tennis.

tenor ['tɛnə*] n (MUS) ténor m; (of speech etc) sens général.

tense [tɛns] a tendu(e); (person) tendu, crispé(e) // n (LING) temps m; ~ness n tension f.

tension ['tɛnʃən] n tension f.

tent [tɛnt] n tente f.

tentacle ['tɛntəkl] n tentacule m.

tentative ['tɛntətɪv] a timide, hésitant(e); (conclusion) provisoire.

tenterhooks ['tɛntəhuks] npl: on ~ sur des charbons ardents.

tenth [tɛnθ] num dixième.

tent: ~ peg n piquet m de tente; ~ pole n montant m de tente.

tenuous ['tɛnjuəs] a ténu(e).

tenure ['tɛnjuə*] n (of property) bail m; (of job) période f de jouissance; statut m de titulaire.

tepid ['tɛpɪd] a tiède.

term [tə:m] n (limit) terme m; (word) terme, mot m; (SCOL) trimestre m; (LAW) session f // vt appeler; ~s npl (conditions) conditions fpl; (COMM) tarif m; ~ of imprisonment peine f de prison; in the short/long ~ à court/long terme; 'easy ~s' (COMM) 'facilités de paiement'; to be on good ~s with bien s'entendre avec, être en bons termes avec; to come to ~s with (person) arriver à un accord avec; (problem) faire face à.

terminal ['tə:mɪnl] a terminal(e); (disease) dans sa phase terminale // n (ELEC) borne f; (for oil, ore etc) terminal m; (also: air ~) aérogare f; (also: coach ~) gare routière.

terminate ['tə:mɪneɪt] vt mettre fin à // vi: to ~ in finir en or par.

termination [tə:mɪ'neɪʃən] n fin f; (of contract) résiliation f; ~ of pregnancy n (MED) interruption f de grossesse.

termini ['tə:mɪnaɪ] npl of terminus.

terminology [tə:mɪ'nɔlədʒɪ] n terminologie f.

terminus, pl termini ['tə:mɪnəs, 'tə:mɪnaɪ] n terminus m inv.

termite ['tə:maɪt] n termite m.

terrace ['tɛrəs] n terrasse f; (row of houses) rangée f de maisons (attenantes les unes aux autres); the ~s (SPORT) les gradins mpl; ~d a (garden) en terrasses.

terracotta ['tɛrə'kɔtə] n terre cuite.

terrain [tɛ'reɪn] n terrain m (sol).

terrible ['tɛrɪbl] a terrible, atroce; (weather, work) affreux(euse); épouvantable; terribly ad terriblement; (very badly) affreusement mal.

terrier ['tɛrɪə*] n terrier m (chien).

terrific [tə'rɪfɪk] a fantastique, incroyable, terrible; (wonderful) formidable, sensationnel(le).

terrify ['tɛrɪfaɪ] vt terrifier.

territorial [tɛrɪ'tɔ:rɪəl] a territorial(e).

territory ['tɛrɪtərɪ] n territoire m.

terror ['tɛrə*] n terreur f; ~ism n terrorisme m; ~ist n terroriste m/f; ~ize vt terroriser.

terse [tə:s] a (style) concis(e); (reply) laconique.

test [tɛst] n (trial, check) essai m; (: of goods in factory) contrôle m; (of courage etc) épreuve f; (MED) examens mpl; (CHEM) analyses fpl; (exam: of intelligence etc) test m (d'aptitude); (: in school) interrogation f de contrôle; (also: driving ~) (examen du) permis m de conduire // vt essayer; contrôler; mettre à l'épreuve; examiner; analyser; tester; faire subir une interrogation (de contrôle) à.

testament ['tɛstəmənt] n testament m; the Old/New T~ l'Ancien/le Nouveau Testament.

test: ~ case n (LAW, fig) affaire-test f; ~ flight n vol m d'essai.

testicle ['tɛstɪkl] n testicule m.

testify ['tɛstɪfaɪ] vi (LAW) témoigner,
déposer.

testimonial [tɛstɪ'məunɪəl] n (reference)
recommandation f; (gift) témoignage m
d'estime.

testimony ['tɛstɪmənɪ] n (LAW)
témoignage m, déposition f.

test: ~ **match** n (CRICKET, RUGBY) match
international; ~ **paper** n (SCOL)
interrogation écrite; ~ **pilot** n pilote m
d'essai; ~ **tube** n éprouvette f.

testy ['tɛstɪ] a irritable.

tetanus ['tɛtənəs] n tétanos m.

tether ['tɛðə*] vt attacher // n: at the end
of one's ~ à bout (de patience).

text [tɛkst] n texte m; ~**book** n manuel
m.

textile ['tɛkstaɪl] n textile m.

texture ['tɛkstʃə*] n texture f; (of skin,
paper etc) grain m.

Thai [taɪ] a thaïlandais(e) // n
Thaïlandais/e; (LING) thaï m; ~**land** n
Thaïlande f.

Thames [tɛmz] n: the ~ la Tamise.

than [ðæn, ðən] cj que; (with numerals):
more ~ 10/once plus de 10/d'une fois;
I have more/less ~ you j'en ai
plus/moins que toi; she has more apples
~ pears elle a plus de pommes que de
poires.

thank [θæŋk] vt remercier, dire merci à;
~ you (very much) merci (beaucoup);
~s npl remerciements mpl // excl merci!;
~s to prep grâce à; ~ful a: ~ful (for)
reconnaissant(e) (de); ~less a ingrat(e);
T~sgiving (Day) n jour m d'action de
grâce.

that [ðæt, ðət] cj que // det ce(cet + vowel
or h mute), f cette; (not 'this'): ~**book**
ce livre-là // pronoun ce; (not 'this one')
cela, ça; (the one) celui(celle); (relative:
subject) qui; (: object) que, prep +
lequel(laquelle); (with time): on the day
~ he came le jour où il est venu // ad:
~ high aussi haut; si haut; it's about ~
high c'est à peu près de cette hauteur; ~
one celui-là(celle-là); what's ~? qu'est-
ce que c'est?; who's ~? qui est-ce?; is
~ you? c'est toi?; ~'s what he said c'est
ce qu'il a dit; ~ is... c'est-à-dire...,
à savoir...; all ~ tout cela, tout ça; I can't
work ~ much je ne peux pas travailler
autant que cela.

thatched [θætʃt] a (roof) de chaume; ~
cottage chaumière f.

thaw [θɔ:] n dégel m // vi (ice) fondre;
(food) dégeler // vt (food) (faire) dégeler;
it's ~ing (weather) il dégèle.

the [ði:, ðə] det le, f la, l' (l' + vowel or h
mute), pl les; (NB: à + le(s) = au(x); de +
le = du; de + les = des).

theatre, theater (US) ['θɪətə*] n théâtre
m; ~-goer n habitué/e du théâtre.

theatrical [θɪ'ætrɪkl] a théâtral(e); ~
company n troupe f de théâtre.

theft [θɛft] n vol m (larcin).

their [ðɛə*] a leur, pl leurs; ~s pronoun
le(la) leur, les leurs; it is ~s c'est à eux;
a friend of ~s un de leurs amis.

them [ðɛm, ðəm] pronoun (direct) les;
(indirect) leur; (stressed, after prep)
eux(elles); I see ~ je les vois; give ~
the book donne-leur le livre.

theme [θi:m] n thème m; ~ **song** n
chanson principale.

themselves [ðəm'sɛlvz] pl pronoun (reflexive) se; (emphatic) eux-
mêmes(elles-mêmes); between ~ entre
eux(elles).

then [ðɛn] ad (at that time) alors, à ce
moment-là; (next) puis, ensuite; (and also)
et puis // cj (therefore) alors, dans ce cas
// a: the ~ **president** le président d'alors
or de l'époque; from ~ on dès lors.

theologian [θɪə'ləudʒən] n théologien/ne.

theological [θɪə'lɔdʒɪkl] a théologique.

theology [θɪ'ɔlədʒɪ] n théologie f.

theorem ['θɪərəm] n théorème m.

theoretical [θɪə'rɛtɪkl] a théorique.

theorize ['θɪəraɪz] vi élaborer une théorie;
(pej) faire des théories.

theory ['θɪərɪ] n théorie f.

therapeutic(al) [θɛrə'pju:tɪk(l)] a
thérapeutique.

therapist ['θɛrəpɪst] n thérapeute m/f.

therapy ['θɛrəpɪ] n thérapie f.

there [ðɛə*] ad là, là-bas; ~, ~! allons,
allons!; it's ~ c'est là; he went ~ il y
est allé; ~ is, ~ are il y a; ~ he is le
voilà; ~ has been il y en a; on/in ~
là-dessus/ -dedans; to go ~ and back
faire l'aller et retour; ~abouts ad (place)
par là, près de là; (amount) environ, à peu
près; ~after ad par la suite; ~fore ad
donc, par conséquent; ~'s = ~ is; ~
has.

thermal ['θə:ml] a thermique.

thermometer [θə'mɔmɪtə*] n thermomètre m.

thermonuclear [θə:məu'nju:klɪə*] a
thermonucléaire.

Thermos ['θə:məs] n ® (also: ~ **flask**)
thermos m or f inv ®.

thermostat ['θə:məustæt] n thermostat m.

thesaurus [θɪ'sɔ:rəs] n dictionnaire m
synonymique.

these [ði:z] pl pronoun ceux-ci(celles-ci) //
pl det ces; (not 'those'): ~ **books** ces livres-
ci.

thesis, pl **theses** ['θi:sɪs, 'θi:si:z] n thèse
f.

they [ðeɪ] pl pronoun ils(elles); (stressed)
eux(elles); ~ **say that...** (it is said that)
on dit que...; ~'d = they had; they
would; ~'ll = they shall; they will;
~'re = they are; ~'ve = they have.

thick [θɪk] a épais(se); (crowd) dense;
(stupid) bête, borné(e) // n: in the ~ of
au beau milieu de, en plein cœur de; it's
20 cm ~ ça a 20 cm d'épaisseur; ~en
vi s'épaissir // vt (sauce etc) épaissir;
~ness n épaisseur f; ~set a trapu(e),
costaud(e); ~skinned a (fig) peu sensible.

thief, thieves [θi:f, θi:vz] n voleur/euse.

thieving ['θi:vɪŋ] n vol m (larcin).

thigh [θaɪ] n cuisse f; ~**bone** n fémur m.

thimble ['θɪmbl] n dé m (à coudre).

thin [θɪn] a mince; (person) maigre; (soup)
peu épais(se); (hair, crowd) clairsemé(e);
(fog) léger(ère) // vt (hair) éclaircir; to ~
(down) (sauce, paint) délayer.

thing [θɪŋ] *n* chose *f*; (*object*) objet *m*; (*contraption*) truc *m*; ~s *npl* (*belongings*) affaires *fpl*; for one ~ d'abord; the best ~ would be to le mieux serait de; how are ~s? comment ça va?

think, *pt*, *pp* **thought** [θɪŋk, θɔ:t] *vi* penser, réfléchir // *vt* penser, croire; (*imagine*) s'imaginer; to ~ of penser à; what did you ~ of them? qu'as-tu pensé d'eux?; to ~ about sth/sb penser à qch/qn; I'll ~ about it je vais y réfléchir; to ~ of doing avoir l'idée de faire; I ~ so je crois or pense que oui; to ~ well of avoir une haute opinion de; to ~ over *vt* bien réfléchir à; to ~ up *vt* inventer, trouver.

thinly ['θɪnlɪ] *ad* (*cut*) en tranches fines; (*spread*) en couche mince.

thinness ['θɪnnɪs] *n* minceur *f*; maigreur *f*.

third [θə:d] *num* troisième // *n* troisième *m/f*; (*fraction*) tiers *m*; (*SCOL: degree*) ≈ licence *f* avec mention passable; a ~ of le tiers de; ~ly *ad* troisièmement; ~party insurance *n* assurance *f* au tiers; ~-rate *a* de qualité médiocre; the T~ World *n* le Tiers-Monde.

thirst [θə:st] *n* soif *f*; ~y *a* (*person*) qui a soif, assoiffé(e).

thirteen ['θə:'ti:n] *num* treize.

thirty ['θə:tɪ] *num* trente.

this [ðɪs] *det* ce(cet + *vowel or h mute*), *f* cette; (*not 'that'*): ~ book ce livre-ci // *pronoun* ce; ceci; (*not 'that one'*) celui-ci(celle-ci); ~ is what he said voici ce qu'il a dit.

thistle ['θɪsl] *n* chardon *m*.

thong [θɔŋ] *n* lanière *f*.

thorn [θɔ:n] *n* épine *f*; ~ bush *n* buisson *m* d'épines; ~y *a* épineux(euse).

thorough ['θʌrə] *a* (*search*) minutieux(euse); (*knowledge, research*) approfondi(e); (*work*) consciencieux(euse); (*cleaning*) à fond; ~bred *n* (*horse*) pur-sang *m inv*; ~fare *n* rue *f*; 'no ~fare' 'passage interdit'; ~ly *ad* minutieusement; en profondeur; à fond; he ~ly agreed il était tout à fait d'accord.

those [ðəuz] *pl pronoun* ceux-là(celles-là) // *pl det* ces; (*not 'these'*): ~ books ces livres-là.

though [ðəu] *cj* bien que + *sub*, quoique + *sub* // *ad* pourtant.

thought [θɔ:t] *pt*, *pp of* **think** // *n* pensée *f*; (*opinion*) avis *m*; (*intention*) intention *f*; ~ful *a* pensif(ive); réfléchi(e); (*considerate*) prévenant(e); ~less *a* étourdi(e); qui manque de considération.

thousand ['θauzənd] *num* mille; ~th *num* millième; one ~ mille; ~s of des milliers de.

thrash [θræʃ] *vt* rouer de coups; donner une correction à; (*defeat*) battre à plate couture; to ~ about *vi* se débattre; to ~ out *vt* débattre de.

thread [θrɛd] *n* fil *m*; (*of screw*) pas *m*, filetage *m* // *vt* (*needle*) enfiler; to ~ one's way between se faufiler entre; ~bare *a* râpé(e), élimé(e).

threat [θrɛt] *n* menace *f*; ~en *vi* (*storm*) menacer // *vt*: to ~en sb with sth/to do menacer qn de qch/de faire.

three [θri:] *num* trois (*m inv*); ~-dimensional *a* à trois dimensions; (*film*) en relief; ~fold *ad*: to increase ~fold tripler; ~-piece suit *n* complet *m* (avec gilet); ~-piece suite *n* salon *m* comprenant un canapé et deux fauteuils assortis; ~-ply *a* (*wood*) à trois épaisseurs; (*wool*) trois fils *inv*; ~-wheeler *n* (*car*) voiture *f* à trois roues.

thresh [θrɛʃ] *vt* (*AGR*) battre; ~ing machine *n* batteuse *f*.

threshold ['θrɛʃhəuld] *n* seuil *m*.

threw [θru:] *pt of* **throw**.

thrift [θrɪft] *n* économie *f*; ~y *a* économe.

thrill [θrɪl] *n* frisson *m*, émotion *f* // *vi* tressaillir, frissonner // *vt* (*audience*) électriser; to be ~ed (with *gift etc*) être ravi; ~er *n* film *m* (*or* roman *m or* pièce *f*) à suspense.

thrive, *pt* **thrived**, **throve** *pp* **thrived**, **thriven** [θraɪv, θrəuv, 'θrɪvn] *vi* pousser or se développer bien; (*business*) prospérer; he ~s on it cela lui réussit; thriving *a* vigoureux(euse); prospère.

throat [θrəut] *n* gorge *f*; to have a sore ~ avoir mal à la gorge.

throb [θrɔb] *n* (*of heart*) pulsation *f*; (*of engine*) vibration *f*; (*of pain*) élancement *m* // *vi* (*heart*) palpiter; (*engine*) vibrer; (*pain*) lanciner; (*wound*) causer des élancements.

throes [θrəuz] *npl*: in the ~ of au beau milieu de; en proie à; in the ~ of death à l'agonie.

thrombosis [θrɔm'bəusɪs] *n* thrombose *f*.

throne [θrəun] *n* trône *m*.

throttle ['θrɔtl] *n* (*AUT*) accélérateur *m* // *vt* étrangler.

through [θru:] *prep* à travers; (*time*) pendant, durant; (*by means of*) par, par l'intermédiaire de; (*owing to*) à cause de // *a* (*ticket, train, passage*) direct(e) // *ad* à travers; to put sb ~ to sb (*TEL*) passer qn à qn; to be ~ (*TEL*) avoir la communication; (*have finished*) avoir fini; 'no ~ way' 'impasse'; ~out *prep* (*place*) partout dans; (*time*) durant tout(e) le(la) // *ad* partout.

throve [θrəuv] *pt of* **thrive**.

throw [θrəu] *n* jet *m*; (*SPORT*) lancer *m* // *vt* (*pt* **threw**, *pp* **thrown** [θru:, θrəun]) lancer, jeter; (*SPORT*) lancer; (*rider*) désarçonner; (*fig*) décontenancer; (*pottery*) tourner; to ~ a party donner une réception; to ~ away *vt* jeter; to ~ off *vt* se débarrasser de; to ~ out *vt* jeter dehors; (*reject*) rejeter; to ~ up *vi* vomir; ~away *a* à jeter; ~-in *n* (*SPORT*) remise *f* en jeu.

thru [θru:] *prep*, *a*, *ad* (*US*) = **through**.

thrush [θrʌʃ] *n* grive *f*.

thrust [θrʌst] *n* (*TECH*) poussée *f* // *vt* (*pt*, *pp* **thrust**) pousser brusquement; (*push in*) enfoncer; ~ing *a* dynamique; (*fig*) qui se met trop en avant.

thud [θʌd] *n* bruit sourd.

thug [θʌg] *n* voyou *m*.

thumb [θʌm] *n* (*ANAT*) pouce *m* // *vt* (*book*) feuilleter; to ~ a lift faire de l'auto-stop, arrêter une voiture; ~ index *n* répertoire *m* (à onglets); ~nail *n* ongle *m* du pouce; ~tack *n* (*US*) punaise *f* (*clou*).

thump [θʌmp] n grand coup ; (sound) bruit sourd // vt cogner sur // vi cogner, frapper.

thunder [θʌndəᵉ] n tonnerre m // vi tonner ; (train etc): to ~ past passer dans un grondement or un bruit de tonnerre ; ~clap n coup m de tonnerre ; ~ous a étourdissant(e) ; ~storm n orage m ; ~struck a (fig) abasourdi(e) ; ~y a orageux(euse).

Thursday [θə:zdɪ] n jeudi m.

thus [ðʌs] ad ainsi.

thwart [θwɔ:t] vt contrecarrer.

thyme [taɪm] n thym m.

thyroid [θaɪrɔɪd] n thyroïde f.

tiara [tɪ'ɑ:rə] n (woman's) diadème m.

tic [tɪk] n tic (nerveux).

tick [tɪk] n (sound: of clock) tic-tac m ; (mark) coche f ; (ZOOL) tique f ; (col): in a ~ dans un instant // vi faire tic-tac // vt cocher ; to ~ off vt cocher ; (person) réprimander, attraper.

ticket [tɪkɪt] n billet m ; (for bus, tube) ticket m ; (in shop: on goods) étiquette f ; (: from cash register) reçu m, ticket ; (for library) carte f ; ~ collector n contrôleur/euse ; ~ holder n personne munie d'un billet ; ~ office n guichet m, bureau m de vente des billets.

tickle [tɪkl] n chatouillement m // vt chatouiller ; (fig) plaire à ; faire rire ; **ticklish** a chatouilleux(euse).

tidal [taɪdl] a à marée ; ~ wave n raz-de-marée m inv.

tiddlywinks [tɪdlɪwɪŋks] n jeu m de puce.

tide [taɪd] n marée f ; (fig: of events) cours m // vt: to ~ sb over dépanner qn.

tidily [taɪdɪlɪ] ad avec soin, soigneusement.

tidiness [taɪdɪnɪs] n bon ordre, goût m de l'ordre.

tidy [taɪdɪ] a (room) bien rangé(e) ; (dress, work) net(nette), soigné(e) ; (person) ordonné(e), qui a de l'ordre // vt (also: ~ up) ranger ; to ~ o.s. up s'arranger.

tie [taɪ] n (string etc) cordon m ; (also: neck~) cravate f ; (fig: link) lien m ; (SPORT: draw) égalité f de points ; match nul // vt (parcel) attacher ; (ribbon) nouer // vi (SPORT) faire match nul ; finir à égalité de points ; 'black/white ~' 'smoking/habit de rigueur' ; to ~ sth in a bow faire un nœud à or avec qch ; to ~ a knot in sth faire un nœud à qch ; to ~ down vt attacher ; (fig): to ~ sb down to contraindre qn à accepter, fixer à qn ; to ~ up vt (parcel) ficeler ; (dog, boat) attacher ; (arrangements) conclure ; to be ~d up (busy) être pris or occupé.

tier [tɪəᵉ] n gradin m ; (of cake) étage m.

tiff [tɪf] n petite querelle.

tiger [taɪgəᵉ] n tigre m.

tight [taɪt] a (rope) tendu(e), raide ; (clothes) étroit(e), très juste ; (budget, programme, bend) serré(e) ; (control) strict(e), sévère ; (col: drunk) ivre, rond(e) // ad (squeeze) très fort ; (shut) à bloc, hermétiquement ; ~s npl collant m ; ~en vt (rope) tendre ; (screw) resserrer ; (control) renforcer // vi se tendre, se resserrer ; ~-fisted a avare ; ~ly ad (grasp) bien, très fort ; ~-rope n corde f raide.

tile [taɪl] n (on roof) tuile f ; (on wall or floor) carreau m ; ~d a en tuiles ; carrelé(e).

till [tɪl] n caisse (enregistreuse) // vt (land) cultiver // prep, cj = until.

tiller [tɪləᵉ] n (NAUT) barre f (du gouvernail).

tilt [tɪlt] vt pencher, incliner // vi pencher, être incliné(e).

timber [tɪmbəᵉ] n (material) bois m de construction ; (trees) arbres mpl.

time [taɪm] n temps m ; (epoch: often pl) époque f, temps ; (by clock) heure f ; (moment) moment m ; (occasion, also MATH) fois f ; (MUS) mesure f // vt (race) chronométrer ; (programme) minuter ; (remark etc) choisir le moment de ; a long ~ un long moment, longtemps ; for the ~ being pour le moment ; from ~ to ~ de temps en temps ; in ~ (soon enough) à temps ; (after some time) avec le temps, à la longue ; (MUS) en mesure ; in a week's ~ dans une semaine ; on ~ à l'heure ; 5 ~s 5 5 fois 5 ; what ~ is it? quelle heure est-il? ; to have a good ~ bien s'amuser ; ~'s up! c'est l'heure! ; I've no ~ for it (fig) cela m'agace ; ~ bomb n bombe f à retardement ; ~keeper n (SPORT) chronomètre m ; ~ lag n décalage m ; (in travel) décalage m horaire ; ~less a éternel(le) ; ~ limit n limite f de temps, délai m ; ~ly a opportun(e) ; ~ off n temps m libre ; ~r n (in kitchen) compte-minutes m inv ; ~-saving a qui fait gagner du temps ; ~ switch n minuteur m ; (for lighting) minuterie f ; ~table n (RAIL) (indicateur m) horaire m ; (SCOL) emploi m du temps ; ~ zone n fuseau m horaire.

timid [tɪmɪd] a timide ; (easily scared) peureux(euse).

timing [taɪmɪŋ] n minutage m ; chronométrage m ; the ~ of his resignation le moment choisi pour sa démission ; ~ device n mécanisme m de retardement.

timpani [tɪmpənɪ] npl timbales fpl.

tin [tɪn] n étain m ; (also: ~ plate) fer-blanc m ; (can) boîte f (de conserve) ; (for baking) moule m (à gâteau) ; ~ foil n papier m d'étain.

tinge [tɪndʒ] n nuance f // vt: ~d with teinté(e) de.

tingle [tɪŋgl] n picotement m ; frisson m // vi picoter.

tinker [tɪŋkəᵉ] n rétameur ambulant ; (gipsy) romanichel m ; to ~ with vt bricoler, rafistoler.

tinkle [tɪŋkl] vi tinter // n (col): to give sb a ~ passer un coup de fil à qn.

tinned [tɪnd] a (food) en boîte, en conserve.

tinny [tɪnɪ] a métallique.

tin opener [tɪnəupnəᵉ] n ouvre-boîte(s) m.

tinsel [tɪnsl] n guirlandes fpl de Noël (argentées).

tint [tɪnt] n teinte f ; (for hair) shampooing colorant.

tiny [taɪnɪ] a minuscule.

tip [tɪp] n (end) bout m ; (protective: on umbrella etc) embout m ; (gratuity) pourboire m ; (for coal) terril m ; (for rubbish) décharge f ; (advice) tuyau m // vt (waiter) donner un pourboire à ; (tilt) incliner ; (overturn: also: ~ over)

renverser ; (*empty: also:* ~ out) déverser ;
~-**off** *n* (*hint*) tuyau *m* ; ~**ped** a (*cigarette*)
(à bout) filtre *inv* ; **steel-**~**ped** à bout
métallique, à embout de métal.

tipple ['tɪpl] *vi* picoler // *n*: **to have a** ~
boire un petit coup.

tipsy ['tɪpsɪ] *a* un peu ivre, éméché(e).

tiptoe ['tɪptəu] *n*: **on** ~ sur la pointe des
pieds.

tiptop ['tɪp'tɔp] *a*: **in** ~ **condition** en
excellent état.

tire ['taɪə*] *n* (*US*) = **tyre** // *vt* fatiguer
// *vi* se fatiguer ; ~**d** a fatigué(e) ; **to be**
~**d of** en avoir assez de, être las(lasse)
de ; ~**dness** *n* fatigue *f* ; ~**less** a
infatigable, inlassable ; ~**some** a
ennuyeux(euse) ; **tiring** a fatigant(e).

tissue ['tɪʃu:] *n* tissu *m* ; (*paper
handkerchief*) mouchoir *m* en papier,
kleenex *m* ® ; ~ **paper** *n* papier *m* de soie.

tit [tɪt] *n* (*bird*) mésange *f* ; **to give** ~ **for
tat** rendre coup pour coup.

titanium [tɪ'teɪnɪəm] *n* titane *m*.

titbit ['tɪtbɪt] *n* (*food*) friandise *f* ; (*news*)
potin *m*.

titillate ['tɪtɪleɪt] *vt* titiller, exciter.

titivate ['tɪtɪveɪt] *vt* pomponner.

title ['taɪtl] *n* titre *m* ; ~ **deed** *n* (*LAW*) titre
(constitutif) de propriété ; ~ **role** *n* rôle
principal.

titter ['tɪtə*] *vi* rire (bêtement).

tittle-tattle ['tɪtltætl] *n* bavardages *mpl*.

titular ['tɪtjulə*] a (*in name only*)
nominal(e).

tizzy ['tɪzɪ] *n*: **to be in a** ~ être dans tous
ses états.

to [tu:, tə] *prep* à ; (*towards*) vers ; envers ;
give it ~ **me** donne-le-moi ; **the key** ~
the front door la clé de la porte d'entrée ;
the main thing is ~ **...** l'important est
de... ; **to go** ~ **France/Portugal** aller en
France/au Portugal ; **I went** ~ **Claude's**
je suis allé chez Claude ; **to go** ~
town/school aller en ville/à l'école ;
pull/push the door ~ tire/pousse la
porte ; **to go** ~ **and fro** aller et venir.

toad [təud] *n* crapaud *m* ; ~**stool** *n*
champignon (vénéneux) ; ~**y** *vi* flatter
bassement.

toast [təust] *n* (*CULIN*) pain grillé, toast *m* ;
(*drink, speech*) toast // *vt* (*CULIN*) faire
griller ; (*drink to*) porter un toast à ; **a
piece or slice of** ~ un toast ; ~**er** *n* grille-
pain *m inv* ; ~**master** *n* animateur *m* pour
réceptions ; ~**rack** *n* porte-toast *m*.

tobacco [tə'bækəu] *n* tabac *m* ; ~**nist** *n*
marchand/e de tabac ; ~**nist's** (**shop**) *n*
(bureau *m*) de tabac *m*.

toboggan [tə'bɔgən] *n* toboggan *m* ;
(*child's*) luge *f*.

today [tə'deɪ] *ad,n* (*also fig*) aujourd'hui
(*m*).

toddler ['tɔdlə*] *n* enfant *m/f* qui
commence à marcher, bambin *m*.

toddy ['tɔdɪ] *n* grog *m*.

to-do [tə'du:] *n* (*fuss*) histoire *f*, affaire *f*.

toe [təu] *n* doigt *m* de pied, orteil *m* ; (*of
shoe*) bout *m* ; **to** ~ **the line** (*fig*) obéir,
se conformer ; ~**hold** *n* prise *f* ; ~**nail** *n*
ongle *m* de l'orteil.

toffee ['tɔfɪ] *n* caramel *m* ; ~ **apple** *n*
pomme caramélisée.

toga ['təugə] *n* toge *f*.

together [tə'gɛðə*] *ad* ensemble ; (*at same
time*) en même temps ; ~ **with** *prep* avec ;
~**ness** *n* camaraderie *f* ; intimité *f*.

toil [tɔɪl] *n* dur travail, labeur *m* // *vi*
travailler dur ; peiner.

toilet ['tɔɪlət] *n* (*lavatory*) toilettes *fpl*,
cabinets *mpl* // *cpd* (*bag, soap etc*) de
toilette ; ~ **bowl** *n* cuvette *f* des W.-C. ;
~ **paper** *n* papier *m* hygiénique ; ~**ries**
npl articles *mpl* de toilette ; ~ **roll** *n*
rouleau *m* de papier hygiénique ; ~ **water**
n eau *f* de toilette.

token ['təukən] *n* (*sign*) marque *f*,
témoignage *m* ; (*voucher*) bon *m*, coupon
m ; **book/record** ~ *n* chèque-livre/disque
m.

told [təuld] *pt, pp of* **tell.**

tolerable ['tɔlərəbl] a (*bearable*) tolérable ;
(*fairly good*) passable.

tolerance ['tɔlərns] *n* (*also:* TECH)
tolérance *f*.

tolerant ['tɔlərnt] *a*: ~ (**of**) tolérant(e) (à
l'égard de).

tolerate ['tɔləreɪt] *vt* supporter ; (*MED,
TECH*) tolérer ; **toleration** [-'reɪʃən] *n*
tolérance *f*.

toll [təul] *n* (*tax, charge*) péage *m* // *vi* (*bell*)
sonner ; **the accident** ~ **on the roads** le
nombre des victimes de la route ; ~**bridge**
n pont *m* à péage.

tomato, ~**es** [tə'mɑ:təu] *n* tomate *f*.

tomb [tu:m] *n* tombe *f*.

tombola [tɔm'bəulə] *n* tombola *f*.

tomboy ['tɔmbɔɪ] *n* garçon manqué.

tombstone ['tu:mstəun] *n* pierre tombale.

tomcat ['tɔmkæt] *n* matou *m*.

tomorrow [tə'mɔrəu] *ad,n* (*also fig*)
demain (*m*) ; **the day after** ~ après-
demain ; ~ **morning** demain matin.

ton [tʌn] *n* tonne *f* (= 1016 *kg*; 20 *cwt*) ;
(*NAUT: also:* **register** ~) tonneau *m* (= 2.83
cu.m; 100 *cu. ft*) ; ~**s of** (*col*) des tas de.

tonal ['təunl] a tonal(e).

tone [təun] *n* ton *m* ; (*of radio*) tonalité *f*
// *vi* s'harmoniser ; **to** ~ **down** *vt* (*colour,
criticism*) adoucir ; (*sound*) baisser ; **to** ~
up *vt* (*muscles*) tonifier ; ~-**deaf** a qui n'a
pas d'oreille.

tongs [tɔnz] *npl* pinces *fpl* ; (*for coal*)
pincettes *fpl* ; (*for hair*) fer *m* à friser.

tongue [tʌn] *n* langue *f* ; ~ **in cheek** *ad*
ironiquement ; ~-**tied** a (*fig*) muet(te) ; ~-
twister *n* phrase *f* très difficile à
prononcer.

tonic ['tɔnɪk] *n* (*MED*) tonique *m* ; (*MUS*)
tonique *f* ; (*also:* ~ **water**) tonic *m*.

tonight [tə'naɪt] *ad, n* cette nuit ; (*this
evening*) ce soir.

tonnage ['tʌnɪdʒ] *n* (*NAUT*) tonnage *m*.

tonne [tʌn] *n* (*metric ton*) tonne *f*.

tonsil ['tɔnsl] *n* amygdale *f* ; ~**litis** [-'laɪtɪs]
n amygdalite *f*.

too [tu:] *ad* (*excessively*) trop ; (*also*) aussi ;
~ **much** *ad* trop // *det* trop de ; ~ **many**
det trop de ; ~ **bad!** tant pis!

took [tuk] *pt of* **take.**

tool [tu:l] *n* outil *m* // *vt* travailler,

ouvrager ; ~ **box/kit** n boîte f/trousse f
à outils.

toot [tu:t] n coup m de sifflet (or de klaxon)
// vi siffler ; (with car-horn) klaxonner.

tooth, pl **teeth** [tu:θ, ti:θ] n (ANAT. TECH)
dent f ; **~ache** n mal m de dents ; **~brush**
n brosse f à dents ; **~paste** n (pâte f)
dentifrice m ; **~pick** n cure-dent m ; **~**
powder n poudre f dentifrice.

top [tɔp] n (of mountain, head) sommet m ;
(of page, ladder) haut m ; (of box, cupboard,
table) dessus m ; (lid: of box, jar) couvercle
m ; (: of bottle) bouchon m ; (toy) toupie
f // a du haut ; (in rank) premier(ère) ;
(best) meilleur(e) // vt (exceed) dépasser ;
(be first in) être en tête de ; on ~ of sur ;
(in addition to) en plus de ; from ~ to toe
de la tête aux pieds ; at the ~ of the list
en tête de liste ; to ~ up vt remplir ;
~coat n pardessus m ; ~ **floor** n dernier
étage ; ~ **hat** n haut-de-forme m ; **~-**
heavy a (object) trop lourd(e) du haut.

topic ['tɔpɪk] n sujet m, thème m ; **~al** a
d'actualité.

top: **~less** a (bather etc) aux seins nus ;
~less swimsuit n monokini m ; **~-level**
a (talks) à l'échelon le plus élevé ; **~most**
a le(la) plus haut(e).

topple ['tɔpl] vt renverser, faire tomber //
vi basculer ; tomber.

topsy-turvy ['tɔp 'sɪtə:vɪ] a,ad sens
dessus-dessous.

torch [tɔ:tʃ] n torche f ; (electric) lampe f
de poche.

tore [tɔ:ə] pt of **tear**.

torment n ['tɔ:mɛnt] tourment m // vt
[tɔ:'mɛnt] tourmenter ; (fig: annoy) agacer.

torn [tɔ:n] pp of **tear** // a : ~ **between**
(fig) tiraillé(e) entre.

tornado, **~es** [tɔ:'neɪdəu] n tornade f.

torpedo, **~es** [tɔ:'pi:dəu] n torpille f.

torpor ['tɔ:pə] n torpeur f.

torque [tɔ:k] n couple m de torsion.

torrent ['tɔrnt] n torrent m ; **~ial** [-'rɛnʃl]
a torrentiel(le).

torso ['tɔ:səu] n torse m.

tortoise ['tɔ:təs] n tortue f ; **~shell**
['tɔ:təʃl] a en écaille.

tortuous ['tɔ:tjuəs] a tortueux(euse).

torture ['tɔ:tʃə] n torture f // vt torturer.

Tory ['tɔ:rɪ] a tory (pl tories),
conservateur(trice) // n tory m/f,
conservateur/trice.

toss [tɔs] vt lancer, jeter ; (pancake) faire
sauter ; (head) rejeter en arrière ; to ~ a
coin jouer à pile ou face ; to ~ up for
sth jouer qch à pile ou face ; to ~ and
turn (in bed) se tourner et se retourner.

tot [tɔt] n (drink) petit verre ; (child)
bambin m.

total ['təutl] a total(e) // n total m // vt
(add up) faire le total de, totaliser ; (amount
to) s'élever à.

totalitarian [təutælɪ'tɛərɪən] a totalitaire.

totality [təu'tælɪtɪ] n totalité f.

totem pole ['təutəmpəul] n mât m
totémique.

totter ['tɔtə] vi chanceler.

touch [tʌtʃ] n contact m, toucher m ;
(sense, also skill: of pianist etc) toucher ;
(fig: note, also: FOOTBALL) touche f // vt

(gen) toucher ; (tamper with) toucher à ; a
~ of (fig) un petit peu de ; une touche de ;
in ~ with en contact or rapport avec ; to
get in ~ with prendre contact avec ; to
lose ~ (friends) se perdre de vue ; to ~
on vt fus (topic) effleurer, toucher ; to ~
up vt (paint) retoucher ; **~-and-go** a
incertain(e) ; it was **~-and-go** whether
we did it nous avons failli ne pas le faire ;
~down n atterrissage m ; (on sea)
amerrissage m ; **~ed** a touché(e) ; (col)
cinglé(e) ; **~ing** a touchant(e),
attendrissant(e) ; **~line** n (SPORT) (ligne f
de) touche f ; **~y** a (person) susceptible.

tough [tʌf] a dur(e) ; (resistant)
résistant(e), solide ; (meat) dur, coriace //
n (gangster etc) dur m ; ~ **luck!** pas de
chance! ; tant pis! ; **~en** vt rendre plus
dur(e) (or plus résistant(e) or plus solide) ;
~ness n dureté f ; résistance f ; solidité f.

toupee ['tu:peɪ] n postiche m.

tour ['tuə] n voyage m ; (also: package
~) voyage organisé ; (of town, museum)
tour m, visite f ; (by artist) tournée f //
vt visiter ; **~ing** n voyages mpl
touristiques, tourisme m.

tourism ['tuərɪzm] n tourisme m.

tourist ['tuərɪst] n touriste m/f // ad
(travel) en classe touriste // cpd
touristique ; ~ **office** n syndicat m
d'initiative.

tournament ['tuənəmənt] n tournoi m.

tour operator ['tuər'ɔpəreɪtə] n organisateur m de voyages.

tousled ['tauzld] a (hair) ébouriffé(e).

tout [taut] vi : to ~ **for** essayer de
raccrocher, racoler ; to ~ **sth (around)**
essayer de placer or (re)vendre qch.

tow [təu] vt remorquer ; '**on** ~' (AUT)
'véhicule en remorque'.

toward(s) [tə'wɔ:d(z)] prep vers ; (of
attitude) envers, à l'égard de ; (of purpose)
pour.

towel ['tauəl] n serviette f (de toilette) ;
(also: tea ~) torchon m ; **~ling** n (fabric)
tissu-éponge m ; ~ **rail** n porte-serviettes
m inv.

tower ['tauə] n tour f ; ~ **block** n tour
f (d'habitation) ; **~ing** a très haut(e),
imposant(e).

towline ['təulaɪn] n (câble m de) remorque
f.

town [taun] n ville f ; to go to ~ aller
en ville ; (fig) y mettre le paquet ; ~ **clerk**
n ≈ secrétaire m/f de mairie ; ~ **council**
n conseil municipal ; ~ **hall** n ≈ mairie
f ; ~ **planner** n urbaniste m/f ; ~
planning n urbanisme m.

towpath ['təupɑ:θ] n (chemin m de)
halage m.

towrope ['təurəup] n (câble m de)
remorque f.

toxic ['tɔksɪk] a toxique.

toy [tɔɪ] n jouet m ; to ~ **with** vt fus jouer
avec ; (idea) caresser ; **~shop** m magasin
m de jouets.

trace [treɪs] n trace f // vt (draw) tracer,
dessiner ; (follow) suivre la trace de ;
(locate) retrouver ; without ~ (disappear)
sans laisser de traces.

track [træk] n (mark) trace f ; (path: gen)
chemin m, piste f ; (: of bullet etc)

trajectoire f; (: of suspect, animal) piste; (RAIL) voie ferrée, rails mpl; (on tape, SPORT) piste // vt suivre la trace or la piste de; to keep ~ of suivre; to ~ down vt (prey) trouver et capturer; (sth lost) finir par retrouver; ~ed a (AUT) à chenille; ~er dog n chien policier; ~suit n survêtement m.

tract [trækt] n (GEO) étendue f, zone f; (pamphlet) tract m; respiratory ~ (ANAT) système m respiratoire.

tractor ['træktə'] n tracteur m.

trade [treɪd] n commerce m; (skill, job) métier m // vi faire du commerce; to ~ with/in faire du commerce avec/le commerce de; to ~ in vt (old car etc) faire reprendre; ~-in (value) n reprise f; ~mark n marque f de fabrique; ~name n marque déposée; ~r n commerçant/e, négociant/e; ~sman n (shopkeeper) commerçant; ~ union n syndicat m; ~ unionist syndicaliste m/f; trading n affaires fpl, commerce m; trading estate n zone industrielle; trading stamp n timbre-prime m.

tradition [trə'dɪʃən] n tradition f; ~s npl coutumes fpl, traditions; ~al a traditionnel(le).

traffic ['træfɪk] n trafic m; (cars) circulation f // vi: to ~ in (pej: liquor, drugs) faire le trafic de; ~ circle n (US) rond-point m; ~ jam n embouteillage m; ~ lights npl feux mpl (de signalisation); ~ sign n panneau m de signalisation; ~ warden n contractuel/le.

tragedy ['trædʒədɪ] n tragédie f.

tragic ['trædʒɪk] a tragique.

trail [treɪl] n (tracks) trace f, piste f; (path) chemin m, piste; (of smoke etc) traînée f // vt trainer, tirer; (follow) suivre // vi traîner; to ~ behind vi traîner, être à la traîne; ~er n (AUT) remorque f; (US: CINEMA) court film de lancement; ~ing plant n plante rampante.

train [treɪn] n train m; (in underground) rame f; (of dress) traîne f // vt (apprentice, doctor etc) former; (sportsman) entraîner; (dog) dresser; (memory) exercer; (point: gun etc): to ~ sth on braquer qch sur // vi recevoir sa formation; s'entraîner; one's ~ of thought le fil de sa pensée; ~ed a qualifié(e), qui a reçu une formation; dressé(e); ~ee [treɪ'ni:] n stagiaire m/f; (in trade) apprenti/e; ~er n (SPORT) entraîneur/euse; (of dogs etc) dresseur/euse; ~ing n formation f; entraînement m; dressage m; in ~ing (SPORT) à l'entraînement; (fit) en forme; ~ing college n école professionnelle; (for teachers) ≈ école normale.

traipse [treɪps] vi (se) traîner, déambuler.

trait [treɪt] n trait m (de caractère).

traitor ['treɪtə'] n traître m.

tram [træm] n (also: ~car) tram(way) m; ~line n ligne f de tram(way).

tramp [træmp] n (person) vagabond/e, clochard/e // vi marcher d'un pas lourd // vt (walk through: town, streets) parcourir à pied.

trample ['træmpl] vt: to ~ (underfoot) piétiner; (fig) bafouer.

trampoline ['træmpəli:n] n trampolino m.

trance [trɑ:ns] n transe f; (MED) catalepsie f.

tranquil ['træŋkwɪl] a tranquille; ~lity n tranquillité f; ~lizer n (MED) tranquillisant m.

transact [træn'zækt] vt (business) traiter; ~ion [-'zækʃən] n transaction f; ~ions npl (minutes) actes mpl.

transatlantic ['trænzət'læntɪk] a transatlantique.

transcend [træn'sɛnd] vt transcender; (excel over) surpasser.

transcript ['trænskrɪpt] n transcription f (texte); ~ion [-'skrɪpʃən] n transcription.

transept ['trænsɛpt] n transept m.

transfer ['trænsfə'] n (gen, also SPORT) transfert m; (POL: of power) passation f; (picture, design) décalcomanie f; (: stick-on) autocollant m // vt [træns'fə:'] transférer; passer; décalquer; to ~ the charges (TEL) téléphoner en P.C.V.; ~able [-'fɔ:rəbl] a transmissible, transférable; 'not ~able' 'personnel'.

transform [træns'fɔ:m] vt transformer; ~ation [-'meɪʃən] n transformation f; ~er n (ELEC) transformateur m.

transfusion [træns'fju:ʒən] n transfusion f.

transient ['trænzɪənt] a transitoire, éphémère.

transistor [træn'zɪstə'] n (ELEC, also: ~ radio) transistor m.

transit ['trænzɪt] n: in ~ en transit; ~ lounge n salle f de transit.

transition [træn'zɪʃən] n transition f; ~al a transitoire.

transitive ['trænzɪtɪv] a (LING) transitif(ive).

transitory ['trænzɪtərɪ] a transitoire.

translate [trænz'leɪt] vt traduire; translation [-'leɪʃən] n traduction f; (SCOL: as opposed to prose) version f; translator n traducteur/trice.

transmission [trænz'mɪʃən] n transmission f.

transmit [trænz'mɪt] vt transmettre; (RADIO, TV) émettre; ~ter m émetteur m.

transparency [træns'pɛərnsɪ] n (PHOT) diapositive f.

transparent [træns'pærnt] a transparent(e).

transplant vt [træns'plɑ:nt] transplanter; (seedlings) repiquer // n ['trænsplɑ:nt] (MED) transplantation f.

transport n ['trænspɔ:t] transport m // vt [træns'pɔ:t] transporter; ~ation [-'teɪʃən] n (moyen m de) transport m; (of prisoners) transportation f; ~ café n ≈ restaurant m de routiers.

transverse ['trænzvə:s] a transversal(e).

transvestite [trænz'vɛstaɪt] n travesti/e.

trap [træp] n (snare, trick) piège m; (carriage) cabriolet m // vt prendre au piège; (immobilize) bloquer; (jam) coincer; to shut one's ~ (col) la fermer; ~ door n trappe f.

trapeze [trə'pi:z] n trapèze m.

trapper ['træpə'] n trappeur m.

trappings ['træpɪŋz] npl ornements mpl; attributs mpl.

trash [træʃ] n (pej: goods) camelote f; (: nonsense) sottises fpl; ~ can n (US) boîte f à ordures.

trauma ['trɔːmə] n traumatisme m; ~tic [-'mætik] a traumatisant(e).

travel ['trævl] n voyage(s) m(pl) // vi voyager; (move) aller, se déplacer // vt (distance) parcourir; ~ agent's n agence f de voyages; ~ler, ~er (US) n voyageur/euse; ~ler's cheque n chèque m de voyage; ~ling, ~ling (US) n voyage(s) m(pl) // cpd (bag, clock) de voyage; (expenses) de déplacement; ~ sickness n mal m de la route (or de mer or de l'air).

traverse ['trævəs] vt traverser.

travesty ['trævəsti] n parodie f.

trawler ['trɔːlə*] n chalutier m.

tray [trei] n (for carrying) plateau m; (on desk) corbeille f.

treacherous ['trɛtʃərəs] a traître(sse).

treachery ['trɛtʃəri] n traîtrise f.

treacle ['triːkl] n mélasse f.

tread [trɛd] n pas m; (sound) bruit m de pas; (of tyre) chape f, bande f de roulement // vi (pt trod, pp trodden [trɔd, 'trɔdn]) marcher; to ~ on vt fus marcher sur.

treason ['triːzn] n trahison f.

treasure ['trɛʒə*] n trésor m // vt (value) tenir beaucoup à; (store) conserver précieusement; ~ hunt n chasse f au trésor.

treasurer ['trɛʒərə*] n trésorier/ère.

treasury ['trɛʒəri] n trésorerie f; the T~ (POL) le ministère des Finances.

treat [triːt] n petit cadeau, petite surprise // vt traiter; it was a ~ ça m'a (or nous a etc) vraiment fait plaisir; to ~ sb to sth offrir qch à qn.

treatise ['triːtiz] n traité m (ouvrage).

treatment ['triːtmənt] n traitement m.

treaty ['triːti] n traité m.

treble ['trɛbl] a triple // n (MUS) soprano m // vt, vi tripler; ~ clef n clé f de sol.

tree [triː] n arbre m; ~-lined a bordé(e) d'arbres; ~top n cime f d'un arbre; ~ trunk n tronc m d'arbre.

trek [trɛk] n voyage m; randonnée f; (tiring walk) tirée f // vi (as holiday) faire de la randonnée.

trellis ['trɛlis] n treillis m, treillage m.

tremble ['trɛmbl] vi trembler; (machine) vibrer; **trembling** n tremblement m; vibrations fpl // a tremblant(e); vibrant(e).

tremendous [tri'mɛndəs] a (enormous) énorme, fantastique; (excellent) formidable.

tremor ['trɛmə*] n tremblement m; (also: earth ~) secousse f sismique.

trench [trɛntʃ] n tranchée f.

trend [trɛnd] n (tendency) tendance f; (of events) cours m; (fashion) mode f; ~y a (idea) dans le vent; (clothes) dernier cri inv.

trepidation [trɛpi'deiʃən] n vive agitation.

trespass ['trɛspəs] vi: to ~ on s'introduire sans permission dans; (fig) empiéter sur; 'no ~ing' 'propriété privée', 'défense d'entrer'.

tress [trɛs] n boucle f de cheveux.

trestle ['trɛsl] n tréteau m; ~ table n table f à tréteaux.

trial ['traiəl] n (LAW) procès m, jugement m; (test: of machine etc) essai m; (hardship) épreuve f; (worry) souci m; to be on ~ passer en jugement; by ~ and error par tâtonnements.

triangle ['traiæŋgl] n (MATH, MUS) triangle m; **triangular** [-'æŋgjulə*] a triangulaire.

tribal ['traibəl] a tribal(e).

tribe [traib] n tribu f; ~sman n membre m de la tribu.

tribulation [tribju'leiʃən] n tribulation f, malheur m.

tribunal [trai'bjuːnl] n tribunal m.

tributary ['tribjutəri] n (river) affluent m.

tribute ['tribjuːt] n tribut m, hommage m; to pay ~ to rendre hommage à.

trice [trais] n: in a ~ en un clin d'œil.

trick [trik] n ruse f; (clever act) astuce f; (joke) tour m; (CARDS) levée f // vt attraper, rouler; to play a ~ on sb jouer un tour à qn; ~ery n ruse f.

trickle ['trikl] n (of water etc) filet m // vi couler en un filet or goutte à goutte; to ~ in/out (people) entrer/sortir par petits groupes.

tricky ['triki] a difficile, délicat(e).

tricycle ['traisikl] n tricycle m.

trifle ['traifl] n bagatelle f; (CULIN) ≈ diplomate m // ad: a ~ long un peu long; **trifling** a insignifiant(e).

trigger ['trigə*] n (of gun) gâchette f; to ~ off vt déclencher.

trigonometry [trigə'nɔmətri] n trigonométrie f.

trilby ['trilbi] n (chapeau m en) feutre m.

trim [trim] n (house, garden) bien tenu(e); (figure) svelte // n (haircut etc) légère coupe; (embellishment) finitions fpl; (on car) garnitures fpl // vt couper légèrement; (decorate): to ~ (with) décorer (de); (NAUT: a sail) gréer; ~mings npl décorations fpl; (extras: gen CULIN) garniture f.

Trinity ['triniti] n: the ~ la Trinité.

trinket ['triŋkit] n bibelot m; (piece of jewellery) colifichet m.

trio ['triːəu] n trio m.

trip [trip] n voyage m; (excursion) excursion f; (stumble) faux pas // vi faire un faux pas, trébucher; (go lightly) marcher d'un pas léger; on a ~ en voyage; to ~ up vi trébucher // vt faire un croc-en-jambe à.

tripe [traip] n (CULIN) tripes fpl; (pej: rubbish) idioties fpl.

triple ['tripl] a triple.

triplets ['triplits] npl triplés/ées.

triplicate ['triplikət] n: in ~ en trois exemplaires.

tripod ['traipɔd] n trépied m.

tripper ['tripə*] n touriste m/f; excursionniste m/f.

trite [trait] a banal(e).

triumph ['traiʌmf] n triomphe m // vi: to ~ (over) triompher (de); ~al [-'ʌmfl] a triomphal(e); ~ant [-'ʌmfənt] a triomphant(e).

trivia ['triviə] npl futilités fpl.

trivial ['triviəl] a insignifiant(e); (commonplace) banal(e); ~ity [-'æliti] n caractère insignifiant; banalité f.

trod [trɔd] pt of **tread**; **~den** pp of **tread**.

trolley ['trɔlɪ] n chariot m; **~ bus** n trolleybus m.

trollop ['trɔləp] n prostituée f.

trombone [trɔm'bəun] n trombone m.

troop [tru:p] n bande f, groupe m; **~s** npl (MIL) troupes fpl; (: men) hommes mpl, soldats mpl; **to ~ in/out** vi entrer/sortir en groupe; **~er** n (MIL) soldat m de cavalerie; **~ing the colour** (ceremony) le salut au drapeau; **~ship** n (navire m de) transport m.

trophy ['trəufɪ] n trophée m.

tropic ['trɔpɪk] n tropique m; **in the ~s** sous les tropiques; **T~ of Cancer/Capricorn** tropique du Cancer/Capricorne; **~al** a tropical(e).

trot [trɔt] n trot m // vi trotter; **on the ~** (fig: col) d'affilée.

trouble ['trʌbl] n difficulté(s) f(pl), problème(s) m(pl); (worry) ennuis mpl, soucis mpl; (bother, effort) peine f; (POL) conflits mpl, troubles mpl; (MED): **stomach etc ~** troubles gastriques etc // vt déranger, gêner; (worry) inquiéter // vi: **to ~ to do** prendre la peine de faire; **~s** npl (POL etc) troubles mpl; **to be in ~** avoir des ennuis; (ship, climber etc) être en difficulté; **to go to the ~ of doing se** donner le mal de faire; **it's no ~!** je vous en prie!; **what's the ~?** qu'est-ce qui ne va pas?; **~d** a (person) inquiet(ète); (epoch, life) agité(e); **~-free** a sans problèmes ou ennuis; **~maker** n élément perturbateur, fauteur m de troubles; **~shooter** n (in conflict) conciliateur m; **~some** a ennuyeux(euse), gênant(e).

trough [trɔf] n (also: **drinking ~**) abreuvoir m; (also: **feeding ~**) auge f; (channel) chenal m; **~ of low pressure** n (GEO) dépression f.

trounce [trauns] vt (defeat) battre à plates coutures.

troupe [tru:p] n troupe f.

trousers ['trauzəz] npl pantalon m; **short ~** npl culottes courtes.

trousseau, pl **~x** or **~s** ['tru:səu, -z] n trousseau m.

trout [traut] n, pl inv truite f.

trowel ['trauəl] n truelle f.

truant ['truənt] n: **to play ~** faire l'école buissonnière.

truce [tru:s] n trêve f.

truck [trʌk] n camion m; (RAIL) wagon m à plate-forme; (for luggage) chariot m (à bagages); **~ driver** n camionneur m; **~ farm** n (US) jardin maraîcher.

truculent ['trʌkjulənt] a agressif(ive).

trudge [trʌdʒ] vi marcher lourdement, se traîner.

true [tru:] a vrai(e); (accurate) exact(e); (genuine) vrai, véritable; (faithful) fidèle.

truffle ['trʌfl] n truffe f.

truly ['tru:lɪ] ad vraiment, réellement; (truthfully) sans mentir; (faithfully) fidèlement; **'yours ~'** (in letter) 'je vous prie d'agréer l'expression de mes sentiments respectueux.'

trump [trʌmp] n atout m; **~ed-up** a inventé(e) (de toutes pièces).

trumpet ['trʌmpɪt] n trompette f; (player) trompettiste m/f.

truncated [trʌŋ'keɪtɪd] a tronqué(e).

truncheon ['trʌntʃən] n bâton m (d'agent de police); matraque f.

trundle ['trʌndl] vt, vi: **to ~ along** rouler bruyamment.

trunk [trʌŋk] n (of tree, person) tronc m; (of elephant) trompe f; (case) malle f; **~s** npl caleçon m; (also: **swimming ~s**) maillot m or slip m de bain; **~ call** n (TEL) communication interurbaine; **~ road** ≈ route nationale.

truss [trʌs] n (MED) bandage m herniaire; **to ~ (up)** vt (CULIN) brider.

trust [trʌst] n confiance f; (LAW) fidéicommis m; (COMM) trust m // vt (rely on) avoir confiance en; (entrust): **to ~ sth to sb** confier qch à qn; **~ed** a en qui l'on a confiance; **~ee** [trʌs'ti:] n (LAW) fidéicommissaire m/f; (of school etc) administrateur/trice; **~ful, ~ing** a confiant(e); **~worthy** a digne de confiance; **~y** a fidèle.

truth, **~s** [tru:θ, tru:ðz] n vérité f; **~ful** a (person) qui dit la vérité; (description) exact(e), vrai(e); **~fully** ad sincèrement, sans mentir; **~fulness** n véracité f.

try [traɪ] n essai m, tentative f; (RUGBY) essai // vt (LAW) juger; (test: sth new) essayer, tester; (strain) éprouver // vi essayer; **to ~ to do** essayer de faire; (seek) chercher à faire; **to ~ on** vt (clothes) essayer; **to ~ it on** (fig) tenter le coup, bluffer; **to ~ out** vt essayer, mettre à l'essai; **~ing** a pénible.

tsar [zɑ:*] n tsar m.

T-shirt ['ti:ʃə:t] n tee-shirt m.

T-square ['ti:skwɛə*] n équerre f en T.

tub [tʌb] n cuve f; baquet m; (bath) baignoire f.

tuba ['tju:bə] n tuba m.

tubby ['tʌbɪ] a rondelet(te).

tube [tju:b] n tube m; (underground) métro m; (for tyre) chambre f à air.

tuberculosis [tjubə:kju'ləusɪs] n tuberculose f.

tube station ['tju:bsteɪʃən] n station f de métro.

tubing ['tju:bɪŋ] n tubes mpl; **a piece of ~** un tube.

tubular ['tju:bjulə*] a tubulaire.

TUC n (abbr of Trades Union Congress) confédération f des syndicats britanniques.

tuck [tʌk] n (SEWING) pli m, rempli m // vt (put) mettre; **to ~ away** vt cacher, ranger; **to ~ in** vt rentrer; (child) border // vi (eat) manger de bon appétit; attaquer le repas; **to ~ up** vt (child) border; **~ shop** n boutique f à provisions (dans une école).

Tuesday ['tju:zdɪ] n mardi m.

tuft [tʌft] n touffe f.

tug [tʌg] n (ship) remorqueur m // vt tirer (sur); **~-of-war** n lutte f à la corde.

tuition [tju:'ɪʃən] n leçons fpl.

tulip ['tju:lɪp] n tulipe f.

tumble ['tʌmbl] n (fall) chute f, culbute f // vi tomber, dégringoler; (with somersault) faire une or des culbute(s) // vt renverser, faire tomber; **~down** a délabré(e) ; ~ dryer n séchoir m (à linge) à air chaud.

tumbler ['tʌmblə*] n verre (droit), gobelet m ; acrobate m/f.

tummy ['tʌmɪ] n (col) ventre m.

tumour ['tju:mə*] n tumeur f.

tumult ['tju:mʌlt] n tumulte m ; ~uous ['tju:mʌltjuəs] a tumultueux(euse).

tuna ['tju:nə] n, pl inv (also: ~ fish) thon m.

tune [tju:n] n (melody) air m // vt (MUS) accorder ; (RADIO, TV, AUT) régler, mettre au point ; to be in/out of ~ (instrument) être accordé/désaccordé ; (singer) chanter juste/faux ; to be in/out of ~ with (fig) être en accord/désaccord avec ; to ~ in (to) (RADIO, TV) se mettre à l'écoute (de) ; to ~ up vi (musician) accorder son instrument ; ~ful a mélodieux(euse) ; ~r n (radio set) radio-préamplificateur m ; piano ~r accordeur m de pianos ; ~r amplifier n radio-ampli m.

tungsten ['tʌŋstn] n tungstène m.

tunic ['tju:nɪk] n tunique f.

tuning ['tju:nɪŋ] n réglage m ; ~ fork n diapason m.

Tunisia [tju:'nɪzɪə] n Tunisie f ; ~n a tunisien(ne) // n Tunisien/ne.

tunnel ['tʌnl] n tunnel m ; (in mine) galerie f // vi creuser un tunnel (or une galerie).

tunny ['tʌnɪ] n thon m.

turban ['tə:bən] n turban m.

turbid ['tə:bɪd] a boueux(euse).

turbine ['tə:baɪn] n turbine f.

turbojet [tə:bəu'dʒɛt] n turboréacteur m.

turbot ['tə:bət] n, pl inv turbot m.

turbulence ['tə:bjuləns] n (AVIAT) turbulence f.

turbulent ['tə:bjulənt] a turbulent(e) ; (sea) agité(e).

tureen [tə'ri:n] n soupière f.

turf [tə:f] n gazon m ; (clod) motte f (de gazon) // vt gazonner ; the T~ n le turf, les courses fpl ; to ~ out (col) jeter ; jeter dehors.

turgid ['tə:dʒɪd] a (speech) pompeux(euse).

Turk [tə:k] n Turc/Turque.

turkey ['tə:kɪ] n dindon m, dinde f.

Turkey ['tə:kɪ] n Turquie f.

Turkish ['tə:kɪʃ] a turc(turque) // n (LING) turc m ; ~ bath n bain turc ; ~ delight n loukoum m.

turmoil ['tə:mɔɪl] n trouble m, bouleversement m.

turn [tə:n] n tour m ; (in road) tournant m ; (tendency: of mind, events) tournure f ; (performance) numéro m ; (MED) crise f, attaque f // vt tourner ; (collar, steak) retourner ; (milk) faire tourner ; (change): to ~ sth into changer qch en // vi tourner ; (person: look back) se (re)tourner ; (reverse direction) faire demi-tour ; (change) changer ; (become) devenir ; to ~ into se changer en ; a good ~ un service ; a bad ~ un mauvais tour ; it gave me quite a ~ ça m'a fait un coup ; 'no left ~' (AUT) 'défense de tourner à gauche' ; it's your ~ c'est (à) votre tour ; in ~ à son tour ; à tour de rôle ; to take ~s se relayer ; to take ~s at faire à tour de rôle ; to ~ about vi faire demi-tour ;

faire un demi-tour ; to ~ away vi se détourner, tourner la tête ; to ~ back vi revenir, faire demi-tour ; to ~ down vt (refuse) rejeter, refuser ; (reduce) baisser ; (fold) rabattre ; to ~ in vi (col: go to bed) aller se coucher // vt (fold) rentrer ; to ~ off vi (from road) tourner // vt (light, radio etc) éteindre ; (engine) arrêter ; to ~ on vt (light, radio etc) allumer ; (engine) mettre en marche ; to ~ out vt (light, gas) éteindre // vi: to ~ out to be... s'avérer..., se révéler... ; to ~ up vi (person) arriver, se pointer ; (lost object) être retrouvé(e) // vt (collar) remonter ; (increase: sound, volume etc) mettre plus fort ; ~around n volte-face f ; ~ed-up a (nose) retroussé(e) ; ~ing n (in road) tournant m ; ~ing circle n rayon m de braquage ; ~ing point n (fig) tournant m, moment décisif.

turnip ['tə:nɪp] n navet m.

turnout ['tə:naut] n (nombre m de personnes dans l') assistance f.

turnover ['tə:nəuvə*] n (COMM: amount of money) chiffre m d'affaires ; (: of goods) roulement m ; (CULIN) sorte de chausson.

turnpike ['tə:npaɪk] n (US) autoroute f à péage.

turnstile ['tə:nstaɪl] n tourniquet m (d'entrée).

turntable ['tə:nteɪbl] n (on record player) platine f.

turn-up ['tə:nʌp] n (on trousers) revers m.

turpentine ['tə:pəntaɪn] n (also: turps) (essence f de) térébenthine f.

turquoise ['tə:kwɔɪz] n (stone) turquoise f // a turquoise inv.

turret ['tʌrɪt] n tourelle f.

turtle ['tə:tl] n tortue marine ; ~neck (sweater) n pullover m à col montant.

tusk [tʌsk] n défense f.

tussle ['tʌsl] n bagarre f, mêlée f.

tutor ['tju:tə*] n (in college) directeur/trice d'études ; (private teacher) précepteur/-trice ; ~ial [-'tɔ:rɪəl] (SCOL) (séance f de) travaux mpl pratiques.

tuxedo [tʌk'si:dəu] n (US) smoking m.

T.V. [ti:'vi:] n (abbr of television) télé f.

twaddle ['twɔdl] n balivernes fpl.

twang [twæŋ] n (of instrument) son vibrant ; (of voice) ton nasillard // vi vibrer // vt (guitar) pincer les cordes de.

tweed [twi:d] n tweed m.

tweezers ['twi:zəz] npl pince f à épiler.

twelfth [twɛlfθ] num douzième ; T~ Night n la fête des Rois.

twelve [twɛlv] num douze ; at ~ à midi ; (midnight) à minuit.

twentieth ['twɛntɪɪθ] num vingtième.

twenty ['twɛntɪ] num vingt.

twerp [twə:p] n (col) imbécile m/f.

twice [twaɪs] ad deux fois ; ~ as much deux fois plus.

twig [twɪg] n brindille f // vt, vi (col) piger.

twilight ['twaɪlaɪt] n crépuscule m.

twill [twɪl] n sergé m.

twin [twɪn] a,n jumeau(elle) // vt jumeler.

twine [twaɪn] n ficelle f // vi (plant) s'enrouler ; (road) serpenter.

twinge [twɪndʒ] n (of pain) élancement m ; (of conscience) remords m.

twinkle ['twɪŋkl] n scintillement m; pétillement m // vi scintiller; (eyes) pétiller.

twin town [twɪn'taun] n ville jumelée.

twirl [twə:l] n tournoiement m // vt faire tournoyer // vi tournoyer.

twist [twɪst] n torsion f, tour m; (in wire, flex) tortillon m; (in story) coup m de théâtre // vt tordre; (weave) entortiller; (roll around) enrouler; (fig) déformer // vi s'entortiller; s'enrouler; (road) serpenter.

twit [twɪt] n (col) crétin/e.

twitch [twɪtʃ] n saccade f; (nervous) tic m // vi se convulser; avoir un tic.

two [tu:] num deux; to put ~ and ~ together (fig) faire le rapport; ~-door a (AUT) à deux portes; ~-faced a (pej: person) faux(fausse); ~-fold ad: to increase ~-fold doubler; ~-piece n (costume m) deux-pièces m inv; ~-piece (swimsuit) n (maillot m de bain) deux-pièces m inv; ~-seater n (plane) avion m biplace m; (car) voiture f à deux places; ~-some n (people) couple m; ~-way a (traffic) dans les deux sens.

tycoon [taɪ'ku:n] n: (business) ~ gros homme d'affaires.

type [taɪp] n (category) genre m, espèce f; (model) modèle m; (example) type m; (TYP) type, caractère m // vt (letter etc) taper (à la machine); ~-cast a (actor) condamné(e) à toujours jouer le même rôle; ~-script n texte dactylographié; ~-writer n machine f à écrire; ~-written a dactylographié(e).

typhoid ['taɪfɔɪd] n typhoïde f.

typhoon [taɪ'fu:n] n typhon m.

typhus ['taɪfəs] n typhus m.

typical ['tɪpɪkl] a typique, caractéristique.

typify ['tɪpɪfaɪ] vt être caractéristique de.

typing ['taɪpɪŋ] n dactylo(graphie) f; ~ error n faute f de frappe; ~ paper n papier m machine.

typist ['taɪpɪst] n dactylo m/f.

tyranny ['tɪrənɪ] n tyrannie f.

tyrant ['taɪərnt] n tyran m.

tyre, tire (US) ['taɪə*] n pneu m; ~ pressure n pression f (de gonflage).

tzar [zɑ:*] n = tsar.

U

U-bend ['ju:'bɛnd] n (AUT) coude m, virage m en épingle à cheveux; (in pipe) coude.

ubiquitous [ju:'bɪkwɪtəs] a doué(e) d'ubiquité, omniprésent(e).

udder ['ʌdə*] n pis m, mamelle f.

UFO ['ju:fəu] n (abbr of unidentified flying object) O.V.N.I. (objet volant non identifié).

ugh [ə:h] excl pouah!

ugliness ['ʌɡlɪnɪs] n laideur f.

ugly ['ʌɡlɪ] a laid(e), vilain(e); (fig) répugnant(e).

UHF abbr of ultra-high frequency.

UHT a (abbr of ultra-heat treated): ~ milk n lait upérisé or longue conservation.

U.K. n abbr see united.

ulcer ['ʌlsə*] n ulcère m; (also: mouth ~) aphte f.

Ulster ['ʌlstə*] n Ulster m.

ulterior [ʌl'tɪərɪə*] a ultérieur(e); ~ motive n arrière-pensée f.

ultimate ['ʌltɪmət] a ultime, final(e); (authority) suprême; ~ly ad en fin de compte; finalement; par la suite.

ultimatum [ʌltɪ'meɪtəm] n ultimatum m.

ultraviolet ['ʌltrə'vaɪəlɪt] a ultraviolet(te).

umbilical [ʌmbɪ'laɪkl] a: ~ cord cordon ombilical.

umbrage ['ʌmbrɪdʒ] n: to take ~ prendre ombrage, se froisser.

umbrella [ʌm'brɛlə] n parapluie m; (fig): under the ~ of sous les auspices de; chapeauté(e) par.

umpire ['ʌmpaɪə*] n arbitre m // vt arbitrer.

umpteen [ʌmp'ti:n] a je ne sais combien de; for the ~th time pour la nième fois.

UN, UNO abbr see united.

unabashed [ʌnə'bæʃt] a nullement intimidé(e).

unabated [ʌnə'beɪtɪd] a non diminué(e).

unable [ʌn'eɪbl] a: to be ~ to ne (pas) pouvoir, être dans l'impossibilité de; être incapable de.

unaccompanied [ʌnə'kʌmpənɪd] a (child, lady) non accompagné(e).

unaccountably [ʌnə'kauntəblɪ] ad inexplicablement.

unaccustomed [ʌnə'kʌstəmd] a inaccoutumé(e), inhabituel(le); to be ~ to sth ne pas avoir l'habitude de qch.

unadulterated [ʌnə'dʌltəreɪtɪd] a pur(e), naturel(le).

unaided [ʌn'eɪdɪd] a sans aide, tout(e) seul(e).

unanimity [ju:nə'nɪmɪtɪ] n unanimité f.

unanimous [ju:'nænɪməs] a unanime; ~ly ad à l'unanimité.

unashamed [ʌnə'ʃeɪmd] a sans honte; impudent(e).

unassuming [ʌnə'sju:mɪŋ] a modeste, sans prétentions.

unattached [ʌnə'tætʃt] a libre, sans attaches.

unattended [ʌnə'tɛndɪd] a (car, child, luggage) sans surveillance.

unattractive [ʌnə'træktɪv] a peu attrayant(e).

unauthorized [ʌn'ɔ:θəraɪzd] a non autorisé(e), sans autorisation.

unavoidable [ʌnə'vɔɪdəbl] a inévitable.

unaware [ʌnə'wɛə*] a: to be ~ of ignorer, ne pas savoir, être inconscient(e) de; ~s ad à l'improviste, au dépourvu.

unbalanced [ʌn'bælənst] a déséquilibré(e).

unbearable [ʌn'bɛərəbl] a insupportable.

unbeatable [ʌn'bi:təbl] a imbattable.

unbeaten [ʌn'bi:tn] a invaincu(e).

unbecoming [ʌnbɪ'kʌmɪŋ] a malséant(e), inconvenant(e).

unbeknown(st) [ʌnbɪ'nəun(st)] ad: ~ to à l'insu de.

unbelief [ʌnbɪ'li:f] n incrédulité f.

unbelievable [ʌnbɪ'li:vəbl] a incroyable.

unbend [ʌn'bɛnd] vb (irg) vi se détendre // vt (wire) redresser, détordre.

unbounded [ʌn'baundɪd] a sans bornes, illimité(e).

unbreakable [ʌn'breɪkəbl] a incassable.

unbridled [ʌn'braɪdld] a débridé(e), déchaîné(e).

unbroken [ʌn'brəukən] a intact(e); continu(e).

unburden [ʌn'bə:dn] vt: to ~ o.s. s'épancher, se livrer.

unbutton [ʌn'bʌtn] vt déboutonner.

uncalled-for [ʌn'kɔ:ldfɔ:*] a déplacé(e), injustifié(e).

uncanny [ʌn'kænɪ] a étrange, troublant(e).

unceasing [ʌn'si:sɪŋ] a incessant(e), continu(e).

uncertain [ʌn'sə:tn] a incertain(e); mal assuré(e); ~ty n incertitude f, doutes mpl.

unchanged [ʌn'tʃeɪndʒd] a inchangé(e).

uncharitable [ʌn'tʃærɪtəbl] a peu charitable.

uncharted [ʌn'tʃɑ:tɪd] a inexploré(e).

unchecked [ʌn'tʃɛkt] a non réprimé(e).

uncle [ˈʌŋkl] n oncle m.

uncomfortable [ʌn'kʌmfətəbl] a inconfortable; (uneasy) mal à l'aise, gêné(e); désagréable.

uncommon [ʌn'kɔmən] a rare, singulier(ère), peu commun(e).

uncompromising [ʌn'kɔmprəmaɪzɪŋ] a intransigeant(e), inflexible.

unconditional [ʌnkən'dɪʃənl] a sans conditions.

uncongenial [ʌnkən'dʒi:nɪəl] a peu agréable.

unconscious [ʌn'kɔnʃəs] a sans connaissance, évanoui(e); (unaware) inconscient(e) // n: the ~ l'inconscient m; ~ly ad inconsciemment.

uncontrollable [ʌnkən'trəuləbl] a irrépressible; indiscipliné(e).

uncork [ʌn'kɔ:k] vt déboucher.

uncouth [ʌn'ku:θ] a grossier(ère), fruste.

uncover [ʌn'kʌvə*] vt découvrir.

unctuous [ˈʌŋktjuəs] a onctueux(euse), mielleux(euse).

undaunted [ʌn'dɔ:ntɪd] a non intimidé(e), inébranlable.

undecided [ʌndɪ'saɪdɪd] a indécis(e), irrésolu(e).

undeniable [ʌndɪ'naɪəbl] a indéniable, incontestable.

under [ˈʌndə*] prep sous; (less than) (de) moins de; au-dessous de; (according to) selon, en vertu de // ad au-dessous; en dessous; **from** ~ sth de dessous or de sous qch; ~ **there** là-dessous; ~ **repair** en (cours de) réparation.

under... [ˈʌndə*] prefix sous-; ~**age** a qui n'a pas l'âge réglementaire; ~**carriage**, ~**cart** n train m d'atterrissage; ~**clothes** npl sous-vêtements mpl; (women's only) dessous mpl; ~**coat** n (paint) couche f de fond; ~**cover** a secret(ète), clandestin(e); ~**current** n courant sous-jacent; ~**cut** n (CULIN) (morceau m de) filet m // vt irg vendre moins cher que; ~**developed** a sous-développé(e); ~**dog** n opprimé m; ~**done** a (CULIN) saignant(e); (pej) pas assez cuit(e); ~**estimate** vt sous-estimer, mésestimer; ~**exposed** a (PHOT) sous-exposé(e); ~**fed** a sous-alimenté(e); ~**foot** ad sous les pieds; ~**go** vt irg subir; (treatment) suivre; ~**graduate** n

étudiant/e (qui prépare la licence); ~**ground** n métro m; (POL) clandestinité f; ~**growth** n broussailles fpl, sous-bois m; ~**hand(ed)** a (fig) sournois(e), en dessous; ~**lie** vt irg être à la base de; ~**line** vt souligner; ~**ling** [ˈʌndəlɪŋ] n (pej) sous-fifre m, subalterne m; ~**mine** vt saper, miner; ~**neath** [ʌndə'ni:θ] ad (en) dessous // prep sous, au-dessous de; ~**paid** a sous-payé(e); ~**pants** npl (Brit) caleçon m, slip m; ~**pass** n passage souterrain; (on motorway) passage inférieur; ~**play** vt minimiser; ~**price** vt vendre à un prix trop bas; ~**privileged** a défavorisé(e), économiquement faible; ~**rate** vt sous-estimer, mésestimer; ~**shirt** n (US) tricot m de corps; ~**shorts** npl (US) caleçon m, slip m; ~**side** n dessous m; ~**skirt** n jupon m.

understand [ʌndə'stænd] vb (irg: like stand) vt, vi comprendre; I ~ that... je me suis laissé dire que...; je crois comprendre que...; ~**able** a compréhensible; ~**ing** a compréhensif(ive) // n compréhension f; (agreement) accord m.

understatement [ʌndə'steɪtmənt] n: that's an ~ c'est (bien) peu dire, le terme est faible.

understood [ʌndə'stud] pt, pp of **understand** // a entendu(e); (implied) sous-entendu(e).

understudy [ˈʌndəstʌdɪ] n doublure f.

undertake [ʌndə'teɪk] vt irg entreprendre; se charger de.

undertaker [ˈʌndəteɪkə*] n entrepreneur m des pompes funèbres, croque-mort m.

undertaking [ˈʌndəteɪkɪŋ] n entreprise f; (promise) promesse f.

underwater [ʌndə'wɔ:tə*] ad sous l'eau // a sous-marin(e).

underwear [ˈʌndəwɛə*] n sous-vêtements mpl; (women's only) dessous mpl.

underweight [ʌndə'weɪt] a d'un poids insuffisant; (person) (trop) maigre.

underworld [ˈʌndəwə:ld] n (of crime) milieu m, pègre f.

underwriter [ˈʌndəraɪtə*] n (INSURANCE) souscripteur m.

undesirable [ʌndɪ'zaɪərəbl] a peu souhaitable; indésirable.

undies [ˈʌndɪz] npl (col) dessous mpl, lingerie f.

undisputed [ʌndɪ'spju:tɪd] a incontesté(e).

undistinguished [ʌndɪs'tɪŋgwɪʃt] a médiocre, quelconque.

undo [ʌn'du:] vt irg défaire; ~**ing** n ruine f, perte f.

undoubted [ʌn'dautɪd] a indubitable, certain(e); ~**ly** ad sans aucun doute.

undress [ʌn'drɛs] vi se déshabiller.

undue [ʌn'dju:] a indu(e), excessif(ive).

undulating [ˈʌndjuleɪtɪŋ] a ondoyant(e), onduleux(euse).

unduly [ʌn'dju:lɪ] ad trop, excessivement.

unearth [ʌn'ə:θ] vt déterrer; (fig) dénicher.

unearthly [ʌn'ə:θlɪ] a surnaturel(le); (hour) indu(e), impossible.

uneasy [ʌn'i:zɪ] a mal à l'aise, gêné(e); (worried) inquiet(ète).

uneconomic(al) [ˈʌniːkəˈnɒmɪk(l)] a peu économique ; peu rentable.
uneducated [ʌnˈsdjukeɪtɪd] a sans éducation.
unemployed [ʌnɪmˈplɔɪd] a sans travail, en chômage // n: the ~ les chômeurs mpl.
unemployment [ʌnɪmˈplɔɪmənt] n chômage m.
unending [ʌnˈɛndɪŋ] a interminable.
unenviable [ʌnˈɛnvɪəbl] a peu enviable.
unerring [ʌnˈəːrɪŋ] a infaillible, sûr(e).
uneven [ʌnˈiːvn] a inégal(e) ; irrégulier(ère).
unexpected [ʌnɪkˈspɛktɪd] a inattendu(e), imprévu(e).
unexploded [ʌnɪkˈspləudɪd] a non explosé(e) or éclaté(e).
unfailing [ʌnˈfeɪlɪŋ] a inépuisable ; infaillible.
unfair [ʌnˈfɛə*] a: ~ (to) injuste (envers) ; ~ly ad injustement.
unfaithful [ʌnˈfeɪθful] a infidèle.
unfamiliar [ʌnfəˈmɪlɪə*] a étrange, inconnu(e).
unfasten [ʌnˈfɑːsn] vt défaire ; détacher.
unfathomable [ʌnˈfæðəməbl] a insondable.
unfavourable, unfavorable (US) [ʌnˈfeɪvərəbl] a défavorable.
unfeeling [ʌnˈfiːlɪŋ] a insensible, dur(e).
unfinished [ʌnˈfɪnɪʃt] a inachevé(e).
unfit [ʌnˈfɪt] a en mauvaise santé ; pas en forme ; (incompetent): ~ (for) impropre (à) ; (work, service) inapte (à).
unflagging [ʌnˈflægɪŋ] a infatigable, inlassable.
unflappable [ʌnˈflæpəbl] a imperturbable.
unflinching [ʌnˈflɪntʃɪŋ] a stoïque.
unfold [ʌnˈfəuld] vt déplier ; (fig) révéler, exposer // vi se dérouler.
unforeseen [ˈʌnfɔːˈsiːn] a imprévu(e).
unforgivable [ʌnfəˈgɪvəbl] a impardonnable.
unfortunate [ʌnˈfɔːtʃnət] a malheureux(euse) ; (event, remark) malencontreux(euse) ; ~ly ad malheureusement.
unfounded [ʌnˈfaundɪd] a sans fondement.
unfriendly [ʌnˈfrɛndlɪ] a froid(e), inimical(e).
unfurnished [ʌnˈfəːnɪʃt] a non meublé(e).
ungainly [ʌnˈgeɪnlɪ] a gauche, dégingandé(e).
ungodly [ʌnˈgɒdlɪ] a impie ; at an ~ hour à une heure indue.
unguarded [ʌnˈgɑːdɪd] a: ~ moment n moment m d'inattention.
unhappiness [ʌnˈhæpɪnɪs] n tristesse f, peine f.
unhappy [ʌnˈhæpɪ] a triste, malheureux(euse) ; ~ with (arrangements etc) mécontent(e) de, peu satisfait(e) de.
unharmed [ʌnˈhɑːmd] a indemne, sain(e) et sauf(sauve).
unhealthy [ʌnˈhɛlθɪ] a (gen) malsain(e) ; (person) maladif(ive).
unheard-of [ʌnˈhəːdɒv] a inouï(e), sans précédent.
unhook [ʌnˈhuk] vt décrocher ; dégrafer.

unhurt [ʌnˈhəːt] a indemne, sain(e) et sauf(sauve).
unicorn [ˈjuːnɪkɔːn] n licorne f.
unidentified [ʌnaɪˈdɛntɪfaɪd] a non identifié(e).
uniform [ˈjuːnɪfɔːm] n uniforme m // a uniforme ; ~ity [-ˈfɔːmɪtɪ] n uniformité f.
unify [ˈjuːnɪfaɪ] vt unifier.
unilateral [juːnɪˈlætərəl] a unilatéral(e).
unimaginable [ʌnɪˈmædʒɪnəbl] a inimaginable, inconcevable.
unimpaired [ʌnɪmˈpɛəd] a intact(e).
uninhibited [ʌnɪnˈhɪbɪtɪd] a sans inhibitions ; sans retenue.
unintentional [ʌnɪnˈtɛnʃənəl] a involontaire.
union [ˈjuːnjən] n union f ; (also: trade ~) syndicat m // cpd du syndicat, syndical(e) ; U~ Jack n drapeau du Royaume-Uni.
unique [juːˈniːk] a unique.
unison [ˈjuːnɪsn] n: in ~ à l'unisson, en chœur.
unit [ˈjuːnɪt] n unité f ; (section: of furniture etc) élément m, bloc m ; (team, squad) groupe m, service m.
unite [juːˈnaɪt] vt unir // vi s'unir ; ~d a uni(e) ; unifié(e) ; (efforts) conjugué(e) ; U~d Kingdom (U.K.) n Royaume-Uni m ; U~d Nations (Organization) (UN, UNO) n (Organisation f des) Nations unies (O.N.U.) ; U~d States (of America) (US, USA) n États-Unis mpl.
unit trust [ˈjuːnɪttrʌst] n (Brit) société f d'investissement.
unity [ˈjuːnɪtɪ] n unité f.
universal [juːnɪˈvəːsl] a universel(le).
universe [ˈjuːnɪvəːs] n univers m.
university [juːnɪˈvəːsɪtɪ] n université f.
unjust [ʌnˈdʒʌst] a injuste.
unkempt [ʌnˈkɛmpt] a mal tenu(e), débraillé(e) ; mal peigné(e).
unkind [ʌnˈkaɪnd] a peu gentil(le), méchant(e).
unknown [ʌnˈnəun] a inconnu(e).
unladen [ʌnˈleɪdn] a (ship, weight) à vide.
unlawful [ʌnˈlɔːful] a illégal(e).
unleash [ʌnˈliːʃ] vt détacher ; (fig) déchaîner, déclencher.
unleavened [ʌnˈlɛvnd] a sans levain.
unless [ʌnˈlɛs] cj: ~ he leaves à moins qu'il (ne) parte ; ~ we leave à moins de partir, à moins que nous (ne) partions ; ~ otherwise stated sauf indication contraire.
unlicensed [ʌnˈlaɪsənst] a non patenté(e) pour la vente des spiritueux.
unlike [ʌnˈlaɪk] a dissemblable, différent(e) // prep à la différence de, contrairement à.
unlikely [ʌnˈlaɪklɪ] a improbable ; invraisemblable.
unlimited [ʌnˈlɪmɪtɪd] a illimité(e).
unload [ʌnˈləud] vt décharger.
unlock [ʌnˈlɒk] vt ouvrir.
unlucky [ʌnˈlʌkɪ] a malchanceux(euse) ; (object, number) qui porte malheur.
unmannerly [ʌnˈmænəlɪ] a mal élevé(e), impoli(e).

unmarried [ʌn'mærɪd] a célibataire.

unmask [ʌn'mɑːsk] vt démasquer.

unmistakable [ʌnmɪs'teɪkəbl] a indubitable ; qu'on ne peut pas ne pas reconnaître.

unmitigated [ʌn'mɪtɪgeɪtɪd] a non mitigé(e), absolu(e), pur(e).

unnatural [ʌn'nætʃrəl] a non naturel(le) ; contre nature.

unnecessary [ʌn'nɛsəsərɪ] a inutile, superflu(e).

unnerve [ʌn'nəːv] vt faire perdre son sang-froid à.

UNO [juːnəʊ] n see united.

unobtainable [ʌnəb'teɪnəbl] a (TEL) impossible à obtenir.

unoccupied [ʌn'ɔkjupaɪd] a (seat etc) libre.

unofficial [ʌnə'fɪʃl] a non officiel(le) ; (strike) ≈ non sanctionné(e) par la centrale.

unorthodox [ʌn'ɔːθədɒks] a peu orthodoxe.

unpack [ʌn'pæk] vi défaire sa valise, déballer ses affaires.

unpalatable [ʌn'pælətəbl] a (truth) désagréable (à entendre).

unparalleled [ʌn'pærəleld] a incomparable, sans égal.

unpleasant [ʌn'plɛznt] a déplaisant(e), désagréable.

unplug [ʌn'plʌg] vt débrancher.

unpopular [ʌn'pɒpjʊlə*] a impopulaire.

unprecedented [ʌn'prɛsɪdəntɪd] a sans précédent.

unpredictable [ʌnprɪ'dɪktəbl] a imprévisible.

unprepossessing ['ʌnpriːpə'zɛsɪŋ] a peu avenant(e).

unpretentious [ʌnprɪ'tɛnʃəs] a sans prétention(s).

unqualified [ʌn'kwɒlɪfaɪd] a (teacher) non diplômé(e), sans titres ; (success) sans réserve, total(e).

unravel [ʌn'rævl] vt démêler.

unreal [ʌn'rɪəl] a irréel(le).

unreasonable [ʌn'riːznəbl] a qui n'est pas raisonnable.

unrelated [ʌnrɪ'leɪtɪd] a sans rapport ; sans lien de parenté.

unrelenting [ʌnrɪ'lɛntɪŋ] a implacable ; acharné(e).

unreliable [ʌnrɪ'laɪəbl] a sur qui (or quoi) on ne peut pas compter, peu fiable.

unrelieved [ʌnrɪ'liːvd] a (monotony) constant(e), uniforme.

unremitting [ʌnrɪ'mɪtɪŋ] a inlassable, infatigable, acharné(e).

unrepeatable [ʌnrɪ'piːtəbl] a (offer) unique, exceptionnel(le).

unrepentant [ʌnrɪ'pɛntənt] a impénitent(e).

unrest [ʌn'rɛst] n agitation f, troubles mpl.

unroll [ʌn'rəʊl] vt dérouler.

unruly [ʌn'ruːlɪ] a indiscipliné(e).

unsafe [ʌn'seɪf] a dangereux(euse), hasardeux(euse).

unsaid [ʌn'sɛd] a: to leave sth ~ passer qch sous silence.

unsatisfactory ['ʌnsætɪs'fæktərɪ] a qui laisse à désirer.

unsavoury, unsavory (US) [ʌn'seɪvərɪ] a (fig) peu recommandable, répugnant(e).

unscathed [ʌn'skeɪðd] a indemne.

unscrew [ʌn'skruː] vt dévisser.

unscrupulous [ʌn'skruːpjʊləs] a sans scrupules, indélicat(e).

unseemly [ʌn'siːmlɪ] a inconvenant(e).

unsettled [ʌn'sɛtld] a perturbé(e) ; instable ; incertain(e).

unshaven [ʌn'ʃeɪvn] a non or mal rasé(e).

unsightly [ʌn'saɪtlɪ] a disgracieux(euse), laid(e).

unskilled [ʌn'skɪld] a: ~ worker n manœuvre m.

unsophisticated [ʌnsə'fɪstɪkeɪtɪd] a simple, naturel(le).

unspeakable [ʌn'spiːkəbl] a indicible ; (bad) innommable.

unsteady [ʌn'stɛdɪ] a mal assuré(e), chancelant(e), instable.

unstuck [ʌn'stʌk] a: to come ~ se décoller ; (fig) faire fiasco.

unsuccessful [ʌnsək'sɛsfʊl] a (attempt) infructueux(euse) ; (writer, proposal) qui n'a pas de succès ; (marriage) malheureux(euse), qui ne réussit pas ; to be ~ (in attempting sth) ne pas réussir ; ne pas avoir de succès ; (application) ne pas être retenu(e) ; ~ly ad en vain.

unsuitable [ʌn'suːtəbl] a qui ne convient pas, peu approprié(e) ; inopportun(e).

unsuspecting [ʌnsə'spɛktɪŋ] a qui ne se méfie pas.

unswerving [ʌn'swəːvɪŋ] a inébranlable.

untangle [ʌn'tæŋgl] vt démêler, débrouiller.

untapped [ʌn'tæpt] a (resources) inexploité(e).

unthinkable [ʌn'θɪŋkəbl] a impensable, inconcevable.

untidy [ʌn'taɪdɪ] a (room) en désordre ; (appearance) désordonné(e), débraillé(e) ; (person) sans ordre, désordonné(e) ; débraillé ; (work) peu soigné(e).

untie [ʌn'taɪ] vt (knot, parcel) défaire ; (prisoner, dog) détacher.

until [ən'tɪl] prep jusqu'à ; (after negative) avant // cj jusqu'à ce que + sub, en attendant que + sub ; (in past, after negative) avant que + sub ; ~ then jusque-là.

untimely [ʌn'taɪmlɪ] a inopportun(e) ; (death) prématuré(e).

untold [ʌn'təʊld] a incalculable ; indescriptible.

untoward [ʌntə'wɔːd] a fâcheux (euse), malencontreux(euse).

untranslatable [ʌntrænz'leɪtəbl] a intraduisible.

unused [ʌn'juːzd] a neuf(neuve).

unusual [ʌn'juːʒʊəl] a insolite, exceptionnel(le), rare.

unveil [ʌn'veɪl] vt dévoiler.

unwavering [ʌn'weɪvərɪŋ] a inébranlable.

unwell [ʌn'wɛl] a indisposé(e), souffrant(e).

unwieldy [ʌn'wiːldɪ] a difficile à manier.

unwilling [ʌn'wɪlɪŋ] a: to be ~ to do ne pas vouloir faire ; ~ly ad à contrecœur, contre son gré.

unwind [ʌn'waɪnd] vb (irg) vt dérouler // vi (relax) se détendre.

unwitting [ʌn'wɪtɪŋ] a involontaire.

unworthy [ʌn'wɜ:ði] a indigne.

unwrap [ʌn'ræp] vt défaire; ouvrir.

unwritten [ʌn'rɪtn] a (agreement) tacite.

up [ʌp] prep: to go/be ~ sth monter/être sur qch // ad en haut; en l'air; ~ there là-haut; ~ above au-dessus; ~ to jusqu'à; to be ~ (out of bed) être levé(e), être debout inv; it is ~ to you c'est à vous de décider, ça ne tient qu'à vous; what is he ~ to? qu'est-ce qu'il peut bien faire?; he is not ~ to it il n'en est pas capable; ~-and-coming a plein d'avenir or de promesses; ~s and downs npl (fig) hauts mpl et bas mpl.

upbringing ['ʌpbrɪŋɪŋ] n éducation f.

update [ʌp'deɪt] vt mettre à jour.

upend [ʌp'ɛnd] vt mettre debout.

upgrade [ʌp'greɪd] vt promouvoir; (job) revaloriser.

upheaval [ʌp'hi:vl] n bouleversement m; branle-bas m; crise f.

uphill [ʌp'hɪl] a qui monte; (fig: task) difficile, pénible // ad: to go ~ monter.

uphold [ʌp'həuld] vt irg maintenir; soutenir.

upholstery [ʌp'həulstəri] n rembourrage m; (of car) garniture f.

upkeep ['ʌpki:p] n entretien m.

upon [ə'pɔn] prep sur.

upper ['ʌpə*] a supérieur(e); du dessus // n (of shoe) empeigne f; the ~ class ≈ la haute bourgeoisie; ~-class a ≈ bourgeois(e); ~most a le(la) plus haut(e); en dessus.

upright ['ʌpraɪt] a droit(e); vertical(e); (fig) droit, honnête // n montant m.

uprising ['ʌpraɪzɪŋ] n soulèvement m, insurrection f.

uproar ['ʌprɔ:*] n tumulte m, vacarme m.

uproot [ʌp'ru:t] vt déraciner.

upset n ['ʌpsɛt] dérangement m // vt [ʌp'sɛt] (irg: like set) (glass etc) renverser; (plan) déranger; (person: offend) contrarier; (: grieve) faire de la peine à; bouleverser // a [ʌp'sɛt] contrarié(e); peiné(e); (stomach) détraqué(e), dérangé(e).

upshot ['ʌpʃɔt] n résultat m.

upside ['ʌpsaɪd]: ~-down ad à l'envers.

upstairs [ʌp'stɛəz] ad en haut // a (room) du dessus, d'en haut // n: there's no ~ il n'y a pas d'étage.

upstart ['ʌpstɑ:t] n parvenu/e.

upstream [ʌp'stri:m] ad en amont.

uptake ['ʌpteɪk] n: he is quick/slow on the ~ il comprend vite/est lent à comprendre.

up-to-date ['ʌptə'deɪt] a moderne; très récent(e).

upturn ['ʌptə:n] n (in luck) retournement m.

upward ['ʌpwəd] a ascendant(e); vers le haut; ~(s) ad vers le haut; and ~(s) et plus, et au-dessus.

uranium [juə'reɪnɪəm] n uranium m.

urban ['ə:bən] a urbain(e).

urbane [ə:'beɪn] a urbain(e), courtois(e).

urchin ['ə:tʃɪn] n gosse m, garnement m; sea ~ n oursin m.

urge [ə:dʒ] n besoin m; envie f; forte envie, désir m // vt: to ~ sb to do exhorter qn à faire, pousser qn à faire; recommander vivement à qn de faire; to ~ on vt aiguillonner, talonner.

urgency ['ə:dʒənsɪ] n urgence f; (of tone) insistance f.

urgent ['ə:dʒənt] a urgent(e); ~ly ad d'urgence, sans délai.

urinal ['juərɪnl] n urinoir m.

urinate ['juərɪneɪt] vi uriner.

urn [ə:n] n urne f; (also: tea ~) fontaine f à thé.

us [ʌs] pronoun nous.

US, USA n abbr see united.

usage ['ju:zɪdʒ] n usage m.

use n [ju:s] emploi m, utilisation f; usage m // vt [ju:z] se servir de, utiliser, employer; she ~d to do it elle le faisait (autrefois), elle avait coutume de le faire; in ~ en usage; out of ~ hors d'usage; it's no ~ ça ne sert à rien; to have the ~ of avoir l'usage de; to be ~d to avoir l'habitude de, être habitué(e) à; to ~ up vt finir, épuiser; consommer; ~d a (car) d'occasion; ~ful a utile; ~fulness n utilité f; ~less a inutile; ~r n utilisateur/trice, usager m.

usher ['ʌʃə*] n placeur m; ~ette [-'rɛt] n (in cinema) ouvreuse f.

USSR n: the ~ l'URSS f.

usual ['ju:ʒuəl] a habituel(le); as ~ comme d'habitude; ~ly ad d'habitude, d'ordinaire.

usurer ['ju:ʒərə*] n usurier/ère.

usurp [ju:'zə:p] vt usurper.

utensil [ju:'tɛnsl] n ustensile m.

uterus ['ju:tərəs] n utérus m.

utilitarian [ju:tɪlɪ'tɛərɪən] a utilitaire.

utility [ju:'tɪlɪtɪ] n utilité f; (also: public ~) service public.

utilization [ju:tɪlaɪ'zeɪʃn] n utilisation f.

utilize ['ju:tɪlaɪz] vt utiliser; exploiter.

utmost ['ʌtməust] a extrême, le(la) plus grand(e) // n: to do one's ~ faire tout son possible.

utter ['ʌtə*] a total(e), complet(ète) // vt prononcer, proférer; émettre; ~ance n paroles fpl; ~ly ad complètement, totalement.

U-turn ['ju:'tə:n] n demi-tour m.

V

v. abbr of verse, versus, volt; (abbr of vide) voir.

vacancy ['veɪkənsɪ] n (job) poste vacant; (room) chambre f disponible; 'no vacancies' 'complet'.

vacant ['veɪkənt] a (post) vacant(e); (seat etc) libre, disponible; (expression) distrait(e).

vacate [və'keɪt] vt quitter.

vacation [və'keɪʃən] n vacances fpl; ~ course n cours mpl de vacances.

vaccinate ['væksɪneɪt] vt vacciner; **vaccination** [-'neɪʃən] n vaccination f.

vaccine ['væksi:n] n vaccin m.

vacuum ['vækjum] n vide m; ~ **cleaner** n aspirateur m; ~ **flask** n bouteille f thermos ♠.

vagary ['veigəri] n caprice m.

vagina [və'dʒainə] n vagin m.

vagrant ['veigrnt] n vagabond/e, mendiant/e.

vague [veig] a vague, imprécis(e); (blurred: photo, memory) flou(e); ~**ly** ad vaguement.

vain [vein] a (useless) vain(e); (conceited) vaniteux(euse); **in** ~ en vain.

valance ['væləns] n (of bed) tour m de lit.

valentine ['væləntain] n (also: ~ **card**) carte f de la Saint-Valentin.

valeting ['vælitiŋ] a: ~ **service** n pressing m.

valiant ['væliənt] a vaillant(e), courageux(euse).

valid ['vælid] a valide, valable; (excuse) valable; ~**ity** [-'liditi] n validité f.

valise [və'liːz] n sac m de voyage.

valley ['væli] n vallée f.

valuable ['væljuəbl] a (jewel) de grande valeur; (time) précieux (euse); ~**s** npl objets mpl de valeur.

valuation [vælju'eiʃən] n évaluation f, expertise f.

value ['væljuː] n valeur f // vt (fix price) évaluer, expertiser; (cherish) tenir à; ~ **added tax (VAT)** n taxe f à la valeur ajoutée (T.V.A.); ~**d** a (appreciated) estimé(e); ~**r** n expert m (en estimations).

valve [vælv] n (in machine) soupape f; (on tyre) valve f; (in radio) lampe f.

van [væn] n (AUT) camionnette f; (RAIL) fourgon m.

vandal ['vændl] n vandale m/f; ~**ism** n vandalisme m; ~**ize** vt saccager.

vanguard ['vænguːd] n avant-garde m.

vanilla [və'nilə] n vanille f // cpd (ice cream) à la vanille.

vanish ['væniʃ] vi disparaître.

vanity ['væniti] n vanité f; ~ **case** n sac m de toilette.

vantage ['vɑːntidʒ] n: ~ **point** bonne position.

vapour, vapor (US) ['veipə*] n vapeur f; (on window) buée f.

variable ['vɛəriəbl] a variable; (mood) changeant(e).

variance ['vɛəriəns] n: **to be at** ~ (**with**) être en désaccord (avec); (facts) être en contradiction (avec).

variant ['vɛəriənt] n variante f.

variation [vɛəri'eiʃən] n variation f; (in opinion) changement m.

varicose ['værikəus] a: ~ **veins** npl varices fpl.

varied ['vɛərid] a varié(e), divers(e).

variety [və'raiəti] n variété f; (quantity) nombre m, quantité f; ~ **show** n (spectacle m de) variétés fpl.

various ['vɛəriəs] a divers(e), différent(e); (several) divers, plusieurs.

varnish ['vɑːniʃ] n vernis m // vt vernir.

vary ['vɛəri] vt, vi varier, changer; ~**ing** a variable.

vase [vɑːz] n vase m.

vast [vɑːst] a vaste, immense; (amount, success) énorme; ~**ly** ad infiniment, extrêmement; ~**ness** n immensité f.

vat [væt] n cuve f.

VAT [væt] n abbr see **value**.

Vatican ['vætikən] n: the ~ le Vatican.

vault [vɔːlt] n (of roof) voûte f; (tomb) caveau m; (in bank) salle f des coffres; chambre forte; (jump) saut m // vt (also: ~ **over**) sauter (d'un bond).

vaunted ['vɔːntid] a: **much-**~ tant célébré(e).

VD n abbr see **venereal**.

veal [viːl] n veau m.

veer [viə*] vi tourner; virer.

vegetable ['vedʒtəbl] n légume m // a végétal(e); ~ **garden** n potager m.

vegetarian [vedʒi'tɛəriən] a, n végétarien(ne).

vegetate ['vedʒiteit] vi végéter.

vegetation [vedʒi'teiʃən] n végétation f.

vehemence ['viːiməns] n véhémence f, violence f.

vehicle ['viːikl] n véhicule m.

vehicular [vi'hikjulə*] a: '**no** ~ **traffic**' 'interdit à tout véhicule'.

veil [veil] n voile m // vt voiler.

vein [vein] n veine f; (on leaf) nervure f; (fig: mood) esprit m.

velocity [vi'lɔsiti] n vélocité f.

velvet ['vɛlvit] n velours m.

vending machine ['vendiŋməʃiːn] n distributeur m automatique.

vendor ['vendə*] n vendeur/euse.

veneer [və'niə*] n placage m de bois; (fig) vernis m.

venerable ['vɛnərəbl] a vénérable.

venereal [vi'niəriəl] a: ~ **disease** (VD) n maladie vénérienne.

Venetian [vi'niːʃən] a: ~ **blind** n store vénitien.

Venezuela [vɛnɛ'zweilə] n Venezuela m; ~**n** a vénézuélien(ne) // n Vénézuélien/ne.

vengeance ['vendʒəns] n vengeance f; **with a** ~ (fig) vraiment, pour de bon.

venison ['vɛnisn] n venaison f.

venom ['vɛnəm] n venin m; ~**ous** a venimeux(euse).

vent [vent] n orifice m, conduit m; (in dress, jacket) fente f // vt (fig: one's feelings) donner libre cours à.

ventilate ['vɛntileit] vt (room) ventiler, aérer; **ventilation** [-'leiʃən] n ventilation f, aération f; **ventilator** n ventilateur m.

ventriloquist [vɛn'triləkwist] n ventriloque m/f.

venture ['vɛntʃə*] n entreprise f // vt risquer, hasarder // vi s'aventurer, se risquer.

venue ['vɛnjuː] n lieu m de rendez-vous or rencontre; (SPORT) lieu de la rencontre.

veranda(h) [və'rændə] n véranda f.

verb [vəːb] n verbe m; ~**al** a verbal(e); (translation) littéral(e).

verbatim [vəː'beitim] a, ad mot pour mot.

verbose [vəː'bəus] a verbeux(euse).

verdict ['vəːdikt] n verdict m.

verge [vəːdʒ] n bord m; '**soft** ~**s**' 'accotements non stabilisés'; **on the** ~ **of doing** sur le point de faire; **to** ~ **on** vt fus approcher de.

verger ['vɜːdʒə*] n (REL) bedeau m.

verification [verɪfɪ'keɪʃən] n vérification f.

verify ['verɪfaɪ] vt vérifier.

vermin ['vɜːmɪn] npl animaux mpl nuisibles; (insects) vermine f.

vermouth ['vɜːməθ] n vermouth m.

vernacular [və'nækjulə*] n langue f vernaculaire, dialecte m.

versatile ['vɜːsətaɪl] a (person) aux talents variés; (machine, tool etc) aux usages variés; aux applications variées.

verse [vɜːs] n vers mpl; (stanza) strophe f; (in bible) verset m.

versed [vɜːst] a: (well-)~ in versé(e) dans.

version ['vɜːʃən] n version f.

versus ['vɜːsəs] prep contre.

vertebra, pl ~e ['vɜːtɪbrə, -briː] n vertèbre f.

vertebrate ['vɜːtɪbrɪt] n vertébré m.

vertical ['vɜːtɪkl] a vertical(e) // n verticale f; ~ly ad verticalement.

vertigo ['vɜːtɪgəu] n vertige m.

verve [vɜːv] n brio m; enthousiasme m.

very ['verɪ] ad très // a: the ~ book which he lent me même que; at the ~ end tout à la fin; the ~ last le tout dernier; at the ~ least au moins; ~ much beaucoup.

vespers ['vespəz] npl vêpres fpl.

vessel ['vesl] n (ANAT. NAUT) vaisseau m; (container) récipient m.

vest [vest] n tricot m de corps; (US: waistcoat) gilet m // vt: to ~ sb with sth, to ~ sth in sb investir qn de qch; ~ed interests npl (COMM) droits acquis.

vestibule ['vestɪbjuːl] n vestibule m.

vestige ['vestɪdʒ] n vestige m.

vestry ['vestrɪ] n sacristie f.

vet [vet] n (abbr of veterinary surgeon) vétérinaire m/f // vt examiner minutieusement; (text) revoir.

veteran ['vetərn] n vétéran m; (also: war ~) ancien combattant; ~ car n voiture f d'époque.

veterinary ['vetrɪnərɪ] a vétérinaire; ~ surgeon n vétérinaire m/f.

veto ['viːtəu] n, pl ~es veto m // vt opposer son veto à.

vex [veks] vt fâcher, contrarier; ~ed a (question) controversé(e).

VHF abbr of very high frequency.

via ['vaɪə] prep par, via.

viable ['vaɪəbl] a viable.

viaduct ['vaɪədʌkt] n viaduc m.

vibrate [vaɪ'breɪt] vi: to ~ (with) vibrer (de); (resound) retentir (de); **vibration** [-'breɪʃən] n vibration f.

vicar ['vɪkə*] n pasteur m (de l'Église anglicane); ~age n presbytère m.

vice [vaɪs] n (evil) vice m; (TECH) étau m.

vice- [vaɪs] prefix vice-; ~chairman n vice-président m.

vice squad ['vaɪsskwɔd] n ≈ brigade mondaine.

vice versa ['vaɪsɪ'vɜːsə] ad vice versa.

vicinity [vɪ'sɪnɪtɪ] n environs mpl, alentours mpl.

vicious ['vɪʃəs] a (remark) cruel(le), méchant(e); (blow) brutal(e); ~ness n méchanceté f, cruauté f; brutalité f.

vicissitudes [vɪ'sɪsɪtjuːdz] npl vicissitudes fpl.

victim ['vɪktɪm] n victime f; ~ization [-'zeɪʃən] n brimades fpl; représailles fpl; ~ize vt brimer; exercer des représailles sur.

victor ['vɪktə*] n vainqueur m.

Victorian [vɪk'tɔːrɪən] a victorien(ne).

victorious [vɪk'tɔːrɪəs] a victorieux(euse).

victory ['vɪktərɪ] n victoire f.

video ['vɪdɪəu] cpd vidéo inv; ~ (-tape) recorder n magnétoscope m.

vie [vaɪ] vi: to ~ with lutter avec, rivaliser avec.

Vienna [vɪ'enə] n Vienne.

view [vjuː] n vue f; (opinion) avis m, vue // vt (situation) considérer; (house) visiter; on ~ (in museum etc) exposé(e); in my ~ à mon avis; in ~ of the fact that étant donné que; to have in ~ avoir en vue; ~er n (viewfinder) viseur m; (small projector) visionneuse f; (TV) téléspectateur/trice; ~finder n viseur m; ~point n point m de vue.

vigil ['vɪdʒɪl] n veille f; ~ance n vigilance f; ~ance committee n comité m d'autodéfense; ~ant a vigilant(e).

vigorous ['vɪgərəs] a vigoureux(euse).

vigour, vigor (US) ['vɪgə*] n vigueur f.

vile [vaɪl] a (action) vil(e); (smell) abominable; (temper) massacrant(e).

vilify ['vɪlɪfaɪ] vt calomnier.

villa ['vɪlə] n villa f.

village ['vɪlɪdʒ] n village m; ~r n villageois/e.

villain ['vɪlən] n (scoundrel) scélérat m; (criminal) bandit m; (in novel etc) traître m.

vindicate ['vɪndɪkeɪt] vt défendre avec succès; justifier.

vindictive [vɪn'dɪktɪv] a vindicatif(ive), rancunier(ère).

vine [vaɪn] n vigne f; (climbing plant) plante grimpante; ~ grower n viticulteur m.

vinegar ['vɪnɪgə*] n vinaigre m.

vineyard ['vɪnjɑːd] n vignoble m.

vintage ['vɪntɪdʒ] n (year) année f, millésime m; ~ wine n vin m de grand cru.

vinyl ['vaɪnl] n vinyle m.

viola [vɪ'əulə] n alto m.

violate ['vaɪəleɪt] vt violer; **violation** [-'leɪʃən] n violation f.

violence ['vaɪələns] n violence f; (POL etc) incidents violents.

violent ['vaɪələnt] a violent(e); ~ly ad violemment; extrêmement.

violet ['vaɪələt] a (colour) violet(te) // n (plant) violette f.

violin [vaɪə'lɪn] n violon m; ~ist n violoniste m/f.

VIP n (abbr of very important person) V.I.P. m.

viper ['vaɪpə*] n vipère f.

virgin ['vɜːdʒɪn] n vierge f // a vierge; she is a ~ elle est vierge; the Blessed V~

la Sainte Vierge; ~ity [-'dʒɪnɪtɪ] n virginité f.

Virgo ['vɜːgəu] n la Vierge; to be ~ être de la Vierge.

virile ['vɪraɪl] a viril(e).

virility [vɪ'rɪlɪtɪ] n virilité f.

virtually ['vɜːtjuəlɪ] ad (almost) pratiquement.

virtue ['vɜːtjuː] n vertu f; (advantage) mérite m, avantage m; by ~ of par le fait de.

virtuoso [vɜːtjuˈəuzəu] n virtuose m/f.

virtuous ['vɜːtjuəs] a vertueux(euse).

virulent ['vɪrulənt] a virulent(e).

virus ['vaɪərəs] n virus m.

visa ['viːzə] n visa m.

vis-à-vis [viːzəˈviː] prep vis-à-vis de.

viscount ['vaɪkaunt] n vicomte m.

visibility [vɪzɪ'bɪlɪtɪ] n visibilité f.

visible ['vɪzəbl] a visible; **visibly** ad visiblement.

vision ['vɪʒən] n (sight) vue f, vision f; (foresight, in dream) vision; ~ary n visionnaire m/f.

visit ['vɪzɪt] n visite f; (stay) séjour m // vt (person) rendre visite à; (place) visiter; ~ing card n carte f de visite; ~ing professor n ≈ professeur associé; ~or n visiteur/euse; (in hotel) client/e; ~ors' book n livre m d'or; (in hotel) registre m.

visor ['vaɪzə*] n visière f.

vista ['vɪstə] n vue f, perspective f.

visual ['vɪzjuəl] a visuel(le); (nerve) optique; ~ aid n support visuel (pour l'enseignement).

visualize ['vɪzjuəlaɪz] vt se représenter; (foresee) prévoir.

vital ['vaɪtl] a vital(e); ~ity [-'tælɪtɪ] n vitalité f; ~ly ad extrêmement; ~ statistics npl (fig) mensurations fpl.

vitamin ['vɪtəmɪn] n vitamine f.

vitiate ['vɪʃɪeɪt] vt vicier.

vivacious [vɪ'veɪʃəs] a animé(e), qui a de la vivacité.

vivacity [vɪ'væsɪtɪ] n vivacité f.

vivid ['vɪvɪd] a (account) frappant(e); (light, imagination) vif(vive); ~ly ad (describe) d'une manière vivante; (remember) de façon précise.

vivisection [vɪvɪ'sekʃən] n vivisection f.

V-neck ['viːnek] n décolleté m en V.

vocabulary [vəu'kæbjulərɪ] n vocabulaire m.

vocal ['vəukl] a (MUS) vocal(e); (communication) verbal(e); (noisy) bruyant(e); ~ chords npl cordes vocales; ~ist n chanteur/euse.

vocation [vəu'keɪʃən] n vocation f; ~al a professionnel(le).

vociferous [və'sɪfərəs] a bruyant(e).

vodka ['vɔdkə] n vodka f.

vogue [vəug] n mode f; (popularity) vogue f.

voice [vɔɪs] n voix f; (opinion) avis m // vt (opinion) exprimer, formuler.

void [vɔɪd] n vide m // a: ~ of vide de, dépourvu(e) de.

voile [vɔɪl] n voile m (tissu).

volatile ['vɔlətaɪl] a volatil(e); (fig) versatile.

volcanic [vɔl'kænɪk] a volcanique.

volcano, ~es [vɔl'keɪnəu] n volcan m.

volition [vəˈlɪʃən] n: of one's own ~ de son propre gré.

volley ['vɔlɪ] n (of gunfire) salve f; (of stones etc) pluie f, volée f; (TENNIS etc) volée f; ~ball n volley(-ball) m.

volt [vəult] n volt m; ~age n tension f, voltage m.

voluble ['vɔljubl] a volubile.

volume ['vɔljuːm] n volume m; ~ control n (RADIO, TV) bouton m de réglage du volume.

voluntarily ['vɔləntrɪlɪ] ad volontairement; bénévolement.

voluntary ['vɔləntərɪ] a volontaire; (unpaid) bénévole.

volunteer [vɔlən'tɪə*] n volontaire m/f // vi (MIL) s'engager comme volontaire; to ~ to do se proposer pour faire.

voluptuous [vəˈlʌptjuəs] a voluptueux(euse).

vomit ['vɔmɪt] n vomissure f // vt, vi vomir.

vote [vəut] n vote m, suffrage m; (cast) voix f, vote; (franchise) droit m de vote // vt (bill) voter; (chairman) élire // vi voter; ~ of censure n motion f de censure; ~ of thanks n discours m de remerciement; ~r n électeur/trice; voting n scrutin m.

vouch [vautʃ]: to ~ for vt se porter garant de.

voucher ['vautʃə*] n (for meal, petrol) bon m; (receipt) reçu m.

vow [vau] n vœu m, serment m // vi jurer.

vowel ['vauəl] n voyelle f.

voyage ['vɔɪdʒ] n voyage m par mer, traversée f.

vulgar ['vʌlgə*] a vulgaire; ~ity [-'gærɪtɪ] n vulgarité f.

vulnerability [vʌlnərə'bɪlɪtɪ] n vulnérabilité f.

vulnerable ['vʌlnərəbl] a vulnérable.

vulture ['vʌltʃə*] n vautour m.

W

wad [wɔd] n (of cotton wool, paper) tampon m; (of banknotes etc) liasse f.

wade [weɪd] vi: to ~ through marcher dans, patauger dans // vt passer à gué.

wafer ['weɪfə*] n (CULIN) gaufrette f; (REL) pain m d'hostie f.

waffle ['wɔfl] n (CULIN) gaufre f; (col) rabâchage m; remplissage m // vi parler pour ne rien dire; faire du remplissage.

waft [wɔft] vt porter // vi flotter.

wag [wæg] vt agiter, remuer // vi remuer.

wage [weɪdʒ] n salaire m, paye f // vt: to ~ war faire la guerre; ~s npl salaire, paye; ~ claim n demande f d'augmentation de salaire; ~ earner n salarié/e; (breadwinner) soutien m de famille; ~ freeze n blocage m des salaires.

wager ['weɪdʒə*] n pari m.

waggle ['wægl] vt, vi remuer.

wag(g)on ['wægən] n (horse-drawn) chariot m; (truck) camion m; (RAIL) wagon m (de marchandises).

wail [weɪl] n gémissement m; (of siren) hurlement m // vi gémir; hurler.

waist [weɪst] n taille f, ceinture f; ~**coat** n gilet m; ~**line** n (tour m de) taille f.

wait [weɪt] n attente f // vi attendre; to lie in ~ for guetter; I can't ~ to (fig) je meurs d'envie de; to ~ behind vi rester (à attendre); to ~ for attendre; to ~ on vt fus servir; ~**er** n garçon m (de café), serveur m; 'no ~**ing**' (AUT) 'stationnement interdit'; ~**ing list** n liste f d'attente; ~**ing room** n salle f d'attente; ~**ress** n serveuse f.

waive [weɪv] vt renoncer à, abandonner.

wake [weɪk] vb (pt woke, ~d, pp woken, ~d [wəuk, 'wəukn]) vt (also: ~ up) réveiller // vi (also: ~ up) se réveiller // n (for dead person) veillée f mortuaire; (NAUT) sillage m; ~**n** vt, vi = **wake**.

Wales [weɪlz] n pays m de Galles.

walk [wɔːk] n promenade f; (short) petit tour; (gait) démarche f; (pace): at a quick ~ d'un pas rapide; (path) chemin m; (in park etc) allée f // vi marcher; (for pleasure, exercise) se promener // vt (distance) faire à pied; (dog) promener; 10 minutes' ~ from à 10 minutes de marche de; from all ~s of life de toutes conditions sociales; ~**er** n (person) marcheur/euse; ~**ie-talkie** ['wɔːkɪ'tɔːkɪ] n talkie-walkie m; ~**ing** n marche f à pied; ~**ing holiday** n vacances passées à faire de la randonnée; ~**ing shoes** npl chaussures fpl de marche; ~**ing stick** n canne f; ~**out** n (of workers) grève-surprise f; ~**over** n (col) victoire f or examen m etc facile; ~**way** n promenade f.

wall [wɔːl] n mur m; (of tunnel, cave) paroi m; ~ **cupboard** n placard mural; ~**ed** a (city) fortifié(e).

wallet ['wɔlɪt] n portefeuille m.

wallflower ['wɔːlflauə*] n giroflée f; to be a ~ (fig) faire tapisserie.

wallop ['wɔləp] vt (col) taper sur, cogner.

wallow ['wɔləu] vi se vautrer.

wallpaper ['wɔːlpeɪpə*] n papier peint.

walnut ['wɔːlnʌt] n noix f; (tree) noyer m.

walrus, pl ~ or ~**es** ['wɔːlrəs] n morse m.

waltz [wɔːlts] n valse f // vi valser.

wan [wɔn] a pâle; triste.

wand [wɔnd] n (also: **magic** ~) baguette f (magique).

wander ['wɔndə*] vi (person) errer, aller sans but; (thoughts) vagabonder; (river) serpenter; ~**er** n vagabond/e.

wane [weɪn] vi (moon) décroître; (reputation) décliner.

wangle ['wæŋgl] vt (col) se débrouiller pour avoir; carotter.

want [wɔnt] vt vouloir; (need) avoir besoin de; (lack) manquer de // n: for ~ of par manque de, faute de; ~**s** npl (needs) besoins mpl; to ~ to do vouloir faire; to ~ sb to do vouloir que qn fasse; to be found ~**ing** ne pas être à la hauteur.

wanton ['wɔntn] a capricieux(euse); dévergondé(e).

war [wɔː*] n guerre f; to go to ~ se mettre en guerre.

ward [wɔːd] n (in hospital) salle f; (POL) section électorale; (LAW: child) pupille m/f; to ~ off vt parer, éviter.

warden ['wɔːdn] n (of institution) directeur/trice; (of park, game reserve) gardien/ne; (also: **traffic** ~) contractuel/le.

warder ['wɔːdə*] n gardien m de prison.

wardrobe ['wɔːdrəub] n (cupboard) armoire f; (clothes) garde-robe f; (THEATRE) costumes mpl.

warehouse ['wɛəhaus] n entrepôt m.

wares [wɛəz] npl marchandises fpl.

warfare ['wɔːfɛə*] n guerre f.

warhead ['wɔːhɛd] n (MIL) ogive f.

warily ['wɛərɪlɪ] ad avec prudence, avec précaution.

warlike ['wɔːlaɪk] a guerrier(ère).

warm [wɔːm] a chaud(e); (thanks, welcome, applause) chaleureux(euse); it's ~ il fait chaud; I'm ~ j'ai chaud; to ~ up vi (person, room) se réchauffer; (water) chauffer; (athlete, discussion) s'échauffer // vt réchauffer; chauffer; (engine) faire chauffer; ~**-hearted** a affectueux(euse); ~**ly** ad chaudement; vivement; chaleureusement; ~**th** n chaleur f.

warn [wɔːn] vt avertir, prévenir; ~**ing** n avertissement m; (notice) avis m; ~**ing light** n avertisseur lumineux.

warp [wɔːp] vi travailler, se voiler // vt voiler; (fig) pervertir.

warrant ['wɔrnt] n (guarantee) garantie f; (LAW: to arrest) mandat m d'arrêt; (: to search) mandat de perquisition.

warranty ['wɔrntɪ] n garantie f.

warrior ['wɔrɪə*] n guerrier/ère.

warship ['wɔːʃɪp] n navire m de guerre.

wart [wɔːt] n verrue f.

wartime ['wɔːtaɪm] n: in ~ en temps de guerre.

wary ['wɛərɪ] a prudent(e).

was [wɔz] pt of **be**.

wash [wɔʃ] vt laver // vi se laver // n (paint) badigeon m; (washing programme) lavage m; (of ship) sillage m; to give sth a ~ laver qch; to have a ~ se laver, faire sa toilette; to ~ away vt (stain) enlever au lavage; (subj: river etc) emporter; to ~ down vt laver à grande eau; to ~ off vi partir au lavage; to ~ up vi faire la vaisselle; ~**able** a lavable; ~**basin** n lavabo m; ~**er** n (TECH) rondelle f, joint m; ~**ing** n (linen etc) lessive f; ~**ing machine** n machine f à laver; ~**ing powder** n lessive f (en poudre); ~**ing-up** n vaisselle f; ~**out** n (col) désastre m; ~**room** n toilettes fpl.

wasn't ['wɔznt] = **was not**.

wasp [wɔsp] n guêpe f.

wastage ['weɪstɪdʒ] n gaspillage m; (in manufacturing, transport etc) déchet m.

waste [weɪst] n gaspillage m; (of time) perte f; (rubbish) déchets mpl; (also: **household** ~) ordures fpl // a (material) de rebut; (heat) perdu(e); (food) inutilisé(e); (land) inculte // vt gaspiller; (time, opportunity) perdre; ~**s** npl étendue f désertique; to ~ away vi dépérir; ~**bin** n corbeille f à papier; (in kitchen) boîte f à ordures; ~ **disposal unit** n broyeur m d'ordures; ~**ful** a gaspilleur(euse); (process) peu économique; ~ **ground** n terrain m vague; ~**paper basket** n corbeille f à papier.

watch [wɔtʃ] n montre f; (act of watching) surveillance f; guet m; (guard: MIL) sentinelle f; (: NAUT) homme m de quart; (NAUT: spell of duty) quart m // vt (look at) observer; (: match, programme) regarder; (spy on, guard) surveiller; (be careful of) faire attention à // vi regarder; (keep guard) monter la garde; to ~ out vi faire attention; ~dog n chien m de garde; ~ful a attentif(ive), vigilant(e); ~maker n horloger/ère; ~man n gardien m; (also: night ~man) veilleur m de nuit; ~ strap n bracelet m de montre.

water ['wɔːtə*] n eau f // vt (plant) arroser; in British ~s dans les eaux territoriales Britanniques; to ~ down vt (milk) couper d'eau; (fig: story) édulcorer; ~ closet n w.-c. mpl, waters mpl; ~colour n aquarelle f; ~colours npl couleurs fpl pour aquarelle; ~cress n cresson m (de fontaine); ~fall n chute f d'eau; ~ hole n mare f; ~ ice n sorbet m; ~ing can n arrosoir m; ~ level n niveau m de l'eau; (of flood) niveau m des eaux; ~ lily n nénuphar m; ~logged a détrempé(e); imbibé(e) d'eau; ~line n (NAUT) ligne f de flottaison; ~main n canalisation f d'eau; ~mark n (on paper) filigrane m; ~melon n pastèque f; ~polo n water-polo m; ~proof a imperméable; ~shed n (GEO) ligne f de partage des eaux; (fig) moment m critique, point décisif; ~-skiing n ski m nautique; ~ softener n adoucisseur m d'eau; ~ tank n réservoir m d'eau; ~tight a étanche; ~works npl station f hydraulique; ~y a (colour) délavé(e); (coffee) trop faible.

watt [wɔt] n watt m.

wave [weɪv] n vague f; (of hand) geste m, signe m; (RADIO) onde f; (in hair) ondulation f // vi faire signe de la main; (flag) flotter au vent // vt (handkerchief) agiter; (stick) brandir; (hair) onduler; ~length n longueur f d'ondes.

waver ['weɪvə*] vi vaciller; (voice) trembler; (person) hésiter.

wavy ['weɪvɪ] a ondulé(e); onduleux(euse).

wax [wæks] n cire f; (for skis) fart m // vt cirer; (car) lustrer // vi (moon) croître; ~en a cireux(euse); ~works npl personnages mpl de cire; musée m de cire.

way [weɪ] n chemin m, voie f; (path, access) passage m; (distance) distance f; (direction) chemin, direction f; (manner) façon f, manière f; (habit) habitude f, façon; (condition) état m; which ~? — this ~ par où or de quel côté? — par ici; to be on one's ~ être en route; to be in the ~ bloquer le passage; (fig) gêner; to go out of one's ~ to do (fig) se donner du mal pour faire; in a ~ d'un côté; in some ~s à certains égards; d'un côté; in the ~ of en fait de, comme; '~ in' 'entrée'; '~ out' 'sortie'; the ~ back le chemin du retour; this ~ and that par ci par-là; 'give ~' (AUT) 'cédez la priorité'.

waylay [weɪˈleɪ] vt irg attaquer; (fig) I got waylaid quelqu'un m'a accroché.

wayward ['weɪwəd] a capricieux(euse), entêté(e).

W.C. ['dʌblju:'si:] n w.-c. mpl, waters mpl.

we [wiː] pl pronoun nous.

weak [wiːk] a faible; (health) fragile; (beam etc) peu solide; ~en vi faiblir // vt affaiblir; ~ling n gringalet m; faible m/f; ~ness n faiblesse f; (fault) point m faible.

wealth [wɛlθ] n (money, resources) richesse(s) f(pl); (of details) profusion f; ~y a riche.

wean [wiːn] vt sevrer.

weapon ['wɛpən] n arme f.

wear [wɛə*] n (use) usage m; (deterioration through use) usure f; (clothing): sports/baby~ vêtements mpl de sport/pour bébés // vb (pt wore, pp worn [wɔː*, wɔːn]) vt (clothes) porter; mettre; (beard etc) avoir; (damage: through use) user // vi (last) faire de l'usage; (rub etc through) s'user; town/evening ~ n tenue f de ville/de soirée; ~ and tear n usure f; to ~ away vt user, ronger // vi s'user, être rongé(e); to ~ down vt user; (strength) épuiser; to ~ off vi disparaître; to ~ on vi se poursuivre; passer; to ~ out vt user; (person, strength) épuiser.

wearily ['wɪərɪlɪ] ad avec lassitude.

weariness ['wɪərɪnɪs] n épuisement m, lassitude f.

weary ['wɪərɪ] a (tired) épuisé(e); (dispirited) las(lasse); abattu(e) // vt lasser // vi: to ~ of se lasser de.

weasel ['wiːzl] n (ZOOL) belette f.

weather ['wɛðə*] n temps m // vt (wood) faire mûrir; (tempest, crisis) essuyer, être pris(e) dans; survivre à, tenir le coup durant; ~-beaten a (person) hâlé(e); (building) dégradé(e) par les intempéries; ~ cock n girouette f; ~ forecast n prévisions fpl météorologiques, météo f; ~ vane n = ~ cock.

weave, pt wove, pp woven [wiːv, wəuv, 'wəuvn] vt (cloth) tisser; (basket) tresser; ~r n tisserand/e; weaving n tissage m.

web [wɛb] n (of spider) toile f; (on foot) palmure f; (fabric, also fig) tissu m; ~bed a (foot) palmé(e); ~bing n (on chair) sangles fpl.

wed [wɛd] vt (pt, pp wedded) épouser // n: the newly-~s les jeunes mariés.

we'd [wiːd] = we had, we would.

wedded ['wɛdɪd] pt,pp of wed.

wedding ['wɛdɪŋ] n mariage m; silver/golden ~ n noces fpl d'argent/d'or; ~ day n jour m du mariage; ~ dress n robe f de mariage; ~ present n cadeau m de mariage; ~ ring n alliance f.

wedge [wɛdʒ] n (of wood etc) coin m; (under door etc) cale f; (of cake) part f // vt (fix) caler; (push) enfoncer, coincer; ~-heeled shoes npl chaussures fpl à semelles compensées.

wedlock ['wɛdlɔk] n (union f du) mariage m.

Wednesday ['wɛdnzdɪ] n mercredi m.

wee [wiː] a (Scottish) petit(e); tout(e) petit(e).

weed [wiːd] n mauvaise herbe // vt désherber; ~-killer n désherbant m.

week [wiːk] n semaine f; ~day n jour m de semaine; (COMM) jour ouvrable; ~end n week-end m; ~ly ad une fois par semaine, chaque semaine // **a,n** hebdomadaire (m).

weep, pt, pp **wept** [wiːp, wɛpt] vi (person) pleurer; **~ing willow** n saule pleureur.

weigh [weɪ] vt,vi peser; to ~ **anchor** lever l'ancre; to ~ **down** vt (branch) faire plier; (fig: with worry) accabler; to ~ **up** vt examiner; **~bridge** n pont-bascule m.

weight [weɪt] n poids m; **sold by** ~ vendu(e) au poids; **~lessness** n apesanteur f; ~ **lifter** n haltérophile m; ~**y** a lourd(e).

weir [wɪə*] n barrage m.

weird [wɪəd] a bizarre; (eerie) surnaturel(le).

welcome ['wɛlkəm] a bienvenu(e) // n accueil m // vt accueillir; (also: **bid** ~) souhaiter la bienvenue à; (be glad of) se réjouir de; to be ~ être le(la) bienvenu(e); **welcoming** a accueillant(e); (speech) d'accueil.

weld [wɛld] n soudure f // vt souder; **~er** n (person) soudeur m; **~ing** n soudure f (autogène).

welfare ['wɛlfɛə*] n bien-être m; ~ **state** n État-providence m; ~ **work** n travail social.

well [wɛl] n puits m // ad bien // a: to be ~ aller bien // excl eh bien!; bon!; enfin!; ~ **done!** bravo!; **get** ~ **soon!** remets-toi vite!; to do ~ **in** sth bien réussir en or dans qch.

we'll [wiːl] = **we will, we shall.**

well: ~**-behaved** a sage, obéissant(e); ~**-being** n bien-être m; ~**-built** a (building) bien construit(e); (person) bien bâti(e); ~**-developed** a (girl) bien fait(e); ~**-earned** a (rest) bien mérité(e); ~**-groomed** a très soigné(e) de sa personne; ~**-heeled** a (col: wealthy) fortuné(e), riche.

wellingtons ['wɛlɪŋtənz] npl (also: **wellington boots**) bottes fpl de caoutchouc.

well: ~**-known** a (person) bien connu(e); ~**-meaning** a bien intentionné(e); ~**-off** a aisé(e), assez riche; ~**-read** a cultivé(e); ~**-to-do** a aisé(e), assez riche; ~**-wisher** n: scores of ~**-wishers** had gathered de nombreux amis et admirateurs s'étaient rassemblés; **letters from** ~**-wishers** des lettres d'encouragement.

Welsh [wɛlʃ] a gallois(e) // n (LING) gallois m; ~**man/woman** n Gallois/e; ~ **rarebit** n croûte f au fromage.

went [wɛnt] pt of **go.**

wept [wɛpt] pt, pp of **weep.**

were [wəː*] pt of **be.**

we're [wɪə*] = **we are.**

weren't [wəːnt] = **were not.**

west [wɛst] n ouest m // a ouest inv, de or à l'ouest // ad à or vers l'ouest; **the W~** n l'Occident m, l'Ouest; **the W~ Country** n le sud-ouest de l'Angleterre; ~**erly** a (situation) à l'ouest; (wind) d'ouest; ~**ern** a occidental(e), de or à l'ouest // n (CINEMA) western m; **W~ Germany** n Allemagne f de l'Ouest; **W~ Indies** npl Antilles fpl; ~**ward(s)** ad vers l'ouest.

wet [wɛt] a mouillé(e); (damp) humide; (soaked) trempé(e); (rainy) pluvieux-

(euse); to get ~ se mouiller; ~ **blanket** n (fig) rabat-joie m inv; ~**ness** n humidité f; '~ **paint**' 'attention peinture fraîche'; ~ **suit** n combinaison f de plongée.

we've [wiːv] = **we have.**

whack [wæk] vt donner un grand coup à; ~**ed** a (col: tired) crevé(e).

whale [weɪl] n (ZOOL) baleine f.

wharf, wharves [wɔːf, wɔːvz] n quai m.

what [wɔt] excl quoi!, comment! // det quel(le) // pronoun (interrogative) que, prep + quoi; (relative, indirect: object) ce que; (: subject) ce qui; ~ **are you doing?** que fais-tu?, qu'est-ce que tu fais?; ~ **has happened?** que s'est-il passé?, qu'est-ce qui s'est passé?; ~**'s in there?** qu'y a-t-il là-dedans?, qu'est-ce qu'il y a là-dedans?; **I saw** ~ **you did/is on the table** j'ai vu ce que vous avez fait/ce qui est sur la table; ~ **a mess!** quel désordre!; ~ **is it called?** comment est-ce que ça s'appelle?; ~ **about doing ...?** et si on faisait ...?; ~ **about me?** et moi?; ~**ever** det: ~**ever book** quel que soit le livre que (or qui) + sub; **n'importe quel livre** // pronoun: **do** ~**ever is necessary/you want** faites (tout) ce qui est nécessaire/(tout) ce que vous voulez; ~**ever happens** quoi qu'il arrive; **no reason** ~**ever** or ~**soever** pas la moindre raison.

wheat [wiːt] n blé m, froment m.

wheel [wiːl] n roue f; (AUT: also: **steering** ~) volant m; (NAUT) gouvernail m // vt pousser, rouler // vi (also: ~ **round**) tourner; ~**barrow** n brouette f; ~**chair** n fauteuil roulant.

wheeze [wiːz] n respiration bruyante (d'asthmatique) // vi respirer bruyamment.

when [wɛn] ad quand // cj quand, lorsque; (whereas) alors que; **on the day** ~ **I met him** le jour où je l'ai rencontré; ~**ever** ad quand donc // cj quand; (every time that) chaque fois que.

where [wɛə*] ad,cj où; **this is** ~ c'est là que; ~**abouts** ad où donc // n: **sb's** ~**abouts** l'endroit où se trouve qn; ~**as** cj alors que; ~**ver** [-'ɛvə*] ad où donc // cj où que + sub.

whet [wɛt] vt aiguiser.

whether ['wɛðə*] cj si; **I don't know** ~ **to accept or not** je ne sais pas si je dois accepter ou non; **it's doubtful** ~ il est peu probable que; ~ **you go or not** que vous y alliez ou non.

which [wɪtʃ] det (interrogative) quel(le), pl quels(quelles); ~ **one of you?** lequel(laquelle) d'entre vous?; **tell me** ~ **one you want** dis-moi lequel tu veux or celui que tu veux // pronoun (interrogative) lequel(laquelle), pl lesquels (lesquelles); (indirect) celui(celle) qui (or que); (relative: subject) qui; (: object) que, prep + lequel(laquelle) (NB: à + lequel = auquel; de + lequel = duquel); **I don't mind** ~ peu importe lequel; **the apple** ~ **you ate/**~ **is on the table** la pomme que vous avez mangée/qui est sur la table; **the chair on** ~ la chaise sur laquelle; **the book of** ~ le livre dont or duquel; **he said he knew,** ~ **is true/I feared** il a dit qu'il le savait, ce qui est vrai/ce que je craignais; after ~ après quoi; in ~ **case** auquel cas; ~ever det: take ~ever book you **prefer** prenez le livre que vous préférez, peu importe lequel; ~ever book you take quel que soit le livre que vous preniez; ~ever way you de quelque façon que vous + *sub*.

whiff [wɪf] *n* bouffée *f*.

while [waɪl] *n* moment *m* // *cj* pendant que; (*as long as*) tant que; (*whereas*) alors que; bien que + *sub*; **for a** ~ pendant quelque temps.

whim [wɪm] *n* caprice *m*.

whimper ['wɪmpə*] *n* geignement *m* // *vi* geindre.

whimsical ['wɪmzɪkl] *a* (*person*) capricieux(euse); (*look*) étrange.

whine [waɪn] *n* gémissement *m* // *vi* gémir, geindre; pleurnicher.

whip [wɪp] *n* fouet *m*; (*for riding*) cravache *f*; (*Brit: POL: person*) chef *m* de file (*assurant la discipline dans son groupe parlementaire*) // *vt* fouetter; (*snatch*) enlever (or sortir) brusquement; ~**ped cream** *n* crème fouettée; ~**round** *n* collecte *f*.

whirl [wə:l] *n* tourbillon *m* // *vt* faire tourbillonner; faire tournoyer // *vi* tourbillonner; ~**pool** *n* tourbillon *m*; ~**wind** *n* tornade *f*.

whirr [wə:*] *vi* bruire; ronronner; vrombir.

whisk [wɪsk] *n* (*CULIN*) fouet *m* // *vt* fouetter, battre; **to** ~ **sb away or off** emmener qn rapidement.

whisker ['wɪskə*] *n*: ~**s** (*of animal*) moustaches *fpl*; (*of man*) favoris *mpl*.

whisky, whiskey (*Irlande, US*) ['wɪskɪ] *n* whisky *m*.

whisper ['wɪspə*] *n* chuchotement *m*; (*fig: of leaves*) bruissement *m*; (*rumour*) rumeur *f* // *vt, vi* chuchoter.

whist [wɪst] *n* whist *m*.

whistle ['wɪsl] *n* (*sound*) sifflement *m*; (*object*) sifflet *m* // *vi* siffler.

white [waɪt] *a* blanc(blanche); (*with fear*) blême // *n* blanc *m*; (*person*) blanc/blanche; ~**bait** *n* blanchaille *f*; ~**collar worker** *n* employé/e de bureau; ~**elephant** *n* (*fig*) objet dispendieux et superflu; ~ **lie** *n* pieux mensonge; ~**ness** *n* blancheur *f*; ~**paper** *n* (*POL*) livre blanc; ~**wash** *n* (*paint*) lait *m* de chaux // *vt* blanchir à la chaux; (*fig*) blanchir.

whiting ['waɪtɪŋ] *n*, *pl inv* (*fish*) merlan *m*.

Whitsun ['wɪtsn] *n* la Pentecôte.

whittle ['wɪtl] *vt*: **to** ~ **away**, ~ **down** (*costs*) réduire, rogner.

whizz [wɪz] *vi* aller (*or* passer) à toute vitesse; ~ **kid** *n* (*col*) petit prodige.

WHO *n* (*abbr of World Health Organization*) O.M.S. *f* (Organisation mondiale de la Santé).

who [hu:] *pronoun* qui; ~**dunit** [hu:'dʌnɪt] *n* (*col*) roman policier; ~**ever** *pronoun*: ~**ever finds** it celui(celle) qui le trouve, (qui que ce soit), quiconque le trouve; **ask** ~**ever you like** demandez à qui vous voulez; ~**ever he marries** qui que ce soit *or* quelle que soit la personne qu'il épouse; ~**ever told you that?** qui a bien pu vous dire ça?, qui donc vous a dit ça?

whole [həul] *a* (*complete*) entier(ère), tout(e); (*not broken*) intact(e), complet(ète) // *n* (*total*) totalité *f*; (*sth not broken*) tout *m*; **the** ~ **of the time** tout le temps; **the** ~ **of the town** la ville tout entière; **on the** ~, **as a** ~ dans l'ensemble; ~**hearted** *a* sans réserve(s), sincère; ~**sale** *n* (*vente f en*) gros *m* // *a* **de gros**; (*destruction*) systématique; ~**saler** *n* grossiste *m/f*; ~**some** *a* sain(e); (*advice*) salutaire; **wholly** *ad* entièrement, tout à fait.

whom [hu:m] *pronoun* que, *prep* + qui (*check syntax of French verb used*); (*interrogative*) qui.

whooping cough ['hu:pɪŋkɔf] *n* coqueluche *f*.

whopping ['wɔpɪŋ] *a* (*col: big*) énorme.

whore [hɔ:*] *n* (*col: pej*) putain *f*.

whose [hu:z] *det*: ~ **book is this?** à qui est ce livre?; ~ **pencil have you taken?** à qui est le crayon que vous avez pris?, c'est le crayon de qui que vous avez pris?; **the man** ~ **son** you rescued l'homme dont *or* de qui vous avez sauvé le fils; **the girl** ~ **sister** you were speaking to la fille à la sœur de qui *or* laquelle vous parliez // *pronoun*: ~ **is this?** à qui est ceci?; **I know** ~ **it is** je sais à qui c'est.

Who's Who ['hu:z'hu:] *n* ≈ Bottin Mondain.

why [waɪ] *ad* pourquoi // *excl* eh bien!, tiens!; **the reason** ~ la raison pour laquelle; ~**ever** *ad* pourquoi donc, mais pourquoi.

wick [wɪk] *n* mèche *f* (*de bougie*).

wicked ['wɪkɪd] *a* mauvais(e), méchant(e); inique; cruel(le); (*mischievous*) malicieux(euse).

wicker ['wɪkə*] *n* osier *m*; (*also*: ~**work**) vannerie *f*.

wicket ['wɪkɪt] *n* (*CRICKET*) guichet *m*; espace compris entre les deux guichets.

wide [waɪd] *a* large; (*region, knowledge*) vaste, très étendu(e); (*choice*) grand(e) // *ad*: **to open** ~ ouvrir tout grand; **to shoot** ~ tirer à côté; ~**-angle lens** *n* objectif *m* grand-angulaire; ~**-awake** *a* bien éveillé(e); ~**ly** *ad* (*different*) radicalement; (*spaced*) sur une grande étendue; (*believed*) généralement; ~**n** *vt* élargir; ~**ness** *n* largeur *f*; ~**open** *a* grand(e) ouvert(e); ~**spread** *a* (*belief etc*) très répandu(e).

widow ['wɪdəu] *n* veuve *f*; ~**ed** *a* (qui est devenu(e)) veuf(veuve); ~**er** *n* veuf *m*.

width [wɪdθ] *n* largeur *f*.

wield [wi:ld] *vt* (*sword*) manier; (*power*) exercer.

wife, wives [waɪf, waɪvz] *n* femme (mariée), épouse *f*.

wig [wɪg] *n* perruque *f*.

wiggle ['wɪgl] *vt* agiter remuer // *vi* (*loose screw etc*) branler; (*worm*) se tortiller.

wild [waɪld] *a* sauvage; (*sea*) déchaîné(e); (*idea, life*) fou(folle); extravagant(e); ~**s** *npl* régions *fpl* sauvages; ~**erness** ['wɪldənɪs] *n* désert *m*, région *f* sauvage; ~**-goose chase** *n* (*fig*) fausse piste; ~**life** *n* faune *f*; ~**ly** *ad* (*applaud*) frénétiquement; (*hit, guess*) au hasard; (*happy*) follement.

wilful ['wɪlful] *a* (*person*) obstiné(e); (*action*) délibéré(e); (*crime*) prémédité(e).

will [wɪl] *auxiliary vb*: **he ~ come** il viendra // *vt* (*pt, pp* **~ed**): **to ~ sb to do** souhaiter ardemment que qn fasse; **he ~ed himself to go on** par un suprême effort de volonté, il continua // *n* volonté *f*; testament *m*; **~ing** *a* de bonne volonté, serviable; **he's ~ing to do it** il est disposé à le faire, il veut bien le faire; **~ingly** *ad* volontiers; **~ingness** *n* bonne volonté.

willow ['wɪləu] *n* saule *m*.

will power ['wɪlpauə*] *n* volonté *f*.

wilt [wɪlt] *vi* dépérir.

wily ['waɪlɪ] *a* rusé(e).

win [wɪn] *n* (*in sports etc*) victoire *f* // *vb* (*pt, pp* **won** [wʌn]) *vt* (*battle, money*) gagner; (*prize*) remporter; (*popularity*) acquérir // *vi* gagner; **to ~ over, ~ round** *vt* gagner, se concilier.

wince [wɪns] *n* tressaillement *m* // *vi* tressaillir.

winch [wɪntʃ] *n* treuil *m*.

wind *n* [wɪnd] (*also MED*) vent *m* // *vb* (*pt, pp* **wound** [waund]) *vt* enrouler; (*wrap*) envelopper; (*clock, toy*) remonter; (*take breath away*: [wɪnd]) couper le souffle à // *vi* (*road, river*) serpenter; **the ~(s)** (*MUS*) les instruments *mpl* à vent; **to ~ up** *vt* (*clock*) remonter; (*debate*) terminer, clôturer; **~break** *n* brise-vent *m inv*; **~fall** *n* coup *m* de chance; **~ing** *a* (*road*) sinueux(euse); (*staircase*) tournant(e); **~ instrument** *n* (*MUS*) instrument *m* à vent; **~mill** *n* moulin *m* à vent.

window ['wɪndəu] *n* fenêtre *f*; (*in car, train, also*: **~ pane**) vitre *f*; (*in shop etc*) vitrine *f*; **~ box** *n* jardinière *f*; **~ cleaner** *n* (*person*) laveur/euse de vitres; **~ frame** *n* châssis *m* de fenêtre; **~ ledge** *n* rebord *m* de la fenêtre; **~ pane** *n* vitre *f*, carreau *m*; **~sill** *n* (*inside*) appui *m* de la fenêtre; (*outside*) rebord *m* de la fenêtre.

windpipe ['wɪndpaɪp] *n* gosier *m*.

windscreen, **windshield** (*US*) ['wɪndskriːn, 'wɪndʃiːld] *n* pare-brise *m inv*; **~ washer** *n* lave-glace *m inv*; **~ wiper** *n* essuie-glace *m inv*.

windswept ['wɪndswɛpt] *a* balayé(e) par le vent.

windy ['wɪndɪ] *a* venté(e), venteux(euse); **it's ~** il y a du vent.

wine [waɪn] *n* vin *m*; **~ cellar** *n* cave *f* à vins, **~ glass** *n* verre *m* à vin; **~ list** *n* carte *f* des vins; **~ merchant** *n* marchand/e de vins; **~ tasting** *n* dégustation *f* (de vins); **~ waiter** *n* sommelier *m*.

wing [wɪŋ] *n* aile *f*; (*in air force*) groupe *m* d'escadrilles; **~s** *npl* (*THEATRE*) coulisses *fpl*; **~er** *n* (*SPORT*) ailier *m*.

wink [wɪŋk] *n* clin *m* d'œil // *vi* faire un clin d'œil; (*blink*) cligner des yeux.

winner ['wɪnə*] *n* gagnant/e.

winning ['wɪnɪŋ] *a* (*team*) gagnant(e); (*goal*) décisif(ive); **~s** *npl* gains *mpl*; **~ post** *n* poteau *m* d'arrivée.

winter ['wɪntə*] *n* hiver *m* // *vi* hiverner; **~ sports** *npl* sports *mpl* d'hiver.

wintry ['wɪntrɪ] *a* hivernal(e).

wipe [waɪp] *n* coup *m* de torchon (*or* de chiffon *or* d'éponge) // *vt* essuyer; **to ~ off** *vt* essuyer; **to ~ out** *vt* (*debt*) régler; (*memory*) oublier; (*destroy*) anéantir; **to ~ up** *vt* essuyer.

wire ['waɪə*] *n* fil *m* (de fer); (*ELEC*) fil électrique; (*TEL*) télégramme *m* // *vt* (*fence*) grillager; (*house*) faire l'installation électrique de; (*also*: **~ up**) brancher; **~ brush** *n* brosse *f* métallique.

wireless ['waɪəlɪs] *n* télégraphie *f* sans fil; (*set*) T.S.F. *f*.

wiry ['waɪərɪ] *a* noueux(euse), nerveux(euse).

wisdom ['wɪzdəm] *n* sagesse *f*; (*of action*) prudence *f*; **~ tooth** *n* dent *f* de sagesse.

wise [waɪz] *a* sage, prudent(e), judicieux(euse).

...wise [waɪz] *suffix*: **time~** en ce qui concerne le temps, question temps.

wisecrack ['waɪzkræk] *n* sarcasme *m*.

wish [wɪʃ] *n* (*desire,*) désir *m*; (*specific desire*) souhait *m*, vœu *m* // *vt* souhaiter, désirer, vouloir; **best ~es** (*on birthday etc*) meilleurs vœux; **with best ~es** (*in letter*) bien amicalement; **give her my best ~es** faites-lui mes amitiés; **to ~ sb goodbye** dire au revoir à qn; **he ~ed me well** il me souhaitait de réussir; **to ~ to do/sb to do** désirer *or* vouloir faire/que qn fasse; **to ~ for** souhaiter; **it's ~ful thinking** c'est prendre ses désirs pour des réalités.

wisp [wɪsp] *n* fine mèche (de cheveux); (*of smoke*) mince volute *f*; **a ~ of straw** un fétu de paille.

wistful ['wɪstful] *a* mélancolique.

wit [wɪt] *n* (*gen pl*) intelligence *f*, esprit *m*; présence *f* d'esprit; (*wittiness*) esprit; (*person*) homme/femme d'esprit; **to be at one's ~s' end** (*fig*) ne plus savoir que faire; **to ~ ad** à savoir.

witch [wɪtʃ] *n* sorcière *f*; **~craft** *n* sorcellerie *f*.

with [wɪð, wɪθ] *prep* avec; **red ~ anger** rouge de colère; **the man ~ the grey hat** l'homme au chapeau gris; **to be ~ it** (*fig*) être dans le vent; **I am ~ you** (*I understand*) je vous suis.

withdraw [wɪθ'drɔː] *vb* (*irg*) *vt* retirer // *vi* se retirer; (*go back on promise*) se rétracter; **~al** *n* retrait *m*; (*MED*) état *m* de manque.

wither ['wɪðə*] *vi* se faner; **~ed** *a* fané(e), flétri(e); (*limb*) atrophié(e).

withhold [wɪθ'həuld] *vt irg* (*money*) retenir; (*decision*) remettre; (*permission*): **to ~ (from)** refuser (à); (*information*): **to ~ (from)** cacher (à).

within [wɪð'ɪn] *prep* à l'intérieur de // *ad* à l'intérieur; **~ sight of** en vue de; **~ a mile of** à moins d'un mille de; **~ the week** avant la fin de la semaine.

without [wɪð'aut] *prep* sans.

withstand [wɪθ'stænd] *vt irg* résister à.

witness ['wɪtnɪs] *n* (*person*) témoin *m*; (*evidence*) témoignage *m* // *vt* (*event*) être témoin de; (*document*) attester l'authenticité de; **to bear ~ to sth** témoigner de qch; **~ box, ~ stand** (*US*) *n* barre *f* des témoins.

witticism ['wɪtɪsɪzm] *n* mot *m* d'esprit.
witty ['wɪtɪ] *a* spirituel(le), plein(e) d'esprit.
wives [waɪvz] *npl of* **wife**.
wizard ['wɪzəd] *n* magicien *m*.
wk *abbr of* **week**.
wobble ['wɔbl] *vi* trembler; (*chair*) branler.
woe [wəu] *n* malheur *m*.
woke [wəuk] *pt*; **~n** *pp of* **wake**.
wolf, wolves [wulf, wulvz] *n* loup *m*.
woman, *pl* **women** ['wumən, 'wɪmɪn] *n* femme *f*; **~ doctor** *n* femme *f* médecin; **~ly** *a* féminin(e); **~ teacher** *n* professeur *m* femme *f*.
womb [wu:m] *n* (*ANAT*) utérus *m*.
women ['wɪmɪn] *npl of* **woman**.
won [wʌn] *pt,pp of* **win**.
wonder ['wʌndə*] *n* merveille *f*, miracle *m*; (*feeling*) émerveillement *m* // *vi*: **to ~ whether** se demander si; **to ~ at** s'étonner de; s'émerveiller de; **to ~ about** songer à; **it's no ~ that** il n'est pas étonnant que **+ *sub***; **~ful** *a* merveilleux(euse); **~fully** *ad* (*+ adjective*) merveilleusement; (*+ vb*) à merveille.
wonky ['wɔŋkɪ] *a* (*col*) qui ne va *or* ne marche pas très bien.
won't [wəunt] = **will not**.
woo [wu:] *vt* (*woman*) faire la cour à.
wood [wud] *n* (*timber, forest*) bois *m*; **~ carving** *n* sculpture *f* en *or* sur bois; **~ed** *a* boisé(e); **~en** *a* en bois; (*fig*) raide; inexpressif(ive); **~pecker** *n* pic *m* (*oiseau*); **~wind** *n* (*MUS*) bois *m*; the **~wind** (*MUS*) les bois; **~work** *n* menuiserie *f*; **~worm** *n* ver *m* du bois.
wool [wul] *n* laine *f*; **to pull the ~ over sb's eyes** (*fig*) en faire accroire à qn; **~len, ~en** (*US*) *a* de laine; (*industry*) lainier(ère); **~lens** *npl* lainages *mpl*; **~ly, ~y** (*US*) *a* laineux(euse); (*fig: ideas*) confus(e).
word [wə:d] *n* mot *m*; (*spoken*) mot, parole *f*; (*promise*) parole; (*news*) nouvelles *fpl* // *vt* rédiger, formuler; **in other ~s** en d'autres termes; **to break/keep one's ~** manquer à/tenir sa parole; **I'll take your ~ for it** je vous crois sur parole; **to send ~ of** prévenir de; **~ing** *n* termes *mpl*; langage *m*; **~y** *a* verbeux(euse).
wore [wɔ:*] *pt of* **wear**.
work [wə:k] *n* travail *m*; (*ART, LITERATURE*) œuvre *f* // *vi* travailler; (*mechanism*) marcher, fonctionner; (*plan etc*) marcher; (*medicine*) faire son effet // *vt* (*clay, wood etc*) travailler; (*mine etc*) exploiter; (*machine*) faire marcher *or* fonctionner; **to be out of ~** être au chômage; **~s** *n* (*factory*) usine *f* // *npl* (*of clock, machine*) mécanisme *m*; **Minister/Ministry of W~s** ministre *m*/ministère *m* des Travaux publics; **to ~ loose** *vi* se défaire, se desserrer; **to ~ on** *vt fus* travailler à; (*principle*) se baser sur; **to ~ out** *vi* (*plans etc*) marcher // *vt* (*problem*) résoudre; (*plan*) élaborer; **it ~s out at £100** ça fait 100 livres; **to get ~ed up** se mettre dans tous ses états; **~able** *a* (*solution*) réalisable; **~er** *n* travailleur/euse, ouvrier/ère; **~ing class** *n* classe ouvrière; **~ing-class** *a* ouvrier(ère);

~ing man *n* travailleur *m*; **in ~ing order** en état de marche; **~man** *n* ouvrier *m*; **~manship** *n* métier *m*, habileté *f*; facture *f*; **~shop** *n* atelier *m*; **~-to-rule** *n* grève *f* du zèle.
world [wə:ld] *n* monde *m* // *cpd* (*champion*) du monde; (*power, war*) mondial(e); **to think the ~ of sb** (*fig*) ne jurer que par qn; **out of this ~** *a* extraordinaire; **~ly** *a* de ce monde; **~wide** *a* universel(le).
worm [wə:m] *n* ver *m*.
worn [wɔ:n] *pp of* **wear** // *a* usé(e); **~out** *a* (*object*) complètement usé(e); (*person*) épuisé(e).
worried ['wʌrɪd] *a* inquiet(ète).
worrier ['wʌrɪə*] *n* inquiet/ète.
worry ['wʌrɪ] *n* souci *m* // *vt* inquiéter // *vi* s'inquiéter, se faire du souci; **~ing** *a* inquiétant(e).
worse [wə:s] *a* pire, plus mauvais(e) // *ad* plus mal // *n* pire *m*; **a change for the ~** une détérioration; **~n** *vt,vi* empirer; **~ off** *a* moins à l'aise financièrement; (*fig*): **you'll be ~ off this way** ça ira moins bien de cette façon.
worship ['wə:ʃɪp] *n* culte *m* // *vt* (*God*) rendre un culte à; (*person*) adorer; **Your W~** (*to mayor*) Monsieur le Maire; (*to judge*) Monsieur le Juge; **~per** *n* adorateur/trice; (*in church*) fidèle *m/f*.
worst [wə:st] *a* le(la) pire, le(la) plus mauvais(e) // *ad* le plus mal // *n* pire *m*; **at ~** au pis aller.
worsted ['wustɪd] *n*: (*wool*) **~ laine** peignée.
worth [wə:θ] *n* valeur *f* // *a*: **to be ~** valoir; **it's ~ it** cela en vaut la peine; **50 pence ~ of apples** (pour) 50 pence de pommes; **~less** *a* qui ne vaut rien; **~while** *a* (*activity*) qui en vaut la peine; (*cause*) louable; **a ~while book** un livre qui vaut la peine d'être lu.
worthy [wə:ðɪ] *a* (*person*) digne; (*motive*) louable; **~ of** digne de.
would [wud] *auxiliary vb*: **she ~ come** elle viendrait; **he ~ have come** il serait venu; **~ you like a biscuit?** voulez-vous *or* voudriez-vous un biscuit?; **he ~ go there on Mondays** il y allait le lundi; **~-be** *a* (*pej*) soi-disant.
wound *vb* [waund] *pt, pp of* **wind** // *n,vt* [wu:nd] *n* blessure *f* // *vt* blesser; **~ed in the leg** blessé à la jambe.
wove [wəuv] *pt of* **weave**; **~n** *pp of* **weave**.
wrangle ['ræŋgl] *n* dispute *f* // *vi* se disputer.
wrap [ræp] *n* (*stole*) écharpe *f*; (*cape*) pèlerine *f* // *vt* (*also*: **~ up**) envelopper; **~per** *n* (*of book*) couverture *f*; **~ping paper** *n* papier *m* d'emballage; (*for gift*) papier cadeau.
wrath [rɔθ] *n* courroux *m*.
wreath, ~s [ri:θ, ri:ðz] *n* couronne *f*.
wreck [rɛk] *n* (*sea disaster*) naufrage *m*; (*ship*) épave *f*; (*pej: person*) loque humaine // *vt* démolir; (*ship*) provoquer le naufrage de; (*fig*) briser, ruiner; **~age** *n* débris *mpl*; (*of building*) décombres *mpl*; (*of ship*) épave *f*.

wren [rɛn] n (ZOOL) roitelet m.

wrench [rɛntʃ] n (TECH) clé f (à écrous); (tug) violent mouvement de torsion; (fig) arrachement m // vt tirer violemment sur, tordre; to ~ sth from arracher qch (violemment) à or de.

wrestle ['rɛsl] vi: to ~ (with sb) lutter (avec qn); to ~ with (fig) se débattre avec, lutter contre; ~r n lutteur/euse; **wrestling** n lutte f; (also: all-in wrestling) catch m; wrestling match n rencontre f de lutte (or de catch).

wretched ['rɛtʃɪd] a misérable; (col) maudit(e).

wriggle ['rɪgl] n tortillement m // vi se tortiller.

wring, pt, pp **wrung** [rɪŋ, rʌŋ] vt tordre; (wet clothes) essorer; (fig): to ~ sth out of arracher qch à.

wrinkle ['rɪŋkl] n (on skin) ride f; (on paper etc) pli m // vt rider, plisser // vi se plisser.

wrist [rɪst] n poignet m; ~ **watch** n montre-bracelet f.

writ [rɪt] n acte m judiciaire; to issue a ~ against sb assigner qn en justice.

write, pt **wrote**, pp **written** [raɪt, rəut, 'rɪtn] vt, vi écrire; to ~ **down** vt noter; (put in writing) mettre par écrit; to ~ **off** vt (debt) passer aux profits et pertes; (depreciate) amortir; to ~ **out** vt écrire; (copy) recopier; to ~ **up** vt rédiger; ~-**off** n perte totale; the car is a ~-**off** la voiture est bonne pour la casse; ~**r** n auteur m, écrivain m.

writhe [raɪð] vi se tordre.

writing ['raɪtɪŋ] n écriture f; (of author) œuvres fpl; **in** ~ par écrit; ~ **paper** n papier m à lettres.

written ['rɪtn] pp of **write**.

wrong [rɔŋ] a faux(fausse); (incorrectly chosen: number, road etc) mauvais(e); (not suitable) qui ne convient pas; (wicked) mal; (unfair) injuste // ad faux // n tort m // vt faire du tort à, léser; **you are** ~ to do it tu as tort de le faire; **you are** ~ **about that, you've got it** ~ tu te trompes; **to be in the** ~ avoir tort; **what's** ~? qu'est-ce qui ne va pas?; **to go** ~ (person) se tromper; (plan) mal tourner; (machine) tomber en panne; ~**ful** a injustifié(e); ~**ly** ad à tort; ~ **side** n (of cloth) envers m.

wrote [rəut] pt of **write**.

wrought [rɔ:t] a: ~ **iron** fer forgé.

wrung [rʌŋ] pt, pp of **wring**.

wry [raɪ] a désabusé(e).

wt. abbr of **weight**.

X Y Z

Xmas ['ɛksməs] n abbr of **Christmas**.

X-ray [ɛks'reɪ] n rayon m X; (photograph) radio(graphie) f // vt radiographier.

xylophone ['zaɪləfəun] n xylophone m.

yacht [jɔt] n yacht m; voilier m; ~**ing** n yachting m, navigation f de plaisance; ~**sman** n yacht(s)man m.

Yank [jæŋk] n (pej) Amerloque m/f.

yap [jæp] vi (dog) japper.

yard [jɑ:d] n (of house etc) cour f; (measure) yard m (= 914 mm; 3 feet); ~**stick** n (fig) mesure f, critère m.

yarn [jɑ:n] n fil m; (tale) longue histoire.

yawn [jɔ:n] n bâillement m // vi bâiller; ~**ing** a (gap) béant(e).

yd. abbr of **yard(s)**.

year [jɪə*] n an m, année f; **every** ~ tous les ans, chaque année; **to be 8** ~**s old** avoir 8 ans; ~**ly** a annuel(le) // ad annuellement.

yearn [jə:n] vi: **to** ~ **for sth/to do** aspirer à qch/à faire, languir après qch; ~**ing** n désir ardent, envie f.

yeast [ji:st] n levure f.

yell [jɛl] n hurlement m, cri m // vi hurler.

yellow ['jɛləu] a, n jaune (m); ~ **fever** n fièvre f jaune.

yelp [jɛlp] n jappement m; glapissement m // vi japper; glapir.

yeoman ['jəumən] n: **Y**~ **of the Guard** hallebardier m de la garde royale.

yes [jɛs] ad oui; (answering negative question) si // n oui m.

yesterday ['jɛstədɪ] ad,n hier (m).

yet [jɛt] ad encore; déjà // cj pourtant, néanmoins; **it is not finished** ~ ce n'est pas encore fini or toujours pas fini; **must you go just** ~? dois-tu déjà partir?; **the best** ~ le meilleur jusqu'ici or jusque-là; **as** ~ jusqu'ici, encore; **a few days** ~ encore quelques jours.

yew [ju:] n if m.

Yiddish ['jɪdɪʃ] n yiddish m.

yield [ji:ld] n production f, rendement m; rapport m // vt produire, rendre, rapporter; (surrender) céder // vi céder.

yodel ['jəudl] vi faire des tyroliennes, jodler.

yoga ['jəugə] n yoga m.

yog(h)ourt, yog(h)urt ['jəugət] n yaourt m.

yoke [jəuk] n joug m.

yolk [jəuk] n jaune m (d'œuf).

yonder ['jɔndə*] ad là(-bas).

you [ju:] pronoun tu; (polite form) vous; (pl) vous; (complement) te, t' + vowel; vous; (stressed) toi; vous; (one): **fresh air does** ~ **good** l'air frais fait du bien; ~ **never know** on ne sait jamais.

you'd [ju:d] = **you had**; **you would**.

you'll [ju:l] = **you will**; **you shall**.

young [jʌŋ] a jeune // npl (of animal) petits mpl; (people): **the** ~ les jeunes, la jeunesse; ~**ish** a assez jeune; ~**ster** n jeune m (garçon m); (child) enfant m/f.

your [jɔ:*] a ton(ta), pl tes; votre, pl vos.

you're [juə*] = **you are**.

yours [jɔ:z] pronoun le(la) tien(ne), les tiens(tiennes); le(la) vôtre, les vôtres; **is it** ~? c'est à toi (or à vous)?; **yours sincerely/faithfully** je vous prie d'agréer l'expression de mes sentiments les meilleurs/mes sentiments respectueux or dévoués.

yourself [jɔ:'sɛlf] pronoun (reflexive) te; vous; (after prep) toi; vous; (emphatic) toi-même; vous-même; **yourselves** pl pronoun vous; (emphatic) vous mêmes.

youth [ju:θ] n jeunesse f; (young man: pl ~**s** [ju:ðz]) jeune homme m; ~**ful** a jeune ; de jeunesse ; juvénile ; ~ hostel n auberge f de jeunesse.

you've [ju:v] = you have.

Yugoslav ['ju:gəu'slɑ:v] a yougoslave // n Yougoslave m/f.

Yugoslavia ['ju:gəu'slɑ:viə] n Yougoslavie f.

Yule [ju:l]: ~ log n bûche f de Noël.

zany ['zeɪnɪ] a farfelu(e), loufoque.

zeal [zi:l] n zèle m, ferveur f; empressement m ; ~ous ['zɛləs] a zélé(e) ; empressé(e).

zebra ['zi:brə] n zèbre m ; ~ crossing n passage m pour piétons.

zenith ['zɛnɪθ] n zénith m.

zero ['zɪərəu] n zéro m ; ~ hour n l'heure f H.

zest [zɛst] n entrain m, élan m ; zeste m.

zigzag ['zɪgzæg] n zigzag m // vi zigzaguer, faire des zigzags.

zinc [zɪŋk] n zinc m.

Zionism ['zaɪənɪzm] n sionisme m.

zip [zip] n (also: ~ fastener, ~per) fermeture f éclair ® // vt (also: ~ up) fermer avec une fermeture éclair ®.

zither ['zɪðə*] n cithare f.

zodiac ['zəudɪæk] n zodiaque m.

zombie ['zɔmbɪ] n (fig): like a ~ l'air complètement dans les vapes, avec l'air d'un mort vivant.

zone [zəun] n zone f ; (subdivision of town) secteur m.

zoo [zu:] n zoo m.

zoological [zuə'lɔdʒɪkl] a zoologique.

zoologist [zu:'ɔlədʒɪst] n zoologiste m/f.

zoology [zu:'ɔlədʒɪ] n zoologie f.

zoom [zu:m] vi: to ~ past passer en trombe ; ~ lens n zoom m, objectif m à focale variable.

NOTES TO THE USER OF THIS DICTIONARY

I. Using the dictionary

In using this book, you will either want to check the meaning of a French word you don't know, or find the French for an English word. These two operations are quite different, and so are the problems you may face when using one side of the dictionary or the other. In order to help you, we have tried to explain below the main features of this book.

The 'wordlist' is the alphabetical list of all the items in large bold type, ie. all the 'headwords'. Each 'entry', or article, is introduced by a headword, and may contain additional 'references' in smaller bold type, such as phrases, derivatives, and compound words. Section 1. below deals with the way references are listed.

The typography distinguishes between three broad categories of text within the dictionary. All items in bold type, large or smaller, are 'source language' references, for which an equivalence in the other language is provided. All items in standard type are translations. Items in italics are information about the words being translated, ie. either labels, or 'signposts' pinpointing the appropriate translation, or explanations.

1. *Where to look for a word*

1.1 Derivatives

In order to save space, a number of derivatives have been listed within entries, provided this does not break alphabetical order. Thus, **pensionnaire** and **pensionnat** are listed within the entry for **pension,** or **caller** and **calling** under **call.** You must remember this when looking for a word you don't find listed as a headword. These derivatives are always listed last within an entry (see also I.2 on entry layout).

1.2 Homographs

Homographs are words which are spelt in exactly the same way, like French **boucher** (to block) and **boucher** (butcher), or English **fine** (nice etc) and **fine** (penalty). As a rule, in order to save space, such words have been treated as one headword only. In the very few cases where this was not possible, either a cross-reference is given (see **pas,** in the French wordlist), or else the presence of a feminine form helps distinguish between two consecutive homograph entries (**boulot** vs **boulot,-te, vu** vs **vu,-e** vs **vue**).

1.3 Phrases

Because of the constraints of space, there can be only a limited number of idiomatic phrases in a pocket dictionary like this one. Particular emphasis is given to verbal phrases like **mettre au point, mettre à jour, prendre feu, faire feu, faire du feu**, etc, and also to basic constructions (see for instance the entries for **apply, agree, apprendre, moment**).

Verbal phrases with the ten or so basic verbs like *faire, mettre, prendre*, etc. are listed under the noun. Other phrases and idioms are listed under the first key word (ie. not a preposition), for instance **filer doux** under **filer**, **d'emblée** under **emblée**.

1.4 Abbreviations and proper names

For easier reference, abbreviations, acronyms and proper names have been listed alphabetically in the wordlist, as opposed to being relegated to the appendices. **M.O.T.** is used in every way like **certificate** or **permit**, **R.E.R.** like **métro**, and these words are treated like other nouns.

1.5 Compounds

Housewife, bicycle track, pare-chocs and **pomme de terre** are all compounds. One-word compounds like 'housewife' are no problem as regards consulting the dictionary, since they can appear only in one place and in strict alphabetical order. When it comes to other compounds, however – hyphenated compounds and compounds made up of separate words – each language presents its own peculiar problems.

1.5.1 French compounds

There are many compounds made up of two or more 'words'. When it comes to checking a French compound, you might not be aware that you are dealing with a compound and not a string of autonomous words, and there might inevitably be some toing and froing between entries.

As spelling is quite set in French, we have listed French compounds under the first word, and grouped them alphabetically within that entry. For instance, **cour martiale** is within the entry for **cour** and comes before the headword **courage**. **Fête mobile** is within the entry for **fête**, and comes before **Fête-Dieu** and **fêter** at the end of the same entry (see also section 2.). Remember that the meaning of a phrase or of a compound can be quite different from that of its elements taken separately, so be prepared to check through an entry thoroughly before giving up.

1.5.2 French 'verbes pronominaux'

Verbs like **se rappeler, se noyer, se promener, s'arroger** are called 'pronominaux' in French because they are used with a 'pronom personnel': je *me* rappelle, tu *te* promènes etc. They must be distinguished from truly reflexive or reciprocal uses like 'il *se* regarde dans la glace' (he is looking *at himself* in the mirror) and 'ils *se* regardaient sans rien dire' (they were looking *at each other* in silence). The 'verbes pronominaux' are intransitive or transitive verbs in their own right: 'se promener' is intransitive like 'flâner', and 's'arroger' transitive in the same way as 'prendre'.

There are no such verbs in English (which has another type of 'compound verb', the phrasal verb, see 1.5.4), where a verb used with 'oneself' is as a rule truly reflexive. Compare for instance the translations for **se noyer** (accidentellement) and **se noyer** (suicide). These verbs have been listed as phrases under the entry for the key word. See for instance the entries for **rappeler, rapporter, ingénier.**

1.5.3 English compounds

Here there is a problem of where to find a compound because of less predictable spelling than is the case with French: is it **airgun, air-gun** or **air gun**? This is why we choose to list them according to strict alphabetical order. Thus **tea set** comes between **tease** and **teashop**. The entries between **tax** and **technical** will provide a good illustration of the system of listing. It has drawbacks, for instance in that **tax-free** and **tax-payer** are separated by **taxi, taxidermist** and three 'taxi' compounds. However, in a short dictionary used by beginners, it has the merit of simplicity and consistency.

1.5.4 English 'phrasal verbs'

'Phrasal verbs' are verbs like **go off, blow up, cut down** etc. Here you have the advantage of knowing that these words belong together, whereas it will take the foreign user some time before he can identify these verbs immediately. They have been listed under the entry for the basic verb (eg. **go, blow, cut**), grouped alphabetically before any other derivative or compound – eg. **pull up** comes before **pulley**. For instance, look up **to back out, to look up** (a word), **to look out.**

1.6 Irregular forms

When looking up a French word, you may not immediately find the form you are looking for, although the word in question has been duly entered in the dictionary. This is possibly because you are looking up an irregular noun or verb form, and these are not always given as entries in their own right. Obviously we have assumed that you know the basics regarding French verb forms, noun plurals and feminine forms. Thus you will be expected to know that 'chantent' is a form of the verb **chanter**, chevaux the plural of **cheval**, and so on. However, in order to help you, we have included the main irregular forms as entries in their own right, with a cross-reference to the basic form.

Thus, if you come across the word 'buvais' and attempt to look up a verb 'buver', you won't find it but what you will find at that place in the wordlist, between **butte** and **buvard,** is the entry **buvais** *etc vb voir* **boire.**

Similarly, **fausse,** and **fasse** are cross-referred to *faux* and *faire* respectively. With past participles, it sometimes happens that in addition to the purely verbal form there is an adjectival or noun use, for instance **connu** or **meublé**. These usages are translated as autonomous words, but they are also cross-referred to the verb whenever appropriate (see for instance entries for **couvert or assis**).

2. *Entry layout*

All entries, however long or complex, are arranged in a very systematic manner. But it may be a little difficult at first to find one's way through an entry like **passer, back, round** or **run** because homographs are grouped together (see 1.2) and the text is run on without any breakdown into paragraphs, in order to save space. Ease of reference comes with practice, but the guidelines below will make it easier for you.

2.1 'Signposting'

If you look up a French word and find a string of quite different English translations, you are unlikely to have much trouble finding out which is the relevant one for the context, because you know what the English words mean, and the context will almost automatically rule out unsuitable translations.

It is quite a different matter when you want to find the French for, say, **lock,** in the context 'we got to the lock around lunchtime', and are faced with an entry that reads 'lock: serrure (f); écluse (f); mèche (f), boucle (f)'. Obviously you can then go to the other side and check what each translation means. But this is time-consuming, and it doesn't always work. This is why we have provided the user with signposts which pinpoint the relevant translation. For instance with **lock,** the entry reads: ... *(of door, box)* serrure *f*; *(of canal)* écluse *f*; *(of hair)* mèche *f*, boucle *f* ...

For the context suggested above, it is now clear that 'écluse' is the right word.

2.2 Grammatical categories and meaning categories

Complex entries are first broken down into grammatical categories, eg.:
lock *n // vt // vi*. Be prepared to go through entries like **run** or **back**
carefully, and you will find how useful all these 'signposts' are. Each
grammatical category is then split where appropriate into the various
meanings, eg.:

> **lock** *n (of door, box)* serrure *f; (of canal)* écluse *f; (of
> hair)* mèche *f*, boucle *f // vt (with key)* fermer à clé;
> *(immobilize)* bloquer *// vi (door etc)* fermer à clé;
> *(wheels)* se bloquer.

3. *Using the translations*

3.1 Gender

All feminine endings for French adjectives have been given on the
English-French side. This may appear to duplicate information given on
the other side, but we feel it is a useful reminder where and when it
matters. The feminine version is given for words like **driver, teacher,
research worker** etc. Remember that the French equivalents of **his,
her, its** or **the** do not behave like their English counterparts: see
section II for more information.

3.2 Plural

We have assumed knowledge on the part of the user of plural formation
in French (see section II), including the plural of compounds. A form
like 'yeux' is given (see entry for **eye**), but in the main, plural forms are
not shown.

3.3 Verb forms

Irregular French verbs appearing as translations have not been marked
as such, and the user should refer to the French verb tables when in
doubt (pp. 507–514).

3.4 Colloquial language

You should as a rule proceed with great caution when handling foreign
language which has a degree of informality. When an English word or
phrase has been labelled *(col)*, ie. colloquial, you must assume that the
translation belongs to a similar level of informality. If the translation is
followed by (!) you should handle it with extreme care, or best avoid it
unless you are with close friends!

3.5 'Grammatical words'

It is exceedingly difficult to give adequate treatment for words like **for, away, whose, which, out, off** etc. in a short dictionary such as this one. We have tried to go some way towards providing as much relevant information as possible regarding the most frequent uses of these words. However, for further information use a good monolingual dictionary of French, especially one for foreign learners, and a good modern French grammar.

3.6 'Approximate' translations and cultural equivalents

It is not always possible to give a genuine translation, when for instance an English word denotes a thing or institution which either does not exist in France, or is quite different. Therefore, only an approximate equivalence can be given, or else an explanation. See for instance **whip, shadow cabinet, C.I.D.**, and on the French-English side **hémicycle, R.E.R., rosette.**

3.7 Alternative translations

As a rule, translations separated by commas can be regarded as broadly interchangeable for the meaning indicated. Translations separated by a semi-colon are not interchangeable and when in doubt you should consult either a larger bilingual dictionary such as the Collins-Robert French dictionary, or a good monolingual French dictionary. You will find however that there are very few cases of translations separated by a semi-colon without an intervening 'signpost'.

II. Notes on French grammar

When you are first confronted with French at school, or if you happen to be at a business meeting where you are the only one speaking little or no French, it may seem to you that French is very different from English. On the other hand, if you stand back and consider a wider range of related and unrelated languages, French can look very close to English.

We have tried here to show some of the main differences, especially with the beginner and the dictionary user in mind, without dwelling on subtleties or aspects of French that are broadly similar to English. Among the greatest obstacles for the beginner are gender, verb forms and tenses, the position of adjectives, the use of prepositions and of course the sounds of French.

1. *Nouns and 'satellite' words (articles, adjectives)*

1.1 Gender

One of the basic differences: 'the table and the knife', but '**la** table et **le** couteau'. Largely unpredictable, this business of gender must be learned as a feature to be remembered with each new word. It is most important to get the article right, and of course the agreement of adjectives and past participles: '**la vieille** maison et **le vieux** chalet'. See also 1.4 (possessive adjectives).

1.2 Articles: le, la, un, du, des etc.

Apart from the problem of gender, there is the question of whether the article is used or not, and French does not always follow the English pattern. For instance you say 'I like wine' but the French say 'j'aime **le** vin'. Conversely, 'my father is a publisher' but 'mon père est éditeur'.

1.2.1 'le, la, les'

(a) In almost all cases where 'the' is not used in English, the article must be used in French. For instance:

apples are good for you   **les** pommes sont bonnes pour la santé
salmon is expensive   **le** saumon est cher
love is not enough   **l'**amour ne suffit pas
he won't stand laziness   il ne tolère pas **la** paresse
France is beautiful   **la** France est belle
he likes skiing   il aime **le** ski

NB. A few names of countries are used without the article in French, like Cuba or Madagascar, Chypre, Malte, Jersey.

(b) use of 'le/la' with parts of the body

Where the possessive is used in English, 'le/la' tends to be used in French (sometimes together with a pronoun):

I broke **my** leg   je **me** suis cassé **la** jambe
Put up **your** hand   levez **la** main
He trod on **my** foot   il **m'**a marché sur **le** pied

(c) à + le, de + le

Remember the contracted forms (shown in the dictionary under **à** and **de**): je vais **au** cinéma, le parapet **du** pont.

1.2.2 'un, une, des'

(a) In structures of the type 'with incredible courage', the article 'un/une' is used in French:

He showed incredible coolness   il a fait preuve d'**un** sang-froid incroyable
A film in appallingly bad taste   un film d'**un** mauvais goût désolant

(b) On the other hand, this article is not used in French in structures equivalent to 'my father is a teacher':

my sister is a nurse   ma sœur est infirmière
he is a sailor's son   il est fils de marin (or: c'est **un** fils de marin, c'est le fils d'un marin)

But this only applies with names of professions and crafts:

his brother is an idiot   son frère est un imbécile

my sister is a very liberated young lady   ma sœur est une jeune fille très émancipée

(c) 'without a pen', 'without bread': no article in French

Where the English uses the article with a so-called 'countable' noun (like 'hat' as opposed to 'milk' or 'water' or 'bread'), the French doesn't: 'sans plume, on ne peut pas écrire', 'un repas sans pain'.

(d) 'des'

Remember to use 'des' in the plural, although there may be no article in English:

friends from Paris have arrived   **des** amis de Paris sont arrivés

1.2.3 'du, de la, des', 'de' = 'some', 'any'

Remember not to confuse 'du' as in 'le titre du livre' and 'du' as in 'j'aimerais du pain' (see entry **de**). Where you have 'some' or 'any' or sometimes nothing in English, the French use 'du' etc., as shown below:

je veux du pain   I want some bread

veux-tu du pain/de la soupe/des cigarettes? Would you like any (or some) bread/soup/cigarettes?

je ne veux pas de pain/soupe/cigarettes   I don't want any bread/soup/
cigarettes

1.3   Adjectives

Apart from the question of gender (subtil-subtile *but* utile, etc.), the
main difficulty is the position of adjectives. As a general rule, they follow
the noun (des plantes marines, un repas délicieux, des volets rouges).
Some adjectives or types of adjectives will always go after the noun (une
maison délabrée, des plantes marines, une robe rouge). Some can also
come before the noun for stylistic effect, without any change in meaning
(un délicieux repas). A few others will usually or always go before the
noun.

Among adjectives usually found before the noun are 'petit, grand,
haut, long, gros; vieux, jeune; bon, mauvais, joli; nouveau, ancien'.
Some like 'premier' are not found after the noun (except maybe in the
odd set phrase). Others like 'brave' or 'ancien' will be found in either
position, but with different meanings. The dictionary makes these
different meanings clear.

1.4   Possessives

1.4.1   Son/sa, mon/ma, ton/ta *vs* his/her/its, my, your

Contrary to what happens in English, the possessive varies according to
the gender of the noun it qualifies. Whether the owner is male or female,
it will be **sa** valise and **son** parapluie. There is no such difference in the
plural: **ses** valises et **ses** parapluies.

1.4.2   Le mien, la mienne, les miens, les miennes etc. *vs* mine etc.

Here again, the form of the possessive depends on the gender and
number of the qualified noun (ie. 'hers' will be **la sienne** if a car – la
voiture – is being referred to, and **le sien** if it's a handbag – le sac). In
the plural (ie. several owners) with a plural noun there is no gender
distinction: les nôtres, les vôtres, les leurs.

1.5   Demonstratives: *ce, ce ...-ci, celui-ci, ceux-ci* etc.

1.5.1   The distinction 'this' vs 'that' is rendered in French by a
demonstrative plus '-ci' or '-là', eg. **ce** garçon-**ci** – this boy; **ce**
garçon-**là** – that boy. However, whereas English always draws the
distinction between 'this' and 'that', the French demonstratives are often
used without the '-ci' and '-là' additions, so that 'ce garçon' may mean
'this boy' or 'that boy'. The main difference is again one of gender:
remember to use 'cette', 'celle' or 'celles' with a feminine noun.

1.6 Comparative and superlative: *plus … que* etc.

1.6.1 The comparative and superlative in French are formed by placing **plus** and **le plus** respectively in front of the adjective or adverb. Eg.: plus grand – bigger; le plus grand – the biggest; plus vite – more quickly; le plus vite – the most quickly.

2. *Verbs*

This is one of the main areas of difficulty for English-speaking learners. There are four major problems. First the variety of endings (je pars, nous part*ons* etc) and the number of irregular or 'semi-irregular' forms. Second, the difference in the formation of negative or interrogative phrases (no equivalent of 'do', 'did' etc. as in 'I didn't go, did you?'). Third, the difference in the use of tenses (eg. no real equivalent of our 'continuous' tense). Fourth the use of 'avoir' or 'être' as auxiliary verbs where English just uses 'to have'.

2.1 Verb forms

The verb tables on pp. 507 to 514 will give you ending patterns for the main regular verbs, plus a list of the most common irregular verbs. There is no substitute for practice on this, but try not to look at these forms as a vast number of separate items to be learnt: there are two basic combining patterns, one relating to the person (a 'nous' form vs a 'vous' form etc), and one relating to the tense. Also, don't learn and practise too many different tenses at once, parrot-fashion. The present, the imperfect, the future, the conditional and the perfect will cater for most of your needs when it comes to expressing yourself in French.

2.2 Negatives and questions

'**ne** (**n'**) + verb form + **pas** (+ past participle)' is the basic pattern of negative verb phrases. 'Je **ne** crois (vraiment) **pas** que …', 'il **n'**est **pas** parti (tout de suite)', il **n'a pas** (tout de suite) répondu'. The one place where no adverb can fit is between 'ne' and the verb form. Otherwise, there are various possible combinations, depending on the adverb and the meaning of the whole sentence.

One easy way to form an interrogative phrase is to use the invariable question form **est-ce que/qu'**…, eg. 'il part demain': '**est-ce qu'**il part demain?'. Alternatively, use the inversion of verb and subject (but only when the subject is a pronoun), eg. 'il part demain': 'part-il demain?'. Very often in spoken French (and, whatever they say to the contrary, for most people), intonation only is used to indicate the question form: 'il part demain?' (voice raised on the last syllable).

2.3 Tenses

2.3.1 There is no equivalent in French of our 'progressive' -ing form (I am reading). When the English has the sense of 'to be in the process of doing ...' it can be translated with the structure 'être en train de' + infinitive. In other cases, the present tense or the imperfect will convey the same meaning: I was living at Rosalie's: j'habitais chez Rosalie; we are seeing him tomorrow: nous le voyons demain.

2.3.2 The two tenses of the past in English (I went there, he has taken it) do not correspond closely to the French. Of the imperfect (j'habitais), the perfect (j'ai répondu) and the past historic (je partis), the last is hardly ever used in spoken French. The perfect is used much more widely than its counterpart in English and it can be used in many cases when the English would use the preterite (*I went, he gave* etc.).

2.3.3 The perfect tense ('passé composé')

The use of 'avoir' as an auxiliary verb is by far the most common, hence it is convenient to concentrate on the few verbs which use 'être'. They are all intransitive and verbs expressing movement or becoming, like *aller, venir; partir, arriver, retourner; descendre, monter, entrer, sortir; naître, mourir, devenir.*

The second thing to remember is that the past participle will occasionally take the marks of gender and/or plural. Thick tomes have been written on the agreement of the past participle, but two basic rules should enable you to cope with most problems. The past participle remains in the form of the masculine singular (j'ai répondu, il a passé) unless: *a*. with a transitive verb, the object precedes the verb – '*les livres* que j'ai lu*s*'; *b*. the auxiliary 'être' is used: '*elle* est parti*e* hier'.

2.3.4 The imperfect ('imparfait')

This is used for an action or state without definite limits in time. Compare for instance 'he lived in London during the war: il habitait à Londres pendant la guerre', 'he stood near the window: il se tenait (il était) près de la fenêtre' and 'they lived here from '64 to '68: ils ont habité ici de 64 à 68', 'he stood up: il s'est levé (il se leva)'.

2.4 The subjunctive ('subjonctif'): je veux qu'il fasse ... *vs* je sais qu'il fait ...

Good command of the present tense of the subjunctive is necessary in order to speak reasonably good French. However, as far as basic communication is concerned, in only a very few cases is the use of the subjunctive essential in order to avoid a misunderstanding. In other words, the use of the subjunctive is a constraint which if ignored will identify you as a poor speaker of French without impairing communication in any significant way.

One instance where ignoring the subjunctive might lead to a misunderstanding is with the verb 'dire': 'dites-lui qu'il vienne' means 'tell him to come', but 'dites-lui qu'il vient' means 'tell him (or her) that he's coming'.

It is not possible to give a simple rule showing when the subjunctive should be used. This dictionary will occasionally show you when a particular construction requires the use of the subjunctive (see for instance English **lest**).

It usually follows a verb + *que* construction where the sentence expresses doubt, a hypothesis rather than a fact, a question (tu veux qu'on y aille?), an interdiction.

It is always used after 'vouloir que ...', 'il faut que ...'. There are also a few conjunctions which always take the subjunctive, usually those which express desire or intention (eg. 'afin que ...', 'de sorte que ...' – 'so that ...').

2.5 The passive

Broadly speaking, the passive voice is similar in French. 'He was dismissed' or 'he has been dismissed' can both be rendered by 'il a été renvoyé'. Note that impersonal uses such as 'I was told that ...' are often best rendered by the 'on' construction: 'on m'a dit que ...' (see entry for French **on**).

Constructions like 'the road is being repaired' are often best translated without using the passive: 'la route est en réparation', 'on est en train de réparer la route'. In cases like 'the book I was given' or 'the book I was given by my brother', where the subject ('I') would in fact be the indirect object in the active voice, the passive cannot be used in French: 'le livre qu'on m'a donné', 'le livre que m'a donné mon frère'.

3. *Personal pronouns*

I, me	**je** voyage, je **me** coiffe, il **me** parle, il **me** voit, il **m'**a vu, et **moi**?
we, us	**nous** voyageons, **nous nous** coiffons, il **nous** parle, il **nous** voit, il **nous** a vus(vues), et **nous**?
he, him	il voyage, **il se** coiffe, je **lui** parle, je **le** vois, je **l'**ai vu, et **lui**?
she, her	**elle** voyage, **elle se** coiffe, je **lui** parle, je **la** vois, je **l'**ai vue, et **elle**?

it	il(elle) est rouge, il(elle) se casse, je le(la) vois, je l'ai vu(e)
they, them	ils(elles) voyagent, ils(elles) se coiffent, je **leur** parle, je **les** vois, je **les** ai vus(vues), et **eux(elles)**?
you (*plural*)	vous voyagez, vous vous coiffez, coiffez-vous, je **vous** parle, je **vous** vois, je **vous** ai vus(vues), et **vous**?
you (*singular*)	*familiar form*: tu voyages, tu te coiffes, coiffe-toi, je **te** parle, je **te** vois, je **t'**ai vu(vue), et **toi**?
	polite form: **vous** voyagez, **vous vous** coiffez, coiffez-vous, je **vous** parle, je **vous** vois, et **vous**?

'Voyager' is an intransitive verb; 'se coiffer' is a reflexive verb ('verbe pronominal'); 'parler' is shown here with an indirect object ('parler à quelqu'un'); 'voir' is shown with a direct object ('voir quelqu'un'); the strong pronoun form is shown last, and is the one used after a preposition ('pour moi', 'après lui', 'devant nous' etc.); the imperative is shown for the 2nd person with the reflexive verb.

When there is a direct and an indirect object, personal pronouns are in the following order (indirect object shown in bold):

me	il **me** le(la) donne, il **me** l'a donné(donnée), il ne **me** l'a pas donné(donnée)
us	il **nous** le(la) donne, il **nous** l'a donné(donnée), il ne **nous** l'a pas donné(donnée)
him, her	je le(la) **lui** donne, je le(la) **lui** ai donné(donnée), je ne le(la) **lui** ai pas donné(donnée)
them	je le(la) **leur** donne, je le(la) **leur** ai donné(donnée), je ne le(la) **leur** ai pas donné(donnée)
you (*plural*)	je **vous** le(la) donne, je **vous** l'ai donné(donnée), je ne **vous** l'ai pas donné(donnée)
you (*singular*)	*familiar form*: je **te** le(la) donne, je **te** l'ai donné(donnée), je ne **te** l'ai pas donné(donnée)
	polite form: je **vous** le(la) donne, je **vous** l'ai donné(donnée), je ne **vous** l'ai pas donné(donnée)

III. French verbs

1. The following tables of irregular verbs are self-explanatory. Unless stated otherwise, if one form only is given, it is the first person singular; if two forms are given, they are the first person singular and the first person plural. If not shown, the second person singular is the same as the first; the second and third person plural are regularly formed on the root of the first person plural (ie. *part*ons, *part*ez, *part*ent).

2. For verbs in '-ir' not appearing in the list of irregular verbs, follow 'finir'. For verbs in '-duire', follow 'conduire'. For verbs in '-andre, -ondre, -perdre, -ordre', follow 'rendre'.

3. Do not forget to use the appropriate pronoun with pronominal verbs: je me rase, il se rase, vous vous êtes coupé.

4. 'Semi-irregular' verbs.

Some verbs are only 'irregular' in a few predictable ways:

4.1 A 'c' will change to a 'ç' before 'o' or 'a' (the corresponding sound remaining [s]): **placer**, nous plaçons, nous plaçâmes.

4.2 A 'g' will change to 'ge' before 'o' or 'a' (the corresponding sound remaining [ʒ]): **bouger**, nous bougeons, nous bougeâmes; **protéger**, nous protégeons, nous protégeâmes.

4.3 An 'l' or a 't' will change to 'll' or 'tt' before 'e(s)' or 'ent', and in the future and conditional tenses (ie. at the end of a syllable): **appeler**, j'appelle, ils appellent, ils appelleront (*but*: nous appelons, j'appelais); **jeter**, je jette, ils jettent, nous jetterons (*but*: nous jetons, je jetais).

4.4 An 'e' will change to 'è' if followed by a consonant sound within the syllable: **geler**, il gèle, ils gèlent, il gèlera (*but*: nous gelons, il gelait); **acheter**, j'achète, ils achètent, ils achèteront (*but*: nous achetons, j'achetais); also: **dépecer, protéger.**

4.5 A 'y' will change to 'i' before 'e(s)', 'ent', and in the future and conditional tenses (ie. at the end of a syllable): **nettoyer**, il nettoie, ils nettoient, ils nettoieront (*but*: vous nettoyez, je nettoyais); also for '-uyer' and '-ayer' verbs (ennuyer, balayer). **Payer** may either retain the 'y' or follow the above changes.

5. The 'temps composés' are formed as follows:

5.1   Perfect ('passé composé'): with 'être' je suis parti, tu es parti etc. (see 'être'); with 'avoir' j'ai couru, tu as couru etc. (see 'avoir')

5.2   Pluperfect ('plus-que-parfait'): j'étais parti etc.; j'avais couru etc.

5.3   Future anterior ('futur antérieur'): je serai parti etc.; j'aurai couru etc.

5.4   Past conditional ('conditionnel passé'): je serais parti etc.; j'aurais couru etc.

5.5   The past anterior ('passé antérieur') – j'eus couru etc. – and the pluperfect subjunctive ('plus-que-parfait du subjonctif') – j'eusse couru etc. – are rarely used.

6. The imperfect subjunctive ('imparfait du subjonctif') is practically obsolete in spoken French and rare in written French. It is recognizable by its 'ss' element – que je fusse, que nous fussions; que j'eusse, que nous eussions etc – and also by the circumflex in the 3rd person singular – qu'il fût, qu'il eût, qu'il allât.

A typical regular verb: 'parler' [paʀle]

PAST HISTORIC		
	ai	[e]
	as	[a]
	a	
parl-		[paʀl...
	âmes	[ɑm]
	âtes	[ɑt]
	èrent	[ɛʀ]

IMPERFECT		
	ais	[ɛ]
	ais	
	ait	
parl-		[paʀl...
	ions	[jɔ̃]
	iez	[je]
	aient	[ɛ]

IMPERATIVE	parle, parlez [paʀl(ə), paʀle]
PAST PARTICIPLE	parlé (parlée) [paʀle]
PERFECT	j'ai parlé, tu as parlé etc.

VERB TABLES

VERB TABLES: 1 Participe présent **2** Participe passé **3** Présent **4** Subjonctif présent **5** Imparfait **6** Futur **7** Conditionnel **8** Passé simple

absoudre 1 absolvant **2** absout(absoute) **3** absous, absout, absolvons **4** absolve, absolvions **5** absolvais, absolvions **6** absoudrai, absoudrons **7** absoudrais, absoudrions **8** absolus, absolûmes

acquérir 1 acquérant **2** acquis(acquise) **3** acquiers, acquiert, acquérons, acquièrent **4** acquière, acquérions **5** acquérais, acquérions **6** acquerrai, acquerrons **7** acquerrais, acquerrions **8** acquis, acquîmes

aller 1 allant **2** allé(allée) **3** vais, vas, va, allons, allez, vont **4** aille, ailles, aille, allions, alliez, aillent **5** allais, allions **6** irai, irons **7** irais, irions **8** allai, allâmes

assaillir 1 assaillant **2** assailli(assaillie) **3** assaille, assaillons **4** assaille, assaillions **5** assaillais, assaillions **6** assaillirai, assaillirons **7** assaillirais, assaillirions **8** assaillis, assaillîmes

asseoir 1 asseyant 2 assis(assise) 3 assieds, assied, asseyons, asseyez, asseyent 4 asseye, asseyions 5 asseyais, asseyions 6 assiérai, assiérons 7 assiérais, assiériez 8 assis, assîmes

atteindre 1 atteignant 2 atteint(atteinte) 3 atteins, atteint, atteignons 4 atteigne, atteignions 5 atteignais, atteignions 6 atteindrai, atteindrons 7 atteindrais, atteindrions 8 atteignis, atteignîmes

avoir 1 ayant 2 eu(eue) 3 ai, as, a, avons, avez, ont 4 aie, aies, ait, ayons, ayez, aient 5 avais, avions 6 aurai, aurons 7 aurais, aurions 8 eus, eûmes

battre 1 battant 2 battu(battue) 3 bats, bats, bat, battons, battez, battent 4 batte, battions 5 battais, battions 6 battrai, battrons 7 battrais, battrions 8 battis, battîmes

boire 1 buvant 2 bu(bue) 3 bois, boit, buvons, buvez, boivent 4 boive, buvions, boivent 5 buvais, buvions 6 boirai, boirons 7 boirais, boirions 8 bus, bûmes

bouillir 1 bouillant 2 bouilli(bouillie) 3 bous, bout, bouillons, bouillent 4 bouille, bouillions 5 bouillais, bouillions 6 bouillirai, bouillirons 7 bouillirais, bouillirions 8 bouillis, bouillîmes

clore 2 clos(close) 3 clos, clôt, closent 4 close 6 clorai 7 clorais

conclure 1 concluant 2 conclu(conclue) 3 conclus, conclut, concluons, concluent 4 conclue, concluions, concluent 5 concluais, concluions 6 conclurai, conclurons 7 conclurais, conclurions 8 conclus, conclûmes

conduire 1 conduisant 2 conduit(conduite) 3 conduis, conduit, conduisons 4 conduise, conduisions 5 conduisais, conduisions 6 conduirai, conduirons 7 conduirais, conduirions 8 conduisis, conduisîmes

connaître 1 connaissant 2 connu(connue) 3 connais, connaît, connaissons 4 connaisse, connaissions 5 connaissais, connaissions 6 connaîtrai, connaîtrons 7 connaîtrais, connaîtrions 8 connus, connûmes

coudre 1 cousant 2 cousu(cousue) 3 couds, coud, cousons 4 couse, cousions 5 cousais, cousions 6 coudrai, coudrons 7 coudrais, coudrions 8 cousis, cousîmes

courir 1 courant 2 couru(courue) 3 cours, court, courons 4 coure, courions 5 courais, courions 6 courrai, courrons 7 courrais, courrions 8 courus, courûmes

couvrir 1 couvrant 2 couvert(couverte) 3 couvre, couvrons 4 couvre, couvrions 5 couvrais, couvrions 6 couvrirai, couvrirons 7 couvrirais, couvririons 8 couvris, couvrîmes

craindre 1 craignant 2 craint(crainte) 3 crains, craint, craignons, craignent 4 craigne, craignions 5 craignais, craignions 6 craindrai, craindrons 7 craindrais, craindrions 8 craignis, craignîmes

croire 1 croyant 2 cru(crue) 3 crois, croit, croyons, croient 4 croie, croyions 5 croyais, croyions 6 croirai, croirons 7 croirais, croirions 8 crus, crûmes

croître 1 croissant 2 crû(crue) 3 croîs, croît, croissons 4 croisse, croissions 5 croissais, croissions 6 croîtrai, croîtrons 7 croîtrais, croîtrions 8 crûs, crûmes

cueillir 1 cueillant 2 cueilli(cueillie) 3 cueille, cueillons, cueillent 4 cueille, cueillions 5 cueillais, cueillions 6 cueillerai, cueillerons 7 cueillerais, cueillerions 8 cueillis, cueillîmes

devoir 1 devant 2 dû(due) 3 dois, doit, devons, doivent 4 doive, devions, doivent 5 devais, devions 6 devrai, devrons 7 devrais, devrions 8 dus, dûmes

dire 1 disant 2 dit(dite) 3 dis, dit, disons, dites, disent 4 dise, disions 5 disais, disions 6 dirai, dirons 7 dirais, dirions 8 dis, dîmes.

dormir 1 dormant 2 dormi 3 dors, dort, dormons 4 dorme, dormions 5 dormais, dormions 6 dormirai, dormirons 7 dormirais, dormirions 8 dormis, dormîmes

écrire 1 écrivant 2 écrit(écrite) 3 écris, écrit, écrivons 4 écrive, écrivions 5 écrivais, écrivions 6 écrirai, écrirons 7 écrirais, écririons 8 écrivis, écrivîmes

être 1 étant 2 été 3 suis, es, est, sommes, êtes, sont 4 sois, sois, soit, soyons, soyez, soient 5 étais, étions 6 serai, serons 7 serais, serions 8 fus, fûmes

faire 1 faisant 2 fait(faite) 3 fais, fais, fait, faisons, faites, font 4 fasse, fassions, fassent 5 faisais, faisions 6 ferai, ferons 7 ferais, ferions 8 fis, fîmes

falloir 2 fallu 3 faut 4 faille 5 fallait 6 faudra 7 faudrait 8 fallut

finir 1 finissant 2 fini(finie) 3 finis, finis, finit, finissons, finissez, finissent 4 finisse, finissions 5 finissais, finissions 6 finirai, finirons 7 finirais, finirions 8 finis, finîmes

fuir 1 fuyant 2 fui 3 fuis, fuit, fuyons, fuient 4 fuie, fuyions, fuient 5 fuyais, fuyions 6 fuirai, fuirons 7 fuirais, fuirions 8 fuis, fuîmes

haïr 1 haïssant 2 haï(haïe) 3 hais, hait, haïssons 4 haïsse, haïssions 5 haïssais, haïssions 6 haïrai, haïrons 7 haïrais, haïrions

joindre 1 joignant 2 joint(jointe) 3 joins, joint, joignons, joignent 4 joigne, joignions 5 joignais, joignions 6 joindrai, joindrons 7 joindrais, joindrions 8 joignis, joignîmes

lire 1 lisant 2 lu(lue) 3 lis, lit, lisons 4 lise, lisions 5 lisais, lisions 6 lirai, lirons 7 lirais, lirions 8 lus, lûmes

luire 1 luisant 2 lui 3 luis, luit, luisons 4 luise, luisions 5 luisais, luisions 6 luirai, luirons 7 luirais, luirions

maudire 1 maudissant 2 maudit(maudite) 3 maudis, maudit, maudissons 4 maudisse, maudissions 5 maudissais, maudissions 6 maudirai, maudirons 7 maudirais, maudirions 8 maudis, maudîmes

mentir 1 mentant 2 menti 3 mens, ment, mentons 4 mente, mentions 5 mentais, mentions 6 mentirai, mentirons 7 mentirais, mentirions 8 mentis, mentîmes

mettre 1 mettant 2 mis(mise) 3 mets, met, mettons 4 mette, mettions 5 mettais, mettions 6 mettrai, mettrons 7 mettrais, mettrions 8 mis, mîmes

moudre 1 moulant 2 moulu(moulue) 3 mouds, moud, moulons

4 moule, moulions **5** moulais, moulions **6** moudrai, moudrons **7** moudrais, moudrions **8** moulus, moulûmes

mourir 1 mourant **2** mort(morte) **3** meurs, meurt, mourons, meurent **4** meure, mourions, meurent **5** mourais, mourions **6** mourrai, mourrons **7** mourrais, mourrions **8** mourus, mourûmes

mouvoir 1 mouvant **2** mû(mue) **3** meus, meut, mouvons, meuvent **4** meuve, mouvions, meuvent **5** mouvais, mouvions **6** mouvrai, mouvrons **7** mouvrais, mouvrions **8** mus, mûmes

naître 1 naissant **2** né(née) **3** nais, naît, naissons **4** naisse, naissions **5** naissais, naissions **6** naîtrai, naîtrons **7** naîtrais, naîtrions **8** naquis, naquîmes

nuire *voir* **luire**

offrir 1 offrant **2** offert(offerte) **3** offre, offrons **4** offre, offrions **5** offrais, offrions **6** offrirai, offrirons **7** offrirais, offririons **8** offris, offrîmes

partir 1 partant **2** parti(partie) **3** pars, part, partons **4** parte, partions **5** partais, partions **6** partirai, partirons **7** partirais, partirions **8** partis, partîmes

peindre 1 peignant **2** peint(peinte) **3** peins, peint, peignons **4** peigne, peignions **5** peignais, peignions **6** peindrai, peindrons **7** peindrais, peindrions **8** peignis, peignîmes

placer 'ç' before a vowel other than 'e' or 'i': 'nous plaçons' etc.

plaire 1 plaisant **2** plu **3** plais, plaît, plaisons **4** plaise, plaisions **5** plaisais, plaisions **6** plairai, plairons **7** plairais, plairions **8** plus, plûmes

pleuvoir 1 pleuvant **2** plu **3** pleut, pleuvent **4** pleuve, pleuvent **5** pleuvait, pleuvaient **6** pleuvra, pleuvront **7** pleuvrait, pleuvraient *NB. 3rd person only*

pourvoir 1 pourvoyant **2** pourvu(pourvue) **3** pourvois, pourvoit, pourvoyons, pourvoient **4** pourvoie, pourvoyions **5** pourvoyais, pourvoyions **6** pourvoirai, pourvoirons **7** pourvoirais, pourvoirions **8** pourvus, pourvûmes

pouvoir 1 pouvant **2** pu **3** peux, peut, pouvons, peuvent **4** puisse, puissions, puissent **5** pouvais, pouvions **6** pourrai, pourrons **7** pourrais, pourrions **8** pus, pûmes

prendre 1 prenant **2** pris(prise) **3** prends, prend, prenons, prennent **4** prenne, prenions, prennent **5** prenais, prenions **6** prendrai, prendrons **7** prendrais, prendrions **8** pris, prîmes

prévoir 1 prévoyant **2** prévu(prévue) **3** prévois, prévoit, prévoyons, prévoient **4** prévoie, prévoyions, prévoient **5** prévoyais, prévoyions **6** prévoirai, prévoirons **7** prévoirais, prévoirions **8** prévis, prévîmes

recevoir 1 recevant **2** reçu(reçue) **3** reçois, reçoit, recevons, reçoivent **4** reçoive, recevions **5** recevais, recevions **6** recevrai, recevrons **7** recevrais, recevrions **8** reçus, reçûmes

rendre 1 rendant **2** rendu(rendue) **3** rends, rend, rendons **4** rende, rendions **5** rendais, rendions **6** rendrai, rendrons **7** rendrais, rendrions **8** rendis, rendîmes

résoudre 1 résolvant 2 résolu(résolue) 3 résous, résout, résolvons 4 résolve, résolvions 5 résolvais, résolvions 6 résoudrai, résoudrons 7 résoudrais, résoudrions 8 résolus, résolûmes

rire 1 riant 2 ri 3 ris, rit, rions, rient 4 rie, riions, rient 5 riais, riions 6 rirai, rirons 7 rirais, ririons 8 ris, rîmes

rompre 1 rompant 2 rompu(rompue) 3 romps, rompt, rompons 4 rompe, rompions 5 rompais, rompions 6 romprai, romprons 7 romprais, romprions 8 rompis, rompîmes

savoir 1 sachant 2 su(sue) 3 sais, sait, savons, savent 4 sache, sachions 5 savais, savions 6 saurai, saurons 7 saurais, saurions 8 sus, sûmes

sentir 1 sentant 2 senti(sentie) 3 sens, sent, sentons 4 sente, sentions 5 sentais, sentions 6 sentirai, sentirons 7 sentirais, sentirions 8 sentis, sentîmes

servir 1 servant 2 servi(servie) 3 sers, sert, servons 4 serve, servions 5 servais, servions 6 servirai, servirons 7 servirais, servirions 8 servis, servîmes

sortir 1 sortant 2 sorti(sortie) 3 sors, sort, sortons 4 sorte, sortions 5 sortais, sortions 6 sortirai, sortirons 7 sortirais, sortirions 8 sortis, sortîmes

souffrir 1 souffrant 2 souffert(soufferte) 3 souffre, souffrons 4 souffre, souffrions 5 souffrais, souffrions 6 souffrirai, souffrirons 7 souffrirais, souffririons 8 souffris, souffrîmes

suffire 1 suffisant 2 suffi 3 suffis, suffit, suffisons 4 suffise, suffisions 5 suffisais, suffisions 6 suffirai, suffirons 7 suffirais, suffirions 8 suffis, suffîmes

suivre 1 suivant 2 suivi(suivie) 3 suis, suit, suivons 4 suive, suivions 5 suivais, suivions 6 suivrai, suivrons 7 suivrais, suivrions 8 suivis, suivîmes

taire 1 taisant 2 tu(tue) 3 tais, tait, taisons 4 taise, taisions 5 taisais, taisions 6 tairai, tairons 7 tairais, tairions 8 tus, tûmes

tenir 1 tenant 2 tenu(tenue) 3 tiens, tient, tenons, tiennent 4 tienne, tenions, tiennent 5 tenais, tenions 6 tiendrai, tiendrons 7 tiendrais, tiendrions 8 tins, tînmes

traire 1 trayant 2 trait(traite) 3 trais, trait, trayons, traient 4 traie, trayions, traient 5 trayais, trayions 6 trairai, trairons 7 trairais, trairions

vaincre 1 vainquant 2 vaincu(vaincue) 3 vaincs, vainc, vainquons, vainquent 4 vainque, vainquions, vainquent 5 vainquais, vainquions 6 vaincrai, vaincrons 7 vaincrais, vaincrions 8 vainquis, vainquîmes

valoir 1 valant 2 valu 3 vaux, vaut, valons 4 vaille, valions, vaillent 5 valais, valions 6 vaudrai, vaudrons 7 vaudrais, vaudrions 8 valus, valûmes

venir 1 venant 2 venu(venue) 3 viens, vient, venons, viennent 4 vienne, venions, viennent 5 venais, venions 6 viendrai, viendrons 7 viendrais, viendrions 8 vins, vînmes

vêtir 1 vêtant 2 vêtu(vêtue) 3 vêts, vêt, vêtons, vêtent 4 vête, vêtions 5 vêtais, vêtions 6 vêtirai, vêtirons 7 vêtirais, vêtirions 8 vêtis, vêtîmes

vivre 1 vivant 2 vécu(vécue) 3 vis, vit, vivons 4 vive, vivions 5 vivais, vivions 6 vivrai, vivrons 7 vivrais, vivrions 8 vécus, vécûmes

voir 1 voyant 2 vu(vue) 3 vois, voit, voyons, voient 4 voie, voyions, voient 5 voyais, voyions 6 verrai, verrons 7 verrais, verrions 8 vis, vîmes

vouloir 1 voulant 2 voulu(voulue) 3 veux, veut, voulons, veulent 4 veuille, voulions, veuillent 5 voulais, voulions 6 voudrai, voudrons 7 voudrais, voudrions 8 voulus, voulûmes *impératif:* veuille, veuillez

IV. The sounds of French

Learning to pronounce French well is, as with all foreign languages, largely a matter of adopting different 'speech habits' from those used in speaking English.

A 'foreign accent' results from using the sounds of one's own language to approximate the sounds of the foreign language. This is particularly tempting when the same letter or letters represent similar sounds in each language. For instance the letter 'i' is used in both French and English, but to represent slightly different sounds in each, and many French speakers are unable to pronounce it in the English manner. It is possible that many do not even realize that the English speaker uses a different sound from the French – hence the typical French pronunciation of 'it is' which sounds to the English speaker as if it were written 'eet eese'.

These are the main ways in which French 'speech habits' differ from the English:

1. Activity of the lips
The lips play a very important part in French. When a vowel is described as having 'rounded' lips, the lips are slightly drawn together and pursed, as when the English speaker expresses exaggerated surprise with the vowel 'ooh!'. Equally, if the lips are said to be 'spread', the corners are pulled firmly back towards the cheeks, tending to reveal the front teeth.

In English, lip position is not important, and vowel sounds tend to merge because of this. In French, the activity of the lips means that every vowel sound is clearly distinct from every other.

2. No diphthongs
A diphthong is a glide between two vowel sounds in the same syllable. In English, there are few 'pure' vowel sounds, but largely diphthongs instead. Although speakers of English may *think* they produce one vowel sound in the word 'day', in fact they use a diphthong, which in this instance is a glide between the vowels [e] and [ɪ]: [deɪ]. In French the

tension maintained in the lips, tongue and the mouth in general prevents diphthongs occurring, as the vowel sound is kept constant throughout. Hence the French word corresponding to the above example, 'dé', is pronounced with no final [ɪ] sound, but is phonetically represented thus: [de].

3. Consonants

Consonants in French are always given their full value. In English, consonants are often pronounced with a degree of laxness that can result in their practically disappearing altogether although not strictly 'silent'. In a relaxed pronunciation of a word such as 'hat', the 't' is often scarcely heard, or is replaced by a 'glottal stop' (a sort of jerk in the throat). Hence a Frenchman sounds unmistakeably foreign to an English speaker if he pronounces the 't' and 'l' in a word such as 'bottle' as energetically as he would in French.

4. Stress

In English, each word has its own particular stress pattern – for instance, the two different stress patterns for the word 'escort' produces two different words, one a noun and one a verb (*an escort bureau, may I escort you*). There is no possibility of this in French, since individual words have no characteristic stress pattern; syllables are stressed only when they occur at the end of the sentence or phrase:

eg. je les ai *vus*
    je les ai vus *hier*
    je les ai vus hier ma*tin*

The stressed syllable is in italics in each case, and all the other syllables are unstressed. This gives French a peculiarly 'staccato' effect, since all unstressed syllables tend to be of about the same length.

Pronunciation of the sounds of French

I. Vowels

as in:	Hints on pronunciation
[a] pa*tte* pl*at a*mour	Pronounced more or less as in English 'pat'.
[ɑ] ba*s* pâ*te*	Longer and further back in the mouth than [a]. This sound resembles the English exclamation of surprise: 'ah!'. Similar to the vowel in English 'car', without the r-sound, but a little shorter.
[ɛ] l*ait* jou*et* m*erci	Similar to the sound in English 'pet', but the lips are slightly further apart. Beware of substituting the English diphthong [eɪ] as in 'pay' when the sound [ɛ] comes at the end of a word

515

[e] *été jouer*	The tongue is held very tense and quite high in the mouth to pronounce a pure [e] sound. Again quite different from English [eɪ] of 'pay'
[ə] *le premier*	The lips are slightly rounded for this vowel, and this is what distinguishes it from the sound in 'butter'
[i] *ici vie lycée*	The lips are well spread towards the cheeks and held very tensely while uttering this sound. Try saying English 'see' with your lips in this position. The sound is however shorter in French than the corresponding English vowel
[ɔ] *mort homme*	The lips must be well rounded, and the sound is half-way between 'u' and 'o' in the English words 'cut' and 'cot'
[o] *mot dôme eau*	A 'pure' vowel with strongly rounded lips. Make sure this sound does not become the diphthong used in English 'bone' and 'low'
[u] *genou roue*	Again, a 'pure' vowel with strongly rounded lips. The lip position is like that used at the beginning of the consonant [w] in English
[y] *rue vêtu*	This sound is often considered the most difficult for English speakers to produce. Round your lips to say [u] (see above), then try to say [i] instead. Easier for Scots: try this sound in 'muesli' or 'Zürich'. There is no [j] sound (as in English 'pure') before this vowel
[œ] *sœur beurre*	Similar to the vowel sound in English 'fir' or 'murmur', but without the 'r' sounded, and with greater lip-rounding
[ø] *peu deux*	To pronounce this vowel, try to say [e] (see above) with strongly rounded lips

Nasal vowels

These are always spelt with a vowel followed by a 'nasal' consonant – *n* or *m*. The production of nasal vowels can scarcely be explained without the help of a teacher or a recording of the sound quality. As a guide, however, the vowel is pronounced by allowing air to come partly down the nose and partly through the mouth, and the consonant disappears altogether. Best tip: ask a native French speaker to say and repeat for

you the words 'mais*on*', 'jard*in*', 'ch*am*bre', 'br*un*', and try to copy
what you hear.

[ã] *l*e*nt* s*ang* d*ans* ⎫

[ɛ̃] mat*in* pl*ein* ⎪ In each case the vowel shown in the phonetic
⎬ symbol is pronounced in the normal way, but air
[ɔ̃] *non* p*ont* ⎪ is allowed to come down the nose as well as
⎪ through the mouth
[œ̃] br*un* *un* ⎭

II. Consonants

Those consonants which are pronounced more or less as in English are
represented phonetically as [b, f, g, k, m, p, v, w]. There is no aspiration
with the production of [b, p, d, t, g, k] in French. Most other consonants
are similar to their English counterparts but slight differences should be
noted:

[d] *d*inde ⎫

[t] *t*en*t*e ⎪ The tip of the tongue touches the upper teeth and
⎬ not the roof of the mouth as in English
[n] *n*on*n*e ⎪

[l] *L*i*ll*e ⎭

[s] *ç*a *t*ous ⎫ As in English, but the tip of the tongue is held
⎬ low, behind the bottom teeth
[z] *z*éro ro*s*e ⎭

[ʃ] *ch*ose ta*ch*e   As in English '*sh*out'

[ʒ] *j*e *g*ilet bei*g*e   As in English 'mea*s*ure', 'bei*g*e'

[j] *y*eux pa*ill*e   As in English '*y*es'

Three consonant sounds are not heard in English:

[ʀ] *r*are veni*r*   For many speakers of English, 'r' is often silent,
eg. 'fa*r*m'. In French, the 'r' is always
pronounced, unless it follows an 'e' at the end of
a word (cherch*er*, berg*er*). Its pronunciation in
French is similar to the final sound of the Scottish
word 'lo*ch*'. If you find this difficult, try thinking
of the sound made when gargling, since the
French [ʀ] is produced at the back of the mouth
in a similar way

| [ɲ] | vigne agneau | Very similar to [nj] as in 'Spaniard' |
| [ɥ] | huile lueur | Like a very rapid [y] (see above) followed by the next vowel sound in the word |

There are two extra symbols used in this dictionary: ° and '. See for instance the entry for *haie*. These symbols mean that no liaison is made before the following vowel:

cf. la haie *vs* l'habitation
les haies *vs* les habitations.

From spelling to sounds

French spelling can be very confusing since one and the same sound can be represented in many different ways in the written word. Conversely, a given letter or group of letters can have different pronunciations depending on its position in the word. You may therefore be surprised to learn that these differences are governed by fairly precise 'rules' that are not difficult to assimilate.

The most important distinction to be drawn is whether the group of letters comes at the end of a word or syllable, or whether the letters are split between two syllables. Eg. in 'ma-tin' the dash represents the break between syllables and you can see that the word consists of two syllables of which the final one ends in 'in', one of the characteristic spellings of the nasal vowel [ɛ̃]. However in 'ma-ti-née', as the dashes show, the 'i' and the 'n' belong to different syllables, and they no longer constitute a single sound. The 'i' has its usual value (as in 'ici'), and the 'n' is pronounced as part of the next syllable.

This example illustrates how one of several French consonants is silent when it occurs at the end of the word or syllable, but is sounded when it begins a word or syllable.

Other consonants which regularly behave in this way at the end of words are:

t	éclat [ekla]	BUT	écla-ter [eklate]
d	chaud [ʃo]	BUT	chau-dement [ʃodmã]
s	des [de]	BUT	dé-sir [deziʀ]
n	vain [vɛ̃]	BUT	vai-nement [vɛnmã]
	matin [matɛ̃]	BUT	mati-née [matine]
m	parfum [paʀfœ̃]	BUT	parfu-mer [paʀfyme]
x	aux [o]	BUT	au-xiliaire [ɔksiljɛʀ]
z	nez [ne]	BUT	zé-zayer [zezeje]
r	aider [ede]	BUT	nous parle-rons [paʀləʀɔ̃]

'm' and 'n' at the end of syllables (but not necessarily at the end of words):

m im-perméable
  [ɛ̃pɛʀmeabl]   BUT i-magination [imaʒinasjɔ̃]
               BUT im-mobile [imɔbil]
n in-cident [ɛ̃sidɑ̃] BUT i-nique [inik]

Typical pronunciation of some French spellings

There are several groups of vowels in French spelling which are regularly
pronounced in the same way, and these can easily be learnt:

spelling	pronunciation	examples
ai	[ɛ] or [e]	maison, marchai (verb form), faire
au	[o]	auberge, landau
eau	[o]	eau, beau, tableau
ou	[u]	fou, oublier
eu	[œ] or [ø]	peur, feu, heureux, feuille
œu	[œ]	sœur, cœur
ue	[y]	rue
		BUT recueil [ʀəkœj]

Added to these are the many groups of letters occurring at the end of
words, where their pronunciation is predictable, bearing in mind the
tendency (see above) of final consonants to remain silent:

typical words	*pronunciation of final syllable*
pas, mât, chat	[ɑ] or [a]
marcher, marchez, marchais, marchait, baie, valet, mes, fumée	[e] or [ɛ]
nid	[i]
chaud, vaut, faux, sot, tôt, Pernod, dos, croc	[o]
bout, bijoux, sous, boue	[u]
fut, fût, crus, crûs	[y]
queue, heureux, bleus	[ø]
en, vend, vent, an, sang, grand, dans	[ɑ̃]
fin, feint, frein, vain	[ɛ̃]
on, pont, fond, avons	[ɔ̃]
brun, parfum	[œ̃]

V. The time

what time is it ?   quelle heure est-il ?

it is ...   il est ..., c'est ...
at what time ?   à quelle heure ?
at ...   à ...

  00.00 minuit
  00.10 minuit dix
  00.15 minuit et quart
  00.30 minuit et demie, minuit trente
  00.45 une heure moins (le) quart

  01.00 une heure du matin
  01.10 une heure dix (du matin)
  01.15 une heure et quart, une heure quinze
  01.30 une heure et demie, une heure trente
  01.45 deux heures moins (le) quart, une heure quarante-cinq, une heure trois quarts
  01.50 deux heures moins dix, une heure cinquante
  01.59 deux heures moins une, une heure cinquante-neuf

  12.00 midi, douze heures
  12.30 midi et demie, midi trente

  13.00 une heure de l'après-midi, treize heures
  01.30 une heure et demie (de l'après-midi), une heure trente, treize heures trente

  19.00 sept heures du soir, dix-neuf heures
  19.30 sept heures et demie (du soir), sept heures trente, dix-neuf heures trente

  23.00 onze heures (du soir), vingt-trois heures
  23.45 onze heures trois quarts, onze heures quarante-cinq, vingt-trois heures quarante-cinq, minuit moins quart

in 20 minutes   dans vingt minutes

20 minutes ago   il y a vingt minutes

wake me up at 7   réveillez-moi à sept heures

1 hour, 20', 45'' une heure, vingt minutes et quarante-cinq secondes

Dates and numbers

1. The date

what's the date today?	quelle est la date d'aujourd'hui?, quel jour sommes-nous?
it's the ...	nous sommes le ..., c'est le ...

1st of February	premier février
2nd of February	deux février
28th of February	vingt-huit février

he's coming on the 7th (of May)	il vient le sept (mai)

NB: use cardinal numbers except for the first day of the month

I was born in 1945
  je suis né en dix-neuf cent quarante-cinq
I was born on the 15th of July 1945
  je suis né le quinze juillet dix-neuf cent quarante-cinq

during the sixties	dans les années soixante
in the twentieth century	au vingtième siècle
in May	en mai
on Monday (the 15th)	lundi (quinze)
on Mondays	le lundi
next/last Monday	lundi prochain/dernier
in 10 days' time	dans dix jours

2. Telephone numbers

I would like Paris 334 22 15
  j'aimerais Paris trois cent trente-quatre / vingt-deux / quinze
give me Paris 302 02 02
  donnez-moi Paris trois cent deux / zéro deux / zéro deux
could you get me Dijon 22 00 79, extension 2233
  pouvez-vous m'appeler Dijon vingt-deux / zéro zéro / soixante-dix-neuf, poste vingt-deux / trente-trois
the Geneva prefix is 022
  l'indicatif de Genève est zéro / vingt-deux

3. Using numbers

he lives at number 10	il habite au dix
it's in chapter 7, on page 7	c'est au chapitre sept, à la page sept
he lives on the 7th floor	il habite au septième (étage)
he came in 7th	il est arrivé (le) septième
a share of one seventh	une part d'un septième
scale 1:25,000	échelle au vingt-cinq millième

Numbers

1	un(une)	1st	premier(première), 1er	
2	deux	2nd	deuxième, 2e *or* 2ème	
3	trois	3rd	troisième, 3e *or* 3ème	
4	quatre	4th	quatrième	
5	cinq	5th	cinquième	
6	six	6th	sixième	
7	sept	7th	septième	
8	huit	8th	huitième	
9	neuf	9th	neuvième	
10	dix	10th	dixième	
11	onze	11th	onzième	
12	douze	12th	douzième	
13	treize	13th	treizième	
14	quatorze	14th	quatorzième	
15	quinze	15th	quinzième	
16	seize	16th	seizième	
17	dix-sept	17th	dix-septième	
18	dix-huit	18th	dix-huitième	
19	dix-neuf	19th	dix-neuvième	
20	vingt	20th	vingtième	
21	vingt et un(une)	21st	vingt-et-unième	
22	vingt-deux	22nd	vingt-deuxième	
30	trente	30th	trentième	
40	quarante	100th	centième	
50	cinquante	101st	cent-unième	
60	soixante	1,000th	millième	
70	soixante-dix			
71	soixante et onze	1/2	un demi	
72	soixante-douze	1/3	un tiers	
80	quatre-vingts	2/3	deux tiers	
81	quatre-vingt-un(-une)	1/4	un quart	
90	quatre-vingt-dix	1/5	un cinquième	
91	quatre-vingt-onze			
100	cent	0.5	zéro virgule cinq, 0,5	
101	cent un(une)	1.5	un virgule cinq, 1,5	
300	trois cents	10%	dix pour cent	
301	trois cent un(une)			
1,000	mille, 1 000	2 + 2	deux plus deux	
1,001	mille un(une)	2 ÷ 2	deux divisé par deux	
5,000	cinq mille, 5 000	2 × 2	deux fois deux	
1,000,000	un million	2 − 2 =	deux moins deux égale ...	

6^2 six au carré, six à la puissance deux ; $20\ m^2$ vingt mètres carrés
6^3 six au cube, six à la puissance trois ; $20\ m^3$ vingt mètres cubes